Enron and Other Corporate Fiascos:
The Corporate Scandal Reader

ABOUT THE EDITORS

NANCY B. RAPOPORT is the Gordon Silver Professor of Law at the William S. Boyd School of Law, University of Nevada, Las Vegas. After receiving her B.A., *summa cum laude,* from Rice University in 1982 and her J.D. from Stanford Law School in 1985, she clerked for the Honorable Joseph T. Sneed on the United States Court of Appeals for the Ninth Circuit and then practiced law (primarily bankruptcy law) with Morrison & Foerster in San Francisco from 1986-1991. She started her academic career at The* Ohio State University College of Law in 1991, and she moved from Assistant Professor to Associate Professor to Associate Dean for Student Affairs and Professor in 1998 (just as she left Ohio State to become Dean and Professor of Law at the University of Nebraska College of Law). She served as Dean of the University of Nebraska College of Law from 1998-2000. She then served as Dean and Professor of Law at the University of Houston Law Center from July 2000-May 2006 and as Professor of Law from June 2006-June 2007, when she left to join the faculty at UNLV.

Her specialties are bankruptcy ethics, ethics in governance, and the depiction of lawyers in popular culture. She has taught Contracts, Sales (Article 2), Bankruptcy, Chapter 11 Reorganizations, Legal Writing, Contract Drafting, and Professional Responsibility. She is admitted to the bars of the states of California, Ohio, Nebraska, Texas, and Nevada and of the United States Supreme Court. In 2001, she was elected to membership in the American Law Institute, and in 2002, she received a Distinguished Alumna Award from Rice University. She is a Fellow of the American Bar Foundation and a Fellow of the American College of Bankruptcy.

She has also appeared in the Academy Award®-nominated movie, *Enron: The Smartest Guys in the Room* (Magnolia Pictures 2005) (as herself). Although the movie garnered her a listing in www.imdb.com, she still hasn't been able to join SAG.

JEFFREY D. VAN NIEL is a native of Columbus, Ohio. He enlisted in the United States Marine Corps immediately after graduating from high school in 1976. After four years of service in the Marines as a scout sniper, he received an Honorable Discharge and joined the Ohio State Highway Patrol. He left the Highway Patrol in 1981 to get a Bachelor's Degree in Criminal Justice at Ohio University in 1983. He started law school in 1984 in lieu of joining the Secret Service (and never looked back). Mr. Van Niel served as Executive Notes Editor for the *Capital University Law Review,* and he was graduated from Capital University Law School in 1987, *cum laude,* having received the honors

* "The" really is capitalized as part of The Ohio State University's official name.

of the *Order of the Curia* and the *Order of the Barristers*. He clerked for Ohio Supreme Court Justice Andrew Douglas after graduation, and then he joined the Cleveland, Ohio law firm of Hahn Loeser ▲ Parks in 1988. When one of the firm's partners became the Ohio Attorney General, Mr. Van Niel followed him to serve in the Ohio Attorney General's Public Utilities Commission Practice Group. He volunteered for a second tour of duty with the Supreme Court of Ohio in 1993 as the Court's Utilities Law Master Commissioner. Moving from Ohio to Nebraska to Houston (to join his wife at each of her academic positions), Mr. Van Niel worked as a consultant until 2004, when he joined the Harris County Community Service and Corrections Department as Staff Counsel. In yet another move to satisfy his wife's wanderlust, this time to Las Vegas, Mr. Van Niel became the a consultant in regulatory and governmental affairs to Nye County in the Yucca Mountain licensing proceeding in October 2007.

Bala Dharan, Ph.D., CPA, is Visiting Professor of Accounting at Harvard Law School and J. Howard Creekmore Professor Emeritus at Rice University. He is also a Vice President at CRA International, a business and litigation consulting firm. He has published widely in major accounting and finance journals, and is the co-author of three textbooks on financial accounting and finance topics. He has been invited three times by the United States Congress to testify on financial reporting, structured finance, and accounting standards. He has extensive litigation and business consulting experience on financial accounting and disclosures, transactions analysis, damages, and valuation issues. He has previously served on the business school faculties at Rice University and Northwestern University, and has been a visiting professor of accounting at the Harvard Business School and at University of California, Berkeley.

CONTRIBUTING AUTHORS (IN ALPHABETICAL ORDER)

JOHN C. COFFEE, JR. is the Adolf A. Berle Professor of Law at Columbia Law School.

CYNTHIA COOPER is the President of Cynthia Cooper Consulting, and she provides consulting and training services in internal audits, internal controls, governance, and ethics.

LYNNE L. DALLAS is a Professor of Law at the University of San Diego School of Law.

BALA G. DHARAN is a Visiting Professor of Accounting at the Harvard Law School and J. Howard Creekmore Professor Emeritus at Rice University. He is also a Vice President at CRA International.

SARAH HELENE DUGGIN is an Associate Professor of Law and the Director, Law and Public Policy Program, at the Columbus School of Law, the Catholic University of America.

JOSÉ M. GABILONDO is an Assistant Professor of Law at the College of Law, Florida International University.

MALCOLM GLADWELL is a staff writer for *The New Yorker* magazine. He is also the author of the books THE TIPPING POINT, BLINK, and OUTLIERS.

KENT GREENFIELD is a Professor of Law and Law Fund Research Scholar at Boston College Law School.

KRISTEN HAYS is a reporter for the *Houston Chronicle*.

KATHERINE R. KRUSE is an Associate Professor of Law at the William S. Boyd School of Law, University of Nevada, Las Vegas.

GEORGE W. KUNEY is the W.P. Toms Professor of Law and the Director of the Clayton Center for Entrepreneurial Law at the University of Tennessee College of Law.

DONALD C. LANGEVOORT is the Thomas Aquinas Reynolds Professor of Law and Co-Director of the Joint Degree in Law and Business Administration at Georgetown University Law Center.

JEFFREY M. LIPSHAW is an Associate Professor of Law at Suffolk University Law School.

DAVID J. LUBAN is a University Professor at Georgetown University Law Center.

JONATHAN R. MACEY is Deputy Dean and the Sam Harris Professor of Corporate Law, Corporate Finance, and Securities Law at Yale Law School.

PETER S. MARGULIES is a Professor of Law at the Roger Williams University School of Law.

COLIN P. MARKS is an Assistant Professor of Law at St. Mary's University School of Law.

STANLEY MILGRAM was a social psychologist at Yale University.

GERALDINE SZOTT MOOHR is the Alumnae Professor of Law at the University of Houston Law Center.

MARLEEN A. O'CONNOR is a Professor of Law at Stetson University College of Law.

FRANK PARTNOY is a Professor of Law at the University of San Diego School of Law.

ANDREW M. PERLMAN is an Associate Professor of Law at Suffolk University Law School.

ROBERT PRENTICE is a Professor in the Information, Risk and Operations Management Department of the McCombs School of Business at the University of Texas at Austin.

NANCY B. RAPOPORT is the Gordon Silver Professor of Law at the William S. Boyd School of Law, University of Nevada, Las Vegas.

ROBERTA ROMANO is the Oscar M. Ruebhausen Professor of Law at Yale Law School and the Director of the Yale Law School Center for the Study of Corporate Law.

MARK A. SARGENT is Dean and Professor of Law at Villanova University Law School.

STEVEN L. SCHWARCZ is the Stanley A. Star Professor of Law and Business at the Duke University School of Law.

DAVID ARTHUR SKEEL, JR. is the S. Samuel Arsht Professor of Corporate Law at the University of Pennsylvania Law School.

JEFFREY D. VAN NIEL is an attorney in Las Vegas, Nevada.

W. BRADLEY WENDEL is a Professor of Law at Cornell Law School.

CHRISTOPHER J. WHELAN is a Visiting Professor at the Washington & Lee University School of Law and the Associate Director of International Law Programs at the University of Oxford.

DUANE WINDSOR is the Lynette S. Autrey Professor of Management at the Jesse H. Jones Graduate School of Management, Rice University.

L. RANDALL WRAY is a Professor of Economics at the University of Missouri–Kansas City.

Enron and Other Corporate Fiascos: The Corporate Scandal Reader

Edited by

Nancy B. Rapoport
Jeffrey D. Van Niel
Bala G. Dharan

Front cover art: Jeffrey D. Van Niel, "Corporate Fiascos: Has Anyone Seen the Boss?"

Back cover art: Jeffrey D. Van Niel, "Enron, Titanic, and the Perfect Storm."

195 Broadway, 9th Floor
New York, NY 10007
Phone Toll Free 1–877–888–1330
Fax (212) 367–6799
foundation-press.com

Printed in the United States of America

ISBN 978–1–59941–336–5

TEXT IS PRINTED ON 10% POST CONSUMER RECYCLED PAPER

CONTENTS

FOREWORD

Enron? Aren't we "over" Enron by now? After all, the company's debacle occurred in 2001, and it's almost 2009 already. The major criminal trials are over, Ken Lay is no longer alive, and Jeff Skilling and Andy Fastow are in prison. The Enron bankruptcy has wound down, and most people who didn't own Enron stock have moved on with their lives. So why do we need a second edition of this book?

In part, we wanted to put out a second edition of this book because our reason for *"Enron I"*—that people would study Enron's failure and learn from it—hasn't really been accomplished. In fact, we've had as many corporate fiascos since Enron as before: for example, we've watched our housing values decline and the availability of credit tighten up due to the subprime mortgage crisis, and we've watched board chairs and lawyers fall from grace (remember the Hewlett-Packard "pretexting" scandal?*) thanks to some very bad decisions. So we've dedicated this second edition to the study of a different issue. Because humans obviously aren't going to stop making large-scale mistakes (also known as "future Enrons"), we decided to study why people continue making the same mistakes over and over. Why *haven't* we learned from Enron? If we can't prevent future Enrons, can we at least learn the warning signs for making Enron-sized mistakes?

This edition of our book is divided into six print chapters and one website: http://www.thecorporatescandalreader.com. The website contains many of the articles from the first edition of the book, as well as some new articles that we think are useful. We'll do our best to keep updating this website with more thoughts and information about various corporate scandals. (As you're studying, keep checking the website for ideas for class discussion and seminar papers!) In Chapter 1 of the print version, we review some of the key issues surrounding Enron, and we wrap up some previously unanswered issues (like who went to prison). Chapter 2 focuses on what conclusions we can draw from the Enron-era abuses, without bringing in other ways of looking at corporate scandals generally. In Chapter 3, we bring in some social science research regarding why smart people can make some extremely dumb decisions. Chapter 4 covers how we might be able to add some structural safeguards to current governance structure. Those safeguards won't prevent Enron-type mistakes, but they might help to reduce the frequency or severity of those mistakes. In Chapter 5, we cover some key ethics issues that crop up in corporate scandals. Finally, in Chapter 6, we turn to some lessons that

* If you don't remember that scandal, take a look at http://news.lp.findlaw.com/legalnews/lit/hewlett-packard/index.html.

we can eke out from the Enron-era abuses, and we explore one of the current corporate scandals—the subprime mortgage crisis.

We hope that you'll find our second edition useful. Many of you will go on to careers that will include leadership roles and other positions of power. If we've helped you become more aware of the types of mistakes that even the smartest people can make, then this book might keep your own organizations out of any subsequent editions of THE CORPORATE SCANDAL READER.

ACKNOWLEDGMENTS

We could not have done this revision without the hard work of many people, including Jennifer Gross, the tenacious Annette Mann, research assistants Emelia Allen, Gabrielle Angle, Robert Arroyo, Nicole Cannizzaro, and Matthew Seaton, and the good folks at Foundation Press, who waited patiently for the manuscript. Extra thanks go to Sharon Ray, who turned the draft into an actual book. I want to thank my wonderful husband, Jeff Van Niel, for his editing (and art) skills, used to great advantage on both editions of this book; my father, Morris Rapoport, who raised me to follow the news; and Steve Errick, now at Wolters Kluwer, who came up with the idea for the Enron book in the first place. I also owe Bala Dharan, my co-editor on the first edition of this book, a huge debt of gratitude for his participation in the project from the very beginning. For me, this book is dedicated to both of my parents, Morris and Shirley Rapoport. Mom was a writer and a reporter and, for my money, one of the very best.

NBR

I want to thank my loving wife, Nancy Rapoport, who invited me to participate in this effort from the beginning. She has been patient and understanding about my hectic schedule and has encouraged me to use what is left of my artistic skills to craft the cover art on this and the first edition of the Enron book. Surprisingly, Nancy appreciates my editing skills and has made use of them since the beginning of our relationship. I have mastered the short sentence. I would also like to thank my exceedingly sweet cat Shadow for her tenacity and perseverance in following her never-ending quest of walking on my keyboard and adding her own edits to our work. Finally, I must thank Grace, the alpha female in our household; without her, ours would be a squeakless habitat.

JDVN

I am grateful to Nancy Rapoport and Jeff Van Niel for the opportunity to work with them on this project. It has been a delight to get to know Nancy personally and experience first-hand the boundless energy and enthusiasm she brings to everything she does. I also want to express my heartfelt thanks to my wife of thirty years, Vidya, and our beloved son, Anand, for their love, encouragement, and support.

BGD

Chapter 1

Background: The Enron-Era Scandals

We admit that we've been obsessed by Enron ever since the first hints of disaster started playing in our then-local newspaper, right around the time that Jeffrey Skilling resigned as Enron's Chief Executive Officer in August 2000. For one thing, we were living in Houston at the time, and Houston was the epicenter of Enron's universe. For another thing, we saw Enron's unraveling as a Greek tragedy: smart people, greed, hubris, and, ultimately, death (both of the company, and of some of the key players, including Ken Lay, who had been the "face" of Enron).

This chapter is designed to give you a flavor of what really happened at Enron. Kristen Hays, one of the top reporters on the Enron saga, walks you through the trials that occurred after the first edition of this book was published. Then we'll take some of the essays from the first edition, all of which will take you through some of the particulars of Enron's story. You'll learn how Enron did its various deals, why various gatekeepers didn't catch the fraud earlier (in particular, what Enron's lawyers perhaps should have considered at the time), and what happened to the "whistleblowers" (if that's what they were). You'll also read some lessons that you could have learned from the Enron disaster. (Too bad that few people actually did learn anything from Enron.)

As you review the essays in this chapter, ask yourself whether you'd have acted any differently back then if you'd been an Enron executive, an accountant who worked on Enron, an in-house or outside lawyer for Enron, or an analyst rating Enron. In subsequent chapters, we explore why your first instinct—"I wouldn't have made those mistakes!"—might not be correct.

As you read this chapter, you're getting just a taste of our authors' analyses of the Enron scandal. The most difficult part of editing the second edition was deciding which pieces from the first edition we'd leave in the print version of this book and which pieces we would have to—reluctantly—consign to the website that accompanies this edition. (Kristen Hays's piece, which follows, is the only new essay included in this chapter. The rest of the essays in this chapter are from the first edition.)

We'd hate for you to miss out on the other great essays that we had to cut, so please see the website for the following essays:

- Steven Harmon Wilson, Ph.D., *Malefactors of Great Wealth: A Short History of "Aggressive" Accounting*
- Edward J. Janger, Brandeis, *Business Ethics, and Enron*
- Jeffrey D. Van Niel & Nancy B. Rapoport, *Dr. Jekyll & Mr. Skilling: How Enron's Public Image Morphed from the Most Innovative Company in the Fortune 500 to the Most Notorious Company Ever*
- Bala G. Dharan & William R. Bufkins, *Red Flags in Enron's Reporting of Revenues and Key Financial Measures*
- John C. Coffee, Jr., *Understanding Enron: "It's About the Gatekeepers, Stupid"*
- Matthew J. Barrett, *Enron and Andersen—What Went Wrong and Why Similar Audit Failures Could Happen Again*
- Jacqueline Lang Weaver, *Can Energy Markets Be Trusted? The Effect of the Rise and Fall of Enron on Energy Markets*
- Dr. Michelle Michot Foss, *Enron and the Energy Market Revolution*
- Charles J. Tabb, *The Enron Bankruptcy*
- Edward J. Janger, *The Enron Bankruptcy: Financial Engineering, Recharacterization, Substantive Consolidation, and Avoidance*
- Douglas G. Baird & Robert K. Rasmussen, *Four (or Five) Easy Lessons from Enron*
- Douglas G. Baird, *Enron and the Long Shadow of Stat. 13 Eliz.*
- Victor B. Flatt, *The Enron Story and Environmental Policy*
- Geraldine Szott Moohr, *An Enron Lesson: The Modest Role of Criminal Law in Preventing Corporate Crime*
- Colleen E. Medill, *Enron and the Pension System*
- John H. Langbein, *What's Wrong with Employer Stock Pension Plans*
- Troy A. Paredes, *Enron: The Board, Corporate Governance, and Some Thoughts on the Role of Congress*
- Roger C. Cramton, *Enron and the Corporate Lawyer: A Primer on Legal and Ethical Issues*
- Deborah L. Rhode & Paul D. Paton, *Lawyers, Ethics, and Enron*
- W. Amon Burton & John S. Dzienkowski, *Reexamining the Role of In-House Lawyers After the Conviction of Arthur Andersen*
- Robert W. Gordon, *A New Role for Lawyers?: The Corporate Counselor After Enron*
- Robert W. Gordon, *Why Lawyers Can't Just Be Hired Guns*
- Susan P. Koniak, *When the Hurlyburly's Done: The Bar's Struggle with the SEC*
- Lawrence J. Fox, *The Academics Have It Wrong: Hysteria Is No Substitute for Sound Public Policy Analysis*
- Jacqueline Lang Weaver, *Lessons for Teaching Energy Law*
- Bala G. Dharan, *Business Education and Corporate Accounting Scandals: Lessons on Accounting Information and Investor Trust*

Enron at Eye Level: A Reporter's View of the Trials

Kristen Hays[*]

On a clear, frigid day in December 2006, former Enron Corp. CEO Jeffrey Skilling surrendered his freedom at a southern Minnesota prison across the road from a frozen cornfield. He wasn't the last ex-Enron executive to go to prison for crimes committed at the onetime corporate jewel that had flamed out in a vicious scandal just five years and 11 days earlier. Nor did he enter the sliding glass door into the foyer of the Federal Correctional Institution in tiny, picturesque Waseca in order to serve a 24-year, four-month term for killing the company he had earnestly professed to love.

But for all intents and purposes, he may as well have entered Waseca as a murderer. His transformation from corporate star to Federal Inmate No. 29296-179 was what thousands of ex-Enron employees who had been left jobless and holding nearly worthless stock had been waiting for. They finally had their pound of flesh from this 53-year-old.

There was a time when Jeff Skilling spoke and people listened. He could move markets, instill fear, and charm analysts taken by his plainspoken nature. He could inspire glowing profiles by journalists impressed by his accomplishments. On this cold day in 2006, though, he was wounded, but not beaten. He reported to prison as ordered, without need of federal officers or shackles, marking the end of an era of corporate scandals that Enron's failure had touched off and repeatedly inflamed. He remained unwavering in his insistence that he had done nothing wrong and that his company had been viciously undercut by a confluence of rapid erosion of market confidence, by a vulnerably low credit rating, by the exposure of questionable financial structures that had been approved by scads of accountants and lawyers, by frightened former friends and colleagues who turned on him to avoid the expensive and losing gamble he had taken with a jury, and by overzealous prosecutors hell-bent on making him pay.

Skilling spent his first two minutes in prison hugging his wife, brother, and longtime assistant. Then the trio who had accompanied him left the building and drove away in a rented silver Jeep Liberty. Skilling made his first trek across the yard of the

[*] Reporter for the HOUSTON CHRONICLE.

college-campus-turned-prison, easily visible in blue jeans and a yellow shirt behind the 10-foot fence topped with barbed wire. The black topcoat he had worn when he walked inside had already been surrendered.

Inmate No. 29296-179 was home.

Exactly five years before Skilling's sentencing, he had been in a Florida hotel room, listening to a disastrous conference call during which Ken Lay failed to convince Wall Street to keep the Enron faith. Skilling had abruptly resigned from Enron in mid-August 2006, ending an 11-year career with Enron that had brought him great wealth and prestige. With Lay's blessing, he had directed Enron's rebirth from a natural gas pipeline company into a ruthless trading juggernaut that seemingly could do no wrong. Though few believed that Skilling had really stepped down to spend time with his family after succeeding Lay as CEO only six months earlier—an oft-used but rarely believed excuse for quitting, in the corporate world—the swirling dust caused by his departure had settled quickly because Lay stepped back into the role, assuring employees and investors that all would be fine. For a while, they believed Lay, who had founded Enron through the merger of his Houston Natural Gas with Nebraska's InterNorth in 1985.

A a week before that conference call, Enron had unveiled its third-quarter 2001 earnings that announced a $638 million loss. Enron hadn't had a quarterly loss since 1997. The company also wiped out $1.2 billion in shareholder equity. Something had to be wrong, but no one could yet grasp what would later become clear: Enron's fabulous success had been undermined by years of schemes to guarantee the appearance of constant growth. When shares hit a high of more than $90 in August 2000, Enron was a success story that the business press and Wall Street showered with praise.

The stock price didn't keep rising as Skilling and Lay said it would. It began to fall steadily, and it kept falling after Lay handed the CEO reins to Skilling in February 2001. Lay stayed on as chairman, but Skilling grew increasingly despondent over the falling price and the departure of members of his inner circle, a smart gang of executives who had become multimillionaires under his wing. The complicated financial structures that had kept much of Enron's massive debt and poorly performing assets off its books were proving unsustainable because they needed a high stock price to stay afloat. New ventures that Skilling had banked on—broadband and retail energy divisions—weren't meeting expectations. The party was coming to an end.

Enron survived Skilling's abrupt departure, a move that infuriated many of his colleagues who thought him selfish for bailing out when things got rough. Lay stepped in to calm investors and employees, and for a few weeks it worked—until the company unveiled its losses. Believers turned into doubters, and a string of desperate moves to survive—drawing down $3 billion in bank loans, ousting Chief Financial Officer Andrew Fastow when banks refused to deal with him any more, accepting an ill-fated offer from Dynegy to buy the company—made no difference. On December 2, 2001, Enron filed what was then the biggest corporate bankruptcy in U.S. history. A day later, thousands of employees poured out of Enron's gleaming downtown Houston headquarters, out of work, with shares worth about as much as Confederate bonds after the Civil War.

Standing before U.S. District Judge Simeon Lake in Houston to be sentenced on October 23, 2006, Skilling professed his innocence. He said the company might have survived if its credit rating had been higher. He said he couldn't understand the conventional wisdom that he had no remorse. He said he had friends, "good men," who had died—his best friend and former Enron vice chairman, Cliff Baxter, of a self-inflicted gunshot wound as the scandal swirled in its early days in January 2002, and Lay of heart disease just six weeks after they were convicted together on May 25, 2006 of participating in a massive fraud that spanned the company's finance, trading, broadband, and retail energy divisions.

An unsympathetic Lake hammered Skilling with multi-decade prison terms for 19 counts of conspiracy, securities fraud, insider trading, and making false statements to auditors. The punishment was just eight months shy of the 25-year term that former WorldCom CEO Bernard Ebbers began serving a month earlier for orchestrating the telecom company's $11 billion accounting fraud.

Had Lay lived, he would have faced a double-digit punishment as well. The disgraced chairman was convicted of six counts of conspiracy, wire fraud, and securities fraud alongside Skilling, and another four counts of bank fraud and making false statements to banks in a separate case tried before Lake rather than a jury. But he hadn't been sentenced or launched an appeal, so seven days before Skilling was sentenced, Lake vacated Lay's convictions, leaving him with a clean record in death.

That left Skilling to receive the most severe punishment of anyone ensnared in the federal government's sprawling investigation. Shortly after the bankruptcy, the Justice Department created an Enron Task Force, bringing in prosecutors from San Francisco, New York, and other cities, many of whom were experienced in Mafia prosecutions that involved getting to the top through underlings. FBI agents trained in accounting and securities fraud also were appointed to the specialized squad.

Of 20 people who entered guilty pleas ranging from obstruction of justice to securities fraud to conspiracy, two later withdrew their pleas and 17 were sentenced. Nine went to prison, with sentences ranging from one to six years. Six received probation, including the only three Enron traders ever charged with manipulating the California power market in 2000 and 2001, when consumers were overcharged billions of dollars for capacity problems largely created by exploiting loopholes in the state's convoluted electricity deregulation system.

But of the 14 indicted who either went to or intended to go to trial—13 individuals and one company, former Enron auditor Arthur Andersen LLP—the Task Force's ultimate record is far from impressive.

Andersen's 2002 conviction was unanimously overturned by the U.S. Supreme Court in 2005.[1] Of six defendants in a 2004 trial centered on a loan that prosecutors said was disguised as an asset sale to allow Enron to book year-end 1999 earnings, one was acquitted, one didn't appeal, and four former Merrill Lynch & Co. executives, each of whom served several months to a year in prison, saw most of their convictions over-

---

[1] *See* Arthur Andersen LLP v. United States, 544 U.S. 696 (2005).

turned by an appeals panel in August 2006.[2] The 2005 trial of five broadband division executives ended with a handful of acquittals and with jurors deadlocked on dozens of other counts after hearing three months of tedious testimony about whether the company's broadband network had ever worked as touted. Of two broadband division executives retried in 2006, one was acquitted while the other was convicted and then cleared by the trial judge, based on the same ruling that overturned the Merrill executives' convictions. He awaits a third trial in 2009. The other three broadband executives in 2008 lost an appeal to throw out most of the remaining, pared-down cases against them. Two await trial in late 2008, and the third in early 2009.

In the Merrill case, a split 5th U.S. Circuit Court of Appeals panel deemed as flawed the prosecution's theory that the defendants deprived Enron of their honest services by participating in sham deals that allowed the company to manipulate its earnings. That same prosecution theory plays a critical role in Skilling's appeal. The Justice Department chose not to appeal the ruling, in order to avoid a final decision before Skilling's appeal.

THE FIRST TRIAL

Arthur Andersen

By the time Andersen went to trial in May 2002, it was clear there wouldn't be much of a firm left if an acquittal was in its future. Andersen disclosed in January that year that its Houston office had destroyed literally tons of Enron-related audit documents, both paper and electronic, in late October and early November 2001, as the Enron scandal burst open. The company was under orders from the U.S. Securities and Exchange Commission to conduct its audits properly and comply with securities laws, having been disciplined for signing off on faulty audits for Sunbeam and Waste Management. The Waste Management case involved inflated earnings from 1993 to 1996, and Andersen had paid a $7 million fine to the SEC earlier in 2001. The Andersen global risk partner who signed the Waste Management-related agreement to toe the line, Gary Goolsby, had repeatedly said the firm had "learned its lesson," according to then-SEC investigator Thomas Newkirk.

As Enron prepared to release its third-quarter earnings in October 2001, Andersen executives in Houston and at the firm's headquarters in Chicago had repeated meetings and conference calls to discuss Enron, and a junior lawyer for the firm, Nancy Temple, took detailed notes. Months later, she would essentially be tried in absentia through those notes, which prosecutors said showed that she was aware of Andersen's past mistakes and that the firm had a signed a permanent pledge to comply with securities laws. Andersen's willingness to sign off on misleading financial statements for Enron, a lucrative client that paid the firm $1 million a week, brought about a third and devastating strike.

---

[2] *See* United States v. Brown, 459 F.3d 509 (5th Cir. 2006).

From the time that Andersen disclosed the document destruction, the firm and its lawyers sought to cut a deal with the Justice Department. On January 15, 2002, the firm fired David Duncan, who had been its lead auditor on the Enron account in Houston, and cast him aside as a rogue who violated company policy.

But the Justice Department wanted an admission from the firm that someone from inside Andersen might have broken the law. Andersen refused, insisting that no one had destroyed documents with criminal intent to thwart investigators. Like other accounting firms, Andersen had a "document retention" policy that called for destruction of drafts and superfluous documents used in audits and retention of the final product. The policy aimed to protect client confidentiality while destroying drafts that showed disagreements in interpretation of accounting rules or that could potentially be misinterpreted in a civil or criminal case.

In mid-March 2002, the firm was indicted for obstruction of justice. Company lawyers appeared in court for Andersen's plea of "not guilty" while hundreds of Houston's Andersen employees gathered outside, wearing "I Am Arthur Andersen" T-shirts, angry that their jobs were threatened when most had never touched an Enron audit. But the damage was done. That same month, companies across the country held annual shareholder meetings and fired Andersen, while entire offices of Andersen auditors worldwide bolted to other firms. The firm—with 28,000 employees in the United States and 85,000 worldwide—was crumbling.

In April 2002, the task force got its first cooperator when David Duncan pleaded guilty to obstruction. But the case wasn't black and white. Much of the trial boiled down to the timing and interpretation of e-mails and discussions of what to retain and what to destroy.

On the government's side at trial was Andrew Weissmann, a well-versed Mob prosecutor from New York; Samuel Buell, another Mob prosecutor from Boston; and Matthew Friedrich, a Virginia prosecutor with ties to Texas. Andersen's frontman was Rusty Hardin, a member of Houston's elite defense bar, with 15 years as a state prosecutor under his belt. Presiding was U.S. District Judge Melinda Harmon, one of the few federal judges in Houston who hadn't needed to recuse herself from Enron matters because of stock ownership or some kind of relationship with someone who worked at the company.

The government said that Andersen deliberately obstructed justice by destroying documents when the firm knew that the SEC was looking into Enron's accounting. Prosecutors said the motive to thwart the investigation was to avoid yet another rebuke and fine from the agency. "Those (Andersen) partners knew the law was coming and those partners made a simple series of choices, which is what this case is all about," Friedrich told the jury in the government's opening statement.

Andersen countered that document destruction took place as per company policy, and there was no criminal intent involved. Hardin said in Andersen's opening statement that e-mails and documents reflected differences between the firm's Chicago headquarters and its Enron team in Houston over how to approach Enron audits, and such internal arguments are expected to be destroyed under the document retention policy. Also, he repeatedly argued that the government's evidence stemmed greatly from reams of documents that were preserved and turned over by Andersen, further bolstering the firm's lack of criminal intent.

Prosecutors sought to show that Andersen knew it was playing with fire with Enron years before the shredding by displaying a parody written by an Andersen partner in 1995 to the tune of the Eagles' "Hotel California." Titled "The Hotel Kenneth Lay-A," the parody lyrics included, "They're livin' it up at the Hotel Cram It Down Ya/When the suits arrive/Bring your alibis." But the partner who wrote it, James Hecker, testified that he penned the parody out of envy that Andersen devoted so many resources to Enron audits while other partners, like himself, had to make do with less in handling books of other companies.

Documents and e-mails dominated the six-week trial, but the chief document was an e-mail that Temple had sent to Andersen partner and practice manager Michael Odom on October 12, 2001. That e-mail said, "It will be helpful to make sure we have complied with the policy," and to remind employees of the document retention policy's existence. During a conference call with Andersen partners on October 20, shortly after the SEC announced that it had opened an informal inquiry into partnerships run by then-Enron Chief Financial Officer Andrew Fastow to conduct asset deals with Enron, Temple twice emphasized compliance with the document retention policy.

Odom did not testify in the trial, but jurors watched a videotape of an October 10, 2001 training session that he had conducted for audit team managers in which he said destruction of documents before litigation is filed is "great" because "whatever might have been of interest to anybody is gone and irretrievable." The document retention policy was central to the training. Coupled with Temple's e-mail sent two days later, the implication was that Odom and Temple urged compliance with the policy as the Enron scandal loomed.

The SEC did not take interest in Enron's finances and accounting until after the company revealed its third-quarter losses (four days after Temple hit "send"). Also, Emily Madison, an Andersen partner, testified that, two days before Odom gave his presentation, she asked him what should be done with documents from the account of a company that had fired Andersen. She said his e-mailed reply was that the policy said "we have no need to retain anything" except papers that support final audit conclusions.

Carl Bass, a partner with Andersen's Professional Standards Group, an elite group of accountants who advised colleagues on sticky issues, said that he didn't take Odom's October 10 presentation as a discreet instruction to destroy documents. Bass's view carried weight because he had a history of being openly critical toward Enron's accounting practices. In fact, Bass had been kicked off Enron's audit team because of complaints from the energy company's top accountants that he was too caustic and "rule oriented."

Patricia Grutzmacher, an accountant on Duncan's Enron audit team, testified that all the team members were required to keep a shred box at their desks for Enron documents because Enron was "very, very concerned about their [sic] confidentiality related to any information."

But at the October 23 meeting, she recalled Duncan as saying, "I'm not telling you to go shred a bunch of documents or anything, but you need to make sure you're in compliance with the policy." Two other accountants testified that Duncan and another partner, Thomas Bauer, had told them about the SEC's informal inquiry earlier that day, but when they heard Duncan advise compliance with the policy at the later meeting, neither linked the two issues as code to destroy documents to keep them out of the SEC's possession. Both said they threw out old handwritten notes, drafts, and extraneous documents.

However, Shane Philpot, another accountant in Andersen's Portland, Oregon office, which oversaw accounting for Portland General Electric, then Enron's Oregon utility, said that he had directed his team to keep all Enron-related audit documents after receiving a reminder of the policy because "it seemed to be the conservative thing to do."

Duncan was the much-anticipated star witness. Tall and unemotional, he said simply when he began testifying, "I obstructed justice." Then he described the events leading up to that conference call and the document destruction. He said he sometimes disagreed with how Enron worded its disclosures, but didn't refuse to sign off on anything. He believed Enron's accounting was proper, though aggressive, and regularly sought input from higher-ups on how to handle Enron matters. And he didn't act on October 12 when Temple sent the e-mail reminding Odom of the policy.

And when he described the October 23, 2001 meeting that he had called to advise of the policy, he said that the mood was calm. He told the staff about the policy and said they should follow it. He didn't wave his arms, raise his voice, or otherwise issue an urgent plea to shred everything and shred it immediately. Members of his staff who testified in the trial backed up his recollections.

"I told them not to do anything more or less than follow the policy," Duncan testified.

He said after he told his staff of the policy, he and they started destroying what they thought were extraneous documents. An Andersen manager who ran the "shred room" in the firm's Houston office said that the Enron team sent much more paper than usual in October, in 18 to 20 footlocker-like trunks. The job overwhelmed the firm's in-house shredding capabilities, so Andersen hired a shredding company to destroy tons of paper.

John Riley, a former SEC corporate finance investigator who handled SEC matters for Andersen, went to Houston on October 26 to look into Enron's accounting. He said he thought he heard a shredder grinding away in the offices of Andersen's Enron audit team and asked Duncan about it. Duncan told him there was an onsite shredder for routine destruction of confidential client information.

"My response to him was: 'Well, this wouldn't be the best time in the world for you guys to be shredding a bunch of stuff," Riley testified. He also referred to Andersen's post-indictment demise when noting that Enron was among the firm's most high-risk clients apt to use aggressive accounting. "We have—or we used to—have lots of max-risk clients," Riley said.

The shredding continued until the firm received a subpoena from the SEC on November 9, 2001. Shannon Adlong, Duncan's assistant, sent an e-mail to the employees instructing, "No more shredding." Duncan said he believed that it was acceptable to destroy documents until the subpoena had been issued.

When Hardin began cross-examining Duncan, he zeroed in on whether Duncan had actually committed a crime by telling his staff to destroy potential evidence to thwart an investigation. The question arose of whether he actually had committed a crime, or had convinced himself that he had done so out of fear that he could face years in prison away from his family, having already been cast aside by his company.

Temple invoked her Fifth Amendment right against self-incrimination by mail and declined to testify. However, in January 2002, she testified before Congress alongside other Andersen executives. "I never counseled any shredding or destruction of documents. I only wish that someone would have raised the question," she said at that time. After her testimony, she learned that she was a target in the Justice Department's investigation. During the trial, outside of the jury's presence, Buell called Temple the government's central witness.

Two other Andersen employees invoked their Fifth Amendment rights not to testify as well: Bauer, one of Duncan's Enron audit lieutenants who oversaw Enron's use of reserves; and Kate Agnew, a manager. Bauer invoked his Fifth Amendment right by letter, but Agnew did so in court, though at a bench conference outside the presence of the jury. Hardin accused prosecutors of using a frightened Agnew to intimidate other potential witnesses who could help the defense by parading her in court to demonstrate that "they had better think long and hard about testifying."

A constant theme throughout the trial was Harmon's alleged favoritism toward the prosecution and frequent open tension with Hardin. She sustained more objections from the prosecution than the defense, and she displayed her temper when Hardin openly challenged her. At one point, she ordered him to sit down, and when he did not comply immediately, a court security officer approached him on her orders to force him to sit down. He sat down when the officer was in front of the bench, a few feet from the defense table.

Enmity also was apparent between Hardin and the prosecution team. He openly referred to them as "whiny little babies" when they complained during bench conferences that Hardin asked improper questions, forcing them to frequently jump up to object. At Hardin's retort, the judge warned him, "I don't want to take draconian measures against you."

The case went to the jury on June 5, and for the first seven days of deliberations, the panel asked no questions or otherwise offered no clues about its deliberations. On the seventh day, the panel sent out a note saying that it was deadlocked. After a 20-minute discussion with lawyers from both sides, and over vehement objections from the defense, Harmon removed a sentence from the Allen Charge that reminds jurors that they must render a not-guilty verdict if "evidence fails to remove reasonable doubt." Then she told jurors it was their duty to agree on a verdict if they can do so "without rendering your conscientious conviction" and sent them back to keep trying.

The next day another note emerged, asking if they had to agree that the same person acted knowingly and with corrupt intent if all believed that someone did, but disagreed on who it was. On June 14, the ninth day of deliberations, Harmon noted that she could not find a parallel case on which to base a ruling, and she decided that jurors could disagree on which individual Andersen employee or employees "acted knowingly and with corrupt intent" as long as all of them believed that someone did. She openly fretted about the ruling, saying she appeared to be breaking legal ground. "I'm kind of in a position of a case of first impression, which is terrifying for a district judge," she said.

The jury returned the next morning, and within half an hour, announced that it had reached a verdict. Guilty. The Enron Task Force had bagged its first conviction.

As a company, Andersen was barely breathing. Its Houston offices were empty, and contents would later be auctioned off. A few hundred workers remained at its headquarters and training center in Chicago, their main task reduced to dealing with myriad pending lawsuits. But the lawyers weren't giving up. At the prosecutors' request, Harmon gave an instruction to the jury that allowed the panel to convict without first finding the presence of criminal intent, and that instruction proved critical in Andersen's appeal.

A three-judge panel of the 5th U.S. Circuit Court of Appeals affirmed the conviction, calling Andersen part of Enron's "supporting cast." Andersen appealed to the U.S. Supreme Court, which unanimously overturned the conviction in June 2005. The 11-page decision written by then-Chief Justice William Rehnquist came just a month after the high court heard arguments.

The opinion said that Harmon had erred in giving that instruction because the jury did not have to find criminal intent and could convict if the firm "honestly and sincerely believed its conduct was lawful."

"Indeed, it is striking how little culpability the instructions required," Rehnquist wrote.

In November 2005, the government decided that it would not re-try Andersen. And in December of that year, Duncan withdrew his guilty plea on the same principle because he had not admitted to criminal intent when he entered his plea. The government agreed to the withdrawal but retained the right to re-indict him as prosecutors feverishly prepared for the Lay/Skilling trial, slated to begin in January 2006. Duncan was on the defense teams' potential witness list, but his refusal to testify fueled their contention that the threat that he might be re-indicted was intended to keep him (and his contention that Enron's accounting was proper) out of the Lay/Skilling case. Duncan was not re-indicted.

Guilty Pleas

After the Andersen trial ended, the Task Force poured all of its energy into Enron itself. The first target was Andrew Fastow, the chief financial officer who used his position to skim millions of dollars for himself, his family, and selected friends through complex financial schemes that also helped Enron manipulate its earnings to show constant growth. The Task Force had uncovered some of these schemes and had filed a criminal complaint against three British bankers in June 2002 to send a message to Fastow and his underlings that they were in the crosshairs.

The indictment alleged that the National Westminster Bank bankers (David Bermingham, Giles Darby, and Gary Mulgrew) took part in a scheme in which Enron would buy their employer's interest in a financial vehicle, but the bankers would tell NatWest that the price was much less than Enron actually paid so that they, Fastow, and a few selected Enron executives could pocket the difference. Of the $20 million that Enron paid, NatWest got $1 million and the remaining $19 million was split among Fastow, the bankers, and related others. The indictment got the attention of Michael Kopper, a managing director under Fastow, who was one of the beneficiaries of the NatWest scheme. He had left Enron in the summer of 2001 to run LJM2, a partnership that Fastow had created to buy Enron assets that Enron wanted to unload. Kopper had pocketed about $16 million from Fastow's schemes, dating back to 1997.

In August 2002, Kopper became the first ex-Enron executive to cut a deal. He pleaded guilty to money-laundering conspiracy and conspiracy to commit wire fraud, and the complaint against him described a string of schemes and identified participants, including "Enron's CFO," the "CFO's wife," former Enron treasurer Ben Glisan Jr., Kopper's domestic partner, Fastow's brother, and several LJM2 employees. The complaint also had a forfeiture allegation, revealing the government's intent to seize contents of bank accounts of the identified participants and a new mansion then under construction for the Fastows in Houston's wealthiest enclave, River Oaks.

Fastow was indicted in October 2002, facing what would grow to 98 counts of fraud, conspiracy, and other crimes. The same month, Timothy Belden, once Enron's top West Coast trader, pleaded guilty to conspiracy to defraud the United States for manipulating California's power market in 2000 and 2001.

More guilty pleas followed. In November 2002, Larry Lawyer, a mid-level broadband executive who had taken a five-figure "gift" from Kopper for his work on one of Fastow's early schemes, pleaded guilty to filing a false tax return for failing to identify the money as income. In February 2003, Jeffrey Richter, a trader who had worked for Belden, pleaded guilty to conspiracy to commit wire fraud and making a false statement to a government agency—lying to the FBI—about his participation in California power market manipulation.

Two months later, in April 2003, former Enron trader John Forney was handcuffed and escorted from American Electric Power's trading offices in Columbus, Ohio, on a charge of conspiracy to commit wire fraud for his part in the California market manipulation. Ten counts of wire fraud aiding and abetting would later be added to his indictment.

At this point, the government's investigation had penetrated Enron's finance and trading divisions. Results of its broadband division probe would be unveiled next.

In March 2003, Kevin Howard, the former CFO of Enron's broadband unit, and Michael Krautz, an in-house accountant for the unit, were indicted on securities fraud, wire fraud, making false statements to the FBI, and conspiracy to commit wire and securities fraud charges. The charges stemmed from participating in a two-part deal in 2000 and 2001 to sell future revenues of a video-on-demand venture with Blockbuster Inc. The venture never made a profit and crumbled in March 2001 when Enron and Blockbuster parted ways.

Then in May 2003, a slew of new indictments were handed down. Five defendants were added to the Howard/Krautz indictment, all former broadband executives accused of overhyping the unit's profitability when its broadband network never surpassed the testing stage and a bandwidth trading venture never got off the ground. These defendants were Joseph Hirko and Kenneth Rice, co-CEOs of the unit; strategist Scott Yeager; software executive Rex Shelby; and Kevin Hannon, former chief operating officer of the division. Each faced multiple counts of conspiracy to commit wire and securities fraud, wire fraud, securities fraud, money laundering, and insider trading. Yeager alone faced more than 100 counts.

Two more names were added to Fastow's indictment: Ben Glisan Jr., the former Enron treasurer whose $5,300 investment in a deal identified in Kopper's complaint brought him a $1 million return; and Dan Boyle, a former finance executive who participated in the Nigerian barge scam. That scam involved a loan from Merrill Lynch & Co., disguised as a sale of three power plants mounted on barges off the coast of Nigeria at the end of 1999 so that Enron could appear to have met quarterly earnings targets. (Enron later repurchased those barges, which rendered the "sale" to Merrill Lynch a disguised loan.) Glisan faced multiple counts of conspiracy to commit wire fraud, conspiracy to commit wire and securities fraud, conspiracy to falsify books and records, and money laundering, while Boyle was charged with conspiracy to commit wire fraud and conspiracy to falsify books and records.

And Fastow's wife, Lea, was indicted in a case all her own on six counts of conspiracy to commit wire fraud, money laundering conspiracy, and filing false tax returns, all charges stemming from helping her husband hide ill-gotten income from the Internal Revenue Service. The indictment said that she endorsed kickback checks from Kopper written to the Fastows' two young sons.

Glisan, who had tried to cut a deal before he was indicted but was turned away by prosecutors who didn't think he was completely truthful, pleaded guilty in September 2003 to conspiracy to commit wire and securities fraud and agreed to serve the maximum five-year sentence in prison. He did not have a cooperation agreement and went straight to prison. His plea stemmed from his creation of the Raptors, four financial structures backed by Enron stock that prosecutors said were used to house poor assets and bad investments that the company wanted to be kept off its books. Glisan would begin cooperating with prosecutors a few months later.

Later that month, more indictments sprang from the deal at the center of the charges against Boyle. Three former Merrill Lynch & Co. executives—Daniel Bayly, head of investment banking for the brokerage; James Brown, head of its asset-lease group; and Robert Furst, a liaison to Enron—were each charged with conspiracy to commit wire fraud and three counts of wire fraud. At the same time, the Justice Department announced that it had struck a non-prosecution agreement with Merrill Lynch itself in which the brokerage firm paid a $80 million fine, acknowledged that some of its employees may have broken the law, and stepped up scrutiny of questionable year-end deals requested by clients. The government also appointed an independent monitor to oversee Merrill's adherence to the terms of the agreement for 18 months.

In October 2003, two more indictments in the barge case emerged: William Fuhs, who worked for Brown, and former in-house Enron accountant Sheila Kahanek were charged with wire fraud and conspiracy to commit wire fraud for helping push through the barge deal.

Also in October 2003, David Delainey, who was head of Enron's trading franchise until February 2001, when he became CEO of the retail energy division, pleaded guilty to insider trading for gaining $4.2 million through stock trades when he knew that Enron's publicly reported results didn't truthfully reveal the wobbly state of the company's finances. Delainey, a Canadian citizen, offered himself up to the U.S. government of his own accord, when he could have remained in Canada and out of the prosecutors' reach. He also gained brief attention in the weeks after Enron went bankrupt, when he gave $10,000 to a fund to help employees who had abruptly lost their jobs and needed financial help.

However, the investigation appeared to stall at that point. Fastow had dug in his heels and remained in "fighting" mode after his wife was indicted. That stance changed in January 2004, opening the door for prosecutors to obtain indictments against Richard Causey, former chief accounting officer; Skilling; and Lay.

Lea Fastow's lawyer, Mike DeGeurin, would later reveal that she convinced her husband to enter into plea talks with prosecutors by late 2003. In mid-January 2004, Andrew Fastow pleaded guilty to two counts of conspiracy to commit wire fraud (related to his LJM2 partnership) as a means for Enron to manipulate earnings, and various other transactions, from which he skimmed at least $45 million. His wife pleaded guilty to a felony count of filing a false tax return.

While Fastow was locked into his plea that included his agreement to serve the maximum 10-year prison term for the two conspiracy counts, prosecutors and Lea Fastow's lawyers had agreed that her deal guaranteed that she would serve five months in prison and five months confined at home. The couple's lawyer wanted to ensure that their prison terms wouldn't overlap, so one parent could be home with their two young sons at all times. That caveat caught the attention of Comedy Central's *The Daily Show.* Sitting next to a graphic that showed a picture of the couple with the catchphrase, "2 Fastows 2 Furious," a play on the movie, *2 Fast 2 Furious,* host Jon Stewart joked, "someone has to teach these kids right from wrong."

But U.S. District Judge David Hittner, who presided over Lea Fastow's case, refused to agree up front that she would receive the punishment that the prosecutors and her lawyers wanted. He accepted her plea, but not the plea deal. He ordered a pre-sentence investigation and reserved the right to impose whatever sentence he saw fit. Lea Fastow also reserved the right to withdraw her plea.

More than a week after Fastow pleaded guilty, Richard Causey was indicted on what would grow to 36 counts of conspiracy to commit wire and securities fraud, securities fraud, wire fraud, insider trading, false statements to auditors, and money laundering. In February 2004, Skilling's indictment followed, on 35 counts of conspiracy to commit wire and securities fraud, securities fraud, insider trading, and making false statements to auditors.

The next month, prosecutors said (in a filing that responded to the pre-sentence investigation for Lea Fastow) that her husband's cooperation had proven critical in securing the indictment against Skilling and was "likely to bear additional fruit," though it did not mention Lay by name. The pre-sentence investigation suggested a 10- to 16-month prison term for Lea Fastow, and she was slated to be sentenced in April 2004. The lower end of that range, suggested by federal sentencing guidelines, could be satisfied by the split of five months in prison and five months confined at home that her lawyers and prosecutors wanted, but Hittner retained the final say over her punishment.

On the day that she was to be sentenced for the felony, Lea Fastow withdrew her guilty plea after Hittner refused to agree to the parameters of the plea deal. Hittner scheduled her trial for June and moved it from Houston to Brownsville to avoid a jury pool tainted by publicity about the tangled plea talks. Later that month, prosecutors dropped the six felony tax and conspiracy counts in her indictment and filed a new misdemeanor charge of filing a false tax form, to which she pleaded guilty in May 2004. The switch automatically limited her punishment to the maximum year in prison for a misdemeanor.

Hittner sentenced her to the maximum and chastised prosecutors for seeking an indictment (charging her with six felonies) that later was traded for a single misdemeanor indictment after her husband's cooperation and guilty pleas had been secured. He said that the switch "might be seen as a blatant manipulation of the federal justice system, and is of considerable concern to this court." Linda Lacewell, who briefly served on the Enron Task Force as the lead Fastow prosecutor, responded that resolution of the Fastows' cases would allow the government to pursue executives higher up the chain of the company.

In July 2004, prosecutors secured an indictment charging Lay with 11 counts of conspiracy to commit wire and securities fraud, securities fraud, bank fraud, and making false statements to banks. The conspiracy and securities fraud counts stemmed from the alleged fraud at Enron, while the bank fraud and false statements counts centered on his personal banking, in which he was accused of reneging on written promises not to use bank loans to buy margin stock.

And unlike all the others who had been indicted or pleaded guilty, Lay gave a press conference—in the same hotel meeting room where Enron had held its last shareholder meeting in 2001—to profess his innocence of any wrongdoing. He also gave several media interviews and appeared on CNN's *Larry King Live.* Whereas Skilling had spoken publicly in the early months of the scandal and then eschewed public statements, Lay broke his silence and opened the verbal floodgates, claiming that he had been betrayed by Fastow and that he had tried in vain to save a dying company in late 2001.

"I continue to grieve, as does my family, over the loss of the company and my failure to be able to save it. But failure does not equate to a crime," Lay declared. "I firmly reject any notion that I engaged in any wrongful or criminal activity. Not only are we ready to go to trial, but we are anxious to prove my innocence."

But 2004 brought more guilty pleas as well. In May, Paula Rieker, the former No. 2 executive in investor relations who became the corporate secretary in September 2001, pleaded guilty to insider trading for selling $629,000 in stock in 2001 when she knew that Enron's broadband division's losses were much higher than publicly disclosed. She had remained employed by Enron until shortly before she entered her plea. She had to return a $130,000 retention bonus to Enron because she took it having said that she had not committed any crimes. In July and August, Rice and Hannon broke from the other broadband defendants and pleaded guilty to securities fraud and conspiracy, respectively. Also in August, Forney pleaded guilty to conspiracy to commit wire fraud in California, and Mark Koenig, former head of investor relations, pleaded guilty to aiding and abetting securities fraud. And in October 2004, former assistant treasurer Timothy DeSpain pleaded guilty to conspiracy to defraud the United States for misleading credit rating agencies about Enron's financial health.

More pleas were yet to come. In July 2005, Christopher Calger, a former vice president, pleaded guilty to conspiracy for pushing through a deal involving an interest in a power plant from which Enron had recorded profits that hadn't yet been earned.

Three days after Christmas, in December 2005, just weeks before he was slated to go to trial alongside Skilling and Lay, Causey broke ranks and pleaded guilty to securities fraud. His plea came shortly after prosecutors had turned over witness statements of his actions at Enron, fueling speculation that, once he saw the evidence against him, he chose to cut a deal and take a smaller sentence rather than risk a jury conviction and a prison term of 20 years or more. Causey also agreed to turn over $1.25 million to the government, a signal that he had little money left after paying lawyers for nearly two years. That turnover of funds led the Lay and Skilling legal teams to claim that his inability to pay for an expensive defense at trial prompted his plea rather than any actual guilt.

Causey agreed to serve seven years in prison, and prosecutors retained the right to recommend reducing his term to five years if they were satisfied with his cooperation. But his late entry into the field of cooperators meant that his value to prosecutors was mainly that he allowed them to simplify the Lay/Skilling case. Without Causey among the defendants, prosecutors could shave weeks from the case, because there would be no need for tedious accounting testimony to prove his guilt.

The last round of guilty pleas came from the first round of defendants charged in an Enron fraud. More than five years after they were initially charged in June 2002, three British former bankers each pleaded guilty to a single count of wire fraud in a case centered on their collusion with Fastow to cheat their onetime employer, National Westminster Bank, of millions of dollars in a deal to sell its interest in a Fastow-run financial structure to Enron.

In the weeks before Enron went bankrupt, the bankers had voluntarily spoken with Britain's Financial Services Authority, which is similar to the Securities and Exchange Commission in the United States, to discuss the complicated deal that Fastow had named for his Houston neighborhood, Southampton. Within months, the FSA closed its inquiry without taking action against the bankers, and they learned through media reports in June 2002 that they had been charged in a criminal complaint. They were indicted in September of that year.

The case against them, however, sat untouched for years after its filing, and that delay prompted Kopper to plead guilty and then lead prosecutors to Fastow. The trio of bankers was not arrested in London until April 2004, and at that time they launched an extradition fight that garnered much attention in Britain. But in the United States, their case was a remnant of the early months of the Enron investigation, and they were of little value to prosecutors as potential cooperators. Both Kopper and Fastow had cut plea deals by that time, leaving the bankers with no one to finger.

They were transported to Houston to face seven counts of wire fraud in July 2006, after they had lost every avenue of their extradition battle. They were given restrictive bonds that required them to stay in the Houston area and which prohibited them from having any contact with each other outside of court, pending trial.

The original indictment alleged that the trio had defrauded the bank by taking money and by depriving it of their honest services. After the Fifth Circuit issued its "honest services" *Brown* opinion, prosecutors wiped the honest services allegations from the indictment, leaving what amounted to straight theft. But in November 2007, less than two months before they were to go to trial in early January 2008, the three men struck plea deals. They agreed to serve 37 months in prison, and the government agreed to support their intention to apply to serve the bulk of their punishment in a United Kingdom prison, once they were incarcerated.

THE ENRON TRIALS

Nigerian Barge

The seven-week trial of the four Merrill executives, Boyle, and Kahanek, which began in September 2004, was the first to involve ex-Enron executives. It also was the first and only Enron case to go after Wall Street figures for joining in a deal that could benefit their employer by pleasing Enron and gaining more business from such a lucrative client.

The case stemmed from Enron's desire to sell three power plants mounted on barges off the coast of Nigeria at the end of 1999 (because Enron had set an earnings target that met or exceeded Wall Street analyst expectations and hadn't yet reached it). Failure to meet or exceed such targets could easily trigger a drop in any company's stock price, which was particularly true in the highly bullish late 1990s. But efforts to sell the barges were unsuccessful, largely because potential buyers were put off by Enron's need to get the deal done before the end of the year, leaving any buyers little time to conduct due diligence. Enron grew more and more desperate to find a buyer, but initially refused requests from rushed potential buyers that bordered, at least, on the unusual: that the energy company promise to repurchase the barges at a later date. Fastow even proposed to an unenthusiastic Kopper that LJM2 step in, as Kopper testified in the trial, so "he would look like a hero to Jeff Skilling."

But at the same time, Jeff McMahon, then Enron's treasurer, pitched a deal to Merrill in which the brokerage would buy the barges for $7 million, and Enron would buy back or resell them within six months and pay Merrill a premium of $7.5 million—plus a $250,000 fee. Merrill agreed. In June 2000, LJM2 bought the barges from Merrill for the predetermined amount, though LJM2 also garnered a promise of its own that Enron would buy the barges back from LJM2 or resell them within months. Enron sold those three barges and six others to AES Corp. for $50 million in the latter half of 2000.

The barge deal was not among the more complicated finance structures that became unsustainable in 2001 and helped to fuel Enron's failure. Even the judge presiding over the barge case, U.S. District Judge Ewing Werlein Jr., referred to the trial as "not a big, high-profile Enron case." But prosecutors portrayed it as a sliver of how Enron did business: The company needed to meet earnings targets, and when it couldn't sell assets legitimately, it joined hands with a willing participant in a scheme to disguise a loan as a sale that would later be unwound. Enron got the penny in earnings-per-share that it needed, and Merrill was assured that its participation would be rewarded with more lucrative business.

The government team consisted of Matthew Friedrich, who was part of the Andersen team; Kathryn Ruemmler, a federal prosecutor in Washington; and John Hemann, a federal prosecutor in San Francisco. Noted Houston defense lawyers Dan Cogdell and William Rosch represented Kahanek and Boyle, respectively; and the Merrill defendants each had New York attorneys retained by the brokerage firm: Richard Shaeffer for Bayly, with Houston's Tom Hagemann; Lawrence Zweifach for Brown; Ira Lee Sorkin for Furst; and David Spears for Fuhs.

Bayly was Merrill's global head and chairman of investment banking. Furst, the former managing director who answered to Bayly, and Bayly were each named in a March 2003 SEC complaint alleging that they aided and abetted securities fraud by helping push through the barge deal. Also named in that complaint were Tom Davis, former executive vice president of Merrill's Corporate and Institutional Client Group, and Schuyler Tilney, Merrill's Enron liaison in Houston, who answered to Davis. Tilney's wife, Beth, had been a top public relations executive and a Lay favorite at Enron. Merrill fired Tilney and Davis in September 2002 when both refused to cooperate with investigators, but neither was charged with crimes. U.S. District Judge Kenneth Hoyt closed the SEC case in March 2006.

All six defendants were charged with one count of conspiracy to commit wire fraud and two counts of wire fraud. Brown also was charged with perjury and obstruction of justice for allegedly lying to a grand jury about the nature of the barge deal. Boyle faced an additional charge of lying to congressional investigators about the deal. Though

Bayly also spoke to congressional investigators and denied knowledge of any promise of a buyback of the assets, he didn't face that additional charge.

Prosecutors said the purported sale was really a loan because Merrill's investment was never at risk. The defendants repeatedly referred to the official paperwork associated with the deal, none of which noted a buyback, but prosecutors said that was exactly the point. The buyback promise was a verbal, under-the-table deal that couldn't be noted in the official paperwork because that would block Enron from booking the profit.

McMahon approached Furst about the deal, and Furst supported it in a memo to Bayly. Brown questioned whether it could be booked as a sale and was concerned that the buyback provision wasn't in writing. He helped convene a committee to examine the deal after Tilney, then Furst's boss, said the deal was important to secure more business from Enron.

Brown told Neal Batson, the examiner for Enron's massive bankruptcy, about his concerns, which Batson noted in an extensive July 2003 report about Enron's dealings with titan banks and brokerages. Viewed in hindsight, Brown's comments to Batson would appear remarkably prescient:

> Well, I raised the matter, you know, if Enron ever in the future fell apart from a credit—just like a credit meltdown or something, and we had been involved in this transaction, in light of the fact that I had these accounting concerns about the transaction, would that somehow create reputational risk for us? Would we have our names in the press?

Brown also made a handwritten list of his concerns, which included "reputational risk, i.e. aid/abet Enron income stmt manipulation," and "no repurchase obligation from Enron," because he thought that a verbal deal had no legal weight. Prosecutors said the list showed that, although Brown had initially voiced concerns, he later went along with the deal, knowing the risk of helping a client manipulate its books.

Internal e-mails that proved critical to the case showed that Davis had approved the deal, Bayly called Fastow, secured verbal assurances of the buyback, and told Brown to close the transaction. Brown assigned Fuhs that duty.

Then Boyle emerged in 2000 to ensure that the barges were bought back or resold as promised. He informed Fuhs via e-mail that a buyer had been found—LJM2—and would purchase the barges at the "agreed upon" price. Prosecutors alleged Kahanek's role centered on her alleged severe reprimand of a colleague for noting the buyback in an internal document, which the government said that she had ordered destroyed to ensure that the loan could be booked as a sale.

The trial focused on e-mails that appeared damning to Brown, Boyle, Furst, and Fuhs, as well as on Bayly's conference call with Fastow. Among the most damaging of the e-mails was one that Brown wrote to another colleague in March 2001, which implicated Bayly and appeared to memorialize the buyback promise, despite his concerns that the deal was problematic. That e-mail, which Brown's lawyers fought hard and in vain to keep out of the jury's purview, referred to a different deal with a different company that also had included a verbal side deal:

> We had a similar precedent with Enron last year, and we had Fastow get on the phone with Bayly and lawyers and promise to pay us back no matter what. Deal was approved and all went well.

An e-mail sent by in-house Enron accountant Alan Quaintance to Boyle and others in June 2000 said that he had discussed the barges with Enron's auditors at Arthur Andersen LLP, and said that they didn't like the deal, which they called a "sham transaction," and were "extremely uncomfortable with us taking a gain."

But prosecutors had little on paper linking Kahanek to any wrongdoing. They had no e-mails written by her that mentioned the buyback. One witness claimed that she had sent an e-mail scolding an intern who had included guarantee language in a document summarizing a proposed deal with another buyer before Merrill stepped up, but the government never presented that e-mail to the jury.

Instead, the government relied on witnesses to portray Kahanek as a willing participant in hiding the truth of the deal from auditors and regulators, several of whom had cut immunity deals with prosecutors. Kahanek did not sign the so-called "deal approval sheet," or DASH, authorizing the transaction, but two former colleagues who did sign that sheet—Amanda Colpean, who held a higher position than Kahanek in Enron's corporate hierarchy, and Eric Boyt, an accountant on Kahanek's team—were among witnesses who testified against her. Boyt had an immunity deal with prosecutors, and Colpean did not. But both claimed that Kahanek knew of the buyback and demanded that it not be mentioned in any deal-related paperwork, so that Enron could account for it as a sale and book the profit.

Colpean testified about the alleged reprimand, saying that Kahanek had yelled at her for jeopardizing the deal by putting the buyback in writing. She said that she had refused to change the document, but was among 11 Enron executives who had signed the DASH that did not include language about the buyback. She insisted that she did not remember signing it, but contradicted herself by saying later that she thought that she would be fired if she didn't.

Neither Fastow nor Bayly testified, so jurors didn't hear details of their conversation during the conference call two days before Christmas 1999. A written summary of what Fastow had told federal investigators about the barge deal that was provided to the defense teams as part of pretrial discovery indicated that his verbal assurances weren't as clear as the indictment had made them sound. That summary showed that Fastow told investigators he did not use the words "guarantee" or "promise" when giving his assurances.

When prosecutors made clear before trial that they would not call Fastow to the witness stand, the defense teams considered summoning him and even sought approval from Werlein to treat him as a hostile witness. But the former CFO never appeared, and prosecutors called Kopper and Ben Glisan, the former treasurer who had already served one-fifth of a five-year term in prison after pleading guilty to conspiracy a year before the trial had started.

Kopper called Fastow both "brilliant" and "very greedy," noting that his former boss skimmed about $45 million in ill-gotten gains from Enron schemes while he himself had pocketed about $16 million. He said that he had kept track of their under-the-table scams on a laptop, which he threw in a dumpster in the latter half of 2001—as the Enron scandal erupted—at Fastow's behest.

He said that Fastow called him in June 2000, when it was time for Enron to buy back or resell the barges from Merrill, and "kind of giggled" about LJM2 stepping in as the buyer. At the time, Kopper was a managing director for both LJM2 and Enron. He said that Fastow had told him that McMahon had promised Merrill would be bought out within six months of buying the barges, and that Enron needed to make good on that pledge to maintain its reputation in the marketplace as a company that kept its word.

In his first public statements about his crimes at Enron, Kopper seemed resigned and walked to and from the witness stand with hunched shoulders. He told the jury that he hoped his testimony and cooperation would convince Werlein, who had taken his guilty plea, to spare him from going to prison.

Glisan presented a sharp contrast, arriving to testify in a green prison-issued jumpsuit and blue canvas shoes. He became involved in March 2000, as the deadline to buy back or resell the barges loomed. Boyle sent an e-mail to executives trying to find a new buyer. That e-mail said that, if no buyer emerged by June 30 that year, Enron would have to restate its fourth-quarter and year-end 1999 financial results to erase the profit from the barge deal. That restatement would "require a level of damage control with Arthur Andersen," then Enron's outside auditor, because the firm's auditors had not been told of any verbal assurance of a buyback.

Glisan, who replaced McMahon as treasurer in March 2000, chimed in with another e-mail in May 2000: "To be clear, (Enron) is obligated to get Merrill out of the deal on or before June 30. We have no ability to roll the structure."

Glisan testified that he felt it was his job to make Enron appear stronger than it was. He said he thought the barge deal was "blatantly wrong" because the buyback assurance meant that Merrill had assumed no risk. He also thought it was odd that Enron worked so hard on such a minor deal for a company that reported $100 billion in revenues in 2000. But he focused on ensuring that Enron kept its promise in order to prevent any gossip on Wall Street that Enron didn't keep its word. "I felt that we were obligated based on Mr. McMahon's guarantee, which I understand was ratified by Mr. Fastow," Glisan testified.

He said that he had asked Furst if Merrill could keep the barges for a while longer after June 30 that year, when Enron had trouble finding another buyer, but he said that Furst had balked at the idea. He also said that he had complained to McMahon that the deal appeared to be "almost an act of desperation," but McMahon replied, "I'm comfortable with handshake deals."

During the trial, Bayly's lawyers called an in-house Merrill attorney, Kathy Zrike, to testify about how she had discussed the barge deal with Bayly, Furst, and Brown and then with Bayly and Davis. She said they discussed whether unwritten assurances that Enron would try to find another buyer made the deal fraudulent, but she saw no reason to block the transaction with Merrill as a temporary purchaser whose interest would be bought later by a third party. She said that Davis had agreed to approve the deal as "a favor" to Enron, and that she had instructed Bayly to talk to a "senior person" at Enron to ensure that the energy company would keep trying to resell the barges.

Through Zrike, the defense sought to show that Bayly relied on legal advice to move forward with the deal, which would challenge the prosecution's contention that he had criminal intent. However, during Friedrich's cross examination, Zrike indicated she wasn't told the entire story in her meetings with the executives involved in the deal. She said she would not have approved it had she known of a verbal promise to buy back the assets in six months if another buyer couldn't be found. "I would have felt it was a sham," she said.

Of the six defendants, three testified—Boyle, Kahanek, and Fuhs.

By far, Kahanek was the most believable, reiterating what several prosecution witnesses had said: She never supported a buyback and was consistently adamant that it not be a part of the deal, calling herself a "broken record" in insisting that Enron couldn't book profit from a sale if a buyback guarantee was part of the deal. She also said the confrontation Colpean described, but didn't document, simply did not happen.

Fuhs's testimony was marked by his lack of recollection or failure to see certain damaging documents sent to him that made the transaction appear to have been a disguised loan. He said he didn't know of a buyback guarantee, only that Enron had promised to keep looking for another buyer. He also did not participate in meetings about the deal, and said his role was limited to shuffling papers and e-mails back and forth.

He said that he didn't see a letter drafted by one of his subordinates that contained language about the buyback and guaranteed return, nor did he notice when Boyle sent it back to him with lines drawn through that language, indicating that it should be struck. He also said that he didn't believe he had ever looked at a letter to Enron that the subordinate had drafted in June 2000 with instructions to wire $7.5 million to a Merrill-controlled bank account by the end of that month.

However, he sent an e-mail to the subordinate saying that he had just spoken to Boyle, who "pre-empted our letter" by telling him that Enron had lined up a buyer—LJM2.

But Boyle contradicted himself, diminishing his credibility. He said he realized, upon receiving Glisan's e-mail in May 2000 noting that Enron was "obligated" to buy Merrill out by June 30, that the barge deal was improper, but he followed through on getting the barges sold by the predetermined deadline. However, he had sent an e-mail to the leader of Enron's barge deal team three days before Glisan's e-mail went out, noting that Enron would have to buy back the barges by June 30 if another buyer couldn't be found. "As you know, ML's decision to purchase the equity was based solely on personal assurances by Enron senior management to ML's vice chairman that the transaction would not go beyond June 30, 2000," Boyle's e-mail said.

He also had written several e-mails in the first half of 2000 reminding the barge deal team of the impending June 30 deadline. He wrote in an e-mail that day to a colleague about a separate deal that "LJM reluctantly bought ML out on Thursday. Still major issue to smooth over with [Andersen] but Furst is happy."

Boyle also was the only participant in the Bayly/Fastow conference call to testify. He said that Fastow had told Bayly and Furst that the barges would be up and running by April 2000 and therefore attractive to other buyers. When asked on cross-examination if he heard Fastow say that Merrill would not own the barges past June 30, 2000, Boyle replied, "I did not hear that statement."

Several potential witnesses whose names came up repeatedly throughout the trial invoked their Fifth Amendment right not to testify, including McMahon and Davis. While McMahon did so by letter, Davis appeared in court, having been summoned by the defense. Neither were ever charged criminally, though in June 2007 McMahon agreed to pay the SEC $300,000 to settle allegations that he violated securities laws by pitching the barge deal to Merrill with the buyback promise, participating in other deals with banks intended to help Enron inflate earnings, and misleading credit rating agencies about Enron's financial health.

When the barge case went to the jury in late October 2004, Werlein had a problem. Two weeks into the trial, the U.S. Supreme Court heard arguments in a case that challenged the federal sentencing system. The issue was whether judges, rather than juries, can consider factors that can increase guideline-recommended prison sentences, such as the number of victims, whether the defendant had any special training, or financial loss from a fraud. The loss factor was the most powerful force in sentence enhancement, because it had the potential to add decades to a prison term, depending on the amount. If a loss was determined to be in excess of $100 million—an easy feat if exposure of a scam sent a company's stock price tumbling—a defendant could face more than 20 years of incarceration.

Also, at the time, the guidelines were mandatory. Those guidelines, imposed in November 1987, were intended to ensure fairness in sentencing, so defendants convicted of similar crimes would receive similar punishments no matter where they were tried. Because they were mandatory, judges had little discretion to impose a shorter sentence, particularly if prosecutors didn't recommend such a downward departure.

That issue gained national attention in March 2004 when Jamie Olis, a former mid-level finance executive for Dynegy, was sentenced to 24 years and four months in prison for six counts of conspiracy to commit mail, wire and securities fraud, wire fraud, mail fraud, and securities fraud. A jury had convicted him of those crimes in November 2003 for helping push through an April 2001 deal that had improperly inflated the company's cash flow. An official from the University of California testified that the institution lost $105 million when Dynegy disclosed the deal in April 2002 (among other bad news affecting the company). Olis's trial lawyers didn't dispute the loss figure, so U.S. District Judge Simeon Lake relied on that testimony in sentencing Olis to 292 months in prison—24 years and four months. Olis's former boss and an in-house Dynegy accountant each had pleaded guilty to conspiracy before Olis had gone to trial, and each of them had only received prison terms of 15 months and 30 days, respectively. No senior Dynegy executives were ever charged, even though some were implicated during the trial, and internal e-mails showed they were aware of the deal when it was concocted and closed.

The 5th U.S. Circuit Court of Appeals later affirmed Olis's convictions, but remanded his case to Lake for resentencing, ruling that it was unreasonable to hold him responsible for the entire loss. In September 2006, Lake re-sentenced Olis to six years in prison. He had already served two years and four months of his term.

In early November 2004, the barge jury acquitted Kahanek and convicted the five men on all counts. The Supreme Court still had not ruled on the sentencing issue, so Werlein took the unusual step of adding a sentencing phase similar to a penalty phase in state courts. He instructed jurors to hear evidence on whether prison sentences should be enhanced, and told the panel it would serve an advisory role to him in terms of sentencing.

Jurors heard testimony from prosecution and defense experts with predictably opposite views on the loss. Prosecutors pegged it at $80 million, though their expert placed it at nearly half that—$43 million—just enough to hike sentences dramatically. Under that scenario, Brown faced the most, up to 33 years in prison for his five counts. The defense expert contended that there was no financial loss to investors or anyone else. The barge deal was never revealed until after Enron went bankrupt, so the deal itself, or its nature, didn't cause the company's stock to fall. The prosecution's theory was that the penny that the deal provided to quarterly earnings was derived from a sham transaction, so shareholders suffered by paying too much for artificially inflated shares.

The jury came up with a loss figure all its own: $13.7 million. The panel didn't explain publicly how it arrived at that number, but it could have included the $12 million pretax profit that Enron had booked from the deal and the $775,000 that Enron had paid in fees to Merrill for participating. If Werlein agreed with the jury's conclusion, that loss amount could lead to a decade or more in prison for the defendants, though they wouldn't face 20 to 30 years or more.

However, the issue became moot in January 2005. The Supreme Court ruled that federal sentencing guidelines were strictly advisory, so judges could consider factors to enhance prison terms from the recommended amounts but retain final say over a punishment they deemed fit.[3]

In pre-sentencing reports, federal probation officers had recommended stiff sentences for the barge defendants: up to 33 years for Brown; in the teens for Bayly, Furst and Boyle; and seven to nine years for Fuhs. But Werlein criticized the government's pursuit of sentences longer than the 10-year maximum that Fastow had agreed to serve for his guilty plea to two counts of conspiracy, given the ex-CFO's central role in myriad frauds at the company. The judge said that the term awaiting Fastow and the five years that Glisan was serving "established some benchmarks" for the barge defendants, and

[3] *See* United States v. Booker, 543 U.S. 220 (2005).

noted that they faced "unjustified disparate sentences" in comparison to others much more involved in Enron crimes. He called the barge deal "rather small and relatively benign in the constellation of Enron frauds" and said, in reference to Bayly, that the fact that someone who was a leader in the investment banking world "goes to prison at all serves as a deterrent effect."

He then sentenced Bayly to two and a half years in prison; Brown and Boyle, three years and 10 months; and three years and a month for Furst and Fuhs.

Throughout the barge trial, prosecutors contended that the barge defendants had robbed Enron of their honest services by participating in a deal that they knew to be a sham, deliberately disguised as an asset sale to help Enron appear to have met its earnings targets. That stance was a stretch of the federal wire fraud statute, because the honest services theory had previously applied when defendants stole, embezzled, took bribes, or otherwise benefited from taking money or property from the alleged victim, deviating from that victim's corporate interests. None of the barge defendants skimmed profits from a deal that helped Enron maintain its illusion of success to investors. The prosecution's use of the honest services theory would come back to haunt the Enron Task Force and the Justice Department in the Merrill defendants' appeals and permeate nearly all of the other Enron cases.

Broadband

In April 2005, the third Enron trial began, with five former executives from its broadband division on trial in essentially two cases sandwiched together. Hirko, Shelby, and Yeager were accused of overhyping capabilities of Enron's broadband network at analyst conferences in January 2000 and January 2001 and of knowing that broadband's abilities were overstated in press releases. The overstatements would help Wall Street tout the stock, enabling the Enron executives to enrich themselves by selling inflated shares. About two weeks of the three-month trial concerned the charges against Howard and Krautz and their role in a two-part deal involving the sale of future revenues in the Blockbuster video-on-demand venture that failed.

The list of 176 counts facing the defendants was staggering. Yeager faced more than 100 charges, most of those money laundering and insider trading. Hirko faced 27; Shelby, 24; and Howard and Krautz each faced 15. All were charged with one overarching conspiracy count that linked the two seemingly disparate cases under the same umbrella of trying to make Enron's financial performance appear much stronger than it was to analysts and investors, thereby maintaining an artificially high stock price.

The prosecution team consisted of Ben Campbell, Lisa Monaco, and Cliff Stricklin, a former Dallas state district judge. The defendants, except for Krautz, each had multiple lawyers. U.S. District Judge Vanessa Gilmore presided.

Prosecutors sought to simplify a hopelessly complicated case by saying it was about lying for profit. But the defense teams challenged the government's view that the broadband network didn't work. The case was bogged down with weeks of intricate, jargon-filled testimony about the technology, giving jurors mind-numbing lessons on the Internet, servers, video streaming, the workings of a fiber optic network, how information goes from one place to another on that network, and so on. The technology defendants testified that the network indeed did work, but was being implemented in phases when the technology bubble that so wowed Wall Street melted down in 2000 and 2001, leaving Enron with a massive, largely unused broadband network that had little commercial value.

Hirko, Shelby, and Yeager all testified, saying they did not lie to investors or overhype the division's capabilities and outlook.

Howard and Krautz each testified that they indeed participated in the deal to sell future revenues, and explained that such transactions, known as monetizations, were common and legal. Prosecutors sought to portray the video-on-demand deal much like the barge deal, with an unwritten buyback promise made to the buyer of those future revenues: a little Oregon Internet company called nCube. But unlike Merrill Lynch, Enron did not buy back or resell nCube's interest in the venture. Instead, nCube lost its money when Enron went bankrupt, and it found itself among the throngs of other Enron creditors.

Although prosecutors had secured guilty pleas from two senior broadband executives—Rice and Hannon—only Rice testified in the trial. He said that he and others had lied about the network's capabilities in order to win Wall Street's support for the broadband venture, which was a departure from Enron's bread-and-butter mission of energy trading.

"We chose to lie about the capabilities of the network," he said. For the January 2000 analyst conference, the presentation by Skilling, Rice, and Hirko sought to convey that Enron was credible in its ability to deliver on promises that its network and software were unmatched by competitors, even those much more well-versed in telecommunications. He also said that an April 1999 press release that described the network as "lit, tested and ready" was inaccurate and was intended to get a big valuation for the division—in the billions of dollars—that would translate to a hefty portion of Enron's stock price.

Rice also referred to the monetization of the video-on-demand deal as "a shot of crack cocaine" that he approved because the unit wasn't earning needed income from actual operations. The unit had been projected to lose money in 2000, but the goal was to ensure that the losses didn't exceed the $60 million that Skilling had told analysts to expect, Rice testified.

In an added subplot, prosecutors portrayed Skilling as leading the charge of overhyping the broadband network as well as the division's aim to jump-start bandwidth trading. Jurors repeatedly watched videotapes of his presentations about the division and its prospects at the analyst conferences. The charges facing Skilling included some counts related to lying to investors, analysts, and employees about the division's capabilities and portraying it as earning income from operations rather than from sales of unused portions of the fiber optic network. Members of Skilling's legal team attended every day, often frustrated at their inability to respond because their client's trial wouldn't come until 2006. Skilling himself tried to sit in on a day when Rice, once a close friend and member of his inner circle at Enron, was slated to testify. He was quickly ordered to leave because he was on one of the many witness lists, and witnesses were sequestered.

But the prosecution's strategy of injecting Skilling into the trial backfired to a certain extent. First of all, Skilling's remarks alternated between telling analysts what the broadband network could do at the time and what it would be able to do in the future. The distinction was critical because Skilling didn't say outright that the network had reached its full potential at the time. Instead, he used phrases such as "we have the potential for" and "we're real optimistic about the outlook for this business" as well as "Enron has already established the superior broadband delivery network." Analysts indeed were impressed, and the company's stock rose to $67 from $54 per share on the day of the conference, and then up to more than $72 the next day.

After nearly four days of deliberations, the jurors told Gilmore that they were deadlocked. The judge gave them 45 minutes to keep trying. The panel then returned with a handful of acquittals for Hirko, Shelby, and Yeager, but insisted that they remained deadlocked on those defendants' remaining counts and all counts against Howard and Krautz. The jury acquitted Yeager of six conspiracy and fraud counts, leaving 109 insider trading and money laundering counts. Hirko was acquitted of 14 insider trading and money laundering counts, and Shelby was acquitted of four insider trading counts.

Stricklin implored the judge to urge the jury to continue deliberations, saying four days of talks wasn't enough, given the complicated nature of the case and reams of evidence presented over three months of testimony. Gilmore agreed that the time devoted to deliberations appeared to be short, but she declined to order that talks resume, and she declared a mistrial and discharged the panel.

In November 2005, the government re-indicted all five defendants on fewer counts and separated them into three cases: Shelby and Hirko; Yeager; and Howard and Krautz. Yeager was re-indicted on just 13 insider trading and money laundering counts; Hirko and Shelby on the conspiracy, wire and securities fraud, and some insider trading counts; and Howard and Krautz, five counts each of conspiracy, fraud, and falsifying books and records. Yeager, Hirko, and Shelby appealed to have all or most charges thrown out, postponing their retrials. But Howard and Krautz faced a jury again in May 2006 in Gilmore's courtroom as the Lay/Skilling trial in Lake's courtroom next door entered its final weeks.

The abbreviated case against them still concerned the same deal, but only the first part of it. The trial centered on the monetization of the video-on-demand venture in the fourth quarter of 2000, but not a repeat of the same process in the first quarter of 2001. The retrial garnered little attention—to the relief of both Howard and Krautz—with the much bigger case involving Enron's top two executives raging next door.

Though the same defense teams represented Howard and Krautz, the prosecution team had changed. Van Vincent, a federal prosecutor from Nashville, and Jonathan Lopez, a federal prosecutor from Miami, had joined the task force in December 2005 and February 2006, respectively. Again, the prosecutors portrayed the deal as a loan disguised as a sale, much like the strategy in the barge case. And again, the defense countered that a buyback wasn't part of the final deal and that Enron never repurchased nCube's interest. Howard and Krautz each faced five counts of conspiracy, fraud, and falsifying books and records.

This time, the jury returned with a verdict that gained little fanfare because it came several days after the Lay/Skilling trial had ended. Krautz was acquitted on all counts, while Howard was convicted on all counts. The verdict on Krautz was read first, and he and his family were visibly relieved, though subdued. At the first "guilty," a stoic Howard simply closed his eyes. His lawyers later contended that the jury played a bit of horsetrading during deliberations, agreeing to free Krautz as long as everyone agreed to convict Howard. However, the same honest services issue that became a critical appeal point for the Merrill defendants in the barge case would later benefit Howard as well.

Skilling and Lay

The epic battle in the Enron saga began January 30, 2006, when Skilling and Lay made the first of four months of daily treks to the courthouse, completely cognizant that a hoard of photographers and videographers aimed to capture every facial expression. Lay arrived almost every day hand in hand with his wife, Linda, with a ready smile and a nod for the cameras. Linda Lay, who studiously took notes on a steno pad throughout the trial, sometimes arrived later, and their children often arrived a few steps behind along with his lawyers. Petrocelli laid out Skilling's routine from the start: the pair would always arrive and leave together. Skilling would be cordial if not inviting, in contrast to the sneering combativeness he displayed upon being indicted, before image-conscious Petrocelli had taken the lead in his defense team. Skilling's camera-shy wife, Rebecca Carter, walked a few lengths behind the pair, as did Skilling's other lawyers, the cameras still angling for her husband as she walked by.

Scores of potential jurors arrived at the federal courthouse to undergo voir dire. Of more than 100 who filed into one of the courthouse's largest courtrooms—two flights up from U.S. District Judge Simeon Lake's ninth-floor courtroom—the judge screened 46, and from those, the legal teams chose 12 jurors and four alternates. Lake had refused pleas from the defense teams to conduct lengthy, one-on-one voir dire and questioned jurors himself in quiet conversations at the bench. Prosecutors and defense lawyers interjected questions, but this was Lake's show. He intended to spend one day on jury selection, and the panel was chosen by day's end.

"I can assure you this will be one of the most interesting and important cases ever tried," he told the entire pool before questioning began. "We are not looking for people who want to right a wrong or provide remedies for those who suffered in the collapse of Enron," he also said.

Four men and eight women were the decision-makers, and two women and two men were alternates. In the late stages of the four-month trial, one of the female alternates would drop out, but the original dozen ended up deliberating.

The next day, the panel listened to hours of opening statements, in which both sides sought to frame what jurors would see and hear for the next several months. Lay sat at a defense table next to his daughter, Elizabeth Vittor, an attorney firmly ensconced in his legal team, which was led by Michael Ramsey, Ramsey's partner Chip Lewis, George "Mac" Secrest, and Dallas civil attorney Bruce Collins. Skilling sat next to Petrocelli. Around the two defense tables that formed a "T" were other "Team Skilling" members from Petrocelli's firm: Randall Oppenheimer, Mark Holscher, Matt Kline, and former Houston U.S. Attorney Ron Wood. Other lawyers also flanked both teams around the defense tables and on a bench in front of the bar.

The prosecution team sat nearer to the jury box: Sean Berkowitz, who had assumed the title of director of the Enron Task Force in mid-2005 and who would cross-examine Skilling; Kathryn Ruemmler, a barge trial veteran who was deputy director of the Task Force; and John Hueston, an Assistant U.S. Attorney who had joined the Task Force in January 2004, with his sights set clearly on Lay. Stricklin was the fourth member of the main team, though the other three dominated the questioning throughout the trial. Other prosecutors and FBI agents who rounded out the team packed the bench in front of the bar on the opposite side of the defense teams as well as in plenty of seats in the gallery.

Dozens of reporters and other interested lawyers filled several rows of courtroom seats as well as an overflow courtroom on the fourth floor, which had an audio and video link to the main courtroom. Writers and bloggers who needed to tap away at keyboards as the action took place were in the overflow room, while those in the courtroom scribbled fervently in notebooks, carefully scrutinizing Skilling and Lay for facial expressions and even the slightest reaction to whatever was said. Anyone looking for animated expressions was disappointed; Skilling sat calmly, his right hand atop his left in his lap with his legs crossed, his face inscrutable. Lay made occasional notes on a legal pad—a habit he maintained throughout the case—and often glanced toward his wife, Linda, seated amongst the Lay family in the first row of the gallery.

"This is a simple case. It is not about accounting. It is about lies and choices," Hueston told the jury, in an attempt to assure that the vast case was one that the jury could easily grasp.

He pinpointed mid-August 2001 as one example among many: illustrating how the government would prove that Skilling and Lay blithely painted falsely rosy public pictures of Enron's health when they knew that the company was rotting from within, unable to sustain years of financial machinations that could no longer hide weaknesses. In August 2001, Skilling abruptly resigned, having succeeded Lay as CEO just six months earlier. Skilling's public reason for resigning was that he wanted to spend more time with his family, but the convenient timing of a departure a few months before Enron failed would be an issue in the case. Lay, who had founded Enron 16 years earlier, stepped back into the CEO role upon Skilling's departure and assured investors that the company was healthy.

"They chose to lie. And when a chief executive officer chooses to lie about the true financial condition of its company, when they choose to conceal important facts from investors, facts that are important for investors to make their own decisions about whether to buy, hold, or sell stock, they commit a crime," Hueston said.

Petrocelli, an accomplished civil attorney spearheading his first criminal case, then stepped in front of the jury box to frame what many saw as an inherently unbelievable defense: Skilling was innocent of fraud because there was no fraud. Instead, zealous prosecutors sought to criminalize normal, though aggressive, business practices.

"Let me tell you right now this man, he never, ever led any criminal conspiracy. He wasn't part of any criminal conspiracy. He didn't know about any criminal conspiracy. He didn't see any criminal conspiracy. And the same is true of that man, Mr. Lay.

"And it's not because they were sitting up in the Office of the Chair while there was this massive fraud of conspiracy swirling around them. It's because it did not happen. I want to be clear: This is not a case of hear no evil, see no evil. This is a case of there was no evil."

Petrocelli recounted Skilling's decision to leave a fabulously successful career at the consultancy McKinsey & Co. to join Enron and make a go of his idea to create a marketplace for natural gas. The idea appealed to Lay, a fervent supporter of deregulation. The idea exploded, creating a market to buy and sell natural gas that grew to all kinds of commodities, such as electricity, pulp, paper, metals, and even weather futures and, in what turned out to be a sad irony, bankruptcy risk protection.

Of the government's cooperators, three—Andrew Fastow, Ben Glisan, and Michael Kopper—were admitted thieves, having skimmed money from Enron through various Fastow-run schemes. The others, Petrocelli said, were law-abiding executives who chose to plead guilty rather than gamble on a costly battle that could lead them to decades in prison if they lost.

Ramsey told the jury that a liquidity crisis killed Enron, rather than fraud. When questions began swirling about Fastow running partnerships that conducted deals with his employer, trust among traders and Wall Street eroded, forcing Enron to post collateral for trades that siphoned what little cash on hand it had.

"What happened was the word or the odor of the wolf got into the flock and the flock stampeded," the attorney said, demonstrating his flair for folksy language. "Enron, which was making a living trading on trust of a phone call, instantaneous execution, [and] high liquidity, had lost the faith of the market and the market killed them."

Over the course of the next four months, 54 witnesses would testify: 25 for the prosecution and 29 for the defense. The government's lineup included eight ex-executives who had pleaded guilty to crimes and another who had struck a deal with the SEC without having been charged with a crime. The star witnesses were the defendants themselves, each of whom testified over several days and faced a few surprise punches from prosecutors. The government avoided making Andrew Fastow a star witness, which would have been a shaky move, given all his baggage. Instead, prosecutors made him part of an ensemble in which others proved more critical and believable.

Despite the deep havoc that Enron's demise wrought for thousands of employees left jobless, the trial did not attract big crowds. Former employees didn't plan vacations to sit in, more than four years later. The courtroom was packed only for the testimony of Skilling, Lay, and Fastow, the most notorious trio in the Enron cast of players and the ones deemed most responsible for the inner putrefaction that fueled the collapse of what was once the nation's seventh-largest company.

First up was Mark Koenig, the former head of investor relations, who had pleaded guilty to aiding and abetting securities fraud in 2004. Koenig said Enron manipulated earnings to ensure that the company met stated income targets, and Skilling and Lay knew it. However, his testimony foreshadowed what other witnesses would say: the top two executives knew of financial skullduggery, but did not overtly order any books to be cooked. There would be no e-mails ordering or discussing schemes to hide Enron's true condition from investors. There would be no meetings in which anyone brazenly concocted fraudulent schemes he knew to skirt the law. There would be no written or spoken orders of secrecy from Skilling or Lay. People in search of such obvious smoking guns would be disappointed, because no smoking guns existed amid what prosecutors presented to be more subtle subterfuge.

For example, Kenneth Rice, once a top trader and CEO of the broadband division, testified that, by early 2001, the unit was bleeding $100 million per quarter without bringing in any significant cash from operations. Instead, that unit over-relied on asset sales to stem losses. Also, its bandwidth trading venture never took off during the burst of the telecom bubble. Yet Skilling, a strong booster for the unit since its conception years earlier, told analysts in March 2001 that the division had "strong growth as far as people, budgets, the whole thing" when "the reality was we were cutting people," Rice said.

Paula Rieker took aim at Lay. Often addressing the jury directly as though she were a seasoned expert witness, she said Enron's board of directors was outraged when they learned in February 2002 that he had sold more than $70 million in Enron stock back to the company in 2001 to pay back some of his loans from the company, even as the enterprise was spiraling downward. She quoted a director who had been particularly supportive of Lay, John Duncan, as saying, "He was using Enron like a damn ATM machine."

Rieker also said Koenig told her that Skilling ordered a two-cent increase to Enron's reported earnings-per-share in the second quarter of 2000 so that the company's results would appear to exceed analyst expectations. However, Koenig didn't go so far in his testimony to say that Skilling had explicitly ordered anything—only that he was authorized to do so.

The distinction was one that would show up often. As other witnesses recounted similar experiences, they said that they had committed deeds that they believed to be ordered from the top, though they didn't hear the orders themselves. Others recounted examples of efforts to hide losses or bad investments to maintain a falsely positive picture to investors.

But a few witnesses packed extraordinarily bruising punches.

David Delainey, once head of Enron's trading franchise and later its flailing retail energy division, who had once harbored hopes of succeeding Skilling as CEO, boiled the company's maverick aggression down to a sentence: "At Enron in Houston, we tended to be pretty fast and loose with our rules." He pleaded guilty in October 2003 to insider trading for selling millions of dollars in stock when he knew about internal earnings manipulation.

He was one of the few who described firsthand a plan concocted at a senior management meeting to hide losses in the retail division by folding its trading function into the company's larger trading enterprise, Enron North America. In late March 2001, the retail division was facing $200 million in losses, and top executives decided during a meeting in Skilling's office to move the division's trading arm into ENA. Delainey said he told his superiors that the move lacked integrity, to which an angry Causey responded, "Isn't this a bona fide operational change?" Delainey said that Skilling simply looked at him and asked, "What do you want to do?"

He took Skilling's question as a veiled order to "get in line" and go along with the plan, though Delainey didn't explicitly say he took it as an order to break the law. "There was no business purpose to this other than to hide the loss, and I knew that was not proper," Delainey said.

The next month, when Enron released its first-quarter 2001 earnings, Skilling told analysts that the move was driven by the retail unit's growth and was intended to combine two like functions in order to increase efficiency. (Causey's 11th-hour guilty plea was to a securities fraud charge stemming from that decision to move retail trading into ENA.)

Delainey also said that he had felt pressure from Skilling to wrongly raid reserves from ENA's trading profits to meet or beat analyst expectations for quarterly earnings, but again, gave no examples of explicit orders from his boss to break the law.

Petrocelli sought to ridicule the idea that Delainey, Skilling, and other top executives conspired to do anything wrong, challenging Delainey's black-and-white recollections.

"As a management team, we did lie. We had a very compelling story that we were telling, and we weren't telling the complete truth," Delainey said.

"What was this Enron story? Is it a story about a criminal conspiracy?," Petrocelli asked, drawing out the word "conspiracy."

"Yes," an unshaken Delainey replied without hesitation.

"Is it a story about fraud?," Petrocelli pressed, drawing out the word "fraud."

"Yes," Delainey replied.

Petrocelli kept pressing Delainey, trying to shake his dogged declaration that the decision to move retail trading into ENA was wrong because it hid losses of one flailing unit in another unit that was awash with profits. "In my memory, that was just about as bad as it could get and as brazen as it could get." Petrocelli kept asking, pointing out that Delainey had initially lied to investigators in an effort to avoid prosecution before he agreed to plead guilty to a crime. But the affable Delainey didn't lose his cool or budge from his stance: "I wish on my kids' lives I had stepped away from that table," he said.

When Fastow took the stand, he lacked the defiant stoicism he had displayed years earlier when he had pleaded not guilty upon being indicted. He looked older, his salt-

and-pepper hair almost completely gray. More lines marked his face. And the courtroom was packed with lawyers, reporters, ex-Enron employees, and interested observers keen to hear his first public statements about Enron since he was ousted years earlier as the engineer of myriad schemes to create Enron's illusion of financial health while pocketing tens of millions of dollars on the side.

He said he set up LJM1—the initials being those of his wife and sons, Lea, Jeffrey and Michael—in 1999 to help Enron lock in profits reported from an investment in an Internet startup firm so that the company wouldn't have to take a loss later if the firm's shares fell. He quoted Skilling as saying, "Get me as much of that juice as you can," when he said he told Skilling he would need to raise more money for the partnership so that it could conduct more deals. The much larger LJM2 followed, which Fastow said was designed to warehouse Enron assets in deals disguised as sales so the company could report the earnings that it wanted to report.

He said that he received "bear hugs" (verbal assurances) from Skilling, guaranteeing that LJM2 wouldn't lose money in buying unsavory Enron assets, like the three power barges at the center of the Nigerian barge trial, or a money-losing power plant in Brazil. Fastow kept no notes or records of these promises other than a copy of a list of deals, dubbed the "Global Galactic," that was marked with initials of only Fastow and Causey.

He also described the Raptors, four financial vehicles that Glisan had created in 2000, which Fastow said Skilling and Lay knew were used to help manipulate Enron's earnings. Backed by company stock, the Raptors helped to lock in gains from asset values or investments while keeping hundreds of millions of dollars in debt off Enron's books. Those Raptors depended on a high Enron stock price in order to be sustainable. As Enron's shares fell, the Raptors crumbled, forcing the company to wipe out $1.2 billion in shareholder equity at the same time that Enron reported $638 million in losses in the third quarter of 2001.

Fastow also went after Lay. He said that he had met with Lay the day after Skilling quit and warned that Enron faced huge write-offs to compensate for grossly overvalued international assets. Skilling had even noted in one document that international assets were bringing in paltry returns and were overvalued by as much as $5 billion. Fastow testified that Lay had misled analysts and credit rating agencies about Enron even though Fastow had briefed him about the company's serious financial situation. In September 2001, Fastow said that he and Lay met with Goldman Sachs & Co. executives to discuss restructuring options for the troubled company, such as a merger or bankruptcy, but no such actions were taken. Fastow said that he had solicited Goldman's advice because the firm wasn't among Enron's lenders, from which he had wanted to hide Enron's true financial condition.

Prosecutors knew that Fastow's own past actions would put his credibility into question, and Hueston put Fastow's sins on display during direct examination. Fastow fought back tears as he recounted that his wife had pleaded guilty to a misdemeanor tax crime and went to prison for a year for signing a joint tax return that had omitted his illegal income from a scheme unrelated to the LJM partnerships. He appeared unable to admit that his wife had committed a crime, saying instead that he was sure she didn't lie to a judge when she pleaded guilty. Instead, he said he misled her when he told her that a series of kickback checks written to her, him, and their two young sons were gifts that she then endorsed and deposited. He stared at the floor in front of the jury box when Hueston displayed those checks on a large screen for the jury. The temper and histrionics for he was known at Enron were gone or deeply buried. Fastow came off as beaten and contrite. He admitted to his greed, lies, cheating, and stealing.

Petrocelli cross-examined Fastow first, launching a merciless attack on Fastow as a liar, thief, and a cad who had let his wife go to prison rather than admit to his own crimes: flashing incredulous looks at the jury, Petrocelli pounded, "Your greed was so great that you allowed your wife to go to prison, didn't you?"

"My actions caused my wife to go to prison, yes," Fastow replied. "I find it very hard myself to think my wife was guilty. I love my wife and I know her. I also find it very difficult to believe that she would ever lie to a federal judge. I accept that in her mind she was guilty, but it was my actions that caused her to go to prison and I'll live with that for the rest of my life."

He admitted to being greedy, sometimes bristling at Petrocelli's aggressive tone. He repeatedly cited a hearing problem in asking Petrocelli to repeat questions when the lawyer would ask one while walking the length of the jury box away from the witness stand. Petrocelli displayed for jurors what he called a "booty list" of fees that Fastow and Kopper had pocketed from the LJM partnerships. Fastow noted that many senior Enron managers benefited financially from his efforts to misrepresent the company's financial health, which he called stealing as well.

"You think he's guilty, right?" Petrocelli asked of Skilling.

"I think we committed crimes together, yes," Fastow replied.

The Global Galactic's journey from Fastow's possession to that of the government also gave Petrocelli plenty of attack fodder. Fastow said that he had destroyed the original, but a copy that Causey had refused to keep turned up in an envelope in a safe-deposit box that Fastow and his wife maintained at a bank. The agreement was with a copy of Fastow's employment agreement in a folder, and he claimed to have no idea how it ended up there.

He acknowledged that his wife found the envelope when she checked the couple's safe-deposit box in April 2004, which happened to be the same month that prosecutors dropped all felony charges against her and substituted a misdemeanor tax crime to which she pleaded guilty. But Fastow said that his wife had left the envelope on his desk, and that he looked inside the envelope a month later and gave the copy of the Global Galactic to his attorney, who passed it on to the government. Petrocelli sought to cast doubt on its authenticity, particularly given the coincidental timing of its discovery.

After four days of Petrocelli's grilling, Fastow appeared worn, slowly opening and closing his eyes as if very tired. He avoided looking at Skilling or Lay during his testimony, instead staring at the floor during breaks.

Ramsey continued the pummeling, also capitalizing on Fastow's crimes and lies. "You are sorry to the core, aren't you?" he asked in a tone dripping with sarcasm. "I'm ashamed to the core," Fastow replied. "I have destroyed my life. And yes, sir, I am sorry to the core."

Ramsey challenged Fastow's account of the meeting with Goldman executives, noting that Goldman was Enron's primary issuer of commercial paper (short-term debt that all companies use for day-to-day expenses and payrolls). Therefore, Goldman was, in fact, one of Enron's crucial lenders.

"Didn't it just cross our mind a little bit that if we tell our major commercial paper broker our secrets, the paper is gonna dry up overnight?" Ramsey asked.

"That's not what I was thinking, sir," Fastow replied.

While both defense attorneys focused on shredding Fastow's already shaky credibility at best, their aggressive verbal assaults had an unintended effect. The supposed financial whiz widely credited with orchestrating Enron's downfall with his schemes emerged having generated some sympathy, however minute. He cried when he acknowledged that his refusal to cut a deal with prosecutors had opened the door to his wife's indictment and subsequent year in prison. He appeared contrite and ashamed when faced with checks that his partner in crime, Michael Kopper, had written to the two Fastow sons. If he had spent years fuming that he was a scapegoat or harbored any desire to take Skilling and Lay down with him, he managed to hide those impulses on the witness stand, presenting himself instead as a beaten man, without any trace of the swagger that he had once enjoyed.

Fastow's appearance attracted a notable observer: former HealthSouth Corp. CEO Richard Scrushy, who was acquitted the previous year of overseeing a $2.7 billion fraud at the Alabama company. He told reporters that he was in Houston on business (just what business, he declined to specify) and he stopped in on the trial during Petrocelli's cross-examination for about an hour while waiting to go to the airport to catch a flight home. He had to watch from the overflow room because he didn't arrive early enough to get a pass guaranteeing him a seat in the packed courtroom.

"I wouldn't believe anything [Fastow] says," Scrushy said in a hallway outside the overflow courtroom. "He's a thief. He was stealing from the company."

Prosecutors intended much of Fastow's testimony to corroborate that of Glisan, who had less baggage and could be seen as a Fastow protégé who was seduced by his former boss's greed. This time, Glisan sat in the witness chair dressed in a jacket and tie rather than prison-issued clothing and added himself to the list of people at Enron who said that they had warned Lay, after Skilling's departure, that the company was in serious trouble. He also said Skilling knew that the company was struggling before he quit.

Glisan, who was still serving a prison term for creating one of the Raptors, presented information about the structure to a committee of Enron's board in May 2000. He said Skilling and Lay, who were at the meeting, heard Causey explain that the Raptors had some "accounting risk," or could raise questions if scrutinized, but that they had been approved by Andersen.

Glisan testified that Skilling told the committee that the Raptor structure was not a deal he would recommend, except that it allowed him to circumvent accounting rules. But on cross-examination, Petrocelli pointed out that Glisan had told a grand jury that Skilling said that he wouldn't enter into the Raptor structure but for accounting rules that require writedowns on assets with values that decline unless they were hedged. Glisan conceded that Skilling didn't say "circumvented" or that the structure was improper.

Glisan further testified on direct examination that Enron's financial difficulties grew worse after Skilling's departure, when Lay told him to feel out credit rating agencies on how large a writedown could be before it would jeopardize the company's already low investment grade rating. A downgrade to a level below investment grade would alert Wall Street that all was not well within Enron, the company would have to pay much higher interests rates for loans critical to its trading franchise, and massive amounts of debt could suddenly come due with little cash to pay up.

Glisan's fishing expedition revealed that the agencies could tolerate no more than $1 billion without a downgrade, so the company limited its writedowns to that amount.

Glisan's testimony clearly struck a nerve with Lay, who told reporters during a mid-afternoon break, "I've never heard so many lies in one day in my whole life."

On cross, Petrocelli didn't turn to the sarcasm or ridicule that had fallen flat when he questioned Delainey. Instead, he highlighted how Glisan had no notes or e-mails to corroborate his recollection that Skilling knew of and participated in fraud. The attorney also questioned Glisan about how he was subpoenaed to appear before a grand jury in Houston on the same day that Skilling made his first appearance in court upon being indicted. After FBI agents had led a handcuffed Skilling into the courthouse, he entered an elevator and encountered Glisan, dressed in prison garb. Asked if he believed that meeting was a coincidence, Glisan replied, "I didn't believe that, no," bolstering Petrocelli's contention that prosecutors had ensured that the two of them would meet in hopes of rattling Skilling.

Glisan also testified about how his five-year prison term was shortened by a year because he had completed a drug and alcohol treatment program available to all non-violent federal inmates. The defense teams had claimed that Glisan gave damaging testimony in exchange for prosecutors who arranged for furloughs and other breaks. He did receive furloughs to meet with investigators and was on furlough to testify in the trial, but he shortened his prison term by the same means offered to other white-collar inmates—15 percent off for good behavior, and completion of the drug and alcohol program.

Collins, one of Lay's lawyers, sought to weaken Glisan's assertion that he had warned Lay in October 2001 that the company was increasingly troubled. On October 23 of that year—the same day of Lay's disastrous conference call with analysts and a day before Enron pushed Fastow out because banks would no longer work with him—Glisan said he told Lay that bankruptcy was inevitable. He described Lay's reaction as non-responsive and somewhat resigned, yet Lay then told employees that the company was doing well financially and operationally.

But as he had with Petrocelli, Glisan—who testified that he often kept detailed notes of meetings—conceded that he had not documented his warning to Lay, nor had he documented his conversations with Skilling. But he noted that he had asked for approval for Enron to seek a $1.5 billion loan from banks and a private $500 million loan, in addition to the $1.5 billion the company already had access to head off financial crisis. Three days later, Enron drew down $3 billion in credit lines from major banks, spurring more questions about the company's stability. Enron responded by saying that the draw-down reflected the banking community's confidence in the company's strength.

Among the prosecution's non-felons was Vince Kaminski, an unimpeachable expert mathematician and economist who once ran an elite risk assessment team at Enron. He said that he had questioned the propriety of LJM1 when it was created in mid-1999 because it was run by Enron's own CFO and was funded partly by Enron stock. Skilling later moved him from the risk assessment group to Enron's trading division. "He said my group acted more like cops, preventing people from executing transactions instead of helping them," Kaminski testified.

More than two years later, Kaminski questioned the Raptors in an October 2001 meeting of executives, including Lay, at a time when the company was increasingly under fire. Kaminski told the group that coming clean was the company's best fighting chance. Lawrence "Greg" Whalley, head of the trading division, gently pushed him from a podium, saying, "Enough, Vince."

Kaminski's testimony augmented that of Sherron Watkins. In early 2002, Congress outed her as a whistleblower for warning Lay, just days after Skilling resigned, that the Raptors constituted fraud. Watkins's infamous memo told Lay that she was "incredibly nervous that we will implode in a wave of accounting scandals."

Both Kaminski and Watkins took aim at Lay's public claims in the fall of 2001 that Enron was healthy. Although Watkins was well known for her efforts to warn Lay of impending doom, Kaminski bolstered the government's contention that Lay heard plenty of additional evidence within Enron's walls that the company was in serious trouble.

As the prosecution's case wound down, the big unanswered question was whether the government would call Causey to the stand. He was among the Big Four on Enron's 50th floor, along with Lay, Skilling, and Fastow. Fastow said that Causey colluded with dirty deals; Delainey said that Causey was in on the big meeting in which executives decided to move the retail unit's trading arm into Enron North America in order to hide losses; Hannon said that Causey was among the executives who heard Skilling say, "They're on to us." Causey was one of two executives designated to ensure that Fastow's LJM deals were proper. Fastow claimed that Causey's initials were on the questionable Global Galactic list of sweetheart LJM deals and that Causey was in charge of the financial statements that Skilling had signed. Causey also was Enron's chief liaison with Arthur Andersen. As the top accountant, Causey was at the center of most allegations facing Lay and Skilling.

But Causey did not testify, either in the prosecution and defense cases in chief or as a rebuttal prosecution witness. As it turned out, Causey's most tangible contribution to the government's case was to allow prosecutors to streamline it by pleading guilty. Had he gone to trial, the case would likely would have delved into weeks of arcane accounting testimony. Without him, the case was simply about whether Lay and Skilling lied.

But the spectre of his testimony also likely helped shape the defenses' strategies, given Causey's ubiquitous presence in so many of the events and meetings presented to the jury. Unlike Fastow, Causey didn't steal from Enron. He didn't draw family members and friends into schemes. His nickname at Enron was the "Pillsbury Doughboy," not so much because of the paunch he had at the time, but more for what many employees described as a friendly demeanor among other ruthless executives. Also, he was hand-in-hand with Lay and Skilling in a united defense for nearly two years. He may not have been as easy to attack, so the defense teams likely would have approached him gingerly, painting him as a victim of government zealousness because he didn't have the resources to fight to exonerate himself.

Throughout the defense case, Petrocelli hinted that he might call Causey to testify. But Causey could have been much more of a liability than an aid to Skilling's defense. The defense teams had repeatedly challenged prosecution witnesses on whether they had accounting expertise to challenge legitimacy of the various financial structures and transactions that prosecutors claimed were vehicles to manipulate Enron's financial statements—even going so far as to challenge actual accountants. Although Causey would have had that expertise, he had admitted to committing a crime by going along with the move of retail's trading function into the larger trading franchise. The jury could have viewed him as owning up to his actions while the other defendants continued denying having done anything wrong.

The prosecution ended its case with a few last shots at Skilling. Among those was a powerful blow centered on Skilling's sale of 500,000 shares of Enron stock—half his Enron holdings—on September 17, 2001, the first day the market re-opened after shutting down upon the September 11, 2001 terrorist attacks. That trade earned him $15.5 million. It was one of 10 improper trades he was alleged to have made, but prosecutors essentially punted on the other nine, choosing to focus on this trade, the largest of them all. And although Lay was never charged with insider trading because he sold his stock back to the company to repay company loans, Skilling sold his shares on the open market.

Skilling had told the SEC in December 2001 that he "agonized" over the sale, but went through with it because he, like millions of other investors, was afraid of how the market would react to the attacks and he wanted to protect his wealth. But prosecutors produced his then-stockbroker, Glenn Ray, who testified that Skilling had called him on September 6, 2001—the Thursday before the attacks—with a request to sell 200,000 Enron shares. Skilling had not told the SEC about his pre-9/11 attempt to sell Enron shares.

Skilling had told Ray that he was no longer an officer at Enron (he had resigned the previous month) and therefore did not have to report trades to the SEC. But Ray first needed a letter from Enron verifying Skilling's new status as a non-officer, so the trade was put on hold so Skilling could get such a letter to him. The letter, dated September 10, didn't get to Ray before the markets closed after the September 11 attacks.

"The market is dropping now," Skilling told Ray on an audiotape of his call to the broker, asking that he sell 500,000 shares when the market reopened on September

17. Brokers typically record such calls for their records. Skilling also told Ray on the call, "You can't do anything if you have material inside information, but that's true for any human being on the planet and that's a decision I have to make." The inference was that Skilling demanded the smaller trade on September 6—and then upped it to 500,000 shares on September 17—because he knew Enron was failing, and with the added uncertainty of the attacks, he wanted to cash out a substantial portion of his holdings based on information that the marketplace lacked.

Prosecutors rested their case on March 28, 2006. In doing so, they dropped three counts against Skilling and one count against Lay, leaving them to face 28 and six counts, respectively. But the case had no obvious smoking guns. It hinged on recollections and interpretations of witnesses and documents without anything that conclusively tied Lay and Skilling to a scheme to defraud investors. In order to convict, jurors would have to put together the pieces of a puzzle that the prosecutors had presented. Moreover, they would have to believe the key prosecution witnesses.

Although the defense teams had their own lineup intended to counter prosecution witnesses, the ones that really counted were Lay and Skilling. Jurors would have to decide whom to believe. The defense teams had complained for months that they couldn't convince critical witnesses to testify, or even speak to them, because they were afraid of being indicted if they cooperated with the defendants. A defense witness list that once had exceeded 200 had been whittled to about 100, but less than a third of the people on the list testified.

Skilling had been known for being emotional and impulsive, quick to slap down what he considered foolishness—or even a simple challenge—with sarcasm and disdain. Early in the trial, jurors heard an audiotape of an infamous April 2001 conference call regarding that year's first-quarter earnings in which Skilling called a hedge fund analyst an "asshole" when the analyst had complained that Enron never released financial statements at the same time that it posted results. In another analyst conference call a month earlier, intended to quell market rumors that Enron was in trouble, Skilling started off telling listeners he was in "a really lousy mood" because he had just returned from a trip to South America. Observers expected multiple blowups and perhaps an angry meltdown or two while Skilling endured cross-examination.

Lay, on the other hand, was expected to charm jurors. His public persona had been more consistently unflappable, which was unsurprising because he was the one at Enron who interacted with politicians and heads of state. Of the two, he was the critical civic and business leader in Houston and a generous charitable donor. In October 2001, the same hedge fund worker who prompted Skilling's profanity challenged Lay during a conference call as Enron was beginning to crumble, and while Lay accused him of trying to drive down Enron's stock price and cut him off, the company's longtime ambassador didn't lose his cool.

When the defense opened its case, Lay's lead lawyer, Michael Ramsey, had been sidelined by a heart condition. Days before the prosecution rested, he had a stent inserted in his chest. The trial continued without the sometime blustery attorney, who missed five weeks of the case recovering from the first procedure and a second week implanting a second stent in his carotid artery to relieve blockage. He would miss Lay's testimony, leaving Mac Secrest to question their client.

The lead-up witnesses to the defendants picked away at parts of the prosecution's case, but all eyes were on the defendants, and Skilling went first.

"I am absolutely innocent," he declared when he took the stand on April 10, launching what would be seven days of testimony. Though admitting that he was somewhat nervous, he was relaxed and conversational under Petrocelli's methodical questioning. At times he was even self-deprecating, joking that his acceptance into Harvard Business School long before he joined Enron was "some huge mistake." He also took on a light professorial tone, seeking to teach jurors about the workings of gas and electricity markets as well as Enron's businesses, and fondly recalling his lead role in bringing his idea of pioneering new trading markets (the "Gas Bank").

He portrayed himself as a man obsessed with Enron, to the point that he ignored his three children, ended his first marriage in divorce, and increasingly took it personally that the company's stock steadily dropped from its August 2000 high of more than $90 a share. He said he quit in August 2001 because he was worn out and had become convinced that he was doing Enron no favors by staying as the share price dropped. But he repeated what he told Congress in 2002—that he left the company certain that it was financially strong. When asked if he had any idea that Enron would implode less than four months later, he replied, "Not in my wildest dreams, no. It's almost inconceivable now what happened."

Skilling also said he never observed or participated in any fraud at Enron and knew of no reason that the company would have to resort to that to succeed. In a staccato fashion, Petrocelli asked if he ever destroyed documents, set up offshore accounts to hid his wealth, or did anything to hide his past behavior or business dealings. Each time Skilling answered "no," sometimes leaning forward to add punch to his denials.

Skilling also had answers for the damaging testimony from prosecution witnesses. About two hours into his direct testimony, he said that he did not remember calling Ray, his broker, the week before the September 11 attacks, asking to sell 200,000 Enron shares, though he remembered arranging to short-sell 800,000 shares of another energy company, AES Corp., in a move that garnered him $15 million. Whether or not he lied about his memory lapse, his claim that he remembered one aspect of the call while forgetting the other rang hollow. It particularly stung because his testimony came within days of his broker's testimony, who was among the prosecution's final witnesses. The moment begged the question of whether he displayed selective recollection, because his failure to tell the SEC about the September 6 call years earlier left him no choice. It also undercut his credibility from the start, because, if he was lying about having forgotten that conversation, he could lie to extricate himself from other allegations as well.

Regarding Fastow's testimony that he had said, "get me as much of that juice as you can" in reference to starting a second LJM partnership, Skilling said that he didn't use the word "juice" in that context. He said that he didn't give Fastow so-called bear hugs—the verbal promises that LJM2 wouldn't lose money in deals with Enron. He also said that he and Causey did not concoct such side agreements, calling Causey a consummate professional and a "conscientious, hard-working guy."

Regarding last-minute increases in earnings per share that prosecution witnesses claimed were added to please him whether or not performance warranted it, Skilling didn't remember the one, and called the other "absurd" because the company's trading profits had already soared past Wall Street expectations.

And, with respect to Delainey's testimony, Skilling said his question about moving the retail unit's trading function into Enron North America was, "Are you sure you want to do this?," rather than "What do you want to do?" as Delainey had testified, the distinction being that his question was a request, not a veiled order.

In terms of the Raptors, Skilling testified that they were protecting gains rather than hiding losses, and that they had been reviewed and approved by in-house and outside lawyers and accountants. Skilling's contention contradicted Glisan and Fastow's view that the Raptors were improper structures designed to help Enron cook its books. But Skilling also acknowledged that Causey had told him that the Raptors would lock in gains as long as Enron's stock price remained above a certain level. Even though Enron's shares fell throughout 2001, Skilling said Causey assured him, shortly before Skilling resigned in August of that year, that solvent Raptors could bail out others that were hurt by the lower stock price, backing up his assumption that Enron was healthy before he left.

When discussing the specific charges against him, Skilling's temper emerged, though he kept it in check. He remained angry not only that he had been demonized, but that his company had been maligned as a hotbed of fraud and lies. In Skilling's view, he was seeking to exonerate the company as well as himself. "We are innocent. By 'we,' I mean Enron Corporation," he said.

Skilling's face-off with Berkowitz began April 17. Bit by bit, Berkowitz sought to undercut Skilling's explanations of allegations described by prosecution witnesses. But the prosecutor also introduced issues unrelated to the charges, challenging Skilling's truthfulness and ethics—a move intended to bolster the government's contention that Skilling didn't adhere to rules or policies, instead doing what he pleased.

For example, the prosecutor noted that Skilling had invested in a photo-sharing business in 2000 and 2001 run by his ex-girlfriend. The company did business with Enron, but Skilling didn't disclose his investment to Lay or Enron's board, as required by the company's code of ethics. Skilling said that he invested $60,000 in the venture, but Berkowitz presented canceled checks and a copy of a wire transfer that showed Skilling's investment was $180,000, or three times that amount.

Skilling sometimes responded to Berkowitz as though he was talking to someone ignorant of the basic tenets of business and risk management. He acknowledged exerting pressure for Enron's divisions to meet earnings targets, but noted that every company did so, and in his view Enron had no issues when it came to hitting projections. When Berkowitz displayed a chart that showed more than $1 billion in reserves were "available for earnings," Skilling, who had denied the allegation that Enron raided reserves to pad earnings, said the prosecutor misunderstood how reserves are calculated, approved, and set and therefore misinterpreted the document. Berkowitz snapped, "Let's move on," to which Skilling responded, "Let's NOT move on."

"I know it is difficult for you to sit here and answer questions, Mr. Skilling, and I know you at times overreact to people who are critical," Berkowitz said, conjuring Skilling's reputation for having little patience with being challenged. "But if you could just let me ask the questions, and we'll move along, Mr. Skilling." Skilling responded by raising his eyebrows and cocking his head, acknowledging the rebuke.

More dust-ups emerged when Skilling challenged Berkowitz's questions about Skilling's insistence that Enron was not a trading company, but rather an intermediary that packaged services for commodity buyers and sellers. When asked why he felt the need to define Enron as a logistics company rather than a trading business during a quarterly conference call with analysts—which prosecutors contended was part of an overall effort to portray Enron as stable rather than risky—an irritated Skilling said the analysts on the call had followed Enron for a decade and needed no such clarification. But after Enron failed, analysts largely claimed that they had relied on Skilling's explanations because they either couldn't figure out how the company made money by perusing financial statements or simply did not study them closely.

Overall, Skilling's testimony was viewed as neither a success or a failure. During cross-examination, he seethed, was occasionally sarcastic, and grew visibly irritated when Berkowitz prevented him from giving expansive answers. But he didn't lose control, raise his voice, or otherwise erupt as expected. Expectations of how he would present himself on the witness stand were likely so low that when he didn't explode, he was viewed as having done little either to help or hurt himself.

Lay would be the polar opposite. Expectations that he would bring his public affability to the witness stand were quickly shattered, even under direct examination. He was prickly and combative, often narrowing his eyes when answering questions, making himself appear defiant rather than contrite. Skilling had clearly been carefully prepared on issues such as body language and communication skills, and he trusted Petrocelli to guide his testimony. Lay charted his own combative course, appearing suspicious of even Secrest's questions and motives. It was as though Lay still believed himself to be the chairman of the board, managing his defense rather than trusting his legal team to manage it.

"I'm not done yet, Mr. Secrest. I told you this is not simple," Lay snapped when Secrest interrupted Lay's unfocused description of what torpedoed Enron in his view—a deadly mixture of bad press, a thieving CFO, and short-sellers who had colluded to drive Enron's stock down at a time when market confidence was waning.

Lay's testimony began well enough. In a conversational and folksy tone, he described his hardscrabble beginnings as the son of a Baptist minister in Missouri, having lived the American dream of gaining wealth and prestige through hard work. "I've not only pursued the American dream, I've achieved it," he said. "I suppose we could say the last few years I've also achieved the American nightmare."

He portrayed himself as scrambling to save Enron from Fastow's betrayal, short-sellers, and damaging publicity that fueled the fire engulfing the company he created and loved. But he wasn't connecting with jurors. His attempts at humor often fell flat, generating laughter or smiles only from his family members in the gallery. When Secrest asked why structures and projects were given such names as Raptor, Lay laughed and said, "Beats the hell out of me." His laughter wasn't infectious.

Lay said that he believed Enron was strong and had a great future when he resumed the role of CEO upon Skilling's departure. He flatly denied that Fastow met with him the next day to tell him about massive looming write-offs from overvalued international assets. He said the September 2001 meeting that he and Fastow had held with Goldman Sachs executives was about Enron's vulnerability to a takeover, not to discuss restructuring or possible bankruptcy. He testified that, in preparing to release Enron's third-quarter earnings results in October 2001, he decided to unwind the Raptors because they were crumbling along with the company's falling stock price.

He also considered Fastow's LJM partnerships to be an "old, dead issue" by the fall of 2001. Fastow had sold his interest in the partnerships to Michael Kopper that summer, so the sticky issue of having the CFO running partnerships that conducted deals with Enron no longer existed. In the days after Enron released third-quarter results, the *Wall Street Journal* published a string of hard-hitting stories that brought the LJM partnerships—and Fastow's lucrative compensation from them—out of the labyrinth of Enron's financial statements and into the public eye. That Fastow no longer ran the partnerships didn't matter. The fact that he had, and that they had acquired Enron assets to Enron's financial benefit, fueled more questions about the propriety of the company's disclosures. But Lay testified that, amid all the "noise" of the LJM partnerships, Enron's accounting was correct. He also said the *Journal's* outing of an older partnership named Chewco that had been run by Kopper posed a more serious problem, because it had been wrongly treated as independent of Enron and would force the company to restate earnings dating back to 1997—a sharp blow at a time when market confidence was slipping away.

Lay was accused of lying to analysts, investors, and employees when he repeatedly assured them throughout the fall of 2001 that all was well at Enron when it wasn't. He testified that he stood by those statements, based on what he knew at the time. But evidence showed that he had received plenty of warnings from employees who questioned the company's financial integrity. In addition to Fastow, Glisan, and Watkins, Lay received an e-mail from a trader who wrote that he thought it was criminal that top management knew that the Raptors were being used to manipulate Enron's books. The company's chief of staff told Lay in an August 2001 e-mail, sent three days after Skilling quit, that the company's unclear financial statements could draw accounting scrutiny. The *Journal's* persistent questions raised red flags. And unnamed employees wrote in an internal online survey in September 2001 that Enron relied on "accounting trickery" and deceptive transactions to meet earnings targets.

Even though Lay was receiving good news too, particularly from the survey that he said had solicited 3,000 responses, he didn't give the bad news top priority, other than the Watkins complaints that received a cursory investigation. When pressed on cross-examination about his failure to look into the negative input, Lay sneered to

Hueston, "The corpse is on the gurney now, Mr. Hueston, and you're carving it up any way you want to carve it up. I didn't have that luxury when I was right in the middle of battle."

At the end of his direct examination, Secrest—either unwittingly or knowingly—lit the fuse of Lay's intense dislike for Hueston, the prosecutor who had stalked him since joining the task force six months before Lay was indicted in 2004. Secrest asked about the final $7.5 million of the more than $70 million in loans that Lay had taken from Enron throughout 2001. Lay had repaid all but that last increment with company stock, claiming that he used stock to repay margin calls because he had collateralized other loans from banks with company shares. He said he tried to repay the last amount, but declared loudly, "John Hueston blocked it."

Another defense witness, attorney Martin Siegel (who worked for Lay in another Enron case), would later testify that Lay had tried to pay that last amount years after the bankruptcy, but the effort fell through because Hueston didn't respond to repayment-related documents sent to him. Hueston joined the task force in January 2004, more than two years after Enron went bankrupt. Berkowitz suggested that the holdup stemmed from Lay's "horse trading" demand that he receive a $1 million insurance policy from Enron in exchange for paying off that last loan, but Siegel said he didn't know what the prosecutor meant by "horse trading." However, Lay never simply wrote a check to Enron in the years before Hueston joined the task force—or before the task force was even formed.

When Hueston stepped up for what would be a bruising cross-examination, Lay shifted slightly in the witness chair, as though shoring himself up for a fight. The prosecutor's first punch indicated that Lay had tried to contact other witnesses regarding testimony during the trial.

"Did you have any conversations to get your story straight for trial?," the prosecutor demanded.

"Can you elaborate on that, Mr. Hueston?," Lay snapped. "I'm not sure what you're talking about."

Hueston obliged, noting that Lay had called two Goldman Sachs executives during the trial to discuss the September 2001 meeting that Fastow had described. Lay acknowledged that he tried to call them in March—the same month that Fastow had testified. Lay said that he was trying to "make sure some facts I had about a meeting were as accurate as they could be," as opposed to Fastow's "fake version of the meeting." Goldman Sachs attorneys advised Lay to stop calling them directly.

In addition, Lay acknowledged that he had tried to contact Vince Kaminski through a friend days before Kaminski testified for the prosecution. Kaminski had described Lay's cold reaction to his suggestion to Lay and other top executives that Enron "come clean" on questionable financial structures, like the Raptors, before the company spiraled into bankruptcy.

Lay claimed that he didn't know Kaminski was going to testify, even though Kaminski's name had been on the prosecution's witness list since the government released its first version in November 2005. And though Kaminski often spoke with Skilling during their days at Enron, he didn't have such a past relationship with Lay. But Lay testified that he was "trying to reconnect with Vince, to talk to him about some issues I wanted to talk to him about." Pressed further, he said he wanted to talk about "risk management" issues.

Those revelations challenged Lay's credibility, in that it appeared that he thought he could ignore the protocol of not speaking to other witnesses in the case, and that he could take care of potentially problematic testimony by calling them rather than let jurors decide whom to believe. Secrest later sought to soften that blow, asking if he had been trying to tamper with witnesses. Lay said he was trying to see if they would meet with his lawyers.

Hueston's assault on Lay grew much more intense when the prosecutor challenged Lay's oft-repeated claim that he repaid $70 million in Enron loans with company stock because he needed cash to satisfy margin calls. He had repeatedly portrayed himself as unloading Enron stock under duress, but had no choice because he had collateralized $100 million in personal loans from banks with company stock. The banks issued margin calls as the share price fell throughout 2001.

"It was a lot more sufficient way to handle this problem than selling on the open market. I found it more convenient to use the line of credit. It was set up to provide me, and other senior executives, with more financial flexibility."

Lay wasn't charged with insider trading, and he said that an internal Enron lawyer had advised him that he couldn't conduct an illegal insider trade by selling company stock back to Enron because the company would have as much information about its workings as Lay did. But Hueston sought to portray Lay as putting his personal needs over those of shareholders and employees, enjoying his ability to obtain massive loans even as the company was spiraling toward failure. In September 2001, Lay encouraged employees to buy more stock, noting that he had bought shares himself. But he didn't say that he had sold many more shares than he had purchased.

When Hueston asked him why he didn't just disclose his stock sales even though regulations didn't require him to do so until the proxy statement was filed, Lay narrowed his eyes and said he had fully complied with the existing regulations at the time. Some jurors rolled their eyes at his response. Lay could have taken a different approach by saying in a contrite tone that he had followed the regulations at the time, but in hindsight it looked like he was hiding something by failing to disclose stock sales that had been intended to bail himself out of financial jams. Instead, he treated Hueston like an irritant, and focused on their one-on-one battle instead of why he was there in the first place—to convince 12 jurors that he was an honest man. Those jurors didn't have ready access to tens of millions of dollars whenever they needed it. Skilling, by contrast, sold his shares on the open market and reported them publicly as required.

Hueston then made rich fodder of Lay's extravagant lifestyle. In the first half of 2001, Lay chartered a boat, the Amnesia, for $200,000 for his wife's birthday party. They paid $4,700 for a two-night stay in a hotel on the French Riviera. They spent $20,000 on an antiquing trip in Mallorca, Spain. His own birthday party at a resort that year cost $12,000, prompting Lay to joke that he cost less than his wife. The joke garnered no laughter from the middle-class jury. Lay said he had no way of knowing that Enron would falter months after he and his family enjoyed those extravagances.

"We could have reduced some living costs, but as I said earlier, we had realized the American dream. We were living a very expensive lifestyle. It was difficult to turn off that lifestyle like a spigot," Lay testified.

Lay finished his six days of testimony professing his love for the company and its employees. He said he had spent half his professional life running Enron, a great company that changed markets around the world. The ending was much like the beginning, when he said Enron's demise was more painful for him than deaths of loved ones.

"I think the most painful thing in my life was watching Enron finally have to go into bankruptcy," Lay said.

The defense case ended with a series of experts who said that it is common for companies to scramble and make last-minute changes to their reported earnings-per-share before reporting quarterly results. One also said that Enron properly reported its move of the retail unit's trading arm into the company's larger trading franchise as a resegmentation, and that nothing in the accounting rules addresses the intent of such a move.

The defense rested on May 8, having called 29 witnesses to testify—seven more than the 22 who testified for the prosecution's case-in-chief. Ramsey returned to court that day after having been out for five weeks. The prosecution followed up with three rebuttal witnesses, bringing the total witness count to 54. But the rebuttal witnesses added little to the government's case.

One in particular, Mike Muckleroy, who was an executive at Enron from the company's inception in 1985 until he was fired in the early 1990s, told jurors that "under certain business exigencies, I have known Mr. Lay not to tell the truth." But he couldn't explain what he meant. Before the trial began, Lake had denied a government request to introduce evidence of an oil trading scandal (the "Valhalla" scandal) that had severely threatened Enron in 1987. In that instance, Enron oil traders had bet wrong on the direction of oil prices, leaving the company to cover massive positions that could have driven it into bankruptcy. The traders also had kept a separate series of books, padding their own pockets with oil trading profits. Muckleroy had cleaned up the mess. Lay had been informed of the traders' actions, but did not fire them because their division was profitable for the company. Lay had later claimed that he was unaware of what they had done, once the scandal was revealed publicly.

Prosecutors wanted to introduce evidence of that scandal to show that Lay had once before claimed public ignorance when he knew of serious internal problems at the company. But Lake refused to allow it because Lay hadn't been criminally charged and the scandal had occurred so many years before Enron failed.

A dozen hours of closing arguments launched on May 15 with Ruemmler saying that the duo had overseen a massive fraud carried out "through accounting tricks, fiction, hocus-pocus, trickery, misleading statements, half-truths, omissions, and outright lies." She said that the defendants were still clinging to cover stories that had been blown during the exhausting trial. She accentuated her point by displaying a quote from Lay's testimony, in which he said rules were important, but "you should not be a slave to the rules, either."

She said that Enron could have come clean when Skilling resigned in August 2001 and Lay resumed the role of CEO. She said that Enron could have told investors that the broadband venture had failed, the retail energy unit was drowning in losses, financial structures dependent on a high stock price were crumbling, and assets had been grossly overvalued. Instead, both Lay and Skilling had assured analysts and investors that Enron was strong, maintaining the story Skilling had told and that Lay would continue telling until the truth finally emerged with Enron's failure.

"They chose to lie," she declared.

The defense teams sought to turn the tables on the government, portraying their clients as victims of overzealous prosecutors bent on finding crimes when there were none so that the top two executives would be punished for one of the biggest corporate scandals in U.S. history. "This was all manufactured after the fact. Because it's Enron. After all, somebody has to pay—it's Enron," Petrocelli said.

He said the government stalked underlings as though Enron was the Mafia, and robbed them of their free will by threatening prosecution that would leave them penniless and possibly facing decades in prison if they didn't acquiesce, plead guilty, and toe the line of the story that the government wanted to tell. He pointed out that prosecutors didn't have tangible proof of wrongdoing through documents, e-mails, or tape recordings, and that, instead, the government had resorted to intimidating former executives into interpreting honest mistakes and normal business practices as crimes.

Petrocelli's tone softened when he told the panel that he felt as though he had held "Jeff's life in my hands" for two years leading up to the trial. The next day, he would have to put his client's fate in the jury's hands.

"Look into his eyes. Look into his soul. See if you see a criminal," the attorney said. He also urged jurors not to broker any deals during deliberations, agreeing to acquit Skilling on some counts because of doubts about his guilt while convicting him of others. "Don't negotiate with his life," Petrocelli said. "Not guilty, not guilty, not guilty—28 times."

Lay's team split its closing argument among Secrest, Lewis, Collins, and Ramsey, leaving their presentation somewhat disjointed, unlike the smooth flow of Petrocelli's argument. Secrest built on Petrocelli's theme, urging jurors to consider that the devastating effects of Enron's failure translated to a fierce motive for the government to make sure the company's top two executives were punished "at any and all costs."

Ramsey took only a few minutes, speaking for the first time since he returned to court after having been sidelined with his heart problems. He said the judge and the American flag represented the United States, not the prosecutors. "You speak for the country when you render a verdict, and render a true verdict. Not guilty. Not guilty. Not guilty," he said.

Berkowitz provided the government's last word, calling the trial an historic case in which the jury must send a message that it's wrong to construct a web of lies and deliberately misleading financial disclosures to maintain an illusion of prosperity. He said that neither Skilling nor Lay tried to ruin Enron, but that they had perpetuated unsustainable fraud that lies could no longer mask.

He said Lay's stock sales in 2001 showed that he had put his needs above those of employees and investors. And when faced with an insider trading allegation, Skilling used the September 11 terrorist attacks to cover his tracks. The prosecutor then reminded all listeners who made up the defendants' jury of their peers: "Administrative managers, dairy farmers, payroll managers, retired engineers, ship inspectors, teachers, apartment marketers, design engineers, roofing salespeople, clerks of the court, personnel managers, retired sales assistants, and dental hygienists."

"You get the final word in this historic case," Berkowitz said. "You get to decide whether they told the truth or they told lies."

Lay's Bank Fraud

With jurors deliberating the fraud and conspiracy case, Skilling hunkered down at his legal team's "war room" in a building across the street from the courthouse, awaiting a verdict. But Lay was on trial again in a three-day case centered on his personal banking.

Lay's original indictment charged him in the Enron case as well as the banking case, which involved one count of bank fraud and three counts of making false statements to banks. The charges stemmed from $75 million in loans that Lay had obtained from three banks, beginning in 1999. He was accused of reneging on agreements with those lenders not to use the money to buy or carry margin stock (stock bought with loans). But Lay did use the money for that purpose, which prompted him to tap the company for loans that he repaid with Enron stock in order to repay those margin calls. Lay repaid all of the bank loans, but the case involved whether he intended to misrepresent how he had planned to use the loans.

Lay's lawyers had called the banking charges "tag-alongs" to the conspiracy and fraud case, to give the government a different way to convict him should he be acquitted in the larger trial. Lay had complained in a speech to Houston business leaders in mid-December 2005 that his legal team's research showed that no one had been charged under the banking laws at the center of the case except him.

In October 2004, Lake severed the banking case from the conspiracy case. Lay's legal team had pushed for an immediate trial on all the charges against him within two months of his indictment, and offered to forego his right to a jury and make the case a bench trial, if that would speed up the process. Lake granted the request in the banking case, but ruled that Lay and Skilling would be tried together in the fraud and conspiracy case. Lay's lawyers then retreated from their speedy-trial push and asked that the banking case be tried two months after the fraud and conspiracy case, prompting prosecutors to ask that it be tried in the spring or early summer of 2005, with or without a jury. Lake offered to try the banking case in a bench trial while the jurors deliberated the fraud and conspiracy case, a proposition to which Lay agreed.

Jury deliberations began May 17, and Lay's second trial began the next day. But the tone of the banking case was much more subdued than the fraud and conspiracy trial. Even when Hueston cross-examined Lay, the enmity between the two had deflated. Prosecutor Robb Adkins told Lake the case involved one simple lie: Lay signed forms for bank loans that stated he would not use the money to buy margin stock, and he used the money to buy margin stock. Lay's lawyer Ken Carroll countered that Lay had no intent to ignore such covenants; moreover, Lay had repaid the loans. If he had been told he was misusing the money, he would have fixed the problem, Carroll said.

The banking case stemmed from federal rules adopted after the 1929 stock market crash that allowed only half of a bank loan to be used to buy stock. The loan documents that Lay had signed noted that rule, which Robb said that Lay had repeatedly violated. James Shelton, who served as Lay's private banker at Bank of America from 1993 through 1998, said that he had advised Lay of the rule. Lay obtained two lines of credit from the bank—one of which was intended for stock purchases—and signed documents agreeing to all regulations for both. Sally Ballard, a secretary for the Lays and the person who paid their bills, testified that Lay actively managed his own finances.

Once again in the witness chair, Lay acknowledged that his use of the loans violated the no-stock-purchases rule. But he said that he didn't intend to skirt any regulations and never got a warning from assistants or lawyers. "I regret I did not have more time to spend on my personal matters and perhaps this is one of the consequences of that," he testified.

The case went to Lake on May 23, and the judge said that he would render his verdict after the fraud and conspiracy jury rendered its verdict.

THE VERDICTS

There wasn't long to wait. Two days later, shortly after 10 a.m., the jury sent word that it had a verdict. Hueston was showing two reporters pictures of his children in his 12-floor office of the federal courthouse when a harried Berkowitz rushed by, saying, "They have a verdict. Judge is going to announce at 11." The reporters ran for the elevators and told their editors a verdict was coming. Soon the wire services, newspaper Web sites, and television stations announced that the end had come and would be announced in less than an hour.

A lunchtime crowd started gathering in front of the courthouse. Although Houston hadn't had its eyes on the trial for the previous four months, the verdict was something that people had anticipated since the company imploded. The legal teams and the defendants filed into the courtroom to await the decision. Skilling's brother, Mark, who was an attorney, was at his right at the defense table with Petrocelli at his left. Lay, however, wanted his wife by his side at the defense table. But Mrs. Lay was not an attorney, unlike Lay's daughter, so Lake did not allow Mrs. Lay to sit next to her husband. Lay instead seated himself on the bench right in front of the bar, his wife at his right, and his daughter at her right. The rest of his family packed the front row in the gallery nearest the jury box, where they had sat throughout the trial. Skilling's children did not attend, nor did his wife.

Barely a sound could be heard except for shuffling footsteps as the jury filed into the courtroom for the last time, taking the seats that they had warmed for four months. The lengthy general verdict form was handed to Lake, who began to read the results for Skilling first.

At the first "guilty" on the single overarching conspiracy count, Skilling's face, and that of his brother, remained inscrutable. Petrocelli's eyes briefly closed, and the attorney appeared grim. Some of the younger lawyers on Skilling's dedicated legal team appeared stunned. Lake said "guilty" 19 times—for one count of conspiracy, 12 counts of securities fraud, one count of insider trading, and five counts of making false statements to auditors. The judge said "not guilty" nine times for nine counts of insider trading.

At hearing his co-defendant's fate, Lay's face went gray, and then his cheeks went red. His wife wept quietly on his right shoulder. Other Lay family members wept or sat in stunned silence. Their emotional reactions continued when Lake got to Lay's own counts in the conspiracy case. At the first "guilty," Lay tossed his head as if taking a blow, clutching his wife's left hand in his right. Five more "guilty" verdicts followed with convictions on all charges: one count of conspiracy, two counts of wire fraud, and three counts of securities fraud.

Lake then rendered his verdict in the banking case: guilty on all four counts. He set a sentencing date of September 11—a date that would eventually be postponed, but appeared to symbolically slap Skilling for saying he had sold half his Enron holdings because of the market's reaction to the September 11, 2001 attacks. Skilling was free to leave on the same $5 million bond he had posted when he was indicted in February 2004. Outside the courthouse, Skilling appeared less daunted than Petrocelli, who tiredly told reporters, "We've just begun to fight." Skilling eyes watered almost imperceptibly when he said he was disappointed, "but that's the way the system works."

Lake's attitude toward Lay visibly changed from that of the impartial judge to one who had just convicted a federal felon. When Lay was indicted, he was granted a $500,000 bond and allowed to keep his passport. Lake immediately ordered that Lay post a $5 million bond and surrender the passport, but Lay didn't have it with him. He and his family waited in the courthouse for more than an hour until the passport could be retrieved and then turned over to authorities. And Lake made Lay's bond more restrictive than Skilling's. Whereas Skilling's bond required him to remain in the continental United States, Lay's new bond prohibited travel outside the 13-county Southern District of Texas and Colorado, where the Lays had property in Aspen.

Lay, who had testified that he was in debt after paying millions in legal fees, didn't have the ready cash to post his bond. His and his wife's children put up their homes as collateral, making for a somber moment as they each raised their right hand before Lake to swear that the property was theirs before signing the paperwork.

Once cleared, Lay left the courthouse, and stepped up to the media microphones after he stepped out the door. Appearing crestfallen, his cheeks still red, Lay said he firmly believed he was innocent of all the charges against him. "We believe that God in fact is in control and indeed he does work all things for good for those who love the Lord." Then he walked away hand in hand with his wife, the pair jostled at the center of a media mob.

LAY'S DEATH

Lay would not live to appeal his convictions or see the inside of a prison cell. In the early morning hours of July 5, 2006, just six weeks after he and Skilling were convicted, he died of heart disease while at one of his vacation homes in Aspen. An autopsy showed he had three severely blocked coronary arteries and that he had suffered at least two heart attacks in the past. Two stents had been implanted to relieve some of the blockage, which reached 90 percent in some areas. His sudden death came as a surprise, because unlike Ramsey, Lay had shown no signs of illness during the lengthy trial or the years leading up to it.

Whether or not Lay maintained a treatment regimen after the trial, in death he would clear his name as far as the law was concerned. His convictions were not final because he had not yet been sentenced, nor had he filed an appeal. A week before Lay had been slated to be sentenced alongside Skilling in October 2006, Lake vacated Lay's convictions.

The government didn't give up. On the day Skilling was sentenced, the government filed a civil forfeiture case, alleging that Lay's crimes had gained him more than $90 million. Prosecutors sought to seize nearly $13 million of that amount, which they said that they could trace to criminal activity. Specifically, the government sought about $10 million in cash and more than $2 million that Lay had used to pay off the mortgage of the $6 million condominium that he shared with his wife. Subsequent filings indicated that both sides tried to reach a settlement that would involve Linda Lay turning over cash in order to keep the dwelling. But no settlement emerged by the time that Werlein denied her May 2007 motion to dismiss the case in November of that year. If the case goes to trial, the government will have to re-prove Lay's guilt because his criminal convictions have been vacated.

THE SENTENCES

Skilling was sentenced to 292 months in prison (24 years and four months). He took the news of his punishment much as he had absorbed his convictions—with an impassive face and no tears. Skilling's sentence is by far the most harsh of any imposed on Enron felons. Of those who pleaded guilty to crimes, sentences range from one to six years in prison for nine of the felons and two to four years' probation for six of them.

Fastow's wife, Lea, received the least prison time—one year for the misdemeanor tax crime, which she finished in July 2005. Her husband received the longest sentence of all the cooperators (six years)—but it was four years fewer than what he had agreed to serve upon pleading guilty, and the lesser term came because of a judge's mercy and a prosecutor's failure to argue that he should stick to the time that Fastow had agreed to serve under his plea deal. Fastow has signaled his intention to enroll in the same drug and alcohol treatment program that Glisan completed. With that, and 15 percent off for good behavior, Fastow will likely be released from prison in four years.

Sentences for the other Enron cooperators fell in the middle of the Fastow bookends. Lake, cognizant of Fastow's shorter term, sentenced Causey in November 2006 to five and a half years in prison, cutting more time from the seven-year maximum than prosecutors had recommended. The same month, Kopper received three years and a month, and Koenig received 18 months, each sentenced by Werlein.

The week before Fastow was sentenced, Hoyt imposed two and a half years for Delainey, who would finish his term at a prison in his native Canada. In June 2007, Gilmore sentenced Hannon to two years and gave Rice two years and three months. The six who received probation when sentenced in 2006 and 2007 were Larry Lawyer, Paula Rieker, Timothy DeSpain, and the three traders—Belden, Richter, and Forney. All received probation for two years except DeSpain, who was given a four-year term.

Despite the havoc wrought on California electricity consumers throughout the state's power crisis in 2000 and 2001, the light sentences for the only three Enron traders ever charged with crimes sparked little notice.

And in December 2006, one of the last guilty pleas entered, that of Christopher Calger, was withdrawn with the prosecutors' blessing. The same problem that prosecutors would face on appeal with usage of the honest services theory was intregal to his plea, so rather than fight that fight, the government backed off.

THE APPEALS

Although the Enron Task Force scored a long list of guilty pleas, most of the appeals have shined a harsh light on the prosecutions. In 2005, amid the first broadband trial, the U.S. Supreme Court unanimously overturned Arthur Andersen LLP's conviction because of the vague jury instruction that Harmon had given at the prosecutors' request. The government's trial record received another stinging blow in August 2006, when the Fifth U.S. Circuit Court of Appeals overturned most of the convictions of the Merrill Lynch defendants in the barge case.

In a 2-1 decision, an appeals panel ruled that prosecutors wrongly stretched a federal wire fraud statute pertaining to honest services. The majority ruled that the deprivation of honest services refers to the taking of money or property by way of theft, embezzlement, or taking bribes. But if such acts do not take place, and the crime in question is in the victim's corporate interest, the majority opinion concluded that the honest services theory doesn't apply. In the barge case, the participants did not take anything, and the deal, sham or not, was in Enron's corporate interest (to meet earnings targets). And because the jury presented a general verdict that did not specify which prosecution theory led to the decision to convict, the possibility that a wrongly applied honest services theory prevailed was what prompted the Fifth Circuit panel to overturn the fraud and conspiracy convictions against Bayly, Brown, and Furst. The fraud and conspiracy convictions against Fuhs were overturned for lack of evidence. The opinion did not obliterate the prosecution's contention that a crime occurred—it just struck down one of the theories that the government used to win the convictions. Brown's convictions for perjury and obstruction of justice were affirmed, and the U.S. Supreme Court denied his request for review.

The Fifth Circuit hinted in June 2006 that a reversal might be coming with rulings that allowed Bayly, Furst, and Fuhs to be released from prison pending the outcome of the appeal. All had begun serving their terms in 2005. Brown didn't receive that early reprieve, but he was released within days of the issuance of the opinion. Though the opinion didn't specifically say he should be re-sentenced for his affirmed convictions, Deputy Attorney General Alice Fisher conceded in a filing that he was entitled to be re-sentenced for the convictions that had stood up on appeal. Under federal sentencing guidelines, the year that he had served would suffice for perjury and obstruction.

In October 2006, Werlein vacated Fuhs's convictions, and Fuhs cannot be retried. But the government plans to retry Bayly, Furst, and Brown with a superseding indictment that erased all mention of honest services.

Court filings by Brown's new legal team—which, for a time, included Dan Cogdell, the lawyer who had represented Kahanek when she was acquitted in the first round—indicate that the government has leaned on Brown to plead guilty to another felony in order to intimidate Bayly and Furst to follow suit to avoid having their former colleague testify against them in a retrial. All three defense teams have entered negotiations to reach a settlement, but none has been willing to allow their clients to plead to a felony. Instead, each team has said that their clients would agree to a civil settlement like those reached by defendants and the SEC. But with Skilling's appeal still ongoing—and its attack of the honest services theory—the government has refused to budge, leaving everyone anticipating a second trial.

Prosecutors in the retrial of Howard and Krautz presented the honest services theory with four of the five counts, and the judge gave jurors an instruction that linked the fifth count—falsifying books and records—to the others. In November 2006, prosecutors conceded that Howard's fraud and conspiracy convictions should be vacated because they were unlikely to stand up on appeal. However, the government argued that the fifth count stood apart and should be upheld. Howard's lawyers countered that the jury instruction that Gilmore had given jurors at the prosecution's request linked it to the tainted counts, so all five should be thrown out. Gilmore agreed and vacated everything in February 2007.

In November 2006, Hirko, Shelby, and Yeager filed their appeals with the Fifth Circuit, which heard arguments in August 2007. Unlike the other appeals, the honest services theory didn't play a part in their arguments.

Samuel Buffone, who represented Yeager alongside Canales in the original trial, argued that the abbreviated money laundering and insider trading case against Yeager should be dismissed because he was acquitted of the overarching conspiracy and wire and securities fraud counts. With his client having been found not guilty of participating in those crimes, Buffone said, the government cannot allege that he sold stock and moved tainted funds among different bank accounts while armed with inside information derived from the conspiracy. Shelby's appellate lawyer, Susan Hays, and Hirko's appellate lawyer, Lawrence Robbins, presented a similar argument coming from a different direction: because their clients were acquitted of money laundering and insider trading counts in the first trial, that left no fraud.

Hirko and Shelby didn't appeal the conspiracy count, so they face a retrial if the government follows through on a second prosecution whether or not the appeals court throws out the fraud and insider trading counts against them.

Doug Wilson, the government's appellate lawyer in the broadband case, countered that Yeager could have known about a scheme to lie about the broadband division's capabilities without participating in it, so the remaining counts against him should stand. And regarding Hirko and Shelby, he argued that the original jury would have acquitted them of conspiracy and fraud had the panel found that no fraud existed.

Members of the three-judge panel that heard the arguments—Patrick Higginbotham, Fortunato Benavides, and Emilio Garza—criticized the government's original case, saying it was too unmanageable, with too many counts. The tangled outcome of a few acquittals, no convictions, and jurors who had hung on more than 100 counts showed that the prosecution had failed to sell the jury on its case, Higginbotham said. Wilson conceded that the original case had "too many counts for the jury to sort through."

Benavides also appeared more open to Yeager's argument than those of Hirko had Shelby. He said that Yeager's acquittals went to the heart of the prosecution's case, while Hirko and Shelby appeared to say that any acquittal would spread. "It seems you can't have it both ways," Benavides said.

However, all three lost their appeals, and their retrials were scheduled for late 2008 and early 2009.

But Kevin Howard prevailed before the Fifth Circuit. Unlike the other broadband defendants, he could seize the Brown ruling because prosecutors presented the honest services theory in his retrial. After Gilmore vacated all his convictions, the government appealed to the Fifth Circuit to restore the fifth count. In January 2008, the Fifth Circuit's Higginbotham, Jerry Smith, and Eugene Davis heard those arguments from Doug Wilson, the government's appellate lawyer, and Lawrence Robbins, who represented Howard on appeal as well as Hirko.

Wilson acknowledged the government's error in asking for the jury instruction that linked Howard's fifth count to others that prosecutors had conceded were tainted by honest services. But he told the panel that Gilmore should not have agreed to issue that instruction, and when she did, the defense should have argued against it. An annoyed Higginbotham told Wilson his stance amounted to arguing that the government's mistake was the defense's fault "for not having stopped me."

Robbins chimed in that the government "should not be relieved of the bed it made for itself."

About a month later in February 2008, the panel ruled 3-0 to uphold Gilmore's decision to vacate all of Howard's convictions. Several months later the government decided to retry him a third time on all five counts in 2009.

The ruling in Howard's case appeared to bode well for Skilling in his pending appeal. Although Howard's case involved a single deal and was much less complicated than Skilling's vast case, the crux of the key argument was remarkably similar: The honest services theory tainted a critical count, and the same kind of linking jury instruction—also requested by prosecutors—could spread the taint to the majority of his other convictions, if not all.

Skilling filed his 239-page appeal in September 2007 and attacked the government's use of the honest services theory to help prove the overarching count of conspiracy to commit wire and securities fraud.

When Skilling was convicted in May 2006, his appeal options did not appear very strong. The "deliberate ignorance" jury instruction that could have applied to him when he took no such stance during the trial was a possible option, as were other arguments, such as Lake's refusal to grant a change of venue or his claims of prosecutorial misconduct.

The Fifth Circuit's honest services opinion, which had issued more than two months after his conviction, provided him with a much more potent weapon. As in the barge case, the Skilling jury returned a general verdict that did not specify which prosecution theory prompted the jury to convict, leaving those convictions vulnerable to attack. Prosecutors presented three theories: honest services fraud, "money or property" wire fraud, and securities fraud. Jurors could take their pick, and the verdict did not indicate which they chose. The same general verdict issue existed in the barge and Howard cases as well.

Lake had denied Skilling's request to remain free on bond pending the outcome of his appeal, so Skilling's legal team, still led by Petrocelli, appealed that ruling to the Fifth Circuit. The afternoon before Skilling was slated to surrender to a federal prison in southern Minnesota on December 12, 2006, the Fifth Circuit issued a stay of his report deadline to allow careful review of his request. About 24 hours later, the Fifth Circuit's Higginbotham issued an order lifting the stay and denying his request. Higginbotham hinted, however, that 14 counts (the majority of his convictions) could be overturned, largely because of the honest services ruling issued in August of that year.

"Our review has disclosed serious frailties in Skilling's conviction of conspiracy, securities fraud, and insider trading, difficulties brought by a decision of this court handed down after the jury's verdict, as well as less formidable questions regarding the giving of a jury instruction on deliberate ignorance," Higginbotham wrote.

But the opinion also hinted that Skilling's convictions on five counts of making false statements to auditors could stand. It said further that Skilling had raised no substantial question that was likely to result in reversal of his convictions on all counts and that any resulting sentence would likely exceed the expected duration of his appeal, so the stay of his surrender date was lifted. Skilling entered the prison shortly after noon on December 13, 2006.

Skilling's appeal brief argued that all 19 counts of which he was convicted should be reversed: one count of conspiracy to commit wire and securities fraud, 12 counts of securities fraud, one count of insider trading, and five counts of making false statements to auditors.

The arguments in the appeal include:

1. *Erroneous theory of honest services fraud.* Unlike Fastow or Kopper, Skilling did not skim money from schemes, take bribes, or otherwise rob Enron of money or property. The government theorized that he could be held liable for defrauding Enron even if his acts were intended to benefit his employer.
2. *Erroneous jury instructions.* Lake's "deliberate ignorance" instruction allowed the jury to infer guilty knowledge on Skilling's part if it found that he had sought to make himself ignorant of suspected criminal conduct. But Skilling's stance throughout the trial was that there was no fraud; therefore, he never tried to hide from discovering any fraud. Lake also denied the prosecutors' request that he modify the instruction by telling the jury that it could find deliberate ignorance as to one of the defendants, but not both. Other challenges to jury instructions include Lake's refusal to explain the concept of materiality in financial statements; his refusal to advise jurors on how to determine if a secret oral side agreement actually eliminated risk in the written documentation of a deal; and his refusal to explain Skilling's reliance on the institutional advice of professional advisers, such as lawyers and accountants, rather than just as if he had personally received such advice.
3. *Community prejudice and truncated voir dire.* Lake refused to move the trial from Houston and refused to allow lawyers to question potential jurors one-on-one. Lake asked most questions at the bench during the five-hour voir dire and screened 46 jurors.
4. *Prosecutorial misconduct.* Petrocelli argued that members of the Enron Task Force had intimidated potential defense witnesses to ensure they did not speak to the defense teams privately or testify on the defendants' behalf, and that the prosecutors had obstructed access to documents.

The honest services attack was widely seen as Skilling's best shot to strike down at least 14 of his 19 convicted counts, particularly with the Fifth Circuit's August 2006 ruling in the barge case. "In *Brown,* this court conducted a comprehensive review of the honest-services case law and identified a clear line distinguishing the type of self-dealing conduct criminalized by the statute from other conduct that, while arguably wrongful, unethical or dishonest, is not the federal crime of honest services fraud," the appeal said. "According to *Brown,* an 'honest services' fraud prosecution will not lie where—as here—the defendant's allegedly 'dishonest conduct' is not 'bribery or self-dealing' at the company's expense, but instead is 'associated with and concomitant to the employer's own immediate interest.'"

Although the honest services theory was presented only alongside the conspiracy count, the appeal argued that other counts were tainted as well. Skilling allegedly traded stock based on insider information that he derived from participating in the conspiracy, so without conspiracy, insider trading would falter. On the securities fraud counts, Lake instructed jurors that, if they found Skilling guilty of conspiracy, he also could be held liable for securities fraud committed by his co-conspirators whether or not he committed acts of securities fraud himself. The appeal said that, without conspiracy, Skilling cannot be held vicariously liable. And with the general verdict, it isn't known whether the jury convicted him of the securities fraud counts because it found that he had committed fraud or because he was held liable for his co-conspirators' acts.

Neither the honest services theory or the linkage jury instruction was presented or given in conjunction with the counts of false statements to auditors. But the appeal has argued that those counts are as tainted as the others because the jury could have found that Skilling or his co-conspirators committed honest-services fraud, and therefore Skilling falsely represented to auditors that there was no fraud at Enron.

The government's response demonstrated a fierce desire to maintain all of Skilling's convictions. In an argument that mirrored an earlier filing that opposed Skilling's request for bail pending appeal, prosecutors argued that the *Brown* holding did not apply to Skilling because he was part of Enron's top management. As such, he defined the company's message and had set the improper and fraudulent corporate goals rather than merely pursuing them, like the Merrill defendants in the barge case. Skilling's appeal countered that the *Brown* decision held that honest services fraud was improperly alleged because the defendants' actions furthered the mutual interest of employer and employee and did not distinguish liability by job title.

As for Skilling's argument that the general verdict made it impossible to know whether jurors had convicted on the honest services theory or one of the other valid theories, the government argued that, if the honest services ruling is found to apply to the conspiracy count, "the error is harmless" because any jury that convicted Skilling of conspiracy to deprive Enron and shareholders of their right to honest services also would have convicted him of conspiracy to commit securities fraud. Therefore, the prosecutors reasoned, the honest services precedent wouldn't apply to Skilling's 18 other convictions.

As for Skilling's other arguments, the government said that Lake properly instructed jurors that they could apply the deliberate indifference instruction to one or both defendants. Even though Skilling contended that no fraud or crime took place at Enron other than crimes by Fastow and his minions, prosecutors said that Skilling, in some instances, testified that he was unaware of any conspiracy or fraudulent activity—in contrast to testimony by government cooperators and other ex-Enron employees. For example, Skilling allowed the creation of the LJM partnerships despite receiving warnings from some executives that Fastow's participation in them raised a conflict of interest. When Kaminski opposed LJM's first transaction, Skilling transferred him from the company's risk assessment and control group, which prosecutors said illustrated Skilling's desire to prevent roadblocks to LJM deals and to avoid hearing about how the partnerships could be used to manipulate Enron's earnings.

Regarding Skilling's change of venue argument, the government said that the jury's decision to acquit Skilling of nine counts of insider trading demonstrated the panel's impartiality. Even though Skilling argued that the acquittals simply reflect how prosecutors chose not to present evidence on those counts, the government said a jury infected with bias fueled by pretrial publicity "would not have bothered to parse the evidence" and determine his guilt on each individual count.

Finally, regarding Skilling's allegations of prosecutorial misconduct, the government noted Lake's efforts to ensure that any witness who may have refused to meet with Skilling's defense team out of fear of reprisal from prosecutors could do so without that fear. The judge issued orders and sent letters to attorneys of potential witnesses offering that assurance.

Petrocelli remained as Skilling's lead lawyer and argued his appeal before a three-judge panel of the Fifth Circuit on April 2, 2008. The lead prosecutors from the trial had long since moved on; Berkowitz and Ruemmler joined different offices of the Latham & Watkins law firm; Hueston had joined Irell & Manella; and Stricklin had become an Assistant U.S. Attorney in Denver. Doug Wilson argued for the government.

Skilling's supporters attended the arguments in New Orleans, including his siblings, several members of Lay's legal team, and Lay's daughter, Liz Vittor. James Brown and his attorneys also sat in, interested in how the appellate ruling bearing his name would play out for a fellow Enron felon.

The honest services issue—Skilling's most powerful weapon and the government's weakest link—easily dominated the limited time. Petrocelli had asked to argue for two hours, but the appellate court unceremoniously shot him down, limiting him and Wilson to the standard 30 minutes each. However, with questions, each side had about 45 minutes.

The panel that heard the Skilling arguments included Jerry Smith, who had served on the Howard appeal panel. He was joined by Edward Prado and U.S. District Judge Alia Ludlum of the Western District of Texas.

Given the time limits, Petrocelli focused his argument solely on honest services. Even if fraud existed, the misuse of that theory taints the convictions, he argued. He went so far as to say, "there was fraud all over this case," which raised eyebrows in the gallery because it sounded as though he was repudiating his stance that no fraud existed, the core of the defense he had presented since he took over Skilling's case more than four years earlier. Afterward, Petrocelli explained to reporters that there was no such reversal, and he used "legalspeak" to push his argument on honest services. Days later he even sent a letter to the Fifth Circuit reiterating that explanation of what he'd said.

Petrocelli also countered a government argument that compared Skilling's case to another involving university basketball coaches who fraudulently ensured that transfer students were eligible to play and assumed they were acting in the institution's best interests in doing so. However, Petrocelli said the university in that case didn't know what the coaches were doing—while Enron's board approved financial structures deemed fraudulent by prosecutors, such as the LJM partnerships and the Raptors.

In response, Wilson said that the board didn't green-light those structures to commit fraud or manipulate financial statements.

When Prado asked if artificially pumping up earnings was in Enron's corporate interests, Petrocelli said yes. And relying on barge and Howard precedents, he noted that even if such actions are crimes, they don't constitute a breach of honest services because the actions are in Enron's corporate interest and don't involve taking money or property.

Later, Smith and Ludlum questioned whether Skilling's insider trading conviction involved self-dealing actions, implying that his profit from that stock sale could be construed as taking money or property, therefore a breach of honest services. Petrocelli argued that such a breach would involve actions unknown to Enron. Skilling sold his stock on the open market. He didn't hide his actions, and he did not have to report the sale to the SEC because he had resigned from Enron nearly a month earlier.

As of this writing, the Fifth Circuit has yet to rule. However, several legal observers expect the panel to overturn at least the conspiracy count and the 12 securities fraud counts because of honest services and the linking instruction. Petrocelli argued that prosecutors linked insider trading to the conspiracy count during closing arguments, saying his insider knowledge stemmed from his participation in the conspiracy.

Either way, the appeal is on its first leg. If counts are thrown out, the government can appeal to the U.S. Supreme Court and seek a final say on the honest services ruling that prosecutors decided to let lie with the *Brown* decision. Or Skilling can appeal as well to throw out whatever is left intact. Eventually the case will likely return to Lake's court for resentencing on whatever counts survive, and possibly a retrial on whatever did not.

For any reporter who covered it, Enron was a story like no other. It was the first in a series of business scandals that brought about more regulatory scrutiny, harsher white-collar sentences, and a sprawling human drama of hubris, tragedy, brilliance, and failure. Covering Enron was all-enveloping, particularly in the early months of the scandal and culminating with the Lay/Skilling trial. However, after that big face-off, most journalists have moved on to other things, and the appeals (except for that of Skilling) have garnered fleeting interest. And plenty of loose ends remain: Three broadband retrials, potentially two barge retrials as Brown's case was severed from that of Bayly and Furst, the forfeiture case against Lay's assets, and of course, the outcome of Skilling's appeal.

However, Enron evokes strong views even now. The word itself remains a metaphor for greed, crime, skirting the rules, and cheating shareholders. There are factions that see Skilling as a selfish crook whose powers of intimidation and break-the-rules attitude fostered a den of fraud amid executives who got rich under his wing and didn't care how they did it. Others assert just as passionately that Enron demonstrated that he is a scapegoat for scandal, where aggressive business practices that once garnered admiration and jealousy could be painted as criminal by others ready to sacrifice him to save themselves from a fate like his.

For a reporter in the middle of covering a case like this that stretches over so many years, the real challenge is to try to view the big picture. Every step, every new indictment, every argument is a piece of a vast puzzle. Enron illustrated the government's power in building incredibly complicated cases, and how its fervor can backfire immensely, as it did in that broadband case and by its widespread use of the honest services theory. Enron also illustrated the difficulty faced by defendants when the landscape of charges against them appears insurmountable and charging into battle is a multimillion-dollar fight. The big headlines may have faded, but the puzzle has yet to be completed.

Enron—The Primer[*]

Jeffrey D. Van Niel

The stage was set for the collapse of the collection of companies known as Enron long before Enron existed.[1] Corporate governance issues, including mismanagement and outright fraud, have plagued our free-market system since it was created. It seems we feel compelled to revisit these same issues once every generation.[2] From my perspective, a company operating in a free market attempts to maximize its profits by taking every advantage of the gaps that exist within and between the various rules and regulations that form the boundaries of that market. Unfortunately, corporate focus has shifted towards the "what can I get away with?" perspective and away from a business model bounded by common sense and ethical norms. The problem with this view is that it ignores the distinction between legal and illegal (and moral and immoral) conduct.

But I digress. Although this text and its updates do not focus exclusively upon Enron and its meteoric rise and fall into bankruptcy, the events surrounding Enron's

---

[*] During the last year, I have helped my wife edit many of the papers gathered together to form this book. Given the breadth of topics in this compilation work, we believed that you, the student, would prefer not to read virtually the same historical recitation of Enron's meteoric rise and crash into bankruptcy in every paper of every chapter in this book. So I have undertaken in this Primer to set forth a coherent, factual statement of the events leading up to the collapse of Enron. In order to make this primer as accurate as possible, I have relied upon and made liberal use of virtually all of the authors' papers in this book. For their research efforts and help in making this primer understandable and accurate, I am particularly grateful for the research of Victor Flatt and Jacqueline Weaver, whose works formed the backbone of this primer, to Bala Dharan for his editing, and to Nancy Rapoport, for her help with the accounting section. *Editors' note:* This essay was included in the first edition of this book. Reprinted by permission.

[1] The company known as Enron was actually several separate companies (Enron Energy Services, Enron Broadband Services, Enron Capital and Trade, later called Enron Wholesale Services, and Enron Transportation Services) that were owned wholly or in part by Enron Inc., *see* Enron Annual Report 2000, *available at* http://www.enron.com/corp/investors/annuals/2000/ar2000.pdf.

[2] "National Student Marketing in the 1970s, OPM in the early 1980s, Lincoln Savings & Loan during the S&L crisis of the 1980s, and the huge BBCI bank failure and fraud of the 1990s." Roger Cramton, *Enron and the Corporate Lawyer: A Primer on Legal and Ethical Issues*, 58 Bus. Law. 143, 143 (2002) (footnotes omitted).

collapse (and the subsequent corporate scandals—and current corporate governance upheaval—that occurred relatively soon thereafter) makes for an excellent learning opportunity. To that end, this primer attempts to set forth, briefly, the political, legal, and energy policy environment within which Enron grew to be what it became—the most influential energy-trading and market-creating company ever seen. The purpose of this primer is to provide you with sufficient background so that you can engage in a basic discussion of the events and circumstances surrounding the collapse of Enron and the most recent crisis of corporate governance. Consequently, I have not provided an exhaustive dissertation on the history and evolution of Enron or of its actions in the California energy crisis (not that we will ever really know ***all*** of the facts and circumstances surrounding the collapse of what was once the seventh largest company in the Fortune 500). The individual essays in this book and your professors will help you study Enron (and "Enron-esque") issues in more detail.

SETTING THE STAGE FOR THE CREATION OF ENRON

Long before electricity or natural gas, people used coal, wood, and various animal fats and oils to heat and light their homes. None of these resources was efficient or clean, and the smell permeated everything. As population centers grew more dense, something needed to change in the manner in which individuals were supplied with heat and light. Soon enough, companies were competing with each other to supply natural gas or other flammable liquids and gases to urban dwellers. Since no company at this time had exclusive rights to serve any of these customers, the streets and rights-of-way were constantly torn up as each company installed its own pipelines to serve its customers. Eventually, municipalities brought this chaotic practice to a halt, and the first monopolistic utilities were born.[3] Delivering electricity to the masses followed a similar competitive infrastructure growth pattern, with wires and power poles filling all of the available space in the rights-of-way. Additionally, the electric industry fought a more fundamental internal war to determine whether to distribute direct current (DC)[4] or alternating current (AC) to the prospective customers. (Light bulbs and small engines run equally well on either power supply.)[5] Eventually, alternating current won out over direct current, because alternating current was capable of being transported longer distances, and electric utilities sprouted across the county.

---

[3] AMY FRIEDLANDER, POWER AND LIGHT: ELECTRICITY IN THE U.S. ENERGY INFRASTRUCTURE 1870-1940 at 81-92 (1996).

[4] Thomas Edison, credited with inventing the incandescent electric light bulb, was a strong advocate of the distribution of direct current electricity, and owned at least one direct current electric company that distributed power to urban dwellers in New York City. *Id.* at 40.

[5] *See, e.g.,* Dennis Bernaal, *Electricity: Transformers and Delivery of Electric Power, in* MACMILLAN ENCYCLOPEDIA OF ENERGY, 392 (John Zumerchik ed., 2001); *see also Direct Current, available at* http://www.sunblock99.org.uk/sb99/people/DMackay/dc.html; WhatIs?Com, *DC, available at* http://whatis.techtarget.com/definition/0,,sid9_gci213659,00.html.

Although local electricity and natural gas distribution systems are functionally similar, providing heat and light to customers, the industries evolved in dramatically different ways. At its most basic level, natural gas is extracted from the ground as a naturally occurring molecule that must be refined to meet certain purity standards before it is considered capable of entry into and transmission in the national interstate pipeline system. You can, if you want, physically track an individual molecule of natural gas through the various pipelines from the well to your house. But, since every molecule of natural gas is fungible, no one makes the effort to physically track individual molecules of gas. Customers simply take what they need from the gas system and pay the bill when it arrives. Natural gas can also be pressurized and stored for long periods of time for later use. An electron of electricity, on the other hand, is created using a process that turns an alternating current generator. Unlike natural gas, technology does not yet permit us to track individual electrons as they pass down an electric wire. Nor can electricity be stored for later use, except through the use of batteries. Fortunately, an electron is an electron, so there is no need to be able to track electrons over the wires. Again, customers simply use what they need and then pay the bill when it arrives.

Functionally speaking, local gas and electricity utilities put their products into the hands of the end-use customer in very similar ways. The product is first produced (either generated or pumped from a well). It is then transported to the local distribution area using a bulk transport system (interstate and intrastate pipelines for gas and interstate and intrastate transmission lines for electricity). Once the product reaches the local distribution area, the local utility converts the product into volumes that can be used by local consumers (reducing the pressure for the gas and reducing the voltages for electricity to voltages usable by individual customers). The local utility then transmits the product to the end-use customer. Functionally speaking, the production chain looks like what you see in Chart A.

1. Natural Gas

During the regulated or monopolistic time in gas history, each aspect of the natural gas delivery chain (well-head, pipeline, local distribution company ("LDC"), end-user/customer) was regulated, with some level of governmental review and price approval and control. The type and number of potential sellers and buyers for the gas were also limited. At that time, only pipeline companies were permitted to sell gas to municipalities for resale to end-users.[6] In that context, the pipelines were filling the merchant and delivery functions in the delivery chain. Similarly, only LDCs, which were frequently municipalities, were permitted to sell gas to the residents and industries within their distribution areas. Within this system, the entity filling the merchant function had an obligation to serve *all* of the customers who requested its service within its area of operations, whether it wanted to or not. In other words, if you ran a pipeline, all of

[6] PAUL W. MACAVOY, THE NATURAL GAS MARKET: SIXTY YEARS OF REGULATION AND DEREGULATION 16 (2000).

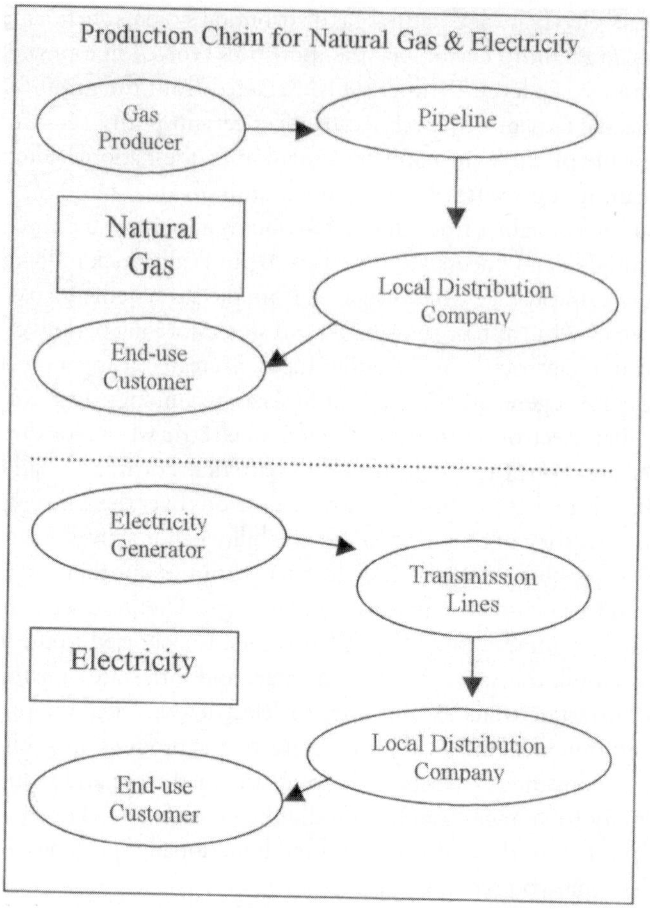

Chart A

the municipalities that tied into your pipeline were your customers and you had to provide them with gas. The same was true for an LDC or a city; it had to serve all of the customers within its area of operations that requested service. The obligation to serve flowed directly from the benefit received by the distributing entity for being the only service provider—i.e., having a monopoly. If you were the only service provider, you had to serve those who sought service.[7] The only part of this production chain that did not have an obligation to serve were the gas producers. They could sell to whom they wanted and withhold supply from those whom they did not want to serve.

The current restructuring of the electric and natural gas energy markets, or deregulation, as it is now known, began as a direct consequence of the oil crisis in the 1970s.

[7] *Id.*

Politically, the government had to do something to prevent a total collapse of the U.S. economy.[8] Restructuring initially began in 1978,

> when Congress passed the Natural Gas Policy Act ("NGPA"), and began the march towards a competitive retail natural gas marketplace.[9] Pursuant to the NGPA, the Federal Energy Regulatory Commission ("FERC") issued several orders both to forcibly open the natural gas industry to competition and to control the competitive behavior of the various industry participants, including the pipelines, marketing and aggregating companies and local gas utilities.[10] Ultimately, FERC issued Order 636, to "promot[e] competition among gas suppliers... [and to] benefit all gas consumers and the nation by 'ensur(ing) an adequate and reliable supply of (clean and abundant) natural gas at the lowest reasonable price.'"[11]

Restructuring efforts for the natural gas delivery chain have now eliminated virtually all of this governmental regulation, and replaced it with market-based economic theory (freedom to choose your supplier of each service, be it product, transportation, or ancillary service). In other words, customers are now generally free to shop for a better price or terms from any supplier they can find.[12] The final and most recent step in this restructuring effort permits residential consumers to purchase their own gas supplies from any number of willing sellers in the marketplace. This step must be accomplished on an individual state-by-state basis, as retail sales are beyond the purview of federal regulation.

---

[8] Susanna McBee, *U.S. Governors Eschew the Old Freebies and Get Serious*, WASH. POST, Aug. 31, 1978, at A5 ("...natural gas pricing bill, which [President Carter] considers a key part of his energy package, and which [State Governors] consider crucial to the nation's economy and thus their own states' well-being.")

[9] 15 U.S.C. §§ 3301-3432 (2001).

[10] *Regulation of Natural Gas Pipelines After Partial Wellhead Decontrol*, Order No. 436 ("FERC Order 436"), 50 FR 42408 (Oct. 18, 1985), FERC Stats. & Regs. (Regulations Preamble 1982-1985) 30,665 (1985), *vacated and remanded*, Associated Gas Distrib. v. FERC, 824 F.2d 981 (D.C. Cir. 1987), *cert. denied*, 485 U.S. 1006 (1988), *readopted on an interim basis*, Order No. 500, 52 F.R. 30334 (Aug. 14, 1987), FERC Stats. & Regs. (Regulations Preambles, 1986-1990) 30,761 (1987), *remanded*, American Gas Ass'n v. FERC, 888 F.2d 136 (D.C. Cir. 1989), readopted, Order No. 500-H, 54 F.R. 52344 (Dec. 21, 1989), FERC Stats. & Regs. (Regulations Preambles 1986-1990) 30,867 (1989), *reh'g granted in part and denied in part*, Order No. 500-I, 55 FR 6605 (Feb. 26, 1990), FERC Stats. & Regs. (Regulations Preambles 1986-1990) 30,880 (1990), *aff'd in part and remanded in part*, American Gas Ass'n v. FERC, 912 F.2d 1496 (D.C. Cir. 1990), *cert. denied*, 111 S.Ct. 957 (1991).

[11] Jeffrey D. Van Niel & Nancy B. Rapoport, *"Retail Choice" Is Coming: Have You Hugged Your Utilities Lawyer Today? (PART I)*, 2002 No. 2 NORTON BANKR. L. ADVISER 2 (citing FERC Order 636, 57 F.R. 13267, 13269 (April 16, 1992), Order on Reh'g, Order 636(A), 57 F.R. 36128 (Aug. 12, 1992), *Order on Reh'g*, Order 636(B), 61 F.R. 61272 (Nov. 27, 1992), *Order on Reh'g*, Order 636(C), 78 FERC 61186 (1997)) [hereinafter *Retail Choice*].

[12] *Id.* at 3.

As a result of these various FERC Orders, any customer seeking to acquire and/or transport natural gas over an interstate pipeline may do so, so long as that customer acquires the necessary transport rights from that pipeline, as Chart B indicates. Moreover, some industrial and large commercial customers currently may, depending upon their state, individually acquire and transport their own natural gas to their facilities, paying the pipelines and LDC only a transport fee to deliver the gas. As individual customers have acquired more and more rights to buy and transport gas on the interstate pipeline system, there has been a corresponding increase in companies willing to perform these services for the customer. These middlemen are known by many names: agents, marketers, brokers, etc. Their function is to ease the burden on individual customers by buying and arranging for the transportation of the gas to the customer or the customer's facility. As a result of these middlemen, the nice, clean contract days of the past are long gone. As reflected in Chart B, contract relationships are now as potentially complex as the number of individuals that may get involved in the transaction. A customer or his broker or marketer can contract directly with any or all aspects of the supply or delivery chain in order to obtain and deliver gas.

2. Electricity[13]

Historically, each electric utility generated virtually all of the power necessary to service the customer needs in its service territory and then transmitted that power to its service territory over transmission lines that it also owned. Since virtually all of these utilities competed with each other for retail customers and service territory, the concepts of free flowing electrons between service territories to enhance competition never entered the, production, construction or transmission development equation. Accordingly, the national electric grid more closely resembles a patchwork quilt than the free-flowing system design of the natural interstate gas pipelines and distribution system.

Although neighboring service territories do interconnect at various points, these interconnections were historically designed only to assist neighboring utilities in case of an emergency, not to facilitate efficient electron flow between, among and across several service territories. Contrary to the gas industry, no national high voltage transmission system exists to enhance the transmission of electricity from region to region across the country. These utility-owned generation, transmission, and distribution assets were constructed and are being maintained at huge expense to the local utility and its customers. Accordingly, requiring these same utilities to give up their monopoly rights and potentially guaranteed profits, not to mention the control and sometimes ownership of their facilities, has been and will be an uphill battle.

---

[13] I took this part of my essay directly from an earlier piece that I co-authored. *See Retail Choice, supra* note 11, at 2. We said it just fine the first time, and I saw no need to reinvent the wheel.

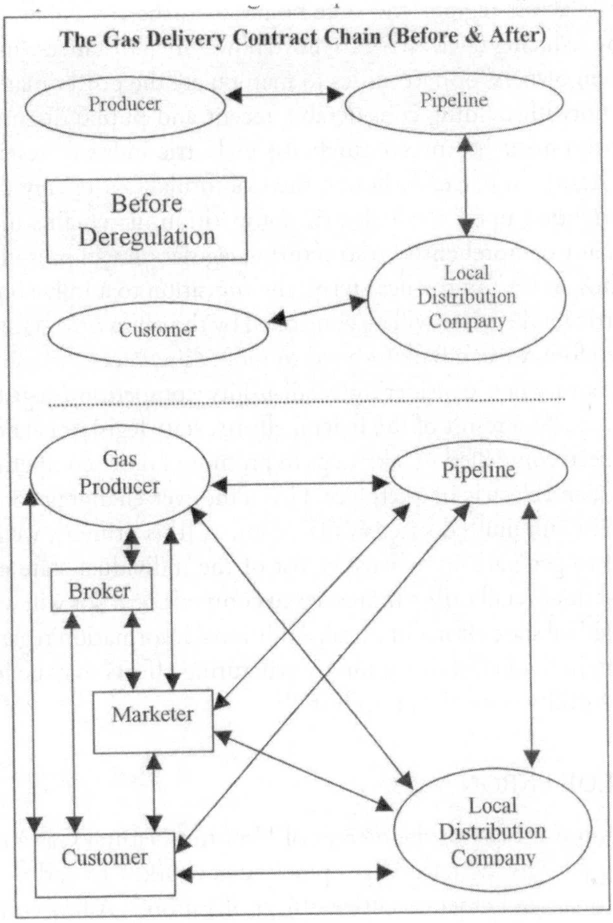

Chart B

The Energy Power Act of 1992 started the competitive march in the electric industry by instructing FERC to order electric utilities to permit third parties to use the utilities transmission assets to transmit ("wheel") blocks of wholesale power through the utilities' service area. Essentially, FERC was requiring the transmission line owners to convert their transmission patchwork quilt into a national freeway system for transmitting electricity across and through states. FERC implemented the Energy Policy Act's mandates by issuing FERC Orders 888 and 889, as well as the Independent System Operator ("ISO") and Regional Transmission Organizations ("RTO") orders, each of which seeks to eliminate constraints on the movement of power across regions and permit non-utility power purchasers to buy and transmit blocks of power over large distances to different regions and states.

The ISO and RTO orders seek to have independent third-party entities operate the high voltage transmission lines in order to facilitate the movement of electricity across regions and state boundaries, thereby enhancing competition by reducing (1) the cost to move power long distances, and (2) the transmission owners' opportunities to manipulate the power markets.

Sadly, notwithstanding considerable recent and public discussion, the federal government has no comprehensive electric industry restructuring policy or statute in place. Although the California . . . [energy crisis] has focused attention upon retail electric competition, it remains highly unlikely that any comprehensive restructuring legislation will pass in the near future. Thus, at least in the near term, the transition to a fully competitive retail electric marketplace will be controlled by the states on a state-by-state basis. Therefore, we can look forward to more differences than similarities between states when considering retail utility competition legislation or programs. . . . As a result of the federal efforts, state legislators and regulators have been compelled to take steps to promote a more competitive local natural gas, and electric marketplace. Given the ever-changing competitive environment and limited space available in . . . [this primer], we have not attempted to generate an exhaustive list of the individual state efforts to open the various retail utility industries to competition. Nor will we discuss these individual state efforts in detail. Additional information regarding the status of an individual state's utility restructuring efforts may be found on each state's utility commission website.[14]

B. THE BIRTH OF ENRON[15]

In 1985, Enron was born of the merger of Houston Natural Gas with Internorth, creating the first nationwide natural gas pipeline network.[16] In early 1986, Ken Lay was named chairman and chief executive officer of Enron.[17] A few years later, Enron began opening overseas offices in England in order to take advantage of the privatization of the United Kingdom's power industry.[18] An extremely ambitious company, Enron

---

[14] *Retail Choice, supra* note 11, at 2-3 (citing Promoting Wholesale Competition through Open Access Non-Discriminatory Transmission Services by Public Utilities, Docket No. RM95-8-000, 888 at 280 (April 24, 1996) 61 Fed. Reg. 21,540 (May 10, 1996), FERC Stats. & Regs. P31,036 (1997), *Order on Reh'g,* Order No. 888(A), 62 Fed. Reg. 12,274 (1997), FERC Stats. & Regs. P31,048 (1997), *Order on Reh'g,* Order No. 888(B), 81 FERC P61,248 (1997), *Order on Reh'g,* Order No. 888(C), 82 FERC P61,046 (1998); *Inquiry Concerning the Commission's Policy on Independent System Operator*, Docket No. PL98-5-000, and *Regional Transmission Organizations*, Docket No. RM99-2-000 (December 20, 1999) 65 Fed. Reg. 12,088 (March 8, 2000), 90 FERC Stats. & Regs. P31,092, *Order on Reh'g,* Order No. 2000(A) 90 FERC Stats. & Regs. P61, 201.

[15] This section has been taken nearly verbatim from an earlier draft by Victor Flatt. Victor B. Flatt, *The Enron Story and Environmental Policy*, 33 ENVTL. L. REV. 10485 (2003).

[16] HOUS. CHRON. ONLINE, *Enron Timeline* (2002), *available at* http://www.chron.com/cs/CDA/printstory.hts/special/enron/1127125 (last visited June 18, 2003) [hereinafter *Enron Timeline*].

[17] *Id.*

[18] *Id.*

pushed the envelope and shifted from the regulated transportation of natural gas to the unregulated energy trading markets, under the impression that there was more money in buying and selling financial contracts linked to the value of energy assets than in actual ownership of physical assets.[19] Jeffrey Skilling entered the scene in 1989, launching a program under which buyers of natural gas locked in long-term supplies at fixed prices.[20] In the following years, Enron continued to expand worldwide, with pipelines in South America and power plants in England and India.[21] Over this period, Enron spent billions of dollars in acquiring and building new sites and companies, even as it tried to shift away from "old market" ideas (like real assets) toward "new market" ideas (Skilling's "asset-lite" philosophy).[22]

At its zenith, Enron was named the "most innovative" company in the United States by *Fortune* magazine *every year* between 1996 and 2001.[23] In mid-August 2000, *Fortune* magazine named Enron as one of the top ten stocks that would last the decade because Enron had so successfully transformed itself from a stodgy gas utility into the largest online broker of energy.[24] Obviously, there is a lot more to the birth and growth of Enron than is represented in this section.

C. THE COLLAPSE OF ENRON[25]

Enron was well known for its aggressive stance on nearly virtually every energy-related issue. Some call that perspective "arrogance." Over time, Enron developed a veritable buffet of financial strategies to skirt and sometimes defy the boundaries of the law, all of which created the façade of profitability.[26] These strategies, which will be discussed

---

[19] Mark Jickling, *The Enron Collapse: An Overview of Financial Issues, Cong. Research Serv.*, (March 19, 2002), *available at* http://fpc.state.gov/documents/organization/9110.pdf (March 28, 2002).

[20] *Enron Timeline*, *supra* note 16.

[21] *Id.*

[22] Lanny J. Davis, *Enron? We're Missing the Point*, WASH. POST, Jan. 6, 2002, at B01 ("Jeffrey K. Skilling actually once boasted about the company's absence of hard assets. He proudly described its approach as 'asset lite,' adding: 'In the old days, people worked for assets. We've turned it around—what we've said is, the assets work for people.'").

[23] David Ivanovich, *Everybody Knows Enron's Name But Pop Icon Status Probably Won't Last,* HOUS. CHRON., Oct. 21, 2002, at 1A; *accord,* PETER C. FUSARO & ROSS M. MILLER, WHAT WENT WRONG AT ENRON: EVERYONE'S GUIDE TO THE LARGEST BANKRUPTCY IN U.S. HISTORY (2002) at 75; *see also* Daniel Altman, *Finding Gems of Genius Among Enron's Crumbs*, N.Y. TIMES, Feb. 3, 2002 at 6A.

[24] David Rynecki, *Ten Stocks to Last the Decade*, FORTUNE, Aug. 14, 2000 at 114, 117.

[25] This section is primarily the result of an earlier draft by Victor Flatt, but some portions are derived from the work of Jacqueline Weaver. Jacqueline L. Weaver, *Can Energy Markets Be Trusted? The Effect of the Rise and Fall of Enron on Energy Markets*, 3 HOUS. BUS. & TAX L. J. (Fall 2003); *see also* Flatt, *supra* note 15.

[26] PUBLIC CITIZEN'S CRITICAL MASS ENERGY & ENVIRONMENTAL PROGRAM, BLIND FAITH: HOW DEREGULATION AND ENRON'S INFLUENCE OVER GOVERNMENT LOOTED BILLIONS FROM AMERICANS (2001), *available at* http://www.law.wayne.edu/mcintyre/text/Blind_Faith_mjm.pdf; *see also* nn. 34-58 and accompanying text.

in more detail later, helped to camouflage and hide Enron's precarious financial position. In fact, Enron's strategies to conceal information regarding its true financial status were so successful that several billion-dollar Wall Street firms registered—or at least feigned—surprise when Enron's house of cards collapsed.[27] What caused the ultimate downfall of Enron? Several issues contributed to Enron's downfall, although two in particular sealed its fate: 1) Enron lived and died by the "deal"—and many of its deals went horribly wrong, losing millions of dollars;[28] and 2) when Enron's sham accounting schemes came to light, the company collapsed, virtually overnight, as people sought to distance themselves from the company and its stock.

Following Enron's collapse, California's deregulation nightmare, energy traders' manipulation of the natural gas and electric indices and swap trades, and the economic and financial effect of the stock market plunge, consumers have become significantly more conservative in their perspectives towards taking on additional risks.[29] The net effect of these events has been a significant slowdown in states' movement towards a fully competitive retail marketplace. In that regard, California has taken steps to reestablish a fully regulated retail environment, effectively killing the first efforts at retail competition for electricity in the U.S.[30]

D. THE GATEKEEPERS' ROLE IN THE COLLAPSE OF ENRON

Regardless of your personal opinion regarding Enron's outside accounting firm, Arthur Andersen ("Andersen"), or Enron's lawyers, Enron was likely not capable of creating and implementing the various schemes used to artificially inflate its earnings without the help of its in-house and outside accountants and its in-house and outside lawyers. It is possible that no single outside law firm knew all that Enron was trying to do. We don't yet know what the lawyers said in advising Enron,[31] although the Third Examiner's Report may reveal more facts.[32] I mention them here, simply to set the

---

[27] *Id.*

[28] Deals "gone bad" include the Dabhol gas-fired power plant in India, the Azurix foray into privatizing water markets in England and Argentina, and Project Braveheart's rush into selling broadband capacity in a glutted market. *See* Weaver, *supra* note 25, at 15, n. 41.

[29] Jeffrey D. Van Niel & Nancy B. Rapoport, *"Retail Choice" Is Coming: Have You Hugged Your Utilities Lawyer Today? (PART II),* 2002 No. 8 NORTON BANKR. L. ADVISER 2 (August 2002) at 1 (citations omitted).

[30] *Id.*, citing Howard Horn, *Unplug Deregulation in Texas,* HOUS. CHRON. at C1 (August 4, 2002).

[31] *See* Neal Batson, Second Interim Report of Neal Batson, Court-Appointed Examiner, *In re* Enron Corp., No. 01-16034 (Bankr. S.D.N.Y. Jan. 21, 2003), *available at* 2003 Extra Lexis 4, 2003 WL 1917445 (stating that the Third Examiner's Report would explore the actions of the professionals in more detail). *Editors' note:* None of the Enron Examiner's Reports released any of the legal advice given by Enron's lawyers.

[32] *Editors' Note:* In fact, in Batson's Third Interim Report, Batson alleges that some of Enron's senior officers kept pertinent information from Andersen in order to get Andersen's approval on the fraudulent deals. *See* Neal Batson, Third Interim Report of Neal Batson, Court-Appointed Examiner, *In re* Enron

stage for their inclusion later in the text. As to Andersen, the laundry list of corporate misdeeds and accounting scandals, fraud, and other issues with which the company was intimately involved belies the argument that the Enron situation resulted from the acts of a single rogue employee (even, say, a Skilling or a Fastow),[33] notwithstanding the Andersen criminal jury's willingness to pin the blame on in-house counsel Nancy Temple.

Accounting Games and Enron[34]

One of the first questions that the public asked, after the Enron scandal came to light, was "why didn't we/the Board of Directors/the market know that Enron's business plan was doomed to fail?" Part of the problem was that Enron used and abused the accounting rules to obscure its true financial condition. Two of the most well known examples of the use and abuse of accounting rules were Enron's use of "special purpose entities" ("SPEs") and its use of "mark-to-market" accounting.

SPEs and mark-to-market accounting are both important parts of many businesses' operations, as are such other traditional accounting tools as pro forma reporting.[35] These tools are not, in themselves, good or evil. It's how they're used that makes them good or evil.

Drug companies and movie studios use SPEs to move the risk of a new product or movie off the balance sheet of the main company. An SPE will let a new or potentially risky project obtain financing, without increasing the risk exposure of the main company.[36] Without SPEs, there would be few new miracle drugs in development, few breakaway hits like *My Big Fat Greek Wedding*[37] (as well as fewer disasters such as phen-fen). SPEs let companies take on more risk than they (or their lenders) might otherwise choose to do. The SPEs let companies move risk off their main (consolidated) balance sheets by creating a separate, independently controlled entity, with a portion of the ownership separate from the main company's ownership.[38] The risk exposure

---

Corp., No. 01-16034 (Bankr. S.D.N.Y. June 30, 2003), Appendix C, at 38-44 [hereinafter Third Examiner's Report].

[33] Among Andersen's most notorious accounting clients are Adelphia Communications, Baptist Foundation of Arizona, Boston Chicken, Global Crossing, McKesson-HBOC, Qwest Communications, Sunbeam, Waste Management, WorldCom, and, of course, Enron. Barbara Lay Toffler & Jennifer Reingold, Final Accounting: Ambition, Greed, and the Fall of Arthur Andersen 1 (2003).

[34] This section is derived in substantial part from an earlier draft by Victor Flatt, but Nancy Rapoport has made significant contributions as well. *See* Flatt, *supra* note 15.

[35] In pro-forma reporting, financial information is reported "as if" certain assumptions applied.

[36] William C. Powers, Jr. et al., Report of Investigation by the Special Investigative Committee of the Board of Directors of Enron Corp., 38 (Feb. 1, 2002), *available at* http://news.findlaw.com/hdocs/docs/enron/sicreport/sicreport020102.pdf [hereinafter Powers Report].

[37] My Big Fat Greek Wedding (IFC Films 2002).

[38] Powers Report, *supra* note 36, at 5.

of the SPE must also be severed from the exposure of the main company, or the SPE's structure becomes nothing more than smoke and mirrors.[39]

Enron violated both of the basic SPE principles. First, the ownership wasn't truly independent.[40] The partnerships that represented the 3% independent ownership of many of Enron's SPEs were partnerships controlled by Enron's Chief Financial Officer, Andrew Fastow. In essence, Fastow-the-CFO-of-Enron was negotiating with Fastow-the-general-partner-of-the-SPE. Not surprisingly, Fastow, not Enron, profited most from the deals that Enron made with the SPEs. Second, Enron guaranteed the SPEs that Enron would make good any losses that the SPEs suffered as a result of the deals with Enron. Therefore, Enron still retained substantial risk exposure and should have disclosed the debt on its consolidated balance sheet.[41]

Enron was able to manipulate reporting, hide debts, and hide poor-performing assets through these related-party transactions.[42] These internal business transactions also allowed Enron to meet its earnings expectations and sustain its stock price. Although GAAP requires detailed disclosure of related-party transactions in financial statements,[43] Enron never disclosed sufficient details to determine exactly how it had structured the SPEs.[44] Enron also failed to report its indebtedness to creditors in guaranteeing the debt of its SPEs.[45] GAAP requires that material indebtedness be disclosed; yet Enron failed to disclose this indebtedness. It remains to be seen whether the court-appointed bankruptcy examiner for the Enron cases finds that Enron failed to make those disclosures on its own or based on advice from its professionals.[46] The Third Examiner's Report, due to be released after this essay has been proofread for publication, may shed some light on that question.

Like its SPEs, Enron misused mark-to-market accounting as well. Under GAAP, an enterprise cannot recognize revenue until the business has substantially completed performance in a bona fide exchange transaction.[47] In essence, mark-to-market accounting lets a company book all expected profits in the first year of a long-term deal. (If, later, the deal does not produce the expected profits, the company is required to restate the original profit figures.) Enron misused mark-to-market in two ways. First,

---

39 *Id.*

40 Walter M. Campbell, *Enron's Aggressive Accounting*, 22 No. 5 FUTURES & DERIVATIVES L. REP. 12 (2002).

41 POWERS REPORT, *supra* note 36, at 14.

42 *Id.* at 4.

43 *Id.* at 179.

44 *Id.* at 178.

45 *Id.* at 197.

46 *Editors' note: See* Third Examiner's Report, *supra* note 32, at Appendix C (role of Enron's officers). The Fourth Examiner's Report discussed the role of some of Enron's other professionals.

47 Manuel A. Rodriguez, *The Numbers Game: Manipulation of Financial Reporting by Corporations and Their Executives*, 10 U. MIAMI BUS. L. REV. 451, 462 (2002) (citing Arthur Levitt, *The Numbers Game: Manipulation of Earnings in Financial Reports*, THE CPA J., Dec. 1998, at 14.).

because the deals that Enron was creating were usually "never before seen" types of deals (like Weather futures and markets in broadband), Enron was free to make up the projected profit figures. Since there were no other competing figures to challenge the profit projections that Enron was using, no one could challenge Enron's figures. Second, even when a deal was going poorly, Enron did not restate the original profit estimates. The first type of misuse is, possibly, understandable. After all, innovative companies *don't* have accurate profit projections for "never before done" deals. The second type of misuse, though, likely constitutes an intentional misrepresentation.

Let's now consider the pro forma reports. Enron used pro formas (and made up the underlying assumptions) to misrepresent its net income from its operations by labeling billion dollar expenditures as "one-time" or "non-recurring" charges.[48] (The memo from Andersen's in-house lawyer, Nancy Temple, to the Andersen partner in charge of the Enron account, David Duncan, dealt with precisely this issue.) Moreover, Enron engaged in active "earnings management," timed to ensure that it made "profits" every quarter. In effect, Enron overstated its restructuring charges to clean up its balance sheet, took a large one-time earnings hit, then reversed some of those charges at a later date and added them back into income in a period where true earnings fell short.[49] Although this type of earnings management is not unheard of in the normal course of businesses, it does not follow GAAP.[50] Excluding the non-recurring items allowed Enron to meet and exceed its estimated earnings when, in actuality, Enron was unable to match investor expectations.

Enron also provided incomplete financial statements as far back as 1996. To be considered "complete," financial statements require several components, including a balance sheet, an income statement, and a statement of cash flow.[51] Enron repeatedly failed to provide these components on a timely basis.[52] The failure to provide such information deprived investors of critically needed information. Decisions based on the income statement alone could not provide the full financial picture necessary to make informed investor decisions. Enron's misleading financial statements distorted the information needed by investors, creditors, and lenders and, ultimately, undermined the credibility of the capital markets.[53]

---

48 *Id.* at 3.

49 *Id.* at 125.

50 *See* Rodriguez, *supra* note 47, at 460-61.

51 *Id.* at 451.

52 CBS.MarketWatch.com, *Enron, OPEC, ChevronTexaco and More*, CBS MarketWatch (2001) ("Enron, accused repeatedly of withholding critical financial information, provided investors Wednesday with a financial update of the company and its plans for the future as it heads toward a merger with Dynegy.").

53 Peter Behr, *Lay Leaves Enron Board; Founder Severs Last Ties to Firm*, WASH. POST, Feb. 5, 2002, at A4 ("Powers told members of the House Financial Services Committee yesterday that the failure of Lay and other directors to police accounting and ethics violations at Enron was "appalling." Disclosures of executives' self-dealing and false financial statements by Enron shattered its credibility with investors and customers, forcing it into bankruptcy.").

If we're generating a laundry list of Enron's accounting abuses, we have to include one that is controversial—stock option grants. The use of stock option grants to compensate employees actually started as a reaction to a $1,000,000 cap on salaries for top-level employees. In order to "pay" those employees more than $1,000,000, Enron (as well as numerous other companies, both established and start-up) granted the employees stock options. Like most of these other companies, Enron did not treat stock option grants to employees as a form of compensation and did not list the grants as expenses. Though not illegal, this practice allows the posting of financial data that is not complete, especially in Enron's case, where stock options represented a very large and important form of employee compensation. Had Enron reported the granting of stock options in the manner proposed by the Financial Accounting Standards Board (FASB), Enron's profits from 1998 through 2000 would have been reduced by approximately $188 million.[54]

Additionally, Enron's auditors were compromised. An auditor examining these transactions should have been able to correctly interpret and understand what had occurred, required the proper reporting of such transactions, and ordered Enron to change its practices for future transactions. That did not happen. The Securities Exchange Commission ("SEC") uses auditing as its primary method of regulation of information and financial documents for large publicly traded companies. The failure of the audits to reveal the problems, therefore, hampered any possible SEC enforcement actions. Enron's auditors also sold Enron some very creative financial structuring advice—advice that allowed Enron to book losses sufficient to prevent Enron from having to pay much income tax for many years, despite the vast profits that Enron was simultaneously reporting to shareholders and the SEC.[55]

The use of large accounting firms simultaneously to perform auditing and non-auditing services created a huge conflict of interest between auditor dependence and company pressures. During 2000, Enron paid a total of $52 million to Andersen: $25 million for auditing services and $27 million for non-auditing (consulting) services. The consulting services provided Enron with advice for structuring its business deals. Andersen estimated that keeping Enron as a client would generate $100 million a year in revenues.[56] In order to satisfy auditing standards, auditors must remain independent. Andersen's extensive consulting work for Enron may well have compromised its independence and its judgment in determining the nature, timing, and extent of audit procedures. Further, the $27 million in consulting fees may also have been lucrative enough to deter Andersen from asking Enron to make revisions to its financial

---

[54] Julie Kosterlitz & Neil Munro, *Full Disclosure*, NAT'L J. (Feb. 23, 2002).

[55] David Cay Johnston, *Wall St. Firms Are Faulted In Report on Enron's Taxes*, N.Y. TIMES, Feb. 14, 2003, at C1.

[56] Reed Abelson & Jonathan D. Glater, *Who's Keeping the Accountants Accountable?*, N.Y. TIMES, Feb. 15, 2002, at C1.

statements.[57] Certainly, Andersen failed to live up to its founder's policy that the firm would always "[t]hink straight, [t]alk straight."[58]

E. ENRON AND THE CALIFORNIA ENERGY CRISIS[59]

It will take years to determine the exact roles played in the California energy markets by the various market participants (independent power generators, energy traders, pipeline capacity owners, the California Independent Service Operator ("ISO"), the California Power Exchange ("PX"), FERC, and state and federal politicians) and other factors, including the retail price caps, drought, and environmental laws. Armed with hindsight and internal Enron legal memoranda detailing the manipulation schemes[60] developed by Enron for use in the California market,[61] we now know that Enron and several other companies successfully "gamed" the California energy markets between 2000 and 2001. During that time, these companies reaped *huge* profits. One-hundred-fifty different companies have been called to task by the FERC over their involvement in these market manipulation schemes.[62]

California sought to restructure its retail energy markets to reduce its energy costs.[63] Eager to be the first state with this new market structure, both of California's state legislative houses unanimously passed the restructuring of the energy market. Sadly, the assumption that a deregulated retail market could not drive prices up and make matters worse was wholly erroneous. The hastily developed legislation restructuring California's energy market was subject to rampant abuse and has since been proven a horrible failure.[64]

---

[57] *Id.*

[58] TOFFLER & REINGOLD, *supra* note 33, at 9.

[59] Large portions of this section come from the work by Jacqueline Weaver, whose detailed discussion of this topic covers nearly 50 pages. Additional contributions to this section were taken from an earlier draft by Victor Flatt. *See* Flatt, *supra* note 15; *see also* Weaver, *supra* note 25.

[60] The schemes Enron developed and used in California may not have been clearly illegal. But if using these schemes did not directly cross the line of illegality, Enron certainly cast its shadow across the line. Indeed, Enron's counsel advised the company of this fact prior to their implementation. *See* Harvey Rice, *Enron Was Told Strategy in California Could be Illegal,* HOUS. CHRON., December 12, 2002, at A1.

[61] On May 6, 2002, memos written by Enron's Oregon lawyers were given to FERC by Enron's bankruptcy attorneys and posted on FERC's website. The memoranda are on the FERC website, http://www.ferc.gov/ferris.htm, in Docket No. PA02-2-000 (last visited June 27, 2003).

[62] Order to Show Cause Why Market-based Rate Authority Should Not Be Revoked, Fed. Energy Reg. Comm'n Rep. (CCH) Docket No. PA02-2-00, 99 FERC P 61,272 (2002), *available at* http://www.ferc.gov/Electric/bulkpower/PA02-2/showcause-06-04-02.pdf.

[63] Mike Stenglein, *The Causes of California's Energy Crisis,* 16 NAT. RESOURCES & ENV'T 237 (2002).

[64] David Penn, *California's Electric Deregulation Debacle and Enron's Bankruptcy in Perspective: an Analysis,* (June 26, 2002), *available at* http://www.appanet.org/pdfreq.cfm?PATH_INFO=/legislativeregulatory/legislation/Pennenron.pdf&VARACTION=GO (last visited June 27, 2003).

A brief history of California's power generation and delivery system is relevant in understanding the complex nature of restructuring California's electric power generation and delivery system. California's energy problems began in earnest in 1973 with rolling brownouts. Utility companies could not build power plants fast enough to keep up with rapid population growth in the west.[65] Finally, environmental pressures to pursue energy conservation and to refrain from building nuclear power plants hampered the growth of new power plants. Under this pressure, in the 1960s, many power plants began burning oil, which was cleaner and cheaper than coal.[66] Unfortunately, the oil embargo and oil shortages of the 1970s resulted in huge cost increases for consumers. California's energy conservation movement continued to promote the use of energy conservation instead of continued power plant construction. Utility companies lacked the broad-based public support needed to justify their continued monopoly status.

The Energy Policy Act of 1992 allowed restructuring of the regulatory landscape and set the stage for deregulation.[67] The 1992 Act required power generators to compete on the wholesale level and allowed states to begin retail competition as well.[68]

After marathon closed-door negotiations, the California legislature unanimously passed deregulation legislation commonly known as AB 1890.[69] The legislation became effective January 1, 1998, and it split California's electricity market into three areas: (1) generation of electricity, (2) transmission of bulk electricity flows, and (3) distribution of the electricity to the retail customer.[70] AB 1890 and CPUC created new rules for selling electricity into California. These new rules included the creation of two non-profit companies, the California PX and the California ISO.[71] The PX provided the marketplace for buying and selling electricity, known as the "wholesale power pool." The ISO managed the day-to-day operations and ensured the reliability of the transmission grid under the supervision of the FERC.[72] Since the PX and the ISO were non-profit companies, with no corresponding profit motive, they were supposed to

---

[65] Jamaca Potts, Book Note, *Power Loss: The Origins of Deregulation and Restructuring in the American Electric Utility System, by Richard F. Hirsh*, 26 HARV. ENVTL. L. REV. 269, 273 (2002).

[66] *Id.*

[67] Timothy P. Duane, Essay, *Regulation's Rationale: Learning from the California Energy Crisis*, 19 YALE J. ON REG. 471, 496 (2002).

[68] A.B. 1890 § 854, 1996 Cal. Stat. 854, codified, in relevant part, at Cal. Pub. Util. Code §§ 330-398.5 (Deering 2001) [hereinafter AB 1890]. Federal jurisdiction over electricity is limited to wholesale transactions and power sales made in interstate commerce, while state jurisdiction over the retail marketplace is exclusive. *See* Transm. Access Policy Study Group v. Fed. Energy Regulatory Comm., 225 F.3d 667, 690-92 (2000).

[69] Duane, *supra* note 67, at 497.

[70] Harvey Wasserman, *California's Deregulation Disaster* (2001), *available at* http://www.nirs.org/mononline/califdereghw.htm (last visited June 27, 2003).

[71] Sam Weinstein & David Hall, *The California Electricity Market—Overview and International Lessons*, Public Services International Research Unit (February 2001), *available at* http://www.psiru.org/reports/2001-02-E-Calif.doc (last visited June 27, 2003).

[72] Stenglein, *supra* note 63, at 237.

prevent one segment of the industry from exercising its market power and manipulating the marketplace. Both the PX and the ISO failed in this effort.

The legislation froze retail rates at levels 10 percent below those in effect in June 1996.[73] Freezing retail rates proved to be one of the two major flaws in California's retail competition experiment. By eliminating the market-based pricing incentives from the retail market, consumers had no incentive to reduce their usage under this new regime. Beginning in May 2000, the demand for electricity began to exceed the supply, causing wholesale costs to skyrocket. The wholesale rates from December 1999 had increased by 938% in December 2000.[74] The retail price freezes affected Pacific Gas & Electric ("PG&E") and other retail power suppliers because they were required to absorb all the high wholesale costs.[75] On April 6, 2001, PG&E, California's largest IOU, filed for Chapter 11 bankruptcy protection.[76]

1. Structural Flaws in the System[77]

Because of its poor design, the California energy market was ripe for the picking, and numerous companies swarmed over that market like buzzards to a kill. From what we know today, several design features of the California system combined to create the crisis: (1) the PX's market design and structure flaws; (2) the ISO's market design and structure flaws, (3) CPUC's prohibition on long-term contracts and other risk-reducing tools; (4) CPUC's forced divestiture of the IOU's generation and the corresponding obligation to serve load in California; (5) FERC's failure to timely respond to the crisis;[78] and (6) the market participants' ability to find and exploit multiple schemes to manipulate the market and extract huge profits from the market.[79] I leave the details of the market design flaws to the individual authors later in this text.

2. Game-Playing in California

California's market design had flaws, but the crisis was caused more precisely by a failure to understand the inherent rationale of regulation or to regulate despite those flaws.[80] Some of Enron's schemes appear to violate ISO rules, which expressly prohibit gaming the system. The ISO tariff prohibits (1) "gaming" (defined as "taking unfair advantage of the rules and procedures") of either the PX or ISO; (2) "taking undue

---

[73] *Id.*

[74] *Id.*

[75] *Id.*

[76] *Id.*

[77] This section is derived from an earlier draft by Victor Flatt. *See* Flatt, *supra* note 15.

[78] Stenglein, *supra* note 63, at 239.

[79] FED. ENERGY REG. COMM'N, FINAL REPORT ON PRICE MANIPULATION IN WESTERN MARKETS I-17 (Mar. 26, 2003).

[80] *Id* at I-12.

advantage" of congestion or other conditions that may affect the grid's reliability or render the system "vulnerable to price manipulation to the detriment of [the ISO Markets'] efficiency"; or (3) engaging in anomalous market behavior, such as "pricing and bidding patterns that are inconsistent with prevailing supply and demand conditions."[81] Contrary to these express prohibitions, Enron and other companies created and tested techniques that did all of the above. These techniques had names like Death Star (a phantom power transfer), Fat Boy (an artificial increase in demand), Ricochet (see Ricochet Chart and description below), Load Shift (megawatt laundering—see Load Shift Chart below) and others to extract huge profits from the California market.[82] Let's look at some of these games in a bit more detail.

Under several of the schemes, companies would intentionally over-schedule power into a transmission and power transfer interface in order to take advantage of the most obvious loophole in the system, in which the ISO would pay congestion relief charges to companies that failed to deliver power to the interface. In other words, the companies would schedule loads for delivery that they had *no intention* of providing, so that they could be paid by the ISO not to deliver that power. Enron called this particular scheme "Load Shift."[83] Chart C illustrates this scheme.

Enron had another game called "Ricochet." Remember: 1) the PX was selling power on an hour-ahead and day-ahead basis, 2) the generators had no obligation to sell their power to the PX or keep it in state, and 3) the ISO had an obligation to import power from out-of-state if there was inadequate power available to meet the expected demands. Using this weakness in the system, Enron and others simply bought power from the PX, shipped it out of state to a confederate, then when prices were high enough in California, wheeled that same power back into California at prices that were sometimes 200 times higher than the price that was paid for the same power earlier that day.[84] See Chart D below. Simply put, Enron and other power suppliers exploited the system.

---

[81] Stoel Rives memo, dated Dec. 6, 2000, at 8, *available at* http://news.findlaw.com/hdocs/docs/enron/stoelrives120800mem.pdf (last visited July 7, 2003) [hereinafter Rives]. A different law firm wrote the second memo to Richard Sanders, assistant general counsel at Enron, after it reviewed the December 8 memo and then met with Enron traders, including the head trader in the Pacific Northwest, Tim Belden. This later memo explained that some of the analysis of the effect of the trading schemes on electricity prices or supplies in the earlier memo was erroneous. Severin Borenstein, an academic expert, concluded that some strategies were pretty clear violations of ISO rules. HOUS. CHRON., May 12, 2002 at 1A, 18A. In August 2002, FERC released a report that attempted to analyze the impact of Enron's trading strategies on Enron's profits and on California's electricity market. Staff Report of Federal Energy Regulatory Commission, *Initial Report on Company-Specific Proceedings and Generic Reevaluations; Published Natural Gas Price Data; and Enron Trading Strategies*, Docket No. PA02-2-2000, Aug. 2002 at 83-100.

[82] We will examine some of these schemes in detail below.

[83] Rives, *supra* note 81, at 5.

[84] *Id.* at 6-7; LOREN FOX, ENRON: THE RISE AND FALL 197-98 (2003).

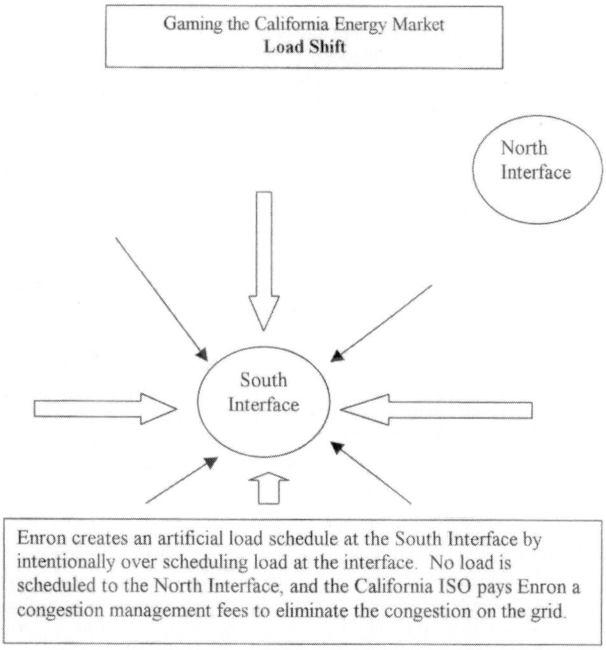

Chart C. Load Shift Chart

3. Other Abuses and Games[85]

One of the most popular abuses employed was "wash trades," "swap trades," or "roundtrip trades." Under this mechanism, there appears to be two purchases and two sales between two market participants. In reality, these trades exist only on paper: no power or money ever changes hands, as the two transactions take place simultaneously and cancel each other out completely. See Chart E below. Electricity was not the only commodity manipulated using the roundtrip trade method; roundtrip trading was also used for natural gas and broadband capacity. Dynegy, AEP, CMS, El Paso, and Williams admitted that some of their traders had engaged in roundtrip trades.[86]

Another abuse arose from withholding generation from the California market.[87] Many felt that, just as traders could profit from market manipulation, power generators could make billions if they could successfully game the system. As reflected in Jacqueline

[85] This section is derived from an earlier draft of Jacqueline Weaver's essay on energy markets. *See* Weaver, *supra* note 25.

[86] Dynegy was the first company to settle with the CFTC over the practice of submitting false data to publications, paying a $5 million fine. Michael Davis, *$5 Million Settlement for Dynegy*, HOUS. CHRON., Dec. 20, 2002, at C1.

[87] The gaming tactics revealed in the Enron memos were those of a trader, not a power generator. Experts believed that electricity suppliers made billions of dollars through two mechanisms: (1) physical withholding, *i.e.*, not running power plants; and (2) economic withholding, *i.e.*, bidding supplies into the

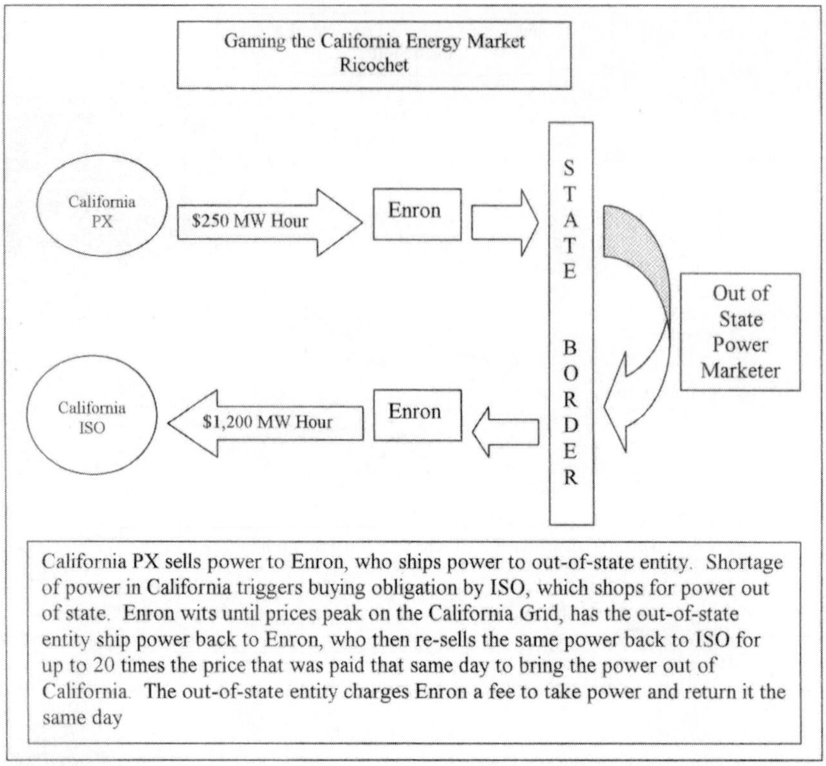

Chart D. Ricochet Chart

Weaver's essay on our webpage, power generators did game the system and reaped obscene profits as a result. Additionally, the market participants saw fit to manipulate the gas and electric trading indices. In other words, companies were reporting erroneous prices for natural gas sold onto the spot markets in California. Given the close tie between the industries—a lot of electricity is generated using natural gas—manipulating the published prices for the spot market would cause significant swings in electric prices.[88]

4. Where Was the FERC?[89]

FERC's role in the California crisis has been correctly criticized in light of this deregulation disaster. Since the major suppliers came from out of state, they were

market only at very high prices or refusing to bid supply into the market David Ivanovich, *Enron Opens a Pandora's Box*, HOUS. CHRON., May 12, 2002 at 1A, 18A (quoting Severin Borenstein).

[88] FERC STAFF REPORT, COMPANY SPECIFIC SEPARATE PROCEEDINGS AND GENERIC REEVALUATIONS; PUBLISHED NATURAL GAS PRICE DATA; AND ENRON TRADING STRATEGIES, Docket No. PA02-2-000, Aug. 2002.

[89] This section is derived from an earlier draft by Victor Flatt. *See* Flatt, *supra* note 15. Jacqueline Weaver also presents a comprehensive discussion of this topic in her essay on energy markets. *See* Weaver, *supra* note 25.

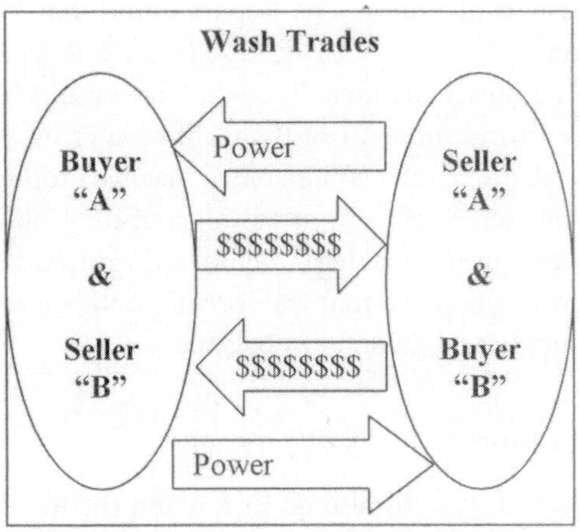

Chart E. Wash Trades Chart

under FERC's ***exclusive*** regulatory jurisdiction. Most important, FERC failed in its duty to deter and discipline the anti-competitive behavior that was driving the pricing increases.[90] FERC was, from the inception of California's deregulation efforts, advised about the potential problems that might arise in that market.[91] It obtained reports as early as 1996 commenting on the potential for price manipulation and weakness in California's deregulation scheme.[92] FERC ignored all of these reports and signed off on California's deregulation plan. A recent report notes how few resources FERC then spent (and currently spends) on controlling anti-competitive behavior in the energy market.[93] FERC blamed on all of the flaws in the design of the California system on the California CPUC, California PX, and California ISO, thus deflecting attention from its own deficiencies and culpability in approving such a system.[94]

Other federal agencies were not so shy when it came to assessing FERC's poor performance in dealing with the California market. In June 2001, the General Accounting Office (GAO) released a report assessing why energy prices in California had increased so dramatically.[95] The report criticized FERC's study of outages, stating that it was not thorough enough to support the conclusions that generators had not withheld supply.[96] In November 2002, the Senate Committee on Governmental Affairs released a report

---

[90] Duane, *supra* note 67, at 516.

[91] Stenglein, *supra* note 62, at 241.

[92] *Id.*

[93] David Ivanovich, *Report Raps FERC Over Enron Schemes*, HOUS. CHRON., November 12, 2002, at 1B.

[94] *Id.*

[95] GENERAL ACCOUNTING OFFICE, ENERGY MARKETS: RESULTS OF STUDIES ASSESSING HIGH ELECTRICITY PRICES IN CALIFORNIA (GAO-01-857) (June 2001).

[96] *Id.*

regarding FERC's oversight of Enron. The Report found that FERC "was no match for a determined Enron."[97]

Had FERC acted in a timely manner, "it could have saved Californians billions of dollars."[98] At the most critical moment of the California crisis, FERC abandoned its role as a regulator, leaving the market vulnerable to massive profiteering.[99] FERC chose to investigate the various schemes being used to game the California energy market only after the disclosure of an internal legal memo at Enron. Sadly, prior to the release of that memo, FERC was convinced that California's problems were merely the result of poor design and a supply and demand imbalance.

5. Enron's Political Clout[100]

As the California market was crumbling, Enron and the in-state power generators launched a public relations campaign to convince the world that California's problems were not the result of market abuse, but instead were a self-inflicted supply and demand imbalance combined with a drought. Simultaneously, these companies flexed their lobbying clout with Vice President Dick Cheney and the FERC commissioners, arguing against imposing wholesale price caps in the California market.[101] As Enron put it, the crisis was created entirely by California's own hand, and California could solve that crisis itself.

Throughout Enron's lifespan, Enron aggressively lobbied Congress, the Commodity Futures Trading Commission ("CFTC"), the SEC, and the FERC for less regulation and oversight. Enron's lobbying success is impressive. Through a series of decisions, FERC authorized "power marketers" like Enron to operate with little oversight in its energy market.[102] Following FERC's decisions freeing Enron from regulatory oversight, Enron petitioned the chairwoman of CFTC, Wendy Gramm, to exempt energy derivatives from regulation. Ms. Gramm initiated rulemaking in favor of Enron's peti-

---

97 U.S. SENATE STAFF REPORT OF COMMITTEE ON GOVERNMENTAL AFFAIRS, COMMITTEE STAFF INVESTIGATION OF FERC'S OVERSIGHT OF ENRON CORP. at 2 (Nov. 12, 2002), *available at* http://www.senate.gov/~gov_affairs/111202fercmemo.pdf.

98 Stenglein, *supra* note 62, at 242 (quoting Senator Feinstein).

99 Duane, *supra* note 67, at 517.

100 This section is derived in part from an earlier draft of Jacqueline Weaver's essay on energy markets and in part from an earlier draft by Victor Flatt. *See* Flatt, *supra* note 15; *see also* Weaver, *supra* note 25.

101 On April 17, 2001, Ken Lay met with Vice President Dick Cheney to discuss the California crisis and reportedly gave Cheney an eight-point memo that advised the administration to reject price caps, even temporary price caps. The day after the meeting, Cheney said price caps would not solve California's problems. Patty Reinert, *FERC to Focus on Enron's Role in Calif. Energy Crisis*, HOUS. CHRON., Feb. 1, 2002 at A1. *See also* U.S. SENATE STAFF REPORT OF COMMITTEE ON GOVERNMENTAL AFFAIRS, COMMITTEE STAFF INVESTIGATION OF FERC'S OVERSIGHT OF ENRON CORP., at 41-46 (Nov. 12, 2002), *available at* http://www.senate.gov/~gov_affairs/111202fercmemo.pdf (regarding Enron's lobbying).

102 MINORITY STAFF COMM. OF GOV'T REFORM, FACT SHEET: HOW LAX REGULATION AND INADEQUATE OVERSIGHT CONTRIBUTED TO THE ENRON COLLAPSE (2002).

tion to be exempt from CFTC oversight.[103] Five weeks after stepping down from her governmental position, Ms. Gramm was named to Enron's board of directors, and she was compensated "between $915,000 and $1.8 million in salary, attendance fees, stock options and dividends over . . . eight years."[104] Coincidence? Perhaps.

Enron's lobbying efforts were so aggressive and successful that "staff members of one Congressional committee asked a lobbyist for an Enron-led industry group to negotiate major aspects of the bill directly with regulators."[105] In 2000, the CFTC was further removed from regulating energy traders when Congress passed the Commodity Futures Modernization Act, which codified the CFTC's decision exempting energy contracts from regulatory oversight.[106]

6. Where Are the Manipulators Now?[107]

The glare of publicity about their gaming, manipulation, and accounting fraud has nearly bankrupted many of the companies involved in the California market and energy trading scandals. Most have now disposed of their energy trading businesses and are trying to preserve the remaining aspects of their companies. By December 2002, one year after the Enron bankruptcy, the stock prices of the companies that once rode the wave of deregulation have, with 3 exceptions, dropped by at least 80% (Dynegy, 97%; El Paso, 87%; Williams, 92%; AES Corp., 82%; Calpine, 87%; Mirant Energy, 93%; Reliant Resources, 88%; Duke Energy, 50%; Enron, 100%; and CMS Energy 60%):[108]

FERC has issued motions to show cause to 150 companies regarding their behavior in the California markets.[109] As of early 2003, it appears that in excess of $3.3 billion in refunds will be given back to California by these companies.[110]

---

[103] *Corrections*, S.F. CHRON., Feb. 1, 2002, at A2 ("A story Jan. 13 reported that Wendy Gramm, when chairwoman of the Commodity Futures Trading Commission in January 1992, led a majority vote in favor of a rule that exempted Enron Corp.'s electricity contracts from CFTC oversight. The vote, in fact, was to initiate the rulemaking in favor of Enron. Final approval of the rule occurred after Gramm had left the board.").

[104] Robert Manor, *Gramms Regulated Enron, Benefited From Ties*, CHI. TRIB., Jan. 18, 2002, at 17N. Senator Phil Gramm, Wendy Gramm's husband, was the senior Republican on the Senate Banking Committee, which participated heavily in the drafting of the 2000 legislation.

[105] Michael Schroeder and Greg Ip, *Out of Reach: The Enron Debacle Spotlights Huge Void in Financial Regulation*, WALL ST. J. Dec. 13, 2001, at A1.

[106] Commodity Futures Modernization Act of 2000, Pub. L. No. 106-554, 114 Stat. 2763 (codified as amended in scattered sections of 7 U.S.C.).

[107] This section is derived from a previous draft by Jacqueline Weaver. *See* Weaver, *supra* note 25.

[108] The data is the decreased stock price from Oct. 15, 2001 to December 2002. John E Olson, *Energy Markets at a Crossroads: Has Deregulation Failed?,* Int'l Ass'n of Energy Economics Conference, Houston, Tex., Dec. 12, 2002.

[109] Order to Show Cause Why Market-based Rate Authority Should Not Be Revoked, Fed. Energy Reg. Comm'n Rep. (CCH) Docket No. PA02-2-00, 99 FERC P 61,272 (2002), *available at* http://www.ferc.gov/Electric/bulkpower/PA02-2/showcause-06-04-02.pdf.

[110] The Administrative Law Judge at FERC reviewing the complaints regarding market manipulation and violations issued an order assessing refunds in the amount of $1.8 billion. That order was reviewed

CONCLUSION

Obviously, Enron's various business dealings, its ability to affect national policy, and its ultimate effect on markets is more complex than this primer reflects. The rest of the text will elaborate on each of these issues, as well as on many other issues (legal issues, business issues, and social and psychological issues). The beauty of Enron as a case study is that it presents so many complex issues—and so many learning opportunities.

by the FERC, and FERC determined that the proper refund amount was more like $3.3 billion. Richard A. Oppel, Jr., *Panel Finds Manipulation By Energy Companies*, N.Y. TIMES, March 27, 2003, at A14.

Enron's Accounting Issues: What Can We Learn to Prevent Future Enrons?

Dr. Bala G. Dharan[*]

Mr. Chairman and members of the Committee, I want to thank you for inviting me to present my analysis of the accounting issues that led to Enron's downfall. I am honored to be given this opportunity.

I am Bala Dharan, Professor of Accounting at the Jesse H. Jones Graduate School of Management, Rice University, Houston. I received my Ph.D. in accounting from Carnegie Mellon University, Pittsburgh. I have been an accounting professor at Rice University since 1982. In addition, I have taught accounting as a professor at Northwestern University's Kellogg School of Management, and as a visiting professor at the Haas School of Business at University of California, Berkeley, and the Harvard Business School. I am also a Certified Public Accountant and a Registered Investment Advisor in the state of Texas. I have published several articles in research journals on the use of financial accounting disclosures by investors.

The Enron debacle will rank as one of the largest securities fraud cases in history. Evidence to date points to signs of accounting fraud involving false valuation of assets, misleading disclosures, and bogus transactions to generate income. I have had several invitations to speak on Enron's accounting issues over the last few months. In my talks and lectures, I am asked two questions most frequently: One, how could this tragedy have happened while the company's management, board of directors, and outside auditors were supposedly watching over for employees and investors? Two, what can we learn from this debacle so that we can avoid future Enrons? Undoubtedly the first question will be the focus of the many investigations currently underway, including your Committee's efforts. In my testimony, I will focus on what we can learn from the accounting issues related to Enron's use of mark-to-market ("MTM") accounting and special purpose entities ("SPEs"). These two issues are very closely related, especially as they were practiced by Enron. In addition, I will address the related accounting issue

[*] BALA G. DHARAN, Testimony, *in* LESSONS LEARNED FROM ENRON'S COLLAPSE: AUDITING THE ACCOUNTING INDUSTRY, S. Doc. No. 107-83, at 87-96 (Feb. 6, 2002), *available at* http://energycommerce.house.gov/107/action/107-83.pdf. *Editors' note:* This essay was included in the first edition of this book. Reprinted by permission.

of pro-forma disclosures, and also how Enron's failed business strategy contributed to the accounting errors. I hope other invited panelists addressing this Committee will talk about the critical roles played by Enron's management, board, auditors, lawyers, consultants, financial analysts, and investment bankers in Enron's fall. I conclude with recommendations for regulatory changes and improvements in the accounting and auditing rules governing special purpose entities, mark-to-market accounting, and financial disclosures in general.

1. LOSS OF INVESTOR TRUST

My analysis of the Enron debacle shows that Enron's fall was initiated by a flawed and failed corporate strategy, which led to an astounding number of bad business decisions. But unlike other normal corporate failures, Enron's fall was ultimately precipitated by the company's pervasive and sustained use of aggressive accounting tactics to generate misleading disclosures intended to hide the bad business decisions from shareholders. The failure of Enron points to an unparalleled breakdown at every level of the usual system of checks that investors, lenders, and employees rely on—broken or missing belief systems and boundary systems to govern the behavior of senior management, weak corporate governance by the board of directors and its audit committee, and compromised independence in the attestation of financial statements by the external auditor.

Enron started its transformation from a pipeline company to a "risk intermediation" company in the 1980s. It adopted a corporate strategy of an "asset-less" company, or a "frictionless company with no assets." The company's Chief Financial Officer said in a 1999 interview to a management magazine (which awarded him a "CFO Excellence Award for Capital Structure Management") that the top management transformed Enron into "one engaged in the intermediation of both commodity and capital risk positions. Essentially, we would buy and sell risk positions." What this description of the company implies is that, unlike any other major company in the U.S., Enron's corporate strategy was virtually devoid of any boundary system that defined the perimeter of what is an acceptable and unacceptable investment idea for managers to pursue. Since any business investment basically involves some risk position, this strategy is not really a strategy at all but an invitation to do anything one pleases. Enron's top management essentially gave its managers a blank order to "just do it," to do any "deal origination" that generated a desired return. "Deals" in such unrelated areas as weather derivatives, water services, metals trading, broadband supply, and power plants could all be justified and approved by managers under this concept of an asset-less risk intermediation company. The company even briefly changed its tagline in a company banner from "the world's leading energy company" (which implies some boundary system for investments) to "the world's leading company." It is no wonder that this flawed business strategy led to colossal investment mistakes in virtually every new area that the company tried to enter.

While bad business strategy and bad investment decisions can and do contribute to a company's fall, it is a company's desperate attempt to use accounting tricks to hide bad decisions that often seals its fate. My analysis of cases of major stock price declines shows that when news of an unanticipated business problem, such as a new product competition or obsolescence of technology, is released to the market, the company's stock price does take a hit, but it often recovers over time if the company takes appropriate and timely management actions. However, when a company loses the trust and confidence of the investing public because of discoveries of accounting wrongdoings, the net result on the company's stock price and competitive position is mostly devastating and long-lasting. This is because accounting reports are the principal means by which investors evaluate the company's past performance and future prospects, and a loss of trust effectively turns away investor interest in the company.

My analysis also suggests that it is not possible to recover from a loss of investor confidence by some quick management actions. Before re-admitting the company to their investment portfolios, investors would demand and seek evidence that the accounting numbers are again reliable, and this process of rebuilding of trust often takes place through several quarters of reliable financial disclosures. If the company's finances are not fundamentally sound to begin with, then it is quite likely that the company would not survive this long trust-recovery phase intact. This is exactly what happened in the case of Enron. Burdened with dozens of failing investments and assets hidden in special purpose entities whose very existence and financing often depended on the high stock price of Enron's shares, the company quickly entered a death-spiral when investors questioned its accounting practices and pushed its share price down to pennies.

2. USE OF PRO-FORMA EARNINGS

Enron's loss of investor faith started with the company's 2001 third quarter earnings release on October 16, 2001. As earnings releases go, this one must rank as one of the most misleading. The news release said, in an underlined and capitalized headline, "Enron Reports Recurring Third Quarter Earnings of $0.43 per diluted shares." The headline went on to reaffirm "recurring earnings" for the following year, 2002, of $2.15 per share, a projected increase of 19% from 2001. But an investor had to dig deep into the news release to know that Enron actually lost $618 million that quarter, for a loss of ($0.84) per share. A net loss of $618 million loss was converted to a "recurring net income" of $393 million by conveniently labeling and excluding $1.01 billion of expenses and losses as "non-recurring."

The practice of labeling certain earnings items as non-recurring or "one-time" has unfortunately become widespread in the U.S. and has corrupted the corporate disclosure environment to the detriment of investors and the public. Companies ranging from General Motors to Cisco mention some form of pro-forma earnings in their earnings disclosures. Of course, there is nothing "one-time" or "non-recurring" about the $1.01 billion of expenses and losses that Enron chose to label as such in its 2001 third quarter earnings release. In other words, neither accountants nor managers could assure that what they call non-recurring would not recur.

My ongoing research also shows that the adoption of pro-forma earnings reporting is often a company's desperate response to hide underlying business problems from its investors. As an example, Enron did not always use pro-forma earnings in its news releases. Its earnings release as late July 24, 2000, for 2000 second quarter did not contain any reference to recurring earnings. In its 2000 third quarter earnings release on October 17, 2000, Enron started using the recurring earnings in the body of the news release. We know from the Enron board's internal report, dated February 1, 2002, that this was also the time when the senior management started worrying about the declining value of many of their merchant investments. By the following quarter, recurring earnings had been elevated by Enron to news headline.

Not all companies, of course, use pro-forma earnings or use them in blatantly misleading ways. Companies like Microsoft do report their earnings without having to resort to misleading pro-forma disclosures. However, we need to ensure that misleading pro-forma disclosures are halted altogether. In a recent speech, the Chairman of the Securities and Exchange Commission has warned companies that pro-forma earnings would be monitored by the SEC for misleading disclosures. However, this does not go far enough. The SEC should recognize all pro-forma disclosures for what they really are—a charade. They may differ from one another in the degree of deception, but the intent of all pro-forma earnings is the same—to direct investor attention away from net income measured using generally accepted accounting principles, i.e., GAAP earnings.

Enron's 2001 third quarter earnings press release, on October 16, 2001, contained another major shortcoming—lack of information about its balance sheet and cash flows. While the company's press release provided information on net income, the company failed to provide a balance sheet. This is inexplicable—we teach in Accounting 101 that the income statement and the balance sheet are interrelated ("articulated") statements. This essentially means that we cannot really prepare one without preparing the other. Not surprisingly, almost every major company's earnings release contains the balance sheet along with its income statement. Financially responsible companies would also provide a cash flow statement. Analysts and investors puzzled with Enron's lack of balance sheet disclosure had to wait until after the markets closed on October 16, 2001, when the senior management disclosed—in response to a question during the earnings conference call—that it had taken a $1.2 billion charge against its shareholders' equity (a balance sheet item), including what was described as a $1 billion correction of an accounting error. The experience suggests, that along with reforms on pro-forma earnings usage, we should mandate a fuller, more complete presentation of financial statements in the earnings news releases so that investors can truly be in a position to interpret the quality and usefulness of the reported earnings numbers.

3. SPECIAL PURPOSE ENTITY ACCOUNTING

3.1. Business Purpose of SPEs

Enron's internal report, released on February 1, 2002, makes clear that Enron used dozens of transactions with special purpose entities ("SPEs") effectively controlled by the company to hide bad investments. These transactions were also used to report over $1 billion of false income. Many of these transactions were timed (or worse, illegally back-dated) just near ends of quarter, so that the income can be booked just in time and in amounts needed to meet investor expectations. However, SPEs were not originally created as mere tools of accounting manipulation. Surprisingly, the SPE industry did start with some good business purpose. Before discussing the accounting issues related to SPE accounting, it would be useful to have a brief description of what these entities are and how they arose.

The origin of SPEs can be traced to the way large international projects were (and are) financed. Let's say a company wants to build a gas pipeline in Central Asia and needs to raise $1 billion. It may find that potential investors of the pipeline would want their risk and reward exposure limited to the pipeline, and not be subjected to the overall risks and rewards associated with the sponsoring company. In addition, the investors would want the pipeline to be a self-supported, independent entity with no fear that the sponsoring company would take it over or sell it. The investors are able to achieve these objectives by putting the pipeline into a special purpose entity that is limited by its charter to those permitted activities only. Thus a common historical use of SPE was to design it as a joint venture between a sponsoring company and a group of outside investors. The SPE would be limited by charter to certain permitted activities only—hence the name. Such an SPE is often described as brain-dead or at least on auto-pilot. Cash flows from the SPE's operations of the project are to be used to pay its investors.

In the U.S., the use of SPEs spread during the 1970s and 1980s to the financial services industry. In the early 1980s, SPEs were used by the financial services firms to "securitize" (market as securities) assets that are otherwise generally illiquid and non-marketable, such as groups of mortgages or credit card receivables. Because they provide liquidity to certain assets and facilitate a more complete market for risk sharing, many SPEs can and do indeed serve a useful social purpose.

3.2. Accounting Purposes of SPEs

These examples illustrate that SPEs can be motivated by a genuine business purpose, such as risk sharing among investors and isolation of project risk from company risk. But as we have seen from the Enron debacle, SPEs can also be motivated by a specific accounting goal, such as off-balance sheet financing. The desired accounting effects are made possible because of the fact that SPEs are not consolidated with the parent if they satisfy certain conditions. The accounting effects sought by the use of SPEs can be summarized into the following types:

1. Hiding of Debt (Off-Balance Sheet Financing). The company tries to shift liabilities and associated assets to an SPE. The main purpose of forming the SPE in this case is to let the SPE borrow funds and not show the debt in the books of the sponsoring entity. The so-called "synthetic leases" are examples of this type of SPE. In the 1980s, SPEs became a popular way to execute synthetic lease transactions, in which a company desiring the use of a building or airplanes tries to structure the purchase or use in such a way that it does not result in a financial liability on the balance sheet. Though Enron's earlier use of SPEs may have been motivated by this objective, the key SPEs formed by Enron since 1997, such as Chewco, LJM1 and LJM2, were intended more for the other accounting objectives described below.

2. Hiding of Poor-Performing Assets. This objective has a major factor in several SPE transactions of Enron. For example, Enron transferred poor-performing investments (such as Rhythms NetConnections) to SPEs, so that any subsequent declines in the value of these assets would not have to be recognized by Enron. In 2000 and 2001 alone, Enron was able to hide as much as $1 billion of losses from poor-performing merchant investments by these types of SPE transactions.

3. Earnings Management—Reporting Gains and Losses When Desired. This accounting objective has also been a fundamental motivation for several of the complicated transactions arranged by Enron with SPEs with names such as Braveheart, LJM1, and Chewco. For example, Enron was able to transfer a long-term business contract—an agreement with Blockbuster Video to deliver movies on demand to an SPE and report a "gain" of $111 million.

4. Quick Execution of Related Party Transactions at Desired Prices. Enron's use of SPEs such as LJM1 and LJM2, controlled by its own senior managers, was specifically intended to do related party transactions quickly and when desired, at prices not negotiated at arms-length but arrived at between parties who had clear conflicts of interest. For example, the Blockbuster deal above was arranged at the very end of December 2000, just in time so that about $53 million of the "gain" could be included in the 2000 financial report. (The rest of the gain, $58 million, was reported in 2001 first quarter.) The purpose of this and several similar transactions by Enron seems to have been to use these transactions with SPEs controlled by its own senior executives to essentially create at short notice any amount of desired income, to meet investor expectations.

There are three sets of accounting rules that permit the above financial statement effects of SPEs. One deals with balance sheet consolidation—whether or not SPEs such as synthetic leases should be consolidated or reported separately from the sponsoring entity. The second deals with sales recognition—when the transfer of assets to an SPE should be reported as a sale. The third deals with related party transactions—whether transfers of assets to related parties can be reported as revenue. Of these, the accounting problem that needs immediate fixing is the one dealing with consolidation of SPEs. This is addressed next. With respect to sales recognition rules and related party transaction rules, the problem may lie more with Enron's questionable accounting and corresponding auditor errors, rather than the rules themselves. However, Enron's revenue recognition from SPE transactions often depended on the so-called mark-to-market accounting rules, which gave Enron the ability to assign arbitrary values to its energy and other business contracts. These rules do have certain problems that need fixing, and this issue is addressed in section 4.

3.3. Consolidation of SPEs

Despite their potential for economic and business benefits, the use of SPEs has always raised the question of whether the sponsoring company has some other accounting motivations, such as hiding of debt, hiding of poor-performing assets, or earnings management. Additionally, the explosive growth in the use of SPEs led to debates among managers, auditors, and accounting standards-setters as to whether and when SPEs should be consolidated. This is because the intended accounting effects of SPEs can only be achieved if the SPEs are reported as unconsolidated entities separate from the sponsoring entity. In other words, the sponsoring company needs to somehow keep its ownership in the SPE low enough so that it does not have to consolidate the SPE.

Thus consolidation rules for SPEs have been controversial and have been hotly contested between companies and accounting standards-setters from the very beginning. In the U.S., the involvement of the Financial Accounting Standards Board ("FASB"), the accounting standards-setting agency, in SPE accounting effectively started from 1977, when the FASB issued lease capitalization rules to control the use of off-balance sheet financing with leases. Corporate management intent on skirting around the new lease capitalization rules appeared to have led to the rapid development of SPEs to do the so-called "synthetic leases." In the first of several accounting rules directed at SPEs, in 1984, the Emerging Issues Task Force ("EITF") of the FASB issued EITF No. 84-15, "Grantor Trusts Consolidation." However, given the rapid growth of SPEs and their ever-widening range of applications, standards-setters were always a step or two behind (and were being reactive rather than proactive) in developing accounting rules to govern their proper use.

The question of whether a sponsoring company should consolidate an SPE took a definitive turn in 1990 when the EITF, with the implicit concurrence of the SEC, issued a guidance called EITF 90-15. This guidance allowed the acceptance of the infamous "three percent rule," i.e., an SPE need not be consolidated if at least three percent of its equity is owned by outside equity holders who bear ownership risk. Subsequently, the FASB formalized the above SPE accounting rule with Statement No. 125, and more recently Statement No. 140, issued in September 2000.

An analysis of the development of the three percent rule suggests that the rule was an ad-hoc reaction to a specific issue faced by the FASB's Emerging Issues Task Force and was intended as a short-term band-aid, but has somehow been elevated to a permanent fix. More importantly, the rule, in many ways, was a major departure from the normal consolidation rules used for other subsidiaries and entities. In the U.S., we generally require full consolidation if a company owns (directly or indirectly) 50 percent or more of an entity. Thus the three percent rule is a major loosening of the normal consolidation rule. The motivation for this seems to have been that the SPEs were restricted in their activities by charter and thus the parent company could claim lack of control. The parent company only had to show that some other investors did indeed join the SPE venture with a significant exposure (signified by the three percent rule) in order to make the SPE economically real and thus take it off the books.

Clearly the accounting for SPE consolidation needs to be fixed, starting with the abandonment of the three percent rule and its replacement with a more strictly defined "economic control" criterion. The need to fix consolidation rules has also been amply recognized by the FASB, which has been working for several years on a comprehensive "consolidation" project. However, the Enron debacle should give our standards-setters the needed push to rapidly complete this critical project and issue new rules for the proper consolidation of SPEs whose assets or management are effectively controlled by the sponsoring company. The rules should emphasize economic control, rather than rely on some legal definition of ownership or on an arbitrary percentage ownership. Economic control should be assumed unless management can prove lack of control.

4. MARK-TO-MARKET ACCOUNTING AND EARNINGS MANAGEMENT

In the U.S., financial assets, such as marketable securities, derivatives, and financial contracts, are required to be reported on the balance sheet at their current market values, rather than their original acquisition cost. This is known as mark-to-market ("MTM") accounting. MTM also requires changes in the market values for certain financial assets to be reported in the income statement, and in other cases in the shareholders' equity as a component of "Accumulated Other Comprehensive Income" ("OCI"), a new line item that was required for all public companies by FASB Statement No. 130 from 1997.

MTM was implemented in FASB Statement No. 115, issued in 1993, for financial assets that have readily determinable market values, such as stocks and traded futures and options. In 1996, FASB Statement No. 133 extended MTM to all financial derivatives, even those that do not have traded market values. For some derivatives, a company may have to use complex mathematical formulas to estimate a market value. Depending on the complexity of the financial contract, the proprietary formulas used by companies for market value estimation may depend on several dozen assumptions about interest rate, customers, costs, and prices, and may require several hours of computing time. This means that it is hard, if not impossible, to verify or audit the resulting estimated market value. Of course, a consequence of this lack of verifiability is that MTM accounting can potentially provide ample opportunities for management to create and manage earnings. Thus MTM accounting represents the classic accounting struggle of weighing the trade-off between relevance and reliability—in this case the relevance of the market value data against the reliability of the data. In the end, the accounting standards-setters took the position that the increased benefit from reporting the market value information on the balance sheet justified the cost of decreased reliability of income statements and the earnings number.

It will be useful to consider an example of how Enron recognized value with MTM accounting, in order to understand how MTM can be easily manipulated by a company to manage earnings, especially with respect to financial contracts that do not have a ready market. Assume that Enron signed a contract with the city of Chicago to deliver electricity to several office buildings of the city government over the next twenty years, at fixed or pre-determined prices. The advantage to the city of Chicago from this "price risk management" activity is that it fixes its purchase price of electricity and allows the city government to budget and forecast future outlays for electricity without having to worry about price fluctuations in gas or electricity markets.

Enron sought and obtained exemptions from regulators to allow it to report these types of long-term supply contracts as "merchant investments" rather than regulated contracts, and obtained permission from accounting standards-setters to value them using MTM accounting. Without MTM, Enron would be required to recognize no revenue at the time the contract is signed and report revenues and related costs only in future years for actual amounts of electricity supplied in each year. However, MTM accounting permits Enron to estimate the net present value of all future estimated revenues and costs from the contract and report this net amount as income in the year in which the supply contract is signed. The idea for such an accounting treatment seems to be based on the notion that the financial contract could have been sold to someone else immediately at the estimated market value, and hence investors would benefit from knowing this amount in the balance sheet and correspondingly in the income statement. Enron used similar MTM procedures not only to value merchant investments on its books but also to determine the selling price, and hence gain on sale, for investments it transferred to the various SPEs it controlled.

A major problem with using MTM accounting for private contracts such as the one described above is that the valuation requires Enron to forecast or assume values for several dozen variables and for several years into the future. For example, the revenue forecasts may depend on assumptions about the exact timing of energy deregulation in various local markets, as well as twenty years of forecasts for demand for electricity, actions of other competitors, price elasticity, cost of gas, interest rates, and so on.

While there are strong conceptual reasons to support MTM accounting, the Enron crisis points to at least some need to revisit and revise the current accounting rules for reporting transactions and assets that rely on MTM values. In particular, MTM rules should be modified to require that all gains calculated using MTM method for assets and contracts that do not have a ready market value should be reported only in "Other Comprehensive Income" in the balance sheet, rather than the income statement, until the company can meet some high "confidence level" about the realization of revenue for cash flows that are projected into future years. Normal revenue recognition rules do require that revenue should be recognized after service is performed, and moreover that revenue should be "realized or realizable," meaning that cash flow collection should be likely. In the absence of satisfying this condition, revenue rules (such as those explained in SEC Staff Accounting Bulletin 101) normally compel a company to wait until service is performed and cash collection probabilities are higher. Extending this logic to MTM accounting would protect the investing public from unverifiable and unauditable claims of gains being reported in the income statement.

5. RECOMMENDATIONS

The Enron meltdown is a result of massive failure of corporate control and governance, and failures at several levels of outside checks and balances that investors and the public rely on, including an independent external audit. In my testimony, I have focused on the accounting issues, and in particular on the possible changes we need to make in these areas in order to prevent future Enrons. My recommendations are summarized below.

1. The SEC, the New York Stock Exchange ("NYSE"), and the Nasdaq should adopt new rules severely restricting the format and use of pro-forma earnings reporting. All earnings communications by companies should emphasize earnings as computed by Generally Acceptable Accounting Standards. Any additional information provided by the company to highlight special or unusual items in the earnings number should be given in such a way that the GAAP income is still clearly the focus of the earnings disclosure.
2. Companies should be reminded by regulators and auditors that the use of terms such as "one-time" or "non-recurring" about past events in earnings communications implies certain promises to investors about future performance, and therefore should not be used except in rare cases.
3. Companies should present a complete set of financial statements, including a balance sheet and a cash flow statement, in all their earnings communications to the general public, in order to permit investors to evaluate the quality of the reported earnings numbers.
4. The FASB needs to accelerate its current project on consolidation accounting, and in particular, fix the consolidation rules in the accounting for Special Purpose Entities to prevent its continued abuse by corporations for earnings management. The current consolidation rules, including the "3 percent" rule for SPEs need to be abandoned and replaced with an "economic control" rule. The new rules need to emphasize economic control rather than rely on some legal definition of ownership or on an arbitrary percentage ownership. Economic control should be assumed unless management can prove lack of control. Similar rules should be extended to lease accounting.
5. The FASB and the SEC need to consider requiring new disclosures on transactions between a company and its unconsolidated entities, including SPEs. In particular, more detailed footnote disclosures on the sale or transfer of assets to unconsolidated entities, recognition of income from such transfers, and the valuation of transferred assets should be required.
6. The mark-to-market accounting methodology, while theoretically sound, needs to be modified in the light of what we have learned from the Enron meltdown. Traditional revenue recognition rules, such as the realization principle, should be extended to the recognition of gains and losses from MTM accounting. Forecasted cash flows beyond two or three years should be presumed to have a low level of confidence of collectibility. Gains resulting from present values of such cash flows should be recorded in the Accumulated Other Comprehensive Income in the balance sheet, rather than the income statement, until the confidence level increases to satisfy the usual realization criterion of collectibility.

Auditors and Analysts: An Analysis of the Evidence and Reform Proposals in Light of the Enron Experience

John C. Coffee, Jr.[*]

I. INTRODUCTION

I want to thank the Committee for inviting me to appear today. Because I realize that you are covering a broad range of issues and have only limited time to listen to any individual witness, I believe that my contribution will be the most useful if I focus on just two issues: (1) What powers, duties, and standards should Congress include in any legislation that establishes a self-regulatory body to oversee the auditing profession? and (2) How should Congress respond to the evidence that conflicts of interest do bias the recommendations and research of securities analysts?

If we focus only on Enron, it cannot prove by itself that there is a crisis or that either auditors or securities analysts have been compromised by conflicts of interest. By itself, Enron is only an anecdote—bizarre, vivid, and tragic as it may be. But Enron does not stand alone. As I elaborated in detail in testimony before the Senate Commerce Committee on December 17, 2001 (and thus will not repeat at any length here), Enron is part of a pattern. As the liabilities faced by auditors declined in the 1990s and as the incentives auditors perceived to acquiesce in management's desire to manage earnings increased over the same period (because of the opportunities to earn highly lucrative consulting revenues), there has been an apparent erosion in the quality of financial reporting. Assertive as this conclusion may sound, a burgeoning literature exists on earnings management, which indicates that earnings management is conscious, widespread and tolerated by auditors within, at least, very wide limits.[1] Objective data also show a decline in the reliability of published financial results. To give only the simplest

[*] John C. Coffee, Jr. & Adolf A. Berle, Auditors & Analysts: An Analysis of the Evidence and Reform Proposals in Light of the Enron Experience (Mar. 5, 2002), *available at* http://banking.senate.gov/02_03hrg/030502/coffee.htm. *Editors' note:* This essay was included in the first edition of this book. Reprinted by permission.

[1] John C. Coffee Jr., *The Acquiescent Gatekeeper: Reputational Intermediaries, Auditor Independence and the Governance of Accounting* (May 2001) (unpublished Columbia Law and Economics working paper No. 0191), *available at* http://papers.ssrn.com/sol3/papers.cfm?abstract_id=270944.

quantitative measure, from 1997 to 2000, there were 1,080 earnings restatements by publicly held companies.[2] Most importantly, there has been a significant recent increase in the number of earnings restatements. Earnings restatements averaged 49 per year from 1990 to 1997, then increased to 91 in 1998, and soared to 150 in 1999 and 156 in 2000.[3] Put simply, this sudden spike in earnings restatements is neither coincidental nor temporary.

Worse yet, the accounting profession is conspicuous by its lack of any meaningful mechanism for internal self-discipline. This void contrasts starkly with the governance structure of the broker-dealer industry, where the National Association of Securities Dealers ("NASD") administers a vigorous and effective system of internal discipline. Because both brokers and auditors ultimately serve the same constituency—i.e., investors—this disparity is unjustifiable.

Put simply, American corporate governance depends at bottom on the credibility of the numbers. Only if financial data is accurate can our essentially private system of corporate governance operate effectively. Today, there is doubt about the reliability of reported financial data—and also about the independence and objectivity of the two watchdogs who monitor and verity that data: namely, auditors and securities analysts.

What should Congress do about the crisis? While there is a case for raising the liabilities that auditors and analysts face, I am fully aware that many are skeptical of private enforcement of law through class and derivative actions. Essentially, this asks a third watchdog—the plaintiff's attorney—to monitor the failings of the first two (auditors and analysts), and plaintiffs' attorneys may have their own disincentives. Also, it may still be too early to ask Congress to revisit the Private Securities Litigation Reform Act of 1995 (the "PSLRA"). Thus, both in my December appearance before the Senate Commerce Committee and again today, I am urging the Congress to give fuller consideration to public enforcement through the creation or strengthening of self-regulatory organizations ("SROs"). An SRO already exists with jurisdiction over securities analysts (i.e., the NASD), but one needs to be created from whole cloth in the case of auditors. Thus, my comments will focus first on the creation of a new SRO for auditors and then how to strengthen the oversight of analysts.

II. AN SRO FOR AUDITORS: SOME SUGGESTED STANDARDS

The governance of accounting is today fragmented and indeed Balkanized among (1) state boards of accountancy, (2) private bodies, of which there are essentially seven, and (3) the SEC, which has broad anti-fraud jurisdiction, but less certain authority

---

[2] George Moriarty & Philip Livingston, *Quantitative Measures of the Quality of Financial Reporting*, FIN. EXECUTIVE, July-Aug. 2001, at 53.

[3] *Id.* 715 of these restatements involved Nasdaq listed companies; 228 involved New York Stock Exchange companies; the rest were listed either on the American Stock Exchange or traded in the over-the-counter market. Premature revenue recognition was found to be the leading cause of restatements.

under Rule 102(e) of its Rules of Practice.[4] Disciplinary authority is particularly divided within the profession. The Quality Control Inquiry Committee ("QCIC") of the SEC Practice Section of the American Institute of Certified Public Accountants ("AICPA") is delegated responsibility to investigate alleged audit failures involving SEC clients arising from litigation or regulatory investigations, but it is charged only with determining if there are deficiencies in the auditing firm's system of quality control. The Professional Ethics Executive Committee ("PEEC") of the AICPA is supposed to take individual cases on referral from the QCIC, but as a matter of "fairness" PEEC will automatically defer, at the subject firm's request, any investigation until all litigation or regulatory proceedings have been completed. In short, the investor's interest in purging corrupt or fraudulent auditors from the profession is subordinated to the firm's interest in settling litigation cheap, uninfluenced by any possible findings of ethical lapses.

Little in this system merits retention. Legislation is necessary to create a body that would have at least the same powers, duties, and obligations as the NASD. In truth, however, the legislation that created the NASD in 1938 (the Maloney Act) is not an ideal model, given its general lack of specific guidance. Rather, model legislation should have the following elements:

1. *Rule-Making Power.* The SRO should be specifically authorized to (1) address and prohibit conflicts of interest and other deficiencies that might jeopardize either auditor independence or the public's confidence in the accuracy and reliability of published financial statements, and (2) establish mandatory procedures, including procedures for the retention of accountants by publicly-held companies and for the interaction and relationship between the accountants and audit committees. This is a broad standard—and deliberately so. It could authorize the SRO to require that auditors be retained and/or fired by the audit committee and not by the company's management. In addition, the SRO should be authorized to affirmatively mandate the adoption and use of new or improved quality control systems, as they from time to time become accepted.

2. *Mandatory Membership.* All outside auditors preparing or certifying the financial statements of publicly-held companies or of companies conducting registered public offerings would be required to be members in good standing, and suspension or ouster from the SRO would render an auditor unable to certify the financial statements of such companies.

3. *SEC Supervision.* SEC approval of the initial registration of such an SRO and of all amendments to its rules would be mandated, just as in the case of the NASD. The SEC would also have authority to amend the SRO's rules in compliance with a statutory "public interest" standard. Finally, the SEC should have authority to sanction, fine, or suspend the SRO and to remove or suspend its officers or directors for cause.

---

[4] 17 C.F.R § 201.102 (1998). The SEC's authority under Rule 102(e) was clouded by the D.C. Circuit's decision in Checkosky v. SEC, 139 F.3d 221 (D.C. Cir. 1998) (dismissing Rule 102(e) proceeding against two accountants of a "Big Five" firm). The SEC revised Rule 102 in late 1998 in response to this decision (see Securities Act. Rel. No. 7593 (Oct. 18, 1998) *available at* 1998 SEC LEXIS 2256 (last visited Jun 18, 2003)), but its authority in this area is still subject to some doubt that Congress may wish to remove or clarify.

4. *Enforcement Powers.* The SRO should have the same authority to impose financial penalties or to suspend or disbar an auditor from membership, or to suspend, disbar, fine, or censure any associated professional. Such fines and penalties should not require proof of fraud, but only a demonstration of negligent or unethical conduct. Subpoena authority should also be conferred, and a failure to cooperate or provide evidence should be grounds for discipline or dismissal.

5. *Duties of Supervisory Personnel.* A common response of organizations caught in a scandal or a criminal transaction is to blame everything on a "rogue" employee. Yet, such "rogues" are often responding to winks and nods from above (real or perceived) or to an organizational culture that encourages risk-taking (Enron is again symptomatic). The federal securities laws impose duties on supervisory personnel in brokerage firms to monitor their employees, and a parallel standard should apply to supervisory personnel in auditing firms.

6. *Governance.* The SRO should have at least a supermajority (say, 66 2/3%) of "public" members, who are not present or recently past employees or associated persons of the auditing industry.

7. *Prompt Enforcement.* The practice now followed by PEEC of deferring all disciplinary investigations until civil litigation and regulatory investigations have been resolved is self-defeating and unacceptable. It might, however, be possible to render the findings and disciplinary measures taken by the SRO inadmissible in private civil litigation.

III. SECURITIES ANALYSTS

A. What Do We Know About Analyst Objectivity?

A number of studies have sought to assess the impact of conflicts of interest upon the objectivity of securities analyst recommendations. Additional evidence was also recently collected at hearings held in June 2001 by the Subcommittee on Capital Markets, Insurance and Government-Sponsored Enterprises of the House Financial Services Committee. This data is probably more germane, and merits greater reliance, than the well-known statistic that an alleged 100:1 ratio exists between the "buy" recommendations and "sell" recommendations made by securities analysts. Although the actual ratio may be somewhat less extreme than 100:1,[5] the real problem with this statistic is that it is not necessarily the product of conflicts of interest. That is, analysts employed by brokerage firms (as all "sell-side" analysts are) have a natural incentive to encourage purchase or sale transactions. For this purpose, "buy" recommendations are more useful than "sell" recommendations, because all clients can buy a stock, but only existing holders can sell, as a practical matter.

[5] A December 2000 Thomson Financial Survey reported that 71% of all analyst recommendations were "buys" and only 2.1% were "sells." Apparently, only 1% of 28,000 recommendations issued by analysts during late 1999 and most of 2000 were "sells." This study also finds that the overall "buy" to "sell" ratio shifted from 6:1 in the early 1990s to 100:1 by sometime in 2000. Of course, this shift also coincided with the Nasdaq bull market of the 1990s.

Other data better illustrates the impact of conflicts of interest on analysts. Among the most salient findings from recent research are the following:

1. *Conflict of Interests.* Several studies find that "independent" analysts (i.e., analysts not associated with the underwriter for a particular issuer) behave differently from analysts who are so associated with the issuer's underwriter. For example, Roni Michaely and Kent Womack found that the long-run performance of firms recommended by analysts who are associated with an underwriter was significantly worse than the performance of firms recommended by independent securities analysts.[6] They further found that stock prices of firms recommended by analysts associated with lead underwriters fall on average in the thirty days before a recommendation is issued, while the stock prices of firms recommended by analysts not so associated with underwriters rose on average over the same period. Finally, the mean long-run performance of buy recommendations made by analysts on non-clients is more positive than the performance of recommendations made on clients—at least for twelve out of fourteen brokerage firms.

Still another study by *CFO Magazine* reports that analysts who work for full-service investment banking firms have 6% higher earnings forecasts and close to 25% more "buy" recommendations than do analysts at firms without such ties.[7] Similarly, using a sample of 2,400 seasoned equity offerings between 1989 and 1994, Lin and McNichols find that lead and co-underwriter analysts' growth forecasts and, particularly, their recommendations are significantly more favorable than those made by unaffiliated analysts.[8]

2. *Pressure and Retaliation.* In self-reporting studies, securities analysts report that they are frequently pressured to make positive buy recommendations or at least to temper negative opinions.[9] Sixty-one percent of analysts responding to one survey reported personal experience with threats of retaliation from issuer management.[10] Similarly, former Acting SEC Chairman Laura Unger noted in a recent speech that a survey of 300 chief financial officers found that 20% of surveyed CFOs acknowledged withholding business from brokerage firms whose analysts issued unfavorable research.[11] This is a phenomenon that is almost certain to be underreported.

This data should not be over-read. It does not prove that securities research or analyst recommendations are valueless or hopelessly biased, but it does tend to confirm what one would intuitively expect: namely, conflicts of interest count, and conflicted analysts behave differently than unaffiliated or "independent" analysts.

---

[6] R. Michaely & K.L. Womack, *Conflict of Interest and the Credibility of Underwriter Analyst Recommendations*, 12 REV. FIN. STUD. 653 (1999).

[7] Stephen Barr, *What Chinese Wall*, CFO (Mar. 2000).

[8] Hsiou-wei Lin & Maureen F. McNichols, *Underwriting Relationships and Analysts' Earnings Forecasts and Investment Recommendations*, 25 J. ACCT. & ECON. 101 (1997).

[9] Jane Cote, *Analyst Credibility: The Investor's Perspective*, 351 J. MANAGERIAL ISSUES (2000).

[10] Debbie Galant, *The Hazards of Negative Research Reports*, INSTITUTIONAL INVESTOR (July 1990).

[11] Laura Unger, *How Can Analysts Maintain Their Independence,* Remarks at Northwestern Law School (Apr. 19, 2001), *available at* http://www.sec.gov/news/speech/spch477.htm.

B. The Regulatory Response

In light of public criticism regarding securities analysts and their conflicts of interest, the National Association of Securities Dealers ("NASD") proposed Rule 2711 ("Research Analysts and Research Reports") in early February 2002.[12] Proposed Rule 2711 is lengthy, complex and has not yet been adopted. Nonetheless, because its adoption in some form seems likely, a brief analysis of its contents seems useful as an introduction to what further steps Congress should consider.

Basically, Rule 2711 does seven important things:

(1) It places restrictions on the investment banking department's relationship with the "research" or securities analyst division of an integrated broker-dealer firms;
(2) It restricts the pre-publication review of analyst research reports by the subject company and investment banking personnel;
(3) It prohibits bonus or salary compensation to a research analyst based upon a specific investment banking services transaction;
(4) It prohibits broker-dealers from promising favorable research or ratings as consideration or an inducement for the receipt of business or compensation;
(5) It extends the "quiet period" during which the broker-dealer may not publish research reports regarding a company in an IPO for which the firm is acting as a manager or co-manager for 40 calendar days from the date of the offering;
(6) It restricts analysts' ability to acquire securities from a company prior to an IPO or to purchase or sell for a defined period before or after the publication of research report or a change in a rating or price target; and
(7) It requires extensive disclosure by an analyst of certain stock holdings or compensation or other conflict of interest relationships.

All of these prohibitions are subject to substantial exceptions and/or qualifications, and it is debatable whether some can be effectively monitored. Only time and experience with proposed Rule 2711 can tell us whether its exceptions will overwhelm the rule. Nonetheless, Rule 2711 represents a serious and commendable effort to police the conflicts of interest that exist within broker-dealer firms that both underwrite securities and provide securities research and recommendations. In this light, the most important question is: what else can or should Congress do? Are there topics or areas that Rule 2711 has not addressed that Congress should address? These are considered below.

C. Congressional Options

The overriding policy question is whether conflicts of interest relating to securities research should be prohibited or only policed. As I will suggest below, this question is not easily answered, because there are costs and imperfections with both options:

---

[12] S. REP. NO. 2002-21 (2002).

1. *Radical Reform: Divorce Investment Banking From Securities Research.* Congress could do what it essentially did a half-century ago in the Glass-Steagall Act:[13] namely, prohibit investment banking firms that underwrite securities from engaging in a specified activity (here, providing securities research to all, or at least certain, customers). Arguably, this is what Congress and the SEC have already proposed to do with respect to the accounting profession: i.e., separate the auditing and consulting roles performed by accountants. Here, the conflict might be thought to be even more serious because the empirical evidence does suggest that the advice given by conflicted analysts is different from the advice given by independent analysts.

But this divestiture remedy is here even more problematic than in the case of the original Glass-Steagall Act. Put simply, securities research is not a self-sufficient line of business that exists on a free-standing basis. To be sure, there are a limited number of "independent" securities research boutiques (Sanford C. Bernstein & Co is probably the best known and most often cited example) that do not do underwriting, but still survive very well. Yet, this is a niche market, catering to institutional investors. Since May 1, 1975 ("Mayday"), when the old system of fixed commissions was ended and brokerage commissions became competitively determined, commissions have shrunk to a razor-thin margin that will not support the costs of securities research. Instead, securities research (i.e., the salaries and expenses of securities research) is essentially subsidized by the investment banking division of the integrated broker-dealer firm. The problematic result is at the same time to subsidize and arguably distort securities research.

This point distinguishes the securities analysts from the accountant. That is, if the auditor is prohibited from consulting for the client, both the auditing and the consulting function will survive. But, in particular because the costs of securities research cannot be easily passed on to the retail customer, a Glass-Steagall divorce might imply that the number of securities analysts would shrink by a substantial fraction.[14] A cynic might respond: why seek to maximize biased research? Yet, if the number of analysts were to fall by, hypothetically, one half, market efficiency might well suffer, and many smaller firms simply would not be regularly covered by any analyst. Hence, the divestiture approach may entail costs and risks that cannot be reliably estimated.

2. *Piecemeal Reform: Policing Conflicts.* Proposed Rule 2711 represents an approach of trying to police conflicts and prevent egregious abuse. The practical ability of regulators to do this effectively is always open to question. For example, although proposed Rule 2711 generally prohibits investment banking officials from reviewing research reports prior to publication, it does permit a limited review "to verify the factual accuracy of information in the research report" (see Rule 2711(b)(3)). It is easy to imagine veiled or stylized communications that signal that the investment banking division is displeased

---

[13] *See* Glass-Steagall Act of 1933, 12 U.S.C. § 36 et. seq. (separating commercial and investment banking).

[14] I recognize that the number of "buy side" analysts employed by institutional investors might correspondingly increase, but not, I think, to a fully compensating degree. Moreover, "buy side" analysts do not publish their research, thus implying increased informational asymmetries in the market.

and will reduce the analyst's compensation at the next regular salary review. Such signals, even if they consist only of arched eyebrows, are effectively impossible to prohibit. Still, at the margin, intelligent regulation may curtail the more obvious forms of abuse.

Although proposed Rule 2711 addresses many topics, it does not address every topic. Some other topics that may merit attention are discussed below, but they are discussed in the context of suggesting that Congress might give the NASD general policy instructions and ask it to fine-tune more specific rules that address these goals:

1. *An Anti-Retaliation Rule.* According to one survey,[15] 61% of all analysts have experienced retaliation—threats of dismissal, salary reduction, etc.—as the result of negative research reports. Clearly, negative research reports (and ratings reductions) are hazardous to an analyst's career. Congress could either adopt, or instruct the NASD to adopt, an anti-retaliation rule: no analyst should be fired, demoted, or economically penalized for issuing a negative report, downgrading a rating, or reducing an earnings, price, or similar target. Of course, this rule would not bar staff reductions or reduced bonuses based on economic downturns or individualized performance assessments. Thus, given the obvious possibility that the firm could reduce an analyst's compensation in retaliation for a negative report, but describe its action as based on an adverse performance review of the individual, how can this rule be made enforceable? The best answer may be NASD arbitration. That is, an employee who felt that he or she had been wrongfully terminated or that his or her salary had been reduced in retaliation for a negative research report could use the already existing system of NASD employee arbitration to attempt to reverse the decision. Congress could also establish the burden of proof in such litigation and place it on the firm, rather than on the employee/analyst. Further, Congress could entitle the employee to some form of treble damages or other punitive award to make this form of litigation viable. Finally, Congress could mandate an NASD penalty if retaliation were found, either by an NASD arbitration panel or in an NASD disciplinary proceeding.

2. *A No-Selling Rule.* If we wish the analyst to be a more neutral and objective umpire, one logical step might be to preclude the analyst from direct involvement in selling activities. For example, it is today standard for the "star" analyst to participate in "road shows" managed by the lead underwriters, presenting a highly favorable evaluation of the issuer and even meeting on a one-to-one basis with important institutional investors. Such sales activity seems inconsistent with the much-cited "Chinese Wall" between investment banking and investment research.

Yet, from the investment banking side's perspective, such participation in sales activity in what makes the analyst most valuable to the investment banker and what justifies multimillion dollar salaries to analysts. Restrict such activities, they would argue, and compensation to analysts may decline. Of course, a decline in salaries for super-stars does not imply a reduction in overall coverage or greater market inefficiency.

Although a "no-selling" rule would do much to restore the objectivity of the analyst's role, one counter-consideration is that the audience at the road show is today limited to

---

[15] Galant, *supra* note 10; Cote, *supra* note 9.

institutions and high-net-worth individuals. Hence, there is less danger that the analyst will overreach unsophisticated retail investors. For all these reasons, this is an area where a more nuanced rule could be drafted by the NASD at the direction of Congress that would be preferable to a legislative command.

3. *Prohibiting the "Booster Shot."* Firms contemplating an IPO increasingly seek to hire as lead underwriter the firm that employs the star analyst in their field. The issuer's motivation is fueled in large part by the fact that the issuer's management almost invariably is restricted from selling its own stock (by contractual agreement with the underwriters) until the expiration of a lock-up period that typically extends six months from the date of the offering. The purpose of the lock-up agreement is to assure investors that management and the controlling shareholders are not "bailing out" of the firm by means of the IPO. But as a result, the critical date (and market price) for the firm's insiders is not the date of the IPO (or the market value at the conclusion of the IPO), but rather the expiration date of the lock-up agreement six months later (and the market value of the stock on that date). From the perspective of the issuer's management, the role of the analyst is to "maintain a buzz" about the stock and create a price momentum that peaks just before the lock-up's expiration.[16] To do this, the analyst may issue a favorable research report just before the lock-up's expiration (a so-called "booster shot," in the vernacular). To the extent that favorable ratings issued at this point seem particularly conflicted and suspect, an NASD rule might forbid analysts associated with underwriters from issuing research reports for a reasonable period (say, thirty days) both before and after the lock-up expiration date. Proposed Rule 2711 stops well short of this and only extends the "quiet period" so that it now would preclude research reports for this first 40 days after an IPO. Such a limited rule in no way interferes with the dubious tactic of "booster shots."

IV. SUMMARY

The most logical and less overbroad route for Congress to take with regard to securities analysts and their conflicts is to pass legislation giving the NASD more specific guidance and instructions about the goals that they should pursue and then instruct the NASD to conduct the necessary rule-making in order to fine tune this approach. NASD penalties might also properly be raised. This approach spares Congress from having to adopt a detailed code of procedure, avoids inflexibility and rigid legislative rules, and relies on the expertise of the SEC and the NASD, as paradigms of sophisticated administrative agencies.

---

[16] This description of the analyst's role (and of the underwriter's interest in attracting "star" analysts) essentially summarizes the description given by three professors of financial economics: Rajesh Aggarwal, Laurie Krigman and Kent Womack. Rajesh Aggarwal et al., *Strategic IPO Underpricing, Information Momentum, and Lockup Expiration Selling*, 66 J. FIN. ECON. 105 (2002).

Enron and the Derivatives World

Frank Partnoy[*]

I am submitting testimony in response to this Committee's request that I address potential problems associated with the unregulated status of derivatives used by Enron Corporation.

I am a law professor at the University of San Diego School of Law. I teach and do research in the areas of financial market regulation, derivatives, and structured finance. During the mid-1990s, I worked on Wall Street structuring and selling financial instruments and investment vehicles similar to those used by Enron. As a lawyer, I have represented clients with problems similar to Enron's, but on a much smaller scale. I have never received any payment from Enron or from any Enron officer or employee.

I. INTRODUCTION AND OVERVIEW

Enron has been compared to Long-Term Capital Management, the Greenwich, Connecticut, hedge fund that lost $4.6 billion on more than $1 trillion of derivatives and was rescued in September 1998 in a private bailout engineered by the New York Federal Reserve. For the past several weeks, I have conducted my own investigation into Enron, and I believe the comparison is inapt. Yes, there are similarities in both firms' use and abuse of financial derivatives. But the scope of Enron's problems and their effects on its investors and employees are far more sweeping.

According to Enron's most recent annual report, the firm made more money trading derivatives in the year 2000 alone than Long-Term Capital Management made in its entire history. Long-Term Capital Management generated losses of a few billion dollars; by contrast, Enron not only wiped out over $70 billion of shareholder value, but also defaulted on tens of billions of dollars of debts. Long-Term Capital Management

[*] Professor of Law, University of San Diego School of Law. Frank Partnoy, Enron & the Derivatives World (Jan. 24, 2002), *available at* http://www.senate.gov/~gov_affairs/012402partnoy.htm (last visited Sept. 4, 2003).

The original testimony has been slightly edited for inclusion in this book. *Editors' note:* This essay was included in the first edition of this book. Reprinted by permission.

employed only 200 people worldwide, many of whom simply went on to start new hedge funds after the bailout, while Enron employed 20,000 people, many of whom have been fired, and many more of whom lost their life savings as Enron's stock plummeted last fall. In short, Enron makes Long-Term Capital Management look like a lemonade stand.

It will surprise many investors to learn that Enron was, at its core, a derivatives trading firm. Nothing made this more clear than the layout of Enron's extravagant new building in which the top executives' offices on the seventh floor were designed to overlook the crown jewel of Enron's empire: a cavernous derivatives trading pit on the sixth floor.

I believe there are two answers to the question of why Enron collapsed, and both involve derivatives. One relates to the use of derivatives "outside" Enron, in transactions with some now-infamous special purpose entities. The other—which has not been publicized at all—relates to the use of derivatives "inside" Enron.

What are derivatives? They are complex financial instruments whose value is based on one or more underlying variables, such as the price of a stock or the cost of natural gas. Derivatives can be traded in two ways: on regulated exchanges or in unregulated over-the-counter ("OTC") markets. My testimony involves the OTC derivatives markets, the focus of Enron's activities.

Sometimes OTC derivatives can seem too esoteric to be relevant to average investors. Even the well-publicized OTC derivatives fiascos of a few years ago—Procter & Gamble or Orange County, for example—seem ages away. But the OTC derivatives markets are too important to ignore, and are critical to understanding Enron. The size of derivatives markets typically is measured in terms of the notional values of contracts. Recent estimates of the size of the exchange-traded derivatives market, which includes all contracts traded on the major options and futures exchanges, are in the range of $13 to $14 trillion in notional amount. By contrast, the estimated notional amount of outstanding OTC derivatives as of year-end 2000 was $95.2 trillion. And that estimate is most likely an understatement. In other words, OTC derivatives markets, which for the most part did not exist twenty (or, in some cases, even ten) years ago, now comprise about 90 percent of the aggregate derivatives market, with trillions of dollars at risk every day. By those measures, OTC derivatives markets are bigger than the markets for U.S. stocks.

Enron may have been just an energy company when it was created in 1985, but by the end it had become a full-blown OTC derivatives trading firm. Its OTC derivatives-related assets and liabilities increased more than five-fold during 2000 alone.

And, let me repeat, the OTC derivatives markets are largely unregulated. Enron's trading operations were not regulated, or even recently audited, by U.S. securities regulators, and the OTC derivatives it traded are not deemed securities. OTC derivatives trading is beyond the purview of organized, regulated exchanges. Thus, Enron—like many firms that trade OTC derivatives—fell into a regulatory black hole.

After 360 customers lost $11.4 billion on derivatives during the decade ending in March 1997, the Commodity Futures Trading Commission began considering whether to regulate OTC derivatives. But its proposals were rejected, and in December 2000 Congress made the deregulated status of derivatives clear when it passed the Commodity Futures Modernization Act. As a result, the OTC derivatives markets have become a ticking time bomb, which Congress thus far has chosen not to defuse.

Many parties are to blame for Enron's collapse. But as this Committee and others take a hard look at Enron and its officers, directors, accountants, lawyers, bankers, and analysts, Congress also should take a hard look at the current state of OTC derivatives regulation. (In the remainder of this testimony, when I refer generally to "derivatives," I am referring to these OTC derivatives markets.)

II. DERIVATIVES "OUTSIDE" ENRON

The first answer to the question of why Enron collapsed relates to derivatives deals between Enron and several of its 3,000-plus off-balance sheet subsidiaries and partnerships. The names of these byzantine financial entities—such as JEDI, Raptor, and LJM—have been widely reported.

Special purpose entities might seem odd to most investors, but they actually are very common in modern financial markets. Structured finance is a significant part of the U.S. economy, and special purpose entities are involved in most investors' lives, even if they do not realize it. For example, most credit card and mortgage payments flow through special purpose entities, and financial services firms typically use such entities as well. Some special purpose entities generate great economic benefits; others—as I will describe below—are used to manipulate a company's financial reports to inflate assets, to understate liabilities, to create false profits, and to hide losses. In this way, special purpose entities are a lot like fire: they can be used for good or ill. Special purpose entities, like derivatives, are unregulated.

The key problem at Enron involved the confluence of derivatives and special purpose entities. Enron entered into derivatives transactions with these entities to shield volatile assets from quarterly financial reporting and to inflate artificially the value of certain Enron assets. These derivatives included price swap derivatives (described below), as well as call and put options.

Specifically, Enron used derivatives and special purpose vehicles to manipulate its financial statements in three ways. First, it hid speculator losses it suffered on technology stocks. Second, it hid huge debts incurred to finance unprofitable new businesses, including retail energy services for new customers. Third, it inflated the value of other troubled businesses, including its new ventures in fiber-optic bandwidth. Although Enron was founded as an energy company, many of these derivatives transactions did not involve energy at all.

A. Using Derivatives to Hide Losses on Technology Stocks

First, Enron hid hundreds of millions of dollars of losses on its speculative investments in various technology-oriented firms, such as Rhythms NetConnections, Inc., a start-up telecommunications company. A subsidiary of Enron (along with other investors such as Microsoft and Stanford University) invested a relatively small amount of venture capital, on the order of $10 million, in Rhythms NetConnections. Enron also invested in other technology companies.

Rhythms NetConnections issued stock to the public in an initial public offering on April 6, 1999, during the heyday of the Internet boom, at a price of about $70 per share. Enron's stake was suddenly worth hundreds of millions of dollars. Enron's other venture capital investments in technology companies also rocketed at first, alongside the widespread run-up in the value of dot.com stocks. As is typical in IPOs, Enron was prohibited from selling its stock for six months.

Next, Enron entered into a series of transactions with a special purpose entity—apparently a limited partnership called Raptor, one of a several of similarly-named entities created by Enron, which was owned by another Enron special purpose entity called LJM1—in which Enron essentially exchanged its shares in these technology companies for a loan, ultimately, from Raptor. Raptor then issued its own securities to investors and held the cash proceeds from those investors.

The critical piece of this puzzle, the element that made it all work, was a derivatives transaction—called a "price swap derivative"—between Enron and Raptor. In this price swap, Enron committed to give stock to Raptor if Raptor's assets declined in value. The more Raptor's assets declined, the more of its own stock Enron was required to post. Because Enron had committed to maintain Raptor's value at $1.2 billion, if Enron's stock declined in value, Enron would need to give Raptor even more stock. This derivatives transaction carried the risk of diluting the ownership of Enron's shareholders if either Enron's stock or the technology stocks Raptor held declined in price. Enron also apparently entered into options transactions with Raptor and/or LJM1.

Because the securities Raptor issued were backed by Enron's promise to deliver more shares, investors in Raptor essentially were buying Enron's debt, not the stock of a start-up telecommunications company. In fact, the performance of Rhythms NetConnections was irrelevant to these investors in Raptor. Enron got the best of both worlds in accounting terms: it recognized its gain on the technology stocks by recognizing the value of the Raptor loan right away, and it avoided recognizing on an interim basis any future losses on the technology stocks, were such losses to occur.

It is painfully obvious how this story ends: the dot.com bubble burst and by 2001 shares of Rhythms NetConnections were worthless. Enron had to deliver more shares to "make whole" the investors in Raptor and other similar deals. In all, Enron had derivative instruments on 54.8 million shares of Enron common stock at an average price of $67.92 per share, or $3.7 billion in all. In other words, at the start of these deals, Enron's obligation amounted to seven percent of all of its outstanding shares. As Enron's share price declined, that obligation increased and Enron's shareholders were substantially diluted. And here is the key point: even as Raptor's assets and Enron's shares declined in value, Enron did not reflect those declines in its quarterly financial statements.

B. Using Derivatives to Hide Debts Incurred by Unprofitable Businesses

A second example involved Enron using derivatives with two special purpose entities to hide huge debts incurred to finance unprofitable new businesses. Essentially, some very complicated and confusing accounting rules allowed Enron to avoid disclosing certain assets and liabilities.

These two special purpose entities were Joint Energy Development Investments Limited Partnership ("JEDI") and Chewco Investments, L.P. ("Chewco"). Enron owned only 50 percent of JEDI, and therefore—under then-applicable accounting rules—could (and did) report JEDI as an unconsolidated equity affiliate. If Enron had owned 51 percent of JEDI, accounting rules would have required Enron to include all of JEDI's financial results in its financial statements. But at 50 percent, Enron did not have to.

JEDI, in turn, was subject to the same rules. JEDI could issue equity and debt securities, and as long as there was an outside investor with at least 50 percent of the equity—in other words, with real economic exposure to the risks of Chewco—JEDI would not need to consolidate Chewco.

One way to minimize the applicability of this "50 percent rule" would be for a company to create a special purpose entity with mostly debt and only a tiny sliver of equity for which the company easily could find an outside investor. Such a transaction would be an obvious sham, and one might expect to find a pronouncement by the accounting regulators that it would not conform to Generally Acceptable Accounting Principles. Unfortunately, there are no such accounting regulators, and there was no such pronouncement. The Financial Accounting Standards Board, a private entity that sets most accounting rules and advises the Securities and Exchange Commission, had not given a satisfactory answer to the key accounting question: what constitutes sufficient capital from an independent source, so that a special purpose entity need not be consolidated?

Since 1982, Financial Accounting Standard No. 57, Related Party Disclosures, has contained a general requirement that companies disclose the nature of relationships they have with related parties, and describe transactions with them. Accountants might debate whether Enron's impenetrable footnote disclosure satisfies FAS No. 57, but clearly the disclosures currently made are not optimal. In 1998, FASB adopted FAS No. 133, which includes new accounting rules for derivatives. Now at 800-plus pages, FAS No. 133's instructions are an incredibly detailed—but ultimately unhelpful—attempt to rationalize other accounting rules for derivatives.

As a result, even after two decades, there is no clear answer to the question about disclosures on related parties. Instead, some early guidance (developed in the context of leases) has been grafted onto modern special purpose entities. This guidance is a 1991 letter from the Acting Chief Accountant of the SEC in 1991, stating:

> The initial substantive residual equity investment should be comparable to that expected for a substantive business involved in similar [leasing]

> transactions with similar risks and rewards. The SEC staff understands from discussions with Working Group members that those members believe that 3 percent is the minimum acceptable investment. The SEC staff believes a greater investment may be necessary depending on the facts and circumstances, including the credit risk associated with the lessee and the market risk factors associated with the leased property.

Based on this letter, and on opinions from auditors and lawyers, companies started pushing debt off their balance sheets into unconsolidated special purpose entities so long as (1) the company did not have more than 50 percent of the equity of the special purpose entity, and (2) the equity of the special purpose entity was at least 3 percent of its total capital. As more companies have done such deals, more debt has moved off balance-sheet, to the point that, today, it is difficult for investors to know if they have an accurate picture of a company's debts. Even if Enron had not tripped up and violated the letter of these rules, it still would have been able to borrow 97 percent of the capital of its special purpose entities without recognizing those debts on its balance sheet.

Transactions designed to exploit these accounting rules have polluted the financial statements of many U.S. companies. Enron is not alone. For example, Kmart Corporation—which was on the verge of bankruptcy as of January 21, 2002, and clearly was affected by Enron's collapse—held 49 percent interests in several unconsolidated equity affiliates. I believe this Committee should take a hard look at these widespread practices.

In short, derivatives enabled Enron to avoid consolidating these special purpose entities. Enron entered into a derivatives transaction with Chewco similar to the one it entered into with Raptor, effectively guaranteeing repayment to Chewco's outside investor. (The investor's sliver of equity ownership in Chewco was not really equity from an economic perspective, because the investor had nothing—other than Enron's credit—at risk.) In its financial statements, Enron took the position that, although it provided guarantees to unconsolidated subsidiaries, those guarantees did not have a readily determinable fair value, and management did not consider it likely that Enron would be required to perform or otherwise incur losses associated with guarantees. That position enabled Enron to avoid recording its guarantees. Even the guarantees listed in the footnotes were recorded at only 10 percent of their nominal value. (At least this amount is closer to the truth than the amount listed as debt for unconsolidated subsidiaries: zero.)

Apparently, Arthur Andersen either did not discover this derivatives transaction or decided that the transaction did not require a finding that Enron controlled Chewco. In any event, the Enron derivatives transaction meant that Enron—not the 50 percent "investor" in Chewco—had the real exposure to Chewco's assets. The ownership daisy chain unraveled once Enron was deemed to own Chewco. JEDI was forced to consolidate Chewco, and Enron was forced to consolidate both limited partnerships—and all of their losses—in its financial statements.

All of this complicated analysis will seem absurd to the average investor. If the assets and liabilities are Enron's in economic terms, shouldn't they be reported that way in accounting terms? The answer, of course, is yes. Unfortunately, current rules allow companies to employ derivatives and special purpose entities to make accounting standards diverge from economic reality. Enron used financial engineering as a kind of plastic surgery, to make itself look better than it really was. Many other companies do the same.

Of course, it is possible to detect the flaws in plastic surgery, or financial engineering, if you look hard enough and in the right places. In 2000, Enron disclosed about $2.1 billion of such derivatives transactions with related entities, and recognized gains of about $500 million related to those transactions. The disclosure related to these staggering numbers is less than conspicuous, buried at page 48, footnote 16 of Enron's annual report, deep in the related party disclosures for which Enron was notorious. Still, the disclosure is there. A few sophisticated analysts understood Enron's finances based on that disclosure; they bet against Enron's stock. Other securities analysts likely understood the disclosures, but apparently chose not to speak for fear of losing Enron's banking business. An argument even can be made—although not a good one, in my view—that Enron satisfied its disclosure obligations with its opaque language. In any event, the result of Enron's method of disclosure was that investors did not get a full picture of the firm's finances.

Enron is not the only example of such abuse; accounting subterfuge using derivatives is widespread. I believe Congress should seriously consider legislation explicitly requiring that financial statements describe the economic reality of a company's transactions. Such a broad standard—backed by rigorous enforcement—would go a long way towards eradicating the schemes companies currently use to dress up their financial statements.

Enron's risk management manual stated the following: "Reported earnings follow the rules and principles of accounting. The results do not always create measures consistent with underlying economics. However, corporate management's performance is generally measured by accounting income, not underlying economics. Risk management strategies are therefore directed at accounting rather than economic performance." This alarming statement is representative of the accounting-driven focus of U.S. managers generally, who all too frequently have little interest in maintaining controls to monitor their firm's economic realities.

C. Using Derivatives to Inflate the Value of Troubled Businesses

A third example is even more troubling. It appears that Enron inflated the value of certain assets it held by selling a small portion of those assets to a special purpose entity at an inflated price, and then revaluing the lion's share of those assets it still held at that higher price.

Consider the following sentence disclosed from the infamous footnote 16 of Enron's 2000 annual report, on page 49: "In 2000, Enron sold a portion of its dark fiber inventory to the Related Party in exchange for $30 million cash and a $70 million note receivable that was subsequently repaid. Enron recognized gross margin of $67 million on the sale." What does this sentence mean?

It is possible to understand the sentence today, but only after reading a January 7, 2002, article about the sale by Daniel Fisher of *Forbes* magazine, together with an August 2001 memorandum describing the transaction (and others) from one Enron employee, Sherron Watkins, to Enron Chairman Kenneth Lay.

Here is my best understanding of what this sentence means.

First, the "Related Party" is LJM2, an Enron partnership run by Enron's Chief Financial Officer, Andrew Fastow. (Fastow reportedly received $30 million from the LJM1 and LJM2 partnerships pursuant to compensation arrangements Enron's board of directors approved.)

Second, dark fiber refers to a type of bandwidth Enron traded as part of its broadband business. In this business, Enron traded the right to transmit data through various fiber-optic cables, more than 40 million miles of which various Internet-related companies had installed in the United States. Only a small percentage of these cables were "lit"—meaning they could transmit the light waves required to carry Internet data; the vast majority of cables were still awaiting upgrades and were "dark." As one might expect, the rights to transmit over dark fiber are very difficult to value.

Third, Enron sold dark fiber it apparently valued at only $33 million for triple that value: $100 million in all—$30 million in cash plus $70 million in a note receivable. It appears that this sale was at an inflated price, thereby enabling Enron to record a $67 million profit on that trade. LJM2 apparently obtained cash from investors by issuing securities and used some of these proceeds to repay the note receivable issued to Enron.

What the sentence in footnote 16 does not make plain is that the investor in LJM2 was persuaded to pay what appears to be an inflated price, because Enron entered into a "make whole" derivatives contract with LJM2 (of the same type it used with Raptor). Essentially, the investor was buying Enron's debt. The investor was willing to buy securities in LJM2, because if the dark fiber declined in price—as it almost certainly would, from its inflated value—Enron would make the investor whole.

In these transactions, Enron retained the economic risk associated with the dark fiber. Yet as the value of dark fiber plunged during 2000, Enron nevertheless was able to record a gain on its sale, and avoid recognizing any losses on assets held by LJM2, which was an unconsolidated affiliate of Enron, just like JEDI.

As if all of this were not complicated enough, Enron's sale of dark fiber to LJM2 also magically generated an inflated price, which Enron then could use in valuing any remaining dark fiber it held. The third-party investor in LJM2 had, in a sense, "validated" the value of the dark fiber at the higher price, and Enron then arguably could use that inflated price in valuing other dark fiber assets it held. I do not have any direct knowledge of this, although public reports and Sherron Watkins's letter indicate that this is probably what happened.

For example, suppose Enron started with ten units of dark fiber, worth $100, and sold one to a special purpose entity for $20—double its actual value—using the above scheme. Now, Enron had an argument that each of its remaining nine units of dark fiber also were worth $20 each, for a total of $180. Enron then could revalue its remaining nine units of dark fiber at a total of $180. If the assets used in the transaction were difficult to value—as dark fiber clearly was—Enron's inflated valuation might not generate much suspicion, at least initially. But ultimately the valuations would be indefensible, and Enron would need to recognize the associated losses.

It is an open question for this Committee and others whether this transaction was unique, or whether Enron engaged in other, similar deals. It seems likely that the dark fiber deal was not the only one of its kind. There are many sentences in footnote 16 regarding other related party transactions.

D. The "Gatekeepers"

These are but three examples of how Enron's derivatives dealings with outside parties resulted in material information not being reflected in market prices. There are others, many within JEDI alone. I have attempted to summarize this information for the Committee. Clearly it is important that investigators question the Enron employees who were directly involved in these transactions to get a sense of whether my summaries are complete.

Moreover, a thorough inquiry into these dealings also should include the major financial market "gatekeepers" involved with Enron: accounting firms, banks, law firms, and credit rating agencies. Employees of these firms are likely to have knowledge of these transactions. Moreover, these firms have a responsibility to come forward with information relevant to these transactions. They benefit directly and indirectly from the existence of U.S. securities regulation, which in many instances both forces companies to use the services of gatekeepers and protects gatekeepers from liability.

Recent cases against accounting firms—including Arthur Andersen—are eroding that protection, but the other gatekeepers remain well insulated. Gatekeepers are kept honest—at least in theory—by the threat of legal liability, but this threat is virtually non-existent for some gatekeepers. The capital markets would be more efficient if companies were not required by law to use particular gatekeepers (which only gives those firms market power), and if gatekeepers were subject to a credible threat of liability for their involvement in fraudulent transactions. Congress should consider expanding the scope of securities fraud liability by making it clear that these gatekeepers will be liable for assisting companies in transactions designed to distort the economic reality of financial statements.

With respect to Enron, all of these gatekeepers have questions to answer about the money they received, the quality of their work, and the extent of their conflicts of interest. It has been reported that Enron paid $52 million in 2000 to its audit firm, Arthur Andersen, the majority of which was for non-audit related consulting services, yet Arthur Andersen failed to spot many of Enron's losses. It also seems that at least one of the other "Big 5" accounting firms was involved in at least one of Enron's special purpose entities.

Enron also paid several hundred million dollars in fees to investment and commercial banks for work on various financial aspects of its business, including fees for derivatives transactions, and yet none of those firms pointed out to investors any of the derivatives problems at Enron. Instead, as late as October 2001, sixteen of seventeen securities analysts covering Enron rated it a "strong buy" or "buy."

Enron paid substantial fees to its outside law firm, which previously had employed Enron's general counsel, yet that firm failed to correct or disclose the problems related to derivatives and special purpose entities. Other law firms also may have been involved in these transactions; if so, they should be questioned, too.

Finally, and perhaps most importantly, the three major credit rating agencies—Moody's, Standard & Poor's, and Fitch/IBCA—received substantial, but as yet undisclosed, fees from Enron. Yet just weeks prior to Enron's bankruptcy filing—after most of the negative news was out and Enron's stock was trading at just $3 per share—all three agencies still gave investment grade ratings to Enron's debt. The credit rating agencies in particular have benefited greatly from a web of legal rules that essentially requires securities issuers to obtain ratings from them (and them only), and at the same time protects those agencies from outside competition and liability under the securities laws. They are at least partially to blame for the Enron mess.

An investment-grade credit rating was necessary to make Enron's special purpose entities work, and Enron lived on the cusp of investment grade. During 2001, it was rated just above the lowest investment-grade rating by all three agencies: BBB+ by Standard & Poor's and Fitch IBCA, and Baa1 by Moody's. Just before Enron's bankruptcy, all three rating agencies lowered Enron's rating two notches, to the lowest investment grade rating. Enron noted in its most recent annual report that its "continued investment grade status is critical to the success of its wholesale business as well as its ability to maintain adequate liquidity." Many of Enron's debt obligations were triggered by a credit ratings downgrade; some of those obligations had been scheduled to mature in December 2001. The importance of credit ratings at Enron and the timing of Enron's bankruptcy filing are not coincidences; the credit rating agencies have some explaining to do.

Derivatives based on credit ratings—called credit derivatives—are a booming business and they raise serious systemic concerns. The rating agencies seem to know this. Even Moody's appears worried, and recently asked several securities firms for more detail about their dealings in these instruments. It is particularly chilling that not even Moody's—the most sophisticated of the three credit rating agencies—knows much about these derivatives deals.

III. DERIVATIVES "INSIDE" ENRON

The derivatives problems at Enron went much deeper than the use of special purpose entities with outside investors. If Enron had been making money in what it represented as its core businesses, and had used derivatives simply to "dress up" its financial statements, this Committee probably would not be meeting here today. Even after Enron restated its financial statements on November 8, 2001, it could have clarified its accounting treatment, consolidated its debts, and assured the various analysts that it was a viable entity. But it could not. Why not?

This question leads me to the second explanation of Enron's collapse: most of what Enron represented as its core businesses were not making money. Recall that Enron began as an energy firm. Over time, Enron shifted its focus from the bricks-and-mortar energy business to the trading of derivatives. As this shift occurred, it appears that some of its employees began lying systematically about the profits and losses of Enron's derivatives trading operations. Simply put, Enron's reported earnings from derivatives seem to be more imagined than real. Enron's derivatives trading was profitable, but not in the way an investor might expect based on the firm's financial statements. Instead, some Enron employees seem to have misstated systematically their profits and losses in order to make their trading businesses appear less volatile than they were.

First, a caveat. During the past few weeks, I have been gathering information about Enron's derivatives operations, and I have learned many disturbing things. Obviously, I cannot testify first-hand to any of these matters. I have never been on Enron's trading floor, and I have never been involved in Enron's business. I cannot offer fact testimony as to any of these matters.

Nonetheless, I strongly believe the information I have gathered is credible. It is from many sources, including written information, e-mail correspondence, and telephone interviews. Congressional investigators should be able to confirm all of these facts. In any event, even if only a fraction of the information in this section of my testimony proves to be correct, it will be very troubling indeed.

In a nutshell, it appears that some Enron employees used dummy accounts and rigged valuation methodologies to create false profit and loss entries for the derivatives Enron traded. These false entries were systematic and occurred over several years, beginning as early as 1997. They included not only the more esoteric financial instruments Enron began trading recently—such as fiber-optic bandwidth and weather derivatives—but also Enron's very profitable trading operations in natural gas derivatives.

Enron derivatives traders faced intense pressure to meet quarterly earnings targets imposed directly by management and indirectly by securities analysts who covered Enron. To ensure that Enron met these estimates, some traders apparently hid losses and understated profits. Traders apparently manipulated the reporting of their real economic profits and losses in an attempt to fit the imagined accounting profits and losses that drove Enron management.

A. Using "Prudency" Reserves

Enron's derivatives trading operations kept records of the traders' profits and losses. For each trade, a trader would report either a profit or a loss, typically in spreadsheet format. These profit and loss reports were designed to reflect economic reality. Frequently, they did not.

Instead of recording the entire profit for a trade in one column, some traders reportedly split the profit from a trade into two columns. The first column reflected the portion of the actual profits the trader intended to add to Enron's current financial statements. The second column, ironically labeled the "prudency" reserve, included the remainder.

To understand this concept of a prudency reserve, suppose a derivatives trader earned a profit of $10 million. Of that $10 million, the trader might record $9 million as profit today, and enter $1 million into "prudency." An average deal would have prudency reserve of up to $1 million, and all of the "prudency" entries might add up to $10 to $15 million.

Enron's prudency reserves did not depict economic reality, nor could they have been intended to do so. Instead, "prudency" was merely a slush fund that could be used to smooth out profits and losses over time. The portion of profits recorded as "prudency" could be used to offset any future losses.

In essence, the traders were saving for a rainy day. Prudency reserves would have been especially effective for long-maturity derivatives contracts, because it was more difficult to determine a precise valuation as of a particular date for those contracts, and any "prudency" cushion would have protected the traders from future losses for several years going forward.

As luck would have it, some of the prudency reserves turned out to be quite prudent. In one quarter, some derivatives traders needed so much accounting profit to meet their targets that they wiped out all of their "prudency" accounts.

Saving for a rainy day is not necessarily a bad idea, and it seems possible that derivatives traders at Enron did not believe they were doing anything wrong. But prudency accounts are far from an accepted business practice. A trader who used a prudency account at a major Wall Street firm would be seriously disciplined, or perhaps fired. To the extent Enron was smoothing its income using prudency entries, it was misstating the volatility and current valuation of its trading businesses, and misleading its investors. Indeed, such fraudulent practices would have thwarted the very purpose of Enron's financial statements: to give investors an accurate picture of a firm's risks.

B. Mismarking Forward Curves

Not all of the misreporting of derivatives positions at Enron was as brazen as "prudency." Another way derivatives frequently are used to misstate profits and losses is by mismarking forward curves. It appears that Enron traders did this, too.

A forward curve is a list of forward rates for a range of maturities. In simple terms, a forward rate is the rate at which a person can buy something in the future.

For example, natural gas forward contracts trade on the New York Mercantile Exchange ("NYMEX"). A trader can commit to buy a particular type of natural gas to be delivered in a few weeks, months, or even years. The rate at which a trader can buy natural gas in one year is the one-year forward rate. The rate at which a trader can buy natural gas in ten years is the ten-year forward rate. The forward curve for a particular natural gas contract is simply the list of forward rates for all maturities.

Forward curves are crucial to any derivatives trading operation because they determine the value of a derivatives contract today. Like any firm involved in trading derivatives, Enron had risk management and valuation systems that used forward curves to generate profit and loss statements.

It appears that Enron traders selectively mismarked their forward curves, typically in order to hide losses. Traders are compensated based on their profits, so if a trader can hide losses by mismarking forward curves, he or she is likely to receive a larger bonus.

These losses apparently ranged in the tens of millions of dollars for certain markets. At times, a trader would manually input a forward curve that was different from the market. For more complex deals, a trader would use a spreadsheet model of the trade for valuation purposes, and tweak the assumptions in the model to make a transaction appear more or less valuable. Spreadsheet models are especially susceptible to mismarking.

Certain derivatives contracts were more susceptible to mismarking than others. A trader would be unlikely to mismark contracts that were publicly traded—such as the natural gas contracts traded on NYMEX—because quotations of the values of those contracts are publicly available. However, the NYMEX forward curve has a maturity of only six years; accordingly, a trader would be more likely to mismark a ten-year natural gas forward rate.

At Enron, forward curves apparently remained mismarked for as long as three years. In more esoteric areas, where markets were not as liquid, traders apparently were even more aggressive. One trader who already had recorded a substantial profit for the year, and believed any additional profit would not increase his bonus much, reportedly reduced his recorded profits for one year, so he could push them forward into the next year, which he wasn't yet certain would be as profitable. This strategy would have resembled the "prudency" accounts described earlier.

C. Warning Signs

Why didn't any of the "gatekeepers" tell investors that Enron was so risky? There were numerous warning signs related to Enron's derivatives trading. Yet the gatekeepers either failed utterly to spot those signs, or spotted those signs and decided not to warn investors about them. Either way, the gatekeepers failed to do their job. This was so even though there have been several recent and high-profile cases involving internal misreporting of derivatives.

Enron disclosed that it used "value at risk" ("VAR") methodologies that captured a 95 percent confidence interval for a one-day holding period, and therefore did not disclose worst-case scenarios for Enron's trading operations. Enron said it relied on "the professional judgment of experienced business and risk managers" to assess these worst-case scenarios (which, apparently, Enron ultimately encountered). Enron reported only high and low month-end values for its trading, and therefore had incentives to smooth its profits and losses at month-end. Because Enron did not report its maximum VAR during the year, investors had no way of knowing just how much risk Enron was taking.

Even the reported VAR figures are remarkable. Enron reported VAR for what it called its "commodity price" risk—including natural gas derivatives trading—of $66 million, more than triple the 1999 value. Enron reported VAR for its equity trading of $59 million, more than double the 1999 value. A VAR of $66 million meant that Enron could expect, based on historical averages, that on five percent of all trading days (on average, twelve business days during the year) its "commodity" derivatives trading operations alone would gain or lose $66 million, a not trivial sum.

Moreover, because Enron's derivatives frequently had long maturities—maximum terms ranged from six to twenty-nine years—there often were not prices from liquid markets to use as benchmarks. For those long-dated derivatives, professional judgment was especially important. For a simple instrument, Enron might calculate the discounted present value of cash flows using Enron's borrowing rates. But more complex instruments required more complex methodologies. For example, Enron completed over 5,000 weather derivatives deals, with a notional value of more than $4.5 billion, and many of those deals could not be valued without a healthy dose of professional judgment. The same was true of Enron's trading of fiber-optic bandwidth.

And finally there was the following flashing red light in Enron's most recent annual report: "In 2000, the value at risk model utilized for equity trading market risk was refined to more closely correlate with the valuation methodologies used for merchant activities." Enron's financial statements do not describe these refinements, and their effects, but given the failure of the risk and valuation models even at a sophisticated hedge fund such as Long-Term Capital Management—which employed "rocket scientists" and Nobel laureates to design various sophisticated computer models—there should have been reason for concern when Enron spoke of "refining" its own models.

It was Arthur Andersen's responsibility not only to audit Enron's financial statements, but also to assess the adequacy of Enron management's internal controls on derivatives trading. When Arthur Andersen signed Enron's 2000 annual report, it expressed approval in general terms of Enron's system of internal controls during 1998 through 2000.

Yet it does not appear that Andersen systematically and independently verified Enron's valuations of certain complex trades, or even of its forward curves. Andersen apparently examined day-to-day changes in these values, as reported by traders, and checked to see if each daily change was recorded accurately. But this Committee—and others investigating Enron—should inquire about whether Andersen did anything more than sporadically check Enron's forward curves.

Even when the relevant risk information is contained in Enron's financial statements, it is unclear whether Andersen adequately considered this information in opining that Enron management's internal controls were adequate. To the extent Andersen alleges—as I understand many accounting firms do—that their control opinion does not cover all types of control failures and necessarily is based on management's "assertions," it is worth noting that the very information Andersen audited raised substantial questions about potential control problems at Enron. In other words, Andersen has been hoisted by its own petard.

But Andersen was not alone in failing to heed these warning signs. Securities analysts and credit rating agencies arguably should have spotted them, too. Why were so many of these firms giving Enron favorable ratings, when publicly available information indicated that there were reasons for worry? Did these firms look the other way because they were subject to conflicts of interest? Individual investors rely on these institutions to interpret the detailed footnote disclosures in Enron's reports, and those institutions have failed utterly. The investigation into Andersen so far has generated a great deal of detail about that firm's approach to auditing Enron, but the same questions should be asked of the other gatekeepers, too. Specifically, this Committee should ask for and closely examine all of the analyst reports on Enron from the relevant financial services firms and credit rating agencies.

Finally, to clarify this point, consider how much Enron's businesses had changed during its last years. Andersen's most recent audit took place during 2000, when Enron's derivatives-related assets increased from $2.2 billion to $12 billion, and Enron's derivatives-related liabilities increased from $1.8 billion to $10.5 billion. These numbers are staggering. Most of this growth was due to increased trading through EnronOnline. But EnronOnline's assets and revenues were qualitatively different from Enron's other derivatives trading. Whereas Enron's derivatives operations included speculative positions in various contracts, EnronOnline's operations simply matched buyers and sellers. The "revenues" associated with EnronOnline arguably do not belong in Enron's financial statements. In any event, the exponential increase in the volume of trading through EnronOnline did not generate substantial profits for Enron.

Enron's aggressive additions to revenues meant that it was the "seventh-largest U.S. company" in title only. In reality, Enron was a much smaller operation, whose primary money-making business—a substantial and speculative derivatives trading operation—covered up poor performance in Enron's other, smaller businesses, including EnronOnline. Enron's public disclosures show that, during the past three years, the firm was not making money on its non-derivatives businesses. Gross margins from these businesses were essentially zero from 1998 through 2000.

To see this, consider the table below, which sets forth Enron's income statement separated into its non-derivatives and derivatives businesses. I put together this table based on the numbers in Enron's 2000 income statement, after learning from the footnote 1, page 36, that the meaning of the "Other revenues" entry on Enron's income statement is—as far as I can tell—essentially "Gain (loss) from derivatives":

Enron's Income from Derivatives and Non-Derivative Businesses (in millions of dollars)

	2000	1999	1998
Non-derivatives revenues	93,557	34,774	27,215
Non-derivatives expenses	94,517	34,761	26,381
Non-derivatives gross margin	(960)	13	834
Gain (loss) from derivatives	7,232	5,338	4,045
Other expenses	(4,319)	(4,549)	(3,501)
Operating income	1,953	802	1,378

This table demonstrates four key facts. First, the recent and dramatic increase in Enron's overall non-derivatives revenues—the statistic that supposedly made Enron the seventh-largest U.S. company—was offset by an increase in non-derivatives expenses. The increase in revenues reflected in the first line of the chart was substantially from

EnronOnline, and did not help Enron's bottom line, because it included an increase in expenses reflected in the second line of the chart. Although Enron itself apparently was the counterparty to all of the trades, EnronOnline simply matched buyers ("revenue") with sellers ("expenses"). Indeed, as non-derivatives revenues more than tripled, non-derivatives expenses increased even more.

Second, Enron's non-derivatives businesses were not performing well in 1998 and were deteriorating through 2000. The third row, "Non-derivatives gross margin," is the difference between non-derivatives revenues and non-derivatives expenses. The downward trajectory of Enron's non-derivatives gross margin shows, in a general sense, that Enron's non-derivatives businesses made some money in 1998, broke even in 1999, and actually lost money in 2000.

Third, Enron's positive reported operating income (the last row) was due primarily to gains from derivatives (the fourth row). (Enron—like many firms—shied from using the word "derivatives" and substituted the euphemism "Price Risk Management.") Excluding the gains from derivatives, Enron would have reported substantially negative operating income for all three years.

Fourth, Enron's gains from derivatives were very substantial. Enron gained more than $16 billion from these activities in three years. To place the numbers in perspective, these gains were roughly comparable to the annual net revenue for all trading activities (including stocks, bonds, and derivatives) at the premier investment firm, Goldman Sachs & Co., during the same periods, a time in which Goldman Sachs first issued shares to the public.

The key difference between Enron and Goldman Sachs is that Goldman Sachs seems to have been up front with investors about the volatility of its trading operations. In contrast, Enron officials represented that it was not a trading firm, and that derivatives were used for hedging purposes. As a result, Enron's stock traded at much higher multiples of earnings than more candid trading-oriented firms.

The size and scope of Enron's derivatives trading operations remain unclear. Enron reported gains from derivatives of $7.2 billion in 2000, and reported notional amounts of derivatives contracts as of December 31, 2000, of only $21.6 billion. Either Enron was generating 33 percent annual returns from derivatives (indicating that the underlying contracts were very risky), or Enron actually had large positions and reduced the notional values of its outstanding derivatives contracts at year-end for cosmetic purposes. Neither conclusion appears in Enron's financial statements or its management's discussion and analysis ("MD&A") section.

IV. CONCLUSION

How did Enron lose so much money? That question has dumbfounded investors and experts in recent months. But the basic answer is now apparent: Enron was a derivatives trading firm; it made billions trading derivatives, created through use of reporting tricks such as mismarking forward curves and managing prudency reserves, while it lost billions on virtually everything else it did, including projects in fiber-optic bandwidth, retail gas and power, water systems, and even technology stocks. Enron used its expertise in derivatives to hide these losses. For most people, the fact that Enron had transformed itself from an energy company into a derivatives trading firm is a surprise.

Enron is to blame for much of this, of course. The temptations associated with derivatives have proved too great for many companies, and Enron is no exception. The conflicts of interest among Enron's officers have been widely reported. Nevertheless, it remains unclear how much top officials knew about the various misdeeds at Enron. They should and will be asked. At least some officers must have been aware of how deeply derivatives penetrated Enron's businesses; Enron even distributed thick multi-volume Derivatives Training Manuals to new employees. (The Committee should ask to see these manuals.)

Enron's directors likely have some regrets. Enron's Audit Committee in particular failed to uncover a range of external and internal financial gimmickry. However, it remains to be seen how much of the inner workings at Enron were hidden from the outside directors; some directors may very well have learned a great deal from recent media accounts, or even perhaps from this testimony. Enron's general counsel, on the other hand, will have some questions to answer.

But too much focus on Enron misses the mark. As long as ownership of companies is separated from their control—and in the U.S. securities market it almost always will be—managers of companies will have incentives to be aggressive in reporting financial data. The securities laws recognize this fact of life, and create and subsidize "gatekeeper" institutions to monitor this conflict between managers and shareholders.

The collapse of Enron makes it plain that the key gatekeeper institutions that support our system of market capitalism have failed. The institutions sharing the blame include auditors, law firms, banks, securities analysts, independent directors, and credit rating agencies.

All of the facts I have described in my testimony were available to the gatekeepers. I obtained this information in a matter of weeks by sitting at a computer in my office in San Diego, and by picking up a telephone. The gatekeepers' failure to discover this information, and to communicate it effectively to investors, is simply inexcusable.

The difficult question is what to do about the gatekeepers. They occupy a special place in securities regulation, and receive great benefits as a result. Employees at gatekeeper firms are among the most highly-paid people in the world. They have access to superior information and supposedly have greater expertise than average investors at deciphering that information. Yet, with respect to Enron, the gatekeepers clearly did not do their job.

One potential answer is to eliminate the legal requirements that companies use particular gatekeepers (especially credit rating agencies), while expanding the scope of securities fraud liability and enforcement to make it clear that all gatekeepers will be liable for assisting companies in transactions designed to distort the economic reality of financial statements. A good starting point before considering such legislation would be to call the key gatekeeper employees to testify.

Congress also must decide whether, after ten years of deregulation, the post-Enron derivatives markets should remain exempt from the regulation that covers all other investment contracts. In my view, the answer is no.

A headline in Enron's 2000 annual report states, "In Volatile Markets, Everything Changes But Us." Sadly, Enron got it wrong. In volatile markets, everything changes, and the laws should change, too. It is time for Congress to act to ensure that this motto does not apply to U.S. financial market regulation.

Business Ethics at "The Crooked E"

Duane Windsor[*]

On December 2, 2001, Enron filed the then-largest corporate bankruptcy in U.S. history, measured by reported assets.[1] (WorldCom filed a larger bankruptcy in 2002.)[2] Enron reported recently that it is the object of some 22,000 claims by various injured stakeholders, totaling $400 billion.[3] This essay assesses what (sadly) passed for "business ethics" at Enron and at other firms associated with Enron; and also examines key public policy and corporate governance reforms for fostering responsible management in the wake of multiple corporate scandals.[4] At Enron, "business ethics" *was* an oxymoron.[5] It

[*] Lynette S. Autrey Professor of Management, Jesse H. Jones Graduate School of Management, Rice University. *Editors' note:* This essay was included in the first edition of this book. Reprinted by permission.

[1] *In re Enron Corp.*, No. 01-16034 (Bankr. S.D.N.Y. 2001).

[2] *In re WorldCom, Inc.*, No. 02-13533 (Bankr. S.D.N.Y. 2002).

[3] Darren Fonda, *Enron: Picking over the carcass*, TIME, Dec. 30, 2001-Jan. 6, 2002 (double issue), at 56. The Enron bankruptcy occurred in declining economic conditions and following on the 9-11 (2001) terrorist attacks on the World Trade Center and the Pentagon, so that tracing the bankruptcy's effects and repercussions are difficult. Economic weakness and accounting irregularities in 2002 resulted in a record bankruptcy year measured as $368 billion in assets. *The year of the falling companies*, HOUS. CHRON., Jan. 2, 2003, at 1B (citing BankruptcyData.com). There were 257 Chapter 11 bankruptcy filings in 2001 by public companies, versus 186 in 2002. *Id.* Over those two years, Chapter 11 filings involved $626 billion in assets. *Id.* Year 2003 may be at least as bad. *Id.*

[4] Martha Stewart, then a member of the NYSE governing board, allegedly engaged in insider trading in ImClone Systems stock. Stewart was indicted, as was her former stockbroker Peter Bacanovic, in early June 2003. Five counts were alleged against Stewart, including obstruction of justice, conspiracy, lying to investigators, and securities fraud. Both defendants pleaded innocent. The SEC filed a civil action for insider trading that would bar Stewart from ever leading a public company. (There was no criminal charge of insider trading.) *See* Erin McClam (Associated Press), *Stewart's denial now part of case: Prosecutors call it securities fraud*, Hous. Chron., June 6, 2003, at 1C, 2C. In late May 2003, NBC televised a film, *Martha Inc.: The Story of Martha Stewart,* based on the book by CHRISTOPHER M. BYRON, MARTHA INC.: THE INCREDIBLE STORY OF MARTHA STEWART LIVING OMNIMEDIA (Wheeler Pub., 2002). Of course, scandals and stock markets go back a long way. In the 1930s, Richard Whitney, a former NYSE president (and apparent confidant of J.P. Morgan), went to prison for theft.

[5] *Cf.* Norman Augustine, *Foreword* to JEFFREY SEGLIN, THE GOOD, THE BAD, AND YOUR BUSINESS: CHOOSING RIGHT WHEN ETHICAL DILEMMAS PULL YOU APART, at vii (2000).

may be, however, that the board of directors was duped, as well as negligent, and that corruption and misconduct were restricted to a handful of key executives.[6] (Ongoing investigations may reveal the truth.) There is no reason on any present evidence to suspect the vast majority of Enron employees—who lost jobs, pensions, and reputations—of any legal or moral indiscretions. In keeping with Machiavelli's advice to *The Prince* to appear honorable always,[7] Enron leadership made a public display of professed ethical standards, corporate citizenship, and consumer welfare innovations having nothing to do with actual motives or conduct.[8] The public display marched with imprudent disregard or perhaps even contempt for customary business morality, fiduciary responsibility, stakeholder responsibility, and in at least some proven instances, law.[9]

The Enron debacle reveals lessons about business leadership, corporate governance, and government regulation. What happened is reasonably clear—in rough outline, if not yet in full detail. Greed and opportunism at the top were, of course, the motive

---

[6] In testimony before the House Committee on Energy and Commerce, Subcommittee on Oversight and Investigations, Robert K. Jaedicke rejected the conclusions concerning the Enron board of the Powers Committee. He argued that a board must rely on cross-checking controls and "the full and complete reporting of information to it" (by management and outside advisors). *See The Role of the Board of Directors in Enron's Collapse: Hearing Before the House Comm. on Energy and Commerce, Subcomm. on Oversight and Investigation*, 107th Cong. 511 (2002) (testimony of Robert K. Jaedicke, Enron Bd. of Dir., Chairman Audit and Compliance Comm.). In Jaedicke's view, the board received regular assurances of legality and appropriateness of transactions and adequacy of internal controls. *Id.* The board may have been overwhelmed by "systemic failure" and had no direct interest in any of the transactions. *Id.* "We could not have predicted that all the controls would fail." *Id.* Jaedicke's view cannot be rejected out of hand. On the contrary, it raises the difficulty that a very stringent standard of vigilance must be defined for the board in ways that mean concretely an utter lack of trust in management and external advisors. By prevailing standards of the time, anything less than a very vigilant board might have been duped; by the same token, the board may also have been negligent.

[7] NICCOLÒ MACHIAVELLI, THE PRINCE 109 (Leo P.S. de Alvarez trans., 1980) (1515).

[8] Steve Salbu, *Foreword* to BRIAN CRUVER, ANATOMY OF GREED: THE UNSHREDDED TRUTH FROM AN ENRON INSIDER, at xii (2002) (noting that *Fortune* surveys for 1996 through 2001 identified Enron as the most innovative U.S. firm).

[9] LARRY A. ELLIOTT & RICHARD J. SCHROTH, HOW COMPANIES LIE: WHY ENRON IS JUST THE TIP OF THE ICEBERG 25 (2002). Salbu calls the effect "bone-chilling." Salbu, *supra* note 8. Enron emphasized principles of "respect, integrity, communications, and excellence." *Id.* These principles were nicknamed RICE internally. CRUVER, *supra* note 8, at 43. Chairman Kenneth L. Lay's letter to the shareholders in the 2001 annual report "contained a lengthy and heady sermon about the integrity and high standards of the Enron culture" and social responsibility and stakeholder protection activities. ELLIOTT & SCHROTH, *supra* at 24. CFO Andrew S. Fastow was named CFO of the Year by *CFO* magazine for innovative financial engineering. *Id.* at 31. Jeffrey K. Skilling was introduced at one conference as the number one CEO in America. D. QUINN MILLS, BUY, LIE, AND SELL HIGH: HOW INVESTORS LOST OUT ON ENRON AND THE INTERNET BUBBLE 48 (2002). Fastow is quoted as stating: "We're going to do the right thing and make money without having to do anything but the right thing." *Id.* at 47 (citing Shaila K. Dewan, *Enron's Many Strands: A Case Study; A Video Study of Enron Offers A Picture of Life Before the Fall*, N.Y. TIMES, Jan. 31, 2002, at C7 (quoting Robert F. Bruner & Samuel E. Bodily, Darden Graduate School of Business Administration, U. of Virginia, *A Video Study of Enron Officers, A Picture of Life Before the Fall* (2002))).

and the modus operandi, respectively.[10] "Enron failed because its leadership was morally, ethically, and financially corrupt."[11] But greed and opportunism are expected of all market actors (if not, strictly speaking, socially encouraged). "Shirking" by managers is at the heart of agency theory. Given shirking, a board can trust management only where trust can be personally confirmed in moral integrity or reasonably reliable (and hence costly) contracts and controls.[12] Why greed and opportunism got so wildly, and widely, out of hand, has not yet been well studied.[13] The interesting possibility is that not only did key actors lack any effective internal moral compass and believe (as must all "Machiavels") that some end justifies any means (and some undoubtedly violated laws), but they may have substituted other values for fiduciary, moral, and legal responsibilities. It is not necessary to dwell on distinctions here—Enron flagrantly violated all of these responsibilities.[14] The Enron value set apparently included an extreme laissez-faire ideology of absolutely "free" (i.e., absolutely unregulated) markets[15]—conceptualized as purely price-volume mechanisms;[16] and a cynical (if arguably valid) view of purchase of influence in government.[17] The Enron organizational history apparently evolved a financial and moral corruption machine, something akin to "victory disease," denying the possibility of failure, and a corporate culture and moral climate ultimately hostile

[10] "Greed is good," proclaimed the character Gordon Gekko (played by Michael Douglas) in the film *Wall Street.* Salbu, *supra* note 9, at xiv (quoting *Wall Street* (20th Century-Fox 1987)).

[11] ROBERT BRYCE, PIPE DREAMS: GREED, EGO, AND THE DEATH OF ENRON 12 (2002).

[12] It is possible to model morally sensitive agents. Douglas E. Stevens & Alex Thevaranjan, *Ethics and Agency Theory: Incorporating a Standard for Effort and an Ethically Sensitive Agent* (Syracuse University Working Paper, Oct. 18, 2002). Carroll suggests that the supply of moral managers could prove thin. Archie B. Carroll, *The Pyramid of Corporate Social Responsibility: Toward the Moral Management of Organizational Stakeholders*, 34.4 BUS. HORIZONS 39, 39-48 (1991).

[13] *Cf.* BRYCE, *supra* note 11, at 8.

[14] *See* Terry L. Price, *The Ethics of Authentic Transformational Leadership*, 14.1 LEADERSHIP QUARTERLY 67, 67-81 (2003) (arguing that leaders may sometimes behave immorally because they are blinded by their own values).

[15] PETER C. FUSARO & ROSS M. MILLER, WHAT WENT WRONG AT ENRON: EVERYONE'S GUIDE TO THE LARGEST BANKRUPTCY IN U.S. HISTORY 2, 20, 28 (2002).

[16] This extreme ideology (by no means unique to Enron) is a profound distortion of the liberal market economy tradition. Adam Smith in THE THEORY OF MORAL SENTIMENTS (1759) and THE WEALTH OF NATIONS (1776) argued that (workably) competitive markets will outperform (unsound) government monopolies and excessive regulation, so that economic self-interest should be free to innovate. *See* James Q. Wilson, *Adam Smith on Business Ethics*, 32.1 CAL. MGMT. REV. 59, 59-71 (1989). But Smith also made important assumptions about the cooperative nature of society, moral education, and moral sympathy for others. Alfred Marshall, in his neoclassical PRINCIPLES OF ECONOMICS (various editions), emphasized ethics in economic behavior. Milton Friedman argued for profit maximization—but with (appropriate) legal and moral "rules of the game" and an early stakeholder conception of the firm. *See* Milton Friedman, *The Social Responsibility of Business*, N.Y. TIMES MAG., Sept. 13, 1970, at 32-33, 122, 126.

[17] Duane Windsor, *Public Affairs, Issues, Management, and Political Strategy: Opportunities, Obstacles, and Caveats*, 1.4 J. OF PUB. AFF. 382, 382-415 (2002).

to business ethics. The evidence lies unavoidably in detailed study of individuals, corporate culture, and ethical climate.

The Enron debacle is the story of two self-destructing firms, Enron and Arthur Andersen—the latter being a supplier of both external and internal auditing[18] and of consulting services also.[19] All the usual suspects were involved: senior management, the board of directors, their accounting advisors (Arthur Andersen) and legal advisors (Vinson & Elkins),[20] and, albeit more distantly, investment banks, commercial banks, and brokerage firms. Professional codes of conduct for accountants and attorneys did not suffice. Although even more distantly, one must also add Congress (which killed a proposed stock option expensing rule), the White House (which had political linkages with Lay), and various regulators (e.g., the SEC, the NYSE, the evidently highly vulnerable California energy framework) as considerations in what turned out to be defective corporate governance and weak regulation. Enron was a political scandal as well as a business failure,[21] and the revelations helped propel sudden passage of the Bipartisan Campaign Reform Act of 2002. Something like a financial and moral corruption machine, commencing with the top management, evolved progressively—almost logically or compellingly as a series of "missteps"[22]—out of the constellation of circumstances at work, both internal and external to Enron. While likely not the most economically important bankruptcy among recent filings, Enron may prove the most interesting—in terms of complexity, sophistication, and breadth of corruption.[23]

The title of this essay draws on a sadly appropriate internal nickname, "The Crooked E"—reportedly passed to a new Enron employee, Brian Cruver, by a friend also

---

[18] CRUVER, *supra* note 8, at 181.

[19] Arthur Andersen was the auditor for WorldCom and also Freddie Mac. The second largest U.S. mortgage finance company announced on June 9, 2003, that it had fired its president (and chief operating officer) for failing to cooperate fully with counsel to the board of directors' audit committee in reviewing earnings statements for 2000, 2001, and 2002. The chairman (and chief executive officer) "retired," and the chief financial officer "resigned." *See* Philip Klein, *Freddie Mac fires president, replaces top executives,* REUTERS (June 9, 2003, 2:06 p.m. ET), *accessed at* http://biz.yahoo.com/rb/030609/financial_freddiemac.12.html (document expired subsequently).

[20] For a discussion of attorneys' roles and duties, see Megan Barnett, *How to account for lawyers: Attorneys are facing more scrutiny in cases of corporate financial fraud,* U.S. NEWS & WORLD REP., Dec. 9, 2002, at 26, 28. The Sarbanes-Oxley Act of 2002 requires the SEC to introduce a rule requiring corporate attorneys to report wrongdoing to superiors. Sarbanes-Oxley Act of 2002, Pub. L. No.107-204, 116 Stat. 745 (codified in scattered sections of 15 U.S.C. & 18 U.S.C.). A Congressional committee recommended criminal charges against Arthur Andersen attorney Nancy Temple. *See* David Ivanovich & Michael Hedges, *Pressure builds on Andersen lawyer, available at* HoustonChronicle.com, http://www.chron.com/cs/CDA/story.hts/special/andersen/1706699 (Dec. 18, 2002).

[21] BRYCE, *supra* note 11, at 6.

[22] FUSARO & MILLER, *supra* note 15, at xi.

[23] U.S. NEWS & WORLD REPORT'S "Rogue of the Year" was Tyco's former CEO Dennis Kozlowski, not Enron's former Chairman Lay. *See* Marianne Lavelle et al., *Rogues of the Year,* U.S. NEWS & WORLD REP., Dec. 30, 2002, at 33 (published in parallel with Jodie Morse & Amanda Bower, *Persons of the Year/Coleen Rowley/Cynthia Cooper/Sherron Watkins,* TIME MAG., Dec. 30, 2002, at 52). Prosecutors charge that Kozlowski obtained $600 million through theft, misuse of loans, and selling of Tyco shares. *Id.*

working there.[24] This characterization may endure as the symbol both of how Enron came to be bankrupt, and of a whole era of shameless corporate scandal uncovered in 2001-2002 and involving a number of other large companies (e.g., Adelphia, Global Crossing, ImClone, Merrill Lynch, Tyco, WorldCom), with Cendant, Sunbeam, and Waste Management being earlier harbingers, and not just in the U.S. (e.g., Allied Irish Bank, and the Korean unit of Lernout & Hauspie Speech Products NV).[25] Xerox improperly recognized some $6 billion in revenues over 1997-2001; and Halliburton was investigated by the SEC for cost overruns when it was headed by now-U.S. Vice President Dick Cheney.[26] The registered mark or corporate logo of Enron was a capital E, with ENRON as the base—the logo tilted 45 degrees leftward of vertical. This logo appeared on business cards as well as a simple tilted E situated outside the Enron headquarters in Houston, Texas.[27] The Enron logo was adapted as a mark for a continuing *Houston Chronicle* newspaper series on "The Fall of Enron" (in Enron red, green, blue) for each article, with the addition of "The Fall of" at the top of the tilted E. The CBS Network[28] premiered (on January 5, 2003) the first made-for-TV movie based ("loosely" would be a polite term) on Cruver's book and titled *The Crooked E: The Unshredded Truth about Enron*—drawing on the subtitle of Cruver's book.[29]

This essay makes a preliminary moral assessment and examines public policy reform proposals. It makes no specific judgments concerning criminal culpability or civil liability. Criminal investigations, civil litigation, and the bankruptcy proceedings are still ongoing and may continue for years. A basic guide for moral responsibility is to avoid harming others (defined here as various stakeholders, including investors) and to meet obvious moral and legal rules of conduct (prohibiting mendacity, fraud, and so on). Enron creditors, employees, investors, and other stakeholders have been badly harmed. Thousands of employees lost their jobs; all employees lost pensions to the degree held in Enron stock; and, as Sherron Watkins cautioned in her one-page

---

[24] CRUVER, *supra* note 8, at 9. A University of Texas at Austin MBA, Cruver joined Enron as a risk trader nine months before its bankruptcy.

[25] ELLIOTT & SCHROTH, *supra* note 9, at 41 (citing a WALL STREET JOURNAL report of April 2001); *see* John Carreyrou, *Lernout Unit Engaged in Massive Fraud to Fool Auditors, New Inquiry Concludes*, WALL ST. J., Apr. 6, 2001, at A3; John Carreyrou, *Lernout Files Complaint with Prosecutors in Seoul,* WALL ST. J., Apr. 26, 2001, at A17.

[26] LOREN FOX, ENRON: THE RISE AND FALL 305 (2003).

[27] The sign was sold at bankruptcy auction for $44,000. Jodie Morse & Amanda Bower, *The Party Crasher*, TIME, Dec. 30, 2002, at 52, 53.

[28] *See* Bill Murphy, *CBS flick shows difficulty of making drama out of Enron*, HOUS. CHRON., Dec. 23, 2002, at 1A.

[29] Lay's attorney, who had warned CBS about misportraying his client, dismissed the film because "[t]he production values were so bad on the thing that it's largely meaningless." *Lay lawyer says movie no big deal,* HOUS. CHRON., Jan. 10, 2003, at Business-4. A number of ex-Enron women employees criticized the depiction of women in the film. Murphy, *supra* note 28, at A1. Arthur Andersen stood convicted on June 15, 2002, of obstruction of justice. Its responsible partner, David Duncan, had pleaded guilty in April 2002 in connection with the shredding of Enron-related documents. Arthur Andersen closed its auditing business in August 2002.

anonymous memo (August 15, 2001) to Chairman Kenneth L. Lay, an Enron resume may prove worthless.[30] A bad business model and self-destructive culture, as appear to have prevailed at Enron, can reflect poor judgment, but not necessarily legal accountability. Long-Term Capital Management self-destructed in 1998 due to bad investment decisions involving Nobel Prize laureates in (financial) economics.[31] There is, however, a vital difference between bad judgment and recklessly gambling with corporate destiny while self-dealing for profit. Moral responsibility occurs at two distinct levels in business leadership. One level is broadly defined: the senior executives of Enron had the same general responsibility of prudent concern for corporate and stakeholder safety as the officers of any ship at sea. At Enron, everything that could go wrong by and large did go wrong. The senior executives of Enron bear the moral responsibility of such blatant negligence.[32] The other level is more narrowly defined: particular individuals at Enron engaged in specific commissions or omissions of moral duty, such as self-dealing and intimidation, or failing to caution employees about sound diversification of pension risk. The sciences of mendacity, deception, hype, fraud, and hypocrisy[33] seem to have become highly developed at Enron's upper levels.

The facts for a systematic and definitive assessment are not completely available in the public record. Congress conducted hearings in February 2002, at which Chairman Kenneth L. Lay, CFO Andrew S. Fastow, Rick Causey (Chief Accounting Officer), Michael Kopper (a key figure in the Chewco arrangement organized by Fastow, and who later pleaded guilty), and Rick Buy (Chief Risk Officer) took Fifth Amendment protection,[34] while former President and CEO Jeffrey K. Skilling, Sherron Watkins, and Robert K. Jaedicke (Chairman, Audit and Compliance Committee) testified. Available are *Houston Chronicle* coverage and a number of books[35] that collectively draw on SEC filings and the Powers Committee report (published February 2, 2002),[36] and a revealing book by an Enron insider.[37] Bryce and Fox conducted interviews with former Enron employees. Watkins has just participated in publishing a book with Mimi

---

[30] MIMI SWARTZ WITH SHERRON WATKINS, POWER FAILURE: THE INSIDE STORY OF THE COLLAPSE OF ENRON at 362 (2003). The same caution logically applies by extension to an Arthur Andersen resume.

[31] FUSARO & MILLER, *supra* note 15, at 36, 43, 118-19.

[32] Henry (Lord) Acton urged that moral responsibility (historically if not legally) must march with power. ACTON, letter to Mandell Creighton, April 5, 1887; *in* ESSAYS ON FREEDOM AND POWER 364 (Gertrude Himmelfarb, ed., 1948). I argue that Acton's principle applies directly to Enron's top leadership.

[33] *Cf.* ELLIOTT & SCHROTH, *supra* note 9, at 12.

[34] BRYCE, *supra* note 11, at 358-59.

[35] *E.g.*, BRYCE, *supra* note 11; ELLIOTT & SCHROTH, *supra* note 9; FOX, *supra* note 26; FUSARO & MILLER, *supra* note 15; MILLS, *supra* note 9.

[36] In mid-October 2001, the Board established a special investigation committee chaired by William C. Powers, Jr., Dean of the University of Texas Law School (Austin), who joined the board temporarily for that purpose. The inquiry was conducted with independent counsel (Wilmer, Cutler & Pickering) and accountants (Deloitte & Touche). The lengthy committee report was filed February 2, 2002.

[37] CRUVER, *supra* note 8.

Swartz.[38] For purposes of this essay, I have relied on the facts set forth in these books: in general, the basic facts seem well-published at this point. There is some range of differing opinions about aspects of the Enron story. There have been criticisms as well as defenses, for example, of Watkins. The ethics of Watkins's whistleblowing will be treated as a separable matter.

A recommended methodology for business ethics diagnosis and action planning comprises four steps or phases in sequence: (1) determine objectively the key facts of a situation; (2) delineate the important issues, principles, and/or stakes involved in the situation; (3) identify options or alternatives for concrete action; and (4) make a decision from among those options, and design and implement a practical action plan.[39] The remainder of the essay following this introduction is accordingly organized into three sections. The immediately following "facts" section marshals the morally relevant information. What happened inside Enron (and, by extension, Arthur Andersen, Vinson & Elkins, and banking partners and brokerages)? Senior executives and directors, and their accounting and legal and financial advisors, faced and apparently disregarded plain moral (and some legal) considerations. The subsequent "issues" section examines issues, principles, and stakes and emphasizes assessment of the constellation of causes (i.e., the etiology) resulting in Enron's bankruptcy. How widespread within Enron was an apparent culture or climate of corruption and misconduct involving fraudulent misrepresentation, self-dealing, and contempt for moral values and Enron's stakeholders? How and why did such corruption occur? In the "reforms" section following the "issues" section, I summarize various reform proposals. How widespread is the phenomenon of corporate corruption in U.S. public companies? A brief concluding section addresses the nature of moral responsibility and business ethics education for managers. What are the implications for corporate governance and government regulation reforms to moderate future repetitions?

SOME MORALLY KEY FACTS

The Enron debacle involves a business judgment story, a legal story, a public policy story, and a blatantly irresponsible business ethics story of moral bankruptcy. Despite an enormous welter of complex details (still being unraveled), the business and moral basics of the Enron debacle seem now reasonably clear in general outline (if not full detail) sufficient to a preliminary assessment.[40] Kenneth L. Lay was head of Enron from November 1985. Jeffrey K. Skilling was President and COO from January 10, 1997, and CEO from February 1, 2001. The senior executives were highly experienced and professionally trained.[41] The head of a public company has a broad responsibility for

---

[38] SWARTZ WITH WATKINS, *supra* note 30.

[39] Kenneth E. Goodpaster, *Illustrative Case Analysis for Consolidated Foods Corporation (A)*, *in* POLICIES AND PERSONS: A CASEBOOK IN BUSINESS ETHICS 500-03 (John B. Matthews et al. eds., 1985).

[40] FOX, *supra* note 26, at vii-xiii (provides a detailed chronology).

[41] Lay was a Ph.D. economist with prior regulatory and executive experience; Skilling was a Harvard MBA (graduating a George F. Baker Scholar, top 5% of his class). *See* BRYCE, *supra* note 11, at 49; Fastow

sound business judgment and selection of reliable subordinates, and a parallel moral responsibility for stakeholders' welfare.[42] The senior executives did not even meet a reasonable standard for prudence and fiduciary responsibility to investors, but focused instead on self-dealing (as predicted by agency theory), and some, at least, engaged in illegal actions. When Skilling took over as COO in 1997, Enron's stock price was about $19.[43] At July 31, 1998, Enron's stock price was about $25.[44] It rose to range around $40 during the second half of 1999. It then jumped during 2000 to a high of about $90 in August 2000, generally sliding thereafter. Both the desire to increase stock price and the desire to restore falling stock price would have been powerful motives for increasingly risky courses of action, from which some number of senior executives and directors personally benefited—even if indirectly.[45] In 2000, Enron became the seventh largest company in the U.S., measured by (apparently inflated) revenues.[46] Between end 1996 and end 2000, employment nearly tripled, from 7,500 to 20,600.[47] The Enron stock price growth strategy followed a reasonable business-judgment path: from pipeline firm to online energy trading to varied trading and online services for a large range of commodities and risks. The result was to make markets in risks; but then, effectively, Enron assumed rather than reduced the risks; the underlying driver was signaled when, in late March 2001, the lobby banner became "From the World's Leading Energy Company—To the World's Leading Company."[48]

In retrospect, the apparent success of Enron was not grounded in economic reality. Skilling's sudden resignation on August 14, 2001, was a key signal of coming difficulties. Key features of the business model were exotic "financial engineering" schemes, aggressive hyping of stock value "stories" to analysts, aggressive accounting manipulations, and apparently unprofitable expansions into trading of more types of commodities and risks.[49] "A videotape of a 1997 party has surfaced, showing Skilling joking that Enron could make 'a kazillion dollars' through an exotic new accounting technique."[50] Flood

---

was a Northwestern MBA. Skilling brought Fastow to Enron in 1990. FUSARO & MILLER, *supra* note 15, at 37. The long-serving chair of the audit and compliance committee was Robert K. Jaedicke, a distinguished accounting professor and former dean of the Stanford business school. The chair of the finance committee was Herbert Winokur, a member in 2001 of the Harvard Corporation—that university's governing body. BRYCE, *supra* note 11, at 268. In addition to an accounting professor, the 2001 board had two former energy regulators and four executives of financial or investment firms. FOX, *supra* note 26, at 309.

[42] If grounded in economic reality, long-run stock price increase arguably could be a win-win outcome for most of the key stakeholders.

[43] BRYCE, *supra* note 11, at 137.

[44] BRYCE, *supra* note 11; FUSARO & MILLER, *supra* note 15, at xiv.

[45] Expansion of shares outstanding would increase the pressure.

[46] Morse & Bower, *supra* note 27, at 55

[47] BRYCE, *supra* note 11, at 134.

[48] CRUVER, *supra* note 8, at 20-21, 26, 3.

[49] Fayez Sarofim, one of Houston's top money managers, declined to invest because he did not understand how Enron made money. *See* BRYCE, *supra* note 11, at 267-269.

[50] Fonda, *supra* note 3, at 56.

and Fowler amplify that Skilling was reading from a script; the authors do not report who prepared the script.[51] Skilling's reading from the script mentioned moving "from mark-to-market accounting to something I call HFV, or hypothetical future value accounting" as the basis for "a kazillion dollars." Enron used thousands of special purpose entities ("SPEs") to place debt off the balance sheet. Some SPEs may have been legitimate, with corrupt practices restricted to a few; but some apparently included "material adverse change" clauses that would precipitate Enron's resumption of obligations under conditions involving, for example, bond status and stock price.[52]

On July 13, 2001, Skilling unexpectedly informed Lay of his intention to resign from Enron as President and CEO.[53] That resignation was effective August 14, 2001, when announced, and Lay resumed the post of President and CEO, in addition to chairmanship. Skilling cited personal (i.e., family) reasons, and Lay publicly described the voluntary departure in these terms. Bryce reports that Skilling conceded to Lay at the July meeting that he was not sleeping, out of his concern for the falling stock price.[54] If the allegation is true, then Lay omitted vital information in his public statement. Moreover, if the allegation is true, then Skilling's resignation marks a dividing line between lying and omitting to tell the whole, unvarnished truth.[55]

On October 15, 2001, there was a surprise restatement involving a $618 million loss for third quarter 2001, $1.01 billion in non-recurring charges (including $287 million for Azurix water operations and $180 million for Enron Broadband Services), and a $1.6 billion reduction of equity.[56] Of the non-recurring charges, $544 million were for various bad investments and early termination of arrangements "with a previously discussed entity"—the latter in fact being entities controlled by CFO Fastow, called LJM (initials for Fastow's wife and children), involving only $35 million in Enron losses but from which Fastow had profited.[57] On October 23, 2001, Fastow went on a leave of absence, replaced as CFO by Jeff McMahon (Enron treasurer, 1998-2000).[58] The October revelation sent Enron sliding down into eventual bankruptcy.[59] A November 8, 2001 restatement reduced earnings of the prior four years by nearly $600 million (by $96 million for 1997, $113 million for 1998, $250 million for 1999, and $132 million for 2000) and disclosed an additional $3 billion in debt obligations. This second restatement also revealed that Fastow had made $30 million from two dozen

---

[51] Tom Fowler & Mary Flood, *Broadband claims investigated as fraud*, HOUS. CHRON., Dec. 29, 2002, at 1A, 24A.

[52] BRYCE, *supra* note 11, at 332.

[53] BRYCE, *supra* note 11, at 285.

[54] *Id.*

[55] Naturally to reveal concerns about stock price is to precipitate a decline.

[56] CRUVER, *supra* note 8, at 116, 117. *See also* Sen. Rep. No. 107-146, at 3 (2002).

[57] CRUVER, *supra* note 8, at 120.

[58] *Id.* at 138.

[59] Rosanna Ruiz, *Watkins, 2 others share Time honor*, HOUS. CHRON., Dec. 23, 2002, at 12A.

deals with LJMs (actually $45 million).[60] The November 19, 2001 restatement (the third in just over a month) further increased the third quarter 2001 losses from $618 million,[61] already raised to $635 million in the November 8, 2001 restatement, to $664 million.[62] It was revealed in the November 19, 2001 restatement that the November 12 downgrade of debt by Standard & Poor's to just above junk status shifted a $690 million note payable into a cash demand obligation due on November 27. Moreover, if debt was downgraded further to junk status and stock price fell below an unspecified price, then Enron would face obligations of $3.9 billion; nearly a fourth would be due to Marlin—an SPE removing debt from Azurix water company.[63] There were looming $18.7 billion in liabilities from derivatives and commodities futures contracts.[64] On November 20 (the next day), Enron stock fell by almost 25% to $6.99.[65] On November 28, Standard & Poor's reduced Enron debt to junk, followed by Moody's and Fitch.[66] Stock price fell that day from $4.11 at the previous close to 60 cents, with 342 million shares changing hands—a record to that point.[67]

Federal investigations have been conducted in Houston and New York (into the role of banks and brokerages), and San Francisco (into the role of Enron and other energy firms in the California energy crisis of 2000 and 2001), as well as by the SEC and the Commodity Futures Trading Commission ("CFTC"). On March 12, 2003, the CFTC filed charges that Enron and Hunter Shively, previously the supervisor of the Enron natural gas trading desk for the central U.S., had manipulated natural gas prices in 2001 and that Enron Online had functioned as an "illegal futures exchange" between September and December 2001 by way of failing to register or inform the CFTC of a change in its approach.[68] As of early January 2003, no sentences had been handed down, as criminal investigations continued.[69] Michael Kopper had pleaded guilty to fraud and money laundering (in connection with Chewco, a SPE organized by Fastow); Timothy Belden (an energy trader working in Portland, Oregon) had pleaded guilty to wire fraud and conspiracy (in connection with California energy trading);[70] Lawrence

---

[60] BRYCE, *supra* note 11, at 328.

[61] October 16 10-Q filing with the SEC.

[62] BRYCE, *supra* note 11, at 329.

[63] *Id.* at 330.

[64] *Id.* at 332.

[65] *Id.* at 331.

[66] BRYCE, *supra* note 11, at 337.

[67] *Id.*

[68] Laura Goldberg, *Gas price charges are filed: Agency alleges manipulation*, HOUS. CHRON., Mar. 13, 2003, at 1B, 4B.

[69] Tom Fowler & Mary Flood, *Task force moving at steady pace: With indictments and guilty pleases in hand, Enron prosecutors expect more charges in second year,* HOUS. CHRON., Jan. 6, 2003, at 1A, 4A.

[70] A report by the California Independent Systems Operator ("ISO") complains that 21 energy companies and publicly owned utilities (including Enron) "*may* [emphasis added here] have engaged in a trading practice known as Death Star, an Enron strategy that earns a profit without selling power." *See*

Lawyer (a finance employee) had pleaded guilty to a false tax report (in not reporting personal earnings from a SPE, allegedly on advice by Kopper).[71] Fastow was indicted in October 2002 on 78, counts including fraud and money laundering. (A superseding indictment followed in May 2003.) In relation to Kopper's guilty plea, indictments were issued against three former British bankers (of National Westminster Bank) for mail fraud. Rick Causey, former Chief Accounting Officer of Enron, was cited (by job title) in a criminal complaint against Fastow for a secret agreement allegedly guaranteeing no loss to Fastow from LJM. Ben Glisan, former treasurer of Enron, was cited (by job title) in a Fastow indictment; and subsequently informed that he is a subject of inquiry by federal prosecutors.[72] Glisan had been an investor in a SPE and had announced he would return huge profits made on a $5,800 investment in Southampton;[73] such profits are a powerful incentive. It was speculated in two newspaper articles that insider trading charges might be brought against Lay (on the basis that his stock sales exceeded requirements for repaying various loans).[74]

Skilling might prove very difficult to prosecute on the perjury charge, as he had voluntarily testified before Congress (albeit without immunity), or about Enron's broadband hyping.[75] Skilling was explicit in his congressional testimony that he had not lied to anyone.[76] In 1997, Enron had acquired Portland General (an electric utility), which had a fiber-optic network along its utility rights of way. A Houston federal grand jury has been investigating whether broadband hype (at January 2000, January 2001, and February 2001 meetings with analysts) by then-Enron Broadband Services ("EBS") CEO Ken Rice and CFO Kevin Howard, and CEO Skilling involved fraud (selling shares while hyping broadband and a proposed deal with Blockbuster that never came to fruition).[77] Following the January 2000 meeting, Enron stock price rose

Harvey Rice, *Report cites others in Enronlike trades*, HOUS. CHRON., Jan. 7, 2003, at 1B. ISO is trying to get the Federal Energy Regulatory Commission ("FERC") to compel return of about $9 billion to California ratepayers, and the claims have not been established conclusively. In May 2002, Enron memos outlined "Death Star, Fat Boy and other questionable—and possibly illegal—strategies." *Id.* at 4B.

71 Tom Fowler & Mary Flood, *Sentencing delayed on partnership tax charges*, HOUS. CHRON., Jan. 24, 2003, at 3C.

72 Bill Murphy & Tom Fowler, *Pressure on Glisan builds up: Former treasurer may see criminal case*, HOUS. CHRON., Dec. 28, 2002, at 1C, 4C.

73 Glisan received about $1.04 million, but paid $412,000 in taxes—he will repay $628,000. Tom Fowler, *Enron treasurer to repay $628,000 from shady deal*, HOUS. CHRON., Dec. 18, 2002, at 1A, 25A. Former Enron lawyer Kristina Mordaunt, in contrast, has claimed she is entitled to earnings on a similar investment. *Id. Editor's note:* On September 10, 2003, Glisan was sentenced to five years in prison, apparently as a result of a plea bargain.

74 Fowler & Flood, *supra* note 69, at 4A; Fonda, *supra* note 3, at 56.

75 Fonda, *supra* note 3, at 56.

76 FUSARO & MILLER, *supra* note 15, at 27.

77 Murphy & Fowler, *supra* note 72. During late April and early May 2003, a Houston federal grand jury issued a six-count indictment against Lea Fastow ("conspiracy to commit wire fraud, money laundering, and making false tax returns") and two reindictments: a 218-count reindictment superseded the

25% that day. (Such price movements are powerful incentives.) In July 2000, Enron announced a twenty-year deal with Blockbuster for video on demand delivered across the Enron fiber-optic network. In August 2000, Enron stock price reached a high of $90.56, after which the price began to decline. On January 2, 2001, stock price was valued at $79.88. At the January 2001 presentation, Skilling told analysts that the Enron stock price should be $126 per share, with EBS having added about $40. In March 2001, the deal with Blockbuster was cancelled.[78] However, defense attorneys have argued that such hype was widespread throughout the market, and prosecution would be difficult.[79] If the defense is correct, then a widespread pattern of puffery can be protection against prosecution (e.g., the dot.com phenomenon).

In December 2002, a dozen New York banks and brokerages agreed to a "global settlement" with the New York Attorney General, the SEC, and other regulatory bodies.[80] The settlement involved some $1.4 billion in fines and another nearly $1 billion over five years to fund independent stock research. About half the fines would go to an investor restitution fund. Investigations concerned improperly bullish research reports to generate investment banking business, with e-mails, for example, revealing that analysts privately derided stocks they publicly recommended, and improper distribution of IPOs to favored executives at companies that were investment banking clients. Merrill Lynch had agreed earlier to pay $100 million to avoid criminal charges.[81]

A brief review of Enron's financial history is highly revealing. Rich Kinder (subsequently a co-founder of Kinder Morgan) was President and COO during 1990-1996

March 2003 indictment of Kevin Howard and Michael Krautz (*see infra* note 79) and added Kenneth Rice, Joseph Hirko, Kevin Hannon, Scott Yeager, and Rex Shelby ("securities fraud, wire fraud and money laundering" in connection with Enron Broadband Services); a 109-count reindictment superseded the October 2002 indictment of Andrew Fastow and added Ben Glisan and Dan Boyle (for conspiracy to manipulate Enron's financial reports). *See Summary of charges in latest 3 indictments filed in the Enron case*, HOUS. CHRON., May 2, 2003, at 17A.

[78] The Braveheart partnership with a Canadian bank CIBC paid for rights to future earnings of the Blockbuster deal, and Enron recorded a $110.8 million gain. *See* BRYCE, *supra* note 11, at 282. On March 12, 2003, this so-called gain resulted in the arrest for fraud of former CFO Kevin Howard and the former senior director of accounting Michael Krautz, both still working at Enron in different positions. (*See supra* note 77 concerning reindictment.) The SEC filed additional civil charges. Howard and Krautz were also charged with conspiring to keep information from Andersen auditors. *See* Kurt Eichenwald, *Fraud Charges Filed Against 2 Employees of Enron Unit*, N.Y. TIMES, Mar. 13, 2003, at C1.

[79] Enron Broadband Services ("EBS") reflected an Enron strategy of becoming a trader of anything. Fowler & Flood, *supra* note 69, at 4A. Enron was being portrayed as the epitome of the "new economy"—the dot.com bubble world that burst. *See* JOEL KURTZMAN & GLEN RIFKIN, RADICAL E: FROM GE TO ENRON—LESSONS ON HOW TO RULE THE WEB (2001).

[80] Ben White, *Wall St. agrees to $1 billion in fines*, HOUS. CHRON., Dec. 20, 2002, at 1A, 14A.

[81] The SEC filed charges on March 17, 2003 (in Federal District Court in Houston) alleging that Merrill Lynch and four former Merrill executives had aided securities fraud at Enron. FOX, *supra* note 26, at 305. Merrill announced that day the finalization of a previously announced agreement with the SEC to pay $80 million in settlements. *See* Kurt Eichenwald, *4 at Merrill Accused of an Enron Fraud*, N.Y. TIMES, Mar. 18, 2003, at C1.

(being succeeded by Skilling). In 1990, Enron revenues were $5.336 billion and net income $202 million (a profit rate of 3.8%, calculated here).[82] In 1996, revenues were $13.289 billion and net income $584 million (a calculated profit rate of 4.4%).[83] Long-term debt rose from $2.982 billion to $3.3 billion, an increase of just over 10%.[84] In 1997, revenues were $20.273 billion (up substantially) and reported net income (before restatement) $105 million (down substantially, and a calculated profit rate of only 0.5%).[85] The actual net income (per the November 8, 2001 restatement) was just $9 million (effectively a zero rate of profit).[86] The continuing low profit rate may have been a driver of aggressive financial engineering and accounting and stock value hype.[87] In 2000, revenues were $100.789 billion (a quintupling of the 1997 turnover), and reported net income (later reduced on restatement) $979 million (a calculated profit rate of just under 1%).[88] Long-term debt rose from $6.254 billion in 1997 (almost doubled over 1996) to $9.763 billion in first quarter 2001.[89] When the material adverse change provisions kicked in, the firm could not obtain enough cash to meet obligations. Skilling stated that there was a "run on the bank," or a liquidity crisis that destroyed trading, the heart of the firm.[90] While this statement is true technically, it does not address causes and responsibilities.

Revenues ballooned in 2001, at $50.129 billion for first quarter, $100.189 billion for second quarter, and $138.718 billion for third quarter.[91] Long-term debt fell to $6.544 billion in 3rd quarter 2001, but short-term debt ballooned from $1.67 billion (end of 2000) to $6.4 billion in November 2001.[92] Net cash from operating activities fell from $4.779 billion in 2000 (basically quadrupled over 1999) to $2.554 billion through the first three quarters of 2001.[93] (Net cash from operating activities had been, with a minor exception in 1995, positive since 1990.) Bryce reports that Enron was taking losses on repurchasing the shares of the failed water company Azurix, buying paper mills, buying into and operating in the metals trading business, and operating Enron

[82] BRYCE, *supra* note 11, at 287 (based on Enron SEC filings).

[83] *Id.*

[84] *Id.*

[85] *Id.*

[86] BRYCE, *supra* note 11, at 287.

[87] *Id.*

[88] *Id.* In early 2002, Petroleum Finance Co. recalculated the 2000 revenue down from $100.8 billion to about $9 billion, doing recalculations for several other trading firms as well. *See* MILLS, *supra* note 9, at 49 (citing *The Ship That Sank Quietly*, THE ECONOMIST, February 16, 2002, at 57).

[89] BRYCE, *supra* note 11, at 287.

[90] FOX, *supra* note 26, at 308; FUSARO & MILLER, *supra* note 15, at 141.

[91] Bryce, *supra* note 11, at 287.

[92] *Id.*

[93] *Id.*

Broadband Services ("EBS").[94] It should be noted that, even as restated at November 8, 2001, net income rose from $590 million in 1998 (reported at $703 million) to $643 million in 1999 (reported at $893 million) to $847 million in 2000 (reported at $979 million).[95] It is the low profit rate (on revenues) that is dramatic information. Restatements did not particularly affect 2001 net income (the changes were minor). Net income (restated) was $442 million for first quarter 2001 (up a little from original report) and $409 million for second quarter 2001 (also up a little from original report).[96] But net income (restated) was negative $635 million for third quarter 2001 (a modest improvement over the original report).[97]

SOME ISSUES, PRINCIPLES, AND STAKES

The moral and public policy interest in Enron lies in the relative sophistication of the schemes created by CFO Fastow (with key details allegedly concealed from the directors and even upper management), the moral and business failings of the senior leadership, the systematic failure of virtually all the conventional checks-and-balances of corporate governance (the board of directors, the accounting and legal advisors, bankers, and brokerages), the apparent promotion or at least toleration of a self-destructive business culture and ethical climate, and the weakness of external political and regulatory checks. It must be borne in mind that Fastow, although indicted, has not been convicted of any charge.

Powers blames senior management (Lay, Skilling, and Fastow by name), the board of directors, Enron's outside advisors, and "a flawed idea, self-enrichment by employees, inadequately-designed controls, poor implementation, inattentive oversight, simple (and not-so-simple) accounting mistakes, and overreaching in a culture that appears to have encouraged pushing the limits."[98]

The report (May 6, 2002) from the Chairman of the Senate Committee on the Judiciary, Senator Leahy, recommending the proposed Corporate and Criminal Fraud Accountability Act of 2002 (S. 2010), stated:

> According to a Report of Investigation commissioned by a Special Investigative Committee of Enron's Board of Directors ("the Powers Report"), Enron apparently, with the approval or advice of its accountants, auditors and lawyers, used thousands of off-the-book [special purpose] entities [or

---

94 BRYCE, *supra* note 11, at 286.

95 *Id.* at 287, 328.

96 *Id.* at 287.

97 *Id.*

98 *See Enron Bankruptcy: Hearing Before the Comm. on Commerce, Sci., and Transp.*, 107th Cong. 2, 5 (2002) (statement of William C. Powers, Jr., Chairman, the Special Investigative Comm. of the Bd. of Dir. of Enron Corp.).

> vehicles] to overstate corporate profits, understate corporate debts and inflate Enron's stock price.
>
> The alleged activity Enron used to mislead investors was not the work of novices. It was the work of highly educated professionals, spinning an intricate spider's web of deceit. The partnerships—with names like Jedi, Chewco, Rawhide, Ponderosa and Sundance—were used essentially to cook the books and trick both the public and federal regulators about how well Enron was doing financially. The actions of Enron's executives, accountants, and lawyers exhibit a 'Wild West' attitude which valued profit over honesty.
>
> . . . [T]he few at Enron who profited appear to be senior officers and directors who cashed out while they and professionals from accounting firms, law firms and business consulting firms, who were paid millions to advise Enron on these practices, assured others that Enron was a solid investment.[99]

In my view, a number of considerations reveal the profound absence of business ethics and fiduciary responsibility within management at Enron. The available evidence reveals imprudent behavior, self-dealing, defects of moral character, company code of conduct relaxation or violation, defects of corporate culture, and defects of corporate governance. Each consideration is addressed in more detail immediately below.

Imprudent Behavior. This book's cover features, appropriately, an image of the *Titanic;* and the introduction by the editors makes reference to the *Titanic.* Like the captain of the *Titanic* steaming a poorly designed and ill-equipped vessel at high speed at night in iceberg waters to achieve a time record for economic gain, Enron's senior management hazarded investors' equity and other stakeholders' welfare by imprudent behavior for personal gain while profiting personally (so far, pending future legal outcomes). A fatally wrong assumption in both instances was that the "ship" was unsinkable. There was no contingency planning for failure of that assumption. Fundamentally, it now appears that the Enron business model was ill-considered and ill-executed, that it functioned in conjunction with deliberately concealed financing manipulations carried out by some managers who profited personally, and that this business model marched with corrupt leadership, hardball tactics applied to stakeholders and regulators, and a dominating culture of aggressive and opportunistic self-dealing. There are now proven instances of illegalities.[100]

Self-Dealing. During the period October 19, 1998 to November 27, 2001, gross proceeds from Enron stock sales were over $270 million for Lou Pai (head, Enron Energy Services), over $184 million for Lay, nearly $112 million for Robert Belfer (a

---

[99] Sen. Rep. No. 107-146, at 2-4 (2002).

[100] "Literal" compliance with accounting principles may not be a sufficient defense against criminal prosecution if creating "a fraudulent or misleading impression." *See* MILLS, *supra* note 9, at 53 (citing Floyd Norris, *An Old Case Is Returning to Haunt Auditors*, N.Y. TIMES, February 4, 2002, at 1).

director), over $76.8 million for Ken Rice (CEO, Enron Broadband Services), nearly $70.7 million for Skilling, and nearly $33.7 million for Fastow.[101] The chair of the audit committee, Robert Jaedicke, sold a little over $840,000; Bryce does not report on stock sales by Winokur (chair of the finance committee). Bryce estimates that for this period, some two dozen Enron executives and directors sold stock for more than $1.1 billion.[102] During the Enron debacle, a change in pension plan administrator caused a blackout period during which employees could not sell holdings for several weeks.[103] The Sarbanes-Oxley Act of 2002 tries to fix this matter.[104]

Defects of Moral Character. Following the Clinton presidential sex scandal, there has been a prevailing view that private behavior is separate from the conduct of high office. Enron revisits the matter of moral character. The Greek historian Plutarch considered that character is exactly to be judged by small details and not great achievements.[105] Cruver characterizes Lay as a politician[106] and Skilling as a risk-taker.[107] The London Metal Exchange levied a fine of $264,000 against Enron for "seriously inadequate" compliance with the exchange's trading rules that "jeopardized confidence" in the exchange.[108] Skilling publicly rebuked an analyst with foul language during a conference call.[109] There have been reported (apparently well-known) office adulteries of Lay (before

---

[101] BRYCE, *supra* note 11, at ix; CRUVER, *supra* note 8, at 131-32.

[102] BRYCE, *supra* note 11, at 7.

[103] FUSARO & MILLER, *supra* note 15, at 115.

[104] Sarbanes-Oxley Act of 2002, Pub. L. No. 107-204, 116 Stat. 745 (codified at scattered sections of 15 U.S.C. & 18 U.S.C.).

[105] JOHN HETHERINGTON, BLAMEY x (The Australian War Memorial and The Australian Government Publishing Service, 1973) (citing Plutarch, *Life of Alexander, in* PLUTARCH'S LIVES (Aubrey Stewart trans., G. Bell & Sons vol. 3 1924)).

[106] CRUVER, *supra* note 8, at 22, 24. John Biggs, the retired chairman, President, and CEO of TIAA-CREF pension funds (TIAA-CREF does *not* separate the positions), and erstwhile candidate for chairmanship of the new Public Company Accounting Oversight Board, has commented: "...Enron's Ken Lay, when asked for a $100,000 donation [to an accounting standards foundation], was bold enough to ask his corporate counsel if it would buy any influence." Scott Burns, *Biggs' loss was no gain for investors*, DALLAS MORNING NEWS, Dec. 1, 2002, at 1H.

[107] CRUVER, *supra* note 8, at 22, 24. It has been reported by a Harvard Business School professor that, in an MBA class, then-student Skilling supported the position that he would keep selling a harmful (even fatal) product for profit maximization unless the government prohibited such conduct. *See* FUSARO & MILLER, *supra* note 15, at 28. I hold such a position to be defective: the role of moral responsibility is to stand between market opportunity and lag in public policy action. But it is also not strictly fair (in isolation) to hold the student's class comment against the later manager: positions may be defended in class for pedagogical purposes (the student was asked the question by the professor in a class setting) without automatically telling against moral character. No known later evidence reverses the initial inference, however.

[108] BRYCE, *supra* note 11, at 286. While small, the amount was the second-largest such fine after that levied against a group of banks involved in the earlier Sumitomo Corporation copper-trading scandal. *Id.*

[109] BRYCE, *supra* note 11, at 268-69; CRUVER, *supra* note 8, at 53-54.

joining Enron), Skilling, Rice, and Pai.[110] An Enron executive told Bryce: "I knew Enron was corrupt when Jeff [Skilling] made his mistress [Rebecca Carter, subsequently Mrs. Skilling] the corporate secretary and the board never said a word about it."[111]

Relaxation or Violation of Codes of Conduct. On two known occasions, Enron faced (in principle) company code of conduct issues concerning Fastow's financial engineering. Chewco, managed by Kopper,[112] was formed in November 1997.[113] There is suspicion that Fastow and/or Kopper may have concealed key information from the directors (or even from Lay and Skilling) or did not receive desirable permissions before embarking on the orgy of perverse SPEs.[114] Chewco was subsequently a significant portion of Enron losses.[115] In June 1999, Fastow's role as manager of LJM received specific waiver of the code of ethics by the board.[116] LJM also passed "scrutiny" by Arthur Andersen and Vinson & Elkins.[117] A reasonable perspective here is what should have concerned a prudent director. It is conceivable that officers and directors were deceived by early signals of success, and that they understood at some later point that a continuation of growth by any possible means was the only path away from potential disaster.

Defects of Corporate Culture. "It was the culture, stupid."[118] Dallas defines "corporate culture" as the set of beliefs and expectations held in common by employees based on shared values, assumptions, attitudes, and norms.[119] Dallas defines "ethical climate" as the manifestation of corporate culture that characterizes the ethical meaning attached by employees to corporate policies, practices, and procedures.[120] Enron has been characterized as "a culture that valued only deal-making and money."[121] Skilling has allegedly said: "Relationships don't matter. Trust doesn't matter."[122] There was hardball intimidation (inside and outside the company), as revealed, for instance, in the

---

[110] BRYCE, *supra* note 11, at 11.

[111] BRYCE, *supra* note 11, at 145.

[112] Evidently to avoid disclosure requirements. FOX, *supra* note 26, at 123.

[113] *Id.* at viii.

[114] BRYCE, *supra* note 11, at 141; FOX, *supra* note 26, at 124; FUSARO & MILLER, *supra* note 15, at 132 (citing the Powers report).

[115] FUSARO & MILLER, *supra* note 15, at 133.

[116] FOX, *supra* note 26, at ix; FUSARO & MILLER, *supra* note 15, at 41; 135.

[117] FUSARO AND MILLER, *supra* note 15, at 135.

[118] BRYCE, *supra* note 11, at 12.

[119] Lynne Dallas, *A Preliminary Inquiry into the Responsibility of Corporations and Their Directors and Officers for Corporate Climate: The Psychology of Enron's Demise*, 35 RUTGERS L.J. (2003), *available at* http://papers.ssrn.com/paper.taf?abstract_id=350341.

[120] *Id.*

[121] Murphy, *supra* note 24, at 15A; *see also* Juin-Jen Chang & Ching-Chong Lai, *Is the Efficiency Wage Efficient? The Social Norm and Organizational Corruption*, 104.1 SCANDINAVIAN J. OF ECON. 27, 27-47 (2002) (arguing that pandemic organizational corruption has a snowballing effect that can overwhelm the expected efficiency incentive effect of wages), *available at* http://papers.ssrn.com/taf?abstract_id=312931.

[122] BRYCE, *supra* note 11, at 124.

California energy crisis; the treatment of external analysts and banks;[123] and the internal performance review system. Such pressure tends to erode anyone's moral compass. The Peer Review Committee ("PRC") process—nicknamed internally "rank and yank"—in effect deliberately drove out the bottom 15% of employees every six months and put others on notice that their careers were in jeopardy.[124] And the "rank and yank" system was itself reportedly corrupt:[125] it was not strictly peer evaluation of performance, but who you knew, accompanied by "horse trading" among managers.[126] "The PRC created a culture within Enron that replaced cooperation with competition."[127]

Defects of Corporate Governance. Corporate governance is a fundamentally weak checks and balances approach, in that it has historically relied on reasonably honest and honorable managers and directors (in the face of agency theory to the contrary). A financial and moral corruption machine emanating from senior management, ensnaring a trusting or negligent board, shaped the corporate culture and ethical climate, and ensnared the auditors, the external attorneys, and to some degree, the politicians and regulators. This machine was built around specific elements: (1) a shared ideology[128] of free markets, deregulation, and innovation; (2) systematic attempts at political influence of legislation and regulation; (3) Lay's philanthropic activities as (perhaps genuine) evidence of corporate citizenship and community leadership;[129] (4) a cynical view that greed is good, personally and for society; (5) strong financial incentives for suborning checks and balances; and (6) hardball tactics. There was a constellation of interlinking elements at work.

The etiology of Enron's stock price bubble and subsequent collapse is gradually coming to light through the multiple investigations underway. Enron began running on a rising stock price treadmill that must steadily accelerate on management and the board[130]—and that ran into adverse economic conditions. Skilling came over to Enron from a partnership at McKinsey, in 1990, when that firm recommended that Enron

---

[123] *Id.* at 224.

[124] CRUVER, *supra* note 8, at xv, 61-64; *see also* Kim Clark, *Judgment day: It's survival of the fittest as companies tighten the screws on employee performance reviews*, U.S. NEWS & WORLD REP., Jan. 13, 2003, at 31 (noting that General Electric, under Jack Welch, used a bottom 10%).

[125] FUSARO & MILLER, *supra* note 15, at 52.

[126] BRYCE, *supra* note 11, at 128; CRUVER, *supra* note 8, at 64.

[127] BRYCE, *supra* note 11, at 129.

[128] Lay, in Spring 1997, was quoted: "We believe in markets. Sometimes there's an aberration. But over time, markets figure out value." *See* BRYCE, supra note 11, at 1 (citing Gary McWilliams, *The quiet man who's jolting utilities*, BUS. WK., June 9, 1997, at 84. The thesis applies, of course, to market valuation of a firm, whether built on economic reality or trickery (the latter presumably delaying discovery).

[129] Lay brokered the deal to keep the Astros baseball team in Houston, reflected in the new Enron Field ballpark (later renamed). He was co-chairman of the Houston host committee for the 1990 Economic Summit of Industrialized Nations, held at Rice University; he was head of the Houston host committee for the 1992 Republican national convention in Houston. BRYCE, *supra* note 11, at 87-88. There has been an Enron Prize for Distinguished Public Service given through Rice University's Baker Institute. BRYCE, *supra* note 11, at 323-24.

[130] *Cf.* FUSARO & MILLER, *supra* note 15, at 73, 78.

go into financial products and services.[131] The shift to mark-to-market accounting began with Skilling at Enron Gas Services Group ("EGSG") and spread to the whole company when he became COO.[132] This accounting in effect simply booked Enron's own internal estimates of what markets were worth, virtually unregulated pro forma estimates.[133] Bryce[134] cites Skilling's employment contract from the 1990 Enron proxy statement: he received cash bonuses ("phantom equity rights") as a percentage of the increase in market value of Enron Finance Corp.[135] These bonuses were worth $10 million at $200 million value and $17 million at $400 million value, relative to his salary of $275,000 (and loan of $950,000).[136] Bryce cites the 1997 proxy statement as revealing additional stock options.[137] Bryce argues that Skilling convinced Lay, the audit committee, and the board of the worth of mark-to-market accounting.[138] The strategic emphasis shifted to revenue growth.[139] On May 17, 1991, the audit committee adopted mark-to-market accounting for EGSG on a motion by the chair (Jaedicke).[140] Enron and Arthur Andersen lobbied the SEC, which granted permission by letter of January 30, 1992, for EGSG only.[141] Enron then introduced the approach a full year earlier than previously discussed with the SEC; Bryce reports that an anonymous auditor told him that, otherwise, the last quarter of 1991 would have been negative.[142] The Commodity Futures Trading Commission ("CFTC"), operating with only three of its five members, approved in late 1992, on recommendation by the chair, a rule exempting energy derivatives contracts from federal regulation.[143] The chair, Wendy Lee Gramm (wife of Senator Gramm of Texas), became a director of Enron in early 1993, shortly after stepping down from the CFTC. Derivatives thus involved no licensing or regulation by the SEC or the NYSE.[144]

It appears that these arrangements were only vaguely disclosed to analysts and investors. The Enron 2000 Annual Report[145] disclosed that there were limited partnerships whose general managing member was an Enron senior officer, but the report did not

131 MILLS, *supra* note 9, at 48.

132 BRYCE, *supra* note 11, at 64-66.

133 *Cf.* ELLIOTT & SCHROTH, *supra* note 9, at 39.

134 BRYCE, *supra* note 11, at 64.

135 *Id.*

136 *Id.*

137 *Id.* at 64-65.

138 *Id.* at 65.

139 *Id.* at 66.

140 BRYCE, *supra* note 11, at 66-67.

141 BRYCE, *supra* note 11, at 67.

142 *Id.*

143 *Id.* at 81.

144 *Id.* at 83; *see also* FUSARO & MILLER, *supra* note 15, at 20 (noting that hedging operations may necessitate secrecy for success, so off-shore operation and non-regulation might be viewed as logical steps).

145 CRUVER, *supra* note 8, at 59-60.

specifically name the officer involved.[146] The report stated that the transactions were regarded as comparable to what could have been negotiated with unrelated third parties.[147] If that were in fact the case, of course, the question should arise as to why unrelated third parties were not being used.

In testimony before Congress, Powers summarized findings concerning transactions between Enron and partnerships controlled by CFO Fastow as follows: "What we found was appalling."[148] Fastow earned at least $30 million, Kopper earned at least $10 million, two others earned $1 million each, and two others earned some hundreds of thousands of dollars each.[149] There were *some* failures to follow accounting rules in these relationships. "We found a systematic and pervasive attempt by Enron's Management to misrepresent the Company's financial condition. Enron Management used these partnerships to enter into transactions that it could not, or would not, do with unrelated commercial entities. Many of the most significant transactions apparently were not designed to achieve bona fide economic objectives. They were designed to affect how Enron reported its earnings."[150] "Essentially, Enron was hedging with itself" through the Raptors, in which—despite appearances of being Fastow-organized partnerships—"only Enron had a real economic stake and . . . [the] main assets were Enron's own stock."[151] Powers cites notes by Enron's corporate secretary of a Finance Committee meeting on the Raptors: "Does not transfer economic risk [away from Enron] but transfers P+L volatility [away from Enron]."[152] The Powers report concludes that the purpose was to allow Enron to avoid reporting losses on investments: "there is no question that virtually everyone, from the Board of Directors on down, understood that the company was seeking to offset its investment losses with its own stock. That is not the way it is supposed to work. Real earnings are supposed to be compared to real losses."[153] Over the period from third quarter of 2002 through third quarter of 2001 (fifteen months), reported earnings were improperly inflated by over $1 billion, and more than 70% of reported earnings for the period were not real.[154]

[146] *Enron Annual Report 2000*, 48 *available at* http://www.enron.com/corp/investors/annuals/2000/ar2000.pdf.

[147] *Id.*

[148] *See Enron Bankruptcy: Hearing Before the Comm. on Commerce, Sci., and Transp.*, 107th Cong. 2 (2002) (statement of William C. Powers, Jr., Chairman, the Special Investigative Comm. of the Bd. of Dir. of Enron Corp.).

[149] *See id.*

[150] *Id.* at 3.

[151] *Id.* at 4. An Enron attorney sent an e-mail (September 1, 2000) to his superiors in the legal department questioning the Raptors as possibly generating a perception of cooking the books, while Arthur Andersen signed off. BRYCE, *supra* note 11, at 231.

[152] *See Enron Bankruptcy: Hearing Before the Comm. on Commerce, Sci., and Transp.*, 107th Cong. 4 (2002) (statement of William C. Powers, Jr.).

[153] *Id.* at 4-5.

[154] *See id.* at 5.

The moral status of Watkins's whistleblowing at Enron is a separable matter, and is treated below as such. Three women whistleblowers were the 2002 *Time* magazine "Persons of the Year": WorldCom auditor Cynthia Cooper; FBI agent Coleen Rowley; and former Enron vice president for corporate development Sherron Watkins.[155] *Time* states: "They took huge professional and personal risks to blow the whistle on what went wrong at WorldCom, the FBI and Enron—and in so doing helped remind Americans what courage and values are all about."[156]

Watkins came to public notice first, in January 2002, when it was leaked that she had communicated with Lay about suspected accounting manipulations at Enron.[157] She had gone to work for Fastow in June 2001, and was assigned to selling assets.[158] In the course of her duties, she discovered off-the-books irregularities.[159] It appears that she began looking for a job, planning to confront Skilling on her last day.[160] Skilling unexpectedly resigned on August 14, 2001.[161]

On August 15, 2001, the day after Skilling's resignation, she sent an anonymous one-page memo to Lay—a memo precipitated by the Raptors.[162] Watkins then saw Cindy Olson, head of Enron Human Resources, who advised her to go to Lay.[163] On August 20, in an interview with *Business Week*, Lay stated there were no issues, "no other shoe to fall."[164] On August 22, 2001, she met with Lay by appointment and gave him a second, detailed seven-page memo and an annotated document concerning a suspect partnership.[165] She advised Lay against using Vinson & Elkins for the inquiry. Lay had Vinson & Elkins look into the issues; the firm reported that SPEs were not a problem.[166] Two days after this meeting, an e-mail from a Vinson & Elkins attorney stated: "Texas

---

[155] *See* Ruiz, *supra* note 59; *see also* Michael J. Gundlach, Scott C. Douglas, & Mark J. Martinko, *The decision to blow the whistle: A social information processing framework,* 28.1 THE ACAD. OF MGMT. REV. 107, 107-23 (2003) (examining decisions to blow the whistle).

[156] TIME 5 (Dec. 30, 2002-Jan. 6, 2003, double issue, vol. 160, no. 27). In June 2002, Cooper had informed the WorldCom board of accounting manipulations inflating 2001 and 2002 profits by $3.8 billion (wildly exceeding Enron manipulations with respect to profits). Ruiz, *supra* note 59, at 1A. Rowley had written the FBI director in May 2002 criticizing bureau failure to act on alleged warning signs received before the 9-11 (2001) terrorist attacks. *Id.*

[157] Morse & Bower, *supra* note 27.

[158] *Id.*

[159] *Id.*

[160] *Id.*

[161] *Id.*

[162] FUSARO & MILLER, *supra* note 15, at 135 (noting that Lay, in addressing Skilling's departure, had invited communications from employees). *See* SWARTZ WITH WATKINS, *supra* note 30, for this short memo.

[163] BRYCE, *supra* note 11, at 294.

[164] CRUVER, *supra* note 8, at 94 (quoting Stephanie Forest's interview of Kenneth Lay in *Business Week*, August 20, 2001).

[165] This action violated the chain of command, as Fastow was Watkins's superior. *See* SWARTZ WITH WATKINS, *supra* note 30.

[166] BRYCE, *supra* note 11, at 298.

law does not currently protect corporate whistle-blowers."[167] Fastow reportedly seized Watkins's office hard drive.[168] She was moved down thirty-three floors from executive level and assigned (in effect) to "special projects" (notoriously the place where people on the way out of a firm are parked temporarily).[169] Cruver reports that Watkins asked for and received a transfer.[170] The attorney's e-mail was brought to Watkins's attention on February 13, 2002. She testified before Congress on February 14.[171] In her testimony, she characterized Lay as a "man of integrity."[172] "Watkins claimed that Lay had been 'duped' by Skilling and Fastow."[173]

Watkins left Enron in November 2002, reportedly to set up a global consulting firm to advise boards on governance and ethics; she reportedly receives up to $25,000 per speaking engagement, and she contracted for half of a $500,000 advance with Houston writer Mimi Swartz to prepare a book entitled *Power Failure.*[174]

Watkins's nomination for anything approaching decent business ethics at Enron is reportedly controversial for some ex-Enron employees. To some Watkins is a hero;[175] to others, she is a villain.[176] Some employees have criticized Watkins for not going to the SEC,[177] and for selling $47,000 in Enron stock in late August and in October[178]—as if anyone who could get out of the stock should have held it. Morse and Bower observe, correctly, in response, that Watkins was the only one to speak up (even internally) at Enron.[179] It is not clear that subordinate managers have strong duties to go public—at high personal cost. New SEC rules for attorneys specifically restricted (under great pressure by attorneys) the duty to report concerns about securities laws violations to management and the board, and excluded the SEC, contrary to what the agency had initially proposed.[180]

---

167 E-mail from Carl Jordan, Vinson & Elkins Associate, to Joe Dilg (August 24, 2001, 07:02 PM), *available at* http://energycommerce.house.gov/107/hearings/02142002Hearing489/tab18.pdf.

168 Morse & Bower, *supra* note 27, at 53.

169 *Id.*

170 CRUVER, *supra* note 8, at 95-96.

171 *The Financial Collapse of Enron—Part 3: Hearing Before the Subcomm. on Oversight & Investigations of the Comm. on Energy and Commerce*, 107th Cong. 14 (2002) (testimony of Sherron Watkins, Vice President of Corporate Development, Enron Corp.).

172 Morse & Bower, *supra* note 27, at 53.

173 FUSARO & MILLER, *supra* note 15, at 142.

174 Morse & Bower, *supra* note 27, at 53, 54.

175 *Id.* at 52.

176 *See* BRYCE, *supra* note 11, at 295 (quoting half a dozen Enron employees saying Watkins was "calculating, vindictive . . . facing almost certain firing by Fastow . . .").

177 Her role was apparently internal only and was leaked to the outside.

178 Morse & Bower, *supra* note 27, at 56.

179 *Id.*

180 *SEC lays down rules for lawyers: Agency tells how to report violations.* HOUS. CHRON., Jan. 24, 2003, at 1C, 3C.

The reader should bear in mind that, arguably, under Texas law (and, in my view, in practice virtually everywhere, regardless of law), a whistleblower is not protected (certainly not well-protected), and should study a classic Harvard Business School case on whistleblowing, "Tony Santino."[181] The classic strategy for dealing with a corporate whistleblower is portrayal as a "disgruntled employee" in order to shift attention and blame. "Santino" (the disguised name of a Harvard MBA graduate), a former Navy aviator, had high standards of courage and values.[182] These standards caused him to lose one job at a defense contractor (what a surprise!), and to have to take a less attractive job at a manufacturing firm—where he was asked basically to falsify a pricing list to customers by faking product specifications with the firm's lab engineers. The case concerns not only courage and values, but equally important practical (or pragmatic) action planning—how to avoid being destroyed while doing the right thing. Ultimately "Santino" resigns while informing his superiors that they are violating the law; his wife (a CPA) divorces him; he winds up working at a third firm after six months without employment. In the case, "Santino" asks a lawyer for advice, and learns that the government is unlikely to prosecute such a minor case; he asks a business school professor (a consultant), who wonders why "Santino" is so impractical. Watkins (who has a husband and children) arguably played her cards very carefully (cards dealt to her by superiors and events), and, in effect, prospered. Her actions will make for a very useful case study of whistleblowing duties and tactics. Temporizing is not automatically a failure of duty or of moral integrity.

REFORM PROPOSALS

Norman Augustine, the ex-CEO of Lockheed Martin, comments in his foreword to Seglin: "Public confidence surveys invariably show [big] business . . . enjoying little public respect—ranking right in there with politicians, the media, and axe murderers."[183] One can point to a long history of executive and corporate misconduct in the U.S.;[184] and, regrettably, this tradition may be expected to recur in both refurbished and exotic new forms.[185]

---

[181] Jeffrey A. Sonnenfeld, *Tony Santino (A)* (October 1, 1981) (field study of a "recent MBA without a stable work history in the private sector who feels that he is being forced to compromise his personal convictions and professional integrity through a violation of the Robinson-Patman Act"), *available for purchase at* http://harvardbusinessonline.hbsp.harvard.edu/b02/en/common/item_detail.jhtml?id=482045.

[182] To draw on *Time's* theme for its "Persons of the Year." *See* Morse & Bower, *supra* note 23, at 52.

[183] SEGLIN, *supra* note 6, at vii.

[184] Michael Satchell, *Scandal as usual: America's economic history is riddled with tales of fraud, swindles, and get-rich-quick schemes*, U.S. NEWS & WORLD REP., Dec. 30, 2002-Jan. 6, 2003 (double issue), at 49.

[185] Barry Minkow's ZZZZ Best Company allegedly would obtain huge profits from insurance repairs of fire and water damage in large buildings. The market valuation rose to $200 million; when the bubble collapsed, the assets were auctioned for $64,000. Minkow was convicted in Dec. 1988 of fraud. *See* Satchell, *supra* note 184, at 49.

There are over 14,000 registered public companies in the U.S.[186] The U.S. economy produces annual output at a value of roughly $10 trillion. In the aftermath of corporate misconduct revelations, the SEC, in summer 2002, required the CEOs and CFOs of the 945 largest U.S. public companies (with greater than $1.2 billion revenues) to sign statements attesting to the accuracy of their firm's financial statements.[187] The strong majority of such officers evidently faced no serious difficulties in doing so.[188] Understandably, investor confidence has been badly shaken—but capital market effects involved a broader context of recession, terrorist sneak attacks and continuing threat, and diplomatic confrontations with Iraq and then North Korea.

Various doubtless useful reform measures have been proposed by the President, the Congress, SEC, NYSE, The Conference Board, and others. Additionally, pursuant to the Sarbanes-Oxley Act of 2002, the U.S. Sentencing Commission is strengthening white-collar crime penalties.[189] These reform measures are necessary (particularly to set standards and penalties and to restore investor confidence), but likely not sufficient to deter all future misconduct. The measures are necessary because there is an inherent conflict of interest between management (and their advisors) and investors and other stakeholders. This conflict of interest is the essence of the agency model,[190] in which amoral actors maximize self-interest. Amoral actors compute cost-benefit estimates of what to do.[191] The problem is not that so many executives and directors are bad; most of them probably calculate that misconduct is not worthwhile (even before Sarbanes-Oxley), and the summer 2002 CEO and CFO signatures attest so. The problem is that, given the sciences of deception and mendacity that can be practiced by executives, it is difficult to know which relatively few apples are bad; and that relaxation of standards or development of exotic new opportunities will entice additional violators into making rational calculations. Regulation is ever caught between the necessity of control to hamper deception and mendacity and the desirability of freedom to innovate, which in turn drives economic development.

Senior executives, directors, and their accounting, consulting, and legal advisors face enormous incentives for corruption and misreporting of performance. These incentives come in three general forms: (1) employment, salary, and bonuses tied (unavoidably) to perceived performance; (2) unnoticed selling of shares at gain, with shares typically in the form of stock options; and (3) ability to issue equity to finance new projects or acquisitions.[192] These incentives encourage efforts directed at rising stock prices, through

---

186 ELLIOT & SCHROTH, *supra* note 9, at 20.

187 FOX, *supra* note 26, at 305.

188 The proportion involving serious restatements might be a rough index of prior concealments and other difficulties. A detailed study would be necessary.

189 Sarbanes-Oxley Act of 2002, Pub. L. No. 107-204, 116 Stat. 745 (codified at scattered sections of 15 U.S.C. & 18 U.S.C.).

190 Prominent in financial economics literature.

191 EDWARD C. BANFIELD, HERE THE PEOPLE RULE: SELECTED ESSAYS 337 (1985).

192 Lucian A. Bebchuk & Oren Bar-Gill, *Misreporting Corporate Performance*, *available at* http://papers.ssrn.com/paper.taf?abstract_id=354141 (Dec. 7, 2002).

both fair and foul means (i.e., any undetected means will serve).[193] The fatal conceit at Enron was that stock prices would rise and that foul means would remain undetected. Significant blame must attach to stock options for senior executives[194]—which Congress strongly resisted prior to recent revelations.[195] Such incentives encourage greater risk taking than is prudent.[196] Biggs notes that, at Intel, only 2% of options go to senior executives; it is younger personnel who should be so motivated.[197] Perhaps straight salary should suffice for senior executives.

President Bush (a Harvard MBA) in statements of March and July 2002 made several proposals for corporate governance reform: (1) Improving financial transparency and disclosure by quarterly investor access to data (which was already supposed to happen) and prompt access to critical data (concealed at Enron). (2) Strengthening of officer responsibilities and penalties as follows: CEO must vouch for disclosures subject to criminal penalties (one could add the CFO); officers cannot profit from errors; officers can lose the right to serve in any corporate leadership positions; officers must report stock activities. (3) Strengthening of auditor independence and oversight as follows: There must be auditor independence and integrity; the authors of accounting standards must be responsive to the needs of investors; and accounting systems should be best practices rather than minimum standards.[198]

The Sarbanes-Oxley Act of 2002 addressed a wide range of matters.[199] Much of the Act involves instructions to the SEC. Other than Title I, the Act is essentially a laundry list of monitoring and control enhancements. Title I established a Public Company Accounting Oversight Board, as a nonprofit corporation (District of Columbia), appointed by and reporting to the SEC, for registration and supervision of public accounting firms engaged in auditing services.[200] Title II addresses measures for auditor independence.[201] Title III ("Corporate Responsibility") addresses audit committees, corporate responsibility for financial reports, improper influence on conduct of audits, conditions for forfeiture of bonuses and profits, bars and penalties for officers and directors, prohibition of insider trades during pension fund blackout periods and rules for blackout notices (a feature of the Enron story), rules of professional responsibility

---

193 As soon as stock prices fell over the past few years, companies began asking investors to approve repricing of options (downward). *See* Timothy G. Pollock, Harald M. Fischer, & James B. Wade, *The role of power and politics in the repricing of executive options*, 45.6 THE ACAD. OF MGMT. J. 1172, 1172-82 (2002). There might as well be no incentive strategy, if employees win whether stock price rises or falls.

194 Burns, *supra* note 106, at 1H.

195 Representative Oxley reportedly opposed stock option expensing rules proposed by the International Accounting Standards Board. *See* ELLIOT & SCHROTH, *supra* note 9, at 36.

196 Burns, *supra* note 106, at 1H.

197 *Id.*

198 President Bush (a Harvard MBA) in statements of March and July 2002.

199 Sarbanes-Oxley Act of 2002, Pub. L. No. 107-204, 116 Stat. 745 (codified at scattered sections of 15 U.S.C. & 18 U.S.C.).

200 *Id.* § 7211-7219.

201 *Id.* § 7231.

for attorneys (to be issued by the SEC), redirection of civil penalties (and donations) to disgorgement funds for investors.[202] Title IV seeks ways to enhance financial disclosures, such as for special purpose entities or transactions involving directors, officers and principal stockholders, to reduce conflicts of interest for executives, to emphasize adequate internal controls, to require corporate code of ethics for senior financial officers, to encourage audit committees to contain at least one financial expert, to enhance SEC review of periodic disclosures, and disclosure of material changes "in plain English."[203] Title V seeks to reduce conflicts of interest for analysts.[204] Title VI directs additional resources and authority to the SEC.[205] Title VII requires certain studies and reports by the GAO (into public accounting industry consolidation and investment banks and financial advisers) and SEC (into credit rating agencies and recent violations of securities laws).[206] Title VIII, the Corporate and Criminal Fraud Accountability Act of 2002, addresses enhancements of various criminal penalties and related matters—directing a review of sentencing guidelines for obstruction of justice and "extensive criminal fraud" by the U.S. Sentencing Commission, and addressing whistleblower protection.[207] Title IX addresses white-collar crime penalty enhancements.[208] Title X is a sense of the Senate that CEOs should sign a firm's federal income tax return.[209] Title XI addresses criminal responsibility for obstruction of justice, and additional authority for the SEC, such as prohibiting individuals from serving as officers or directors.[210]

The Conference Board's Blue Ribbon Commission on Public Trust and Private Enterprise issued its final report on recommended corporate governance approaches.[211] The report recommended (rather than required) as alternatives formal separation of Chairman and CEO roles[212] or a "Lead Independent Director" or a "Presiding Director" to control information flow, board agenda, and board schedule, with the non-management directors[213] encouraged to meet frequently.[214] John Biggs, the now-retired chairman,

---

[202] *Id.* § 7241.

[203] *Id.* § 7261.

[204] *Id.* § 78o-6.

[205] *Id.* § 78kk.

[206] *Id.* § 7201.

[207] 18 U.S.C. § 1501 (2003).

[208] *Id.* § 1341.

[209] *Id.*

[210] *Id.* § 1512.

[211] The Conference Bd., Comm'n on Pub. Trust & Private Enter., *available at* http://www.conference-board.org/pdf_free/758.pdf (last modified January 9, 2003).

[212] *Id.* at 15. Note that Chairman and CEO roles had been separated at Enron for years between Lay and Skilling.

[213] *Id.* A substantial majority of the board must be independent directors.

[214] *Id.*

president, and CEO of TIAA-CREF, dissented from the separation recommendation.[215] The NYSE recommends only that a majority of directors be independent. Generally speaking, Enron's board met these standards. There are no real tests or standards for independence, any more than professional codes affected the conduct of accountants and attorneys in the Enron situation.

CONCLUSION

There is a philosophy holding that moral values are private choices and that markets, in combination with democratic public policy process, will resolve all important matters. The Enron debacle should be an object lesson that such philosophy may have its practical limits. Enron leadership substituted private choices for moral and legal responsibilities and strove to suborn public policy process. We may expect new methods of evading laws and regulations after some period of time has passed and new opportunities for wealth pursuit by any means arise.[216] The pressures and opportunities are organic to a dynamic marketplace.[217] Recent events occurred mostly (not exclusively) in the new frontier industries of energy trading and telecommunications. It is infeasible fully to regulate a complex economy. The reform proposals noted in the previous section are perfectly obvious—leading to the question of why they were not in place before the recent scandals. In the long run, ultimate reliance must be placed on the moral character of executives and directors.[218] External regulation is penultimate only. There are always pressures of various types to relax vigilance and concern. The purpose of voluntary morality—truly professional conduct, properly conceived—is to separate the marketplace and public policy so that economic actors regulate themselves. At Enron, it appears that key actors regarded public policy as just another kind of marketplace for dealmaking and markets as amoral machinery.[219] The view of Adam Smith is significant: he felt that natural moral sympathy for others could be improved more rapidly by moral education.[220] Even today, some significant proportion of business schools cannot show that they require ethics education of newly minted MBAs.[221] The response to recent corporate scandals by the American Association of Collegiate Schools of Business ("AACSB"), the key accrediting body (comprised of business school deans acting collectively), has been to consider moving ethics to the top of a list

---

215 *Id.* at 35. The positions of Chairman and CEO are combined at TIAA-CREF.

216 ELLIOT & SCHROTH, *supra* note 9, at 15.

217 The Italian offices of Sotheby's (London auctioneers) reportedly were smuggling old masters out of Italy. *See* PETER WATSON, SOTHEBY'S: THE INSIDE STORY (1997).

218 *Cf.* ELLIOT & SCHROTH, *supra* note 9, at 49.

219 Wilson, *supra* note 16, at 59-71 (arguing that market capitalism is an amoral mechanism: its chief virtue, and not a negligible one, is that, on balance, it alleviates over time widespread poverty more effectively than other alternative social arrangements).

220 *Id.*; *see also supra* text accompanying note 12.

221 Salbu, *supra* note 9, at xiii.

of important topics, while declining to endorse any necessity of a required course in business ethics and fostering development of school codes of conduct for faculty and students. The question arises as to why ethics was not at the top before recent corporate scandals. The AACSB prefers to let business schools choose between a required course and the "infusion" of ethics education into other courses—e.g., strategy, finance, marketing—without specifying who should handle such instruction.[222] The infusion approach is already suspect: "B-school assurances that ethics are examined throughout the curriculum sound hollow, if not downright laughable, to most students and recent M.B.A. graduates."[223]

---

[222] See e-mail from author to AACSB & The Academy of Management, *An Open Letter on Business School Responsibility* (Oct. 8, 2002) (on file with author and available to the reader via e-mail at odw@ rice.edu.)

[223] Salbu, *supra* note 8, at xiii.

Enron and Ethical Corporate Climates

Lynne L. Dallas[*]

With substantial inquiry concerning what individual Enron directors and officers knew or what they should have known, little attention has been directed to examining the institutional structure at Enron that may have spawned the unethical behavior—and to assessing responsibility for that structure. By institutional structure, I refer to Enron's ethical climate, which is a manifestation of its culture. Corporate culture is defined as a "complex set of common beliefs and expectations held by members of the organization," which are based on shared value, assumptions, attitudes, and norms.[1] The corporation's ethical climate refers to the ethical meaning attached by employees to organizational policies, practices and procedures. These policies, practices, and procedures influence moral awareness, the criteria used in moral decision-making, whether morals will have priority over other values, and moral behavior.

I. SOCIAL CONTEXT IS IMPORTANT TO INDIVIDUAL ETHICAL/UNETHICAL DECISION-MAKING

There is considerable reluctance to make directors liable for a legal violation committed by others. The assumption is that fault for such illegal decision-making lies solely in the individual characteristics of the persons committing the violations. Research makes clear, however, that "individual characteristics alone are insufficient to explain moral and ethical behavior."[2] One commentator summarizes this research as follows:

---

[*] Professor of Law, University of San Diego School of Law, San Diego.

This essay is based on one of my articles: *A Preliminary Inquiry into the Responsibility of Corporations and Their Officers and Directors for an Ethical Corporate Climate: The Psychology of Enron's Demise*, 35 RUTGERS L. J. 1 (2004). *Editors' note:* This essay was included in the first edition of this book. Reprinted by permission.

[1] Vicky Arnold & James C. Lampe, *Understanding the Factors Underlying Ethical Organizations: Enabling Continuous Ethical Improvement*, 15 J. APPLIED BUS. RES. 1, 2 (1999).

[2] Bart Victor & John B. Cullen, *The Organizational Bases of Ethical Work Climates*, 33 ADMIN. SCI. Q. 101, 103 (1988).

> Theory and research related to the situational effects on ethical/unethical behavior offer strong support for situational variables having a profound effect on ethical/unethical behavior in most people. The clear implication is that it is inappropriate for organizations to rely totally on individual integrity to guide behavior. . . . Therefore, organizations must provide a context that supports ethical behavior and discourages unethical behavior.[3]

Although this research does not relieve the individual violator of responsibility, it does widen the net of responsibility to those responsible for the environment in which decision-making occurs. Having the persons responsible for a corporation's unethical climate bear some of the blame, thus giving them an incentive to improve their corporation's climate, is particularly important in a world where the actions of a few employees can have severe, adverse consequences.

While the social context of decision-making is extremely important, more attention has been given to the components of individual ethical decision-making and moral reasoning processes. An examination of these components and processes reveal, however, an important role for social context.

II. COMPONENTS OF INDIVIDUAL ETHICAL/UNETHICAL DECISION-MAKING AND THE IMPORTANCE OF SOCIAL ENVIRONMENT

James Rest, in his important publication *Moral Development: Advances in Research Theory*, identified four inner cognitive-affective processes that he called components in ethical decision-making. They are: (1) "moral awareness," which is awareness that an ethical issue exists, thus a situation is interpreted as raising moral issues; (2) "moral decision-making," which is deciding what course of action is morally sound; (3) "moral intent," which refers to deciding that moral values should take priority over non-moral values in the decision; and (4) "moral behavior," which constitutes executing and implementing the moral decision.[4]

The first component, moral awareness, is affected by the moral intensity of the issue involved. Two factors that are relevant to moral intensity are social consensus and social proximity. These factors suggest that corporations affect the moral awareness of their employees. Social consensus is defined by Thomas M. Jones as "the degree of social agreement that a proposed act is evil (or good)."[5] Kenneth D. Butterfield states that it is "the individual's perception of social consensus within the individual's relevant social

---

[3] Linda Klebe Trevino, *Ethical Decision-Making in Organizations: A Person-Situation Interactionist Model*, 11 ACAD. MGMT. REV. 601, 614 (1986).

[4] James R. Rest, *The Major Components of Morality*, in MORALITY, MORAL BEHAVIOR, AND MORAL DEVELOPMENT 24, 24-36 (William M. Kurtines & Jacob Gewirtz eds., 1984).

[5] Thomas M. Jones, *Ethical Decision-Making by Individuals in Organizations: An Issue-Contingent Model*, 16 ACAD. MGMT. REV. 366, 375 (1991).

sphere that is most important to determining whether an individual will recognize a moral issue."[6] His empirical study confirms that:

> [M]oral awareness is more likely to be triggered when an individual perceives a social consensus within the organization/profession that the activity in question is ethically problematic. Thus, although previous normative and descriptive writings have tended to suggest that ethical decision-making is an individual or personal process . . . research suggests that, in organizational contexts, it is very much a social process. If a decision-maker perceives that others in the social environment will see an issue as ethically problematic, she or he will be more likely to consider the ethical issues involved.[7]

Thus, the corporation plays an important role in determining the degree to which its employees are aware of ethical issues.

The corporation also affects moral awareness by influencing the moral intensity of an issue resulting from social proximity. Social proximity refers to the "feeling of nearness (social, cultural, psychological, or physical) that the moral agent has for victims (beneficiaries) of the evil (beneficial) act in question."[8] Moral awareness or sensitivity includes the "awareness that the resolution of a particular dilemma may affect the welfare of others."[9] Business practices and procedures determine the degree to which consequences of business decisions are made salient to the employee as decision-maker. Does the corporation, for example, require managers to "explicitly report on potential consequences" (both beneficial and non-beneficial) to corporate stakeholders of his or her decisions?[10] Is the employee evaluated on the basis of these consequences? Because an employee's perceptions and interpretations of particular situations affect his or her emotions, an understanding of the consequences of business decisions may create empathy, and thus moral awareness, in employees.

Management's framing of issues in ethical or moral terms may also affect the moral awareness of employees. For example, corporate norms at Ford dictated that employees deciding on the recall of the Ford Pinto not refer to the "problem" of the Pinto "bursting into flames" and killing people, but rather refer to the "condition" of the Pinto as "lightening up." Butterfield found a significant relationship between ethical issue framing and moral awareness for those actions that are viewed by participants as ethically ambiguous. These findings indicate that the corporation, through issue

[6] Kenneth D. Butterfield et al., *Moral Awareness in Business Organizations: Influences of Issue-Related and Social Context Factors*, 53 HUM. REL. 981, 990, 999 (2000).

[7] *Id.* at 1001.

[8] Jones, *supra* note 6, at 376.

[9] Alice Gaudine & Linda Thorne, *Emotions and Ethical Decision-Making in Organizations,* 31 J. BUS. ETHICS 175, 179 (2001).

[10] Butterfield et al., *supra* note 7, at 989.

framing, may have an impact on employees in situations that employees view as ethically ambiguous.

With respect to component two, moral decision-making (deciding what is the moral course of action), Rest offers two approaches that suggest the importance of social context to individual ethical/unethical decision-making. The social norms approach suggests that individuals determine the appropriate course of action by reference to social norms. According to this approach, "moral development is a matter of acquiring a number of social norms and being set to have those norms activated by specific situations."[11] Corporations have an important impact on the social norms adopted by employees. Perceived practices and procedures of corporations reflect workplace norms that involve ethics and that include "the perceived prescriptions, proscriptions and permissions regarding moral obligations" in the corporation.[12] For example, as discussed later in this article, various social norms operating in Enron's workplace influenced the employees' unethical decision-making.

The second approach to moral decision-making focuses on cognitive development. Lawrence Kohlberg developed a theory of moral development in which persons progress in moral reasoning through three stages. The stages reflect how persons interact with their environment, think about ethical dilemmas, and determine what is fair and just. For persons reasoning at the first two stages, social environment has a profound effect on individual decision making. According to Kohlberg, persons progress to higher stages of moral reasoning by experiencing ethical dilemmas and being exposed to higher-stage reasoning. Thus, corporations may increase the moral reasoning levels of their employees through work tasks, training programs, and education. Rest reports that such moral development programs do produce "modest but significant gains."[13] Training programs of particular use to employees are those that center on ethical dilemmas that are likely to arise in their jobs and workplaces. Rest also notes that programs "emphasizing peer discussion of controversial moral dilemmas" are particularly effective."[14]

Lastly, the third and fourth components of ethical decision making involve following through with what a person reasons to be morally sound. There is "moral intent," which is the decision to give priority to morals over competing values and "moral behavior," which is to actually engage in the execution and implementation of a moral decision.

A number of contextual factors encourage or discourage an employee from giving priority to morals and actually following through with a moral decision. First, general role expectations within the business environment can influence the ethics of decision-making. Bommer claims that employees are "ethical segregationists" in that they often apply different sets of values to work and home.[15] Bommer claims that "managerial

---

[11] *See supra* note 5, at 31.

[12] Victor & Cullen, *supra* note 3, at 101.

[13] JAMES R. REST, MORAL DEVELOPMENT: ADVANCES IN RESEARCH AND THEORY 177 (1986).

[14] *Id.*

[15] Michael Bommer et al., *A Behavioral Model of Ethical and Unethical Decision-Making,* 6 J. BUS. ETHICS 265, 268 (1987).

decisions will correspond more closely to the humanistic, religious, cultural, and societal values of the society-at-large only when these values are made part of the job environment."[16]

A second factor is the employee's assessment of personal responsibility for corporate decision-making. Unethical behavior is more likely when responsibility is diffuse or attributed to others higher in the corporation. Through its expectation of employees and its policies and practices, the corporation determines whether and to what extent employees are held personally responsible for corporate decisions.

Third, the corporate environment influences whether empathy-based moral motives are encouraged or discouraged. Martin Hoffman notes that "[m]ature empathy... reflects a sensitivity to subtle differences in the severity and quality of consequences that different actions might have for different people, and it may therefore contribute to informed moral judgments about behavior."[17] Empathy may also increase the receptiveness of an individual to justice principles such as equality and fairness. Business practices and policies enhance employee empathy when they encourage employees to consider the consequences of their decisions on other stakeholders and facilitate extensive communication between employee decision-makers and those who will bear the consequences of their decisions.

Fourth, an important social factor in an employee's moral behavior is his or her choice of referent—or persons after whom his or her behavior is modeled. Referents in the work environment may be higher-level officials who are viewed as organizational heroes, direct supervisors, or peers. The differential association theory explains that unethical behavior is learned by employees while observing and interacting with members of primary groups such as peers and managers. Employees either internalize the primary group's definition of unethical behavior through a socialization process, or adopt it through peer pressure, and act on that basis. The beliefs and values of referents often are better predictors of behavior than the employee's own individual beliefs. In addition, the opportunity for unethical behavior is a necessary condition for unethical behavior. In this regard "corporate policies are moderating variables in controlling opportunity."[18]

In conclusion, while the wider social environment, individual personality traits, and the nature of specific ethical issues are important to the ethics of employee decision-making, the corporation itself creates a social environment that can increase or decrease the likelihood of ethical decision-making.

---

[16] *Id.*

[17] Martin L. Hoffman, *Empathy, Its Limitations, and Its Role in a Comprehensive Moral Theory*, in MORALITY, MORAL BEHAVIOR, AND MORAL DEVELOPMENT 283, 297 (William M. Kurtines & Jacob L. Gerwirtz eds., 1984).

[18] O.C. Ferrell & Larry G. Gresham, *A Contingency Framework for Understanding Ethical Decision-Making in Marketing*, 49 J. MARKETING 87, 92 (1985).

III. ASCERTAINING CORPORATE CLIMATES AND THEIR EFFECT ON EMPLOYEE ETHICAL/UNETHICAL DECISION-MAKING

A. Methods of Ascertaining Ethical Climates

Ethical climates can be ascertained and studied. A number of methodologies exist for determining a corporation's ethical climate. Employee questionnaires are the most common. These questionnaires may focus on the main goals and values of the corporations, elicit information on the beliefs of top executives, supervisors, and peers, inquire about ethical and unethical behavior engaged in by employees or observed by them in the workplace (either generally or by specific categories), find out the employees' perceptions of whether their colleagues are ethical or unethical, and ascertain the corporation's commitment to, and support of, ethical behavior through questions about its policies, practices, and procedures.

B. Victor and Cullen's Ethical Climate Questionnaire

Bart Victor and John Cullen have developed a classification of ethical climates that has been widely used by academic researchers. They characterize corporate climates according to whether or not participants use egoism (instrumentalism), benevolence, or principle as the main ethical criterion. These decision criteria are defined in terms of whether the goals are "maximizing self-interest, maximizing joint interests [benevolence], or adherence to principle."[19] Most corporate climates have at least minimal degrees of caring and instrumentalism.

C. The Effect of Climates on Ethical/Unethical Decision-Making

A corporation's climate is important to decision-making by employees. One study, based on responses to projective vignettes, found that ethical climates measured by questions such as "what are the opinions of your colleagues concerning the ethicality of X," were positively related to ethical decision-making. Another study of twenty-two large mall department stores found that stores with well-defined codes of ethics and organizational values experienced less employee theft. In addition, a survey of employees from different companies found that an ethical compliance program that was values-driven resulted in lower observed instances of unethical conduct.

In terms of Victor and Cullen's climate classification system, Wimbush proposes that the instrumental (egoism) climate will foster unethical behavior. He explains:

> This is expected to occur because only in an ethical climate based on an egoistic decision-making criterion would people most likely act in ways to promote their own exclusive self-interest regardless of laws, rules, or the impact their decisions have on others. . . . The deleterious effect of the decision-maker's decisions on others could mean, for example, taking from

[19] Victor & Cullen, *supra* note 3, at 104.

> others what is rightfully theirs or intentionally not providing adequate or truthful information.[20]

These expectations are confirmed by Victor and Cullen's survey of employees in a number of corporations. They found that "[e]mployees were more satisfied with the ethics of their company when they observed greater levels of caring [benevolence]... and lower levels of instrumentalism [self-interest]."[21] Wimbush notes that without organizational policies encouraging ethical behavior the perception of workers may be that "anything goes as long as the organization's desired level of productivity is achieved."[22]

A recent study also used Victor and Cullen's classification system. It found that ethical climates have an important impact on an employee's perception of the nature of his or her relationship with the corporation that may, in turn, affect employee conduct. The study focused on "covenantal" relationships between employees and corporations, which are "based on mutual commitment to the welfare of the other party, as well as allegiance to a set of shared values, which may be expressed in the mission and objectives of the organization."[23] Covenantal relationships were contrasted with "transactional" employment relationships where the contract is based on an economic exchange in which the relationship "is limited to the offering of . . . skills and abilities that are instrumental to the outcomes sought by both parties."[24] The study found that employees' perception of the corporation's climate affects whether they believe they have a covenantal relationship with their corporation. Employees' perceptions of climates in which the ethical criterion was egoism were negatively associated with their beliefs in a covenantal relationship with the corporation. Benevolent and principle work climates were positively associated with the employee belief that a covenantal relationship existed. The covenantal relationship is deemed to encourage employees "to engage in proactive behaviors, such as organizational citizenship behaviors, that promote the long-run interest of the organization."[25]

IV. FACTORS RELEVANT TO ETHICAL CORPORATE CLIMATES

Factors relevant to an ethical climate include the corporation's mission statement and code of ethics, the criteria for business decisions, the words and actions of leaders, the handling of conflicts of interest, the reward system, the guidance provided to employees

---

[20] James C. Wimbush & Jon M. Shepard, *Toward an Understanding of Ethical Climate: Its Relationship to Ethical Behavior and Supervisory Influence*, 13 J. BUS. ETHICS 637, 641 (1994).

[21] Victor & Cullen, *supra* note 3, at 117.

[22] Wimbush & Shepard, *supra* note 21, at 641.

[23] Tim Barnett & Elizabeth Schubert, *Perceptions of the Ethical Work Climates and Covenantal Relationships*, 36 J. BUS. ETHICS 279, 287 (2002).

[24] *Id.* at 280.

[25] *Id.* at 287.

concerning dealing with ethical issues, and the monitoring system. The relevance of the reward system to an ethical climate is briefly discussed below.

The type of reward system that is used appears to affect the likelihood of ethical decision-making. Two systems are identified: outcome-based systems and behavior-based systems. In an outcome-based system, employees are evaluated only on the basis of the outcome of their efforts, such as sales volume or profits booked. In a behavior-based system, consideration is also given by supervisors to the methods or techniques used by employees to achieve the desired outcomes. In a study comparing these systems, behavior-based systems were found to be associated with more ethical decision-making and a more ethical corporate climate.

Whether the compensation system is perceived by employees to be fair also appears to contribute to an ethical climate within the corporation. Doeringer notes the importance of fair compensation to the employees' perceptions of the legitimacy and the morality of corporate authority. He writes that "[t]he importance placed on fairness is related less to the possibility that pay inequities will result in lower effort among disgruntled employees than to a larger concern with creating a set of corporate values that will be perceived as legitimate and moral by the work force."[26]

By placing unrealistic expectations on employees and threatening them with dire personal consequence for not meeting certain ends, management places its relationship with employees on a transactional basis grounded in egoism. They fail to provide a climate for the maintenance of a covenantal relationship in which there is a mutual commitment to the welfare of the other party and allegiance to a shared set of values consistent with social responsibility.

Reward systems can also become unfair and, therefore, increase the likelihood of unethical conduct by tending to politicize the compensation and promotion system. An example is ranking employees at various levels, with those at the bottom rank being first in line for firing. These systems tend to magnify employee insecurity and increase the amount of employee time devoted to currying favor with superiors. Other adverse consequences include decreasing the likelihood of employees communicating problems to supervisors, less accountability for superiors who are not challenged by their employees, and over-confidence on the part of the more powerful managers. Moreover, for those department heads who are successful in attracting and motivating good employees, an intra-departmental rating system risks losing lower-ranked employees to less successful departments where they will be ranked higher. The system is unfair for several reasons: it discourages teamwork, which is a necessary component of many corporate jobs; it punishes the more successful manager who is able to attract good employees and motivate them; it requires the ranking of employees who often make incommensurable contributions to the success of a company; and it politicizes the compensation process. When Enron, for example, adopted its "rank and yank" system, it was observed that

[26] Peter B. Doeringer, *The Socio-Economics of Labor Productivity*, in MORALITY, RATIONALITY, AND EFFICIENCY 108, 108-09 (Richard M. Coughlin ed., 1991).

the "most visible consequence was the large amount of time people spent at the local Starbucks, buttering up superiors and bad mouthing peers."[27]

V. ENRON'S CLIMATE

Without extensive surveys and interviews of Enron's employees, it is not possible to give a definitive account of Enron's climate. A review of journalist accounts of Enron, however, indicates that many factors were present that did not support and encourage an ethical climate.

The officers and employees of the company viewed laws and company rules as something to get around or change if the rules did not serve the company's purpose of making money. As one employee explained, "Our job was to take advantage of the law to make as much money as we can."[28]

The employees were expected to work around the laws and company rules to make money. The law and rules were viewed as hindering innovation, creativity, and the entrepreneurial spirit rather than being a necessary foundation for them. Former CEO Jeffrey Skilling encouraged disrespect of rules and company authority. Skilling "set employees loose, encouraging them to push the edge of every rule, even without their supervisors' knowledge."[29] A particularly egregious example is an Enron employee who used $30 million worth of company hardware and enlisted the help of 380 Enron employees to develop a trading system that Skilling, then CEO, was on record as opposing. The employee was not reprimanded because the trading system made money. Current and former employees state that by 2001, "Enron had become less a company than a collection of mercenaries. . . ."[30] An Enron trader claimed that "[t]here wasn't anything they wouldn't try to make money at."[31] The lack of adult restraint apparently spilled over into relations among employees at Enron's offices.

Enron supported and encouraged unethical/illegal behavior by maintaining a reward system that was highly political. The following is a description of how the system apparently worked. The company formed a twenty-person Personnel Review Committee ("PRC") to rank over 400 Enron vice presidents and a number of its other managers. There were substantial differences in bonuses among rankings and the possibility of firings for those with the lowest rankings. Every six months the PRC process would begin, requiring managers to obtain evaluations from supervisors, peers, and subordinates. The PRC could only rank by unanimous consent, which gave members of the PRC the incentive to lobby for favorable rankings for their employees. Andrew Fastow, Enron's chief financial officer ("CFO"), was willing to hold up the PRC for days to get what

---

27 James Lardner, *Why Should Anyone Believe You?*, Business 2.0, at 47 (Mar. 2002).

28 David Streitfeld & Lee Romney, *Enron's Run Tripped by Arrogance, Greed; Profile: A Lack of Discipline and A Drive to Bend the Rules Were Key Factors in the Meltdown*, L.A. Times, Jan. 27, 2002, at A1.

29 *Id.*

30 *Id.*

31 *Id.*

he wanted. The members who were not successful in negotiating for their employees would lose employees to other divisions and would often receive lower future evaluations themselves. One journalist noted that members developed "entourages" or "fiefdoms" of loyal employees who gravitated to them because of their ability to protect them in the PRC process.[32] As a result, the managers who emerged to run Enron's new businesses were not necessarily the most competent in those businesses, but they were the most competent in playing the game for power and recognition at Enron.

The system ensured that the powerful players would not be held accountable. Facing precarious futures but the possibility of huge bonuses, employees were fearful of criticizing powerful players. For example, members of the risk assessment group who reviewed the terms and conditions of deals were fearful of retaliation in the PRC from persons whose deals they were reviewing. Internal auditors at Enron may also have felt these pressures because some of them were placed under the authority of the separate business units they audited rather than under the jurisdiction of Enron's central internal auditing officer. In addition, those officers who dealt with the special purpose entities were required to negotiate, on behalf of Enron, with their bosses who had conflicts of interest with respect to these entities. Certain Enron officers, including CFO Fastow, were particularly feared by employees for their vicious retaliations. Enron's culture was described as "ruthless and reckless... that lavished rewards on those who played the game, while persecuting those who raised objections."[33] Employees reported that what resulted was a "yes-man" culture in which it became very important to be in the "in-group." As one former employee stated, "One day, you are viewed with favor, and the next day you are not. You know who is in the in-crowd and who is not.... You want to continue to be liked in that organization. You do everything you can do to keep that."[34] This system placed considerable power in top management. Some employees feared, for example, that "not giving enough to the chairman's favorite political candidate could send their careers into a dive."[35] An Enron former executive officer reported the effect of such an environment on CEO Skilling:

> Over the years, Jeff changed. He became more of a creature of his own creation. His hubris came to outweigh some of the more attractive parts of his personality. He became more intolerant, more opinionated, and more bombastic. Jeff was always right, and that got worse. He had a little bit of a God syndrome.[36]

Skilling's arrogance translated into an "institutional arrogance." Unthinking loyalty, homogeneity, and the rejection of outsiders characterized the system. Some employees

---

[32] Joshua Chaffin & Stephen Fidler, *Enron Revealed To Be Rotten to the Core*, FIN. TIMES (London), Apr. 9, 2002, at 30.

[33] *Id.*

[34] Joe Stephens & Peter Behr, *Enron's Culture Fed Its Demise*, WASH. POST, Jan. 27, 2002, at A01.

[35] *Id.*

[36] Evan Thomas et al., *Every Man for Himself*, NEWSWEEK, Feb. 18, 2002, at 26-27.

noted how "loyalty required a sort of groupthink" and that you had to "keep drinking the Enron water."[37] One aspect of the loyalty was that problems were "papered over."[38] A myth was perpetuated that "there were never any mistakes."[39] The culture was self-perpetuating. As one young employee in the risk assessment group, which was mainly staffed by inexperienced MBAs, noted:

> If your boss was fudging, and you have never worked anywhere else, you just assume that everybody fudges earnings. . . . Once you get there and you realized how it was, do you stand up and lose your job? It was scary. It was easy to get into "Well, everybody else is doing it, so maybe it isn't so bad."[40]

Enron's socialization process was referred to as "Enronizing," and people who did not fit in were referred to as "damaged goods" or "shipwrecks."[41]

The lack of accountability is also reflected in the failure of the reward system to consider the manner in which profits were booked. According to former employees, "[e]mployee commissions were tied to the projected profits on long-term deals, with little concern for how the transactions actually worked."[42] Former employees from all divisions reported that "their units routinely engaged in aggressive accounting and financial manipulation, designed to conceal losses and make their operations appear highly profitable."[43] Over-estimations of profits and under-estimations of costs were endemic to the organization. Top management exerted substantial pressure. In discussing Enron's derivative traders, Frank Partnoy, in his Congressional testimony, noted "Enron derivative traders faced intense pressure to meet quarterly earnings targets imposed directly by management and indirectly by securities analysts who covered Enron" and that these traders "apparently manipulated the reporting of their 'real' economic profits and losses in an attempt to fit the 'imagined' accounting profits and losses that drove Enron management."[44] Insiders called the company "The Crooked E," which was "a word-play on [the company's] slanted logo and business practices."[45]

The reward system, which ranked employees against each other and which offered substantial bonuses, also did not encourage team work or caring among employees. The system discouraged sharing of power, authority, or information. As one employee

---

[37] Stephens & Behr, *supra* note 35.

[38] Bethany McLean et al., *Why Enron Went Bust*, Fortune, Dec. 24, 2001, at 62.

[39] *Id.*

[40] John Byrne et al., *The Environment Was Ripe For Abuse*, Bus. Wk., Feb. 25, 2002, at 118.

[41] Johnnie L. Roberts et al., *Enron's Dirty Laundry*, Newsweek, Mar. 11, 2002, at 26.

[42] Chaffin & Fidler, *supra* note 32.

[43] *Id.*

[44] *Testimony of Frank Partnoy at the Senate Enron Hearings,* 21 Futures & Derivatives L. Rep. No. 11, Feb. 2002, at 10.

[45] Chaffin & Fidler, *supra* note 33.

stated, "People became proprietary about their deals. . . . Why should I help Johnny if I'm rated against Johnny?"[46] The system was "heavily built around star players."[47] A former employee reported that "I locked my desk every night so my colleagues wouldn't steal my work."[48] Enron traders were "afraid to go to the bathroom because the guy sitting next to them might use information off their screen to trade against them."[49]

Enron attracted individuals who wanted to make a lot of money fast. The competitive atmosphere was reflected in Skilling's personality which reportedly thrived "on one-upmanship and didn't mind trying to embarrass the less-quick-witted or anyone who challenged him."[50] Civility was apparently also not valued at Enron.

Enron had a code of ethics and company-stated values that were referred to as RICE, standing for Respect, Integrity, Communication, and Excellence. These values were not adopted after widespread company discussions; rather, they were personally selected by Kenneth Lay. The values were displayed on banners in the lobby of Enron's Houston headquarters and appeared on various items that were given as inspirational gifts to employees. Enron employees said, however, that Lay's interests were "limited to actions that boosted the company's bottom line—and ultimately its stock price."[51] Moreover, in terms of honesty and communication, Lay's statements to employees and the public prior to Enron's filing for bankruptcy on October 24, 2001, are problematic. On August 24, 2001, he stated, "The company is probably in the strongest and best shape it has ever been."[52] On September 26, 2001 he stated that Enron is "fundamentally sound," its third quarter is "looking great," and "we're well-positioned for a very strong fourth quarter."[53] And on October 16, 2001, Lay stated "Our 26% increase in [profits] shows the strong results of our core wholesale and retail energy businesses and our natural gas pipelines."[54]

In addition, although Enron had a code of ethics, an anonymous hotline, and required new employees to sign the code, the Enron board waived the conflicts of interest provision in its code of ethics regarding related party transactions with special purpose entities. Moreover, the board members themselves had conflicts of interest.

The climate of Enron came from the top and was probably a long time in the making. It is significant that on the day when internal Enron whistleblower, Sherron Watkins, met with Lay to discuss her allegations of accounting irregularities, Enron's outside law firm delivered a memo to Enron on the "possible risks associated with discharging (or

---

[46] Streitfeld & Romney, *supra* note 29.

[47] Byrne et al., *supra* note 41.

[48] Streitfeld & Romney, *supra* note 29.

[49] McLean, *supra* note 39, at 61-62.

[50] Roberts et al., *supra* note 42, at 25.

[51] Chaffin & Fidler, *supra* note 33.

[52] Lardner, *supra* note 28, at 46.

[53] Rushworth M. Kidder, *Ethics at Enron*, Institute for Global Ethics, ETHICS ONLINE, Jan. 21, 2002, *available at* http://www/rider.edu/planc/coursed/us.pol/Enron?ethics.htm (last visited Sept. 13, 2002).

[54] Lardner, *supra* note 28, at 46.

constructively discharging) employees who report allegations of improper accounting practices."[55]

After Enron's problems had become public and just before it filed for bankruptcy, Lay knew what to do. In September 2001, Lay sent out an employee survey, which, in comparing the corporation to the way it had been a year before, found that forty-two percent of Enron employees viewed the company as more self-serving, thirty-seven percent as less trustworthy, and thirty-nine percent as more arrogant. He wrote to employees: "Enron's values will have more importance in each employee's evaluation and feedback. . . . We are all responsible for how we treat our coworkers and customers."[56] It was, however, too little, too late.

The Enron climate did not encourage and support ethical behavior. At most, Enron adopted a compliance-based approach. It clearly did not adopt a values-based approach that would have encouraged employees to follow not only the letter, but also the intent, of laws. Enron also did not encourage compliance with its own rules, which supported an attitude that made it much more likely that employees would not only break company rules, but the law as well.

Although concern with quarterly earnings is an aspect of the current business environment that seeks to enhance shareholder value, Enron's culture was focused not so much on shareholder well-being, or on the well-being of other stakeholders, but on individual self-interest. Every six months, the entire organization geared up for performance reviews and consideration of bonuses. The PRC process affected decision-making throughout the organization at other times. The emphasis on individual bonuses detracted from concern for the impact of business decision-making on Enron's stakeholders. This individual self-interested climate created a situation where monitoring was extremely important. But because of the cavalier attitude towards rules modeled by top management, and, at most, a compliance-based approach to laws and rules, the likelihood of effective monitoring at Enron was substantially reduced.

Enron's top management conveyed the impression that all that mattered was for employees to book profits. Although nothing is wrong with a profit objective, Enron placed this objective above all others. Moreover, the focus was on "paper," and not real profits. Aggressive accounting was encouraged and condoned. Unfortunately, this was also encouraged by the broader business environment in which Enron operated. In addition, Enron placed unreasonable pressures on its employees to book profits, possibly to increase the value of top management's stock options. This exclusive focus on profits and these pressures increased the likelihood of illegal/unethical conduct at Enron.

Enron further eroded the likelihood of ethical behavior by failing to make employees responsible for their decisions. Their responsibility was to "do the deal." Once the deal was closed, employees were rewarded without consideration of how the deal would work out in practice. The emphasis was on appearances and not on real performance. Moreover, the reward structure encouraged the pervasive "fudging" of accounting

---

[55] Peter Behr & Susan Schmidt, *Enron CEO Knew of Deals' Risk*, WASH. POST, Feb 20, 2002, at A1.

[56] Streitfeld & Romney, *supra* note 29.

numbers throughout the organization. The ranking system increased the emphasis on individual self-interest and diminished teamwork (or a caring environment) among coworkers and the expression of empathy. The size of the bonuses also contributed to accounting transgressions and added to the viciousness of retaliations, which diminished open discussions of problems and accountability within the organization.

The ranking system and the PRC unanimity rule also increased the political nature of the system that created an unfair compensation system. Considerable power was placed in top management. Moreover, the system placed power in the hands of individuals who were willing to devote the necessary energies to office politics and political maneuvering. The net effect of such a system was to decrease the likelihood that employees would raise objections to the unethical/illegal conduct of powerful players because power, not real performance, was the driving force of the organization.

Enron socialized new employees to go along with the unethical/illegal behavior of their supervisors. The conduct was pervasive. With so many inexperienced employees, these employees understandably came to believe that ethics has nothing to do with business.

Although Enron had a code of ethics, which is a factor in an ethical climate, Enron's board of directors waived compliance with it on a number of occasions to permit conflicts of interest transactions by Enron's CFO. The lack of concern for conflicts of interest was also evident in the reward system for members of the risk management group and the association of Enron's internal auditors with business units. Additionally, a number of Enron's directors who waived the conflicts of interest rules also had conflicts of interests.

Enron has been described as having an arrogant climate. Such a climate is prone to greater homogeneity because differing views are not valued. This homogeneity can exaggerate the impact of various decision-making biases. Groups that are homogeneous experience group polarization that can result in more risk-adverse behavior or riskier decisions. At Enron, risky decisions were the norm and high risk was encouraged and supported by the lack of contrary views being expressed. To the extent that unethical/illegal activity is considered risky, such a climate can enhance the probability of unethical/illegal behavior. Moreover, this type of climate is likely to exaggerate the egocentric bias that "refers to the tendency for individuals to assume that others are more like them than is actually the case."[57] As a result, Enron's top management and its traders did not take account of the risk preferences of its shareholders, employees, and consumers. In addition, once Enron managers perceived Enron to be at risk, according to prospect theory, they were likely to adopt more risky strategies as they perceived themselves to be choosing between options that represented losses. Also, corporations with arrogant climates are likely to have less accountable employees due to the confirmation bias, which is the "tendency of group members to seek information that confirms their ini-

---

[57] Lynne L. Dallas, *The New Managerialsim and Diversity on Corporate Boards of Directors*, 76 TULANE L. REV. 1363, 1402 (2002).

tial opinions."[58] Moreover, homogeneous groups are more likely than heterogeneous groups to rely on shared information, that is, information that they have in common. These tendencies adversely affect information-seeking processes and are likely to result in inadvisable decision-making.

VI. FINAL ANALYSIS AND RECOMMENDATIONS

Ethics and ethical compliance systems require consideration of (a) organizational values, (b) the nature of organizational decision-making, (c) the values and behavior of the organization's leaders, (d) the organization's reward system, (e) the handling of conflicts of interest, (f) the availability of ethical guidance for employees, and (g) the organization's monitoring system. These factors are relevant to the promotion of an ethical climate.

Concerning organizational values, the organization must highly value ethics and ethical behavior. Ethics must be as important as, if not more important than, profits. The organization must value business decisions that take into consideration their consequences to organizational stakeholders. Finally, the organization must take a values-based rather than a compliance-based approach to ethical compliance, which means that the organization places importance not only on compliance with the law and company rules, but also compliance with their intent.

The nature of decision-making within the organization is also relevant to the promotion of an ethical climate. In an ethical climate ethical standards influence decision-making. Business standards are taken into account in day-to-day decision-making by all employees, and business issues are framed in ethical terms. Employees are encouraged to consider the consequences of their decisions on stakeholders and to assume responsibility for those consequences. Employees understand that their role is to consider ethical standards and the consequences of their business decisions on corporate stakeholders. Employees recognize that business decisions are based on compliance with the intent as well as the letter of the law and organizational policies.

The values and behavior of leaders are also relevant to the promotion of an ethical climate. In an ethical climate, leaders view their ethical responsibilities as being as important as, if not more important than, their other organizational responsibilities. Leaders model ethical behavior. For example, ethical leaders are truthful with the organization's stakeholders. They promote communications among employees throughout the organization of information and concerns, both good and bad. They are consistent in words and in actions in encouraging and supporting ethical behavior and discouraging unethical behavior within the organization. In this regard, they do not place on employees unreasonable expectations that may increase the likelihood of unethical/illegal conduct within the organization.

With respect to conflicts of interest, the organization enhances its ethical climate by determining organizational structure, appointments, and benefits with attention

[58] *Id.*

to actual or potential conflicts of interest. The organization must have policies that prohibit directors, officers, and employees from taking actions or having interests that make it difficult for them to act in the best interest of the organization.

The organization's reward structure promotes an ethical climate when employee compensation and promotion decisions take into account compliance with ethical standards. Ethical behavior is rewarded and unethical behavior punished. The reward structure also promotes an ethical climate when it provides a behavior-based system that not only considers employee outcomes (production) but also the manner in which those outcomes are achieved. The reward structure must also be perceived as fair by employees. It must not provide the prime motivation for employees and must not detract from the employee's attention to the real business of the organization. In addition, the compensation of leaders must include an assessment of the ethical/unethical behavior of the units that they oversee. Finally, employee compensation must not reflect retaliation for the good faith reporting of violations of ethical standards to appropriate persons within the organization.

In terms of the availability of ethical guidance to employees, the organization increases the likelihood of having an ethical climate when it adopts a code of ethics that provides guidance to employees in their decision-making. The code is most effective when it contains guidance for common ethical dilemmas faced by employees and when it is distributed to all employees, including managers and lower-level employees. The corporation increases the likelihood of having an ethical climate when it encourages and supports open discussions of ethics and ethical compliance among employees. Moreover, employees must know from whom to seek guidance within the organization concerning ethically ambiguous situations and must be encouraged to do so. The organization must emphasize training for employees, for both top managers and low-level employees, which programs are most effective when they provide opportunities for employee discussions and role playing, deal with business ethical dilemmas relevant to the employees involved, and make employees self-aware of factors leading to unethical/illegal decision-making.

As for the organization's monitoring system, an organization supports an ethical climate by having a person with high status and authority within the organization who has primary responsibility for gathering information, monitoring, and reporting on ethics and ethical compliance within the organization. This individual would also be responsible for recommending any changes in the corporation's policies and practices as they relate to ethics and ethical compliance.

An ethical climate is also supported by having the organization's board of directors, or a board committee, periodically review reports on ethics and ethical compliance within the organization, and having the board or its committee discuss and make decisions, when necessary, concerning organizational personnel, policies and practices relating to ethics and ethical compliance.

In addition, the organization enhances the likelihood of an ethical climate when it periodically makes self-assessment of its values, ethical climate, and ethical compliance record. This would involve conducting employee surveys that apply to the organization as a whole and separate surveys of employees in subunits, different job classifications, and hierarchical levels. These employee surveys would cover perceptions of organizational values, the nature of organizational decision-making, the values and behavior of leaders, conflicts of interest, reward structure, employee guidance, and monitoring and assessing the nature and extent of violations of ethical standards. In addition to employee surveys, the organization might conduct exit interviews and employee focus groups to assess ethics and ethical compliance and would periodically interview and survey organizational stakeholders.

The organization would also provide a method for employees to report anonymously violations of the code. It would require employees to periodically acknowledge their understanding and compliance with the organization's code of ethics. In addition, the organization's leaders would periodically certify that:

a. Ethical behavior is highly valued in the organization and is as important as, if not more important than, profit-seeking behavior;
b. The organization's climate encourages and supports ethical decision-making by employees;
c. Employees know that their decisions should comply with the intent as well as the letter of the law and company policies;
d. Ethical decision-making is rewarded, and unethical decision-making punished; and
e. A reasonably system is in place to review, monitor and if necessary, modify the corporation's climate.

Finally, the organization, when deemed advisable, would seek outside audits and advice on the organization's ethics and ethical compliance.

Based on these recommendations, the law does not go far enough in ensuring that corporations have ethical climates. It focuses almost exclusively on the adoption of a code of ethics by corporations and the disclosure of any waiver of the code. In the wake of Enron, Congress passed the Sarbanes-Oxley Act of 2002.[59] The Sarbanes-Oxley Act directed the Securities and Exchange Commission ("SEC") to promulgate rules and regulations that require public corporations to disclose whether or not they have a code of ethics for senior financial officers and, if they do not, to disclose the reasons why they do not have such a code. The Act also requires the SEC to promulgate rules that provide for prompt disclosure of any waivers of code standards. The Act defines codes of ethics to include "standards [that] are reasonably necessary to promote . . . honest and ethical conduct."[60]

In addition, the SEC in 2003 adopted rules required by the Sarbanes-Oxley Act that provide that reporting companies adopt a code of ethics and disclose any waivers (explicit or implicit) of the code. Consistent with the Sarbanes-Oxley Act, the SEC

---

[59] Pub. L. No. 107-204, § 406, 116 stat. 745, 789-790 (to be codified at 15 U.S.C. § 7265).

[60] *Id.*

requires the code of ethics to provide for "(1) Honest and ethical conduct, including the ethical handling of actual or apparent conflicts of interest between personal and professional relationships; (2) Full, fair, accurate, timely, and understandable disclosure in reports and documents that a registrant files with . . . the Commission and in other public communications . . . ; [and] (3) Compliance with applicable governmental laws, rules and regulations."[61]

Similarly, the New York Stock Exchange ("NYSE") has proposed to the SEC rules that require companies listed on the NYSE to adopt a code of ethics and disclose any waiver of the code.[62] The NYSE proposed rules require the code of ethics to cover a number of topics, namely, conflicts of interest, corporate opportunities, confidentiality, fair dealing, protection and proper use of company assets, and compliance with laws, rules, and regulations.

A limitation of the Sarbanes-Oxley Act is that it requires the code of ethics to cover only senior financial officers. The Act does not require the code of ethics to apply to directors, other senior executive officers, or lower-level employees of the corporation. The SEC, in its rules applicable to reporting companies, has expanded this coverage to include the corporation's chief executive officer. The NYSE, in its proposed rules, has gone further, however, in requiring listed companies to have a code of ethics that applies to directors, officers, and lower-level employees.

While having a code of conduct is likely to contribute to ethical behavior within an organization, it is the least effective means of decreasing the likelihood of unethical conduct when it is compared to the following: organizational consistency between ethical policies and actions, rewarding ethical behavior and punishing unethical behavior, ethical executive leadership, and open discussions of ethics within the organization. To some extent provisions included within a code of ethics that relate to compliance with the code goes some of the way in assuring that there is consistency between the organization's ethical policies and actions, some connection between rewards and unethical/ethical behavior, ethical behavior by executives, and an open discussion of ethics in the organization. The SEC rules, for example, require the code to provide for "prompt internal reporting of violations of the code to an appropriate person or persons identified in the code" and "accountability for adherence to the code."[63] The NYSE rules provide that corporations must proactively encourage ethical behavior by encouraging employees to report illegal or unethical behavior and consult with appropriate personnel about the best course of action when in doubt. The company must also ensure that "employees know that the company will not allow retaliation for reports made in good

---

[61] Disclosure Required By Sections 406 and 407 of the Sarbanes-Oxley Act of 2002, SEC Release No. 33-8177 (Jan. 23, 2003).

[62] NYSE Corporate Accountability and Listing Standards Committee, Recommendations Submitted for SEC Approval (2002); Self Regulatory Organizations; Notice of Filing of Proposed Rule Change and Amendment Nol. 1 Thereto by the New York Stock Exchange, Inc. Relating to Corporate Governance, SEC Release 34-47672 (April 11, 2003).

[63] Disclosure Required By Sections 406 and 407 of the Sarbanes-Oxley Act of 2002, SEC Release No. 33-8177 (Jan. 23, 2003).

faith."[64] These compliance provisions, however, do not explicitly address organizational consistency, reward systems, ethical leadership by executives, and an open discussion of ethics throughout the organization. Moreover, no mention is made of the use of employee questionnaires or surveys to ascertain corporate climate, and there is no provision for leader certification of important ethical climate measures. There are also no guidelines that state that employees should consider the consequences of their decision on stakeholders, that the employee reward system should be fair, or that feedback on organizational conduct should be obtained from organizational stakeholders.[65]

Finally, the Sarbanes-Oxley Act also directed the U.S. Sentencing Commission to reevaluate its sentencing guidelines as applied to organizations. It has solicited comments regarding whether the U.S. Sentencing Guidelines should encourage organizations to foster ethical cultures to ensure more than technical compliance which "can potentially circumvent the purpose of the law or regulation."[66] Ethicists would answer this in the affirmative. They stress the importance to organizational ethics of a values-based approach to compliance where the intent as well as the letter of the law is important. A climate that supports and encourages technical compliance alone will likely increase the probability of illegal conduct within the organization. The Commission has also sought public comments regarding what an "effective program to prevent and detect violations of law" should consist of. The Guidelines should provide that:

> The organization must periodically assess its employees' perceptions of organizational values, the nature of organizational decision-making, the values and behavior of leaders, the reward system, and employee guidance and monitoring systems in encouraging and supporting compliance with the letter and intent of laws and company policies.

Moreover, the Commission should add the following bracketed language to its Guidelines on appropriate organizational conduct:

> The organization must have taken reasonable steps to achieve compliance with its standards:
>
> [a] By utilizing monitoring and auditing systems reasonably designed to detect [and decrease the likelihood of violations of law and company policies] by its employees and other agents;

---

[64] NYSE Corporate Accountability and Listing Standards Committee, *Recommendations Submitted for SEC Approval* (2002).

[65] The only reference to fairness is that which is legally problematic. The NYSE rules state that "[e]ach employee would endeavor to deal fairly with the company's customers, suppliers, competitors and employees." Unfairness consists of taking advantage through "manipulation, concealment, abuse of privileged information, misrepresentation of material facts, or any other unfair dealing practice."

[66] Advisory Group on Organizational Guidelines to the United States Sentencing Commission, REQUEST FOR ADDITIONAL PUBLIC COMMENT REGARDING THE U.S. SENTENCING GUIDELINES FOR ORGANIZATIONS (2002).

[b] [By making a periodic self-assessment of its ethical climate];

[c] By having in place and publicizing a reporting system whereby employees and other agents could report [to an independent ombudsman] [violations of law and company policies] by others within the organization without fear of retribution;

[d] [By requiring employees to periodically acknowledge their understanding and compliance with the organization's code of ethics; and]

[e] [By having the corporate CEO and CFO certify, to their knowledge and after reasonable inquiry, that:

(1) Ethical behavior is as highly valued in the organization and is as important as, if not more important than, profit-seeking behavior; (2) the organization's climate encourages and supports ethical decision-making by employees; (3) employees know that their decisions should comply with the intent as well as the letter of the law and company policies; (4) ethical decision-making is rewarded, and unethical decision-making punished, within the organization; and (5) a reasonable system is in place to review, monitor, and if necessary, modify the corporation's ethical climate.]

VII. CONCLUSION

This paper has shown that corporate climates influence ethical/unethical decision-making by employees. In addition, ethical climates are ascertainable and there is considerable agreement about many of the factors that create and support ethical climates.

It is clear that, given Enron's climate, it was only a matter of time before Enron would have imploded. Thus, Congress and other regulatory organizations are justifiably directing their attention to codes of ethics and ethical climates. This paper has argued, however, that to assure legal and ethical decision-making, a corporation has to do more than merely adopt a code of ethics and disclose any waiver of it.

Giving attention to ethical climates will contribute to organizational compliance programs by eliciting employees' perceptions of ethics and ethical compliance within the organization. This inquiry adds an additional dimension to legal compliance programs. By focusing on ethical climates, the organization can take steps to decrease the likelihood of unethical/illegal decision-making that, as the demise of Enron and other corporations amply demonstrates, has devastating consequences for employees, shareholders, creditors, and the economy as a whole.

Everything I Needed to Know About Enron I Learned in Kindergarten (and Graduate School)

George W. Kuney[*]

INTRODUCTION

Something went wrong at Enron. Whether phrased in terms of a failure of gatekeepers[1] or an aggressive culture of greed based upon bending the rules,[2] the root causes of the problems at Enron were social in nature. And, if the restatement of financial statements at a variety of other companies[3] and other similar business collapses and restructurings that followed[4] are indicators, these problems probably were not and are not isolated in the remains of the fallen energy-trading giant.

[*] George W. Kuney is an Associate Professor of Law and the Director of the Clayton Center for Entrepreneurial Law at the University of Tennessee College of Law. He holds a J.D. from the University of California's Hastings College of the Law and an M.B.A. from The University of San Diego. Prior to joining the faculty of the University of Tennessee, he was a partner in a large West Coast law firm where his practice focused on business, restructuring, and insolvency. He thanks Matthew Stearns for his factual research regarding Enron, Gena Lewis for her legal research and development of the notes and problems that conclude this piece, and German translation, and Donna C. Looper for insightful analysis and editorial assistance in the preparation of this article. All statements in this article are statements of opinion based upon the facts and opinions as reported or stated in the works of others, as cited. *Editors' note:* This essay was included in the first edition of this book. Reprinted by permission.

[1] *See, e.g.,* John C. Coffee, Jr., *Understanding Enron: "It's About the Gatekeepers, Stupid,"* 57 Bus. Law. 1405, 1405 (2002) ("Properly understood, Enron is a demonstration of gatekeeper failure, and the question it most sharply poses is how this failure should be rectified.").

[2] *See, e.g.,* Anita Raghavan, Kathryn Kranhold & Alexei Barrionuevo, *Full Speed Ahead: How Enron Bosses Created a Culture of Pushing Limits,* Wall St. J., Aug. 26, 2002, at A1 ("When Enron Corp. was riding high, Chief Financial Officer Andrew Fastow had a Lucite cube on his desk supposedly laying out the company's values. One of these was communication, and the cube's inscription explained what that meant: When Enron says it's going to 'rip your face off,' it said, it will 'rip your face off.' It was a characteristic gesture inside Enron, where the prevailing corporate culture was to push everything to the limits: business practices, laws and personal behavior.").

[3] *See* Huron Consulting Group, *An Analysis of Restatement Matters: Rules, Errors, Ethics, For the Five Years Ended December 31, 2002* (2002), *available at* http://www.huronconsultinggroup.com/uploadedFiles/Huron_RestatementStudy2002.pdf (last visited June 2, 2003).

[4] For example, *see* Neil H. Aronson, *Symposium: Enron: Lessons and Implications: Preventing Future Enrons: Implementing the Sarbanes-Oxley Act of 2002,* 8 Stan. J. L. Bus. & Fin. 127 (2002).

In response to Enron's collapse, there has been an outpouring of sentiment—from the press, the public, and Congress—in support of change. The passage and implementation of the Sarbanes-Oxley Act[5] and other developments will continue to provide an opportunity for a major cultural change in corporate governance.

This essay briefly reviews the facts underlying the Enron debacle.[6] It then describes some of the lessons that can be learned from this chain of events. Reasonable minds can differ on these lessons, but all of the lessons should be borne in mind by the players in corporate America and those who advise them. Drastic revisions of accounting and legal rules and standards are probably not necessary in order to prevent "another Enron"—strictly hewing to existing standards is sufficient. The rules did not fail at Enron; those who were supposed to follow and enforce them failed.

A BRIEF REVIEW OF THE FACTS

Enron was a public company whose shares traded on the New York Stock Exchange ("NYSE"). At its peak stock price of just over $90 a share, Enron was the seventh largest United States corporation in terms of market capitalization.[7] Since Enron's stock was publicly traded, the company was regulated by the Securities and Exchange Commission ("SEC").[8] Enron's officers and directors had a fiduciary duty to the company's investors

---

[5] *See* Sarbanes-Oxley Act of 2002, PL 107-204, 116 Stat. 745 (HR 3763, July 30, 2002) [hereinafter Sarbanes-Oxley].

[6] All factual statements in this article are based upon reports of others and allegations contained in government indictments. *See, e.g.,* PERMANENT SUBCOMMITTEE ON INVESTIGATIONS, COMMITTEE ON GOVERNMENTAL AFFAIRS, THE ROLE OF THE BOARD OF DIRECTORS IN ENRON'S COLLAPSE, S. REP. NO. 107-70 (2002) [hereinafter Report on Board of Directors], *available at* http://news.findlaw.com/hdocs/docs/enron/senpsi70802rpt.pdf (last visited June 2, 2003); NEAL BATSON, THE SECOND INTERIM REPORT OF NEAL BATSON (2003) [hereinafter Batson Report], *available at* 2003 extra lexis 4; WILLIAM C. POWERS, RAYMOND S. TROUBH, HERBERT S. WINOKUR, REPORT OF INVESTIGATION BY THE SPECIAL INVESTIGATIVE COMMITTEE OF THE BOARD OF DIRECTORS OF ENRON CORP. (2002) [hereinafter Powers Report], *available at* http://www.chron.com/content/news/photos/02/02/03/enron-powers report.pdf (last visited June 2, 2003). To the extent that these facts are proven or construed to be otherwise, the author does not dispute those conclusions or contentions. The lessons and opinions stated in this essay are based upon the alleged facts as stated, and if those alleged facts are incorrect, the lessons and conclusions drawn from those alleged facts may need to be adjusted accordingly.

[7] *See* Report on Board of Directors, *supra* note 6 ("At the time of Enron's collapse in December 2001, Enron Corporation was listed as the seventh largest company in the United States, with over 100 billion in gross revenues and more than 20,000 employees worldwide."); *see also* Batson Report, *supra* note 6 ("Until the fall of 2001, Enron was one of the largest companies in the world.").

[8] *See* Batson Report, *supra* note 6, at 54 ("A public company like Enron, in addition to complying with the literal GAAP rules and publishing financial statements that fairly present its financial position, results of operations and cash flows in accordance with GAAP, must also comply with the federal securities laws mandating disclosure."); *see also* Report on Board of Directors, *supra* note 6, at 11 ("Steady revelations since October 2001 have raised questions about numerous aspects of the company's operations from its extensive undisclosed off-the-books dealings... to an April 2002 SEC filing announcing that the

and potential investors to, among other things, record and disclose accurate financial numbers to the investing public in accordance with SEC regulations.[9]

A host of parties in interest, from government prosecutors[10] to Enron's Bankruptcy Examiner, Neal Batson,[11] have alleged that Andrew Fastow, other officers, Arthur Andersen ("Andersen") accountants, and various lawyers devised schemes to defraud the investing public with the ultimate goals of: (1) making Enron appear more financially successful than it actually was, (2) artificially inflating Enron's stock price, (3) avoiding government regulations both to gain undeserved benefits and to avoid legally proper costs, and (4) obtaining personal enrichment. Further, the government claims that Enron's officers attempted to achieve these goals by: (1) engaging in fraudulent transactions involving special purpose entities ("SPEs"), (2) filing false and misleading financial statements with the SEC, (3) making false statements concerning the health of Enron's underlying business model, and (4) exercising control over both the main company and the "independent" SPEs for personal benefit.[12]

In essence, much of the alleged fraud revolves around the creation and management of "off balance sheet" partnerships (Chewco, LMJ1, LMJ2, et al.).[13] Enron allegedly used these SPE partnerships to (1) inflate revenues via sham "left-hand to right-hand"

---

company's financial statements were unreliable and the book value of its assets would have to be written down as much as 24 billion....").

[9] *See* Report on Board of Directors, *supra* note 6, at 5 ("Among the most important of Board duties is the responsibility the Board shares with the company's management and auditors to ensure that the financial statements provided by the company to its shareholders and the investing public fairly present the financial condition of the company. This responsibility requires more than ensuring the company's technical compliance with generally accepted accounting principles.").

[10] Government prosecutors most recently have handed down indictments against eight former Enron executives, including Andrew Fastow's wife. These indictments also include new charges against Fastow himself. *See* Mary Flood et al., *The Fall of Enron: Fastow's Wife, 6 Others Surrender to Federal Authorities: Charges grow for ex-Enron execs,* Hous. Chron., May 2, 2003, at A1 ("Enron prosecutors took a big step forward Thursday by winning indictments against eight more former executives on scores of criminal counts, adding more counts against former Chief Financial Officer Andrew Fastow. One of the eight charged was Fastow's wife, Lea.").

[11] For example, *see* Batson Report, *supra* note 6, at 56 ("The Examiner has found that Enron used SPEs to engineer its financial statements so that they diverged materially from Enron's actual economic condition and performance.")

[12] *See* Report on Board of Directors, *supra* note 6, at 3 (alleging the following failures on the part of Enron's Board of Directors: fiduciary failure, high-risk accounting, inappropriate conflicts of interest, extensive undisclosed off-the-books activity, excessive compensation, and lack of independence).

[13] *See* Eric Berger, Mary Flood & Tom Fowler, *The Fall of Enron: Report Details Enron's Deception: Examiner Cites Auditors, Lawyers, and Banks as Part of Scheme,* Hous. Chron., March 6, 2003, at B1 ("It is against federal criminal law for executives to knowingly make false material representations about the company's financial condition to the public. The examiner [Neal Batson] several times specifically states Enron broke Securities and Exchange Commission rules, and in the case of special purpose vehicle and prepay transactions, materially misrepresented its financial condition. 'I think the fact he used the word 'materially' is important. It expresses his belief that there is a substantive violation of the criminal law,' said Jacob Frenkel, a former federal prosecutor and SEC lawyer in Washington D.C.").

transactions and (2) conceal debt.[14] This combination allowed the firm to state fictitiously high earnings.[15] In theory, the liabilities of these SPEs can be left off of the company's consolidated balance sheet if outside investors own 3% or more of the SPE's equity and have the power to control the disposition of the asset in the SPE.[16] Enron allegedly achieved this necessary equity investment both by (1) creating sham entities to provide the capital, and (2) issuing "equity," to outside investors, that closely resembled the intrinsic characteristics of a debt instrument.[17] Additionally, the officers are accused of making false and misleading statements concerning the SPEs and Andersen's accounting procedures to the board, the SEC, and securities analysts.[18]

For example, in 1993, Enron and the California Public Employee Retirements System ("CalPERS") formed a $500M joint venture, JEDI, to make energy investments.

---

[14] *See* Batson Report, *supra* note 6, at 15 ("Two factors drove Enron's management of its financial statements: (i) its need for cash and (ii) its need to maintain an investment grade credit rating. Enron was reluctant to issue equity to address these needs for fear of an adverse effect on its stock price and was reluctant to incur debt because of possible adverse effects on its credit ratings.").

[15] For example, Neal Batson, the examiner appointed by the Bankruptcy Court to investigate Enron's prepetition activities, describes how Enron, through the use of SPEs and aggressive accounting practices, so engineered its reported financial position and results of operations that its financial statements bore little resemblance to its actual financial condition or performance. *See* Batson Report, *supra* note 6, at 15.

[16] *See* William W. Bratton, *Enron and the Dark Side of Shareholder Value,* 76 TUL. L. REV. 1275, 1306-07 (2002) ("There is also a critical SEC rule—three percent of the SPE's total capital must come from an outside equity investor who must in addition have the power to control the disposition of the asset in the SPE. This means that the outside equity holder must hold at least a majority of the SPE's equity. In addition, the outside equity holder's capital must be *at risk*—the originator can't guarantee the investment's results. Finally, a legal determination as to the bankruptcy remote status of the SPE from the transferor also must be made."); *see also* Powers Report, *supra* note 6, at 39 ("The SEC staff has taken the position that 3% of total capital is the *minimum* acceptable investment for the substantive residual capital, but that the appropriate level for any particular SPE depends on various facts and circumstances.").

[17] *See* Bratton, *supra* note 16, at 1307 ("Enron used Fastow's limited partnerships as a means to stay in compliance with the SPE rules. Fastow's entities served as the outside equity investor—the source of the qualifying three percent—for SPEs, which served no economic purpose other than to pump up Enron's accounting earnings.").

[18] *See* Batson Report, *supra* note 6, at 15 ("The Examiner has concluded that, through pervasive use of structured financing techniques involving SPEs and aggressive accounting practices, Enron so engineered its reported financial position and results of operations that its financial statements bore little resemblance to its actual financial condition or performance. This financial engineering in many cases violated GAAP and applicable disclosure laws, and resulted in financial statements that did not fairly present Enron's financial condition, results of operations or cash flows."); *see also* Report on Board of Directors, *supra* note 8, at 3 ("The Enron Board failed to safeguard Enron shareholders and contributed to the collapse of the seventh largest public company in the United States, by allowing Enron to engage in high-risk accounting, inappropriate conflict of interest transactions, excessive undisclosed off-the-books activities, and excessive executive compensation. The Board witnessed numerous indications of questionable practices by Enron management over several years, but chose to ignore them to the detriment of Enron shareholders, employees and business associates.... The Enron Board of Directors knowingly allowed Enron to conduct billions of dollars in off-the-books activity to make its financial condition appear better than it was and failed to ensure adequate public disclosure of material off-the-books liabilities that contributed to Enron's collapse."); *see also* Powers Report, *supra* note 17, at 41 ("The participation of an Enron employee as a principal of Chewco appears to have been accomplished without any presentation to, or approval by, Enron's Board of Directors").

CalPERS owned 50% of the JEDI equity, thus allowing Enron to treat JEDI as a *bona fide* SPE.[19] However, in 1997, as part of its investment into JEDI II, CalPERS decided to liquidate its JEDI investment, and Fastow apparently proposed the creation of a new SPE, Chewco, to buy CalPERS's stake for $383M.[20] However, Chewco was basically an Enron-controlled entity, which would violate the "spirit" of the rule requiring a 3% *outside* equity investment and outside control over deposition of the assets involved.[21]

Enron's primary accounting and auditing firm, Andersen, aided in the creation and management of these SPEs.[22] Further, Andersen's Houston office was accused of shredding potentially damning documents relating to the developing Enron scandal in fall 2001.[23] Obstruction of justice charges followed, and Andersen weathered the trial in poor shape. After its conviction, Andersen notified the SEC that it would cease to audit public companies,[24] and consequently shut down its audit practice.[25] Now run by Brian

---

[19] Batson Report, *supra* note 6, at 15.

[20] *See* Powers Report, *supra* note 6, at 43-44 ("In 1997 Enron considered forming a $1 billion dollar partnership with CalPERS called 'JEDI II'. Enron believed that CalPERS would not invest simultaneously in both JEDI and JEDI II, so Enron suggested it buy out CalPERS's interest in JEDI. Enron and CalPERS attempted to value CalPERS's interest (CalPERS retained an investment bank) and discussed an appropriate buy-out price. In order to maintain JEDI as an unconsolidated entity, Enron needed to identify a new limited partner. Fastow initially proposed that he act as the manager of, and an investor in, a new entity called 'Chewco Investments'—named after the Star Wars character 'Chewbacca.' . . . Enron ultimately reached an agreement with CalPERS to redeem its JEDI limited partnership interest for $383 million. In order to close that transaction promptly, Chewco was formed as a Delaware limited liability company on very short notice in early November 1997.").

[21] *See* Powers Report, *supra* note 6, at 41-42 ("Enron Management and Chewco's general partner could not locate third parties willing to invest in the entity. Instead, they created a financing structure for Chewco that—on its face—fell at least $6.6 million (or more than 50%) short of the required third party equity. Despite this shortfall, Enron accounted for Chewco as if it were an unconsolidated SPE from 1997 through March 2001.").

[22] For example, *see* Batson Report, *supra* note 6, at 39 ("Enron carefully designed its FAS 140 technique with advice from Andersen and Enron's lawyers, with the goal that the asset transfer would qualify for sale treatment under GAAP despite the fact that sale treatment did not reflect the economic substance of the transaction. In fact, Andersen discussed the basic template for the FAS 140 technique with SEC staff accountants in 1999, who indicated that non-consolidation of the SPE and sale treatment were consistent with existing GAAP. The Examiner concluded in the September Report, however, that Enron's failure to disclose the nature of its obligations to repay principal and interest under the debt associated with the transactions was not in compliance with GAAP.").

[23] *See* C. William Thomas, *The Rise and Fall of Enron*, 4/1/02 J. ACCT. 41 (2002), *available at* http://www.aicpa.org/pubs/jofa/apr2002/thomas.htm (last visited June 3, 2003) ("To make matters worse for it, and to the astonishment of many, Andersen admitted it destroyed perhaps thousands of documents and electronic files related to the engagement, in accordance with 'firm policy,' supposedly before the SEC issued a subpoena for them. . . . The firm fired David B. Duncan, partner in charge of the Enron engagement, placed four other partners on leave and replaced the entire management team of the Houston office.").

[24] *See Texas Board Revokes Andersen's License,* N.Y. TIMES, Aug. 17, 2002, at C14 ("Andersen told the Securities and Exchange Commission after the June verdict that it would stop auditing public companies by Aug. 31.").

[25] *See* Jonathan D. Glater, *Last Task at Andersen: Turning Out the Lights,* N.Y. TIMES, Aug. 30, 2002, at C3.

Marsal of the Chicago-based financial restructuring firm Alvarez & Marsal, Andersen is a shell of its former self and exists primarily as a "bundle of accounts receivable, leases and hundreds of Enron-related and other lawsuits."[26] By October 2002, Andersen had "sold off most of its units and shuttered most of its offices."[27] Its principal remaining asset is a 105-acre training facility in St. Charles.[28]

Several of Andersen's accountants and consultants resigned from the firm to work directly for Enron.[29] This had the effect of "blurring the line" between where Enron stopped and its supposedly independent auditing firm started.[30]

Enron's primary legal counsel, the independent law firm of Vinson & Elkins, has thus far escaped the wrath of the government prosecutors.[31] The firm's precise role in the Enron scandal is unclear, but it is logical to assume that (1) the firm knew of the existence of these SPEs, and (2) the firm advised Enron on the acceptability or unacceptability of these entities.[32] However, the nature and quality of that counsel is not entirely clear, so it is uncertain if the firm "checked off" or "rubber-stamped" decisions, reports, and opinions regarding the SPEs or if the Enron officers continued to use the entities in spite of warnings by the law firm counseling Enron against using those

---

26 Mike Comerford, *The Lone Gem in Andersen's Fading Empire St. Charles Campus Rethinks Mission,* CHI. DAILY HERALD, April 29, 2003, at B1 [hereinafter Comerford].

27 *Andersen Holds Almost-Out-of-Business-Sale,* CHI. TRIB. 4 (Oct. 2, 2002).

28 *See* Comerford ("Its main asset is the 150-acre training facility in St. Charles, a former women's college complete with dormitories, food service and recreational facilities.").

29 *See* Flynn McRoberts, *Ties to Enron Blinded Andersen: Firm Couldn't Say "No" to Prized Client,* Chi. Trib., Sept. 3, 2002, *available at* 2002 WL 26770980 ("Inside the gleaming Houston headquarters of Enron Corp., it could be hard to distinguish between the energy traders and the Andersen people checking their books. . . . The potential conflicts were only worsened . . . by the close relationships Andersen employees had with the many alumni of the firm who had taken jobs at Enron.").

30 Of course, the line between Enron and its accountants was not the only line that may have been blurred, *see* Batson Report, *supra* note 6, at 51 ("Enron and its accounting firm Andersen were also aggressive participants in the GAAP standard-setting process").

31 Civil litigation may be another matter, however. Several class action lawsuits have been filed against Enron on behalf of shareholders and employees. On December 19, 2002, the judge hearing one of these suits denied Vinson and Elkins's motion to dismiss itself from the suit. *See* Batson Report, *supra* note 6, at 11-12 (fn. 36); *see also Federal Court Rules to Keep Most Defendants in Enron Shareholder's Lawsuit,* Yahoo! Finance (2002), *available at* http://216.239.37.100/search?q=cache:WqznSD1aAVYJ:biz.yahoo.com/prnews/021220/dcf050_1.html (last visited June 3, 2003) ("The federal judge handling the Enron Corp. securities lawsuit ruled today [Dec. 20, 2002] against several major financial institutions, law firms and the Arthur Andersen accounting firm, substantially denying most defendants' motions to be dismissed from the case. . . . Judge Harmon denied in their entirety the motions of . . . Enron's corporate legal counsel, Vincent [sic] and Elkins . . . 'This decision confirms the validity of our legal claims against the major defendants and leaves in the case defendants with resources to pay substantial compensation to the class,' said William Lerach, senior partner at Milberg, Weiss, Bershad, Hynes, & Lerach.").

32 *See* Powers Report, *supra* note 6, at 173 ("Derrick says that he and Lay both recognized there was a downside to retaining V&E [Vinson & Elkins to investigate Sherron Watkins's letter] because it had been involved in the Raptor and other LJM transactions.").

entities.[33] It appears, however, that the lawyers played a significant role in the creation and management of the SPEs.[34] It is unclear if and when the firm will be forced to produce its relevant documents and testimony. As a practical matter, it is unlikely that the firm or its partners will face legal liability before the completion of the legal actions against the former Enron officers.[35]

Enron conducted investment-banking transactions with many, if not most, of Wall Street's leading firms. The various firms helped create the SPEs, and some of the firms even invested their own capital in the entities.[36] These investments helped Enron meet the necessary level of outside equity investment levels necessary for these SPEs to pass initial legal muster.[37] The investment-banking firms' potential legal liability is largely

---

[33] The Powers Report maintains that Vinson & Elkins shared responsibility for Enron's failure to adequately disclose related party transactions. *See* Powers Report, *supra* note 6, at 178 ("We found significant issues concerning Enron's public disclosures of related-party transactions. Overall, Enron failed to disclose facts that were important for an understanding of the substance of the transactions.... We believe that the responsibility for these inadequate disclosures is shared by Enron Management, the Audit and Compliance Committee of the Board, Enron's in-house counsel, Vinson & Elkins, and Andersen.").

[34] For instance, *see* Batson Report, *supra* note 6, at 39 ("Enron carefully designed its FAS 140 technique with advice from Andersen and Enron's lawyers, with the goal that the asset transfer would qualify for sale treatment under GAAP despite the fact that sale treatment did not reflect the economic substance of the transaction. . . . Enron frequently obtained the legal opinions Andersen required. These opinions, however, were limited in scope and analyzed only certain steps and specific entities, rather than the transaction in its entirety. In many of the FAS 140 Transactions, the Examiner believes that legal isolation was not achieved.").

[35] *But see* Batson Report, *supra* note 6, at 129, 131 ("The 'avoidance actions' that are covered by this report are potential claims of the Debtors to avoid, as constructively fraudulent transfers or preferential transfers, payments of money or transfers of property, and to recover the amount avoided. The transfers analyzed by the Examiner as potentially avoidable . . . or (iv) were paid to certain professionals providing legal services to the Debtors or to the Creditors' Committee. . . . [T]he Examiner is in the process of analyzing whether Enron's law firms, accounting firms, banks, investment advisors and others may be considered insiders for the purposes of the application of the avoidance provisions of the Bankruptcy Code.").

[36] Permanent Subcommittee on Investigations, Committee on Governmental Affairs, Report on Fishtail, Bacchus, Sundance, and Slapshop: Four Enron Transactions Funded and Facilitated by U.S. Financial Institutions, S. Prt. 107-82, at 2 (2003), *available at* http://levin.senate.gov/enronreport0102.pdf (last visited June 3, 2003) ("The cumulative evidence from the three Subcommittee hearings demonstrates that some U.S. financial institutions have been designing, participating in, and profiting from complex financial transactions explicitly intended to help U.S. public companies engage in deceptive accounting or tax strategies. This evidence also shows that some U.S. financial institutions and public companies have been misusing structured finance vehicles, originally designed to lower financing costs and spread investment risk, to carry out sham transactions that have no legitimate business purpose and mislead investors, analysts, and regulators about the companies' activities, tax obligations, and true financial condition.").

[37] For an example of how banks helped structure transactions and the effect of these transactions on Enron's financial statements, debt ratio, and cash flow, *see* Batson Report, *supra* note 6, at 99 ("Citibank had formed Caymus Trust and funded it with $6 million of 'equity' and $194 million of debt. Enron guaranteed Caymus Trust's obligation to repay the debt to Citibank by entering into a Total Return Swap with Caymus Trust. Enron treated the transfer of the Fishtail Class C equity as a sale to Sonoma and recorded income equal to the $112 million of gain it believed existed in the trading business. The Examiner believes that this transaction did not constitute a 'true sale,' and therefore should have been recorded as a loan. Because of the consolidation of Fishtail and the failure of the transfer of its equity to Sonoma to

related to the prolonged "buy" ratings that the firms issued for Enron stock while it was declining in price.[38] This exposure is related to a conflict of interest problem that was (and some would say is) apparently widespread throughout the industry. The same firms that were competing for Enron's lucrative investment-banking fees were also the firms that provided equity investment ratings for Enron's stock.[39] Theoretically, an ethical wall separated the investment-banking operations from the securities analysis practice, but this separation appears not to have been strictly maintained.[40] Obviously, a firm has a large incentive to issue generous equities ratings, which generate demand for a stock, drive up its price, and please the company's officers, many of whom own the stock or stock options, and who in turn direct the flow of investment-banking business to the firms that issue the "buy" ratings in the first place.

LESSON ONE: THE FRAUD WAS NOT COMPLEX

Anyone who has investigated securities frauds upon the public will report that these frauds and attempts at fraud are, at root, not that complex. They play upon two fundamental tendencies that lie at the core of many people's behavior: greed and laziness.[41] Dangling the promise of vast returns on a passive investment, based upon a supposed new development[42] or inside information, appears to be a lure that vast numbers of otherwise intelligent people cannot resist.

---

qualify as a sale, Enron overstated its income in its financial statements by $112 million and understated its debt by $200 million. It also received $208 million of year-end cash flow, $200 million of which it recorded as cash flow from operating activities rather than financing activities.").

[38] *See* William S. Lerach, *Plundering America: How American Investors Got Taken for Trillions by Corporate Insiders, the Rise of the New Corporate Kleptocracy*, 8 STAN. J.L. BUS. & FIN. 69, 115 (2002) ("These banks were not just peddling Enron's worthless securities. Following repeal of Glass-Steagall, these banks were Enron's commercial lenders, its commercial joint venture partners, its investment bankers selling its securities to the public, and its derivative trading counter-parties—all the while, constantly issuing cheerleading analysts' reports about Enron, stressing the skill and integrity of its management, the quality of its balance sheet and reported earnings and its future prospects for strong profit growth.").

[39] *See* Lerach, *supra* note 38, at 115 ("Instead of playing their traditional role as underwriters—gatekeepers to protect the public—prestigious banking firms, including J.P. Morgan Chase, CitiGroup, CS First Boston, Merrill Lynch, CIBC, Deutsche Bank, and Barclays Bank became business partners with Enron, intertwining themselves in every aspect of Enron's business.").

[40] For example, *see id.* ("Top officials of several Wall Street banks . . . secretly invested with Enron's corrupt (now indicted) CEO in the secret partnerships Fastow ran, which did billions of dollars of deals with Enron, enabling these partnerships to loot Enron. These bank executives secretly took equity positions in those partnerships which self-dealt in Enron's assets. These partnerships produced fantastic returns for these investors. . . .The lowest return on a deal was 150%. The highest was 2,500%.").

[41] Some label these traits "Temptation." Douglas G. Baird & Robert K. Rasmussen, *Four (or Five) Easy Lessons from Enron*, 55 VAND. L.REV. 1787 (2002) [hereinafter Easy Lessons]. (In other contexts, I have also termed them laziness and self-interest, which could also be called utility maximization, the desire for as much good from as little effort as possible.).

[42] *See, e.g.*, ROBERT ZUCCARO, DOW 30,000 BY 2008: WHY IT'S DIFFERENT THIS TIME (Palisade Literary Press 2001) (This book's title is indicative of the "new development" scenario.).

Neither greed nor laziness is that dangerous in isolation. But together, when indulged in by large numbers of people, they lead to stock market, and other market, bubbles.[43] Enron is not the only example, of course. Consider the New Era bankruptcy in Philadelphia. There, the debtor had convinced over 180 charities and institutions of higher education and 150 individual donors that, if they deposited funds in the debtor's accounts, those funds would be matched—i.e. provided with a 100% return—by anonymous donors.[44] Eventually, as with all such things, the scheme collapsed.[45]

The old saying holds: If it sounds too good to be true, it probably is. So when it sounds too good, it is time for officers, directors, attorneys, accountants, analysts, and investors to start asking tough questions and start demanding answers that make sense.

As Douglas Baird has pointed out, "Enron was not a Ponzi scheme."[46] Like Charles Ponzi, however, Enron offered investors an irresistible combination: huge returns on investments, coupled with the allure of a seemingly heretofore undiscovered business opportunity.[47] Ponzi promised investors returns of more than 50% in 90 days, returns enabled by Ponzi's discovery of "a lucrative arbitrage opportunity in postal coupons."[48] Due to the fluctuating value of currencies after WWI, the value of postal coupons varied from country to country, because the exchange rates for such coupons had been set in 1906.[49] A coupon bought in a country with a depressed currency could be redeemed for greater value in a country whose currency was worth more.[50] In truth, Ponzi wasn't investing in postal coupons at all but was rather paying off earlier investors with subsequent investors' money.[51]

Although Enron did not literally use subsequent investors' money to pay off earlier investors, Enron and Charles Ponzi share some striking similarities, not the least of which is that Enron's business plan also presented a "lucrative arbitrage opportunity." Conservatives "point to insufficient market competition as the cause of the failure" of

---

[43] *See* Larry E. Ribstein, *Market vs. Regulatory Responses to Corporate Fraud: A Critique of the Sarbanes-Oxley Act of 2002*, 28. J. Corp. L. 1, 19 (2002) ("Indeed, almost 300 years ago the South Sea Bubble, the high tech of its day, lured investors with, among other things, the hope of riches from the new world, only to collapse amid recriminations against directors and 'stock-jobbers.'"); *see also* Frederick Lewis Allen, *Only Yesterday: an Informal History of the 1920s in America* (1931), *available at* http://xroads.virginia.edu/~Hyper/Allen/ch11.html (last visited June 3, 2003) (describing the Florida Real Estate Bubble of the 1920s).

[44] *See* Evelyn Brody, *The Limits of Charity Fiduciary Law*, 57 Md. L. Rev. 1400, 1491 (1998) ("Created by John Bennett in 1989, the Foundation for New Era Philanthropy had been inviting selected charities to contribute funds—but only for a short period. At the end of six months, New Era would return the 'contributed' amount, plus a matching amount of money from anonymous donors.").

[45] *Id.* at 1492-94.

[46] *See* Easy Lessons, *supra* note 41, at 1809.

[47] *Id.* at 1787-92.

[48] *Id.* at 1787.

[49] *Id.*

[50] *Id.*

[51] *Id.*

Enron,[52] but such a claim must bear a degree of irony, since Enron itself was a market, or at least a "market-maker."[53] Indeed, Enron claimed to be a firm that "excelled at creating new markets"[54] and sought to become "a pure financial intermediary"[55] consisting of a "proprietary market place in which Enron matched up energy producers, carriers, and users," and which "Enron was expanding . . . to cover anything which could be traded—pulp, paper, metals, even broadband services."[56]

Market-makers like Enron enable "buyers and sellers to find each other at low cost, eliminating wasted resources through a reduction in transaction costs. The entrepreneur who creates such a market can capture as profit a fair portion of the benefit the initial buyers and sellers enjoy by finding each other."[57] Unlike Ponzi, who never invested in the postal coupons he was supposedly trading, Enron actually did make markets.[58] The problem with being in the business of making markets, however, is that such a business is adverse to competition. Markets cannot be kept secret and can be replicated by competitors at little cost.[59] Thus, "profits are [quickly] competed away."[60]

Making a small profit on each trade was fundamentally not in keeping with Enron's corporate culture, in which "the principals saw themselves in a tournament" where "their job was not just to make money, but to make the most money—to be the superstar firm."[61] Winning the tournament meant "destroying the next firm and much of industrial organization with it, and always delivering good numbers."[62] To deliver these good

---

[52] Lawrence A. Cunningham, *Sharing Accounting's Burden: Business Lawyers in Enron's Dark Shadows*, 57 BUS. LAW. 1421 (2003) [hereinafter Cunningham].

[53] *See* Easy Lessons, *supra* note 41, at 1790.

[54] *Id.* at 1789.

[55] Bratton, *supra* note 16, at 1287.

[56] *Id.*; *see* Report on Board of Directors, *supra* note 6, at 6 ("It [Enron] had received widespread recognition for its transition from an old-line energy company with pipelines and power plants to a high-tech global enterprise that traded energy contracts like commodities, launched into new industries like broadband communications, and oversaw a multibillion dollar international investment portfolio. One of Enron's key corporate achievements during the 1990s was creation of an online energy trading business that bought and sold contracts to deliver energy products like natural gas, oil or electricity. Enron treated these contracts as marketable commodities comparable to securities or commodities futures, but was able to develop and run the business outside existing controls on investment companies and commodity brokers."); *see also* Batson Report, *supra* note 6, at 16 ("Starting out as a company that had a concentration in natural gas pipelines, it [Enron] became over time a company that depended less on pipelines and transportation and more on *energy trading and investing in new technologies and businesses.*") (emphasis added).

[57] *See* Easy Lessons, *supra* note 41, at 1790.

[58] *Id.*

[59] *Id.*

[60] *Id.*

[61] Bratton, *supra* note 16, at 1286.

[62] *Id.* at 1286-87.

numbers, Enron embarked upon a course that would lead to its becoming best known "as a company that cooked its books."[63] As Lawrence A. Cunningham notes,

> At the core of the Enron debacle are accounting chicanery related to off-balance sheet financing and related party transactions plus colossal failures of board oversight. In its penumbra are auditing conflicts of interest that may be pervasive, incentivized board members posing as independent directors who could be more widespread than is known, law firms apparently asleep at the deal, and political donations and influence peddling that is almost certainly more common than polite politicians prefer to pretend.[64]

Enron has provoked "controversial questions about the values and structures constituting and legitimating American corporate governance, market capitalism, and the globalization of markets and trade."[65] William Lerach, the high-profile plaintiffs' lawyer, observed that, a "few years ago, few could have foreseen the carnage that has recently roiled our securities markets."[66] However, it is not so much that few could have foreseen Enron's collapse and the burst of the stock market bubble, but rather that few wanted to foresee such problems. Like a stock market bubble or a Ponzi scheme, Enron offered investors the opportunity to get rich quick with little effort. Offer people an opportunity for easy money, and you offer them a powerful incentive to believe: Greed. Coupled with laziness (here, in the guise of a fundamental disinclination to raise questions),

---

[63] *See* Easy Lessons, *supra* note 41, at 1791; *see also* Powers Report, *supra* note 6, at 4 ("This personal enrichment of Enron employees, however, was merely one aspect of a deeper and more serious problem. . . . Many of the most significant transactions apparently were designed to accomplish favorable financial statement results, not to achieve *bona fide* economic objectives or to transfer risk. . . . Other transactions were implemented—improperly we are informed by our accounting advisors—to offset losses. They allowed Enron to conceal from the market very large losses resulting from Enron's merchant investments by creating an appearance that those investments were hedged—that is, that a third party was obligated to pay Enron the amount of those losses—when in fact that third party was simply an entity in which only Enron had a substantial financial stake.").

[64] Cunningham, *supra* note 52, at 1426; *see also* Batson Report, *supra* note 6, at 11 ("In the months immediately following Enron's disclosures, allegations surfaced of securities fraud, accounting irregularities, energy market price manipulation, money laundering, breach of fiduciary duties, misleading financial information, ERISA violations, insider trading, excessive compensation and wrong doing by certain of Enron's bankers.").

[65] Faith Stevelman Kahn, *Bombing Markets, Subverting the Rule of Law: Enron, Financial Fraud, and September 11, 2001*, 76 Tul. L. Rev. 1579, 1634 (2002). There are, perhaps, good reasons for these questions. *See* Report on Board of Directors, *supra* note 6, at 11 ("Steady revelations since October 2001 have raised questions about numerous aspects of the company's operations, from its extensive undisclosed off-the-books dealings, often with companies run by Enron personnel, to an April 2002 SEC filing announcing that the company's financial statements were unreliable and the book value of its assets would have to be written-down as much as $24 billion, to its apparent intention to manipulate the California energy market, to tax strategies which apparently included Enron's ordering its tax department to produce billions of dollars in company earnings through the use of complex tax shelters.").

[66] Lerach, *supra* note 38, at 70.

this combination led investors' belief in the implausible.[67] Fraud is easy when people want to believe. It is time to reaffirm the duty of skepticism of all the watchdogs and gatekeepers that failed to watch and bark,[68] including the investors themselves.

LESSON TWO: AVOID A CULT OF PERSONALITY

Leaders of legendary reputations who have actively participated in the creation of their image rarely produce long-term benefits to a company or other organization.[69] One is tempted to look at Mao, Stalin, Marcus Brutus, Kim Jong Il, and other governmental figures whose organizations became too wrapped up in the leader and his self-reflected glory to focus on long-term success and benefit to the stakeholder.[70] But one need not go beyond recent business headlines.[71] Think of Jack Welch, Bill Gates, Martha Stewart.

GE finally ousted Welch in 2001 after disclosures relating to aggressive and questionable earnings management.[72] That ouster possibly freed the company from Welch's focus on GE Capital's growth at the expense of other units.

---

[67] *See* Report on Board of Directors, *supra* note 6, at 12 ("During their Subcommittee interviews, the Enron Directors seemed to indicate that they were as surprised as anyone by the company's collapse. But a chart produced at the Subcommittee hearing marks more than a dozen incidents over three years that should have raised Board concerns about the activities of the company.").

[68] Harold S. Peckron, *Watchdogs that Failed to Bark: Standards of Tax Review After Enron,* 5 FLA. TAX REV. 853 (2002).

[69] For a post-modern view, see Jeanne L. Schroeder, *The Four Discourses of Law: A Lacanian Analysis of Legal Practice and Scholarship* 79 TEX. L. REV. 15, 29 (2000) ("The master signifier is the one signifier that gives meaning to the shifting chain of signifiers. . . . In order to serve this function, the master signifier itself must be totally devoid of meaning. . . . The master signifier itself is the signifier without any signified that can serve as the starting point of the chain. . . . Consequently, within the context of the chain, it has no separate meaning of its own, but is defined by the entire chain of signifiers to which it relates. . . . The classic example of master signifiers [is] political masters who rule through a cult of personality. . . .").

[70] For example, *see* Andrew Roberts, *Lenin's Legacy of Shame*, Daily Mail 8 (1994) ("Political heroes have been deified before, but Lenin was accorded a reputation for infallibility that had not existed since the Roman Empire. It led directly to the cult of personalities which later surrounded Stalin, Hitler, Mao Tse-tung and still exists with Kim Il-Sung in North Korea today [now deceased and replaced by his son Kim Jong Il]. Camps designed especially for the liquidation of political enemies were pioneered by Lenin long before Stalin came to power. They were later to destroy millions of Russian lives in degradation, slavery, torture, and were copied by Hitler and Mao.").

[71] *See* Gary Strauss, *Tyco Events Put Spotlight on Director's Role,* USA TODAY Sept. 16, 2002, at B3, *available at* http://www.usatoday.com/money/industries/manufacturing/2002-09-15-tyco-direct_x.htm (last visited June 3, 2003).

[72] *See* Ameet Sachdev, *Scandal and Upheaval: Corporate America's Image Suffers from Probes, Charges, and Andersen's Convictions,* CHI. TRIB., Dec. 31, 2002, at B1, *available at* 2002 WL 104502193 ("Who would have guessed that a business icon such as Jack Welch, the former CEO of General Electric Co., would come under scrutiny for his retirement perks? A dalliance with the then-editor of the *Harvard Business Review* caused his wife to file for divorce, which led to the revelations of GE picking up the expenses at his Manhattan apartment, including food, wine, cook, and waitstaff. In addition, GE allowed Welch to

Microsoft's antitrust case could probably have been resolved faster, with smaller overall legal bills, and with better image management had Bill Gates not been as personally involved in the case and had he been more prepared to be a sympathetic or appealing witness.[73]

And Martha Stewart, a former stockbroker, was brought down as a tippee in an insider trading scam that threatens the goodwill she built up in her company, in spite of her widely reported tendency to have a personal style 180 degrees opposed to the happy, industrious homemaker to whom she was supposed to appeal.[74] These leaders' behaviors were not focused on their company's long-term success, but rather on their own images, agendas, and short-term gains. As one columnist has said, avoid the iconic CEO—or at least the iconic CEO/Chairman of the Board who dominates the officers and directors: "Seek the anonymous plodder."[75]

Charisma and leadership are important in upper management, but these qualities must be balanced with strong self- and company-assessment skills. Senior management needs to make sure that it does not unquestioningly believe its own press. Hubris is not a character flaw reserved only for Greek tragedies or Shakespearean histories. The danger of a cult of personality is not isolated in the cult of an individual leader.

The cult of personality can be a cult of corporate personality, creating a damaged corporate culture. Enron was the Elvis of energy corporations and was to become "far and away the most vigorous agent of change in its industry."[76] The company was formed in 1985 from the merger of a natural gas and a pipeline company. However, the merger that had created Enron saddled the corporation with debt, and deregulation had taken away Enron's exclusive rights to its pipelines.[77] Kenneth Lay, Enron's CEO, needed a "new and innovative business strategy to generate profits and cash flow."[78] The strategy was engineered by Jeffrey Skilling, whose "revolutionary solution to Enron's credit, cash and profit woes" was to reconceive the company as a virtual corporation, or a "gas bank" (in which Enron would buy gas from a network of suppliers and sell it to a network of consumers, contractually guaranteeing both the supply and the

---

use the company's Boeing 737 jets and provided tickets to sporting and entertainment events. After the publicity, Welch agreed to pay GE nearly $2.5 million each year for the perks.").

73 For example, *see* Michael J. Martinez, *Trial and Error? Did "Attitude" or "Faith" Cause Microsoft's Downfall?* Associated Press, *at* http://abcnews.go.com/sections/tech/DailyNews/microsoft000612.html (last visited June 3, 2003).

74 *See* Ameet Sachdev, *Scandal and Upheaval: Corporate America's Image Suffers from Probes, Charges, and Andersen's Convictions*, Chi. Trib., Dec. 31, 2002, at B1 ("Even the doyenne of domesticity, Martha Stewart, wound up gracing magazine covers—not for her cooking but because of insider trading allegations.").

75 Marianne Jennings, *Remembering the "Business" in Business Ethics*, Wash. Post, Aug. 25, 2002, at B07, *available at* 2002 WL 25998598.

76 Scott Sherman, *Enron Uncovering the Uncovered Story*, Colum. Journalism Rev. 2228 March/April 2002.

77 William C. Thomas, *The Rise and Fall of Enron*, J. Acct. April 2002, at 41 (2002), *available at* http://www.aicpa.org/pubs/jofa/apr2002/thomas.htm (last visited June 3, 2003).

78 *Id.*

price, charging fees for the transactions, and assuming the associated risks).[79] Through Skilling's innovation, Enron "created both a new product and a new paradigm in the industry—the energy derivative."[80]

Skilling transformed not only Enron's business plan, but also its employees, through the active recruitment of the "best and brightest traders," and through the awarding of "merit based bonuses that had no cap, permitting traders to 'eat what they killed.'"[81] Skilling also instituted the creatively named "rank and yank" employee evaluation system, which "became known as the harshest employee ranking system in the country," where employees who failed to produce large profits were fired.[82] Under "rank and yank," "fierce internal competition prevailed and immediate gratification was prized beyond long-term potential."[83] Just as Skilling transformed Enron's internal culture, so did one of Skilling's earliest hires transform Enron's finances. Andrew Fastow, Enron's CFO, oversaw the corporation's "financing by ever more complicated means."[84]

Lay, Skilling, and Fastow were not anonymous plodders; rather, they took actions and made innovations that transformed a staid energy company into a "new economy" rock star. For this transformation, they and the corporation were lionized. Insiders in the industry voted Enron *Fortune*'s "Most Innovative Company" for six years running.[85] *Business Week* named Lay one of the "25 Top Managers" of 2000, while *Worth*'s survey

---

[79] Thomas, *supra* note 77; *see* Batson Report, *supra* note 6, at 16 ("By the mid-1990s, Enron's business and business model changed dramatically. . . . In its 2000 Annual Report, Enron described its four business segments: Wholesale Services, Energy Services, Broadband Services, and Transportation Services. . . . Wholesale Services created trading markets in gas, oil, electricity and other energy products and provided price risk management and other related services."); *see also* Report on Board of Directors, *supra* note 6, at 6 ("It [Enron] had received widespread recognition for its transition from an old-line energy company with pipelines and power plants, to a high-tech global enterprise that traded energy contracts like commodities, launched into new industries like broadband communications, and oversaw a multi-billion dollar international investment portfolio.").

[80] Thomas, *supra* note 77, at 2.

[81] *Id.*; *see* Report on Board of Directors, *supra* note 6, at 52 ("One Board member said during his interview that Enron's philosophy was to provide 'extraordinary rewards for extraordinary achievement'; others claimed that the company was forced to provide lavish compensation to attract the best and brightest employees.").

[82] Thomas, *supra* note 77, at 42.

[83] *Id.*

[84] Thomas, *supra* note 77. And enriching himself in the process. *See* Powers Report, *supra* note 6, at 166-67 ("Fastow, as CFO, knew what assets Enron's business units wanted to sell, how badly, and how soon they wanted to sell them, and whether they had alternative buyers. He was in a position to exert great pressure and influence, directly or indirectly, on Enron personnel who were negotiating with LJM. We have been told of instances in which he used that pressure to try to obtain better terms for LJM, and where people reporting to him instructed business units that LJM would be the buyer of the assets they wished to sell. . . . This situation led one Fastow subordinate, then-Treasurer Jeff McMahon, to complain to Skilling in March 2000. . . . Skilling has said he recalls the conversation focusing only on McMahon's compensation. Even if that is true, it still may have suggested that Fastow's conflict was placing pressure on an Enron employee.").

[85] Sherman, *supra* note 76, at 24.

of the "50 Best CEOs" included Lay and Skilling, with Skilling ranked second.[86] As Scott Sherman states, "The print media coverage of Enron's top executives was pure hagiography."[87]

Enron and its executives do illustrate the perils of conspicuous innovation and hype. "Skilling's relentless push for creativity and competitiveness . . . fostered a growth-at-any-cost culture, drowning out voices of caution and overriding all checks and balances."[88] Although not as glamorous, the tortoise can win over the hare, and corporations should seek, if not anonymous plodders, then rigorous, methodical individuals to balance charismatic, hard-charging leadership, and should maintain an internal culture that is consistent with notions of responsible stewardship, appropriate disclosure, and maximization of long-term shareholder value.[89] Of all the fabled corporate leaders of the last decade, perhaps the closest to this model is Berkshire Hathaway's Warren Buffett. Berkshire Hathaway, a holding company, is thinly staffed. Buffett focuses on value investing, using quantitative analysis, seeking to acquire companies that are worth more than their market capitalization and that are leaders in currently out-of-favor market segments. Instead of ousting prior management after an acquisition, Buffett largely leaves that management in place, not insisting that they run the business differently from the way they did before the acquisition.[90] Although widely heralded and recognized, Buffett is a picture of solid Midwestern business values and quantitative methods, and the successes that those values and methods can bring—not a charismatic, grandstanding leader that seeks the limelight.

---

[86] *Id.* at 25.

[87] *Id.*; WEBSTER'S THIRD NEW INT'L DICTIONARY 1019 (1986) (defines "hagiography" as "1 a: biography of saints: saint's lives"). A bit ironic, since the Powers Report concluded that, when it came to Enron's management, "no one was minding the store." *See* Powers Report, *supra* note 6, at 166.

[88] Tom Fowler, *The Pride and the Fall of Enron*, HOUS. CHRON. Oct. 20, 2002, at A1, *available at* http://www.chron.com/cs/CDA/printstory.hts/special/enron/1624822 (last visited June 3, 2003); *see* Powers Report, *supra* note 6, at 27-28 ("The tragic consequences of the related party transactions and accounting errors were the results at many levels and by many people: a flawed idea, self-enrichment by employees, inadequately defined controls, poor implementation, inattentive oversight, simple (and not-so-simple) accounting mistakes, and overreaching in a culture that appears to have encouraged pushing the limits.").

[89] *See* Batson Report, *supra* note 6, at 13 ("This Report concludes that: . . . certain transfers made to Lay, certain other Enron employees and certain professionals can be avoided as constructively fraudulent transfers and preferential transfers."); *see also* Report on Board of Directors, *supra* note 6, at 49-50 ("Enron provided its executives with lavish compensation. On more than one occasion, it paid tens of millions of dollars to a single executive as a bonus for work on a single deal. Stock options were distributed in large numbers to executives. . . . Mr. Lay alone accumulated more than 6.5 million options on Enron stock. In 2000, Mr. Lay's compensation exceeded $140 million, including $123 million from exercising a portion of his Enron stock options. . . . One example of the Compensation Committee's lavish compensation philosophy, combined with its failure to conduct adequate compensation oversight, involves its May 1999 decision to permit Mr. Lay to repay company loans with company stock. . . . In the one-year period from October 2000 to October 2001, Mr. Lay used the credit line to obtain over $77 million in cash from the company and repaid the loans exclusively with Enron stock.").

[90] *See generally* Roger Lowenstein, BUFFETT, THE MAKING OF AN AMERICAN CAPITALIST (1995).

LESSON THREE: ARTIFICIAL ENTITIES ARE ABOUT STEWARDSHIP

CEOs, CFOs, officers, and those attorneys and accountants who advise the company, remember: It is *not* your money! The modern corporation—or limited liability company, partnership, business trust, or other juristic entity formed to conduct business—is an incredible tool for collecting and deploying the capital of a diverse group of owners,[91] many of whom are not, and have no interest in being, involved in the day-to-day operations of a business.[92] The corporation is run by its directors, who select officers, for the benefit of the shareholders (or, when the corporation is operating in the zone of insolvency, for the benefit of creditors and shareholders).[93] The role of the officers and

---

[91] *See* William W. Bratton & Joseph A. McCahery, *Protecting Investors in a Global Economy: Incomplete Contracts Theories of the Firm and Comparative Corporate Governance*, 2 THEORETICAL INQUIRIES L. 745, 750 (2001) ("Market corporate governance systems are characterized by dispersed equity holding, a portfolio orientation among equity holders, and a broad delegation to management of discretion to operate the business. . . . Their shareholders can cheaply reduce their risks through diversification. Relative to shareholders in blockholder systems, they receive high rates of return. Market systems deep trading markets facilitate greater shareholder liquidity); *see also* Ann E. Conaway, *Reexamining the Fiduciary Paradigm at Corporate Insolvency and Dissolution: Defining Directors Duties to Creditors*, 20 DEL. J CORP. L. 1, 113 (1995) ("Generally, stockholders own and indirectly manage the corporation through equity securities of common stock."); *see, e.g.*, Margaret M. Blair and Lynn A. Stout, *A Team Production Theory of Corporate Law* 85 VA. L. REV. 247, 248 (1999) ("Contemporary discussions of corporate governance have come to be dominated by the view that public corporations are little more than bundles of assets collectively owned by shareholders."); *see also* Phillip I. Blumberg, *The Corporate Entity in an Era of Multinational Corporations*, 15 DEL. J. CORP. L. 283, 326 (1990) ("The traditional concept of the corporation as a separate juridical unit clashes violently with reality when applied, not merely to simple corporations with shares owned by individual investors, but to corporations that are members of a corporate group. In such cases, the 'corporation' and the enterprise are no longer identical. The enterprise is no longer being conducted solely by a single corporation but collectively by the coordinated activities of numerous interrelated corporations under common control.").

[92] *See* Stephen M. Bainbridge, *The Board of Directors as Nexus of Contracts*, 88 IOWA L. REV. 1, 3 (2002) ("Shareholders, who are said to "own' the firm, have virtually no power to control either its day-to-day operations or its long-term policies. Instead, the firm is controlled by its board of directors and subordinate managers, whose equity stake is often small [in comparison to the company's total market capital]"); *see also* Susan Jacqueline Butler, *Models of Modern Corporations: A Comparative Analysis of German and U.S. Corporate Structures*, 17 ARIZ. J. INT'L & COMPARATIVE L. 555, 589 (2000) ("The power to manage the corporation is generally vested in the directors who delegate the day-to-day business to the officers."); *see also* Derek Murphy, *Corporate Governance: The Conflict Between Money and Morality*, 32 HKLJ 233, 234 (2002) ("The financial contributors—the shareholders—rely upon the skill, integrity and resourcefulness of those to whom they have delegated the task of running the business: the company's management and its Board of Directors.").

[93] *See* Ira M. Millstein and Paul W. MacAvoy, *The Active Board of Directors and Performance of the Large Publicly Traded Corporation*, 98 COLUM. L. REV. 1283 (1998); *see also* BLACK'S LAW DICTIONARY 166 (7th ed. 1999) ("board of directors: 1. The Governing body of a corporation, elected by the shareholders to establish corporate policy, appoint executive officers, and make major business and financial decisions."); Rev. Model Bus. Corp. Act § 8.01; *see also* Margaret M. Blair and Lynn A. Stout, *A Team Production Theory of Corporate Law*, 85 VA. L. REV. 247, 262 (1999) ("The owner is understood to delegate residual control rights to her agents (in the corporate context, the board of directors) who in turn are charged with managing the assets in the principal's interest, perhaps through several more layers of delegation.").

directors is to protect and grow the business,[94] not to personally profit at the expense of the stakeholders.[95] Like Caesar's wife, they should strive to be beyond reproach.[96]

The use of stock option incentive programs and the mid-1980s to 1990s' shift away from paying dividends and to retaining earnings at the corporate level appear to have increased the temptation to lose sight of this principle of stewardship.[97] With more resources on hand and an immediate, personal reward for creating short-term market gains in the stock's secondary market, positive reinforcement for behavior that falls short of the fiduciary standards applicable to officers and directors may have clouded

---

94 *See* Gregory Scott Crespi, *Rethinking Corporate Fiduciary Duties: The Inefficiency of the Shareholder Primacy Norm*, 55 SMU L. Rev. 141 (2002) (summarizing "the conventional understanding among modern courts and commentators" as: fiduciary duties of corporate officers and directors "run exclusively to the corporations' common shareholders, and that other financial claimants of the corporation, such as its bondholders and preferred shareholders, are generally entitled only to enforcement of their express contractual rights. When corporate directors and officers . . . make decisions within the remaining zone of discretion . . . they are regarded as subject to a fiduciary duty to maximize shareholder wealth."); *see also* Francis v. United Jersey Bank, 432 A.2d 814, 824 (1981) ("In general, the relationship of a corporate director to the corporation and its stockholders is that of a fiduciary. Shareholders have a right to expect that directors will exercise reasonable supervision and control over the policies and practices of a corporation."); Rest. 2d. Agency § 387 ("Unless otherwise agreed, an agent is subject to a duty to his principle to act solely for the benefit of the principal in all matters connected with his agency.").

95 *See infra* notes 105-135 and accompanying text for a detailed discussion of the fiduciary duties of directors and officers; *see also* Butler, *supra* note 92, at 590 ("[T]he duty of loyalty generally requires managers to maximize investors' wealth rather than their own and creates a duty of fair dealing in self-interested transactions. When a conflict arises, it is the management's obligation not to enrich themselves at the corporation's expense."); Murphy, *supra* note 92, at 233 ("It is trite law that directors stand in a fiduciary relationship with their company. They have duties to act in good faith in the interests of the company; they must exercise powers for a proper purpose; and they must avoid conflicts of interest. They must not improperly use information obtained through their position to gain an advantage for themselves or someone else or cause detriment to the corporation."); *see* William Meade Fletcher, 3 FLETCHER CYCLOPEDIA OF PRIVATE CORP. § 837.50 (2002) ("This fiduciary duty runs to shareholders and the corporation, and not to fellow officers or directors except to the extent they are shareholders.").

96 Or, alternatively, they should behave like Platonic Guardians, *see* Stephen M. Bainbridge, *The Board of Directors as Nexus of Contracts*, 88 IOWA L. REV. 1, 33 (2002).

97 For an argument from the 1990s arguing for the increased use of stock options, *see* Charles M. Elson, *The Duty of Care, Compensation, and Stock Ownership*, 63 U. Cin. L. Rev. 649, 691 (1995) ("The outside directors must not remain mere observers of the corporate pecuniary interests, but must become active equity participants. If a director's personal capital is potentially affected by inept or corrupt management, that director is much less likely to acquiesce passively to such a group."). For the opposite view, *see* Jeffrey N. Gordon, *What Enron Means for the Management and Control of the Modern Business: Some Initial Reflections,* 69 U. CHI. L. REV. 1233, 1235 (2002) (arguing that Enron "undermines the corporate governance mechanism, the monitoring board, that has been offered as a substitute for unfettered shareholder access to the market for corporate control. In particular, the board's capacity to protect the integrity of financial disclosure has not kept pace with the increasing reliance on stock price performance in measuring and rewarding managerial performance."); *see also* Lerach, *supra* note 38, at 80 ("This explosion of new 'high growth' public companies, plus an executive-compensation system based on meeting predetermined earnings and stock-price appreciation targets, with stock options to be exercised and sold quarterly, created very powerful incentives to falsify results.").

the view of the stewardship model.[98] Stewardship remains the law, however, as well as the fundamental bedrock principle that makes modern corporate capitalism possible.[99] If the public loses its faith that the corporate stewards are acting primarily in the company's and shareholders' best interests, investment falters, the stock market plunges, and it becomes difficult to restart the country's stalled economic engine that, in good times, is fueled by healthy demand from both businesses and consumers.[100]

Enron demonstrates the consequences of lost faith. Trust was essential to the success of Enron's business, and once "there was doubt about the company's ability to perform as a counterpart" to transactions involving "trading in sophisticated energy and other derivatives," both Enron "and the cash flow and profits it generated, rapidly evaporated."[101] Enron relied on "dubious, and at times outrightly fraudulent, accounting

---

[98] *See* Gordon, *supra* note 97, at 1242 ("Recruitment of directors who are qualified to be board members of a large public company may require substantial compensation, especially for directors on time-consuming high-profile committees such as the audit committee. Yet high levels of compensation may compromise director independence, since a director's sharp questioning of senior management may lead to subtle pressures against his/her renomination. Moreover, stock-based director compensation may enhance the board's vigor as a shareholder agent but also increase its ambivalence about uncovering embarrassing facts that will reduce the share price."); *see also Who Dropped the Ball,* FRONTLINE: BIGGER THAN ENRON, *available at* http://www.pbs.org/wgbh/pages/frontline/shows/regulation /watchdogs/ (last visited June 3, 2003) ("In recent years, executives' compensation packages have included large grants of stock options . . . making them even more sensitive to the short-term performance of the company's stock. . . . Although the company's board of directors is supposed to represent the interests of the shareholders, some charge that in recent years they either have been asleep at the wheel or have been seduced by company management. Critics charge that sitting on a corporate board has turned into a lucrative venture with directors receiving consulting fees, sales contracts, donations to their favorite charities, and other assorted side deals that have the potential to compromise their objectivity and make them beholden to management, rather than the other way around.").

[99] *See* T. Jackson Lyons, 3 MS PRAC. ENCYCLOPEDIA MS LAW § 22:168 (2003) ("The fiduciary duties of officers and directors have affirmative obligations. Silence, or concealment, when one ought to speak because of the duty of utmost loyalty and good faith is actionable and the fiduciary may be held liable for any personal benefit or harm to the corporation.").

[100] *See* Kahn, *supra* note 65, at 1585-87 ("By the spring and summer of 2002, concern about the implications of Enron's sudden collapse had escalated into profound, nearly pervasive anxiety about the veracity of corporate reporting and the integrity of corporate governance systems supporting it. . . . Commentators coined the terms 'Enronitis,' and 'the Cockroach theory' to make light of the very serious fact that confidence in the accounting, auditing, disclosure, investment banking, credit ratio, and managerial oversight systems supporting the integrity of the capital markets had been grossly undermined by Enron's failure and the conduct of many of its principals and outside counselors. In the following months, both the capital markets and the general economy teetered at the edge of crisis. . . .").

[101] *Id.* at 1589; *see* Powers Report, *supra* note 6, at 3 ("The LJM1-Chewco-related restatement, like the earlier charge against earnings and reduction of shareholders' equity, was very large. It reduced Enron's reported net income by $28 million in 1997 (of $105 million total), by $133 million in 1998 (of $703 million total), by $248 million in 1999 (of $893 million total), and by $99 million in 2000 (of $979 million total). The restatement reduced reported shareholders' equity by $258 million in 1997, by $391 million in 1998, by $710 million in 1999, and by $754 million in 2000. It increased reported debt by $71 million in 1997, by $561 million in 1998, by 685 million in 1999, and by $628 million in 2000. Enron also revealed, for the first time, that it had learned that Fastow received more than $30 million

and disclosure practices, including the immediate recognition of profits on long-term sales contracts of speculative, future value."[102] These faulty systems of "accounting, auditing, and disclosure breached its [Enron's] investors' and employees' rightful expectations of financial transparency."[103]

Enron was seriously destabilized by disclosures of self-dealing transactions involving a raft of side deals connected to "two limited partnerships of which Enron's CFO, Andrew Fastow, was the manager of the general partner."[104] Not only did these deals put $30 million dollars into Fastow's pocket, they also resulted in "an overstatement of Enron's earnings over four years of at least $591 million."[105] The company "used its own high-flying common stock to surmount the sticking point" whenever "economics had gotten in the way of a result it wanted."[106] While employees and investors bore the

---

from LJM1 and LJM2. These announcements destroyed market confidence and investor trust in Enron. Less than one month later, Enron filed for bankruptcy.").

[102] Kahn, *supra* note 65, at 1589; *see* Batson Report, *supra* note 6, at 15 ("The Examiner has concluded that, through pervasive use of structured finance techniques involving SPEs and aggressive accounting practices, Enron so engineered its reported financial position and results of operations that its financial statements bore little resemblance to its actual financial condition or performance.").

[103] Kahn, *supra* note 65, at 1591; *see* Batson Report, *supra* note 6, at 53, 54, 55 ("As discussed in detail . . . despite Enron's extraordinary efforts to comply with the GAAP rules, in many cases the Examiner has been unable to find a sufficient basis under even the rules-based GAAP standards to support Enron's reported financial accounting . . . the Examiner has concluded that Enron's reporting of many of the SPE transactions did not comply with applicable GAAP rules in the first instance. This failure resulted in Enron's financial statements during the periods it engaged in these transactions not fairly presenting in all material respects its financial position, results of operations and cash flows in accordance with GAAP. . . . The Examiner concludes that, quite apart from questions of whether its accounting for particular SPE transactions was proper, Enron failed in several key respects to provide adequate disclosure to the marketplace for facts and circumstances that were critical to an understanding of its financial condition, operating results and cash flows.").

[104] Bratton, *supra* note 16, at 1305; *see* Powers Report, *supra* note 6, at 8-9 ("In 1999, with Board approval, Enron entered into business relationships with two partnerships in which Fastow was the manager and an investor. The transactions between Enron and the LJM partnerships resulted in Enron increasing its reported financial results by more than a billion dollars, and enriching Fastow and his co-investors by tens of millions of dollars at Enron's expense.").

[105] Bratton, *supra* note 16, at 1305.

[106] Bratton, *supra* note 16, at 1320; *see* Batson Report, *supra* note 6, at 21-22 ("An Enron manager who actively participated in the design and implementation of many of Enron's structured finance transactions confirmed how well he appreciated the importance of financial engineering in a self evaluation memorandum prepared sometime after the close of the 2000 fiscal year. He began the memorandum by pointing out his own contribution to Enron's funds flow and its balance sheet from 1995 through 2000: '. . . While the funds flow metric allows Enron to maintain its current debt rating assuming a certain balance sheet capital structure, of equal importance is the maintenance of that capital structure and maintaining debt ratios which have been generally in the 40% range overt the past five years. To maintain our credit rating, if Enron were to finance itself primarily or solely through simpler, on-balance-sheet reported structures, 40% of each transaction would be funded by the issuance of new debt and 60% through retained earnings or new equity. . . . For 2000, I was responsible for the Global Finance team that generated approximately $5.5 billion of overall off-balance sheet financing. . . . The value of avoiding $6.1 billion of equity dilution

brunt of the collapse of Enron stock in 2001, many of Enron's "senior-level insiders had already banked huge financial windfalls."[107] Enron's Chairman and CEO, Kenneth Lay, sold off millions of dollars of Enron stock in 2001 without disclosing the sales.[108] Had he done so, the sales might have "aroused greater scrutiny and concern about what was occurring at Enron.... Greater transparency might also have led to management, operational and reporting reforms that might have resolved the problems at Enron before they proved terminal."[109] Instead, as Lay was liquidating his own stock, throughout the late summer and early fall of 2001, he "reassured Enron employees about the positive financial prospects of the firm and even suggested that they would benefit from purchasing more Enron stock."[110]

Such actions undermine confidence in both corporations and markets, since strong markets "depend on healthy investor psychology."[111] When the "fraudsters and charlatans gain prominence, excesses rage and burned investors shy away from markets."[112] Enron was itself a market, and what holds true for Enron holds true for the stock market as well: "no one can believe anything asserted by a firm that covers up losses by entering into sham derivative contracts with itself."[113] Investors won't invest in a market that looks "like the Bulgarian stock market,"[114] and corporate officers like Kenneth Lay and Andrew Fastow not only defraud investors, but fundamentally undermine confidence in the market itself.

---

is difficult for me to quantify although, as a shareholder, I know it's reflected in the valuation given the avoided dilution of earnings per share.").

[107] Kahn, *supra* note 65, at 1594; *see* Powers Report, *supra* note 6, at 3 ("Enron employees involved in the partnerships were enriched, in the aggregate, by tens of millions of dollars they should never have received.").

[108] Kahn, *supra* note 65, at 1594.

[109] *Id.* at 1595.

[110] *Id.* at 1594; for instance, *see* Batson Report, *supra* note 6, at 6 ("In an earnings release on October 16, 2001, Kenneth Lay . . . while expressing confidence in Enron's 'strong earnings outlook,' announced, among other things, that Enron was taking 'after-tax-non-recurring charges' of $1.01 billion in the third quarter."). Lay may be paying back some of his ill-gotten gains, however. *See* Batson Report, *supra* note 6, at 131 ("The Examiner's preliminary conclusions are as follows: Enron has a cause of action under Section 548(a)(1)(B) of the Bankruptcy Code (i.e., constructively fraudulent conveyance) against Lay to recover transfers in excess of $74 million made in the year prior to the Petition Date arising out of certain loans made by Enron to Lay and which Lay repaid Enron with Enron stock at a time when Enron was presumed to be insolvent. . . . Enron has a cause of action under Section 547 of the Bankruptcy Code (i.e., preference) against certain employees of the Debtors arising out of Enron's accelerated payments, totaling $53 million, under two deferred compensation plans, made in a 30-day period (commencing on October 30, 2001), at a time when Enron was presumably insolvent.").

[111] Lerach, *supra* note 38, at 120.

[112] *Id.* at 122.

[113] Bratton, *supra* note 16, at 1320.

[114] *See* Lerach, *supra* note 38, at 122.

LESSON FOUR: OFFICERS AND DIRECTORS MUST KNOW AND FULFILL THEIR DUTIES OR FACE LIABILITY

It is black-letter law that the directors and officers of a corporation have fiduciary duties owed to the corporation's stockholders.[115] This statement means that they appoint management, determine management's compensation, and review and approve major investment and operational decisions made by management. In doing so, they must exercise due care and maintain loyalty to the corporation and its stockholders. If they fail in these obligations, they risk liability to the corporation, its shareholders, and its creditors.[116]

An officer may owe a similar set of fiduciary duties to the corporation and its stockholders within the scope of his or her employment, as delegated by the board of directors.[117] Persons simultaneously serving as directors and officers will be held to the standards applicable to directors, and the scope of their responsibilities as officers does not limit the scope or breadth of their duties as directors.

A. The Duty of Care

The duty of care has two component parts: a decision-making duty and an oversight duty. The decision-making duty of care itself has two elements within its scope: (1) the duty to be informed of all material information that is reasonably available before making a decision, and (2) the duty to use reasonable care in making the decision itself.[118]

---

[115] When the corporation approaches the zone of insolvency, these fiduciary duties are enhanced and the class of beneficiaries expands beyond stockholders to include creditors. *See* Credit Lyonnais Bank Nederland, N.V. v. Pathe Communications Corp., 1991 WL 277613, 17 Del. J. Corp. L. 1099, 1991 Del. Ch. LEXIS 215 (Del. 1991). Upon bankruptcy they may even expand further to encompass all "parties in interest," a nebulous description indeed.

[116] This liability may be non-dischargeable in a subsequent bankruptcy by the director or officer. *See* Nahman v. Jacks (In re Jacks), 266 B.R. 728 (B.A.P. 9th Cir. 2001) (applying California trust fund doctrine); Flegel v. Burt & Assocs., P.C. (In re Kallmeyer), 242 B.R. 492 (B.A.P. 9th Cir. 1999). By characterizing the trust fund doctrine as one that imposes an express trust, corporate creditors that succeed on a breach of fiduciary duty claim against a director may bring an adversary proceeding in the director's bankruptcy case and have the debt declared non-dischargeable, *i.e.*, determined to be a debt that will *survive* the bankruptcy case and continue to be enforceable against the debtor-director. The non-dischargability of a breach of fiduciary duty claim must be timely and affirmatively sought by the creditor through the bankruptcy adversary proceeding process or the claim will be time barred. *See* 11 U.S.C. § 523(c); *see also* Fed. R. Bankr. P. 4004 & 4007 (statute of limitations and procedure for dischargability actions); Katherine S. Kruis, Esq., *The Time Limitation for Objecting to Discharge of Debts: A Trap for the Unwary*, 26 Cal. Bankr. J. 55 (2001).

[117] Del. Code Ann. tit. 8, § 141(a) ("The business and affairs of every corporation . . . shall be managed by or under the direction of a board of directors."); *cf.* In re Ben Franklin, 225 B.R. 646, 652 n.10 (Bankr. N.D. Ill. 1998) ("No fiduciary duty governing management of a corporation's affairs can be imposed on persons who have no authority to manage those affairs.").

[118] Smith v. Van Gorkom, 488 A.2d 858, 872-74 (Del. 1985).

The oversight duty requires that directors exercise reasonable care in overseeing and monitoring the performance of corporate officers and the corporation's business.

B. The Duty of Loyalty

The duty of loyalty is even easier to understand than the duty of care. Directors are to act in good faith in the best interest of the corporation and are not to engage in self-dealing or usurp corporate opportunities. If a director desires to engage in a self-dealing transaction or to take advantage of a business opportunity that the corporation would otherwise have the chance to pursue, the director may do so if, after full disclosure of all material facts: (1) the transaction is approved by a majority of the disinterested members of the board of directors, or (2) the transaction is ratified by a wholly disinterested stockholder vote.[119] Absent one of those two conditions being satisfied, the director will bear the burden, in a subsequent lawsuit, of demonstrating that the transaction is objectively and intrinsically fair.[120]

C. The Business Judgment Rule

The business judgment rule is a doctrine creating a rebuttable presumption that a board's decision is one made on an informed basis, with a good-faith belief that the action was taken in the best interests of the corporation.[121] Absent evidence contradicting some portion of this presumption, or a showing that one or more directors with a conflicting interest participated in the decision-making, a reviewing court will not substitute its own judgment for that of the board.[122]

The principal area in which the business judgment rule's protections may be lost involves non-disinterested directors. If a board is dominated or controlled by one or more directors with an undisclosed conflicting interest, the protection of the rule may not apply.[123] Additionally, if the board is predominantly composed of members with a financial interest in the transaction, the business judgment rule may not apply.[124]

The business judgment rule is a shield for directors facing claims of breach of the decision-making duty of care. It does not apply to the duty of loyalty if a director

---

[119] DEL. CODE ANN. tit. 8, § 144; CAL. CORP CODE § 310 (1990).

[120] Mills Acquisition Co. v. MacMillan, Inc., 559 A.2d 1261, 1280 (Del. 1989). Delaware's authorization of an exculpatory provision to limit monetary damages for a breach of the duty of care does not apply to breaches of the duty of loyalty or improper self-dealing. DEL. CODE ANN. tit. 8, § 102(b)(7)(i), (iv). By contrast, California's enabling statute contains no such express limitation. *See* CAL. CORP. CODE § 204(a)(10)(1990).

[121] *See* CAL. CORP. CODE § 309(a) (1990); Briano v. Rubio, 46 Cal. App. 4th 1167, 54 Cal. Rptr. 2d 408 (1996); Polk v. Good, 507 A.2d 531, 536 (Del. Super. Ct. 1986); Brant v. Hicks, Muse & Co. (In re Healthco International, Inc.), 208 BR 288, 302-07 (Bankr. D. Mass 1997).

[122] *Id.*

[123] *See* Cede & Co. v. Technicolor, Inc., 634 A.2d 345, 363, *modified*, 636 A.2d 956 (Del. 1994).

[124] *See* AC Acquisition Co. v. Anderson, Clayton & Co. 519 A.2d 103, 111 (Del. Ch. 1986).

pursues a self-interested transaction without either disinterested director approval or stockholder ratification, in each case after full disclosure of all material facts. The business judgment rule does not apply at all to a claim for usurpation of corporate opportunity. If the business judgment rule does not apply to an alleged breach of the duty of loyalty, then the intrinsic or fundamental fairness standard applies, and the non-disinterested director bears the burden of proof that the transaction was both substantively and procedurally fair.[125]

Here's the point: The business judgment rule is a rule for the courtroom; directors should not rely upon it in the boardroom. Although it may apply and protect them if their decisions are later challenged, prudent directors should assume that the rule will not apply and should therefore conduct themselves accordingly, *i.e.*, they should, at all times, exercise the duty of care of a reasonable person in:

(a) gathering information,
(b) assessing alternatives and potential outcomes, and
(c) making decisions,
(d) all in good faith, and
(e) *either:*
 (i) in a disinterested fashion, or
 (ii) with full disclosure of all conflicts of interest, subject to approval by a majority of disinterested directors or stockholder ratification.

If a lawsuit later arises, the protections of the business judgment rule should supplement an otherwise strong decision-making record.

Finally, a director or officer should not take refuge by resigning from the board or company upon learning of a difficult circumstance or wrongful action. One might especially wish to avoid the example of Jeffery Skilling, who purportedly told Kenneth Lay that he [Skilling] was resigning from Enron for personal reasons, which included his desire to spend more time with his children, and his being kept up at night by Enron's falling stock price.[126] As a director, although one is not irrevocably committed for the ultimate long haul, one has taken on a duty of stewardship to supervise and manage a

---

[125] Cinerama, Inc. v. Technicolor, Inc., 1991 WL 111134, at *8-12, (Del. Ch. 1991), *aff'd in part, rev'd in part sub nom* Cede & Co. v. Technicolor, Inc., 634 A.2d 345 (Del. 1993), *modified*, 636 A.2d 956 (Del. 1994) (explaining business judgment rule as a rule that imposes the burden of proof on the plaintiff and, as an alternative, the entire fairness standard of review as imposing the burden of proof on the defendant director). The inquiry into *substantive* fairness focuses on the terms of the transaction and asks, were these terms fair to the corporation? The *procedural* fairness inquiry focuses on whether there was full disclosure and appropriate approval by disinterested directors. To achieve *both* substantive and procedural fairness, boards often employ a committee of disinterested directors to negotiate the transaction with the interested director (or the entity representing his or her interest) and then approve the transaction by a majority of the disinterested members of the entire board.

[126] *See* David Barboza, *Enron's Many Strands: the Former Chief*, N.Y. Times, Aug. 22, 2002 at C1 ("In a summary of an interview with lawyers last January, Mr. Lay said that Mr. Skilling told him that he wanted to spend more time with his three children. When he was pressed, the summary stated: 'Skilling said he

corporation. Suddenly resigning when the going gets rough is not an action consistent with this notion of stewardship.[127] Further, the protections of the business judgment rule have been held to apply only to director action, not to director inaction, at least under Delaware law.[128] Doing nothing or resigning upon discovery of problems or wrongdoing will rarely be appropriate and should not relieve a director from liability when the plane crashes after he or she bails out.

The behavior of Enron's executives will no doubt become enshrined in that most telling of legends: the cautionary tale. Like Icarus, who flew too close to the sun and perished as a result, Enron's executives will continue to be held up to the business and legal community as examples of what *not* to do. The completion of the cautionary Enron legend will have to await the conclusion of lengthy, civil, criminal, regulatory, and bankruptcy proceedings. The Powers Report "rightly faults Enron's board for defective ongoing monitoring of the LJM transactions,"[129] and Powers himself concluded that "Enron's board of directors breached the fiduciary duty of care it owed to the company's shareholders."[130] By having a "material financial interest in the transactions between Enron and the investment partnerships he created and managed," Andrew Fastow more than likely breached the duty of loyalty.[131] Even managers who did not benefit monetarily from Enron's transactions with suspect partnerships may have breached the duty of care. Jeffrey Skilling supposedly surrounded himself with "yes men," and it "would be reasonable to argue that the 'yes men,' if they were corporate officers, breached the duty of care by invariably saying yes instead of adequately investigating, monitoring and ensuring compliance with the law."[132] Enron's former CEO, Kenneth Lay, may have breached the duty of care by being out of touch and unfamiliar with

was under a lot of pressure and felt that Enron's stock price was dropping and he could not do anything about it. Skilling was taking Enron's stock price personally and could not sleep at night.'")

[127] *See* Xerox v Genmoora Corp., 888 F.2d 345 (5th Cir. 1989) (analogizing resignation on the eve of corporate transaction to a pilot bailing out of a commercial airplane after pointing it at a mountain; it is an insufficient defense that one is not at the controls at the moment of impact).

[128] Rabkin v. Philip A. Hunt Chem. Corp., 1987 WL 28436, at *3, LEXIS 522, *3 (Del. Ch. 1987) (The business judgment rule "has no role where directors have either abdicated their functions, or, absent a conscious decision, failed to act.").

[129] Bratton, *supra* note 16, at 1332; *see* Powers Report, *supra* note 6, at 24 ("In sum, the Board did not effectively meet its obligation with respect to the LJM transactions.").

[130] Cheryl L. Wade, *Corporate Governance and the Managerial Duty of Care*, 76 ST. JOHN'S L. REV. 767, 780 (2002); *see* Powers Report, *supra* note 6, at 22 ("With respect to the issues that are the subject of this investigation, the Board of Directors failed, in our judgment, in its oversight duties. This had serious consequences for Enron, its employees, and its shareholders.").

[131] Wade, *supra* note 130, at 781; *see* Powers Report, *supra* note 6, at 18 ("Fastow was Enron's Chief Financial Officer and was involved on both sides of the related-party transactions. What he presented as an arrangement intended to benefit Enron became, over time, a means of both enriching himself personally and facilitating manipulation of Enron's financial statements. Both of these objectives were inconsistent with Fastow's fiduciary duties to Enron and anything the Board authorized.").

[132] Wade, *supra* note 130, at 781; *see* Powers Report, *supra* note 6, at 19 ("Individually and collectively, Enron's management failed to carry out its substantive responsibility for ensuring that the transactions

many aspects of his own company.[133] The highly competitive, win-at-all-costs culture that Enron fostered "risked the kinds of managerial breaches and possibly criminal conduct that occurred."[134] Enron's leaders "averted their eyes from the manifest implications of their own actions" and as they "stepped across the line to fraud, their belief system trumped reality."[135]

D. The More Organizational Layers, the More Opportunity for Rot

Max Weber's theory of bureaucracy involved the primacy of a social structure that allocated resources according to a set of rules and qualifications, rather than according to rank or status. Bureaucracy was to provide a fair and uniform set of gatekeepers. The theoretical, ideal form of bureaucracy, however, has never materialized. Flawed versions of the model have prevailed. These include the internal governance structure of a corporation and the regulation of that corporation and the information that it discloses to the public by the interaction of officers, directors, lawyers, accountants, and the Securities and Exchange Commission, among others.

In organizational structures like this, there is much to gain by maintaining as "flat" a system as possible. Each layer of bureaucrats and gatekeepers inhibits clear and accurate communication and the institutional transparency necessary to root out wrongdoing. A series of Byzantine layers also provides the gatekeepers at each level with more opportunity to indulge in self-dealing. An organization chart that must be printed in "landscape" mode is desirable when one seeks to increase transparency and decrease opportunities for wrongdoing and self-dealing.

The remedy for incompetent or self-dealing management is supposed to be the oversight of a competent and adequately informed board of directors, the major features of which are "independent directors, specialized committees (especially an

---

were fair to Enron—which in many cases they were not—and its responsibility for implementing a system of oversight and controls over the transactions with the LJM partnerships.").

[133] Wade, *supra* note 130, 781-82; *see* Powers Report, *supra* note 6, at 19 ("For much of the period in question, Lay was the Chief Executive Officer of Enron and, in effect, the captain of the ship. As CEO, he had ultimate responsibility for taking reasonable steps to ensure that the officers reporting to him performed their oversight duties properly. He does not appear to have directed their attention, or his own, to the oversight of the LJM partnerships. Ultimately, a large measure of the responsibility rests with the CEO.").

[134] Wade, *supra* note 130, at 782.

[135] Bratton, *supra* note 16, at 1332. For example, *see* Report on Board of Directors, *supra* note 6, at 13 ("While the evidence indicates that, in some instances, Enron Board members were misinformed or misled, the Subcommittee investigation found that overall the Board received substantial information about Enron's plans and activities and explicitly authorized or allowed many of the questionable Enron strategies, policies and transactions now subject to criticism. Enron's high-risk accounting practices, for example, were not hidden from the Board. The Board knew of them and took no action to prevent Enron from misusing them. . . . Enron's extensive off-the-books activity was not only well known to the Board, but was made possible by Board resolutions authorizing new unconsolidated entities, Enron preferred shares, and Enron stock collateral that was featured in many of the off-the-books deals.").

audit committee) consisting exclusively of independent directors to perform crucial monitoring functions, and clear charter of board authority."[136] On the face of it, Enron's board of directors was a model board, consisting of fourteen members, only two of whom were insiders. The prestigious and qualified directors included the former Chairperson of the Commodity Futures Trading Commission and a former United Kingdom Secretary of State.[137] Enron's Audit Committee had a state-of-the-art charter, giving the committee the power to do everything, from oversee the company's reporting procedures and internal controls, to the power to hire and "retain other accountants, lawyers, or consultants."[138] Both the Board and the Audit Committee, however, were "undermined by side payments of one kind or another."[139] Furthermore, the use of "political contributions to friends and allies of the directors, larger contributions to institutions the directors were associated with, and a lavish equity package for the directors either chloroformed or corrupted Enron's Board."[140] The Board maintained that things were going well; so well, in fact, that the proposal to "suspend the corporate ethics code to permit conflicted transactions by a senior executive, an extraordinary request—did not stir the antennae."[141]

---

136 Gordon, *supra* note 97, at 1241; *see* Report on Board of Directors, *supra* note 6, at 5 ("In the United States, the Board of Directors sits at the apex of a company's governing structure. A typical Board's duties include reviewing the company's overall business strategy; selecting and compensating the company's senior executives; evaluating the company's outside auditor; overseeing the company's financial statements; and monitoring overall company performance. According to the Business Roundtable, the Board's 'paramount duty' is to safeguard the interests of the company's shareholders.").

137 Lerach, *supra* note 38, at 106; *see* Report on Board of Directors, *supra* note 6, at 8 ("The Subcommittee interviews found the Directors to have a wealth of sophisticated business and investment experience and considerable expertise in accounting, derivatives, and structured finance.").

138 Gordon, *supra* note 97, at 1241.

139 *Id.* at 1242.

140 Lerach, *supra* note 38, at 106; *see* Report on Board of Directors, *supra* note 6, 51-52 ("At the May 7 hearing, the expert witnesses testified that the independence and objectivity of the Enron Board had been weakened by financial ties between Enron and certain Directors. . . . A number of corporate governance experts contacted by the Subcommittee staff identified these financial ties as contributing to the Enron Board's lack of independence and reluctance to challenge Enron management. . . . Robert H. Campbell . . . testified that 'consulting arrangements with directors are absolutely incorrect, absolutely wrong' because directors are already paid a substantial fee to be available to management and provide their perspective on company issues. The three experts at the May 7 hearing also criticized the compensation paid to the Board members, noting that $350,000 per year was significantly above the norm and that much of the compensation was in the form of stock options, which enabled the Board members to benefit from stock gains, without risking investment loss.").

141 Gordon, *supra* note 97, at 1242; *see* Report on Board of Directors, *supra* note 6, at 24 ("The Enron Board's decision to waive the company's code of conduct and allow its Chief Financial Officer (CFO) Andrew Fastow to establish and operate off-the-books entities designed to transact business with Enron was also highly unusual and disturbing."); *see also* Powers Report, *supra* note 17, at 156. ("At bottom, however, the need for such an extensive set of controls said something fundamental about the wisdom of permitting the CFO to take on this conflict of interest. The two members of the Special Committee participating in

If a corporate bureaucracy is meant to function as a system of gatekeepers and checks ensuring honesty and preventing fraud, then the malfunction of that system is illustrated not only by the failure of Enron's board, but also by the failure of Enron's professional gatekeepers: the accountants, lawyers, and bankers who serviced the energy tracking giant.[142] Enron's accounting firm, Author Andersen, was a disaster; for awash "in 27 million in consulting fees on top of 25 million in audit fees at Enron, Andersen, as 'business consultant,' helped structure the very transactions that [it was] to later audit."[143] Enron's lawyers "held themselves out as having special expertise to help put together the kinds of complex structured financial transactions that created million [sic] and millions of dollars of false profits for Enron."[144] Worst of all, however, were the banks. Some of the nation's most prestigious financial institutions "made at least six billion dollars in concealed loans to Enron,"[145] enabling the corporation to hide its debt and maintain its investment grade credit rating. With the help of its bankers, Enron raised billions of dollars in fresh capital from investors in the four years before it went bankrupt.[146]

---

this review of the Board's actions believe that a conflict of this significance that could be managed only through so many controls and procedures should not have been approved in the first place.").

142 Lerach, *supra* note 38, 108-117; *see* Powers Report, *supra* note 6, at 148 ("Oversight of the related-party transactions by Enron's Board of Directors and Management failed for many reasons. . . . Enron's outside auditors supposedly examined Enron's internal controls, but did not identify or bring to the Audit Committee's attention the inadequacy in their implementation.); *see also* Report on Board of Directors, *supra* note 8, at 3 ("The Board also failed to ensure the independence of the company's auditor, allowing Andersen to provide internal audit and consulting services while serving as Enron's outside auditor.").

143 Lerach, *supra* note 38, at 108. For example, *see* Batson Report, *supra* note 6, at 39 ("Enron carefully designed its FAS 140 technique with advice from Andersen and Enron's lawyers, with the goal that the asset transfer would qualify for sale treatment under GAAP despite the fact that sale treatment did not reflect the economic substance of the transaction.").

144 Lerach, *supra* note 38, at 113. For example, *see* Powers Report, *supra* note 6, at 190 ("Enron had an obligation to disclose the 'amount of [Fastow's] *interest* in the transaction(s)' (emphasis added), not just his income. The lawyers apparently searched for and embraced a technical rationale to avoid that disclosure.").

145 Lerach, *supra* note 38, at 114. For example, *see* Batson Report, *supra* note 6, at 65-66 ("The financial institutions—specifically, Citibank and JPMorgan—played significant roles in facilitating the Prepay Transactions. They helped Enron structure the transactions, providing the funding either directly or indirectly, and assisted in forming the conduit entities Andersen and Enron deemed necessary to the transactions. Both Citibank and JPMorgan knew that Enron accounted for its obligations under the Prepay Transactions as liabilities from price risk management activities rather than debt. They also believed that Enron reported the cash as cash flow from operating activities rather than financing activities. Nevertheless, both lenders recognized that the Prepay Transactions were essentially loans.").

146 Lerach, *supra* note 38, at 114. Actually, Enron informed its banks of the extent of its debt on November 19, 2001. *See* Batson Report, *supra* note 6, at 9-10 ("On November 19, 2001, the same day Enron filed its third quarter financial statements, senior Enron executives met with certain of Enron's bankers at the Waldorf Astoria hotel in New York City. Enron's objectives for the meeting were to restore creditor confidence, relive its liquidity crisis and discuss its proposed merger with Dynegy, Inc. During this meeting, Enron informed its bankers that, while the debt reflected on its third quarter 2001 balance

Enron is thus paradigmatic of the systemic problem of failed bureaucracy. A "flatter" corporate structure, and a consequently higher level of transparency, might have prevented, or at least revealed, the problems in the corporation. Smaller committees, like smaller classes in graduate schools, allow for more questioning, more searching inquiries; they allow participants a level of intimacy and comfort that allows them to display their ignorance, to question current practices, and to engage in higher quality learning and decision-making.[147]

The problem with Kafkaesque systems of gatekeepers and gates is not only that they shield the system from outside penetration,[148] but also that the gatekeepers tend

---

sheet under GAAP was $12.978 billion, Enron's 'debt' . . . was 38.094 billion. Thus, as Enron noted, $25.116 million of debt was 'off-balance-sheet,' or in some cases reflected on the balance sheet, but classified as something other than debt.").

[147] Professor Warren C. Neal, Director of the Center for Corporate Governance at the University of Tennessee College of Business Administration, Remarks at the Clayton Center for Entrepreneurial Law, the University of Tennessee College of Law, Knoxville, Tennessee (March 24, 2003) (emphasizing the use of small committees and sub-committees to improve the quality of the processes of board deliberation and inquiries of management as a means of improving the quality of corporate governance in U.S. corporations).

[148] The author refers to the following passage from Kafka's *Trial:*

> "Don't deceive yourself," said the priest. "What am deceiving myself in?" said K.
>
> "You're deceiving yourself in the court," said the priest, "the introductory writings on the law speak to this deception: A gatekeeper stands before the law. A man from the country comes to the gatekeeper and asks entry into the law. But the gatekeeper says, he cannot guarantee him entry. The man considers and then asks, whether he might enter later. "It's possible," says the gatekeeper, "but not now." Since the door to the law stands open as always and the gatekeeper walks off to the side, the man bends down in order to see through the gate, and into the interior. When the gatekeeper sees that, he laughs and says: "If it tempts you so, try it then, to go in despite my forbidding it. See here though: I am powerful. And I am only the least of the gatekeepers. From chamber to chamber, however, stand gatekeepers, one more powerful than the other. Already the sight of the third is more than even I can bear." The man from the country had not expected such difficulties, the law should be open to each and always he thinks, but as he now looks more closely at the gatekeeper in his fur coat, his big pointed nose, the long, thin, black tartan beard, he decides, he'd better wait until he gets permission to enter. The gatekeeper gives him a stool and lets him sit down beside the door. There he sits for days and years. He makes many attempts to be let in, and tires the gatekeeper out with his requests. The gatekeeper more often holds small interrogations with him, asks him all about his home and about much else besides, they are however disinterested questions, like great lords ask, and at the end he tells him again as always, that he cannot let him in. The man, who had provisioned himself more than adequately for his trip, expends everything, regardless of its value, in order to bribe the gatekeeper. That one accepts everything, but adds, "I'm only accepting it, so that you won't think that you've wasted something." Over the course of many years, the man observes the gatekeeper almost without interruption. He forgets the other gatekeepers, and this first one seems to him to be the only impediment to entry into the law. He curses the unlucky coincidence out loud in the early years, in the later, when he's old, he grumbles only to himself. He becomes childish, and since during the course of his years-long study of the gatekeeper, he has come to recognize even the fleas in his fur coat, he asks the fleas as well to help him and persuade the gatekeeper. Finally the light in his eyes becomes dim, and he knows not, whether it is really becoming darker around him, or if his eyes deceive him. But in the darkness he now recognizes well

to become friendly with each other and to realize that mutually profitable relationships may spring up within guarded walls. Gatekeepers may not let outsiders in, but, as Enron illustrates, gatekeepers are also not to be trusted to refrain from pillaging that which they are supposed to guard, let alone to continue to watch the other watchers of the gates.

E. Leverage: Great High, Heavy Hangover

All the technical accounting and legal explanations aside, what was the purpose of Enron's SPEs?[149] As Neil Batson points out, the problem was not so much Enron's use of SPEs as Enron's *misuse* of them.[150] ("There is nothing improper about the use of structured finance and SPEs to achieve and report business results. Enron, however, used structured finance to report results it had not achieved.")[151] Enron hid debt. It hid leverage. Leverage is not bad in and of itself. Leverage is a tool that can be used to boost returns on equity and reward debt holders with an appropriate rate of interest for the use of their funds.[152] Enron's actual debt-to-equity ratio was on the order of 90%,[153] but for a period, Enron did not report this true figure. Had Enron reported

---

> a light that inextinguishably breaks forth from the door of the law. He will not live much longer. Before his death the experiences of the whole time all coalesce in his mind into a single question, that until now he had not asked the gatekeeper. He beckons to him, for he can no longer raise his stiffening body. The gatekeeper must bend down deeply to him, for the difference in height has changed very much in the man's favor. "What do you want to know now," asks the gatekeeper. "You are insatiable." "All strive toward the law," says the man, "how come no one except me has requested entry in so many years." The gatekeeper recognizes that the man is already at his end, and in order to reach his fading hearing, he bellows at him, "No one else could gain entry here, for this entrance was meant only for you. I'll go now and close it."

Franz Kafka, *Der Prozess, in* FRANZ KAFKA: DIE ROMANE 259, 432-34 (1963) (original translated to English from German).

[149] For a thorough discussion of SPEs, tax review standards, and Enron's accounting practices, *see* Harold S. Peckron, *Watchdogs that Failed to Bark: Standards of Tax Review After Enron*, 5 FLA. TAX REV. 853, 903, 910, 913 (2002) ("Using off-the-books partnerships and maddeningly opaque accounting . . . Enron shielded about 500 million in debt. That helped keep Enron's credit rating high . . . assuming arguendo that some of the Enron special purpose entities that shifted debt off the balance sheet met the realistic possibility standard, still their ethical impact on third parties (e.g. shareholders, creditors, etc.) should have been considered. . . . For instance is it ethically necessary now to consider the impact of the debt-shifting special purpose entity shelter on the publicly traded company's stock price. The creation of special purpose entities . . . acted as tax shelters and off-balance sheet financing vehicles. . . .").

[150] *See* Batson Report, *supra* note 6, at 49-50.

[151] *Id.*

[152] For a thorough discussion of leverage and its benefits, see Robert E. Scott, *The Truth About Secured Financing*, 82 CORNELL L. REV. 1436, 1448-1456 (1997).

[153] *See Testimony of Robert Roach, Chief Investigator: Permanent Subcommittee on Investigations: the Role of Financial Institutions in Enron's Collapse*, at 2, *available at* http://govt-aff.senate.gov/072302roach.pdf (last visited June 5, 2003) ("With the inclusion of the prepays as debt, Enron's debt to equity ratio would have risen from about 69% to about 96%. Its debt to total capital ratio would have risen from 40% to

the true figure, the risk associated with such a high degree of leverage would have been factored into the stock price, which would have declined to reflect a more accurate risk premium.[154]

A company's degree of leverage must be accurately assessed and reported at all times, and officers, directors, accountants, and attorneys must be attuned to the possibility that hidden debt and other liabilities are boosting a company's or a unit's reported returns.[155] For those who benefit from high returns, such as managers of strategic business units and others compensated or promoted based upon their unit's performance, the temptation is always there to over-report revenue and under-report expenses and debt. As Ronald Regan once said, in another context, "Trust, but verify." The comment is apt in the corporate governance arena as well.[156]

CONCLUSION

The Enron debacle: A concentration of phenomena that, taken together, led to a huge financial collapse. The lessons that can be learned from Enron are many, but they are all simple, fundamental points learned by (or at least taught to) every accounting,

---

49%."); *see also* Paul Sperry, *Did Enron insiders smell trouble in '98?: Heavy stock selling began 4 years ago, as company's overseas debt piled up*, WorldNetDaily.com, *available at* http://www.worldnetdaily.com/news/article.asp?ARTICLE_ID=26085 (last visited June 5, 2003) ("Over the same period, Enron's debt-to-equity ratio continued to climb, from 78 percent to 91 percent.").

[154] This was precisely what Enron wanted to avoid, however. *See* Batson Report, *supra* note 6, at 15, 18-19 ("Two key factors drove Enron's management of its financial statements: (i) its need for cash and (ii) its need to maintain an investment grade credit rating. Enron was reluctant to issue equity to address these needs for fear of an adverse effect on its stock price and was reluctant to incur debt because of a possible adverse effect on its stock ratings. Moreover, Enron's use of market-to-market . . . accounting created a large gap between net income and funds flow from operations. . . . By 1999, Enron's Wholesale Services was by far the most significant of Enron's business segments. . . . In order to continue the growth of this business, Enron needed to trade with other market participants without being required to post collateral. Thus, the continued success of Enron's entire business was dependent upon the continued success of its Wholesale Services business segment, which in turn was dependent upon Enron's credit ratings for its senior unsecured long-term debt.").

[155] *See* Batson Report, *supra* note 6, at 54 ("A public company like Enron, in addition to complying with the literal GAAP rules and publishing financial statements that fairly present its financial position, results of operations and cash flows in accordance with GAAP, must also comply with the federal securities laws mandating additional financial disclosure.").

[156] Leverage also has an effect on the legal duties owed by officers and directors. As a company approaches bankruptcy or operates in the zone of insolvency, the fiduciary duties normally owed to shareholders alone shift to include both shareholders and creditors as beneficiaries. This creates a conflict of interest so great that it may be impossible to serve both sets of interests. With few exceptions, when a corporation's balance sheet is leveraged, the creditors and stockholders have fundamentally different stakes and motivations: Stockholders over-value risk (that is the point of leverage) while creditors undervalue it. *See* John D. Ayer & Michael L. Bernstein, *Bankruptcy In Practice* 137 (ABI 2002) (presenting explanation of this conflict of interest and illustrating it with risk-adjusted balance sheet presentation). Stockholders of insolvent corporations—who face the highest risks—always stand to gain from delayed liquidation; it gives them more time for their risk to pay off. *Id.* If a business has debt, this conflict of interest is guaranteed to exist.

business, and law student. Fraud is not complex. If it sounds too good to be true, it probably is. Retain a healthy sense of skepticism and engage in critical analysis of any report or conclusion. Recognize the role of a corporate steward, gatekeeper, or watchdog, and discharge the duties of that role faithfully. Do not establish incentive systems that create conflicts of interest. Prefer flat, transparent organizational structures. Avoid cults of individual or corporate personality. Watch your leverage. Design corporate boards that are, in fact, capable of discharging their fiduciary duties, after reasonable investigation in a disinterested fashion. All you ever needed to know about avoiding another Enron-style situation, you learned in kindergarten—or at least in graduate school.

Enron, Titanic, *and* The Perfect Storm*

*Nancy B. Rapoport***

> [Former Enron CEO Jeffrey] Skilling offered a hypothesis for what brought Enron down, calling it a "perfect storm" of events.
>
> He speculated that questions raised about the quality of Enron's accounting and about self-dealing caused a loss of confidence in the financial community. That led to Enron's debt being downgraded.
>
> That downgrade, he said he was told by an Enron executive after he left, meant Enron couldn't access several billion dollars of back-up credit lines. A liquidity crunch followed, he said, even though Enron was solvent and highly profitable.
>
> —Laura Goldberg, *Houston Chronicle*[1]

---

* Originally published at 71 FORDHAM L. REV. 1373 (2003). Reprinted by permission. *Editors' note:* This essay was included in the first edition of this book. Reprinted by permission.

** Dean and Professor of Law at the University of Houston Law Center. All views expressed in this essay are mine alone, and not those of the University of Houston or its faculty, staff, or administration. I want to thank Emily Chan-Nguyen, Kelli Cline, Luddie Collins, Bala Dharan, Patrick Flanagan, Jimmy Halvatzis, Susan Hartman, Michele Hedges, Morris & Shirley Rapoport, Harriet Richman, Jeff Van Niel, and Michelle Wu. I also want to thank the students in my 2002 Seminar on *Special Issues in Ethics:* Sara Alonso Oliver, Justin Berg, Alison Chien, Doug Du Bois, Trevor Fish, Patrick Flanagan (who gets thanked twice, because he was also one of the cite-checkers for this article), Kim Havel, Cathy Helenhouse, Colin Moore, Sandy Oballe, Kevin Powers, Barry Rienstra, Ron Smeberg, and Tiffany Toups.

1 Laura Goldberg, *Did No Wrong, Skilling Says: Defends His Role in Enron Fall*, HOUS. CHRON., Jan. 17, 2002, *available at* http://www.chron.com/cs/CDA/story.hts/special/enron/dec01/1183520; *see also Good Morning America* (ABC television broadcast, Feb. 7, 2002) ("All eyes will be on former CEO Jeff Skilling. Skilling blames Enron's collapse on an unfortunate collision of events—the perfect storm. Congressional investigators point out he was at Enron's helm at the time."). Of course, now everyone—and I mean everyone—has latched onto this "perfect storm" metaphor. *See, e.g.*, Federal Document Clearing House, Worldcom CEO John Sidgmore Testifies Before the U.S. Senate Committee on Commerce, Science and Transportation, July 30, 2002, *available at* 2002 WL 1753183, at *3 (statement of John Sidgmore, CEO, WorldCom) ("Several factors . . . converged to create, I'll use Mr. Legere's words, a kind of perfect storm—and I guarantee you we did not rehearse this—that ripped through the telecommunications industry.");

> Of course, we now know the extraordinary combination of circumstances that existed at that time which you would not meet again in 100 years; that they should all have existed just on that particular night shows, of course, that everything was against us.
>
> —Second Officer Charles Lightoller, *RMS Titanic*[2]

> I had some misgivings about calling [my book] *The Perfect Storm,* but in the end I decided that the intent was sufficiently clear. I use perfect in the meteorological sense: a storm that could not possibly have been worse.
>
> —Sebastian Junger[3]

Much has been written about the Enron fiasco, from scholarly articles[4] to popular books,[5] and I'm sure that much more will be written about the deals that brought the company down, the arrogance of some of the main players, and the ethical and moral

---

Federal Document Clearing House, *Harming Patient Access to Care: The Impact of Excessive Litigation,* July 17, 2002, *available at* 2002 WL 1584492, at *3 (statement of Richard Anderson, CEO, The Doctor's Company) ("The combination of these factors created . . . the perfect storm . . . for medical liability insurers."); Federal Document Clearing House, *House Committee on Education and the Workforce Holds a Hearing on Enron's Benefits Plan and its Compliance With Laws on Employer-Sponsored Pension Plans,* Feb. 7, 2002, *available at* 2002 WL 203240, at *12 (statement of Teresa Ghilarducci, Associate Professor of Economics, University of Notre Dame) ("The 1990s was the perfect storm for pensions to increase."); Federal Document Clearing House, *U.S. Senate Judiciary Committee Holds Hearing on Accountability Issues: Lessons Learned From Enron's Fall,* Feb. 6, 2002, *available at* 2002 WL 188865, at *11-12 (statement of Christine Gregoire, Attorney General, Washington State) ("In Washington [State,] we feel like Enron has been the gathering of the perfect storm. First, they gouged our consumers and rate payers with highly questionable power prices last year. And now, sadly, they have defrauded our investors and others across the nation.").

One of the coolest things that can happen to a law professor happened to me after I first published this article in the *Fordham Law Review.* I sent a copy to Sebastian Junger, author of THE PERFECT STORM. He read it and said that I was correct in my understanding of the "perfect storm" concept. Thank you, Mr. Junger!

[2] WALTER LORD, THE NIGHT LIVES ON 47 (1987) [hereinafter THE NIGHT LIVES ON].

[3] SEBASTIAN JUNGER, THE PERFECT STORM: A TRUE STORY OF MEN AGAINST THE SEA xiv (1997).

[4] *See, e.g.*, Michelle Chan-Fishel, *After Enron: How Accounting and SEC Reform Can Promote Corporate Accountability While Restoring_Public Confidence*, 32 ENVTL. L. REP. 10965 (2002); Timothy P. Duane, *Regulation's Rationale: Learning from the California Energy Crisis*, 19 YALE J. ON REG. 471 (2002); Marisa Rogoway, *Recent Developments, Proposed Reforms to the Regulation of 401(k) Plans in the Wake of the Enron Disaster*, 6 J. SMALL & EMERGING BUS. L. 423 (2002); Marissa P. Viccaro, *Can Regulation Fair Disclosure Survive the Aftermath of Enron?*, 40 DUQ. L. REV. 695 (2002).

[5] *See, e.g.*, DIRK J. BARREVELD, THE ENRON COLLAPSE: CREATIVE ACCOUNTING, WRONG ECONOMICS OR CRIMINAL ACTS? A LOOK INTO THE ROOT CAUSES OF THE LARGEST BANKRUPTCY IN U.S. HISTORY (2002); ROBERT BRYCE, PIPE DREAMS: GREED, EGO, AND THE DEATH OF ENRON (2002); LOREN FOX, ENRON: THE RISE AND FALL (2002); PETER C. FUSARO & ROSS M. MILLER, WHAT WENT WRONG AT ENRON: EVERYONE'S GUIDE TO THE LARGEST BANKRUPTCY IN U.S. HISTORY (2002).

issues that seemed to come to light only after the story broke in the media.[6] Enron's collapse, along with the failures of such other mega-businesses as WorldCom and Global Crossing,[7] triggered new legislation[8] and introduced such heretofore arcane acronyms as "SPEs" into the general lexicon.[9] The metaphor most used to describe Enron's quick descent into chapter 11 has been the "perfect storm."

That "perfect storm" metaphor irks me no end. I maintain, and this essay is designed to illustrate, that what brought Enron down—at least as far as we know—wasn't a once-in-a-lifetime alignment of elements beyond its control. Rather, Enron's demise

---

6 One of the reasons that I'm sure more will be written is that I'm working on such a project: ENRON: CORPORATE FIASCOS & THEIR IMPLICATIONS (with Bala G. Dharan).

7 Take a look at the largest bankruptcies, in terms of approximate stated liabilities, in the past twelve months [2001-02]: WorldCom (7/02 bankruptcy filing) ($43 billion, including $2 billion more in liabilities discovered after the bankruptcy filing); Enron (12/01) ($32 billion); NTL, Inc. (5/02) ($23.4 billion); Adelphia (6/02) ($18.6 billion); Global Crossing (1/02) ($12.4 billion); KMart (1/02) ($10.2 billion). *See* American Bankruptcy Institute, *A Look Inside the Mega-Case,* 10th Annual Southwest Bankruptcy Conference, Sept. 12-15, 2002; Bill Atkinson, *Kmart Files Chapter 11 Bankruptcy; No. 3 Discounter Cites Weak Economy, Tough Competition; 'Couldn't Pay the Bills'; Swift Move Surprises; $2 Billion Loan to Aid Firm's Reorganization*, BALT. SUN, Jan. 23, 2002, at 1A ("The Troy, Mich.-based firm listed $17 billion in assets and $11.3 billion in liabilities. . . . [A]lthough Kmart's bankruptcy is large, it pales in comparison to the largest bankruptcy in history, filed last month by Enron Corp . . . [which] listed $49 billion in assets and $31.2 billion in debts."); Julie Creswell, *Going For Broke; Crash! There Goes Another Company into Bankruptcy. How Did We Get Here? (Long Story.) Are We on the Mend? (Don't Bet on It.)*, FORTUNE, Feb. 18, 2002, *available at* 2002 WL 2190302; Lorrie Grant, *Discounter Hopes for Fast Reorganization*, USA TODAY, Jan. 23, 2002, at B02 ("Kmart listed $16.28 billion in assets and $10.34 billion in debts."); Andrew Leckey, *Bankruptcies Leave Investors in the Lurch*, CHI. TRIB., Aug. 27, 2002, *available at* 2002 WL 2689322; Alexandra R. Moses, Chern Yeh Kwok, & Thomas Lee et al., *Retailer Kmart Files for Bankruptcy; Officials Plan to Close Some Stores, Reorganize*, ST. LOUIS POST-DISPATCH, Jan. 23, 2002, at A1 ("[Kmart] has $10.25 billion in debt."); Chris Reidy, *Kmart Tumbles Discount Retail Chain in Record Chap. 11 Filing*, BOSTON GLOBE, Jan. 23, 2002, at C1 ("In its bankruptcy filing, Kmart and its US subsidiaries listed $17 billion in total assets at book value and total liabilities of $11.3 billion as of the quarter ended Oct. 31."); Gary Young, *Major Bankruptcies Filed in New York City*, 228 N.Y. L.J. 5 (Aug. 1, 2002).

8 *See, e.g.*, Sarbanes-Oxley Act of 2002, Pub. L. No. 107-204, 116 Stat. 745, Corporate and Criminal Fraud Accountability Act of 2002, Pub. L. No. 107-204, 116 Stat. 800 (codified at 18 U.S.C. § 1348, 1514A, 1519-20) [hereinafter Sarbanes-Oxley]; *Framework for Enhancing the Quality of Financial Information Through Improvement of Oversight of the Auditing Process,* 67 Fed. Reg. 44964-01 (proposed July 5, 2002) (to be codified at 17 C.F.R. pt. 210, 229).

9 If you don't believe me, just do a search in WESTLAW or LEXIS on "SPEs" and see how many documents you get, especially documents dated after October 2001, when the Enron disaster began to break. A search of major newspaper articles (Westlaw database NPMJ) for the terms "special purpose entity" or "special purpose entities" during the year 1999 yielded zero results. The first article in this database appeared in October 2001 and a search of 2002 now yields over 328 results (as of the second week in October 2002, with more being added daily).

was a synergistic combination of human errors and hubris: a *"Titanic"*[10] miscalculation, rather than a "perfect storm."[11]

I. WHY *TITANIC* IS A BETTER METAPHOR FOR ENRON'S EVENTUAL DOWNFALL THAN IS *THE PERFECT STORM*

The story of the *Titanic* is well-known. The ship was, at the time of its maiden (and only) transatlantic voyage, the largest in the world, carrying a microcosm of society.[12] The glitterati of the United States and Europe were on board, as were hundreds of immigrants trying to make their way to a new land. The ship was built with watertight compartments that extended from the keel up several decks (some to D Deck and some to E deck); she also had a double bottom for extra protection.[13] She was designed to float with any two consecutive compartments flooded and even with three of the first five compartments (out of sixteen) flooded,[14] thanks to electronic doors that could be closed by a single command.[15] And she was touted as "unsinkable," at least in some press reports.[16]

But sink she did, based upon a series of miscalculations, no single one of which might have proved fatal, but all of which, taken together, doomed the ship. In a chapter of his follow-up book to *A Night to Remember*, called *The Night Lives On,*[17] Walter Lord enumerates the many individual mistakes made that night:

---

[10] And, no, it wasn't the Leonardo DiCaprio movie (TITANIC (20th Century Fox 1997)) that first piqued my interest in the ship's history. I've been fascinated by it for probably thirty or so years. Among other things, I'm a member of the Titanic Historical Society, and I probably own virtually every book and movie about the ship. If you're wondering if I'm a bit obsessed with the ship and its tale, you're right. But everyone needs a hobby.

[11] I've used the *Titanic* comparison once before. *See, e.g.*, Mike Tolson, *The Fall of Enron/'Convenient whipping boy'/Enron Scandal Offers Fodder for Wide Range of Groups Seeking a Symbol for Their Cause*, HOUS. CHRON., Mar. 3, 2002, at 26, *available at* 2002 WL 3245488. Others have also made the comparison between Enron and the *Titanic*. *See* Edward J. Cleary, *Lessons For Lawyers From The Enron Debacle*, BENCH & B. MINN., Apr. 2002, at 16 (footnotes omitted) (quoting George F. Will, *Indignation Over Enron is Just the Beginning,* WASH. POST, Jan. 16, 2002) ("Given that Enron employee pensions were decimated with, as one commentator noted, the employees "locked in steerage like the lower orders on the *Titanic*, and given that many state pension funds were among the casualties, both state and national public officials will be forced to act."); Martha Neil, *Partners at Risk*, 88 A.B.A. J. 44 (Aug. 2002) ("The collapse of Enron might give partners at law firms reason to ponder another epic disaster: the sinking of the *Titanic*.").

[12] WALTER LORD, A NIGHT TO REMEMBER 1 (1997) [hereinafter A NIGHT TO REMEMBER].

[13] *Id.* at 174-75. She did not, however, have a double hull. *Id.*

[14] *Id.* at 26.

[15] *Id.* at 8.

[16] *Id.* at 175.

[17] THE NIGHT LIVES ON, *supra* note 2.

- the calm sea, which meant that the lookouts couldn't see any waves breaking against the bergs;[18]
- the numerous, apparently ignored ice warnings from ships already crossing the Atlantic Ocean that were using the same route as the *Titanic;*[19]
- the lack of any systematic procedure to deliver ice and weather warnings from the Marconi telegraph room to the bridge;[20]
- the fact that the lookouts' binoculars had been lost earlier in the trip;[21]
- the failure of the *Titanic's* officers to urge Captain Smith (or each other) to take a more cautious approach to travel, based on the calm sea and rapidly dropping temperature;[22]
- not enough lifeboats for the number of souls aboard;[23]
- Captain Smith's failure to hold lifeboat drills[24] or to do more than a perfunctory test of the ship's braking speed and maneuverability;[25]
- First Wireless Operator Phillips's famous response to an ice warning from the *Californian* (the ship that, according to some accounts, was closest to the *Titanic* when it sunk), "Shut up, shut up . . . I am working Cape Race";[26]
- the fact that lookout Frederic Fleet spotted the berg too late to stop the ship or otherwise to avoid the berg;[27]
- First Officer Murdoch's decision to port around the berg rather than ramming it head-on, a counterintuitive action that might have saved the ship;[28] and
- the *Californian's* decision not to come to the aid of a vessel in enough obvious distress to fire white distress rockets (apparently visible to the *Californian's* crew) at several intervals.[29]

The list of miscalculations goes on and on.[30] But Walter Lord tells it best:

---

18 *Id.* at 47.

19 *Id.* at 48-53.

20 *Id.* at 53.

21 *Id.* at 60.

22 *Id.* at 53-54.

23 *Id.* at 72-80.

24 A NIGHT TO REMEMBER, *supra* note 12, at 42.

25 THE NIGHT LIVES ON, *supra* note 2, at 56.

26 *Id.* at 58.

27 *Id.* at 59-60.

28 *Id.* at 59.

29 *Id.* at 134-59.

30 And so have I, at some social gatherings, as my very indulgent husband can attest.

> Given the competitive pressures of the North Atlantic run, the chances taken, the lack of experience with ships of such immense size, the haphazard procedures of the wireless room, the casualness of the bridge, and the misassessment of what speed was safe, it's remarkable that the *Titanic* steamed for two hours and ten minutes through ice-infested waters without coming to grief any sooner.
>
> "Everything was against us?" The wonder is that she lasted as long as she did.[31]

The Perfect Storm, on the other hand, describes a combination of meteorological bad luck and human miscalculation, born less of arrogance than of desperation. Granted, Billy Tyne, captain of the *Andrea Gail,* made a fatal mistake by sailing into the storm,[32] but he did "what ninety percent of us would've done—he battened down the hatches and hung on."[33] Although the signs were clear that bad weather was coming, the sheer magnitude of the storm was far beyond the experience (or imagination) of any of the ship captains in the large area covered by the storm, and each of them had to make a quick decision:

> [The weather bulletin describing Hurricane Grace] reads like an inventory of things fishermen don't want to hear. . . . Every boat in the swordfish fleet receives this information. Albert Johnston, south of the Tail, decides to head northwest into the cold water of the Labrador Current. . . . The rest of the sword fleet stays far to the east, waiting to see what the storm does. They couldn't make it into port in time anyway. The *Contship Holland,* a hundred miles south of Billy, heads straight into the teeth of the thing. Two hundred miles east, . . . the Liberian-registered *Zarah,* also heads for New York. Ray Leonard on the sloop *Sartori* has decided not to head for port; he holds to a southerly course for Bermuda. The *Laurie Dawn 8* keeps plowing out to the fishing grounds and the *Eishin Maru 78,* 150 miles due south of Sable Island, makes for Halifax harbor to the northeast. Billy can either waste several days trying to get out of the way, or he can stay on-course for home. The fact that he has a hold full of fish, and not enough ice, must figure into his decision.[34]

Billy Tyne's decision proved wrong, and the *Andrea Gail* lost all six hands aboard.[35] *Titanic* lost over 1,500 souls, with only 705 saved.[36] Both events were tragic. But only

---

[31] THE NIGHT LIVES ON, *supra* note 2, at 61.

[32] Special thanks to Boyd Henderson for reminding me, at a luncheon, that some human error contributed to the fate of the *Andrea Gail.*

[33] JUNGER, *supra* note 3, at 124 (quoting Captain Tommie Barrie, of the ship *Allison*).

[34] *Id.*

[35] *Id.* at 186.

[36] A NIGHT TO REMEMBER, *supra* note 12, at 176.

the *Titanic* can trace the loss of life directly to human arrogance.[37] When I compare the two tragedies in light of Jeffrey Skilling's claim that the fall of Enron was based on factors outside of the company's control—an economic "perfect storm"—I find that Skilling's claim falls flat.

II. HOW A FAILURE OF CHARACTER CAN TURN "PERFECT STORMS" INTO *TITANIC* MISTAKES

I'm not going to rehash the mechanics of the various Enron deals here. Others have done a good job of describing the problems with the deals,[38] with the Board's lack of oversight of the deals,[39] and with the general culture of Enron that encouraged aggressive risk-taking and short-term profits.[40] We obviously don't know enough about the deals or the people yet to reach any final conclusions, so my comments are going to concentrate on one theme—character. If we are to believe that there is a single root cause of the Enron mess (an arguable point at best in such a complicated situation), failure of character gets my nomination.

Character and leadership are inextricably linked.[41] When the leaders are engaging in self-dealing and side deals,[42] and the supervisors of those leaders are also engaging

---

[37] The Golden Age's love of, and faith in, science contributed to the tragedy as well, as some of the miscalculations that Captain Smith made were based on the scientific advances in ship design.

[38] *See, e.g.*, WILLIAM C. POWERS, JR., ET AL., REPORT OF INVESTIGATION BY THE SPECIAL INVESTIGATIVE COMMITTEE OF THE BOARD OF DIRECTORS OF ENRON CORP., 2002 WL 198018 (CORPSCAN 1980818 (ENRON)) [hereinafter Powers Report]. The Powers Report is also available at http://i.cnn.net/cnn/2002/LAW/02/02/enron.report/powers.report.pdf. There is also a lot of good Congressional testimony on the subject. *See, e.g.*, Federal Document Clearing House, *Strengthening Accounting Oversight: Hearing Before the Subcomm. on Commerce, Trade and Consumer Protection of the House Comm. on Energy and Commerce,* June 26, 2002, *available at* 2002 WL 1381127 (statement of Bala G. Dharan, J. Howard Creekmore Professor of Management, Rice University); Federal Document Clearing House, *U.S. Senate Governmental Affairs Committee Holds a Hearing on the Collapse of Houston-based Enron Corporation,* Jan. 24, 2002, *available at* 2002 WL 93421 (statement of John Langbein, Professor of Law, Yale Law School); Federal Document Clearing House, *Deregulating Capital Markets, Outline of the Testimony of Professor John C. Coffee, Jr., before the Subcommittee on Telecommunications and Finance of the House Commerce Committee,* Nov. 14, 2002, *available at* 2002 WL 1381127 (statement of John C. Coffee, Jr., Columbia University).

[39] *See* SENATE PERMANENT SUBCOMMITTEE ON INVESTIGATIONS OF THE COMMITTEE ON GOVERNMENTAL AFFAIRS, 107TH CONG., THE ROLE OF THE BOARD OF DIRECTORS IN ENRON'S COLLAPSE, July 8, 2002, *available at* http://www.access.gpo.gov/congress/senate/senate12lp107.html [hereinafter Senate Print].

[40] *See, e.g.*, Tom Fowler, *The Pride and the Fall of Enron,* HOUS. CHRON., Oct. 20, 2002, at A25 [hereinafter *The Pride and the Fall*] ("[One manager, told that a deal would take a year, said,] 'I haven't got a year. If I can't do it in three months I won't do it because my bonus depends on it'" since "bonuses were based on the total value of the deal, not the cash it brought in."); Greg Hassell, *The Fall of Enron/The Culture/Pressure Cooker Finally Exploded,* HOUS. CHRON., Dec. 9, 2001, at 1.

[41] Mary C. Daly, *Panel Discussion on Enron: What Went Wrong?,* 8 FORDHAM J. CORP. & FIN. L. 1, S28 (2002) ("What the literature teaches is that the ethical behavior is taught from the top down . . . . It is management's commitment to ethical standards that sets the tone.").

[42] The self-dealing by former Enron CFO Andrew Fastow was, apparently, approved by Enron's Board of Directors when the Board waived its ethics rules (more than once) to allow Fastow to head two

in side deals,[43] and the gatekeepers are approving those side deals,[44] what should the rank and file be thinking? Given the magnitude of the potentially illegal profits made by CFO Andrew Fastow and CEO Jeffrey Skilling,[45] and the sense of entitlement that Enron encouraged,[46] it must have taken significant strength of character to resist getting on that gravy train. And yet, several people did resist. Who resisted, and why?

By now, those following the Enron case know that Sherron Watkins tried to alert CEO Kenneth Lay to serious concerns that she had about Enron's deals:

> Shortly after Enron announced Skilling's unexpected resignation on August 14, 2001, Watkins sent a one-page anonymous letter to Lay. The letter stated that "Enron has been very aggressive in its accounting—most notably the Raptor transactions." The letter raised serious questions concerning the accounting treatment and economic substance of the Raptor transactions (and transactions between Enron and Condor Trust, a subsidiary of Whitewing Associates), identifying several of the matters discussed in this Report. It concluded that "I am incredibly nervous that we will implode in a wave of accounting scandals." Lay told us that he viewed the letter as thoughtfully written and alarming.[47]

---

partnerships that would be negotiating with Enron. *See, e.g.*, Letter from Max Hendrick, III, Vinson & Elkins, to James V. Derrick, Jr., Enron [Re: Preliminary Investigation of Allegations of an Anonymous Employee] (Oct. 15, 2001), *available at* 2001 WL 1764266 (CORPSCAN); *see also* Senate Print, *supra* note 39, at 23-24; Powers Report, *supra* note 38, at *68-71.

43 The Enron Board apparently had several directors who also had consulting agreements with Enron, enabling a form of double-dipping. *See* Senate Print, *supra* note 39, at 51-55.

44 *See* Powers Report, *supra* note 38, at *10 ("There was an absence of forceful and effective oversight by Senior Enron Management and in-house counsel, and objective and critical professional advice by outside counsel at Vinson & Elkins, or auditors at Andersen.").

45 *Fastow Charged With Fraud, Conspiracy in Enron Case*, WASH. POST, Oct. 3, 2002, at A01; April Witt & Peter Behr, *Dream Job Turns Into a Nightmare; Skilling's Success Came at High Price*, WASH. POST, July 29, 2002, at A01; *see also* Senate Print, *supra* note 39, at 24, 34-36; Powers Report, *supra* note 38, at *3, 10.

46
> Enron employees who mastered the art of trading and deal-making could earn fantastic sums. Annual bonuses were as high as $1 million. Shortly after each bonus time, a new crop of silver Porsches—the most favored status symbol at Enron—would appear in the company garage. "I remember one trader going crazy because his bonus was only $500,000. He was cursing and screaming and throwing things at his desk," one former Enron employee recalls. "He thought because he was so brilliant, they should be paying him a lot more."

Hassell, *supra* note 40, at 1.

47 Powers Report, *supra* note 38, at 79. Note the new standards of behavior imposed on company attorneys by Sarbanes-Oxley:

> Not later than 180 days after the date of enactment of this Act, the Commission shall issue rules, in the public interest and for the protection of investors, setting forth minimum standards of professional conduct for attorneys appearing and practicing before the Commission in any way in the representation of issuers, including a rule—

Watkins later told Lay that she had written the letter and met with him regarding her concerns.[48] Lay referred the matter to Enron's General Counsel, James Derrick, a former Vinson & Elkins partner.[49] Derrick in turn asked Vinson & Elkins, one of Enron's key outside law firms, to conduct a preliminary review of the situation—but not to review the underlying transactions that Watkins had discussed in her letter.[50] Within the confines of Derrick's request, Vinson & Elkins conducted an investigation (interviewing Watkins, among others).

V&E concluded that "none of the individuals interviewed could identify any transaction between Enron and LJM that was not reasonable from Enron's standpoint or that was contrary to Enron's best interests." On the accounting issues, V&E said that both Enron and Andersen acknowledge[d] "that the accounting treatment on the Condor/Whitewing and Raptor transactions is creative and aggressive, but no one has reason to believe that it is inappropriate from a technical standpoint." V&E concluded that the facts revealed in its preliminary investigation did not warrant a "further widespread investigation by independent counsel or auditors," although the firm did note that the "bad cosmetics" of the Raptor related-party transactions, coupled with the poor performance of the assets placed in the Raptor vehicles, created "a serious risk of adverse publicity and litigation."[51]

One observation: Vinson & Elkins's undertaking of the investigation had certain restrictions, including Enron's request not to review the bona fides of the underlying

---

(1) requiring an attorney to report evidence of a material violation of securities law or breach of fiduciary duty or similar violation by the company or any agent thereof, to the chief legal counsel or the chief executive officer of the company (or the equivalent thereof); and

(2) if the counsel or officer does not appropriately respond to the evidence (adopting, as necessary, appropriate remedial measures or sanctions with respect to the violation), requiring the attorney to report the evidence to the audit committee of the board of directors of the issuer or to another committee of the board of directors comprised solely of directors not employed directly or indirectly by the issuer, or to the board of directors.

Sarbanes-Oxley Act of 2002 § 307, 15 USC § 7245 (West Supp. 2002). After a whole slew of parties filed objections to the SEC's Proposed Rule regarding attorney conduct (with many of the objections focused on the "noisy withdrawal" provisions of the Proposed Rule, *see* http://www.sec.gov/rules/proposed/s74502.shtml), the SEC apparently abandoned the "noisy withdrawal" provision in its final rule, *see* http://www.sec.gov/news/press/2003-13.htm. As of this writing, I have only seen the press release regarding the final rule, not the actual text of the rule.

The days of taking an issue only partially up the chain of command are over, at least for publicly traded companies. But haven't lawyers always had the responsibility of taking matters all the way up the chain of command? *See* MODEL RULES OF PROF'L CONDUCT R. 1.13 (2002). I wonder whether Ms. Watkins, as an accountant, had a similar duty under her profession's ethics rules. If she did have such a duty, and she didn't go all the way to the Board of Directors (and beyond) with her concerns, was she really a whistleblower? (Mind you, what she did took some guts, even though she was not a whistleblower in the true sense.)

[48] Powers Report, *supra* note 38, at 79.

[49] *See* Ellen Joan Pollock, *Anderson: Called to Account: Enron Lawyers Face Congress Over Their Role,* WALL ST. J., Mar. 15, 2002, at C13 (noting that Derrick used to be a partner at Vinson & Elkins).

[50] Powers Report, *supra* note 38, at 79.

[51] *Id.* at *80.

transactions.[52] We don't know what sort of give and take occurred between Enron and Vinson & Elkins about the usefulness of such a request.[53] At some point, thanks to the ability of Enron's chapter 11 management to waive the attorney-client privilege,[54] we may learn more. But I have to admit, right off the bat, that I have a hard time

---

[52] *Id.* at *79. "The result of the V&E review was largely predetermined by the scope and nature of the investigation and the process employed . . . . The scope and process of the investigation appear to have been structured with less skepticism than was needed to see through these particularly complex transactions." *Id.* at *81 (footnote omitted).

[53] Jordan Mintz, Enron Global Finance's General Counsel, has stated that Vinson & Elkins "fulfilled its professional duties" in terms of the advice it gave to Enron. Laura Goldberg, *Enron's Words as Relevant as Deeds/Reports May Have Told Partial Truths*, HOUS. CHRON., Feb. 11, 2002, at 1. Because of Vinson & Elkins's ties to Enron's General Counsel James Derrick, though, Mintz hired a separate firm, Fried, Frank, Harris, Shriver & Jacobson, to review the deals of which Watkins had complained. Rone Tempest, *Enron Counsel Warned About Partnerships Probe: Company's Legal Executive Asked Opinion of Law Firm in April. Congressional Investigators Say It Was to 'Halt This Practice,'* L.A. TIMES, Jan. 31, 2002, at C1. I'm not yet ready to get on the bandwagon that denounces all of Enron's lawyers.

[54] The principal case involving privilege in the bankruptcy context is, of course, Commodity Futures Trading Commission v. Weintraub, 471 U.S. 343, 358 (1985) ("[W]e hold that the trustee of a corporation in [a chapter 7] bankruptcy has the power to waive the corporation's attorney-client privilege with respect to pre-bankruptcy communications."). Weintraub answered the question of how much control a chapter 7 trustee had over the corporation's attorney-client privilege. *Id.* Subsequent cases have answered the question about how far the Weintraub holding could go in a chapter 11 context. *See, e.g.*, Am. Metrocomm Corp. v. Duane Morris & Heckscher LLP, 274 B.R. 641, 654-56 (Bankr. D. Dela. 2002) (stating that debtor-in-possession controls attorney-client privilege, and debtor-in-possession can request documents from attorneys even if attorneys raise work product privilege as a defense); *In re* Bame, 251 B.R. 367, 370, 374 (Bankr. D. Minn. 2000) (converting chapter 11 case to chapter 7 case; holding that chapter 7 trustee can access the post-petition, pre-conversion communications between the debtor-in-possession and its lawyers because the privilege is held by the estate, and not by the debtor-in-possession); Whyte v. Williams (In re Williams), 152 B.R. 123, 129 (Bankr. N.D. Tex. 1992) ("The liquidating trustee [under a confirmed chapter 11 plan] controls the power to waive or invoke the evidentiary privileges that arise in connection with the causes of action transferred to the liquidating trust under Article 25.5 of the confirmed plan."); *see also* S. Air Transp., Inc. v. SAT Group, Inc., 255 B.R. 706, 711 (Bankr. S.D. Ohio 2000) (citations omitted).

> The Court agrees that a corporate fiduciary is precluded from asserting privileges to protect his own interests that are adverse to those of the corporation. Corporate officers must "exercise the privilege in a manner consistent with their fiduciary capacity to act in the best interests of the corporation and not of themselves individually."

Id. The interesting part about the privilege issue in the Enron bankruptcy context is whether Steve Cooper (the restructuring expert currently running Enron) is going to waive the privilege in order to get information from the various law firms that represented Enron and then, if the information gives rise to a cause of action against any of Enron's lawyers, use that very information to pursue them in bankruptcy court. Mr. Cooper can also pursue Enron's officers and directors using that privileged information, as the privilege belongs to the client (Enron) and not to any of the client's employees. I've been following the work of the Severed Enron Employees Coalition in the pursuit of the prepetition bonuses paid to certain Enron executives on the theory that the bonuses were fraudulent conveyances. Severed Enron Employees Coalition v. N. Trust Co., No. 02-0267 (S.D. Tex. complaint, filed Jan. 24, 2002). Any privileged advice, on the order of "Should we pay this person a retention bonus? What will we get in terms of a benefit for the retention bonus?," could be helpful in this regard.

believing that Vinson & Elkins, or any of Enron's other law firms, knowingly advised Enron to do anything that was clearly illegal. The real issue is how Enron handled the grey areas of the law, based on the advice of all of its lawyers (both its in-house and outside counsel).

Watkins wasn't the lone voice questioning Enron's deals; others, including Enron Global Finance's General Counsel Jordan Mintz, were concerned about the structure and disclosure of the various deals.[55] Apparently, Fastow and Skilling didn't brook disagreement willingly. Those who objected often found themselves the subject of pressure, downright abuse, and exile.[56]

I'd like to put forward one striking similarity between the *Titanic* and Enron: a failure of meaningful communication stemming from a belief that someone else had "taken care of it." Here's how a recent newspaper article described the problem:

> [S]ince most only saw their part of the business, they assumed the problems were isolated. . . . "You understood your piece of the business and maybe what the guy next to you did, but very few understood the big picture. . . . That segmentation allowed us to get work done very quickly, but it isolated that institutional knowledge into the hands of very few people."[57]

Certainly, the Powers Report describes the failure of follow-through regarding several of the Enron deals—the failure to ascertain if the checks and balances, supposedly part of each deal's structure, were in place and working.[58] As John Coffee explains,

---

[55] *See, e.g.*, Senate Print, *supra* note 39, at 28 n.81 (quoting an internal memorandum from Mintz):

> [T]he Company needs to improve both the process it follows in executing such transactions and implement improved procedures regarding written substantiation supporting and memorializing the Enron/LJM transactions . . . . [F]irst is the need for the Company to implement a more active and systematic effort in pursuing non-LJM sales alternatives before approaching LJM . . . ; the second is to . . . impose a more rigorous testing of the fairness and benefits realized by Enron in transacting with LJM.

Id.; *see also* Dan Feldstein, *Skilling Says He Did No Wrong / Lawyer Told Not to Stick Neck Out*, HOUS. CHRON., Feb. 8, 2002, at 1 (describing how Fastow tried to bully Mintz into blessing irregularities in certain Enron deals).

[56] *See, e.g.*, *The Pride and the Fall*, *supra* note 40, at 27A (listing three people—Andersen partner Carl Bass, former Enron CFO (after Fastow) Jeff McMahon, and former Merrill Lynch analyst John Olson—who were demoted (Olson was fired) after criticizing the aggressive Enron deals and accounting methods); *see also* Editorial Desk, *Not Quite a Whistle-Blower*, N.Y. TIMES, Feb. 15, 2002, at A20; Andy Geller, *"I Believe Mr. Skilling and Mr. Fastow Duped Mr. Lay"—Enron VP Rips Duo Before Congress*, N.Y. POST, Feb. 15, 2002, at 9; Susan Schmidt, *CEO Was 'Misserved' At Enron, Hill Told; Former Executive Blames Other Top Managers*, WASH. POST, Feb. 15, 2002, at A01; Peter Spiegel, *The Architect of Enron's Downfall: Internal Probe Reveals Andy Fastow as a CFO who Bullied Staff and Even Wall Street Banks, Enriching Himself by More than Dollars 45m in the Process*, FIN. TIMES, May 21, 2002, at A20.

[57] *See, e.g.*, *The Pride and the Fall*, *supra* note 40, at 27A. Remember that those "very few people" included members of the Board of Directors, which waived Enron's ethics rules more than once to allow self-dealing by some of Enron's executives. *See supra* note 42.

[58] *See* Powers Report, *supra* note 38, at *18-28.

> Enron . . . furnish[es] ample evidence of a systematic governance failure. Although other spectacular securities frauds have been discovered from time to time over recent decades, they have not generally disturbed the overall market. In contrast, Enron has clearly roiled the market and created a new investor demand for transparency. Behind this disruption lies the market's discovery that it cannot rely upon the professional gatekeepers—auditors, analysts, and others—whom the market has long trusted to filter, verify and assess complicated financial information. Properly understood, Enron is a demonstration of gatekeeper failure, and the question it most sharply poses is how this failure should be rectified.[59]

Failures of gatekeeper professionals aren't new. The savings and loan crisis, which also represented a significant gatekeeper failure, occurred a mere twenty years ago;[60] the Salomon Brothers Treasury bonds trading scandal occurred just ten years ago.[61]

It's certainly possible that many of the legal and accounting professionals (the in-house and the outside professionals) who advised Enron assumed that Enron's own businesspeople were doing the follow-through; moreover, many of those same professionals may well have thought that it was not the lawyers' or accountants' "place" to bill Enron for continued checks of the system. (I know nothing about the training of accountants, so I'm going to limit the rest of this discussion to the training of lawyers.) If the lawyers saw themselves as morally independent from Enron, rather than morally interdependent, then they might well have believed that it was Enron's job, not theirs,

---

[59] John C. Coffee, Jr., *Understanding Enron: It's About the Gatekeepers, Stupid,* 57 BUS. LAW. 1403 (2002) (footnote omitted).

[60] Now that I wear bifocals, twenty years just doesn't seem that long ago. *Editors' note:* No more bifocals, but LASIK doesn't take away years of living—just some myopia.

[61] Daly, *supra* note 41, at S25-S28; Federal Document Clearing House, *U.S. Senate Committee on Commerce, Science and Transportation Holds a Hearing on Enron Bankruptcy,* Dec. 18, 2001, *available at* 2001 WL 1623334 (statement of John Coffee, Columbia University) ("Well, when a debacle like Enron occurs, the critical question for Congress and for regulators is to ask, as you've been beginning to ask, where were the gatekeepers; where were the watchdogs? . . . Here, all failed, and all failed fairly abysmally.").

> The fallout from [the savings and loan] scandal included a Justice Department action against the prestigious New York firm of Kaye, Scholer, Fierman, Hays & Handler. Kaye, Scholer and partner Peter Fishbein were said to have gone beyond mere aggressive lawyering, and more than one observer viewed their representation as akin to aiding and abetting, while others attributed any errors to simple inattentiveness. Ultimately, the case was settled, with the firm and its malpractice carrier paying $41 million in settlement, and the Keating lawyers paid for their alleged sins, notwithstanding their ability to spread the loss to other lawyers via malpractice insurance coverage.

Jeffrey W. Stempel, *Embracing Descent: The Bankruptcy of a Business Paradigm for Conceptualizing and Regulating the Legal Profession,* 27 FLA. ST. U. L. REV. 25, 111-12 (1999) (footnotes omitted). For a wonderful discussion of the Kaye, Scholer firm and the savings and loan crisis, see David B. Wilkins, *Making Context Count: Regulating Lawyers After Kaye, Scholer,* 66 S. CAL. L. REV. 1147 (1993). As Clarence Darrow apparently said, "History repeats itself, and that's one of the things that's wrong with history." The Quotations Home Page, *available at* http://www.geocities.com/~spanoudi/topic-h3.html#history.

to ensure follow-through. A more complex explanation is that cognitive dissonance—well-documented in social science literature and applied to lawyers by, among others, David Luban—prevented the lawyers from seeing some of these deals more clearly. My hunch is that both concepts (a mistaken belief in moral independence, rather than interdependence, and the effects of cognitive dissonance) played a part in any failures by the gatekeepers.

A. "Moral Independence" Versus "Moral Interdependence" as an Explanation

For the longest time, lawyers have done everything they could to distinguish the client's ends from the means that the lawyers used to achieve those ends. This "moral independence" theory has been used to justify everything from lawyers who take on unpopular causes to lawyers who facilitate shady deals, even though the original theory was never intended to justify shady deals.[62]

Several scholars have recognized, though, that the complexity of modern legal practice forces lawyers to take a more active role in shaping not just the clients' advice but the clients' deals and litigation as well.[63] Richard Painter's "moral interdependence" theory

---

[62] According to a study by Erwin Smigel, lawyers'

> independence derived from two sources. First, "they . . . 'represent' the law and must therefore separate themselves from the client." Second, the commodity they sold was "[i]ndependent legal opinion." Smigel observed that "client[s] desire that a firm maintain its autonomy" so that they can obtain the best advice. Moreover, as the large firms grew older, they increased their number of clients and moved away from fundamentally relying on one or a few clients. This shift "strengthened . . . a firm's ability to retain its independence" because "no one client provid[es] enough income to materially or consciously influence the law office's legal opinion."

Russell G. Pearce, *Lawyers as America's Governing Class: The Formation and Dissolution of the Original Understanding of the American Lawyer's Role,* 8 U. CHI. L. SCH. ROUNDTABLE 381, 406 (2001) (footnotes omitted) [hereinafter Governing Class] (quoting ERWIN O. SMIGEL, THE WALL STREET LAWYER: PROFESSIONAL ORGANIZATION MAN? (1964)).

The fun part about the history of the bar's independence theory is its link with the robber barons of yesteryear. *See, e.g.*, Thomas L. Shaffer, *The Profession as a Moral Teacher*, 18 ST. MARY'S L.J. 195, 222-23 (1986) [hereinafter *Moral Teacher*]; Thomas L. Shaffer, *The Unique, Novel, and Unsound Adversary Ethic,* 41 VAND. L. REV. 697, 703-04 (1988). As Russell Pearce points out,

> In becoming hired guns, elite lawyers abandoned the traditional governing class ideology. They were no longer acting as a disinterested political leadership capable of discerning and pursuing the common good. Instead, they were advocates of private interests. They had violated professionalism's taboo on acting as a servant of big business and could no longer claim the special tie to the public good which distinguished them from those in business.

Pearce, *Governing Class, supra*, at 400-10.

[63] Richard W. Painter, *The Moral Interdependence of Corporate Lawyers and Their Clients*, 67 S. CAL. L. REV. 507, 511, 544-45 (1994); *see also id.* at 526 ("Joint decisionmaking by lawyer and client has become both efficient and prudent.") (footnote omitted).

of the lawyer-client interaction is a more realistic view of the lawyer's modern role, especially when it comes to complex transactions or complex litigation.[64]

When you overlay the lawyer's moral interdependence on top of a cutthroat culture, you get Enron (and WorldCom, and Tyco, etc.). We still don't know a lot of the facts behind Enron's various deals, including what the various lawyers said, Enron's response to that advice, or how much the accountants' advice contradicted (or supported) the lawyers' advice. But we do know that the structure of Enron itself encouraged a constant pushing of the outside of the envelope.[65] Enron encouraged a "me, first" structure, not a cooperative one.

> "Enron sought to redefine the rules of the industry," said Robert Bruner, a professor at the University of Virginia who has made a case study of Enron's culture. "It was a culture of challenge and confrontation."
>
> . . . .
>
> [Former CEO Jeffrey] Skilling also is responsible, many insiders say, for creating a mercenary, cutthroat culture to stoke the fires beneath the enterprise. One of the hallmarks of the Skilling regime was a performance review process that employees called "rank and yank." The evaluations compared the performance of employees against one another, with the bottom 15 percent getting axed every year.
>
> The evaluations were done by asking employees to judge others' performance. They did so knowing their own promotions and survival hung in the balance.
>
> "Because of that, you never helped one another," said one former Enron employee. "Everyone was in it for themselves. People stabbed you in the back."
>
> Teamwork, once a source of strength, started to disappear.
>
> "It was every man for himself," a former Enron executive said.
>
> What sense of teamwork survived "rank and yank" was undermined by Enron's reward system, which seemed to place no value on group goals but lavishly rewarded individual accomplishment. An employee who could

---

[64] For example, the Powers Report points out that, with respect to preparing the various disclosure forms that Enron filed, "[w]hile accountants took the lead in preparing the financial statement footnote disclosures, lawyers played a more central role in preparing the proxy statements, including the disclosures of the related-party transactions." Powers Report, *supra* note 38, at 84. This interdependence is by no means limited to the lawyers who worked on Enron's deals. *See Governing Class*, *supra* note 62, at 408-09 (citing Robert A. Kagan and Robert Eli Rosen, *On the Social Significance of Large Law Firm Practice*, 37 STAN. L. REV. 399 (1985) and Robert L. Nelson, *Ideology, Practice, and Professional Autonomy: Social Values and Client Relationships in the Large Law Firm*, 37 STAN. L. REV. 503 (1985)). Both the Kagan & Rosen study and the Nelson study are well worth reading.

[65] I first saw this phrase in TOM WOLFE, THE RIGHT STUFF 12 (1979).

close big deals got big bonuses and promotions. Those who couldn't were shown the door.[66]

Let's take this moral interdependence theory one step further. Add to the theory (1) Enron's culture, and (2) the personality traits of a large number of lawyers (whether or not they ever had Enron as a client), and you have a disaster just waiting to happen. Susan Daicoff has summarized the literature on lawyers' personality traits quite nicely in a series of articles.[67] Lawyers tend to have certain personality characteristics that contribute to their need to "win." They "appear to be more competitive, aggressive, and achievement-oriented, and overwhelmingly Thinkers (instead of Feelers). . . . Lawyers are more often motivated by a need for achievement than are others, which includes a need to compete against an internal or external standard of intelligence."[68] No matter which way you slice it, these gatekeepers were too closely involved with their client[69] to be able to stand up and say, "You shouldn't do that." At some point, we need lawyers to say, "The law lets you do it, but don't. . . . It's a rotten thing to do."[70]

B. Cognitive Dissonance as an Explanation

Even if the gatekeepers weren't so closely involved with the client, there's yet another reason for their failure to protest the deals that were on (or over) the edge: cognitive dissonance. My sociologist friends[71] tell me that moral development alone—which is an individual trait—can't explain how an individual will react to a particular situation.[72]

---

[66] Hassell, *supra* note 40. For a masterful compendium of the theories surrounding community norms in monitoring and shaping the roles of lawyers, see W. Bradley Wendel, *Nonlegal Regulation of the Legal Profession: Social Norms in Professional Communities*, 54 VAND. L. REV. 1955 (2001) [hereinafter *Social Norms*].

[67] *See, e.g.*, Susan Daicoff, *Lawyer, Know Thyself: A Review of Empirical Research on Attorney Attributes Bearing on Professionalism*, 46 AM. U. L. REV. 1337 (1997) [hereinafter *Know Thyself*]; Susan Daicoff, *(Oxymoron?) Ethical Decisionmaking by Attorneys: An Empirical Study*, 48 FLA. L. REV. 197, 217-18 (1996).

[68] *Know Thyself, supra* note 67, at 1408-09 (footnotes omitted). According to Daicoff, law students come into law school hard-wired with these traits. *Id.* at 1349-50. Imagine my relief at knowing that law school didn't "ruin" them.

[69] *See, e.g., supra* notes 49-50 and accompanying text.

[70] Sol M. Linowitz, *Moment of Truth for the Legal Profession,* Address at the University of Wisconsin Law School (Oct. 24, 1997), *in* 1997 WIS. L. REV. 1211, 1214-15 ("I believe Elihu Root once again had it exactly right when he told a client: "The law let[s] you do it, but don't . . . . It's a rotten thing to do.").

[71] Special thanks go to Julia McQuillan, who guided me through the literature and theories in her field.

[72] *Cf.* Julia McQuillan & Julie Pfeiffer, *Why Anne Makes us Dizzy: Reading Anne of Green Gables from a Gender Perspective*, 16 MOSAIC 34/2, June 2001, at 19 ("In an attempt to explain variation within sex categories, sociologists have argued that external social structures (our actual experiences in the world) organize our behavior more than socialization (how we've been told to behave).").

The situation itself will interact with the traits of the individual, and both the person's individual traits and his situation will affect an outcome.[73]

Peer pressure is one such particular influence. There are some well-regarded studies showing that even relatively obvious physical conclusions, such as the distance from one point to another or the length of a line, can become subject to "groupthink," placing peer pressure on the unbelieving minority to conform to the wrong-headed thinking of the majority.[74] And if hard-wired concepts, such as size and location, are manipulable by the particulars of the situation, what about the fuzzier concept of behavior?

Stanley Milgram's studies on the willingness of experimental subjects to inflict pain (electrical shocks) on complete strangers can give us a glimpse into how powerful the effect of a particular situation can be. In Milgram's best-known study, the actual subject was asked to give a series of progressively more severe shocks to someone who was posing as a fellow experimental subject. Although the actual subject usually agonized about administering the shocks, he went ahead and administered them nonetheless.[75]

In analyzing Milgram's experiment, Lee Ross and Richard Nisbett concluded that the powerful structure of the situation—the authority figure setup; the calm tones of the experimenter standing next to the subject who was administrating the shocks; the experimenter's repetition of the phrases, "The experiment requires that you continue; you have no choice"—served to overcome the subjects' expressed desire to stop the experiment before reaching the "severe shock" stage.[76] Most of the subjects were stymied by uncertainty and couldn't overcome the social pressure of the situation. It's not that the subjects were sadists. But the structure of the situation prevented them from acting on their own reluctance to continue the shocks.

David Luban has also described the Milgram experiment and has pointed out that almost two-thirds of the subjects in Milgram's experiments actually did go all the way

---

[73] The thought that moral development alone can predict a person's behavior without regard to the particular situation is called the "fundamental attribution error." *See* DAVID J. LUBAN, THE ETHICS OF WRONGFUL OBEDIENCE, *in* ETHICS IN PRACTICE: LAWYERS' ROLES, RESPONSIBILITIES, AND REGULATION 94, 101 (Deborah L. Rhode ed., 2000) [hereinafter WRONGFUL OBEDIENCE]; *see also* Lee M. Johnson, et al., *General Versus Specific Victim Blaming*, 142 J. OF SOC. PSYCHOL. 249 (Apr. 2002) ("The fundamental attribution error occurs when individuals overemphasize personal attributes and discount environmental attributes in their judgments of others"); LEE ROSS, THE INTUITIVE PSYCHOLOGIST AND HIS SHORTCOMINGS: DISTORTIONS IN THE ATTRIBUTION PROCESS, IN 10 ADVANCES IN EXPERIMENTAL SOCIAL PSYCH. 173 (Leonard Berkowitz ed., 1977); *see generally* DAVID C. FUNDER, PERSONALITY JUDGMENT: A REALISTIC APPROACH TO PERSONAL PERCEPTION (1999).

[74] LEE ROSS & RICHARD E. NISBETT, THE PERSON AND THE SITUATIONS: PERSPECTIVES OF SOCIAL PSYCHOLOGY 30 (1991) ("Our most basic perceptions and judgments about the world are socially conditioned and dictated.") (citing Sherif's "autokinetic effect" studies and Asch's "comparison lines" studies).

[75] *Id.* at 56-57.

[76] One of Milgram's later variations on the study involved changing the setting from Yale to an inner-city, run-down, suspicious-looking lab in another town. He recorded approximately the same results, no matter the setting. *See id.* at 55.

to 450 volts.[77] He posits that a "corruption of judgment" stemming from cognitive dissonance caused two-thirds of the subjects of Milgram's experiments to "kill" the learner:

> [T]he key to understanding Milgram compliance lies in features of the experimental situation. . . . The teacher moves up the scale of shocks by 15-volt increments, and reaches the 450-volt level only at the thirtieth shock. Among other things, this means that the subjects never confront the question "Should I administer a 330-volt shock to the learner?" The question is "Should I administer a 330-volt shock to the learner given that I've just administered a 315-volt shock?" It seems clear that the latter question is much harder to answer. . . .
>
> Cognitive dissonance theory teaches that when our actions conflict with our self-concept, our beliefs and attitudes change until the conflict is removed. . . . Cognitive dissonance theory suggests that when I have given the learner a series of electrical shocks, I simply won't view giving the next shock as a wrongful act, because I won't admit to myself that the previous shocks were wrong.[78]

Luban's most important point is that lawyers aren't immune to the effects of cognitive dissonance. He does a masterful job of linking the *Berkey Photo-Inc. v. Eastman Kodak Co.*[79] case and Stanley Milgram's experiments on obedience to explain how very well-intentioned lawyers can find themselves slipping into serious breaches of ethics. For those who aren't familiar with this case, Brad Wendel describes it nicely:

> The lawyers representing Kodak had retained an economist as an expert witness, expecting that he would testify that Kodak's domination of the market was due to its superior technological innovations, not to anticompetitive behavior. The plaintiff's counsel requested any documents pertinent to the expert's testimony, Kodak's lawyer's resisted, and ultimately a magistrate ordered production of numerous documents including interim reports prepared by the economist. At the economist's deposition, one of Kodak's lawyers stated that he had destroyed the interim reports, which were somewhat unfavorable to Kodak's defense. The lawyer even filed an affidavit in a subsequent discovery dispute in the case, stating under oath that the documents had been destroyed. In fact, the lawyer had not destroyed the documents, but had hidden them in his office and withheld them from

---

[77] WRONGFUL OBEDIENCE, *supra* note 73, at 97 ("In reality, 63 percent of subjects complied all the way to 450 volts. Moreover, this is a robust result: it holds in groups of women as well as men, and experimenters obtained comparable results in Holland, Spain, Italy, Australia, South Africa, Germany, and Jordan. . . .") (footnote omitted).

[78] *Id.* at 102 (footnotes omitted).

[79] 74 F.R.D. 613 (S.D.N.Y. 1977).

> production. The affidavit was perjurous. The fallout was a calamity for the firm. Kodak fired it and hired one of its arch-rivals to defend the antitrust case. The firm paid its client over $600,000 to settle Kodak's claims related to its conduct of the litigation. It lost Kodak's business, which had accounted for approximately one-fourth of the firm's billings and had employed thirty lawyers full-time. The partner who had coordinated the firm's preparation of the economist's testimony was released from the firm and spent twenty-seven days in jail for contempt of court.[80]

In his discussion of the *Berkey-Kodak* case, Luban relates the following episode:

> Joseph Fortenberry, the associate working for [Mahlon Perkins, the partner representing Kodak], knew that Perkins was perjuring himself and whispered a warning to him; but when Perkins ignored the warning, Fortenberry did nothing further to correct his misstatements. "What happened" recalls another associate, "was that he saw Perkins lie and really couldn't believe it. And he just had no idea what to do. I mean, he . . . kept thinking there must be a reason. Besides, what do you do? The guy was his boss and a great guy!"[81]

Fortenberry's comments highlight how fledgling lawyers will take many social cues from those more experienced lawyers whom they respect.[82] Of course, the pressure that the senior lawyers have to keep their clients, maintain their billings, and compete

[80] W. Bradley Wendel, *Morality, Motivation, and the Professionalism Movement*, 52 S.C. L. REV. 557, 606-07 (2001) (footnotes omitted); *see also* Walter Kiechell III, *The Strange Case of Kodak's Lawyers*, FORTUNE, May 8, 1978, at 188. If I were a superstitious sort, I'd worry about the fact that one of the two "smoking guns" in the case was Exhibit 666. *Id.* I am *not* making this up.

[81] WRONGFUL OBEDIENCE, *supra* note 73, at 95 (footnotes omitted).

[82] Cognitive dissonance isn't limited to outside counsel. In a study of inside counsel, Hugh and Sally Gunz found that the lawyers' advice was not always independent from the direction that the company itself intended to go:

> From a practitioner standpoint, the model highlights issues surrounding the nature of the advice that organizations can expect to obtain from their in-house counsel when placed in positions of ethical conflict. In our original study of OPC [organizational professional conflict], we suggested that an important implication of our findings was that in-house counsel might not necessarily always provide disinterested professional advice. In their different ways, the Technician and Organization Person might produce superficially helpful advice, which could, under certain circumstances, be dangerously misleading. The Technician, for example, may deliver clever but myopic solutions, and the Observer could well misjudge a situation and remain silent inappropriately. But the Advisor, by avoiding the "cop" aspect of the Lawyer role (in the sense that there is no implication that he or she intends to report the situation to the next level higher within the organization, or to a regulator outside the organization), stays closer to the Lawyer's advice. So the model, as revised, suggests an even greater variety of potential responses than in its initial L[awyer], T[echnician], and O[bserver] form, underlining yet more firmly the need to avoid making simplistic assumptions about the nature of the advice in-house counsel provide their employer[s].

with other elite lawyers at other firms (who are all too happy to steal clients away), is relentless pressure indeed. But if the more senior lawyers can't withstand the pressure, then who will teach the fledgling lawyers to resist?

III. WHERE DO WE GO FROM HERE?

If we want lawyers to spend more time understanding themselves and their relationship to their clients, then we're going to have to lead from the top, with judges, partners, bar associations, and other senior lawyers all singing the same tune. It won't be sufficient for law professors to warn students against the temptations and pressures of law practice. As a matter of fact, it's depressing how little influence law professors have on their students' understanding of legal ethics.

Larry Hellman's study on cognitive dissonance in a legal ethics class is proof of the need to have top lawyers do the preaching, not law professors.[83] Hellman asked the students in his ethics course to keep diaries of possible ethics violations that they observed while working for lawyers during the semester, and those students recounted bad lawyering in an astonishing variety of forms—neglect, incompetence, conflicts of interest, and the like.[84] If we want to train newly minted lawyers to be ethical, it's just not enough for law professors to talk the talk. We must join forces with the lawyers and judges in the "real world," those who can walk the walk.

Lawyers need to behave as true counselors to their clients, rather than as hired guns who are just following orders. Society needs us to take on the role of the social conscience (or, if that sounds too darn highfallutin', the role of the grease that helps society run). As David Luban has pointed out,

> If lawyers have special responsibilities to legal justice, that is not because they are divinely elected, or better and holier that [sic] the rest of us. It is because of how their role fits into an entire division of social labor. Lawyers represent private parties before public institutions, or advise private parties about the requirements of public norms, or reduce private transactions to a publicly-prescribed form, or ratify that transactions are in compliance with public norms. To say that they have special duties of fidelity to those norms is no more ecstatic and supernatural than saying that food-preparers have heightened duties to ensure their hands are clean. It is their social role, not the brush of angels' wings on their foreheads, that requires [food service workers] to wash their hands every time they go to the bathroom.[85]

Hugh P. Gunz & Sally P. Gunz, *The Lawyer's Response to Organizational Professional Conflict: An Empirical Study of the Ethical Decision Making of In-House Counsel*, 39 AM. BUS. L.J. 241, 279-80 (2002) (footnotes omitted).

[83] Lawrence K. Hellman, *The Effects of Law Office Work on the Formation of Law Students' Professional Values: Observation, Explanation, Optimization*, 4 GEO. J. LEGAL ETHICS 537 (1991).

[84] *Id.* at 601-05.

[85] David Luban, *Asking the Right Questions*, 72 TEMP. L. REV. 839, 849-50 (1999).

We used to be better at setting good examples, or so I've heard. In the "golden days" that Tom Shaffer recounts, some of the lawyers that he observed set wonderful examples for their newly minted lawyer colleagues. In my favorite article of his, *The Profession as a Moral Teacher,* he tells story after story of lawyers who did the right thing.[86] The constant choice of ethical over unethical behavior helped mold the lawyer that Shaffer eventually became:

> [Those two partners in my former law firm] were philosophically and temperamentally different and . . . practiced law in different ways. That they were so much alike in these moral matters said something about their personal character, of course, but, in view of their personal differences, it also said something about the way the firm practiced law—about the way the firm functioned as the profession (for me) and, as the profession, functioned (for me) as a moral teacher. It was not, that is, an apprenticeship, in which I was learning my craft, and the morals of my craft, from a master—or at least it didn't seem, then, that it was. It was the profession (the law firm) that was the moral teacher. . . . It was even more like the moral formation a person gets from family, town, and church. Which is to say that, here, code depended on character.[87]

From his experience as a young lawyer, Shaffer took the moral lesson that a lawyer should also be a gentleman.[88] Tom Shaffer's view of the "gentlemanly" lawyer, of course, has its critics,[89] including Shaffer himself.[90] And yet, we do understand the concept

---

[86] *Moral Teacher, supra* note 62, at 214-17.

[87] *Id.* at 216-17.

[88] Thomas L. Shaffer, *On Being a Professional Elder,* 62 NOTRE DAME L. REV. 624, 630-31 (1987) [hereinafter *Professional Elder*] ("When character is in place, fortified by 'a few rules' that have to do with professional craft, the professional person becomes dependable. Professional character is the connection between virtue and craft. The convention has been to describe that connection with the word gentleman.") (footnotes omitted). If you haven't read Tom Shaffer's work on this topic, you should. For a quick shortcut—not to be confused with reading Shaffer's work—Leslie Gerber has created a good primer. *See* Leslie E. Gerber, *Can Lawyers Be Saved? The Theological Legal Ethics of Thomas Shaffer,* 10 J.L. & RELIGION 347 (1994).

[89] *See, e.g.*, Ann Bartow, *Still Not Behaving Like Gentlemen*, 49 U. KAN. L. REV. 809, 810-11 (2001); Susan Daicoff, *Asking Leopards to Change Their Spots: Should Lawyers Change? A Critique Of Solutions to Problems with Professionalism by Reference to Empirically-Derived Attorney Personality Attributes*, 11 GEO. J. LEGAL ETHICS 547, 582-83 (1998); William J. Wernz, *Does Professionalism Literature Idealize the Past and Over-Rate Civility? Is Zeal a Vice or a Cardinal Virtue?*, 13 PROF. LAW. 1 (2001) (disputing the claim that "back then"—whenever "then" was—lawyers were more professional and more civil).

[90] Thomas L. Shaffer, *The Gentleman in Professional Ethics*, 10 QUEEN'S L.J. 1, 11 (1984).

> The 19th century gentleman in North America gave us slavery, Manifest Destiny, the theft of half of Mexico, the subjugation of women, the exploitation of immigrant children, Pinkerton detectives, yellow-dog contracts, and the implacable genocide of American Indians. You could

that he's trying to express:[91] that of a lawyer who understands her role in society as more than just a mere scrivener or functionary, and who tries always to take the moral high ground.[92]

What happens when we don't set the right example? We can call doing the right thing "behaving like gentlemen," or we can use some other, less "loaded" phrase. If we don't exert some leadership and emphasize the role of character in the practice of law, some very smart lawyers will continue to do stupid things, and some clients will continue to do stupid (or venal) things. Some of these people will even trot out the hoary (and discredited) old saw that they were "just following orders."[93]

So how do we encourage lawyers to withstand peer pressure and client pressure, especially in those grey areas in which the lawyer gives advice akin to "it's an aggressive interpretation of the law" and the client chooses to use that aggressive interpretation, even at the risk of later litigation? Remember, we're not talking about lawyers who deliberately counsel clients to flout the law. Rather, we're talking about lawyers who say that a particular interpretation could go either in favor of the client or against it.

Personally, I like Russ Pearce's idea that we create a new Model Rule 1.0. His Model Rule 1.0 would provide that "lawyers are morally accountable for their conduct as

---

> make a case . . . that the gentleman's ethic is not worth taking seriously. If the gentleman has left the professions, the best thing for us would be to bar the door lest he get back in.

Id.; *see also* Thomas L. Shaffer, *Inaugural Howard Lichtenstein Lecture in Legal Ethics: Lawyer Professionalism as a Moral Argument*, 26 GONZ. L. REV. 393, 400 (1991); *Professional Elder*, *supra* note 88, at 633-34.

91 Edward McGlynn Gaffney, Jr., *In Praise of a Gentle Soul, Remarks at the Annual Banquet of the Journal of Law and Religion* (Oct. 14, 1993), *in* 10 J.L. & RELIGION 279, 284 (1993/1994).

> The acid test of [Tom Shaffer's] reliance on the ethics of gentlemen is whether it, too, is not flawed at its core. Is it not by definition limited to males, and does it have any space for minorities? Only one like Shaffer, who by decades of living like a gentleman himself and reflecting carefully on that ethic, could have come to the conclusion that the ethic of the gentleman-lawyer has greater possibilities for the subversion of patriarchy than the ABA's model of professionalism.

Id. (footnotes omitted).

92 Bill Hodes points out that "[t]he acid test of ethical lawyering is rarely what to do in the face of crisis—a client shows you the buried bodies or drops a bloody knife on your desk or commits perjury or destroys or hides material property asked for in discovery." W. William Hodes, *Accepting and Rejecting Clients—The Moral Autonomy of the Second-to-the-Last Lawyer in Town*, 48 U. KAN. L. REV. 977, 978 (2000) (citing the classic cases of People v. Belge, 372 N.Y.S. 2d 798 (N.Y. Crim. Ct. 1975) (buried bodies), State v. Olwell, 394 P.2d 681 (Wash. 1964) (bloody knife), Nix v. Whiteside, 475 U.S. 157 (1986) (perjury), and Berkey Photo, Inc. v. Eastman Kodak Co., 74 F.R.D. 613 (S.D.N.Y. 1977) (work product)). For a wonderful discussion of how social norms affect lawyering, see *Social Norms*, *supra* note 66.

93 *See, e.g.*, Tom Fowler, *Ex-Andersen auditor defended / Aide: Boss was told to shred files*, HOUS. CHRON., Mar. 7, 2002, at 1 ("An assistant to the Arthur Andersen lead partner who handled the Enron account said she believes her boss was just following orders when he told workers to destroy Enron-related documents last fall."); Marcy Gordon, *SEC, Informal Wall Street System Failed to Detect Enron Failure, Report Finds*, ASSOCIATED PRESS NEWSWIRES, Oct. 7, 2002, Westlaw, Allnewsplus Library (Fastow's lawyer contends that his client was just following orders).

lawyers."[94] That rule hits the question of moral interdependence head on, and it provides a powerful reminder that "just following orders" is the weakest of excuses.[95]

We can blame part of Enron's downfall on the economy. We can blame part of it on corporate misbehavior, on board malfeasance, and on pure greed. We can blame part of it on a structure that allowed gatekeepers and reputational intermediaries—the board, the accountants, and the lawyers—to rely on the other two categories to understand the overall picture of what Enron was doing. We can even blame the Enron employees who chose to place too much Enron stock in their own 401(k) plans, thereby betting twice with the same money.[96] But one thing we can't blame is fate. Enron's collapse wasn't due to a "perfect storm" of mere coincidence—the collapse was caused by humans and their hubris. We need to ensure that hubris doesn't blind us to the first rule of leadership: It's all about character.

---

[94] Russell G. Pearce, *Model Rule 1.0: Lawyers are Morally Accountable*, 70 FORDHAM L. REV. 1805, 1807-08 (2002). Pearce points out that Model Rule 1.0 would not take sides in current disputes regarding the lawyer's role. What it would do is move the debates regarding the lawyer's moral duties, like that between Freedman, who favors zealous representation, and Luban, Rhode, and Simon, who favor some significant limits on that representation, to the center of the bar's legal ethics conversations. While the bar currently pays some slight attention to these issues, Model Rule 1.0 would move them to a more prominent place in the bar's official deliberations and continuing legal education courses, as well as in the efforts of the conscientious lawyer to explore her own moral accountability.

[95] I'm not sure how one might enforce a Model Rule 1.0, but at least Pearce is heading in the right direction.

[96] *See, e.g.*, Mark Davis, *The Fallout of a Fallen Enron; Too Much Company Stock in 401(k); Plans Poses Risk*, KAN. CITY STAR, Jan. 20, 2002, at A1; Kaja Whitehouse, *401(k) Woes? Might Be Your Own Fault*, DOW JONES NEWS SERV., Jan. 18, 2002, Westlaw, Allnewsplus Library. Of course, the freeze on selling stock as the value of the stock spiraled downward also had something to do with the losses in the employees' 401(k) plans. *See, e.g.*, Davis, *supra*; Editorial, *Enron and Frontier Justice Fear of Angry Workers Sends Energy Trading Firm to New York to File for Bankruptcy*, PORTLAND OREGONIAN, Dec. 4, 2001, at D06.

Chapter 2

Why Didn't Studying Enron Fix the Problem?

Now that you've reviewed some of the Enron "basics" in Chapter 1 (and, we hope, taken a gander at some of the essays on our website), let's take a more philosophical view regarding Enron's spectacular failure. Would additional required disclosures have helped the various stakeholders discover Enron's fraud? Perhaps more disclosures wouldn't have helped at all. Perhaps the question doesn't go to the *quantity* of disclosure but, instead, to the *quality* of the disclosure.

Even the best disclosure likely wouldn't have stopped the fraud from happening in the first place, though. A clever criminal isn't going to stop planning or trying to execute the perfect crime just because there is a risk that he might get caught. After all, a *really* smart criminal is willing to bet that he won't get caught. That's one of the reasons that this chapter also examines how we might alter the behavior of the people in and around a company that has lost its ethical compass.

As you read the essays in this chapter, think about the practical applications of the ideas that our authors are suggesting. Put yourself in the place of someone who has just become a company's chief executive officer or chief legal officer. Which of these ideas might work no matter what type of company you're in? Are there some ideas that will work better for privately held companies? Publicly held companies? Mom-and-Pop companies? Don't forget to think about various sectors, too. For example, law firms aren't immune from scandal. Would any of these ideas work in law firms?

As we segue from Chapter 1 to Chapter 3, we hope that you'll spend some time in this chapter thinking about the structures of organizations—its way of organizing its bones, muscles, and nerves. A healthy structure isn't, by itself, sufficient for a body or an organization, but it's sure a great place to start.

Icarus and American Corporate Regulation[*]

David Arthur Skeel, Jr.[**]

Nearly all of America's most important federal corporate regulation has been enacted in the wake of corporate scandals, while state lawmakers have tended to regulate on a more continuous basis. After exploring the historical evolution of America's two-track regulatory structure for corporate law, this article considers the most recent cycle of scandal and reform. The article (1) assesses the likely effectiveness, that is, the merits of the recent Sarbanes-Oxley Act and other recent governance reforms; (2) considers the mode of American regulation, in particular, the reliance on courts and federally imposed mandatory rules, in contrast to the more norms-based approach used in England for important issues such as takeover regulation; and (3) concludes by briefly considering the scope of American corporate law and the role of corporate ethics.

INTRODUCTION

When the American corporate scandals hit—Enron, then Global Crossing, Adelphia, and finally WorldCom—two of the most frequently asked questions were: have there ever been scandals like these before?, and, if so, are there any similarities between today's scandals and the corporate crises of the past? The first question was easily answered: yes, there certainly were major scandals before Enron and WorldCom. The second, however, turns out to be much more subtle; it goes to the very heart of America's peculiar two-track mode of corporate governance, with its division of authority between federal and state regulation. To a remarkable extent, American corporate regulation has proceeded scandal by scandal.

---

[*] Originally published at 61 Bus. Law. 155 (2005).

[**] S. Samuel Arsht Professor of Corporate Law, University of Pennsylvania. This Article was first prepared for a "Good Governance" conference in Amsterdam (April 2005). I am grateful to my commentor, Bill Bratton, to the participants at the conference, and to Robert Prentice for helpful comments.

To appreciate the links between scandal and regulation, it is useful to begin by briefly describing two of the most spectacular corporate scandals—scandals long forgotten by most Americans yet central to much of the discussion that follows.[1] In the 1860s, Philadelphia banker Jay Cooke was probably the most famous businessman in America.[2] At the outset of the Civil War, he pioneered a revolutionary new strategy for selling government debt—a strategy that relied on extensive advertising and door-to-door sales of the bonds—which he used to raise millions of dollars for the Union cause. Buying government debt, he argued, wrapping his appeals in the flag, "would strike terror to the rebels and greatly help" the war effort.[3] After the war, he used the same technique to finance the nation's second transcontinental railroad, the Northern Pacific. But Cooke got in over his head, continuing to throw money at the railroad even when everyone else (including his own partners) had concluded it was too risky, and acquiring more and more of the railroad's stock. Like Ken Lay of Enron in our own era, Cooke had close ties to the American president, Ulysses S. Grant; in fact, Grant was staying at Cooke's Philadelphia house the night before the railroad venture and Cooke's bank imploded, ushering in a depression known as the Panic of 1873.

Fast forward sixty years to the 1920s. Samuel Insull—a Chicago electricity magnate who'd gotten his start serving as Thomas Edison's right hand man—was a business superstar known to millions in Chicago and beyond as a yachtsman and benefactor who built a forty-two floor building to house the Chicago Civic Opera Company.[4] Like Bernie Ebbers and WorldCom, Insull embarked on a relentless expansion program in the 1920s, acquiring electricity companies and other businesses as far away as Maine. To disguise the empire's increasingly precarious finances, Insull, like Enron, erected an elaborate holding company structure that included several parent corporations and a maze of subsidiaries, some of which had substantial assets and some of which didn't. When the empire came crashing down in 1932, it was described by some as the "biggest business failure in the history of the world";[5] and it inspired one of Franklin Roosevelt's most famous campaign speeches, a call for action against the "Ishmael or Insull whose hand is against every man's."[6]

With each of these scandals, as with our more recent corporate collapses, the highflying businessmen at the heart of the scandals were not alone. Cooke and Insull

---

[1] The scandals discussed below are described in much more detail in DAVID SKEEL, ICARUS IN THE BOARDROOM: THE FUNDAMENTAL FLAWS IN CORPORATE AMERICA AND WHERE THEY CAME FROM (2005) [hereinafter "SKEEL, ICARUS IN THE BOARDROOM"].

[2] Cooke's rise and subsequent failure are discussed in detail in *id.* at 29-45.

[3] *Id.* at 29 (quoting Cooke).

[4] Insull's principal innovation was "massing production"—keeping his generators running around the clock in order to reduce the per-unit costs of production. For further discussion, see *id.* at 80-89.

[5] FORREST MCDONALD, INSULL vii (1962).

[6] Franklin D. Roosevelt, *New Conditions Impose New Requirements upon Government and Those Who Conduct Government, in* THE PUBLIC PAPERS AND ADDRESSES OF FRANKLIN D. ROOSEVELT 742, 755 (Samuel I. Rosenman, ed.; New York: Random House, 1938).

personified a breakdown in accountability that pervaded all of American corporate and financial life. Indeed, Insull's lawyers successfully defended him in his 1934 criminal trial by, as his biographer puts it, portraying Insull as "an infirm and aged sometime public benefactor persecuted for the sins of his generation."[7]

As devastating as they have been, the massive scandals also have a crucial silver lining; in each case, public outrage has forced lawmakers to step in. This pattern, as it turns out, lies at the heart of American corporate governance. For the past century, American corporate regulation has consisted of periodic, dramatic regulatory interventions by federal lawmakers after a major scandal, together with more nuanced ongoing regulation by the states.

The first two parts of this Article will try to explain how and why this pattern emerged. I start by describing how scandals have inspired nearly all of our most important federal regulation of corporate and financial life. I then turn to the very different role played by the states, focusing most extensively on Delaware, the nation's de facto regulator of state corporate law.

After exploring America's two-track regulatory structure, I consider the implications of the current regulatory framework. This final part 1) assesses the likely effectiveness—that is, the merits—of the recent Sarbanes-Oxley Act[8] and other recent governance reforms; 2) considers the mode of American regulation—in particular, the reliance on federally imposed, mandatory rules, in contrast to the more norms-based approach used for important issues such as takeover regulation in England; and 3) concludes by briefly considering the scope of American corporate law and the role of corporate ethics.

I. ICARUS EFFECT SCANDALS AND FEDERAL REFORM

Each of America's great corporate scandals, from Jay Cooke's 1873 collapse to the 2002 corporate scandals, can be traced to the confluence of the same three general factors. I refer to these factors elsewhere as "Icaran," and to the scandals that they have made possible as "Icarus Effect" scandals.[9] Icarus, for those who may have forgotten their Greek mythology, was a boy who was given wings made of wax and feathers by his father. Although Icarus was warned not to fly too close to the sun, he became intoxicated with his newfound powers, flew higher and higher and, when the wax holding the feathers in place melted, fell to his death.[10]

The first of the three factors—and the one that most closely fits the Icarus theme—is risktaking. Although we tend to associate risktaking with the garages and Silicon Valley coffee shops where the newest innovations are percolating, it also can be found in the

[7] McDonald, *supra* note 5, at 319.

[8] Pub. L. No. 107-204, 116 Stat. 745 (2002) [hereinafter "SOXA"].

[9] Skeel, Icarus in the Boardroom, *supra* note 1, at 4, 7.

[10] Interestingly, in some accounts of the Icarus myth, Icarus is also warned not to fly too low, in order to avoid the spray from the sea's waves. As with executive risk-taking, this account suggests, there are dangers in both directions.

boardrooms of America's largest corporations. To rise to the top of the corporate ladder, an executive must win "probationary crucibles" at each step on the way up.[11] The executives who succeed tend to be self confident and willing to take risks. The takeover wave of the 1980s magnified this tendency by creating more managerial mobility than ever before, as new managers were brought in to run target companies; and even companies that hadn't been taken over searched for charismatic CEOs.[12]

The structure of managerial compensation further reinforced the incentive to take risks. Much of $14.7 million that the average CEO of an S&P 500 firm took home in 2000[13] came from stock options, which reward risk, since options are all upside and no downside: they promise a big payoff if the company's stock price goes up, but there's no cost to the CEO if she gambles with the company's business and the stock price plummets.

Risktaking isn't necessarily a bad thing, of course. Much of American corporate governance is designed to encourage managers to take appropriate risks.[14] But if risktaking—and perhaps more importantly, financial manipulation—isn't reined in, it can have catastrophic consequences.

The second factor is competition. Competitive markets are also good, but they too can reinforce managers' incentives to take risks. Americans have long rebelled against concentrated economic power, in favor of industries with a multitude of competing companies. In this kind of marketplace, a marketplace where monopolies like Microsoft are the exception rather than the rule, the success of a business innovator attracts competitors. If an innovative company's profits are eroded by the influx of competitors, its managers may be tempted to respond by taking increasingly misguided and even illegal risks, or disguising their precarious finances, as they attempt to replicate their early success.

The final factor is manipulation of the corporate form. The ability to tap huge amounts of capital in enterprises that are set up as corporations, together with the large number of people whose livelihood depends in one way or another on the business, means that an Icaran executive who takes excessive or fraudulent risks may jeopardize the financial lives of thousands of employees, investors, and suppliers of the business.

---

[11] *See* ROBERT JACKALL, MORAL MAZES: THE WORLD OF CORPORATE MANAGERS 40 (1988) (describing "probationary crucibles").

[12] This tendency, and the attention lavished on celebrity CEOs, is explored in detail in RAKESH KHURANA, SEARCHING FOR A CORPORATE SAVIOR: THE IRRATIONAL QUEST FOR CHARISMATIC CEOS (2002).

[13] Cited in LUCIEN BEBCHUK & JESSE FRIED, PAY WITHOUT PERFORMANCE: THE UNFULFILLED PROMISE OF EXECUTIVE COMPENSATION 1 (2004).

[14] Since shareholders can diversify their investments, they benefit if managers are willing to take risks that have a positive net present value for the company. Encouraging sensible risk taking has long been one of the principal justifications for the business judgment rule, which discourages second-guessing of managerial decision-making. *See, e.g.,* Joy v. North, 692 F.2d 880 (2d Cir. 1982), *cert. denied,* 460 U.S. 1051 (1983) (explaining the rationale). The problem comes when executives begin taking risks that have a negative net present value. Historically, these gambles have all too often been accompanied by deceptions that are designed to disguise from investors the risks being taken.

The corporate form itself can also multiply the opportunities for mischief. By permitting corporations to hold the stock of other corporations in the late nineteenth century, lawmakers gave corporate managers the ability to tuck some of the assets of a business in one corporate entity and other assets elsewhere.[15] This corporate smoke and mirrors figured prominently in the collapse of Samuel Insull and other utility empires in the 1930s, and it was equally central to Enron's managers' efforts to keep investors in the dark as they ratcheted up the gas company's risks.[16]

American business history can be seen—at its simplest level—as an ongoing cat-and-mouse game between regulators, whose job is to rein in excesses in the three areas just described; and business leaders, who push back against regulatory strictures in order to promote flexibility and innovation.

Under ordinary circumstances, business leaders usually have the upper hand, due to the relentless logic of interest group politics. Corporate managers are intensely interested in the regulatory landscape and they are backed by the coffers of the corporation itself. They also are well-organized, through groups such as the Chamber of Commerce and the Business Roundtable. Although ordinary Americans have a great deal at stake overall, their stake is far more thinly spread. Even now, when more than half of all Americans own stock, most of us have a relatively small overall stake in corporate America. As a result, ordinary Americans are much less likely than corporate managers to focus on the contours of corporate regulation; and even when they do, collective action problems interfere with their efforts to translate their concerns into effective regulation.[17] Mobilization is costly, and ordinary Americans generally do not have enough at stake to justify a campaign for reform.

The influence of managers is reflected both in state lawmaking and in the legislation that is enacted by Congress. In the 1990s, for instance, business leaders pushed through two separate federal reforms that were designed to make it harder to bring securities law claims against companies that are alleged to have made misstatements to the markets.[18]

---

[15] New Jersey led the way, passing a corporate law statute in 1889 that permitted corporations to own stock in other corporations (thus reinforcing a 1888 court decision). *See, e.g.*, SKEEL, ICARUS IN THE BOARDROOM, *supra* note 1, at 63.

[16] Enron's misuse of special purpose entities (SPEs) is described in vivid detail in BETHANY MCLEAN & PETER ELKIND, THE SMARTEST GUYS IN THE ROOM: THE AMAZING RISE AND SCANDALOUS FALL OF ENRON (2003).

[17] The literature on collective action is enormous. The wellspring is MANCUR OLSON, THE LOGIC OF COLLECTIVE ACTION (1971), which explores in detail the political disadvantage large diffuse groups have as compared to small groups whose members have a significant stake. The literature is surveyed in David A. Skeel, Jr., *Public Choice and the Future of Public Choice-Influenced Legal Scholarship*, 50 VAND. L. REV. 647 (1997).

[18] *See* Private Securities Litigation Reform Act of 1995, Pub. L. No. 104-67, 109 Stat. 737 (imposing enhanced pleading requirements and providing more protection for forward looking information); Securities Litigation Uniform Standards Act of 1998, Pub. L. No. 105-353, 112 Stat. 3227 (preventing most securities fraud class actions from being pursued in state court).

But corporate scandals instantly transform the political calculus. The outrage provoked by a wave of scandals galvanizes public opinion in favor of sweeping corporate reforms that simply would not be possible in a more placid corporate and financial environment. America's most important corporate regulation has always been enacted in the wake of stunning Icarus Effect collapses.[19]

. . . .

Most recently, we have Enron and WorldCom to thank for the Sarbanes-Oxley Act of 2002, the recent stock exchange reforms, and Eliot Spitzer's settlement with the securities industry.[27] The Sarbanes-Oxley Act focused most extensively on the accounting industry and on the responsibility of top corporate executives. With accounting, the most glaring problem was a pervasive conflict of interest: the auditors of the nation's largest companies usually provided consulting services as well; this gave the auditors a huge disincentive to conduct a tough audit, for fear that an unhappy client might direct its consulting business elsewhere. (At Arthur Andersen, the poster child for this problem, second-guessing Enron would have jeopardized roughly $25 million a year in consulting business).[28] The corporate responsibility reforms address this concern by

---

[19] The pattern outlined in the text is similar to the interest group transformation described in Douglass North's work. *See, e.g.,* LANCE E. DAVIS & DOUGLASS C. NORTH, INSTITUTIONAL CHANGE AND ECONOMIC GROWTH (1971). Bill Bratton & Joe McCahery characterize the same dynamic as bringing the median voter's perspective to the fore. William W. Bratton & Joseph A. McCahery, The Content of Corporate Federalism (unpublished manuscript, 2004), available at http://repositories.cdlib.org/cgi/viewcontent.cgi?article=1091&context=berkeley_law_econ.

[27] For good overviews and analysis of the Sarbanes-Oxley Act, see, e.g., Lawrence A. Cunningham, *The Sarbanes-Oxley Yawn; Heavy Rhetoric, Light Reform (and It Just Might Work),* 36 CONN. L. REV. 915 (2003); Larry E. Ribstein, *Market vs. Regulatory Responses to Corporate Fraud: A Critique of the Sarbanes-Oxley Act of 2002,* 28 J. CORP. L. 1 (2002).

As discussed in more detail in Part III(A), infra, the New York Stock Exchange added a series of independence requirements. The boards of directors of listed firms must have a majority of independent directors, and they must have independent compensation and nomination committees. *See, e.g.,* NYSE LISTED CO. MANUAL 303A.01 (majority of independent directors); 303A.04 (independent nominating committee); 303A.05 (independent compensation committee). NASDAQ added somewhat similar requirements. NASDAQ Rules 4200(a)(15), 4350(c).

Under the Spitzer settlement, the major investment banks were required to pay $900 million in fines, to subsidize $450 million in research by independent securities analysts, and to create a stronger wall of separation between a bank's securities analysts and investment bankers. For further discussion, see, e.g., SKEEL, ICARUS IN THE BOARDROOM, *supra* note 1, at 180-82.

[28] For a good discussion of the conflict, see John C. Coffee, Jr., *Understanding Enron: It's About the Gatekeepers, Stupid,* 57 BUS. LAW. 1403 (2002). One recent empirical study concludes that companies whose auditors also performed significant amounts of consulting services for the same client were not significantly more likely to later restate their financial results. Other evidence suggests that consulting business did distort the auditing process, however, and even auditors whose firm did not provide substantial consulting business for a client may well have been influenced by the prospect that consulting opportunities might increasingly come their way. The recent studies are reviewed in detail in JOHN C. COFFEE, JR., GATEKEEPERS: THE ROLE OF THE PROFESSIONS AND CORPORATE GOVERNANCE (Clarendon Lectures in Management Studies, 2007).

prohibiting the Big Four accounting firms from providing consulting services to their audit clients;[29] the reforms also established a new, more independent accounting regulator.[30] Turning to corporate executives, the law's most controversial provision requires every public company to establish an internal control system designed to make sure that every part of the business provides accurate financial information.[31] The CEO and CFO are required to certify its periodic financial statements, and to report on the company's internal controls.[32] These reforms—which are discussed further in Part III of the Article—were so clearly inspired by the recent scandals that they might well be called the [F]uture Enron [P]revention [A}ct.[33]

Scandals also have served as the lightning rod for more targeted reforms. In the 1940s, Richard Whitney, head of the New York Stock Exchange, was discovered to have embezzled several million dollars from the exchange. The outrage provoked by his misbehavior enabled SEC Chairman William Douglas to orchestrate a major restructuring of the exchange.[34] In the early 1970s, the Watergate investigators uncovered evidence that many of America's leading corporations had set aside slush funds for bribing foreign officials. Congress responded to the widespread anger by enacting the Foreign Corrupt Practices Act, which forbids companies from paying foreign officials.[35]

Each of these reforms followed the same pattern as the more pervasive legislation in the 1930s and in 2002: a shocking scandal galvanizes attention, neutralizing the influence that corporations have under ordinary circumstances; Congress (or, in the case of the Whitney scandal, regulators) quickly responds by enacting reforms that are demanded by ordinary Americans. It is these reforms that provide the federal regulatory infrastructure for the decades that follow.

II. SMOOTHING THE SKIDS: DELAWARE AND STATE REGULATION

For the past seventy years, nearly all of the scandal-based reforms have come from federal lawmakers and regulators. How, then, do the states fit into the regulatory picture? In the beginning, the states handled nearly all of corporate law, due to the fact that they were the ones who doled out corporate charters. But the state role shifted sharply

---

29 SOXA, § 201.

30 SOXA, §§ 101-109 (establishing Public Accounting Oversight Board consisting of five independent members, two of which are to be certified public accountants).

31 SOXA, § 404.

32 SOXA, § 302.

33 The emphasis on Enron is particularly evident in provisions such as a whistleblowing provision that requires the audit committee to establish a hotline for complaints such as those raised by Sherron Watkins at Enron. SOXA, § 301(m)(4).

34 The Whitney scandal and the stock exchange reforms it facilitated are described in [JOEL SELIGMAN, THE TRANSFORMATION OF WALL STREET: A HISTORY OF THE SECURITIES AND EXCHANGE COMMISSION AND MODERN CORPORATE FINANCE] 167-79 [(1982)].

35 Pub. L. No. 95-213, 91 Stat. 1494 (1977) (codified in 15 U.S.C. §§ 78m(b), 78dd-1, 78dd-2). For a good discussion of the origins and political background of the legislation, see BRATTON & MCCAHERY, *supra* note 19, at 45-47.

at the end of the nineteenth century. Since then, the states' regulatory role has looked quite different from the federal interventions described in Part I.

The key period in early American business history—the moment when the federal and state roles shifted toward the modern pattern—came in the 1880s and 1890s, with the emergence of the so-called corporate trusts. In 1882, John D. Rockefeller bought out all of his significant competitors in the oil industry and assembled them into the corporate behemoth known as Standard Oil. After Rockefeller successfully cobbled together his giant trust, the trust strategy was employed in one industry after another.[36] By the end of the decade, roughly 100 different trusts had already been formed. The trusts were not America's first large scale corporations; this honor belonged to the railroads, as we have seen. But with the trusts, big business seemed to be coming of age.

The emergence of large-scale corporations met with serious resistance at both the state and federal levels. Many states had maximum capital limitations, which were designed to keep corporate growth in check.[37] State attorneys general also challenged expansion, particularly by railroads, as *ultra vires*—that is, as not within the corporation's power.[38] In 1890, Congress entered the fray by enacting the Sherman Act, which prohibited any "contract, combination in the form of trust or otherwise, or conspiracy, in restraint of trade or commerce," as well as "any attempt to monopolize" trade or commerce.[39]

. . . .

Over time, another factor loomed largest of all and came to define the state role in corporate regulation. By the late nineteenth century, American business had become increasingly mobile, thanks to the advent of railroads, the telegraph, and other new forms of communication and transportation. If a state developed a reputation for aggressively policing the large corporations located within its borders, the corporations might move elsewhere. As political scientists Jacob Hacker and Paul Pierson have argued, the threat of relocation gave businesses structural power.[47] As a result, even states that weren't competing to offer business-friendly corporate laws were reluctant to pursue policies that

---

[36] Because a corporation could not own the stock of other corporations, Rockefeller initially could not simply buy the stock of his competitors. To circumvent this limitation, he set up a trust arrangement. The shareholders of the constituent companies retained their stock, but ceded voting authority to a trust controlled by Rockefeller. *See, e.g.*, SKEEL, ICARUS IN THE BOARDROOM, *supra* note 1, at 59-60.

[37] In Massachusetts, for instance, mechanical, mining and manufacturing corporations were prohibited from having more than $1 million in capital. *See, e.g.*, Margaret M. Blair, *Locking in Capital: What Corporate Law Achieved for Business Organizers in the Nineteenth Century*, 51 UCLA L. REV. 387, 389 n.3 (2003).

[38] In the 1870s and 1880s, many of these state challenges were successful. The battles are described in detail in MORTON J. HORWITZ, THE TRANSFORMATION OF AMERICAN LAW, 1870-1960: THE CRISIS OF LEGAL ORTHODOXY 82-86 (1992).

[39] Sherman Anti-Trust Act, ch. 647, 26 Stat. 209 (1890) (codified at 15 U.S.C. §§ 1-7).

[47] Jacob S. Hacker & Paul Pierson, *Business Power and Social Policy: Employers and the Formation of the American Welfare State*, 30 POL. & SOC. 277, 290 (2002) (explaining the states' failure to enact significant welfare protections).

confronted big business head on. It was this political reality that laid the groundwork for the role that state lawmakers still play in contemporary corporate law.[48]

The states' abandonment of the fight against corporate combinations shifted the campaign against corporate monopoly from the states to Congress and federal regulators. Two decades later, a trust-busting campaign led by Teddy Roosevelt would firmly establish federal regulators as the principal guardians of competition in American industry.[49] One effect of the transition to federal oversight (which we will revisit later) was to separate antitrust issues from the rest of corporate law.

The core terms of internal governance are still regulated by the states. Until 1913, New Jersey was the Liberia of corporate law, the clear winner in the competition to persuade large corporations to fly under the state's flag. But New Jersey dropped out of the picture in 1913, due to the presidential aspirations of Woodrow Wilson.[50] Delaware took over and has made sure ever since that it will not repeat its forerunner's mistake.[51]

Whereas federal law provides the market infrastructure, regulates disclosure, and deputizes the principal outside watchers, state corporate law focuses on the internal affairs of the corporation—in particular, on the relations among shareholders, managers and directors. This includes everything from fiduciary duty and shareholder voting rights, to the standards for effecting mergers and other transactions. Although Delaware

---

[48] Notice that this argument is somewhat different from the standard focus in the corporate charter competition literature on the fact that the state of incorporation governs the internal affairs of the corporations it charters. The structural power that corporations have would remain even if the internal affairs doctrine were reversed, since it stems from a company's physical presence in the state. For a somewhat similar intuition, see Ernest L. Folk, III, *Some Reflections of a Corporation Law Draftsman,* 42 CONN. BAR J. 409, 418-19 (1968) (questioning the "irrational conviction" that a strict corporate law statute would discourage businesses from doing business in a state).

[49] Roosevelt's campaign against the corporate trusts, which began with a Sherman Act challenge in 1902 to the Northern Securities Corporation that had been formed by J.P. Morgan, is described in SKEEL, ICARUS IN THE BOARDROOM, *supra* note 1, at 68-69.

[50] While serving as president of Princeton, Woodrow Wilson ran a successful campaign for governor of New Jersey on a platform calling for more stringent regulation of corporations. As his U.S. presidential campaign geared up, he began promoting a group of laws known as the Seven Sisters that were designed to re-invigorate state antitrust enforcement in New Jersey. The reforms were enacted while Wilson awaited his inauguration as president in 1913. For a more detailed discussion of Delaware's displacement of New Jersey as the state of choice for major corporations, see, e.g., Christopher Grandy, *New Jersey Corporate Chartermongering,* 1875-1929, 49 J. ECON. HIST. 677 (1989); William E. Kirk, III, *A Case Study in Legislative Opportunism: How Delaware Used the Federal-State System to Attain Corporate Pre-Eminence,* 10 J. CORP. L. 233 (1984).

[51] Delaware's implicit promise not to repeat New Jersey's sudden shift in focus is reinforced by a provision in Delaware's state constitution that requires any change to the corporate laws to be passed by a two-thirds majority of the General Assembly. Del. Const. art. IX, § 1. Delaware's most important commitment, however, is the fact that the state relies on its chartering business for a very large percentage—fifteen to twenty percent—of its revenues. Roberta Romano has labeled the commitment that stems from Delaware's dependence on its corporate revenue the "genius" of American corporate law. ROBERTA ROMANO, THE GENIUS OF AMERICAN CORPORATE LAW (1993).

has been the most important corporate law regulator since 1913, the moment that defined Delaware's current pre-eminence came in 1967, when Delaware passed a major overhaul of its general corporation law. Spear-headed by Samuel Arsht, who is viewed by many as the father of Delaware corporate law, the 1967 reforms expressly authorized cashout mergers and expanded corporations' right to indemnify their directors against liability claims.[52]

. . . .

Painting with a very broad brush, then, American corporate law consists of two parallel and interlocking systems, state corporate law and the federal over- and under-lay.[68] Congress has tended to intervene crisis by crisis, following years of relative silence with dramatic intervention in the crucible of a wave of major corporate scandals. Delaware and other states regulate in a more continuous fashion, generally promoting flexibility and innovation.

III. THE ROAD AHEAD: GOOD, BAD AND POINTS IN BETWEEN

America's peculiar two-track regulatory system, with its allocation of responsibilities between Congress and the states, is hardly inevitable. Even before the Nader campaign in the 1970s, there were several serious efforts to federalize corporate law, first under Teddy Roosevelt in the early twentieth century, and then again during the New Deal.[69] Nor are the existing allocations of authority stable. The recent corporate responsibility reforms—with their independence and compliance program requirements, which move well beyond the traditional federal focus on disclosure and policing fraud—intrude deeply into the traditional domain of state corporate law oversight. And even before the recent reforms, the overlaps between federal insider trading and misdisclosure actions, on the one hand, and state fiduciary duty litigation, on the other, have been steadily increasing.[70]

---

[52] Perhaps I'm getting a little carried away here—I have Arsht's family to thank for the chair that I hold at the University of Pennsylvania. But by any yardstick, Arsht was a (and arguably, the) major player in the 1967 amendments, and in promoting the revisions. Bratton & McCahery note that the portion of Delaware's revenues that came from chartering had dropped to 7% as of the early 1960s, but that Delaware's success in attracting corporations soared after the 1967 Act. Bratton & McCahery, *supra* note 19, at 21-22.

[68] The SEC obviously also plays an important role in the developing the contours of American corporate law. The boundaries of SEC oversight are set by Congressional legislation, but the SEC plays an ongoing role in articulating the standards for proxy voting and on other issues.

[69] The initiatives are described in SKEEL, ICARUS IN THE BOARDROOM, *supra* note 1, at 71-72 (Roosevelt call for federal incorporation in 1907); Seligman, *supra* note [27], at 205-09 (New Deal efforts to promote federal incorporation).

[70] *See, e.g.*, Robert Thompson & Hillary Sale, *Securities Fraud as Corporate Governance: Reflections Upon Federalism,* 56 VAND. L. REV. 859 (2003) (arguing that state law duty of care issues are increasingly litigated under Rule 10b-5 of the federal securities laws).

What should we make of the two-track system that American history and politics have given us? Let me conclude by offering three sets of observations about the way that corporate law is made and enforced in the United States.

A. Crisis Legislation Comes With No Guarantees

The first lesson our history teaches is that crisis legislation comes with no guarantees. Each of the major waves of corporate scandal has reflected a breakdown in American corporate and financial life. The silver lining has been the overwhelming pressure on lawmakers to pass structural reform. But the fact that Congress steps into the fray doesn't necessarily mean that Congress will solve the problems revealed by the corporate collapse.[71]

The remarkable success of the New Deal reforms may have made us too optimistic in this respect. The securities acts and banking reforms of the 1930s greatly enhanced the transparency of the American securities markets and replaced the Wall Street banks with a new set of "watchers"—companies' auditors and, in time, the securities analysts who covered them.

The recent Sarbanes-Oxley Act and the new stock exchange rules that accompanied it, by contrast, are more of a mixed bag. As noted earlier, many of the new rules are aimed at the accounting industry, including provisions that forbid the Big Four firms from providing consulting services to their audit clients; and others that set up a new independent oversight board for the accounting industry.[72] These are the best of the new reforms, a welcome (though partial) solution to the conflicts that bedeviled the accounting industry during the 1990s.[73]

At the other end of the spectrum, the stock exchanges have salted their listing rules with a spate of new independence requirements, starting with the obligation that listed companies have a majority of independent directors on their boards. Most firms will not be hurt by these requirements, and some might be helped, but the existing empirical data suggest that the changes won't make much of a difference.[74] Delaware's judges

---

[71] For a much stronger version of this point, see Larry E. Ribstein, *Bubble Laws,* 40 HOUS. L. REV. 77 (2003). Unlike my analysis, which suggests that post-scandal reforms are often necessary, Ribstein argues that bubble laws frequently stifle economic growth.

[72] *See supra* notes 29-30 and accompanying text.

[73] In my own view, Congress should have gone still further, and required that the stock exchanges rather than the companies themselves select the company's auditor. The problem with permitting the company to select its auditor—even when a disinterested audit committee does the selecting—is that the auditor inevitably views the company as its client. For a more detailed discussion, see SKEEL, ICARUS IN THE BOARDROOM, *supra* note 1, at 188-89.

[74] *See, e.g.,* Roberta Romano, *The Sarbanes-Oxley Act and the Making of Quack Corporate Governance,* 114 YALE L.J. 1521 (2005) (summarizing studies); Bernard S. Black, *Shareholder Activism and Corporate Governance in the United States, in* 3 THE NEW PALGRAVE DICTIONARY OF ECONOMICS AND THE LAW 459, 463 (Peter Newman ed., 1998) (noting that "there is no compelling evidence that greater board independence improves overall firm performance").

rightly complain, moreover, that these provisions run roughshod over state lawmakers' traditional authority over internal governance issues.[75] The new standards for directorial independence create a danger that boards will be subject to different definitions of independence in different contexts—one standard for stock exchange listing, another for state fiduciary duty oversight.

By far the most controversial reform is section 404, a new requirement that companies establish an internal control system.[76] Corporate America is complaining bitterly about the cost of putting the required controls in place, which for many companies amounts to millions of dollars a year.[77] If the expense assures that accurate financial information is produced at every level of the company, the cost will be worth it. And costs are likely to decline once the compliance programs are put in place—the largest expense is the cost of getting the program up and running in the first instance. But the efficacy of the new programs remains to be seen. There is a risk that the new requirements will simply add up to more internal bureaucracy—that companies will hire a new internal compliance officer and essentially keep doing what they were doing before. There is also a risk that companies will focus narrowly on the financial compliance called for by the reform, while ignoring other kinds of potential misbehavior within the firm.[78]

A major question raised by the fact that the reforms reach far into the heart of traditional corporate governance functions is whether these rules should apply to non-American companies.[79] The commitment to comply with American disclosure obligations has traditionally been an important benefit to European companies of listing on the American exchanges. But the new reforms mandate a "one size fits all" approach on governance issues for which there is not an single, optimal approach for every firm. The most sensible way to apply the new rules to non-U.S. companies would be to treat them as disclosure obligations, rather than mandatory rules. European companies should be required to disclose the independence (or not) of their directors and the nature of

---

[75] For a good statement of this concern by a corporate law scholar, see, e.g., Stephen Bainbridge, *The Creeping Federalization of Corporate Law,* 26 REGULATION 32 (Spring 2003).

[76] In addition to the company's obligation to establish and report on its "internal control structure and procedures . . . for financial reporting," the auditor is required to "attest to, and report on, the assessment made by the management of the issuer." SOXA, § 404(b). The auditor attestation requirement has dramatically increased the costs of recent audits.

[77] *See, e.g.,* Bob Fernandez, *Firms Surprised by the Cost to Keep Ledgers Honest,* PHILA. INQ., April 13, 2005, at A1, A6 (citing a survey finding that the average cost of compliance for the largest companies was $4.36 million in 2004).

[78] Congress also indulged its penchant for moralistic criminal legislation by adding a slew of new corporate crimes to the criminal code, and ratcheting up the penalties for others. I have criticized these provisions elsewhere. David Skeel & William Stuntz, *Christianity and the (Modest) Rule of Law,* 8 U. PA. J. CONST. L. 809 (2006) (manuscript on file with The Business Lawyer).

[79] The SEC has delayed implementation of section 404 for foreign companies, as well as small and mid-sized American firms. But as of this writing, the Commission takes the position that foreign companies eventually will be required to fully comply. *See, e.g.,* William H. Donaldson, *We've Been Listening,* WALL ST. J., March 29, 2005, at A14.

their internal controls. But they shouldn't be forced to adopt a U.S.-style structure as the price for listing shares on U.S. markets.[80]

Much more troublesome than the reforms that Congress passed were the ones it didn't. Congress did almost nothing to address two of the most obvious problems highlighted by the corporate scandals. The first is runaway compensation, and in particular, the perverse incentives created by injecting huge amounts of stock options into executives' pay.[81] Options are a one way ratchet, with an unlimited upside but little downside for executives who pump the company's stock price. But nothing was done to remove the existing tax incentives for granting options.[82] Second is the risk to employees whose retirement plans are now invested in the stock market. At the least, employees should be required to diversify their investment, to prevent a reprise of the financial devastation suffered by Enron and WorldCom employees whose retirement accounts were loaded with company stock. Lawmakers also need to give more serious thought to the need to provide at least limited protection for the funds that investors have in market-based pension plans.[83]

In Delaware, the principal legacy of the scandals seems to be the newly emerging good faith duty and the possibility that Delaware will subject directorial compensation to closer scrutiny than in the past. It is important to note that this response to the scandals has come in Delaware's courts, rather than through a statutory reform effort. This is significant for at least two related reasons. First, because the judicial process takes time, even in Delaware, the principal cases are being decided long after the initial outrage at

[80] Many foreign companies that are currently listed on U.S. exchanges are considering delisting in order to avoid the new mandates. Under the securities laws, companies are required to continue complying unless they have less than three hundred U.S. shareholders. For an argument that this requirement should be relaxed if the company makes a reasonable buyout offer to its U.S. shareholders, see Robert Pozen, *How to Break Free From an American Listing,* FIN. TIMES, Feb. 13, 2004, at 17.

[81] For more detailed discussion of the compensation problem, see, e.g., SKEEL, ICARUS IN THE BOARDROOM, *supra* note 1, at 152-54; BEBCHUK & FRIED, *supra* note 13. A new study by Kees Cools found that the best predictors of whether a company was likely to be required to restate its financials in the 1990s were the amount of options based compensation is provided its executives, the amount of media attention the company received, and the percentage increase in its average earnings targets. *See, e.g.,* Kees Cools, *Ebbers Rex,* WALL ST. J., March 22, 2005, at B2 (describing the study).

[82] Under an Internal Revenue Code provision put in place in 1993—ironically, in an effort to curb managerial compensation—companies are permitted to deduct a maximum of $1 million per year of compensation for each executive as a business expense. The deduction is lost for amounts in excess of $1 million. But Congress excluded stock and stock options from the ceiling, which encourages companies to use these forms of compensation rather than cash. Internal Revenue Code, 26 U.S.C. § 162(m) (2000).

Reversing the tax incentive to use option and stock-based compensation might also cool off overall levels of compensation, since companies would lose their tax deduction for compensation of any sort that exceeded the ceiling amount (currently $1 million per year).

[83] Several possible insurance strategies are discussed in SKEEL, ICARUS IN THE BOARDROOM, *supra* note 1, at 212-14.

the scandals has passed.[84] As a result, there is much less pressure for a radical response now. Second, Delaware's fiduciary duty jurisprudence has a self-correcting quality. It is open-ended enough so that the courts can incorporate new concerns without dramatically altering its prior precedent.[85]

In short, in the 2000s, as in the 1930s, the most dramatic reforms have come from Congress because Congress faces intense public pressure to address breakdowns in corporate America. The shortcomings of the recent reforms vividly illustrate the point made at the outset of this section—that the pressure Congress faces to act after a scandal does not guarantee that the reforms that are passed will be ideal. But each of the great corporate scandals has reflected a breakdown in corporate oversight, which suggests, at the least, that Congress is likely to be aiming at the right target when it steps in. As a result, scandal reforms generally will make things better rather than worse overall, which is a fair assessment of the recent reform efforts.

. . . .

C. Corporate Ethics and the (Narrow) Scope of Corporate Law

The final implication of the historical evolution of American corporate governance lies in the contemporary scope of corporate law. Over the last century, the domain of American corporate law has steadily shrunk. Antitrust, labor law, and environmental regulation—all of which are integral to corporate life—were each separated from corporate law at various points in the twentieth century.[97] In America, corporate law now means internal governance issues such as fiduciary duties and decision-making on fundamental transactions, and not much else. This balkanization is also reflected in the academic world, where most corporate law scholars do not specialize in areas like environmental or employment law.

Although the narrow scope of corporate law is in many respects a historical accident, as we have seen, it has had profound implications for American corporate governance. Limiting the field of inquiry to the agency relations among shareholders, directors, and officers has reinforced the emphasis on the profit-making role of corporations. Corporate managers can't ignore their employees or environmental obligations, but

[84] The waning sense of outrage may be part of the explanation for the Delaware chancery court's recent decision in the Disney case, which found no liability despite an almost complete lack of oversight of CEO Michael Eisner's decision to give Michael Ovitz $140 million in termination benefits. In re Walt Disney Co. Derivative Litigation, No. Civ. A. 15452, 2005 WL 2056651 (Del. Ch. Aug. 9, 2005).

[85] For an extended analysis of this attribute of Delaware corporate law, see Kahan & Rock, *supra* note 67 (arguing that Delaware's emphasis on common law adjudication is an effective strategy for keeping Congress at bay).

[97] One could add corporate reorganization to this list, too. *See, e.g.*, David A. Skeel, Jr., Debt's Dominion: A History of Bankruptcy Law in America (2001) (describing the severing of corporate reorganization from corporate and securities practice in the 1930s, and the partial reintegration in the 1980s and 1990s).

the regulatory structure treats these concerns as peripheral to the core functions of corporate governance.

This emphasis on profits, and on shareholders as the managers' principal constituency, has a tremendous upside benefit: it provides an appropriate focus for managerial decision making.[98] But the narrow scope of corporate law may also have abetted some of the excesses of the 1990s. The prevailing ethos of the bubble years assumed that managers, directors, and shareholders were (and should be) motivated entirely by self-interest.[99] Managers were encouraged to focus solely on the company's stock price not just by the structure of corporate law, but also by compensation arrangements that relied on stock options as the principal form of executive pay. Unfortunately, the relentless appeal to self-interest—narrowly defined in terms of stock price— too often forced basic ethical considerations out.

What would it take to bring a healthier focus to American corporate life? Let me conclude by offering three simple suggestions. The first is to reform the regulatory rules that contributed to the corporate scandals, as discussed earlier.[100] So long as the tax code rewards companies for compensating their executives with stock options rather than cash, there will be structural pressures for managers to continue focusing narrowly on stock price. Altering the regulatory incentives that encouraged misbehavior should therefore remain a top priority.

The second is to insist on a broader perspective on corporate law, one that looks beyond the narrow confines of shareholder, director, and manager relations.[101] I don't mean to suggest that directors' fiduciary duties should encompass not only shareholders, but also employees, suppliers and other constituencies, as advocates of a "team production" approach to corporate law have proposed.[102] The problem with inviting directors

---

[98] And conversely, expecting managers to focus on a broader range of constituencies could actually undermine their accountability, as noted below. As will quickly become clear, I do not share Milton Friedman's famous view that "there is one and only one social responsibility of business—to use its resources and engage in activities designed to increase its profits [for shareholders]." MILTON FRIEDMAN, CAPITALISM AND FREEDOM 133 (1962); Milton Friedman, *A Friedman Doctrine—The Social Responsibility of Business is to Increase its Profits,* N.Y. TIMES, Sept. 13, 1970 (Magazine), at 33. But I agree that managers should view the company's shareholders as their primary constituency.

[99] For a postmortem critique of the assumption that "people are selfish, constantly calculating to their own advantage, with no thought of others," see Robert J. Shiller, *How Wall Street Learns to Look the Other Way,* N.Y. TIMES, Feb. 8, 2005, at A25.

[100] *See supra* notes 82-85 and accompanying text.

[101] A fascinating recent article that takes a similar perspective is Adam Winkler, *Corporate Law or the Law of Business?: Stakeholders and Corporate Governance at the End of History,* 67 LAW & CONTEMP. PROBS. 109 (2004). Winkler argues that if we construe corporate law broadly to include the full range of regulation that comprises the "law of business," it is not nearly so narrowly focused on shareholders' interests as is often believed.

[102] *See, e.g.,* Margaret M. Blair & Lynn A. Stout, *A Team Production Theory of Corporate Law,* 85 VA. L. REV. 247 (1999).

to abandon their focus on shareholders is that directors who are told to be loyal to many constituencies are too likely to prove loyal to none. The effect—as we saw with the "other constituency" statutes enacted during the takeover wave of the 1980s[103]—is to give the directors unfettered discretion, since nearly any decision they wish to make can be defended as benefiting one or more constituencies.[104] But policy makers and corporate scholars need to pay greater heed to areas like labor law, antitrust, and campaign finance that often do not even figure in discussions of corporate regulation. Although directors' principal internal responsibility is to the company's shareholders, the company's compliance with its obligations to employees, creditors, and other third parties should be central to our assessment of corporate performance.[105]

Third is simply integrating ethics into the existing emphasis on self-interest, starting with our law and business school classrooms and continuing into corporate life itself. There are many reasons to believe that simply announcing a policy of ethical behavior will not by itself change the ethical tone of the company. If compensation and promotion practices are closely tied to bottom line performance measures, they will undercut the company's code of ethics by signaling that the code is simply window dressing. Corporate ethics also requires that executives practice what they preach. "[I]t probably is necessary," as Don Langevoort puts it, "that senior management display in their own actions the sort of other-regarding behaviors they want to see from their agents."[106] Only if the company's values are reflected in the executive suite and in the expectations created throughout the firm will the recent emphasis on ethics prove more than a temporary fad.

The lessons just described are not a cure-all that will end corporate misbehavior and single-handedly usher in a new, permanent era of corporate and financial health. For better and worse, the historical cycle of periodic waves of Icarus Effect scandals followed by a federal regulatory response is part of the inevitable push and pull of American business. In the name of flexibility and innovation, corporate leaders push back against the regulatory constraints imposed in the aftermath of scandals (a process now well underway, as reflected in the continuing debates over Sarbanes-Oxley's internal controls requirement), and changes in business create new challenges for reining in abuses stemming from the familiar pattern of risktaking, competition and misuse

---

103 For a discussion and critique of the constituency statutes, see William J. Carney, *Does Defining Constituencies Matter?*, 59 U. Cinn. L. Rev. 385 (1990).

104 The classic discussion of the dangers of managerial discretion is Adolph A. Berle, Jr., *Corporate Powers as Powers in Trust,* 44 Harv. L. Rev. 1049 (1931).

105 An important contribution of the recent book The Anatomy of Corporate Law is to reintroduce these kinds of considerations into the analysis of corporate law. Reinier Kraakman et al., The Anatomy of Corporate Law (2004) (including agency costs between the corporation and third parties such as employees and creditors within its model for corporate law). As noted above, Adam Winkler has also argued for a broader conception of the "law of business." Winkler, *supra* note 101.

106 Donald C. Langevoort, *Monitoring: The Behavioral Economics of Corporate Compliance with Law,* 2002 Colum. Bus. L. Rev. 71, 110.

of the corporate form. But whether the next round of corporate scandals comes later or sooner will depend in no small part on how fully regulators and businesses respond to what we have learned from the most recent breakdown in American corporate and financial life.

Efficient Capital Markets, Corporate Disclosure, and Enron[*]

Jonathan R. Macey[**]

INTRODUCTION

The market capitalization of Enron Corporation declined by $63 billion in the one-year period between January 2001 and January 2002.[1] In practical terms, this means that someone who invested in Enron, Inc. for a comfortable retirement "nest egg" in 2001—say 3000 shares worth about $250,000—would barely have enough money to buy a major home appliance a scant year later.[2] Ironically, Enron's shares were thought prior to January 2001 to experience relatively low volatility.

The collapse of Enron dealt a stunning blow, not only to people's wallets and a once-formidable U.S. corporation, but also to a number of conventional theories and core beliefs within the legal academy. The theories and beliefs challenged by the Enron debacle include the following: (1) the U.S. corporate governance system is the best in the world; (2) the U.S. system of corporate disclosure is the best in the world; and (3) the U.S. capital markets, particularly the markets for large corporations such as those listed on the prestigious New York Stock Exchange (NYSE), are highly efficient.

Following a brief corporate history of Enron, Parts I, II, III, and IV of this Article discuss, in turn, what remains of each of these conventional academic theories in the wake of Enron's collapse. My principal conclusions are as follows: Initially, with respect to U.S. corporate governance, the collapse of Enron reveals the fundamental tradeoff between objective and proximate monitoring by corporate directors, auditors, rating

---

[*] Reprinted by permission of the Cornell Law Review and the author. Jonathan R. Macy, *Efficient Capital Markets, Corporate Disclosure, and Enron,* 89 CORNELL L. REV. 394 (2004).

[**] J. DuPratt White Professor of Law and Director, John M. Olin Program in Law and Economics, Cornell Law School. The author thanks Michael Heiss and the seminar participants in the Cornell Law School Faculty workshop series for helpful comments.

[1] *See* Gary Katz, *Enron*, CBC NEWS ONLINE, Feb. 2002, *at* http://www.cbc.ca/news/features/enron.html.

[2] *See id.*

agencies, analysts, and others.[3] Second, the collapse of Enron demonstrates that disaster ensues when supposedly neutral and objective corporate monitors are "captured" by the firms they are supposed to monitor. Third, the U.S. system of corporate governance relies on these objective monitors more than other corporate governance systems, and is therefore more vulnerable when such monitors fail, as was the case with Enron. The downfall of Enron also illustrates both the importance of corporate governance to corporate performance, and the inherent susceptibility to corruption present in any system of corporate governance.

Further, from an international perspective, one is tempted to ask whether the Enron debacle could happen in Europe or Japan or whether it demonstrates a vulnerability unique to the U.S. system of corporate governance. I have three observations to make on this issue. First and foremost, the Enron fiasco demonstrates the acute pressure felt by U.S. corporate management to produce superior performance results. As discussed later in this Article, Enron's financial maneuvering, which led to the company's massive 2001 restatement of earnings, was prompted only in 1997 when Enron came under significant pressure from investors. Essentially, Enron's corporate performance was consistent for a considerable period of time prior to 1997.[4] However, between 1996 and 1997, the firm's profits and return on equity each declined by ninety percent.[5] The sudden deterioration in performance pressured management to engage in transactions that increased revenue and moved debt off of the firm's balance sheet.[6] This intense pressure on corporate management is unique to the U.S. system of corporate governance.

Second, outside the United States, management's incentives to succumb to the creative accounting gimmicks that Enron employed are significantly weaker. From an international perspective, Enron's collapse demonstrates the strength of the U.S. system of corporate governance, namely the intensely competitive environment in which U.S. management teams operate. In the vast majority of cases, this environment causes management to work extremely hard, producing superior results in response to increased pressure.

However, in rare cases like Enron, the "pressure-cooker" environment leads managers of U.S. corporations and their advisors to take shortcuts and mislead investors about corporate performance. Independent monitors are supposed to deal with these "rare cases" by identifying cheaters and publicly announcing their wrongdoings. One

---

[3] This monitoring tradeoff is developed in more detail in my article co-authored with Arnoud Boot. . . . *See* Arnoud W.A. Boot & Jonathan R. Macey, *Monitoring Corporate Performance: The Role of Objectivity, Proximity, and Adaptability in Corporate Governance*, 89 CORNELL L. REV. 356, 357-60 (2004).

[4] *See* Anthony H. Catanach, Jr. & Shelley Rhoades-Catanach, *Enron: A Financial Reporting Failure?*, 48 VILL. L. REV. 1057, 1058-60, tbls. 2, 3 (2003).

[5] *Id.* at tbl. 3 (showing decline in profit margin ratio from 4.27% in 1996 to 0.43% in 1997 and in return on equity from 15.26% in 1996 to 1.57% in 1997).

[6] Such financial alchemy began in 1997 with the establishment of special purpose entities. *See* WILLIAM C. POWERS, JR. ET AL., REPORT OF INVESTIGATION BY THE SPECIAL INVESTIGATIVE COMMITTEE OF THE BOARD OF DIRECTORS OF ENRON CORP. 36-40, *at* http://news.findlaw.com/hdocs/docs/enron/sicreport/sicreport020102.pdf (Feb. 1, 2002) [hereinafter Powers Report].

of the principal lessons to be gleaned from Enron's collapse is that the U.S. system for monitoring corporate management has itself become corrupt.

Third, the Enron catastrophe puts considerable pressure on the traditional law and economics model of corporate disclosure. According to this model, firms have strong incentives to disclose information in order to distinguish themselves from poorly performing rivals.[7] Fear of negative sanctions prevents firms from misrepresenting their corporate performance.[8] Part III of this Article considers these issues. It appears that, at least in some cases, the traditional law and economics model of corporate disclosure should be replaced by a prisoners' dilemma model, in which all firms have incentives to engage in minor cheating, in the hope that excessive cheating—which would cause investors to distrust the system—will not be the end result.

In Part IV of this Article, I consider Enron's implications for the Efficient Capital Markets Hypothesis (ECMH). The ECMH posits that share prices of publicly traded companies change quickly to reflect new information, such as changes in the financial condition of the company.[9] In particular, the "semistrong" form of the ECMH posits that share prices react quickly to reflect publicly available information.[10] The collapse of Enron dealt a blow to the ECMH. Because Enron had massive amounts of debt loosely hidden under a complicated matrix of thousands of special purpose entities structured as partnerships and usually organized offshore, the market was unable to penetrate the "cloud cover" of these accounting gimmicks to uncover Enron's true economic conditions.

Enron's board of directors apparently knew of these entities for at least four years prior to the company's collapse and, further, that the "aggressive" accounting techniques employed by Enron's accounting firm helped bury these facts.[11] The semistrong form of the ECMH remains intact after Enron's collapse only because public disclosures by Enron showed that the company was very strong. The special purpose entities hid Enron's true financial condition so that the company's books indicated that Enron was in far better shape than it truly was, and one would "have had to do an almost impossible inspection to know" the true financial condition of the company.[12]

Unfortunately, while the ECMH remains more or less intact after Enron as a theoretical academic construct, it is not obvious what relevance, if any, the theory still holds. Part IV of this Article details the exceedingly poor performance in the Enron case of the institutions and infrastructures that drive markets to function efficiently. Thus, another key lesson from the collapse of Enron is that improving traditional mechanisms

---

7 *See* Frank H. Easterbrook & Daniel R. Fischel, *Mandatory Disclosure and the Protection of Investors*, 70 VA. L. REV. 669, 674 (1984).

8 *See id.* at 677.

9 *See Some Anomalous Evidence Regarding Market Efficiency*, 6 J. FIN. ECON. 95, 96-97 (1978) [hereinafter *Anomalous Evidence*].

10 *See id.* at 97.

11 *See* Katz, *supra* note 1.

12 *Id.*

of market efficiency provides a very effective way of reducing the probability that such debacles will occur in the future. In particular, improving market participants' ability to short stock and to buy and sell single stock index futures will provide effective "early warning systems" to alert the public and regulators of companies riddled with financial fraud.

. . .

II. ENRON AND U.S. CORPORATE GOVERNANCE

Monitoring is the central, defining feature of any system of corporate governance. Corporate monitors come in a variety of forms, including directors, auditors, credit rating agencies, stock market analysts, takeover firms, arbitrageurs, large shareholders, and outside lenders.[34] One may even view customers and suppliers as monitors because of their ability to observe management quality and send effective signals to the market regarding management's performance.

Arnoud Boot and I have identified in a different article what we regard as a fundamental tradeoff encountered when evaluating the ability of a monitor to improve a corporate governance system: the tradeoff between objectivity and proximity.[35] We posit a model of corporate governance that captures this tradeoff, such that those designing corporate governance systems must choose a system that features one of these characteristics or the other, but not both.[36]

Alternatively, we argue that certain corporate governance systems, such as the one in place in Italy, feature neither attribute, but have proven to be successful nonetheless.[37] Without either proximity or objectivity to guarantee the effective monitoring and discipline of management, investors will be reluctant to invest, and firms will be required to turn to internal sources of finance. Despite its obvious costs, such a system has hidden virtues. In particular, it provides strong incentives for managers to make the firm-specific human capital investments necessary to develop specialized skills.[38]

A. Proximity

In systems of corporate governance similar to those that exist in Germany and the Netherlands, one often finds intimate, sustained, intensive, and finely textured monitoring of management, either by significant shareholders or by largely autonomous, entrenched boards of directors—supervisory boards—who enjoy close proximity to

---

[34] *See* Boot & Macey, *supra* note 3, at 357.

[35] *See id.* at 357-60.

[36] *Id.* at 357.

[37] *See id.* at 385-88; Jonathan R. Macey, *Italian Corporate Governance: One American's Perspective*, 1998 COLUM. BUS. L. REV. 121, 140.

[38] *See* Macey, *supra* note 37, at 142-43.

the firms they monitor.[39] Through their participation in decisionmaking and real-time supervision of management activity, these significant shareholders and supervisory boards inevitably become insiders and are frequently captured by the firms they are monitoring. Participation in the decisionmaking process not only requires readier access to information than that needed by outside monitors, such as takeover artists, arbitrageurs, credit rating agencies, and analysts, but also establishes the conditions by which incumbent management will likely capture the monitors. Capture occurs when the ostensible monitor loses its independence and adopts the perspective of the management team being supervised. The gradual resulting loss of the ability to evaluate the firms' performance in an objective manner mitigates the informational advantage that these insiders enjoy.[40]

B. Objectivity

By contrast, far less monitoring comes from directors, large shareholders, or others in close proximity to the firm's managers in the United States' system of corporate governance. Rather, a variety of outside forces and institutions, including credit rating agencies, investment banking analysts, and especially those in the market for corporate control, substitute for direct shareholder involvement. In such a system, considerable distance exists between monitors (investors) and management. Without the kind of "proximity" described above, investors may be unable to obtain timely, reliable information about management.[41]

In theory, this shortage of information could negatively impact the effectiveness of corporate governance systems in regimes in which monitors lack close proximity to management. This is especially true in the United States, as monitoring is generally ex post and evaluative rather than ex ante and proactive.[42] However, the U.S. system also benefits from this lack of proximity, because the distance between U.S. investors and firms in which they invest brings with it a high degree of objectivity not present in corporate governance systems in which the proximity of monitoring subjects them to the risk of capture.[43] This objectivity increases the probability that the outside monitors will sanction corrupt or underperforming managers.

---

39 *See* Edward S. Adams, *Corporate Governance After Enron and Global Crossing: Comparative Lessons for Cross-National Improvement*, 78 IND. L.J. 723, 762-63 (2003).

40 *See* William W. Bratton & Joseph A. McCahery, *Comparative Corporate Governance and the Theory of the Firm: The Case Against Global Cross Reference*, 38 COLUM. J. TRANSNAT'L L. 213, 232 (1999).

41 *See id.* at 223 (reasoning that, in a market system like the United States', "[m]anagement has superior information respecting investment policy and the firm's prospects, but this information tends to be either soft or proprietary and therefore cannot credibly be communicated to actors in trading markets").

42 *See* Boot & Macey, *supra* note 3, at 359.

43 *See* Bratton & McCahery, *supra* note 40, at 224 ("[A]lthough market system shareholders and their outside-director agents cannot access full information about firm operations, their very distance from operations. . . . makes them relatively immune to capture by the management interest and assures objective evaluation of the information they do receive.").

C. Adaptability

Our discussion of proximity and objectivity makes two points. First, effective monitoring of corporate management cannot exist unless the monitors possess the characteristics of either proximity or objectivity. Second, there is a tradeoff between proximity and objectivity that prevents a corporate governance system from providing monitoring that is both proximate and objective.

Investors shy away from investing in systems in which monitors are neither proximate nor objective because they know they will be unable to protect themselves from opportunistic management behavior. Such pathological corporate governance systems, which are economic hallmarks of developing countries, must adapt to survive. These adaptations, which generally involve internal sources of finance, have benefits that are not obvious at first glance, such as encouraging firm and asset-specific capital investments.[44]

D. The Role of Shareholders

Direct shareholder involvement might solve the problem of corporate governance. In the United States, however, direct shareholder involvement is mitigated by the fact that share ownership is relatively diverse, which limits shareholders' involvement to periodic interference through proxy fights, hostile takeovers, or other mechanisms designed to mobilize shareholders.[45] Thus, involvement by small-stakes shareholders exists more in theory than in practice.[46]

In Continental Europe, concentrated ownership is more prevalent,[47] but this does not readily translate into more shareholder control. In some Western and Southern European countries, such as Germany, cross holdings and pyramid structures shield

---

[44] *See generally* Rafael La Porta et al., *Corporate Ownership Around the World*, 54 J. FIN. 471 (1999) (demonstrating that diverse ownership through shareholding has been limited in developing economies); Erik Berglöf & Ernst-Ludwig von Thadden, *The Changing Corporate Governance Paradigm: Implications for Transition and Developing Countries, available at* http://www.worldbank.org/research/abcde/washington_11/pdfs/berglof.pdf (preliminary draft) (noting the closely held nature of firms in developing countries and some benefits of such concentrated ownership).

[45] Shareholder control generally becomes more powerful when financial difficulties and managerial control problems emerge. In those circumstances, we often observe a concentration of shareholdings. *See generally* Andrei Shleifer & Robert W. Vishny, *Large Shareholders and Corporate* Control, 94 J. POL. ECON. 461 (1986) (demonstrating that when larger shareholders believe that incumbent management is performing poorly and the firm could be run better by new managers, the large shareholders have greater incentive to either acquire more shares or to monitor and negotiate with current management to increase performance).

[46] *See* John C. Coffee, Jr., *The SEC and the Institutional Investor: A Half-Time Report*, 15 CARDOZO L. REV. 837, 848, 906-07 (1994) (stating that, as of 1991, over 50% of outstanding stock in U.S. companies was held by institutional investors, who did not regularly exert influence over management decisions because such investors are "inclined to rely more on exit than voice" to protect their investment).

[47] *See* Bratton & McCahery, *supra* note 40, at 218 n.8 (comparing the share dispersion in the U.S. with several foreign countries).

firms from shareholders.[48] Also, nonexecutive directors, or supervisory boards in a two-tier system, protect management from direct shareholder involvement.[49] This is particularly true in certain Continental European countries, like the Netherlands and—to a lesser extent—Germany, where relatively autonomous supervisory boards operate semi-independently of shareholders and effectively shield management from direct shareholder involvement.[50] Thus, direct shareholder control over management is actually quite limited in many European countries, just as it is in the United States.[51]

The Enron collapse illustrates the basic tradeoff at the core of the Boot-Macey theory of corporate governance.[52] In theory, Enron had both proximate monitors—its directors—as well as numerous objective monitors: outside auditors, bankers, credit rating agencies, and, of course, the cadre of stock market analysts who followed Enron. None of these monitors did their jobs effectively because the corporation captured both the proximate and the objective monitors.

Enron's Board clearly trusted management too much and did not adequately understand or question the self-dealing transactions between top managers and the corporation. However, such faith on the part of proximate managers is unsurprising. The more troubling question is why Enron's ostensibly objective monitors did such a poor job.

E. Analysts

Incredibly, in October 2001, despite the stock price having fallen by fifty percent in the previous six months and articles in the financial press calling Enron's financial

---

48 See Janis Sarra, *Corporate Governance in Global Capital Markets, Canadian and International Developments*, 76 TUL. L. REV. 1691, 1722 (2002).

49 Deeply entrenched in U.S. law is an emphasis on the duties that directors and officers owe to shareholders. *See, e.g.,* Revlon, Inc. v. MacAndrews & Forbes Holdings, Inc. 506 A.2d 173, 182 (Del. 1986) (finding that "[a] board may have regard for various constituencies in discharging its responsibilities, provided there are rationally related benefits accruing to the stockholders"); L.A. Hamermesh, *The Shareholder Rights By-Law: Doubts from Delaware*, 5 CORP. GOVERNANCE ADVISOR 9 (1997) ("Delaware fully supports the proposition, dismissed in some quarters as myopic, that the business and affairs of a Delaware for profit stock corporation are to be managed so as to maximize the value of the investment of one group and one group only, its stockholders."); *see also* Margaret M. Blair & Lynn A. Stout, *A Team Production Theory of Corporate Law*, 85 VA. L. REV. 247 (1999) (arguing the controversial point of view that American corporate law should require directors to act in the interest of the firm, and not solely in the interest of shareholders). This focus mimics Continental European corporate governance arrangement. For example, Dutch corporate law explicitly states that directors should serve the interests of the firm as an entity. *See* Winfried van den Muijsenbergh, *Corporate Governance: The Dutch Experience*, 16 TRANSNAT'L LAW. 63, 65 (2002).

50 *See* Thomas J. André, Jr., *Some Reflections on German Corporate Governance: A Glimpse at German Supervisory Boards*, 70 TUL. L. REV. 1819 (1996); Muijsenbergh, *supra* note 49, at 65.

51 Shareholder control is very real in cases where no separation exists between ownership and control, as one would expect in the case of family businesses. *See* Shleifer & Vishny, *supra* note 45, at 462. Nevertheless, the corporate governance debate focuses not on these businesses but rather on large public firms characterized by a separation of ownership and control.

52 *See* discussion *supra* Part II.A, B.

statements "impenetrable,"[53] all sixteen analysts tracked by Thomson Financial/First Call rated Enron a "buy," and thirteen called it a "strong buy."[54] Worse, in November 2001—less than a month prior to Enron's bankruptcy filing, and after it had been disclosed that the SEC was investigating Enron's accounting practices—eleven of the thirteen analysts following Enron still recommended that the public purchase the stock, and only one recommended selling it.[55] Clearly, the analyst community was worthless to Enron investors.

The problem with the analysts' recommendations is not difficult to grasp. Investment banks pressure the analysts they employ to give positive ratings to companies tracked by issuers because positive ratings boost stock prices and generate capital for their investment banking clients. The case of investment banking analyst Chung Wu perhaps best illustrates this problem. UBS Paine Webber, Wu's employer, fired him on the same day that he recommended some of his clients sell Enron stock.[56] UBS Paine Webber administered the Enron employee stock option plan and had a "strong buy" position on Enron three days before the firing and re-affirmed the "strong buy" rating immediately after firing Wu. Shares of Enron stock were trading for $36 per share on the day Wu was fired.[57] Three months later, Enron had collapsed.

The Wu anecdote demonstrates that analysts cannot effectively serve as corporate monitors. Analysts cannot act objectively when the very companies they are supposed to monitor capture their employers. A recent study by Roni Michaely and Kent Womack, comparing analysts' recommendations of companies taken public by the broker-dealer firms that employed the analysts with recommendations by analysts at disinterested broker-dealers, produced similar conclusions.[58] Specifically, the study demonstrated

---

[53] *See* Bethany McLean, *Is Enron Overpriced?*, FORTUNE, Mar. 5, 2001, at 122, 123.

[54] *See The Watchdogs Didn't Bark: Enron and the Wall Street Analysts: Hearing Before the Sen. Comm. on Gov't Affairs*, 107th Cong. (2002) (statement of Charles L. Hill, Director of Research, Thomson Financial/First Call) ("[O]n the eve of Enron's third quarter 2001 earnings report, [thirteen] broker analysts had a strong buy[,] . . . three had a buy, and none had a hold, sell, or strong sell.").

[55] *Id.* at 55. According to Mr. Hill,

> [b]y November 12, almost a month after Enron had announced a $1.2 billion write-off that Ken Lay could not explain on a conference call, almost a month after the Wall Street Journal reported Enron executives stood to make millions from Enron partnerships, [three] weeks after the CFO was fired, [two] weeks after Enron announced it was being investigated by the SEC, and [four] days after Enron announced that it had overstated [four] years of earnings by $600 million . . . there were still eight analysts with a strong buy, three with a buy, one with a hold, and one with a strong sell.

Id.

[56] *See* Richard A. Oppel, Jr., *The Man Who Paid the Price for Sizing Up Enron*, N.Y. TIMES, Mar. 27, 2002, at C1.

[57] *See id.*

[58] *See* Roni Michaely & Kent L. Womack, *Conflict of Interest and the Credibility of Underwriter Analyst Recommendations*, 12 REV. FIN. STUD. 653-57 (1999).

that stocks recommended by underwriter-affiliated analysts performed significantly worse than stocks recommended by independent analysts.[59]

Not surprisingly, "buy" recommendations have been the norm on Wall Street for some time. While two-thirds of all analysts' recommendations are either "buy" or "strong buy," less than two percent of such recommendations are either "sell" or "strong sell."[60]

The rules regulating analysts must be reformed in order to regain investors' trust in the U.S. corporate governance system. Recently, the SEC approved changes in the rules concerning management and disclosure of conflicts of interest between research and invest-banking activities.[61] These new rules limit the amount of compensation analysts can receive and restrict their ability to trade the securities they analyze.[62] Furthermore, the SEC's new rules prohibit offering favorable research to attract business, and they require disclosure of analysts' ownership or interests in a client company.[63]

F. Credit Rating Agencies

If anything, the major credit rating agencies—Standard & Poor's and Moody's— performed even worse than financial analysts during the Enron debacle. Neither Standard & Poor's nor Moody's downgraded Enron's debt below investment grade status until November 28, 2001, four days before the firm's bankruptcy, when the company's share price had plunged to a paltry sixty-one cents.[64] Although credit rating agencies' loss of independence and analysts' conflicts of interest stem from two different sources, the result is the same: these supposedly outside monitors do not perform the corporate governance role on which investors rely.

Downgrades to below investment grade ratings are problematic because they become self-fulfilling prophecies.[65] For most publicly traded companies, such downgrades make bankruptcy a foregone conclusion because they signal that the company can no longer

---

[59] *See id.*

[60] *See* Lewis Braham, *Stock Ratings That Won't Give You the Runaround*, Bus. Wk., Sept. 17, 2001, at 110.

[61] *See* Press Release, New York Stock Exchange, *SEC Approves Sweeping Changes in Rules Regarding Research Analysts* (May 8, 2002), *at* http://www.nyse.com/press/1043881801503.html; Self Regulatory Organizations; Order Approving Proposed Rule Changes by the National Association of Securities Dealers, Inc. and the New York Stock Exchange, Inc. and Notice of Filing and Order Granting Accelerated Approval of Amendment No. 2 to the Proposed Rule Change by the National Association of Securities Dealers, Inc. and Amendment No. 1 to the Proposed Rule Change by the New York Stock Exchange, Inc. Relating to Research Analyst Conflicts of Interest, Exchange Act Release No. 34-45908, 67 Fed. Reg. 34968-01 (May 10, 2002).

[62] *Id.* at 34970.

[63] *Id.* at 34969.

[64] Thomas S. Mulligan & Nancy Vogel, *Collapse of Merger Pushes Enron to Brink of Ruin: Bankruptcy Filing Is Likely as Stock Value Withers and Bonds Fall to "Junk" Status*, L.A. Times, Nov. 29, 2001, at A1.

[65] *See id.* (noting that Moody's and Standard & Poor's cut Enron's ratings "knowing that they probably were pronouncing a death sentence").

raise the debt necessary to support its operations. Thus, when such a company receives a downgrade from a credit rating agency, it will be unable to attract the credit needed to finance its operations: suppliers and trading counter-parties demand payment in advance, and the firm collapses because its creditors cut off liquidity. Many other companies' public debt goes into technical default upon a downgrade below a certain rating level, usually investment grade. A downgrade directly prompts bankruptcy for such a company because defaulting on its debt obligations triggers the company's obligation to repay hundreds of millions of dollars of debt.[66]

Because a rating downgrade effectively functions like a corporate nuclear bomb, credit rating agencies are extremely reluctant to use their power to downgrade a company's debt. This, in turn, undermines the efficacy of credit ratings as a corporate governance device. For Enron, the corporation's $250 million in rated senior unsecured debt had declined in value from ninety cents to thirty-five cents on the dollar in the month preceding its downgrade. In other words, the market rejected the investment grade rating on Enron's debt before the credit rating agencies exercised their power to downgrade it.

G. The Market for Corporate Control

Some Chicago School economists have argued that market forces alone, particularly the market for[67] corporate control, can resolve the problem of corporate accountability. Henry Manne, for example, has asserted that "Enron is a predictable consequence of rules that inhibit the efficient functioning of the market for corporate control." He suggests that the takeover market is the most efficient mechanism not only for disciplining inefficient management, but also for reducing the incidence of corporate scandals caused by managers with low morals. The market for corporate control is an extremely powerful corporate governance device, and, in my view, the cornerstone of U.S. corporate governance. However, the market for corporate control is not capable of dealing with recent corporate governance problems involving artificially inflated earnings, profits, and other measures of corporate performance.[68]

The market for corporate control exerts powerful disciplinary pressure on underperforming management in that share prices will lag in companies with slothful or corrupt management. These depressed share prices present attractive investment opportunities for entrepreneurial corporate raiders, who profit by purchasing a controlling

---

[66] This was in fact the case with regard to some Enron credit agreements. *See* Sean J. Griffith, *Afterword and Comment: Towards an Ethical Duty to Market Investors*, 35 CONN. L. REV. 1223, 1238 (2003).

[67] Henry G. Manne, *Bring Back the Hostile Takeover*, WALL ST. J., June 26, 2003, at A16; *see also* Paolo Mastrolilli, *Interview with Milton Friedman*, LA STAMPA, June 25, 2002 (Del 10/7/2002 Sezione: Economia Pag. 3) (on file with author) (proposing that solution "for corrupt or incompetent managers comes from competition for control of the company").

[68] *See* E.S. Browning, *Investor Confidence Remains Fickle*, WALL ST. J., Sept. 9, 2002, at C1 ("Scandals at Enron, WorldCom, Global Crossing, Tyco International, Adelphia Communications, ImClone Systems and a host of other companies have raised questions about whether corporate earnings reports and corporate executives can be trusted.").

interest in underperforming companies and installing more competent and motivated management.[69]

However, the market for corporate control only disciplines bad management when the target firm's share prices are underperforming relative to their potential. Accounting fraud, however, causes share prices to be artificially inflated, rather than depressed. Consequently, the takeover entrepreneurs who drive the market for corporate control have no incentive to utilize the takeover market to monitor and discipline managers who successfully employ questionable accounting practices to overinflate their companies' share prices.[70] In fact, the prospect of accounting fraud impedes the market for corporate control because the danger that such fraud exists deprives potential outside bidders of the ability to know with certainty the value of the assets they might be acquiring. More fundamentally, the market for corporate control depends on efficiency in the capital markets, but if share prices do not reflect managers' actual performance, the market for corporate control cannot effectively discipline corporate management.

H. Accounting Firms

Accounting firms, like stock analysts and credit rating agencies, have proven to be rather ineffective objective monitors of corporate governance due to capture problems not unlike those that plague analysts.

Accounting firms would appear to be ideal objective monitors from an outsider's perspective. A significant client like Enron represents only a tiny fraction of global revenues for even the largest accounting firms. Consequently, it seems illogical for a massive accounting firm like Arthur Andersen to risk its reputation by sacrificing its independent judgment in order to please a single miscreant client like Enron.[71]

However irrational it was for Arthur Andersen to become captured by Enron, capture may not have seemed irrational to the individual Arthur Andersen partners auditing Enron. Because partners in big accounting firms have only one client, their professional success depends upon the quality of the relationships they form with their clients' top managers. Accounting debacles like Enron's were inevitable in an environment that rewards audit partners who are captured by their client and punishes those who report negative information about their clients through the proper corporate channels.

Arthur Andersen partners assigned to the Enron account ignored their own specialists' advice, which would have stopped Enron from falsifying its financial records.[72] Furthermore, when Andersen accounting specialists concluded that some of Enron's

---

69 *See* Schleifer & Vishny, *supra* note 45, at 462 (noting that the raider benefits when the share prices of the target firm rise to reflect the improved earnings generated by the new management team).

70 *See id.*

71 *See* Easterbrook & Fischel, *supra* note 7, at 675.

72 Kurt Eichenwald with Floyd Norris, *Early Verdict on Audit: Procedures Ignored*, N.Y. Times, June 6, 2002, at C6 (noting that "Andersen's top accounting specialists had concluded that some of Enron's most questionable accounting practices were improper, only to have their conclusions overridden by Andersen's Houston office").

practices were improper, they were overridden by the Houston office and, in some instances, were taken off the Enron account altogether if the firm disagreed with their decisions or their portrayal of Enron in a less-than-positive light.[73]

Thus, Arthur Andersen demonstrated that audit teams assigned to large accounts may be willing to risk their firms' reputations because doing so is extremely profitable for the individual partners. Moreover, Arthur Andersen's frightening acquiescence to Enron's aggressive accounting practices, its failure to warn the market about Enron's precarious financial situation, and its inability to adequately explain what went wrong in its handling of the Enron account are symptoms of a problem afflicting the entire accounting profession.

For decades, the accounting profession flourished because investors demanded honest, independent scrutiny of companies' financial records. Companies subjected themselves to this scrutiny because it was necessary to attract outside capital.[74] Because internal accounting services would cost only a fraction of the price of an outside auditor, the strong market demand for outside auditors is best explained by outside investors' willingness to pay more for securities issued by companies whose books have been independently audited. In other words, the economic justification for the accounting profession is that reputational capital—auditors' reputations for honesty and integrity—makes companies' securities more valuable.[75]

In the past, accounting firms would approve companies' financial records only if they conformed to the high standards imposed by the accounting profession. Investors trusted accountants because they knew that sloppy or corrupt accounting firms would not stay in business for long. Accounting firms believed that the long-term deterioration of their reputation from doing slipshod or fraudulent work significantly outweighed any possible short-term gains obtained by cutting corners.[76] For this reason, companies subjected themselves to public audits, thereby sending a strong signal to investors that their financial house was in order. More importantly, auditors would dismiss companies that refused to comply with the their demands for reporting transparently and simply. As I have noted elsewhere, being fired by an accounting firm sent a strong negative signal to investors that often devastated the company and led to the dismissal of top management.[77]

---

[73] *See id.* (providing anecdotal evidence, not unlike the Chung Wu story described above in Part II.E, about the silencing of lower-level Anderson auditors who refused to sign off on certain dubious Enron transactions).

[74] *See* Easterbrook & Fischel, *supra* note 7, at 675.

[75] *See id.*

[76] *See id.*

[77] John C. Coffee, Jr., *Understanding Enron: "It's About the Gatekeepers, Stupid,"* 57 BUS. LAW. 1403, 1411 (2002) (noting that such firing causes "embarrassment" to the company); Jonathan Macey & Hillary A. Sale, *Observations on the Role of Commodification, Independence and Governance in the Accounting Industry*, 48 VILL. L. REV. 1167, 1169 (2003) (being fired by an accounting firm "often would both devastate a company and lead to the dismissal of top management").

Unfortunately, in recent years, the balance of power between accounting firms and their clients has shifted dramatically, reducing the clout of accounting firms and empowering their client companies instead. This change threatens to undermine the investing public's faith in the quality of financial reporting. Further, if left unchecked, this shift in power will undermine the integrity of the financial markets because perceived inaccuracies in a company's financial records will prompt investors to either charge prohibitive rates to compensate for the uncertain risk of investment, or else cease investing altogether.

Moreover, the exclusive relationship between audit partner and client, upon which the partner's career largely depends, makes the partner particularly susceptible to client capture.[78] Thus, even though Arthur Andersen was deemed "independent" because Enron accounted for less than one percent of Andersen's total billings, Enron accounted for all of the billings of the lead partner assigned to Enron and for several members of his audit team.[79] Further, Arthur Andersen's management in Chicago apparently relied solely on the captured audit team for information about the client.[80] Though not an uncommon practice among accounting firms, this disproportionate reliance on the particular audit team assigned to a client gives investors ample reason to worry about the quality and uniformity of these firms' financial reporting practices.[81] Arthur Andersen's top management fired David Duncan, the lead Enron audit partner, and placed three other partners also involved with Enron on administrative leave for violating the firm's "reasonable good judgment" policy.[82] This disciplinary action may not have been necessary, however, if Andersen's top management had itself exercised "reasonable good judgment" in its supervision of the Enron audit team. Preventing the recurrence of Enron-like financial disasters requires improved internal monitoring and control in accounting firms.

Enron damaged investors' faith in the integrity of financial markets, and particularly in the U.S. system of corporate disclosure. That system will not function properly until a lead audit partner can confidently fire a dishonest client without jeopardizing his career.

To fix the system, reform is needed. The state pension funds in New York and North Carolina have proposed a scheme which would award their brokerage business only to firms that make structural changes to reduce conflicts of interest.[83] Other institutional

---

78 *See supra* notes 71-72 and accompanying text.

79 *See* Ken Brown & Ianthe Jeanne Dugan, *Sad Account: Andersen's Fall From Grace Is a Tale of Greed and Miscues,* Wall St. J., June 7, 2002, at A1.

80 *See* In re Enron Corp. Sec. Derivative and ERISA Litig., 235 F. Supp. 2d 549, 679 (S.D. Tex. 2002); Macey & Sale, *supra* note 77, at 1179-82.

81 *See* Macey & Sale, *supra* note 77, at 1181-82.

82 *See* Ken Brown et al., *Paper Trail: Andersen Fires Partner It Says Led Shredding of Enron Documents,* Wall St. J., Jan. 16, 2002, at A1.

83 Charles Gasparino, *Two Big States Tell Wall Street: Reform, or Else!*, Wall St. J., June 7 2002, at C1.

investors should likewise pressure intermediaries to reform.[84] The elimination of ties between analysts' compensation and the ratings they issue or the business they attract is one important and viable change. Analysts' compensation could instead be based on the quality and accuracy of the analysts' forecasts as compared to their competitors. Such a compensation scheme would reduce the proclivity toward the current "herd" behavior in analysts' recommendations.[85] Regulation is unlikely to be effective in this context, and so investment banks and other "sell side" financial intermediaries must adapt their services to a changing market environment. If firms do not change, the demand for their analysts' services probably will erode demonstrably.

III. ENRON AND CORPORATE DISCLOSURE

The basic economic model of pre-Enron corporate disclosure is relatively easy to construct. Economic theory as it relates to disclosure dictates that high-quality corporations seeking to attract capital have strong incentives to distinguish themselves from rivals because investors that cannot distinguish high- from low-quality issuers will not pay more for securities from high-quality issuers.[86] In other words, inadequate disclosure will force issuing corporations to pay higher capital costs. Under this theory, antifraud rules prevent low-quality firms from making misrepresentations that cause investors to mistakenly believe that they are high-quality firms.[87]

A. Mandatory v. Enabling Rules

However, the fact that high-quality firms have incentives to disclose truthful information about themselves to lower their costs of capital and that low-quality firms have incentives to refrain from committing fraud does not imply that such disclosures should be made mandatory by law. It is not obvious why disclosure should be mandatory when disclosure itself is costly and firms appear to internalize the costs of making inadequate disclosure. However, existing theoretical and empirical economic studies provide no more than weak support for mandatory disclosure.[88] Recent research indicates that making the disclosure of certain information—such as audited balanced sheets, audited profit and loss statements, proxy information prior to shareholder meetings, and details on insider transactions—mandatory resulted in significant positive abnormal returns

---

[84] Because of their significant economic clout, institutional investors such as pension funds may occupy key positions in the drive for reform. *See id.*

[85] *See* John C. Coffee, Jr., *What Caused Enron? A Capsule Social and Economic History of the 1990's*, 89 CORNELL L. REV. [101, 129-30] (2004) (discussing the herd behavior phenomenon in the context of professional money managers).

[86] *See* Easterbrook & Fischel, *supra* note 7, at 683-85.

[87] *See id.*

[88] William H. Beaver, *The Nature of Mandated Disclosure*, *in* RICHARD A. POSNER & KENNETH E. SCOTT, ECONOMICS OF CORPORATION LAW AND SECURITIES REGULATION 316 (1980).

to shareholders in the range of sixteen to eighteen percent.[89] This research suggests that mandatory disclosure may benefit firms, either by solving the collective action problems described below, or by assisting firms who want to make certain disclosures about themselves to make these disclosures more credible to investors.

One argument supporting mandatory disclosure states that externalities will lead to inadequate disclosure without sufficient regulation.[90] Externalities are economic side effects, arising when contracting parties' actions affect third parties, who cannot be charged or compensated for the benefits or costs they receive.[91] Pollution is a classic example of an externality: Smoke generated by a factory may impose health costs and cleanup costs on nearby residents who receive no compensation for bearing such costs. Polluters benefit from externalities if their production costs are lower than if polluters had to bear the total costs of their activities, including those incurred by third parties.

Corporate disclosures generate substantial externalities when they aid investors and other entities dealing with or competing against the disclosing firm. If, for example, disclosure helps competitors evaluate whether a particular product manufactured by the disclosing firm is successful, it "may provide information to other firms about their chances of success in similar product developments . . . . [and] might even obviate their having to expend resources on product developments."[92] In such a case, there will be little incentive to disclose because the disclosing firm is not compensated for the benefits that its disclosure confers on other firms.[93]

It is unclear, however, whether externalities support or weaken the case for mandatory disclosure. Mandatory disclosure ostensibly is warranted in this context because absent regulation, firms will decline to make certain disclosures for fear of passing benefits on to competitors.[94] Requiring disclosure under these conditions would be highly inefficient if the benefits to competitors were so great that they caused firms to halt product development.[95] Firms would refrain from developing new products if such developments were costly and competitors could "free-ride" on the firms' required disclosures.[96] Thus, the case for mandatory disclosure remains indeterminate.

Further, some investors will read and benefit from a corporation's disclosure but ultimately decide not to invest. Such noninvesting free-riders may acquire valuable information without paying the costs of disclosure, while current shareholders are

---

[89] MICHAEL GREENSTONE, PAUL OYER, & ANNETTE VISSING-JÖRGENSEN, MANDATED DISCLOSURE, STOCK RETURNS, AND THE 1964 SECURITIES ACTS AMENDMENTS 2 (Oct. 2003) (unpublished manuscript, on file with author).

[90] *See* Beaver, *supra* note 88, at 319.

[91] *See id.* at 320.

[92] *Id.*

[93] *Id.*

[94] *See* Easterbrook & Fischel, *supra* note 7, at 685-86.

[95] *See* Beaver, *supra* note 88, at 320.

[96] *Id.*

stuck with those disclosure costs and without any influx of new capital.[97] As a result, a suboptimal level of information will be disclosed unless such disclosure is made mandatory. However, it is unclear why companies and their investors should have to bear these disclosure costs, which inure in part to third parties.

A further economic justification for mandatory disclosure is that an excessive level of searching for corporate financial information will be conducted without it. Absent mandatory disclosure, investors will engage in duplicative and inefficient searches for information about public companies.[98] In contrast, requiring companies to disclose this information publicly would clearly eliminate inefficiency. However, if investors value the information, they would, presumably, be willing to pay for it, and companies would have incentive to produce it if, as Easterbrook and Fischel suggest, they can provide it more efficiently than investors.[99]

The final argument for mandatory disclosure of corporate information is that it would alleviate managers' incentives to suppress valuable information that is unfavorable.[100] Because traditional antifraud rules do not affirmatively require firms to make disclosures, firms must only be accurate in their disclosure if they choose to disclose information at all. Mandatory disclosure might subject all firms to antifraud laws, thereby solving the problem of managers suppressing unfavorable information. On the other hand, investors might prefer to delay the release of unfavorable information in order to give management the time necessary to counter its effects. For example, before disclosing the fact that a company has lost a major client or customer, the firm may want some time to marshal its sales force to launch a search for a replacement. The loss of the customer's orders may free up some of the company's productive capacity, and if a new customer can be found, the effects of the loss of the first customer can be mitigated. If the announcement is made prematurely, though, it can harm morale and lead to an unwarranted loss of confidence in the firm, making it hard to replace the lost business.

The Enron debacle revealed a number of deficiencies in the classic economic models of disclosure policy. Obviously, the assumption that firms generally will disclose negative information about themselves must be re-examined. More fundamentally, the assumption that investors will not invest in companies that fail to disclose sufficient information about their financial condition likewise needs to be reevaluated. Market and regulatory forces may punish firms that do not make adequate disclosures about themselves in fact as well as in theory, but the prospect of receiving such punishment is apparently neither harsh nor immediate enough to deter the worst offenders.

---

[97] *See id.* at 320-21 (explaining that, in such shareholder externality contexts, "current shareholders bear the costs of disclosure, yet prospective shareholders share in the benefits of disclosure (i.e., they are free riders)").

[98] *See* Easterbrook & Fischel, *supra* note 7, at 681-82.

[99] *See id.* at 682.

[100] *See* John C. Coffee, Jr., *Market Failure and the Economic Case for a Mandatory Disclosure System*, 70 VA. L. REV. 717, 722 (1984).

In the following subsections, I make two additional contributions to the economic theory of mandatory disclosure, both of which relate to the economics of trust in the financial and capital markets.

B. Externalities

Externalities cause under-reporting, such as where firms unrelated to Enron are punished for Enron's wrongdoing. As noted above, externalities can lead to both overproduction and underproduction: positive externalities cause underproduction because firms producing the externality go uncompensated, whereas negative externalities cause overproduction because firms producing the externality never pay the costs they impose on third parties.[101]

Enron's misleading financial statements created an unequivocal negative externality. While they benefited Enron and its management for a time, these statements clearly tended to harm other firms, particularly those in the energy trading sector, by diminishing investors' confidence in the accuracy of the financial reporting of these companies.[102] Investors naturally are concerned that other companies have managers and disclosure policies like Enron's. Put differently, Enron's actions harmed other companies by diminishing the degree to which investors and lenders trust corporate disclosure. Because Enron did not fully internalize the costs of its disclosure policies, they did not deter its conduct. Failure to account for this negative effect of misleading disclosures constitutes a deficiency in the standard law and economics model.

C. Collective Action Problems

The current economic model of disclosure also fails to account for the collective action problem, similar to a prisoners' dilemma, faced by corporations like Enron when they establish disclosure policies.[103] The prisoners' dilemma, which models a problem

---

[101] *See supra* notes 88-91 and accompanying text.

[102] Capital is scarce. To the extent that Enron's misleading financial statements made the company look more profitable, financially secure and promising than the facts warranted, Enron's access to capital, and its cost of capital, would have been better and cheaper relative to its competitors than it deserved.

[103] *See* Barry Nalebuff, *Prisoners' Dilemma, in* 3 THE NEW PALGRAVE DICTIONARY OF ECONOMICS AND THE LAW 89-94 (Peter Newman ed., 1998). In the original version of the prisoners' dilemma, police arrest two suspects on suspicion of armed robbery and separate them for interrogation. Each prisoner must choose whether to confess and implicate the other suspect or to remain silent. If neither prisoner confesses, police and prosecutors can obtain a criminal conviction only for carrying a concealed weapon. If one prisoner confesses, the government can obtain convictions on both the weapons charge and on the far more serious charge of armed robbery. A prisoner can obtain a drastic sentence reduction by confessing, but if one prisoner refuses to confess and his partner-in-crime confesses, the prisoner who refuses to talk will receive a particularly harsh sentence. In other words, no matter what the other prisoner does, a suspect can improve his own position by confessing and implicating the other suspect. However, the prisoners would obtain the best collective result if both remained silent. See infra note 104 for a chart depicting the outcome under the various scenarios described here.

faced by groups or individuals unable to cooperate with each other, is the best-known construct of game theory in the social sciences.[104] Without cooperation, individuals and companies pursue their own, rational self-interest, making suboptimal decisions from the perspective of the group as a whole.

Applying this framework to corporate disclosure policy, two hypothetical companies, Enron and Exron, which are identical in every way, must each choose between having highly transparent and honest—"good"—disclosure policies and having highly opaque and obfuscatory—"bad"—policies. Simultaneously pursuing a good disclosure policy produces a better result for both companies, but each company can benefit individually by adopting a bad disclosure policy, provided the other company adopts a good one. The worst outcome for either company would be to adopt a good disclosure policy if the other company adopts a bad disclosure policy. In a world of limited capital, each company can benefit at the expense of the other company by making false or misleading disclosures to convince investors that their securities are worth more than those of the other company. An initially honest company can narrow this differential only by engaging in fraudulent conduct to counteract other firms' fraudulent conduct.

In particular, both firms would disclose a certain acute problem if they were completely honest with the investing public. If such disclosures were made, neither firm would suffer relative to the other, although the share prices of both firms would decline. However, the market punishes the firm and its managers as soon as they make the disclosure. Therefore, if Enron discloses the information but Exron does not, then the market will punish Enron immediately, but Exron will emerge unscathed. In monetary terms, Enron's stock would drop from, say, $100 per share to, say, $25 per share, while Exron's shares will stay, for the time being, at $100 per share. Similarly, if Exron discloses the information but Enron does not, Exron's stock will drop to $25, and Enron's stock will remain at $100.

Thus, both firms have incentives not to disclose because each firm will obtain the best possible outcome if it refrains from disclosing and the other firm makes the disclosure. However, each firm will suffer the worst possible outcome if it discloses and the other firm hides the information.

Unfortunately, if neither firm makes the appropriate disclosure, market participants generally will come to distrust the public disclosure of reporting companies, and the value of both investments will shrink, say, to $30 per share. But if both firms make the

---

[104] *See id.* The following chart reflects the jail sentence each suspect described in note 103 supra would receive under the four possible scenarios:

Prisoner's Dilemma

	Prisoner 1 Confesses:	Prisoner 1 Doesn't Confess:
Prisoner 2 Confesses:	Prisoner 1: 10 Years Prisoner 2: 10 years	Prisoner 1: 25 Years Prisoner 2: 3 Years
Prisoner 2 Doesn't Confess:	Prisoner 1: 3 years Prisoner 2: 25years	Prisoner 1: 1 year Prisoner 2: 1 year

appropriate disclosure, share prices will only drop to $50 per share because investors and other market participates will be confident that all of the negative information about the company has been circulated. The following table illustrates these outcomes:

Prisoner's Dilemma and Disclosure

	Enron discloses:	Enron doesn't disclose:
Exron discloses:	Enron: $50 Exron $50	Enron: $ 100 Exron: $25
Exron doesn't disclose:	Enron $25 Exron: $100	Enron: $30 Exron: $30

The problem becomes more pronounced when one moves the example from a two-firm theoretical construct to the real world, in which there are hundreds of thousands of public companies. Share prices remain high so long as investors trust the overall integrity of the public disclosure system. If investors come to distrust the system, however, then share prices will collapse, and all firms will suffer. Firms that commit to making public disclosure about themselves have strong incentives to "cheat" by making false, partial, or misleading disclosures. Whereas cheating by a small number of firms will benefit those firms if confidence in the system as a whole remains generally high, cheating by a large percentage of reporting companies will cause share prices to collapse because investors will no longer trust the market.

If all public companies made binding agreements to report fully, fairly, and honestly, the best of all possible prisoner's dilemma disclosure outcomes for both firms and society would result. This scenario maximizes firms' pool of available capital and contributes to low cost of capital and the high quality of capital markets. However, each firm can benefit at the expense of its rivals by cheating slightly on its promise to make full and fair disclosure of material information, thereby making itself look comparatively better and further lowering its cost of capital. Therefore, cheating on disclosure is the dominant, "maxi-min," strategy: it is the only way to obtain the maximum benefit—producing the lowest cost of capital—when one firm alone makes misleading disclosures, but at the same time it is the only way to avoid the worst, i.e., "minimum," outcome, which results if one firm is honest but all other firms cheat.

Thus, honest firms face something akin to a prisoners' dilemma when establishing their disclosure policies. Dishonest rivals can benefit at the expense of honest firms by making false or incomplete disclosures, but widespread cheating will eventually cause the system to collapse under the weight of its own dishonesty. In this context, regulation of public disclosure is necessary to solve the prisoners' dilemma facing public companies because a severe punishment for false reporting will eliminate firms' incentive to cheat. Recent empirical research supports the conclusion that mandatory disclosure may benefit investors by reducing agency costs.[105]

---

[105] *See* Greenstone, Oyer, & Vissing-Jórgensen, *supra* note 89.

IV. ENRON AND MARKET EFFICIENCY

Issues of market efficiency are closely connected to issues of disclosure, and therefore assumptions about the reasons for market efficiency inform our views about disclosure.

Securities markets function efficiently when share price fully reflects information about the issuer.[106] In economists' terms, an efficiency model where prices reflect all information until the point at which the marginal costs of using the information outweigh the attainable profits is the most sensible.[107] Securities markets are described as "weak form" efficient if share prices reflect only the information implied by historical prices, "semi-strong" efficient if securities prices reflect all publicly available information about the company, and "strong form" efficient if securities prices reflect all information—both public as well as private inside information.[108]

Virtually no support exists for the "strong" form of the efficient capital markets hypothesis (ECMH), which makes sense because insiders can earn significant, abnormal returns by trading on non-public information. On the other hand, there is considerable support for the "weak" and "semi-strong" forms of the ECMH.[109] In particular, studies have shown that mutual fund managers relying on publicly available information do not outperform the market indices.[110]

Market efficiency protects shareholders and saves them money: efficient share prices that reflect all available information permit shareholders to buy and sell shares at fair, unbiased prices in reliance on publicly listed prices. As a result, shareholders need not incur the cost of ferreting out information about the companies in which they invest.

Put differently, average shareholders cannot be expected to understand the arcane world of corporate accounting and finance. Prices must therefore be efficient in order to encourage average people to rely on the information content of securities prices. To the extent that the market is efficient, share prices would protect investors without the need to read lengthy and impenetrable disclosure documents.

What does Enron reveal about the efficiency of the market? From one perspective, Enron's collapse casts some serious doubts on the efficiency of the market. After all,

---

[106] *See* Beaver, *supra* note 88, at 328 ("[T]he market is efficient with respect to a given piece of information if prices act as if everyone possessed that information and were able to interpret its implications for security prices").

[107] *See* Eugene F. Fama, *Efficient Capital Markets: II*, 46 J. FIN. 1575 (1991) ("[An] economically more sensible version of the efficiency hypothesis says that prices reflect information to the point where the marginal benefits of acting on information (the profits to be made) do not exceed the marginal costs." (citation omitted)); *Anomalous Evidence*, *supra* note 9, at 96 ("A market is efficient with respect to information set out if it is impossible to make economic profits by trading on the basis of information set out.").

[108] *See* Eugene F. Fama, *Efficient Capital Markets: A Review of Theory and Empirical Work*, 25 J. FIN. 383, 388 (1970); *Anomalous Evidence*, *supra* note 9, at 97.

[109] *See* Stephen A. Ross et al., *Corporate Finance, reprinted in part in* FOUNDATIONS OF CORPORATE LAW 45, 51-58 (Roberta Romano ed., 1993).

[110] *Id.* at 57 (noting that this is indicative of and "consistent with semistrong-form and weak-form efficiency").

the company's shares fell from over $85 per share in September 2000 to just over $25 per share in 2001, to almost zero in 2002.[111] Had the market for Enron stock been efficient, share prices would have reflected the related-party transactions commencing in 1997.

In fact, CalPERS wanted to cash in its JEDI I stake in September 1997 because of its concerns about the conflict of interest transactions. Rather than liquidate JEDI I, Enron looked for another party to invest $383 million in CalPERS' place. Enter Chewco Investments, created specifically for that purpose.[112] This does not deflate the "semi-strong" form of the ECMH, however, because CalPERS received material nonpublic information—not included in the "semi-strong" form of efficiency—during its negotiations with Enron about its JEDI I investment.

On the other hand, analyst Jim Chanos began scrutinizing Enron's financial statements in September 1990 and proceeded to trade at the height of Enron's success.[113] Chanos realized that Enron, which was trading at sixty times its earnings, was vastly overvalued.[114] Moreover, using publicly available documents, Chanos calculated that Enron was earning only seven percent on its capital, as compared to an average cost of capital of ten percent.[115]

A September 2000 article in the now-defunct Texas edition of the *Wall Street Journal* inspired Chanos to look more closely into Enron's financial condition.[116] The article questioned the quality of stated earnings at Enron and a number of other companies with large energy trading departments and pointed out that investors may not realize that Enron's large reported profits were in the form of large, unrealized noncash gains that could be wiped out by changes in market conditions.[117] For example, Enron had booked $747 million in unrealized gains from trading activities during the second quarter of 2000—far exceeding its $609 million pretax earnings.[118] In other words,

---

[111] For a particularly colorful chart of Enron's share price over time, see the Milberg Weiss Bershad Hynes & Lerach Web site, http://www.enronfraud.com/pdf/enron_chart2.pdf (last visited Dec. 20, 2003); http://stocks.tradingcharts.com/stocks/charts/ENE/M (last visited Dec. 20, 2003).

[112] *See* POWERS REPORT, *supra* note 6, at 44-45.

[113] Jonathan R. Laing, *The Bear That Roared: How Short-Seller Jim Chanos Helped Expose Enron*, BARRON'S, Jan. 28, 2002, at 18.

[114] *See id.* Chanos reasoned that Enron should trade more like a hedge fund than an energy company because it relied on trading for more than eighty percent of its earnings, and in that case many other, better-performing hedge funds' shares were priced attractively relative to Enron's. *See id.*

[115] *See id.*

[116] *See Lessons Learned from Enron's Collapse: Auditing the Accounting Industry: Hearing Before the House Comm. on Energy and Commerce*, 107th Cong. 72 (2d Sess. 2002) (testimony of James Chanos, President, Kynikos Assoc., Ltd.).

[117] *See* Jonathan Weil, *Energy Traders Cite Gains, but Some Math Is Missing*, WALL ST. J., TEX. J., Sept. 20, 2000, at T1, *available at* 2000 WL-WSJ 26610344; *see also* POWERS REPORT, *supra* note 6, at 11 ("Enron sold assets to [certain SPEs] that it wanted to remove from its books. These transactions often occurred close to the end of financial reporting periods."); *id.* at 12-13.

[118] *See* Weil, *supra* note 117.

Enron would have suffered a quarterly loss without these unrealized gains, rather than the 26% increase in earnings it actually reported.[119]

Enron's financials did not reveal that two-thirds of the company's debt was not disclosed on its balance sheet. However, its annual and quarterly reports reveal that an unnamed Enron "senior officer" supervised several limited partnerships engaged in numerous transactions with the company, all of which removed assets from Enron's books while providing Enron with revenue.[120] For this reason, Chanos singled out Enron, then trading at $80 per share, at his firm's annual "Bears in Hibernation" meeting in February 2001.[121]

The market's apparent inability to translate the signal sent when Skilling, Enron's former President and Chief Operating Officer, resigned in December 2000 demonstrates another hole in the ECMH.[122] Moreover, Enron share prices remained high in the first quarter of 2001, even after Bethany McLean's article titled "Is Enron Overpriced?" questioned Enron's "impenetrable" accounting practices.[123]

Not all of the evidence surrounding Enron's share price collapse points towards market inefficiency, however. In particular, the market price provided a far better signal of Enron's decline than the ratings posted by both credit rating agencies and analysts. Nevertheless, analysts' continued "buy" recommendations, even after the Company disclosed that its last five years of earnings needed to be restated, indicates that analysts were more concerned with currying favor with issuers than distributing honest ratings.

Enron insiders' sale of more than a billion dollars of Enron stock in the years preceding the company's collapse provides further proof that the strong form of the ECMH is not valid.

CONCLUSION

The history of capital markets regulation is largely a series of regulatory responses to problems already corrected by market forces.[124] While it is easy to say that the irresponsible and lawless actions that led to Enron's collapse should not be repeated, it is considerably more difficult to discern the appropriate measures to prevent another monumental collapse. The most forceful and effective action thus far has been initiated

---

[119] *See id.*

[120] The identity of this partner was revealed in October 2001 to be Andrew Fastow, Enron's CFO. *See id.*

[121] *See id.*

[122] *See* McLean, *supra* note 26, at 58 (describing Skilling's resignation as "what should have been the clearest signal yet of serious problems").

[123] McLean, *supra* note 53.

[124] For an insightful analysis of lessons that one should not derive from Enron's collapse, see C. Evan Stewart, *Caveat "Reformers": Lessons Not To Be Learned from Enron's Collapse*, 34(8) BNA SECURITIES REGULATION LAW REPORT ANALYSIS AND PERSPECTIVE 310, Feb. 25, 2002.

not by regulators, legislators, or academics, but by investors.[125] Enron, along with the "steady stream of accounting scandals, corporate chicanery and questionable practices at Wall Street firms," has damaged investors' confidence in the market.[126] Further, the unscrupulous conduct of senior executives has wounded the business community as a whole.[127] Interestingly, as reported in a recent poll, eighty-four percent of U.S. investors believe that dubious accounting practices are responsible for U.S. markets' dismal performances this year, much more than the war in Iraq or terrorism concerns.[128] Moreover, a staggering seventy-one percent of U.S. investors think questionable accounting practices are widespread in business.[129] Consequently, investors are less prone to invest in stocks or mutual funds than before.[130] Thus, the corruption among corporate executives and analysts is hindering the growth and recovery of our market.[131]

Investors doubt the fundamental fairness of American capital markets to a greater extent now than anytime since the Great Depression. Firms in search of capital will have to address investors' concerns about the market honesty or face capital costs so high that the prospects for meaningful economic recovery all but disappear. Meaningful reform, in my view, will require fewer technical disclosure rules. Such technical disclosure requirements provided the blueprint for Enron's financial fraud, where accounting rules were employed to hide the company's debt through off-balance sheet limited partnerships. Rather, investors need disclosure that is simple, clear and informative.[132] The current, highly technical accounting system is easy to manipulate because of its complexity, and firms will take advantage of this fact because of the intense pressure to produce a profit.[133] Regulators should streamline and simplify the stupefying disclosure rules that Enron so easily manipulated.

The oligopolistic nature of the accounting, credit rating, and investment banking industries impedes meaningful reform in these sectors. Without independent analysts,

---

[125] *See, e,g,.* Nick Evans, *Enronitis, Witch-hunts, and Financial Hypochondria,* EUROMONEY, Mar. 2002, at 42 (describing Krispy Kreme's immediate announcement to restructure the financing of a factory after a *New York Post* article warned investors that Krispy Kreme planned to finance the factory with off-balance sheet transactions).

[126] Gretchen Morgenson, *What If Investors Won't Join the Party?,* N.Y. TIMES, June 2, 2002, § 3, at 1.

[127] Patrick McGeehan, *Goldman Chief Urges Reforms in Corporations,* N.Y. TIMES, June 6, 2002, at C1.

[128] Morgenson, *supra* note 126.

[129] University of Michigan Monthly Consumer Confidence Report, *at* http://www.sca.isr.umich.edu/main.php.

[130] *See* Morgenson, *supra* note 126.

[131] McGeehan, *supra* note 127.

[132] *See* Stewart, *supra* note 124, at 310. This disclosure must clearly delineate the assumptions used to make claims regarding valuations, and it must also explain which valuations are based on qualitative judgments.

[133] *See* McGeehan, *supra* note 127.

investors lose faith in the system.[134] At this writing, there are only four functional accounting firms, two dominant credit rating agencies, and a handful of "bulge bracket"[135] investment banks in an industry that is "overly dominated" by these established firms.[136] These firms may not have sufficient incentives to thoroughly reform themselves until they are forced to face an increased level of rigorous competition. Rather than piling on new laws to regulate the financial markets, regulators should devise strategies to encourage more market competition.

---

[134] *See id.*

[135] "Bulge bracket" is Wall Street jargon for the most elite investment banks. The term refers to the banks in an underwriting syndicate responsible for selling the largest amounts of the issuer's securities and whose names appear first on prospectuses and "tombstone" ads. Ayako Yasuda, *Do Bank-Firm Relationships Affect Bank Competition in the Corporate Bond Underwriting Market?* (Jan. 10, 2003) (Wharton School Working Paper), *at* http://finance.wharton.upenn.edu/~rlwctrpapers/0302.pdf.

[136] *Redesign Flaws: Investment Banking*, ECONOMIST-JAPAN.com, http://www.economistjapan.com/2002/20021116/cont_e02.html (last visited Dec. 20, 2003).

Enron, Intelligence, and the Perils of Too Much Information[*]

Malcolm Gladwell[**]

1

On the afternoon of October 23, 2006, Jeffrey Skilling sat at a table at the front of a federal courtroom in Houston, Texas. He was wearing a navy-blue suit and a tie. He was fifty-two years old, but looked older. Huddled around him were eight lawyers from his defense team. Outside, television-satellite trucks were parked up and down the block.

"We are here this afternoon," Judge Simeon Lake began, "for sentencing in United States of America versus Jeffrey K. Skilling, Criminal No. H-04-25." He addressed the defendant directly: "Mr. Skilling, you may now make a statement and present any information in mitigation."

Skilling stood up. Enron, the company he had built into an energy-trading leviathan, had collapsed into bankruptcy almost exactly five years before. In May, he had been convicted by a jury of fraud. Under a settlement agreement, almost everything he owned had been turned over to a fund to compensate former shareholders.

He spoke haltingly, stopping in mid-sentence. "In terms of remorse, Your Honor, I can't imagine more remorse," he said. He had "friends who have died, good men." He was innocent—"innocent of every one of these charges." He spoke for two or three minutes and sat down.

Judge Lake called on Anne Beliveaux, who worked as the senior administrative assistant in Enron's tax department for eighteen years. She was one of nine people who had asked to address the sentencing hearing.

"How would you like to be facing living off of sixteen hundred dollars a month, and that is what I'm facing," she said to Skilling. Her retirement savings had been wiped out by the Enron bankruptcy. "And, Mr. Skilling, that only is because of greed, nothing but greed. And you should be ashamed of yourself."

---

[*] Originally published at THE NEW YORKER 44 (Jan. 8, 2007). Reprinted by permission.

[**] Staff writer for *The New Yorker* magazine.

The next witness said that Skilling had destroyed a good company, the third witness that Enron had been undone by the misconduct of its management; another lashed out at Skilling directly. "Mr. Skilling has proven to be a liar, a thief, and a drunk," a woman named Dawn Powers Martin, a twenty-two-year veteran of Enron, told the court. "Mr. Skilling has cheated me and my daughter of our retirement dreams. Now it's his time to be robbed of his freedom to walk the earth as a free man." She turned to Skilling and said, "While you dine on Chateaubriand and champagne, my daughter and I clip grocery coupons and eat leftovers." And on and on it went.

The Judge asked Skilling to rise.

"The evidence established that the defendant repeatedly lied to investors, including Enron's own employees, about various aspects of Enron's business," the Judge said. He had no choice but to be harsh: Skilling would serve two hundred and ninety-two months in prison—twenty-four years. The man who headed a firm that *Fortune* ranked among the "most admired" in the world had received one of the heaviest sentences ever given to a white-collar criminal. He would leave prison an old man, if he left prison at all.

"I only have one request, Your Honor," Daniel Petrocelli, Skilling's lawyer, said. "If he received ten fewer months, which shouldn't make a difference in terms of the goals of sentencing, if you do the math and you subtract fifteen per cent for good time, he then qualifies under Bureau of Prisons policies to be able to serve his time at a lower facility. Just a ten-month reduction in sentence . . . ."

It was a plea for leniency. Skilling wasn't a murderer or a rapist. He was a pillar of the Houston community, and a small adjustment in his sentence would keep him from spending the rest of his life among hardened criminals.

"No," Judge Lake said.

2

The national-security expert Gregory Treverton has famously made a distinction between puzzles and mysteries. Osama bin Laden's whereabouts are a puzzle. We can't find him because we don't have enough information. The key to the puzzle will probably come from someone close to bin Laden, and until we can find that source bin Laden will remain at large.

The problem of what would happen in Iraq after the toppling of Saddam Hussein was, by contrast, a mystery. It wasn't a question that had a simple, factual answer. Mysteries require judgments and the assessment of uncertainty, and the hard part is not that we have too little information but that we have too much. The C.I.A. had a position on what a post-invasion Iraq would look like, and so did the Pentagon and the State Department and Colin Powell and Dick Cheney and any number of political scientists and journalists and think-tank fellows. For that matter, so did every cabdriver in Baghdad.

The distinction is not trivial. If you consider the motivation and methods behind the attacks of September 11th to be mainly a puzzle, for instance, then the logical response is to increase the collection of intelligence, recruit more spies, add to the volume of information we have about Al Qaeda. If you consider September 11th a mystery, though, you'd have to wonder whether adding to the volume of information would only make things worse. You'd want to improve the analysis within the intelligence community; you'd want more thoughtful and skeptical people with the skills to look more closely at what we already know about Al Qaeda. You'd want to send the counterterrorism team from the C.I.A. on a golfing trip twice a month with the counterterrorism teams from the F.B.I. and the N.S.A. and the Defense Department, so they could get to know one another and compare notes.

If things go wrong with a puzzle, identifying the culprit is easy: it's the person who withheld information. Mysteries, though, are a lot murkier: sometimes the information we've been given is inadequate, and sometimes we aren't very smart about making sense of what we've been given, and sometimes the question itself cannot be answered. Puzzles come to satisfying conclusions. Mysteries often don't.

If you sat through the trial of Jeffrey Skilling, you'd think that the Enron scandal was a puzzle. The company, the prosecution said, conducted shady side deals that no one quite understood. Senior executives withheld critical information from investors. Skilling, the architect of the firm's strategy, was a liar, a thief, and a drunk. We were not told enough—the classic puzzle premise—was the central assumption of the Enron prosecution.

> "This is a simple case, ladies and gentlemen," the lead prosecutor for the Department of Justice said in his closing arguments to the jury:
>
> "Because it's so simple, I'm probably going to end before my allotted time. It's black-and-white. Truth and lies. The shareholders, ladies and gentlemen, . . . buy a share of stock, and for that they're not entitled to much but they're entitled to the truth. They're entitled for the officers and employees of the company to put their interests ahead of their own. They're entitled to be told what the financial condition of the company is.
>
> "They are entitled to honesty, ladies and gentlemen."

But the prosecutor was wrong. Enron wasn't really a puzzle. It was a mystery.

3

In late July of 2000, Jonathan Weil, a reporter at the Dallas bureau of the *Wall Street Journal,* got a call from someone he knew in the investment-management business. Weil wrote the stock column, called "Heard in Texas," for the paper's regional edition, and he had been closely following the big energy firms based in Houston—Dynegy, El Paso, and Enron. His caller had a suggestion. "He said, 'You really ought to check out Enron and Dynegy and see where their earnings come from,'" Weil recalled. "So I did."

Weil was interested in Enron's use of what is called mark-to-market accounting, which is a technique used by companies that engage in complicated financial trading. Suppose, for instance, that you are an energy company and you enter into a hundred-million-dollar contract with the state of California to deliver a billion kilowatt hours of electricity in 2016. How much is that contract worth? You aren't going to get paid for another ten years, and you aren't going to know until then whether you'll show a profit on the deal or a loss. Nonetheless, that hundred-million-dollar promise clearly matters to your bottom line. If electricity steadily drops in price over the next several years, the contract is going to become a hugely valuable asset. But if electricity starts to get more expensive as 2016 approaches, you could be out tens of millions of dollars. With mark-to-market accounting, you estimate how much revenue the deal is going to bring in and put that number in your books at the moment you sign the contract. If down the line, the estimate changes, you adjust the balance sheet accordingly.

When a company using mark-to-market accounting says it has made a profit of ten million dollars on revenues of a hundred million, then, it could mean one of two things. The company may actually have a hundred million dollars in its bank accounts, of which ten million will remain after it has paid its bills. Or it may be guessing that it will make ten million dollars on a deal where money may not actually change hands for years. Weil's source wanted him to see how much of the money Enron said it was making was "real."

Weil got copies of the firm's annual reports and quarterly filings and began comparing the income statements and the cash-flow statements. "It took me a while to figure out everything I needed to," Weil said. "It probably took a good month or so. There was a lot of noise in the financial statements, and to zero in on this particular issue you needed to cut through a lot of that." Weil spoke to Thomas Linsmeier, then an accounting professor at Michigan State, and they talked about how some finance companies in the nineteen-nineties had used mark-to-market accounting on subprime loans—that is, loans made to higher-credit-risk consumers—and when the economy declined and consumers defaulted or paid off their loans more quickly than expected, the lenders suddenly realized that their estimates of how much money they were going to make were far too generous. Weil spoke to someone at the Financial Accounting Standards Board, to an analyst at the Moody's investment-rating agency, and to a dozen or so others. Then he went back to Enron's financial statements. His conclusions were sobering. In the second quarter of 2000, $747 million of the money Enron said it had made was "unrealized"—that is, it was money that executives thought they were going to make at some point in the future. If you took that imaginary money away, Enron had shown a significant loss in the second quarter. This was one of the most admired companies in the United States, a firm that was then valued by the stock market as the seventh-largest corporation in the country, and there was practically no cash coming into its coffers.

Weil's story ran in the *Journal* on September 20, 2000. A few days later, it was read by a Wall Street financier named James Chanos. Chanos is a short-seller—an investor who tries to make money by betting that a company's stock will fall. "It pricked up my ears," Chanos said. "I read the 10-K and the 10-Q that first weekend," he went on, referring to the financial statements that public companies are required to file with federal regulators. "I went through it pretty quickly. I flagged right away the stuff that was questionable. I circled it. That was the first run-through. Then I flagged the pages and read the stuff I didn't understand, and reread it two or three times. I remember

I spent a couple hours on it." Enron's profit margins and its return on equity were plunging, Chanos saw. Cash flow—the life blood of any business—had slowed to a trickle, and the company's rate of return was less than its cost of capital: it was as if you had borrowed money from the bank at nine-percent interest and invested it in a savings bond that paid you seven-percent interest. "They were basically liquidating themselves," Chanos said.

In November of that year, Chanos began shorting Enron stock. Over the next few months, he spread the word that he thought the company was in trouble. He tipped off a reporter for *Fortune,* Bethany McLean. She read the same reports that Chanos and Weil had, and came to the same conclusion. Her story, under the headline "IS ENRON OVERPRICED?," ran in March of 2001. More and more journalists and analysts began taking a closer look at Enron, and the stock began to fall. In August, Skilling resigned. Enron's credit rating was downgraded. Banks became reluctant to lend Enron the money it needed to make its trades. By December, the company had filed for bankruptcy.

Enron's downfall has been documented so extensively that it is easy to overlook how peculiar it was. Compare Enron, for instance, with Watergate, the prototypical scandal of the nineteen-seventies. To expose the White House coverup, Bob Woodward and Carl Bernstein used a source—Deep Throat—who had access to many secrets, and whose identity had to be concealed. He warned Woodward and Bernstein that their phones might be tapped. When Woodward wanted to meet with Deep Throat, he would move a flower pot with a red flag in it to the back of his apartment balcony. That evening, he would leave by the back stairs, take multiple taxis to make sure he wasn't being followed, and meet his source in an underground parking garage at 2 A.M. Here, from "All the President's Men," is Woodward's climactic encounter with Deep Throat:

"Okay," he said softly. "This is very serious. You can safely say that fifty people worked for the White House and CRP to play games and spy and sabotage and gather intelligence. Some of it is beyond belief, kicking at the opposition in every imaginable way."

Deep Throat nodded confirmation as Woodward ran down items on a list of tactics that he and Bernstein had heard were used against the political opposition: bugging, following people, false press leaks, fake letters, cancelling campaign rallies, investigating campaign workers' private lives, planting spies, stealing documents, planting provocateurs in political demonstrations.

"It's all in the files," Deep Throat said. "Justice and the Bureau know about it, even though it wasn't followed up."

Woodward was stunned. Fifty people directed by the White House and CRP to destroy the opposition, no holds barred?

Deep Throat nodded.

The White House had been willing to subvert—was that the right word?—the whole electoral process? Had actually gone ahead and tried to do it?

Another nod. Deep Throat looked queasy.

And hired fifty agents to do it?

"You can safely say more than fifty," Deep Throat said. Then he turned, walked up the ramp and out. It was nearly 6:00 a.m.

Watergate was a classic puzzle: Woodward and Bernstein were searching for a buried secret, and Deep Throat was their guide.

Did Jonathan Weil have a Deep Throat? Not really. He had a friend in the investment-management business with some suspicions about energy-trading companies like Enron, but the friend wasn't an insider. Nor did Weil's source direct him to files detailing the clandestine activities of the company. He just told Weil to read a series of public documents that had been prepared and distributed by Enron itself. Woodward met with his secret source in an underground parking garage in the hours before dawn. Weil called up an accounting expert at Michigan State.

When Weil had finished his reporting, he called Enron for comment. "They had their chief accounting officer and six or seven people fly up to Dallas," Weil says. They met in a conference room at the *Journal*'s offices. The Enron officials acknowledged that the money they said they earned was virtually all money that they hoped to earn. Weil and the Enron officials then had a long conversation about how certain Enron was about its estimates of future earnings. "They were telling me how brilliant the people who put together their mathematical models were," Weil says. "These were M.I.T. Ph.D.s. I said, 'Were your mathematical models last year telling you that the California electricity markets would be going berserk this year? No? Why not?' They said, 'Well, this is one of those crazy events.' It was late September 2000, so I said, 'Who do you think is going to win? Bush or Gore?' They said, 'We don't know.' I said, 'Don't you think it will make a difference to the market whether you have an environmentalist Democrat in the White House or a Texas oil man?" It was all very civil. "There was no dispute about the numbers," Weil went on. "There was only a difference in how you should interpret them."

Of all the moments in the Enron unravelling, this meeting is surely the strangest. The prosecutor in the Enron case told the jury to send Jeffrey Skilling to prison because Enron had hidden the truth: You're "entitled to be told what the financial condition of the company is," the prosecutor had said. But what truth was Enron hiding here? Everything Weil learned for his Enron exposé came from Enron, and when he wanted to confirm his numbers the company's executives got on a plane and sat down with him in a conference room in Dallas.

Nixon never went to see Woodward and Bernstein at the *Washington Post*. He hid in the White House.

4

The second, and perhaps more consequential, problem with Enron's accounting was its heavy reliance on what are called special-purpose entities, or S.P.E.s.

An S.P.E. works something like this. Your company isn't doing well; sales are down and you are heavily in debt. If you go to a bank to borrow a hundred million dollars, it will probably charge you an extremely high interest rate, if it agrees to lend to you at all. But you've got a bundle of oil leases that over the next four or five years are almost certain to bring in a hundred million dollars. So you hand them over to a partnership—the S.P.E.—which you have set up with some outside investors. The bank then lends a hundred million dollars to the partnership, and the partnership gives the money to you. That bit of financial maneuvering makes a big difference. This kind of transaction did not (at the time) have to be reported in the company's balance sheet. So a company could raise capital without increasing its indebtedness. And because the bank is almost certain the leases will generate enough money to payoff the loan, it's willing to lend its money at a much lower interest rate. S.P.E.s have become commonplace in corporate America.

Enron introduced all kinds of twists into the S.P.E. game. It didn't always put blue-chip assets into the partnerships-like oil leases that would reliably generate income. It sometimes sold off less than sterling assets. Nor did it always sell those assets to outsiders, who presumably would raise questions about the value of what they were buying. Enron had its own executives manage these partnerships. And the company would make the deals work—that is, get the partnerships and the banks to play along—by guaranteeing that, if whatever they had to sell declined in value, Enron would make up the difference with its own stock. In other words, Enron didn't sell parts of itself to an outside entity; it effectively sold parts of itself to itself—a strategy that was not only legally questionable but also extraordinarily risky. It was Enron's tangle of financial obligations to the S.P.E.s that ended up triggering the collapse.

When the prosecution in the Skilling case argued that the company had misled its investors, they were referring, in part, to these S.P.E.s. Enron's management, the argument went, had an obligation to reveal the extent to which it had staked its financial livelihood on these shadowy side deals. As the Powers Committee, a panel charged with investigating Enron's demise, noted, the company "failed to achieve a fundamental objective: they did not communicate the essence of the transactions in a sufficiently clear fashion to enable a reader of [Enron's] financial statements to understand what was going on." In short, we weren't told enough.

Here again, though, the lessons of the Enron case aren't nearly so straightforward. The public became aware of the nature of these S.P.E.s through the reporting of several of Weil's colleagues at the *Wall Street Journal*—principally John Emshwiller and Rebecca [Smith]—starting in the late summer of 2001. And how was Emshwiller tipped off to Enron's problems? The same way Jonathan Weil and Jim Chanos were: he read what Enron had reported in its own public filings. Here is the description of Emshwiller's epiphany, as described in Kurt Eichenwald's "Conspiracy of Fools," the definitive history of the Enron debacle. (Note the verb "scrounged," which Eichenwald uses to describe how Emshwiller found the relevant Enron documents. What he means by that is "downloaded.")

It was section eight, called "Related Party Transactions," that got John Emshwiller's juices flowing.

After being assigned to follow the Skilling resignation, Emshwiller had put in a request for an interview, then scrounged up a copy of Enron's most recent SEC filing in search of any nuggets.

What he found startled him. Words about some partnerships run by an unidentified "senior officer." Arcane stuff, maybe, but the numbers were huge. Enron reported more than $240 million in revenues in the first six months of the year from its dealings with them.

Enron's S.P.E.s were, by any measure, evidence of extraordinary recklessness and incompetence. But you can't blame Enron for covering up the existence of its side deals. It didn't; it disclosed them. The argument against the company, then, is more accurately that it didn't tell its investors enough about its S.P.E.s. But what is enough? Enron had some three thousand S.P.E.s, and the paperwork for each one probably ran in excess of a thousand pages. It scarcely would have helped investors if Enron had made all three million pages public. What about an edited version of each deal? Steven Schwarcz, a professor at Duke Law School, recently examined a random sample of twenty S.P.E. disclosure statements from various corporations—that is, summaries of the deals put together for interested parties—and found that on average they ran to forty single-spaced pages. So a summary of Enron's S.P.E.s would have come to a hundred and twenty thousand single-spaced pages. What about a summary of all those summaries? That's what the bankruptcy examiner in the Enron case put together, and it took up a thousand pages. Well, then, what about a summary of the summary of the summaries? That's what the Powers Committee put together. The committee looked only at the "substance of the most significant transactions," and its accounting still ran to two hundred numbingly complicated pages and, as Schwarcz points out, that was "with the benefit of hindsight and with the assistance of some of the finest legal talent in the nation."

A puzzle grows simpler with the addition of each new piece of information: if I tell you that Osama bin Laden is hiding in Peshawar, I make the problem of finding him an order of magnitude easier, and if I add that he's hiding in a neighborhood in the northwest corner of the city, the problem becomes simpler still. But here the rules seem different. According to the Powers report, many on Enron's board of directors failed to understand "the economic rationale, the consequences, and the risks" of their company's S.P.E. deals—and the directors sat in meetings where those deals were discussed in detail. In "Conspiracy of Fools," Eichenwald convincingly argues that Andrew Fastow, Enron's chief financial officer, didn't understand the full economic implications of the deals, either, and he was the one who put them together.

"These were very, very sophisticated, complex transactions," says Anthony Catanach, who teaches accounting at the Villanova University School of Business and has written extensively on the Enron case. Referring to Enron's accounting firm, he said, "I'm not even sure any of Arthur Andersen's field staff at Enron would have been able to understand them, even if it was all in front of them. This is senior-management-type stuff. I spent two months looking at the Powers report, just diagramming it. These deals were really convoluted."

Enron's S.P.E.s, it should be noted, would have been this hard to understand even if they were standard issue. S.P.E.s are by nature difficult. A company creates an S.P.E. because it wants to reassure banks about the risks of making a loan. To provide that reassurance, the company gives its lenders and partners very detailed information about a specific portion of its business. And the more certainty a company creates for the lender—the more guarantees and safeguards and explanations it writes into the deal—the less comprehensible the transaction becomes to outsiders. Schwarcz writes that Enron's disclosure was "necessarily imperfect." You can try to make financial transactions understandable by simplifying them, in which case you run the risk of smoothing over some of their potential risks, or you can try to disclose every potential pitfall, in which case you'll make the disclosure so unwieldy that no one will be able to understand it. To Schwarcz, all Enron proves is that in an age of increasing financial complexity the "disclosure paradigm"—the idea that the more a company tells us about its business, the better off we are—has become an anachronism.

5

During the summer of 1943, Nazi propaganda broadcasts boasted that the German military had developed a devastating "super weapon." Immediately, the Allied intelligence services went to work. Spies confirmed that the Germans had built a secret weapons factory. Aerial photographs taken over northern France showed a strange new concrete installation pointed in the direction of England. The Allies were worried. Bombing missions were sent to try to disrupt the mysterious operation, and plans were drawn up to deal with the prospect of devastating new attacks on English cities. Nobody was sure, though, whether the weapon was real. There seemed to be weapons factories there, but it wasn't evident what was happening inside them. And there was a launching pad in northern France, but it might have been just a decoy, designed to distract the Allies from bombing real targets. The German secret weapon was a puzzle, and the Allies didn't have enough information to solve it. There was another way to think about the problem, though, which ultimately proved far more useful: treat the German secret weapon as a mystery.

The mystery-solvers of the Second World War were small groups of analysts whose job was to listen to the overseas and domestic propaganda broadcasts of Japan and Germany. The British outfit had been around since shortly before the First World War and was run by the BBC. The American operation was known as the Screwball Division, the historian Stephen Mercado writes, and in the early nineteen-forties had been housed in a nondescript office building on K Street, in Washington. The analysts listened to the same speeches that anyone with a shortwave radio could listen to. They simply sat at their desks with headphones on, working their way through hours and hours of Nazi broadcasts. Then they tried to figure out how what the Nazis said publicly—about, for instance, the possibility of a renewed offensive against Russia—revealed what they felt about, say, invading Russia. One journalist at the time described the propaganda analysts as "the greatest collection of individualists, international rolling stones, and slightly batty geniuses ever gathered together in one organization." And they had very definite thoughts about the Nazis' secret weapon.

The German leadership, first of all, was boasting about the secret weapon in domestic broadcasts. That was important. Propaganda was supposed to boost morale. If the Nazi leadership said things that turned out to be misleading, its credibility would fall.

When German U-boats started running into increasingly effective Allied resistance in the spring of 1943, for example, Joseph Goebbels, the Nazi minister of propaganda, tacitly acknowledged the bad news, switching his emphasis from trumpeting recent victories to predicting long-term success, and blaming the weather for hampering U-boat operations. Up to that point, Goebbels had never lied to his own people about that sort of news. So if he said that Germany had a devastating secret weapon it meant, in all likelihood, that Germany had a devastating secret weapon.

Starting from that premise, the analysts then mined the Nazis' public pronouncements for more insights. It was, they concluded, "beyond reasonable doubt" that as of November, 1943, the weapon existed, that it was of an entirely new type, that it could not be easily countered, that it would produce striking results, and that it would shock the civilian population upon whom it would be used. It was, furthermore, "highly probable" that the Germans were past the experimental stage as of May of 1943, and that something had happened in August of that year that significantly delayed deployment. The analysts based this inference, in part; on the fact that, in August, the Nazis abruptly stopped mentioning their secret weapon for ten days, and that when they started again their threats took on a new, less certain, tone. Finally, it could be tentatively estimated that the weapon would be ready between the middle of January and the middle of April, with a month's margin of error on either side. That inference, in part, came from Nazi propaganda in late 1943, which suddenly became more serious and specific in tone, and it seemed unlikely that Goebbels would raise hopes in this way if he couldn't deliver within a few months. The secret weapon was the Nazis' fabled V-1 rocket, and virtually every one of the propaganda analysts' predictions turned out to be true.

The political scientist Alexander George described the sequence of V-1 rocket inferences in his 1959 book "Propaganda Analysis," and the striking thing about his account is how contemporary it seems. The spies were fighting a nineteenth-century war. The analysts belonged to our age, and the lesson of their triumph is that the complex, uncertain issues that the modern world throws at us require the mystery paradigm.

Diagnosing prostate cancer used to be a puzzle, for example: the doctor would do a rectal exam and feel for a lumpy tumor on the surface of the patient's prostate. These days, though, we don't wait for patients to develop the symptoms of prostate cancer. Doctors now regularly test middle-aged men for elevated levels of PSA, a substance associated with prostate changes, and, if the results look problematic, they use ultrasound imaging to take a picture of the prostate. Then they perform a biopsy, removing tiny slices of the gland and examining the extracted tissue under a microscope. Much of that flood of information, however, is inconclusive: elevated levels of PSA don't always mean that you have cancer, and normal levels of PSA don't always mean that you don't—and, in any case, there's debate about what constitutes a "normal" PSA level. Nor is the biopsy definitive: because what a pathologist is looking for is early evidence of cancer—and in many cases merely something that might one day turn into cancer—two equally skilled pathologists can easily look at the same sample and disagree about whether there is any cancer present. Even if they do agree, they may disagree about the benefits of treatment, given that most prostate cancers grow so slowly that they never cause problems. The urologist is now charged with the task of making sense of a maze of unreliable and conflicting claims. He is no longer confirming the presence of a malignancy. He's predicting it, and the certainties of his predecessors have been replaced with outcomes that can only be said to be "highly probable" or "tentatively estimated." What medical progress has meant for prostate cancer—and, as the physician H. Gilbert Welch argues in his book "Should I Be Tested for Cancer?," for virtually every other cancer as well—is the transformation of diagnosis from a puzzle to a mystery.

That same transformation is happening in the intelligence world as well. During the Cold War, the broad context of our relationship with the Soviet bloc was stable and predictable. What we didn't know was details. As Gregory Treverton, who was a former vice-chair of the National Intelligence Council, writes in his book "Reshaping National Intelligence for an Age of Information": "Then the pressing questions that preoccupied intelligence were puzzles, ones that could, in principle, have been answered definitively if only the information had been available: How big was the Soviet economy? How many missiles did the Soviet Union have? Had it launched a 'bolt from the blue' attack?" These puzzles were intelligence's stock-in-trade during the Cold War.

With the collapse of the Eastern bloc, Treverton and others have argued that the situation facing the intelligence community has turned upside down. Now most of the world is open, not closed. Intelligence officers aren't dependent on scraps from spies. They are inundated with information. Solving puzzles remains critical: we still want to know precisely where Osama bin Laden is hiding, where North Korea's nuclear-weapons facilities are situated. But mysteries increasingly take center stage. The stable and predictable divisions of East and West have been shattered. Now the task of the intelligence analyst is to help policymakers navigate the disorder. Several years ago, Admiral Bobby R. Inman was asked by a congressional commission what changes he thought would strengthen America's intelligence system. Inman used to head the National Security Agency, the nation's premier puzzle-solving authority, and was once the deputy director of the C.I.A. He was the embodiment of the Cold War intelligence structure. His answer: revive the State Department, the one part of the U.S. foreign-policy establishment that isn't considered to be in the intelligence business at all. In a post-Cold War world of "openly available information," Inman said, "what you need are observers with language ability, with understanding of the religions, cultures of the countries they're observing." Inman thought we needed fewer spies and more slightly batty geniuses.

6

Enron revealed that the financial community needs to make the same transition. "In order for an economy to have an adequate system of financial reporting, it is not enough that companies make disclosures of financial information," the Yale law professor

Jonathan Macey wrote in a landmark law-review article that encouraged many to rethink the Enron case. "In addition, it is vital that there be a set of financial intermediaries, who are at least as competent and sophisticated at receiving, processing, and interpreting financial information . . . as the companies are at delivering it." Puzzles are "transmitter-dependent"; they turn on what we are told. Mysteries are "receiver dependent"; they turn on the skills of the listener, and Macey argues that, as Enron's business practices grew more complicated, it was Wall Street's responsibility to keep pace.

Victor Fleischer, who teaches at the University of Colorado Law School, points out that one of the critical clues about Enron's condition lay in the fact that it paid no income tax in four of its last five years. Enron's use of mark-to-market accounting and S.P.E.s was an accounting game that made the company look as though it were earning far more money than it was. But the I.R.S. doesn't accept mark-to-market accounting; you pay tax on income when you actually receive that income. And, from the I.R.S.'s perspective, all of Enron's fantastically complex maneuvering around its S.P.E.s was, as Fleischer puts it, "a non-event": until the partnership actually sells the asset—and makes either a profit or a loss—an S.P.E. is just an accounting fiction. Enron wasn't paying any taxes because, in the eyes of the I.R.S., Enron wasn't making any money.

If you looked at Enron from the perspective of the tax code, that is, you would have seen a very different picture of the company than if you had looked through the more traditional lens of the accounting profession. But in order to do that you would have to be trained in the tax code and be familiar with its particular conventions and intricacies, and know what questions to ask. "The fact of the gap between [Enron's] accounting income and taxable income was easily observed," Fleischer notes, but not the source of the gap. "The tax code requires special training."

Woodward and Bernstein didn't have any special training. They were in their twenties at the time of Watergate. In "All the President's Men," they even joke about their inexperience: Woodward's expertise was mainly in office politics; Bernstein was a college dropout. But it hardly mattered, because coverups, whistle-blowers, secret tapes, and exposés—the principal elements of the puzzle—all require the application of energy and persistence, which are the virtues of youth. Mysteries demand experience and insight. Woodward and Bernstein would never have broken the Enron story.

"There have been scandals in corporate history where people are really making stuff up, but this wasn't a criminal enterprise of that kind," Macey says. "Enron was vanishingly close, in my view, to having complied with the accounting rules. They were going over the edge, just a little bit. And this kind of financial fraud—where people are simply stretching the truth—falls into the area that analysts and short-sellers are supposed to ferret out. The truth wasn't hidden. But you'd have to look at their financial statements, and you would have to say to yourself, What's that about? It's almost as if they were saying, 'We're doing some really sleazy stuff in footnote 42, and if you want to know more about it ask us.' And that's the thing. Nobody did."

Alexander George, in his history of propaganda analysis, looked at hundreds of the inferences drawn by the American analysts about the Nazis, and concluded that an astonishing eighty-one percent of them were accurate. George's account, however, spends almost as much time on the propaganda analysts' failures as on their successes. It was the British, for example, who did the best work on the V-1 rocket problem. They systematically tracked the "occurrence and volume" of Nazi reprisal threats, which is how they were able to pinpoint things like the setback suffered by the V-1 program in August of 1943 (it turned out that Allied bombs had caused serious damage) and the date of the Nazi V-1 rocket launch. K Street's analysis was lackluster in comparison. George writes that the Americans "did not develop analytical techniques and hypotheses of sufficient refinement," relying instead on "impressionistic" analysis. George was himself one of the slightly batty geniuses of K Street, and, of course, he could easily have excused his former colleagues. They never left their desks, after all. All they had to deal with was propaganda, and their big source was Goebbels, who was a liar, a thief, and a drunk. But that is puzzle thinking. In the case of puzzles, we put the offending target, the C.E.O., in jail for twenty-four years and assume that our work is done. Mysteries require that we revisit our list of culprits and be willing to spread the blame a little more broadly. Because if you can't find the truth in a—even a mystery shrouded in propaganda—it's not just the fault of the propagandist. It's your fault as well.

7

In the spring of 1998, Macey notes, a group of six students at Cornell University's business school decided to do their term project on Enron. "It was for an advanced financial-statement-analysis class taught by a guy at Cornell called Charles Lee, who is pretty famous in financial circles," one member of the group, Jay Krueger, recalls. In the first part of the semester, Lee had led his students through a series of intensive case studies, teaching them techniques and sophisticated tools to make sense of the vast amounts of information that companies disclose in their annual reports and S.E.C. filings. Then the students picked a company and went off on their own. "One of the second-years had a summer-internship interview with Enron, and he was very interested in the energy sector," Krueger went on. "So he said, 'Let's do them.' It was about a six-week project, half a semester. Lots of group meetings. It was a ratio analysis, which is pretty standard business-school fare. You know, take fifty different financial ratios, then lay that on top of every piece of information you could find out about the company, the businesses, how their performance compared to other competitors."

The people in the group reviewed Enron's accounting practices as best they could. They analyzed each of Enron's businesses, in succession. They used statistical tools, designed to find telltale patterns in the company's financial performance—the Beneish model, the Lev and Thiagarajan indicators, the Edwards-Bell-Ohlsen analysis—and made their way through pages and pages of footnotes. "We really had a lot of questions about what was going on with their business model," Krueger said. The students' conclusions were straightforward. Enron was pursuing a far riskier strategy than its competitors. There were clear signs that "Enron may be manipulating its earnings."

The stock was then at forty-eight—at its peak, two years later, it was almost double that—but the students found it over-valued. The report was posted on the Web site of the Cornell University business school, where it has been, ever since, for anyone who cared to read twenty-three pages of analysis. The students' recommendation was on the first page, in boldfaced type: "Sell."

A Revisionist View of Enron and the Sudden Death of "May"[*]

Frank Partnoy[**]

I. INTRODUCTION

This Article makes two points about the academic and regulatory reaction to Enron's collapse. First, it argues that what seems to be emerging as the "conventional story" of Enron, involving alleged fraud related to Special Purpose Entities (SPE), is incorrect. Instead, this Article makes the revisionist claim that Enron is largely a story about derivatives—financial instruments such as options, futures, and other contracts whose value is linked to some underlying financial instrument or index.[1] A close analysis of the facts shows that the most prominent SPE transactions were largely irrelevant to Enron's collapse, and that most of Enron's deals with SPEs were arguably legal, even though

* Originally published at 48 VILL. L. REV. 1245 (2003). Reprinted by permission.

** Professor of Law, University of San Diego School of Law. I am grateful to George Benston, Bill Bratton, Bill Carney, Jeannette Filippone, Peter H. Huang, Don Langevoort, Shaun Martin, Steven Schwarcz and John Tishler for comments on a draft of this Article, and to Andrew Kenis for help in the editorial process.

1 The two basic categories of derivatives are options and futures, although these instruments can be combined to create more complex financial instruments, including swaps and other structured derivatives. Derivatives can be traded in two ways: on regulated exchanges or in unregulated over-the-counter (OTC) markets. The size of derivatives markets typically is measured in terms of the notional values of contracts. Recent estimates of the size of the exchange-traded derivatives market, which includes all contracts traded on the major options and futures exchanges, are in the range of $13 to $14 trillion in notional amount. *See* ALFRED STEINHERR, DERIVATIVES: THE WILD BEAST OF FINANCE 153 (rev. ed. 2000). By contrast, the estimated notional amount of outstanding OTC derivatives as of June 2002 was $128 trillion. *See* Press Release, Bank for International Settlements, Acceleration of OTC Derivatives Market Activity in the First Half of 2002 (Nov. 8, 2002), *at* http://www.bis.org/publ/otc_hy0211.pdf. In other words, OTC derivatives markets, which for the most part did not exist twenty (or, in some cases, even ten) years ago, now comprise about ninety percent of the aggregate derivatives market, with trillions of dollars at risk. Measured by notional amount, value at risk, or any other measure, OTC derivatives markets are bigger than the markets for U.S. stocks.

disclosure of those deals did not comport with economic reality.[2] To the extent SPEs are relevant to understanding Enron, it is the derivatives transactions between Enron and the SPEs—not the SPEs themselves—that matter. Even more important were Enron's derivatives trades and transactions other than those involving the SPEs. This first point about derivatives is important to the literature studying the relationship between finance and law: legal rules create incentives for parties to engage in economically equivalent, unregulated transactions, and financial innovation creates incentives for parties to increase risks (to increase expected return) outside the scope of legal rules requiring disclosure.[3]

Second, this Article argues that the regulatory response to Enron was in large part misguided because it focused too much on the conventional story. If the conventional story about Enron is incorrect—and Enron instead is largely a story about derivatives—then the prescriptions that follow from Enron's collapse, if any, should relate to the regulation and disclosure of derivatives. Interestingly, Congress—in a little-noticed provision of the Sarbanes-Oxley Act of 2002, Section 401(a)—sought to implement precisely such an approach, directing the Securities and Exchange Commission (SEC) to adopt new regulations requiring that annual and quarterly financial reports filed with the SEC disclose "all material off-balance sheet transactions . . . that may have a material current or future effect on financial condition [of the company filing]."[4] The SEC originally proposed disclosure regulations based on this heightened "may" standard, but in its final release reverted to a lower "reasonably likely" standard, with specific rules governing tabular disclosure of particular transactions.[5] Surprisingly, the SEC

---

[2] *See The Fall of Enron: How Could It Have Happened?; Hearing Before the Senate Comm. on Gov't Affairs*, 107th Cong. 58-74 (Jan. 24, 2002) (statement of Frank Partnoy, Professor of Law, University of San Diego Law School) [hereinafter Partnoy, Testimony], *available at* http://govt-aff.senate.gov/012402partnoy.htm; *see also* NEIL BATSON, SECOND INTERIM REPORT, COURT-APPOINTED EXAMINER, IN RE ENRON, DOC. NO. 9551 (Mar. 5, 2003), *available at* http://www.elaw4enron.com.

[3] Merton H. Miller began arguing during the 1980s that financial innovation was driven by regulatory changes. *See* Merton H. Miller, *Financial Innovation: The Last Twenty Years and the Next*, 21 J. FIN. & QUANTITATIVE ANALYSIS 459, 460 (1986); *see also* MERTON H. MILLER, MERTON MILLER ON DERIVATIVES 1-14, 52-53 (1997). More recently, scholars have been citing "regulatory arbitrage" as a significant force in international regulatory competition. *See* Peter H. Huang & Michael S. Knoll, *Corporate Finance, Corporate Law and Finance Theory*, 74 S. CAL. L. REV. 175, 190-91 (2000); Amir N. Licht, *Regulatory Arbitrage for Real: International Securities Regulation in a World of Interacting Securities Markets*, 38 VA. J. INT'L L. 563 (1998); Roberta Romano, *The Need for Competition in International Securities Regulation*, 2 THEORETICAL INQ. L. 387, 387 (2001).

[4] Sarbanes-Oxley Act of 2002 § 401(a), Pub. L. No. 107-204, 116 Stat. 745 (2002) (emphasis added). Section 401(a) became the new Section 13(j) of the Securities Exchange Act. This "may" provision covered disclosure of the type related to Enron's derivatives deals with the SPEs, but also included disclosure related more generally to Enron's trading of derivatives to the extent the fair value of its derivatives was not fully reflected as an asset or liability in a company's financial statements. See Disclosure in Management's Discussion and Analysis about Off-Balance Sheet Arrangements and Aggregate Contractual Obligations, Securities Act Release No. 33-8182, Securities Exchange Act Release No. 34-47264, 2003 SEC LEXIS 227, *4 (Jan. 28, 2003) [hereinafter SEC Release Nos. 33-8182, 34-47264].

[5] "Reasonably likely" is the standard generally applicable to contingent disclosure in Management's Discussion and Analysis of Results and Operations (MD&A). *See* SEC Release Nos. 33-8182, 34-47264, *supra* note 4, at *6.

promulgated these "reasonably likely" regulations even though Congress, in debating Sarbanes-Oxley, already had considered and rejected the "reasonably likely" approach. This second point about regulatory response is important to the literatures studying both mandatory disclosure and the relationship between Congress and administrative agencies: not only did interested private actors quickly capture the agency rule-making process,[6] but they were able to persuade the agency to revive an interpretation the legislature already had considered and rejected.

Scholarship addressing the collapse of Enron should incorporate these two points. To date, the debate among legal academics[7] has been framed by the two hundred-plus page report by the Special Committee of Enron's Board of Directors, which was commissioned to study Enron's SPE transactions,[8] and by the related congressional hearings and proposals, which culminated in Sarbanes-Oxley. The essential facts from these sources are well known.[9]

In the first law review article addressing the collapse of Enron, William Bratton assessed four possible "causation stories" about Enron's collapse.[10] One of those stories was "Enron as Derivative Speculation Gone Wrong." In this story, Bratton cautioned scholars not to draw too many conclusions about Enron until more facts were known about the firm's trading in derivatives.[11] Since then, most commentators on Enron have focused primarily on a handful of people and transactions—the company's senior

---

[6] *See* George Stigler, *A Theory of Economic Regulation,* 2 Bell J. Econ. & Mgmt. Sci. 3, 3 (1971); James Q. Wilson, *The Politics of Regulation, in* The Politics of Regulation 357, 369 (James Q. Wilson ed., 1980).

[7] *See, e.g.*, William W. Bratton, *Enron and the Dark Side of Shareholder Value*, 76 Tul. L. Rev. 1275 (2002); Jeffrey N. Gordon, What *Enron Means for Management and Control of the Modern Business Corporation: Some Initial Responses*, 69 U. Chi. L. Rev. 1233 (2002); Larry E. Ribstein, *Market vs. Regulatory Responses to Corporate Fraud: A Critique of the Sarbanes-Oxley Act of 2002*, 28 J. Corp. L. 1 (2002); Douglas G. Baird & Robert K. Rasmussen, *Four (or Five) Easy Lessons from Enron*, 55 Vand. L. Rev. 1787 (2002); John C. Coffee, Jr., *What Caused Enron?: A Capsule Social and Economic History of the 1990s*, Columbia Law and Econ. Working Paper No. 214 (2003); John C. Coffee, Jr., *Understanding Enron: "It's About the Gatekeepers, Stupid,"* Columbia Law and Econ. Working Paper No. 207 (2002); Donald C. Langevoort, *Managing the "Expectations Gap" in Investor Protection: The SEC and the Post-Enron Reform Agenda*, 48 Vill. L. Rev. 1139 (2003); Steven L. Schwarcz, *Rethinking the Disclosure Paradigm in a World of Complexity*, 2004 U. Ill. Law Rev. 1 (2004).

[8] *See* Enron Corp. Form 8-K, Exhibit 99.2, *Report of Investigation by the Special Investigative Committee of the Board of Directors of Enron Corp.*, at 77 (Feb. 1, 2002) [hereinafter *Special Report*], *available at* http://www.enron.com/corp/investors/sec; *see also* Gordon, *supra* note 7, at 1240 (assessing Enron's use of SPEs).

[9] In a nutshell, three radically different characters—the professorial founder Kenneth Lay, the free-market consultant Jeffrey Skilling, and the brash financial whiz Andrew Fastow—converted a small natural gas producer into the seventh largest company in the United States. On the way, they generated fabulous wealth for Enron shareholders, employees and especially insiders, who cashed out more than $1.2 billion before the company spectacularly fell into bankruptcy. The thousands of layoffs, the imploded retirement plans, the controversy surrounding political contributions, the details of Enron executives' personal lives and the role of now infamous SPEs have been part of public debate since 2001.

[10] Bratton, *supra* note 7, at 1299-1332.

[11] *Id.* at 1302-03.

executives (Lay, Skilling and especially Fastow) and a small number of SPEs (JEDI, Chewco, the LJM partnerships and the Raptors)—concluding that these SPEs were designed to inflate Enron's income and hide its debt and that the unraveling of those deals led Enron to restate its financial statements during 2001, and then to its collapse.[12] Scholars also have focused primarily on regulatory changes directed at these issues: increased penalties for fraud; new requirements for independent corporate directors, audit committees and accountants; and new disclosure requirements.

The two points in this Article suggest that the key to understanding Enron's collapse is to reframe this discussion in terms of the complexity of the financial instruments—derivatives and off-balance sheet transactions—that drove Enron's major businesses.[13] Unfortunately, even after intense media scrutiny, congressional hearings and other government investigations, most of the firm's derivatives dealings remain unpenetrated. Even after Enron's bankruptcy, the firm's own officials were unable to grasp enough detail to issue an annual report in 2002; even with the help of a new team of accountants from PricewaterhouseCoopers, they simply could not add up the firm's assets and liabilities.[14] This Article's claim is that those details are central. If scholars are to understand the implications of Enron's collapse, they must begin by revisiting the conventional story about Enron.

Section II describes how Enron used and disclosed derivatives. Much of the relevant information about Enron's derivatives transactions was disclosed in Enron's financial reports, albeit in an unclear manner. Other derivatives were disclosed in summary form, based on SEC rules suggesting tabular presentation. Enron's risk exposure to derivatives was disclosed in limited ways, but arguably was consistent with prevailing standards of practice, which required disclosure of only "reasonably likely" contingencies. Overall, Enron's disclosure practices were driven by accounting rules and did not necessarily comport with economic reality.[15]

Section III analyzes the regulatory approach to derivatives disclosure. Enron's trading businesses and financial innovations were driven by a rules-based regulatory system

---

[12] *See* Enron Corp. Form 8-K, *Special Report*, *supra* note 8, at 77; Gordon, *supra* note 7.

[13] Financial economist Myron Scholes described Enron as one of the few non-financial services companies that was sufficiently sophisticated in such financial instruments to compete with banks and securities firms. *See* Myron Scholes, *Derivatives in a Dynamic Environment*, 88 AMER. ECON. REV. 350, 360 (1998) ("Product standardization will erode profits more quickly than in the past because more diverse entities, such as General Electric, Enron, or accounting firms, can compete in providing financial services using financial technology.").

[14] Other firms, such as Dynegy, encountered similar problems, particularly with respect to the valuation of derivatives using methodology based on forward curves. *See* Dynegy Inc. Form 10-K (Feb. 14, 2003), *available at* http://dynegy.com/downloads/Dynegy20030214_10KA.pdf; *see also* Warren Buffett, *What Worries Warren*, FORTUNE, Mar. 3, 2003, at 1-3 (describing problems associated with derivatives valuation); *Avoiding a "Mega Catastrophe,"* FORTUNE, Mar. 17, 2003, at 82-87.

[15] Enron's Risk Management Manual explicitly stated a preference for accounting reality: "Reported earnings follow the rules and principles of accounting. The results do not always create measures consistent with underlying economics. However, corporate management's performance is generally measured by accounting income, not underlying economics. Risk management strategies are therefore directed at accounting rather than economic performance." Enron Corp. Risk Management Manual (on file with author).

in which derivatives were largely unregulated, even when they were economically equivalent to regulated financial instruments. The SEC's "reasonably likely" standard did not require disclosure of financial contingencies that are important to the assessment of derivatives-related risks. Moreover, the SEC's rules-based tabular disclosure regulations create perverse disclosure incentives. Congress recognized the limitations of such a system and proposed a lower-threshold "may" standard, but the SEC reverted to "reasonably likely," supplemented by rules-based tabular disclosure. This disclosure regime has two flaws: it sets the bar too low for derivatives disclosure, and it creates unwarranted incentives for parties to make tabular disclosure (and not other disclosure) even if it is not useful. In general terms, efficient and fair financial regulation should treat derivatives as it treats economically equivalent financial instruments (including equivalent regulated securities). Accordingly, this Article suggests that in this context standards based on economic reality are generally preferable to rules based on accounting reality, and that the standards for derivatives disclosure should be higher than that for other MD&A disclosure, as Congress originally intended in enacting Section 401(a).

II. A REVISIONIST VIEW OF ENRON

This section assesses the importance of derivatives in understanding Enron. Enron used derivatives in transactions with other corporations and partnerships to borrow money "off-balance sheet" and to fund various SPEs. Derivatives were central to the SPE transactions; without derivatives, Enron could not have achieved the purposes it intended: inflating profits and hiding debt. Moreover, other derivatives deals—with outside parties other than the well-known SPEs—were even more important to Enron's collapse.

The collapse of Enron does not necessarily lead to a conclusion that equity capital markets were inefficient, or that high equity valuations were unwarranted.[16] Instead, Enron's high equity valuations through 2000 might rationally have been based, at least in part, on Enron's ability to exploit the rules-based regulatory environment applicable to debt and derivatives,[17] thereby securing an unusually low cost of capital, given Enron's risks. Enron used financial innovation to reduce a range of direct regulatory costs: it reduced reported taxable income; it issued preferred and other hybrid securities in place of equity (and debt); it engaged in financial innovation to avoid specific rules in

[16] *See* Gordon, *supra* note 7, at 1240 (noting that "Enron disturbs the efficient market hypothesis").

[17] The over-the-counter (OTC) derivatives markets are subject to limited disclosure requirements based on particularized rules. For example, companies generally are not required to include swap transactions as assets or liabilities on their balance sheets. Prior to Sarbanes-Oxley, the rules applicable to OTC derivatives required only that companies disclose summary details, in tabular form, about their derivatives transactions in the footnotes to their financial statements. *See generally* Frank Partnoy, *The Shifting Contours of Global Derivatives Regulation*, 22 U. Pa. J. Int'l Econ. L. 421 (2001). The standard for disclosing contingencies related to derivatives in MD&A was relatively high ("reasonably likely"). *See* SEC Release Nos. 33-8182, 34-47264, *supra* note 4, at *6. In addition, other regulatory exceptions applied to disclosure of derivatives, including exceptions based on the nature and purpose of particular instruments, allowing such hedging with OTC derivatives. *See* Accounting for Derivatives Instruments and Hedging Activities, Statement of Financial Accounting Standards No. 133 (Fin. Accounting Standards Bd. 1998).

the natural gas and electricity markets. It also used derivatives to satisfy the rules-based regulatory regime associated with credit ratings,[18] thereby reducing its cost of capital. In other words, Enron's collapse is evidence of inefficiencies in the rules-laden debt and derivatives markets more than it is evidence of inefficiencies in equity markets. As Enron lost the ability to exploit the relevant rules during 2001, the value of its residual equity claims collapsed.

The key factor sustaining Enron's ability to secure a low cost of capital was an investment grade credit rating (e.g., BBB+ from Standard & Poor's), which the major credit rating agencies gave to Enron's debt from 1995 until November 2001.[19] The rating agencies received information during this period indicating that Enron was engaging in substantial derivatives and off-balance sheet transactions, including both non-public information and information disclosed in Enron's annual reports. But they maintained an investment grade rating based in part on the assumption that Enron's off-balance sheet transactions were appropriately excluded from Enron's debt and should not matter in calculating related financial ratios because they were non-recourse to Enron.[20] In reality, Enron's derivatives converted its off-balance sheet debt into billions of dollars of recourse debt, depending—among other things—on Enron's stock price. If Enron's credit rating had reflected the company's actual debt levels during this period (i.e., had been sub-investment grade), its cost of capital would have been much higher, and its equity valuations would have been much lower. In sum, derivatives enabled Enron to exploit inefficiencies in debt and derivatives rules, thereby artificially (if only temporarily) inflating the value of its residual equity claims.

A. Derivatives and the SPEs

A complete description of Enron's use of derivatives transactions with SPEs is well beyond the scope of this Article (or any article—the bankruptcy examiner's report detailing such transactions already runs to several thousand pages[21]). Instead, this section briefly will analyze the role of derivatives in a few of Enron's most prominent SPEs.[22]

---

[18] For a description of this regulatory regime, see Frank Partnoy, *The Siskel and Ebert of Financial Markets?: Two Thumbs Down for the Credit Rating Agencies*, 77 WASH. U. L.Q. 619, 648-54 (1999).

[19] *Rating the Raters: Enron and the Credit Rating Agencies, Hearing Before the Senate Comm. on Gov't Affairs*, 107th Cong. 7-10 (Mar. 20, 2002) (statement of Ronald M. Barone, Managing Director, Standard and Poor's), *available at* http://www.senate.gov/~gov_affairs/072302barone.pdf.

[20] Enron listed billions of dollars of off-balance sheet debt in its informal non-public presentations to the rating agencies. *See id.* at 13. In describing these additional obligations to the credit rating agencies, Enron included what it called a "Kitchen Sink Disclaimer," stating that "Enron does not recommend using this analysis for anything other than illustrative purposes and for the purpose of concluding that the off-balance sheet obligations are not material to Enron's consolidated credit analysis. Cigarette smoking may be harmful to your health." *See* Jeffrey McMahon, Enron Corp. Credit Conference Credit Profile, Jan. 29, 2000, at 12 (copy on file with author).

[21] *See* BATSON, *supra* note 2.

[22] SPEs do not necessarily touch the OTC derivatives markets, and SPEs need not enter into derivatives deals with related (or non-related) entities. SPEs and SPE transactions are common in modern financial

First, Enron used derivatives with the LJM1 and Raptor SPEs to hide losses suffered on technology stocks. Second, Enron used derivatives with the JEDI and Chewco SPEs to hide debt incurred to finance new businesses. The common theme in these transactions was that, without these derivatives,[23] Enron's SPE "schemes" would not have worked.

1. Using Derivatives to Hide Losses on Technology Stocks

First, Enron used derivatives to hide hundreds of millions of dollars of losses on its speculative investments in various technology-oriented firms, such as Rhythms Net Connections, Inc., a start-up telecommunications company.[24] Through a subsidiary, Enron invested $10 million in Rhythms NetConnections, an Internet service provider and potential competitor of Netscape, the company whose initial public offering (IPO) had marked the beginning of the Internet boom in 1995.[25] Enron bought shares of Rhythms NetConnections at less than $2 per share.[26]

Rhythms NetConnections issued stock to the public in an initial public offering on April 6, 1999, during the heyday of the Internet boom, at $21 per share; by the end of the day, the shares were trading at $69 per share.[27] Enron suddenly had a $300 million gain. Enron's other venture capital investments in technology companies also increased in value at first, alongside the widespread run-up in the value of dot-com stocks. As was typical in IPOs, Enron was prohibited from selling its stock for six months.[28] Because these stocks were carried in Enron's "merchant portfolio," changes in the value of the positions resulted in volatility on its balance sheet, and unwanted gains and losses on its income statement.

Enron engaged in a series of derivatives transactions designed to reduce this volatility and lock in its profits, as well as to capture the value of futures contracts on its own stock. Specifically, Enron entered into a series of transactions with an SPE, LJM Swap Sub L.P., which was owned by another SPE, LJM1. In those transactions Enron essentially exchanged its shares in Rhythms NetConnections for a loan, ultimately, from LJM1.[29] These deals were structured as derivatives instead of as loans or sales, because Enron would have been required to record a loan as debt and would have been required to pay tax on a sale (and prior to six months from the IPO date, would not

markets and they offer numerous economic benefits, including non-recourse financing, separation of financial risks and creation of new markets. For example, credit card and mortgage payments frequently flow through SPEs, and financial services firms typically use such entities as well. *See generally* STEVEN L. SCHWARCZ, STRUCTURED FINANCE: A GUIDE TO THE PRINCIPLES OF ASSET SECURITIZATION (3d ed. 2002).

[23] These derivatives included price swap derivatives, as well as call and put options.

[24] *Special Report*, *supra* note 8, at 77.

[25] *See id.*

[26] *See id.*

[27] *See id.*

[28] *See id.* This provision was known as a "lock-up."

[29] *See id.* at 78-79.

have had the right to sell, because of the lock-up provision). A derivatives deal did not incur such regulatory consequences.

Enron's transactions with another group of SPEs, the Raptors, worked in a similar fashion. Enron attempted to minimize the appearance of losses in its investments in technology companies by creating SPEs as "accounting hedges."[30] The critical element in this strategy was a series of derivatives transactions between Enron and the Raptors.

In three of the Raptors, Enron funded the SPE by giving it contingent derivatives based on restricted stock and stock contracts at below market value, in exchange for a promissory note.[31] Most of the derivatives transactions that followed, essentially put options on Enron's stock, allowed the Raptors to keep any increases in value of the technology stocks, but required them to pay Enron the amount of any future losses.[32] Because the Raptors' assets consisted almost entirely of Enron stock, the more the value of the technology stocks declined, the more Enron stock would need to be sold to meet their obligations.[33] As more Enron stock was sold to meet the obligations related to the derivatives contracts, the Raptors would have less money available to repay the promissory note to Enron.[34]

As a result, Enron continued to bear the economic risk in the transactions.[35] The performance of the underlying technology investments was irrelevant to the other investors in the Raptors because they were guaranteed a return.[36] Enron recognized a gain on the technology stocks by recognizing the value of the Raptor loans right away, and it avoided recognizing on an interim basis any future losses on the technology stocks, were such losses to occur (which, of course, they did).[37]

In all, Enron had derivative instruments on 54.8 million shares of Enron common stock at an average price of $67.92 per share, or $3.7 billion total— all publicly disclosed in Enron's 2000 annual report.[38] In other words, at the start of these deals, Enron's derivatives obligations amounted to seven percent of all of its outstanding shares. As Enron's share price declined, that obligation increased and Enron's shareholders were substantially diluted. Yet even as the Raptors' assets and Enron's shares declined in value, Enron did not reflect those declines in its financial statements because its derivatives transactions fell outside rules that required Enron to record such losses.

---

[30] *See id.* at 97.

[31] *See id.* at 97-98.

[32] *See id.* at 107-08.

[33] See *id.* at 97.

[34] *See id.* at 97-98, 110-11.

[35] *See id.* at 97.

[36] *See id.* at 103-04.

[37] *See id.* at 97.

[38] Enron 2000 Annual Report 2, 44 n.11 (2001), *available at* http:// www.enron.com/corp/investors/annuals/2000/ar2000.pdf (last visited Mar. 21, 2003) [hereinafter Annual Report] (Enron's 2000 Annual Report to Shareholders).

2. Using Derivatives to Hide Debt

A second example involved Enron using derivatives with SPEs to hide debt incurred to finance new businesses. Essentially, some very complicated and unclear accounting rules allowed Enron to avoid disclosing certain assets and liabilities.

Two of these SPEs were Joint Energy Development Investments Limited Partnership (JEDI) and Chewco Investments, L.P. (Chewco). Enron owned only fifty percent of JEDI and, therefore, under applicable accounting rules, could (and did) report JEDI as an unconsolidated equity affiliate. If Enron had owned fifty-one percent of JEDI, accounting rules would have required Enron to consolidate all of JEDI's financial results in its financial statements.[39]

One way to minimize the applicability of this rule would be for Enron to create an SPE with mostly debt and only a tiny sliver of equity, say, $1 worth, for which the company easily could find an outside investor. One might expect to find a pronouncement by accounting regulators that such a transaction would not conform to Generally Acceptable Accounting Principles (GAAP). However, there was no such pronouncement. The Financial Accounting Standards Board, the private entity that set most accounting rules and advises the SEC, had not answered the accounting question of what would constitute sufficient capital from an independent source, so that an SPE would not need to be consolidated.[40]

Instead, beginning in 1982, Financial Accounting Standard (FAS) No. 57, Related Party Disclosures, contained a general requirement that companies disclose the nature of relationships they had with related parties and describe transactions with them.[41] In 1991, the Acting Chief Accountant of the SEC attempted to clarify this requirement in a guidance letter issued in the context of leases.[42]

---

[39] JEDI, in turn, was subject to the same rules. JEDI could issue equity and debt securities, and as long as there was an outside investor with at least fifty percent of the equity—in other words, with real economic exposure to the risks of Chewco—JEDI would not need to consolidate Chewco.

[40] Nor are other derivatives-related accounting rules very helpful. In 1998, FASB adopted FAS No. 133, which included new accounting rules for derivatives. ACCOUNTING FOR DERIVATIVES INSTRUMENTS AND HEDGING ACTIVITIES, Statement of Financial Accounting Standards No. 133, *supra* note 17. Now at 800-plus pages, FAS 133's instructions are an incredibly detailed set of rules, describing particularized instances when derivatives need not be disclosed, but do not answer the question of what would constitute sufficient outside capital.

[41] RELATED PARTY DISCLOSURES, Statement of Financial Accounting Standards No. 57 (Fin. Accounting Standards Bd. 1982). Enron's footnote disclosure arguably satisfied the letter of FAS 57, although the disclosures were neither clear nor forthcoming.

[42] This letter stated:

> The initial substantive residual equity investment should be comparable to that expected for a substantive business involved in similar [leasing] transactions with similar risks and rewards. The SEC staff understands from discussions with Working Group members that those members believe that 3 percent is the minimum acceptable investment. The SEC staff believes a greater investment may be necessary depending on the facts and circumstances, including the credit risk associated with the lessee and the market risk factors associated with the leased property.

Based on this letter, and on opinions from auditors and lawyers, companies began incurring off-balance sheet debt through unconsolidated SPEs where (1) the company did not have more than fifty percent of the equity of the SPE, and (2) the equity of the SPE was at least three percent of the total capital.[43] Under these rules, Enron would have been able to borrow ninety-seven percent of the capital of its SPEs without consolidating that debt on its balance sheet.

Because Enron could not find a truly independent investor to provide three percent equity, it entered into a derivatives transaction with Chewco similar to the one it entered into with the Raptors. However, it structured the transaction as a swap, effectively guaranteeing repayment to Chewco's outside investor. (Consequently, the investor's sliver of equity ownership in Chewco was not really equity from an economic perspective, because the investor had nothing—other than Enron's credit—at risk.) In its financial statements, Enron took the position that although it provided guarantees to unconsolidated subsidiaries, those guarantees did not have a readily determinable fair value, and management did not consider it reasonably likely that Enron would be required to perform or otherwise incur losses associated with these guarantees.[44] That position enabled Enron to avoid recording the guarantees.[45]

The effect of the derivatives transaction was that Enron—not the "investor" in Chewco—had the economic exposure to Chewco's assets. Ultimately, the ownership daisy chain unraveled once Enron was deemed to own Chewco. Then JEDI was forced to consolidate Chewco, and Enron was forced to consolidate both limited partnerships—and all of their losses—in its financial statements.[46]

Nearly a year before this unraveling, Enron disclosed some of the information related to these transactions in its public filings. In its 2000 annual report, Enron disclosed about $2.1 billion of such derivatives transactions with related entities, and recognized gains of about $500 million related to those transactions.[47] A few sophisticated analysts seemed to understand Enron's transactions based on that disclosure, and they bet against Enron's stock.[48] Other securities analysts either did not understand (or read) the disclosures, or chose not to speak, perhaps because of conflicts of interest related to Enron's substantial banking business.

See Partnoy, Testimony, *supra* note 2; *see also* Bratton, *supra* note 7, at 1306 n.118 (describing GAAP authorities for the letter).

[43] This provision was generally referred to as the "three percent rule."

[44] Annual Report, *supra* note 38, at 39 n.3, 48 n.15.

[45] Even the guarantees listed in the footnotes to Enron's financial statements were recorded at only ten percent of their nominal value. *Id.* at 48 n.15.

[46] *See Special Report*, *supra* note 8, at 2-3, 42 (describing circumstances surrounding consolidation of Chewco, and subsequent financial impact on Enron's financial statements).

[47] Annual Report, *supra* note 38, at 48 n.16.

[48] *See* Richard W. Stevenson & Jeff Gerth, *Enron's Collapse: The System; Web of Safeguards Failed as Enron Fell*, N.Y. TIMES, Jan. 20, 2002, at A1.

In sum, Enron did numerous derivatives deals with its SPEs, thereby enabling it to inflate income, avoid losses, and hide debt. Enron at least partially disclosed many of the relevant material facts about these deals. To the extent these SPEs are relevant to the debate about Enron, it is the derivatives deals with those SPEs—the put options and contingent contracts with the Raptors and the swaps related to JEDI and Chewco—that are of greatest importance.

B. Other Derivatives Use

Not only is the "conventional story" about Enron and the SPEs suspect—in that derivatives were the key to the SPEs—but the SPEs were not especially important to Enron's collapse. Instead, it was derivatives and off-balance sheet transactions other than those involved in the SPEs that were of primary importance. Issues related to those deals should be the focus of academic and regulatory inquiry into Enron's collapse.

If the SPEs, even with the derivatives deals, were not significant to Enron's publicly reported financial statements, then why did Enron collapse? One possible explanation is that investors simply lost confidence in the company and rushed to sell their shares, no longer trusting Enron's financial statements. However, this explanation ignores the role of sophisticated investors who closely followed Enron and were willing to buy the company's stock when they perceived it to be undervalued. Enron's officers had several months after analysts began questioning the firm's SPEs in which to disclose additional information showing that the company was in reasonable financial condition. Yet Enron's stock price declined steadily throughout 2001, and the most significant short-term declines were not based on new negative information.[49]

Instead, a more plausible reason for the decline in the value of Enron's stock was that Enron had engaged in numerous other derivatives deals to inflate reported profits, to reduce reported debt and to make it appear that Enron was sufficiently creditworthy to justify the investment grade credit rating necessary to sustain its derivatives trading business. As it became more likely that the credit rating agencies would downgrade Enron to sub-investment grade, Enron's stock price fell. The largest single-day decline was the day the credit rating agencies finally confirmed the downgrade, when shareholders learned that Enron's access to capital would become too limited and costly to sustain its derivatives trading operation.

As with the SPE transactions, a complete description of Enron's other derivatives is well beyond the scope of this Article.[50] Instead, this section will briefly analyze Enron's

---

[49] *See* FRANK PARTNOY, INFECTIOUS GREED: HOW DECEIT AND RISK CORRUPTED THE FINANCIAL MARKETS 330-41 (2003).

[50] Enron's bankruptcy examiner has written hundreds of pages detailing how Enron used derivatives to borrow money without recording debt on its balance sheet. *See* BATSON, *supra* note 2. Enron used two strategies—end-of-year deals and prepaid swaps—to inflate reported profits and reduce reported debt, again within the parameters of a rules-based regulatory approach to accounting and disclosure. For example, in December 1999, Enron "sold" an interest in some Nigerian barges mounted with electricity generators to Merrill Lynch, which agreed to "buy" Enron's interest in the barge after Enron CFO Andy Fastow orally

use of derivatives other than in transactions with SPEs. First, Enron's financial statements disclosed extensive use of derivatives, although the disclosures were not especially useful because they did not go beyond disclosures required by rule. Second, there is evidence that Enron's profits were due primarily to derivatives trading. Enron did not disclose the contingent risks associated with its trading businesses, but SEC disclosure rules arguably did not require such disclosure.

Even accounting for the effect of the previously discussed SPEs, as reflected in Enron's restated financials in November 2001, Enron was in strong financial condition. Its net income, even as restated, had been positive and increasing since 1993.[51] Enron's last years were especially profitable, and the company's net income for 2000, even as restated, was nearly a billion dollars.[52]

Likewise, the balance sheet value of Enron's equity was positive and increasing throughout this period. In 2000, even as restated, Enron's equity was recorded at more than $10 billion.[53] Compared to its reported equity, Enron's reported debt was at reasonable levels; even as restated, Enron's debt-equity ratio was roughly 1.0 during 1999 and 2000, and had declined substantially since 1997.[54]

Enron's bankruptcy examiner concluded that Enron's actual debt was more than double the amount reported in its financial statements.[55] Such high debt levels likely would not have warranted an investment grade rating, given Enron's capital structure and financial performance. But neither should such high debt levels have been a surprise to anyone who closely examined Enron's financial statements. Enron's 2000 annual report alone makes it clear that Enron had incurred substantial additional leverage and had significantly increased its risk exposure in various derivatives markets.

First, even a cursory examination of Enron's balance sheet reveals remarkable disclosures of Enron's new derivatives deals, cleverly labeled "price risk management activities."[56] For 2000, Enron reported price risk management activities as its most significant asset ($12.0 billion, up from $2.2 billion in 1999).[57] Enron also reported price risk management activities as its most significant liability ($10.5 billion, up from

promised that by June 2000 Enron would "make sure Merrill Lynch was relieved of its interest." Richard A. Oppel Jr., *U.S. Studying Merrill Lynch in Enron Deal*, N.Y. TIMES, July 27, 2002, at C1 (quoting Enron executive Alan Quaintance, Jr.). This year-end deal was designed to enable Enron to recognize a profit during 1999. Enron also did $8 billion of "prepaid swaps" with J.P. Morgan Chase and Citigroup. These prepaid swaps were loans from an economic perspective, but Enron recorded the loan proceeds as cash flow from operations, based on accounting rules. *See* Richard A. Oppel Jr. & Kurt Eichenwald, *Citigroup Is Linked to a Deal that Let Enron Skirt Rules*, N.Y. TIMES, July 23, 2002, at C4.

51 *See* Enron Corp., Form 10-Ks, 1993-2001.

52 *See* Enron Corp. Form 8-K, Special Report, *supra* note 8, at 4.

53 *See id.*

54 *See id.*

55 *See* BATSON, *supra* note 2.

56 *See* Annual Report, *supra* note 38, at 36 (describing accounting for "price risk management activities" as including forwards, swaps, options and energy transportation contracts).

57 *See id.* at 32 (discussing assets from price risk management activities).

$1.8 billion in 1999).[58] Since the previous year, derivatives assets and liabilities had increased more than five-fold.

The same conclusions are apparent from Enron's income statement, which reports $7.2 billion of "other revenues"[59] and explains, in a footnote, that "other revenues" consists of unrealized (i.e., "mark-to-market") gains on price risk management activities (i.e., derivatives trading).[60] In aggregate, Enron's revenues and expenses each tripled from 1998 to 2000.[61] But Enron's net income increased only marginally during the same period; by 2000, net income was less than one percent of total revenues.[62]

Enron's non-derivatives businesses were not performing well in 1998 and were deteriorating through 2000. Enron's non-derivatives businesses made some money in 1998, broke even in 1999 and lost money in 2000.[63] Enron officials represented that it was not a trading firm, and that derivatives were used primarily for hedging purposes, and Enron's stock traded at much higher multiples of earnings than other trading-oriented firms. But Enron's financial statements did not support such representations.

Accounting regulations did not require additional disclosure related to derivatives in Enron's financial statements. Instead, specific rules suggested tabular disclosure of various types in footnotes to financial statements. Enron included tabular disclosure of its price risk management activities in terms of notional amount, fair value, and counterparty risk.[64] But Enron did not include in the footnotes to its financial statements a description of possible contingencies related to its price risk management activities.

---

[58] *See id.* at 33 (discussing liabilities from price risk management activities). Much of the growth in both assets and liabilities was due to increased trading through EnronOnline, Enron's internet-based trading platform. EnronOnline's assets and revenues were qualitatively different from Enron's other derivatives trading. Whereas Enron's derivatives operations included speculative positions in various contracts, much of EnronOnline's operations purported to match buyers and sellers. Accordingly, a portion of the "revenues" associated with EnronOnline arguably did not belong in Enron's financial statements. But even without these additions, Enron's liabilities from derivatives trading were substantial and increasing.

[59] *See id.* at 31 ("Revenues, other" category). Interestingly, Enron reported notional amounts of derivatives contracts as of December 31, 2000, of $21.6 billion. *Id.* at 38 (listing total of columns "Fixed Price Payor, Notional Amounts" and "Terms"). Either Enron was generating thirty-three percent annual returns from derivatives (indicating that the underlying contracts were very risky), or Enron actually had much larger positions and somehow reduced the notional values of its outstanding derivatives contracts at year-end for reporting purposes. Enron's financial statements do not explain this issue.

[60] *See id.* at 36 ("Unrealized gains and losses from newly originated contracts, contract restructurings and the impact of price movements are recognized as 'other revenues.'"); *see also* Baird & Rasmussen, *supra* note 7, at 1801-02 (describing Enron's substantial trading activities).

[61] *See* Annual Report, *supra* note 38, at 31. Enron's gains from price risk management activities from 1998 to 2000 ($16 billion) were roughly comparable to the annual net revenue for all trading activities (including stocks, bonds and derivatives) at the investment firm, Goldman Sachs & Co., during the same periods, a time in which Goldman Sachs first issued shares to the public. *See* Partnoy, Testimony, *supra* note 2.

[62] *See* Annual Report, *supra* note 38. Enron's consolidated statement of cash flows similarly reflected the importance of price risk management activities. *See id.* at 34.

[63] *See* Partnoy, Testimony, *supra* note 2.

[64] *See* Annual Report, *supra* note 38, at 38-39.

Instead, Enron included some information about such contingencies in the Management's Discussion and Analysis, section of its annual report, where it disclosed in tabular form—as suggested by SEC rule—a range of "value at risk" (VAR) estimates related to its derivatives risk exposure. Enron's VAR methodologies captured a ninety-five percent confidence interval for a one-day holding period, and therefore did not cover worst-case scenarios for Enron's trading operations.[65] Nevertheless, Enron's disclosure arguably satisfied SEC rules, which permitted companies to comply with existing risk disclosure requirements by reporting such VAR estimates.

Enron reported high and low month-end values for its trading, but not interim values or averages, and therefore had incentives to smooth its profits and losses at month-end.[66] Enron did not report its maximum VAR during the year, or give qualitative information about worst-case scenarios, and therefore did not report how much risk its traders were taking.

Even so, Enron's reported VAR figures were remarkable. In 2000, Enron reported VAR for what it called "commodity price" risk—which included natural gas derivatives trading—of $66 million, more than triple its 1999 value.[67] Enron reported VAR for equity trading of $59 million, more than double the 1999 value.[68] A VAR of $66 million meant that Enron expected, based on historical averages, that on five percent of all trading days (on average, twelve business days during the year) its commodity derivatives trading operations would gain or lose $66 million. Enron's highest end-of-month commodity price risk VAR estimate was $81 million (almost ten percent of Enron's reported net income for 2000).[69] These VAR estimates were higher than virtually any other company, including other trading firms.

Because Enron's derivatives frequently had long maturities—maximum terms ranged from six to twenty-nine years[70]—there often were not prices from liquid markets to use as benchmarks in valuing and assessing the derivatives. For those long-dated derivatives, professional judgment was important to valuation. For a simple instrument, Enron might calculate the discounted present value of cash flows using Enron's borrowing rates. But more complex instruments required more complex methodologies. For example, Enron completed over five thousand weather derivatives deals, with a notional value of more than $4.5 billion,[71] and many of those deals could not be valued without professional judgment. Enron disclosed that it relied on "the professional judgment of experienced business and risk managers" in assessing worst-case scenarios not covered

---

[65] *See id.* at 28.

[66] *Id.*

[67] *Id.*

[68] *Id.*

[69] *Id.*

[70] *Id.* at 38.

[71] *Id.* at 39.

by its VAR methodologies.[72] But Enron did not report any qualitative information about worst-case scenarios, nor did regulations require that it do so.

Moreover, there is substantial evidence that Enron's VAR disclosures underestimated the firm's derivatives risks because they were based on inaccurate internal estimates of the variables used to value its derivatives.[73] Enron's derivatives traders faced intense pressure to meet quarterly earnings targets imposed directly by management and indirectly by securities analysts who covered Enron. To ensure that Enron met these estimates, some traders manipulated the reporting of their "real" economic profits and losses in an attempt to fit the "imagined" accounting profits and losses reflected in Enron's financial statements. First, traders smoothed income using "prudency" reserves, dummy accounts that led to false profit and loss entries for the derivatives Enron traded.[74] Second, traders mismarked the forward curves used to determine the current value of derivatives trades.[75] Both methods reduced the apparent volatility of Enron's trading businesses, making Enron's derivatives trading appear less risky.

---

[72] *Id.* at 38.

[73] Consider the following statement in Enron's 2000 Annual Report: "In 2000, the value at risk model utilized for equity trading market risk was refined to more closely correlate with the valuation methodologies used for merchant activities." *Id.* at 28. Enron's financial statements do not describe these refinements, and their effects, but given the recent failure of the risk and valuation models at other firms, including Long-Term Capital Management, there should have been reason for concern when Enron referred to "refining" its own models.

[74] *See generally* PARTNOY, *supra* note 49, Chapter 10; *see also* Partnoy, Testimony, *supra* note 2 (describing use of prudency reserves). Enron's derivatives traders kept records of their profits and losses. For each trade, a trader would report either a profit or a loss, typically in spreadsheet format. Instead of recording the entire profit for a trade in one column, some traders split the profit from a trade into two columns. The first column reflected the portion of the actual profits the trader intended to add to Enron's current financial statements. The second column, labeled the "prudency" reserve, included the remainder.

To understand this concept of a "prudency" reserve, suppose a derivatives trader earned a profit of $10 million. Of that $10 million, the trader might record $9 million as profit today, and enter $1 million into "prudency." An average deal would have "prudency" of up to $1 million, and all of the "prudency" entries might add up to $10 to $15 million. The portion of profits recorded as "prudency" could be used to offset any future losses. "Prudency" reserves were especially effective for long-maturity derivatives contracts, because it was more difficult to determine a precise valuation as of a particular date for those contracts, and any "prudency" cushion would have protected the traders from future losses for several years going forward. In sum, "prudency" reserves smoothed Enron's trading profits and losses, thereby reducing apparent volatility.

[75] *See generally* PARTNOY, *supra* note 49, Chapter 10. A forward curve is a list of "forward rates" for a range of maturities. In simple terms, a forward rate is the rate at which a person can buy something in the future. For example, natural gas forward contracts trade on the New York Mercantile Exchange (NYMEX). A trader can commit to buy a particular type of natural gas to be delivered in a few weeks, months or even years. The rate at which a trader can buy natural gas in one year is the one-year forward rate. The rate at which a trader can buy natural gas in ten years is the ten-year forward rate. The forward curve for a particular natural gas contract is simply the list of forward rates for all maturities.

Forward curves are used to determine the value of a derivatives contract today. Like any firm involved in trading derivatives, Enron had risk management and valuation systems that used forward curves to generate profit and loss statements. However, some Enron traders selectively mismarked their forward

If Enron had been making money in what it represented as its core businesses, its substantial derivatives risks should not have been so important. Even after Enron restated its financial statements on November 8, 2001, it could have clarified its accounting treatment, consolidated its debt and assured analysts and investors that it was a viable ongoing concern. But it could not. Why not?

The answer requires a revision of the conventional view of Enron's collapse. What Enron represented as its core business was not making money, even as Enron's stock price was rising during the late 1990s. Recall that Enron began as an energy firm. Over time, Enron shifted its focus from the bricks-and-mortar energy business to the trading of derivatives. As this shift occurred, some of Enron's employees began misrepresenting the profits and losses of Enron's derivatives trading operations. Enron's derivatives trading was profitable, but was much more volatile than it appeared based on Enron's financial reports. Although Enron was a bricks-and-mortar company when it was created in 1985, by the end it had become primarily a derivatives trading firm, dependent on access to low-cost capital (and, therefore, on its own investment grade credit rating).

Enron's trading operations were not regulated by U.S. securities or commodities regulators, and the over-the-counter (OTC) derivatives it traded fell outside the scope of U.S. securities law. OTC derivatives trading also was beyond the reach of organized, regulated exchanges. Thus, Enron—like many firms that trade OTC derivatives—fell into a regulatory black hole.[76] The absence of regulation might not have mattered if investors had been aware of the firm's risks. But Enron's key gatekeepers[77]—including the

---

curves, typically in order to hide losses. (Traders are compensated based on their profits, so if a trader can hide losses by mismarking forward curves, he or she is likely to receive a larger bonus.) These losses ranged in the tens of millions of dollars for certain markets. For more complex deals, a trader would use a spreadsheet model of the trade for valuation purposes and tweak the assumptions in the model to make a transaction appear more or less valuable.

Certain derivatives contracts were more susceptible to mismarking than others. Traders typically would not mismark contracts that were publicly traded—such as the natural gas contracts traded on NYMEX—because quotations of the values of those contracts would be publicly available. However, because the NYMEX forward curve has a maturity of only six years, a trader would be more likely to mismark a ten-year natural gas forward rate. At Enron, forward curves remained mismarked for as long as three years. From a disclosure perspective, such a strategy would have had a similar effect to the use of prudency reserves.

[76] The Commodity Futures Trading Commission began considering whether to regulate OTC derivatives in 1997, but its proposals were rejected, and in December 2000, Congress made the deregulated status of derivatives clear when it passed the Commodity Futures Modernization Act. As a result, during its final year, Enron operated in a largely unregulated market. Commodity Futures Modernization Act, S. 2697, 106th Cong. (2000); H.R. 4541, 106th Cong. (2000). *See also* Michael Schroeder, *Lugar in Senate Charges CFTC, SEC Impede Bill to Deregulate Derivatives*, WALL ST. J., June 22, 2000, at C26 (describing legal and regulatory uncertainty and legislation proposed to reduce it).

[77] *See generally* Coffee, *Understanding Enron: "It's About the Gatekeepers, Stupid," supra* note 7. Commentators also have blamed Arthur Andersen, Enron's auditor, although they have not directly addressed the accountants' role in disclosures related to Enron's derivatives. Arthur Andersen was responsible not only for auditing Enron's financial statements, but also for assessing Enron management's internal controls on derivatives trading. When Arthur Andersen signed Enron's 2000 annual report, it expressed approval in general terms of Enron's system of internal controls during 1998 through 2000. *See* Annual Report,

major credit rating agencies—either failed to spot the numerous risk disclosures related to Enron's derivatives trading, or spotted these disclosures but did not respond.

In sum, the story of Enron's collapse is not what at first appears. The firm was a highly-leveraged derivatives trading firm and it collapsed when its credit rating finally reflected that fact. The scholarly and regulatory response to Enron's collapse should reflect this understanding. Given this revised view, the next section assesses the specific regulatory response to Enron's failure to disclose more information about its use of derivatives.

III. THE REGULATORY RESPONSE TO ENRON'S USE OF DERIVATIVES

What lessons can be drawn from Enron's collapse about the type of regulation that should govern derivatives disclosure? Specifically, should regulation be weighted toward rules or standards,[78] and at what level of required disclosure should any rules or standards be aimed?

Securities regulation—like most regulation—generally is a combination of blended rules-standards with some "rules" (e.g., various types of tabular form disclosure) and some "standards" (e.g., the "reasonably likely" threshold for MD&A), with varying levels of required disclosure, depending on the type of information. Congress, the SEC, and international regulators have suggested that the weighting should be toward standards, yet disclosure regulation in practice—particularly as it relates to derivatives—has been highly rules-based. Recently, Congress and the SEC have disagreed about the appropriate level of disclosure.

This section concludes that Enron's collapse was strong evidence of the substantial inefficiencies associated with a rules-based disclosure regime, specifically rules based on accounting reality rather than economic reality. It further suggests that the SEC should move, as Congress expressly intended in passing Section 401(a) of Sarbanes-Oxley, toward a standards-based regime designed to capture more disclosure of financial contingencies related to derivatives.

A. Market-Based Responses

The analysis of derivatives disclosure in MD&A raises, in a specific context, the question scholars have asked for decades—whether regulators should mandate disclosure at

supra note 38, at 30. Yet it does not appear that Arthur Andersen systematically and independently verified Enron's valuations of certain complex trades, or even of its forward curves. *See* Partnoy, *supra* note 49, Chapter 10. Arthur Andersen apparently examined day-to-day changes in these values, as reported by traders, and checked to see if each daily change was recorded accurately. But Andersen only sporadically checked Enron's forward curves and did not confirm that the values Enron had recorded reflected fair market values. *See id.*

[78] As a general matter, rules are formal or mechanical and depend on uncontested facts, whereas standards are flexible and depend on context.

all. Enron's derivatives disclosure practices are a challenging example for the theoretical literature on mandatory disclosure.[79]

One possible regulatory response to Enron's collapse is no response at all. According to the argument supporting this approach, market participants, post-Enron, will pressure companies to disclose relevant facts about their financial contingencies, including derivatives risks, and companies that do not make demanded disclosures will suffer a higher cost of capital and lower share valuation. For example, Larry Ribstein has argued that the markets will correct Enron-related problems, because investors and analysts now will understand where and how to look for the relevant information, and companies will have a model to follow in deciding how much to disclose.[80]

However, if the argument of Section II of this Article is correct—and many market participants have fundamentally misunderstood Enron's collapse, even more than a year after the company's bankruptcy—it seems unlikely that the same people will have the ability to assess, and therefore have the incentives to demand, appropriate and relevant information. Moreover, given the pace of financial innovation, even sophisticated financial analysts are unlikely to know precisely which questions to ask, or to be able to determine whether an answer is accurate or complete.[81] Perhaps most importantly, restrictions on shorting stock create asymmetric incentives, because sophisticated investors can easily buy shares to profit from positive information not reflected in market prices, but find it more difficult and costly to sell shares to profit from negative information.[82]

Moreover, pre-Enron market failures are likely to continue if certain structural conditions in the market persist. First, disclosure related to derivatives positions is

---

[79] The early assessments of the effects of mandatory disclosure did not consider the disclosure of complex financial contingencies. *See* George J. Benston, *Required Disclosure and the Stock Market: An Evaluation of the Securities Exchange Act of 1934*, 63 AM. ECON. REV. 132, 144-45 (1973); Irwin Friend & Randolph Westerfield, *Required Disclosure and the Stock Market: Comment*, 65 AM. ECON. REV. 467, 471 (1975); Gregg A. Jarrell, *The Economic Effects of Federal Regulation of the Market for New Securities Issues*, 24 J.L. & ECON. 613, 615-21 (1981); Joel Seligman, *The Historical Need for a Mandatory Corporate Disclosure System*, 9 J. CORP. L. 1, 2 (1983); George J. Stigler, *Public Regulation of Securities Markets*, 37 J. BUS. 117, 120-24 (1964).

[80] *See* Ribstein, *supra* note 7, at 43-53.

[81] For example, analysts have admitted that they are incapable of deciphering derivatives disclosures. In response to a question raised at an International Swaps and Derivatives Association conference, Ethan M. Heisler, a Vice President at Salomon Brothers, expressed skepticism that even sophisticated securities analysts could draw anything of value out of financial disclosures about derivatives: "[S]how me an equity analyst who has taken the disclosures that you currently have on derivatives and made any kind of meaningful use out of those disclosures. I would challenge you to find it. I have never seen it." *Derivatives Accounting Disclosure and Market Surveillance,* International Swaps and Derivatives Association Conference 7 (Sept. 25, 1996). Steven Schwarcz has suggested a related point: that some transactions may be so complex that they simply cannot effectively be disclosed. *See* Schwarcz, *Rethinking the Disclosure Paradigm in a World of Complexity, supra* note 7.

[82] *See* Andrei Shleifer & Robert Vishny, *The Limits of Arbitrage*, 52 J. FIN. 35, 42 (1997); Charles M. Jones & Owen A. Lamont, *Short Sale Constraints and Stock Returns*, CRSP Working Paper No. 533 (2001), *available at* http://www.ssrn.com.

costly, and those costs are not reduced by the collapse of Enron; indeed, the cost of derivatives disclosure is greater if market participants are more concerned about such disclosures. Second, it is not necessarily easier for market participants to assess derivatives disclosure (or non-disclosure) post-Enron; they have similar technological capacity and access to information.[83] Moreover, the gap between what managers know and what shareholders understand[84] could persist if both issuers and investors become more sophisticated. Third, the collective action problems associated with a diffuse investor base have not changed. Any individual investor, even a large sophisticated one (such as a hedge fund), will not be able to appropriate much of the gains from investigating a firm's derivatives risks. Fourth, the regulatory exemptions applicable to certain types of derivatives (e.g., the Commodity Futures Modernization Act[85]) and the limited disclosure requirements associated with accounting pronouncements related to derivatives (e.g., FAS 133) will continue to permit companies to avoid disclosure even in the face of market pressure. There has not been much pressure since Enron's collapse to reverse the CFMA exemptions for OTC derivatives or otherwise to create regulations with incentives for companies to disclose more information about their use of complex financial instruments.[86]

In sum, if the benefits and costs of disclosure pre- and post-Enron's collapse are similar, disclosure practices—and the effects of those practices—are likely to be similar. Consider the question of whether Enron's managers would make different disclosure decisions regarding derivatives today. According to SEC rules, Enron's managers were required to decide whether it was "reasonably likely" that a particular contingency would occur. Given the volatility in the markets where Enron participated, would managers choose to disclose the potential losses associated with a particular market change? Under a rules-based system, where the SEC specifically provides guidance regarding the kind of tabular disclosure that will satisfy its disclosure requirements, managers would be likely to make precisely those disclosures. If other companies were making such disclosures—and only such disclosures—managers of any given company would have a disincentive to make additional disclosures. Moreover, the most important contingencies would not definitively be described as "reasonably likely."

Tabular disclosure of the type suggested by SEC rules is unlikely to be useful, either to individual investors or securities analysts, and therefore is unlikely to promote price transparency and accuracy. Tabular disclosure is both complex and inevitably outdated, given the rapid pace of financial innovation.

---

[83] For example, Regulation Fair Disclosure ("Reg FD")—which requires managers to disclose non-public information publicly (and simultaneously)—remains in effect. *See* 17 C.F.R. § 243.100-243.103 (2001).

[84] Much of this information was publicly available in early 2001. *See, e.g.,* Bethany McLean, *Is Enron Overpriced?,* Fortune, Mar. 5, 2001, at 122 (questioning Enron's high stock valuation based on public disclosures).

[85] Commodity Futures Modernization Act of 2000, Pub. L. No. 106-554, 114 Stat. 2763.

[86] Indeed, the pressure from various market participants has been in the opposite direction.

Rules-based tabular disclosure would improve market efficiency if analysts found the information useful in evaluating companies. Unfortunately, rules-based tabular disclosure is quickly outdated and does not include enough information to enable even the most sophisticated securities analysts to assess the risks associated with a company's complex financial contingencies. The evidence supporting this conclusion is merely anecdotal, but is consistent with the well-established theory that financial market innovation is designed to avoid legal rules and outpace regulation.[87]

Congress recognized the potential for market failure in this area and accordingly provided in Section 401(a) of Sarbanes-Oxley that a broad-based standard would apply to issuer disclosures related to off-balance transactions, derivatives, and other contingent financial contracts. Specifically, Section 401(a) provided that the SEC must promulgate rules requiring issuers to file quarterly and annual reports disclosing

> all material off-balance sheet transactions, arrangements, obligations (including contingent obligations), and other relationships of the issuer with unconsolidated entities or other persons, that may have a material current or future effect on financial condition, changes in financial condition, results of operations, liquidity, capital expenditures, capital resources, or significant components of revenues or expenses.[88]

Before assessing the regulations promulgated by the SEC pursuant to Section 401(a), it is useful to place this legislation in context, among the regulatory apparatus governing disclosure of financial contingencies. The theory supporting these regulations is inconsistent with the notion that market pressure alone will create incentives for companies to make adequate disclosures, and that market participants will be able to decipher those disclosures. Instead, Item 303(a) of Regulation S-K identifies a basic and overriding requirement of MD&A to "provide such other information that the registrant believes to be necessary to an understanding of its financial condition, changes in financial condition and results of operations."[89]

The SEC long has recognized the importance of a narrative discussion in MD&A, and, prior to Sarbanes-Oxley, MD&A regulations reflected a standard of "reasonably likely to have a material effect."[90] In 1987, the SEC noted that:

> numerical presentations and brief accompanying footnotes alone may be insufficient for an investor to judge the quality of earnings and the likeli-

---

[87] *See* Miller, *supra* note 3, at 460.

[88] Pub. L. No. 107-204, § 401(a), 116 Stat. 745 (2002) (emphasis added).

[89] Regulation S-K, Item 303(a).

[90] *See, e.g.*, Notice of Revision of Proposed Amendment to Guide 22 of the Guides for Preparation and Filing of Registration Statements under the Securities Act of 1933 and Revision of Proposed Adoption of Guide 1 to the Guides for Preparation and Filing of Reports and Registration Statements under the Securities Exchange Act of 1934, Securities Act Release No. 33-5443, 39 Fed. Reg. 829 (Dec. 12, 1973).

> hood that past performance is indicative of future performance. MD&A is intended to give the investor an opportunity to look at the company through the eyes of management by providing both a short and long-term analysis of the business of the company.[91]

In other words, the SEC recognized the power and importance of narrative in supplying investors and analysts with information and analysis they otherwise might not receive, and the SEC endorsed the benefits of a disclosure regime that was weighted more to standards than rules. The theory was that narrative disclosure would be important and useful both because it is more accessible to investors and analysts, and therefore is more likely to be reflected in market prices. The theory also suggested that narrative disclosure would be more likely to reflect accurately management's assessment of their company's future earnings—the key information in most financial valuation models—than numerical or tabular information.

In 1989, the SEC began requiring that managers make specific disclosures of financial contingencies and off-balance sheet arrangements when a particular "trend, demand, commitment, event or uncertainty" was "reasonably likely."[92] If management determined that the contingency was not reasonably likely to occur, no disclosure was required.[93]

As a separate component of the discussion of results of operations, management was required to discuss "any known trends or uncertainties that have had or that the registrant reasonably expects will have a material favorable or unfavorable impact on net sales or revenues or income from continuing operations."[94] These disclosure requirements were more like standards than rules. For example, the SEC noted that "[t]he discussion and analysis shall focus specifically on material events and uncertainties known to management that would cause reported financial information not to be necessarily indicative of future operating results."[95] Management was to discuss both new matters that will have an impact on future results and matters that previously had an impact on reported operations, but were not expected to have an impact on future operations.

The key question relevant to such MD&A disclosure is whether the "reasonably likely" standard is optimal in terms of expected costs and benefits. "Reasonably likely" is a term of art and necessarily is subject to a range of interpretations and actions by

---

91 Concept Release on Management's Discussion and Analysis of Financial Condition and Results of Operations, Securities Act Release No. 6711, 52 Fed. Reg. 13715 (Apr. 17, 1987).

92 Management's Discussion and Analysis of Financial Condition and Results of Operations; Certain Investment Company Disclosures, Securities Act Release No. 6835, 54 Fed. Reg. 22427 (May 18, 1989).

93 If management could not make a determination about whether the contingency was "reasonably likely," then management needed to make an "objective" evaluation of the consequences of the contingency. Under this second prong, management was required to disclose the contingency, unless [it] determined that the consequences were "not reasonably likely" to occur. *See id.; see also* In the Matter of Bank of Boston Corp., Admin. Proc. File No. 3-8270, 1995 SEC LEXIS 3456, at *11 (Dec. 22, 1995) (applying "reasonably likely" standard).

94 Regulation S-K, Item 303(a)(3)(ii).

95 Regulation S-K, Item 303(a), Instruction 3.

managers. Economically rational managers will assess the expected benefits and costs of making particular disclosure. If managers are acting exclusively in shareholders' interests, they will disclose all financial contingencies, even absent the disclosure requirement, where the benefits of doing so (to the shareholders) exceed the costs. Accordingly, a disclosure requirement would matter only if managers either (1) misperceive how the disclosure would affect shareholder value, or (2) are not acting in shareholders' interests. With respect to the first instance, managers might be risk averse with respect to financial disclosures. With respect to the second instance,[96] economically rational managers would only disclose if the personal benefit was greater than the personal cost.

Given the low starting point of disclosure of financial contingencies, most disclosure would likely have a negative price effect in the short-run, unless the market already was discounting the uncertainty associated with potential undisclosed financial contingencies. Conversely, not disclosing financial contingencies in such an environment would lead to a higher share valuation. Accordingly, managers operating in such an environment would have an incentive to decide that contingencies were not "reasonably likely" if their direct compensation would increase by more than the expected penalty associated with making such a disclosure. Given the standards-based nature of the regulation, the probability of a criminal prosecution for a decision about "reasonably likely" would be a low probability event. Likewise, the probability of personal liability would be low for such a decision, given insurance coverage and the high expected costs to plaintiffs litigating such a suit (as compared to a suit alleging more serious non-disclosure or fraud). Under such circumstances, management's disclosure might be suboptimal.

Although the MD&A contingent disclosure standards arguably require a level of disclosure beyond GAAP, the penalties for failing to make such disclosures are not high, even if the most significant cases hold defendants in violation of securities law. For example, in *In the Matter of Caterpillar, Inc.*, the SEC found that Caterpillar had violated Section 13(a) of the Exchange Act by failing to disclose the importance of its Brazilian subsidiary to Caterpillar's earnings.[97] Caterpillar argued that disclosure was not required under GAAP, but the SEC found that the MD&A rules required disclosure, even if GAAP did not. The question did not involve OTC derivatives or complex off-balance sheet transactions, but the principles were the same, and managers did not suffer any serious consequences.

Similarly, in *United States v. Simon*,[98] Judge Henry Friendly found that accountants who technically had complied with GAAP could nevertheless be held criminally liable if the disclosures created a fraudulent or misleading impression among shareholders. In

---

[96] A complete analysis of the second instance is beyond the scope of this Article. The behavioral economics literature suggests that the interests of managers and shareholders might diverge under such circumstances. *See generally* Donald C. Langevoort, *Selling Hope, Selling Risk, Some Lessons for Law from Behavioral Economics About Stockbrokers and Sophisticated Customers*, 84 CAL. L. REV. 627 (1996).

[97] In the Matter of Caterpillar, Inc., Securities Exchange Act Release No. 34-30532, 1992 SEC LEXIS 786 (Mar. 31, 1992).

[98] 425 F.2d 796 (2d Cir. 1969).

Simon, a footnote in Continental Vending's annual report had resembled the opaque disclosures in footnote 16 of Enron's 2000 annual report. As Judge Friendly put it, "The jury could reasonably have wondered how accountants who were really seeking to tell the truth could have constructed a footnote so well designed to conceal the shocking facts."[99] But the principles articulated in *Simon* did not increase expected costs much because few prosecutions for similar conduct followed that case (moreover, the defendants paid small fines and later were pardoned by President Richard Nixon).[100]

Although the regulations requiring "reasonably likely" disclosures are drafted using standard-like language, the SEC also has provided rules-based guidance by suggesting specific ways of disclosing various contingencies using tabular forms of presentation. With respect to complex financial contingencies, the SEC even has recommended particular methodologies (e.g., Value-at-Risk). By suggesting tabular forms of presentation, the SEC effectively has converted the standards into rules. Tabular forms of presentation discourage managers from providing other information because non-standard disclosures are not comparable across companies. Analysts examining disclosure of financial contingencies can compare notional values and at risk statistical measurements from dozens of companies with relative ease. But as the methods of disclosure specified in rules inevitably become less relevant due to financial innovation, and as registrants seek ways of minimizing the costs of disclosure, those disclosures become less useful. Tabular presentation rules are likely to lead to lock-in, creating incentives for managers to avoid disclosing information about contingencies in addition to that required in tabular form.

In such circumstances, one would predict that companies such as Enron would substantially increase their off-balance sheet transactions, as well as their exposure to financial contingencies, without making additional disclosures. For example, given the choice between debt, which must be disclosed in the balance sheet, and an economically equivalent financial derivative such as a prepaid swap, which need be disclosed only in summary tabular form, rational managers would choose the disclosure with the lower regulatory cost. More importantly, managers would have an incentive to *shift* to complex financial contracting to the extent these contracts were economically equivalent to other contracts, but were governed only by a "reasonably likely" standard. In such instances, managers would not have an incentive to disclose more than the tabular disclosure suggested by the SEC. Enron's disclosures described in Section II are consistent with such incentives.

In sum, a relatively low standard, such as "reasonably likely," is not likely to cover the financial contingencies most relevant to assessing a company involved in derivatives trading or complex risk management activities. The SEC has converted even this relatively low-level standard into a set of less useful rules by providing guidance regarding tabular disclosure. Even if market incentives alone would lead managers to make adequate disclosures of complex financial contingencies, the presence of tabular disclosure rules will pervert this incentive. In such an environment the regulatory incentives overwhelm

[99] *Id.* at 807.

[100] Floyd Norris, *An Old Case Is Returning to Haunt Auditors*, N.Y. Times, Mar. 1, 2002, at C1.

market incentives, the level of disclosure will be suboptimal, and market prices will not reflect the risks associated with a firm's complex financial contingencies.

B. The SEC's Response

In a January 2002 release, the SEC restated its position on the "reasonably likely" standard:

> Registrants are reminded that identification of circumstances that could materially affect liquidity is necessary if they are "reasonably likely" to occur. This disclosure threshold is lower than "more likely than not." Market price changes, economic downturns, defaults on guarantees, or contractions of operations that have material consequences for the registrant's financial position or operating results can be reasonably likely to occur under some conditions.[101]

The SEC focused on the need for improved MD&A disclosure in three specific areas of concern: (1) liquidity and capital resources, including off-balance sheet arrangements; (2) certain trading activities involving non-exchange traded contracts accounted for at fair value; and (3) relationships and transactions with persons or entities that derive benefits from their non-independent relationships with the registrant or the registrant's related parties. The implication was that the SEC believed there were problems with this standard, as applied, but that these problems could be resolved with a simple warning.

Market participants, legislators and their staffs were well aware that the SEC was attempting to improve the level of disclosure by "reminding" registrants of their previously-existing obligations under the "reasonably likely" standard. With this SEC release as a backdrop, Congress held numerous hearings on Enron and began debating the provisions that would become Sarbanes-Oxley.

In early 2002, Congress explicitly considered continuing to apply the extant "reasonably likely" standard for disclosure of off-balance sheet transactions, but rejected this standard after months of deliberations. The legislative history on this point is clear. The bill that became Sarbanes-Oxley was introduced in the House of Representatives on February 14, 2002; on April 24, 2002, the House considered and passed proposed legislation that included a "reasonably likely" standard for off-balance sheet transactions.[102] But on July 15, 2002, the Senate amended that proposal to add the language

---

[101] Commission Statement About Management's Discussion and Analysis of Financial Condition and Results of Operations, Securities Act Release No. 33-8056, 67 Fed. Reg. 3746 (Jan. 22, 2002), *available at* http://www.sec.gov/rules/other/33-8056.htm.

[102] *See* 148 Cong. Rec. H1544 (daily ed. Apr. 24, 2002). The House record states:

SEC. 6. IMPROVED TRANSPARENCY OF CORPORATE DISCLOSURES.

(a) MODIFICATION OF REGULATIONS REQUIRED.

in Section 401(a), changing "reasonably likely" to "may."[103] Several Senate committees held hearings on the issue of off-balance sheet transactions, including derivatives, during the months before both houses passed the final legislation in July 2002, and the legislative history is replete with references to problems associated with the disclosures related to Enron's off-balance sheet transactions and derivatives.[104] Indeed, the Senate Committee on Governmental Affairs, and its Permanent Subcommittee on Investigations, conducted a detailed investigation of such transactions and the disclosures related to those transactions from January 2002 until the July 2002 vote on Sarbanes-Oxley, and various senators expressed serious concerns about these issues during this period.[105] In sum, Congress had the opportunity to weigh the costs and benefits of both the "reasonably likely" and "may" standards, and it opted for the latter after months of hearings, debate, and opportunity for public and private comment.

The legislative history does not make it clear specifically what Congress intended by the use of "may." Reference to the ordinary meaning of the term "may" is not especially useful; a typical dictionary definition states that "may" is "used to indicate

---

> The Commission shall revise its regulations under the securities laws pertaining to the disclosures required in periodic financial reports and registration statements to require such reports to include adequate and appropriate disclosure of—
>
> (1) the issuer's off-balance sheet transactions and relationships with unconsolidated entities or other persons, to the extent they are not disclosed in the financial statements and are *reasonably likely* to materially affect the liquidity or the availability of, or requirements for, capital resources, or the financial condition or results of operations of the issuer. . . .

Id. (emphasis added).

[103] *See* 148 Cong. Rec. S6734 (daily ed. July 15, 2002). The Senate report states:

> SEC. 401. DISCLOSURES IN PERIODIC REPORTS.
>
> (a) DISCLOSURES REQUIRED.—
>
> Section 13 of the Securities Exchange Act of 1934 (15 U.S.C. 78m) is amended by adding at the end the following:
>
> . . .
>
> (j) OFF-BALANCE SHEET.—Not later than 180 days after the date of enactment of the Public Company Accounting Reform and Investor Protection Act of 2002, the Commission shall issue final rules providing that each annual and quarterly financial report required to be filed with the Commission shall disclose all material off-balance sheet transactions, arrangements, obligations (including contingent obligations), and other relationships of the issuer with unconsolidated entities or other persons, that may have a material current or future effect on financial condition, changes in financial condition, results of operations, liquidity, capital expenditures, capital resources, or significant components of revenues or expenses.

Id. (emphasis added).

[104] For a listing of hearings held by the U.S. Senate Committee on Governmental Affairs, see its website at http://govt-aff.senate.gov/hearings02.htm.

[105] *See* FINANCIAL OVERSIGHT OF ENRON: THE SEC AND PRIVATE-SECTOR WATCHDOGS, REPORT OF THE STAFF TO THE SENATE COMM. ON GOV'T AFFAIRS 3 n.2 (Oct. 8, 2002), at http://govt-aff.senate.gov/100702watchdogsreport.pdf.

a certain measure of likelihood or probability."[106] There are two possible interpretive approaches. First, Congress might have used "may" to indicate that it was implementing a new standard to be used in assessing whether particular contingency disclosures were required. Second, Congress might have used "may" to indicate that it was importing whatever appropriate measure of likelihood or probability the SEC later would deem appropriate, thereby delegating to the SEC the authority to articulate the precise contours of the standard. Under either possibility, it is clear that Congress already had considered—and rejected—the "reasonably likely" standard and instead used "may" in Section 401(a) to describe a different standard applicable to disclosure of complex financial contingencies.

In proposing new rules in response to Section 401(a), the SEC indicated its belief that in using the word "may" Congress intended to work a dramatic change in the disclosure standard applicable to financial contingencies. The proposed rules state:

> We read the legislative mandate in the Sarbanes-Oxley Act as suggesting a lower disclosure threshold for prospectively material information related to off-balance sheet arrangements. Instead of adopting the "reasonably likely" standard, it directs us to adopt a rule to require disclosure of items that "may" have a material current or future effect. We believe that an appropriate interpretation of the disclosure threshold is best captured by the concept of "remoteness." Accordingly, the proposals would require disclosure of off-balance sheet arrangements under circumstances where management concludes that the likelihood of the occurrence of a future event and its material effect is higher than remote. In other words, an off-balance sheet arrangement "may" have a current or future material effect, and disclosure would be required, unless management determines that the occurrence of an event and the materiality of its effect is outside of the realm of reasonable possibility.[107]

The SEC proposed "not remote" and "reasonably possible" as standards consistent with Congress's intent in using "may." "Not remote" and "reasonably possible" (like "reasonably likely") are terms of art, and they are long-standing probability thresholds used in financial disclosure.[108] By using a "not remote" (or "reasonably possible") standard, the SEC indicated in its proposed rules that managers should increase the quantity and quality of disclosures with respect to financial derivatives and off-balance

---

106 WEBSTER'S II NEW RIVERSIDE DICTIONARY 734 (1984).

107 Disclosure in Management's Discussion and Analysis about Off-Balance Sheet Arrangements, Contractual Obligations and Contingent Liabilities and Commitments, Securities Act Release No. 33-8144, Securities Exchange Act Release No. 34-46767, 2002 SEC LEXIS 2810 (Nov. 4, 2002).

108 *See* ACCOUNTING FOR CONTINGENCIES, Statement of Financial Accounting Standard No. 5, ¶ 3 (Fin. Accounting Standards Bd. 1975).

sheet transactions.[109] These comments were consistent with the legislative history of Sarbanes-Oxley and the numerous Congressional hearings related to Enron's use of derivatives.

The SEC received four dozen comment letters in response to the proposed release, most of which arrived on December 9, 2002, the deadline for comments.[110] The vast majority of the comment letters—including letters from several associations of accountants and lawyers, as well as the "Big Four" accounting firms and several prominent law firms—argued that the SEC should effectively replace the word "may" in Section 401(a) with "reasonably likely."[111]

The "Big Four" accounting firms argued in separate letters that the proposed "not remote" standard would confuse investors and create inconsistencies in financial statement disclosures.[112] For example, Ernst & Young argued that "[i]n our view, 'reasonably

---

[109] In supporting its proposed rules, the SEC concluded that:

> The proposed disclosure would be required if management determines either that an off-balance sheet arrangement is material in the current period or that it may become material in the future. Disclosure would not be required for off-balance sheet arrangements where the likelihood of either the occurrence of an event, or the materiality of its effect, is remote.

Disclosure in Management's Discussion and Analysis about Off-Balance Sheet Arrangements, Contractual Obligations and Contingent Liabilities and Commitments, Securities Act Release No. 33-8144, Securities Exchange Act Release No. 34-46767, 2002 SEC LEXIS 2810, at 35 (Nov. 4, 2002). The SEC further stated that:

> Under the proposed disclosure threshold, management first must identify and carefully review the registrant's direct or indirect guarantees, retained interests, equity-linked or -indexed derivatives and obligations (including contingent obligations) that are not fully reflected on the face of the financial statements. Second, management must assess the likelihood of the occurrence of any known trend, demand, commitment, event or uncertainty that could either require performance of a guarantee or other obligation, or require the registrant to recognize impairment. If management concludes that the likelihood of occurrence is remote, then no disclosure would be required under the proposed rules. If management cannot make that determination, it would have to evaluate objectively the consequences of the known trend, demand, commitment, event or uncertainty on the assumption that it will come to fruition. Disclosure then would be required unless management concludes that likelihood of the event having a material effect is remote.

Id. at 41.

[110] Several letters arrived after the December 9, 2002 deadline.

[111] Indeed, one commenter explicitly suggested that the SEC "replace" the word "may" in the statute (something the SEC, an agency, obviously did not have the power to do), asserting that the drafting process had been rushed. *See* Comments of Jerry W. Powell, General Counsel and Secretary, Compass Bancshares, Inc., 2002 SEC Comment LEXIS 2101, at *11 (Dec. 9, 2002) ("We encourage the Commission to replace the word "may" as it appears in the sixth line of paragraph (a)(4)(i)(C) of proposed Item 303 of Regulation S-K with the words "is reasonably likely to" in order to align the disclosure threshold of other similar information.").

[112] *See, e.g.,* Comments of KPMG LLP, 2002 SEC Comment LEXIS 2099, at 9-10 (Dec. 9, 2002). KPMG argued that the standard would:

> confuse investors and other financial statement users who are unlikely to understand that different probability thresholds attach to different disclosures within the same item; imply that off-balance

likely' is a more appropriate interpretation of 'may' than is 'not remote' as the SEC has proposed."[113] Several associations of lawyers argued—sometimes quite creatively—that the SEC could appropriately implement a "reasonably likely" standard as a response to the language in Sarbanes-Oxley,[114] and that such a standard would be preferable.[115]

> sheet arrangements are inherently more significant and vulnerable than on-balance sheet items (an inference that we believe may be misleading since risk of loss applies equally to on- and off-balance sheet items); and create inconsistency with the historical purpose of MD&A to discuss the business through the eyes of management, which may consider remote outcomes, but which is more likely to manage based on reasonably likely outcomes.

Id.; *see also* Comments of PricewaterhouseCoopers LLP, 2002 SEC Comment LEXIS 2107, at 8 (Dec. 9, 2002) ("While we note the use of the word 'may' in the Sarbanes-Oxley Act, we do not believe that the intent was to further lower the threshold and thereby overwhelm the reader with information that may not be useful to an understanding of the issuer's operations if it is not at least reasonably likely that there will be an impact on the registrant."); Comments of Deloitte & Touche LLP, 2002 SEC Comments LEXIS 2097, at 12 (Dec. 9, 2002) ("We believe the proposed disclosure threshold would require highly speculative judgments and would be burdensome to issuers and investors because it would result in overly voluminous disclosure of information that is of questionable relevance to investors."); Comments of Ernst & Young LLP, 2002 SEC Comment LEXIS 2100, at 2 (Dec. 9, 2002) (making similar arguments in favor of "reasonably likely" instead of "may"); Comments of William F. Ezzell, CPA, Chairman, Bd. of Directors, & Barry C. Melancon, CPA, President and CEO, Am. Institute of Certified Public Accountants, 2002 SEC Comment LEXIS 2298, at 2-4 (Dec. 9, 2002) (same).

113 Comments of Ernst & Young LLP, 2002 SEC Comment LEXIS 2100, at 2 (Dec. 9, 2002).

114 *See* Comments of Gerald S. Backman, Chairman, Comm. on Sec. Regulation, Bus. L. Section, N.Y. State Bar Ass'n, 2002 SEC Comment LEXIS 2296, at 2, 11 (Dec. 13, 2002) ("We urge the Commission to change the proposed 'remoteness' disclosure threshold for off-balance sheet arrangements and transactions to the existing 'reasonably likely' threshold applicable to other MD&A disclosures. Sarbanes-Oxley Section 401(a) does not use, and we do not believe it requires, a remoteness standard. . . . If the statute intended possibility, it would have used the word 'could' which indicates possibility, in the place of 'may' which is '[u]sed to indicate a certain measure of likelihood or possibility.'") (citation omitted); Comments of Stanley Keller, Chair, Comm. on Fed. Regulation of Sec., Bus. L. Section, Am. Bar Ass'n, 2002 SEC Comment LEXIS 2546, at 13 (Dec. 31, 2002) ("We do not believe that the statute's use of the term 'may' requires a departure from current MD&A standard of 'reasonably likely,' particularly as construed by the Commission, and we are concerned that such a low standard will undermine the usefulness of the disclosure for investors while greatly increasing the cost of compliance.") (citation omitted); Comments of Charles M. Nathan, Jr., Chair, Comm. on Sec. Regulation, & Steven J. Slutzky, Ad Hoc Subcomm., Comm. on Sec. Regulation, Ass'n of the Bar of the City of N.Y., 2002 SEC Comment LEXIS 2094, at 14-15 (Dec. 9, 2002) ("The word 'may' in the Sarbanes-Oxley Act allows for a broad range of meanings in the context of the threshold for disclosure. This range certainly includes the 'reasonably likely' disclosure threshold currently applicable throughout MD&A, and, absent a legislative history requiring otherwise, 'may' should be presumed to have a meaning consistent with the existing disclosure threshold throughout MD&A. . . . Furthermore, while the legislative history of the Sarbanes-Oxley Act does refer to the fact that there was testimony that enhanced disclosures concerning off-balance sheet arrangements are necessary to prevent future Enron-type problems, there is no suggestion that manipulation of the MD&A disclosure threshold itself led to any of the well-publicized accounting failures of recent history or that it creates loopholes that undercut clear disclosure.").

115 *See* Comments of Stanley Keller, Chair, Comm. on Fed. Regulation of Sec., Bus. L. Section, Am. Bar Ass'n, 2002 SEC Comment LEXIS 2546, at 13 n.6 (Dec. 31, 2002) ("By placing the burden on management to determine that a contingent event is not reasonably likely to have a material effect, the

Various associations of financial executives, investment advisers and analysts also argued that the proposed standard would confuse and overwhelm investors by requiring companies to deliver too much information.[116]

The Financial Accounting Policy Committee of the Association for Investment Management and Research—an association of 61,000 financial analysts, portfolio managers and other investment professionals—submitted comments opposing a "reasonably likely" standard,[117] as did a few individuals.[118] But the vast majority of the comments specifically endorsed reverting to a "reasonably likely" standard.

The SEC responded in its final rules by abandoning the "not remote" standard in favor of "reasonably likely." The SEC stated a belief that the "reasonably likely" threshold

current MD&A standard of probability already provides an appropriate standard of probability for disclosure."); Comments of Gerald S. Backman, Chair, Comm. on Sec. Regulation, Bus. L. Section, N.Y. State Bar Ass'n, 2002 SEC Comment LEXIS 2296, at 2-3 (Dec. 13, 2002) ("In addition, we are not aware of any problem with the reasonably likely standard, and there has been no showing of any basis to justify a change in that standard. It would not be sound disclosure policy to introduce a different standard into MD&A, which could mislead investors. Finally, the lower threshold could result in information overload, and the additional disclosures would not provide investors with information management uses to manage the company."); *see also id.* at 12 ("There should be one standard for everything in MD&A. . . .").

116 *See* Comments of Karen L. Barr, General Counsel, Inv. Counsel Ass'n of Am., 2002 SEC Comment LEXIS 2109, at 7 (Dec. 10, 2002) ("Moreover, we are concerned that the use of the 'remote' standard could result in voluminous information and overwhelm the reader."); Comments of Frank H. Brod, Chair, Comm. on Corp. Reporting, & David H. Sidwell, Chair, SEC Subcomm., Comm. on Corporate Reporting, Fin. Executives Int'l, 2002 SEC Comment LEXIS 2293, at 2 (Dec. 20, 2002) ("We believe lowering the threshold for MD&A disclosure from 'reasonably likely' to 'more than remote' will result in less meaningful disclosures because there will be a vast increase in the quantity of disclosures, the very extent of which will outweigh meaningful disclosures about higher probability matters."); Comments of Karen Doggett & Broc Romanek, Co-Chair, Subcomm. on Off-Balance Sheet Arrangements, Am. Soc'y of Corp. Secretaries, 2002 SEC Comment LEXIS 2294, at 3 (Dec. 18, 2002) ("To summarize, the application of a 'higher than remote' standard could have several unintended results, including a disproportionate emphasis on off-balance arrangements over other portions of MD&A that are more material to a particular issuer, and too much information about off-balance sheet obligations so that an investor would struggle to determine which are most likely to have negative impact."); Comments of Sullivan & Cromwell, 2002 SEC Comment LEXIS 2114, at 2 (Dec. 9, 2002) (arguing that the proposed rules "will result in voluminous disclosures that are more likely to confuse and overwhelm investors than provide important information that will enable investors to make informed investment decisions").

117 Comments of Jane Adams, Chair, Fin. Accounting Policy Comm. & Rebecca McEnally, Ph.D., CFA, Vice-President, Advocacy, Ass'n for Inv. Mgmt. and Research (Dec. 31, 2002), *available at* http://www.sec.gov/rules/proposed/s74202/jadams1.htm.

118 *See, e.g.,* Comments of Robert G. Beard, 2002 SEC Comment LEXIS 2057, at 3 (Nov. 25, 2002) ("The 'remote' disclosure threshold appears to be most consistent with Sarbanes-Oxley. Off-balance sheet transactions are permitted under relatively aggressive accounting standards in that accounting recognition is not required by the obligor or guarantor even if such obligor/guarantor may be ultimately liable for a significant portion of the indebtedness of the special purpose entity. For that reason, a stricter disclosure threshold is warranted. Also, given the complex nature of these transactions, the unsophisticated investor deserves an explanation of the potential risks even if such risks appear remote at the time. The remote standard allows investors to make judgments on potentially material adverse consequences to the registrant that are not required to be recognized or possibly even disclosed in the financial statements.").

"best promotes the utility of the disclosure requirements by reducing the possibility that investors will be overwhelmed by voluminous disclosure of insignificant and possibly unnecessarily speculative information."[119] The SEC did not describe which investors it believed would be overwhelmed, and it did not conclude that securities prices would not reflect this information because some investors would be overwhelmed.[120]

The SEC also noted, "we are mindful of the potential difficulty that registrants would have faced in attempting to comply with the 'remote' disclosure threshold set forth in the Proposing Release. We also believe that our use of a consistent disclosure threshold throughout MD&A will preclude the potential confusion that could result from disparate thresholds."[121] However, the SEC did not weigh these costs against the expected benefits associated with a more inclusive disclosure standard. The SEC concluded that "[w]e have found no express reference in the legislative history conclusively demonstrating Congress' intent in using the word 'may.'"[122] However, the SEC did not mention the numerous references in the legislative history to the problems associated with derivatives and disclosure of derivatives, nor did it mention the Senate's rejection of the "reasonably likely" standard.

The SEC's final regulations also included a rules-based provision that management make tabular disclosure regarding "(1) long-term debt obligations; (2) capital lease obligations; (3) operating lease obligations; (4) purchase obligations; and (5) other long-term liabilities reflected on the registrant's balance sheet under GAAP."[123] However, tabular disclosure was not explicitly required or suggested for derivatives or contingent contracts in other categories.[124] Thus, the SEC shifted the regulatory regime toward rules-based tabular disclosure.

---

[119] Disclosure in Management's Discussion and Analysis about Off-Balance Sheet Arrangement and Aggregate Contractual Obligations, Securities Act Release No. 33-8182, Securities Exchange Act Release No. 34-47264, 68 Fed. Reg. 5982, 5985 (Feb. 5, 2003). Sophisticated analysis, not individual investors, are the target audience for these kinds of disclosures. According to a survey by Ernst & Young, the length of an average annual report had increased from thirty-five pages, when FASB first began setting accounting rules, to sixty-four pages in the early 1990s; the number of footnotes increased from four to seventeen. Ray J. Groves, *Here's the Annual Report. Got a Few Hours?*, WALL ST. J., Aug. 4, 1994, at A12. Few individual investors can read or understand the basics of an average annual report, much less the complexities of contingent disclosures related to derivatives.

[120] In fact, such information is precisely the type that would be most useful to sophisticated investors and analysts, whose activities are reflected in securities prices.

[121] Disclosure in Management's Discussion and Analysis about Off-Balance Sheet Arrangement and Aggregate Contractual Obligations, Securities Act Release No. 33-8182, Securities Exchange Act Release No. 34-47264, 68 Fed. Reg. 5982, 5985 (Feb. 5, 2003).

[122] *Id.*

[123] *Id.* at 5986.

[124] The SEC included a standards-based requirement stating that management must provide other information that it believes to be necessary for investors to understand both the company's off-balance sheet arrangements and the material effects of these arrangements on its financial condition. This "catch all" standard is intended to capture any "reasonably likely" events that otherwise would not fall into a particular category covered by the regulation. Whether this standard is effective depends on the extent to

To apply the "reasonably likely" test, management first must "identify and critically analyze" the company's off-balance sheet arrangements.[125] Second, management must assess the likelihood of the occurrence of "any known trend, demand, commitment, event or uncertainty that could affect an off-balance sheet arrangement."[126] If management concludes that the known trend, demand, commitment, event or uncertainty is "not reasonably likely to occur," then no disclosure is required.[127] If management cannot make that determination, it must make disclosure unless it determines that even if the contingency were to occur, a material change in the company's financial condition was "not reasonably likely to occur."[128] In other words, management has two bites at the "reasonably likely" apple: one when determining whether the contingency would be "reasonably likely," and another when determining whether a material effect of any contingency that did occur would be "reasonably likely."

Even those groups advocating a "reasonably likely" standard have suggested that specific rules-based requirements are inappropriate. For example, Sullivan & Cromwell, a law firm that represents several derivatives dealers, noted its belief that

> the Commission should adopt a more flexible and less proscriptive approach, requiring companies to discuss in general terms the level and significance of off-balance sheet arrangements as well as the Company's reasons for pursuing such arrangements and specific disclosure in reasonable detail on those significant off-balance sheet arrangements according to current standards of MD&A disclosure.[129]

Similarly, the European Commission stated, "[a]ccordingly, there is a primordial need for an appropriate accounting treatment of arrangements and transactions whose (whole or partial) purpose is to remove from an entity's balance sheet liabilities or assets. Such accounting must reflect the economic substance of the transactions and arrangements. This should follow a principles-based approach."[130]

---

which the SEC enforces it. This catch-all provision is consistent with the SEC's more general approach to MD&A disclosure, requiring that companies disclose facts even if accounting rules do not require disclosure. *See generally* Cautionary Advice Regarding Disclosure, Securities Act Release No. 33-8040, 66 Fed. Reg. 65,013 (Dec. 17, 2001); Commission Statement About Management's Discussion and Analysis of Financial Condition and Results of Operations, Securities Act Release No. 33-8056, 67 Fed. Reg. 3746 (Jan. 25, 2002).

[125] Disclosure in Management's Discussion and Analysis About Off-Balance Sheet Arrangement and Aggregate Contractual Obligations, Securities Act Release No. 33-8182, Securities Exchange Act Release No. 34-47264, 68 Fed. Reg. 5982, 5983 (Feb. 5, 2003).

[126] *Id.*

[127] *Id.*

[128] *Id.*

[129] Comments of Sullivan & Cromwell, 2002 SEC Comment LEXIS 2114, at 2-3 (Dec. 9, 2002).

[130] Comments of Alexander Schaub, Director-General, European Comm'n (Dec. 9, 2002), *available at* http://www.sec.gov/rules/proposed/s74202/aschaub1.htm.

The tabular disclosure rules do not cover many important financial contingencies. For example, consider the class of instruments known as credit derivatives, whose value is based on credit ratings. Many of Enron's off-balance sheet contracts depended, explicitly or implicitly, on the level of its credit rating. Enron did not disclose relevant and material information about these contracts, except to note in its 2000 annual report that its "continued investment grade status is critical to the success of its wholesale business as well as its ability to maintain adequate liquidity."[131] Presumably, Congress and the SEC would want to encourage or require such disclosure, but the application of the new rules to such disclosures remains unclear.

Disclosure of "reasonably likely" contingencies would not likely have prevented the problems associated with Enron. Indeed, Enron arguably was in compliance with the newly-enacted SEC regulations. In assessing the firm's financial contingencies at the end of 2000, management would not have considered a scenario in which Enron's stock price would decline by more than half to be "reasonably likely." Accordingly, management would not have needed to disclose details about Enron's derivatives contracts with the SPEs. Nor would it have been "reasonably likely" that the volatility of commodity prices in 2000 would continue. Moreover, management's assessment is required to be objectively "reasonable" only as of the time the assessment is made.[132] As of any particular time, the reasonableness of a decision about whether a particular contingency is "reasonably likely" will be based on the relevant price histories for the relevant variables and predictions about how those variables are likely to change in the future. Such disclosures necessarily will exclude "worst case" scenarios. To the extent traders are not accurately reporting the volatility of their portfolios; they can provide managers with excuses to make more limited disclosures. In other words, a "reasonably likely" standard creates incentives to report profits and losses that are relatively smooth, so that "reasonably likely" disclosures will be relatively limited. In such an environment, systemic risks will increase, because investors will not have accurate information about the risk distributions of a company's derivatives trading, and companies will not disclose much useful information about their derivatives risk exposure.

C. Is "Reasonably Likely" a Permissible Construction of "May"?

Finally, whatever the wisdom of the SEC's "reasonably likely" standard, it is unclear whether it will survive judicial review. In the event of a challenge to the regulations promulgated pursuant to Section 401(a), a court would perform the established two-step analysis governed by *Chevron U.S.A., Inc. v. NRDC*[133] in evaluating the SEC's

[131] Annual Report, *supra* note 38, at 27.

[132] *See* Management's Discussion and Analysis of Financial Condition, Securities Act Release No. 33-6835, 54 Fed. Reg. 22,427, at 22430 (May 24, 1989).

[133] 467 U.S. 837 (1984).

interpretation of Sarbanes-Oxley.[134] First, the court would consider whether the statute clearly resolves the issue. If the court determined that Congress has spoken clearly in Section 401(a), then the court (and the SEC) must "give effect to the unambiguously expressed intent of Congress."[135] Second, if the statute does not resolve the issue, the court would accept the SEC's interpretation so long as it reflects a "permissible construction of the statute."[136]

Would the SEC's interpretation withstand this analysis? There are persuasive arguments that the answer is likely to be no. Courts applying *Chevron* analysis typically assess the comparative expertise of legislatures and agencies (and courts).[137] But arguments about deference and comparative expertise matter less where Congress explicitly has considered and rejected the *exact* language of the interpretation the agency ultimately adopts. Even if Section 401(a)'s language is ambiguous, so that Congress has not spoken clearly, the SEC's interpretation is unlikely to be a "permissible construction" if it simply reverts to language already considered and rejected by Congress.[138]

Courts generally interpret "may" in a permissive way, as in "maybe."[139] A few courts have construed "may" as "shall," but only when the context or subject matter of the legislation made it clear such a meaning was intended.[140] Of course, Congress might clarify the issue through new legislation, but the failure of Congress expressly to reject

---

[134] *See id.* at 842-45; *see also* FDA v. Brown & Williamson Tobacco Corp., 529 U.S. 120, 132-33 (2000) (applying *Chevron* analysis in assessing whether Congress granted Federal Food and Drug Administration jurisdiction to regulate tobacco products).

[135] *Chevron*, 467 U.S. at 843.

[136] *Id.*

[137] *See, e.g.,* Daniel B. Rodriguez, *The Positive Political Dimensions of Regulatory Reform*, 72 WASH. U.L.Q. 1, 133-38 (1994) (assessing arguments regarding relevant expertise of legislatures, agencies and the judiciary).

[138] The issue is complicated by two unique problems. First, "may" includes within its definition the meaning specifically encompassed by the term ultimately used in the regulation. Second, the standard for judging the agency interpretation—whether it was reasonable—is also subsumed within the words in the regulation.

[139] *See, e.g.,* People v. Hoehl, 568 P.2d 484, 486 (Colo. 1977); La Bove v. Employers Ins. Co., 189 So. 2d 315, 317 (La. Ct. App. 1966). For example, in *People v. Hoehl*, the court rejected the dictionary definition of "may" in favor of a definition similar to the one adopted by the SEC. *See Hoehl*, 568 P.2d at 486. The relevant statute provided that "a person commits child abuse if he knowingly, intentionally, or negligently, and without justifiable excuse, causes or permits a child to be placed in a situation that may endanger the child's life or health." *Id.* The court indicated that if the word "may" in the clause "may endanger the child's life or health" were strictly construed according to the dictionary definition (in that case, "be in some degree likely"), the statute would be unconstitutional on its face, because "virtually any conduct directed toward a child has the possibility, however slim, of endangering a child's health." *Id.* To preserve the constitutionality of the statute, the court rejected the dictionary definition and created its own definition of "may" as meaning a "reasonable probability." *See id.*

[140] *See* United States v. Lexington Mill & Elevator Co., 232 U.S. 399, 411 (1914) (considering meaning of "may" as mandatory); Bloom v. Texas State Bd. of Examiners of Psychologists, 475 S.W.2d 374, 377 (Tex. Civ. App. 1972) (same).

the SEC's final regulations need not indicate Congressional acquiescence in the SEC's interpretation.[141]

The weeks between November 2002 (when the SEC, following Congress's directive in using "may," proposed rules requiring disclosure unless a contingency was "remote") and January 2003 (when the SEC adopted final rules requiring disclosure only if a contingency was "reasonably likely") were an active time for financial lobbyists. The evidence that formed the basis for the SEC's change in view is scant, but the weight of opinion favoring the change was heavy. Public choice scholars looking for recent examples of agency capture will feast on the SEC's final response to Section 401(a) of Sarbanes-Oxley.

IV. CONCLUSION

The reasons for Enron's collapse should affect the normative conclusions of scholars, and the standard account of these reasons is incomplete. At its core, Enron was a derivatives trading firm; it made billions trading derivatives, but it lost billions on virtually everything else it did. Enron used its expertise in derivatives to hide these losses. For most people, the fact that Enron had transformed itself from an energy company into a derivatives trading firm is a surprise, although there were many clues buried in its financial statements.

The collapse of Enron suggests that regulations applicable to derivatives disclosure should change in two ways. First, regulations should treat derivatives like economically equivalent financial instruments. In other words, they should become more standard-like, and create incentives for corporate managers to make disclosures consistent with economic reality, not accounting reality. Second, the SEC should follow Congress's intent in Section 401(a) of Sarbanes-Oxley and encourage additional disclosure of contingencies related to derivatives. At minimum, courts should prevent the SEC from reverting to a disclosure standard Congress explicitly rejected.

---

[141] *See* Sierra Club v. EPA, 540 F.2d 1114, 1126 (D.C. Cir. 1976).

Getting the Word Out About Fraud: A Theoretical Analysis of Whistleblowing and Insider Trading[*]

Jonathan R. Macey[**]

INTRODUCTION

Over the past five years, it appears that whistleblowing has become fashionable. Whistleblowers, who traditionally have been considered tattletales and otherwise viewed with suspicion,[1] have recently enjoyed a distinct rise in popularity. As *Salon* observed not long ago:

> In recent years, aided in part by movies like "The Insider," whistle-blowers have attained the status of folk heroes. "It's become popular to protect whistle-blowers—that's never happened before," says Danielle Brian, executive director of the Project on Government Oversight, a nonprofit public interest group dedicated to exposing governmental corruption and

---

* Reprinted from MICHIGAN LAW REVIEW, June 2007, Vol. 105, No. 8. Copyright 2007 by The Michigan Law Review Association.

** Sam Harris Professor of Corporate Law, Securities Law and Corporate Finance, Yale University. I am grateful for comments from Bruce Ackermand, Ian Ayres, Henry Hansmann, Oona Hathaway, Al Klevorick, Henry Manne, Dan Markovitz, and Geoffery Miller; and from participants in the Harvard Law School Workshop in Law and Economics and the Yale Law School Faculty Workshop. Stephanie Bidermann, Sachin Shivaram, and Johanna Spellman, Yale Law School class of 2007, and Robin Preussel, Yale Law School class of 2006, provided valuable research assistance.

1 In the past whistleblowing was viewed as radical and vaguely subversive, if not downright disloyal and unpatriotic. *See, e.g.*, FREDERICK ELLISTON ET AL., WHISTLEBLOWING: MANAGING DISSENT IN THE WORKPLACE (1985); DAVID W. EWING, FREEDOM INSIDE THE ORGANIZATION: BRINGING CIVIL LIBERTIES TO THE WORKPLACE (1977); WHISTLEBLOWING: SUBVERSION OR CORPORATE CITIZENSHIP? (Gerald Vinten ed., 1994); Frederick A. Elliston, *Civil Disobedience and Whistleblowing: A Comparative Appraisal of Two Forms of Dissent*, 1 J. BUS. ETHICS 23 (1982); Brian Martin, *Whistleblowing and Nonviolence*, 24 PEACE & CHANGE 15 (1999); Joyce Rothschild & Terance D. Miethe, *Whistleblowing as Resistance in Modern Work Organizations: The Politics of Revealing Organizational Deception and Abuse*, *in* RESISTANCE AND POWER IN ORGANIZATIONS 252-73 (John M. Jermier et al. eds., 1994).

mismanagement that works closely with whistle-blowers and that advocates for them.[2]

Time magazine called 2002 "The Year of the Whistleblower," honoring "inside do-gooders who risked their careers"[3] to expose, among other things, how the FBI lost a key terrorism suspect before the terrorist attacks of September 11, 2001, and how Enron misled investors through phony accounting treatment of off-balance sheet transactions. There is even a National Whistleblower Center, a nonprofit group dedicated to helping whistleblowers in their efforts "to improve environmental protection, nuclear safety, and government and corporate accountability."[4]

It is still probably the case that whistleblowing is "a form of organizational dissent."[5] But the recent positive publicity for whistleblowers suggests that whistleblowing is now viewed with less suspicion—and whistleblowers as less politically motivated and more altruistic—than was true in the past. Whistleblowers are now thought of as an integral component of the recently re-regulated system of corporate governance that is supposed to result in better monitoring and control of managerial misconduct (agency costs) in large, publicly held corporations.[6] Tip-offs from insiders have been described as "by far the most common method of detecting fraud."[7]

The purpose of this Article is to suggest that whistleblowing and one particular kind of insider trading—namely insider trading on the basis of information about corporate corruption, corporate fraud or other illegal corporate conduct—are analytically and functionally indistinguishable as responses to corporate pathologies such as fraud and

---

[2] Eric Boehlert, *The Betrayal of the Whistle-blowers*, SALON, Oct. 21, 2003, http://dir.salon.com/story/news/feature/2003/10/21/whistleblower/index.html.

[3] *Id.*

[4] For information about the National Whistleblower Center, see About NWC, http://www.whistleblowers.org/html/about_nwc.html (last visited Feb. 17, 2007) ("The primary goal of the Center is to ensure that disclosures about government or industry actions that violate the law or harm the environment are fully heard, and that the whistleblowers who risk their careers to expose wrongdoing are defended. The Center's mission is to strengthen the rights of whistleblowers and to help make their underlying claims known to the public in order to safeguard the welfare of the American people.").

[5] Brian Martin & Will Rifkin, *The Dynamics of Employee Dissent: Whistleblowers and Organizational Jiu-Jitsu*, 4 PUB. ORG. REV. 221, 221 (2004).

[6] The centerpiece of the new corporate governance regime is the Sarbanes-Oxley Act of 2002, Pub. L. No. 107-204, 116 Stat. 745 (codified in scattered sections of 11, 15, 18, 28 and 29 U.S.C. (Supp. III 2003)). This bill contains significant protections for private sector whistleblowers. *See infra* text accompanying notes 108-115. Upon signing the bill into law, President George W. Bush observed that "today I sign the most far-reaching reforms of American business practices since the time of Franklin Delano Roosevelt. . . . This law says to every dishonest corporate leader: 'You will be exposed and punished. The era of low standards and false profits is over. No boardroom in America is above or beyond the law.'" George W. Bush, Remarks on Signing the Sarbanes-Oxley Act of 2002 (July 30, 2002), in 38 WEEKLY COMP. PRES. DOC. 1283, 1284 (Aug. 5, 2002).

[7] *A Price Worth Paying?*, ECONOMIST, May 21, 2005, at 71, *available at* http://www.economist.com/business/displayStory.cfm?story_id=3984019.

corruption. This, in turn, explains why whistleblowers are sometimes viewed with suspicion and distrust, not only by their colleagues but also by regulators and journalists.

When giant businesses like Enron, Adelphia, or WorldCom are brought to their knees by whistleblowers, innocent people are harmed. The innocent employees, small suppliers, local communities, and philanthropic organizations that depended on these firms suffer as much, if not more, than the firm's largely diversified investor base. These groups single out the whistleblower as the source of their trouble. Revelations by whistleblowers can be embarrassing to regulators, prosecutors, and others who are supposed to be alert for fraudulent corporate activity.

Conversely, it also is the case that inside traders sometimes have fared surprisingly well in the courts. In particular, in cases where insider trading leads to the same revelations about incipient fraud as whistleblowing would, courts can be remarkably accepting of such trading.[8]

In this Article, I advance the theory that both whistleblowing and insider trading are best analyzed as involving rights in the same inchoate intellectual property: valuable information. Whether one has the right to blow the whistle on somebody else and whether one has the right to trade on the basis of nonpublic information ultimately depends on whether the person engaging in the conduct has a rightful property interest in the information he or she is using. If so, then the conduct, whether characterized as whistleblowing or insider trading, should be not only legally permissible, but affirmatively encouraged. By contrast, in situations where the person doing the trading or the whistleblowing has no legitimate property interest in the information, the behavior should be illegal.

Part I offers a definition of whistleblowing and a history of the government's efforts to encourage the practice, including an analysis of perhaps the most famous case of whistleblowing: Sherron Watkins and Enron. Part II compares insider trading and whistleblowing. This comparison explains the traditional antipathy and suspicion toward whistleblowers. In Part III, I explore whistleblowing and insider trading as phenomena that often occur in tandem. Part IV demonstrates why whistleblowers lack credibility and explains that verifying the assertions of nontrading whistleblowers is likely to be very costly. In Part V, I discuss the implications of a property-rights regime for insider trading and whistleblowing, as well as the legal regimes dealing with each. I then show how insider trading on negative information, when properly regulated, is a superior substitute for whistleblowing. The argument here is not that insider trading should be generally permitted or that such trading is universally beneficial to shareholders, companies, or society. Rather, the argument is that the limited and tightly regulated ability to "sell short" can credibly signal to the market that the trader has negative information about a company.[9] Part VI considers why, in light of this analysis, we

---

[8] *See* Dirks v. SEC, 463 U.S. 646 (1983) (finding that petitioner had not violated antifraud provisions of securities laws by sharing inside information obtained from a tipper whose purpose was to expose fraud).

[9] Selling short involves selling shares that one does not own with the intention of profiting by "covering the short position," which entails buying the shares more cheaply in the future when the price declines.

observe such radically different treatment of whistleblowers and inside traders. In Part VII, I look at the distributional concerns of insider trading and of whistleblowing for the investors of a company, exploring who actually pays for these practices and their effects on the company. Part VIII explains why the private contracting process within firms is not likely to permit the sort of trading advocated here, thereby making it necessary to accomplish the result by regulation rather than by intrafirm contracting. Part IX briefly discusses blackmail as a method for reacting to confidential or secretive information about corporate fraud and compares this reaction to that of whistleblowing and insider trading.

I. DEFINING WHISTLEBLOWING

A whistleblower is an employee or other person in a contractual relationship with a company who reports misconduct to outside firms or institutions, which in turn have the authority to impose sanctions or take other corrective action against the wrongdoers.[10] While some definitions of whistleblowing require that the misconduct be reported to people outside the organization, other definitions also include reporting misconduct up the chain of command within an organization.[11] Where one is blowing the whistle against an entire way of doing business or against people at or near the very top of a company, as was the case with Enron, reporting the behavior up the chain of command is not actually whistleblowing. After all, it is hardly whistleblowing to report misconduct to the very people engaged in the misconduct. But where the misconduct involved is that committed by public officials, instead of individuals in the private sector, disclosure to those outside the organization may constitute a crime if the information is classified pursuant to administrative action or subject to an executive order of confidentiality.[12]

---

[10] BLACK'S LAW DICTIONARY 1627 (8th ed. 2004) (defining whistleblower as "[a]n employee who reports employer wrongdoing to a governmental or law-enforcement agency"); John A. Gray, *Is Whistleblowing Protection Available Under Title IX?: An Hermeneutical Divide and the Role of Courts*, 12 WM. & MARY J. WOMEN & L. 671, 671 (2006).

[11] For example, whistleblowing has been defined in one statute as conduct that involves disclosure of information by an employee or applicant which the employee or applicant reasonably believes evidences—

> (i) a violation of any law, rule, or regulation, or
>
> (ii) gross mismanagement, a gross waste of funds, an abuse of authority, or a substantial and specific danger to public health or safety,
>
> if such disclosure is not specifically prohibited by law and if such information is not specifically required by Executive order to be kept secret in the interest of national defense or the conduct of foreign affairs.

5 U.S.C. § 2302(b)(8)(A) (2000); *see generally* C. Fred Alford, WHISTLEBLOWERS: BROKEN LIVES AND ORGANIZATIONAL POWER (2001).

[12] *Cf.* 5 U.S.C. § 2302(b)(8)(A) (2000) (allowing personnel action if disclosed information is prohibited by law or required by Executive order to be kept secret).

A. Our Venerable Tradition of Compensating Whistleblowers

The origins of whistleblowing legislation in the United States can be traced to the False Claims Act, enacted in 1863 to reduce the incidence of fraud among the suppliers of munitions and other war materials to the Union government during the Civil War.[13] Significantly, the act authorizes payments to whistleblowers of a percentage of any money recovered or damages won by the government in cases of fraud that the whistleblower's evidence helped expose.[14] The act allows whistleblowers, called "relators," to bring qui tam actions on behalf of the government against those alleged to have submitted false claims to the government.[15] As with modern whistleblower statutes, the False Claims Act also protects whistleblowers from wrongful dismissal.[16]

The False Claims Act was not widely utilized until far-reaching amendments to the act in 1986 made it an attractive weapon to combat fraud in virtually any program involving federal funds.[17] Although originally intended to deter the submission of fraudulent invoices by defense contractors, the False Claims Act now covers every industry that deals with the federal government.[18] The act provides for whistleblowers to be reinstated to their jobs with seniority, double back pay, interest on back pay, compensation for discriminatory treatment, and legal fees.[19] Additional federal legislation bars reprisals against those who expose government corruption.[20]

Congress adopted further whistleblower protection for public employees in 1989 when it passed the Whistleblower Protection Act of 1989 ("WPA").[21] The WPA is an anti-retaliation statute that prohibits the federal government from retaliating against employees who blow the whistle on public sector misconduct and that provides a means of redress for employees.[22] The Office of the Special Counsel and the Merit Systems

---

[13] False Claims Act, ch. 67, 12 Stat. 698 (1863) (current provisions contained in 31 U.S.C. §§ 3729-3731 (2000)).

[14] 31 U.S.C. § 3730(d)(1) (2000).

[15] 31 U.S.C. § 3730(b). "Qui tam" is an abbreviation of the Latin phrase "qui tam pro domino rege quam pro se ipso in hac parte sequitur," which means "who brings action for the king as well as himself." Qui tam actions date back to at least the fourteenth century. Vermont Agency of Natural Res. v. United States ex rel. Stevens, 529 U.S. 765, 774 (2000) (citing Prior of Lewes v. De Holt (1300), reprinted in 48 Selden Society 198 (1931)).

[16] 31 U.S.C. § 3730(h) (2000).

[17] Pub. L. No. 99-562, §§ 3, 4, 100 Stat. 3154 (codified at 31 U.S.C. §§ 3729-3731 (2000)).

[18] 31 U.S.C. § 3729(a) (2000).

[19] 31 U.S.C. § 3730(h) (2000).

[20] 5 U.S.C. § 2302(b)(8) (2000). Harassment and dismissal of whistleblowers and the revelation of widespread waste and fraud in defense contracting led Congress to strengthen the position of whistleblowers in 1989. Whistleblower Protection Act of 1989, Pub. L. No. 101-12, 103 Stat. 32 (codified at 5 U.S.C. §§ 1211-1219, 1221, 1222, 3352 (2000)).

[21] Whistleblower Protection Act of 1989, Pub. L. No. 101-12, 103 Stat. 32 (codified at 5 U.S.C. §§ 1211-1219, 1221, 1222, 3352 (2000)).

[22] 5 U.S.C. §§ 1213, 1214 (2000).

Protection Board are charged with upholding the WPA.[23] Employees can obtain protection as whistleblowers either by making disclosure to a special counsel, the inspector general of an agency, another employee designated by an agency head to receive such disclosures, or to any other individual or organization.[24]

Thus, employees who work for companies that deal with the government or who are themselves in government jobs have incentives to disregard internal channels, such as the internal audit function, and file whistleblower actions in court. The so-called "qui tam" provision of the federal False Claims Act enables an individual with knowledge that someone has filed a false claim involving payment by the government to file a qui tam action in court.[25] When such an action is filed, the government takes responsibility for investigating the allegation.[26]

Where the fraud is successfully prosecuted, the whistleblower is eligible to receive a bounty of at least fifteen percent of the final recovery,[27] which for large frauds can amount to tens of millions of dollars merely for having brought a false claim to the government's attention. The burden of proving the false claim must be met by the government: "[t]he whistleblower has to do nothing other than file the qui tam action."[28]

Thus, while it is tempting to distinguish whistleblowing from insider trading on the grounds that the motivations of whistleblowers are more "pure," this does not appear to be the case. Here the point is not that inside traders are particularly virtuous. Of course they aren't. Rather the point is that whistleblowers are often motivated by the financial returns associated with whistleblowing in the same way that inside traders are motivated by the financial returns associated with trading. Consistent with this intuition, the federal statutes regulating whistleblowing for public corruption are specifically designed to provide economic incentives for whistleblowers. And at least some whistleblowers have profited richly from qui tam actions. In the fiscal year 2005, for example, federal whistleblowers were awarded $166 million, up from $108 million in 2004.[29] In one particular case, the various government settlements from the myriad investigations into HealthSouth Corporation's alleged fraud against Medicare and other federally-insured

---

[23] *Id.* §§ 1212, 1214.

[24] *Id.* § 1213(a)(2).

[25] 31 U.S.C. § 3730 (2000).

[26] *Id.*

[27] *Id.* § 3730(d)(1).

[28] Jonathan Figg, *Whistleblowing*, INTERNAL AUDITOR, Apr. 2000, at 30, 36.

[29] Press Release 05-595, U.S. Dep't of Justice, Justice Department Recovers $1.4 Billion in Fraud & False Claims in Fiscal Year 2005; More Than $15 Billion Since 1986, Nov. 7, 2005, http://www.usdoj.gov/opa/pr/2005/November/05_civ_595.html [hereinafter Press Release 05-595]; U.S. Dep't of Justice, Civil Division, Fraud Statistics—Overview, October 1, 1986-September 30, 2004 (Mar. 4, 2005) [hereinafter Fraud Statistics—Overview].

health care programs yielded $327 million in fines payable to the U.S. government.[30] Of this amount, $76 million in recoveries was attributable to four qui tam law suits.[31] Five relators received $12.6 million for their contributions to the HealthSouth litigation.[32] More generally, recoveries resulting from all qui tam and non-qui tam cases brought under the False Claims Act from 1986 to 2004 total $13.5 billion.[33] Whistleblower rewards for qui tam cases exceeded $1.4 billion during this period.[34]

B. Self-Interested Behavior and Whistleblowing

As noted above, a whistleblower is someone who observes criminal behavior and alerts a competent authority. The term naturally conjures up images of concerned citizens frantically blowing whistles to thwart muggings and bank robberies on Main Street, U.S.A.[35] Yet even where whistleblowers do not engage in whistleblowing for money, there often are other self-interested motivations behind this ostensibly altruistic behavior. Disgruntled employees are more likely to engage in whistleblowing than other employees, and revenge is often a common feature in whistleblower cases.[36] Thus, it does not appear possible to distinguish whistleblowing from insider trading by portraying whistleblowers as wholly altruistically motivated in contrast to inside traders.[37]

---

[30] Press Release 05-595, supra note 29. In that case, the government alleged as follows:

> HealthSouth, the nation's largest provider of rehabilitative medicine services, engaged in three major schemes to defraud the government. The first, comprising $170 million of the settlement amount, resolved Health South's [sic] alleged false claims for outpatient physical therapy services that were not properly supported by certified plans of care, administered by licensed physical therapists or for one-on-one therapy as represented. Another $65 million resolved claims that HealthSouth engaged in accounting fraud which resulted in overbilling Medicare on hospital cost reports and home office cost statements. The remaining $92 million resolved allegations of billing Medicare for a range of unallowable costs, such as lavish entertainment and travel expenses incurred for HealthSouth's annual administrators' meeting at Disney World, and other claims. Government-initiated claims accounted for $251 million of the settlement amount, with the remaining $76 million attributable to four qui tam law suits.

Id.

[31] *Id.*

[32] *Id.*

[33] Fraud Statistics—Overview, *supra* note 29.

[34] *Id.*

[35] Dan Ackman, *Sherron Watkins Had Whistle, But Blew It*, FORBES.com, Feb. 14, 2002, http://www.forbes.com/2002/02/14/0214watkins.html.

[36] *See* William De Maria, *The Victorian Whistleblower Protection Act: Patting the Paws of Corruption* 13 (May 3, 2002) (unpublished manuscript, on file with author) ("[I]nformants disclose important and socially useful information for all sorts of reasons ([e.g.,] revenge) . . ."), *available at* http://www.uow.edu.au/arts/sts/bmartin/dissent/documents/DeMaria_Viclaw.pdf.

[37] Although there is a potential financial benefit to whistleblowing, it is generally difficult to demonstrate that such financial benefit is the primary motivating factor rather than just a contributing one. By contrast, in the case of insider trading, the primary motivation often is to profit from the inside information.

1. *Sherron Watkins—A Paradigmatic Whistleblower?*

Sherron Watkins, the iconic whistleblower, does not remotely fit the traditional definition and imagery associated with a whistleblower.[38] She did write a memorandum articulating some of her concerns about the "suspicions of accounting improprieties" at Enron.[39] But she gave this document to the company's then-CEO, Kenneth Lay, later a criminal defendant in various fraud and insider trading cases related to Enron's collapse.[40] Then, on the basis of Lay's vague assurances that he would look into the wrongdoing, she did nothing; her memorandum was not made public until Congressional investigators released it six weeks after Enron filed for bankruptcy—long after the company and its stock price had collapsed.[41]

Critical to understanding Ms. Watkins's role as a self-interested whistleblower is understanding her objectives in writing the whistleblower letter. To do this, it is necessary to parse the letter that Watkins anonymously e-mailed to Lay. The opening line makes it clear that Watkins's objective is to retain her employment and to protect her pension savings. The Watkins letter begins by asking, "Has Enron become a risky place to work? For those of us who didn't get rich over the last few years, can we afford to stay?"[42] Far from whistleblowing, the letter suggests ways that the company can unwind its problems, without the need to notify investors or regulators of the massive improprieties going on in the company. She adds: "I am incredibly nervous that we will implode in a wave of accounting scandals. My eight years of Enron work history will be worth nothing on my resume, the business world will consider the past successes as nothing but an elaborate accounting hoax."[43]

Moreover, Watkins clearly identified herself with the management team that created the scandal, as much as with the Enron investors who were devastated by the collapse of the company. For example, she expresses concern that unhappy employees were aware of the company's improper accounting practices and could possibly seek revenge on the company by exposing the fraud.[44] Watkins observes that many shareholders "bought [Enron common stock] at $70 and $80 a share looking for $120 a share and now they're at $38 or worse."[45] She also observes that she and other employees "are under too much

---

Highlighting wrongdoing may merely be a fringe benefit. It does appear, however, to be naïve to assume that whistleblowers are altruistic or that they as a group have a "moral edge" on inside traders.

[38] *See* Ackman, *supra* note 35. Besides being hailed as one of *Time* magazine's People of the Year in 2002, a reporter once observed that Watkins "has been hailed as a whistle-blower so often it's starting to sound like part of her name." *Id.*

[39] *Id.*

[40] *Id.*

[41] *Id.*

[42] E-mail from Sherron Watkins to Kenneth Lay, Enron Chairman (Jan. 20, 2002), http://www.itmweb.com/f012002.htm.

[43] *Id.*

[44] *Id.*

[45] *Id.*

scrutiny and there are probably one or two disgruntled 'redeployed' employees who know enough about the 'funny' accounting to get us in trouble."[46]

Watkins's letter reveals that she was well aware that the company was engaged in accounting fraud, and that the financial statements of the company did not fully represent to investors and regulators the true condition of the company. For example, Watkins observed, "[W]e have had a lot of smart people looking at this and a lot of accountants including AA & Co. have blessed the accounting treatment. None of that will protect Enron if these transactions are ever disclosed in the bright light of day."[47]

This suggests that Watkins was not only self-interested, but she also realized that there were material accounting issues that had not been disclosed. Rather than disclose these issues, she advocated attempting to correct the problems secretly, which she analogized to "robbing [a] bank in one year and trying to pay it back two years later."[48] In other words, the Watkins letter is more consistent with an effort by Watkins to distance herself from the fraud, but to continue to participate in the cover-up, in hopes that the entire mess would somehow blow over and life could return to normal.

Acting in a manner entirely consistent with the model of rational, self-interested behavior, Watkins attempts to quantify the risks and rewards of continuing to mask the company's ongoing fraud by assessing the probability of getting caught. She argues that if "[t]he probability of discovery is low enough and the estimated damage too great; then therefore we [should] find a way to quietly and quickly reverse, unwind, write down these positions/transactions."[49] Alternatively, she advises that if "[t]he probability of discovery is too great, the estimated damages to the company too great . . . we must quantify [and] develop damage containment plans and disclose."[50] Her biggest concern is detection. She fears that "[t]oo many people are looking for a smoking gun,"[51] and she fully understood that Enron was "'a crooked company.'"[52]

2. Analyzing Sherron Watkins's Actions

The point here is not to vilify Sherron Watkins. Rather, the purpose of this detailed review of Sherron Watkins's "whistleblowing" is to emphasize the point that Ms. Watkins did not do anything to expose the ongoing financial irregularities and accounting fraud. It is doubtful that Ms. Watkins properly can be characterized as a whistleblower. As I observed earlier, reporting fraud to the very people engaged in the misbehavior is hardly whistleblowing. Even if Ms. Watkins could be thought of as a whistleblower, she must be described as an unsuccessful one. This is unsurprising given that the only

---

46 *Id.*

47 *Id.*

48 *Id.*

49 *Id.*

50 *Id.*

51 *Id.*

52 *See id.*

person to whom Ms. Watkins directed her whistleblowing was Enron CEO Kenneth Lay, who was later convicted of multiple felonies for misrepresenting Enron's financial condition.

More importantly, regardless of whether Ms. Watkins's activities technically constitute whistleblowing, it is impossible to describe her motives as being more altruistic than inside traders. Clearly, there were many motivations for her actions, including concerns about self-preservation, her savings, her reputation, and about the undiversified human capital investment she had made in Enron.

The complexity that characterizes Sherron Watkins's motives is probably quite typical. Whatever distinctions one might be able to draw between whistleblowers and inside traders, it is not possible to distinguish these two activities on the basis of the motives of the actors. Since the activities cannot be distinguished on the basis of motive, and they cannot be distinguished on the basis of consequences, one is left to wonder what fuels our intuition that whistleblowing is desirable while insider trading on the same set of information is so abhorrent.[53]

Most, but not all, whistleblowing is tolerated. There is an exception to the general rule favoring whistleblowing when a whistleblower reveals confidential information that she has a legitimate legal duty not to disclose. But this, as shown below, is precisely the context in which insider trading is illegal. My point is that, as with whistleblowing, insider trading should be prohibited only in cases in which whistleblowing is prohibited, that is, in those cases in which the would-be trader has a legitimate legal duty to keep the information confidential and otherwise to refrain from acting on the information.

But, while the legal system ostensibly excoriates inside traders, the law protects whistleblowers from retaliation by their employers by making it illegal for any public company to "discharge, demote, suspend, threaten, harass, or in any other manner discriminate against an employee" because of any lawful provision of information about suspected fraud.[54]

---

[53] Despite the recent surge in popularity, whistleblowers and whistleblowing still face image problems not demonstrably different from the image problems faced by people accused of insider trading. For example, one whistleblower, Jesselyn Radack, a former legal adviser to the Justice Department's Professional Responsibility Advisory Office, observes being called "traitor," "turncoat," and "terrorist sympathizer." Jesselyn Radack, *Whistleblowing: My Story*, THE NATION, July 4, 2005, at 8, 24. She was so described after advising the criminal division of the FBI that any interrogation of "American Taliban" John Walker Lindh outside of the presence of his lawyer would be unethical. The FBI ignored Radack's advice and interrogated Lindh when he did not have the benefit of legal counsel. Radack claims a number of e-mails she had written explaining her legal position determining that Lindh had a right to a lawyer while being interrogated had been destroyed after the judge in the Lindh case ordered that all the documents be turned over to the court. Radack then turned whistleblower, disclosing the existence of the missing e-mails to *Newsweek*. Radack claims that she believed this was permitted by the Whistleblower Protection Act. Writing about the incident, Radack observes that "[w]histleblowers are stereotyped as disgruntled employees, troublemakers and snitches. The conscientious employee is often portrayed as vengeful, unstable or out for attention." *Id.*

[54] 18 U.S.C. § 1514A (Supp. III 2003).

II. INSIDER TRADING AS WHISTLEBLOWING

Sometimes, insider trading accomplishes precisely the same public policy objectives as whistleblowing is intended to accomplish. When this occurs, we should protect insider trading under the venerable common law doctrine that like cases should be treated alike. In this Part, I demonstrate that sometimes insider trading is the functional equivalent of whistleblowing. Such insider trading accomplishes the same goals as whistleblowing but much more effectively. Such insider trading might be called "high-powered whistleblowing."

Insider trading involves buying or selling securities (or derivatives, such as puts, calls, or futures) on the basis of material, nonpublic information.[55] In this Article, I limit my discussion of insider trading to the narrow context in which such trading occurs in a situation in which whistleblowing could also occur.[56]

In this whistleblowing context, insider trading occurs when the potential whistleblower has bad news about a company. The conduct that replaces the whistleblowing may involve selling shares short,[57] selling single-stock futures contracts, or purchasing put options or selling call options—all strategies that permit traders to profit on the basis of price declines.

Insider trading on the basis of information about an ongoing fraud necessarily leads to the exposure of that fraud. It is not profitable for an inside trader simply to sell or to sell short shares in the company involved in the fraud without revealing or causing the underlying information to be revealed. While it might seem that mere selling without disclosure might be a profitable strategy for insiders because such selling drives share prices down, this is not the case.[58] In efficient capital markets,[59] transacting in financial

---

[55] It also is possible to trade shares in rival firms on the basis of material inside information. For example, when an employee in a company obtains good (or bad) news about her company's prospects, she may sell (or buy) shares in rivals, particularly in markets with high levels of concentrations and barriers to entry. *See generally* Ian Ayres & Joseph Bankman, *Substitutes for Insider Trading*, 54 Stan. L. Rev. 235, 235-94 (2001).

[56] For a broad defense of insider trading as an efficient mechanism for compensating management, *see* Henry G. Manne, Insider Trading and the Stock Market (1966).

[57] Short selling occurs when somebody sells shares that she does not own by first borrowing such shares, and delivering them to the purchaser. The short seller must, at some point, repurchase the shares. The short seller's goal is for the price of the shares being sold to decline so that they can be repurchased at a lower price, thereby enabling the seller to profit from a decline in the price of the stock. A short seller's profit is the price at which the stock are sold minus the cost of buying the shares plus the commissions and expenses (interest) associated with borrowing the stock until the short position is covered.

[58] Daniel R. Fischel & David J. Ross, *Should the Law Prohibit "Manipulation" in Financial Markets?*, 105 Harv. L. Rev. 503, 519-21 (1991).

[59] The proposition that stock markets are efficient has been formalized in the well-known "Efficient Capital Markets Hypothesis" (ECMH). For a discussion of the ECMH, which posits that a market is efficient if the prices of the assets traded in that market fully reflect all available information relevant to the pricing decision, *see* Jonathan R. Macey, An Introduction to Modern Financial Theory 38 (2d ed. 1998); Burton G. Malkiel, A Random Walk Down Wall Street (8th ed. 2004); and Burton G. Malkiel, The Efficient Markets Hypothesis and Its Critics, J. Econ. Persp., Winter 2003, at 59. The

assets, whether buying or selling, will not affect the underlying values of those assets unless such transactions reveal information. This is because the prices of securities and other financial assets reflect, at any given time, all publicly available information relevant to the price of that asset.[60]

Because trades that lack information content will not affect prices, insiders cannot profit merely by selling—they must also reveal information for prices to adjust. As with whistleblowing, insider trading on whistleblower information must result in the information about a fraud being revealed. If the information turns out to be unreliable, prices will not adjust, and the insider will lose the transaction costs associated with his investment. These costs can be substantial if the insider is selling short as well as liquidating his current holdings.[61] For this reason, short selling is likely to be a far more credible signal than whistleblowing: the talk involved in whistleblowing is cheap, while the trading involved in short selling is costly to the short seller whose information about the underlying company is erroneous.

Such short selling can create perverse incentives, particularly the incentive that top managers might have to cause harm to their firms in order to make private gains on declines in the company's shares. But these perverse incentives do not pose a problem in cases where insider trading is done by employees who have no power to affect the strategic decisions of the firm, either because they no longer are employed by the company or because they work in a low-level capacity that does not involve strategic decision-making. For this reason, in my view, regulation should be enacted that permits low-level insiders such as rank-and-file employees to trade on the basis of material, nonpublic information under certain conditions.[62]

---

semi-strong form of the ECMH posits that current securities prices "fully reflect public knowledge . . . and that efforts to acquire and analyze this knowledge cannot be expected to produce superior investment results." JAMES H. LORIE, PETER DODD & MARY HAMILTON KLIMPTON, THE STOCK MARKET: THEORIES AND EVIDENCE 56 (Myron S. Scholes ed., 2d ed. 1985).

[60] Mere trading does not affect share prices. Rather, trading only affects share prices to the extent that the trading reveals new information about the returns to investors in the underlying asset. For example, the available evidence indicates that large block trades adjust rapidly to reflect new information contained in the sale of the block. Larry Y. Dann et al., *Trading Rules, Large Blocks and the Speed of Adjustment*, 4 J. FIN. ECON. 3 (1977).

[61] Short selling is so costly that very few shares are actually sold short. Robert J. Shiller, *From Efficient Markets to Behavioral Finance*, J. ECON. PERSP., Winter 2003, at 83, 101. For example, studies show that less than two percent of all stocks had short interest of more than five percent of outstanding shares. Patricia M. Dechow et al., *Short Selling, Fundamental Analysis, and Stock Returns*, 61 J. FIN. ECON. 77, 87 (2001). In addition to the complex tax issues associated with short selling, traders who sell short must pay daily accruing interest for the shares they borrow in order to deliver to the purchaser of the shares that have been sold short. *Id.* at 80. Also, short sellers generally do not receive interest on the funds received from selling stock short and these funds do not reduce outstanding margin balances. *Id.*; *see also* Short Sales, Exchange Act Release No. 50,103, 69 Fed. Reg. 48,008 (Aug. 6, 2004).

[62] Such regulation should cover trading by employees who have not had any role in the underlying conduct on which the trading is based.

As with whistleblowing, insider trading requires that the person engaged in the conduct have a pre-existing relationship with the company. In fact, liability for insider trading requires that there be a pre-existing relationship of trust and confidence that the defendant-insider has breached by trading.[63] To be a whistleblower requires a similar sort of relationship. And, of course, at a bare minimum, both whistleblowing and insider trading require that the whistleblowers and the traders actually have some information not generally known that is of interest to others.

Tying these various strands together, we see that whistleblowers and insiders share the same basic defining characteristics: (a) they are informational intermediaries; (b) they have information not widely known or not already reflected in share prices; and (c) they are in a pre-existing contractual or quasi-contractual relationship with the source of the information.[64] As a descriptive matter, the only meaningful difference between inside traders and whistleblowers is that whistleblowers speak rather than trade their information. This distinction may appear vast, but, when analyzed realistically, it is far from clear that this is a difference with much, if any, moral significance. And, as shown below, it also is far from clear that these activities can be distinguished on the basis of their economic impact on third parties.

A. *Dirks v. SEC*

The starting point for any analysis of the relationship between whistleblowing and insider trading is *Dirks v. SEC*.[65] This case is interesting for two reasons. First, the case involves the efforts of a failed whistleblower who passed on tips about company fraud to the defendant. Second, *Dirks* suggests that whistleblowers and inside traders are likely to have similar motivations for their behavior. Whether their underlying motivation is revenge, profit-seeking, or some complex combination of reasons does not appear relevant to our analysis of the social desirability of the behavior.

A brief review of the facts: On March 6, 1973, Raymond Dirks, a securities analyst at the investment bank Hawkins Delafield, received a tip from Ronald Secrist, a disgruntled former officer of Equity Funding of America.[66] Secrist's tip alleged that the assets of Equity Funding, a diversified corporation primarily engaged in selling life insurance and mutual funds, were vastly overstated as the result of a massive, ongoing series of fraudulent corporate practices.[67] Secrist also told Dirks that he and others had tried to convey his information about the fraud at Equity Funding to various regulatory agencies, including the SEC and the New York State Insurance Commissioner's

---

[63] *See* United States v. O'Hagan, 521 U.S. 642 (1997); Dirks v. SEC, 463 U.S. 646 (1983); Chiarella v. United States, 445 U.S. 222 (1980).

[64] *See infra* Table 1.

[65] 463 U.S. 646 (1983).

[66] *Id.* at 648-49.

[67] *Id.*

Office.[68] None of the agencies followed up on these accusations.[69] Secrist urged Dirks to verify the fraud and to disclose it publicly.[70] Secrist did not attempt to blackmail Equity Funding.

At oral argument in the Supreme Court, the SEC took the position that Dirks's obligation to disclose would not be satisfied by reporting the information to the SEC.[71] In its brief to the Court, the SEC took an inconsistent position, speaking favorably of a "safe harbor" rule under which an investor would satisfy his obligation to disclose by reporting the information to the Commission and then waiting a set period of time before trading.[72] However, as noted by Justice Blackmun in dissent, since no such safe harbor rule was in effect, "persons such as Dirks have no real option other than to refrain from trading."[73]

The prohibition on insider trading was unfortunate in *Dirks*. If the legal restrictions against insider trading had been successful in deterring Raymond Dirks from acting on the tip he had received from Ronald Secrist, it would have prolonged a massive ongoing fraud. Clearly, prohibiting insider trading would have been inefficient in this context, which is why the Supreme Court rejected the SEC's legal theory and overturned the Commission's sanctions against Raymond Dirks.

B. Lessons from *Dirks*

The *Dirks* case illustrates that insider trading has at least one clear advantage over whistleblowing: it provides a significantly more credible signal the information is true. Talk is cheap. When, as is often the case, the whistleblower is a disgruntled employee, people are less inclined to believe the whistleblower's story. This is particularly true in a situation like that of Equity Funding, or Enron, where the corporation is highly regarded and has significant resources with which to respond to the whistleblower's allegations. In *Dirks* (and there is no reason to assume that this result should not be generalized), insider trading worked where whistleblowing did not. The constellation of facts that produced the litigation in *Dirks* demonstrates that insider trading on negative information has certain decisive advantages over whistleblowing. For instance, insider trading does not require that the person in possession of knowledge of the wrongdoing be able to persuade a government official to take action before the wrongdoing can be confronted. The insider need only convince herself that she is right in her own

---

[68] *Id.* at 649, 669 n.2.

[69] *Id.* at 649.

[70] *Id.*

[71] *Id.* at 661 n.21 (quoting Transcript of Oral Argument at 27, *Dirks*, 463 U.S. 646 (No. 82-276)).

[72] *Id.* at 678 n.17 (Blackmun, J., dissenting) (citing Brief for Respondent at 43-44, *Dirks*, 463 U.S. 646 (No. 82-276)).

[73] *Id.*

assessment of the situation before acting.[74] This, of course, means that insider trading on whistleblower information obviates the credibility problem that typically plagues whistleblowers.

It is true that in the important subset of cases involving government corruption, whistleblowers can bring their own lawsuits in the form of qui tam actions. But litigation is costly and time-consuming, and plaintiffs in qui tam actions must confront the bureaucratic hurdles of court procedure, hurdles that need not be confronted by those who simply trade.[75] Thus, at least in some cases, insider trading has the advantage of involving a faster and more certain payoff for the insider in possession of whistleblower information than whistleblowing does. This is because, unlike whistleblowers, inside traders do not have to rely on government officials, who are often poorly motivated or inept, in order to profit from the information they have acquired. Similarly, unlike whistleblowers, inside traders do not have to wait for the litigation process to run its course, which may take years to produce a recovery or settlement.

III. INSIDER TRADING AND WHISTLEBLOWING: IS THE COMBINATION THE NORM?

Dirks v. SEC, described in the previous section, involved the simultaneous use of both whistleblowing and insider trading (via tipping) in a very effective manner, where effectiveness is measured by the success in revealing the fraud. The claim that insider trading and whistleblowing are closely linked is bolstered by the extent to which these activities are conducted simultaneously. Insider trading and whistleblowing both require possession of material, nonpublic information, and both trading and whistleblowing

---

[74] If the insider who trades turns out to be wrong in her belief about the existence of an ongoing fraud, then she may lose money on her trading. Moreover, like any insider who trades, the insider who believes she is trading on information about an ongoing fraud has an obligation not to trade on the basis of legitimate nonpublic information unrelated to any fraud. Thus, in my view, while it should be permissible for an insider to trade on the basis of information about an ongoing fraud, it is, and should continue to be, illegal for an insider to trade on the basis of legitimate material, nonpublic information such as information about a decline in earnings or a downturn in sales.

[75] Under the False Claims Act, the whistleblower first files a lawsuit against the individual or business association charged with defrauding the government under seal. 31 U.S.C. § 3730(b)(2) (2000). Copies of the complaint must be served on the Department of Justice, along with a written disclosure of all material evidence and information in the whistleblower's possession so that the Federal Government is able to investigate the claim prior to deciding whether to intervene. *Id.* The Department of Justice is then supposed to investigate the case and decide whether to intervene in the lawsuit. § 3730(b)(3)-(4). While the statute provides for sixty days for the Department of Justice to make up its mind whether to sue, this period can be and often is extended at the request of the government in the court in which the complaint was filed. *Id.* If the Government declines to intervene, the whistleblower may continue to pursue the litigation on her own. § 3730(c)(3). If the Government decides to intervene, the whistleblower receives a slightly smaller percentage of any recovery: if the Government intervenes, the whistleblower is entitled to between fifteen to twenty-five percent of the proceeds of the action or settlement, plus expenses and attorneys' fees. § 3730(d)(1). If the Government does not intervene, the whistleblower is entitled to between twenty-five and thirty percent of the proceeds plus expenses and attorneys' fees. § 3730(d)(2).

are consistent with the rational self-interest of the people engaging in these activities. Thus it should not be surprising that in cases such as *Dirks*, these activities are carried on simultaneously.

For example, Sherron Watkins, who was widely portrayed as a heroine for calling attention to accounting irregularities at Enron,[76] engaged in trading on the basis of the information contained in her whistleblower memorandum, and, in doing so, may have violated insider trading laws.[77] During her Congressional testimony about her role in uncovering the financial and accounting fraud at Enron, Watkins revealed that soon after warning Enron CEO Kenneth Lay that the company was about to "implode in a wave of accounting scandals," she sold a large block of her shares in order to avoid impending losses.[78] That sale violated the current interpretation of SEC Rule 10b-5, the regulation prohibiting insider trading, which makes it illegal to buy or sell securities "on the basis of material nonpublic information about that security," where doing so involves the breach of a pre-existing duty of trust to maintain the confidentiality of such information.[79]

Of course it is not possible to acquire data on the specific incidences of insider trading by people with whistleblower information since people trading on the basis of material, nonpublic information do not advertise their transactions. However, Sherron Watkins's near incrimination under the laws prohibiting insider trading is not without precedent.

In addition to the Watkins and the Dirks examples, the classic insider trading/whistleblower sequence (and even accusations of blackmail) is reiterated in the example of Ted Beatty at Dynegy, another Houston energy company.[80] Mr. Beatty, angry at Dynegy when he was overlooked for a promotion, resigned from the company. When he left, he took with him incriminating documents that suggested questionable accounting at the company in a transaction called Project Alpha. The information revealed by Mr. Beatty caused several high-ranking Dynegy officers to resign almost immediately and led to the fraud investigations of energy traders at several companies. The information also resulted in an SEC suit against Dynegy for securities fraud. Dynegy ultimately

---

[76] *E.g.*, Esther Addley, *Women: Let's hear it for our women of the year; A totally arbitrary, personal and partial look at the women who have delighted, impressed and inspired us in 2002*, GUARDIAN (London), Dec. 20, 2002, at 6; Arianna Huffington, *If women ran corporate America*, SAN DIEGO UNION-TRIBUNE, May 15, 2003, at B13.

[77] *See, e.g.*, Bruce Nichols, *Enron witness became pariah: Whistle-blower in case details response after her meeting with Lay*, DALLAS MORNING NEWS, Mar. 16, 2006, at 1D.

[78] The Financial Collapse of Enron—Part 3: Hearing Before the Subcomm. on Oversight & Investigations of the H. Comm. on Energy & Commerce, 107th Cong. 50 (2002) (testimony of Sherron Watkins), available at http://energycommerce.house.gov/107/action/107-89.pdf.

[79] 17 C.F.R. § 240.10b5-1 (2006).

[80] *See* Jathon Sapsford & Paul Beckett, *Informer's Odyssey: The Complex Goals and Unseen Costs of Whistle-Blowing—Dynegy Ex-Trainee Encounters Short-Sellers and Lawyers, Fears Being Blackballed—Seeking Justice and a Payday*, WALL ST. J., Nov. 25, 2002, at A1.

suffered the complete collapse of its equity and consented to a $3 million SEC civil fine, selling all of its major assets in order to survive.[81]

Following a pattern of conduct virtually identical to the one followed by Ronald Secrist in the *Dirks* case, Mr. Beatty tipped his information about Dynegy to another analyst, Jack Pitts, of the New York investment fund, Steadfast Capital.[82] Steadfast, like Raymond Dirks's clients, sold Dynegy's stock short.[83] Shortly before trading, Mr. Pitts, the tippee, wrote an e-mail to his tipper, Mr. Beatty, observing that "any sign of dubious accounting at Dynegy would 'make investors' fears go crazy and take the stock into a tailspin.'"[84] Again, it was the combination of whistleblowing and insider trading that led to the exposure of fraud.

IV. CREDIBILITY, PAYOFFS AND RELIANCE ON OTHER MECHANISMS OF CORPORATE GOVERNANCE

The *Dirks* case and the Beatty incident both illustrate parallels between insider trading and whistleblowing where the information being used pertains to fraud or other corporate misconduct. In both cases, it appears trading was more successful than whistleblowing in revealing the fraud. Given the complexity of whistleblowers' motives, their inability to make a credible commitment about the veracity of their information, and the necessity for bureaucratic investigation of the information being disclosed, it is not surprising that whistleblowing is often unsuccessful.

An important distinction between whistleblowing and insider trading relates to how each of these activities interacts with other institutions of corporate governance and informational gatekeepers, particularly Wall Street industry analysts and the SEC. Whistleblowing, to be effective, requires that other institutions of corporate governance also function effectively, because whistleblowing is not self-effectuating. Specifically, unlike inside traders, whistleblowers must first convince regulators, financial analysts, or some other corporate governance intermediary of the validity of their claims before their actions can gain traction. Thus, the effectiveness of whistleblowing largely depends on the integrity and efficacy of these other institutions. In light of the historical unreliability of institutions of corporate governance, the need to rely on these institutions is a serious disadvantage for whistleblowing relative to insider trading. Again, the *Dirks* case provides a useful illustration of the point.

A. The Failure of External Corporate Governance Mechanisms

Stock market analysts were quite bullish on Equity Funding, the company whose fraud Ronald Secrist was attempting to reveal. Shortly before Equity Funding collapsed,

81 *Id.*

82 *Id.*

83 *Id.*

84 *Id.*

an analyst at the investment banking firm Cowen & Co. issued a report recommending that investors buy Equity Funding "for aggressive accounts."[85] An analyst at Burnham & Co., Inc. opined that Equity Funding was "an excellent value" and rated the Company "a Buy."[86]

Analysts were not only touting Equity Funding, they also engaged in active efforts to defend the stock against Secrist's efforts at whistleblowing. On March 26, 1973, the day before the New York Stock Exchange halted trading in Equity Funding, the analyst at Hayden, Stone, Inc. who was responsible for covering the company circulated a memorandum announcing that "rumors have been circulating which have affected Equity Funding's stock."[87] The analyst reported that his well-regarded investment bank had "checked these rumors, and there appears to be no substance to any of them."[88] It turns out that the analyst "had checked with insurance regulators in various states and each one said they had no present intention of conducting any inquiries" into Secrist's allegations of fraud at Equity Funding.[89] The SEC showed a similar lack of interest in investigating Equity Funding until investors tipped by Secrist began trading on the information he gave them. Secrist testified that Equity Funding employees who had attempted to notify the SEC of the wrongdoing at the company had been "brushed aside with a comment that that's a ridiculous story."[90] Worse still, whistleblowing employees "also found that the information was sometimes relayed back to Equity Funding, and that 'they were placed in personal jeopardy as a result of having gone'" to the SEC.[91]

Attempts by Dirks to tip Equity Funding's outside auditors were similarly ineffective. During the course of his investigation of Equity Funding, Dirks met with the company's auditors "in an attempt to spread word of the fraud and bring it to a halt."[92] When Dirks learned that Equity Funding's auditors were about to release certified financial statements for the company, he "contacted them and apprised them of the fraud allegations, hoping that they would withhold release of their report and seek a halt in the trading of [Equity Funding] securities."[93] Instead, the auditors "merely reported Dirks' allegations to . . . management."[94]

Despite the fact that whistleblowers had contacted the SEC and state insurance officials as early as 1971, Equity Funding's chairman—one of the principal architects of the fraud—testified that, prior to March 1973, when Secrist's insider trading caused

---

[85] Brian Trumbore, *Wall Street History: Ray Dirks and the Equity Funding Scandal*, STOCKSANDNEWS.COM, Feb. 6, 2004, http://www.stocksandnews.com/searchresults.asp?Id=1573&adate=2/6/2004.

[86] *Id.*

[87] *Id.*

[88] *Id.*

[89] *Id.*

[90] Brief for the United States as Amicus Curiae in Support of Reversal, Dirks v. SEC, 463 U.S. 646 (1983) (No. 82-276), *available at* http://www.usdoj.gov/osg/briefs/1982/sg820094.txt.

[91] *Id.*

[92] *Id.*

[93] *Id.* (alteration in original).

[94] *Id.*

Equity Funding's stock price to collapse, he had "received no questions from auditors, state regulatory authorities, or federal regulatory authorities that suggested 'they suspected there was a fraud at Equity Funding.'"[95]

B. The Failure of the Media to Expose Corporate Fraud

Journalists often perform no better than regulators in facilitating the efforts of whistleblowers. In fact the rationale given by the *Wall Street Journal* for declining to write a story about the fraud at Equity Funding usefully reveals a general problem for journalists seeking to publish information tipped by whistleblowers: namely, the lack of a means to verify the credibility of the information being provided by the whistleblower:

> [D]uring the entire week that Dirks was in Los Angeles investigating Equity Funding, he was also in touch regularly with William Blundell, the *Wall Street Journal*'s Los Angeles bureau chief. Dirks kept Blundell up to date on the progress of the investigation and badgered him to write a story for the *Wall Street Journal* on the allegations of fraud at Equity Funding. Blundell, however, was afraid that publishing such damaging rumors supported only by hearsay from former employees might be libelous, so he declined to write the story.
>
> [Dirks] provided Blundell with "the substance of all he knew," including his "notes" and the "names" of all witnesses. Nevertheless, given the "scope of the fraud," Blundell doubted that it could have been "missed by an honest auditor" and discounted the entire allegation.[96]

C. Whistleblowers' Failure to Communicate

The cautious reactions to information provided by whistleblowers are not necessarily a result of sloth or venality on the part of regulators, market analysts, journalists, or others. Rather, the suspicion attached to whistleblowers is justified by the dubious motives that often accompany their actions. For example, Ronald Secrist, the tipper who pointed Raymond Dirks to the Equity Funding fraud, was reported to have tipped Dirks because he was "upset over his small Christmas bonus."[97] Similarly, Ted Beatty, the Dynegy tipper, began his whistleblowing because Dynegy failed to give him "the promotion he felt he deserved."[98]

In addition, it is by no means clear that the highly cautious reactions one often observes in response to whistleblowers' information is a particularly inefficient response to whistleblowing. In order to gauge the efficiency of ignoring whistleblowing, one must

---

[95] *Id.*

[96] *Id.* (first alteration in original) (internal citations omitted).

[97] Trumbore, *supra* note 85.

[98] Sapsford & Beckett, *supra* note 80.

compare the costs of ignoring the whistleblowing information with the benefits, which come in the form of conserving resources that otherwise would be wasted in pursuing the false charges of disgruntled employees and other malcontents. The question of whether the costs of such caution in response to whistleblowers' complaints exceed the benefits of investigating the merits of the allegations remains an empirical issue for which data is scarce if not nonexistent. One thing that is known, however, is that the cost-benefit calculations associated with ignoring whistleblowers may be different for bureaucrats and financial intermediaries than for society as a whole. Bureaucrats are inherently risk-averse. They benefit little from validating a whistleblower's complaint, and risk a lot if they make a blunder. Thus, bureaucratic incentives may lead to whistleblowers' claims being met with an excess of caution.

Of course, when analysts and other corporate governance intermediaries have incentives to bias their recommendations and analyses in favor of companies and to ignore fraud, whistleblowers will face even greater obstacles in trying to convince people that what they are saying is true. As I have observed in a previous article: "[t]he problem with the analysts' recommendations is not difficult to grasp. Investment banks pressure the analysts they employ to give positive ratings to companies tracked by issuers because positive ratings boost stock prices and generate capital for their investment banking clients."[99]

Thus gatekeepers such as stock market analysts and bureaucrats have much to lose and little to gain from crediting whistleblowers' accusations.

D. The Effects of These Failures on Whistleblowing: The Relative Payoffs of Whistleblowing and Insider Trading

This analysis reveals a major defect with whistleblowing. Besides providing a more credible signal than whistleblowing, insider trading does not rely on the efficacy of other institutions of corporate governance in order to be effective. As these other corporate governance institutions become more effective, however, the need for whistleblowing also declines. This, in turn, indicates that whistleblowing is least effective when it is most needed, which is during times when the basic institutions of corporate governance are not functioning independently or effectively.

Predictably, the market's response to whistleblowing and insider trading reflects the higher value associated with trading than whistleblowing. The Beatty incident at Dynegy and the *Dirks* case both suggest the monetary payoff for trading is higher than the payoff for either whistleblowing or tipping, at least in the private sector, where there are no statutes that provide monetary incentives for whistleblowers. In both cases it appears that the tippees receiving the information and trading on it fared much better than the tippers who provided them with the information and attempted to inform regulators of the problems they had discovered. Mr. Beatty was assured by the people he approached with his information about Dynegy that his assistance in their trading

---

[99] Jonathan R. Macey, *Efficient Capital Markets, Corporate Disclosure, and Enron,* 89 CORNELL L. REV. 394, 404 (2004).

activities "would earn him big money."[100] Subsequent press reports of Mr. Beatty's activities, however, reveal that "no such payout has materialized," and that Mr. Beatty is now "unemployed and in financial stress."[101] Raymond Dirks became a celebrity. Ironically, his efforts to cooperate with the SEC led to his being prosecuted by the SEC for insider trading.[102] If he had confined his activities to tipping, and had not attempted to inform the SEC of his concerns about Equity Funding, it is likely that he would have avoided prosecution.

V. INSIDER TRADING, WHISTLEBLOWING, PROPERTY RIGHTS, AND LAW

Insider trading can accomplish the same socially desirable results as whistleblowing. An important difference between insider trading and whistleblowing is that whistleblowing is strictly regulated and constrained by the need for whistleblowers to have their claims validated by some sort of public institution like an administrative agency or a prosecutor. This required mediation by an outside organization is a controlling mechanism to ostensibly restrict the flow of frivolous or inappropriate whistleblowing. As shown above, the problem with this process is not so much that it may generate too many whistleblower complaints, but that it may generate too few, and those that are generated are sometimes still inappropriately discounted.

A. The Law of Insider Trading and Its Foundations in Property Rights

By contrast, there is no mediating public institution in place to monitor and control insider trading on whistleblowing information. There are, of course, legal restrictions on insider trading in place, but these restrictions are aimed at eliminating insider trading, and do not have the intention of facilitating insider trading on whistleblower-type information.

Completely eliminating or even relaxing the rules against insider trading would predictably result in an oversupply of insider trading. Some mechanism or interpretive rule is needed to distinguish among the various sorts of inside (material, nonpublic) information, and also to permit market participants to determine what sort of information may be utilized in trading and what sort of information must remain confidential.

Current court interpretations of the SEC rules related to insider trading provide a very promising starting point for developing an interpretive rule about when insider trading is appropriate in the whistleblowing context. Here the argument proceeds in three steps. First, the legal prohibition against insider trading does not bar all trading that occurs when one trader has an informational advantage over her counterparty. Rather, the rule requires that trading on the basis of such an informational advantage be the result of a breach of fiduciary duty for it to be illegal.

---

[100] Sapsford & Beckett, *supra* note 80.

[101] *Id.*

[102] Dirks v. SEC, 463 U.S. 646, 650-51 (1983).

Second, basing legal responsibility for insider trading on the breach of fiduciary duty provides a basis for establishing and allocating property rights in nonpublic information. Information belongs to somebody, usually the company that is the source of the information. Where trading on this information involves the misappropriation (or theft) of such information, a breach of duty occurs. Conversely, trading does not involve the breach of a duty when the trader is not violating the property rights of any other person or entity by trading.

Third, applying the above analysis of fiduciary duties and property rights to trading on the basis of whistleblower information suggests that there is no basis upon which to ban such trading. Information about an ongoing fraud or other criminal activity should not be considered the property of the firm that is engaged in the fraud. Trading on the basis of such information, therefore, should not be considered a breach of fiduciary duty. Put simply, while companies clearly have a valid interest in maintaining the confidentiality of legitimate corporate information, such as their strategic plans, their earnings, their acquisition plans and other activities, they have no valid interest in maintaining the confidentiality of information about fraud or other illegal activities that might be used in whistleblowing.

The rules against insider trading are meant to protect public companies and investors from theft of information that properly belongs to them. Insiders such as executives or directors, and "temporary insiders" such as attorneys, accountants, financial printers, and investment bankers routinely obtain confidential information about a company in the course of their work. The insider trading rules are intended to prevent both these permanent and temporary insiders from abusing their positions of trust by trading in violation of their legal duties of confidentiality.

The Supreme Court clearly articulated the fiduciary underpinnings of insider trading regulations in *Chiarella v. United States*.[103] The defendant in this case, Vincent Chiarella, was a financial printer whose employer, Pandick Press, was routinely hired by companies seeking to acquire other companies. These acquirers needed the services of a printer to manufacture the disclosure documents that would accompany their offers to acquire other companies. Chiarella traded on the basis of his advance knowledge of the information contained in the disclosure documents that he was printing. In so doing, he breached a fiduciary duty not to his trading partners—he owed no fiduciary duties to them—but rather to the bidding firms that were the sources of the information and to his employer, both of whom had relied on Chiarella to keep the information in his possession confidential. In the Court's view, unless Chiarella had a fiduciary obligation requiring him to keep the information he had acquired confidential, his trading did not constitute insider trading, despite the fact that he clearly possessed advantageous, nonpublic information.[104]

---

[103] 445 U.S. 222, 231 (1980).

[104] Chiarella clearly breached a fiduciary duty to his employer, Pandick Press, when he traded on information that he had promised, as a condition of his employment, to keep confidential. However, because

B. Legal Lessons for Trading on Whistleblower Information: Creating Incentives

Here the parallel to whistleblowing is clear. Insider trading is regulated in order to *maintain* the confidentiality of legitimate corporate information. Whistleblowing is encouraged in order to *prevent* information about fraud and corruption from remaining confidential. In both the insider trading context and the whistleblowing context, the key issue is the extent to which the applicable law provides the appropriate incentives. In the case of insider trading, the focus is on providing incentives for people to maintain the confidentiality of legitimate corporate information that is meant to be used only for a corporate purpose and not for the private benefit of inside traders. In the case of whistleblowing, the focus is on providing incentives for people to reveal information about wrongdoing.

No rational person would consider the disclosure of some material, nonpublic information about a company's strategic plans to be legitimate whistleblowing. It is, therefore, mysterious why anyone would consider information about an ongoing corporate fraud to be bona fide corporate information that a company could legitimately require its employees to keep confidential. Since it seems irrational to prevent people from disclosing such information, it also seems irrational to prevent people from trading on the basis of this sort of whistleblower information.

From a legal perspective, insider trading is illegal only when such trading is based on material, nonpublic information and the person doing the trading has breached a fiduciary duty by trading. From a property rights perspective, the same inquiries into whether a person owes and has breached fiduciary duties by trading define and allocate the nature of the property interest in the information being exploited through trading. This is because one cannot owe a fiduciary duty, such as a duty to refrain from trading or to keep information confidential, unless the person to whom such an obligation is owed enjoys a property interest in such information.

Consistent with this analysis and going back at least to John Locke, information acquired through legitimate means, such as one's own labor, is the property of the person who has acquired it.[105] One has a presumptive right to use information acquired in this way.[106] As Hernando de Soto has powerfully illustrated, the economic justifications for clearly defining property rights, as well as for extending such rights to people who have made legitimate acquisitions, is that doing so provides the best set of incentives to maximize the value of such information. As Locke was concerned with the underutilization of land enclosed by England's landed gentry, de Soto's concern is with what he described as "dead" assets, a term he used to describe the undisclosed and

---

the government had not presented this theory of liability to the jury, the Court held that Chiarella could not be convicted for trading in breach of a fiduciary relationship of trust and confidence. *Id.* at 236-37.

[105] JOHN LOCKE, TWO TREATISES OF GOVERNMENT bk. II, ch. V, at 285-302 (Peter Laslett ed., 3d ed., Cambridge Univ. Press 1988) (1690).

[106] Alan Strudler, *Moral Complexity in the Law of Nondisclosure*, 45 UCLA L. REV. 337, 375 (1997).

unregistered assets of those operating outside of the highly corrupt, over-bureaucratized formal economies of undeveloped countries.[107]

The implications are clear: failure to allow insider trading on the basis of whistleblower information will lead to the same sort of underutilization of assets as the failure to legalize property rights in underdeveloped sectors of the world. Just as in the case of ill-defined property rights in de Soto's native Peru, the failure to recognize the rights of people in possession of corporate whistleblower information to profit from that information will lead to underutilization of such information and to inefficiency.

Applying this analysis to the legal restrictions on insider trading yields at least three reasons why certain insiders should be permitted to trade on whistleblower information. First, insider trading is only illegal when it involves the breach of a fiduciary duty, and there is no fiduciary duty to maintain the confidentiality of information about an ongoing fraud. Second, from a property rights perspective, a company committing fraud cannot claim a legitimate corporate interest in maintaining the ongoing confidentiality of information relating to its fraud. Finally, applying the sort of economic analysis that de Soto applies in the development context yields the conclusion that insider trading on whistleblower information should be encouraged because, just as it is socially desirable to encourage the efficient utilization of assets in the economy, it is also efficient to encourage activities that will not only lead to the exposure of corporate fraud, but also actually discourage such fraud by raising the probability that it will be exposed.

Still another incentive-based justification for permitting insider trading on the basis of whistleblower information is that doing so is likely to decrease the time required for the information to be revealed to the public. Insiders may trade knowing that the information they are using will come out eventually. As long as insider trading is illegal, however, there exists a powerful disincentive to reveal that they are trading. Legitimizing their property rights in whistleblower information by making insider trading on the basis of such information legal would not only have the obvious effect of encouraging more such trading, but it also would encourage traders to disclose or otherwise take steps to make public the information in their possession. This in turn would accelerate the exposure of the fraud and other wrongdoing that was the subject of the trading.

C. What Kind of Information Qualifies as Whistleblower Information?

In addition to limiting the identity of who can trade on whistleblower information, there remains the issue of what sort of information is the proper subject of trading and what is not. Here the analysis is greatly facilitated by analogy to protections afforded to corporate whistleblowers by the Sarbanes-Oxley Act. Sarbanes-Oxley provides protection for information "regarding any conduct which the employee reasonably believes

---

[107] HERNANDO DE SOTO, THE MYSTERY OF CAPITAL: WHY CAPITALISM TRIUMPHS IN THE WEST AND FAILS EVERYWHERE ELSE (2000); *see also* Richard Pipes, PROPERTY AND FREEDOM (1999). For an extremely useful comparison of the work of Locke and de Soto, on which this paragraph draws, see Donald A. Krueckeberg, *The Lessons of John Locke or Hernando de Soto: What if Your Dreams Come True?,* 15 HOUSING POL'Y DEBATE 1 (2004), *available at* http://content.knowledgeplex.org/kp2/cache/documents/38182.pdf.

constitutes a violation of . . . any provision of Federal law relating to fraud against shareholders."[108] Thus, just as not every disclosure by self-proclaimed whistleblowers is protected activity, neither should every trade by an insider be subject to the defense that it involved protected whistleblowing. Nevertheless, the category of protected activity is broad for whistleblowers,[109] and it should be no less broad for inside traders.

Whistleblower disclosures to nongovernmental agencies including the news media have long been protected by the Department of Labor under statutory provisions that are virtually identical to the provisions protecting whistleblowers in Sarbanes-Oxley.[110] Permitting whistleblowers to communicate in a slightly different way, by trading, seems like a modest extension of this current policy.

Sarbanes-Oxley contains protections for whistleblowers who mistakenly believed that their employers were engaged in illegal conduct. Specifically, an employee's whistleblower disclosures are protected as long as they are based on the employee's "reasonable belief" that the employer has engaged in fraudulent or illegal conduct. Under Sarbanes-Oxley, the employee is under no obligation to show that her allegations are meritorious.[111]

The problem associated with the transmittal of erroneous information pertaining to a corporation's activities is far less acute in the whistleblower context than for insider trading for two reasons. First, where an insider engages in trading on the basis of whistleblower information—regardless of whether that trading consists of short-selling, selling call options or single-stock futures, or buying put options—the insider must risk her own capital, betting that there will be a decline in the value of the company's share price when the whistleblower information is revealed. This means that, regardless of whether the insider is acting in good faith, it is costly for an insider to trade on the basis of erroneous information, because doing so involves a substantial risk that the insider will suffer trading losses. Second, whistleblowing involves moral hazard problems that do not exist in the insider trading context. Specifically, because it is illegal for employers to retaliate against whistleblowers, employees have an incentive to invent issues about which they can whistleblow in order to obtain job security that they

---

108 18 U.S.C. § 1514A(a) (Supp. III 2003).

109 STEPHEN M. KOHN ET AL., WHISTLEBLOWER LAW: A GUIDE TO LEGAL PROTECTIONS FOR CORPORATE EMPLOYEES 79 (2004).

110 *See* Gutierrez, ARB No. 99-116, ALJ No. 98-ERA-19, 2002 WL 31662915, at *1-2, 4-5 (Dep't of Labor Nov. 13, 2002), *also available at* http://www.oalj.dol.gov/PUBLIC/ARB/DECISIONS/ARB_DECISIONS/ERA/99_116A.ERAP.PDF (finding that, in addition to contacting members of Congress, communicating with reporters and a public interest organization, leading to the whistleblower being quoted in three "prominent" newspapers, was a protected activity designed to "publicly reveal information" about misconduct).

111 The standard was articulated in Halloum, ARB No. 04-068, OALJ No. 2003-SOX-0007, 2004 WL 5032613, at *13 (Dep't of Labor Mar. 4, 2004), *also available at* http://www.oalj.dol.gov/PUBLIC/WHISTLEBLOWER/DECISIONS/ALJ_DECISIONS/SOX/03SOX07A.HTM ("A belief that an activity was illegal may be reasonable even when subsequent investigation proves a complainant was entirely wrong. The accuracy or falsity of the allegations is immaterial; the plain language of the regulations only requires an objectively reasonable belief that shareholders were being defrauded to trigger the [Sarbanes-Oxley] Act's protections.").

would not otherwise have. Employers will be reluctant to fire whistleblowers because doing this risks not only civil penalties, but criminal sanctions under section 1107 of Sarbanes-Oxley.[112]

In addition, Congress, in order to make it "easier for an individual . . . to prove that a whistleblower reprisal has taken place," held that for a whistleblower to obtain relief in the form of reinstatement or damages for alleged retaliation, he need not show that "the whistleblowing was a . . . factor in a personnel action."[113] Indeed, the whistleblower need not even show that the whistleblowing was a substantial motivating or predominant factor in any action taken against him.[114] Instead he need only show a tenuous correlation: merely showing that the official taking the action knew that whistleblowing had taken place and acted within a time period after such whistleblowing that "a reasonable person could conclude that the disclosure was a factor in the personnel action."[115]

The analysis up to this point has demonstrated that there are built-in incentives that limit the extent to which people will engage in insider trading on the basis of erroneous whistleblower information. These safeguards do not similarly constrain whistleblowers. The analysis also indicates that only certain information should be the subject of insider trading. This information, which is the same information that might assist in an investigation of a violation of law, is the sort of information which we should encourage whistleblowers to disclose. The fact that we are able to determine the sort of information that qualifies for whistleblower protection demonstrates that we can also determine the sort of information that is the proper subject for protected insider trading.

However, the analysis here does not yield the conclusion that anybody in possession of material information about an ongoing corporate fraud should be able to trade on such information. As suggested above, the information must have been obtained in some legitimate manner. Thus it is necessary, as Locke puts it, that such property rights be allocated to information and other assets that are the product of one's "honest industry."[116] This suggests that the right to engage in insider trading on the basis of whistleblower information ought not be allocated to people who actually are participating in the fraud, because those who generate or participate in generating information about an ongoing fraud have not acquired such information as the result of their" honest industry," and are not entitled to profit from exploiting such information.[117] Similarly,

---

[112] Section 1107(a) of Sarbanes-Oxley amends 18 U.S.C. § 1513 to provide that: "[w]hoever knowingly, with the intent to retaliate, takes any action harmful to any person, including interference with the lawful employment or livelihood of any person, for providing to a law enforcement officer any truthful information relating to the commission or possible commission of any Federal offense, shall be fined under this title or imprisoned not more than 10 years, or both." 18 U.S.C. § 1513 (Supp. III 2003).

[113] 135 CONG. REC. 4508, 4513 (1989).

[114] *Id.*

[115] *Id.*

[116] LOCKE, *supra* note 105, at 31 ("[J]ustice gives every man a title to the product of his honest industry.").

[117] In an interview, Dean Henry Manne, when asked about the corporate scandals at Enron and Global Crossing, indicated that insider trading, if permissible, would have prevented these and other

from an economic perspective, permitting participants in a fraudulent scheme within a corporation to trade on such information could have the undesirable effect of providing additional incentives for miscreants to commit fraud.

VI. WHISTLEBLOWERS AND INSIDER TRADING: SOME DIFFERENCES

Whistleblowing and insider trading are complements, not substitutes. A system that permitted both whistleblowing and insider trading on whistleblowing information would do a better job of ferreting out wrongdoing than a system that permitted only one practice and not the other. The legitimacy of payments to whistleblowers is well-established and uncontroversial. The legitimacy of insider trading is, of course, far more contested.

The previous Part stressed certain advantages insider trading has over whistleblowing. Insider trading is self-effectuating. Inside traders receive prompt compensation for revealing corporate fraud. By contrast, private sector whistleblowers are merely protected from retaliation by law. Even in the public sector, where statutes provide for payments to whistleblowers, compensation for whistleblowing is highly uncertain and requires the whistleblower to wait years, if not decades. Insider trading on whistleblower information, however, is not without problems of its own. Thus, as discussed below, insider trading will never replace whistleblowing as a device for dealing with corporate wrongdoing.

A. The Need for Public Securities Markets

One problem with insider trading as a corporate governance device is that it is only effective in companies whose shares are publicly traded. There may be no insider trading opportunities for whistleblowers where the fraud or wrongdoing discovered by the whistleblower took place in government agencies or in privately held businesses. However, this shortcoming of insider trading can be easily overstated. First, the observation that it is not possible to engage in insider trading in agencies and firms with no publicly traded shares does nothing to undermine the argument that insider trading on whistleblower information can be of value in revealing fraud in companies whose shares are publicly traded. Second, drawing from what Ian Ayres and Joseph Bankman have observed, when insiders cannot trade in their own company's stock, they may be able to use the information to trade instead in the stock of their firm's rivals, suppliers, customers, or the manufacturers of complementary products.[118] Ayres and Bankman

---

frauds, saying, "I don't think the scandals would ever have erupted if we had allowed insider trading . . . because there would be plenty of people in those companies who would know exactly what was going on, and who couldn't resist the temptation to get rich by trading on the information, and the stock market would have reflected those problems months and months earlier than they did under this cockamamie regulatory system we have." Larry Elder, Commentary, *Legalize Insider Trading?*, WASH. TIMES, June 15, 2003, http://www.washtimes.com/commentary/20030615-112306-2790r.htm.

[118] Ayres & Bankman, *supra* note 55.

refer to this form of trading as trading in stock substitutes. These scholars observe that trading in stock substitutes may be quite profitable, and Heather Tookes has shown that insider trading in competitors often is a more profitable trading strategy for insiders than trading shares in their own firm.[119]

Ayres and Bankman do not consider the possible role of insider trading as a substitute for whistleblowing. Clarifying the law to permit insider trading in stock substitutes would dramatically expand the usefulness of insider trading on whistleblower information. For example, where a municipal worker has information about fraud in the allocation of construction contracts, she could sell stock in the contractor prior to blowing the whistle.[120]

B. The Timing Problem

An additional theoretical problem with insider trading is that the ability to engage in insider trading on any sort of information, including (but not limited to) whistleblower information, may create perverse incentives for the person in possession of the whistleblower information to delay revealing the information in order to complete her trading. Legalizing insider trading in material, nonpublic information about corporate fraud, or any other whistleblower information, is inefficient to the extent that such legalization provides incentives for traders to delay disclosure until the point at which the information would otherwise be disclosed.[121]

The question of the extent to which such delays would occur is an empirical one for which no data are available. However, while delays in the disclosure of whistleblower information do represent potential social costs inherent in the proposed regime, there are significant benefits on the other side of the ledger that are very likely to outweigh such costs.

Foremost among these advantages is the fact that permitting insider trading on whistleblower information would lead to the disclosure of information that otherwise would not be divulged at all. Since complete nondisclosure of whistleblower information is clearly worse than a mere delay in disclosure of such information, it is highly probable that the benefits of permitting insider trading on the basis of whistleblower information outweigh the costs.

---

119 Heather Tookes, *Information, Trading and Product Market Interactions: Cross-Sectional Implications of Insider Trading* (2004) (unpublished manuscript, on file with author).

120 Clearly it should be illegal for a government official involved in the investigation or prosecution of activity, either in the public sector or the private sector, to engage in any sort of trading on the basis of that information. The ability to engage in such trading would present a profound moral hazard, as the government official would have incentives to bring cases against innocent companies in order to benefit from stock price movements around the time of the announcement of contemplated regulatory action.

121 Henry Manne has suggested there is no problem here because insider trading enables investors to receive "virtual" full disclosure in the form of immediate and correct price adjustments. *See* Henry G. Manne, *The Case for Insider Trading*, WALL ST. J., Mar. 17, 2003, at A14.

Even if there is a delay in disclosure while insiders trade, this delay must be evaluated in light of the fact that there also is an inevitable delay in disclosure whenever a whistleblower engages in whistleblowing without concomitantly engaging in insider trading. Moreover, as described in more detail below, insider trading tends to push prices in the "correct" direction even before the revelatory disclosures are made. In contrast, when whistleblowing occurs unaccompanied by trading, there may be no change in share values prior to the public disclosure of information.

VII. WHO PAYS FOR WHISTLEBLOWING AND INSIDER TRADING: FAIRNESS WORRIES AND DISTRIBUTIONAL ISSUES

The above discussion presented an analysis that favored allowing insider trading on the basis of whistleblower information from instrumentalist and efficiency perspectives. Insider trading also raises important distributional concerns. In particular, at first blush it might appear that one advantage whistleblowing has over insider trading is that, since its impact is distributed more evenly over a corporation's population of shareholders, it is more "fair" than insider trading.

A. Fairness

At the outset, I wish to emphasize that no claim is being made here that those who trade on the basis of an informational advantage are particularly virtuous. These folks are not heroes. No claim is made that they are. Rather, the claim is simply that those who trade on the basis of inside information about an ongoing corporate fraud cannot be said categorically to be morally inferior to someone like Sherron Watkins who engages in self-serving whistleblowing. This, of course, is not because those who engage in insider trading are commendable, but rather because those who engage in whistleblowing are not. Nevertheless, it is far from clear that insider trading of the sort described here should be banned on fairness grounds.[122]

It is important to recognize at the outset that the traders being discussed here deserve to be able to sell their shares ahead of other shareholders. From a fairness perspective, perhaps the best way to conceptualize the issue is by analogizing the shareholders in a company riddled with fraud to the ethical dilemma that confronts the crew of a sinking ship with a grossly insufficient supply of life rafts. Selling shareholders are a bit like crew members who learn about a crisis on board ship in the course of their duties some time

[122] Louis Kaplow and Steven Shavell argue that legal policy analysis should be guided by reference to the well-being of individuals, and that legal rules should not guided by notions of fairness except to the extent that these fairness notions affect individuals' well-being. LOUIS KAPLOW & STEVEN SHAVELL, FAIRNESS VERSUS WELFARE 27 (2002). Of course, under this approach, one need not address the issues of fairness raised by analytical devices such as Kant's categorical imperative or the veil-of-ignorance construct. Under the Kaplow-Shavell approach, insider trading of the kind I describe in this Article should be encouraged because it unambiguously leads to improvements in the welfare of individuals. However, in this portion of the Article my aim is to show that insider trading of the kind I describe is best characterized as "fair" in Kantian or Rawlsean terms as well as "efficient" in Pareto terms.

before their fellow passengers. Should the crew members be able to use this information to save themselves by securing a place on a life raft before the passengers?

Focusing on the differences between the employees (crew) and the outside investors (passengers) suggests that in the corporate context, the answer to this question generally will be yes. This is because, unlike outside investors, the rank-and-file employees are unable to diversify their investments in the companies in which they work, and thus they suffer disproportionately from the effects of major corporate scandals. In particular, workers, unlike outside investors, have undiversifiable investments in their own human capital. Trading on the basis of inside information related to an ongoing corporate fraud that is going to destroy the company at least permits an employee to recoup some of this lost investment.

When corporations like Cendant, Enron, and Equity Funding implode, the rank-and-file workers are often the hardest hit. When Enron filed for bankruptcy protection, more than 4500 workers lost their jobs.[123] In the fall of 2001, as the problems at Enron gradually revealed themselves, "the company swiftly collapsed, taking with it the fortunes and retirement savings of thousands of employees."[124] The Enron rank-and-file employees have had a very difficult time securing comparable employment elsewhere, even years after the collapse of the company.[125] In contrast with the executives at the top, who participated in the fraud and made millions, "most former Enron employees who had nothing to do with the fraud at the company," have not fared well at all.[126]

Like 25.6% of companies with 5000 or more employees, most (sixty percent)[127] of Enron employees had their retirement money as undiversified investments in Enron

---

[123] Kristen Hays, *Midlevel Enron Corp. Executive Pleads Guilty to Filing False Fax Return*, ABILENE REPORTER-NEWS, Nov. 27, 2002, http://www.texnews.com/1998/2002/texas/texas_Midlevel_1127.html.

[124] Simon Romero, *10 Enron Players: Where They Landed After the Fall*, N.Y. TIMES, Jan. 29, 2006, at 9.

[125] Simon Romero, *Hard Times Haunt Enron's Ex-Workers; Few Find Jobs of Equal Stature Years After Company's Collapse*, N.Y. TIMES, Jan. 25, 2006, at 1.

[126] *Id.*

[127] Ari Weinberg, *The Post-Enron 401(k)*, FORBES.COM, Oct. 20, 2003, http://www.forbes.com/2003/10/20/cx_aw_1020retirement.html. Enron had 11,000 employees in its 401(k) plan. *See* Michael W. Lynch, *Enron's 401(k) Calamity*, REASON ONLINE, Dec. 27, 2001, http://www.reason.com/ml/ml122701.shtml (noting that "[i]n early 2001, Enron decided to contract out its 401(k) administration to an outside company"). This transfer required that Enron's 401(k) accounts be frozen. Thus, for a certain period of time in October and November 2001 employees could not move their retirement funds out of Enron stock. There is a dispute about whether the accounts were frozen for twelve trading days, (from October 26, 2001 through November 12, 2001), as the Company claims, or for a longer period. One employee has alleged that his account was frozen on September 26, 2001. A separate law suit alleges that accounts were frozen beginning on October 17, 2001. The period when the accounts were frozen, whatever the precise dates actually were, was a time of extreme upheaval at Enron. On October 16, 2001, the Company announced that it had to take a $1.1 billion charge for bad investments. On October 22, the SEC announced an informal investigation into Enron's accounting practices. On October 29, Moody's downgraded its ratings of Enron's debt. On October 31, the SEC announced that its investigation was formal. On November 8, Enron restated its financial results for every year since 1997. On October 26,

stock,[128] despite the fact that these employees had other alternatives.[129] "Enron, like many other public companies, matched pretax 401(k) contributions with its own stock and limited the ability of employees to sell that stock."[130] Given the undiversified nature of employees' investment in Enron stock, and the inability of Enron employees to diversify, it does not appear to be unfair to permit these employees to sell and to sell short when in possession of material, nonpublic information about their company. Other investors can avoid the firm-specific risk of an implosion at Enron by holding a diversified portfolio of securities. Workers cannot avoid this risk. The only way for them to mitigate the risk is by trading on the basis of inside information.

Permitting certain rank-and-file insiders to trade on the basis of their informational advantage about the ongoing fraud at Enron would be entirely fair. Workers are at a disadvantage relative to other shareholders because they are unable to diversify their human capital investment in the companies they work for. Rules enabling these people to trade would be consistent with Rawls's idea that resources ought to be arranged so that they inure "to the greatest benefit of the least advantaged."[131] This suggests that Rawls could endorse precisely the sort of involuntary disadvantage that results from insider trading when such disadvantage benefits the worst-off.

Rawls's veil of ignorance generates the same conclusion about the fairness of insider trading. To generate principles of justice, Rawls suggests that we imagine what rules of social ordering rational, self-interested people would choose from behind a veil of ignorance. Rational shareholders in large public companies would agree ex ante to permit innocent insiders to trade on the basis of whistleblower information because these insiders cannot diversify in any other way. Self-interested investors also would agree to permit this sort of insider trading because it reduces the probability that fraud will occur by increasing the probability that such fraud would be found out.

It is undeniable that insider trading, by definition, involves unequal treatment. To the extent that fairness is defined as equal outcomes, then the insider trading I describe, along with all other trading, would be banned. More troubling is the fact that the trading I describe also involves inequality of opportunity, because the insiders have access to whistleblower information that is not available to their trading partners. However, as Frank Easterbrook and Daniel Fischel ably have explained, in the corporate context at least, fairness does not mean equal treatment because fairness and equality are not the

2001, the day Enron claims it froze its 401(k) accounts, its stock was trading at $13.81 per share. By the time 401(k) investors could sell again, the stock was at $9.98. *Id.*

128 *See generally* Corey Rosen, *Questions and Answers About Enron, 401(k)s, and ESOPs*, THE NATIONAL CENTER FOR EMPLOYEE OWNERSHIP, Jan. 2002, http://www.nceo.org/library/enron.html.

129 *See Enron and Beyond: Enhancing Worker Retirement Security: Hearing Before the Subcomm. on Education and the Workforce*, 107th Cong. 12 (2002) (statement of Douglas Kruse, Ph.D., Professor, School of Management and Labor Relations, Rutgers University) ("Most participants, interestingly, in ESOPs and other employer stock plans are in companies that also maintain diversified pension plans.").

130 Weinberg, *supra* note 127.

131 JOHN RAWLS, A THEORY OF JUSTICE 83 (1971); *see also* Daniel Markovits, *How Much Redistribution Should There Be?*, 112 YALE L.J. 2291, 2326-29 (2003).

same thing.[132] Fairness, for investors, requires the pursuit of policies that maximize the value of investments ex ante.[133] Easterbrook and Fischel illustrate the point as follows: given a choice between two ventures, one that provides a payoff of $10 to every one of a firm's ten investors, and one that provides a payoff of $40 to five of the ten investors but nothing to the remaining five, a firm's board should choose the latter venture. This is because the total expected (ex ante) return from the latter investment is $200, while the expected return from the former investment is only $100. As Easterbrook and Fischel observe, if unequal distribution is necessary to make the overall returns higher, then the company is required to choose inequality.[134] This illustration maps perfectly onto the whistleblower issue. Barring insider trading on whistleblower information would eliminate the inequality that results from the insider's trading on an informational advantage, but it also would eliminate the substantial gains to all investors associated with the ex ante reduction in the incidence of fraud. Thus, because shareholders "unanimously prefer legal rules under which the amount of gains is maximized, regardless of how the gains are distributed,"[135] insider trading on the basis of whistleblower information is fair to investors under any coherent notion of the meaning of the term "fair."

Finally, with respect to fairness, I hasten to acknowledge that the "pure" whistleblower (should such a thing exist) is a Good Samaritan.[136] Insiders, on the other hand, decidedly cannot be described as Good Samaritans. Nevertheless, nobody has ever seriously suggested that one is legally required to be a Good Samaritan. The issue, in other words, is not whether insider trading on whistleblower information should be applauded; the issue is whether the conduct should be considered criminal. At a minimum, this decision should be left to investors themselves, who, after full disclosure, should be allowed to decide for themselves whether they want to invest in a public company that permits insider trading on the basis of whistleblower information.

B. Distributional Concerns

Intuitively, whistleblowers' impact is uniform across all shareholders, while insiders' trading differentially affects those (buying) shareholders who are unfortunate enough to be the counterparties of the insiders who are selling on whistleblower information. However, this intuition is wrong because it falsely assumes that those trading with insiders in possession of whistleblower information are harmed. In fact, the outsiders who are the whistleblower information traders' counterparties likely benefit from the insider trading here. This is because selling by insiders in possession of whistleblower information will,

---

[132] FRANK EASTERBROOK & DANIEL R. FISCHEL, THE ECONOMIC STRUCTURE OF CORPORATE LAW 110 (1991).

[133] *See id.*

[134] *Id.* at 111.

[135] *Id.* at 124.

[136] *See generally* Judith Jarvis Thomson, *A Defense of Abortion*, 1 PHIL. & PUB. AFF. 47, 62 (1971) (defining a Good Samaritan as someone who goes "out of his way, at some cost to himself, to help").

to the extent that it has any effect at all on share prices, drive down those prices, thereby benefiting their counterparties by driving down their acquisition costs.

The downward pressure on share prices caused by insider trading will benefit ordinary investors, whom I define as investors who do not purport to trade on information not already impounded in share prices, but instead buy and sell shares either to adjust their portfolios or because of changes in patterns of consumption and investment over their life cycle. The critical point here is that such traders are not induced by insider selling to buy: they would have bought anyway. As such, they are made better off, not worse off, by any informed sales by insiders because such sales drive down the price at which the insiders' counterparties are able to buy. The effect of insider trading on true outsiders just described is depicted in the chart below.

The assumption is that, all else being equal, in the absence of any prohibition on insider trading there will be more such trading than there would be otherwise. This greater incidence of insider trading would cause share prices to fall more precipitously than they would fall otherwise. Alternatively, if enforcement of the law is "perfect" in the sense that all inside traders are caught and punished, there will be no such trading, and share prices will adjust only when the fraud or other corporate misconduct that is the subject of the whistleblowing is revealed to the public, at which time there will be a dramatic drop in share prices. Finally, where there are prohibitions on insider trading on the basis of whistleblower information, but those prohibitions are imperfectly enforced, share prices will respond to insider trading, but less dramatically than they would respond if such trading were condoned.

Distributional Effects of Insider Trading Regulation About Corporate Misconduct

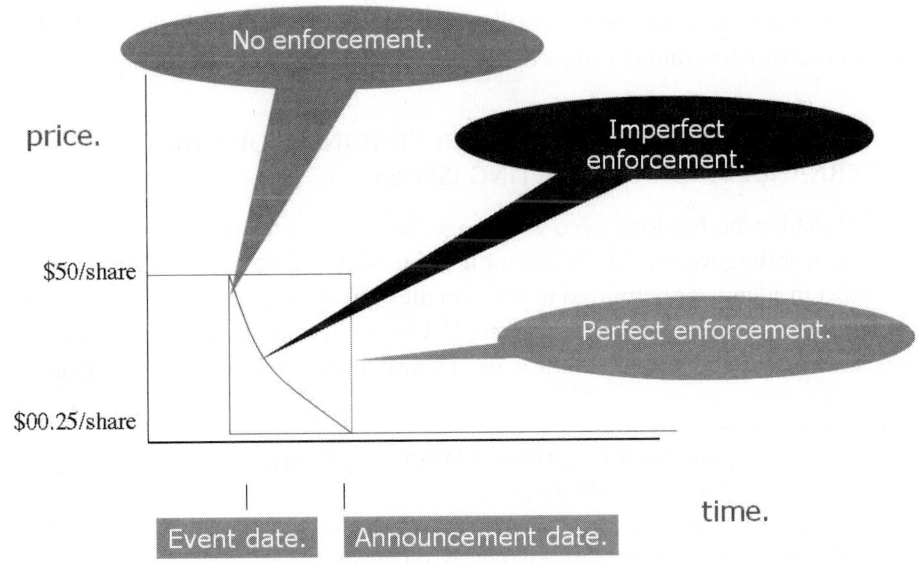

As depicted in the graph, because share prices fall most dramatically when insider trading is permitted, this is the legal regime that most benefits buyers. It is also clear that people who trade prior to the commencement of the fraud are not affected. And, of course, people who trade after the fraud is announced are similarly unaffected by the insiders' trading.

The above discussion of the distributional effects of insider trading on whistleblower information is incomplete because it ignores the real possibility that if insider trading on whistleblower information were permitted, then insiders might delay exposing an ongoing fraud in order to allow themselves time to trade on such information. This possibility, as noted above, also affects the analysis of the efficiency characteristics of trading on whistleblower information. However, from a distributional perspective, it is by no means clear that a delay in revealing an ongoing fraud or other corporate misconduct hurts a company's existing shareholders. Rather, such shareholders benefit as long as the conduct goes undetected, because as long as this is the case, share prices remain high. Shareholders who manage to use any extra time to sell their shares clearly benefit.

It is also the case that if insider trading is illegal and the only avenues that insiders have for dealing with fraud or corporate misconduct are blackmail and whistleblowing, the delay in the release of information about corporate misconduct is likely to be even longer than it will be if insiders are permitted to trade. Most importantly, from both an efficiency standpoint and a distributional standpoint, insider trading on whistleblower information is likely to lead to less corporate misconduct because the possibility that such insider trading will occur increases the probability that corporate fraud will be detected, thereby leading to a reduction in the incidence of such fraud.

This reduction in fraud makes all shareholders better off, whether viewed from a distributional perspective or an efficiency perspective. Thus, while there is some ambiguity about the distributional effects of insider trading on whistleblower information, the argument that insider trading has distributional benefits for true outsiders, which is the class of shareholders thought most deserving of protections, is quite compelling.

VIII. WHISTLEBLOWING AND INSIDER TRADING: CORPORATE GOVERNANCE AND CONTRACTING ISSUES

Whistleblowing has long been encouraged as a means to reduce the incidence of fraud against the government. At common law, insider trading was tolerated: managers and other insiders were permitted to trade on the basis of nonpublic information unless specifically forbidden to do so by contract.[137] Corporate charters are silent both on the issue of insider trading[138] and on the issue of whistleblowing. This is surprising on both

[137] Goodwin v. Agassiz, 186 N.E. 659 (Mass. 1933); Todd A. Bauman, Comment, *Insider Trading at Common Law*, 51 U. CHI. L. REV. 838 (1984).

[138] *See* Dennis W. Carlton & Daniel R. Fischel, *The Regulation of Insider Trading*, 35 STAN. L. REV. 857 (1983) (noting that corporate charters do not prevent insider trading).

counts—it is surprising that corporate charters do not bar trading on inside information, and it also is surprising that corporate charters do not encourage whistleblowing by offering monetary rewards to whistleblowers like the ones provided for in federal whistleblower statues such as the False Claims Act.

The foregoing analysis, however, explains both of these phenomena. As for insider trading, the analysis here suggests it is not in shareholders' interests to bar all sorts of insider trading. Insider trading on whistleblower information should not be banned: it should be encouraged. On the other hand, where insider trading involves the misappropriation of information that is the property of shareholders or the company itself, insider trading must be banned, as is the case where there is insider trading in advance of the announcement of a tender offer or of corporate earnings. Suppose for example that a corporate officer accepts a bribe in exchange for information that a company was about to repurchase a large block of its own shares at a premium above the current market price. This information is then used by the person paying the bribe to purchase stock in the company, thereby driving up the price that the company must pay to acquire its own shares.[139] This sequence of events involves the theft of valuable information that is in the nature of a property right.

Current law permits insider trading when, and only when, such trading is consistent with traders' fiduciary duties of care and loyalty to the company. Fiduciary duties are the mechanism employed by the law to identify and allocate property rights in the information that provides the basis for trading. Fiduciary duties therefore replace contractual rules where contracting is too costly. Since insider trading can arise in a widely divergent set of circumstances, and because corporations and their agents do not have perfect foresight and thus are unable to anticipate all future situations in which insider trading might occur, it would be extremely costly to draft a corporate contract that specified with precision what sorts of trading are banned. So instead of trying to specify ex ante every possible situation in which insider trading should be banned, we have a rule that prohibits trading that involves breaches of fiduciary duties and theft of intellectual property.

The "contracting cost" explanation of why we do not observe provisions in corporate charters or bylaws barring insider trading does not explain why we do not observe provisions in corporate contracts that specifically permit whistleblowing, provide protections, and authorize monetary rewards for whistleblowers. One possibility is that venal and corrupt corporate managers prevent these sorts of charter provisions from being implemented because they want to discourage whistleblowers from revealing their illegal acts. This explanation is highly unlikely for two reasons. First, while it is undoubtedly the case that there are a few corporate managers who are dishonest, there

---

[139] *Cf.* FMC Corp. v. Boesky, 573 F. Supp. 242 (N.D. Ill. 1987), *modified*, 852 F.2d 981 (7th Cir. 1988), *remanded to* 727 F. Supp. 1182 (N.D. Ill. 1989) (addressing a corporation suing an arbitrageur for insider trading on information about a corporate recapitalization that would distribute cash to shareholders in exchange for reducing their equity stakes in the company in order to give managers a larger share of the corporation's equity, on the theory that the corporation had to pay more to acquire the shareholders' equity because insider trading drove up the price of the company's shares).

are many more who are honest. Such managers would be able to signal their integrity by providing job security and bounties for whistleblowers. Thus, it might not be surprising that some firms decide not to provide such protections, but it is quite curious that none did until Sarbanes-Oxley required them to do so.

The Sarbanes-Oxley Act of 2002 contains two sets of provisions addressing issues involving corporate whistleblowers. One set of provisions are the whistleblower procedures mandated by Sarbanes-Oxley section 301, which requires audit committees to establish internal whistleblowing procedures pursuant to Securities Exchange Act Rule 10A-3.[140] The second set of provisions is contained in Sarbanes-Oxley section 806, which adds a panoply of whistleblower protections to Title 18 of the U.S. Code.[141]

Rule 10A-3 of the Exchange Act requires the New York Stock Exchange, NASDAQ, and other stock market self-regulatory organizations to compel the audit committees of listed companies to establish formal procedures for responding to whistleblowers' complaints regarding accounting and auditing issues.[142] Audit committees must establish procedures for dealing with both external complaints from any sources and internal complaints from employees. Companies must provide a mechanism for receiving and processing confidential, anonymous submissions by employees of concerns regarding questionable accounting or auditing matters.

Section 806 of Sarbanes-Oxley establishes safeguards for employee whistleblowers who report certain sorts of corporate misconduct. Section 806 provides protections for any employee who either: (a) files, testifies, participates in, or otherwise assists in any proceeding relating to an alleged violation of the mail, wire, bank, or securities laws; or (b) provides information or assists in an investigation regarding any conduct that the employee "reasonably believes" constitutes a violation of the mail, wire, bank, or securities laws.[143] Employees are protected by section 806 if they report information to a federal regulatory or law enforcement agency, any member or committee of Congress, any person with supervisory authority over the employee, or any other person who has "the authority to investigate, discover, or terminate misconduct."[144] Additionally, section 806 prevents employees who file complaints with the Secretary of Labor from being discharged, demoted, suspended, threatened, harassed, or discriminated against as a result of that involvement.[145] Civil remedies for violations of section 806 include reinstatement, back pay with interest, and attorneys' fees.[146]

Second, it is curious why firms emerging from bankruptcy, firms going public for the first time, or firms whose original financing came from venture capitalists did not try to improve their access to the capital markets and the terms of their initial financ-

---

[140] 15 U.S.C. § 78j-1 (Supp. III 2003).

[141] 18 U.S.C. § 1514A (Supp. III 2003).

[142] 17 C.F.R. 240.10A-3 (2006).

[143] 18 U.S.C. § 1514A (Supp. III 2003).

[144] *Id.*

[145] *Id.*

[146] *Id.*

ing by introducing whistleblower protections such as the ones contained in Sarbanes-Oxley. In all likelihood, such provisions were not adopted by companies because they do not enhance shareholder welfare. It would be an exaggeration to say that providing protections for whistleblowers is devoid of benefits. Rather, the point is simply that it appears likely that companies generally decide on their own not to provide for protections for whistleblowers because the cost of maintaining such provisions outweighs the benefit.

One significant cost of installing whistleblower protections of the kind described in Sarbanes-Oxley is the cost of evaluating a whistleblower complaint. Particularly where bounties are involved, as noted above, there are likely to be several false complaints for every valid one. The risk of receiving false complaints is compounded when one takes into account the fact that disgruntled former employees, especially those who have been terminated, are likely to bring whistleblower complaints in order to try to obtain reinstatement and/or back pay.[147] It is also likely that terminated employees will attempt to extract a measure of revenge on former supervisors, particularly those responsible for the employees' termination.[148]

Evidence of concern about false whistleblower complaints is contained in the provisions of Sarbanes-Oxley Act itself, which requires OSHA to dismiss any whistleblower complaint without conducting an investigation unless the complainant can make a "prima facie showing" that his or her whistleblowing activities constituted at least "a contributing factor" in any alleged unfavorable personnel action. Even if the complainant succeeds in making this prima facie showing, Sarbanes-Oxley does not permit OSHA to investigate a whistleblower's complaint "if the employer demonstrates, by clear and convincing evidence, that the employer would have taken the same unfavorable personnel action in the absence of that behavior."

The high costs of investigating a whistleblower's complaints and the problems of false and retaliatory complaints, coupled with what may, in fact, be a low incidence of corporate fraud, make it likely that the costs of whistleblower provisions outweigh the benefits. These costs appear to be the best explanation for why companies did not adopt whistleblower protections such as the ones mandated by Sarbanes-Oxley before they were required to do so by statute.

IX. WHISTLEBLOWING AND INSIDER TRADING ARE NOT BLACKMAIL

Like whistleblowing and insider trading, requests for blackmail payments reflect an effort to traffic in intellectual property. In particular, in all three cases, there is

---

[147] The problem of distinguishing among whistleblower complaints is likely exacerbated by the fact that whistleblowers often are mavericks who may have personality conflicts with supervisors anyway.

[148] Thus it is not surprising that whistleblowers are viewed with some moral ambiguity: "To some, whistle blowing is considered to be an ultimate expression of accountability. To others, whistle blowing is the spiteful behavior of disgruntled employees and an act of organizational disloyalty." AM. SOC'Y FOR PUB. ADMIN., POSITION STATEMENT ON WHISTLE BLOWING (1979), http://ethics.iit.edu/codes/coe/amer.soc.public.admin.a.html.

information that somebody wants to conceal and somebody else wants to bring to the light of day. Scholars have gone to great lengths to try to explain the harm in blackmail.[149] My goal here is not to add to the existing theories of how blackmail is different from or similar to other crimes. The primary reason that blackmail has posed such an analytical problem for scholars is because it involves the combination of two acts: threatening to reveal a secret and demanding money (presumably) to keep the secret, neither of which, standing alone, is illegal.[150] Rather my point is simply that blackmail does not share the benign, welfare-enhancing characteristics that link insider trading and whistleblowing. In particular, whereas whistleblowing and insider trading inevitably lead to the discovery and exposure of pathological behavior, the payment and acceptance of blackmail lead to the continued concealment of the unacceptable behavior. This suggests that blackmail is a less desirable practice than either insider trading or whistleblowing. While insider trading and effective whistleblowing lead to the exposure of wrongdoing, successful blackmail leads to the continued cover-up of wrongdoing.[151]

Blackmailers are accurately perceived as sleazy and corrupt. Their conduct is clearly illegal. By contrast, whistleblowers are occasionally viewed as brave and altruistic, and inside traders, while viewed somewhat more ambivalently than whistleblowers, seem to hold a position in the moral order somewhere between blackmailers and whistleblowers.

CONCLUSION

Insiders who know or suspect corporate wrongdoing can respond in one of three ways: by whistleblowing, by insider trading, or by blackmailing the wrongdoers. This Article has advanced the argument that insider trading on the basis of information about corporate wrongdoing is more like whistleblowing than it is like blackmail. Unlike blackmail, in order for insider trading on information concerning corporate misconduct to be successful, the information that underlies such trading must be revealed or else the share price of the company engaged in the wrongdoing will not fall and the insider will not profit. By contrast, a successful blackmail strategy will result in a payoff to the blackmailer that will keep the information quiet forever. Thus, insider trading on whistleblower information, like whistleblowing itself, results in the release of information about corporate misconduct.

The argument here is not that all insider trading should be condoned. In fact the opposite is true. The analysis here applies only to a very narrow subset of inside information—information about corporate misconduct that would be the proper cause

---

[149] Jennifer Gerarda Brown, *Blackmail as Private Justice*, 241 U. PA. L. REV. 1935 (1993); James Lindgren, *Unraveling the Paradox of Blackmail*, 84 COLUM. L. REV. 670 (1984); Henry E. Smith, *The Harm in Blackmail*, 92 NW. U. L. REV. 861 (1998).

[150] Glanville L. Williams, *Blackmail*, 1954 CRIM. L. REV. (Eng.) 79, 163.

[151] This is not to say that blackmail involves only costs and no benefits. To the extent that the possibility of blackmail deters the undesirable conduct that is the subject of the blackmail, there are benefits. The social costs of blackmail, however, clearly outweigh the private benefits to the blackmail contract.

for whistleblowing. Trading on nonpublic information about legitimate corporate news, whether the news is good or bad, is and should be illegal. The prohibition of this sort of insider trading is efficient because it protects valuable property rights in information. By contrast, corporations and corporate miscreants have no legitimate property-based expectation in keeping information about an ongoing misconduct confidential. Permitting insider trading on the basis of such information would, in a variety of contexts, provide the strongest incentives for people to seek out and expose such corporate wrongdoing.

Table 1

Definition	**Whistle-blowing**	**Insider Trading**	**Blackmail**
Pre-existing contractual or quasi-contractual relationship of trust/confidence	Yes	Yes	No
Trading/Whistling/Blackmail demand involves breach of duty	No	No	No
Information becomes reflected in securities prices	Yes	Yes	No
Motivations of actor	Highly Varied	Highly Varied	Venal
Informational intermediaries	Yes	Yes	No
Actions impose distributional harm	Yes	Yes	No
Actions lead to corrective measures	Yes	Yes	No
De minimis problem	No	Yes	Yes
Verification Problem	Yes	No	Yes

Enron: A Brief Behavioral Autopsy[*]

Robert Prentice[**]

I. INTRODUCTION

People see what they want to see in the Enron (Global Crossing/WorldCom/etc.) corporate corruption scandal. Conservatives see a triumph of capitalism.[1] Those of a more liberal persuasion see stark limitations of capitalism.[2] Republicans blame the scandal on Democrats.[3] Democratic leaders, unsurprisingly, blame it on Republicans.[4] This is an example of the confirmation bias, the tendency of people to gather and process information in a manner that fits their preexisting viewpoints.[5] When an ambiguous

* Originally published at 40 AM. BUS. L.J. 417 (2003). Reprinted by permission.

** Ed and Molly Smith Centennial Professor of Business Law, University of Texas at Austin.

1 Conservatives see in the Enron saga a triumph of capitalism in that the government did not bail Enron out when it collapsed. *See, e.g.*, Robert L. Borosage, *Enron Conservatives*, THE NATION, Feb. 4, 2002, at 4 (noting that Bush administration Treasury Secretary Paul O'Neill called Enron's rise and fall a "triumph of capitalism").

2 *See, e.g.*, Kris Zickert, *Nationalize All Utilities*, THE OREGONIAN, Mar. 16, 2002, at E5 (arguing that the Enron debacle illustrates "the inherent corruption of capitalism").

3 *See, e.g.*, Peter Beinart, *Backward*, THE NEW REPUBLIC, July 22, 2002, at 6 (noting that Republicans are suggesting that former President Clinton is "to blame for today's corporate scandals").

4 *See, e.g.*, Anne E. Kornblut, *Bush Team Defends SEC Chief on Business Scandals*, BOSTON GLOBE, July 8, 2002, at A3 (noting that Senate Majority Leader Tom Daschle had blamed the Bush administration for fostering a "cozy, permissive relationship" of lax regulations toward corporate America that contributed to Enron and other scandals)

5 In testing a hypothesis, people tend to preferentially select information that supports their point of view. *See* SCOTT PLOUS, THE PSYCHOLOGY OF JUDGMENT AND DECISION MAKING 232-33 (1993) (noting several studies confirming the confirmation bias); Michael E. Doherty et al., *Pseudodiagnosticity*, 43 ACTA PSYCHOLOGICA 111, 118 (1979) (finding that people are unskilled in detecting potentially disconfirming information); Joshua Klayman & Young-Won Ha, *Confirmation, Disconfirmation, and Information in Hypothesis Testing*, 94 PSYCHOL. REV. 211, 225 (1987) (arguing that the confirmation bias is better understood as a "positive test strategy" which generally well serves as a broad heuristic, although it can lead to systematic errors or inefficiencies); Matthew Rabin, *Psychology and Economics*, 36 J. ECON. LIT. 11, 26 (Mar. 1998) ("People tend to misread evidence as additional support for initial hypotheses.").

article on the death penalty is shown to different groups of people, the confirmation bias will cause both supporters and opponents of the death penalty to tend to view the article as supporting their (opposite) points of view.[6] And so it is with corporate misdeeds.[7]

It should come as no surprise, then, that business law professors generally view the Enron scandal as evidence that business law and business ethics should have more of a presence in business school curricula—both graduate and undergraduate.[8] The quantity and quality of business ethics instruction must improve.[9] The business school commitment to teaching business ethics must change from the current token attempts[10] that often mirror Enron's token commitment to its famed "RICE" code of ethics.[11]

Nor should it be a surprise that I, having recently read an insider's account of the Enron saga—Brian Cruver's *Anatomy of Greed: The Unshredded Truth From an Enron Insider*[12]—see in the Enron scandal support for my attempts in recent years to apply

---

[6] *See generally* Charles G. Lord et al., *Biased Assimilation and Attitude Polarization: The Effects of Prior Theories on Subsequently Considered Evidence*, 37 J. PERSONALITY & SOC. PSYCHOL. 2098, 2108 (1979) (exploring this phenomenon).

[7] Coffee recently pointed out that Enron "is becoming a virtual Rorschach test in which each commentator can see evidence confirming what he or she already believed." John C. Coffee, Jr., *Understanding Enron: "It's About the Gatekeepers, Stupid,"* 57 BUS. LAW. 1403, 1403 (2002). As may be deduced from his title, Coffee finds problems with the financial system's gatekeepers—auditors, attorneys, and other reputational intermediaries—at the core of the Enron debacle. *Id.* Other academic commentators' conclusions also likely reflect their predispositions. *See, e.g.*, William W. Bratton, *Enron and the Dark Side of Shareholder Value*, 76 TUL. L. REV. 1275(2002), *available at* http://papers.ssrn.com/abstract=301475 (arguing that the Enron scandal teaches that an unhealthy commitment to maximization of share prices exacerbates old pathologies that have traditionally caused corporate financial frauds); Lawrence A. Cunningham, *Sharing Accounting's Burden: Business Lawyers in Enron's Dark Shadows*, 57 BUS. LAW. 1421 (2002) (concluding that a major lesson of the Enron scandal is that lawyers must know more about accounting); Jeffrey N. Gordon, *What Enron Means for the Management and Control of the Modern Business Corporation: Some Initial Reflections*, 69 U. CHI. L. REV. 1233 (2002) (drawing several lessons from the Enron scandal, including the need to restructure the accounting profession and increase the true independence of boards of directors).

[8] *See* Robert A. Prentice, *An Ethics Lesson for Business Schools*, N.Y. TIMES, Aug. 20, 2002, at A21 [hereinafter Prentice, Business Schools] (arguing that Enron and other recent scandals involve breaches of law more than ethical lapses and demonstrate the need to teach more business law in business schools).

[9] *See* Eric Orts, *Law Is Never Enough to Guarantee Fair Practice*, FIN. TIMES, Aug. 23, 2002, at 9 (arguing that the Enron collapse demonstrates the need for teaching ethics to business managers).

[10] *See* Amitai Etzioni, *When It Comes to Ethics, B-Schools Get an F*, WASH. POST, Aug. 4, 2002, at B4 (alleging that current business school efforts to teach ethics are token only and claiming that more needs to be done).

[11] RICE stood for Respect, Integrity, Communication, and Excellence. *See generally* Gregory J. Millman, *New Scandals, Old Lessons: Financial Ethics After Enron*, FIN. EXECUTIVE, July 1, 2002, at 16 (noting that Enron had a code of ethics, but not a culture of ethics).

[12] BRIAN CRUVER, ANATOMY OF GREED: THE UNSHREDDED TRUTH FROM AN ENRON INSIDER (2002). As its forward by my colleague Steve Salbu indicates, *Anatomy of Greed* is intentionally in the tradition of Michael Lewis's *Liar's Poker*—an insider's tale of an important business scandal emblematic of the excesses of an era, breezily written with vivid language, liberally sprinkled with sexual references and

behavioral decision theory[13] to legal issues in an attempt to create more realistic policy prescriptions than have been derived from the Chicago School law and economics reasoning that has dominated the interdisciplinary approach to legal analysis in recent years.[14]

In this essay, I will attempt to use the disclosures of Cruver's book and other sources[15] and the insights of behavioral research to argue that law and economics theory has two

descriptions of sophomoric activity, and featuring characters who are colorful and greedy to the point of being caricatures. *Id.* at xi.

[13] A major portion of behavioral decision theory derives from the seminal work of Amos Tversky and Daniel Kahneman. In their experiments and those of their followers, substantial evidence has been produced that most people are prone to using various "heuristics and biases" in their thinking that prevents them from reasoning as economists often presume that rational people would. *See generally* MAX BAZERMAN, JUDGMENT IN MANAGERIAL DECISION MAKING (4th ed. 1998); REID HASTIE & ROBYN M. DAWES: RATIONAL CHOICE IN AN UNCERTAIN WORLD: THE PSYCHOLOGY OF JUDGMENT AND DECISION MAKING (2001); RESEARCH ON JUDGMENT AND DECISION MAKING (William M. Goldstein & Robin M. Hogarth eds., 1997); JUDGMENT UNDER UNCERTAINTY: HEURISTICS AND BIASES (Daniel Kahneman, Paul Slovic & Amos Tversky eds., 1982).

[14] *See, e.g.*, Robert A. Prentice & Jonathan J. Koehler, *A Normality Bias in Legal Decision Making*, 88 CORNELL L. REV. 583 (2003) (reporting results of an empirical study on biases that affect legal decision making); Robert A. Prentice, *Contract-Based Defenses in Securities Fraud Litigation: A Behavioral Analysis*, 2003 U. ILL. L. REV. 337 (applying behavioral insights to argue that the law should protect securities investors, and other consumers, from fraud even if they have contractually waived that protection); Robert A. Prentice, *Whither Securities Regulation? Some Behavioral Observations Regarding Proposals for Its Future*, 51 DUKE L.J. 1397 (2002) [hereinafter Prentice, *Whither Securities Regulation*] (using behavioral insights to critique recent proposals to deregulate securities markets); Robert A. Prentice, *The Case of the Irrational Auditor: A Behavioral Insight into Securities Fraud Litigation*, 95 NW. U. L. REV. 133 (2000) [hereinafter Prentice, *Irrational Auditor*] (citing substantial behavioral literature in critiquing court rulings that presume auditors are rational and that it is irrational for auditors to audit carelessly); Robert A. Prentice, *The SEC and MDP: Implications of the Self-Serving Bias for Independent Auditing*, 61 OHIO ST. L.J. 1597 (2000) [hereinafter Prentice, *SEC and MDP*] (using behavioral insights to caution against allowing auditors to engage in substantial nonaudit activity for audit clients); Robert A. Prentice & Mark E. Roszkowski, *"Tort Reform" and the Liability "Revolution": Defending Strict Liability in Tort for Defective Products*, 27 GONZ. L. REV. 251 (1991-1992) (using behavioral literature to gain insight into product liability law); Mark E. Roszkowski & Robert A. Prentice, *Reconciling Comparative Negligence and Strict Liability: A Public Policy Analysis*, 33 ST. LOUIS U. L.J. 19 (1988) (same).

[15] Cruver's book is just one of many that will be written about this scandal; among those already published are: DIRK J. BARREVERD, THE ENRON COLLAPSE: CREATIVE ACCOUNTING, WRONG ECONOMICS, OR CRIMINAL ACTS? (2002); PETER C. FUSARO & ROSS M. MILLER, WHAT WENT WRONG AT ENRON: EVERYONE'S GUIDE TO THE LARGEST BANKRUPTCY IN U.S. HISTORY (2002); RICHARD J. SCHROTH & A. LARRY ELLIOTT, HOW COMPANIES LIE: WHY ENRON IS JUST THE TIP OF THE ICEBERG (2002). Another exceedingly useful accounting of the Enron fiasco appeared in a five-part series in the *Washington Post. See* Peter Behr & April Witt, *Visionary's Dream Led to Risky Business*, WASH. POST, July 28, 2002, at A1; April Witt & Peter Behr, Dream *Job Turns Into a Nightmare*, WASH. POST, July 29, 2002, at A1; Peter Behr & April Witt, *Concerns Grow Amid Conflicts*, WASH. POST, July 30, 2002, at A1; April Witt & Peter Behr, Losses, *Conflicts Threaten Survival*, WASH. POST, July 31, 2002, at A1; Peter Behr & April Witt, *Hidden Debts, Deals Scuttle Last Chance*, WASH. POST, Aug. 1, 2002, at A1. And, needless to say, the single most important document for those attempting to understand what happened at Enron is the Powers Report, commissioned by Enron's board and named after the committee's head, Dean William Powers of the University of Texas School of

major shortcomings. First, it tends to ignore the behavioral decision literature that demonstrates clearly that law and economics is built on a raft of inaccurate assumptions that can lead to faulty policy prescriptions.[16] Second, it does damage by eliminating any space in its adherents' scheme of thinking for ethics and morality.[17] After addressing these points, I will briefly explore the steps Congress has recently taken to address the implications of the Enron scandal.[18] Ultimately, I hope to shed a modest amount of illumination upon the Enron scandal and to introduce the reader to the field of behavioral decision theory.[19]

II. LAW AND ECONOMICS VS. BEHAVIORAL DECISION THEORY

For twenty years, law and economics has been the dominant interdisciplinary school of thought in the legal academy.[20] Recently, several scholars, including myself, have imported behavioral decision theory into legal analysis, often in response to perceived limitations inherent in Chicago School law and economics analysis. Unsurprisingly, and perhaps illustrative of the confirmation bias, I find support for the value of behavioral decision theory in the Enron Scandal.

A foundational principle of law and economics analysis is that people behave rationally.[21] This assumption leads law and economics scholars, including some who currently

---

Law. *See* WILLIAM C. POWERS, JR. ET AL., REPORT OF INVESTIGATION BY THE SPECIAL INVESTIGATIVE COMMITTEE OF THE BOARD OF DIRECTORS OF ENRON CORP. (Feb. 1, 2002), *available at* http://www.chron.com/content/news/photos/02/02/03/enron-powersreport.pdf (the "Powers Report").

[16] *See infra* notes 20-82 and accompanying text.

[17] *See infra* notes 83-116 and accompanying text.

[18] *See infra* notes 116-131 and accompanying text.

[19] This is not the first article to discuss behavioral decision theory in the pages of this journal. *See, e.g.,* Royce de R. Barondes, *Professionalism Consequences of Law Firm Investment in Clients: An Empirical Assessment*, 39 AM. BUS. L.J. 379, 440 n.174 (2002) (making a passing reference to some of the key behavioral decision literature); M. Neil Browne & Nancy K. Kubasek, *A Communitarian Green Space between Market and Political Rhetoric about Environmental Law*, 37 AM. BUS. L.J. 127, 140 n.61 (1999) (noting in passing some important behavioral concepts and their implications for environmental law); Larry DiMatteo, *A Theory of Efficient Penalty: Eliminating the Law of Liquidated Damages*, 38 AM. BUS. L.J. 633, 703-06 (2001) (using behavioral factors as part of a broad critique of the law of liquidated damages); Daniel T. Ostas, *Deconstructing Corporate Social Responsibility: Insights from Legal and Economic Theory*, 38 AM. BUS. L.J. 261, 292-96 (2001) (using behavioral insights to question traditional economic assumptions of rationality and exogenous preferences). Other members of the Academy of Legal Studies in Business have written in a behavioral vein. *See, e.g.*, Hal R. Arkes & Cindy Schipani, *Medical Malpractice v. the Business Judgment Rule: Differences in the Hindsight Bias*, 73 OR. L. REV. 587 (1994) (analyzing the impact of the hindsight bias on the contrasting rules for judicial review of decisions of doctors and directors).

[20] The birth of the law and economics movement is often traced to the publication of Richard Posner's seminal work. *See* RICHARD A. POSNER, ECONOMIC ANALYSIS OF LAW (1st ed. 1973). Posner's book was inspired by earlier works, including Ronald Coase, *The Problems of Social Cost*, 3 J.L. & ECON. 1 (1960) (using economic principles to analyze nuisance law), and Guido Calabresi, *Some Thoughts on Risk Distribution and the Law of Torts*, 70 YALE L.J. 499 (1961) (analyzing the economic logic of tort law).

[21] *See* Posner, *supra* note 20, at 3. *See also* Roger G. Noll & James E. Krier, *Some Implications of Cognitive Psychology for Risk Regulation*, 19 J. LEGAL STUD. 747, 750-51 (1990) (summarizing key assumptions

sit on the federal bench, to various policy conclusions. For example, it leads them to conclude that companies will fully and honestly disclose all relevant financial information because companies that do so can raise capital more cheaply.[22] It leads them to conclude that we should assume that auditors always act honestly because (they make the further assumption) the only rational way for auditors to act is honestly for the reason that their reputation for honesty is their most valuable asset.[23] In its unvarnished form, this rationality assumption leads to the conclusion that the Enron scandal could not have happened, because it was completely irrational for the companies' officers to mislead, commit fraud, help their employer commit corporate suicide, and court lengthy prison sentences. Had they thought rationally about where their actions would take Enron Corporation, Kenneth Lay, Jeff Skilling, Andy Fastow, and other Enron leaders likely would have acted much differently than they did. Their actions did create fabulous personal wealth, but they are not in situations they wish to be in today.

In a series of articles, I have pointed out that the foundational assumption that people make decisions as if they are homo economicus ("Chicago Man")[24] is indisputably wrong.[25] Therefore, I have argued, the notion that auditors will act rationally, that corporate managers will act rationally, and that their firms will act rationally is simply wrong. I have predicated much of my argument upon a stream of behavioral decision literature commenced many years ago by Amos Tversky and Daniel Kahneman called generally the "heuristics and biases" literature. The essential notion is that rather than act as Chicago Man theoretically does, most people make many decisions that are affected by various heuristics (mental short-cuts) and biases (mental tunnels) that lead them to results that are often less than optimal.[26]

For example, in arguing that it is quite plausible that auditors would not act rationally in auditing their clients, I pointed to a number of these heuristics and biases:

---

of the standard model); W. Kip Viscusi, *Individual Rationality, Hazard Warnings, and the Foundations of Tort Law*, 48 RUTGERS L. REV. 625, 636 (1996) (observing that the "foundation of economic analysis of choice is based on the rationality of individual decision making.").

[22] *See, e.g.*, Stephen Choi, *Regulating Investors Not Issuers: A Market-Based Proposal*, 88 CAL. L. REV. 279 (2000). Choi's essential notion is that because it is rational for companies and other players in the financial markets to disclose fully and fairly and because sophisticated investors can and do bargain for the amount of risk they are willing to bear regarding fraud and carelessness, the financial markets should be fully deregulated. *Id.* At 282-83.

[23] *See, e.g.*, Melder v. Morris, 27 F.3d 1097, 1103 (5th Cir. 1994) ("[A]ccounting firms—as with all rational economic actors—seek to maximize their profits . . . . [Therefore,] it seems extremely unlikely that [defendant audit firm] was willing to put its professional reputation on the line by conducting fraudulent auditing work for [its client].").

[24] *See* Daniel McFadden, *Rationality for Economists?*, 19 J. RISK & UNCERTAINTY 73, 76, 83 (1999) (coining the phrase "Chicago Man" to denote the rational actor of the Chicago School law and economics movement as contrasted to "K-T Man," the severely limited decision maker described by Kahneman and Tversky's research).

[25] *See supra* note 13.

[26] *See* MASSIMO PIATELLI-PALMARINI, INEVITABLE ILLUSIONS: HOW MISTAKES OF REASON RULE OUR MINDS 19 (1994).

- First, the evidence has long been clear that people (unlike Chicago Man) are, at best, boundedly rational in that they "seldom have complete and perfectly accurate information and never have perfect capacity to process that information rationally."[27]
- Second, people often display rational ignorance in that, unlike Chicago Man, they often choose to make decisions based on much less than full information. They willingly "satisfice" rather than optimize their decision making outcomes.[28]
- Third, people tend to be subject to the confirmation bias in that they seek out and process information in such a way as to confirm pre-existing beliefs rather than in a more optimally neutral manner.[29]
- Fourth, people are often subject to the hindsight bias, the tendency to regard things that have occurred as having been relatively predictable and obvious.[30] This is related to the notion of curse of knowledge—the fact that knowledge can affect judgment. For example, peer reviewers are more likely to evaluate a particular audit procedure negatively if they are told of allegations that the auditor lacked independence.[31]
- Fifth, most people (again, unlike Chicago Man) are subject to cognitive dissonance, meaning that once they have committed themselves to a particular position or belief, "the subsequent discovery of information that indicates harmful consequences flowing from that commitment directly threatens their

---

[27] Prentice, *Irrational Auditor, supra* note 14, at 143. The concept of bounded rationality derives from the works of Herbert Simon and James March back in the 1950s. *See generally* James G. March, *Bounded Rationality, Ambiguity, and the Engineering of Choice*, 9 BELL J. ECON. 587, 590 (1978); HERBERT A. SIMON, ADMINISTRATIVE BEHAVIOR xxiv (2d ed. 1957).

[28] Prentice, *Irrational Auditor, supra* note 14, at 144-45. To "satisfice" is to follow the first satisfactory solution that presents itself, rather than attempt to find the optimal solution. It is a decision making process that is sensible given the constraints humans typically face in making decisions, but would be suboptimal if the constraints were removed, as they are in many economists' hypothetical worlds. *See* JAMES G. MARCH, BOUNDED RATIONALITY, AMBIGUITY, AND THE ENGINEERING OF CHOICE, IN DECISION MAKING: DESCRIPTIVE, NORMATIVE, AND PRESCRIPTIVE INTERACTIONS 33, 40 (David E. Bell et al. eds., 1988). This concept, an aspect of bounded rationality, also derives from the work of March and Simon. *See* JAMES G. MARCH & HERBERT A. SIMON, ORGANIZATIONS 171 (2d ed. 1993).

[29] Prentice, *Irrational Auditor, supra* note 14, at 145-47. Because of the confirmation bias, even trained scientists tend to find articles that agree with their positions to be of higher quality than articles that disagree with their positions. *See* Jonathan J. Koehler, *The Influence of Prior Beliefs on Scientific Judgments of Evidence Quality*, 56 ORGANIZATIONAL BEHAV. & HUM. DECISION PROCESSES 28, 47 (1993).

[30] Prentice, *Irrational Auditor, supra* note 14, at 147-49. *See also* Jonathan D. Casper et al., *Juror Decision Making, Attitudes, and the Hindsight Bias*, 13 LAW & HUM. BEHAV. 291, 308 (1989) (noting that jurors generally have difficulty disregarding ultimate outcomes even when instructed to do so).

[31] *See* John C. Anderson et al., *Evaluation of Auditor Decisions: Hindsight Bias Effects and the Expectation Gap*, 14 J. ECON. PSYCHOL. 711, 722 (1993).

self-concept as good, worthwhile individuals. Thus, cognitive processes will work to suppress such information if at all possible."[32]

- Sixth, most people suffer memory limitations, including a tendency to remember things as they wish to remember them and to be overconfident in the accuracy of their memories.[33]
- Seventh, people tend to be influenced by overoptimism and overconfidence.[34] Thus, for example, people tend to overestimate their own knowledge and ability to make accurate judgments.[35]
- Eighth, people's judgments (unlike those of Chicago Man) tend to be subject to framing effects in that their answers are affected by how problems are framed.[36] Thus, by properly framing their presentation, sophisticated fraudsters have more luck fooling auditors.[37]
- Ninth, most people (unlike Chicago Man) tend to be affected by the representativeness heuristic, the tendency to judge probabilities via nonstatistical methods, for example, by relying on salient examples rather than base rates.[38] For example, people in the market for a new car tend to rely more heavily on the salient example of a friend who had a bad experience with a particular model of car than on a comprehensive survey by a consumer magazine.[39]
- Tenth, people tend to be insensitive to the source of information, crediting information even after they have evidence that its source is not credible.[40] Even trained auditors tend to overweigh client explanations for suspicious accounting entries.[41]

---

[32] Donald C. Langevoort, *Where Were the Lawyers? A Behavioral Inquiry Into Lawyers' Responsibility for Clients' Fraud*, 46 VAND. L. REV. 75, 102-03 (1993) [hereinafter Langevoort, *Where Were the Lawyers?*]. *See generally* LEON FESTINGER, A THEORY OF COGNITIVE DISSONANCE (1957); Prentice, *Irrational Auditor, supra* note 14, at 149-50.

[33] Prentice, *Irrational Auditor, supra* note 14, at 151-52. *See generally* Jonathan B. Holmes et al., *The Phenomenology of False Memories: Episodic Content and Confidence*, 24 J. EXPERIMENTAL PSYCHOL. 1026, 1027 (1988) (noting that people "often rate their false memories with high degrees of confidence.").

[34] Prentice, *Irrational Auditor, supra* note 14, at 152-56.

[35] *See* Lyle A. Brenner et al., *Overconfidence in Probability and Frequency Judgments: A Critical Examination*, 65 ORGANIZATIONAL BEHAV. & HUM. DECISION PROCESSES 212, 218 (1996).

[36] Prentice, *Irrational Auditor, supra* note 14, at 156-57.

[37] Karim Jamal et al., *Detecting Framing Effects in Financial Statements*, 12 CONTEMP. ACCT. RES. 85, 102 (1995) ("Despite their motivation, training, and experience, over half . . . of the audit partners who participated in this study were deceived by management's frame.").

[38] Prentice, *Irrational Auditor, supra* note 14, at 158-63.

[39] *See* Richard E. Nisbett et al., *Popular Induction: Information Is Not Necessarily Informative, in Judgment Under Uncertainty, supra* note 13, at 101, 109.

[40] Prentice, *Irrational Auditor, supra* note 14, at 160-61.

[41] *See* Mark E. Peecher, *The Influence of Auditors' Justification Processes on Their Decisions: A Cognitive Model and Experimental Evidence*, 34 J. ACCT. RES. 125, 137-39 (1996).

- Eleventh, people's judgments are affected by the anchoring and adjustment heuristic;[42] if auditors start with their clients' numbers, for example, their judgment is anchored on those numbers and they tend not to correct adequately for new information.[43]
- Twelfth, the self-serving bias means, among other things, that people's judgments, including judgments of fairness, tend to be influenced by their self-interest. Even if people are trying to be fair, what seems fair to them is inevitably influenced by what is in their own best interests.[44] Thus, the more revenue an auditor gains from a client, the more difficult it is for that auditor to withstand the client's request for improper accounting treatment.[45]
- Thirteenth, people's judgments tend to be influenced by sunk cost effects in that while economists say it is irrational to allow sunk costs to influence judgments, people do so every day.[46]
- Fourteenth, people are subject to time-delay traps in that they have difficulty appreciating the long-range implications of decisions. Therefore, they tend to value immediate over delayed gratification.[47]
- The time-delay trap is related to a fifteenth concept, bounded willpower. Even when they appreciate the long-range implications of activities such as smoking or drinking, people often lack the willpower to refrain from those activities.[48]

While even this lengthy laundry list of human decisional foibles is far from complete, it should substantially undermine the Chicago Man model of the rational actor that is fundamental to much of law and economics analysis. I was able in my article on auditors to tap into a huge stream of empirical literature by accounting professors that demonstrated the applicability of these various heuristics and biases to the decisions

---

[42] Prentice, *Irrational Auditor,* supra note 14, at 163-66.

[43] *See* D. Eric Hirst & Lisa Koonce, *Audit Analytical Procedures: A Field Investigation*, 13 CONTEMP. ACCT. RES. 457, 467 (1996).

[44] Prentice, *Irrational Auditor, supra* note 14, at 168-70.

[45] *See generally* Prentice, *SEC and MDP, supra* note 14, at 1597 (arguing that because of the self-serving bias, we should be leery of allowing audit firms to increase their streams of nonaudit revenue from clients).

[46] Prentice, *Irrational Auditor, supra* note 14, at 171-76. Honoring sunk cost effects can irrationally lead to escalation of commitment—the pouring of more and more resources into a deteriorating situation. *See generally* Max H. Bazerman et al., *Escalation of Commitment in Individual and Group Decision Making*, 33 ORGANIZATIONAL BEHAV. & HUM. PERFORMANCE 141, 150 (1984).

[47] Prentice, *Irrational Auditor, supra* note 14, at 176-79. Time-delay traps arguably have a lot to do with criminal activity in that wrongdoers tend to be unable to appreciate fully the long-term costs of their acts and tend to discount future consequences disproportionately. *See generally* MARGARET FRY, ARMS OF THE LAW 82-84 (1951).

[48] Prentice, *Irrational Auditor, supra* note 14, at 179-80.

made every day by auditors.[49] My point was not that auditors are always irrational, just that it is irrational to assume that they are always rational, especially in the face of specific evidence of an audit failure.[50]

If individuals do not act rationally, then their organizations will tend toward irrationality as well. Although I did not give this subject full treatment, I noted three points in my article on auditors. First, the behavioral literature is clear that people's decision making is shaped by heuristics and biases when they act on behalf of organizations as well as when they act on their own behalf.[51] Second, I noted that Professor Langevoort has demonstrated that structural and behavioral factors tend to make corporations systematically overoptimistic.[52] Third, I noted the phenomenon of subgoal pursuit—the tendency of heads of subunits within organizations to act as advocates of their own subunit's best interests at the expense of the interests of the larger organization.[53]

III. A BEHAVIORAL LOOK AT ENRON'S COLLAPSE

According to traditional economic analysis, regulation of Enron was unnecessary because Enron, like other rational actors, would voluntarily act honestly in order to reduce long-term costs of raising capital,[54] and its officers would not derail promising individual careers by engaging in financial fraud.[55] The facts disclosed by Cruver's *Anatomy of Greed* illustrate that the behavioral factors that I have highlighted carry

---

[49] *Id.* at 139-81.

[50] *Id.* at 217-19.

[51] *Id.* at 181.

[52] *Id.* at 182-83. *See generally* Donald C. Langevoort, *Organized Illusions: A Behavioral Theory of Why Corporations Mislead Stock Market Investors (and Cause Other Social Harms),* 146 U. PA. L. REV. 101 (1997)

[53] Prentice, *Irrational Auditor, supra* note 14, at 184. *See generally* John C. Coffee, Jr., *Beyond the Shut-Eyed Sentry: Toward a Theoretical View of Corporate Misconduct and an Effective Legal Response,* 63 VA. L. REV. 1099, 1135 (1977) (discussing subgoal pursuit).

[54] It is rational to act honestly because full and fair disclosure does reduce capital costs. *See, e.g.,* Richard Frankel et al., *Discretionary Disclosure and External Financing,* 70 ACCT. REV. 135, 149 (1995) (finding that firms accessing capital markets are more likely to disclose information than firms not doing so); Mark Lang & Russell Lundholm, *Cross-Sectional Determinants of Analyst Ratings of Corporate Disclosure,* 31 J. ACCT. RES. 246, 269 (1993) (reporting a study finding that firms issuing securities tend to disclose more information than firms not issuing securities); CHRISTIAN LEUZ & ROBERT E. VERRECCHIA, THE ECONOMIC CONSEQUENCES OF INCREASED DISCLOSURE 33 (July 1999) (unpublished manuscript on file with author) (finding in a study of German companies that a switch from the traditional German system to a fuller reporting regime, such as in the United States, appeared to allow them to "garner economically and statistically significant benefits.").

[55] Top managers are usually forced to resign when accounting irregularities occur. *See, e.g.,* Ehsan H. Feroz et al., *The Financial and Market Effects of the SEC's Accounting and Auditing Enforcement Releases,* 29 J. ACCT. RES. 107, 108 (1991) (finding that 72% of the companies targeted for accounting irregularities between 1982 and 1989 fired or received the resignation of top managers). More recently, they have also been doing the "perp walk" on national television. *See* Beth Piskora, *Stocks Back Down,* N.Y. POST, Aug. 2, 2002, at 33 (noting the arrest of WorldCom CFO Scott Sullivan).

substantial explanatory power regarding the Enron scandal. They help explain why neither Enron nor its officers acted rationally.

First, and perhaps foremost, is the self-serving bias. People tend to see that which they wish to see because their judgments are heavily if unconsciously influenced by self-interest.[56]

> A growing body of behavioral research indicates that acting contrary to one's self interest is not a natural or easy thing. It is not just that people consciously say: "I'm looking out for me; screw the other guy," although they sometimes do. Rather, a menu of cognitive biases and limits on rationality affect how people perceive, process, and remember information, and, consequently, how they choose among alternative actions, assess risk, and make many other types of decisions.[57]

The self-serving bias worked particular evil at Enron. Cruver explains why:

> Enron, more than any other "energy" company, dealt in commodities and derivative structures and deal terms that were far too unusual to have an established price. It was an issue of liquidity: if the deal required a price on something that was rarely bought and sold (making it illiquid), and there wasn't much of an established market, then the price had to be made up.[58]

When Enron employees valued proposed deals, which affected the numbers Enron could put on its books, which in turn determined whether or not employees met their bonus targets, which in turn determined whether millions of dollars in bonuses were paid to the very people who were deciding what the numbers should be, even assuming good faith (and at least some of the Enron officers must have been acting in good faith), the self-serving bias must have had an impact. This is especially so because Enron employees were often not choosing between legitimate Option A and legitimate Option B; rather, "the prices were pulled from [someone's ass] because there was nowhere else to get them!"[59]

Second, when Cruver learned of the Enron system and saw the huge potential for abuse, he was comforted by the fact that Enron's own division of Risk Assessment and Control (RAC) was responsible for reviewing the deals and their attached numbers. Given the novelty and complexity of Enron's ever evolving business ventures, RAC

---

[56] *See* George Loewenstein, *Behavioral Decision Theory and Business Ethics: Skewed Trade-Offs Between Self and Others, in* CODES OF CONDUCT: BEHAVIORAL RESEARCH INTO BUSINESS ETHICS 214, 221 (David M. Messick & Ann E. Tenbrunsel eds., 1996) ("[P]eople tend to conflate what is personally beneficial with what is fair or moral.").

[57] Prentice, *SEC and MDP, supra* note 14, at 1603 (citations omitted).

[58] CRUVER, *supra* note 12, at 80.

[59] *Id.*

should have been more wary, but the behavioral phenomenon of overconfidence raised its ugly head. Throughout Enron, employees believed they were the best and brightest and the hubris of officers such as Skilling and Fastow clearly played a role in the company's downfall.[60] At RAC, for example, Cruver reports, "people had built up a tough outer shell—and it was a shell that would be tough to crack. It was like [RAC] believed they already had everything under control."[61]

Third, consider the behavioral factors that propel companies toward overconfidence. Even when company officials intend to be honest, they often produce overly optimistic financial figures for a variety of behavioral reasons. In another article, I summarized Professor Langevoort's thesis in this way:

> Langevoort essentially argues that (a) due to natural concerns about raises, promotions, and terminations within the corporate structure, good news flows to the top more quickly than bad news; (b) corporate cultures often operate to cause managers to misperceive risks and to harbor unrealistically optimistic beliefs about the corporation's prospects; (c) heuristics, such as cognitive conservatism and decision simplification, coupled with groupthink, encourage corporate management groups to underestimate risk and otherwise unrealistically view the firm's competitive environment; (d) for various reasons, optimists tend to be hired and to advance faster through corporate ranks, and the resulting overoptimism coupled with the human being's natural illusion of control leads to a "can do" culture that ignores reality; (e) once executives commit to a course of action, which they often do based on sketchy, preliminary information, it is psychologically difficult for them to change course; (f) self-serving inferences causing company managers to see what they wish to see are pervasive in business; and (g) all factors can coalesce to cause upper level managers to place a recklessly positive spin on information they receive from lower levels.[62]

This systematic tendency toward over optimism was especially strong at Enron due to the fact that (a) potential bonuses were literally "unlimited,"[63] and (b) Enron adopted an aggressive employee review system—a semiannual weeding out known as the "rank and yank."[64] In this unique employee evaluation system, every six months 15% of employees were to be given unsatisfactory ratings that largely doomed their careers at

---

[60] *See generally* Malcolm Gladwell, *The Talent Myth*, NEW YORKER, July 22, 2002, at 28 (arguing that Enron's obsession with hiring the "best and the brightest" and giving them nearly unlimited discretion helped cause its downfall).

[61] CRUVER, *supra* note 12, at 77.

[62] Prentice, *Irrational Auditor, supra* note 14, at 182-83.

[63] CRUVER, *supra* note 12, at 68 ("There was literally no cap on the size of the bonus.").

[64] *Id.* at 61-62 (the process's formal name was the "Peer Review Committee (PRC), but it was widely known within the firm as 'rank and yank'").

Enron. These behavioral factors led to a very simple situation where, despite its well-known RICE code of ethics, the real rule was an unwritten one: NO BAD NEWS.[65]

Fourth, the problem of subgoal pursuit permeated Enron. Cruver himself was hired into a start-up group, as noted earlier, to begin marketing derivatives that would protect clients from risk that might come if firms that owed them money went bankrupt. According to Cruver,

> if you were futzing along in a stagnant area within Enron, then the fastest way to break out and make zillions was to start a new group. Waterston had done just that, pitching our credit-risk idea to Skilling and getting a green light. Waterston knew that such an all-or-nothing strategy would be high risk and that such adventures had a 95% failure rate, but hey, he was in his late thirties so this was his time.[66]

Thus, because of subgoal pursuit, individual units of Enron tackled huge, risky projects and a number of them—a large power plant in Dabhol, India, a large power plant in South America, a large water business (Azurix) in England—went under, helping drag Enron down.[67] The risk profiles of the individual units did not match the optimal risk profile for Enron itself.

Fifth, cognitive dissonance played a role in Enron's demise. Enron proclaimed itself the best corporation in the world. Enron's CEO repeatedly told critics that they "just didn't get it."[68] Enron's employees believed that they were the '90s version of the "Masters of the Universe" who roamed Wall Street in the 1980s.[69] With those beliefs firmly held and repeatedly expressed, it became extremely difficult for Enron employees to process contrary information. Professor Langevoort has explained how cognitive dissonance

---

[65] According to Cruver, he had the following exchange with his anonymous Deep Throat-like source, "Mr. Blue": He leaned in:

> "There was an unwritten rule . . . a rule of 'no bad news.' If I came to them with bad news, it would only hurt my career."
>
> "Bad news about what?"
>
> "About Enron's deals—how little sense they made, how they would lose money, how they were run by unqualified egomaniacs."

Id. at 176.

[66] *Id.* at 65. Gladwell, *supra* note 60, at 30 gives another example. A young Enron employee thought that Enron should develop an online gas trading business and set about to do it. "Kitchin's qualification for running EnronOnline, it should be pointed out, was not that she was good at it. It was that she wanted to do it, and Enron was a place where stars did whatever they wanted." *Id.*

[67] CRUVER, *supra* note 12, at 75.

[68] Bethany McLean, *Why Enron Went Bust*, FORTUNE, Dec. 24, 2001, at 58 (noting that anyone who challenged Enron was told by its leaders that they "just didn't get it").

[69] Of course, these Masters of the Universe have been painted brilliantly by Michael Lewis and Tom Wolfe. *See* MICHAEL LEWIS, LIAR'S POKER (1989) (factual account); TOM WOLFE, THE BONFIRE OF THE VANITIES (1987) (fictional account).

makes it hard for lawyers who have taken public positions to accept critical information about their clients.[70] I have made a similar case regarding auditors who have certified their clients' financial statements as full and fair.[71] Similarly, it was extremely difficult for employees of "the world's greatest company" to see its flaws. As Cruver explained, after he learned from his supervisor Middleton that many Enron deals were inflated in value so that officers could make their bonuses,

> I had to assume [Middleton] was right about the underlying cause of the inflated deals, but I wasn't so sure about the effect. Maybe people were trying to push these deals past him, but surely someone in charge within RAC or at Arthur Andersen had control of the overall situation. This company was profitable, and you can't just pull profits out of thin air.[72]

Of course, we know now that Enron was pulling these profits out of thin air, but no Enron employee would want to believe this, nor be prone to question when their CEOs were repeatedly telling them that nothing was wrong. Certainly there should have been some seeds of doubt planted when CEO Skilling resigned, but when Kenneth Lay resumed the CEO position and assured the employees and the world that "[t]here are no accounting issues, no trading issues, no reserve issues, no previously unknown problem issues . . . . There is no other shoe to fall,"[73] they would tend to believe the company line. In addition to cognitive dissonance, part of the problem was anchor and adjustment—employees' beliefs were anchored on the vision of Enron as an invincible corporate giant and new information would tend not to be processed in such a way as to move employees sufficiently far from that belief. Even stock analysts whose beliefs were anchored on Enron as a success had great difficulty adjusting as negative news continued to stream in; Cruver and a stock analyst friend of his who followed Enron called it "intellectual inertia,"[74] but it was simple anchoring and adjustment reinforced by cognitive dissonance.

A related problem is a behavioral phenomenon known as the false consensus effect that causes honest people to impute their honest motives to others.[75] Those Enron employees who were honest would not tend to believe that some of their colleagues and bosses could be dishonest.[76] Finally, people have a basic inability to tell when they

---

[70] *See* Langevoort, *Where Were the Lawyers?, supra* note 32, at 102-03.

[71] *See* Prentice, *Irrational Auditor, supra* note 14, at 150

[72] CRUVER, *supra* note 12, at 84.

[73] *Id.* at 94 (quoting a *Business Week* interview with Kenneth Lay).

[74] *Id.* at 125.

[75] *See generally* Colin F. Camerer, *Individual Decision Making, in* THE HANDBOOK OF EXPERIMENTAL ECONOMICS 587, 612-13 (John H. Kagel & Alvin E. Roth, eds., 1995) (explaining the phenomenon); Lee Ross et al., *The "False Consensus Effect:" An Egocentric Bias in Social Perception and Attribution Processes*, 13 J. EXPERIMENTAL & SOC. PSYCHOL. 279 (1977) (same).

[76] *See* Prentice, *Whither Securities Regulation, supra* note 14, at 1462 (discussing the false consensus effect in the context of securities investing).

are being deceived.[77] Enron employees desperately wanted to believe Ken Lay—he was, after all, a family man[78] so they did, to their ultimate regret.

I could go on. I haven't even touched upon the auditors,[79] the lawyers,[80] or the bankers.[81] There's enough in the Enron saga to keep behavioral psychologists and organizational behavior theorists up to their eyeballs in case studies for years to come. The point I seek to make is that behavioral decision theory has substantial explanatory power in the Enron debacle.[82]

---

[77] *See* EVELIN SULLIVAN, THE CONCISE BOOK OF LYING 206 (2001) ("In scientifically conducted experiments, the success rate of people being asked to sort out lies from truth, say by watching people on videotape either lying or telling the truth, has been shown to be poor.").

[78] After one of Lay's pep talks to the Enron employees, a colleague reported to Cruver: "Linda Lay was there, and he introduced her. He's amazing. He's just so sincere, and you can really trust that everything is going to be fine. He's a family man . . . . We gave him a huge standing ovation." CRUVER, *supra* note 12, at 93.

[79] The obvious point that I have made in earlier articles is that it will be difficult even for auditors who are trying to be honest to judge their client's situation objectively when the auditors have an overwhelmingly strong financial motive to keep the audit client happy. Enron's auditor, Arthur Andersen, was making more than $50 million a year in fees from Enron (more from consulting than from auditing), and expected soon to be making $100 million annually. One cannot escape the conclusion that Andersen's collective judgment was affected by the self-serving bias, because several officials inside Andersen realized the legal risks presented by Enron's aggressive accounting practices. *See generally* Delroy Alexander et al., *Ties to Enron Blinded Andersen*, CHI. TRIB., Sept. 3, 2002, at N1 (detailing various problems making it difficult for Andersen to maintain the required auditor's skepticism).

[80] Like the auditors, many of Enron's law firms had huge financial ties to Enron that made it difficult for the individual lawyers in those firms to overcome the self-serving bias. For example, Enron was Vinson & Elkins's single largest client, paying it $36 million in 2001. *See* Julie Mason, *Legal Counsel Scrutinized*, HOUSTON CHRON., Mar. 8, 2002, at A22.

[81] Consider that Merrill Lynch was involved with Enron in at least seven different capacities. It underwrote Enron stock and bond deals, raised capital for Enron's special purpose entities, invested in those entities, partnered with Enron in floating three power plants, loaned Enron money, was a counterparty in various Enron energy derivatives trades, and, notwithstanding all of those ties, purported to provide independent securities analysis of Enron stock to investors. *See* Paula Dwyer et al., *Merrill Lynch: See No Evil?*, BUS. WK., Sept. 16, 2002, at 68, 69 (detailing these relationships). One may legitimately question whether Merrill Lynch could provide unbiased analysis of Enron's stock under such conditions.

[82] To explore just one more example, consider Andy Fastow and Michael Kopper. The clearest evidence of criminal conduct to surface thus far in the Enron probes relates to CFO Fastow and his assistant Kopper, who profited enormously by investing in and operating various "special purpose entities" designed to allow Enron to move debt off its books. Fastow apparently took around $40 million at Enron's expense. Kopper recently pled guilty and agreed to reimburse the government for $12 million that he had pocketed. *See* Bill Murphy, *Go-getter Rose Quickly, Raked in Cash*, HOUSTON CHRON., Aug. 22, 2002, at Bus. 1 (detailing Kopper's plea). Holman Jenkins recently delved into the psychological literature to suggest that Fastow and Kopper were not conscious criminals, but instead victims of their own poor decision making. Holman Jenkins, *How Could They Have Done it?*, WALL ST. J., Aug. 28, 2002, at A15. Jenkins noted that behavioralists Max Bazerman and David Messick have pointed out that "[u]nethical business decisions may stem not from the traditionally assumed [rational] trade-off between ethics and profits . . . but from psychological tendencies that foster poor decision making." David M. Messick & Max H. Bazernan, *Ethical Leadership and the Psychology of Decision Making*, 37 SLOAN MGMT. REV., Winter 1996, at 9, 18. I believe that it is possible that Fastow and Kopper deluded themselves into thinking that they deserved the extra millions they were salting away. After

IV. LAW AND ECONOMICS VERSUS BUSINESS ETHICS

Not only is law and economics largely a failure in its attempts to produce descriptive and predictive accuracy; it inevitably carries an unfortunate normative aspect. Borrowing a point from Charles Pouncy,[83] I note that as traditional economic theory, premised on the notion that man is a creature who maximizes his personal utilities (primarily reduced to monetary units), gains purchase in business schools, law schools, and elsewhere, it carries the strong implicit message that this is the way people should act. As Pouncy observes, "economic rationality acts as a cultural contaminant, devaluing other moral and cultural considerations. . . ."[84] In the economic rationality assumption, economic optimization is the key yardstick, "but economic optimization in no way guarantees that the allocation of resources will be the 'best or most favorable' in a moral or political sense."[85]

> If economic actors are taught to value ethical and moral behavior by their families, religious institutions, or MBA programs, then it is reasonable to expect these values to be observed in economic decision-making. However, if economic actors have been taught by their culture to value their personal well-being, narrowly defined in terms of finance and/or status, above all else, then market principles suggest that ethics and morality may be traded-off for goods that are more utility maximizing.[86]

Despite a well-publicized code of ethics (that was observed mainly in the breach), Enron, as described by Cruver, was an organization where money was the only yardstick

all, they were being creative; they were taking chances on Enron's behalf. It is possible that they rationalized that they deserved the money, much as Cruver later rationalized continuing to fly first class and eat at the finest restaurants on Enron's tab even as the company in its final days urged cost-cutting by employees. *See infra* note 110 and accompanying text. While traditional economic literature assumes that people commit crimes because the expected benefits exceed the expected costs, *see* RICHARD A. POSNER, ECONOMIC ANALYSIS OF LAW 242 (5th ed. 1998), "the reality is that people usually slide into crime not as the result of a single rationally-weighed cost-benefit decision, but because of a series of small irrational decisions to experiment with drugs, join a gang, or the like." Prentice, *Irrational Auditor, supra* note 14, at 177.

[83] *See* Charles R.P. Pouncy, *The Rational Rogue: Neoclassical Economic Ideology in the Regulation of the Financial Professional,* 26 VT. L. REV. 263 (2002) [hereinafter Pouncy, *Rational Rogue*]; Charles R.P. Pouncy, *Contemporary Financial Innovation: Orthodoxy and Alternatives,* 51 SMU L. REV. 505 (1998).

[84] Pouncy, *Rational Rogue, supra* note 83, at 264. Indeed, Pouncy notes that "[t]he decisional structure envisioned by neoclassical economic theory leaves little room for the operation of ethics and morality in its model-building project." *Id.* at 281.

[85] *Id.* at 274. Pouncy also observes that "[w]hen market processes are deemed to yield optimal results, optimality and the efficiency construct upon which it is based become proxies for ethics and morality." *Id.* at 276

[86] *Id.* at 280. Although I believe that MBAs' ethical views are largely established before they reach graduate school and that it is difficult to alter them dramatically by business ethics courses, *see* Prentice, Business Schools, *supra* note 8, at A21, there is some evidence that business students' ethics do deteriorate as they go through school. *See* Etzioni, *supra* note 10, at B4 ("A recent Aspen Institute study of about 2,000 graduates of the top 13 business schools found that B-school education not only fails to improve the moral character of students, it actually weakens it.").

and ethics had little place in anyone's decisional calculus. This mindset started at the top with Kenneth Lay, who once said: "I don't want to be rich, I want to be world-class rich."[87] He achieved his objective. The primacy of personal wealth continued with Enron's 401(k) plan handout for employees that featured George Bernard Shaw's observation that "[l]ack of money is the root of all evil."[88] It was continually drummed into employees with the "rank and yank" review process. Those who didn't make their numbers were demoted and destroyed, and those who did make their numbers received bonuses so fabulous that Houston luxury car dealers knew to come to Enron to exhibit their wares every bonus period.[89] The centrality of money was cemented with the stock options that allowed Tom White to leave Enron to be Secretary of the Army, salvaging $14 million in severance payments and stock payments,[90] and allowed other Enron officers to profit in the tens of millions and even hundreds of millions of dollars.[91] While amassing huge personal fortunes, these officers presided over a company where, Cruver points out, although there was a code of ethics, "[t]he reality was that perception led the way."[92]

As William Bennett has observed, "capitalism requires capitalists with moral and ethical tethers."[93] Unfortunately, Cruver paints a picture of an organization where the only thing that really counted was money and where the code of ethics was only window dressing.[94] When corporate officers only talk the talk and do not walk the walk, codes of ethics are essentially meaningless.[95] Indeed, ethical action may well have been suspect inside the Enron machine, for "[w]hen economic rationality takes on the imprimatur of truth, human behavior that is inconsistent with economic rationality becomes suspect both as irrational, in the sense that it operates at odds with consensus reality, and immoral, in that it is less likely to result in an efficient solution, a moral imperative in an economic theory based on presumed scarcity."[96]

---

[87] CRUVER, *supra* note 12, at 23.

[88] *Id.* at 3 (emphasis added).

[89] *Id.* at 68.

[90] *Id.* at 69.

[91] Among the individuals who sold Enron stock just during the class action period of the initial shareholder suit filed against Enron, Lay sold $184 million, Robert Belfer $111 million, Rebecca Mark $82 million, Lou Pai $270 million, Jeff Skilling $70 million, Andy Fastow $33 million, Ken Harrison $75 million, etc., etc. *Id.* at 131-32.

[92] *Id.* at 40.

[93] William J. Bennett, *Capitalism and a Moral Education*, CHI. TRIB., July 28, 2002, at C9.

[94] Ott has pointed out the distinction in many organizations between espoused values and values-in-use. J. STEVEN OTT, THE ORGANIZATIONAL CULTURE PERSPECTIVE 44-45 (1989). In Enron, there was a stark distinction between the two.

[95] Pouncy, *Rational Rogue, supra* note 83, at 364 ("The teaching of this and similar studies is that ethical intervention by means of codes or training is only effective when the organization actively enforces its ethical proscriptions, and leaders of the organization model appropriate ethical behavior."), citing inter alia Anusorn Singhapakdi & Scott J. Vitell, *Analyzing the Ethical Decision Making of Sales Professionals*, J. PERS. SELLING & SALES MGMT., Fall 1999, at 1.

[96] Pouncy, *Rational Rogue, supra* note 83, at 292.

Ultimately, Enron illustrates Pouncy's point that "[i]ndividuals will find it difficult to 'do the right thing' when the right thing is not among the options presented by the institutional processes in which they are participating."[97] A theory known as social proof provides that we all tend to take our cues for proper behavior from those around us.[98] Social proof helps account for the success of laugh tracks on TV shows,[99] mass suicides,[100] and the tendency of bystanders not to help a person in peril when others seem unconcerned.[101] Watching others for cues has been shown to guide decisions to sign form contracts ("if everyone else is signing this, it must be okay"),[102] to return a lost wallet,[103] to engage in promiscuous sexual activity in a safe versus unsafe manner,[104] and to engage in various other forms of activity.[105] Social proof causes securities analysts

---

[97] *Id.* at 322.

[98] *See* ROBERT B. CIALDINI, INFLUENCE: SCIENCE AND PRACTICE 114-66 (Rev. ed. 1993) (explaining and illustrating the social proof concept); Robert Axelrod, *An Evolutionary Approach to Norms*, 80 AM. POL. SCI. REV. 1095, 1105 (1986) ("The actions of others provide information about what is proper for us, even if we do not know the reasons."); Robert H. Frank, *The Political Economy of Preference Falsification: Timur Kuran's Private Truths, Public Lies*, 34 J. ECON. LIT. 115, 119 (1996) ("[O]ur cognitive capabilities are limited, and without heavy reliance on social proof no one could manage even to get through the day.").

[99] John Mariotti, *Understanding Influence and Persuasion*, THE INDUSTRY STANDARD, Apr. 5, 1999, at 126.

[100] *Id.* (noting that the Jonestown mass suicide can be linked to social proof). Empirical studies have also linked social proof to suicide. *See, e.g.*, Ann F. Garland & Edward Zigler, *Adolescence Suicide Prevention: Current Research and Social Policy Implications*, (Special Issue) 48 AM. PSYCHOLOGIST 169, 174 (1993) (noting a social imitation effect that increases suicide likelihood when others have modeled the behavior and thereby lowered taboo against suicide); David P. Phillips & Lundie L. Carstensen, *The Effect of Suicide Stories on Various Demographic Groups, 1968-1985*, 18 SUICIDE & LIFE-THREATENING BEHAV. 100, 108 (1988) (finding that "nearly all demographic groups displayed a rise in suicides after publicized suicide stories.").

[101] *See* BIBB LATANE & JOHN M. DARLEY, THE UNRESPONSIVE BYSTANDER: WHY DOESN'T HE HELP? 125 (1968) (making this point about the famous Kitty Genovese case in which dozens of people witnessed or heard a series of attacks on a young woman in New York City, yet no one intervened).

[102] G. Richard Shell, *Fair Play, Consent and Securities Arbitration: A Comment on Speidel*, 62 BROOK. L. REV. 1371 (1996) ("To the extent customers think about [clauses in form contracts] at all, my guess is that they say to themselves: 'There are a lot of people like me . . . and they all signed this contract, too. Some of them must have given it some thought even if I am too busy to do so. It must be OK.'").

[103] Harvey A. Hornstein et al., *Influence of a Model's Feeling about His Behavior and His Relevance as a Comparison Other on Observers' Helping Behavior*, 10 J. PERSONALITY & SOC. PSYCHOL. 222, 225 (1968) (finding that people are more likely to return an apparently lost wallet intact when they have a model of someone similar to them doing so).

[104] Bram P. Buunk & Arnold B. Bakker, *Extradyadic Sex: The Role of Descriptive and Injunctive Norms*, 32 J. SEX RES. 313, 317 (1995) (finding in two studies that the perceived conduct of others had an important impact on whether individuals chose to engage in extramarital sexual relations); Robert W. Winslow et al., *Perceived Peer Norms, Casual Sex, and AIDS Risk Prevention*, 22 J. APP. SOC. PSYCHOL. 1809, 1821 (1992) (finding that perceptions of the behavior of one's peers had more impact on college students' sexual activity than did knowledge about AIDS).

[105] *See* LARRY M. BARTELS, PRESIDENTIAL PRIMARIES AND THE DYNAMICS OF PUBLIC CHOICE 110 (1988) (finding that favorable poll results cause people to evaluate a candidate more positively); Albert Bandura

to initiate and abandon coverage of certain firms,[106] so it is little wonder that it affects the actions of employees who are hired into a corrupt corporate culture.[107]

Organizations such as Enron reap what they sow. They usually become victims of the ethical corner-cutting that they encourage their employees to practice against competitors.[108] Thus, Lou Pai made (up) his numbers, took $350 million in compensation, and walked out the door leaving Enron with numerous projects that in reality were losing money.[109]

Cruver himself was a quick study in the Enron culture. When Enron's financial difficulties became apparent and the company urged economy measures in travel expenditures, Cruver tells us that "[p]ersonally, I continued taking business-related trips, staying in the best hotels and eating in the best restaurants."[110] He rationalized flouting the advisory with an "everyone does it" and an "I was working hard so I deserved it."

et al., *Vicarious Extinction of Avoidance Behavior*, 5 J. PERSONALITY & SOC. PSYCHOL. 16, 20 (1967) (reporting results of study finding that children's fear of dogs was not reduced by seeing a dog in a positive light, but was reduced by seeing other children interact nonanxiously with a dog); Robert B. Cialdini et al., *A Focus Theory of Normative Conduct: Recycling the Concept of Norms to Reduce Littering in Public Places*, 58 J. PERSONALITY & SOC. PSYCHOL. 1015, 1025 (1990) (finding that people's beliefs about others' littering affected their own practices); David D. Kirkpatrick, *Book Agent's Buying Fuels Concern on Influencing Best-Seller List*, N.Y. TIMES, Aug. 23, 2000, at C1 (noting that social proof can affect book buying activity).

[106] Hayagreeva Rao et al., *Fool's Gold: Social Proof in the Initiation and Abandonment of Coverage by Wall Street Analysts*, 46 ADMIN. SCI. Q. 502, 521 (2001) (reporting the results of a study indicating that "research departments of investment banks and brokerage firms were more likely to adopt a focal firm for coverage when peers had recently adopted it."). Similarly television networks take cues from each other in programming, introducing shows aimed at taking advantage of the success of competitors even though conventional industrial organization theory implies that firms should differentiate their products instead. *See* Sushil Bikhchandani et al., *A Theory of Fads, Fashion, Custom, and Cultural Change as Information Cascades*, 100 J. POL. ECON. 992, 1010 (1992), citing Robert E. Kennedy, *Strategy Fads and Strategic Positioning: An Empirical Test for Herd Behavior in Prime-Time Television Programming* (Harvard Business School, Division of Research Working Paper, 1997).

[107] Asch's classic studies demonstrate how overpoweringly persuasive social proof can be. Subjects asked whether line A is the same length as line B, line C, or line D often give an obviously incorrect response when confederates of the experimenter have previously given the same obviously wrong answer. *See* Solomon E. Asch, *Opinions and Social Pressure*, SCI. AM., Nov. 1955, at 31, 31-35. *See also* Richard A. Crutchfield, *Conformity and Character*, 10 AM. PSYCHOLOGIST 191, 196 (1955) (replicating Asch's study with female subjects—Asch had studied only males); Morton Deutsch & Harold B. Gerard, *A Study of Normative and Informational Social Influences Upon Individual Judgment*, 51 J. ABNORMAL & SOC. PSYCHOL. 629, 632 (1955) (replicating Asch's results under conditions of anonymity).

[108] Two other obvious recent examples include WorldCom and Tyco. WorldCom was brought low by the excessive financial frauds of its CFO, the same frauds that had made it seem a success in the first place. *See generally* Jonathan Moules, *WorldCom Trial Net Cast Wider*, FIN. TIMES, Sept. 5, 2002, at 24 (noting that WorldCom's former CFO Scott Sullivan had pled "not guilty" in federal court to charges of securities fraud). Tyco, another high-flying firm, was apparently looted by its insiders. *See generally* Kevin McCoy & Gary Strauss, *Kozlowski, Others Accused of Using Tyco as 'Piggy Bank,'* USA TODAY, Sept. 13, 2002, at 1B (noting that former CEO Kozlowski and others had been charged with stealing at least $600 million from the company).

[109] CRUVER, *supra* note 12, at 80.

[110] *Id.* at 73.

When Enron's bankruptcy filing became imminent, Cruver remembered an Enron program allowing employees to order Dell computers to enable them to improve their computer skills. Employees were to repay a portion of the purchase price after leaving the firm, unless Enron was forced to terminate their employment for business reasons. Realizing that such a termination was about to take place, Cruver "decided it was time to get a free computer." He then ordered a new computer at no cost to himself; the next day Enron suspended the program.[111]

When Enron laid Cruver off and then mistakenly continued to pay him, he went through various machinations to lay his hands on the checks and to cash them, rationalizing that Enron would not be able to make the severance payments he had been promised when hired and promising himself that he would stop accepting the mistaken paychecks when the amount exceeded his promised severance package.[112] He and friends who were beneficiaries of the same mistake agreed to keep quiet about the mistake and to pocket the funds as long as possible.[113]

Cruver then started selling Enron memorabilia on e-Bay.[114] There may have been nothing really wrong with that until he started selling Enron e-mails to which he had been privy.[115] These were e-mails that embarrassed Enron and it appears that Cruver was still accepting the mistaken paychecks at that point, so he should have owed a more sensitive duty of loyalty.[116]

Finally, of course, Cruver gained at Enron's expense by writing his book and selling the attendant movie rights. We can be glad he did, I suppose. The victim of his disloyalty was so richly deserving.

V. SARBANES-OXLEY

Congress responded to Enron and similar scandals by passing the Sarbanes-Oxley Act[117] in July 2002. If economic actors are rational, Sarbanes-Oxley should solve most corporate financial fraud problems. After all, Sarbanes-Oxley addresses the incentive structure of virtually all the important actors in what experts have called the "corporate reporting supply chain"[118]—officers, directors, auditors, attorneys, and securities analysts.

---

[111] *Id.* at 196-97.

[112] *Id.* at 248, 256-58.

[113] *Id.* at 252.

[114] *Id.* at 297-98.

[115] *Id.* at 298-99.

[116] e-Bay later pulled Cruver's listing, apparently after threats of litigation from Enron. *Id.* at 300.

[117] Sarbanes-Oxley Act of 2002, Pub. L. No. 107-204, 116 Stat. 746-810 (2002)(codified as amended in 15 U.S.C. §§ 7201-7266 and scattered sections of 18 U.S.C.). Sarbanes-Oxley's text is available on the Internet at various sites. *See, e.g.*, http://news.findlaw.com/hdocs/docs/gwbush/sarbanesoxley072302.pdf.

[118] *See* Samuel A. DiPiazza, Jr. & Robert G. Eccles, Building Public Trust: The Future of Corporate Reporting 48 (2002).

For example, Sarbanes-Oxley requires CEOs and CFOs to certify each periodic report containing financial statements that is filed with the SEC and subjects them to criminal penalties for knowing or willful violations.[119] It also requires them to reimburse their companies for any bonus or other incentive-based compensation received during a period in which their employer must restate its accounts due to misconduct (even if the CEO and CFO are not involved).[120] The law punishes any corporate official who fraudulently influences, coerces, manipulates, or misleads the company's auditors.[121] And, Sarbanes-Oxley requires officers (and directors) to promptly report their trading activity in their company's shares[122] and requires the SEC to require issuers to establish codes of ethics for senior financial officers.[123]

Sarbanes-Oxley increases the requirements for public companies' audit committees (all members must be independent and at least one must be a "financial expert"),[124] and gives those audit committees increased authority (such as the power to hire and supervise the company's independent auditors).[125] Increased authority likely will lead to increased liability, which is designed to focus the directors' attention to a greater degree than the Enron directors were engaged.[126]

Sarbanes-Oxley ends the audit profession's self-regulation, creating the Public Company Accounting Oversight Board (PCAOB) and charging it with registering public accounting firms that audit public companies; adopting auditing, quality control, ethics, independence, and other standards for the profession; inspecting accounting firms to ensure compliance; and sanctioning violators.[127] The PCAOB's powers are broad, and Congress has required that its rules prohibit independent audit firms from offering most nonaudit services to audit clients in order to eliminate the serious conflicts of interest that were manifest in the Arthur Andersen-Enron relationship.[128]

In Sarbanes-Oxley, Congress requires the SEC to issue minimum standards of professional conduct for attorneys that will require them to report evidence of violations of securities laws or breaches of fiduciary duty to the client's chief legal counsel or CEO and, if these parties do not respond appropriately, to the firm's audit committee.[129]

---

[119] 15 U.S.C. § 7241 (2002) (civil provision) and 18 U.S.C. §§ 1341, 1343 (2002) (criminal provision).

[120] 15 U.S.C. § 7244

[121] *Id.* § 7242.

[122] *Id.* § 78p.

[123] *Id.* § 7264.

[124] *Id.* § 7265.

[125] Pub. L. No. 107-204, Title III, § 301 (2002).

[126] *See Stampede to Sign Up for New Oath Law*, LLOYD'S LIST, Aug. 15, 2002, at 1 (noting that Sarbanes-Oxley will likely expose audit committee members to greater personal liability than they faced before).

[127] 15 U.S.C. §§ 7211-7219.

[128] *Id.* § 7231.

[129] *Id.* § 7245.

Additionally, to minimize the tendency of financial analysts to skew their advice in order to gain underwriting and other business for their firms, Sarbanes-Oxley requires the SEC to issue rules designed to protect the objectivity and independence of securities analysts.[130] Investment bankers are not to have the right to preapprove analysts' reports and recommendations nor to supervise them or set their compensation. Analysts are protected from retaliation and threats from investment bankers in their firms, and securities analysts are also required to disclose compensation that might prejudice their objectivity.[131]

VI. CONCLUSION

In the provisions described above and others, Congress in Sabanes-Oxley took salutary action against corporate fraud. Rational wrongdoers should be deterred. Of course, rational wrongdoers would have been deterred by the civil and criminal provisions already on the books that will likely send Enron's Michael Kopper and Andy Fastow, WorldCom's Scott Sullivan, Tyco's Dennis Kozlowski, and others to jail.[132] Unfortunately perhaps, it is not a rational world and the behavioral insights offered in this paper help us realize why these frauds occur in the first place and let us know that even beneficial legislation like Sarbanes-Oxley offers no panacea.

Nonetheless, Sarbanes-Oxley may be applauded for at least three reasons that are consistent with the behavioral literature. First, in several ways (limiting auditor provision of nonaudit services and isolating securities analysts from investment bankers, for example), Sarbanes-Oxley minimizes existing conflicts of interest in a way that should reduce the pervasive influence of the self-serving bias. Henceforth, auditors and securities analysts who wish to be honest will have an easier time of it than they have had in the past.[133]

Second, although some of Sarbanes-Oxley's provisions largely duplicate current rules[134] and others merely increase already severe penalties,[135] the passage of this high-profile law implicates three related biases—the vividness bias (people tend to perceive as more dangerous risks that are based on emotionally interesting information

[130] *Id.* §§ 78o-6, 78u-2.

[131] *Id.*

[132] Knowingly or recklessly making false representations or omissions in connection with the sale of securities was already punishable under the 1934 Securities Exchange Act, for example. Section 10(b) of the 1934 Act prohibits such conduct in violation of SEC rules. 15 U.S.C. § 78j(b) (2002). Rule 10b-5 implements that provision. 17 C.F.R. § 240.10b-5 (2001). Section 32 of the Act provides that any intentional violation of any 1934 Act provision or rule issued thereunder is a criminal offense. 15 U.S.C. § 78ff (2002). The maximum penalty for individuals was already 10 years in jail and/or a fine of $1 million. *Id.*

[133] Through a different mechanism, Sarbanes-Oxley also helps issuers' employees to do the right thing by providing protection for whistleblowers. 18 U.S.C. § 1514A (2002).

[134] Section 807 of Sarbanes-Oxley punishes fraud in connection with any security of a public company, largely duplicating § 10(b) of the 1934 Act.

[135] Section 1106 of Sarbanes-Oxley increases the criminal penalties for violating provisions of the 1934 Securities Exchange Act from an already stiff maximum punishment of a fine of $1,000,000 and/or 10 years in jail for an individual to a fine of $5,000,000 and/or 20 years in jail.

rather than more probative abstract data),[136] the availability bias (people tend to perceive as more dangerous risks that they can readily recall),[137] and the saliency bias (people tend to perceive as more dangerous risks that are illustrated by colorful, dynamic or other distinctive stimuli).[138] Some worry that the public generally overestimates vivid, salient risks, such as those stemming from nuclear power or cancer, in part because they are readily available for recollection because of broad coverage in the media.[139] The forceful and highly-publicized Congressional declaration that CEOs must do that which they were already bound to do (certify accurate financial statements), supplemented by some rather vivid "perp walks," will likely serve to concentrate executives' attention in a more effective manner than has been accomplished in the past.[140]

Third, Sarbanes-Oxley sends a message regarding the law's resolve. Just as law often reflects society's underlying values, law can cause those values to change.[141] Sarbanes-Oxley will likely influence in a beneficial direction what both businesspeople and others view as acceptable business behavior in the future.

---

[136] *See generally* PLOUS, *supra* note 5, at 125-27 (discussing the vividness effect).

[137] *See generally* ROBYN M. DAWES, EVERYDAY IRRATIONALITY 99-107 (2001) (discussing studies of the availability bias).

[138] *See generally* Shelley E. Taylor, *The Availability Bias in Social Perception and Interaction, in* JUDGMENT UNDER UNCERTAINTY, *supra* note 13, at 190, 192 (defining the saliency bias).

[139] *See* Christine Jolls et al., A *Behavioral Approach to Law and Economics, in* BEHAVIORAL LAW AND ECONOMICS 13, 37-38 (Cass R. Sunstein ed., 2000) (discussing how the public's perception of risk is heavily influenced by vivid, available anecdotes). *See also* Harry S. Gerla, *The "Reasonableness" Standard in the Law of Negligence: Can Abstract Values Receive Their Due?*, 15 U. DAYTON L. REV. 199, 200-11 (1990) (discussing how these three biases can affect jury decision making).

[140] *Yummies for the CEO*, ST. LOUIS POST-DISPATCH, Sept. 10, 2002, at B6 ("The sight of executives being walked in handcuffs in front of TV cameras also has a deterrent effect. More 'perp walks' and people may decide that crime doesn't pay.").

[141] *See* Thomas Donaldson & Thomas W. Dunfee, TIES THAT BIND: A SOCIAL CONTRACTS APPROACH TO BUSINESS ETHICS 95-96 (1999):

> Outside sources may influence the development of norms. Law, particularly when it is perceived as legitimate by members of a community, may have a major impact on what is considered to be correct behavior. Thus, the U.S. Corporate Sentencing Guidelines may be expected to influence perceptions of appropriate structures and policies for assigning managerial responsibility pertaining to corporate social responsibility. Conventional wisdom holds that U.S. law has influenced changes in ethical norms pertaining to racial or gender-based discrimination and also as to the legitimacy of insider trading.

See also Mark Kelman, *Consumption Theory, Production Theory, and Ideology in the Coase Theorem*, 52 S. CAL. L. REV. 669, 695 (1979) (observing that "perhaps society learns what to value in part through the legal system's descriptions of our protected spheres"); Eric A. Posner, *Law, Economics, and Inefficient Norms*, 144 U. PA. L. REV. 1697, 1731 (1996) ("[L]aws inevitably strengthen or weaken social norms by signaling an official stance toward them . . . .").

Chapter 3

Human Nature and Corporate Scandals

In the last chapter, you've thought about how the structure of an organization might make it easier or harder to defraud. Ah, if only structure took care of all the problems! In this chapter, we want to introduce you to some research concerning human behavior. We believe that how an organization's structure looks on paper can tell you very little about how the people in that organization might behave. (After all, Enron had a Code of Ethics, at least on paper: take a look at it here: http://www.thesmokinggun.com/graphics/packageart/enron/enron.pdf.)

Here's what Enron said about itself, on page 4 of its July 2000 Code of Ethics:

> **Values**
>
> *Respect*
> We treat others as we would like to be treated ourselves. We do not tolerate abusive or disrespectful treatment. Ruthlessness, callousness and arrogance don't belong here.
>
> *Integrity*
> We work with customers and prospects openly, honestly and sincerely. When we say we will do something, we will do it; when we say we cannot or will not do something, then we won't do it.
>
> *Communication*
> We have an obligation to communicate. Here, we take the time to talk with one another . . . and to listen. We believe that information is meant to move and that information moves people.
>
> *Excellence*
> We are satisfied with nothing less than the very best in everything we do. We will continue to raise the bar for everyone. The great fun here will be for all of us to discover just how good we can really be.

OK—you can stop laughing now. You can see that, on paper, Enron looked like a wonderful place to work. We're sure that there were many people at Enron who actually behaved in accordance with these espoused values. Unfortunately, some of Enron's employees made a mockery of those values. "Respect"? Not hardly. Enron allowed (even encouraged) its energy traders to run roughshod over the rest of the company; a more snide, nasty, and ethically challenged group of folks would be hard to find. (You can listen to the traders' transcripts at http://www.npr.org/templates/story/story.php?storyId=5180594.) "Integrity"? Let's just say that openness, honesty, and sincerity weren't Enron's hallmarks. We could go on and on, but then you'd never get to read this chapter.

It's possible that Ken Lay and some of the other Enron executives truly believed that Enron was following its written statement of values. This chapter explores how smart people can fool themselves on a regular basis—fool themselves into thinking that, even when they're doing something wrong, what they're doing is perfectly all right. You'll read about the classic Milgram study on cognitive dissonance, and you'll also read Andrew Perlman's article discussing work on social pressure, which should give you some insight into how people at Enron (and elsewhere) could go along with some very shameful behavior, even though they "knew better" at the time. Then you'll take a look at David Luban's integration of these social science concepts into the world of practicing lawyers and at Marleen O'Connor's integration of these concepts into the world of Enron's board.

Ultimately, we want you to think about those times that you've been pressured into doing something that you knew was wrong. Were there patterns of thought that helped ease your way into making the mistake of saying "yes" to something that should have been a "no" from the start? What might you have done differently to have prevented yourself from justifying bad behavior? (Don't worry: each of us has done things that we knew, in retrospect, was wrong. We feel your pain. And we won't tell.)

Behavioral Study of Obedience (1963)[*]

Stanley Milgram[**]

Obedience is as basic an element in the structure of social life as one can point to. Some system of authority is a requirement of all communal living, and it is only the man dwelling in isolation who is not forced to respond, through defiance or submission, to the commands of others. Obedience, as a determinant of behavior, is of particular relevance to our time. It has been reliably established that from 1933-45 millions of innocent persons were systematically slaughtered on command. Gas chambers were built, death camps were guarded, daily quotas of corpses were produced with the same efficiency as the manufacture of appliances. These inhumane policies may have originated in the mind of a single person, but they could only be carried out on a massive scale if a very large number of persons obeyed orders.

Obedience is the psychological mechanism that links individual action to political purpose. It is the dispositional cement that binds men to systems of authority. Facts of recent history and observation in daily life suggest that for many persons obedience may be a deeply ingrained behavior tendency, indeed, a prepotent impulse overriding training in ethics, sympathy, and moral conduct. C. P. Snow (1961) points to its importance when he writes:

> When you think of the long and gloomy history of man, you will find more hideous crimes have been committed in the name of obedience than have ever been committed in the name of rebellion. If you doubt that, read William Shirer's "Rise and Fall of the Third Reich." The German Officer Corps were brought up in the most rigorous code of obedience . . . in the name of obedience they were party to, and assisted in, the most wicked large scale actions in the history of the world [p. 24].

---

[*] This sudy is reprinted with the permission of Mrs. Milgram.

[**] Stanley Milgram (1933-1984) was a social psychologist who, among other things, conducted the "small world" experiment (of "six degrees of separation" fame) and the experiment described in this essay.

While the particular form of obedience dealt with in the present study has its antecedents in these episodes, it must not be thought all obedience entails acts of aggression against others. Obedience serves numerous productive functions. Indeed, the very life of society is predicated on its existence. Obedience may be ennobling and educative and refer to acts of charity and kindness, as well as to destruction.

GENERAL PROCEDURE

A procedure was devised which seems useful as a tool for studying obedience (Milgram, 1961). It consists of ordering a naive subject to administer electric shock to a victim. A simulated shock generator is used, with 30 clearly marked voltage levels that range from 15 to 450 volts. The instrument hears verbal designations that range from Slight Shock to Danger: Severe Shock. The responses of the victim, who is a trained confederate of the experimenter, are standardized. The orders to administer shocks are given to the naive subject in the context of a "learning experiment" ostensibly set up to study the effects of punishment on memory. As the experiment proceeds the naive subject is commanded to administer increasingly more intense shocks to the victim, even to the point of reaching the level marked Danger: Severe Shock. Internal resistances become stronger, and at a certain point the subject refuses to go on with the experiment. Behavior prior to this rupture is considered "obedience," in that the subject complies with the commands of the experimenter. The point of rupture is the act of disobedience. A quantitative value is assigned to the subject's performance based on the maximum intensity shock he is willing to administer before he refuses to participate further. Thus for any particular subject and for any particular experimental condition the degree of obedience may be specified with a numerical value. The crux of the study is to systematically vary the factors believed to alter the degree of obedience to the experimental commands.

The technique allows important variables to he manipulated at several points in the experiment. One may vary aspects of the source of command, content and form of command, instrumentalities for its execution, target object, general-social setting, etc. The problem, therefore, is not one of designing increasingly more numerous experimental conditions, but of selecting those that best illuminate the *process* of obedience from the sociopsychological standpoint.

Related Studies

The inquiry bears an important relation to philosophic analysis of obedience and authority (Arendt, 1958; Friedrich, 1958; Weber, 1947), an early experimental study of obedience by Frank (1944), studies in "authoritarianism" (Adorn, Frenkel-Brunswik, Levinson, & Sanford, 1950; Rokeach, 1961), and a recent series of analytic and empirical studies in social power (Cartwright, 1959). It owes much to the long concern with *suggestion* in social psychology, both in its normal forms (e.g., Binet, 1900) and in its clinical manifestations (Charcot, 1881). But it derives, in the first instance, from direct observation of a social fact; the individual who is commanded by a legitimate authority ordinarily obeys. Obedience comes easily and often. It is a ubiquitous and indispensable feature of social life.

METHOD

Subjects

The subjects were 40 males between the ages of 20 and 50, drawn from New Haven and the surrounding communities. Subjects were obtained by a newspaper advertisement and direct mail solicitation. Those who responded to the appeal believed they were to participate in a study of memory and learning at Yale University. A wide range of occupations is represented in the sample. Typical subjects were postal clerks, high school teachers, salesmen, engineers, and laborers. Subjects ranged in educational level from one who had not finished elementary school to those who had doctorate and other professional degrees. They were paid $4.50 for their participation in the experiment. However, subjects were told that payment was simply for coming to the laboratory, and that the money was theirs no matter what happened after they arrived. Table 1 shows the proportion of age and occupational types assigned to the experimental condition.

Personnel and Locale

The experiment was conducted on the grounds of Yale University in the elegant interaction laboratory. (This detail is relevant to the perceived legitimacy of the experiment. In further variations, the experiment was dissociated from the university, with consequences for performance.) The role of experimenter was played by a 31-year-old high school teacher of biology. His manner was impassive, and his appearance somewhat stern throughout the experiment. He was dressed in a gray technician's coat. The victim was played by a 47-year-old accountant, trained for the role; he was of Irish-American stock, whom most observers found mild-mannered and likable.

Table 1
Distribution of Age and Occupational Types in the Experiment

20-29 years Occupations	*n*	30-39 years *n*	40-50 years *n*	Percentage of total (occupations)
Workers, skilled and unskilled	4	5	6	37.5
Sales, business, and white-collar	3	6	7	40.0
Professional	1	5	3	22.5
Percentage of total (Age)	20	40	40	

Note: Total $N = 40$.

Procedure

One naive subject and one victim (an accomplice) performed in each experiment. A pretext had to be devised that would justify the administration of electric shock by the naive subject. This was effectively accomplished by the cover story. After a general introduction on the presumed relation between punishment and learning, subjects were told:

> But actually, we know *very little* about the effect of punishment on learning, because almost no truly scientific studies have been made of it in human beings.
>
> For instance, we don't know how *much* punishment is best for learning—and we don't know how much difference it makes as to who is giving the punishment, whether an adult learns best from a younger or an older person than himself—or many things of that sort.
>
> So in this study we are bringing together a number of adults of different occupations and ages. And we're asking some of them to be teachers and some of them to be learners.
>
> We want to find out just what effect different people have on each other as teachers and learners, and also what effect *punishment* will have on learning in this situation.
>
> Therefore, I'm going to ask one of you to be the teacher here tonight and the other one to be the learner.
>
> Does either of you have a preference?

Subjects then drew slips of paper from a hat to determine who would be the teacher and who would be the learner in the experiment. The drawing was rigged so that the naive subject was always the teacher and the accomplice always the learner. (Both slips contained the word "Teacher.") Immediately after the drawing, the teacher and learner were taken to an adjacent room and the learner was strapped into an "electric chair" apparatus.

The experimenter explained that the straps were to prevent excessive movement while the learner was being shocked. The effect was to make it impossible for him to escape from the situation. An electrode was attached to the learner's wrist, and electrode paste was applied "to avoid blisters and burns." Subjects were told that the electrode was attached to the shock generator in the adjoining room.

In order to improve credibility the experimenter declared, in response to a question by the learner: "Although the shocks can be extremely painful, they cause no permanent tissue damage."

Learning Task

The lesson administered by the subject was a paired-associate learning task. The subject read a series of word pairs to the learner, and then read the first word of the pair along with four terms. The learner was to indicate which of the four terms had originally been paired with the first word. He communicated his answer by pressing one of four switches in front of him, which in turn lit up one of four numbered quadrants in an answer-box located atop the shock generator.

Shock Generator

The instrument panel consists of 30 lever switches set in a horizontal line. Each switch is clearly labeled with a voltage designation that ranges from 15 to 450 volts. There is a 15-volt increment from one switch to the next going from left to right. In addition, the following verbal designations are clearly indicated for groups of four switches going from left to right: Slight Shock, Moderate Shock, Strong Shock, Very Strong Shock, Intense Shock, Extreme Intensity Shock, Danger: Severe Shock. (Two switches after this last designation are simply marked XXX.)

Upon depressing a switch: a pilot light corresponding to each switch is illuminated in bright red; an electric buzzing is heard; an electric blue light, labeled "voltage energizer," flashes; the dial on the voltage meter swings to the right; various relay clicks are sounded.

The upper left-hand corner of the generator is labeled Shock Generator, Type ZLB, Dyson Instrument Company, Waltham, Mass. Output 15 Volts-450 Volts. Details of the instrument were carefully handled to insure an appearance of authenticity. The panel was engraved by precision industrial engravers, and all components were of high quality. No subject in the experiment suspected that the instrument was merely a simulated shock generator.[1]

Sample Shock

Each naïve subject is given a sample shock on the shock generator, prior to beginning his run as teacher. This shock is always 45 volts, and is applied by pressing the third switch of the generator. The shock is applied to the wrist of the naive subject, and has its source in a 45-volt battery wired into the generator. This further convinces the subject of the authenticity of the generator.

Shock Instructions

The subject is told to administer a shock to the learner each time he gives a wrong response. Moreover—and this is the key command—the subject is instructed to "move

---

[1] A related technique, making use of a shock generator, was reported by Buss (1961) for the study of aggression in the laboratory. Despite the considerable similarity of technical detail in the experimental procedures, both investigators proceeded in ignorance of the other's work. Milgram provided plans and photographs of his shock generator, experimental procedure, and first results in a report to the National Science Foundation in January 1961. This report received only limited circulation. Buss reported his procedure 6 months later, but to a wider audience. Subsequently, technical information and reports were exchanged.

one level higher on the shock generator each time the learner flashes a wrong answer." He is also instructed to announce the voltage level before administering a shock. This serves to continually remind subjects of the increasing intensity of shocks administered to the learner.

Preliminary and Regular Run

Pretests revealed that the procedure of reading words and administering shocks requires some practice before it can be handled smoothly. Therefore, immediately preceding the regular run, the teacher is given a preliminary series of 10 words to read to the learner. There are 3 neutral words in the practice series (i.e., words that the learner answers correctly), so that shocks are administered for 7 of the words, with the maximum shock at 105 volts (moderate shock). Almost all subjects master the procedure by the time the preliminary run is over.

Subjects are then presented with a second list, and are told that the procedure is the same as for the first list; the experimenter adds, however:

> When you get to the bottom of the list, repeat it over again, and continue giving shocks, until the learner has learned all the pairs correctly.

The experimenter instructs the subject to start from 15 volts and increase the shock level one step each time the learner gives a wrong answer.

Feedback from the Victim

In all conditions the learner gives a predetermined set of responses to the word pair test, based on a schedule of approximately three wrong answers to one correct answer. In the present experimental condition no vocal response or other sign of protest is heard from the learner until Shock Level 300 is reached. When the 300-volt shock is administered, the learner pounds on the wall of the room in which he is bound to the electric chair. The pounding can be heard by the subject. From this point on, the learner's answers no longer appear on the four-way panel.

At this juncture, subjects ordinarily turn to the experimenter for guidance. The experimenter instructs the subject to treat the absence of a response as a wrong answer, and to shock the subject according to the usual schedule. He advises the subjects to allow 5-10 seconds before considering no response as a wrong answer, and to increase the shock level one step each time the learner fails to respond correctly. The learner's pounding is repeated after the 315-volt shock is administered; afterwards he is not heard from, nor do his answers reappear on the four-way signal box.

Experimenter Feedback

At various points in the experiment the subject may turn to the experimenter for advice on whether he should continue to administer shocks. Or he may indicate that he does not wish to go on. It was important to standardize the experimenter's responses to these inquiries and reactions.

If the subject indicated his unwillingness to go on, the experimenter responded with a sequence of "prods," using as many as necessary to bring the subject into line.

Prod 1: Please continue *or* Please go on.
Prod 2: The experiment requires that you continue.
Prod 3: It is absolutely essential that you continue.
Prod 4: You have no other choice, you *must* go on.

The prods were always made in sequence: Only if Prod 1 had been unsuccessful, could Prod 2 be used. If the subject refused to obey the experimenter after Prod 4, the experiment was terminated. The experimenter's tone of voice was at all times firm, but not impolite. The sequence was begun anew on each occasion that the subject balked or showed reluctance to follow orders.

Special prods. If the subject asked if the learner was liable to suffer permanent physical injury, the experimenter said:

> Although the shocks may be painful, there is no permanent tissue damage, so please go on. [Followed by Prods 2, 3, and 4 if necessary.]

If the subject said that the learner did not want to go on, the experimenter replied:

> Whether the learner likes it or not, you must go on until he has learned all the word pairs correctly. So please go on. [Followed by Prods 2, 3, and 4, if necessary.]

Dependent Measures

The primary dependent measure for any subject is the maximum shock he administers before he refuses to go any further. In principle this may vary from 0 (for a subject who refuses to administer even the first shock) to 30 (for a subject who administers the highest shock on the generator). A subject who breaks off the experiment at any point prior to administering the thirtieth shock level is termed a *defiant* subject. One who complies with experimental commands fully, and proceeds to administer all shock levels commanded, is termed an *obedient* subject.

Further Records

With few exceptions, experimental sessions were recorded on magnetic tape. Occasional photographs were taken through one-way mirrors. Notes were kept on any unusual behavior occurring during the course of the experiments. On occasion, additional observers were directed to write objective descriptions of the subjects' behavior. The latency and duration of shocks were measured by accurate timing devices.

Interview and Dehoax

Following the experiment, subjects were interviewed; open-ended questions, projective measures, and attitude scales were employed. After the interview, procedures were undertaken to assure that the subject would leave the laboratory in a state of well being. A friendly reconciliation was arranged between the subject and the victim, and an effort was made to reduce any tensions that arose as a result of the experiment.

RESULTS

Preliminary Notions

Before giving an account of the experimental results, it is instructive to consider how persons predict others will perform when commanded to administer powerful shocks to another person. Fourteen Yale seniors, all psychology majors, were provided with a detailed description of the experimental situation. They were asked to reflect carefully on it, and to predict the behavior of 100 hypothetical subjects. More specifically, they were instructed to plot the distribution of obedience of "100 Americans of diverse occupations, and ranging in age from 20 to 50 years," who were placed in the experimental situation.

There was considerable agreement among the respondents on the expected behavior of hypothetical subjects. All respondents predicted that only an insignificant minority would go through to the end of the shock series. (The estimates ranged from 0 to 3%; i.e., the most "pessimistic" member of the class predicted that of 100 persons, 3 would continue through to the most potent shock available on the shock generator—450 volts.) The class mean was 1.2%. The question was also posed informally to colleagues of the author, and the most general feeling was that few if any subjects would go beyond the designation Very Strong Shock.

Result of Experiment I

Subjects Accept Situation

With few exceptions subjects were convinced of the reality of the experimental situation, that they were administering shocks to another person, and the most potent shocks were extremely painful. In the post-experimental interview subjects were asked: "How painful to the learner were the last few shocks that you administered to him?" Subjects were instructed to indicate their answers on a printed 14-point scale ranging from "Not at all painful" to "Extremely painful.") The modal response was 14 (Extremely painful) with the mean at 13.42.

Signs of Extreme Tension

Many subjects showed signs of nervousness in the experimental situation, and especially upon administering the more powerful shocks. In a large number of cases the degree of tension reached extremes that are rarely seen in sociopsychological laboratory studies. Subjects were observed to sweat, tremble, stutter, bite their lips, groan, and dig their fingernails into their flesh. These were characteristic rather than exceptional responses to the experiment.

One sign of tension was the regular occurrence of nervous laughing fits. Fourteen of the 40 subjects showed definite signs of nervous laughter and smiling. The laughter seemed entirely out of place, even bizarre. Full-blown, uncontrollable seizures were observed for 3 subjects. On one occasion we observed a seizure so violently convulsive that it was necessary to call a halt to the experiment. The subject, a 46-year-old encyclopedia salesman, was seriously embarrassed by his untoward and uncontrollable behavior. In the post-experimental interviews, subjects took pains to point out that they were not sadistic types, and that the laughter did not mean they enjoyed shocking the victim.

Distribution of Scores

It had been conjectured that persons would not, in general, agree to administer shocks beyond the level designated as Very Strong Shock. The distribution of maximum shocks for this experiment is shown in Table 2. The obtained distribution of scores deviates radically from the prediction.

Upon command of the experimenter, each of the 40 subjects went beyond the expected break-off point. No subject stopped prior to administering Shock Level 20. (At this level—300 volts—the victim kicks on the wall and no longer provides answers to the teacher's multiple-choice questions.)

Of the 40 subjects, 5 refused to obey the experimental commands beyond the 300-volt level. Four more subjects administered one further shock, and then refused to go on. Two broke off at the 330-volt level, and 1 each at 345, 360, and 375 volts. Thus a total of 14 subjects defied the experimenter. It is instructive to reprint their remarks at the point of defiance, as transcribed from the tape recordings:

> [0124] I think he's trying to communicate, he's knocking. . . . Well it's not fair to shock the guy . . . these are terrific volts. I don't think this is very humane . . . . Oh, I can't go on with this; no, this isn't right. It's a hell of an experiment. The guy is suffering in there. No, I don't want to go on. This is crazy. [Subject refused to administer more shocks.]

> [0123] He's banging in there. I'm gonna chicken out. I'd like to continue, but I can't do that to a man. . . . I'm sorry I can't do that to a man. I'll hurt his heart. You take your check. . . . No really, I couldn't do it.

These subjects were frequently in a highly agitated and even angered state. Sometimes, verbal protest was at a minimum, and the subject simply got up from his chair in front of the shock generator, and indicated that he wished to leave the laboratory.

Table 2
Distribution of Breakoff Points

Verbal designation and voltage indication	Number of subjects for whom this was maximum shock
Slight Shock	
15	0
30	0
45	0
60	0
Moderate Shock	
75	0
90	0
105	0
120	0
Strong Shock	
135	0
150	0
165	0
180	0
Very Strong Shock	
195	0
210	0
225	0
240	0
Intense Shock	
255	0
270	0
285	0
300	5
Extreme Intensity Shock	
315	4
330	2
345	1
360	1
Danger: Severe Shock	
375	1
390	0
405	0
420	0
XXX	
435	0
450	26

Of the 40 subjects, 26 obeyed the orders of the experimenter to the end, proceeding to punish the victim until they reached the most potent shock available on the shock generator. At that point, the experimenter called a halt to the session. (The maximum shock is labeled 450 volts, and is two steps beyond the designation: Danger: Severe Shock.) Although obedient subjects continued to administer shocks, they often did so under extreme stress. Some expressed reluctance to administer shocks beyond the 300-volt level, and displayed fears similar to those who defied the experimenter; yet they obeyed.

After the maximum shocks had been delivered, and the experimenter called a halt to the proceedings, many obedient subjects heaved sighs of relief, mopped their brows, rubbed their fingers over their eyes, or nervously fumbled cigarettes. Some shook their heads, apparently in regret. Some subjects had remained calm throughout the experiment, and displayed only minimal signs of tension from beginning to end.

DISCUSSION

The experiment yielded two findings that were surprising. The first finding concerns the sheer strength of obedient tendencies manifested in this situation. Subjects have learned from childhood that it is a fundamental breach of moral conduct to hurt another person against his will. Yet, 26 subjects abandon this tenet in following the instructions of an authority who has no special powers to enforce his commands. To disobey would bring no material loss to the subject; no punishment would ensue. It is clear from the remarks and outward behavior of many participants that in punishing the victim they are often acting against their own values. Subjects often expressed deep disapproval of shocking a man in the face of his objections, and others denounced it as stupid and senseless. Yet the majority complied with the experimental commands. This outcome was surprising from two perspectives: first, from the standpoint of predictions made in the questionnaire described earlier. (Here, however, it is possible that the remoteness of the respondents from the actual situation, and the difficulty of conveying to them the concrete details of the experiment, could account for the serious underestimation of obedience.) But the results were also unexpected to persons who observed the experiment in progress, through one-way mirrors. Observers often uttered expressions of disbelief upon seeing a subject administer more powerful shocks to the victim. These persons had a full acquaintance with the details of the situation, and yet systematically underestimated the amount of obedience that subjects would display.

The second unanticipated effect was the extraordinary tension generated by the procedures. One might suppose that a subject would simply break off or continue as his conscience dictated. Yet, this is very far from what happened. There were striking reactions of tension and emotional strain. One observer related:

> I observed a mature and initially poised businessman enter the laboratory smiling and confident. Within 20 minutes he was reduced to a twitching, stuttering wreck, who was rapidly approaching a point of nervous collapse.

> He constantly pulled on his earlobe, and twisted his hands. At one point he pushed his fist into his forehead and muttered: "Oh God, let's stop it." And yet he continued to respond to every word of the experimenter, and obeyed to the end.

Any understanding of the phenomenon of obedience must rest on an analysis of the particular conditions in which it occurs. The following features of the experiment go some distance in explaining the high amount of obedience observed in the situation.

1. The experiment is sponsored by and takes place on the grounds of an institution of unimpeachable reputation, Yale University. It may be reasonably presumed that the personnel are competent and reputable. The importance of this background authority is now being studied by conducting a series of experiments outside of New Haven, and without any visible ties to the university.
2. The experiment is, on the face of it, designed to attain a worthy purpose—advancement of knowledge about learning and memory. Obedience occurs not as an end in itself, but as an instrumental element in a situation that the subject construes as significant and meaningful. He may not be able to see its full significance, but he may properly assume that the experimenter does.
3. The subject perceives that the victim has voluntarily submitted to the authority system of the experimenter. He is not (at first) an unwilling captive impressed for involuntary service. He has taken the trouble to come to the laboratory presumably to aid the experimental research. That he later becomes an involuntary subject does not alter the fact that, initially, he consented to participate without qualification. Thus he has in some degree incurred an obligation toward the experimenter.
4. The subject, too, has entered the experiment voluntarily, and perceives himself under obligation to aid the experimenter. He has made a commitment, and to disrupt the experiment is a repudiation of this initial promise of aid.
5. Certain features of the procedure strengthen the subject's sense of obligation to the experimenter. For one, he has been paid for coming to the laboratory. In part this is canceled out by the experimenter's statement that:

    > Of course, as in all experiments, the money is yours simply for coming to the laboratory. From this point on, no matter what happens, the money is yours.[2]

6. From the subject's standpoint, the fact that he is the teacher and the other man the learner is purely a chance consequence (it is determined by drawing

[2] Forty-three subjects, undergraduates at Yale University, were run in the experiment without payment. The results are very similar to those obtained with paid subjects.

lots) and he, the subject, ran the same risk as the other man in being assigned the role of learner. Since the assignment of positions in the experiment was achieved by fair means, the learner is deprived of any basis of complaint on this count. (A similar situation obtains in Army units, in which—in the absence of volunteers—a particularly dangerous mission may be assigned by drawing lots, and the unlucky soldier is expected to hear his misfortune with sportsmanship.)

7. There is, at best, ambiguity with regard to the prerogatives of a psychologist and the corresponding rights of his subject. There is a vagueness of expectation concerning what a psychologist may require of his subject, and when he is overstepping acceptable limits. Moreover, the experiment occurs in a closed setting, and thus provides no opportunity for the subject to remove these ambiguities by discussion with others. There are few standards that seem directly applicable to the situation, which is a novel one for most subjects.
8. The subjects are assured that the shocks administered to the subject are "painful but not dangerous." Thus they assume that the discomfort caused the victim is momentary, while the scientific gains resulting from the experiment are enduring.
9. Through Shock Level 20 the victim continues to provide answers on the signal box. The subject may construe this as a sign that the victim is still willing to "play the game." It is only after Shock Level 20 that the victim repudiates the rules completely, refusing to answer further.

These features help to explain the high amount of obedience obtained in this experiment. Many of the arguments raised need not remain matters of speculation, but can be reduced to testable proportions to be confirmed or disproved by further experiments.[3]

The following features of the experiment concern the nature of the conflict which the subject faces.

10. The subject is placed in a position in which he must respond to the competing demands of two persons: the experimenter and the victim. The conflict must be resolved by meeting the demands of one or the other; satisfaction of the victim and the experimenter are mutually exclusive. Moreover, the resolution must take the form of a highly visible action, that of continuing to shock the victim or breaking off the experiment. Thus the subject is forced into a public conflict that does not permit any completely satisfactory solution.
11. While the demands of the experimenter carry the weight of scientific authority, the demands of the victim spring from his personal experience of pain and suffering. The two claims need not be regarded as equally pressing and

[3] A series of recently completed experiments employing the obedience paradigm is reported in Milgram (1964).

legitimate. The experimenter seeks an abstract scientific datum; the victim cries out for relief from physical suffering caused by the subject's actions.

12. The experiment gives the subject little time for reflection. The conflict comes on rapidly. It is only minutes after the subject has been seated before the shock generator that the victim begins his protests. Moreover, the subject perceives that he has gone through but two-thirds of the shock levels at the time the subject's first protests are heard. Thus he understands that the conflict will have a persistent aspect to it, and may well become more intense as increasingly more powerful shocks are required. The rapidity with which the conflict descends on the subject, and his realization that it is predictably recurrent may well be sources of tension to him.
13. At a more general level, the conflict stems from the opposition of two deeply ingrained behavior dispositions: first, the disposition not to harm other people, and second, the tendency to obey those whom we perceive to be legitimate authorities.

Unethical Obedience by Subordinate Attorneys: Lessons From Social Psychology[*]

Andrew M. Perlman[**]

INTRODUCTION

Consider the plight of a lawyer—fresh out of law school with crushing loan debt and few job offers—who accepts a position at a medium-sized firm. A partner asks the young lawyer to review a client's documents to determine what needs to be produced in discovery. In the stack, the associate finds a "smoking gun" that is clearly within the scope of discovery and spells disaster for the client's case. The associate reports the document to the partner, who without explanation tells the associate not to produce it. The associate asks the partner a few questions and quickly drops the subject when the partner tells the associate to get back to work.

We would like to believe that the young lawyer has the courage to ensure that the partner ultimately produces the document. We might hope, or expect, that the lawyer will report the issue to the firm's ethics counsel, if the firm is big enough to have one, or consult with other lawyers in the firm, assuming that she has developed the necessary relationships with her colleagues despite her junior status.

In fact, research in the area of social psychology suggests that, in some contexts, a subordinate lawyer will often comply with unethical instructions of this sort.[1] This basic, but crucial, insight into human behavior suggests that there is often a significant

[*] Reprinted with permission of the *Hofstra Law Review Association.* Andrew M. Perlman, *Unethical Obedience by Subordinate Attorneys: Lessons From Social Psychology,* 36 HOFSTRA L. REV. 451 (2007).

[**] Associate Professor of Law, Suffolk University Law School. B.A., Yale College; J.D., Harvard Law School; LL.M., Columbia Law School. Several friends and colleagues have given me valuable suggestions for this Article, including Lisa Aidlin, Thomas Blass, Robert Keatinge, Sung Hui Kim, Jeffrey Lipshaw, and John Steele. I also benefited enormously from the assistance of research librarian Ellen Delaney and from comments and questions during presentations at Cumberland and Suffolk Law Schools and at the Hofstra Legal Ethics Conference. I also received very useful insights from several students in my professional responsibility classes at Suffolk.

[1] *See infra* Parts II and III. Although there is limited research on whether lawyers tend to obey authority figures, there is no reason to think that attorneys are somehow immune from the pressures that lead to obedience. *See, e.g., infra* note 80.

gap between what the legal ethics rules require and how lawyers will typically behave. Indeed, lawyers will too often obey obviously unethical or illegal instructions or fail to report the wrongdoing of other lawyers.[2]

This article explores what lessons we can learn from social psychology regarding a lawyer's willingness to comply with authority figures, such as senior partners or deep-pocketed clients, when they make unlawful or unethical demands. Part II reviews some of the basic literature in social psychology regarding conformity and obedience, much of which emphasizes the importance of context as a primary factor in predicting people's behavior.[3]

Part III contends that lawyers frequently find themselves in the kinds of contexts that produce high levels of conformity and obedience and low levels of resistance to illegal or unethical instructions. The result is that subordinate lawyers, like the attorney in the initial example, will find it difficult to resist a superior's commands in circumstances that should produce forceful dissent.

Part IV proposes several changes to existing law in light of these insights, including giving lawyers the benefit of whistleblower protection, strengthening a lawyer's duty to report the misconduct of other lawyers,[4] and enhancing a subordinate lawyer's responsibilities upon receiving arguably unethical instructions from a superior.[5] These proposals, however, are ultimately less important than the insights that underlie them. Namely, by gaining a deeper understanding of social psychology, the legal profession can more effectively prevent and deter attorney misconduct.

II. BASIC LESSONS FROM SOCIAL PSYCHOLOGY ABOUT CONFORMITY AND OBEDIENCE

Studies on conformity and obedience suggest that professionals, whom we would ordinarily describe as "honest," will often suppress their independent judgment in favor of a group's opinion or offer little resistance in the face of illegal or unethical demands.[6] These studies demonstrate that we ascribe too much weight to personal-

---

[2] *See* MODEL RULES OF PROF'L CONDUCT R. 5.2(a)-(b) (2007) (subjecting subordinates to the Rules of Professional Conduct unless the supervisory lawyer's instructions reflect a "reasonable resolution of an arguable question of professional duty"); MODEL RULES OF PROF'L CONDUCT R. 8.3(a) (2007) (requiring a lawyer to report another lawyer's misconduct if that conduct "raises a substantial question as to that lawyer's honesty, trustworthiness or fitness as a lawyer").

[3] As explained in more detail in Part II, social context plays a significant role in human behavior. *See* LEE ROSS & RICHARD E. NISBETT, THE PERSON AND THE SITUATION xiv (1991) ("[W]hat has been demonstrated through a host of celebrated laboratory and field studies is that manipulations of the immediate social situation can overwhelm in importance the type of individual differences in personal traits or dispositions that people normally think of as being determinative of social behavior.").

[4] MODEL RULES OF PROF'L CONDUCT R. 8.3(a) (2007).

[5] MODEL RULES OF PROF'L CONDUCT R. 5.2(b) (2007).

[6] Although there is a growing legal ethics literature that draws on social psychology, there is surprisingly little scholarship that draws on social psychology to explain the particular problem of wrongful obedience among lawyers. For a few notable exceptions, see MILTON C. REGAN, JR., EAT WHAT YOU KILL: THE FALL

ity traits like honesty,[7] and that contextual factors have far more to do with human behavior than most people recognize.[8] Social psychologists have called this tendency to overemphasize individual personality differences and underestimate the power of the situation "the fundamental attribution error."[9] Indeed, a number of experiments have amply demonstrated that situational forces are often more powerful predictors of human behavior than dispositional traits like honesty.

A. Foundational Studies on Conformity

The importance of context is apparent from a number of experiments related to conformity, the most celebrated of which is a 1955 study by Solomon Asch.

Asch wanted to determine how often a group member would express independent judgment despite the unanimous, but obviously mistaken, contrary opinions of the rest of the group.[10] To make this determination, Asch designed a study involving two cards similar to those shown below.[11]

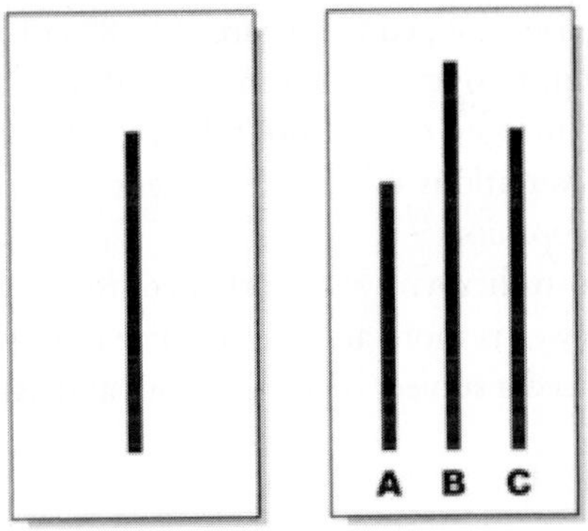

OF A WALL STREET LAWYER 307, 323-24 (2004); David J. Luban, *The Ethics of Wrongful Obedience,* in ETHICS IN PRACTICE: LAWYERS' ROLES, RESPONSIBILITIES, AND REGULATION 94, 95 (Deborah L. Rhode ed., 2000); Sung Hui Kim, *The Banality of Fraud: Re-Situating the Inside Counsel As Gatekeeper,* 74 FORDHAM L. REV. 983, 1001-26 (2005).

[7] *See generally* JOHN M. DORIS, LACK OF CHARACTER: PERSONALITY AND MORAL BEHAVIOR (2002) (arguing that context explains far more about human behavior than individual differences in character traits). For a detailed examination of the importance of context in determining lawyer behavior, *see* Regan, *supra* note 6, at 4-6, 10, 294-95, 302-04.

[8] ROSS & NISBETT, *supra* note 3, at 4.

[9] *Id.* (citation omitted); *see also* Doris, *supra* note 7, at 93.

[10] Solomon E. Asch, *Opinions and Social Pressure,* SCI. AM., Nov. 1955, at 31, 32. Solomon E. Asch, *Opinions and Social Pressure,* SCI. AM., Nov. 1955, at 31, 32.

[11] *Id.* This image appears at http://en.wikipedia.org/wiki/Image:Asch_experiment.png (last visited Jan. 20, 2008).

In one version of the study, the experimenter told the subject that he was about to participate in a vision test and asked the subject to sit at a table with four other individuals who were secretly working with the experimenter.[12]

All five people were shown the two cards and asked to identify which line in the card on the right (A, B, or C) was the same length as the line shown in the card on the left.[13] Each person was asked his opinion individually and answered out loud,[14] with the subject of the experiment going near the end.[15] After each person had answered, a new set of cards was produced, and the participants were once again asked their opinions.[16]

During the initial rounds, all of the confederates chose the obviously right answer.[17] Not surprisingly, under this condition, the subject also chose the right answer.[18]

In some subsequent rounds, however, Asch tested the subject's willingness to conform by prearranging for the confederates to choose the same wrong answer.[19] Even though the four confederates were obviously mistaken, subjects of the experiment nevertheless provided the same wrong answer as the confederates 35.1% of the time,[20] with 70% of subjects providing the wrong answer at least once during the experiment.[21]

Most importantly, Asch found that the introduction of certain variables dramatically affected conformity levels. For example, Asch found that conformity fell quickly as the confederate group size dropped from three (31.8% of the answers were wrong) to two (13.6% were wrong) to one (3.6% were wrong), but did not increase much in groups larger than seven (maxing out at about 37%).[22] Moreover, conformity fell by more than 50% in most variations of the experiment when one of the confederates dissented from the group opinion.[23]

Not surprisingly, other studies have shown that conformity levels increase when (as is true in the law) the answer is more ambiguous. For example, in studies pre-dating Asch's, Muzafer Sherif placed a subject in a dark room and asked the person to look at

---

[12] Asch, *supra* note 10, at 32.

[13] *Id.*

[14] *Id.* All of the subjects were male college students. Subsequent work has revealed that women are, under certain circumstances, even more susceptible to conformity than men. *See, e.g.,* Alice H. Eagly & Carole Chrvala, *Sex Differences in Conformity: Status and Gender Role Interpretations,* 10 PSYCHOL. OF WOMEN Q. 203, 217 (1986).

[15] Asch, *supra* note 10, at 32.

[16] *Id.*

[17] *Id.*

[18] *Id.*

[19] *Id.*

[20] *Id.* at 35.

[21] PHILIP ZIMBARDO, THE LUCIFER EFFECT: UNDERSTANDING HOW GOOD PEOPLE TURN EVIL 263 (2007). Some subjects always went along with the wrong answer, while other subjects never chose the wrong answer. Still others chose the wrong answer occasionally. Overall, though, the "wrong" answer was given thirty-five percent of the time. Asch, *supra* note 10, at 33, 35.

[22] Asch, *supra* note 10, at 35.

[23] *Id.* at 34-35.

a projected spot of light and guess how far it moved.[24] Notably, the light did not move at all, but only appeared to move due to an optical illusion called the autokinetic effect.[25] The precise extent of the perceived movement was thus impossible for subjects to determine objectively.[26]

In one variation of the experiment, a subject gave individual assessments and was subsequently put in a room with a confederate, whose opinion intentionally varied from the subject's.[27] As expected, the subject's assessments quickly came into line with the confederate's or (when the subject was placed in a group) with the group's.[28] Thus, Sherif found that questions with ambiguous answers tended to produce more conformity, because people were understandably less certain of their original assessments.

The Asch and Sherif studies offer compelling evidence—also supported by more recent experiments—that a group member's opinion is easily affected by the group's overall judgment.[29] Critically, the studies also reveal that this effect varies considerably, depending on situational variables, such as the level of ambiguity in the assigned task, the number of people in the group, the status of the person in the group (e.g., high status people feel more comfortable offering a contrasting view), and the existence of dissenters.[30] The situation, in short, has a powerful effect on human behavior.

B. Foundational Studies on Obedience

Not long after Asch's provocative study, Stanley Milgram focused on a different but related question: When will people follow the unethical or immoral orders of an authority figure?[31]

The answer turned out to be both surprising and alarming. Milgram found that, under the right conditions, an experimenter could successfully order more than sixty percent of people to administer painful and dangerous electric shocks to an innocent, bound older man with a heart condition, despite the man's repeated pleas to be let go.[32]

---

24 MUZAFER SHERIF, THE PSYCHOLOGY OF SOCIAL NORMS 95-96 (1973).

25 *Id.* at 91-92.

26 *Id.* at 92.

27 *Id.* at 93.

28 *Id.* at 100-08; *see also* Muzafer Sherif, *A Study of Some Social Factors in Perception, in* 27 ARCHIVES OF PSYCHOLOGY 5, 32-41 (R.S. Woodworth ed., 1935).

29 ROSS & NISBETT, *supra* note 3, at 33 (explaining that "studies [have] demonstrated again and again that arbitrarily constructed groups, even ones that hold no long-term power to reward conformity or punish dissent, can exert potent conformity pressures").

30 *Id.* at xiv (noting that "what has been demonstrated through a host of celebrated laboratory and field studies is that manipulations of the immediate social situation can overwhelm in importance the type of individual differences in personal traits or dispositions that people normally think of as being determinative of social behavior").

31 For a discussion of the differences between conformity and obedience, *see infra* Part III.

32 STANLEY MILGRAM, OBEDIENCE TO AUTHORITY: AN EXPERIMENTAL VIEW 55-57, 60 (1974).

These results came out of Milgram's brilliantly staged and oft-cited experiment. It typically[33] began with a subject and a secret accomplice of the experimenter drawing lots to determine who would be a "teacher" and who would be a "learner" in a study that the subject believed to be about the learning process.[34] In fact, the experiment had nothing to do with learning theory, and the drawing was "rigged so that the subject was always the teacher and the accomplice always the learner."[35]

The teacher (the subject) and the learner (the accomplice) were then taken to another room where the teacher watched the experimenter connect electrical wires to the learner.[36] The experimenter explained that the teacher was soon going to have to ask the learner a series of questions and that, after each wrong answer, the teacher was going to have to administer an electric shock through the attached wires using a generator in another room.[37]

After the experimenter applied a gel that was supposed to help the electrical current flow to the learner without causing blistering or burning,[38] the learner (in one version of the study) informed the experimenter and the teacher that he had a heart condition.[39] The experimenter explained that, although the shocks might be painful, they would not be dangerous.[40] While in the teacher's presence, the experimenter then strapped the learner to a chair to ensure that he could not break free.[41] The teacher/subject was subsequently brought back to the original room and placed in front of the electric shock generator.[42]

The experimenter instructed the teacher to ask the learner questions through an intercom (the subject could not see the learner in this variation of the experiment) and to shock the learner for each wrong answer, starting with 15 volts.[43] With every additional wrong answer, the experimenter explained that the teacher had to increase the shock by one increment on the generator, with each increment producing an extra 15 volts of electricity.[44] The generator, which was clearly marked, went as high as 450

---

[33] Milgram conducted many versions of this experiment, but the variation described here is among the most commonly described.

[34] Milgram, *supra* note 32, at 18-19.

[35] *Id.* at 19.

[36] *Id.*

[37] *Id.* at 19-21.

[38] *Id.* at 19.

[39] *Id.* at 55-57.

[40] *Id.* at 56.

[41] *Id.* at 19.

[42] *Id.* at 3.

[43] *Id.* at 20-21, 28.

[44] *Id.* at 20-21.

volts.[45] At 375 volts, the generator read: "Danger: Severe Shock," and between 435 and 450 volts, the generator's label simply indicated "XXX."[46]

Unbeknownst to the teacher, the learner was not actually attached to the generator and was instructed to provide numerous wrong answers through a nearby key pad.[47] Milgram's objective was to measure how long the teachers would continue to follow the experimenter's orders to apply the shocks.[48]

In the initial stages, nearly all of the subjects/teachers willingly applied the lowest level of shocks on the generator. But as the experiment continued, the learner/confederate produced increasingly loud and forceful objections to the experiment, including (as time went on) requests to be let out of the experiment and complaints about heart pain.[49] Eventually, the learner refused to answer and became ominously silent.[50] The subject, of course, had no idea that these objections and protests were pre-recorded and played at precise points during the experiment.

Despite the learner's pleas to be released, his complaints about heart pain, his refusals to answer, and his eventual silence, Milgram found that the majority of subjects complied with the experimenter's instructions fully, including repeated applications of the 450 volt shock lever. A startling sixty-five percent of subjects obeyed the instructions to the bitter end in this scenario.[51]

Critically, Milgram, like Asch and Sherif before him, found that context was essential. Obedience varied a great deal depending on a number of situational factors, such as whether the learner was in the same room as the teacher,[52] whether the person issuing the orders was in the same room as the teacher,[53] whether subjects assisted a confederate with the shocks instead of administering the shocks themselves,[54] and whether someone dissented (such as when the experiment occurred in a group setting).[55]

Milgram's findings have been replicated throughout the world, with similar results in both genders, different socioeconomic groups, and different countries.[56] Moreover,

---

45 *Id.* at 28.

46 *Id.*

47 *Id.* at 19-20, 22.

48 *Id.* at 23-24, 26.

49 *Id.* at 22-23, 56-57.

50 *Id.* at 23.

51 *Id.* at 60. In fact, compliance levels varied and were even higher in other versions of the experiment. *Id.* at 35, 60-61, 119.

52 *Id.* at 34-36.

53 *Id.* at 59-60, 62.

54 *Id.* at 119, 121-22.

55 *Id.* at 118-21.

56 *Id.* at 5, 170 (socioeconomic groups), 62-63 (gender), 170-71 (international replications).

because of new ethics guidelines that make Milgram's work difficult to reproduce today,[57] his work still stands as one of the most significant contributions to our understanding of human obedience to authority. We know from his work that, given the right situation, most people will follow orders that they would ordinarily consider blatantly immoral.

C. The Power of the Situation

The basic point of these studies is not that people are social conformists, mindless followers of authority, or latent sadists. Indeed, the studies do not suggest that "people are disposed to obey authority figures unquestioningly."[58] Rather, the point is that "manipulations of the immediate social situation can overwhelm in importance the type of individual differences in personal traits or dispositions that people normally think of as being determinative of social behavior."[59] As a result, "subtle features of . . . [the] situation . . . prompt[] ordinary members of our society to behave . . . extraordinarily."[60]

The importance of context is clear. Asch's studies showed that a single variable, such as reducing the number of people in the group or introducing a dissenting group member, could dramatically reduce conformity levels.[61] Milgram also found that the existence of a dissenter could reduce obedience and that other factors, such as placing the experimenter outside of the room or moving the "learner" into the same room as the subject, produced a similar effect.[62] Social psychologists, in short, have found that conformity and obedience are heavily context-dependent and that social forces play a much greater role—and dispositional traits a much weaker role—in determining human behavior than most people assume.

III. SITUATIONAL CONFORMITY AND OBEDIENCE: IMPLICATIONS FOR LAWYER BEHAVIOR

Conformity and obedience are different in subtle but important ways. According to Milgram, "[o]bedience to authority occurs within a hierarchical structure in which the actor feels that the person above has the right to prescribe behavior. Conformity regulates the behavior among those of equal status . . . ."[63] So, for example, the discov-

---

57 SHELLEY E. TAYLOR ET AL., SOCIAL PSYCHOLOGY 228 (11th ed. 2003). There are also other reasons to expect that a similar experiment could not be fully replicated today, including the increasing sophistication of subjects and the expense of such work. *See* David J. Luban, *Milgram Revisited,* 9 RESEARCHING LAW (Am. B. Found., Chi., Ill.), Spring 1998, at 1, 6. Nevertheless, a partial replication was recently conducted and produced results very similar to Milgram's. Jerry Burger, *Replicating Milgram,* APS OBSERVER, Dec. 2007, available at http://www.psychologicalscience.org/observer/getArticle.cfm?id=2264.

58 ROSS & NISBETT, *supra* note 3, at 58.

59 *Id.* at xiv.

60 *Id.* at 56.

61 *See supra* notes 10-30 and accompanying text.

62 Milgram, *supra* note 32, at 34-36, 59-60, 62.

63 *Id.* at 114.

ery hypothetical primarily implicates issues of obedience, because a superior is issuing an order to a subordinate. The hypothetical would implicate conformity if the young lawyer saw her colleagues at the firm concealing "smoking guns" and consequently followed their lead without being instructed to do so. Despite the differences in the two concepts, both of them can exist in many law practice settings.

A. SITUATIONAL FACTORS THAT PRODUCE CONFORMITY IN LAW PRACTICE

Recall that numerous factors contribute to conformity, including the size of the group, the level of unanimity, the ambiguity of the issues involved, group cohesiveness, the strength of an individual's commitment to the group, the person's status in the group, and basic individual tendencies, such as the desire to be right and to be liked.[64]

Many of these factors frequently exist in law practice.[65] For instance, lawyers often have to tackle problems that contain many ambiguities of law and fact. Even questions that, at first, seem to have well-settled answers are often susceptible to an analysis that can make the answers seem unclear. Indeed, law students are trained to perform this particular art of legal jiu jitsu.[66]

Given the uncertainty of many legal answers and lawyers' expertise in identifying (or manufacturing) those uncertainties, lawyers are especially susceptible to the forces of conformity. For example, the subordinate in the initial discovery hypothetical may review the discovery rules and find language that could theoretically (though implausibly) support the partner's position, particularly if she perceives that other lawyers at the firm are engaging in similar behavior.[67] Thus, despite her initial belief about the document's discoverability, she might begin to believe that her original view was either a product of inexperience or a failure to appreciate fully all of the nuances about how discovery works in practice.[68] She might consequently come to think that her initial view was wrong, even though it was quite clearly right. And if the document's discoverability

---

[64] *See supra* notes 22-30 and accompanying text.

[65] Obviously, law practice occurs in a wide range of environments, and each setting produces its own constraints and social forces that profoundly influence attorney behavior. *See generally* Andrew M. Perlman, *A Career Choice Critique of Legal Ethics Theory*, 31 Seton Hall L. Rev. 829 (2001). Thus, the analysis offered here is not universally applicable.

[66] *See, e.g.*, Duncan Kennedy, *Legal Education and the Reproduction of Hierarchy*, 32 J. Legal Educ. 591, 595-96 (1982).

[67] Again, obedience and conformity are related, but distinct, forces. Technically, conformity is an effect that occurs in groups, whereas the original hypothetical primarily concerns obedience. *See supra* note 63 and accompanying text.

[68] One recent study suggests that the social forces that produce conformity actually affect one's subjective perception of a situation and do not simply push someone to conform for the sake of fitting in with the group. Gregory S. Berns et al., *Neurobiological Correlates of Social Conformity and Independence During Mental Rotation*, 58 Biological Psychiatry 245, 251 (2005). For a useful summary of the experiment, see Zimbardo, *supra* note 21, at 264-65. The study implies that the associate may truly believe that the partner is right and will not consciously recognize that she is engaging in an act of conformity.

fell into an area that was even slightly grey instead of black and white, the tendency to conform would be even greater.[69]

The hierarchical structure of lawyering also makes conformity more likely. Studies suggest that strong conformity forces exist even in "arbitrarily constructed groups . . . that hold no long-term power to reward conformity or punish dissent."[70] Lawyers, however, work in groups that are not arbitrarily constructed and actually do hold long-term power to reward conformity or punish dissent. Attorneys typically work in settings where other group members, such as senior partners or corporate executives (e.g., in-house counsel jobs), control the professional fates of subordinates, a condition that increases the likelihood of conformity.[71] So, for example, the young lawyer in the initial hypothetical would feel a powerful, though perhaps unconscious, urge to conform, especially given that she had trouble finding a job and faced significant financial burdens.

Social status also affects conformity. There is evidence that people with more social prestige feel more comfortable deviating from the prevailing opinion.[72] By contrast, a person with a lower status, such as the junior law firm associate in the hypothetical, will be more likely to conform to protect her more vulnerable position.

Unanimity also encourages conformity, and unanimity is common among lawyers who are working together on the same legal matter. Studies have shown that zealous advocacy tends to make lawyers believe that the objectively "correct" answer to a legal problem is the one that just so happens to benefit the client.[73] This tendency causes teams of lawyers to agree on many issues, making it even more difficult for dissenting voices to be heard. So in the discovery example, the absence of a dissenting voice would make the subordinate more likely to assume that her initial position was incorrect or, at the very least, not worth pursuing.

The point here is not that lawyers will always conform to the views of superiors or colleagues. Plenty of lawyers express their own beliefs, even under very difficult circumstances.[74] The claim is that powerful social forces exist in many law practice settings that make conformity more likely than most people would expect.

---

[69] *See, e.g.*, Wash. State Physicians Ins. Exch. & Ass'n v. Fisons Corp., 858 P.2d 1054 (Wash. 1993).

[70] ROSS & NISBETT, *supra* note 3, at 33.

[71] *See* Perlman, *supra* note 65, at 834-39; *see also* Kim, *supra* note 6, at 1005-06, 1008 (describing the particularly strong social forces that act on in-house counsel).

[72] *See, e.g.*, Cass R. Sunstein, *Conformity and Dissent* 12 (Univ. of Chi. Law Sch. Pub. Law & Legal Theory Working Paper Series, Paper No. 34, 2002), available at http://www.law.uchicago.edu/academics/publiclaw/resources/34.crs.conformity.pdf; *see also* Sherif, supra note 28, at 42.

[73] *See, e.g.*, Donald C. Langevoort, *Where Were the Lawyers? A Behavioral Inquiry Into Lawyers' Responsibility for Clients' Fraud*, 46 VAND. L. REV. 75, 95-111 (1993).

[74] *See, e.g.*, Meyerhofer v. Empire Fire & Marine Ins. Co., 497 F.2d 1190, 1192-93 (2d Cir. 1974) (describing a junior associate who resigned from his job and reported his firm's misconduct to the Securities and Exchange Commission); Jane Mayer, *The Memo: How an Internal Effort to Ban the Abuse and Torture of Detainees Was Thwarted*, NEW YORKER, Feb. 27, 2006, at 32, 32 (describing Alberto Mora's defiance of his superiors in an attempt to stop the torture of detainees at the Guantanamo Bay prison); Douglas

B. Situational Factors that Produce Obedience in Law Practice

Law practice also tends to produce excessive obedience. To understand why this happens, consider just a few of the key variables that affected obedience in Milgram's experiments: (1) the existence of a plausible legitimate reason for the wrongful conduct (in Milgram's experiment, it was to study the learning process); (2) the use of positive language to describe the negative behavior (e.g., the shocks help the person to learn); (3) the presentation of rules that, on their face, seem benign (e.g., hit the lever when the learner gives a wrong answer); (4) the creation of some kind of verbal or contractual obligation to help (e.g., the experimenter asked participants to agree to follow certain procedures before starting the experiment); (5) the assignment of specific roles (e.g., teacher/learner); (6) the physical separation of the person carrying out the orders and the victim (e.g., the learner being in an adjoining room); (7) the close proximity of the person issuing the orders and the person following them (e.g., the experimenter being in the same room as the subject); (8) the blurring of responsibility or the assignment of responsibility to someone else (e.g., when a subject asked the experimenter who was responsible for the fate of the bound man, the experimenter told the subject that the experimenter, not the subject, was responsible); (9) the incremental nature of the experiment (e.g., starting with only fifteen volts and increasing the shocks by small increments); (10) the social prestige of the setting (e.g., Milgram's initial experiment occurred in a laboratory at Yale University);[75] and (11) the elimination of dissent (e.g., Milgram found that, when the experiment was done in groups, the presence of a dissenter dramatically reduced obedience).[76]

Many of these factors exist in law practice. First, lawyers can usually frame unethical or illegal requests in ways that fit the first and second factors. For example, the partner who requested the withholding of the smoking gun document could articulate a legitimate reason for the request, such as "it's not within the scope of discovery" or "it's arguably privileged," even though neither statement is objectively accurate. The partner could also explain that withholding the document will produce the salutary effect of promoting zealous advocacy and advancing the client's cause. In these ways,

---

McCollam, *The Trials of Jesselyn Radack,* AM. LAW., July 1, 2003, at 19-21 (describing Jesselyn Radack's defiance of superiors in the Justice Department regarding the Department's tactics in questioning John Walker Lindh, the so-called American Taliban).

[75] Obedience levels dropped when Milgram moved the experiment to a rundown office building unaffiliated with Yale. Milgram, *supra* note 32, at 66-70 (noting a reduction in obedience from sixty-five percent to forty-eight percent when the study was moved from Yale to a rundown office building that had no apparent ties to the University). Although Milgram's particular results were not statistically significant, subsequent studies reveal that the status of the authority figure is a factor that influences obedience. Zimbardo, *supra* note 21, at 275-76.

[76] Social psychologists have offered many explanations for Milgram's results, but the explanations described here are some of the most common. *See* Zimbardo, *supra* note 21, at 273-75. For a slightly different list, see Philip G. Zimbardo, *A Situationist Perspective on the Psychology of Evil: Understanding How Good People Are Transformed into Perpetrators, in* THE SOCIAL PSYCHOLOGY OF GOOD AND EVIL 21, 27-28 (Arthur G. Miller ed., 2004).

the authority figure—in this case, a partner—could give the subordinate a seemingly plausible explanation for refusing to disclose the document and argue that it promotes a positive outcome (factors one and two respectively).

The partner could also frame the instruction as part of litigation's unwritten "rules of the game" (factor three).[77] In this way, the demand appears entirely benign. Moreover, the consequences may also appear inconsequential. Unlike Milgram's experiments, where obedience resulted in painful electric shocks to a man with a heart condition, compliance in many (but not all)[78] lawyering contexts produces far less dire consequences. For instance, in the discovery example, the lawyer is "merely" withholding a document as part of the discovery "game" that all lawyers play,[79] not causing somebody physical pain or risking someone's life. The seemingly benign nature of the request can enhance the subordinate's willingness to obey.

This factor is likely to have more weight if the subordinate has little litigation experience and does not have the necessary expertise to question the partner's authority. In contrast, if the subordinate has handled numerous document productions and has a strong experiential basis to know that the partner's request is impermissible, the subordinate is less likely to give the partner's demand a benign gloss. Of course, even when it is absolutely clear that the partner's behavior is unethical or illegal, the subordinate may still comply if some of the other factors favoring obedience are present.[80]

---

[77] *See, e.g.*, Wash. State Physicians Ins. Exch. & Assoc. v. Fisons Corp., 858 P.2d 1054, 1074-85 (Wash. 1993) (remanding the case for the imposition of sanctions on attorneys who had abused the judicial process by failing to disclose a smoking gun document in discovery); *see also* Kimberly Kirkland, *Ethics in Large Law Firms: The Principle of Pragmatism*, 35 U. MEM. L. REV. 631, 718-19, 724 (2005) (concluding from her study of large law firm litigators that they frequently "view zealous advocacy as an affirmative moral obligation" and view the ideal of litigation as "a game well-played").

[78] *See, e.g.*, Balla v. Gambro, 584 N.E.2d 104, 107 (Ill. 1991) (describing the firing of an in-house counsel after he warned the company's president that one of the company's products could cause "death or serious bodily harm to patients").

[79] Discovery is a "game" in both an academic and layman's sense. From an academic perspective, discovery has an interesting game theory dimension. For a very nice discussion of game theory's implications for discovery in the context of a subordinate lawyer, see David McGowan, *Politics, Office Politics, and Legal Ethics: A Case Study in the Strategy of Judgment*, 20 GEO. J. LEGAL ETHICS 1057, 1071-75 (2007). But discovery is also a game in the more ordinary sense of the word. Namely, lawyers frequently think of the process not so much as a method for discovering the truth, but as a game that needs to be won. *See generally* Robert L. Nelson, Essay, *The Discovery Process as a Circle of Blame: Institutional, Professional, and Socio-Economic Factors that Contribute to Unreasonable, Inefficient, and Amoral Behavior in Corporate Litigation*, 67 FORDHAM L. REV. 773, 794-95 (1998).

[80] For a recent real world illustration of this effect, see Qualcomm Inc. v. Broadcom Corp., No. 05cv1958-B, 2008 WL 66932, at *13 n.10 (S.D. Cal. Jan. 7, 2008); *see also* Regan, *supra* note 6, at 4-6, 294, 323-24 (emphasizing the role that social context played in a lawyer's failure to disclose pertinent information); Lawrence J. Fox, *I'm Just an Associate . . . At a New York Firm*, 69 FORDHAM L. REV. 939 (2000) (offering a realistic account of a subordinate who is asked to bury discovery documents); Luban, *supra* note 6, at 95-96 (describing a subordinate's complicity with a partner's obvious perjury to a federal judge).

Factors four (an agreement to help the authority figure) and five (the presence of assigned roles) also frequently exist in law practice. The lawyer-client relationship itself is essentially an agreement to help clients achieve their goals (factor four). When combined with the common perception that a lawyer's morality is distinct from individual morality (i.e., role differentiation),[81] lawyers are more apt to view arguably legal conduct as part of their job as an advocate (factor five). Thus, subordinates, such as the associate in the discovery example, will view the authority's instructions as part of the agreement to help the client, with the mindset of role-differentiation only adding to the belief that any moral consequences are not the subordinate's primary concern.[82]

The effect that role has on judgment is nicely illustrated by a study involving 139 auditors at major accounting firms. The auditors were given hypothetical accounting scenarios and asked to assess the accounting in each situation.[83] Roughly half of the accountants were asked to assume that they were retained by the firm that they were auditing, while the rest were supposed to assume that they had been hired by an outside investor who was considering making an investment in the company.[84] On average, the auditors were significantly more likely to find that the company's financial reports complied with generally accepted accounting standards when they played the role of the company's accountant than when they played the role of the investor's accountant.[85] Their assigned roles, in other words, heavily influenced their perspectives.

Another factor that contributes to obedience is that attorney misbehavior will typically affect victims who are more remote in time and place than the victims in Milgram's experiments (factor six). For example, the failure to produce a smoking gun document will affect an adverse party, but in a much more indirect way than the application of an electric shock. Similarly, assisting a company's financial fraud (e.g., the Enron scandal) will primarily harm shareholders and lower level employees, people with whom lawyers have little contact.[86] Because a lawyer will perceive these harms to be less immediate and proximate than someone suffering painful electric shocks in an adjoining room,

---

[81] David Luban, Lawyers and Justice: An Ethical Study 104-47 (1988) (describing and criticizing this view); Richard Wasserstrom, *Lawyers as Professionals: Some Moral Issues,* 5 Hum. Rts. 1, 3-4 (1975) (same).

[82] *See generally* Zimbardo, *supra* note 21 (describing his well-known Stanford Prison Experiments, in which he demonstrated the substantial impact that social role has on behavior); *see also* Kim, *supra* note 6, at 1012 (making a similar point); David Luban, *Integrity: Its Causes and Cures,* 72 Fordham L. Rev. 279, 292-93 (2003) (reviewing the social psychology literature, including Professor Zimbardo's work, that highlights the extent to which role influences behavior).

[83] *Id.* at 1009-10 (citing Don A. Moore et al., *Conflict of Interest and the Unconscious Intrusion of Bias* (Harv. Bus. Sch. Negotiations, Orgs. & Mkts. Unit, Working Paper No. 02-40, 2002)).

[84] *Id.* at 1009.

[85] *Id.* at 1009-10; *see also* Ross & Nisbett, *supra* note 3, at 72-75 (describing partisans' inability to view a given situation objectively); Linda Babcock et al., *Biased Judgments of Fairness in Bargaining,* 85 Am. Econ. Rev. 1337, 1339-42 (1995) (finding that lawyers' assessment of the value of a case varies dramatically depending on which side they are assigned to represent); Langevoort, *supra* note 73, at 95-111.

[86] Kim, *supra* note 6, at 1033 (making this point in the context of securities fraud).

this factor favors obedience in the lawyering context even more strongly than what Milgram found in many of his experiments.

Not only will the victims of legal misconduct be relatively remote, but the person issuing the orders will be nearby. Milgram found that obedience increased when the authority figure and the subordinate were in the same room and decreased when the experimenter issued orders using a tape recorder or from another location.[87] For lawyers, the authority figure who issues the instruction will typically be a colleague or a client with whom the subordinate has a great deal of contact and who may exercise considerable power regarding the subordinate's future at the firm, thus further adding to the likelihood of obedience (factor seven).[88]

Subordinates may also discount their responsibility for their conduct (factor eight) by shifting moral responsibility to the person issuing the orders. Indeed, when Milgram's subjects asked who was responsible for what happened in the laboratory, the experimenter said that he (the experimenter) was ultimately responsible for any harm to the learner.[89] This shifting of responsibility is especially likely in the legal ethics context, where Model Rule 5.2(b) states that "[a] subordinate lawyer does not violate the Rules of Professional Conduct if that lawyer acts in accordance with a supervisory lawyer's reasonable resolution of an arguable question of professional duty."[90] Given the ambiguity of so many legal and ethical duties, subordinates will frequently find that a supervisory lawyer's instructions reflect a "reasonable resolution of an arguable question of professional duty."[91] Thus, subordinate lawyers are likely to believe that responsibility for their actions ultimately lies with superiors.

Another significant factor that contributed to obedience in Milgram's subjects was the incremental nature of the experiment (factor nine).[92] Each new shock was only modestly larger than the last, making it difficult for subjects to distinguish morally what they were about to do from what they had already done.[93] This phenomenon of justifying past actions in a way that makes conduct of a similar type in the future seem ethical is known as cognitive dissonance.[94] In Milgram's experiment, it meant that obedience was more likely at higher voltages because subjects had already complied with shocks at lower voltages.[95]

In one of the few articles to describe in detail the implications of Milgram's work for legal ethics, Professor David Luban contends that the incremental nature of the experi-

---

[87] Milgram, *supra* note 32, at 59-62.

[88] Kim, *supra* note 6, at 1003-04, 1011 (making a similar observation).

[89] Milgram, *supra* note 32, at 7-8.

[90] MODEL RULES OF PROF'L CONDUCT R. 5.2(b) (2007).

[91] *See* Luban, *supra* note 57, at 5 (making a similar point).

[92] Milgram, *supra* note 32, at 20-21.

[93] *Id.* at 149; *see also* Luban, *supra* note 57, at 8.

[94] Luban, *supra* note 57, at 8.

[95] Milgram, *supra* note 32, at 149.

ment offers the best explanation for the obedience that Milgram observed.[96] Luban explains that "[b]y luring us into higher and higher level shocks, one micro-step at a time, the Milgram experiments gradually and subtly disarm our ability to distinguish right from wrong."[97]

Professor Luban is clearly right that obedience in Milgram's experiments occurred, in part, because the experimenter made seemingly benign initial requests followed by gradually larger requests for punishment.[98] Nevertheless, the incremental nature of the experiment probably did not play the decisive role that Luban suggests. Although each step up on the shock generator was only fifteen volts, subjects did not experience each step in precisely the same way. In fact, some of the shocks were meaningfully different from the shocks that had come before. For example, the learner eventually requested to be let go at 150 volts, making any additional shocks quite different in effect. Indeed, when subjects resisted Milgram's commands, more did so at this point in the experiment than at any other time.[99] Moreover, the learner's complaints about heart pain and his subsequent ominous silence made additional shocks clearly distinguishable from the shocks that the subjects had already administered. Thus, cognitive dissonance and the incremental nature of the experiment were important, but clearly not the only—or even the primary—factors.

In fact, Professor Luban offers an example that illustrates the limited explanatory force of increments. In the famous *Berkey-Kodak* case, an associate failed to report the blatant lying of a respected senior colleague.[100] Luban contends that the associate's obedience reflected the kind of incremental "corruption-of-judgment" that produced obedience in Milgram's experiments.[101] Namely, the associate's loyalty to his lying superior was the "end of a slippery slope, beginning with lawful adversarial deception and culminating with lies, perjury, and wrongful obedience."[102]

The problem is that, even if a contentious discovery process had preceded the lying, there is quite a leap from engaging in contentious discovery to helping a partner lie to a federal judge. The *Berkey-Kodak* case, according to Professor Luban's own account, involves a large jump on the legal ethics equivalent of the shock generator from a small shock to a potentially lethal one. Such a jump is not consistent with Luban's

---

[96] Luban, *supra* note 6, at 103.

[97] *Id.* Professor Luban also pointed out how this force can affect law practice, such as in the discovery context. He explained that an initial attempt to avoid producing a document can lead to more and increasingly problematic attempts to resist the production of relevant information, leading ultimately to the type of situation described in the initial hypothetical. *Id.* at 106.

[98] Milgram, *supra* note 32, at 20-21.

[99] *Id.* at 35-37 (noting that in this version of the experiment, five of the fifteen people who disobeyed the experimenter did so at 150 volts, the point at which the "learner" demanded to be let go); *see also* Doris, *supra* note 7, at 50 (making a similar observation).

[100] Luban, *supra* note 57, at 4.

[101] *Id.* at 9.

[102] *Id.*

contention that subordinates follow orders as a result of a gradual corruption of judgment. Of course, increments play a role in excessive obedience, but such obedience can readily occur in cases like *Berkey-Kodak* without increments, assuming other forces are present.[103]

Social prestige (factor ten) is another of those forces.[104] Many law firms, especially larger firms, are held in high esteem among lawyers. These firms are thus likely to produce the same social forces that Yale University produced in Milgram's subjects.[105] Moreover, smaller firms can also produce the same effect, especially if the superior is an experienced and respected partner.[106]

Finally, the partner in the example is the only person to offer an opinion, so the subordinate has not heard any dissent regarding the partner's interpretation. The absence of dissent (factor eleven) is yet another force that favors obedience.[107]

In addition to the factors that contributed to obedience in Milgram's experiment, there is one factor that favors obedience in the lawyer situation that did not exist for Milgram: professional and financial self-interest.[108] In Milgram's experiments, subjects were told that they could keep the modest amount of money that they had been given, even if they refused to continue with the experiment.[109] Moreover, their professional

---

[103] Professor Luban also argues that "[t]he Achilles' heel of situationism is explaining why anyone deviates from the majority behavior." Luban, *supra* note 6, at 101; Luban, *supra* note 82, at 295-96 (making a similar point). In fact, this Achilles' heel can only be found on a straw man version of situationism. Situationists do not claim that context fully explains all human behavior or that everyone will act the same way in the same situation. Doris, *supra* note 7, at 25 (asserting that neither he nor any situationist he knows of maintains that "correlations between measurable dimensions of situations and single behaviors typically approach 1.0"); *id.* at 46 (acknowledging that dispositional differences provide a partial explanation for why some people did not comply with the experimenter's commands in Milgram's experiments). Rather, situationists make more modest claims, such as that dispositional traits are far less important than most people realize and that context is a much more significant determinant of human behavior than people typically believe. *Id.* at 24-25.

[104] Milgram, *supra* note 32, at 66-70 (noting a reduction in obedience from sixty-five percent to forty-eight percent when the study was moved from Yale to a rundown office building that had no apparent ties to the University). *But see supra* note 75.

[105] Milgram, *supra* note 32, at 66-70.

[106] Luban himself offers a nice description of this phenomenon in the context of the Berkey-Kodak case, *see* Luban, *supra* note 6, at 95-96, though he does not ultimately identify it as a force that could impact the associate's behavior independently of his corruption of judgment theory.

[107] *See, e.g.,* Kim, *supra* note 6, at 1021 (making this point in the in-house counsel context); *see also* Ross & Nisbett, *supra* note 3, at 41 (explaining why people who witness, or find themselves in, a potentially dangerous situation will fail to act if other people also fail to do so). There are, of course, many other forces that contribute to obedience that were not part of Milgram's experiment. For example, a superior can increase obedience by demeaning the intended victim. Milgram, *supra* note 32, at 9. Thus, the common tendency among lawyers to demonize an opponent or the opponent's lawyers makes it more likely that a subordinate will carry out an unethical command that adversely affects that opponent.

[108] Kim, *supra* note 6, at 1027 (describing this self-serving bias).

[109] *See* Milgram, *supra* note 32, at 14-15 (showing the newspaper announcement that was used to recruit subjects).

fortunes were in no way affected by whether they complied. In contrast, a subordinate lawyer has a lot to lose by refusing to obey: a job. The subordinate's concern for her job, particularly a junior lawyer who may have had few other professional opportunities, is likely to be substantial. Thus, this factor also weighs heavily in favor of compliance and suggests that lawyers might be even more likely to comply than the subjects of Milgram's experiments.

There is, however, one factor that weighs against the hypothetical lawyer's compliance: obedience could lead to monetary sanctions or disbarment. If the lawyer believes that she faces a real chance of discipline, she arguably would be more likely to resist the partner's demands. The powerful concern for professional survival might trump the other social forces that favor obedience and conformity and make compliance less likely than in Milgram's experiments, where subjects had no equivalent incentive to dissent.

There are three problems with this view. First, it assumes that the subordinate will recognize that the partner's demands implicate her ethical duties. The reality is that, given the forces at work, she may easily begin to question her initial opinion and view the partner's opinion as, at the very least, justifiable.[110] This tendency to interpret the situation so that it does not implicate one's ethical or moral responsibility is sometimes called ethical fading.[111] Specifically, the actor reinterprets the situation in such a way that the ethical nature of the situation fades from view. If the subordinate does not even identify the ethics issue, the concern for professional survival cannot override the social forces favoring conformity and obedience.

Second, even if the subordinate recognizes the ethical dilemma, she is not likely to be terribly concerned about discipline. Rule 5.2 only imposes discipline if the superior's instructions were clearly unethical. So unless the instruction is blatantly impermissible, the subordinate is not likely to fear any disciplinary consequences.

Third, even if the instruction is blatantly unethical or illegal, a lawyer may still not fear discipline, at least in the discovery context. Bar discipline for this sort of misconduct occurs rarely, and sanctions are usually far below what would be necessary to discourage this sort of behavior.[112]

---

[110] Luban, *supra* note 6, at 95-96 (describing this phenomenon in the context of the *Berkey-Kodak* case).

[111] Ann E. Tenbrunsel & David M. Messick, *Ethical Fading: The Role of Self-Deception in Unethical Behavior,* 17 SOC. JUST. RES. 223, 224-25 (2004); *see also* Kim, *supra* note 6, at 1026-29 (citing additional studies that have reached a similar conclusion); Luban, *supra* note 82, at 280 (observing that "hundreds of experiments reveal that when our conduct clashes with our prior beliefs . . . our beliefs swing into conformity with our conduct, without our ever noticing").

[112] *See* John S. Beckerman, *Confronting Civil Discovery's Fatal Flaws,* 84 MINN. L. REV. 505, 572-73 (2000) (noting the general reluctance of courts to refer discovery violations to disciplinary authorities); Bruce A. Green, *Policing Federal Prosecutors: Do Too Many Regulators Product Too Little Enforcement?,* 8 ST. THOMAS L. REV. 69, 90 (1995) (citing Commission on Evaluation of Disciplinary Enforcement, Am. Bar Ass'n, Report to the House of Delegates 36 (1991)). It is too early to tell whether the recent sanctions for discovery abuses in the recent high profile case of Qualcomm Inc. v. Broadcom Corp., No. 05cv1958-B, 2008 WL 66932, at *13 n.10 (S.D. Cal. Jan. 7, 2008), will have any impact on lawyers' behavior.

The case of *Washington State Physician Insurance Exchange & Associates v. Fisons Corp.* is illustrative.[113] The original plaintiff in that case was a child who had suffered seizures and permanent brain damage after taking medicine that Fisons manufactured.[114] The plaintiff's discovery requests called for all documents related to a particular ingredient in the medicine and any information that Fisons had about that ingredient's dangerousness in children.[115] Despite these requests, the defense lawyers relied on a contorted and frivolous rationale for not turning over documents that proved that Fisons knew about the ingredient's toxicity in children.[116]

After an anonymous copy of the smoking gun emerged, the trial court considered and rejected any sanctions against the company or its lawyers.[117] The trial court relied heavily on the notion that "the conduct of the drug company and its counsel was consistent with the customary and accepted litigation practices of the bar of [the county] and of [Washington] state."[118] The Washington Supreme Court reversed that determination,[119] but the ultimate sanction for the lawyers was an out-of-court settlement of a mere $325,000,[120] a small fraction of the fees that the firm had generated from the case. Put simply, the defense lawyers received a slap on the wrist for a rather blatant discovery violation that was similar to the one in the initial hypothetical.

Finally, the risks of sanctions and discipline are no higher (and may be lower) than the risks associated with making the report. Many lawyers in this circumstance would be concerned not only about losing their current jobs, but about whether a report of this sort might make it difficult to get jobs in the future once they were labeled as whistleblowers.

To summarize, the hypothetical associate faces considerable pressures to conform and obey and few risks from compliance and obedience. Even if the misconduct is uncovered, a risk that may be rather small, she is unlikely to face any punishment that will adversely affect her career. The ultimate and disturbing result is that she is prone to obey the partner who has issued the unethical and illegal command.

IV. IMPLICATIONS FOR THE LAW OF LAWYERING

The challenge for legal ethicists is to counter the social forces that contribute to excessive conformity and obedience. In one of the few efforts to address that challenge, Professor Luban has suggested that, by educating lawyers about their own tendencies to obey authorities, they might be better able to resist an order to commit illegal or

---

[113] 858 P.2d 1054 (Wash. 1993).

[114] *Id.* at 1058.

[115] *Id.* at 1080-83.

[116] *Id.* at 1079-84.

[117] *Id.* at 1074-75.

[118] *Id.* at 1078.

[119] *Id.* at 1085.

[120] Stuart Taylor, Jr., *Sleazy in Seattle,* AM. LAW., Apr. 1994, at 5, 5.

unethical conduct.[121] Unfortunately, there is little evidence that this so-called "enlightenment effect" holds much promise, at least in this particular context.[122]

There are some steps, however, that might make a difference in some cases. Rather than offering an exhaustive list of potential remedies, the following proposals are illustrations of how social psychology could play a more active role in debates about professional regulation.[123]

A. Providing Whistleblower Protections for Attorneys

Currently, some states do not offer whistleblower protections for lawyers.[124] In those jurisdictions, lawyers who are fired after disclosing illegal conduct have no legal recourse against their employers. This lack of whistleblower protection is unwise, given that it reinforces the already strong social forces that weigh against defiance in such circumstances.[125]

The problem is amply illustrated by the well-known Illinois case, *Balla v. Gambro, Inc.*,[126] in which Gambro's general counsel, Mr. Balla, learned that his company was selling dialyzers for dialysis machines that were not within federal specifications and that could cause potentially serious medical complications.[127] After Balla unsuccessfully urged Gambro not to put the dialyzers on the market, Gambro fired Balla.[128] Balla

---

[121] Luban, *supra* note 6, at 116 ("Perhaps the best protection [for lawyers against the forces described in Milgram's experiments] is understanding the . . . insidious way [those forces] work on us."); *see also* Deborah L. Rhode, *Ethics by the Pervasive Method,* 42 J. LEGAL EDUC. 31, 47 (1992) (suggesting that exposure to Milgram's work might help law students avoid unethical behavior).

[122] Thomas Blass, *The Milgram Paradigm After 35 Years: Some Things We Now Know About Obedience to Authority, in* OBEDIENCE TO AUTHORITY: CURRENT PERSPECTIVES ON THE MILGRAM PARADIGM 35, 50-53 (Thomas Blass ed., 2000) (drawing on several studies and concluding that "[b]eing enlightened about the unexpected power of authority may help a person stay away from an authority-dominated situation, but once he or she is already in such a situation, knowledge of the drastic degree of obedience authorities are capable of eliciting does not necessarily help free the individual from the grip of the forces operating in that concrete situation"). Despite this lack of evidence, I share Professor Luban's intuition that enlightening lawyers about this tendency is worthwhile. I show my students a video of the Milgram experiments on the last day of class in the hope that it might make some difference at some point in their professional lives.

[123] For an excellent analysis of social psychology's implications for the regulation of lawyers who represent publicly traded companies, *see* Kim, *supra* note 6, at 1034-75.

[124] *See, e.g.,* Balla v. Gambro, Inc., 584 N.E.2d 104, 107 (Ill. 1991).

[125] Kim, *supra* note 6, at 1042-44, 1064-71 (arguing that securities lawyers should receive whistleblower protection under the Sarbanes-Oxley Act for reasons similar to those described here); Douglas R. Richmond, *Professional Responsibilities of Law Firm Associates,* 45 BRANDEIS L.J. 199, 257 (2007) (arguing in favor of whistleblower protection for lawyers).

[126] *Balla,* 584 N.E.2d at 104.

[127] *Id.* at 106.

[128] *Id.*

subsequently revealed the defects to the Federal Food and Drug Administration and sued for retaliatory discharge under the state's whistleblower statute.[129]

The Illinois Supreme Court rejected Balla's claim, explaining that whistleblower statutes exist to protect employees who might otherwise be reluctant to report corporate malfeasance.[130] The court's primary rationale was that, since lawyers in Illinois already had an ethical obligation to report misconduct like the selling of the defective dialyzers, Mr. Balla did not need whistleblower protection.[131]

On its face, the Illinois Supreme Court's logic is sound. If the whistleblower statute is unclear regarding its application to lawyers and if the purpose of the statute would not be furthered by applying it to attorneys, Balla should not receive protection.

The problem is that the court's opinion rested on a flawed assumption about human behavior. Social psychology suggests that lawyers in Balla's situation would find it difficult to disclose information of the sort described in the opinion, especially without whistleblower protection. First, lawyers like Balla are unlikely to put much stock in the ethical obligation that the court referenced. The rule is ambiguous, and the various forces described earlier can lead a lawyer to interpret the rule as not requiring disclosure. Moreover, there are very few instances where lawyers have been disciplined for failing to disclose information under similar circumstances. Thus, any fear of discipline would be overshadowed by what the lawyer had to lose (i.e., a job) by reporting the misconduct and by other situational forces, such as Balla's distance from the prospective victims, his proximity to his bosses, the hierarchical structure of a corporation, and the presumptive absence of dissent.

Balla's refusal to comply given these variables was notable (and one of the reasons the case is so widely reported), but there is no reason to think that his response was typical. Given similar circumstances, lawyers will face considerable pressure to conceal a client's harmful conduct and to develop legal justifications for that concealment. The reality, in other words, is that lawyers—like most people—face significant social pressures that make it difficult to resist a client's insistence on harmful and potentially illicit courses of conduct, even if a duty to report exists. Justice Freeman, in his dissent, stated this point convincingly:

> . . . . [T]o say that the categorical nature of ethical obligations is sufficient to ensure that the ethical obligations will be satisfied simply ignores reality. Specifically, it ignores that, as unfortunate for society as it may be, attorneys are no less human than nonattorneys and, thus, no less given to the temptation to either ignore or rationalize away their ethical obligations when complying therewith may render them unable to feed and support their families.

---

[129] *Id.*

[130] *Id.* at 108.

[131] *Id.* at 108-09.

> I would like to believe, as my colleagues apparently conclude, that attorneys will always "do the right thing" because the law says that they must. However, my knowledge of human nature, which is not much greater than the average layman's, and, sadly, the recent scandals involving the bench and bar of Illinois are more than sufficient to dispel such a belief. Just as the ethical obligations of the lawyers and judges involved in those scandals were inadequate to ensure that they would not break the law, I am afraid that the lawyer's ethical obligation to "blow the whistle" is likewise an inadequate safeguard for the public policy of protecting lives and property of Illinois citizens.
>
> As reluctant as I am to concede it, the fact is that this court must take whatever steps it can, within the bounds of the law, to give lawyers incentives to abide by their ethical obligations, beyond the satisfaction inherent in their doing so. We cannot continue to delude ourselves and the people of the State of Illinois that attorneys' ethical duties, alone, are always sufficient to guarantee that lawyers will "do the right thing." In the context of this case, where doing "the right thing" will often result in termination by an employer bent on doing the "wrong thing," I believe that the incentive needed is recognition of a cause of action for retaliatory discharge, in the appropriate case.[132]

Justice Freeman got it exactly right. The court should have acknowledged how human beings are likely to behave, discounted the ethical obligation to disclose, and affirmed the value of whistleblower protection. Of course, the existence of whistleblower protection will not ensure that all lawyers reveal information about a client's illicit actions, but such protection could make a difference in some cases by weakening the significant psychological forces that weigh against such disclosures.

B. Enforcing the Duty to Report Misconduct

Most states impose on attorneys a duty to report another lawyer's misconduct if the misconduct implicates the lawyer's trustworthiness, honesty, or fitness to practice law.[133]

The problem with the rule is that most lawyers, especially subordinates, are not eager to report the misconduct of other attorneys. For instance, the associate in the discovery example may find it difficult to report the partner, even if she were convinced that the partner had engaged in an intentional and egregious discovery violation that reflected on the partner's trustworthiness or honesty.[134] As Part III explained, the subordinate is

---

[132] *Id.* at 113 (Freeman, J., dissenting).

[133] Model Rules of Prof'l Conduct R. 8.3(a) (2007).

[134] *See, e.g.,* Luban, *supra* note 6, at 95 (describing an associate's failure to report a partner's obvious perjury in a well-known case).

likely to feel considerable pressure to obey the authority figure and to be complicit in the authority's misconduct. It would take an unusual subordinate to not only resist that temptation, but to take the next step of reporting the superior to the bar.[135]

Part of the problem is that Rule 8.3, like the disclosure duty in Illinois, is rarely enforced. The vast majority of states do not have a single reported case where a lawyer was disciplined under this rule.[136] As a result, lawyers are willing to run the very negligible risk of discipline in order to avoid having to report another attorney to the bar.

One potential solution is to increase enforcement of the rule so that lawyers perceive a greater threat to their own professional well-being if they fail to report the misconduct of other attorneys under Model Rule 8.3. Indeed, Illinois's experience with this rule suggests that modest increases in enforcement can have a discernable effect on reporting. After the Illinois Supreme Court issued an opinion that disciplined a lawyer under Rule 8.3,[137] Illinois's bar disciplinary authorities observed a substantial increase in Rule 8.3 reports.[138]

The increase in Illinois implies that the fear of discipline can prompt lawyers to report misconduct that they otherwise would have swept under the rug.[139] Thus, increased enforcement of Rule 8.3 can also help to weaken the social forces that would ordinarily encourage lawyers, especially subordinate lawyers, to ignore perceived misconduct.

C. Strengthening the Responsibilities of Subordinate Lawyers

Another Model Rule that impacts the conduct of subordinate lawyers is, unsurprisingly, the rule written specifically for subordinate lawyers—Rule 5.2. That rule states that "[a] subordinate lawyer does not violate the Rules of Professional Conduct if that lawyer acts in accordance with a supervisory lawyer's reasonable resolution of an arguable question of professional duty."[140] The rule essentially permits a lawyer to carry out a superior's orders as long as those orders constitute a reasonable interpretation of the relevant ethical obligation.

---

135 *See* Meyerhofer v. Empire Fire & Marine Ins. Co., 497 F.2d 1190, 1192-93 (2d Cir. 1974) (describing the actions of a junior associate who resigned from his firm and reported the firm's misconduct to the Securities and Exchange Commission).

136 *See* Fred C. Zacharias, *What Lawyers Do When Nobody's Watching: Legal Advertising as a Case Study of the Impact of Underenforced Professional Rules,* 87 IOWA L. REV. 971, 999 & n.134 (2002) (noting the lack of enforcement of this rule).

137 In re Himmel, 533 N.E.2d 790, 794-95 (Ill. 1988).

138 Leonard E. Gross, *Legal Ethics for the Future: Time to Clean Up Our Act?,* 77 ILL. B.J. 196, 198 n.26 (1988).

139 Mary T. Robinson, *A Lawyer's Duty to Report Another Lawyer's Misconduct: The Illinois Experience,* 2007 SYMP. ISSUE PROF. LAW. 47, 49-50 (observing an increase in reporting after Himmel); Patricia A. Sallen, *Combating Himmel Angst,* 2007 SYMP. ISSUE PROF. LAW. 47, 49-50 (describing a similar phenomenon in Arizona).

140 MODEL RULES OF PROF'L CONDUCT R. 5.2(b) (2007).

On its face, the rule makes sense. After all, why should a lawyer face discipline for following the arguably ethical and legal orders of a superior?

But as with the *Balla* decision, the rule rests on a questionable assumption about human behavior. By allowing a lawyer to avoid responsibility for "reasonable resolutions of an arguable question of professional duty," the rule opens the door to interpreting a wide range of instructions as "arguably" ethical. For example, the subordinate in the discovery example is likely to understand her ethical obligations through the distorted prism of what the partner wants, leading her to construe the discovery issue as "arguable" and the partner's resolution of it as "reasonable." This tendency, referred to earlier as ethical fading,[141] suggests that the typical subordinate attorney will conclude that Rule 5.2 applies and that she can carry out the partner's commands without fear of professional discipline.[142]

One possible solution is to repeal Rule 5.2(b) to make it clear that subordinates have an independent duty to assess whether a particular course of action is ethical and legal.[143] Of course, the "just following orders" defense could still be raised as a mitigating factor when determining the appropriate punishment.[144] But it should not allow a lawyer to avoid discipline entirely. Indeed, such a defense is generally rejected in most other contexts.[145] Moreover, by putting subordinates on notice that they have an independent duty to question a superior's orders, subordinates would be less likely to assume that a superior's actions are permissible and more likely to offer resistance to unethical or illegal commands.[146]

V. CONCLUSION

More than forty years of research into social psychology has revealed that, under certain conditions, we will conform to group opinions and obey authorities who issue illegal instructions. If a majority of people are willing to apply dangerous electric shocks to a bound older man with a heart condition just because someone with a lab coat says so, there is every reason to believe that lawyers will frequently obey their superiors when instructed to perform unethical or illegal tasks.

By drawing on a tiny fraction of social psychology research, this Article suggests some steps that the profession can take to weaken the social forces that produce excessive

---

141 *See supra* note 111 and accompanying text.

142 *See* Luban, *supra* note 57, at 5 (making a similar point).

143 *See* Carol M. Rice, *The Superior Orders Defense in Legal Ethics: Sending the Wrong Message to Young Lawyers,* 32 WAKE FOREST L. REV. 887, 931-34 (1997) (making a similar proposal). *But see* Richmond, *supra* note 125, at 213 (endorsing Rule 5.2(b)).

144 *See* Rice, *supra* note 143, at 889 n.5, 912-14; *see also* Richmond, *supra* note 125, at 212.

145 *See* Rice, *supra* note 143, at 904-14.

146 Of course, this approach cannot counter the ethical fading phenomenon. A lawyer will only consider reporting another lawyer if she recognizes the ethical issue.

obedience and conformity. These suggestions, however, have important limitations, such as the problem of ethical fading.[147] Nevertheless, they hint at a much broader project, one that draws on the very rich literature in social psychology to address various causes of attorney misconduct.

[147] *See supra* note 111 and accompanying text.

Milgram Revisited[*]

David J. Luban[**]

. . . .

In legal ethics, I think most lawyers would agree about the single biggest discrepancy between the law in books—the profession's ethics codes—and the law in action. The ethics codes are almost entirely *individualist* in their focus. They treat lawyers (clients, too, for that matter) largely as self-contained decision-makers. In fact, however, lawyers increasingly work in and for organizations. The A[merican] B[ar] F[oundation]'s demographic studies of the legal profession are instructive on this subject. While most lawyers continue to practice in small firms, and sole practitioners still form the largest single subset of the profession, the trend is toward organizational practice. The profession as a whole is becoming younger, with a median age of around 35. Younger lawyers are substantially less likely to strike out on their own than older lawyers were, and a higher percentage of them work for large law firms.

The importance of these trends for legal ethics can hardly be exaggerated. Psychologists, organization theorists, and economists all know that the dynamics of ethical decision-making change dramatically when the individual works in an organizational setting. Loyalties become tangled and personal responsibility gets diffused. Bucks are passed and guilty knowledge bypassed. Chains of command not only tie people's hands, they fetter their minds and consciences as well. Reinhold Niebuhr called one of his

[*] Originally published in RESEARCHING LAW: AN ABF UPDATE 1 (Volume 9, No. 2, Spring 1998). Reprinted with permission; www.americanbarfoundation.org.

[**] David J. Luban is the second recipient of the W. M. Keck Foundation Award and Lectureship in Legal Ethics and Professional Responsibility. He presented the address at the Luncheon of The Fellows of the American Bar Foundation, Nashville, Tennessee, February 1, 1998. Luban is Frederick J. Haas Professor of Law and Philosophy, Georgetown University Law Center. Luban has published more than 100 articles on various topics in law and philosophy, and he is the author of *Lawyers and Justice: An Ethical Study* (Princeton University Press, 1988), *Legal Modernism* (University of Michigan Press, 1994), the co-author of *Legal Ethics* (Foundation Press, 1992), and the editor of *The Good Lawyer: Lawyers' Roles and Lawyers' Ethics* (Rowan & Allanheld, 1983) and *The Ethics of Lawyers* (Dartmouth Publishing, 1994).

books *Moral Man, Immoral Society,* and I suggest that for students of ethics no topic is more important than understanding whatever truth this title contains.

My own students, I might add, think about it constantly and without any prompting. No dilemma causes them more anxiety than the prospect of being pressured by their boss to do something they disapprove of. Not only do they worry about losing their jobs if they defy the boss to do the right thing, they also fear that the pressures of the situation might undermine their ability to know what the right thing is.

Some in this room remember one of the most painful examples of this phenomenon, the *Berkey-Kodak* antitrust litigation in 1977. In the heat of adversarial combat, an admired senior litigator for the large New York law firm representing Kodak snapped. For no apparent reason, he lied to his opponent to conceal documents from discovery, then perjured himself to a federal judge to cover up the lie. Eventually he owned up, resigned from his firm, and served a month in prison. Perhaps this sounds like an instance of chickens coming home to roost for a Rambo litigator. But by all accounts, the partner was an upright and courtly man, the diametrical opposite of a Rambo litigator.

The associate working for him knew that the partner had perjured himself, but kept silent. "What happened . . . ," recalls another associate, "was that he saw [the partner] lie and really couldn't believe it. And he just had no idea what to do. I mean, he . . . kept thinking there must be a reason. Besides, what do you do? The guy was his boss and a great guy."[1]

Notice the range of explanations here. *First,* the appeal to hierarchy: the guy was his boss. *Second,* to personal loyalty: the guy was a great guy. *Third,* to helplessness: the associate had no idea what to do. *Fourth,* the associate couldn't believe it. He kept thinking there must be a reason. The last is an explanation of a different sort, suggesting that the associate's own ethical judgment was undermined by the situation he found himself in.

As a matter of fact, the same may be said of the partner. He wasn't the lead partner in the litigation; he belonged to a team headed by a newcomer to the firm, an intense, driven, focused, and controlling lawyer. In a situation of supreme stress, the perjurious partner's judgment simply failed him.

In *Berkey-Kodak,* neither the partner nor the associate received an explicit order to break the rules, but sometimes lawyers do. What guidance does the law in books give when this happens? ABA Model Rule 5.2 denies the defense of superior orders to a subordinate lawyer ordered to behave unethically, but the second half of the rule states that a subordinate may defer to "a supervisory lawyer's reasonable resolution of an arguable question of professional duty." The problem is that the pressures on subordinate lawyers may lead them to misjudge when a question of professional duty is arguable and when the supervisor's resolution of it is reasonable. Remember the associate in the *Kodak* case, who "kept thinking there must be a reason" when he heard his supervisor perjure himself before a federal judge. This was not even close to an arguable question, and there's nothing reasonable about perjury—but the very fact that it was the associate's respected supervisor who committed, it undermined his own confidence that he

---

1 Steven Brill, *When a Lawyer Lies,* ESQUIRE, Dec. 19, 1979, at 23-24.

understood what was reasonable and what was not. When that happens, the defer to-your-boss-when-it's-reasonable half of the rule will seem more salient to the associate than the bright-line prohibition on wrongful obedience.[2]

In the spirit of the Bar Foundation, I want to see what we can learn about wrongful obedience from the most celebrated effort to study it scientifically—Stanley Milgram's experiments conducted at Yale thirty-five years ago. Even though these experiments are very well-known, I will begin by reminding you of what Milgram did and what he discovered.

Imagine, then, that you answer Milgram's newspaper advertisement, offering $20 if you volunteer for a one-hour psychology experiment.[3] When you enter the room, you meet the experimenter, dressed in a gray lab coat, and second volunteer, a pleasant, bespectacled middle-aged man. Unbeknownst to you, the second volunteer is, in reality, a confederate of the experimenter.

The experimenter explains that you will be participating in a study of the effect of punishment on memory and learning. One of you, the learner, will memorize word-pairs; the other, the teacher, will punish the learner with steadily-increasing electrical shocks each time he makes a mistake. The experimenter leads you to the shock-generator, a formidable machine with thirty switches, marked from 15 volts to 450. Above the voltages labels are printed. These range from "Slight Shock through "Danger: Severe Shock"; they culminate in an ominous-looking red label reading "XXX" above 435 and 450 volts. Both volunteers experience a 45-volt shock. Then they draw lots to determine their role. The drawing is rigged so that you become the teacher. The learner mentions that he has a mild heart problem, and the experimenter replies rather nonresponsively that the shocks will cause no permanent tissue damage. The learner is strapped into the hot seat, and the experiment gets underway.

The learner begins making mistakes, and as the shocks escalate he grunts in pain. Eventually he complains about the pain, and at 150 volts announces in some agitation that he wishes to stop the experiment. The man in the gray coat says only, "The experiment requires that you continue." As you turn up the juice, the learner begins screaming. Finally, he shouts out that he will answer no more questions. Unflapped, the experimenter instructs you to treat silences as wrong answers. You ask him who will take responsibility if the learner is injured, and he states that he will. You continue.

As the experiment proceeds, the agitated learner announces that his heart is starting to bother him. Again, you protest, and again the man in the lab coat replies, "The experiment requires that you continue." At 330 volts, the screams stop. The learner falls ominously silent, and remains silent until the bitter end—540 volts.

But it never actually gets to the bitter end, does it? You may be excused for thinking so. In a follow-up study, groups of people heard the Milgram setup described. They were asked to guess how many people would comply all the way to 450 volts, and to predict

---

[2] *See* Carol M. Rice, *The Superior Orders Defense in Legal Ethics: Sending the Wrong Message to Young Lawyers,* 32 WAKE FOREST L. REV. 887 (1997).

[3] Milgram actually offered $4, but this was in 1960 dollars.

whether they themselves would. People typically guessed that at most one teacher out of a thousand would comply—and no one believed that they themselves would.

In reality, 63 percent of subjects complied all the way. Moreover, this is a robust result: it holds in groups of women as well as men, and experimenters obtained comparable results in Holland, Spain, Italy, Australia, South Africa, Germany, and Jordan; indeed, the Jordanian experimenters replicated the 63 percent result not only among adults, but among seven-year-old children.

Milgram was flabbergasted. He and other researchers ran dozens of variations on the experiment, which I won't describe, although I'll mention some of them shortly. His battery of experiments, which lasted for years and ultimately involved more than a thousand subjects, stands even today as the most imaginative, ambitious, and controversial research effort ever undertaken by social psychologists. No one will ever undertake anything like it again, for three reasons that should be of interest to you, as patrons of social science research. First, so many commentators thought the experiments themselves were immoral (because of what they put the subjects through) that ethical rules on human experimentation were changed. There is no chance that Milgram would be allowed to conduct the experiments today.

Second, the experiments were extraordinarily expensive, at least by social psychology standards. The phony shock generator is not exactly a superconducting supercollider—it's actually more like a prop from *The Bride of Frankenstein*—but social psychology research doesn't attract big science dollars.[4] Third, and finally, deceptive social psychology experiments have become a victim of their own success. Today's subjects are more sophisticated than Milgram's: they expect to be duped. Their expectations are so likely to game the experiments, that today's researchers are pretty much compelled to devise strategy-proof, nondeceptive research programs.

The Milgram experiments place moral norms in conflict. One is what I'll call the *performance principle:* the norm of obeying authority, coupled with the norm of doing your job. The other is the *no-harm principle:* the prohibition on torturing, harming, and killing innocent people. In the abstract, we might think, only a sadist or a fascist would subordinate the no-harm principle to the performance principle. But the Milgram experiments seem to show that what we think in the abstract is dead wrong. As deans used to say in law school orientations, look to your left and look to your right. Two out of every three people in this room would electrocute you if a laboratory technician ordered them to.

The question is why. At this point, I'm going to run through several explanations of the Milgram results. None of them fully satisfies me. . . .

Each of these explanations focuses on a different aspect of human personality, and I'll label them accordingly. There is, first, Milgram's own explanation. He describes the mentality of compliant subjects as an *agentic state*—a state in which we view ourselves as mere agents or instruments of the man giving the orders. The terminology is entirely

---

[4] I am tempted to suggest funding as a materialist explanation for why social psychologists have turned to research on cognition, which can be done on the cheap with pencil-and-paper questionnaires.

familiar to lawyers, of course, because it is agency principles that govern the relationship between lawyer and client.

The problem with this explanation is that it merely relabels the question rather than answering it. *Why* do we turn off our consciences and "go agentic" when an authority figure starts giving us orders? Saying "because we enter an agentic state" is no answer; it's reminiscent of Moliere's physician, who explains that morphine makes us sleepy because it possesses a "dormative virtue."

Admittedly, Milgram's subjects usually offered the agentic explanation in their debriefing. But as we all know, "I was just following orders" is often an insincere rationalization. Even if the subjects offered it sincerely, we shouldn't accept it at face value, because people aren't very gifted at explaining our own behavior.

Indeed, one of Milgram's experiments dramatizes this fact. Many of Milgram's subjects insisted that they went along with the experiment only because the learner had consented. To test their explanation, Milgram ran a variation in which the learner expressly reserved the right to back out of the experiment whenever he wanted. He did this out loud, in the presence of the teacher and the experimenter. But even so, 40 percent of the subjects followed the experimenter's orders to the bitter end despite the learner's protests; three-fourths of the subjects proceeded long after the point where the learner withdrew his consent. We simply can't take subjects' own explanations for their obedience at face value.

If the *Agentic Personality* doesn't explain Milgram's results, how about the *Authoritarian Personality?* A group of researchers in the early 1950s devised a famous questionnaire to measure the cluster of personality traits that they believed characterize supporters of fascist regimes—traits that included an emotional need to submit to authority, but also an exaggerated and punitive interest in other people's sexuality, and a propensity to superstition and irrationalism. They called this measure the *F-scale—'F'* for fascist.

Interestingly, Milgram's compliant subjects had higher F-scores than his defiant subjects.[5] Indeed, isn't it mere common sense that authoritarians are more obedient to authority? Unfortunately, the answer is no. For one thing, subsequent research has largely discredited the authoritarian personality studies. The F-scale turns out to be a good predictor of racism but a bad predictor of everything else politically interesting about authoritarianism.[6] For another, people who volunteer for social psychology experiments are generally low-F, which makes Milgram's subjects, at best, atypical authoritarians.[7] For a third, high-F individuals typically mistrust science, so it rather begs the question to assume that they regard the experimenter as an authority. Finally, remember that the

[5] Alan C. Elms & Stanley Milgram, *Personality Characteristics Associated with Obedience and Defiance Toward Authoritative Command,* 2 J. EXPERIMENTAL RES. IN PERSONALITY 282 (1966).

[6] John J. Ray, *Why the F Scale Predicts Racism: A Critical Review,* 9 POLITICAL PSYCHOLOGY 671 (1988).

[7] It is unclear whether the compliant Milgram subjects were high-F compared with the population at large, or only compared with the defiant subjects. The latter alternative is fully compatible with the compliant subjects being normal, or even low-F, compared with the population at large.

F-scale measures other things besides emotional attachment to hierarchy. We might as well call high-F something other than the Authoritarian Personality: we might call it the Superstitious Personality, or even the Perverted Prude Personality. In that case, the explanation only raises new questions. Why should Perverted Prudes or believers in alien abduction be specially prone to obedience?

Some researchers, perhaps with the Perverted Prude in mind, argued that the true explanation for Milgram's results is the *Sadistic Personality:* The experimenter's orders remove our inhibitions and permit us to act on our repressed urge to hurt other people for pleasure.

The problem is that there is no evidence that we *have* such an urge. None of Milgram's compliant subjects seemed to take even the slightest pleasure in administering punishment, and many of them seemed downright agonized. They protested, they bit their lips until they bled, they broke into sweat or hysterical giggles. One went into convulsions. Milgram writes, "I observed a mature and initially poised businessman enter the laboratory smiling and confident. Within 20 minutes he was reduced to a twitching, stuttering wreck, who was rapidly approaching a point of nervous collapse. . . . At one point he pushed his fist into his forehead and muttered: 'Oh God, let's stop it.' And yet he continued to respond to every word of the experimenter, and obeyed to the end."[8] This hardly describes a sadist at work.

And, as it happens, the researchers who proposed the Sadistic Personality had an ax to grind.[9] They claimed, based on Rorschach tests done on the Nuremberg defendants and Adolf Eichmann, that every last one of the top Nazis was a psychopath. Like Professor Goldhagen today, they wanted to show that there was nothing ordinary about Hitler's executioners, nothing banal about Nazi evil. Their interest in Milgram seemed largely a competitive interest in shoring up their own theory of Nazism.

But their studies were flawed and their argument fallacious. Without interviews and other evidence of clinical pathology, Rorschach diagnoses are quack psychiatry; in any case, the researchers used a discredited method to analyze their Nazi Rorschachs. More basically, Rorschach diagnoses are based on deviations from statistical norms—and Milgram compliance *is* the statistical norm! To say in clinical terms that two-thirds of adults are sadists is arithmetically impossible, like saying that all the children are above average.[10]

A very different kind of explanation grows out of the cognitive psychology of the past three decades. Much of this research has revolved around the claim that we all rely on heuristics—rules of thumb—to make everyday judgments. Life is too short for us

---

[8] Stanley Milgram, *Behavioral Study of Obedience,* 67 J. Abnormal & Social Psych. 371, 375-77 (1963).

[9] Florence Miale & Michael Selzer, The Nuremberg Mind: The Psychology of the Nazi Leaders (1975); Michael Selzer, *The Murderous Mind,* N. Y. Times Magazine, Nov. 27, 1977, at 35-40.

[10] *See, e.g.,* Stephen W. Hurt et al., *The Rorschach,* in Integrative Assessment of Adult Personality (Larry E. Beutler & Michael R. Berren, eds., 1995), at 202; Eric Zillmer et al., in Integrative Assessment of Adult Personality, at 73-76, 94; 1 John E. Exner, Jr., The Rorschach: A Comprehensive System, Basic Foundations (1993), at 330.

to be Cartesian rationalists, thinking everything through to the bottom, and natural selection is not kind to Cartesian rationalists. Instead, evolution statistically favors creatures who make snap judgments by applying largely reliable rules.

One of these is what might be called the *Trust Authority* heuristic. And this suggests that what drives Milgram's compliant subjects is not the Agentic Personality, nor the Authoritarian Personality, nor the Sadistic Personality, but the *Trustful Personality.* Indeed, some of Milgram's subjects said in their debriefings that they went along with the experimenter because they were sure he knew what he was doing. Remember the *Berkey-Kodak* associate, who "kept thinking there must be a reason" for the partner to lie. Ordinarily, we do well to follow the Trust Authority heuristic, because authorities usually know better than lay people. At times, though, even the best heuristic fails—and Milgram devised one such situation.

This is a sophisticated explanation, but I think that Milgram's own data refutes it. In one experiment, Milgram pairs two experimenters with a naive subject who draws the role of teacher. One experimenter announces that a second volunteer, the learner, has canceled his appointment. After some discussion of how they are going to meet their experimental quota, one of the experimenters decides that he himself will take the learner's place, the other giving the orders. Like the learner in the basic setup, the experimenter in the hot seat begins complaining, and at 150 volts demands to be released. Indeed, he follows the entire schedule of complaints, screams, and ominous silence.

Surely, if subjects were relying on the Trust Authority heuristic, the fact that one of the authorities was demanding that the experiment stop should have diminished compliance.[11] Here, however, the usual two-thirds of the subjects complied to 450 volts. Apparently, it isn't deference to the experimenters' superior knowledge that promotes obedience.

Perhaps the most radical suggestion is that nothing in the subjects' personalities accounts for their compliance. The so-called situationist view holds that situational pressures, not personalities, account for human behavior. Indeed, situationists argue that attributing behavior to personality is one of the fundamental delusions to which human beings are prey—it is, in their terminology, the "fundamental attribution error." Situationists point out that small manipulations of Milgram's experimental setup are able to evoke huge swings in compliance behavior. For example, in some experiments Milgram placed the teacher on a team with other "teachers," who were actually actors working for Milgram. When the fellow teachers defied the experimenter, compliance plunged to 10 percent, but when they uncomplainingly delivered the shocks, compliance shot up to 90 percent. Obviously, variation like this arises from the situation, not from the subjects' personalities.[12]

---

[11] Indeed, in another version of the experiment, in which two experimenters disagreed about whether the teacher should go on shocking the volunteer learner, all of the "teachers" broke off the experiment.

[12] A clear and forceful statement of situationism may be found in LEE ROSS & RICHARD E. NISBETT, THE PERSON AND THE SITUATION: PERSPECTIVES OF SOCIAL PSYCHOLOGY (1991).

As a consequence, situationists argue that the only reliable predictor of how any given person will behave in a situation is the baseline rate for the entire population. The person's observable character traits are by and large irrelevant. But then why does anyone deviate from the majority behavior? This question is the Achilles heel of situationism. The other theories struggled to explain Milgram's two-thirds compliance rate. Situationists have to explain why one-third of the subjects defy the experimenter.

Their explanation is that people perceive situations differently from each other: the defiant minority simply must not perceive the experiment in the same way as the compliant majority.[13] Yet I find this explanation a little too convenient, particularly because there is no evidence to back it up. Just what do the defiant subjects perceive in the experiment that their compliant brethren perceive differently? Without an answer to this question, and evidence to support it, it seems to me that the situationist challenge fails.

And yet I agree that the key to understanding Milgram compliance lies in features of the experimental situation. The feature I want to focus on is the slippery-slope character of the electrical shocks. The teacher moves up the scale of shocks by 15-volt increments, and reaches the 450-volt level only at the thirtieth shock. This means that the subjects never confront the question, "Should I administer a 330-volt shock to the learner?" Their question is, "Should I administer a 330-volt shock to the learner *given that I've just administered a 315-volt shock?"* It seems clear that the latter question is much harder to answer. As Milgram himself pointed out, to conclude that administering the 330-volt shock is wrong is to admit that the 315-volt shock was probably wrong, and perhaps *all* the shocks were wrong.[14]

The theory of cognitive dissonance holds that when our actions conflict with our beliefs, the beliefs change to fit the action. We are all pro se defense lawyers in the court of conscience.[15] Cognitive dissonance theory suggests that when I have given the learner a series of electrical shocks, I simply won't view giving the next shock as a wrongful act, because I won't admit to myself that the previous shocks were wrong.

Let me examine this line of thought in more detail. Moral decision-making requires more than adhering to sound principles, like the no-harm principle. It also requires good judgment, by which I mean knowing which actions violate a moral principle and which do not. Every lawyer understands the difference between good principles and good judgment—it is the difference between knowing a rule of law and being able to apply it to particular cases. As Kant first pointed out, you can't teach good judgment through general rules, because we already need judgment to know how rules apply. Judgment is therefore always and irredeemably particular.

---

[13] *Id.* at 11-13.

[14] STANLEY MILGRAM, OBEDIENCE TO AUTHORITY (1974) at 149.

[15] I take the lawyer metaphor from Roderick M. Kramer & David M. Messick, *Ethical Cognition and the Framing of Organizational Dilemmas: Decision Makers as Intuitive Lawyers,* in CODES OF CONDUCT: BEHAVIORAL RESEARCH INTO BUSINESS ETHICS (David M. Messick & Ann E. Tenbrunsel, eds., 1996), at 59.

Let's assume that most of Milgram's subjects do accept the no-harm principle and agree in the abstract that it outweighs the performance principle. *They still need good judgment to know at what point the electrical shocks violate the no-harm principle.* Virtually no one thinks that the slight tingle of a 15-volt shock violates the no-harm principle: if it did, medical researchers would violate the no-harm principle every time they take blood samples from volunteers. Only two of Milgram's thousand subjects refused to give any shocks at all.

But how can 30 volts violate the no-harm principle if 15 volts didn't? And if a 3D-volt shock doesn't violate the no-harm principle, neither does a shock of 45 volts. Of course we know that slippery slope arguments like this are bad logic. At some point, the single grains of sand really do add up to a heap, and at some point shocking the learner really should shock the conscience as well. But it takes good judgment to know where that point lies. Unfortunately, cognitive dissonance generates enormous psychic pressure to deny that our previous obedience may have violated a fundamental moral norm. That denial requires us to gerrymander the boundaries of the no-harm principle so that the shocks we've already delivered don't violate it. However, once we've smudged the bright line, it becomes virtually impossible to judge that the next shock, only imperceptibly more intense, crosses the border from the permissible to the forbidden. By luring us into higher and higher level shocks, one micro-step at a time, the Milgram experiments gradually and subtly disarm our ability to distinguish right from wrong. Milgram's subjects never need to lose, even for a second, their faith in the no-harm principle. Instead, they lose their capacity to recognize that administering an agonizing electrical shock violates it.

What I am offering here is a *corruption-of-judgment* explanation of the Milgram experiments. The road to Hell turns out to be a slippery slope, and the travelers on it really do have good intentions—they "merely" suffer from bad judgment. The corruption-of-judgment theory fits in well with one of the other classic experiments of social psychology—Freedman and Fraser's 1966 demonstration of the so-called foot-in-the-door effect. A researcher posing as a volunteer asks homeowners for permission to erect a large, very ugly "Drive Carefully!" sign in their front yards. The researcher shows the homeowners a photo of a pleasant-looking home completely obscured by the sign. Unsurprisingly, most homeowners refuse the request—indeed, the only real surprise is that 17 percent agree to take the sign.

Within one subset of homeowners, however, three out of four agree to take the sign. What makes these homeowners different? Just one thing: two weeks previously, they had agreed to place a small, inconspicuous Be A Safe Driver sticker in their windows. Apparently, once the public service foot insinuated itself in the door, the entire leg followed.[16] Perhaps what is surprising is only that such a small foot could provide an opening for such a large leg. The slippery slope from sound judgment to skewed judgment is a lot steeper than we may have suspected.

---

[16] Jonathan L. Freedman & Scott C. Fraser, "Compliance without Pressure: The Foot-in-the-Door Technique," 4 *J. Personality & Social Psych.* 195 (1966).

Let me conclude by returning to the *Berkey-Kodak* case and seeing what light the corruption-of-judgment theory may shed on it. The theory suggests that we should find the partner's and associate's misdeeds at the end of a slippery slope, beginning with lawful adversarial deception and culminating with lies, perjury, and wrongful obedience. Following this lead, one fact leaps out at us: *the misdeeds occurred near the end of a high-stakes discovery process.*

Every litigator knows that discovery is one of the most contentious parts of civil litigation. Civil discovery is like a game of Battleship. One side calls out its shots—it files discovery request—and the other side must announce when a shot scores a hit. It makes that announcement by turning over a document. There are two big differences. First, unlike Battleship, it isn't always clear when a shot has scored a hit. Lawyers get to argue about whether their document really falls within the scope of the request. They can argue that the request was too broad, or too narrow, or that the document is privileged, or is attorney work product. Second, unlike Battleship, lawyers don't get to peek at the opponent's card after the game. When the opponent concludes that a shot missed her battleship, she makes the decision ex parte—she doesn't have to announce it to her adversary, who may never learn that a smoking-gun document (the battleship) was withheld based on a debatable legal judgment.

Every litigation associate goes through a rite of passage: She finds a document that seemingly lies squarely within the scope of a legitimate discovery request, but her supervisor tells her to devise an argument for excluding it. As long as the argument isn't frivolous, there is nothing improper about this, but it marks the first step onto the slippery slope. For better or for worse, a certain kind of innocence is lost. It is the moment when withholding information, despite an adversary's reasonable request, starts to feel like zealous advocacy rather than cheating. It is the moment when the no-deception principle encoded in Model Rule 8.4(c)[17] gets gerrymandered away from its plain meaning. But like any other piece of elastic, the no-deception principle loses its grip if it is stretched too often. Soon, if the lawyer isn't very careful, every damaging request seems too broad or too narrow; every smoking-gun document is either work product or privileged; no adversary ever has a right to "my" documents. At that point the fatal question is not far away: *Is lying really so bad when it is the only way to protect my documents from an adversary who has no right to them?* If legitimate advocacy marks the beginning of this particular slippery slope, *Berkey-Kodak* lies at its end.

I certainly don't mean to suggest that corruption of judgment is inevitable in organizations or in the adversary system. But neither do I have a fail-safe remedy to protect lawyers from the optical illusions of the spirit that adversarial ethics, authority, and cognitive dissonance engender. Perhaps the best protection is understanding the illusions themselves, their pervasiveness, the insidious way they work on us.

One of Milgram's compliant subjects wrote him a year after the experiment,

---

[17] The rule reads: "It is professional misconduct for a lawyer to engage in conduct involving dishonesty, fraud, deceit or misrepresentation."

> What appalled me was that I could possess this capacity for obedience and compliance to a central idea, . . . even at the expense of another value, i.e., don't hurt someone else who is helpless and not hurting you. As my wife said, "You can call yourself Eichmann."[18]

It's hard to believe that this man will obey orders unreflectively in the future.

Although I've argued that wrongful obedience has roots deep within human nature, I don't mean to suggest that this lets anyone off the hook. The temptation to obey is like any other temptation. It is perfectly natural to give in to it—that's why they call it temptation!—but of course being perfectly natural excuses nothing. There's a story about a politician caught taking a bribe who announced at his press conference, "My constituents would be ashamed of me if I turned down so much money for such a small favor!"—as if resisting temptation is irrational if only it's tempting enough. But he was confused: We don't excuse a politician for taking a bribe just because it's a million dollars rather than a hundred.[19]

The point is that to understand all is emphatically not to forgive all. But if I am right, to understand all may well put us on guard against doing the unforgivable. Social science needs no higher justification than that.

---

[18] MILGRAM, OBEDIENCE TO AUTHORITY, at 54.

[19] On this point, see Ferdinand Schoeman, *Statistical Norms and Moral Attributions,* in RESPONSIBILITY, CHARACTER, AND THE EMOTIONS 287 (Ferdinand Schoeman ed., 1987); HANNAH ARENDT, EICHMANN IN JERUSALEM: A REPORT ON THE BANALITY OF EVIL 295 (rev. ed. 1963) ("[S]ome American literati have professed the naive belief that temptation and coercion are really the same thing, that no one can be asked to resist temptation. . . . [W]hen so much money is at stake, who could possibly resist?").

The Enron Board: The Perils of Groupthink[*]

Marleen A. O'Connor[**]

One Enron director could have made a difference.

—William Patterson, AFL-CIO[1]

INTRODUCTION

The Enron debacle is one of the United States' most disastrous business failures.[2] One of the striking features of Enron's collapse was the firm's abrupt and dramatic transformation from what appeared to be a very prosperous company to a bankrupt enterprise in less than three months. Wall Street uniformly portrayed Enron as a successful corporation that had transitioned from an old-economy energy company to a high-tech global enterprise. Specifically, from 1998 to 2000, Enron's gross revenues rose from $31 billion to more than $100 billion, making it the seventh largest company by

** Professor, Stetson University College of Law; Associate Director, International Institute for Corporate Governance and Accountability, George Washington University Law School; oconnor@law.stetson.edu. I would like to thank William Bratton, Stephen Bainbridge, Claire Dickerson, and Jill Fisch for their insightful comments. I would also like to thank Sharon Gisclair for her word processing support and Pam Burdett for her library assistance.

1 Matthew Benjamin, *Cardboard Board,* U.S. NEWS & W. RPT., Apr. 18, 2002, at 28, 30.

2 For a detailed history and examination of the causes of the fall of Enron, *see, e.g.,* William W. Bratton, *Enron and the Dark Side of Shareholder Value,* 76 TUL. L. REV. 1275 (2002). For other articles on the corporate governance aspects of Enron, see Samuel Bodily & Robert F. Bruner, Enron, 2001 (Graduate School of Business Administration, University of Virginia 2002); Lawrence Cunningham, *Sharing Accounting's Burden: Business Lawyers in Enron's Dark Shadows* (Boston College Working Paper 2002); Jeffrey N. Gordon, *What Enron Means for the Management and Control of the Modern Business Corporation: Some Initial Reflections,* 69 U. CHI. L. REV. 1233 (2002); Faith Stevelman Kahn, *Bombing Markets, Subverting the Rule of Law: Enron, Financial Fraud, and September 11, 2001,* 76 TUL. L. REV. 1579 (2002); *Panel Discussion: Enron: What Went Wrong?,* 8 FORD. J. CORP. & FIN. L. S1 (2002).

market capitalization of the Fortune 500.[3] In October 2001, however, Enron shocked Wall Street by revealing a $544 million charge to earnings and a $1.2 billion reduction of shareholder equity. Investor confidence plummeted when the media reported that the charge and write-down stemmed from transactions with partnerships that Enron's Chief Financial Officer controlled.[4] One month later, market faith collapsed when Enron acknowledged that the transactions with the related-party partnerships allowed Enron to inflate its earnings for the last five years and keep billions of dollars of contingent liabilities off its balance sheet.[5] The decline in Enron's stock price caused credit rating agencies to downgrade their assessments of Enron. Within weeks, this crisis of confidence led Enron to file bankruptcy.[6] As a result of Enron's collapse, thousands of employees lost their jobs and retirement savings,[7] while shareholders lost billions of dollars.

---

[3] *See, e.g.*, Bethany McLean, *Why Enron Went Bust*, FORTUNE, Dec. 24, 2001, at 32.

[4] For a detailed description of how these related-party transactions worked, *see* Bratton, *supra* note 2; Kurt Eichenwald, *Deal at Enron Gave Insiders Fast Fortunes*, N.Y. TIMES, Feb. 5, 2002, at A1.

In brief, Enron used many Special Purpose Entities (SPEs), through which the transferor transfers an asset to the SPE in exchange for payment other than SPE equity. The SPE usually raises the money to pay for the asset through outside borrowing or providing the transferor with its own note. Firms using SPEs are not required to consolidate these entities on their financial statements providing that (1) an outside investor funds at least three percent of the SPE's equity (2) the transferor does not "control" the SPE, and (3) the transferor gives an opinion concerning the "bankruptcy remote" status of SPE. In one case, Chewco, Enron could not find a three percent equity investor to replace CalPERS. This led Jeffrey Skilling, the CEO at Enron for the first six months of 2001, to use a hidden loan by Enron to fund the Chewco equity. In the fall of 2001, Enron recognized that Chewco did not qualify for nonconsolidation, decreasing Enron's earnings by $405 million and raising its liabilities by $628 million. To solve the equity problem that arose in Chewco, Fastow set up two related-party partnerships, LJM1 and LJM2, to serve as the three percent outside equity investor in SPEs set up by Enron. Many of the transactions with these related-party partnerships were used to manipulate Enron's reported earnings.

Many firms frequently use SPEs as vehicles for off-balance sheet securitization of financial assets such as accounts receivables. Thus, we need to take caution in any reform of these vehicles post-Enron. *See, e.g.*, Steven L. Schwarcz, *Enron and the Use and Abuse of Special Purpose Entities in Corporate Structures*, 70 U. CIN. L. REV. 1309 (2002).

[5] On November 8, Enron issued restated earnings disclosing that "financial statements for these periods and the audit reports relating to the year-end financial statements for 1997 through 2000 should not be relied upon." BODILY & BRUNNER, *supra* note 2, at 39. Enron revealed that the restatement was necessary to correct accounting errors connected with the $1.2 billion write down in shareholder's equity and to consolidate three off-balance sheet entities. *Id.* On November 19, Enron filed its third quarter earnings report with the SEC; three items shocked Wall Street as well as Dynegy, a possible merger partner. First, Enron owed $690 million to a partnership as a result of Enron's lower credit rating. Second, Enron had less funds than forecasted. Third, Enron would owe $3.9 billion from other partnerships if its credit rating fell further. Enron warned that fourth-quarter earnings would be less than expected. On November 28, rating agencies downgraded Enron to "junk status" and the deal was off with Dynegy. *Id.*

[6] *See, e.g.*, Wendy Zellner & Stephanie Anderson Forest, *The Fall of Enron*, BUS. WK., Dec. 17, 2001, at 33.

[7] On October 17, 2001, Enron management locked down its 401(k) plan for employees, which had been sixty percent invested in Enron stock. Despite the fact that employees were not allowed to sell the

This article concentrates on the Enron Board's role in the scandal for three reasons. First, although Enron was one of numerous recent corporate meltdowns,[8] it captured the public's attention in a unique way.[9] That is, Enron serves as a "perfect storm"[10] metaphor that the checks and balances in the American system of corporate governance are not working the way they should. Second, although other corporate watchdogs failed in Enron, the board serves as the primary protection in the corporate governance system.[11] Analysis of the Enron Board's role, however, has implications to understand the lack of diligence by other corporate gatekeepers such as analysts,[12] auditors,[13] outside counsel,

---

declining Enron stock, officers and directors are accused of unloading $1 billion over a three-year period. *See, e.g.*, Reed Abelson, *Enron Board Comes Under A Storm of Criticism*, N.Y. TIMES, Dec. 16, 2001, at BU4; Leslie Wayne, *Before Debacle, Enron Insiders Cashed in $1.1 Billion in Shares*, N.Y. TIMES, Jan. 13, 2002, at A1.

[8] Other scandals, such as Waste Management, Sunbeam, and Cendant, preceded Enron and others followed, such as *Global Crossing, Audits & Bubbles*, THE WASHINGTON POST, Feb. 3, 2002, at B.06 [hereinafter Audits & Bubbles] (bankrupt after booking long-term contracts as revenue immediately); Tyco, *see, e.g.*, Ellen Simon, *Tyco's Directors Could Sue Ex-CEO*, THE STAR-LEDGER, July 7, 2002 (former CEO Dennis Kozlowski accused of using company money to buy paintings, a New York apartment, and a house; directors accused of acting like "lapdogs."); George Mannes, *Adelphia Filing Details Intricate Financial Web, at* www.TheStreet.com (May 24, 2002) (directors unaware of related-party transactions); WorldCom, reports on new scandal, the WorldCom's fraud—the largest in corporate history, dealt with a simple accounting issue; they capitalized $3.8 billion in expenses. The fraud later turned out to be $7.1 billion. *See, e.g.*, Elisabeth Douglass et al., *Global Crossing Hurt by Board's Cronyism*, LOS ANGELES TIMES, Feb. 24, 2002, at C1 (board compromised by cronyism and chronic instability; in last three years thirty directors on board ranging from eight to seventeen members).

[9] For perceptive discussion of the public's sustained outrage over Enron, *see* Cheryl Wade, *Comparisons Between Enron and Other Types of Misconduct: Compliance with Law and Ethical Decision Making as the Best Form of Public Relations*, 1 SEATTLE J. SOC. JUS. 97 (2002) (comparing public reaction to Enron to corporate misdeeds involving harms from tobacco, the Ford/Firestone controversy, and racial discrimination at Texaco).

[10] Many commentators have used this phrase to refer to the proliferation of corporate scandals. *See, e.g.*, John A. Byrne et al., *How to Fix Corporate Governance,* BUS. WK., May 6, 2002, at 68.

[11] Congressional hearings reported: "[Enron] represents a colossal failure of virtually every mechanism that is supposed to provide checks and balances on which the integrity of our capital markets depend. And in that system, the board of directors is supposed to provide the first line of defense by overseeing the conduct of management." FINANCIAL COLLAPSE OF ENRON CORPORATION: HEARING BEFORE THE SUBCOMM. ON OVERSIGHT & INVESTIGATIONS OF THE COMM. ON ENERGY & COMMERCE, 107th Cong. 7 (2002), *available at* http://energycommerce.house.gov/107/action/107-88.pdf. [hereinafter Enron Hearings].

[12] For criticism of the role of analysts in pumping up Enron's stock prices, *see, e.g.*, Joseph Fuller & Michael C. Jensen, *Just Say No to Wall Street* (Harvard Business School Working paper 2002), available at http://ssrn.com; Leslie Wayne, *Congress' Scrutiny Shifts to Wall Street and Its Enron Role*, N.Y. TIMES, Feb. 19, 2002, at A1.

[13] *See, e.g.*, Sean M. O'Connor, *The Inevitability of Enron and the Impossibility of "Auditor Independence" Under the Current Audit System* (Working Paper 2002), available at http://ssrn.com; Robert A. Prentice, *The Case of the Irrational Auditor: A Behavioral Insight Into Securities Fraud Litigation*, 95 NW. U. L. REV. 133 (2005).

institutional investors,[14] credit rating agencies,[15] journalists, investment bankers, and regulators. Finally, subsequent investigations of the Enron Board provide detailed documentation about the specifics of the Enron Board's decision making processes, providing a rare glimpse into actual boardroom dynamics.[16] These accounts suggest that a significant factor contributing to Enron's demise was the Enron Board's approval of and failure to monitor the related-party transactions.[17] Although the Enron Board's waivers of the company's ethics code to allow these deals were unusual events, the

[14] Diana B. Henriques, *CalPERS Knew of Problem But Kept Silent*, N.Y. TIMES, Feb. 5, 2002, at 1. CalPERS board's also had conflicts of interest—five members of the board owned stock also owned by CalPERS and received political campaign contributions from companies in which they invested. Sharon L. Crenson & Martha Mendoza, *Problems at Pension Fund Giant*, MARKET NEWS INT'L, July 18, 2002.

[15] *See, e.g.*, Patrick Caragata, *Protecting Public Confidence in the Market Place*, 10 BOARDROOM, July/ August 2002, at 1 (through Oct. 2001, Goldman Sachs, CSFB, UBS Warburg, and Salomon Smith Barney rated Enron a "strong buy"; Merrill Lynch rated Enron a "buy.").

[16] We know little about what actually goes on in boardrooms because minutes of board meetings are not publicly available. DEL. CODE. ANN. TIT. 8, § 220 (shareholders can inspect corporate records if they show proper purpose). In the future, institutional shareholders may use these types of statutes to make directors more accountable.

Thus, I use Enron for this case study because of information available in the Powers Report, Congressional hearings, and the Senate Report. *See infra* note 17. Congress is currently evaluating the boards of other scandals.

[17] *See, e.g.*, WILLIAM POWERS JR., BOARD OF DIRECTORS OF ENRON, REPORT OF THE SPECIAL INVESTIGATIVE COMMITTEE OF ENRON (Feb. 1, 2002) [hereinafter Powers Report], *available at* http://news.findlaw.com/hdocs/docs/enron/sicreport; SENATE GOVERNMENTAL AFFAIRS COMMITTEE, THE ROLE OF THE ENRON BOARD IN THE COLLAPSE OF ENRON CORPORATION 1 (May 7, 2002); U.S. SENATE PERMANENT SUBCOMMITTEE ON INVESTIGATIONS, THE ROLE OF THE BOARD OF DIRECTORS IN ENRON'S COLLAPSE (Report 107-70, July 8, 2002) [hereinafter Senate Report].

William Bratton provides a subtle and complex account of the fall of Enron that includes the related-party transactions in conjunction with three factors. Bratton, *supra* note 2. First, Bratton explains that the Enron SPEs involved funding with Enron's own stock in return for debt instruments of the SPEs. The proper accounting treatment required an increase in shareholders' equity as the notes were paid. Enron, however, booked the notes issued by the SPEs as assets on its balance sheet and increased its shareholders' equity immediately. This improper accounting led Enron to reduce shareholders' equity by $1.2 billion. *Id.*

Second, Enron's "asset-light strategy" involved forming SPEs with Enron's own stock as a fall back. Specifically, Enron used LJM-related SPEs as counterparties in equity swaps, so that if the stock Enron held in its merchant portfolio decreased, the SPEs would have to pay Enron. When Enron's stock price fell, Enron was issuing its own common stock to cover its income statement loss. Bratton notes: "This one may not do under the most basic rules of accounting, indeed, under the most basic rules of capitalism." *Id.* Enron executives concealed this series of transactions from the Board. *Id.*

Third, as Enron's stock declined beginning October, 2001, contract contingencies began to trigger $4 billion of off balance sheet debt. Enron did not disclose this debt until November, 19, 2001; this led to credit agencies downgrading Enron. *Id.*

In summarizing the fall of Enron, Bratton explains: "Had Enron suffered no reverses in its basic business and no crisis of confidence, the contingencies respecting the $4 billion of obligations that pushed Enron into Chapter 11 might never have occurred. . . . We can pare down the account by coupling the crisis of confidence and the hidden $4 billion of obligations as primary causes." *Id.*

Enron Board's actions serve as a case study of boardroom politics that may influence other corporate boards to varying degrees.[18]

This article responds to a question many commentators have debated in the aftermath of Enron: How could the Board let it happen? Why was the Enron Board fooled by the emperor's new clothes? The Enron Board consisted of experienced and intelligent people.[19] The Enron directors followed many of the best practices for good corporate governance, achieving acclaim as one of the five best boards in corporate America.[20] In addition, corporate commentators hailed the landmark decision of *Smith v. Van Gorkom*[21] as requiring independent directors to ask management hard questions.[22] So why did the Enron Board neglect to make these inquiries despite the presence of significant red flags? Why were these sophisticated, bright directors duped by such objectively defective proposals? Have the best practices of corporate governance been more myth than reality?

To understand the Enron Board's role in the firm's demise, this article examines the literature from social psychology on small group decision making.[23] In the last few years, corporate governance scholars have turned away from the dominance of neoclassical economics toward social psychology to focus on how cognitive imperfections such as ego and self-deception distort decision making. Although social psychology depends

---

[18] *See, e.g.*, Benjamin, *supra* note 1 (Ken Bertsch of TIAA-CREF stating that Enron suggests boards may still serve as rubber stamps); Ralph Whitworth, *Self-Governance in the Wake of Enron: What Must Change*, DIRECTORS' MONTHLY, July 2002, at 13-14 (same).

[19] The Enron Board consisted of fourteen directors; Robert Belfer (since 1983); Norman Blake (since 1993); Ronnie Chan (since 1996); John Duncan (since 1985); Wendy Gramm (since 1993); Robert Jaedicke (since 1985); Kenneth Lay (since 1985); Charles Lemistre (since 1985); John Mendelson (since 1999); Paul Perraz Pereira (since 1995); Frank Savage (since 1999); Jeffrey Skilling (since 1997); John Wakeham (since 1994); Herbert Winokur (since 1985). Enron Proxy Statement (Mar. 27, 2001), *available at* http://edgar-online.com. Ken Lay was Board chairman and CEO; Jeffrey Skilling was a board member from 1997 until August 2001, when he resigned from Enron. The Enron Board consisted of one Asian American woman, one Hispanic man, one Asian man, and one African American man. The Enron directors had impressive qualifications: former chairperson of the executive committee of Gulf & Western, Industries; former chairperson of the U.S. Commodity Futures Trading Commission; former Secretary of State for Energy of the United Kingdom; Professor of Accounting and former Dean of the Stanford Business School. Enron Proxy Statement (2000), *available at* www.edgar-online.com.

[20] Thomas R. Horton, *Groupthink in the Boardroom*, SOME THINGS CONSIDERED 9, Winter, 2002.

[21] 488 A.2d 858 (Del. 1985) (directors breached due care by approving decision to sell company in a two-hour meeting, held on short notice, relying only on oral report from CEO and failing to ask questions). For a recent symposium on this case *see Symposium: Van Gorkom and the Corporate Board: Problem, Solution, or Placebo?*, 96 NW. U. L. REV. 447 (2002).

[22] *See, e.g.*, Lynne Stout, *In Praise of Procedure: An Economic and Behavioral Defense of Smith v. Van Gorkom and the Business Judgment Rule*, 96 NW. L. REV. 675, 690 (2002).

[23] The behavioral law and economics movement relies on much of the literature in social psychology. For a general overview of behavioral law and economics, *see* BEHAVIORAL LAW AND ECONOMICS (Cass R. Sunstein ed., 2000); Donald Langevoort, *Behavioral Theories of Judgment and Decision Making in Legal Scholarship: A Literature Overview*, 51 VAND. L. REV. 1499 (1998); Christine Jolls et al., *A Behavioral Approach to Law and Economics*, 50 STAN. L. REV. 1471 (1998).

on laboratory studies that may not fully approximate real world settings,[24] this research offers a much more realistic approach than the rational actor model for evaluating the role of directors. Social psychology shows that groups are generally better than individuals in making many of the types of decisions made by boards. This research also reveals, however, that groups can suffer from behavioral defects similar to those that affect individuals. While human frailties are magnified in groups, groups can also succumb to their own distinct patterns of cognitive faults.[25]

Using the lens of social psychology, this article seeks to shed light on the debate about whether the recent corporate scandals involve only "a few bad apples" or whether corporate governance is "rotten to the core."[26] Without empirical data, we cannot know whether either position has validity. In the absence of statistical evidence, this article surmises that both explanations are inadequate. On the one hand, we should not accept the story that there are only "a few bad apples," given the proliferation of corporate meltdowns and the widespread knowledge required within many of the corporations for the problems to occur. On the other hand, we need to resist the cynical view that most corporate actors are corrupt. Although the scandals appear to involve some greedy, deceptive individuals, we should not generalize their motivations to others in the corporate governance system.

Social psychology teaches that people are fallible. Specifically, good corporate actors can make bad decisions when placed in certain situations. They can do so without guilt, however, because self-serving biases allow them to rationalize their behavior to maintain self-esteem.[27] Societal and corporate norms foster this rationalization process so that corporate actors can continue to think of themselves as honorable people. This perspective explains why many boards have learned to go through the motions of good corporate procedures, but nevertheless continue to fail to challenge managers when necessary. Although actors falling under the influences of cognitive defects may be less morally blameworthy than first appears, behavioral biases should not serve as a legal defense for poor behavior. This would allow genuinely corrupt actors to assert disingenuous defenses that courts would not be able to distinguish from those involving honest, good faith behavior. Rather, an understanding of cognitive biases is useful in evaluating the potential of corporate governance reforms to change the dysfunctional norms present in some boardrooms. Specifically, effective reform requires not only

---

[24] *See, e.g.*, Jennifer Arlen, *The Future of Behavioral Economics of Law*, S. VAND. L. REV. 1765 (1998).

[25] Donald C. Langevoort, *Taking Myths Seriously: An Essay for Lawyers*, 74 CHG.-KENT L. REV. 1569, 1577 (2000) [hereinafter Langevoort, *Myths*] (noting the relationship is controversial).

[26] *See* Cover, *The Crisis in Corporate Governance*, BUS. WEEK, May 6, 2002, http://www.businessweek.com/magazine/toc/02_18/B3781govern.htm; Cover, *Wall Street: How Corrupt is it?*, BUS. WEEK, May 13, 2002, http://www.businessweek.com/magazine/toc/02_19/B3782magazine.htm.

[27] For an overview of issues pertaining to corporate morality, *see, e.g.*, Donald C. Langevoort, *Organized Illusions: A Behavioral Theory of Why Corporations Mislead Stock Market Investors (and Cause Other Social Harms)*, 146 U. PA. L. REV. 101 (1997) [hereinafter Langevoort, *Illusions*].

implementing new procedures, but also eliminating the behavioral barriers that jeopardize their effectiveness.

This article uses social psychology to build a case study for how the Enron Board may have been affected by a significant impediment to group deliberation called "groupthink." As this article explains in more detail below, Irving Janis, the creator of this theory, described groupthink as "a mode of thinking that people engage in when they are deeply involved in a cohesive in-group, when the members' striving for unanimity overrides their motivation to realistically appraise alternative courses of actions."[28] According to Janis, groupthink causes members of a group to unconsciously generate shared illusions of superiority that hinder critical reflection and reality testing.[29] For these reasons, groupthink leads groups to make faulty judgments. With an understanding of groupthink, we can see that the Enron Board did not prevent the Enron debacle because of psychological processes that lead cohesive boards to avoid seriously scrutinizing managerial policy. Thus, examination of the cognitive factors surrounding the Enron Board's decision making is significant because such human foibles may affect other corporate boards.[30]

Part I provides background by reviewing the role of the board of directors in light of the social psychology literature on group decision making. This Part details how several of the requirements needed to obtain the optimal benefits from peer group decision making are not present in some boardrooms. Specifically, despite reforms to include more independent directors on corporate boards, CEOs retain much influence over board decision making. Even in the absence of this dominance, however, information

---

[28] IRVING JANIS, VICTIMS OF GROUPTHINK 78 (1978) [hereinafter JANIS, VICTIMS]. For other literature on groupthink *see, e.g.*, IRVING JANIS, GROUPTHINK (1982); IRVING JANIS, GROUPTHINK: PSYCHOLOGICAL STUDIES OF POLICY DECISIONS AND FIASCOES (1982); Irving Janis & Leon Mann, *Decision-Making Context, in Decision Making* (1977); Won-Woo Park, *A Review of Research on Groupthink*, 3 J. OF BEH. DECISION MAKING 203 (1987); Jeanne Longley & Dean G. Pruitt, *Groupthink: A Critique of Janis's Theory*, in 1 REV. OF PERSONALITY AND SOC. PSYCHOL. 74 (1980); R. Aldag & S. Fuller, *Beyond Fiasco: A Reappraisal of the Groupthink Phenomenon and a New Model of Group Decision Processes*, 3 PSYCHOL. BULL. 113 (1993); Richard Cline, *Detecting Groupthink: Methods for Observing the Illusion of Unanimity*, 2 COMM. Q. 38 (1990); Ronald Sims, *Linking Groupthink to Unethical Behavior in Organizations*, 11 J. BUS. ETHICS 651 (1992); Peter Tetlock et al., *Assessing Political Group Dynamics: A Test of the Groupthink Model*, 3 J. PERSONALITY & SOC. PSYCHOL. 63 (1992); Matt Turner et al., *Threat, Cohesion, and Group Effectiveness: Testing a Social Identity Maintenance Perspective on Groupthink*, 5 J. PERSONALITY & SOC. PSYCHOL. 63 (1992); Christopher Neck & Gregory Moorhead, *Groupthink Remodeled: The Importance of Leadership, Time Pressure, and Methodical Decision-Making Procedures*, 48 HUM. REL. 537 (1995).

[29] JANIS, VICTIMS, *supra* note 28, at 68.

[30] Several corporate scholars have noted that groupthink is prevalent in boardrooms. *See, e.g.*, James D. Cox & Harry L. Munsinger, *Bias in the Boardroom: Psychological Foundations and Legal Implications of Corporate Cohesion*, 48 J.L. & CONTEMP. PROBS. 82, 99 (Summer 1985); Jayne Barnard, *Institutional Investors and the New Corporate Governance*, 69 N.C. L. REV. 1135 (1991). As one corporate governance commentator remarks: "It's always been interesting to me that you take these intelligent, accomplished, honorable people, and somehow you put them around a boardroom table and their IQ points drop 50 percent and their spines fly out the room." *All Things Considered, Nell Minow Discusses How Companies Can Restore Investor Confidence* (NPR radio broadcast, July 2, 2002).

constraints diminish director's ability to perform their monitoring role. Specifically, social psychology warns that even the most honest, hard-working, independent directors may inevitably lack the psychological objectivity necessary to scrutinize managerial policy. With this perspective, Part I analyzes how rising stock prices may create a more difficult situation for corporate governance to address (and are thus potentially more dangerous) than declining stock prices. Indeed, the recent corporate scandals suggest that a bubble stock market may lull boards into a false sense of security.

Although this article focuses on the problem of groupthink, Part II examines two related, but distinct, negative aspects of group decision making called "polarization" and "cascades." Polarization refers to the strong tendency of like-minded people deliberating in groups to move toward extreme consequences.[31] Specifically, polarization shows that groups make riskier decisions than those made by individuals acting alone. A cascade involves a process whereby an entire group quickly comes to share a view, which may be false, because some people in the group appear to accept the belief. While polarization and cascades are helpful in developing a fuller account of board deliberations, this article maintains that groupthink may more accurately reflect the social dynamics of the Enron Board's failure to properly monitor the related-party transactions. Each of these theories, however, is a form of "group-mindlessness," that is, a process whereby persons adjust their behavior in response to their impressions of other group members. Thus, polarization, cascades, and groupthink may have each contributed to the Enron Board's decisions regarding the related-party transactions. Social psychology emphasizes that when several factors come together, they can multiply group biases so that the effect is much greater than simply adding the factors together.[32]

Part III presents the case study of how groupthink by Enron's board contributed to dramatically negative business consequences. In applying the groupthink theory, this Part analyzes evidence about the Enron's board's deliberations found in the Report Prepared by the U.S. Senate Permanent Subcommittee on Investigations (Senate Report),[33] Enron's Special Committee (Powers Report),[34] and Congressional hearings. These investigations reveal that the Enron directors "were as surprised as anyone by the company's collapse."[35] Indeed, it appears that the Enron Board was one of the last to know about the firm's problems.[36] Likewise, in many other business failures, execu-

[31] For discussion of polarization in the corporate law literature, *see, e.g.*, John C. Coffee, Jr., *No Soul to Damn: No Body to Kick: An Unscandalized Inquiry Into the Problem of Corporate Punishment*, 79 MICH. L. REV. 386, 395 (1981); Lynne L. Dallas, *The Relational Board: Three Theories of Corporate Boards of Directors*, 22 J. CORP. L. 1 (1996) [hereinafter Dallas, *Relational*]; Cass Sunstein, *Deliberative Trouble? Why Groups Go to Extremes*, 110 YALE L.J. 71 (2000).

[32] COX & MUNSINGER, *supra* note 30, at 104.

[33] SENATE REPORT, *supra* note 17.

[34] POWERS REPORT, *supra* note 17.

[35] SENATE REPORT, *supra* note 17, at 12.

[36] RALPH NADER ET AL., TAMING THE GIANT CORPORATION 17 (1976) (compare the board to "cuckolds" who are "often the last to know when the dominant partner—management—has done something illicit.").

tives explain that they could not comprehend how they could let it happen; that is, they felt swept along in disregarding warning signs and believing irrational predictions. Groupthink explains how and why this happens.

Part IV discusses the reforms recently passed by the New York Stock Exchange (NYSE) to improve board decision making in terms of their potential to prevent groupthink.[37] This Part is skeptical that these reforms will end the era of laxity when directors fail to ask hard questions.[38] While these reforms empower directors with better tools for decision making, they do not go far enough. In the end, we need directors who are bold and courageous enough to say that the emperor has no clothes. To facilitate this behavior, this Part proposes two reforms based on the literature aimed at preventing groupthink. First, Part IV recommends establishing and rotating the role of the devil's advocate on the board. The devil's advocate role formalizes the right to challenge managers in a manner that does not undermine the independent directors' collegial relationships with corporate insiders. This reform provides independent directors with the "power to act," but it does not assure that they have the "will to act."[39] To assure more directors have the "will to act," the second proposal seeks to increase diversity on corporate boards by appointing directors with "outsider values." By increasing diversity, this reform reduces the existing homogeneity that can lead to groupthink.[40] In this regard, several institutional investors promote diversity on boards to foster divergent thinking that may contribute to board effectiveness and ultimately shareholder value. Of course, formalizing the role of the devil's advocate and increasing diversity on the board are not cure-alls for the various cognitive biases that influence directors. Admittedly, there is no simple solution. Even with these reforms, time and informational constraints will continue to limit what we can expect from boards. Along with the NYSE reforms, however, the implementation of these two methods to prevent groupthink may play a significant role in reducing the conformity pressures that inhibit candid discussion in the boardroom.

In Part V concludes that the proliferation of recent corporate scandals should lead corporate law professors to engage in critical self-reflection about how and what we teach in our business courses. As professors, we influence the ways students perceive the corporate world and their lives as corporate attorneys. We need to find a way to get past the prevailing cynical accounts of corporate governance and overcome the public disillusionment with corporate actors. On the one hand, we should not provide students with a picture of human behavior as solely self-interested because this dark

---

[37] Report of the New York Stock Exchange Corporate Accountability and Listing Standards Committee, approved August 1, 2002; set for approval by the SEC on September 6, 2002.

[38] Jean Strouse, *Capitalism Depends on Character*, N.Y. TIMES, July 7, 2002, at 9.

[39] *See, e.g.*, Shannon Turnbull, *Crumbling Corporate Governance Myths*, 704 J. OF CORP. DIRS. ASS'N OF AUSTL. 5 (2002), *available at* http://www.thecorporatelibrary.com/special/turnbull/turnbull10.html (distinguishing the "power to act" versus the "will to act").

[40] I use the term "diversity" broadly to mean gender, race, class, ethnicity, age, national origin, sexual orientation, and socio-economic background.

view can become a self-fulfilling prophecy.[41] On the other hand, we do not want to foster blind faith in corporate actors, either. Rather, we should encourage "cautious trust," a perspective that is both realistic and idealistic at the same time.[42] To achieve these goals, Part V calls on corporate law professors to emphasize corporate morality in teaching their courses. To include ethics in business courses, this Part recommends that we teach students about social psychology so that they can recognize and avoid the various cognitive biases present in corporate cultures. This perspective is important for corporate attorneys to fulfill their new obligations to report corporate wrongdoing to the board under the Sarbanes-Oxley Act.[43] Specifically, unless transaction lawyers overcome cognitive limits, they will fail to appreciate red flags indicating potential corporate wrongdoing. Part V urges that an effective teaching tool to convey the essence of these behavioral traps is to tell morality stories such as the one offered by the tale of the Enron Board.

I. SOCIAL PSYCHOLOGY AND THE MONITORING FUNCTION OF CORPORATE BOARDS

A. Small Group Decision Making and Boards

Corporate boards serve three roles. First, their most important function is to monitor firm performance to prevent managerial self-dealing and shirking.[44] Second, board members provide advice and guidance to senior managers in making major policy decisions.[45] Finally, the board serves a relational function, whereby board memberships provide links to various corporate stakeholders.[46]

Recently, corporate law scholars have turned to the literature in social psychology on small group decision making to evaluate the deliberative processes of boards. This literature provides support for the requirement in corporate statutes that the board meet as a collective body because groups make better decisions than individuals in evaluative assignments.[47] For these tasks, groups provide more reliable decisions, generate fewer errors, and uncover more mistakes than individuals.[48] To explain these results, social psychologists theorize that groups curb individual weaknesses by offering different

---

41 *See, e.g.*, Jeffrey Rachlinski & Cynthia Farina, *Cognitive Psychology and Optimal Government Design*, 87 CORN. L. REV. 549, 554 (2002).

42 Jerry L. Mashaw, *Deconstructing Debate, Reconstructing Law*, 87 CORN. L. REV. 682 (2002).

43 Sarbanes-Oxley Act of 2002, Pub. L. No. 107-204, sec. 307, 116 Stat. 745, 784.

44 *See, e.g.*, MELVIN A. EISENBERG, THE STRUCTURE OF THE CORPORATION 140-48 (1976).

45 *See, e.g.*, JAY W. LORSCH & ELIZABETH MCIVER, PAWNS OR POTENTATES: THE REALITY OF AMERICA'S CORPORATE BOARDS (1989).

46 Dallas, *Relational, supra* note 31, at 1-3.

47 STEPHEN M. BAINBRIDGE, CORPORATION LAW AND ECONOMICS (2002) (reviewing studies where groups outperform individuals for problems with one clear answer, logical problem-solving, complex problem involving over twenty variables, and complex decisions making under conditions of high uncertainty).

48 *See, e.g.*, *id.*, at 10; Robert J. Haft, *Business Decisions by the New Board: Behavioral Science and Corporate Law*, 80 MICH. L. REV. 1 (1981); Donald C. Langevoort, *The Human Nature of Corporate*

perspectives, arousing greater attention to the issues, and correcting random errors among members.[49] Thus, these studies provide support for the board's role in overseeing managers' plans.[50]

Social psychology offers evidence that changing the processes used in group decision making can improve the outcome.[51] Specifically, studies indicate that groups make better decisions when: (1) the group consists of equal status peers, (2) the group has nondirective leadership, (3) members feel free to ask questions, and (4) members have assigned roles in small task groups. To promote better decision making by boards, institutional shareholders have pushed for various reforms for over a decade.[52] For example, boards size has decreased[53] and many boards have committees of independent directors that focus on auditing, nominating directors, and compensation. This comports with the findings discussed above that small task groups and assigned evaluative roles allow groups to make better decisions. Current boardroom practices, however, fail in a critical respect. Specifically, the next section examines how many boards do not consist of equal status peers who have impartial leadership because the CEO dominates the board.[54]

B. Factors Impeding Peer Group Decision Making on Boards

CEO-dominated boards may fail to monitor managers in the shareholders' best interests because independent directors may be beholden to the CEO in six ways.[55] First, devising a definition of "independence" that ensures that directors criticize management when necessary is not feasible. Most definitions of independence include the absence of employment, family relationships, and consulting contracts with the company. The goal of these definitions is to remove financial ties other than stock ownership.[56] With respect to stock ownership, corporate governance scholars suggest that firms provide

Boards: Law, Norms, and the Unintended Consequences of Independence and Accountability, 89 GEO. L.J. 797, 782 (2001).

49 *See, e.g.*, HAFT, *supra* note 48, at 10.

50 BAINBRIDGE, *supra* note 47, at 210.

51 Barnard, *supra* note 30, at 1170.

52 For an overview, *see, e.g.*, Robert A.G. MONKS & NELL MINOW, CORPORATE GOVERNANCE (1995).

53 *See, e.g.*, Theodore Eisenberg & Stefan Sundgren, Larger *Board Size, Decreasing Firm Value, and Increasing Firm Insolvency*, 48 J. FIN. ECON. 35 (1998). *But see* BAINBRIDGE, *supra* note 47, at 42-43 (finding studies inconclusive and arguing large board size may be better). As a result of these reforms, the average size for corporate boards is eleven directors. *See Korn/Ferry's New Study Tracks 25 Years of Change in America's Corporate Boardrooms*, BUS. WIRE, Sept. 24, 1998.

54 *See, e.g.*, Cox & Munsinger, *supra* note 30, at 92; Lynne L. Dallas, *Proposals for Reform of Corporate Boards of Directors: The Dual Board and Board Ombudsperson*, 54 WASH & LEE L. REV. 91, 93 (1997) [hereinafter Dallas, *Ombudsperson*].

55 Alan Greenspan, Speech at Stern School of Business (NYU, Mar. 26, 2002). A leading article that first espoused this notion is Victor Brudney, *The Independent Director—Heavenly City of Potemkin Village*, 95 HARV. L. REV. 597 (1982).

56 Charles M. Elson, *Director Compensation and the Management-Captured Board: The History of a Symptom and a Cure*, 50 SMU L. REV. 127 (1996).

director compensation in stock, rather than the current practice of using stock options.[57] Stock options allow directors to benefit on the upside when the stock price increases, but not to experience the pain caused when the stock price falls. To assure that directors share in the downside, some corporate governance experts suggest that directors hold the stock for the tenure of their terms. Other commentators go further and argue that directors should not be paid in stock because it contributes to short-term thinking and ties directors to only one corporate stakeholder to the detriment of other stakeholders, especially employees.[58] The social psychology literature on small group decision making confirms these views about director stock ownership; that is, groups do not obtain the benefits of peer group decision making if members receive contingent compensation based on short-term stock prices.[59]

Second, another factor that reduces independence is that many directors receive side payments in the form of corporate philanthropy to their pet charities[60] [as well as] consulting contracts.[61] As a matter of human nature, such financial ties can redirect loyalty away from shareholders and toward managers.[62] Jeff Gordon explains that managers can use such side payments to threaten directors with "low visibility sanctions" if they do not concur with the CEO's wishes.[63] This is in contrast to the "high visibility sanction" of not renominating a dissenting director to the board. Because low visibility sanctions do not appear on analysts' radar screens,[64] Gordon surmises that these side payments may undercut director independence to an even greater extent than the threat of dismissal from the board.

The third factor that diminishes the equal peer status of boards is when the CEO serves as the chairperson of the board; this is the case in three out of the four largest corporations.[65] Through this position, the CEO establishes the agenda at board meetings and controls the quantity and timing of the information presented to other directors at meetings. Social psychology warns that members of a group tend to conform their opinions to what they perceive the leader of the group wants to hear.[66]

---

57 Charles Elson, *The Bad Board Booby Trap*, DIRECTORS MONTHLY, Mar. 2001.

58 Marleen A. O'Connor, *Union Pension Power and the Shareholder Revolution* (1999) (unpublished article prepared for The Second National Heartland Labor-Capital Conference (Apr. 29-30, 1999), *available at* http://www.heartlandnetwork.org/conference4_99/downloads/OConnor.pdf).

59 HAFT, *supra* note 48, at 12-13.

60 *See, e.g.*, Faith Stevelman Kahn, *Pandora's Box: Managerial Discretion and the Problem of Corporate Philanthropy*, 44 UCLA L. REV. 579 (1997); Symposium, *Corporate Philanthropy*, 28 STETSON L. REV. 1 2000; Symposium, *Corporate Philanthropy, Law, Culture, Education, and Politics*, 41 N.Y.L. SCH. L. REV. 753 (1997).

61 *See generally* Benjamin, *supra* note 1 (former SEC Chairperson Arthur Levitt states: "A whole panoply of seductions bind the interest of the board members to the CEO rather than to shareholders.").

62 *Id.*

63 Gordon, *supra* note 2, at 12.

64 *Id.*

65 Benjamin, *supra* note 1.

66 Haft, *supra* note 48, at 13.

Fourth, despite nominating committees that consist entirely of independent directors, these committees are sympathetic to the CEO's views about the "right type of person" to serve as a director.[67] Indeed, many independent directors on the nominating committees consist of current and former CEOs who may favor maintaining a system that benefits them. Social psychology indicates that the independent directors are likely to feel strong loyalty to their appointer.[68] In looking for directors who will "fit in," nominating committees usually seek people who have accommodating demeanors and avoid those who are irritable and overly opinionated.[69] In this regard, the usual nominations are the CEO's social or business acquaintances—leading to the clubby nature of boards. As a result of this cronyism, corporate boards are quite homogeneous, consisting mostly of white males, in their mid-fifties, who are predominately Protestant and Republican.[70] Social psychologists explain that the common background and social ties among group members can gradually lead to an in-group bias. Specifically, the cultural cohesiveness on corporate boards can stifle directors' willingness to dissent.[71]

Fifth, many independent directors serve for long terms—over twenty years.[72] On the upside, long terms for directors foster collegiality that promotes the notion of "fictive friendship" among directors. To a certain degree, cohesiveness is essential to promote good working relationships among board members. On the downside, the presence of such "fictive friendships" on the board creates social norms that make it inappropriate for the independent directors to challenge their "friends."[73] Specifically, these continuing relationships can lead to too much conformity among group members, which decreases their willingness to engage in critical analysis.[74]

Finally, although many compensation committees consist of independent directors, CEOs still retain considerable leverage over this issue. Here again, part of the problem stems from stacking the compensation committee with current and former CEOs who have a vested interest in perpetuating the status quo. Although compensation committees rely on outside consultants, many CEOs still select the consulting firm and have leverage over its opinions by providing other consulting opportunities.[75] Indeed, some compensation committee members publicly have stated that they are influenced by

---

[67] *See, e.g.*, Cox & Munsinger, *supra* note 30, at 98; Langevoort, *Human Nature, supra* note 48, at 780.

[68] Haft, *supra* note 48, at 10.

[69] Langevoort, *Human Nature, supra* note 48, at 782.

[70] *See, e.g.*, James D. Westphal & Edward J. Zajac, *Who Shall Govern? CEO/Board Power, Demographic Similarity, and New Director Selection*, 40 ADMIN. SCI. Q. 60 (1995).

[71] Cox & Munsinger, *supra* note 30, at 92.

[72] *Id.* at 98.

[73] *Cf.* Donald C. Langevoort, *Selling Hope, Selling Risk: Some Lessons for Law from Behavioral Economics About Stockbrokers and Sophisticated Customers*, 84 CAL. L. REV. 627, 654-55 (1996) [hereinafter Langevoort, *Selling Hope*] (discussing "fictive friendships" between brokers and investors).

[74] Haft, *supra* note 48, at 9.

[75] *See, e.g.*, Uma V. Sridharan, *CEO Influence and Executive Compensation*, 31 FIN. REV. 51 (1996) (the more influence CEO has over the board, the higher the CEO pay).

O.[76] The CEO's domination leads some boards to allot more time and energy ..pensation issues, rather than to assuring the integrity of the company's financial reporting system.[77]

Thus, while institutional shareholders have achieved some success in pushing for reforms, these efforts fall far below those needed to achieve peer group decision making. Perhaps this is why empirical evaluation shows that implemented reforms do not correlate with improved financial performance.[78] For example, although many institutional shareholders assume that independent directors will increase firm value, no empirical evidence supports this position, and some evidence points the other way.[79] The existing statistical studies may not capture the nature of the shareholder revolution for two reasons. First, despite the lack of data showing that shareholder proposals alone improve the bottom line, shareholders use governance practices as important factors in evaluating the quality of management. Second, even though the actual number of shareholder proposals that change governance practices are low, managers are not likely to seek to install defensive tactics through the articles of incorporation because they know that shareholders will veto such measures.[80]

C. The Business Judgment Rule: Increasing Directors' Duties

The business judgment rule protects directors from liability for decisions made without fraud or self-dealing. The reason behind the business judgment rule is that courts should not judge board decisions with hindsight bias. Hindsight bias causes people to evaluate events as being easily foreseeable.[81] The business judgment rule encourages risk-taking by managers, which benefits shareholders holding diversified portfolios. Thus, courts dismiss shareholder suits for breach of the duty of care by applying the business judgment rule if they can find "any rational business purpose" for the decision. The

---

[76] *See, e.g.*, Todd Perry & Marc Zenner, *CEO Compensation in the 1990s: Shareholder Alignment or Shareholder Expropriation?*, 35 WAKE FOREST L. REV. 123, 135-36 (2000); Carol J. Loomis, *This Stuff is Wrong*, FORTUNE, June 25, 2001, at 72.

[77] Byrne et al., *supra* note 10, at 68 (Oracle compensation committee met twenty-four times; entire board met five times).

[78] *See, e.g.*, Bernard Black, *Shareholder Activism and Corporate Governance in the United States*, CORP. GOV. ADVISOR 14 (Jan./Feb. 1999) ("One could hardly say that institutional investor activism is a bad thing. But the best reading of the currently available evidence is that institutional investors activism does not significantly affect firm performance, and cannot substitute for the discipline provided by an active market for corporate control.").

[79] *See, e.g.*, Sanjai Bhagat & Bernard Black, *The Uncertain Relationship Between Board Composition and Firm Performance*, 54 BUS. LAW. 921 (1999). This evidence may indicate that inside directors play an important role in strategic decision making. April Klein, *Firm Performance and Board Committee Structure*, 41 J.L. & ECON. 195 (1992).

[80] *See* Black, *supra* note 78, at 16.

[81] *See, e.g.*, Jeffrey Rachlinski, *A Positive Psychological Theory of Judging in Hindsight*, 65 U. CHI. L. REV. 571 (1998).

theory is that free markets will weed out those firms making too many bad decisions, rather than having a court play this role. Social psychology also lends support to the business judgment rule because external review of group decision making would harm the interpersonal relationships among board members that are necessary for boards to function.[82] This threat to cohesiveness also offers a rationale as to why corporate law does not distinguish among directors for liability purposes.

After *Smith v. Van Gorkom*,[83] boards use more rigorous decision making procedures in order to avoid liability for breach of the duty of due care. As a result of these ritualized procedures, it is generally noted that directors take their duties more seriously by working harder preparing for and participating at meetings. By requiring directors to ask questions, *Van Gorkom* reduces directors' "costs of confrontation" by allowing them to "sugarcoat" their questions by appealing to the law as the reason for their inquiries, rather than distrust of management.[84]

Another case increasing the responsibilities of directors is *In re Caremark*. While this case does not require directors to implement compliance programs to monitor firms, many boards have implemented these procedures. Examined through the lens of the business judgment rule, good faith attempts by the board to monitor management are sufficient. The *Caremark* opinion explicitly states a high threshold for directors' liability: "Only a sustained or systematic failure . . . to exercise oversight—such as an utter failure to attempt to assure a reasonable information and reporting system exists—will establish the lack of good faith that is a necessary condition to liability." Thus, lack of good faith is not demonstrated by a single instance of faulty monitoring, but rather through prolonged neglect. By imposing this duty, fiduciary law also reduces the directors' "costs of confrontation" by allowing them to implement compliance programs in a manner that does not undermine collegiality among independent directors and managers.

Courts give directors the benefit of the business judgment rule only when there is an absence of self-dealing. In cases of conflict-of-interest transactions, the interested fiduciary has the burden of proving that the transaction is "fair," which means that the terms are similar to those obtained in an arm's-length deal. In Delaware, prior approval or ratification by disinterested directors or disinterested shareholders provides the interested directors with the benefit of the business judgment rule. Thus, the plaintiff needs to prove that the transaction amounts to "waste," i.e., no quid pro quo. Other states, however, take a different approach and shift the burden of proving the unfairness of the transaction to the plaintiff when the interested director obtains disinterested director or shareholder approval.

Social psychology offers a partial explanation for these rules. With regard to conflict-of-interest transactions presented to the board for prior approval, the social dynamics of the boardroom make it uncomfortable for disinterested directors to deny a colleague access to a proposed project. Independent directors may be biased toward endorsement

---

[82] BAINBRIDGE, *supra* note 47, at 49 ("every man for himself" phenomenon).

[83] 448 A.2d 858 (Del. 1985).

[84] Stout, *supra* note 22, at 690.

of these deals because voting "no" is akin to saying "I do not trust you" to the manager proposing the deal. It is even more difficult, however, for disinterested directors to refuse to ratify a completed project because lack of approval subjects the interested director to serious risks of shareholder litigation. Given that directors pursuing conflict-of-interest transactions may rely on the mutual trust of fellow board members to approve deals that favor the director, social psychology supports the need for courts to scrutinize these business decisions for fairness.

Cases such as *Van Gorkom* and *Caremark* increased the proliferation of good corporate governance practices in boardrooms, but these reforms have not succeeded in overcoming the dysfunctional norms of many boardrooms. In other words, some independent directors may be motivated by the desire to get along and gain approval of those to whom they feel accountable—senior managers, not shareholders. Specifically, board members know that renomination to the board depends on "appropriate performance," which means they need to conform their behavior to the "cult of politeness." While it is appropriate to give weight to senior executives' views, this is qualitatively different than the CEO's domination of the board. Under current boardroom norms, directors' criticism of the CEO signals disloyalty or "no confidence" in the CEO. Given time and information constraints, independent directors may seek to fulfill their board duties by making satisfactory, rather than optimal decisions. In other words, given the human nature to prefer the "least effort" solution, independent directors who lead hectic, overloaded lives may take the easy road when faced with complex decisions and simply smile and nod during board meetings. Another reason for this behavior is that if directors say "no" to managers, they face the immediate risk of jeopardizing their "friendship" with managers, which may lead to the loss of side payments. Going along with managers' policies may hurt shareholders, who the directors have probably never met, but these negative consequences often occur later. Given this "time delay trap," independent directors, like most human actors, may choose short-run gratification. These behavioral tendencies cause boards to rarely (1) vote other than unanimously on issues of importance to the CEO, (2) seek information outside the communication channels provided by the CEO, and (3) discuss issues of accountability or the premises upon which the board operates. As a result, board meetings tend to resemble "endless pep rallies," rather than necessary conversations about corporate strategies.

D. Bubble Governance and the Dangers of Tournaments

1. Independent Directors' Schemas

Even if directors were financially independent of managers, doubt remains about how well they can perform their monitoring role because they have limited information and meet only a few times a year. Given these constraints, psychological weaknesses may impair independent directors' abilities to perform their monitoring function in a vigilant manner. Specifically, questions exist about how "cognitively independent" directors are from managers' views and perceptions. To explain, we need to consider the perspective of the independent director in deciding whether to join a board. In making this initial decision, the director needs to assess whether to trust the senior executives of the firm. Given that most independent directors are successful people with demanding schedules, an individual director may seek to minimize the time and information required to evaluate this complex decision. Thus, the independent director may use initial impressions as short cuts to form mental roadmaps about the corporation.[85] Social psychology refers to this process as using a heuristic device known as a "schema."[86] The director may develop an overall favorable impression or schema of top management when she does not see any surface problems in the firm, but perceives that the senior executives have impressive track records and other respected gatekeepers associate with the corporation.[87] In addition, since the CEO effectively appoints the director, social psychology suggests that an individual tends to develop favorable views of others who can promote her goals.[88]

Once an independent director makes the commitment to trust senior managers, the director may be reluctant to change this initial impression despite warning signs. This is because people tend to interpret new information in a manner to confirm the status quo.[89] Specifically, once people have made some voluntary commitment to a person or course of behavior, there is a strong subconscious need to maintain consistency in the face of subsequent events in order to continue to justify the original commitment to themselves and others.[90] Social psychologists refer to this as "cognitive conservatism."[91] Social psychology explains that when people face information that indicates that their initial decision was wrong, they may rationalize it away or ignore it. This is the well-accepted notion of "cognitive dissonance," that is, the tendency to reduce psychological inconsistencies.[92] The tendency for "cognitive dissonance" is likely to be strong when a person's commitment is made public, such as that of an independent director's decision to join a board.[93]

Although an independent director's schema evolves throughout her term on the board, this schema remains substantially derived from the insiders' perspectives.[94] In this way, inside directors, particularly the CEO, have considerable influence in

---

[85] *See, e.g.*, ELLIOT ARONSON, THE SOCIAL ANIMAL 136-37 (6th ed. 1992).

[86] Donald C. Langevoort, *Where Were the Lawyers? A Behavioral Inquiry into Lawyers' Responsibility for Clients' Fraud*, 46 VAND. L. REV. 75, 98 (1993) [hereinafter Langevoort, *Where*].

[87] *Id.*

[88] Langevoort, *Where*, *supra* note 86, at 99.

[89] ARONSON, *supra* note 85, at 118.

[90] *Id.* at 202-03.

[91] Langevoort, *Where*, *supra* note 86, at 100.

[92] *See, e.g.*, *id.* at 103.

[93] *Id.* at 102-03.

[94] Donald C. Langevoort, *The Epistemology of Corporate-Securities Lawyering: Beliefs, Biases and Organizational Behavior*, 63 BROOK L. REV. 629, 637 (1997) [hereinafter Langevoort, *Epistemology*].

setting the tone within the boardroom.[95] In addition, as the next section details, the CEO plays a primary role in establishing the corporate culture. Corporate cultures may influence directors because they are dependent upon insiders' views of the firm.[96] In this way, independent directors may lose their outsider perspective, that is, their "cognitive independence," by falling prey to the cognitive influences permeating the corporate belief system.[97] Importantly, the independent director may not receive sufficient warnings from the other corporate gatekeepers to change this favorable schema. Specifically, outside lawyers, accountants, and consultants undergo similar processes in developing schemas of a particular firm.[98] Thus, these corporate watchdogs may also adopt the corporation's biases because they are also dependent upon much "derivative information-gathering" from insiders.[99]

Directors' lack of psychological independence poses particular problems when the firm's stock price is rising. It is much easier for directors to ask questions when the stock price is dropping. Thus, good corporate governance practices serve as a "floor"—if the company performs poorly, it is more likely that the board will dismiss the CEO.[100] When the firm's financial statements indicate success, directors may be reluctant to question managers about details.[101] Thus, rising stock prices may cause directors to be less diligent, posing serious problems for corporate governance in a bubble stock market.

2. *Superstars and Loss Framing*

To examine how senior executives influence corporate cultures, this section examines the economic literature on compensation and promotion practices. Many large firms in competitive environments structure internal labor markets through promotion processes whereby employees' success depends upon their relative positions in competition with their colleagues.[102] As an example, Enron used the "rank and yank" system

---

[95] *See, e.g.*, Dallas, *Relational, supra* note 31, at 5 (discussing the two-process theory of influence; group members experience conformity pressures due to normative and informational social influences).

[96] Langevoort, *Epistemology, supra* note 94 at 639.

[97] *Id.* at 643.

[98] *See* Prentice, *supra* note 13; Langevoort, Epistemology, supra note 94.

[99] Langevoort, *Human Nature, supra* note 48, at 813.

[100] *Directors' Monthly*, 23 CORP. GOV. REV. 1 (Jan. 1999) (Ken West, TIAA-CREF).

[101] Evidence shows that boards with a majority of independent directors have a higher chance of removing a CEO for poor results, but are less likely to remove the CEO if the firm's stock price is above average. Michael S. Weisbach, *Outside Directors and CEO Turnover*, 20 J. FIN. ECON. 431 (1988).

[102] *See, e.g.*, Donald C. Langevoort, *Ego, Human Behavior and Law*, 81 VA. L. REV. 853 (1995) [hereinafter Langevoort, *Ego*]. For an overview of tournaments, *see, e.g.*, MARC GALANTER & THOMAS PALAY, TOURNAMENT OF LAWYERS: THE TRANSFORMATION OF THE BIG LAW FIRM (1991). *See, e.g.*, David B. Wilkins & G. Mitu Gulati, *Reconceiving the Tournament of Lawyers: Tracking, Seeding, and Information Control in the Internal Labor Markets of Elite Law Firms*, 84 VA. L. REV. 1581 (1998) [hereinafter Wilkins & Gulati, *Tracking*]; David B. Wilkins & G. Mitu Gulati, *Why Are There So Few Black Lawyers in Corporate Law Firms? An Institutional Analysis*, 84 CAL. L. REV. 493 (1996). These tournaments can lead to second-generation discrimination against minorities and women. *See infra* notes 473-81.

whereby workers evaluated each other; those falling at the bottom of the curve were fired, while those at the top were given large bonuses. Many firms use similar practices to establish what is in essence a tournament—a key determinate of a corporation's culture.[103] At Enron, the tournament structure led to a "gladiator"[104] or survival-of-the-fittest corporate culture where employees attempted to defeat not just outsiders, but each other.[105] Although managers used the rhetoric of "team building," the Enron tournament promoted the notion of the star player.

Under a tournament structure, an employee who excels, or a "superstar," is generally rewarded with less supervision and oversight.[106] Yet, to retain her status, the superstar must continuously outdo herself and others. In such a competitive environment, the constant "what have you done for me lately?" stress may lead the superstar to worry that she may lose her status.[107] Social psychologists explain that when people perceive that they may lose existing benefits, they may take greater risks to keep the benefit than they would to obtain it in the first place. This is called a "loss frame." Under a loss frame, superstars may take greater risks to maintain their current status and their long-run concerns for their reputation diminish. This willingness to take greater risks to prevent the loss of superstar status can lead to a vicious cycle where the superstar continually takes larger risks to maintain her status.

In addition, Donald Langevoort writes how superstars tend to be "high-ego" or "high-mach" employees who may suffer from an overconfidence bias.[108] Due to this overconfidence, such "high-mach" types are slow to recognize problems as attributable

---

The economic model of tournament theory explains why firms do not reward workers for their current productivity. Instead, many large firms, including large law firms, provide an implicit promise for employees to compete with their colleagues for promotions to positions with higher pay and security. Importantly, these firms do not promote every qualified worker, but only a pre-set number based on relative performance. Tournament theorists explain that when the costs of monitoring workers is high, firms can avoid these expenses by simply putting workers in competition with each other and promoting the best performers. Thus, workers compete in a "multiround" tournament, which includes practices such as tracking, seeding, and information control typically found in sporting events and other kinds of formal competitions. Donald C. Langevoort, *The Organizational Psychology of Hyper-Competition: Corporate Irresponsibility and the Lessons of Enron*, 70 GEO. WASH. L. REV. 968 (2002) [hereinafter Langevoort, *Hyper-Competition*] (on file with University of Cincinnati Law Review).

[103] *See, e.g.*, Kimberly D. Krawiec, *Accounting for Greed: Unraveling the Mystery of the Rogue Trader*, 79 ORE. L. REV. 301, 330 (2000). Under this peer-review process, a group of twenty employees voted unanimously to judge Enron employees. The top five percent ranked superior received bonuses sixty-six percent higher (and much larger stock option grants) than those ranked excellent, the next thirty percent.

[104] William Bratton used this term to refer to Enron's corporate culture during his talk at Tulane Law School in April, 2002.

[105] McLean, *supra* note 3.

[106] Krawiec, *supra* note 103, at 312 (superstar has less supervision thus the superstar can take larger risks).

[107] *See* Amos Tuersky & Daniel Kahneman, *The Framing of Decisions and the Psychology of Choice*, 211 SCI. 453, 454 (1981).

[108] Langevoort, *Hyper-Competition*, *supra* note 102 ("ultimate tournament survivor is a hard core narcissist").

to their mistakes. Self-serving biases may allow the superstar to see failure as an incident of bad luck, but success as proof of superior talents.[109] In extreme cases where the superstar is engaged in serial decision making, this overconfidence may lead to serious problems. Specifically, rather than change course when a long-term project begins to fail, executives may take greater risks and throw even more good money after bad in the hope that their luck will change. This cognitive bias is known as the "optimism-commitment whipsaw."[110]

With this perspective, we can see how executives who achieve success may get caught in "encore trap" because maintaining their superstar status depends on meeting or exceeding analysts' predictions about next quarters' earnings.[111] Successful executives reveal that they continue to work hard long after making their millions. After they attain a certain amount of wealth, the additional compensation does not affect everyday life and the money itself means little.[112] Rather, the main motivation for superstars is the excitement of "the game" and the chance to test oneself as a "major player."[113] The level of compensation is merely a way to "keep score" as a measure of one's winnings.[114] One corporate governance commentator noted that this mentality leads to the concept of the "trophy wife."[115] In this way, the company's stock price goes deeply to its executives' sense of identity and self-worth.[116] The recent scandals suggest that some CEOs sought to retain their status by "hyping [their] way to stock market stardom."[117] That is, these executives manipulated accounting rules through complex financial maneuvers to create "virtual wealth"—paper profits that do not contribute to real productivity gains in the long-term.

To further understand how tournaments may foster pathological behavior, we can analyze how corporate cultures contribute to executives rationalizing away ethical violations. Specifically, Langevoort emphasizes that tournament structures may defeat firms' attempts to implement compliance programs to ensure ethical behavior.[118] Employees may rationalize cutting corners because the corporate culture is perceived as unfair. Langevoort offers two factors contributing to this perception. First, exorbitant CEO

---

[109] MAX BAZERMAN, JUDGMENT IN MANAGERIAL DECISION MAKING 96 (3d ed. 1994).

[110] Barry Staw, *The Escalation of Commitment to a Course of Action*, 6 ACAD. MGMT. REV. 577, 580 (1981).

[111] THOMAS R. HORTON, THE CEO PARADOX: THE PRIVILEGE AND ACCOUNTABILITY OF LEADERSHIP 66 (2001).

[112] *Id.* at 330.

[113] Krawiec, *supra* note 103, at 314.

[114] AL DUNLAP, MEAN BUSINESS 98 (1997).

[115] HORTON, *supra* note 111, at 66.

[116] Donald Langevoort, *The Organizational Psychology of Hyper-competition: Corporate Irresponsibility and the Lessons of Enron* (Working Paper 2002) [hereinafter Langevoort, Hyper-competition].

[117] *Audits & Bubbles*, supra note 8, at b.06.

[118] Donald C. Langevoort, *Monitoring: The Behavioral Economics of Inducing Agents' Compliance With Legal Rules* (Working Paper 2002), *available at* http://ssrn.com [hereinafter Langevoort, Monitoring].

pay may lead employees to believe that senior executives sanction self-serving behavior.[119] Specifically, the CEO sets the tone for ethical behavior at the firm. An employee may feel that if the CEO uses his power in a self-serving manner, it is acceptable for the employee to do the same. Second, employees may feel the tournament is not fair because its demands are too stringent. An employee may come to view her corporation's efforts to foster an ethical climate as insincere given the dog-eat-dog pressures to perform, internally from the tournament and externally from the stock market.[120] Such competitive pressures may lead employees to rationalize overly aggressive actions in a manner that allows them to think that they behaved honorably, or should be blameless for the consequences of their decisions. Facilitating these rationalizations, Langevoort explains that firms using tournaments infuse their corporate cultures with military and sports rhetoric to simultaneously inculcate competitiveness and loyalty.[121] Such metaphors allow employees to see questionable moral conduct as merely the type of combative action needed to win the "war" or the "game."[122] Thus, these metaphors can aid employees in making rationalizations by viewing corporate ethics codes in a cynical way to avoid guilt.

This explanation of how corporate cultures promote processes whereby corporate actors rationalize away unethical actions does not mean that such actors should necessarily be let off the hook for bad behavior. Rather, the goal is to shed light on the powerful dynamics that flow from tournaments and the corporate cultures they create. This Part emphasizes doubt about how "independent" directors remain because they are subject to "contagious biases"[123] of the prevailing corporate belief system. To explore these issues further, the next Part focuses on two cognitive biases that may impede board decision making: polarization and cascades. As mentioned previously, these two theories overlap in some respects with the groupthink theory discussed in Part III. Thus, Part II serves as a prelude to a fuller account of the Enron Board's deliberations that follows in Part III.

II. POLARIZATION AND SOCIAL CASCADES

Polarization and social cascades raise serious problems for board deliberation.[124] Polarization refers to how group deliberation pushes a group, and its individual members,

---

[119] *Id.*

[120] *Id.*

[121] Langevoort, *Myths*, *supra* note 25, at 1592.

[122] *Id.*

[123] *Id.* at 647.

[124] Corporate governance scholars have recognized the problems relating to polarization. *See, e.g.*, Dallas, *Ombudsperson*, *supra* note 54, at 107. Stephen Bainbridge, however, states that the tendency for groups to make riskier decisions than individuals benefits shareholders who hold diversified portfolios. BAINBRIDGE, *supra* note 47, at 156.

toward increased risk-taking.[125] Prior to social psychologists examining group decision making, the generally accepted belief was that groups move toward the center of the members' positions held prior to group discussion.[126] Empirical evidence, first produced by J.A.F. Stoner in 1962, shows that groups have a strong tendency to take extreme positions. Specifically, Stoner asked several groups to make unanimous choices between safe and risky decisions, including a low-return, high-security stock or a high-return, lower security stock. The members of the group made initial decisions individually and then discussed their choices in a group. Twelve out of the thirteen groups chose the riskier alternatives. Importantly, after group deliberations, individual's private opinions also changed to favor the riskier positions.[127] In explaining why polarization occurs, an individual's need for conformity does not provide a complete answer because group members do not converge on the mean result of their individual opinions.[128] Instead, two factors account for polarization. First, when groups consist of like-minded members, the argument pool becomes limited and "persuasive arguments"[129] based on rhetoric currently favored in the culture become significant.[130] Second, social influence comes into play because people like to maintain certain self-perceptions.[131] For example, if an individual likes to think of herself as more risk prone than average, she may shift her position to favor even more risk after hearing other members in the group espouse risky positions. Thus, when like-minded members of a group favor risk, then group deliberations can produce quite extreme decisions due to polarization.[132]

The polarization story may offer help in explaining the Enron Board's role in the fall of Enron. Specifically, the Enron CEOs, Jeffrey Skilling and later Ken Lay, may have acted as "polarization entrepreneurs" by creating enclaves of like-minded people to monitor them on the Board. The Enron Board probably shared a limited argument pool—hearing many arguments in favor of taking risks and few counter positions. In this regard, arguments for increased risk-taking to produce shareholder value in the new economy may have had a rhetorical advantage in pushing the Enron Board to approve the related-party transactions. In addition, given the strong risk-taking norm present in the Enron culture, individual board members may have wanted to hold themselves out to others as people who are not afraid to take risk. Thus, individual board members may have shifted their initial positions to take even greater risks upon hearing the views of other Enron Board members.

---

125 Note that the "risky shift" does not result when groups make certain types of decisions such as whether one should marry or travel with a medical condition. Sunstein, *supra* note 31.

126 *Id.*

127 *Id.*

128 *Id.*

129 *Id.*

130 For example, cultural norms make it hard to argue for reducing sentences for drug crimes. *Id.*

131 *Id.*

132 *Id.* ("enclaves of people, inclined to risky business practices, might move sharply in that direction as a consequence of internal deliberations.").

Related to the polarization concept is the theory of cascades, which can also lead groups to take extreme positions. As a result of cascades, groups end up with a shared perception—which may not be true—because other people seem to hold a particular view. The distinctive feature of cascades is a snowballing effect. Specifically, as members of a group with low thresholds start to favor a position, members with higher thresholds come to share this view in a cascade-like process, reaching a "tipping" point where group consensus forms.[133] Similar to polarization, cascades occur for informational and reputational reasons. In the case of an informational cascade, group members who lack information rely on the opinions of others in making up their own minds. In contrast, reputational cascades occur because members may publicly take a stand or remain silent in order to maintain their reputations with other members of the group, although their private perceptions may vary.[134] Cascades differ from polarization because cascades can occur without group deliberation. In addition, polarization can result from each group member reaching an extreme position independently, rather than through a cascade-like process.

The cascade effect may have played a role in influencing the Enron directors. Specifically, as one director spoke in favor of approving the related-party transactions, other directors may have joined for informational reasons, because they did not know what to think or for reputational reasons, to maintain the esteem of the other board members.

These two negative aspects of group decision making—polarization and cascades—are important to our understanding of interactions in the boardroom. This article maintains, however, that groupthink, which is related but distinct from polarization and cascades, provides a more descriptive account of the Enron Board's role in Enron's collapse. As noted previously, however, groupthink encompasses the same ideas as polarization and cascades; thus each of these biases may have been present in the Enron boardroom.

III. THE ENRON BOARD AND GROUPTHINK THEORY

A. The Groupthink Phenomenon

In the 1970s, Irving Janis developed the groupthink theory by examining how small, high-level groups of government officials used faulty decision-making procedures that resulted in fiascoes in U.S. policy. Specifically, in formulating this theory, Janis examined how various groups of Presidential advisors interacted in making strategic decisions, such as those leading to the attack at the Bay of Pigs, the unpreparedness of the U.S. for the attack on Pearl Harbor, the escalation of the Vietnam War, and the Watergate cover-up.[135] Analyzing the social dynamics of these groups of advisors, Janis produced

---

133 *Id.* at 77 ("where a rivulet ends up as a flood.").

134 *Id.*

135 JANIS, VICTIMS, *supra* note 28, at 25.

case studies to show how cohesive groups can make serious miscalculations about both the practical and moral consequences of their decisions.[136]

Janis emphasized that under the influence of groupthink, groups believe that their goals are based on ethical principles and they stop questioning the morality of their behavior. This tendency may foster overoptimism, lack of vigilance, and sloganistic thinking about out-groups. At the same time, groupthink causes members to ignore negative information by viewing messengers of bad news as people who "don't get it." As a result, Janis explained that group members engage in self-censorship to repress dissent: "When groupthink tendencies become dominant, the members try to avoid saying anything that might disturb the smooth surface unanimity that enables the members to feel confident that their policies are correct and bound to succeed."[137] In addition, a group suffering from groupthink tends to arrive at a decision before realistically appraising the available courses of action.

Janis was a firm believer that good procedures lead to better decisions. Groupthink causes a deterioration in the quality of group deliberation, thus the probability of the group reaching a successful decision diminishes. Groupthink usually produces faulty decisions, but Janis noted that groupthink is helpful in making routine decisions because it saves time. In addition, groupthink does not necessarily lead to disasters because some groups under this influence may fortuitously avoid negative results.[138] Interestingly, within the same group, groupthink can occur in making one decision, but not another. As an example, Janis referred to how groupthink influenced President Kennedy's inner circle of advisors in formulating strategic plans leading to the Bay of Pigs, whereas the members avoided the same errors when deliberating during the Cuban Missile Crisis.[139]

Of course, just because a group decision fails does not mean that it was the result of groupthink or any other type of defective decision making.[140] Bad decisions result from other common causes of human error as well, such as information overload, fatigue, prejudice, ignorance, and bickering, as well as various individual and group behavioral biases. Beyond these types of errors, however, groupthink can affect cohesive groups in a way that they develop a strong concurrence-seeking tendency suppressing critical inquiry.

Although Janis's groupthink theory is well-accepted in the field of social psychology, empirical tests have produced mixed results as to the theory's validity.[141] The nature of some of the predicates for groupthink make Janis's hypotheses difficult to test in controlled laboratory settings. Specifically, cohesiveness is the most important condition

---

[136] *Id.*

[137] *Id.* at 37.

[138] *Id.*

[139] JANIS, VICTIMS, *supra* note 28, at 14.

[140] *Id.* at 11.

[141] *See, e.g.*, Marceline B.R. Koorn et al., *Managing Group Decision making Processes: Individual Versus Collective Accountability and Groupthink*, 2 INT'L. J. CONFLICT MGMT. 91 (1991).

for groupthink to occur, but because of its elusive and multifaceted nature, cohesiveness is difficult to replicate in studies. Researchers, however, have developed several case studies to support the basic notions of groupthink.[142] Yet, much more empirical and theoretical work is needed to clarify the groupthink theory, especially the relationships between the variables.

When Janis first developed the groupthink theory, it struck a responsive chord because of the tendency for spectacular failures to captivate the public's attention. Many are intrigued by Janis's intentional use of the Orwellian sounding term "groupthink," which echoes notions of "doublethink" from the novel *1984.* (Indeed, doublethink seems to apply to boards because some directors are "more equal" than others. In addition, we use the term "election" to describe how directors obtain board seats.) As a result of the popularity of the concept of groupthink, some people use the term loosely and indiscriminately, as an expression to explain any type of bad decision made by a group. This lack of analysis appears in some newspaper accounts about Enron that refer to the result as a product of groupthink without much evaluation.[143] Before applying the groupthink label, however, Janis cautioned that one must carefully look for three antecedent conditions and eight symptoms. This Part examines the three antecedent conditions: (1) a cohesive group, (2) structural faults in decision making, and (3) situational context. Then, this Part discusses the eight symptoms of groupthink: (1) sense of invincibility, (2) belief in inherent morality of goals, (3) collective rationalization, (4) stereotyping of out-groups, (5) appearance of unanimity, (6) self-censorship, (7) pressure on dissenters, and (8) self-appointed mind-guards.[144] These symptoms overlap in some respects and reflect three categories: (1) the first two symptoms stem from overconfidence, (2) the next two symptoms reflect the biased way members perceive issues, and (3) the last four represent pressures for conformity.

As this Part discusses the various components of the groupthink theory, it applies these factors to the Enron Board's decision making regarding the related-party transactions. In building a case study of groupthink, Janis warns that major fiascoes resulting from apparent errors of judgment invite controversies about what happened and why. For this reason, Janis emphasized that, for each antecedent factor and symptom, a case study should construct a solid foundation by examining contemporary and retrospective reports by the group members themselves. Following this guidance, this Part relies primarily on the Enron directors' statements in the Powers Report, the Senate

---

[142] *See generally* Park, *supra* note 28.

[143] A few newspaper accounts of Enron mention groupthink in passing without further explanation. *See, e.g.*, Carl Franklin, *Beware of the Ostrich Factor*, SUNDAY BUS., Jan. 13, 2002; Allan Sloan, *Who Killed Enron?*, NEWSWEEK, Jan. 21, 2002, at 20; Jeffrey Sonnenfeld, *How Go-Along Boards Jam Up Firms, The Forum*, USA TODAY, Feb. 6, 2002, at A13.

[144] *See generally*, JANIS, GROUPTHINK, *supra* note 28. Past studies have veered away from the original groupthink model to suggest that additional factors are needed to explain why groupthink occurs within small groups. Some of the variables that have been suggested to complement Janis's original framework are group polarization, individual dominance, group cognitions, and time pressure on group decision making.

Report,[145] and Congressional hearings (subsequent investigations).[146] Janis noted, however, that where such direct evidence does not exist, case studies may appropriately make inferential leaps by using other sources of information. Accordingly, for many of the antecedent conditions and symptoms of groupthink, this Enron case study relies on general boardroom norms and journalists' accounts of Enron to bolster the direct proof. This Part also uses this indirect evidence to supply support for three symptoms (sense of invulnerability, pressure on dissenters, and self-appointed mind guards), where firsthand proof is not available at this time. Although direct proof does not exist for these symptoms, Janis emphasized that case studies do not need to include all eight symptoms. In developing a case study, Janis stressed the need to look at broader social and cultural forces to understand group dynamics. For this reason, this case study seeks to evaluate how the "new-economy" myth and a bubble stock market may have affected the Enron Board's decision making. Researchers explaining the groupthink theory also incorporate other behavioral tendencies in case studies of groupthink. As mentioned previously, groupthink is related to other insights about group dynamics, such as polarization and cascades. This Part explores how these parallel theories, as well as individual behavioral biases, are complementary to groupthink and may reinforce groupthink tendencies. Thus, where applicable, this Part explores other social-psychological phenomena that may overlap or blend into the groupthink phenomenon.

B. Antecedent Conditions of Groupthink

1. Cohesiveness

a. Theory

The first, and most important, antecedent condition of groupthink is cohesiveness. Janis described cohesiveness as involving a "we-feeling" that produces a "warm clubby atmosphere."[147] What was striking about Janis's groupthink theory is that he showed how too much cohesiveness in groups can have a detrimental impact on decision making. By fostering an environment of camaraderie, Janis explained that cohesiveness may cause a group to avoid facing hard questions in order to avoid conflict so that the group quickly reaches a consensus.

---

[145] During April 2002, the Subcommittee staff interviewed thirteen past and present Enron Board members, none of whom had previously been interviewed: Robert A. Belfer, Blake, Chan, Duncan, Gramm, Jaedicke, LeMasitre, Mendelsohn, Perira, Savage, Wakeham, Walker, and Winokur; all appeared voluntarily and were represented by the same counsel. SENATE REPORT, *supra* note 17, at 2-3.

[146] The Powers Report reflected information gathered from the interviews of Enron directors; during Congressional hearings, five Enron directors testified; and the Senate Report contains information gathered from other directors. *See* POWERS REPORT, *supra* note 17.

[147] JANIS, VICTIMS, *supra* note 28, at 142. Janis further explains: "[T]he more amiability and esprit de corps among the members of a policy making in-group, the greater the danger that independent critical thinking will be replaced by groupthink, which is likely to result in irrational actions directed against outgroups." *Id.*

At the outset, it is important to note that cohesiveness is one of the most studied, yet controversial, topics in social psychology. Importantly, groupthink can develop when groups are only moderately cohesive.[148] A generally accepted principle is that cohesiveness stems from all the forces motivating members to stay in the group. Cohesiveness may arise because the members have strong affective ties. As an example, Janis pointed to the off-duty socializing of the military officers before the attack on Pearl Harbor.[149] Affective ties, however, are not necessary for groupthink to occur. Rather, cohesiveness of the group may flow from functional ties. As an example, Janis noted that the inner circle of Nixon advisors had much internal competition, but were bound together through loyalty to Nixon.[150]

In discussing functional ties, Janis emphasized that three factors contribute to cohesiveness because they provide incentives for members to remain in the group. First, cohesiveness arises when members share a sense of belonging to a powerful, protective group. Second, homogeneity of the members' social backgrounds, ideologies, and cultural backgrounds promotes cohesiveness.[151] Finally, cohesiveness develops when members have significant admiration for the group leader and the group has achieved success in the past. Through attachment to a high-prestige group, members satisfy the human need to verify their self-worth.[152]

General boardroom norms indicate that many boards of Fortune 500 companies have a high level of cohesiveness for two reasons.[153] Directors note that the identity of other board members is the most important factor in joining a board. Not only do directors enjoy associating with other successful people,[154] directors provide each other with access to key informal and social networks that promote career advancement.[155] Indeed, many commentators state that boards remain "good ol' boys clubs" where insider bargains are struck. In addition, boards are high status groups described as "elite private clubs

---

[148] *Id.* at 197 ("If the group is moderately or highly cohesive, I tentatively suggest that every executive who participates in group decision is ostensibly susceptible to groupthink.").

[149] *Id.* at 257.

[150] *Id.* at 211-13.

[151] *See, e.g., id.* at 259; Cox & Munsinger, *supra* note 30, at 105.

[152] Cox & Munsinger, *supra* note 30, at 98.

[153] *See, e.g.,* Dallas, *Relational, supra* note 31, at 6. *But see* Martin Lipton & Jay Lorsch, *A Modest Proposal for Improved Corporate Governance*, 48 BUS. LAW. 59, 65 (1992) (directors very busy and spend little time together; thus, "most boards are not a cohesive group able to work well together toward a common purpose.").

[154] Cox & Munsinger, *supra* note 30, at 94.

[155] When asked why he accepted a directorship, one director quickly responded "Vanity." Edmond Warner, *The Inside View: Time to Declaw An Old Pet*, THE GUARDIAN, Mar. 9, 2002, at 1.24. As Lynne Dallas explains: "Corporate boards are groups characterized by their ability to provide valuable benefits to their members; . . . Board members are primarily motivated to serve on boards because of the identity of other board members." Lynne Dallas, *Ombudsperson, supra* note 54, at 109; *see also* Barry Baysinger & Robert E. Hokisson, *The Composition of Boards of Directors and Strategic Control: Effects on Corporate Strategy*, 15 ACAD. MGMT. REV. 72, 72-73 (1990).

with a rubber stamp."[156] The enhanced self-esteem derived from being singled out for membership in a select group motivates many directors to join boards.[157] Thus, both (1) the motives and rewards that encourage directors to serve on boards, and (2) the process used to select independent directors interact to form cohesive groups.

b. Application to Enron

Direct evidence of the Enron Board's cohesiveness is found in the Senate Report and Congressional hearings. The Senate Report stated, "Enron Board members uniformly described internal board relations as harmonious."[158] One Enron director went so far as to testify during Congressional hearings: "Personally, I believe while we may have initially just been a collection of individuals, we have now evolved into a very cohesive and collegial group."[159] The Senate Report noted that the Enron directors characterized their working relationship with Enron management as "good."[160] Specifically, the Enron directors indicated they had possessed great respect for senior Enron officers, trusting their integrity and competence.[161]

This cohesiveness among the Enron directors does not appear to stem from affective ties. Specifically, although some of the directors had close personal relationships with the CEO, Ken Lay,[162] the Senate Report stated that the directors had "very little interaction or communication" outside Enron Board meetings.[163] Rather, the Enron Board's cohesiveness flowed from three factors: (1) a high degree of homogeneity among the Enron Board members, (2) financial incentives for the Enron Board to bond together, and (3) a corporate culture that promoted loyalty to the Enron senior executives.

First, the common backgrounds as well as the long terms of the Enron directors were conducive to producing a clubby atmosphere in the Enron Boardroom. The board members had similar social, educational, and career backgrounds of the power elite in corporate America.[164] In addition, many of the independent directors served for extensive terms (over twenty years),[165] setting the stage to develop cohesiveness from attachments to the group itself.

Second, several types of financial incentives may have promoted a sense of solidarity among Enron Board members and a strong affiliation to the group itself. Enron Board

---

[156] *See, e.g.*, Langevoort, *Human Nature*, *supra* note 48, at 79.

[157] Cox & Munsinger, *supra* note 30, at 99.

[158] SENATE REPORT, *supra* note 17, at 8.

[159] *Enron Hearings*, *supra* note 11, at 21.

[160] SENATE REPORT, *supra* note 17, at 8.

[161] *Id.*

[162] *Id.*

[163] *Id.* at 10.

[164] Enron Proxy Statement, 2000, *supra* note 19.

[165] *See supra* note 19.

members were among the most highly compensated directors in the world; most of this compensation consisted of Enron stock options.[166] As a result, some board members were large stockholders of Enron[167] many making hundreds of thousands of dollars, and a few making more than a million dollars in sales of Enron stock.[168] In addition, ten of the fifteen most recent independent directors had conflicts stemming from side payments.[169] Several Enron directors had conflicts of interest involving donations by Enron or Enron executives to several of the directors' pet charities.[170] Other conflicts resulted from consulting or legal work that Enron had with directors or their firms.[171] Note: the Audit Committee members received these types of side payments, which may have clouded their judgments.[172]

Finally, media reports noted the "cult-like" atmosphere at Enron.[173] Specifically, Enron employees reported being "fanatically loyal" to the CEOs, Jeffrey Skilling and later Ken Lay.[174] One Enron employee asserted: "[E]very time Skilling spoke, I'd believe everything he'd say."[175] In describing this loyalty, one former Enron executive went so far as to analogize Enron to the Taliban.[176] This intense allegiance to Enron managers within the Enron corporate culture may have permeated the boardroom.

Thus, direct evidence, as well as boardroom norms and journalists' accounts, indicate that the most important antecedent condition for groupthink—cohesiveness—may have existed among the Enron directors. Analysis of the other two antecedent factors reveals that they may have also been present in the Enron Board's decision making.

---

166 SENATE REPORT, *supra* note 17, at 11 (the total cash and equity compensation of Enron Board members in 2000 was valued by Enron at about $350,000 or more than twice the national average of $138,000).

167 Sonnenfeld, *supra* note 143, at A13 (directors were large shareholders; Robert Belfer, $2 billion as Enron investor, holding more shares than any other individual; Enron director's Frank Savage's firm, Alliance Capital, was Enron's firm's largest shareholder with 43 million shares).

168 *Enron Hearings*, *supra* note 11, at 8.

169 *Id.*

170 *See, e.g.*, Daniel Kadlec et al., *Power Failure*, 158 BUS. SOURCE ELITE 68 (Dec. 10, 2001) (John Mendelsohn, president of a cancer clinic given about $600,000 by Enron and CEO Lay; Charles LeMaistre ran the cancer clinic now headed by Mendelsohn for eighteen years.).

171 *Id.* Lord John Wakeham, a former parliamentarian in England, received $72,000 in Enron consulting fees in 2000. *Id.* John Urquhart, a former General Electric executive and Enron Board member until May 2001, made nearly $200,000 a year consulting for Enron. John Barber's oil and gas firm did more than $30 million in business with Enron in 2000. *Id.*

172 Wendy Gramm is Director of the Mercatus Center; Enron has given the Mercatus Center $50,000. *See, e.g.*, Joanne S. Lubin, *Inside, Outside Enron, Audit Committee is Scrutinized*, WALL ST. J., Feb. 1, 2002, at C1; Ronald E. Berenbein, *The Enron Ethics Breakdown: The Conference Board*, 15 EXEC. ACT., Feb 2002. For John Mendelson's conflict, *see id.*

173 Joe Stephens & Peter Behr, *Enron's Culture Fed its Demise*, WASH. POST, Jan. 27, 2002, at A01.

174 *Id.*

175 *Id.*

176 *Id.*

2. Structural Faults in the Organization

a. Theory

The second antecedent condition for groupthink to develop concerns structural faults in the group's decision making processes. These structural faults may involve (1) inadequate decision making procedures, and (2) a lack of impartial leadership.[177] With respect to inadequate decision making procedures, Janis emphasized that an important impediment to groups' decision making is the reliance on faulty information given by outside experts. In some instances, where different groups rely on each other for information, Janis noted the possibility of collective groupthink by interlocking groups. In examining the United States' lack of precautions for the attack on Pearl Harbor, Janis discussed how the Navy, Army, and War Council each demonstrated groupthink inclinations that magnified these same tendencies by the other groups. Specifically, under the influence of groupthink, members suppressed their personal doubts. Thus, the interlocking groups reciprocally indulged in the withholding of information, intensifying each group's inclination toward groupthink.[178] In this way, a circular form of social learning took place whereby each of these groups discounted the negative information it possessed, because the other groups failed to show apprehension.[179]

Janis stated that impartial leadership also leads to structural faults. Leaders are impartial when they strongly state their own views at the beginning of meetings and discourage dissent.

b. Application to Enron

In reviewing the Enron Board's actions, four structural faults stand out for emphasis. First, as noted at the beginning of this article, other corporate gatekeepers failed to detect the problems at Enron, such as analysts, auditors, outside counsel, lead lenders, institutional investors, credit rating agencies, journalists, investment bankers, and regulators. With respect to this widespread breakdown of corporate checks and balances, collective groupthink may have influenced these interlocking groups. Specifically, each of the corporate watchdogs in the Enron scandal may have downplayed red flags and avoided greater vigilance because the other groups appeared to maintain positive schemas of Enron.

Second, the Enron Board relied on the involvement of Enron's outside auditor, Arthur Andersen.[180] The Senate Report revealed that Arthur Andersen (and Enron managers) were aware of problems for months and withheld this information from the

---

[177] JANIS, VICTIMS, *supra* note 28, at 183. Janis argued that this groupthink conditions infers "the leader does not feel constrained by any organizational tradition to avoid pushing for his own preferred policies." Closed leaders do not encourage divergent opinions from group members, do not emphasize the importance of reaching a wise decision, and states his or her opinion at the outset of the meeting. *Id.*

[178] *Id.* at 100.

[179] Langevoort, *Where, supra* note 86, at 107.

[180] POWERS REPORT, *supra* note 17, at 167 n.3.

Enron Board.[181] In addition, Andersen had a conflict of interest in advising Enron on structuring the related-party transactions because Enron was Andersen's largest client and Andersen employees routinely went to work for Enron.[182] Andersen also obtained significant consulting fees from Enron and served as Enron's internal auditor for two years. During Congressional hearings, the Enron directors stated that these potential conflicts by the outside auditor did not cause apprehension. This lack of concern is understandable, given that the prevailing norm among directors at the time accepted auditor conflicts as routine by the oligopoly of the then-existing Big Five accounting firms. When questioned about the evidence of Enron's "high risk" accounting, the Enron directors emphasized that Enron's auditor had given the company a clean audit opinion each year. In addition, the Audit Committee relied on the fact that they offered Andersen personnel an opportunity to present information to them without management present.[183] The Enron directors reported that they could not recall occasions when Andersen disclosed reservations about particular transactions or accounting practices at Enron.[184] Revealing an important aspect of the Enron corporate culture, an Enron employee stated: "[A]nyone who questioned suspect deals quickly learned to accept assurances of outside lawyers and accountants."[185]

Third, structural faults existed in how Enron employees negotiated the related-party transactions with Fastow, Enron's CFO (the managing partner of the general partners of the limited partnerships investing the special purpose entities set up to transact with Enron). Specifically, contrary to the Enron Board's request for compliance controls, Enron employees working on the related-party deals reported to Fastow and sat next to Enron workers negotiating on Enron's behalf. The Powers Report found that in at least thirteen instances, Fastow pressured Enron employees to obtain better terms for his partnerships.[186] According to the Powers Report, "[s]imply put, there was little of separation and independence required to enable Enron employees to negotiate effectively against LJM2."[187] With respect to the Enron Board's control procedures to review the related-party transactions, the Powers Report notes that in many instances, "officers interpreted their roles very narrowly . . . [and] [n]o one in Management stepped forward to address the issues as they arose, or to bring the apparent problems to the Board's attention."[188]

Finally, Congressional hearings indicated that the Enron Board lacked impartial leadership. As with most boards, the CEO, Ken Lay, appointed many of the Enron

---

181 SENATE REPORT, *supra* note 17, at 15-20.

182 *Id.* at 24.

183 *Id.* at 10.

184 *Id.* at 14.

185 McLean, *supra* note 3, at 33.

186 POWERS REPORT, *supra* note 17, at 67-69.

187 *Id.* at 67.

188 *Id.* at 10.

directors[189] and served as chairperson of the Enron Board.[190] In addition, the Enron Board did not have a practice of meeting without Enron management present.[191] The Senate Report noted that Lay and Skilling usually attended Executive, Finance, and Audit Committee meetings, as well as full Board meetings. Lay also attended many Compensation Committee meetings; one indication of Lay's influence on the Enron Board is the level of his compensation, which was quite high, even by current standards.[192]

3. Situational Context

a. Theory

The final antecedent condition for groupthink focuses on the group's need to make consequential policy decisions during a time of high stress.[193] Janis emphasized that groupthink is a problem for high-level decision makers making important, as opposed to routine, decisions. Janis found that this condition occurs when a group needs to formulate policies that contradict prevailing ethical standards, including individual member's own moral codes. When faced with the sacrifice of moral values, group members recognize that they risk threats of social condemnation as well as self-disapproval. In this difficult situation, each member may encounter personal feelings of shame and guilt, which lower self-esteem. To block these negative emotions, each member will turn to the others in the group for rationalizations to avert the potential loss of honor. Thus, Janis explained that groupthink is a defensive mode for coping with decisional stress. In particular, Janis emphasized that the role of threatened self-esteem pushes members of the group toward quick consensus as a form of social support.

To promote this rationalization process, Janis stated that the group may become a source of moral consolation that nurtures the shared belief that "we are a wise and good group." That is, members turn to group concurrence to ease anxieties aroused from violating ethical standards.[194] This may lead the members to view group consensus as the criterion for judging the efficacy, as well as the morality, of the group's decision. For these reasons, members avoid raising ethical concerns that imply that this "fine group of ours, with its humanitarianism and its high-minded principles, might be capable of adopting a course of action that is inhumane and immoral."[195] In addition, members seek to reassure themselves with the idea that "you can't make an

---

[189] Joseph Nocera, *System Failure*, FORTUNE, June 20, 2002, at 62, 72.

[190] Enron Form 10k (Spring 2001) *available at* http://www.edgar-online.com.

[191] SENATE REPORT, *supra* note 17, at 10.

[192] Lay received $141 million in 2000—ten times the average of CEO compensation of the top 200 CEOs. Enron Hearings, supra note 11, at 18-19. In fairness, the average CEO compensation for the top ten companies was $169 million. *Id.*

[193] JANIS, VICTIMS, *supra* note 28, at 86.

[194] *Id.* at 203.

[195] *Id.* at 20.

omelet without breaking some eggs."[196] In this way, Janis explained that cohesiveness causes "hardhearted actions by soft-headed groups." As an example, Janis explains how Nixon's advisors became dependent upon the group to maintain their morale during the Watergate cover-up.[197]

b. Application to Enron

The subsequent investigations provide several examples that the antecedent factor of situational context may have been present in the Enron Board's deliberations. Specifically, the Enron Board waived the company's ethics code three times within sixteen months to allow the CFO to serve as general partner of the entities that Enron used as conduits for much of its highly complicated and controversial financial maneuvering.[198] These waivers by the Enron Board were unusual events. During Congressional hearings, the Enron directors could not identify a precedent for the waivers, stating that they were "unaware of any company that had its CFO running a private equity fund on the side."[199] In addition, corporate governance experts testified that they never heard of a public company ratifying a similar proposal.[200] Indeed, one former CEO commented, "In my wildest dreams, I can't imagine how a director can sit there and approve that."[201] That CEO stated that not only would he have voted against the transaction, he would have resigned the next day if the board approved it. In addition, an internal memo at Arthur Anderson noted, "Why would any director in his or her right mind ever approve such a scheme?"[202] Nevertheless, the Senate Report notes, "[Enron] Board approval proved easy to obtain" with few questions asked.[203]

The Enron directors testified that they made the decisions to waive the ethics code for two reasons. First, although the Enron Board members realized that significant risks were present regardless of what decision they made, they felt the benefits outweighed the costs. On the one hand, the Enron Board noted the advantages flowing to Enron because Fastow's expertise could lead to efficiencies in structuring deals between Enron and the related-party partnerships.[204] On the other hand, Enron directors recognized the disadvantage stemming from the risk of public criticism for approving the related-party transactions.[205]

---

196 *Id.* at 203.

197 JANIS, GROUPTHINK, *supra* note 28, at 210-11.

198 *Id.* at 27.

199 *Enron Hearings, supra* note 11.

200 *Id.* at 6.

201 *Id.*

202 SENATE REPORT, *supra* note 17, at 25-26.

203 *Id.* at 28.

204 POWERS REPORT, *supra* note 17, at 67.

205 *Id.* at 151 (risks arising from Fastow's conflict of interest could create a poor public appearance).

Second, the Enron Board members testified that they had established controls to mitigate the conflicts.[206] In response, the Powers Report chastised the board: "At bottom, however, the need for such an extensive set of controls said something fundamental about the wisdom of permitting the CFO to take on this conflict of interest."[207]

Thus, the Enron Board may have believed it was necessary "to break some eggs" by waiving Enron's ethics code to allow the related-party transactions to assure Enron's continued success. In sum, the antecedent factors of groupthink—cohesiveness, structural faults, and situational context—appear to have been present in the Enron Boardroom. Next, this Part examines how the Enron Board demonstrated the symptoms of groupthink.

C. Symptoms of Groupthink

1. *Illusion of Invulnerability*

a. Theory

The first symptom of groupthink is the group's feeling of invincibility, which creates overconfidence and leads to excessive risk-taking. Specifically, group members may come to believe that they can do no wrong, particularly when the group is powerful and has achieved past success. Essentially, the idea is, if the leader and everyone else in the group decides that the plan is appropriate, then the plan is bound to succeed, even if it is quite risky, because luck is on the group's side.[208] As an example, Janis referred to the sense of "unlimited confidence" Kennedy's advisors had in planning the Bay of Pigs invasion. Janis noted that the advisors had tremendous faith in Kennedy because "[e]verything had broken right for him. Everyone around him thought he had the Midas touch and would not lose."[209] This "buoyant optimism" centered on the promise of bold, new ideas and the "euphoria of the new day." Thus, Janis summarized the attitude as "everything is going to work out all right because we are a special group."[210]

In general, individuals tend to be overly optimistic about (1) risky events that they have little control over, and (2) their own talents and abilities.[211] Indeed, successful people can become so overconfident that they resist evaluating the boundaries to their power and the losses that may arise if their luck does not hold.[212] This cognitive bias is known as the "winner's curse."[213] Within groups, successful individuals can spread this bias to others through a process called "emotional contagion." Indeed, this bias

---

[206] POWERS REPORT, *supra* note 17, at 29.

[207] *Id.* at 68.

[208] JANIS, VICTIMS, *supra* note 28, at 36.

[209] *Id.*

[210] *Id.* at 132; *see also* Langevoort, *Illusions*, *supra* note 27, at 143-45.

[211] BAZERMAN, *supra* note 109, at 95.

[212] JANIS, VICTIMS, supra note 28, at 37.

[213] *See, e.g.*, RICHARD H. THALER, THE WINNER'S CURSE: PARADOXES AND ANOMALIES OF ECONOMIC LIFE (1992).

may be so contagious that it leads to a type of "group narcissism."[214] This tendency for excessive optimism is present in many corporate cultures because it relieves stress[215] and fosters a "can do" atmosphere. Such optimism can turn into a self-fulfilling prophecy because it promotes higher morale and aggressiveness among employees.[216] This theory is used to explain how executives' overly-optimistic views of their firms' future lead to large takeover premiums.[217]

This ego-centric bias, however, has a dark side when it causes organizational members to ignore indications that point toward limits to their competence. Specifically, the illusion of invincibility affects a person's perceptions pertaining to risk-assessment. In general, powerful psychological influences are necessary to overcome the risk-aversion most individuals have. Motivated by financial incentives and loss framing, however, individuals, as well as groups may turn to rationalizations that allow them to view large risks as reasonable.[218] Bolstered by overconfidence, groups may underestimate the severity of risk posed by their decisions. In this way, groupthink has important similarities to polarization, discussed in Part II.

b. Application to Enron

Examination of direct sources revealed no evidence that the Enron directors felt invincible. Such bald-faced statements of superiority by individuals are rare, even among high-ego types. During Congressional hearings, however, one senator stated: "The [Enron] Board . . . succumbed to the Enron ether of invincibility, superiority and gamesmanship in manipulating Enron's financial statements to keep the Enron stock price soaring."[219]

The direct evidence, however, does indicate that the Enron directors approved of Enron's overall strategic plans, which were extraordinarily ambitious. Enron's "asset-light" policy required an intense focus on Enron's credit rating, cash flow, and debt burden. To accomplish these objectives, the Enron directors supported management's methods of using complicated transactions with convoluted financing and accounting structures.[220] Although the Enron directors denied it, the Powers Report criticized Enron for engaging in "significant transactions that were apparently designed to accomplish favorable financial statement results, not to achieve bona fide economic objectives to transfer risk."[221]

---

214 Langevoort, *Myths, supra* note 25, at 1578.

215 *See* Langevoort, *Hyper-Competition, supra* note 102.

216 *Id.*

217 Matthew Hayward & Donald C. Hambrick, *Explaining the Premiums Paid for Large Acquisitions: Evidence of CEO Hubris*, 42 AMIND. SCI. Q. 103, 120 (1998).

218 Langevoort, *Selling Hope, supra* note 73, at 641.

219 *Enron Hearings, supra* note 11, at 2; SENATE REPORT, *supra* note 17, at 8.

220 SENATE REPORT, *supra* note 17, at 8.

221 POWERS REPORT, *supra* note 17, at 4.

Providing indirect support that the Enron Board displayed the symptom of invincibility, journalists' accounts reflect that the Enron corporate culture was well-known for its high level of hubris. Specifically, four factors indicate that an illusion of invulnerability permeated the Enron corporate culture and may have influenced the Enron Board's decision making. First, Enron compiled an extraordinary track record. For example, *Fortune* magazine voted Enron as the most innovative company for five years running.[222] Skilling once boasted "Enron has reported 20 straight quarters of increasing income. There's not a trading company in the world that has that kind of consistency."[223] Thus, the Enron culture promoted the belief that its employees' conquests stemmed from talent, rather than luck.[224]

Second, this impressive performance led to a superstar culture of "we're above everyone else"[225] at Enron. As evidence, Enron described itself as "the world's leading company."[226] Indeed, the culture of arrogance was so extreme that Skilling once told a group of utility executives: "I'm going to eat your lunch."[227]

Third, the Enron culture promoted the idea that Enron was "untouchable."[228] This sense of untouchability arose from Enron's position as one of corporate America's top political contributors.[229] Prior to Enron's fall, these political investments appeared to reap large benefits for Enron. For example, Enron was the largest contributor of George W. Bush's career and President Bush referred to Lay as "Kenny Boy."[230] As evidence of Enron's political influence, Lay was the only energy executive to advise Vice President Dick Cheney in framing the Administration's energy policy.[231] Most importantly, Enron received an exemption of its trading activities from federal regulation.[232] Thus, the Enron culture promoted the concept that Enron had purchased vast political power.

Fourth, Enron's culture of hubris encouraged breaking the rules and taking extreme risks.[233] One reporter noted, "The common theme is hubris, an overweening pride,

---

[222] Patrap Chatterjee, *Enron: Pulling the Plug on the Global Power Broker*, CORPWATCH, Dec. 13, 2002.

[223] McLean, *supra* note 3, at 32.

[224] Langevoort, *Hyper-competition, supra* note 116, at 8.

[225] BODILY & BRUNNER, *supra* note 2, at 48.

[226] McLean, *supra* note 3, at 28.

[227] *Id.*

[228] Rick Bragg, *Enron's Collapse: Workers*, N.Y. TIMES, Jan. 20, 2002, at 1.

[229] Enron spent $10.2 million between 1997 and 2000. *See, e.g.*, Albert R. Hunt, *A Scandal Centerpiece: Enron's Political Connections*, WALL ST. J., Jan. 17, 2001, at A15.

[230] In running for governor, Bush received $774,000 from Enron managers and $312,000 from Enron, *see e.g.*, Chatterjee, *supra* note 222, at 28; Howard Fineman & Michael Isikoff, *Lights Out: Enron's Failed Power Play*, NEWSWEEK, Jan. 21, 2002, at 15.

[231] *See, e.g.*, Stephen Labaton, *Enron's Collapse: The Lobbying*, N.Y. TIMES, Jan. 19, 2002, at 1.

[232] The Commodity Futures Modernization Act included an exemption for energy trading companies. *See, e.g.*, Bratton, *supra* note 2.

[233] Bill Mann, *Enron as Icarus*, THE MOTLEY FOOL, Nov. 30, 2001, at 19.

which led people to believe they can handle increasingly exotic risk without danger."[234] This over-optimism, however, also had a dark side. Through the "rank and yank" tournament structure, the Enron culture placed intense pressure upon employees to improve Enron's glowing track record.[235] This competitive atmosphere may have provided Enron employees with the rationalization that aggressive tactics were merely part of the game.[236] In describing the Enron culture, an Enron officer stated, "You can break the rules, you can cheat, you can lie, but as long as you make money, it's all right."[237] As an example, one Enron employee received a promotion after violating company policy in making an investment that turned out to be successful.[238] As one reporter summed up the corporate culture:

> [B]ut what made Enron successful—innovation and daring—got the company into trouble when it decided in its arrogance that it could "financialize" almost anything. Feeling it could do no wrong, the company too often pursued unprofitable markets, obscured the costs and stiff-armed anyone who asked for an explanation.[239]

The Enron culture of invincibility may have infected the Enron Board, which had been hailed as one of the five best corporate boards.[240] It is human nature for directors to allow such praise to cloud their judgments, especially when their corporation has a track record as glowing as Enron's. This is true especially in light of the time constraints on the Enron Board; as is typical of most boards, the Enron Board met five times a year in regular meetings and occasionally in special meetings.[241] The Finance Committee and the Audit and Compliance Committee each met for one to two hours before the board meeting.[242] Enron directors varied in how much time they spent reading the materials and preparing for Board meetings, with the reported preparation time for each meeting ranging between two hours and two days.[243] Given these constraints, many Enron Board members probably relied on the objective evidence of Enron's rising

---

234 *Id.* ("It bred a culture of breathtaking arrogance that Enron could do the impossible.").

235 *See, e.g.*, Stephens & Behr, *supra* note 173, at A01.

236 Langevoort, *Selling Hope, supra* note 73, at 664 ("experience the happy confluence of higher share price and lower moral anxiety").

237 *Id.*

238 Stephens & Behr, *supra* note 173, at A01.

239 *Id.*

240 Horton, *supra* note 20, at 9.

241 *See e.g.*, SENATE REPORT, *supra* note 17, at 9. The Board normally held five regular meetings during the year, with additional special meetings as needed. Board meetings usually lasted two days, with the first day devoted to Committee meetings and a board dinner and the second day devoted to a meeting of the full Board. *Id.*

242 POWERS REPORT, *supra* note 17, at 158 n.3.

243 SENATE REPORT, *supra* note 17, at 9.

stock price to simplify and reduce to manageable proportions the many complex factors involved in approving the related-party transactions. Simply put, Enron's high stock prices generated a culture of optimism and the Enron Board may have felt it should not interfere with Enron's extraordinary achievements.

2. *Belief in Inherent Morality of the Group*

a. Theory

Another symptom of groupthink, related to the first symptom of invincibility, is a belief in the group's inherent morality.[244] One social scientist explains, "The feeling is that we are good guys and our decisions are in everyone's best interests. We are doing this to benefit everyone."[245]

b. Application to Enron

The Powers Report and Congressional hearings provide direct support for the view that the Enron Board demonstrated this symptom. Before reviewing this evidence, this section provides background by examining two aspects of the Enron corporate culture: (1) the belief that the Enron strategy would improve the world, and (2) society's view of top Enron executives as heroes.

First, Enron set out to enhance societal welfare by reducing the role of government and changing the nature of markets.[246] Specifically, Enron inculcated the belief that it was leading a revolution that would change the world. Indeed, Enron's former CEO Jeffrey Skilling not only stated, "[W]e're the good guys,"[247] he went so far as to say, "[W]e're on the side of the angels."[248] Both Skilling and Lay were true believers that deregulation was the key to improving society. Analysts reported that conferences with Enron executives had the flavor of revival meetings where the Enron executives' pitch rested on a "near-fundamentalist faith in the self-regulating efficiency of the market."[249] One journalist described Enron as an "evangelical cult," with Ken Lay as its "messiah."[250] Another newspaper account stated that Skilling was like a "religious zealot who couldn't stop repeating his favorite mantra as the solution to all the world's problems."[251]

---

[244] JANIS, VICTIMS, *supra* note 28, at 88.

[245] *Id.* at 178.

[246] *See, e.g.*, *Fallen Idols*, ECONOMIST, May 4, 2002, at 11; Mann, *supra* note 233; Kadlec et al., *supra* note 170, at 68; Sloan, *supra* note 143, at 19.

[247] *OnLine Extra: Q & A with Enron's Skilling*, BUS. WK. ONLINE, Feb. 12, 2001.

[248] *Id.*

[249] Bethany McLean, *Is Enron Overpriced?*, FORTUNE, Mar. 5, 2001, at 32.

[250] Pratap Chatterjee, *Enron: Pulling the Plug on the Global Power Broker*, CORPWATCH, Dec. 13, 2001.

[251] *Id.*

Enron's deregulation strategy was part of its portrayal as a new-economy maverick. Pushing the view that Enron was making business history, Skilling stated, "[t]here's only been a couple of times in history when these costs of interaction have radically changed. One was the railroads, and then the telephone and the telegraph."[252] Skilling claimed there were no limits to its "asset-light" strategy[253] to reduce Enron's dependence on hard assets so that Enron would serve as a market intermediary, trading everything from water futures to weather contracts.[254] Enron cast its competition as "stick-in-the-mud"[255] companies that didn't "get it." Skilling once stated, "These big companies will topple over from their own weight."[256]

This account of the Enron corporate culture sheds light on the direct evidence. Congressional hearings noted that the Enron Board needed to "exercise heightened vigilance when a company is pursuing unfamiliar or new territory.[257] These hearings indicated, "[i]t appears that the [Enron] board of directors continued to perform its duties as if Enron were still an old-line conservative energy company, at a time when it appears they should have been far more probing, given Enron's metamorphosis into an energy trading company."[258] This is easy to say in hindsight. The sense of mission generated by the idea that Enron was leading a revolution may have provided Enron Board members with rationalizations to allow the related-party transactions to proceed. In addition, the popularity of "new era economics" in the financial press served as a short cut justification for many sophisticated people in making business decisions in the bubble economy.[259] Specifically, the dot-com boom started a cultural change in the outside financial community that supported and encouraged the distortion of basic business values by using new financial metrics.[260] The Senate Report indicated that the Enron Board may have been influenced by this "new era" thinking. One Enron director stated, "I think all of us understood that these [were] highly structured, new kinds of transactions . . . [that would allow Enron] to be at the beginning of these transactions . . . ."[261] Another Enron director echoed these sentiments, stating these transactions were "relatively new" and had "not been done by many companies in the

---

[252] Jerry Useem, *And Then, Just When You Thought the "New Economy" Was Dead*, BUS. 2.0 (Aug. 2001), www.business2.com.

[253] *See* Bill Bratton's description of Enron as a "virtual corporation." Bratton, *supra* note 2, at 1280.

[254] For an innovative discussion on virtual corporations, *see* Claire Moore Dickerson, *Spinning Out of Control: The Virtual Organization and Conflicting Governance Vectors*, 59 U. PITT. L. REV. 759 (1998).

[255] *The History of Enron* (NPR radio broadcast, Jan. 22, 2002).

[256] McLean, *supra* note 3, at 34.

[257] *Enron Hearings*, *supra* note 11, at 5.

[258] *Id.* at 6.

[259] Langevoort, *Human Nature, supra* note 48; *see generally* Langevoort, *Myths, supra* note 25 (people unconsciously impose an order on their environment through myths that serve as "anxiety buffers").

[260] *See, e.g.,* Tim Race, *Ashamed to Be an Executive*, N.Y. TIMES, July 1, 2002.

[261] SENATE REPORT, *supra* note 17, at 19-20.

world."[262] Given the time and information constraints on the board, some Enron directors may have believed that the new economy propelled Enron's success. Such framing may have reduced the cognitive complexity involved in evaluating the complex financial structures used to build Enron's house of cards.[263]

Second, American culture portrayed the CEOs of Enron, Skilling and then Lay, as modern day heroes.[264] In times of economic transition, business executives become "larger-than-life leaders" because they are the engines of social change as they push through the massive transformations that society periodically undertakes.[265] At the beginning of the 1900s, Andrew Carnegie, John D. Rockefeller, and Henry Ford became legends. In the past few years, the shareholder value mantra made Wall Street heroes out of financial wizards who could do magic with share prices.[266] Enron was "laser focused"[267] on shareholder value at a time when many people viewed higher, short-term stock prices as an unequivocal virtue.[268] Indeed, Enron had televisions in its elevators to allow employees to monitor stock prices at all times.[269] As a result of

---

[262] *Id.* at 20.

[263] Thus, in describing Enron, one commentator noted: "It looked like the quintessential instance of bubble governance: a pliant board, lulled into false sense of security by a rising stock price, a successful management team and a stable of high-profile advisors." Andrew Hill, *Enron's Demise Has Taken the Shine Off Boardroom Tables*, FIN. TIMES, May 30, 2002, at 22.

[264] *See, e.g.*, Jennifer G. Hill, *Deconstructing Sunbeam—Contemporary Issues in Corporate Governance*, 67 U. CIN. L. REV. 1099 (1999) ("the cult of the charismatic CEO continues to have a powerful, but potentially dangerous hold on U.S. commercial psyche . . ."); Michael Maccoby, *Narcissistic Leaders: The Incredible Pros, The Inevitable Cons*, 78 HARV. BUS. REV. 69 (2002) (superstars, such as Bill Gates and Jack Welch, "the world's business personalities are increasingly seen as the makers and shapers of our public and personal agendas."). The Enron debacle and other scandals seem to have ended the era of CEO as heroes. A more significant contributor to the fall of executives as gods was the action of firefighters and police officers on September 11, 2002. As one journalist noted: "It is difficult not to contrast the professionalism of modestly paid firefighters and police doing their duty on September 11 with the secretive and squirrelly behavior of six and seven figure CEOs who failed at their duty with Enron." Bruce Nussbaum, *Can You Trust Anybody Anymore?*, BUS. WK., 31, 31, Jan. 28, 2002.

[265] Maccoby, *supra* note 264, at 70.

[266] *Id.; see generally*, MARJORIE KELLY: THE DIVINE RIGHT OF CAPITAL: DETHRONING THE CORPORATE ARISTOCRACY (2002) (shareholder worship of CEOs who inflated stock prices).

[267] Enron Annual Report 2000, at 2 *available at* http://www.enron.com/corp/investors/annuals/2000/ar2000.pdf.

[268] Maccoby, *supra* note 264, at 70. Commentators noted:

> As stock options became an increasing part of executive compensation, and managers who made great fortunes on options became the stuff of legends, the preservation or enhancement of short-term stock value became a personal (and damaging) priority for many a CEO and CFO. High share prices and earnings multiples stoked already amply endowed managerial egos.

Fuller & Jensen *supra* note 12, at 2; *see also* Jeremy Kahn, *Accounting in Wonderland; Down the Rabbit Hole with G.E.'s Books*, FORTUNE, Mar. 19, 2001, at 37.

[269] *Enron Hearings, supra* note 11, at 2.

Enron's success, the financial and popular press lionized Enron executives.[270] Kenneth Lay achieved icon status as part of the elite corporate royalty. Viewing themselves as "revolutionaries" that lived the rule of "creative destruction," some Enron executives went so far as to describe themselves as being like Gandhi and Martin Luther King.[271] Thus, journalists described the senior Enron managers as "self-proclaimed masters of the universe."[272]

This background sets the stage to review the direct evidence. The Powers Report and congressional hearings reveal that the Enron Board relied on the Enron managers' reputations in making the decisions to approve and monitor the related-party transactions. Significantly, one director testified that the Enron Board approved the deals because Enron executives were "some of the most creative and talented people in business."[273] One Enron director stated, "We truly believed we had hired some of the best and brightest in the industry. National independent publications lauded the Enron officers for their intelligence, leadership, and creativity."[274] Perhaps the Enron Board believed the CEO-worship hype and approved the related-party transactions in the belief that such decisions were warranted to allow the heroes of Enron to continue making business history.

3. Collective Rationalization

a. Theory

Another symptom of groupthink is the group's efforts to rationalize away red flags that would otherwise lead members to revise their positions.[275] This symptom of collective rationalization demonstrates a mindset of "hear no evil, see no evil, speak no

---

[270] *See, e.g., Fallen Idols*, ECONOMIST, May 4, 2002, at 11.

[271] Bill Mann, *Enron as Icarus*, THE MOTLEY FOOL, Nov. 30, 2001, at 19; *see generally* Maccoby, *supra* note 264, at 70 (Consider how an executive at Oracle describes CEO Larry Ellison: "The difference between God and Larry is that God does not think he is Larry.").

[272] Peter Coy & Emily Thornton, *Enron: Running on Empty*, BUS. WK., Dec. 10, 2001 at 80. In the past, Al Dunlap, a.k.a. "Chainsaw Al" or "Rambo in pinstripes," was also viewed as a hero. *Exit Bad Guy*, ECONOMIST, June 20, 1998, at 70. Dunlap's accounting gimmickry at Sunbeam lead to his demise as he attempted to repeat his success at Scott Paper. John A. Byrne, How *Al Dunlap Self-Destructed: The Inside Story of What Drove Sunbeams, Board to Act*, BUS. WK., July 6, 1998, at 58.

[273] *Enron Hearings*, *supra* note 11, at 4.

[274] *Id.* at 2.

[275] JANIS, VICTIMS, *supra* note 28, at 45. Individuals can also suffer from a similar phenomenon. Donald Langevoort explains: "When people voluntarily commit themselves to a certain position, attitude or belief, the subsequent discovery of information that indicates harmful consequences flowing from that commitment directly threatens their self-concept as good, worthwhile individuals. Thus, cognitive processes will work to suppress such information if at all possible." Langevoort, *Where, supra* note 86, at 102-03; *see also* Langevoort, *Human Nature, supra* note 48, at 826 (path dependence leads people to throw good money after bad); Langevoort, *Illusions, supra* note 27, at 143 (self-serving beliefs—"people naturally see what they want to see").

evil." As discussed previously, social psychology explains that red flags indicate the need for change and that it is human nature to preserve the status quo in order to reduce stress under the "illusion of normalcy."[276] That is, groups can interpret negative data in a way that supports the maintenance of previously agreed upon policies through "cognitive conservatism."[277]

Given sunk costs and serial decision making, groups suffering from illusions of invulnerability may engage in what Janis called the "irrational escalation of commitment." This is the so-called "optimism-commitment whipsaw" discussed previously, whereby decision makers ignore red flags as instances of bad luck and intensify their efforts in the hope that their luck will change. To avoid the potential loss of self-esteem from facing up to the situation, groups suffering from this bias may not only stay their course, but also increase their level of commitment by throwing even more resources at the problem.[278] As an example, Janis pointed to the Johnson administration's failure to recognize that the United States was failing in its attempt to win the Vietnam War.[279] Instead, through a series of decisions, Johnson's advisors responded by continuing to escalate the United States' commitment by employing more troops and resources.

As discussed previously, independent directors often make decisions to trust the CEO of the company in deciding to accept a board seat. This initial determination to rely on the CEO, however, creates the possibility of cognitive dissonance because facing up to negative information may lead to an ego-threatening realization that the independent director originally had poor judgment. This cognitive dissonance may lead the independent directors to be less diligent in their monitoring role in three ways. First, independent directors are likely to accept managers' explanations at face value without making an effort to otherwise investigate the accuracy of these statements.[280] Second, directors may subconsciously choose to forego seeking information that indicates that the initial choice to join the board was a bad decision. Thus, independent directors may not take the time to comb through the preparation materials prior to board meetings to look for proof that managers are failing. Finally, independent directors may fail to heed warning signs that suggest that such trust should not continue.[281] Post-commitment, these independent directors may tend to dismiss suspicious information by relying on the other independent directors who appear not to worry. This fosters an unfortunate cycle when the other independent directors share the same biases.

In addition, Langevoort explains the concept of "motivated influence," which may play a role in independent director's perceptions.[282] Discovering a red flag would put the director in the unpleasant position of having to question the integrity of a "friend."

---

276 Langevoort, *Myths, supra* note 25, at 1575.

277 JANIS, VICTIMS, *supra* note 28, at 45.

278 Langevoort, *Selling Hope, supra* note 73, at 645.

279 JANIS, VICTIMS, *supra* note 28, at 97.

280 Prentice, *supra* note 13, at 163 (auditors accept client's explanations).

281 Langevoort, *Selling Hope, supra* note 73, at 693.

282 Langevoort, *Monitoring, supra* note 118.

Rather than risk destroying the managers' trust, independent directors may give managers the benefit of the doubt and favor an interpretation that avoids negative inferences. Once such rationalizations occur, the independent may not notice a red flag.[283] Perceiving some evidence of problems, independent directors may honestly, but mistakenly believe that these are minor setbacks, drawing on collective myths of invulnerability derived from the salience of past achievements.

It may take quite a long time for a board that has rationalized away red flags to recognize that a strong possibility of failure is imminent. By the time reality hits, the "commitment-whipsaw" bias tends to reduce the time interval of the failure and increase the acuteness of the firm's collapse.[284] In other words, when the board finally perceives how bright red the flags actually are, the firm may be very deep in the Big Muddy. Social psychologists call this the "last-period problem."[285]

b. Application to Enron

The Senate Report indicates several examples of different types of collective rationalizations used by the Enron Board to ignore red flags. Before reviewing these collective rationalizations, it is important to note that the Senate Report included thirteen red flags over two years that the Enron Board should have seen.[286] This led one senator to state: "[T]he board had ample knowledge of the dangerous waters in which Enron was swimming, and it didn't do anything about it."[287] Perhaps this is too easy to say in hindsight. Social psychology provides a more subtle, nuanced account of the Enron Board's failure to respond to red flags. Fastow and other Enron managers may have shrewdly framed the Enron Board's decisions in a manner that the directors perceived Enron's situation in a loss frame;[288] that is, Fastow may have emphasized that without these related-party deals, Enron could lose its superstar status. Given the salience of Enron's stellar track record, the optimism-commitment may have led the Enron Board to continue to grant waivers of the ethics code despite indications that they needed to change course. Despite warnings over this two-year period, the Enron directors continued to grant waivers of the firm's ethics code to allow additional related-party transactions—three waivers of the ethics code within two years—providing evidence of the so-called "optimism-commitment whipsaw."

---

283 *Id.*

284 Langevoort, *Epistemology, supra* note 94, at 645.

285 *Id.*

286 POWERS REPORT, *supra* note 17, at 148 ("The Board was denied important information that might have led it to take action, but the Board also did not fully appreciate the significance of some of the specific information that came before it."); *Enron Hearings, supra* note 11, at 3 (staff identified over a dozen red flags).

287 *Enron Hearings, supra* note 11, at 30.

288 *Cf.* Prentice, *supra* note 13, at 156 (citing studies where half of the auditors were decided by management's frame).

This section reviews six of the red flags discussed in the Senate Report in historical sequence and suggests reasons why the Enron directors may have ignored this mounting evidence about the related-party transactions. First, the Enron directors downplayed their role in Congressional hearings. Specifically, several Enron directors refused to admit that they "waived" the Enron code of conduct, but rather referred to the action as "ratification of the Office of the Chairman."[289] This statement indicates that the Enron Board members rationalized away the degree of their responsibility for the decisions.

Second, the Enron Board encountered a warning signal during the outside auditors' presentation on the second related-party deal. Specifically, Arthur Andersen reported to the Enron Board that the most significant hazard of the transaction was "accounting risk."[290] Anderson ranked the different risk factors with "H" for high, "M" for medium and "L" for low.[291] Anderson highlighted that one of the major risks of the deal was that authorities would challenge the accounting treatment used, giving the factor an "H." The Enron Board failed to inquire what this conspicuous signal entailed. During Congressional hearings, an Enron director said that he viewed the "H" for "high risk" accounting as really meaning an "I" for "important"[292] providing evidence of the nature of the rationalization used to minimize the negative implications of this information.

Third, although Audit Committee monitoring was a critical control for the related-party transactions, the Powers Report found that the Audit Committee treated this issue by "cursory reviews," as "brief items on the agenda,"[293] which lasted only ten to fifteen minutes. No Enron Board member recalled asking to review the documents for the related-party transactions, such as the private placement memorandum or other marketing materials used to attract investors to the limited partnerships.[294] The subsequent investigations fault the Enron Board for failing to ask probing questions despite obvious risks and warning signals. For example, the Audit Committee did not question whether the Enron managers followed the control procedures and whether these mechanisms achieved the goal of protecting Enron against transactions that were overly generous to Fastow. These actions suggest that the Enron Board engaged in "see no evil" rationalization. That is, if the Enron directors scrutinized the deals in greater detail, such behavior would have served as a "relationship-threatening act of defiance" that human nature tends to avoid.[295] One Enron Board member testified that he re-

---

[289] SENATE REPORT, *supra* note 17, at 25 n.59 (In the case of the LJM partnerships, Lay approved waiving the code of conduct prohibition for Fastow, but also asked the Enron Board to ratify his decision, even though Board concurrence was not explicitly required by company rules.).

[290] POWERS REPORT, *supra* note 17, at 158.

[291] SENATE REPORT, *supra* note 17, at 16.

[292] *Enron Hearings, supra* note 11, at 14, 23, 53.

[293] POWERS REPORT, *supra* note 17, at 162.

[294] SENATE REPORT, *supra* note 17, at 16 (they would have learned two other senior Enron financial officers who worked for Fastow participated in LJM2, although they did not seek a waiver of the ethics code).

[295] Langevoort, *Selling Hope, supra* note 73, at 683.

ceived the memorandum in the mail, offering him the opportunity to invest in one of the deals, but he threw it away without reading it.[296] The Enron director may have avoided reading the document because he did not want to look for indications that his original decision to approve these deals was made poorly.

Fourth, the Enron Board failed to see Skilling's abrupt departure for "personal reasons" in August 2001—after only six months of serving as CEO, but three months before the beginning of Enron's abrupt decline—as a red flag.[297] Journalists reported after Enron's demise that the resignation was "bizarre" because Skilling gave up a $19.9 million severance package and $2 million in loan forgiveness.[298] During Congressional hearings, the Enron directors stated that they did not view this event as a danger signal. Yet, it is important to recognize that the other corporate watchdogs also failed to recognize this red flag. After Skilling left, Ken Lay stepped back into the role of CEO, and reported that there were "[a]bsolutely no accounting issues, no trading issues, no reserve issues, no previously unknown problem issues,"[299] behind Skilling's departure. Lay had such credibility on Wall Street that most people believed him.[300] In the aftermath of Enron, one reporter stated, "What's astonishing is that even in the face of this dramatic—and largely inexplicable—event, people were still willing to take Enron at its word."[301] Thus, the Enron Board may have engaged in the type of "hear no evil" collective rationalization with respect to Skilling's resignation.

Fifth, during Congressional testimony, the Enron directors stated that they left the board meeting in early October 2001 (the beginning of Enron's quick, downward spiral), believing that Enron was "still on track,"[302] even though the Enron Board learned about an anonymous employee letter warning of company problems. The outside counsel, Vinson & Elkins, indicated that their preliminary study of the employee's concerns did not deserve additional inquiry. Relying on this presentation, the Enron directors did not ask to review the original letter, or the Vinson & Elkins report on the parameters of the investigation, until Enron began to collapse.[303] Social psychology explains that to ask for such documentation would indicate a lack of trust, not only in the outside counsel, but also in the CEO. Again, this suggests that the Enron Board failed to heed this red flag using the "hear no evil" collective rationalization.

Finally, at this same meeting, the Enron directors learned about an $800 million earnings charge from the termination of one of the related-party deals, known as Raptors. During Congressional testimony, the Enron directors testified they were not concerned

---

[296] SENATE REPORT, *supra* note 17, at 28.

[297] *Id.* at 12.

[298] *Id.* at 31.

[299] POWERS REPORT, *supra* note 17, at 97.

[300] Alex Berenson, *Enron's Collapse: The Chairman*, N.Y. TIMES, Jan. 23, 2002, at 16.

[301] BODILY & BRUNNER, *supra* note 2.

[302] SENATE REPORT, *supra* note 17, at 12.

[303] *Id.* at 48.

about the termination of this deal because it was a "one-time event." This "one-time" rationalization is commonly used to trivialize problems as being insignificant because they will not reoccur.[304]

During this October 2001 meeting, the Enron Board later testified that Lay told them of the $800 million charge to terminate Raptors, but not the $1.2 billion equity write-down. The Enron directors learned about the write-down by reading a *Wall Street Journal* article following Lay's disclosure to financial analysts on October 17th.[305] Several directors reported that this was the event that made them realize that Enron was in trouble, or recognition of the "last period problem." By this time however, it was too late because Enron was deep in the Big Muddy, beginning its intense and abrupt downward cycle, lasting only three months before Enron filed for bankruptcy.

The subsequent investigations provide direct evidence that the Enron Board may have been swept away by a "see no evil" norm in approving the related-party transactions.[306] The Enron directors were probably unaware of how much they were relying on shared rationalizations in order to appraise these highly risky ventures as safe.

4. Out-Group Stereotypes

a. Theory

The fourth symptom of groupthink is the group's stereotyping of rivals, which can apply to outsiders as well as to members of the group itself. Through such negative stereotyping, the group fosters the belief "either you are with us or against us." Janis explained that this stereotyping process causes cohesive groups to view those opposing the decision, either within the group or outside the group, as weak-minded for "not getting it."[307]

---

[304] Langevoort, *Epistemology, supra* note 94, at 643.

[305] *Senate Report, supra* note 17, at 48.

[306] In addition, journalists' accounts reveal that many others within Enron and outside Enron show evidence of collective rationalization. Specifically, an atmosphere of "puffery," and "winking" arose surrounding Enron and within Enron. With respect to analyzing the financial disclosures for the related-party transactions, analysts seemed to bury their heads in the sand. Specifically, analysts accepted statements that the details of these deals were "confidential" because Enron "did not want information to get into the market." Bodily & Brunner, *supra* note 2, at 38 ("[it was] Enron culture that contained the seeds of its collapse, a culture of highly questionable financial engineering, misstated earnings and persistent efforts to keep investors in the dark."); McLean, supra note 3, at 38 ("Enron's aggressive culture, which had been an asset during the company's transformation, became a liability as questions about Enron's credibility increased.").

[307] Janis, Victims, *supra* note 28, at 230. With respect to experts advising the group, members may stereotype these experts as slowing down decision making tasks. For example, Ronald Sims notes that group leaders may disparage an accountant by making sport of fastidiousness as "fussiness." Sims, *supra* note 28, at 27. Perhaps this explains, in part, Arthur Andersen's role. In addition, the old accounting rules were said to be ill-equipped to measure the new economy companies.

Within the group, deviants face intense social disapproval and may become outcasts. As an example, Janis discussed how this stereotyping behavior was used by the inner circle of President Kennedy's advisors in planning the Bay of Pigs fiasco.[308] Some members of this group represented the military and supported the use of force through bold, brutal rhetoric. In addition, the military members insinuated that Kennedy's supporters were soft-headed idealists. Afterward, some members stated that they failed to voice disapproval of the decision to invade Cuba during these planning sessions because they feared seeming "unvirile" or "unmasculine" in front of the military advisors.[309]

Viewed in a similar light, we can see why intelligent, experienced directors who monitor firms on a part-time basis may be unwilling to challenge management's business acumen. Most people, but particularly professionals, do not want to risk embarrassment by displaying their ignorance in public.[310] This leads some individuals to subconsciously avoid such humiliation by pretending to understand the complicated issues at hand; they concur, but in reality they are relying on the trust in their "friends."[311] Thus, independent directors may try to avoid appearing unsophisticated in the presence of management when discussing complex financial matters. Shrewd CEOs and senior managers may manipulate this cognitive weakness by using tough rhetoric to pressure independent directors to act like they "get it" and accept dubious proposals.[312]

b. Application to Enron

Subsequent investigations contain evidence that this stereotyping symptom may have influenced the Enron Board. In order to place this information in context, this section reviews journalists' accounts of Enron's reputation for publicly humiliating those who asked too many questions, from the outside financial community and within Enron itself.

Externally, Enron had a "we're smarter than you guys" attitude toward analysts.[313] Specifically, one analyst reported, "When you question them in detail, they get offended."[314] For example, when an analyst questioned Skilling, he replied: "Our business is not a black box. It's very simple to model. People who raise questions are people who have not gone through it in detail. We have explicit answers, but people want to throw rocks at us."[315] Thus, until its downfall, Enron denied that its financial statements were complicated; anyone who couldn't understand its business just didn't "get

[308] JANIS, VICTIMS, supra note 28, at 14.

[309] *Id.* at 41.

[310] Langevoort, *Selling Hope, supra* note 73, at 656.

[311] *Id.* at 653.

[312] *Id.* at 657.

[313] Zellner & Forest, *supra* note 6, at 30.

[314] Kadlec et al., *supra* note 170, at 68.

[315] McLean, *supra* note 3, at 33.

it."[316] Skilling also had a reputation of taking more extreme measures if the questioner persisted. For example, when the first reporter began to ask how Enron really made its money, Skilling told her the questions were "unethical" and hung up the phone.[317] In another instance, when Enron executives distributed the firm's balance sheet, but not the income statement during an analysts' meeting, one analyst asked to see the missing financial statement. Skilling responded by calling this analyst an "asshole"; no one asked any more questions after that exchange.[318] As one analyst summed up the situation, "[Enron] had Wall Street beaten into submission."[319]

Internally, Enron had a reputation for stereotyping its employees that stemmed from the "rank and yank" tournament structure. As one Enron employee stated: "If you didn't act like a light bulb came on pretty quick, Skilling would dismiss you."[320] Thus, Enron employees reported: "[Y]ou either got with the system or you were out the door."[321] Another worker noted: "One day, you are viewed with favor, and the next day you are not. You know who is in the in-crowd and who is not. You want to continue to be liked in that organization. You do everything you can do to keep that."[322]

Given this corporate culture of stereotyping rivals, we can turn to the Powers Report for evidence of this symptom in the Enron boardroom. The Powers Report stated:

> The Board authorized the Rhythms transactions and three of the Raptor transactions. It appears that many of its members did not understand those transactions—the economic rationale, the consequences, and the risks. Nor does it appear that they reacted to warning signs in those transactions as they were presented, including the statement to the Finance Committee in May 2000 that the proposed Raptor transaction raised a risk of "accounting scrutiny." . . . As complex as the transactions were, the existence of Fastow's conflict of interest demanded that the Board gain a better understanding of the LJM transactions that came before it, and ensure (whether through one of its committees or through use of outside consultants) that they were fair to Enron.[323]

---

[316] *Id.*

[317] *Id.* at 33; Felicity Barringer, *10 Months Ago, Questions on Enron Came and Went With Little Notice*, N.Y. TIMES, Jan. 28, 2002, at A11.

[318] *Special Report, Enron, The Amazing Disintegrating Firm,* ECONOMIST, Dec. 8, 2001, at 61.

[319] John Byrne, *At Enron, The Environment Was Ripe for Abuse*, BUS. WK., Feb. 25, 2002.

[320] *Id.*

[321] Rick Bragg, *Enron's Collapse: Workers*, N.Y. TIMES, Jan. 20, 2002, at 1.

[322] Stephens & Behr, *supra* note 173, at A01. Thus, managers worried about their advancing age in a culture which had many young upstarts. Skilling was made CFO at the age of thirty-six. Older executives feared their superiors would see them as too conservative, pushing them to demonstrate extreme risk-taking. Id.

[323] POWERS REPORT, *supra* note 17, at 23.

The Powers Report also noted that the Raptor deal was "an extremely complex transaction, presented to the [Enron Board] by advocates who conveyed confidence and assurance that the proposal was in Enron's best interests, and that it was in compliance with legal and accounting rules."[324] Thus, we see hints that the Enron Board members may have faced pressure to put up a front during these meetings, acting as if they "got it." In addition, Enron's culture of negative stereotyping may have affected the Enron Board's willingness to inquire about the complicated related-party transactions for fear of being seen as afraid of risk. That is, the Enron directors may not have wanted to appear "soft" on risk-taking or like "old-time dinosaurs" who could not adapt to "new economy" thinking. If a board member did have the courage to raise issues, [he] may have quickly backed down upon meeting the type of rebuff the Enron management gave to people who asked too many questions.

5. *Illusion of Uniformity*

a. Theory

Under this symptom of groupthink, the appearance of a group consensus pressures members to accept decisions.[325] Of course, a certain degree of concurrence seeking is necessary for any group to reach a decision. Janis, however, distinguished the type of concurrence seeking in groupthink as being extreme and premature. Similar to the cascade phenomenon discussed previously, once a sufficient number of members of the group appear to favor a proposal, others sense "which way the wind is blowing" and adopt the same view.[326] Group leaders can pressure this type of quick concurrence, by simply stating, "it appears the group has reached a consensus." Such a comment may lead to self-censorship by group members for fear of "rocking the boat." This self-censorship increases the illusion that silence means consent.[327] In extreme cases, this tendency can lead to situations that many in the organization know are problems, but are afraid to discuss openly. Management theorists refer to such topics as "moose issues."

b. Application to Enron

With respect to the symptom of the appearance of unanimity, the Senate Report noted, "[Enron Board members] said that Board votes were generally unanimous and could recall only two instances over the course of many years involving dissenting votes."[328] Thus, the subsequent investigations revealed no indication that the Enron

---

[324] *Id.* at 166.

[325] JANIS, VICTIMS, *supra* note 28, at 83.

[326] HAFT, *supra* note 48, at 37-38.

[327] JANIS, VICTIMS, *supra* note 28, at 167.

[328] SENATE REPORT, *supra* note 17, at 8.

directors challenged management, even though some directors lost millions of dollars from their investments in Enron stock.[329] In addition, the Powers Report stated:

> [T]here's no question that virtually everyone, from the Board of Directors on down, understood that the company was seeking to offset its investment losses with its own stock. That is not the way it is supposed to work. Real earnings are supposed to be compared to real losses. . . . As a result of these transactions, Enron improperly inflated its reported earnings for a 15-month period—from the third quarter of 2000 through the third quarter of 2001—by more than $1 billion. This means that more than 70 percent of Enron's reported earnings for this period were not real.[330]

This comment implied that the financial manipulation relating to the related-party deals developed into a "moose" issue within Enron. Other indications support the proposition that the Enron Board may have also been influenced by the Enron culture, which showed strong signs of the illusion of uniformity. For example, one Enron executive remarked, "You had to keep drinking the Enron water"; while another stated you had to "drink the Kool-Aid."[331] As a telling indicator of the symptom of unanimity, an Enron employee from the Enron Energy Services division (EES) reported, "EES knowingly misrepresented EES' earnings . . . . This is common knowledge among all the EES employees, and is actually joked about. . . . Enron must investigate all these going ons."[332]

6. *Self-Censorship*

a. *Theory*

The sixth symptom of groupthink is self-censorship by members of the group.[333] This symptom demonstrates the members' psychological need for excessive concurrence seeking. Specifically, members may remain silent even if they disagree, or they may soft-pedal their disagreements when the group appears to favor a decision. Group members conform to the group opinion rather than suffering the costs of being the lone objector and "sticking out like a sore thumb."[334] Simply put, if everyone else in the

---

[329] Robert Belfer, the largest Enron shareholder, lost $600-$700 million and his family lost $2 billion. Carrie Johnson, *Enron Director Robert Belfer Gave Away Millions*, LINCOLN J. STAR, May 9, 2002, at 3.

[330] Testimony of William C. Powers, Jr., Chairperson of the Special Investigative Committee of the Board of Directors of Enron Corporation, Before the Committee on Financial Services, United States House of Representatives, Feb. 4, 2002, at 4.

[331] Stephens & Behr, *supra* note 173, at A1.

[332] *Id.*

[333] JANIS, VICTIMS, *supra* note 28, at 34.

[334] Candice Predergast, *A Theory of "Yes Men"*, 83 AM. ECON. REV. 757, 769 (1993) (tell supervisors what they want to hear).

group is against you, the easiest approach is to "put up and shut up."[335] Thus, members may publicly agree, or remain silent even when they privately disagree. In essence, they "go along to get along." This symptom points to the pressures for conformity in boardrooms. With boards, this pressure may flow from the hierarchical relationship directors have with the CEO. An individual director may comply with a decision as a form of obedience to her appointer.

b. Application to Enron

The subsequent investigations provided evidence of two instances that the Enron Board may have engaged in self-censorship. In addition, journalists' accounts of Enron's corporate culture support the inference that this symptom appeared in the boardroom.

First, the most dramatic indication that the Enron directors engaged in self-censorship comes from the Audit Committee's failure to ask how much money Fastow and other executives made from the related-party transactions. For the first year, the Enron Board relied on Skilling to review the amount of income and asked no questions. In October 2000, after learning about the multiple, high dollar transactions the related-party partnerships had with Enron, the Finance Committee asked the Compensation Committee to conduct a one-time review of Fastow's earnings from these deals. This led an Enron director to ask a senior compensation officer to provide data on all Section 16(b) officers; the director did not tell the officer that he wanted information about Fastow "to avoid office gossip."[336] After failing to receive the information after requesting it twice, the director let the matter drop.[337] Thus, one year later, despite the Finance Committees directive, the Compensation Committee failed to learn about Fastow's significant levels of compensation from the related-party transactions.[338]

The Enron Board found out about the large benefits Fastow reaped at Enron's expense by reading the newspaper. After Enron's October 2001 disclosure, journalists investigated the related-party deals and reported that Fastow earned $30 million. This led an Enron director to have Enron's general counsel draft specific questions to ask Fastow about this matter. The Enron Board sent a written memorandum to Fastow, which began with the deferential phrase "we very much appreciate your willingness to visit with us."[339] During Congressional testimony, an Enron director noted that in the meeting following this letter, Fastow admitted receiving $45 million, but never provided information about his partnerships' rates of return to the Enron Board. The Enron Board, however, placed Fastow on leave after this conversation.[340]

---

[335] Sims, *supra* note 28, at 134.

[336] SENATE REPORT, supra note 17, at 35.

[337] *Id.*

[338] *Id.*

[339] *Id.* at 36.

[340] *Id.*

When asked during the Congressional hearings why the Enron directors did not pursue the issue about Fastow's compensation more assertively, some directors reported that they felt such questions were "inappropriate" or "intrusive."[341] In response, the Powers Report stated that this "reticence" was unreasonable given that the Enron Board merely had asked for Fastow's tax returns.[342] Such reluctance, however, may have arisen from the "fictive friendships" that arise in boardrooms; social norms do not allow one to inquire into a "friend's" financial situation. In addition, Congressional hearings criticized the Enron Board for being "obsequious" in questioning Fastow after the media brought Fastow's compensation to the Enron Board's attention.[343] The Enron directors' courtesy toward Fastow, then being shocked after reading the newspapers, may indicate extreme self-censorship by Enron Board members.

These indications that the Enron Board engaged in self-censorship are bolstered by the "kill the messenger" norm present within the Enron culture. Specifically, journalists' accounts provide three examples of how Enron employees knew that conveying negative news could destroy their careers because co-workers would jeopardize their reviews under the "rank and yank" system. First, one Enron employee remarked, "You don't object to anything, the whole culture at the vice-president level and above just became a yes-man culture."[344] Second, an employee reported, "People perpetuated the myth that there were never any mistakes. It was astounding to me."[345] Finally, an Enron employee stated that under the "rank and yank" tournament, "[p]eople went from being geniuses to idiots overnight."[346] Thus, direct evidence, as well as the Enron corporate culture, indicates that the Enron directors may have engaged in self-censorship.

7. Direct Pressure on Dissenters

a. Theory

Under this symptom of groupthink, members use common forms of social pressure against individuals who question the group's judgment in order to ease their own anxiety and guilt about the merits of a dubious decision.[347] Because each member wants to stay in the group, the others have sanctioning power over deviants. For example, group members place direct pressure on a dissenter by labeling the person as "not a good team player."[348] Additionally, the group leader can downplay criticism through power statements such as, "I'm sure that the dissenter isn't trying to upset the apple

---

[341] POWERS REPORT, *supra* note 17, at 173.

[342] *Id.*

[343] *Enron Hearings*, *supra* note 11, at 64-65.

[344] Byrne, *supra* note 319, at 45.

[345] McLean, *supra* note 3, at 362.

[346] BODILY & BRUNNER, *supra* note 2, at 48.

[347] JANIS, VICTIMS, *supra* note 28, at 39-40.

[348] JANIS, VICTIMS, *supra* note 28, at 56.

cart."[349] More extreme pressure on dissenters can produce a culture of fear that leads to the classic corporate "yes man."[350]

As an example, Janis discussed how the inner circle of President Johnson's Administration pressured dissenters who questioned the escalation of the Vietnam War.[351] During these sessions, members described the dissenter as losing his "effectiveness," as a "has been" who would ultimately face banishment from power. The inner circle of the Johnson Administration allowed some disagreement, but only if it was presented in a detached manner by using humor. But, even in these instances, the good-natured objector had to accept collegial jokes made at his expense. For example, the inner circle of the Johnson Administration commonly referred to one disagreeing member as "Mr. Stop the Bombing."[352] Janis emphasized that the weak presence of this subdued criticism served to facilitate the group's rationalization, that after accepting and appraising opposing views, the process they used in making their decisions was sound.[353]

b. Application to Enron

Although no direct evidence exists at this time that Enron managers pressured the independent directors, the subsequent investigations reveal two indications of this type of pressure on others.[354] First, the Powers Report detailed how Fastow attempted to coerce Enron workers who dealt with the related-party partnerships to gain better terms for himself.[355] One Enron employee complained to Skilling in March of 2000, stating that he received a smaller bonus after disagreeing with Fastow about a matter pertaining to the related-party partnerships.[356] In general, Enron employees described Fastow as a "prickly, even vindictive man, prone to attacking those he didn't like in Enron's group performance reviews."[357] Specifically, an Enron employee stated, "[Fastow] was such a cut-throat bastard that he would use it against you. . . . He could filibuster and hold up the group for days, because every decision had to be unanimous."[358] Second,

---

349 Sims, *supra* note 28, at 87.

350 This raises the classic issue related to whistleblowers; why don't people blow the whistle more often or sooner? Is it pressure from pressure of colleagues or the fear of losing money from their stock options? One answer to the dilemma may be to allow whistle blowers to sell short.

351 JANIS, VICTIMS, *supra* note 28, at 99.

352 *Id.* at 115.

353 *Id.* at 12.

354 In other cases, journalists reported that an analysts who expressed apprehension about Enron was fired from his brokerage firm. In another situation, the media indicated that Fastow tried to have a lawyer fired for negotiating too hard for Enron. Tom Hamburger & John Emshwiller, *Enron Officials Sought Lawyer's Dismissal Over Negotiations with Outside Partnership*, WALL ST. J., Feb. 6, 2002, at A3.

355 POWERS REPORT, *supra* note 17, at 166.

356 *Id.*

357 Zellner & Forest, *supra* note 6, at 30.

358 *Id.*

Congressional testimony indicated that Arthur Andersen may have faced coercion from Enron managers to approve the related-party transaction.[359] The Senate Report notes that Andersen marked its risk analysis of Enron as a client as "maximum" because "management pressures were very significant."[360] At Enron's request, an Andersen employee on an audit team faced reassignment after asking too many questions.[361]

With regard to pressure on the Enron Board, Fastow made several presentations to the Enron Board to get the related-party transactions approved. Thus, Fastow's reputation for manipulating the "rank and yank" system may have influenced the Enron directors.[362] Although subsequent investigations do not reveal that Enron Board caved in to managerial pressure, perhaps there was no need for this type of action because the directors did not express any objections in the first place.

8. Self-Appointed Mindguards

a. Theory

The last symptom of groupthink is the emergence of self-appointed mindguards, that is, members who take it upon themselves to protect the group from adverse information.[363] The mindguard performs the role of "thought homogenizer" by informing others in the group that the leader is not open to criticism or by running to the leader to act as a "mole" any time a member shows signs of dissent.

b. Application to Enron

With respect to self-appointed mindguards on the Enron Board, the subsequent investigations do not provide any direct signs that an individual Enron Board member or Enron manager performed this role. The Senate Report, however, noted that Fastow was so confident that the Enron Board would approve the second waiver of the ethics code, that he completed much of the negotiations for the transaction prior to asking the Enron Board for approval.[364] Similar to the symptoms of direct pressure on dissenters, the presence of Enron managers during the board meetings approving the related-party deals, may have served as self-appointed mindguards. In addition, perhaps no such mindguards were needed because the Enron Board quickly approved these deals.

In sum, this Part reveals that the Enron Board's actions fit a specific pattern of concurrence seeking behavior in face-to-face groups, when the "we-feeling" of solidarity is running high. Thus, group processes may have been subtly at work, preventing the

---

359 *Enron Hearings, supra* note 11, at 25.

360 SENATE REPORT, *supra* note 17, at 18.

361 *Enron Hearings, supra* note 11, at 4.

362 John Schwartz, *As Enron Purged Its Ranks, Dissent Was Swept Away*, N.Y. TIMES, Feb. 4, 2002, at C1.

363 JANIS, VICTIMS, *supra* note 28, at 78.

364 SENATE REPORT, *supra* note 17, at 28.

members of the Enron Board from debating the real issues posed and from carefully appraising its serious risks. Perhaps some Enron directors did not realize that other directors shared their negative opinions, and these directors did not wish to provoke conflict with the CEO. This case study of the Enron Board shows that groupthink is an error that can diminish abilities of some of the most intelligent people in our society—the prestigious, independent directors of publicly-held corporations. Without empirical evaluation, we cannot know the extent to which groupthink is a problem for boards in general. This case study, however, suggests that many boards may be susceptible to this phenomenon under certain conditions. In addition, the Enron debacle raises questions about how well our corporate governance system monitors "superstar" performance by executives motivated by stock options to play "the numbers game"[365] in a bull market[366] dominated by "irrational exuberance."[367]

The purpose of this Enron case study is to expand the awareness of groupthink and the other biases that impair directors' cognitive abilities to monitor managers. The next Part examines recent reform efforts in terms of their chances of reducing the probability of groupthink and other biases arising in boardrooms.

IV. REFORMING CORPORATE BOARDS TO PREVENT GROUPTHINK

As lawmakers and regulators contemplate reforming corporate boards to prevent the next Enron from happening, it is easy to be skeptical about such efforts for two reasons. First, suspicion stems from corporate lobbyists' efforts, such as the Business Roundtable,[368] and from self-regulatory arbitrage between the NYSE and NASDAQ,[369] that prevents much needed reforms from taking place—such as expensing stock

---

[365] *See, e.g.*, Arthur Levitt, *The Numbers Game*, at http://www.sec.gov/news/speech/speecharchive/1998/spch220.txt. In addition, Former SEC Chairperson Arthur Levitt warned:

> Increasingly, I have become concerned that the motivation to meet Wall Street earnings expectations may be overriding common sense business practices. Too many corporate managers, auditors and analysts are participants in a game of nods and winks . . . As a result, I fear that we are witnessing an erosion in the quality of earnings, and therefore, the quality of financial reporting. Managing may be giving way to manipulation; Integrity may be losing out to illusion.

SEC Chairman Arthur Levitt, *Concerned That Quality of Corporate Financial Reporting is Eroding, Announces Action Plan to Remedy Problem* (SEC News Release), at 1998 WL 779351 (SEC).

[366] For an in depth critique of the dangers of shareholder value maximization, *see* LAWRENCE E. MITCHELL, CORPORATE IRRESPONSIBILITY: AMERICA'S NEWEST EXPORT (2001).

[367] ROBERT SCHILLER, IRRATIONAL EXUBERANCE (1999) (discussing how shareholder engage in herd behavior to push up stock prices).

[368] Arianna Huffington, *My What Big Teeth You Have*, SALON, July, 2002, http//archive.salon.com/news/col/huff/2002/07/11/businessroundtable/index_np.html.

[369] The NASDAQ rules are considered less stringent than the NYSE rules and the NASDAQ has been accused of self-regulatory arbitrage in that companies may delist from the more stringent rules of the NYSE and list with NASDAQ. The NASDAQ rules emphasize independence of the audit committee and also require shareholder approval for equity-based compensation.

options.[370] Second, for the reforms that succeed in passing, apprehension arises because social psychology suggests that it is difficult to change norms.[371] Indeed, one of the main lessons of Enron is that boardroom dynamics are difficult to prescribe because structural solutions are easily subverted, negating the impact on substance.[372] Thus, reforms in the wake of Enron may result in corporate lawyers leaving behind even more extensive paper trails to document compliance with hollow rituals. Undoubtedly, some independent directors will fail to take the spirit of the NYSE Rules to heart. This is because of the human tendency for independent directors to use ego-protecting and stress-reducing techniques to view the corporate scandals as attributable to bad luck or character flaws that do not affect them.[373] Thus, suffering from self-serving biases, these directors may view these reforms as necessary for other directors who lack diligence. These directors may view the reforms as not applicable to their own situations because they perceive themselves as performing their duties in an above-average manner.[374]

Effective corporate boards require independent directors who can overcome the cognitive biases prevalent within corporate cultures that prevent them from performing their monitoring role effectively. This Part concludes that although many of the changes in corporate governance are useful, these structural reforms may not go far enough because good governance does not stem from procedures alone. Rather, transformation of the powerful psychological forces operating within boardrooms is necessary so that directors do not tune out at board meetings, dulled by repetition of the same old scripted gatherings.

In seeking to change boardroom dynamics, this Part turns to the social psychology literature on preventing groupthink to discuss two reform proposals: (1) formalizing the role of devil's advocate,[375] and (2) increasing diversity on corporate boards.[376] Before reviewing these proposals to prevent groupthink, this Part first discusses the Enron director's potential liability under state law for breach of the fiduciary duty of due care. This Part then examines the recently enacted New York Stock Exchange proposals for

---

[370] *See, e.g.*, Amy Borrus & Paula Dwyer, *To Expense or Not to Expense*, BUS. WK., July 29, 2002, at 44. A few companies are signaling their use of good corporate governance practices by treating stock options as expenses voluntarily. Mary Deibel, *Restoring Trust in Corporate America*, SAN DIEGO UNION TRIB., July 21, 2002 (Coca-Cola, The Washington Post, and Bank One).

[371] *See* Jeffrey J. Rachlinski, *The "New" Law and Psychology: A Reply to Critics, Skeptics, and Cautious Supporters*, 85 CORNELL L. REV. 739 (2000).

[372] Statement of Nell Minow, Corporate Accountability and Listing Standards, NYSE, Apr. 15, 2002.

[373] Langevoort, *Where, supra* note 86, at 112-13.

[374] Robert Prentice, *The Case of the Irrational Auditor: A Behavioral Insight into Securities Fraud Litigation*, 95 NW. L. REV. 133, 153 (2000).

[375] I have found two other corporate scholars advocating this proposal. Barnard, *supra* note 30, at 1170; Haft, supra note 48, at 7.

[376] For another corporate scholarship law advocating this position, *see* Steven Ramirez, *Diversity and the Boardroom*, 6 STAN. J.L. BUS. & FIN. 85 (2000).

boardroom reforms (NYSE Rules)[377] with regard to their potential to curb cognitive biases that influence independent directors.

A. Shareholder Suits Against Enron Directors for Breach of the Duty of Due Care

The Senate Report criticized the Enron Board, stating that "[t]he failure of any Enron Board member to accept any degree of personal responsibility for Enron's collapse is a telling indicator of the Board's failure to recognize its fiduciary obligations."[378] Groupthink theory provides an explanation for this behavior. Specifically, groupthink literature explains that "de-individualization" through group processes results in individuals becoming less self-aware, and more inclined to go along with group decisions. Rather than taking personal responsibility for their own actions, de-individualized people view responsibility as diffused, or distributed to the group as a whole. This leads individual group members to feel that they bear no individual responsibility for the consequences of the group's decisions. Thus, social psychology provides an explanation for why the Enron directors did not appear to have guilt, despite the fact that their lack of vigilance led to so much harm.

In reviewing the Enron directors' liability for breach of the duty of due care, it is important to note that Langevoort explains that "ego" in particular "frustrates law's attempt to channel behavior in particular directors . . . . We cannot expect people to respond fully to legal rules that ask them to modify their actions upon spotting danger signs, when perceiving such signs would provoke the stress of an ego threat."[379] Langevoort maintains that cognitive biases void the good faith standard of most of its legal meaning. Specifically, Langevoort states that "good faith, honesty of views means little if ego makes it easy to believe it with utmost sincerity in the wisdom and efficacy of ones' own actions however self serving."[380] As stated previously, however, the Enron case study in Part III does not seek to let the Enron Board off the hook legally by providing the rather lame excuse of groupthink for two reasons. First, to do so would allow truly pathological boards to try to fake this defense. Second, social psychology

---

377 Report of the New York Stock Exchange Corporate Accountability and Listing Standards Committee (June 6, 2002); New York Stock Exchange Corporate Accountability and Listing Standards Committee, June 6, 2002. The NYSE approved these rules on August 1, 2002 and the SEC is scheduled to make a decision on September 6, 2002. The Business Roundtable decision in 1988 found that the SEC cannot initiate changes on the exchanges. For an overview, see Stephen M. Bainbridge, *The Short Life and Resurrection of SEC Rule 19c-4*, 60 WASH. UNIV. L.Q. 565 (1991). The exchanges, however, can submit such reforms to the SEC for approval. If the SEC could initiate such changes it could prevent the regulatory arbitrage between the NYSE and NASDAQ.

378 SENATE REPORT, *supra* note 17, at 49.

379 Langevoort, *Ego, supra* note 102, at 856.

380 *Id.* at 876.

warns that people, including judges and jurors, are poor judges of whether someone is telling the truth.[381]

Shareholder litigation against the Enron Board depends on whether shareholders can rebut the strong presumption of the business judgment rule. If they can, a court must determine whether the Enron directors acted with due care under *Smith v. Van Gorkom*[382] and fulfilled their duties under *In re Caremark*.[383] Specifically, a court first needs to evaluate whether to apply the business judgment rule, and if it does not, whether the Enron Board breached its duty by waiving Enron's ethics code to allow the related-party transactions to go forward. Then, judicial consideration turns to whether the Enron Board failed in its fiduciary obligations to monitor these deals.

With respect to the initial decision to approve the related-party transactions,[384] the most important factor that a court needs to evaluate is the minimal amount of time that the Enron Board took to make this highly unusual type of decision. For the first waiver, the entire board meeting lasted one hour, yet the Enron Board considered several other weighty issues besides the ethics code waiver to allow the LJM1 proposal to go forward.[385] On the other hand, there is evidence pointing toward application of the business judgment rule. Specifically, the Enron Board members received written materials three days before the special meeting. Although the Enron directors stated that they relied on a fairness opinion from a reputable investment bank for the deal, as dictated by *Smith v. Van Gorkom*,[386] this opinion was not obtained until two months after the Enron Board's approval. The Enron Board followed similar practices in approving the second waiver as well.[387]

Next, a court needs to evaluate whether the Enron Board's monitoring of the transactions complied with the requirements of *In re Caremark*. A court may find that the Enron directors failed to satisfy *Caremark* duties because the Audit Committee's reviews

---

[381] Hal R. Arkes & Cindy A. Schipani, *Medical Malpractice v. the Business Judgment Rule: Differences in Hindsight Bias*, 73 OR. L. REV. 587, 588 (1994).

[382] 488 A.2d 858 (Del. 1985). Bratton notes that Enron is an Oregon corporation, but that Delaware law will be persuasive. Bratton, *supra* note 2.

[383] 698 A.2d 959 (Del. Ch. 1996)

[384] In approving the related-party transactions, William Bratton states: "there was no prima facie breach of fiduciary duty bound up in the Fastow deal at the time the Enron Board approved it." Bratton, *supra* note 2; *but see* Joann S. Lublin & John R. Emshwiller, *Enron Board's Actions Raise Liability Questions*, WALL ST. J., Jan. 17, 2002, at C1 (suggesting liability may be possible).

[385] Other matters included resolutions authorizing a major stock split, an increase in the shares in the company's stock compensation plan, the purchase of a new corporate jet, and an investment in a Middle Eastern power plant. Mr. Lay also discussed a reorganization underway at Enron. SENATE REPORT, *supra* note 17, at 24.

[386] *Id.* at 27.

[387] In approving the second waiver of the ethics code to allow LJM2, the Finance Committee of the Enron Board did review the transaction, after what the Chairperson of the Finance Committee described as "a vigorous discussion." Then the entire Enron Board approved it. POWERS REPORT, *supra* note 17, at 75-76.

only lasted a few minutes and the Enron Board failed to heed red flags—such as "high risk" accounting practices. On the other hand, a court may give the Enron directors the benefit of the doubt because the outside auditor did not voice explicit disapproval about particular transactions or accounting practices at Enron.[388] Although it is hard to predict the outcome of shareholder litigation against the Enron directors in light of the available evidence to date, the political dynamics of the public's outrage over Enron and the support from the highly critical Senate Report may increase the Enron shareholders' chances of success.[389] This article counsels, however, that judges need to be careful not to evaluate the Enron directors' actions too harshly in the light of post-bubble hindsight. In addition, the court needs to recognize that most independent directors are successful individuals who have hectic and stressful schedules; such people need to rely on others for advice in fulfilling their complicated and multiple duties in their part-time positions as directors.

Whether or not the state law action by shareholders against the Enron directors and officers is successful, courts may play a useful role in shaming the Enron directors for poor decisions. Corporate governance scholars have emphasized that Delaware cases provide morality stories designed to shame directors into vigilant monitoring.[390] Social psychology, however, warns that these shaming tactics have difficult cognitive hurdles to overcome. Specifically, this scholarship suggests that shaming may be an ineffective tool because independent directors may not recognize the wrongfulness of their behavior because cognitive processes minimize the effect of ego-threatening information.[391]

Whether change stems from shaming or other reasons, the proliferation of corporate scandals may lead to changes in some boardrooms.[392] As directors engage in self-evaluation post-Enron, journalists suggest that directors are attending more board meetings and asking more questions. In addition, director search firms report that

---

[388] Viewed in this light, a court may stress the time limitations faced by the Enron Board, and find it reasonable for the directors to rely on the reports from outside accountants and legal counsel in approving and monitoring the highly technical related-party transactions.

[389] *See, e.g.*, Adam Zagorin, *Enron's Board Games*, 160 BUS. SOURCE ELITE 16, July 15, 2002. On the other hand, the Enron directors' lawyers criticized the Senate Report for using "very selective use of the evidence" and "an unfair and unwarranted characterization of facts to reach a predetermined outcome." Kathryn Kranhold & Michael Schroeder, *Questioning the Books: Enron Directors Are Faulted in Senate Report*, ASIAN WALL ST. J., July 9, 2002, at A4 (quoting lawyer for former Enron directors). The directors' lawyer also stated: "Senate is setting a far higher standard for directors than is normally understood." *Id.*; *see also*, *Enron Board: We Were Mislead*, CNN MONEY, May 7, 2002.

[390] On the role of shaming, *see* Edward B. Rock, *Saints and Sinners: How Does Delaware Corporate Law Work?*, 44 UCLA L. REV. 1009 (1997); David A. Skeel, Jr., *Shaming in Corporate Law*, 149 U. PENN. L. REV. 1811 (2001).

[391] Langevoort, *Ego, supra* note 102, at 856.

[392] NAT'L ASS'N OF CORP, DIRS., RECOMMENDATIONS TO CONGRESS (2002), http://www.nacdonline.org/nacd/enron_recommendations.asp.

they are looking for "independent thinkers,"[393] but that it is more difficult to persuade directors to accept board seats.[394] Such signs show that independent directors may have learned the post-Enron lesson that it is not acceptable to simply nod in approval and later claim "I didn't know," or "I didn't understand," or "no one told me." To ensure that such actions are not transitory responses, the next section reviews how the recently adopted NYSE Rules[395] seek to ensure the independence of the board from managerial domination.

B. Corporate Governance Proposals to Reform the Board

1. The NYSE Exchange Rules

a. New Definition of Director Independence

The NYSE Rules require that independent directors must comprise a majority of the board.[396] This provision will not lead to much change because currently seventy-five percent of publicly-held companies have more than a majority of independent directors.[397] The NYSE Rules also formulate a tighter definition of independence for board members and require increased disclosure of this independence.[398] In determining whether a director is independent, the NYSE Rules require boards to review whether each director has "any material relationship with the company, either directly or as a partner, shareholder, or officer of an organization that has a relationship with the company."[399] The NYSE Rules do not provide a general definition of a "material relationship," but make a per se conclusion in several instances that require a five year cooling-off period. This cooling-off period applies to directors who were employees of the company, or of its independent auditor, and for directors who are or were employees of any company whose compensation committee includes an executive officer of the

---

[393] Post-Enron Boards are taking steps to find more independent thinkers. Mike McNamee et al., *Turn Up the Heat on Board Cronyism, Mr. Grasso*, BUS. WK., Apr. 22, 2002, at 36 (Korn/Ferry International, a director recruiter reports that searches for candidate up thirty percent and "no one wants lapdogs.").

[394] Emily Thornton & Louis Lavelle, *It's Getting Tough to Fill a Boardroom,* Bus. Wk., July 29, 2002, at 80.

[395] Report of the New York Stock Exchange Corporate Accountability and Listing Standards Committee 6 (June 6, 2002), at http://www.myse.com/abouthome.html/query=/about/report.html [hereinafter NYSE Rules].

[396] The prior NYSE Rules only required at least three independent directors and that the audit committee consist of at least three independent directors. For criticism of this proposal *see,* Stephen M. Bainbridge, *A Critique of the NYSE's Director Independence Listing Standards* (Working Paper 2002), available at http://ssrn.com (one size does not fit all).

[397] NAT'L ASS'N OF CORP, DIRS., PUBLIC COMPANY CORPORATE GOVERNANCE SURVEY 2001-2002, http://www.nacdonline.org/publications/ (based on 5,000 proxies).

[398] NYSE Rules, *supra* note 395, at 6-7.

[399] *Id.* at 6.

enterprise making the independence inquiry, and for the immediate family members of these individuals.

The NYSE Rules eliminate some of the types of financial connections that can impair directors' independence. Yet, the NYSE Rules do not affirmatively prohibit some side payments to directors, such as charitable contributions and consulting contracts. As noted previously, CEOs can use these side payments to sanction dissenting directors in a manner that is beyond analysts' radar screens. The NYSE Rules provide that directors' fees must be the sole compensation that audit committee members receive,[400] but do not extend this broad prohibition to other directors. Thus, this standard is less stringent than those adopted by many institutional shareholders that try to ensure that independent directors' compensation is only from payment as a director. Importantly, as discussed previously, even if reforms removed these financial ties to management, directors may remain "psychologically dependent" upon managers.

b. Empowering Independent Directors: Outside Meetings and Lead Director

The NYSE Rules seek to empower outside directors by requiring them to meet at regularly scheduled meetings without management and to publicly designate a lead director to chair these sessions. The NYSE Rules recognize that these requirements allow greater and more frank discussion of management.[401] By compelling such regular meetings, the NYSE Rules seek to reduce the independent directors' "costs of confrontation," by "preventing any negative inference from . . . calling such executive sessions."[402]

Thus, the NYSE Rules attempt to create structures that allow independent directors to voice their opinions freely and frequently outside the presence of management. This provision does not, however, address the aversion of independent directors to confront management face-to-face by asking tough questions. Thus, independent directors may find it easy to criticize managers behind closed doors, but still melt when sitting in front of corporate executives.

The NYSE Rules' use of the lead director position differs from many shareholder proposals calling for lead directors in two ways. First, under the NYSE Rules the lead director is only responsible for conducting the outside meetings, but the NYSE Rules do not require the lead director to perform this role during full board meetings.[403] In addition, the lead director under the NYSE Rules is not accountable to the board for succession planning, a critical issue for good corporate governance practices. In this

---

[400] In addition, the NYSE Rules provide that the chair and voting methods of the audit committee cannot hold more than 20 percent of the company's stock. *See supra* note 377.

[401] NYSE Rules, *supra* note 395, at 8.

[402] *Id.*

[403] Most calls for lead directors make this director responsible for calling board meetings, setting the agenda, leading discussions, and calling in outside experts. *See, e.g.*, Martin Lipton & Jay W. Lorsch, *A Modest Proposal for Improved Corporate Governance*, 48 BUS. LAW. 59, 70 (1992); Gayle Mattson, *The Effective Lead Director*, 23 THE CORP. BOARD 1 (July/Aug. 2002). Directors favor (seventy-two percent) having a lead director, according to a recent survey by McKinsey & Co. FIN. TIMES, May 28, 2002.

way, the NYSE Rules do not entirely avoid an important antecedent condition of groupthink, the lack of impartial leadership.

c. Empowering Committees

The NYSE Rules require companies to have an audit committee, a nominating or corporate governance committee, and a compensation committee, each comprised solely of independent directors. This reform enhances board decision making by assigning evaluative roles to small groups. The NYSE Rules seek to reduce the boards' dependence upon managers for information by allowing these committees to control the hiring of outside consultants. By reducing independent directors' reliance on insiders for information, this requirement reduces the structural faults in decision making, an antecedent condition of groupthink.

The NYSE Rules require each listing firm's audit committee to review more information on the auditor's independence. In addition, the NYSE Rules expand the audit committee's review of financial information by mandating quarterly meetings with management, internal auditors, and independent auditors. The NYSE Rules also require listing firms to have a nominating or corporate governance committee that includes oversight of evaluation processes for senior managers. By requiring these types of reviews, the NYSE Rules reduce the independent directors' "costs of confrontation" that impair collegiality at the board level.

Importantly, the NYSE Rules require shareholder approval of equity-based compensation for managers to serve as a check over the CEO's influence over compensation committees. While this reform may help to curb executive compensation where institutional shareholders play an active role, this reform falls below that suggested by corporate governance leaders. Many commentators assert that corporations should treat stock options as expenses. Others go further, to suggest the elimination of executive compensation in either stock or stock options because this leads managers to take a short-term view that ignores constituents other than shareholders.

d. Director Evaluation

The NYSE Rules require that these three committees have written charters and conduct annual self-assessments. By requiring periodic reviews, these provisions help to prevent "loss framing" by ensuring that change is part of the psychological mix of these committees. Literature on small group decision making, however, warns against such self-evaluations because it can undo the peerage of the group.[404] Specifically, this scholarship suggests that peer groups punish individual loafing by subtle pressure, rendering such formal evaluation unnecessary.[405]

---

[404] Haft, *supra* note 48, at 20 (relying on Oliver Williamson's position that evaluation among individuals in groups creates a hierarchy rather than a peer group).

[405] *Id.*

2. *Institutional Shareholders' Agenda Post-Enron*

The NYSE Rules are fairly standard reforms that have been espoused by institutional shareholders for many years. Such reforms may help in changing boardroom dynamics somewhat, but the most important reforms, such as allowing shareholders to nominate directors,[406] have not received adequate attention. This is the most important reform needed to change the CEO-dominated board. This article asserts that the NYSE should allow shareholders to nominate board candidates on managers' proxy statements to allow true corporate democracy. For other reforms, the institutional shareholders need to continue to push corporations to internalize the evolving best practices in corporate governance. Such reforms should be left to institutional shareholders to implement a case-by-case basis because command-and-control legislation is inadequate given that "one size does not fit all."[407] However, in many cases when shareholders' resolutions pass, management frequently ignores them. Given that Delaware courts may hold that binding bylaw amendments are invalid,[408] the NYSE Rules should require that shareholder proposals that pass for three years become binding.

a. Banning Related-Party Transactions for Senior Executives

Shareholder proposals should forbid related-party transactions for the senior officers of publicly-held corporations, or at least require shareholder approval for such transactions. This proposal would deny a manipulative manager the ability to place undue pressure upon the "fictive friendships" on the board that make it difficult to vote against these transactions.

b. Separating the Positions of CEO and Board Chair

The benefits of group deliberation exist only if the board consists of an equal-status peer group. Although the NYSE Rules require a lead director to chair outside meetings, this is a second-best solution. Separating the position of CEO from the Chairperson of

---

406 Using shareholder nomination committees or institutional investor associations to nominate board members would go much further in fostering fundamental changes in boardroom dynamics. *See, e.g.*, Ronald J. Gilson & Reineer Kraakman, *Reinventing the Outside Director: An Agenda for Institutional Investors*, 43 STAN. L. REV. 863 (1991). As an alternative, when a shareholder proposal gets a majority vote and is still rejected by the directors, in the next proxy the shareholders should have the option to nominate one director candidate. At other times, shareholders who hold at least five percent of the stock should have the right to nominate a single director for inclusion in the company's proxy materials. Statement of Nell Minow, *supra* note 372; Damon Silvers, Associate General Counsel, AFL-CIO, Presentation to the New York Stock Exchange Special Committee on Corporate Accountability and Listing Standards, May 23, 2002, A6-7 (shareholders with ten percent of the shares should have access to management's proxy statement to nominate candidates. Allow shareholders with five percent to have access to the proxy statement for shareholder proposals that the SEC currently deems to constitute ordinary business.).

407 Bainbridge, *supra* note 396.

408 *See, e.g.*, John C. Coates, IV & Bradley C. Faris, *Second-Generation Shareholder Bylaws: Post-Quickturn Alternatives*, 56 BUS. LAW. 1323 (2001).

the board would reduce the CEO's influence over the board, thereby creating impartial leadership, which would reduce the possibility of groupthink.[409]

In a recent study by McKinsey & Co. of 180 U.S. directors representing 500 companies, more than two-thirds favored separating the CEO position from that of Chairperson of the board. Such reforms may be difficult because CEOs resist giving up this power, although this practice is followed in the U.K.[410] Of course, even in cases where shareholders succeed in separating the CEO and board chairperson positions,[411] the CEO can still wield much power.

c. Term Limits

Currently, only five percent of large, publicly-held companies use terms limits for directorships.[412] On the one hand, an advantage of term limits is that they prevent the type of cohesiveness on boards that leads to groupthink. On the other hand, term limits poses two disadvantages. First, term limits prevent long-term relationships from developing; such relationships foster moral behavior because people care about how others perceive them. Second, term limits may not be efficient in some cases where directors need time to acquire human capital to perform their roles properly. For these reasons, institutional shareholders are best positioned to balance the benefits of substantial expertise on boards against the costs of groupthink on a firm-by-firm basis.

C. Suggested Reform Proposals to Prevent Groupthink

To aid independent directors in avoiding the various cognitive biases that permeate corporate boardrooms, this section considers two reform proposals from the literature on preventing groupthink. First, boards should assign a different director at each meeting to serve as a formal devil's advocate.[413] Second, boards should seek greater diversity of director candidates. Both reforms attempt to reduce conformity pressures on boardrooms and foster critical analysis of managers' policies.

---

409 For commentary favoring this view, *see, e.g.*, JAY W. LORSCH & ELIZABETH MACIVER, PAWNS OR POTENTATES: THE REALITY OF AMERICA'S CORPORATE BOARDS 194-85 (1989); Monks & Minow, *supra* note 52, at 185-86. *But see* James A. Brickley et al., *Leadership Structure: Separating the CEO and Chairman of the Board*, 3 J. CORP. FIN. 189 (1997) (lose efficiency in separating CEO and Chairperson).

410 Brickley et al., *supra* note 409, at 189.

411 *See e.g.*, Jared Sandberg, *Questioning the Book-Congress Begins WorldCom—An Already Tarnished Board Also Faces Tough Questions Over Accounting Fiasco*, WALL ST. J., June 28, 2002, at A3 (CEO Ebbers gave chief executives of the companies he wanted to acquire the Chairperson position; but it was only "ceremonial.").

412 The Conference Board reports that only five percent of companies have term limits. Carolyn Kay Brancato & D. Jeanne Patterson, *Board Diversity in U.S. Corporations*, CONFERENCE BOARD REPORT 12 (1999).

413 I want to thank Adam Winkler for encouraging me to emphasize this reform proposal.

1. Rotating the Position of Devil's Advocate

Janis, the originator of groupthink, suggested that one of the most important methods to prevent groupthink is to formalize the role of the devil's advocate and rotate this position among group members at each meeting.[414] Janis noted that this technique may stimulate more open discussion on controversial issues when the group consists of people with different status and power, such as that existing on corporate boards. Specifically, the devil's advocate role gives each member "an unambiguous assignment to present his arguments as cleverly and convincingly as he can, like a good lawyer, challenging the testimony of those advocating the majority position."[415] Thus, Janis suggested that the devil's advocate serve as a discussion leader for the group, who does not express his own views, but rather encourages questions and protects any emerging minority. In order to prevent too much confrontation stemming from this role, Janis emphasized that the devil's advocate should not be rude or strident in pressing for alternative points of view. Rather, Janis emphasized that the most effective performers would be "truly devilish" by raising questions in a conventional, low-key style, such as "haven't we perhaps overlooked . . . ? shouldn't we give some thought to . . . ?"[416]

Frank discussion can be confrontational and many people have a natural tendency to shy away from interpersonal conflict. Through formalizing the role of the devil's advocate, however, this proposal provides a defense mechanism for independent directors who are reluctant to challenge the "culture of politeness" in corporate boardroom in three ways. First, this proposal seeks to change director's self-perception; that is, a director who has this assignment does not perform well if she does not ask hard questions. Thus, this proposal allows independent directors to discuss topics that were formally considered taboo. Second, the devil's advocate role reduces the independent directors' fears about sounding self-righteous. Finally, when the devil's advocate does not understand an issue, she can seek clarification on behalf of the other directors. In this way, the devil's advocate does not suffer any humiliation for admitting that she does not "get it."[417]

Rotating the position among different directors at every meeting may prevent "domestication of the devil."[418] By requiring each director to assume this rule, it is less likely that managers can label a questioning director as a disloyal team member who should be shut out of the loop. In addition, publishing the rotation schedule for the devil's advocate would allow other directors to channel questions about upcoming sensitive issues to that person in advance.

---

[414] JANIS, VICTIMS, *supra* note 28, at 267.

[415] *Id.* at 215.

[416] *Id.* at 268.

[417] I thank Claire Moore Dickerson for pointing out this important advantage of the devil's advocate role.

[418] JANIS, VICTIMS, *supra* note 28, at 268.

Laboratory tests on the use of the devil's advocate highlight certain advantages and disadvantages from using this technique. On the positive side, these studies confirm that the devil's advocate role improves group performance.[419] Specifically, laboratory studies find that groups using a devil's advocate generate better assumptions and recommendations than groups employing unstructured debates. On the negative side, these studies reveal that the devil's advocate has three drawbacks. First, this technique increases the amount of time that groups take to make decisions.[420] Second, some studies confirm that the devil's advocate role can become a mere formality that does not produce authentic dissent.[421] Finally, laboratory explorations show that the devil's advocate may increase tension within the group, which may impair the ability of groups to work together in the future.[422] These studies indicate that the effectiveness of this reform may depend on how the first director fulfills her role because it may set the norm for other directors to follow. To avoid these drawbacks, director training programs should use role playing to demonstrate how to effectively use the devil's advocate role to avoid groupthink in the boardroom. In addition, these training programs should teach independent directors about other cognitive biases to raise awareness of red flags that may indicate poor performance by managers.

2. Diversity on the Board

One of the main lessons of the groupthink theory is that social homogeneity on corporate boards harms critical deliberation. Social scientists posit that the best way to avoid groupthink is to prevent enclaves of like-minded people from making group decisions. Thus, this scholarship suggests that reform proposals should discourage groupthink by promoting more diversity on boards in terms of gender, race, class, ethnicity, age, national origin, sexual orientation, and socio-economic background, as well as expertise and temperament.[423] Specifically, studies on social psychology indicate that diversity may promote more independent thinking on boards because diversity

---

[419] *See, e.g.*, Dan N. Stone et al., *Formalized Dissent and Cognitive Complexity in Group Processes and Performance*, 25 DECISION SCI. 243 (1994). The devil's advocate role is often compared to the use of dialectic inquiry, another method to formalize dissent. Under the dialectic inquiry method, proponents of a plan and a counterplan engage in a structured debate to highlight the reasonableness of the assumptions underlying each plan. *Id.* at 245.

[420] *Id.* at 245.

[421] Charlan Nemeth et al., *Devils' Advocate Versus Authentic Dissent: Stimulating Quantity and Quality*, 31 EUR. J. SOC. PSYCHOL. 707 (2001).

[422] David M. Schweiger et al., *Experiential Effects of Dialectical Inquiry, Devil's Advocacy, and Consensus Approaches to Strategic Decision Making*, 32 ACAD. MGMT. J. 745 (1989).

[423] With respect to the Enron Board, thirteen of the fourteen members were men; three of the men appear to be minorities (Hispanic, African American, and Asian). The one Asian woman on the board shared the same socio-economic background. *Supra* note 19. As management scholars explore the role of emotions in corporate life, they are beginning to study issues concerning different temperament. *See, e.g.*, Sigal Barsade et al., *To Your Heart's Content: A Model of Affective Diversity in Top Management Teams*, 45 ADM. SCI. Q. 802 (2000).

directors may hold "outsider values." That is, diversity may enhance board effectiveness because different life experiences may lead to different perceptions of social reality.[424] Although directors who add various types of diversity can achieve the goal of preventing groupthink, this Part concentrates on including more women on corporate boards, but also discusses the need for more minority candidates when the research on women board members applies.

In the past, shareholder activists viewed promoting diversity on boards as a corporate social responsibility issue. Increasingly, Enron and September 11th have facilitated the process of convergence, whereby corporate social responsibility issues "cross over" to become corporate governance practices.[425] Diversity has been the leading crossover issue, supported by CalPERS,[426] TIAA-CREF,[427] and the Council of Institutional Investors, Lens, and the NACD.[428] Shareholder proposals calling on companies to increase racial and gender diversity on their boards have received the highest levels of approval among the social policy resolutions—nearly nineteen percent.[429] Given the demand for more "independent thinkers" on boards and the decline in the pool of traditional candidates as they become more reluctant to accept board positions,[430] nominating committees may look to a more diverse group of candidates to serve as directors.

Indeed, the recent scandals may provide an opportunity for women because some firms seek to restore investor confidence by appointing more women to the board for two reasons. First, sensing they are not one of the "good ol' boys," women may perceive wrongdoing more easily and may be more willing to speak out when necessary.[431] Second, a common perception is that women generally have a moral authority that they may bring to the board service to encourage more ethical conduct. Studies in social psychology offer some support for the view that adding more women to the

---

[424] *See, e.g.*, Patricia Hill Collins, *Learning From the Outsider Within: The Sociological Significance of Black Feminist Thought*, 33 SOC. PROBS. (Dec. 1986).

[425] Carolyn Brancato suggests that institutional shareholders are intervening a new stage of activism to consider issues previously thought of as promoting corporate social responsibility. CAROLYN KAY BRANCATO, INSTITUTIONAL SHAREHOLDERS AND CORPORATE GOVERNANCE 87 (1997). For example, CalPERS recently pulled its investments from several Asian countries based on poor labor practices. *Post-Enron Observations on Corporate Governance*, CORP GOV NEWS, May 2002.

[426] CALPERS, DOMESTIC PROXY VOTING GUIDELINES (1999), http://www.calpers-governance.org/principles/domestic/voting/page01.asp.

[427] TIAA-CREF, POLICY STATEMENT ON CORPORATE GOVERNANCE.

[428] NAT'L ASS'N OF CORP. DIRS., CORPORATE GOVERNANCE SURVEY, http://www.thecorporatelibrary.com/docs/tiaa-cref%20policy%C20stmnt%C20on%C20corp% 20gov.html (last visited June 11, 2003).

[429] Meg Voorhes, *Social Proposals Get New Levels of Support*, CORP. SOC. ISSUES RPTR., May 2002, at 1-3 (diversity proposal at EMC received thirty-two percent shareholder vote).

[430] *See, e.g.*, Susan Stellin *Executive Life; Directors Ponder New Tougher Roles*, N.Y. TIMES, June 30, 2002 at 3-16; *see also, The Fading Appeal of the Boardroom*, ECONOMIST, Feb. 10, 2002.

[431] *See, e.g.*, Kelly Pate, *Corporate Woes Spell Opportunity for Women*, DEN. POST, Aug. 2, 2002, at C-01; Mary Williams Walsh, *Preparing A Corps For Women For Corporate Social Responsibility*, N.Y. TIMES, Aug. 13, 2002, at C-1.

board may offset some behavioral biases in existing boards that are predominately male. Overall, women are less affected than men by the over-optimism bias that leads to excessive risk-taking.[432] In addition, studies indicate that business women may have a higher degree of moral development than male executives.[433] Thus, post-Enron, the traditional "old boys' network" may give way to searching beyond the power elite to include others with different views.

a. Promoting Directors With "Outsider Values" on Corporate Boards

A recent Conference Board report maintains that diversity on boards enhances shareholder value because the additional experience and knowledge bases brought about such diversity contributes to profit generation.[434] Although statistical data does not exist for showing that the presence of diversity on boards increases firm performance, the Conference Board found it noteworthy that the top Fortune 10 companies in terms of profitability all have a woman on their boards, and eight out of these ten have more than one woman on their boards.[435] In the past, three economic considerations pushed senior managers to widen their horizons about the types of people who provide the "right fit" on corporate boards. First, some corporations consider the notion of "market reciprocity"; if women make up half the consumer base of a corporation, then that corporation's board should have proportional representation.[436] Second, corporate boards recognize that cultural diversity is important in the global economy to attract business from other parts of the globe. Finally, some firms place women and minorities on their boards for a less virtuous reason, as a method to mitigate against discrimination litigation.[437]

Competing empirical results, as well as corresponding theoretical arguments, exist with regard to the influence of diversity on group performance. Some research indicates some negative aspects from introducing diversity into group decision making. These studies show that heterogeneity creates distance between group members, which makes interpersonal relations based on trust less likely. Offering a more hopeful view, some studies have found that initially homogeneous groups had higher quality processes than heterogeneous groups, but over time heterogeneous groups adapt to acquire processes at or above the level of homogeneous groups.[438] Going through this adjustment process may

---

432 In other words, the commonly held view by women that men have "big egos" has empirical support from social psychology studies. *See supra* notes 108-10 and accompanying text.

433 Prentice, *supra* note 13, at 194 n.351 (female accountants score higher).

434 CAROLYN KAY BRANCATO & D. JEANNE PATTERSON, BOARD DIVERSITY IN U.S. CORPORATIONS: BEST PRACTICES FOR BROADENING THE PROFILE OF CORPORATE BOARDS 12 (1999).

435 *Id.* at 8.

436 *Id.*

437 *Id.* at 9.

438 John Oetzel, *Explaining Individual Communication Process in Homogeneous and Heterogeneous Groups Through Individualism*, 25 HUMAN COMM. RES. 202 (1998).

be worthwhile because some research shows that heterogeneity enhances the breadth of perspective, cognitive resources, and general problem-solving ability of group decision making. No clear consensus exists on how heterogeneity influences group performance, and thus more research is needed to explore this important issue. Specifically, this topic has many implications for corporate governance beyond the boardroom. Firms have shifted their organizational structures away from individual responsibility toward focusing on teams of employees. For this reason, much more research is needed in light of globalization and changing demographics of the workforce.[439]

Empirical studies evaluating the gender composition of small groups found that mixed-gender groups have a higher tendency to avoid group-think, whereas groups composed of one gender have a higher probability of succumbing to this phenomenon.[440] Evaluation of mixed-gender groups posits that such groups also have different interaction styles than groups composed of a single gender. Specifically, groups made up of all men or all women have extreme positions on several stereotypic, gender-related variables. These findings show that women in small groups perform socio-emotional roles and men behave consistently with task-oriented roles.[441]

In the 1970s, Rosabeth Moss Kanter surmised that gender influences are proportional to the gender composition of the group.[442] Subsequent studies of small groups support this proposition. Specifically, gender and race do not affect group decision making unless the percentage of women and minorities in the group rises above the critical level of twenty percent. Thus, having one woman or minority candidate on an average board consisting of eleven people may not produce the efficiency benefits of diversity. One sole woman director sums up these findings by describing her boardroom experience: "[I]t's like going into a [men's] locker room where everybody all of a sudden shuts up."[443]

Studies of the "small world of the corporate elite"[444] in corporate America are pessimistic about the progress made so far in promoting outsider values on corporate boards.[445] This cynicism stems from the fact that directors who represent diversity on corporate boards [could] share the same values as the old, homogeneous group.[446] Perhaps, directors representing diversity learn to assure incumbent boards that they will "fit in" and not cause trouble. In this way, some corporate scholars warn that the power elite creates an illusion of diversity by selecting women and minorities who share the

---

439 *Symposium, Issue on Group Diversity*, EUROPEAN J. WORK AND ORG. PSYCHOL. (1997).

440 Marceline B.R. Kroon et al., *Group Versus Individual Decision Making: Effects of Accountability and Gender on Groupthink*, 23 SMALL GROUP RESEARCH 427 (1992).

441 *Id.* at 30.

442 ROSABETH MOSS KANTER, MEN AND WOMEN OF THE CORPORATION 102 (1977).

443 2001 CATALYST CENSUS OF WOMEN BOARD DIRECTORS 22 [hereinafter CATALYST REPORT].

444 Min Yoo et al., *The Small World of the Corporate Elite*, 27 DIRECTORSHIP 4 (Nov. 2001) (4.6 degrees of separation between directors for Fortune 1000 corporations; 3.7 degrees between each board).

445 *Id.* at 192.

446 *Id.* at 6.

same ideologies of the existing CEOs.[447] Arguably, increasing the number of women and minorities above the twenty percent level may change these social dynamics to allow diversity directors to feel comfortable in sharing outsider values.

Although homogeneity on the board can lead to too much cohesiveness, some level of collegiality is desirable because it promotes a well-functioning board. In the past, corporate governance scholars have argued against having constituency directors or cumulative voting because it increases confrontation in boardrooms.[448] In addition, corporate governance scholars have cautioned that too many independent directors on a board may weaken the trust needed among the CEO and board members, which is conducive to giving the CEO advice about strategic planning.[449] Viewed in this light, a possible argument against diversity is that heterogeneity on boards may lead to too much confrontation in the boardroom. However, in light of Enron, corporate boards should worry less about a new director's ability to "fit in" and more about whether the candidate will think independently, speak out on difficult subjects, and provide diverse perspectives for tactical and strategic decisions. Social psychology literature on preventing groupthink also offers a rebuttal to the American perspective that views the German board structure, which provides employees with membership, as inefficient due to heterogeneity.[450] Given the potential drawback of heterogeneity, however, this article maintains that director training programs should focus on diversity training[451] to overcome the potential biases directors may have in working with people who are "different." The next section focuses on the glass ceiling problem preventing women from obtaining more board seats.

b. Promoting More Women on Corporate Boards

The 2001 Catalyst Census of Women Board Directors reports that in the United States the percentage of women on boards is 12.4 percent, up from 11.7 percent in 2000 and 11.2 percent in 1999.[452] Eighty-seven percent of Fortune 500 companies have at least one woman on their boards, up from eighty-six percent in 2000 and eighty-four percent in 1999. Thirty-five percent have one or more African-American directors (male or female) and eleven percent have one or more Hispanic board members (male

---

447 RICHARD L. ZWEIGENHAFT & G. WILLIAM DOMHOFF, DIVERSITY IN THE POWER ELITE: HAVE WOMEN AND MINORITIES REACHED THE TOP? 192 (1998).

448 Haft, *supra* note 48, at 23-24.

449 Langevoort, *Human Nature, supra* note 48, at 813 (citing James D. Westphal, *Collaboration in the Boardroom: Behavioral and Performance Consequences of CEO-Board Social Ties*, 42 ACAD. MGMT. J. 7 (1999)).

450 HENRY HASSMANN, WORKER OWNERSHIP (1999). For comparative research using the groupthink concept see Theo Postma & Han Van Ees, *On the Functions of Supervisory Boards in the Netherlands* (Working Paper 2002) (Cooperation leads to higher potential for groupthink).

451 Langevoort, *Human Nature, supra* note 48, at 800.

452 CATALYST REPORT, *supra* note 443, at 1.

or female).[453] Women of color hold 2.6 percent of the board seats of Fortune 500 companies.[454] This report found that women directors are not as likely as men to serve on the important committees of boards, such as auditing, nominating, and compensation committees.[455] Women directors, however, are more likely to serve on corporate social responsibility committees.[456] While the percentage of women on boards has increased recently, progress is slow. At the current rate, the percentage of women in top leadership positions will not exceed the critical level of 25 percent until 2020.

Why do we have so few women on corporate boards? CEOs generally state that they have a hard time identifying female candidates.[457] In response, the Conference Board suggests that nominating committees need to look beyond the CEOs of Fortune 1000 companies because currently there are only eleven female CEOs of these firms. Using a broader perspective, many qualified women are "in the pipeline" to be selected for board service.

i. Women Managers

Women now make up fifty percent of managerial and specialized professional positions in organizations in the United States. Studies of top executives reveal that women scored higher than men in many indices of leadership, including those related to the bottom line.[458] Women excelled in interpersonal skills commonly associated with feminine styles of management that are increasingly recognized as important in today's organizations, which stress customer service. Specifically, women managers performed better than men on giving feedback, rewarding and motivating individuals and teams, and acting with integrity. Women also scored higher than men on maintaining productivity, producing quality work, meeting project deadlines, generating new ideas, and moving projects forward.[459] Despite these findings, surveys show that senior managers (eighty-one percent men) viewed actions such as focusing on results and taking charge as positive indications for men, but as negative factors for women. This gender difference stems from societal and organizational norms about leadership. Specifically, corporate rhetoric espouses that leaders should focus on team-building, but the notion of the senior manager as an emotionally restrained, command-and-control type still prevails.

---

[453] BRANCATO & PATTERSON, *supra* note 434, at 14.

[454] CATALYST REPORT, *supra* note 443, at 1.

[455] Diana Bilimorai & Sandy Dristin Piderity, *Board Committee Membership: Effects of Sex-Based Bias*, 37 ACAD. MGMT. 1453 (1994).

[456] BRANCATO & PATTERSON, *supra* note 434, at 30.

[457] Diana Bilimoria, *Women Directors: The Quiet Discrimination*, 16 THE CORP. BOARD 10 (July 17, 1995).

[458] Deborah M. Merrill-Sands & Deborah M. Kolb, *Women as Leaders: The Paradox of Success*, 9 CGO INSIGHTS, Apr. 2001, http://www.simmons.edu/gsm/cgo/insights_9.pdf.

[459] *Id.*

In analyzing gender differences in organizations, Catalyst reports that these differences arise because corporate environments were designed by and for men and presumably geared toward their behavior and responsive to their needs.[460] In a Catalyst survey of Fortune 1000 CEOs, eighty-two percent of the male CEOs responding to survey points to the lack of experience as holding women back and sixty-four percent of these male CEOs believe that women have not been in the pipeline long enough to hold board positions.[461] Many executives, however, tend to disagree with this "pipeline" argument; these executives suggest that male stereotyping (fifty-two percent women and twenty-five percent men) and exclusion from informal networks (forty-nine percent women and fifteen percent men) are the reasons why women have not broken through the glass ceiling.[462] Interestingly, while senior executives perceived the need for organizations to change to include women (seventy-six percent women and eighty percent men), more women than men think they also need to share responsibility in adapting to corporate cultures (seventy-three percent women and sixty-one percent men).[463]

To understand these gender norms in more detail, the next section discusses literature on second-generation discrimination in the workplace. Although a detailed examination of this topic is beyond the scope of this article, this section outlines how tournament structures may operate to exclude women.

ii. Second Generation Discrimination: Tournaments and Gladiator Corporate Cultures

Scholars studying gender and race discrimination state that organizations have eradicated most blatant types of discrimination, but subtle forms still prevail.[464] This type of gender discrimination stems from norms that appear gender-neutral on their face, but operate to hurt women.[465]

---

[460] DEBRA MEYERSON & JOYCE FLETCHER, DISAPPEARING ACTS 129 (1999).

[461] CATALYST, WOMEN IN CORPORATE LEADERSHIP: PROGRESS AND PROSPECTS 36 (1996). This is the first large-scale research study of women who have made it to senior management in the largest companies. This study reports that seventy-two percent of these women are married; sixty-four percent have children; eighty-seven percent are part of career couples; married women contribute an average of sixty-eight percent of their household income; and three-quarters provide over half of the total household income, making them the primary "breadwinners" of the family.

[462] *Id.* at 39.

[463] *Id.*

[464] Susan Sturm, *Second Generation Employment Discrimination*, 101 COLUM. L. REV. 458 (2001).

[465] In one example, an organization concerned about high turnover of women and difficulty in recruiting women found that some of the problems arose because the corporate culture had a norm of allowing people to call meetings on an informal basis at any time. This norm operated to the detriment of women, but men also found the norm disruptive. Identifying this issue and changing the norm benefited all employees in the organization and thus improved organizational effectiveness. *Id.* at 472.

In another article,[466] this author considers how tournaments structures lead to "gladiator" corporate cultures that tend to exclude women. Specifically, tournaments foster winner-take-all combat, reflecting a distinctly male view of the world. As a result of global competitive pressures, tournaments have led to longer working hours in the United States. American employees now work more hours than employees in any other advanced industrialized country, including Japan.[467] Thus, under the pressures of the tournament, successful workers give up on a balanced life and resort to total obsession with the rewards from work. Joan Williams, a leading work and family scholar, documents that eighty-five percent of woman are mothers, but ninety-three percent of mothers work less than fifty hours a week during their key career building years.[468] In addition, mothers who seek alternative work arrangements are frequently branded as "unprofessional" for lacking sufficient commitment to their firms. Thus, tournaments and gladiator corporate cultures naturally tend to exclude employees, especially mothers, concerned with the well-being of their children.

Moving beyond the ideology of the corporate gladiator stemming from the tournament structure will not be easy for two reasons. First, scholars studying tournament structures report that a firm may use gender and race as factors in their decision making about employee promotion without hurting the bottom line.[469] When firms invest scarce training and mentoring resources in average men as opposed to average women, they can do so without impeding the firm's ability to produce the small number of high quality senior executives that it needs to succeed in the future. Thus, these scholars suggest that firms may engage in second-generation discrimination against women and minorities, but may not lose out to other firms that have similar practices in the competitive marketplace.

Second, many workers, especially men, may not work these long hours just for the money. Joan Williams surmises that the incentive to stay in the tournament stems from ego, that is, the need to feel one is a "major player."[470] This points to the need not only to change tournament structures, but also the norms that drive employees to engage in these survival-of-the-fittest competitions to the detriment of all else life has to offer.

Scholars seeking to prevent this subtle form of gender discrimination emphasize that command-and-control legislation will not work because each organization develops its own corporate culture with distinct norms. Instead, scholars such as Susan Sturm recommend that firms hire intermediaries such as Catalyst to investigate the norms prevalent within their corporate cultures that operate to the disadvantage of women and minorities. Such organizations have the expertise to question employees to find out about these workplace

---

[466] Marleen A. O'Connor, *Sustainable Corporate Governance and Flexible Labor Markets: Recognizing the Family as A Corporate Stakeholder* (copy on file with University of Cincinnati Law Review).

[467] Joan Williams, *The Family-Hostile Corporation*, 70 GEO. WASH. L. REV. 921 (2002).

[468] *Id.*

[469] *See, e.g.*, Wilkins & Gulati, *supra* note 102, at 1584.

[470] Williams, *supra* note 467; *see also* Marc Galanter & Thomas Palay, *Large Law Firm Misery, It's the Tournament, Not the Money*, 52 VAND. L. REV. 953 (1999).

norms and to suggest changes aimed at eliminating subtle discriminatory forces.[471] As a reform proposal, this article suggests that institutional shareholders encourage corporations to consider using such intermediaries as part of their overall efforts to promote diversity on their boards. In this regard, Catalyst offers a hopeful note by reporting that it cannot determine which comes first, but corporations with many women executives and board members tend to have progressive work and family programs.[472]

In sum, this Part suggests two methods to prevent groupthink in boardrooms: formalizing the role of the devil's advocate and increasing diversity on boards. The next Part considers how corporate law teachers need to adjust their teaching post-Enron to incorporate perspectives from business ethics and social psychology.

V. CONCLUSION: CORPORATE SCANDALS AND THE ROLE OF CORPORATE LAW PROFESSORS[473]

> Our schools of business must be principled teachers of right and wrong, and not surrender to moral confusion and relativism.
>
> —President George W. Bush[474]

Heeding President Bush's call, business school professors have engaged in a debate about the need to emphasize business ethics in their courses to prevent future corporate scandals.[475] As a result, accounting education is undergoing major revisions and other business school professors are rethinking their approaches.[476] While many business professors favor introducing more ethical content in their teaching, others state that they have no personal responsibility to teach morality. Some business school professors go so far as to rationalize that the problem is really a legal one. Thus, they seek to shift the blame to law school professors. This article asserts that law school professors share this responsibility with business school professors. The corporate law academy, however, shows little sign of serious discussion about such issues post-Enron. Such a debate is crucial, however, for corporate lawyers to fulfill their obligations to report wrongdoing to the board under the recently enacted Sarbanes-Oxley Act.[477] Thus, this article calls on fellow corporate law professors to rethink how we teach business courses, especially the basic course in business associations.

---

[471] Sturm, *supra* note 464, at 464.

[472] BRANCATO & PATTERSON, *supra* note 434, at 8.

[473] I also call this part "My *Jerry Maguire* mission statement." I was inspired to write this conclusion after watching the movie.

[474] Remarks by the President on Corporate Responsibility, www.whitehouse.gov/news/releases.

[475] *See* Michael Lissack's website, "Business Schools and Ethics," for comments, at http://isce/edu/wwwboard/wwwboard.html (last visited Aug. 12, 2003).

[476] *See, e.g.*, Laurie Winslow, *Accountants, Students Discuss Accounting Fraud at Tulsa, Okla., Conference*, KRTBN: TULSA WORLD., Oct. 5, 2002.

[477] *See supra* note 43.

Specifically, we need to ask whether the theories we advocate are justifiable in light of the proliferation of corporate scandals. Do we teach fiduciary law as a mere contractual term void of moral content? Do we promote cynical theories of motivation for corporate actors that treat economic rewards as the only goal? Have we fostered a self-destructive era of selfishness and greed, where business lawyers see ethics as an unwanted invasion into corporate life? Do we preach unfettered capitalism and sinister views of government regulation? Do we emphasize techniques of financial manipulation to promote short-term stock prices at the expense of making long-term investments for real productivity gains? By failing to criticize the status quo within corporate governance scholarship and at our own law schools, do we inadvertently provide role models for our students to act like good corporate "yes men?" That is, does our professional behavior signal that it is safer to "bow to authority," rather than jeopardize one's career through "rocking the boat by making waves?"

Corporate law professors need to focus more on teaching business ethics because this aspect of corporate law has not been emphasized in the last decade. Instead, law and economics has dominated corporate law discourse with the myth that human beings are only motivated by self-interest.[478] The dissonance between the language of law and economics and the reality of human nature has had a distorting impact on both lawyering and the legal process. In contrast, for the past fifteen years, Progressive Corporate Law (PCL) scholars have opposed the hegemony of the neoclassical law and economics movement by emphasizing that corporate actors should focus on serving the public interest rather than just shareholder value. Specifically, PCL scholars advocated the need to view corporate executives as moral beings, rather than just rational, economic actors who narrowly focus on short-term stock prices.[479] Mainstream scholars rejected and marginalized the ideas of the PCL movement to the point that some espoused "the end of corporate law."[480] As proof of their victory, these scholars emphasize that the U.S. model of corporate governance is sweeping the globe. Unfortunately, the "dark side of

[478] Donald C. Langevoort, *Behavioral Theories of Judgment and Decision Making in Legal Scholarship: A Literature Review*, 51 VAND. L. REV. 1499, 1526 (1998) ("central rhetorical construct of rational man evokes an image of an institutionally controlled world; or the image of the rational actor as the ideal type reflects the ego-centric self-image of lawyers?").

[479] *See generally* PROGRESSIVE CORPORATE LAW (Lawrence E. Mitchell ed., 1993).

[480] *See, e.g.*, Henry Hansmann & Reinier Kraakman, *The End of History for Corporate Law*, 89 GEO. L.J. 439, 441 (2001); *see also* ROBERT HAMILTON, THE LAW OF CORPORATIONS IN A NUTSHELL 72 (5th ed. 2000) ("As this is written at the end of the Twentieth Century, it seems that the social responsibility debate has ended. Laissez faire and the goal of profit maximization appear to have carried the day."); Stephen M. Bainbridge, *Book Review: Community and Statism: A Conservative Contractarian Critique of Progressive Corporate Law Scholarship*, 82 CORN. L. REV. 856 (1997). For criticism of this view, *see* Margaret Blair, *Post-Enron Reflections on Comparative Corporate Governance*, 14 J. OF INTERDISC. ECON. 113 (2003) (Enron causes loss of confidence U.S. corporate governance leads to long-term economic development); Kent Greenfield, *September 11 and the End of History For Corporate Law*, 76 TUL. L. REV. 1409(2002); William W. Bratton, *Never Trust a Corporation*, 70 GEO. WASH. L. REV. 876, 876 (2002) ("[T]he norm of shareholder value maximization was carried forth to the world as America's greatest gift to global economy since mass production itself.").

shareholder value"[481] is beginning to appear as well, as we witness corporate scandals similar to Enron proliferating around the world.[482]

It is easy to dismiss these observations as appearing naïve in light of the widespread cynicism about corporate ethics. After all, Enron itself had a detailed ethics code. And many remain skeptical after President Bush's call for "a new era of integrity in corporate America"[483] because his past business practices raise questions of unethical dealings.[484] Social psychology, however, warns that relentless cynicism about corporate governance may turn to a self-fulfilling prophecy. The recent corporate scandals will lead many academics and practitioners to jump on the "corporate morality" band wagon, but this author maintains that we need to keep a steady focus on this crucial issue, rather than let it drop when stock prices rise.

Unfortunately, a cynical model of the corporate actor has dominated the thinking about the nature of the fiduciary duties owed by corporate actors over the last twenty years. Recent scholarship on fiduciary law stresses enforcement through threats from shareholder suits or reputational sanctions. This presents a rather sterile view of fiduciary duty because it supports the idea that "honesty is the best policy" as an appeal to self-interest. Instead, we need to emphasize the value of fidelity for its own sake. To stress only obtaining economic rewards and avoiding negative sanctions from being "a good fiduciary" denies us the sense of intrinsic satisfaction we can receive from honorable behavior. Displacing rational self-interest, some legal scholars assert that the prime motivation for human action is the quest for meaning to fulfill moral obligations.[485] Thus, we need to focus more on positive emotions as motivations for behavior in corporate life. Specifically, corporate law scholars need to celebrate the joy, excitement, and flow of everyday worklife in communicating the basic doctrines of corporate governance to their students.

The current reforms of boardroom processes stress empowering independent directors to act on their ethical impulses. We should be careful about placing too much emphasis upon the procedural aspects of corporate governance, however, because it may send a counterproductive message that focuses on decorum, rather than actual propriety itself. In order for these reforms to succeed, much still depends on whether an individual director's conscience dictates appropriate behavior.

---

481 Bratton, *supra* note 2.

482 *See, e.g.*, Claire Dickerson, *The Ozymandius Effect Applied to Executive Behavior: Are We Shocked—Shocked!* (Working Paper for the 3rd Annual Workshop on Corporations and Capitalism, Osgoode Law School, Sept. 2002); Jean Eaglesham & Nikki Tait, *UK-Style Enron 'Is Possible'*, FIN. TIMES, May 27, 2002.

483 See Remarks by the President, *supra* note 474. Bush's ten-point plan to increase corporate accountability includes a doubling of prison sentences for financial fraud, increased funding for the SEC, etc.

484 *See, e.g.*, Paul Krugman, *Steps to Wealth*, N.Y. TIMES, July 1, 2002, at A-17 (hard to talk about "character" as "questions about Harken Energy pile up").

485 Edward L. Rubin, *Public Choice, Phenomenology, and the Meaning of the Modern State: Keep the Bathwater, But Throw Out the Baby*, 87 CORN. L. REV. 309 (2002).

Although behavioral law and economics has done much to expand our thinking about the complexity of human actors, we still have much work to do concerning how we can teach fiduciary law in a manner that promotes ethical conduct in corporate life. We know that rules and process controls cannot cover every situation that arises for corporate fiduciaries. In seeking to fill in the gaps and make sense of a situation, a fiduciary will feel stress and anxiety. To avoid these negative feelings, executives will search for rationalizations to continue to think of themselves as just and honorable people. Corporate cultural norms can provide these rationalizations so that executives can engage in questionable conduct without feeling guilt. Thus, developing corporate reforms for board decision making involves not only articulating goals and procedures, but also confronting the various cognitive biases that influence individuals and groups, which jeopardize their effectiveness.

How can we overcome the cynicism about reform procedures that leads to such rationalizations? We should focus not only on structural issues, but also on individual integrity, because it takes character to have the courage to tell the emperor he has no clothes. A fiduciary must resolve many issues through the exercise of sensitive internal dialogue. The director may ask, "Am I the type of person who seeks to benefit from the inherent uncertainty involved in reviewing the transaction?" Or, "Am I the type of fiduciary who resists temptation and chooses the common good?" A director struggling with her conscience turns to fiduciary norms for guidance about what is "right." At this point, fiduciary norms affect directors' value choices by removing a source of rationalization for questionable conduct.

For these reasons, corporate law professors need to revive the moral tradition of fiduciary law that has been lost to the narrow, value-free economic analysis of fiduciary duty.[486] These rhetorical differences play an important role in constituting our moral and social worlds. Specifically, the way we talk about fiduciary obligation is crucial because the most distinguishing characteristic of fiduciary law is its operation as a system of moral education that promotes and reinforces trust and honesty in commercial transactions. The sermon-like style of fiduciary rhetoric captivates our moral consciousness and contributes to an understanding of fiduciary obligation in ways that reason alone cannot. In its true essence, fiduciary duty seeks to embody a complex value system that penetrates everyday life by appealing to our ears and hearts. This moral appeal offers an experience, an invitation for reflection. In this way, fiduciary rhetoric seeks to intrude into the psyches of fiduciaries to create feelings of guilt for violation of duty and feelings of honor for upholding the tradition. This language encourages readers to internalize the message, to change their ways of thinking and being. In this way, fiduciary discourse has a complex psychological appeal that speaks to our better side to desire noble aspirations, while simultaneously reprimanding our other side by instilling fear of fiduciary breach.

---

[486] Marleen A. O'Connor, *How Should We Talk About Fiduciary Duty? Directors' Conflict-of-Interest Transactions*, 61 GEO. WASH. L. REV. 954 (1993).

How can we, as corporate governance teachers, ensure that future corporate executives and business lawyers receive ethical training? Currently, corporate law casebooks do not offer much in terms of teaching about ethics and corporate social responsibility.[487] Reciting Justice Cardozo's "punctilio of an honor the most sensitive" and discussing grand theories of business ethics leads some students to give you cynical stares, while others go to sleep. How do we convey ethical lessons about corporate morality to young, ambitious students in a way that captures their minds and hearts and in a manner that they can use in practicing corporate law?

Rather than just using aspirational language to inspire good business lawyers, Langevoort emphasizes that we need to equip students with lessons from social psychology.[488] We need to emphasize that, although deliberate wrongdoing exists, in many cases cognitive biases operating within corporate cultures may lead individuals to have good faith misperceptions of problems. Social psychology suggests that to the extent that corporate cultures place individuals in certain situations, good people will make bad decisions, but they can do so without guilt through rationalizations.

Offering guidance on how to communicate the literature in social psychology to students, Langevoort suggests examining the role of myths or storytelling in educating business lawyers.[489] Langevoort emphasizes that it is necessary to provide a "good story to overcome the more dysfunctional forms of myth and rationalization that put such a hard protective coating over the pursuit of self-interest."[490] Specifically, teaching fiduciary duty caselaw as morality stories has the capacity to influence students' affective responses.[491] This is important because fiduciary duty must be heartfelt. In this way, students can see the issues in more depth, emotionally as well as intellectually. Thus, corporate law professors need to explore the use of metaphors, stories, myths, language, and rituals to communicate the guiding values of business ethics.

This case study of the Enron directors' role in the scandal aims to serve as a story that allows students to see how honest, smart individuals can succumb to cognitive biases prevailing in corporate cultures. More importantly, perhaps students and lawyers will use this case study as a parable to tell themselves and their clients to avoid these behavioral defects in the first place.

---

[487] For criticism of these current modes of teaching corporate law, *see* Lynn P. Q. Johnson, *The Social Responsibility of Law Professors*, 76 TUL. L. REV. 1483 (2002); Theresa Maynard, *Law Matters, Lawyers Matter*, 76 TUL. L. REV 1501 (2002); Kent Greenfeld, *There's A Forest in Those Trees: Teaching About the Role of Corporations in Society*, 34 GA. L. REV. 1011 (2000); Kellye Y. Testy, *Adding Value(s) To Corporate Law: An Agenda for Reform*, 34 GA. L. REV. 1025, 1042 (2000) (questioning whether outside directors really provide "outsider" perspectives).

[488] Langevoort, *Epistemology, supra* note 94, at 630.

[489] Langevoort, *Myths, supra* note 25, at 1568.

[490] *Id.* at 1569.

[491] Edward Rock, *Saints and Sinners: How Does Delaware Corporate Law Work?*, 44 UCLA L. REV. 1009, 1047 (1997).

Chapter 4

Corporate Scandals and Corporate Governance

Now that you've had a chance to consider the dual issues of what might really have gone wrong at Enron (Chapter 2) and how human nature may have contributed to the fiasco (Chapter 3), it's time to think a bit more deeply about how legislation and a corporation's governance structure might make it more difficult to ferret out fraud. Let's spend some time thinking about Congress's response to the scandals at Enron and WorldCom, among others.*

After you've had the opportunity to think a little bit about the relationship of Sarbanes-Oxley to the ability of gatekeepers to uncover corporate misdeeds, it will be time for you to consider whether there are better ways to get corporations to toe the ethical line. Finally, at the end of this chapter, you'll have a chance to read the words of a true hero: Cynthia Cooper, the accountant who uncovered the fraud at WorldCom. In the first of two excerpts from her book, she describes how some of the employees at WorldCom talked themselves into participating in the fraud.

While you read the essays in this chapter, think about what might happen if you were a Chief Executive Officer who gave your employees the directive to maximize earnings for the shareholders. How far might your employees go to follow these orders?** How can you keep them on the right side of the ethical line?

---

* If you'd like to read the entire text of Sarbanes-Oxley, you can find it here: http://fl1.findlaw.com/news.findlaw.com/hdocs/docs/gwbush/sarbanesoxley072302.pdf.

** One of the arguments that Jeff Skilling is making in his Fifth Circuit appeal, which you can find at http://online.wsj.com/public/resources/documents/skillingappeal.pdf, is that he acted at all times in the way that he thought that Enron had wanted him to act (the "honest services" issue). *See id.* at 61-80.

September 11th and the End of History for Corporate Law[*]

Kent Greenfield[**]

September 11th changed everything, or so it seems. The attack and subsequent war has brought about a reexamination of airline regulation, immigration policies, privacy rights, the Middle East peace process, and the nation's defense strategy, among other things. Those of us who live in the United States were jarred from a sense of security that perhaps was false in any event. The future is going to be different than we expected in many ways.

The direct blame for the attacks has descended on a score of hijackers and their alleged leaders in international terrorist organizations. Indirect blame has been placed on everything from lax airport security, the lack of dependable intelligence about terrorists, the openness of our society, and the hatred of some for democracy and freedom.

It is only natural for people to interpret the tragedy and subsequent events in light of their own interests and perspective. The apparent unity of experience and emotion that the events of September 11th brought upon us will undoubtedly fade as time passes. Those who suffered personal losses will bear the horrible weight of those losses for much longer than the rest of us. Those of us who were fortunate enough to avoid direct harm and who avoided losing a loved one (though the stories of near misses are ubiquitous and unsettling) will filter and interpret and analyze the events of September 11th by our own lights. It will be only natural that physicians will think about the public-health implications. Police officers will think about the consequences for public safety and law enforcement. Politicians will think about how to address the political ramifications. Business people will think about the significance of the attacks on the economy. Lawyers will think about the legal implications.

[**] Associate Professor of Law and Law Fund Research Scholar at Boston College Law School. J.D., University of Chicago; A.B., Brown University. The author wishes to thank the organizers of and participants in the Tulane Law School conference, "Socio-Economics and Corporate Law: The New Corporate Social Responsibility," for their excellent feedback. The author also thanks the faculty of the University of Connecticut School of Law for their very helpful comments during a faculty colloquium in February 2002.

I am a law professor. More precisely, I am a professor of corporate law. So how does a corporate law professor think about September 11th? For the first few hours and days and weeks, probably much like everyone else, with a mix of horror, fear, patriotism, self-doubt, sadness, empathy, and powerlessness. Slowly, however, I started seeing it through my own particular lens and started to think about the role of corporations in all of this.

At first glance, it seems obtuse (or heartless, or worse) to talk about corporate law in connection with those horrible acts of terrorism in New York and Washington, D.C. Upon reflection, however, I have come to believe that there are things that can and should be said about that day that relate to corporations and how we regulate them. It is of course obtuse (or heartless, or worse) to say that corporations or corporate law caused the events of September 11th. But I believe it is correct to say that corporations and corporate law helped create the context in which the tragedy could occur and helped create the contours of the nation's response to it.

SEPTEMBER 11TH AS MARKET FAILURE

Consider the fact that very quickly after the attacks, many commentators pointed fingers at allegedly lax airport security. At the time of this writing, it is unclear whether security personnel failed in their jobs at the three airports from which the hijacked flights departed. By most accounts, the hijackers used pocketknives or box cutters to hijack the planes, and airline regulations did not bar passengers from carrying such tools as of that morning.[1] But it does not require a leap of logic to assert that the hijackings could have been prevented by a more attentive security staff (isn't it unusual to have several passengers carrying box cutters on the same flight?) or security regulations and policies that made safety a higher priority (why didn't airlines bar passengers from carrying box cutters?).

One possible reason for poor security on September 11th was that air travelers did not want better security. Traditional economic theory would suggest that the market, given force through the choices of profit-maximizing airline corporations, should have provided what the consumers desired. If travelers wanted better, less sieve-like security, they would have demanded it, and the cost of airfares would have been increased in order to pay for it. Perhaps consumers did not in fact want security that would have prevented the hijackings. One cannot disprove this notion by pointing to the behavior of travelers, the airlines, or regulators after September 11th. Travelers may be experiencing "hindsight bias" and demanding more safety now even though they have never desired it before.[2]

---

[1] Evan Thomas & Mark Hosenball, *Bush: 'We're at War,'* NEWSWEEK, Sept. 24, 2001, at 26.

[2] *See* Greg Schneider et al., *Air Travel Has New Look for Holidays,* WASH. POST, Nov. 18, 2001, at A1. For a description of hindsight bias, see Christine Jolls et al., *A Behavioral Approach to Law and Economics,* 50 STAN. L. REV. 1471, 1523-26 (1998). Even if travelers are demanding more security than ever before, the market still seems unable to provide it efficiently. To use my home airport, Boston's Logan Airport, as an example, there were notable and embarrassing lapses in security even after September 11th. In one

I doubt, however, that this traditional economic story is correct as an empirical matter. I would suppose that if travelers before September 11th had known that the tragedy that occurred was a real possibility, they would have been willing to pay something more for their tickets to ensure that air travel was safer and that airplanes could not be hijacked and flown into skyscrapers. If this is true, then there was a fundamental market failure, and such failure contributed to the tragedy of September 11th. September 11th was thus not just a story of how fanatic zealots used the openness of a society against it. It is also a story of the failure of the market to provide what people actually desired.[3]

Why, then, was there a market failure? Why didn't the airlines provide better safety? Or more fundamentally, why didn't the free market provide better safety?

Airport security on September 11th was largely the responsibility of airlines themselves.[4] The airlines contracted out the responsibilities of staffing the security checkpoints to firms that paid their workers little more than minimum wage, which made it difficult to attract the best people. Because of the low pay, many of the screeners had to work at some other job as well, making them exhausted and unable to concentrate effectively. Many of the contractors did not offer health insurance or paid sick days. As a result, according to the *New York Times,* "many screeners report[ed] to work sick and struggled to remain alert."[5] Before September 11th, training of checkpoint screeners often consisted of watching a videotape and receiving about one hour of on-the-job training. The fact that some security firms are responding to the September 11th tragedy by proposing increases in the wages of the screeners gives credence to the notion that the screeners' low pay had negative implications for security in the first place.

The belief that there was a market failure is bolstered by the fact that one of the first public responses to the attacks was a move to make airport security a function of the federal or state government. In other words, because the airlines could not be trusted to provide what consumers wanted, many believed that the government must step in. Barely two months after the attacks, the federal government federalized the screening function.[6]

---

instance, travelers were able to board a flight without going through any screening at all. The screener had left his post for a break, and no one replaced him. Robert Rudolph et al., *Hijackers Didn't Have to Hide Their Weapon of Choice—Security Now Bans Knives, But Some Say Enforcement Is Lax,* STAR-LEDGER (Newark, N.J.), Oct. 7, 2001, at 1.

[3] Even after September 11th, the airlines have been unable to provide the level of security that travelers desire. *See* Alan Levin & Debbie Howlett, *Airlines' Security Assailed,* USA TODAY, Nov. 6, 2001, at 1A. "Transportation Secretary Norman Mineta, reacting to a spate of recent airport security breakdowns, accused airlines Monday of failing to take security seriously . . . ." *Id.* In just five days in early November 2001, the Federal Aviation Administration had to evacuate passengers from eight different airport terminals because of major security breaches. *Id.*

[4] Greg Hitt & Jeanne Cummings, *Reregulation: Terror Attack Reverses a Two-Decade Drive to Shrink Government,* WALL ST. J., Sept. 26, 2001, at A1.

[5] Steven Greenhouse, *Worker Finds Gains at Airport Are Mixed,* N.Y. TIMES, Oct. 22, 2001, at A16.

[6] Judy Keen, *'Aggressive' Air Security Coming in Phases,* USA TODAY, Nov. 20, 2001, at A8.

Consider why screeners' wages were so low to begin with. As noted above, it is not likely that they were low because travelers were unwilling to pay slightly more for airline tickets so that the security firms could pay for good training and decent wages for screeners. The market failed, in that respect. I would suppose that in this case the market failure was in large part an information failure. To use myself as an example, I did not know that airport security was the responsibility of the airlines, and I travel often. I assumed travel was safe. I assumed that someone—the government, really—made sure that airport security was tight and that planes could not purposefully be flown off course for more than an hour and then into a building.[7]

But the market failure was more than an information failure. Even if I had known that screeners were so poorly paid and trained, my options would have been extremely limited. I could not have volunteered to pay more for my air travel in exchange for more security. A travel agent would have chuckled at such a request. I could not have sought out a safer airline, because all the airlines (at least in the United States) provided basically the same apparent level of safety.

Why, then, did United Airlines, or American Airlines, or any of the others, not market itself as safer than its competitors? In other words, why did competition not make airlines safer? The answer is that such a claim would have had little meaning to travelers. Because most travelers assumed air travel was safe, it would have been difficult to make believable claims of one airline's distinctiveness on that ground. It was cheaper to compete on the basis of ticket cost, or convenience of schedules, or on-time arrivals. Similarly, contractors providing the security for the airlines did not have good incentives to compete on the basis of their ability to provide better security. Contractors paying their employees more to provide better safety would be putting themselves at a competitive disadvantage. Because safety improvement would not be apparent to the ultimate customer, the airlines would be uninterested in paying the contractors more so that these contractors could pay the screeners more.

Finally, one might wonder why shareholders of United and American and other airlines failed to demand that the airlines provide safer air travel. In hindsight, better security might have been a good financial investment. Airlines have suffered dramatic financial losses because of the drop in the number of passengers who were willing to travel by air. According to the *Wall Street Journal,* United Airlines alone was losing $20 million a day six weeks after the disaster.[8]

There are a number of reasons why shareholders did not prevent the disasters. Many of the airlines' shareholders simply did not know that they held airline stock. Their

---

[7] In all fairness, a number of reports in the years and months leading up to September 11th focused on the poor quality of airport security. AVIATION SEC.: TESTIMONY BEFORE THE SUBCOMM. ON AVIATION OF THE HOUSE COMM. ON TRANSP. AND INFRASTRUCTURE, 106th Cong. 3-4 (2001), *available at* http://www.gao.gov/new.items/d11165t.pdf (last visited June 13, 2002) (statement of Gerald L. Dillingham, Director, Physical Infrastructure Issues). The fact that nothing was done strengthens the notion that there was a fundamental market failure in the provision of safe air travel.

[8] Michael J. McCarthy & Susan Carey, *UAL's New CEO Brings Turnaround Skills from Stint at Weyerhaeuser,* WALL ST. J., Oct. 30, 2001, at B1.

shares might have been held in trust, with an institution, or in a pension fund. Another possibility is that the airlines' shareholders held the same assumptions as many of the rest of us: that air travel was safe and that there was no need to worry that such a disaster could occur. Lastly, and most likely, shareholders simply might not have thought about it. Shareholders of large, publicly traded companies are not typically managers; the management of the firm is in the hands of the board and senior employees.

If shareholders had wanted to affect the level of safety on the airlines, the best they could have done (in the real world) was to sell their stock. But even that would have been pointless, because the company would have no way of knowing that the reason that any shareholder sold her stock was to protest poor security or to avoid the possibility of future losses stemming from an air disaster. A sale of one's shares, then, would not affect company policy. The best such a sale could do was to protect the shareholder from any potential losses stemming from a disaster. Any shareholder who declined to sell her stock was therefore implicitly or explicitly making a wager that cheap, imperfect security was a better investment than more expensive, less imperfect security.

SEPTEMBER 11TH, EXTERNALITIES, AND "ENABLINGISM"

It is important to note that the law, and most corporate law scholars as well, assume that shareholders make this very calculation. Because shareholders can learn about companies from information freely available and can sell stock in a fluid securities market, it is assumed that those who hold a company's stock voluntarily accept the risk/return ratio of that security. And it is also assumed that shareholders only really care about making money. Shareholder preferences are assumed to be homogenous, and the law and market is arranged in such a way as to make sure that the management hews close to the shareholders' one assumed concern, making money. All this is a legal fiction, to be sure, but a fiction that allows corporate law to be characterized as "voluntary."[9] Everyone else involved in the firm is also assumed to be consenting to their involvement in a meaningful way. This is what the law and economics scholars mean when they say a corporation is a "nexus of contracts." No one is coerced into taking part in the firm. If the parties dislike the terms of the "contract," they can leave. Shareholders can sell their shares, employees can quit, managers can find a different company to manage, suppliers can sell their goods elsewhere, and creditors can sell their bonds. The contract, it is said, does not affect anyone not a party to it. In economic terms, the claim is that the corporate "contract" does not create any externalities.[10]

September 11th helps show the flaw in this argument. To say that the decisions of the airlines concerning the safety of air travel do not affect anyone external to the decision-makers themselves is ludicrous. The bad decisions of the airlines about safety

---

[9] Frank H. Easterbrook & Daniel R. Fischel, The Economic Structure of Corporate Law 12 (1991) ("The corporation is a voluntary adventure.").

[10] *Id.* at 17 ("The corporation's choice of governance mechanisms does not create substantial third party effects.").

certainly had many horrible effects on thousands who had no real, meaningful way to affect the decision-making of the airlines before September 11th. Said positively, safer air travel would have inured to the benefit not only of the decision-makers of the company (management and shareholders) but also to employees, customers, and sadly, the workers in the World Trade Center and the Pentagon, the passengers on the doomed flights, and numerous brave firefighters and police officers. The people working in the World Trade Center and the Pentagon could not have "paid" anything for better airline security. They were totally and utterly shut out of the decision-making about airline security. Their only route of influence, before the fact, was through the government. And the government had already ceded the corporations the right to police themselves in many important respects. The airlines were trusted to provide something that they had little incentive to provide, beyond whatever minimum level was necessary to make travelers feel safe (whether they were or not).

This notion that corporations regularly create externalities is not a new one. My point here, and the point often overlooked in corporate law doctrine, is that the corporate "contract" itself makes these externalities possible, even likely. Lawrence Mitchell calls the corporation an "externalizing machine," and one of the reasons it is such is because of corporate law.[11] By centralizing power in management, limiting the involvement of other stakeholders in corporate decision-making, and imposing a requirement that the firm's management look after the interests of the shareholders first and foremost, the law has created an entity that is virtually guaranteed to shed as many costs and risks onto others as it can.[12] If a corporation can make money by polluting a river, the rules of corporate governance make it more likely that the corporation will do so. If a corporation can make money by paying its workers low wages or making them work in unsafe conditions, the rules of corporate governance make it more likely that the corporation will do so. If a corporation can make money by creating a harmful product, whether a toy, a car, or air travel, the rules of corporate governance make it more likely that the corporation will do so. By law and norm, the corporation cares about one thing, money. Anything that is not money is set aside unless it is in service of that one thing. Instead of creating a governance system that would help internalize the concerns of society in general, or of customers, or of employees, the system of

---

[11] LAWRENCE MITCHELL, CORPORATE IRRESPONSIBILITY: AMERICA'S NEWEST EXPORT 49-65 (2001).

[12] Another reason why corporations are such great externality creating entities is the dominance of Delaware as the source of corporate law. Because of the state-law-based nature of corporate law, and because of the internal affairs doctrine, Delaware is able to dominate the "market" in the provision of corporate law. Delaware can provide the law of corporate governance even for corporations without offices, employees, sales, or any other significant involvement in the state. To the extent that "contracts" of corporate governance have effects on the states where the corporations do business but are not incorporated, such effects constitute externalities. Those other states have little ability to affect the corporate governance of those corporations, and Delaware has little interest in internalizing the interests of those other states. This problem is made worse by the quasi-constitutional status of the internal affairs doctrine after CTS and Amanda. *See* CTS Corp. v. Dynamics Corp. of Am., 481 U.S. 69 (1987); Amanda Acquisition Corp. v. Univ. Foods Corp., 877 F.2d 496 (7th Cir. 1989).

corporate governance in the United States sets up shareholder interests as supreme and centralizes decision-making so that those interests are served. Other stakeholders are left to depend on mechanisms external to the firm—contract and regulation—both seriously imperfect, to protect their interests.[13]

Another central claim of traditional corporate scholars is that because everyone's involvement in the firm is voluntary, the law should simply be enabling. "Enablingism" is indeed now considered the "dominant statutory mode," meaning that corporate law generally eschews mandatory provisions and allows the participants to choose the terms of the corporate "contract" that best serve their collective interests.[14] The notion that voluntary arrangements optimize collective utility is a central underlying tenet of much of corporate law. The role of the law is thus limited, in general, to establishing waivable default rules that most parties would choose if they actually sat down at a table and negotiated terms. The government should not place its finger on the scale to assist one or another party in setting the terms of the corporate contract. To do so either causes the agreement to shift away from the optimal contract, which by definition is what the parties would agree to absent government intervention, or forces the parties to expend time, effort, and money to readjust other terms in the contract to make up for the advantage imposed by the government. Even worse than the government stepping in at the formation of the corporate "contract" is government intervention after the terms are set. Adjusting the contract through regulation changes people's settled expectations, and makes it even more costly for the parties to recalibrate their arrangement.[15]

This justification for "enablingism" is so appealing that it has been the dominant normative prescription for corporate law for several decades and has had a significant effect on positive law. There is much that is problematic in this account, however, only some of which can be touched on here. One fundamental problem with this account is the belief that default rules do not have any real meaning, other than as a starting point to negotiation. Increasingly, studies show that default rules have remarkable staying power, even when they are not in fact what people would negotiate in the absence of those rules.[16] This is in part because people take cues about their own behavior and beliefs from what the law suggests. More concretely, because the law sets shareholders as supreme within the firm, it is much more likely that they (indeed, other stakeholders as well) will believe that they deserve that superiority.

---

[13] For the limits of both the contractual and regulatory remedy, see generally Kent Greenfield, *The Place of Workers in Corporate Law,* 39 B.C. L. Rev. 283 (1998), and Christopher D. Stone, Where the Law Ends: The Social Control of Corporate Behavior (1975).

[14] *See* Lewis D. Solomon et al., Corporations: Law and Policy 7 (4th ed. 1994) (noting that corporate law is based on state law and that "enablingism" is the "dominant statutory mode").

[15] Easterbrook & Fischel, *supra* note 9, at 32-34 (discussing "latecomer" terms).

[16] Russell Korobkin, *The Status Quo Bias and Contract Default Rules,* 83 Cornell L. Rev. 608, 664-75 (1998) (stating that status quo bias prevents contracting parties from bargaining around default rules, even when doing so is in their best interests); Ian Ayres & Robert Gertner, *Strategic Contractual Inefficiency and the Optimal Choice of Legal Rules,* 101 Yale L.J. 729, 746-59 (1992) (discussing legal implications of high costs of contracting around default rules).

Another fundamental flaw in this account of "enablingism" is that it takes as given the appropriateness of utility (measured by the satisfaction of preferences) as the guiding principle within law in general and corporate law in particular. An argument that government should stand aside to allow negotiating parties to maximize their collective preferences depends on the notion that the satisfaction of preferences should be the organizing principle of public policy. Of course, whether utilitarianism should be the touchstone for law is an age-old debate that rages still.[17] Suffice to say, however, that it may indeed be the case that corporate law, like other areas of the law, could choose to advance public virtues, such as human dignity or fairness or compassion or equality or autonomy, in addition to utility.

The difficulty in the "enablingism" account that I want to focus on, however, goes to the heart of the assertion that contractarianism optimizes the interests of the various parties to the deal. Because law is supposed to stand aside, the contract that results depends upon the power of the parties going into the negotiation. The resulting "contract" defining the terms of corporate governance thus mirrors the preexisting market power of the various parties. To say that a contract optimizes the interests of the various parties may be true in the sense that it allows the parties to improve on what would be their lot without such a contract. But it emphatically is not the case that all contracts are fair, just, supportive of human dignity, or consistent with the interests of society as a whole. We cannot say that a contract that depends on preexisting entitlements is just or fair unless we know that those preexisting entitlements are just and fair. We take this notion as almost self-evident in large areas of the law. For example, people in the United States cannot (even freely) enter into employment contracts that will pay them less than the minimum wage or will subject them to racial or sexual harassment.[18] However self-evident elsewhere, the concept that fairness and justice and public welfare may include more than the mere satisfaction of preferences seems to be forgotten by contractarian corporate scholars.

The externality creation aspect of the corporate law can now be tied into the "enablingism" point. Because the law largely stands aside in the formation of the corporate governance "contract," the parties with power, the shareholders and managers, can largely agree to whatever arrangement will benefit them. They can externalize the cost of the contract onto those who have less power to do anything about it. Because corporate law reinforces market power rather than ameliorates it, those who have less market power to begin with, such as workers and communities, are cemented into their position.

The law might appear neutral in that it merely gives force to what parties to the corporate "contract" would bargain for anyway. But that is simply another way of saying that the law should use market power as the predominant guide for public policy, and such an assertion is highly contestable and far from neutral. Imagine a scholar who

---

[17] *See* LOUIS KAPLOW & STEVEN SHAVELL, FAIRNESS VERSUS WELFARE (2002); Joseph William Singer, *Something Important in Humanity,* 37 HARV. C.R.-C.L. L. REV. 103 (2002).

[18] *Cf.* Elinor Burkett, *'God Created Me to Be a Slave,'* N.Y. TIMES, Oct. 12, 1997, (Magazine), at 56 (describing phenomenon of some people selling themselves into slavery).

advocated that individuals should be free from discrimination on the basis of sex, race, or sexual orientation only if they were willing and able to pay for such freedom. Such an assertion would be very controversial and could hardly be defended on the ground that the law was simply choosing a neutral baseline—market power—as the basis for public policy. Instead, in such a legal regime, it would be almost mundane to note that the discrimination would itself be an externality of the choice of legal rule. Similarly, when corporate law scholars argue for legal rules that say that a stakeholder's ability to protect herself in the relationship depends on her contractual rights, that simply is another way of saying that she gets only those rights she can pay for. Such "enablingism" is hardly neutral. It uses the law to bolster the power of those who are already powerful and allows the costs of the enterprise to be externalized onto the less powerful stakeholders who have less ability to pay for their own protection.

SEPTEMBER 11TH AND THE MYTH OF THE FREE MARKET

The rhetoric of enablingism is quintessentially that of free-market and laissez-faire economics. The government should simply create the context in which private parties can negotiate to their mutual benefit.[19] The aftermath of September 11th makes it clear that this free-market rhetoric has few genuine adherents and certainly does not describe the society in which we live.

As a normative matter, the demand for greater government oversight of air travel reveals, as mentioned above, that the market cannot be trusted to produce and deliver many things that people truly desire. Corporations may be good at making money, but they are not as capable of providing things that take a long time to produce, things that cannot be provided without many of us working together, things that cannot be easily reduced to a monetary value, or things that are valued by people with no money. It is as if the public understood, almost innately, what my students sometimes do not. Government regulation, in this context of air travel, but also in any number of areas, is often necessary to enhance liberty. Without government regulation, many of us would not be free to travel safely, or to work in a safe workplace, or to buy a home in an integrated neighborhood.

September 11th also reveals as false the rhetoric of the free market as a positive matter. Even though the law assumes that shareholders of public companies voluntarily accept the risk/return ratio of the securities they hold, lobbyists for the airlines were on Capitol Hill literally hours after the disaster, asking for massive government assistance.[20] The government bailed out the airlines to the tune of $15 billion, and through the Fall of 2001 also entertained various entreaties from travel agents, hotel chains, insurance

[19] I have written elsewhere that this fixation on contract within corporate law is a throwback to *Lochner*, in that it assumes a private sphere insulated from government regulation. Kent Greenfield, *Using Behavioral Economics To Show the Power and Efficiency of Corporate Law as Regulatory Tool,* 35 U.C. DAVIS L. REV. 581, 591-601 (2002).

[20] Keith L. Alexander, *The View from the Ground: Delta's Reaction to Sept. 11 Illustrates the Airline Industry's Violent Change,* WASH. POST, Dec. 30, 2001, at H1.

companies, and even soybean farmers, among others.[21] In fact, within a few weeks of the September 11th tragedy, President Bush and his Commerce Secretary met privately with fifteen insurance executives, who asked for help not because the tragedy would hurt the industry, which has assets of more than $3 trillion, but because they worried about future attacks.[22] Bush's willingness to meet with corporate executives so soon after the tragedy might be explained in part by the fact that the insurance industry had given $1.6 million to Bush's 2000 campaign, making it Bush's tenth-largest contributor.[23] In any event, it is quite clear that the insurance executives were not asking for the government to allow the market to work. Just the opposite.

Indeed, it is more than a bit ironic that the contractarian, free-market rhetoric is so strong within corporate law scholarship, when so few firms, executives, or shareholders would sign on to such rhetoric outside the limited area of corporate governance. To be sure, corporations depend mightily on government assistance to survive and make money. I am speaking not only of the billions of dollars a year that go into export subsidies, price supports, tax concessions, and other examples of "corporate welfare." I refer also to the very infrastructure of the market, which is in large part a creation of government and government regulation.[24]

One of the arguments often made in favor of shareholder primacy within corporate law is that other stakeholders of the firm will be able to protect themselves through the legislative and regulatory processes. This argument only works, it seems to me, if the nonshareholder stakeholders have some comparative advantage in the legislature or regulatory agencies. One of the lessons from September 11th is that the comparative advantage, to the extent it exists, sits on the other side of the ledger.[25]

After September 11th, airlines laid off thousands of employees and received billions of dollars of government money in the bailout.[26] Another of the public responses to the tragedy was a renewed attention to an economic stimulus plan. Less than six weeks after September 11th, the *Wall Street Journal* reported that the House of Representatives had scheduled a vote on an economic stimulus package that would result in the United States Treasury sending checks worth hundreds of millions of dollars directly to profit-

---

[21] *See* Stephen Labaton & Joseph B. Treaster, *Insurers Push for Cap on Future Payouts,* N.Y. TIMES, Oct. 22, 2001, at B7.

[22] *Id.*

[23] Jacob B. Schlesinger & John D. McKinnon, *Hands Out: Bush Tax Cuts Send Corporate Lobbyists into a Feeding Frenzy,* WALL ST. J., Feb. 2, 2001, at A1.

[24] *See* Paulette Olson & Dell Champlin, *Ending Corporate Welfare As We Know It: An Institutional Analysis of the Dual Structure of Welfare,* 32 J. OF ECON. ISSUES 759, 759 (1998) (noting that corporate welfare is estimated to cost federal government between $170 and $200 billion each year).

[25] Christopher Stone made this point thirty years ago. *See* Stone, *supra* note 13.

[26] Brad Foss, *United Airlines' Frank Ads Get Mixed Reviews,* L.A. TIMES, Oct. 22, 2001, at C5. United Airlines laid off 20,000 workers after September 11th. *The List—Terror's Aftermath: Layoffs,* BUS. WK., Oct. 8, 2001, at 10. In October 2001, United's national ad campaign included commercials in which employees of United gave testimonials of the company's resurgence, saying things such as "we're Americans, and this is not gonna beat us down," and "if we stick together, we can get through this."

able corporations.[27] Under the plan adopted by a House committee, Chevron could receive over $300 million, General Electric almost $700 million, and General Motors over $800 million.[28] Incredibly, IBM would receive a check for almost $1.5 billion, and Ford Motor Company would stand to gain over $2.3 billion.[29] The *Wall Street Journal* reported that the proposal to send lump-sum payments to corporations was added in the House Ways and Means Committee "with little debate, after quiet and effective lobbying by U.S. multinational companies."[30] The free market be damned.

SEPTEMBER 11TH AND THE END OF HISTORY

Nine months before the tragedies of September, two of the leading scholars in corporate law, Henry Hansmann and Reinier Kraakman, published an article arguing that the "ideology" of shareholder primacy has become so dominant in the United States and globally that we are experiencing the "end of history" for corporate law.[31] There are both descriptive and normative claims imbedded in Hansmann and Kraakman's thesis.[32] Perhaps the aftermath of September 11th proves their descriptive claim in one respect. There is little doubt that corporations are fixated on profit maximization, even if it takes government intervention to achieve it. September 11th also makes it appear that the government, too, is dedicated to protecting shareholder interests.

But Hansmann and Kraakman's normative claims are more vulnerable, and the aftermath of September 11th helps reveal their weaknesses. The arguments for shareholder primacy depend on the notion that corporations that look after shareholder interests benefit society more than corporations that look after other interests. Hansmann and Kraakman make this point explicitly, saying that "[a]ll thoughtful people" agree that business should be "organized and operated to serve the interests of society as a whole, and that the interests of shareholders deserve no greater weight in this social calculus than do the interests of any other members of society."[33] This admission is to their credit, because it is not often acknowledged by corporate law scholars. Hansmann and Kraakman never fully explain, however, why they believe shareholder primacy is best for society. The jump from corporate welfare to social welfare is performed by way of simple assertion:

---

[27] John D. McKinnon & Shailagh Murray, *Companies Could Reap Big Tax Refunds from House Bill,* WALL ST. J., Oct. 23, 2001, at A28.

[28] *Id.*

[29] *Id.*

[30] *Id.*

[31] Henry Hansmann & Reinier Kraakman, *The End of History for Corporate Law,* 89 GEO. L.J. 439 (2001).

[32] *Id.*

[33] *Id.* at 441.

> The point is simply that now, as a consequence of both logic and experience, there is convergence on a consensus that the best means to this end (that is, the pursuit of aggregate social welfare) is to make corporate managers strongly accountable to shareholder interests and, at least in direct terms, only to those interests.[34] This is simply the trickle-down theory reapplied to corporate law. What is good for shareholders is good for corporations. What is good for corporations is good for society.

I believe the real reasons for shareholder supremacy have absolutely nothing to do with any testable assertions that we are better off as a society. The most contractarians really say is that we are better off as an economy. Hansmann and Kraakman say that comparison across countries "lends credence to the view that adherence to the standard [shareholder as supreme] model promotes better economic outcomes."[35] That itself is highly contestable. But even if it is true, it does not prove the point that needs to be made. Not even the most evangelical economists equate success as an economy with success as a society. Indeed, one can imagine a very affluent society in which people are personally and socially insecure, where the poor have almost no chance of receiving a decent education, where one-fourth of all children are born into poverty,[36] where men of color have a greater chance of spending four years in jail than four years in college.[37]

Even if the claim is that shareholder primacy makes macro-economic sense, much turns on which economic touchstone one considers. The poverty rate for children in the United States is almost four times that of France.[38] Income inequality is worse in the United States than in any other developed nation, is at its worst since World War II, and is getting even worse.[39] Real wage growth in the United States is negative over the past thirty years.[40] Typical working people in the United States make less in real terms now than their parents did during the Nixon administration.[41]

It is worth considering Germany, where corporations are organized in such a way so that shareholders are not supreme. There, the law requires that companies organize their workplaces under the oversight, review, and guidance of work councils and that large companies reserve one-half of their supervisory boards to employee representatives.[42]

---

[34] *Id.*

[35] *Id.* at 450.

[36] David Wessel & Jacob M. Schlesinger, *U.S. Economy's Report Card: Not All A's,* WALL ST. J., May 5, 1997, at A2.

[37] Paul D. Butler et al., *Promoting Racial Equality,* 9 J.L. & POL'Y 347, 350 (2001) (providing comments of Professor Paul D. Butler).

[38] LAWRENCE MISHEL ET AL., STATE OF WORKING AMERICA 2000-2001, at 393 tbl. 7.14 (2001).

[39] *Id.* at 124 (noting that the hourly earnings of typical U.S. production worker, in constant dollars, is almost twenty cents less in 1999 than in 1973).

[40] *Id.*

[41] *See* Wessel & Schlesinger, *supra* note 36, at A2.

[42] MICHEL ALBERT, CAPITALISM VS. CAPITALISM 110-12 (Paul Haviland trans., 1993).

The latter codetermination requirement puts workers within the decision-making structure at the top of the firm's hierarchy.[43] Meanwhile, workers share power at the level of the actual workplace, in the form of committees similar to British work councils. According to Michel Albert, "All issues of concern to the workforce are referred to these councils: training, redundancies, schedules, methods of payment, work patterns etc."[44] This allocation reflects the German notion that "dialogue between partners is the indispensable oil that keeps the wheels of business turning and reduces the likelihood of destructive social friction."[45] "The company is seen by all its members as a community of interests, a true partnership."[46]

Of course, from the standpoint of shareholders and short-sighted managers, codetermination and work councils are by definition inefficient. It is thus unsurprising that those who support shareholder primacy criticize this model on grounds of inefficiency. But of course from the perspective of the workers, these councils make the company a more efficient instrument for furthering and protecting the interests of workers.

Hansmann and Kraakman say that this labor-oriented model of corporate governance "has steadily lost power as a normative ideal."[47] They say that "[t]he growing view" is that worker participation in corporate decision-making produces "inefficient decisions, paralysis, or weak boards" and that these "costs" likely outweigh "any potential benefits that worker participation might bring."[48] Instead, workers must depend on contract law, "supplemented by appropriate labor market regulation," to protect them, as it is "evidently superior" to worker participation in resolving conflicts between the firm and its workers.[49]

Hansmann and Kraakman appear to believe that these claims are relatively self-evident. It is worth noting, however, when it is said that the worker involvement model is obsolete, that Germany provides for its workers much better than the United States does. Of all the great industrialized nations, Germany has the shortest working week and the highest wages.[50] What's more, the gap between the best-paid and the lowest-paid workers is not as wide as in other countries.[51] Germany is much more egalitarian than the United States or even France.[52]

---

[43] Since 1976, German firms with more than 2000 workers must allocate one-half of the seats on the company's supervisory board to employees. *Id.* at 112.

[44] *Id.*

[45] *Id.*

[46] *Id.*

[47] Hansmann & Kraakman, *supra* note 31, at 445.

[48] *Id.*

[49] *Id.* at 446.

[50] Albert, *supra* note 42, at 100.

[51] *See id.* at 114.

[52] *Id.*

Essentially, what we know is that a shareholder-oriented model does a better job of protecting shareholders. A worker-oriented model does a better job of protecting workers. Which does a better job with the economy or with society as a whole? Note that it is very difficult to make cross-cultural comparisons on that ground. But that is exactly what Hansmann and Kraakman purport to do.

In any event, it is worth emphasizing that Germany's version of power sharing at times gives it more flexibility in responding to economic crises. During the recession years of 1981 and 1982, employers and trade unions agreed to keep wages down, so as to maintain the viability of companies that would otherwise be in distress.[53] In some cases, the workers even agreed to salary cuts.[54] Because the cuts were negotiated rather than imposed, workers could continue to feel as if they were partners in their firms rather than merely hired hands. According to Albert, the resulting economic recovery "was extraordinarily vigorous."[55]

When one boils down the assertion that shareholder primacy is better for society, or for the economy, what is really said is that shareholder supremacy is better for corporations. Hansmann and Kraakman say that with the globalization of business, companies organized in different ways have increasingly come into direct competition. They assert, without citation, that "it is now widely thought" that firms following the model of shareholder supremacy "have the upper hand" in these competitions.[56] They argue that shareholder-oriented firms "can be expected to have important competitive advantages" over firms organized under other legal regimes.[57] These advantages include, apparently, access to capital at lower cost, "stronger incentives" to reorganize in ways that are "managerially coherent" (meaning, I suppose, without worker involvement), and the ability to abandon "inefficient investments" more quickly.[58]

Note that the list of competitive advantages relate not to the economy as a whole but to the ability of the corporation to maximize shareholder advantage. The abandonment of inefficient investments, for example, is simply another way of saying that the company can close a plant or lay off workers with less concern for the workers. Managerial coherence, I suppose, means the ability of management to control the operation of the firm with less concern for the presumed inefficiency of worker involvement. Access to capital at lower cost is simply another way of saying that shareholders will appreciate being supreme, thank you very much.

The structure of their argument is tautological: the shareholder-oriented model is superior because it is better at maximizing shareholder welfare. Hansmann and Kraakman's argument thus shows only that shareholder-oriented firms will beat out other firms, if the measuring stick for the competition is shareholder advantage. Their argu-

[53] *Id.* at 115.

[54] *Id.*

[55] *Id.*

[56] Hansmann & Kraakman, *supra* note 31, at 450.

[57] *Id.*

[58] *Id.* at 450-51.

ment does not prove, however, that shareholder-oriented firms are better than other firms on any other basis.

Even so, the claim that shareholder supremacy is good for corporations is contestable as well. Here I do not mean that the argument is contestable in the mundane sense that if corporations act as good citizens they will benefit their shareholders, and to benefit their shareholders they must be mindful of whether their workers, customers, creditors, and communities are happy. The argument is contestable in the far more fundamental sense that serving shareholder interests may not maximize the value of the firm, even in economic terms. Because of limited liability and because of the diversification of shareholder portfolios, shareholders are largely indifferent as to the well-being of any given corporation the stock of which they hold. I have written about this elsewhere.[59] For now, suffice to say that many, even most, shareholders of a particular firm may not have its interests at heart. First of all, shareholders often feel no real connection to the firm. They may not even know they own stock in a firm, much less feel any real "ownership" of it. Most people who hold stock in a company in any given moment did not ever contribute money to the firm. They bought the stock from someone who bought the stock from someone who bought the stock from someone who bought the stock from someone who bought the stock from an investment banker who bought it from the company.

Second, because most shareholders invest in a number of different companies and thus have diversified portfolios, they are therefore risk neutral with respect to the decisions of any specific company.[60] Diversified shareholders want management of any particular company to make decisions that maximize the expected value of the results, even if the results also are highly variable.[61] Shareholders will prefer risky decisions, which gamble on high payoffs but risk bankruptcy, over decisions that provide lower expected returns but have less risk of pushing the firm into financial distress.[62]

Workers, however, have every incentive to make sure that the companies they work for survive and thrive.[63] Employees are not diversified in their labor investment because they typically work for one or two employers at a time and may have invested much time and effort to develop firm-specific human capital.[64] Workers are not risk neutral;

---

[59] Greenfield, *supra* note 13, at 305-11.

[60] *Id.*

[61] *Id.* at 308.

[62] As Easterbrook and Fischel state, "the investor wants to maximize the value of his holdings, not the value of a given stock." Easterbrook & Fischel, *supra* note 15, at 28.

[63] Greenfield, *supra* note 13, at 309.

[64] *Id.; cf.* BARBARA EHRENREICH, NICKEL AND DIMED: ON (NOT) GETTING BY IN AMERICA (2001). Ehrenreich chronicles her experiences working in low-level jobs around the country. One of the things that is striking about her account is that even in the most mundane jobs, such as hotel maid, waitress, and sales clerk, the amount of firm-specific or job-specific knowledge is quite high. I am thankful to Joseph Singer for pointing out this insight in conversation.

as to their employment, they are risk averse.[65] Rather than being indifferent as to the liquidation risk of the company they work for, they care deeply about their firm's financial health because they face harsh consequences from unemployment if their firm suffers.[66] If their company fails, workers typically lose a great deal. They not only lose their jobs but also the value of any firm-specific skills and sometimes a good portion of retirement or pension benefits. (Consider the recent Enron bankruptcy.[67]) In contrast to shareholders, workers prefer that management not make decisions with a high variance, even when such decisions have a high expected return. Workers instead want decisions that value stability, even with a lower-expected total return.

Workers' interests may thus function as a better placeholder for the best interests of the firm. Because shareholders are largely indifferent as to the possibility of any single firm failing, managers who make decisions according to what is good for the shareholders will bring about the failure of their companies more often than managers who make decisions based on what is good for a broader mix of stakeholders. If one really cares what is better for a specific firm, it is not so clear that shareholders' desires should dominate, at least if we define "what is better for the firm" to include survival.[68]

Finally, workers have continuing relationships with firms in ways most shareholders do not. Because of this relationship, taking account of workers' interests can inure to the firm's benefit in yet another way, by building "positive reciprocity." This is simply a fancy term for the notion that people largely respond to others in the way they are treated. There is almost no room for this effect to occur in the company's relationship with most shareholders, because the contribution of capital is usually an isolated act performed by someone who bought stock from the firm years previously. Workers, however, can "give back" to the firm when they are treated well.[69] For example, when workers believe they are treated fairly by their employers, they are more productive and obey firm rules at a much higher rate than when they feel they are mistreated.[70] The employment relation is not a zero-sum game.

One can show evidence of this effect even at a macroeconomic level. Even though the rate of union membership is about three times higher in Germany than in the United States, the number of days lost to strikes in Germany is about 1/20 of the U.S. total.[71] Indeed, Germany has the lowest level of strike activity in the Western world.

---

[65] Greenfield, *supra* note 13, at 309.

[66] *Id.* (citing Marleen A. O'Connor, *The Human Capital Era: Reconceptualizing Corporate Law to Facilitate Labor—Management Cooperation,* 78 CORNELL L. REV. 899, 908 n.26 (1993)).

[67] Ellen E. Schultz, *Enron Workers Face Losses on Pensions, Not Just 401(k)s,* WALL ST. J., Dec. 19, 2001, at C1.

[68] Greenfield, *supra* note 13, at 309.

[69] *See* Gillian Lester, *Careers and Contingency,* 51 STAN. L. REV. 73, 135 (1998).

[70] *Id.*

[71] Albert, *supra* note 42, at 122-23. In 1988, West Germany lost 28,000 working days to strikes; the United States lost 12,215,000, France lost 568,000, and Britain lost 1,920,000. *Id.* at 123.

When all is said and done, all one can say persuasively is that a shareholder-oriented model of corporate law is better for shareholders. It is quite difficult to say it is better for society as a whole, or for the economy, or for other stakeholders. It is even difficult to say it is better for the firm itself.

So then, how do we organize corporate law? We may have to go back to questions of the first order. What is clear, at least, is that if we want to help workers, rather than shareholders, we should organize corporate law very differently. Or if we valued stability, or equality, or any number of other public principles, we would organize corporate law very differently. In any event, corporate law should be seen not as a narrow, private law field for the acolytes of law and economics. Rather, it should be debated as if it were a part of larger social and macroeconomic policy. Perhaps the United States is productive and affluent enough that we would want to "spend" a little in opportunity costs to "buy" stability and safety and social harmony. Corporate law produces the fabric of governance of our most important and powerful institutions other than government. Instead of using corporate law to accentuate the antagonisms in society, perhaps we would want to craft a method of corporate governance that builds harmony and partnership.

Michel Albert wrote his important book almost a decade ago, but it is even more relevant today. One passage in particular is worth quoting at length:

> As the world becomes a more and more uncertain place, immaterial factors like trust and belonging are increasingly important. It becomes essential for all corporate enterprises to ensure that their members play the same game by the same rules, share the same views and fit into the same patterns, so that in the end decisions can be taken by consensus and energies can be mobilized naturally, spontaneously. Stability at home is all the more valuable when uncertainty and instability are abroad; far from stifling change and adaptability, domestic harmony can be turned to competitive advantage.[72]

September 11th reminds us of the importance of building connections, of reaching out to build community. Unfortunately, the aftermath of the tragedies indicates that government and corporations may be more interested in allowing the few who already have a great deal to aggrandize even more. Perhaps we would want to use the government to create bonds among us, to encourage discussion, to facilitate the sharing of power. Corporate law can be an important part of this process, but only if shareholder primacy is abandoned. If we did so, we could experience the beginning of a new history for corporate law.

---

[72] *Id.* at 113.

The Sarbanes-Oxley Act and the Making of Quack Corporate Governance[*]

Roberta Romano[**]

It's hard to argue logic in a feeding frenzy . . . .[1]

I. INTRODUCTION

The Sarbanes-Oxley (SOX) Act of 2002,[2] in which Congress introduced a series of corporate governance initiatives into the federal securities laws, is not just a considerable change in law, but also a departure in the mode of regulation. The federal regime

[*] Reprinted by permission of The Yale Law Journal Company, Inc., and The William S. Hein Company. Roberta Romano, *The Sarbanes-Oxley Act and the Making of Quack Corporate Governance,* 114 YALE L.J. 1521 (2005).

[**] Allen Duffy/Class of 1960 Professor of Law, Yale Law School; Research Associate, National Bureau of Economic Research; Fellow, European Corporate Governance Institute. Earlier versions of this Article were presented as a plenary lecture at the Twentieth Annual Conference of the European Association of Law and Economics; the Matthews Lecture at the University of Mississippi School of Law; the Harald Voss Memorial Lectures at the Institute for Law and Finance of Johann Wolfgang Goethe-Universität in Frankfurt; the Vienna University of Economics and Business Administration and UNCITRAL Forum für Internationales Wirtschaftsrecht in Vienna; the University of Pennsylvania Institute of Law and Economics Roundtable; the Centre for European Policy Studies Roundtable on Corporate Governance Reform in the EU; the Kirkland & Ellis LLP Corporate Law and Economics Workshop; and workshops at the John F. Kennedy School of Government and the Columbia, University of Chicago, University of Denver, University of Iowa, University of North Carolina, and University of Virginia Law Schools. In addition to participants at those presentations, I would like to thank Jennifer Arlen, Cary Coglianese, John Core, Alan Gerber, Marcel Kahan, April Klein, Jonathan Macey, Paul Mahoney, and Mathew McCubbins for helpful comments.

[1] Jim Drinkard, *Scandal Publicity Drives Accounting Bill Forward*, USA TODAY, July 25, 2002, at 10A (internal quotation marks omitted) (quoting Senator Phil Gramm).

[2] SOX, Pub. L. No. 107-204, 2002 U.S.C.C.A.N. (116 Stat.) 745 (to be codified in scattered sections of 15 and 18 U.S.C.). Politicians heralded the Act as the most important financial market legislation since the initiation of federal securities regulation in the 1930s. *E.g.,* 148 CONG. REC. S7356 (daily ed. July 25, 2002) (statement of Sen. Corzine) (claiming that the legislation "may be the most important step" taken since the enactment of the securities laws); Remarks on Signing the Sarbanes-Oxley Act of 2002,

had until then consisted primarily of disclosure requirements rather than substantive corporate governance mandates, which were traditionally left to state corporate law. Federal courts had, moreover, enforced such a view of the regime's strictures, by characterizing efforts of the SEC to extend its domain into substantive corporate governance as beyond its jurisdiction.[3] SOX alters this division of authority by providing explicit legislative directives for SEC regulation of what was previously perceived as the states' exclusive jurisdiction.

SOX was enacted in a flurry of congressional activity in the runup to the midterm 2002 Congressional elections after the spectacular failures of the once highly regarded firms Enron and WorldCom. Those firms entered bankruptcy proceedings in the wake of revelations of fraudulent accounting practices and executives' self-dealing transactions. But many of the substantive corporate governance provisions in SOX are not in fact regulatory innovations devised by Congress to cope with deficiencies in the business environment in which Enron and WorldCom failed. Rather, they may more accurately be characterized as recycled ideas advocated for quite some time by corporate governance entrepreneurs. In particular, the independent-director requirement and the prohibition of accounting firms' provision of consulting services to auditing clients had been advanced as needed corporate law reforms long before Enron appeared on any politician's agenda.[4] That is not, of course, unique or surprising, because Congressional initiatives rarely are constructed from whole cloth; rather, successful law reform in the national arena typically involves the recombination of old elements that have been advanced in policy circles for a number of years prior to adoption.[5]

There is no rigorous theory of how policy proposals come to the forefront of the legislative agenda, but the political science literature identifies shifts in national mood and turnover of elected officials, coupled with focusing events, as key determinants that open "policy windows" for policy entrepreneurs to link their proposed solutions to a

---

38 WEEKLY COMP. PRES. DOC. 1283, 1284 (July 30, 2002) (calling the legislation the "most far-reaching reforms of American business practices since the time of Franklin Delano Roosevelt").

[3] *See* Bus. Roundtable v. SEC, 905 F.2d 406 (D.C. Cir. 1990) (striking down an SEC action to require one share, one vote through its stock exchange rulemaking authority).

[4] *See, e.g.*, Stephen M. Bainbridge, *A Critique of the NYSE's Director Independence Listing Standards*, 30 SEC. REG. L.J. 370, 377-81 (2002) (comparing the post-SOX exchange rules that expanded on the SOX audit committee mandate to the abortive ALI corporate governance project of the 1980s). Efforts to separate auditing from consulting services were not new: Congress considered the issue in the 1970s. *See* SUBCOMM. ON REPORTS, ACCOUNTING, & MGMT. OF THE SENATE COMM. ON GOVERNMENTAL AFFAIRS, 95TH CONG., IMPROVING THE ACCOUNTABILITY OF PUBLICLY OWNED CORPORATIONS AND THEIR AUDITORS (Comm. Print 1977). More recently, under Arthur Levitt's term as chairman, the SEC vigorously pursued the issue in two rulemaking processes in 1999 and 2000. *See* Revision of the Commission's Auditor Independence Requirements, 65 Fed. Reg. 76,008 (Dec. 5, 2000) (codified at 17 C.F.R. §§ 210.1-02, 240.14a-101 (2004)); Audit Committee Disclosure, Exchange Act Release No. 34-42,266, 64 Fed. Reg. 73,389 (Dec. 30, 1999) (codified in scattered sections of 17 C.F.R. pts. 210, 228-29, 240 (2004)). Exchange rules requiring independent audit committees were adopted in tandem with the 1999 rulemaking proceeding.

[5] JOHN W. KINGDON, AGENDAS, ALTERNATIVES, AND PUBLIC POLICIES 151, 192, 209-11 (1984).

problem.[6] At least two of those three elements were without question present to create the window of opportunity for advocates of the corporate governance provisions included in SOX: As indicated in Table 1, in 2002 there was a shift in public mood regarding big business,[7] coinciding with the high-profile corporate scandals causing significant displacement and financial distress, as well as a sharp decline in the stock market.

There was no turnover of elected officials prior to the enactment of SOX, the third element thought to be important in propelling proposals onto the legislative agenda. However, it was widely perceived in the media that members of Congress were motivated by reelection concerns when a statute was hurriedly enacted in the summer prior to the midterm elections, after months of languishing in committee, following heightened attention on corporate malfeasance as the WorldCom scandal erupted post-Enron.[8] The suggestion from the media was that the priority of members of Congress was to enact something, with the specific content of less concern and importance.[9]

The failure of Enron, then, provided the occasion for implementation of corporate governance initiatives that were already in the policy soup. What is perhaps most striking is how successful policy entrepreneurs were in opportunistically coupling their corporate governance proposals to Enron's collapse, offering as ostensible remedies for

---

[6] *Id.* at 20-21, 170-72, 206-08.

[7] As indicated in Table 1, the proportion of the public having either a great deal or quite a lot of confidence in big business in 2002—20%—was the lowest percentage in more than a decade and represented a substantial drop from the relatively high level of confidence—an average of 29%—over the prior five years, 1997 to 2001, as reported by the Gallup Organization. It is also more than 10% lower than the average, 24%, over the period 1990 to 1996, and 20% below the average of 26% for the decade 1990 to 2001. It is quite probable that the two variables, public opinion toward business and stock prices, are integrally related—that is, when the stock market is doing well the public's perception of business is positive, and when the market drops it is negative, whether or not the change in price is related to corporate scandals. There is some credence to this conjecture: The correlation between the S&P 500 Composite Index and the percentage of the public expressing a great deal of confidence in business is significantly positive (at less than 5%), ranging between 0.55 and 0.59, depending on whether the S&P is measured at the end of the month preceding the poll, the end of the month in which the poll was taken, or the average of the two months. S&P 500 data are available at S&P, http://www.standardandpoors.com (last visited Apr. 27, 2005).

[8] The House Committee on Financial Services held its first hearing on Enron in December 2001 and reported a bill, which was passed shortly after its introduction, in April 2002. The Senate did not act on the House bill until after the WorldCom bankruptcy filing in July 2002. For an example of the media's perception that election concerns figured prominently in the consideration of SOX, see David E. Sanger, *Bush, on Wall St., Offers Tough Stance*, N.Y. TIMES, July 10, 2002, at A1 (reporting a speech by President Bush to Wall Street on his approach to the corporate scandals and noting that the "Democrats have now seized on [the need for drastic legislative change in response to the corporate scandals] as a crucial issue for the November elections," while emphasizing how "partisan the battle has become").

[9] *E.g.*, Shailagh Murray & John D. McKinnon, *Senate Passes Tough Fraud Bill in Unanimous Vote*, WALL ST. J., July 11, 2002, at A1. As one television reporter put it, "This was a stampede. . . . The House Republicans dropped their opposition to this legislation because there was simply too much pressure on them to pass something." *World News Tonight* (ABC television broadcast, July 24, 2002) (reporting of Linda Douglass).

Table 1
Gallup Public Opinion Polls of Confidence in Big Business, 1990-2003

Poll	Date	Sample Size	Percent expressing "great deal (quite a lot) of confidence" = total of both categories
Gallup	Aug. 1990	1241	9 (16) = 25
Gallup	Feb. 1991	1012	11 (15) = 26
Gallup	Oct. 1991	1009	7 (15) = 22
Gallup	Mar. 1993	1003	7 (16) = 23
Gallup/CNN/USA Today	Mar. 1994	1036	9 (17) = 26
Gallup/CNN/USA Today	Mar. 1995	1008	8 (13) = 21
Gallup/CNN/USA Today	Mat 1996	1019	7 (17) = 24
Gallup/CNN/USA Today	July 1997	1004	11 (17) = 28
Gallup/CNN/USA Today	June 1998	1003	11 (19) = 30
Gallup/CNN/USA Today	July 1998	1035	13 (18) = 31
Gallup/CNN/USA Today	June 1999	1016	11 (19) = 30
Gallup	June 2000	1021	9 (20) = 29
Gallup/CNN/USA Today	June 2001	1011	10 (18) = 28
Gallup/CNN/USA Today	June 2002	1020	7 (13) = 20
Gallup/CNN/USA Today	June 2003	1029	8 (14) = 22

Note: Poll data were obtained from the iPoll databank of The Roper Center for Public Opinion Research at the University of Connecticut.

future "Enrons" reforms that had minimal or absolutely no relation to the source of that firm's demise. The most opportunistic coupling in response to Enron's collapse was the Bipartisan Campaign Reform Act of 2002[10] (a campaign finance reform measure that had been stalled prior to the scandal), because Enron's campaign contributions had nothing to do with Enron's financial collapse, nor were there allegations to that effect.

This Article does not, however, analyze the peculiar disjuncture between the substantive corporate governance provisions of SOX and the source of Enron's failure. Rather, it evaluates SOX's substantive governance provisions and the political dynamics that produced them from the perspective of the substantial body of empirical accounting and

[10] Bipartisan Campaign Reform Act of 2002, Pub. L. No. 107-155, 2002 U.S.C.C.A.N. (116 Stat.) 81 (to be codified in scattered sections of 2 and 36 U.S.C.).

finance literature related to those provisions.[11] The existence of a literature that addresses the efficacy of some of the SOX mandates highlights an even more troubling feature of the legislative process than the opportunistic packaging of initiatives as preventatives for future Enrons when their relationship to the problem at hand was, at best, attenuated. The gist of the literature, that the proposed mandates would not be effective, was available to legislators while they were formulating SOX. Yet it went unnoticed or was ignored. With the scholarly literature [that was] at odds with the proposed governance mandates being treated as though it did not exist, the quality of decisionmaking that went into the SOX legislative process was, to put it mildly, less than optimal.

The substantive corporate governance mandates in SOX that are the focus of this Article consist of the provisions that require independent audit committees, restrict corporations' purchases of nonauditing services from their auditors, prohibit corporate loans to officers, and require executive certification of financial statements.[12] In contrast to provisions in SOX entirely within the bounds of traditional federal securities regulation, such as the direction for increased disclosure of off-balance-sheet transactions,[13] or outside the scope of issuer regulation, such as the creation of a new public board

---

[11] The fact that SOX codified ideas that had been circulating in policy circles over many years has two salutary consequences for such an analysis: Research motivated by prior policy debates bears on the SOX initiatives, and variations in firms' practices related to the SOX initiatives permit cross-sectional analyses that shed light on the probable efficacy of the legislation.

[12] One substantive corporate governance provision—the forfeiture of CEO and CFO bonus, incentive, and equity compensation in the event of a material restatement of the company's financials, *see* SOX, Pub. L. No. 107-204, § 304, 2002 U.S.C.C.A.N. (116 Stat.) 745, 778 (to be codified at 15 U.S.C. § 7243)—is not discussed because, although much research exists on executive compensation, it is not helpful for evaluating the efficacy of the provision. (The research does not bear on the relation between the form of compensation and accounting misconduct.) Studies with results tangentially related to the issue are Jap Efendi et al., *Why Do Corporate Managers Misstate Financial Statements? The Role of Option Compensation, Corporate Governance, and Other Factors* (May 17, 2004) (unpublished manuscript), *available at* http://ssrn.com/abstract=547922 (finding that CEOs of firms restating earnings had a higher number of "in-the-money stock" options then managers of nonrestating firms); and Shane A. Johnson et al., *Executive Compensation and Corporate Fraud* (Apr. 16, 2003) (unpublished manuscript), *available at* http://ssrn.com/abstract=395960 (finding that executives of firms charged with accounting fraud had higher equity-based compensation than executives at matched firms). There may well be unintended negative consequences of this initiative. During the debates over SOX, for example, some members of Congress contended that the federal legislation limiting the tax deduction for managerial compensation to one million dollars unless performance based caused firms to increase managers' stock and option compensation, the increased use of which was now being identified as the reason for the accounting misconduct by the managers of Enron and other scandal-plagued firms. *E.g.*, 148 Cong. Rec. S6628 (daily ed. July 11, 2002) (statement of Sen. Gramm). This scenario further indicates the extreme difficulty of regulating compensation effectively: Firms will adapt their contracts, while the adaptations come at a cost (because the previously unregulated contracts optimized the compensation mix). *See infra* note 47 and accompanying text. The SOX forfeiture provision, for example, appears to have resulted in an increase in fixed-salary compensation. *See* Daniel A. Cohen et al., *The Sarbanes Oxley Act of 2002: Implications for Compensation Structure and Risk-Taking Incentives of CEOs* (July 2004) (unpublished manuscript), *available at* http://ssrn.com/abstract=568483. It is therefore altogether possible that, as with the governance mandates discussed in this Article, the forfeiture provision will not function as Congress anticipated.

[13] SOX § 401(j), 2002 U.S.C.C.A.N. (116 Stat.) at 786 (to be codified at 15 U.S.C. § 78m(j)).

to oversee auditors,[14] the substantive corporate governance provisions overstep the traditional division between federal and state jurisdiction, although they did not have to do so. They could have been formulated as disclosure mandates.[15] Had that been done, those provisions would have fallen within the conventional regulatory apparatus. Instead, they were imposed as substantive mandates, a different and more costly regulatory approach. Moreover, none of the fifty states nor the District of Columbia, whose corporate laws governed the matters covered by the new SOX provisions, mandated the practices that Congress did in SOX. It is instructive that the SOX initiatives are not to be found in any state corporation codes. The message of the empirical finance and accounting literature is that this absence is not fortuitous, because the literature suggests that the mandates will not provide much in the way of benefit to investors.

The fact that the literature indicates that the corporate governance provisions in SOX are ill-conceived raises the puzzling question of why Congress would enact legislation that in all likelihood will not fulfill its objectives. Simply put, the corporate governance provisions were not a focus of careful deliberation by Congress. SOX was emergency legislation, enacted under conditions of limited legislative debate, during a media frenzy involving several high-profile corporate fraud and insolvency cases.[16] These occurred in conjunction with an economic downturn, what appeared to be a free-falling stock market, and a looming election campaign in which corporate scandals would be an issue. The healthy ventilation of issues that occurs in the usual give-and-take negotiations over competing policy positions, which works to improve the quality of decisionmaking, did not occur in the case of SOX. That is because the collapse of Enron and its auditor, Arthur Andersen, politically weakened key groups affected by the legislation, the business community and the accounting profession. Democratic legislators who crafted the legislation relied for policy guidance on the expertise of trusted policy entrepreneurs, most of whom were closely aligned with their political party. Insofar as those individuals were aware of a literature at odds with their policy recommendations, they did not attempt to square their views with it. Nor did legislators of either party follow up on the handful of comments that hinted at the existence of studies inconsistent with those recommendations. Republican legislators, who tended

---

[14] *Id.* § 101, 2002 U.S.C.C.A.N. (116 Stat.) at 750-53 (to be codified at 15 U.S.C. § 7211).

[15] The loan prohibition, for example, was adopted without discussion or debate on the Senate floor in an amendment offered by Senators Charles Schumer and Dianne Feinstein. In both the Senate and House bills, there was a loan provision in the traditional form of a disclosure requirement. Corporate and Auditing Accountability, Responsibility, and Transparency Act of 2002, H.R.3763, 107th Cong. § 6(a)(2) (2002); 148 CONG. REC. S6689-90 (daily ed. July 12, 2002).

[16] The media coverage appears to have had an impact on Congressional deliberations. The debates are replete with members of Congress referring to newspaper editorials and articles criticizing Congressional action or inaction, presumably as a means of rationalizing their positions. *See, e.g.*, 148 CONG. REC. S6692 (daily ed. July 12, 2002) (statement of Sen. Craig) (referring to a *Wall Street Journal* editorial); *id.* at H1547-48 (daily ed. April 24, 2002) (statement of Rep. Jones of Ohio) (referring to a *Washington Post* editorial). Senator Gramm, a reluctant supporter of the legislation, referred to its high profile and noted that it was impossible "[i]n the environment" in which Congress was operating to correct what he considered serious flaws in the legislation. *Id.* at S7353 (daily ed. July 25, 2002) (statement of Sen. Gramm).

to be more sympathetic to the regulatory concerns of accountants and the business community, dropped their bill for the Democrats', determining that it would be politically perilous to be perceived as obstructing the legislative process and portrayed as being on the wrong side of the issue.

The central policy recommendation of this Article is that the corporate governance provisions of SOX should be stripped of their mandatory force and rendered optional for registrants. The findings of the empirical literature are consistent with the view that the more efficacious corporate and securities law regimes are the product of competitive legal systems, which permit legal innovations to percolate from the bottom up by trial and error, rather than being imposed from the top down by regulators or corporate governance entrepreneurs, who are far removed from the day-to-day operations of firms.[17] In that regard it is important to point out that the bulk of the provisions of competitive corporate codes are enabling, permitting firms to tailor their internal organization to their specific needs. The best path to ameliorating the misguided Congressional promulgation of substantive governance mandates through SOX is to conform them to the states' enabling approach to corporate law. A plausible mechanism to reduce the probability of future policy blunders on the scale of SOX is to routinize a requirement of periodic review for any legislation enacted in emergencies or similar crisis-like circumstances.

I. EVALUATING THE SUBSTANTIVE CORPORATE GOVERNANCE MANDATES IN SOX

A considerable body of corporate finance and accounting research bears on the efficacy of the substantive corporate governance mandates of SOX. This Part briefly reviews the relevant empirical literature, which indicates that the data do not support the view that the SOX initiatives will improve corporate governance or performance.[18]

A. Independent Audit Committees

Section 301 of SOX requires all listed companies to have audit committees composed entirely of independent directors, as defined by Congress.[19] The rationale for

---

[17] *See* ROBERTA ROMANO, THE ADVANTAGE OF COMPETITIVE FEDERALISM FOR SECURITIES REGULATION (2002).

[18] A detailed analysis of the studies summarized in this Part can be found in Roberta ROMANO, THE SARBANES-OXLEY ACT AND THE MAKING OF QUACK CORPORATE GOVERNANCE 12-102 (Yale Int'l Ctr. for Fin., Working Paper No. 04-37, 2004), *available at* http://ssrn.com/abstract=596101.

[19] SOX § 301, 2002 U.S.C.C.A.N. (116 Stat.) at 775-77 (to be codified at 15 U.S.C. § 78j-1(m)). To qualify as independent, the director may not "accept any consulting, advisory or other compensatory fee from the issuer" nor be an "affiliated person of the issuer or any subsidiary." *Id.* 2002 U.S.C.C.A.N. (116 Stat.) at 776. State law had no such requirement, although it encouraged the use of independent directors, while as of 1999 the stock exchanges required listing firms to have completely independent audit committees. *See* Audit Committee Disclosure, Exchange Act Release No. 34-42,266, 64 Fed. Reg. 73,389 (Dec. 30, 1999) (codified in scattered sections of 17 C.F.R. pts. 210, 228-29, 240 (2004)). For

the rule is that such directors can be expected to be effective monitors of management and thereby reduce the possibility of audit failure, because their financial dependence on the firm is limited to directors' fees (misstating earnings will not, for example, increase their income as could be the case for insiders with bonus compensation related to earnings). Congress also mandated disclosure of whether any of those directors are "financial expert[s]," along with an explanation—for firms with no expert on the audit committee—of why no committee members are experts.[20]

A large literature has developed on whether independent boards of directors improve corporate performance. Across a variety of analytical approaches, the learning of that literature is that independent boards do not improve performance and that boards with too many outsiders may, in fact, have a negative impact on performance.[21] There are fewer studies of the relation between audit committee composition and firm performance (four in total).[22] None of these studies has found any relation between audit committee independence and performance, using a variety of performance measures including both accounting and market measures as well as measures of investment strategies and productivity of long-term assets.

While not as extensive as the literature on board composition and performance, many more studies have examined the impact of the independence of audit committees on the probability of financial statement misconduct than on performance. Table 4 (in the Appendix) compiles the findings of studies on audit committee independence.[23] The

a review of the relation between the SOX provisions and preexisting law, see ROMANO, *supra* note 19, at 14-16. In implementing the SOX audit committee independence provisions, which require the delisting of any firm that does not comply with them, the SEC eliminated exemptions contained in the pre-SOX listing standards. *See* Standards Relating to Listed Company Audit Committees, Securities Act Release No. 33-8220, Exchange Act Release No. 34-47,654, 68 Fed. Reg. 18,788 (Apr. 16, 2003) (codified in scattered sections of 17 C.F.R. pts. 228-29, 240, 249, 274 (2004)).

[20] SOX § 407, 2002 U.S.C.C.A.N. (116 Stat.) at 790 (to be codified at 15 U.S.C. § 7265). SOX's substantive corporate governance mandates in this context are expressed as directions to the SEC to adopt rules rendering the governance provisions mandatory.

[21] For literature reviews, see Sanjai Bhagat & Bernard Black, *The Uncertain Relationship Between Board Composition and Firm Performance*, 54 BUS. LAW. 921 (1999); and Roberta Romano, *Corporate Law and Corporate Governance*, 5 INDUS. & CORP. CHANGE 277 (1996).

[22] Julie Cotter & Mark Silvester, *Board and Monitoring Committee Independence*, ABACUS, June 2003, at 211, 228-29; April Klein, *Firm Performance and Board Committee Structure*, 41 J.L. & ECON. 275, 287-301 (1998); Nikos Vafeas & Elena Theodorou, *The Relationship Between Board Structure and Firm Performance in the UK*, 30 BRIT. ACCT. REV. 383, 398 (1998); Charlie Weir et al., *Internal and External Governance Mechanisms: Their Impact on the Performance of Large UK Public Companies*, 29 J. BUS. FIN. & ACCT. 579, 606 (2002).

[23] The studies are KIRSTEN L. ANDERSON ET AL., BOARDS OF DIRECTORS, AUDIT COMMITTEES, AND THE INFORMATION CONTENT OF EARNINGS (Univ. of Del. John L. Weinberg Ctr. for Corporate Governance, Working Paper No. 2003-04, 2003), *available at* http://ssrn.com/abstract=444241; Lawrence J. Abbott et al., *The Effects of Audit Committee Activity and Independence on Corporate Fraud*, 26 MANAGERIAL FIN. 55 (2000); Mark S. Beasley, *An Empirical Analysis of the Relation Between the Board of Director Composition and Financial Statement Fraud*, 71 ACCT. REV. 443 (1996); Mark S. Beasley et al., *Fraudulent Financial Reporting: Consideration of Industry Traits and Corporate Governance Mechanisms*, 14 ACCT. HORIZONS 441 (2000); Jean Bédard et al., *The Effect of Audit Committee Expertise, Independence, and Activity on Aggressive*

definition of independence used by researchers is the same as that adopted by Congress in SOX, which excludes individuals employed by or otherwise affiliated with the issuer or a subsidiary or those receiving consulting or other compensatory fees from the issuer (other than for director service).[24] The measures of financial statement misstatements are abnormal accruals,[25] financial statement restatements and fraud, SEC actions, third-party or contract fraud allegations, and stock market responses to unexpected earnings ("earnings informativeness"). The question raised by this research, from the perspective of the SOX mandate on audit committee composition, is whether Congress has accurately matched a problem with a solution.

Of the sixteen studies collected in Table 4, ten (including the four studies of explicit performance measures already noted) do not find that complete independence of the audit committee improves performance—a finding equally consistent whether performance is measured conventionally or by the existence of accounting improprieties—and one study reports inconsistent results (under one model formulation, independence improves performance, but not under all other models tested).[26] The data are mixed

---

Earnings Management, AUDITING: J. PRAC. & THEORY, Sept. 2004, at 13; Cotter & Silvester, *supra* note 23; April Klein, *Audit Committee, Board of Director Characteristics, and Earnings Management*, 33 J. ACCT. & ECON. 375 (2002); Klein, *supra* note 23; Dorothy A. McMullen & K.Raghunandan, *Enhancing Audit Committee Effectiveness*, J. ACCT., Aug. 1996, at 79; Hatice Uzun et al., *Board Composition and Corporate Fraud,* FIN. ANALYSTS J., May/June 2004, at 33; Vafeas & Theodorou, *supra* note 23; Weir et al., *supra* note 23; Biao Xie et al., *Earnings Management and Corporate Governance: The Role of the Board and the Audit Committee*, 9 J. CORP. FIN. 295 (2003); Lawrence J. Abbott et al., *Audit Committee Characteristics and Financial Misstatement: A Study of the Efficacy of Certain Blue Ribbon Committee Recommendations* (Mar. 2002) (unpublished manuscript), *available at* http://ssrn.com/abstract=319125; Anup Agrawal & Sahiba Chadha, *Corporate Governance and Accounting Scandals* (Sept. 2004) (unpublished manuscript), *available at* http://ssrn.com/abstract=595138; and Andrew J. Felo et al., *Audit Committee Characteristics and the Perceived Quality of Financial Reporting: An Empirical Analysis* (Apr. 2003) (unpublished manuscript), available at http://ssrn.com/abstract=401240.

[24] SOX § 301, 2002 U.S.C.C.A.N. (116 Stat.) at 775-77 (to be codified at 15 U.S.C. § 78j-1(m)(3)). To the extent that the statutory language does not cover relatives of officers, the studies' definition is broader because they exclude relatives, following the SEC's definition of independence in its proxy disclosure rules. *See* Schedule 14A, Item 7, 17 C.F.R. § 240.14a-101 (2004) (referencing items 401 and 404 of Regulation S-K, *id.* §§ 229.401, . 404). All but five of the studies use this definition. For details on the exceptions, *see* ROMANO, *supra* note 19, at 18 n.36.

[25] Accruals are an accounting convention to recognize changes in value (revenues and expenses) independent of when cash flows into and out of the firm. Accounting researchers have developed econometric models to determine firms' expected accruals. The difference between the model estimates and actual accruals, called abnormal accruals, is considered a proxy for earnings management, a practice by which firms manipulate their reported accounting figures to smooth out earnings across reporting years. Although earnings management is often consistent with generally accepted accounting principles, the SEC considers it inappropriate. *See, e.g.*, Arthur Levitt, Remarks at the New York University Center for Law and Business (Sept. 28, 1998), *available at* http://www.sec.gov/news/speech/speecharchive/1998/spch220.txt (remarks as then-SEC chairman).

[26] In addition, three of the five studies reporting that completely independent committees improve performance are unreliable and are not a source for valid inferences because of methodological flaws. *See* ROMANO, *supra* note 19, at 32-34 (discussing the methodological flaws in the 2000 Abbott et al., Beasley et al., and McMullen and Raghunandan studies).

on whether even a committee with a majority of independent directors improves performance,[27] but the issue for SOX is whether complete independence improves on the effect of a majority-independent committee, not the efficacy of a majority of independent directors.

A few studies find that having a director with financial expertise improves performance and, more specifically, that complete independence is less significant than expertise with respect to the relation between audit committee composition and accounting statement quality.[28] These results are notable in that SOX does not mandate the presence of a financial expert on the audit committee (it has only a disclosure requirement regarding financial expertise on the committee), while it does mandate completely independent audit committees.

It should be noted that these studies, as with all regression analyses, cannot demonstrate causality. For example, the finding of statistical significance for director expertise in relation to financial statement restatements can be considered evidence that directors with expertise are effective monitors of accounting controls and audit quality—the rationale for reforming corporate governance in this regard. But it is also possible that firms that are better managed, and hence less likely to restate their financial statements, choose to have independent directors with expertise. That is, a finding of significance may be a function of self-selection and not of the efficacy of the corporate governance mechanism. Accordingly, if selection effects explain the study results, then that would strengthen the case against the mandate.[29]

The compelling thrust of the literature on the composition of audit committees, in short, does not support the proposition that requiring audit committees to consist solely of independent directors will reduce the probability of financial statement wrongdoing or otherwise improve corporate performance. Not only is that the case for the overwhelming majority of studies, but also, and more importantly, that is so for the studies using the more sophisticated techniques. It should further be noted that, using conventional confidence standards with properly specified statistical tests, false positives—statistically significant results—can be expected five percent of the time, even though there is no significant relation between variables. Indeed, a commonly

---

[27] *Compare* Klein, *supra* note 24 (finding that firms whose audit committees have at least a majority of independent directors have significantly smaller abnormal accruals, although finding no significant relation between abnormal accruals and completely independent committees), *with* Xie et al., *supra* note 24 (finding no relation between proportion of independent directors and accruals), and Agrawal & Chadha, *supra* note 24 (finding no relation between proportion of independent directors and earnings restatements).

[28] *E.g.*, Agrawal & Chadha, *supra* note 24; Felo et al., *supra* note 24.

[29] Some (but not all) studies seek to test whether the alternative self-selection interpretation is correct. Agrawal and Chadha, for example, who find that expertise but not independence improves accounting performance, test for causality by examining whether operating performance varies across the firms restating their financials and the nonrestaters in their study. Agrawal & Chadha, *supra* note 24. The reasoning of the test is that operating performance is a proxy for management quality. Because Agrawal and Chadha find that operating performance is not significantly related to the presence of a director with financial expertise, they conclude that the causality in their data runs from expert director absence to restatement and not the reverse.

expressed concern regarding literature reviews that is not applicable to these data is that significant results are overstated because papers finding insignificant relations between the variables of interest typically do not get published in academic journals (the "'file drawer' problem"[30]). In the audit committee literature, by contrast, the finding of insignificance was considered important enough by journal editors to merit publication, and it is easy enough to grasp that significant results in a small number of papers could well be false positives, the product of random error.

B. Provision of Nonaudit Services

Section 201 of SOX prohibits accounting firms from providing specified nonaudit services to firms that they audit.[31] The banned services include financial information system design and implementation, appraisal or valuation services, internal auditing services, investment banking services, legal and expert services unrelated to the audit, brokerage services, and actuarial services. Although this provision is included in SOX's cluster of provisions directed at the accounting profession, it is, in fact, a substantive corporate governance mandate. Congress is substituting its judgment regarding what services a company can purchase from its auditor for that of corporate boards or shareholders. The rationale for the ban was that the receipt of high fees for nonaudit services compromises auditor independence by providing auditors with a financial incentive to permit managers to engage in questionable transactions or accounting practices in the audit.

SOX's nonaudit services prohibition had a history: In 2000, the SEC required registrants to disclose the amounts paid to auditors for audit- and nonaudit-related services, and some nonaudit services were identified as compromising the auditor's independence and therefore prohibited (because the securities laws require issuers' financials to be certified by independent auditors).[32] This outcome was the best that then-SEC Chairman Arthur Levitt could obtain after a multiyear effort in which he failed to generate sufficient political support for a total ban on auditors' provision of nonaudit services. A further factor in Levitt's settling for a more limited ban than he originally sought was that the Clinton Administration was about to turn over, and, as a consequence, his term as chairman

---

[30] T.D. Stanley, *Wheat from Chaff: Meta-Analysis as Quantitative Literature Review*, J. ECON. PERSP., Summer 2001, at 131, 146.

[31] SOX, Pub. L. No. 107-204, § 201, 2002 U.S.C.C.A.N. (116 Stat.) 745, 771-72 (to be codified as section 10A(g) of the Securities Exchange Act, 15 U.S.C. § 78j-1(g)).

[32] Revision of the Commission's Auditor Independence Requirements, 65 Fed. Reg. 76,008, 76,011, 76,055-56, 76,084-85, 76,087 (Dec. 5, 2000) (codified at 17 C.F.R. §§ 210.1-02, 240.14a-101 (2004)). Two services that the SEC had proposed to ban but had been unable to include in the final rule because of significant opposition (financial information system design and implementation, internal audit outsourcing) were included in the SOX prohibition. Of the nine services prohibited by the rule, seven were already restricted under SEC guidelines and under professional rules of conduct promulgated by the American Institute of Certified Public Accountants (AICPA). As noted in ROMANO, *supra* note 19, at 41, state law does not restrict firms' purchase of services from their auditors, but directors could be subject to liability ex post for any such decision that proved wrongful under fiduciary standards.

would soon end (the compromise was reached and the rule issued in November 2000).[33] The compromise was not due to Levitt's being a political novice or being inept: He skillfully used the media in the debate over the auditor independence rule to undermine the private-sector entities he had established to study and regulate auditor independence (the Independence Standards Board and the Panel on Audit Effectiveness) when it became evident that they would not recommend restricting nonauditing services.[34]

Because the provision of nonaudit services by auditors had been subject to persistent efforts at elimination by the SEC prior to SOX's prohibition, numerous studies have sought to gauge whether the provision of such services by the external auditor compromises audit quality (the rationale advanced for banning the practice). The variables most frequently used to measure the importance of nonaudit services to the auditing firm are the fee ratio (the ratio of nonaudit to total fees or to audit fees paid to the external auditor) and total fees (the sum of nonaudit and audit fees paid to the external auditor); others include fee measures that adjust the amounts by client to construct a proxy for the client's importance to the auditor and percentile ranks, by auditor, of a firm's nonaudit and audit fees.[35] Higher values of the various fee variables are considered to represent a nonindependent auditor (that is, the potential for auditor compromise is expected to depend directly on the fees received for nonaudit services). Several variables are used to measure audit quality, including abnormal accruals, measures of earnings

---

[33] *See* Sandra Sugawara, *Accounting Firms, SEC Agree on Audit Rule*, WASH. POST, Nov. 15, 2000, at E1 (reporting a compromise reached over the "controversial" rule that Levitt "ha[d] been pushing to get enacted before the end of the Clinton administration").

[34] *See* Zoe-Vonna Palmrose & Ralph S. Saul, *The Push for Auditor Independence*, REGULATION, Winter 2001, at 18, 22 (recounting, according to members of the Panel on Audit Effectiveness, how Levitt and the SEC staff used the press to generate public support for their position and to counter findings by the Panel and the Independence Standards Board that there was a lack of evidence of a problem regarding nonaudit services). The Panel on Audit Effectiveness (also referred to as the O'Malley Panel after its chairman, Shaun O'Malley) was created by the Public Oversight Board, a self-regulatory organization of the accounting profession, to review the audit process at the request of Levitt. He requested the Panel as part of his effort to prohibit nonaudit services, at the same time that he requested the stock exchanges to appoint a blue-ribbon committee to undertake a similar review. *See, e.g.*, 1 ACCOUNTING REFORM AND INVESTOR PROTECTION: HEARINGS BEFORE THE SENATE COMM. ON BANKING, HOUS., AND URBAN AFFAIRS, 107th Cong. 71 (2002) [hereinafter *Senate Hearings*] (prepared statement of David S. Ruder, SEC Chairman, 1987-1989).

[35] Because the SEC only recently began requiring disclosure of auditor fees, *see* Auditor Revision of the Commission's Auditor Independence Requirements, 65 Fed. Reg. at 76,008 (requiring disclosures in proxies filed after the rule's effective date of February 5, 2001), many of the studies are relatively recent, and the data are limited (the earliest available data are expenditures from fiscal year 2000). The SEC required information on auditing and nonauditing fees to be disclosed from 1978 to 1982, and some other countries have required such disclosure for many years. A few studies make use of those alternative data sources.

conservatism,[36] earnings surprises,[37] financial statement restatements, and issuance of qualified audit opinions.

The findings of the studies on nonaudit services are collected in Table 5 (in the Appendix).[38] The overwhelming majority of the studies (nineteen of twenty-five) suggest that SOX's prohibition of the purchase of nonaudit services from an auditor is an

---

[36] Conservatism refers to a longstanding accounting principle of accelerating expenses and deferring revenues (attained in practice by requiring a higher level of verification for revenue recognition), which results in lower profits than would otherwise be reported; hence reported earnings are "conservative." The principle has been operationalized in empirical research by measuring whether bad news is incorporated in financial reports (and hence in stock prices) more rapidly than good news.

[37] Earnings surprises refer to a firm's exactly meeting or narrowly beating analysts' forecasted earnings and are considered to be evidence of earnings management.

[38] The studies are RICK ANTLE ET AL., THE JOINT DETERMINATION OF AUDIT FEES, NON-AUDIT FEES, AND ABNORMAL ACCRUALS (Yale Sch. of Mgmt., Working Paper No. AC-15, 2002), available at http://ssrn.com/abstract=318943; PELHAM GORE ET AL., NON-AUDIT SERVICES, AUDITOR INDEPENDENCE AND EARNINGS MANAGEMENT (Lancaster Univ. Mgmt. Sch., Working Paper No. 2001/014, 2001), *available at* http://www.lums.co.uk/publications/viewpdf/000126; Hollis Ashbaugh et al., *Do Nonaudit Services Compromise Auditor Independence? Further Evidence*, 78 ACCT. REV. 611 (2003); Hyeesoo Chung & Sanjay Kallapur, *Client Importance, Nonaudit Services, and Abnormal Accruals*, 78 ACCT. REV. 931 (2003); Allen T. Craswell, *Does the Provision of Non-Audit Services Impair Auditor Independence?*, 3 INT'L J. AUDITING 29 (1999); Allen Craswell et al., *Auditor Independence and Fee Dependence*, 33 J. ACCT. & ECON. 253 (2002); Mark L. DeFond et al., *Do Non-Audit Service Fees Impair Auditor Independence? Evidence from Going Concern Audit Opinions*, 40 J. ACCT. RES. 1247 (2002); Michael J. Ferguson et al., *Nonaudit Services and Earnings Management: U.K. Evidence*, 21 CONTEMP. ACCT. RES. 813 (2004); Michael Firth, *Auditor-Provided Consultancy Services and Their Associations with Audit Fees and Audit Opinions*, 29 J. BUS. FIN. & ACCT. 661 (2002); Richard M. Frankel et al., *The Relation Between Auditors' Fees for Nonaudit Services and Earnings Management*, 77 ACCT. REV. (Supplement: Quality Earnings Conf.) 71 (2002); William R. Kinney Jr. et al., *Auditor Independence, Non-Audit Services, and Restatements: Was the U.S. Government Right?*, 42 J. ACCT. RES. 561 (2004); David F. Larcker & Scott A. Richardson, *Fees Paid to Audit Firms, Accrual Choices, and Corporate Governance*, 42 J. ACCT. RES. 625 (2004); Clive S. Lennox, *Non-Audit Fees, Disclosure and Audit Quality*, 8 EUR. ACCT. REV. 239 (1999); Lynn M. Pringle & Thomas A. Buchman, *An Examination of Independence in Fact When Auditors Perform Nonaudit Services for Audit Clients*, 6 ACCT. ENQUIRIES 91 (1996); J. Kenneth Reynolds & Jere R. Francis, *Does Size Matter? The Influence of Large Clients on Office-Level Auditor Reporting Decisions*, 30 J. ACCT. & ECON. 375 (2001); Divesh S. Sharma & Jagdish Sidhu, *Professionalism vs Commercialism: The Association Between Non-Audit Services (NAS) and Audit Independence*, 28 J. BUS. FIN. & ACCT. 595 (2001); Agrawal & Chadha, *supra* note 24; Mukesh Bajaj et al., Auditor Compensation and Audit Failure: An Empirical Analysis (Feb. 27, 2003) (unpublished manuscript), *available at* http://ssrn.com/abstract=387902; Carol Callaway Dee et al., *Earnings Quality and Auditor Independence: An Examination Using Non-Audit Fee Data* (Jan. 28, 2002) (unpublished manuscript), *available at* http://ssrn.com/abstract=304185; Jere R. Francis & Bin Ke, *Do Fees Paid to Auditors Increase a Company's Likelihood of Meeting Analysts' Earnings Forecasts?* (May 21, 2003) (unpublished manuscript, on file with author); Nicole Thorne Jenkins, *Auditor Independence, Audit Committee Effectiveness, and Earnings Management* (Jan. 31, 2003) (unpublished manuscript, on file with author); Gopal V. Krishnan, *Are Audit and Nonaudit Services Associated with the Delayed Recognition of Bad News?* (Mar. 27, 2004) (unpublished manuscript), *available at* http://ssrn.com/abstract=457960; Vivian Li et al., *Non-Audit Services and Auditor Independence: New Zealand Evidence* (Sept. 2003) (unpublished manuscript), *available at* http://ssrn.com/abstract=452260; K. Raghunandan et al., *Are Non-Audit Fees Associated with Restated Financial Statements? Initial Empirical Evidence* (Apr. 11, 2003) (unpublished manuscript), *available at* http://ssrn.com/abstract=394844; and

exercise in legislating away a nonproblem. The majority (fifteen) find no connection between the provision of nonaudit services and audit quality. One finds no connection when the auditors are the Big Five (including Arthur Andersen) accounting firms (the firms of concern to Congress in enacting SOX, because they audit nearly all large public companies). And three find that nonaudit services improve audit quality (and two of the fifteen that find no relation also find that audit quality improves in at least one model specification), which directly contradicts the rationale for the SOX prohibition.[39]

Of the remaining six studies, five find that audit quality is compromised, while one finds that audit quality is compromised in only one of several model specifications. However, the results of the initial and leading study by Frankel et al., which found that audit quality (measured by abnormal accruals) is compromised by the purchase of nonaudit services, are not robust.[40] Numerous studies, summarized in Table 5, have redone the analysis of Frankel et al., refining the model in a variety of ways. These include, among others, controlling for factors known to affect the audit performance measure used in the original study and using auditor independence measures that take account of the importance of the client to the auditor. When the model is refined by any of those methods, the original results do not hold up. As a consequence, valid policy inferences cannot be drawn from the Frankel et al. study. This could also be true for the other studies finding a significant inverse relation between nonaudit fees and audit quality. Less prominent than the Frankel et al. study but using the same methodology, those studies have not been the objects of further research.[41]

The conclusion that audit quality—and hence auditor independence—is not jeopardized by the provision of nonaudit services is compelling not only because it is the finding of the vast majority of studies but also because it is the result of the studies using the most sophisticated techniques, as well as those whose findings are most robust to alternative model specifications. The absence of a systematic inverse relation between nonaudit fees and audit quality (across all measures of audit quality) in the scholarly literature is consistent with the Panel on Audit Effectiveness's failure to identify a single instance of a compromised audit by auditors providing nonaudit services in its field study of auditor independence.[42] That finding no doubt contributed to the Panel's

---

Caitlin Ruddock et al., *Non-Audit Services and Earnings Conservatism: Is Auditor Independence Impaired?* (Apr. 2004) (unpublished manuscript), *available at* http://ssrn.com/abstract=303343.

[39] A theoretical example that could explain why audit quality might improve because of a nonaudit service is a client who hires the auditor to install an inventory control system; if the system is effective, those nonaudit fees would lead to lower abnormal accruals. *See* ANTLE ET AL., *supra* note 39, at 9.

[40] Frankel et al., *supra* note 39.

[41] For a caveat regarding the appropriate inference to draw from one of the two studies finding that nonaudit fees compromise audit quality using an alternative measure of audit quality (issuance of a qualified opinion), acknowledged by the author, see ROMANO, *supra* note 19, at 78. In this regard, it should also be noted that the most sophisticated study of qualified opinions (DeFond et al., *supra* note 39) did not find an association.

[42] The Panel conducted in-depth reviews of the quality of 126 audits of public firms conducted by 28 offices of the 8 largest audit firms; in 37 of these engagements (29%) the auditor also provided a nonaudit service other than tax work. PANEL ON AUDIT EFFECTIVENESS, PUB. OVERSIGHT BD., REPORT AND RECOM-

decision, as well as to that of the Independence Standards Board, not to recommend banning the provision of nonaudit services and to opt instead for bolstering the audit committee function by proposing that audit committees be composed of independent and financially literate directors.

C. Executive Loans

Section 402(a) of SOX prohibits corporations from arranging or extending credit to executive officers or directors (unless the corporation is a financial institution offering credit in the ordinary course of business and the terms of the credit are the same as those offered to the public).[43] Loans became a focus of Congressional attention in the wake of disclosures that executives at Enron, WorldCom, Tyco International, and Adelphia Communications had obtained extremely large loans (in some cases in the hundreds of millions of dollars), personally benefiting from firms whose shareholders and employees suffered devastating financial losses. The ban was introduced at the end of the legislative process in the Senate as a floor amendment substitute for a provision that was drafted and reported out of the Senate committee as a disclosure measure. The blanket prohibition has engendered concern among practitioners, because it appears to prohibit standard compensation practices thought to be uncontroversial and beneficial, such as the purchase of split-dollar life insurance policies and the arrangement with brokers or other financial institutions for employees' cashless exercise of stock options under incentive compensation plans.[44]

In contrast to other SOX corporate governance provisions, this initiative had not been a component of recent policy discussions; the permissibility of such transactions had been settled state law for decades without generating scholarly controversy.[45] As is true of all the SOX mandates, this provision is in conflict with the state law approach.

MENDATIONS ¶¶ 1.14, 5.17 (2000). The reviewers identified no case of a negative impact on an audit's quality and concluded that in one-quarter of the cases the nonauditing services had a positive impact on the effectiveness of the audit. *Id.* ¶ 5.18. While the Panel's report therefore found no evidence that nonaudit services impaired independence in fact, it noted that "many people" were concerned that such services could impair independence or give the appearance of the potential for impaired independence. *Id.* ¶ 5.20. The studies summarized in Table 5 examine whether independence is impaired in fact. For a note on the smaller number of studies that have been directed at the issue of perception, see ROMANO, *supra* note 19, at 45 n.90.

[43] SOX, Pub. L. No. 107-204, § 402(a), 2002 U.S.C.C.A.N. (116 Stat.) 745, 787 (to be codified at 15 U.S.C. § 78m(k)).

[44] Sean A. Power, *Sarbanes-Oxley Ends Corporate Lending to Insiders: Some Interpretive Issues for Executive Compensation Surrounding the Section 402 Loan Prohibition*, 71 UMKC L. REV. 911, 924-35 (2003). In a split-dollar life insurance policy, the company pays the premiums and is reimbursed out of the policy's payout to the officer upon its expiration at the officer's retirement or death.

[45] Even critics of the twentieth-century trend toward enabling provisions on executive loans did not advocate a return to an absolute prohibition of such transactions but rather argued for disclosure and limits on loans in specific contexts. *E.g.*, Jayne W. Barnard, *Corporate Loans to Directors and Officers: Every Business Now a Bank?*, 1988 WIS. L. REV. 237, 274-76. For a discussion of the state law on executive loans, see ROMANO, *supra* note 19, at 87-88.

In this regard, a practical reason for permitting executive loans should be noted: It is extremely difficult to regulate managerial compensation, because if one form of compensation is restricted, managers can renegotiate their contracts to make up for the loss, undoing the legislative intent.[46] As a result, regulation of compensation, such as the federal loan ban, can be expected to alter the form that compensation takes but is not likely to result in a reduction in total pay, and it comes at a cost: Investors have to increase another component of the manager's pay package to make up the loss in utility from the removal of the now-restricted compensation option. Moreover, the dollar value of the component that is increasing will be higher than that of the one forgone. That is because, had the manager valued an increase in the unrestricted component more highly than the lost compensation (the loan), the latter would not have been part of the original compensation package in the first place.

Given that the extension of credit to corporate officers under state corporate law has not been a contentious topic for decades, it is not surprising that there is an absence of empirical research on the practice. Motivated by the spotlight thrown on executive loans in the scandals leading to SOX and by its ban on the practice, a recent study sought to measure the efficacy of executive loans by analyzing whether they accomplish the purpose of increasing managerial stock ownership, thereby aligning managerial incentives with shareholder interests.[47] Table 6 (in the Appendix) summarizes the study's results. The bulk of the sample loans were made to assist in stock purchases and stock option exercises, with a much smaller set consisting of relocation loans. The data are consistent with the fact that most loans' purpose is one of incentive alignment: There is an increase in executives' equity ownership after the extension of credit to purchase stock or to exercise stock options, although the increase is small relative to loan value.[48]

---

[46] *See, e.g.*, Cohen et al., *supra* note 13, at 19 (finding that after SOX, firms decreased CEOs' incentive compensation and increased their nonforfeitable fixed salaries, thereby providing insurance to managers for increased risk); Tod Perry & Marc Zenner, *Pay for Performance? Government Regulation and the Structure of Compensation Contracts* 19-20 (June 2000) (unpublished manuscript), *available at* http://ssrn.com/abstract=60956 (finding that firms changed the mix of managerial compensation to reduce salaries and increase incentive pay to adapt to Congress's limitation on the tax deductibility of non-performance-based compensation over one million dollars).

[47] Kuldeep Shastri & Kathleen M. Kahle, *Executive Loans*, 39 J. FIN. & QUANTITATIVE ANALYSIS 791 (2004).

[48] On average, a loan enabling a manager to buy one hundred shares of stock increases the manager's ownership by eight shares. Shastri and Kahle find that a higher number of options are exercised in their sample than in a study of the effect of stock option plans on managerial stock ownership, Eli Ofek & David Yermack, *Taking Stock: Equity-Based Compensation and the Evolution of Managerial Ownership*, 55 J. FIN. 1367 (2000). They attribute the difference to the presence of the loans: In their view, the loans permit the managers to hold onto more shares after exercise because they do not need to sell shares to pay taxes and the exercise price. Shastri & Kahle, *supra* note 48, at 808. That would again suggest that the loans are functioning as desired, increasing management stock ownership. But it should be noted that Shastri and Kahle do not evaluate the cost effectiveness of the loan program (that is, whether there is a cheaper mechanism to increase stock ownership than through a stock option or purchase loan program).

Because executive loans in many cases appear to serve their purpose of increasing managerial stock ownership, thereby aligning managers' and shareholders' interests, the blanket prohibition of executive loans in SOX is self-evidently a public policy error. The provision in the original Senate bill, which was consistent with the conventional federal regulatory approach, required disclosure of executive loans but did not prohibit them. Such an approach would have been far less problematic than the final legislative product, from the perspective of shareholder welfare. It would have had the effect of facilitating the termination of loans most unlikely to benefit shareholders, by highlighting their presence to investors who could then put those loans' elimination on a corporate governance agenda (in the many states where they would otherwise not be involved because shareholder approval of loans is not required). Instead, the legislation is a blunderbuss approach that prohibits all loans, whether or not they are useful in facilitating the shareholders' objective of providing a sought-after incentive effect.

D. Executive Certification of Financial Statements

Section 302 of SOX requires the CEO and CFO to certify that the company's periodic reports do not contain material misstatements or omissions and "fairly present" the firm's financial condition and the results of operations.[49] The certification requirement contains substantive corporate governance mandates. It imposes on the signing officers the responsibility for establishing and maintaining internal controls and for evaluating the effectiveness of those controls, along with the duty to disclose to the audit committee any deficiencies in the internal control design or any fraud involving any officer or employee with a significant role in the company's internal controls. The officers' signature certifies both the undertaking of those tasks and the veracity of the financial information. Section 404 contains a related filing requirement, a management report attested to by the external auditor assessing the internal controls.[50] A third provision, section 906(a), is a new criminal statute that enumerates penalties for knowingly violating a certification requirement similar to that of section 302.[51]

The certification provision, in contrast to the other corporate governance provisions that have been discussed, is a less explicit infringement on state corporate law: Although it is a corporate governance mandate—it imposes duties on corporate officers—the required certification accompanies the filing of federally mandated documents that are

---

[49] SOX, Pub. L. No. 107-204, § 302, 2002 U.S.C.C.A.N. (116 Stat.) 745, 777-78 (to be codified at 15 U.S.C. § 7241). Paralleling the audit committee mandate, this mandate directs the SEC to adopt rules to implement it.

[50] *Id.* § 404, 2002 U.S.C.C.A.N. (116 Stat.) at 789 (to be codified at 15 U.S.C. § 7262).

[51] *Id.* § 906(a), 2002 U.S.C.C.A.N. (116 Stat.) at 806 (to be codified at 15 U.S.C. § 1350). The two sections—section 906(a) and section 302—differ in the certification language and covered reports. *See, e.g.*, Lisa M. Fairfax, *Form over Substance?: Officer Certification and the Promise of Enhanced Personal Accountability Under the Sarbanes-Oxley Act*, 55 RUTGERS L. REV. 1, 18-20 (2002).

not part of the state corporate law regime.[52] Nor is this an entirely new type of federal requirement, although its specific form is of recent vintage. Prior to the enactment of SOX, the SEC imposed a certification requirement on the largest public firms.[53] This requirement was one of the proposals advanced by President Bush in his response to the Enron scandal, a ten-point plan to make corporate executives more accountable to investors that had been announced in March 2002.[54] But even before the promulgation of the SEC rule, CEOs and CFOs had always been required to sign the annual report and were liable for knowingly filing fraudulent reports as well as for inadequate internal controls.[55]

As indicated in Table 7 (in the Appendix), two studies have sought to measure the efficacy of the SEC's rule requiring executive certification of the financials of the largest firms, as a means of evaluating SOX's expansion of the requirement to all firms, by examining stock price reactions to timely and untimely certifications.[56] The research

---

[52] Given the mandatory federal reporting and disclosure requirements, there was no room (or need) for state law to develop reporting requirements for publicly traded corporations, although a few states required corporations to provide shareholders with annual reports and financial statements. *E.g.*, CAL. CORP. CODE § 1501 (West 1990 & Supp. 2004). Before the enactment of the federal securities regime in the 1930s, the New York Stock Exchange (NYSE) mandated financial disclosures; the federal disclosure regime displaced those listing requirements. *See* Paul G. Mahoney, *The Exchange as Regulator*, 83 VA. L. REV. 1453, 1466 (1997). After SOX was enacted, California expanded its disclosure requirements to include, among others, SOX-related items such as nonaudit services and loans to directors. *See* Roy J. Schmidt et al., *Compliance with the New California Disclosures Act: Issues and Tips*, WALL ST. LAW., Nov. 2002, at 11. For a brief discussion of the implications for state corporate law of the SOX certification requirements, see ROMANO, *supra* note 19, at 94-95.

[53] Order Requiring the Filing of Sworn Statements Pursuant to Section 21(a)(1) of the Securities Exchange Act of 1934, File No. 4-460 (June 27, 2002), *available at* http://www.sec.gov/rules/other/4-460.htm.

[54] *See* Remarks at the Presentation of the Malcolm Baldridge National Quality Awards, 38 WEEKLY COMP. PRES. DOC. 370 (March 7, 2002) (outlining proposals to improve corporate responsibility); Press Release, White House, President's Ten-Point Plan (Mar. 7, 2002), *available at* http://www.whitehouse.gov/infocus/corporateresponsibility/index2.html.

[55] *See* Fairfax, *supra* note 52, at 20-42 (discussing prior law regarding signatures on financial statements). Section 102 of the Foreign Corrupt Practices Act requires public corporations to establish internal controls adequate to ensure that "transactions are recorded as necessary" to permit the preparation of financial statements in accordance with "generally accepted accounting principles." Foreign Corrupt Practices Act, Pub. L. No. 95-213, §102, 1977 U.S.C.C.A.N. (91 Stat.) 1494, 1494-95 (1977) (codified as amended at 15 U.S.C. § 78m(b) (2000)). Although the impetus for that legislation was to prohibit sensitive foreign payments, the language imposing obligations on firms is not limited to the accounting for bribe-related transactions.

[56] The studies are BEVERLY HIRTLE, FED. RESERVE BANK OF N.Y., STAFF REPORT NO. 170, STOCK MARKET REACTION TO FINANCIAL STATEMENT CERTIFICATION BY BANK HOLDING COMPANY CEOS (2003), *available at* http://ssrn.com/abstract=425002; and Utpal Bhattacharya et al., *Is CEO Certification of Earnings Numbers Value-Relevant?* (Nov. 2002) (unpublished manuscript), *available at* http://ssrn.com/abstract=332621. The methodology, which evaluates the impact of specific policies on the welfare of investors by examining changes in stock returns (commonly referred to as an "event study"), is widely used and well accepted in financial economics. For an overview of the technique, see, for example, Sanjai Bhagat & Roberta Romano, *Event Studies and the Law: Part I: Technique and Corporate Litigation*, 4 AM. L. & ECON. REV. 141 (2002).

question is whether the SEC requirement of certification provided new information to investors about firms' financial conditions—as the literature puts it, was the requirement "value relevant"?—and more specifically, did a failure to comply, or early compliance, provide information to investors?

The informational effect of the requirement is ambiguous because the results of the two studies are inconsistent. As Table 7 indicates, one study finds that the certification requirement had no impact, suggesting that investors did not obtain new information about firms from their failure to certify—that is, that the earnings certification required by the SEC was a "nonevent."[57] But the other study finds that for a subset of firms considered to be informationally opaque (bank holding companies), early certification provided new, and positive, information to the market.

Two points should be made that caution against generalization from the study finding no effect. First, the small number of firms that failed to certify in time limits the power of the test. Second, by the time the SEC issued the earnings certification order, the market had, in all likelihood, adjusted stock prices for an "Enron effect," reducing the value of firms with opaque financial statements and numerous off-balance-sheet transactions, and many firms had reacted by voluntarily increasing their disclosure to provide more transparent reports.[58] It is therefore possible that in the future, under different market circumstances (for example, in a time of less investor scrutiny of firms), a failure to certify earnings might provide new information about the firm. But a similar caution applies against generalizing from the study finding a price impact. It is an open question whether the positive reaction was a one-time effect or whether in the future certification will continue to provide new information to investors about financial firms.

The contrary findings of the two event studies of the certification requirement render it difficult to draw any definitive conclusion regarding the efficacy of the provision for improving the ability of investors to distinguish between high- and low-quality firms. There is a need for considerably more research in order to draw strong inferences.[59] But one policy approach that would reconcile the results would be to render the certification regime optional. That would permit firms for which there is a benefit to engage in special certifications rather than the conventional financial statement signatures (for example, opaque firms such as bank holding companies) to do so. Such an approach is supported by the considerable compliance costs associated with certification that have

[57] In other words, the market could predict which firms would not be able to certify their earnings. Many of the noncertifiers were well-known scandal firms, such as Enron and WorldCom, that were not expected to certify and firms in financial distress that had restated their earnings in the past year.

[58] The SEC order was issued in June 2002. Firms that had opaque balance sheets like Enron experienced stock price declines in the fall of 2001 upon the revelation of Enron's accounting problems. *See* ROMANO, *supra* note 18, at 58-59.

[59] In addition to the difficulty of drawing definitive policy implications from the studies regarding the informative efficacy of the certification requirement, it should be noted that the studies do not address whether certification will alter management's behavior to reduce the occurrence of accounting misconduct in the first place. Only studies with a longer window will afford such a test.

been reported or anticipated:[60] Firms would select into the regime when the burden of compliance was more likely to produce a positive payoff to their investors.

II. THE POLITICAL ECONOMY OF THE SOX CORPORATE GOVERNANCE MANDATES

The brief review of the empirical literature suggests that a case does not exist for the principal corporate governance mandates in SOX. The decisive balance of research indicates that those mandates will not benefit investors. The policy implication of the literature presents a puzzle: What were the political dynamics that produced legislation in which Congress enacted a set of mandates that in all likelihood will not achieve the professed goal of the legislation, an improvement in investor welfare?

Although much of the research reviewed in this Article was not available to Congress during its deliberations, at the time there were sufficient findings on independent audit committees and nonaudit services to at least give pause about, if not caution against, the legislation's approach.[61] That this literature was not even cursorily addressed is indicative of the poor quality of decisionmaking that characterized the enactment of the SOX corporate governance mandates. The corporate governance mandates stemmed from the intricate interaction of the Senate Banking Committee chairman's response to the suggestions of policy entrepreneurs and party politics in an election cycle coinciding with spectacular corporate scandals, a sharp stock market decline, and the consequent political collapse of the interest groups (the accounting profession and the business community) whose policy position was most consistent with the empirical literature. Moreover, those circumstances contributed to a perception of a crisis, and SOX was enacted under procedures applicable to emergency legislation. After detailing how those dynamics reveal a Congress inattentive to the governance provisions and hence unaware of the disconnect between legislative means and ends, this Part considers (and rejects) characterizing the provisions' adoption as an act of costless window dressing. SOX stands as an exemplar of low-quality legislative decisionmaking in the context of a crisis, a feature that has been repeated on other occasions when the federal government has intervened in financial markets (the subject of Section E).

Legislators' lack of awareness or disregard of the empirical literature, which resulted in low-quality decisionmaking, have to be realistically evaluated, however. Even with a committee system permitting specialization, legislators cannot be expected to have

---

[60] *See* Patricia A. Vlahakis, *Takeover Law and Practice 2003, in* 2 35th ANNUAL INSTITUTE ON SECURITIES REGULATION 673, 799-800 (PLI Corporate Law & Practice, Course Handbook Series No. B-1396, 2003) (describing the costly impact of the certification requirement on acquisitions of private and foreign corporations); Adrian Michaels, *Costs Rise as US Businesses Act To Meet Governance Laws*, FIN. TIMES (London), Apr. 25, 2003, at 15 (discussing a survey indicating that the cost of being a public company doubled after SOX); *infra* notes 188-194 and accompanying text.

[61] Several of the sources cited in this Article with publication dates after 2002 were circulating in manuscript form before 2002, including the one paper cited by a witness (Lynn Turner) in support of the prohibition on nonaudit services, *see infra* note 180.

extensive technical expertise: There are numerous demands on their time, and they must rely on staff and the information provided by interested parties.[62] Without doubt, therefore, some of the shortcomings of SOX's corporate governance mandates should be assigned to legislative staff. Whether that failure was due to staff members' ideological commitments, a lack of the technical skill necessary to evaluate the literature, or a combination of the two is unknown. But members of Congress select their staff, and in that regard, they bear responsibility for the poor performance of those individuals.

A. Background

SOX was adopted in July 2002, slightly less than a year after the Enron scandal broke, amid a tanking stock market. A flurry of Congressional hearings were held on the company's collapse, its causes, and potential legislative solutions, commencing in December 2001 and continuing beyond the enactment of the legislation.[63] The House passed a bill in April 2002, after the House Financial Services Committee had held seven hearings on Enron and proposed legislation. But legislation was not considered by the Senate until shortly after WorldCom's collapse in July 2002. Only one of the corporate governance mandates adopted in SOX appeared in the House bill, a more limited restriction on the provision of nonaudit services by auditors than what was enacted.[64] The other mandates, along with a more stringent prohibition on nonaudit services, were introduced in the Senate.

---

[62] As John Kingdon notes (in a study of voting in the U.S. House of Representatives in 1969), legislators rarely rely on printed material in their voting decisions, and instead rely on other members of Congress, particularly trusted, like-minded committee members, for voting cues. JOHN W. KINGDON, CONGRESSMEN'S VOTING DECISIONS 74-90, 210-11 (3d ed. 1989). In the case of SOX, the committee members whom one would expect to be informed were, as discussed in the text, neither informed nor attentive to the literature relevant to the governance mandates. This fact is perhaps explained in part by their not being on notice of the need to be so informed, because the mandates appeared in the Senate bill that was drafted after the conclusion of the Senate hearings. The late appearance of the mandates would also have made it difficult for the other major influences on voting besides fellow legislators identified in Kingdon's research—constituents and interest groups, *id.* at 17, 20, 22-23—to communicate the relevant information to legislators (had they been aware of the literature).

[63] The Law Library of Congress identifies more than forty Enron-related hearings held by ten different House and Senate committees from December 2001 to February 2003. Law Library of Cong., Enron Hearings, http://www.loc.gov/law/guide/enronhrgs.html (last visited Apr. 27, 2005).

[64] *See* Corporate and Auditing Accountability, Responsibility, and Transparency Act of 2002, H.R. 3763, 107th Cong. § 2(c) (2002). This bill was introduced and referred to committee on February 14, 2002, ordered reported on April 16, reported to the House on April 22, and passed on April 24. One of the mandates, the executive certification requirement, was rejected by the House committee (by a vote of 29-30 on the ranking Democrat's motion to amend the Republican bill). H.R. REP. NO. 107-414, at 25 (2002). That requirement, as well as a more expansive prohibition on nonaudit services, was included in the House Democrats' bill. Comprehensive Investor Protection Act of 2002, H.R. 3818, 107th Cong. § 2 (2002); 148 CONG. REC. H1574 (daily ed. Apr. 24, 2002) (amendment no. 5, offered by Rep. LaFalce (the ranking Democrat) as a substitute for the Republican bill). Finally, as noted earlier, the House bill required disclosure of executive loans, as opposed to the prohibition adopted on the Senate floor. H.R. 3763 § 6(a)(2).

Some important institutional detail should be noted before examining the legislative process in the Senate. First, in 2002 the Republicans controlled the House, and the Democrats controlled the Senate. The House bill was a Republican bill, although many Democrats voted for it.[65] The Senate Democrats substituted their bill for the House bill when the legislation was brought up on the Senate floor. Second, the Enron scandal was followed by revelations of accounting fraud and insider self-dealing at several large corporations, nearly all of which were thereafter pushed into bankruptcy: Adelphia Communications, Global Crossing, Tyco International, and WorldCom. Third, and coincident with the revelation of other corporate scandals, the stock market declined sharply throughout the time frame in which Congress was considering the SOX legislation. The economy had come out of a recession several months earlier, but employment continued to decline through July 2002 from its pre-recession peak in February 2001.[66]

The environment in which Congress enacted SOX can be best understood by reference to Figure 1. The figure plots the daily closing price of the S&P 500 composite index from two months before Enron's revelation of its earnings restatement through two months after the enactment of SOX; the other major indices exhibited a similar pattern. After declining from July 2001 through shortly before Enron's financial restatements and collapse in the fall of that year, the market plunged starting in April 2002, with the S&P reaching bottom in July 2002. The low point, which represented more than a one-third loss in value of the index over the preceding year, occurred on the day before the conference committee reported out a bill (July 23), which was also the second trading day after the bankruptcy filing of WorldCom (it filed on a weekend). Congress was therefore operating in an environment in which investor losses were staggering. A subsequent study by the GAO indicated that one well-known measure of investor sentiment, which was inaugurated in 1996, was at its lowest recorded level in June and

[65] The vote on the bill's adoption was 334 to 90. 148 CONG. REC. H1592 (daily ed. Apr. 24, 2002). There were three votes on amendments, two of which were much closer votes following party lines. *See id.* at H1574 (recording a 39-318 vote on the question of creating a government agency to conduct audits of public companies); *id.* at H1588-89 (recording a 202-219 vote on the Democrats' substitute bill, which included a certification requirement); *id.* at H1591-92 (recording a 205-222 vote on the Democrats' amendment, which contained provisions endorsed by President Bush that were not in the bill of the Republicans, who were likely to view the items as within the SEC's authority). The one vote sponsored by the Democrats regarding instructions to be provided to the members of the conference committee also followed party lines. *Id.* at H4846 (daily ed. July 17, 2002) (recording a 207-218 vote on the Democrats' motion to require House conferees to accept certain provisions of the Senate bill not in the House bill).

[66] The National Bureau for Economic Research (NBER), the nonprofit research organization that is the official arbiter of the U.S. business cycle, identified a recession's start in March 2001 (the end of the peak of the prior expansion that began in March 1991) and its end in November 2001 (the trough in economic activity). *See* BUS. CYCLE DATING COMM., NBER, THE NBER'S RECESSION DATING PROCEDURE (2003), *available at* http://www.nber.org/cycles/recessions.html. Note that employment rose slightly from July through November 2002 and then, with the exception of January, declined until September 2003. *Id.*

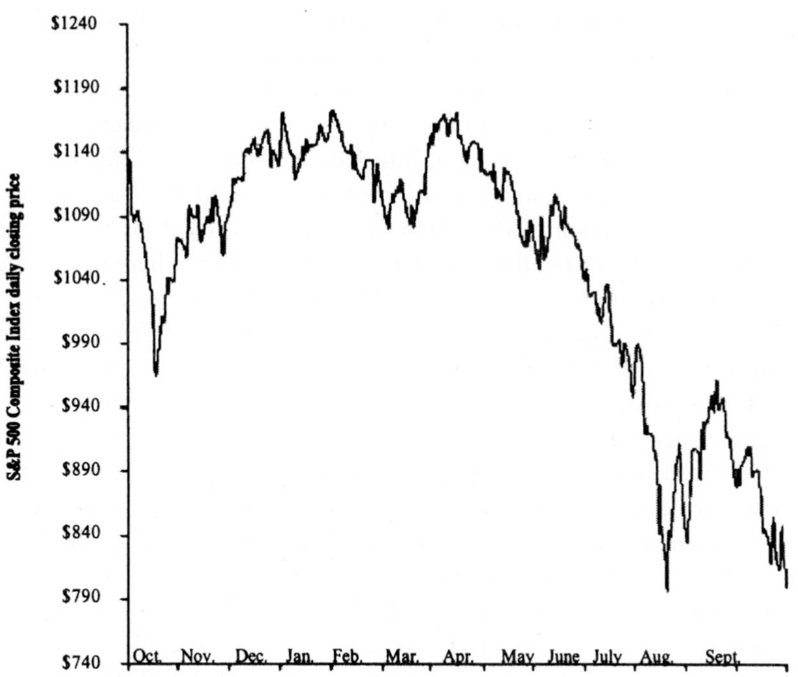

Figure 1. S&P 500 Composite Index Closing Price, September 2001 to October 2002

Note: Data for the figure come from Global Financial Data, S&P 500 Composite Price Index (w/GFD Extension), available at http://www.globalfinancialdata.com.

July 2002.[67] Members of Congress, not surprisingly, were attentive to the situation: Senators explicitly referred to the steep stock market decline in July as a rationale for the need for legislative action.[68] That response was certainly not out of the ordinary.

---

[67] GAO, NO. GAO-03-138, FINANCIAL STATEMENT RESTATEMENTS: TRENDS, MARKET IMPACTS, REGULATORY RESPONSES, AND REMAINING CHALLENGES 32-34 (2002) (citing the UBS/Gallup Index of Investor Optimism, a survey-based index of investor sentiment). The GAO attributed the loss of investor confidence to accounting scandals growing out of the large number of financial statement restatements. The investor confidence indices of the International Center for Finance at the Yale School of Management did not, however, register a consistent decline over that period. *Id.* at 37. The "one-year" and "crash" confidence indices increased over the period, and the "buy on dip" confidence index remained unchanged for institutional investors but declined for individual investors. *Id.* at 37-38.

[68] *E.g.*, 148 CONG. REC. S6558 (daily ed. July 10, 2002) (statement of Sen. Reid) ("[T]he stock market dropped again today almost 300 points. We need to do something to reestablish credibility and to reestablish . . . confidence . . . . This legislation goes a long way toward that end."); *id.* at S6622 (daily ed. July 11, 2002) (statement of Sen. Nelson of Florida) (commenting favorably on the "timing" of an amendment to the Sarbanes bill to enhance the SEC's sanctioning authority, among other provisions, and noting that "yesterday when the market dropped almost 300 points, . . . [it was] a reflection . . . that confidence is sinking"); *id.* at S6744 (daily ed. July 15, 2002) (statement of Sen. Allen) ("[I]n today's

As Stuart Banner notes, most new major securities regulation in the United States, as well as the United Kingdom, has followed stock market crashes.[69]

The downward spiral in the stock market ceased after the conference committee reported its bill, but the upward drift was only temporary: By October 2002, the S&P was back to about where it had been in July. Consequently, it is difficult to attribute the change in market direction upon the conference committee's conclusion to the market's positive assessment of the substantive provisions of SOX; if that had been the case, the upturn following the conference report should not have been temporary. The same interpretive difficulty is presented by Senator Phil Gramm's more jaded take on the legislation: In supporting the conference report, he noted that investors should have been reassured that the bill being enacted was not worse.[70] Event studies of the progress of the legislation present inconsistent (and largely insignificant) results, except for the significantly negative market reaction at the time of the WorldCom bankruptcy filing, which overlapped with the start of the conference committee's deliberations.[71] But whether one considers the reconciliation across chambers as stemming a negative market assessment of previously introduced legislation as too lenient (the Democrats' view of the market decline after the House action in April and that of one event study) or too strict (Gramm's view of the market decline during the Senate deliberations and that of another event study), in either scenario the upturn should not have faltered. This leads me to conclude that the declining stock price pattern before enactment is best explained as a reflection of investors' assessment of market fundamentals and not of the legislation moving through Congress.

A possible interpretation of the resumption of the market decline soon after SOX's enactment is that the market's initial positive evaluation of the legislation changed to a negative one. Insofar as public opinion poll data are informative on such matters—given that such polls do not solely measure the views of investors—they are at best murky. In polls taken during and after the Senate's deliberations but before the conference report,

---

climate, with the stock market dropping again today, . . . it is axiomatic that there is a pressing need for accounting reform . . . . The bill, as it is presented, is a very good bill.").

[69] Stuart Banner, *What Causes New Securities Regulation? 300 Years of Evidence,* 75 WASH. U. L.Q. 849, 850 (1997). The SOX governance mandates and Banner's observation are consistent with the results of an interesting model of news media bias by David Baron, in which issues receiving media attention produce increased regulation. DAVID P. BARON, PERSISTENT MEDIA BIAS (Stanford Graduate Sch. of Bus., Research Paper No. 1845, 2004), *available at* http://ssrn.com/abstract=516006. The model depends on a median-voter model of politics and the assumption, supported by empirical evidence, that the news media is biased toward the left, a bias Baron translates into the regulatory context as supporting more stringent regulation.

[70] 148 CONG. REC. S7354 (daily ed. July 25, 2002) (statement of Sen. Gramm) ("If people on Wall Street are listening to the debate and trying to figure out whether they should be concerned about this bill, I think they can rightly feel that this bill could have been much worse. I think if people had wanted to be irresponsible, this is a bill on which they could have been irresponsible and almost anything would have passed on the floor of the Senate.").

[71] For a discussion of event studies of the enactment of SOX, see ROMANO, *supra* note 19, at 102-14.

a majority of respondents indicated that they thought the Senate's bill would have a minor effect or no effect on reducing corporate wrongdoing. Shortly after the legislation was enacted, a majority said it would have a major effect; yet one month later, there was a shift back, as a smaller percentage (a bare majority) opined that the legislation would make a difference.[72] The inconclusiveness of the polling data bolsters the view that the market trend during the legislation's consideration and after its enactment is best understood as randomly fluctuating in line with market fundamentals rather than evincing investors' reactions to SOX.[73] Of course, members of Congress did not have the benefit of hindsight, and rightly or wrongly, with an election looming, they interpreted the market decline from April through July 2002 as requiring legislative action.

B. The Legislative Process

The corporate governance mandates were neither a principal nor a subsidiary focus of legislative consideration. With the exception of the restriction on the provision of nonaudit services by auditors, for all practical purposes they were not even discussed. The legislation in both houses was considered within a narrow time frame: Only one day, for instance, was allocated for the House's consideration of the Financial Services Committee's bill. The Senate debate, which lasted a week, was conducted under a Republican press for a cloture motion that succeeded, restricting the time for legislative

[72] The "Polling the Nations" database, which consists of more than 14,000 surveys conducted by more than 700 polling organizations in the United States and other countries from 1986 to the present using scientifically selected random samples, contained five questions asking respondents' views on the effect of the proposed or enacted legislation on corporate misconduct or corporate corruption. The results were as follows:

Poll	Field Dates, 2002	Sample Size	Major effect	Minor (no effect)
Newsweek	July 11-12	1000	26%	48% (14%)
Newsweek	July 17-19	1004	27%	48% (14%)
Gallup/CNN/USA Today	July 29-31	1003	66%	30%
NBC News/WSJ	Sept. 3-5	1011	50%	44%

Three polls asked whether respondents thought the legislation would have a "major" effect or a "minor/no" effect. The figures for the NBC News/*Wall Street Journal* poll were obtained using slightly different language. Half of the respondents were asked whether it would make a "real difference" or "not make a real difference" (the figures cited in the table above). The other half were asked whether, when the legislation was enacted, "enough will have been done" (24%) or "more should be done" (71%). Data were obtained from Polling the Nations, http://www.orspub.com (last visited Apr. 27, 2005).

[73] Peter Wallison has advanced another plausible explanation of the stock market's movement, also unrelated to SOX: its reaction to an anticipated war in Iraq. *See* Peter J. Wallison, Sarbanes-Oxley: A Review (May 5, 2004) (unpublished manuscript), *available at* http://www.aei.org/docLib/20040506_WallisonIntroduction.pdf.

consideration as well as permissible amendments.[74] Hence, the usually key role of committees in the formulation of legislation was virtually absolute, and in the committees, the Democrats' drafting was heavily informed by the views of former SEC Chairman Levitt and his former SEC chief accountant Lynn Turner.[75]

In a remarkable turn of events, Levitt was able to revive his agenda for accounting regulation (particularly the prohibition on nonaudit services), which had failed less than two years earlier when confronted with bipartisan congressional support for the accounting profession's position against Levitt's proposals.[76] Levitt had ready-made solutions for perceived problems with the accounting profession. In conjunction with his longtime support of and affiliation with the Democratic Party, his background in the securities industry and as a regulator who took on the accounting profession made

---

[74] After cloture is invoked, debate on a bill is limited to "a maximum of thirty additional hours . . . before a vote must be taken." SAMUEL KERNELL & GARY C. JACOBSON, THE LOGIC OF AMERICAN POLITICS 228 (2d ed. 2003).

[75] For example, in introducing the bill and summarizing its content, the floor manager, Senator Paul Sarbanes, referred to Levitt's testimony regarding the kind of regulatory board that was needed. 148 CONG. REC. S6331 (daily ed. July 8, 2002) (statement of Sen. Sarbanes). In introducing and describing his committee's bill, the floor amendment to SOX containing the criminal provisions discussed *infra* Subsection II.B.2, Senator Patrick Leahy stated that Levitt and his predecessor as SEC chairman supported the provision expanding the statute of limitations for private securities actions. 148 CONG. REC. S6440 (daily ed. July 9, 2002) (statement of Sen. Leahy); *see also id.* at S6525 (daily ed. July 10, 2002) (statement of Sen. Wellstone) (discussing his support in 2000 of Levitt's failed effort to restrict nonaudit services and characterizing Sarbanes's bill as largely implementing that agenda ("[Levitt's] solution looked a lot like what is in this bill.")). The ranking House Democrat, Representative John LaFalce, also acknowledged his debt to Levitt and his staff. *E.g.*, H.R. 3763—THE CORPORATE AND AUDITING ACCOUNTABILITY, RESPONSIBILITY, AND TRANSPARENCY ACT OF 2002: HEARINGS BEFORE THE HOUSE COMM. ON FIN. SERVS., 107th Cong. 163 (2002) [hereinafter *House CARTA Hearings*] (statement of Rep. LaFalce) (noting that Turner discussed and approved LaFalce's bill's provisions); THE ENRON COLLAPSE: IMPLICATIONS TO INVESTORS AND THE CAPITAL MARKETS: HEARINGS BEFORE THE SUBCOMM. ON CAPITAL MKTS., INS., AND GOV'T SPONSORED ENTERS. OF THE HOUSE COMM. ON FIN. SERVS., 107th Cong. 19 (2002) [hereinafter *Enron Hearings II*] (statement of Rep. LaFalce) (urging consideration of Levitt's recommendations). Levitt's influence on the Democrats' legislation was widely reported in the press. *E.g.*, Michael Schroeder, *Arthur Levitt Finds Himself on the Outs*, WALL ST. J., Nov. 29, 2002, at A4 (noting Levitt's "strong role in formulating" the accounting provisions and his former staff's help in drafting the Democrats' bill).

Barbara Sinclair discusses how the legislative process has come to vary considerably from the textbook view of a bill's progress within one committee's tight control, which underscores more starkly the influence exerted by the Senate Banking Committee chairman with respect to the governance mandates in SOX. *See* BARBARA SINCLAIR, UNORTHODOX LAWMAKING: NEW LEGISLATIVE PROCESSES IN THE U.S. CONGRESS 10-26, 36-41, 48-56, 70-81 (2d ed. 2000) (describing lawmaking processes since the 1970s in which bills are referred to multiple committees, bypass committees entirely, are included in omnibus legislation, are subject to marathon amendment sessions on the Senate floor and complex or restrictive rules on the House floor, and are drafted in legislative summits attended by the President and party leaders rather than committee chairs). It should be noted that with the exception of House consideration under a restrictive rule, the other features that she considers common, albeit "unorthodox" from the textbook perspective, were not part of SOX's legislative process.

[76] *See supra* notes 33-35 and accompanying text.

him a natural and trusted source for advice and guidance among Democrats.[77] To understand how the governance mandates appeared in SOX, this Section examines the floor debates, which establish legislators' general lack of interest in, and inattention to, the mandates. The next Section then identifies the source of the mandates at an earlier point in the legislative process, the committee hearings, which served as the incubator for policy entrepreneurs' proposals that resonated with the key legislator.

1. The Debate in the House

The majority party exercises strict control over the legislative process in the House, and the adoption of Representative Michael Oxley's Financial Services Committee bill was no exception: The Republican Party shepherded the bill through the floor with one day of debate. In that debate, Democrats objected to the absence of provisions that subsequently appeared in the Senate bill. Two of these were substantive corporate governance mandates, the expansion of prohibited nonaudit services and the certification requirement, both of which appeared in a House Democratic bill that was offered as a substitute amendment and defeated on the floor. But the bill passed with broad bipartisan support. For most Democrats, the easy calculation was that in their upcoming reelection campaigns, a vote against the Republican legislation on the grounds that the bill was not "tough enough" and that they had voted for a preferable alternative that had been defeated might be difficult to explain.[78]

As indicated in Table 2, at no point in the House debate did anyone mention audit committee independence or executive loans, the subjects of the SOX corporate governance mandates most intrusive on state law jurisdiction, nor did those mandates appear in House Democrats' bills.[79] In fact, few representatives participated in the debate at

---

[77] *See* ARTHUR LEVITT WITH PAULA DWYER, TAKE ON THE STREET: WHAT WALL STREET AND CORPORATE AMERICA DON'T WANT YOU TO KNOW: WHAT YOU CAN DO TO FIGHT BACK 3-4, 7, 10 (2002) (describing his political background, including his father's elected position as a Democratic state comptroller of New York and his own fundraising efforts for Bill Clinton's 1992 presidential campaign and lobbying activities for the American Stock Exchange). Levitt was a textbook policy entrepreneur, with the appropriate expertise, connections, persistence, and readiness to seize the opportunity presented, as described in KINGDON, *supra* note 5, at 189-91.

[78] A similar dynamic eventually operated in the Senate. Senate Republicans, who had to make an analogous calculation, voted for the Democratic bill and, it should be noted, did not have the opportunity for an up-or-down vote on their own bill as a substitute, as did the House Democrats. *See infra* Subsection II.B.2.

[79] The House bill contained a provision requiring disclosure of executive loans. *See supra* note 65. The minority views included in the report accompanying the House bill in April, however, objected to the bill's not having any provision restricting the definition of directors' independence to exclude their acting as "consultants," citing in support the views of Turner, former SEC chief accountant under Levitt. HOUSE COMM. ON FIN. SERVS., CORPORATE AND AUDITING ACCOUNTABILITY, RESPONSIBILITY, AND TRANSPARENCY ACT OF 2002, H.R. REP. NO. 107-414, at 49-50 (2002). The substitute bill offered by the Financial Services Committee's ranking Democrat, Representative LaFalce, had a provision that instructed the SEC to adopt rules requiring independent directors to be nominated by nominating committees consisting solely of independent directors, with the definition to follow that used by stock exchanges in their

Table 2
Congressional Debates on SOX

A. Senate: Sarbanes Bill, July 8-12, 15, 2002

Issue	No. Speakers
Audit Committee Independence	8
Restriction on Non-audit Services	21
Loans to Officers	6
Certification of Financials	9
Accounting Profession Regulator	21
Statute of Limitations for Class Actions	7
Accounting for Stock Options	13
Stock Analysts	10
Executive Forfeiture of Bonuses	6
Increased Criminal Penalties	23
Total speaking on any issue	53

B. House of Representatives: Oxley Bill, April 24, 2002

Issue	No. Speakers
Restriction on Non-audit Services	15
Certification of Financials	6
Accounting Profession Regulator	24
Stock Analysts	8
Executive Forfeiture of Bonuses	9
Total speaking on any issue	47

C. House of Representatives: Judiciary Committee Bill, July 16, 2002

Issue	No. speakers
Certification of Financials	7
Statute of Limitations for Class Actions	6
Civil Penalties	3
Increased Criminal Penalties	13
Total speaking on any issue	21

D. House of Representatives: Motion on Conference Committee Instructions, July 17, 2002

Issue	No. speakers
Certification of Financials	1
Statute of Limitations for Class Actions	6
Accounting for Stock Options	3
Stock Analysts	1
Increased Criminal Penalties	6
Total speaking on any issue	19

Notes: Data for the table were tabulated from the *Congressional Record.* Speakers may be counted in more than one panel as appropriate. All speakers in Panel D were also speakers in Panel B. Eleven of the speakers in Panel C were also speakers in Panel B. Seven of the speakers in Panel C were also speakers in Panel D.

all; of those who did, virtually all were members of the Financial Services Committee that had produced the bill.

As Table 2 indicates, the issue that attracted the most attention during the House debate was the creation of an accounting industry regulator. Given the absence of corporate governance provisions in the House Financial Services Committee's draft legislation, this is unexceptional, because the creation of a new regulator (as advocated by then-SEC Chairman Harvey Pitt) was the bill's most significant alteration of the status quo. The table shows a related pattern, however, when action in the Senate three months later triggered further activity on the legislation in the House: None of the governance provisions that had been introduced in the Senate bill was even mentioned in the House debate over the Senate bill.[80]

rules on audit committees. *See* HOUSE COMM. ON RULES, PROVIDING FOR CONSIDERATION OF H.R. 3763, CORPORATE AND AUDITING ACCOUNTABILITY, RESPONSIBILITY, AND TRANSPARENCY ACT OF 2002, H.R. REP. NO. 107-418, at 35 (2002).

[80] Over two days of consideration, House members raised neither the Senate's additions of the governance provisions regarding audit committees and loans nor the differences between the Senate and House bills on the matters earlier debated in the House (regarding restrictions on nonaudit services and the new overseer of the accounting profession). Rather, the issues debated paralleled the issues debated in the Senate, discussed *infra* Subsection II.B.2. The July 16 floor debate summarized in Panel C of Table 2 concerned a House Judiciary Committee bill drafted by the Republicans in response both to the House Democrats' bill, which was similar to the bill of the Democrat-controlled Senate Judiciary Committee (being enacted in the Senate at the time), and to remarks by President Bush calling for harsher criminal sanctions for securities fraud. Much of the debate on that day consisted of Democrats objecting to what they considered to be improper political maneuvering by Republicans to rush the Republicans' bill to the floor and prevent a vote on the Democrats' alternative. The July 17 floor debate in Panel D of Table 2 was over a motion by the Democrats to instruct the House members of the conference committee to support the Senate version over that of the House with respect to extending the statute of limitations for private securities actions and certain other criminal and civil provisions; that motion was defeated on a party-line vote of 207 to 218. 148 CONG. REC. H4846 (daily ed. July 17, 2002).

Political scientists have characterized House floor debate as for "public consumption" rather than for persuasion of members on the other side of an issue.[81] Even from that perspective, the lack of reference to the corporate governance reforms that were included in the final bill is notable, because it indicates that members of Congress did not consider those provisions to be matters that would serve either to justify their votes or to demonstrate to constituents how legislation was solving the "Enron problem." The governance provisions therefore would appear to have been of principal interest to corporate governance policy entrepreneurs, individuals "inside the Beltway," at least as far as House members were concerned.

2. The Debate in the Senate

While committee deliberations are conventionally considered key to the making of legislation, floor action is often more important for shaping legislation in the Senate than in the House.[82] This is because Senate rules permitting nongermane amendments and filibusters provide individual senators with considerable ability to affect—and delay—legislation. To obtain an orderly and timely consideration of a bill, the party leadership therefore "routinely negotiate[s] unanimous consent agreements" that determine what amendments will be allowed and what other procedures will be followed.[83]

That process changes with a successful cloture motion, because once cloture is invoked, debate and amendments are severely restricted.[84] Because under the Senate rules a cloture motion requires the vote of three-fifths of the Senate, the leadership of both parties typically must agree on the content of a bill (and line up support from enough party members) to sustain a successful cloture motion. In the absence of the successful cloture motion on SOX, a more extensive unanimous consent agreement would have been necessary instead. Such an agreement might have been difficult to achieve, given the many members seeking to attach their issues to the legislation.[85] The successful cloture motion's limitations on the Senate debate over SOX accordingly meant that matters unresolved in committee would never reach the floor and that compromises in

---

[81] KERNELL & JACOBSON, *supra* note 76, at 229.

[82] *See, e.g., id.*

[83] *Id.* at 228.

[84] Only amendments that are germane to the bill are permissible once cloture is invoked. This contrasts with the ordinary Senate procedures, by which any amendment can be added to a bill. Under House rules for considering a bill, by contrast, amendments must be germane. *Id.* at 227, 229.

[85] Because everyone recognized that a bill would be enacted given the perceived public demand for action, a large number of senators saw the amendment process as an opportunity to implement favored initiatives. For a sense of the problem, *see*, for example, 148 CONG. REC. S6633 (daily ed. July 11, 2002) (statement of Sen. Gramm) (responding to a senator proposing to debate all amendments for half an hour each). Senator Gramm explained,

> [W]e have 36 Republicans who want to offer an amendment. My amendment is next on the list. I am the ranking member of this committee, and it appears I am not going to get an opportunity to offer an amendment. . . . There are 58 Democrat amendments.

committee could not be recrafted without unanimous agreement. As a consequence, none of the governance mandates in the committee bill, nor the one mandate included as a floor amendment, was subject to any scrutiny on the floor.

a. The Committee Compromise and Impetus to Cloture

The Senate bill was drafted by the Democrats, but the Republicans had some input because their support was needed to move the legislation. Because the Democrats had a bare floor majority of one vote, major legislation such as SOX required some degree of bipartisan support in committee to have any possibility of success on the floor (let alone for legislation to proceed to an expedited vote with the Senate operating under cloture). The authorization for up to two members of the new accounting regulator's board to be (or to have been) certified public accountants is the most prominent instance of the Republicans' ability to affect the legislation.

The inclusion of practicing accountants on the new regulator's board was of particular concern to Senator Michael Enzi, a Republican who was the only certified public accountant in the Senate and a member of the Banking, Housing, and Urban Affairs Committee; his support of the Democratic bill, which was crucial to its reaching the floor, depended on that provision's inclusion. Legislation had been stalled in the Senate committee because the Democrats who controlled the Senate favored greater regulation than the Republicans, but a Democratic bill that passed on a party-line vote in committee was not considered likely to succeed on the floor. Accounts of the Senate committee deliberations indicate that it took until the end of May for the committee chairman, Senator Paul Sarbanes, to draft a bill acceptable to all of the Democrats on the committee and another month to reach agreement with Enzi.[86] Their compromise ended the committee stalemate because Enzi had been sponsoring the alternative Republican bill, and his shift in support brought over other members of his party. That

> . . . If we sat here and tried to do [all of them]—and some of them having to do with things such as the Ninth Circuit Court of Appeals and bankruptcy law—we would literally spend 3 or 4 months.

Id. Senator Sarbanes also explained,

> I know there are a lot of amendments pending, but we have now been on this legislation a full week. . . .
>
> There are a number of amendments that are relevant to the bill but not germane. Once cloture is invoked, they will fall. I know that is a matter of some concern to those who are proposing those amendments, but I do not know how we can handle this differently and move along towards a resolution.
>
> In addition . . . there are also amendments that are not even relevant . . . .
>
> I am frank to say to my colleagues, I do not see how we can progress and move towards a final vote and resolution on this issue without invoking cloture this morning.

Id. at S6684 (daily ed. July 12, 2002) (statement of Sen. Sarbanes).

[86] *See* David S. Hilzenrath et al., *How Congress Rode a 'Storm' to Corporate Reform*, WASH. POST, July 28, 2002, at A1.

action enabled Sarbanes to achieve a bipartisan, albeit nonunanimous, committee vote in favor of his bill and bring it to the Senate floor.[87]

Still, the Republicans' input into the committee draft was peripheral. Republican committee members submitted more than one hundred proposed amendments to Sarbanes's bill, stalling its progress, and the compromise with Enzi released the bill without including the substance of those proposals.[88] The dispute between the parties over the regulatory sweep of the bill (with the Republicans favoring a narrower bill similar to that passed by the House) was the reason action in the Senate was protracted compared to the House, whose rules enable the majority party to implement its will.[89]

During the course of the legislative process, however, the Republicans' strategy changed from what the press characterized as delaying tactics and efforts to kill the bill to attempts to expedite action. After the bill reached the floor, the Republican leadership sought a cloture motion (and thereby supported the bill's adoption), although they had opposed the bill throughout the committee process. The Republicans' explanation for the shift was that they expected to be better positioned to influence the legislation in the conference committee, which would have to reconcile the Senate bill with the House bill that they preferred.[90]

---

[87] The committee vote was 17 to 4; 6 of the 10 Republicans on the committee voted for Sarbanes's bill. On the floor, Enzi acknowledged Sarbanes's compromise on the accounting board's composition. *See* 148 CONG. REC. S6338 (daily ed. July 8, 2002) (statement of Sen. Enzi).

[88] Hilzenrath et al., *supra* note 89; *Senate Democrats Forced To Lower Expectations on Accounting Reform Bill*, SEC. WK., May 27, 2002, at 1. Most of the amendments were offered by the ranking minority member, Senator Gramm, who was opposed to Sarbanes's bill. *See* Douglas Turner, *SEC Chief To Impose 'Stringent' Rules on Accountants*, BUFFALO (N.Y.) NEWS, May 24, 2002, at A9 (explaining that Gramm, who "opposes increased regulation of the accounting business," introduced 77 of 123 amendments to the bill at the "last minute").

[89] The Republicans also had a larger margin of control in the House than the Democrats did in the Senate (although it was still a narrow one).

[90] *See, e.g.*, 148 CONG. REC. S6684 (daily ed. July 12, 2002) (statement of Sen. Gramm). Gramm explained,

> [W]e need to pass a bill. We are going to conference with a House bill that is substantially different from this bill. . . . The amendments that are being offered now are largely non-germane. . . .
>
> It is very important that we get on with our business and that we pass this bill. I intend to vote for it today. I do not think it is the bill we need in the end, but it gets us to conference where we can get the bill we need in the end. I urge my Republican colleagues to vote for it, not because in the end they are for this version but because they want to do something. We need to bring this debate to a close. . . .
>
> So I urge my colleagues to vote to end the debate.

Id. The agreement on the expanded statute-of-limitations provision producing the cloture vote, *see infra* note 111 and accompanying text, further illustrates this description of the Republicans' position. The first person to mention the possibility of a cloture motion on the floor of the Senate was Enzi, a Republican, in his initial remarks on the legislation on the first day of debate. *See* 148 CONG. REC. S6340 (daily ed. July 8, 2002) (statement of Sen. Enzi) ("As we get into this bill, there are virtually no limits on what amendments can be put on—at least unless there is a cloture motion. I hope people will recognize the need to have something done, the need to get it done quickly, and not try and make this a vehicle for everything they ever thought needed to be done with corporations.").

But the calculation of a better outcome in conference does not explain why the Republicans sought to expedite the legislative process—after all, the bill would end up in conference whether it took a week or a month on the Senate floor. The political science literature suggests an answer: Emergency legislation is more likely to be considered under restrictive rules such as a cloture motion than is other legislation. Political scientists attribute that finding to legislators' having high discount rates in such a context; that is, in a situation calling for emergency action, legislators have strong preferences for "earlier rather than later passage."[91] The hypothesis that SOX was emergency legislation has plausibility in explaining the Republican switch that led to the agreement on cloture.

Initially, Enron's collapse in the fall of 2001 generated a crisis situation and a media frenzy, as every Congressional committee that could find some jurisdictional basis held a hearing on the scandal. But by April, the sense of an emergency had lessened, such that the members of the Senate Banking Committee did not feel any urgency to agree on a bill in response to the House action. Indeed, even after Sarbanes took several months to craft a bill that met bipartisan committee approval, it appeared that the bill would not progress. The best that Senate Majority Leader Thomas Daschle could do was to try to schedule a vote on the bill for sometime after the August recess, and legislators opposed to the bill expressed the view that "Enron's moment as a galvanizing issue ha[d] quickly passed."[92] When the WorldCom scandal broke on June 26, the political environment changed dramatically once again, and Daschle, now predicting eighty votes in support of the bill, was able to move it up on the calendar for a July vote. Senator Gramm, the ranking Republican on the committee, who opposed the bill and had earlier thought the feeding frenzy was over and the movement for legislation stopped, now did not even attempt to stem the bill's progress to the floor and a vote.[93] This chain of events suggests that circumstances had altered senators' perception of the situation to be one calling for emergency action.[94] The Senate thereupon moved on the legislation rapidly, agreeing to cloture after having taken no action on the House bill for months.

b. Action on the Floor

As detailed in Table 2, only one of the corporate governance mandates (the restriction on nonaudit services) was the focus of significant debate on the Senate floor. It was one of two provisions in the House bill that Senate Democrats had flatly rejected and that were consequently a matter of controversy in the Senate; the other was the

---

[91] Keith Krehbiel, *Legislative Organization*, J. ECON. PERSP., Winter 2004, at 113, 125.

[92] Stephen Labaton & Richard A. Oppel Jr., *Enthusiasm Waning in Congress for Tougher Post-Enron Controls*, N.Y. TIMES, June 10, 2002, at A1.

[93] Hilzenrath et al., *supra* note 89.

[94] This view is also held by legislators. For instance, Senator Jon Corzine, a member of the Banking Committee, was described as having "said the [Senate] bill would have lost momentum without WorldCom and the other scandals that followed Enron." Spencer S. Hsu & Kathleen Day, *Senate Vote Spotlights Audit Reform and Sarbanes*, WASH. POST, July 15, 2002, at A1.

accounting regulator. The House bill left the organizational structure of the new accounting regulator as a matter for the SEC to determine and maintained the language of the SEC's existing rule restricting nonaudit services, simply adding two services to the list.[95] Although most of the senators mentioning matters in the table did so in laundry list statements of support for the bill, Republicans also expressed a preference for the form that the nonaudit services and accounting regulator provisions took in the House bill. The House provisions dovetailed with then-SEC Chairman Pitt's proposals for regulatory reform, which had been vetted with the accounting profession; accordingly, the accounting profession supported the House legislation. That process created an additional barrier to reaching a compromise, because the failure of Arthur Levitt's regulatory effort a few years earlier was attributed to Pitt's successful advocacy, as counsel to the accounting profession, which orchestrated political support for the industry against the SEC. No doubt the Democrats' displeasure with Pitt—and the Republicans' support for him—was a factor contributing to their differing positions on both the organization of the entity regulating accounting and the nonaudit services provision.[96] It is possible that the parties' positions might have been otherwise had there been a different SEC chairman or if Democrats had controlled the executive branch.

The debate over the nonaudit services prohibition was, therefore, in large part a replay of a battle over the regulation of the accounting industry fought two years earlier when Levitt was SEC chair. But the environment this time was markedly different. There was a media frenzy, heightened by a sharply declining stock market and high-profile accounting frauds and business failures, in the middle of an election year. For example, the major network evening news coverage between January and July 2002 contained 613 stories on business, of which 471 (77%) were about corporate scandals;

---

[95] The two services now proscribed by Congress (internal audit and financial information systems) were not included in the rule the SEC adopted in 2000 because of opposition by the accounting profession. In the atmosphere of corporate scandals, the profession now acquiesced in the ban, and the House bill proscribed the services in its codification of the SEC rules. The House Democrats objected that the Republican bill "include[d] no real limits on the non-audit services" and that it "reference[d] the existing SEC rules in a way that includes only the limited restrictions that the SEC currently places," "codifying existing regulatory carve-outs" and "mak[ing] no change in existing law." HOUSE COMM. ON FIN. SERVS., CORPORATE AND AUDITING ACCOUNTABILITY, RESPONSIBILITY, AND TRANSPARENCY ACT OF 2002, H.R. REP. NO. 107-414, AT 48 (2002). The Senate bill enumerated all of the nonaudit services restricted by the SEC rule along with internal audit and financial information systems. It also relocated the rulemaking authority regarding those services to the new accounting regulator. In addition, the Senate bill did not leave the details of the accounting regulator to the SEC but established them itself, giving the SEC only the power to appoint the members of the new entity's board.

[96] In this regard, the House Republicans generally sought to delegate as much authority as possible to the SEC to organize the regulation of the accounting profession, while the Democrats' objective was to create an entity with greater independent authority and to provide it with instructions about its role. Despite the House Republicans' ability to exercise strict control over the legislative process, the antagonism toward Pitt was so intense that, at the committee hearings, Democrats successfully insisted that he be sworn in as a witness. That posture irritated Republicans, who contended that formal swearing-in was conventionally reserved for witnesses representing organizations under investigation. *See Enron Hearings II, supra* note 77, at 2-9.

of those stories, 195 connected corporations to Congress (individual members or the institution itself), while 188 connected corporations to the Bush Administration. These figures compare to a total of 489 business stories, of which only 52 (11%) were about scandals, in the same period the prior year.[97] Moreover, more than 80% of the scandal-related stories looked to government action to address the problem.[98] In this charged atmosphere, Levitt's earlier reform proposals now seemed prescient (at least to the Democrats for whom Levitt was a source of expertise), and the accounting industry had lost its public credibility with the audit failures.[99]

There was a near-total absence of discussion on the Senate floor of the other three corporate governance mandates—the independent audit committee provisions, the executive loan ban, and the certification requirement—that were included in the Senate but not the House bill. Table 2 makes clear that legislators perceived those provisions as unproblematic. Only a minority of senators (twenty-eight) referred to any of those provisions on the floor, and nearly all those references were part of laundry lists, in which senators expressed support for the legislation by enumerating specific provisions in the bill.[100] Besides the two House provisions altered by the Senate bill as noted earlier, the other topics commonly raised on the floor as indicated in Table 2 were raised either in conjunction with consideration of a Senate Judiciary Committee amendment to the bill or individual senators' attempts to propose amendments to the bill that the leadership would not permit. One of the more contested failed amendments involved the efforts of Senators John McCain and Carl Levin to add a provision on the accounting treatment of stock options. Given a lack of consensus on the issue, the leadership had agreed not to include such a provision in the bill because it could have threatened adoption of legislation.[101] This was not a partisan controversy: To obtain support in

[97] Video clip: Karlyn H. Bowman, *Sarbanes-Oxley and Public Opinion After Enron and WorldCom, Presentation at Sarbanes-Oxley: A Review* (May 5, 2004) [hereinafter Bowman], *available at* http://www.aei.org/events/eventID.809,filter.all/event_detail.asp (follow "Video" link, at 00:13:45) (discussing data compiled by the Media Research Center).

[98] *Id.*

[99] *See Top of Their Game: Lobby Leaders in 2002*, LEGAL TIMES, Dec. 16, 2002, at 14 (noting that the accounting industry's "lobbying effectively stopped the day WorldCom hit"). The impact of media pressure on the Congressional bandwagon for the Levitt-Turner approach is apparent in Senator Gramm's floor remarks. While criticizing the bill's prohibition of an enumerated set of nine nonaudit services, in contrast to his proposal that would have left the decision to the new accounting regulator, Gramm referred to having "read editorials" that said the provision "makes the bill tougher, but I don't think it makes it better," 148 CONG. REC. S6335 (daily ed. July 8, 2002) (statement of Sen. Gramm). He also lamented "that the media has decided that the tougher bill is the bill with more mandates." *Id.* at S6333.

[100] The number twenty-eight eliminates double counting of senators who referred to more than one of the governance provisions in their remarks; no senator referred to all four mandates. ROMANO, *supra* note 19, at 134 n.261. For details on the distribution of senators' remarks, including the discussion of the conference committee report (not tabulated), *see id.* Two of the six Senate references to loans in Table 2, Panel A were references to the disclosure requirement in the bill and bore no relation to its final form as a loan prohibition.

[101] For an overview of Congress's involvement in the nearly decade-old controversy over the accounting treatment of stock options, *see id.* at 138 n.268.

committee from members of his own party, Senator Sarbanes had agreed to eliminate a provision in his original bill on the expensing of stock options.[102]

The Senate Judiciary Committee bill (the Leahy Amendment) consisted of provisions involving criminal penalties (because these were not within the Banking Committee's jurisdiction), protection for whistleblowers, and a provision extending the statute of limitations for private securities fraud actions.[103] The statute-of-limitations extension overruled a Supreme Court decision[104] setting the statute of limitations, which had been left unchanged by Congress's 1995 private securities litigation reform despite lobbying at the time by the SEC and the plaintiffs' bar to overturn the decision. The Democratic Senate majority bundled the statute-of-limitations provision with the bill's extensions of criminal penalties for securities fraud, which enjoyed broad support. In contrast to the penalty provisions, the civil statute-of-limitations provision was controversial and had a partisan tinge, given Republicans' general support for and Democrats' opposition to litigation reform that restricted liability—positions that paralleled the perspective of key party constituencies, the business community for the Republicans and the plaintiffs' bar for the Democrats.[105] The measure, understandably, was not in the Republican-controlled House's version of the criminal penalty bill. The 1995 securities reform legislation was bipartisan legislation (it withstood a veto by President Clinton), although it had been vigorously opposed by the plaintiffs' bar, which was said to have influenced the President's action.[106] After the Republicans gained the White House in

---

[102] Hilzenrath et al., *supra* note 89.

[103] The criminal certification requirement was added by another Senate Judiciary Committee proposal, known as the Biden-Hatch Amendment.

[104] Lampf v. Gilbertson, 501 U.S. 350 (1991).

[105] For a discussion of these groups' campaign contributions, especially with regard to conference committee members, *see* Romano, *supra* note 19, at 193-98. The Senate Judiciary Committee voted against a Republican amendment to exclude the provision expanding the statute of limitations on a 7-11 party-line vote (with one Republican crossover), and then approved, by voice vote, an amendment lowering the bill's expansion of the statute of limitations, from the earlier of three years from the date of the discovery of the fraud or five years from the date of the fraud, to the earlier of two years from the date of the discovery of the fraud or five years from the date of the fraud. S. REP. NO. 107-146, at 22 (2002). The 1995 Securities Litigation Reform Act and Supreme Court decisions cutting back on liability were mentioned by witnesses during the hearings as factors contributing to the accounting scandals. *E.g.*, *2 Senate Hearings*, *supra* note 35, at 1008 (statement of Howard Metzenbaum, Chairman, Consumer Fed'n of Am.); 2 *id.* at 1018-19 (statement of Damon A. Silvers, Assoc. Gen. Counsel, AFL-CIO). A related proposal promoted by the same witnesses, to reestablish aiding-and-abetting liability under the federal securities laws (which would have similarly overturned a Supreme Court decision left intact by the 1995 law that was of interest to the plaintiffs' bar), was not included in the bill. *E.g.*, 2 *id.* at 1008 (statement of Howard Metzenbaum); 2 *id.* at 1018-19 (statement of Damon Silvers). Given the omission from the bill of the one provision and not the other, it is most plausible to conclude that there was not sufficient support among senators of either party for such an expansion of liability, and that the latter provision was excluded to ensure the legislation would move forward.

[106] The President's veto was unexpected. William Lerach, one of the leading securities class action plaintiffs' lawyers, met with Clinton at a political dinner the weekend before the veto, but White House

2001, Senate Democrats blocked litigation reform initiatives,[107] and many Republican legislators and the business community viewed the effort to "repeal" the 1995 limitations on securities litigation (the only litigation initiative that had been adopted at the federal level) with considerable ire.

The inclusion of the statute-of-limitations provision provided an opening for a Republican legislative maneuver leading to cloture. Senator Gramm moved to separate the statute-of-limitations provision from the other provisions in the Leahy Amendment, which he was able to do as a matter of right under the Senate rules. This move jeopardized the bill's progress. Shortly thereafter, the two sides reached an agreement to clarify the language regarding the extension of the statute of limitations and to file a cloture motion on the bill, and the division of the Leahy Amendment was withdrawn.[108]

In the limited time for consideration of the bill following the cloture motion, a few amendments agreed to by both parties were added on the floor without debate, including the prohibition of loans to executives. There was no discussion of that amendment when it was offered by Senator Charles Schumer: It was immediately unanimously agreed to without a roll-call vote.[109] A few days earlier in a speech on Wall Street, President Bush had called on corporate boards to prevent officers from receiving company loans.[110] Schumer referred to the President's remarks when introducing the amendment,[111] and just why the President made the suggestion is unknown. Perhaps he was seeking to immunize himself from criticism of loans that he had received when he was in business.[112] But whatever the reason, his remarks appear to have been a decisive

officials stated that the two did not discuss the legislation. *See* Neil A. Lewis, *Securities Bill Becomes Law as the Senate Overrides Veto*, N.Y. Times, Dec. 23, 1995, at 39.

[107] Clinton had vetoed other tort reform legislation passed by the Republican Congress, *See* Don Van Natta Jr. with Richard A. Oppel Jr., *Memo Linking Political Donation and Veto Spurs Federal Inquiry*, N.Y. Times, Sept. 14, 2000, at A1, and President Bush ran on tort reform, among other issues, *See* Leslie Wayne, *Trial Lawyers Pour Money into Democrats' Chests*, N.Y. Times, Mar. 23, 2000, at A1. When the Democrats took control of the Senate in 2001, tort reform was "written off as dead" by lobbyists. Leslie Wayne, *Senate Shifts, So Lobbyists Who Seek To Influence Its Legislation Scramble To Shift, Too*, N.Y. Times, June 9, 2001, at A16.

[108] *See* 148 Cong. Rec. S6534 (daily ed. July 10, 2002) (motion dividing the Leahy Amendment); *id.* at S6535 (colloquy between Sens. Sarbanes and Gramm) (linking the division and cloture motions); *id.* at S6538 (statement of Sen. Gramm) (describing agreement).

[109] *Id.* at S6690 (daily ed. July 12, 2002). Because the Senate was operating under the cloture time limits, this was essentially the only way new amendments could be made to the bill.

[110] *See* Press Release, White House, Summary: A New Ethic of Corporate Responsibility (July 9, 2002), *available at* http://www.whitehouse.gov/news/releases/2002/07/20020709.html. The White House's press release on the issue did not seem to indicate that the President was seeking a statutory rather than a voluntary termination of loans to executives, because his "call" to cease the practice was addressed to corporate compensation committees. The part of the release addressed to Congress was a request for action on a proposal for additional funds for the SEC.

[111] 148 Cong. Rec. S6690 (daily ed. July 12, 2002) (statement of Sen. Schumer).

[112] In an attempt to tie Bush to the corporate scandals, some Democrats had picked up on press reports that pointed out that he had received loans as a corporate officer in the 1980s. *E.g.*, *id.* at S6608 (daily ed.

factor in the inclusion of this provision, because such a provision had previously been rejected by the Banking Committee. Senator Sarbanes, the manager (and drafter) of the legislation, stated, when introducing the bill on the Senate floor, that the Banking Committee did not "go [as] far" as prohibiting loans to executives, as some had argued, but instead opted for a disclosure requirement, because "[s]ome testified there are some good reasons" for providing loans to officers "on occasion."[113]

The near-total absence of considered discourse on SOX's governance provisions in the Senate is consistent with the characterization of the corporate governance issues as being "below the radar screen" and "inside the Beltway." In the limited time frame available for legislative debate, senators did not focus any attention on the corporate governance provisions. Thus, as in the House, legislators who could not possibly be informed on technical issues and who felt that they had to act under the pressure of mounting corporate accounting scandals simply accepted the bill that was presented. That bill consisted of measures advocated by policy entrepreneurs (former government officials aligned largely with one political party), as filtered by the Banking Committee chairman. Many of those individuals were advancing proposals that they had previously advocated and that they believed would improve the quality of financial reporting, despite a virtually complete lack of data supporting their beliefs. With little attention accorded to the proposals in the committee hearings and even less attention on the floor, the disjuncture between the recommended policies and the empirical literature was never even acknowledged, as might have been possible if the legislative process had not been operating in a crisis atmosphere.[114]

The policy entrepreneurs on whom the Democrats relied in the context of the highly publicized and time-restricted deliberation over SOX—Arthur Levitt, the former SEC chairman, and Lynn Turner, who had been chief accountant during Levitt's tenure—are the key to understanding why Congress enacted a series of provisions that are ill-matched to fulfill their stated objectives. During Levitt's term as chairman, empirical research

July 11, 2002) (statement of Sen. Byrd) ("I ask . . . to have printed in the Record an article from today's *Washington Post* titled 'Bush Took Oil Firm's Loans as Director'; and an article from today's *Washington Times* titled 'Cheney Named in Fraud Suit.'" (capitalization altered)).

[113] *Id.* at S6332, S6332-33 (daily ed. July 8, 2002) (statement of Sen. Sarbanes).

[114] The committee hearings are discussed *infra* Section II.C. Corporate governance proposals were often suggested in witnesses' written statements but not emphasized in their oral testimony, and consequently such proposals did not receive much attention from the legislators participating in the hearings. The Chamber of Commerce lobbied against several provisions of the bill, *see, e.g.*, Letter from R. Bruce Josten, Executive Vice President, Government Affairs, U.S. Chamber of Commerce, to Members of the United States Senate (July 15, 2002) [hereinafter Chamber Senate Letter], *available at* http://www.uschamber.com/issues/letters/2002/020715s2673.htm (discussing the Public Company Accounting Reform and Investor Protection Act of 2002), but when WorldCom collapsed, the lobbying process shut down, and the Republicans, who had up to then taken seriously the business community's objections, reversed course and accepted the Democrats' bill. *See Top of Their Game*, *supra* note 102. As one commentator put it, "[T]he Chamber [of Commerce] called on Congress to be 'cautious' in its final considerations of the measure. Congress' answer: fat chance in an election year." Peter Mayberry & Jessica Franken, *Legislation Targets Stock Scandals*, Nonwovens Industry, Sept. 2002, at 20, 22.

was accorded little weight in the setting of regulation. This fact is made plain by the SEC's response while he was chairman to the Panel on Audit Effectiveness's failure to find that the provision of nonaudit services compromised audit quality. In the release on the proposed auditor independence rules restricting nonaudit services, the agency summarily dismissed the concern raised by the accounting profession that, in light of the Panel's report, there was no evidence of a connection between the provision of nonaudit services and accounting fraud or audit compromise. The SEC stated that "[s]tudies cannot always confirm what common sense makes clear."[115] The Panel, it should be recalled, was created at Levitt's request. Not surprisingly, a statute informed by Levitt's perspective would not be responsive to the concerns of a literature that did not fit with his preconceptions.

c. Why Did the Republicans Support the Democrats' Bill?

The difficult political environment provides the context for why the Republicans voted for a bill influenced by Democratic policy advisers whose views were at odds with their own political viewpoint and that of important constituents. That environment would have limited Republicans' ability to use the empirical literature supporting their position, had they recognized or assimilated it. But there was another important factor affecting the Republicans' resolve to maneuver against the Democrats' bill. A united business community can be a powerful political force, although its political clout is often misunderstood and overstated,[116] but SOX was not, in the end, a unifying issue. The business community split over the Senate bill: The Business Roundtable, whose membership consists of large corporations, supported that bill, while the Chamber of Commerce, which has many small-firm members,[117] did not.

The different positions of the business umbrella organizations on the Senate bill can plausibly be explained by the disparity in expected compliance costs for the organizations' members regarding the accounting and certification measures: The small and

---

[115] Revision of the Commission's Auditor Independence Requirements, 65 Fed. Reg. 43,148, 43,155 (July 12, 2000).

[116] Mark Smith has carefully demonstrated that when business unites behind legislation, labor tends to be united on the other side. As a consequence, if business "wins" it is because public opinion and election outcomes are tilting toward business's policy position and not because of financial leverage exerted by business over legislators. MARK A. SMITH, AMERICAN BUSINESS AND POLITICAL POWER: PUBLIC OPINION, ELECTIONS, AND DEMOCRACY (2000). As Smith details, issues that unify business tend to be ideological (the issue separates liberals and conservatives), partisan (the issue separates Democrats and Republicans), and salient (the issue is highly visible to the public). Thus, Smith finds that in these issue contexts, direct resources or forms of power wielded by business (through campaign contributions and lobbying capacity) do not explain legislative outcomes, but public opinion polls reflecting attitudes toward business and the partisan composition of elected lawmakers do.

[117] The overwhelming majority of the Chamber's members are small firms, although larger firms provide more of the organization's revenues (because dues are payable on a sliding scale) and have dominated its board of directors. *Id.* at 49. Smith considers the Chamber's positions "in their entirety" to "demonstrate a reasonable balance between big and small business." *Id.*

medium-sized firms that are the membership base of the Chamber of Commerce were expected to find it far more costly to meet the proposed legislative mandates than large firms.[118] Accordingly, the Chamber supported an amendment proposed by Senator Gramm to permit the new accounting regulator to exempt small businesses from the nonaudit services prohibitions (it was not enacted).[119] A further source of divergence between the positions of the Business Roundtable and the Chamber of Commerce may have been the accounting scandals' concentration among the largest public corporations. Roundtable members may have thought that by supporting the legislative proposal perceived to be tougher on corporate crime and accountability, they would be distancing themselves in the public mind from scandal-tinged firms, a factor of little moment to smaller businesses.

When core constituents are divided on an issue, there is no obvious winner or loser for a legislator to support. With the media criticizing the Republicans' bill, compared to the Democrats' bill, as too lax toward corporate wrongdoers (accountants and executives), the split among key business constituents gave Republicans little reason to insist on their bill and risk alienating other constituents, individuals whose pension and stock portfolios had declined precipitously in the wake of the corporate scandals.

It is possible that many Senate Republicans had closer connections to the Chamber than to the Roundtable (because all states have many Chamber members) and voted for the Democratic bill consistent with their stated reason for seeking its quick adoption, to get to conference and negotiate a final bill closer to the House bill that the Chamber preferred. But there were some other plausible benefits for Republicans from expediting the process. The issue of corporate accountability that was implicated by the accounting scandals was considered a Democratic issue, and Republicans feared that Democrats would gain in the midterm elections if no legislation was enacted and Republican candidates could be portrayed as "soft" on corporate crime.[120] In addition,

---

[118] For example, several members of Congress expressed concern that the nonaudit services prohibition would adversely affect small businesses, which relied on their outside accountants more for a variety of services than [did] large firms. *E.g.*, 148 Cong. Rec. S6335 (daily ed. July 8, 2002) (statement of Sen. Gramm); *id.* at S6339 (statement of Sen. Enzi); *id.* at S6693 (daily ed. July 12, 2002) (statement of Sen. Santorum). For evidence that the expectation that SOX would be costlier for small firms was correct, see *infra* notes 188-193 and accompanying text.

[119] Letter from R. Bruce Josten, Executive Vice President, Government Affairs, U.S. Chamber of Commerce, to Members of the United States Senate (July 11, 2002), *available at* http://www.uschamber.com/issues/letters/2002/020711s2673a.htm ("Support Senator Gramm's Amendment to S. 2673"). Gramm's amendment was introduced with the stated purpose of "provid[ing] the Board with appropriate flexibility in applying non-audit services restrictions to small businesses." 148 Cong. Rec. S6537-38 (daily ed. July 10, 2002) (amendment no. 4184 to division 1 of amendment no. 4174). The amendment was introduced in conjunction with Gramm's motion to divide the Leahy Amendment, as an amendment to the amendment calling for the division. *Id.* But the amendment was never voted on in the wake of the compromise that followed Gramm's motion: Gramm withdrew his amendments in exchange for the agreement to vote on cloture. *See supra* note 111 and accompanying text.

[120] *E.g.*, Amy Borrus & Mike McNamee, *Accounting: Congress Only Looks like It's Getting Tough*, Bus. Wk., Apr. 29, 2002, at 51. Democrats actively sought to associate Republicans, and especially the Bush

an expedited process limiting the time spent considering the bill would provide one less reason for the public to have a negative view of Congress. Political scientists have found that public opinion is least approving of Congress when members engage in open partisan debate and conflict over legislation—that is, attitudes toward Congress are influenced not simply by the policies produced but by the processes that make those policies.[121] Limited consideration and quick floor passage of the bill curtailed partisan debate and shifted discussion of the issues out of the public spotlight. Electoral concerns were thereby addressed at the cost of a comprehensive consideration of the implications of the legislation.

It is far from clear how realistic the Republicans' expectation of achieving a better result in the conference committee was at the time of the floor debate: Some studies by political scientists, for example, have suggested that the Senate has the upper hand in conference.[122] But whatever the merits of the strategy, with hindsight, the calculation proved to be seriously mistaken. The conference compromise strategy unraveled as a rapidly changing environment made the political landscape considerably more hostile to the Republicans' less regulation-oriented position once the conference committee

---

Administration, with corporate crime. *E.g.*, 148 CONG. REC. S6749 (daily ed. July 15, 2002) (statement of Sen. Grassley). Grassley explained,

> I have heard . . . during . . . news conferences . . . Democrats wishing to use Enron and WorldCom events very much as, I think, political issues. I think maybe the Democrats are hoping for a "November storm" in which our economy is weak and no progress is made on accounting reforms.
>
> . . . [T]he distinguished majority leader on "Face the Nation" recently attributed the current crisis to the alleged "permissive" attitude in the Bush administration towards business.

Id. For a summary of efforts to connect the Bush Administration to the corporate scandals and suggestions about why the scandal-stoking efforts failed, see ROMANO, *supra* note 19, at 131-32 & nn.254-57.

[121] John R. Hibbing & James T. Smith, *What the American Public Wants Congress To Be, in* CONGRESS RECONSIDERED 45, 46-52, 58-63 (Lawrence C. Dodd & Bruce I. Oppenheimer eds., 7th ed. 2001). It should be noted that the idea that partisan debate produces negative consequences may be limited to modern Congresses (the data from which the hypothesis is derived and tested are from post-World War II Congresses, so the relation may not hold historically). Moreover, many members of Congress appear to behave as if this were not true, because they often engage in intensive partisan debate.

[122] For a review of studies indicating Senate dominance in conference, *see* WILLIAM J. KEEFE & MORRIS S. OGUL, THE AMERICAN LEGISLATIVE PROCESS: CONGRESS AND THE STATES 181-82, 204 nn.35-39 (8th ed. 1993). The studies reviewed do not provide much in the way of a theoretical explanation for this phenomenon, except to note that, in the appropriations context in some of the studies, the Senate is required to move second. Keefe and Ogul caution that it is difficult to tell who "wins" given the complexity of legislation. Other political scientists emphasize that the Senate's rules give it an advantage in conference: The greater power of individual senators to hold up legislation translates into a supermajority vote necessary for that chamber's adoption of the conference's output, compared to only a majority in the House. Barbara Sinclair, *The New World of U.S. Senators, in* CONGRESS RECONSIDERED, *supra* note 124, at 1, 17. But it is most likely impossible for there to be any long-term, predictable, systematic institutional difference in conference success rates. That is because the losing chamber would become cognizant of that fact and adapt its legislative strategies to offset the disadvantage, such as by revising the initial content of proposed bills to alter the nature of the conference bargaining process to its advantage or by otherwise redesigning its procedural rules.

convened. That is, events overtook them: Intensive scrutiny by the media, calling for government action and attacking the House bill as inadequate,[123] took a toll in the wake of additional revelations of accounting irregularities at WorldCom, its subsequent bankruptcy filing, and the continued tanking of the stock market. Members of Congress feared that there might be additional revelations of corporate misconduct that would further depress the market and make corporate scandals a potent reelection issue. Internal polls indicated that public confidence was dropping, which contributed to Republican concern that any delay in acting on corporate governance legislation (i.e., not adopting the Democrats' bill) would be "politically perilous."[124] As a lobbyist for the Chamber of Commerce, which opposed the Senate bill, put it, "When the WorldCom scandal hit, it became, to me, a bit of a—a very different attitude and atmosphere, if not a political tsunami . . . ."[125]

These factors—a media frenzy and the precipitous drop in the stock market, in conjunction with reelection concerns—led the conference committee to act quickly and report a bill virtually identical to the Senate bill, with only a few minor changes (such as inclusion of the House's lengthier criminal sanctions).[126] That is, the Republicans capitulated to the Democrats' bill. As House Minority Leader Richard Gephardt put it, the Republicans' action was "an unconditional surrender."[127] This may well have been a prudent decision for Republicans from the perspective of their electoral ambitions. As commentators have suggested, the electoral gains Republicans made in the 2002 election were due to national security (especially September 11) being the public's dominant concern rather than, as had been expected, corporate scandals, which were thought to be an issue favoring the Democrats.[128] The enactment of SOX may have contributed to a shift in public focus by removing corporate scandals from the public policy agenda.

---

[123] *E.g.*, Editorial, *Mr. Oxley Punts*, WASH. POST, Apr. 24, 2002, at A28. The intensified national network news coverage of the corporate scandals framed the issue as a "national and systemic problem" rather than one of "individual or corporate misdeeds," thus necessitating government action. Bowman, *supra* note 100.

[124] Gail Russell Chaddock, *Congressmen, Too, Feel Pocketbook Panic*, CHRISTIAN SCI. MONITOR, July 25, 2002, at 2.

[125] *World News Tonight*, *supra* note 10 (remarks of R. Bruce Josten, Executive Vice President, Gov't Affairs, U.S. Chamber of Commerce). For a discussion of lobbying expenditures on SOX, see ROMANO, *supra* note 19, at 198-201.

[126] Business groups advocated three changes to the bill: The two that limited the applicability of the certification requirement were adopted in conference, but the third, to eliminate the statute-of-limitations extension, was not. Hilzenrath et al., *supra* note 89.

[127] Jim Drinkard, *Deal Reached on Business Reform*, USA TODAY, July 25, 2002, at 1A.

[128] *E.g.*, Alan Ehrenhalt, *The Vast Right-Wing Conspiracy and How It Grew: Thoughts on Thirty Years of Politics, Remarks for the American Enterprise Institute's Bradley Lecture Series* (Nov. 3, 2003), *available at* http://www.aei.org/events/eventID.476,filter./event_detail.asp.

C. The Role of Policy Entrepreneurs

Given the general lack of interest in the SOX corporate governance mandates shown by legislators during the floor debate, to understand how those mandates came into being one must examine the deliberation process of the committees with legislative jurisdiction: the House Financial Services Committee and the Senate Banking Committee. Congressional hearings serve multiple functions in the formulation of public policy, often educating the public about proposed legislation more than legislators. As this Section details, public policy entrepreneurs, who were mostly former government officials, and the Senate Banking Committee chairman, Senator Sarbanes, were key formulators of SOX's corporate governance provisions. This may not have been fortuitous, because government officials (present and former) were the group consulted most often by the originating committees during the legislative process in seven House and ten Senate committee hearings held from December 2001 to April 2002, as indicated in Table 3. Virtually all of these individuals were associated in some capacity with the SEC.

Two important differences between the Senate and House committees' hearings should be noted at the outset, because they suggest why the Senate bill would have been more likely to contain governance mandates than the House bill, even controlling for the difference in majority party. First, while two House committee hearings were held on draft legislation (the majority and the minority bills), no Senate committee hearing was held on any bill, including the bill introduced on the floor.[129] By holding hearings on specific legislative proposals, the House process tightly focused witnesses' remarks. By contrast, Senate witnesses could range far more freely, because they were not directed to comment on particular bills. This may well have affected policy entrepreneurs' effectiveness, because they had greater ability to set the agenda of their testimony and could thereby more actively seek to shape legislative policy.

Second, the composition of the witnesses differed across the chambers. Remarkably, the Senate committee heard no witnesses from the business community, in contrast to the House, even though business was an anticipated object of regulation and ostensibly among the potential beneficiaries of the legislation. The business community would, for instance, benefit from any improvement in the quality of auditing accomplished by legislation. Instead, the Senate was more focused on the accounting profession; it heard from a larger number of accounting industry regulators and members than did the House.[130] Of course, it should be noted that witness lists are obviously not random.

---

[129] Most of the ten hearings the Senate committee held on Enron-related concerns focused on issues that were ultimately included in the reported bill, such as the structure of a new oversight agency for accountants and the prohibition on nonaudit services.

[130] Because all five of the Senate witnesses from the accounting industry were affiliated with the AICPA and testified on the same panel, the industry was not as well represented as it might appear. By segregating all of the industry's testimony into one session, with individuals expressing one institution's policy perspective, the potential impact of the testimony on senators and the public (through the media covering the hearings) was subtly diluted. By contrast, accounting regulators were also grouped together on panels, but they testified over several sessions, and consequently there was a greater opportunity for legislators to assimilate their positions and for the media to showcase their perspective. It should be noted

Table 3
Witnesses at Hearings of the Senate Banking, Housing, and Urban Affairs Committee and the House Financial Services Committee, 2001-2002

Witness Type	House hearing	House minority hearing	Senate hearing
Academics and policy analysts	1	1	6
Accounting industry	1	0	5
Accounting regulators	0	0	6
Business groups	3	0	0
Consumer groups	1	0	1
Enon/Arthur Andersen officials	3	0	0
Federal government officials (current or former)	6	2	10
Institutional investors	3	0	2
Other[1]	1	0	5
Securities analysts	1	0	2
Securities industry	1	0	1
Unions[2]	1	1	1
Total Witnesses	22	4	39

Notes: Data for the table were tabulated from *House CARTA Hearings, supra* note 77, and *Senate Hearings, supra* note 35. The House committee hearings were held on December 12, 2001; February 4 and 5, 2002; and March 13 and 20, 2002; the witnesses at the committee's hearing on Global Crossing on March 21, 2002 (one government official and seven executives from the company and industry) are not included in the table. The Democratic House minority held a hearing on April 9, 2002. The Senate committee hearings were held on February 12, 14, 26, and 27, 2002 and March 5, 6, 14, 19, 20, and 21, 2002. Two House witnesses (a government official and an Arthur Andersen official) appeared at two different House hearings and are therefore counted twice.

[1] The House witness in this category was an attorney. The Senate witnesses in this category were the former head of the FDIC, an accountant; an investment banker who chaired the Blue Ribbon Committee on Improving the Effectiveness of Corporate Audit Committees; a lawyer who served on the Blue Ribbon Committee; an accountant/investment bank partner who was deputy chair of the 1978 Cohen Commission on accounting; and an accountant who chaired the Panel on Audit Effectiveness.

[2] The union witness was invited to the House committee hearing at the request of the ranking minority member.

Committees select their witnesses. The presence or absence of a specific class of witnesses in a chamber is a conscious choice related to specific policy objectives.[131] The

---

that the SEC chief accountants are classified in Table 3 as government officials, not accounting regulators. Thus, the number of accounting regulators testifying (as compared to industry representatives) is even higher than appears in the table.

[131] Institutional differences may also have been a factor: In the House, as noted, the majority party exercises far greater control over the legislative process than in the Senate. Thus, the selection of witnesses

choice is significant because a hearing provides an opportunity to showcase potential legislation and may therefore be "orchestrated to make a record for (or against) a particular proposal."[132] Given that the chambers were controlled by different political parties, it is not surprising that their witnesses differed or that the corporate governance mandates were introduced in the Senate process, because the parties' policy objectives differed.[133]

1. Executive Loans

The origin of the executive loan provision in the Senate bill is the easiest of the corporate governance mandates to trace. At the initial Senate hearing, one witness expressed concern about executive loans. This was former SEC Chairman Richard Breeden, who recommended that all loans be disclosed in corporate proxies and, when above a specified amount, subject to shareholder approval.[134] This resonated with

---

might be expected to be more one-sided in the House than in the Senate. In this regard, it is instructive that the House minority demanded a hearing, which they had of right under the House rules. *House CARTA Hearings*, *supra* note 77, at 127 (statement of Rep. LaFalce). The focus of that hearing was a comparison of the Democrats' bill with that of the majority. It was held after the full committee's hearings were completed, immediately before the committee was to mark up the Republican bill. By contrast, the Senate minority expressed its satisfaction with the hearings conducted by Senator Sarbanes. *E.g.*, 148 CONG. REC. S6333 (daily ed. July 8, 2002) (statement of Sen. Gramm) ("I would like to say for the record that no one can object to the hearings we had, the approach the chairman has taken."); *id.* at S6338 (statement of Sen. Enzi) ("Had it been my choice to call the witnesses, I would have chosen nearly every person who testified.").

[132] KERNELL & JACOBSON, *supra* note 76, at 225. Hearings may also be used "to generate publicity for committee members as well as issues." *Id.* The hearings of other committees (not summarized in Table 3) investigating Enron's collapse, which summoned as witnesses Enron executives whom they knew would invoke their Fifth Amendment rights, tend to fall in this latter category.

[133] There was, in fact, little overlap between the House and Senate witnesses. Only six of sixty-three witnesses testified before both the House and Senate committees. Five were current or former government officials: Harvey L. Pitt (then the SEC chairman), Roderick M. Hills (SEC chairman, 1975-1977), and Lynn E. Turner (SEC chief accountant, 1998-2001, during Arthur Levitt's term as chairman) testified to both chambers' committees; Richard C. Breeden (SEC chairman, 1989-1993) and David M. Walker (comptroller general of the United States, serving a fifteen-year term as head of the GAO, to which he was appointed in 1998) testified at a Senate committee hearing and at the hearing held at the request of the minority of the House committee. The sixth witness, union official Damon A. Silvers (associate general counsel, AFL-CIO), testified to both committees, although his appearance before the House committee was specifically identified as having been at the request of the ranking minority member. Not included among the six are two organizations that were represented by different individuals in the two chambers, the Consumer Federation of America (whose representative for the Senate hearing was the chairman, a former senator) and TIAA-CREF. However, TIAA-CREF's Senate witness, Chairman John Biggs, appears to have been called not as a representative of that specific institutional investor but as a corporate governance expert because of his participation on the Blue Ribbon Committee (along with the other witness on his panel) and the Public Oversight Board (the other members of which testified on a subsequent Senate panel). *See* 1 *Senate Hearings*, *supra* note 35, at 342 (statement of Sen. Sarbanes).

[134] 1 *id.* at 62 (prepared statement of Richard Breeden). Breeden also suggested prohibiting the use of stock to repay loans. No other witnesses included the regulation of loans in their prepared statements.

Senator Sarbanes, who proceeded to ask six other witnesses (witnesses on two panels considered to have expertise in corporate governance) what they thought of Breeden's testimony regarding loans. Only one witness, former Democratic Senator Howard Metzenbaum, representing the Consumer Federation of America, thought that loans to officers should be banned.[135] The other witnesses queried—a prominent corporate governance attorney and representatives of institutional investors and the AFL-CIO—expressed support only for a disclosure provision.[136] Indeed, one of the witnesses noted that company loans originated for the legitimate purpose of assisting relocations and argued that it would "get[] very messy" if Congress were to say, "[Y]ou cannot ever lend money to an employee."[137]

The importance of the difference across the chambers in structuring witness testimony is well illustrated by the testimony on executive loans: Breeden was also a witness at the House hearing on the minority bill, but he did not mention the issue of executive loans in his House testimony.[138] His written statement responded to specific questions posed by the committee to the witnesses in advance, none of which explicitly mentioned loans. Although the questions mentioned corporate governance and disclosure of conflicts of interests, Breeden did not take the opportunity to include a recommendation regarding loan disclosure in any of his responses. Because his testimony to the House occurred two months after he had testified to the Senate, whatever the reason for the omission, it was not because the issue had not occurred to him. It is possible that Breeden did not refer to loans because the House bill contained a loan disclosure provision, but he specifically addressed other provisions in the bill to commend or criticize their inclusion, so that would not appear to be a satisfactory explanation for the omission. This suggests an additional possibility: Corporate loan regulation was not high on Breeden's agenda. Indeed, disclosure of executive loans was only one of a number of proposals that Breeden had suggested to the Senate committee, and he raised one of those other ideas in his written House responses.[139] Sarbanes mulled over Breeden's proposal regarding

---

[135] 2 *id.* at 1024 (statement of Howard Metzenbaum).

[136] 1 *id.* at 370 (statements of John H. Biggs, Chairman, TIAA-CREF, and Ira M. Millstein, Attorney and Co-Chairman, Blue Ribbon Comm. on Improving the Effectiveness of Corporate Audit Comms.); 2 *id.* at 1024, 1026 (statement of Sarah Teslik, Executive Dir., Council of Institutional Investors); 2 *id.* at 1025 (statement of Damon A. Silvers, Assoc. Gen. Counsel, AFL-CIO); 2 *id.* at 1026 (statement of Thomas A. Bowman, President, Ass'n for Inv. Mgmt. & Research).

[137] 2 *id.* at 1026 (statement of Sarah Teslik).

[138] In the House hearings, executive loans came up only once, at an early hearing held before a bill had been drafted (and before Breeden's testimony to the Senate), when a representative asked Pitt whether he thought a "more efficient disclosure mechanism" was needed for insiders selling stock back to their companies and, more generally, for all executive loans. *Enron Hearings II*, *supra* note 77, at 44 (statement of Rep. Bentsen). Pitt replied that the SEC needed to take a closer look, because more disclosure might be needed, and that the agency probably had sufficient authority to take care of disclosure issues, but he added that he could "understand why Congress might deem it appropriate to legislate here." *Id.* (statement of Harvey Pitt).

[139] Among Breeden's other proposals were moving to multiyear contracts for auditors with serious periodic review, instituting a cooling-off period before public corporations could hire a member of the outside audit team for a senior financial position, and requiring accounting firms to have independent boards of direc-

executive loans with other witnesses and adopted that approach in his bill, paralleling the provision in the House bill, which was neither inspired nor discussed by Breeden (nor any other House witness).

Whether Sarbanes would have included a disclosure provision if he had foreseen its transformation into an outright ban on the Senate floor cannot be ascertained in hindsight. It is probable that the prohibition would have been included as an amendment to the Senate bill even had there been no provision touching on loans. Given the timing of the President's remarks, it is unlikely that any senator would have objected, and the subject matter would surely have been deemed germane. But it is ironic that the avenue facilitating its inclusion—the loan disclosure provision—was an idea that appealed more to the committee chairman than to its originator, Richard Breeden, for whom it was one, and in all likelihood not the most important, of a series of proposals, most of which were not pursued by the committee.

2. *Independent Audit Committees*

The origin of the Senate provision requiring independent audit committees is a bit harder to trace than that of the loan provision. The composition of the audit committee was a concern emphasized by former SEC Chairman Roderick M. Hills in both chambers' earliest hearings, although his specific proposal was to require that members of the audit committee be appointed by nominating committees consisting exclusively of independent directors.[140] It should be noted that the initial stock exchange requirement of an audit committee occurred on his watch as SEC chairman, in 1974, in the wake of a corporate scandal involving sensitive payments to foreign officials.[141] Hills perceived his recommendation as being a timely and necessary follow-up to that legislation, that is, as the provision of a "legislative endorsement" or of a more formal legal status for audit committees.[142]

Other witnesses on the Senate panel with Hills also referred to the importance of independent audit committees or to a vague need to "enhance" their independence,

---

tors. 1 *Senate Hearings, supra* note 35, at 62, 65 (statement of Richard Breeden). Only the first of these was mentioned in his House statement, in response to a question regarding mandatory rotation. *House CARTA Hearings, supra* note 77, at 476 (statement of Richard Breeden). In response to a question regarding what corporate governance reforms were necessary, Breeden suggested disclosure of waivers of company ethics or conflicts codes and of any conflict of interest involving a senior officer. *Id.* at 473. Breeden was not the only witness to refer to a cooling-off period in the Senate hearings, and it was included in the bill.

[140] *House CARTA Hearings, supra* note 77, at 263 (statement of Roderick Hills); 1 *Senate Hearings, supra* note 35, at 83 (prepared statement of Roderick Hills).

[141] 1 *Senate Hearings, supra* note 35, at 78 (prepared statement of Roderick Hills). The foreign payment scandal also produced federal legislation, the Foreign Corrupt Practices Act of 1977, Pub. L. No. 95-213, 1977 U.S.C.C.A.N. (91 Stat.) 1494 (codified in scattered sections of 15 U.S.C.), which prohibited such payments and required public companies to adopt a system of internal controls.

[142] 1 *Senate Hearings, supra* note 35, at 92 (letter from Roderick M. Hills to Steve Harris, Majority Staff Dir., Senate Comm. on Banking, Hous., & Urban Affairs); *see also House CARTA Hearings, supra* note 77, at 48 (statement of Roderick Hills).

but they did not provide specific proposals.[143] In later sessions, however, witnesses made more concrete recommendations on independence similar to the provisions included in the Senate bill. Most notably, Lynn Turner stated that the stock exchange rules permitting exceptions to the requirement that all audit committee members be independent should be eliminated.[144] Another former SEC chief accountant, Michael Sutton, also recommended requiring completely independent audit committees.[145] The third former SEC chief accountant who testified on the panel, Walter Schuetze, stated that Enron's problems were inherent to current accounting rules (that assets and liabilities are not marked to market) rather than due to lack of auditor independence or oversight. He also provided copies of his articles discussing how accounting ought to be reformed, one of which referred to another article's "excellent discussion and analysis" of why the presence of independent audit committees cannot improve the quality of an audit.[146] He did not, however, challenge his copanelists' recommendations on audit committee composition, nor was he asked for his views on that matter, and the suggestion in his articles that independent audit committees would not alleviate the problem was not picked up by any senator. It was simply ignored.

The recommendation of the other two former SEC chief accountants regarding audit committee independence was not ignored, however. Senator Sarbanes, for example, stated at the outset of the Senate hearing that came after their testimony that suggestions had been "brought to [the committee's] attention to require stock exchanges to toughen board and committee independence standards."[147] The objective of that subsequent hearing was, in fact, "to consider numerous corporate governance issues raised by recent

---

[143] *E.g.*, 1 *id.* at 67 (written statement of Richard Breeden) (suggesting that states should "enhance audit committee independence" but offering no specific proposal); 1 *id.* at 73 (written statement of David S. Ruder, SEC Chairman, 1987-1989) (noting that the role of the audit committee is "particularly important" but providing no specific proposal); 1 *id.* at 75 (written statement of Harold M. Williams, SEC Chairman, 1977-1981) (noting the "need[] to address," among other topics, the composition of the board and audit committees but advancing no specific proposal).

[144] 1 *id.* at 198-99 (statement of Lynn Turner). Turner also advocated changing the definition of independence to prohibit payments on behalf of a director to charitable organizations. Audit committee independence did not come up in his testimony to the House, but his proposals to eliminate exceptions from the stock exchange rules on audit committee independence and to modify the definition of director independence were included in his written statement. *House CARTA Hearings*, *supra* note 77, at 288 (written statement of Lynn Turner).

[145] Sutton did not refer to this recommendation in his oral remarks but opined in his written statement that audit committees "should be made up of entirely independent directors." 1 *Senate Hearings*, *supra* note 35, at 243 (written statement of Michael H. Sutton, SEC Chief Accountant, 1995-1998). The written recommendation was picked up by Senator Zell Miller, who asked another witness, a corporate governance expert, what he thought of it. 1 *id.* at 362 (statement of Sen. Miller) (addressing Ira Millstein) ("Yesterday, Mr. Sutton went so far as to recommend that the audit committee ought to be made up entirely of independent directors. What do you think about that?").

[146] 1 *id.* at 291 (lecture given by Walter P. Schuetze, SEC Chief Accountant, 1992-1995); *See* 1 *id.* at 189-91 (statement of Walter P. Schuetze).

[147] 1 *id.* at 342 (statement of Sen. Sarbanes).

corporate difficulties," and among the issues Sarbanes identified as receiving "widespread attention" was the independence of directors and audit committees.[148] That day's panel was composed of two witnesses called as experts on corporate governance: Ira Millstein, a prominent corporate lawyer who was co-chair of the Blue Ribbon Committee on Improving the Effectiveness of Corporate Audit Committees, and John Biggs, the chief executive of the activist institutional investor TIAA-CREF who was a member of the Blue Ribbon Committee and the Public Oversight Board.

Neither of the corporate governance expert witnesses' statements referred to audit committee composition. When asked whether audit committees should consist solely of independent directors, both witnesses replied that that was already the practice (a reason, presumably, for their not addressing the matter in their prepared remarks).[149] Millstein had recommended requiring (through the SEC's encouragement of a new stock exchange listing requirement) a substantial majority of the board, and all the members of the nominating and compensation committees, to be independent.[150] In this regard, Millstein echoed the position of former SEC Chairman Hills concerning the need for independent nominating committees. But a more relevant comparison is the similarity of his approach to policy proposals with that of former Chairman Levitt. Millstein in his testimony never referred to the existence of a literature at odds with his position on board independence, of which he was fully aware, given that he had coauthored an article at variance with the literature on the point.[151] The literature was instead treated as though it did not exist. The committee bill did not follow his further suggestions, however; it focused solely on audit committee composition.

As with the issue of executive loans, Sarbanes also asked the witnesses on the second panel devoted to corporate governance their views on the need to strengthen audit committee independence, referring to Hills's testimony regarding the relation between audit and nominating committees. The reaction of this panel was similar to that of the prior panel. None of the witnesses offered specific responses directed at the composition

---

148 1 *id.* at 341.

149 1 *id.* at 362 (statement of Ira Millstein) (stating that independence is already required by stock exchanges); 1 *id.* (statement of John Biggs) (stating that independence is "pretty standard now").

150 1 *id.* at 354, 362 (statement of Ira Millstein). Although Congress did not pick up on this suggestion, the stock exchanges thereafter amended their listing requirements to require listed companies to have a majority of independent directors on their boards and completely independent nominating and compensation committees. Self-Regulatory Organizations, NYSE and NASD, Order Approving Proposed Rules Changes, Exchange Act Release No. 34-48,745, 68 Fed. Reg. 64,154 (Nov. 4, 2003) (approving NYSE Final Rule, Final Corporate Governance Listing Standards (to be codified at NYSE Listing Manual § 303A) and NASD Amendments to Rules 4200 and 4350(c)).

151 Ira M. Millstein & Paul W. MacAvoy, *The Active Board of Directors and Performance of the Large Publicly Traded Corporation*, 98 COLUM. L. REV. 1283, 1296-98 (1998).

of the audit committee.[152] But in written documents provided to the committee, they recommended requiring that a majority of the board be independent.[153]

Finally, four Senate witnesses raised the independence of the audit (or nominating) committee in their testimony, but only one actually recommended complete independence of the audit committee, and that was a circumspect recommendation.[154] An equal number of witnesses emphasized the need for audit committee members to have greater auditing, finance, and accounting expertise.[155] None of the witnesses expressed

---

[152] Their written statements referred to tightening the definition of independence, as had Millstein's testimony. 1 *Senate Hearings*, *supra* note 35, at 354, 362 (statement of Ira Millstein) (advocating standardizing the definition of director independence to the stock exchange definition for the audit committee, which followed the Blue Ribbon Committee's definition); 2 *id.* at 1040 (prepared statement of Howard M. Metzenbaum, Chairman, Consumer Fed'n of Am.) (advocating that stock exchanges adopt the entire independence recommendation of the Blue Ribbon Committee); 2 *id.* at 1057 (response of Sarah Teslik to written questions of Sen. Akaka) (advocating tightening the independence definition). Their responses to Sarbanes's question regarding audit committee independence were not directly on point: Metzenbaum's response was to suggest that a procedure be developed whereby "outside sources" would recommend whom to put on the audit committee, rather than have management select them, while Teslik's response was to suggest having audit committees select the auditor and certify their firm's financials. 2 *id.* at 1022-23 (statement of Sarah Teslik).

[153] 2 *id.* at 1040 (prepared statement of Howard Metzenbaum) (recommending that exchanges be pressed to adopt a listing requirement that a majority of the board be independent, and tighter definitions of independence); 2 *id.* at 1048 (prepared statement of Thomas A. Bowman, President and CEO, Ass'n for Inv. Mgmt. & Research) (recommending requiring that at least half of the directors be independent, along with board rather than management appointment of the members of the audit, nominating, and compensation committees); 2 *id.* at 1057 (response of Sarah Teslik to written questions of Sen. Akaka) (recommending requiring that two-thirds of the board be independent). Arthur Levitt also expressed the opinion that stock exchanges should adopt listing standards requiring a majority of independent directors on boards, but he did not advocate that as a legislative reform. 1 *id.* at 14 (statement of Arthur Levitt).

[154] 2 *id.* at 533 (statement of Joel Seligman, Dean, Wash. Univ. Sch. of Law) (stating that he was "struck by the testimony" of Hills and recommending strengthening the independence of the audit committee and creating an independent nominating committee to appoint the audit committee); 2 *id.* at 554-55 (prepared statement of David M. Walker, Comptroller Gen. of the United States, GAO) (including, in a list of questions Congress needed to consider, whether independence rules for audit committees were adequate); 2 *id.* at 876 (prepared statement of Robert E. Litan, Vice President & Dir., Econ. Studies Program, The Brookings Inst.) (noting that the "best" available option for increasing auditors' incentives to improve performance was to require all members of audit committees to be independent but cautioning that this option was not perfect because management influences who is on the committee and because committees would have to spend much more time than in current practice and be compensated more highly); 2 *id.* at 968 (prepared statement of L. William Seidman, former Chairman, FDIC, and former Chairman, Resolution Trust Corp.) (noting there are many independence rules in place for audit committees, arguing for the need to take care not to unduly burden those committees because doing so would reduce the availability of good directors to serve, and recommending independent nominating committees).

[155] *See* 2 *id.* at 691 (statement of Arthur R. Wyatt, Professor of Accountancy, Emeritus, Univ. of Ill., and former Chairman, AICPA Accounting Standards Executive Comm. & Int'l Accounting Standards Comm.); 2 *id.* at 819 (statement of James G. Castellano, Chairman, AICPA); 2 *id.* at 826 (statement of Olivia F. Kirtley, former Chairman, AICPA, and retired Vice President and CFO, Vt. Am. Corp.); 2 *id.* at 920 (statement of John C. Whitehead, Co-Chair, Blue Ribbon Comm., former Co-Chairman, Goldman Sachs & Co., and former Deputy Sec'y of State).

the slightest awareness of a literature bearing on whether director independence (on the audit committee or on the board as a whole) or expertise matters for either audit quality or corporate performance. It is therefore understandable that an audit committee independence requirement was viewed as unproblematic: The idea had been advanced by former high-ranking government officials who were well regarded by many members of the Senate Banking Committee, the committee chairman found the idea attractive, and the committee never had to confront the inconvenient reality that there was a relevant literature whose learning was starkly at odds with this regulatory focus. As far as the committee was concerned, the literature did not exist.

Again, a comparison with the more focused House hearings is instructive. In the House hearings, only a few witnesses raised the issue of audit committee independence, and none advocated requiring a majority of independent directors on the board.[156] Hills testified to the House committee as he had to the Senate committee, and although he again emphasized the importance of the audit committee, his proposal focused on the nominating committee, noting his concern that an audit committee could not be independent unless it was appointed by an independent nominating committee.[157] In the House hearings, only one witness suggested a need for completely independent audit committees, and a few witnesses emphasized a need for greater expertise.[158] Again, no witness referred to or indicated any awareness of the existence of a scholarly literature on director independence. In addition, two witnesses who were asked by House Democrats for their opinion of Hills's testimony did not directly endorse his position.[159]

---

[156] The written statement of the witness representing TIAA-CREF noted the organization's position in favor of majority-independent boards and completely independent audit, compensation, and nominating committees, but the statement did not include requiring director independence in its list of needed reforms. *House CARTA Hearings*, *supra* note 77, at 399, 401 (prepared statement of Peter C. Clapman, Senior Vice President & Chief Counsel, Corporate Governance, TIAA-CREF).

[157] *Id.* at 55 (testimony of Roderick Hills). On this occasion Hills also noted that Enron, as it happened, had an independent nominating committee. *Id.*

[158] *Id.* at 11 (statement of Barry C. Melancon, President and CEO, AICPA) (stating that audit committees "should be composed of outside directors with auditing, accounting, or financial expertise"); *id.* at 104 (statement of Philip B. Livingston, President and CEO, Fin. Executives Int'l) (advocating tougher requirements for financial expertise for audit committee members); *id.* at 113, 388-408 (statement and written testimony of Jerry J. Jasinowski, President, Nat'l Ass'n of Mfrs.) (indicating support for the idea in the ranking Democrat's bill on independent nominating committees, while opining that legislation might not be necessary, but not including, in the written testimony, any proposed reforms regarding any board committee's independence, although stating that audit committee members should have expertise); *id.* at 229 (prepared statement of Ted White, Dir. of Corporate Governance, CalPERS) (advocating requiring more than one audit committee member with expertise).

[159] *Id.* at 76 (testimony of Harvey L. Pitt, Chairman, SEC) (responding, to a question from Representative LaFalce for his opinion on Hills's testimony regarding independent nominating committees, that he considered the suggestion "constructive" and noting that the SEC had asked the stock exchanges to "come forward with corporate governance standards"); *id.* at 118 (statement of Franklin D. Raines, Chairman and CEO, Fannie Mae, and Chairman, Corp. Governance Task Force, Bus. Roundtable) (responding, to a question from Representative Carolyn Maloney, for his opinion on Hills's testimony regarding the need to give "legal status" to audit committees and to have independent audit committees appointed by

No doubt, the difference in testimony and emphasis on audit committee independence across the chambers reflects the difference in party control: This was not a top concern of Republicans in the House, and the witnesses they called either were also not interested in the issue or determined it was best to direct their attention to matters the majority deemed a priority. In fact, even the ranking Democrat, Representative John LaFalce, who considered reform of boards' and audit committees' independence a top priority, in contrast to the Republicans who did not mention the issue, indicated that he believed legislation was unnecessary because committee independence was within the SEC's rulemaking authority.[160] Accordingly, the difference in agenda control and dynamics across the chambers on the issue of audit committee independence sheds light on the difference in the content of the chambers' bills: No witnesses before the House explicitly advocated legislation on independent audit committees, fewer witnesses raised the issue there than in the Senate, and the House committee chairman did not latch onto the idea as worthy of pursuit.

3. Executive Certification of Financial Statements

The origin of the executive certification requirement can be related briefly, because it presents a similar pattern to the other two provisions, although it was a focus of less attention. In the Senate, former SEC chief accountant Turner was the first to recommend the requirement, which he noted was a practice followed in foreign jurisdictions.[161] Thereafter, three other witnesses expressed support for a certification requirement as an incentive device to improve reporting.[162] These endorsements were volunteered,

---

independent nominating committees, that audit committees already have status in corporations; objecting to designating any committee as independent of the board; and noting that audit committees "should be populated by independent directors" and that directors should be appointed by board nominating committees). The Business Roundtable's Statement on Corporate Governance advocates that a "substantial majority" of the board be independent, although it considers appropriate a less restrictive definition of independence for the full board than the stock exchanges require for audit committee members. *Id.* at 339 (written statement of the Bus. Roundtable).

[160] *See id.* at 4, 55 (statement of Rep. LaFalce). Thus there was no provision regarding audit committee composition in LaFalce's substitute bill. *See* HOUSE COMM. ON RULES, PROVIDING FOR CONSIDERATION OF H.R. 3763, CORPORATE AND AUDITING ACCOUNTABILITY, RESPONSIBILITY, AND TRANSPARENCY ACT OF 2002, H.R. REP. NO. 107-418, at 7 (2002).

[161] 1 *Senate Hearings*, *supra* note 35, at 199 (statement of Lynn Turner).

[162] 2 *id.* at 943 (prepared statement of Charles A. Bowsher, Chairman, Pub. Oversight Bd., and former Comptroller Gen. of the United States) (stating that management should have to attest to compliance with internal controls in an annual SEC document, which the auditor would review, as a procedure to improve the quality of audits); 2 *id.* at 1023, 1041 (testimony and prepared statement of Sarah Teslik) (stating that the CEO and the audit committee should have to sign financials to make them think twice, just as individuals do when signing tax returns); 2 *id.* at 1068 (statement of Harvey Pitt) (stating that the SEC intended to implement the President's directive to require executive certification of financials in order to improve financial reporting by increasing individual accountability for disclosure). In addition, one witness, who advocated more frequent financial reporting despite objections that the information would be unaudited, referred to the Administration's proposal to require certification of quarterly as well

because Senator Sarbanes did not seek other witnesses' views on Turner's proposal. Sarbanes's lack of follow-up on Turner's suggestion may well have been a function of a lack of interest in the recommendation. The certification requirement was, in fact, the one governance mandate to which Sarbanes did not refer in his remarks on the Senate floor during the deliberations on SOX. A week after Turner's testimony, President Bush announced a ten-point plan for improving corporate responsibility, which included a similar certification requirement, and the SEC indicated that it intended to implement that proposal on its own.[163] These comments were, without doubt, critical to the certification requirement's inclusion in the committee bill, given Sarbanes's low level of personal interest in it. The legislative history notes that the bill "in effect" adopted Bush's proposal, while crediting the precise formulation to Senator Zell Miller,[164] who was a crucial committee vote in Sarbanes's effort to produce a bipartisan bill.[165]

In contrast to the Senate, only one witness at the House hearings raised the issue of executive certification of financials. That witness was once again Turner, who now endorsed the Administration's suggestion of certification in response to questions by ranking member LaFalce on how to improve auditor independence and on the need to restructure audit committees.[166] The House hearing was held after the President had announced his corporate responsibility proposals, but also after the Republicans had drafted their bill, which did not include a certification provision. Because the President's proposal did not require legislative action—the SEC could (and did) implement it under its own rulemaking authority—the House Republicans did not have to amend their bill for the proposal to move forward. Nor did Republicans need to include a certification requirement in their legislation to distinguish themselves from the Administration, which might have been a concern for Democrats.

In fact, many of the points in President Bush's ten-point plan did not require legislative action because they were hortatory or could be executed by the SEC (and some were already on the SEC's agenda).[167] Four of Bush's ten points did call for action,

as annual financials as one that might mitigate the objection, depending on the sanctions, even though the quarterly data would still be unaudited. 2 *id.* at 878 (prepared statement of Robert E. Litan, Vice President and Dir., Econ. Studies Program, The Brookings Inst.).

[163] 2 *id.* at 1068 (statement of Harvey Pitt); Press Release, *supra* note 55.

[164] S. REP. NO. 107-205, at 25 (2002).

[165] Hilzenrath et al., *supra* note 89. As noted in ROMANO, *supra* note 19, at 150 n.294, 163 n.326, 184 n.364, Miller appears to have been the median voter on the committee, the voter whose preferences determine the outcome in standard political science voting models of two-party systems.

[166] *House CARTA Hearings*, *supra* note 77, at 55 (testimony of Lynn Turner). Although at the time LaFalce expressed skepticism about whether certification would be adequate, *id.* at 56 (statement of Rep. LaFalce), the only other reference to a certification requirement in the House hearings was by the congressman himself, when he referred in passing to such a provision's inclusion in the bill that he had just introduced at the April hearing called at his request, *id.* at 129.

[167] These included a call for investors' access to necessary information on a quarterly basis, a call for investors' "prompt access to critical information," a call for the "authors of accounting standards" to be responsive to investors' needs, a call for auditors to compare firms' accounting systems with "best practices" and not "minimum standards," and the statement that "[i]nvestors should have complete confidence in the

which the SEC began to implement, but in contrast to the certification requirement, these proposals also appeared in the House bill: the call for an independent regulatory board for accountants (Harvey Pitt's plan), the SEC's ban on officers who "abuse their power" from serving on corporate boards, forfeiture of executive bonuses based on financial statements if the statements were false, and more timely disclosure of insider trading.[168]

A plausible conjecture explaining the difference between the House bill's posture on these provisions and on the certification requirement is that the U.S. Chamber of Commerce supported the forfeiture provision and the officer ban but was concerned about the certification requirement.[169] The Chamber sent a letter on the House bill the day of the floor debate expressing opposition to any amendment that would weaken or repeal the 1995 legislation that made private securities lawsuits more difficult to pursue.[170] Because the letter did not voice any concern regarding any provision in the bill, it is plausible to assume that the Republicans had factored in the Chamber's position in crafting their bill, and that the noticeable absence of a certification requirement—which was included in the ranking Democrat's bill paralleling the plank in the President's corporate governance program—reflected the Chamber's position at the time. This explanation is purely conjectural, however, because the Chamber took a public position on those issues in conjunction with its lobbying effort on the Senate's bill, at which time it expressed support for the forfeiture, officer ban, and certification provisions.[171]

independence and integrity of companies' auditors." Press Release, *supra* note 55. It should be noted that the rather vaguely formulated point regarding investor confidence in auditors was articulated differently in President Bush's speech that introduced the plan: In his remarks he called on the SEC to do "more to guard against conflicts of interest, requiring, for example, that an external auditor not be permitted to provide internal audits to the same client." Remarks at the Presentation of the Malcolm Baldridge National Quality Awards, *supra* note 55, at 372. As discussed earlier, the accounting profession had agreed to that restriction. *See supra* note 98.

168 Corporate and Auditing Accountability, Responsibility, and Transparency Act of 2002, H.R. 3763, 107th Cong. (2002); Press Release, *supra* note 55.

169 *See* Thomas S. Mulligan, *Reaction to Pitt's Proposal Is Mixed*, L.A. TIMES, June 28, 2002, at C4 (describing concern over whether the certification requirement was workable on the part of the president of the Chamber and other business leaders).

170 Letter from R. Bruce Josten, Executive Vice President, Government Affairs, U.S. Chamber of Commerce, to Members of the House of Representatives (Apr. 24, 2002), *available at* http://www.uschamber.com/issues/letters/2002/020424hr3763.htm. This issue was also raised in two letters to the Senate during its consideration of the legislation. Chamber Senate Letter, *supra* note 117; Letter from R. Bruce Josten, Executive Vice President, Government Affairs, U.S. Chamber of Commerce, to Members of the United States Senate (July 11, 2002), *available at* http://www.uschamber.com/issues/letters/2002/020711s2673c.htm.

171 Mulligan, *supra* note 175; Chamber Senate Letter, *supra* note 117. The Chamber opposed the Senate bill's prohibition on the provision of nonaudit services by auditors and its institution of the new accounting regulator as duplicative or in conflict with the SEC's oversight. Chamber Senate Letter, *supra* note 117. The Chamber had expressed opposition to Pitt's specific proposal for a new accounting oversight entity, which was unveiled after the House enacted its bill but prior to the Senate's action. Walter Hamilton, *SEC's Oversight Proposal Derided*, L.A. TIMES, June 21, 2002, at C1.

Still, representatives of the Chamber had earlier voiced concern over the certification requirement but not the other two proposals.

4. *Provision of Nonaudit Services*

The restriction of auditors' provision of nonaudit services attracted considerably more attention from witnesses in both chambers than the other mandates, because it had a history as a political issue. This would appear to have been an issue of greater concern to the Democrats than the Republicans, because the hearings in their control had a much higher number (as well as proportion) of witnesses speaking to the issue: thirty Senate witnesses compared to fourteen House witnesses, three of whom testified at the minority's hearing. But only about half of the witnesses addressing the issue in either chamber expressed a view supporting prohibition or a more restrictive approach to the matter than the accounting profession's position, which was embodied in the House Republicans' bill.[172] The testimony of the witnesses does not have to be examined, however, to identify the policy entrepreneur behind the nonaudit services provision. Its source, as mentioned earlier, was Arthur Levitt, who led the SEC's initiative on the issue two years before.

Levitt was able to advance his agenda of a total ban on the provision of nonaudit services by auditors now that the accounting profession had landed in Congress's cross hairs with the apparent involvement in Enron's financial statement fraud of its auditor, Arthur Andersen. Levitt and Turner displayed the skills of expert legislative-agenda-setting entrepreneurs: Through their testimony during the hearings (and additional off-stage communication, including considerable media exposure), they were able to link the scandal with Levitt's position on auditors' provision of consulting services and with the accounting profession's successful opposition to his agenda to ban such services while he was SEC chairman. Members of Congress who had supported the accounting industry against Levitt's efforts to ban nonaudit services in the rulemaking process less than two years earlier hastily abandoned that position in the aftermath of Enron.[173] But in contrast to the other corporate governance mandates, the testimony on this provision underscores the problematic relation between entrepreneurial policymaking, issue salience, and the quality of legislative decisionmaking implicated by SOX. Three of the witnesses who opposed expanding the restrictions on nonaudit services made reference to data—that there was no evidence that the provision of nonaudit services

---

[172] For details regarding the classification of the witnesses' positions, see ROMANO, *supra* note 19, at 166 n.333.

[173] *E.g.*, 2 *Senate Hearings*, *supra* note 35, at 1061 (statement of Sen. Bunning) ("I was one of those who urged [Levitt] to slow down a little on the auditor independence issue. I thought he was trying to ram a major rule through and taking side in an industry fight without the proper vetting. Though I still think that we were moving just a little too fast at the time, I think that we must have a true auditor independence. Although the firms have split off their consulting arms, we should codify that split into law. If you audit someone, you should not be able to do their business consulting.").

compromises audit quality—to support their position.[174] However, only one of the witnesses testifying in favor of prohibition or greater restrictions on nonaudit services even acknowledged the existence of empirical findings contrary to that position, let alone attempted to distinguish them.

The position of that witness, Lee Seidler, was unique: He had served on a 1978 AICPA commission that did not prohibit consulting services because it found no evidence that such services compromised audits, and he had been asked to testify on a panel with the chairman of the more recent Panel on Audit Effectiveness, which had reached the same conclusion. In contrast to other witnesses, circumstances appear to have compelled Seidler to address the data inconsistent with his policy stance, but he did so obliquely: He stated, in support of his position to restrict nonaudit services, that his "conclusion [was] not based on empirical evidence."[175] It should be noted that

---

[174] Of sixty-three witnesses in the seventeen hearings held by the House and the Senate committees, only five witnesses referred to any data on the relation between nonaudit services and audit quality. The three witnesses opposing greater regulation who referred to data showing that audits were not compromised by nonaudit services were a Senate witness from a Big Four accounting firm representing the AICPA, the professional accounting organization, 2 *id.* at 822, 864 (statement of James E. Copeland, CEO, Deloitte & Touche) (testifying for the AICPA that "several recent studies" had "demonstrated that there is no correlation between the provision of nonaudit services and audit failures," referring to the findings in the report of the Panel on Audit Effectiveness and to DeFond et al., *supra* note 39); a House witness from a policy institute, *House CARTA Hearings*, *supra* note 77, at 12 (statement of James K. Glassman, Resident Fellow, Am. Enter. Inst.) (citing an article by members of the Panel on Audit Effectiveness, Palmrose & Saul, *supra* note 35, to indicate that "the issue of auditor independence has been extensively studied with almost no empirical evidence of abuse"); and another Senate witness, the chairman of the Panel on Audit Effectiveness and former chairman of Price Waterhouse, 2 *Senate Hearings*, *supra* note 35, at 683 (statement of Shaun F. O'Malley, Chairman, Panel on Audit Effectiveness) (summarizing the Panel's finding of no instances of nonaudit services affecting audits or impairing audit performance but noting that a survey indicated that there was a perception of such an effect). A fourth witness, discussed *infra* note 181, recognized that data existed but took a contrary position in support of the prohibition. After his testimony, a fifth witness, Turner, submitted a copy of Frankel et al., *supra* note 39, in support of the restriction, 1 *Senate Hearings*, *supra* note 35, at 302 (letter from Lynn Turner to Steven B. Harris, Staff Dir. and Chief Counsel, Senate Comm. on Banking, Hous. & Urban Affairs). Turner submitted the study to the Senate a few days after his testimony to refute what he had noted in his written testimony—that there were those who "have suggested" that there is no "'smoking gun' that provides a basis for changes in regulation and laws." *Id.*

The Frankel et al. study was, in fact, the only study on any of the mandates mentioned by any member of Congress in the congressional debates over and the seventeen hearings leading up to SOX. Representative Maloney entered in the record an "MIT, Michigan State and Stanford study" that was "cited in *Business Week*" that "showed that companies that use their auditors as consultants tend to manage earnings" and argued "that steps need to be taken statutorily." House *CARTA Hearings*, *supra* note 77, at 90 (statement of Rep. Maloney). She did so in response to testimony of then-SEC Chairman Pitt on an unrelated question that she had asked him. In response to her question whether he supported mandatory rotation of accounting firms, Pitt had stated that studies showed that most "frauds occur in the first 2 years of an audit-client relationship." *Id.* at 89 (statement of Harvey Pitt).

[175] 2 *Senate Hearings*, *supra* note 35, at 687 (statement of Lee J. Seidler, Deputy Chairman of the 1978 AICPA Comm'n on Auditors' Responsibilities and Managing Dir. Emeritus, Bear Stearns). In his written statement, Seidler referred to the Panel on Audit Effectiveness's report, as well as a similar finding by the 1978 Cohen Commission on which he had served, that the "theory [that consulting services

other witnesses who advocated a prohibition, such as Levitt, were, without question, fully aware of both reports, but one would not have known that from their testimony. The lack of candor is embarrassing.

Legislators only compounded the problem, however, by failing to follow up on the rare occasional references that were inconsistent with the direction in which the legislation was heading. The passing references by three witnesses to studies at odds with prohibiting nonaudit services were ignored. This fact is striking because the accounting profession was not yet considered politically radioactive at the time of the hearings, in contrast to the situation when the conference committee convened.

The adoption of the nonaudit services restriction illustrates the critical entrepreneurial role of the committee chairman. With the bulk of his career in the public sector and a very liberal voting record,[176] Senator Sarbanes's priors would make him favorably disposed to greater regulation of business, such as the use of mandates rather than disclosure as the corporate governance approach for SOX, and to adoption of a nonaudit services prohibition that was stricter than the House's (i.e., Pitt's SEC's) version. It is altogether understandable why the few references to data inconsistent with the recommendations to restrict nonaudit services by witnesses such as Levitt, who for the most part shared Sarbanes's worldview, did not enter into the senator's calculation and influence his adoption of their recommendations. Because the objective was to produce a bill that was acceptable to his party and that would get through the Senate, Sarbanes also had to be open to compromise on at least some hotly disputed issues regarding the regulation of the accounting profession (such as permitting accountants to serve on the new accounting regulator's board) and the expensing of stock options. Having forged a sufficient compromise in committee on those matters, on the contested issue of nonaudit services he was able to adopt the policy recommendation closest to that of Levitt, the expert whose judgment he trusted. On the shape of the other corporate governance provisions, and particularly audit committee independence, Sarbanes had

---

compromised audit quality] was not supported by empirical evidence"; he therefore offered an alternative "theory" that the problem was created not by the provision of consulting services but by the receipt of fees. *Id.* at 733-34. The contention makes no sense, because the auditors in the Panel's data set received fees for their nonaudit services, so the effect of the fees was captured in the analysis (and of course, all of the scholarly research discussed in the text uses fee data to study the question). It should be noted that when Turner submitted the Frankel et al. study (then an unpublished manuscript) to the committee after his testimony in support of his position on prohibition, he did not attempt to distinguish, let alone refer to, the empirical literature inconsistent with his position.

176 Senator Sarbanes began his career in public service in 1966, after a few years of law practice. Richard A. Oppel Jr., *A Point Man on Corporate Change*, N.Y. TIMES, July 14, 2002, §3 (Money & Business), at 2. His "lifelong pursuit" was of "liberal economic policies," Hsu & Day, *supra* note 97, and he was perceived as a "formidable liberal force" by the media, Oppel, *supra*. For a comparison of his ideological position with that of other legislators, as calculated by political scientists from his voting record, see ROMANO, *supra* note 19, at 171-72 & nn.342-43, 175 & n.349. Sarbanes's liberal ideological score places him to the left of the median member of his party, both in the chamber and on his committee, and therefore to the left of the full chamber and committee medians.

even greater room to maneuver as the drafter of the legislation, given its low visibility during the legislative process.

It should be noted that then-SEC Chairman Pitt sought to limit the scope of the nonaudit services regulation by advocating caution and waiting to ascertain the impact of the SEC's recently adopted rule on nonaudit services.[177] In extensive testimony before both the House and Senate committees, he endorsed neither the independent audit committee requirement nor the executive loan ban, although several provisions in SOX originated in his agenda (in particular, the new accounting regulator and the certification requirement). However, many of the witnesses who advocated those policy proposals were former SEC officials, and the proposals were typically extensions of agendas they had advanced at the agency. Accordingly, in the assessment of one former SEC commissioner who is critical of SOX, the SOX corporate governance mandates are the successful culmination of a multidecade effort by the agency's personnel to assert authority over public corporations in areas long considered the jurisdiction of the states.[178] Pitt's position on those issues was simply at variance with longstanding institutional objectives that, in the crisis environment in which the legislation was drafted, resonated with the Senate Banking Committee chairman.

D. Were the SOX Governance Mandates Symbolic Politics or Window Dressing?

The SOX corporate governance mandates were not carefully considered by Congress; in particular, they were not evaluated in light of the empirical literature questioning their efficacy. Before drawing policy inferences from this apparent mismatch of means and ends, there is a remaining question to address: Would Congress still have adopted those mandates had members been alerted that they were not likely to improve audit quality or otherwise benefit investors? An affirmative response would require viewing the SOX mandates as symbolic politics or, more cynically, as window dressing of particular importance in an election year. Though this is certainly a possible explanation, descriptively it does not accord well with the legislators' behavior.

The contention from a symbolic politics perspective is that despite the mandates' known probable ineffectiveness, their enactment provided an expressive or symbolic benefit: Congress's demonstration to a concerned public that it was remedying a serious problem. There is a fundamental flaw in this argument, however. If the rationale for supporting the governance provisions were symbolic, then we would expect legislators to have claimed some credit for those provisions (in contrast to other provisions or the

---

177 *See, e.g.*, 2 *Senate Hearings*, *supra* note 35, at 1070 (statement of Harvey Pitt).

178 *See* ROBERTA S. KARMEL, REALIZING THE DREAM OF WILLIAM O. DOUGLAS—THE SECURITIES AND EXCHANGE COMMISSION TAKES CHARGE OF CORPORATE GOVERNANCE 1, 12-16, 25, 36-37, 42, 50, 52 (Brooklyn Law Sch. Pub. Law & Legal Theory Research Paper Series, Research Paper No. 7, 2004), *available at* http://ssrn.com/abstract=525522 (relating SOX provisions to the history of thwarted SEC initiatives to regulate corporate governance matters, such as director independence and compensation, shareholder voting, fiduciary duties, and the accounting and legal professions).

more general symbol of passing any legislation, regardless of its content).[179] That is, senators and representatives should have been widely publicizing the corporate governance mandates in their floor speeches on the bill, or focusing on those initiatives when questioning witnesses at hearings, to communicate to their constituents how they were solving problems through those features of the legislation.

Yet as Table 2 and the discussion of the progress of those provisions through the hearings indicate, members of Congress did not do so. In fact, far more speakers addressed the provisions enhancing criminal penalties for corporate misconduct and establishing a regulator for the accounting profession than three of the governance mandates combined, with only the restriction on nonaudit services attracting attention equal to that of the provisions for a new accounting regulator. The attention to that provision, in all probability, is better explained by its being a revision of what was only a two-year-old compromise on a controversy between the accounting profession, which had been backed by members of Congress, and the SEC, rather than by its saliency to voters and its usefulness as a symbol.

Indeed, the increased criminal sanctions fit more squarely with a characterization as symbolic politics (if there was an aspect of symbolic politics in the enactment of SOX): They were highlighted by half of the legislators taking part in the legislative debate and are consistent with a pattern of Congress's raising criminal penalties in election years.[180] In addition, the criminal penalties were perceived as a central component of the legislation by the media. Opinion polls administered by the press seeking the public's view of the efficacy of the legislation moving through the Senate to deal with corporate misconduct referred specifically to its tightening of criminal sanctions.[181]

---

[179] In a classic of American politics, David Mayhew described the election-related activities of members of Congress of "advertising," "credit-claiming," and "position taking," which are important for reelection in order to identify the incumbent with benefits to constituents and with popular messages containing little content or controversy. DAVID R. MAYHEW, CONGRESS: THE ELECTORAL CONNECTION 49-76 (1974). While the activities he identifies—roll-call votes, signatures on discharge petitions, bill amendments—may be easier for constituents to inform themselves about than the floor speeches considered here, the symbolic effect is the same, and there were essentially no opportunities to engage in those other activities with respect to SOX (amendments were severely restricted, and there were few roll-call votes).

[180] For example, in 1990, during the escalating cost of the bailout of the savings and loan industry, Congress enacted enhanced banking crime penalties, even though it had increased banking crime sanctions in the banking reform package only a year before. And from 1982 to 1994 Congress enacted increased criminal sanctions in most election years (albeit for violent rather than white-collar crimes). Brian T. FitzPatrick, *Congressional Re-Election Through Symbolic Politics: The Enhanced Banking Crime Penalties*, 32 AM. CRIM. L. REV. 1, 13-15, 39-40 & n.229 (1994). Increasing criminal penalties is arguably symbolic politics because, as several reputable scholars have contended, the severity of sanctions does not appear to be among the most influential factors affecting crime rates. *See id.* at 2 nn.2-3. Vik Khanna puts a further spin on the symbolic politics explanation of corporate criminal legislation: He maintains that such laws satisfy Congress's need to react to a public outcry over corporate scandals at minimal cost to corporations. That is, corporations prefer such legislation because, he contends, it deflects liability from individual officers to entities and avoids more detrimental forms of legislative responses, such as facilitating private civil litigation. Vikramaditya S. Khanna, *Corporate Crime Legislation: A Political Economy Analysis*, 82 WASH. U. L.Q. 95, 97-98 (2004).

[181] For summaries of the polls, see *supra* note 74. While before enactment the overwhelming majority of respondents expected the legislation to have either a minor effect or no effect on corporate misconduct,

Given the substantial stock losses of members of the voting public in the corporate scandals, from a legislator's perspective, claiming that corporate executives would be sent to jail for lengthy intervals would be eminently more useful as a reelection vehicle than highlighting a provision rearranging the source of accounting firms' income.

One could instead disregard the legislators' choice of emphasis and express the cynical view of SOX as window dressing that deliberately offered ineffective solutions to a gullible public in order to benefit corporations or accountants, contending that many of the mandates were not that different from the prevailing state of the law. Executives had to sign SEC filings prior to SOX, the stock exchanges required independent audit committees, and the SEC had prohibited most of the nonaudit services banned by SOX. An observer could contend, along with Senator Gramm, that SOX was not a terrible regulatory outcome compared to what could have been enacted, and go further than the senator to contend that it was therefore costless window dressing.

In my judgment, however, that would be an incorrect assessment, even if much worse legislation could have been produced and was avoided and if the legislation is, in that respect, accurately characterized as symbolic. This is because the mandates are not costless (as one would expect legislation that is intentionally symbolic to be). In particular, compliance costs to meet the certification requirement appear to be considerable, especially for smaller firms. For example, a recent survey of companies' projected expenditures to meet the SOX internal controls provisions by the financial officers' professional organization shows that companies with annual revenues over $5 billion projected external consulting, software, and additional audit fees of $2.9 million per company, compared to a projection of $222,200 by companies with annual revenues under $25 million.[182] Taking the revenue thresholds as a benchmark, smaller companies' projected outlays as a proportion of revenue are an order of magnitude greater than larger companies' (0.009 compared to 0.0006). Another survey, of firms going private, reported that the cost of being public more than doubled after SOX, rising on average from $900,000 to $1.95 million, with the increase attributed primarily to higher

---

thereafter the proportion expecting an effect increased. Of course, to the extent that the public did not come to hold the view that Congress's proposed solution solved the problem at hand, it would have been difficult for members of Congress to obtain an electoral benefit from claiming to have crafted a solution.

[182] The survey was conducted by Financial Executives International (FEI), the professional organization of CFOs, treasurers, and controllers. FEI, FEI Survey on Sarbanes-Oxley Section 404 Implementation (Jan. 2004) (unpublished document), *available at* http://www.fei.org/download/Section404_summary.pdf; *see also Large Companies Expect To Spend Millions To Meet SOXA Internal Controls Requirements*, 36 Sec. Reg. & L. Rep. (BNA) 315 (Feb. 16, 2004) (reporting the results of the FEI survey). Large companies projected an average expense of roughly $1.8 million on 35,000 hours of "internal manpower" to satisfy the requirements, whereas small companies expected to incur an "average of 1,150 people hours" (the data-for-dollar conversion was not provided). FEI, *supra*, at 1. The results should be read with considerable caution because fewer small firms responded than did large firms (ten compared to sixty-one firms, or three percent compared to twenty percent of solicited participants, respectively), and it is unclear to what extent the survey responses represent one-time start-up costs of creating adequate compliance systems.

audit, insurance, and outside-director fees.[183] These data indicate that SOX imposed a far more significant burden on small than on large firms.

Smaller firms are also experiencing indirect costs from business disruption and quality control issues raised by having to find new auditors from the ranks of small and mid-sized accounting firms, because Big Four accounting firms have been dropping their smaller clients due to staffing shortages and the increased time and cost of audits under SOX.[184] In addition, small firms are more likely to be burdened by the mandates on audit committee composition. A recent study by James Linck et al., for instance, finds that after SOX, the size of boards and the proportion of directors that are independent significantly increased for all firms, but that the effect was disproportionately experienced by small firms (which before SOX had fewer outside directors than did large firms).[185] The study also finds that smaller-sized firms' expenditures on directors' compensation appear to have massively increased. It reports two measures of expenditures for a small sample of firms stratified by size: The cash compensation that medium-sized firms paid to outside directors increased from $21,688 to $40,783 between 2001 and 2004 (the effective date for compliance with most SOX rules), and small firms' compensation to outside directors increased from $7.25 per $1000 in net sales to $9.76 over the same period, compared to a trivial increase ($0.20) for large firms.[186] Furthermore, SOX appears to have affected the rate at which small firms stay

---

[183] Stanley B. Block, *The Latest Movement to Going Private: An Empirical Study*, J.Applied Fin., Spring 2004, at 36, 37. Block does not provide revenue data for the sample firms, so these firms' figures cannot be compared precisely with the FEI survey data, in which the reported cost increase was smaller. In all likelihood, Block's sample would fall at the smaller end of the FEI survey: Block's sample's median market capitalization was $61.7 million, and twenty-seven firms had negative earnings over the prior year. In addition, a survey by a law firm estimated that the cost of being a public company increased 90% the year after SOX and found that the increase disproportionately affected small and mid-cap firms. Thomas E. Hartman, Foley & Lardner LLP, The Increased Financial & Non-Financial Costs of Staying Public 6, 15 (2004), *available at* http://www.aei.org/docLib/20040505_Hartman.pdf. Moreover, in a follow-up survey, the law firm found that costs continued to increase substantially (by 130%) in 2004, although given the low response rate, the figures must be treated with great caution. Thomas E. Hartman, Foley & Lardner LLP, The Cost of Being Public in the Era of Sarbanes-Oxley 2 (2004), *available at* http://www.foley.com/files/tbl_s31Publications/FileUpload137/2017/Public% 20Study%C20Results%FINAL.doc.pdf.

[184] *See* Lynnley Browning, *Sorry, the Auditor Said, but We Want a Divorce*, N.Y. Times, Feb. 6, 2005, § 3 (Money & Business), at 5.

[185] James S. Linck et al., Effects and Unintended Consequences of the Sarbanes-Oxley Act on Corporate Boards 16-18 (March 2005), *available at* http://ssrn.com/abstract=687496.

[186] *Id.* at 25-26.

public.[187] But it should be noted that the costs imposed by SOX on all public firms appear to be substantial.[188]

In addition to direct compliance costs, there are some costs that are difficult to quantify but that could prove to be substantial, such as the contraction in financing opportunities for small and mid-sized businesses, as public firms are deterred from acquiring private and foreign firms (because the acquisition will make the acquirer responsible for certifying the accuracy of the entity's not-yet-certified books and records) or as those firms do not go public because of the SOX mandates.[189] To the extent that acquirers' transaction risk has increased because of the certification requirement, the efficiency of the market for corporate control could be affected—a potentially serious, and unintended, cost of the legislation.

Finally, there are also potential long-run costs for U.S. stock exchanges and consequently U.S. investors from fewer foreign listings, as foreign firms shift to the principal competitor venue—the London exchange—to avoid SOX. The cost and difficulty for foreign firms of complying with SOX's requirements may well be greater than for smaller U.S. firms, or at least much less worthwhile when balanced against the benefit obtained from a U.S. listing. This is not simply speculation, because many foreign firms are contemplating delisting.[190] U.S. investors, as well as exchanges, would be

---

[187] *See* Ellen Engel et al., *The Sarbanes-Oxley Act and Firms' Going-Private Decisions* 2-3 (May 2004) (unpublished manuscript), *available at* http://ssrn.com/abstract=546626 (finding that going-private transactions almost doubled after SOX, with smaller firms particularly affected). A study by the accounting firm Grant Thornton comparing going-private transactions the year before and the year after SOX similarly found that the number of companies seeking to go private increased (by 30%) post-SOX, while deal size decreased substantially (the median deal size decreased by half). CONO FUSCO, GRANT THORNTON LLP, SARBANES-OXLEY: A REVIEW: PANEL III: DO THE COSTS OF THE ACT OUTWEIGH THE BENEFITS? 8 (2004), *available at* http://www.aei.org/docLib/20040505_Fusco.pdf. Grant Thornton suggests that the change is due to SOX's having increased the cost of remaining public for small companies. *Id.* at 1-11. Moreover, according to Stanley Block's survey, the most common reason for going private was to avoid the cost of being public (30%), and the frequency of that response as the reason was higher for firms going private post-SOX (60%). Block, *supra* note 189, at 37. The second-most-frequent reason, top management time, was also related to SOX: Survey respondents indicated that this factor became "especially burdensome" after SOX due to the certification requirement. *Id.*

[188] In the financial officers' association survey, for example, the projected increase in external audit fees from the new requirement—that auditors attest to management's certification of internal controls—was similar across firm size, averaging a 38% increase. FEI, *supra* note 188, at 2.

[189] *See supra* notes 61, 193. As David Silk and David Katz note, SOX has "beyond question" increased the risks to acquirers of doing deals. David M. Silk & David A. Katz, *Doing Deals 2004: Keeping Pace with a Rapidly Changing Market, in* TAKEOVER LAW AND PRACTICE 2003, at 1139, 1267 (PLI Corporate Law & Practice, Course Handbook Series No. B0-025Q, 2004).

[190] *See* Daniel Epstein, *Goodbye, Farewell, Auf Wiedersehen, Adieu ...*, WALL ST. J., Feb. 9, 2005, at A10 (discussing how European companies with U.S. cross-listings are investigating delisting because of costly compliance under SOX). Congress explicitly refused to exempt non-U.S. firms from SOX, although other federal regulations do not apply equally to domestic and foreign firms. Although the SEC thus cannot exempt foreign firms, under pressure from foreign regulators, and perhaps to stem the tide of delistings and new listings of foreign companies in London rather than New York, the agency has indicated that it will consider delaying the statute's effective date for foreign firms and revising a rule that prevents delisted

disadvantaged by such a trend, because while they will still be able to purchase such firms' shares abroad, transaction costs will be higher. (Besides higher trading fees, the transactions will not be in U.S. dollars.)

More important, the extent of the full cost of the SOX governance mandates still cannot be ascertained because much depends on the SEC's implementation of the mandates and on whether it will be able to use SOX as a springboard to assert a more expansive regulatory authority. This is a real possibility. The SEC's implementation of the audit committee independence rules has already raised operating costs for small companies beyond those of the previous regime, by restricting the stock exchanges' exclusion for small businesses and provision for exceptions from complete independence within a board's discretion.[191] In addition, the SEC has recently proposed a significant incursion into corporate governance that mandates shareholder nomination of directors under specified circumstances, an initiative that utterly disregards state law and has no connection to Congress's specific derogation of state law in the corporate governance provisions in SOX.[192]

Finally, the form of the mandates in SOX, compared to their prior permutations, creates a set of hidden costs that further renders problematic the innocuous window-dressing interpretation. The audit committee composition and nonaudit services requirements have now been codified, whereas before SOX they were contained in stock exchange and SEC rules. It is far easier to revise exchange or agency rules than to amend a federal statute if dynamic business conditions regarding organizational or accounting practices necessitate a rule change or if it turns out that a chosen rule was mistaken. In sum, given the available information, it is not credible to characterize SOX's governance mandates as no- or low-cost window dressing whose adoption made sense in order to calm the media frenzy over corporate scandals, even if more costly governance proposals could be imagined.

E. Placing SOX in Context: Financial Legislation in Times of Crisis

The dismal saga of the SOX governance mandates demonstrates that Congressional lawmaking in times of perceived emergency offers windows of opportunity to well-positioned policy entrepreneurs to market their preferred, ready-made solutions when there is little time for reflective deliberation. The low quality of Congressional decisionmaking regarding the inclusion of the mandates in SOX is not, however, unique or necessarily surprising when it comes to financial regulation. Much of the expansion of federal regulation of financial markets has followed a similar pattern, occurring after significant economic turmoil. Although this pattern has been noted by many, it has not

firms from also deregistering, thereby subjecting foreign firms to SOX even if they are no longer publicly traded on a U.S. exchange. *See id.*

[191] *See* Standards Relating to Listed Company Audit Committees, Securities Act Release No. 33-8220, Exchange Act Release No. 34-47,654, 68 Fed. Reg. 18,788, 18,795 (Apr. 16, 2003) (codified in scattered sections of 17 C.F.R. pts. 228-29, 240, 249, 274 (2004)).

[192] Security Holder Director Nominations, 68 Fed. Reg. 60,784 (Oct. 23, 2003).

been systematically examined or explained, either empirically or theoretically. I offer no explanation here beyond observing the relationship and the parallel between SOX and the circumstances of the initial federal forays into financial market regulation.

The Future Trading Act of 1921,[193] the first federal statute regulating commodity futures markets, was enacted in the wake of the most severe recession in the United States up to that time. Farm prices collapsed and farm foreclosure rates increased as the United States eliminated price controls and European agricultural products returned to the world market with the end of World War I.[194] In this economically depressed environment, farm groups that had been lobbying to end commodity speculation for many years succeeded in obtaining legislation (although not the absolute prohibition they sought). They had helped to elect a new Republican majority in Congress, which enacted the legislation even though, at hearings, opponents of the legislation (grain trade witnesses, including a professor of agricultural economics) provided a cogent explanation of the economics of speculation and the grain market that made plain the proponents' fundamentally flawed understanding of the problem and its solution.[195]

But even had economic theory and econometric techniques been as sophisticated and widespread then as they are today, it would have been to little avail given the political circumstances: Many legislators were hostile to the grain market, paralleling their constituents' views. Hence, there were some genuine electoral concerns, and legislators spent much of the hearings impugning the personal integrity of witnesses critical of market regulation rather than addressing the substance of their testimony.[196] As a consequence, the 1921 legislation that regulated futures trading was not a solution even remotely addressing the problem at hand. That is because short selling and grain middlemen were generating more accurate grain prices rather than contributing to the farmers' economic plight, which was due to an increased supply of grain. Not surprisingly, the agricultural crisis persisted for many years thereafter.

The federal securities laws enacted in the 1930s were a prominent piece of the New Deal legislation that was a response to the 1929 stock market crash and the Great Depression. In contrast to SOX, this legislation was enacted after a crisis of considerable duration, following multiyear Senate hearings, in conjunction with a critical election that changed the administration and Congress. The Pecora hearings (named after the committee's counsel, Ferdinand Pecora) were orchestrated to develop an explanation of the market

---

[193] Future Trading Act of 1921, ch. 86, 42 Stat. 187.

[194] *See* Roberta Romano, *The Political Dynamics of Derivative Securities Regulation*, 14 YALE J. ON REG. 279, 286-87 (1997).

[195] *Id.* at 294. The far more sophisticated analyses of modern economic theory and empirical research indicate that the legislation's opponents' analyses were correct.

[196] For examples of such conduct at the hearings, see *id.* at 294-95. It should be noted that opponents of regulation outnumbered proponents at the first hearings because the committees had permitted all interested parties to testify; under the influence of committee members supporting the legislation, the number of witnesses was restricted at subsequent hearings. *Id.* at 292. Prior to the election of 1920, when they helped elect a Republican majority, farm groups had supported independent farm party candidates. As the farm recession continued into 1922, Republicans lost several seats to farmer-backed candidates, although their national defeat has been explained as a function of the success of the Progressive Party. *Id.* at 288.

crash as having been caused by market manipulation, fraud, and abuse by financial firms, in order to implement an agenda for market regulation.[197] Pecora was without question a founding and prototype policy entrepreneur for financial market regulation.

Present-day research has shown that market manipulation, fraud, and abuse were not widespread leading up to the crash.[198] In fact, consistent with that research's findings, much of the Pecora hearings focused on data "irrelevant to an investigation of the causes of the crash"—financiers' large salaries and income tax returns—rather than identifying the occurrence of widespread abuses.[199] In the extended financial crisis following the 1929 crash, electoral change, combined with Pecora's effective advocacy, led to the implementation of far-reaching legislation that had eluded proponents of market regulation during the Hoover Administration.[200] But this is yet another case, tracking the futures regulation of 1921, of a remedy not directed at solving an economic problem: The securities legislation did not restart the economy or reinvigorate the stock market, because the principal source of the 1930s economic crisis was catastrophic mistakes in monetary policy. Moreover, a persuasive case can be made that the benefit of the federal regulatory regime produced by the Pecora hearings has not been worth the cost.[201]

Stuart Banner's historical research suggests that these examples are not exceptions but rather are the template for financial regulation. Examining the conditions for securities market regulation in the eighteenth and nineteenth centuries in the United Kingdom and United States, he reports that legislation was adopted only after stock market declines, which, by 1837, coincided with economic contractions.[202] Banner contends that the reason for the association is that deep-seated popular suspicion of speculation comes in bad financial times to dominate otherwise popular support for markets, resulting in the expansion of regulation.[203] That is to say, financial exigencies embolden critics of markets to push their regulatory agenda. They are able to play on the strand of popular opinion that is hostile to speculation and markets because the

---

[197] Joel Seligman, an advocate of the federal regulation, characterizes the Pecora hearings as having an "obvious political purpose": to "diminish [the majority of the voters'] faith in the nation's financial institutions." JOEL SELIGMAN, THE TRANSFORMATION OF WALL STREET: A HISTORY OF THE SECURITIES AND EXCHANGE COMMISSION AND MODERN CORPORATE FINANCE 2 (1995).

[198] For a summary of the literature, see ROMANO, *supra* note 18, at 44-45. Although there was no such scholarly literature at the time that could have countered Pecora's highly orchestrated hearings, given the political climate any inconsistent data would no doubt have been ignored, as occurred with SOX and with the Future Trading Act.

[199] SELIGMAN, *supra* note 203, at 2. The Enron hearings, *see supra* note 138, more closely resemble this aspect of the Pecora hearings than do those conducted by the SOX originating committees, which were not principally investigatory in focus.

[200] SELIGMAN, *supra* note 203, at 2-18.

[201] *See* ROMANO, *supra* note 18, at 14-45.

[202] STUART BANNER, ANGLO-AMERICAN SECURITIES REGULATION: CULTURAL AND POLITICAL ROOTS, 1690-1860, at 257 (1998). His discussion of legislation in the United States includes state regulation.

[203] As Banner puts it, in good times, people do not complain about speculators because "too many people have been making too much money to favor regulation," and so legislation does not get introduced. Banner, *supra* note 70, at 851.

general public is more amenable to regulation after experiencing financial losses. A regulatory agenda, in short, does not generate popular support in a booming market. Due to greater sophistication in our understanding of market processes, there is far less popular suspicion of trading speculation today than in prior centuries. But we can still identify in Banner's formula for new regulation—the conjunction of the impact of a stock market downturn on public attitudes and the presence of political entrepreneurs with off-the-shelf regulatory proposals (Banner's ever-present critics of free markets)—a pattern largely consistent with the making of SOX.[204]

To be sure, as Banner reports, not all stock market declines in the eighteenth and nineteenth centuries resulted in new regulation.[205] This has also been true in more recent times: The October 1987 stock market break—the largest one-day decline in market history up to then—was not followed by a significant increase in regulation. The SEC did attempt to use the crisis to further its agenda and obtain control over financial derivative markets, which it had sought for decades, but legislation expanding its regulatory jurisdiction was not forthcoming.[206] In contrast to the legislative situations in the 1930s and in the debate over SOX, the 1987 market break was not coincident with scandal or revelations of corporate misconduct.[207] However, the significance of this factor is difficult to gauge, because no such scandals accompanied the 1920 futures regulation either. Financial turmoil thus appears to be a necessary but not sufficient condition for the enactment of market regulation, and the quality of federal legislative decisionmaking in such an environment has consistently left much to be desired.

---

[204] A similar dynamic—the public's conflicting and changing views of speculation as either immoral gambling or legitimate commercial enterprise—is also present in the context of futures trading (as opposed to Banner's focus on securities markets), as detailed IN ANN FABIAN, CARD SHARPS, DREAM BOOKS, & BUCKET SHOPS: GAMBLING IN 19TH-CENTURY AMERICA (1990). Larry Ribstein makes a related argument: Stock market bubbles facilitate fraud, and therefore, when investors' gains disappear as the bubble bursts and frauds are revealed, increased market regulation typically follows. Larry E. Ribstein, *Bubble Laws,* 40 HOUS. L. REV. 77, 80-81 (2003).

[205] *E.g.*, Banner, *supra* note 70, at 850.

[206] Those products are under the jurisdiction of the Commodity Futures Trading Commission (CFTC) and are subject to a less restrictive regulatory regime. The efforts of the SEC to shift jurisdiction from the CFTC before the market crash are summarized in Romano, *supra* note 200, at 356-59. The SEC intensified that effort after the 1987 crash, maintaining that derivatives (and its lack of regulatory authority over them) contributed to the crash. The SEC's failure was not, however, due to legislators' consideration of economic research on the issue. Rather, the status quo of dispersed regulatory authority was matched by divergent Congressional committee jurisdictions, which legislators protected, in keeping with the opposing financial market interests they represented. *See id.* at 359-77.

[207] The insider trading scandals of the 1980s began more than a year earlier, with the indictment of Dennis Levine in May 1986, *see* Nathaniel C. Nash, *An Insider Scheme Is Put in Millions*, N.Y. TIMES, May 13, 1986, at A1, and the indictment and plea bargain of Ivan Boesky in November 1986, *see* James Sterngold, *Boesky Said To Aid Inquiry by Taping of Wall St. Talks*, N.Y. TIMES, Nov. 18, 1986, at A1. Congress increased the penalties for insider trading in 1984 and 1988. *See* Insider Trading and Securities Fraud Enforcement Act of 1988, Pub. L. No. 100-704, 1988 U.S.C.C.A.N. (102 Stat.) 4677 (codified in scattered sections of 15 U.S.C.); Insider Trading Sanctions Act of 1984, Pub. L. No. 98-376, 1984 U.S.C.C.A.N. (98 Stat.) 1264 (codified in scattered sections of 15 U.S.C.).

III. POLICY IMPLICATIONS

The analysis of the empirical literature and the political dynamics relating to the SOX corporate governance mandates indicates that those provisions were poorly conceived, because there was no basis to believe they would be efficacious. Hence, there is a disconnect between means and ends. The straightforward policy implication of this chasm between Congress's action and the learning bearing on it is that the mandates should be rescinded. The easiest mechanism for operationalizing such a policy change would be to make the SOX mandates optional, i.e., statutory default rules that firms could choose whether to adopt. An alternative and more far-reaching approach, which has the advantage of a greater likelihood of producing the default rules preferred by a majority of investors and issuers, would be to remove corporate governance provisions completely from federal law and remit those matters to the states. Finally, a more general implication concerns emergency legislation. It would be prudent for Congress, when legislating in crisis situations, to include statutory safeguards that would facilitate the correction of mismatched proposals by requiring, as in a sunset provision, revisiting the issue when more considered deliberation would be possible.

A. Converting Mandates into Statutory Defaults

Were the SOX corporate governance mandates treated as defaults, corporations would be able to opt out by shareholder vote. In this way, for example, small firms for which the audit committee composition, nonaudit services, and certification requirements pose substantial costs would be able to sidestep coverage—in contrast to larger firms with lower compliance costs, whose owners might perceive an attractive cost-benefit ratio from the mandates and wish to retain them. This would be the easiest way to revamp Congress's misconceived corporate governance provisions, because it could be done by the SEC under its general exemptive authority, without Congressional action.[208]

---

[208] *See* 15 U.S.C. § 78mm (2000). It is, however, exceedingly unlikely that the SEC would exercise its exemptive authority regarding SOX requirements for all firms. At the outset, when it began to implement the statute, it did not appear that the SEC would contemplate doing so even on a narrow basis for small firms, as exemplified by the agency's implementation of SOX's independent audit committee requirement. Prior to SOX, the stock exchange rules that mandated completely independent audit committees gave boards the discretion to have a nonindependent director on the committee. The SEC's implementation of SOX not only restricted that discretion, but also rejected even a de minimis exception, proposed by issuers, that would have exempted trivial sums paid directly to a director or relatives or the business with which the director was affiliated (because the SEC's definition of independence prohibits both indirect and direct payments to the director). Standards Relating to Listed Company Audit Committees, Securities Act Release No. 33-8220, Exchange Act Release No. 34-47,654, 68 Fed. Reg. 18,788, 18,792-93 (Apr. 16, 2003) (codified in scattered sections of 17 C.F.R. pts. 228-29, 240, 249, 274 (2004)). The SEC adopted the position of union and public pension funds, which opposed any exception, even though SOX specifically provided the agency with exemptive authority regarding the statutory definition of independence of audit committee members for "particular relationship[s]" as it deemed fit, SOX, Pub. L. No. 107-204, § 301, 2002 U.S.C.C.A.N. (116 Stat.) 745, 775-76 (to be codified at 15 U.S.C. § 78j-1(m)(3)(C)). Thus, when presented with the opportunity to mitigate the effect of Congress's misconceived mandate on audit committee independence, the SEC in fact compounded the error.

State corporate law consists principally of enabling provisions that operate as defaults from which firms opt out if tailoring better suits their organizational needs. Firms can therefore particularize their corporate charters, as well as pick the state code that best matches their requirements, so as to minimize the cost of doing business, thereby increasing the return to their investors. The defaults incorporated in state codes are those expected to be selected by the vast majority of firms, which further reduces transaction costs (because most firms need not incur the cost of particularizing their charters). Transforming the SOX mandates into optional defaults for firms would move the federal regime closer to the state law approach to corporate governance.

From a transaction-cost-reducing perspective on corporate governance regulation, it is questionable whether all, or even most, of the SOX mandates would be chosen by a majority of firms and, consequently, whether they should be structured as opt-in or opt-out default provisions. Some pertinent facts lend support to an opt-in approach. States, for instance, could have enacted similar requirements to SOX as statutory defaults, but none chose to do so. Indeed, in the case of executive loans, state corporation codes contained the opposite substantive default rule, specifying the criteria for undertaking such transactions. The most reasonable and straightforward inference to draw is that there was no demand for the SOX mandates: If there had been a significant demand, then the provisions would have appeared in at least some state codes.

In addition, despite state corporation codes' silence, firms could have declined to purchase nonaudit services from auditors, refused to make executive loans, and created completely independent audit committees (prior to the stock exchange requirement of such committees). Many firms chose not to do so, and the literature suggests they had good reasons: Completely independent audit committees add no significant benefit over majority-independent committees (and the benefit from even majority-independent committees is an open question), purchasing nonaudit services from auditors does not diminish audit quality, and executive loan programs can serve bona fide purposes that benefit shareholders. Were the SOX mandates rendered optional, firms that found them

However, there has been a political backlash, intensified by the high costs of SOX compliance, regarding several post-SOX expansive regulatory initiatives (unrelated to SOX) undertaken by the SEC by a nonunanimous vote of the commissioners. In the aftermath of the 2004 election, the backlash has taken the form of questioning the wisdom of reappointing current SEC Chairman William Donaldson. Donaldson, in turn, has announced the formation of an advisory committee to examine the impact of SOX on small firms. Jackie Calmes & Deborah Solomon, *Snow Says 'Balance' Is Needed in Enforcing Sarbanes-Oxley Law*, WALL ST. J., Dec. 17, 2004, at A1. He also appears to have altered his position on a controversial initiative on shareholder access, because the regulation's promulgation has been delayed. At the same time that he announced the advisory committee's formation, however, Donaldson said that the SEC had no current plans to review the statute's impact on larger firms. In addition, the senior staff's view is that cost-benefit analysis of SOX provisions is inappropriate. Alison Carpenter, *Complete, Current Section 404 Disclosure Will Lessen Negative Reaction, Experts Say*, 3 Corp. Accountability Rep. (BNA) 62 (Jan. 21, 2005) (reporting on a panel at which Alan Beller, director of the SEC's corporate finance division, responded to a panelist's proposed cost-benefit analysis of the certification requirements in section 404 of SOX by stating that it was "wrong to focus on analyzing the costs and benefits"). It is therefore highly doubtful that the agency will undertake a full-fledged review of the SOX requirements, particularly if Donaldson's actions are considered sufficient by the administration to justify his retention despite important constituents' opposition.

beneficial would be unaffected, because they could continue to follow the SOX strictures.[209] For example, firms that did not wish to purchase nonaudit services from their auditors could follow such a policy without its being mandated, and to demonstrate a continuing commitment to that policy, they could opt into the federal default provision.[210]

B. Returning Corporate Governance to the States

The absence of state codes or corporate charters tracking the SOX mandates further suggests that board composition, the services that corporations purchase from their auditors, and their credit arrangements with executives—the substance of the SOX mandates—are not proper subjects for federal government action, let alone mandates. Accordingly, rendering them optional would not be as optimal as outright repeal.[211] The states and the stock exchanges are a far more appropriate locus of regulatory authority for those governance matters than Congress and its delegated federal regulatory agents.[212] They are closer to the affected constituents (corporations and investors) and

---

209 The menu approach is consistent with research suggesting that the optimal composition of the board, and hence the audit committee, varies with firm characteristics and, in particular, that firms operating in more complex or uncertain environments benefit from the presence of inside and affiliated directors (individuals with firm-specific knowledge) and therefore from less independent audit committees (because committee composition is a function of board composition). *See* April Klein, *Economic Determinants of Audit Committee Independence*, 77 Acct. Rev. 435, 438-39, 445, 447-50 (2002) (providing theoretical and empirical support for variation in audit committee independence by firm characteristics, such as growth opportunities).

210 Even before SOX, there were firms that appear to have followed such a practice voluntarily. For example, many firms in the Kinney et al. study of audit firms' services did not purchase any of the subsequently prohibited nonaudit services from their auditors, and a small number of firms purchased no nonaudit services, including the tax- and audit-related services the purchase of which SOX continued to permit. Kinney et al., *supra* note 39, at 574-75. It is possible, however, that those firms were not deliberately shunning the use of their auditor as required by SOX, but simply had no need for such services. For a discussion of nuances in the choice between opt-in or opt-out default provisions because of asymmetrical effects of the state law charter amendment process on managers and shareholders, see Romano, *supra* note 19, at 209-12 & nn.405-08.

211 A basis for rendering optional the certification requirement is the disparate event study data that suggest that only some firms' investors benefited from the information provided by the certification. *See supra* Section I.D. One cannot draw any inference from the absence of such a provision in state codes because the regulation of audited financial statements has been a matter of federal, not state, law since the 1930s. Given its relation to the federal filing requirement, in contrast to the recommendation to repeal the other federal corporate governance mandates, the certification provision should be maintained as part of the federal regulatory system, albeit rendered optional.

212 For a more detailed explanation of why state competition for corporate charters is preferable to exclusive federal regulation, see, for example, Roberta Romano, The Genius of American Corporate Law (1993). The SEC's exercise of authority over exchange rules would need to be eliminated or severely restricted for the stock exchanges to become an effective source of corporate governance standards. This is because the SEC now uses its authority to force the exchanges to adopt uniform standards that it considers desirable, which undermines the benefit of exchange-based governance stemming from the market-based incentives for competing exchanges to offer rules that enhance the value of listed firms. A better approach to exchange standards regarding corporate governance is that taken by the London Stock Exchange, which

are less likely to make regulatory mistakes. This is because they operate in a competitive environment: Corporations choose in which state to incorporate and can change their domicile if they are dissatisfied with a legal regime, just as corporations choose, and can change, their trading venue.[213] Moreover, any regulatory mistakes made will be less costly, because not all firms will be affected.

Regulatory competition offers an advantage over a single regulator because it provides regulators with incentives and the necessary information to be accountable and responsive to the demands of the regulated. That is because there is a feedback mechanism in a competitive system that indicates to decisionmakers when a regime needs to be adapted and penalizes them when they fail to respond: the flows of firms out of regimes that are antiquated and into regimes that are not.[214] This is an important regulatory characteristic in the corporate context, because firms operate in a changing business environment, and their regulatory needs concomitantly change over time.

There are incentives for states to seek to retain more locally incorporated corporations rather than fewer and therefore to respond to a net outflow of firms: States receive annual

---

follows a "disclose and explain" approach: Listed firms are required to disclose whether they comply with a code of best practices or, if they do not comply, to explain why they do not. SOX's audit committee expert provision, section 407, takes a similar form. It is difficult to determine the explanation for the difference in approach between the U.K. and U.S. exchanges, given the institutional differences in the regulatory and market environments. That is, it is not clear whether the difference is due to the SEC's preferences (because the agency can impose its desired form of listing mandates through its oversight authority) or to the presence of multiple exchanges, the competition among which could foster a product-differentiation strategy in which an exchange benefited from adopting mandatory standards through which listed firms could signal quality to investors. However, Jonathan Macey and Maureen O'Hara contend that stock exchanges such as the NYSE no longer provide a reputational function (at least for domestic firms), which undercuts the latter explanation. Jonathan R. Macey & Maureen O'Hara, *The Economics of Stock Exchange Listing Fees and Listing Requirements*, 11 J. FIN. INTERMEDIATION 297, 301-03 (2002).

[213] Until recently, it was difficult to delist from the NYSE. *See, e.g.*, David Alan Miller & Marci J. Frankenthaler, *Delisting/Deregistration of Securities Under the Securities Exchange Act of 1934*, INSIGHTS: CORP. & SEC. L. ADVISOR, Oct. 2003, at 7 (noting the further easing of NYSE delisting requirements in 2003); A.C. Pritchard, *Markets as Monitors: A Proposal To Replace Class Actions with Exchanges as Securities Fraud Enforcers*, 85 VA. L. REV. 925, 992 (1999) (noting the recent dilution of the NYSE delisting rule, which, in contrast to other exchanges, required shareholder approval for delisting). By contrast, a corporation could avoid the federal regime by moving its operations to a foreign country or going private, but these are considerably more costly strategies than the paper transactions required to change domicile or stock exchange listing.

[214] *E.g.*, ROMANO, *supra* note 18, at 49. It should be noted, in this regard, that states can act more quickly than Congress. For instance, the Delaware legislature responded to *Smith v. Van Gorkom*, 488 A.2d 858 (Del. 1985), considered an undesirable corporate law decision on director liability, 1.5 years after the holding, whereas Congress has averaged 2.4 years when reversing judicial opinions invalidating federal statutes. ROMANO, *supra* note 218, at 239 n.140. Although the wisdom of the overruling is questionable, the Supreme Court's decision on the statute of limitations overturned by SOX was decided in 1991, more than a decade before its statutory reversal. That time frame for a reversal is consistent with the data in William Eskridge's comprehensive study of congressional reversals of Supreme Court decisions interpreting federal statutes: The average (mean) reversal occurred twelve years after the decision, with sixty-eight percent occurring more than two years after the decision. *William N. Eskridge, Jr., Overriding Supreme Court Statutory Interpretation Decisions*, 101YALE L.J. 331, 338 tbl.1, 424 app. I, 450 app. III (1991).

franchise fee payments, and an important political constituency, the local corporate bar, profits from local incorporations.[215] Exchanges, similarly, prefer more listings to less, because listing fees are a major source of revenue.[216] While even a monopoly regulator is interested in increasing the number of firms subject to its regulatory authority,[217] the SEC has principally done so not by trying to induce a voluntary increase in registrants by improving its regulatory product but by either aggressively interpreting the scope of its authority to include previously unregulated entities or lobbying Congress for a statutory expansion of jurisdiction.[218] Competing regulators, by contrast, can increase the number of firms under their jurisdiction solely by providing a product of higher value to firms. Thus, states can be expected to be more effective in setting the appropriate corporate governance default rules than Congress or the SEC. They have a greater incentive to get things right.

C. Providing Safeguards in Emergency Legislation

While this Article is focused on recommendations for rectifying the specific policy blunders wrought by SOX, there is a more general policy concern: how to improve emergency financial market legislation. Recommending restraint, such as resisting an immediate legislative response in favor of more deliberate proceedings, while perhaps more satisfactory from a policymaking standpoint, is simply not in the realm of the feasible. Members of Congress cannot be expected to take no action in times of financial exigency, given the election cycle. Retaining one's public office is an understandably powerful motivating force, and financial crises are often accompanied by a media frenzy searching for scapegoats that plays into public discontent and generates expectations of government solutions (as occurred with SOX).[219] A more plausible recommendation is for lawmakers crafting emergency legislation to include, as a matter of legislative convention, procedural safeguards to ensure that expanded regulation will be revisited

---

[215] Romano, *supra* note 218, at 28.

[216] *See* Macey & O'Hara, *supra* note 218, at 308 (noting that forty percent of NYSE revenues in 1998 were from listing fees).

[217] *See, e.g.*, William A. Niskanen, Jr., Bureaucracy and Representative Government 38-41 (1971) (describing bureaucrats' tendency to maximize budgets).

[218] For example, the SEC recently proposed to regulate hedge funds, although they are not a public investment vehicle. *See* Judith Burns, *SEC May Widen Hedge-Fund Rules*, Wall St. J., Apr. 29, 2004, at D9. It lobbied Congress successfully in the 1960s to expand its regulation of firms trading in over-the-counter markets and unsuccessfully from the 1970s through the 1990s to include stock-based financial derivatives in its jurisdiction. *See* Seligman, *supra* note 203, at 293-323 (describing SEC activities leading up to the 1964 amendments expanding registration requirements to firms traded over the counter); Romano, *supra* note 200, at 354-67 (describing the SEC's failed efforts to shift regulatory jurisdiction over financial derivatives to itself from the CFTC).

[219] There is considerable empirical evidence that the Congressional agenda corresponds closely to what can be called the "'public agenda,'" the issues considered most pressing in the public's mind (as measured by opinion polls). Bryan D. Jones & Frank R. Baumgartner, *Representation and Agenda Setting*, 32 Pol'y Stud. J. 1, 3 (2004).

when more sober assessment is possible—after markets have settled, the individuals who engaged in actual misconduct have been punished, and scandals have receded a bit.

There are a number of strategies for implementing a regime of safeguards, and the most appropriate mechanism may well vary with statutory specifics. But one time-tested procedural mechanism that would routinize the review of emergency legislation is for such legislation to include sunset provisions. Sunset refers to periodic review of regulatory programs, with termination possible if not renewed by Congress. It came to the fore in the 1970s as a means of increasing Congressional oversight of the executive branch and has often been applied in nonemergency legislative contexts.[220] It has specifically been used in financial market regulation: The federal regulator of commodities futures was created as a sunset agency, subjecting it to a periodic reauthorization process.[221] Sunset is not without its own implementation difficulties (such as inflexibility in the scheduling of reviews and the creation of workload problems for Congress), which could impede effective review.[222] In addition, review of provisions like the SOX governance mandates might not be as straightforward as review of federal spending programs for which the sunset concept was devised. But such a review would nonetheless mitigate the problem of quasi-permanent regulatory blunders produced by emergency legislation that burdens financial markets, thereby impeding capital development and growth, without any discernible compensating benefit.

An alternative approach that would avoid some of the implementation difficulties that congressional review would entail would be to impose the sunset renewal inquiry on the agency designated to implement emergency legislation instead. Under such an approach, the SOX governance mandates, for example, would have to be reviewed by the SEC according to a timetable fixed by the statute creating those requirements, such as at an interval of three or four years thereafter. After its review, the SEC would have to recommend to Congress the statute's renewal (which could include suggestions for amendment). Without such renewal, the statute would be automatically repealed. To exercise greater control over the administrative review, Congress could require the agency to provide it with a written report documenting the review process and justifying the decision. More important, to ensure compliance in spirit as well as form with the sunset provision, Congress could specify that the agency must collect and consider the relevant academic research bearing on the regulation undergoing review, with that analysis included in the required report to Congress. Such a process would not only force the agency to confront a literature that might be at odds with preconceived regulatory

---

[220] *See* JOEL D. ABERBACH, KEEPING A WATCHFUL EYE: THE POLITICS OF CONGRESSIONAL OVERSIGHT 27-28 (1990) (describing how strife between the legislative and executive branches during the Nixon Administration generated a number of legislative reform proposals directed at improving oversight, one of which was sunset legislation).

[221] *See* ROMANO, *supra* note 200, at 353.

[222] For a discussion of the competing concerns about institutional and individual power by members of Congress regarding oversight that caused the sunset concept to "fade[] away" politically, see ABERBACH, *supra* note 226, at 207.

notions but would also improve legislators' ability to evaluate effectively whether the agency's decision on renewal was cost justified.

The probability is no doubt low that an agency administering emergency legislation that expands its jurisdictional authority will recommend that the legislation be permitted to lapse. An intermediate path between sunset review conducted by Congress and review by the SEC would be for emergency legislation, as a matter of course, to establish a blue-ribbon outside advisory committee, consisting of academic experts and representatives from industry and the investor community, to be appointed by the President and the ranking party leaders in Congress within the statute's sunset time frame. The statute would designate the committee to undertake the entire sunset inquiry and report directly to Congress, or to evaluate the relevant academic literature and the efficacy of the agency's implementation and administration of the emergency statute in a written document that the agency would use as a basis for making a recommendation to Congress. Because an agency can be expected to be predisposed to renew legislation for which it has expended effort on developing an administrative apparatus, an independent expert advisory committee should be a more objective assessor of the relevant literature. Such a committee would therefore be more likely than agency review, even with detailed instructions from Congress on its conduct, to improve on the quality of decisionmaking in the ex post review process compared to that undertaken when legislating in crisis mode.

CONCLUSION

This Article has examined the substantive corporate governance mandates adopted by Congress in the wake of the Enron scandals. An extensive empirical literature suggests that those mandates were seriously misconceived, because they are not likely to improve audit quality or otherwise enhance firm performance and thereby benefit investors as Congress intended. In the frantic political environment in which SOX was enacted, legislators adopted proposals of policy entrepreneurs with neither careful consideration nor assimilation of the literature at odds with the policy prescriptions. The specific policy implication drawn from this Article's analysis of the scholarly literature and political dynamics is that the mandates should be rescinded, either by transforming them into statutory defaults that apply to firms at their option or by removing them completely and redirecting jurisdictional authority to the states. The more general implication is the cautionary note that legislating in the immediate aftermath of a public scandal or crisis is a formula for poor public policymaking (at least in the context of financial market regulation). The high salience of events forestalls a careful and balanced consideration of the issues, providing a window for action by the better-positioned, not the better-informed, policy entrepreneurs. This is a particular concern because legislation drafted in a perceived state of emergency can be difficult to undo. It took more than sixty years to repeal the Glass-Steagall Act, the New Deal financial market regulation that is now widely recognized as having greatly contributed to the banking debacle of the 1980s. The problem would be mitigated by routinizing the inclusion in emergency legislation of a provision for revisiting the legislation to determine whether continuation is warranted at a later date when more deliberative reflection is possible.

Congressional repeal of SOX's corporate governance mandates is not on the near-term political horizon. Officeholders would not want to be perceived as revising rules that are supposed to diminish the likelihood of corporate accounting scandals. The alternative of treating SOX as a set of default rules could be implemented by the SEC under its general exemptive authority, but it is improbable that the agency will do so in a comprehensive way, in part because it is still stinging from being perceived as lagging behind state regulators in finding and prosecuting entire financial industry sectors for alleged misconduct.[223] It is therefore important to work to educate the media, the public, political leaders, and agency personnel regarding the reality that Congress committed a public policy blunder in enacting SOX's corporate governance mandates and that there is a need to rectify the error.

[223] *E.g.*, Steve Bailey, Op-Ed, *Asleep at the Switch*, BOSTON GLOBE, Oct. 24, 2003, at D1 ("As the scandals roll out across Wall Street and beyond . . . the question 'Where was the Securities and Exchange Commission?' is becoming part of the lexicon. . . . It has been left to New York Attorney General Eliot Spitzer to uncover one problem after another in the securities business and to show the SEC and its boss, William Donaldson, what regulation is all about."); Editorial, *Feds Flubbed Mutual Fund Oversight*, NEWS TRIB. (Tacoma, Wash.), Nov. 5, 2003, South Sound, at B6 ("Asleep-at-the-wheel federal regulators have helped give 95 million American investors something they don't need—yet another major stock market scandal to worry about. . . . Congress should find out how the SEC allowed a scandal of this magnitude to slip under its radar screen for so long—and require the agency to shape up."). As mentioned *supra* note 214, pressure from legislators and the administration, responding to constituents dissatisfied with the SEC, has led the SEC to create a committee that will report in a year on whether SOX's applicability to small firms should be modified, but more broad-based exemptions are not on the agency's agenda.

APPENDIX

Table 4
Studies on Audit Committee Independence*

Study	Sample	Performance Measure	Findings
Klein (1998)	485 S&P firms, 1992; 486 S&P firms, 1993	Return on assets; Jensen Productivity measure; 1-year raw market return	No association with percent independent and any measure; no stock market effect for change in composition of committee
Cotter and Silvester (2003)	109 large Australian firms, 1997	Market value	No association
Vafeas and Theodorou (1998)	250 U.K. firms, 1994	Market to book ratio, stock return and accounting measures	No association
Weir, Laing, and McKnight (2002)	311 firms from 1996 Times1000 (U.K.)	Tobin's Q	No association
Klein (2002)	692 S&P firms, 1992-93	Abnormal accruals	No association with 100% independent; negative relation with majority independent or percent independent
Chtourou, Bédard, and Courteau (2001)	300 firms, 1996	Abnormal accruals	No association with 100% independent; negative association with high accruals with percent independent who are also not managers of other firms
Xie, Davidson, and DaDalt (2003)	282 S&P 500 firms, 1992, 1994, 1996	Abnormal accruals	No association; negative association with proportion of investment bankers or other corporate officers on committee

Study	Sample	Performance measures	Findings
Agrawal and Chadha (2003)	159 pairs of firms, 2000-01	Earnings restatements	No association with percent independent or 100% independent; Negative relation with financial expert on committee
Beasley (1996)	75 firms, 1980-91; 26 pairs with audit Committees	Financial statement fraud	No association with percent independent
Abbott, Parker, and Peters (2002)	129 pairs of firms, 1991-99	Financial reporting misstatements or fraud	Negative relation with 100% independent or absence of financial expert on committee
Abbott, Park, and Parker (2000)	78 pairs of firms, 1980-96	Financial statement fraud	Negative relation with variable combining 100% independent and 2 meetings a year
Beasley et al. (2000)	66 firms in high technology, health care and financial services industries, 1987-97	Financial statement fraud	Univariate test: Negative relation for 100% independent in two of three industries
McMullen and Raghunandan (1996)	51 firms with financial problems pre-1989; 77 control firms	SEC enforcement action or quarterly earnings restatement	Univariate test: Negative relation for 100% independent and for presence of accounting expert on committee
Uzun et al. (2004)	133 firms accused of fraud from 1978-2001 paired with no-fraud firms	Allegations of third-party and government contract fraud, financial statement fraud, and regulatory violations	No association for percent independent; positive association for percent of "grey" (affiliated) directors

Felo, Kristhnamurty, and Solieri (2003)	119 firms, 1992-93; 130 firms, 1995-96 (77 firms in both periods)	Financial analysts' score for quality of financial reporting	No association with percent independent; positive relation with proportion of financial experts on committee in 1995-96; no association with expert with accounting background; change in score from 1992-93 to 1995-96 positively related to percentage experts in 1992-93 and to change in number of experts over the period
Anderson, Deli, and Gillan (2003)	1,241 firms, 2001	Stock market response to unexpected earnings (earnings informativeness) Earnings response significantly related to board independence with	Earnings response significantly related to board independence with no incremental significance of audit committee independence

Notes: Jensen productivity is the change in market value and equity minus a benchmark return on investment, defined as the change in net property, plant and equipment multiplied by the firm's cost of capital (assumed to be 8%); Tobin's Q is the ratio of a firm's market value to the replacement cost of its assets (proxied for by total assets).

[1] The studies in this table are cited *supra* notes 23-24. Jensen productivity is the change in market value and equity minus a benchmark return on investment, defined as the change in net property, plant, and equipment multiplied by the firm's cost of capital (assumed to be 8%). Tobin's Q is the ratio of a firm's market value to the replacement cost of its assets (proxied for by total assets). The results reported for Bjdard et al., *supra* note 24, differ from those reported in ROMANO, *supra* note 19, at 22, because the results in the published article, cited herein, are the opposite of those in the working paper, Sonda Marrakchi Chtourou et al., *Corporate Governance and Earnings Management* (Apr. 2001) (unpublished manuscript), *available at* http://ssrn.com/abstract=275053, cited in Romano, *supra* note 19, at 22. The model estimated in the article differs from that of the working paper in the following ways: elimination of all governance variables except for those related to the audit committee; inclusion of a dummy variable for an audit committee with 50%-99% independence; elimination of an interaction variable for audit committee independence and level of activity; a different definition of audit committee activity; inclusion of economic variables correlated with earnings management, such as negative cash flows; and the use of a multinomial regression model using low earnings management firms as the base comparison, rather than a logistic model.

Table 5
Studies on the Provision of Nonaudit Services[1]

Study	Sample	Independence Measure	Audit Quality Measure	Findings
Agrawal & Chadha (2003)	159 pairs of firms, 2000-2001	Fee ratio; nonaudit fees over $1 million	Earnings restatements	No association
Antle et al. (2002)	2443 U.K. firm-years, 1994-2000; 1430 U.S. firms	Audit fees; nonaudit fees; fee ratio	Discretionary accruals (simultaneous estimation of accruals and fees)	Negative relation between nonaudit fees and accruals; positive association between audit fees and accruals; accruals do not explain fees; positive relation between fees; no significant associations in nonsimultaneous estimation; ratio insignificant (nonsimultaneous estimation)
Ashbaugh et al. (2003)	3170 firms (1666 firms in earnings tests)	Fee ratio; total fees; audit fees; nonaudit fees	Discretionary accruals (controlled for performance); earnings surprises or small increases	Association between ratio and accruals is only for income-decreasing accruals; negative relation between audit fees and total fees and small increases; no other systematic significant associations
Bajaj et al. (2003)	100 pairs of firms, 2001-2002	Fee ratio; total fees; nonaudit fees; audit fees	Securities class actions alleging accounting improprieties	No association; higher fee ratio and nonaudit fees for sued firms for subset of 33 firms with the largest stock price drop over class period
Chung & Kallapur (2003)	1871 clients of Big Five firms	Client importance (ratio of nonaudit and of total fees to total revenues); also estimated at local-office level	Discretionary accruals	No association; if use Frankel et al.'s model, positive association between ratio and accruals only for smallest group of firms
Craswell (1999)	885 Australian firms, 1984; 1477 in 1987; 1079 in 1994	Fee ratio	Qualified opinion	No association

Craswell et al. (2002)	1062 Australian firms, 1994; 1045 in 1996	Client fee ratio, measured at both national firm and local office level	Qualified opinion	No association
Dee et al. (2002)	203 S&P 500 firms	Fee ratio	Level of discretionary accruals	Positive association
DeFond et al. (2002)	1158 firms (96 received first-time going concern reports)	Fee ratio; nonaudit fees; audit fees; total fees; client importance fee ratio and fees; unexpected ratio and fees	Going concern audit reports (simultaneous model estimated as robustness check)	No association
Ferguson et al. (2003)	610 U.K. firms, averaged 1996-1998	Fee ratio; nonaudit fees; decile ranking of client's nonaudit fees by regional office	Discretionary accruals; news report of analyst criticism or regulatory investigation into accounting; restatements or adjustments under 1999 U.K. accounting rule change	Positive association for all measure pairs except for decile ranking and news report
Firth (2002)	1112 U.K. firms on International Stock Exchange, 1996	Nonaudit fees Standardized by total assets of client	Qualified opinion	Negative association (higher ratio reduces probability of qualified opinion)
Francis & Ke (2003)	1588 firms (5208 quarterly earnings observations)	Fee ratio; total fees; nonaudit fees; dummy for ratio greater than .5; percentile ranking of dollar amount of nonaudit fees and of total fees	Earnings surprises (controlling for large negative earnings)	Association between ratio and surprises only for firms with large negative earnings; no other associations
Frankel et al. (2002)	3074 firms (2012 firms in earnings tests)	Fee ratio; percentile ranking of client's nonaudit fees; total fee; audit fees	Discretionary accruals; earnings surprises or small increases	Positive association between ratio and nonaudit fees rank and accruals and surprises; negative association between audit fees rank and accruals; total fees rank insignificant
Gore et al. (2001)	4779 U.K. firm-years, 1992-1998	Fee ratio	Discretionary accruals	No association for Big Five firms; positive association for non-Big Five firms

Study	Sample	Independence Measure	Audit Quality Measure	Findings
Jenkins (2003)	303 Fortune 1000 firms, 2000-2001	Fee ratio; percentile ranking by auditor of nonaudit fees, total fees, and audit fees	Discretionary accruals	Positive association for absolute accruals; negative for directional accruals when variables measuring audit committee effectiveness and its interaction with audit fees are included in model, but when audit committees are effective, no relation between fees and accruals; negative relation for income decreasing accruals, negative for income increasing accruals when performance controlled
Kinney et al. (2003)	432 restating and 512 nonrestating firm fee years, 1995-2000; 289 pairs (76 pairs for first restatement year)	Nonaudit fees by type of service; audit fees	Earnings restatements	No association with prohibited nonaudit service fees; negative relation with tax services (permitted) fees; positive relation with audit fees and miscellaneous nonaudit services fees (permissibility ambiguous); no association in paired sample tests
Krishnan (2003)	5430 firm years, 2000-2001	Total fees; fee ratio; audit fees; nonaudit fees; client importance; unexpected ratio and fee measures	Earnings conservatism	Greater conservatism for high-fee clients than for low-fee clients (total fees, audit fees, and nonaudit fees); no association for fee-ratio or client importance measures
Larcker & Richardson (2004)	3424 firms, 2000-2001	Fee ratio; client importance; abnormal client importance fees	Discretionary accruals	No association; positive association for 8.5% of sample using fee ratio and nondirectional or negative constrained accruals, which group has poor corporate governance features; negative relation using client importance measures and nondirectional and constrained accruals
Lennox (1999)	837 U.K. firms, 1988-1994	Fee ratio; nonaudit fees	Qualified opinion	No association; positive association in one specification (nonaudit services increase audit quality)

Li et al. (2003)	177 large New Zealand firms, 1999; 224 in 2000; 243 in 2001	Nonaudit fees; fee ratio; client importance (total client fees to total revenues)	Qualified or Modified opinion	No association; positive association in one year in one specification (higher nonaudit fees increase probability of qualified opinion)
Pringle & Buchman (1996)	47 bankrupt firms, 1978-1982	Fee ratio	Qualified opinion	No association
Raghunandan et al. (2003)	3591 firms (of which 110 issued restated financials); some tests on 84 pairs of Firms	Unexpected fee ratio; unexpected audit fees; unexpected nonaudit fees	Financial restatements	No association
Reynolds & Francis (2001)	6747 client firms at 499 offices of Big Five firms, 1996 (4952 for accruals; 2439 for Going concern opinion tests)	Client influence (ratio of client log sales to total client sales of local office)	Discretionary and total accruals; volatility of accruals; going concern opinions	Client dependence associated with decreased client discretion (lower accruals) and in some specifications higher rate of going concern opinions; no association if national rather than local office used for influence calculation
Ruddock et al. (2003)	4708 Australian firm-years, 1993-2000	Fee ratio; ratio scaled by assets	Earnings conservatism	No association
Sharma & Sidhu (2001)	49 bankrupt Australian firms, delisted 1989-1996	Fee ratio	Going concern opinion	Negative association

[1] The studies in this table are cited *supra* note 39. 2000 data unless otherwise indicated. Earnings surprises are defined as earnings meeting or just beating the consensus analysts' forecast (that is, an indicator variable for a zero- or one-cent difference between reported earnings and forecast). Small increases are earnings greater than surprises. Fee ratio is the ratio of nonaudit fees to total fees (in Antle et al., Pringle and Buchman, and Li et al. the denominator is audit fees; Bajaj et al. use both denominators). Jenkins uses the ratio of audit fees to total fees, but for consistency in comparison of the results across studies, the table reports the results as if she had used the same fee ratio as the others (it reverses the sign of the results in the paper). Total fees are the total of nonaudit and audit fees. Client importance computes the fee measures (fee ratio, nonaudit fees, or total fees) in relation to the auditor's total U.S. revenue. The Craswell et al. fee ratio is the ratio of client audit or client nonaudit fees to total fees.

Table 6
Study of Executive Loan Programs (Shastri & Kahle, 2004)[1]

Type of loan (number in sample)	Mean loan amount (% secured)	Mean interest rate	Findings on incentive alignment hypothesis
Stock purchase (334)	\$2,5000,000 (63.6%)	6.057%	Ownership increases; much higher increases for managers with low stock ownership
Stock option purchase (246)	\$1,700,000 (78.4%)	6.187%	Ownership increases
Relocation (91)	\$770,000 (75.3%)	3.910%	No effect on ownership

[1] The study in this table is cited supra note 48. It used a sample of 70 firms issuing loans to executives from 1996 to 2000, for a total of 2018 person-year observations, of which 700 are observations of executives with outstanding loans and 1469 are person-year observations for ownership calculations. Percent secured for stock and option purchase loans is fraction secured by stock; for relocation loans, percent secured is fraction secured by assets (purchased house).

Table 7
Event studies on Executive Certification of Financials[1]

Study	Sample	Findings
Bhattacharya et al. (2002)	902 firms required to certify (of these, 22 noncertifiers)	No significant abnormal returns to any portfolio; noncertifiers did not experience abnormal trading volume or volatility; firm characteristics not significantly related to magnitude of abnormal return
Hirtle (2003)	42 bank holding companies (all certified by deadline)	Positive abnormal returns on certification date; portfolio result driven by early certifiers (when subdivided by certification date, only early certifiers' returns are significant); firm characteristics of opacity related to size of abnormal return but not to timing of certification

[1] The studies in this table are cited supra note 57.

Financial Moral Panic! Sarbanes-Oxley, Financier Folk Devils, and Off-Balance-Sheet Arrangements[*]

José M. Gabilondo[**]

INTRODUCTION

The firm has come undone.[1] The break-up started as an idea in finance, where options pricing and transaction cost analysis traced the firm's fault lines with theoretical implications about how the firm funds itself.[2] Then, traders went to work, turning

---

[**] Assistant Professor, College of Law, Florida International University, Miami, Florida, jose.gabilondo@fiu.edu.; B.A., Harvard University, 1987; J.D., University of California, Boalt Hall School of Law, 1991.
The allocative and distributional constraints of an acknowledgement notwithstanding, I must thank my College of Law chums for their gifts to my earlier drafts: Heather Hughes (voice), Jerry Markham (financial history), Peggy Maisel (purpose), Charles Pouncy (theory), and Howard Wasserman (sociology). I am also grateful for the thoughtful comments of George Mundstock (University of Miami School of Law) and Roger Schechter (George Washington University School of Law) and to John Gordon (Boston College School of Law) for the Tantra of Bluebook. Thanks also to my dedicated research assistants, Henry Chaverra, Jeff Hochberg, Lina Husseini, and Tony Montesano, Janet Reinke (our law librarian), and the other Law Library staff for their research support. All errors are my own.

[1] Instead of thinking of it as a solid entity, see the firm as a cipher and accounting rules as the symbol system that constitutes and decodes the cipher. Accounting theorists see the firm this way. *See, e.g.*, Jim Donegan & Shyam Sunder, CONTRACT THEORETIC ANALYSIS OF OFF-BALANCE SHEET FINANCING, J. Acct. Auditing & Fin., March 1989, at 203, 204 ("From the representational faithfulness perspective, the firm is seen as a collection of economic facts; accounting methods are evaluated by their ability to produce numbers and disclosures that approximate these facts as closely as possible.") (citations omitted). The "facts" are value propositions about cash flows and contingencies. The law of financial reporting is the syntax and the grammar of this language and each financial report is a novel utterance. A good transactional lawyer is a finance semiotician too. *See* generally Lawrence A. Cunningham, SEMIOTICS, HERMENEUTICS, AND CASH: AN ESSAY ON THE TRUE AND FAIR VIEW, 28 N.C. J. Int'l L. & Com. Reg. 893, 894-95 (2003) (arguing that a hermeneutic approach to accounting would facilitate the convergence of national accounting standards).

[2] Two major insights that in particular helped to atomize the firm's cash flows were options pricing and transaction cost economics. In 1973, a paper by Fischer Black and Myron Scholes transformed finance

these financial insights into self-sustaining markets where firms could meet their needs for liquidity and capital with complex products.[3] Here, securitization and other forms of disintermediation made funds more mobile[4] and helped to "complete" the financial markets.[5] Understandably, the Securities and Exchange Commission (SEC)

---

by demonstrating a mathematical approach to pricing options and corporate liabilities. Fischer Black & Myron S. Scholes, THE PRICING OF OPTIONS AND CORPORATE LIABILITIES, 81 J. Pol. Econ. 637 (1973). A new part of financial speech, options pricing let traders estimate the value of bundles of financial risk which had previously been held hostage to whole asset forms. In other words, the Black-Scholes model helped to demonstrate that an option is the smallest unit of financial contingency. *See infra* note 185 for an example of an options pricing analogy for the federal government's risk with respect to federally-insured deposits. Maturing after options pricing, transaction cost economics provided an intellectual foundation for increased scrutiny of the "make-or-buy" problem as applied to funding. *See* Ronald Coase, THE NATURE OF THE FIRM (1937), *reprinted in* THE NATURE OF THE FIRM: ORIGINS, EVOLUTION, AND DEVELOPMENT 18 (Oliver Williamson ed., 1990) (illuminating how a firm's organizational structure reflects the decisions by a firm to economize on costs by sometimes internalizing factors of production and, at other times buying them in the open market); *see also* Oliver Williamson, THE ECONOMIC INSTITUTIONS OF CAPITALISM 2-12 (1985) (putting the 1937 article in the context of the analytical approaches which developed in its wake). *See infra* notes 257-61, 275-78 and accompanying text for recommendations to reduce the transaction costs of gathering information about firms' effective capital structure in order to promote greater investor understanding of firm funding. *See generally* Charles R.P. Pouncy, *Contemporary Financial Innovation: Orthodoxy and Alternatives*, 51 SMU L. REV. 505, 551-54 (1998) (arguing that the Efficient Capital Markets Hypothesis, modern portfolio theory, the Modigliani-Miller theorem about optimal capital structure, and options pricing provided the rationale for wide use of new financial products).

[3] When used to describe a firm, "liquidity" means the firm's ability to satisfy its payment obligations as they become due. *See* U.S. COMPTROLLER OF THE CURRENCY, LIQUIDITY: COMPTROLLER'S HANDBOOK 1 (2001), available at http://www.occ.treas.gov/handbook/liquidity.pdf. Prudential regulation of depository institutions has the most systematic approach to firm liquidity. *See generally* Jarl Kallberg & Kenneth Parkinson, CORPORATE LIQUIDITY: MANAGEMENT AND MEASUREMENT (1993). *See* Pouncy, *supra* note 2, at 527-34, 569-71 (showing how competition and interest in speculation led to intermediation in firm funding through swaps, derivatives, money market instruments, and securitization)

[4] "Funding" refers to how the firm finances its activities. *See* LIQUIDITY: COMPTROLLER'S HANDBOOK, *supra* note 3, at 9-22 (summarizing liquidity sources and distinguishing between retail and wholesale funding sources). In general, funding relates to the liabilities and equity accounts on the right hand side of the balance sheet. An operational rather than legal concept, funding refers to how the firm stays afloat as an obligor. To appreciate what funding means to transactional lawyers, visit The Bond Market Association, Funding, http://www.bondmarkets.com/funding (last visited Feb. 18, 2006). "Disintermediation" means any substitution in the funding market by one liquidity or capital source for another. *See* LIQUIDITY: COMPTROLLER'S HANDBOOK, *supra* note 3, at 1-2 (explaining how the shift from retail to wholesale funding by banks has increased their overall liquidity risk). À la Coase, transaction cost efficiencies drive these substitutions. For example, the commercial paper market took off because high-quality borrowers could borrow more cheaply by issuing their own paper to investors rather than by getting a bank loan. *See* John P. Judd, *Competition Between the Commercial Paper Market and Commercial Banks*, Econ. Rev. (1st Q. 1979), at 39. Similarly, transaction accounts with nonbank financial institutions have diverted customer deposits from banks, now scrambling for low-cost funding. (Deposits were the manna of bank funding because they were cheap.) *See, e.g.*, Robert Litan, The Revolution in U.S. Finance: Past, Present, and Future, Remarks Before The American College, Bryn Mawr, Pennsylvania (Apr. 30, 1991) (explaining how receivables securitization transformed the flow of funds between financial intermediaries) (copy on file with author).

[5] A complete market is one in which all commodities and claims can be traded. WILLIAM H. BEAVER, FINANCIAL REPORTING: AN ACCOUNTING REVOLUTION 38-39 (3d ed. 1998). *See also* Mario Draghi et al.,

and accounting regulators did not keep pace with these dynamic shifts.[6] Before these shifts, readers of financial reports could look to the balance sheet as a rough proxy for a firm's net worth.[7] But as firm managers turned increasingly to "off-balance-sheet" (OBS) arrangements like swaps and special purpose vehicles, the balance sheet lost its faithfulness as a public financial report.[8] Investors outside of the charmed circle of the financially initiated were lost.

The gap between what public financial reports say about funding and how the cash actually moves in and out of firms became apparent with some highly publicized losses at Enron and other large firms, many of which involved cash flow games.[9] A Greek chorus of indignant legislators, disgruntled investors, and evasive regulators blamed the losses on rogue managers and officers at these firms. These cads had broken the rules of

---

Transparency, Risk Management and International Financial Fragility, at 1 (Harv. Bus. Sch. Working Paper No. 03-118, 2003) ("The role of swaps and other privately negotiated derivative instruments is to complete financial markets, thus increasing the ability of individuals, financial institutions, corporations and governments to manage risk.").

[6] This is another example of the point that "[c]ontemporary financial innovation is a dance between the regulator and the regulated." Pouncy, *supra* note 2, at 546 (showing how heterodox economic theory reveals a wider range of public risks from derivatives and financial innovation generally than does orthodox economics). Pouncy notes how firms mitigate the costs of regulation through tactical innovation:

> Kane has characterized this process as the "regulatory dialectic." This process is a continual struggle between regulators and the regulated in which regulatory policy is confronted with financial innovation designed to circumvent the policy. Regulatory policy is then adjusted to counteract the circumventive innovation, which, in turn, induces another innovative response. This process is also known as Goodhart's Law, which concludes that "basing a policy upon a recognized statistical relationship will bring about a policy-induced change in the relationship."

Id. (footnotes omitted) (citing Edward J. Kane, MICROECONOMIC AND MACROECONOMIC ORIGINS OF FINANCIAL INNOVATION, IN FINANCIAL INNOVATION 5-6 (William L. Silber ed., 1975)); *see also infra* notes 262-75 and accompanying text for a critical evaluation of the agency's knowledge base.

[7] *See infra* notes 107-14 and accompanying text to appreciate the scope of the balance sheet.

[8] State law, the certificate of incorporation, or a bond covenant may let other corporate constituencies vote on fundamental questions of capital structure. *See* JERRY W. MARKHAM & THOMAS LEE HAZEN, CORPORATE FINANCE: CASES AND MATERIALS 156-220 (2004). It is, however, the firm's managers who run its day-to-day funding, including the use of off-balance-sheet arrangements.

[9] In addition to Enron, recent prominent corporate scandals have included Dynegy (misrepresentation of cash flows on its statement of cash flows), Global Crossing (potential phantom transactions with no economic substance), Adelphia (three billion dollars in questionable loans), Tyco (charges of tax evasion and evidence tampering), WorldCom (significant accounting irregularities), Xerox Company (accounting irregularities), Arthur Andersen (obstruction of justice claim), KPMG (auditing malfeasance), ImClone (insider trading), and Merrill Lynch & Company (deceptive securities analysis). *See generally* Jerry W. Markham, *Accountants Make Miserable Policemen: Rethinking the Federal Securities Laws*, 28 N.C.J. INT'L L. & COM. REG. 725, 773-86 (2003) (reviewing asset write-downs, rising earnings restatements, and other accounting irregularities leading to market and Securities and Exchange Commission (SEC) interventions). For a bibliography of over one hundred legal, administrative, and congressional documents related just to Enron, the most notorious of these scandals, see Stephanie Burke, *The Collapse of Enron: A Bibliography of Online Legal, Governmental and Legislative Resources,* Apr. 15, 2002, http://www.llrx.com/features/enron.htm.

the game, said the chorus. A special fury went to the auditors who had given the rogues cover under financial accounting. In this blame narrative, financiers became folk devils who threatened virtuous wealth accumulation by retail investors and others. (Much of what was "lost" was unrealized value created by these rogues in the first place using the same accounting practices, but more about this later.) The pattern of losses across firms cast doubt on the financial reporting model overall, including the statement of cash flows, a financial report which had previously stood in relatively good repute.[10]

Financial moral panic! A moral panic starts with some bit of reality and then mushrooms into a movement for reform as sensationalist media reports fuel populist outrage over wrongdoing.[11] In a moral panic, "[s]tatements that would . . . mark the speaker as hyperbolic or paranoid suddenly acquire the status of incontestable fact, while skeptics are pitied for their callous denial."[12] In this nervous climate, Congress passed the Sarbanes-Oxley Act of 2002 (Sarbanes-Oxley or Act).[13] Moral panic legislation blames social problems on bad people rather than bad structures and the Act bears these hallmarks by casting corporate officials and auditors as deviants. In this case, casting financiers as miscreants substituted for a more nuanced examination of whether the law of financial reporting adequately mapped firms' true capital structure in light of the dynamic funding shifts of the past thirty years.[14]

To Congress's credit, the Act roused the SEC from its slumber over accounting. Specifically, the Act directed the agency to require publicly-registered firms to say more about these curious "off-balance-sheet" items, which had previously escaped much substantive disclosure.[15] Under the baleful glare of Congress, the SEC adopted

---

[10] The balance sheet is built on generally accepted accounting principles (GAAP), the basis for financial accounting. *See* Markham, *supra* note 9, at 765-68 (reviewing the development of generally accepted auditing standards (GAAS) and GAAP).

[11] *See infra* notes 32-53 and accompanying text for an explanation of moral panic and moral panic analysis.

[12] PHILIP JENKINS, MORAL PANIC: CHANGING CONCEPTS OF THE CHILD MOLESTER IN MODERN AMERICA 7 (1998) (analyzing the moral panics from 1890s-1990s about the sexual abuse of minors). To understand the analogy drawn in this Article, substitute "financier" for "child molester."

[13] Sarbanes-Oxley Act of 2002, Pub. L. No. 107-204, 116 Stat. 745 (codified at 15 U.S.C. §§ 7201-66 (Supp. II 2002).

[14] By the law of financial reporting I mean only federal securities laws, not state laws that impose financial reporting requirements.

[15] Sarbanes-Oxley Act of 2002 § 401(a), 15 U.S.C. § 7261(c)(1) (Supp. II 2002), added § 13(j) to the Securities Exchange Act of 1934, which required the SEC to amend its rules to require each annual and quarterly financial report required to be filed with the SEC to disclose:

> all material off-balance sheet transactions, arrangements, obligations (including contingent obligations), and other relationships of the issuer with unconsolidated entities or other persons, that may have a material current or future effect on financial condition, changes in financial condition, results of operations, liquidity, capital expenditures, capital resources, or significant components of revenues or expenses.

15 U.S.C. § 78m(j) (Supp. II 2002).

a rule that selectively increases the transparency of firms' effective capital structure by making them consider the financial impact of some types of OBS arrangements.[16] When reporting to Congress on the rule's efficacy and the current structure of the OBS market, though, the SEC admitted that market transparency problems persist.[17] Given the ongoing gap between publicly-reported funding and funding as the daily practice of survival by firms, do public financial reports say enough about how a firm finances itself? Not yet. Much of what led to Enron and the other losses continues.[18] What is needed is a technical legal approach rather than the now-familiar "perp" walk on the nightly news.

Like Marabunta,[19] scholars have descended upon the Act's provisions about corporate governance, the audit process, and accounting generally. My own ant-like contribution to this debate is to frame the Act in terms of financial moral panic, to point out how this legislative approach limited the Act's efficacy in predictable ways, and to recommend changes to reduce, if possible, the risk of future financial moral panics. Indeed, as noted, post-Enron scholarship ought to restore a factual rather than moral approach to complex financial transactions.[20]

---

[16] SEC Final Rule: Disclosure in Management's Discussion and Analysis about Off-Balance Sheet Arrangements and Aggregate Contractual Obligations, Exchange Act Release No. 34-47264 (Jan. 28, 2003), available at http://www.sec.gov/rules/final/33-8182.htm, codified at 17 C.F.R. §§ 228-29, 249 (2005).

[17] *See* OFFICE OF THE CHIEF ACCOUNTANT, SEC, REPORT AND RECOMMENDATIONS PURSUANT TO SECTION 401(C) OF THE SARBANES-OXLEY ACT OF 2002 ON ARRANGEMENTS WITH OFF-BALANCE SHEET IMPLICATIONS, SPECIAL PURPOSE ENTITIES, AND TRANSPARENCY OF FILINGS BY ISSUERS 40 (2005), http://www.sec.gov/news/studies/soxoffbalancerpt.pdf [hereinafter SEC Report]. *See also infra* notes 225-34 and accompanying text about the SEC's conclusion that opacity persists with respect to the transparency of firms' OBS dealings.

[18] *See* Frank Partnoy, *A Revisionist View of Enron and the Sudden Death of "May,"* 48 VILL. L. REV. 1245, 1264 (2003) (arguing that Sarbanes-Oxley failed to appreciate the significance of risk from OBS derivatives to the Enron crisis):

> Moreover, pre-Enron market failures are likely to continue if certain structural conditions in the market persist. First, disclosure related to derivatives positions is costly, and those costs are not reduced by the collapse of Enron; indeed, the cost of derivatives disclosure is greater if market participants are more concerned about such disclosures. Second, it is not necessarily easier for market participants to assess derivatives disclosure (or non-disclosure) post-Enron; they have similar technological capacity and access to information. Moreover, the gap between what managers know and what shareholders understand could persist if both issuers and investors become more sophisticated.

Id. (emphasis added) (footnotes omitted).

[19] Also called the New World Army Ants, the *marabunta* travel in hordes and devour agricultural land. *See* New World Army Ants, http://www.armyants.org (last visited Feb. 19, 2006); La Marabunta, http://www.lamarabunta.org/ (last visited Feb. 19, 2006) (Spanish-language site for ant enthusiasts).

[20] *See* Partnoy, *supra* note 18, at 1247 (arguing that regulatory responses to Enron based on the idea that fraud rather than financial complexity of derivatives led to Enron are misguided). Such scholarship has already been developed with respect to securitization, which suffered guilt-by-association to the extent that it was associated with Enron's OBS practices. *See* Steven L. Schwarcz, *Securitization Post-Enron*, 25 CARDOZO L. REV. 1539, 1568-74 (2004) (clarifying the value of securitization); Steven L. Schwarcz, *Enron and the Use and Abuse of Special Purpose Entities in Corporate Structures,* 70 U. CIN. L. REV. 1309, 1318

With an argument used historically by the Left, Part I explains how financial moral panic was the zeitgeist for the Act.[21] In a financial moral panic, false cause obscures a more complete understanding of cause-in-fact by blaming what are really routine market losses on individuals deemed to have acted in exceptionally opportunistic ways. The Act's legislative history shows how financiers came to be viewed as folk devils and financial predators. Framed this way, their misconduct would distract investors and others from ambient economic anxieties about the ongoing market risk of unrealized gain in financial assets, an anxiety made more acute during a price bubble. Unfortunately, structural economic insecurity transcends individual misconduct. Indeed, this insecurity is intrinsic to our economic system.

Turning from cultural studies to financial reporting, Part II explains, again, why the balance sheet no longer reflects a firm's financial position.[22] The aim here is to provide a critical counterpoint to the prevailing view that financiers at Enron and other firms destroyed "real" shareholder value, often with bogus deals involving off-balance-sheet arrangements. Indeed, managers' fiduciary duties to shareholders may have obliged these managers to use such arrangements (and, indeed, may continue to do so) for the sake of increasing residual return. To show how better cash flow reporting may have stemmed these losses, this Article discusses the statement of cash flows, a relative late-comer to the financial reporting model. This is part of a plea for reporting a firm's effective capital structure to improve the overall usefulness of public reports to financial reporting's diverse constituencies, i.e., investors, financial regulators, managers, auditors, and information intermediaries.[23] More granular disclosure would benefit investors (even though it might increase firms' reported volatility) by reminding investors of the unavoidable uncertainty of future financial states of the world. Part III then discusses the SEC's OBS disclosure rule.[24] In truth, despite its substantial limitations, the rule contributes to the evolution of financial reporting because the rule makes firms say more about their effective capital structure.[25] But more is needed.

(2002) ("Ultimately, the greatest danger of the Enron debacle is our possible overreaction, and consequent over-regulation."); *see also* William W. Bratton, *Enron and the Dark Side of Shareholder Value*, 76 TUL. L. REV. 1275, 1283 (2002) ("[T]he rogue characterization serves a double function—it deflects attention from the respectable community's own business practices. This Article aspires to counterbalance with a picture of Enron's collapse that deemphasizes the rogue to focus on the regular."); Steven L. Schwarcz, *Rethinking the Disclosure Paradigm in a World of Complexity*, 2004 U. ILL. L. REV. 1, 18-19 (challenging the efficacy of mere disclosure of extremely complex financial instruments because disclosure will not produce a critical mass of investors who understand the transaction reasonably promptly).

[21] *See infra* notes 54-104 and accompanying text.

[22] *See infra* notes 122-34, 217-24 and accompanying text.

[23] Beaver notes that financial reporting balances the interests of five distinct constituencies: investors choosing between alternative investment portfolios, financial reporting regulators concerned about capital formation and resource allocation, firms' managers interested in increasing shareholder wealth and their own, auditors who need financial information to certify a firm's financial reports, and information intermediaries involved in searching out and processing "raw" financial data. *See* Beaver, *supra* note 5, at 150-56.

[24] *See infra* notes 187-216 and accompanying text.

[25] *See infra* notes 198-203 and accompanying text.

Part IV recommends some technical improvements to these technical problems.[26] First, the SEC should require firms to disclose a transparency ratio on the balance sheet which suggests the magnitude of OBS items not otherwise disclosed.[27] Revealing the fact of nondisclosure would seem to be a corollary of disclosure.[28] Such a financial transparency ratio would reduce the information gap between firm insiders and outsiders without too much reporting "noise." Second, the SEC should require the reporting of more firm-level information about cash flow to help market intermediaries further disaggregate the firm's cash flows into tradable units. The SEC could do this through the statement of cash flows.[29] If adopted, these suggestions would increase transparency, enabling traders and other financial intermediaries to further complete funding markets.[30] Also, the SEC should institutionalize market-wide surveillance of effective capital structure to increase the agency's in-house knowledge about funding trends. So informed, the SEC could better mitigate future financial moral panics by responding to

---

[26] *See infra* notes 245-80 and accompanying text.

[27] I use the word "firm" broadly to mean any business that consumes financial capital. So that includes corporations, partnerships, limited liability entities, business trusts, and other forms of business organization. Federal securities laws require any firm with $10 million or more in assets and five hundred or more owners of any class of equity securities to register with the SEC. Securities Exchange Act of 1934, 15 U.S.C. §§ 78a-78ll (2002). Registrants include the country's largest corporations, thus including those listed on the exchange and over-the-counter securities markets. My comments about financial reporting obligations under federal securities law apply only to registrants, but the economic arguments in the Article apply to all firms.

[28] There are three kinds of knowledge: what one knows, what one knows that one does not know, and what one does not know that he does not know. The distinction reflects the behavioral assumption that "human behavior is intendedly rational, but only limitedly so . . . ." HERBERT A. SIMON, ADMINISTRATIVE BEHAVIOR: A STUDY OF DECISION-MAKING PROCESSES IN ADMINISTRATIVE ORGANIZATION xxiv (1961).

[29] In considering cash flow, I join others who note the value of liquidity disclosures. *See* Matthew J. Barrett, *The SEC and Accounting, in Part Through the Eyes of Pacioli*, 80 NOTRE DAME L. REV. 837, 863-65 (2005) (praising the value of the liquidity risk disclosures required to be made by Item 303 of Regulation S-K); Cunningham, *supra* note 1, at 924-30 (arguing that increased accounting focus on the statement of cash flows would facilitate international convergence of accounting standards); Jack Friedman, *Chapter 11 Financial Reporting Rules for Debtors: The Impact on Creditors, Shareholders, New Investors, and the Bar*, 9 EMORY BANKR. DEV. J. 257, 266 (1992) (noting creditor interest in increased disclosure of cash flow information about debtors); Henry T. C. Hu, *Faith and Magic: Investor Beliefs and Government Neutrality*, 78 TEX. L. REV. 777, 854-60 (2000) (arguing that mutual funds should be subject to the same general liquidity disclosures currently required for publicly-registered companies); Stanley Siegel, *The Coming Revolution in Accounting: The Emergence of Fair Value as the Fundamental Principle of GAAP*, 42 WAYNE L. REV. 1839, 1850 (1996) (arguing that recent accounting pronouncements recognize the increasing relevance of cash flow calculations).

[30] Accounting considers financial reporting from two distinct but related perspectives: financial reporting as an information tool in the service of market efficiency and financial reporting as a measurement device for a firm's financial characteristics. *See* Beaver, *supra* note 5, at 76-77. An informational view evaluates the adequacy of financial reports in terms of their marginal informational value to decision-making about the firm. *Id.* A measurement view strives for fidelity between a firm's financial reports and its financial essence. *Id.* Although the recommendations made in Part IV have informational consequences, the thrust of this Article is to measure the firm as a financial item in a more comprehensive fashion.

fear with facts. Part V points out that there will always be an Enron and that, therefore, transactional law faculty should proselytize students (and seek curricular rents from deans) in order to increase the transactional and financial sophistication of law students, who could then better inject sobriety into future panics.[31]

I. FINANCIAL MORAL PANIC: FINANCIERS AS PREDATORS

Congress passed the Act after a hue and cry went up about investor and employee losses caused by accounting irregularities at several national firms.[32] Typical of moral panic legislation, the Act focused on bad actors rather than on bad structures.[33] In particular, the thorny issue that the Act and the prior Congressional hearings dodged was the extent of economic insecurity intrinsic to an economy such as ours, in which most people's wealth takes the form of unrealized gain in financial assets. As discussed in the following section, displacement of this sort is par for a moral panic. What was novel about this one was the symbiotic (and ambivalent) relationship between the moral discourse against the market and the critics' psychological and financial investment in the market itself. Let me start by explaining moral panic and moral panic analysis.

A. Moral Panic and Moral Panic Analysis

Moral panic theory claims that the media, moral entrepreneurs, government authorities, and special interest groups (including values communities) often react to a perceived threat to a fundamental social interest by invoking a deviant to blame for the perceived threat.[34] Stanley Cohen, now a sociologist at the London School of

---

[31] This Article grew out of teaching the Dynegy case (mentioned *supra* note 9 and discussed *infra* notes 150-53 and accompanying text) in my corporate finance course at the College of Law. The case resonated with my conclusion from my time in Washington, D.C. during the Enron hearings that the law has not adequately thematized useful legal standards about how firms fund themselves. The two notable exceptions to this conclusion are the prudential regulation of banks and the net capital rule for broker-dealers (discussed *infra* notes 182-85, 263 and accompanying text), two examples of a federal interest in firm funding. I began writing this Article to identify OBS arrangements which would be presumptively material under the applicable disclosure standards. Deductive presumptions develop in common law after a period of gestation through inductive adjudication. I had wanted to shortcut that process, since presumptions can add legal certainty to compliance and can help judges faced with adjudicating the materiality of complex OBS items. My research, however, did not turn up enough aggregate data about effective capital structure to let me articulate a presumption about the materiality of OBS items. So, I offer the financial transparency ratio discussed herein, *infra* notes 248-56 and accompanying text, as a basis for a future presumption about materiality. I leave the project of building presumptions to the future, my own as well as that of colleagues, critics, and allies.

[32] *See supra* note 9 listing some of the more prominent examples of the losses attributed to accounting irregularities.

[33] *See infra* notes 95-104 and accompanying text.

[34] *See* STANLEY COHEN, FOLK DEVILS AND MORAL PANICS xxxi (3d ed. 2002). Cohen notes a concurrent use of the term by another researcher control (Jock Young), and assumes that both traced the idea of moral panic to Marshall McLuhan. *Id.*; *see generally* MARSHALL MCLUHAN, UNDERSTANDING MEDIA: THE

Economics, introduced the moral panic concept to analyze nervous British reactions to public brawling between two youth groups in Britain: the Mods and the Rockers.[35] He defined a moral panic as a situation in which a

> condition, episode, person or group of persons emerges to become defined as a threat to societal values and interests; its nature is presented in a stylized and stereotypical fashion by the mass media; the moral barricades are manned by editors, bishops, politicians and other right-thinking people; [and] socially accredited experts pronounce their diagnoses and solutions.[36] Reviewing the deployment of the concept over its busy thirty-year life, Cohen recently identified seven classic social situations which trigger a moral panic.[37] What the triggers have in common is that they are perceived by the usual authorities (Church, state, the family or their diverse proxies) to threaten the social or moral order: young, working class violent males;[38] school violence;[39] recreational drug use;[40] child abusers, Satanists, and pedophiles;[41] popular dissemination of sexual and violent content; welfare cheats and single mothers;[42] and refugees and asylum seekers. Though comprehensive, this

EXTENSIONS OF MAN (1964). Other British sociologists like Stuart Hall also popularized the idea, which formed part of the cultural studies movement. *See infra* note 68 and accompanying text for Hall's argument about the racialized construction of mugging. *See generally* Michael Tonry, *Rethinking Unthinkable Punishment Policies in America*, 46 UCLA L. REV. 1751, 1782-84 (1999) (reviewing the original clash between the Mods and the Rockers leading to early moral panic analysis).

35 *See* Cohen, *supra* note 34, passim.

36 *See id.* at 1.

37 *See id.* at viii-xxi. Most of these situation predicates have generated legal scholarship applying moral panic analysis.

38 *See, e.g.*, John M. Hagedorn, *Gang Violence in the Postindustrial Era*, 24 CRIME & JUST. 365, 376 (1998) (noting tendency to construct male gangs as deviant during a moral panic).

39 *See, e.g.*, Aaron H. Caplan, *Public School Discipline for Creating Uncensored Anonymous Internet Forums*, 39 WILLAMETTE L. REV. 93, 112-20 (2003) (noting moral panic over use of Internet by teenagers).

40 *See, e.g.*, Kathleen Auerhahn, *The Labor Market and the Origins of Antidrug Legislation in the United States*, 24 LAW & SOC. INQUIRY 411, 411-16 (1999) (using moral panic analysis to explain how anti-drug legislation acts to manage the formation of class interests); Theodore Caplow & Jonathan Simon, *Understanding Prison Policy and Population Trends*, 26 CRIME & JUST. 63, 85-86 (1999) (noting that drug trafficking and child abuse have recently produced moral panics).

41 *See, e.g.*, Amy Adler, *The Perverse Law of Child Pornography*, 101 COLUM. L. REV. 209, 232 (2001) (noting moral panic in connection with child abuse); John Comaroff & Jean Comaroff, *Policing Culture, Cultural Policing: Law and Social Order in Postcolonial South Africa*, 29 LAW & SOC. INQUITY 513, 514-16 (2004) (explaining a moral panic in South Africa in response to occult-related violence).

42 *See* Megan Weinstein, *The Teenage Pregnancy "Problem": Welfare Reform and the Personal Responsibility and Work Opportunity Reconciliation Act of 1996*, 13 BERKELEY WOMEN'S L.J. 117, 144 (1998) (noting moral panic in response to teen sexual activity); Rachael Knight, Comment, *From Hester Prynne to Crystal Chambers: Unwed Mothers, Authentic Role Models, and Coerced Speech*, 25 BERKELEY J. EMP. & LAB. L. 481, 486 (2004) (analogizing to moral panic to explain the treatment of unwed mothers).

is not an exhaustive list. Crime triggers much moral panic.[43] Sexual and gender minorities are also favorite targets of moral panics.[44]

In each of these cases, an incident or pattern catalyzes pre-existing social anxiety and an ad hoc issues movement is born. The media fans the flames through sensationalist and reductionist news stories.[45] As Cohen notes, identifying a "folk devil" to blame takes the place of cooler consideration of multivariate causes which may have contributed to the original trigger.[46] Usually, a hasty legal reform results from the panic. Driven as it is by irrationality, the reforms usually miss the point of the original problem and suffer from disproportionality.[47]

A remedial move made by socially conscious critics, moral panic theory contests the "folk devil" construction of the problem and reframes it, instead emphasizing structural causes. Thus, moral panic theory reveals the unstated ideological interests at work in a particular framing of a problem by allowing us "to identify and conceptualize the lines of power in any society, the ways we are manipulated into taking some things too seriously and other things not seriously enough."[48] In discussing the Mods and the Rockers, Cohen lists the two key aspects of a moral panic which moral panic theory targets, i.e., an ideological slant and false causation:

> [T]he point [of moral panic analysis] was to expose social reaction not just as over-reaction in some quantitative sense, but first as tendentious (that is, slanted in a particular ideological direction) and second, as misplaced or displaced (that is, aimed—whether deliberately or thoughtlessly—at a target which was not the 'real' problem).[49]

While a moral panic fixates on individual deviants, moral panic analysis tries to refocus the policy debate on the web of institutions, ideological interests, and other

---

[43] *See, e.g.*, Sarah Eschholz, *The Media and Fear of Crime: A Survey of the Research*, 9 J. LAW. & PUB. POL'Y 37, 46-52 (1997) (analyzing the relationship between media coverage of crime and fear of crime); Daniel M. Filler, *Silence and the Dimension of Megan's Law*, 89 IOWA L. REV. 1535, 1581-88 (2004) (noting disparate impact on African Americans of Megan's Laws requiring registration of persons convicted of sexual offenses); Neil Gilbert, *Advocacy Research and Social Policy*, 22 CRIME & JUST. 101, 105 (1997) (noting in connection with rape that research conducted by issue advocates may contribute to sensationalized reporting); Joseph E. Kennedy, *Monstrous Offenders and the Search for Solidarity Through Modern Punishment*, 51 HASTINGS L.J. 829, 860-86 (2000) (using moral panic idea to explain the selected increase in criminal punishment in the United States during the 1980s and 1990s).

[44] *See* Nancy J. Knauer, *Homosexuality as Contagion: From the Well of Loneliness to the Boy Scouts*, 29 HOFSTRA L. REV. 401, 438, (2000) (using moral panic to explain heteronormative reprisal to expressions of same-sex identity); Marc S. Spindelman, *Reorienting Bowers v. Hardwick*, 79 N.C. L. REV. 359, 446 (2001) (linking constitutional validation of criminal homosexual sodomy statute to moral panic about AIDS).

[45] *See* Cohen, *supra* note 34, at 1.

[46] *Id.* at xxii.

[47] *Id.; see also* Jenkins, *supra* note 12.

[48] *See* Cohen, *supra* note 34, at xxxv.

[49] *Id.* at xxxi.

drivers that work in concert to recast social anxieties into a discourse about bad people rather than bad conditions.[50] Moral panic theory must evolve in light of changes in media structure and in reaction to complementary theories of social construction and cultural studies, of which moral panic was an important harbinger.[51] By extending the analysis beyond the usual authorities and the usual suspects,[52] my aim is to expand the reach of moral panic arguments into financial legislation as well.[53]

B. Financial Moral Panic: When Financiers Become "Folk Devils"

Financial moral panic is the expression in the explicitly economic sphere of the more general form of moral panic. The public discourse about the scandals discussed in this Article was framed in the familiar terms of a moral panic. In this panic narrative, rogue managers and auditors threatened public confidence in a vital public good—the capital market—risking the solvency of every investor's financial future. A national auto de fe against financial heresy, the Congressional hearings leading up to the Act opened on this tone.[54] Consistent with popular accounts of accounting scandals, the legislative

---

[50] *Id.* at xxii:

> To point to the complexities of the relationship between social objects and their interpretations is not a 'criticism' but the whole point of studying deviance and social control. Some trivial and harmless forms of rule-breaking can indeed be 'blown out of all proportion.' And yes, some very serious, significant and horrible events—even genocide, political massacres, atrocities and massive suffering—can be denied, ignored or played down. Most putative problems lie between these two extremes—exactly where and why calls for a comparative sociology of moral panic that makes comparisons within one society and also between societies.

[51] *See* Angela McRobbie & Sarah L. Thornton, *Rethinking 'Moral Panic' for Multi-Mediated Social Worlds*, 46 BRIT. J. SOC. 559, 560 (1995).

> Although both the original model of moral panics and the reformulations which introduced notions of ideology and hegemony were exemplary interventions in their time, we argue that it is impossible to rely on the old models with their stages and cycles, univocal media, monolithic societal or hegemonic reactions. The proliferation and fragmentation of mass, niche and micro-media and the multiplicity of voices, which compete and contest the meaning of the issues subject to 'moral panic,' suggest that both the original and revised models are outdated in so far as they could not possibly take account of the labyrinthine web of determining relations which now exist between social groups and the media, 'reality' and representation.

Id. Cohen notes that theories of social construction, media and cultural studies, and the idea of the "risk" society followed the sociology of moral panic analysis. *See* Cohen, *supra* note 34, at xxii-xxvi.

[52] *See supra* notes 37-44 and accompanying text.

[53] Security panic analysis is another extension of the moral panic concept. Security panic arguments explain repressive intrusions in civil liberties on perceived threats to national security, typically from non-citizens or other outsiders. *See* Adrian Vermeule, *Libertarian Panics*, 36 RUTGERS L.J. 871 (2005).

[54] In Inquisition history, the auto de fe was a public spectacle in which the Crown and Inquisition authorities convened in the town square to discipline those who had been convicted by Inquisition authorities for violating religious law. *See* JEAN PLAIDY, THE SPANISH INQUISITION 147-59 (1967). In Spain, the auto de fe helped to consolidate a central national identity by imposing a uniform regulation across geographically and culturally disparate communities. *Id.* at 87-103.

history of the Sarbanes-Oxley Act similarly reflects the reception of the blame narrative.[55] Some witnesses did testify to the technical nature of the accounting problems which underlay Enron,[56] but these voices were outnumbered by the gnashing of teeth over lapses in professional ethics. Imputing a simple intent to Congress's 535 independent

---

[55] Notice the invocation of sensationalist media accounts typical of a panic in the opening statement of the Committee Chair, Senator Sarbanes:

> The stunning collapse of Enron has cast a long and dark shadow over our capital markets, crowding other important stories off the business pages and creating widespread anxiety. Headlines like: "Worries of More Enrons To Come Give Prices A Pounding," *The New York Times*, January 30; and "Nervous and Scandal-Shy Investors Hold Prices Down," *The New York Times*, February 6, have become routine. *The Baltimore Sun* just 2 days ago has: "Investors Squeamish Amid Turmoil." And you can pick up virtually any paper in the country and see comparable headlines.
>
> . . . As *The Washington Post* put it, if one company "issued make-believe accounts, why should anyone believe that dozens of other companies aren't practicing the same deception?"

Accounting Reform and Investor Protection: Hearings on the Legislative History of the Sarbanes-Oxley Act of 2002: Accounting Reform and Investor Protection Issues Raised by Enron and Other Public Companies Before the S. Comm. on Banking, Hous., and Urban Affairs, 107th Cong. 1-2 (2002) (opening statement of Chairman Paul S. Sarbanes) [hereinafter Hearings], *available at* http://www.access.gpo.gov/congress/senate/senate05sh107.html (follow "TEXT" or "PDF" hyperlinks corresponding to S. Hrg. 107-948).

Chairman Sarbanes's focus on media triggers reflects the ongoing value of Cohen's point about the role of the media in a moral panic:

> The student of moral enterprise cannot but pay particular attention to the role of the mass media in defining and shaping social problems. The media have long operated as agents of moral indignation in their own right: even if they are not self-consciously engaged in crusading or muck-raking, their very reporting of certain "facts" can be sufficient to generate concern, anxiety, indignation or panic. When such feelings coincide with a perception that particular values need to be protected, the preconditions for new rule creation or social problem definition are present.

See Cohen, *supra* note 34, at 7.

[56] One witness explicitly warned that merely focusing on bad actors would not resolve the structural problems with financial reporting:

> You will hear or have heard many suggestions for improvement to our system of financial reporting and audits of those financial reports. Some will say that auditor independence rules need to be strengthened. That external auditors should not be allowed to do consulting work and other nonaudit work for their audit clients. That external audit firms should be rotated every 5 years or so. That oversight of auditors needs to be strengthened. That punishment of wayward auditors needs to be more certain and swift, and so on and on. In my opinion, those suggestions, even if legislated by Congress and signed by the President, will not fix the underlying problem.
>
> The underlying problem is a technical accounting problem. The problem is rooted in our rules for financial reporting. Those financial reporting rules need deep and fundamental reform. Unless we change those rules, nothing will change. Today's crisis as portrayed by the surprise collapse of Enron is the same kind of crisis that arose in the 1970's when Penn Central surprisingly collapsed and in the 1980's when hundreds of savings and loan associations collapsed, which precipitated the S&L bailout by the Federal Government. There will be more of these crisis [sic] unless the underlying rules are changed.

HEARINGS, *supra* note 55, at 189-90 (statement of Walter Schuetze, Chief Accountant, U.S. Securities and Exchange Commission, 1992-95). For example, some of what came out in the hearings was that Enron seemingly complied with accounting requirements. *Id.* at 577 (prepared statement of Joel Seligman, Dean

members often seems farfetched, but not so with respect to the sentiment that the corporate officials and auditors in question had behaved wantonly.[57] Though stopping short of phrenology, the floor debate from the Act contains numerous aspersions about chief executive officers, chief financial officers, and accountants—the folk devils of this financial moral panic.[58] (Lawyers played a key role in the media construction of this moral panic,[59] confirming their complicity in feeding a moral panic which they were also in a position to critically evaluate.[60])

---

and Professor, Washington University School of Law) ("The off balance sheet transactions that Enron employed were made in accordance with generally accepted accounting standards.").

[57] As one legal commentator put it:

> Congress jumped into the Enron media circus by holding almost thirty Enron-related media hearings within three months of that company's bankruptcy. Those hearings in many ways resembled a McCarthy-era witch hunt against suspected communists. Enron executives were likened to the terrorists who struck America on September 11, 2001. . . . Great theater, but such histrionics had been little seen since Joseph McCarthy left the Senate.
>
> Witnesses who did appear to testify were berated, badgered, mocked, and cut off if their answers were not what the congressional examiner wanted to hear. One member of Congress insisted on only yes or no answers to complicated, convoluted questions that assumed a guilty answer.

JERRY W. MARKHAM, A FINANCIAL HISTORY OF MODERN U.S. CORPORATE SCANDALS: FROM ENRON TO REFORM 93 (2005).

[58] *See* 148 Cong. Rec. S6734, S6750 (daily ed. July 15, 2002) (statement of Sen. Grassley) ("We ought to be correcting the situation so that people have confidence and so that crooks who are running our corporations and doing these things that are evidenced here. When I say 'crooks running our corporations,' I mean the ones who would do this sort of thing to their stockholders and to the country and to the economy—so that they cannot get away with that in the future."). Blaming these individuals for the losses also required explaining these losses in moral rather than market terms, a point that I make below. *See infra* notes 61-87 and accompanying text.

[59] Given that law professors now form part of the chattering class that comments in the media about legal controversies, Erwin Chemerinsky's observations on the ethical duties of law professors in this role bear repeating:

> Consider the first duty of a commentator to be competent. While lawyers may have a sense of how ordinary criminal investigations work and how ordinary trials are conducted, political proceedings are a hybrid of legal process and political determinations. . . .
>
> . . . .
>
> There also appeared to be added pressures on commentators to speculate on cases occurring in the political, rather than legal, arena. . . .
>
> . . . .
>
> It is more difficult in political commentary to compartmentalize one's opinion from legal description. Therefore, it is even more important that commentators in the political arena be aware of their biases and make full disclosure of them to the media and public.

Erwin Chemerinsky & Laurie Levenson, *The Ethics of Being a Commentator III*, 50 MERCER L. REV. 737, 748-50 (1999) (arguing for the adoption of a voluntary code of ethics for legal commentators).

[60] In a moral panic, lawyers can function as the disease or the cure:

> The legal system, in the conventional wisdom, should be immune to such hysteria, and indeed, should act as a rational and calming force. All too often, however, the creation of a moral panic depends on the complicity and active participation of the legal system. Legal actors—police,

However, the actual social interest at stake in the scandals rarely appeared publicly during the hearings. The structural interest which these scandals really threatened was a shared "consensus reality" about the nature of prosperity, financial value creation, and economic stability.[61] At present, our consensus reality about wealth rests on unrealized gain as an important store of value.[62] To some extent, the New Deal laid the groundwork for the current "consensus reality" in which even lower-middle-class workers rest their future on unrealized gain in financial assets.[63] This view seems to have become the

---

> prosecutors, defense attorneys, expert witnesses, judges, juries—have in various ways, the power to affirmatively fuel the creation of institutionalized hysteria . . . .

Susan Bandes, *The Lessons of Capturing the Friedmans: Moral Panic, Institutional Denial, and Due Process*, 2 Law, Culture & Human. 293 (2007) (arguing that legal actors fueled moral panic about the prosecution of Arnold and Jesse Friedman for sexual abuse of minors).

[61] Consensus reality explains the nature of perceived reality as the result of implicit or explicit agreement between social participants into a contract about what the state of the world is. *See* Thomas S. Kuhn, The Structure of Scientific Revolutions 10-12 (1970) (noting how theoretical challenges to dominant paradigms are opposed by incumbent academics that stand to lose reputation by the reception of the new idea). The idea implies that the experience of reality is contingent and open to paradigm shifts.

[62] For example, in a paper based on the Federal Reserve triennial survey of consumer finances, a researcher notes "a striking pattern of growth in family income and net worth between 1998 and 2001" by offsetting the unrealized appreciation in consumers' investment holdings against the large increase in liquidated debt of U.S. households. *See* Ana M. Aizcorbe et al., *Recent Changes in U.S. Family Finances: Evidence from the 1998 and 2001 Survey of Consumer Finances*, 89 Fed. Res. Bull. 1, 1 (2003) ("The level of debt carried by families rose over the period, but the expansion in equities and the increased values of principal residences and other assets were sufficient to reduce debt as a proportion of family assets.").

[63] The New Deal itself was no moral panic because the legislative remedies were proportional to the scope of the economic crisis. Another difference is that the New Deal deemphasized individual wrongdoing and emphasized structural reform, unlike Sarbanes-Oxley, which focused on increasing criminal penalties for certain white-collar offenses. In his history of the New Deal, Robert Leuchtenburg describes how the Depression put the nation on a crash course with class consciousness by bringing out some of the contradictions about market distribution:

> The persistence of the depression raised questions not merely about business leadership but about capitalism itself. When so many knew want amidst so much plenty, something seemed to be fundamentally wrong with the way the system distributed goods. While the jobless wore threadbare clothing, farmers could not market thirteen million bales of cotton in 1932. While children trudged to school in shoes soled with cardboard, shoe factories in Lynn and Brockton, Massachusetts, had to close down six months of the year. . . . While people went without food, crops rotted in the fields. . . . Western ranchers, unable either to market their sheep or feed them, slit their throats and hurled their carcasses into canyons. In the plains states, breadlines marched under grain elevators heaped high with wheat.

William E. Leuchtenburg, Franklin D. Roosevelt and The New Deal 1932-1940, at 22-23 (1963) (footnotes omitted) (analyzing Roosevelt's role in institutionalizing New Deal programs). Hunger and need planted the seeds of collective action:

> In February 1933, thousands of former members of barter groups seized the county-city building in Seattle. In the Blue Ridge, miners smashed company store windows and storekeepers were given the choice of handing out food or having it seized. Unemployed workers in Detroit invaded self-service groceries in groups, filled their baskets, and left without paying. Iowa leagues of the unemployed enlisted jobless gas and light workers to tap gas and electric lines. In Des Moines,

dominant way that investors conceptualize their wealth.[64] Granted, the most notorious of these accounting scandals, Enron's bankruptcy, did result in significant realized losses to shareholders, creditors, and employees.[65] Much of the most sensationalist reporting, however, related to unrealized losses.[66] As reported in the media, the alarm over these

> workers boarded streetcars in groups of ten or twenty and told the cowed conductors to "charge the fares to the mayor." In Chicago, a group of fifty-five was charged with dismantling an entire four-story building and carrying it away brick by brick.

Id. at 25 (footnotes omitted).

[64] In the 1960s a split began developing between technical analysts who measured firm profitability with information other than net income and investors who focused on short-term earnings. *See* BEAVER, *supra* note 5, at 4 ("In the late 1960s the perspective shifted from economic income measurement to an 'informational' approach."). Investors, however, continued to look at earnings:

> Initially, American investors were concerned primarily with the net worth, book value or physical assets of the firm. Investors then relied on income return, dividends and yield as a measure of the firm's worth. Following World War II, high taxes on ordinary income and tax rates which favored capital gains shifted investors [sic] attention from dividends to earnings. . . . During the 1960s, instant growth in earnings became the single most important indicator of a stock's worth in the eyes of the investment community.

Wendy Nelson Espeland & Paul M. Hirsch, *Ownership Changes, Accounting Practice and the Redefinition of the Corporation*, 15 ACCT. ORGS. & SOC. 77, 84 (1990) (making a hermeneutic argument that accounting methods facilitated the financial conglomerate movement of the 1960s).

[65] A realized loss means the loss of an actual out-of-pocket outlay of cash or some other liquid resource. In contrast, stock appreciation is unrealized gain until the stock is reduced to cash through sale. "Losing" share appreciation is an unrealized loss. To put it in another way, your consumer debt is your lender's unrealized gain, although collateral may reduce your lender's market risk. *See* LAWRENCE REVSINE ET AL., FINANCIAL REPORTING AND ANALYSIS 48-50, 805 (1999).

Who lost what in Enron? Enron's ten largest shareholders lost about $11 billion (Alliance Premier Growth, Fidelity Magellan, AIM Value, Putnam Investors, Morgan Stanley Dividend Growth, Janus Fund, Janus Twenty, Janus Mercury, Janus Growth and Income). MICHAEL COVEL, TREND FOLLOWING: HOW GREAT TRADERS MAKE MILLIONS IN UP OR DOWN MARKETS 122 (2004). Several public retirement funds incurred realized losses. *See, e.g.*, University of California, Update on the UC's Enron Investments and Lawsuits, http://www.universityofcalifornia.edu/news/enron/q&a.html (last visited Feb. 19, 2006) (announcing a realized loss of $115.5 million on shares purchased for $68.50 or $71.34 and sold for an average price of $5.33). Other large losses (indicated here in parentheses) included the Kansas Public Employees Retirement System (about $1 million), the City of Fort Worth Retirement Fund (nearly $1 million), the Teacher Retirement System of Texas (realized losses of $23.3 million; unrealized losses of $12.4 million), the Georgia Teachers Retirement System ($79 million), the New York City Pension Fund ($110 million), and the Ohio State Pension Fund ($114 million). *See* Turtle Trader, Hall of Shame, http://www.turtletrader.com/hall-of-shame.html (last visited Feb. 19, 2006). For many of the large public retirement funds, the losses were relatively insignificant as compared with the overall fund size, indicated here in parentheses: Pennsylvania Public School Employees' Retirement System ($50 billion) lost $59 million, less than 0.25%; New York State Pension Fund ($112 billion) lost $58 million; Pennsylvania State Employees' Retirement System ($24.7 billion) lost $10.6 million; York County, Pennsylvania and City Employee Pension Funds ($182 million) lost $1.26 million; and the State of West Virginia ($5.4 billion) lost $1 million. *Id.*

[66] Enron employees who had invested in Enron stock suffered significant losses of unrealized value, which became realized only when the employees sold their shares later. Enron blocked these employees who had chosen to invest their shares in Enron from selling these shares during an eleven-day period in the fall of 2001. *See Hearings on the Enron Collapse and Its Implications for Worker Retirement Security, Part II Before*

unrealized losses threatened the ongoing viability of the consensus reality built around unrealized gain. To recapitulate, protecting the consensus reality was the (unstated) social interest at stake in the media construction of the scandals, the hearings, and the Act, i.e., the anxiety driver in Cohen's model about moral panic.[67]

In a general moral panic, though, economic anxiety is displaced away from the market and onto social issues.[68] My point in this Part of the Article is to show that in a financial moral panic the economic anxiety stays in the economic sphere but plays out in a new form. Put another way, the logic of the financial moral panic must explain the losses caused by the scandals without undermining the basic optimism in capital markets overall. Since indifferent markets could not be blamed for these investment and employment losses, bad people would have to be. A parody of Calvinist predestination, causation in this instance explained financial losses in terms of personal morality, not market movements, as reflected in the moral critiques of accounting scandals issued at the time.[69]

---

the H. Comm. on Educ. and the Workforce, 107th Cong. 104 (2002) (statement of Mikie Rath, Benefits Manager, Enron Corp.), *available at* http://edworkforce.house.gov/hearings/107th/fc/fchearings.htm (follow "Serial No. 107-42 (PDF, 6.6M)" hyperlink). Enron's retirement plan gave its staff twenty investment options, including mutual funds, a Schwab account, and Enron stock. *Id.* Enron matched contributions only to its Enron stock. *Id.* Participants could trade the stock in their accounts daily, with the exception of the matching contributions of Enron stock, which could not be traded before the plan participant reached the age of fifty. *Id.* In the first week of October, Enron mailed its employees a notice that, due to a change in the plan service provider, a trading suspension would be in effect for eleven trading days, from October 29 to November 13, 2001. *Id.* On October 16, 2001, Enron announced a $618 million third-quarter loss, beginning a downward price spiral in its stock. Press Release, Enron Corp., Enron Reports Recurring Third Quarter Earnings of $0.43 Per Diluted Share; Reports Non-Recurring Charges of $1.01 Billion After-Tax; Reaffirms Recurring Earnings Estimates of $1.80 for 2001 and $2.15 for 2002; and Expands Financial Reporting (Oct. 16, 2001), *available at* http://www.enron.com/corp/pressroom/releases/2001/ene/68-3QEarningsLtr.html. On October 10, Enron stock was selling for $35 a share. By October 26 it had fallen to $15 and by November 20 it had fallen to $7 per share. By the end of November, Enron stock was selling for fewer than fifty cents a share. The lockout occurred during this price drop. Blackout periods routinely occur when plans change service providers or when companies merge. Such periods are intended to ensure that account balances and participant information are transferred accurately. Blackout periods will vary in length depending on the condition of the records, the size of the plan, and number of investment options. While there are no specific ERISA rules governing blackout periods, plan fiduciaries are obliged to be prudent in designing and implementing blackout periods affecting plan investments.

[67] Clearly there is a tradeoff between increasing the allocative efficiency for firms (for example, by letting them off the hook in terms of their legal duties to their employees) and the distributional equity objective of increasing economic security for these same employees. That conundrum drives the panic.

[68] Stuart Hall noted the link between economic insecurity and moral panic. He showed how underlying economic anxiety was displaced into an anxiety about "muggings" by black, working class men. *See generally* STUART HALL ET AL., POLICING THE CRISIS: MUGGING, THE STATE, AND LAW AND ORDER (1978) (using moral panic analysis to explain racialized construction of street crime in response to economic insecurity).

[69] This statement by a political action group that advocates for middle- and working-class families is an example of a moral theory of financial loss:

> Corporate scandals have taken money directly out of the pockets of millions of Americans. The Institute for America's Future has found that individual retirement accounts have lost over $175 billion. American Family Voices has determined that public pension funds across America have lost

In truth, a greater challenge to the current consensus reality about unrealized wealth comes from the prevalence of economic insecurity in U.S. households, not primarily from rogue financiers. Consider the sobering facts behind the real estate bubble. After a period of flat rates of homeownership, homeownership did increase from around 60% in the early 1990s to more than 65% by 2000.[70] Home mortgage debt increased too.[71] As the real estate price bubble increased home equity, households converted this (unrealized) home equity gain into liquidity by pledging their unrealized equity as collateral in refinancing and equity lines of credit.[72] At the same time, the subprime mortgage market grew from $35 billion in 1994 to $140 billion in 2001.[73]

The net result of these trends in homeownership, refinancing, and equity draws is that during the last thirty years, U.S. homeowners' equity has actually dropped from 68.3% to 55%.[74] Of course, financing consumption has become more expensive as the cost of living has increased, seen most dramatically in the 350% increase between 1977 and 1998 in health insurance rates.[75] During this same period average household income went up just 17%.[76] Not surprisingly, foreclosure rates on single-family homes

---

> at least $6.4 billion. And over one million workers have lost their jobs as their looted companies tumbled into bankruptcy. . . . While all this went on, company insiders cashed in. . . . No wonder that working families are saying that enough is enough: we can do better.

See American Family Voices, Corporate Recklessness Report, http://www.americanfamilyvoices.org/pdf/cost.pdf (on file with Author). The website says that the purpose of American Family Voices is to be "a strong voice for middle and low income families on economic, health care, and consumer issues." *Id.*

[70] *See* Wenli Li, *Moving Up: Trends in Homeownership and Mortgage Indebtedness*, BUS. REV. (Fed. Reserve Bank of Phila.), 1st Q. 2005, at 28, *available at* www.phil.frb.org/files/br/brq105wl.pdf (analyzing home ownership and financing trends using consumer and banking data).

[71] *Id.*

[72] For example, in 2003, homeowners liquidated $312 billion in equity through refinancing and equity lines of credit. *See* Federal Deposit Insurance Corporation, FDIC Outlook: In Focus This Quarter: The U.S. Consumer Sector, http://www.fdic.gov/bank/analytical/regional/ro20044q/na/2004winter_01.html (scroll to "Households Use Home Equity to Increase Cash Flow") (summarizing trends in economic indicators reflecting consumer income, wealth, and consumption).

[73] Mortgage indebtedness is measured with a loan-to-value ratio that compares the amount of the loan with the value of the property. *See generally* FRANK FABOZZI & DESSA FABOZZI, THE HANDBOOK OF FIXED INCOME SECURITIES 485 (4th ed. 1995). The higher the ratio—i.e., the greater the amount of the loan to the property being financed—the greater the degree of the borrower's leverage. The median loan-to-value ratio for mortgage indebtedness rose from 15% in 1984 to over 35% in 2001. Li, *supra* note 70, at 32.

[74] *See* Javier Silva, *A House of Cards: Refinancing the American Dream*, DEMOS, Jan. 9, 2005, http://www.demos.org/pubs/AHouseofCards.pdf (concluding that much of the cash flow from refinancing and equity lines of credit obtained between 2001 and 2003 went to cover living expenses and pay down consumer credit). Demos is a public policy institute that studies economic insecurity and advocates for interventions to reduce it. *See* Demos—A Network for Ideas & Action, About Demos, http://www.demos.org/page2.cfm (last visited Feb. 19, 2006).

[75] John S. James, *Institute of Medicine Calls for Universal Health Insurance by 2010*, AIDS TREATMENT NEWS, Jan. 15, 2004, http://www.aidsnews.org/2004/01/IOM.html.

[76] *Id.*

have increased nine-fold since the 1950s and threefold since the 1980s.[77] It would seem that economic insecurity is a staple of many U.S. households, despite the nominal bubble in asset prices.[78]

Against this background of ambient economic insecurity, the narrative about rogue officers who robbed workers of their life savings is poignant but no less misleading for being so. An explanation of these financial losses in terms of individual misconduct misses the point. After all, it was the same accounting and business practices here repudiated that had created much of the wealth and many of the jobs whose evaporation had triggered the financial moral panic in the first place.[79] In fact, Enron, in particular, had become a poster firm for "best practices" in financial engineering, associated

---

[77] *See* Peter J. Elmer & Steven A. Seelig, *The Rising Long-Term Trend of Single-Family Mortgage Foreclosure Rates* 2 (Fed. Deposit Ins. Corp., Working Paper No. 98-2, 1998), available at www.fdic.gov/bank/analytical/working/98-2.pdf. Foreclosures increase the risk of crime and other socially disruptive activity. *See* Dan Immergluck & Geoff Smith, *The Impact of Single-Family Mortgage Foreclosures on Neighborhood Crime* (Jan. 31, 2005) (conference paper, Federal Reserve Bank of Chicago), *available at* http:// www.chicagofed.org/cedric/files/2005_conf_paper_session1_immergluck.pdf; *see also* Michael Powell, *A Bane Amid the Housing Boom: Rising Foreclosures*, WASH. POST, May 30, 2005, at A1 (noting recent increases in foreclosure rates in forty-seven states, observing the disproportionate amount of foreclosures on lower-income homeowners, and asking whether federal home ownership initiatives are hurting rather than helping this community)

[78] Financial innovation may significantly increase the fragility of firms. *See* Pouncy, *supra* note 2, at 566. One approach to reducing the economic insecurity imposed on others by this type of firm fragility is to build in limits to financial innovation to reduce the potential social costs of failure. Taking a different tack, my approach sees the regulation of financial risk-taking as a separate field from the human services regulation needed to provide a safety net for investors when firms come apart. The recommendations made in this Article do nothing to reduce the structural condition of economic insecurity. Rather, these recommendations suggest that financial reports ought to more fully express the natural volatility involved in capital investment instead of airbrushing risk out of financial reports. Sobering annual reports may better pierce investment euphoria than those currently allowed under financial reporting. Identifying the regulatory provisions—i.e., Social Security, education, unemployment insurance, housing benefits—to insulate vulnerable persons from the social costs of financial innovation is beyond the scope of this Article. However, for these recommendations to contribute more to vulnerable constituencies, provisioning for the social costs is essential.

[79] No doubt, it produces cognitive dissonance to admit that one may owe her employment security to questionable accounting practices:

> Earnings management distorts the allocation of resources in the economy, especially in periods of high financial valuations. When hiring and investment decisions are observable [in the market], bad managers hire and invest too much in order to mimic good managers. When they are caught and forced to restate, their firms shrink quickly.

Simi Kedia & Thomas Philippon, *The Economics of Fraudulent Accounting 23* (Nat'l Bureau of Econ. Research, Working Paper No. 11573, 2005), *available at* http://pages.stern.nyu.edu/~tphilipp/papers/sktp.pdf. *See* also Daniel Gross, *The Crime: Slow Job Growth. A Suspect: Enron*, N.Y. TIMES, Sept. 11, 2005, § 3, at 3 (suggesting that aggressive earnings management explained much of the job growth in recent years). In a similar vein, when students in my class complain about receiving a grade they feel is lower than deserved I am tempted to ask whether they also complain when receiving an examination grade they feel is higher than they deserve. So far I have resisted the temptation.

with the production of financial wealth.[80] This poignant narrative about investor and worker losses also reflects a common misconception about the nature of unrealized appreciation in financial assets. Again, most of what Enron employees lost was unrealized value, which, for example, the federal income tax laws do not tax as income.[81] Evoking tulip bulbs, Enron reminded us of the ephemeral nature of unrealized gain, striking a chord since such gain makes up much of our wealth.[82] Would a retirement based on unrealized appreciation in corporate equities be rosy? Maybe not, given the nature of market risk. John Kenneth Galbraith argues that during a price bubble, a collective psychology built on denial of financial realities sets in with investors.[83] The psychology leads to financial speculation and concomitant disaster.[84] Financial moral panic is a defense mechanism of this mind set. More specifically, my point is that panics of this type deny the unavoidable underlying volatility of financial assets, of which capital market investment is simply the most popular example.[85] Moreover, although framed in terms of class injury to Enron workers who lost unrealized value, the class discourse around the corporate scandals silenced other more fundamental phrasings

[80] One commentator who put the Enron question into a market structure perspective noted that:

> This story is not, however, simply about moral hazard, or a few bad agents, but rather about the general evolution of the practices used to define the rights to income derived from the productive assets of corporations . . . . As a leading innovator in its field, pressing into the gray areas of corporate practice to more aggressively engineer its financial structures, Enron provides a convenient case of best practice in modern industrial evolution. In light of its bankruptcy this may seem unusual, but it should be remembered that the practices which led to its collapse had previously been praised as visionary.

Eric Hake, *Financial Illusion: Accounting for Profits in an Enron World*, 39 J. ECON. ISSUES 595, 596-97 (2005) (emphases added).

[81] The inability or unwillingness to distinguish between the loss of unrealized value and cash losses occurred throughout the hearings. *See, e.g.*, HEARINGS, *supra* note 55, at 3-4 (statement of Sen. Richard C. Shelby) ("Unfortunately, Enron is only the tip of the iceberg. Some experts have estimated that investors lost over $200 billion over the last 6 years due to earnings restatements and to lost market capitalization following audit failures."); *Id.* at 7 (statement of Sen. Debbie Stabenow) ("In fact, in Michigan, the Genessee County Employees Pension Fund lost $370,000 on Enron's fall, and I know that there were hundreds of thousands of dollars that were lost in other pension funds, not to mention the employees who lost their life savings.").

[82] In the 17th century, Holland was seized with a speculative investment fever over tulips, leading to a major financial crisis there. *See* CHARLES KINDLEBERGER, MANIAS, PANICS, AND CRASHES: A HISTORY OF FINANCIAL CRISIS 109-11 (2000). The tulip has become the official flower of financial historians.

[83] *See* JOHN KENNETH GALBRAITH, A SHORT HISTORY OF FINANCIAL EUPHORIA 1-17 (1993) (arguing that collective psychological mechanisms contribute to financial crises by, inter alia, discouraging criticism of financial speculation).

[84] This psychology is the collective behavioral expression of the financial instability some scholars cite as a cause of financial innovation. *See* Pouncy, *supra* note 2, at 566-67 (analyzing Minsky's financial instability thesis that cyclical fragility in the finance sector leads to financial innovation). Bounded rationality *en masse* like this should give us pause when wondering about privatizing Social Security.

[85] Airbrushed financial statements help to lull investors into this mindset.

of the economic insecurity in question.[86] Queen for a day or investor for life—how salient is the difference for many?[87]

When deviants are singled out to bear the blame for structural problems this way, it is the Left which turns to moral panic analysis to contest the moral framing of the problem.[88] While used by the sex Left, the penological Left, and the racial Left to address conventional deviancy,[89] moral panic analysis has not been deployed by legal scholars to parse finance law. This is another expression of the tendency in contemporary legal scholarship to match particular critical methods with substantive political projects,

---

[86] E.M. Forster evokes this silenced constituency when introducing Leonard Bast, the protagonist in *Howard's End*, a class novel set in Edwardian England:

> We are not concerned with the very poor. They are unthinkable and only to be approached by the statistician or the poet. This story deals with gentlefolk, or with those who are obliged to pretend that they are gentlefolk.
>
> The boy, Leonard Bast, stood at the extreme verge of gentility. He was not in the abyss, but he could see it, and at times people whom he knew had dropped in, and counted no more. He knew that he was poor, and would admit it; he would have died sooner than confess any inferiority to the rich. This may be splendid of him. But he was inferior to most rich people, there is not the least doubt of it. He was not as courteous as the average rich man, nor as intelligent, nor as healthy, nor as lovable. His mind and his body had been alike underfed, because he was poor, and because he was modern they were always craving better food. Had he lived some centuries ago, in the brightly coloured civilizations of the past, he would have had a definite status, his rank and his income would have corresponded. But in his day the angel of Democracy had arisen, enshadowing the classes with leathern wings, and proclaiming, "All men are equal—all men, that is to say, who possess umbrellas," and so he was obliged to assert gentility, lest he slipped [sic] into the abyss where nothing counts, and the statements of Democracy are inaudible.

E.M. FORSTER, HOWARD'S END 38-39 (Penguin Books 2000) (describing class consciousness in Edwardian England linked to an estate, Howard's End).

[87] Queen for a Day was a popular 1950s "sob show" in which working-class women competed for having the most economically miserable life, as determined by an audience applause meter. The winning Cinderella would receive prizes and weep while being crowned and robed. As its producer noted, "Sure 'Queen' was vulgar and sleazy and filled with bathos and bad taste. . . . That was why it was so successful. It was exactly what the general public wanted. . . . And the TV audience cried their eyes out, morbidly delighted to find there were people worse off than they were, and so they got what they were after." MAXENE FABE, TV GAME SHOWS 120-30 (1979) (quoted in Shawn Hanley, QUEEN FOR A DAY (Dec. 16, 1996) (unpublished manuscript, *available at* http://history.sandiego.edu/gen/projects/hanley/queen.html) (internal quotation marks omitted).

[88] *See* COHEN, *supra* note 34, at xxxi:

> It is obviously true that the uses of the concept to expose disproportionality and exaggeration have come from a left liberal consensus. This empirical project is concentrated on (if not reserved for) cases where the moral outrage appears driven by conservative or reactionary forces. For cultural liberals (today's "cosmopolitans"), this was an opportunity to condemn moral entrepreneurs, to sneer at their small-mindedness, puritanism or intolerance; for political radicals, these were easy targets, the soft side of hegemony or elite interests.

Id.

[89] *See supra* notes 38-44 (see cited legal scholarship applying moral panic analysis to the social control of conventional folk devils).

thereby freezing the movement of a critical style across ideological camps.[90] Moral panic analysis has, however, no natural affinity with either the Left or the Right, given that mobs can form anywhere along the political spectrum. So, moral panic analysis may critique statutes which favor interests anywhere along the majoritarian spectrum. As in any panic, a financial moral panic is another opportunity to consider the social construction of deviancy, although the folk devils in question may not belong to the usual suspects.[91] To the extent that it challenges popular legislation, effective moral panic analysis is coherently (and persuasively, I think) anti-democratic.

But where was the economic Left to object to the ideological framing of the corporate scandals? Students of constitutional law should be aware of the historic role of federal courts in silencing proponents of Left-based radical approaches to economic

---

[90] *See* Edward L. Rubin, *The New Legal Process, the Synthesis of Discourse, and the Microanalysis of Institutions*, 109 HARV. L. REV. 1393, 1398-1403 (1996) (noting the historic divide between critical approaches such as law and economics and outsider jurisprudence). Rubin notes that there is no intrinsic antagonism between—in this case—law and economics and alterity jurisprudence:

> An obvious explanation is the divergent political predilections that gave rise to each movement, but the correspondence between their political positions and their methodologies is not logically required. That is, economic analysis is not necessarily the exclusive instrument of the political right, nor deconstruction the instrument of the left; political debate could have been carried out within either methodological framework.

Id. at 1401-02. He looks to scholarship (as do I) as a place where academics can integrate methodologies without the bondage of history:

> In fact, it is remarkable how disconnected the two movements are, given that they have developed in the same academic institutions, published in the same scholarly journals, and shared a common concern with law and legal institutions.
>
> . . . Because any synthesis of these movements is likely to occur at the level of scholarly discourse, and not at the level of substantive political positions, real possibilities for synthesis emerge primarily in this methodological realm.

Id. at 1412. I tried doing so in *Sending the Right Signals: Using Rent-Seeking Theory to Analyze the Cuban Central Bank*, 27 HOUS. J. INT'L L. 483, 484-525 (2005) ("Identifying the governance structure of rent-seeking deals between central banks and their constituencies shows how private creditor interests impact the workings of financial regulations. To that end, using opportunism to model institutional and individual action makes [critical] theory more relevant, especially that of liberals, progressives, and deconstructionists on the left (island [Cuba], diaspora, and elsewhere).").

[91] Pointing out the social construction of financial elites as deviants does not suggest that all folk devils suffer equally. We know that they do not. The sociology of law makes clear that governmental social control is regressive, falling most heavily on the most socially and economically marginalized. *See* DONALD BLACK, THE BEHAVIOR OF LAW 16-30 (1976) (expressing law as a series of postulates that describe the incidence of social control). Nor do I suggest that the financiers convicted during this round-up had not broken *some* law. Given the pattern of prosecutorial retreat into obstruction of justice charges when the evidentiary burdens of substantive offenses were too high, the legal violations, however, may not have been of financial law. Even financial witch hunts, though, must conform to procedural requirements. *See* Arthur Andersen LLP v. United States, 125 S. Ct. 2129 (2005) (unanimously reversing prosecution on obstruction of justice charge due to defective jury instructions).

insecurity.[92] The ongoing effect of this silencing is that the United States—unlike many other industrialized economies—lacks a robust economic Left from which to frame economic questions in more explicitly structural terms, an ironic market failure in the marketplace of ideas.[93] Also, the otherwise left-leaning moral panic analysts may object less when it is financiers who fall prey to social stigma.[94]

In the absence of any meaningful opposition to the blame narrative, Congress acted accordingly. Since the evil calling for Congress's attention was framed as mischief by officials and auditors, the Act ended up with a punitive rather than technical focus. The traditional focus of federal securities law is disclosure.[95] However, only three of Sarbanes-Oxley's sixty-six substantive provisions address disclosure.[96] Instead, criminalizing corporate and managerial activity is the overriding purpose of the Act; three titles are dedicated to fraud and criminal penalties.[97] Targeting folk devils, the Act increased

---

[92] Indeed, the American judicial campaign against the economic left has been singularly effective. *See, e.g.,* Whitney v. California, 274 U.S. 357 (1927) (conviction for political organizing on behalf of the Communist Party); Abrams v. United States, 250 U.S. 616 (1919) (upholding conviction of anarchists); Debs v. United States, 249 U.S. 211 (1919) (convicting Eugene Debs for anti-war speech made after a strong 1916 run for President).

[93] Today one can speak of the economic Left in the United States only apocryphally because, in terms of institutionalized economic views, our system has only a party of the center, a party of the right, and elements of the far right. To invoke "the left," therefore, without explicit qualification is to move the political spectrum rightward. *See* Matt Bai, *The Framing Wars*, N.Y. TIMES MAG., July 17, 2005, at 38 (profiling Professor George Lakoff, who studies how framing of political issues affects the efficacy of political advocacy). For a prominent counterexample that attempts to institutionalize a Left perspective in the legal academy, see generally LEFT LEGALISM/LEFT CRITIQUE (Wendy Brown & Janet Halley eds., 2002).

[94] Brown and Halley note that a willingness to consider radical uncertainty is an essential part of critique. Applying financial moral analysis to discourses purporting to address distributional problems is part of a richer critique of economic life:

> For part of what it means to dissect the discursive practices that organize our lives is to embark on an inquiry whose outcome is unknown, and the process of which will be radically disorienting at times. . . . Indeed, one of our worries about legalism pertains to its impulse to call the question too peremptorily. . . . It was *through* the process of subjecting political and philosophical idealism to critique that Marx found his way to dialectical materialism and political economy, but a careful reading of this early work makes clear that Marx did not know in advance where his critiques would take him . . . .

LEFT LEGALISM/LEFT CRITIQUE, *supra* note 93, at 27.

[95] *See* THOMAS LEE HAZEN, THE LAW OF SECURITIES REGULATION 740 (4th ed. 2002) (stating that "federal securities law's exclusive focus is on full disclosure").

[96] In addition to the rule discussed here, Sarbanes-Oxley amended the previous requirement that certain individuals with controlling interests in a registrant disclose change in control transactions involving the firm. See 15 U.S.C. § 78(p) (2000 & Supp. II 2002). Also, the law charged the SEC with rulemaking to ensure that registrants disclose whether audit committees include anyone who is a financial expert. *See id.* § 7265 (Supp. II 2002). The law does provide for additional review of registrant disclosures by SEC staff, but the section does not impose a new disclosure requirement. *See id.* § 7266 (Supp. II 2002).

[97] *See* Corporate and Criminal Fraud Accountability Act of 2002 § 802, Pub. L. No. 107-204, 116 Stat. 800 (codified at 18 U.S.C. §§ 1519-20 (Supp. II 2002) (Title VIII of Sarbanes-Oxley); White-Collar Crime Penalty Enhancement Act of 2002 § 903, Pub. L. No. 107-204, 116 Stat. 805 (amending 18 U.S.C. § 1341 (2000 & Supp.)) (Title IX of Sarbanes-Oxley); and Corporate Fraud Accountability Act

the liability of the chief financial officer (CFO) by requiring the CFO to attest to the accuracy of periodic reports under pain of criminal prosecution.[98] Moreover, by setting up the Public Company Accounting Oversight Board, the Act puts auditors squarely in the sights of the SEC, now empowered to increase its criminal and disciplinary action over a profession that had previously been largely self-regulated.[99] Again, this emphasis on individual criminality reflects the influence of moral panic in the legislative process. Consistent with the national mood, financiers convicted in related prosecutions have received heavy sentences, in particular the contumaciously intransigent ones who refused to plea bargain.[100] Other prosecutions and civil actions brought against corporate

of 2002 § 1102, Pub. L. 107-204, 116 Stat. 807 (amending 18 U.S.C. § 1512 (2000 & Supp. II 2002)) (Title XI of Sarbanes-Oxley).

[98] For example, the Act requires the CFO to attest to the accuracy of the firm's financial reports. 15 U.S.C. § 7241(a)(2)-(3) (Supp. II 2002). It requires that:

> the principal financial officer or officers, or persons performing similar functions, certify in each annual or quarterly report filed or submitted under either such section of such Act that—
>
> . . . .
>
> (2) based on the officer's knowledge, the report does not contain any untrue statement of a material fact or omit to state a material fact necessary in order to make the statements made, in light of the circumstances under which such statements were made, not misleading; . . .
>
> (3) based on such officer's knowledge, the financial statements, and other financial information included in the report, fairly present in all material respects the financial condition and results of operations of the issuer as of, and for, the periods presented in the report . . . .

Id. Failure to comply with the attestation requirement exposes a chief financial officer to imprisonment for up to 20 years and fines of up to $5 million. 18 U.S.C. § 1350 (Supp. II 2002). The new requirements extend the chief financial officer's previous duty to ensure the accuracy of financial reports. *See* Joseph F. Morrissey, *Catching the Culprits: Is Sarbanes-Oxley Enough?*, 2003 COLUM. BUS. L. REV. 801, 841-44 (pointing out that chief financial officers and chief executive officers already had to attest to the accuracy of financial reports under securities law requirements that predated Sarbanes-Oxley); Marie Leone, *Command and Controllers: Sarbanes-Oxley May Bring New Risks to the CFO's Office, But It's Raising the Profile of the Once-Faceless Company Controller*, CFO.com, July 14, 2003, http://www.cfo.com/article.cfm/3009814/c_3036076?origin=archive (considering alternative reporting structures in the firm to comply with the CFO's new statutory liabilities).

[99] *Cf.* Richard I. Miller & Michael R. Young, *Financial Reporting and Risk Management in the 21st Century*, 65 FORDHAM L. REV. 1987, 2010-17 (1997) (showing how computer-based financial reporting creates new liabilities and defenses for auditors).

[100] *See 3 Sentenced for Enron Deal*, N.Y. TIMES, May 13, 2005, at C12 (noting three-year and ten-month sentence of Enron finance official Boyle and three-year and one-month sentences of Merrill Lynch bankers Furst and Fuhs in earnings management transaction); Associated Press, *Adelphia Founder Gets 15-Year Term; Son Gets 20*, MSNBC.com, June 20, 2005, http://msnbc.msn.com/id/8291040/ (discussing fifteen-year prison sentence of John Rigas and twenty-year sentence of son, Timothy Rigas, for securities fraud involving use of cash management systems and nondisclosure of OBS transactions); Associated Press, *Ex-Tyco CEO Dennis Kozlowski Found Guilty*, MSNBC.com, June 17, 2005, http://www.msnbc.msn.com/id/8258729 (noting that Kozlowski and his former finance chief Swartz face up to thirty years in prison); *Federal Judge Imposes Harsh Prison Sentence on Defendant Convicted After Testifying in His Own Defense*, White Collar Crime Alert (Blank Rome LLP), Oct. 2005, http://www.blankrome.com/Publications/whitecollar/WhiteCollar1004-6.pdf (suggesting a tendency of judges to impose increased punishment on defendants who testify on their own behalf and are later convicted); Mary Flood, *2 Enron Case Figures Avoid Long Jail Terms*, HOUSTON CHRON., Apr. 22, 2005, at A1 (noting three-year and ten-month prison sentence of Merrill Lynch

officials have also tried to expand the concept of financial loss beyond the previous legal definition.[101] Constructing the problem in question in terms of corporate rogues has also dovetailed with the SEC's self-concept as an enforcement agency, rather than as a knowledge center about capital market structure.[102]

Granted, public floggings do deter misconduct, but they are not likely to solve the technical problems about financial reporting.[103] These problems continue.[104] Part IV offers technical recommendations for these problems which would contribute to fi-

banking and finance staff Brown and Bayly); Bruce Nichols, *For Former Dynegy Exec, Prison Takes Turn for Worse*, DALLAS MORNING NEWS, Jan. 31, 2005, at 4A (discussing transfer of Dynegy trader Jamie Olis to medium-security prison based on his twenty-four-year sentence for a complex cash flow arrangement that mischaracterized financing cash flow as operating cash flow); Andrew Ross Sorkin, *Ex-Banking Star Given 18 Months for Obstruction*, N.Y. TIMES, Sept. 9, 2004, at A1 (discussing eighteen-month prison sentence of Frank Quattrone for obstruction of justice); Stephen Taub, *Rite Aid Exec, 76, Gets 10 Years in Prison*, CFO.com, Oct. 18, 2004, http://www.cfo.com/article.cfm/3305191/c_3305215?f=archives&origin=archive (discussing ten-year prison sentence for accounting fraud and obstruction of justice); *see generally Determining the Reasonableness of an Upward Departure in a Fraud Case*, White Collar Crime Prof Blog, http://lawprofessors.typepad.com/whitecollarcrime_blog/2005/06/upward_departur.html (June 18, 2005) (discussing *United States v. Meeker*, 411 F.3d 736 (6th Cir. 2005), which departed from the fifty-one to sixty-three month prison sentence for investment fraud under the Sentencing Guidelines to impose an eighty-four-month sentence based on thirty letters from victims, twenty-six of which were not disclosed to the defendant).

101 *See, e.g.*, Memorandum of *Amicus Curiae* United States Chamber of Commerce Concerning Interpretation of "Loss," United States v. Bayly, CR. No. H-03-363 (S.D. Tex. Mar. 25, 2005) (arguing that common law and civil securities law standard for loss should control the construction of "loss" under the Federal Sentencing Guidelines), *available at* http://www.uschamber.com/nclc/caselist/issues/securities.htm (follow "View brief" hyperlink under "'Loss Causation' in Criminal Sentencing"). Securities law does recognize a civil action for unrealized loss, but only if the disclosure of the misrepresentation caused the loss. 15 U.S.C. § 77l(b) (2000 & Supp. II 2002) (allowing an action for loss measured as "the depreciation in value of the . . . security" resulting from a misrepresentation).

102 Consider the emphasis on enforcement from the SEC's website discussion on institutional mission: "Crucial to the SEC's effectiveness . . . is its enforcement authority. Each year the SEC brings hundreds of civil enforcement actions against individuals and companies for violations of the securities laws." U.S. Securities and Exchange Commission, How the SEC Protects Investors, Maintains Market Integrity, and Facilitates Capital Formation, http://www.sec.gov/about/whatwedo.shtml (last visited March 2, 2006). Later I urge the SEC to reconsider its self-concept more in terms of regulatory intelligence about capital market structure. *See infra* notes 262-80 and accompanying text, suggesting the formation of a capital structure surveillance unit at the SEC to supplement and inform enlightened enforcement of the securities laws.

103 The Public Company Accounting Oversight Board

> is supposed to fix the system and force accountants to be policeman in their audits. Does anyone seriously believe that this board will be able to monitor the auditing of thousands of public companies to assure that accountants are acting as policemen, rather than accountants? Of course it cannot, but investors are still being deceived into believing that it will. The Enron debacle and the telecom and dotcom implosions, as well as continuing scandals, by now should have removed any doubts as to the hollowness of the assurance that full disclosure protects investors. That was an impossible dream, and Sarbanes-Oxley only adds more smoke to this vision.

Markham, *supra* note 9, at 799.

104 *See* William H. Beaver, *What Have We Learned from the Recent Corporate Scandals That We Did Not Already Know?*, 8 STAN. J.L. BUS. & FIN. 155, 163 (2002) (analyzing corporate scandals in the context

nancial transparency for lay investors.[105] But, first, I must address some of the technical dynamics behind the hazy moral construction outlined in the previous Part.

II. FROM MORALIZING TO FINANCIAL TRUTH: CORRECTING THE MYOPIA OF THE BALANCE SHEET

Many of the losses which triggered the financial moral panic involved the failure to disclose significant OBS liabilities and the related failure to book loan income as such, rather than as operating cash flow. In other words, neither the balance sheets of these firms nor their statements of cash flows adequately reflected the firms' true capital structure. Understanding why this gap developed requires appreciating the appeal of OBS arrangements to managers, who gravitate to the OBS sector for both fiduciary and self-serving reasons.[106] Using examples of the cash flow games played by Enron and Dynegy, below I explain why a disclosure standard based on effective capital structure would result in more transparency about a firm's risk.

A. The Discrete Charm of Off-Balance-Sheet Arrangements

The balance sheet is supposed to be a point-in-time snapshot of a firm's net worth and capital structure, i.e., the mixture of the debt and equity instruments that finance the firm. Net worth is calculated by netting the reporting firm's claims to value against the claims of others on the firm.[107] The balance sheet "recognizes" these claims by estimating their total value and aggregating like claims into analytically unified categories of asset claims, liability claims, and equity claims.[108] Shown on the left side of the balance sheet, "Assets" are the firm's claims on others. These claims are listed by declining

---

of capital markets research on financial reporting discretion). Professor Beaver notes how the emotional climate of the corporate scandal has impeded a more technical approach to the issues:

> At this stage, there has been a great deal of rhetoric and outrage but relatively little analysis. There has been pressure for rapid responses in the absence of fully understanding the causes of the problems and how they are linked to structural defects in the financial reporting-corporate governance environment. Without these links, it is possible that, in spite of an increase in legislation and regulation, the same problems will reappear.

Id. at 168; *see also* Partnoy, *supra* note 18, at 1264 for a concurrence.

[105] *See infra* notes 245-80 and accompanying text.

[106] For a sophisticated but friendly explanation of the balance sheet, see Walter Schuetze, *What are Assets and Liabilities? Where is True North? (Accounting that My Sister Would Understand)*, 37 ABACUS J. ACCT., FIN. & BUS. STUD. (2001) (emphasizing that balance sheet values should be based on cash or cash-equivalent values).

[107] *See* FIN. ACCOUNTING STANDARDS BD., STATEMENT of FINANCIAL ACCOUNTING CONCEPTS NO. 6: ELEMENTS of FINANCIAL STATEMENTS (1985), *available at* http://www.fasb.org/pdf/con6.pdf.

[108] In accounting, "recognition" means reporting the value of an item in a financial report. *See* Thomas R. Dyckman et al., *Intermediate Accounting 36* (5th ed. 2001). Mandatory recognition is more invasive than mere disclosure. The new disclosure rule requires only disclosure, not recognition.

liquidity.[109] Shown at the top of the right side of the balance sheet, "Liabilities" are third parties' credit claims on the firm. They are listed by maturity and relative priority.[110] The difference between "Assets" and "Liabilities" is called "Shareholder's Equity" and appears under the "Liabilities" section in the right-hand column.[111] The owners' account, shareholder's equity is the residue that would be left for the firm's owners in a hypothetical liquidation after satisfaction of creditors' claims.[112] By convention, the "Assets" equals the sum of the "Liabilities" and "Equity" accounts.[113] The firm's balance sheet also includes the assets and liabilities of any other entity controlled by the firm.[114] Most registrants use the annual 10K form filed with the SEC as their balance sheet.

---

[109] Accounting definitions sound somewhat metaphysical. "Assets are probable future economic benefits obtained or controlled by a particular entity as a result of past transactions or events." STATEMENT of FINANCIAL ACCOUNTING CONCEPTS NO. 6, *supra* note 107, at 6. Asset claims may be choses in possession, i.e., an asset claim may be a building, or, more commonly, choses in action, such as a debt obligation against another, requiring further action to reduce the chose to a liquid form. Liquidity when used with regard to an asset claim—rather than to an obligor as a whole—means the ease with which the asset may be converted into cash or its equivalent. *See generally* LIQUIDITY: COMPTROLLER'S HANDBOOK, *supra* note 4, at 9-13.

[110] "Liabilities are probable future sacrifices of economic benefits arising from present obligations of a particular entity to transfer assets or provide services to other entities in the future as a result of past transactions or events." *See* STATEMENT OF FINANCIAL ACCOUNTING CONCEPTS NO. 6, *supra* note 107, at 6. Liability entries should also tell a reader something about a firm's funding style. Does the firm issue long- or short-term debt? Will its payment obligations mature over time or all at once? The answers to these questions help a reader appreciate the funding philosophy of the firm.

[111] "Equity . . . is the residual interest in the assets of an entity that remains after deducting its liabilities." *Id.* The real value of asset and liability claims is unclear because neither is marked-to-market to reflect liquidation value. Most firms value assets at historic cost rather than replacement cost. Firms book liabilities at par, i.e., nominal, value rather than reflecting what creditors would accept to settle the claim (which would be a mark-to-market approach to liabilities). So the value of Shareholders' Equity is intrinsically variable.

[112] In truth, though, the varieties of accounting methods used by the balance sheet make it hard to estimate a firm's actual liquidation value without more detail about assets and liabilities.

> The accounting and reporting model under Generally Accepted Accounting Principles is actually a mixed-attribute model. Although most transactions and balances are measured on the basis of historical cost, which is the amount of cash or its equivalent originally paid to acquire an asset, certain assets and liabilities are reported at current values either in the financial statements or related notes. For example, certain investments in debt and equity securities are currently reported at fair value, receivables are reported at net realizable value, and inventories are reported at the lower of cost or market value.

See HEARINGS, *supra* note 55, at 561 n.13 (prepared statement of David M. Walker, Comptroller General of the United States, General Accounting Office).

[113] This is called the fundamental accounting equation. PAUL D. KIMMEL ET AL., FINANCIAL ACCOUNTING 12 (1998).

[114] Part of the OBS sector had started with an early accounting pronouncement that clarified when a firm had to consolidate legally separate entities on its balance sheet. AM. INST. OF CERTIFIED PUB. ACCOUNTANTS, ACCOUNTING RESEARCH BULLETIN NO. 51: CONSOLIDATED FINANCIAL STATEMENTS (1959)

The numbers on the balance sheet matter dearly. If they hint at illiquidity or capital shortfalls, the firm may have to pay more for credit, face the white-hot glare of regulators, or trigger adverse contractual rights of demanding counterparties. For example, some credit covenants let a creditor sue if the borrowing firm's (balance sheet) debt to equity ratio drops below a contractually-set point.[115] To mitigate these business risks, the careful manager optimizes the presentation of information on the balance sheet. For example, firms may reclassify debt from short-term to long-term in order to improve their liquidity ratios.[116] Shifting numerical values only in the assets column (left-hand side), only in the liabilities column (right-hand side), or only between the liability and the equity accounts (both on the right-hand side) does not change the overall size of the balance sheet.[117] To modify the size of the visible balance sheet, managers must move off the balance sheet, using reporting discretion which is customary in accrual accounting.[118] For example, the classification of operating leases is subject to significant discretion.[119] The generalized practice of funding with OBS items leads

(requiring consolidation of a legally separate entity when the reporting firm had a controlling financial interest, including majority voting interest). Consolidation eliminates the risk of surprise from an OBS item because the reporting firm absorbs the OBS entity for reporting purposes. The issues presented in this discussion arise with respect to unconsolidated entities.

[115] *See* ILEEN B. MALITZ, THE MODERN ROLE OF BOND COVENANTS 15-26 (describing bond covenants creditors use to limit wealth expropriation by owners and managers).

[116] *See* JEFFREY GRAMLICH ET AL., BALANCE SHEET MANAGEMENT: THE CASE OF SHORT-TERM OBLIGATIONS RECLASSIFIED AS LONG-TERM DEBT, 39 J. Acct. Res. 283 (2001) (documenting significant debt reclassifications of 220 firms to smooth out balance sheet liquidity and leverage measures).

[117] None of these moves disturbs the basic stability of the fundamental accounting equation that "Assets" equals the sum of "Liabilities" plus "Equity."

[118] A prominent accounting theorist notes:

> The term used in the research literature is earnings management, rather than some pejorative phrase, such as earnings manipulation. . . . Discretion in financial reporting can be used to signal or convey additional information management has that is not publicly available. Hence, it may be benign rather than sinister . . . earnings management does not necessarily imply a violation of Generally Accepted Accounting Principles (GAAP). There is a range of discretion within the boundaries of judgment that is permitted, in fact required, under GAAP-based accrual accounting.

See BEAVER, *supra* note 5, at 163.

[119] Booked off-the-balance sheet, the lease shows up in neither the asset or liability column. But recognizing the item on the balance sheet increases book assets by the value of the item and book liabilities by debt in respect of the lease. Constructive capitalization better reflects a firm's effective capital structure. *See* Eugene A. Imhoff et al., *Operating Leases: Impact of Constructive Capitalization*, ACCOUNTING HORIZONS, Mar. 1991, at 51 (showing effects on net income and balance sheet of constructively capitalizing unrecorded operating leases). The Securities and Exchange Commission estimates that U.S. corporate issuers may owe as much as $1.25 trillion in non-cancelable OBS operating leases. *See* SEC Report, *supra* note 17, at 4.

finance practitioners to distinguish between a firm's "book leverage" and its "financial leverage."[120] Some arrangements are hard to classify as on- or off-balance-sheet.[121]

Managers may seek shelter from balance sheet disclosure both for fiduciary and opportunistic reasons.[122] Conducting a transaction off the balance sheet gives managers more flexibility by reducing the discipline of oversight from creditors or owners who

---

[120] A fundamental aspect of capital structure, leverage is the ratio of debt financing to equity financing; in other words, the extent to which owners use creditors' resources to increase the firm's operating base and the owners' residual upside gain. Financial accounting calculates "book" leverage with generally accepted accounting principles. A more economic observer measures the firm's effective leverage (also called financial leverage) on the basis of actual financial power. Obviously, book and financial leverage diverge. Finance classes teach students about financial leverage. *See* RAY H. GARRISON ET AL., MANAGERIAL ACCOUNTING 796-97 (11th ed. 2006).

[121] The treatment of leases is a good example of how items with potential OBS implications were treated. The problem with a lease is that it may be a true lease or, instead, a disguised property interest that belongs on the balance sheet. Between 1939 and 1959, the main source of accounting rules was the AICPA's Committee on Accounting Procedure, which produced Accounting Research Bulletins (ARB). The AICPA first addressed lease accounting in 1949. *See* AM. INST. OF CERTIFIED PUB. ACCOUNTANTS, ACCOUNTING RESEARCH BULLETIN NO. 38 (1949) [hereinafter ARB No. 38] (superseded by AM. INST. OF CERTIFIED PUB. ACCOUNTANTS, ACCOUNTING RESEARCH BULLETIN NO. 43: RESTATEMENT AND REVISION OF ACCOUNTING RESEARCH BULLETINS (1953)). ARB No. 38 laid down only a loosely defined standard about the problem. Later lease accounting pronouncements refined these principles to increase the accuracy of financial reporting with respect to leases. Identifying when a lease had to be reflected on the balance sheet, i.e., capitalized, or could be located off the balance sheet remained a contentious issue for the next forty years. *See* FIN. ACCOUNTING STANDARDS BD., STATEMENT OF FINANCIAL ACCOUNTING CONCEPTS NO. 13: ACCOUNTING FOR LEASES (1976) (clarifying when leases must be capitalized on the balance sheet); FIN. ACCOUNTING STANDARDS BD., STATEMENT OF FINANCIAL ACCOUNTING STANDARDS NO. 23: INCEPTIONS OF THE LEASE (1978) (noting when capitalization must be done at the beginning of a lease); FIN. ACCOUNTING STANDARDS BD., STATEMENT OF FINANCIAL ACCOUNTING STANDARDS NO. 91: ACCOUNTING FOR NONREFUNDABLE FEES AND COSTS ASSOCIATED WITH ORIGINATING OR ACQUIRING LOANS AND INITIAL DIRECT COSTS OF LEASES (1986) (identifying which costs need not be reflected on the balance sheet); and FIN. ACCOUNTING STANDARDS BD., STATEMENT OF FINANCIAL ACCOUNTING STANDARDS NO. 98: ACCOUNTING FOR LEASES (1988). The issue is still not definitively resolved.

[122] It is no accident that these items are invisible. Consider this comment on the OBS items targeted by the new disclosure rule:

> The [OBS entities] that this interpretation covers are currently invisible, by design. There is no simple or reliable way for analysts or investors to judge which companies are most likely to be affected. Clues might be found in the management's discussion and analysis, but not enough to enable financial statement users to reliably estimate how the interpretation will affect companies' financial statements. This new interpretation might cause very few changes in corporate balance sheets, because companies that would have to consolidate their SPEs under the requirements of this interpretation might already be taking steps to shut down or sell their interests prior to the effective date. This scenario would avoid the embarrassment for the sponsors of presenting what they never professed to own. The other alternative is that Interpretation 46(R) might cause significant adverse adjustments to companies' balance sheets and create technical defaults in loan covenants.

Jalal Soroosh & Jack T. Ciesielski, *Accounting for Special Purpose Entities Revised: FASB Interpretation 46(R)*, CPA J., July 2004, at 30, 37, *available at* http://www.nysscpa.org/cpajournal/2004/704/essentials/p30.htm.

would be able to monitor publicly-reported financial details.[123] Common fiduciary motivations include managing the firm's book leverage, credit rating, or risk profile for the sake of protecting the trading value of the firm's shares.[124] For example, an OBS deal may boost the firm's book income me without worsening the firm's book leverage.[125] A firm may deduct the OBS debt interest from some special purpose entities on its federal taxes without having to report the underlying liability on its balance sheet.[126] Firms also use OBS partnerships to optimize the tax value of their research and development expenditures.[127] Segregating a business project off-balance-sheet insulates the firm from the risk of loss from the investment. Stealth funding through OBS arrangements may avoid covenants limiting investment in new business opportunities in bank loan documents, bondholder indenture agreements, or a firm's certificate of incorporation.[128] Such deals may, however, violate explicit contractual duties of good faith and fair dealing.[129]

---

[123] In this sense, using OBS activities increases the value of a manager's "switching options" to reallocate resources between investment. *Cf.* George Triantis, *Financial Slack Policy and the Laws of Secured Transactions*, 29 J. LEGAL STUD. 35, 3, (2005) ("As a general proposition, managers are much more prone to take actions that increase their welfare (for example, perquisite consumption or empire building) or the welfare of their shareholders (for example, share repurchases or high-risk investments) if they have cash at their disposal."). The disclosure recommendations made in Part IV may reduce the value of these options by providing more detail about cash flow to external constituencies of the firm. *See* Part IV.A.

[124] *See generally* WILLIAM BEAVER, PERSPECTIVES ON RECENT CAPITAL MARKET RESEARCH, 77 Acct. Rev. 453, 466-68 (2002) (concluding that it is difficult to isolate the primary motive for discretionary behavior by managers over reporting earnings because managers have multiple motives for such conduct). *Cf.* Anthony J. Luppino, *Stopping the Enron End-Runs and Other Trick Plays: The Book-Tax Accounting Conformity Defense*, 2003 COLUM. BUS. L. REV. 35 (arguing that accounting practices should be conformed to tax standards to avoid characterizing transactions differently for tax and financial accounting purposes).

[125] *See generally* Fred D. Campobasso, *Off-Balance-Sheet Financing Can Generate Capital for Strategic Development*, HEALTHCARE FIN. MGMT., June 2000, *available at* http://www.findarticles.com/p/articles/mi_m3257/is_6_54/ai_62929196 (noting return and liquidity advantages to using synthetic leases, sale-and-leaseback, and joint venture arrangements to finance real estate operations).

[126] *See* David Mangefrida & E. Ray Beeman, *Recent IRS Securitization Ruling Signals Analytical Shift in Distinguishing Between Sales and Financings*, INVESTMENT LAW., Oct. 1998, at 5 (explaining ability to characterize the lease as sale or financing).

[127] *See generally* Douglas Shackelford & Terry Shevlin, *Empirical Tax Research in Accounting*, 31 J. ACCT. & ECON. 321 (2001); Terry Shevlin, *Taxes and Off-Balance-Sheet Financing: Research and Development Limited Partnerships*, 62 ACCT. REV. 480 (1987).

[128] *Cf.* In re Explorer Pipeline Co., 781 A.2d 705 (Del. Ch. 2001) (holding that corporation's decision to enter into an OBS operating lease was not subject to a supermajority provision found in the corporation's certificate of incorporation); *see also* Samir El-Gazzar et al., *The Use of Off-Balance Sheet Financing to Circumvent Financial Covenant Restrictions*, 4 J. ACC. AUDITING FIN. 217 (1989) (analyzing forty-three addenda to leases which contained debt covenants to examine how firms use OBS arrangements to modify covenant-based restrictions).

[129] For example, a court has been unwilling to expand the concept of good faith with respect to balance sheet debt. *See* Metro. Life Ins. Co. v. RJR Nabisco, Inc., 716 F. Supp. 1504, 1507-08 (S.D.N.Y. 1989) (rejecting plaintiff's request to imply a covenant of good faith and fair dealing into a bond indenture which did not impose debt limits on the defendant-issuer). The use of OBS debt, however, may warrant wider

Apart from fiduciary brinksmanship for the sake of shareholders, managers may also use an OBS arrangement for their own opportunistic ends, which may be antithetical to the interests of their principals, i.e. shareholders. When executive compensation is pegged to balance sheet ratios such as return on assets, return on equity, and debt-to-equity, a manager would likely prefer, all else being equal, an OBS deal which increases his compensation by improving one of these ratios.

Undisclosed OBS arrangements bear on conflicts between a firm's competing claimants, including the stockholder-bondholder conflict over the firm's exposure to financial risk.[130] OBS cash flow may also increase existing agency costs for shareholders.[131] Management accounting will carefully monitor these arrangements to the extent that they are material to the decisions faced by a firm's managers.[132] Some firm outsiders

---

consideration for a creditor, although careful bond counsel would draft covenants taking into account the existence of OBS items.

[130] Bondholders enjoy legal priority over stockholders to only a liquidated amount, i.e., the principal and interest on the bonds in question. *See* MALITZ, *supra* note 115, at 3-4 (explaining the conflict of interest between creditors and owners of a corporation). Stockholders recover only after satisfaction of these liquidated claims, but they keep whatever is left over, i.e., the residual upside. These adverse rights lead to a class conflict in the corporation over risk and investment: stockholders may prefer a low probability, high investment return because they collect the residue; contra, bondholders may prefer a high probability, low investment return because they get paid first and gain nothing from risk in excess of what is required for a return of their capital. When OBS liabilities increase the residual upside, these liabilities let the firm leverage the bondholders' money free of the contractual protections for which the bondholders bargained. This is the private firm version of the financing moral hazard in banks. *See infra* note 185. Conversely, OBS assets may inure to the benefit of the bondholder to the extent that the OBS asset may be used to fund the bondholder's fixed claim on firm assets.

[131] Cash flow from an OBS item intensifies the agency problem over free cash flow because it is harder for corporate stakeholders to monitor activities sourced off-the-balance sheet. The new OBS disclosure rule could reduce the agency costs for the shareholder if the disclosure helps to monitor the agent's opportunism by revealing the nature of the free cash flow more accurately. *Cf.* George G. Triantis, *Organizations as Internal Capital Markets: The Legal Boundaries of Firms, Collateral, and Trusts in Commercial and Charitable Enterprises*, 117 HARV. L. REV. 1102 (2004) (modeling a firm as an internal capital pool in which legal restrictions on liquidity restrict managerial discretion, including the freedom to consume perquisites). So, apart from the opportunity cost of liquidity, i.e., foregone investment return, restraining managers' opportunism is a governance reason why shareholders might prefer to limit a firm's liquidity. For an empirical analysis of how free cash flow impacts managerial decision-making, see John Paul Broussard et al., *CEO Incentives, Cash Flow, and Investment*, FIN. MGMT., July 1, 2004, at 51 (analyzing different incentives for chief executive officers to encourage them to invest excess cash flow for the benefit of shareholders).

[132] To the extent that OBS items may impact the firm, its management accounting will track the risk. *See* GARRISON ET AL., *supra* note 120, at 9:

> Financial accounting is mandatory; that is, it must be done. Various outside parties such as the Securities and Exchange Commission (SEC) and the tax authorities require periodic financial statements. Managerial accounting, on the other hand, is not mandatory. A company is completely free to do as much or as little as it wishes. No regulatory bodies or other outside agencies specify what is to be done, or, for that matter, whether anything is to be done at all. Since managerial accounting

such as institutional creditors may also bargain for this type of information.[133] Financial databases, an important public source of firm-level information, however, usually lack much information about OBS items.[134]

To illustrate the motivations that lead corporate officials to use OBS arrangements, the next section discusses cash flow games used by two companies implicated in the accounting controversies that led to the Act, Enron and Dynegy.

B. Cash Flow Games

The purpose of this particular Enron strategy was for Enron to receive liquidity from a bank without increasing the firm's financial ratios by having to report a liability on the Enron balance sheet.[135] At this time, Enron needed to maintain its credit standing to avoid a negative funding spiral.[136] If its credit rating were to drop, some energy trading counterparties would stop dealing with the firm, depriving it of operating cash flow.[137] Worse still, if Enron's credit dropped below investment grade, trading counterparties would demand more collateral (taxing liquidity further), the interest cost of some

> is completely optional, the important question is always, "Is the information useful?" rather than, "Is the information required?"

Id. If the information is useful to the firm's managers, ought it not be revealed to investors and other market intermediaries?

[133] *See* Raghuram Rajan & Andrew Winton, *Covenants and Collateral as Incentives to Monitor*, 50 J. FIN. 1113 (1995).

[134] *See* Imhoff et al., *supra* note 119, at 63 (finding that financial databases of Dun and Bradstreet, Value Line, and Compact Disclosure did not reflect the value of legally binding OBS operating lease commitments in firms' financial information).

[135] Many of Enron's solvency problems dealt with how the firm financed its transformation from an energy company to a derivatives trading platform in which—towards the end—ninety percent of firm revenues came from trading in increasingly esoteric financial derivatives like bandwidth and pollution-emission credits. *See* Ronald Fink, *Beyond Enron: The Fate of Andrew Fastow and Company Casts a Harsh Light on Off-Balance-Sheet Financing*, CFO, Feb. 2002, *available at* http://www.findarticles.com/p/articles/mi_m3870/is_2_18/ai_83045541.

[136] As has been noted:

> Enron was acutely aware of the importance of its credit ratings. In its 1999 annual report, Enron management stated that the company's "continued investment grade status is critical to the success of its wholesale business as well as its ability to maintain adequate liquidity." . . . An investment grade rating was needed not only to keep down credit costs but also because various trigger provisions for support of [off-balance sheet entities] would be activated in the event of a ratings downgrade.

See MARKHAM, *supra* note 57, at 100.

[137] *See* THE ROLE OF THE FINANCIAL INSTITUTIONS IN ENRON'S COLLAPSE, BEFORE THE PERMANENT SUBCOMM. ON INVESTIGATIONS OF THE S. COMM. ON HOMELAND SECURITY AND GOVERNMENTAL AFFAIRS, 107th Cong. 220 (2002) (prepared statement of Robert L. Roach, Counsel & Chief Investigator, Permanent Subcomm. on Investigations), app. A, *Accounting Treatment of Prepays: Effect of Enron's Financial Statement*, at A-2 to A-4 [hereinafter Accounting Treatment of Prepays], *available at* http://www.gpo.gov/congress/senate/senate12sh107.html (Click "TXT" or "PDF" links under "S. Hrg. 107-618—The Role of the Financial Institutions in Enron's Collapse").

variable rate debt would increase, some payment obligations would become accelerated, and Enron would be locked out of the commercial paper market, hence worsening the firm's illiquidity spiral.[138]

Finessing these funding demands with its financial reporting duties, Enron arranged a series of "prepays" which gave the firm more than $8 billion in financing over six years.[139] Given their true economic nature as loans, Enron ought to have reported the prepays as bank loans on its balance sheet that generated financing cash flow rather than operational cash flow—on the statement of cash flows.[140] Had Enron reported the prepays this way, credit ratios which determined the firm's ongoing credit access would have deteriorated. Indeed, the debt-to-equity ratio would have risen from about 69% to about 96%, and the debt-to-total-capital ratio would have increased from about 40% to 49%.[141]

The mechanics of the transaction are a bit more complicated.[142] Again, Enron wanted to borrow money without reporting a loan on its balance sheet. So Enron structured the deal as a pair of commodities trades. The would-be lender—in this case, the bank—wanted to make a loan but did not want to speculate in commodities. Ordinarily Enron would reflect a loan from a bank on the firm's balance sheet as a liability and report the cash inflow on the firm's statement of cash flows as a financing cash flow. But another of Enron's preferences about this transaction was to keep the firm's debt-to-equity ratio as low as possible (lenders will charge more to lend to a firm with a high debt-to-equity ratio). Of course, an accounting question arises as to whether these arrangements are a trade or a loan, which would entail adverse balance sheet consequences.[143]

In order to avoid classifying the transaction as a loan, Enron inserted a sham counterparty between Enron and the bank.[144] In this way, Enron converted the loan from the bank into two sales contracts. In the deal, the bank would "buy" a fixed amount of

---

138 *Id.* at A-5.

139 *See* THE ROLE OF THE FINANCIAL INSTITUTIONS IN ENRON'S COLLAPSE, BEFORE THE PERMANENT SUBCOMM. ON INVESTIGATIONS OF THE S. COMM. ON HOMELAND SECURITY AND GOVERNMENTAL AFFAIRS, 107th Cong. 16 (2002) (prepared statement of Robert L. Roach, Counsel & Chief Investigator, Permanent Subcomm. on Investigations) [hereinafter *Role of the Financial Institutions*], *available at* http://www.gpo.gov/congress/senate/senate12sh107.html (Click "TXT" or "PDF" links under "S. Hrg. 107-618—The Role of the Financial Institutions in Enron's Collapse"). Of this amount, Chase Manhattan Bank provided $3.7 billion and Citigroup provided $4.8 billion. *Id.*

140 *Id.* at 14.

141 *Id.* at 17; *see also Accounting Treatment of Prepays, supra* note 137, at A-4.

142 *See* Second Interim Report of Neal Batson, Court Appointed Examiner at 58-67 & app. E, In re Enron Corp., No. 01-16034 (Bankr. S.D.N.Y. Jan. 21, 2003), *available at* http://www.enron.com/corp/por/examiner2.html.

143 A loan compensates the lender for credit risk and the commodity value of money. A trade compensates the trader for price risk in the commodity. Settlement does expose a trader to the counterparty's credit risk incidentally, but it is the (upside) commodity price risk and not the counterparty credit risk which induces the risk-taking.

144 *See* ROLE OF THE FINANCIAL INSTITUTIONS, *supra* note 139, at 14-15.

commodities from the sham counterparty. Next, Enron would "sell" that same amount of commodities to the sham counterparty. So far these were two commodity contracts with only incidental credit risk (although the net effect of the deal was that Enron had sold commodities to the bank).

In order to keep the bank from bearing the commodity price risk in the sales, Enron also entered into a swap with the bank.[145] In the swap, the bank would exchange the market value of the commodities for the price agreed to in the original sale to the counterparty.[146] If the price of the commodities had decreased (by the time the bank went to sell the commodities) the swap made the bank whole at the original prices.[147] If the price of the commodities had increased (by the time that the bank went to sell the commodities) the swap terms required the bank to transfer that upside to Enron, which would give the bank only the original fixed prices.[148] Using the OBS swap, thus gave the bank the credit risk which it wanted without exposing the bank to commodity price risk.[149] Why would the bank enter into this deal? The bank wanted and received the loan interest and fees from what was really an effective loan.

Another energy company (and Enron trading counterparty), Dynegy, also used creative accounting to turn financing into operational cash flow, at least as a financial reporting matter. In 2001, securities analysts compared Dynegy's accrual-based earnings with its operating cash flow and concluded that the operating cash flow did not seem to sustain the share price of Dynegy stock.[150] The company needed more operating cash flow to support the trading price of its stock.[151] To reassure (and mislead) its critics, Dynegy generated phantom operational cash flow using OBS arrangements that were later deemed loans as a matter of law.[152] As with the Enron prepays, the disclosure of loan rather than operating cash flow (i.e., effective capital structure) would have depressed Dynegy's share price, reduced the firm's credit access, and triggered a negative funding spiral like the one described above for Enron. As part of the SEC's order to institute cease-and-desist proceedings, Dynegy agreed to restate its 2001 financial statements to more accurately reflect the firm's effective capital structure.[153]

---

[145] *Id.*

[146] *Id.*

[147] *See id.*

[148] *See id.*

[149] *See id.* at 15.

[150] *See* Katrina M. Miltich, *A Slap on the Wrist:* Dynegy, Inc. v. Securities and Exchange Commission, 28 N.C. J. INT'L L. & COM. REG. 983, 984-85 (2003) (reviewing the facts and major legal issues in the Dynegy matter).

[151] *See In re* Dynegy Inc., Exchange Act Release No. 34-46537 (Sept. 25, 2002), *available at* http://www.sec.gov/litigation/litreleases/lr17744.htm. *See generally* Miltich, *supra* note 150, at 983.

[152] James Olis, the financier who designed the arrangement, now faces a twenty-four-year sentence. *See* Nichols, *supra* note 100. *Editors' note:* Olis's sentence was later reduced to 6 years.

[153] *See* Miltich, *supra* note 150, at 986.

C. The Materiality of Effective Capital Structure

Given the gap, then, between the foreseeably misleading financial reports prepared by managers and the realties of the cash flow games which these reports seek to address, what should financial reporting law do? Mapping a firm's effective capital structure is the counter-move to the earnings management practices made possible by the accounting discretion. So, financial reporting law should encourage more comprehensive measurement of a firm's effective capital structure.[154] This would mean reflecting more of a firm's volatility in messier financial reports. Like the shadows in Plato's allegory about the cave, public financial reports can only convey a highly selective approximation of a firm's financial reality, but increased reported volatility would be more accurate.[155]

The existing literature on effective capital structure focuses on mapping effective debt, although understanding effective equity belongs to effective structure analysis too.[156] All effective debt analysis involves reconstructing the whole from the part.[157] For example, much like proving the existence of a black hole by observing its gravitational pull on matter, effective debt can be backed out by comparing income tax returns (which claim business interest deductions from both "book" and effective liabilities) and the balance sheet (which includes only "book" debt).[158] Undisclosed debt exists to the extent that

---

[154] A suggestion made during the SEC's administrative rule-making about OBS items epitomizes what effective capital structure is:

> The Management Discussion and Analysis should provide a pro forma capital structure showing the full effects of all off balance sheet financing entities. The common stock equity of the company should be recast to show the *pro forma level of common equity* that exists once the debt related aspects of the special purpose entity are factored in. . . .
>
> . . . The Management Discussion and Analysis should also show the potential effects that imputed debt service from the special purpose entity may have on the covenants in the various financing agreements for the company. . . . [T]he full effects should be shown.

See Letter from Kevin M. Bronner, Ph.D, to Jonathan G. Katz, Secretary of the U.S. Securities and Exchange Commission (Nov. 13, 2002), *available at* http:// sec.gov/rules/proposed/s74202/kmbronner1.htm (emphases added).

[155] Apart from any limitations in the reports themselves, public disclosures are only as complete as their underlying markets: "Given that many of the assets and claims reported on the financial statements are represented by imperfect or incomplete markets, ... the 'ideal' that financial statements are attempting to represent is not clear conceptually." BEAVER, *supra* note 5, at 4. For an explanation of Plato's allegory about bounded rationality, *see* S. Marc Cohen, The Allegory of the Cave, http://faculty.washington.edu/smcohen/320/cave.htm (last updated July 8, 2002).

[156] The federal government's position as a stand-by source of equity capital to bail out insured depositors of failed banks is an example of effective equity.

[157] The forensic accounting exercises in which Congressional subcommittees engaged when reconstructing Enron's effective balance sheet are an example of effective debt analysis. *See supra* note 141 and accompanying text.

[158] One team of researchers inferred the level of OBS debt by comparing public firms' SEC filings with their federal income taxes. Lillian F. Mills & Kaye J. Newberry, *Firms' Off-Balance Sheet Financing: Evidence from their Book-Tax Reporting Differences* (January 5, 2004), *available at* http://ssrn.com/abstract=49474

the tax interest deductions suggest debt greater than the book debt.[159] Debt rating agencies approximate effective capital structure when considering the impact of OBS items on a credit rating.[160] Capitalizing OBS leases into the equity account rather than as a liability may better reflect the all-in cost of OBS items.[161] Investors, though, lack the time and resources needed to infer true capital structure.

Comprehensively measuring cash flow is a key aspect of effective capital structure. A firm manages its day-to-day liquidity on the basis of financial cash flow.[162] Though valuable, financial cash flow is hard to square with the balance sheet and the income statement, which use different accounting methods to present financial information.[163] Examples like the cash flow games played by Enron illustrate the gap between tracking financial cash flow and reported cash flow. Instead of financial cash flow, the statement of cash flows reflects accounting cash flow, the best publicly available proxy for a firm's

(later published as Lillian F. Mills & Kaye J. Newberry, *Firms' Off-Balance Sheet and Hybrid Debt Financing: Evidence from their Book-Tax Reporting Differences*, 43 J. ACCT. RES. 251 (2005)).

[159] *Id.*

[160] These OBS factors include: operating leases, pension obligations, debt of joint ventures and unconsolidated subsidiaries, guarantees, receivables that have been factored or sold with recourse, potential legal judgments or settlements of lawsuits, and other contingent liabilities, including environmental cleanup liabilities. STANDARD AND POOR'S, CREDIT POLICY UPDATE: FACTORING OFF-BALANCE SHEET FINANCING INTO THE RATINGS PROCESS 1-2 (April 15, 2002) (on file with author) (reviewing Standard and Poor's rating criteria for off-balance sheet items) (available to registered Standard and Poor's users at http://www.standardandpoors.com). As per the Efficient Capital Markets Hypothesis (ECMH), it is specialized intermediaries that first analyze raw financial data and then internalize it by buying or selling securities in the open market or preparing market intelligence for use by other investors. The market internalizes the information as trading prices begin to internalize the information. Debt rating agencies serve this function for OBS items by treating operating lease expenses as a permanent part of a firm's effective capital structure.

[161] *See* Steve C. Lim, Steven C. Mann & Vassil T. Mihov, *Market Evaluation of Off Balance Sheet Financing: You Can Run but You Can't Hide* 2 (Dec. 1, 2003), *available at* http://papers.ssrn.com/sol3/papers.cfm?abstract_id=474784 (comparing the impact of OBS operating lease financing on a firm's debt cost for 6800 U.S. issuers). The study examined whether credit ratings reflected this aspect of the firms' effective capital structure. *Id.* The authors compared two valuation approaches to the OBS items: treating the OBS item as a current liability or as permanent part of the company's capital. *Id.* They concluded that the perpetuity approach resulted in a higher actual cost, which better reflected the true cost of the leases. *Id.*

[162] Cash is fungible. From a cash management perspective, then, it makes no difference whether a cash inflow or outflow arises on or off the balance sheet.

[163] The main reporting formats are: the balance sheet, the income statement, the statement of changes in equity, and the statement of cash flows. *See generally* DYCKMAN ET AL., *supra* note 108, at 118-219. For a good summary of these financial reports (including the statement of cash flows), see SEC Report, *supra* note 17, at 11-14. These reports may use historical price information or current market values to price assets, may calculate asset and liability values using either cash methods or accrual methods, typically make no adjustment for the time value of money when considering cash flows in different periods, and, finally, may use different probability thresholds to determine whether an item needs to be disclosed at all. At best, these varied measures can provide only an impressionistic rendering of the dynamically shifting financial values that make up a firm. In this sense, cash flow intrudes into the neat formalisms of forward projection and financial reporting.

financial cash flow.[164] Tracking accounting cash flow has many virtues, as shown by the SEC's wide use of this technique to explain the OBS sector to Congress,[165] the use of cash flow to measure firm profitability,[166] the use of cash flow analysis by credit agencies,[167] and the pedagogical value of cash analogies.[168] Of course, uncertainty

---

[164] Accounting cash flow refers to a public representation of a firm's financial cash flow that conforms to generally accepted accounting principles. Ongoing debates about the advantages of a cash-flow tax rather than an income tax refer to accounting cash flow. *See* Chris Edwards, *Replace the Scandal-Plagued Corporate Income Tax with a Cash-Flow Tax, in* AFTER ENRON: LESSONS FOR PUBLIC POLICY 283 (William Niskanen ed., 2005) (Edwards argues that cash-flow tax would eliminate many of the current distortions of corporate income caused by the income tax).

[165] In its statutorily required (15 U.S.C. § 7261) report, the SEC stressed the reporting value of cash flow: "What presents difficulties for investors, as well as the market as a whole, is a lack of information about potential positive and negative cash flows." *See* SEC Report, *supra* note 17, at 5. The Report also used cash flow scenario analysis throughout. *See id.* at 59 (using cash flow scenario analysis to estimate the value firm's obligations under employee defined-benefit plans); *id.* at 65 (estimating the value of cash flows from capital leases); *id.* at 67 (using cash flow scenario analysis to estimate the value of contingent obligations); *id.* at 89 (using cash flow to measure the impact of purchase and sale obligations of filers).

[166] *See* BEAVER, *supra* note 5, at 5 (noting the trend in security valuation away from earnings measurement and towards discounted cash flow valuation). A 1994 survey of chief financial officers reported a moderate increase (54% to 62%) of officers who made maximizing cash flow a top priority from a previous survey. *CFO Forum: King Cash*, INSTITUTIONAL INVESTOR (AM. ED.), Sept. 1994, at 93. Increasingly, CFOs use cash flow based measures to determine employee compensation. *See* Stephen Gates, CFO 2000: THE GLOBAL CFO AS STRATEGIC BUSINESS PARTNER 13 (Conference Bd. 1998) (conducted interviews and surveys of chief financial officers regarding composition of the CFO function). Chief financial officers have called for increased use of cash flow in earnings rather than net income. *See* Barney Jopson, *CFO Urges Cashflow as New Measure*, FINANCIAL TIMES (London, England), Apr. 21, 2005, at 22. Some theorists agree. *See* Pablo Fernández, *Cash Flow Is a Fact. Net Income Is Just an Opinion* 1 (Mar. 18, 2004), *available at* http://ssrn.com/abstract=330540 ("A company's net income is a quite arbitrary figure obtained after assuming certain accounting hypotheses regarding expenses and revenues. On the other hand, the cash flow is an objective measure, a single figure that is not subject to any personal criterion."). Some qualify the value of cash flow information over accrual earnings by pointing out that cash flow data is more relevant for firms experiencing rapid growth or decline, but that accrual earnings say more about a firm during a steady period of the firm's life. *See* Divesh Shankar Sharma & Errol Iselin, *The Decision Usefulness of Reported Cash Flow and Accrual Information in a Behavioral Field Experiment*, 33 ACCT. & BUS. RES. (U.K.) 123 (2003) (noting that information about a firm's cash flows may be useful only for a firm facing solvency problems).

[167] Reflecting the value of cash flow analysis, credit rating agencies note the importance of cash flow in their rating decisions. *See Hearings on the Current Role and Functions of Credit Rating Agencies in the Operation of the Securities Markets Before the Securities and Exchange Commission* 113 (Nov. 15, 2002) (testimony of Leo C. O'Neill, President, Standard & Poor's), *available at* http://www.sec.gov/news/extra/credrate/credrate111502.txt ("The information that we get, in most cases, is corporations, projections, call it what you will, their view of their future cash requirements, how their capital spending is going to go, what their cash flow is going to be to support that . . .").

[168] Analogizing to cash also helps to explain some income tax concepts. Students seem to find it easier to understand cash consideration than other forms of property. When explaining the tax implications of a transaction with noncash consideration, I encourage students to restate the consideration on both sides as cash and to analyze the issue restated that way. The tax effects of the notional cash exchange will generally mirror the tax effects of the actual noncash transactions. For example, to simplify the analysis in the case,

limits the ability to project future cash flow.[169] The statement of cash flows nets cash inflows and cash outflows for a time period between two balance sheets.[170] The statement does not reflect accrual losses or gains.[171] Rather, it reflects only accounting cash outflows and inflows.[172] The statement lets a reader compare accrual-based earnings or balance sheet values with accounting cash flow, sourced on- or off-balance-sheet. Any single financial indicator has its limits and this is also true for measures that track cash flow.[173] Publicly revealing more about financial cash flow would lead to the appearance

---

restate as cash the consideration in Philadelphia Park Amusement Co. v. United States, 126 F. Supp. 184 (Ct. Cl. 1954), which addresses income recognition and basis for taxable exchanges.

[169] As Beaver notes:

> A common approach to valuation of complex claims under uncertainty is to take a valuation model derived from certainty, such as the discounted cash flow model, and to replace each variable in that formula with the expected value of that variable to reflect the uncertainty . . . . In a multiperiod setting, characterizing the present value or price of a complex claim in terms of discounting expected cash flow [under uncertainty] at expected rates of return is not possible in general.

See BEAVER, *supra* note 5, at 60-61; *id.* at 49 (noting the Financial Accounting Standards Board's preference for accrual earnings over cash flow).

[170] Cash flow discounting may actually refer to any of ten different methodologies for valuation. *See* Pablo Fernández, *Equivalence of Ten Different Methods for Valuing Companies by Cash Flow Discounting*, 1 INT'L J. FIN. EDUC. 141, 142-43 (2005), *available at* http://www.senatehall.com/getfile.php?file=paper140.pdf (identifying ten alternative cash flow discounting methods).

[171] Accrual accounting records resource inflows and outflows based not on actual cash flows, but instead on the basis of whether a firm's legally-enforceable rights (or obligations with respect to outflows) have vested. *See* DYCKMAN ET AL., *supra* note 108, at 33-34. A firm's statement of income identifies what the firm's net profit or loss position was during a specific period, typically one year's economic activity. The income statement provides a bridge between a firm's balance sheet at the beginning of the period in question and the balance sheet at the end of the reporting period. A typical income statement reflects various different measures of income, typically accrual income plus other adjustments. Some measures try to reconcile accrual earnings with cash flow by adding back to accrual earnings accounting adjustments that do not reflect actual funds outlays. For example, accounting goodwill is a wasting asset for which a firm "accounts" by allocating a portion of the deemed waste in goodwill in each accounting period, i.e., amortization of goodwill. So, since accrual earnings reflect the amortization of goodwill, all else being equal, they will be lower than actual cash earnings for the same period. One approach to reconcile book earnings to cash flow is to add back the amount of amortized goodwill to the accrual amount.

[172] An accrual loss would occur when the ultimate value of an asset or receivable turns out to be less than its book value. *See generally* DYCKMAN ET AL., *supra* note 108, at 40-41. Assume that a firm books an account receivable on the asset side of its balance sheet for $100. If the firm collects only $80 on the account, the deficit gives rise to an accrued loss reflected only on the income statement. The statement of cash flows would reflect an operating inflow of $80. Conversely, if a firm collects $120 in exchange for investment securities booked on the asset side of the balance sheet for $100, the firm books a gain in the income statement of $20. The amount reflected as an investment cash flow is $120.

[173] Accrual accounting makes possible the economic matching of the expenses and revenues from a project. *See* BEAVER, *supra* note 5, at 2 ("Reporting cash receipts and cash disbursements will not properly match, and some form of accrual accounting is called for."); *see also* Cunningham, *supra* note 1, at 928 (noting limitations of cash flow reporting).

of volatility for firms.[174] Part IV recommends changes to make the statement of cash flows more useful as a public financial report by reflecting volatility, which is currently airbrushed out of the statement.

The statement of cash flows was the last major financial report to become widely used by firms.[175] Ever reactive on accounting matters, the SEC began to mandate the

---

[174] Agreeing with this view, an accounting study group considering the future balance sheet urged more cash flow-based analysis and disclosure, despite the resulting appearance of volatility:

> The balance sheet of the future will be a more flexible instrument, able to adapt to a wide variety of industries and circumstances. . . .
>
> . . . [It] would permit the display of different kinds of numbers—either in a range, or presented as alternatives. This approach could be used to portray cash transactions for which audit assurance is highest, the historical cost allocations of prior cash transactions, [and] market values from actual arms'-length transactions . . . .
>
> . . . [W]e recognize that financial reports prepared in this fashion would *appear* to be considerably more volatile, complex and subjective than the financial reports we are accustomed to scrutinizing today. . . .
>
> . . . [I]t is the *illusion* of exactitude that carries with it the false perception that financial reports are relatively stable and easily comparable. . . . [We] believe the current emphasis on reducing volatility, complexity, and subjectivity and on seeking a greater degree of comparability needs tempering. The world, the economy, and the business environment are in a constant state of flux and any financial reporting system that tries to distill all the data contained in increasingly complex financial statements into one verifiable, static number such as GAAP EPS [earnings per share] flies in the face of reality.

AM. ASSEMBLY, COLUMBIA UNIV., THE FUTURE OF THE ACCOUNTING PROFESSION 11, *available at* http://www.americanassembly.org/programs.dir/report_file.dir/accounting_report_report_file_future%20of%C20the%C20accounting% C20profession%C20report%final.pdf.

[175] At the time of the New Deal, firms did not use the statement of cash flows widely, although accounting teachers had thought of a statement of the sources and uses of funds, and some firms were already voluntarily disclosing liquidity information. *See* Karl Käfer & V.K. Zimmerman, *Notes on the Evolution of the Statement of Sources and Applications of Funds*, 1 INT'L. J. ACCT. EDUC. & RES. 89-121 (1965) (tracing statement from emergence in the early 1900s through the early 1960s in UK and USA; the book contains an anthology of essays tracing the development of public financial reporting). Large railroad concerns were the first to include these statements in their financial statements. *Id.* A turn-of-the-century financial columnist, Thomas Warner Mitchell, was probably the first to publish systematic analyses of the sources and uses of funds by companies in the United States. *See* CORPORATE FINANCIAL REPORTING AND ANALYSIS IN THE EARLY 1900S 191-215 (Richard P. Brelf ed., 1986) (analyzing liquidity changes by the International Paper Company, the Tennessee Coal, Iron, and Railroad Company, and the Chicago and Alton Railroad Company). *See also* Cunningham, *supra* note 1, at 216-20 (discussing the development of the cash flow statement in the United Kingdom and Germany). Voluntary disclosures of cash flow information seems to be a pattern elsewhere too. *See* Christian Leuz, *The Development of Voluntary Cash Flow Statements in Germany and the Influence of International Reporting Standards*, 52 SCHMALENBACH BUS. REV. 182 (2000) (showing how German firms voluntarily reported cash flow information before any legal requirement to do so). U.S. Accounting authorities started requiring a statement of cash flows in 1971. For a comprehensive survey of cash flow products—especially in the United Kingdom—see T.A. LEE, TOWARDS A THEORY AND PRACTICE OF CASH FLOW ACCOUNTING (1986) (reviews history of cash flow accounting, accounting for goodwill and enterprise income, and the use of cash flow accounting to track firm profitability).

disclosure of cash flow information by firms for the first time after an agency study recommended the mandatory disclosure of accounting cash flow.[176] During this same period cash flow became a popular way of valuing the firm.[177] In 1985, the Financial Accounting Standards Board (FASB) began to adopt cash flow valuation for selected situations, starting with the treatment of pensions.[178] Only in 1987 did FASB require the disclosure of accounting cash flow in a firm's financial reports. Beginning in that year, firms had to report cash flow classified according to whether it was related to

---

[176] In 1971, the Accounting Principles Board of the American Institute of Certified Public Accountants issued Opinion 19, recommending the inclusion of a "Statement of Changes in Financial Position" in a firm's financial statements. AM. INST. OF CERTIFIED PUB. ACCOUNTANTS, ACCOUNTING PRINCIPLES BOARD OPINION NO. 19: REPORTING CHANGES IN FINANCIAL POSITION (1972). The main objective of Opinion No. 19 was to "summarize the financing and investing activities of the entity, including the extent to which the enterprise has generated funds from operations during the period." *Id.* at ¶ 4 (quoted in J.W. Giese & T.P. Klammer, *Achieving the Objectives of APB Opinion No. 19*, J. ACCOUNTANCY, Mar. 1974, at 54-55). Research conducted after the adoption of Accounting Principles Board Opinion No. 19 found substantial noncompliance with the requirements. *See* Giese & Klammer, *supra*, at 54, 57 (concluding from a financial reporting study of fifty Fortune 500 firms that one-half of the firms did not properly label the sources and uses of funds). German firms also failed to comply with cash flow reporting requirements after it became a duty to make the disclosures. *See* Günther Gebhardt & Aaron Heilmann, *Compliance with German and International Accounting Standards in Germany: Evidence From Cash Flow Statements, in* THE ECONOMICS AND POLITICS OF ACCOUNTING 218 (Leuz et al. eds., 2004) (documenting that a majority of firms failed to report operating, investing, and financing cash flows as required by IAS7, the cash flow standard of the International Accounting Standards Board, and GAS2, the German accounting standard on cash flow). One reason for the belated recognition of cash is the accounting profession's historic preference for measures based on accrual earnings over cash flow indicators as a measure of firm value. *See* FIN. ACCOUNTING STANDARDS BD., STATEMENT OF FINANCIAL ACCOUNTING CONCEPTS NO. 1: OBJECTIVES OF FINANCIAL REPORTING BY BUSINESS ENTERPRISES ¶ 44 (1978), *available at* http://www.fasb.org/pdf/con1.pdf. "Information about enterprise earnings and its components measured by accrual accounting generally provides a better indication of enterprise performance than does information about current cash receipts and payments." *Id.* This subordination of cash flow to accrual measures has hindered the comprehensive financial reporting of a firm's balance sheet and OBS sectors.

[177] For an example of how law has incorporated cash flow analysis, consider how judges in Delaware dissenter's appraisal proceedings rely on cash flow discounting. *See generally* Joseph Evan Calio, *New Appriasals of Old Problems: Reflections on the Delaware Appraisal Proceeding*, 32 AM. BUS. L.J. 1 (1994) (documenting the increase in use of cash flow discounting by judges since a 1983 case authorized the use of any generally accepted financial valuation technique).

[178] *See* Siegel, *supra* note 29, at 1851 (noting the adoption of cash flow valuation by the Financial Accounting Standards Board for pensions in 1985 and employee benefit plans in 1990). The Financial Accounting Standards Board (FASB) has been wryly commissioned the "SEC's SPE (Special Purpose Entity)" because of its funding value. *See* George Mundstock, *The Trouble with FASB*, 28 N.C. J. INT'L. L. & COM. REG. 813, 834 (2003). "The SEC liked, and likes, having an off-budget source of financing for activities that it otherwise would be required to fund. FASB is the SEC's SPE (Special Purpose Entity)." *Id.*

operating,[179] investing,[180] or financing[181] activity, a classification to which I return in my recommendations.

Of firms, only banks come close to disclosing their effective capital structure because they must report their OBS positions to their banking supervisors.[182] In these reports, the bank calculates its effective capital structure by converting OBS items into their balance sheet equivalents. Many of these items are credit exposures to borrowers, so conversion means that the bank adds these notional asset values to its balance sheet,

---

[179] Operating cash flow reflects net cash flow from a firm's core business, sales in the context of a merchandising concern, interest rate differentials and fee income in the context of a depository institution, capital return in the context of a registered broker-dealer, and the net return on underwriting in the context of an insurance company. *See generally* EUGENE BRIGHAM & MICHAEL EHRHARDT, FINANCIAL MANAGEMENT THEORY AND PRACTICE 40-41 (10th ed. 2002). Operating cash flow tells a reader of a firm's financial statements how much liquidity arose or was consumed by the firm's core business. *Id.* In this sense, operating cash flow may be the best indicator of trends in a firm's going concern value. Operating cash flow may be calculated with either the direct or indirect method, which presents operating activities in different ways but leads to the same net cash flow from operations. *See* DYCKMAN ET AL., *supra* note 108, at 1189. The indirect method derives the same net operating cash flow amount by adjusting net income for items whose operating cash flow and income effects are unequal. If the company chooses to report operations cash flow under the direct method, the firm must also include a supplemental schedule showing the reconciliation of earnings and net operating cash flows, i.e., a schedule of the indirect method. *Id.*

[180] Investment cash flow reflects both the cash flow from a firm's position-taking in investment markets—just like any other investor in the capital market—as well as the net cash effects of investing in (or liquidating) assets that support the firm's core business. DYCKMAN, *supra* note 108, at 1191-92. So, for example, investment cash flow reflects the net return on a firm's securities portfolio. Investment cash flow also reflects allocations of cash to buy physical plant, depreciable equipment, franchises, and other capital assets whose income is included in operating cash flow.

[181] Financing cash flow reflects the firm's cash position as a borrower and lender in the capital market. *Id.* at 1192.

[182] Since 1913, all state member banks of the Federal Reserve System must file "call" reports of financial condition with their respective regulator. *See* Federal Reserve Act of 1913, Pub. L. No. 63-43, 38 Stat. 251 (codified as amended in scattered sections of 12 U.S.C.); 12 U.S.C. § 632 (2000). The Federal Financial Institutions Examination Council coordinates the collection and dissemination of the call report, which says much about banks' OBS items. *See* Fed. Fin. Inst. Examination Council, Consolidated Reports of Condition and Income for a Bank With Domestic and Foreign Offices, Schedule RC-L Derivatives and Off Balance Sheet Items (June 30, 2005), *available at* http://www.ffiec.gov/PDF/FFIEC_forms/FFIEC031_20050630_f.pdf. Schedule RC-L distinguishes between OBS assets and OBS liabilities. Consider the Comptroller of the Currency's tough love advice to its banks on this point:

> A gap report that does not include off-balance-sheet interest rate positions does not fully measure a bank's interest rate risk profile. All material positions in off-balance-sheet instruments whose value can be affected by interest rates should be captured in a gap report. Such instruments include interest rate contracts, such as swaps, futures, and forwards; option contracts, such as caps, floors, and options on futures; and firm forward commitments to buy or sell loans, securities, or other financial instruments.

U.S. COMPTROLLER OF THE CURRENCY, INTEREST RATE RISK: COMPTROLLER'S HANDBOOK 78 (1997), *available at* http://www.occ.treas.gov/handbook/irr.pdf.

which must still balance even as adjusted.[183] Because prudential regulation imposes composition requirements on bank capital, e.g., Tier 1 and Tier 2 capital requirements, bank regulators say that the bank faces a "capital charge" on the formally OBS item.[184] Banking supervisors demand that banks reveal their effective capital structure in regulatory reports because of the spillover risks from bank failure and because federally-insured banking exposes the federal government to liquidity risk.[185] Private firms do not directly expose the federal government to such risk and, hence, are not subject to the same degree of transparency.[186]

III. SLOUCHING TOWARDS TRANSPARENCY IN SARBANES-OXLEY

Faced with the transactional complexities discussed in Part II, above, Congress turned away from a more detailed look at financial reporting requirements and, instead, penalized individuals. Sarbanes-Oxley did, however, add some transparency about effective capital structure, namely a direction to the SEC to require firms to better disclose OBS arrangements. After noting the SEC's reluctance to engage seriously with accounting, this Part analyzes the new OBS rule, which is a step in the right direction. It contributes to financial literacy by legally classifying some types of OBS arrangements.[187] Nevertheless, the SEC—and I—conclude that more is needed.

A. Retreating to Accounting in Law

No statute explicitly charges the SEC with developing accounting standards. The New Deal's Securities Act and the Exchange Act gave the SEC authority over accounting

---

[183] The fundamental accounting equation still holds for this notional balance sheet.

[184] Extra prudent through asymmetry, prudential regulation does not generally give regulatory capital credit, i.e., count an item as equity capital, for OBS commitments from a third party to contribute risk capital to a depository institution. Instead, banking regulators tend to give capital credit only for "a dollar on the barrel." Interview with Dr. Roger Tufts, Capital Department, Office of the Comptroller of the Currency, in Washington, D.C. (June 16, 2005) (on file with author).

[185] Regulation protects bank solvency because of the federal government's contingent exposure from insurance for customer deposits. Financially speaking, the Federal Deposit Insurance Corporation (FDIC) bears residual loss when banks become insolvent. In this sense, the FDIC is short a put on the national portfolio of the depositor institution, creating an appealing moral hazard for bank owners, who bear only the residual upside in this lopsided deal. (A "put" is a legal obligation to buy an asset for a fixed price. By ensuring depositor obligations, it is as though the FDIC has promised to "buy" the assets of a failed bank in exchange for assuming its depositor obligations.) Given its short exposure, the federal government makes banks hike up their skirts with respect to OBS items. For that reason, bank regulators require banks to maintain enough capital to meet even OBS exposures.

[186] The limited liability of corporations and other forms of business organization, however, certainly produces social costs that are sometimes borne by the federal government.

[187] As discussed in Part IV, standardizing information about the firm's constituent cash flows would help both investors and firms.

standards.[188] These authorities specifically extend to the form and use of the balance sheet.[189] Instead of using this authority directly, the SEC has let private standard setters make accounting pronouncements, often at the cost of sound accounting principles.[190]

---

188 The Securities Act and the Exchange Act give the SEC parallel authority over accounting. Securities Act of 1933 § 19, 15 U.S.C. § 77s (2000 & Supp. II 2002); Securities Exchange Act of 1934 § 13, 15 U.S.C. § 78m (2000 & Supp. II 2002). The SEC's new OBS rule requiring disclosure of OBS arrangements which affect a registrant's liquidity and capital resources is based in part on these essentially parallel grants of authority. Although Congress passed these laws during a national panic, that situation was not a moral panic—financial or otherwise—because the scope of the New Deal's state-building was proportional to a generalized and serious economic crisis. For a good general discussion of the early history of the SEC's use of accounting, *see* THE SEC AND ACCOUNTING: THE FIRST 50 YEARS (Robert H. Manheim & Mayes E. Leech eds., 1984) (Not surprisingly, given my thesis, the twelve essays make virtually no mention of the off-balance sheet sector or cash flow disclosures and their utility as regulatory indicators.).

189 The Securities Act provides:

> Among other things, the Commission shall have authority, for the purposes of this title . . . , to prescribe the form or forms in which required information shall be set forth, the items or details to be shown in the balance sheet and earning statement, and the methods to be followed in the preparation of accounts, in the appraisal or valuation of assets and liabilities, in the determination of depreciation and depletion, in the differentiation of recurring and nonrecurring income, in the differentiation of investment and operating income, and in the preparation, where the Commission deems it necessary or desirable, of *consolidated balance sheets or income accounts* of any person directly or indirectly controlling or controlled by the issuer, or any person under direct or indirect common control with the issuer.

15 U.S.C. § 77s (2000 & Supp. II 2002) (emphasis added). The SEC's authority under the Exchange Act is essentially identical except that the provision also grants authority to deconsolidate the balance sheet of a registrant: "The Commission may prescribe . . . the methods to be followed . . . in the preparation . . . of separate and/or consolidated balance sheets or income accounts of any person directly or indirectly controlling or controlled by the issuer, or any person under direct or indirect common control with the issuer . . . ." *Id.* § 78m(b)(1) (emphasis added).

190 *See* Mundstock, *supra* note 178, at 817 ("Accounting, like commercial law, developed before courts and legislatures became involved in business affairs. While commercial law became an object for the state, accounting principles thus far have not." (footnotes omitted)). The endowment effect is one of the reasons for the trend cited by Professor Mundstock:

> Another factor that has contributed to the SEC's ongoing abdication of responsibility over accounting principles is worth noting: People have a natural tendency to belittle expertise that they do not possess. The SEC has been composed primarily of lawyers. Lawyers do not want to be bothered by accounting, which they view as merely "technical." Hence, the SEC has been willing to leave accounting to the accountants.

Id. at 827. Professor Mundstock notes the importance of institutional self-interest in standard setting:

> To summarize the history of private standard-setting in America: the players [including accountants] acted in their own self-interest . . . . Independence really has meant isolation and irrelevance. The central feature of the resulting accounting standards is the flexibility notion: accounts need not be right, merely acceptable. . . . When faced with controversy, particularly critiques from business interests, the private standard setter has either reorganized or capitulated. The SEC's institutional interests—combined with the distaste for accounting shared by most lawyers—have prevented the SEC from playing a proper role in the setting of accounting principles.

Id. at 839.

This hands-off policy delayed adequate regulation of OBS arrangements, which vexed fundamental accounting assumptions.[191] In fact, the FASB did not address how firms ought to treat securitized assets—one type of OBS item—until 1996.[192] Although the early and continued focus of legislative attention after Enron was on financier misconduct, former SEC Commissioner Richard Breeden introduced the idea of requiring disclosure of firms' OBS arrangements into the public record on the very first day of the hearings.[193] Some firms had voluntarily reported some of their OBS arrangements after Enron's problems had come to light, but by then it was clear that more was needed in terms of regulation.[194] Adopting Breeden's suggestion, Congress directed the SEC to address the OBS sector by studying it and amending its rules to increase the public disclosure of OBS arrangements.[195] After rulemaking, the SEC amended its forms and rules to require managers to discuss OBS information in the management's discussion and analysis of the annual report.[196] Under the new requirement, registrants must also

---

[191] *See* Donegan & Sunder, *supra* note 1, at 210:

> Under our current system of financial reporting, articulation between stocks on the balance sheet and flows on the statements of income and changes in cash flow is both incomplete and imperfect; the unavoidable lapses in articulation [i.e., mistakes and lack of correspondence between items on the balance sheet and flow statements] are critical to understanding the OBSF [off-balance-sheet financing] problem. . . .
>
> . . . How to construct correspondent variables, and under what conditions it is appropriate to abandon the task of articulation, are questions that lie at the heart of the major problems in standardizing accounting practice including OBSF.

Id. at 208. For example, market movements may change an OBS asset to a liability, and then back again. Consider a swap. When in-the-money, it is an asset to the swapholder. When out-of-the-money, it becomes a liability to the same counterparty. *See, e.g.*, U.S. COMPTROLLER OF THE CURRENCY, AN EXAMINER'S GUIDE TO INVESTMENT PRODUCTS AND PRACTICES 90 (1992) (advising bank examiner to determine whether a bank's swap position increases or reduces risk).

[192] FIN. ACCOUNTING STANDARDS BD., STATEMENT OF FINANCIAL ACCOUNTING STANDARDS NO. 125: ACCOUNTING FOR TRANSFER AND SERVICING OF FINANCIAL ASSETS AND EXTINGUISHMENT OF LIABILITIES (1996). Implementation problems, though, led to a substitute pronouncement. *See* FIN. ACCOUNTING STANDARDS BD., STATEMENT OF FINANCIAL ACCOUNTING STANDARDS NO. 140: ACCOUNTING FOR TRANSFER AND SERVICING OF FINANCIAL ASSETS AND EXTINGUISHMENT OF LIABILITIES (2000) (creates a safe harbor for qualifying special purpose entities which need not be consolidated on a reporting firm's balance sheet). The direction of accounting pronouncements is towards keeping the balance sheet and selectively recognizing and disclosing certain OBS items. *See also* FIN. ACCOUNTING STANDARDS BD., STATEMENT OF FINANCIAL ACCOUNTING STANDARDS NO. 133: ACCOUNTING FOR DERIVATIVE INVESTMENTS AND HEDGING ACTIVITIES (1998), *available at* www.fasb.org/pdf/fas133.pdf.

[193] *See* HEARINGS, *supra* note 55, at 62 (prepared statement of Richard C. Breeden, Chairman, U.S. Securities and Exchange Commission, 1989-1993).

[194] *See* Fink, *supra* note 135 (describing how El Paso Corp. consolidated an OBS subsidiary, how Electronic Data Systems began to voluntarily report its OBS debt in its quarterly financial statements, and how PeopleSoft was considering book consolidation of a research and development subsidiary).

[195] *See supra* note 15 for the language of the new statutory reporting requirement.

[196] *See* SEC Final Rule, *supra* note 16. These are changes to Regulations S-B and S-K, which contain many of the SEC's financial disclosure requirements for registrants. *See* 17 C.F.R. § 228.303(c) (2005)

file a Form 8-K whenever they assume a direct financial obligation related to an OBS item.[197]

The OBS rule does not require recognition of OBS items on the balance sheet, the income statement, or the statement of cash flows in the sense of financially complete measurement and disclosure of the item. Instead, the rule merely requires the firm to discuss the fact of OBS items in sufficient detail.[198] As reflected in the Conference Report,[199] which introduced H.R. 3763 (later enacted into law as the Act), Congress specifically expected the SEC to expand the disclosure requirements for registrants' OBS arrangements, but it is not clear whether the current rule has done so. For example, the OBS rule requires firms to disclose OBS items only if they are "reasonably likely" to impact the firm, a disclosure standard which gives reporting firms broad leeway.[200] Originally, the SEC had proposed a disclosure threshold lower (i.e., one that would lead to more disclosure) than the standard generally used for material events, but the final rule abandoned this approach, substituting a "reasonably likely" for a "more than remote" standard.[201] The "reasonably likely" threshold of probability for disclosure defeats some of the purpose of the rule by letting firms off the hook in terms of disclosing their effective capital structure.[202] As well noted, the SEC's adoption of a relatively

(part of Regulation S-B); *id.* § 229.303(a)(4) (2005) (part of Regulation S-K). A similar requirement was imposed on the Exchange Act financial disclosures for foreign private issuers. *Id.* § 249.220(f) (2005) (foreign private issuers use Form 20-F to file an annual report with the SEC); *id.* § 249.240(f) (2005) (qualified Canadian issuers use Form 40-F).

Publicly-registered companies must file public reports. Securities Exchange Act of 1934 §§ 13, 15(d), 15 U.S.C. §§ 78m, 78o(d) (2000 & Supp. II 2002); *see also* 17 C.F.R. § 229.303(a)(4)(i) (2005).

[197] [omitted by original author]

[198] For example, the information required by Item 301 to be included on the balance sheet, the statement of income, and the statement of cash flows are subject to this standard of disclosure. 17 C.F.R. § 229.301 (2005). This information is "recognized" in the accounting sense that the impact of the information is reflected in the firm's reported financial position. In contrast, disclosure of the mere existence of an item without further elaboration of its significance provides less information to readers of financial reports and leaves it to the discretion of corporate officials to decide the materiality.

[199] The Act:

> requires the Commission to revise its regulations under the securities laws to *expand* the disclosure requirements for the financial reports and registration statements of public companies, so that they provide adequate and appropriate disclosure of certain of an issuer's off-balance sheet transactions.

H.R. Rep. No. 107-414, at 40 (2002) (emphasis added).

[200] *See* SEC Final Rule, *supra* note 16, codified at 17 C.F.R. § 229.303(a)(4)(i) (2005).

[201] In a January 2002 statement, the SEC indicated that "reasonably likely" is a lower disclosure threshold than "more likely than not." *See* Commission Statement About Management's Discussion and Analysis of Financial Condition and Results of Operations, Exchange Act Release No. 33-8056, 67 Fed. Reg. 17 (Jan. 22, 2002), *available at* http://www.sec.gov/rules/other/33-8056.htm.

[202] *See* Partnoy, *supra* note 18, at 1278 (arguing that even under the subsequent OBS reporting requirements Enron managers need not have disclosed much of their OBS activity if they concluded that the financial downside of this activity was more remote than "reasonably likely"):

weak disclosure standard reflects successful rent-seeking by issuers, finance firms, and accounting firms whose separate liquidity, business, and liability-reduction interests converged in this rulemaking project.[203]

Notwithstanding the widespread criticisms of accounting rules and auditors during the financial moral panic, the new rule turns directly to existing accounting standards and incorporates them by reference.[204] Specifically, the rule defines an OBS arrangement as one of four items: a guarantee obligation captured by the definition in FASB Interpretation No. 45;[205] a retained or contingent interest in assets transferred to an

---

Disclosure of "reasonably likely" contingencies would not likely have prevented the problems associated with Enron. Indeed, Enron arguably was in compliance with the newly-enacted SEC regulations. In assessing the firm's financial contingencies at the end of 2000, management would not have considered a scenario in which Enron's stock price would decline by more than half to be "reasonably likely." Accordingly, management would not have needed to disclose details about Enron's derivatives contracts with the SPEs. Nor would it have been "reasonably likely" that the volatility of commodity prices in 2000 would continue.

[203] *Id.* To the extent that a company's true financial leverage exceeds its book leverage, a company's funding costs would increase. So issuers interested in retaining freedom to manage the balance sheet tactically defend managerial discretion over OBS disclosures. Investment banks that collect transaction costs, i.e., fees, to plan and implement complex OBS deals would defend their business line. The OBS rule bears on the liability of accountants by setting out the scope of required disclosures, so accountants have a mixed interest in the rule. A standard which unambiguously establishes disclosure requirements immunizes accounting firms from pressure by issuers interested in particular reporting treatments that may be inconsistent with the standard. On the other hand, accountants have different levels of risk-aversion too, and those with an appetite for more risk might prefer a rule with leeway to go out on a limb in terms of whether and how OBS items are booked or disclosed. Most of the comments from accounting firms noted the need for clarity. One of the advantages for legal and financial scholarship of federal rulemaking under the Administrative Procedure Act is that the comment process leaves a written record of rentseeking by affected constituencies. These comments make it possible to document—and sometimes infer—the motives of affected constituencies.

[204] The regulatory definition uses the definitions established by three accounting pronouncements: FIN. ACCOUNTING STANDARDS BD., FASB INTERPRETATION NO. 45: GUARANTOR'S ACCOUNTING AND DISCLOSURE REQUIREMENTS FOR GUARANTEES, INCLUDING INDIRECT GUARANTEES OF INDEBTEDNESS OF OTHERS (2002) (hereinafter FIN 45), *available at* http://www.fasb.org/pdf/fin%2045.pdf; STATEMENT OF FINANCIAL ACCOUNTING STANDARDS NO. 133, *supra* note 192; FIN. ACCOUNTING STANDARDS BD., FASB INTERPRETATION NO. 46: CONSOLIDATION OF VARIABLE INTEREST ENTITIES (2003) (hereinafter FIN 46), *available at* http://www.fasb.org/pdf/fin%2046.pdf. *See* Item 303(a)(4)(ii) of Regulation S-K, 17 C.F.R. § 229.303(a)(4)(ii) (2005). The definition is cross-referenced in several forms and rules. *See, e.g.*, Form 8-K, Item 2.03, Instruction 1, *available at* http://www.sec.gov/about/forms/form8-k.pdf. The SEC had first proposed a rule discussing the new disclosure requirements. *See* SEC Proposed Rule: Disclosure in Management's Discussion and Analysis About Off-Balance Sheet Arrangements, Contractual Obligations and Contingent Liabilities and Commitments, Securities Exchange Act Release No. 33-8144, 67 Fed. Reg. 68054 (Nov. 4, 2002), *available at* http://www.sec.gov/rules/proposed/33-8144.htm. In response to the proposed rule, most commenters asked the SEC to define OBS items more precisely. Disagreement about the type of financial arrangements this definition should capture were the most common remark made by persons and institutions who submitted comments during the proposed rule's public comment period.

[205] 17 C.F.R. § 229.303(a)(4)(ii)(A) (2005).

unconsolidated entity;[206] an obligation referenced to the registrant's stock which is excluded from FASB Statement of Financial Accounting Standards No. 133;[207] or an obligation in a variable interest entity as defined by FASB Interpretation No. 46 (FIN 46).[208] In particular, by internalizing FIN 46, the OBS rule does draw some relatively bright lines about the interests subject to consolidation.[209] However, the standard leaves open important legal questions because the Interpretation's criteria go to the heart of the meaning of an equity interest in a firm.[210] As a result, the legal use of this accounting standard also internalizes interpretive ambiguity, as noted by the SEC.[211]

These regulatory definitions of OBS arrangements, however, follow the pattern of the financial contracts involved in Enron. Essentially, it was these types of obligations which led to Enron's liquidity problems,[212] raising the question of whether the rule

---

206 *Id.* at § 229.303(a)(4)(ii)(B).

207 *Id.* at § 229.303(a)(4)(ii)(C).

208 *Id.* at § 229.303(a)(4)(ii)(D).

209 For example, FIN 46 increases the minimum amount of third-party equity required in a special purpose entity to keep the entity off the sponsoring firm's books to ten percent from the previous floor of three percent. FIN 46, *supra* note 204, ¶ E-23. Before this interpretation, a firm could avoid consolidating any SPE if at least three percent of the equity was owned by separate investors. SPEs that had an effective external equity of less than three percent contributed to Enron's downward liquidity spiral. FIN 46 also creates some safe harbors for entities and arrangements that need not be consolidated. FIN 46 excludes the following legal forms from consolidation on a reporting firm's balance sheet: qualifying special purpose entities as defined by STATEMENT OF FINANCIAL ACCOUNTING STANDARDS NO. 140, *supra* note 192, certain pension plans, not-for-profit entities, certain entities with interests in variable interest entities created before December 31, 2003, entities meeting the definition of a "business" under the standard, and certain other entities. FIN 46, *supra* note 204, ¶ 4.

210 The interpretation requires a firm to consolidate any firm that is a variable interest entity, which includes any entity in which the equity investor lacks one or more of the following three incidents: 1) the direct or indirect ability to make decisions that effect the success of the firm; 2) the obligation to absorb the entity's expected losses; or 3) the right to receive the entity's residual gains. FIN 46, *supra* note 204, ¶ 14. As firms further unbundle risk, the question arises about the extent to which the firm retains any residual risk or whether that residual risk has been farmed out to other investors using OBS arrangements. For this reason, by turning FIN 46 into positive law, the OBS rule sets the stage for judicial adjudications to determine equity as an accounting matter. Those will be interesting cases to observe.

211 In its report to Congress, the SEC noted the ambiguity about this accounting standard as used in the OBS rule. *See* SEC Report, *supra* note 17, at 92 ("Although Interpretation No. 46(R) constitutes an improvement over the previously existing consolidation guidance, a number of interpretive questions remain. Many users of Interpretation No. 46R [sic] find it theoretically and practically challenging to apply."). This is the converse situation to the FASB's de facto role as disclosure monitor:

> In principle, the jurisdiction of the FASB was said to be the setting of financial accounting standards, whereas the jurisdiction of the SEC was said to be disclosure. Yet the distinction has never been well-defined, and, as a practical matter, the distinction is not operational. The standards of the FASB typically also include disclosure requirements.

BEAVER, *supra* note 5, at 12.

212 Enron guaranteed several investment contracts to investors who had provided the nominal outside capital for the special purpose entities, e.g., Raptor, which Enron used to shift liabilities off the balance sheet. Obligations pegged to Enron common stock were one of the main triggers of the company's downward

leaves financial reporting ready to fight the last war but not the next one.[213] Moreover, given the disclosure threshold adopted by the SEC, Enron might not have even had to disclose these particular OBS arrangements.[214] Nor would these new requirements have required disclosure of the cash flow games that led to the highly publicized prosecution of officials at Adelphia Communications.[215] In other words, what is required to be disclosed is only a subset of the OBS arrangements described previously.[216]

Despite their under-inclusiveness, the attempt to codify the meaning of OBS arrangements in the federal securities regime is a good first step. This is no mean feat, because the OBS sector is where the wild things are.[217] A brief summary of the major

---

liquidity spiral. As Enron's share price dropped, the company's obligations to provide additional consideration to investors holding these obligations increased, causing a liquidity drain for the company. Many of the special purpose vehicles described in the Powers report were variable interest entities. Relative to these three financial contracts, retained and contingent interests played a smaller role in Enron, although accounting for retained interests has been a longstanding issue in connection with securitizations by banks.

[213] Beaver notes as much:

> Certainly, the accounting for Special Purpose Entities (SPEs) that was at the heart of the problems with Enron's financial reporting is being revisited and rightly so. However, a revision in this accounting standard represents a specific fix for a problem involved in a specialized type of transaction and does not in itself address broader issues. For example, obtaining the effects of *off-balance sheet financing* via derivative transactions is a much more pervasive and difficult problem to address.

BEAVER, *supra* note 104, at 164 (emphasis added).

[214] Professor Partnoy concurs:

> Disclosure of "reasonably likely" contingencies would not likely have prevented the problems associated with Enron. Indeed, Enron arguably was in compliance with the newly-enacted SEC regulations. In assessing the firm's financial contingencies at the end of 2000, management would not have considered a scenario in which Enron's stock price would decline by more than half to be "reasonably likely."

Partnoy, *supra* note 18, at 1278.

[215] *See* Triantis, *supra* note 131, at 12.

[216] *See infra* notes 217-24 and accompanying text for a partial taxonomy of OBS arrangements.

[217] Like the joke about the five blind men and the elephant, what is considered off-balance-sheet depends on whom you ask:

> Once upon a time, there were five blind men who had the opportunity to experience an elephant for the first time. The first approached the elephant and, upon encountering one of its sturdy legs, stated, "Ah, an elephant is like a tree." The second, after exploring the trunk, said, "No, an elephant is like a strong hose." The third, grasping the tail, said, "Fool! An elephant is like a rope!" The fourth, playing with an ear, stated, "No, more like a fan." And the fifth, leaning against the animal's side, said, "An elephant is like a wall." The five then began to argue loudly about who had the more accurate perception of the elephant.
>
> The elephant, tiring of all this abuse, suddenly reared up and stomped on all of the men. He continued to trample them until they were nothing but bloody lumps of flesh. Walking away, the elephant said, "It just goes to show that you can't depend on first impressions. When I first saw them I didn't think they'd be any fun at all."

Brad Templeton's Rec.Humor.Funny, Leading the Blind, http://www.netfunny.com/rhf/jokes/88q2/11950.html (last visited Feb. 27, 2006). What is the moral of this story? Well, beware the all too real consequences of a market practice that you have failed to describe properly.

OBS arrangements is in order here. Many OBS arrangements are voluntary, i.e., contractual, arrangements.[218] Banks have long made contingent credit commitments to borrowers that may not be reflected on the balance sheet, e.g., a depository institution's letters of credit, financial guarantees, and other loan commitments.[219] Firms use affiliated trusts, limited liability partnerships, and limited liability companies to avoid recognizing financial activity on the balance sheet.[220] Firms active in real estate may keep leases and synthetic leases[221] off the balance sheet to reduce the reported firm size and its effective leverage. Sometimes a contract substitutes for a special purpose vehicle; for example, "take-or-pay" and "throughput" contracts require periodic payments for goods or services without regard to whether the buyer takes delivery or actually uses the services.[222] Another OBS entity, the special purpose entity (SPE), is a separate legal person designed to serve a single purpose, for example, to hold assets or liquefy receivables.[223] Other OBS liabilities include forward and futures contracts lawsuits and

---

[218] The broadest construction of the phrase would capture executory contracts, employment agreements, licenses, royalty contracts, pension commitments, and guarantees to customers under contracts. *See* SEC Final Rule, *supra* note 16. The SEC narrowed the reach of the rule by limiting OBS items to those determined as such under certain accounting statements. *Id.* But this produces regulatory renvoi: the legal scope of these pronouncements has yet to be determined. *See supra* notes 209-11 and accompanying text.

[219] *See* CHRIS J. BARLTROP & DIANA MCNAUGHTON, 2 BANKING INSTITUTIONS IN DEVELOPING MARKETS: INTERPRETING FINANCIAL STATEMENTS 13 (World Bank 1992) (classifying banks' OBS exposures, including credit substitutes and contingent liabilities). Assets and asset expectancies may be OBS too. The same contingent credit commitments of the depository institutions described above become assets of the lender once the borrower has drawn down on the credit line. As a credit intermediary, the function of a bank is to trade in products which reflect the holding preferences of other market participants with respect to the term and liquidity characteristics of assets and liabilities. One example of such a product is the bank's commitment to extend credit to a (contingent) borrower in the event that this borrower fails to make payment on another contractual obligation. If the contingency ripens and the borrower draws down on the credit line, this credit exposure of the bank shows up as an asset on its balance sheet. In this sense, asset expectancies may also be OBS.

[220] See Mei Feng, Jeffrey D. Gramlich & Sanjay Gupta, *Special Purpose Entities: Empirical Evidence on Determinants and Earnings Management* (Jan. 9, 2006), *available at* http://papers.ssrn.com/sol3/papers.cfm?abstract_id=717301.

[221] The best of both worlds, a synthetic lease lets the lessor depreciate the asset as though she owned it without recognizing the debt that true ownership would have entailed. *See* John Murray, *Off-Balance-Sheet Financing: Synthetic Real Estate*, 24 MICH. REAL PROP. REV. 5 (1997).

[222] *See generally* Soroosh & Ciesielski, *supra* note 122.

[223] SPEs are perhaps the OBS arrangement which has generated the most public and regulatory interest as of late due to Enron. Enron made wide use of special purpose entities (SPEs). It would transfer assets to the SPE, immediately recognize a financial accounting gain on the transfer as though sold at arm's-length, defer the recognition of any losses on the transferred assets, and reduce its book leverage by shifting debt in respect to the assets off of the firm balance sheet. This worked well until the value of Enron stock fell, triggering contractual commitments that taxed the firm's liquidity.

other kinds of liabilities in the form of derivatives, e.g., credit derivatives.[224] Even this partial taxonomy suggests the breadth of the OBS sector.

B. Persistent Opacity in the Off-Balance-Sheet Sector

The Act also required the SEC to report on the efficacy of its rulemaking to increase the transparency of OBS arrangements.[225] Separately, the Act also directed the SEC to report on the existing market structure of OBS arrangements.[226] (In a sense, the market structure report was intended to serve as a demonstration of the efficacy of the new reporting requirements.) The SEC filed a single report to Congress addressing both issues.[227] Despite noting modest improvements in transparency, the report concluded that inadequate disclosure of OBS arrangements persisted.[228] For example, the SEC concluded that financial transparency problems exist with regard to the reporting of firms' investments in other entities,[229] of contingent obligations and guarantees,[230]

---

[224] A forward contract is a present contractual duty to perform at some future date. *See* INTEREST RATE RISK: COMPTROLLER'S HANDBOOK, *supra* note 182, at 96-98. A futures contract is a forward contract that trades on a federally registered commodities exchange market. *Id.* at 93-95. A credit derivative is a contract that obligates a counterparty to indemnify a lender in the event of a credit loss on a loan to a third party borrower. *See generally* OCC Bulletin, U.S. Comptroller of the Currency, OCC 96-43: Credit Derivatives (Aug. 12, 1996).

[225] Sarbanes-Oxley Act of 2002 § 401(c)(1), 15 U.S.C. § 7261(c)(1) (Supp. II 2002).

[226] *Id.* § 401(c)(2)(E), 15 U.S.C. § 7261(c)(2)(E) (Supp. II 2002).

[227] *See* SEC Report, *supra* note 17, at 91-98.

[228] The difficulty that I had locating anecdotal and aggregate information about the OBS sector for this Article leads me to join the following SEC conclusion about the ongoing underinclusiveness of adequate financial information about the OBS sector:

> Nevertheless, it appears that issuers may not have identified all of the off-balance sheet arrangements that are required to be discussed in the OBS section of MD&A. Further, the Staff believes—based in part on the difficulties faced in gathering the data necessary for the Study and Report—that the quality of the issuer disclosures provided in the off-balance sheet section of MD&A can and should be improved.

Id. at 98.

[229] The Staff notes that, due to the varying placement of the disclosures and the different levels of disclosures required [for investments], it may sometimes be difficult for investors to fully comprehend the extent of an issuer's involvement with equity method investments and to compare such involvements across issuers. As a result, the Staff acknowledges that the values reported . . . may be understated. *Id.* at 40.

[230] "The Staff noted during its analysis of the filings that disclosures about contingent obligations vary widely in terms of format and location in the filing. As a result, the data for contingent obligations was difficult to collect in a consistent manner across issuers." *Id.* at 69.

of derivatives,[231] and with respect to firms' OBS arrangements generally.[232] These conclusions may understate the scope of the problem because the sample that provided the filings for the study does not represent the universe of most active users of OBS arrangements.[233] The ongoing opacity of the OBS sector may also be due to the SEC's decision not to require firms to disclose comprehensive information about the unconsolidated entities with which a firm had OBS transactions.[234] Because more is needed in the way of material financial disclosures, Part IV of this Article recommends disclosures to further implement the disclosure objectives of the Act.

It is too early to comprehensively map the ultimate impact of the OBS rule, but changes have already occurred. While disclosing information about these arrangements may reduce the cost of capital for some securities issuers,[235] capital costs have, in fact,

---

[231] Despite the disclosures required by the accounting standards and the Commission's rules, there is still often a perceived lack of transparency as to an issuer's market risk exposures, use of derivatives and the potential impact of those derivatives. . . .

> . . . .
>
> . . . [A]s a result of conducting the Study of filings by issuers, the Staff notes that it is often difficult to determine the total dollar amounts that are on the balance sheet related to derivatives. This difficulty stems from the fact that derivatives may be presented as separate line items on the balance sheet, or alternatively, included as a component of some broader category (e.g., other assets).

Id. at 80-81.

[232] "In many cases, it is obvious whether the commitment in question is, indeed, on the issuer's balance sheet (e.g., debt). However, in some cases, the Staff notes that whether the item is on or off the balance sheet remains unclear." *Id.* at 90.

[233] *See* SEC Report, *supra* note 17, at 27-29. The study sample was based on the 100 issuers with the largest capitalization and 100 randomly selected issuers. *Id.* The sample selection methodology used by the SEC did not target the actual users of OBS arrangements. The pattern is that firms with greater financial risk tend to use OBS arrangements more than firms with less leverage. The managerial reasons for optimizing the balance sheet discussed earlier explain why this is so. Had the SEC been sensitive to effective capital structure, the sample might have been targeted more carefully to identify the firms with the greatest tendency to use OBS arrangements, i.e., highly indebted firms interested in reducing the appearance of leverage. Consequently, a sampling methodology that better targeted active users of OBS arrangements would probably have revealed an even greater degree of opacity in financial reporting.

[234] The SEC's proposed rule had required disclosure of assets and liabilities of unconsolidated entities with which a firm had OBS arrangements. SEC Proposed Rule, *supra* note 204. In the Final Rule, however, the SEC receded from this requirement:

> We have eliminated one aspect of the proposed disclosure requirements after considering the public commentary. The amendments do not require a registrant to disclose the nature and amount of the total assets and total obligations of an unconsolidated entity that conducts off-balance sheet activities on behalf of the registrant. Commenters indicated that it might be impracticable to obtain, monitor or evaluate information about unconsolidated entities that are unaffiliated with the registrant.

See SEC Final Rule, *supra* note 16.

[235] *Cf.* Douglas Diamond & Robert Verrecchia, Disclosure, *Liquidity, and the Cost of Capital*, 46 J. FIN. 1325, 1328-32 (1991) (making a mathematical argument that for large firms disclosure of financial information may add value by reducing the potential information asymmetry with investors, who might otherwise refrain from holding the securities of those firms).

increased for some firms after their disclosure of the existence of OBS arrangements.[236] If the past is prologue, firms will certainly minimize the compliance costs of the new rule by restructuring their transactions to avoid disclosures which adversely impact their capital and liquidity activities, leading to a fresh round of financial legerdemain and regulatory reprisal.[237] Overall, firms will likely reduce their OBS activities, especially to avoid the stigma of reporting previously undisclosed liabilities.[238] Some firms are considering the joint venture as an alternative to other OBS arrangements.[239] Without

---

[236] *See, e.g.*, Andrew Osterland, *Reining In SPEs: New Rules for Special-Purpose Entities May Result in Bigger Corporate Balance Sheets*, CFO.com, May 1, 2002, http://www.cfo.com/printable/article.cfm/3004484?f=options (describing credit downgrade and fifty percent price drop of share price of Adelphia Communications Corp. after it disclosed OBS debt in previously unconsolidated special-purpose entities).

[237] The SEC noted that some companies had already done so:

> In anticipation of the implementation of Interpretation No. 46 and Interpretation No. 46(R), a number of entities restructured arrangements with potential VIEs [variable interest entities] such that they would not require consolidation. Disclosures of such restructurings were noted in the [SEC report] sample companies. The Staff also is aware anecdotally that many arrangements with potential VIEs were restructured such that the entity either would not be considered a VIE or such that no party would be required to consolidate the VIE.

See SEC Report, supra note 17, at 92.

This is another example of the "dance between the regulator and the regulated." Pouncy, *supra* note 2, at 546. Compliance by restructuring transactions or entities is common with respect to accounting standards. For example, FASB passed STATEMENT OF FINANCIAL ACCOUNTING STANDARDS NO. 13 [hereinafter SFAS No. 13], *supra* note 121, to increase the reporting of OBS operating leases. SFAS No. 13 required firms to include a lease on the balance sheet if the lease possesses any of the following four attributes: the lease transfers ownership of the leased asset to the lessee; the lease lets the lessee purchase the leased asset for a below-market price; the lease is not cancelable for 75% or more of the lease's economic life; or the present value of the minimum lease payments on the lease are at least 90% of the leased asset's value. *Id.* Evidence suggests that firms restructured the terms of their capital leases to avoid triggering SFAS No. 13's capitalization requirements. *See* Eugene A. Imhoff, Jr. & Jacob K. Thomas, *Economic Consequences of Accounting Standards: The Lease Disclosure Rule Change*, 10 J. ACCT. & ECON. 277 (1988) (showing how firms modified capital leases to avoid the new disclosure requirement).

[238] As noted by accounting researchers:

> This new interpretation might cause very few changes in corporate balance sheets, because companies that would have to consolidate their SPEs under the requirements of this interpretation might already be taking steps to shut down or sell their interests prior to the effective date. This scenario would avoid the embarrassment for the sponsors of presenting what they never professed to own. The other alternative is that Interpretation 46(R) might cause significant adverse adjustments to companies' balance sheets and create technical defaults in loan covenants.

Soroosh & Ciesielski, *supra* note 122, at 37.

[239] *See, e.g.*, Marie Leone, *Off-Balance-Sheet Deals: C'est la Vie?*, CFO.com, Jan. 1, 2003, http://www.cfo.com/article.cfm/3007774?f=related (discussing how some corporations look to joint ventures to substitute for investments in securitizations, synthetic leases, and unconsolidated entities which must now be disclosed under the OBS rule).

the cost-savings formerly available through OBS arrangements, firms may pass on increased credit costs to their customers.[240]

This new regulatory change and the ensuing OBS market structure shift may also impact the internal management structure of the firm.[241] For example, consider the emergence of the CFO function as a reaction to the increased tactical significance of a firm's funding activities. Today, the CFO provides strategic decision support for other managers rather than merely overseeing what were formerly the more ministerial functions of the treasurer and comptroller.[242] Unlike the comptroller, a CFO may have significant apparent authority to bind the firm in complex financing transactions. Poised as a convenient folk devil, when a scandal occurs, the CFO is often the first officer to be blamed, fired, and, at times, prosecuted for violations of federal securities

---

240 Some banks act as conduit sponsors on behalf of clients. By requiring the sponsor banks to consolidate some previously OBS debt onto the balance sheet, banks face regulatory capital charges. The incidence of this cost does not stay with the bank, however. As one bank manager commented, "If we cannot maintain [these loans] off balance sheet, at a minimum our clients' costs will go up . . . . Worst case, we cut their line." Brett Nelson, *A Blue Summer For Off-Balance-Sheet Lenders?*, FORBES.COM, Apr. 11, 2003, http://www.forbes.com/2003/04/11/cz_bn_0411banks.html (quoting Bradley Schwartz, managing director of asset-backed conduits at J.P. Morgan Chase, which administers $17 billion in conduits).

241 Patterns of leverage influence how a firm organizes its financial management. For example, firms with high leverage appoint a Chief Risk Officer to manage risk enterprise-wide. *See* André P. Liebenberg & Robert E. Hoyt, *The Determinants of Enterprise Risk Management: Evidence from the Appointment of Chief Risk Officers*, 6 RISK MGMT. & INS. REV. 37, 45 (2003).

242 Typically an accountant, the comptroller acts with actual authority, has some general knowledge of the firm's overall financial position, and reports to an officer. Generally a corporate treasurer maintains custody of accounts, manages relationships with creditors, services debt, and coordinates investment. *See* JAMES D. WILLSON ET AL., CONTROLLERSHIP: THE WORK OF THE MANAGERIAL ACCOUNTANT 19-20 (6th ed. 1999) (discussing relationship between treasurer, controller, and chief financial officer). The comptroller forecasts the raising and utilization of liquidity, reconciles bank account balances, and manages internal control systems with respect to receipts and disbursements. *Id.* at 604-11 A small firm may not separate the treasurer and the controller function. *Id.* Many firms have brought the comptroller under a Chief Financial Officer (CFO) to respond to the growing market and legal demands of funding. Christine H. Andersen, *The CFO Transformation: From Chief Accountant to Change Agent*, AME INFO, May 23, 2005, http://www.ameinfo.com/60697.html (emphasizing the role of the current CFO as an enterprise-wide risk manager); BOOZ ALLEN HAMILTON, CFO THOUGHT LEADERS: ADVANCING THE FRONTIERS OF FINANCE 9-10 (2005) (cross-industry study of the CFO function at global firms concluding that increasingly, CFOs act as change agents rather than accountants). The CFO's functions include both overseeing the firm capital structure and the preparation of its internal and external financial reports. In addition to these functions, a CFO typically also oversees asset investment, accounting, risk management, dividend policy, incentive design, tax policy, and cost aspects of compensation policy. *See* Thomas Copeland, *The Expanding Role of the CFO*, WEEKLY TOYO KEIZAI (JAPAN), Sept. 1, 2001, *available at* http://ssrn.com/abstract=717703. Increasingly, the CFO engages more substantively in decision-support at the executive level than previously and less in controlling and reporting transactions. *See* GATES, *supra* note 166, at 26 (conducting interviews and surveys of chief financial officers regarding composition of the CFO function). Anecdotal evidence suggests that a growing number of chief executive officers served previously as CFOs. *See* Copeland, *supra*.

laws. The Act's attestation requirements contribute to this tendency by increasing both the CFO's significance and liability.[243]

Despite the Congressional mandate, additional funding, the agency's extensive research on the issue, and intense public pressure, the SEC could not definitively estimate the size of the OBS sector. If the SEC could not get this information, how could an investor make an informed investment decision about these firms? The purpose of the financial transparency ratio suggested in Part IV is to relate potentially material, undisclosed management accounting data about OBS arrangements to the balance sheet for the benefit of the wider investing public.[244]

IV. CONFORMING FINANCIAL REPORTING LAW TO FUNDING VÉRITÉ

Given the ongoing opacities in the OBS market discussed above, more is needed. I recommend that the SEC take two regulatory actions to satisfy its duties under the Act to increase financial disclosures.[245] First, the SEC should make registrants include a financial transparency ratio on their balance sheet that lets readers know the magnitude of what is not otherwise being disclosed about OBS items. This transparency ratio would act as an interface between the managerial accounting information (available only to firm insiders) and the financial accounting information required to be released by federal securities law as such. The transparency ratio would alert investors to risks the current information asymmetry makes difficult to evaluate.[246] Second, the SEC should exercise its statutory authorities over accounting to make the statement of cash flows more useful as a public financial report by introducing some categories, including a distinction between operating cash flow and other types. Finally, a bureaucratic reform is in order too. The SEC should make policy research about trends in effective capital structure a routine part of its job, rather than a dramatic interruption of the agency's perceived core functions. That way, the SEC could proactively deal with future funding shifts and their financial reporting implications and, thereby, stem future financial moral panics with facts instead of speculation.[247] Being more aggressively self-informed

---

[243] *See supra* note 98 for attestation requirements.

[244] *See supra* notes 248-56 and accompanying text (for a ratio that would tell investors about the magnitude of management accounting data that is not disclosed in financial accounting reports).

[245] These recommendations further the SEC's policy initiatives set out in its study of OBS arrangements. *See* SEC Report, *supra* note 17, at 98-105. In particular, disclosures of a balance sheet to OBS ratio and funding dynamics that are presumptively material (i.e., the two specific recommendations in this Part of the Article) would further consistency of financial disclosures, one of the four major initiatives discussed in this section of the Report.

[246] Although the substance of the information would not be internalized into the decision-making process of a market participant, the investors would be aware of the fact of the information.

[247] Making recommendations that are capable of being implemented is part of the institutional microanalytic approach in law. "[T]he microanalysis of existing institutions is more practical, at least in the short run, and more amenable to the specifically legal approach of framing recommendations to existing

about funding practices would reduce the SEC's risk of reputational slight through congressional prodding after celebrated disasters.

A. Reducing the Public Information Gap with a Financial Transparency Ratio

Being able to determine the inclusiveness of a firm's reported financial position is presumptively material. Firms must now disclose any OBS arrangements material to a firm's liquidity or capital resources.[248] To link the GAAP[249] balance sheet to a firm's effective capital structure, the SEC should require registrants to put a financial transparency ratio on the balance sheet. The ratio would add marginal value with respect to undisclosed items or to the materiality of a firm's OBS portfolio in the aggregate.[250] Inspired by the leverage ratios used in financial analysis, a transparency ratio would reflect the proportion of, on the one hand, information required to be disclosed under current disclosure standards to, on the other hand, undisclosed information about contingencies known to the firm through its managerial accounting but not required to be revealed under current regulatory reporting thresholds.[251] In so doing, the ratio would lessen information gaps between well-informed firm insiders, moderately-informed institutional investors, and uninformed public shareholders by signaling how much management accounting data escapes disclosure in public reports prepared using financial accounting rules.[252] This proposal avoids the risk of excess disclosure for complex transactions which has been persuasively noted.[253]

policymakers." Rubin, *supra* note 90, at 1431 (arguing that institutional microanalysis can synthesize the historically separate critical disciplines such as alterity jurisprudence and law and economics).

[248] *See* SEC Final Rule, *supra* note 16.

[249] *See supra* note 10.

[250] In other words, the ratio would reflect the dollar volume of OBS arrangements, which taken singly would not rise to the level of materiality that currently triggers disclosure under the OBS rule. A firm may have several OBS positions, no single one of which materially impacts the firm's liquidity or capital. Yet when added together the sum of OBS positions becomes material. The ratio would reveal the potential scope of such a risk.

[251] Finance ratios use financial statement data to understand and predict firm performance. *See* William Beaver, *Financial Ratios as Predictors of Failure, in Empirical Research in Accounting: Selected Studies*, 1966, at 71-111 (Sidney Davidson ed., 1967). *See also* KALLBERG & PARKINSON, *supra* note 3, at 23-31 (summarizing types of financial ratios used to evaluate a firm's liquidity). Financial leverage measures the amount of debt to equity in a firm's capital structure. Operating leverage attempts to assess the degree to which a firm's operating costs are fixed. Meaningfully estimating operating leverage is difficult. *Id.* at 75. A firm may calculate its leverage ratios for internal use differently from leverage ratios intended for public dissemination.

[252] *See supra* notes 130-34 and accompanying text (regarding information asymmetries).

[253] *See* Steven L. Schwarcz, *Rethinking the Disclosure Paradigm in a World of Complexity*, 2004 U. ILL. L. REV. 1, 18-19 (2004) (challenging the sufficiency of disclosure of complex deals because the disclosure will not yield enough investors who understand the transaction in time to impact market prices). He calls these "disclosure-impaired transactions." *Id.* at 30.

Such a ratio promotes transparency without risking disclosure logorrhea of irrelevant data or requiring firms to disclose sensitive information about specific financial claims.[254] To the extent that the ratio draws attention to undisclosed information, this proposal might reduce trading liquidity in a firm's securities. At its simplest, the ratio would compare the size of the reported balance sheet to a pro forma balance sheet—based on confidential management accounting information—that reflected a financial rather than accounting definition of leverage. In other words, the numerator of the ratio would be the GAAP balance sheet and the denominator would be an effective balance sheet.[255] To calculate such a ratio would require auditors to systematically review confidential management accounting data and to put it in the context of publicly available information. A ratio of 1:1 would signal perfect transparency. The lower the ratio, e.g., 1:2, the less the amount of financial transparency in the firm's public financial reports. A low financial transparency ratio might signal dubious financial reporting motives.[256] (For example, a firm may want to hide a higher leverage ratio or a concentration of debt contracts coming due for renegotiation.) By reminding the reader of financial statements of the limits of the balance sheet, the ratio would provide fair notice that an investor may need to poke around in a firm's financial reports. Changes in the ratio would also alert a reader as to whether a firm was changing its fundamental strategy with respect to the transparency of its funding practices.

B. Using Cash Flow Reporting to Further Disaggregate the Firm

Adding some reporting granularity to the statement of cash flows would help investors and other market intermediaries to evaluate a firm's funding position by reducing the transaction costs of monitoring the firm's cash flows.[257] Doing this would further

---

[254] The SEC justified its adoption of the "reasonably likely" threshold for disclosure in part on the fear that a lower standard would generate too much information: "We believe that the 'reasonably likely' threshold best promotes the utility of the disclosure requirement by reducing the possibility that investors will be overwhelmed by voluminous disclosure of insignificant and possibly unnecessary speculative information." *See* SEC Final Rule, *supra* note 16, at 7. In that same vein, a prominent scholar of securitizations and their disclosure implications believes that disclosure of enough information to understand certain OBS deals would overwhelm readers of financial reports. *See* Schwarcz, *supra* note 253, at18-19 (challenging the sufficiency of disclosure of complex deals because the disclosure will not yield enough investors who understand the transaction in time to impact market prices). He calls these "disclosure-impaired transactions." *Id.* at 30.

[255] The denominator could include the four arrangements listed in the OBS rule. Managers would still use their own judgment when deciding whether an item met the materiality threshold for disclosure, but the practice of calculating the ratio would complement the OBS rule.

[256] *See supra* note 118 and accompanying text. Research also notes that financial transparency may be correlated with creditworthiness. For example, more creditworthy firms are willing to disclose debt on the balance sheet, while firms interested in managing their credit rating more carefully may prefer OBS financing.

[257] *See* BEAVER, *supra* note 5, at 6 (noting that the value of accounting disclosures depends on the processing costs of the data to the user).

the SEC's stated policy of encouraging disclosure of material information about funding.[258]

The statement of cash flows distinguishes between investment, operational, and financing cash flows.[259] However, the statement currently blurs two streams of investment cash flow that would have more informational value if unbundled: (1) that from investment in assets related to a firm's core functions; and (2) that due to investments in other than operational assets. By separating operational investment cash flow from market investment cash flow, the classification would let the reader distinguish between investment required by the firm's core activities and that from the firm's activities as a speculative investor in the market. Such a distinction would help an investor to appreciate whether cash flow is attributable to business decisions about operations or to speculative investment decisions.

Since the statement of cash flows reflects the impact of much OBS activity,[260] comparing the volume of cash flow overall to a firm's risk capital in the form of a ratio would reflect the effective ability of a firm to leverage risk capital into liquidity. Abnormally high cash flow leverage ratios—or unusual trends in a firm's cash flow leverage ratio—could signal risk from OBS activities.[261]

C. Exploiting the SEC's Comparative Advantage to Conduct Capital Structure Market Surveillance

The financial moral panic revealed technical gaps in the SEC's capital structure knowledge, an agency whose institutional structure emphasizes disclosure and enforce-

---

[258] In response to a petition from several accounting firms, the SEC had—before the OBS rulemaking—issued a statement calling for improvement of the quality of disclosure of OBS arrangements and clarifying the scope of registrants' then-duties under Regulation S-K, Item 303. Commission Statement about Management's Discussion and Analysis of Financial Condition and Results of Operations, Release Nos. 33-8056, 34-45321 (Jan. 22, 2002), *available at* http://www.sec.gov/rules/other/33-8056.htm. This guidance emphasized the cause and effect relationship between OBS activity and a firm's solvency and liquidity:

> [R]egistrants should consider describing the sources of short-term funding and the circumstances that are reasonably likely to affect those sources of liquidity. . . .
>
> . . . .
>
> If the registrant's liquidity is dependent on the use of off-balance sheet financing arrangements, such as securitization of receivables or obtaining access to assets through special purpose entities, the registrant should consider disclosure of the factors that are reasonably likely to affect its ability to continue using those off-balance sheet financing arrangements.

Id. (footnotes omitted).

[259] For a discussion of the statement of cash flows, *see* SEC Report, *supra* note 17, at 11-14.

[260] *See supra* note 170-71, 179-81 and accompanying text.

[261] So, for example, Enron's cash flow games described in Part II.B might have been reflected through such ratio analysis.

ment.[262] This enforcement emphasis means that the contours of current law determine the agency's effective knowledge base.[263] A more institutionally pervasive focus on capital market structure would complement the SEC's current approaches.[264] The General Accounting Office recently noted these limits:

> Both SEC and industry officials agree that the current level of human capital and budgetary resources has strained SEC's capacity to address current and evolving market issues. Industry officials generally hold SEC staff in high regard and said that SEC does a good job overall. However, industry officials also said that they would like to see SEC devote more effort to evolving and ongoing areas . . . .[265]

Although the agency has conducted special industry studies to cover self-diagnosed technical gaps, it failed to do so in time to deal with the crises in the OBS sector.[266] Accordingly, the Act directs the SEC to increase its technical expertise not just with

---

[262] For example, the focus of the Division of Enforcement—a historically and increasingly prominent function at the SEC—requires market knowledge only as needed to supplement legal claims in an enforcement action. In contrast, the few units that interact with firms regularly know the most about market structure.

[263] Some exceptions are worth noting. The Office of Risk Management (Division of Market Regulation) monitors compliance by registered broker-dealers with the liquidity requirements of the net capital rule for broker-dealers. This Office has rich firm-level knowledge that could usefully be synthesized into a better understanding of broker-dealer market structure. *See generally* Michael P. Jamroz, *The Net Capital Rule*, 47 BUS. LAW. 863 (1992) (describing in significant detail how the net capital rule ensures the liquidity of broker-dealers). When I worked in the Office of Compliance Inspections and Examinations (OCIE), I was enriched by regular and comprehensive contact with broker-dealers, securities exchanges, clearing and depository entities, and other financial intermediaries. *See generally* John H. Walsh, *Right the First Time: Regulation, Quality, and Preventive Compliance in the Securities Industry*, 1997 COLUM. BUS. L. REV. 165, 177-78 (1997) (describing OCIE's statutory authorities and programs).

[264] Respectful of the agency staff's commitment to capital markets, I make these recommendations in the spirit of preserving the agency's reputation as a jewel of the New Deal.

[265] GENERAL ACCOUNTING OFFICE, SEC OPERATIONS: INCREASED WORKLOAD CREATES CHALLENGES, GAO-02-302, at 24 (2002) (finding that securities market structure changes had dramatically increased the volume and complexity of the SEC's workload and recommending increased capacity for the agency). *See also* HEARINGS, *supra* note 55, at 620.

[266] *See, e.g.*, SEC. & EXCH. COMM'N, THE OCTOBER 1987 MARKET BREAK (1988) (analyzing the causes of market volatility that led to a thirty percent loss in the value of traded common stocks); SEC. & EXCH. COMM'N, U.S. DEP'T OF THE TREASURY & BD. OF GOVERNORS OF THE FED. RESERVE SYS., JOINT REPORT ON THE GOVERNMENT SECURITIES MARKET (1992) (examining government securities market structure and considering regulatory approaches after a bidding regularity in the government securities auction); Report of Investigation Pursuant Regarding the Nasdaq Stock Market, Inc., Securities Exchange Act Release No. 51163 (Feb. 9, 2005), *available at* http://www.sec.gov/litigation/investreport/34-51163.htm (investigating market maker practices in the over-the-counter market). The pattern is that crises trigger self-directed studies of a particular market problem.

respect to OBS arrangements but also securities violators and violations,[267] enforcement actions,[268] and credit rating agencies,[269] suggesting the need for the SEC to retool its market structure knowledge generally.[270] The Act's directions to the General Accounting Office to conduct capital market studies more typically in the SEC's bailiwick raise questions of whether the SEC has already lost some reputational capital with Congress.[271]

Congress has enabled the agency to update its institutional mission by increasing its appropriation and reducing the transaction costs of hiring technical experts. First, Congress gave the SEC pay parity with depository institution regulators, who have long been able to pay staff more than the salaries on the General Service scheduler.[272] More recently, Congress increased the SEC's flexibility in hiring accountants, economists, and securities analysts.[273] Increased resources without a more comprehensive market structure approach to capital structure surveillance will not, however, solve the regulatory reporting problems highlighted by these scandals.[274] Therefore, to deal with this problem the SEC should establish a research and analysis unit (or reconfigure existing institutional resources) to exploit the SEC's existing knowledge base and to add to it

---

[267] Sarbanes-Oxley Act of 2002 § 703, 15 U.S.C. § 7201 note (GAO Study and Report Regarding Consolidation of Public Accounting Firms) (2000 & Supp. II 2002).

[268] *Id.* § 704.

[269] *Id.* § 702.

[270] Congress's direction to the SEC to conduct these studies suggests a critique of how the agency has handled the make-buy problem as applied to certain knowledge about capital market structure. The make-buy problem takes a different form in the context of a federal agency. Statutes determine the agency's freedom to determine what goes on and what stays out, i.e., its institutional structure.

[271] Sarbanes-Oxley requires the Comptroller General to study the impact of requiring mandatory rotation of registered accounting firms (Sarbanes-Oxley Act of 2002 § 207), the impact of the consolidation of accounting firms on public audit quality (Sarbanes-Oxley Act of 2002 § 701) and the relationship of investment banks and their advisors earnings management by private firms (Sarbanes-Oxley Act of 2002 § 705). Tasking the GAO with studies that fit squarely within the SEC's jurisdiction may reflect a desire not to burden the SEC with more studies. But one wonders whether Congress doubted whether the SEC had enough internal knowledge, capital and willingness to address these questions, which bear importantly on market structure, or whether the GAO studies reflect a desire to have independent analysis with which to critically evaluate the performance of the SEC.

[272] Previously, Congress had exempted the Federal Reserve Board, the Office of the Comptroller of the Currency, the Office of Thrift Supervision, the Federal Deposit Insurance Corporation, and the National Credit Union Administration from statutory ceilings on staff compensations. Financial Institutions Reform, Recovery and Enforcement Act of 1989, Pub. L. No. 101-73, §§ 805, 1105, 1202, 1203, 1206, 103 Stat. 183 (codified as amended in scattered sections of 12 & 15 U.S.C.). In response to vigorous SEC advocacy, Congress extended the same pay parity privileges to the SEC. Investor and Capital Markets Fee Relief Act, Pub. L. No. 107-123 § 8, 115 Stat. 2390 (2002).

[273] Accountant, Compliance, and Enforcement Staffing Act of 2003, Pub. L. No. 108-44, 117 Stat. 842. The law allows the SEC to appoint these staff to the excepted service rather than the competitive service, which restricts employer discretion to redeploy or discharge staff more than the excepted service.

[274] A small number of economists in the Office of Economic Analysis participate in a wide variety of regulatory, surveillance, and enforcement functions. This office needs more financial economists specifically trained in monitoring trends in firms' effective capital structure.

by closely following trends in effective capital structure.[275] This the SEC can do with the approval of a majority of commissioners before Congress acts remedially again.[276] Such a unit could best exploit the agency's informational advantage about how firms finance themselves.[277] The SEC's § 401(c) report[278] is an example of the kind of aggregate market structure analysis that should be a routine matter for the agency.

At present, decisions about materiality are left to individual public companies, subject to adjudication to determine whether with the benefit of hindsight a registrant properly evaluated the materiality of a particular financial fact.[279] Given the recurring funding situations faced by firms, though, some financing practices are presumptively material, as a matter of effective capital structure. However, judges, lawyers, and investors do not have the benefit of market-wide data when interpreting materiality. Armed with such market-wide knowledge, the SEC could provide more interpretive advice in the context of market structure as a whole. Information intermediaries like investment advisors and business newspapers would disseminate this information to a wider investing public. Better capital structure surveillance would also help the SEC

---

[275] Drawing again on bank regulation, I urge the SEC to disrupt the Weberian logic of its current departmental structure and to consider the usefulness of an inter-divisional approach to capital structure surveillance. The Capital Steering Committee (Capital Steering) of the Comptroller of the Currency (Comptroller) is an example of an inter-divisional process that targets OBS items. Like any complex government bureaucracy, the Comptroller is functionally divided into a legal division, banking supervision divisions, a special unit that looks at regulatory capital policy, international divisions, and risk management divisions. Recognizing that OBS funding crosses these organizational units, the Comptroller has a standing inter-divisional process in Capital Steering to bring together legal, risk, and supervisory perspectives when ruling on national banks' funding practices. Capital Steering meets regularly to review proposals for funding products submitted by national banks. In the meeting, capital policy staff explain the funding products—many of which are OBS items—in order to educate staff from other divisions. By institutionalizing information sharing about the frontiers of national banks' OBS activities, Capital Steering keeps the Comptroller's knowledge base about funding current.

[276] Institutional theory about innovation in government bureaucracy, however, indicates that the suggestion to form a capital structure analysis unit will not be adopted. *See generally* OLIVER WILLIAMSON, THE MECHANISMS OF GOVERNANCE 219-49 (1996) (identifying structural institutional forces that restrict innovative change).

[277] For example, in 2000, the SEC received nearly 100,000 separate filings by issuers describing securities products and transactions, a cornucopia of data about financial market structure. *See* GENERAL ACCOUNTING OFFICE, *supra* note 265 (finding that securities market structure changes had dramatically increased the volume and complexity of the SEC's workload and recommending increased capacity for the agency). The Division of Corporate Finance has the most complete knowledge base about financing trends because the unit reviews prospectuses about new securities. A Weberian bureaucracy, the Division divides prospectus review by industry such that few staff know more than one industry well.

[278] *See* SEC Report, *supra* note 17.

[279] A presumption encourages uniformity in an area that few investors and other market participants understand, lets registrants rebut this presumption in circumstances in which the financing trend does not materially impact a firm's liquidity or capital, and preserves judicial discretion to determine when a rebuttal of the presumption is justified. This approach is also consistent with the tacit recognition in financial reporting law that certain events are deemed to be so material to a firm that a public issuer must file a Form 8-K as required by 17 C.F.R. § 240.13a-11 (2005).

to exercise its oversight duties over the new Public Company Accounting Oversight Board created by the Act.[280]

V. THERE WILL ALWAYS BE AN ENRON (PROLEGOMENON)

We live in an economy organized around market risk, in which unrealized gain in financial assets will continue to be the chief store of wealth. Preserving the dignity of investors requires clearer disclosure about the market risk of unrealized gain, sobering though such disclosure may be. Not that any of this will prevent future financial disasters. So long as there are firms trying to economize on funding efficiencies (for both fiduciary and opportunistic motives), traders willing to help, and investors looking for a financial return, there will always be an Enron.[281]

Given this structural implication of the rules of the game, it would behoove the legal profession to produce lawyers who are more financially fluent. Hindsight tells the repeat players in law school—law professors and deans—that some students may have a calling for transactional finance. These students are generally underserved by the current curriculum at many law schools.[282] Forced to take a random walk through the first year of law school, they typically begin upper-level courses without the basic analytical methods in finance, accounting, and game theory. Increasingly, these methods inform the performance expectations for an effective transactional lawyer, especially

---

[280] The Public Company Accounting Oversight Board (PCAOB) is a private non-profit organization. It oversees public company audits by developing audit standards, inspecting accounting firms, investigating and disciplining auditors, and conducting disciplinary proceedings. *See* Sarbanes-Oxley Act of 2002 §§ 101, 107, 15 U.S.C. §§ 7211, 7217 (2000 & Supp. II 2002). The SEC appoints Board members, approves Board rules and professional standards, approves the Board's budget, and acts as an appellate body for disciplinary actions and disputes arising from the Board's inspection reports. *See generally* Richard I. Miller & Paul H. Pashkoff, *Regulations Under the Sarbanes-Oxley Act*, J. ACCOUNTANCY, Oct. 2002, at 33, *available at* http://www.aicpa.org/PUBS/JOFA/oct2002/miller.htm (summarizing the implications of the Act for the auditing profession). To date, the Board has registered 1522 audit firms. *See* PCAOB, Registered Public Accounting Firms, http://www.pcaobus.org/Registration/Registered_Firms.pdf (last visited Feb. 28, 2006). Eventually the Board expects to have 200 full-time staff. *See Accounting Under Sarbanes-Oxley: Are Financial Statements More Reliable? Before the H. Comm. on Financial Services*, 108th Cong. 4 (2003) (testimony of William J. McDonough, Chairman, Public Company Accounting Oversight Board), *available at* http://purl.access.gpo.gov/GPO/LPS47468. This was the first hearing that Congress convened after the Act to review its implementation. Congress then held a second hearing to review progress further. *Hearings on Sarbanes-Oxley: Two Years of Market and Investor Recovery Before the H. Comm. on Financial Services*, 108th Cong. (2004), *available at* http://purl.access.gpo.gov/GPO/LPS56380.

[281] That conclusion is implied in the idea of the "regulatory dialectic." *See* Pouncy, *supra* note 2, at 546.

[282] One exception is the positive trend in legal education towards increased training for law students in transactional law in the development of analytical methods courses. *See, e.g.*, HOWELL E. JACKSON ET AL., ANALYTICAL METHODS FOR LAWYERS (1989) (assembles game theory, accounting, finance, statistics, and other transactional methodologies for use in a first-year or upper-level law school course). An elective first-year methods class at Harvard Law School uses this book, a fitting penance from the institution that helped to fossilize the Langdellian approach in the first place.

one who will be advising a chief financial officer, poised as the office is to bear liability and calumnies, especially after recent history's devilish depiction of this corporate official. For these students, fewer brambles and more financial analytic methods are needed. In closing, I call on my transactional law colleagues to foster more integration of analytical financial methods into a basic legal education. Such an approach might produce more transactional lawyers capable of spotting and stemming future financial moral panics.

Jiminy Cricket for the Corporation: Understanding the Corporate "Conscience"[*]

Colin P. Marks[**]

I. INTRODUCTION

In Disney's classic retelling of the fable *Pinocchio*, soon after being granted life by the Blue Fairy, Geppetto's wooden boy is assigned a conscience in the form of the talking insect, Jiminy Cricket.[1] The implication of this assignment is clear: as Pinocchio is not yet a real boy, he does not possess a conscience and must rely on an external voice (Jiminy Cricket) to tell him right from wrong. Throughout the movie, Pinocchio gets into a number of misadventures, including some debacles resulting from ignoring his assigned conscience (including one in which he is half-transformed into an ass).[2]

In this sense, Pinocchio makes an appropriate analogy for the modern American for-profit corporation. Like Pinocchio, the corporation is an artificial entity created by humans. It is then given "life," so to speak, by the state in which it is incorporated, and it interacts with the individuals and society around it. Also like Pinocchio, corporations have often found themselves embroiled in misadventures, seemingly from acting without a conscience. Other commentators have characterized corporations as soulless,[3] analogizing

---

[**] Assistant Professor of Law, St. Mary's University School of Law. J.D., University of Houston Law Center; B.S. University of Missouri–Columbia. Prior to accepting a position at St. Mary's University, Professor Marks was an associate in the trial department of Baker Botts, L.L.P., Houston, Texas, where he concentrated in areas of commercial law and attorney-client privilege. The author would like to acknowledge the hard work and assistance of his research assistants, Myles Bentsen, Jason Goss, and David Gregorcyk, in writing this Essay as well as to thank Professor Reynaldo Valencia of St. Mary's University School of Law for his support and feedback. The author would also like to thank his wife Jill, daughter Savannah, and son George for their love and support.

[1] *See generally* PINOCCHIO (Walt Disney Pictures 1940).

[2] *See id.*

[3] LAWRENCE M. FRIEDMAN, A HISTORY OF AMERICAN LAW 134 (3d ed. 2005).

them to the tin man of the Wizard of Oz[4] (who has no heart) or the Jewish Golem, which can only mindlessly carry out the instructions slipped into its mouth on a piece of paper.[5] But are corporations truly without any sort of conscience, or do they also have a "Jiminy Cricket"—an external voice that influences them to act in a way that could be deemed "right" or "good?" The question is a difficult one, in part because defining what is "right" is such a subjective task. But if we view corporate behavior more broadly, to turn the question to what causes corporations to engage in conduct that benefits society, we understand that some external force or forces must direct the corporation. This Article seeks to analyze the external forces that curb or drive corporate behavior as they relate to activities that benefit society in the context of having a "conscience."

Part II of this Article examines the corporation from an historical perspective, tracking its evolution from a small number of specially chartered organizations with a limited, publicly oriented purpose, to the modern, highly regulated profit-making organizations of today. Part III examines whether the modern corporation can have a conscience and what that term means with regard to such an artificial entity. Part IV identifies three driving forces behind what will be termed corporate behavior that is beneficial to society: behavior driven by legal compliance; behavior that also benefits the corporation; and behavior that is seemingly driven by altruistic (or semi-altruistic) motives. Part V reflects upon how these categories can be used to evaluate corporate behavior.

II. EVOLVING PURPOSE OF THE CORPORATION

Before delving into the task of categorizing the basis of corporate behavior, it is useful to reflect upon how the modern corporation evolved in America. This is more than a mere academic exercise, as it is important to understand what role the corporation has played in American history in order to understand its current status.[6] And this status is essential to understanding what drives corporate behavior.

A. Historical Underpinnings of the Corporation

Though the earliest forms of the corporation can be traced as far back as Roman times,[7] the modern corporation did not begin to take on its current form in America until the mid-to-late 19th century, with the emergence of general incorporation stat-

---

[4] Lawrence E. Mitchell & Theresa A. Gabaldon, *If I Only Had a Heart: Or, How Can We Identify a Corporate Morality*, 76 TUL. L. REV. 1645, 1646-47 (2002).

[5] LAWRENCE E. MITCHELL, CORPORATE IRRESPONSIBILITY: AMERICA'S NEWEST EXPORT 44 (2001); RALPH ESTES, TYRANNY OF THE BOTTOM LINE: WHY CORPORATIONS MAKE GOOD PEOPLE DO BAD THINGS 21 (1996).

[6] *See, e.g.*, Sarah H. Duggin & Stephen M. Goldman, *Restoring Trust in Corporate Directors: The Disney Standard and the "New" Good Faith*, 56 AM. U. L. REV. 211, 219 (2006) (reviewing the development of the corporation in America to explain how the law has struggled with holding directors accountable).

[7] 1 WILLIAM MEADE FLETCHER, FLETCHER CYCLOPEDIA OF THE LAW OF CORPORATIONS § 1 at 3 (Carol A. Jones ed., 2006); Douglas Arner, *Development of the American Law of Corporations to 1832*, 55 S.M.U. L. REV. 23, 25 (2002).

utes.[8] The earliest forms of the corporation in America came by specific charters from the states in the late 18th century, which were carried over from the colonial days when corporations obtained charters directly from the King of England.[9] Corporations were formed with limited purposes (and even time limits) within which they could operate.[10] The typical corporation would be formed to complete some specific task, such as to build a canal or bridge, and would only be given a charter for a period of five, twenty, or thirty years.[11] The number of corporations was also extremely limited, with only 335 granted in the entire 18th century, 181 of which were granted between 1796 and 1800.[12] Most of these corporations were chartered for some specific aspect of the public good, such as building utilities, and very few were for manufacturing purposes.[13]

The early limitations placed upon corporations were in large part a result of the inherent distrust that the public had for the corporation.[14] Corporations at that time were monopolistic by their very nature because they maintained exclusive control over some public asset or business opportunity.[15] The public was also concerned about the concentration of wealth that was centered in a corporation.[16] As Justice Brandeis recounted in his dissent in the chain store tax case of *Louis K. Liggett Co. v. Leeu*,[17]

> There was a sense of some insidious menace inherent in large aggregations of capital, particularly when held by corporations. So at first the corporate privilege was granted sparingly; and only when the grant seemed necessary in order to procure for the community some specific benefit otherwise unattainable.[18]

But although public suspicion of corporations may have remained,[19] economic necessity altered the limited grant of the corporate privilege in the 19th century.

---

[8] FRIEDMAN, *supra* note 3, at 130, 390; Susan P. Hamill, *From Special Privilege to General Utility: A Continuation of Willard Hurst's Study of Corporations*, 49 AM. U. L. REV. 81, 84-85, 104-06 (1999).

[9] Hamill, *supra* note 8, at 88 ("Corporations always have been creatures of statute, requiring a formal recognition normally evidenced by a corporate charter issued by a sovereign person or government.") (citation omitted); *see also* FRIEDMAN, *supra* note 3, at 129-30.

[10] FRIEDMAN, *supra* note 3, at 131-32.

[11] *Id.*

[12] *Id.* at 129; Fletcher, *supra* note 7, § 2 at 8 ("The cloud of disfavor under which corporations labored in America was not dissipated until near the end of the eighteenth century, and during the last 11 years of that period, the total number of charters granted did not exceed 200.").

[13] FRIEDMAN, *supra* note 3, at 130-32, 134 (noting that a "mere handful" of these early corporations were established for manufacturing purposes); ESTES, *supra* note 5, at 22-24.

[14] FRIEDMAN, *supra* note 3, at 132.

[15] *Id.*

[16] Louis K. Liggett Co. v. Lee, 288 U.S. 517, 549 (1933) (Brandeis, J., dissenting).

[17] 288 U.S. 517 (1933).

[18] *Id.* at 549 (Brandeis, J., dissenting).

[19] *Id.*

One of the most significant changes was the shift of granting corporate status via special charter by the state legislatures to the enactment of general incorporation statutes. At the start of the 19th century, corporations were still relatively rare, and the special charter system made sense.[20] But as the country grew, the practice of issuing special charters became burdensome.[21] As legal historian Lawrence Friedman describes,

> In theory, the special charter system was a good way to control corporations. But the demand for charters, in the end, got to be too heavy. By the 1840s and 1850s, it would have swamped the legislatures, if the process had not become so routine. Even so, state session laws bulged with special charters. Time was wasted in the drudge work of issuing, amending, and extending hundreds of charters. In the rush, there was little time to supervise those charters that perhaps needed supervision.[22]

To combat this problem, states began enacting general incorporation statutes.[23] In 1809, Massachusetts passed a general incorporation act for manufacturing companies, and New York soon followed with its own general incorporation statute in 1811.[24] By the 1850s, over twenty states had passed general incorporation statutes,[25] and by 1875, general incorporation laws were available in virtually every state.[26]

Even though general incorporation laws were available, the special charter system did not entirely disappear, and, indeed, many incorporators still chose the special charter route.[27] Although most every state had a general incorporation statute or law by 1875, only eighteen states had prohibited special charters.[28] The reasons for electing to incorporate by special charter varied from concerns over lack of prestige of being incorporated under a general incorporation statute to more seedy motives, such as securing favorable arrangements from the state that would not be available to others.[29] Ultimately, concerns over such behavior and a weakening of confidence in

---

[20] FRIEDMAN, *supra* note 3, at 134.

[21] Margaret M. Blair, *Locking in Capital: What Corporate Law Achieved for Business Organizers in the Nineteenth Century*, 51 UCLA L. REV. 387, 426 (2003) (noting that by the 1820s, demand by business people for corporate charters was growing rapidly).

[22] FRIEDMAN, *supra* note 3, at 134.

[23] *Id.*; Blair, *supra* note 21, at 425-26.

[24] Blair, *supra* note 21, at 425-26; *see also* FRIEDMAN, *supra* note 3, at 134 (noting that New York is generally credited as the first to enact a general incorporation law for business corporations).

[25] Blair, *supra* note 21, at 426.

[26] Hamill, *supra* note 8, at 123.

[27] FRIEDMAN, *supra* note 3, at 135.

[28] Hamill, *supra* note 8, at 123.

[29] *Id.*; FRIEDMAN, *supra* note 3, at 135 (commenting that "[t]here were unscrupulous incorporators, and there were recurrent bribery scandals.").

public officials, led to state constitutional prohibitions on special charters.[30] However, the practice continued in many states early into the 20th century.[31]

During the 19th century, the corporate form as we know it today also began to take shape. The basic characteristics of a corporation—entity status with perpetual life, separation of ownership from management, and limited liability—all began to take hold in the minds of American jurists and scholars.[32] Justice Marshall expressed the early 19th century view of the corporation in the seminal case of *Dartmouth College v. Woodward*.[33] In *Dartmouth College*, the Supreme Court was faced with whether the state of New Hampshire could unilaterally alter the charter originally granted to Dartmouth College's trustees by the British Crown in 1769.[34] In 1816, New Hampshire passed an act that attempted to transform Dartmouth College into Dartmouth University.[35] The most significant part of the act altered the mode of governance provided in the college's original charter by increasing the size of the board of trustees from twelve to twenty-one and provided that the new members would be appointed by the governor.[36] The existing trustees objected and brought suit, claiming that the New Hampshire act violated the Contract Clause of the United States Constitution.[37]

The Supreme Court agreed with the trustees and found that the charter was in fact a contract between Dartmouth College and the state.[38] In the course of his analysis, Justice Marshall set forth what it meant legally to be a corporation, stating,

> A corporation is an artificial being, invisible, intangible, and existing only in contemplation of law. Being the mere creature of law, it possesses only those properties which the charter of its creation confers upon it, either expressly or as incidental to its very existence. These are such as are supposed best calculated to effect the object for which it was created. Among the most important are immortality, and, if the expression may be allowed, individuality; properties, by which a perpetual succession of many persons are considered as the same, and may act as a single individual. They enable a corporation to manage its own affairs, and to hold property without the perplexing intricacies, the hazardous and endless necessity, of perpetual

---

[30] FRIEDMAN, *supra* note 3, at 135; Hamill, *supra* note 6, at 123-27.

[31] Hamill, *supra* note 8, at 127-29.

[32] FRIEDMAN, *supra* note 3, at 135; HERBERT HOVENKAMP, ENTERPRISE AND AMERICAN LAW 1836-1937 49-50 (1991); Dartmouth College v. Woodward, 17 U.S. 518, 636 (1819).

[33] 17 U.S. 518 (1819).

[34] *Id.* at 624-26.

[35] *Id.* at 626.

[36] *Id.*; R. Kent Newmyer, *John Marshall as a Transitional Jurist:* Dartmouth College v. Woodward *and the Limits of Omniscient Judging*, 32 CONN. L. REV. 1665, 1666 (2000).

[37] *Dartmouth College*, 17 U.S. at 626-27.

[38] *Id.* at 627 ("It can require no argument to prove that the circumstances of this case constitute a contract.").

> conveyance for the purpose of transmitting it from hand to hand. . . . By these means, a perpetual succession of individuals are capable of acting for the promotion of the particular object, like one immortal being. But this being does not share in the civil government of the country, unless that be the purpose for which it is created. Its immortality no more confers on it political power, or a political character, than immortality would confer such power or character on a natural person. It is no more a state instrument than a natural person exercising the same powers would be.[39]

Justice Marshall's opinion essentially became the starting point for the developing law of corporations.[40] Though the decision in *Dartmouth College* did not specifically analyze a business corporation, most scholars understood that the result was intended to go beyond simply a small college charter.[41] The Court's ultimate conclusion was that a charter was a valid contract that could not be unilaterally altered by the state in violation of the Contract Clause, just as the state could not unilaterally alter a contract with an individual.[42]

Although some predicted that the *Dartmouth College* case signified a sweeping change in the relationship between the state and the corporation, its effect on corporate law turned out to be less significant.[43] As Justice Story had pointed out in his concurrence in *Dartmouth College*, if the state wished to alter the terms of a corporate charter after granting such charter, such authority "must be reserved in the grant."[44] Apparently, the states took this advice to heart, as the reservation of grant authority soon became a part of multiple state incorporation statutes.[45] Though reservation rights effectively overruled *Dartmouth College*, in actuality, the states exercised little control over their

---

[39] *Id.* at 636.

[40] *See* Gregory A. Mark, *The Personification of the Business Corporation in American Law*, 54 U. CHI. L. REV. 1441, 1450 (1987) (noting that the language and structure of Justice Marshall's opinion were followed throughout the nineteenth century); Arner, *supra* note 7, at 50 (stating that Marshall's opinion, as modified by Justice Story's concurrence, became the "starting point by Joseph Angell and Samuel Ames in their Treatise on the Law of Private Corporations Aggregate") (citation omitted).

[41] Friedman, *supra* note 3, at 136.

[42] *Dartmouth College*, 17 U.S. at 643-46.

[43] Friedman, *supra* note 3, at 137.

44 *Dartmouth College*, 17 U.S. at 712 (Story, J. concurring).

> In my judgment it is perfectly clear that any act of a legislature which takes away any powers or franchises vested by its charter in a private corporation or its corporate officers, or which restrains or controls the legitimate exercise of them, or transfers them to other persons, without its assent, is a violation of the obligations of that charter. If the legislature mean[s] [sic] to claim such an authority, *it must be reserved in the grant.*

Id. (emphasis added).

[45] Friedman, *supra* note 3, at 137; Mark, *supra* note 40, at 1454 ("The legislatures immediately began to include clauses reserving to the state the power to amend or repeal the charters that they granted.").

corporate creations[46]—an expected result, given that the very nature of general incorporation (and the subsequent increased number of corporations) militated against the state legislatures' ability to regulate individually each corporation created.[47] By the close of the 19th century, charter-based regulation had failed, and corporate behavior began to be governed by more general regulations.[48]

B. The Development of Corporate Law in the Late Nineteenth and Twentieth Centuries

With the advent of the corporation transforming from a special franchise of the state to a private business organization, state control over each individual corporation diminished.[49] By the close of the 19th century, shareholders, rather than the state, became responsible for disciplining corporate managers and directors, but the standard of manager accountability had gradually declined throughout the 19th century.[50] As Herbert Hovenkamp recounts, "by 1890 those in control of the corporation were legally answerable for virtually nothing but illegality, clearly ultra vires acts . . . or gross negligence."[51] The environment for investors was also turbulent during the late 19th century. As Lawrence Friedman describes, "[t]he investment market was totally unregulated; no SEC [Security Exchange Commission] kept it honest, and the level of morality among promoters was painfully low, to put it mildly. . . . The investing public was unmercifully fleeced."[52] Change, however, was coming.

1. The Curbing of Corporate Behavior

Throughout the late 19th century and continuing through to modern day, much of corporate law was developed through a pattern of public outcry followed by legislative action. In some cases, this outcry over corporate behavior was precipitated by a single event, but in other cases, a general distrust of corporate power initiated the action. An example of the latter can be found in the development of the antitrust laws.

At the close of the 19th century, the public's distrust of the amount of power held by corporations was increasing.[53] The growth of major corporations after the Civil War increased the long-held fear of monopoly, particularly amongst farmers, workers, and small businessmen.[54] In response to these fears, the Sherman Act was passed as

---

[46] Mark, *supra* note 40, at 1454 .

[47] *Id.*

[48] *Id.* at 1445; HOVENKAMP, *supra* note 32, at 56.

[49] HOVENKAMP, *supra* note 32, at 56.

[50] *Id.*

[51] *Id.*

[52] FRIEDMAN, *supra* note 3, at 391; Duggin & Goldman, *supra* note 6, at 222 (quoting Friedman).

[53] FRIEDMAN, *supra* note 3, at 346.

[54] FRIEDMAN, *supra* note 3, at 346; HOVENKAMP, *supra* note 32, at 241.

a means of breaking-up the so-called "trusts," which were viewed as restricting trade and competition.[55] The Sherman Act's early history was shaky, with courts narrowly interpreting the Act.[56] However, under President Theodore Roosevelt, enforcement of the Act received a boost, and subsequent victories in the Supreme Court as well as the establishment of the Federal Trade Commission ("FTC") and passage of the Clayton Act helped to transform the antitrust laws into meaningful regulations.[57] Today, antitrust concerns are not near the level of hysteria that evoked the regulation, but the laws arguably have more of a real effect.[58] As historian Lawrence Friedman has noted, early in American history, individuals such as "John D. Rockefeller could swallow up competitors at will; the modern merger barons must humbly beg permission."[59]

Whereas the antitrust movement was in reaction to a fear of the economic power of the corporation, more often corporate law has developed as a reaction to everyday corporate behavior.[60] A classic example is in the development of the food and drug laws. Although individual states had their own regulations, Congress was compelled to pass such laws in the wake of Upton Sinclair's 1906 novel *The Jungle*, which described in graphic detail the hellish conditions of meatpacking plants in Chicago.[61] The novel generated such disgust and public outcry that President Theodore Roosevelt hired investigators who confirmed much of the novel, and the Food and Drug Act swiftly sailed through Congress.[62]

This pattern of curbing unethical corporate behavior continued throughout the 20th century.[63] For example, around the same time as the Food and Drug Act's passage, Congress passed worker's compensation and safety regulation laws, largely in reaction to safety concerns over the operation of the railroads.[64] Additionally, Congress enacted The Securities Exchange Act of 1933[65] and the Securities Exchange Act of 1934[66] in order to address abuses in the issuance and trading of securities, which were seen as

---

[55] *Id.* As Friedman notes, the use of the word "trust" was a vestige, as holding companies were actually used, rather than trusts, to put monopolies together. *Id.*

[56] LAWRENCE M. FRIEDMAN, AMERICAN LAW IN THE 20TH CENTURY 55 (2002) [hereinafter "FREIDMAN, 20TH CENTURY"].

[57] *Id.* at 55-59; FRIEDMAN, *supra* note 3, at 349.

[58] FREIDMAN, 20TH CENTURY, *supra* note 56, at 392-93.

[59] FRIEDMAN, *supra* note 3, at 349.

[60] FRIEDMAN, *supra* note 3, at 392 ("The law of corporations, as such, deals less with the economic power of corporations than with their everyday behavior.").

[61] FRIEDMAN, 20TH CENTURY, *supra* note 56, at 60-61; *see also* U.S. Food and Drug Administration, *The 1906 Food and Drugs Act and Its Enforcement, available at* http://www.fda.gov/oc/historyoffda/section1.html (crediting Sinclair's book as the final precipitating force behind a comprehensive food and drug law).

[62] FRIEDMAN, 20TH CENTURY, *supra* note 56, at 60-61.

[63] FRIEDMAN, *supra* note 3, at 559-61.

[64] FRIEDMAN, 20TH CENTURY, *supra* note 56, at 62.

[65] 15 U.S.C.A. §§ 77a-77aa (West 2006).

[66] *Id.* §§ 78a-78mm.

helping to cause the great stock market crash of 1929.[67] More recently, much of the Sarbanes-Oxley Act was passed as a response to the latest spate of corporate scandals that plagued the beginning of the 21st century.[68] A general theme that seems to have developed through these regulations is that corporations cannot be trusted to police or regulate themselves, and, therefore, external regulations.

2. The Relationship between Management and Shareholders

At the close of the 19th century, corporate managers and directors were virtually answerable for nothing short of illegal or *ultra vires* acts. But beginning in the mid-19th century, courts began to recognize a method by which shareholders could sue the corporate directors—the derivative suit. The derivative suit, or stockholder's suit, is an action typically brought by shareholders on behalf of the corporation against "a third party (usu[ally] a corporate officer) because of the corporation's failure to take some action against the third party."[69] Shareholder challenges to *ultra vires* acts were first recognized in the 1830s and 1840s, but the derivative suit did not begin to emerge until the 1850s.[70] Eventually, as *ultra vires* challenges became less relevant,[71] the derivative suits began to focus on the duties that the directors of a corporation owed to the corporation itself.

The derivative suit as it relates to the duties owed by corporate directors to the shareholders and corporation itself initially emerged from the law of trusts.[72] The basis of the relationship was that corporate management was a trustee, or guardian, of every shareholder and thus was bound by a fiduciary duty to the corporation and its shareholders.[73] As the trustee model evolved, this fiduciary obligation emerged as having two basic components: a duty of loyalty and a duty of care.[74] The duty of loyalty required that the directors place the corporation before their own interests,[75] but the duty of care was more difficult to define, as courts struggled with what level of discretion

---

[67] Duggin & Goldman, *supra* note 4, at 222; Sec. & Exch. Comm'n v. Capital Gains Research Bureau, Inc., 375 U.S. 180, 186 (1963) ("A fundamental purpose, common to these statutes, was to substitute a philosophy of full disclosure for the philosophy of *caveat emptor* and thus to achieve a high standard of business ethics in the securities industry.").

[68] Geoffrey Christopher Rapp, *Beyond Protection: Invigorating Incentives for Sarbanes-Oxley Corporate and Securities Fraud Whistleblowers*, 87 B.U. L. REV. 91, 92 (2007).

[69] BLACK'S LAW DICTIONARY 475 (8th ed. 2004); Model Business Corporation Act § 7.40(1) (2003) ("'Derivative proceeding' mean a civil suit in the right of a domestic corporation . . . ."); *see also* FRIEDMAN, *supra* note 3, at 393; LARRY E. RIBSTEIN & PETER V. LETSOU, BUSINESS ASSOCIATIONS 514 (4th ed. 2003).

[70] HOVENKAMP, *supra* note 32, at 60-61; FRIEDMAN, *supra* note 3, at 393 (noting that the concept received a "push" by the Supreme Court in Dodge v. Woolsey, 59 U.S. 331 (1856)).

[71] FRIEDMAN, *supra* note 3, at 396.

[72] Duggin & Goldman, *supra* note 3, at 223.

[73] *Id.*; FRIEDMAN, *supra* note 3, at 393.

[74] Duggin & Goldman, *supra* note 6, at 224.

[75] *Id.*; Meinhard v. Salmon, 164 N.E. 545, 546 (N.Y. 1928) (describing the duty of loyalty as requiring "the punctilio of an honor the most sensitive.").

corporate managers should be given in running the company.[76] The ultimate standard that emerged was the business judgment rule.

The business judgment rule essentially frees management to run the corporation as it sees fit.[77] Under the rule, directors cannot be held liable to shareholders for mere errors in judgment, no matter how gross those errors were, so long as the decisions were made in good faith and in the ordinary course of business.[78] The effect of the rule is that it prevents courts and shareholders from second-guessing the business decisions of directors.[79] The interplay of the duty of care and the limits of the business judgment rule are well illustrated in the case of *Dodge v. Ford Motor Co.*[80]

In *Dodge*, the plaintiffs, primarily led by brothers John and Horace Dodge, who were minority shareholders in Ford Motor Company, brought suit against the directors.[81] Prior to the suit, Ford had enjoyed many years of success, which enabled Ford to pay special dividends totaling $41 million from December 1911 through October 1915, as well as a regular dividend of five percent per month on the existing $2,000,000 capital.[82] However, in 1916, Henry Ford, who owned 58% of the Ford Motor Company stock, declared that no more special dividends would be paid and that the earnings would instead be put back into the company.[83] Henry Ford announced his motive in a press release to the city of Detroit, stating,

> My ambition . . . is to employ still more men; to spread the benefits of this industrial system to the greatest possible number, to help them build up their lives and their homes. To do this, we are putting the greatest share of our profits back into the business.[84]

Based on this and other comments by Henry Ford, the plaintiffs sued to enjoin Ford from expanding its operations by building a smelting plant and to compel Ford to issue a special dividend of 75% of the $54 million surplus.[85] After a hearing, the lower court agreed with the plaintiffs, enjoined Ford Motor Company's use of the surplus to expand its operations, and ordered a special dividend to be issued.[86]

---

[76] HOVENKAMP, *supra* note 32, at 62 ("During the second half of the [nineteenth] century a deep division emerged in state courts over the appropriate standard for directors' exercise of their business judgment.").

[77] FRIEDMAN, *supra* note 3, at 396.

[78] HOVENKAMP, *supra* note 32, at 62; FRIEDMAN, *supra* note 3, at 396.

[79] Duggin & Goldman, *supra* note 6, at 225.

[80] 170 N.W. 668 (Mich. 1919).

[81] *Id.* at 669.

[82] *Id.* at 670.

[83] *Id.* at 671.

[84] *Id.*

[85] *Id.* at 672-74.

[86] *Id.* at 677-78.

On appeal, the Michigan Supreme Court rejected the plaintiffs' claims that Ford Motor Company had illegally expanded beyond the authorized amount of capital provided by statute and also rejected the plaintiffs' claim that the expansion of the corporation's business into a smelting plant was *ultra vires*.[87] Nonetheless, the court initially seemed sympathetic to the plaintiffs' claims that Ford's expansion and withholding of special dividends were primarily for humanitarian, rather than business reasons.[88] In reviewing Henry Ford's testimony and legal precedence, the court stated,

> His testimony creates the impression, also, that he thinks the Ford Motor Company has made too much money, has had too large profits, and that, although large profits might be still earned, a sharing of them with the public, by reducing the price of the output of the company, ought to be undertaken. We have no doubt that certain sentiments, philanthropic and altruistic, creditable to Mr. Ford, had large influence in determining the policy to be pursued by the Ford Motor Company—the policy which has been herein referred to.
>
> . . . .
>
> There should be no confusion (of which there is evidence) of the duties which Mr. Ford conceives that he and the stockholders owe to the general public and the duties which in law he and his codirectors owe to protesting, minority stockholders. A business corporation is organized and carried on primarily for the profit of the stockholders. The powers of the directors are to be employed for that end. The discretion of directors is to be exercised in the choice of means to attain that end, and does not extend to a change in the end itself, to the reduction of profits, or to the nondistribution of profits among stockholders in order to devote them to other purposes.[89]

Despite this statement, however, the court went on to reverse the lower court's injunction on the expansion of Ford's business operations, holding that the court should not "interfere with the proposed expansion of the business. . . . The judges are not business experts."[90] In upholding the directors' decision to expand, the court noted that this goal did not appear to harm the interests of the shareholders.[91] Though the court reversed the injunction, it did affirm a portion of the trial court's order requiring a distribution

---

[87] *Id.* at 679-81. At the time, Michigan had in effect a statute limiting the amount of capital stock for a corporation organizing under Michigan law to $25 million, which was later increased to $50 million. *Id.* at 679-80. The Michigan Supreme Court found that the statute did not limit the amount of capital a corporation could amass after formation. *Id.* at 680.

[88] *Id.* at 683 ("It is the contention of plaintiffs that the apparent effect of the plan is intended to be . . . to continue the corporation henceforth as a semi-eleemosynary institution and not as a business institution.").

[89] *Id.* at 683-84.

[90] *Id.* at 684.

[91] *Id.*

of approximately $20 million of the cash surplus, finding that even with some of the money being diverted to the expansion of operations, the surplus was great enough that it was the directors' duty to distribute "a very large sum of money to stockholders" in the form of a dividend.[92] Thus, the *Dodge* case demonstrates both the duty of care owed by corporate directors through the affirmation of the special dividend, and the application of the business judgment rule, through the reversal of the injunction against expansion.[93]

Although the *Dodge* court used the business judgment rule to justify expenditures on business expansion, the rule has been applied in a variety of other areas. As one commentator has noted,

> Pursuant to the Rule, courts generally defer to decisions taken by corporate directors, whether they relate to mergers and acquisitions, paying out of dividends, charitable donations, or executive compensation, as long as: (1) a business decision was made, (2) in good faith, (3) after the director reasonably informed herself, and (4) the director had no financial interest in the decision at issue.[94]

Courts continue to struggle with the exact application of the business judgment rule,[95] but the result, in most cases, is that corporate management is, at least legally, not liable for its good faith business decisions. This liberalization of the business judgment rule has given somewhat more discretion to the corporate managers than to the shareholders who technically own the company.[96]

This phenomenon was famously announced by Adolph Berle and Gardiner Means in their 1932 book, *The Modern Corporation and Private Property*.[97] The Berle-Means thesis argues that the sharp division between corporate ownership and control has led to

---

[92] *Id.* at 685 (citations omitted).

[93] As an interesting side note, some of Ford's motives may not have been as altruistic as articulated. The principle plaintiffs in the case, the Dodge brothers, were originally the manufacturers of the Ford chassis but in 1912, Ford started making its own chassis. RIBSTEIN & LETSOU, *supra* note 69, at 383. It appears Ford was attempting to undercut the prices of his stockholders and competitors as well as deny them dividends which were in effect helping fund the competition. After this case, Ford announced he would sell a $250 automobile and was then able to purchase the Dodge brothers' stock for $25 million (down $10 million from the Dodge brothers' initial asking price). *Id.*

[94] D.A. Jeremy Telman, *The Business Judgment Rule, Disclosure, and Executive Compensation*, 81 TUL. L. REV. 829, 831-32 (2007) (internal citations omitted).

[95] *Id.* at 833-39 (noting the confusion over the business judgment rule as either an evidentiary presumption, standard of review, or abstention doctrine); *see also* Stephen M. Bainbridge, *The Business Judgment Rule as Abstention Doctrine*, 57 VAND. L. REV. 83, 84 (2004).

[96] HOVENKAMP, *supra* note 32, at 63.

[97] ADOLF A. BERLE, JR. & GARDINER C. MEANS, THE MODERN CORPORATION AND PRIVATE PROPERTY 119-25 (17th prtg. 1950); FRIEDMAN, 20TH CENTURY, *supra* note 56, at 390.

management becoming the effective owners of a corporation.[98] The implicit economic problem of the thesis is that corporate managers could act in their own self-interests or for some purpose other than profit maximization and thus not act in the interest of the owners of the corporation, *i.e.* the shareholders.[99] Minority shareholders of large corporations could not efficiently monitor the managers; thus, such abuses could go unchecked.[100] This concern helped bring about federal reforms, such as the federal proxy regulations.[101] However, while the Berle-Means thesis remains a widely cited work, it is not without its critics.[102] Shareholders are not entirely powerless, as Lawrence Freidman has noted, because they "can vote with their feet, so to speak; and when share prices fall, and stockholders sell, management is in deep, deep trouble."[103] As I will discuss below, this concern for share price and profit is a limiting factor on corporate managers who wish to spend the firm's money on charitable causes.[104]

III. DEFINING "CONSCIENCE" AS IT RELATES TO "GOOD" BEHAVIOR

With a firm grasp of the corporation's historical roots and evolution, we can turn to the task of understanding what it means for a corporation to have a "conscience." BLACK'S DICTIONARY defines "conscience" as: "[t]he moral sense; the faculty of judging the moral qualities of actions, or of discriminating between right and wrong; . . . The sense of right and wrong inherent in every person by virtue of his existence as a social entity; good conscience being a synonym of equity."[105] WEBSTER'S offers a slightly different definition: "knowledge or feeling of right and wrong; the faculty, power, or principle of a person which decides on the lawfulness or unlawfulness of his actions, with a compulsion to do right; moral judgment that prohibits or opposes the violation of a previously recognized ethical principle."[106] From these definitions, we can glean two main themes: 1) a conscience involves the ability to make a choice based on a moral sense or feeling; and 2) a conscience involves the ability to determine right from wrong and comport behavior accordingly. These themes pose some interesting hurdles

---

98 BERELE & MEANS, *supra* note 97, at 119-25; FRIEDMAN, 20TH CENTURY, *supra* note 56, at 390.

99 RIBSTEIN & LETSOU, *supra* note 69, at 254-55; FRIEDMAN, 20TH CENTURY, *supra* note 56, at 390; HOVENKAMP, *supra* note 32, at 306.

100 RIBSTEIN & LETSOU, *supra* note 69, at 255.

101 *Id.* at 269.

102 William W. Bratton, *Berle and Means Reconsidered at the Century's Turn*, 26 J. CORP. L. 737, 737-38, 754-55 (2000); FRIEDMAN, 20TH CENTURY, *supra* note 56, at 390.

103 FRIEDMAN, 20TH CENTURY, *supra* note 56, at 390.

104 *See infra* Part III.

105 BLACK'S LAW DICTIONARY 209 (abridged 6th ed. 1991). Interestingly, the more recent eighth edition of Black's Law Dictionary is less nuanced, defining "conscience" more concisely as "[t]he moral sense of right or wrong; esp., a moral sense applied to one's own judgment and actions." BLACK'S LAW DICTIONARY 322 (8th ed. 2004). I have chosen to use the more detailed definition provided in the sixth edition.

106 WEBSTER'S NEW UNIVERSAL UNABRIDGED DICTIONARY 387 (2d ed. 1979).

when applying the term to a corporation. First, given that the quality of having a moral sense or feeling is generally human, can "conscience" even be applied to a non-human corporation? And, given the subjective nature of right and wrong, what does it mean for a corporation to choose "right?"

A. Can Corporations Make "Conscience" Choices?

Most definitions of a "conscience" involve a uniquely human characteristic to determine right from wrong based on an internal "feeling" or "moral sense." But, corporations are obviously not human. Indeed, from their inception, corporations have been viewed by the public as soulless.[107] It has been feared that a corporation's perpetual life, large size, and limited liability could act to "aggregate the worst urges of whole groups of men," with no sense of morality to temper its powers.[108] Lawrence Mitchell has analogized the corporation to Rabbi Judah Loew's *Golem*, stating that, like the *Golem*, "which came to life to protect the Jewish people once the right words were inserted into its ear, the modern American corporation knows only one thing [profit maximization]. . . So we have the paradox of having created an artificial creature with all of the rights of natural persons to formulate and pursue ends that give its life meaning, but without the ability to choose and pursue those ends."[109] Or, if we return to the analogy at the beginning of this Article, the corporation is akin to Pinocchio, in that it is an artificial entity, created by man.[110] However, even if a corporation is "soulless," it is made up of and run by human beings.[111] And, though the corporation does not have a "conscience" in the traditional sense,[112] clearly, corporations do make choices that have an effect, positive or negative, on society.

---

[107] FRIEDMAN, *supra* note 3, at 134.

[108] *Id.*

[109] MITCHELL, *supra* note 5, at 44.

[110] *See id.* at 43 ("[Corporations] are special kinds of people; people created not by God but by law and humans. As such, and in contrast to the Enlightenment vision of autonomous man, they have only the ends given to them by their creators.").

[111] FRIEDMAN, *supra* note 3, at 134; Milton Friedman, *The Social Responsibility of Business*, *in* THE ESSENCE OF FRIEDMAN 36-37 (Kurt R. Leube ed., 1987) (noting that corporate responsible behavior must refer to the corporate executives); *see also* MITCHELL, *supra* note 5, at 13, 43-44.

[112] *Cf.*, Friedman, *supra* note 111, at 36. Milton Friedman, in discussing whether "business" can have responsibilities, urges that they cannot, at least not in the traditional sense, stating:

> What does it mean to say that "business" has responsibilities? Only people can have responsibilities. A corporation is an artificial person and in this sense may have artificial responsibilities, but "business" as a whole cannot be said to have responsibilities, even in this vague sense.

Id.

1. The Individual in the Corporation

So, are these choices driven purely by the whims and conscience of management? Probably not, as corporate managers can still be held accountable for their actions. Though an individual may wish to act generously with corporate funds, he or she cannot treat corporate monies and possessions as his or her own without running afoul of several laws.[113] For instance, in *Worthington v. Worthington*,[114] Henry R. Worthington, president of a corporation which manufactured and sold hydraulic machinery, agreed to donate equipment to Columbia University's hydraulic laboratory.[115] In a letter agreeing to the donation, Henry Worthington used language that appeared to indicate that he personally was willing to donate the machinery and asked that the donation be identified with his father's name.[116] The corporation sued to recover the value of the equipment from Henry Worthington, claiming the donation was not an authorized expenditure.[117] The court agreed, finding that despite the fact that Henry Worthington was the corporation's president and a large shareholder, he could not, "by virtue of his office, give away the [corporation's] property."[118] The court clearly took issue with the express individual gratification that Henry Worthington received from the donation, as articulated by his own words in a letter to Columbia University.[119]

What may have played an even larger role in the decision, however, was the failure to have the corporation approve and endorse the action, so that the donation would appear to be one based upon the business judgment of the corporation.[120] Indeed, in

---

113 *See, e.g.*, Rice v. Wheeling Dollar Sav. & Trust Co., 130 N.E.2d 442, 449 (Ohio C.P. 1954) (holding that contribution, at insistence of officers and directors, to a charitable corporation in memory of president's mother without notification to all shareholders, was an unsanctioned use of corporate funds). *Cf.* Theodora Holding Corp. v. Henderson, 257 A.2d 398, 403-04 (Del. Ch. 1969) (holding that where president placed his own interest above that of the company's by selling a stock exchange seat previously purchased with corporate funds for personal profit, president was accountable to the company for the profit made). Though the *Theodora* court found that the business judgment rule did not protect the president for the sale of a stock exchange seat at a personal profit, it held the rule did protect a large gift made to a charitable foundation. *Id.* at 405.

114 Henry R. Worthington v. Worthington, 91 N.Y.S. 443 (N.Y. App. Div. 1905).

115 *Id.* at 444-45.

116 *Id.* at 444.

117 *Id.* at 445.

118 *Id.* at 444-45.

119 *Id.* at 445.

> It was a laudable and commendable thing for the defendant to make the gift, not only for the purpose of promulgating knowledge in mechanical engineering, but in perpetuating his father's memory. In doing this, however, he was obligated to use his own property, and not that of another. . . . [T]here is nothing in the record which would justify a finding that any action was taken by *the corporation* which could be construed into its giving the materials and making the expenditure as a gift.

Id. (emphasis added).

120 *Id.*; *see also In re* Caremark Int'l Inc. Derivative Litig., 698 A.2d 959, 967-68 (Del. Ch. 1996) (noting that the business judgment rule is process oriented).

other scenarios, even when the benefit to the corporation has been speculative, courts have been reluctant to interfere with the business affairs of a corporation. An example of such reluctance can be seen in the oft-cited case of *Shlensky v. Wrigley*.[121] In *Shlensky*, the plaintiff, a minority shareholder of the Chicago National League Ball Club (which operated the Cubs' home baseball park of Wrigley Field), sued the directors for failing to install lights at Wrigley Field for night games.[122] For those unfamiliar with baseball, Wrigley Field was, at the time of the lawsuit, as it is today, located in a heavily residential neighborhood on the north side of Chicago.[123] At the time of the suit, Wrigley Field was the only major league park not equipped with lights, and so night games could not be played.[124] The plaintiff alleged that the decision not to install lights was costing the corporation revenues that would have resulted from the increase in attendance during night games, and that the decision not to install the lights was not based on financial welfare or interests of the corporation.[125] Instead, the plaintiff claimed the decision was based on the personal position of the president, Philip K. Wrigley, that the installation of lights and night baseball games would have a "deteriorating effect upon the surrounding neighborhood."[126] Despite the plaintiff's allegations, the appellate court refused to reverse the trial court's dismissal of the case, based in part upon the business judgment rule.[127] Instead, the court found that the directors' actions could be consistent with the best interests of the corporation, stating,

> [W]e are not satisfied that the motives assigned to Philip K. Wrigley, and through him to the other directors, are contrary to the best interests of the corporation and the stockholders. For example, it appears to us that the effect on the surrounding neighborhood might well be considered by a director who was considering the patrons who would or would not attend the games if the park were in a poor neighborhood. Furthermore, the long run interest of the corporation in its property value at Wrigley Field might demand all efforts to keep the neighborhood from deteriorating.[128]

---

[121] Shlensky v. Wrigley, 237 N.E.2d 776 (Ill. App. Ct. 1968).

[122] *Id.* at 777.

[123] RIBSTEIN & LETSOU, *supra* note 69, at 378.

[124] *Shlensky*, 237 N.E.2d at 777.

[125] *Id.* at 778.

[126] *Id.* Wrigley was also allegedly motivated by his view that baseball was a "daytime sport." *Id.*

[127] *Id.* at 780.

[128] *Id.* As an aside, lights were eventually installed at Wrigley Field. As Larry Ribstein and Peter Letsou note, rather sarcastically:

> The inexorable tide of progress finally brought lights to Wrigley Field in 1988. The first night game was scheduled for August 8, 1988. . . . Cub greats Billy Williams and Ernie Banks threw out the first pitches. Thunderstorms accompanied by fierce dramatic lightening stopped the game in the fourth inning. Speculation as to the cause of the storm is beyond the scope of this book.

Ribstein, *supra* note 69, at 380.

As can be seen in the *Shlensky* case, courts can be, and often are, reluctant to interfere with the decisions of the directors, even when the motives may appear purely altruistic.[129] Indeed, as will be explored later, many activities that appear altruistic in fact can benefit the corporation as well.[130] Furthermore, many modern state rules, with regard to corporate giving, have removed the need of a court to find a business purpose by essentially sanctioning charitable donations and protecting corporate directors from scrutiny so long as their decisions are made in good faith.[131]

In practice, corporate giving is, essentially, free of any legal restrictions.[132] Although directors can often justify charitable donations and the like under the business judgment rule, legal impediments are not their only concern. At the end of the day, the corporation must make a profit.[133] The individuals who run a corporation may very well wish to act with their own conscience but can, and often are, limited by the mandate that the corporation maximize shareholder wealth.[134] But, is shareholder wealth or profit maximization necessarily a bad thing?[135] The degree to which directors should seek to maximize the profits of the corporation versus engaging in socially responsible behavior is the subject of much debate.

---

129 Greene County Nat. Farm Loan Ass'n v. Fed. Land Bank of Louisville, 57 F. Supp. 783, 789 (W.D. Ky. 1944); A. P. Smith Mfg. Co. v. Barlow, 98 A.2d 581, 586-87 (N.J. 1953) (holding that corporate power to make reasonable charitable contributions exists even apart from express statutory provisions).

130 *See infra* Part IV.B.

131 *See, e.g.*, Del. Code Ann. Tit. 8, § 102(b)(7) (2006) (allowing corporations to eliminate or limit the personal liability of a director to a corporation or stockholder for breach of fiduciary duty except in limited circumstances such as, *inter alia*, acts or omissions not in good faith). Soon after Delaware enacted this statute, other states followed, and now all fifty states have similar provisions. *See also* Duggin & Goldman, *supra* note 6, at 233-34; Einer Elhauge, *Sacrificing Corporate Profits in the Public Interest*, 80 N.Y.U. L. REV. 733, 767-68 (2005) (noting that "[t]wenty-four states (including Delaware) authorize 'donations for the public welfare or for charitable, scientific, or educational purposes.'"); Revised Model Bus. Corp. Act §§ 3.02(13), (15) (2002) (authorizing donations "further[ing] the business and affairs of the corporation," and donations for "charitable, scientific or educational purposes.").

132 David L. Engel, *An Approach to Corporate Social Responsibility*, 32 STAN. L. REV. 1, 16-17 (1979) ("As a practical matter, the business judgment defense is unlikely to fail in the absence of conflicts of interest, extraordinary amounts of profit foregone, or some other affirmative suggestion of bad faith.") (citation omitted).

133 MITCHELL, *supra* note 5, at 11 (noting that "*profit* is essential to corporate survival") (emphasis in original).

134 *Id.* at 44.

135 *See generally* Stephen M. Bainbridge, *In Defense of the Shareholder Wealth Maximization Norm: A Reply to Professor Green*, 50 WASH. & LEE L. REV. 1423 (1993) (arguing that corporate decision makers cannot, or at the very least should not, attempt to serve the interest of two masters, *i.e.* shareholders and nonshareholders).

2. Conscience and the Corporate Social Responsibility Debate

The corporate social responsibility ("CSR") debate began as early as the 1930s,[136] but has garnered much attention over the past 20 years.[137] At one far end of the debate is the view that the only responsibility corporate directors have is to make a profit for their shareholders. The economist Milton Friedman championed this view, writing, that, in a free economy, "there is one and only one social responsibility of business—to use its resources and engage in activities designed to increase its profits so long as it stays within the rules of the game, which is to say, engages in open and free competition, without deception or fraud."[138] The flip side of this argument is that corporations—which owe their very existence, including characteristics such as limited liability, to society—owe a reciprocal duty to nonshareholders and to society.[139]

Complicating the CSR debate is that the term itself can mean different things.[140] As Cynthia Williams has noted, "[l]egal academics have struggled to produce useful definitions of CSR, and in that effort may be well advised to look to management literature."[141] This management literature classifies CSR into four types, "(1) the economic responsibility to be profitable; (2) the legal responsibility to abide by the laws of society; (3) the ethical responsibility to do what is right, just, and fair; and (4) the philanthropic responsibility to contribute to various kinds of social, educational, recreational, or cultural purposes."[142] Other definitions are not as broad, however, and some scholars exclude from CSR activities that tend to benefit the corporation, even if it costs the corporation money in the short-term.[143] Ultimately, how CSR is defined and whether it is right or wrong for a company to engage in CSR activities is not within the scope of this Article. What is important, however, is what the CSR debate

---

[136] Jill E. Fisch, *The "Bad Man" Goes to Washington: The Effect of Political Influence on Corporate Duty*, 75 FORDHAM L. REV. 1593, 1601 (2006) (crediting Merrick Dodd for the scholarly roots of the CSR discussion in 1932).

[137] Lawrence E. Mitchell, *Roles of Corporations and Corporate Officers*, 99 AM. SOC'Y INT'L L. PROC. 265, 265 (2005) (noting that the phrase CSR has only developed as an aspect of public debate since the early 1990s).

[138] MILTON FRIEDMAN, CAPITALISM AND FREEDOM 133 (1962); *see also* Milton Friedman, *supra* note 111, at 36-38.

[139] William T. Allen, *Our Schizophrenic Conception of the Business Corporation*, 14 CARDOZO L. REV. 261, 265 (1992). Allen describes two characterizations of the corporation. The first is a property model, whereby the corporation is viewed as the property of the shareholders, and his view epitomizes the Friedman view of CSR and the corporation. The second view is of the corporation as a social institution, "tinged with a public purpose." *Id.*; *see also* Fisch, *supra* note 136, at 1601-02.

[140] Veronica Besmer, *The Legal Character of Private Codes of Conduct: More Than Just a Pseudo-Formal Gloss on Corporate Social Responsibility*, 2 HAST. BUS. L.J. 279, 280 (2006) (noting that CSR means different things to different people).

[141] Cynthia A. Williams, *A Tale of Two Trajectories*, 75 FORDHAM L. REV. 1629, 1647, n.54 (2006).

[142] *Id.* (emphasis omitted) (quoting Dirk Matten & Andrew Crane, *Corporate Citizenship: Toward an Extended Theoretical Conceptualization*, 30 ACAD. MGMT. REV. 166, 167 (2005)).

[143] Engel, *supra* note 132, at 9; *see* also, Milton Friedman, *supra* note 11, at 40-41.

represents, *i.e.,* recognition that corporations have the ability *to choose* to engage, or not engage, in behavior that benefits some entity, group, or individual other than just the corporation itself.

But, returning to the initial question of whether corporations can have a conscience, do corporations engage in this behavior based on an internal "feeling" or "moral sense?" Even though corporate managers can make decisions based on such human qualities, it may not be the case that what one corporate manager chooses to do is based on the same "moral sense" as other decision-makers within the company.[144] And, even if those managers wish to act based on their own internal moral senses or feelings of what is right or wrong, other factors, such as making a profit, also influence corporate behavior. The factors that influence corporate behavior will be discussed in more detail below, but with regard to having a conscience, it appears that a corporation is indeed without an internal conscience in the literal sense. But as I have already discussed, corporations do make social choices and those choices are influenced by external factors stemming, at least in part, from the corporation's status as a social entity (if we borrow from the BLACK'S definition). So, perhaps the corporation does not have an internal conscience, but like Pinocchio, it has an external one. Instead of Jiminy Cricket, though, the corporation's "conscience" is a complex combination and interaction of social and market forces, as well as the individual consciences of its corporate managers and directors.

B. What is "Good" Corporate Behavior?

Because a conscience involves determining right from wrong, some definition of what is "right", (or if we synonymously use the term "good," what is good) corporate behavior is in order. After all, one person's saint is another person's sinner.[145] Take, for example, the imaginary ABC Corporation, which makes a decision to recognize same-sex marriages under its benefits plan. Although ABC Corporation could certainly justify its decision as a recruiting tool, many people might decry the decision as immoral or wrong, while others would celebrate it as progressive and good. Further, questions about the nature of "good" behavior could be raised by activities that appear to be altruistic because they don't seem to benefit the corporation's bottom line, such as philanthropic giving to charities unrelated to the corporation. As the CSR debate demonstrates, whether corporations should even be delving into areas other than activities that profit the corporation is debated. Given that a corporation does not have the ability to tell "right" from "wrong," and as the individuals who run the company and own the company, *i.e.* management and shareholders, may have pluralistic moral senses giving varying answers to what is "right" and "wrong," how can a corporation comport its behavior accordingly?

---

[144] *See* Fisch, *supra* note 136, at 1603 ("The corporation cannot readily adopt the moral perspective of its individual constituents. . . . various corporate stakeholders may have differing moral perspectives"). Fisch further notes that corporate managers' ethical views may not mirror those of society. *Id.*

[145] Milton Friedman, *supra* note 111, at 40 (noting, with regard to arguments for corporate managers to act socially responsibly, that "one man's good is another's evil").

If we rely on such concepts as defining a conscience, there is no way to reconcile a conscience and the corporation. But if we look at the end result of pressures to produce "good" behavior, we can see a theme of behavior that benefits some entity, person, or group other than just the corporation. Thus, corporations may not know right from wrong, but corporations do act upon pressures to help or benefit some aspect of society, be it global, national, statewide, municipality, or even a smaller demographic or group. So, again, if we turn to the view that a corporation is a social entity, based on its status as such, it can and does comport its behavior to act, perhaps not based on what is right or wrong, but upon pressures to act to benefit some aspect of society other than itself (though not mutually exclusive of benefiting itself). Thus, the view of a corporation as a social entity, returns us to the conclusion that corporations act, not based upon an internal conscience, but based upon an external conscience made up of many interacting factors.

IV. A CATEGORICAL APPROACH TO WHAT DRIVES THE CORPORATE CONSCIENCE

To review briefly, I have traced the evolution of the corporation in the late 18th century from a relative few, specially chartered associations generally organized to complete projects for the public good, to the modern profit making behemoths of modern America. Along the way, corporations have been subjected to regulation, often in response to public outcry against perceived abuses of power. This corporate evolution has also resulted in a general separation of ownership and control, though that is not to say that corporate mangers act completely free from external pressures such as to make a profit. With regard to the corporate "conscience," while corporations do not have one in the traditional sense of the word, the corporation is run by corporate managers who can act based upon their own sense of morals, but that alone does not account for corporate behavior that benefits society as a whole. Nonetheless, corporations do tend to act based upon the decisions of management as they interact with other factors. I have grouped these factors into three main categories: 1) acts that benefit society and that also benefit the corporation, but which flow from legal compliance; 2) acts that benefit society and that also benefit the corporation, but which do not flow directly from legal compliance; and 3) acts that benefit society and that also benefit the corporation, based on altruistic (or semi-altruistic, for those who do not believe in pure altruism) motives alone.[146] I will discuss each in turn below.

---

[146] Professor Cynthia Williams uses a similar categorical approach to explain why corporations engage in social responsibility initiatives. Williams, *supra* note 141, at 1644. Professor Williams divides her explanation into four possible reasons: 1) law compliance; 2) market driven; 3) politically motivated; and, 4) intrinsic motivations. *Id.* at 1644-46. Though my second category could easily be broken down into market-driven and politically motivated to similarly mirror Professor Williams' approach, for the purpose of identifying what motivates the corporate conscience, I believe these are actually part of the larger category of actions beneficial to the corporation as well as society.

A. Compliance with the Law

The first category involves actions that have a positive effect on society and which are compelled by law. Historically, we have seen corporations grow from a relative few organizations with special charters that were monitored by the state to the numerous generally chartered organizations of today. Along the way, corporate abuses, or at least perceived abuses of power, have led to reactions by the government in the form of laws meant to curb egregious corporate behavior.[147] Modern corporations are faced with a number of laws and regulations affecting their behavior, from environmental laws to SEC regulations to employment laws. Although legal compliance may not seem to involve a decision of the conscience, in fact, compliance with the law is very much a choice. If we accept that the law is generally a society-imposed form of morality—of what is right and wrong—then compliance represents a choice of the conscience.[148] Though we like to think of individuals as acting in compliance with the law out of a sense of morality, punishment and deterrence certainly play a part, and, just as individuals break the law for a variety of reasons, so do corporations.

One reason corporations break the law is simple: profit.[149] The lure of profits may cause a corporation to engage in a cost-benefit analysis, weighing what is a small fine for what may seem like rather innocuous behavior against maximizing profits.[150] And to a degree, if society imposes too small a fine, the prohibited behavior must not be deemed that bad in the first place.[151] In addition to the level of punishment, the risk of getting caught plays a factor in a corporation's willingness to violate the law. As Daniel Ostas notes, some regulations "are not effectively enforced either because violators find it possible to conceal their acts or because society provides insufficient resources to prosecute violations."[152]

---

147 *See supra* part II.B.1.

148 Engel, *supra* note 132, at 37 ("If the legislature has purported to attach civil or criminal liability to (or to retain such liability for) a particular piece of behavior, then there is, under our assumptions, a public consensus that such behavior should be reduced."); Daniel T. Ostas, *Cooperate, Comply, or Evade? A Corporate Executive's Social Responsibilities With Regard to Law*, 41 AM. BUS. L.J. 559, 565 (2004) (citations omitted) (noting that under a "Public Interest Theory" of regulation, "[r]egulators regulate in the public interest and regulations reflect the aspirations of a democratic society.").

149 Estes, *supra* note 5, at 104 (quoting former SEC chief of enforcement Stanley Sporkin that, "[i]n many instances where people are not lining their own pockets you can only explain corporate crime in terms of 'produce or perish.'").

150 Ostas, *supra* note 148, at 573-74.

151 Frank H. Easterbrook & Daniel R. Fischel, *Antitrust Suits by Targets of Tender Offers*, 80 MICH. L. REV. 1155, 1177, n.57 (1982) ("[M]anagers do not have an ethical duty to obey economic regulatory laws just because the laws exist. They must determine the importance of these laws. The penalties Congress names for disobedience are a measure of how much it wants firms to sacrifice in order to adhere to the rules . . . managers not only may but also should violate the rules when it is profitable to do so."). *But see* Cynthia A. Williams, *Corporate Compliance with the Law in the Era of Efficiency*, 76 N.C. L. REV. 1265, 1266-70 (1997-1998) (criticizing an "efficient breach" approach to regulatory law).

152 Ostas, *supra* note 148, at 567. David Engel breaks corporate non-compliance with regulatory laws down into three reasons:

Take the hiring of illegal immigrants as an example. Under the Immigration Reform and Control Act of 1986, Title 18 of the United States Code imposes fines for employers who knowingly employ at least ten illegal immigrants; employers in violation of the Code may also be imprisoned for up to five years.[153] Even though these penalties have been in place since 1986, enforcement has since been in steady decline.[154] As one commentator has pointed out, "[i]n the ten-year period from 1992 to 2002, the number of investigations of employers of illegal aliens declined seventy percent, from 7053 to 2061, on-site job arrests of illegal aliens declined from 8027 to 451, and the fines imposed on employers declined from 1063 to thirteen—a staggering ninety-nine percent decrease."[155] With such scarce enforcement, it is easy to see how a corporation could choose to employ illegal immigrants at lower wages and to take the seemingly low risk of getting caught rather than decreasing its bottom line by having to pay higher wages to legal workers.[156]

But even when the societal stakes should be high, corporations can fail to meet legal standards based on a concern for profits. For instance, in the wake of a March 2005 explosion in a BP refinery in Texas City, Texas, BP conducted a self-audit of its process safety culture at all of its U.S. refineries.[157] Though the study was not intended to measure legal compliance or to assess the causes of the Texas City explosion,[158] the results of some of the surveys of employees give interesting insights into the perception of where BP's primary concerns were with regard to safety processes (which can certainly implicate legal requirements). For instance, in response to a question regarding whether process safety was compromised by short-term financial goals, thirty percent of the Texas City refinery operators and forty-five percent of a Toledo, Ohio refinery's operators said it was compromised.[159] Similarly, thirty-three percent of Texas City operators

---

> (1) the corporate acts may not be detected; (2) the transaction costs of establishing liability may exceed the amount nominally due successful private plaintiffs or the potential benefit perceived by the public prosecutor; or (3) the nominal liability may bankrupt the corporation, in which case the rule of limited liability will protect the shareholders.

Engel, *supra* note 132, at 39.

[153] 8 U.S.C. § 1324(a)(3)(A) (2000).

[154] Hugh Alexander Fuller, *Immigration, Compensation and Preemption: The Proper Measure of Lost Future Earning Capacity Damages After* Hoffman Plastic Compounds, Inc. v. NLRB, 58 BAYLOR L. REV. 985, 1003 (2006) (citing Donald L. Barlett & James B. Steele, *Who Left the Door Open?*, TIME, Sept. 20, 2004, at 51, 52); Bob Herbert, *Who's Getting the New Jobs*, N.Y. TIMES, July 23, 2004, at A23; Louis Uchitelle, *I.N.S. Is Looking the Other Way As Illegal Immigrants Fill Jobs*, N.Y. TIMES, March 9, 2000, at C1.

[155] *See* Fuller, *supra* note 154, at 1003.

[156] *See id.* (noting that "penalties will not deter illegal immigration if they are never imposed.").

[157] THE REPORT OF THE BP REFINERIES SAFETY REVIEW PANEL 17 (January 2007) (on file with author). [In the interest of full academic disclosure, the author, in his previous employment, briefly worked on portions of the independent safety review that was the basis of this report, but took no part in the formulation, dissemination, or review of the survey questions cited.]

[158] *Id.* at 14.

[159] *Id.* at 64.

and forty-two percent of Toledo operators agreed that process safety was secondary to achieving production goals.[160] Even though these numbers are by no means a majority of the employees, the survey represents a significant portion of people with an inside view "from the trenches,"[161] and demonstrates how the financial bottom line could affect a corporation's cultural attitude toward compliance.

The above discussion has focused on decisions to comply or not comply with the law. However, corporations can also flirt with non-compliance by acting in the gray areas of the law. "Loopholes" in the law may allow corporations to comply with the letter, if not the spirit, of a law. Vague or ambiguous language in a law may leave a regulation open to a variety of interpretations, and that vagueness or ambiguity can lead to abuses.[162] Those abuses stem from "[c]reative compliance" with the law, *i.e.,* the ability to legally achieve the same ends as criminal action by manipulating and exploiting the legal system.[163] This area presents an interesting cross-road for the corporate conscience, as it does not deal with out-and-out illegality, but rather with a decision to comply with the letter of the law but not with the spirit of the law.[164]

The accounting scandal that precipitated Enron's collapse provides an excellent example of "creative compliance." One of the keys to Enron's ability to state such high profits was its use of mark-to-market accounting. Under normal accounting methods, revenue recognition occurs after a service has been provided (or mostly provided) and payment has been received.[165] Under the mark-to-market accounting method, however, Enron was able to recognize revenue even before a service was provided, allowing Enron "to report expected benefits from future transactions into current period income."[166] Enron coupled the mark-to-market accounting with an aggressive interpretation of

---

[160] *Id.* at 65. Similar numbers were also reported for maintenance/craft technicians. *Id.* at 64-65. The surveys covered three other refineries in Whiting, Indiana, Cherry Point, Oregon, and Carson, California. *Id.* The results for these refineries were much more favorable to BP's commitment to process safety. *Id.* However, contractors tended to have a much less favorable view of BP's commitment to process safety, with 39-60 percent agreeing that production goals took precedence over process safety. *Id.*

[161] Management uniformly answered the question more favorably to BP's commitment to process safety. *Id.* However, the report's ultimate conclusion was that "BP has not adequately established process safety as a core value across its five U.S. refineries." *Id.* at 65.

[162] Ostas, *supra* note 148, at 567. Ostas notes a fundamental difference between compliance with the law and cooperation with the law, stating that "compliance embodies a less expansive duty than does cooperation. At its heart, the distinction highlights the difference between the letter and the spirit of the law. One complies with the letter of the law; one cooperates with the law's spirit." *Id.* at 566.

[163] Doreen McBarnet, *After Enron Will "Whiter Than White Collar Crime" Still Wash?*, 46 BRIT. J. CRIMINOLOGY 1091, 1092 (2006).

[164] Ostas, *supra* note 148, at 566. Another interesting twist on this concept involves the corporation's ability to influence the law. Fisch, *supra* note 136, at 1604-05. Through political influence, corporations have the ability to change laws with which they do not want to comply. *Id.* at 1610.

[165] Bala G. Dharan & William R. Bufkins, *Red Flags in Enron's Reporting of Revenues and Key Financial Measures*, *in* ENRON: CORPORATE FIASCOS AND THEIR IMPLICATIONS 102 (Nancy B. Rapoport & Bala G. Dharan eds., 2004).

[166] *Id.* at 101-02.

what constituted trades, adopting a "merchant model" of revenues.[167] Under the "merchant model," an entity, such as a retailer, could account for the entire selling price of products in its possession because it is deemed to take the risk of selling the goods in its possession.[168] Enron used this model to account for the entire selling price of its energy trades, rather than just accounting for the trading or brokerage fees as was more customary.[169] Despite the potential for abuse in such accounting practices, Enron had actually obtained approval from the SEC to use the mark-to-market accounting method in January of 1992.[170] The result, however, was that Enron reported "enormously inflated performance, high share values, otherwise unsustainable credit ratings, and huge recompense for executives in both performance related pay and share options."[171]

Just because actions are compelled by the law does not mean that they are devoid of choice. Profit weighs a clear role in the decisions of some corporations to engage in, or refrain from, illegal activities. Though some may argue that a cost-benefit analysis is appropriate with regard to legal compliance, it would be difficult to fault a corporation for choosing compliance. Even Milton Friedman has caveated that the responsibility of businessmen to make as much money as possible is to be done "while conforming to the basic rules of the society, both those embodied in law and those embodied in ethical custom."[172] And even when a corporation is practicing "creative compliance," as in the Enron example above, the spirit of the law may be broken by doing what is not arguably illegal, but still in violation of the underlying rules of society embodied in ethical custom.

B. Acts that Benefit both Society and the Corporation

This category includes behavior that has a positive effect on society but that also benefits the corporation and that goes beyond mere legal compliance. At the most basic level, charitable donations tend to fall in this category.[173] Corporations are eligible for a tax deduction on the donations, reaping the benefits of good public relations with a

---

[167] *Id.*

[168] *Id.* at 103.

[169] *Id.* The accounting for just the brokerage fee of the trade is known as the "agent model" because an "'agent' is someone who provides a service to the customer (such as facilitating the purchase of an airline ticket), but does not really take up the risks of possession and the risks of collection." *Id.*

[170] *Id.* at 104.

[171] McBarnet, *supra* note 163, at 1095; Dharan & Bufkins, *supra* note 165, at 103 (estimating that revenues were increased as much as fifty times through use of these accounting methods). Of course, Enron involved much more than mere creative compliance to maximize shareholder profits, as there was also a large degree of self-dealing.

[172] Milton Friedman, *supra* note 111, at 37.

[173] Rikki Abzug & Natalie J. Webb, *Rational and Extra-Rational Motivations for Corporate Giving: Complementing Economic Theory with Organization Science*, 41 N.Y.L. SCH. L. REV. 1035, 1039 (1997) (noting that "economists tend to believe that nearly all donations benefit the corporation in some way.") (citation omitted).

relatively small output of money when compared to the company's net profits. However, though a large donation of the corporation's profits would likely not be worth the tax deduction or the benefits from positive public relations, few corporations give more than a very small percentage of their profits to charity,[174] despite the Federal Tax Code allowing for a deduction for up to ten percent.[175]

Some corporate giving also contains an ulterior motive beyond the obvious benefits to the corporation and goodwill obtained. Again, Enron provides a good example of the motives behind charitable donations. Despite its other questionable dealings, Enron was known for its charity, annually disbursing one percent of its pretax earnings to worthy causes, which totaled $12 million in 2001.[176] Enron's giving was so extensive that, after its fall, many of the beneficiaries of its generosity, including the United Way, the YMCA, and local Houston arts and theater programs felt its absence keenly.[177] Although Enron's charity clearly benefited the community, there was also a benefit to Enron; the most obvious benefit being the goodwill and positive public relations that Enron enjoyed as a good "corporate citizen." Even though Enron was able to take tax deductions for its charity, there may have also been a more sinister motive behind Enron's largesse. Following Enron's fall, many questioned whether Enron was giving money, both to charitable organizations as well as political contributions, to avoid closer scrutiny of its operations.[178] Viewed cynically, Enron's generosity was intended to influence people with the power to help or hurt the company.[179] As accounting professor Ralph Estes surmised, "[m]ost of the rationale is that somehow it will pay off on the bottom line . . . It's calculated to pay a dividend, and these actions can keep the wolves from the door."[180] In other words, the benefit gained by charitable activities, whether it be through a reduction in the costs of defending the corporation's actions before the government, an avoidance of governmental regulations, or a reduction in property damage at the hands of activists, makes-up for or exceeds the costs to the corporation.[181]

---

[174] SPECIAL REPORT: PHILANTHROPY 2005, *Smarter Corporate Giving,* BUSINESS WEEK, November 28, 2005, at 72 (noting that giving in 2004 by corporations equaled 1.2 percent of total corporate profits, which was the average for the previous forty years). Corporate giving in the United States in 2006 reportedly only accounted for 4.3 percent of the total contributions made to charities in 2006, while 75.6 percent came from individuals. *Report: Most U.S. giving done by individuals*, CINCINNATI BUS. COUR., June 25, 2007.

[175] I.R.C. § 170(b)(2) (2006).

[176] Allan Turner, *Enron's Fall Shakes Up Nonprofit Community*, HOUS. CHRON., Dec. 7, 2001, at A1.

[177] *Id.* (collecting accounts of Enron's corporate giving as well as the efforts of its individual employees).

[178] Alan Clendenning, *Critics Question Enron's Charitable Donations: Company and Lay Contributed to Wide Range of Causes*, ST. LOUIS POST-DISPATCH, Jan. 27, 2002, at A4.

[179] *Id.*

[180] *Id.* (quoting Dr. Ralph Estes, accounting professor emeritus at American University).

[181] NEIL H. JACOBY, CORPORATE POWER AND SOCIAL RESPONSIBILITY: A BLUEPRINT FOR THE FUTURE 194-97 (1973).

> Rational enterprise managers judge the yield of outlays for social purposes by their long-run effect upon profits. They measure the return on the "investment" in each social program. Each social

Other than charitable donations, corporations have developed a number of other ways to help society while adding to the company's bottom line and/or reputation. For instance, one modern trend is the integration of marketing campaigns for products with prominent charities or social causes.[182] A small sampling of such ventures was recounted in November of 2006 in *The New York Times*:

> Saks Fifth Avenue is selling a leather jacket from Kenneth Cole this holiday season for $795, and a percentage of the sales price will be donated to Help USA, a group that fights homelessness.
>
> Bath & Body Works is selling an Elton John scented candle for $16.50, with 10 percent of each sale, or $2, going to the Elton John AIDS Foundation.
>
> Gap, Apple Computer and Motorola are offering limited-edition red-colored products to benefit the AIDS charity (Product) RED. Gap gives 50 percent of the profits from sales; Apple gives $10 for each iPod Nano; and Motorola $17 for each phone.[183]

The (RED)® campaign is an excellent example of this trend and of corporate behavior that has a positive effect on society while benefiting the corporation. The (RED)® campaign is the brain child of musician Bono and California politician Bobby Shriver.[184] The concept is simple: manufacturers make product lines tied to the (RED)® campaign, for instance a red Motokrzr® phone, and give a portion of the profits to the Global Fund to Fight AIDS.[185] The idea is that, rather than a one-time charitable donation, because the companies are making a profit from the sale of the (RED)® products, the

---

> outlay is tested by a cost/benefit analysis. Among the benefits may be a reduction in the costs of defending the firm's actions before the legislative or executive agencies of government, an avoidance of onerous governmental regulations, or a reduction in property damage at the hands of activists. Social pressures generate costs, the amount of which can be minimized by appropriate corporate outlays.

Id. at 196.

[182] Craig and Marc Kielburger, *Cause-tied Marketing Not Perfect*, TORONTO STAR, July 16, 2007, at World and Comment (noting that cause-related marketing is an "increasingly effective way to reach savvy consumers."); John Hall Scripps, *Firm, Non-profits Both Benefit From Cause Marketing*, FORT WAYNE J. GAZETTE, July 13, 2007, at 3E; Michael Barbaro, *Candles, Jeans, Lipsticks: Products With Ulterior Motives*, N.Y. TIMES, Nov. 13, 2006, at F33 ("[R]etailers across the country are putting philanthropy at the center of their product lines, whether it is clothes, books or shoes."). Michael E. Porter and Mark R. Kramer have described corporations' attempts at creating value for both society and themselves as a "shared value" stating, "The essential test that should guide [corporate social responsibility] is not whether a cause is worthy but whether it presents an opportunity to create shared value—that is, a meaningful benefit for society that is also valuable to the business." Michael E. Porter & Mark R. Kramer, *The Link Between Competitive Advantage and Corporate Social Responsibility*, HARV. BUS. REV., HBR Spotlight, Dec. 2006, at p. 8.

[183] Barbaro, *supra* note 182, at F33.

[184] Louise Story, *Want to Help Treat AIDS in Africa? Buy a Cellphone*, N.Y. TIMES, Oct. 4, 2006, at C8.

[185] *Id.*

donations will be sustained.[186] Participants include Gap, Armani Exchange, Motorola, Converse, Apple, and American Express.[187] There have, however, been some concerns raised over the transparency of the donations in the (RED)® campaign,[188] and though the concept seems sound, time will tell whether abuses destroy the public benefit to such campaigns.

The move by many corporations to go "green" (adopt environmentally friendly practices) often offers another example of actions that benefit society and the corporation. Corporations that offer "green" products or services hope to cash-in on an environmentally conscious consumer base.[189] Additionally, as with the (RED)® campaign, corporations get the public relations benefit of claiming that they are helping the environment.[190] But, the "green" movement goes beyond appealing to the consumer's desire to help the environment. Many corporations see a direct benefit in the energy savings themselves.[191] For instance, a standard feature in new Wal-Mart stores is to have a series of skylights in the roof to reduce energy costs for lighting.[192] Such "green" construction is seen as a way that many companies can reduce the environmental impacts of operations.[193] Other companies are reducing their energy footprint and saving money through other means; for example, Marriott Hotel's use of compact fluorescent light bulbs to save 65% on hotel lighting costs.[194] Beyond the benefits to the corporation in energy savings and to public relations, some states have also created incentives for

---

186 *Id.*

187 *Id.*; Barbaro, *supra* note 182, at F33.

188 Scripps, *supra* note 182, at 3E (noting concerns over transparency in accounting and how the proceeds of products are funneled to the Global Fund). *Cf.* Kielburger, *supra* note 182, at 2 (noting that the campaign has spent over four times as much in advertising than it has raised).

189 Paul Davidson, *Getting Gold Out of Green: Companies Learn Eco-friendliness Helps Bottom Line*, USA TODAY, April 19, 2007, at 7A.

190 This has led to some concerns that corporations are "'greenwashing,' or using environmentalism to polish their corporate images." *Id.* Consumers concerned over the climate-friendliness of companies can obtain a global scorecard which ranks companies based, among other things, on "what they have done to reduce their impact on the climate, [and] their stances on global-warming legislation." MSNBC News Services, *Companies Get Ranked on Global Warming: Canon, Nike Among the Best; Apple, eBay, Levi Strauss Among Worst*, June 19, 2007, *available at* https://www.msnbc.msn.com/id/19315109/ (describing it as a "pocket-sized scorecard produced by a new nonprofit, Climate Counts, and based on 22 criteria developed with help from experts.").

191 *Id.*; Daniel Franklin, *A change in climate; The greening of corporate* responsibility, *in Just good business: A special report on corporate social responsibility*, THE ECONOMIST, Jan. 19, 2008, at 14 ("Beyond the lofty talk, reducing a company's output of greenhouse gasses and encouraging 'responsible' use of resources can also mean cutting waste and saving money."); Jim Downing, *Go Green to Save Some Green; Wal-Mart Seeks Ways to Cut Electricity Usage*, FORT WAYNE J. GAZETTE, April 30, 2007, at 4C.

192 Downing, *supra* note 191, at 4C.

193 Brian D. Anderson, *Legal and Business Issues of Green Building*, 79 WIS. LAW. 10, 11 (2006); Rick Rothacker, *Environmentally Friendly Projects: Buildings growing Wachovia, BofA part of push to cut the ecological impact of doing business*, CHARLOTTE OBSERVER, May 2, 2007, at 1D.

194 Davidson, *supra* note 189, at 7A.

environmentally friendly corporations.[195] For instance, Wisconsin has enacted "Green Tier" legislation, which is designed to promote "superior environmental performance" by businesses.[196] The Wisconsin legislation creates a two-tier market-based incentive program for environmentally responsible businesses.[197] Also, on the federal level, the U.S. has given tax credits in the past to renewable-energy producers, though the failure to renew the credit in some years has made the credit unpredictable.[198] Still, there is a belief among many that a federal level of control is inevitable, be it through incentives or strict controls.[199] Even such federal controls have the potential to create big business, however, in the form of carbon credits, *i.e.,* credits that can be bought on the open market that are awarded to businesses for the tons of carbon dioxide that are *not* emitted.[200] Such legislation would provide another potential money making angle for corporations that choose to go "green."[201]

In all of the situations described above, however, the question is: if there is a benefit to the corporation, why are the above mentioned activities even a choice? After all, it would seem that if choosing to pair with the (RED)® campaign or to switch all of your business's light bulbs over to compact fluorescent light bulbs will save or make your business money, then why isn't everyone taking those actions? What sort of choice is being made? Again, turning a profit, even if just in the short-term, can be an obstacle. Many corporate managers feel pressure to make short-term earnings. According to a survey conducted by authors Dominic Dodd and Ken Favaro for their book, THE THREE TENSIONS, "nearly two-thirds (63 percent) of the managers in our survey said that the capital markets are biased toward short-term earnings."[202] Thus, if a venture requires a large up-front outlay of capital, such as some energy-saving steps, or if the return is

---

[195] *See, e.g.*, WIS. STAT. § 299.83 (2007) (setting out Green Tier legislation intended to create incentives for businesses with superior environmental performance). Similarly, Oregon has established a Green Permits program which offers reduced inspection frequency, among other benefits, as an incentive to encourage firms to adopt an environmental management system. OR. DEP'T OF ENVTL. QUALITY, THE OREGON GREEN PERMITS PROGRAM GUIDE 4-1 (2000).

[196] WIS. STAT. § 299.83; Linda H. Bochert & Mary Woolsey Schlaefer, *Achieving Environmental Excellence: Green Tier Legislation*, 78 WIS. LAW. 8, 9 (2005).

[197] Bochert & Schlafer, *supra* note 194, at 9.

[198] *Sunlit Uplands: Wind and Solar Power are Flourishing, Thanks to Subsidies*, THE ECONOMIST, June 2, 2007, *in Cleaning up: A Special Report on Business and Climate Change*, at 16-19.

[199] *Everybody's Green Now: How America's Big Companies Got Environmentalism*, THE ECONOMIST, June 2, 2007, *in Cleaning up: A Special Report on Business and Climate Change*, at 6.

[200] *Trading Thin Air: The Carbon Market is Working, but not Bringing Forth as Much Innovation as had Been Hoped*, THE ECONOMIST, June 2, 2007, *in Cleaning up: A Special Report on Business and Climate Change*, at 8.

[201] Of course, any compulsory legislation would belong in the first category. I have included "green" legislation in the second category only to the degree that it is incentive based as opposed to compulsory.

[202] DOMINIC DODD & KEN FAVARO, THE THREE TENSIONS 71 (2007).

speculative, it is understandable how some corporate managers might delay or decline to enter into such ventures.[203]

C. Altruistic (or Semi-Altruistic) Acts

The third and final category involves corporate behavior that benefits society and is initiated by altruistic motives. Of course, the very term "altruistic" can be controversial. The term "altruism" means an "unselfish concern for the welfare of others."[204] However, one could argue that no action, be it by a corporation or an individual, is completely unselfish.[205] I do not intend to enter into such a philosophical debate, and so, for the purposes of this Article, I will use the term more loosely to cover behavior that is motivated by something other than a solid and foreseeable benefit to the corporation.

Even given this broad definition, it can be hard to categorize corporate behavior as "altruistic." Corporate managers are influenced and pressured to maximize profit. Some privately held corporations, however, have made altruistic behavior a part of their corporate culture. This behavior is often initiated by specific persons within the organizations who have taken stands based on their own beliefs as to how a corporation should behave—in other words, people who, in effect, act as individual "Jiminy Crickets" for the corporation. For instance, many a hungry fast-food fan is aware that Chick-fil-A is not open on Sundays.[206] The reason: Chick-fil-A's founder and chairman, S. Truett Cathy, is a devout Christian.[207] His beliefs have led him to close on Sundays, "a time in the quick service industry that normally generates 20 percent of revenue."[208] Even though the company also admits that its Sunday closures are a useful incentive in hiring and retaining employees,[209] it is clear that the real motivation for Sunday closures is S. Truett Cathy's desire to worship on Sundays. As Mr. Cathy expressed in response to a question about what he would like his greatest legacy to the organization to be:

---

[203] *Id.* at 72 (noting that, of those surveyed, 27 percent often, and 54 percent sometimes, cut spending on R&D, marketing, or IT to safeguard short-term earnings and 13 percent often, and 64 percent sometimes, delayed a project, even if it would be profitable for the same reason).

[204] WEBSTER'S UNIVERSAL COLLEGE DICTIONARY (1997).

[205] Indeed, a recent study suggests that undertaking unselfish acts releases chemicals in the brain that activate some of the same pleasure centers in your brain as food and sex. *To your brain, altruism's as good as sex: Even paying taxes can trigger pleasure centers, study says*, REUTERS, June 14, 2007, *available at* http://www.msnbc.msn.com/id/19235071/.

[206] *See* Chick-fil-A, corporate website, http://www.chick-fil-a.com/Closed.asp (last visited March 23, 2008).

[207] Miles Davis & Leyland M. Lucas, *Principle before Profits: An Interview with S. Truett Cathy*, NEW ENGLAND J. OF ENTREPRENEURSHIP, April 1, 2007, at 27; Thuy-Doan Le, *A Day of Rest: Religious Choice May Sacrifice Sales but Build Customer Loyalty*, THE SACRAMENTO BEE, April 15, 2006, at D1.

[208] Davis & Leyland, *supra* note 207, at 27; Ben Werner, *Chick-fil-A Founder Shares his Philosophy*, THE COLUMBIA (SC) STATE, April 18, 2007.

[209] Le, *supra* note 207.

> I think the greatest contribution would be the fact that we're closed on Sunday. We've done that for 60 years. And there are times when you mention Chick-fil-A, yeah, that's the place that's closed on Sundays. And it gives us opportunity to explain well sure, you can't go eat at Chick-fil-A because they're closed on Sunday to respect the Lord's Day. "Honor the Lord's Day and keep it holy." It's a special day that the Lord has given Man. We need that day off, it's to honor God. We just need a day off to think about the little things that are important. And that's the bottom line.[210]

Thus, though there may be some incidental benefits to the decision to close on Sundays, the real motivation behind the decision is not a profit- or benefit-seeking motive, but rather a religiously based decision.

Ben & Jerry's ice cream offers another example of a corporation that has engaged in behavior for reasons other than profit.[211] Ben & Jerry's was started by Ben Cohen and Jerry Greenfield in Burlington, Vermont, in 1978.[212] From its inception, Ben & Jerry's used milk from local dairy farmers that was growth-hormone-free. The company partnered early-on with non-profit organizations to offer job training to disadvantaged people.[213] In addition, Ben & Jerry's set-up a compensation plan through which all staff earned at least twenty percent of the salary of the highest paid employee and committed 7.5 percent of its pre-tax profits to philanthropic causes.[214] Even though Ben & Jerry's was bought by food giant Unilever in 2000, the deal included a promise by Unilever to keep in place Ben & Jerry's corporate philanthropic philosophy as well as to commit

---

[210] Davis & Leyland, *supra* note 207, at 31. Interestingly, when asked about corporate social responsibility and whether the responsibility of a corporate manager is to the stockholders or shareholders, Mr. Cathy responded:

> You should be honest to your stockholders. Look at it the way they practice in the Navy where the captain's always the last one to depart from the ship. If you got a sinking ship, it is the captain who leaves last. I felt that in business it's the same way, you got to be responsible to the stockholders—unlike a business owner I heard about. He took his money and left the company in bad shape. He shouldn't have walked off, leaving his business in trouble. He did all he could to leave the scene. You should take care of the stockholders, those who invest their life savings in it and trust in the company. They shouldn't be disappointed by the person they're trusting in, with mistake and no protection really, but that's the stock market. But it gets back to biblical principles. Treat others like you like to be treated, be honest and be truthful. These are the basic things that are expected of an individual.

Id. at 30.

[211] EMILY ROSS & ANGUS HOLLAND, 100 GREAT BUSINESSES AND THE MINDS BEHIND THEM 353 (Sourcebooks, Inc. 2006) (2004) (noting that Ben & Jerry's is the first company to make a profit while acting like a non-profit organization).

[212] *Id.*

[213] *Id.* at 353-55.

[214] *Id.* at 355. Ben & Jerry's also "set up all manner of revenue streams into nonprofit activities . . . [and] offered staff extended maternity and paternity leave and allowances for de facto and gay couples." *Id.*

a percentage of profits to charity.[215] And since the takeover, Ben & Jerry's still boasts that the company's annual reports continue to "evaluate achievement on social and environmental goals, including assessments by an external auditor."[216]

That is not to say that only privately held corporations can fall into this altruism category. For instance, Robert Galvin, a former senior officer with Motorola, described an instance where his company forfeited profits based upon principles of integrity and respect for other people.[217] His anecdote recalls an instance around 1950, when Motorola had the opportunity to enter into a microwave contract with a South American government.[218] The contract would have meant a significant, but not enormous, increase in the company's profit margin.[219] But it came to the company's attention that the South American government was trying to play fast and loose with where the money was going, and Motorola suspected that the contract would ultimately result in cash being funneled to some of that country's generals.[220] Motorola refused to enter into the contract and, furthermore, according to Galvin, would never solicit that government again, despite the profit that Motorola could have made.[221]

Does this anecdote really represent an instance of altruistic behavior? Galvin admits that, though the company did not take that contract, it "made so much more money honorably over the next twenty years while [the] anecdote was still fresh in people's minds,"[222] indicating that the reputation boost and subsequent positive effect it had on the company's bottom line was worth any short-term profit Motorola could have made by entering into a contract with a corrupt government. So does this sort of conduct really belong in the previous category? Perhaps not; according to Galvin, Motorola's decision, or perhaps more accurately, the decision of its officers, was not based on what was profitable or legal but on what the company held as a core value of right and wrong.[223]

---

215 *Id.* at 355-56. According to Ben & Jerry's website, it donates "over $1.1 million" a year to charity and donated $1.6 million in 2006. *See* http://www.benjerry.com/foundation/ (last visited March 23, 2008); *see also Company Profile for Ben & Jerry's*, March 30, 2007, *available at* http://www.benjerry.com/our_company/press_center/press/.

216 *50 for History*, HR MAGAZINE, Dec. 1, 2005, at 10.

217 Robert W. Galvin, *Corporate Social Responsibility is Not a Challenge, in* IS THE GOOD CORPORATION DEAD? SOCIAL RESPONSIBILITY IN A GLOBAL ECONOMY 254 (John W. Houck & Oliver F. Williams eds., 1996).

218 *Id.*

219 *Id.* at 255.

220 *Id.* at 254-55. This occurred prior to enactment of the Federal Corrupt Practices Act ("FCPA"). *Id.* at 258; 15 U.S.C. §§ 78dd-1, 78dd-2 (2006).

221 Galvin, *supra* note 217, at 255.

222 *Id.*

223 *Id.* at 258. Galvin notes that although the conduct in question in the anecdote would now be illegal, he believes that the legality was irrelevant because, as he puts it, "I know right from wrong and practice what is right, regardless of the law." *Id.*

Another company that has recently made headlines with its seemingly progressive corporate culture is American Apparel, Inc., which specializes in selling T-shirts.[224] American Apparel's claim to fame is that all of its merchandise is manufactured in Los Angeles, California rather than overseas.[225] American Apparel's founder, Dov Charney, has made it his company's goal to prove that T-shirts can be made profitably in the U.S.A. while still paying a decent wage to employees and providing good working conditions.[226] Indeed, American Apparel has not just settled for manufacturing in the U.S.A., but also has offered benefits beyond a "decent" wage. Along with workers on average $12.50 an hour,[227] American Apparel offers a number of perks, such as health insurance, paid vacations, free English classes (the workers are predominantly Hispanic), subsidized bus passes, lunches, legal assistance as well as yoga, massage and counseling.[228] American Apparel has announced a stock plan under which the average employee would receive 540 shares in the company.[229] All of this is part of Charney's vision to present a "sweatshop free" product which has reaped rewards for the company.[230] American Apparel reported $80 million in sales in 2003[231] and that number grew to $300 million in 2006.[232]

The sweatshop free vision is more than just an altruistic tag-line, however; it is also the heart of American Apparel's business model. By keeping manufacturing in the U.S., Charney claims he is better able to respond to market demands as well as ensure quality control.[233] The generous pay and benefits also helps to attract and retain workers. As Charney himself has noted, "It's not a marketing ploy, necessarily, it's about taking care of people that are taking care of the company. And it's also a capitalistic ploy, because they can say, 'Well, you know, someone works at another factory, they make

---

[224] *See* American Apparel website, *available at* http://americanapparel.net/. American Apparel, Inc. trades on the American Stock Exchange (AMEX) as APP.

[225] SUZANNE BERGER, HOW WE COMPETE: WHAT COMPANIES AROUND THE WORLD ARE DOING TO MAKE IT IN TODAY'S GLOBAL ECONOMY 201-202 (2006); Rob Walker, *Conscience Undercover*, N.Y. TIMES, Aug. 1, 2004 at Section 6, p. 18; Interview by John Blackstone with Dov Charney, creator of American Apparel company ("To a T," Feb. 4, 2007) on CBS Sunday Morning.

[226] BERGER, *supra* n. 225, at 203.

[227] *Id.* at 202; Walker, *supra* n. 225 (quoting a $13 per hour wage).

[228] BERGER, *supra* n. 225, at 202-03; Linda Baker, *Made in the U.S. of A.?*, Salon.com, Feb. 11, 2004.

[229] Interview by John Blackstone with Dov Charney, creator of American Apparel company ("To a T," Feb. 4, 2007) on CBS Sunday Morning.

[230] BERGER, *supra* n. 225, at 203. *American Apparel Registers Record-Breaking Sales*, BUS. WIRE, Dec. 10. 2002.

[231] Jenny Strasburg, *Made in the U.S.A.*, SAN FRANCISCO CHRON., July 4, 2004, at Business p. J1.

[232] Interview by John Blackstone with Dov Charney, creator of American Apparel company ("To a T," Feb. 4, 2007) on CBS Sunday Morning.

[233] Interview by John Blackstone with Dov Charney, creator of American Apparel company ("To a T," Feb. 4, 2007) on CBS Sunday Morning.; BERGER, *supra* n. 225, at 203; Marisa Katz, *Millionaire in a T-shirt*, Israel Business Arena, Nov. 16, 2004 (noting that Charney briefly outsourced in the beginning to Mexico but that the quality control created issues that off-set the savings in cheaper labor).

$2 less or $5 less an hour,' and they're 'Oh, at American Apparel, you have medical insurance.'"[234] The sweatshop-free tagline has also been a marketing point itself, which may be a large part of the company's success.[235] Thus, as with the Motorola example above, although corporate behavior may have its genesis in an altruistic or semi-altruistic motive, ultimately, it is the concept's profitability that makes it sustainable. As Charney himself has noted, "'If you've got a company where everybody wins, that company will be around for awhile.'"[236]

D. Blurring the Lines

As the Motorola anecdote and American Apparel business model both demonstrate, it is often difficult to identify the main motivating factor behind corporate behavior that is beneficial to society. Though the Foreign Corrupt Practices Act was not yet in place, Motorola may have felt that it was treading into a gray legal area, or at least one that could eventually cause the company legal headaches. Additionally, as Galvin noted, the corporation saw a long-term benefit based on refraining to do business. American Apparel is motivated to provide a sweatshop-free product, but that same tagline has helped sell the shirts and thus made the product profitable. Identifying what motivates such corporate behavior is difficult without more information from the companies themselves,[237] and even then, we may well be suspect of their explanations, which may be nothing more than a public relations spin. On the other hand, corporate managers may be doing the opposite, attempting to offer legitimate beneficial results for the corporation to justify their own desire to engage in altruistic behavior.[238]

In reflecting upon the above factors, it is important to note that they are just that; factors. They very well may not be mutually exclusive, but rather, interact in a complex way to produce socially beneficial corporate behaviors. And though I have used examples to identify behaviors based upon driving factors, it is certainly open for debate about whether, and to what degree, corporate behavior is based upon one of these categories.

---

[234] Interview by John Blackstone with Dov Charney, creator of American Apparel company ("To a T," Feb. 4, 2007) on CBS Sunday Morning.

[235] *Id.*; BERGER, *supra* n. 225, at 202-03; Shannon McMahon, *Made in Downtown L.A.; American Apparel's progressive practices winning over customers*, San Diego Union-Tribune, Dec. 18, 2004, at Business, p. C-1 ("American Apparel's socially conscious vibe is still what first strikes a chord with consumers.").

[236] McMahon, *supra* n. 235 (quoting Dov Charney).

[237] As Professor Williams notes in discussing her own categorical approach to CSR initiatives, "[d]istinguishing between these explanations is difficult without access to information about companies' internal decision-making processes, which will require more in-depth interviews and case studies; there are undoubtedly multiple explanations for this relatively new phenomenon." Williams, *supra* note 141, at 1647.

[238] Abzug & Webb, *supra* note 173, at 1041 (noting that, with regard to giving, because managers cannot separate their individual interests from occupational decision-making, managers "may maximize their own utility").

V. JUDGING THE CORPORATE CONSCIENCE

It is tempting, when looking at the above categories, to use them as a checklist for good corporate behavior. For instance, if a corporation is generally abiding by the laws and occasionally donating money to charity, then we could be conclude that the corporation is acting as an acceptable corporate citizen, even if it does not engage in altruistic acts. Just as we could conclude that any individual John Doe who generally abides by the law[239] and who occasionally gives money to a local charity (but enjoys the tax write-off) could be deemed a good citizen. But such an approach over-simplifies the analysis. Continuing with the John Doe example, Doe, a single unattached man, could also be having an affair with his best friend's fiancée. Many would consider this rather morally reprehensible though completely legal. Corporations can also engage in behavior that, though legal, can be seen as immoral and affect our view of their corporate citizenship. Returning to the hypothetical of the corporation that chooses to recognize same-sex partnerships, whether the corporation is considered to have made a right or wrong choice is a highly individualized question.

These factors, though are not useless in evaluating corporate behavior. Quite the contrary. Someone may well look at a situation and make his own determination of what the motivating factor should be behind socially beneficial actions. Law and economics proponents may well argue that no corporate act should be based on the altruistic category, and proponents of CSR will likely promote decision-making based in that same category (though perhaps not exclusively). But whatever the moral base of the individual judging corporate behavior, understanding what motivates corporate behavior is important in understanding how to change or curb corporate misbehavior.

VI. CONCLUSION

The corporation has evolved extensively from its roots in America as a specially chartered association organized to accomplish some public good, to the modern profit-making entities of today. Along the way, abuses of corporate power, whether real or perceived, have resulted in regulations aimed at curbing corporate behavior. Furthermore, the separation of ownership from control in the corporation, articulated in the Berle-Means thesis, has led to debates over the roles and duties of corporate managers. This separation of control from ownership has also helped to shape the debate over whether, and to what degree, corporate managers should cause the corporation to engage in socially beneficial behaviors.

Though these individuals who run the corporation have a conscience, the corporation itself does not have one, in the traditional sense of the word. The corporation is an artificial entity, soulless and devoid of the ability to reflect upon its actions. However, like the wooden boy, Pinocchio, corporate behavior is directed by its own Jiminy Cricket, *i.e.* external factors. These external factors of legal compliance, corporate benefit and even altruism (even if it is manifested through a controlling corporate manager), often

[239] Though we would probably tend to forgive the errant minor violation, such as a traffic ticket.

act in conjunction to produce corporate behaviors that ultimately benefit some aspect of society. While more empirical research is needed to understand to what degree each of these factors affects corporate behaviors, through understanding these factors, we may begin to understand why corporations act as they do and how corporate misbehaviors may be curbed in the future.

Sarbanes-Oxley, Jurisprudence, Game Theory, Insurance and Kant: Toward a Moral Theory of Good Governance[*]

Jeffrey M. Lipshaw[**]

I. INTRODUCTION

Congress enacted the Sarbanes-Oxley Act of 2002[1] in direct response to the spate of corporate scandals in late 2001 and 2002, including as the poster child the previously high-flying Enron.[2] Since then, legal practitioners, even in public companies with no taint of the recent corporate scandals, have struggled with the application of Sarbanes-Oxley and the various regulations it required the Securities and Exchange Commission to issue.

Perhaps because practicing lawyers are overwhelmed merely with ensuring their clients are in technical compliance with the statute and regulations, and academic lawyers are removed from the day-to-day business of corporate managers and directors in fulfilling their obligations to the corporate stakeholders, little rigorous thought has been given to whether the corporate governance provisions of the statute are accomplishing what they were intended to do, and if not, why. Up until the great governance crisis of the

---

[*] Originally published at 50 WAYNE L. REV. 1083 (2005). Reprinted by permission.

[**] Adjunct Professor, Indiana University School of Law–Indianapolis. Senior Vice President, General Counsel & Secretary, Great Lakes Chemical Corporation. A.B., 1975, University of Michigan; J.D., 1979, Stanford University. I owe thanks to a number of people who looked at the thesis of this paper at various early stages and encouraged me to keep at it or shared materials: Douglas Baird, Robert Weisberg, Joseph Grundfest, Andrew Achenbaum, Steven Newborn, Lynn Stout, Anthony Tarr, Ira Millstein, Carter Emerson, Jennifer McElroy Fahey and Karen Witte Duros. I owe a debt of gratitude to Susan Neiman, Director of the Einstein Forum, Potsdam, Germany, whose moving insights about making sense of the gap between the "is" and the "ought" and our subsequent correspondence made me realize how much philosophy could account for what I, a mere practitioner, observed from day to day. She truly is, at least as to the subject of evil, the ironic embodiment of the principle "those who can, do; those who can't, teach." Finally, I have been privileged to observe and provide legal advice to the patient and wise independent directors of Great Lakes Chemical Corporation since 1999. Their character, as a group and to a person, provided the intuitive basis for my thesis.

[1] Pub. L. No. 107-204, codified at 15 U.S.C. SS7201 et seq. (2003) and sections of 18 U.S.C.

[2] At the same time, stories were breaking about abuses at WorldCom, Adelphia Communication, Qwest, Global Crossing and other companies. *See generally* S. Rep. No. 107-205 (2002).

early third millennium, much of the debate, captured mostly in shareholder proposals over specific aspects of corporate governance (poison pills, classified boards, cumulative voting, supermajority requirements), has been about the relationship between those variations of governance and the equity value of the firm.[3] Shareholder advocates argued such measures reduced value; corporate boards argued the opposite. But nobody has ever seriously doubted the relationship of governance to value, and it was natural for Congress to address a perceived concern over confidence in the public markets by enacting laws intended to enhance responsible corporate governance.[4]

Yet, if in a moment of quiet reflection, the harried practitioner had thought about it, he or she would have been intrigued, if not unsettled, by the apparent disconnection between what the law is supposed to accomplish versus what much of it and its regulatory progeny require. In functional terms, if the desired output of responsible corporate governance is y, and the various reforms (independence standards, internal control certifications, bans on the extension or arranging of credit in the form of personal loans to officers or directors, audit committee financial experts, etc.) are inputs x1, x2, x3, x4, etc., is there any credible basis for believing there is a function y = f(x) relating the inputs to the output, individually or taken as a group?

As a practitioner, my intuition was there was not, at least in the application of most of these rules.[5] Much of Sarbanes-Oxley is directed at the specific abuses of the 2001-2002 corporate implosions, whether or not the resulting specific prescriptions were meaningful to the vast majority of public companies. Those rules intended to dictate a certain set of behaviors had a compliance effect, but not necessarily what the reformers

---

[3] *See, e.g.*, Paul A. Gompers, Joy L. Ishii & Andrew Metrick, *Corporate Governance and Equity Prices* (2002) (unpublished manuscript, Ctr. for Financial Institutions Working Papers 02-32, Wharton Sch. Ctr. for Fin. Inst., Univ. of Pa.), *available at* http://ideas.repec.org/p/wop/pennin/02-32.html (last visited Feb. 22, 2005); Lucian Arye Bebchuk, John C. Coates IV & Guhan Subramanian, The *Powerful Antitakover Force of Staggered Boards: Theory, Evidence & Policy*, 54 STAN. L. REV. 887 (2002).

[4] "Clearly, the ethical breakdowns, and in some cases, criminal behavior in the most recent corporate scandals broke fundamental bonds of trust with investors. . . . These scandals clearly illuminated the need for a new commitment to higher standards of corporate governance and accounting and regulatory oversight." John A. Thain, Chief Executive Officer, New York Stock Exchange, Remarks at the Economic Club of New York City (May 27, 2004) (transcript available from the New York Stock Exchange).

[5] This is not to say that every provision of Sarbanes-Oxley reflects poor law or policy. Most of the heartburn and debate is not over the governance provisions, but the Section 404 internal control certification and attestation requirement. Paul Volcker & Arthur Levitt, Jr., *In Defense of Sarbanes-Oxley*, WALL STREET JOURNAL, June 14, 2004, at A16. Volcker and Levitt cite a survey of 153 directors by Corporate Board Member finding that 60% think the effect of the law has been positive for their companies, and more than 70% see it as positive for their boards. They also defend the cost-benefit calculus of the intense one-time and continuing focus on internal controls (for companies exceeding $5 billion in revenue, the one-time cost is estimated to average $4.7 million, and the continuing annual cost is expected to be $1.5 million). *Id.*

That aspect of the statute is outside of the scope of this article, but in my brief experience, it is providing an operational benefit, whether or not it is cost-justified. Similarly, some of the financial reporting requirements, such as the reconciliation of GAAP and pro-forma statements in Section 401(b)(2) and later SEC rules, have had a positive impact.

sought, which was the day-to-day operation of corporate management in a way that takes appropriate fiduciary account of shareholder (or other stakeholder) interests.

In this paper, I contend first that the frustrations with Sarbanes-Oxley have their basis in the jurisprudence underlying the statute—the presence or absence of articulated policies and principles underlying the specific rules. I assess the law under modern positivist and naturalist theories, and point out ironies in its ultimate application. Second, I contend there is a more fundamental issue. Neither the law, nor one of the most cogent theories of non-legal norms—Eric Posner's application of game theory and signaling to principles—accounts fully for the moral aspect of corporate board service and ethical decision-making. I critique the economic model with a real world example of a wealthy director's assessment of his potential gain versus potential exposure, particularly in view of the limitations of directors' and officers' insurance. I suggest there is a moral theory that explains compliance outside of law or economics, and that the directors operate simultaneously under moral, legal and economic dictates. Finally, I contend social policy and legal training that in turn fail to recognize the importance of moral bearing on corporate governance will very likely miss the intended objective of good governance: more thoughtful, independent focus by boards on their fiduciary obligations to corporate stakeholders.

II. JURISPRUDENCE, SARBANES-OXLEY AND THE REFORM OF CORPORATE GOVERNANCE

A. The Jurisprudential Ironies of Sarbanes-Oxley

Enron was a natural gas pipeline company whose principal executives transformed it into a marketer and trader of energy, often in the form of derivative contracts. In 1998, Enron's share price was approximately $20; it peaked at almost $90 in 2000; with the revelation of significant losses and write-offs in October 2001, the share price sank to the $20 range; on December 2, 2001, the company filed for Chapter 11 protection, and thereafter the stock was almost worthless.[6] Over the next seven months, in a frenzied atmosphere, both houses of Congress introduced and passed legislation. The House and Senate bills were reconciled in a conference report filed on July 24, 2002. The House agreed to the report in a 423-3 vote and the Senate in a 99-0 vote, and President Bush signed it on July 30, 2002.[7]

---

[6] *Timeline of Enron's Collapse, available at* http://www.washingtonpost.com/ac2/wp-dyn?pagename=article&contentId=A25624-2002Jan10&notFound=true; Enron 5 year stock performance, available at http://www.augsburg.edu/home/business/ (click link for Enron slides) (last visited Feb. 25, 2005).

[7] A thorough review of the political process leading up to the passage of the Act is contained in Roberta Romano, *The Sarbanes-Oxley Act and the Making of Quack Corporate Governance* (2004), *available at* http://ssrn.com/abstract=596101 (Last visited Mar. 3, 2005). The article assesses the effectiveness of the legislation on its own terms, apart from its genesis in the Enron scandal. Professor Romano concludes Sarbanes-Oxley is ill-conceived legislation on its own terms, because the pre-existing data on the specific types of provisions imposed by Sarbanes-Oxley show no meaningful correlation between the kinds of reforms enacted and surrogates for better governance.

Whether or not they addressed the root cause of the Enron collapse and other scandals, and regardless whether they would be effective, most of the governance proscriptions of Sarbanes-Oxley were a direct response to the pathologies making news at the time. While Congress purported to address the general subject of restoring faith in corporate governance,[8] the governance provisions of the statute largely tied back to specific sins.

- The Enron audit committee passed without objection on off-balance sheet special purpose entities created to transfer debt and improve earnings, resulting in earnings restatements and a billion dollar write-off: Section 301(a) (audit committee independence), Section 401 (disclosure of material off-balance sheet transactions) and Section 407 (disclosure whether the audit committee contains at least one financial expert).[9]
- Enron's CEO and CFO each signed the shareholder letters and MD&A in the periodic SEC reports, but claimed to have lacked knowledge of the financial reporting misstatements because they relied on subordinates: Section 302 (CEO and CFO certification of periodic financial reports, including a certification that an internal disclosure process control exists).[10]
- Enron executives cashed in stock options and sold stock during a period that employees could not transfer 401(k) money out of the Enron stock fund, and while the CEO was encouraging employees to buy stock: Section 306 (ban on insider trading during pension blackouts).[11]
- Enron, Adelphia, WorldCom, Qwest, AES, and Global Crossing all made millions of dollars in personal loans to their executive officers: Section 402 (banning companies from extending or arranging credit in the form of personal loans to directors or officers).[12]
- The Enron CFO took a personal financial interest in a number of the Enron off-balance sheet entities. The board twice waived the conflict of interest

[8] In reporting the bill back from committee, Senator Sarbanes stated: "Regrettably, in my view, unless we come to grips with this current crisis in accounting and corporate governance, we run the risk of seriously undermining our long-term world economic leadership. . . . I believe the vast majority of our business leaders and those in the accounting industry are decent, hard-working, and honorable men and women. They are, in a sense, tarnished by the burden of these scandals. But trust in markets and in the quality of investor protection, once shaken, is not easily restored, and I believe that this body must act decisively to reaffirm the standards of honesty and industry that have made the American economy the most powerful in the world. That is what this legislation does, and that is why I urge its adoption by my colleagues." 148 CONG. REC. S6330 (daily ed. July 8, 2002).

[9] DIRECTOR'S ALERT, BOARDROOMS IN A POST-ENRON WORLD 20 (May 2002) *available at* http://www.directorsalert.com) (hereinafter BOARDROOMS).

[10] *Id.* at 11.

[11] *Id.* at 18. See also S. Rep. 107-205.

[12] *Id.*

policy for the CFO: Section 406 (imposing the requirement of a code of ethics for senior financial officers and the disclosure of waivers of the code).[13]

My aim is not to critique every aspect of Sarbanes-Oxley and its regulatory progeny. This is instead a jurisprudential and philosophical reaction to some of those particular aspects of the legislation that regulate oversight of the corporation by its directors. Seen from the perspective of the predominant jurisprudential schools of thought, how does law incorporate the social or moral aims of a society? And how did Sarbanes-Oxley succeed on that score?

1. The Positivist Ironies

a. Hart's Rules and Morals

H.L.A. Hart offered the modern positivist view: the law as it exists may be, and often is, distinct from the law as it morally ought to be.[14] To Hart, law was foremost a system of rules, notwithstanding that general rules were incurably incomplete and that penumbral cases might need to be decided by reference to social aims.[15] Hart distinguished law from other means by which individuals might be bound by defining and identifying both primary and secondary rules. Primary rules are those which regulate behavior, bestow rights or impose duties and obligations. Rules differ from orders because they are normative: they set a standard for behavior that goes beyond the mere threat to impose the standard. A rule becomes law, not merely because it is accepted as binding (as might be the case in primitive communities), but because some group of secondary rules (which are accepted as binding a priori) confers validity on the rules.[16] Hart's term for these secondary rules is "rule of recognition." Hart recognized, however, that rules have "open texture:" for example, an ordinance may ban "vehicles" in a public park. While there may be little doubt the rule, at its core, bans an automobile or a diesel truck, a judge may have to decide, and Hart supposed this was based on social aims outside the law, whether an electric golf car, a bicycle, or a toy truck is covered by the rule.[17] In any event, whatever the source of the interpretation, the judge would be creating law as much as a legislature in enacting a statute.

---

[13] BOARDROOMS, *supra* note 9, at 15. *See also* S. Rep. 107-205.

[14] H.L.A. Hart, *Positivism and the Separation of Law and Morals*, 71 HARV. L. REV. 593, 606 (1958) ("Rules that confer rights, though distinct from commands, need not be moral rules or coincide with them. . . . [A]t many points, it is apparent that the social acceptance of a rule or standard of authority (even if it is motivated only by fear or superstition or rests on inertia) must be brought into the analysis and cannot itself be reduced to the two simple terms. Yet nothing in this showed the utilitarian insistence on the distinction between the existence of law and its 'merits' to be wrong.").

[15] *Id.* at 607-09.

[16] H.L.A. HART, THE CONCEPT OF LAW 89-96 (1961).

[17] Hart, *supra* note 14, at 607. In referring to the incorporation of social aims, Hart was taking note of the legal realists of the early twentieth century, who criticized the "formalist" notion that the result could be derived or discovered deductively without reference to social norms.

b. The Commands of Sarbanes-Oxley

From the positivist point of view, Sarbanes-Oxley is a rule that imposes an obligation on corporate directors not to repeat the sins of the Enron and WorldCom debacles. And public companies have duly obeyed, like drivers at stop signs in empty intersections at three a.m., often out of compliance for compliance's sake, and not for salutary benefit that should result from compliance. Consider the following responses to the positive law of Sarbanes-Oxley:

- The prohibition on the extension or arranging of credit by a company in the form of a personal loan to an officer or director (which took immediate effect on July 30, 2002) caused a flurry of questions, analysis, concern and legal memoranda around heretofore uncontroversial employee benefits like travel advances, incidental personal use of company credit cards, personal use of company cars, relocation payments subject to reimbursement, stay and retention bonuses subject to reimbursement, indemnification advances, deferred compensation, tax indemnity payment to overseas-based officers, relocation bridge loans, cashless stock option exercises, and 401(k) plan loans.[18]
- Proxy statements for 2004 annual meetings contained myriad and often indistinguishable corporate codes of conduct and ethical standards for senior financial officers.[19]
- CEOs and CFOs (to their knowledge) re-certify financial statements under Sections 3022[20] and 906,[21] despite the fact that the latter statute, carrying criminal penalties of up to $1,000,000 and ten years imprisonment, makes no provision for any immaterial failure of full compliance with all of the 10-K and 10-Q rules.

It is a fair observation that these rules were obeyed because, and only because, they were duly authorized under the jurisprudential rule of recognition.

To the extent there were "open textures"—like whether the personal loan ban covered a cashless stock option exercise—very few had anything to do with the aim of promoting better governance. Fewer still will ever be litigated. And, as discussed in the next section, the bare nature of the commands, responding to specific sins, left the door wide open for reinterpretation by the SEC. The new commands arose out of the SEC staff's own assessment of social aims, whether or not it corresponded with that of Congress.[22]

---

[18] *See* Memorandum from 25 major law firms (October 15, 2002) (on file with the author).

[19] The 2004 proxy statements of the companies sampled *infra* at note 34 provide examples of the references to senior financial officer codes of ethics.

[20] 15 U.S.C. § 7241 (2003).

[21] 18 U.S.C. § 1350 (2003).

[22] The core of the positivist-naturalist debate can be seen in the question whether the "principles" behind the SEC's reinterpretation of certain provisions were part of the law, as Dworkin would contend,

2. *The Naturalist Ironies*

a. The Naturalism of Fuller and Dworkin

The great naturalists of the 20th century were Lon Fuller and Ronald Dworkin. Each resisted the positivist thesis that law is divorced from morality—arguing that a putative law can only be law when infused with some semblance of moral content. Hence, principles that surround the rules and give them context are "law."[23]

Dworkin focused primarily on understanding how judges made law. He distinguished rules (e.g., "you will have a member of the audit committee who is independent of management and is an expert in generally accepted accounting principles") from "principles" or norms (e.g., generalized statements like "the board's obligation is to maximize long-term shareholder value" or "a director has a duty of loyalty to the corporation") and from "policies," i.e., standards for a societal goal to be reached in some aspect of the community (e.g. "we need to restore investor trust in the governance of publicly-held corporations").[24] To Dworkin, the policies and principles relied on by the judge, as much as the rules, were part of the law.

b. ACFEs and the Confused Legislation of Rules

From the standpoint of the naturalists, Sarbanes-Oxley bears out Professor Dworkin's distinction among rules, principles, and policies, but with an ironic reversal. Sarbanes-Oxley contains rules that clearly have dictated particular behaviors, and a legislative history that reflects moral outrage and the direction for a policy, but, at least as to governance, very few Dworkinian principles. It is hardly rare for legislation to arise out of policies embodying community standards or social norms, but invariably the legislation states principles or principle-like rules and permits judges to wrestle with

---

or merely the backdrop to a morality-neutral command, as Hart would contend. *See infra* note 26. The layering-on of principles (and possible inconsistencies) between legislative and administrative intent certainly give traction to Hart's contention that the law is no more than the statutes and regulations. In theory, there may be principles or policies that are as much a part of the law as the statute and regulations themselves, but the difficulty in reconciling the two levels of intent may make them so difficult to determine as to be useless.

Indeed, as discussed at note 75, *infra*, it is that very conflict that led Kant, despite his belief in a transcendental basis for deciding issues of right and wrong, to accept the dictates of positive law. Jeremy Waldron, *Kant's Legal Positivism*, 109 HARV. L. REV. 1535, 1546 (1996) ("The premise of Kant's account is that, in the absence of legal authority, we must expect that individuals will disagree about right and justice and that this disagreement will lead to violent conflict. The task of the legislator is to put an end to this conflict by replacing individual judgments with the authoritative determinations of positive law.") The irony is that if a statement of positive law is the only way to express a community norm, the legislature needs to beware of too much specificity in what it asks for: it may get exactly what it wants, and no more.

[23] Lon L. Fuller, *Positivism and Fidelity to Law—A Reply to Professor Hart*, 71 HARV. L. REV. 630 (1958).

[24] Ronald M. Dworkin, *The Model of Rules*, 35 U. CHICAGO L. REV. 14, 22-23 (1967).

the application to specific facts.[25] Where the issue is not whether law incorporates community notions of morality; indeed, the legislative history suggests the sponsors and supporters of Sarbanes-Oxley had the highest moral aims. Rather the issue is whether a legislature, without setting forth a general policy or principle, can be effective in creating rules that in fact guide parties to the desired social or moral outcome.

I will focus on one particular provision where, instead of stating a policy or principle, Congress tried to capture its concern in a rule: the requirement that the company disclose whether it has at least one audit committee financial expert ("ACFE") on the audit committee.[26]

Section 407 of Sarbanes-Oxley required the SEC to issue rules that would require public companies "to disclose whether or not, and if not, the reasons therefor, the audit committee of that issuer is comprised of at least one member who is a financial expert, as such term is defined by the Commission." Congress required the SEC, in defining "financial expert" to consider:

> [W]hether a person has, through education and experience as a public accountant or auditor or principal financial officer, comptroller, or principal accounting officer of an issuer, or from a position involving the performance of similar functions—
> (1) an understanding of generally accepted accounting principles;
> (2) experience in—
> (A) the preparation or auditing of financial statements of generally comparable issuers; and
> (B) the application of such principles in connection with the accounting for estimates, accruals and reserves;
> (3) experience with internal accounting controls; and
> (4) an understanding of audit committee functions.

The ACFE requirement originated in the Senate version. The Banking Committee reported it had "received testimony about the important role played by the audit committee in corporate governance. The Committee believes the effectiveness of the audit

[25] *Id.* at 28 (noting the courts construed Section 1 of the Sherman Act to modify the phrase "restraints of trade" with the word "unreasonable," allowing the provision to function logically as a rule but substantively as a principle: "a court must take into account a variety of other principles and policies in determining whether a particular restraint in particular economic circumstances is unreasonable.")

[26] This is not the only instance in which either the SEC or practitioners have attempted to convert a rule announced by Sarbanes-Oxley into a more flexible principle. For example, the SEC extended the Section 406 requirement of a code of ethics for financial officers, despite the unambiguous language of the statute to CEOs, because it was "logical" to do so. Final Rule: Disclosure Required by Sections 406 and 407 of the Sarbanes-Oxley Act of 2002, Exchange Act Release No. 33-8177, *available at* http://www.sec.gov/rules/final/33-8177.htm (Last visited Mar. 3, 2003) (hereinafter SEC Release). CEOs and CFOs routinely certify the full compliance of 10-Ks and 10-Qs under the criminal Section 906, 18 U.S.C. S1350 (2003), no doubt on advice of counsel that courts will read a rule of material compliance into the statute. *See also, supra* note 18 and accompanying text, regarding the interpretation of the ban on the extension or arranging of credit.

committee depends in part on its members' knowledge of and experience in auditing and financial matters. . . . In defining 'financial expert,' the SEC shall consider whether a person understands GAAP and financial statements, has experience auditing financial statements, has experience with internal accounting controls, and understands audit committee functions."[27]

As required by Section 407, the SEC issued final regulations defining the audit committee financial expert.[28] Despite the clearly restrictive legislative intent and prescriptive statutory language, the SEC expanded the definition of an ACFE to include someone who had experience "overseeing or assessing the performance of companies or public accountants with respect to preparation, auditing or evaluation of financial statements."[29] In its final rule release, the SEC stated:

We recognize that many people actively engaged in industries such as investment banking and venture capital investment have had significant direct and close exposure to, and experience with, financial statements and related processes. Similarly, professional financial analysts closely scrutinize financial statements on a regular basis. Indeed, all of these types of individuals often hold positions that require them to inspect financial statements with a healthy dose of skepticism.[30]

The SEC also extended ACFE status to those who had experience actively supervising someone in the positions described in the statute.[31] Without modification or interpretation, this covered every CEO who ever "supervised" a CFO. But the SEC staff, apparently not willing to attribute a "healthy skepticism" to every CEO, took a narrow view of active supervision:

> . . . . The term "active supervision" means more than the mere existence of a traditional hierarchical reporting relationship between supervisor and those being supervised. Rather, we mean that a person engaged in active supervision participates in, and contributes to, the process of addressing, albeit at a supervisory level, the same general issues regarding preparation, auditing, analysis or evaluation of financial statements as those addressed by the person or persons being supervised. We also mean that the supervisor should have experience that has contributed to the general expertise necessary to prepare, audit, analyze or evaluate financial statements that is at least comparable to the general expertise of those being supervised. A principle [sic] executive officer should not be presumed to qualify. A principal executive officer with considerable operations involvement, but

---

[27] S. Rep. 107-205.

[28] SEC Release, *supra* note 26.

[29] 17 C.F.R. § 229.401(h)(3)(iii). Section 401(h)(3)(i),17 C.F.R. § 229.401(h)(3)(i), tracked the experience requirement of the statute ("education and experience as a principal financial officer, principal accounting officer, controller, public accountant or auditor or experience in one or more positions that involve the performance of similar functions").

[30] SEC Release, *supra* note 26.

[31] 17 C.F.R. § 229.401(h)(3)(ii).

> little financial or accounting involvement, likely would not be exercising the necessary active supervision.[32]

The SEC also permitted a catch-all for "other relevant experience" but in such case required the company to disclose in the proxy what that is.[33]

It is clear that the drafters of Section 407 thought: (1) Enron's financial managers pulled the wool over the eyes of the audit committee; (2) this occurred because the audit committee lacked the technical competence to understand how Enron's managers manipulated the financial reporting; and (3) the goal of better corporate governance would be served by the inclusion of at least one GAAP/auditing technician on every public company audit committee. To test whether the statute and regulations made audit committees more technically adept, I reviewed the proxy statement audit committee disclosures for 2003 and 2004 (before and after the ACFE rule took effect) for forty-two publicly-traded companies.[34] I distinguished among designated ACFEs as follows:

- Directors who clearly had a technical grounding in GAAP present or former auditors, CPAs, or chief financial officers (GAAP Technicians);
- Directors who were only described as present or former CEOs (CEOs);[35]
- Directors who had backgrounds as investment bankers, venture capitalists or financial analysts (Financial Skeptics).

Of the 42 companies in the sample:

- All chose to designate and disclose an ACFE (despite the invitation in the regulation to disclose the reasons why a company might not have one).

---

[32] SEC Release, *supra* note 26 (emphasis added).

[33] 17 C.F.R. § 229.401(h)(3)(iv) and instructions to Item 401(h).

[34] I identified my random but unscientific sample of audit committee disclosures as every available 2003 and 2004 definitive Schedule 14A filing on EDGAR for those companies ranking 781 to 800, 881 to 900, and 981 to 1000 in the 2004 Fortune 1000 (it seemed to me these companies were likely to be more "typical" than the mega-corporations at the top end of the rankings). That yielded 42 companies, ranging in revenues from $1.7 billion down to $1.2 billion, that had filed the Schedule 14As: DST Systems, Genzyme, Chesapeake Energy, Abercrombie & Fitch, UST, LSI Logic, Pride International, Graphic Packaging, Amerus Group, Dentsply International, Cenveo, Ohio Casualty, Pacer International, Warnaco, Georgia Gulf, Dade Behring Holdings, Belo, Arch Coal, C.R. Bard, Trinity Industries, CKE Restaurants, Ivax, Banta, Building Material Holdings, Holly, Earthlink, Blyth, Select Medical, Fairchild Semiconductor, Piedmont Natural Gas, Valhi, Federal Signal, Donaldson, Joy Global, Goody's Family Clothing, Coca-Cola Bottling, Stewart & Stephenson Services, Plum Creek Timber, NBTY, GenCorp, XTO Energy and Career Education

[35] The author's anecdotal experience is that almost all present and former CEOs would say they actively supervised their CFOs, but very few, when pressed, would be able to demonstrate the required GAAP and financial statement expertise. Because the regulation does not require the board to disclose how it decided that the CEOs were active supervisors to the extent they became GAAP experts, versus being merely operational, as distinguished in the staff's explanation, I have assumed this is the basis for the designation, but I also assume that almost all were not GAAP Technicians as either Congress or the SEC intended.

- Nine companies, or 21%, took the step of adding at least one GAAP Technician as a new board member in 2003 and designating that individual as ACFE.[36]
- Sixteen companies, or 38%, already had at least one GAAP Technician as an audit committee member, and simply designated that individual as ACFE.[37] One additional company had a GAAP Technician on the committee who continued to serve but designated a CEO, also continuing to serve, as the ACFE.
- Sixteen companies, or 38%, had no GAAP Technicians on the committee in 2003, and had made no personnel changes as of the 2004 proxy. Of those companies, three designated exclusively one or more incumbent Financial Skeptics; six designated exclusively one or more incumbent CEOs; and one designated an assortment of both.[38]

Nine companies, or 21%, actually took steps to comply with the core intention of the legislation. The remainder were equally split between those companies to whom the statute was irrelevant (or, more accurately, the source of another administrative chore) because they were already compliant with the core intention, or because they did not see a need, based on their interpretation of the statute and the SEC's rules, to change what they were already doing.

By the time the original conception was expressed as a specific and prescriptive rule, reinterpreted by the SEC as a principle, expressed again in the regulation as a rule itself needing significant interpretation, and then finally applied in practice, it is no wonder audit committees were only marginally more adept technically than before the entire exercise was begun. Congress, like a micromanaging CEO, gave instructions rather than dictating a policy or principle. In the absence of a policy or principle, the SEC tried to create one and then embody it in another set of rules. And corporate boards and their legal advisors, particularly in view of the difficulty of finding audit committee members who were true GAAP technicians and the cost in time and energy of making significant changes to the board, threw their hands in the air.

Congress' moral and social aim was better governance through more intense, knowledgeable and skeptical review of financial statement manipulation. It is highly likely

---

[36] Of those companies, one appeared to be newly public in 2003 and simply appointed three GAAP Technicians as its Audit Committee

[37] Presumably on the principle that misery loves company, seven of the sixteen, or almost half, nevertheless identified either CEOs or Financial Skeptics as additional ACFEs. Two of the companies, for some reason, though apparently compliant, did not state that the apparent GAAP Technician was an ACFE.

[38] Of the remaining companies which did not change the composition of the audit committee and had no GAAP Technicians in either 2003 or 2004, two neither designated ACFEs nor explained why they had not. The remainder I had difficulty characterizing as CEOs (in the sense they would have had the possibility of supervising a CFO or controller) or Financial Skeptics (in the sense of an investment banker, venture capitalist, or financial analyst). These ACFEs included a developer/consultant, a non-CEO executive, and a strategy consultant.

that audit committees, no matter how constituted, are reviewing financial statements more intensely and more skeptically (whether or not, based on the ACFE data, they are doing it more knowledgeably).[39] It is equally likely that this more intense review is not necessarily occurring because audit committees universally consist, as Congress intended, of more GAAP Technicians.

In short, the Sarbanes-Oxley rules may be the tail of the morality dog if they work, but it is most likely the rules are more effective as bark.[40] It is certainly possible that judges called upon to resolve issues of fact or law in cases actually litigated under Sarbanes-Oxley will call upon notions of morality and social custom, and that the debate between positivists and naturalists (whether those principles are part of the "law") will continue. But Congress did no favor in legislating reform as specific rules, and the SEC did no favor in a number of its regulations. It is no surprise that the resulting interpretations of the underlying norm are scattered and inconsistent.[41]

B. The Locus of Corporate Behavior and the Role of Law

The ironies shown by both positivist and naturalist analyses of Sarbanes-Oxley still do not, however, offer a fully satisfactory explanation of the significant gap between the underlying aim of Sarbanes-Oxley and its implementation by even well-meaning and benevolent boards. I contend the disconnection demonstrates something even more

---

[39] According to a PricewaterhouseCoopers Management Barometer Survey, after the corporate scandals and the enactment of Sarbanes-Oxley, some 88% of senior executives report that directors at their companies are expected to have more input on a variety of issues, 73% say their boards will be more vocal on risk identification and risk management, 63% have made changes or improvements in the skill sets of their audit committees, 72% say their company has established a whistle-blower complaint process, as required by Sarbanes-Oxley, even though the provision is not yet in effect, and some 57% of audit committees have performed a self-assessment in the twelve months preceding March 2004. Dennis M. Nally, Chairman & Senior Partner, PricewaterhouseCoopers LLP, The New Realities: Corporate Governance, Accountability, and Confidence, Address to the General Audit Management Conference, Institute of Internal Auditors (Mar. 23, 2004), *available at* http://www.pwc.com/images/gx/eng/about/svcs/grms/DennisNallySpeech.pdf (last visited Feb. 22, 2005). In particular, compare the 63% of managers who report changes or improvements in "skill sets" of audit committees (it is unclear whether this includes changes in membership) to the 21% of companies in the author's unscientific sample who made changes to membership to add GAAP Technicians).

[40] Romano, *supra* note 7, at 162-65, considers whether the enactment of Sarbanes-Oxley constituted symbolic politics, and I take the term to be pejorative. I distinguish symbolic politics, i.e., ineffective or misdirected legislation intended to calm an angry electorate, from the moral "standard of care" that good legislation would imply.

[41] Contrast policies and principles recommended by other commentators in reaction to the Enron abuses: "The CEO [sic] is the most critical element in the entire governance process. Boards must be aware of the tone at the top and how that filters down within the ranks. Does the CEO live up to his or her own principles and foster a culture of integrity?" BOARDROOMS, *supra* note 9 at 10; "The selection, compensation and evaluation of a well-qualified and ethical CEO is the single most important function of the board. . . . The CEO should be a person of integrity who takes responsibility for the corporation adhering to the highest ethical standards." THE BUSINESS ROUNDTABLE, PRINCIPLES OF CORPORATE GOVERNANCE 2, 8 (May 2002) (hereinafter BRT Principles).

fundamental about the relationship of law, morality, and self-interest. Even the legal naturalists' attempt to redeem law by infusing it with the moral content of principles is protective of the discipline of law, but fails to account for the true regulators of conduct, which may well be neither legal rules nor legal principles. Judges will apply principles only in the most pathological cases. In each litigated case, a court will derive or modify the norm from, and apply a rule to, a particularly pathological set of facts. That circumstance is wholly removed from the real world of director and management conduct. The life of better governance will be in boardrooms and management suites. Very little will be decided in public or private litigation.

So what is the role of the law?

III. SELF-INTEREST, MORALITY AND CORPORATE GOVERNANCE

I am hardly the first to suggest there are significant non-legal norms regulating and explaining behavior, even in the context of governing corporations. From the standpoint of good policy, however, it is important to identify the right ones. If a certain pattern of behavior were best explained by social psychology, economic or legal disincentives would probably not be effective.

Of all the alternative ways to approach social norms, one of the most cogent is Eric Posner's general model of non-legal cooperation.[42] Nevertheless, I want to take issue with Professor Posner's suggestion that the model is the best (or only) way to explain why we (including corporate directors) behave well, even when there are no legal sanctions or they are unavailable as a practical matter.[43] I argue the behavior of good corporate governors is rooted in a dualistic philosophy underlying our simultaneous adherence or non-adherence to legal rules and moral standards, rather than in a model of law or economic self-interest (and whether that particular interest is rooted in preservation of wealth or reputation).

---

[42] ERIC A. POSNER, LAW AND SOCIAL NORMS (2000). *See also* Melvin A. Eisenberg, *Corporate Law and Social Norms*, 99 COLUM. L. REV. 1253, 1258-64 (1999) (summarizing various models of obligational and non-obligational social norms).

[43] I find game theory to be intuitively appealing as a model of behavior (even if its usefulness for non-mathematicians, at least, is limited beyond the lessons from simple two-person games). Posner's use of it to explain what might otherwise be seen as principled behavior has some cynical appeal, at least to anyone who has ever served on the board of a non-profit or religious institution. My objection to the thesis stems from a disagreement that "methodologically sterile" philosophical or phenomenological explanations of principled behavior are less valid than sociological or economic explanations. *Id.* at 191-92. For a critique of the Posner thesis on its own terms, *see* W. Bradley Wendel, *Mixed Signals: Rational-Choice Theories of Social Norms and the Pragmatics of Explanation*, 77 IND. L. J. 1 (2002).

But none of law, economics, or philosophy has an exclusive claim on explanations for principled behavior. *See* Sharon Begley, *Researchers Seek Roots of Morality in Biology, With Intriguing Results*, WALL STREET JOURNAL, June 11, 2004, at B1 (describing biological research into the source of the intuition that rationally indistinguishable alternatives are morally different; e.g. throwing a person off a sinking life boat to save the others is inherently evil while flipping a switch so that a runaway train kills one person rather than five is morally neutral).

A. Corporate Governance and the Economic Model of Non-Legal Principles

Posner's thesis, rooted in game theory, is that "people engage in behavioral regularities in order to show that they are desirable partners in cooperative endeavors."[44] Consider the application of the model to principled or ethical behavior in the context of Enron and Sarbanes-Oxley.

The argument is that people acting in their rational self-interest face powerful incentives to claim to be principled in the ordinary sense of the word, that is, never to cheat in the cooperative relationships to which they belong. Having claimed to be principled, people must act consistently with the demands of principle, lest they be immediately perceived as bad types. At the same time, people will cheat when the short-term gains outweigh the long-term reputational costs.[45]

Hence, Posner and I agree a director may well not be guided by the dictates of Sarbanes-Oxley, or the dictates of his legal fiduciary obligations. Posner, however, would account for principled behavior by the director's desire to preserve his reputation for the next iteration of the directorship game or some other real-world benefit. A director does the right thing without legal compulsion, because he recognizes, consciously or subconsciously, that he profits in the long-run by preserving his reputation for being principled.

It is hard to argue that there is no insight to be derived from economic self-interest and game-theory models. Of course we are motivated by self-interest and we take action in anticipation of the reactions by other players in this iteration of the game or the next. I believe, although I cannot prove, that notions of doing the right thing, regardless of economic self-interest, are a powerful extra-legal force in governing behavior.[46]

1. The Case of the Wealthy Outside Director

A wealthy director joins as an outside director on the board of a mid-sized public company (say, $2 billion in market capitalization). He or she has already made a fortune worth $100 million, and not all of it is protected from creditors. None of that wealth arose from or was attributable to the success of the company on whose board the director serves. While he believes in the competence and integrity of the management team, he also knows that it is not atypical, if there were a restatement of a prior year's

---

[44] *Id.* at 5.

[45] *Id.* at 191.

[46] This article does not fully address, and I will reserve for discussion in a future work, Judge Richard Posner's attack on any kind of jurisprudential thinking that invokes moral philosophy. For a thorough and cogent defense of philosophy in response to the law and economics movement and Posner's "pragmatism," *see* John Mikhail, Note, *Law, Science and Morality: A Review of Richard Posner's The Problematics of Moral and Legal Theory,* 54 STAN. L. REV. 1057 (2002). Martha Nussbaum has also challenged the movement's philosophical foundations. Martha C. Nussbaum, *Flawed Foundations: The Philosophical Critique (of a Particular Type of) Economics*, 64 U. CHICAGO L. REV. 1197 (1997). In what follows, I belatedly take up her invitation, in the context of real-world corporate governance, to "[sit] down with the arguments of eminent predecessors to see what can be learned from their years of labor." *Id.* at 1214.

earnings, for a company's stock price to drop twenty or thirty percent in hours or days. If that were to happen, there is a good chance he would be a defendant in a securities class action on behalf of the shareholders who lost $400 million to $600 million in aggregate market value. He receives $60,000 per year in director and committee fees, and a reasonable number of stock options.

In this section, I argue that, if, in the exercise of his rational self-interest, he were to compare the typical forms of insurance available to officers and directors against his theoretical exposure and what he has to lose, he would not serve. It may well be that board service for wealthy outside directors (and ethical behavior as part of that service), like golf club memberships and vacation homes, cannot be explained in all cases merely on rational economic grounds.[47]

a. The Director's Risk Profile

State corporation codes permit corporations to indemnify their officers and directors against liability for their acts or omissions on behalf of the corporation.[48] Most corporate charters or bylaws require such indemnification to the fullest extent permissible under the governing law. Officers and directors are entitled to indemnification for liability and defense costs (other than in shareholder derivative actions) if their acts were in good faith, they reasonably believed the acts to be in or not opposed to the best interest of the corporation, and as to allegedly criminal acts, they had no reason to believe the acts were unlawful.[49] In a direct action by the corporation or a shareholder derivative action (the form of action in which a shareholder would assert a breach of fiduciary duty to the corporation), the officer or director would be indemnified even if the company or shareholder alleged a breach of such duty. Nevertheless, in Delaware, for example, the officer or director found to be liable would be indemnified only to the extent the court determined to be fair (i.e., officers and directors would not generally be entitled to indemnification if it were established that they violated their duties to the corporation).[50]

State corporation laws also give the corporation the power to purchase insurance on behalf of its officers and directors against liabilities arising out of their service in those capacities ("D&O insurance").[51] There is a relatively limited number of insurance carriers offering D&O insurance to publicly-traded corporations, and there is substantial

---

[47] I have no present basis, other than casual observation and informal polling of colleagues, for assessing how typical this hypothetical is, but judging from the background descriptions of the audit committee members in the forty-two companies reviewed in connection with the ACFE requirement, not to mention all the other directors profiled in those proxy statements, it seems likely to me it is not atypical.

[48] *See, e.g.*, DEL. CODE ANN. Tit. 8, § 145 (2004).

[49] *Id.*, § 145(a).

[50] *Id.*, § 145(b).

[51] *Id.*, § 145(g).

concentration in the largest carriers.[52] Coverage is usually arranged in "stacks" or "layers" of primary insurance and excess insurance. Hence, the primary coverage may, for example, have maximum limits of $25 million, the next layer is $10 million excess of the first $25 million, the next is $5 million excess of $35 million, and so on.

The terms of coverage for primary coverage are, at their core, fairly standard.[53] In most cases, the corporation's assets stand behind its obligation to indemnify the officers and directors, and the D&O insurance does nothing more than reimburse the corporation for the amounts it is required to spend to defend and indemnify the officers and directors. Most D&O policies call this "Side B" or "Coverage B" or "Indemnifiable Loss."[54] Under this coverage, the corporation forwards indemnity and defense costs, and submits a claim to the insurer for reimbursement in excess of the deductible. Any loss in excess of the total limits of insurance is payable by the corporation.[55]

The insurance carrier will also step in when the corporation cannot or will not reimburse an individual officer or director under the corporate charter and bylaws or the applicable state corporation law. These circumstances include claims of behavior that fall outside of the bounds of the indemnification statutes, shareholder derivative actions, and cases where the corporation refuses or is unable to make good on its in-

---

[52] "Capacity" in the insurance business, at least insofar as the insured is concerned, means the amount that an insurer (usually referred to by brokers as a "market") will make available to the insured. For D&O insurance placed in 2004, the total amount of insurance capacity theoretically available to a typical insured was between $900 million and $1 billion (of which the typical insured would be trying to secure $50 million or so). Four insurance groups, ACE/CODA, AIG, Arch and XL, accounted on average for about 40% of this capacity. AON FINANCIAL SERVICES GROUP, INC., INSURANCE MARKET OVERVIEW MATERIALS (2004) (on file with the author) (hereinafter *Aon Market Data*).

[53] The significant points of difference in coverage at the primary level relate to (i) the ability of the carrier to rescind the policy for fraud or misrepresentation in the application, and (ii) exclusions from coverage for fraud, criminal acts, or self-dealing. Differences in coverage are more apparent at higher layers of excess coverage, particularly as to whether the so-called Side A coverage, which protects the personal assets of individual directors and officers when corporate indemnification is not available, "drops down" if underlying carriers will not pay.

[54] AIG AMERICAN INTERNATIONAL COMPANIES, Executive Organization Liability Insurance Policy, Form 75011 (2/00) (hereinafter *AIG Policy*), at 1 (on file with the author).

[55] In the past, so-called "Side C" or "entity" coverage has been available, which protected the corporation itself when it was named as the defendant in a securities fraud claim (typically, (1) the corporation gives earnings guidance on an analyst call, then announces shortly thereafter that it has agreed with the SEC to restate earnings for a prior period, (2) the price of the corporation's stock plummets on the announcement, and (3) the inevitable series of class actions are filed within days naming the corporation as a control person as well as its officers and directors). Beginning with the 2003 renewal season, D&O policies began limiting the availability of Side C coverage. If both the corporation and individual directors and officers were named, and the corporation were solvent, the coverage would fall under Side B as to that which the corporation would be required to indemnify the directors and officers, but the corporation itself would have no coverage for its liability, if any. Insurers began offering a "pre-determined allocation" under which the insurer and corporation agree in advance, regardless of any later proofs, liability findings, or settlement, that a percentage of the loss is attributable to the corporation. This pre-determination allocation ranged from zero to fifty percent. The incentive to the corporation was a reduction in premium.

demnification obligation due to bankruptcy or financial distress. Most D&O policies call this "Side A" or "Coverage A" or "Non-Indemnifiable Loss."[56] Side A coverage is intended to protect the personal assets of officers and directors, reimburses for defense and indemnity costs, and has no deductible (i.e., it covers from the first dollar of exposure). Nevertheless, the policy has limits, and any loss payable in excess of the insurance limits is the responsibility of the individual officer or director.

b. The Limits of D&O Insurance

For rational officers and directors, the only meaningful coverage is Side A. If the corporation has assets to stand behind the individual, and is willing to do so, there is no individual exposure. For outside directors in particular, there are three significant concerns: (1) prior bad acts or omissions on the part of company officers, not disclosed in the application for insurance, will be attributed to outside directors for purposes of rescinding the Side A coverage;[57] (2) the insurance company will assert exclusions to coverage for acts that would be covered by the policy, but for the exclusion,[58] and (3) the insurance company simply refuses to pay or, in the event of a bankruptcy, creditors

---

[56] *Id.* at 1.

[57] One of the significant current battlegrounds is whether a misrepresentation or omission in the D&O insurance application can be attributed to all insureds, whether or not they were aware of the misrepresentation or omission. The insurer's argument, in a nutshell, is that but for the application misrepresentation, it never would have issued the policy to any of those covered. Recent decisions have gone both ways. In re Health South Ins. Litig., 308 F. Supp. 2d 1253 (N.D. Ala. 2004) (holding there was severability of the application); Cutter & Buck, Inc. v. Genesis Ins. Co., 306 F. Supp. 988, *mot. to amend den.*, 2004 WL 1274736 (W.D. Wash. 2004) (holding the policy was rescinded as to all insureds). Many D&O policies contain an express "severability" clause to deal with the problem. Nevertheless, most policies are now offering only limited severability, and the knowledge of present and past CEOs and CFOs is still attributable, under the policy terms, to innocent outside directors, for purposes of rescission claims. Moreover, under the law of some states, knowledge of the misrepresentation or omission may be irrelevant to the rescission claim, making even the limited saving clause worthless. Assume that the CFO is aware that the earnings from Year 1 will need to be restated, but does not disclose it in the application that will cover all or part of Year 2. In Year 2, the company announces a restatement of Year 1 earnings. Because D&O insurance applications incorporate by reference prior 10-Ks and 10-Qs, the knowledge of that material omission could be attributed to our wealthy director. If the corporation is or might become financially distressed, our wealthy outside director would need to be concerned that the Side A coverage might be rescinded. In the hard insurance market of 2003, this was fairly common even as to Side A coverage. In the softer market of 2004, many policies provided full severability on the Side A coverage. Aon Market Data, *supra* note 52.

[58] Most D&O policies contain exclusions for certain personal conduct of officers or directors, in particular with respect to claims that those individuals took illegal profits, advantage or remuneration, or whose acts were deliberately fraudulent or criminal. These clauses may be ameliorated from the insureds' standpoint by proof requirements (e.g., the insurer may not deny coverage merely on an allegation of wrongdoing, but only on a final adjudication or specific written admission of the wrongdoing) or by express severability provisions. AIG Policy, *supra* note 54, at 8.

of the corporation argue that the proceeds of Side B coverage should be collected on behalf of the corporation and used to pay general creditor claims.[59]

The corporation may hold $25, $50, $100 million or more in traditional Side A/ Side B coverage, but our wealthy director, presumably well-advised, will know there is still a significant possibility of exposure, not remediable by insurance, to his personal assets in the case of a catastrophic corporate event, bankruptcy, or the ensuing class actions (the only thing about which he truly worries). There is "side A only" coverage available, with director-friendly rescission and exclusion provisions and which covers only outside directors (Side A) with no proceeds to the corporation merely for the reimbursement of indemnified claims (Side B), but on a limited basis and like credit, available only to those who probably do not need it (i.e., the insurance is obtainable on a showing of a strong balance sheet and practices that indicate sound financial reporting and corporate governance).[60]

---

[59] Assume a corporate crisis (like Tyco) where the old board, including our wealthy director, is swept out, and a new CEO and board come in. It is conceivable that the corporation, though capable of indemnifying our wealthy director or paying defense costs, under shareholder pressure or otherwise, might simply refuse.

Recall also that policies generally have one combined limit for Side A and Side B claims. Assume, as has occurred in several cases, the corporation goes into bankruptcy. It is highly likely that creditors will seek to have the proceeds of the policy directed to the Side B coverage, and thus available for payment of general creditor claims. In re Boston Reg'l Med. Ctr, Inc., 285 B.R. 87, 2002 Bankr. LEXIS 866 (D. Mass. 2002).

In either case, our wealthy director ought to be concerned about how much coverage, either for defense or indemnity, would be available in a major corporate crisis. The primary policies attempt to ameliorate these concerns with "order of payment" and "waiver of bankruptcy" clauses.

> Bankruptcy or insolvency of [the company] or any [individual officers or directors] shall not relieve the Insurer of its obligations hereunder. The coverage provided under this policy is intended as a matter of priority to protect the [individual officers and directors] such that, in the event of bankruptcy of the [company], the Insurer shall first pay Loss under Coverages A and C [which cover individuals for outside board service undertaken at the request of the company] prior to paying Loss under Coverage B.

AIG Policy, Endorsement 10, *supra* note 54.

Nevertheless, there is substantial question whether those clauses would hold up as against the general creditors in a dispute whether Side A or Side B should be invoked. *Boston Reg'l*, 285 B.R. at 92 n.5 ("I reject the suggestion by the nominal defendants that BRMC's indemnity coverage is ultimately a protection for the officers, directors, and trustees, not a corporate protection, and therefore cannot be interposed to defeat the right of the officers, directors, and trustees to payment. The insureds with respect to indemnity coverage are the entities who are obligated to pay claims for indemnification. The coverage enables them to pay the claims for indemnity *without depleting their own resources in doing so*. This coverage inures in part to the benefit of the entity's officers, directors, and trustees, but the coverage is the entity's, and it inures in no small part the entity itself by protecting the assets of the entity.") (emphasis in original).

[60] The "gold standard" of such excess D&O coverage has been a policy known as a "difference-in-conditions" policy issued by the Bermuda-based insurer ACE/CODA. It provides the following significant benefits:

- The company is not named as an insured; hence there would be no dispute in bankruptcy as to the entitlement of company creditors to benefit from the proceeds.

Such coverage, if obtainable, will be comforting to our wealthy director, but it is nevertheless generally only a fraction of the total insurance coverage obtained by the company. So while a mid-sized public company might carry a total of $50 to $75 million in D&O coverage, only ten to twenty percent would generally be in the form of effective excess "Side A only" coverage.[61]

2. *Financial Gain as Explanation*

The decision of our wealthy director to continue to serve, in view of the exposure to his personal net worth, simply cannot be explained purely in terms of economic self-interest. The possibility of gain from director fees or stock-based compensation simply cannot match the possibility of exposure, even if the probabilities of uninsured loss are low.[62]

- It drops down if the underlying insurer is financially unable to pay or if the loss is covered by the company's charter, bylaws, or other agreements and the company simply refuses to pay.
- It covers punitive and exemplary damages (allowed under Bermuda law).
- It pays defense costs even if there is an allegation that the individual acted in a way that would invoke the personal conduct exclusions.
- The policy may not be rescinded by the insurer based upon the restatement of, or any misstatement or error in, any financial statements of the company contained in the application.

CORPORATE OFFICERS & DIRECTORS ASSURANCE LTD., CODA PREMIERSM DIRECTORS AND OFFICERS LIABILITY EXCESS AND DIFFERENCE-IN-CONDITIONS POLICY (2003) (hereinafter CODA Policy) (on file with the author). In the "hard market" of 2003, while other D.I.C. policies were available, none contained the clarity and favorability to insureds of the CODA policy. In 2004 the market has softened, and more competitive policies are available. Aon Market Data, *supra* note 52.

It is possible, for a price, to negotiate coverage in almost any configuration, and a logical question is why not just buy "Side A only" coverage beginning at the primary layer. Although it does occur, it is not common. The premium reduction offered for this versus the traditional Side A/Side B is not substantial, and the resulting "Side A only" coverage is almost illusory because the conditions of non-indemnifiable loss are so rarely met (i.e., the corporation is insolvent or otherwise will not defend or indemnify the officer or director).

[61] For all U.S. public companies, with assets, sales and market cap between $1 billion and $5 billion, the mean amount of total D&O insurance coverage in 2003 was approximately $65 million, and the median and mode were $50 million. *Id.*

[62] *See* Lynn A. Stout, *In Praise of Procedure: An Economic and Behavioral Defense of Smith v. Van Gorkom and the Business Judgment Rule*, 96 NW. L. REV. 675, 678-80 (financial "carrots" are notably missing from the boardroom).

I suggest there is a gap between the law and directors' perception of legal liability. A group of highly regarded law professors has made both academic and popular press arguments that the actual risk of director liability, where directors exercise a modicum of care, is low. *See* Bernard Black, Brian Cheffins & Michael Klausner, *Liability Risk for Outside Directors: A Cross-Border Analysis, Working Paper*, 2004, *available at* http://ssrn.com/abstract=557070 (last visited Feb. 22, 2005). For a version of the same argument intended for the directors themselves, *see* John R. Engen, *Worried About Shareholder Suits? Fuhgedaboudit!*, CORP. BOARD MEMBER, Mar./Apr. 2004, at 20-25 (interview with Black, Cheffins & Klausner).

Nevertheless, recent publicity around directors' proposed personal contributions to civil settlements in the Enron and WorldCom matters ($13 million and $18 million, respectively, apart from D&O insurance contributions) have reignited real concerns in the corporate community over the financial risk of serving

There is at least some anecdotal evidence of this proposition. A retired public company CFO who had cashed out a substantial equity stake upon the sale of his company served on the board (and the audit committee, although not as the chairman) of a mid-sized public company. The corporation had $50 million in first dollar non-indemnifiable loss coverage under a standard Side A/SideB policy, and another $10 million excess layer under a CODA Policy. Based on publicly available information about his previous company, it was generally supposed the retired director's net worth was at least three times the total amount of coverage and eighteen to twenty times the CODA coverage. His annual fees totaled approximately $30,000 and his stock-based compensation was almost worthless. The director qualified as an ACFE, but stated that he would resign from the audit committee if he were the only designated ACFE. He insisted, despite all law to the contrary (including an express regulatory safe harbor[63]), that he was more exposed to liability if he was the only ACFE.[64] His personal counsel's proposed solution was to have him resign from all public company boards, and the company's general counsel suggested the real issue was whether the director should serve at all, much less on the audit committee (i.e., the expressed concern about ACFE status was not rational). Nevertheless, the director continued to serve both on the board and the audit committee, largely because of his loyalty to the company.[65]

---

on a board. Gretchen Morgenson, *10 Ex-Directors from WorldCom to Pay Millions*, N.Y. TIMES, Jan. 6, 2005, at A1; Kurt Eichenwald, *Ex-Directors of Enron to Chip In on Settlement*, N.Y. TIMES, Jan. 8, 2005, at C1; *see also* Memorandum from Peter A. Atkins, Skadden, Arps, Slate, Meagher & Flom LLP, *WorldCom/ Enron Settlements—Implications for Directors* (Jan. 2005) (on file with the author) ("The likely impact will be that demands for personal contributions from director defendants as a condition to the settlement of securities class actions will become more frequent in the cases where the adequacy of the directors' oversight is at issue—including in circumstances far less dramatic than WorldCom or Enron.")

It may well be, at least insofar as it relates to the rationality of service on a public company board, the perception is the reality. As the Skadden memorandum notes, "In assessing the impact of the WorldCom and Enron proposed settlements, as a threshold matter directors should understand what this development is not about. It is not about the 'law'—these proposed settlements do not make or change any law applicable to director conduct." *Id.* To draw in this instance on game theory, studies in the utility function support the idea that a wealthy director's continued service on a board, where he perceives his net worth is at risk, is not economically rational. People do not always make their decisions based on a current assessment of the risk/benefit but rather on how their situations arose or were described. "People who are winners often want to avoid risk—witness the winning poker player who wants to go home." MORTON D. DAVIS, GAME THEORY: A NON-TECHNICAL INTRODUCTION (1983), *citing* Daniel Kahneman & Amos Tversky, *The Psychology of Preferences*, SCIENTIFIC AMERICAN 160-73 (Jan. 1982).

[63] 17 C.F.R. § 229.401(h)(4)(ii) ("The designation or identification of a person as an audit committee financial expert pursuant to this Item 401 does not impose on such person any duties, obligations or liability that are greater than the duties, obligations and liability imposed on such person as a member of the audit committee and board of directors in the absence of such designation or identification").

[64] This may explain instances of the designation of multiple ACFEs in addition to GAAP Technicians on other audit committees. *See supra* notes 34-38 and accompanying text.

[65] Interviews and telephone interviews with a public company director and outside counsel (names withheld but on file with the author, Feb. 15, 2004 and shortly thereafter).

If service by a wealthy director itself is not economically rational, then it is little stretch to conclude the decision-making that occurs during service will not necessarily be dictated by the economic self-interest of the director.

3. Preservation of Reputation as Explanation

It is impossible to refute the philosophical basis of the Posner model of the economic basis for principles—particularly the notion that people, including wealthy directors, will cheat as an economic matter, and are deterred only by rational calculation of the long-term harm to their reputations—any more than the Enlightenment rationalists and empiricists could "prove" the superiority of their epistemologies, or Hart or Fuller could "prove" the superiority of their conflicting explanations of the nature of law. One must step back from the model and decide whether it is a philosophy that comports with one's observation of the workings of the world. Hence, I take issue with Posner's very premise, rather than the cogency of his explanation.

This has already been the subject of debate among economists. Posner anticipates my objection in his answer to Amartya K. Sen, who argued, as do I, that people are motivated by real principle, and not just economic self-interest disguised as principle.[66] Sen, the 1998 Nobel Laureate in economics, took issue with the prevailing rational theory of preference, arguing that economic theory failed sufficiently to account for the behavior he termed "commitment."

One way of defining commitment is in terms of a person choosing an act that he believes will yield a lower level of personal welfare to him than an alternative that is also available to him. Notice that the comparison is between anticipated welfare levels, and therefore this definition of commitment excludes acts that go against self-interest resulting purely from a failure to foresee consequences.[67]

Sen argued that commitment "drives a wedge between personal choice and personal welfare, and much of traditional economic theory relies on identity of the two."[68] Sen notes the exercise of commitment may well be limited in the selection of private goods (he excepts the occasional exotic acts such as "the boycotting of South African avocados or the eschewing of Spanish holidays"), but that it is more likely to operate in questions about the use of public goods—those which more than one of us may use.[69] Service, and decision-making, on a corporate board invite the same model of commitment as the use of public goods. Directors are already faced with the allocation of resources and profits as among various constituencies—shareholders, employees, management and

---

[66] Amartya K. Sen, *Rational Fools: A Critique of the Behavioral Foundations of Economic Theory*, 6 PHIL. AND PUB. AFF. 317 (1977) (a transcript of the Herbert Spencer Lecture, delivered at Oxford University in Oct., 1976).

[67] *Id.* at 327.

[68] *Id.* at 329.

[69] *Id.* at 330.

the board itself. There can be little doubt Sen would have questioned the application to a corporate board of an economic model based solely on rational self-interest.

Posner responded, as one economist to another, highlighting not truth but problems of econometrics:

> The problem with Sen's argument . . . is that simply assuming that people operate out of principle and rational calculation gives one less methodological purchase than the ordinary rational choice assumptions do, without, as far as I can tell, compensating for this loss by producing a methodological gain.[70]

In short, maybe Sen is right, but how would he ever prove it?[71]

I wish to take up the argument where Sen left off, warning "against viewing behavior in terms of the traditional dichotomy between egoism [rational self-interest] and universalized moral systems such as utilitarianism. Groups intermediate between oneself and all, such as class and community, provide the focus of many actions involving commitment."[72] Posner is not the first social philosopher to object to irresolvable dichotomies as satisfactory answers. An answer, if not a rebuttal, is that there is longstanding philosophic precedent for accepting irresolvable dichotomies or antinomies (contradictions or inconsistencies between two apparently reasonable principles or laws, or between conclusions drawn from them[73]) as answers, and as I contend in the next section, that is an equally plausible way to understand why we operate simultaneously under moral principles, on one hand, and either law or economic interest, on the other.[74]

---

[70] Posner, *supra* note 42, at 192.

[71] In a reply to Martha Nussbaum's critique, *supra* note 46, Cass Sunstein argues for a reconciliation of economists and philosophers, focusing on the ability of economic analysis to assess the efficacy of the positive or prescriptive aspects of law. He defines the "prescriptive" work of economics as something less than full-fledged normative assessment of what the law should be. "Economists are . . . helpful in giving accounts of how law comes into being and in showing the best way to achieve specified ends. At the more normative [i.e., prescriptive] level, they are most helpful in showing that if some X is the goal, some instrument Y will or will not achieve it." Cass R. Sunstein, *On Philosophy and Economics*, 19 QUINNIPIAC L. REV. 333, 334 (2000) (bracketed explanation is mine).

As I noted at the outset of the paper, the positive law of Sarbanes-Oxley assumes some function of X—its governance provisions—that is intended to produce an outcome Y. I do not doubt if we can agree on a measurable surrogate for Y, economic analysis is useful in assessing the efficacy of X. Indeed, my argument in the first half of this paper, based on my small sample, suggests that if Y was more technical GAAP competence on audit committees, the statute did nothing other than impose additional cost on 38% of the companies (which were already compliant), and get ignored (with the help of the SEC) by another 38%. What I am suggesting in the second half of the paper is that the law is not the sole model for what drives directors, and neither is economics, whether in the form of financial or reputation gain—and that policy focused as such is likely to have a limited impact.

[72] *Id.* at 344 (bracketed explanation is mine).

[73] WEBSTER'S NEW WORLD DICTIONARY OF AM. ENGLISH, 3d Coll. Ed. (1988).

[74] As we will see in the next section, Posner simply assumes away the philosophic point of Kant's metaphysics of morals. We are physical beings subject to the natural world of cause-and-effect, of hunger

B. A Moral Theory of Good Governance

1. A Philosophical Approach to Moral Behavior

Having taken issue with law or economic self-interest as sufficient models for the regulation of corporate governance, I argue instead that the common thread of the obligation we perceive, whether as a practice of acceptance or an enforceable sanction under a system of law, springs more often from the strictures of the heart than economic interest or legal compulsion.[75] The positivists and naturalists at least acknowledge that morality (versus self-interest) plays a role in judicial decision-making, even if they do not agree whether morality is a necessary element of the law.[76] The critical connection

---

and desire, of greed and fear, and the same time free and autonomous moral agents with the power to will an end, whether or not it is in our self-interest. As one writer describes it:

> Of all [intentional] actions the question can be asked: Why do that? This question asks not for a cause or explanation, but for a reason. Suppose someone asks me why I struck an old man in the street. The answer 'Because electrical impulses from my brain precipitated muscular contractions, and this resulted in my hand making contact with his head' would be absurd and impertinent, however accurate as a causal explanation. The answer 'Because he annoyed me' may be inadequate in that it gives no good reason, but it is certainly not absurd. Reasons are designed to justify action, and not primarily to explain it. They refer to the grounds of an action, the premises from which an agent may conclude what to do.

Roger Scruton, *Kant, in* GERMAN PHILOSOPHERS 69-70 (1982). Posner assumes all questions need be answered with causal explanations. I am contending that people are capable of acting for reasons, and those are the premises to which we must refer in reforming corporate governance. *See also* Nussbaum, *supra* note 46, at 1202-03 ("One corollary of the recognition of qualitatively distinct ends is the recognition of contingent moral dilemmas, conflicts in which one cannot satisfy all the distinct claims that legitimately demand recognition. . . . It seems reasonable to think that the recognition of such contingent conflicts is both an important part of daily life, influencing behavior in ways we think are significant, and also an important part of a normative account of social rationality.").

[75] I am subject to the well-earned accusation that what follows in the text regarding Kant is oversimplified and unsubtle. The categorical imperative was Kant's way of establishing there was a basis in reason for a universal "ought principle" underlying any moral action; in the words of Jeremy Waldron, that the action was removed from any individual's "material interest or the exigencies of survival." Waldron, *supra* note 22, at 1546-48. Waldron explains the extrapolation from the philosophy of individual moral choice to legal or political philosophy: in the real world, where there are opposing views of duty, but the community needs a single standard, only a statement of positive law will suffice. "When one thinks about justice, one must recognize that others are thinking about justice and that one's confidence in the objective quality of one's own conclusions is matched by other's confidence in the objective quality of theirs." *Id.* at 1566. I am less concerned about Kant's insight into how and why we create positive law than I am his insights into how we might operate simultaneously recognizing the dictates of the community's positive law and our individual notions of the moral law. In this, I have taken particular inspiration from the work of, and discussion with, Susan Neiman. *See* SUSAN NEIMAN, EVIL IN MODERN THOUGHT: AN ALTERNATIVE HISTORY OF PHILOSOPHY (2002).

[76] Indeed, Hart alludes to, but does not expressly reference, the categorical imperative, in distinguishing what Kant would call the moral law—that imperative which may be derived from the application of practical reason—from the binding and governmental rules that jurisprudence scholars call "law." Hart compares derivations of moral "oughts," whether from ends we take *a priori* and transcending reason, or as the result of values imposed by the empirical world in which we live, but contends under any moral standard, it is possible for a law to be itself reprehensible and still a law. Hart, *supra* note 14, at 624-26.

between Sarbanes-Oxley and good governance is not its awkward and ineffective attempt to translate principles into rules, but the bully-pulpit it provides for the moral law, as Kant would have used the term.

When we try to explain how law impacts the vast majority of transactions in which the law only loosely binds the parties and is rarely enforced, and not believing that economics or self-interest rule all action, we are still hard-pressed to understand the debate between legal positivists and naturalists. The positivists are correct in observing that law may only be expressed in rules (particularly secondary rules that inform the authority of the primary rules); the naturalists are correct in observing that notions of morality and other community norms may influence the legislative or judicial pronouncements of a rule. But each is concerned only with the impact of morality on the pathological situations where law regulates, treating all other transactions with as little regard as "primitive communities hav[ing] only primary rules, [which] are binding entirely because of practices of acceptance."[77]

There is no more compelling statement of the philosophic basis for non-binding practices of acceptance than Kant's statement of the categorical imperative:

> I do not, therefore, need any far-reaching penetration to discern what I have to do in order that my will may be morally good. Inexperienced in the course of the world, incapable of being prepared for all of its contingencies, I only ask myself: Canst thou also will that thy maxim should be a universal law? If not, then it must be rejected, and that not because of a disadvantage accruing from it to myself or even to others, but because it cannot enter as a principle into a possible universal legislation, and reason extorts from me immediate respect for such legislation. I do not yet indeed discern on what this respect is based (this the philosopher may inquire), but at least I understand this, that it is an estimation of the worth which far outweighs all worth of what is recommended by inclination [by "inclination" Kant means self-interest in any tangible or intangible way], and that the necessity of acting from pure respect for the practical law [by practical law, Kant means the moral law derived from practical reason] is what constitutes duty, to which every other motive must give place, because it is the condition of a will being good in itself, and the worth of such a will is above everything.[78]

As an example of the categorical imperative, Kant asks whether if in distress, I may make a promise without intending to keep it. It may be prudent to lie to extricate

---

[77] Dworkin, *supra* note 24, at 21.

[78] IMMANUEL KANT, FUNDAMENTAL PRINCIPLES OF THE METAPHYSICS OF MORALS (Thomas K. Abbott, trans., 1785), in BASIC WRITINGS OF KANT (Allen W. Wood, ed., 2001), 161 (bracketed explanations are mine). In particular, the reference to practical law invokes Kant's basic metaphysical distinction: in practical matters, reason is capable of letting us decide what we ought to do—it makes no claims as to truth or falsity. As to the assessment of truth, reason that takes us beyond experience or possible experience is "pure." It seeks unconditioned knowledge of the world—to view the world from a point of view other than the observer.

myself from the distress. It may be equally prudent not to lie because I can foresee the long-run consequence of lying will be worse than the present distress. But even a prudent act based on the fear of consequences is not moral. A moral act is one whose principle we would wish to be observed by anyone in a similar circumstance. I would will truth-telling as a universal law not because of its advantage to me, but because if I were to will lying as the law, I would destroy the value of promise-making.[79]

In the transactional world, more often than might be thought in the academic world, parties take advantage of legal principles, yet often do not take full advantage of legal rights, and their behavior is not fully a matter of risk-benefit analysis or the prediction of outcomes under well-understood legal principles.[80] Our sense of the Golden Rule (a subset of Kant's categorical imperative) not only provides a moral basis for avoiding false promises, but keeps us, in many cases, from requiring full victory, even when we have a basis for it.[81]

2. *The Antinomy of Law and Morality*

That tension between positive law rights and duties, on one hand, versus that which we feel morally inclined nevertheless to do, on the other hand, is an antimony of which law and morality are the contradictory prongs.[82] We simultaneously recognize and

[79] *Id.* at 160-61. For a modern and deliberately non-academic take on a similar process for making moral judgments, see STEPHEN L. CARTER, INTEGRITY (HarperPerennial, 1997). Though his short reference to this passage from Kant misses the deeper point, *id.* at 33-34, Professor Carter's message to those who are neither saints nor evildoers is essentially that proscribed by Kant. Integrity means being controlled by a sense of duty, discerning what that duty is, acting on what one has discerned, even at personal cost, and saying openly that one is doing so. *Id.* at 7-9.

[80] "The courts and legislatures have attempted to do what corporations have often been reluctant to do on their own—establish corporate souls by defining corporate values. . . . I believe the essence of the solution lies in believing that a corporation does have a soul and that one of the primary responsibilities of management is to bring the external actions of the corporation—its operating self—into harmony with its soul—its inner self, its values, its ethics—so that the corporation can achieve wholeness. Leaders must face the ultimate responsibility of articulating the values that breathe a soul into the corporation and define it for everyone to understand." B. Kenneth West, Chairman and Chief Executive Officer, Harris Bankcorp, Inc., *Remarks to the Center for Ethics and Corporate Policy* (Oct. 1987) (on file with the author).

[81] *See* Stout, *supra* note 62, at 687-92 (the social institution of the board of directors is built on the expectation of director altruism; the focus on procedure under *Van Gorkom* encourages altruistic behavior by reducing its cost); *see also* Lisa Bernstein, *Opting Out of the Legal System: Extra-contractual Relations in the Diamond Industry*, 21 J. LEGAL STUD. 115 (1992), which analyzes commitment and dispute resolution in terms of, among other things, game theory for a repetitive game. What, to me, is even more intriguing is her discussion of the role of Jewish law, ethics, and custom, which she never fully reconciles with the economic theory.

[82] The debate over the relationship between law and morality generally is bounded by the reference of law to morality—either it does not (positivism, determinacy) or it does (naturalism, coherence). I am suggesting here a more general antinomy of law and morality in the individual circumstance that accounts for both—we simultaneously operate under systems of determinate law and moral imperative (even in the same transaction) because both are necessary but neither is sufficient. Reference to antinomies in law and political theory are not new. *See, e.g.*, William A. Edmundson, *The Antinomy of Coherence and Determinacy*, 82 IOWA L. REV. 1 (1996); ROBERTO UNGER, KNOWLEDGE AND POLITICS 91(1975) ("A system of laws or

commit to positive legalisms (whether comprised of rules or principles or both) and to the rejection of those legalisms in favor of practices of acceptance where there is a perceived gap between the moral law and the positive law. Thus, it is not enough to reconcile positive law with the infusion of morality or principles so as to distinguish us from primitive communities. I suggest instead that standards of behavior operate all the time, sometimes consistently with and sometimes in derogation of that which the theorists recognize as law, and those standards may well have authority, even in the most developed communities, solely as a result of practices of acceptance. This is what explains corporations' resistance to, and willingness to bend, to and beyond the breaking point, the literal strictures of Sarbanes-Oxley, for example, in the designation of ACFEs.

But positive law may well be a far more subtle influence on conduct than realized.[83] A primary regulator of behavior even in complex legal environments, like governance, will not be law at all, but practices of acceptance based on some form of Kant's categorical imperative. In that case, the importance of law is neither in the adoption of rules nor the judicial application of norms, but in the pronouncement of a duty. Perhaps the most significant aspect of Sarbanes-Oxley, after all, is the "bark:" the community's directive to each moral person that he or she consider the principle of his or her actions, and whether he or she would be willing, in Kant's formulation, to make that principle a universal law of nature.[84]

3. *Policy Implications*

a. Regulation

Lawmakers should reconsider the underlying assumption that behavior is wholly explicable by legal or economic models. Legal theorists accept that we are more modern (i.e., less primitive) when we move beyond rules that are binding merely because they are accepted by tribal or community custom to rules that are binding because they are part of a system conferring authority. The jurisprudence is consistent with more general assumptions about the directionality of modernization.[85] One of the great deceivers

---

rules (legal justice) can neither dispense with a consideration of values in the process of adjudication, nor be made consistent with such a consideration. Moreover, judgments about how to further general values in particular rules (substantive justice) can neither do without rules, nor be made compatible with them.") I am, however, focusing on the microcosm of individual action, not the macrocosm of political theory.

[83] *But cf.* Rex R. Perschbacher & Debra Lyn Bassett, *The End of Law*, 84 BOSTON U. L. REV. 1 (2004) (the "privatization" of law—i.e., the increasing trends to non-judicial dispute resolution, judicial discretion—is destroying the "certain role of legal norms in the process of law").

[84] Here, I suppose, whether because of the time in which I live, the context of this analysis, or merely that I am more optimistic, I am less concerned than Kant about the need for positive law as the only way to avoid violence, and more willing to let opposing views contend, so long as there are core policies or principles that are, if not universal, then almost so. I contrast this, for example, with the field of international law, in which there is a real possibility of violence if a positive law does not prevail.

[85] Ferdinand Tönnies, the German sociologist and colleague of Max Weber, published the seminal *Gemeinschaft und Gesellschaft* (Community and Society) in 1887. "Tönnies developed the concepts of

arising from the pace of technological change and access to information is that we have changed—the dialectic proceeds apace. I suggest that below the veneer of our modern structures, there is little new under the sun.[86] Hence, if our behaviors are not wholly regulated by law, nor wholly predictable by game theory, incentives and disincentive based on law and economics may well miss the intended mark.

I propose a return to a more circumspect role for the law. Let federal securities law regulate what it regulates well: the disclosure to investors of that information we deem useful to them in deciding whether to buy or sell public market securities. Let judges decide state law issues of fiduciary principles either as positivists or naturalists, but in either case as the agents responsible for case-by-case application of policies and principles.

Finally, if the law is to operate at all in the vast majority of non-litigated and non-pathological circumstances, let it operate as a general endorsement of our common understanding of the universal duties of company managers and directors. There are aspects of governance reform (largely not included in the prescriptions of Sarbanes-Oxley) that directors would agree are good, as evidenced (at least anecdotally) by the enthusiasm with which they have been embraced in the business community. These include the adoption of clear charters and governance procedures, the designation of lead independent directors and the institution of regular independent director executive sessions, the adoption of board nomination and retention criteria, and board and committee performance self-evaluations.[87] The self-regulatory organizations under the SEC's

---

Gemeinschaft and *Gesellschaft* by elaborate analyses of their empirical prototypes: kinship, neighborhood, town and spiritual community are prototypes of the former; contractual relationships, collectives based on common interests, and special purpose associations are prototypes of the latter. . . . He saw the transition from a predominantly *Gemeinschaft*-like social order to a predominantly *Gesellschaft*-like social order primarily as a consequence of increasing commercialization together with the rise of modern state and the progress of science." Rudolf Heberle, *Tönnies, Ferdinand*, INTERNATIONAL ENCYCLOPEDIA OF THE SOCIAL SCIENCES, VOL. 16 (David Sills, ed.) 98-102 (1968). For a brief summary of the different sociological approaches to distinguishing the traditional and modern, *see* ALEX INKELES & DAVID H. SMITH, BECOMING MODERN 15-35 (1974).

[86] The most cursory review of the sociological models belies the strict dichotomy of primitive and modern. According to Tönnies, "[e]mpirically pure *Gemeinschaft* is impossible, because all *Gemeinschaften* have rational aspects; likewise, pure *Gesellschaft* is impossible, because man's social conduct can never be entirely determined by intellect and reason. Any concrete social entity, therefore, is only more or less Gemeinschaft-like or more or less *Gesellschaft*-like." Heberle, *supra* note 84, at 100.

Philosophy provides a different insight, as well, to this perception of the inexorable passage from primitive or traditional to modern. Hegel rejected Kant's dualism between is and ought, as well as his insistence that the gap between the empirical (the real) and the rational (the transcendental) was permanent: "The gap is not metaphysical but a product of history. Kant's misery was self-imposed, for the dualism he located in the structure of reality could be overcome." Neiman, *supra* note 74, at 87. It is hard to deny that we are more modern: ". . . . the fact that we can barely stand to read descriptions of things we would have brought our children to watch a few centuries earlier marks an advance in human consciousness that seems hard to reverse." *Id.* at 99. We are more modern, but the dualism is still meaningful.

[87] The Business Roundtable is an association of CEOs of large corporations. In May 2002, while news of the scandals was breaking and Congress was considering legislation, the Roundtable published

jurisdiction (NYSE and NASDAQ) were adopting these measures before the Enron debacle—and there is no reason not to continue to endorse reforms that create more transparent, more responsive, more organized, and more thoughtful governance.[88]

b. Training Lawyers

There is also a policy implication for the training of corporate lawyers. The lawyer's instinct to win the argument, and to be right, are ingrained in our culture and our law. This is no surprise, philosophically speaking. Kant's fundamental critique of pure reason was that it was incapable of establishing a priori truth when it went beyond experience or possible experience. Put another way, our reason wants to take us to a place where there is no "methodological purchase" (to use Eric Posner's term) because it seeks a conclusion that is final and unconditioned—the First Cause, the Immovable Mover.[89] That the conclusion cannot be proved does not make it true or false; it is beyond the world of experience and hence not provable. Our culture and law are embedded with polarities—setting stretch goals but also meeting our commitments, Republicans and Democrats, the rational basis test and strict scrutiny, winning and losing, regard for life and a woman's right to choose—that leave us uncomfortable when they cannot be resolved. Our reason wants a final reconciliation of polarities—for example, does the law incorporate morality or not?—when the answer, however unsatisfactory it may be, is we must simply live with the polarity. And finally, the serenity of acceptance of

---

a set of principles "to assist corporate management and boards of directors in their individual efforts to implement best practices of corporate governance, and also to serve as guideposts for the public dialogue on evolving governance standards." BRT Principles, *supra* note 41, at vi. The twenty-eight pages of the BRT Principles are, unlike Sarbanes-Oxley or its regulatory progeny, largely a statement of policies and principles, organized around subjects like the roles of the board, the CEO and management, board composition and leadership, committee organization, board operations, evaluation of board and management, and relationships with stockholders, employees, communities and government. BRT Principles, *passim. See also* John F. Olson & Michael T. Adams, *Composing a Balanced and Effective Board to Meet New Governance Mandates*, 59 BUS. LAW. 421, 448-51 (2004) (ten ground rules for selecting a board that can balance shareholder interests and competing constituencies, the business and strategies of the corporation, and the more intense regulatory scrutiny).

[88] Romano, *supra* note 7 at 167-73, proposes the SEC consider establishing the governance requirements under Sarbanes-Oxley as defaults, from which companies could opt out. That strikes me as helpful, although the number of governance requirements under Sarbanes-Oxley pale in comparison to those imposed by the SROs without an opt-out alternative. NEW YORK STOCK EXCHANGE, LISTED COMPANY MANUAL, § 303A (2003); NASDAQ MARKETPLACE RULES (2004), *available at* http://www.nasdaq.com/about/RecentRuleChanges.stm (last visited Feb. 22, 2005).

[89] This is particularly evident in positivism, which seeks to identify the principle that makes a law a law. If a secondary rule must validate a primary rule, what validates the secondary rule? And how does one keep from falling into an infinite regress? Compare the "basic norm" of Hans Kelsen (an "ought-statement" not itself a positive legal norm, basic to the authority of law, but not anywhere posited) to Hart's rules of recognition (those rules—a constitution, the divine right of kings, for example—accepted by society as the basis for authority). MARK TEBBIT, PHILOSOPHY OF LAW: AN INTRODUCTION 39-44 (2002).

the permanence of the dichotomy versus the instinct to resolve the problem is itself an irresolvable polarity.

This is fine for philosophers, but how does it impact anything going on in the real world? I will not add to the criticisms of training of lawyers by the case method, because I do not think it should be abandoned, or the adversarial system, which is certainly better than violence or trial by ordeal. F. Scott Fitzgerald said "the test of a first-rate intelligence is the ability to hold two opposed ideas in the head at the same time, and still retain the ability to function."[90] I am suggesting that corporate lawyers need to be moral leaders as well, which may mean applying a standard other than law, but not to the abandonment of law, and sometimes in the same transaction or even the same meeting. This means accepting simultaneously applicable, and perhaps contradictory, standards, despite the demand of reason that it not be so.

When we hold directors' colleges, like those at Duke or Stanford, we do not teach just the technicalities of directorship. We teach the theory and practice of more transparent, more responsive, more organized, and more thoughtful governance. Primary and continuing education of corporate lawyers needs to focus not just on, for example, the limitation of liability, but on counseling that appeals to sources other than the law. It is fine to know the business judgment rule, or the indemnification statute, or the *Basic Inc. v. Levinson*[91] test of materiality. It is necessary for lawyers to know, and thus necessary to teach them, the "front page of the *Wall Street Journal*" test as well.[92]

IV. A PHILOSOPHICAL CODA

With regard to morality, Kant's contribution is the antinomy of freedom—we operate as autonomous individuals with the freedom to act or not act, while at the same time we are physical beings subject to the natural world of cause and effect. As a leading Kant scholar has recently observed, it is dualism that makes Kant's philosophy so compelling more than two hundred years after its publication:

> Kant offered a metaphysic of permanent rupture. The gap between nature and freedom, is and ought, condition all human existence. . . . Integrity requires affirming the dissonance and conflict at the heart of experience. It means recognizing we are never, metaphysically, at home in the world. This affirmation requires us with the mixture of longing and outrage that few

[90] *Available at* http://www.quotationspage.com/quote/90.html (last visited Mar. 3, 2005).

[91] 485 U.S. 224 (1988).

[92] I recall watching a trial training video featuring Irving Younger years ago. After teaching the technique of throwing the opposing lawyer off-balance with the little-used "motion to dismiss on the opening statement," Younger paused and said something like, "now whether that's the right thing to do, and whether that's the kind of person you want to be, is up to you." This was advice for the sublimated warfare that is litigation.

> will want to bear. Kant never lets us forget either the extent of our limits or the legitimacy of our wish to transcend them.[93]

In this article, I have used the attempt of Sarbanes-Oxley to regulate governance to question the effectiveness of legal or economic theory, both of which are models of the world of self-interest and consequences, to explain and solve the problems they confront. More basically, I am questioning whether either can be fully understood, as a philosophy that explains our actions, as an "either-or." I suggest the truth about the role of law in regulating our conduct lies somewhere in a dualism our jurisprudence has yet to acknowledge.

---

[93] NEIMAN, *supra* note 75, at 80.

Of Bad Apples and Bad Trees: Considering Fault-Based Liability for the Complicit Corporation[*]

Geraldine Szott Moohr[**]

Corporate crime is not new. For over 100 years, individual officers and employees of business firms and occasionally firms themselves have been charged and convicted of crimes. Nonetheless, corporate crime entered the public consciousness in a new way after Enron, and unfolding corporate and business scandals have kept it there. Another new element is that business entities, executives, and employees are now caught in the cross hairs of recently emerging trends that make it easier to convict.[1] Adding to the pressure, those injured by recent corporate malfeasance face significant hurdles in pursuing civil remedies[2] and they, along with regulators, legislators, and executive branch officials, have turned to the criminal system for redress.

In response to corporate malfeasance, federal authorities sought to restore investor confidence, largely by using criminal laws to go after the "bad apples."[3] Congress wove

[*] Originally published at 44 AM. CRIM. L. REV. 1343 (2007). Reprinted by permission.

[**] Alumnae Law Center Professor of Law, University of Houston Law Center, J.D., American University. I am grateful to Darren Bush, Joan Krause, Ken Rosen, Joe Sanders, and Rich Saver for their conversation and comments about this topic. I also thank the conference participants, as well as Roger Sherman, Mon Yin Lung, and student research assistants, Megan Kemp and Andrew Trexler, for their valuable and timely help.

[1] The federal criminal code now provides broad statutes that are readily applied to conduct once confined to civil suits. *See, e.g.*, 18U.S.C. §§ 1343, 1346 (2007) (criminal statute for mail fraud). The code also provides multiple iterations of offenses that expose actors to layered charges based on a single course of conduct. *See, e.g.*, United States v. Stewart, 433 F.3d 273 (2d Cir. 2006) (upholding conviction for false statements, obstruction, and defendant Bacanovic's perjury). Corporate defendants, whether individuals or corporate bodies, now face a well-developed, sophisticated sentencing scheme. *See* U.S. SENTENCING GUIDELINES MANUAL ch. 8 (2005).

[2] *See* Christine Hurt, *The Undercivilization of Corporate Law*, U. OF Il. LAW & ECON. RES. PAPER NO. LE07-005 (2007), http://ssm.com/abstract=965871 (discussing why civil remedies may be more appropriate than criminal prosecutions for corporate misconduct); Geraldine Szott Moohr, *An Enron Lesson: The Modest Role of Criminal Law in Preventing Corporate Crime*, 55 FLA. L. REV. 937, 969-71 (2003) [hereinafter Moohr, *An Enron Lesson*].

[3] *See* DEPARTMENT OF JUSTICE, FACT SHEET: CORPORATE FRAUD TASK FORCE (August 9, 2006) http://www.usdoj.gov/opa/pr/2005/August/05_opa_434.htm (citing restoring confidence to the marketplace

heightened penalties and new crimes into the regulatory reforms of the Sarbanes-Oxley Act,[4] and the executive branch instituted an aggressive enforcement strategy.[5] As a result, hundreds of officers and employees of well-known, generally respected business firms have been charged and convicted.[6] Many of those individuals, executives, and employees were bad apples who had acted for personal monetary gain.[7] These cases illustrate the classic conundrum of corporate law that the corporation, which can act only through human agents, can fall victim to those agents. But some corporations were also implicated in criminal conduct, indicating the presence of bad trees. Between 2003 and 2006, federal prosecutors found sufficient criminal evidence to indict thirty-one "bad trees," although none was prosecuted.[8] Such enforcement efforts against corporations and the prosecution of Arthur Andersen have given new urgency to the long-standing debate about punishing corporate entities. These cases indicate that the prosecutorial focus might profitably include not only the "bad apples" but also the "bad trees."

This essay does not revisit the question of *whether* to hold corporations liable for the crimes of their agents, but addresses when and how it is appropriate to do so. I suggest that when a corporation encourages or induces criminal conduct, the firm should be held criminally liable. How might corporations be held criminally liable? Although

---

as one of the Bush Administration's Corporate Fraud Task Force's main goals) [hereinafter FACT SHEET]; President's Remarks on Signing the Sarbanes-Oxley Act of 2002, 2 PUB. PAPERS 1319 (July 30, 2002) ("This law says to every dishonest corporate leader: you will be exposed and punished; the era of low standards and false profits is over; no boardroom in America is above or beyond the law."). Following the savings and loan scandals of the 1980s, President George H.W. Bush similarly pursued the bad apple strategy. *See* Mary Kay Ramirez, *The Science Fiction of Corporate Criminal Liability: Containing the Machine Through the Corporate Death Penalty*, 47 ARIZ. L. REV. 933, 953 n.115 (2005) ("We will not rest until the cheats and chiselers and the charlatans spend a large chunk of their lives behind the bars of a federal prison." (quoting President George H.W. Bush)).

[4] *See* Sarbanes-Oxley Act of 2002, Pub. L. No. 107-204, 116 Stat. 745 (2002); Moohr, *An Enron Lesson*, *supra* note 2, at 940-51 (reviewing criminal provisions of the Sarbanes-Oxley Act).

[5] *See generally* Kathleen F. Brickey, *Enron's Legacy*, 8 BUFF. CRIM. L. REV. 221 (2004) (summarizing Department of Justice response to the corporate fraud crisis, which included task forces, real-time enforcement, and reliance on cooperating witnesses).

[6] *See* Kathleen F. Brickey, *Major Corporate Fraud Prosecutions, March 2002-December 2005* (unpublished manuscript on file with author) (listing fifty-two firms that had major corporate fraud prosecutions filed against them between 2002 and 2005). These prosecutions involve crimes that require proof of culpability, most usually based on some type of fraud. *See generally id.*

[7] *See, e.g.*, David Lieberman & Michel McCarthy, *Adelphia Founder, Son Are Convicted*, USA TODAY, July 9, 2004, at B1 (reporting prosecutors' allegations John and Timothy Rigas defrauded shareholders of $3.2 billion); Floyd Norris, *Tyco to Pay $3 Billion in Settlement*, N.Y. TIMES, May 16, 2007, at C1 (stating that the Tyco case became synonymous with corporate excess because CEO Kozlowski used corporate funds to support a lavish lifestyle). More mundane examples of employees acting for personal monetary gain include embezzlement by employees and commercial bribery.

[8] *See* Leonard Orland, *The Transformation of Corporate Criminal Law*, 1 BROOK. J. CORP., FIN. & COM. L. 45, 57 (2006) (finding federal prosecutors agreed to defer or not to prosecute thirty-one firms between 2003 and 2006, when heightened enforcement began). Business firms faced indictment for securities fraud, mail and wire fraud, and tax fraud, as well as for obstruction and false statements. *Id.* at 52 n.41.

the much critiqued doctrine of respondeat superior could be used, this essay explores the mechanism of accomplice liability, a long-standing doctrine of criminal law. The analysis is developed in three parts.

Part I briefly traces the current enforcement effort to show how it has focused largely on individual bad apples. It goes without saying that agents who commit an offense should be held responsible and face punishment. But a review of the forces exerted on executives and employees in the corporate setting reveals that the story is not so straightforward. Bad trees produce bad apples. Characteristics of a complicit corporate tree are identified through a recent Fifth Circuit case, *United States v. Brown*.[9] The facts of *Brown* illustrate how executives and employees can be encouraged, even induced, to engage in unlawful conduct by firm policies and executive directives.

Part II considers how basic principles and elements of accomplice liability apply to corporate firms. Applying the standards of accomplice liability and the traditional offense of aiding and abetting, a firm is complicit in a crime when its policies and directives encourage, induce, or otherwise aid the commission of a crime by an executive or employee.

The final discussion in Part III evaluates fault-based liability of corporate bodies, assessing the benefits of using accomplice liability and identifying issues that might constrain its use. That discussion indicates that the interests of fairness, deterrence, and the problems associated with respondeat superior criminal liability support using accomplice liability doctrine to hold a firm criminally liable for fault-based conduct that encourages corporate crime.

This proposal may satisfy no one. Those who advocate criminal penalties for corporations will note that this proposal limits the number of possible corporate defendants. Those who advocate against criminal penalties for corporations will note that it provides a firm doctrinal basis with which to evaluate blame and assign responsibility. Even so this paper may begin a long-overdue discussion of alternate ways of dealing with deviant corporations.

I. THE CURRENT ENFORCEMENT EFFORT—A SEARCH FOR BAD APPLES

As of May 2004, the current enforcement effort had resulted in over 1000 convictions, almost all of them individuals.[10] Defendants included chief executives, chief financial officers, and those who founded and led their companies. Although some escaped with light penalties because of plea bargains and cooperation agreements, other executives and employees received unprecedented penalties for non-violent first-offenses. In one case, prosecutors recommended an eighty-five-year sentence for a chief financial officer

---

[9] 459 F.3d 509 (5th Cir. 2006).

[10] From the inception of the Corporate Task Force in 2002 to May 31, 2004, prosecutors have secured over 1000 corporate fraud convictions, including convictions of over 100 CEOs and presidents in 600 filed cases, more than thirty CFOs and 100 vice-presidents, and charged more than 1300 defendants. *See* FACT SHEET, *supra* note 3.

who had not disclosed fraudulent conduct that occurred under another executive.[11] Others were sentenced to serve what amounted to life sentences.[12] Yet by definition a corporate crime "takes two," the individual agent who commits the crime and the corporate entity.

In contrast to the recent past, even when the putative target of an investigation is a firm, prosecutors now seem more interested in individuals.[13] Between 2003 and 2006, thirty-one firms avoided prosecution, and in slightly over half of those cases individuals were indicted.[14] A former prosecutor put it bluntly: firms now help convict their ex-employees.[15] Under Department of Justice policy, firms can avoid prosecution by cooperating with investigators, which means turning over documents and results of in-house investigations that inevitably implicate those who worked on the matter under investigation. In response to significant criticism, the policy has recently been adjusted.[16] It remains to be seen whether the tacit understanding that a firm can avoid indictment

---

[11] *See* United States v. Adelson, 441 F. Supp. 2d 506, 507 (S.D.N.Y. 2006).

[12] Bernie Ebbers of WorldCom received a sentence of twenty-five years, Jeffrey Skilling of Enron received twenty-four years, John Rigas of Adelphia and Stuart Wolff, of Homestore.com, Inc. received fifteen years, and Sanjay Kumar of Computer Associates received twelve years. *See* United States v. Ebbers, 458 F.3d 110, 129-130 (2006) (upholding the reasonableness of Ebbers' twenty-five-year sentence); Peter Henning, *White Collar Crime Sentences after Booker: Was the Sentencing of Bernie Ebbers Too Harsh?,* 37 McGEORGE L. REV. 757, 762 (2006); Alexi Barrionuevo, *Skilling Sentenced to 24 Years,* N.Y. TIMES, Oct. 24, 2006 at C1; *Ex-Chief Gets 15 Years,* N.Y. TIMES, Oct. 13, 2006 at C9; Michael J. de la Merced, *Ex-Leader of Computer Associates Gets 12-year Sentence and Fine,* N.Y. Titans, Nov. 3, 2006 at C3.

[13] *Compare* Julie Rose O'Sullivan, *Professional Discipline for Law Firms? A Response to Professor Schneyer's Proposal,* 16 GEO. J. LEGAL Brims 1, 19-20 (2002) (discussing how employees may be more likely to escape indictment than firms) *with* Orland, *supra* note 8, at 45 (stating that the routine disposal of corporate misconduct through deferred or no prosecution agreements constitute a "sea change" in the way the federal government responds to serious corporate misconduct).

[14] *See* Orland, *supra* note 8, at 86-87 (illustrating that, since 2003, individuals at eighteen firms were indicted).

[15] *See* Larry Ribstein, *A Former Prosecutor Shares His Secrets,* IDEOBLOG, April 21, 2006, http://busmovie.typepad.com/ideoblog/2006/04/a_fonner_prosec.html (quoting former prosecutor David Anders).

[16] DOJ policy, based on the Thompson Memorandum, practically required firms to waive work-product and attorney-client privilege. The policy was vigorously criticized by courts, commentators, and Congress. *See* United States v. Stein, 435 F. Supp. 2d 330 (S.D.N.Y. 2006); JOHN HASNAS, TRAPPED: WHEN ACTING ETHICALLY IS AGAINST THE LAW 51-55 (2006); Lisa Kern Griffin, *Compelled Cooperation and the New Corporate Criminal Procedure,* 82 N.Y.U. L. REV. 311, 350-352 (2007); William S. Laufer, *Corporate Prosecution, Cooperation, and the Trading of Favors,* 87 IOWA L. REV. 643, 648 (2002) (noting trend toward "reverse whistleblowing" by corporations who identify employees and offer evidence against them in return for leniency for the, corporation). Congress considered legislation that would limit this practice. *See* Attorney Client Privileges Protection Act of 2006. S. 30 109th Cong. § 3014(b) (2006). In response, the Justice Department issued new guidelines in December, 2006. Memorandum from Paul J. McNulty, Deputy Attorney General, to Heads of Department Components and U.S. Attorneys on Principles of Federal Prosecution of Business Organizations, at 16 (2006), *available at* http://lawprofessors.typepad.com/whitecollarcrime_blog/files/mcnulty_memo.pdf.

and/or prosecution by fully cooperating with investigators, providing privileged material, and incriminating former executives and employees can be reversed.[17]

One reason for targeting individuals rather than firms is the view that corporate crime is a simple manifestation of the principal-agent problem that is inherent in corporate governance.[18] Under this view, executives and employees invariably act in their own self-interest, and their pursuit of individual goals is the primary reason for corporate crime. The firm's obligation is thus to monitor its agents to prevent executives and employees from pursuing their own goals. The corporation is rather helpless, engaged in the Sisyphean task of controlling the conduct of its agents. When corporate crime occurs, the corporation's fault rests on an omission, a failure to control its agents who have agendas of their own.[19] This conception of corporate crime essentially excuses the corporate entity. If the offense is primarily that of a deviant employee, the corporation bears less responsibility, suffers little moral opprobrium, and is not blameworthy. Thus it is not entirely appropriate to charge the corporation with the offense.

While powerful, the assumption that corporate crime begins and ends with the ethical and moral lapses of executives and employees is not completely or always accurate.[20] Moral content can be found in the ethos of an organization,[21] and corporate policies can manifest fault and the deservedness of corporate punishment.[22] In many instances of corporate crime, the interests of the firm and the individual are aligned, and agents act, however misguidedly, for the benefit of the firm as well as for themselves. In these cases, the principal-agent conception tends to obscure the corporation's responsibility for the offense. The following discussion shows that the reality of corporate crime differs from assumptions about the ultimate responsibility of individual bad apples. Individuals commit criminal acts even when the interests of principals and agents converge, and firms can encourage unlawful conduct through executive directives and corporate policies.

---

[17] *See* Lynnley Browning, *Some Lawyers Urge More Safeguards on Rights in Corporate Fraud Cases,* N.Y. TIMES, March 8, 2007, at C3 (reporting that former prosecutors criticized the McNulty memorandum).

[18] *See* RICHARD A. POSNER, ECONOMIC ANALYSIS OF THE LAW § 12.1-12.4 (1972); Richard S. Saver, *Medical Research Oversight from the Corporate Governance Perspective: Comparing Institutional Review Boards and Corporate Boards,* 46 WM. & MARY L. REV. 619 (2004) (summarizing principal/agent problem and risks of managerial opportunism).

[19] *See* Kimberly D. Krawiec, *Organizational Misconduct: Beyond the Principal-Agent Model,* 32 FLA. ST. U. L. REV. 571, 597-98 (2005) (suggesting that current law over-relies on the principal-agent model of organizational misconduct); Jonathan R. Macey, *Agency Theory and the Criminal Liability of Organizations,* 71 B.U. L. REV. 315, 319 (1991) (stating that corporate actors engage in criminal activity to advance their careers).

[20] *See* David A. Westbrook, *Corporation Law After Enron: The Possibility of a Capitalist Reimagination,* 92 GEO. L.J. 61, 97 (2003) (concluding that the conventional morality tale, "bad people at the top stole the company while good people were not watching" does not adequately explain Enron's collapse).

[21] *See generally* Pamela H. Bucy, *Corporate Ethos: A Standard for Imposing Corporate Criminal Liability,* 75 MINN. L. REV. 1095 *passim* (1991) [hereinafter Bucy, *Corporate Ethos*].

[22] *See generally* PETER A. FRENCH, COLLECTIVE AND CORPORATE RESPONSIBILITY (1984).

A. The Bad Apples—Executives and Employees

A close look at the employment relationship and the institutional workplace setting complicates the story about bad apples. Generally speaking, the corporate context and its mandate to generate income for shareholders tend to constrain independent thinking, and institutional forces present in organizations and specific firm policies tend to influence the values and behavior of executives and employees.[23]

More specifically, personal characteristics of business executives and employees can also contribute to misconduct within a firm. Optimistic, independent, risk-taking individuals are highly valued by business firms that seek people with these traits. But even positive characteristics can mutate into an excessive self-regard when firms reward bold, decisive management styles that, ironically, lead to arrogant over-confidence that can eventually harm the firm.[24] Otherwise law-abiding executives and employees often do not perceive that they are embarking on criminal conduct because they conceive themselves as ethical actors.[25] Yet another personal trait is the human tendency to interpret rules sympathetically, which can evolve into more pernicious conduct.[26]

An institutional environment can also exert forces that undercut personal values and subvert law-abiding instincts. For instance, work that involves a team effort can lead an individual to unquestioningly support the group and never to develop a sense of personal responsibility for decisions made by the group. A law-abiding individual who sees a colleague or superior engage in unethical or wrongful conduct will experience cognitive dissonance. Although the discomfort could be alleviated by challenging the conduct, in a group setting it is more likely for the person to adjust his or her own standards to match those of the colleague and the group.[27]

---

[23] *See* LAWRENCE E. MITCHELL, CORPORATE IRRESPONSIBILITY: AMERICA'S NEWEST EXPORT 43-44 (2001) (stating that individuals working for a corporate entity are animated by the corporation which "takes away their individual capacitates for self-determination") [hereinafter MITCHELL, CORPORATE IRRESPONSIBILITY]. I have surveyed personal and institutional factors that serve as barriers to effective deterrence in a recent article. *See* Geraldine Szott Moohr, *The Prospects of Deterring Corporate Crime,* 2 J. BUS. & TECH. L. 25 (2007).

[24] *See* John C. Coffee, Jr., *Beyond the Shut-Eyed Sentry: Toward a Theoretical View of Corporate Misconduct and an Effective Legal Response,* 63 VA. L. REV. 1099, 1103, 1105-06 (1977) (identifying a "recurring management style—overzealous, action-oriented, and characterized by a remarkably low level of risk aversion"). Commentators seek to explain this tendency by applying the insights of behavioral economics. *See, e.g.,* Donald C. Langevoort, *Organized Illusions: A Behavioral Theory of Why Corporations Mislead Stock Market Investors (and Cause Other Social Harms),* 146 U. PENN. L. REV. 101, 139-40 (1997) (explaining cognitive bias of over-optimism that under-emphasizes downside risk and over-emphasizes probability of gain and individual ability); *see also* Larry E. Ribstein, *Market vs. Regulatory Responses to Corporate Fraud: A Critique of the Sarbanes-Oxley Act of 2002,* 28 J. CORP. L. 1, 19-21 (2002).

[25] *See* John M. Darley, *On the Unlikely Prospect of Reducing Crime Rates by Increasing the Severity of Prison Sentences,* 13 J.L. & POL'Y 189, 200 (2005).

[26] *See id.* at 199 (describing how bending the rules once can "establish a pattern of rule bending that makes it harder to resist bending the rules in the future").

[27] *See* Nancy Rapoport, *Enron, Titanic, and the Perfect Storm, in* ENRON: CORPORATE FIASCOS AND THEIR IMPLICATIONS 927, 942 (Nancy Rapoport & Bala G. Dharan eds., 2004) (arguing in a corporate atmosphere, there is enormous "peer pressure on the unbelieving minority to conform to the wrong-headed thinking of the majority").

Moreover, the obligation to obey the law at work may conflict with a competing social goal, the legal and ethical obligation of loyalty to one's employer. Loyalty is a strong cultural value that has long been enforced through common law and more recently through contract.[28] The strength of the obligation is illustrated by the community's ambivalence about whistle blowers, even when their value is obvious.[29] The duty of loyalty is also reflected in the obligations of fiduciaries and is the genesis of the federal crime of honest services fraud.[30] As a social value, the duty of loyalty encourages employees to develop significant bonds with their workgroup and supervisors, who have authority over pay and termination, rather than to remote shareholders. As a result, executives and employees view the group to whom they have formed loyalty bonds as the object of their obligations.[31] Thus they substitute the interests of their department or their conception of the firm for the interests of shareholders.

Finally, specific policies of a firm can influence a person's conduct and even form patterns of behaving. Salary structures and bonus policies that emphasize performance

---

[28] *See* RESTATEMENT (SECOND) OF AGENCY § 387 (1958) ("Unless otherwise agreed, an agent is subject to a duty to his principal to act solely for the benefit of the principal in all matters connected with his agency."); MARK A. ROTHSTEIN & LANCE LIEBMAN, EMPLOYMENT LAW 1005-1030 (6th ed. 2007) (presenting post employment obligations of employees based on common law duty of loyalty); Benjamin Aaron & Matthew Finkin, *The Law of Employee Loyalty in the United States,* 20 COMP. LAB. L. & POL'Y J. 321, 321 (1999) ("[T]he law of individual employment in the United States grew out of the English law of master and servant, a law of a domestic relationship in which many of the respective obligations were legally imposed."). *See also generally* Katherine V.W. Stone, *The New Psychological Contract: Implications of the Changing Workplace for Labor and Employment Law,* 48 UCLA L. REV. 519, 519 (2001) ("The U.S. system of labor and employment law that originated in the New Deal period is built upon the assumption of long-term attachment between employer and employee."); Michelle Jacobs, *Loyalty's Reward—A Felony Conviction: Recent Prosecutions of High-Status Female Offenders,* 33 FORDHAM. URB. L.J. 843 (2006).

[29] *See* Miriam A. Cherry, *Whistling in the Dark? Corporate Fraud, Whistleblowers, and the Implications of the Sarbanes-Oxley Act for Employment Law,* 79 WASH. L. REV. 1029, 1051 (2004) ("[N]ot only has the law been generally unsympathetic to whistleblowers, but so have co-workers and others outside the organization who do not support a decision to report wrongdoing."); *id.* at 1052 (noting the "extreme societal disapproval" of whistleblowers).

[30] 18 U.S.C. § 1346 (2007).

[31] It is not always clear to whom executives and employees are obligated. In the classic principal-agent view of corporate governance, shareholder interests are primary and the board's obligation is to maximize shareholder interests by monitoring management. Thus, executives and employees are also obligated to serve the interests of shareholders. *See* Alan J. Meese, *The Team Production Theory of Corporate Law: A Critical Assessment,* 43 WM. & MARY L. REV. 1629, 1631 (2002). At the other end of the spectrum, stakeholder models view the corporation's purpose as serving not only the interests of shareholders but also other constituents of the firm such as bondholders and employees. *See* Stephen M. Bainbridge, *Director Primacy: The Means and Ends of Corporate Governance,* 97 NW. U. L. REV. 547, 549 (2003). Meanwhile, other alternative theories suggest that the board, in running the corporation, acts not as the mere agent of shareholders but as a mediating hierarch among the firm's factors of production, *see* Margaret M. Blair & Lynn A. Stout, *Director Accountability and the Mediating Role of the Corporate Board* 79 WASH. U. L.Q. 403 (2001), or as a Platonic guardian serving as the nexus of contracts for the corporation; thus, although contractually obligated to maximize wealth for shareholders, the board nonetheless has considerable discretion in running the firm and deciding which interests to favor in day-to-day governance. *See* Bainbridge, *supra,* at 552-74.

goals—rather than how the goal is achieved—provide incentives to achieve company objectives with no counter-weight for consideration of ethical implications or legality.[32] Surveys indicate that unethical conduct is likely to occur when the corporation pushes for profits too aggressively.[33] Generous salaries and awards of stock options align the interests of executives and shareholders and encourage aggressive tactics designed to increase the value of the company's stock.[34] Studies also show that the behavior of superiors at a firm influences those who work for them, even far down the corporate ladder.[35]

Although none of the insights catalogued in this discussion excuses criminal conduct, they do add to our understanding of corporate crime. The symbiotic relation between the values of a firm and the values of those who work within it can lead to misguided notions about "doing the right thing."[36] That understanding about the influence of the corporate setting and a firm's specific policies challenges the bad-apple theory. Simply stated, bad apples are sometimes the fruit of bad trees.

B. The Corporate Entity as a Bad Tree

Bad apples, in fact, are not always rogue employees off on a frolic of their own. One of Enron's infamous transactions, as related in *United States v. Brown*,[37] provides a useful illustration.[38] The Fifth Circuit decision is an important contribution to the

---

[32] *See* Lynne L. Dallas, *A Preliminary Inquiry into the Responsibility of Corporations and Their Officers and Directors for Corporate Climate: The Psychology of Enron's Demise,* 35 RUTGERS L.J. 1, 34-35 (2003) (presenting research showing that compensation based on outcomes, like reaching profit goals, is inimical to ethical decision making).

[33] *See* MARSAHLL B. CLINARD, CORPORATE ETHICS AND CRIME 69-70 (1983).

[34] *See* William W. Bratton, *Enron and the Dark Side of Shareholder Value,* 76 TUL. L. REV. 1275, 1326-32 (2002) (detailing relation between corporate compensation and risk taking behavior as one cause of Enron failure); *see also* MITCHELL, CORPORATE IRRESPONSIBILITY *supra* note 23, at 4-11 (stating that the link between executive salaries and stock price creates serious risks to the firm and the community).

[35] *See* CLINARD, *supra* note 33, at 132 (discussing how research indicates that behavior and philosophy of top management was identified as the primary reason for illegal conduct of employees).

[36] *See* Coffee, *supra* note 24, at 1105-06 (characterizing employee motives to benefit the firm as "benevolent misconduct"); Kurt Eichenwald, *Even if Heads Roll, Mistrust Will Live On,* N.Y. TIMES, Oct. 6, 2002, § 3, at 1 (expressing view of Professor John Darley that "fairly decent people" should not be put under such hidden pressures).

[37] *See* United States v. Brown, 459 F.3d 509 (5th Cir. 2006) (vacating convictions of four Merrill Lynch employees for conspiracy to commit wire fraud and two substantive wire fraud counts). *See also* KURT EICHENWALD, CONSPIRACY OF FOOLS 292-96 (2005) (discussing the transaction).

[38] Similar conditions existed at other firms, engendering similar behavior. *See* Alex Berenson, *CA Says its Founder Aided Fraud,* N.Y. TIMES, Apr. 14, 2007, at C1 (reporting on corporate culture at Computer Associates); Floyd Norris & Diana B. Henriques, *3 Admit Guilt in Falsifying CUC's Books,* N.Y. TIMES, June 15, 2000, at C1 (explaining that fraud at Cendant was a result of "a culture that had been developing over many years" that was ingrained in employees by superiors); *see also* BARBARA LEY TOFLER & JENNIFER REINGOLD, FINAL ACCOUNTING: AMBITION, GREED AND THE FALL OF ARTHUR ANDERSEN (2003); Leslie Griffin, *Whistleblowing in the Business World,* in CORPORATE FIASCOS AND THEIR IMPLICATIONS 209, 218 (Nancy Rapoport & Bala G. Dharan, eds., 2004) (recounting similar situation at WorldCom).

debate about honest services fraud and for that reason merits attention.[39] It is presented here, however, to illustrate the role played by a corporate entity in the unlawful acts of its agents.

The appellants in *Brown* were Merrill Lynch employees[40] who had worked with Enron executives to execute the sale to Merrill Lynch of three power-generating barges that were moored off the coast of Nigeria.[41] The transaction was not, however, a bona fide sale; instead, Enron had successfully parked an unproductive asset. When Enron posted the transaction as a sale, rather than the loan it was, it inflated its annual earnings by twelve million dollars, enabling the firm to meet the earnings goal that it had forecast for the year.[42] The government charged that the Merrill defendants conspired to cause Enron employees to breach their duty to provide honest services to Enron; the breach occurred when the Enron employees did not disclose the full truth about the transaction.[43] The court held that the alleged scheme fell outside the scope of honest services fraud because the Enron employees had not deprived the firm of their honest services.[44] Indeed, the Enron employees had behaved exactly as the company wished.[45]

---

[39] The decision joins the long litany of federal court decisions that have struggled with honest services fraud. *See, e.g.,* United States v. Rybicki, 354 F.3d 124 (2d Cir. 2003) (en banc); United States v. Brumley, 116 F.3d 728 (5th Cir. 1997) (en banc). The *Brown* decision has already had ramifications on convictions within the Fifth Circuit. *See* United States v. Howard, 471 F. Supp. 2d 772 (S.D. Tex. 2007) (relying on reasoning of Brown to vacate conviction of Kevin Howard, former Chief Financial Officer of Enron Broadband Services). Jeffrey Skilling relied on *Brown* to argue against incarceration pending his appeal. *See* United States v. Skilling, Cr. No. H-04-025-02, 2006 WL 3030721 (S.D. Tex. Oct. 23, 2006) (denying motion for bond).

[40] The four Merrill employees who appealed had been tried with two Enron employees. Sheila Kahnek, the Senior Director in Enron's APACHI energy division was acquitted and Daniel Boyle, Enron Vice-President of Global Finance, was convicted and did not appeal. *Brown,* 459 F.3d at 517.

[41] *Id.* at 514.

[42] Recording the transaction as a sale inflated earnings because Enron had not really divested itself of the barges; it had promised that it would buy the barges back from Merrill, which it did. Merrill made $ 775,000 on its investment, a fifteen percent return on the $ 7 million it paid for the barges and a $250,000 advisory fee. The defendants were also charged with violating the securities laws, 15 U.S.C. § 78m(b)(2), (b)(5) and 78ff, and 17 C.F.R. § 240.13b2-1. *Id.* at 516.

[43] It is worth noting the attenuated nature of the charges. The Merrill defendants did not owe Enron or its shareholders a duty to provide honest services, so they could not be charged directly with honest services fraud. *Id.* at 534-35 (DeMoss, J., concurring in part and dissenting in part) (registering concern about coupling conspiracy with honest services fraud).

[44] *Id.* at 522. Because the jury had returned a general verdict that did not distinguish between property fraud and honest services fraud, the court vacated the conviction. *Id.* at 523. Thus the court did not address the government's second argument, that the firm had been defrauded of property—the loss of fees and bonuses. This question will apparently be taken up in the planned retrial of the defendants. *See* Kristen Hays, *Judge Orders Retrials in Enron Barge Case,* HOUS. CHRON., Apr. 4, 2007, at Dl (reporting intention of prosecutors to retry the Brown defendants).

[45] *See Brown,* 459 F.3d at 522 (defendants' dishonest conduct was "associated with and concomitant to the employer's immediate interest").

As the court put it, "however benighted that understanding . . . all were driven by the concern that Enron would suffer absent the scheme."[46] Although they were paid bonuses for completing the deal,[47] the Enron employees had not otherwise personally benefited; the purpose of their work on the barge transaction was to benefit Enron and not to surreptitiously enrich them.[48] The employees were not bad apples; they had performed in the interest of the firm, and their interests—in advancement and pay—were aligned with those of the firm.

It is worthwhile to consider further the *Brown* illustration. High-level officers of the firm were intimately involved in the deceptive transaction and the earnings misstatement. They planned the deal and directed managers to execute it, and the Chief Financial Officer finalized the agreement in a long conference call.[49] An imprimatur by senior executives encouraged employees to engage in the deception. Policies of the firm also contributed to the wrongful conduct.[50] In addition to generous salaries, the firm routinely awarded bonuses based on performance and contributions to corporate profits and apparently was not overly concerned with long-term effects of the deals.[51] In addition to this carrot, the firm wielded a heavy stick in its "rank and yank" evaluation system. The evaluations compared the performance of employees against one another, listing them from top to bottom; those who landed in the bottom fifteen percent were dismissed.[52] Evaluating employees so they know even colleagues who are performing

---

[46] *Id.*

[47] *Id.* (noting that increased personal bonus was "a promise of the corporation" and thus did not create a conflict of interest between the employees and the firm).

[48] The court carefully delineated its holding:

> [W]here an employer intentionally aligns the interests of the employee with a specified corporate goal, where the employee perceives his pursuit of that goal as mutually benefiting him and his employer, and where the employee's conduct is consistent with that perception of mutual interest, such conduct is beyond the reach of the honest services fraud theory of fraud as it has hitherto been applied.

United States v. Brown, 459 F.3d 509, 522 (5th Cir. 2006).

[49] *Id.* at 514-15 (relating that senior officer Jeff McMahon, Enron's then-Treasurer, initiated the transaction at Andrew Fastow's request and Vice-President Daniel Boyle worked with Merrill to complete the deal).

[50] Enron's corporate culture and its specific policies are now well documented. *See generally* BETHANY MCLEAN & PETER ELKIND, THE SMARTEST GUYS IN THE ROOM: THE AMAZING RISE AND SCANDALOUS FALL OF ENRON (2003); ROBERT BRYCE, PIPE DREAMS: GREED, EGO AND THE DEATH OF ENRON (2002); KURT EICHENWALD, CONSPIRACY OF FOOLS (2005); PETER C. FUSARO & ROSS M. MILLER, WHAT WENT WRONG AT ENRON (2002); MIMI SWARTZ & SHERRON WATKINS, POWER FAILURE: THE INSIDE STORY OF THE COLLAPSE OF ENRON (2003).

[51] *See* Tom Fowler et al., *The Fall of Enron: A Year Ago, Enron's Crumbling Foundation was Revealed to All When the Company Reported its Disastrous Third-Quarter Numbers. Its Growth-at-Any-Cost Culture Led it to Bankruptcy—and Ignominy: The Pride and the Fall,* HOUS. CHRON., Oct. 20, 2002, at A1 (noting how bonuses were based on the total value of the deal, rather than actual income the deal produced).

[52] *See* Greg Hassell, *The Fall of Enron: The Culture: Pressure Cooker Finally Exploded,* HOUS. CHRON., Dec. 9, 2001, at A1 (reporting that fellow employees judged others' performance); *see also* Moohr, *An Enron Lesson, supra* note 2, at 966 (providing commentary on this system).

well will be terminated encourages them to follow unquestioningly the directives of superiors. Finally, Enron's corporate culture was driven by an emphasis on bold, risky deals that brought high returns, but implicitly fostered behavior that skirted the line of legality.[53]

Consummation of the phantom sale of the barges, from initiating the transaction to preparing the annual financial statement, involved several Enron departments and, presumably, many employees at different levels of responsibility. Moreover, the firm embraced the deal, using it for its benefit. The transaction was apparently valuable enough that Enron paid Merrill an advisory fee in addition to the promised interest on their investment.[54]

Neither the Fifth Circuit's decision[55] nor this analysis condones or justifies the unethical conduct of individuals in devising and consummating a sham transaction that misstated earnings. In a more perfect world, one would expect mid-level managers to refuse to participate in a course of conduct they knew was deceptive. Given the dynamics of the Enron workplace, however, it is not surprising that executives and employees would engage in conduct that benefits the firm and themselves. In these circumstances, "the fact that the scapegoats may not be completely innocent does not mean they cannot be scapegoats."[56]

II. THE FIRM AS A COMPLICIT ACTOR

A firm that engages in conduct described in *Brown* does more than merely fail to counteract the natural tendencies of agents who are subject to pressures of the organizational setting. In this case, it is not difficult to identify proactive corporate conduct. Corporate policies constructed incentives that aligned the interests of executives, employees, and the firm. Officers of the firm instigated and finalized the unlawful course of conduct, and corporate policies rewarded employees for engaging in it. What implications flow from a firm's involvement in the crime of an agent? The doctrine of accomplice liability provides a reference point.

A. Accomplice Liability

The doctrine of accomplice liability and the crime of aiding and abetting rest on the moral intuition that those who participate in the commission of a crime are as blameworthy as those who commit the offense and are as deserving of punishment. Accomplice liability has an ancient origin that attests to the soundness of its grounding

53 *See* Nancy B. Rapoport, *Enron and the New Disinterestedness—The Foxes Are Guarding the Henhouse,* 13 AM. BANKR. INS. L. REV. 521, 532 (2005) (providing an example of top executives tolerating fraudulent deals).

54 *See* United States v. Brown, 459 F.3d 509, 516 (5th Cir. 2006) (noting payment of an advisory fee of $ 250,000 and a fifteen percent profit of $ 550,000).

55 *See id.* at 522 ("We do not presume that it is in a corporation's legitimate interests ever to misstate earnings—it is not.").

56 *See* Westbrook, *supra* note 20, at 92.

in moral intuitions about blame.[57] Thus, accomplice liability simply "rounds out" or completes the definitions of criminal offenses.[58] The crime of aiding and abetting applies generally to a criminal code, so all offenses include both primary actors and accomplices.[59]

Unlike conspiracy,[60] accomplice liability is not a crime in itself; rather it is a method for holding an actor responsible for a substantive offense.[61] Criminal liability of the accomplice thus is dependent on or derives from a crime committed by another person. The person who helps another individual, referred to as the primary party, commit fraud is also guilty of fraud, and is punished as if he or she had committed the target offense.[62] Holding an individual guilty for a crime actually committed by somebody else would seem to offend principles of criminal law. Note however, that liability is neither strict nor vicarious; the accused must have engaged in conduct—some act of encouragement or assistance, with a culpable state of mind—a desire that the criminal act succeed.[63]

---

[57] *See* United States v. Peoni, 100 F.2d 401, 402 (2d Cir. 1938) (noting in an opinion written by Learned Hand that the theory was used in homicides in the fourteenth century and in treason, robbery and arson in the sixteenth). Perhaps because of this long pedigree, and because the doctrine comports with intuitions of justice, its specific rationale is not well-documented. Yet, it is unlikely accomplice liability would have survived were it inconsistent with societal objectives. *See* Sanford H. Kadish, *Complicity, Cause and Blame: A Study in the Interpretation of Doctrine,* 73 CAL. L. REV. 323, 329 (1985) (arguing that "[a]ttributing blame is a pervasive human phenomenon").

[58] *See* GEORGE FLETCHER, RETHINKING CRIMINAL LAW § 8.6 (1978) (noting that every crime has built into it a penumbral orbit of liability for those who aid in committing an offense).

[59] The federal statute simply states that a person who "aids, abets, counsels, commands, induces, or procures" the commission of an offense "is a principal." *See* 18 U.S.C. § 2 (2007). The federal offense of aiding and abetting was formulated in 1901 to avoid the complexities of the common law categories of accessories. *See* F.W. Standefer v. United States, 447 U.S. 10, 15-16 (1980) (recounting historical antecedents of the aiding and abetting statute). 18 U.S.C. § 2 also applies to criminal provisions that appear in other sections of the federal code. *See* Cent. Bank of Denver, N.A. v. First Interstate Bank of Denver, N.A., 511 U.S. 164, 190 (1994) (holding that "an aider and abettor of a criminal violation of any provision of the 1934 Act, including § 10(b), violates 18 U.S.C. § 2").

[60] Accomplice liability is somewhat similar to a conspiracy that ends with successful completion of the target offense. Both crimes are concerned with the danger of group criminality and, under the *Pinkerton* rule, both rely on a rough theory of agency. *But see* FLETCHER, *supra* note 58, § 8.5.4(B) (noting the "neighboring concept" of conspiracy is "sharply distinguished" from accomplice liability).

[61] *See* United States v. Petty, 132 F.3d 373, 377 (7th Cir. 1997) ("In a sense, the essential elements of aiding and abetting serve as a substitute for the defendant's actual physical participation in the crime.").

[62] Concern has been registered about treating the accomplice and the primary party as subject to equal punishment and about holding all accomplices to the same standard, no matter how minimal their aid. *See* Adam Harris Kurland, *To "Aid, Abet, Counsel, Command, Induce, or Procure the Commission of an Offense": A Critique of Federal Aiding and Abetting Principles,* 57 S.C. L. REV. 85 (2005). That critique is of less concern, however, when the accomplice is the party that induced or led the course of conduct. *See* Joshua Dressler, *Reassessing the Theoretical Underpinnings of Accomplice Liability: New Solutions to an Old Problem,* 37 HASTINGS L. J. 91, 114 (1985) (critiquing agency idea and formulating alternate explanation based on causation).

[63] The elements of the offense are: (1) knowledge of the illegal activity that is being aided and abetted, (2) a desire to help that activity succeed, and (3) some act of helping. *See* United States v. Irwin, 149 F.3d 565, 570 (7th Cir. 1998).

As to conduct, the accomplice need not physically participate in actual commission of the crime, as long as the accomplice provided some type of aid. The common denominator of various kinds of possible aid is encouraging the primary actor.[64] Blame attaches because without such aid, the primary party might not have chosen to engage in the conduct or might have abandoned it.[65] Culpability of the accomplice is found in the intention to help—to encourage or influence or otherwise assist—the primary actor who engaged in the criminal conduct.[66] In sum, although liability of the accomplice for the target offense is dependent on another, fault and blame are justified by the accomplice's personal conduct and culpability.

B. The Corporation As an Accomplice

Corporate criminal liability on this theory has a familiar ring.[67] Like corporate law and the doctrine of respondeat superior, accomplice liability rests on a relationship between parties, between principal and agent.[68] Under the respondeat superior standard, the individual employee or executive plays the role of agent; the firm is the principal.[69] When the agent acts on behalf of the principal within the scope of his or her authority, the principal is responsible, under civil and criminal law, for those acts and their consequences. Accomplice liability is based on the same premise: the acts of one person can, in certain circumstances, redound to another person. For this purpose, the principal is the person who actually committed the crime. Thus, the corporation plays the role of the "agent" who acts for the principal, the executive or employee who engages in criminal conduct.[70] The roles of the corporation and employee/executive are the reverse of roles played in the business world and for fixing responsibility under

[64] *See* Kadish, *supra* note 57, at 345 (noting that this element requires that the secondary party is aware of the accomplice's assistance).

[65] *See id.* at 345-46 (noting also that courts have found the accomplice guilty even when the primary party was unaware of the assistance).

[66] *See id.* at 346-49 (noting the distinction between the accomplice's intent and the mens rea of the target crime).

[67] Aiding and abetting is no stranger to corporate liability. *See* Cent. Bank of Denver N.A. v. First Interstate Bank of Denver, N.A., 511 U.S. 164, 181 (1994) (holding that a private plaintiff may not maintain an aiding and abetting suit under § 10(b)). The aiding and abetting statute may be applied to criminal violations of § 10(b). *Id.* at 190. The Private Securities Litigation Reform Act restored aiding and abetting liability in SEC enforcement actions. *See* Private Securities Litigation Reform Act of 1995 § 104(0, 15 U.S.C. § 78t (2003).

[68] Professor Kadish suggests that intentional aiding and abetting is based on the notion of agreement or consent, which makes the principal liable for the acts of another person. *See* Kadish, *supra* note 57, at 355; *see also* Dressler, *supra* note 62, at 111 (critiquing agency idea and formulating alternate explanation based on causation); Robert Weisberg, *Reappraising Complicity*, 4 BUFF. CRIM. L. REV. 217, 222-31 (2000) (surveying justifications for accomplice liability).

[69] *See infra* text accompanying notes 90-94 (discussing operation of respondeat superior theory in criminal law).

[70] *Cf.* Nye & Nissen v. United States, 336 U.S. 613, 619 (1949) (presenting circumstance of an agent of the firm aiding and abetting the criminal conduct of corporation).

respondeat superior doctrine. Nevertheless, accomplice liability is consistent with an underlying characteristic of corporate crime, the involvement of two separate parties.

To paraphrase Learned Hand, the firm in *Brown* acted as an accomplice because it associated itself with the venture, participated in it as in something that it wished to bring about, and sought by that action to make it succeed.[71] Liability flows from the elements of the crime of aiding and abetting: the government must establish an actus reas, conduct that encourages the primary party to commit the offense, and a mens rea, a desire, purpose, or intention that the primary party acts.

The actus reas of accomplice liability is broad and encompasses almost any act that helps, encourages, or induces another person to commit a crime. The corporation encourages, aids, or assists in the criminal act when an executive officer, who speaks for and embodies the firm, directs a subordinate to commit the crime.[72] It is not always possible to identify a managerial agent who is authorized to speak for the firm, and a second means of acting fills that gap. As Professors Bucy and French have argued, a firm can also act through self-executing policies.[73] Corporate criminal liability may be based on its affirmative policies and on failure to adopt preventive policies after misconduct has occurred.[74] Of the seven factors Professor Bucy identified as indicating a problematic corporate ethos, two are especially useful here.[75] They may be restated as (1) corporate goals that value profits and ignore the means by which they are achieved; and (2) a reward structure that creates an incentive for criminal conduct.

The rationale for including the reward structure applies also to other corporate policies. Compensation schemes are self-executing policies that upon adoption op-

---

[71] *See* United States v. Peoni, 100 F.2d 401, 402 (2d Cir. 1938) (noting that "[a]ll the words used—even the most colorless, 'abet'—carry an implication of purposive attitude toward it").

[72] *Cf.* Model Penal Code §2.07(1)(c) (Proposed Official Draft 1962). The Model Penal Code drafters rejected the respondeat superior approach and substituted conduct by the board or high managerial agents because it is "reasonable to assume that their acts are in some substantial sense reflective of the policy of the corporate board." *See id.* § 2.07 cmt. at 339-40; *see also* Elizabeth K. Ainslie, *Indicting Corporations Revisited: Lessons of the Arthur Andersen Prosecution,* 43 AM. CRIM. L. REV. 107 (2006) (recommending that federal courts draft a jury instruction based on the Model Penal Code standard).

[73] *See* Bucy, *Corporate Ethos, supra* note 21; FRENCH, *supra* note 22.

[74] Professors Fisse and Braithwaite are associated with the view that the firm's failure to prevent crime or to adopt policies after a crime has occurred are indicators of corporate fault. *See generally* BRENT FISSE & JOHN BRAITHWAITE, CORPORATIONS CRIME AND ACCOUNTABILITY 113 (1993) (stating that corporate responsibility may be based on corporate intentionality reflected in corporate policies); Brent Fisse, *Corporate Criminal Responsibility,* 15 CRIM. L. J. 166, 173-74 (1991); Brent Fisse, *Restructuring Corporate Criminal Law: Deterrence, Retribution, Fault, and Sanctions,* 56 S. CAL. L. REV. 1141 (1983); *see also* William S. Laufer, *Corporate Bodies and Guilty Minds,* 79 EMORY L. J. 647, 665-68 (1994) (summarizing approaches to finding corporate culpability) [hereinafter Laufer, *Corporate Bodies*].

[75] *See* Bucy, *Corporate Ethos, supra,* note 21, at 1146. The remaining five indicators of a suspect corporate ethos addressed the failure of the firm to prevent individuals from committing crimes, *id.,* and are similar to those identified by Professor Fisse. *See supra* note 74. Professor Laufer has persuasively argued that a firm's failure to prevent or rectify criminal conduct fails to address criminal culpability at the time of the illegal act. *See* Laufer, *Corporate Bodies, supra,* note 74 at 669 (including corporate ethos theory in this observation).

erate without human intervention, aside from those actions necessary to apply it.[76] Other policies, such as evaluation systems, similarly apply automatically and similarly can motivate criminal conduct. It seems reasonable to consider such self-executing policies as actions of the firm, and the firm as responsible for their consequences.[77] Corporate policy regarding profit maximization, as noted earlier, also affects executives and employees, and in effect justifies and ratifies questionable acts. Again, it is not unreasonable to consider such policies as acts that encourage and abet the individual in the commission of the offense.

Accomplice liability is not premised on strict liability. The actor must have provided help or encouragement with the intention to or desire that the target offense occur. In theory, the intention element is the heightened mens rea of specific intent, that the accomplice provided aid with the purpose of facilitating the crime.[78] In practice, the standard is less rigorous, because fact finders may infer intent from the accomplice's conduct.[79] Thus, the conduct—in this case the policies of the firm—is assessed to determine if it provides indicia of intent.

In sum, a plausible argument can be made that, under the longstanding criminal doctrine of accomplice liability, corporations may be charged with substantive criminal offenses. The following discussion begins the consideration of whether there are reasons for doing so.

III. CONSIDERING FAULT-BASED LIABILITY FOR COMPLICIT CORPORATIONS

Corporate criminal liability involves two legal doctrines, corporate governance and criminal law theory, and each field presents significant barriers to imposing punishment on a corporate entity.[80] Notwithstanding the merits of that theoretical debate, controlling the behavior of powerful corporate entities seems as imperative today as it

---

[76] *See* FRENCH, *supra* note 22, at 58 (discussing corporate policies as broad, general principles rather than detailed statements of methods).

[77] *See id.* at 44 ("[W]hen a corporate act is consistent with an instantiation or implementation of established corporate policy, then it is proper to describe it as having been done for corporate reasons, as having been caused by a corporate desire coupled with a corporate belief and so, in other words, as corporate intentionality.").

[78] *See* United States v. Raper, 676 F. 2d 841 (D.C. Cir. 1982) (upholding defendant's conviction for aiding and abetting because of his intent to aid his co-defendant).

[79] *See* United States v. Irwin, 149 F. 3d 565, 571 (7th Cir. 1998). The court noted that conduct and intentionality are "intertwined," and when the natural consequence of aid is to further the crime and help it succeed, the jury is entitled to infer that the defendant intended by his assistance to further the crime. *Id.; see also Raper,* 676 F.2d at 849 (intent established if the defendant knowingly participated in the offense "in a manner that indicated he intended to make it succeed").

[80] There is a rich commentary on the issue, in addition to the articles cited in the previous footnotes. For a review of these issues, see H. Lowell Brown, *Vicarious Criminal Liability of Corporations for the Acts of their Employees and their Agents,* 41 LOY. L. REV. 279 (1995). For comprehensive treatments, see WILLIAMS S. LAUFER, CORPORATE BODIES AND GUILTY MINDS; THE FAILURE OF CORPORATE CRIMINAL LIABILITY

was in 1909 when the Supreme Court adopted respondeat superior criminal liability for corporations.[81] Despite advances in regulatory systems, the threat of punishment remains a necessary back-up to regulatory enforcement.[82] Thus, rather than revisit the debate over whether to hold corporations criminally liable, this discussion begins from where we are. A rough societal consensus appears to view criminal penalties for corporate misconduct as appropriate, evidenced by the longstanding respondeat superior doctrine and by public support for aggressive prosecution policies.[83] Yet current white collar enforcement efforts are marked by an absence of corporate prosecutions. This is somewhat surprising because corporations may be readily convicted under the doctrine of respondeat superior for offenses committed by executives and employees.

The following analysis considers an alternate method of holding corporations responsible when a crime is committed by an individual who is not a rogue agent, but who has acted in the interest of the firm as well as in his or her own interest. In that circumstance, a corporation that encourages or induces criminal conduct because it wants it to occur is complicit in the crime. The following discussion considers two justifications for fault-based corporate liability: intuitions about just desserts from criminal law theory, and deficiencies of respondeat superior liability.

A. Criminal Law Theory

The most compelling reason for punishing complicit corporations echoes the justification for punishing accomplices: an accomplice is worthy of blame. Accomplice liability, although it derives from the crime of an agent, is based on the conduct and culpability

(2006); KIP SCHLEGEL, JUST DESSERTS FOR CORPORATE CRIMINALS (1990); CELIA WELLS, CORPORATIONS AND CRIMINAL RESPONSIBILITY (2d ed. 2001).

Several other recent articles, published since Enron burst upon the scene, present valuable perspectives. *See* Patricia S. Abril & Ann Morales Olazabal, *The Locus of Corporate Scienter,* 2006 COLUM. BUS. L. REV. 81 (2006); David Hess, et al., *The 2004 Amendments to the Federal Sentencing Guidelines and Their Implicit Call for a Symbiotic Integration of Business Ethics,* 11 FORDHAM J. CORP. & FIN L. 725 (2006); Donald C. Langevoort, *Resetting the Corporate Thermostat: Lessons from the Recent Financial Scandals about Self-Deception, Deceiving Others and the Design for Internal Controls,* 93 GEO. L.J. 285 (2004).

For commentary from the utilitarian perspective of law and economics, see Daniel R. Fischel & Alan O. Sykes, *Corporate Crime,* 25 J. LEGAL STUD. 319 (1996); V.S. Khanna, *Corporate Criminal Liability: What Purpose Does it Serve?,* 109 HARV. L. REV. 1477 (1996).

For retributive approaches, see Lawrence Friedman, *In Defense of Corporate Criminal Liability,* 23 HARV. J.L. & PUB. POL'Y 833 (2000) (concluding that expressive function of criminal law justifies corporate criminal liability); Andrew Taslitz, *The Expressive Fourth Amendment: Rethinking the Good Faith Exception to the Exclusionary Rule,* 76 MISS. L.J. 483 (2006) (utilizing retributive view of corporate criminal liability in context of police departments).

[81] New York Cent. & Hudson River R.R. Co. v. United States, 212 U.S. 481, 495-96 (1909).

[82] *See* GEORGE P. FLETCHER, BASIC CONCEPTS OF CRIMINAL LAW § 11.4 (1998) (noting the pragmatic utility of using criminal sanctions to influence social behavior of corporations).

[83] As reaction to the Andersen indictment indicated, some part of the business community is undoubtedly less sanguine about the prospect of corporate liability. *See generally* Kathleen F. Brickey, *Andersen's Fall From Grace,* 81 WASH. U. L. Q. 917 (2003).

of the corporate actor.[84] The corporation acts through its policies and executive directives and is culpable because of its own intentionality regarding the commission of the offense. Properly applied, accomplice liability is congruent with criminal law theory, which premises guilt on the choice to engage in prohibited conduct.

As the discussion so far has shown, a corporate culture can encourage agents to act unlawfully. Specific firm policies, such as compensation schemes, can induce criminal behavior when they provide incentives that motivate criminal conduct. Moreover, when supervisors "encourage their subordinates to meet targets by any means necessary," they abet; when a firm "provide[s] assistance and resources, it aids."[85] An obvious way to deter firms from aiding and abetting fraud and other criminal acts of their executives and employees is to exact criminal penalties.

In addition, failing to punish a complicit actor who has induced another to act seems less than fair.[86] The harsh penalties for convicted white collar offenders, especially those who do not plead or cooperate, make the failure especially troubling. Make no mistake, aid and encouragement by the corporation does not excuse individual executives and employees; it may, however, indicate that a firm has contributed to a corporate crime. In these circumstances, just as it is fair to hold an accomplice liable, it is fair to hold the corporation criminally liable.

Key Point

When all responsible parties are not fairly charged, a sense of disquiet arises in the specific community affected by criminal acts and enforcement efforts. Sound criminal enforcement principles counsel against creating perceptions of unfairness in those who work in the corporate world. Unfairness breeds resentment and cynicism that can undercut the goal of encouraging law-abiding conduct and impede effective enforcement.[87] People are also more likely to informally enforce the law among their peers when they view the law and its enforcement as fair, an important tool in preventing future misconduct.[88] Furthermore, individuals and corporate entities who respect the criminal

---

[84] *See* Laufer, *Corporate Bodies, supra* note 74, at 665-73 (critiquing various methods of identifying genuine corporate culpability).

[85] *See* David Luban, *Contrived Ignorance,* 87 GEO. L.J. 957, 964 (1999).

[86] *See* Coffee, *supra* note 24, at 1106 (suggesting that "basic concepts of fairness argue for some limits on the degree to which corporate officials seeking to benefit (and perhaps actually benefiting) the corporation should be held liable in order to deter others").

[87] *See* PAUL H. ROBINSON & JOHN M. DARLEY, JUSTICE, LIABILITY & BLAME 157 (1995) (noting that some obey the law because they generally respect it); Gerard E. Lynch, *The Role of Criminal Law in Policing Corporate Misconduct,* 60 LAW & CONTEMP. PROBS. 23, 44-46 (1997) (noting that criminal enforcement impacts the law-abiding, rather than the criminal, community); Tom R. Tyler & John M. Darley, *Building a Law-Abiding Society: Taking Public Views About Morality and the Legitimacy of Legal Authorities Into Account When Formulating Substantive Law,* 28 HOFSTRA L. REV. 707, 708 (2000).

[88] *See* Paul H. Robinson & John M. Darley, *The Utility of Desert,* 91 NW. U. L. REV. 453, 468 (1997) (stating that when the criminal justice system is viewed as morally credible and legitimate, individuals are likely to defer to the authority of the law—even in the absence of a strong internalized norm and in marginal situations where conduct is ambiguous or of borderline criminality).

justice system are more likely to obey the law even when they do not completely share the particular societal norm about the issue.[89]

Accomplice liability also meets utilitarian goals of deterrence and prevention in a more direct way. A person who offers encouragement and incentives for another to engage in a crime makes it more likely that the harm the law seeks to avoid will occur. Encouragement given by a second party makes it less likely that the primary actor will change his or her mind and abandon the endeavor. Even-handed enforcement that includes all guilty parties provides a more just and effective deterrence mechanism.

B. Respondeat Superior Doctrine

A second set of factors that support fault-based criminal liability relate to problematic issues raised by use of the respondeat superior doctrine. The respondeat superior theory of strict and vicarious liability provides a powerful method of imposing punishment on a corporate body.[90] Under this doctrine, a corporation is guilty of the criminal act of an agent if the agent acted within the scope of his or her authority and for the benefit of the firm. Had the individual agents in *Brown* been found guilty, the firm could have been convicted. Even if prosecutors were to have used the more restrictive Model Penal Code formulation of respondeat superior, the corporation in *Brown* would face conviction.[91] Given this ready remedy, moving to a fault-based system may seem rather counter-intuitive.

Respondeat superior, however, is an infirm theory on which to base criminal punishment. Its fatal flaw is its inconsistency with a basic requirement of criminal law: the accused must engage in conduct with appropriate culpability, and these elements must concur in time.[92] This basic flaw of respondeat superior criminal liability is evidenced by current federal policies that soften its full effect. The Department of Justice considers compliance programs and other preventive actions in deciding whether to indict; and the Sentencing Guidelines consider such factors when devising punishment. Both policies take into account the efforts firms had made to ensure their executives and

---

[89] *See* TOM R. TYLER, WHY PEOPLE OBEY THE LAW 104-09 (1990) (drawing a relation between fair procedures and a respect for the law).

[90] *See* New York Cent. & Hudson River R.R. Co. v. United States, 212 U.S. 481, 495-96 (1909) (arguing that without a respondeat superior theory of liability "many offenses might go unpunished and acts be committed in violation of law"); *see also* United States v. Union Supply Co., 215 U.S. 50, 55 (1909) (stating that corporations are "as capable of a 'willful' breach of the law" as are individuals) (citation omitted).

[91] *See* MODEL PENAL CODE § 2.07 (1)(c) (Proposed Official Draft 1962)). A corporation may be convicted of the commission of an offense if the commission of the offense was authorized, requested, commanded, performed or recklessly tolerated by the board of directors or by a high managerial agent acting on behalf of the corporation within the scope of his office or employment. *Id.*

[92] *See* Laufer, *Corporate Bodies, supra* note 74, at 668-73 (critiquing other models of assigning criminal liability to corporations for failing to meet this requirement).

employees acted in accordance with the law.[93] As Professor Laufer has noted, the two policies reflect a basic antipathy toward use of respondeat superior criminal liability.[94] In practice, the policies have also shifted the risk of indictment to the executives and employees and away from the firm.

Using the doctrine of accomplice liability rather than respondeat superior increases the burden of establishing corporate guilt, making it more difficult to convict a corporation. The elements of aiding and abetting—assistance, encouragement, inducement, undertaken with a desire that the crime occur—must be proved beyond a reasonable doubt. Only those firms that had engaged in such conduct would be "eligible" for criminal treatment, thus reducing the chance of indictment.[95] A proposal that would reduce the pool of corporate defendants may cause one to wonder why fault-based criminal liability is preferable to respondeat superior liability.[96] As it turns out, several considerations support that preference.

C. A Preference for Fault-Based Corporate Criminal Liability

Accomplice liability, unlike respondeat superior, is based on fault. One reason for preferring it is that a fault-based conviction is more credible than the strict and vicarious liability of respondeat superior. Evidence must indicate that the organization encouraged and induced commission of a crime with the desire that the offense be committed. Proof of accomplice liability shows why the organization deserves punishment. This kind of conviction cannot be readily dismissed as due to the bad luck of catching a prosecutor's attention.[97] Fault-based criminal liability, which punishes the obviously

---

[93] *See* U.S. SENTENCING GUIDELINES MANUAL ch. 8; (outlining the charging guidelines for organizations). Similarly, the Model Penal Code offers an affirmative defense if a corporate officer employed due diligence to prevent the crime. *See* MODEL PENAL CODE § 2.07(5) (Proposed Official Draft 1962). Proposals for a good faith defense are in the same vein. *See generally* Ellen S. Podgor, *A New Corporate World Mandates a "Good faith" Affirmative Defense,* 44 AM. CRIM. L. REV. 1537 (2007).

[94] *See* William S. Laufer & Alan Strudler, *Corporate Intentionality, Desert, and Variants of Vicarious Liability* 37 AM. CRIM. L. REV. 1285, 1302-03 (2000) (stating that the federal charging guidelines indicate the DOJ has renunciated criminal liability under the respondeat superior doctrine) [hereinafter Laufer & Strudler, *Corporate Intentionality*].

[95] Lowering the chance of indictment could have the unintended consequence of removing the incentive to monitor and control executives and employees, now provided by respondeat superior liability. However, the Sentencing Guidelines, which reduce punishment of firms that have effective compliance programs, would continue to provide an incentive to monitor employees. U.S. SENTENCING GUIDELINES MANUAL § 8C2.5(f).

[96] Although not the purpose of the proposal, a fault-based system also reduces the power of prosecutors to leverage cooperation and plea agreements from firms. *See supra* text accompanying notes 13-17. Conversely, it may expose those corporations that are indicted to harsher collateral consequences because an indictment on this theory presupposes crime by the corporate entity, not just responsibility for the crime of an agent.

[97] *See* Brickey, *supra* note 83 at 942-45 (recounting accounting firm's reaction and public relations campaign to pressure the government not to prosecute). Many of the deferred and no-prosecution agreements

guilty, thus provides another reason for the preference; it would enhance the moral force of white collar criminal law.[98]

The clarity of the legal standard—aiding in the commission of a crime is a crime—also has the positive effect of educating the business public, an effect that is not possible under respondeat superior. As trials and appellate decisions provide examples of conduct that constitutes aiding and abetting, firms will learn what to avoid and how to adjust policies so they do not encourage or induce criminal acts. The improved clarity of the standard can bring more effective deterrence; when corporate actors know the rules and understand the conduct to be avoided, it is easier for them to avoid breaking the law.

In contrast to a particularly unfair aspect of respondeat superior liability, a fault-based system is not over-inclusive. Under the theory of strict and vicarious liability, a firm can be liable even when its policies forbade the conduct at issue, and convictions have been upheld even when the firm's benefit was dubious.[99] Firms may be liable when the crime was not tolerated or ratified by an officer, when the organization made good efforts to monitor, and when the firm had not been complicit. The patent unfairness of strict and vicarious liability is striking and can be counterproductive.[100] Fault-based liability removes this arbitrary aspect of vicarious and strict liability. In addition, a clear, transparent standard for criminal liability produces a more efficient deterrent mechanism. The threat of liability in these circumstances can cause firms to engage in cumbersome oversight protocols, or over-deterrence. When firms know what type of conduct is likely to expose them to criminal liability, wasteful efforts may be reduced.

Basing corporate criminal liability on fault-based accomplice liability does not solve all the problems associated with corporate criminal liability under respondeat superior. For instance, the respondeat superior standard is underinclusive because it requires that an identifiable agent committed a crime. Fault-based liability under accomplice liability doctrine does not address this aspect of respondeat superior because aiding and abetting, like respondeat superior, also requires the commission of an underlying offense by a human agent.[101] A more exhaustive analysis of accomplice liability and the

---

include provisions that prohibit the firm from asserting innocence by making contradictory comments about the agreement. *See* Orland, *supra* note 8, at 72, 86-87.

[98] Professor Robinson notes that using respondeat superior, which is devoid of moral force, may have the long-term effect of reducing the moral condemnation in cases against individuals. *See* PAUL H. ROBINSON, CRIMINAL LAW § 7.2 (1997) (stating that "[e]very conviction is made slightly less condemnable when a conviction is imposed without personal blame").

[99] *See e.g.,* United States v. Hilton Hotel, 467 F.2d 1000, 1004 (9th Cir. 1972) ("[A] corporation is liable for acts of its agents within the scope of their authority even when done against company orders."); United States v. Sun-Diamond Growers of Cal., 138 F.3d 961 (D.C. Cir. 1998) (affirming conviction of firm even though it was defrauded by its agent's bribery scheme).

[100] *See* Laufer & Strudler, *Corporate Intentionality, supra* note 94, at 1312 (stating that "no rational person would respect a system that is fundamentally unfair; a system that metes out undeserved punishment is unfair").

[101] *See supra* text accompanying notes 57-66 (discussing offense). Courts have addressed the problem of underinclusivity through the collective knowledge doctrine. *See* United States v. Batik of New Eng., 821 F.2d 844, 856 (1st Cir. 1987) ("Corporations compartmentalize knowledge, subdividing the elements of

crime of aiding and abetting may reveal infirmities in that doctrine that make it less suitable in the circumstances outlined here. Finally, fault-based liability also does not address another serious issue, the legitimacy of the underlying criminal offense. As in *Brown*,[102] broad and vague criminal fraud statutes can result in treating civil wrongs as crimes.[103]

In the end, the benefits of fault-based convictions will depend on the context in which they are used. For instance, in some types of crimes, such as those that threaten public health and safety, respondeat superior may be a more appropriate basis of conviction than fault-based liability.[104] Nor does this proposal impinge on the ability of enforcers to charge a firm directly.[105]

A final consideration bears remark. Failing to address the bad tree of corporate complicity and continuing to target only individual bad apples can create a false impression among the public. Trials, plea bargains, and accompanying headlines about arrested and convicted executives and employees may generate the perception that misconduct at business firms is an exceptional occurrence, committed only by deviant persons. As

---

specific duties and operations into smaller components. The aggregate of those components constitutes the corporation's knowledge of a particular operation."); United States v. T.I.M.E.-D.C., Inc., 381 F. Supp. 730, 738-39 (W.D. Va. 1962) ("[K]nowledge acquired by employees within the scope of their employment is imputed to the corporation."); *see also* Luban, *supra* note 85, at 963 (stating that collective knowledge doctrine "teeters on the brink of quack metaphysics or mystical science fiction").

102 United States v. Brown, 459 F.3d 509 (5th Cir. 2006)

103 *See* sources cited *supra* note 39 (noting recent case law); *see also* John C. Coffee, Jr., *The Metastasis of Mail Fraud: The Continuing Story of the "Evolution" of a White-Collar Crime,* 21 Am. Crim. L. Rev. 1, 3 (1983) ("[T]he reach of the statute continues to be extended further into sensitive areas not previously thought to be subject to the criminal law of fraud."); Peter J. Henning, *Maybe It Should Just Be Called Federal Fraud: The Changing Nature of the Mail Fraud Statute,* 36 B.C. L. Rev. 435 (1995); Geraldine Szott Moohr, *Mail Fraud and the Intangible Rights Doctrine: Someone to Watch Over Us,* 31 Harv. J. on Legis. 153, 156 (1994); Julie R. O'Sullivan, *The Federal Criminal Code Is a Disgrace: Obstruction Statutes as a Case Study,* 96 J. Crim. L. & Criminology 643, 660-65 (2006); Ellen S. Podgor, *Mail Fraud: Opening Letters,* 43 S.C. L. Rev. 223 (1992).

104 Public welfare offenses merit strict and vicarious liability because of the imperative to protect the public from harm in those situations in which it cannot protect itself. Usually these situations involve highly regulated industries such as food and drugs. As *malum prohibitum* crimes, they are punished lightly and do not stigmatize the entity as a deviant felon. *See* Morissette v. United States, 342 U.S. 246 (1952) (reviewing the need to protect the public from the dangers of unregulated industries and noting the light penalties of regulatory violations).

105 For instance, federal prosecutors recently announced a plea bargain with Purdue Pharma, Inc. for the felony offense of intentional fraud and misbranding drugs under which the company will pay fines of $600 million. Although three executives were charged with misdemeanors, no human agent was charged with the felony. *See* Barry Meier, *Narcotic Maker Guilty of Deceit Over Marketing,* N.Y. Times, May 11, 2007, at A1.

The case is also interesting because the United States Attorney in charge of the case indicated in an interview that the action was justified in part by the firm's "corporate culture." *See* Interview with John L. Brownlee, United States Attorney for the Western District of Virginia and Dr. Sidney Wolfe, director of health research at Public Citizen, *The NewsHour with Jim Lehrer* (Public Broadcasting System broadcast May 11, 2007) *available at* http://www.pbs.org/newshour/bb/health/jan-june07/oxycontin_05-11.html.

we now know, serious misconduct at firms is not confined to the first-wave scandals at Enron, WorldCom, and Adelphia.[106] The continuing litany of scandals indicates that causes of misconduct are more likely to be systemic and ongoing.[107] For the executive branch, with the cooperation of the judiciary, to give the impression that convicting individual executives and employees will eliminate the risk of criminal conduct borders on deception.

The egregious facts in *Brown*, which included directives from a chief financial officer and unlawful posting of the sham transaction, make it an easy case in which to charge the firm. Accomplice liability is not, however, limited to cases in which the firm engaged in an illegal act because the conduct of aiding and abetting need not be unlawful in itself. Accomplice liability could be used when corporate conduct, in the guise of policies, encourages criminal behavior. This liability is not as broad as it might appear. There is a natural limit to liability because conviction also requires proof of culpability, an intention that the crime occur.

On the practical front, implementing change to the status-quo may not be possible. Change requires courts and enforcers to maneuver around public outrage about corporate crime,[108] the comfort corporations find in deferred prosecution agreements, and the efforts of the business community to avoid criminal responsibility.[109] Nevertheless, recent developments indicate that it is time to think about a theory that bases corporate

---

[106] In the weeks before this conference convened, newspapers reported yet more criminal conduct at large firms. *See* Loren Steffy, *Haven't We Learned Anything?*, HOUS. CHRON., Feb. 9, 2007, at D1 (reporting the backdating of stock option awards); Jenny Anderson, *S.E.C. Is Looking at Stock Trading*, N.Y. TIMES, Feb. 6, 2007, at A1 (examining the investigation into advance tips to clients); Jenny Anderson & Michael J. de la Merced, *13 Accused of Trading As Insiders*, N.Y. TIMES, March 2, 2007, at C1 (outlining an insider trading scheme). For academic treatment of problems in the securities industry, see Vincent Di Lorenzo, *Does the Law Encourage Unethical Conduct in the Securities Industry?*, 11 FORDHAM J. CORP. & FIN. L. 765, 772-73 & nn.21-25 (2006) (listing unethical business practices in the securities industry).

[107] *See generally* MITCHELL, CORPORATE IRRESPONSIBILITY, *supra* note 23 (detailing the growth of American corporate criminality); *see also* Bratton, *supra* note 34, at 1283 (noting that criminal prosecutions of rogue employees deflects attention from problematic business practices); Westbrook, *supra* note 20, at 92 (noting that punishing the bad apples is "something of a distraction"); *see generally* Jill E. Fisch & Ken Rosen, *Is There a Role for Lawyers in Preventing Future Enrons?*, 48 VILL. L. REV. 1097 (2003).

[108] *See* Henry Allen, *Ken Lay's Last Evasion: To Some, CEO is Cheating Them One Last Time*, WASH. POST, July 6, 2006, at C1 (detailing public reaction to Lay's death and suggesting it shows a "frustrated craving for revenge"); Came Johnson & Brooke A. Masters, *Cook the Books, Get Life in Prison: Is Justice Served?*, WASH. POST, Sept. 25, 2006, at A1 (noting that death of convicted Enron founder Ken Lay induced profanity-laden outrage from shareholders who felt cheated because Lay escaped punishment); *see also* Fischel & Sykes, *supra* note 80, at 346 ("The sentencing guidelines, like the broader phenomenon of corporate criminal liability, cannot be reconciled with any rational policy of the criminal law or of optimal penalties.").

[109] *See e.g.*, Carrie Johnson, *Plan Unveiled to Scrap A Sarbanes-Oxley Rule*, WASH. POST, Dec. 20, 2006, at D1; Came Johnson, *Accounting for the Future*, WASH. POST, Mar. 9, 2007, at D1 (four accounting firms press for relief from regulatory oversight); Stephen Labaton, *Officials Reject More Oversight of Hedge Funds*, N.Y. TIMES, Feb. 23, 2007, at A1; Floyd Norris, *Winds Blow for Rollback of Regulation*, N.Y. TIMES, Dec. 1, 2006, at C1. A day before this conference was convened, high-level executives and government officials

criminal liability on the actual conduct and culpability of a firm and that would create a fairer, more effective, and more complete response to corporate crime.

CONCLUSION

The relationship between a collective body, such as a corporation, and the individuals who comprise it raises difficult questions about respective responsibility. The Nuremberg Charter established that individual actors should not escape responsibility for crimes committed on behalf of the state, another kind of collective body. On the other hand, shielding the corporation from responsibility for acts of its executives and employees that were encouraged by the firm is also problematic. Fairness to both the firm and individual agents requires that a corporation should neither escape criminal liability nor be held criminally responsible simply because it is a collective body.

Holding a corporation responsible for its complicit conduct in encouraging commission of an offense meets the demand of just deserts. It also is consistent with deterrence goals; if the corporation is not held responsible for its complicity in crime, unlawful conduct is likely to continue, albeit with a different set of individual actors. Further, fault-based criminal liability for complicit corporations avoids the negative aspects of respondeat superior liability, which includes unfairness to some firms. Credible and transparent convictions of corporations through fault-based liability will enhance the moral force of criminal law and respect for the criminal justice system. Given these considerations, failing to hold the corporation criminally responsible when it has aided and encouraged a criminal act is misguided.

---

met to discuss the report of a blue ribbon panel convened to consider the effect of Sarbanes-Oxley. *See* Came Johnson, *Wall Street, Washington Huddle on U.S. Markets,* Wash. Post, Mar. 14, 2007, at D1.

Extraordinary Circumstances: The Journey of a Corporate Whistleblower[*]

Cynthia Cooper[**]

THE SLIPPERY SLOPE

> Sow a thought, reap an action; sow an action, reap a habit; sow a habit, reap a character; sow a character, reap a destiny.
>
> —Scottish author Samuel Smiles

It's October, 2000 . . . . The accounting team at WorldCom has just closed the company's books for the third quarter. David Myers is shocked by the numbers. Line cost expense—what the company pays to lease telecommunications lines and to originate and terminate telephone calls, its single largest expense—is too high by hundreds of millions of dollars, driving earnings well below Wall Street expectations. Someone must have made an error. But where?

David is a Mississippi boy who's done well for himself. Tall with a slim build, he played basketball in high school and earned a degree in accounting from the University of Mississippi in Oxford. He started his career in public accounting with Ernst & Whinney (now Ernst and Young), one of the country's most prestigious firms, and then moved into industry with Lamar Life Insurance in Jackson, the state capital. Hardworking and friendly, David quickly moved forward professionally.

Things have been going well for him. He's happily married with three children, two from a previous marriage. In his early 40s, David has been able to achieve some financial security for his family. By working hard and putting in long hours, he's moved up the corporate ladder to Senior Vice President, commanding an annual salary close to a quarter of a million dollars. As the Controller, he reports directly to Scott Sullivan, the Chief Financial Officer, and has hundreds of finance employees under his charge.

---

[*] From CYNTHIA COOPER, EXTRAORDINARY CIRCUMSTANCES: THE JOURNEY OF A CORPORATE WHISTLEBLOWER.

[**] President of Cynthia Cooper Consulting, providing consulting and training services in internal audits, internal controls, governance, and ethics.

David joined WorldCom in 1995. In his first years with the company, the stock soared. By 1999, when the stock hit a record high, his stock options were worth over $15 million. David has received some $700,000 in pre-tax profit by exercising his options. He and his wife moved into a lake-front home in an upscale neighborhood, and purchased a home for his wife's parents, but David has held the remainder of his options.

Now that potential wealth seems at risk of evaporating. The highflying bull market of the 1990s is on a fast downhill slide. The Internet stock bubble that burst in March, 2000 is about to be followed by a less publicized but much larger and more devastating collapse: Telecom. The entire sector is in disarray, but many in the industry believe the problems are temporary. Still, the figures glaring back at David are far worse than expected. Are the numbers he sees an error or a train wreck in progress?

David isn't looking forward to presenting such bad news to his boss Scott Sullivan, especially since he has no idea why the numbers are so abysmal. But he knows he can't put it off. WorldCom soon has to release its quarterly earnings to the public. He walks through the halls joining the building where the accountants work with the one housing the executive suite, where Bernie and Scott have large adjacent corner offices. As he walks through the double glass doors to the suite, he sees the lighted bookcases he's seen so many times on his way in, filled with company memorabilia Bernie has collected over the years, including items marking each acquisition.

David takes a deep breath and walks into Scott's office. The glass windows taking up the entire wall behind Scott's desk provide a beautiful view of the small man-made lake, fountain, and walking trail below. But David is in no mood to admire the view. He might as well get right to it: The numbers are bad. He can't explain why. His department has checked and re-checked them. The accountants can't find any errors.

Scott isn't happy. This is unacceptable news. Surely, someone made a mistake. David is sent back to his office to go through the numbers again, or do whatever it takes to find and fix the errors. He asks several of his accountants to retrace their steps, but even the second time around, they find no mistakes. He returns to Scott with the news, but Scott still refuses to accept the numbers, insisting there's a mathematical mistake.

Management is now only days away from having to release financial results to the public. Scott and David know that if they report these results, WorldCom will not meet the earnings guidelines executives previously issued. The stock price will get hammered, and analysts will downgrade their opinions, which could send the company into a downward spiral. And WorldCom depends on its high stock price to acquire companies.

The pressure is intense and building every hour. What are we going to do, David asks Scott? Scott is at a dangerous crossroads. He rationalizes that the cost of telling the truth is too high. In any case, there must be an error, he thinks, and it'll surely correct itself the following quarter. Change the numbers, he instructs David. Reduce line-cost expense so that the company can meet earnings guidance. "While [Scott] didn't believe that this was the right and appropriate thing to do," David later recalled, he said "this is what we needed to do at the time."

Scott's instructions are stressful for David. But David has always felt loyal to his boss, so he, too, rationalizes. This will be temporary. There must be an error. Scott is sure of it. Either way, WorldCom is just going through a tough time. The industry will soon turn around.

To change the financial statements, David will have to pull several of his mid-level accountants into the plan. David and Scott are at high enough levels in the company that they don't actually make accounting entries in the system. The trusted inner circle will have to grow.

David decides to relay Scott's message to his right-hand lieutenant, an accounting director named Buford (Buddy) Yates. David trusts Buddy. They've been friends for many years, having worked together at Lamar Life. Buddy joined WorldCom in 1997. With a stocky build and gray hair, some say he can be like a bulldog—he isn't afraid to speak his mind and doesn't mince words, turning gruff at times. This time is no exception. Buddy can't believe what he's hearing. Is Scott really serious? Very much so, David tells him.

David then turns to Betty Vinson and Troy Normand, two mid-level accountants who report to Buddy and playa key role in compiling the financial results. They'll be able to analyze the details, help decide which specific accounts to adjust, and physically make changes in WorldCom's accounting system.

Like Buddy, Troy and Betty are extremely uncomfortable with Scott's request. This is beyond tweaking—to meet earnings expectations, they'd have to make adjustments in the hundreds of millions of dollars with no support and only the hope that the problem would correct itself. They're feeling upset and pressured, but there's little time to think things through—the company has to release its earnings to the public. All three are their families' primary breadwinners. Not following orders could mean losing jobs that aren't easily replaceable in Jackson, Mississippi. Begrudgingly, they decide to go along with the plan—this once.

The three split the work load. Buddy and Troy work on one side of the accounting entries, deciding which liability accounts can be reduced. Betty works on the other side, doing the same for expense accounts.

Because there are estimates in accounting, especially during acquisitions, companies sometimes overstate liabilities and expenses. This has to be corrected once the exact numbers have been determined, though some companies choose to leave them in place, creating what's known in accounting, disapprovingly, as rainy-day "cookie-jar reserves." These are the accounts that Betty, Buddy, and Troy are drawing down, but they don't have a legitimate business rationale. They're just drawing down reserves by whatever amount is necessary to meet earnings. "I just really pulled some [accounts] out of the air," Betty will recall.

Once the changes have been made, David takes Scott the adjusted financial statements. Now they're exactly what the boss wants to see, but David is worried that his accountants may jump ship. Both Betty and Troy have told him that they're contemplating resigning from the company. Buddy is also growing upset. They love their jobs and have been devoted to WorldCom, working long hours and often taking work home to continue through the night—whatever it took to get the job done. But now, it seems, they're being forced to walk away.

Scott offers a solution—the company will reduce earnings guidance going forward so that, in the future, no one will have to make bad entries. David is relieved to hear the news. He asks Scott if he would mind personally reassuring the three accountants. Hearing it from someone so senior to them may make a difference.

Scott agrees to meet with the accountants. Buddy doesn't attend, but Betty and Troy are anxious to hear what Scott has to say. When they arrive at his office, he invites them to sit in the executive seating area in front of his desk. Employees usually sit around the large conference table, but the sofa and chairs make for a homier, more intimate setting.

Scott knows all too well what's at stake, and he pours it on thick and heavy. He appeals to their loyalty. He flatters. He assures Betty and Troy that the false entries were a one-time thing, since earnings guidance will be lowered. He thanks them for their hard work and apologizes that they had to do this. In any case, he still believes that the numbers in the initial statement were simply wrong and will correct themselves come next quarter.

"This is a situation where you have an aircraft carrier out in the middle of the ocean and its planes are circling up in the air," Scott tells the two accountants, according to David's recollection, "and what you want to do, if you would, is stick with the company long enough to get the planes landed to get the situation fixed . . . . Then if you still want to leave the company, then that's fine, but let's stick with it and see if we can't change this."

Troy tells Scott that he's "scared" and doesn't want to find himself "in a position of going to jail for [Scott] or the company." Scott "said that he respected our concern," Troy would later recall, but that "we weren't being asked to do anything that he believed was wrong . . . but that if it later was found to be wrong, that he would be the person going to jail, not me."

As Troy and Betty discuss the meeting on the way back to their offices, Troy wonders if maybe he's making too much out of this. After all, Scott's very smart and highly regarded. He must know what he's doing. Still, in the end, he and Betty decide that they don't feel any more comfortable. Not wanting to be pulled any further into Scott's scheme, they think about resigning.

On October 26, 2000, the same day that WorldCom issues a press release announcing the third quarter financial results, Troy writes a formal letter of resignation addressed to Buddy and David: "Due to the circumstances surrounding the third quarter 2000 close, I feel I have no choice but to resign. I have chosen not to participate in the recommended course of action and have also decided not to take any future risk. "

Betty composes a similar letter. "Dear Buddy, this letter is to serve as notice of my resignation from WorldCom effective today. The actions proposed regarding quarter close entries has necessitated this action. If needed, I can assist with any transition issues that may arise. My income situation is such that I request we . . . work out an equitable arrangement regarding some sort of salary and benefits continuation until I can obtain other employment, because I feel that upper management has forced my decision surrounding my resignation. This is not the course of action that I prefer, but feel I must take. It has truly been a pleasure working for you."

Betty and Troy decide to hold their letters to see if the company will lower earnings guidance as Scott promised. On November 1, 2000, five days later, WorldCom sends out a press release lowering future guidance. Scott has kept his word. But will the revised guidance be low enough to keep them from having to make these types of entries again?

Day after day, their letters unsent, outside pressure begins to weaken Troy and Betty's resolve. "Me and my wife had lost a set of twins in early 2000," Troy would explain. "Subsequent to that—I was the only income earner in the family. [Then] she had a miscarriage, and . . . soon thereafter she got pregnant once again. And I was scared to leave as the sole provider of my family." Doubts begin to grow in Betty's mind too. She's also the primary breadwinner. She has a young daughter and is worried that, in her mid-forties, it will be tough to find a comparable position. "I thought about it for a while, and I believed what Scott said, that this would be a one-time thing, go ahead and get through it," she later recalled. "I liked my job. These quarter close entries were so much removed from what I did every day, I liked the people I worked with, and I really wanted to stay there."

As 2000 draws to a close, David and the accountants discover bad news: Scott's prediction that the problem would reverse itself in the fourth quarter hasn't come true. What's worse, the new lower guidance still isn't enough to prevent doctoring the results. Once again, the four accountants find themselves forced to choose—blow the whistle and come forward with the truth, resign and say nothing, or make the entries and hope things will turn around next quarter.

Once again, Troy and Betty search the company's books for liability accounts they can reduce to offset the higher-than-expected line costs and lower-than-expected earnings. But such accounts are nearly depleted by now; this is the last quarter they can draw down excess in liability accounts to meet earnings. If the telecom market doesn't make a drastic change for the better in the first quarter of 2001, Scott will have to come up with a new plan. Surely things will turn around by then and this will be the last quarter they're asked to make unsupported entries. But the end of the next quarter shows this was wishful thinking. The expected turnaround is nowhere in sight. Since the previously lowered accounts no longer have any excess amounts to draw down, Scott instructs his staff to employ a new scheme—count the excess line costs as capital assets instead of expenses. The cost of capital assets, like facilities and equipment, is written off over a much longer period than the cost of operational expenses like these line costs, which must be expensed in the month they are incurred. Scott's plan will spread the costs over a much longer period, buying the company time for a turnaround.

As quarters pass, the accountants commit themselves further and further to a path of deceit. Almost a year has passed since Betty and Troy wrote their resignation letters. Still, the letters are unsent. Each quarter, David and his three accountants hope for better news, but the telecommunications sector continues to deteriorate. At home, life goes on with husbands, wives, and children, and, at times, the accountants can focus on other things—the parts of their jobs they love, their children's activities. But still, shelved in a corner of their minds, their actions weigh heavier and heavier, taking a physical and emotional toll. Buddy eventually visits an attorney to discuss his options, but ultimately doesn't take any action. Betty struggles to sleep and begins losing weight.

It's October, 2001. David is reviewing the company's results for the third quarter. Things are getting worse, not better. For the first time during David's tenure with the company, WorldCom is not making a profit.

"Scott, how are we going to stop this?" David asks, desperate for a solution.

Hearing no good answers, he realizes in his heart that, for the foreseeable future, nothing will change. He has begun to feel deeply depressed. He withdraws and becomes distant from his family, and no longer wants to go out and visit with friends.

Eventually, David starts thinking of taking his own life. Maybe it would be better to just end it all, he thinks. He punches the accelerator of his BMW to see how much speed it will take before spinning out of control. He watches the speedometer rise to 80, 90, 100, 115 miles per hour. But he always takes his foot off the gas pedal. It's no good. Taking his life is not the answer to his problems.

David's increasingly dark moods have not gone unnoticed by his wife Lynn. As they look out over the calm lake behind their home, the scene is peaceful, but Lynn is tense. She's been watching her husband, the man she adores and loves deeply, suffer under the extraordinary stress of his job. David hasn't told her what's going on at work, but a wife can tell when something is terribly wrong. She misses the old David. She and her son need him to come back.

"You're somewhere else," she says. "We have a baby. You work all the time. Why not quit?"

David tries to comfort her. He explains that he can't quit yet, but he doesn't share with her the real reason for his distress. With Lynn's encouragement, David finally goes to see a doctor and begins taking an antidepressant. It helps his moods, but it can't fix the source of his anguish.

David ponders various options, but there seems to be no good way out of his dilemma. It's too late to quit. He's already participated in the deception; if it ever comes out, the road will lead back to him. He still feels loyalty to Scott, and an obligation to Buddy, Betty, and Troy, whom he's talked into seeing this through. His team depends on him. He can't just leave them to deal with this.

Plus he has a wife and baby to support. His $240,000 salary would be virtually irreplaceable in Jackson. If things turn around, maybe, down the road, he can leave. Then he can start a new life, maybe go into business for himself, and finally be free of all this. But the slippery slope leaves few options.

Chapter 5

Ethics and Governance

For those of you who are law students, this chapter should help you think about the single most important issue of your careers: how do you make sure that you do the right thing? We know that lawyers often identify with their clients' needs. In fact, we'd want lawyers to do just that—to have a real passion for their clients' cases. But at some point, your desire to do the best job for your client might just be outpaced by your temptation to be "the smartest" or "the first" lawyer to come up with a particular idea. After all, being the first person to come up with a new argument or a novel transaction can make or break your career.

Most of the time, those new arguments or transactions are perfectly fine and are just what the client needs. Sometimes, though, the arguments or transactions fall on the wrong side of the ethical line. (We know, we know. Those ethical lines are often very hard to pin down.) The temptation to be the smartest guy[*] in the room[**] is a hallmark of one of our favorite movies, THE DEVIL'S ADVOCATE (Warner Brothers Pictures 1997). In that movie, the Devil (using the name "John Milton," ironically) tries to lure a lawyer to his "team" by promising him all sorts of goodies, including the ability to win every trial. Even after the lawyer supposedly learns his lesson near the end of the movie, and even after he outsmarts the Devil, the Devil has the last word, as he ropes the lawyer in for a second time, stating: "Vanity, definitely my favorite sin."[***]

Vanity is just a part of what may drive lawyers to cross the line between ethical and unethical behavior. We believe that hard-wired cognitive errors (remember Chapter 3?) also play a significant role. Take a look at the essays in this chapter and ask yourself whether, if you represented a client who wants you to cross that ethical line, you'd be able to resist temptation.

---

[*] And yes, we use "guy" in its non-sexist, applicable-to-any-gender way.

[**] *Cf.* BETHANY MCLEAN & PETER ELKIND, THE SMARTEST GUYS IN THE ROOM: THE AMAZING RISE AND SCANDALOUS FALL OF ENRON (2003).

[***] http://www.imdb.com/title/tt0118971/quotes.

Lawyers in the Perfect Storm[*]

Mark A. Sargent[**]

I. INTRODUCTION

People steal. People cheat. Then they lie about it. When they can steal, cheat, and lie in a big way, they do it. When people can steal, cheat, and lie behind the protective facade of the corporation, they *really* do it. The concentration of wealth and power in public corporations, when combined with the separation of ownership and control and the consequent diminishment of accountability, creates, almost by definition, a gigantic moral hazard. This is nothing new. So why should we be startled or even particularly troubled by the wave of corporate scandals for which the word "Enron" is a convenient shorthand?

History shows us that corporate scandals have developed symbiotically with the corporation, from the antics of the railroad barons of the mid-nineteenth century through the scandals of today. To suggest that there was a golden age of corporate probity, in which the norms governing the behavior of managers were somehow more stringent than today's norms, may be indulging a fantasy. Economics, as well as history, should preclude such fantasies. Neoclassical theory of the firm teaches that while the public corporation is a useful nexus of contracts,[1] it is abuse-prone, because the separation of ownership and control inevitably produces substantial agency costs.[2] The managers of

[**] Dean and Professor of Law, Villanova University School of Law. I would like to thank Dean Dennis R. Honabach for the invitation to deliver this paper at the 2003 Foulston Siefkin Lecture, and the participants in the Villanova Faculty Workshop who commented on a draft. Thanks also to Jason Acevedo for his research assistance. Mistakes are my own.

[1] This basic principle derives from Ronald Coase, *The Theory of the Firm*, 4 ECONOMICA (N.S.) 386 (1937). The legal consequences of the principle are elaborated in Frank H. Easterbrook & Daniel R. Fischel, *The Corporate Contract*, 89 COLUM. L. REV. 1416 (1989), which also cites much of the leading economic and legal literature.

[2] The classic article on agency costs is Michael C. Jensen & William H. Meckling, *Theory of the Firm: Managerial Behavior, Agency Costs and Ownership Structures*, 3 J. FIN. ECON. 305 (1976).

such firms, each of which is a rational *homo economicus*, and a person who does not have the same interests as the owners of the firm, tend to maximize their own utility rather than that of the shareholders by self-dealing and shirking, through devices both subtle and blatant, such as undue risk avoidance, conflict-of-interest transactions or (my favorite) consumption of excess perquisites. Indeed, the central problem of corporate law has been that of defining how agency costs can be controlled, and everyone recognizes that the task is not an easy one.[3]

It also may be that at least some of the recent cases were unique examples of unusually bad corporate governance, not a general failure of corporate governance. As Professor John Coffee pointed out,

> Enron's governance structure was *sui generis*. Other public corporations simply have not authorized their chief financial officer to run an independent entity that enters into billions of dollars of risky and volatile trading transactions with them; nor have they allowed their senior officers to profit from such self-dealing transactions without broad supervision or even comprehension of the profits involved. Nor have other corporations incorporated thousands of subsidiaries and employed them in a complex web of off-balance sheet partnerships.[4]

The problem presented by Enron may simply be one of determining why some boards are so much worse than others, not whether there has been some systemic breakdown of corporate governance.

So why be surprised about Enron and its progeny, and why believe that something fundamental has been altered, requiring major changes in our system of corporate governance? One answer may be that the scale, rapidity and pervasive impact of these corporate collapses seem unprecedented and radical. The dimension of the collapses, however, can be partially accounted for by the violent bursting of the economic bubble on which some of these companies rose, particularly technology firms such as WorldCom and Global Crossing, rather than defects in corporate governance, which may never have been detected if rising markets continued to mask all sins. But the burst bubble does not account for all of the current disenchantment. The widespread disillusion-

---

[3] There are, of course, different schools of thought about how and the extent to which corporate law should play a role in controlling agency costs. For a concise explanation of the different approaches of the neo-classical, managerialist, transaction cost and political theory schools, see WILLIAM A. KLEIN & JOHN C. COFFEE, JR., BUSINESS ORGANIZATION AND FINANCE 172-78 (8th ed. 2000).

[4] John C. Coffee, Jr., *Understanding Enron: "It's About the Gatekeepers, Stupid,"* 57 BUS. LAW. 1403, 1403-04 (2002). For more detailed discussion of the implications of Enron's extraordinarily bad corporate governance, see generally Jeffrey N. Gordon, *What Enron Means for the Management and Control of the Modern Business Corporation: Some Initial Reflections*, 69 U. CHI. L. REV. 1233 (2002). For an insider's view of Enron's unusually dysfunctional corporate culture, see MIMI SWARTZ WITH SHERRON WATKINS, POWER FAILURE: THE INSIDE STORY OF THE COLLAPSE OF ENRON (2003). Watkins was the key whistle-blower at Enron.

ment caused by the bubble bursting was exacerbated by a pervasive sense of deceit and corruption in the highest reaches of corporate America.

Most disturbing has been the sense of systems failure, of a thorough breakdown of all the mechanisms designed to control agency costs, to prevent corporate managers from using other peoples' money in their own interests to the massive detriment of shareholders, employees, home communities and everyone else affected by their behavior. It may be that Enron was unusual, but it had many successors in disaster, suggesting that something about the failure was systemic, and not idiosyncratic. The world of Enron and the others was a world swept by a perfect storm[5] in which regulatory restraints, fiduciary obligation, market discipline, contractual incentives and professional gatekeepers all simultaneously failed to produce their intended beneficial effects.

My principal goal in this paper is to consider the contribution to the perfect storm of one particular group of gatekeepers, the lawyers who represented Enron and the other corporate malefactors. I will then offer some tentative conclusions about the potential usefulness of the attorney whistle-blowing rules Congress has required the Securities and Exchange Commission (SEC) to adopt in response to its perception of those lawyers' ethical and professional failures. Consideration of the lawyers' failures, however, must be contextualized by first trying to understand the other failures that constituted the perfect storm.

II. THE PERFECT STORM

A. The Failure of Law

The elements of this perfect storm are by now clear. First, the federal regulatory framework inherited from the New Deal to ensure that public companies produce and

[5] The term "perfect storm" is taken from the bestseller about an unusually violent storm in the Atlantic Ocean and the fate of fishermen caught in it. SEBASTIAN JUNGER, THE PERFECT STORM: A TRUE STORY OF MEN AGAINST THE SEA (1997). Dean Nancy B. Rapoport, however, writes that the "'perfect storm' metaphor [as applied to Enron] irks me to no end," apparently because it was used by an Enron executive in a self-exculpatory manner. Nancy B. Rapoport, *Enron, Titanic and The Perfect Storm*, 71 FORDHAM L. REV. 1373, 1375 (2003). She maintains "that what brought Enron down—at least as far as we know—wasn't a once-in-a-lifetime alignment of elements beyond its control. Rather, Enron's demise was a synergistic combination of human errors and hubris; a *Titanic* miscalculation, rather than a 'perfect storm.'" *Id.* I think Dean Rapoport is taking her metaphors a little too seriously. The term "perfect storm" is not used here to suggest that this was some sort of unique event that just "happened" to Enron. It is used here as a metaphor, through which the simultaneous and virtually complete failures of both external regulatory and internal self-regulatory systems (in some cases because of human error and hubris, and in others because of the defects in those systems) can be compared to the concatenation of weather forces that produced Junger's perfect storm. My use of the metaphor is not an attempt to deflect responsibility from the pirates (to continue the nautical metaphors ad nauseam) whose arrogance and dishonesty ultimately sunk Enron. Furthermore, while quibbling about metaphors is perhaps a little silly, I would suggest that insistence on comparison of the Enron debacle to the tragicomedy of human errors in the sinking of the *Titanic* underestimates the importance of the systemic failures that allowed the malign leadership of Enron to produce such an enormous disaster.

disseminate accurate, material information into the marketplace about the companies' financial condition failed to extract the kind of information needed to allow the market to detect the fundamental problems with Enron and the other corporations that so suddenly turned success into disaster. The reasons why the mandatory disclosure system administered by the SEC failed are numerous and complex. They range from the inherent difficulty of contending with determined and sophisticated fraud, to the excessive plasticity of accounting standards that allowed the financial condition of issuers to be obscured in an apparently legal manner,[6] to the atrophy of the auditing function that was supposed to ensure the quality of the information fed into the disclosure system,[7] to a market euphoria that kept attention away from the danger signals,[8] to the limitations of an SEC not equal to its oversight and enforcement responsibilities.[9]

Second, reliance on the concept of fiduciary duty, a legally enforceable obligation designed to protect shareholders from the self-seeking behavior of corporate officers and directors, seems to have been misguided, at best. The duty of loyalty imposed little restraint on officers who extracted huge sums from the company for their personal benefit in the form of "loans," cash payments or lavish perks,[10] rammed through lucra-

---

[6] *But see* William W. Bratton, *Enron and the Dark Side of Shareholder Value*, 76 TUL. L. REV. 1275, 1340-48 (2002) (arguing that the primary problem was not primarily with the substance of the accounting rules, but with Enron's failure to follow them). *Cf.* Daniel Altman, *Enron Had More Than One Way to Disguise Rapid Rise in Debt*, N.Y. TIMES, Feb. 17, 2002, at A1 (citing Enron's use of existing accounting rules to avoid treating swap exchanges as debt); Floyd Norris & Joseph Kahn, *Rule Makers Take on Loopholes That Enron Used in Hiding Debt*, N.Y. TIMES, Feb. 14, 2002, at A1 (citing Enron's use of the "Three Percent Rule" to keep the liabilities of its special purpose entities out of its financial statements as debt). These analyses show how Enron apparently followed the existing rules to produce highly undesirable results. The argument has also been made that certain questionable accounting decisions had been made, and were justifiable, because other companies in the same industry were allegedly doing the same thing. WorldCom, Inc., for example, apparently treated "line charges" (charges for using other phone networks) as capital expenses rather than operating costs, allowing the company (allegedly) to claim $5 billion in profit during a three-year period in which it was losing money. In pleading not guilty to fraud charges, WorldCom's former CFO asserted this "everybody was doing it" defense. *See also* Brooke A. Masters, WorldCom *Officer Pleads Not Guilty; Sullivan's Trial Put Off Until 2004,* WASH. POST, Apr. 23, 2003, at E01.

[7] For discussion of this problem, see *infra* notes 33-38 and accompanying text.

[8] Coffee, *supra* note 4, at 1412. In particular, market euphoria compromises or even destroys the effectiveness of gatekeepers such as auditors, lawyers and securities analysts, as Professor Coffee pointed out:

> Indeed, in an atmosphere of euphoria in which stock prices ascend endlessly and exponentially, gatekeepers are largely a nuisance to management, which does not need them to attract investors. Gatekeepers are necessary only when investors are cautious and skeptical, and in a market bubble, caution and skepticism are largely abandoned.

Id.

[9] *See* STAFF OF SENATE COMM. ON GOV'T AFFAIRS, 107TH CONG., FINANCIAL OVERSIGHT OF ENRON: THE SEC AND PRIVATE-SECTOR WATCHDOGS 29-68 (Comm. Print 2002) [hereinafter FINANCIAL OVERSIGHT REPORT] (evaluating the SEC's performance with respect to Enron).

[10] The most notorious recent example of this behavior is perhaps that of Adelphia Communications, where the founders of a public company used their control over the board to secure approval of millions of dollars worth of unjustifiable personal loans and other benefits to the CEO and his family. The CEO

tive conflict-of-interest transactions,[11] manipulated financial data to prop up the stock price to boost the value of their options, or dumped their stock before the bad news of their mismanagement or financial deception became public.[12] Similarly, the duty of care had little impact on the directors of these corporations, particularly independent directors, who allowed all of this malfeasance to take place on their watch.[13]

---

has challenged this characterization of his dealings with the corporation. *See* Andrew Ross Sorkin, *Fallen Founder of Adelphia Tries to Explain*, N.Y. TIMES, Apr. 7, 2003, at C1.

[11] The conflict of interest transactions benefiting Enron senior executives, and approved at their request, are by now well-known. For analysis of how senior executives benefited from such transactions and how they deceived the board of directors (which also failed in its oversight functions), see the report prepared by a special board committee chaired by William F. Powers, Jr., *Report from the Special Investigative Committee of the Board of Directors of Enron Corp., to the Members of the Board of Directors* 148-77 (Feb. 1, 2002), *available at* http://news.findlaw.com/hdocs/docs/enron/sicreport020102.pdf [hereinafter Powers Report]. Particularly questionable was the Enron Board's willingness to suspend the corporation's own code of ethics in order to avoid the conflict of interest rules that would have precluded board approval of certain major transactions that benefited the chief financial officer. *See also* A. LARRY ELLIOTT & RICHARD J. SCHROTH, HOW COMPANIES LIE 100-01 (2003).

[12] Whether officers or directors (particularly independent directors) will be held liable under the federal securities laws for such insider trading, however, remains to be seen as of this writing. In the case of *In re Enron Corp. Securities, Derivative, and ERISA Litigation*, 235 F. Supp. 2d 549 (S.D. Tex. 2002), the court dismissed shareholders' claims that the independent directors of Enron sold stock based on inside information about the company's financial condition. The court found that the complaint nowhere asserted facts giving rise to a strong inference of scienter for any of the independent directors.

[13] For strong criticism of the performance of the Enron Board of Directors, see PERMANENT SUBCOMM. ON INVESTIGATIONS OF THE COMM. ON GOVERNMENTAL AFFAIRS UNITED STATES SENATE, 107TH CONG., THE ROLE OF THE BOARD OF DIRECTORS IN ENRON'S COLLAPSE (Comm. Print 2002) [hereinafter ROLE OF THE BOARD REPORT]. The report concluded:

> [M]uch that was wrong with Enron was known to the Board, from high risk accounting practices and inappropriate conflict of interest transactions, to extensive undisclosed off-the-books activity and excessive executive compensation. . . . [T]he Enron Board failed to provide the prudent oversight and checks and balances that its fiduciary obligations required and a company like Enron needed. By failing to provide sufficient oversight and restraint to stop management excess, the Enron Board contributed to the company's collapse and bears a share of the responsibility for it.

Id. at 59.

The extent to which the independence of the Enron Board, and its willingness to exercise its monitoring function, was compromised by personal and financial ties between supposedly independent directors and key executives remains to be determined. *See* Richard W. Stevenson & Jeff Gerth, Safeguards *Failed to Detect Problems at Enron,* N.Y. TIMES, Jan. 20, 2002, at A1.

The ability of a board of directors to meet its fiduciary obligations of care, furthermore, can be compromised when the officers and their professional advisers do not provide the board with the information it needs to do its job, particularly when they are motivated to withhold data that might reveal their conflicts of interest. This may have been why the board of Global Crossing failed to "comprehensively address the implications of [certain questionable] transactions, in the aggregate, for the company's overall financial position, until it was too late to take remedial action if it chose to do so." *See* Report of the Special Committee on Accounting Matters to the Board of Directors of Global Crossing Ltd., Global Crossing's Response to Olafson's Allegations 15 (Feb. 18, 2003) (on file with author) [hereinafter Global Crossing Report].

B. Market Failure

The perfect storm involved more, however, than a failure of law, whether it was federal securities law or state law of fiduciary obligation. It was also a case of market failure, which, for some, is a more serious problem. Critics of regulatory intervention into corporate governance insist, after all, that the problem of agency costs is best resolved through a combination of market discipline and private contracting.[14]

1. The Limitations of Market Discipline

Corporate managers are disciplined, some argue, by the operation of the market for corporate control, which compels managers to maximize shareholder value at the risk of losing control.[15] There was always an element of overstatement in these theories of market discipline because the takeover phenomenon has been explained in different ways that have nothing to do with the disciplinary hypothesis,[16] but, the limitations of

---

Professor Jeffrey N. Gordon has argued, however, that among the Enron Board's principal governance failures was its willingness to approve an "opaque" disclosure policy while also authorizing a managerial compensation strategy highly dependent on stock price changes that, as a result of Enron's opaque disclosures, did not reflect material information about the issuer, while itself declining to intensely monitor the company's highly complex operations and financial practices. Jeffrey N. Gordon, *Governance Failures of the Enron Board and the New Information Order of Sarbanes-Oxley, Columbia Law School Center for Law and Economic Studies*, 35 CONN. L. REV. 1125 (2003).

[14] The body of contractarian thought that emphasizes the efficiency of private contracting as opposed to government intervention in corporate governance through mandatory, as distinct from enabling, rules derives from Ronald Coase, *The Problem of Social Cost*, 3 J.L. & ECON. 1 (1960). A comprehensive elaboration of the contractarian approach to corporate law is FRANK H. EASTERBROOK & DANIEL R. FISCHEL, THE ECONOMIC STRUCTURE OF CORPORATE LAW (1991).

For a critical analysis of the contractarian approach, see John C. Coffee, Jr., *Contractual Freedom in Corporate Law: Articles & Comments; The Mandatory/Enabling Balance in Corporate Law: An Essay on the Judicial Role*, 89 COLUM. L. REV. 1618 (1989).

[15] The pioneering article arguing that the disciplinary impact of the market for corporate control is an important means of controlling agency costs is Henry G. Manne, *Mergers and the Market for Corporate Control*, 73 J. POL. ECON. 110 (1965). Empirical evidence supporting the thesis that corporate takeovers have the effect of replacing poor managers can be found in Kenneth J. Martin & John J. McConnell, *Corporate Performance, Corporate Takeovers, and Managerial Turnover*, 46 J. FIN. 671 (1991).

For an argument that recognition of takeovers as a method of monitoring management performance requires a rule of managerial passivity in response to a hostile tender offer, see Frank H. Easterbrook & Daniel R. Fischel, *The Proper Role of a Target's Management in Responding to a Tender Offer*, 94 HARV.L. REV. 1161 (1981). For versions of this argument that recognize the importance of the monitoring influence of the market for corporate control, but argue against a rule of pure passivity, see Ronald J. Gilson, *Seeking Competitive Bids Versus Pure Passivity in Tender Offer Defense*, 35 STAN. L. REV. 51 (1982). *See also* Lucian A. Bebchuk, *The Case for Facilitating Competing Tender Offers: A Reply and Extension*, 35 STAN. L. REV. 23 (1982).

[16] For an excellent overview of the literature and excerpts from some of the key articles, see ROBERTA ROMANO, FOUNDATIONS OF CORPORATE LAW 221-57 (1993). It has been argued that the recent wave of corporate fraud is at least partially attributable to the demise of the hostile takeover as a disciplinary mechanism because of the wave of antitakeover regulation in the 1980s and 1990s. *See* Larry E. Ribstein, *Market v. Regulatory Responses to Corporate Fraud: A Critique of the Sarbanes-Oxley Act of 2002*, 28 J. CORP. L. 1,

market discipline as a means of aligning managerial and shareholder interests became particularly obvious in light of the gross misbehavior of corporate managers in the recent debacles.

Also obvious are the limitations of the theory that firms' private incentives to disclose accurate information are sufficient to ensure transparency in corporate disclosure. Undoubtedly, most firms recognize that deceptive disclosure is costly, because eventually it will be detected, diminishing the firm's credibility and producing uncertainty about the value of its securities. The uncertainty discount will then increase its cost of raising capital. Supposedly, this private incentive for truth-telling is so powerful that it renders a government-mandated disclosure system unnecessary.[17] The incentive to disseminate accurate information may be sufficient in most cases, but recent experience suggests that the private incentives for deception can be equally powerful, at least under some circumstances. Those circumstances include situations in which senior managers can benefit enormously in the short term from increases in the stock price, even if those increases are short-lived. They include cases of over-optimism, in which managers believe that future improvements in operations or financial condition will eventually resolve the problems that are inadequately disclosed or even misrepresented.[18] Most important, perhaps, are the situations in which secretiveness, truth-trimming and even outright deception have become part of the corporate culture, so that public dissembling becomes entirely normative. This may seem irrational, but we know from the insights of behavioral economics that in the financial world the irrational can seem perfectly rational.[19] It seems obvious from recent experience that the irrational has

55 (2002). Professor Ribstein argues that the recent spate of corporate fraud was not caused by market failure, but by prior regulatory intervention into corporate governance that gutted the effectiveness of an important market mechanism of managerial discipline. Professor Ribstein has extended that critique of prior regulatory interventions to a critique of the most recent Congressional response to the market excesses of the last few years. He suggests that the post-Enron legislation may be similar to the misconceived regulatory responses to the bursting of previous market bubbles. *See* Larry E. Ribstein, *Bubble Laws*, 40 HOUS. L. REV. 77, 79 (2003) ("In each case, regulation was passed without due consideration either to the benefits or costs of regulation, and it likely constrained the market's recovery from the crash.").

[17] The leading articles arguing that SEC-mandated disclosure under the Securities Act of 1933 for new issues was superfluous were Greg A. Jarrell, *The Economic Effects of Federal Regulation of the Market for New Securities Issues*, 24 J.L. & ECON. 613 (1981) and George J. Stigler, *Public Regulation of the Securities Markets*, 37 J. BUS. 117 (1964). *See also* George Benston, *Required Disclosure and the Stock Market: An Evaluation of the Securities Exchange Act of 1934*, 63 AM. ECON. REV. 132 (1973) (finding that SEC-mandated disclosure under the Securities Exchange Act by already-public companies was of no apparent value to investors). *See generally* John C. Coffee, Jr., *Market Failure and the Economic Case for a Mandatory Disclosure System*, 70 VA. L. REV. 717 (1984). Professor Coffee's rejoinder is more sanguine about the benefits of the system. *See also* Frank H. Easterbrook & Daniel R. Fischel, *Mandatory Disclosure and the Protection of Investors*, 70 VA. L. REV. 669 (1984) (critiquing the alleged benefits of the mandatory disclosure system).

[18] For a concise analysis of the cognitive biases that produce over-optimism and poor decisions among corporate managers, see Dan Lovallo & Daniel Kahneman, Delusions *of Success: How Optimism Undermines Executives' Decisions*, HARV. BUS. REV., July-Aug. 2003, at 59-61.

[19] The leading texts in the emerging field of "behavioral finance" are HERSH SHEFFRIN, BEYOND GREED AND FEAR: UNDERSTANDING BEHAVIORAL FINANCE AND THE PSYCHOLOGY OF INVESTING (2000); ANDREI SHLEIFER, INEFFICIENT MARKETS: AN INTRODUCTION TO BEHAVIORAL FINANCE (2000). An interesting application

seemed rational to at least some corporate managers, with disastrous consequences for the quality of corporate disclosure.

2. Stock Option Compensation and Perverse Incentives

Even more obvious has been the failure of the principal contractual mechanism for controlling agency costs: executive stock options. Stock option compensation seemed a brilliant, non-regulatory solution to the problem of how to provide managers with the incentive to maximize shareholder value. One commentator has described the premises of stock option compensation succinctly, albeit ironically, when he explained that "[o]nce endowed with a generous grant of these magical instruments, a senior executive would no longer think of himself as a mere hired hand but as a proprietor who had the long term health of the firm at heart. That was the theory, anyway."[20] Instead of being a shirking, risk-avoiding bureaucratic time-server, interested only in his own salary and perks and not in maximizing shareholder value, the manager/option-holder would profit with the shareholder from the increased value the now-entrepreneurial manager's efforts would generate.

While stock option arrangements can be complex, the basic agreement is simple, as the following description shows:

---

of these theories is ROBERT SHILLER, IRRATIONAL EXUBERANCE (2000). Professor Donald C. Langevoort has drawn upon the insights of behavioral finance to question the basic premises of the efficient market hypothesis, upon which most theories of market discipline depend. For an exposition of that thesis and its significance for regulation of public corporations and securities markets, see Ronald J. Gilson & Reinier Kraakman, *The Mechanisms of Market Efficiency*, 70 VA. L. REV. 549 (1984). Langevoort proposes instead an inefficient market hypothesis, which would form the basis for what he calls "behavioral securities regulation," which would acknowledge the cognitive biases of both persons involved in issuing securities and investors. Donald C. Langevoort, *Taming the Animal Spirits of the Stock Market: A Behavioral Approach to Securities Regulation*, 97 NW. U. L. REV. 135, 140 (2002). *But see* Stephen J. Choi & Adam C. Pritchard, *Behavioral Economics and the SEC*, 56 STAN. L. REV. 1 (2003) (University of Michigan John M. Olin Center for Law & Economics, Working Paper No. 03-002, *available at* http://ssrn.com/abstract_id=389560). The authors argue that recognition of behavioral biases within securities markets should not necessarily lead to greater regulatory intervention in those markets, because regulators (particularly monopolistic regulators such as the SEC) suffer from their own behavioral biases.

[20] John Cassidy, *The Greed Cycle: How the Financial System Encouraged Corporations to Go Astray*, THE NEW YORKER, Sept. 23, 2002, at 64, 68. This article is an excellent journalistic account of the perverse effects of the stock option compensation arrangements of the 1990s. For further analysis of those effects and their damage to both shareholder and social welfare, see also LAWRENCE E. MITCHELL, CORPORATE IRRESPONSIBILITY 8-9, 109-11, 223-25 (2001). These critiques fly in the face of much conventional wisdom that favored the use of stock option compensation.

For examples of the literature on executive compensation questions, including the role of stock option compensation, see EXECUTIVE COMPENSATION AND SHAREHOLDER VALUE (Jennifer Carpenter & David Yermack eds., 1999). For arguments that the largest component of directors' compensation should be in the form of stock options, see Charles M. Elson, *The Duty of Care, Compensation, and Stock Ownership*, 63 U. CIN. L. REV. 649, 652-53 (1995). For a concise survey of the arguments pro and con regarding stock option compensation, see Randall Thomas & Kenneth Martin, *The Determinants of Shareholder Voting on Stock Option Plans*, 35 WAKE FOREST L. REV. 31, 40-46 (2000).

> An executive stock option is a legal contract that grants its owner the right to buy a stock in his or her company at a certain price (the "strike price") on a certain date in the future. Take a company with a stock price of fifty dollars that grants its chief executive the right to buy a million shares three years hence at the current market price. Assume the stock price rises by ten per cent each year, so that after three years it is trading at about sixty-six dollars and fifty cents. At that point, the chief executive can "exercise" his option and make the company sell him a million shares at fifty dollars. Then he can sell the shares in the open market, and clear a profit of sixteen and a half million dollars.[21]

Stock option arrangements thus blew off the ceiling on potential executive compensation to managers' delight. They were equally delightful from the corporation's standpoint. Stock options did not have to be treated as an expense for accounting purposes, unlike executive salaries, allowing corporate earnings to be goosed upward.[22]

Beginning around 1990, stock options began to take off as the principal method of compensating senior executives, dwarfing cash salary payments in significance.[23] Once installed throughout corporate America, stock option arrangements caused executive compensation to balloon wildly. The gross disproportion between senior executive pay and that received by everyone else caused plenty of controversy,[24] but that was only one problem. Serious as it was, it merely formed a backdrop to the most dangerous dilemma: stock option programs not only failed to meet their avowed goal of aligning managerial and shareholder interests, they created perverse incentives for abusing shareholders.

---

[21] Cassidy, *supra* note 20, at 68.

[22] The question of whether options should be expensed to reduce earnings became controversial in the 1990s, but no meaningful change in the rule was achieved. *See* Faith Stevelman Kahn, *What Are the Ways of Achieving Corporate Social Responsibility?: Bombing Markets, Subverting the Rule of Law: Enron, Financial Fraud, and September 11, 2001*, 76 TUL. L. REV. 1579, 1605 n.73 (2002) (including the authorities cited therein). Post-Enron, however, serious consideration of changing the accounting rule began. *See infra* note 33.

[23] *See* David M. Schizer, *Executives and Hedging: The Fragile Legal Foundation of Incentive Compatibility*, 100 COLUM. L. REV. 440, 442 (2000); Richard H. Wagner & Catherine G. Wagner, *Recent Developments in Executive, Director, and Employee Stock Compensation Plans: New Concerns for Corporate Directors*, 3 STAN. J.L. BUS. & FIN. 5, 6-7 (1997).

[24] For a thorough critique of this disproportion and its effects, even before the post-1990 boom in stock option compensation, see GRAEF S. CRYSTAL, IN SEARCH OF EXCESS (1991). For a more recent critique of the gap and its economic and social effects, see Susan J. Stabile, *One for A, Two for B, and Four Hundred for C: The Widening Gap in Pay Between Executives and Rank and File Employees*, 36 U. MICH. J.L. REFORM 115 (2002). There is some evidence, however, that the recession that began in 2001 has begun to reduce average CEO compensation, both because of reduced payouts of performance-related bonuses and because so many stock options are under water. *See* Louis Lavell et al., *Executive Pay*, BUS. WEEK, Apr. 21, 2003, at 86 (reporting a thirty-three percent decline in average CEO pay packages). Shareholders have also begun to use the SEC proxy mechanism to challenge executive compensation arrangements. *See* Amy Borrus & Michael Arndt, *Labor Strikes Back*, BUS. WEEK, May 26, 2003, at 46.

For example, some corporations indulged in the practice of repricing executives' stock options so that they would still be able to exercise their options profitably when the stock price fell.[25] Managers thus benefited whether the stock price went up or down, although the shareholders only profited when the price went up. It was a kind of "heads I win, tails you lose" scenario, in which the notion that options made managers' and shareholders' interests congruent became laughable. Even in the absence of repricing, the use of stock options created an incentive to use accounting devices designed to prop up the stock price.[26] It should also be noted that compensation schemes other than stock option arrangements can have similarly perverse effects. Enron, for example, used a program of one-time cash bonus payments to senior executives (its "Performance Unit Plan") as a reward for hitting stock-price targets. Apparently over $320 million of such cash payments were made during the year preceding Enron's bankruptcy, the time when the company was making some of its most misleading accounting decisions and financial disclosures in order to meet stock-price expectations[27] in the short term just long enough to allow quick and highly profitable option strikes while the public shareholders were left holding the bag when the price fell.

The use of option repricing thus ensured that the stock option compensation would fail to meet its avowed purpose: giving managers a strong personal incentive to maximize the value of the assets under their control and hence the stock price for the benefit of the shareholders. Even worse than repricing, however, was the incentive that stock option compensation created for managers to manipulate and falsify financial disclosures to raise the stock price to keep or put their options in the money.

Enron's deceptive accounting has received lots of attention because of its subtlety and scale. The company's unorthodox and dubious use of special purpose entities for more than securitizing specific corporate assets (a relatively common corporate financing

---

[25] Naturally, this practice has excited criticism. *See* Charles M. Yablon, Overcompensating: *The Corporate Lawyer and Executive Pay*, 92 COLUM. L. REV. 1867, 1880 (1992) (reviewing GRAEF S. CRYSTAL, IN SEARCH OF EXCESS (1991)). Note, however, that such repricing apparently has been relatively uncommon. *See* Tod Perry & Marc Zenner, *CEO Compensation in the 1990s: Shareholder Alignment or Shareholder Expropriation?*, 35 WAKE FOREST L. REV. 123, 124 (2000). Perry and Zenner point out, however, that companies may avoid repricing because it might be embarrassing when publicly disclosed, but that they achieve much the same effect by issuing new options at a lower strike price ("reloading"). *Id.* at 141.

[26] *See* Thomas & Martin, *supra* note 20, at 44.

> Stock option compensation may lead managers to manipulate earnings or other accounting figures so as to insure that the company meets or exceeds analysts' expectations and that the company's stock price rises. Executives holding options also have a tendency to avoid dividends and engage in share repurchases. This raises important questions about whether managers are running the company to increase the value of their stock options or to raise the value of the common stock held by the shareholders.

Id.

[27] *See* Kurt Eichenwald, *Enron Paid Huge Bonuses in '01: Experts See a Motive for Cheating*, N.Y. TIMES, Mar. 1, 2002, at A1.

technique)[28] created a distorted picture of the corporation's financial condition. This is just one example of how Enron managers kept the stock price floating on a column of hot air.[29] Enron also indulged in accounting practices very familiar to corporate CFOs, such as reporting revenues prematurely or speculatively, as the company did with risky derivative contracts that might not pay off in an indefinite future. Critics of corporate accounting practices have identified a host of similar games that have been played to give a misleadingly positive picture of the corporation's financial condition in order to keep the stock price up and options in the money. Some examples include adding fanciful items to revenue, treating a one-time payment from the sale of an asset

---

[28] A "special purpose entity" (SPE) is used in the process of asset securitization, which is a form of corporate debt financing designed to protect the whole range of the borrower's assets from the claims of the lenders in that financing, and confine potential liability to specified assets. This is achieved by placing a pool of assets, such as commercial leases or consumer receivables, in a separate entity, the SPE. The lender who lends on the strength of the cash flow from that pool of assets has recourse only to those assets in the event of the default, not the other assets of the originator. For a detailed analysis, see Steven L. Schwarz, *The Alchemy of Asset Securitization*, 1 STAN. J.L. BUS. & FIN. 133, 133-34 (1994), and STEVEN L. SCHWARZ, STRUCTURED FINANCE, A GUIDE TO THE PRINCIPLES OF ASSET SECURITIZATION § 1:1 (3d ed. 2002). For a concise guide to the legal considerations in structuring special purpose entities to ensure that the originator remains "bankruptcy remote," see Steven L. Schwarz, *Structured Finance: The New Way to Securitize Assets*, 11 CARDOZO L. REV. 607, 621-26 (1990).

[29] Indeed, Professor Schwarz has argued that Enron's use of SPEs was significantly different from that of normal asset securitization, and failed to provide the transfer of risk (and hence bankruptcy remoteness) that would prevent these highly risky transactions from burying Enron itself under the SPEs' liabilities in the event of default:

> To the extent securitization is used to keep debt off a company's balance sheet, it superficially resembles Enron's use of SPEs. But there are important differences because securitization, unlike the Enron-SPE transactions, unambiguously transfers risk from the company to the SPE and its investors; and transfer of risk is, and should be, central to the accounting determination of non-consolidation. In Enron's SPE transactions, it was at least debatable whether risk was shifted on the hedged assets owned by Enron; although Enron had the right to require the SPEs to buy these assets at a pre-determined price should their values fall, that right was precarious because the SPEs were capitalized solely with Enron stock. Thus, when Enron's asset and stock values simultaneously fell, the SPEs were unable to perform their hedges. In contrast, a company originating a securitization transaction transfers actual risk by selling financial assets—including the risk of non-payment or delayed payment associated with such assets—to the SPE.

Steven L. Schwarz, *Fifteenth Annual Corporate Law Symposium: Corporate Bankruptcy in the New Millennium: Enron, and the Use and Abuse of Special Purpose Entities in Corporate Structures*, 70 U. CIN. L. REV. 1309, 1315-16 (2002).

Professor Schwarz also points out that the allocation of risk in conventional SPE asset securitization is fully disclosed so that lenders can assess their loan risk and investors in the originating company can assess the significance of the SPE for the value of the originator's equity securities. In Enron, disclosure about the SPEs was either intentionally minimized to hide the conflicts of interest that pervaded their SPE arrangements (a case of fraud), or, more fundamentally, "Enron's structured finance transactions were so complex that disclosure is necessarily imperfect—either oversimplifying the transactions or providing detail and sophistication beyond the level of an ordinary investor in Enron's securities." *Id.* at 1316-17. In either case, the Enron SPE disclosures (or non-disclosures) deeply impaired the market's ability to assess Enron's financial condition.

or other windfall as if it were ongoing income, failing to record liabilities in whole or in part, treating ongoing liabilities as a special charge, and shifting current expenses or liabilities to a later period. Some companies treated operating expenditures as capital expenditures, the cost of which can be spread over years, rather than being reflected in the current period.[30] The temptation to use such chicanery to maintain the stock price was exacerbated during the market bubble, when soaring stock prices and price-earnings multiples imposed tremendous pressure on managers to keep up with the market at all costs. The perceived pressure from Wall Street to report positive earnings to sustain the market price was, for some companies such as HealthSouth, Xerox and WorldCom, so irresistible that the financial misrepresentations were not even subtle.[31]

All of these accounting tricks were available to corporate managers eager to keep their options not just profitable, but extraordinarily profitable. The possibility of not just wealth, but immense wealth, for the average CEO or senior executive created an ongoing moral hazard, an Alice-in-Wonderland universe in which debt disappeared mysteriously, revenue popped up out of rabbit holes, stock prices possessed only a theoretical relationship to earnings, financial statements could say whatever management wanted them to say, and lordly compensation came to feel like an entitlement. Perhaps the perspective of hindsight lends too much of an air of inevitability to the malign effects

---

[30] For a survey of these and other accounting tricks, see HOWARD SCHILIT, FINANCIAL SHENANIGANS: HOW TO DETECT ACCOUNTING GIMMICKS AND FRAUD IN FINANCIAL STATEMENTS 63-175 (1993) (describing the "seven shenanigans" of corporate accounting). For a discussion of how easily pro forma accounting, in particular, can be manipulated to produce such results, see ELLIOTT & SCHROTH, *supra* note 11, at 37-42. For an example of how one company used several of these devices, see *In re Arthur Andersen LLP*, Exchange Act Release No. AE-1405, 2001 WL 687561,June 19, 2001; *SEC v. Arthur Andersen LLP*, Exchange Act Release No. AE-1410, 2001 WL 687562, June 19, 2001. In this pre-Enron case, Waste Management used improper capitalization of expenses, a failure to amortize and improper reserve techniques. *See also* Mark Maremont, *Xerox Overstated Pretax Income by $1.41 Billion, Filing Reveals*, WALL ST. J., July 1, 2002, at A3 (reporting Xerox's inappropriate acceleration of revenues from long-term equipment leases).

[31] A particularly egregious example of this kind of blatant and relatively straightforward lying that came to light after Enron was that of HealthSouth Corp. Beginning in 1997, HealthSouth executives began to be concerned about the gap between HealthSouth's actual earnings per share and Wall Street's earnings' expectations. According to the criminal information filed by federal prosecutors against company executives, the defendants regularly used various accounting devices to overstate (in 2002) the company's cash by $300 million and total assets by $1.5 billion. The former CFO pled guilty to those charges. *See Former CFO of HealthSouth to Plead Guilty to Fraud; SEC Sues Over $1.4 Billion Scam*, 35 SEC. REG. & L. REP. (BNA) No. 12, at 504 (Mar. 24, 2003).

Xerox similarly overstated its profits by $1.4 billion over four years, a period during which senior executives gained millions by selling Xerox shares and being paid bonuses for meeting profit targets. *See* Floyd Norris, *6 Former Xerox Executives to Pay $22 Million*, N.Y. TIMES, June 6, 2003, at C1.

A special report commissioned by WorldCom and prepared by Wilmer Cutler & Pickering showed that WorldCom made repeated efforts to boost revenue to meet Wall Street expectations through an exercise called "Close the Gap." The company apparently recorded revenues from transactions that had not yet been approved and reported revenue from one-time transactions while telling investors no such revenue had been included. The report alleges that the CEO, Wolfgang Ebbers, was directly involved in these activities. *See* Rebecca Blumenstein & Susan Pulliam, *WorldCom Report Finds Ebbers Played Role in Inflating Revenue*, WALL ST. J., June 6, 2003, at A1.

of the stock option compensation practices of the 1990s, but it seems that options had an enormous influence on the kinds of accounting and disclosure practices which led so many investors, and the market in general, to overvalue so many companies.

These practices also led, some would argue, to a problem even more fundamental than inadequate disclosure. The argument is similar to the one frequently heard in the 1980s during the heyday of hostile corporate takeovers, to the effect that an obsession with maintaining the stock price at a high level (to forestall tender offers at a premium) leads to short-term planning and decision-making, to the long-term detriment of the corporation. Here, the argument would be that over-reliance on stock option compensation also has led to an equally unhealthy preoccupation with short-term maintenance of stock prices.[32] A possible response to both of these arguments might be that if the firm really was sacrificing the long-term interests of the corporation for short-term benefits in an unjustifiable way, the market would recognize that fact and discount the price of the firm's securities appropriately. This answer presumes, however, that the market has sufficient information about the firm to make such a discount, certainly a questionable presumption these days. An additional problem is whether the market is sufficiently efficient to process the information rationally, a questionable presumption in light of the insights of behavioral finance into market behavior. There is at least an important question as to whether the widespread use of very substantial stock option compensation has created a short-term bias that needs to be explored. Whether the experience of the last couple of years will lead to significant changes in both compensation and accounting practices relating to stock option compensation remains to be seen.[33]

---

[32] For critical discussion of the impact of an excessively short-term focus on earnings in corporate America, see MITCHELL, *supra* note 20, at 116-19.

[33] There is some evidence of a shift from the use of stock options as incentive compensation to the use of restricted shares and so-called "performance" shares. Restricted shares do not have to be set against earnings and do not dilute common shares, and not as many have to be issued as with options. They convert to full shares after a three- to five-year period and, unlike options, retain some value even if the stock price falls. Performance shares are granted only when specified performance goals are met. *See* Robert D. Hof, *Stock Options Aren't the Only Option*, BUS. WEEK, Apr. 14, 2003, at 60.

Professor Brian Hall has argued that compensation in the form of stock as opposed to stock options is preferable for several reasons:

> The problem isn't that stock options don't have any downside risk. The problem is that they have so much. They have value when granted and can fall out of the money very quickly and end up worth nothing. Then boards feel pressure to either reprice them or give additional grants to make up the difference—practices we all hate, for good reasons. Stock is much less fragile—it never falls under water and creates no repricing pressures. Stock is also more transparent to shareholders and to the board, which helps them make better decisions. Stock is also more understandable to a lot of executives. There's no need to rely on a highly complex model to understand its value. Accounting rules have skewed compensation awards in favor of options for far too long. Once we start treating options as a real expense, we're going to see a lot more stock and a lot fewer options.

Charles Elson (moderator), *Roundtable: What's Wrong With Executive Compensation?*, HARV. BUS. REV., Jan. 2003, at 69, 73.

The accounting question is whether companies will voluntarily choose or will be required to deduct the value of stock options from earnings. In the summer of 2002, the Coca-Cola Company announced

C. The Failure of Gatekeepers

Market discipline and legal obligations are not the only constraints on the self-serving and deceptive behavior of corporate managers. Independent professionals also function as gatekeepers, performing functions that help ensure the accuracy and reliability of the information disseminated by the firm into the marketplace. The failures of auditors and securities analysts to perform those functions with respect to Enron and its progeny is by now well known, and has led to the destruction of one of the world's largest accounting firms and a massive legal settlement by some of the leading securities firms.

The auditing profession owes its status as a profession to the requirement of the federal securities laws, beginning in 1933, whereby issuers of securities provide financial statements certified by independent auditors. The new legal requirement of independence gave auditors leverage against domination by their corporate clients, and the ability to make disinterested decisions and reach conclusions on the basis of their expert knowledge of generally accepted accounting principles and auditing standards.[34] The purpose of the legislative mandate for auditor independence was to provide an external check on the quality of financial disclosure by management. The presumption, naturally, was that auditors would, in fact, act independently. Auditors were given a significant incentive to do so through the establishment of liability for them under the anti-fraud provisions of the federal securities laws. The apparent failure of Arthur Andersen in the Enron case to act as any kind of real check on management's approach to financial accounting, and, rather, to facilitate misleading financial disclosures,[35] suggests that other incentives can overwhelm the auditors' incentives to act independently.

---

that it would voluntarily treat management stock options as an expense. *See* Floyd Norris & Sherri Day, Coke *to Report Stock Options as an Expense*, N.Y. TIMES, July 15, 2002, at A1. A major shift in this direction would have a significant impact on the calculation of corporate earnings. It has been estimated that if companies treated options as a cost, "the earnings per share of the companies in the Standard & Poors 500 stock index would have been 20 percent lower in 2001 than they actually were . . . ." David Leonhardt, *Options Calculus: Who Gets it Right?*, N.Y. TIMES, Mar. 30, 2003, § 3, at A1. As companies have begun voluntarily to expense stock option costs, furthermore, controversy has arisen over the proper methodology for calculating the cost that should be reported. *Id.*

As of this writing in the summer of 2003, the question of whether companies will be required to expense the value of stock option compensation remains. The Federal Accounting Standards Board backed off from adopting such a requirement in the mid-1990s, see *supra* note 20, but on March 12, 2003 announced a study of accounting for stock options, expected to be completed by March 2004, which will address the issue. *See FASB Votes to Start Major Project on Accounting for Stock Compensation*, 35 SEC. REG. & L. REP. (BNA) No. 11, at 463 (Mar. 17, 2003). For a summary of the current debate over the desirability of and appropriate methodology for expensing options, see *Witnesses at House Hearing on Options Disagree at Every Turn on Expensing Options*, 35 SEC. REG. & L. REP. (BNA) No. 23, at 35 (June 9, 2003).

[34] *See* THOMAS K. MCCRAW, PROPHETS OF REGULATION 188-92 (1984). McCraw describes how the mutually beneficial relationship of federal securities regulation and the accounting profession evolved, and how it fostered the independence, reputation and growth of the profession.

[35] The extent of Arthur Andersen's failure is by now well-established. *See* FINANCIAL OVERSIGHT REPORT, *supra* note 9, at 28 ("One of the major concerns about Andersen as the auditor of Enron has been that it did not exhibit sufficient independence and objectivity in discharging its responsibilities . . . . Enron's auditor failed to discharge its role of verifying the accuracy of Enron's books."). A committee of indepen-

The other incentive cited most frequently has been accounting firms' interest in obtaining consulting work from companies they are auditing. In at least some cases, the consulting work is more lucrative than auditing work, creating an incentive for the firm to be compliant with or even facilitative of the clients' desire to stretch or even exceed the boundaries of generally accepted accounting principles or auditing standards. Recognition of that clash of incentives has drawn considerable attention, resulting in changes in law and practice designed to mitigate the conflict.[36] Most problematic, however, is the possibility that the culture of auditing may have changed even without reference to the desire to generate or preserve consulting business.[37] One of the indirect

dent directors of Enron also concluded that "Andersen did not fulfill its professional responsibilities in connection with its audit of Enron's financial statements." Powers Report, *supra* note 11, at 24. *See also* Bratton, *supra* note 6, at 1287 (Enron's auditors "manifestly should have refused to give a favorable opinion on Enron's financials. . . . It is clear that Enron had captured its auditor, denuding the relationship of its necessary adversary aspect."). For discussion of the actual accounting violations, see *id.* at 1342. Professor Bratton points out that in most cases either Enron or Andersen, or both, simply failed to follow the existing rules. *Id.* at 1348. In other cases, the rules were followed, but the rules were defective substantively and need reconsideration. *See also* Floyd Norris & Kurt Eichenwald, *Fuzzy Rules of Accounting and Enron*, N.Y. TIMES, Jan. 30, 2002, at C1 (citing the need to develop more effective rules).

[36] The Sarbanes-Oxley Act § 201(a), Pub. Law No. 107-204, 116 Stat. 745 (codified at 15 U.S.C. § 78j-l(g)-(h)), sets out a new list of non-audit services that auditors are proscribed from providing. The SEC adopted rules effective May 6, 2003 implementing those proscriptions, including a prohibition on financial information systems design and implementation services; a prohibition on internal audit outsourcing services; and a restriction on certain types of "expert" services. Strengthening the Commission's Requirements Regarding Auditor Independence, Exchange Act Release No. 33-8183, 68 Fed. Reg. 6006, 6009-10 (Mar. 31, 2003). Note, however, that an auditor may still provide financial information system design and implementation, as well as internal outsourcing services, if it is reasonable to conclude that the results of the service will not be subject to audit procedures during an audit of the client's financial statements. *Id.* at 6011. The new rules also create a requirement for pre-approval by the audit committee of audit and non-audit services to be provided. *Id.* at 6010. These measures fall far short of the full severance of auditing and non-auditing services some thought to be necessary. *See, e.g.*, Nanette Byrnes et al., *Accounting in Crisis*, BUS. WEEK, Jan. 28, 2002, at 44, 46 (urging a bar on consulting services to audit clients). Note, however, that all of the Big Five accounting firms have placed their own restrictions on the sale of consulting services to their clients, particularly internal audit services. *See* Jonathan D. Glater, *Deloitte Is Last Big Audit Firm to Revamp Consulting Business*, N.Y. TIMES, Feb. 6, 2002, at C1.

The Sarbanes-Oxley Act also added new requirements for rotation of audit partners after five years (§ 203), selection of auditors by board audit committees (§ 202), more detailed reporting by auditors to boards (§ 206), and the presence of a "financial expert" on the audit committee (§§ 204, 407).

[37] For an argument by the former head of the ethics consulting unit at Arthur Andersen that a firm once renowned for its revenue became so obsessed with generating revenue and internal competition over fees that it abandoned its own ethical principles, see BARBARA LEY TOFFLER WITH JENNIFER REINGOLD, FINAL ACCOUNTING: AMBITION, GREED AND THE FALL OF ARTHUR ANDERSEN (2003). For discussion of how Andersen became complicit with the fraud being perpetrated by the corporation's executives, with respect to whom they became "part of the family," see ELLIOTT & SCHROTH, *supra* note 11, at 89-99, and of how they accepted Enron executives' spurious materiality arguments regarding earnings overstatements, see Noam Scheiber, *Peer Revue: How Arthur Andersen Got Away With It*, NEW REPUBLIC, Jan. 28, 2002, at 19, 20.

Recognition of the sins of Andersen, however, should not preclude recognizing the many failures of a similar type by other large accounting firms. *See, e.g.*, Floyd Norris, *Ernst Partners Accept Limits on Audits*,

effects of over-reliance on stock option compensation may have been the corruption of the auditing function, as auditors faced extraordinary pressure from managers to approve questionable treatments of earnings and debt to sustain the stock price. When this took place during a stock market boom in which rising prices covered all sins, the risk of liability may have seemed slim to auditors eager to preserve positive relationships with managers, repeat business and a reputation for being "reasonable." This attitude resulted in a tendency to go along, rather than to resist managers insisting on questionable accounting treatment and financial disclosures. There was also a conflict between a firm's interest in maintaining its reputation for auditing integrity and individual partners' desires to maximize their income within the firm, when a partner's income is heavily dependent on billings from one client.[38] Whatever the reason, it seems clear that auditors were frail obstacles, at best, to the degradation of financial disclosure that became epidemic in the scandals of 2002.

The impact of conflicts of interests seems even more obvious in the case of securities analysts. A major settlement initiated by the New York State Attorney General involving several major securities firms was the response to the practice of touting stocks of companies with whom the analysts' firms had a significant investment banking relationship, regardless of the analysts' negative view of those issuers. The practice of tying analysts' compensation to revenues generated by investment banking business significantly distorted analysts' incentives to provide disinterested, critical reports on the issuers they were evaluating, and induced them to delude the investing public with essentially false analyses.

Once again a conflict of interest undermined an incentive to act independently of the issuer of securities. Securities analysts, theoretically, have a strong incentive to provide accurate information and advice. If what they offer is deemed unreliable, presumably its market value will diminish. This dynamic alone should have been sufficient to ensure analysts' probity, especially when the incentive was protected from erosion by the supposed wall between the analysis and investment banking functions in their firms. Apparently, the incentives created by the prevailing compensation system were sufficient in many cases to render the incentive to tell the truth less powerful than it should have been.[39]

N.Y. TIMES, Apr. 25, 2003, at C1 (describing settlement of SEC allegations that auditors approved the financial statements of CUC International when they knew that they did not conform to GAAP).

[38] *See* Larry E. Ribstein, *Market v. Regulatory Responses to Corporate Fraud: A Critique of the Sarbanes-Oxley Act of 2002*, 28 J. CORP. L. 1, 13-14 (2002). Ribstein also considers the possibility that the auditor may be afflicted in those circumstances by a "self-serving bias" that prevents recognition of problems, rather than affirmative dishonesty. *Id.*

[39] In response to this problem, on February 20, 2003 the SEC adopted Regulation AC which requires research reports to contain certifications by the research analyst that: (i) "the views expressed in the report accurately reflect [the analyst's] personal views;" and (ii) "[the analyst must] disclose whether or not the analyst received compensation or other payments in connection with [the analyst's] specific recommendations or views." Regulation AC, Exchange Act Release No. 33-8193; 34-47384, 17 C.F.R. § 242 (2003). Note, however, that Regulation AC does not impose substantive requirements on research analysts regard-

The failures of auditors and securities analysts as gatekeepers are notorious. Relatively less attention has been paid, however, to the lawyers and law firms who advised the fallen corporations. To be sure, some of those lawyers have come in for their share of scrutiny and criticism, and some are enmeshed as defendants in civil litigation brought on behalf of shareholders. Bolstering the role of lawyers in forestalling corporate law-breaking also has become the focus of federal legislation.[40] But lawyers do not seem to have figured in the same relatively simple morality plays as the auditors and the securities analysts. While their behavior has raised serious questions, the answers to those questions about lawyers are not transparently obvious. This is because the lawyers' roles were more complex and ambiguous.

Auditors' roles, when boiled down to their essence, are straightforward. They must play a quasi-adversarial role versus their auditing clients. Their job is not to help the managers of the company achieve their goals. The auditors' responsibility is to protect the investing public by casting a dispassionate, disinterested eye on management's accounting and financial disclosures and placing their own reputation on the line by certifying the corporate financial statement. They function, in essence, as reputational intermediaries, drawing on their professional reputations to vouch for their auditing client's financial disclosures.[41] Similarly, the securities analysts' job is to pierce through the appearance projected by the corporation and to be the one who says, "The emperor has no clothes!" Their relationship to the issuer of securities must be more detached than that of the auditor, and their responsibility flows not to corporate management but to those members of the investing public who rely on their analysis. To the extent that conflicts of interest led auditors and analysts to place currying favor with corporate managers ahead of their clear obligations to investors, they failed their essential

---

ing the content of their research reports or their manner of compensation. The new rules thus fall short of mandating the separation of research and investment banking function.

A major enforcement action spearheaded by the Office of the Attorney General of the State of New York and joined by the SEC and other regulators, however, led to a settlement in 2003 with ten major securities firms that not only extracted in excess of $1.4 billion from those firms, but required those firms to substantially sever the links between research and investment banking, particularly with respect to analysts' compensation. *See* Joint Press Release of the SEC, the State of New York Attorney General, NASAA, the NASD and, the NYSE, Ten of Nation's Top Investment Firms Settle Enforcement Actions Involving Conflicts of Interest Between Research and Investment Banking, *at* http:// www.sec.gov/news/press/2003-54.htm (Apr. 28, 2003); SEC Press Release, Statement Regarding Global Settlement Related to Analyst Conflict of Interest, at http://sec.gov/news/speech/spch042803com.htm (Apr. 28, 2003). For discussion and comments, see Stephen Labaton, *10 Wall St. Firms Settle with U.S. in Analyst Inquiry*, N.Y. TIMES, Apr. 29, 2003, at A1.

It is likely that the parties to this settlement will also face private claims from investors. For an argument that analysts' undisclosed conflicts of interest should give rise to liability for securities fraud, see Jill I. *Gross, Securities Analysts' Undisclosed Conflicts of Interest: Unfair Dealing or Securities Fraud?,* 2002 COLUM. BUS. L. REV. 631.

[40] *See infra* text accompanying notes 98-110.

[41] *See* Ribstein, *supra* note 38, at 13 (regarding the auditing firm's incentive not to forfeit their "reputational bonds").

tasks. In other words, to the extent they became advocates, they failed as auditors and analysts.

That, of course, is the basic difference between the auditors' roles and the role of lawyers that makes lawyers' participation in the perfect storm of systems failures more ambiguous, and not the subject of a simple morality tale. Lawyers are advocates. They have obligations to act on behalf of the corporate client that make their role quite different from the quasi-adversarial role of an auditor and entirely different from the detached, arm's-length function of a securities analyst.[42] Because auditors and analysts are not advocates for the corporation, their decision to act *as if they were advocates* amounted to a betrayal of the public interests they were supposed to serve. It cannot be said that the lawyers in Enron and the other cases, who were in fact supposed to be advocates for their corporate clients, similarly betrayed a public interest simply by virtue of acting on behalf of their clients. That conclusion, however, does not end the analysis. Assumption of the obligations of advocacy does not excuse a lawyer from other obligations.

Lawyers acting in the context of public companies are not only advocates. They are also gatekeepers. They stand at the approaches to the capital markets. As the auditor constrains access to the markets by its power to certify financial statements, and the analyst by its power to make investment recommendations, the company's lawyer has the duty, and at least some power, to constrain unlawful behavior by the company as it seeks access to capital. The lawyer can control market access by withholding cooperation from the potential wrongdoer.[43] She can refuse to do necessary legal work, provide legal opinions or otherwise refuse to associate the law firm's name with the questionable transaction. This will make it difficult for the client to complete the mechanics of the transaction; the lawyer's refusal to vouch for the client by acting as a reputational intermediary will make the transaction less valuable to third parties or less likely to be approved by other professional gatekeepers, higher level corporate decisionmakers or regulators.[44] In addition, a lawyer can act as a gatekeeper more affirmatively by blowing the whistle, reporting the problem to a higher level within the corporate entity or externally to regulators such as the SEC. In many respects, the lawyer-as-gatekeeper in a corporate/securities context has to maintain the type of "healthy skepticism"[45] toward

---

[42] For an example of how an analyst completely lost his detachment from the company he researched, see Landon Thomas, Jr., *Ex-Analyst Was Too Close to Tyco, N.A.S.D. Says*, N.Y. TIMES, May 29, 2003, at C1 (The Merrill Lynch analyst "went so far as to refer to himself as a loyal Tyco employee and joked that he was indirectly paid by the company.").

[43] See generally works by Professor Reinier Kraakman elaborating this definition of "gatekeeper." Reinier H. Kraakman, *Gatekeepers: The Anatomy of a Third-Party Enforcement Strategy*, 2 J.L. ECON. & ORG. 53 (1986); Reinier H. Kraakman, *Corporate Liability Strategies and the Costs of Legal Controls*, 93 YALE L.J. 857 (1984).

[44] With respect to the concept of gatekeeper as "reputational intermediary," see Ronald J. Gilson & Reinier H. Kraakman, *The Mechanisms of Market Efficiency*, 70 VA. L. REV. 549, 612-21 (1984).

[45] For an authoritative statement of this obligation by a leading securities practitioner, see A.A. Sommer, Jr., *The Emerging Responsibilities of the Securities Lawyer, Address to the Banking, Corporation & Business*

management that should also be characteristic of the auditor. The lawyer thus has both an obligation to the client and a public obligation.

Here is where the complexity lies. Lawyers are both advocates and gatekeepers, with obligations running both to the client (of a very specific kind) and to the public (of a more indeterminate type). Their relationship with the client is thus both one of trust and confidence and one that can be adversarial. This duality can produce conflict within the attorney-client relationship, and multiplies the opportunity for failure. Section 307 and the implementing rules reflect the apparent belief that the existing rules governing the attorney-client relationship made it more likely that lawyers would fail as gatekeepers by not imposing upon them the responsibility to report, in some way, unlawful behavior they confronted in the course of their representation. By creating more robust whistle-blowing obligations for lawyers, the section 307 rules attempt to fortify lawyers' positions as gatekeepers. This legislative and regulatory response, however, presumes that the problem in Enron and the other cases was primarily one of insufficient incentives (or legal obligations) to blow the whistle.

That is a questionable presumption. If we look more closely at these cases, we may conclude that lawyers' contributions to the debacles had less to do with the failures as whistle-blowers, but with different, and more fundamental problems to which the section 307 rules do not really respond. If we can understand more precisely how lawyers failed in these cases we can then determine whether the legal response to the perceived failures of corporate lawyering embodied in section 307 of the Sarbanes-Oxley Act and the SEC rules makes sense.

III. HOW DID THE LAWYERS FAIL?

Lawyers can be said to have contributed to the perfect storm in at least three basic ways. First, in some cases, they acted as partners in crime with the malefactors in the executive suite and on the board. Second, in others they provided legitimate advice on legal transactions that turned out to have very bad consequences. Third, in yet other cases, they were "merely" negligent, failing in their basic obligation to their clients to provide competent legal advice. In considering these three different scenarios, the question should be asked whether the presence of a more robust whistle-blowing obligation would have made a material difference.

A. Partners in Crime

There apparently were situations in the recent cases where lawyers actively and intentionally participated in the wrongdoing perpetrated by corporate managers. Those

Law Section, N.Y. State Bar Association (Jan. 24, 1974), *reprinted in* LARRY D. SODERQUIST & THERESA A. GABALDON, SECURITIES REGULATION 617-619 (4th ed. 1999). For a similar statement by two of the leading securities law academics in an authoritative treatise, see LOUIS LOSS & JOEL SELIGMAN, FUNDAMENTALS OF SECURITIES REGULATION 1384 (4th ed. 2001). The securities lawyer should ask "searching questions" about the client's disclosures. *Id.*

lawyers apparently knew that managers were deliberately falsifying disclosures; deceiving the board of directors, regulatory agencies or the investing public; misappropriating assets of the corporation or otherwise illegally self-dealing. These lawyers knowingly facilitated the managers' efforts through the use of their legal expertise in order to benefit themselves. In other words, some lawyers may have chosen to be partners in crime. Given the complexities of the corporate and securities laws, such active connivance by lawyers played a big role in helping corporate managers achieve illicit ends. An example in point may be the general counsel of Tyco International Ltd., who was criminally indicted for allegedly covering up a conflict of interest transaction benefiting the chief executive officer and taking for himself an unauthorized $14 million "loan."[46] Another example may be that of the general counsel of an Enron subsidiary who, according to the SEC, directly participated in and benefited from investments in the conflict of interest transactions with affiliates created by Enron.[47] We may also include in this category situations in which there was a less direct, but equally real benefit to the lawyers involved. The best example is the legal advice, drafting services, and "true sale" opinions delivered by Vinson & Elkins in connection with the special purpose entities created by Enron executives.[48] Vinson & Elkins's participation was a crucial

---

[46] Otis Bilodeau, *After Tyco, the Role of GCS Is Under Scrutiny*, RECORDER, Sept. 26, 2002, at 3; Jonathan D. Glater, *Lawyer Caught in Tyco Tangle Leaves Friends Wondering*, N.Y. TIMES, Sept. 24, 2002, at C1. As of this writing the prosecution against Mark Belnick, the former general counsel of Tyco, remains unresolved. For a more detailed discussion of Belnick's actions and the SEC's allegations against him, see Laurie P. Cohen, *How a Tyco Lawyer Channeled Windfall into Unlikely Cause*, WALL ST. J., June 4, 2003, at A1.

[47] Miriam Rozen, *Allegations Swirl Around Former Enron In-Houser*, TEX. LAW., Feb. 4, 2002, at 21.

[48] Vinson & Elkins's involvement in the construction of Enron special purpose entities has given rise to the claim that the firm is primarily liable for securities fraud under section 10(b) of the Securities Exchange Act of 1934, Pub. Law No. 107-204, 116 Stat. 784 (codified as amended at 15 U.S.C. § 7245). *See* In re Enron Corp. Secs., Derivative & ERISA Litig., 235 F. Supp. 2d 549, 656-69 (S.D. Tex. 2002). The plaintiff's claim is that the law firm's level of participation in the transactions and knowledge of fraudulent conduct was so extensive that it amounted to much more than mere aiding and abetting, for which there is no private cause of action for liability. Cent. Bank v. First Interstate Bank, 511 U.S. 164 (1994). The complaint alleges that "Vinson & Elkins was not merely a drafter, but essentially a co-author of the documents it created for public consumption, concealing its own and other participants' actions." *In re Enron Corp.*, 235 F. Supp. 2d at 704. This was but one of the allegations in the complaint:

> Among the complaint's [other] specific allegations of acts in furtherance of the [deceptive] scheme are that the firm's involvement in negotiation and structuring of the illicit partnerships and off-the-books SPEs, whose formation documentation it drafted, as well as that of the subsequent transactions of these entities. It advised making Kopper manager of Chewco so that Enron's involvement in and control of the SPE would not have to be disclosed, drafted "true sales" opinions that Lead Plaintiff asserts were essential to effect many of the allegedly fraudulent transactions. Vinson & Elkins was materially involved in the New Power IPO, and it structured and provided advice on the Mahonia trades, all actions constituting primary violations of § 10(b). In other words, it "effected the very" deceptive devices and contrivances that were the heart of the alleged Ponzi scheme.

Id. at 705. The court found in *In re Enron Corp.* that the foregoing allegations (and others) stated a claim under § 10(b) and denied Vinson & Elkins' motion to dismiss. *Id.* For discussion of how the assertion of primary liability under § 10(b) was designed as an alternative to the aiding-and-abetting argument

element in the execution of transactions with officers that involved massive conflicts of interest and inadequate public disclosures and which the law firm allegedly knew were fraudulent. The law firm did not invest directly in the transactions, but its participation helped preserve its lucrative relationship with the key officers of one of its largest clients.[49] Purposefully facilitating transactions harmful to the corporation and investors (and preparing misleading disclosures about them)[50] to protect an advantageous relationship with corporate officers crosses the line of mere negligence. A lawyer who does that becomes a partner in crime, and may become liable as a primary violator, and not simply as aider and abettor of client wrongdoing. Whether that actually happened in the case of Vinson & Elkins and Enron remains to be seen as the facts are developed in litigation. To the extent that it happened, however, it is truly bad.

It is bad, naturally, because no one wants to see lawyers, especially those whose actions affect hundreds of millions of dollars of wealth, deliberately engaged in illegality or criminality, particularly when such behavior benefits the lawyer, directly or indirectly. We would find it instructive to ask why such behavior surfaced in elite law firms and general counsels' offices where, theoretically, there are significant internal and external incentives and restraints that should preclude such a thing. This is the type of question we ask about white-collar crime in general, of which this is a specific example.

But, important as such questions may be, the kind of behavior I have just described does not raise novel or even interesting questions about the nature of the lawyer's role

---

eliminated by *Central Bank*, see David E. Rovella, *Milberg Guns for Enron's Lawyers*, NAT'L L.J., Apr. 15, 2002, at A1. Vinson & Elkins has denied that its involvement in the questionable transactions amounted to legal malpractice, let alone fraud. *See* Otis Bilodeau, *V&E Shoots Back*, LEGAL TIMES, Feb. 11, 2002, at 17 (emphasizing lack of knowledge of any fraudulent conduct and lack of responsibility for accounting determinations). Others have also defended the firm, arguing that "the issues surrounding the Enron work turned on judgment calls based on incomplete information" rather than "obvious fraud." John Schwartz, *Troubling Questions Ahead for Enron's Law Firm*, N.Y. TIMES, Mar. 12, 2002, at C1.

While the factual issues in *In re Enron Corp.* remain to be resolved, the allegations, if true, would show that the firm went beyond "mere" malpractice, and truly became a "partner in crime" with its client.

[49] Enron was Vinson & Elkins's top client, accounting for more than seven percent of the firm's $450 million in annual revenue. Mike France et al., *One Client, Big Hassle*, BUS. WEEK, Jan. 28, 2002, at 38. The plaintiffs in *In re Enron Corp.* alleged that "Vinson & Elkins chose to engage in illegal activity for and with its client in return for lucrative fees." 235 F. Supp. 2d at 704-05.

[50] For criticism of Vinson & Elkins's advice regarding the disclosures made by Enron about its SPEs, see the Powers Report, *supra* note 11, at 26 ("Vinson & Elkins should have brought a stronger, more objective and critical voice to the disclosure process."). For specific and highly critical discussion of Vinson & Elkins's role in preparing public disclosures about insiders' interests in Enron's related-party transactions, see *id.* at 178-203. The Report concluded that "the responsibility for these inadequate disclosures is shared by Enron Management, the Audit and Compliance Committee of the Board, Enron's in-house counsel, Vinson & Elkins, and Andersen." *Id.* at 178.

Even more serious charges of active complicity in generating misleading financial disclosures led to indictment of the former general counsel of HBO & Co., who allegedly helped design and execute an elaborate plan to increase revenue artificially by as much as 500% prior to the company's merger with McKesson Corp. The Justice Department called this its first-ever securities fraud indictment of a general counsel. Jason Hoppin, *Corporate GC Indicted in Fraud Case*, LEGAL INTELLIGENCER, June 6, 2003, at 4.

or the relationship of a lawyer's obligations to the client and her duty to the public. No one would suggest that a lawyer knowingly and affirmatively furthering a fraudulent or otherwise illegal scheme is doing anything consistent with a professional obligation to a client. The decision of a lawyer to share in a client's illegality or criminality does not suggest that there is anything wrong with the rules of professional conduct, or that there is a structural problem in the rules governing representation of a public corporation. Such a decision does not involve a question of what the law permits or requires (which should be clear), but of why a lawyer chooses to disobey the law. In short, to the extent the scandals are about lawyers purposely furthering their clients' wrongdoing we have a problem not of law, but of morality or psychology or the sociology of the profession. This problem is certainly important to explore, but it is not necessarily a problem of whistle-blowing. If a lawyer has decided to be partners in crime, a legal obligation to blow the whistle is the least of his concerns. He has already crossed a crucial line, and is not likely to inform on himself.

B. Legal Transactions, Bad Consequences

The partners-in-crime scenario should seem relatively clear. A second scenario is based not on the assumption that some lawyers were participating in anything illegal. Rather, they were engaged in structuring transactions that were entirely legal, but which ultimately had bad consequences. Was the lawyers' participation in structuring those transactions, which presumably needed expert legal advice, somehow problematic?

There are many examples of such "legal" transactions that produced, singly or cumulatively, bad effects. One of the bitterest consequences of the Enron collapse was the destruction of most of the value in ordinary employees' 401(k) plans, which were concentrated in Enron stock.[51] Exacerbating this problem was the company's policy of partially restricting employees from selling their own shares.[52] The employee ben-

[51] At Enron, employees concentrated sixty-two percent of their assets in Enron stock. Jeremy Kahn, *When 401(k)s Are KO'd*, FORTUNE, Jan. 7, 2002, at 104. This level of concentration was relatively high; in October 2001 only thirty percent of the $71 billion invested in 1.5 million 401(k) plans was invested in the stock of the sponsoring company. *Id.* (citing report by Hewitt Associates). Many financial experts believe, however, that even twenty-five percent concentration of assets in employer stock is too high, because most employees would benefit from greater diversification. *How Well Do 401(k) Plans Work, and Who Benefits Most From Them? (Winter 2003)*, *available at* http://knowledge.wharton.upenn.edu. Such diversification, however, was not illegal. It was also not unique at the time. *See* Steven Greenhouse, *Response to 401(k) Proposals Follows Party Lines*, N.Y. TIMES, Feb. 2, 2002, at C1 (quoting Senator Jon Corzine discussing similar examples of concentration at Sunbeam and Waste Management).

[52] Enron employees were prohibited from selling stock contributed to their 401(k) by the company until they were fifty years old. *See* Press Release, Joe Lieberman Press Office, Retirement Insecurity: 401(k) Crisis at Enron (Feb. 5, 2002), *available at* http://www.senate.gov/~lieberman/newsite/press/01101/2002102708.html. They were also prohibited from selling their stock during a controversial moratorium or "lock-down" period for at least two weeks while Enron was changing its outside administrator. *Id.* Enron stock was exceptionally volatile during this period, and only senior executives faced no restrictions in selling their stock. Steven Greenhouse & Stephen Labaton, *Enron Executives Say They Debated Freeze on Pension*, N.Y. TIMES, Feb. 6, 2002, at A1.

efits lawyers who permitted such concentration and restrictions, however, apparently provided correct legal advice. Are they responsible for what may now appear to be the negative effects of overly-permissive legal rules and of Enron executives' and trustees' administration of those rules to the detriment of their employees?[53] A similar question may be asked about the lawyers who set up the stock option compensation plans that now seem to have created perverse incentives rather than an alignment of shareholder and managerial interests.[54]

What about the lawyers who obtained exemptions for Enron from registration under the Investment Company Act of 1940[55] and the Public Utility Holding Company Act?[56] Registration under either act could have subjected Enron to a much higher level

[53] For critical discussion of Enron executives' promotion of employees' 401(k) investment in Enron stock, see Lieberman Press Release, *supra* note 52 ("Enron's top management repeatedly promoted its stock through internal publications and communications, even when executives must have known the company was a house of cards."). Enron executives have also been criticized for not delaying the lock-down or "black-out" period when they knew that a prohibition on selling would exacerbate employees' losses. Greenhouse & Labaton, *supra* note 52. Both the Labor Department and private plaintiffs have initiated action against the 401(k) plan's trustees because of their failure to warn plan participants about serious problems with Enron's accounting and its impending financial crisis. Steven Greenhouse, *U.S. Pressing for Trustees of Enron Plan to Step Down*, N.Y. TIMES, Feb. 11, 2002, at A1. *See also* Kathy Chen & Theo Francis, *Questioning the Books: Enron Official Failed to Warn Participants of 401(k) Plan*, WALL ST. J., Feb. 6, 2002, at C1 (citing argument that trustees also should have stopped offering Enron stock as an investment option and using it as a matching contribution). Whether managers of Enron or the 401(k) plan's trustees violated their fiduciary duties in aggressively pushing investment in Enron or in failing to disclose material risks remains to be seen. The role of their lawyers in advising on their sales practices and disclosure policies also deserves to be explored.

[54] *See supra* text accompanying notes 20-33.

[55] 15 U.S.C. § 80a-6 (2000). For discussion of the exemption order issued by the SEC, see FINANCIAL OVERSIGHT REPORT, *supra* note 9, at 57-60. While finding that the "initial grant of the exemption itself . . . was not clearly erroneous and had some Congressional support," the Report expressed concern with "the SEC's lack of any means to monitor the continued appropriateness of the exemption." *Id.* at 60. For Enron's application for the exemption order, see Enron Corp., Notice of Application for Exemption Under the Investment Company Act of 1940, Exchange Act Release No. IC-22515, SEC File No. 812-10150 (Feb. 14, 1997). For the SEC's order, see In the Matter of Enron Corp., Exchange Act Release No. IC-22560, SEC File No. 812-10150 (Mar. 13, 1997).

While the Report indicates that the correctness or wisdom of the SEC's decision to issue the exemption order may be debatable, it does not suggest that there was anything inappropriate about Enron's decision to apply for the order, the disclosures made in its application or the legal arguments made by its lawyers. The lawyers involved thus seemed merely to have helped their client push the limits of the applicable law, but not do anything illegal. This is an excellent example of how "normal" lawyering within the boundaries of the law can produce bad consequences.

[56] 15 U.S.C. § 79c (2000). Over a period of ten years, Enron and/or its subsidiaries obtained exemptions under the Act or determinations by the SEC staff that the activities they intended to engage in would not bring them under the definition of "public utility holding company." FINANCIAL OVERSIGHT REPORT, *supra* note 9, at 48. The Report does not find these exemptions to have been wrongfully granted, although it does take the agency to task for delaying action on pending applications, because the delay apparently allowed Enron to collect higher rates during the period of pendency than it would have been able to collect if the application had been acted upon quickly. *Id.* at 56-57. It also criticizes the SEC for

of regulatory scrutiny than it received under the Securities Exchange Act of 1934.[57] In fact, Enron's ability to fall between regulatory tools can be cited as one of the reasons it was able to conduct its business in such an unusual, deceptive, and risky manner.[58] Were the attorneys, who made the legal arguments that led to at least arguably correct, if ultimately unfortunate, administrative decisions to exempt Enron from regulation, doing anything inappropriate?

The same thing might be asked about the lawyers who structured Enron's byzantine tax shelter transactions, creating tax issues so complex "that the I.R.S. lacked the capacity to deal with them."[59] These "structured" tax transactions were used not only to generate massive tax deductions, but also as a basis for reporting future tax savings as current income.[60] While the tax opinions from major law firms supporting those transactions, as well as the information disclosed to the IRS and the public about them, have been severely criticized,[61] can it be said definitively that the lawyers involved

"the lack of coordination between the SEC and FERC [which] permitted Enron to take full advantage of gaps and overlaps in the agencies' jurisdictions." *Id.* at 57. Enron's lawyers thus seem to have been both creative and persistent in the typical lawyerly endeavor of exploiting the limitations of the various regulatory schemes applicable to their client.

[57] Pub. L. No. 107-204, 116 Stat. 771, 790, 807 (codified as amended at 15 U.S.C. § 78(a)-(mm)).

[58] For critical discussion of the consequences of granting an exemption under the Investment Company Act of 1940, see John Berlau, *Investigative Report: Who Cleared That Enron Exemption?,* INSIGHT ON THE NEWS, Mar. 4, 2002, at 15; Stephen Labaton, *Exemption Won in '97 Set Stage for Enron Woes,* N.Y. TIMES, Jan. 23, 2002, at A1. It should be noted that Enron also was able to avoid regulation under the Commodities Future Trading Commission by supporting legislation exempting energy trading that was enacted in 2000. *See* Richard W. Stevenson & Jeff Gerth, *Web of Safeguards Failed as Enron Fell,* N.Y. TIMES, Jan. 20, 2002, at 1.

[59] David Cay Johnston, *Wall St. Firms Are Faulted in Report on Enron's Taxes,* N.Y. TIMES, Feb. 14, 2003, at C1.

[60] For an excellent summary of the issues associated with Enron's tax transactions, see Mike France, *The Rise of the Wall Street Tax Machine,* BUS. WEEK, Mar. 31, 2003, at 84. The key to these transactions was highly complex exchanges of assets between Enron and its SPEs not only to generate future tax savings, but to convert those notional savings into current income. France reports that "the 12 tax avoidance transactions the company did from 1995 to 2001 produced $2.02 billion in tax savings—and were then converted into $2.079 billion in current income." *Id.* France's data is derived from a report by the staff on the Joint Committee on Taxation. *See generally* STAFF OF SENATE COMM. ON FINANCE, 107TH CONG., REPORT OF INVESTIGATION OF ENRON CORPORATION AND RELATED ENTITIES REGARDING FEDERAL TAX AND COMPENSATION ISSUES, AND POLICY RECOMMENDATIONS (Comm. Print 2003), *available at* http://www.access.gpo.gov/congress/joint/jcs-3-03/vol1/.

[61] See critical comments by Professors Susan P. Koniak, Gregory A. Plesko, and Jeffrey Gramlich quoted in Peter Behr & Carrie Johnson, *Enron Probes Now Focus on Tax Deals,* WASH. POST, Jan. 21, 2003, at E01. *See also* France, *supra* note 60 (quoting Professor Sheldon D. Pollack). These and other critics have not only questioned the legality of claiming deductions by both Enron and the SPE on the same transaction, and treating tax savings as current income, but also the quality of disclosure regarding those decisions. Without full disclosure of the sleight-of-hand in such conversions, the statement of income is likely to give a misleading picture of the company's profitability.

A particularly troublesome aspect of the tax opinions provided in these transactions was the incestuous relationship among the law firms providing the opinions and the investment bankers or accounting firms promoting the transactions to the clients. The tax opinion is "likely compromised," according to Professor

were doing anything more than helping the client minimize tax liability within the applicable rules?[62]

Let's assume, for the sake of argument, that the opinions and advice provided by Enron's tax counsel were legitimate, in that they were not compromised by deceit, conflict of interest or even incompetence. Does that mean that there is nothing left to say about what these lawyers did?

One can envision a theory of lawyering that requires lawyers to take a very long view of what the potential negative consequences of legal transactions might be for persons other than their clients, or for the public interest in the abstract. Application of such a robust theory of "green" lawyering, as it has been called in a provocative article by Professor David Luban,[63] could provide a response to the problem of "legal transactions, bad consequences," which is something different from intentionally assisting clients in performing unlawful acts (the partners-in-crime scenario), and even willful blindness to those acts (which could be simply another version of the partners-in-crime scenario).[64] In both of these versions of the partners-in-crime scenario the lawyers' duty of non-cooperation should be obvious, although lawyers too frequently justify willful ignorance with highly dubious versions of the "I didn't know" excuse.[65] A truly "green" conception of lawyering, while it would certainly require avoidance of

---

Ronald Pearlman, when the person providing the opinion "is involved in selling the shelter, when that person is paid up front, and when that person's time and effort are invested in putting the shelter together." Paul Braverman, *The Bleeding Edge*, AM. LAW., June 2003, at 94, 97 (discussing criticism of the role of the law firm McKee Nelson Ernst & Young in shelter transactions). These opinions raise a question of whether the lawyers were involved in ordinary transactional cost engineering and tax minimization (raising the "legal transaction, bad consequences" problem), or whether the lawyers were so compromised by conflicts of interest as to become partners in crime. For discussion of the possible moral effects of providing opinions that play so close to the line, see *infra* text accompanying notes 91-93.

[62] Crucial to the consummation of these transactions were opinion letters provided by major law firms such as King & Spalding and Akin Gump Strauss Hauer & Feld on the legality of the tax treatment claimed for the transaction. *See* France, *supra* note 60, at 84-85, 87. Presumably, the attitude of the firms involved was summarized by Robert J. Hermann, former Enron in-house tax counsel, who said, "'People can disagree on what works within the written rules. . . . If you know the rules, you don't have to break the rules, you just use them. That's what lawyers and accountants do.'" Behr & Johnson, *supra* note 61. While it may be that the legal opinions were legitimate means to achieving the legitimate goal of tax minimization, there is a question of whether it was possible for a firm to give an objective, independent opinion when it was involved in the development of the transaction. France, *supra* note 60, at 87. Akin Gump has responded to such a suggestion by asserting that it had the "informal consent" of both parties to the transaction. *Id.* For further discussion of the significance of client consent, see *infra* text accompanying note 87.

[63] *See generally* David Luban, *The Social Responsibilities of Lawyers: A Green Perspective*, 63 GEO. WASH. L. REV. 955 (1995).

[64] For further discussion of this scenario, see *infra* text accompanying notes 89-97.

[65] *See* Luban, *supra* note 63, at 980.

> When I talk with practicing lawyers or law students about rules forbidding lawyers from knowingly doing something improper on behalf of clients, the retort is invariably that you never really *know*. . . . Ironically, lawyers who pride themselves on their common sense practicality, and who usually have no patience for philosophical abstractions and paradoxes, suddenly embrace a wildly

partners-in-crime behavior,[66] would go further by requiring a lawyer advising or opining on legal transactions, and engaged in legal minimization of regulatory or tax burdens, to think holistically about the social effects of her actions as part of a system of coordinated actions by others (including the client). She should "take personal responsibility for the systemic consequences to which [her] actions contribute, even if [her] contribution to those consequences is minimal,"[67] or, I should say, legal. In this "green" view, a lawyer who does not attend to the social consequences of participation in the clients' activities would be socially irresponsible, and hence unethical. Presumably, a system of ethical rules that required such a view of lawyers' responsibilities would mitigate the "legal transactions, bad consequences" problem.

Requiring lawyers to serve as the social conscience of the client, however, obviously raises fundamental questions about the nature of the attorney-client relationship and the traditional presumption of the primacy of the client's claim on the lawyer's loyalties. It is entirely consistent with that claim to demand that a lawyer avoid participating in a client's wrongdoing, even passively through contrived ignorance or convenient blindness. It is more difficult, however, to ask a lawyer to serve two masters when the client is not acting wrongfully, and when the other "master" is so poorly defined. For this ethical reorientation to work, the "green" lawyer would have to resolve questions of definition (what is the public interest—or the third-party interest—for which lawyers must also be advocates?), standard-setting (what consequences other than legality raise an issue for the lawyer?), balancing (how are client interests and public interests to be balanced?), and foreseeability (what should a lawyer do when the social consequences of a cause of action are murky or debatable in principle?).[68]

> implausible standard of knowledge as Cartesian certainty—roughly, equating knowledge with infallibility—whenever "knowing" something would prove inconvenient.

Id.

[66] See Professor Luban's discussion of the lawyers' "contrived ignorance" in the O.P.M. client fraud case of the 1980s, in which the law firm closed millions of dollars of fraudulent loan transactions on behalf of its client, and did not blow the whistle, despite its awareness of client fraud in connection with previous loans it had closed. *Id.* at 981.

[67] *Id.* at 956.

[68] Professor Luban recognizes the foreseeability problem when he points out that "criticizing lawyers because they did not take incalculable long-term effects into account during their representation of clients seems suspiciously like the specious wisdom of twenty-twenty hindsight." *Id.* at 978. He cites as an example the criticism of M&A lawyers during the hostile takeover heyday of the 1980s. Can it be assumed that if hostile takeovers were bad for the economy and society, then M&A lawyers representing bidders were socially irresponsible? If takeovers turned out to be beneficial, productivity-enhancing transactions, were the M&A lawyers representing entrenched management the socially irresponsible ones? Acknowledging this conundrum, Luban concludes

> [g]iven the immense uncertainties involved in macro-economic forecasting, however, it would be preposterous to hold the lawyers morally responsible for "getting it wrong." And if lawyers cannot be expected to get it right, they may as well give their clients the benefit of the doubt . . . .
>
> There really is no reply to this excuse, for in many instances it is absolutely right.

Id. at 979.

In the absence of the adoption of some theory of "green" lawyering, however, what can we say about lawyers who were pretty much doing what business lawyers usually do—solving business problems with legal technology, lowering the costs of regulatory compliance and advising their clients about what the law permits?[69] If that is all they did, was their contribution to the perfect storm culpable in a way that demands regulatory response, particularly in the form of a stronger whistle-blowing mandate?

C. "Merely" Negligent

Lawyers may also have contributed to the perfect storm in an entirely familiar way—through bad lawyering. At least some of the lawyers who could have made a difference simply performed their jobs below an acceptable level of professional competence. Perhaps the best known examples of malpractice in the recent scandals were the special investigations conducted by Simpson Thacher & Bartlett for Global Crossing and Vinson & Elkins for Enron in response to the allegations of whistle-blowers. In both cases, the negligence was compounded, or even caused, by the firms' conflict of interest. In a report[70] commissioned by independent directors of Global Crossing, the law firm Coudert Brothers found that Simpson Thacher's investigation of serious allegations about accounting and disclosure irregularities "failed to satisfy its professional responsibilities to Global Crossing."[71] According to the report, Simpson Thacher failed to obtain critical documents and interview key executives involved in the questionable transactions,[72] failed to inform the outside auditor of the allegations in a timely fashion,[73] and neglected to pursue the investigation vigorously.[74] While Coudert Brothers found that the transactions were legitimate, if of little value to the company, and that Simpson Thacher did not intend to conceal any wrongdoing, the

---

The situation of M&A lawyers is analogous to that of lawyers who constructed executive stock option compensation plans that created perverse incentives and 401(k) plans allowing excessive concentration of assets and limiting liquidity. How can lawyers be expected to have foreseen the negative effects of legal transactions that most people thought actually were good for stockholders and employees? When the foreseeability problem is taken into account, the notion of "green" lawyering does not seem to pose a real solution to the problem of "legal transactions, bad consequences" as I have defined it. It does, however, offer a much needed corrective to the more passive, ambiguous form of acting as a partner in crime which seems to have been endemic in the recent cases. There is an interesting question of whether the lawyers' role in structuring deals, providing opinions and formulating disclosures falls into the category of "legal transactions, bad consequences," or "contrived ignorance" of wrongful client behavior.

[69] On the concept of the lawyer as "transaction cost engineer," see Ronald J. Gilson, *Value Creation by Business Lawyers: Legal Skills and Asset Pricing*, 94 YALE L.J. 239 (1984). For elaboration of the concept, see Mark A. Sargent, *What Does It Take? The Hallmarks of the Business Lawyer*, BUS. L. TODAY, July/Aug., 1996, at 11.

[70] *See* Global Crossing Report, *supra* note 13.

[71] *Id.* at 47.

[72] *Id.* at 37.

[73] *Id.* at 45.

[74] *Id.* at 40-41.

firm also found that Global Crossing "suffered significant injuries as a result" of the inadequacy of the investigation.[75] The report concluded that "causes of action may be asserted against [Simpson Thacher] for malpractice and breach of fiduciary duty."[76] This mess, the report argues, resulted at least in part from the conflict of interest created by a Simpson Thacher partner serving as Global Crossing's acting general counsel while remaining a partner during the investigation.[77]

That a conflict of interest produced an inadequate special investigation is even more apparent in the case of Vinson & Elkins's investigation into the by-now famous allegations of whistle-blower Sherron Watkins.[78] The firm conducted a highly limited investigation into serious allegations about conflicts of interest and accounting problems in Enron's transactions with the numerous affiliated partnerships in which senior officers invested.[79] Vinson & Elkins's investigation consisted of a review of the relevant documents and interviews with some, but not all, of the officers involved in the trans-

---

[75] The Global Crossing Report concluded that the inadequate investigation and the delays it created "deprived the Company of the benefit of audited 2001 financial statements," which had a negative impact on the valuation of the company in bankruptcy. *Id.* at 45. In addition, the Report concluded that the whistle blower's allegations "have subjected the Company to reputational damage and adverse regulatory scrutiny it would have been able to avoid or mitigate if Simpson Thatcher & Bartlett had done its job." *Id.*

[76] *Id.* at 47

[77] *Id.* at 42.

> Brandon served in dual, concurrent capacities. His loyalty did not run exclusively to the company. It also ran to Simpson Thatcher & Bartlett, the law firm of which he remained a partner while he worked as the Company's Acting General Counsel. This circularity precipitated a conflict of interest when Olafson's allegations were not adequately investigated by Simpson Thacher & Bartlett.

Id. Simpson Thacher has vigorously contested the Global Crossing Report's allegations. In a statement to the press, the firm asserted that

> [t]he report is inaccurate and makes no sense. It unfairly faults Simpson Thacher for not inquiring thoroughly into accounting allegations that the committee itself and the outside auditors have concluded are meritless. It suggests that Simpson, not the company, had the responsibility to bring these allegations to the attention of the auditors. But it ignores the fact that, at our first opportunity, we advised the company to make this disclosure to the auditors. The company chose not to follow our advice.

Simpson Thacher: Report "Makes No Sense," LEGAL TIMES, Mar. 17, 2003, at 17. Simpson Thacher has also disputed the Report's claim that the bankrupt company could have been able to obtain audited financial statements but for the firm's allegedly inadequate investigation, and claimed that it was retained only to do an informal, purely internal investigation that the officers back-burnered as Global Crossing approached bankruptcy. Otis Bilodeau, *For Two Elites, a Family Feud,* LEGAL TIMES, Mar. 17, 2003, at 1.

For critical discussion of Simpson Thacher's performance in this matter, see Michelle Cottle, *Private Practice: Why No One Blames the Lawyers*, NEW REPUBLIC, Oct. 14, 2002, at 12; Susan P. Koniak, *Who Gave Lawyers a Pass?*, FORBES, Aug. 12, 2002, at 58.

[78] Letter from Sherron Watkins, to Kenneth L. Lay, Chief Executive Officer, Enron Corp. (Aug. 14, 2002), *available at* http:// news.findlaw.com/hdocs.enron/docs/enron/empltr2lay82001.pdf [hereinafter Watkins Letter]. The letter was originally anonymous.

[79] For detailed (and highly critical) discussion of this investigation see Roger C. Cramton, *Enron and the Corporate Lawyer: A Primer on Legal and Ethical Issues*, 58 BUS. LAW. 143, 162-67 (2002).

actions, as well as its own lawyers and two partners of Arthur Andersen.[80] The firm apparently agreed with the CEO of Enron that there would be no second-guessing of Arthur Andersen's accounting advice, and that there would be neither detailed analysis of the transactions in question, nor a discovery-style inquiry.[81] While Vinson & Elkins ultimately found some conflicts of interest in the arrangements, and that their "bad cosmetics"[82] created "a serious risk of adverse publicity and litigation," the firm concluded that "the facts disclosed do not, in our judgment, warrant a further widespread independent investigation by outside counsel and auditors."[83]

Serious questions can be raised about whether an investigation so circumscribed from the outset could support such a positive conclusion.[84] It is not clear that such a pollyannaish determination would have been reached if a thorough, professionally competent investigation had been conducted. Particularly remarkable was the firm's apparent willingness to base its conclusion on the finding that "none of the individuals interviewed could identify any transaction between Enron and LJM that was not reasonable from Enron's standpoint or contrary to Enron's best interests,"[85] despite the personal interest the same individuals had in the transactions. Even more clear-cut was the law firm's utter insensitivity to the problems identified by Watkins in her letter to the CEO that triggered the investigation: "Can't use V & E due to conflict, they provided some 'true sale' opinions on some of the deals."[86] Vinson & Elkins's willingness to provide allegedly disinterested reassurance to its client about deals in which it

---

[80] The limited, "preliminary" nature of the investigation is stated in the report setting forth Vinson & Elkins' conclusions. See Letter from Max Hendrick III, Vinson & Elkins, L.L.P., to James V. Derrick, Jr., Executive Vice President and General Counsel, Enron Corp. (Oct. 15, 2001), 2001 WL 1764266, at 2 [hereinafter Hendrick Letter]. *See also* Powers Report, supra note 11, at 80 (describing the limited scope of the investigation).

[81] Hendrick Letter, *supra* note 80, at 1.

[82] *Id.* at 9.

[83] *Id.* at 8.

[84] *Id.* at 6. Vinson & Elkins apparently drew solace from the fact that "the individuals interviewed were virtually uniform in stating that LJM provided a convenient alternative equity partner with flexibility," and that "both the awkwardness and potential for conflict of interest should be eliminated on a going-forward basis as a result of Mr. Fastow's divestment of his ownership interest in the LJM partnerships." *Id.* It is not clear why the recognition of a putative business purpose and the elimination of future conflicts of interest should have reconciled the firm to relying on the judgment of individuals who were so obviously conflicted.

[85] Watkins Letter, *supra* note 78, at 6.

[86] "True sale" opinions are essential to the securitization of assets. A law firm must opine that the assets to be securitized have "truly" been sold to the entity that will hold them. The opinion should not be given unless the firm can make the legal determination that the assets have been separated from the originator who wants to securitize them. If they have not been legally severed, and the originator enters bankruptcy, the assets will be included within the bankrupt's estate, and the bondholders who relied on the assets for security will lose that security. For discussion of the problems with the true sale opinions issued by Vinson & Elkins and other firms for Enron's benefit, see Otis Bilodeau, *New Questions over Lawyering in Enron "True Sale" Opinions at Issue in Probe of Controversial Deals*, Legal Times, Sept. 30, 2002, at 1.

provided an essential legal opinion[87] is hardly consistent with its basic obligations to the client of loyalty and due care.[88]

More generally, to the extent that attorneys for public corporations failed to advise their boards about conflicts of interest in officers' self-dealing transactions such as sweetheart loans, usurpation of corporate opportunities, spurious bonuses and excessive compensation, they were negligent in meeting their professional obligations to the board which, after all, is the embodiment of their client, not the officers who hired them. To put it another way, the attorneys' failure to blow the whistle internally on wrongdoing by corporate officers and other senior employees was simply negligence. If that negligence injured the corporate client, those lawyers would be subject to negligence actions brought by newly independent boards, shareholders in derivative actions, or receivers in bankruptcy asserting the corporation's claims for the benefit of the creditors. We may conclude, therefore, that part of the lawyers' contribution to the perfect storm was essentially an epidemic of bad, negligent lawyering.

When the negligence explanation is joined to the other two possible descriptions of the role of lawyers in the perfect storm—partners in crime, and legal transactions, bad consequences—we have a multi-faceted description of the lawyers' contribution to the systems breakdowns that afflicted corporate America. That description, however, does not adequately explain the full range of lawyers' failures in Enron and its successors.

IV. THE COMMON THREAD: "SEE NO EVIL"

At the extremes, the culpability of lawyers who contributed to the frauds and breaches of fiduciary duty characteristic of Enron and its successors is clear. When lawyers knowingly and intentionally participate in and facilitate clients' wrongful acts, and benefit either directly from the ill-gotten gains or indirectly through fees, they have crossed the line. Civil and, where appropriate, criminal liability can only be expected. In deciding what to do about such cases there is no moral conundrum, theoretical problem or legal/doctrinal issue. There is only the specific problem of establishing the facts in individual cases and the more general problem of figuring out why there was so much of this behavior in the profession.

---

[87] Vinson & Elkins's willingness to provide such reassurances about transactions in which it played such a crucial role is especially remarkable in light of its own acknowledgment that the accounting treatment for the transactions was "creative and aggressive." The law firm has defended its undertaking of the investigation on the ground that the client exercised its right to waive any conflict of interest on the part of the firm. Professor Cramton has argued, however, that the waiver on behalf of the corporate client may have been given by the CEO and the general counsel, both of whom were implicated in the misconduct alleged by Watkins, thus invalidating the waiver. Professor Cramton argues further that even if the consent was valid, the firm's investigation failed to meet "the objective standard that the lawyer reasonably believe the representation will not be adversely affected by the lawyer's conflict of interest." Cramton, *supra* note 79, at 164. For a summary of Vinson & Elkins's various defenses of its work for Enron, see Otis Bilodeau, *V&E Shoots Back*, LEGAL TIMES, Feb. 11, 2002, at 17.

[88] For discussion of failure to report wrongdoing to the board as both negligence and an ethical violation, and citation of the relevant sources, see Cramton, *supra* note 79, at 154-56.

At the other extreme, those lawyers who provided legitimate advice on transactions that generated bad consequences would seem to have little culpability, absent a "green" reformation of legal ethics. If the bad consequences flowed from defects in the legal rules permitting the transactions, or if they reflected bad business judgment by the clients, or if the clients manipulated the transactions in a way not anticipated by the lawyer, there is little for which the lawyer can be held accountable.

In between those extremes, however, there is much that needs further analysis. Between the extremes, for example, are the following scenarios:

1. Willful refusal to recognize wrongful behavior by the client, particularly when the client relationship is lucrative. Such contrived ignorance is a passive, although perhaps ambiguous, version of the partners-in-crime scenario. Vinson & Elkins's role in the structuring of and preparing disclosures about Enron's SPEs may be a case in point.
2. Pushing the envelope in providing advice and legal opinions on transactions at the edge of legality, particularly when the opinion provider is conflicted by multiple roles in the transaction. The opinions provided by Akin Gump and Nelson McKee on Enron's (and others') tax shelter transactions are cases in point.
3. Negligent representation that involves inadequate inquiry into questionable transactions, particularly when the lawyer is compromised by a conflict of interest, as was the case in different ways in Simpson Thacher's investigation of Global Crossing and Vinson & Elkins's investigation of Enron's affiliate transactions.
4. Negligent failure to fully inform and warn boards of directors of the dangers inherent in corporate transactions from which the officers will benefit (Enron, Adelphia).

All of these scenarios led to injuries to the corporations the lawyers served, as well as their shareholders. Whether such behavior will subject the lawyers involved to civil or criminal liability under the federal securities laws, malpractice liability, or liability on other grounds remains to be seen. What is interesting about these scenarios, however, is their common thread. The reluctance, or inability, of lawyers to recognize, confront and act upon questionable or even wrongful acts by their clients was a failure on their part. In many of these cases, sophisticated lawyers seemed determined to see no evil.

The determination to see no evil is nothing new, and has been recognized before. It seems to have been endemic among the lawyers involved in the savings and loan collapses of the 1980s.[89] The tendency to see no evil also has many causes. It may be

[89] See Judge Stanley Sporkin's famous *cri de coeur* in *Lincoln Savings & Loan Ass'n v. Wall*, 743 F. Supp. 901, 920 (D.D.C. 1990):

> The questions that must be asked are:
>
> Where were these professionals, a number of whom are now asserting their rights under the Fifth Amendment, when these clearly improper transactions were being consummated?

a problem of social cognition, which arises when a lawyer has internalized the client's worldview, or ego-identified with the client, preventing the lawyer from seeing the world as it really is.[90] It may in some cases be a result of the compartmentalization of legal work by a large company that prevents one law firm from having a complete picture of what is actually going on, assigning different firms pieces of complex transactions, or different transactions in a series of deals. The rapid turnover of deals, the haste to produce public disclosure, and delegation by large, busy firms of important work to inexperienced lawyers[91] may all produce blind spots, particularly when the client's work was extraordinarily complex and novel, as was Enron's.

Some blindness is entirely purposeful. It is a kind of structural or role-blindness, a suspension of judgment about what a client does that allows the lawyer to disclaim any responsibility, on the theory that the lawyer is providing only a narrow "technical" opinion on the law, and that what the client does with it is the client's decision and responsibility. There are a couple of problems with this theory. First of all, it presumes disingenuously that the lawyer is playing a limited, passive role in the structuring of the transactions and deciding how to handle them. As Enron's lawyers' active promotion of the company's tax shelters shows, this is sometimes not the case.[92] Even if those cases represent an unusually blatant conflict between promoting deals and providing allegedly disinterested opinions on those deals, it is not at all unusual for transactional lawyers

---

Why didn't any of them speak up or disassociate themselves from the transactions?

Where also were the outside accountants and attorneys when these transactions were effectuated?

What is difficult to understand is that with all the professional talent involved (both accounting and legal), why at least one professional would not have blown the whistle to stop the overreaching that took place in this case.

For analyses of the role of lawyers in the savings and loan cases, see Symposium, *The Attorney-Client Relationship in a Regulated Society*, 35 S.TEX. L. REV. 571 (1994) and In the Matter of Kaye, Scholer, Fierman, Hays and Handler: *A Symposium on Government Regulation, Lawyers' Ethics, and the Rule of Law*, 66 S. CAL. L. REV. 977 (1993).

[90] The problem of how the dynamics of social cognition influence lawyers' ability to recognize and respond to wrongdoing by clients has been analyzed in great detail by Professor Donald Langevoort. *See* Donald C. Langevoort, *Where Were the Lawyers? A Behavioral Inquiry into Lawyers' Responsibility for Clients' Fraud*, 46 VAND. L. REV. 75, 95-110 (1993).

[91] A case in point may be a two-page letter agreement amending a loan agreement that was drafted by a fourth-year associate at Vinson & Elkins relating to the transfer of $6.6 million from Enron to Chewco Investments, a major Enron affiliate. Once Arthur Andersen became aware of the letter, it determined that Chewco's putatively off-balance sheet liabilities would have to be consolidated with Enron's, with disastrous consequences for Enron. *See* Powers Report, *supra* note 11, at 52-53. For discussion of Vinson & Elkins's role in preparing this letter agreement, see Douglas McCollam, *V&E's Smoking Gun*, AM. LAW., Mar. 2002, at 20. Vinson & Elkins has denied that it had the responsibility for disclosing the fatal side agreement to the auditor. *Letter: Misunderstanding V&E's Role,* AM. LAW., Mar. 6, 2002, at 15 (letter of Harry Reasoner). Regardless of what Vinson & Elkins was required to do for purposes of determining any malpractice liability, there is an interesting question of whether a more experienced lawyer would have recognized the dangerous implications of the letter agreement and raised a question with the client and/or the auditor.

[92] *See supra* notes 60-61.

to play a lead role in devising deal structures. Attorneys know exactly what their clients are doing because their advice makes it possible. Furthermore, that theory embodies a stunted view of the lawyer's role. Instead of providing independent professional judgment, which should be the professional norm, some "lawyers take the position that they must do everything that the client's managers want them to do, providing the conduct is permitted by law."[93] The problem with this definition of the lawyer's role, as Professor Roger Cramton has pointed out, is that "by constantly going to the edge of the law and taking a very permissive view of what the law permits, these lawyers gradually adopt a mindset that ignores and may eventually assist the client's managers in illegality that harms third persons and the client entity."[94] The lawyer who becomes used to walking on the edge, and leaving the client to face the risk of liability, dulls his sensitivity to the permeability of the line between the legal and illegal, the moral and immoral, and becomes, gradually but inevitably, a blind man whose stock in trade is his own blindness.

The most important reason for blindness to wrongdoing, however, is simpler. Seeing evil is costly. Because it is costly, people tend to avoid seeing evil. If they see it, they convince themselves they did not see it, or at least pretend they did not. If they cannot pretend, they begin the process of rationalization, for which human beings have an almost infinite capacity. They conclude that the problem was not really that bad, that the problem was anomalous, or localized and not systemic, or, optimistically, that the problem will take care of itself, disappear over time, or never be discovered. People, including lawyers whose professional training should prevent it, fall back on these devices when they come to appreciate the true costliness of seeing evil.

The costliness has many levels, and needs to be understood as something more than a threat to lawyers' or law firms' greed. There is, for example, an emotional cost. Recognition that a client is asking one to participate in, approve, or cover up questionable or wrongful acts will jar even a cynical lawyer's sense of the ordinary air of legitimacy that surrounds our everyday professional life. Suddenly, the people who seemed to be reliable, trustworthy and well-intentioned colleagues are now "problems." Awkward accusations and embarrassment seem inevitable. Reluctance to deal with such problems, especially ones that require confrontation with the client, is common when the lawyer's instinct is to present the client with solutions, not problems. The lawyer wants to appear as a problem solver who has internalized the values and goals of the firm, not a bomb-thrower. Similarly, a lawyer's status with the firm depends on his ability not just to attract clients, but to keep them happy. Recognition of a "problem," therefore, creates emotionally fraught role-strain within the attorney-client relationship and status anxiety for lawyers operating within firms. That some lawyers conclude that it is better not to see anything is not surprising.

Another emotional cost may be anxiety about injury, both to one's *amour propre* and one's external reputation. It may be exquisitely painful for some lawyers to admit that

---

[93] Cramton, *supra* note 79, at 173.

[94] *Id.*

they have become involved with something questionable.[95] It may be impossible for them to admit that their advice (or that of their partners) was tainted by a conflict of interest, that their opinion letter pushed the limits of the law too far, or that they failed to pursue an issue or an investigation as vigorously as they should. Recognition that their involvement contributed materially to a client's wrongdoing may be too much for some lawyers to bear. They also might not be able to bear thinking about the potential threat to their professional reputation. Because these emotional costs are so high, some lawyers will consciously or unconsciously close their eyes to the problem and indulge in all manners of rationalization. The short-term benefit will be outweighed by the long-term cost, but for some, this is not the sphere of rational decision-making, despite lawyers' training in dispassionate analysis.

Other costs are economic, but even these are complex. Recognition of a problem may result in a loss of "sunk costs." By the time a serious problem is recognized, the lawyer and her firm may have sunk considerable amounts of time into a transaction or an ongoing relationship with a client. That time and its attendant expenses may be never paid if the lawyer surfaces problems that might unravel the transaction or even the client. If the sunk costs are considerable, lawyers may decide that keeping silent and hoping it all works out for the best are the only options. This concern about sunk costs would be particularly intense, for example, for the law firms engaged in promoting corporate tax shelters, because their investment is not just in specific transactions but in a whole line of business involving many clients. This is especially true when it starts to become clear that the essence of the law firm's services entailed serious conflicts of interest and opinions at the outer edge of plausibility.

The question of economic cost is also complicated by the potentially conflicting interests of individual lawyers representing problematic clients and the law firm as a whole.[96] A lawyer whose book of business and personal income is dominated by the problematic client is going to bear a disproportionate share of any loss generated by alienating the client or killing a deal or series of deals. While no firm wants to alienate a client or compromise sources of revenue, the firm's other sources of revenue will make the losses more bearable. The firm thus may have a more objective appreciation of the long-term risks for the firm, which might be much greater than the short-term risk to the individual lawyer of losing his major client. Hence, law firms may be particularly

---

[95] Langevoort, *supra* note 90, at 102-03. As Professor Langevoort put it,

> When people voluntarily commit themselves to a certain position, attitude or belief, the subsequent discovery of information that indicates harmful consequences flowing from that commitment directly threatens their self-concept as good, worthwhile individuals. Thus cognitive processes will work to suppress such information if at all possible.

Id.

[96] A similar point has been made about conflicts within accounting firms between the interests of an individual partner or partners and the firm, using the behavior of the partners in Arthur Andersen's Houston office, who were highly dependent on Enron revenues: "Andersen's Houston office gambled with the reputation of the partnership as a whole in order to maintain the revenue flow from their profit center." Bratton, *supra* note 6, at 1350-51.

vulnerable when a partner in charge is more anxious about loss to himself than the potential cost to the firm. Of course, this distinction evaporates when the problematic client is also one of the firm's major clients. Firms in that situation then tend to think like partners in charge, and begin making calculations about the comparative risk of relatively certain short-term losses versus larger, but more speculative long-term losses.

The final aspect of the question of economic cost is perhaps the simplest. Some lawyers simply cannot stand to see their greed unfulfilled. Surrounded by corporate princes rolling in wealth often created as if by magic, they fall prey to the corruption of envy, as the princes' lawyers ask "why not me?" Their sense of entitlement makes it very hard indeed to take the actions that would destroy their dreams of wealth.

This discussion should not end, however, with simplistic, censorious assumptions about the prevalence of personal greed, although there was apparently plenty of that.[97] The tragedy of the lawyers' failures in these cases is that many of the lawyers involved were not consumed with greed, but were simply doing their best, often under great pressure and uncertainty, to keep their firms afloat by trying to feed the large law firms' endless appetite for billable hours and fees. The economic demands of sustaining a large law firm had a gradually corrosive effect, numbing not just a lawyer's sense of decency but also his own sense of self-preservation as he succumbs to avoidance of the truth and rationalization of his client's and his own legal and moral failures.

V. THE REGULATORY RESPONSE: FORCING THEM TO SEE

A. Section 307 and the SEC Rules

In the summer of 2002, Congress enacted section 307 of the Sarbanes-Oxley Act.[98] Section 307 directs the SEC to issue rules setting forth minimum standards of professional conduct for attorneys appearing and practicing before the Commission in any way in the representation of issuers, which includes attorneys advising corporations registering securities with the SEC, hence all public companies.[99] Those standards were to include a rule requiring such attorneys to report evidence of a "material violation" of securities law or breach of fiduciary duty or similar violation by the company

---

[97] Professor Langevoort also cautions against simplistic assumptions of venality (or stupidity) on the part of lawyers, arguing that "venality competes not so much with stupidity as with honest, even good faith behavior that only in hindsight seems incredible." Langevoort, *supra* note 90, at 78. For Langevoort, the key obstacles to lawyers' recognition of clients' wrongful acts are the "blind spots" created by lawyers' problems of social cognition, as he argues for recognition of

> the possibility that lawyers have a diminished cognitive capacity to appreciate the likely harm flowing from their client's actions. Both ego and stress can induce blind spots. By the time the lawyer actually becomes aware of the wrong, his or her complicity already is fixed. Denial and rationalization ensue. Only at the very late stages, if at all, is there something like a conscious cover-up.

Id.

[98] Sarbanes-Oxley Act § 307, Pub. L. No. 107-204, 116 Stat. 784 (codified at 15 U.S.C. § 7245).

[99] 17 C.F.R. § 205.2(a) (2003).

or any agent to the chief legal counsel or CEO.[100] That rule also was to require the attorney to report the evidence to the audit or other appropriate committee or to the board as a whole if the chief legal counsel or CEO does not appropriately respond to the evidence.[101]

In November 2002, the SEC proposed rules implementing the Congressional mandate for so-called "up the ladder" reporting that included a complex set of definitions, standards and procedures.[102] The Commission went beyond that mandate, however, and also proposed a so-called "noisy withdrawal" requirement.[103] If the attorney representing an issuer reports the matter all the way up the ladder within the issuer and does not receive an appropriate response from the issuer's directors, and if the material violation is ongoing or about to occur and is likely to result in substantial injury to the issuer or an investor, the attorney will be required to withdraw from the representation and notify the Commission that such withdrawal was made for "professional considerations."[104]

As might be expected, the SEC's proposed rules, particularly the noisy withdrawal provisions, provoked an outpouring of formal letters of comment from the bar (mostly con) and the legal academy (mostly pro).[105] The rules, as finally adopted by the Commission on January 23, 2003,[106] included somewhat modified versions of the up-the-ladder provisions but did not include the proposed noisy withdrawal provisions. Instead, the SEC deferred decision on its initial proposal and proposed an alternative that would still require the attorney to withdraw for "professional considerations," but require the *issuer* to report the withdrawal to the SEC. That proposal is still pending as of this writing.

B. Forcing Them to See

How will section 307 force lawyers to see the evil they would prefer not to see? It aims to do so by making not seeing more costly than seeing. By imposing an affirma-

[100] Sarbanes-Oxley Act § 307(1).

[101] Sarbanes-Oxley Act § 307(2).

[102] *See* Proposed Rule: Implementation of Standards of Professional Conduct for Attorneys, Exchange Act Release Nos. 33-8150,34-46868 and IC-25829 (Nov. 21, 2002), 67 Fed. Reg. 1670 (Dec. 2, 2002), *available at* www.sec.gov/rules/proposed/33-8150.htm. The only alternative to the process of reporting to the chief legal counsel or executive officer and to the audit committee or board is reporting to a "Qualified Legal Compliance Committee" composed of non-employee directors, if the issuer has established such a committee. Commodity and Securities Exchanges, 17 C.F.R. §§ 205.1(k), 205.3(c) (2003).

[103] *See* Proposed Rule: Implementation of Standards of Professional Conduct for Attorneys, Exchange Act Release Nos. 33-8150,34-46868 and IC-25829 (Nov. 21, 2002), 67 Fed. Reg. 1670 (Dec. 2, 2002), *available at* www.sec.gov/rules/proposed/33-8150.htm.

[104] *See id.*

[105] The comment letters are available at www.sec.gov/rules/proposed/s74502.shtml.

[106] *See* Final Rule: Implementation of Standards of Professional Conduct for Attorneys, Exchange Act Release Nos. 33-8185,34-47276, IC-25919 (Jan. 29, 2003), 68 Fed. Reg. 6296 (Feb. 6, 2003), *available at* www.sec.gov/rules/proposed/33-8185.htm.

tive whistle-blowing obligation and applying sanctions to lawyers who fail to meet that obligation, the rules are intended to make it more difficult to indulge in willful ignorance, negligent evasion, and insensitivity to their own conflicts of interest that constituted the great middle range of lawyers' failures I have just described.

More concretely, the existence of this obligation may spur the creation of internal systems within law firms for identifying potential client wrongdoing and responding more self-consciously and with more levels of review. Systems of that type may reduce the vulnerability of law firms to the poor decisions of partners whose individual stakes in a client have compromised their objectivity. In other words, the rules may lead to the establishment of institutional bulwarks against avoidance and rationalization.

The rules are likely to have their greatest influence in ambiguous situations involving lawyers' passivity. Presumably, the reporting mandate would make it more difficult to fall back on protestations of ignorance of client wrongdoing. The rules would not have much effect[107] on a lawyer who has decided to participate in a client's misdeeds and share in their benefits, but it may influence those who have half-convinced themselves that they and their clients are not doing anything wrong.

While the rules seem to impose new constraints on lawyers' discretion, they actually seem intended to empower lawyers in their roles as both advocates and gatekeepers. The up-the-ladder internal reporting requirement directly addresses the tendency of lawyers from outside firms to identify the senior managers who hired them as the client, rather than the board. It also provides some check on the apparent tendency of some general counsel to maintain insufficiently critical detachment from officers and other senior managers, preventing them from giving the board the frank advice it needed to perform its own monitoring function.[108] To the extent that senior managers controlled the lawyers, such lawyers failed to meet their obligations as advocates for the corporation, the real client. The up-the-ladder reporting requirement, therefore, does not do any violence to the confidence and trust a corporate client should be able to place in its advocate, and might make lawyers more effective advocates for the real client by making sure that those involved in violating the law know that their lawyers ultimately will have to raise questions with disinterested decision makers. The apparent futility of the few attempts by lawyers and others to raise questions internally in the recent cases[109] suggests that the whistle-blower's position needs to be fortified. Lawyers

---

[107] *See* Proposed Rule: Implementation of Standards of Professional Conduct for Attorneys, Exchange Act Release Nos. 33-8186, 34-47282, IC-25920 (Jan. 29, 2003), 68 Fed. Reg. 6324 (Feb. 6, 2003), *available at* www.sec.gov/rules/proposed/33-8186.htm.

[108] The alleged failure of the Tyco general counsel to disentangle himself from the CEO's self-dealing, and to advise the board properly, helped lead to his indictment. *See* Thomas, *supra* note 42. James V. Derrick, Jr., Enron's general counsel, also has been criticized for being too deferential to the CEO and CFO who were most involved in the questionable self-dealing transactions with Enron's affiliated entities. *See* Miriam Rozen, *An Unenviable Position*, TEX. LAW., Feb. 1, 2002, at 1.

[109] For example, key Enron executives apparently wanted an in-house lawyer fired because he attempted to negotiate vigorously on behalf of the corporation in dealings with an affiliated entity in which the CFO (their supervisor) had a major personal interest. Tom Hamburger & John Emshwiller, *Enron Officials Sought Lawyer's Dismissal over Negotiations with Outside Partnership*, WALL ST. J., Feb. 6, 2002,

may even find that this leverage is helpful, because it seems clear that they cannot use the defense of futility to a charge of breach of fiduciary duty when it is clear that they should have withheld cooperation and raised questions up the ladder.[110]

By attempting to compel lawyers to represent their clients more effectively, the up-the-ladder requirement is also intended to make them more effective gatekeepers. By honoring their obligation to convey evidence of wrongdoing to disinterested decision makers charged with considering the evidence, the rules theoretically will enable, indeed require, the board to take appropriate and timely action. The board's action will not only protect the corporation from potential liability, but also will help protect the shareholders and the investing public from fraud and the consequences of senior managers' breaches of fiduciary duty. The presence of a noisy withdrawal requirement, furthermore, would provide an ultimate fail-safe, designed to ensure that boards confronted with a serious problem actually meet their responsibility to do something about it.

All of that seems to be the theory behind the section 307 rules as originally proposed. They were intended to force lawyers to see, or at least give them an incentive to see, and to do something about what they see. This goal is laudable. The rules are a worthy experiment, but before declaring the experiment a success we should spend some time speculating about the rules' potential efficacy and importance.

VI. SPECULATION AND CONCLUSIONS

In speculating about section 307 rules, it may be helpful to ask three questions. First, how do the rules compare to other possible approaches to preventing the types of lawyer failures that surfaced in Enron and the other cases? Second, are there internal problems with the rules that will make them less effective than they could be? Third, will the rules have unintended, perverse consequences that will make lawyers even less effective as gatekeepers and a positive influence on corporate governance?

A. Are There Better Approaches?

If we could design from scratch a legal framework that would make lawyers more accountable and better gatekeepers, what would it be? It might include a whistle-blowing rule that includes both an up-the-ladder reporting requirement and a noisy withdrawal

at A3. When that lawyer's supervisor, the general counsel of Enron Global Finance, raised serious questions about both the conflicts of interest and accounting in that and other transactions in which senior officers had stakes, he was essentially ignored. Richard A. Oppel, Jr., *Lawyer at Enron Warned Officials of Dubious Deals,* N.Y. TIMES, Feb. 7, 2002, at A1. A junior accountant at HealthSouth also had little luck in getting the company's auditor to take seriously his claims that the company was falsifying assets. *See* Carrick Mollenkamp, *Missed Signal: Accountant Tried in Vain to Expose HealthSouth Fraud,* WALL ST. J., May 20, 2003, at A1.

[110] *See In re* American Cont'l Corp./Lincoln Sav. & Loan Secs. Litig., 794 F. Supp. 1424, 1453 (D. Ariz. 1992) ("Jones Day contends that it would have been futile to act on these fiduciary obligations because those controlling ACC/Lincoln would not have responded. Client wrongdoing, however, cannot negate an attorney's fiduciary duty.").

mandate, but other aspects might be more important. While a whistle-blowing rule addresses the see-no-evil problem, it does not address the partners-in-crime problem. The key to reducing that behavior would require Congressional enactment of an aiding and abetting liability provision under the anti-fraud provisions of the federal securities laws that would legislatively overrule *Central Bank*.[111] In addition, there would need to be a broader range for primary liability under the federal securities laws than currently exists.[112] These changes would create a greater disincentive for intentional participation in client wrongdoing. A lawyer who has decided to engage in such behavior, as argued above,[113] is not likely to blow the whistle on a client when that would mean blowing the whistle on herself. Fear of liability to private plaintiffs as to SEC enforcement action would be far more significant.

A fear of that kind of liability would also create greater incentives for avoiding the various types of see-no-evil behavior. While avoiding recognition of client wrongdoing may not itself provide a basis for primary liability, it could conceivably be characterized as aiding and abetting under a legislatively-revived theory of such liability. Once again, the fear of either private liability or public enforcement may have more of a deterrent effect than a whistle-blowing requirement. That fear of liability under the federal securities law would have a bracing effect on lawyers tempted to give questionable disclosures a pass.

It is also worth noting that section 307 and the SEC rules have an inherently limited scope. There is no reporting requirement unless there is evidence of some kind of violation of law. Even if this standard is broadly construed, the reporting obligation would have no impact on the legal transactions, bad consequences problem that arises when there is no law violation, but somehow the client's use of the lawyer's expertise produces malign results. To the extent that this is a problem, section 307 is no answer, because it is useful only when the lawyer confronts behavior such as fraud or self-dealing. Section 307 and the SEC rules thus do not embody a belief that the corporate lawyer should recognize a duty to be the critical, public conscience of the client. It can be debated whether a green revolution in lawyers' ethics is desirable, but it is indisputable that section 307 does not start one.

B. Internal Problems with the Rules

As of this writing, the SEC has not yet determined whether it will adopt the proposed noisy withdrawal requirement. If it does not, the impact of the up-the-ladder

---

[111] For discussion of the holding in *Central Bank* and an argument for statutory overruling of the decision in order to reestablish liability for damages in aiding and abetting cases, see Cramton, *supra* note 79, at 169-70.

[112] The scope of primary liability for securities fraud on the part of lawyers is currently quite limited. For analysis, see *id.* at 170-73. That range should at least include primary liability when the attorney drafts false representations relied upon by investors, even though he does so anonymously, if the attorney is aware of their falsity. The courts are divided on this issue. *Id.* at 169.

[113] *See supra* text accompanying note 50.

requirement will not be as profound as Congress and the SEC hoped. An up-the-ladder reporting requirement may not have much influence without the threat of mandatory noisy withdrawal behind it. Lawyers may take their obligations seriously, but if the board or key members of the board are unwilling (or unable) to respond constructively to an attorney-whistle blower's allegations, only the threat of required noisy withdrawal will wake them up. This observation is not a conclusion that requiring noisy withdrawal is necessarily a good idea, because requiring it might make the perverse consequences described in the next subsection even more likely. It is a prediction, however, that the up-the-ladder requirement alone may not have much effect on lawyers' behavior.[114]

The effectiveness of the up-the-ladder reporting requirement may be compromised by the ambiguity of its key triggering provision. The language of that provision leaves much wiggle room for interpreting away the lawyer's obligation to report up the ladder. It is theoretically an objective standard for determining when an attorney has an obligation to report up the ladder, but the language is complex and confusing. If an attorney concludes that there is credible evidence that would make it unreasonable for a prudent and competent attorney not to conclude that it is reasonably likely that a material violation has occurred, is ongoing or is about to occur, the attorney will have

---

[114] The potential tension between the SEC's present permissive disclosure rule and state rules that are more restrictive of disclosure of client information was seen recently in a proposed interim formal ethics opinion issued in July 2003 by the Washington State Bar Association. *The Effect of the SEC's Sarbanes-Oxley Regulations on Washington Attorney's Obligations Under the RPCs*, Washington State Bar Association, Proposed Interim Formal Opinion (2003), *available at* http://www.wsba.org/formalopinion.doc. The opinion warned Washington lawyers not to disclose to the SEC information that the SEC's rules would permit them to disclose, unless the disclosure is also allowed by the state's own professional conduct rules. Those rules permit disclosure of client confidence only to "prevent the client from committing a crime." *Id.* The opinion also states that a Washington attorney cannot avoid this limitation by claiming to be complying in good faith with the SEC's rules, if the attorney acts contrary to the opinion. *Id.* The SEC General Counsel responded to the Washington opinion with a public statement to the effect that the Supreme Court has consistently upheld the authority of federal agencies to implement rules of conduct that diverge from and supersede state laws addressing the same conduct. He also argued that an attorney who discloses client information in good faith reliance on the SEC rule will also have a good faith exemption from the state's non-disclosure rule under the preemption doctrine. Letter from Giovannia P. Prezioso, General Counsel, SEC, to J. Richard Manning, President, Washington State Bar Association and David W. Savage, President-Elect, Washington State Bar Association (July 23, 2003), *available at* http://www.sec.gov/news/speech/spch072303gpp.htm.

The question of the relationship between permissive or mandatory external disclosure rules under the SEC and state rules governing disclosure of client information is complex, in part because of the great variation in the state rules. For a discussion of the variations, see Cramton, *supra* note 79, at 156-58. For a discussion of the background to the American Bar Association's (ABA) struggles with this issue, see Larry P. Scriggins, *Legal Ethics, Confidentiality, and the Organizational Client*, 58 BUS. LAW. 123 (2002). In August of 2003 the ABA finally amended Rule 1.6 of the Model Rules of Professional Conduct to follow the lead of many states in allowing the disclosure of client information when the lawyer believes such disclosure necessary to prevent fraud injurious to a third party's financial interests. *See* Press Release, ABA, ABA Adopts New Lawyer Ethics Rules (Aug. 12, 2003), *available at* http://www.abanet.org/media/aug03/081203_1.html. The ABA's initiative on this point may make the SEC feel less obligated to adopt a mandatory noisy withdrawal rule.

an obligation to report the evidence of the violation. The words "credible," "material" and "reasonably likely" leave plenty of room for judgment, or self-serving rationalization, depending upon how you look at it. The use of the double negative in the formulation of the standard, furthermore, could create interpretive haze useful to justify inaction.[115] Some lawyers may not need much haziness in order to conclude that they do not have any obligation to take action.

C. The Possibility of Perverse Consequences

Assume for the sake of argument that the section 307 rules actually work. The lawyers and clients come to believe that the rules effectively compel lawyers to be much more aggressive about reporting corporate wrongdoing, making it much more likely that the wrongdoing will become public. The hope, of course, is that lawyers will become more effective gatekeepers, ultimately reducing the amount of self-dealing and securities fraud perpetrated by the managers of public corporations. It is worth considering the possibility, however, that imposing a reporting requirement with teeth, particularly a noisy withdrawal requirement, may have the opposite effect.

Managers concerned about the possibility of exposure by their lawyers may tend to marginalize the role of lawyers in their activities. Corporate managers may exclude lawyers from their most sensitive discussions. They may divide legal work among a larger number of firms, creating a compartmentalization that prevents anyone from developing a sense of the whole picture. Once a new type of transaction is developed with lawyers' assistance, clients may exclude lawyers from future iterations, as the client manipulates the transaction in ways the lawyers would not have expected or approved. Managers also may engage in even more determined efforts to hide the true facts from their lawyers. The net result is that lawyers might have less of an opportunity to influence their clients' actions positively than they do now.

Law firms themselves may even attempt to reduce the possibility that they would encounter something that they would have to report. Firms are likely to establish "§ 307 committees" and procedures that routinize consideration of whether there might be reportable evidence of a material violation upon which the firm would be compelled to act. That would seem to be a good thing. It would seem, however, that firms, and their risk managers, are likely to use these committees and procedures to find ways of avoiding the situations in which they would have the uncomfortable responsibility of blowing a whistle. For example, firms might circumscribe more narrowly the scope of their representation. They may decline to take on tasks that require substantial due diligence. They may increasingly define themselves as providing highly specific technical advice rather than independent professional judgment. This would indeed be a perverse consequence. The goal of the section 307 rules is to give lawyers an incentive to withhold cooperation from client wrongdoing and increase the risk of public exposure, thus making it more difficult and costly for clients to act wrongly. If lawyers' fear

[115] *See* 17 C.F.R. § 205.2(e) (2003).

of having to turn whistle-blower causes them to absent themselves from the kinds of situation in which their duty of non-cooperation and reporting might be significant, little will have been accomplished. Indeed, they might become less effective gatekeepers than they were.

It is too early, however, to predict that these perverse consequences will ensue, or, if they do, whether their effects will be marginal. The dismal record of lawyers in Enron and its successors, and their material contribution to the systems failure I have called the perfect storm, suggests that the existing framework of legal rules and lawyers' private incentives for doing right are inadequate in the context of representing public companies. The process of practical adaptation by both law firms and clients to the section 307 rules should tell us, before too long, whether anything has changed.

*Some Realism About Professionalism: Core Values, Legality, and Corporate Law Practice**

*Christopher J. Whelan***

INTRODUCTION

There have long been tensions between the high ideals of professionalism, the ideology of libertarianism, and the realities of commercialism in law practice.[1] Traditionally, lawyers have been called upon to be professional—entailing some public service ideal—despite also making a living out of the law.[2] While the need to make a living has always threatened to conflict with the aspirations of professionalism,[3] the transformation of the structure and organization of the legal profession in recent decades has increased this threat.[4] Large law firms, the subject of this Article, "now inhabit a universe whose

* Originally published at 54 BUFF. L. REV. 1067 (2007). Reprinted by permission of the author and the Buffalo Law Review.

** Associate Director, International Law Programmes and Member, Faculty of Law, University of Oxford; Visiting Professor of Law, Washington & Lee University School of Law; Barrister, Three Paper Buildings, Temple, London.

I would like to thank Richard L. Abel, Albert V. Carr, Anthony Harris, Lyman P. Q. Johnson, Peter C. Kostant, David Millon, Blake D. Morant, and W. Bradley Wendel for helpful comments on earlier drafts. Comments were also received from Vinson & Elkins. Thanks to Linda Olsen and Nathaniel Parker for research assistance.

[1] John H. Wigmore, *Introduction* to ORRIN N. CARTER, ETHICS OF THE LEGAL PROFESSION, at xxi (1915) ("[i]n the dominant attitude, the Law is no more than a trade, an occupation, a business . . . .").

[2] ROSCOE POUND, THE LAWYER FROM ANTIQUITY TO MODERN TIMES 5 (1953) (defining professionals as "a group . . . pursuing a learned art as a common calling in the spirit of a public service—no less a public service because it may incidentally be a means of livelihood. Pursuit of the learned art in the spirit of a public service is the primary purpose.").

[3] The classic studies are those by Jerome Carlin. *See* JEROME E. CARLIN, LAWYERS ON THEIR OWN: A STUDY OF INDIVIDUAL PRACTITIONERS IN CHICAGO (1962); JEROME E. CARLIN, LAWYERS' ETHICS: A SURVEY OF THE NEW YORK CITY BAR (1966); JEROME E. CARLIN, LAWYERS ON THEIR OWN: THE SOLO PRACTITIONER IN AN URBAN SETTING (1994).

[4] *See* RICHARD L. ABEL, AMERICAN LAWYERS (1989). For especially good accounts of this phenomenon, *see* ROBERT L. NELSON, PARTNERS WITH POWER: THE SOCIAL TRANSFORMATION OF THE LARGE LAW FIRM

governing laws are those of the market."[5] Alongside this transformation has been the "uncontrolled expansion of libertarian ideology into lawyers' common consciousness."[6] This also threatens to undermine professionalism by denying any public obligation other than to serve the client. It has become, arguably, the "standard conception" of the lawyer's role[7] and the dominant ideology of legal practice.

I. CHALLENGING CORE VALUES

A. Libertarianism

A libertarian ideology "privatizes the lawyer's role,"[8] and makes lawyers "private agents for private parties . . . ; our loyalties to clients must be absolute and undivided."[9] Libertarians endorse "the traditional ethic,"[10] first set out in the 1908 Canons of Professional Ethics: to give "entire devotion to the interest of the client, warm zeal in the maintenance and defense of his rights and the exertion of [the lawyer's] utmost learning and ability."[11] Zealousness, it is claimed, is "the fundamental principle of the law of lawyering."[12] It is proclaimed in Canon 7 of the Model Code: "A Lawyer Should Represent a Client Zealously Within the Bounds of the Law,"[13] and in the preamble to the Model Rules: "the lawyer's obligation zealously to protect and pursue a client's legitimate interests, within the bounds of the law."[14]

A libertarian, client-centered ideology threatens to undermine professionalism by denying any public obligation other than to serve the client. It can also become a "slippery slope" to excessive zeal and uncontrolled instrumentalism.[15] The libertarian ethic demands that lawyers do everything legally permissible to achieve their client's

(1988); LAWYERS' IDEALS/LAWYERS' PRACTICES: TRANSFORMATIONS IN THE AMERICAN LEGAL SYSTEM (Robert L. Nelson et al. eds., 1992).

[5] MILTON C. REGAN, JR., EAT WHAT YOU KILL: THE FALL OF A WALL STREET LAWYER 42 (2004).

[6] Robert W. Gordon, *A Collective Failure of Nerve: The Bar's Response to Kaye Scholer*, 23 LAW & SOC. INQUIRY 315, 320 (1998)

[7] *See, e.g.*, DAVID LUBAN, LAWYERS AND JUSTICE: AN ETHICAL STUDY (1988); DEBORAH L. RHODE & DAVID LUBAN, LEGAL ETHICS 87-89 (3d ed. 2001).

[8] Gordon, *supra* note 6, at 321.

[9] *Id.* at 320.

[10] Monroe H. Freedman, *The Ethical Danger of "Civility" and "Professionalism,"* 6 CRIM. JUST. J. 17, 17 (1998).

[11] CANONS OF PROF'L ETHICS EC 15 (1908). *See generally* Susan D. Carle, *Lawyers' Duty to Do Justice: A New Look at the History of the 1908 Canons*, 24 LAW & SOC. INQUIRY 1 (1999).

[12] Freedman, *supra* note 10, at 17 (citing GEOFFREY C. HAZARD, JR. & W. WILLIAM HODES, THE LAW OF LAWYERING: A HANDBOOK ON THE MODEL RULES OF PROFESSIONAL CONDUCT 17 (Supp. 1988)).

[13] MODEL CODE OF PROF'L RESPONSIBILITY CANON 7 (1980).

[14] MODEL RULES OF PROF'L CONDUCT PMBL. para. 9 (2003).

[15] *See* David Luban, *Milgram Revisited*, RESEARCHING LAW, Spring 1998, at 1, 9.

objectives, including using any law or procedural mechanism, regardless of its purpose, to the client's advantage.[16]

The ideology is at its most powerful when the lawyer perceives that there is no choice but to do whatever will assist the client. As Alan Dershowitz said: "What a defense attorney 'may' do, he must do, if it is necessary to defend his client."[17] While the ideology begins with a compelling and powerful image of the criminal lawyer as "the fearless advocate who champions a client threatened with loss of life and liberty by government oppression,"[18] it has been extended to civil litigation[19] and beyond.[20] Corporate lawyers may have a "moral imperative . . . to defy or undercut the law."[21] Of course, the libertarian model is only one of several posited for lawyers.[22] Some have argued that the context of legal practice is crucial,[23] and concern has also been expressed as to whether or not such a model should apply to corporate transaction lawyers.[24]

B. Commercialism

In the context of large firm practice, a law firm's "sheer size . . . makes it difficult to achieve a consensus on values beyond the common denominator of revenues and

---

[16] *See* MONROE H. FREEDMAN, LAWYERS' ETHICS IN AN ADVERSARY SYSTEM, 43-49 (1975); Abbe Smith, *Defending: The Case for Unmitigated Zeal on Behalf of People Who do Terrible Things*, 28 HOFSTRA L. REV. 925 (2000); Harry I. Subin, *The Criminal Lawyer's "Different Mission": Reflections on the "Right" to Present a False Case*, 1 GEO. J. LEGAL ETHICS 125, 128 (1987).

[17] ALAN M. DERSHOWITZ, REASONABLE DOUBTS 145 (1996).

[18] Geoffrey C. Hazard, Jr., *The Future of Legal Ethics*, 100 YALE L.J. 1239, 1243 (1991).

[19] *See, e.g.*, Spaulding v. Zimmerman, 116 N.W.2d 704, 710 (Minn. 1962) (stating that there is no duty to notify the other side in a personal injury claim of an immediate life-threatening condition). For a critique of this case, *see* Roger C. Crampton & Lori P. Knowles, *Professional Secrecy and Its Exceptions: Spaulding v. Zimmerman Revisited*, 83 MINN. L. REV. 63 (1998).

[20] *See, e.g.*, Robert J. Condlin, *Bargaining in the Dark: The Normative Incoherence of Lawyer Dispute Bargaining Role*, 51 MD. L. REV. 1 (1992) (discussing ethical considerations in negotiations); Geoffrey C. Hazard Jr., *How Far May a Lawyer Go in Assisting a Client in Legally Wrongful Conduct?*, 35 MIAMI L. REV. 669 (1981); Gerald B. Wetlaufer, *The Ethics of Lying in Negotiations*, 75 IOWA L. REV. 1219, 1255-61 (1990) (discussing loyalty and zeal as justification for lying in negotiations).

[21] Robert W. Gordon, *A New Role for Lawyers?: The Corporate Counselor After Enron*, 35 CONN. L. REV. 1185, 1191-92 (2003).

[22] *See, e.g.*, Ted Schneyer, *Moral Philosophy's Standard Misconception of Legal Ethics*, 1984 WIS. L. REV. 1529.

[23] *See* David B. Wilkins, *Making Context Count: Regulating Lawyers After Kaye, Scholer*, 66 S. CAL. L. REV. 1145 (1993).

[24] *See* Robert W. Gordon, *Why Lawyers Can't Just be Hired Guns*, IN ETHICS IN PRACTICE: LAWYERS' ROLES, RESPONSIBILITIES, AND REGULATION 42 (Deborah L. Rhode ed., 2000); Abram Chayes & Antonia H. Chayes, *Corporate Counsel and the Elite Law Firm*, 37 STAN. L. REV. 277 (1985); Robert A. Kagan & Robert Eli Rosen, *On the Social Significance of Large Law Firm Practice*, 37 STAN. L. REV. 339 (1985).

profit."[25] For the large firm lawyer, "eat what you kill" has become the dominant ethic.[26] According to Milton C. Regan, Jr., dramatic forces have "irrevocably transformed elite law firm practice over the past quarter century."[27] He cites three structural factors that have affected large firm practice in particular.

First, there has developed a "tournament of lawyers,"[28] a competition whereby lawyers compete with each other to make partner.[29] Even after making partner, it appears that the tournament continues, as partners compete with each other for compensation, status, and continued employment in order to survive.[30]

Secondly, lawyers' practice has become increasingly specialized and lawyers may resolve issues and problems differently depending upon that specialty.[31] According to this view, "[m]uch of law practice consists of informal understandings about matters such as what arguments are considered within the bounds of good faith, acceptable levels of aggressiveness, the scope of disclosure requirements, how to interact with regulatory agencies, and what constitutes due diligence."[32] In short, "[o]ver time, the shared experiences of practitioners in a particular specialty lead them to develop norms of acceptable behavior."[33]

Thirdly, lawyers often work with colleagues inside and outside the firm in teams, working on increasingly large and complex projects. Members of the team can become a "significant reference group."[34] Teams can shape individual perceptions; members reinforce for one another "the idea that their framework for interpreting events is accurate and reasonable."[35]

The growth in competition in the legal marketplace, within the law firm and beyond, has increased the instability of large firm practice. Law firms seek to find and retain

---

[25] REGAN, *supra* note 5, at 39.

[26] *See generally id.*

[27] *Id.* at 4.

[28] MARC GALANTER & THOMAS PALAY, TOURNAMENT OF LAWYERS: THE TRANSFORMATION OF THE BIG LAW FIRM (1991).

[29] *See also* David B. Wilkins & G. Mitu Gulati, *Reconceiving the Tournament of Lawyers: Tracking, Seeding, and Information Control in the Internal Labor Markets of Elite Law Firms*, 84 VA. L. REV. 1581 (1998).

[30] *See* REGAN, *supra* note 5. A tournament may extend beyond the firm, via the "ethics of grabbing and leaving." ROBERT W. HILLMAN, LAW FIRM BREAKUPS: THE LAW AND ETHICS OF GRABBING AND LEAVING 145 (1990). Some lawyers are discarded from one firm while others are recruited from other firms. *Id.*

[31] *See* REGAN, *supra* note 5, at 40.

[32] *Id.* at 39.

[33] *Id.* at 40.

[34] *Id.* at 41.

[35] *Id.* at 41-42.

clients, while clients shop around for law firms[36] and lawyers.[37] These "legal beauty contests"[38] threaten to undermine the professionalism of lawyers.

C. Professionalism and Core Values

Alongside these growing tensions and threats there has been a focus on the so-called "core values" of the legal profession.[39] According to former ABA President Philip S. Anderson, there are four "core principles" in the legal profession.[40] First, "[t]he practice of law is a learned profession."[41] It requires specialized training, and the "lawyer must gain an understanding of the shared values of the profession."[42] Second, a lawyer must be independent. The "lawyer must zealously represent the client;"[43] strict confidentiality must be maintained; and conflicts of interest must be "avoided absolutely."[44] The lawyer must "control the advice given to a client because the lawyer's judgment must be based solely on the legal and factual circumstances attending a matter and not on untoward influences of another sort."[45] Third, "[t]he practice of law must be governed by ethical principles."[46] Lawyers must be regulated "to ensure competence and ethical conduct."[47] Regulation "promotes the concept that a lawyer serves the public interest in addition to the client."[48] Fourth, "[a] lawyer has an obligation to the public in addition to obligations to a particular client, and a lawyer has responsibility to respect the concept of the rule of law."[49] The "legal profession, operating within the rule of law

---

36 *See* Kagan & Rosen, *supra* note 24, at 423.

37 See Carl D. Liggio, *The Changing Role of Corporate Counsel*, 46 EMORY L.J. 1201, 1210 (1997); Milton C. Regan Jr., *Foreword: Professional Responsibility and the Corporate Lawyer*, 13 GEO. J. LEGAL ETHICS 197, 198 (2000); Robert Eli Rosen, *The Inside Counsel Movement, Professional Judgment and Organizational Representation*, 64 IND. L.J. 479 (1989).

38 Kenneth D. Agran, *The Treacherous Path to the Diamond-Studded Tiara: Ethical Dilemmas in Legal Beauty Contests*, 9 GEO. J. LEGAL ETHICS 1307, 1307 (1996).

39 *See* Susan P. Koniak, *The Law Between the Bar and the State*, 70 N.C. L. REV. 1389 (1992) (referring to the bar's "constitutional norms").

40 Philip S. Anderson, *Remarks*, 18 DICK. J. INT'L L. 43, 44 (2000).

41 *Id.*

42 *Id.* (emphasis added).

43 *Id.*

44 *Id.*

45 *Id.* (emphasis added).

46 *Id.*

47 *Id.*

48 *Id.* at 45.

49 *Id.* at 44 (emphasis added).

and a transparent system of justice, strengthens the disparate institutions of the world's governments and reenforces [sic] the fabric of society."[50]

For some, focusing on core values has been a positive development: "[i]t is in the public interest to preserve the core values of the legal profession."[51] Core values are "essential to the competent, responsible, and effective delivery of legal services to clients."[52] They are said to be universal in character, transcending national borders.[53] For example, an independent legal profession "is an essential means of safeguarding human rights in face of the power of the state and other interests in society.[54] Core values reflect the high ideals of professionalism.[55] As Anderson put it, the core values of the legal profession mean that the "profession of law is more than a job; it is a high calling."[56]

The legal community, however, is facing a "spiritual crisis that strikes at the heart of professional pride."[57] The core values of the legal profession are said to be under

---

[50] *Id.* at 45. Anderson hoped for "universal agreement" on these principles and they seem to capture the common ground. *See, e.g.*, James W. Jones & Bayless Manning, *Getting at the Root of Core Values: A "Radical" Proposal to Extend the Model Rules to Changing Forms of Legal Practice*, 84 MINN. L. REV. 1159, 1189, 1196 (2000) (noting that "core values include preserving the independence of professional judgment; assuring competence in the delivery of legal services; maintaining client confidences; maintaining truthfulness and fair dealing in relations with clients, tribunals, and others; abiding by the rules of tribunals; assisting in providing access to justice and improving the justice system; and providing a framework to support the ethical behavior of individual lawyers.").

[51] American Bar Association, Center for Professional Responsibility, Recommendations, available at http://web.archive.org/web/20050211015424/ (this document is no longer available on the American Bar Association's web page, but is has been archived on the Waybackmachine's web page; go to Internet Archive: Waybackmachine, at http://www.archive.org/web/web.php, in the search field, enter http://www.abanet.org/cpr/mdprecom10f.html, then in the results, click on Oct. 09, 2002). Among the core values are:

a. the lawyer's duty of undivided loyalty to the client;
b. the lawyer's duty competently to exercise independent professional judgment for the benefit of the client;
c. the lawyer's duty to hold client confidences inviolate;
d. the lawyer's duty to avoid conflicts of interest with the client;
e. the lawyer's duty to help maintain a single profession of law with responsibilities as a representative of clients, an officer of the legal system, and a public citizen having special responsibility for the quality of justice[;] [and]
f. the lawyer's duty to promote access to justice.

Id.

[52] Jones & Manning, *supra* note 50, at 1179.

[53] *See* Anderson, *supra* note 40.

[54] CODE OF CONDUCT FOR LAWYERS IN THE EUROPEAN UNION 5 (1998), available at http://www.ccbe.org/doc/En/code2002_en.pdf.

[55] *See Professionalism Symposium*, 52 S.C. L. REV. 443 (2001).

[56] Anderson, *supra* note 40, at 45; *see also Professional Responsibility: Report of the Joint Conference*, 44 A.B.A. J. 1159, 1162 (1958) ("Private legal practice, properly pursued is . . . itself a public service."); Symposium, *Can the Ordinary Practice of Law be a Religious Calling?*, 32 PEPP. L. REV. 373-559 (2005).

[57] ANTHONY T. KRONMAN, THE LOST LAWYER: FAILING IDEALS OF THE LEGAL PROFESSION 2 (1993).

attack.[58] Some have questioned their role and whether, in the future, the profession can and should preserve them.[59] While some have argued that core values should be preserved by lawyers, including in-house counsel,[60] others have not. According to Nathan M. Crystal, reliance on core values in debates about legal ethics reflects an anti-market, anti-competitive attitude of the bar; reliance "has rhetorical appeal but is fundamentally misleading."[61] Deborah L. Rhode and Paul D. Paton observe that "[t]he challenges of maintaining independent judgment are compounded in a competitive market where powerful clients can shop for expedient advice."[62] According to Richard L. Abel, "[a]lthough the 'independence' of lawyers remains an unquestioned shibboleth, it may express nostalgia more than it describes contemporary reality."[63]

D. Core Values in Context: Large Law Firm Corporate Law Practice

But what are the contemporary realities in large, law firm practice? Given the tensions between professionalism, libertarianism, and commercialism, how do large firm corporate lawyers "identify, frame, and resolve ethical questions?"[64] If core values exist, what form do they take and how should they be characterized?

Addressing these questions requires empirical data on "the dynamics of professional behavior in the legal workplace,"[65] something that is not readily available or easy to obtain. As a result, not surprisingly perhaps, "[o]ne of the big problems is that we mostly rely on post-hoc horror stories about what has gone wrong and use those stories to analyze the nature of the problem."[66] Such was the case, par excellence, with

---

[58] Rupert Woolf, former President of the CCBE: "we will need to defend the core values of the profession, namely independence, autonomy, self-regulation and respect for the rule of law." *A Message from the President*, 1 CCBE GAZETTE 1 (2001) (on file with the author).

[59] *See* Jones & Manning, *supra* note 50, at 1179.

[60] *See* Anderson, *supra* note 40; see also Mary C. Daly, The Cultural, Ethical, and Legal Challenges in Lawyering for a Global Organization: The Role of the General Counsel, 46 EMORY L.J. 1057 (1997).

[61] Nathan M. Crystal, *Core Values: False and True*, 70 FORDHAM L. REV. 747, 748 (2001).

[62] Deborah L. Rhode & Paul D. Paton, *Lawyers, Ethics, and Enron, in* ENRON: CORPORATE FIASCOS AND THEIR IMPLICATIONS 625, 642 (Nancy B. Rapoport & Bala G. Dharan, eds., 2004).

[63] ABEL, *supra* note 4, at 9; *see also* Jones & Manning, *supra* note 50, at 1179 ("The prototype of the independent general practitioner/litigator—although continuing to resonate as a kind of mythic paradigm within the legal profession—was, in reality, no longer representative of what most American lawyers actually do.").

[64] REGAN, *supra* note 5, at 4.

[65] Robert L. Nelson, *Professionalism from a Social Science Perspective*, 52 S.C. L. REV. 473, 479 (2001).

[66] *Id.* at 479.

Enron's bankruptcy[67] and "spectacular fall from grace."[68] It spawned a legal literature which has become, according to Donald C. Langevoort, "voluminous, both in terms of official investigations and academic commentary."[69] Its "greatest legacy"[70] was the Sarbanes-Oxley Act, which empowered the Securities and Exchange Commission (SEC) to issue rules "setting forth minimum standards of professional conduct for attorneys appearing and practicing before the Commission."[71]

Therefore, it might appear that there is little left to learn about Enron. In fact, Enron remains an important case study because of the exhaustive and highly authoritative Final Report of Neal Batson, the Court-Appointed Examiner (the Examiner) in the Enron bankruptcy case.[72] Batson was appointed on May 22, 2002; the Final Report was published on November 3, 2003.[73] He was authorized to investigate all transactions involving special purpose vehicles or entities (SPEs) created or structured by—or at the behest of—Enron and certain of its affiliates and those individuals, institutions, and professionals involved therein.[74] What was new in Batson's Report[75] was that it detailed

---

[67] For an accessible overview of the story of Enron's bankruptcy, *see* BRIAN CRUVER, ANATOMY OF GREED: THE UNSHREDDED TRUTH FROM AN ENRON INSIDER (2002). For a journalistic perspective on Enron's bankruptcy, *see* KURT EICHENWALD, CONSPIRACY OF FOOLS (2005).

[68] Julie Rawe, *The Case Against Ken Lay*, TIME, July 19, 2004, at 62, 63 (quoting U.S. Deputy Attorney General James Comey).

[69] Donald C. Langevoort, *Technological Evolution and the Devolution of Corporate Financial Reporting*, 46 WM. & MARY L. REV. 1, 2 n.2 (2004). Books on Enron have become "their own cottage industry." *See* Jeffery D. Van Niel & Nancy B. Rapoport, *Dr. Jekyll & Mr. Skilling*, *in* ENRON: CORPORATE FIASCOS AND THEIR IMPLICATIONS, *supra* note 62, at 77, 87; *see also id.* at 87 n.36 (A search of Amazon.com in May 2003, using an "Enron" search, found in excess of fifty publications).

[70] Rawe, *supra* note 68, at 62, 63.

[71] Sarbanes-Oxley Act of 2002, Pub. L. No. 107-204, 116 Stat. 745 § 307, 15 U.S.C. § 7245 (2002).

[72] Final Report of Neal Batson, Court-Appointed Examiner, In re Enron Corp., No. 01-16034 (Bankr. S.D.N.Y., Nov. 4, 2003) [hereinafter Final Report], *available at* http://www.enron.com/corp/por/examinerfinal.html (last visited Oct. 18, 2006); *see also* Charles J. Tabb, *The Enron Bankruptcy*, *in* ENRON: CORPORATE FIASCOS AND THEIR IMPLICATIONS, *supra* note 62, at 303, 310 (discussing the trend in cases of alleged corporate wrongdoing to appoint examiners for investigative purposes).

[73] Final Report, *supra* note 72, at 1.

[74] *Id.*

[75] The Examiner published three Interim Reports. The first, filed Sept. 21, 2002, examined six SPE transactions; the second, submitted on Jan. 21, 2003, focused on substantially all Enron's material SPE transactions identified to date; the third, submitted on June 30, 2003, focused primarily on certain persons and entities that might have responsibility for Enron's misuse of its SPE structures. *See* Final Report, *supra* note 72, at 2-6. In the Interim Reports, the Examiner found evidence from which a factfinder could conclude that certain senior officers of Enron breached their fiduciary duties by causing Enron to enter the SPE transactions that were designed to manipulate Enron's financial statements and that resulted in the dissemination of materially misleading financial information. *See id.* at 4. The Final Report constituted the fourth and final report together with the prior reports.

the specific role played by Enron's attorneys in aspects of Enron's "development, use, approval, oversight and disclosure of the SPEs."[76]

Enron retained "hundreds of outside law firms."[77] "Outside attorneys were chosen based upon the level of expertise within the law firm and its availability."[78] The Examiner, however, specifically considered the role of Enron's in-house attorneys and two of its outside law firms, Vinson & Elkins and Andrews & Kurth.[79] He examined the evidence which could form the basis of claims, as well as the several possible defenses to such claims.

The Examiner's investigation was exhaustive. It cost over $100 million, "almost certainly the most expensive inquiry of its nature in U.S. history."[80] It was undertaken by Batson and a team of professionals from his firm of Alston & Bird.[81] The team included over thirty-five partners and counsel, thirty-three associates, and four contracted attorneys.[82] The Examiner subpoenaed documents from forty-six law firms.[83] He conducted interviews and reviewed testimony (presented to the SEC, in the numerous Senate and House committees that investigated Enron,[84] in the course of litigation,[85]

---

[76] Final Report, *supra* note 72, at 22; *see also id.* app. C (discussing the role of Enron's attorneys and other persons and entities that may have liability).

[77] *Id.* app. C, at 15 n.17 (quoting sworn statement of Rex Rogers, Vice President and Associate General Counsel); *see also id.* at 48.

[78] *Id.* app. C, at 15 (quoting testimony of Carol Lynne St Clair, former Assistant General Counsel, Enron and Scott Matthew Sefton, former General Counsel, Enron).

[79] *See id.* at 48. Andrews & Kurth (presently Andrews Kurth) was founded in 1902. It has seven offices, including one in London, 400 attorneys, an international clientele, and it "represents the vital interests of established companies and emerging businesses around the globe." Andrews Kurth LLP, http://akllp.com/ (last visited Oct. 18, 2006). This Article focuses on Vinson & Elkins as the larger of the two, and as Enron's "primary outside law firm." Other large law firms referred to in the Final Report include Shearman & Sterling, *id.* app. C, at 69, Kirkland & Ellis, *id.* app. C, at 116, 125-27, 147 n.651, Fried, Frank, Harris, Shriver & Jacobson, *id.* app. C, at 127, 147, 157-58, and Bracewell & Patterson, *id.* app. C., at 147 n.651.

[80] Anthony Lin, *Enron Examiner Billed Estate for $100 Million*, N.Y. L.J., Dec. 5, 2003, *available at* http://www.law.com/jsp/article.jsp?id=1069801691295.

[81] R. Neal Batson is a partner, Chair of the American College of Bankruptcy, member of the National Banking Conference, and former member of the Advisory Committee on the Federal Rules of Bankruptcy Procedure. *See* Tabb, *supra* note 72, at 310. Alston & Bird is another large law firm. Founded in 1893, it has about 700 lawyers, though no offices abroad. Alston & Bird LLP, http://www.alston.com/index.cfm?fuseaction=main (last visited Oct. 18, 2006).

[82] *See* Lin, *supra* note 80, at 1.

[83] *See* Tabb, *supra* note 72, at 311.

[84] *See, e.g.,* The Financial Collapse of Enron—Part 2: Hearing Before the Subcomm. on Oversight and Investigations of the H. Comm. on Energy and Commerce, 107th Cong. (2002). This Senate subcommittee had up to twenty staff people "trying to unravel Enron," according to Mr. Peter Deutsch. *Id.* at 4; *see also* Lessons Learned from Enron: Hearing Before the Subcomm. on Investigations of the S. Comm. on Government Affairs 107th Cong. (2002).

[85] For example, United States v. Arthur Andersen LLP, Transcript of the Proceedings, No. H-02-121, May 6-June 5, 2002 (S.D. Tex. 2002); United States v. Glisan, Cr. No. H-03-3628 (S.D. Tex., Filed

and from about 300 witnesses[86]), the Powers Report,[87] millions of e-mails,[88] and Vinson & Elkins billings. More than forty million pages of documents were amassed[89] in the Enron litigation.[90] The Examiner obtained material that is "off limits to litigants," because it was obtained subject to confidentiality agreements.[91]

The Final Report itself, including Appendices, is 1,114 pages in length.[92] Appendix C, dealing exclusively with the role of Enron's attorneys, is nearly 250 pages. When the Final Report was published, it was described as "a remarkable (though very complex) case study by an independent, well-funded team of lawyers. It provides a look at the world of high-end business and corporate lawyers of the type we almost never get in public, not even in a malpractice trial."[93]

Enron's attorneys generally played a "vital role in Enron's access to the capital markets"[94] by analyzing the structure of the SPE transactions, documenting them, and providing opinions on various transactions. According to the Examiner, "an attorney's willingness to provide certain legal opinions was, as a practical matter, crucial to Enron's ability to complete the FAS 140 Transactions."[95] Without these opinions, Enron would probably not have proceeded with the transactions.[96]

FAS 140 Transactions were structured finance transactions that were designed to comply with either FAS 125 or its successor, FAS 140.[97] These transactions were a key

---

Sept. 10, 2003). Several class action lawsuits were filed on behalf of shareholders and employees. *See* Final Report, *supra* note 72, at 17 n.35.

[86] *See* Richard Acello, *Enron Lawyers in the Hot Seat*, A.B.A. J., June 2004, at 22.

[87] *See* WILLIAM C. POWERS, JR., ET AL., REPORT OF INVESTIGATION BY THE SPECIAL INVESTIGATIVE COMMITTEE OF THE BOARD OF DIRECTORS OF ENRON CORP. (2002) [hereinafter POWERS REPORT], *available at* http://news.findlaw.com/hdocs/docs/Enron/sicreport/.

[88] *See Panel Four: Rule 37 and/or a New Rule 34.1: Safe Harbors for E-Document Preservation and Sanctions*, 73 FORD. L. REV. 71, 78 (2004) (noting that one of the databases Batson's team put together contained 7,366,177 e-mail messages).

[89] *See id.* at 78. For a readily-accessible source of various Enron-related documents, *see* www.enron.com/corp/por/supporting.html (last visited Oct. 18, 2006).

[90] *See* Newby v. Enron Corp., 310 F. Supp.2d 819, 833 (S.D. Tex. 2004).

[91] Lin, *supra* note 80, at 2.

[92] The Final Report, together with the Interim Reports, total over 4,000 pages in length. *See* Final Report, *supra* note 72.

[93] William Freivogel & Lucian Pera, *Enron Watch/Sarbanes-Oxley,* ETHICS AND LAWYERING, Dec. 2003, http://www.ethicsandlawyering.com/Issues/1203.htm.

[94] Final Report, *supra* note 72, at 114.

[95] *Id.* app. C, at 27.

[96] The opinions were required so that Andersen could account for these transactions in the way certain Enron officers required. *Id.* app. C, at 31.

[97] *Id.* app. C, at 26 n.67; *see also* ACCOUNTING FOR TRANSFERS AND SERVICING OF FINANCIAL ASSETS AND EXTINGUISHMENTS OF LIABILITIES, STATEMENT OF FIN. ACCOUNTING STANDARDS NO. 125 (Fin. Accounting Standards Bd. 1996) [hereinafter FAS 125]; ACCOUNTING FOR TRANSFERS AND SERVICING OF FINANCIAL ASSETS AND EXTINGUISHMENT OF LIABILITIES—A REPLACEMENT OF FASB STATEMENT 125, STATEMENT OF

technique Enron officers used to enhance Enron's reported financial condition, results of operations, and cash flow. In 2000, for example, FAS 140 Transactions increased reported income by $350 million, increased cash flow by more than $1 billion, and kept more than $1 billion off Enron's balance sheet.[98]

Enron officers were often more concerned with justifying a desired result rather than making the correct or best decision.[99] To achieve this, they used accounting rules that did not directly address the accounting question at issue, but provided an argument to justify an aggressive position. They also searched for reasons to avoid public disclosure. The obtaining of professional opinions or advice in the process was "merely . . . a necessary procedural step"[100] used "to justify questionable decisions rather than as a tool to assist them in reaching a considered business decision based upon the risks."[101]

In most of its FAS 140 Transactions, Enron asked its outside attorneys to provide an opinion letter that Arthur Andersen, its auditor, would use to satisfy the isolation requirements of FAS 140.[102] If Andersen was not satisfied that the asset had been legally isolated, Enron could not record a gain from the transfer of the asset. It would have to reflect a debt on its balance sheet and record the proceeds of the transaction as a cash flow from financing activities.[103]

According to the Examiner, Enron needed opinions from a law firm because "a determination about whether the isolation criterion has been met to support a conclusion regarding surrender of control is largely a matter of law. This aspect of surrender of control, therefore, is assessed primarily from a legal perspective."[104] Vinson & Elkins provided Enron with true issuance opinion letters in relation to Project Cornhusker, and in a number of similar transactions in 1997, 1998, and 1999. It knew Enron would provide these opinions to Andersen to support the accountancy treatment Enron sought.[105] Enron was permitted to provide Andersen with a copy of each FAS 140 opinion and Andersen was permitted to use the opinion "solely as evidential support

FIN. ACCOUNTING STANDARDS NO. 140 (Fin. Accounting Standards Bd. 2000). The standards distinguishes between transfers that are sales and those that are secured borrowings. In FAS 140 transactions, Enron obtained funds—"monetized"—a variety of otherwise illiquid assets, "removing those assets from its balance sheet while at the same time retaining control over them with a view towards better timing the final sale of those assets." Final Report, supra note 72, app C, at 26

98 *See* Final Report, *supra* note 72, app. B, at 85 (discussing the role of Arthur Anderson).

99 *See* Final Report, *supra* note 72, at 94.

100 *Id.*

101 *Id.* at 99.

102 *See id.* app. C, at 28.

103 *See id.*

104 The Audit Issues Task Force of the Auditing Standards Board, *AU Section 9336: Interpretations of Section 336, Using the Work of a Specialist:* (AU § 9336) (AICPA, Professional Standards) (interpretations of Using the Work of a Specialist, Statement on Auditing Standards No. 73 (Am. Inst. of Certified Pub. Accountants 1994) (AU, § 336). This interpretation was cited by Enron's Examiner in the Final Report. Final Report, *supra* note 72, app. C, at 28 n.71.

105 Final Report, *supra* note 72, app. C, at 31.

in determining the appropriate accounting and financial reporting treatment of the transactions."[106]

Rendering legal opinions is an important part of general practice. Opinions can be used not only to interpret the law or to analyze the legal nature of a particular transaction or relationship. They can also be employed as a defensive strategy—a form of insurance. An opinion can be used to argue that actions taken were technically correct. If that is contested, it at least shows that the action was arguably correct and taken in good faith. Opinions thus are useful in negotiations to compromise or settle a dispute, and to avoid a case going to court. In a financial reporting context, legal opinions can be used to challenge auditors who might take a different view of the nature of a transaction or relationship.

Attorneys often render opinions concerning compliance by their clients with federal securities laws: "legal opinions are often essential to the completion of the transaction, and the parties and the investing public look to the opinion as the authoritative statement that the matters opined upon are in order."[107] Delivering legal opinions is a manifestation of the lawyer's gatekeeper role: "the legal opinion of the reputational intermediary is deemed trustworthy because the parties know that the attorney has a greater stake in its own reputation than in the particular transaction."[108] Opinions have to be from outside counsel to indicate that the opinion is independent of the client: "independence of the attorney is critical to the gatekeeping function."[109]

In the classic phrase of Judge Henry Friendly,

> [i]n our complex society . . . the lawyer's opinion can be [an] instrument for inflicting pecuniary loss more potent than the chisel or the crowbar . . . . Congress equally could not have intended that men holding themselves out as members of these ancient professions [the accounting and legal professions] should be able to escape criminal liability on a plea of ignorance when they have shut their eyes to what was plainly to be seen or have represented a knowledge they knew they did not possess.[110]

Under Texas law, an attorney can commit legal malpractice by giving an erroneous legal opinion.[111] Although lawyers' responsibilities can vary significantly depending on

---

[106] *Id.* app. C, at 31 n.83 (internal quotations omitted).

[107] Attorney's Conduct in Issuing an Opinion Letter Without Conducting an Inquiry of Underlying Facts Failed to Comport With Applicable Standards of Conduct, Exchange Act Release No. 17831, 22 SEC Docket 1200 (June 1, 1981), *available at* http://www.sec.gov/info/municipal/mbonds/bc.htm.

[108] Christine Hurt, *Counselor, Gatekeeper, Shareholder, Thief: Why Attorneys Who Invest in Their Clients in a Post-Enron World Are "Selling Out," Not "Buying In,"* 64 OHIO ST. L.J. 897, 928 (2003).

[109] *Id.* at 929.

[110] United States v. Benjamin, 328 F.2d 854, 863 (2d Cir. 1964).

[111] Kimleco Petroleum, Inc. v. Morrison & Shelton, 91 S.W.3d 921, 923 (Tex. App. 2002); *see also* Final Report, *supra* note 72, app C, annex 1, at 26 n.67.

the identity of the opinion recipient,[112] if the recipient is the client, the opinion giver has a "paramount duty, based on the professional responsibility of the attorney to the client,"[113] and the principles which apply to giving opinions "should apply with even more force."[114]

The principles are that the attorney who prepares or reviews a legal opinion should "exercise good professional judgment and give careful and thoughtful attention to the language and meaning of the opinion, as well as any factual investigation and legal research necessary to support the opinion."[115] The duty to "conduct a reasonable investigation of the relevant facts to support the decision" is "fundamental."[116]

E. Questions, Aims, and Findings

This Article focuses on the role played by Vinson & Elkins, "the outside law firm Enron turned to with the greatest frequency on a wide range of matters."[117] Founded in Houston in 1917, it is, by any definition, a large law firm. It had, during the period of this case study, more than 800 attorneys organized into seventy core practice areas.[118]

Vinson & Elkins views itself as a global law firm. It has offices in ten cities in the United States and abroad, including Beijing, Dubai, London, Moscow, and Singapore. It was one of the first U.S. law firms to establish a multi-national partnership under the rules of the English Law Society.[119] It is a firm that takes pride in itself. Its website noted that seventy-two of its lawyers appeared in the 2001-02 edition of *Best Lawyers in America* and that it ranked consistently as "one of the leading law firms of the world."[120] Shortly after the date the Final Report was published, it described itself as "among the world's major law firms . . . . The firm's clients include the governments of sovereign nations and North American states, as well as cities and municipalities, public

---

112 State Bar of Texas, Business Law Section, *Report of the Legal Opinions Committee Regarding Legal Opinions in Business Transactions*, 15-16 (1992) [hereinafter *Texas Report*]; *see also* Final Report, *supra* note 72, app. C, annex 1, at 26-28.

113 *Texas Report, supra* note 112, at 16.

114 Final Report, *supra* note 72, app. C, annex 1, at 30.

115 *Texas Report, supra* note 112, at 14.

116 *Id.* at 38-39.

117 Final Report, *supra* note 72, app. C, annex. 1, at 21.

118 *Id.* app. C, at 21 n.47.

119 *See* http://www.vinson-elkins.com/firm_overview/firm_overview.cfm (last visited Jan. 16, 2004).

120 Vinson & Elkins LLP, Firm Overview, http://www.vinson-elkins.com/overview/overview.asp (last visited Oct. 20, 2006). Later in 2004, the website stated that Vinson & Elkins had over 750 lawyers and that ninety-five of them appear in the 2003-04 edition. *See* Vinson & Elkins LLP, Rankings/Awards, http://www.vinson-elkins.com/overview/rankings.asp (last visited Oct. 20, 2006).

and private companies from around the world, domestic and international financial institutions, entrepreneurial enterprises and individuals."[121]

Since then, its "General Firm Rankings" include the following: "ranked #1 in the world by number of deals in *Infrastructure Journal*'s 2003 Half-Year League Tables;" *Euromoney* "named four V&E partners in its The Best of the Best 2002, which identifies the worlds leading 25 practitioners across 13 areas of law," and named the firm as "The World's Leading Energy Law Firm;" Thomson Financial ranks the firm "among the top three law firms worldwide in dollar value of Worldwide Equity Issuance by U.S. Issuers for the first half of 2003" and "among the top five law firms worldwide in dollar value of 2002 Initial Public Offerings by U.S. Issuers;" *The American Lawyer* ranks the firm's corporate practice area "first in the nation for IPOs worldwide."[122] As the firm itself puts it, "[w]hen it comes to handling the biggest corporate deals, Vinson & Elkins ranks high among the elite international law firms."[123]

Vinson & Elkins also takes pride in its culture. It emphasizes that the firm "operates on the premise that good attorneys are first good citizens."[124] The firm's "First Principles" include a commitment "to the highest ethical standards, both in our service to clients and in our personal lives."[125] In large law firms, such as Vinson & Elkins, the credentials of attorneys, in terms of core values such as learning and competence, are not normally a significant issue.[126] Similarly, in the Enron case at least, there were few, if any, issues of confidentiality or lawyer conflicts.[127] The focus in this Article, therefore, is on other core values which lie at the heart of legal professionalism, particularly the exercise of independent professional judgment and respect for the rule of law.

Independence is said to be at the heart of Western legal professionalism. According to the Council of the Bars and Law Societies of the European Union (CCBE), an independent legal profession "is an essential means of safeguarding human rights in

---

[121] Vinson & Elkins LLP, Firm Overview, http:// web.archive.org/web/20040204170954/http://www.vinson-elkins.com/firm_overview/firm_Overview.cfm (last visited Oct. 20, 2006) (Vinson & Elkins's current *Overview* no longer contains the exact quote contained in this Article).

[122] Including Joseph C. Dilg, Vinson & Elkins's Enron relationship partner, referred to later in the context of this case study. Vinson & Elkins LLP, Rankings/Awards, http://www.vinson-elkins.com/overview/rankings_detail.asp?title=Best+of+the+Best (last visited Oct. 20, 2006).

[123] Vinson & Elkins LLP, Rankings/Awards, http://www.vinson-elkins.com/overview/rankings_detail.asp?title=Corporate+Control+Alert (last visited Oct. 20, 2006).

[124] Vinson & Elkins LLP, Firm Overview, http://web.archive.org/web/20040204170954/http://www.vinsonelkins.com/firm_ overview/firm_overview.cfm (last visited Oct. 20, 2006). The website now refers to "First Principles," including a commitment to "the highest ethical standards." Vinson & Elkins LLP, First Principles, http://www.vinson-elkins.com/overview/overview_pages.asp?page_name=First%20Principles (last visited Oct. 20, 2006).

[125] *Id.*

[126] Though see text accompanying note 236 below, where the lack of legal and business experience is briefly addressed.

[127] There may, of course, have been conflicts between managers and the corporation.

[the] face of the power of the state and other interests in society."[128] In representing a client, a lawyer should exercise independent professional judgment,[129] free from undue influence by the client. The "lawyer's judgment must be based solely on the legal and factual circumstances attending a matter and not on untoward influences of another sort."[130]

Respect for the rule of law is similarly valued.[131] According to David B. Wilkins, "standard rule-of-law values" are invoked and followed by the "traditional model" of legal ethics.[132] It is the lawyer's responsibility to respect the rule of law and to operate within it. Doing so is a central part of the lawyer's public obligation:[133] "The lawyer is, by vocation, committed to the law."[134] Compliance with regulation also promotes the concept that a lawyer serves the public interest, in addition to the client.[135]

The Article explores these two key core values of the legal profession in the context of the relationship between Vinson & Elkins and Enron (Part II). The analysis suggests that core values do play a significant role in corporate law practice but in unexpected ways. Therefore, I argue that core values need to be re-conceptualized (Part III). On the one hand, they promote a professionalism ideology that has an impact on the lawyer-client relationship. On the other hand, somewhat surprisingly, this ideology serves to undermine the public interest role implicit in professionalism. The reason is that lawyers define their role in terms of the law, of what the law allows, and predictions of what the law will be. Corporate lawyers are legal realists. The problem of their behavior is not one of deviance—breaking the rules—but of compliance—delivering legality.

Therefore, some realism about professionalism is needed (Part IV). The regulation of corporate lawyers is less a problem of lawyers as professionals than it is a problem of law and its capacity to control. This analysis has significant implications for the regulation of lawyers, law firms, and the legal profession.

II. CORE VALUES IN CONTEXT

The principles underpinning legal opinion practice resonate with key core values of the legal profession, such as the exercise of independent professional judgment, basing

---

128 CODE OF CONDUCT FOR LAWYERS IN THE EUROPEAN UNION R. 1.1 (1998), *available at* http://www.ccbe.org/doc/En/code2002_en.pdf. According to the American Bar Association, an independent legal profession is "an important force in preserving government under law." MODEL RULES OF PROF'L CONDUCT PMBL. para. 11 (2003).

129 *See* MODEL RULES OF PROF'L CONDUCT R. 2.1 (2003); *see also* MODEL CODE OF PROF'L RESPONSIBILITY CANON 5 (1980).

130 Anderson, *supra* note 40, at 44.

131 *See* CODE OF CONDUCT FOR LAWYERS IN THE EUROPEAN UNION R. 1.1 (1998), available at http://www.ccbe.org/doc/En/code2002_en.pdf.

132 *See* David B. Wilkins, *Legal Realism for Lawyers*, 104 HARV. L. REV. 468, 473 (1990).

133 Anderson, *supra* note 40, at 44.

134 Gordon, *supra* note 21, at 1200.

135 Anderson, *supra* note 40, at 45.

that judgment solely on the legal and factual circumstances attending the matter and not on untoward influences of another sort, and operating within the rule of law. In this Part, I explore these core values in the practical context of this case study and of the Vinson & Elkins lawyer and Enron client relationship.

A. Client Influence

Large clients can put enormous economic pressure overtly and covertly on employees and their advisers, inside and outside. The compensation system for corporate officers in many large corporations is set by "financial metrics . . . as a means of aligning the interests of management with those of shareholders."[136] In fact, Enron's system of compensation was not only tied to Enron's reported financial results, it "placed the highest emphasis" on them.[137] The Enron compensation structure "depended heavily on the reported financial performance of the company."[138]

The former Vice President of Tax characterized how Enron found the transactions originating in the tax department—where officers and employees understood the important nexus between stock price and compensation: "kind of like cocaine—they got kind of hooked on it."[139] In the three-year period between 1998-2000, a group of twenty-one officers received in excess of $1 billion in the form of salary, bonus, and gross proceeds from sales of Enron stock; in 2000, Kenneth Lay received compensation valued at over $33 million and Jeffrey Skilling over $17 million.[140]

According to Lay's Chief of Staff, the compensation system produced

> [a] near mercenary culture which encourages organizations to hide problems (until those problems have become very big), discourages cooperation and teamwork, and drives off people who demand at least a modicum of civility in their work environment.[141]

It appears that the compensation system also "proved to be an overpowering motivation for implementing SPE transactions that distorted Enron's reported financial results."[142] The Enron compensation program, however, "was not atypical in scope or design as compared to programs of other large public companies at the time."[143] The motivation to manipulate earnings and cash flows is not atypical either, nor is the "allure" of the SPE transactions.[144]

---

136 Final Report, *supra* note 72, at 90.

137 *See id.*

138 *Id.* at 92.

139 *Id.* at 90 n.164.

140 *Id.* at 91.

141 *Id.* at 90 (e-mail from Steven J. Kean to Kenneth Lay, Enron, Aug. 17, 2001, at 1).

142 *Id.* at 91.

143 *Id.* at 92.

144 *See id.* at 93.

Enron put economic pressure on outsiders as well. Analysts reported pressure from superiors not to issue or publish negative comments or research, "due to the importance of Enron as an investment banking client."[145] A specific example involved Merrill Lynch which, in April 1998, had been excluded as a manager for an upcoming $750 million common stock offering because Enron's senior management was angry with the reports and comments of John Olson, Merrill Lynch's equity analyst covering Enron. After a call from Merrill Lynch's Chief Executive Officer to Enron's CEO, Merrill Lynch was added as a manager for the offering. One month later, Olson was fired and replaced with an analyst "with a better opinion of Enron's stock."[146] Merrill Lynch's revenues from Enron increased from $3 million in 1998 to $40 million in 1999.

Andrew Fastow, Enron's Chief Financial Officer, in particular, was perceived to have used his and Enron's authority to exert pressure. Several bank representatives described the pressure he exerted on them to invest in LJM.[147] Apparently, banks understood that investing in LJM would "help their prospects for securing business with Enron."[148] Fastow also had final authority on the evaluations and bonuses of individuals negotiating on Enron's behalf in the LJM transactions.[149] As a result, the perception was that they "might shrink" from their responsibility to vigorously protect Enron's interests.[150]

Of course, bankers and employees are not under a duty to exercise independent judgment in the same way as professionals such as Vinson & Elkins and Arthur Andersen are supposed to. That does not mean professionals are not subject to client pressure. Apparently, "very few people [were] betting on" a "very junior person" who made trouble by questioning the Condor transaction being employed by Andersen "after January 1st."[151]

The concept of independence lies at the "foundation of the public accounting profession, and the critical importance of auditor independence is widely accepted."[152] Although Andersen regarded itself as independent within the rules,[153] the Examiner questioned whether Andersen consistently maintained, in fact, the "independence in mental attitude" required under professional standards.[154] Indeed, by using its economic

---

145 *Id.* at 101 n.192 (Jill Sakol, fixed income analyst, Credit Suisse First Boston).

146 *Id.*

147 *See id.* app. C, at 169 n.778 (Jeffrey M. McMahon, Enron employee).

148 *Id.* app. C, at 169 n.780 (McMahon).

149 For a discussion of the Enron "culture," *see* ROBERT BRYCE, PIPE DREAMS: GREED, EGO, AND THE DEATH OF ENRON 12 (2002).

150 *See* Final Report, *supra* note 72, app. C, at 169 (McMahon); see also id. app. C, at 169 n.777.

151 *Id.* at 102 (e-mail from Joel Ephross, Assistant General Counsel, Enron, to Fernando Tovar, Vinson & Elkins, Dec. 3, 1999).

152 *Id.* app. B, at 31.

153 *See id.* app. B, at 36.

154 *See id.* app. B, at 37. The standard is set out in The Second General Standard of GAAS: "In all matters relating to the assignment, an independence in mental attitude is to be maintained by the auditor or auditors." Codification of Auditing Standards and Procedures, Statement on Auditing Standards No. 1 § 220.01 (Am. Inst. Of Certified Pub. Accountants 1972); *see also* Final Report, *supra* note 72, at 32.

power, Enron officers were able to pressure third parties, including professionals, to accommodate Enron's financial statement objectives. In many instances, use of economic power "appears responsible for overcoming concerns about reputational risk or other reservations by these third parties."[155]

Could this have been because of the close personal and financial links between professionals and client? Between 1989 and 2000, "at least 86 Andersen accountants left Andersen to join Enron, some of whom became key executives in Enron's accounting and treasury functions."[156] The fees Andersen received from Enron were rising rapidly in the period shortly before Enron's bankruptcy: $26.5 million in 1998; $46.4 million in 1999; and $47.9 million in 2000.[157] The majority of these fees came from attesting Enron's internal controls and financial statements and from consulting on the SPE transactions.[158] Enron was described by Andersen as its largest client "by a wide margin in Fiscal 1999."[159]

Vinson & Elkins had personal and financial links with Enron similar to, or possibly even greater than, those of Andersen. As many as 20 Vinson & Elkins lawyers joined Enron,[160] most notably James V. Derrick. Derrick had practiced general business law with Vinson & Elkins from 1971 before joining Enron as General Counsel in 1991.[161] During the first few months after Enron Global Finance (EGF) was created in the third quarter of 1999, its legal department was partly staffed with attorneys loaned from Vinson & Elkins and Andrews Kurth.[162] Each attorney in EGF Legal reported to the General Counsel of EGF Legal.[163] Although they were loaned, they continued to bill as outside counsel.[164]

Like Andersen, Vinson & Elkins received a rapidly increasing level of fees from Enron between 1997 and 2001. Indeed, the fees more than doubled from just over $18.5 million in 1997 to over $42 million in 2000.[165] Apparently, Enron represented 7% of Vinson & Elkins revenue, while only 1% of Andersen's.[166] On this basis, if any

---

155 Final Report, *supra* note 72, at 94.

156 *Id.* at 39.

157 *Id.* The Examiner put Andersen's fees from its engagement with Enron during 2000 at around $54 million. *Id.* app. B, at 9; *see also id.* app. B, at 28-31. In February 2001, 113 Andersen professional personnel were deployed. *Id.* app. B, at 9.

158 *See id.* at 39.

159 *Id.*

160 *See* Brenda Sapino Jeffreys, *V&E Closes Book on Enron,* LEGAL TIMES, Mar. 11, 2002, at 16.

161 *See* Final Report, *supra* note 72, app. C, at 16 n.20.

162 *See id.* app. C, at 19 (Joel Ephross, Senior Counsel, Enron Global Finance).

163 *See id.*

164 *See id.* app. C, at 19 n.37.

165 The figures for Vinson & Elkins LLP each year were as follows: 1997: $18,586,479; 1998: $26,645,963; 1999: $37,840,290; 2000: $42,789,338; 2001: $36,368,833. *Id.* app. C, at 21.

166 *See* CRUVER, *supra* note 67, at 287.

of the professionals should have succumbed to Enron's pressure, it should have been Vinson & Elkins (or other outside attorneys[167]).

It is significant, therefore, that the Examiner did not criticize Vinson & Elkins for a failure of "independence in mental attitude" or for shrinking under economic pressure. Neither overt nor covert economic client pressure appears to have unduly influenced the exercise of Vinson & Elkins' attorneys' professional judgment. There can, however, be other, more subtle, factors which may significantly influence how professional judgment is exercised. The first relates to the complexity of the transactions in which Enron was engaged.

B. Complexity

Vinson & Elkins (and Andrews & Kurth) were asked to provide for Enron the opinion letters that Andersen would use to satisfy the isolation requirements of FAS 140 in part because these transactions were not simple ones. They would not have been needed had the transactions not been complex. Vinson & Elkins had been provided with a copy of Andersen's internal memorandum dated April 1998, which confirmed that "[t]ransactions that would not require a legal letter are limited to transactions such as the simple sale of equity or debt securities."[168] An Andersen publication[169] which accompanied the memorandum emphasized that opinions on whether assets transferred met the requirements of FAS 125 (the predecessor of FAS 140), which was in effect for many of the transactions, "must be from counsel . . . with sufficient expertise . . . to make the determination . . . whether the transaction would be viewed as a sale and not as a secured borrowing if the seller enters bankruptcy."[170]

Vinson & Elkins knew, therefore, that it was being asked for opinions in the context of complex transactions. However, part of Enron's strategy was to embrace complexity. Indeed, "[t]he 'tangled web' created by the complexity and magnitude of the [SPE] structures was extraordinary."[171]

To give an opinion on the nature of a transaction, and to determine, in particular, whether transferred financial assets have been isolated and put presumptively beyond the reach of the transferor and its creditors, could require the attorney to make a number of judgments: can the transferor revoke the transfer; into what kind of bankruptcy or other receivership might a transferor or SPE be placed; would a transfer of financial

[167] Andrews & Kurth's fees rose even more rapidly than Vinson & Elkins, during the same period, though from a much lower base. In 1997, fees were just less than $1 million. By 2000, they had grown to well over $9 million. The figures each year were as follows: 1997: $991,053; 1998: $2,355,399; 1999: $6,644,267; 2000: $9,740,414; 2001: $9,269,594. Final Report, *supra* note 72, app. C, at 25.

[168] *Id.* app. C, at 28 (emphasis added) (quoting an Andersen FAS 125 Memorandum dated Apr. 27, 1998, 66).

[169] FINANCIAL ASSETS AND LIABILITIES, SALES, TRANSFERS AND EXTINGUISHMENTS: INTERPRETATION OF FASB STATEMENT 125. *See* Final Report, *supra* note 72, app. C, at 28 n.72.

[170] Final Report, *supra* note 72, app. C, at 28 n.72.

[171] *Id.* app. C, at 82, n.140 (citing Sir Walter Scott, Marmion, Canto VI, Stanza 17 (1808) ("Oh what a tangled web we weave when first we practice to deceive!")).

assets be likely to be deemed a true sale in law; and is the transferor affiliated with the transferee?[172] In Enron's case, the attorney would also be faced with Enron officers' frequent use of "misleading terms and jargon in connection with Enron's SPE transactions [which] appears to have obscured their economic substance."[173]

C. Analysis

Project Cornhusker closed on March 27, 1998. In June 1998, the Enron client "relationship partner" at Vinson & Elkins, Joseph C. Dilg, received a memorandum voicing the concerns of other Vinson & Elkins attorneys regarding the Cornhusker true issuance opinions. According to the memo,

> [b]ased upon Enron's desire to recognize gain in two separate quarters, it appears that . . . the event that must have resulted in the recognition of the gain was the transaction between Northern Plains and NBIL1 (as to which we gave no opinion). Only [that] part of the transaction . . . was structured to 'straddle' the first and second quarter . . . . This fact suggests that, for opinion purposes, we and the accountants focused on the wrong part of the transaction.[174]

A meeting had also been held between Dilg and several other Vinson & Elkins attorneys involved in the SPE transactions raising concerns should Vinson & Elkins be asked to give a true sale opinion.[175]

In other words, Vinson & Elkins became concerned that the true issuance opinion might not be responsive to the intent or purpose for which the true sale opinion [was] required.[176] Unless a true sale opinion could be rendered on the transaction prior to the share issuance—that is, the transfer of a financial asset to NBIL—the requirements of FAS 125, and its replacement, FAS 140, would not be addressed.

According to one of those present at the meeting,

> [t]he purpose of the meeting was to bring to Mr. Dilg's attention that there were transactions involving true issuance opinions; that we had this issue of whether or not true issuance opinions were responsive to FAS-125. We wanted to be sure that he as the Enron client relationship partner was aware of this. We thought that the issue should be confirmed at high levels on something like this.[177]

---

[172] *See* Final Report, *supra* note 72, app. C, at 27 (citing FAS 125, ¶ 23).

[173] *Id.* app. C, at 94.

[174] *Id.* app. C, at 37 (quoting Stephen Tarry).

[175] *See id.*

[176] *See id.* app. C, at 30 n.80 (Vinson & Elkins memorandum).

[177] *Id.* app. C, at 38 (quoting from David Keyes's sworn statement) (emphasis added).

Dilg asked about the size and financial impact of these transactions at the meeting, and at some point, Vinson & Elkins became aware of the "substantial financial impact" that these transactions could have on Enron's financial statements.[178]

During the same period, another Vinson & Elkins attorney held discussions with several partners about disclosure issues raised by Enron's FAS 140 transactions. He was concerned that Enron was obtaining an increasing percentage of its earnings from appreciation of its merchant assets. One of the concerns he raised was the nature of the "Total Return Swap" (TRS) part of the transaction: Enron was not shifting the risk of loss (or, for that matter, the reward of gain) from assets being transferred.[179] In addition, Enron's obligation under the TRS to pay the loan raised liquidity issues. This attorney also estimated that the impact of these transactions on Enron's financial statements was "significant,"[180] and that at least one senior officer at Enron knew about this.[181]

Thus, there were two main concerns. First, unless a true sale opinion could be given (in regard to the contribution of the financial assets to NBIL), a true issuance by NBIL would accomplish little in regard to the isolation of its financial assets from the original transferor.[182] Secondly, and as a corollary to this, the two separate transfers must "each qualify as sales" under FAS 140; otherwise, NBIL could not sell something which it did not own.[183]

Whether or not the treatments were permitted under accounting rules, there was also the issue of proper disclosure in Enron's "Management's Discussion and Analysis of Financial Condition and Results of Operations" (MD&A).[184] Enron's MD&A appeared in Enron's Forms 10-K and 10-Q filed with the SEC. What action did Vinson & Elkins take to reflect its concerns?

D. Action

One response was to add to its true issuance opinion an assumption: that a court would not recharacterize the entire transaction, when viewed in its entirety, as a loan.[185]

---

178 *See id.* app. C, at 32.

179 "Using a TRS rather than a guarantee was one of Enron's favorite techniques to avoid disclosure." Final Report, *supra* note 72, at 97.

180 Final Report, *supra* note 72, app. C, at 41 (quoting Scott Wulfe of Vinson & Elkins).

181 *See id.* app. C, at 42.

182 *See id.* app. C, at 31 n.81 (analysis of Kimberly Scardino, an Andersen accountant).

183 *See id.* (emphasis added).

184 17 C.F.R. § 229.303 (2004). In the Management's discussion and analysis of financial condition and results of operations (MD&A), companies provide a description of their operations and any initiatives during the relevant year. The aim should be to give investors an opportunity to look at the company through the eyes of management by providing both a short and long-term analysis of the business of the company. *See* http://www.sec.gov/rules/interp/33-6835.htm (last visited Oct. 21 2006).

185 *See* Final Report, *supra* note 72, app. C, at 34-35. Specifically, the Cornhusker opinion letter contained the assumptions that a court would not

The firm did this to "put people on notice" that they were "not giving a true sale opinion."[186] Such a recharacterization would not be acceptable in a true sale opinion—it would be assuming away the very issue that a true sale opinion purported to address: whether the transaction was really a sale or a loan.

In the Cornhusker opinion, Vinson & Elkins also referred to the TRS element of the transaction: it "is basically to make the Lenders whole in the event NBIL2 is unable to repay principal, interest, fees and other amounts owed to the Lenders . . . . The Total Return Swap is similar in function to a guaranty . . . ."[187] Vinson & Elkins did the same thing on other FAS 140 Transactions, such as Project Churchill.[188] It specifically opined that, in the event of a bankruptcy of NBIL, Enron, Northern Plains, or any other consolidated subsidiary of Enron, the Bankruptcy Court could conclude that the Class B Membership Interest would not be the property of these entities.[189]

Vinson & Elkins's attorneys also contacted both Enron and Andersen directly to question whether Andersen fully understood that no true sale opinion was being given.[190] They had repeatedly told Enron and Andersen that Andersen had asked for the wrong opinion when it requested its true issuance opinions.[191] One attorney put it like this: "[F]rom a lawyer's perspective, he [Keyes, a different Vinson & Elkins attorney] didn't think what they [Andersen] were asking for was what his reading of the corporate rules required."[192] "Andersen apparently acknowledged that it was aware that no such opinion was being given."[193]

All these matters—the opinion letters and the disclosure issues—came to a head with a meeting in June 1998 between Joseph C. Dilg, Vinson & Elkins's Enron relationship partner, and James V. Derrick, Enron's General Counsel. Prior to the meeting, Dilg was briefed on the issues.[194] He was concerned that the SPE "transactions which were generating income were different than receiving fees from pushing gas through a pipeline or other types of things."[195] In other words, these were not fees resulting from normal operating activities.

> (i) recharacterize the issuance of the Class B Membership Interest by NBIL . . . as a loan to NBIL supported by a security interest in [its] Class B Membership Interest, or (ii) recharacterize the [t]ransactions as a loan to Northern Plains supported by a security interest in the [financial assets].

Id. app. C, at 35 n.99.

[186] *Id.* app. C, at 35 (from David Keyes's sworn statement).

[187] *Id.* app. C, at 33-34 n.93; *see also id.* at 36 n.106.

[188] *See id.* app. C, at 36 n.106.

[189] *See id.* app. C, at 35 n.105.

[190] *See* Final Report, *supra* note 72, app. B, at 91.

[191] *See id.* app. C, at 31.

[192] *Id.* app. C, at 34 n.98 (referring to Ronald T. Astin of Vinson & Elkins, who is referring to David Keyes).

[193] *Id.* app. B, at 91.

[194] *See id.* app. C, at 37-43.

[195] *Id.* app. C, at 49.

Dilg understood that his partners had two concerns on the opinion letters. The first was whether a true issuance opinion was sufficient for the accounting purposes of the transaction. The second concern revolved around the need to clarify and focus Enron on the qualification in the opinion that the overall transaction would not be recharacterized as a loan. Dilg also testified that he wanted Derrick to be aware that it might cost the company a "fair amount of money to restructure transactions to satisfy us" should Vinson & Elkins be asked to render a different opinion which it could not do professionally without such restructuring.[196]

E. Deference and the Division of Professional Labor

It appears that Vinson & Elkins deferred to the expertise and sophistication of Andersen, of Enron, and of Enron's in-house counsel. There was a division of professional labor. Indeed, one Vinson & Elkins attorney would later testify that the decision to give true issuance opinions ultimately was based on numerous assurances given by Andersen (and Enron) that these were what was required:

> [I]n cases where we issue a true issuance opinion, that's the opinion that we were asked for . . . I mean they were the accountants, they understood what they wanted and based on what she [Debra Cash, Andersen] said, I had . . . no reason to think that was not reasonable from an accounting criteria standpoint. They were the accountants there.[197]

Sometime after the June 1998 meeting, Derrick told Dilg that he had visited with Enron's Chief Accounting Officer, who had "checked with the higher-ups within Arthur Andersen. I [Dilg] took it to be their technical people, and that they had focused on the opinions and they knew what they were and that they felt the opinions were satisfactory for their purposes."[198] For Dilg, that was "the end of the matter."[199] He no longer had any doubts in his mind; the assurances from both Enron and Andersen were sufficient. Dilg told the Vinson & Elkins attorney that they "understood the nature"[200] of Vinson & Elkins's opinions. Further projects and transactions were undertaken and closed.[201] "Both Andersen and Enron continued to ask only for true issuance, not true sale, opinions up until mid-2001."[202] Thus, Vinson & Elkins delivered the opinions, sometimes despite "misgivings, but based on Andersen's assurances" that all that was required was a "true issuance opinion" for FAS 140 Transactions.[203]

---

196 *Id.* app. C, at 44 n.155.

197 *Id.* app. C, at 33 n.92.

198 *Id.* app. C, at 46 (quoting Joseph C. Dilg).

199 *Id.*

200 *Id.*

201 *Id.* app. C, at 46-47.

202 *Id.* app. B, at 91.

203 *Id.* app. C, at 33.

Andersen, of course, was one of the "Big 5" accounting firms, one of the world's biggest. Enron's General Counsel, a former Vinson & Elkins partner, considered his in-house legal department to be a "world-class" in-house law firm.[204] It consisted of approximately 250 attorneys,[205] most of whom had between eight and seventeen years of legal experience when they joined Enron.[206] Each of Enron's business units had its own legal department supervised by a general counsel. Each general counsel reported to the head of the business unit as well as to Enron's General Counsel.[207] There were weekly meetings of the major business units' general counsel and monthly conferences which included the general counsel of overseas entities.[208] These meetings provided, among other things, a forum for attorneys to raise issues and concerns.[209]

Moreover, the Enron Board of Directors itself was hardly "lightweight"; "by all appearances, Enron's board looked great . . . . The directors reflected a wide range of business, finance, accounting, and government experience."[210] Kenneth Lay had a Ph.D. in economics; Jeffrey Skilling graduated with an MBA from Harvard, where he was in the top five percent of his class. The outside directors of the Board included "a group of men and women who were highly successful in their professional careers,"[211] including four with Ph.D.s, one with an honorary doctorate, two medical doctors who each served as president of one of the world's leading cancer treatment centers, two law school graduates, twelve who had served as chief executive officers, a Dean of Stanford University School of Business, a member of the House of Lords in the United Kingdom who had served under then Prime Minister Margaret Thatcher, and a former Chair of the Commodity Futures Trading Commission.[212] Enron's General Counsel, James Derrick, apparently "had a lot of confidence . . . in senior management."[213]

Vinson & Elkins deferred to in-house counsel and to Enron when it expressed concerns about other matters, too. One example was its concern about the legal issues raised by the involvement of Michael Kopper in Chewco.[214] Vinson & Elkins advised

---

[204] *See id.* app. C, at 16.

[205] *Id.* app. C, at 15.

[206] *Id.* app. C, at 16.

[207] *See id.* app. C, at 17.

[208] *See id.* app. C, at 18.

[209] *See id.*

[210] Troy H. Paredes, *Enron: The Board, Corporate Governance, and Some Thoughts on the Role of Congress, in* ENRON: CORPORATE FIASCOS AND THEIR IMPLICATIONS, *supra* note 62, at 495, 504.

[211] Final Report, *supra* note 72, at 56-57.

[212] *See id.* at 57.

[213] *Id.* app. C, at 130 n.571.

[214] Chewco was formed by Enron in late 1997 to acquire the California Public Employee Retirement System's (CalPERS) 50% limited partnership interest in JEDI. JEDI had been created in 1993 to make energy investments. Enron was the other 50% partner and did not want to purchase CalPERS' interest directly because that would require JEDI to be consolidated on Enron's financial statements. Kopper, at the time a vice president in Enron's Global Capital department, was made the managing partner of

Enron that investment by an "executive officer"—such as Andrew Fastow—would have to be disclosed in Enron's public filings. When Vinson & Elkins was presented with a proposed structure that placed Kopper as manager and owner of Chewco, Enron did not deem Kopper to be an "executive officer" as defined by SEC rules.[215] When a Vinson & Elkins attorney discussed the issue with Enron's in-house attorneys, he was told that all the necessary action "would be handled by in-house counsel."[216]

Similarly, Vinson & Elkins had concerns regarding the Raptor 1 and its "distribution feature" that was critical to the maintenance of LJM2's three percent equity position—and its remaining at risk throughout the life of the structure and therefore off Enron's balance sheet. Those concerns were deflected because it was seen as an accounting issue. Vinson & Elkins "received confirmation from Enron that the accounting was appropriate."[217] Checking and making sure that "everybody's comfortable with the accounting and then . . . it doesn't sound like a legal issue."[218]

The approach taken by Vinson & Elkins in deferring to Andersen is further illustrated by its investigation of the Watkins "whistleblower" letter.[219] The letter raised accounting issues, but another issue raised was whether to bring in an outside auditor. The conclusion was not to retain one. Part of the reason for this may have been the "attendant focus of the media on Enron, [which] would be 'fairly drastic.'"[220] But it was also determined that Vinson & Elkins would not "second guess" Andersen or "dig down" into the transactions.[221] Rather, Vinson & Elkins wanted to make sure that Andersen "had the proper facts, that they had all of the facts that they needed to make the review, and that they were comfortable with their accounting decisions. But we were

Chewco. His involvement raised conflict of interest questions under Enron's Code of Conduct, which provided that, in such circumstances, his involvement should be only with the approval of the Board. The Board was never presented with Kopper's role in Chewco. Rather, Chewco was characterized by Fastow as an "unaffiliated" entity to the Enron Board. An additional issue that proved critical to the Chewco transaction was the requirement that outside investors supply 3% of the equity at risk. It was a violation of this requirement which, when discovered by Andersen in November 2001, led to the consolidation of Chewco and JEDI and the restatement of Enron's accounts for the period 1997 through 2001. *Id.* app C, at 108-10. More details regarding the Chewco transaction can be found in the lengthy judgment of the court in In re Enron Corp. Secs., 235 F. Supp. 2d 548, 613-73 (S.D. Tex. 2002).

[215] Final Report, *supra* note 72, app. C, at 112.

[216] *Id.* app. C, at 113.

[217] *Id.* app. C, at 163-64 n.744.

[218] *Id.* app. C, at 141.

[219] Memorandum from Sherron Watkins to Kenneth Lay (Aug. 15, 2001), *available at* http://energycommerce.house.gov/107/hearings/02142002Hearing489/tab10.pdf (last visited Oct. 21, 2006). *See generally* Leslie Griffin, *Whistleblowing in the Business World, in* ENRON: CORPORATE FIASCOS AND THEIR IMPLICATIONS, *supra* note 62, at 209; Memorandum from Sherron Watkins to Kenneth Lay (Aug. 22, 2001), *available at* http://energycommerce.house.gov/107/hearings/02142002Hearing489/tab11.pdf (last visited Oct. 21, 2006).

[220] Final Report, *supra* note 72, app. C, at 165 (according to Max Hendrick's sworn statement on July 8, 2003).

[221] *Id.*

not in a position to second-guess Arthur Andersen's ultimate professional judgment or the accounting issues involved."[222]

The Vinson & Elkins investigation therefore was limited to determining whether there were any facts about the various structures "that Enron management or Andersen did not have that might warrant further investigation of the matters."[223] Vinson & Elkins did not seek to "re-build the disclosure process."[224] In any case, when Vinson & Elkins interviewed Andersen partners to discuss Watkins' letter, the partners explained that "the accounting analysis conducted in each of the transactions . . . was complex and aggressive."[225] However, they were "comfortable with the accounting on Raptors"[226] and Andersen was "aware of the put option [in LJM] and was comfortable with it and the fee arrangement."[227] Regarding LJM, the partners stated that "technically" the investment and the return was proper.[228] The accounting treatment may have looked "facially questionable," but it satisfied the technical requirements."[229] Similarly, in answer to the question of whether there was a valid business purpose for the put, Andersen relied on Enron's representation that a good business reason existed.[230] No wonder Vinson & Elkins concluded that "Enron and Andersen acknowledge that the accounting treatment is aggressive, but no reason to believe inappropriate from a technical standpoint."[231] And, "[n]otwithstanding the bad cosmetics, Enron representatives uniformly stated that the Condor and Raptor vehicles were clever, useful vehicles that benefited Enron."[232]

A division of professional labor, and deference to the expertise and authority of others, meant that Vinson & Elkins attorneys may not have been fully apprised of the situation. Indeed, it might have meant that no one was.

F. Black Holes

Gaps in knowledge and information affect the exercise of professional judgment. Enron's in-house business units' general counsel held meetings weekly or monthly. They provided a forum for, amongst other things, attorneys to raise issues and concerns.[233]

---

[222] *Id.* app. C, at 165 n.754 (quoting Dilg's testimony before Congress).

[223] *Id.* app. C, at 165-66.

[224] *Id.* app. C, at 166.

[225] *Id.* app. C, at 174.

[226] *Id.* app. C, at 174-75.

[227] *Id.* app. C, at 175.

[228] *Id.* app. C, at 175 n.820.

[229] *Id.*

[230] *Id.*

[231] Final Report, *supra* note 72, app. C, at 176.

[232] *Id.* app. C, at 177.

[233] *Id.* app. C, at 18.

Yet, Enron's in-house attorneys failed to identify the concerns which the Examiner identified regarding Enron's SPE transactions at any of these meetings.[234] In fact, the issue of the true issuance opinions may have been raised by Vinson & Elkins with one of Enron's in-house attorneys.[235]

Not all attorneys are experienced, and some may never be experienced enough. Two lawyers involved in one of the structures probably had insufficient experience with such transaction structures to appreciate the significance of a "side letter" which established a reserve account that violated a three percent equity requirement (to avoid consolidation).[236] Even Joseph C. Dilg, aware of Vinson & Elkins's concerns about income generated by what did not appear to be normal operating activities, found it difficult to challenge once assurances had been made. As Dilg put it, he did not "think we knew enough about the overall business to tell them how they ought to write it."[237]

Indeed, in Enron's case, it is not clear that even the Board knew enough about the business, either. Vinson & Elkins' "reporting-up" its concerns to the Board might not have made much difference. First, it appears that the SPE transactions were structured so that Board approval was not needed and Enron Board policies, such as those on Risk Management, Guaranty, and asset divestiture, were not breached.[238] Furthermore, "particularly in circumstances involving complex matters and obfuscation by officers of a company, there are limitations to a board serving as an effective check in the area of oversight."[239]

The outside directors at Enron in particular were not involved in and did not have intimate knowledge of the day-to-day operations and may not have recognized the "red flags" regarding the SPE transactions as indicators of wrongful conduct.[240] Several factors may have contributed to this: Enron officers' use of misleading terms and confusing jargon; the presentation of information in a manner that obfuscated the substance of those transactions; the length of meetings and the number of agenda items; and the size of the Board (unusually large, diminishing the feeling of personal responsibility).[241]

It is not only gaps in information which can undermine judgments. The outside directors in fact were provided with "voluminous information,"[242] but not all this information was helpful. Sometimes there was so much information provided to the

---

[234] *Id.*

[235] *Id.* app. C, at 34.

[236] *Id.* app. C, at 114 (referring to the JEDI structure).

[237] *Id.* app. C, at 49.

[238] Final Report, *supra* note 72, at 121-24.

[239] *Id.* at 119-20.

[240] *Id.* at 58-59.

[241] "The independence and objectivity of the Enron Board may have been weakened by financial ties . . . which affected a majority of the outside Board members . . . ." PERMANENT SUBCOMM. ON INVESTIGATIONS OF THE COMM. ON GOV'T AFFAIRS, THE ROLE OF THE BOARD OF DIRECTORS IN ENRON'S COLLAPSE, S. Rep. No. 107-70, at 54 (2002).

[242] Final Report, *supra* note 72, at 59.

Finance Committee that it was, according to one former Enron director, "numbing rather than elucidating."[243] "[T]he outside directors did not understand important aspects about Enron's use of SPE transactions."[244]

Regarding the MD&A, 10-K, and 10-Q filings, although Vinson & Elkins's attorneys were consulted by Enron's in-house attorneys on disclosure matters, it was only on an "episodic" basis;[245] they saw some but not all.[246] Furthermore, they were probably not told of Enron's expectations about the scope of their involvement in Enron's public disclosures.[247] Enron's in-house counsel's expectations for Vinson & Elkins's review of SEC filings "was very general . . . there was no specific instructions [sic] other than review and give us your comments."[248] The input of various Vinson & Elkins' attorneys working on the various SPE transactions was not solicited.[249] In any case, where specific transactions were discussed in a filing, not necessarily the entire document, but parts only, were sent by in-house attorneys or other groups in Enron to the Vinson & Elkins attorney who worked on that transaction for that attorney's review.[250] Moreover, as the attorney told Dilg, even when they did see the 10-Ks and 10-Qs, "since they were part of the overall financial statements, we had very limited ability to comment, et cetera."[251]

Enron knew, or should have known, that Vinson & Elkins was not devoting significant time to its review of SEC filings and that it was not, contrary to what Derrick

---

[243] *Id.* at 127 (quoting Robert A. Belfer).

[244] *Id.* at 132. The Examiner did conclude there was evidence that they were in possession of facts regarding the LJM1/Rhythms Hedging Transaction and certain of the LJM2/Raptors Hedging Transactions necessary to conclude neither of them had a rational business purpose and that they acted in bad faith and in breach of their fiduciary duty of good faith in authorizing and approving the transactions. *Id.* at 59, 61. In these transactions, Enron transferred substantial value for non-economic hedges, meaning the value of each hedge to Enron was based solely on the value of the securities and cash that Enron itself had transferred to the hedging vehicles, providing Enron with no economic value but only a financial statement benefit, and that they acted in bad faith and in breach of their fiduciary duty of good faith in authorizing and approving the transactions. *Id.* at 59, 61. On Jan. 7, 2005, it was announced that ten former outside directors of Enron had agreed personally to contribute $13 million to a $168 million settlement (apparently reached in Oct. 2004, but kept confidential). The contribution reported equals ten percent of their pre-tax profit from Enron stock sales. These directors were not alleged to have been active participants in any underlying fraud. Further, a court had previously dismissed claims against them for alleged insider dealing. *See* http://www.friedfrank.com/cmemos/050113_worldcom%20enron.pdf (last visited Oct. 21, 2006).

[245] Final Report, *supra* note 72, app. C, at 84.

[246] *Id.* app. C, at 168 n.771 (citing sworn statement of Joseph C. Dilg, referring to Ronald T. Astin).

[247] *Id.* app. C, at 85.

[248] *Id.* app. C, at 86 (quoting the sworn statement of Rex Rogers, Vice President and Associate General Counsel, Enron).

[249] *See id.* (citing the sworn statement of Rogers).

[250] *Id.* (citing the sworn statement of Rogers).

[251] *Id.* app. C, at 168 n.771 (quoting the sworn statement of Joseph C. Dilg, referring to Ronald T. Astin).

testified was his impression, "fully involved in ensuring that Enron's public disclosures were adequate."[252] Vinson & Elkins typically received Enron's financial statements two to three days before filing, so they had "very limited opportunities to comment on them."[253] Vinson & Elkins invoices confirmed all of this.[254]

However, as a result of interaction with Vinson & Elkins, Enron did add new language to its public disclosure. "[N]either the new language nor other information . . . adequately informed shareholders or creditors of the elements of these transactions that Vinson & Elkins had recognized and brought to Enron's attention."[255] However, it was Vinson & Elkins that had brought it to their attention. It had not been passive about the matter and it did respond to the challenge.

Indeed, where Vinson & Elkins did raise disclosure points about certain SPE transactions and felt that disclosure was mandatory, the Examiner found no evidence that Enron ever refused to make such a disclosure. Moreover, as we have seen, Vinson & Elkins, contrary to what was believed prior to the Examiner's Final Report,[256] did not, with the single exception of Project Sundance Industrial, issue true sale opinions. Indeed, it had expressly refused to do so, for example, when Enron requested it do so in Raptor III.[257]

As the firm saw it, it issued "non substantive consolidation opinions,"[258] together with "no recharacterization" assumptions ("to put people on notice"[259]). The "problem" was however, as one Vinson & Elkins attorney put it, that "most disclosure questions are judgmental in nature and it's rare that one is a completely open and shut situation."[260]

G. (Dis)Honest Differences of Opinion

There can be honest—as well as dishonest—differences of opinion about the nature of transactions and the application of regulatory requirements. Vinson & Elkins had to exercise judgment on disclosure questions in partnership with others. Where it made

---

[252] *Id.* app. C, at 84.

[253] *Id.* app. C, at 172 (citing to the sworn statements of Hendrick and Dilg). Note that Vinson & Elkins' involvement in proxy statements was "more involved." *Id.* (citing to the sworn testimony of Joseph Dilg).

[254] *See id.* app. C, at 87.

[255] *Id.* app. C, at 32.

[256] *See* Jill E. Fisch & Kenneth M. Rosen, *Is There a Role for Lawyers in Preventing Future Enrons?*, 48 VILL. L. REV. 1097, 1110 (2003). The error may have come from the Watkins whistleblower letter, which urged that Vinson & Elkins should not be retained to undertake an investigation of her allegations "because it had rendered true sale opinions." Final Report, *supra* note 72, app. C, at 161 n.724).

[257] *See* Final Report, *supra* note 72, app. C, at 162 n.735 (citing to sworn statement of Mark Spradling).

[258] *Id.* app. C, at 162 (quoting the sworn statement of Astin).

[259] *See id.* app. C, at 35 (quoting the sworn statement of David Keyes).

[260] *Id.* app. C, at 87 n.339 (quoting the sworn statement of Astin).

disclosure recommendations to Enron rather than mandatory requirements, there was little it could do when Enron decided not to make so full a disclosure.

Acknowledgment that there may be honest differences forces us to re-appraise what it means to exercise independent professional judgment. The legal standard of care applicable to attorneys is that of the "reasonably prudent attorney."[261] So, if there is "more than one possible decision or course of conduct available to an attorney of reasonable prudence," there should be no liability. The standard allows "some latitude in making strategic and tactical decisions."[262]

That there is more than one way of looking at it is confirmed already, somewhat ironically, by the opinion shopping Vinson & Elkins undertook. It obtained the opinions of "law school professors and practitioners on several matters as to which the Examiner took testimony."[263]

Independent professional judgment does not mean consensus. Vinson & Elkins understood, erroneously, that Andrews & Kurth was issuing true sales opinions after it had taken over most of the FAS 140 Transactions in late 1998.[264] Although it was concerned about the credibility of those opinions, it did not raise it with Enron, concluding "that the issue with the Andrews & Kurth true sale opinions were a matter of professional judgment."[265] Vinson & Elkins concluded that this was a "matter of professional disagreement and that Vinson & Elkins could not say that an attorney acting within the standard of care would not give the opinions."[266] In other words, there was not something "so fatally wrong with the opinion that we didn't think a reasonable lawyer could give it."[267]

There is no evidence that Enron transferred its opinion business to Andrews & Kurth as a form of opinion shopping, though some have suspected it.[268] However, Andrews & Kurth was less questioning of Enron. Unlike Vinson & Elkins, it did not raise with Enron or Andersen whether or not a true issuance opinion was responsive to the requirements of FAS 140. What is particularly significant, however, is that despite common misperception, according to the Examiner, neither Vinson & Elkins nor Andrews & Kurth, with one exception, provided true sale opinions.

---

[261] *See id.* app. C, annex. 1, at 8.

[262] *See id.*

[263] Final Report, *supra* note 72, at 14 n.26.

[264] *See id.* app. C, at 171. Between 1998 and 2001, Enron closed more than thirty FAS 140 Transactions; Andrews & Kurth represented Enron in twenty-eight of them. Andrews & Kurth issued twenty-four opinions after late 1998; only one was a true sale opinion (the same number as Vinson & Elkins). *Id.* app. C, at 53 n.181.

[265] *See id.* app. C, at 171 n.795 (citing the sworn statement of Astin).

[266] *Id.* app. C, at 89 (citing the sworn statement of Astin).

[267] *Id.* (quoting the sworn statement of Astin).

[268] Gordon, *supra* note 21, at 771 ("If one firm balked at approving a deal, as [Vinson & Elkins] occasionally did, Enron managers would go across town to another, more compliant firm, such as Andrews & Kurth."). Andrews & Kurth provided only a single true sale opinion (and twenty-three true issuance opinions).

It was not until another project, Iguana, in late 1999, that Andersen "appears to have understood the import of the true issuance/true sale distinction and the 'no recharacterization' assumption contained in Vinson & Elkins's true issuance opinion letters."[269] A meeting between Vinson & Elkins and Andersen was held where the legal opinion was discussed. Apparently, Enron's in-house attorneys were not happy, as one Vinson & Elkins attorney noted in an e-mail:

> I think I am blamed by some of the inside Enron attorneys, . . . for drawing this distinction to AA's attention, as it could jeopardize Enron's FAS 125 transactions. The Enron theory is, apparently, that relations with AA must be carefully managed and that AA is a sophisticated organization that can read opinions and draw their own conclusion. I have believed that it is our professional duty to call the attention of a third party recipient to the meaning and scope of our opinion, especially in a situation where we do not believe that the recipient has a correct understanding of what it says in relation to the purpose for which the opinion is requested.[270]

Later, however, referring to his e-mail, this attorney testified that this was not an accurate statement of the firm's professional duty. He stated, "I don't think that's a correct statement of legal opinion practice and I—I'm reasonably confident that what I meant by that was that I shouldn't affirmatively mislead somebody . . . ."[271] As we have seen, Enron's FAS 140 Transactions were structured finance transactions that "were intended to comply" with either FAS 125 or its successor, FAS 140.[272] The accounting on the transactions was "creative" and "aggressive."[273] Crucial to the accounting treatment was the matter of the "isolation" of financial risks and rewards from the reporting company. The isolation criteria, however, were a "matter of law,"[274] a legal assessment,[275] hence the need for an opinion letter. Compliance, however, can take several forms.

H. Technical Compliance

In the Cornhusker transaction, a true issuance opinion was given despite Vinson & Elkins's attorneys' concerns over the opinion. An internal Vinson & Elkins memorandum identified the concerns:

---

[269] Final Report, *supra* note 72, at 47.

[270] *Id.* app. C, at 47 n.169 (quoting the sworn statement of David Keyes, Vinson & Elkins) (emphasis added).

[271] *Id.* app. C, at 47 n.169 (emphasis added).

[272] Final Report, *supra* note 72, at 18 n.38.

[273] *Id.* app. C, at 177-78 (citing to letter dated Oct. 15, 2001 from Max Hendrick III to James V. Derrick).

[274] *Id.* app. C, at 27.

[275] *See id.* app. C, at 27-28.

> Although the true issuance opinion is rendered at the step following the transfer of financial assets into the issuer, we believe that rendering a true issuance opinion based exclusively on the relevant state statute concerning issuances of ownership interests, while technically correct, may not be responsive to the intent or purpose for which the true sale opinion is required. In light of this position, while we may continue to render true issuance opinions in transactions that are modeled on earlier true issuance transactions, we believe it may be better to render true sale opinions at the step preceding the issuance, rather than true issuance opinions, for the following reasons: Such opinion is more responsive to the requirements of FAS 125 and its replacement, FAS 140 . . . .[276]

The view that the opinion could be technically correct, despite not responding to regulatory requirements, was shared by others, critics of Vinson & Elkins and Enron. The Examiner found that the financial statements produced failed to disclose the substance of the FAS 140 transactions but added the words: "regardless of whether the accounting was technically correct."[277] Similarly, Watkins, who believed, wrongly as it turned out, that Vinson & Elkins had issued true sale opinions, nevertheless thought that the accounting was "technically" correct.[278] Given its reluctance to issue even a true issuance opinion in Project Cornhusker, how could Vinson & Elkins issue a true sale opinion in Project Sundance Industrial?

I. True Sale Opinion: Project Sundance Industrial[279]

Project Sundance Industrial (PSI) was the third of four separate, but related, transactions that involved Enron's forest products business during late 2000 and 2001. In PSI, Enron formed Sundance Industrial Partners L.P. (Sundance) to acquire the forest products business. Salomon Brothers, a wholly owned subsidiary of Citigroup, was a limited partner in Sundance.

Salomon was to contribute $28.5 million in initial equity investment. However, Enron asked Salomon to (i) contribute $8.5 million in cash to Sundance, (ii) to purchase for $20 million a 0.01% equity interest in Sonoma I, LLC, an entity in another of the four transactions, and (iii) to immediately contribute the Sonoma equity interest to Sundance. As a result, Enron recorded the $20 million of income from gain on sale of the interest.

Had the $20 million equity interest in Sonoma been contributed directly to Sundance (which had been the "original, and more direct, approach to the transaction"[280]) Enron could not recognize the gain. Enron's purpose in structuring the two-step process was

---

[276] *Id.* app. C, at 30 n.80 (author unknown) (emphasis added).

[277] Final Report, *supra* note 72, at 21.

[278] *Id.* app. C, at 165.

[279] The following description is taken from *id.* app. C, at 72-81.

[280] *Id.* app. C, at 74-75 (citing to the sworn statement of Mark Spradling of Vinson & Elkins).

thus to enable Enron to recognize the $20 million gain in earnings. Vinson & Elkins, which represented Enron in PSI, understood that to be the purpose,[281] but still gave a true sale opinion regarding the Sonoma interest to Salomon. As discussed further below, the Examiner concluded that there was no true sale of this interest.

Drawing a distinction between technical correctness and purpose may help to explain this. The first technically correct matter was that Sundance contributed equity sufficient for Enron to treat Sundance as an equity method investee rather than a consolidated subsidiary for accounting purposes. However, the question remains as to why Vinson & Elkins gave a true sale opinion knowing that Enron's purpose in structuring the two-step process was to enable Enron to recognize the $20 million gain in earnings.[282]

Vinson & Elkins was not unconcerned with the nature of the transaction. Salomon would acquire the Sonoma equity interest and, immediately or shortly following that sale, contribute it to the capital of Sundance. An immediate transfer by Salomon to an affiliate of Sonoma was contrary to at least one essential element of a sale—that the risks and rewards of the equity interest had shifted from Sonoma to Salomon. But that was not the only essential element.[283] According to one Vinson & Elkins attorney,

> [w]e emphasize that we believe it is necessary for the transaction to reflect the assumption by SBHC [Salomon] of real risks and benefits of ownership of the Sonoma A that survive the transfer of the Sonoma A interest to Sundance. Any court reviewing the transaction would examine the substance and reality of the transaction rather than its mere form in order to assess whether the characterization chosen by the transaction parties would be respected—in short, . [sic] [w]e believe the current structure lacks several elements we believe would be necessary in order for us to render an opinion that a sale truly occurs under the current transaction documents described above.
>
> In order for us to render a true sale opinion on this transaction, each of the following elements must be present:
>
> The transaction must not be pre-wired (the option given to SBHC to contribute cash or the Sonoma A must be real).
>
> The transaction must have a commercial purpose for both parties (other than simply favorable tax or accounting, although favorable tax and accounting treatment doesn't adversely impact a transaction with another purpose.[sic]
>
> Any transaction retained by SBHC must continue to possess aspects of risk and rewards of ownership with regard to the Sonoma A (that is, SBHC must have some continued ownership characteristics with regard to the asset it purchased).[284]

---

281 *Id.* app. C, at 75.

282 *See id.* app. C, at 75.

283 *Id.* app. C, at 76.

284 *Id.* app. C, at 75-76, (quoting a memorandum written Astin).

Yet, Vinson & Elkins focused only on the technical issue of how to ensure that the risks and rewards had transferred to Salomon, something Salomon was very keen to avoid. Accordingly, Vinson & Elkins had put and call rights added so that both Sundance and Salomon could force each other to re-transfer the interest back to Salomon.

These rights were the subject of intensive negotiation,[285] with Vinson & Elkins insisting on them being "real" and "really exercisable."[286] For Vinson & Elkins, the "puts and calls are what is necessary for us to give our opinion regarding true sale matters."[287] Vinson & Elkins refused to remove the risk from Salomon "since we are already at the wall on the opinion."[288] In the end, in July 2001, the month after the transaction closed on June 1, 2001, Vinson & Elkins gave the true sale opinion.[289]

The Examiner was critical of this decision:

> [T]he circumstances surrounding the inclusion of the sale at the last minute, the persistent attempts of Salomon Holding to extinguish any risk of ownership of the Sonoma Class A Interest, and the difficulty that Vinson & Elkins had in negotiating the put and call provision belie that either Salomon Holding or Enron had any true business purpose in this transaction.[290]
> He concluded that "information available to Vinson & Elkins, including the conduct of the parties, indicates that the only purpose of the sale of the Sonoma Class A Interest to Salomon Holding was to permit Enron to recognize the accounting benefit, a purpose which Astin [a Vinson & Elkins attorney] understood."[291]

Vinson & Elkins was aware of one of the essential elements of a true sale: that the transaction must have a commercial purpose for both parties. This was one of the factors highlighted in a November 2000 internal Vinson & Elkins draft document entitled "Selected True Sale and Non-Consolidation Criteria":

> 21. Overall Business Purpose. The transferor should be motivated by bona fide business benefits in consummating the structured finance transaction . . . apart solely or primarily from achieving a perceived accounting, tax or other "structured" result for the transaction. Once this test is met, a transferor should be free to structure the transaction in the most advantageous manner consistent with applicable law and accounting principles . . . .

---

[285] *Id.* app. C, at 77 (quoting the sworn statement of Astin).

[286] *Id.* app. C, at 77 n.291 (quoting the sworn statement of Astin).

[287] *Id.* app. C, at 77 n.289 (quoting an email dated May 29, 2001 from Astin).

[288] *Id.* app. C, at 77 (quoting an email dated May 29, 2001 from Astin).

[289] *Id.* app. C, at 78 n.297.

[290] *Id.* app. C, at 81 (emphasis added).

[291] *Id.* Vinson & Elkins attorneys were also criticized for their tax opinions on similar grounds, that they were aware that various transactions had no identified business purpose. *Id.* app. C, at 91-107

> 26. Surrounding Facts Consistent with Assumptions. It may not be reasonable to rely on recitations set out in the documents, if the statements or conduct of the parties to the transactions are inconsistent with the recitations.[292]

What happened in this true sale opinion was that Vinson & Elkins, despite the conduct of the parties, Salomon especially, which indicated very clearly a desire to eliminate any risk of ownership,[293] made an assumption "that each party, including Salomon Holding, had a valid business purpose for entering into the transaction."[294] This was spelled out in the Sundance opinion letter, as was the reliance placed by Vinson & Elkins on officers' certificates and representations.[295] Vinson & Elkins made clear that it had deferred to the representations of the client (or what it perceived to be the client).

J. Creative Compliance

The true sale opinion in Project Sundance Industrial was a classic attempt at "creative compliance."[296] Creative compliance is achieved via several strategies; for example, advantageous interpretations of grey areas, seeking out loopholes in specific rules, or dreaming up devices which regulators had not even thought of, let alone regulated. Creative compliance allows claims that regulations have been complied with, while any downside from compliance is avoided. It relies on a formalist approach whether the form of law is narrow and specific, or broad and open-ended; whether the law is expressed as rules or as standards or principles. The rule can be manipulated; the lack of rule can be exploited using a formalist critique—the "where does it say I cannot do that?" approach. Such an approach can in turn often lead to the production of rules, which can then be manipulated.[297]

In the regulation of accounting, in tax, and in many other areas, the claim that what has taken place is perfectly legal is a powerful tool of resistance and a substantial challenge to regulators;[298] hence the importance, once again, of the attorney. The provision of true issuance opinions can be seen as creative compliance, as can other examples.

---

[292] *Id.* app. C, at 80 n.304 (emphasis added).

[293] *See id.* app. C, at 81; *see also id.* app. C, at 79.

[294] *Id.* app. C, at 81 n.305.

[295] *Id.* "We wish to point out that we have not made any investigation or inquiry of any Party or of the books and records of any Party. Rather, we have relied on officer's certificates and representations in the Transaction Documents as to such factual matters as we have deemed appropriate for the purposes of this opinion."

[296] *See* Doreen McBarnet & Christopher Whelan, *The Elusive Spirit of the Law: Formalism and the Struggle for Legal Control*, 54 MOD. L. REV. 848 (1991).

[297] *See id.* Rules can emerge through guidelines and clearances as well as case law.

[298] *See* DOREEN MCBARNET & CHRISTOPHER WHELAN, CREATIVE ACCOUNTING AND THE CROSS-EYED JAVELIN THROWER (1999); *see also* Doreen McBarnet, Syd Weston & Christopher J. Whelan, *Adversary Accounting: Strategic Uses of Financial Information by Capital and Labour*, 18 ACCT. ORG.& SOC 81 (1993).

K. LJM2

In relation to Fastow's interest in LJM2, Jordan Mintz, General Counsel to Enron Global Finance, decided "with assistance from Vinson & Elkins,"[299] that Enron did not have to disclose it in the Proxy Statement filed in 2001. Enron avoided this by creative compliance with the wording of the law requiring disclosure, where "practicable," of the related party's interest.[300] Enron decided that it was not practicable to quantify it and, in so doing, Mintz "placed enormous technical reliance on the word 'practicable' contained in the relevant SEC regulation."[301]

Vinson & Elkins was involved in that analysis, as a result of which the Proxy Statement filed one year earlier, in 2000, specifically mentioned Fastow and that he had a "promoted interest that grew the more successful LJM2 was."[302] However, because the transactions had not been settled or liquidated, it was deemed not practicable to determine the amount of that distribution.

In 2001, however, attorneys knew that Fastow believed LJM would be closed down if his supervisors knew the amount he had received from LJM entities.[303] It turns out he received at least $18 million in distributions and $2.6 million in management fees, a portion of which was received during 2000.[304] Thus, the Statement in 2001 raised more difficult issues for Vinson & Elkins. The starting point was that Enron would have to disclose the compensation Fastow earned from his position in LJM.[305] Fastow wished to avoid this. A meeting was then arranged between in-house and Vinson & Elkins attorneys in January 2001. The agenda, arguably, was creative compliance: "the number one item on our list is to resolve the 'where practicable' language . . . . We need to be 'creative' on this point within the contours of Item 404[306] so as to avoid any type of stark disclosure, if at all possible."[307]

The view of the Vinson & Elkins attorney was that Fastow's "interest wasn't choate or determinable and, therefore, was not to be disclosed under the securities laws."[308] The amounts Fastow received were subject to "clawback" provisions and therefore not "practically determinable."[309]

---

[299] Final Report, *supra* note 72, at 98.

[300] *See* 17 C.F.R. § 229.404(a) (2006).

[301] Final Report, *supra* note 72, at 98 n.183.

[302] *Id.* app. C, at 149-50 (quoting sworn statement of Astin).

[303] *Id.* app. C, at 151.

[304] *Id.* app. C, at 153-54 n.689.

[305] *Id.* app. C, at 150 (e-mail from Jordan Mintz, Enron, to Rex Rogers, Enron, Nov. 28, 2000).

[306] *See* 17 C.F.R. § 229.404(a) (2006).

[307] Final Report, *supra* note 72, app. C, at 151 (e-mail from Mintz to Rogers & Ronald T. Astin, Vinson & Elkins, Jan. 16, 2001, and forwarded to Rob Walls, Deputy General Counsel Enron & James Derrick, General Counsel Enron, the same day).

[308] *Id.* app. C, at 152 n.678 (quoting sworn statement of Walls).

[309] *Id.* app. C, at 155 (quoting sworn statement of Astin).

This conclusion was not arrived at lightly. The attorney was asked: "Is this one of those things that's technically the law, but not the spirit of [the] law?" He replied, "No. This is the spirit of the law and technically the law."[310] There is no stronger claim to be "perfectly legal," but is it actually an accolade to creative compliance?[311] Subsequently, he billed over eight hours on the issue prior to the Proxy Statement being filed on March 27, 2001. The Statement recorded Fastow's involvement in LJM2, and his entitlement to receive a percentage of the profits of LJM2, depending upon the performance of its investments.[312]

While an in-house attorney described the level of disclosure as a "close call,"[313] the Vinson & Elkins attorney confirmed his comfort with it.[314] Shortly after this, the in-house attorney unilaterally sought further advice regarding several issues relating to LJM from another outside law firm, Fried, Frank, Harris, Shriver & Jacobson LLP.[315] There was a difference of opinion. Fried Frank concluded that the prior disclosures were "incomplete";[316] that issues remained relating to the existing structures and prior transactions that "warranted review and possibly fuller disclosure";[317] and that the conclusion—that the interest need not be disclosed because the transactions had not been settled and therefore disclosure was not "practicable—to be too aggressive."[318]

The Enron case study suggests that none of the ideologies of legal practice satisfactorily explains Vinson & Elkins's relationship with Enron. This is not to say that professional ideals, libertarian ideologies, or commercial realities played no part. Elements of all three—and tensions between them—can be found. However, the case study may go some way to de-mystifying them in the context of large firm practice. It suggests a new way of conceptualizing core values in that context with implications for professional and other lawyer regulation.

---

[310] *Id.* app. C, at 152 n.678 (quoting sworn statement of Walls, referring to Astin's answer to Wall's question).

[311] Another example of creative compliance involved the role played by Kopper in the Chewco and LJM transactions respectively. Enron's in-house attorneys decided that Enron did not have to disclose Kopper's involvement as the general partner of Chewco because, although he was a vice president, he was not an "executive officer" of Enron, as defined under applicable SEC rules. Final Report, *supra* note 72, at 98. In relation to LJM, a "where does it say I can't do that?" approach was adopted. Kopper had resigned as an Enron employee so that he could buy Fastow's interest in LJM and LJM2 in 2001. As a former employee of Enron the approach was, "[i]f [it is] not absolutely required" do not do it, so that the transformation of LJM to a "true third-party would seem to be more complete if we exclude the phrase." *Id.* at 98-99.

[312] Final Report, *supra* note 72, app. C, at 155 n.696.

[313] *Id.* app. C, at 157 (quoting the sworn statement by Astin).

[314] *Id.*

[315] *Id.* app. C, at 127 n.547.

[316] *Id.* app. C, at 157 (quoting the sworn statement of James H. Schropp of Fried Frank).

[317] *Id.* app. C, at 158 (quoting the sworn statement of Schropp of Fried Frank).

[318] *Id.*

III. RE-CONCEPTUALIZING CORE VALUES

After Enron, critics, reformers, and regulators have all called for large firm corporate transaction lawyers to be more professional, to re-focus their moral compass, and, in terms of core values, to exercise more independent professional judgment and to show greater respect for the rule of law. Some have recommended that they perform specific public roles such as gatekeeper, watchdog, or whistleblower.[319] Ultimately, they should be prepared to withdraw quietly or, perhaps, noisily.

An extensive literature has developed on the role of the lawyer as "gatekeeper," sometimes referred to as "watchdog."[320] The former term was first used to describe the role of professionals in capital markets.[321] It refers broadly to professionals playing the role of "unbiased intermediaries between issuers and regulators, and to prevent corporate misconduct."[322] Gatekeepers, it is said, lend their professional reputation to transactions and "the market recognizes that the gatekeeper has a lesser incentive to lie than does its client."[323] Thus, the gatekeeper's assurance or evaluation is more "credible."[324]

Although some have advocated that lawyers should act as gatekeepers in some contexts,[325] others have questioned it.[326] According to John C. Coffee, Jr., "[p]roperly understood, Enron is a demonstration of gatekeeper failure, and the question it most

---

[319] There have been similar calls regarding in-house counsel. Sung Hui Kim, *The Banality of Fraud: Re-situating the Inside Counsel as Gatekeeper*, 74 FORDHAM L. REV. 983 (2005). There are exceptions. In the wake of Enron, Sarbanes-Oxley and European accounting scandals, the European Union has proposed a new law to regulate the EU audit professions. According to one commentator, "Europe's response to the Sarbanes-Oxley Act has been a craven submission to an American obsession with regulating ethics." Carl Mortished, *There Is Nothing New Under the Sun, Particularly in Accountancy*, THE TIMES (LONDON), May 12, 2004, at Business 26.

[320] In the watchdog role, the professional assumes, in Chief Justice Burger's view, a "public responsibility transcending any employment relationship with the client." This role assumes "total independence from the client at all times and requires complete fidelity to the public trust." United States v. Arthur Young & Co., 465 U.S. 805, 817-18 (1984). *See generally* Peter C. Kostant, *Breeding Better Watchdogs: Multidisciplinary Partnerships in Corporate Legal Practice*, 84 MINN. L. REV. 1213 (2000).

[321] The term is attributed to Reinier H. Kraakman, *Corporate Liability Strategies and the Costs of Legal Controls*, 93 YALE L.J. 857 (1984). For a comprehensive review, *see* Peter B. Oh, *Gatekeeping*, 29 J. CORP. L. 735 (2004).

[322] Bonnie Fish, *Pointing the Finger at Professionals: The Responsibility of Lawyers and Other Gatekeepers for Corporate Governance Failures, in Corporate Governance and Securities Regulation in the 21st Century* 97-98 (Poonam Puri & Jeffrey Larsen eds., 2004).

[323] John C. Coffee Jr., *Understanding Enron: "It's About the Gatekeepers, Stupid,"* 57 BUS. LAW. 1403, 1405 (2002).

[324] *Id.*

[325] *See, e.g.*, Kostant, *supra* note 320; Wilkins, *supra* note 23; David B. Wilkins, *Who Should Regulate Lawyers?*, 105 HARV. L. REV. 799 (1992) (securities lawyers are in the best position to ensure fidelity to the law); Fred Zacharias, *Lawyers as Gatekeepers*, 41 SAN DIEGO L. REV. 1387 (2004).

[326] *See, e.g.*, Fish, *supra* note 322, at 126; *see also id.* at 111-17 (explaining "Why Lawyers Make Lousy Gatekeepers").

sharply poses is how this failure should be rectified."[327] He argues that boards of directors became "prisoners" of their professional gatekeepers.[328] Sarbanes-Oxley now provides an "invigorated role for lawyers as gatekeepers"[329] and is based on the "model of attorney as gatekeeper, with the premise that forcing attorneys to provide more information to corporate decisionmakers will improve the resulting quality of corporate decisions."[330] Coffee argues that only if the board's agents properly advise and warn can the board function effectively.[331]

Others have advocated that the lawyer's role be extended, in appropriate circumstances, to include whistleblowing.[332] While a gatekeeper would withdraw [its] services in certain circumstances, a whistleblower would go further and explain why [it] did so. The SEC, under Sarbanes-Oxley, proposed a whistleblowing—or "noisy withdrawal"—rule. Under section 205.3(d), an attorney would not only withdraw, but notify the SEC in writing of [his] withdrawal in cases where the issuer's officers and directors failed to respond appropriately to violations that threatened substantial injury to the issuer or investors. Alternatively, the issuer itself would be required to disclose its counsel's withdrawal as a material event.[333] The ABA opposed this proposal on the ground that it would drive a wedge into the attorney-client relationship.[334]

Under Sarbanes-Oxley, reporting "up the ladder" of a material violation of law, or breach of fiduciary duty, is required. Unless the issuer has established a Qualified Legal Compliance Committee, the attorney must report to the Chief Legal Officer (CLO) of the issuer, or both the CLO and the Chief Executive Officer (CEO) of the issuer. The rule requires the attorney to evaluate the appropriateness of the response and to report the matter to the audit committee, another committee of independent directors, or to the full board of directors if the reporting attorney does not reasonably believe that the CLO or CEO has provided an appropriate response within a reasonable time. The rule is also clear that a reporting attorney may not rely completely on the assurance of the CLO that no violation has occurred or that the issuer is undertaking an appropriate

---

[327] Coffee, *supra* note 323, at 1405; *see also* William W. Bratton, *Enron, Sarbanes-Oxley and Accounting: Rules Versus Principles Versus Rents*, 48 VILL. L. REV. 1023, 1024 (2003) ("In our self-regulatory system of corporate law, the job of insisting on trustworthy numbers devolves in the first instance on the gatekeepers."); John C. Coffee, Jr., *The Attorney as Gatekeeper: An Agenda for the SEC*, 103 COLUM. L. REV. 1293 (2003).

[328] JOHN C. COFFEE, JR., GATEKEEPERS: THE ROLE OF THE PROFESSIONS IN CORPORATE GOVERNANCE (2006).

[329] Fisch & Rosen, *supra* note 256, at 1099.

[330] *Id.* at 1101.

[331] Coffee, *supra* note 328.

[332] *See* Griffin, *supra* note 219; Kostant, *supra* note 320; Richard W. Painter, *Toward a Market for Lawyer Disclosure Services: In Search of Optimal Whistleblowing Rules*, 63 GEO. WASH. L. REV. 221 (1995).

[333] 17 C.F.R. § 205.3(d) (2006).

[334] REPORT OF THE AMERICAN BAR ASSOCIATION TASK FORCE ON CORPORATE RESPONSIBILITY 53 n.94 (2003).

response.[335] Deference is not a defense. No longer should [reporting attorneys] be able to deny responsibility for accounting fraud just because they are not accountants; hence the recommendation that corporate lawyers, in order to fulfill this desired role, should be competent in accounting.[336]

Some have gone further and proposed a new role for corporate lawyers. Gordon, for example, rejects the "adversary-advocate" role, which he calls the "bar's standard construction of the corporate lawyer's role" and proposes what is, in essence, the functional equivalent of the traditional English barrister's role.[337] In short, the Enron case has been used to support calls for reform in order to revive the high ideals of lawyering.[338]

In hindsight, of course, it is regrettable that Vinson & Elkins did not take more steps than it did. Attorneys could have provided a "check and balance against the Enron officers' wrongdoing."[339] They could have apprised Enron's General Counsel or Board when they "knew of conduct that could result in Enron disseminating materially misleading financial information."[340] When they were concerned about the "propriety" of the SPE transactions, they could have "refused to render legal services."[341]

But the case study suggests that there should be some realism about professionalism. It challenges some of the assumptions about professional core values and the role they play in practice. It therefore calls into question most, and maybe all, of these prescriptions.

A. Independent Professional Judgment

Scholars have noted that the actions of large firm corporate lawyers are not easily distinguishable from those of their clients;[342] that "[i]ndependence from the client . . .

---

[335] Sarbanes-Oxley Act of 2002, Pub. L. No. 107-204, 116 Stat. 745 (2002) (codified in scattered sections of 15, 18 U.S.C.); see also Implementation of Standards of Professional Conduct for Attorneys, 17 C.F.R. pt. 205.

[336] Lawrence A. Cunningham, *Sharing Accounting's Burden: Business Lawyers in Enron's Dark Shadows*, 57 BUS. LAW. 1421 (2002); *see also* RAPOPORT & DHARAN, *Enron and the Business World, in* ENRON: CORPORATE FIASCOS AND THEIR IMPLICATIONS, *supra* note 62, at 96 (arguing that "[p]art of the solution must include a working knowledge of each other's fields."); *see also id.* at 301.

[337] Gordon, *supra* note 21, at 763. Gordon proposes a "separate professional role for a distinct type of lawyer, the Independent Counselor, with a distinct ethical orientation, institutionalized in a distinct governance regime of ethical codes, liability and malpractice rules, special statutory duties and privileges, and judicial rules of practice." *Id.* at 786.

[338] *See generally id.*

[339] Final Report, *supra* note 72, at 114.

[340] *Id.*

[341] *Id.* Under Texas Rules, withdrawal may be required if there is knowledge of wrongful conduct, even if approved at the highest level of an organization. TEX. RULES OF PROF'L CONDUCT § 1.12(b).

[342] *See* Richard W. Painter, *The Moral Interdependence of Corporate Lawyers and Their Clients*, 67 S. CAL. L. REV. 507 (1994).

is generally not a legitimate aspiration for the bar."[343] Sophisticated, well-advised and economically powerful clients may well dominate the lawyer-client relationship. This follows not only from their financial power, but from their access to non-financial resources—human and technical, in-house and outside. Typically, with corporate clients, it is corporate management who "defines the objectives of the representation, identifies the responsibilities for which the lawyer has been retained and determines whether the lawyer's performance has been acceptable."[344] Add to this a compensation culture which rewards officers if the company's financial matrices look good, and client's officers may put pressure on outsiders, including professional advisers. The result, to say the least, is that the professional ideal of independent professional judgment is under threat.

Large clients, like Enron, can manipulate lawyers and law firms. They have access to many outside law firms and can pick and choose as they wish. They can use litigation lawyers rather than transactional lawyers in order to get the advice they want.[345] They can hire and fire at will. It is unlikely that any single law firm or lawyer has a complete picture of the client's activities.[346] Black holes exist—and can be made to exist—making it difficult to perform a gatekeeper or watchdog role. Specialization by lawyers is routine too. While Gordon says lawyers should ask whether they can "conscientiously and ethically do their jobs and exercise their functions as fiduciaries" when "access to the big picture is prevented," the Enron case study suggests that this is an unrealistic question in practice.[347] While the "it isn't my job" response to criticism may be "alarming,"[348] the "lack of joint ownership of issues" is a fact of large law firm and corporate life. Wrongdoing, therefore, might be easily missed, overlooked, or insufficiently evident. Without sufficient knowledge or information, it is difficult to challenge the client, particularly when the standard requires a "business purpose" test. In this context, it is

---

[343] Evan A. Davis, *The Meaning of Professional Independence*, 103 COLUM. L. REV. 1281, 1281 (2003).

[344] Fisch & Rosen, *supra* note 256, at 1123. Professional regulation makes clear that the client to whom lawyers owe their duties is the corporation, not the officers. TEX. RULES OF PROF'L CONDUCT § 1.12(a). This distinction is "sometimes misunderstood by corporate lawyers," Hazard & Hodes *supra* note 12, at 394, and, it appears, by the courts. *See* William H. Simon, *Whom (Or What) Does the Organization's Lawyer Represent?: An Anatomy of Intra-client Conflict*, 91 CAL. L. REV. 57 (2003). In the Enron case, the Examiner wondered if the attorneys lost sight of the distinction. Final Report, *supra* note 72, at 115. It has been argued that the Rule is "extremely narrow" and is "too vague to offer meaningful guidance for lawyers whose corporate clients have managers that might be harming the corporation, or acting in a manner that might impute liability to the corporation." Peter C. Kostant, *Sarbanes-Oxley and Changing the Norms of Corporate Lawyering*, 2004 MICH. ST. L. REV. 541, 544-45. (referring to Model Rule 1.13, upon which the Texas Rule 1.12 is based).

[345] *See* William H. Simon, *From the Trenches and Towers: the Kaye Scholer Affair*, 23 LAW & SOC. INQUIRY 243, 270-73 (1989).

[346] And, of course, lawyer-client confidentiality can be used as a cloak to protect the client from the full picture ever emerging. This is both a regulatory challenge and an enforcement challenge.

[347] Gordon, *supra* note 21, at 771.

[348] RAPOPORT & DHARAN, *Enron and the Business World, in* ENRON: CORPORATE FIASCOS AND THEIR IMPLICATIONS, *supra* note 62, at 95.

the client that sets the agenda and controls the objectives; law firms respond, and do so in the context of a division of professional labor.

But the case study yields some surprises. While the combination of a libertarian ideology and rampant commercialism would lead many to predict unconfined "partisan zeal,"[349] especially since law is not "objective, consistent and legitimate,"[350] this was not the case. Vinson & Elkins was not simply a "hired gun" for Enron.

There was little or no direct evidence of a particular attorney's actual knowledge of wrongful conduct by an Enron officer. Indeed, attorneys denied having such knowledge.[351] Such knowledge is necessary for malpractice[352] and aiding and abetting breaches of fiduciary duties liabilities. Although he found circumstantial evidence from which a fact-finder could infer knowledge,[353] the Examiner also noted some of the counter-arguments Vinson & Elkins could employ in relation to FAS 140 Transactions:

> that it had no duty to question the subject matter of the opinion requested by Andersen;
>
> that, although they had no duty to do so, Vinson & Elkins attorneys informed both Andersen and Enron of the firm's belief that Andersen was asking for the wrong opinion; that it was assured that, from an accounting standpoint, the opinions requested by Enron and Andersen were then opinions needed to support the legal isolation requirements of FAS 140.[354]

With regard to the Sundance Industrial true sale opinion, Vinson & Elkins assumed there was a valid business purpose. While questioning this, the Examiner acknowledged that Vinson & Elkins could argue that it was entitled to rely on the assumption. Vinson & Elkins made the assumption clear in its opinion. In any case, the transfer of the Sonoma A Interest to Salomon Holding was a true sale. It also added the "no recharacterization" assumption to its opinion; it specifically referred to the TRS element; and it had put and call options added to the transaction. It was only then that it provided a true sale opinion.

On other occasions, Vinson & Elkins refused to give true sale opinions, sometimes despite a specific request to do so.[355] It played a role in Enron providing fuller disclosure, and it asked questions constantly about its role. It sought to double-check with Enron and Andersen that a true issuance opinion was sufficient. It received reassurances from

---

[349] Wilkins, *supra* note 132, at 474.

[350] *Id.*

[351] Final Report, *supra* note 72, app. C, at 1.

[352] *See* TEX. GOV'T CODE ANN. § 84.004 (2005). The rule addresses the attorney's role when the attorney represents an organization, such as a corporation, and learns that a representative commits a violation of a legal obligation which might reasonably be imputed to the organization.

[353] Final Report, *supra* note 72, app. C, at 2.

[354] *Id.* at 179-80.

[355] *Id.* at 162 n.735.

high levels within the client organization and it deferred to their professional judgment, expertise, and authority.

Vinson & Elkins put the client first, but it did not do everything it was asked to do. Nor was commercialism unconfined. For whatever reason, Enron began to switch its FAS 140 opinion work to Andrews & Kurth in late 1998. As a result, the latter's fees rose substantially thereafter.[356] Meanwhile, Vinson & Elkins' fees peaked in 2000 and declined in 2001 by over $6.5 million (14%).

In short, the core value of independent professional judgment manifestly did play a role in this particular lawyer-client relationship. Of course, professional core values—reputation, competence and expertise, judgment, independence, confidentiality, and so on—are market values. As Andersen's own lawyers put it in 2001, "Andersen Legal knows that for a lawyer his professionalism, independence and integrity are his key assets."[357] So, it may be that commercial rather than professional values were at play here. In addition, there is a legitimate fear that managers shopping around for compliant lawyers will induce a race to the bottom.[358] But the case study suggests that decision-making—and regulation—about the core value of independent professional judgment can be safely left to the market: clients, investors, creditors, third parties, the insurance industry, and other market actors.

The Examiner had another theory to explain attorneys' perceived "failure[s]": that "some of [the] attorneys saw their role in very narrow terms, as an implementer, not a counsellor."[359] Lawyers "seemed to focus only on how to address a narrow question or simply to implement a decision (or document a transaction)."[360] This will now be explored in the context of the second key core value.

B. Delivering Legality: Respect for the Rule of Law

Professional regulation seeks to foster "confidence in the rule of law."[361] Lawyers act for their clients "within the bounds of the law,"[362] and "each member of society is entitled to have his conduct judged and regulated in accordance with the law."[363]

---

[356] *See supra* note 167.

[357] Alberto Terol, Patrick Bignon & Tony Williams, *Andersen Legal's Approach to the New Economy, in The Internationalization of the Practice of Law*, 423, 429 (Jens Drolshammer & Michael Pfeifer eds., 2001). Before the demise of Andersen, "Andersen Legal [had] approximately 3,400 lawyers working in 36 countries worldwide . . . [and a turnover of $528 million]." *Id.* at 428. The same authors comment: "To suggest that law is not already a business is bizarre." *Id.* at 428.

[358] Gordon, *supra* note 21, at 779.

[359] Final Report, *supra* note 72, at 115. Although the Examiner gives examples in support of these theories mainly in connection with Enron's in-house attorneys, I believe he meant to include Vinson & Elkins as well.

[360] *Id.*

[361] *See, e.g.*, MODEL RULES OF PROF'L CONDUCT PMBL. ¶ 6 (2003).

[362] MODEL CODE OF PROF'L RESPONSIBILITY CANON 7 (1980).

[363] *Id.* EC 7-1.

Thus, lawyers may help the client achieve lawful objectives by any "legally permissible means";[364] the advocate may urge "any permissible construction of the law favorable to his client, without regard to his professional opinion as to the likelihood that the construction will ultimately prevail."[365] There are limits, but they are minimal. A belief that conduct is or will be unlawful entitles the lawyer to withdraw.[366] And while, under the Code, a lawyer may not assert "a position in litigation that is frivolous"[367] under the Rules, a belief that the client's position will not ultimately prevail does not make an action frivolous.[368]

The emphasis, therefore, is very much on the lawyer furthering the client's objectives as determined by the client.[369] Thus, the lawyer may continue with the representation even if the client pursues a course of conduct "contrary to the lawyer's advice";[370] and "[a] lawyer shall not intentionally [f]ail to seek the lawful objectives of his client through reasonably available means."[371] The "rule-of-law" rhetoric is summed-up by the following: "In the final analysis . . . the lawyer should always remember that the decision whether to forego legally available objectives or methods because of non-legal factors is ultimately for the client and not for himself."[372]

Large law firms—and the bar generally—argue that core values should be protected because they serve both the client and the public interest.[373] The case study, by contrast, reinforces the argument that the core value of respect for the rule of law might be counter-productive and against the public interest.[374]

Large law firms embrace complexity, like their clients. What made the Enron bankruptcy possibly the "most complex" in history[375] was the corporate group structure. When it filed for bankruptcy in December 2001, so did its thirteen affiliates.[376] Court

---

[364] *Id.*

[365] *Id.* EC 7-4.

[366] *Id.* DR 7-101(B)(2).

[367] *Id.* EC 7-4.

[368] MODEL RULES OF PROF'L CONDUCT R. 3.1 cmt. 2 (2003).

[369] *Id.* R. 1.2(a).

[370] MODEL CODE OF PROF'L RESPONSIBILITY EC 7-5 (1980).

[371] *Id.* DR 7-101(A)(1).

[372] *Id.* EC 7-8 (emphasis added).

[373] Terol et al., *supra* note 357, at 429. Hans-Jurgen Hellwig, the current CCBE President, was reported as criticizing the leading City of London law practices for being "hypocritical in their approach to 'core values.'" Linda Tsang, *Lawweek: What the legal journals are reporting this week*, THE TIMES (London), Nov. 2, 2004, at Law 13.

[374] *See* Richard L. Abel, *Why Does the ABA Promulgate Ethical Rules?*, 59 TEX. L. REV. 639, 685 (1981); Christopher J. Whelan, *Ethical Conflicts in Legal Practice: Creating Professional Responsibility*, 52 S.C. L. REV. 697, 724 (2001).

[375] Tabb, *supra* note 72, at 303.

[376] The venue for the Enron bankruptcy was the Southern District of New York because an Enron affiliated company petitioned for voluntary bankruptcy just prior to Enron's filing. *Id.* at 305.

documents revealed that the "affiliated group had more than 4,000 direct and indirect subsidiaries."[377] But group structures are the norm, not the exception, and such complexity of form and complexity of transaction simply increases the need for lawyers to traverse the various legal minefields. One of the reasons in-house counsel use outside counsel is because they need assistance in complex matters.[378]

To meet client needs and objectives and to make their services competitive, large law firms also embrace innovation, precedent-setting, and creativity. Corporate clients are themselves legal constructs. Law is treated as the "raw material to be worked upon"[379] to further the client's objectives, including creative compliance: using the law to escape or to manage unwelcome regulation. A survey of the large law firms mentioned in the Examiner's Final Report, together with the firm that served as official counsel for the Creditors' Committee, shows that Vinson & Elkins is typical in delivering legality in this way.

All the firms emphasise their capacity and competence to engage with complexity. Indeed, Milbank Tweed, Hedley & McCloy was chosen as official counsel because of its experience with large-scale bankruptcy and "its expertise in structured finance and derivatives transactions."[380] The firm itself confirms this view. The Corporate Governance Group "regularly advise boards and committees on their most difficult and complex transactions and problems."[381] Its Global Corporate Group has "in-depth and practical experience" in a range of transactions including "other complex, cutting-edge transactions" and can provide "expert assistance."[382]

Shearman & Sterling points out that many of the securitization transactions it describes "involved complex tax and accounting issues" and that "[w]ith its global presence, local law expertise and creative problem-solving approach, [it] is uniquely qualified to help clients structure, document and complete complex securitization and derivatives transactions."[383]

Corporate clients are also highly innovative. That Enron was exceptionally so was well known for years before the bankruptcy. It was named "the most innovative company in

---

[377] *Id.* at 303 n.1.

[378] Michele M. Hedges, *General Counsel and the Shifting Sea of Change, in* ENRON: CORPORATE FIASCOS AND THEIR IMPLICATIONS, *supra* note 62, at 539, 550.

[379] Doreen McBarnet, *Law and Capital: The Role of Legal Form and Legal Actors*, 12 INT'L. J. SOC. L. 231, 238 (1984).

[380] Tabb, *supra* note 72, at 322. Interestingly, Milbank refers to its "extensive experience in the bankruptcy proceedings of Enron." Statement from Milbank's web site that has since been updated or removed. A printout of the statement is on file with author. Milbank was referred to in Regan's book, *Eat What You Kill. See generally* REGAN, *supra* note 5.

[381] http://www.milbank.com/en/PracticeAreas/GeneralCorporate_alpha.htm.

[382] *Id.*

[383] Statement from Shearman & Sterling's web site that has since been updated. A printout of the statement is on file with author. An updated, though similar, statement can be found at http://www.shearman.com/strucfinance/financial/.

the United States by Fortune magazine every year between 1996 and 2001."[384] Large firm lawyers reflect this characteristic too.

Shearman & Sterling is proud about its involvement in "a great number of highly innovative transactions" noting that it has "won various 'deal of the year' awards."[385] It has worked on the "largest, most complex structured finance transactions ever completed in the bank and capital markets."[386] The Securitization and Derivatives Group emphasizes its "creative and innovative approach" and its "work with clients to develop novel structured finance products."[387] Indeed, "[s]tructuring innovative transactions that provide unique benefits for major U.S. and non-U.S. corporations is the hallmark [of the firm]."[388] The firm was a "key participant in one of the first issuances of medium-term notes by a special purpose vehicle that had previously issued only receivables-backed commercial paper."[389] Its attorneys in New York, San Francisco, London, Paris, and Germany "designed the unprecedented financing" of 20th Century Fox's new films.[390] It has "pioneered the development of off-balance-sheet transactions . . . ."[391] The firm "works closely with clients to develop novel structured finance products that lower financing costs and achieve the specific legal, tax, corporate and financial objectives of all transaction parties."[392]

Bracewell & Patterson "regularly advise[s] issuers and underwriters in the development and use of innovative securities, structures and techniques . . . . Our lawyers are often called upon to develop novel financing structures and techniques to finance leveraged buyouts and other negotiated or hostile transactions."[393] Milbank claims to be a "leader in creating and applying innovative securitization techniques . . . ."[394] Its tax lawyers' expertise puts the firm "on the cutting edge of market practice."[395]

---

[384] Jeffrey D. Van Niel, *Enron—The Primer, in* ENRON: CORPORATE FIASCOS AND THEIR IMPLICATIONS, *supra* note 62, at 3, 11.

[385] Statement from Shearman & Sterling's web site that has since been updated or removed. A printout of the statement is on file with author.

[386] http://www.shearman.com/practices/detail.aspx?practiceid=37ada582-d0d9-485b-b457-106bd86bbc95.

[387] Statement from Shearman & Sterling's web site that has since been updated. A printout of the statement is on file with author. An updated, though similar, statement can be found at http://www.shearman.com/practices/detail.aspx?practiceid=37ada582-d0d9-485b-b457-106bd86bbc95.

[388] http://www.shearman.com/strucfinance/financial/.

[389] http://www.shearman.com/strucfinance/assetbackedpaper/.

[390] Statement from Shearman & Sterling's web site that has since been updated or removed. A printout of the statement is on file with author.

[391] http://www.shearman.com/strucfinance/leasing/.

[392] http://www.shearman.com/practices/detail.aspx?practiceid=37ada582-d0d9-485b-b457-106bd86bbc95.

[393] http://www.bracepatt.com/practices/practice_detail.asp?practiceID=000006132140.

[394] http://www.milbank.com/en/PracticeAreas/SecuritizationStructuredFinance_alpha.htm.

[395] http://www.milbank.com/en/PracticeAreas/Tax_alpha.htm.

A precedent that is created by a law firm is, by any definition, atypical (until others copy it). "Monetization" is a good example. The term was used in "numerous presentations to the Enron board,"[396] but it did not have a precise definition. Board members had "unclear or conflicting understandings of the meaning of this term."[397] Indeed, Joseph C. Dilg testified that "I recall in discussion that we had . . . some conversations about the term monetization, whether anybody really knew what monetization meant . . . ."[398] Now, Vinson & Elkins refers to it on [its] website as something it can offer clients.[399] But so does Shearman & Sterling, for whom asset monetization is described as "a specialty."[400] It has represented Citibank, Deutsche Bank, and Donaldson, Lufkin & Jenrette in the "monetization of client assets through bank and capital market financings and related credit and equity derivatives."[401] The precedent has become the norm. According to Bracewell & Patterson,

> [o]ver the past 20 years . . . many businesses have, for a variety of reasons, rejected traditional forms of debt capital and turned to more creative methods of finance such as monetizations and other types of off-balance sheet finance. As these new debt structures evolve, our firm remains at the forefront though its representation of both the users and providers of these innovative products.[402]

Creativity is routine in large firms too. According to Shearman & Sterling, "In today's marketplace, derivatives are an integral part of many structured transactions designed to achieve complex regulatory, tax, capital, accounting, risk management and financing objectives."[403] Milbank's Leveraged Finance Practice lawyers work as a team whose depth and experience across a range of substantive legal disciplines "enhances our ability to find creative solutions to our client's business challenges."[404]

---

[396] Final Report, *supra* note 72, at 105.

[397] *Id.* at 106.

[398] *Id.* at 106 n.209.

[399] Statement from Vinson & Elkins's web site that has since been updated or removed. A printout of the statement is on file with author

[400] Statement from Vinson & Elkins's web site that has since been updated or removed. A printout of the statement is on file with author

[401] Statement from Vinson & Elkins's web site that has since been updated or removed. A printout of the statement is on file with author

[402] Statement from Vinson & Elkins's web site that has since been updated or removed. A printout of the statement is on file with author

[403] http://www.shearman.com/Practices/Detail.aspx?practiceID=5d1ad7d4-52f6-4589-a0ad-061a9cd49197.

[404] http://www.milbank.com/en/PracticeAreas/SecuritizationStructuredFinance_alpha.htm.

Shearman & Sterling has "created structures . . . in jurisdictions in which legal impediments had previously made such transactions impractical."[405] It represented the arranger in a lease financing for Mazda: "The transaction combined a leasing structure with innovative derivative products employed to overcome certain enforceability limitations under Japanese law."[406]

Kirkland & Ellis will deliver "the crucial legal opinions on matters such as bankruptcy consolidation, true sale, and tax treatment."[407] It also implicitly guarantees the success of its creative compliance. It states that it can obtain preliminary views from rating agencies regarding "novel issues on a 'no-name' basis.[408] These informal contacts can greatly assist clients in planning a novel securitization."[409]

Precedent-setting, therefore, is standard large law firm fare: what is typical is atypicality. Large law firms outsell each other on creativity, innovation, and the ability to deal with complexity. However, they are all "routine." Any one of the above firms could have written the following (in fact, it was Milbank):

> We are routinely involved in the structuring and development of pilot projects, model contracts and cutting edge transactions that often become the market precedent for subsequent transactions . . . . [We are able] to devise creative and cost-efficient solutions to the issues that arise in these complex transactions . . . . We seek to achieve our clients' business goals while being sensitive to client preferences as to the identity and number of individuals involved in any particular aspect of the transaction.[410]

Even the "good" firms adopt similar rhetoric. Fried Frank, the firm that regarded the accounting rationale of Enron's non-disclosure to be "too aggressive," describes [itself] as an "international law firm" which "[is] continuing to provide innovative and imaginative solutions to complex business and legal problems in the twenty-first century."[411] Solutions seem clearly to encompass creative compliance: "At Fried Frank, we are best known for—and take great pride in—our ability to craft sophisticated solutions for complex issues and intricate business transactions, frequently creating the precedents that others follow";[412] and zeal: "Innovative and creative on behalf of our clients, our attorneys all demonstrate an unwavering commitment to client service and

---

[405] Statement from Shearman & Sterling's web site that has since been updated or removed. A printout of the statement is on file with author.

[406] *Id.*

[407] http://www.kirkland.com/practiceAreas/subPracticeMain.aspx?Corporate&practiceAreaH4AssetID=81978444&praticeAreaH4ID=234&subPracticeAreaH4AssetID=82031444&subPracticeAreaH4ID=805.

[408] *Id.*

[409] *Id.*

[410] http://www.milbank.com/en/PracticeAreas/SecuritizationStructuredFinance_alpha.htm.

[411] http://www.ffhsj.com/new_ffhsj.htm (last visited Feb. 1, 2005) (emphasis added).

[412] *Id.* (emphasis added).

to the achievement of our clients' objectives."[413] Even the Examiner's own firm, Alston & Bird "provides creative solutions to client challenges . . . . In each of [more than a dozen legal] service areas, we offer clients a track record virtually second to none in precedent-setting work and successful results."[414]

In short, complexity, innovation, and creativity, in order to solve—or prevent—client problems, are the routine daily work that constitutes large firm corporate law practice. The core values of independence and respect for the rule of law legitimize such work, including creative compliance, and it is the large law firm and its clients which have the resources to take advantage. Creative compliance advances the interests of the client but, if it results in legal policy failing, then it is, on the face of it, against the public interest.

IV. SOME REALISM ABOUT PROFESSIONALISM

It is a truism that there will never be another Enron, for Enron is no more; nor is Andersen. But there is still Vinson & Elkins. Whether or not Vinson & Elkins is ultimately found liable under any of the various potential claims, the firm, by and large, appears to have escaped relatively unscathed.[415] Most of the Vinson & Elkins attorneys involved with Enron as a client appear still to be with the firm. The Enron relationship partner, Joseph C. Dilg, is now Vinson & Elkins's Managing Partner.

This Article has not sought to address legal liabilities as such, nor, by implication, ask whether Vinson & Elkins should or should not be blamed. It has not reviewed in detail all the transactions in which Vinson & Elkins played a role[416] and it has not tried to unravel the "problem" at Enron. Rather, it has focused on the core values and ideologies of professionalism, libertarianism, and commercialism, and the tensions between them. It has focused on legal opinion practice and the provision of opinions by Vinson & Elkins. The Final Report provides so much detail about the Vinson & Elkins-Enron relationship that, while it is only a single law firm-client case study, it provides invaluable insights into the context of large law firm practice.

---

[413] *Id.* (emphasis added).

[414] http://www.alston.com/index.cfm?fuseaction=service (last visited Feb. 15, 2005).

[415] Vinson & Elkins is a defendant in the Enron multistate litigation. In re Enron Corp. Sec., Derivative & ERISA Litig., 235 F. Supp.2d 549, 564 (S.D. Tex. 2002). In June 2006, it was announced that the firm had agreed to pay $30 million to Enron Corp's estate. Michael Orey, *Lawyers: Enron's Last Mystery?*, BUSINESSWEEK ONLINE, June 1, 2006, http://businessweek.com/investor/content/may2006/pi20060531_972686.htm (last visited Sept. 11, 2006). The settlement included the return of $10.5 million in fees earned by the firm in the three months before the bankruptcy. The firm also waived its claim for $3.9 million in fees billed to Enron. John Roper, *Vinson & Elkins settles with Enron for $30 million*, HOUSTON CHRONICLE, June 2, 2006, at A1, *available at* http://www.chron.com/cs/CDA/printstory.mpl/special/Enron/3921779.

[416] While it has touched on most of the transactions, it has totally ignored the tax opinions provided by Vinson & Elkins. The Examiner was critical of these, stating that the various transactions had no identified business purpose. *See* Final Report, *supra* note 72, app. C, at 91-107. For a full review of the tax issues, *see generally* STAFF OF JOINT COMM. ON TAXATION, 108TH CONG. (Comm. Print 2003).

On the surface, prior to the bankruptcy, Enron appeared to be a typical, large corporation. The Board was "top-notch," highly respected and, no doubt, envied by others. It had all the proper committees and policies in place. The compensation structure "was not atypical in scope or design as compared to programs of other large public companies at the time."[417] The motivations were normal too, including the manipulation of earnings and cash flows and the "allure" of the SPE transactions.[418] Enron was advised by the "best" professionals: a "Big 5" accounting firm, a "world-class"[419] in-house legal department, and "hundreds of [outside] law firms"[420] which, like Vinson & Elkins, are amongst the "Best Lawyers in America."[421] As far as the market was concerned, Enron was much admired.[422] Its shares were being recommended right up to the last moment.[423] Whatever the shortcomings in the public disclosure documents of Enron, few analysts spotted them, despite their professed expertise.[424] In short, Vinson & Elkins's relationship with Enron, when viewed in this context, was, to all intents and purposes, probably not atypical.

Indeed, Enron itself is atypical mainly through the lens of hindsight. The bankruptcy was a horror story, but what we know about Enron, its officers, employees, and advisers from the Examiner's Final Report is a "post-hoc horror stor[y] about what ha[d] gone wrong."[425] Liabilities in such circumstances may well follow, depending on how the evidence is presented and received and what expert's opinion the fact-finder prefers. What did follow Enron, however, was a rush to judgment and a voluminous legal literature in which the tensions between professionalism, libertarianism, and commercialism were, once again, to the fore.[426]

---

[417] Final Report, *supra* note 72, at 92.

[418] *Id.* at 93.

[419] *Id.* app. C, at 16.

[420] *Id.* app. C, at 15 (quoting sworn testimony of Rex Rogers); Id. app. C, at 48.

[421] Vinson & Elkins Rankings and Awards, *supra* note 120.

[422] In 2000, *Fortune* ranked Enron 25th among "the world's most admired companies." Nicholas Stein, *The World's Most Admired Companies*, FORTUNE, Oct. 2, 2000, at 184.

[423] *See* Final Report, *supra* note 72, at 83 n.142.

[424] *See* David Millon, *Who "Caused" the Enron Debacle?*, 60 WASH. & LEE L. REV. 309, 321 (2003) ("Despite the steady decline in Enron's share price during 2001, analysts following the company continued to be optimistic about its prospects."). To see what the analysts said, *see id.* at 321-24. *See also* Final Report, *supra* note 72, at 83 n.142 ("We're pretty much pounding the table on Enron right now today [June 2001]. It's a company with the best fundamentals in the industry. But right now we think it also has compelling valuation at these levels.") (quoting Raymond Niles of Salomon Smith Barney). *But see* Bala G. Dharan & William R. Bufkins, *Red Flags in Enron's Reporting of Revenues and Key Financial Measures, in* ENRON: CORPORATE FIASCOS AND THEIR IMPLICATIONS, *supra* note 62, at 97, 98, (analyzing "several forensic accounting red flags" in Enron's financial statements). *See also* THE ESSAYS OF WARREN BUFFETT: LESSONS FOR CORPORATE AMERICA (Lawrence A. Cunningham ed., 2001).

[425] Nelson, *supra* note 65, at 479.

[426] Gordon, *supra* note 21, at 768-74 (reviewing "Some Excuses for What the Lawyers Did.").

In this Article, by contrast, assumptions have been questioned about key core values that exist in the context of current large firm practice. Professionalism, libertarianism, and commercialism may all play a significant part in legal practice, but they need to be de-mystified as do the everyday realities of large firm practice. Large firm corporate law practice routinely comprises complexity, creativity, and precedent-setting. It involves structuring transactions, designing contracts, and avoiding unwelcome regulations. It also entails making judgments in a world where there can be honest—and dishonest—differences of opinion between sets of professionals and others about how to achieve objectives which are determined predominantly by the client.

The Enron case study reminds us that law, whatever its form, is material which can be worked upon. Corporate lawyers are legal realists and working on the law is what they do. To control this kind of lawyer behavior requires a shift in the spotlight, away from the specifics of professional regulation and the law of lawyering, for that is too narrow a focus, and onto the law itself more generally. What should be the regulatory response to creative compliance? How can law prevent the exploitation of "regulatory black hole[s]"[427] or grey areas? How can law prevent lawyers from being lawyers, formalist in an indeterminate legal world? Are large firm lawyers and their clients, via creative compliance, beyond legal control?[428]

In the Enron case, as in most legal practice one would hope, there seems to be little evidence of flagrant breaches of law or professional regulation by Vinson & Elkins or other outside counsel.[429] Law firms and in-house legal departments may have a commitment to ethical behavior; they are increasingly turning to ethics advisors and "compliance specialists."[430] The greatest challenge to regulators therefore is not the professional regulation of corporate lawyers' core values—the market can do that. Nor is it to expect lawyers to behave ethically,[431] despite libertarianism or commercialism. Getting lawyers to be "good" is not a problem of professionalism; it is not a problem of professional regulation; rather, it is a problem of the law itself. What is needed is law which can reduce the supply and demand for creative compliance, and can overcome the barriers to effective enforcement.[432] While it may be relatively easy to catch and

---

427 It has been argued that Enron collapsed partly because of derivatives, "a regulatory black hole." Frank Partnoy, *Enron and the Derivatives World, in* ENRON: CORPORATE FIASCOS AND THEIR IMPLICATIONS, *supra* note 62, at 169, 170.

428 *See* McBarnet & Whelan, *supra* note 296, at 848.

429 There is little doubt that creative accounting in the Enron case went beyond creative compliance to flagrant abuses and fraud.

430 Elizabeth Chambliss & David B. Wilkins, *The Emerging Role of Ethics Advisors, General Counsel, and Other Compliance Specialists in Large Law Firms*, 44 ARIZ. L. REV. 559, 559 (2002).

431 *See generally* Sharon Dolovich, *Ethical Lawyering and the Possibility of Integrity*, 70 FORDHAM L. REV. 1629 (2002).

432 Intriguingly, an attempt to criminalize creative compliance, in the context of lawyers providing advice on the options available to clients seeking financing options for their long-term medical needs, was in effect for only 216 days. *See* Lisa Schreiber Joire, *After New York State Bar Association v. Reno: Ethical Problems in Limited Medicaid Estate Planning*, 12 GEO. J. LEGAL ETHICS 789 (1999). I am grateful to

convict professional deviants who break clear laws, what kind of law can control those who claim that their actions are perfectly legal, and in compliance with the law?

What is needed appears to be a new kind of law, whereby professionals (and others) internalize its norms. The case study suggests that enforcement of legal norms may be more difficult when corporate lawyers adhere to professional core values. The goal of the new law is somehow to make its enforcement unnecessary. Some might characterise this kind of law as "soft law"; others have created the term "transcendental regulation."[433] The real challenge is to identify what form such "transcendental regulation" could take.

Dean Eveland for referring me to this article. Of course, there are non-legal and non-market mechanisms of control which, in the context of law practice, might be far more important. *See* W. Bradley Wendel, *Nonlegal Regulation of the Legal Profession: Social Norms in Professional Communities*, 54 VAND. L. REV. 1955, 1956-57 (2001); Whelan, supra note 374, at 698; Edward B. Rock, *Saints and Sinners: How Does Delaware Corporate Law Work?*, 44 UCLA L. REV. 1009, 1011 (1997).

[433] *See* Whelan, *supra* note 374, at 725-26. Transcendental regulation transcends legal form and cuts through the foundations of creative compliance. The phrase arose out of the work of McBarnet and Whelan, *supra* note 296, at 873.

Professionalism as Interpretation[*]

W. Bradley Wendel[**]

I. INTRODUCTION AND OVERVIEW OF THE ARGUMENT

It is a truism that lawyers were the but-for cause of many of the corporate scandals that came to light in the summer of 2002. Without the participation of lawyers and other professionals, the fraudulent transactions that had distorted the financial statements of Enron, Global Crossing, WorldCom, and other public corporations could not have closed in their original form. But factual causation is one thing; responsibility is another. There has been no shortage of public condemnation of the role of lawyers in facilitating corporate wrongdoing. When the last scandal of this magnitude—the savings and loan crisis of the 1980s—became widely known, a federal judge famously asked "Where . . . were the . . . attorneys"?[1] Judge Sporkin's *cri de coeur* has become a convenient shorthand used by scholars of the legal profession who believe, as I do, that lawyers have failed to take seriously their responsibility as professionals while representing wealthy corporate clients. Lawyers have not yet been subjected to the kind of Congressional grilling that officers like Kenneth Lay and Jeffrey Skilling endured.[2] And

[*] Reprinted by special permission of Northwestern University School of Law, Northwestern University Law Review. W. Bradley Wendel, *Professionalism as Interpretation,* 99 Nw. U. L. Rev. 1167 (2005).

[**] Associate Professor of Law, Cornell Law School. Thanks to Greg Cooper, Roger Cramton, Sarah Cravens, Tim Dare, Bob Gordon, Peter Joy, Doug Kysar, Jeff Rachlinksi, Tanina Rostain, Leila Sadat, Emily Sherwin, Nancy Staudt, Dennis Tuchler, Richard Tur, Rob Vischer, Chuck Wolfram, and the participants at the First International Conference on Lawyers' Ethics at the University of Exeter (U.K.) (organized by Kim Economides and Julian Webb) and a Washington University School of Law faculty workshop for their perceptive and helpful comments. I am additionally grateful to Lonny Hoffman and the students in the University of Houston Law Center's innovative legal scholarship colloquium for their excellent responsive papers.

[1] Lincoln Sav. & Loan Ass'n v. Wall, 743 F. Supp. 901, 920 (D.D.C. 1990); *see also Accountability Issues: Lessons Learned from Enron's Fall: Hearing Before the Senate Comm. on the Judiciary,* 107th Cong. 37-38, 47 (2002) (statement of Susan P. Koniak, ironically echoing Judge Sporkin's question).

[2] Susan P. Koniak, *When the Hurlyburly's Done: The Bar's Struggle with the SEC,* 103 Colum. L. Rev. 1236, 1237 (2003) ("[T]he lawyers have, however, largely escaped responsibility for their role in this nation's latest spate of corporate fraud . . . .").

certainly no law firm has suffered the fate of Enron's auditor, Arthur Andersen, which was convicted of obstruction of justice for attempting to thwart an SEC investigation and subsequently went out of business.[3] Nevertheless, it is appropriate to ask the hard questions about the role of lawyers in the most recent wave of corporate scandals, as well as in other cases in which legal advice was sought by clients who appeared in hindsight to have been interested only in evading the law.

This Article is not a polemic against the rotten state of lawyers' ethics. It is probably true to some extent that "[p]erverse incentives, not declines in ethics, cause scandals."[4] When it comes to the role of lawyers, however, it is impossible to talk about incentives—perverse or otherwise—without having a very clear jurisprudential understanding of how lawyers ought to interpret and apply complex and ambiguous legal norms to their clients' transactions. In particular, we ought to investigate the responsibility of lawyers, acting in their capacity as representatives of clients, vis-à-vis the maintenance of a stable framework of legal norms. Do lawyers bear any responsibility for the system, or may they take a merely instrumental stance toward the law, treating it as something to be evaded or nullified through careful planning? If the technical requirements of law can be evaded to the client's benefit and the detriment of others, is there anything in the lawyer's role that prohibits her from assisting the client?

In this Article, I wish to defend what I call the interpretive attitude of professionalism. Professionalism is a stance toward the law which accepts that a lawyer is not simply an agent of her client (although the lawyer-client relationship is obviously governed by the law of agency). Rather, in carrying out her client's lawful instructions, a lawyer has an obligation to apply the law to her client's situation with due regard to the meaning of legal norms, not merely their formal expression.[5] A professional lawyer must respect the achievement represented by law: the final settlement of contested issues (both factual and normative) with a view toward enabling coordinated action in our highly complex, pluralistic society. The attitude of professionalism has both negative and positive aspects.

---

[3] *See* BARBARA LEY TOFFLER & JENNIFER REINGOLD, FINAL ACCOUNTING: AMBITION, GREED, AND THE FALL OF ARTHUR ANDERSEN 221-22 (2003).

[4] John C. Coffee, Jr., *What Caused Enron? A Capsule Social and Economic History of the 1990s*, 89 CORNELL L. REV. 269, 278 (2004); *see also* William W. Bratton, *Enron and the Dark Side of Shareholder Value*, 76 TUL. L. REV. 1275, 1329-32 (2002) (arguing that the most plausible story of Enron's fall requires understanding the workplace "tournament" culture, which created a bias toward winning and an inability to perceive reality accurately); Donald C. Langevoort, *The Organizational Psychology of Hyper-Competition: Corporate Irresponsibility and the Lessons of Enron*, 70 GEO. WASH. L. REV. 968 (2002) (discussing cognitive psychological research on the production of firm cultures that tend to lead managers to block out distracting concerns, like ethical issues).

[5] Compare the principle of dynamic statutory interpretation, which requires an interpreter to construe a text "in light of [its] present societal, political, and legal context." William N. Eskridge, Jr., *Dynamic Statutory Interpretation*, 135 U. PA. L. REV. 1479, 1479 (1987). It is also similar to the principle of purposivism, familiar in legal ethics from the work of William Simon and David Wilkins. *See* William H. Simon, *The Ideology of Advocacy: Procedural Justice and Professional Ethics*, 1978 WIS. L. REV. 29, 62-90; David B. Wilkins, *Legal Realism for Lawyers*, 104 HARV. L. REV. 468, 505-15 (1990). Differences between these approaches will be apparent in the application of the attitude of professionalism to cases.

In the negative aspect, this obligation of respect means that a lawyer must treat legal norms as precluding the moral and other reasons that would otherwise justify or require a different action in the circumstances.[6] Conversely, the positive aspect is the demand that a lawyer should take a certain attitude toward the law, manifesting her recognition that the law is legitimate—that is, worthy of being taken seriously, interpreted in good faith with due regard to its meaning, and not simply seen as an obstacle standing in the way of the client's goals.[7]

Law is an achievement, but not one that will persist without custodians and defenders. It is the job of lawyers to maintain the institution in good working order, instead of subverting it.[8] As Jeremy Waldron puts it, any attempt to circumvent the law should be accompanied by feelings of distaste and dishonor,[9] not pride in defeating something that is regarded as an adversary. In addition, this obligation of custodianship demands that lawyers provide a public, reasoned justification for an interpretation of legal texts—one which is plausible in light of the interpretive understandings of a professional community.

Professionalism stands in opposition to the view of many lawyers that excellence in lawyering means engaging in "creative and aggressive" structuring of transactions for the benefit of clients, even though the transactions are designed to evade regulatory requirements enacted to protect investors. The quoted language, "creative and aggressive,"

---

[6] For a more elaborate defense of this position, *see* W. Bradley Wendel, *Civil Obedience*, 104 COLUM. L. REV. 363 (2004).

[7] *See* STEVEN J. BURTON, JUDGING IN GOOD FAITH 17, 35-37, *passim* (1992); Thomas D. Morgan & Robert W. Tuttle, *Legal Representation in a Pluralist Society*, 63 GEO. WASH. L. REV. 984 (1995). As Robert Gordon argues:

> [T]here is a difference between trying to game and manipulate a system as a resistance movement or alienated outsider would, and to engage in a committed and good faith struggle within the system to influence it to fulfill what a good faith interpreter would construe as its best values and purposes.

Robert W. Gordon, *A New Role for Lawyers?: The Corporate Counselor After Enron*, 35 CONN. L. REV. 1185, 1200

[8] The obligation on the part of lawyers to maintain the institution of law can be understood as an instance of the Rawlsian natural duty to support just institutions. *See* JOHN RAWLS, A THEORY OF JUSTICE 114-17, 333-37 (1971). For a defense of the Rawlsian position, *see* Jeremy Waldron, *Special Ties and Natural Duties*, 22 PHIL. & PUB. AFF. 3 (1993). In much of his work on legal ethics, Robert Gordon argues for a position very similar to the Rawlsian natural duty to support the basically just legal system of our country:

> Lawyers have, I think, fallen into the habit of thinking that maintaining the integrity of the legal framework is always someone else's problem . . . . But, of course, the order of rules and norms, policies and procedures, and institutional actors and roles that make up the legal system . . . [are] only as effective as voluntary compliance can make it; for if people routinely start running red lights when they think no cop is watching (or hire lawyers to keep a lookout for the cops, and to exhaust the resources of traffic courts arguing the lights were green), the regime will collapse.

Robert W. Gordon, *A Collective Failure of Nerve: The Bar's Response to Kaye Scholer*, 23 LAW & SOC. INQUIRY 315, 321 (1998).

[9] JEREMY WALDRON, LAW AND DISAGREEMENT 101 (1999).

which is often used by lawyers as a term of approbation, comes from the report issued by Enron's long-time outside counsel, Vinson & Elkins, in response to the concerns raised by Enron finance executive Sherron Watkins.[10] The firm, investigating transactions its own lawyers had worked on, despite the glaring conflicts of interest,[11] determined that the only problem with the structure and accounting treatment of the transactions was potentially one of public relations. The subtext of this response was that creativity and aggressiveness is a positive value in sophisticated business counsel. Interestingly, Watkins's letter itself used the word "aggressive" to describe the company's accounting, but she used the term with a decidedly more negative connotation—suggesting that Enron had obscured the economic substance of transactions to the point that the accounting treatment was no longer reliable.[12]

It is relatively easy to say, in the abstract, that lawyers should not be "too aggressive" or should exercise judgment with due regard to the meaning of legal norms. I hope to show that these general standards of professionalism have content when applied to actual transactions that fall within the zone of professional judgment. In many of the Enron transactions, an attitude of professionalism would have required the lawyers to refuse to issue opinion letters where the transactions violated substantively meaningful legal and accounting standards, even though the transactions arguably complied with formal legal rules—albeit "aggressively."[13] In other words, a lawyer would be required to prevent the kind of abuse that is colorfully illustrated by a former Enron employee:

> Say you have a dog, but you need to create a duck on the financial statements. Fortunately, there are specific accounting rules for what constitutes a duck: yellow feet, white covering, orange beak. So you take the dog and

---

[10] *See* LOREN FOX, ENRON: THE RISE AND FALL 259 (2003). Sherron Watkins was a vice president for corporate development in the finance department of Enron at the time she wrote a letter to Kenneth Lay warning that the company might "implode in a wave of accounting scandals." *See id.* at 247-48. The complete Watkins letter is included as an appendix to her book. *See* Letter from Sherron Watkins, Enron Employee, to Kenneth Lay, Chairman and C.E.O., Enron, *reprinted in* MIMI SWARTZ & SHERRON WATKINS, POWER FAILURE: THE INSIDE STORY OF THE COLLAPSE OF ENRON 361-62 (2003) (regarding Enron Accounting Practices).

[11] WILLIAM POWERS, JR., ENRON CORP., REPORT OF INVESTIGATION BY THE SPECIAL INVESTIGATIVE COMMITTEE OF THE BOARD OF DIRECTORS OF ENRON CORP. 176-77 (2002) [hereinafter POWERS REPORT] ("The result of the V&E review was largely predetermined by the scope and nature of the investigation and the process employed. . . . The scope and process of the investigation appear to have been structured with less skepticism than was needed to *see* through these particularly complex transactions."); Roger C. Cramton, *Enron and the Corporate Lawyer: A Primer on Legal and Ethical Issues*, 58 BUS. LAW. 143 (2002).

[12] *See* POWERS REPORT, *supra* note 11, at 4-5 (stating committee's conclusion that certain related-party transactions lacked economic substance and were entered into solely for the purpose of manipulating Enron's financial statements).

[13] *See* William W. Bratton, *Enron, Sarbanes-Oxley and Accounting: Rules Versus Principles Versus Rents*, 48 VILL. L. REV. 1023, 1044 (2003) (distinguishing regulatory arbitrage from strategic noncompliance, and defining the latter as "action under an interpretation of the law in conflict with the stated interpretation of the regulator").

> paint its feet yellow and its fur white and you paste an orange plastic beak on its nose, and then you say to your accountants, "This is a duck! Don't you agree that it's a duck?" And the accountants say, "Yes, according to the rules, this is a duck." Everybody knows that it is a dog, not a duck, but that does not matter, because you have met the rules for calling it a duck.[14]

It is not surprising that the rules of financial accounting would have criteria for duck-ness, but a point often escapes non-lawyers about the nature of rule-based reasoning: no matter how clear a rule appears to be, it will always be ambiguous enough to be manipulated. That is, unless the rule is interpreted in light of non-textually bound interpretive conventions and practices, applied through the informed judgment of a decisionmaker rather than through the text itself.[15] Professionalism, in a nutshell, instructs lawyers not to participate in the hocus-pocus of turning dogs into ducks, and is therefore a principle for regulating the exercise of interpretive judgment.

Similarly, when several internal government memos came to light which seemed to provide a blueprint for evading domestic and international legal prohibitions on torture, two prominent commentators referred to them as "standard lawyerly fare, routine stuff."[16] This characterization, however, begs the question of what attitude lawyers ought to take toward the law. One of the memos counseled the government that mistreatment of prisoners amounts to torture only under extremely unusual circumstances, and that the abuse of prisoners may be justified by criminal law doctrines such as self-defense and necessity.[17] This advice is far from "routine stuff," because it relied on a highly artificial—one might say "creative and aggressive"—reading of the governing law. It is difficult to resist the temptation to pun and call the reasoning "tortured," because it so clearly reveals the author's determination to come up with any argument, however plausible, that the law against torture does not apply to detainees at Guantánamo Bay. The overwhelming reaction by experts in criminal, international, constitutional, and military law has been that the legal analysis in the government memos was so distorted

---

[14] BETHANY MCLEAN & PETER ELKIND, THE SMARTEST GUYS IN THE ROOM: THE AMAZING RISE AND SCANDALOUS FALL OF ENRON 142-43 (2003) (quoting an unidentified former Enron employee).

[15] *See* LEO KATZ, ILL-GOTTEN GAINS: EVASION, BLACKMAIL, FRAUD, AND KINDRED PUZZLES OF THE LAW ix-x (1996) (arguing that legal practice is pervaded by opportunities for "avoision," or clever transactional structuring that straddles the line between legitimate penalty avoidance and illegitimate evasion); Steven L. Schwarcz, *Enron and the Use and Abuse of Special Purpose Entities in Corporate Structures*, 70 U. CIN. L. REV. 1309, 1317 (2002) (claiming that due to the complexity of structured-finance transactions, "Enron's investors . . . must, to some extent, rely on the business judgment of Enron's management").

[16] *See* Eric Posner & Adrian Vermeule, *A "Torture" Memo and Its Tortuous Critics*, WALL ST. J., July 6, 2004, at A22.

[17] *See* Memorandum from Jay S. Bybee, Assistant Attorney General, to Alberto R. Gonzales, Counsel to the President (Aug. 1, 2002), *available at* The George Washington University National Security Documents On-Line Archive, http://www2.gwu.edu/~nsarchiv/NSAEBB/NSAEBB127/index.htm (last visited Dec. 6, 2004) [hereinafter Aug. 1 OLC Memo].

that the lawyers' advice was incompetent.[18] Given that the memos were prepared by agencies, such as the Office of Legal Counsel, that traditionally employ some of the ablest lawyers in government, it is unlikely that the authors lacked technical legal skills. The explanation for the deficiencies in reasoning is more likely that the authors did not want to regard the law as constraining their client's ends, so they approached the law in an excessively adversarial stance, in effect adopting the attitude that they would make the law say what they wanted it to say. Like the metaphorical process of turning dogs into ducks, this is an example of how lawyers can violate the obligation of professionalism when interpreting the law and counseling clients.

This Article belongs to a subgenre of legal ethics scholarship that examines the lawyer's responsibility as a law-interpreter and private law-giver when representing clients in transactional and counseling matters.[19] To the extent a lawyer is justified in taking an adversarial stance toward the law in litigation, that justification depends on procedural checks to safeguard against exploitation or misapplication of law.[20] A considerable degree of impartiality in the proceedings as a whole is insured by three factors: the opposing lawyer's brief, the judge's experience (and the diligence of law

[18] *See, e.g.,* Kathleen Clark & Julie Mertus, *Torturing the Law*, WASH. POST, June 20, 2004, at B3 (criticizing "stunning legal contortions" in memos); Adam Liptak, *Legal Scholars Criticize Memos on Torture*, N.Y. TIMES, June 25, 2004, at A14 (quoting Harold Koh calling the memos "embarrassing" and Cass Sunstein's opinion that the legal analysis was "very low level, . . . very weak, embarrassingly weak, just short of reckless"); Ruth Wedgewood & R. James Woolsey, *Law and Torture*, WALL ST. J., June 28, 2004, at A10 (concluding that memos "bend and twist to avoid any legal restrictions" on torture and ignore or misapply governing law). For an example of what can only be either blatant incompetence or highly tendentious advocacy, consider that the torture memos' discussion of executive power in wartime never even mentions, let along provides a persuasive distinction of, the steel seizure case, *Youngstown Sheet & Tube Co. v. Sawyer*, 343 U.S. 579 (1952), which is the leading Supreme Court decision on separation of powers in this context.

[19] For other examples, *see* Sanford Levinson, *Frivolous Cases: Do Lawyers Really Know Anything at All?*, 24 OSGOODE HALL L.J. 353 (1986); Stephen L. Pepper, *Counseling at the Limits of the Law: An Exercise in the Jurisprudence and Ethics of Lawyering*, 104 YALE L.J. 1545 (1995).

[20] The Model Code, which was frequently criticized for assimilating all lawyering activities to adversarial litigation, actually recognizes quite plainly the importance of context. "Where the bounds of law are uncertain, the action of a lawyer may depend on whether he is serving as advocate or adviser." MODEL CODE OF PROF'L RESPONSIBILITY EC 7-3 (1981). Taking a narrow, technical, or instrumental attitude toward the law is appropriate only (if at all) in adversarial litigation, and only where the lawyer has a good faith belief that her interpretation of the law is supported by existing norms or by a reasonable argument for extension, modification, or reversal of existing law. *Id.* at EC 7-4. In adversarial litigation, this highly partisan stance toward the law may be justified by the effect on the tribunal of opposing partisan presentations: "[T]he advocate, by his zealous preparation and presentation of facts and law, enables the tribunal to come to the hearing with an open and neutral mind and to render impartial judgments." *Id.* at EC 7-19. The attorney as adviser, however, is bound to render a professional opinion as to the applicability of law, interpreted from the point of view of an impartial tribunal. *Id.* at EC 7-5. The modern law governing lawyers preserves these distinctions. *Compare* MODEL RULES OF PROF'L CONDUCT R. 2.1 (2002) [hereinafter MODEL RULES] (stating that an attorney as adviser must use independent professional judgment and render candid advice), with MODEL RULES, *supra,* R. 3.1 (stating that a lawyer representing client in litigated matter may assert any nonfrivolous legal argument).

clerks), and the requirement that lawyers disclose adverse authority and not make material misstatements of law.[21] When the lawyer represents a client outside the litigation context, however, these procedural constraints on partisanship are absent. In counseling and transactional representation, the only constraint on the assistance the lawyer may provide to the client is provided by the law itself, as interpreted by the lawyer on whose client the law is expected to act as a constraint.[22] Thus, a lawyer may be tempted to apply the law as the client wishes it to be, as distinct from as it actually is. As I will argue, this problem cannot be avoided by clarifying the law, because part of the nature of language is its inability to capture the full range of meaning that a text must bear. In other words, there is no such thing as a self-interpreting legal text that regulates the actions of lawyers or clients apart from the exercise of interpretive judgment by a community of professionals. As a consequence, the law cannot operate as a device to settle normative conflict and coordinate activity without a commitment on the part of law-interpreters to respect the substantive meaning standing behind the formal expression of legal norms.[23]

Part II of this Article begins the argument for professionalism by critically examining the prevailing wisdom of many scholars and practicing lawyers, which can be labeled legal realism, law-as-price, or the Holmesian bad man view of law. The position I criticize essentially permits the lawyer to assist the client in planning around the law without regard to the possibility that a legal restriction ought to be interpreted as a legitimate restriction on the client's activities. By "legitimate" I mean that the law has normative significance as such in the client's practical deliberations (conducted through the means of a lawyer, naturally, if the law is too complex to be understood without legal training and experience). The view I criticize would regard the law as functioning in practical reasoning as only one cost among many, and not as the expression of a view that individuals should, or should not do something. The jurisprudential problem with that position is that it undermines the social function of law, which is to establish settlement and coordination in a broad sense.

The terms settlement and coordination are familiar in the legal theory literature,[24] but I use them slightly idiosyncratically to mean a more robust or substantively meaningful

---

[21] For the duty of candor to the tribunal, *see* MODEL RULES, *supra* note 20, R. 3.3(a)(1) (stating that a lawyer may not make material misstatements of fact or law to the tribunal), and *id.* R. 3.3(a)(2) (stating that a lawyer may not fail to disclose to the tribunal controlling adverse legal authority).

[22] Pepper, *supra* note 19, at 1549, 1566-67.

[23] Although superficially this requirement may *seem* objectionable, because it requires the lawyer to imagine herself in the position of a judge, the law governing lawyers actually does require lawyers to adopt this interpretive stance when advising clients. *See* MODEL RULES, *supra* note 20, R. 2.1. This rule requires lawyers to exercise "independent professional judgment" and render "candid advice," which means that the lawyer must provide advice from a standpoint that is independent of the client's interests. As the comments to the rule recognize, this advice may be unpleasant for the client to hear, but lawyers are nevertheless professionally obligated to deliver bad news in the appropriate circumstances. *See id.* R. 2.1 cmt. 1.

[24] *See infra* note 53 and accompanying text. The term "coordination problem" has a technical, narrower use in game theory. Coordination games are those in which the interests of the players do not conflict

resolution of a normative conflict. Suppose there is disagreement about an important public policy issue, such as whether a certain type of corporate transaction must be fully disclosed in a company's financial statements or, even, whether some humiliating and degrading interrogation techniques should be allowed when questioning suspected terrorists. If this disagreement cannot be settled by deliberation and debate, people turn to the law for resolution, in order to enable them to cooperate on common projects without becoming mired in the same normative dispute. It is critical to this settlement process that the law be interpreted as having a substantive meaning that depends in part on legal texts, but which is not exhausted by texts. If the form alone of an enacted law determined its meaning for the purposes of constraining lawyers' interpretive activities, then it would be practically impossible to achieve settlement, because given sufficient cleverness and resources, lawyers can almost always structure their clients' activities around purely formal rules. Using the law to achieve settlement, and therefore the possibility of mutually beneficial social interactions, requires that lawyers approach the law with the intent to recover the meaning of the law, rather than simply to manipulate formal features of legal texts. Thus, Part II will continue by considering a simple example of how different interpretive stances or attitudes can yield different meanings for legal texts.

The straightforward statute in Part II will serve as an analogy for the exponentially more complex schemes of regulation applicable to the practical contexts we will consider in Part III, namely the problem of identifying tax shelters, the abuse of legal and accounting rules by Enron, and the attempt by the Bush administration to avoid legal restrictions on torture. This Part also takes up in more detail the arguments against textualist theories of interpretation. Although I argue against textualism, it is important to emphasize that this Article is located firmly within the positivist tradition, in particular the incorporationist strand associated with Professor H.L.A. Hart. The interpretive attitude that professionalism requires lawyers to take toward the law is not a demand of ethics considered apart from the law. Rather, it is part of the law in the sense that lawyers and judges employ it to determine what the law actually is, as opposed to what it should be. In jurisprudential terms, the rule of recognition of the American legal system incorporates non-textual sources, including interpretive principles that differentiate between legitimate and abusive applications of rules. The instrumental stance toward law is actually ruled out by the interpretive practices of courts and lawyers, but in addi-

---

(in contrast to prisoners' dilemma games), but where the games have more than one Nash equilibrium. The parties are jointly better off adopting one of the equilibrium strategies, but in the absence of a means to communicate their strategy, the parties may not reach the beneficial equilibrium result. *See* DOUGLAS G. BAIRD ET AL., GAME THEORY AND THE LAW 36-42 (1994). I use the term coordination problem in a different sense, but one which is common in jurisprudence. "[A] coordination problem is any cost that results from moral disagreement or from uncertainty about how others will resolve questions about what they are morally permitted, required, or forbidden to do." Larry Alexander, *"With Me, It's All Er Nuthin": Formalism in Law and Morality*, 66 U. CHI. L. REV. 530, 534 (1999). The cost associated with moral disagreement is simply the inability of disputants to move beyond argument and reason-giving, into action that is socially permitted.

tion, one could make a normative argument based on the settlement and coordination function of law. The settlement achieved by law is not merely a form of words that establishes some minimal logical constraint on the range of possible meanings that can be ascribed to the utterance. Rather, it is a substantive response to a normative conflict, which functions in practical reasoning by displacing the reasons that would otherwise count in favor of a contrary action. Thus, to the extent individuals and lawyers share the need to resolve conflict and work together on common projects, they have a sufficient moral reason to respect the meaning of legal norms.

Part III concludes with the application of this theory of legal ethics to the cases of tax shelters, special-purpose entity transactions in Enron, and the Justice Department's memos on the domestic and international law of torture. In each of these cases, the governing legal texts are consistent with a formal interpretation, in which the client is permitted to do something, and a substantive interpretation, in which the client's acts would be prohibited. Although lawyers in all three cases have attempted to justify the formally plausible result, their interpretations would not be accepted in a community of lawyers and judges who are motivated to ascertain the actual meaning of the governing legal standards. Indeed, the only reason the lawyers in all of these cases may have been comfortable arguing for the formally plausible interpretation is that they expected some degree of secrecy, either through the audit lottery (in the case of tax shelters), the cover provided by byzantine transactions and obfuscated disclosures (the Enron manipulations), or geographic isolation and covert activities (the interrogations at Guantánamo Bay and Abu Ghraib). The correlation between a lack of transparency and aggressively instrumental interpretations of law suggests that the public justifiability of a legal interpretation is a significant component of its legitimacy. The veil of secrecy having been stripped from these interpretations, we can criticize the lawyers not in first-order moral terms, but for having misapplied and distorted the law governing their clients' conduct.

II. PROFESSIONALISM VS. THE HOLMESIAN BAD MAN STANCE

The principal target of my argument is the position that lawyers are permitted to take a "Holmesian bad man" interpretive attitude toward legal norms, regarding them as obstacles to be planned around, or even costs to be incurred in the course of pursuing the projects of one's clients.[25] Oliver Wendell Holmes defined the content of the law in terms of a prediction about how legal officials might decide particular cases, which he illustrated through the metaphor of a "bad man" who is interested only in avoiding legal penalties that might attach to his conduct. The problem with the perspective of the bad man is not that it is descriptively inaccurate—surely many people, including lawyers, do care about the law only insofar as it might impose sanctions on them—but that it is jurisprudentially unsatisfying. The bad man's perspective is only one of many

[25] *See* Oliver Wendell Holmes, Jr., *The Path of the Law*, 10 HARV. L. REV. 457, 459-62 (1897).

standpoints that one may adopt toward the law,[26] and it is far from self-evident that it is the best perspective to employ when describing the relationship between lawyers and the law. The choice of an interpretive standpoint is a normative one, and there must be an argument for why one ought to adopt the perspective of the bad man if that perspective is to do any justifying work in jurisprudence. As Ronald Dworkin rightly observes, a participant in a social practice does not regard the practice and its constitutive rules as simply given, but assumes it serves some interest or purpose.[27] The focus of a theory of lawyering must therefore be on the purpose of the legal system and, correspondingly, the value of having officially licensed and regulated lawyers who represent clients in matters requiring legal advice, judgment, and skill.[28] The argument must be "normative all the way down," with a theory of democracy justifying a theory of the function of law, which in turn justifies a conception of the lawyer's role.

Lawyers facing serious criticism from regulators or academics for their roles in client malfeasance usually defend themselves and their extremely narrow interpretive attitude by appealing to the lawyer-client relationship and their duties as fiduciaries of clients. Their duties, say lawyers, are limited to protecting client interests by providing competent representation and keeping secrets, and most certainly do not include serving as a gatekeeper or quasi-regulator of their clients' transactions.[29] This defense misses the point, however, that the lawyer-client relationship is itself created by the legal system

---

[26] *See* William Twining, *The Bad Man Revisited*, 58 CORNELL L. REV. 275 (1973).

[27] RONALD DWORKIN, LAW'S EMPIRE 47 (1986). Dworkin uses the term "the interpretive attitude" to describe the standpoint of participants in a practice who seek to impose some meaning on the practice, and to see it in its best light. *Id.* at 46-48. In this Article I will make a more general reference to plural interpretive attitudes, which need not be identical with Dworkin's constructive interpretation theory of law. I believe Dworkin is right in taking seriously the perspective of participants in a social practice, or those who take what Hart calls an internal point of view toward the rules of a practice. *See* H.L.A. HART, THE CONCEPT OF LAW 56, 88-91 (2d ed. 1994). Dworkin's use of the singular term "interpretive attitude" is too strong, however, because people governed by the rules of certain complex social practices may be able to adopt one of several reasonable stances toward the rules—e.g., attitudes of resistance, cautious acquiescence, enthusiastic embrace, and so on. The attitude one takes toward the rules is a significant jurisprudential question, and because I disagree with some aspects of Dworkin's theory of law, it is important to note this terminological distinction.

[28] *Cf.* JOSEPH RAZ, *The Problem About the Nature of Law*, *in* ETHICS IN THE PUBLIC DOMAIN: ESSAYS IN THE MORALITY OF LAW AND POLITICS 179, 184-87, 192-93 (1994) (arguing against taking a narrow "lawyer's perspective," which eliminates consideration of the lawyer's relationship with other institutions such as courts, legislatures, administrative agencies, and various intermediate associations); Cass R. Sunstein & Adrian Vermeule, *Interpretation and Institutions*, 101 MICH. L. REV. 885 (2003) (recommending that theories of interpretation take into account the institutional competence of the interpreter).

[29] *See, e.g.*, Am. Bar Ass'n, *Statement of Policy Adopted by the American Bar Association Regarding Responsibilities and Liabilities of Lawyers in Advising with Respect to the Compliance by Clients with Laws Administered by the Securities and Exchange Commission*, 31 BUS. LAW. 543 (1975); James A. Cohen, *Lawyer Role, Agency Law, and the Characterization "Officer of the Court,"* 48 BUFF. L. REV. 349 (2000); Evan A. Davis, *The Meaning of Professional Independence*, 103 COLUM. L. REV. 1281 (2003); Jill E. Fisch & Kenneth M. Rosen, *Is There a Role for Lawyers in Preventing Future Enrons?*, 48 VILL. L. REV. 1097 (2003); Lawrence J. Fox, *The Fallout from Enron: Media Frenzy and Misguided Notions of Public Relations Are No*

and imposes duties on lawyers to the extent (and only to the extent) those duties are justified by the social function of the law. Lawyers are not judges, who are institutionally charged with the task of remaining impartial, but they are also not clients, who may be permitted to approach the law from a partisan and self-interested perspective. The role of lawyer is something of an amalgam of the judges' and clients' roles, serving as a bridge between the biased position of the client and the ideally neutral position of the judge.[30]

Lawyers are fiduciaries, but not only caretakers of their clients' interests—they are also custodians of the law in an important sense.[31] Thus, they have a responsibility to build the interests of third parties into their interpretation of law, even when working on behalf of private clients. This is not to say that lawyers have a responsibility toward something amorphous like "the public interest"—indeed, disagreement about the nature of the public interest is precisely what makes law necessary in the first place.[32] Rather, the lawyer's responsibility is toward the law, and to what it represents as a mechanism

---

Reason to Abandon Our Commitment to Our Clients, 2003 U. ILL. L. REV. 1243, 1243-59. For example, the joint submission of numerous large law firms argued as follows:

> An attorney to an issuer . . . is ethically bound to act as a legal counselor to, and at times an advocate for, that issuer, is not independent or required to be, and only in very limited circumstances provides advice that may be relied on by the investing public.

Letter from 79 Law Firms to Jonathan G. Katz, Secretary, Securities and Exchange Commission 2 (Apr. 7. 2003), *available at* http://www.sec.gov/rules/proposed/s74502/79lawfirms1.htm. Harry Reasoner, the managing partner of Vinson & Elkins, one of Enron's principal outside law firms, defended his firm's conduct in similar terms, punting responsibility for ensuring that transactions had economic substance to Enron's accountants. "There is a misunderstanding of what outside counsel's role is," he said. "We would have no role in determining whether, or what, accounting treatment was appropriate." John Schwartz, *Enron's Many Strands: The Lawyers: Troubling Questions Ahead for Enron's Law Firm*, N.Y. TIMES, Mar. 12, 2002, at C1. For a thorough analysis of the tension between competing conceptions of the lawyer's role, which came to a head over the *National Student Marketing* case, *see* Simon Lorne, *The Corporate and Securities Adviser, The Public Interest, and Professional Ethics*, 76 MICH. L. REV. 423 (1978).

[30] Robert W. Gordon, *The Ideal and the Actual in the Law: Fantasies and Practices of New York City Lawyers*, 1870-1910, *in* THE NEW HIGH PRIESTS: LAWYERS IN POST-CIVIL WAR AMERICA 51 (Gerard W. Gawalt ed., 1984). This hybrid role has long been accepted as a description of the duties of a prosecutor. *See, e.g.*, H. Richard Uviller, *The Neutral Prosecutor: The Obligation of Dispassion in a Passionate Pursuit*, 68 FORDHAM L. REV. 1695 (2000).

[31] German law recognizes a similar duty on the part of a lawyer to serve as a custodian of the law—*ein Pfleger des Rechts*. The foundation of the German judicial system is an obligation on the part of all actors within the system, including lawyers, to take care of the law. Thus, a lawyer is referred to as *ein unabhängiges Organ der Rechtspflege*—an independent institution in the administration of justice. *See* Bundesrechtsanwaltsordnung, v. 5.8.2004 (BGBl. I S.565) (as last amended by art. 4 (18) of Zuletzt geändert durch Gesetz zur Modernisierung des Kostenrechts (Kostenrechtsmodernisierungsgesetz), v. 5.5.2004 (BGBl. I S.718)). Thanks to Dennis Tuchler for pointing out this parallel and to Jens Damman for the citation to the German lawyer-licensing statute.

[32] *See* Geoffrey P. Miller, *Government Lawyers' Ethics in a System of Checks and Balances*, 54 U. CHI. L. REV. 1293, 1294 (1987) (arguing that "an agency attorney acts unethically when she substitutes her individual moral judgment for that of a political process which is generally accepted as legitimate").

to coordinate social activity through private ordering (as opposed to active intervention by state officials), despite deep and persistent normative disagreement. Although lawyers usually become almost apoplectic at the suggestion that they have any responsibility toward the legal system or the law as such, it is impossible to justify allowing lawyers to approach the law like Holmes's bad men under an institution-sensitive theory of law and lawyering.

A. Rational Instrumentalism?

Contemporary defenders of the Holmesian bad man interpretive attitude often identify with the law and economics movement.[33] Of course, an affinity for law and economics does not make one pro-Enron; indeed, sophisticated neoclassical economic theory may even support something like the attitude of professionalism. As Kenneth Arrow points out, contracts, markets, and transactions depend on relationships of trust and confidence.[34] It is impossible to draft contracts with enough specificity to handle every situation that could conceivably arise in the course of a commercial relationship. Thus, the parties depend on one another not to behave opportunistically. "Every contract depends for its observance on a mass of unspecified conditions which suggest that performance will be carried out in good faith without insistence on sticking literally to its wording."[35] In relational contracting, the parties rely on the repeated nature of their interactions to safeguard against opportunistic behavior.[36] A similar dynamic

---

[33] *See, e.g.*, the well-known argument of Judge Easterbrook and Professor Fischel:

> [M]anagers do not have an ethical duty to obey economic regulatory laws just because the laws exist. They must determine the importance of those laws. The penalties Congress names for disobedience are a measure of how much it wants firms to sacrifice in order to adhere to the rules; the idea of optimal sanctions is based on the supposition that managers not only may but also should violate the rules when it is profitable to do so.

Frank H. Easterbrook & Daniel R. Fischel, *Antitrust Suits by Targets of Tender Offers*, 80 MICH. L. REV. 1155, 1177 n.57 (1982); *see also* Stephen McG. Bundy & Einer Elhauge, *Knowledge About Legal Sanctions*, 92 MICH. L. REV. 261 (1993) (assuming that the law is relevant to actors only insofar as it imposes a cost on prohibited behavior). Cynthia Williams uses the term "law-as-price" conception to label this interpretive attitude. *See* Cynthia A. Williams, *Corporate Compliance with the Law in the Era of Efficiency*, 76 N.C. L. REV. 1265, 1267 (1998). The law-as-price theory is somewhat different because it expands the Holmesian bad man predictive orientation toward law into a distinctive theory of entitlement. According to law-as-price, one has a *right* to violate the law which can be obtained simply by "purchasing" the associated penalty, or willingly incurring a risk of the penalty. *Id.* at 1268. This difference is immaterial for the purposes of this Article, because both the Holmesian bad man predictive account of law and the law-as-price theory of entitlement are predicated on the same jurisprudential error, which I will discuss in detail here.

[34] Kenneth J. Arrow, *Social Responsibility and Economic Efficiency*, 21 PUB. POL'Y 303, 314 (1973).

[35] *Id.*; *see also* Pepper, *supra* note 19, at 1553-54 (noting that it would become vastly more expensive and cumbersome to regulate through law if lawyers took a Holmesian bad man stance toward the law).

[36] Stuart Macaulay, *Non-Contractual Relations in Business: A Preliminary Study*, 28 AM. SOC. REV. 55 (1963).

limits dishonesty in small communities where the participants may encounter one another in a future commercial relationship and where information about misconduct can be inexpensively disseminated.[37] In one-shot interactions in larger and more impersonal communities, the parties must use a different mechanism to ensure against exploitation; in this case economic theory uses the concept of lawyers as reputational intermediaries to explain why a lawyer or law firm would avoid being too aggressive in structuring transactions.

The services of gatekeepers, such as transactional lawyers and auditing firms, signal to the market that the client's representations are fair and accurate.[38] Gatekeepers can perform this function because their principal stock in trade is a reputation for probity, built up over years of "vouching" for clients by representing them in transactions. A gatekeeper firm would squander this reputation by vouching for a client whose representations were dishonest, so its association with a client is a credible signal of the client's honesty. Because gatekeepers have less to gain from dishonesty than clients do, they have a powerful incentive to monitor the client's conduct for dishonesty, to avoid losing valuable credibility. In effect the gatekeeper becomes a quasi-regulator, ensuring that deals are reached on the basis of accurate information.

Nevertheless, the relational-contracting and gatekeeper ideas still concede something significant to the Holmesian bad man model, namely their bleak vision of professionals as essentially self-interested, amorally pragmatic actors who take a purely instrumental approach to the law.[39] In the economic vision of professional ethics, there is only one reason to follow the law or to be honest in contractual relationships: fear of sanctions.[40]

---

[37] *See, e.g.*, Lisa Bernstein, *Private Commercial Law in the Cotton Industry: Creating Cooperation Through Rules, Norms, and Institutions*, 99 MICH. L. REV. 1724 (2001); Lisa Bernstein, *Opting out of the Legal System: Extralegal Contractual Relations in the Diamond Industry*, 21 J. LEG. STUD. 115 (1992); David Charny, *Nonlegal Sanctions in Commercial Relationships*, 104 HARV. L. REV. 373 (1990).

[38] *See, e.g.*, John C. Coffee, Jr., *The Attorney as Gatekeeper: An Agenda for the SEC*, 103 COLUM. L. REV. 1293 (2003); John C. Coffee, Jr., *Understanding Enron: "It's About the Gatekeepers, Stupid,"* 57 BUS. LAW. 1403 (2002); Coffee, *supra* note 4, at 279-97; Theodore Eisenberg & Jonathan R. Macey, *Was Arthur Andersen Different? An Empirical Examination of Major Accounting Firm Audits of Large Clients*, 1 J. EMPIRICAL LEGAL STUD. 263 (2004); Ronald J. Gilson & Robert H. Mnookin, *Disputing Through Agents: Cooperation and Conflict Between Lawyers in Litigation*, 94 COLUM. L. REV. 509 (1994); Ronald J. Gilson, *Value Creation by Business Lawyers: Legal Skills and Asset Pricing*, 94 YALE L.J. 239 (1984); Reinier Kraakman, *Gatekeepers: The Anatomy of a Third-Party Enforcement Strategy*, 2 J.L. ECON. & ORG. 53 (1986); Reinier Kraakman, *Corporate Liability Strategies and the Costs of Legal Controls*, 93 YALE L.J. 857 (1984).

[39] *See* Brian Leiter, *Holmes, Economics, and Classical Realism*, *in* THE PATH OF THE LAW AND ITS INFLUENCE: THE LEGACY OF OLIVER WENDELL HOLMES, JR. 285 (Steven J. Burton ed., 2000).

[40] *Cf.* Holmes, *supra* note 25, at 462 ("The duty to keep a contract at common law means a prediction that you must pay damages if you do not keep it—and nothing else."). The instrumental attitude toward law may be characterized, in jurisprudential terms, as reducing conduct rules to decision rules. *See* Meir Dan-Cohen, *Decision Rules and Conduct Rules: On Acoustic Separation in Criminal Law*, 97 HARV. L. REV. 625 (1984). Rules are analytically separable into two categories: conduct rules, which are addressed to individuals and which permit or forbid certain actions; and decision rules, which are addressed to officials and regulate the act of passing judgment. Although these categories are conceptually distinct, it is possible to run them together in practice, and conceive of conduct rules as being entirely a function of decision

Sanctions may come in the form of official, state-imposed punishments or non-legal penalties such as the loss of business opportunities. Regardless of form, the avoidance of sanctions is the sole reason to refrain from exploiting other parties in a transaction or from treating legal rules as inconveniences to be planned around. As Holmes so memorably put it, this attitude toward the law "stinks in the nostrils of those who think it advantageous to get as much ethics into the law as they can."[41] His mocking tone shows his disdain for anyone who regards the law as legitimate, and therefore a reason for acting. Economic theory has no place for actors who are guided by legal norms because they regard them as having moral force in their own right.

But what would be the normative argument for taking a purely instrumental stance toward the law? It cannot be the observation that the world is full of Holmesian bad men, which would be a simplistic version of G.E. Moore's naturalistic fallacy.[42] The most promising argument in favor of instrumentalism relies on libertarian premises—the fundamental moral significance of human freedom, and the concomitant requirements that any restrictions on liberty imposed by the state be justified by reasons shared by the object of coercion, general, knowable in advance of acting, and no broader than necessary to accomplish their purpose. Indeed, a deep insight of modern legal ethics theory, characteristic of the work of William Simon and Robert Gordon, is the extent to which the prevailing attitudes of practicing lawyers toward the law reflect the assumption that the purpose of the legal system is to delineate a sphere of individual autonomy which is protected against interference by other individuals or the state.[43] But Simon and Gordon have not only recognized that this foundation is unsound—they, along with David Luban and others, have completely demolished it.[44] In brief, they argue the following.

rules. *See id.* at 632. The Holmesian bad man attitude focuses interpretation solely on decision rules—i.e., when will a judge determine that I have violated the law? The attitude prescribed by professionalism focuses interpretation on conduct rules—i.e., what does the law require?

[41] Holmes, *supra* note 25, at 462.

[42] G.E. MOORE, PRINCIPIA ETHICA 13 (1903). The naturalistic fallacy in ethics is the reduction of propositions of ethics (e.g., "you ought to do X") to observations about what people actually do ("people do X") or what they believe with respect to what they should do ("people think it is good to do X"). The problem is that reduction to propositions about the natural world *seems* to squeeze the normativity out of ethical propositions, because ethical activities like valuing are different from observing, describing, and other scientific activities. Moore expressed this concern with his famous "open question" argument. If one says, "X is good because it produces happiness," it is always an open question why one ought to produce happiness. One major challenge in ethics is to avoid the naturalistic fallacy without an inflationary metaphysics that relies on entities like Moore's supersensory quality of goodness. *See generally* HILARY PUTNAM, ETHICS WITHOUT ONTOLOGY (2004).

[43] *See* WILLIAM SIMON, THE PRACTICE OF JUSTICE 30-37 (1998) (calling this the "Libertarian Premise"); Robert W. Gordon, *Why Lawyers Can't Just Be Hired Guns, in* ETHICS IN PRACTICE: LAWYERS' ROLES, RESPONSIBILITIES, AND REGULATION 42, 47 (Deborah L. Rhode ed., 2000) (describing "libertarian-positivist view"). For the best known defense of the minimal state, grounded in the value of autonomy, see ROBERT NOZICK, ANARCHY, STATE, AND UTOPIA (1974).

[44] *See* DAVID LUBAN, LAWYERS AND JUSTICE 167-69 (1988); David Luban, *The Lysistratian Prerogative: A Response to Stephen Pepper*, 1986 AM. B. FOUND. RES. J. 637.

First, the autonomy of the client is not some kind of moral trump card over the lawyer's own moral agency, which would require reasoning about the permissibility of the client's ends quite apart from considerations of the client's autonomy. Second, citizens are not entitled to autonomy as such, but only to a just measure of autonomy that is compatible with the rights of others. Third, liberty is only one value among others that a decent legal system would seek to protect. Fourth, lawyers participate to such a great extent in interpreting and applying the law that legal restrictions on client autonomy can hardly be said to be impartial and general. And finally, even if autonomy were the most important thing, its exercise depends on a stable framework of legal norms and institutions, which is undercut by instrumentalist approaches to the law.

The other principal argument for taking an instrumental stance toward the law mistakenly overgeneralizes from the paradigm of adversarial litigation.[45] The most shopworn aphorism in legal ethics is that a lawyer's primary duty is to "represent a client zealously within the bounds of the law."[46] Lawyers who seize on this maxim as a justification for interpreting the law as Holmesian bad men often elide the distinction between acting as an advocate in litigation and acting as a counselor or transactional engineer. Ask a securities lawyer why she opposes a requirement to report out evidence of client fraud, and she is likely to mention the principle of zealous representation, seemingly unaware that this phrase, as originally stated in the Model Code, applied only to representation in litigation. For good reason, however, a lawyer's attitude toward the law must vary according to the context in which she is representing a client.

A well prepared adversary and a fully informed tribunal are institutional features that counter excessive adversarial zeal in litigation and ensure that legal norms are applied in an impartial manner. In litigation, the judge serves as the custodian of the law, and as long as she is adequately informed and not misled, the parties' lawyers are justified in leaving to the judge the responsibility for taking care of the law. But transactional lawyering lacks the essential elements of litigation: an impartial referee, orderly procedures, rules for obtaining, introducing, and excluding evidence, and a competent opposing party. It is so different from adversarial litigation that one wonders why anyone has ever thought to analogize the role of lawyer from one context to the other.[47] Whatever psychological enthusiasm a lawyer might feel for her client's cause, the kind of zealous representation a lawyer may provide in counseling and transactional practice is circumscribed by a heightened obligation not to treat the law instrumentally. In effect, the legal system has delegated the judge's caretaker function to the lawyer in cases where the lawyer's interpretation of the law is not subject to review by an impartial referee.

---

[45] *See* BERNARD WOLFMAN ET AL., STANDARDS OF TAX PRACTICE § 201.2, at 43-44 (3d ed. 1995) (arguing that filing a tax return should not be analogized to an adversarial proceeding); William H. Simon, *The Kaye Scholer Affair: The Lawyer's Duty of Candor and the Bar's Temptations of Evasion and Apology*, 23 LAW & SOC. INQUIRY 243 (1998) (noting the litigation mindset that spilled over into the representation of Charles Keating in a regulatory matter, which caused the law firm to take an inappropriately adversarial stance toward government regulators).

[46] MODEL CODE OF PROF'L RESPONSIBILITY Canon 7 (1980).

[47] *See* LUBAN, *supra* note 44, at 56-66.

The arguments in this Article are an attempt to provide a secure jurisprudential foundation for this "caretaker" theory of the authority of law and of legal interpretation—a model of lawyering which treats legal norms legitimately, as reasons in themselves that bear on a lawyer's practical deliberation.[48] In this view, legal rules are not only legitimate reasons for action but preclude recourse to ordinary first-order moral reasons, including the value of client autonomy. Legal norms preempt other reasoning because the law itself arises from recognition of deep and persistent disagreement, resulting from a plurality of worthwhile human goods, values and forms of life, empirical uncertainty, divergent evaluative standpoints, and what Hume called the circumstances of justice—moderate scarcity and limited benevolence.[49] Many goods, such as health care, education, and the protection of safety and property, can be realized only by cooperation with others, so every person has an interest in working together with other members of the society in order to satisfy her desires for these goods.[50] At the same time, people disagree with one another, either about the best way to obtain basic goods (means-ends rational disagreements), constraints that should be placed on others' efforts to satisfy their desires (disagreements about rights); or even fundamental disagreements about whether people should be permitted to live particular kinds of lives (substantive disagreements about goods).[51] These conditions mean that much normative disagreement is in good faith; people are not simply maneuvering in the public domain to grab the biggest piece of the pie for themselves (although of course this happens), but are often motivated by

---

[48] *See* Wendel, *supra* note 6, at 364. The summary here is extremely abbreviated, and many details of the position are explained in the prior Article.

[49] *See* WILLIAM A. GALSTON, LIBERAL PLURALISM 5-6, 28-35 (2002); AMY GUTMANN & DENNIS THOMPSON, DEMOCRACY AND DISAGREEMENT 21-23 (1996); STUART HAMPSHIRE, INNOCENCE AND EXPERIENCE 30-33 (1989); ALASDAIR MACINTYRE, AFTER VIRTUE 6-11 (2d ed. 1984); THOMAS NAGEL, *The Fragmentation of Value, in* MORTAL QUESTIONS 128-41 (1979); NICHOLAS RESCHER, PLURALISM: AGAINST THE DEMAND FOR CONSENSUS 76-78 (1993); WALDRON, *supra* note 9, at 175-79; Isaiah Berlin, *The Pursuit of the Ideal, in* THE CROOKED TIMBER OF HUMANITY 1 (1990); Morgan & Tuttle, *supra* note 7.

[50] JOHN FINNIS, NATURAL LAW AND NATURAL RIGHTS 149, 154-56, 231-33, 248-51 (1980). I do not take a position as to whether the basic aspects of human well-being are those postulated by Finnis. *See id.* at 85-90. It would be possible to generate a somewhat different list by emphasizing basic human *capabilities*, as opposed to goods, for example. *See* MARTHA C. NUSSBAUM, SEX AND SOCIAL JUSTICE 39-42 (1999); *see also* Amartya Sen, *Equality of What?, in* CHOICE, WELFARE AND MEASUREMENT 353-69 (1982) (arguing that basic human capabilities, rather than basic social goods, ought to be used as the basis of the measurement of welfare). It is interesting that many of the goods described by Finnis overlap with the capabilities identified by Nussbaum—consider life, health, play, and practical reason, for instance. Rather than focusing on marginal differences among lists of basic values or capabilities, this account assumes that some set of goods is constitutive of human flourishing and that at least some of those goods can be realized only in an organized society. It is worth emphasizing, though, that I am not using "public goods" in the sense the term is used in economics—i.e., goods such as clean air or national defense from which it is impossible to exclude users—but in a broader sense, to stand for the various sorts of good things in social life that cannot be accomplished by individuals acting alone.

[51] I refer to this dual aspect of human nature, as sociability and disputatiousness, as the "Grotian problematic," following J.B. Schneewind's treatment of Hugo Grotius. *See* J.B. SCHNEEWIND, THE INVENTION OF AUTONOMY 70-73 & *passim* (1998).

the belief that their proposed rules for social ordering are those most likely to maximize social well being.[52]

In many cases, parties to the normative disagreement share a desire for an at least provisional settlement of the issue, enabling coordinated activity notwithstanding the intractable dispute. "Settlement" here means not only termination of the dispute, but taking a position on the normative issue that is robust enough to serve as the basis for coordinated activity. If there were a normative disagreement about, say, whether certain methods of interrogation run afoul of laws prohibiting torture, government officials whose conduct is regulated need to ascertain not only the words of the relevant law, but their meaning. They care about more than what the words say; they want to know whether they will be allowed to use interrogation technique T on detainee D. The parties turn to an impartial, third-party procedural mechanism—the law—because they share the desire for peaceful cooperation and settlement, but cannot reach agreement through deliberation and debate alone.[53] Because the law permits them to do better at realizing their interest in cooperation than they would on their own, and because it is adopted through procedures that meet a threshold standard of fairness and respect for the parties to the normative disputes, the law has authority in the domain of the disagreement and precludes practical reasoning on the basis of the reasons that were relevant to the underlying controversy.[54] This is essentially the argument for the negative aspect of professionalism, which preempts recourse to reasons that would otherwise require a different action in the circumstances, where a legal norm is in force. The positive aspect of professionalism flows from the same conception of the authority of law, and requires lawyers to interpret legal norms in such a way that the law can continue to perform its coordination and settlement functions.

---

[52] LARRY ALEXANDER & EMILY SHERWIN, THE RULE OF RULES: MORALITY, RULES, AND THE DILEMMAS OF LAW 12 (2001) ("[T]he road to the nasty, brutish, and short lives of the Hobbesian state of nature does not require people motivated solely by selfishness and predatory opportunism . . . ."). Some political theorists specify as a constraint on permissible deliberation the requirement that participants in public debate "recogniz[e] that an opponent's position is based on moral principles about which people may reasonably disagree . . . ." GUTMANN & THOMPSON, *supra* note 49, at 82. One might also make an empirical claim that people do in fact disagree in good faith. My point is somewhat different. It is the conceptual claim that the reasons we have for disagreement are such that people could disagree in good faith, although it is also possible for people to be merely spiteful and avaricious.

[53] *See* ALEXANDER & SHERWIN, *supra* note 52, at 11-15; HENRY M. HART, JR. & ALBERT M. SACKS, THE LEGAL PROCESS: BASIC PROBLEMS IN THE MAKING AND APPLICATION OF LAW 1-4 (William N. Eskridge, Jr. & Philip P. Frickey eds., 1994); Larry Alexander & Frederick Schauer, *On Extrajudicial Constitutional Interpretation*, 110 HARV. L. REV. 1359 (1997).

[54] This conception of the authority of law is derived from Joseph Raz's normal justification thesis. *See* JOSEPH RAZ, THE MORALITY OF FREEDOM 53 (1986); Joseph Raz, *Introduction to* AUTHORITY 1, 12-13 (Joseph Raz ed., 1990). It is substantially influenced by Jeremy Waldron's use of the Razian normal justification thesis ("NJT"). *See* WALDRON, *supra* note 9, at 95-96. Both are discussed in considerably more detail in Wendel, *supra* note 6. I am making stronger claims for the force of the NJT than Raz would accept, but I believe they are consistent with Waldron's expansive use of Raz's conception of authority.

Before working through the defense of this position in detail, it may be helpful to take a preliminary look at some examples of how changes in an interpretive attitude in turn alter judicial decisions or the advice given to clients. As the examples should make clear, the approach to legal interpretation that flows from this conception of legal ethics is different from other methods of interpretation, particularly textualism.[55] Legal texts alone cannot achieve the settlement that is the function of law because they are never self-interpreting. Indeed, a pervasive textualist style of interpretation may be positively correlated with abusive interpretations of law that create costly externalities.[56] Texts instead must be interpreted in light of interpretive understandings of the relevant community of lawyers and judges. The most important features of professionalism as a style of interpretation are twofold: first, it avoids the policy preferences or first-order moral beliefs of interpreters; and second, it resists manipulation of the form of legal norms to defeat their substantive meaning. Professionalism, as defended here, does not instruct lawyers to act in the public interest, which may be internally incoherent and normatively contested. Rather, it instructs lawyers to be guided by what the public has come up with as its laws, through the process of legislation, administrative rulemaking, and adjudication. Professionalism is grounded in fidelity to a society's laws, but it is critical that law not be understood narrowly or formalistically. Rather, the law must be interpreted in a way that ensures it will continue to have the capacity to coordinate social action against a background of persistent first-order normative disagreement.

B. An Introductory Example: Text vs. Meaning

Professionalism makes reference to "substantive meanings" of legal norms, as opposed to their mere formal expression. One natural objection to this position is that legal norms do not have a substantive meaning apart from their textual form. The following brief example of an ethical dilemma in lawyering demonstrates that the meaning of

---

[55] For some of the most important contributions to this debate, *see* Stephen Breyer, *On the Uses of Legislative History in Interpreting Statutes*, 65 S. CAL. L. REV. 845 (1992); Frank H. Easterbrook, *Statutes' Domains*, 50 U. CHI. L. REV. 533 (1983); Frank H. Easterbrook, *Text, History, and Structure in Statutory Interpretation*, 17 HARV. J.L. & PUB. POL'Y 61 (1994); William N. Eskridge, Jr. & Philip P. Frickey, *Statutory Interpretation as Practical Reasoning*, 42 STAN. L. REV. 321 (1990); William N. Eskridge, Jr., *The New Textualism*, 37 UCLA L. REV. 621 (1990); Daniel A. Farber, *Statutory Interpretation and Legislative Supremacy*, 78 GEO. L.J. 281 (1989); Daniel A. Farber, *The Inevitability of Practical Reason: Statutes, Formalism, and the Rule of Law*, 45 VAND. L. REV. 533 (1992) [hereinafter Farber, *Inevitability*]; John Manning, *Constitutional Structure and Statutory Formalism*, 66 U. CHI. L. REV. 685 (1999); Richard J. Pierce, Jr., *The Supreme Court's New Hypertextualism: An Invitation to Cacophony and Incoherence in the Administrative State*, 95 COLUM. L. REV. 749 (1995); Frederick Schauer, *Statutory Construction and the Coordinating Function of Plain Meaning*, 1990 SUP. CT. REV. 231; Cass R. Sunstein, *Interpreting Statutes in the Regulatory State*, 103 HARV. L. REV. 405 (1989); Adrian Vermeule, *Legislative History and the Limits of Judicial Competence: The Untold Story of Holy Trinity Church*, 50 STAN. L. REV. 1833 (1998).

[56] *See* Noël B. Cunningham & James R. Repetti, *Textualism and Tax Shelters*, 24 VA. TAX. REV. 1 (2004) (observing correlation between increased incidence of abusive tax shelters and belief in textualist styles of interpretation, prevalent among professional tax advisers).

even the simplest legal norms—in this case a simple statute—depends on interpretive understandings that are not captured in texts themselves. If a reader is persuaded in this case that non-textual conventions and practices of legal reasoning are actually relevant to determining the applicable law, then the only remaining step in the argument for professionalism is to establish the wrongfulness of ignoring them.

The Miserly Railroad

The Northern Atlantic Railroad asks its general counsel whether it must make an expensive modification to its locomotives. It is concerned that a new federal statute may mandate retrofitting the locomotives with an automatic coupling device.[57]

The relevant statutory language reads:

> On and after the first day of January, nineteen hundred and ninety-eight, it shall be unlawful for any such common carrier to haul or permit to be hauled or used on its line any car used in moving interstate traffic not equipped with couplers coupling automatically by impact, and which can be uncoupled without the necessity of men going between the ends of the cars.

The railroad's vice president of engineering tells the general counsel that for technical reasons, it is much more difficult to equip locomotives, as opposed to ordinary cars, with automatic coupling devices. She points out that the statute requires automatic couplers on "cars," which in the ordinary parlance of railroad workers would not be understood to include locomotives. (She actually overheard a snippet of dialogue in which one employee at a switching yard asked, "Are there any cars on that track?" and was told, "Nope, just a locomotive.") Moreover, the examples used to illustrate the definition of "car" in the Oxford English Dictionary all refer to conveyances that are pulled by a locomotive: passenger car, sleeping car, coal car, freight car, and so on. Her argument is supported by the statute's use of the verb "haul," of which "car" is an object—locomotives are not hauled; they do the hauling. The general counsel also remembers reading in law school a case involving the theft of an airplane, in which the Supreme Court noted that the operative term "vehicle" did not "evoke in the common mind" the image of an airplane.[58] What advice should the general counsel give to the railroad regarding compliance with the statute?

In this case, the content of the law on point is facially uncertain, if law is understood as a property of legal texts alone. The apparent uncertainty is the result of linguistic ambiguity or vagueness (does the term "car" encompass locomotives?). I suspect, however, that readers have already concluded that this case does not actually involve any

---

[57] This problem is based on *Johnson v. Southern Pacific Co.*, 196 U.S. 1 (1904), *rev'g* 117 F. 462 (8th Cir. 1902), two casebook classics illustrating issues in statutory interpretation, but I freely embellished many of the facts.

[58] McBoyle v. United States, 283 U.S. 25 (1931) (interpreting a statute criminalizing "transporting in interstate commerce a motor vehicle, knowing the same to have been stolen").

serious uncertainty and that the railroad must equip the locomotives with automatic couplers.[59] What justifies this conclusion? The answer to any question of legal interpretation is ultimately provided by the conventions and practices of legal reasoning, which form the basis for the exercise of informed, sound "situation sense," prudence, practical reasoning, or judgment.[60]

Legal reasoning begins with the text of statutes and the holdings of cases, but it does not end there. Indeed, a judge or lawyer might commit the vice of "hypertextualism" by pretending that the language of a statute, dictionary definitions, and rules of syntax are sufficiently determinate to produce an objective interpretation of a text.[61] Although the statute in the railroad case uses the word "car," the legislature may have intended to require coupling devices on locomotives as well (perhaps after hearing testimony about the frequency of locomotive-car coupling accidents), and only a myopic fixation on the literal language of the statute would cause an interpreter to miss this apparent meaning of the text. Moreover, statutory language, definitions of words, canons of construction, and so on, might create as much interpretive freedom as more expansive methods like purposivism or intentionalism, thereby permitting the interpreter to impose her own policy preferences on the text, under the guise of rendering an objective reading. Fortunately, in both of these styles of legal reasoning, there are second-level principles that have developed in any given domain of law that stabilize and regulate interpretation.[62]

---

[59] *Cf.* Frederick Schauer, *Easy Cases*, 58 S. CAL. L. REV. 1567 (1985) (arguing that doctrinal, factual, and linguistic factors may make a particular outcome easy for competent lawyers to predict).

[60] "Situation sense" is a term favored by Karl Llewellyn. *See* KARL LLEWELLYN, THE COMMON LAW TRADITION: DECIDING APPEALS 60-61, 268-85 (1960). Anthony Kronman uses the Aristotelian terms "prudence" (as a translation of *phronesis*) and "practical wisdom" to convey a similar notion. *See* ANTHONY T. KRONMAN, THE LOST LAWYER (1993); Anthony T. Kronman, *Alexander Bickel's Philosophy of Prudence*, 94 YALE L.J. (1985). Modern commentators on statutory interpretation favor the term "practical reason." *See*, e.g., Eskridge & Frickey, *supra* note 55; Farber, Inevitability, *supra* note 55; *see also* Burton, *supra* note 7, at 6 n.9 (citing sources). One might even use the term "pragmatism," as popularized by Richard Posner, among others. *See, e.g.,* Richard Posner, *Pragmatic Adjudication, in* THE REVIVAL OF PRAGMATISM 235 (Morris Dickstein ed., 1998). I will use the term judgment throughout the Article, but it should be understood that I am appealing to this vigorous tradition of legal theory, whatever label a particular writer chooses. And I intend as well to appeal (without elaboration, because of the constraints of space and relevance) to the work of critics within moral philosophy who *see*k to establish objective truths of ethics while making room for contextual judgment. *See, e.g.,* PUTNAM, *supra* note 42.

[61] Pierce, *supra* note 55, at 750-52.

[62] *See, e.g.,* MELVIN ARON EISENBERG, THE NATURE OF THE COMMON LAW (1988); Owen M. Fiss, *Objectivity and Interpretation*, 34 STAN. L. REV. 739 (1982); Pepper, *supra* note 19, at 1585-87 (summarizing a series of factors and distinctions that define the bounds of the law). Owen Fiss refers to the norms of an interpretive community as "disciplining rules," *see* Fiss, *supra*, at 744-45, but this imprecise use of the term "rules" has created unnecessary confusion, as is evident in Fiss's debate with Stanley Fish. *See* Stanley Fish, *Fish vs. Fiss*, 36 STAN. L. REV. 1325 (1984). Fish makes an infinite regress argument, noting that if these interpretive norms were indeed rules, they would stand in need of interpretation, requiring further meta-disciplining-rules. *See id.* at 1326, 1334. Instead of rules, Fish believes an interpretive community is constituted by "interpretive assumptions and procedures [that] are so widely shared in a community

The word "car" in isolation does inform whether the railroad is required to equip its locomotives with automatic couplers; if anything, it suggests a counterintuitive negative response. Starting with the text of the statute does tell us something; under this particular statute the railroad is not required to equip cars with air brakes, doors that can be opened from the inside, or some other useful safety feature. But the text still leaves interpretive puzzles. What about the absence of the term "locomotive" ? Congress could easily have drafted the provision to read "any car or locomotive . . . not equipped with couplers coupling automatically by impact." Under the canon of construction known as *expressio unius est exclusio alterius*,[63] an interpreter should infer from the inclusion of the term "car" and the absence of the term "locomotive" that Congress intended the statute not to apply to locomotives. Of course, as Karl Llewellyn demonstrated in one of the best known critiques of formalism, every canon of statutory construction has an opposing canon, which should be used "when the context dictates."[64] In this case, if the context so dictates, one could argue that locomotives should be included from the opposing canon that the statute may comprehend cases beyond those specifically mentioned in the text, particularly if it is apparent that the statute has a purpose (such as protecting the safety of railroad workers) that would be advanced by requiring couplers on locomotives.[65] Similarly, the lawyer might argue either that statutes in derogation of the common law rule (which would not have required couplers on locomotives) should be strictly construed, or that remedial statutes (which would require the couplers) should be construed liberally to accomplish their purpose.[66] And these are only principles of interpretation based on the language of a statute.

---

that the rule appears to all in the same (interpreted) shape." *Id.* at 1327. Fiss's argument, read carefully, is that there are "interpretive assumptions and procedures" that are widely shared within a community. Apparently Fiss actually does not disagree with Fish at all, and Fish has simply seized on Fiss's use of the word "rule" to argue against a position that Fiss does not hold.

[63] A NORMAN J. SINGER, SUTHERLAND STATUTORY CONSTRUCTION § 47.23, at 216-17 (5th ed. 1992). This was one of the arguments made by the court of appeals in this case. *See* Johnson v. S. Pac. Co., 117 F. 462, 466 (8th Cir. 1902) ("This striking omission to express any intention to prohibit the use of engines unequipped with automatic couplers raises the legal presumption that no such intention existed. . . .").

[64] Karl N. Llewellyn, *Remarks on the Theory of Appellate Decision and the Rules or Canons About How Statutes Are to Be Construed*, 3 VAND. L. REV. 395, 401-06 (1950). A notorious example of a court disregarding the expressio unius canon is *Church of the Holy Trinity v. United States*, 143 U.S. 457, 458, 463 (1892), in which a statute making it a crime to assist "the importation or migration of any alien" contained exceptions for certain categories of workers, such as lecturers, actors, and domestic servants, but said nothing about "brain toilers" and "ministers of the gospel." The Court nevertheless held the statute inapplicable to an elite New York City church which had arranged for the entry of its new rector from England.

[65] In reversing the Eighth Circuit, the Supreme Court relied heavily on congressional intention and the purpose of the statute. *See* Johnson v. S. Pac. Co., 196 U.S. 1, 14-17 (1904).

[66] The court of appeals opinion discusses these opposing canons. *See Johnson*, 117 F. at 464-65 ("[C]ounsel for the plaintiff persuasively argues that this is a remedial statute . . . and should be liberally construed, to prevent the mischief and advance the remedy"); *id.* at 466 ("A statute which thus changes the common law must be strictly construed.").

There are also policy-based aids to construction, such as the rule of lenity, which provides that an ambiguous criminal statute should be read narrowly.[67] The case mentioned by the railroad's vice president, involving the theft of an airplane, can arguably be justified on this basis. Furthermore, we can ascribe a variety of hypothetical intentions to Congress (in the absence of clear legislative history).[68] Perhaps Congress wanted to improve safety for railroad workers, even though it would impose high costs on the railroads, in which case couplers should be required on locomotives. On the other hand, the statute may have represented a compromise between workplace-safety advocates and the railroad industry, in which case it fairly should be read as requiring couplers only on non-locomotive cars.[69]

---

[67] 3 Singer, *supra* note 59, §59.03, at 102-05. The court of appeals also relied on the rule of lenity. *Johnson*, 117 F. at 467.

[68] Interpretation by ascription of intention is a disfavored methodology in modern jurisprudence, owing to powerful critiques by Dworkin and others. *See* Dworkin, *supra* note 27, at 313-27; Antonin Scalia, A Matter of Interpretation 29-32 (1997); Waldron, *supra* note 9, at 124-29; Easterbrook, *supra* note 55; Eskridge & Frickey, *supra* note 55, at 325-32; Stephen F. Williams, *Restoring Context, Distorting Text: Legislative History and the Problem of Age*, 66 Geo. Wash. L. Rev. 1366 (1998). Briefly, the problems with imputing intentions to a multi-member representative body are that there is no speaker or actor to whom to ascribe an actual unitary intention, and that constructing a fictional unitary intention by combining the intentions of individual legislators is doomed to failure because of theoretical difficulties involved in Identifying and cumulating the mental states of dozens, if not hundreds of legislators. Each legislator may have had a variety of mental states with respect to the proposed legislation—enthusiastic support, cautious assent, isolated qualms, serious reservations, or utter indifference. Legislators also may be moved by motives of rent-*see*king, party loyalty, or logrolling, without regard to the content of the provision under consideration. *See* Daniel A. Farber & Philip P. Frickey, Law and Public Choice (1991). Specifically with respect to intention regarding interpretation, a legislator may hope that an interpreter would read the text in a particular way, even though she fully expected a different interpretation to gain acceptance. Even if we could Identify the intentions of individuals, the actual text voted on by the majority may represent the intention of none of the individuals, because of the way preferences are registered in an assembly. Attempting to divine collective intention from legislative history is no less problematic, because of the malleability of legislative history and the multiplicity of interpretations that can be supported by the relevant history documents such as committee reports and remarks made on the floor by supporters and opponents of the bill. Interpreting statutes by selecting bits and pieces of legislative history has often been criticized as tantamount to "looking over a crowd and picking out your friends." Patricia Wald, *Some Observations on the Use of Legislative History in the 1981 Supreme Court Term*, 68 Iowa L. Rev. 195, 214 (1983); *see also* Conroy v. Aniskoff, 507 U.S. 511, 519 (1993) (Scalia, J., concurring). For an attempt to restore some jurisprudential significance to the lawmaker's intent, *see* Alexander & Sherwin, *supra* note 52, at 98-117.

[69] For a sophisticated discussion of the effect on interpretation of the lawmakers' and enforcement officials' understanding of the remedial purpose of a statute, *see* Pepper, *supra* note 19, at 1570-71. The scheme which limited couplers to non-locomotive cars might be an example of what Dworkin would call a "checkerboard" statute, which seems to resolve the dispute in an arbitrary or unprincipled way. *See* Dworkin, *supra* note 27, at 178-84. Dworkin believes he is tapping into a generally shared intuition that checkerboard statutes are objectionable because we would prefer ex ante that our preferred legal norm be either adopted or rejected, but not compromised. "Even if I thought strict liability for accidents wrong in principle, I would prefer that manufacturers of both washing machines and automobiles be held to that standard than that only one of them be." *Id.* at 182. But leaving aside obvious checkerboards like a statute that made abortion legal on Mondays but illegal on Tuesdays, it is not clear that all legislative compromises like Dworkin's products liability statute are unprincipled. There may be good reasons for imposing strict

As in most legal cases, it is possible to argue both positions in the railroad case. This is the point at which analysis of statutory interpretation often resorts to metaphors of weighing and balancing to capture the process of exercising judgment. The trouble with these tropes is that the process of comparison they suggest creates an illusion of precision which in turn encourages unrealistic expectations about the objectivity of judging. To put it another way, judgment sometimes functions as a black box in legal theory—one result or another mysteriously pops out of the decisionmaking machinery, but the process itself is opaque to third-party observation and criticism. Sophisticated legal theorists do not use judgment in this way, however. In every serious account of legal interpretation, the interpreter's judgment must be transparent—that is, available for public observation and criticism. Requiring the interpreter to justify her judgment to the public defends the judgment's objectivity against the critique that the interpreter is simply imposing her own policy preferences on the law.

For example, Ronald Dworkin is the most enthusiastic proponent of a thoroughgoing interpretive approach to law, and he is quite clear that his hypothetical interpreter, the superhuman judge Hercules, must exercise judgment with respect to an external standard. Hercules's standard is the best justification of a legal speech-act (a judicial decision or the enactment of a statute) where "best" is understood in terms of the coherence of the principles underlying the act (i.e., as reasons explaining and justifying the act) with a political community's ideals of integrity, fairness, and political due process.[70] Dworkin refers to this external constraint as integrity, and offers integrity as a criterion for others to judge whether Hercules has exercised his judgment correctly. Other theorists construct a framework of criteria, rebuttable presumptions, or a continuum of complementary interpretive methodologies.[71] However these external checks on interpretive discretion are constructed, they are essential to guard against both rampant subjectivity by the interpreter, and ex post evaluations of the propriety of an interpretation that would not have been as clear ex ante.[72]

liability on automobile manufacturers but not washing machine manufacturers. (Perhaps washing machines are easier for users to inspect for defects, or the expected cost of accidents is not as high, as compared with automobiles.) In the railroad case, if for some reason it is significantly more expensive to install couplers on locomotives, or if the operation of automatic couplers on locomotives creates some new danger that would not be present if they were used only on non-locomotive cars, the exclusion of locomotives from the coupler requirement would not be a checkerboard statute in Dworkin's sense.

[70] DWORKIN, *supra* note 27, at 337-38, 345-46.

[71] *See* Eskridge, *supra* note 5, at 1496-97 (proposing continuum in which text controls where it provides determinate answers, but history, social and legal context, and evolutive context assume more importance as textualist interpretations become more contestable); Esklrldge & Frickey, *supra* note 55, at 352-53 (proposing "funnel of abstraction" in which interpreter begins with statutory text and tests potential interpretations for historical accuracy and conformity to contemporary circumstances and values); Pepper, *supra* note 19, at 1607-09 (relying on moral perception and character to constrain the exercise of judgment).

[72] *Cf.* Schwarcz, *supra* note 15, at 1313 (suggesting that some of the decisions of accountants and lawyers in the Enron transactions may look bad ex post, but at the time were defensible exercises of discretionary judgment).

To these models of judgment I would add a critical jurisprudential element: interpretation is not a function of a single judicial or lawyerly mind, acting alone.[73] Rather, it is a community-bound enterprise, in which the criteria for reasonable exercise of judgment are elaborated intersubjectively, among an interpretive community that is constituted by fidelity to law. These criteria are available to provide a justification of a decision.[74] As Anthony Kronman correctly points out, a person characterized by good judgment "is not someone who from time to time merely makes certain strikingly appropriate oracular pronouncements."[75] Rather, a person of good judgment can, if called upon to do so, provide a reasoned explanation of her decision.[76] This explanation is a public phenomenon, in the sense that the interpreter is appealing to shared community standards for evaluating the appropriateness of interpretation. In this way, the interpreter's discretion is constrained by public norms regulating the understanding of legal texts.[77] The meaning of these texts therefore becomes a property of the community,

---

[73] Gerald Postema, *"Protestant" Interpretation and Social Practices*, 6 LAW & PHIL. 283 (1987).

[74] *See* BURTON, *supra* note 7, at 19-22 (arguing that the rule of law demands that judges be able to justify their decisions on the basis of reasons about what the law is, as opposed to what they think it should be); WILLIAM TWINING, KARL LLEWELLYN AND THE REALIST MOVEMENT 205 (1973) (discussing Llewellyn's arguments in *The Common Law Tradition*).

[75] Anthony T. Kronman, *Living in the Law*, 54 U. CHI. L. REV. 835, 849 (1987).

[76] HART & SACKS, *supra* note 53, at 143. I do not take a position on whether professionals consciously rely on these criteria when exercising judgment. One influential account of professional judgment emphasizes the extent to which this knowledge is tacit, although it can be given structure through reflection. *See* DONALD A. SCHÖN, THE REFLECTIVE PRACTITIONER: HOW PROFESSIONALS THINK IN ACTION (1983). Others have pointed to research showing that if it is possible to specify criteria for the exercise of judgment, one generally does better by following a mechanical decision procedure than by committing the ultimate decision to the discretion of a professional. KATZ, *supra* note 15, at 14-16. What matters for the purposes of this argument is that legal judgments can be objective to the extent they are justified through publicly available reasons.

[77] This observation is not limited to legal rules, but can be generalized to all linguistic assertions, because language itself can never capture all of the shared understandings that are necessary to make communication intelligible. Even the seemingly clearest possible assertion, such as *"68 + 57 = 125,"* can be understood only in light of intersubjective assumptions about the permissible use of language. SAUL A. KRIPKE, WITTGENSTEIN ON RULES AND PRIVATE LANGUAGE (1982). In our community, the "+" sign is understood to denote addition, but there is no reason, internal to the utterance *"68 + 57 = 125,"* that the "+" sign could not denote "quaddition," that is, the operation "add the two quantities if both are less than 57, otherwise return the value 5." This observation does not mean that "*68 + 57 = 125*" has no determinate meaning, only that its meaning is not a function solely of the symbols written on the page, nor of other facts such as past usage of the "+" symbol, dispositions to use it in a certain way, or intentions. The "quaddition" interpretation is ruled out only by interpretive understandings shared by the community of language-users who wish to communicate with each other, which understandings are internalized and followed unconsciously by members of the community. It is nevertheless the case that "*68 + 57 = 125*" is objectively true. But why cannot one argue that the community is actually engaging in "quinterpretation," which follows interpretive understandings that yield the true proposition, *"68 + 57 = 5"*? Kripke's insight is that the principle of interpretation itself cannot announce that it is not a principle of quinterpretation, and moreover there cannot be another meta-principle ruling out quinterpretation within the legal system because that meta-principle itself must be interpreted.

which confers the ultimate authority on legal norms, and the community's standards are legitimate to the extent they respect the purpose of law, which is to enable people to live peacefully together, flourish, and achieve their common ends.

A textualist might respond that I have assumed too hastily that judgment is necessary. Perhaps the plain language of the statute provides sufficient determinacy to accomplish the settlement of normative disputes that is the function of law. One might also make the argument from the authority of law by noting that legal norms are legitimate only to the extent they are enacted by fair procedures, and in the case of legislation, fair procedures involve a majority vote on a particular form of words embodied in the resolution under discussion.[78] But the argument from authority shows only that "the product of legislation" is entitled to respect, not that the product of legislation is simply a text, the interpretation of which is confined to the literal language of the enactment. Even Jeremy Waldron, who makes the argument from authority powerfully, concedes that "statutes need interpretation [and] the words of the enactment (and their 'plain meaning') are often insufficient to determine the statute's application."[79] For Waldron, the important thing is that the interpretive process begin with the sense that there is a single, definitive proposal under discussion, and that the meaning of the proposal should be recovered by beginning with the text of the enactment. Suppose in the railroad case that the legislature had responded to a series of lurid reports of accidents and resulting public outcry. In the course of considering some response, it became apparent that workers were injured by attaching locomotives to cars as well as by hooking non-locomotive cars together. The course of discussion in the legislature reveals that all members of the assembly were concerned with this problem in toto, although the members disagreed on other points, such as whether to make new safety measures mandatory or voluntary.[80] In that instance, is there any doubt that the word "car" should be interpreted to include locomotives? This interpretation is not undermined by the reasons for treating the enactment as authoritative, because the legislative response was aimed at settling some disagreement other than a disagreement over whether the word "car" should

---

To avoid an infinite regress, it is necessary to take a normative stance on interpretation that is rooted in something external to the system of rules (or language, law, or anything else) that we are considering. This pattern of argument leads to the conclusion, in jurisprudence, that legal texts themselves cannot perfectly constrain interpretation in all cases. Nevertheless, the theory of law advanced here is still positivistic, because the law is capable of identification without resort to moral argumentation. For this definition of positivism, see Jules Coleman, *Negative and Positive Positivism, in* MARKETS, MORALS AND THE LAW 3, 4-5, 16 (1998). Dworkin resists the argument that a positivist theory can rely on a norm that is accepted as part of a legal system because of "a sense of appropriateness developed in the profession." Ronald Dworkin, *The Model of Rules I, in* TAKING RIGHTS SERIOUSLY 14, 24 (1977). But I follow Jules Coleman in believing that a rule of recognition may take account of interpretive conventions or practices. *See* Jules Coleman, *Authority and Reason, in* THE AUTONOMY OF LAW: ESSAYS ON LEGAL POSITIVISM 287 (Robert P. George ed., 1996); *see also* H.L.A. Hart, Postscript, in HART, *supra* note 27, at 237, 241-42.

[78] WALDRON, *supra* note 9, at 25, 77-82.

[79] *Id.* at 79.

[80] *See* ALEXANDER & SHERWIN, *supra* note 52, at 114-15 (arguing that the lawmaker's purposes can provide context that makes interpretation determinate in some cases).

include locomotives. Thus, one should not assume that the functional argument for the authority of law necessarily entails a textualist interpretive methodology; in fact, it may support a broader purposivist approach to statutory meaning.[81]

These higher-order norms regulating the exercise of judgment are legitimate, and have authority to the exclusion of ordinary moral reasons, to the extent they enable the law to fulfill its function of optimizing people's ability to work together to achieve common projects.[82] The law would fail at this end if one of two conditions obtained: (1) it were impossible for a representative of a client to discern the content of the law, or (2) it were permissible for individual legal interpreters, such as lawyers, to manipulate the formal expression of legal norms to make them mean anything at all. Thus, returning to our examples, if it is apparent that the purpose of the statute in the railroad case is to prevent accidents caused by workers getting their hands caught in manual coupling mechanisms, there will be good grounds for interpreting the statute to require automatic couplers on locomotives. Naturally, a contrary purpose may be apparent—perhaps, as suggested previously, the statute was a compromise between advocates of a comprehensive reform of railroad safety regulations and those who preferred a more cautious, incremental approach. In that case, one might make a reasonable argument for not requiring the automatic couplers on locomotives. But the crucial term here is "reasonable." The demand is, in any event, for a reasoned elaboration of an interpretation of legal texts. Appealing only to formal features like the statutory text is not a reasoned elaboration, absent some argument why the form alone ought to have dispositive importance in the particular case.[83]

Finally, it is worth observing that judgment is also necessary in common-law reasoning because it is impossible fully to specify meta-rules that capture the complexity of legal interpretation. The decisionmaker must consider texts, principles, and facts, as well as subsidiary norms such as rules of legal salience (which point to aspects of the facts that are germane to the decision), considerations of weight and priority among competing norms, and the possibility of justified departures from previously sanctioned

[81] *See* William N. Eskridge, Jr., *The Circumstances of Politics and the Application of Statutes*, 100 COLUM. L. REV. 558, 566 (2000) (reviewing WALDRON, *supra* note 9); Lawrence M. Solan, *Private Language, Public Laws: The Central Role of Legislative Intent in Statutory Interpretation*, 93 GEO. L.J. 427 (2005) ("At the very least [legislative history] can help us to determine whether the difficulty in applying the statute results from an unfortunate choice of statutory language to effectuate a legislative goal that is very clear once one investigates the matter.").

[82] HART & SACKS, *supra* note 53, at 146-48.

[83] Kripke's interpretation of Wittgenstein makes a similar point in a different way, noting that for utterances to be said to conform to a rule, they must not only conform to assertability conditions, but also that there is some point, within the community of language-users, of making this type of utterance under these conditions. *See* KRIPKE, *supra* note 77, at 92; *see also* BARBARA HERMAN, THE PRACTICE OF MORAL JUDGMENT 83-84 (1993) (discussing rules of moral salience, which specify features of a situation that are relevant to the exercise of moral judgment, and noting that not just any rules count as rules of moral salience); Schauer, *supra* note 55, at 251 (asserting that members of linguistic communities not only share the ability to make sense of utterances, but do the same things with linguistic understandings).

interpretations. Consider a famous example of the interplay between facts and rules in case interpretation, from Karl Llewellyn's *Bramble Bush*:

> What are *the facts*? The plaintiff's name is Atkinson and the defendant's Walpole. The defendant, despite his name, is an Italian by extraction, but the plaintiff's ancestors came over with the Pilgrims. The defendant has a schnauzer-dog named Walter, red hair, and $30,000 worth of life insurance. . . . The defendant's auto was a Buick painted pale magenta. He is married. His wife was in the back seat, an irritable, somewhat faded blonde. She was attempting back-seat driving when the accident occurred. He had turned around to make objection. In the process the car swerved and hit the plaintiff. The sun was shining; there was a rather lovely dappled sky low to the West. The time was late October on a Tuesday. The road was smooth, concrete. It had been put in by the McCarthy Road Work Company.[84]

It does not take more than a couple of weeks of law school for a first-year student to learn to winnow out the relevant facts from an example like this. But what has the student learned? Surely not a system of rules that can be applied deductively (e.g., "if the dispute involves an auto accident, road conditions may be relevant but not the plaintiff's ethnic ancestry"), because any set of rules would quickly become too complex to learn and apply. For example, the identity of the construction company may or may not be legally salient, depending on whether the case involves allegations that the design of the road contributed to poor visibility. Life insurance may matter if this is a case in which the collateral source rule is an issue. Even the ethnic background of the plaintiff and defendant might conceivably matter if the auto accident had been only the precursor to a violent argument in which insults were exchanged, and out of which the plaintiff claims infliction of emotional distress.[85] Some knowledge of the law is necessary to know which facts are relevant, but the relevance-making relationship between law and facts is not constituted by rules.[86] Instead of rule-application,

---

[84] KARL LLEWELLYN, THE BRAMBLE BUSH 48 (1951).

[85] *See, e.g.,* Taylor v. Metzger, 706 A.2d 685 (N.J. 1998) (recognizing cause of action for intentional infliction of emotional distress arising out of racial epithets uttered in an employment setting).

[86] *See* Michael S. Moore, *Torture and the Balance of Evils*, 23 ISR. L. REV. 280, 287-88 (1989) (arguing that moral knowledge of the domain of consequentialist calculation is needed before it is possible to proceed to consider consequences in moral reasoning); *cf.* HERMAN, *supra* note 83, at 75 ("An agent who came to the [Kantian Categorical Imperative] procedure with no knowledge of the moral characteristics of actions would be very unlikely to describe his action in a morally appropriate way."). Note that Moore does not subscribe to an intuitionist view, in which knowledge of the domain of consequentialist calculation is something mysterious and ineffable; rather, he reviews numerous rigorous standards (such as the act/omission and intended/foreseeable distinctions, the pre-existing peril doctrine, and Judith Jarvis Thomson's principle of redirecting harms) which justify the boundary between permissible and impermissible use of consequences in moral reasoning. Moore, *supra*, at 299-308. Moore boils these down to the standard threefold analysis of criminal law culpability, *id.* at 308-09, but the application of these criteria still calls for the exercise of judgment, as opposed to deductive reasoning. The point is not that the student's judgment

this reasoning process involves the exercise of informed professional judgment, which can be justified on the basis of rules and standards, but which is always incompletely specified, or underdetermined by rules and standards. Lawyers acquire and internalize these higher-order norms through professional education, and follow them largely unconsciously within a given interpretive community.

C. Hard Cases and Right Answers

Building on this last point, and to anticipate a common objection to this line of reasoning, it is important to emphasize that I am not denying the existence of "hard cases," where the relevant legal texts and interpretive practices underdetermine the result.[87] In *The Legal Process,* Hart and Sacks confidently assert that "[u]nderlying every rule and standard . . . is at least a policy and in most cases a principle [which is] available to guide judgment in resolving uncertainties about the arrangement's meaning."[88] Although I share their belief that underlying purposes, policies, and principles are available to guide judgment, the passage quoted is made too strong by the singular nouns—a policy, a principle. Many legal rules and standards serve multiple, sometimes conflicting purposes. In addition, purpose is not the only key to a statute's meaning—the express language of the statute may be in conflict with its purpose, and there may be other indications, such as legislative history and context, that cut against the interpretation suggested by the apparent purpose (even if there is only one). For these reasons, there are a great many cases in which a competent judge or lawyer, reasoning in good faith, could reach result A or result B, and be deemed by a competent observer to have performed her job adequately.[89] An observer might disagree with B, and believe that A was the better result, but nevertheless concede that B was within the range of plausible, justifiable results.[90]

---

in my example, or the ascription of responsibility in Moore's, is incapable of being justified or theorized, but that the precise nature of reasoning process is often opaque to the person exercising judgment.

[87] *See* ALEXANDER & SHERWIN, *supra* note 52, at 115-16; BURTON, *supra* note 7, at xii, 5-12, 47-48, 79-80. The term "hard cases" is associated with Dworkin's debate with Hart. *See* Ronald Dworkin, *Hard Cases, in* DWORKIN, *supra* note 77, at 81.

[88] HART & SACKS, *supra* note 53, at 148.

[89] Kent Greenawalt, *Discretion and the Judicial Decision: The Elusive Quest for the Fetters That Bind Judges,* 75 COLUM. L. REV. 359, 368-69 (1975).

[90] I do not believe it is possible to define "plausible" legal arguments in mathematical terms—e.g., whether a 10% chance, a 30% chance, and so on, is necessary before we can deem an interpretation of law plausible. These numbers create an illusion of precision by masking the uncertainty and guesswork that goes into coming up with the number. Instead, the plausibility standard should be understood in terms of an attitude or conviction on the part of the lawyer who offers the interpretation and may be fleshed out with reference to a kind of hypothetical reasonable observer. Plausibility certainly requires more than passing the proverbial straight-face test. One possible heuristic is that if a lawyer would be comfortable making the argument to the judge for whom she clerked, a professor she respects, or a colleague who is known for her good sense and judgment, the argument is plausible. If the lawyer could stand behind an

For example, consider a municipal ordinance that bans vehicles in excess of 6000 pounds from residential streets. The ordinance is intended to reduce wear and tear on municipal streets, as well as prevent accidents caused by heavy trucks driving in residential neighborhoods. Does the ordinance apply to monster sport-utility vehicles like the Ford Excursion and Cadillac Escalade?[91] Not only do large SUVs fall within the prohibition created by the literal language of the statute, but they pose many of the same dangers; they are within the "mischief" sought to be remedied by the statute, as British lawyers would say.[92] On the other hand, these ordinances were mostly enacted before the widespread craze for SUVs, particularly the subgenre of gigantic vehicles that weigh as much as commercial trucks. The drafters of the ordinances probably did not intend to target vehicles that are owned primarily for personal use. Moreover, the law is generally quite lenient on SUVs, granting their owners special tax breaks and their manufacturers exemptions from passenger car fuel economy standards.[93] Thus,

---

interpretation, take pride in it, and offer it to a third party the lawyer respects for her sound judgment, then the interpretation is plausible.

I recognize that it can be difficult to give a rigorous logical account of the distinction between a plainly implausible legal argument (say, one with only a 1% chance of success) and a clearly plausible one (say, one with a 98% chance of success), just as it is difficult to differentiate formally between a heap of stones and a non-heap. *See* Sorites Paradox, *in* THE CAMBRIDGE DICTIONARY OF PHILOSOPHY 864 (Robert Audi ed., 2d ed. 1999); Jeremy Waldron, *Vagueness in Law and Language: Some Philosophical Issues*, 82 CAL. L. REV. 509 (1994). But law does not lend itself to bivalent logic (i.e., heap vs. non-heap, or frivolous vs. non-frivolous) and always demands the exercise of judgment. Further support for this assertion must await the arguments in Part III. As a preliminary matter, even if we are uncertain whether we need three, four, five, or *n* stones to make a heap, it does not mean that there are no such things as heaps. Moore, *supra* note 86, at 332. By analogy, even if we may be unsure on the margins whether an argument is frivolous, we should not conclude that there is no such thing as a frivolous argument.

In some contexts the law governing lawyers does adopt pseudo-mathematical standards for plausibility or frivolousness. For example, Treasury Department Circular 230, regulating practice before the Internal Revenue Service, permits a lawyer to sign a tax return only where each position in the return has a "realistic possibility of being sustained on its merits." *See* 31 C.F.R. § 10.34(a) (2004). "Realistic possibility" is further defined as "approximately a one in three, or greater likelihood" of being sustained on the merits. *Id.* § 10.34(d)(1); *see also* ABA Comm. on Ethics and Prof'l Responsibility, Formal Op. 352 (1985) (also adopting a "realistic possibility" standard); ABA SPECIAL TASK FORCE REPORT ON FORMAL OPINION 85-352, *reported in* 39 TAX LAW. 635, 638 (1986) (stating that a position with a 5% to 10% chance of success on the merits would not have a realistic possibility of success, while one with a one in three chance would). As suggested previously, I believe these numbers only obscure the issue by deflecting attention away from the lawyer's attitude toward the interpretation. "Realistic possibility" seems better defined in terms of something like "confident endorsement" or whether the lawyer would be comfortable putting her reputation for sound judgment on the line by standing behind the interpretation.

[91] *See* Andy Bowers, *California's SUV Ban*, SLATE, (Aug. 4, 2004), *at* http://slate.msn.com/Id/2104755.

[92] *See* Heydon's Case, 76 Eng. Rep. 637, 638 (Ex. 1584).

[93] *See* Union of Concerned Scientists, *Tax Incentives: SUV Loophole Widens, Clean Vehicle Credits Face Uncertain Future*, *at* http://www.ucsusa.org/clean_vehicles/cars_and_suvs/page.cfm?pageID=1280 (last visited Aug. 4, 2004).

one could plausibly argue that the most reasonable interpretation of the ordinance would not apply to SUVs.

What is critical in hard cases is that the judge argues for A or B on the basis of what might be called "internal" legal reasons, and do so in a way that is respectful of the social function of law.[94] In order to respect the law, these justifications must be based on reasons that could be advanced publicly in an adversarial process in which reasons are given in support of one's position.[95] It is not necessary that all interpreters agree on the result, as long as the result is justifiable in principle on the basis of internal legal reasons. Internal legal reasons are simply those grounds (texts, principles that are fairly deemed to underlie and justify legal rules, interpretive practices, hermeneutic methods, and so on) that are properly regarded in a professional community as appropriate reasons to offer in justification of a result. In the SUV case, the arguments back and forth were offered on the basis of reasons such as the underlying policies (reducing wear and tear on streets), traditional canons of statutory construction (the mischief rule), and interpretive practices that place a single text in a broader legal context (observing the solicitude for SUVs in environmental and tax law). Perhaps it is most natural to define internal legal reasons negatively, as excluding extraneous factors such as a bribe, gratitude for a party's support in a judicial election, information excluded by evidentiary rules, the flip of a coin, or what the judge ate for breakfast.[96] Providing a positive definition of internal legal reasons is a major task of analytic jurisprudence, and the next Part will consider how seemingly esoteric academic debates can actually have a great deal of practical significance in shaping the way lawyers understand their role in relation to the law.

Before moving on to that discussion, however, it is necessary to consider a seeming inconsistency between the demands of professionalism in litigation versus transactional and counseling contexts. In an easy case, a lawyer is not justified in urging a court to

---

[94] In fairness to Hart and Sacks, they recognize the problem of indeterminacy:

> It may even be said that more than one answer is permissible, in the sense that if one answer had been conscientiously reached and generally accepted a reviewing court might well think it ought not to be upset, even though its own answer would have been different as an original matter.

HART & SACKS, *supra* note 53, at 149. Fairly or not, however, *The Legal Process* has become known as the *locus classicus* of the attribution-of-purpose method of statutory interpretation, and Hart and Sacks are usually understood to have relied on an assumption that a statute, case, or legal doctrine has a single purpose standing behind it. *See, e.g.,* Eskridge & Frickey, *supra* note 55, at 333-37. I do want to make clear that I do not subscribe to the interpretation of Hart and Sacks that assumes a single purpose lying behind a regime of legal rules and standards.

[95] *See* MICHAEL IGNATIEFF, THE LESSER EVIL: POLITICAL ETHICS IN AN AGE OF TERROR 49-53 (2004) (arguing that the rule of law does not require invariance, but does require public justification).

[96] The familiar reference to "what the judge had for breakfast" as a basis for judicial decisions is a caricature of American legal realism. Most realists believed that judicial decisions fell into predictable patterns, influenced by various social forces. Only a small faction of realists argued that the reasons for judicial decisions were completely idiosyncratic, a claim whose plausibility is undermined by the ability of lawyers to predict judicial decisions with a fair degree of reliability. *See generally* Brian Leiter, *American Legal Realism, in* THE BLACKWELL GUIDE TO PHILOSOPHY OF LAW AND LEGAL THEORY (Martin Golding ed., 2004).

adopt a spurious interpretation of law; neither is she permitted to structure a transaction in order to take advantage of an illegitimate construction of applicable legal rules. The law governing lawyers—both the state bar disciplinary rules and the law of civil procedure—prohibits advancing frivolous legal arguments.[97] In a hard case, however, it is an implication of professionalism that a lawyer may advocate for an interpretation in litigation that she would be prohibited from adopting as the basis for legal advice to a client or the structure of a transaction. There are such contextual distinctions in the law of lawyering, most notably in the Securities and Exchange Commission's regulations implementing the Sarbanes-Oxley Act. This Act requires lawyers in some cases to report information "up the ladder" within a corporation where they reasonably believe their client is committing certain wrongful acts, but do not require reporting up where the lawyer is representing the client in litigation over the wrongful act.[98] The distinction may nevertheless be incoherent if it amounts to a requirement that the lawyer assert, in litigation, an interpretation of the law that she would be prohibited from relying upon in transactional representation.[99]

It is important to note that my distinction between the transactional and litigation contexts is not an ontological or epistemological claim that the law is actually different in these contexts, or that it may be more easily recovered in one setting than the other. The applicable law and the process of interpretation are the same in both settings. The difference is, in hard cases, the responsibility to serve as a custodian of the law is primarily the judge's, with limited coordinate duties on lawyers to avoid advancing frivolous legal arguments, withholding adverse legal authority missed by the adversary, falsifying evidence, or permitting perjury to taint the record.[100] The lawyer is justified in advancing an aggressive or novel interpretation of law in litigation, as long as there is some good faith basis for the argument, because the judge is always in a position to reject it. Metaphorically, the lawyer in a litigated matter may aim somewhat less accurately at the law, and trust the procedures of adjudication to ensure the right result in the end. A judge, or a lawyer in a transactional matter must take more care and aim more precisely. The law is the same in both cases, but the responsibility for getting it right shifts among the various actors in the legal system, depending on the degree of procedural checking that is available.[101]

---

[97] *See* MODEL RULES, *supra* note 20, R. 3.1; RESTATEMENT (THIRD) OF THE LAW GOVERNING LAWYERS § 110 (2000); FED. R. CIV. P. 11.

[98] *Compare* 17 C.F.R. § 205.3(b)(2)-(3) (2003) (duty to report where representing issuer in non-litigation context), *with* 17 C.F.R. § 205.3(b)(7)(ii) (no duty to report up where lawyer retained "[t]o assert, consistent with his or her professional obligations, a colorable defense on behalf of the issuer . . . in any investigation or judicial or administrative proceeding relating to such evidence of a material violation").

[99] Thanks to Dennis Tuchler and Emily Sherwin for raising this problem with me.

[100] For these litigation-related duties, *see* MODEL RULES, *supra* note 20, R. 3.1 (frivolous legal arguments), R. 3.3(a)(1), (3) (perjury), R. 3.3(a)(2) (adverse legal authority), R. 3.4(b) (falsifying evidence).

[101] *Cf.* WOLFMAN ET AL., *supra* note 45, § 204.2.2, at 77 (noting that the ABA's opinion on tax advising *seems* to require a lawyer to weigh the relevant authorities just as a court would when considering the issue). The claim that a lawyer's "caretaker" responsibility varies by the degree of procedural checking is

Transactional and planning situations are distinctive precisely because there is no impartial referee to resist the lawyer's client-centered construction of the law. The lawyer is the sole legal interpreter and is therefore, in effect, a law-giver from the client's point of view. As such, the lawyer has the power to shape the law for good or for ill. As Spider-Man observed, with great power comes great responsibility, for if the lawyer does not internalize the judicial virtues of impartiality and objectivity, the law will be distorted by partisan zeal where no neutral third party can check this tendency. In litigation, the lawyer's partisan stance and greater flexibility to advance aggressive or novel interpretations of legal rules makes the law itself more flexible and adaptable. If similar interpretive license were permitted in transactional work, however, the legal system would lose some of the virtues identified with the rule of law, such as stability, predictability, and certainty. Legal theory must always balance the need for growth and change with the values of stability and resistance to manipulation. The distinction between transactional and litigation-related representation is one way to strike this balance.

III. ARGUMENTS FOR PROFESSIONALISM

A. Identification and Interpretation of Legal Norms

I have been defending the view that the social function of law is the settlement of uncertainty and normative conflict, and this requires a system of legal norms that can be identified without reference to the truth of moral beliefs. This is an argument about the nature of law. Even if one accepts this account of the nature of law, however, there can be further controversy over the law in a given case.[102] The law on a particular issue must be sufficiently determinate such that the matter may be resolved by reference to the law, rather than to any of the reasons that were at stake in the underlying normative disagreement. The question of the identity of the law, as opposed to the nature of law, is case-specific and interpretive. It can be stated concisely in one of the following ways: "What does it mean to say that a proposition of law is true?"[103] or "With respect to some action, is it legally permitted?"

The controversy about the law can also be understood in terms of criteria for the objectivity of legal decisions. If a judge decides that there is a constitutional right to same-sex marriage, or to obtain an abortion, or to use marijuana for the purpose of alleviating pain, the question naturally arises whether the decision is just the judge's

---

also supported by IRS regulations which permit lawyers to take more aggressive or adversarial positions in tax filings as long as they are adequately disclosed to the IRS. *See* 31 C.F.R. § 10.34(a) (2002) (Circular 230 Regulating Practice Before the Treasury).

[102] Hart drew this distinction, which he accused Dworkin of blurring. *See* HART, *supra* note 77, at 247-48. Waldron explicitly connects the problem of interpretation with the authority of law: "If enacted law is to settle at least some cases at the level of particularity at which they present themselves, a rule of recognition will need to provide a basis for specifying not only which proposal, but *which version* of a given proposal, has been enacted." WALDRON, *supra* note 9, at 39.

[103] *See* DENNIS PATTERSON, LAW & TRUTH 3 (1996).

subjective belief about what the law ought to be, or whether it is in fact an accurate report on what the law is, or at least a defensible judgment where the legal issue could have more than one plausible resolution.[104] Most attempts to understand the nature of objectivity in legal reasoning have addressed the predicament of a judge who must decide a case, or a critic of a judicial decision.[105] With respect to an interpretive question in law, if there is an objective or determinate right answer, a range of plausible right answers, or at least a wrong answer, then it is possible to criticize the judge for making a mistake. If there is no such thing as objectivity or determinacy in law, however, the law does not provide a standpoint for criticizing the judge.

Lawyers too, must worry about whether legal interpretation can be objective or determinate, because when they act in a representative capacity, they enable or limit their clients' enjoyment of legal entitlements.[106] If a client has a legal right to disinherit his son for opposing the war in Vietnam,[107] but his lawyer refuses to draft a will with this effect because of her moral disagreement with the client's desire, the lawyer has blocked the client's enjoyment of a right that the legal system would recognize if asserted—namely, the right to cut his son out of his inheritance. The client may be able to find another lawyer to draft the will, but regardless of whether the client eventually gets his wish, one could ask whether the original lawyer acted wrongly vis-à-vis the client's legal entitlement. The first step in that analysis would be to ascertain the content of the law of wills. For example, in Louisiana a parent can disinherit a child for only one of ten enumerated "just causes," which must be set forth specifically in the will.[108] Unless the hypothetical occurred in Louisiana, however, the testator's freedom is virtually unrestricted, except by pretermitted heir statutes, which require that the will expressly state the intent to disinherit the son.[109] In a state with such a statute, the lawyer may believe her refusal to cooperate with the client to be morally justified, and she may

---

[104] *See* Fiss, *supra* note 62, at 742.

[105] The most helpful discussions include KENT GREENAWALT, LAW AND OBJECTIVITY (1992); JOHN RAWLS, POLITICAL LIBERALISM 110-16 (1993); Jules L. Coleman & Brian Leiter, *Determinacy, Objectivity, and Authority, in* LAW AND INTERPRETATION 203 (Andrei Marmor ed., 1995); Andrei Marmor, *Three Concepts of Objectivity, in* POSITIVE LAW AND OBJECTIVE VALUES 112 (2001); Gerald J. Postema, *Objectivity Fit for Law, in* OBJECTIVITY IN LAW AND MORALS 99 (Brian Leiter ed., 2001).

[106] EISENBERG, *supra* note 62, at 10 ("[I]n the vast majority of cases where law becomes important to private actors, as a practical matter the institution that determines the law is not the courts, but the legal profession . . . ."); *see also* RESTATEMENT (THIRD) OF THE LAW GOVERNING LAWYERS § 23 cmt. c (2000) ("Lawyers who exercise their skill and knowledge so as to deprive others of their rights or to obstruct the legal system subvert the justifications of their calling.").

[107] Richard Wasserstrom, *Lawyers as Professionals: Some Moral Issues*, 5 HUM. RTS. 1, 7-8 (1975) (using this example to illustrate the tension between legal entitlements and ordinary moral reasons).

[108] *See* Max Nathan, Jr., *An Assault on the Citadel: A Rejection of Forced Heirship*, 52 TUL. L. REV. 5, 12 (1977). None of the grounds stated would encompass Wasserstrom's hypothetical—they cover situations such as the child "rais[ing] his hand to strike a parent" or an adult child failing to communicate with a parent, without just cause, for two years. *See* LA. CIV. CODE ANN. art. 1621 (West 2001).

[109] *See* WILLIAM M. MCGOVERN, JR., WILLS, TRUSTS AND ESTATES § 3.6 (1988).

further believe that her moral obligation not to assist the client outweighs her moral obligation to obey the law. But as long as she is a competent lawyer, she will not deny that the governing law would have permitted the client to disinherit his son.

This is obviously an exceptionally simple example,[110] but it illustrates what is at stake for lawyers in the attempt to characterize objectivity in legal interpretation: If the objectively correct interpretation of an applicable legal norm is that the client has a right to do X, then the lawyer in an existing lawyer-client relationship must justify her refusal to assist the client in doing X in moral terms. On the other hand, if one cannot say objectively that legal norms permit the client to do X, then the lawyer has no burden to justify her refusal morally—she can appeal instead to an interpretation of the law. Notice that the will example assumes the lawyer is motivated not to assist her client. The possibility that law is indeterminate creates a different, but equally serious ethical problem if the lawyer is motivated to do anything at all for her (presumably high-paying) client. If one cannot say objectively that the client is not legally entitled to do Y, and Y is a socially harmful thing to do, then the lawyer may assist her client doing Y to cause a significant amount of harm, and there is no legal standpoint from which we can criticize the lawyer for helping the client do Y.

In order to determine whether lawyers are subject to criticism from the point of view of the law, we must first determine what the law is with respect to the transaction in which the lawyer's services are being employed. Except in simple examples like the railroad case or the Louisiana will hypothetical, ascertaining the law in real world situations is not a matter of reading unambiguous statutory language and applying the rule it announces to a case within the core of the statute's plain meaning.[111] Finding the relevant rule is a much more complicated interpretive exercise in most cases, because of familiar problems with the use of verbally formulated rules to guide conduct. In

---

[110] Simple examples are sometimes useful to argue against the view that all legal texts present serious problems of indeterminacy. *See* BURTON, *supra* note 7, at 9-10 nn.20-21 (citing extensive collection of Critical Legal Studies sources urging that indeterminacy is a pervasive and unavoidable aspect of legal interpretation). Although it is possible to overgeneralize from easy cases, it is nevertheless worth noting that there are practically infinite examples that can be offered of uncontroversial interpretation of legal norms. *See, e.g.*, Lawrence B. Solum, *On the Indeterminacy Crisis: Critiquing Critical Dogma*, 54 U. CHI. L. REV. 462 (1987). The strongest form of the indeterminacy claim—that "doctrinal inconsistency necessarily undermines the force of any conventional legal argument"—is fairly straightforwardly refuted by stating propositions such as, the "first paragraph of this essay does not slander Gore Vidal." *Id.* at 471-72 (citing Clare Dalton, An Essay in the Deconstruction of Contract Doctrine, 94 Yale L.J. 997 (1985)); *cf.* PUTNAM, *supra* note 42, at 116-19 (arguing against the view that interpretation is called for in every case).

[111] For the terminology of "core" meaning, *see* H.L.A. Hart, *Positivism and the Separation of Law and Morals*, 71 HARV. L. REV. 593, 607 (1958). In Hart's words,

> [i]f we are to communicate with each other at all, and if, as in the most elementary form of law, we are to express our intentions that a certain type of behavior be regulated by rules, then the general words we use . . . must have some standard instance in which no doubts are felt about its application.

Id. at 607.

Hart's well known formulation, legal rules have an "open texture."[112] That is, rules do not determine the scope of their own application, but there must always be something (another rule perhaps, or a conventional practice in the relevant community) that picks out the instances of some phenomenon falling under the rule.[113]

It is tempting to respond that a legal judgment is objectively true if it corresponds with something "out there," like "what the law really is" in a particular case. In general, correspondence theories of truth are widely believed to be fatally flawed, for a number of reasons, one of which is particularly relevant to the attempt to use correspondence as a criterion for legal objectivity.[114] Suppose we wish to know whether the sentence "the cat is on the mat" is true. The correspondence theory of truth says it is true if the sentence p ("the cat is on the mat") corresponds to a state of affairs in the world W (cat on mat), in some kind of appropriate correspondence-relationship C, whatever that may be. Schematically, we can represent this truth condition as pCW. Now, have we got it right? Does p correspond to W in the right way? This is to ask the question whether pCW itself is true, which suggests there may be some property of the world W' to which pCW may or may not correspond. So pCW is true if pCWCW'. Then it is open for us to ask whether pCWCW' is true. We are thus faced with an infinite regress in which there is no foundational fact-and-correspondence relationship about which we cannot in principle ask whether it is true. Something else must serve as criteria of truth, such as coherence with other beliefs, or a normative community practice of manifesting agreement with the speaker who utters "there is a cat on the mat" under certain conditions.[115]

In legal reasoning, if there is any vagueness, open-texture, or uncertainty in the law, however, it is an open question whether the judgment corresponds to the law as it is. The sentence "the judgment corresponds to the law" is itself contestable, and the attempt to specify truth conditions for that sentence leads us down the same path of infinite regress. In other words, the correspondence relationship is impossible to pin down using only the concept of correspondence. We need something else to give genuine content to the notion of a truth-making relationship between an interpretation, on the one hand, and legal texts, practices, and conventions, on the other. Figuring out the nature

---

[112] HART, *supra* note 27, at 124-36.

[113] *Id.* at 126. Another way to make this point is to distinguish between two categories of rules: conduct rules, which are addressed to citizens and permit or forbid certain acts, and decision rules, which are addressed to officials and regulate what these officials do when they apply or interpret the law. *See* Dan-Cohen, *supra* note 40, at 627. As Dan-Cohen argues, "[t]he proper relationship between decision rules and their corresponding conduct rules is not a logical or analytic matter." *Id.* at 629. Rather, one must make a normative argument about the kinds of decision rules we want, in light of the relevant policies and values. The position advanced in the following textual discussion differs from Dan-Cohen's model of the relationship between decision rules and conduct rules in that it does not concede the existence, as a logical matter, of a rule that can be both a conduct rule and a decision rule. *Cf. id.* at 631.

[114] This discussion is drawn from SIMON BLACKBURN, SPREADING THE WORD: GROUNDINGS IN THE PHILOSOPHY OF LANGUAGE 224-29 (1984).

[115] *See* ALEXANDER & SHERWIN, *supra* note 52, at 113-14.

of that "something else" has been a major preoccupation of analytic jurisprudence. It is certainly an issue that arises in connection with the argument for professionalism, because a lawyer who adheres to the Holmesian bad man position would deny the status of "law" to the considerations I claim should be relevant to legal interpretation by transactional lawyers.

In jurisprudential terms, the problem can be stated in terms of Hart's concept of a rule of recognition. In Hart's account, a legal system is "mature" rather than "primitive" to the extent it is characterized by a union of primary and secondary rules.[116] Primary rules impose obligations, create rights or permissions, and in other ways guide the day-to-day activities of citizens. Secondary rules, by contrast, are rules respecting what can be done with primary rules—they provide for orderly, formal change in primary rules, permit adjudication of disputes that arise under primary rules, and so on. The most important of these secondary rules, essential to the concept of a legal system, is a rule which provides binding criteria for legal officials who must identify primary rules in order to interpret and apply the law. This is the rule of recognition.[117] It specifies general characteristics of primary rules that identify some as law and the rest as non-law. In the simplest case, the rule of recognition might state that any act passed by both houses of Congress and signed by the President is law in the United States. A more complex case might involve conditions for the valid interpretation of law. For example, in the railroad case discussed in Part II, the issue was whether the requirement of equipping "cars" with automatic couplers applied to locomotives. The text of the statute was clear, but there was controversy over whether the word "car" includes locomotives. The applicable rule of recognition included multiple, conflicting sub-rules governing the interpretation of statutes, such as "remedial statutes should be construed liberally" and *expressio unius est exclusio alterius.* In this case, the rule of recognition acknowledges both interpretive principles as validly part of the system of legal interpretation (as opposed to a mere policy argument about the kind of statute it would be desirable to have), but does not resolve the conflict between them.

The structure described by Hart gives rise to a paradox, however, because the rule of recognition cannot depend for its validity on any other rule; otherwise the infinite regress problem would recur.[118] His ingenious solution is to deny that there are legal rules or other norms that require officials to follow the rule of recognition. The rule of recognition, instead, comes into existence because it is practiced, in the sense that officials regard it as a standard for critically evaluating their own and others' conduct.[119] For this

---

[116] HART, *supra* note 27, at 91-94. Hart's term "primitive" is perhaps unfortunate, but he uses it primarily as a thought experiment, not a characterization of any actual human society. A primitive legal system, as Hart uses the term, would be a small, closely knit community in which people knew each other and shared a thick set of values, so that they could effectively govern themselves by simple methods of social control. *Id.* at 92.

[117] *Id.* at 94-95, 100.

[118] Scott J. Shapiro, *On Hart's Way out, in* HART'S POSTSCRIPT: ESSAYS ON THE POSTSCRIPT TO THE *CONCEPT OF LAW* 149, 150-53 (Jules Coleman ed., 2001).

[119] *Id.* at 154; HART, *supra* note 27, at 116-17; Ronald Dworkin, *The Model of Rules II, in* DWORKIN, *supra* note 77, at 46, 49.

reason, moral and policy considerations can play a role in legal reasoning, as long as there is a conventional practice among legal officials of making decisions with reference to these criteria.[120] Moral and policy reasons in effect become incorporated into law, to the extent that legal officials, acting as interpreters of the law, take the attitude that they are relevant to working out the law as it is, as opposed to as it should be. For example, in common law adjudication moral reasons enter into the definition of concepts such as reasonableness in torts and unconscionability in contracts. An "exclusive" rule of recognition that screened out moral reasons from consideration by legal officials would be unable to account for this feature of the common law. The convergence by officials on a standard for identifying legal norms, and the internal attitude that officials take toward the rule as a reason for action, are the criteria for legality. A further rule whose credentials as a legal rule would themselves stand in need of certification by the rule of recognition is unnecessary.

Because it is a product of conventional behavior by officials and the attitude of acceptance of the rule as a guide to conduct, the rule of recognition need not be formally expressed as a rule, or written down in any authoritative legal document.[121] Thus, one might wonder whether legal judgments can be objective, if they have no foundation other than social practices. Specifically in regard to this Article, one might wonder whether the interpretive stance of professionalism is validated as a legal standard by the applicable rule of recognition, whether it is just my subjective policy preference or, as a third possibility, whether it is an objectively binding principle of legal interpretation that is not validated by the rule of recognition. It is important at this juncture not to overstate the requirements for a judgment to be objective. Even a strong conception of objectivity need not require something like Platonic forms or correspondence with the fabric of the universe to underwrite the truth of a proposition. Rather, objectivity in law need be only moderately domain-specific, meaning that the characteristics of an objective judgment in the natural sciences will differ in some respects from that which makes a judgment objective in art criticism, basketball officiating, or faculty hiring decisions.[122]

An objective judgment in any endeavor must have certain characteristics: (1) independence from the subjectivity of the judging subject, openness to the subject matter, and willingness to base judgments on the subject itself, not personal idiosyncrasies; (2) amenability to evaluation of the correctness of judgments, or standards for assessing judgments; and (3) invariance across judging subjects.[123] A decision to follow a norm

---

[120] This is known as "soft" or "inclusive" positivism. *See* W.J. WALUCHOW, INCLUSIVE LEGAL POSITIVISM (1994); Jules Coleman, *Incorporationism, Conventionality, and the Practical Difference Thesis*, 4 LEGAL THEORY 381 (1998); E. Philip Soper, *Legal Theory and the Obligation of a Judge: The Hart/Dworkin Dispute*, 75 MICH. L. REV. 473 (1977). Hart accepted inclusive positivism in the posthumously published Postscript to *The Concept of Law*. *See* Hart, *supra* note 77, at 247-48.

[121] HART, *supra* note 27, at 101-03.

[122] *See* Postema, *supra* note 105, at 100.

[123] *Id.* at 105-09; *see also* RAWLS, *supra* note 105, at 110-12; Fiss, *supra* note 62, at 744 (objectivity implies that an interpretation can be measured against a set of norms that transcend the judging subject).

that is capable of serving as a Hartian rule of recognition satisfies these criteria—in Hart's words, political officials "manifest their own acceptance" of the rule of recognition,[124] acknowledging that whether a norm counts as a rule of recognition is independent of the official's subjectivity. The official also acknowledges that the rule of recognition is a product of the shared acceptance of the norm, which indicates acceptance of standards for evaluating the correctness of this judgment. Finally, there must be a high degree of invariance in officials' acceptance of the norm, or there would be a general collapse in the efficacy of the legal system.[125] As Hart recognized, there may be some disagreement at the margins of a rule of recognition, but as long as there is a "normally concordant" practice of identifying law with reference to certain criteria, one exists.[126]

For Hart, whether a rule of recognition exists is an empirical question.[127] The content of the rule of recognition is an empirical question as well.[128] One can ascertain the existence and content of a rule of recognition by reading cases, doing legal sociology, or employing some other method appropriate to discovering facts about a community's practices. One thing an observer might discover is that interpretive practices by judges, lawyers, legislators, and scholars frequently make reference to principles to justify a conclusion that X is a true proposition of law. In contrast with rules, which have a binary, all-or-nothing character,[129] principles are reasons in support of a judge's decision, but not conclusive reasons in the way that rules are. Two principles can conflict, and one can outweigh another, while both remain parts of the legal system; by contrast, when two rules conflict, one of the rules must persist while the other is abandoned.[130] Ronald Dworkin contends that Hart's rule of recognition has no place for principles, and thus fails to explain the reasoning behind judicial decisions which are based on principles as well as rules. For example, in *Henningsen v. Bloomfield Motors*,[131] the court's decision to impose liability for breach of warranty on a car manufacturer, notwithstanding lack of privity of contract and contractual disclaimers of the warranty, was justified

---

124 HART, *supra* note 27, at 102.

125 *Id.* at 103-04.

126 *Id.* at 109-10.

127 *Id.* at 110. Dworkin criticizes Hart for arguing that social rules are constituted by behavior while admitting that rules can be uncertain at the margins. Dworkin, *supra* note 119, at 54. The Hartian distinction between the core and penumbra of rules can explain this apparent anomaly, because the core of a rule of recognition will exist as long as it works most of the time, with only a few marginal uncertainties.

128 HART, *supra* note 27, at 150 ("Which form of omnipotence . . . our Parliament enjoys is an empirical question concerning the form of rule which is accepted as the ultimate criterion in identifying the law.").

129 Dworkin, *supra* note 77, at 24.

130 *Id.* at 26-27. In his response to Dworkin contained in the Postscript to *The Concept of Law*, Hart refers to this feature of principles as their "non-conclusive" character. Hart, *supra* note 77, at 261. He argues that Dworkin exaggerates this distinction between rules and principles, and that there are many instances in which two legal rules conflict and one is held to outweigh the other. Hart also points out that in cases where a principle conflicts with a rule and the principle prevails, the rule is not abandoned. *Id.* at 262.

131 161 A.2d 69 (N.J. 1960).

on the basis of a balancing of competing reasons which existed outside any legal text such as a statute, rule, or judicial opinion.[132] These reasons included the importance of freedom of contract and voluntary assumption of duties, which tended to support the defendant, and the public's interest in being protected from dangerous products, which supported the plaintiff's position.

Principles in the Dworkinian sense are not the kind of extra-legal moral arguments that one might make to criticize the law for being wrongheaded; rather, they exist within the law and can serve as a link in the chain of an internal justificatory argument.[133] (In *Henningsen*, the Chrysler Corporation would presumably be horrified at the prospect that it could be forced to pay money to an injured person solely on the basis of some judge's beliefs about right and wrong. To legitimately expropriate money from Chrysler, perhaps forcibly, the decision must be based on the kind of reasons that ordinarily justify the use of coercive force.) Because they are part of the law, lawyers can no more ignore these principles than they can omit express statutory or common-law rules from their reasoning process.[134] Thus, my claim that lawyers appeal to extra-textual norms constraining their interpretive activities can be understood as an appeal to Dworkinian principles, which mandate an attitude of respect toward the law and legal interpretation. "[I]n most contexts lawyers can fairly readily tell the difference between making good-faith efforts to comply with a plausible interpretation of the purposes of a legal regime, and using every ingenuity of his or her trade to resist or evade compliance."[135] This observation seems to reflect the presence of a special class of Dworkinian principles within the legal system, which are what I term attitudes or stances adopted by officials, and quasi-officials such as lawyers, toward the law. In jurisprudential terms, my argument is that a reasonable rule of recognition actually does, and must include not only considerations of pedigree (i.e., whether the legislature enacted a particular text or whether a judge decided a case) but also extra-textual interpretive norms that specify which of several textually supportable interpretations are consistent with the social function of the law.[136]

The opposing argument from the Holmesian bad man perspective is that a lawyer need not counsel and assist the client within the bounds of law as defined by good faith efforts and plausible interpretations—rather, the lawyer need only respect arguable or

---

[132] Dworkin discusses *Henningsen* at Dworkin, *supra* note 77, at 23-24.

[133] *Id.* at 35, 44; Dworkin, *supra* note 87, at 85, 115. Hart contended that judges exercise law-making power in cases that lay far out in the penumbra of rules. *See* Hart, *supra* note 27, at 135, 145.

[134] Dworkin argues that principles do not have the same pedigree as judicial decisions and statutes—rather, they are a product of a "sense of appropriateness developed in the profession." Dworkin, *supra* note 77, at 40. Hart responds that there is no reason why principles cannot be identified by pedigree criteria, "in that they have been consistently invoked by courts in ranges of different cases as providing reasons for decision." Hart, *supra* note 77, at 265.

[135] Gordon, *supra* note 43, at 48.

[136] I am grateful to Emily Sherwin for pressing me to clarify some ambiguities in this discussion.

non-frivolous constructions of legal norms.[137] Which of these interpretive stances is the right one to take toward legal norms? One way to answer this question is to determine whether courts require clients to arrange their affairs to comply with the law interpreted in light of substantive principles, values, and social interests. In other words, we can make a descriptive argument for a particular rule of recognition that takes into account interpretive norms, stances, and attitudes. However, descriptive arguments cannot settle with finality the question of whether the attitude of professionalism is a part of our legal system.

One could read every case and conduct exhaustive empirical sociological research and never know the answer for sure. There are two reasons for this. The first is that the rule of recognition, like any legal rule, is characterized by its open texture.[138] There may be a situation in which there is factual uncertainty regarding the content of the rule of recognition, and in that situation some institution will be called upon to make an unconstrained choice about the specific contours of the ultimate rule for identifying law. There are no rules requiring one result or another—as Hart puts it, "at the fringe of these very fundamental things, we should welcome the rule-sceptic."[139] The second is the now-familiar infinite regress problem. No amount of rules and meta-rules can settle an interpretive question with finality. Hart grounded the rule of recognition in social practices to avoid the regress problem, and we might take the same way out with respect to professionalism. A more promising approach, therefore, would be to provide an extra-legal justification for professionalism—one based on the nature and function of law, and therefore the reasons for treating legal directives as authoritative. In other words, we would be giving a normative rather than a conceptual or descriptive argument for positivism.[140]

Philosophers of law ask the conceptual question "what distinguishes law from other means of social ordering?"[141] because law does a distinctive kind of work. My claim has been that the function of law is to secure the conditions necessary for cooperation and

---

137 *See* Gordon, *supra* note 7, at 1194-97. David Luban argues that Holmes invented his image of the lawyer advising a "bad man" client in order to make a jurisprudential point about the separability of law and morality. *See* David Luban, *The Bad Man and the Good Lawyer: A Centennial Essay on Holmes's The Path of the Law*, 72 N.Y.U. L. REV. 1547, 1562 (1997). Holmes can therefore be understood as making the same point as Dworkin—if a norm is not part of the legal system, a judicial decision based on that norm is not legitimate from the point of view of a client who is bound by it. Dworkin's response, of course, is very different from Holmes's, for instead of insisting on a bright-line separation of law and morality, Dworkin enthusiastically incorporates morality into law.

138 HART, *supra* note 27, at 151.

139 *Id.* at 154. As Jules Coleman reconstructs Dworkin's argument against Hart's social rules thesis, "if there is substantial controversy [over the content of the rule of recognition], then there cannot be convergence of behavior sufficient to specify a social rule." Coleman, *supra* note 77, at 15.

140 *See, e.g.,* ALEXANDER & SHERWIN, *supra* note 52, at 1; Dworkin, *supra* note 119, at 50-52; Jeremy Waldron, *Normative (or Ethical) Positivism*, in HART'S POSTSCRIPT: ESSAYS ON THE POSTSCRIPT TO THE CONCEPT OF LAW, *supra* note 118, at 410.

141 *See* JOHN FINNIS, NATURAL LAW AND NATURAL RIGHTS 11-15 (1980).

the realization of collective goods, notwithstanding deep and persistent disagreement over values, ends, conceptions of the good, and the application of moral principles to practical situations. In order to do this work, law must have certain characteristics.[142] It is tempting to say that the law must be uncontroversial,[143] but in anything outside the core of the application of legal norms, common experience shows that the law is anything but uncontroversial. In any event, the requirement that the law be uncontroversial is usually interpreted as a constraint on a legal system's rule of recognition. Namely, the rule of recognition must be capable of formulation without reference to the content of moral principles. Significantly, this constraint on the rule of recognition does not preclude the use in legal reasoning of moral principles that have become incorporated into legal norms.[144]

Preclusion of the content of moral norms is necessary to avoid slipping back into the disagreement that required authoritative settlement by law. But the preclusion of non-legal considerations that is the consequence of the negative aspect of professionalism requires a lawyer to exclude moral principles from her interpretive process only to the extent those principles are not recognized as part of law by the relevant interpretive community. In addition, the positive aspect of professionalism requires that the social function of law guide a lawyer's interpretive judgment. For this reason, interpretive communities have evolved, and ought to evolve, higher-order standards for differentiating artificial, abusive transactions that comply only formally with legal rules from those transactions that comply substantially with the law.

I suppose a lawyer could argue that she is unconcerned with the effective functioning of the law because it is a problem for legislators, rulemakers, or judges, but not for

---

[142] *See* Joseph Raz, *Authority, Law, and Morality, in* ETHICS IN THE PUBLIC DOMAIN 210, 226-27 (1994). As Raz argues:

> [A]ssume that the maintenance of orderly social relations is itself morally valuable. Assume further that a legal system can be the law in force in a society only if it succeeds in maintaining orderly social relations. A necessary connection between law and morality would then have been established, without the legal validity of any rule being made, by the rule of recognition, to depend on the truth of any moral proposition.

Some philosophers believe that soft or inclusive positivism is vulnerable to Raz's authority argument, because the law could not perform its coordination function if those subject to its directives were called upon to evaluate the truth of moral propositions incorporated into law. *See, e.g.,* Kenneth Einar Himma, *Law's Claim of Legitimate Authority, in* HART'S POSTSCRIPT: ESSAYS ON THE POSTSCRIPT TO *THE CONCEPT OF LAW*, *supra* note 118, at 271, 274-75. As mentioned above, professionalism as a theory of legal ethics is a variety of soft positivism, because it permits reference to moral beliefs to the extent there is a conventional practice among legal officials of referring to these beliefs in legal reasoning. This position does not run afoul of Raz's authority argument because affected citizens are not required to ascertain whether a moral proposition is true, only whether officials have referred to it in the past when explaining and justifying a legal decision.

[143] *See* Coleman, *supra* note 77, at 9-11 (explaining that this account of legal positivism is probably Dworkin's target in *The Model of Rules I*, Dworkin, *supra* note 77, but that there is another characteristic of positivism, namely its conventionalism, that is plausible).

[144] *Id.* at 15-16; *see also* Joseph Raz, *Incorporation by Law*, 10 LEGAL THEORY 1 (2004).

her or her client. This attitude, however, would be self-defeating and even irrational. Again picking up on an argument by Robert Gordon, the response to this lawyer is that she must be concerned about the effective functioning of the law, because without it, neither she nor her client could realize their own interests. The market economy presupposes a background of stable law, custom, and enforcement that enforces private ordering.[145] Even if a lawyer and client were concerned only with pursuing their own narrow interests, paradoxically it is only possible to behave self-interestedly within a framework of other-regarding obligations. A lawyer might evade regulatory requirements by aggressive structuring of transactions in one case, but cause long-run damage by eroding the capability of the legal system to facilitate the functioning of financial markets. The lawyer cannot be indifferent to this long-term damage and still claim to be making an ethical argument about the obligations of her role, because it is in the nature of ethical arguments that they must be generalizable to relevantly similar situations.[146] It may be true that a lawyer could game the system once without causing catastrophic damage, but this is impermissible free-riding on the cooperation of others. Thus, any plausible ethical argument—i.e., one that is worthy of the respect of similarly situated others—must take account of the consequences of widespread manipulation of formal legal norms.

B. Professionalism in Practice

This Article has developed a jurisprudential argument for the position that lawyers ought to be guided by the informed judgment of a professional community of lawyers, judges, and other interpreters, who are committed to using the legal system to perform its social function of coordinating valuable social activity. Legal texts alone cannot accomplish this coordination, because it is always possible for clever lawyers to manipulate formal norms to accomplish results that are at odds with the evident purpose of the regime of legal norms. Thus, if the law respecting any area of economic activity is to possess sufficient stability to coordinate action, lawyers who counsel and advise clients, and structure transactions, must do so in a way that could be publicly justified to other members of the relevant community. Significantly, the law already works in the way I have been recommending.[147] Although there are numerous examples to offer, including the law of frivolous litigation[148] and the implicit norms of good faith

---

[145] Gordon, *supra* note 43, at 49; Gordon, *supra* note 7, at 1198-99.

[146] *See, e.g.*, T.M. SCANLON, WHAT WE OWE TO EACH OTHER 153 (1998).

[147] As Milton Regan observes,

> [m]uch of law practice consists of informal understandings about matters such as what arguments are considered within the bounds of good faith, acceptable levels of aggressiveness, the scope of disclosure requirements, how to interact with regulatory agencies, and what constitutes due diligence.

MILTON C. REGAN, JR., EAT WHAT YOU KILL: THE FALL OF A WALL STREET LAWYER 39 (2004).

[148] *See, e.g.*, William Schwarzer, *Sanctions Under the New Federal Rule 11—A Closer Look*, 104 F.R.D. 181 (1985).

dealing observed in various commercial communities,[149] I will concentrate on three examples—the economic substance doctrine in the law of taxation, the law governing the complex special-purpose entity (SPE) transactions that were used by Enron, and the legal advice provided by government lawyers on the application of domestic and international prohibitions on torture to the interrogation of detainees in the war on terrorism.

1. Tax Shelters

One of the recurring problems in the law of taxation is that the tax laws may be defeated through manipulation, that is, by structuring transactions in a way that creates artificial tax consequences.[150] The difficult analytical question is obviously how to define "manipulation" or "artificial," and this question only arises because it is possible for a transaction to comply with formal legal norms while somehow failing to satisfy the substantive standards or principles that those formal norms attempt to express. The difficulty is perhaps particularly acute in tax law, which supposedly does not concern itself with whether the taxpayer's intent in entering into a transaction was to avoid taxes[151] but it must be faced in any complex regulatory arena in which a client may seek the assistance of a lawyer to avoid a legal prohibition or penalty through careful planning. The danger of manipulation results from the familiar dichotomy between form and substance, or rules and standards, in legal norms.[152] Briefly, the distinction depends on the conceptual possibility of divergence between the action mandated (or prohibited) by a rule and the action mandated (or prohibited) by the rule's background justification.[153] A legal norm in the form of a rule permitting only people age sixteen

---

[149] *See supra* note 29 and accompanying text.

[150] David P. Hariton, *Sorting out the Tangle of Economic Substance*, 52 TAX LAW. 235, 236 (1999) (noting that tax lawyers have tried to devise rules so that "business transactions do not permit some taxpayers to avoid tax at the expense of others in a way that was not intended by the political system"); Joseph Isenbergh, *Musings on Form and Substance in Taxation*, 49 U. CHI. L. REV. 859, 863 (1982); David A. Weisbach, *Formalism in the Tax Law*, 66 U. CHI. L. REV. 860, 860 (1999) ("[T]axpayers have been able to manipulate the rules endlessly to produce results clearly not intended by the drafters.").

[151] Alan Gunn, *Tax Avoidance*, 76 MICH. L. REV. 733, 735 (1978).

[152] *See*, e.g., Louis Kaplow, *Rules Versus Standards: An Economic Analysis*, 42 DUKE L.J. 557 (1992); Duncan Kennedy, *Form and Substance in Private Law Adjudication*, 89 HARV. L. REV. 1685 (1976); Weisbach, *supra* note 150. Leo Katz denies that there is anything distinctively legal about this distinction and argues that loopholes in the law result from a similar form/substance dichotomy in morality, which is simply reflected in the structure of law. Leo Katz, *Form and Substance in Law and Morality*, 66 U. CHI. L. REV. 566, 567 (1999).

[153] *See* FREDERICK SCHAUER, PLAYING BY THE RULES: A PHILOSOPHICAL EXAMINATION OF RULE-BASED DECISIONMAKING IN LAW AND IN LIFE 53-55 (1991). The terminology of background justification and the driver's license example, are from a contemporaneous article by Schauer. *See* Frederick Schauer, *Rules and the Rule of Law*, 14 HARV. J.L. & PUB. POL'Y 645, 648-49 (1991); *see also* Schauer, *supra* note 55, at 236. Significantly, the phenomenon of divergence between the result mandated by a general rule and what would be required after full attention to all the relevant features of a situation is not limited to following

or older to obtain a driver's license is plainly justified by reasons of public safety, but the rule is both over-inclusive and under-inclusive with respect to this background justification. The rule may prevent mature, careful fifteen-year-olds from driving (over-inclusiveness) as well as permitting reckless, dangerous twenty-year-olds to obtain a license (underinclusiveness). One response to this problem is to permit a decisionmaker to rely directly on the background justification, by casting the norm in the form of a standard. In our example, the relevant norm expressed as a standard might be that only competent, mature drivers may obtain a license.

The distinction between rules and standards creates two sets of mirror-image risks facing the regulator. Expressing a norm in a standard-like way entails the loss of benefits associated with rules, such as ease of application, error reduction, constraint on the decisionmaker's discretion (and therefore power), and especially values of ex ante predictability and certainty of application.[154] By contrast, expressing the norm in a rule-like way entails the loss of the benefits associated with standards, such as sensitivity to the fit between the outcome of the legal decision and the background justification of the norm, and greater ex post contextualization and particularization of the result, resulting in a more just result as between the parties.

In tax law, rules are generally favored for the additional reason that many transactions are structured carefully in order to capture tax benefits, even if the tax treatment of the given transaction was never foreseen or intended.[155] In particular, a transaction with economic substance and a business purpose may be structured in a "funny" way in order to take advantage of a tax benefit that was not foreseen by Congress.[156] The transaction is not a sham, because it has economic substance and would have been undertaken anyway, for business reasons. But the form of the transaction is artificial, and highly tax-sensitive. Given the sensitivity of transactional structure to tax consequences, there seems to be a heightened need for predictability in tax law as opposed to, say, tort law, where many actors are less likely to be influenced by the precise form of legal norms. Still, there must be limits on the extent to which the formal (or rule-based) treatment of a transaction can diverge from the substantive (or standard-based) approach—too great a divergence and the system will be unfair as between similarly

legal rules. A similar dynamic exists in moral philosophy; indeed, a well known criticism of Kantian ethics is that the emphasis by Kant on moral rules distorts the nature of moral judgment by directing an agent to ignore morally relevant details of a problem. *See* HERMAN, *supra* note 83, at 74-75.

[154] SCHAUER, *supra* note 153, at 135-66; *see also* Antonin Scalia, *The Rule of Law as a Law of Rules*, 56 U. CHI. L. REV. 1175 (1989).

[155] *See, e.g.,* Yosha v. Commissioner, 861 F.2d 494, 497 (7th Cir. 1988) (Posner, J.) ("There is no rule against taking advantage of opportunities created by Congress or the Treasury Department for beating taxes. . . . Many transactions are largely or even entirely motivated by the desire to obtain a tax advantage."); Hariton, *supra* note 150, at 237 (noting the general presumption that the taxpayer "should not be denied beneficial tax results which she stumbles upon, or even *see*ks out, in the course of her legitimate business dealings, even if those results are obviously unanticipated, unintended, or downright undesirable").

[156] Michael L. Schler, *Ten More Truths About Tax Shelters: The Problem, Possible Solutions, and a Reply to Professor Weisbach*, 55 TAX L. REV. 325, 337-40 (2002).

situated taxpayers.[157] There is accordingly great pressure to differentiate between real transactions, undertaken in the ordinary course of a taxpayer's business for legitimate business purposes, and the artificial transactions, with all their Rube Goldberg complexity, set up with no purpose other than to generate tax benefits. The result of this tension has been considerable confusion in the courts, which have applied a variety of substance-over-form doctrines in cases in which a textualist style of interpretation would effectively reward sophisticated evasion of the substantive meaning of the tax laws.[158]

One way to distinguish between real and artificial transactions and their tax consequences is to rely on the informed judgment of members of the relevant professional community. As Mark Gergen observes, "[g]ood tax lawyers know when they are pushing hard at the edge of the envelope."[159] After observing the difficulty in arriving at determinate standards of tax motive and economic substance, which would enable courts to deny a positive result to a taxpayer who had complied formally with the rules, he falls back on professional judgment to formulate a "disclaimer" that could be attached to any analysis of form and substance in tax law:

> A determination that an action is tax motivated or insubstantial is neither a necessary nor a sufficient condition for denying a positive tax result to which the actor claims he is entitled under tax law. There may be other grounds for rejecting the actor's position. These standards do not displace other forms of reasoning. Further, some tax motivated or insubstantial actions are respected. As for which are respected and which are not, that is difficult to say. Do not always expect to find a rule or principle to sort them out. In a novel case the best guide may well be professional common knowledge.[160]

Similarly, tax lawyer Peter Canellos claims that everyone in the relevant community knows the difference between creative tax planning and bogus tax shelters, even though shelters are designed to mimic real transactions.[161] In tax sheltering, "promoters attempt to apply a patina of substance to a transaction that is formal and unreal," while legitimate tax practitioners plan real business transactions with a business purpose, in light of the possibility of obtaining tax advantages.[162] As Canellos recognizes, all of these terms are

---

[157] Hariton, *supra* note 150, at 236.

[158] *See* Cunningham & Repetti, *supra* note 56, at 21-25 (reviewing business purpose and substance-over-form doctrines); Allen D. Madison, *The Tension Between Textualism and Substance-over-Form Doctrines in Tax Law*, 43 SANTA CLARA L. REV. 699, 722-36 (2003) (summarizing sham transaction and recharacterization doctrines).

[159] Mark P. Gergen, *The Common Knowledge of Tax Abuse*, 54 SMU L. REV. 131, 136 (2001).

[160] *Id.* at 138.

[161] Peter C. Canellos, *A Tax Practitioner's Perspective on Substance, Form and Business Purpose in Structuring Business Transactions and in Tax Shelters*, 54 SMU L. REV. 47, 51-52 (2001) ("[E]xperienced tax professionals can usually readily distinguish tax shelters from real transactions. . . .").

[162] *Id.* at 50.

subject to a challenge that they be defined more precisely: What makes a transaction real or unreal? What is the difference between a patina of substance and creative structuring? Ever more elaborate rules cannot provide the answers, however. Professional judgment is an irreducible aspect of the analysis, even though it may be possible to set out some standards or criteria that are germane to the exercise of judgment.[163]

Appeals to professional judgment lead to a predictable reaction—charges of unprincipled decisionmaking, arbitrariness, non-transparency, and a departure from the ideal of objectivity in law.[164] Critics are apt to cite, disparagingly, Justice Stewart's comment about hard-core pornography, that he cannot define it, but he knows it when he sees it.[165] But recall the previous discussion of judgment and objectivity. A judgment in this domain (e.g., "that is a tax shelter, not a legitimate transaction") can be objective as long as the decisionmaker is willing to base judgments on the subject itself, not personal idiosyncrasies, is willing to be open to evaluation of the correctness of her judgment, and makes a decision that exhibits some degree of invariance across judging subjects.[166] This kind of limited domain-specific objectivity can be secured by constraining all-things-considered contextual judgments using more specific criteria which are developed over a series of analogous cases. In the tax example, the taxpayer will not be denied tax benefits as long as the transaction has a legitimate business purpose. This standard can be defined further based on criteria such as:

- the way the transaction was marketed and sold—i.e., whether it was pitched by specialized tax professionals and marketed to the tax or finance department of a corporation, or instead developed by outside investment advisors or internal operations departments and marketed in terms of business or financing opportunities, rather than tax savings;
- the involvement of real or extraneous parties—i.e., whether it included real buyers and sellers, with financing at market rates, or accommodation parties such as foreign subsidiaries or partnerships;

---

163 *Id.* at 53-54 ("Although in theory the line between a tax shelter and an aggressively structured real transaction may appear difficult to draw, in actuality the distinction is rather easy to establish when the transaction involves most of the tax shelter elements described above.").

164 The tax context provides several examples. *See* ACM P'ship v. Commissioner, 157 F.3d 231, 265 (3d Cir. 1998) (McKee, J., dissenting) ("I can't help but suspect that the majority's conclusion . . . is, in its essence, something akin to a 'smell test.'"); Isenbergh, *supra* note 150, at 874-76 (criticizing the economic substance doctrine in taxation as an "essentially aesthetic response" which violates the principle that tax rules should be interpreted narrowly and in accordance with the form, not the substance, of transactions); Id at 882 ("It is not uncommon for professors to regard—and teach—the process of legal interpretation as a vehicle for their own aesthetic preferences."). In legal theory generally, see Farber, *Inevitability*, *supra* note 55, at 541-47, for a summary of critiques.

165 Jacobellis v. Ohio, 378 U.S. 184, 197 (1964) (Stewart, J., concurring). For an interesting, sympathetic interpretation of Justice Stewart's reasoning, *see* Paul Gewirtz, *On "I Know It When I See It,"* 105 YALE L.J. 1023 (1996). Gewirtz's essay is a defense of what he calls nonrational elements of judicial reasoning, such as judgment and character, and I think he is correct that these qualities can be described as excellences or virtues. *See id.* at 1033.

166 Postema, *supra* note 105, at 105-09.

- the use of a series of highly choreographed steps; and
- whether the workings of the transaction were concealed (and thus reliant upon the audit lottery) or publicly disclosed.[167]

Assuming that these evaluative criteria are generally shared within the relevant community, the judgment of legitimate business purpose is sufficiently objective.

I am hedging here a bit with the term "relevant" community. Canellos's article on tax shelters identifies two vastly different communities of practitioners—the tax bar and the tax shelter bar.[168] "Real" tax practitioners structure transactions that are otherwise legitimate in a way that maximizes tax advantages; they are concerned with their reputation and status, and often become involved with high-profile organizations such as the tax sections of the ABA and the New York State Bar Association, which are dedicated to improving the tax law. They consider exercising professional judgment as a stock in trade.[169] Tax shelter practitioners, on the other hand, set up artificially contrived deals,

[167] Canellos, *supra* note 161, at 51-55. These criteria suggest that the community's evaluation—that a transaction exhibits either legitimate tax avoidance or illegitimate tax evasion—is to a considerably degree path dependent. *See* KATZ, *supra* note 15, at 57-73. As Katz puts it, there are deontological features of a situation that should not be exploited merely to achieve, in a roundabout way, an outcome that is more desirable from a consequentialist perspective. *Id.* at 57. This latter, specific principle does not appear to add much to the persons-as-ends formulation of the Kantian categorical imperative. *See* IMMANUEL KANT, GROUNDING FOR THE METAPHYSICS OF MORALS, at 36 (James W. Ellington trans., 1981) (1785) ("Act in such a way that you treat humanity . . . always at the same time as an end and never simply as a means."). I am also uneasy about the reduction of deontological morality to path-dependent evaluations, because a strict deontologist would not approve of violating moral duties by any means. In the puzzles Katz considers, the actor would be subject to criticism for violating the rights of another either directly or indirectly, if both options had the effect of treating a person as a mere means, in violation of that form of the categorical imperative. *See* KATZ, *supra* note 15, at 1-9 (posing numerous hypotheticals). The more promising solution to the problems Katz considers is the distinction between regarding norms (legal or moral) either instrumentally or as legitimate reasons, which is the position defended here. This is closer to the deontologist's strategy of approving of actions only if they are done out of motives of duty. *See* KANT, *supra*, at 9-10. For an insightful discussion of the problem of constructing maxims of action that do not beg the questions against puzzles like Katz's, *see* HERMAN, *supra* note 83, at 217-24. As Herman argues, considerations of value bear on the description of actions and the construction of maxims. If this is correct (and I believe it is), it provides a sufficient account of the choice-worthiness of a particular end and the path by which it is achieved, leaving nothing puzzling about Katz's cases.

[168] Canellos, *supra* note 161, at 55-57; *see also* Joseph Bankman, *The Business Purpose Doctrine and the Sociology of Tax*, 54 SMU L. REV. 149, 150 (2001) (elaborating on Canellos's sociological analysis of the two tax bars); Richard Lavoie, *Deputizing the Gunslingers: Co-Opting the Tax Bar into Dissuading Corporate Tax Shelters*, 21 VA. TAX. REV. 43, 46 (2001) (arguing that "[m]any lawyers involved in corporate tax-shelter activity are deeply troubled by the role they play"). Nancy Staudt suggested in conversation that this informal sociology of the profession may not be entirely accurate, but for the purposes of my normative argument, it is essential only to establish that different communities *could* exist, and that one may do better than the others, in virtue of the values lying behind the legal system. On the descriptive argument, I am not an expert in tax law, and must defer to others, who apparently disagree on the boundaries around the various communities and the norms to which they are committed. *See also infra* notes 174-77, and accompanying text, for a qualification on the ascription of intentions to communities.

[169] This description, particularly the elitism and emphasis on the exercise of judgment, calls to mind Anthony Kronman's lawyer-statesman. *See* ANTHONY T. KRONMAN, THE LOST LAWYER (1993).

care little about their reputation for probity and judgment, and provide legal opinions as a fig leaf for sheltering transactions that are widely derided by real practitioners. So which of these is the relevant community? If we specify real tax practitioners and then derive evaluative criteria from their shared norms, are we not engaging in circular reasoning? The shared norms of the tax shelter bar and the criteria they would generate for identifying abusive transactions (if any) would presumably look very different from those listed above. But why follow the interpretive principles of the tax bar, not the tax shelter bar? Or, why regard oneself as a member of the interpretive community that is constituted by fidelity to those norms? In theory, a lawyer may decide to remove herself from the tax bar and join the tax shelter bar, which recognizes a different set of standards of interpretation.[170] Even if the authority of a community's disciplining rules do not depend on assent to those norms,[171] it seems open to practitioners to opt out of the community and opt into a different community, with a different set of disciplining rules.

A different way to frame this objection might be to claim that the requirement of professionalism in interpretation only gains authority by bootstrapping. That is, the obligation imposed by the attitude of professionalism is a function of the relevant interpretive community and the standards it recognizes for evaluating the correctness of legal judgments (i.e., "although purely formal norms seem to permit X, the law as correctly interpreted prohibits X"). At the same time, I seem to be claiming that a lawyer ought to associate himself with the interpretive community that recognizes the attitude of professionalism and shun other communities that do not. What is the source of this meta-obligation? If the response were, "the obligation of professionalism," that would indeed be bootstrapping. But the correct response is given instead in terms of the social function of law: a relatively stable, determinate framework of legal rights and obligations is necessary to permit ordered cooperation among people who disagree on just about everything except the need to reach settlement of disagreements.

If lawyers were permitted to adopt a Holmesian bad man interpretive attitude (or to opt into a community which recognized that attitude as a proper interpretation of the relevant law), then the law would end up having no boundaries at all, no constraining capacity, and therefore no ability to create authoritative settlement. This conclusion may sound unduly apocalyptic, but experience with practices such as tax sheltering shows that lawyers can always plan around formal legal norms, given sufficient resources and creativity. Purely formal constraints such as legislation, rulemaking, and enhanced

---

[170] *See* ARTHUR ISAK APPLBAUM, ETHICS FOR ADVERSARIES 45-60 (1999) (discussing the possibility that even if the role of doctor were constituted with certain obligations, a practitioner might opt to become a "schmoctor" with different obligations, and that the concept of a role cannot prevent this kind of maneuver); Katharine T. Bartlett, *Feminist Legal Methods,* 103 HARV. L. REV. 829, 855 (1990) (arguing that there are multiple, overlapping communities to which one may belong, and that privileging the dominant community tends to preserve the status quo); *cf.* HERMAN, *supra* note 83, at 222-23 (arguing that the form of maxims, for the purpose of consideration of conformity with the categorical imperative, is given by an agent's regulative standards or projects).

[171] Fiss, *supra* note 62, at 746.

enforcement will never be sufficient to eliminate abuses because lawyers are involved in constructing the bounds of the law.[172] As Robert Gordon rightly observes, there are resources for strategic manipulation within any set of adjudicative or administrative rules and procedures.[173] As a result, the effectiveness of the law depends on constraints exogenous to formal legal norms.

Before moving on, however, we must consider one final objection.[174] I have discussed "the community" and its interpretive practices as if it were a thing to which an intention can be straightforwardly ascribed. In one sense, this is just a convenient fiction—communities don't have practices or disciplining rules; community members follow these norms. The community's standards can be located by observing convergent behavior by community members,[175] but the community itself is not an intentional being. On the other hand we speak quite naturally of collective intentions and norms and attribute these mental states to groups.[176] In this case, we mean literally that the group intends something and are no longer using collective intention as a metaphor. Moreover, we do so even in the absence of some formal procedure, such as taking a poll that reveals the intentions of individuals and aggregates them into a collective intention. Without formal procedures we may reach a premature and incorrect conclusion about the group's intention,[177] so we must regard an ascription of group intention as potentially revisable, but talking as though the group has an intention is not incoherent. In the example here, it may turn out that the elite tax bar is more tolerant of tax shelters than its more outspoken members would admit. This, however, is an empirical challenge to the norms of a particular group, not a conceptual impediment to the general practice of imputing intentions to a collective body.

---

[172] *Cf.* Susan P. Koniak & George M. Cohen, *In Hell There Will Be Lawyers Without Clients or Law*, *in* ETHICS IN PRACTICE: LAWYERS' ROLES, RESPONSIBILITIES, AND REGULATION 177, 180 (Deborah L. Rhode ed., 2000) ("Good lawyers understand that the ethical practice of law involves lawyers simultaneously shaping legal boundaries and recognizing the real limits to this manipulation.").

[173] Gordon, *supra* note 43, at 45.

[174] I am indebted to Dennis Tuchler for pressing me to consider this problem.

[175] HART, *supra* note 27, at 108-09.

[176] Solan, *supra* note 81. I am aware of the extensive social-choice literature which purports to show that there is no such thing as "the collective will" with respect to some outcome. *See* KATZ, *supra* note 15, at 60-67 (citing studies and examples). Accepting that there is no single collective will prior to some kind of aggregation procedure such as voting, it may nevertheless be the case that a collective sense of the meaning of a scheme or rule emerges over time, as a series of test cases is decided, as members of the group debate among themselves about how to resolve hypothetical disputes, and so on. These collective understandings are often embodied in the form of uniform responses to paradigmatic cases and can be extended to new situations by drawing analogies and distinctions. Although this process is most familiar in common law reasoning, it is arguably a feature of moral reasoning as well. *See* ALBERT R. JONSEN & STEPHEN TOULMIN, THE ABUSE OF CASUISTRY (1988).

[177] Solan, *supra* note 81.

2. *Structured-Finance Transactions at Enron*

Enron had a problem. It had an ambitious plan for growth that required billions of dollars in cash, but it could not raise cash through conventional methods like selling stock or borrowing from banks. The reason was simple—additional borrowing would harm its credit rating and issuing additional equity would hurt the price of its stock, which would be unthinkable in a company driven by the need to constantly increase its share price.[178] The markets it had created in natural gas and wholesale electricity were maturing and profits from trading were diminishing in response to increasing competition.[179] Moreover, Jeffrey Skilling's insistence that the company use mark-to-market accounting placed tremendous pressure on corporate managers to show constant revenue growth, even if that meant sacrificing cash flow.[180]

These incentives explain the motivation for most of the convoluted transactions devised by Chief Financial Officer Andy Fastow. Fastow's innovation, if you can call

---

178 McLEAN & ELKIND, *supra* note 14, at 92-94, 150-51, 154-55, 161, 236-37, 296, 318; POWERS REPORT, *supra* note 11, at 36-37; Second Report of Neal Batson, Court-Appointed Examiner 15-22 (Jan. 21, 2003) [hereinafter, Second Batson Report]; Frank Partnoy, *A Revisionist View of Enron and the Sudden Death of "May,"* 48 VILL. L. REV. 1245, 1250 (2003) ("The key factor sustaining Enron's ability to secure a low cost of capital was an investment grade credit rating . . . which the major credit rating agencies gave to Enron's debt from 1995 until November 2001."); Schwarcz, *supra* note 15, at 1309-10.

179 Douglas G. Baird & Robert K. Rasmussen, *Four (or Five) Easy Lessons from Enron*, 55 VAND. L. REV. 1787, 1801-02 (2002); Bratton, *supra* note 4, at 1299-1300.

180 Mark-to-market accounting permits a company to book as revenue the entire estimated value of a stream of income from an asset. Cash will continue to flow in the door over the entire productive life of the asset, but all of the revenue will be realized in the quarter in which it was booked. Not only was this method highly susceptible to abuse in the form of fiddling with the estimated value of an asset, but it also amplifies the pressure from Wall Street to show continuing growth. Because realizing all the future profits when the asset is booked makes one quarter's revenue figures look good, it makes it that much harder to show growth in the subsequent quarter. *See generally* HOUSE COMM. ON ENERGY & COMMERCE, LESSONS LEARNED FROM ENRON'S COLLAPSE: AUDITING THE ACCOUNTING INDUSTRY, H.R. DOC. NO. 107-83, at 87 (Feb. 6, 2002) (statement of Bala G. Dharan) (claiming that mark-to-market accounting, as applied to private contracts for the sale of assets that do not have readily ascertainable market values, requires a great deal of guesswork and assumptions about dozens of variables); *id.* at 76 (statement of James S. Chanos) (explaining that under mark-to-market accounting, if assumptions are not borne out and assets actually decline in value, the reporting company must adjust their book value downward, but in practice there is a powerful incentive to do new deals and book the value of those new deals, using questionable assumptions, to mask the effect of the previous decline in asset values); Second Batson Report, *supra* note 178, at 22-28 (noting that mark-to-market accounting can create a "quality of earnings" problem, because earnings are recognized long before the activity generates any cash); *id.* at 29-32 (explaining how a transaction to provide video on demand, with content supplied by Blockbuster, resulted in recognized gain of $53 million, even though Enron did not have the technology to deliver the content, which Blockbuster in any event could not obtain from the studios); McLEAN & ELKIND, *supra* note 14, at 39-41, 126-29; Bratton, *supra* note 4, at 1303-04 (observing that no market sets values for over-the-counter derivatives, so values must be obtained from economic models; since Enron was at the cutting edge of creating new derivative products, generally accepted approaches to valuation did not exist); Schwarcz, *supra* note 15, at 1309 n.2 (quoting e-mail communication between an accounting professor at Duke's business school and the author, a highly sophisticated scholar of structured finance, which incidentally illustrates how complex these transactions can be).

it that, was to use techniques of structured financing and asset securitization to accomplish two principal goals: first, to borrow money while keeping debt off the books; and second, to enable Enron to book the long-term value of a deal immediately under mark-to-market accounting rules.[181] Significantly, Fastow's corporate finance department set up transactions to milk them for beneficial accounting treatment—in terms of the substantive economics of the business, they did nothing at all. This observation is crucial to evaluating the duties of the lawyers who were employed to provide the documentation for the transactions.[182]

Many of the Fastow transactions have become well known by names such as Chewco, LJM1 and LJM2, and the Raptors. These names refer to special purpose entities (SPEs) which were set up as part of the deals. SPEs are often used in the process of asset securitization, in which the owners of some asset convert a stream of income over time into something that could be repackaged as a security and sold immediately to investors in the capital markets.[183] For example, a bank with many outstanding mortgage loans is entitled to receive monthly payments over the life of those loans, but it may wish to convert those payments into a lump sum in cash that it can use immediately. To do so, it "bundles" the mortgages and transfers them to an SPE, which issues tradable financial instruments (mortgage-backed securities), offered to investors at a discount relative to the present value of the stream of payments. The investors make money because they paid less for the securities than the income over time is worth. The bank is happy because it has converted a formerly illiquid asset into cash.

The investors in these transactions are often investment banks who deal with large corporations on a regular basis, and in Enron's case they were subjected to a fair amount of bullying by Fastow.[184] The banks and other institutional investors would often contribute funds directly to an SPE created for the deal, which in turn purchased the asset from its owner. In all of these transactions, the SPE is supposed to be independent

---

[181] Structured finance techniques can be used for legitimate business purposes, such as enabling a company to obtain lower-cost financing, transferring risk to parties who are better able to evaluate it, and permitting the owner of illiquid but valuable assets to use them to obtain financing. *See, e.g.,* HOUSE COMM. ON ENERGY & COMMERCE, *supra* note 180, at 92-93 (statement of Bala G. Dharan); Steven L. Schwarcz, *The Alchemy of Asset Securitization,* 1 STAN. J. L. BUS. & FIN. 133 (1994).

[182] Stephen Pepper offers the interesting observation that sophisticated clients may enjoy the benefit of access to "more" law to the extent they can initiate the discussion of the legal effect of a particular course of action. *See* Pepper, *supra* note 19, at 1581-82. Fastow's experience with accounting gimmickry gave him an advantage in the lawyer-client relationship, because he was able to suggest intricate, law-evading transactions that might superficially comply with formal legal rules. By comparison, a less sophisticated client who simply asked a lawyer to design a structure to accomplish some financial objective within the constraints of financial accounting rules might obtain access to "less" law because the lawyer may not think of the elaborate structures that someone like Fastow devised. As Pepper notes, the distinction between Fastow and the hypothetical unsophisticated client may not make a difference for the ethical analysis if the law respecting the transactions is the same in both instances. The lawyer's ethical obligation in either case is to give advice with respect to the law, and Fastow's superior ability to manipulate the law means only that the lawyer may have to push back harder against his determination to avoid legal regulation.

[183] *See generally* MCLEAN & ELKIND, *supra* note 14, at 157-59.

[184] *Id.* at 162-65.

of the seller of the assets. But to be deemed independent, it actually need only have three percent of its equity owned by a party unaffiliated with the seller.[185] (If the SPE is independent, it need not be "consolidated"—i.e., reported on the financial statements of the company that transferred assets to the SPE.) Thus, if Citibank or J.P. Morgan contributed $3 million to an SPE and Enron contributed $97 million, Enron would be permitted to transfer assets to the SPE and book the transaction as a bona fide sale to an independent party. This situation was very much preferable, from Enron's perspective, to a $100 million loan from the bank, which would have had an adverse effect on Enron's credit rating.

Although the legal and accounting requirements for transactions with unconsolidated, off-balance-sheet SPEs are not terribly rigorous, Enron had a hard time complying even with those.[186] Or, to put it differently, Enron was not interested in consummating a genuine transfer of assets to a truly independent entity. Its motivation was rather to continue to realize the economic benefits of owning the asset, preferably as operating income as opposed to a one-time profit, but to move any debt associated with the acquisition of the asset off its balance sheet.[187] In order to accomplish this goal, Enron officers and employees, with the assistance of accountants and lawyers, attempted to structure transactions that conformed to the letter of financial accounting rules, while aggressively pushing the boundaries of permissibility. To return to the image which opened this Article, the lawyers and accountants were directed to create a duck, even though the transactions (in more than one sense!) were a dog.

The duck-creating rules for SPE transactions can be summarized very briefly as follows:[188]

---

[185] Bratton, *supra* note 4, at 1306 n.118 (citing SEC and GAAP authorities for the three-percent rule, and noting that while the SEC has consistently denied that the three-percent rule is a bright-line test, it is generally understood as such by accountants).

[186] Eventually Enron employed so many SPEs that it was impossible to find investors with capital representing three percent of the valuation of all of the off-balance-sheet vehicles. *See* MCLEAN & ELKIND, *supra* note 14, at 166, 189; POWERS REPORT, *supra* note 11, at 41 (explaining that the "Chewco" partnership was created because Enron managers were having a hard time finding outside investors to finance a buyout of the JEDI joint venture).

[187] Second Batson Report, *supra* note 178, at 36-39 (motivation for SPE transactions); MCLEAN & ELKIND, *supra* note 14, at 368-69 (abuse of recurring vs. nonrecurring distinction); Schwarcz, *supra* note 181, at 142-43 (legitimate use of off-balance-sheet financing).

[188] *See generally* FIN. ACCOUNTING STANDARDS BD., ACCOUNTING FOR TRANSFERS AND SERVICING OF FINANCIAL ASSETS AND EXTINGUISHMENTS OF LIABILITY—A REPLACEMENT OF FASB STATEMENT NO. 125 (2000) (statement of Financial Accounting Standards No. 140). Several reports prepared under the supervision of the bankruptcy court provide useful summaries of the applicable financial accounting standards. *See, e.g.*, Report of Harrison J. Goldin, Court-Appointed Examiner in the Enron North America Bankruptcy Proceeding, Respecting His Investigation of the Role of Certain Entities in Transactions Pertaining to Special Purpose Entities (Nov. 14, 2003), *available at* http://www.enron.com/corp/por/supporting.html (last visited June 29, 2004) [hereinafter Goldin SPE Report]. For the relevant legal standards, see STEVEN L. SCHWARCZ, STRUCTURED FINANCE: A GUIDE TO THE PRINCIPLES OF ASSET SECURITIZATION (2d ed. 1993).

- The SPE must be "bankruptcy remote" from the originating company (e.g., Enron), so that the originating company's credit risks do not affect the risks associated with owning the securities of the SPE.[189]
- Bankruptcy remoteness depends, in turn, on the genuine transfer of the economic risks and benefits associated with the assets from the originating company to the SPE.[190] In other words, the transfer must be a "true sale."[191]
- If the SPE is not truly independent (i.e., bankruptcy remote) from the originating company, the assets and liabilities of the SPE must be consolidated on the financial statements of the originating company.[192] Fleshing out the requirement of independent ownership, financial accounting standards set a minimum of three percent for the equity that must be contributed by entities unaffiliated with the originating company.[193]
- The independence of an SPE can be compromised by the originating company retaining control over the asset; this can be accomplished through side deals, such as loan guarantees, between the originating company and the SPE, and may be shown by the originating company's attempt to recognize gains in the value of the SPE as earnings on its own balance sheet.[194]

Notice, however, that these norms are subject to manipulation or gaming by lawyers who may be motivated to comply with them only formally. A complete analysis of the appropriateness of the Enron transactions would have to give additional content to those rules by tapping into the understandings of the relevant interpretive community, which are germane to the exercise of interpretive judgment by lawyers and accountants. These principles are relevant to interpretation and can constrain the exercise of judgment, but only if the lawyer engaged in the process of interpretation belongs to a community that is interested in maintaining a stable, publicly accessible framework for cooperative activity. A lawyer who belongs to Andy Fastow's interpretive community

---

[189] Schwarcz, *supra* note 181, at 135.

[190] Second Batson Report, *supra* note 178, app. C at 9-11; POWERS REPORT, *supra* note 11, at 14; Bratton, *supra* note 4, at 1306-07 (citing numerous GAAP authorities); Schwarcz, *supra* note 181, at 141.

[191] Second Batson Report, *supra* note 178, at 37-38.

[192] POWERS REPORT, *supra* note 11, at 38-39 (claiming that consolidation is a presumptive requirement, and the presumption can be overcome only if two conditions are met, namely independence of ownership and control of the SPE).

[193] *See supra* note 185.

[194] Second Batson Report, *supra* note 178, app. C at 12-13, 20-23; POWERS REPORT, *supra* note 11, at 36-37; Christine E. Earley et al., *Some Thoughts on the Audit Failure at Enron, the Demise of Andersen, and the Ethical Climate of Public Accounting Firms*, 35 CONN. L. REV. 1013, 1019-20 (2003) (detailing side agreement between Enron and Michael Kopper, an Enron employee whose involvement need not be disclosed as a related-party transaction, guaranteeing loan from Barclay's Bank to Kopper, for the purpose of acquiring a three-percent interest in Chewco, an SPE run by Andy Fastow); Schwarcz, *supra* note 181, at 136. Enron used complex financial devices, such as a transaction it called a Total Return Swap, to retain the benefits of an asset transferred to an SPE. Second Batson Report, *supra* note 178, app. C at 16-18.

might be interested only in securing short-term economic benefits for her client, or worse, for an individual agent of her client. As I have argued, however, this interpretive stance cannot be given a normative justification that reaches all the way down to the bedrock of the social function of the law. If, on the other hand, a lawyer is interested in exercising judgment in a way that has plausible ethical foundations, she will probably discover that the interpretive community recognizes certain norms that differentiate artificially created ducks from real ducks—that is, distinguishing between transactions that are motivated only by the attempt to create accounting results and those that have a real economic substance. In addition to the rules for duck-ness, there are principles regulating interpretation that sort ducks from dogs dressed up as ducks, including:

- One of the benefits of SPE financing is "disintermediation," or the reduction of transaction costs by removing intermediaries such as banks from the financing process.[195] A transaction involving multiple intermediaries and a highly complex series of steps is unlikely to result in the transaction cost savings that usually justifies SPE transactions.
- Because SPE transactions can benefit both the originating company and investors in the SPE, one would expect a legitimate transaction to be fully disclosed in a sufficiently clear manner. One of the recurring themes of the commentary on the Enron transactions is the opacity of the disclosures.[196] An undisclosed transaction or one that is camouflaged in layers of obfuscating legalese should alert lawyers and accountants that something is fishy.[197]
- Additional caution is warranted when other aspects of the transaction are aggressive. For example, in the LJM transactions, Enron capitalized the SPEs with $1.2 billion of its own common stock, in exchange for notes issued by the SPEs. This is a once-disfavored funding mechanism, and GAAP requires that Enron reduce shareholder equity in the amount of the newly issued

---

[195] Schwarcz, *supra* note 15, at 1315.

[196] *See, e.g.*, POWERS REPORT, *supra* note 11, at 192; Bratton, *supra* note 4, at 1281 (calling financial statements "famously opaque"). The reaction of James Chanos, a sophisticated Wall Street hedge fund manager, is typical: "We read the footnotes in Enron's financial statements about these transactions over and over again, and . . . we could not decipher what impact they had on Enron's overall financial condition." Chanos, *supra* note 180, at 73; *see also* SWARTZ & WATKINS, *supra* note 10, at xi-xiii, 331 (reporting anecdote of Houston financial advisor who did not recommend Enron stock because he could not make sense of its financial statements and Warren Buffett's statement that he never understood how Enron made money). Indeed, the complexity of some of the SPE transactions, such as the "Raptor" hedges, made it difficult even for internal Enron managers to know how a given business unit was performing. *See* Baird & Rasmussen, *supra* note 179, at 1804-06.

[197] I take the point that some structured finance transactions can be so complex that disclosure is necessarily imperfect—either it oversimplifies the transaction or it provides so much detail that it goes over the head of most investors. *See* Schwarcz, *supra* note 15, at 1316-17. When a transaction becomes this complicated, the clarity of the disclosure language, by itself, is an insufficient indication of abuse. In a case like this, however, professionals have a heightened obligation of inquiry and should rely even more heavily on other factors to guide their interpretation of the relevant legal and accounting standards.

shares until the SPE pays down the notes.[198] Use of this kind of capitalization scheme, and the failure of Enron to account for the transaction properly, should have put professionals on notice that other aspects of the transaction should be scrutinized carefully.

- The financial accounting system in general is intended to provide transparent, accurate, easily understood information to managers, creditors, and investors regarding the financial condition of the reporting company.[199] If it appears that managers are valuing complexity for its own sake, it could be a red flag warning to lawyers and accountants that the transaction is intended to manipulate the numbers on the company's financial statements, rather than accomplish some economically useful end.

Like the disciplining rules that differentiate between legitimate structuring to capture favorable tax treatment from bogus tax shelters, these principles of interpretation are not binary, all-or-nothing rules. There is no algorithmic way to capture the process of reasoning from these principles to a correct application of the law to an SPE transaction. For this reason, there may be hard cases in which competent lawyers disagree over whether a given transaction is permissible, and there may be cases in which some lawyers are more aggressive than others in pushing the boundaries of the rules. This is as it should be. My claim is not that the appropriately constrained judgment of interpretive communities produces a single right answer in every case. Rather, the limit on lawyers' creativity that prevents it from degenerating into undue aggressiveness is the requirement of public justifiability. A lawyer must be prepared, in principle, to articulate a reason why the legal treatment (for tax, accounting, bankruptcy, etc., purposes) of a transaction is legitimate, in light of the end sought to be advanced by the regulatory regime in question. In the case of the Enron SPE transactions reviewed in the Powers and Batson reports, there is simply no plausible justification available. Fastow and his confederates had manipulated the techniques of structured financing to produce spurious accounting results which had no relationship whatsoever to the underlying economics of the transactions. Their abuse was abetted by the Holmesian bad man attitudes of lawyers and accountants, who in effect agreed with Fastow that if the rules do not explicitly prohibit an act, it is permissible.

3. Legal Restraints on Torture

The invasion of Afghanistan in the wake of the September 11 attacks resulted in the capture of numerous detainees with possible al-Qaeda affiliation, who might have possessed information on the structure of the organization, personnel, or even future terrorist attacks. The Bush administration was therefore faced with an urgent question regarding the limits it should impose on interrogation techniques. Officials in the Department of Defense and advisers to the president naturally turned to lawyers

---

198 Bratton, *supra* note 4, at 1314-15.

199 Second Batson Report, *supra* note 178, app. B at 3-5.

to interpret and apply the domestic and international legal norms governing the treatment of prisoners.[200] The resulting memos, prepared by the Justice Department's Office of Legal Counsel, were leaked to the press and quickly dubbed the "torture memos." They were eventually disclosed by the White House and are now widely available in electronic form.[201] The memos consider a wide range of legal issues, from whether the Geneva Convention protections afforded to prisoners of war extend to suspected Taliban or al-Qaeda detainees, to whether the President's power as Commander in Chief could be limited by an act of Congress criminalizing mistreatment of prisoners. One of the most notorious memos concluded that certain methods of interrogation might be cruel, inhuman, or degrading, yet fall outside the definition of prohibited acts of torture.[202] Moreover, even if an act were deemed torture, the memo concluded that it might be justified by self-defense or necessity.

Contrary to the suggestion by one of the authors of the memos that critics are implying that it is taboo even to ask legal questions about torture,[203] I do not perceive anything inherently wrong with the administration's decision to seek advice on the application of the law governing torture. The law governing what may be done to a given class of prisoners is quite complex, involving the overlapping norms of international, military, domestic criminal, and constitutional law. As government officials considered the interrogation of detainees ex ante, they could reasonably have worried that an act that did not appear to an ordinary observer to constitute torture might nevertheless contravene some technical legal rule. For example, the Geneva Convention on the

---

[200] There is considerable uncertainty in the law of lawyering over the identity of the client represented by federal government lawyers. As one commentator put it, on any given day the lawyer's client might be identified as a particular agency, an agency official, the executive branch of the government, the United States as a whole, or the public interest. *See* Catherine J. Lanctot, *The Duty of Zealous Advocacy and the Ethics of the Federal Government Lawyer: The Three Hardest Questions*, 64 S. CAL. L. REV. 951, 955 (1991). Specifically with regard to the Office of Legal Counsel ("OLC"), there is controversy over how the role of OLC lawyers should be understood, with positions arrayed on a continuum between litigation-style advocacy on the one hand, and neutral judge-style reasoning on the other. *See* John O. McGinnis, *Models of the Opinion Function of the Attorney General: A Normative, Descriptive, and Historical Prolegomenon*, 15 CARDOZO L. REV. 375 (1993); Randolph D. Moss, *Executive Branch Legal Interpretation: A Perspective from the Office of Legal Counsel*, 52 ADMIN. L. REV. 1303, 1305-06 (2000). It should be clear that my sympathies lean toward the latter extreme, what Moss calls the "neutral expositor" model. In terms of the client-identity question, though, there is less controversy that OLC lawyers in particular, as opposed to government lawyers in general, owe their loyalty and obligation to render candid advice to an identifiable government official, namely the President. Moss, *supra*, at 1316-17. Thus, when I use the term "client" in this section I refer to the President and his top-level advisors.

[201] Two useful collections of the memos are FindLaw, *at* http://news.findlaw.com/hdocs/docs/dod/62204index.html (last visited Dec. 7, 2004), and the National Security Archive at George Washington University, *at* http://www2.gwu.edu/~nsarchiv/NSAEBB/NSAEBB127/index.htm (last visited Dec. 7, 2004).

[202] *See* Aug. 1 OLC Memo, *supra* note 17.

[203] *See* Liptak, *supra* note 18 (quoting John Yoo's statement that "[s]ome critics of the Justice Department's work seem to assume that it is politically incorrect to ask the meaning of a publicly enacted law").

treatment of prisoners of war prohibits "outrages upon personal dignity, in particular, humiliating and degrading treatment,"[204] which conceivably might be interpreted to include what domestic law enforcement personnel would regard as relatively innocuous interrogation tactics. The Army runs a school that teaches intelligence officers how to extract information from unwilling detainees, and although it trains soldiers to "lie . . . prey on a prisoner's ethnic stereotypes, sexual urges and religious prejudices," it nevertheless also claims to respect governing legal norms against torture, as opposed to harsh interrogation techniques.[205] To put the point in Hartian terms, the language of any prohibition on torture will contain a core prohibition of clearly immoral acts, with a penumbra of application to cases in which the immorality is not clear.[206] Thus, it is not immoral to seek legal advice on how to avoid the prohibition on a plainly immoral act, as long as the actor intends to commit a morally permitted, but possibly legally prohibited act.

It is also important to be careful about the role of moral and policy considerations in the process of giving legal advice. John Yoo, one of the principal drafters of the torture memos, has argued that the Justice Department lawyers were not asked to consider policy or moral issues.[207] From this fact about the instructions given to the lawyers, Yoo seeks to infer the conclusion that moral and policy considerations should be somehow hermetically separated from legal advice. As Yoo argues: "[T]he memo sought to answer a discrete question: What is the meaning of 'torture' under the federal criminal laws? What the law permits and what policymakers chose to do are entirely different things."[208] True enough, but it may be the case that "[w]hat the law permits" cannot be determined without reference to moral considerations. Consider, for example, the analysis of the necessity defense to federal criminal liability under the statute implementing the international Convention Against Torture.[209] The Justice Department's memo on the Convention concludes that a necessity defense should be available to a charge of having violated the federal statute.[210] On the standard formulation of the necessity defense, the trier of fact is called upon to decide whether the actor promoted

[204] *See* Geneva Convention (III) Relative to the Treatment of Prisoners of War, *opened for signature* Aug. 12, 1949, art. 3(1)(c), 6 U.S.T. 3316, 75 U.N.T.S. 135.

[205] *See* Sanford Levinson, *"Precommitment" and "Postcommitment": The Ban on Torture in the Wake of September 11*, 81 TEX. L. REV. 2013, 2025 (2003) (quoting Jess Bravin, *Interrogation School Tells Army Recruits How Grilling Works; 30 Techniques in 16 Weeks, Just Short of Torture; Do They Yield Much?*, WALL ST. J., Apr. 26, 2002, at A1).

[206] *See* HART, *supra* note 27, at 144-47.

[207] *See* John C. Yoo, *A Critical Look at Torture Law*, L.A. TIMES, June 6, 2004, at B11.

[208] *Id.*; *see also* Posner & Vermeule, *supra* note 16 ("[T]he Justice Department lawyers . . . were not asked for moral or political advice . . . .").

[209] The federal statute implementing the convention is 18 U.S.C. §§ 2340-2340A (2000). The full title of the relevant convention is Convention *Against Torture and Other Cruel, Inhuman or Degrading Treatment or Punishment*, G.A. Res. 39/46, 39 U.N. GAOR, Supp. No. 51, U.N. Doc. A/39/51 (1984) [hereinafter *Convention Against Torture*].

[210] *See* Aug. 1 OLC Memo, *supra* note 17, at 39-41.

higher-valued goods at the expense of lesser values; if so, the act was justified by the necessity.[211] This evaluation in effect incorporates moral values by reference into the application of legal rules, because "[t]he actor and the court that judges him must know what is good and bad, beneficial and harmful, and it must know comparatively what sorts of things are worse than others."[212] Moreover, to the extent courts and other legal officials have consistently invoked moral considerations to justify their decisions, they are deemed part of law by the rule of recognition prevalent in the legal system.[213] When the lawyers were asked to interpret the law governing torture, there was no way for them to avoid dealing with moral and policy issues.[214]

Similarly, some of the government lawyers' arguments make sense only from an artificially narrow perspective, focused only on particular legal texts divorced from their historical and policy contexts. Administration officials referred repeatedly to the novel nature of the conflict with al-Qaeda, implying that the law ought to be interpreted less rigorously.[215] This argument is blocked, however, by specific provisions in the international law against torture. The 1984 Convention Against Torture contains

---

[211] *See* WAYNE R. LAFAVE, Criminal Law § 5.4(a) (3d ed. 2000). The authors of the memos followed this formulation of the necessity defense. *See* Aug. 1 OLC Memo, *supra* note 17, at 39-40; Working Group Report on Detainee Interrogations in the Global War on Terrorism 25-26 (March 6, 2003), *available at* http://www.cdi.org/news/law/pentagon-torture-memo.pdf [hereinafter Working Group Report].

[212] Moore, *supra* note 86, at 286. Joseph Raz argues that the law does not incorporate morality by reference in this case, because the decisionmaker is already required to take moral considerations into account; the law merely reiterates that it does not *exclude* moral considerations from the decision. *See* Raz, *supra* note 144. Whether one prefers to *see* the issue as non-exclusion or incorporation, the point remains that the interpretation of the law as such requires reference to moral values.

[213] *See* Hart, *supra* note 77, at 265.

[214] In any event, it is highly disingenuous for Yoo to defend the memos by claiming that lawyers were not asked to give policy advice when the memos contain extensive discussion of policy issues. *See, e.g.,* Memorandum from Jay S. Bybee to Alberto R. Gonzales and William J. Haynes 25-28 (Jan. 22, 2002). The discussion of necessity, in particular, specifically acknowledges that "the purpose behind necessity is one of public policy." Aug. 1 OLC Memo, *supra* note 17, at 40; Working Group Report, *supra* note 211, at 25.

[215] *See, e.g.,* the statements of White House Counsel Gonzales accompanying the release of the memos:

> America today does face a different kind of enemy in al Qaeda and its affiliates. And we face an enemy that targets innocent civilians, and we have *see*n certainly graphic evidence of that in recent days. We face an enemy that lies in the shadows, an enemy that doesn't sign treaties, they don't wear uniforms, an enemy that owes no allegiance to any country, they do not cherish life. An enemy that doesn't fight, attack or plan according to accepted laws of war, in particular Geneva Conventions.

Press Briefing, White House Counsel Judge Alberto Gonzales (Jun. 22, 2004), *available at* http://www.whitehouse.gov/news/releases/2004/06/20040622-14.html; *see also* Draft Memorandum from Alberto R. Gonzales to the President 3 (Jan. 25, 2002) ("[T]his is a new type of warfare—one not contemplated in 1949 when [the Geneva Convention] was framed . . . ."). Again it is ironic to read defenders of the administration arguing that lawyers should engage only in formalistic "legal" interpretation, while at the same time invoking historical and policy-based considerations in support of their own legal arguments.

a non-derogation provision, which bluntly states that "[n]o exceptional circumstances whatsoever, whether a state of war or a threat of war, internal political instability or any other public emergency, may be invoked as a justification of torture."[216] The non-derogation language was included specifically to prevent states from attempting to define a category of crimen exceptum, or crimes so dangerous to society that law enforcement officials should be permitted extraordinary latitude.[217] The enactment history of the 1984 Convention shows that an argument from the unprecedented nature of the conflict with al-Qaeda is simply going to be a nonstarter. States frequently try to justify torture as a reasonable self-defense measure against an extraordinary threat, which is precisely why the non-derogation provision was included in the Convention. Calling this a "policy" argument, and then trying to argue that the government had not asked for policy advice, misses the point that it may be impossible to ascertain the content of the law without reference to policy considerations.

Not only did the government lawyers exclude moral, policy, and historical considerations from their analysis, but they ignored other clearly relevant legal texts and traditional techniques for interpreting texts. In other words, even if the lawyers believed they were justified in adopting a textualist style of interpretation, they did a lousy job at textualism. Consider, for example, the memorandum which concluded that an act constitutes torture under a federal statute only if, inter alia, the actor specifically intended to cause severe physical mental pain or suffering, with "severe" defined in terms of other federal statutes defining a medical emergency for the purpose of establishing a right to health benefits.[218] To put it mildly, it is peculiar to make an argument analogizing "severe pain" for the purposes of a statute prohibiting torture with another statute defining an emergency as involving a "serious dysfunction of any bodily organ or part." The health benefits statute notes, almost in passing, that in an emergency the patient will exhibit symptoms including severe pain. This is not a definition of severe pain in terms of organ dysfunction. It is a definition of emergency in terms of organ dysfunction with possible accompanying severe pain. Imagine a definition of "winter" as "a season whose manifestations include snow, ice, and cold weather." It does not follow from that definition that cold weather is weather in which there is snow—obviously enough it can be cold outside and not snowing. Similarly, a person can experience severe pain (and be entitled to health benefits under the statute) without being in imminent jeopardy of organ failure or dysfunction.

The government lawyers would not have made this definitional mistake if they had used a different set of texts for their argument by analogy. In addition to the statute under consideration, implementing the 1984 Convention Against Torture, the U.S.

---

216 *Convention Against Torture*, *supra* note 209, art. 2(2). In ratifying the treaty, the United States stated reservations to the definition of torture (evidently to exempt capital punishment from the reach of the Convention) but it did not state any reservations to the non-derogation provision in Article 2(2). *See* Levinson, *supra* note 205, at 2014-16.

217 *See* EDWARD PETERS, TORTURE 6 (2d ed. 1996).

218 *See* Aug. 1 OLC Memo, *supra* note 17, at 5-6 (citing the health benefits statutes).

Immigration and Naturalization Service adopted regulations implementing the Convention, permitting aliens otherwise subject to removal to apply for an exemption on the ground that he or she would be subject to torture if returned or extradited to another country.[219] The regulations define torture as "any act by which severe pain or suffering . . . is intentionally inflicted."[220] Unsurprisingly, there is a substantial body of cases interpreting the term "torture" in the context of immigration proceedings,[221] none of which were cited in the Justice Department memo. Perhaps these cases are distinguishable, but their omission is striking in the context of an analysis of the term "severe pain" in a torture-related statute. Surely they are better analogies for the criminal prohibition on torture than the statute authorizing health benefits for patients experiencing a medical emergency.

This kind of crabbed argumentation strongly suggests that the lawyers had a motive other than providing their client with an impartial and objective analysis of the law. There is nothing wrong with advising a client to take a novel or creative position under existing law, in the hope that a legal official might treat the client's position favorably. If transactional lawyers were permitted to give only the most conservative legal advice, a significant avenue for legal change would be closed off. If a lawyer's advice is creative and the client's position is unlikely to prevail, however, the lawyer owes an obligation to explain this clearly to the client, so that the client can decide whether to incur the risk of an unfavorable ruling.[222] One of the striking things about the whole set of Justice Department memos is that they do not acknowledge how far out of the mainstream their position is, with respect to executive power, the application of international legal norms, the construction of federal statutes, and other legal issues they address. Two of the defenders of the government lawyers argue, in effect, that the position taken in the memos, particularly with respect to executive power, is so cutting edge that it has wrongly been thought crazy rather than innovative.[223] The trouble with this defense is that nowhere in the memos do the authors flag the argument as a challenge to received wisdom. Instead, it is presented without qualification, almost blandly, as a factual report on what the law is, not what it might be if the innovative arguments of the authors were accepted.

As suggested previously, the explanation for the poor quality of the legal analysis in the memos may be the attitude that the lawyers were instructed— perhaps expressly,

---

[219] *See* 8 C.F.R. § 208.11-208.3 (1999).

[220] *Id.* § 208.18(a)(1).

[221] *See, e.g.*, Zubeda v. Ashcroft, 333 F.3d 463, 472 (3d Cir. 2003) (stating that rape can constitute torture); Al-Saher v. INS, 268 F.3d 1143, 1147 (9th Cir. 2001) (stating that electric shocks to the genitals, beatings, and suspension from rotating ceiling fans can constitute torture).

[222] The state bar disciplinary rules in effect in most jurisdictions require a lawyer to "explain a matter to the extent reasonably necessary to permit the client to make informed decisions regarding the representation." MODEL RULES, *supra* note 20, R. 1.4(b).

[223] *See* Posner & Vermeule, *supra* note 16 (arguing that the "conventional view" of executive power "has been challenged in recent years by a dynamic generation of younger scholars," including John Yoo).

but likely tacitly—to adopt when analyzing legal restrictions on torture. According to published reports, the administration repeated the mantra "forward-leaning" to describe the type of advice it wanted.[224] Lawyers were expected to take risks, think outside the box, and in effect approach the law from an adversarial point of view, rather than as a set of legitimate reasons upon which to act. This direction from the "client" is quite likely to have biased the lawyers' advice by causing them to adopt a Holmesian bad man attitude toward the law. If this stance is troublesome in the context of taxation and financial accounting, it seems almost monstrous when applied to law that is aimed at protecting the most fundamental aspects of human dignity. The obvious context and purpose of certain categories of law compels individuals and lawyers not just to avoid violations, but to "avoid avoidance." That is, some kinds of laws command citizens, in effect, not to calibrate their actions finely in close proximity to legal boundaries. Jeremy Waldron offers a nice example: "Someone for whom the important question is 'How much may I flirt with my student before it counts as harassment?' is already poorly positioned with regard to the concerns underlying harassment law."[225] In the case of harassment, as well as torture, the nature of the prohibited activity exerts a feedback effect on the attitude that one should take when interpreting the law. It is not "routine lawyerly stuff" at all to ignore these interpretive norms; rather, the intelligibility of the law depends on them.

I want to make clear a perhaps unsettling implication of the lawyer's duty to apply the law as it actually is, as opposed to the way the lawyer would like it to be. If the law, properly interpreted, prohibits a certain interrogation technique, then it is irrelevant if a government official would prefer a more "forward-leaning" approach to dealing with detainees. But, if the law permits a technique, such as the use of "stress positions," sleep deprivation, or bombardment by lights and sound,[226] then the lawyer's belief that these techniques are morally wrong should be excluded from the lawyer's analysis of the law. The law governing lawyers permits (but does not require) a lawyer to advise a client on the basis of relevant "moral, economic, social and political factors."[227] Thus, there is nothing wrong with saying to the client, in effect, "That is legal but it is a rotten thing to do." (That was exactly the reaction of the State Department to the White House Counsel's advice that the Geneva Conventions did not apply to the conflict in Afghanistan.[228]) If the client has heard that advice, however, and still decides to go forward with a course of action that the lawyer finds morally wrong, the lawyer's

---

[224] *See* Tim Golden, *After Terror, a Secret Rewriting of Military Law*, N.Y. TIMES, Oct. 24, 2004, at A1.

[225] Waldron, *supra* note 90, at 535-36 n.66.

[226] *See* Levinson, *supra* note 205, at 2027 (quoting Bravin, *supra* note 205, at A1 (discussing military's protocols for conducting harsh investigations)); Don Van Natta, Jr., *Questioning Terror Suspects in a Dark and Surreal World*, N.Y. TIMES, Mar. 9, 2003, at A1 (reporting on interrogation techniques used by U.S. personnel).

[227] MODEL RULES, *supra* note 20, R. 2.1; *see also* Pepper, *supra* note 19, at 1563-64.

[228] *See* Memorandum from William H. Taft IV to Counsel for the President (Feb. 2, 2002).

obligation is to assist the client, regardless of her moral objection. The reason is the settlement and coordination function of the law that is the centerpiece of this approach to legal ethics.

People disagree in good faith over the morality of harsh interrogation techniques, even outright torture, and the scope of cases in which it should be permissible. Judge Posner has argued that no one should be in a position of public responsibility who doubts that, if the stakes are high enough, torture is permissible.[229] Naturally there are others who maintain that torture is never permissible, even in so-called "ticking bomb" cases.[230] Then there are a variety of middle-ground positions, including doubts about the generalizability of the ticking bomb hypothetical,[231] and attempts to qualify the limited permissibility of torture with various democratic process controls.[232] There are undoubtedly cases on which all would agree that torture is wrong, but there are circumstances in which thoughtful and fully informed citizens would reasonably disagree about the moral acceptability of a certain technique, or whether it deserves the normatively laden ascription "torture." Because of the shared interest in working together on the common project of national defense within a constitutional framework that protects human rights, individuals have set up a system of legal procedures for resolving these normative conflicts. Insofar as they are engaging in practical, rather than theoretical reasoning, they have a second-order moral reason to respect the law's position on one of these questions.[233] No matter how serious or strongly felt the lawyer's moral objection to the law, the law nevertheless dictates what is permissible in the context of the attorney-client relationship, absent some kind of catastrophic moral horror.[234] Even if

---

[229] Richard A. Posner, *The Best Offense*, NEW REPUBLIC, Sept. 2, 2002, at 28, 30; *see also* Mark Bowden, *The Dark Art of Interrogation,* ATLANTIC MONTHLY, Oct. 2003, at 51, 76 ("[C]oercion is an issue that is rightly handled with a wink[;] . . . it should be banned but also quietly practiced.").

[230] *See, e.g.,* Oren Gross, *The Prohibition on Torture and the Limits of the Law, in* TORTURE (Sanford Levinson ed., 2004); Henry Shue, Torture, 7 Phil. & Pub. Aff. 124 (1978); Anthony Lewis, Making Torture Legal, N.Y. REV. BOOKS, July 15, 2004, at 4.

[231] *See, e.g.,* Moore, *supra* note 86; *see also* Winfried Brugger, *May Government Ever Use Torture? Two Responses from German Law,* 48 AM. J. COMP. L. 661 (2000).

[232] *See, e.g.,* ALAN M. DERSHOWITZ, WHY TERRORISM WORKS (2002) (proposing "torture warrants" to subject interrogations to judicial oversight); MICHAEL IGNATIEFF, THE LESSER EVIL: POLITICAL ETHICS IN AN AGE OF TERROR (2004) (arguing for constraints like transparency and accountability).

[233] For the terminology of first- and second-order reasons, and the argument for the authority of law, *see* Wendel, *supra* note 6, at 365, 376-84.

[234] To the obvious rejoinder that torture is a paradigmatic case of a catastrophic moral horror, the response is that it is true in some cases. The politically motivated torture of opponents of the government in order to silence dissent, or the wholly gratuitous torture of innocent detainees, would count as a catastrophic moral horror, and no legal permission to engage in these acts would preempt the lawyer's first-order moral reasons not to take part in it. But the cases we are concerned about here do not fall within the core of clear moral catastrophes because one could believe in the permissibility of using coercive or pain-inducing interrogation techniques in some cases, on some suspects, given a sufficiently compelling justification. In order to be warranted in "opting out" of the authority of law, a lawyer must believe not only that the law is wrong, but that anyone who disagrees is completely failing to function as a moral

the lawyer believes, as many do, that the present climate of fear has made us too willing to discard humanitarian considerations, lawmaking is a democratic process, and the lawyer's conscience cannot trump the result of fair procedures where the law on point is clear. As a private citizen, the lawyer is free to lobby or protest the law; the lawyer may withdraw from representing the client; and the lawyer may employ legal channels (with the client's consent, of course) on behalf of the client to attempt to change the law. But the negative aspect of professionalism, which is an implication of the authority conception of legal ethics, precludes reference to first-order moral reasons, except to the extent they are incorporated into law or made relevant to the interpretation of law by the conventional practices of courts and lawyers.

III. CONCLUSION

In response to public criticism of the role of lawyers in the corporate scandals which came to light in 2002, lawyers argued that they were simply responding rationally to the competitive pressures of the marketplace. Similarly, one excuse offered by apologists for the so-called torture memos is that the lawyers were responding to administration pressure to think "outside the box" in the war on terrorism. In both of these cases, we are supposed to grant normative significance to the fact that clients desire aggressive and creative lawyers who are willing to walk right up to the line between legality and illegality, and even push the boundaries if necessary. Lawyers and accountants have described how clients demand, "Show me where it says I can't do that,"[235] when professionals raise concerns about suspicious transactions. In the end, however, it is not for clients to say what the law is. If the client demands that the lawyer paste an orange plastic beak on a dog and call it a duck, the lawyer's response must be that the rules may appear to permit creating ducks out of dogs, but that the law properly interpreted would characterize the creature as a dog. Legal rules are not self-interpreting, and a conclusion about what the law says, with respect to some transaction, depends on the interpretive attitude that one takes toward the rules. The instrumentalist attitude, which treats the law as merely an obstacle to be planned around, cannot be justified in terms of the social function of law, which is to permit people to coordinate their activities in a complex, highly legalistic society. Recognizing this function of law, professional

agent, or is "massively, corruptly, stupidly wrong," as I have previously put the point. *See id.* at 417 n.190. A community is justified in shunning a citizen whose moral beliefs are so clearly beyond the pale that it would be impossible to engage in cooperative, peaceful coexistence with the individual. To the extent a person's views are wrong, but not so wrong that the person should be shunned, those views are part of the background of normative debate that makes it necessary to establish democratic and legal procedures in order to facilitate cooperative endeavors. Thus, lawyers acting in a representative capacity are obligated to respect the resolution achieved by the legal system, with respect to positions that are within the range of good faith moral disagreement.

[235] *Cf. Fundamental Causes of the Accounting Debacle at Enron: Show Me Where It Says I Can't: Summary of Testimony Before the House Comm. on Energy and Commerce*, 107th Cong. (Feb. 6, 2002) (statement of Roman L. Weil), available at http://gsb.uchicago.edu/pdf/weil_testimony.pdf.

communities have developed what we can refer to as disciplining rules, principles of interpretation, or regulative norms that stabilize interpretation and permit discrimination between legitimate and illegitimate constructions of law. Lawyers reasoning on the basis of these disciplining rules, can articulate criteria for the exercise of professional judgment, which are justified on the basis of the purposes standing behind the regime of law that applies in a given domain.

This Article has set out a theory of legal ethics which is grounded in fidelity to the law. Professionalism, in the sense we have been discussing here, does not mean that the lawyer's responsibility is to do right on an all-things-considered basis. Nor is the lawyer acting as an individual moral agent, doing right by her own lights. The lodestar here is always an interpretation of applicable legal norms. Because we disagree in good faith and, in many cases intractably, it is unrealistic to expect the process of moral reasoning alone to provide a stable framework for cooperative social activity. The law has authority to the extent it permits us to move beyond moral disagreement and settle on a common framework for action. As a corollary to this theory of authority, lawyers must not be permitted to unsettle the settlement, and to evade the requirements that have been laid down by a procedural mechanism for resolving moral conflict. The Holmesian bad man attitude toward the law would have exactly that effect. For this reason, it is an unacceptable interpretive stance to take toward the law.

Law as Rationalization: Getting Beyond Reason to Business Ethics[*]

Jeffrey M. Lipshaw[**]

> [T]here is a natural and unavoidable dialectic of pure reason, not one in which a bungler might be entangled through lack of acquaintance, or one that some sophist has artfully invented to confuse rational people, but one that irremediably attaches to human reason, so that even after we have exposed the mirage it will still not cease to lead our reason with false hopes, continually propelling it into momentary aberrations that always need to be removed.
>
> —Immanuel Kant[1]

I. INTRODUCTION

This article attempts to reconcile philosophically how we approach and deal with the difference between law and ethics in business decisions, particularly when argumentation of the law may tell us only what is required or permitted, on the one hand, as against what ethical duties or responsibilities might demand, on the other.

Sometimes the issue of ethical duty is wholly internal to the individual and lacks clear legal implications. For example, many years ago, R.J. Reynolds had recently purchased Kentucky Fried Chicken (KFC). One of the lawyers for KFC quietly told me how uncomfortable it was to work for a tobacco company. I thought about it. How would

---

[*] Originally published at 37 U. Tol. L. Rev. 959 (2006). Reprinted by permission.

[**] Visiting Associate Professor of Law, Tulane University Law School. I have been aided immeasurably by comments from Brian Bix, Wilson Parker, Sidney Shapiro, Alan Calnan, Dennis Sasso, Larry Kramer, Frank Snyder, Robin Bradley Kar, David McGowan, and two unnamed readers who reviewed a prior version for an academic press and noted a number of flaws I hope I have corrected. In addition, in the fall of 2005, a group at the Wake Forest University School of Law, which in addition to Professors Shapiro, Calnan, and Parker included Michael Curtis, Ronald Wright, Graham Strong, Mark Hall, and John Korzen, conducted a number of sessions around readings on law and economics. Those sessions helped me immensely.

[1] Immanuel Kant, Critique of Pure Reason 386-87 (Paul Guyer & Allen W. Wood trans., 1998).

I react? Would my moral qualms about the sale and marketing of tobacco cause me to consider changing jobs? At the time, I had young children. Imagine the conflicting duties. My wife and children rely on my income, and because of my job, are settled in a community. Do my moral concerns about contributing to the success of a tobacco company outweigh the difficulties I might cause to my family if I change jobs? How might I go about making and justifying this decision?

Sometimes there is the same issue of internal conscience with broader moral, if not legal ramifications. For example, the manufacturer of automotive components had a committee of engineers and lawyers known as the Product Integrity Committee. Its job was to investigate claims of product defects and to determine whether, in fact, there was a defect, and if necessary, to recommend broad warranty campaigns or even product recalls. Determining that federal law required a recall involved a two-step analysis. First, was there a defect? Second, did the defect pose an unreasonable risk to highway safety? Often, there was, at least in theory, a defect, but even that inquiry had gray areas. The more difficult question was whether the company believed the defect posed an unreasonable risk to highway safety. This issue was not so simple as merely to issue a recall for every suspected failure. Specifically, if one recalled 400,000 vehicles for an illusory or inconsequential defect, and it took the dealer three hours to replace the part at, say, $35 per hour, the cost to the component part company could be in excess of $40 million, often for a part that was originally sold for a few cents. In those circumstances, how did one, balance the conflicting duties to the public and those of financial prudence?

As a second illustration, a chemical company manufactured flame retardant additives for plastics. There was no question that the product, by preventing furniture fires, or fires in television or computer or printer housings, saved lives. But there were unresolved questions (all subjected to scientific study by the industry and environmental groups) about the environment impact of the product—its pervasiveness and persistence in the environment, its ability to accumulate in the body, and its toxicity, if any. There the issue was slightly different. Specifically, thousands of jobs and livelihoods depended on the production of the product. On both sides of the environmental debate, there were legitimate concerns and arguments. Moreover, how did one make a utilitarian judgment as to the greatest good when weighing short-term benefits and long-term costs were almost impossible to calculate?

The foregoing examples invoke one broad set of conflicting duties and responsibilities, roughly described as the difficult choice: harm to someone is inevitable, and the decision is where it will fall. Recently, Delphi Corporation, the automotive parts company created as a spin-off from General Motors, became the largest corporate bankruptcy in the history of the United States automotive industry.[2] Delphi hired Robert "Steve" Miller, a chief executive described as "Mr. Fix-It for American industry, stepping in to help large, once-dominant businesses confront and manage ugly reali-

---

[2] Jeffrey McCracken, *Reassembling Delphi*, WALL ST. J., Oct. 17, 2005, at B1.

ties, sorting through hard choice about wage cuts or plant closures or termination of pension plans."[3]

The reverse of the difficult choice is the situation in which it is not clear that any real harm will result, but there is tremendous conflict between people or organizations, with an overwhelming drive to prove that one side is correct. I observed the drawn out battle over what often seemed to be ephemeral territories in corporate and law firm life: central office versus the outlying branches; support functions versus line management; debates between business units over fixed cost allocations that had no impact on the corporate bottom line; lawyers who viewed business clients as rash, sloppy, and unthinking opportunists, and business clients who viewed lawyers as impediments to accomplishing anything.

Consider these issues (and hundreds more like them) faced in business and everyday life and how they might be addressed within the legal academy. Imagine my surprise, returning after an absence of a quarter-century to academic exegesis on the law, to find the dominance that economic thinking, as a subset of a more general scientific or naturalistic world view, now has.[4] Although one must give credit to the subtleties that behavioral economics and the old and new institutional economics seek to add to the simpler models of economic actors as wholly rational calculators of their best interest, the idea that science could explain, predict, or direct an ethical decision—an almost transcendental moment of exquisite judgment—was just plain counter-intuitive.

Moreover, it seemed possible, even commonplace, to adopt a utilitarian ethic in this circumstance, and justify harm to others by concern for the greater good. Specifically, if we do not sacrifice the jobs of X number of employees, many persons times X will suffer. It is possible to make those decisions with all the moral insight of Judge Posner's memorable allusion to the internal decision-making process of the rational economic actor, which is to say: none.[5] We might as well be speaking not about the mind and soul of a human being, but of a frog.[6]

There is a thread that connects the examples of ethical or moral dilemma in business decision making, and invoking social science does not adequately describe it or provide guidance. The issue goes to the dignity and discipline of the answer. This is not to say that I or anyone else has access to the literal mind of God, or as a next best alternative,

---

[3] *Id.*

[4] *See generally* Douglas G. Baird, *The Future of Law and Economics: Looking Forward: An Introduction*, 64 U. CHI. L. REV. 1129 (1997) (discussing the impact of economics on the law).

[5] RICHARD A. POSNER, ECONOMIC ANALYSIS OF LAW 17 (6th ed. 2003).

[6] *Id.*

> The basic assumption, that human behavior is rational, seems contradicted by the experiences and observations of everyday life. The contradiction is less acute when one understands that the concept of rationality used by the economist is objective rather than subjective, so that it would not be a solecism to speak of a rational frog. Rationality means little more than a disposition to choose, consciously or unconsciously, an apt means to whatever ends the chooser happens to have.

Id.

a derivation from natural law, by which the answers to these questions magically appear in a moment of blinding insight. However, it is a disservice not to expose lawyers to world views other than the purely scientific, and teach secular thinking, developed over centuries, that probes fundamental questions of duty in a way that is just as rigorous, disciplined, and deserving of respect, as the application of formulas, algorithms, and cost curves to the data of experience. In this world in which bad things happen and the laws of economics operate inexorably, we may make decisions about what to do in a way that is more morally acceptable (even if not easier) than counting noses and minimizing the cost of severance.[7]

Let me lay out what I believe are the roots of the problem. In the first instance, studying law is a descriptive enterprise about what we may do, but it is closely aligned with, or overlaps with, or perhaps is identical with what we ought to do. From the first day of torts, contracts, and civil procedure, we ask the question: what is the law governing this issue? If a party fails to perform the contract, will he held be liable for damages? If a person is sitting in the stands at a baseball game and is hit by a broken bat, does he have a claim for damages against the baseball club? And, if the facts alleged in the complaint do not articulate a recognized cause of action, what are the procedural options?

However, there is also an ongoing normative aspect, in which we either judge the law itself against some other standard—justice, fairness, efficiency—or compare the result of the law to the result we would expect from our sense of morality. In a classic case used to illustrate the concept of a unilateral contract, one in which the offer makes it clear that it may be accepted only by completion of performance and not by a counter-promise, the offeror, knowing that the offeree is knocking at the door, calling out that he is prepared to complete the performance, the offeror revokes the offer, and the offeree is left without recourse.[8] One must ask students to consider whether that result comports with their own sense of justice. Indeed, later developments in the binding effect of a promise on which the offeree reasonably relies to his detriment make it clear there was a normative issue at play.[9]

None of the foregoing has changed much in law school in the last hundred years. What has changed over that period is the inter-disciplinary way we think about and

---

[7] For evidence that rational actor theory continues to live on in the legal academy, and, indeed, is applied to questions of professional responsibility (if not ethics), *see* David McGowan, *Some Realism About Parochialism: The Economic Analysis of Legal Ethics* (San Diego Legal Studies, Paper No. 07-20, 2005), *available at* http://ssrn.com/abstract=819984. One cannot accuse Professor McGowan of incipient Platonism in elevating rational actor to a theory of everything. Rather, I would call his approach pragmatic defeatism because if we can never agree on values (his characterization, not mine), we are better off simply calculating the consequences of a particular policy. I also take issue with the assertion that being forced to do a cost-benefit analysis of a policy "forces one to look at all sides of a question." *Id.* Indeed, this becomes an easy, if not particularly rigorous or satisfying, epistemology: "[Cost-benefit analysis] forces you to ask how you know what you claim to know, which pushes thinking toward consequences and away from concepts. Such consequentialist reasoning is necessary to accommodate the conflicts of interests heterogeneous societies always have." *Id.*

[8] *See* Petterson v. Pattberg, 161 N.E. 428, 429-30 (1928).

[9] *See, e.g.*, Drennan v. Star Paving Co., 333 P.2d 757 (Cal. 1958).

study law.[10] Here is the irony, or dilemma, that we face. The study of law as social science imputes science, and I am comfortable that the descriptive and explanatory enterprise is perfectly amenable to scientific structures. We may be awed by the order observed in nature (the philosophical term is "teleology," which implies ends or purposiveness to the universe),[11] but that is a wholly different inquiry from the question: what caused the phenomenon that inspired such awe? "Intelligent design" is a perfectly acceptable matter of discussion for religion or secular philosophy, but it is unacceptable for science.[12] Nevertheless, the hybrid discipline that is academic law has never satisfactorily defined the distinction between its fit into modern interdisciplinary social science and the oft-cited mission to educate lawyers as problem-solvers. Hence, it is all well and good for Judge Posner to suggest even a rational frog would make sense as the subject of economic modeling,[13] but does that model or any other model purporting to be science aid the frog in making ex ante decisions about what it ought to do?

In a letter to Stanford Law School alumni, Dean Larry Kramer addressed the issue of educating lawyers in an increasingly inter-disciplinary academic environment. Citing both "a weakness of traditional legal training,"[14] and an education that remains "too narrow and technical,"[15] Dean Kramer's vision is ambitious:

> [T]his is about more than enhanced skills training or keeping up with the Jones[es]. Lawyers are actors in all of the most important aspects of governing a liberal democratic society. The world needs lawyers with the perspective and vision to make positive contributions to the problems we face, and who can do so with responsibility and comprehension, not merely by settling into the role of lawyer/advocate.[16] Is the scientific study of law prepared to educate lawyers?[17] Do our current academic endeavors encourage responsibility as well as comprehension, and if so, by what standard?

Whether or not he intended it that way, Dean Kramer captured the tensions that result from academic law's transition to inter-disciplinary scholarship from its professional

---

[10] Jeremy A. Blumenthal, *Law and Social Sciences in the Twenty-First Century*, 12 S. CAR. INTERDISC. L.J. 1, 7-24 (2002).

[11] SUSAN NEIMAN, THE UNITY OF REASON: RE-READING KANT 81 (1994).

[12] *See* Thomas Nagel, *Secular Philosophy and the Religious Temperament*, http://www.law.nyu.edu/clppt/program2005/readings/secular_philosophy.pdf (last visited Oct. 6, 2005).

[13] POSNER, *supra* note 5, at 17.

[14] Larry D. Kramer, *Creating Interdisciplinary Education*, 71 STAN. LAW. 3, 3 (2005).

[15] *Id.*

[16] *Id.*

[17] When I refer to the study of law as "science," I mean primarily the scholarship of the last forty years or so, including the Wisconsin law and society school, the predominance of law and economics, and the recent development of so-called "empirical" approaches.

trade school roots.[18] Comprehension includes the "what" and "why" of the law—as I tell my students, not just the instrumental approaches one takes as the lawyer for a party, but understanding what is happening from our standpoint as historians, philosophers, economists, linguists, and social critics. Does the comprehension of the "what" and "why," without more, teach responsibility? It teaches what we might do, but that is a far cry from teaching what we ought to do.

Responsibility implies ethics: not the comprehension of what the law is, but the consideration of what we ought to do, which in turn the law may or may not address. Moreover, if academic law is, in the words of one legal philosopher, the subject of "technological colonization,"[19] how do we address the "ought?" Following more than a century of critique by consequentials, pragmatists, realists, and positivists on the extent to which the positive law incorporates natural law truths about what we ought to do, by and large, legal realism and positivism dominate current thought.[20] The law is a social institution, perhaps informed, in moral societies by morality, but not necessarily. To suggest as Professor Ronald Dworkin does, that there is an accessible but transcendental codification of right and wrong, leaves us wondering why we should merely accept his version of the "deep structures" of law.[21]

That we continue to debate the interrelationship of law and morality is prima facie evidence of conflation and confusion between the two. There is a distinction between the ability of the social science models of the law to aid in the construction of policy, versus the ability of those models to provide the basis for secular ethics. Indeed, that is the begged question in Judge Posner's set of assumptions. Even granting that rationality means nothing more than the ability to choose the means to an end, whence comes the end? The synergistic effect of legal positivism, an interdisciplinary approach to law, and the "human sciences,"[22] arguably, is a presumption of a consequentialist view

---

[18] *See* Brian Leiter, *Why Is It So Easy to Get Tenure in Law Schools?*, http://leiterreports.typepad.com/blog/2004/06/why_is_it_so_ea.html (last visited Sept. 29, 2005). *See also* A.B.A., AN EDUCATIONAL CONTINUUM, REPORT OF THE TASK FORCE ON LAW SCHOOLS AND THE PROFESSION: NARROWING THE GAP 3 (1992) ("The transition during this century from a clerkship/mentoring system of educating lawyers to reliance on professional schools in a university setting has been traced by many observers to the acceptance of the Langdellian appellate case-method, which views the study of law as an academic science.").

[19] Linda Ross Meyer, *Is Practical Reason Mindless?*, 86 GEO. L.J. 647, 673-74 (1998).

[20] Natural law, legal positivism, and legal realism are succinctly summarized in three essays: Brian Bix, *Natural Law Theory, in* A COMPANION TO PHILOSOPHY OF LAW AND LEGAL THEORY 223-40 (Dennis Patterson ed., 1996); Jules L. Coleman & Brian Leiter, *Legal Positivism, in* COMPANION TO PHILOSOPHY, *supra*, at 241-60; Brian Leiter, *Legal Realism, in* COMPANION TO PHILOSOPHY, *supra*, at 261-80.

[21] Ronald Dworkin, *Hart's Postscript and the Character of Political Philosophy*, 24 OXFORD J. LEGAL STUD. 1, 12-13 (2004); Dennis Patterson, *Dworkin on the Semantics of Legal and Political Concepts*, Mar. 15, 2005, http://ssrn.com/abstract=688781; Jeffrey M. Lipshaw, *Freedom, Compulsion, Compliance and Mystery: Reflections on the Duty Not to Enforce a Promise,* 3 LAW, CULTURE & THE HUMANITIES 82 (2007), *available at* http:// ssrn.com/abstract=742844.

[22] *See* IAN SHAPIRO, THE FLIGHT FROM REALITY IN THE HUMAN SCIENCES 2 (2005) ("quantitative and formally oriented social sciences that are principally geared toward causal explanation"). That the social science approach is married to the dictates of positive law is suggested in one argument for the preferability

of morality, if any view at all.[23] This article does not critique movements like law and economics but deals with how we, as complex humans, might rigorously explore the ex ante issues of "ought" from a non-consequentialist perspective.[24] Indeed, I propose ethics as the deontological ex ante: not knowing what the consequences will be, and not being, in every instance, mere rational frogs, what ought to be our ends?[25]

However, particularly after the corporate scandals grouped under the rubrics "Enron" and "WorldCom," there are voices groping for a way to articulate a secular "ought" which goes beyond mere rational calculation.[26] This article explores that moment of

---

of a broader behavioral science approach over rational choice theory. "[O]ne can analyze the appropriate legal command in any given circumstance without a grand, overarching theory of behavior so long as one has a due regard for the relevant decision-making capabilities of the actors in that specific setting." Russell B. Korobkin & Thomas S. Ulen, *Law and Behavioral Science: Removing the Rationality Assumption from Law and Economics*, 88 CAL. L. REV. 1051, 1057-58 (2000).

[23] *See* Anita Bernstein, *Whatever Happened to Law and Economics?*, 64 MD. L. REV. 303, 311-15 (2005) (describing the debate among advocates of differing consequentialist theses-efficiency versus wealth maximization versus welfare). Professor Bernstein also aptly characterizes the black box that is the mind of the rational frog of Judge Posner's metaphor: "We believe the frog pursues her own ends, but we have nothing but her behavior to look at when we seek support for that belief." *Id.* at 311. Judge Posner hardly invented the concept of consequentialist morality; it was David Hume who most famously observed that reason is slave to our passions. For a comparison of Posnerian and Humean skepticism, *see* Martha C. Nussbaum, *Still Worthy of Praise*, 111 HARV. L. REV. 1776, 1776 (1998) ("Reading Richard Posner's [*'Problematics'* article] is something like reading Hume's *Treatise* with the Hume removed: like, that is, encountering the implausibly mechanistic picture of human personality and the defiant debunking of reason's pretensions without at the same time, and inseparably, encountering the gentle, playful, and many-colored mind, thoroughly delighted by reason and human complexity, incomparably deft in argument, that again and again soars beyond and dives beneath the rigid structures it has erected for itself.").

[24] Professor Bernstein observes that consequential theory is more focused on the ex ante policy-making perspective: "those who make law ought to strive to improve welfare not so much by reaching the right answer in a particular dispute but by writing doctrine that would foster the goods that law and economics says we all pursue: efficiency, wealth-maximization, welfare, better-offedness, or what you will." Bernstein, *supra* note 23, at 326. Professor Bernstein cites several "ex post" antagonists to consequentialism: corrective justice theorists, who emphasize compensation over deterrence in tort law, retribution tradition in criminal law, and "the embrace of Kantian theory within legal theory." *Id.* at 327.

[25] As I discuss *infra* notes 119-124 and accompanying text, behavioral economics seeks to temper the assumptions of rationality by assuming, among other things, that human beings are only rational within bounds, and do not calculate the consequences of their actions by "heuristics," the process of trial-and-error, and the development of rules of thumb. DANIEL H. COLE & PETER Z. GROSSMAN, PRINCIPLES OF LAW AND ECONOMICS 65-67 (2004). *See also* Christine Jolls, Cass R. Sunstein, & Richard Thaler, *A Behavioral Approach to Law and Economics*, 50 STAN. L. REV. 1471, 1471 (1998). Cass Sunstein has contended that the development of morality itself is the result of heuristics. Cass R. Sunstein, *Moral Heuristics*, 28 BEHAV. & BRAIN SCI. 531, 531 (2005). It is important to note the distinction between a social scientific approach that seeks to explain morality versus the attempt to articulate universal moral principles that we might observe but not be able to explain through empirical study. *See, e.g.*, John Mikhail, *Moral Heuristics or Moral Competence? Reflections on Sunstein*, 28 BEHAV. & BRAIN SCI. 557 (2005) (Mikhail's response to Sunstein's article).

[26] I note two articles that raised interesting questions on this subject from the 2003 corporate law symposium at the University of Cincinnati. Donald Langevoort approached the question of intra-corporate

transcendence in the application of a rule, and the question of what, if not religion, guides us? To use the jargon of the physical or social scientist, data suggests that purposes and ends make a significant difference in the world. Even pragmatists, want to believe there is something out there beyond the cold parsing of positivist classification; in a charming phrase, they seek to dispense with "theory guilt," even though they feel compelled to theorize philosophically why they ought not to feel guilty.[27] To others, pragmatism has a feel of so much question-begging (even if on a day-to-day basis it is so, well, pragmatic).[28] Yet, nowadays much of the serious epistemic wrestling in the law is left to legal scholars with a particular religious outlook, who are willing to engage in public reconciliation of those deeply held beliefs with the modern legal scholarship.[29]

This article argues that the confusion between the "is" and the "ought" of law begins with a fundamental confusion over the extent to which even scientific knowledge is possible. The first task is to disentangle the proto-science and ethics of the law. This entails unpacking the workings of reason itself in the scientific effort of comprehension and normative effort of responsibility. In Larry Kramer's terms, comprehension of the law as social science is critical for policy.[30] If we fail to create rigorous predictive theories, the use of law as a social curative is mere gambling. But we need to be very careful in positing those things we know a priori, for fear of clothing a deontological source as a conclusion in scientific jargon. Claims of knowledge are the essence of science, but those claims are always contingent and not necessary, and, at least in theory, are capable of disproof by contrary empirical data.[31] Although claims of what we ought to do are equally capable of purported universality, they are never capable of disproof, and, hence, never of knowledge. In other words, if there is already a teleological aspect to science—that the empirical world may be made intelligible by operation of our reason—then it is not surprising that other less universal assumptions about ends (e.g., that welfare or wealth maximization ought to trump fairness in determining policy) seep into what purports to be the descriptive study of law.

---

candor—clearly an issue of ethics—within a broader treatment of agency law. *See, e.g.*, Donald C. Langevoort, *Agency Law Inside the Corporation: Problems of Candor and Knowledge*, 71 U. CIN. L. REV. 1187, 1188 (2003). Marleen O'Connor addressed the question who, if anyone, is responsible for teaching ethics and values (like candor). Marleen O'Connor, *The Enron Board: The Perils of Groupthink*, 71 U. CIN. L. REV. 1233, 1315-16 (2003).

[27] Catharine Pierce Wells, *Why Pragmatism Works for Me*, 74 S. CAL. L. REV. 347, 357-58 (2000).

[28] In her biting critique of law and economics, Professor Bernstein contends that, as its ability to be coherent as a scientific theory has come under attack, law and economics has morphed in various ways. Bernstein, *supra* note 23, at 322. In particular, she observes that "Judge Posner sought to recharacterize law and economics as a subset of 'pragmatism,' jettisoning for his purpose more familiar philosophical understandings of this word." *Id.* For another view of how Judge Posner's pragmatism is significantly more doctrinaire in its conclusions than other forms, *see* Jeffrey M. Lipshaw, *Contingency & Contracts: A Philosophy of Complex Business Transactions*, 54 DEPAUL L. REV. 1077, 1120-26 (2005).

[29] *See infra* notes 161-166.

[30] Larry D. Kramer, *Creating Interdisciplinary Education*, 71 STAN. LAW. 3, 3 (2005).

[31] *See, e.g.*, McLean v. Arkansas Bd. of Educ., 529 F. Supp. 1255, 1267 (E.D. Ark. 1982).

Having established the bounds of what we may know as scientific truth, the second task is to articulate a basis for ethics, or what Dean Kramer calls responsibility. If theory-driven social science is bad for science, it is also bad for how we conceptualized about ethics. It suggests either that morality can be scientifically derived, or presumes, if we are to think about the "ought" of responsibility, the result is some form of consequentialism.[32] However, therein lies the problem with the conflation of science and morality in the law. Specifically, it is an empirical reality that when we search for purposes and ends (assuming that we have not pragmatically dispensed with the need for the search), most often it is a schizophrenic exercise. We recognize there is mystery, and perhaps universal truths, but, at the same time we clearly understand, despite a lifetime of searching of effort, that we are doomed to fail in anything but the faintest approach to an answer. In the face of that fatalistic realization, we search anyway. As social scientists in this hybrid realm do, we loathe the very idea that we may be incapable of clear and ultimate answers to our hardest cases.

Is there a way to articulate, much less teach, responsibility? Here, I want to learn from, but reach beyond, Kant. Kant knew that he could not state the categorical imperative as a matter of truth. What he drew from the transcendental was practical reason, the ability of the mind to derive ends as a matter of duty that was free of all physical desires and material inclinations.[33] Although Kant articulated applications of the categorical imperative, his greatest contribution was the architectonic, the structure of moral thought.[34] We are left to fill in what practical reason demands in each instance. And one person's duty can be another's dogmatic horror. To conceptualize the categorical imperative as a guide to action in each specific instance is to beg the question. We cannot prove it, but the universality of first assumptions tells us there is something else, and it is the source of all judgments.

It is fashionable to pick apart the work of Ronald Dworkin, particularly when he knows precisely what constitute our rights,[35] yet the liberal values he espouses, and wants us to admire in the law, are ones we often share.[36] However, we are unwilling to take as a given, merely on his, or on anyone else's word, that those values are the ones that must be embedded in positive law to make it legitimately law. Nevertheless, scholars continue to explore the mystery, usually without acknowledging it as such—in attempts to find unified theories of contract,[37] to put economic structure around

---

[32] Steven SCHAFERSMAN, HOW DO HUMANISTS FIND MEANING, PURPOSE, VALUES, AND MORALS IN LIFE?, http://www.freeinquiry.com/humanists-meaning.html (last visited May 1, 2006).

[33] IMMANUEL KANT, THE METAPHYSICS OF MORALS 20-22 (Mary Gregor trans. & ed., Cambridge Univ. Press 1996) (1800).

[34] *Id.* at 31-34.

[35] *See generally* RONALD DWORKIN, TAKING RIGHTS SERIOUSLY (1977).

[36] *See* RONALD DWORKIN, LAW'S EMPIRE 274-75 (1986) (responding to the skeptical arguments against liberalism "as a philosophical system combining metaphysical and ethical ideas").

[37] Nathan Oman, *Unity and Pluralism in Contract Law: Contract Theory*, 103 MICH. L. REV. 1483, 1505 (2005) (citing Jody S. Kraus, *Reconciling Autonomy and Efficiency in Contract Law: The Vertical Integration Strategy*, 11 PHIL. ISSUES 420, 422 (2001)).

altruism,[38] or in the notion that the remedies of torts satisfy a human need for justice and balance.[39]

What I have been trying to do is help revive the dignity of secular and universal discussion about teleology—the notion that we are hard-wired to see purposes and ends and intelligibility in all things.[40] I am interested in the indeterminacy that rests at the core of all attempts to know or to decide or to judge. That is to say, I wish to illuminate, recognizing I will never explain, that moment when we fit, or do not fit, data into a pre-existing model. That was Kant's enterprise in the Critique of Judgment—showing the transcendence of either determining or reflecting judgments: there is no rule for the application of a rule.[41] It is a wholly unscientific project, because while I puzzle with it, and struggle with it, at the same time I know I can never resolve it. The sheer volume of writing on the subject indicates that there is some overlap between law and morality, and therefore it is not far-fetched to suggest lawyers who are not also ethicists may unduly emphasize the legal over the moral.[42]

Arguably, when we understand the extent to which reason incorporates ends into scientific inquiry, we are more circumspect in claiming what is true or good as a matter of science, and more humble and reflective, if no less principled, concerned, or passionate in making claims about what is right. Indeed, the process of legal argumentation is gasoline on the fire of rationalization. Whether or not we have an experiential basis for so concluding, our reason drives us, out of what needs for comfort, security, reassurance, wholeness, to conclusions about truth. We are consumed with proving that we are right, whether or not it comports with truth. The resort to law to resolve disputes is precisely this process of justification. In the typical business conflict, what the economists perceive as opportunism may instead be the rationalization of the current "is" to what we desire that it ought to be.

The real answer is that judgment, particularly when it comes to ethics, is not purely an exercise in reason. There is no rule for the application of a rule. This article argues that modern natural law theories falter in their ability to speak to us as the basis for an ethical code, not because there is anything particularly troubling about the behav-

---

38 *See generally id.*

39 ALAN CALNAN, A REVISIONIST HISTORY OF TORT LAW 241-76 (Carolina Academic Press 2005) (1959).

40 *See generally* IMMANUEL KANT, CRITIQUE OF JUDGMENT (Warner S. Pluhar trans., Hackett Publishing Co. 1987) (1800).

41 *Id.*

42 I think the most articulate expression of this is Martha Nussbaum's *Still Worthy of Praise.* She captures what I think are both the limits and the opportunities of this project:

> Probably argument rarely persuades people to depart altogether from their most settled views. What it more commonly does, however, is to bring to the surface a part of one's moral view that has been obscured or inconsistently applied. Frequently the systematic power of ethical theory is a great help in this sort of argument, ordering what is until then disordered, rendering explicit what is nameless and thus easily denied or effaced.

Nussbaum, *supra* note 23, at 1793.

ior they advocate (unlike the normative implications of rational choice or behavioral economic theory). The real problem is the answer "because I said so" in the secular sensibility. Any claim to insight into natural law as a matter of knowledge has stepped beyond that which can be argued. So to argue, á la Dworkin, that something in the empirical world, like law, is only considered law if one buys his noumena, seems beyond argument. Epistemologically, it is far less satisfying, to conclude we must live with the questions rather than the answers, but at least that is an intellectually honest answer that resonates with thoughtful people. Thus, this article evaluates the concept of a defeasible intuitionism—one that acknowledges the mystery at the core of these issues, and provides a basis for constructive and inferential dialogue about the "ought."

Is it possible to make a universal claim about ethics? Arguably, yes, but only in the very broadest sense and with a humble insight into what is right (or even dictated by natural law), versus what is articulated by rule.[43] Yet believing one has access to the "ought" as though it were truth brings us right back around to dogmatism or absolutism.[44] This article provides a basis for a reflective intuitional ethics, as distinct from law, in the conscious, conscientious, and persistent effort to overcome rationalization. That is not to say we are never right. Instead, it is to say that ethics involves being open to truth rather than justification. An answer lies in the philosophy of second-person relationships. But merely understanding such relationships as conferring a unique status to make claims and demands on another is insufficient for distinguishing law from ethics. Significantly, claims, demands, and their defenses are still creations of reason, and therefore subject to the dark side of reason: dogmatism and rationalization. There is something to our non-inferential intuitions about others and that reason is capable of explaining them away, or justifying action not in accord with the intuition. Only through a direct second-person understanding of others do we avoid justification.

II. FROM REASON TO LAW'S RATIONALIZATION

> Bernard Nussbaum, a senior partner at Wachtell, Lipton, Rosen & Katz in New York City, became Counsel to the President in 1993. He resigned in March, 1994, due to the political fallout after having counseled the President and First Lady to resist the Justice Department's attempt to search the office of Vincent Foster immediately after Foster's suicide. "Asserting a lawyer's prerogative to control information, Nussbaum insisted that he review all the documents in Foster's office first, in order to decide whether any of them should be kept confidential. . . . Months later, when Nussbaum

---

[43] I have previously visited the subject of the inadequacy of rules in the context of corporate governance. *See generally* Jeffrey M. Lipshaw, *Sarbanes-Oxley, Jurisprudence, Insurance, Game-Theory and Kant: Toward a Moral Theory of Good Governance*, 50 WAYNE L. REV. 1083 (2005). For a less theoretical statement of the same point, see the advertisement for the services of PriceWaterhouseCoopers suggesting that rules, such as those set forth in Sarbanes-Oxley, must defer to principles we think "on a macro level." "Can everyone be expected to do the right thing?*" PWC Advertisement, WALL ST. J., Sept. 27, 2005, at A13.

[44] Lipshaw, *supra* note 43, at 1108-12.

appeared before the [Senate] committee, he professed bewilderment at the fuss his obstruction had provoked. Virtually any lawyer would have done as he did, he said, with unfortunate plausibility."[45] Nussbaum claimed his resignation was the "result of [a] controversy generated by those who do not understand, nor wish to understand the role and obligations of a lawyer, even one acting as White House Counsel."[46]

How could a lawyer as brilliant and accomplished as Bernard Nussbaum make such a calamitous misjudgment? To answer the question, one must go back to the very process by which our minds (particularly legal minds) make sense of the world, or, in the most general sense, how we recognize what is and what ought to be. Part of what we do, whether as lawyers, physical scientists, or social scientists, is to engage in what is commonly referred to as a descriptive exercise. Indeed, we often disclaim any aspect of normativity in the exercise. I can hear a chief executive officer or a law firm senior partner saying "don't tell me what I ought to do—tell me what the law is." We view that as a legitimate request, perceiving that we are capable of describing acts and consequence based on a model of the world that is the legal system. Nussbaum followed a rich, century-old tradition of Langdellian or Holmesian legal science and did his best not only to advocate for his client, but to predict, to the best of his ability, how a court of law (as opposed to public opinion) would ultimately characterize the act of resisting the Justice Department investigation.[47]

Today, academic law is different than it was in the days of Langdell and Holmes. Although we still teach doctrine, we regularly seek to explain the law in a cross-disciplinary fashion, using the models of physical and social science—economics, psychology, and anything else that might bring enlightenment to bear. So we seek to explain, to theorize, to find causal connections like social scientists, but we do so in the context of a discipline whose practitioners are also required to advise their clients on what they ought to do. As a result, it is necessary to understand the process by which the very way we think may cause us to confuse the descriptive exercise with the normative.

While this article discusses what we might know objectively and what we might not, and about distinctions in our ability to make claims of truth in matters of nature versus matters of morality, it does not seek to get bogged down in an analysis of the various "-isms" into which my own philosophy may fall.[48] Kant scholar Susan Neiman argues that despite the epistemological quandaries driving modern philosophy,

---

[45] William H. Simon, *The Confidentiality Fetish*, ATLANTIC MONTHLY, DEC. 1, 2004, at 113.

[46] *Id.*; Letter from Bernard W. Nussbaum, White House Counsel, to the Honorable Bill Clinton, President of the United States (Mar. 5, 1994), *available at* http://www.resignation.com/15.html.

[47] For more on Holmesian legal science, *see* Robert J. Cosgrove, *Damned to the Inferno? A New Vision of Lawyers at the Dawning of the Millennium*, 26 FORDHAM URB. L.J. 1669, 1689 (1999).

[48] For a compact summary of the classifications of modern ethical philosophy, *see* Stephen Darwall et al., *Toward Fin de Siècle Ethics: Some Trends, in* MORAL DISCOURSE & PRACTICE: SOME PHILOSOPHICAL APPROACHES 3 (Stephen Darwall et al. eds., 1997).

the "natural, urgent and pervasive" questions arise out of our "demand that the world be intelligible" as a matter of practical and theoretical reason.[49] And despite the heavily epistemological focus in what follows, I agree with her general conclusion: "The question of whether this is an ethical or metaphysical problem is as unimportant as it is undecidable, for in some moments it's hard to view as a philosophical problem at all."[50] Obviously, this article does not argue that there is no objective knowledge, even in matters of nature. Rather, it grapples with a practical problem—what should we do? Common sense suggests that there is a significance difference in the objectivity possible as between nature and morality, but at the margins it is less so than we might otherwise think. This becomes more confused because moral judgments feel like they ought to be describable in terms of truth or falsity.

This article claims no victory or easy answers in attempting to sort this out. Indeed, more than two hundred years ago, David Hume wryly observed the problem of conflating what is with what we contend ought to be:

> [T]he author proceeds for some time in the ordinary ways of reasoning, and establishes the being of a God, or makes observations concerning human affairs; when of a sudden I am surpriz'd to find, that instead of the usual copulations of propositions, is, and is not, I meet with no proposition that is not connected with an ought, or an ought not.[51]

Nussbaum made the jump from "is" to "ought" in just this way. He saw the world as it was through the eyes of a lawyer, and moved immediately to the conclusion that "is" bespoke "ought:" legal justification would serve as general justification of an action.[52] Arguably, within the four walls of the offices where he and his clients discussed the response to the controversy, he was reasoned, persuasive, and truly believed himself to act within the legal and ethical bounds of a lawyer's professional canons. His fundamental failure was not a legal error, indeed, he may have been entirely correct, nor even a political one. The real problem was that he persuaded himself he was right, because his reason told him what ought to be the legal result, and that effort was a massive exercise in self-deception, not because he was wrong about the law, but because he was wrong about the world.

The very process by which we reason to conclusions (or, like lawyers, create argumentation in support of our positions) is capable of exacerbating difficult decisions or disputes. Although reason is capable of allowing us to solve problems, it is also capable of rationalization, justification, and in the end, self-deception. When we add to this mix the possibility of jumping from what we claim to be an impartial description of what is to often unstated presumptions about what is either good or right, we go to the

---

[49] SUSAN NEIMAN, EVIL IN MODERN THOUGHT: AN ALTERNATIVE HISTORY OF PHILOSOPHY 5-7 (2002).

[50] *Id.* at 7.

[51] DAVID HUME, A TREATISE ON HUMAN NATURE 521 (Ernest C. Mossner ed., 1985) (1739).

[52] Nussbaum, *supra* note 23, at 1790.

heart of the dilemma of business ethics. The point of business is utilitarian: to maximize something we have concluded is a good—profits, productivity, sales, or share price, to name a few. But the business game has rules, and companies espouse values, and the question is whether we are capable of justifying whatever conclusion we want when there is a tension between the right and the good. This article argues that to find a way to go beyond reason and rational calculation as a means of ethical decision-making, lawyers need to reflect on their own capabilities of rationalization.

Reason does not serve only to tie together the bits of empirical data that create scientific knowledge. It is also the underpinning of our effort to see, to rationalize, and to justify the world as a whole. Even if we no longer engage in theodicy, is it possible that the same reason that could justify God's creation of the best of all possible worlds might also justify our own internal re-creations? Arguably, the answer is yes, and that skill in reasoned justification, the forte of the lawyer, is capable of creating the kind of troubling gap between the law and ethics that brought down Nussbaum's career as a White House Counsel.

A. Knowledge and Belief Distinguished

In his Critique of Pure Reason, Kant argued that synthetic a priori knowledge, that accessible to us only through reason and not experience, was possible.[53] Indeed, he argued that such a priori knowledge was necessary even for a skeptic like Hume to pose the question "how do we know?"[54] But Kant reached a surprisingly nuanced conclusion: the only things we can judge to be true are those which, in the first instance, are the subjects of our experience (or possible experience).[55] Knowledge comes about through the operation of our sensibility, our perception of objects in the world, and our understanding, the way our minds sort and process the objects of our sensibility.[56] The way we perceive that experience is shaped by certain concepts, which together constitute our understanding that we could not have acquired from experience: unity, causation, substance, plurality, among others.[57] In short, in the first part of the Critique of Pure Reason, entitled the "Transcendental Analytic," Kant deduces that, subjectively, we are able to order and explain our experience only with an already ingrained take on the world.[58] Moreover, he deduces there is objective knowledge: we observe a world that can be different than it appears to us, and which exists independently of our perspective on it.[59] Kant rejects the pure idealistic notion that everything happens for a reason,

---

[53] KANT, *supra* note 1, at 143-46.

[54] *Id.* at 146-48.

[55] *Id.* at 103.

[56] *Id.* at 172.

[57] Kant called these "categories." *Id.* at 212.

[58] *Id.* at 399 ("The form of judgments (transformed into a concept of the synthesis of intuitions) brought forth categories that direct all use of the understanding in experience.").

[59] *Id.* at 219-329.

that there is either a specific or a general Providence knowable to us objectively.[60] But in the world of experience, there is an objective law of causality: as to empirical events in time and space, everything that happens is bound by cause and effect.[61]

Kant claims that reason is something independent from our faculty of understanding or cognition, which orders the impressions conveyed to us by our sensibility.[62] Reason is not "a genuine source of concepts and judgments that arise solely from it and thereby refer it to objects."[63] Instead, it is the faculty by which we derive rules that explain what we perceive, and the logical conditions underlying those rules.[64] Also, reason's goal, whether or not it is even possible, or tied to empirical reality, is to reach the unconditioned proposition—a process Kant describes as reason's "vain but confident treasure hunting."[65]

Often, we will see the terms "constitutive principles" and "regulative principles."[66] A statement like, "All molecules are composed of atoms" is a constitutive principle. It is a proposition that asserts a claim of knowledge, and in this instance, "is a principle of the possibility of experience and of the empirical cognition of objects of sense."[67] Moreover, the constitutive principle is a proposition about how the empirical world works, and suggests more than mere perception of the world, which is the application of our a priori intuitions to our sense perceptions. The processes by which we may arrive at constitutive principles are regulative principles, the rules by which we reason, whether or not that reasoning is ultimately borne out by correspondence with the real world.[68] "Thus the principle of reason is only a rule prescribing a regress in the series of conditions for given appearances, in which regress it is never allowed to stop with an absolutely unconditioned."[69]

May one's reason, the regulative principle, lead one to assert a constitutive claim that goes beyond what we presently know? Kant answers yes, and that should be apparent to anyone who has ever engaged in speculation ranging from the mundane to the apparent ability to fathom the mind of God.[70] Application of the regulative principle beyond what we presently know is certainly something of which our minds are capable. The regulative principle of reason:

---

[60] *Id.* at 116.

[61] *Id.* at 304-05.

[62] *Id.* at 387-89.

[63] *Id.* at 242.

[64] *Id.*

[65] *Id.* at 398 (explaining the distinction between the faculty of cognition and the faculty of reason, which is thinking). *See also* 1 HANNAH ARENDT, THE LIFE OF THE MIND 53-65 (1977).

[66] KANT, *supra* note 1, at 45.

[67] *Id.* at 520.

[68] *Id.* at 520-21.

[69] *Id.* at 520.

[70] *Id.*

> is a principle of the greatest possible continuation and extension of experience, in accordance with which no empirical boundary would hold as an absolute boundary; thus it is a principle of reason, which as a rule, postulates what should be effected by us in the regress, but does not anticipate what is given in the object prior to any regress.[71]

As discussed later in this article, this is the basis by which scientific or theoretical reason allows us to hypothesize what might be versus what we currently believe is. But may one's reason establish the truth of a constitutive claim that goes beyond any experience or possible experience? Kant answers no, because of the paradox inherent in the infinite regress. Indeed, proving the existence of the infinite, the Unconditioned (or God) as a constitutive principle is the ultimate conflation of constitutive and regulative principles. The use of reason to propose constitutive principles beyond experience or possible experience is, as Kant notes, "the ascription of objective reality to an idea [i.e., the infinite regress to the Unconditioned] that merely serves as a rule."[72]

B. Narrowing the Gap

Susan Neiman argues it is the same process of reason that propels us to claims of knowledge in science, and imperatives of action in morality.[73] For Neiman, reason is a regulative process in both instances; it may establish constitutive claims only in matters of experience or possible experience.[74] "Theoretical reason's success is crucially dependent on the cooperation of the world. Practical reason, by contrast, can achieve its ends alone. We do not control the forces of nature, but we do control our wills."[75]

Is scientific inquiry itself wholly objective? The answer is: only as a matter of degree. It is an illusion to believe that descriptive study is somehow superior to moral inquiry because the reasoning process is more objective.[76] Scientific inquiry itself swirls around a paradox of reason.[77] Science is the search for knowledge (or constitutive principles) through reason, but ultimate knowledge, the final Unconditioned proposition—is impossible to obtain.[78] As Neiman explains, "[r]eason's drive to seek the Unconditioned is absolutely necessary; for it is an analytic proposition that once the conditioned is given, a regress in the series of all of its conditions is set us as a task. . . ."[79] Yet, therein

---

[71] *Id.*

[72] *Id.* at 521.

[73] Neiman, supra note 11, at 125-29.

[74] *Id.*

[75] *Id.* at 128.

[76] *Id.* at 62-70.

[77] *Id.*

[78] *Id.* at 64.

[79] *Id.* at 63.

lies the paradox because within the very experience that science seeks to explain, there is no end to the conditions ("all the way down").[80]

It is reason that supplies the regulative principle that purports to say we begin with an intelligible world. As Susan Neiman notes, "[f]or as we have seen, the knowledge that every event has a cause is useless without the idea that human reason is capable of tracing the series of causes to a point at which the events that make up the world become intelligible."[81] In other words, the essence of the paradox is that it is not a necessary conclusion that nature match up with reason's insistence on ultimate intelligibility. Significantly, "[w]e cannot ensure that nature's conclusions—the conditioned given of the experienced world—have adequate grounds in a series of conclusions that, as a whole, is fully explicable. But reason has a right and a need to assume this to be the case."[82] Neiman argues that the drive to science is teleological, and necessarily requires the assumption of order and systematicity.[83] Whether or not the scientist admits it, the process of scientific reason, in presuming intelligibility, presumes something like a purposive "wise and omnipotent author."[84]

Moreover, while the knowledge claims of science are tied to what is confirmable in the real world, it takes reason's ability to conceive of what ought to be to posit any hypothesis that goes beyond mere cognition of the world as it is.[85] Neiman suggests:

---

[80] There is debate about the origins of this allusion, but you see it regularly when a philosopher wants to make a visual statement about infinite regress. *See Turtles All the Way Down, at* http://en.wikipedia.org/wiki/Turtles_all_the_way_down. Stephen Hawking popularized one version of it:

> A well-known scientist (some say it was Bertrand Russell) once gave a public lecture on astronomy. He described how the Earth orbits around the sun and how the sun, in turn, orbits around the centre of a vast collection of stars called our galaxy.
>
> At the end of the lecture, a little old lady at the back of the room got up and said: "What you have told us is rubbish. The world is really a flat plate supported on the back of a giant tortoise."
>
> The scientist gave a superior smile before replying, "What is the tortoise standing on?"
>
> "You're very clever, young man, very clever," said the old lady. "But it's turtles all the way down."

STEPHEN W. HAWKING, A BRIEF HISTORY OF TIME 1 (1988).

[81] NEIMAN, *supra* note 11, at 64.

[82] *Id.*

[83] *Id.* at 82.

[84] *Id.* at 81. *Cf.* STEVEN D. SMITH, LAW'S QUANDARY (2004), discussed *infra* note 167. One of Professor Smith's proposed answers to the question "why do we continue to talk as though the law requires a particular result?" is found in the chapter "Authors Wanted," *id.* at 126-53, and his invocation of Joseph Vining's mysticism on the subject in "The Transcendent Author," *Id.* at 173-74. This concept is really a parallel description of this same paradox between the constitutive goal of knowledge and the regulative and teleological impulse of reason. With all due respect, I disagree with the conclusion Justice Scalia reaches in his review of Law's Quandary: that, out of academic correctness, Professor Smith has shied away from simply identifying this transcendent author as God. *See* Antonin Scalia, *Review of Law's Quandary*, 157 FIRST THINGS 37, 46 (2005). As discussed below, the attribution of authorship to God as a matter of belief is wholly acceptable, but claiming it as knowledge is not.

[85] KANT, *supra* note 1, at 540-41.

> The capacity to demand explanations of experience requires the capacity to go beyond experience, for we cannot investigate the given until we refuse to take it as given. To ask a question about some aspect of experience, we must be able to think the thought that it could be otherwise. Without this thought, we cannot formulate even the vaguest why.[86]

Karl Popper captured the regulative power of reason inherent in the scientist's conjecture, noting that "[w]hat the great scientist does is boldly to guess, daringly to conjecture, what these inner realities are like. This is akin to myth making . . . . The boldness can be gauged by the distance between the world of appearance and the conjectured reality, the explanatory hypothesis."[87] Thus, our inquiry into what is, is forever shaped by our minds' construction of what ought to be.

The way we reason about moral ends is remarkably similar. Notably, Kant's unique contribution to practical reason was his conclusion that we are capable of reasoning our way to moral ends (versus the empiricist's view that ends are solely determined by our desires or inclinations).[88] Reason's relentless, yet ultimately futile, drive toward the Unconditioned—the regulative principle seeking to assert constitutive claims—is the same drive that explains the regulative principles of morality. Kant's basic metaphysical distinction is as follows: in practical matters, reason is capable of letting us decide what we ought to do—it makes no claims as to truth or falsity.[89] But, the claim is stronger than that: reason is capable of determining moral ends, even if those ends are not borne out by experience.[90]

---

[86] NEIMAN, *supra* note 11, at 59.

[87] Karl Popper, *The Problem of Demarcation, in* PHILOSOPHY: BASIC READINGS 275, 278-79 (Nigel Warburton ed., 3d ed. 1999).

[88] In Kant's moral formulation, the ends derived through reason are categorical imperatives—statements of the "ought" that apply universally, regardless of person or circumstance. The first is so well-known that it is not just a categorical imperative, but is generally referred to as "the Categorical Imperative:" act in a way that the principle of your action would be, by your will, a universal law of nature. IMMANUEL KANT, GROUNDWORK OF THE METAPHYSICS OF MORALS 31-36 (Mary Gregor trans., 1997). The second, known as the Formula of Humanity, is to act so as to treat humanity whether in my own self or in that of another, always as an end, and never as a means only. As we must respect the autonomous rational agent that is our own self, we treat others as autonomous beings, and ends in themselves. "Beings the existence of which rests not on our will but nature, if they are beings without reason, still have only a relative worth, as means, and are these for called things, whereas rational beings are called persons because their nature already marks them out as an end in itself." *Id.* at 37. Finally, every rational being must act as if he or she were both a sovereign and a member of a kingdom of ends. This recognizes that each of us has a free and autonomous will that is sovereign for us, but which is required to see others, also having free and autonomous will also as ends. Yet, reciprocally, as to that other, we are the end contemplated by the other's sovereign will. We are thus obligated, even while recognizing that the kingdom of ends is an unattainable ideal, to attempt to achieve it. *Id.* at 40-41.

[89] IMMANUEL KANT, Selections *from Critique of Practical Reason, in* BASIC WRITINGS OF KANT 225-26 (Allen W. Wood trans., 2001).

[90] NEIMAN, *supra* note 11, at 115.

C. From Reason to Self-Deception

Kant cautions against overconfidence both about claims of knowledge and claims of morality.[91] Where the power of our reason causes us to confuse what ought to be with what is, we engage in what Kant calls "transcendental illusion."[92] In that case, reason deceives us by casting subjective illusions as objective truth.[93] If one misunderstands the principles of pure reason "and takes them to be constitutive principles of transcendent cognition, then they produce a dazzling but deceptive illusion, persuasion and imaginary knowledge, and thus also eternal contradictions and controversies."[94] This caution equally applies when we try to determine whether we have undertaken particular action out of moral duty or material inclination.[95] Neiman writes, "[p]ractical reason, like theoretical reason, has a natural tendency to illusion, which leads to its misuse in subtle and spurious exercises that we today call rationalizations."[96] Therefore, the lesson is: be humbler about the claims of knowledge because the reason that derives them is no different than the reason that derives moral ends. Further, when we are humbler about the claims of knowledge, we might be more confident in the claims of duty.

There is a substantial and concentrated body of philosophical and psychological literature on self deception,[97] but here the focus is on the question how, when we persuade ourselves that we know something as a matter of fact or duty to a theoretical or moral certainty, do we know we are not fooling ourselves? The philosopher David Sanborn provides an epistemic "why" of rationalization.[98] Sanborn gives the example of a man who has told himself his new car is a bargain to justify his pleasure in having bought it, and Sanborn uses it to demonstrate the gap between the irrational pleasure that is honest and a justifying "thirst for rationality [that] is a major source of lies."[99] These invented reasons are ostensible, which Sanborn distinguishes from the more paradigmatic view of self-deception:

---

[91] KANT, *supra* note 1, at 386-90.

[92] *Id.* at 385-86.

[93] *Id.* at 386. This aspect of reason is, in Kant's view, neither good nor bad. It simply is.

[94] *Id.* at 621-22.

[95] *Id.* at 165.

[96] NEIMAN, *supra* note 11, at 125.

[97] In addition to the other sources cited, *see, e.g.*, PERSPECTIVES ON SELF-DECEPTION (Brian P. McLaughlin & Amélie Oksenberg Rorty eds., 1988); SELF-DECEPTION AND SELF-UNDERSTANDING: NEW ESSAYS IN PHILOSOPHY AND PSYCHOLOGY (Mike W. Martin ed., 1985); Mike W. MARTIN, SELF-DECEPTION AND MORALITY (1986); ALFRED R. MELE, SELF-DECEPTION UNMASKED (2001); SELF & DECEPTION (Roger T. Ames & Wimal Dissanayake eds., 1996); SELF-DECEPTION & PARADOXES OF RATIONALITY (Jean-Pierre Dupuy ed., 1998); Robert Audi, *Self-Deception, Action, and Will*, 18 ERKENNTIS 133 (1982); W.J. Talbott, *Intentional Self-Deception in a Single Coherent Self*, 55 PHIL. & PHENOMENOLOGICAL RES. 27 (1995).

[98] David Sanborn, SELF-DECEPTION AS RATIONALIZATION, IN PERSPECTIVES ON SELF-DECEPTION 157 (Brian P. McLaughlin & Amélie Oksenberg Rorty eds., 1988).

[99] *Id.* at 157 (quoting T. Penelhum, Pleasure and Falsity, 1 Am. Phil. Q. 81 (1964)).

> The car buyer invents the belief that his new car is a bargain. The lie, which here has the thirst for rationality as a source, is the second-order belief that one believes the car to be a bargain. The car-buyer somehow really knows that the car is not a bargain, but he deceives himself into thinking that it is.[100]

In contrast, what makes a reason ostensible is not that it is necessarily false (indeed, in Sanborn's example, we are to assume that the buyer can in fact demonstrate support for his belief that the car is a bargain); rather, it is ostensible because the reason is a rationalization to cover for other more honest reasons (like I just want it!).[101]

Often, self-deception may consist not of persuading oneself that the false is true, or vice versa, or even of holding inconsistent belief. I contend the very process of rationalization, whereby we adopt anticipating and ostensible beliefs (versus the honest but perhaps irrational ones), constitutes self-deception.

Sanborn claims there can be no self-deception that is free of rationalization, but notes his qualms about the role of rationalization in making that very assertion: "Those who defend theories often provide striking examples of rationalization. Although the defender of the theory thinks he regards the theory as adequate because he thinks there are no genuine counterexamples, his treatment of putative counterexamples is actually heavily biased by his fondness for the theory."[102]

Legal scholars have posited at least two answers to the epistemological question: how do we know whether we are fooling ourselves? One is to give up on epistemology altogether. Pragmatists, by and large, reject the inquiry either because they deny the existence of an external reality accessible only by reason, or if they do not deny it, they do not believe it has any value in addressing the problems of contingency.[103]

Others retreat to the apparent objectivity of science. Consider the writing of Judge Richard Posner, who has the courage to articulate a philosophy to which others do not publicly accede, would, arguably, take Kant at his word, and claim that the use of reason in the pursuit of knowledge or truth is legitimate, but its employment in the pursuit of moral ends is not.[104] This is borne out in Judge Posner's own oddly inconsistent treatment of reason. He clearly grasps (and articulates) a Kantian view of the regulative nature of

---

100 *Id.* at 158.

101 *Id.* at 158-59. Sanborn offers a more general description of ostensible reasons: "Generally, one's attitude A is an ostensible reason for one's attitude B when one overestimates how much one's having attitude A contributes to the reason for one's having attitude B." *Id.* at 160. Last weekend, I bought myself a pair of $300 Bose Noise-Canceling headphones, without telling my wife, who was out of town. I knew that she would not understand why I bought them; indeed, would consider it irresponsible on my part. I resolved simply not to tell her, but was found out when the anti-fraud department of the credit card company called to confirm the purchase (because the store had punched in the wrong expiration date). When I was called out, I had a number of ostensible reasons for the purchase (they made sense if I was traveling, my old headphones were uncomfortable, etc.), all of which were ostensible to the real reason: I thought they were cool.

102 *Id.* at 163-64.

103 Thomas F. Cotter, Legal *Pragmatism and the Law and Economics Movement*, 84 GEO. L.J. 2071, 2075-76 (1996).

104 *Id.*

reason in science. "Neither logic nor any empirical protocol guarantees truth. So even scientific knowledge is tentative, revisable—in short, fallible."[105] However, Posner gives more credit to reason's power than Hume, who denied any ability of a priori reason in scientific explanation.[106] To Hume, ideas were merely copies of our sense impressions, and had no utility for explanation of physical events.[107] Posner endorses reason's power to theorize, but that power is only valid when "it is about observable phenomena and 'real' (physically existing), entities, [and] can be tested by comparing the predictions generated by the theory with the results of the observations."[108] So far, Posner might well be a Kantian: Kant would agree that the application of theoretical reason to matters other than experience is an exercise in theodicy, not science.

Judge Posner departs from Kant in the ability of reason to dictate moral ends, in what he calls "academic moralism," particularly in contrast to science.[109] This hits at the heart of ethics, and of the conflation of science and morality in the law. Notwithstanding his concession to the mere regulative power of reason in science, there is little doubt that Judge Posner endorses a fundamental distinction between the power to know through reason and the power to decide through reason what we ought to do. Under Judge Posner's analysis, it must follow that theoretical reason in science may allow us to approach the truth, but practical reason in morality cannot. However, as discussed above, the process and structure of reason, as applied to issues of science or morality, are the same. The difference is the role of nature, and, in matters of science, whether it corresponds with reason's hypotheses.

D. Legal Discourse as Rationalization

Rationalization of conduct, or remaking the "ought" to comport with the "is," may well be another description of what lawyers do. But, what is the dark side of that process? We may bias our perception of the "is" of sensibility and understanding by virtue of our ought-belief. We view the world, or more particularly others, in the way we believe it or they ought to be. We fail to see malfeasance because we do not believe others are capable of it, or to see the reality of our own mistakes or failures because we ourselves ought not to fail or be mistaken. Or, we may blame the world or others for the state of the "is." We do not change the heteronomous "is" of inclination but justify our complacency in not acting according to the ought-belief to which reason directs us. In Sanborn's car-buyer example, what the buyer knows as the "ought" is that he does not need the car, but that he might rationalize the "ought" to conform with the "is" of his material desire. In other words, he harmonizes the "is" and the "ought" not by changing the "is," overcoming his inclination, but by finding a way to articulate an "ought" consistent with the inclination.

---

105 RICHARD A. POSNER, LAW, PRAGMATISM, AND DEMOCRACY 6 (2003).

106 HUME, *supra* note 51, at 121-25.

107 *Id.*

108 RICHARD A. POSNER, PROBLEMATICS OF MORAL AND LEGAL THEORY 13 (1999).

109 *Id.* at 7.

The moral problem is that we recognize, at some level, consciously or unconsciously, there is a universal law we would legislate for ourselves: we know we are engaging in spin. That is, our opponents or the moral issues themselves are obstacles to the fulfillment of our inclinations and desires. We justify the "is" of our inclinations against the "ought" of our duty. This is the justification exercise of reason writ small; writ large it would involve a complex exercise of legal reasoning to demonstrate why we were, after all, right. Indeed, we may attribute a malevolent or mistaken ought-belief to others. We hold our derivation of the "ought" as superior, and attribute bad faith or malevolence to others when they appear not to concur in it. We need only consider Sanborn's account of the possibility of rationalization and self-deception in theory, or position, defense. How often do we attribute malevolence to our intellectual opponents, and they back to us, when we know certainly that we operate only in good faith and in the pursuit of truth?

Bernard Nussbaum's dilemma, which combined the "we-they" of politics and the argumentation of the law, displayed a number of these characteristics. Specifically, Nussbaum and the Clintons saw the world legally, and presumed the way they thought the world ought to work was the way it did work.[110] Rather than concluding perhaps he had done something wrong, Nussbaum continued, long after his resignation, to justify what he did.[111] It was certainly consistent with Sanborn's characterization: we were right, and our opponents were politically motivated.

In *What is Wrong with Self-Deception?*, Marcia Baron acknowledges the pervasiveness, indeed, necessity in some instances, of self-deception: "self-deception is, for most of us, virtually indispensable. And this is the case not merely because there are episodes in most lives in which we cannot bear to face the truth; it has more to do with the opacity of self-knowledge."[112] Yet, her description of the move from the benign to the wrong is nuanced and touches of our exegesis of reason. Knowing ourselves is a struggle, and sometimes self-knowledge only occurs as a result of the very "instability of the state of self-deception."[113] Indeed, the role of reason in reconciling the "ought" with the "is" is at the heart of her defense: "Self-deception is a sort of extension of something that we all do, and couldn't but do [ ]: we pick a story, though not just any story, to make sense out of our lives."[114] Moreover, how self-deception transforms from a benign exercise to one that is less so is at the heart of the distinction between the process of law and the process of ethics:

Self-deception's greatest evils do not lie in deceiving oneself in the first place, but in refusing to call into question one's beliefs (or "stories"), and in struggling to maintain

---

[110] *See generally* Simon, *supra* note 45.

[111] *The Role of a Counsel*, HARV. L. BULL., Spring 2003, http://www.law.harvard.edu/alumni/bulletin/2003/spring/feature_1-side.html (last visited Jan. 12, 2006).

[112] Marcia Baron, *What is Wrong with Self-Deception?*, *in* PERSPECTIVES ON SELF-DECEPTION, *supra* note 98, at 431, 441.

[113] *Id.*

[114] *Id.* at 442.

those beliefs; or in refusing to engage in self-scrutiny, a refusal often conjoined with a tendency not to notice that what one does or how one lives has profound and far-reaching effects on others.[115]

If rationalization as self-deception has any benign aspect for law, it is that we have at least created institutions in which the parties may tell a third party the stories they have created for themselves to justify what they are doing, and often, why, in the case of conflict one is right and the other is wrong.[116] That the rationalization of one's position through litigation is legal does not mean it is necessarily ethical. The distinction lies in one's willingness, as an individual or a business, to question the product of one's own reason or rationalization: to defeat self-deception.[117]

E. Skepticism and Illusions of Certainty

If we accept the Kantian epistemological model, consider how little difference there is between knowledge and belief, as least as constructed by reason. Reason's essence is the derivation of the conditions to any proposition, but reason is not bound by experience in that process. Moreover, there is a common teleological aspect as between the application of reason to determining knowledge, and reason's derivation of moral ends. Hence, the only real difference between scientific and moral methodology is the ability to demonstrate that any proposition that is the product of reason can be disproved by falsifying evidence that is not merely another product of reason. To put it otherwise, reason's application of regulative principles, how things ought to be may not match the reality of the world, but nothing constrains reason's derivation of what we ought to do. Whether as a matter of science or a matter of morality, reason's desire is to reconcile the "is" of the world that comes to us through sensibility and understanding and the "ought" that reason is capable of determining apart from any tie to experience.

Moreover, if we accept a more generalized epistemology of self-deception, that it is practical reason turning to that "subtle and spurious exercise" of rationalization of the "ought" and the "is," then how do we distinguish, if at all, between rationalization as self-deception in the pursuit of science (employing theoretical reason) from that of moral reasoning (employing practical reason)? What then of a social science discipline, like many comprehensive approaches to law, that purports to be capable of constitutive claims of knowledge devoid of any regulative or normative principles? And, what of the same discipline when its practitioners must come to terms with moral ends? Is it possible that the "is" of comprehension might be conflated with the "ought" of responsibility? In an exercise of epistemic self-deception, might that failure to act responsibility be

---

115 *Id.* at 443-44.

116 Jeffrey M. Lipshaw, *The Bewitchment of Intelligence: Language and Ex Post Illusions of Intention*, 78 TEMP. L. REV. 99, 149 (2005).

117 *Id.* at 150 ("I have no illusion about creating a legal model that is based on an underlying assumption that perfect knowledge and rationality will eliminate conflict. In my experience, that is not the way the world works. I hope instead the inevitable conflict is resolved as reasoned discourse, between parties who recognize each other as rational subjects, and not objects to be dominated.").

justified or rationalized in light of desires or inclinations, whether defense of a theory, the obstruction of an investigation, or the need to make the financial targets for the current quarter?

Particularly in a discipline like law that purports to make claims of descriptive truth and regulative imperative, to what extent does reason itself cause the conflation of dogma and belief, on the one hand, and science and truth, on the other? Indeed, we might conclude well-developed reason is as capable of illusion as it is of insight, Kant's transcendental illusion is more the rule than the exception, and that we regularly, in life, law practice, and academic pursuit, deceive ourselves by mistaking belief for knowledge, and knowledge for belief.[118]

Kant recognized the urge of unrestrained metaphysical meandering as the road to a dogmatic creed, deceived in its belief that it alone had reached the Unconditioned, but wholly or partially untethered to experience. Therefore, it is not particularly surprising that radical skepticism and dogmatism, as the products of attempts to build or deconstruct systematic metaphysics continue in the name of social science. Between the extremes of systematic metaphysics and radical skepticism, our sensibility of the empirical world is often impacted by reason's tendency to the Unconditioned, and our morality directed not to transformation of the social order, but to justification of the world and ourselves as they are. Nothing exempts the social scientist from this process.

To be fair, we must examine the question "why be ethical?" and whether science might be useful in answering the question. One of Judge Posner's great contributions to this dialogue is that he will say in print what others may believe about what is achievable through scientific explanation about human behavior, but decline, perhaps because the implications are so disturbing. Hence, the debate between rational actor economics and behavioral economics is instructive. Behavioral economic theorists acknowledge people do not always act in accordance with what seem to be the assumptions of rational actor theory, and seek a set of assumptions that more accurately account for human irrationality.[119] In response, rational actor theorists note that by attempting to explain everything, you end up with a theory of nothing.[120] This is not to say that Judge Posner does not have his own unified theory of behavior: the concept of "fairness," for example, "can be made precise, and explained, and subsumed under

---

[118] I am not going to claim that every exercise in law as social science is an exercise in illusion. Cass Sunstein, for example, has tried to reconcile economists and philosophers, focusing on the ability of economic analysis to assess the efficacy of the positive or prescriptive aspects of law. He defines the "prescriptive" work of economics as something less than full-fledged normative assessment of what the law should be. "Economists are . . . helpful in giving accounts of how law comes into being and in showing the best way to achieve specified ends. At the more normative level, they are most helpful in showing that if some X is the goal, some instrument Y will or will not achieve it." Cass R. Sunstein, *On Philosophy and Economics*, 19 QUINNIPIAC L. REV. 333, 334 (2000).

[119] *See* Jolls, Sunstein, & Thaler, *supra* note 25, at 1474.

[120] Richard A. Posner, *Rational Choice, Behavioral Economics, and the Law*, 50 STAN. L. REV. 1551, 1560-61 (1998).

a broad conception of rationality, with the aid of the evolutionary biology of positive and negative altruism."[121]

Nevertheless, the problem of science and the "ought" remains. Not surprisingly, Posner has made that almost imperceptible jump from positive to normative analysis, the move from "is-is not" to "ought-ought not," that Hume questioned.[122] If our theory of the "is" posits rational behavior, and we observe the "is not" of what appears to be anomalous, then we ought to explain it. Here is Posner's description of the thinking process: "Faced with anomalous behavior, the rational-choice economist, unlike the behavioral economist, doesn't respond, 'Of course, what do you expect?' Troubled, puzzled, challenged, he wracks his brains for some theoretical extension or modification that will accommodate the seeming anomaly to the assumption of rationality."[123] Indeed, the notion that we "ought" to explain it, to wrack our brains for an explanation is another demonstration of the regulative nature of reason at work. Unless we have a pre-existing idea that people ought to be rational, we would not wrack our brains to explain the anomaly.

But in the rational-choice theory espoused at least by Judge Posner, "ought" goes beyond that imbedded in epistemology, and turns quickly to the ends derivable by practical reason: "One might have thought that behavioral economics had at least one clear normative implication: that efforts should be made through education and perhaps psychiatry to cure the cognitive quirks and weakness of will that prevent people from acting rationally with no offsetting gains."[124] By this account, if behavioral economics teaches us anything positively, it is that all of our flaws, including that stubborn notion of fairness, are curable by education and psychiatry.

III. THE MYSTERY OF ETHICAL JUDGMENT

A. Judging is Different than Knowing

Kant was the first to observe that judging is not the same as knowing.[125] It is not mere application of our faculty of cognition to the real world (i.e., the application of rules like causality or substance so that we might order our sensible perceptions). Instead, judgment is "the faculty of subsuming under rules, i.e., of determining whether something stands under a given rule . . . or not."[126] Nor is judgment an exercise in the kind of logic that constitutes the employment of reason, or the derivation of the conditions of propositions through logic. The attempt to set rules for the application of rules leads to an infinite regress. If you try to determine what circumstances fit within

---

[121] *Id.* at 1561.

[122] *See* HUME, *supra* note 51.

[123] Posner, *supra* note 120, at 1567.

[124] *Id.* at 1575.

[125] *See* KANT, *supra* note 89, at 278-79.

[126] KANT, *supra* note 1, at 268.

a rule, setting another rule merely leads to another rule to another rule to another rule, all the way down. Hence, according to Kant, "the power of judgment is a special talent that cannot be taught but only practiced."[127]

Consequently, there is no rule for the application of a rule. Indeed, if Kant captured anything in the interplay between rules and examples, it is the battle that law professors undertake with their first year students. In the hoary law school test-taking methodology of IRAC ("issue-rule-application-conclusion"), the real exercise of judgment is the A of application, not the mere memorization of rules. It is as though, seeking to derive through the power of logic a universal statement of a rule, the law student commits precisely the errors Kant anticipates. The student may have all the hornbook and study aid rules memorized, "yet can easily stumble in their application, either because he is lacking in natural power of judgment (though not in understanding), and to be sure understands the universal in abstracto but cannot distinguish whether a case belongs in concreto under it, or also because he has not received adequate training for this judgment through examples and actual business."[128]

Moreover, there is a difference between the kind of judgment (namely, pattern finding in experience) we undertake in science, and the kind of judgment we make when we decide that a particular circumstance falls within a more general legal, moral, or ethical rule. Where the general is given, the process by which we determine that a particular instance falls under it is called "determinant" judgment.[129] Where the particular is given and the universal rule must be found, the judgment is termed "reflective judgment."[130] Kant appreciates the power of the inference of ends to inanimate nature; even though nature gives us no reason to believe that its various components relate to each other as means to ends, the very inference of causality implies an order we can never prove.[131] There is no necessity to nature other than our ordering brings to it:

> [N]ature, regarded as mere mechanism, could have fashioned itself in a thousand other different ways without lighting precisely on the unity based on a principle like this, and . . . accordingly, it is only outside the conception of nature, and not in it, that we may hope to find some shadow of ground a priori for that unity.[132]

Kant stresses that this inference of ends ("teleology") is by analogy only. We are merely engaged in deriving, through use of reflective judgment, those laws that appear to govern an objective, yet blindly operating, world. Suggesting there really is a con-

---

[127] *Id.*

[128] *Id.* at 269. Whether Kant had in mind a greater emphasis on clinical education in the modern law schools, the point here is that law professors should not see this solely as a problem of the student.

[129] KANT, *supra* note 89, at 279.

[130] *Id.*

[131] *Id.* at 314-15.

[132] *Id.* at 315.

scious design to nature "would mean that teleology is based, not merely on a regulative principle, directed to the simple estimate of phenomena, but is actually based on a constitutive principle available for deriving natural products from their causes; with the result that the concept of an end of nature now exists for the determinant, rather than the reflective judgment."[133] In summary, the reflective judgment is the usual process of induction tied to experience. It goes beyond what we can know to say that the rule that we have derived by induction from experience truly is, an intelligent design, one with conscious purpose and ends in mind (i.e., a "constitutive" principle or one of real knowledge).

Determinant judgment is even more slippery. It is an exercise by which we now attach a particular example to the general rule. Our reason has conceived of an order, an end, a system into which this example falls, but nature is random and fortuitous, and it may not turn out that way. Obviously it is a contradiction to suggest we can both know and not know an end in nature. And, the answer is that we cannot know. Thus, Kant distinguishes the more speculative essence of the determinant judgment from the reflective judgment. The moment of judgment, the sense of fit to an end, "is transcendent for the determinant judgment if its object is viewed by reason—albeit for the reflective judgment [inferring a pattern from events] it may be immanent in respect of objects of experience."[134] As Professor Linda Meyer notes:

> The key step, the perception of relevance, is not predetermined by the rule. That perception of relevance is driven by a deeper sense of "fit" or "sense of fairness" that is not reducible to rules and remains in the background, expressible only through metaphor or analogy, tangible only in connection with concrete examples. We point to fit or sense, but we cannot give a rule for it.[135]

There is no given path between the statement of any rule, including a legal rule, and its application in a particular circumstance. Something else enters the equation, and that is what we next explore as a matter of law and ethics.

B. Distinguishing Legal Rules and Ethical Standards

To judge, we need a rule to apply. But, let us first distinguish the rules of law from the rules of ethics. In the process by which we reason our way to legal conclusions in matters of private law, we might, but are never required to, ask the question "what ought?" as a matter of universal application. Certainly, in the realm of public law this question might be construed to invite a debate along the well-trod lines of Hart, Fuller, Raz, and Dworkin: to be considered law, does it incorporate some kind of moral base

---

133 *Id.* at 316.

134 *Id.* at 336.

135 Linda Meyer, *Between Reason and Power: Experiencing Legal Truth*, 67 U. Cin. L. Rev. 727, 745 (1999).

line, or is it merely the positive law?[136] But when one is faced with a moral dilemma as to which the only relevant law is private, the issue is different. While the law may have a significant bearing on one's decision because of the belief in the value of adherence to law, the determination what the law requires may differ significantly from the decision what one ought to do.

Regardless of one's position on the positivist-naturalist debate, it is difficult to deny this bit of legal realism: at least in matters of private law, the statement of the applicable law in a particular instance is the result of someone's exercise of determinant judgment. Indeed, whether we look at the parties' positions, or court's decision, the argumentation of law is one in which we look at what is or has been, and by the exercise of determinant judgment, decide whether the general rules of legal entitlement govern the particular instance. In that exercise, we have taken the general rule of legal entitlement as a surrogate for what ought to be and shown how it governs what has happened or what will happen. Most lawyers will work their entire careers without reflecting on the philosophical essence of law, but very few will pass even a day without exercising determinant judgment about what the law in a particular circumstance is.

But there is no rule for the application of a rule. Consequently, the process of determinant judgment must be influenced by something outside the rule itself. In the context of business decision or business conflict, it is entirely possible we are influenced by the desire to find a universal statement of "what ought." However, when we consider the application of the legal rules (the general principles) to the circumstances (the particular), we are more likely influenced by our own instrumental and consequential ends. Indeed, the process of law when directed at the redemption of our particular wants and needs is, above all, a process of justification. We will justify those ends by making an argument that says this particular rule ought to govern, but that is simply another way of saying what the law in the particular circumstance is.[137] Put another way (reflecting Kelsen's Pure Theory of Law), the process of legal argumentation is simply the identification of the legal consequence that flows from a particular set of facts. That, and nothing else, is the positive law.

However, having reached, even provisionally, a determination of the positive law (i.e., the legal "ought" in Kelsen's terms that constitutes the positive law), the question remains "what ought" by appeal to a universal moral standard that may or may not match the legal "ought." Within the legal academy, one view, epitomized by Richard Posner, suggests scientific methodology provides the optimum general rules through the process of induction (as if to say "we have determined that we are all better off when we adopt legal rules that maximize welfare over those concerned with fairness"). The competing view, epitomized by Ronald Dworkin, asserts that there is a single

---

[136] The classic essays by these legal philosophers are widely anthologized, but can be found together in JOEL FEINBERG & HYMAN GROSS, LAW IN PHILOSOPHICAL PERSPECTIVE, SELECTED READINGS 46, 65, 157, 181 (1977).

[137] *See* Jeffrey M. Lipshaw, *Freedom, Compulsion, Compliance and Mystery: Reflections on the Duty Not to Enforce a Promise,* 3 LAW, CULTURE & THE HUMANITIES 82 (2007), *available at* http:// ssrn.com/ abstract=742844 (discussion of Hans Kelsen's positivism).

right answer (determinable through the exercise of reason) to every difficult question of the "ought."[138] Neither approach tells us how to decide in the moment of judgment. Indeed, the dangers in that moment are polarities of transcendental illusion: the subtle and spurious rationalizations of which reason is capable either in the name of science, at one pole, or morality, at the other.

There is a moment of judgment, in which no rule, logic, or showing of the predictive power of a particular economic model can tell us what to do. In science, theoretical reason acts as a regulative mechanism pushing us, untethered to experience, to predictions of what will be; in the Kantian epistemology, what makes it science is its tie to experience or possible experience. Even in knowledge, we can never reach the Unconditioned, but we can approach it, and theoretical reason may be trumped (i.e., falsified) by experience. In morality, practical reason drives us to what ought to be, and we are able to reason to ends by deciding whether the principles governing our action are universals, ones we would apply to anybody in this circumstance. In either case, the concern is about the thirst for rationality that creates lies, and the assertion of ostensible reasons for an act we ought or ought not to undertake. As an ex ante source to which we might turn to decide what to do, law only answers to the question "what are we entitled to do?" Ex post, it is primary a means for justifying what we did by reference to what we were entitled to do. In making judgment about actions, we need to separate the questions of "what is" from "what ought," and do so without conflating the two.

C. Finding an Ethical Standard

The core problem of reflection on ethics is that it invokes a philosophical dilemma: how do we make judgments reconciling the right and the good? If doing right, being virtuous, or abiding our duties, always coincided with an increase in our happiness and the amount of good in the world, there would be no problem. Whether they realize it or not, business managers confront this issue all the time. For example, most contemporary businesses would say that they are concerned not just with financial or operating performance but with values. Indeed, if performance (the accomplishment of the good) and values (the accomplishment of the right) are placed on horizontal and vertical axes, the dilemma does not occur with the coincidence of the right and the good, but in the troubling state of affairs when they do not match. Regardless how he operated in practice, Jack Welch, the former chairman and chief executive officer of General Electric, claimed, in so many words, that there was no place in the organization for the executive who accomplished the good but not the right.[139]

Ethical decision-making would be less troubling if every case of incongruity between the right and the good were at the extremes. In an ideal world, the wrongs would be so clear that any resort to justification by the good would be irrelevant. However, the real world is not so accommodating. Consider the following hypothetical:

---

[138] *See generally* DWORKIN, *supra* note 36.

[139] NOEL TICHY & STRATFORD SHERMAN, CONTROL YOUR DESTINY OR SOMEONE ELSE WILL 229-30 (1992).

> The company has two valuable and high-potential employees, Jack and Stephanie. They are managing the critical launch of the company's newest product, one upon which the future of the company rides.
>
> An internal audit reveals that the two have been using Jack's company credit card to purchase personal items that have no conceivable connection to the company (a new DVD recorder, for example). The human resources manager confronts Jack, who admits that his personal finances had gotten out of control, that it was a bad mistake, but he was desperate, and at some point, intended to repay it. Jack says that he told Stephanie what he was doing, learned that she also was in bad financial straits, and lent the card to her. Jack is terminated for cause immediately and escorted out of the building, and does not contest the termination.
>
> The human resources manager then confronts Stephanie. Stephanie first admits that she used the card, then claims later that she did not, and that Jack purchased the items for her, without her knowing the source of the funds. Over the next two days, as the manager investigates the situation, Stephanie consults with a lawyer, who insists that the company does not have a basis for a termination with cause. In order to get the matter behind him, the manager agrees that Stephanie will be allowed to sign a routine separation agreement and mutual release, and to receive two weeks' severance pay, half of the amount to which she would have been entitled under the company policy.
>
> Friends of Jack complain that concessions made to Stephanie are not right, and that there has been unfair and unequal treatment of the two: if Jack was terminated for cause, Stephanie should have been as well.

Was it wrong, or even unethical, for the human resources manager to have treated Jack and Stephanie differently, merely because Stephanie "lawyered up?" In the context of business ethics, when we try to decide what we ought to do two problems arise. First, what is the ultimate aim of our deliberation? Is our task to determine a duty and to act in accordance with it? Was it the manager's obligation to determine his duty (in this case, of justice) and to do what is right regardless of the consequence (e.g., the drain on his time by fighting the termination with cause issue with Stephanie)? Or, are we obliged to determine the good or bad that will result from our decision, and choose on that basis? In the latter instance, is it permissible to conclude that Jack, notwithstanding his serious violation of the rules, is a valuable employee and the ultimate good in his contribution to the success of the company outweighs the need for discipline?

All of this falls under the rubric of practical reason, the method by which we go about making decisions, not about whether something is true or false, but about what we ought to do. According to Aristotle's practical reason, we look for and act on those virtues that are the mean between polar values;[140] in Kant's deontological practical rea-

[140] *See generally* Lawrence B. Solum, *Virtue Jurisprudence: A Virtue-Centered Theory of Judging*, 34 METAPHILOSOPHY 178 (2003).

son, in which we derive broad and immutable duties prescribed by the moral law and follow their dictates regardless of consequences;[141] in utilitarian ethics, we deny there is any "right" other than the "good" and view the issue solely in terms of maximizing whatever is good in actual experience.[142]

Even if we agree on the standard employed to make the ethical decision, what is the decision-making methodology? How do you go about, on a day-to-day basis, deciding whether duty prevails over consequence? As explored above, there are several possible errors when we reason our way from broad statements of what is right or what is good. For example, even though Kant suggests, in principle, that our duties under the moral law are determinable by the exercise of practical reason, consider the distance between theory and practice. First, our duty is our ultimate freedom from the pulls, inclinations, and desires of the physical world. Once we determine our duty as the rule we would make universal in that circumstance, we have determined good for its own sake, not for any instrumental reason. But, as Kant concedes, we cannot explain how freedom is possible without circularity or antinomy. Second, we cannot be sure that our determination emanates from practical reason and duty or from some underlying inclination. Third, there is always the possibility of transcendental illusion. We mistake the universality of the practical rule for a statement of epistemological truth. That is the road by which reason can lead to rationalization which, in turn, may constitute self-deception.

"I know it when I see it." Although, we can never quite get to "it," "it" nevertheless informs our decisions. "It" does seem to suggest that we manage to apply basic notions of concepts like fairness, justice, or mercy, even if we cannot always articulate precisely how we are doing it. In the face of a difficult decision, "we sleep on it." We do not make progress in sorting through conflicting values by more thought, as much as by isolating that one bothersome tickle at the innermost core of our concern.

Various ethical traditions have tried to make the "it" more concrete without suggesting there is an algorithm by which we might calculate the correct decision. There is a real appeal to virtue ethics. The Aristotelian notion of the golden mean pulsates with common sense. But, for the actor making the decision, virtue ethics beg the question. In one sense (and not surprisingly having been first articulated by Aristotle) virtue ethics are the product of inductive through reflective judgment. Evaluating the data, the best decisions tend to have been made by virtuous people. Thus, we are best off having virtuous people continue to make our critical judgments.[143]

---

[141] *See* Stephen Darwall, *Introduction, in* DEONTOLOGY 1, 1-6 (Stephen Darwall ed., 2003).

[142] *Id.* at 1.

[143] I do not mean to give short shrift to virtue ethics and virtue jurisprudence. The classic modern defense of virtue ethics is G.E.M. Anscombe's classic essay *Modern Moral Philosophy*, in which she urges the abandonment of deontology as the basis for modern moral and ethical philosophy in favor of one that looks to particular virtues. Hence, we would not ask "was that wrong?" or "did she do something she ought not to have done. Instead, we would simply consider a particular virtue, like being just, or being kind, or truthful, or chaste, and measure the person's action against that virtue. *See generally* G.E.M. Anscombe, *Modern Moral Philosophy, in* A. MARTINICH & DAVID SOSA, ANALYTIC PHILOSOPHY: AN ANTHOLOGY 381-92 (2001). Professor Lawrence Solum suggests we turn to virtue ethics as the basis of jurisprudence. He finds

Similarly, modern natural law theory may strike some as an unsatisfying basis for ethics, not because there is anything particularly troubling with the behavior its theorists advocate (unlike the normative implications of rational choice or behavioral economic theory). The real problem is the answer, "because I said so," in the modern sensibility. Moreover, natural law fundamentally presumes, a link between the right and the good, that virtue leads to happiness, and that is simply too much for the modern sensibility. Epistemologically, it is far less satisfying to embrace the idea that we simply must live with the questions rather than the answers. However, the latter is at least an intellectually honest answer that resonates with thoughtful people.

1. Appeal to Natural Law

If one already adheres to a particular body of, or approach to, religious or natural law, it is easy to be influenced by specific dictates given authoritatively by representatives of that body of thinking, whether the church or Ronald Dworkin. The conundrum is as follows: despite one's conviction that there are universalities available to him by intuition, he continues to rebel at religious or natural law dictates. And he asks himself "why?"

At the outset, it is necessary to clarify what is meant by natural law. As Brian Bix points out, we use natural law to describe two separate modes of thought. First, there is the traditional view that natural law is something "higher" than mere positive law, is just, true, unchanging over time and universal, and is accessible by human reason.[144] The second is the "modern" view, although, as discussed below, it would be incorrect to suggest that the traditional view has no modern adherents. Modern natural law theorists deny the positivist claim that there is a necessary separation between law and morality. This discussion focuses particularly on Ronald Dworkin because of the clarity of his claim that judges fit their present decisions to previous cases, and justify the present decision within acceptance moral boundaries.[145] In either case, it is important to wrestle with what seems to be the blocking issue: not just that we talk about answers to hard moral and legal cases as if there were a single answer already determined by some omniscient Author and merely discoverable by efforts of reason, but the conclusion there is such a single answer.

The fair approach is to consider the most articulate contemporary discussions of traditional and modern natural law, and to determine how far one may travel along the paths they suggest, and where one should turn away. So let us briefly turn to them.

---

a middle way between utilitarian and deontological conceptions of what is moral as follows: in applying rules to facts in difficult cases, what we need to do is entrust the decision to virtuous judges. *See generally* Solum, *supra* note 140. Robert Audi's critique of virtue ethics resonates with me: "many morally reflective people . . . find that determining what conduct is virtuous requires going beyond virtue ethics and appealing to principles or standards not clearly implicit in any pure virtue ethics." ROBERT AUDI, THE GOOD IN THE RIGHT 197 (2005).

[144] Bix, *supra* note 20, at 224.

[145] *Id.* at 234-37.

i. Modern Natural Law and the Single Right Answer

Ronald Dworkin is perhaps the most articulate advocate of "modern" natural law. In *Objectivity and Truth: You Better Believe It*[146] and in a sequel available online,[147] Dworkin addresses the modern skepticism toward truth, morality, and responsibility. From the first paragraph, he confronts the skeptical view of objective truth.[148] Are our most "confident convictions about what happened in the past or what the universe is made of or who we are or what is beautiful or who is wicked" mere conventions? Do we deceive ourselves into believing we have discovered "some external, objective, timeless, mind-independent world" or are all of our most universal moral truths things "we have actually invented ourselves, out of instinct, imagination and culture?"[149] Dworkin's answer, consistent with his theory of the law in *Law's Empire,*[150] is that there are objective moral truths, but that inquiry into the metaphysics from which they might derive is not productive.

Although Dworkin uses hot button issues like genocide or abortion, it is effective to think in more mundane, yet equally troubling examples, like the question whether to continue manufacturing the flame retardant described in the Introduction. Dworkin distinguishes what he terms "internal skepticism" from "external skepticism." Internal skepticism is an attitude to which we are entitled if we are engaged in making moral decisions. Dworkin views the skepticism as "internal" because the skeptic acknowledges that some moral decisions are right and some are wrong, some are better and some are worse; the internal skeptic plays the game of moral judgment, but is not skeptical as to the very possibility of moral judgment at all.[151] "An internally skeptical position, then, denies some group of familiar positive claims and justifies that denial by endorsing a different positive moral claim—perhaps a more general or counterfactual or theoretical one."[152] In the example of the flame retardant, we may believe we have reached the right answer by resolving the situation in favor of continuing to manufacture and save present lives, but others can be skeptical of the conclusion because they hold a contrary view of morality.

Nevertheless, Dworkin would insist there is a single right answer to the issue, even if we are uncertain what it is. Here, Dworkin distinguishes between uncertainty, which he holds to be a valid, if weaker, position than either a positive or negative view on an

---

[146] *See generally* Ronald Dworkin, *Objectivity and Truth: You Better Believe It*, 25 PHIL. & PUB. AFF. 87 (1996).

[147] *See generally* Ronald Dworkin, *Truth and Responsibility and Morality as Interpretation*, http://www.law.nyu.edu/clppt/program2005/readings/Hedgehogs_ 2and4.pdf.

[148] Dworkin, *supra* note 146, at 87.

[149] *Id.*

[150] RONALD DWORKIN, LAW'S EMPIRE (1986).

[151] In *Law's Empire,* Dworkin makes this distinction as to the question of interpretation: an internal skeptic may be skeptical of an interpretive conclusion, but does not question the validity of making any interpretative judgments. *Id.* at 78-79. He applies the thesis to moral judgment explicitly in *Objectivity.* Dworkin, *supra* note 146, at 89-94.

[152] *Id.* at 90.

issue, and indeterminacy, which he rejects as a valid philosophical position. Indeterminacy is of two kinds. It is first person if you decide that because you cannot make up your mind, there is no determinable right answer. It is third person, if while observing a dispute between others, you conclude that it is simply not possible to determine who has the better of the argument. Although Dworkin may change his mind on abortion, for example, depending on his mood or the argument, and one may go back and forth on the flame retardant issue, that merely means we are uncertain about the right answer, not that there is no determinable right answer.[153]

To get to Dworkin's ultimate claim about the objective truth of "moral facts," we still need to work through what he calls "external skepticism." External skepticism is not a moral position, but a metaphysical one: it rejects the belief "that one interpretation of some text or social practice can be on balance better than others, that there can be a 'right answer' to the question which is best even when it is controversial what the right answer is."[154] Dworkin coins the phrase "archimedean" to dispute external skeptics who "purport to stand outside a whole body of belief, and to judge it as a whole from premises or attitudes that owe nothing to it."[155]

It is important to understand what Dworkin is rebutting. It is not the radical skeptic who claims to have no basis for making any moral judgments at all. In a paraphrase of the "liar paradox" inherent in the statement "there is no truth" (i.e., if the statement is true, then the statement itself must be false), Dworkin disposes quickly of this radical skepticism.[156] The more difficult issue is that of the so-called selective archimedean, who believes first-order moral propositions like "abortion is wicked" or "genocide is wrong," but is skeptical of any metaphysical basis on which one might contend those first-order propositions are objectively true.[157] As a result, a selective archimedean might agree that genocide is wrong but deny the truth of the second-order statement: it is always and objectively the case that genocide is wrong. This is primarily a response to post-moderns, who assert rightness or wrongness in specific contexts, but deny any basis for saying, ultimately, that one may make objective judgments about right and wrong.

Dworkin collapses the first-order and second-order propositions together, and contends that the second-order proposition is meaningless, because any moral proposition itself makes a claim that it is an objective truth. He does not seek to refute the skeptical response to the second-order proposition, as much as simply to announce an alternative: morality is so deeply imbued in our experience of the real world, which we ought to just accept it as a thing in itself, and disdain further metaphysics.[158]

In the follow-on chapter to *Objectivity,* Dworkin continues to view moral propositions either as, or akin to, objective facts. He proposes a "quotidian" view of meta-ethics

---

[153] *Id.* at 129-31.

[154] DWORKIN, *supra* note 150, at 80.

[155] Dworkin, *supra* note 146, at 88.

[156] *Id.* For a brief summary of the paradox, *see* ROGER SCRUTON, MODERN PHILOSOPHY 5-6 (1994).

[157] Dworkin, *supra* note 146, at 92-94.

[158] *Id.* at 128.

and moral theory, one insisting "that the traditional questions of moral philosophy, including the question whether moral values are real and whether people can achieve moral knowledge, are intelligible and can be answered only if we understand them as ordinary, everyday substantive moral questions."[159] He offers an involved epistemology of morality, including a comparison of scientific reasoning to moral reasoning, all of which seems to assume ab initio that there are "moral facts," but they may not have the same "causal relationships" as scientific facts. All of this seems to assume that noumena are knowable as truth.[160] If it there is an objective truth, we may be uncertain about it, but it does not negate its existence.

ii. Contemporary Application of Traditional Natural Law

A casual review of the literature leads to the conclusion that the introduction of metaphysics into contemporary consideration of law and ethics within the legal academy is largely the province of writers who are willing to engage in public reconciliation of deeply-held religious beliefs and the scholarship of the law. For example, one will find a significant body of Catholic reaction to issues of law and economics,[161] corporate law,[162] or justice generally.[163] There are arguments, based in Jewish tradition, that the

---

[159] Dworkin, *supra* note 147, at 2.

[160] Lipshaw, *supra* note 137, at 18-19.

[161] Mark A. Sargent, *Utility, the Good & Civic Happiness: A Catholic Critique of Law & Economics*, 44 J. CATH. LEGAL STUD. 35, 37 (2005).

> A Catholic jurisprudence may draw on different sources of inspiration such as Scripture, natural law, Thomas Aquinas, the Magisterium of the Church, Catholic social thought, or any combination of those approaches; but all presume the knowability of the Good. While recognizing that no human social, political, or legal arrangements in the fallen world can embody the Good, Catholic thought hardly shares the indifference to ends central to the utility maximization norm. A Catholic jurisprudence ultimately will be about ends. It will make judgments about the values implicit in those ends, and will critique and prescribe legal rules on the basis of those judgments. Nothing could be less like law and economics.

Id.

[162] Susan J. Stabile, *A Catholic Vision of the Corporation* 40 (St. John's Univ. School of Law, Paper No. 07-0018, 2005), *available at* http://ssrn.com/abstract=761605 (footnotes omitted).

> [A]ll religions support communitarian values, pointing "the way beyond ourselves to a deeper connection, both to others and to something sacred, immortal, and timeless . . . [motivating people] toward a sense of wholeness from which they are inspired to serve humanity." Thus, the notion of the common good and of the need for all human institutions to promote that common good is not unique to Catholic Social Thought. Catholic Social Thought contributes uniquely to the discussion, however, because it has a much more organized and well-developed body of social teachings, embodied in numerous papal encyclicals and other documents over the years, than do other religions.

Id.

[163] *See generally* Amelia J. Uelman, *An Explicit Connection Between Faith and Justice in Catholic Legal Education: Why Rock the Boat?*, 81 U. DET. MERCY L. REV. 921 (2004).

law must have some fundamental and universal source, beyond merely the expression of human beings.[164] There are reconciliations of contract law and Christian conscience based in Mormon theology.[165] There is an initial and obvious answer to the attempt to use religion or traditional natural law as the basis for a set of business ethics: whether or not the doctrine states universal principles or claims that it is universal (and remember that "catholic" means universal), we grow up sectarian. One can respect another's right to believe, and even the belief itself, but not believe it.[166]

However, if there is any scholar whose attempt to grapple with traditional natural law in a contemporary setting might appeal to the secular seeker, it is Professor Steven Smith. His *Law's Quandary* asks if we all are now legal positivists and realists, who believe that the law is what the judge says it is, based on all the predilections, prejudices, mores, and standards prevalent at the time of the decision, why do we continue to speak of the law as though it were something that existed before the onset of the present dispute, and which must, upon discovery through argument and application, inexorably apply to the present matter?[167] What is particularly appealing about Smith's approach is that, while he is clearly a devoted Christian, his humility and openness to the intellectual struggle shines through. His essay, *Hollow Men: Law and the Declension of Belief,* is as forthright and articulate defense of the contemporary vitality of belief itself, if not belief in a traditional natural law.[168]

---

[164] David Novak, *Law: Religious or Secular?*, 86 VA. L. REV. 569, 594 (2000).

> But if law is to intelligently order our interpersonal desires in such a way that the common good is properly served, how could that law be the product of the desires of any of those who need to be governed by it? Thus it must come from the will of someone not governed by it. Once there is an externally imposed law on our desires, here is a god of some sort or other. It would seem that we only want to obey someone generically different from and superior to ourselves. Thus, for example, once we discover our parents are generically similar to ourselves, that they are mortal like us and we like them, we have already divested them of the godlike status they had in our infancy. We now honor and respect them because of the command of the everlasting God, who is different in kind both from us and from them and thus prior to their claims on us. The question, then, is not a god or no-god. The question is *whose god.*

Id.

[165] *See* Val D. Ricks, *Contract Law and Christian Conscience*, 2003 BYU L. REV. 993, 993.

[166] At least in some religious traditions, there is an overlap between religious dogma and the claim to natural law, as in the philosophy of Thomas Aquinas. *See* Bix, *supra* note 20, at 225-27. Also, the mission statement of the Ave Maria School of Law states: "Ave Maria School of Law affirms Catholic legal education's traditional emphasis on the only secure foundation for human freedom—the natural law written on the heart of every human being. We affirm the need for society to rediscover those human and moral truths that flow from the nature of the human person and that safeguard human freedom." Ave Maria School of Law Mission Statement, http://www.avemarialaw.edu/prospective/philosophy/phil1.cfm (last visited Jan. 10, 2006).

[167] SMITH, *supra* note 84, at 62-64.

[168] *See generally* Steven D. Smith, *Hollow Men: Law and the Declension of Belief* (Univ. San Diego, Research Paper No. 06-03, 2005), *available at* http://ssrn.com/abstract=672681.

A brief reconstruction of Smith's argument, in a slightly different order, follows. Unlike reasoning, emotion, or sociability, all of which human beings share with other species or beings, human have the unique capability to believe. Indeed, Smith argues, what makes us uniquely human is our capacity to believe, which itself reflects "our distinctive relation to truth—not just truth in the sense of mundane fact . . . but to Truth in the upper case."[169] In light of this predicate, loss of belief or an inability to believe makes us less human—hollower, as it were.[170] Smith sees the decline of belief in the modern age largely as the result of the predominance of the naturalistic or scientific world view.[171] As we have seen, if no theory in science is ever final, then suggesting anything is final or eternal is subject to question, leaving us with a belief system anchored in doubt.

Smith posits four reactions to the challenge to constitutive religious or natural law belief claims: apologetics, abandonment, screening, or the most significant, the declension of belief itself (a type of "lowered expectations" strategy to the whole idea of belief).[172] The declension strategy Smith assesses is the "pragmatic turn": to the extent belief, or the idea of Truth are useful to us, there is some reason for them to exist.[173] He concludes the strategy is ultimately self-contradictory.[174] The value of faith lies in its intrinsic not its instrumental value. Believing something merely because it is useful to do so, and not because it is true, "necessarily involves the believer—or the half-believer—in self-deception, or at least in a sort of Orwellian double-think."[175] The point Smith wants to make in *Law's Quandary,* which he repeats and enhances in *Hollow Men,* is that the reason for our talk of the law, even in an age of legal positivism and realism, as though it were natural law is that there is a transcendent Author, God, who writes the natural law. Yet, he expresses a vision for Christian jurisprudence—that this element of the law that seems to presuppose an ascertainable Truth is an avenue by which "we may glimpse 'the dearest freshness deep down things.'"[176]

Ironically, Smith's claims, though based in more traditional natural law, are humbler and more revealing than Dworkin's. Smith identifies the apparent paradox of our continuing need to believe (and the logical next step, that there is a Truth in which we may believe) in an age when belief no longer suffices as a means of explanation, and the idea of Truth is at best difficult.[177]

---

[169] *Id.* at 2.

[170] *Id.* at 3.

[171] *Id.* at 5.

[172] *Id.* at 6-9.

[173] *Id.* at 9-10.

[174] *Id.* at 15.

[175] *Id.*

[176] *Id.* at 30.

[177] *Id.* at 3.

Is it possible to articulate a secular transcendentalism, an acknowledgment of mystery that takes one to the edge of belief, but not to the more concrete faith of a Christian? Likely that is the natural import of reason's regulative practices: we propose order and purpose because, well, we just propose order and purpose. As Dworkin suggests, we cannot stand outside of reason to understand reason. Indeed, returning again to Kant's wisdom on this subject, we presume a God because of "the dearest freshest deep down things" or perceive that the world is "charged with the grandeur of God." This is the basis for the argument from design, the proof of God Kant said "always deserves to be named with respect."[178]

But our presumptions about God or Truth need to remain beliefs, and hence one might continue to recoil whenever a person tells him, as though it were Truth, what God is thinking or what God wants or what God does as though the person just finished an in-depth conversation with God (or nowadays, received a message on his Blackberry from God). Kant recognized that even though we can, and indeed, must presuppose a "unique wise and all-powerful world author," we have nevertheless not extended our cognition beyond the field of possible experience "[f]or we have only presupposed a Something, of which we have no concept at all of what it is in itself (a merely transcendental object) . . . ."[179] Kant anticipates the seeker who asks, "[y]et may I regard purpose-like orderings as intentions by deriving them from the divine will, though of course mediately through dispositions toward them set up in the world?"[180] The answer is yes, you can, but you can never know that is the case: "where you do perceive purposive unity, it must not matter at all whether you say, "God has wisely willed it so," or "Nature has wisely so ordered it."[181]

So I ask again, "but may I say that I know this ordering to be true as a matter of God's law or universal natural law?" While Kant acknowledges the continuing aim "to seek out the necessary and greatest possible unity of nature," even "to have the idea of a highest being to thank for this so far as we can reach it," the answer is no.[182] Whether it is Dworkin's voice or the voice of a prophet claiming to be the intermediary with natural law or God's law, and as much as that belief is hardwired into us, and makes us human, one cannot blindly accept the intermediate's articulation of the dictates of either law as Truth.[183]

---

[178] KANT, *supra* note 1, at 579-80.

[179] *Id.* at 619.

[180] *Id.* at 620.

[181] *Id.*

[182] *Id.*

[183] Professor Ronald White's analysis of one of the greatest speeches in American history reflects an appreciation of the relationship between reason and dogmatism. In his Second Inaugural Address, Lincoln posed the theological conundrum that both North and South "read the same Bible, and pray to the same God" yet "[t]he prayers of both could not be answered; that of neither has been answered fully." RONALD C. WHITE, JR., LINCOLN'S GREATEST SPEECH 114 (2002). Professor White focuses particularly on Lincoln's reaction to contemporary attempts to justify slavery through recourse to the Bible: "Lincoln was aware

Although this article discusses Martin Buber in greater detail in the next section, his insight on our ability to dictate, much less teach, rules as the source of ethics is helpful at this point. Buber discusses the education of character, and considers the impact of teaching moral rules as though they were equivalent to the axioms of algebra. He explains that envy, bullying, or lying are wrong, and the reaction from his students tells him: "I have made the fatal mistake of giving instruction in ethics, and what I said is accepted as current coin of knowledge; nothing of it is transformed into character-building substance."[184] But he observed:

> After all, pupils do want, for the most part, to learn something, even if not overmuch, so that a tacit agreement becomes possible. But as soon as my pupils notice that I want to educate their characters I am resisted precisely by those who show most signs of genuine independent character: they will not let themselves be educated, or rather, they do not like the idea that somebody wants to educate them. And those, too, who are seriously laboring over the question of good and evil, rebel when one dictates to them, as though it were some long established truth, what is good and what is bad; again how hard it is to find the right way.[185]

Buber is onto something universal: intuitively, we understand how difficult it is to make good judgments, and that there is no rule for the application of a rule. Like the scientist creating the hypothesis as a product of reflective judgment, and not the mass of underlying data, or the judge, as a matter of determinant judgment, deciding that this case represents a particular example of a general rule, we know the right decisions are too nuanced to be dictated to us. In either case, traditional or modern natural law, what arguably drives thoughtful people to skepticism or pragmatism is the implausibility of the single answer.

2. The Promise of Intuitionism

I. The Right Versus the Good

Nevertheless, we have a strong sense of right and wrong—suggesting a single answer—that immediately calls into question the resort to skepticism or pragmatism. Calling it a sense of right and wrong implies the very objectivity and truth that underlies natural and religious law. How then do we make our way through the apparent paradox? As free rational agents we legislate to ourselves, but are restrained by norms. We acknowledge the general rules of law, but the need for the exceptions of equity. In addition, we

---

that religion, because of its appeal to the absolute, is capable of the most awful pretension by clothing immediate causes with ultimate sanction." *Id.* at 115.

[184] MARTIN BUBER, BETWEEN MAN AND MAN 124 (Ronald Gregor-Smith trans., Routledge Classics 2002) (1947).

[185] *Id.* at 124-25.

acknowledge that the capacity to believe makes us human, but rebel against the claim that belief equates to truth or knowledge. We see the power of reason in allowing us to conceive, in science and morality, the possibility of what ought to be, unconstrained by what is, and yet understand the power of reason to drag into transcendental illusion, rationalization, dogmatism, and self-deception.

If there is any common theme regardless of the standard by which we make the judgment, it is that we so often turn not just to the product of reason and reflection, but to an intuitive sense. Even Judge Posner, who espouses a pragmatic skepticism that denies moral universals, nevertheless appeals to an intuitive practical reason as the basis for deciding cases: "anecdote, introspection, imagination, common sense, intuition (due apparently to how the brain structures perceptions, so that, for example, we ascribe causal significance to acts without being able to observe—we never do observe—causality), empathy, imputation of motives, speaker's authority, metaphor, analogy, precedent, custom, memory, 'induction' (the expectation of regularities, related both to intuition and to analogy), 'experience.'"[186]

G.E. Moore provoked a century-long debate over the idea of "intuitionism," an ethical philosophy that addresses the difficulty of applying broader principles to specific instances, either as a matter of utilitarianism or consequentialism, which focus on the maximization of the good and the minimization of the bad, or deontology with its array of conflicting duties that constitute the "right."[187] W.D. Ross rejected Moore's consequentialism, and argued that the aim of ethics is not necessarily the good, but doing what is right, and further disagreed with Moore's claim that the ultimate "right" was doing that which increased the good.[188] Ross's intuitionism was based on a list of prima facie duties: fidelity, reparation, justice, gratitude, beneficence, self-improvement, and non-injury.[189] The duties are prima facie because each indicates a moral reason for action, but the act may not reflect our final duty because of competing duties that might override the first.[190] An example is the person who breaks a promise (the duty of fidelity to one's word) to meet a friend for breakfast because her child is ill and needs attention (the duty of non-injury)[191] "The central idea underlying the Rossian notion of a prima facie duty is that of a duty which is—given the presence of its ground—ineradicable but overridable."[192]

Ross's contribution to intuitionism is two-fold. First, there is the deontological intuition itself—that, contrary to Moore's contention, it just cannot be that the right equals only that which produces the good in a utilitarian sense. Obviously, we will never resolve the issue, but Ross's appeal to a common sense that we perceive duties

---

[186] Richard A. Posner, *The Jurisprudence of Skepticism*, 86 MICH. L. REV. 827, 838 (1988).

[187] For a summary history of intuitionism, *see* AUDI, *supra* note 143, at 5-39.

[188] W.D. Ross, *From The Right and the Good, anthologized in* DEONTOLOGY 55, 57-58 (Stephen Darwall ed., 2003).

[189] *Id.* at 59.

[190] *Id.* at 58-59.

[191] *Id.*

[192] AUDI, *supra* note 143, at 23-24.

not necessarily co-extensive with their consequences is at least as compelling as Judge Posner's opposing view. Note the emphasis:

> [W]e have to ask ourselves whether we really, when we reflect, are convinced that this is self-evident, and whether we really can get rid of our view that promise-keeping [as one example of a prima facie duty] has a bindingness independent of the productiveness of maximum good. In my own experience I find that I cannot, in spite of a very genuine attempt to do so; and I venture to think that most people will find the same. . . ."[193]

Second, Ross, more than the utilitarians, directly addresses the process by which we decide among all the conflicting parameters, and does so in a way that is consistent with what we have observed about judgment. Specifically, Ross asks why, if we are permitted to weigh all of the consequences of an act, we should not also be able to weigh the prima facie duties before coming to a conclusion about our actual duty.[194] Moreover, whether we were to weigh duties or consequences, even knowing beforehand the extent of the good or bad consequences, "there is no principle by which we can draw the conclusion that it is on the whole right or on the whole wrong."[195] Indeed, though not explicit, it is clear that Ross draws on the Kantian exposition of judgment: "the judgement as to the rightness of a particular act is just like the judgement as to the beauty of a particular natural object or a work of art."[196] Judgment of right and wrong is not a simple calculation (there is no rule for the application of a rule); "both in [the case of beauty] and in the moral case we have more or less probable opinions which are not logically justified conclusions from the general principles that are recognized as self-evident."[197]

Recently, Robert Audi sought to reinvigorate a Rossian intuitionism that is reflective and flexible.[198] That is, intuitions are non-inferential, which we simply come to know or to believe; but intuitions are fallible (they may be wrong), defeasible (one can come to see they are wrong by circumstances or another intuition), and provide an irreducible plurality of basic moral principles which associate with different grounds for duty.[199] However, Audi's intuitionism is Kantian in its approach to conflicting duties.[200] Ross's meta-theory held that all prima facie duties were accorded equal weight,

---

[193] Ross, *supra* note 188, at 73.

[194] *Id.* at 56-57.

[195] *Id.* at 67.

[196] *Id.*

[197] *Id.*

[198] *See* Audi, *supra* note 143, at 47-48.

[199] *Id.* at 40-41. Audi claims that Rossian intuitionism is commonly misunderstood as positing "indefeasible justification . . . for any cognition constituting a genuine intuition." *Id.* at 30.

[200] Audi is not the only philosopher to attempt to bring the broad, and seemingly inflexible, principles of the categorical imperative down to everyday moral decisions. Christine Korsgaard also argues for the defeasibility of "ideal" Kantian prescriptions in the non-ideal world, focusing particularly on Kant's

and the determination of overriding duties was a matter of practical wisdom and rules of thumb.[201] If not adopting all of Kant's moral philosophy, Audi takes the view that the Rossian duties might nevertheless be systematized by over-arching moral theory.[202] Audi chooses, if not all of Kant's own ramifications, the universality and intrinsic ends formulations of the Categorical Imperative.[203] Finally, Audi moderates Rossian intuitionism not only with defeasibility of the intuition of duties, but with something that is expressly non-deontological: consideration of intrinsic value, the good or bad that may be the consequences of the action.[204] Again, Audi position is grounded in what to a non-philosopher, or perhaps to an Aristotelian, would seem like ordinary good sense: there must be some way to incorporate the notions of human flourishing—good or bad consequences—at the same time we consider our duties.[205]

Ii. Intuitionism Distinguished

Of course, the objection to intuitionism is obvious. If we have conflicting intuitions, how is my intuition any different from your natural law or religious dogma? What makes mine right and yours wrong? However, we find ourselves moved by a concept of defeasible intuitionism, one that acknowledges the mystery at the core of these issues, and provides a basis for constructive and inferential dialogue about the "ought." That, however, leads us to the most difficult concept of all: how might we go about finding grounds to defeat what comes to us intuitively, to sort through what is merely suppressed, or not-so-suppressed, desire or inclination, what may be the transcendental

---

infamous and counter-intuitive dictum that the duty to tell the truth overrides the duty to save someone from a pursuing murderer. "The Formula of Humanity and its corollary, the vision of a Kingdom of Ends, provide an ideal to live up to in daily life as well as a long-term political and moral goal for humanity. But it is not feasible always to live up to this ideal, and where the attempt to do so would make you a tool of evil, you should not do so." Christine M. Korsgaard, *The Right to Lie: Kant on Dealing with Evil*, originally published at 15 PHIL. & PUB. AFF. 325 (1986), *anthologized in* DEONTOLOGY, *supra* note 141, at 212, 230. Nevertheless, Susan Neiman suggests that we ought not ascribe to Kant this level of rigidity in the application of the categorical imperative. "The 'play-room' that Kant . . . maintains to be necessary in observing the moral law extends not only to an open-endedness in the very examples that the Groundwork may have seemed to determine categorically, such as lying and suicide. . . . Further, those very circumstances on which nearly every ethical decision turns are described by Kant as empirical and hence not a part of ethics proper, which must be a priori." NEIMAN, *supra* note 11, at 123.

[201] AUDI, *supra* note 143, at 92-93.

[202] *Id.* at 83.

[203] *Id.* at 90-94.

[204] *Id.* at 121-38.

[205] *Id.* at 159.

> The intrinsically good and the intrinsically bad kinds of things in question can be non-inferentially and intuitively known to be good or to be bad, as some of the principles that reflect them can be non-inferentially and intuitively known to be true. And, without the burden of having to maximize any value, moral agents can see themselves as realizing the good in fulfilling their obligations.

Id.

illusion of dogmatism, and what may truly be an intuition of ethical rightness, fairness, or justice.

The appeal of moderate intuitionism is its very reasonableness. However, the knife-edge on which we walk is creeping dogmatism (i.e., the danger in believing that one has access to the "ought" as though it were knowledge and not belief). The problem with walking the knife-edge is that it is difficult not to wander off, and the concentration it takes to keep one's consistent balance may be too much to ask. Recall again the difficulties of this approach to ethics: we are going to acknowledge intuition, but refrain from calling the moral insight either fact or truth, and the source of that insight will always remain a mystery to us. Indeed, that is the paradox that seems to want to reify itself in natural law as an accessible truth: on one hand, we rely on intuitions emanating from a mysterious source that cannot be deemed truth or knowledge, and, on the other hand, we will act on those intuitions which seem to us to have aspects of universality (i.e., the natural law as applied to the circumstances before us).

The latter issue can only be resolved by a conscious effort to defeat the power of our own reason, and that effort must involve our relationship with others. Reason as a source of universalisms may as much lead to transcendental illusion, rationalization, or self-deception as to an acceptable universal moral rule. The inherent common sense of virtue ethics is inadequate either to explain or to prescribe in difficult situations, particularly where the continuum of extreme to extreme wherein the mean should be found is not overly clear, as in conflicts between the good and the better, or between two evils. Audi and others have proposed a defeasible and reflective intuitionism, but what is the source of the intuition? Must it not be some variant of natural law, just, true, unchanging over time and universal, and accessible by human reason? Indeed, have we staked out a position that tries to be everywhere and is in fact nowhere, skeptical equally of science and received morality?

It is a fair question to ask what differs between this view of access to ethical decision making through intuition, and Dworkin's insistence that there are objective and knowable moral facts or truths. I do not agree with his contention that it is bad philosophy to consider the epistemology of morality,[206] and conclude instead that there is something different between the objectivity of knowledge we can test in nature, and the moral conviction that seems to us objective and yet can never be proved or disproved. Dworkin's answer to the mystery at the core (or "all the way down") is the mirror-image of the radical skeptic (which was considered earlier). The radical skeptic claims there is nothing all the way down; Dworkin says there has to be something, so you might as well assume it is in the quotidian moral proposition itself.

To understand why Dworkin's path is unsatisfying as a basis for ethics (i.e., one's moral propositions just are what he believes they are, from a first person standpoint, and what he might assess as correct from a third person standpoint), we must look once again to reason itself. Dworkin acknowledges something about reason and morality: "We cannot climb outside of morality to judge it from some external archimedean tribunal,

---

[206] Dworkin, *supra* note 146, at 139.

any more than we can climb out of reason itself to test it from above."[207] Consequently, we employ reason as best we can within the confines of morality to determine true propositions, understanding that we cannot test what we accept as objective truth, any more than we can test reason.

As Professor Zangwill, a commentator on *Objectivity,* observed, this is simply the mirror-image of archimedean skepticism.[208] A skeptic believes, but can never prove, that there is no a priori basis for any moral truth. Dworkin claims that a moral proposition is because it is and always has been and always will be, and that is objective, eternal and unchanging truth. While Dworkin's view about what is true is more satisfying than the skeptic's, there is no basis to conclude Dworkin's first-order propositions as products of reason are not the subject of transcendental illusion, rationalization, and self-deception.

Let us return to the issue whether we should make the flame retardant. Suppose through the exercise of reason we conclude we should. Suppose additionally we call on Professor Dworkin for his advice on the ethics of our decision, and he tells us we are wrong, not just because we disagree, but because it is an objective truth that corporations ought not to be making products whose side effects can injure unknowing non-users, and the users of products protected by the flame retardants ought to find another solution. Why is that not a misunderstanding of the fruits of reason? It seems that we are justified in responding: "you have worked this through in your own mind, employing your faculty of reason, and have come to a non-empirical conclusion that you have then mistaken for constitutive principles of transcendent cognition, what you think is knowledge, but which is dazzling but deceptive illusion, persuasion and imagination."

IV. A SECOND PERSON APPROACH TO GETTING BEYOND REASON

Understanding the role of reason, its capability for rationalization and self-deception, is what focuses us on ethics rather than law. The process of ethics is not just one of reason. Instead, it is the application of determinant judgment (which is distinct from either theoretical or practical reason) in which the application of the general to the particular is guided by our most fundamental intuitions about virtue. But the application of judgment, the determination of duty, is the essence of our personal autonomy, our freedom to legislate for ourselves the rule we would make universal. How, then, do we avoid transcendental illusion; mistaking the universality of the practical rule for a statement of epistemological truth? Also, how can we have confidence that our well-reasoned arguments are not rationalization and self-deception?

The answer is that we can never be sure. The answer lies somewhere in this same paradox of that which cannot be proved and is yet self-evident—the maddening ques-

---

207 *Id.* at 128.

208 Nick Zangwill, *Zangwill Reviews Dworkin*, BROWN ELECTRONIC ARTICLE REV. SERVICE (BEARS) (Dec. 2, 1996), http://www.brown.edu/Departments/Philosophy/bears/9612zang.html (providing commentary on Ronald Dworkin, *Objectivity and Truth: You'd Better Believe It*, 25 PHIL. & PUB. AFF. 87 (1996)).

tion why, if a Designer chose to design the universe, did the Designer leave just enough evidence of the lack of a design to give the skeptics the basis for the counter-argument? Indeed, for all of our confidence that we know surely what is right and what is wrong (at least in the clear cases), we remain open to a smidgen of doubt. Most moral dilemmas are not as clear as genocide in Bosnia. That is why they are dilemmas. Thus, we permit our intuitions to be defeasible. But how?

The problem, in Kantian terms, begins with the process of legislating for ourselves our own morality as autonomous agents. As Kant recognized, there is no guarantee that each of us will reach the same conclusions. This solipsistic figure, seeking out the universal law, in the case of Kant's moral everyman, or Judge Hercules, in Dworkin's vision of the law, is a subject, and nothing compels the incorporation, or even understanding, of the views of another. Even the second articulation of the categorical imperative, the Law of Humanity, is directed at each agent's responsibility within himself, and not to addressing another in the second person. We are to treat others never as means only, but always as ends—others are to be subjects, and worthy of the same respect we would accord ourselves. Because so much about our moral judgment resides in personal autonomy, the check must lie in our relationship with others, not as objects to be analyzed, but as other subjects each making his own judgments, some of which may not only conflict with ours, but may be better. If one's own autonomy is first-person, and one's analytic relationship with others and the world is third-person, then the relationship with another moral agent must be second person.

The second-person relationship is already the subject of some discussion within the legal academy. Significantly, Robin Bradley Kar, taking from the work of Stephen Darwall, has attempted to reconcile the "hard" or exclusive positivism of Joseph Raz with the "soft" or inclusive positivism of H.L.A. Hart.[209] Briefly, the debate is this: Hart's positivism identified primary law, the law that affects us from day to day, as that which is issued pursuant to the Rule of Recognition—the social convention under which certain norms are recognized as law. Hart seemed to say that moral considerations could be part of primary law, so long as the Rule of Recognition allowed for it. On the other hand, Raz viewed law as law only when it provided a reason for acting or not acting exclusive of any moral consideration. In other words, law would be meaningless as a basis for action if it merely mapped precisely on the independent moral reasons, and would be irrational if it contradicted other good moral reasons for acting. "The claim to legal authority is based on the thought that the reasons law provides replace the reasons that otherwise apply to us because acting on the former will enable us more fully to comply with the latter than we will by acting on the basis of them directly."[210]

---

[209] *See generally* Robin Bradley Kar, *How an Understanding of the Second Personal Standpoint Can Change Our Understanding of the Law* (Loyola-LA Legal Studies Paper No. 2005-16, 2005), *available at* http://ssrn.com/abstract=782525. Professor Kar insightfully distinguishes between the first person perspective of reflection, and the objective view of the world that is inherent in a third person perspective. In particular, the third person view is the one we undertake when we undertake science.

[210] Jules L. Coleman & Brian Leiter, *Legal Positivism, in* A COMPANION TO PHILOSOPHY OF LAW AND LEGAL THEORY 241, 255 (Dennis Patterson ed., 1999).

Professor Kar's project is to suggest that Hart can be seen implicitly to have incorporated Raz's theory of authority without abandoning the position that moral considerations can be incorporated into the law. To do this, Professor Kar proposes a view of legal positivism that incorporates a second person perspective, one that is neither the pure self-reflection of the moral agent, nor the detached perspective of the third-party observer. "The second personal perspective is the perspective from which we address one another with claims and grievances, or respond to such claims with apology, excuse or justification."[211] Rather than focusing solely on the role legal reasons (as opposed to all other reasons) might play in the first person reflection of the actor, Professor Kar would justify the role of the law as reason for action from a second person perspective: "the law provides us with exclusionary reasons for action, which can have genuine and distinctive practical effects in our lives, insofar as the breach of a legal obligation—however identified—gives some other person or group the second personal standing to raise a legal claim for non-compliance."[212]

We need to distinguish a second person relationship in matters of law—the resolution of claims and grievances—and ethics—the consideration of the other in deciding what we ought to do. The second person perspective is critical to overcoming rationalization and self-deception in making ethical decisions; it is wholly distinct from the justification of law as law by reference to the second person perspective. Arguably, what Professor Kar sees as second person is not really second person at all. In Kelsen's view, the basic norm is a priori (i.e., one we must assume at the outset, apart from any experience in the world) and "a hypothetical judgment that expresses the specific linking of a conditioning material fact with a conditioned consequence."[213]

In assessing the claim of another person as the basis for acting, the first person actor is really making a scientific third person assessment of the likelihood that another will succeed when that person invokes the adjudicative process. That may well reconcile Hart and Raz, but nothing in the theory compels the actor to consider the position of the second person as a check against rationalization and self-deception. Indeed, considering the possible legal claims and grievances of the second person may be nothing more than an invitation to justify our inclinations and desires by means of the invocation of legal rules. There is nothing in the process that forces us to reconsider our intuitions about the normative rightness of our position.

Indeed, if we look at Stephen Darwall's account of the second person relationship, we get an idea of what it answers and what it does not.[214] The essence of the concept is that there is something different and fundamental in the authority of one person to

---

[211] Kar, *supra* note 209, at 2.

[212] *Id.* at 31.

[213] HANS KELSEN, INTRODUCTION TO THE PROBLEMS OF LEGAL THEORY 23 (Bonnie Litschewski Paulson & Stanley L. Paulson trans., 2002).

[214] *See* Stephen Darwall, *Respect and the Second-Person Standpoint, Presidential Address to the Central Division of the American Philosophical Association* (Apr. 24, 2004), *available at* http://www.lsa.umich.edu/philosophy/philosophy_detail/0,2874,19777%255Farticle% 255F35269,00.html.

demand or claim respect and dignity from another that is distinguishable from what is essentially a third person contemplation about the respect and dignity owing to persons generally. Moreover, this relationship is as a priori and synthetic as any categorical imperative: "To be a person just is to have the authority to address demands as a person to other persons, and to be addressed by them, within a community of mutually accountable equals."[215]

But Darwall's construct of the second-person standpoint bears the same relationship to specific second-person obligations as Kant's categorical imperative bears to specific moral decisions generally. In other words, it establishes the idea that there is a basis for making second-person claims and demands, without suggesting how one might go about determining what one's obligations to the other are. The parallels are particularly evident when Darwall accounts for the second-person standpoint within Kant's writings on ethics.[216] Self-love, "the 'natural' 'propensity' to take 'subjective determining grounds' of the will to have normative significance"[217]—can be cured by one's own contemplation of the moral law. When we consider whether we would legislate the principle as a universal rule of nature, we will conclude that our subjective grounds are not in accord with what we ought to do. Self-conceit, on the other hand, is the fantasy "that one has a standing to make claims and demands on others that others do not have."[218] This problem cannot be cured merely by one's internal reflection; the fantasy will be broken only by making the agent accountable to another agent's claims and demands.

From all of this, we have only gotten through the issue of standing, either legally or morally. What about the second-person claim itself? It is not surprising that Darwall's account was attractive to Professor Kar, because it seems to cast the second-person relationship as one of right to make claims and demands on another is essentially legal. It focuses on the rights of the aggrieved party more than it does the question what the actor ought to do. With the same authority the sergeant issues a drill order, in reaction to a particular circumstance, A makes a claim of dignity and respect on B. What is B supposed to do?

Darwall's structure leaves us hanging: in exercises of rationalization and self-deception, where A and B employ reason to claim and defend against claims, albeit of a second-person nature. At times, we are debating pure issues of fact: If we raise prices, how will our competitors respond? In an initial public offering, how many shares will we be able to sell and at what price? What was the cause of the factory fire? Will the acquisition be accretive to share price? Those matters are properly the subject of argumentation, a particular kind of communication.[219] However, practical questions of what we ought to do are different, because, unlike questions of fact, the answers depend on our interests,

---

[215] *Id.* at 9. Darwall contends the authority to make claims on one another is second-personal "all the way down." *Id.*

[216] *See generally id.*

[217] *Id.*

[218] *Id.*

[219] *See* JÜRGEN HABERMAS, TRUTH AND JUSTIFICATION 269 (Barbara Fultner trans., 2003).

and are not testable against experience. If being ethical means facing down one's own interests (whether material interests or one's stake in one's own vision of what ought to be), we know how difficult that will be. Reason's regulative nature inclines us to always believe we are dealing in truth, whether or not experience will bear it out.

How do we respond to the second-person claim, to make judgments what we ethically ought to do, rather than simply to determine that to which we are legally entitled? If we have learned anything so far, it is that all the science in the world will not tell how to choose. In addition, we are too humble to believe that we have access to a single correct answer (as if it were truth) as posited by the modern natural law theorists and are unsatisfied epistemologically simply to rely on the judgment of virtuous people, as posited by the virtue ethicists. Then, we are left only with a continuing mystery at the heart of judgment, and defeasible intuitionism by which we make non-inferential judgments to guide our ethical choices.

A. Truth, Argumentation, and Justification

Attempting to establish the normative as truth, as though it were science, is at its most benign, futile, and at its worst, self-deceptive. As Dennis Patterson argued, law, as means of adjudication (i.e., as an institutional way of having a third party determine what two or more opposing parties ought to do), is an exercise in language, and consists of argumentation.[220] It may consist of civilized discourse, but at its heart, adjudication, from the parties' perspective, is an argument about events that took place in the past, in which the parties and their lawyers tell narratives justifying why each of them is right. There is no need to see the circumstance from the other party's point of view, except as a tactical or strategic matter. Within the bounds set by the procedural and evidentiary rules, any argument, regardless how ostensible, is permitted.

One can adopt what sounds like a postmodern attitude toward truth, and contend there is nothing but the subjective (as Patterson is wont to argue[221]). The implication of this is the complete denial of any universals obtainable through reason or intuition, but that is not a necessary conclusion. Reason itself, by its regulative nature, demands that we pursue the conditions of propositions "all the way down" in pursuit of an unattainable Unconditioned, the "truth." Where reason pursues matters of experience or possible experience, we have at least some basis for calling what we conclude "knowledge."

---

[220] DENNIS PATTERSON, LAW & TRUTH 181 (1996).

> I have argued that law is a practice of argument. As such, propositions of law do have not "grounds." The essence of law is legal argument: the forms of legal argument are the culturally endorsed modes for showing the truth of propositions of law. It is in the use of these forms that the practice is to be understood. Their use in practice *is* the law.

Id.

[221] "If developments in philosophy of language, epistemology, and metaphysics in the last half century teach us anything, it is that meaning arises from human practices and that no practice or discourse enjoys a privileged position vis-à-vis others. Philosophy, the queen of the sciences, is now a local endeavor." *Id.* at 181-82.

However, in ethics we deal with the "ought" of responsibility, and separating it from the "is" of comprehension (as through law as social science) is critical. Thus, Patterson's argument that truth is a misplaced objective for the normative is convincing. Also, the process by which the resolution of dispute is played out is in the medium of language, whether in law or ethics, is compelling.

The question is whether there are defeasible universals of which we are capable, so long as we do not deceive ourselves into believing they represent knowledge. Litigating parties do not seek to determine what is right, but only to persuade the judge that each is right.[222] "The parties are not committed to the cooperative search for truth, and they can pursue their interest in a favorable outcome through 'the clever strategy of advancing arguments likely to win consensus.'"[223] Put another way, each party argues the rule to apply is the one that will benefit the respective party. Because there is no rule for the application of a rule, we are really arguing that a universal-transcendental-idealized norm requires the application of the rule in our favor. That is a process that may or may not produce justice, but will always involve justification. And where justification involves rationalization, there lies the possibility of the thirst for rationality creating lies.

B. Law, Subjects and Objects

There needs to be a way to test whether we are rationalizing the "ought" to conform to our inclinations and desires, rather than changing what we to do to correspond with the "ought." It is possible that our litigation claims are ostensible reasons, and if we believe them, we are engaged in self-deception. We need to delve deeper into the nature of the second-person relationship, and consider how we leave ourselves open to the possibility there is merit in what our opponent (real or imagined) asserts.

To accomplish this, ironically, we need to get beyond reason, and consider the role of intuition. We have intuitions about the right, and the issue is whether the intuition is one based in reality and justice, or instead in self-deception and justification. Searching for a basis of our intuition in truth, or grounding the basis for our intuition in argument is misdirected. The first is futile and the second reinforces whatever tendency we might have to avoid reality and to justify. We are entitled to our strong intuitions about moral choice; we are not entitled to a view that they are eternally infallible or indefeasible. How do we walk that line? Not easily. One way to begin is to consider, when encountering contrary intuitions, the source of the contrary intuition as subject rather than object.

---

[222] JÜRGEN HABERMAS, BETWEEN FACTS AND NORMS 233 (William Rehg trans., 1998). In discussing the legislative process, Habermas observed:

> No doubt one can use moral discourse of application as a model for investigating legal discourses, for both have to do with the logic of applying norms. But the more complex validity dimension of legal norms prohibits one from assimilating the legitimacy of legal decisions to the validity of moral judgments.

Id. at 233.

[223] *Id.* at 231.

Another is to consider the role of virtues, like humility, not to supplant but to mediate what Kant described as the tendency of reason to dogmatism.[224]

Alternatively, the next section considers Martin Buber and the concept of "dialogue." Notwithstanding his status as one of the foremost philosophers and theologians of the twentieth century, Buber has a reputation as a mystic, yet he is circumspect in his "mystical" claims and concerned not so much about any person's relationship with God, as with relationships with each other.

1. I and You

Because looking to Buber for insight into business law and ethics is, no doubt, a long stretch to many, it is important at the outset to make clear what this is not about. Ironically, *I and Thou,* the primary statement of Buber's philosophy, is not revered as a Jewish document because its fame spread as the result of acclaim by Protestant theologians.[225] Moreover, it claimed no access to mystical insight. Walter Kaufmann observed, "[w]hat is much more remarkable is that a sharp attack on all talk about God and all pretensions to knowledge about God—a sustained attempt to rescue the religious dimension of life from the theologians—should have been received so well by theologians."[226]

If Darwall is correct in seeing the second-person relationship as critical to ethics, but one believes at the same time that reason turned back upon itself as rationalization is corrupting of ethics (whether or not it is civilized as a matter of dispute resolution), then Buber articulates the second-person "all the way down."[227] If this argument is religious, so be it, but if that is the case, then every attempt to deal with the a priori (unless, of course, we choose to simply deny the apparently a priori) is religious. But if, as Darwall claims, the second person authority to make claims and demands just is and yet falls legitimately into secular philosophy, rather than commonly-held notions of what is religious, so too the ensuing discussion of the second-person relationship that may provide a check on self-deception. No wonder Walter Kaufmann observed about *I and Thou:* "The book does not save, or seek to prop up, a tradition. Even less does it aim to save any institution. It speaks to those who no longer believe but who wonder whether life without religion is bound to lack some dimension."[228]

---

[224] *See* Daniel Statman, *Modesty, Pride And Realistic Self-Assessment*, 42 PHILOSOPHICAL Q. 420 (1992).

[225] Walter Kaufmann, *I and You: A Prologue to* MARTIN BUBER, I AND THOU 20 (Walter Kaufmann trans., 1970).

[226] *Id.* at 20-21.

[227] Buber's own "conversion" was the result of having had a conversation with a young man who had sought Buber's advice out of despair. While Buber recalls that he was friendly, and conversed "attentively and openly," he had returned from a morning of traditional "religious" experience (no doubt a morning prayer service), but met with the young man "without being there in spirit." The irony was not lost on Buber. *See* BUBER, *supra* note 184, at 15-17.

[228] Kaufmann, *supra* note 225, at 32.

Buber's philosophy is second-person all the way down because he takes the second-person relationship to its epistemic limit, one beyond even the power of reason to make claims and demands and to respond. Buber sees our relationships, not as the world acting upon us or other acting upon us, but in the very pairing of us and the world or others. Hence, the third person relationship is not merely "I" and "It." Instead, it is symbolized in language by a word pair "I-It." Similarly, the second-person relationship is not "I" and "You." The relationship itself is a basic word composed of "I-You."[229]

The "I-You" relationship is the unmediated second-person relationship.[230] It is the pure encounter between two beings.[231] It is not "I" making claims or demands on "you." A claim or demand is conceptual. "Nothing conceptual intervenes between I and You, no prior knowledge and no imagination; and memory itself is changed as it plunges from particularity into wholeness. No purpose intervenes between I and You, no greed and no anticipation; and longing itself is changed as it plunges from the dream into appearance. Every means is an obstacle. Only where all means have disintegrated encounters occur."[232] Buber must have intended this as a reference to Kant's Formula of Humanity: there we are obliged always to treat humanity, in ourselves and others, as an end also and never only as a means. The pure encounter of I and You has no element of means—You are purely an end.[233]

Were Buber to expect us to live our lives in a way that the pure encounter of I-You predominates, this would be a journey into a never-never land of mysticism. That is not his expectation. The third-person relationship with the world as experience is the "I-It." When we experience the world, the experience occurs in our processing of the experience—generally it is not a matter of relation with experience. Buber suggests we might be in a state where it seems as though we have an I-You relation with nature. His example is the contemplation of a tree. (I do not have an emotional response generally to trees; my example would have been a sunset.) Significantly, we sense the world not as an observer of third-party experience, but as actually having a relation with the thing being observed.[234] As Walter Kaufmann observed, "[e]ven when you treat me only as a means I do not always mind. A genuine encounter can be quite exhausting, even when it is exhilarating, and I do not always want to give myself."[235] Buber noted:

---

[229] *See* BUBER, *supra* note 225, at 53-54. There is an important point here. The title of the work in German is Ich und Du. German, like French or Spanish, but unlike English, has a formal "you" (Sie) and an informal "you" (Du). Du is the form of address between friends and lovers. Kaufmann, *supra* note 225, at 14. As Walter Kaufmann noted, "Du is spontaneous and unpretentious, remote from formality, pomp, and dignity." *Id.* Nevertheless, the original translations of the work were by theologians, who focused on its religious aspect, and the informal you of relationships became the formal "Thou" in English that is evocative of God. *See generally id.* at 14-15.

[230] BUBER, *supra* note 225, at 62.

[231] *Id.*

[232] *Id.* at 62-63

[233] *See generally id.*

[234] *See generally id.* at 58

[235] Kaufmann, *supra* note 225, at 17.

"Genuine contemplation never lasts long; the natural being that only now revealed itself to me in the mystery of reciprocity has again become describable, analyzable, classifiable—the point at which manifold systems of laws intersect."[236] However, it is, possible to live a life defined entirely by the I-It, and that is a life in which our own reason is paramount, and the thirst for rationality that creates lies is born. We are able to move back and forth from "It-world" to "You-world," and this is the way we check the process of reason.

> One cannot live in the pure present: it would consume us if care were not taken that it is overcome quickly and thoroughly. But in pure past one can live; in fact only there can a life be arranged. One only has to fill every moment with experiencing and using, and it ceases to burn.
>
> And in all the seriousness of truth, listen: without It a human being cannot live. But whoever lives only with that is not human.[237]

We cannot live without the It-world, and we have no ability to move forward in it without reason. We can justify our positions by reason and never leave the world of experience. In addition, we can hear and respond to the second-person claims and demands of others, and never truly enter into an event of relation. We may have discourse in which we analyze and justify assertions of truth or normative rightness, and still never experience a second-person relation. Oftentimes, we will contemplate the circumstances, and conclude that we do not want to enter into such a relation, either personally or in our business and professional lives.

It seems to me, however, that a business or professional life, as much as a personal life, is fraught with the possibility of transcendental illusion, of mistaking knowledge for belief, or vice versa. In the world of I-It, there is no other acting as a check on the product of our own reason, because every It is an object or obstacle with which we must deal. Recall Kant's skepticism about whether we might ever be able to know if our determination of the "ought" in a particular circumstance is the product of practical reason, or our own material inclinations.[238] It is possible that what we learn during the process of litigation can shed light on our own motivations. However, without some fundamental change in perspective, our response in the context of litigation stands a good chance of being rationalization all the way down. For just a fleeting moment, we need to stand in relation to another, see that other not as an It but a You, and consider the implications on our choice of action.

2. *Dialogue*

In *Between Man and Man,* Buber plants his feet firmly in this world. Buber is rightly called a theologian, and his writing is no doubt more lyrical than is common for the

---

[236] BUBER, *supra* note 225, at 68.

[237] *Id.* at 85.

[238] *See supra* note 95.

hard-headed world of business. But if we take religious dogma as the ultimate in deeply-held belief, and consider what Buber suggests about dialogue in that context, we ought to be able, a fortiori, to draw conclusions about secular beliefs no less deeply held. The essence of dialogue is rooted in a relationship between one person and another, and that relationship transforms the nature of the communication. "Moreover it is completed not in some "mystical" event, but in one that is in the precise sense factual, thoroughly dovetailed into the common human world and the concrete time-sequence."[239] Moreover, dialogue does not occur when one perceives another in his capacity as observer or onlooker: the person observed "is for them an object separated from themselves."[240] In dialogue, he perceives in the other person "something, which I cannot grasp in any objective way at all, that 'says something' to me."[241] How he receives this something is a matter of real speech (not a metaphor for speech), and is second-personal in a way that is even more fundamental than the second-person authority described by Darwall.[242]

This is the heart of the mystery that lies beyond reason. Buber has touched on our ability to employ reason to rationalize and justify when he observes:

> Each of us is encased in an armour whose task is to ward off signs. Signs happen to us without respite, living means being addressed, we would need only to present ourselves and to perceive. But the risk is too dangerous for us, the soundless thunderings seem to threaten us with annihilation, and from generation to generation we perfect the defence apparatus.[243]

The moment of intuition, reality untarnished by self-deception, occurs in moments that "stir the soul to sensibility."[244] Buber's lyricism is the synthesis of all the foregoing discussion: an intuitional sense, derived from a second person relationship, that the world is something other than what I have rationalized and justified it to be. "It can neither be interpreted nor translated, I can have it neither explained nor displayed; it is not a what at all, it is said into my very life; it is no experience that can be remembered independently of the situation, it remains the address of that moment and cannot be isolated, it remains the question of a questioner and will have its answer."[245] We check our tendency to self-deception not by argumentation (which as an exercise of reason is subject to the same tendency) or even by understanding and responding to an authoritative second-person claim or demand, but by the inexplicable intuitive insight we obtain only by hearing and accepting what something says to us. We are not required

---

239 Buber, *supra* note 184, at 5.

240 *Id.* at 11.

241 *Id.*

242 *Id.* at 11-12.

243 *Id.* at 12.

244 *Id.*

245 *Id.* at 14.

to satisfy the questioner, but only to hear the question: "[t]he basic movement of the life of dialogue is the turning towards the other."[246]

It is interesting to consider how pragmatic Buber is on the subject of dialogue, particularly as contrasted with monologue. The problem with monologue is not (as we have seen) a failure in richness of visions and thoughts. If monologue is reason, and is checked in the empirical world by correspondence to empirical reality, in matters of ethics, dialogue is a way we might test the validity of the principles we, in our freedom, legislate for ourselves. It is not inconsistent with Kantian freedom and autonomy to observe: "[h]e who is living the life of monologue is never aware of the other as something that is absolutely not himself and at the same time something with which he nevertheless communicates."[247] Dialogue is a relationship in which we hear the questions of another; it is not altruism and it is not love.[248] Indeed, Buber concludes his introduction to dialogue by confronting the question whether he has articulated an other-worldly mysticism, and not a way of approaching this world. He acknowledges he has selected his examples as paradigm ("for this reason I appear to draw my tales from the province which you term the 'intellectual'"). He is, however, concerned not with the pure, but with the mundane break-through.[249]

3. *Dialogue as the Source of Business Ethics*

How could the process of making difficult business decisions possibly be informed by the philosophy of Martin Buber? Buber raises the question himself by asking, "You ask with a laugh, can the leader of a great technical undertaking practise the responsibility of dialogue?" and answers, "He can."[250] This section poses some hypothetical situations, and considers the role of Buberian dialogue in them. In questions of ethics, we are always dealing with both the right and the good. They embody the critical distinction in Kant between autonomy and instrumentality, respectively. In everyday life, our needs (the good) are fulfilled by instrumental relationships all the time. Physical and economic laws are discernible that govern the satisfaction of what Kant calls our inclinations (our tangible and intangible needs). The principle of microeconomics that a rational firm

---

[246] *Id.* at 25.

[247] *Id.* at 23.

[248] *Id.* at 24.

> This man of modern philosophy, however, who in this way no longer thinks in the untouchable province of pure ideation [who takes up nature and addresses it in his own thought], but thinks in reality—does he think in reality? Not solely in a reality framed by thought? Is the other, whom he accepts and receives in this way, not solely the other framed by thought, and therefore unreal? Does the thinker of whom we are speaking hold his own with the bodily fact of otherness?

Id. at 32.

[249] *Id.* at 41.

[250] *Id.* at 44.

shuts down the plant when the marginal cost exceeds the marginal revenue is morally neutral (but socialists or critical legal theorists, for example, may disagree).

The real value of Robert Audi's reconciliation of "the good in the right" is the idea that real-world ethics cannot merely be the elevation of duty over consequence; there must be some accommodation of principle to pragmatics. Hence, the "ought" of business must be based on consequence as well as duty. As in the case of Jack and Stephanie, the credit card abusers, there is no perfect justice. However, we might, define achievable justice as the appropriate reconciliation of the "is" and the "ought." If the world is not as we believe it ought to be, we may react to the gap in several ways. We may work to close the gap. Or we may justify the gap. But, if we recognize there is a gap between the is and the ought, we must reconcile it somehow. The reconciliation may direct itself outward in action, or inward in contemplation, or both. We can close the gap by moving the world as it is outwardly closer to the way it ought to be. We may consider the views of others and conclude that our view of the "ought" needs to change. But the process of achievable justice is always distinct from justification: that smug self-satisfaction in the way things are, and, indeed, the proof by means of social science methodology that way things are is the way they ought to be. Nor is justice the knee-jerk rejection of anything that is merely because it is or has been that way in favor of a personal vision of what ought to be.

The following section proposes an addition to the mix by which we make difficult ethical judgments, not just consideration of Rossian duties and intrinsic value (i.e., the determination of the good or bad that may result from acting out of a perceived duty). We have an intuitive sense of the extent to which we are rationalizing and justifying that might become apparent to us when we consider not just the claims and demands of, but our very relationship to, another.

I. Difficult Choices

> A troubled company hires a new CEO. Within the first several weeks, it becomes clear to her that the demand for the company's product has diminished almost overnight (like buggy whips or mainframe computers or VCRs) because of the rapid appearance of a superior substitute. She determines there is no option but to write off some assets and sell others. The consequence will be that 2,000 people will be laid off, but for 8,000 others, the business and their jobs have a chance to survive.

This situation suggests another difficult choice between the good and the right. There is no perfect answer, and there are moral qualms in any course of action, even if legally justifiable. It is an illusion (indeed, a dangerous one at times) if the "is" or "ought" prevails automatically, and moral error if there is no struggle to reconcile them. It is an abdication of responsibility in the world of experience not to consider the need to reduce staff if conditions warrant, and to act on the need. On the other hand, the moral question is: are they people or things to you morally at the time the real world makes you do that? How do you handle the layoffs? Do you provide outplacement? Is the severance sufficient? Have you developed your employees so they have transferable marketable skills? Take the example regarding the toxicity of the flame retardant chemicals. To what extent is the decision motivated by short-term earnings versus scientific evidence? To what extent is the view of the evidence itself tainted by the outcome you want it to show?

ii. Opportunism

> Your client is a large Atlantic City hotel/casino. It has a non-binding letter of intent under which a frozen yogurt shop owner will close her operation in Newark and take space in the hotel. The negotiations have been going on for six months but no final binding agreement has ever been signed. The corporate development officer of the owner of the hotel/casino says "We have just come up with a more synergistic alternative to fill the space, and, now that we think about it, it's really a better deal. Is there any reason why we can't do it?"[251]

At least, in economic theory "the fundamental function of contract law . . . is to deter people from behaving opportunistically toward their contracting parties, in order to encourage the optimal timing of economic activity and (the same point) obviate costly self-protective measures."[252] The preceding hypothetical is from a New Jersey case in which the court held the hotel and casino liable on a theory of promissory estoppel, even though a definitive agreement (one that presumably would have embodied the promise) had never been executed. I once argued to my contracts class that the case, even if correctly decided on its particularly egregious facts, should not be expanded to impose the gray standards of reasonable reliance on the kinds of pre-contractual investments a sophisticated party might make in a complex business deal. But the law on that subject is relatively indeterminate and results hard to predict, even under law and economics.[253]

Does this situation invoke an ethical issue? It is arguable whether the law should or should not incorporate the doctrine of promissory estoppel in this situation, but I have no problem in concluding, were I part of the hotel and casino management, that we were ethically bound to our word, and that, in any event, taking the position that we were wholly without any responsibility, legally or otherwise, because there was no completed contract would have been wrong. Part of my intuition in this particular case has to do with the relative size of the parties. Specifically, I do not have the same

---

251 *See, e.g.*, Pop's Cones, Inc. v. Resorts Int'l Hotel, Inc., 704 A.2d 1321 (N.J. Super. Ct. App. Div. 1998).

252 POSNER, *supra* note 5, at 94-95.

253 *See generally* Lucien Arye Bebchuk & Omri Ben-Shahar, *Precontractual Reliance*, 30 J. LEGAL STUD. 423 (2001).

intuition about pulling out of a deal well into the negotiation in say, a merger of equals between two very large companies where there is no legal obligation to close.

> The beloved manager of a plant in a small town in Alabama dies in a freak boating accident over the Memorial Day weekend. It turns out he had already been "managed out" of the organization and his severance package was dependent on his staying with the company for a transitional six-month period. By dying, he has technically not fulfilled the condition of the severance package. His company-sponsored life insurance is, however, available to his young widow.

I was faced with this issue. Our divisional vice president of human resources asked me to get involved in defending the decision a business unit human resources director had made to deny the severance benefit to the widow, and to leave her only with the life insurance benefits (the theory being that, by dying, the manager failed to fulfill his end of the deal). I listened to the situation, and argued that it was untenable for us to be taking that position, regardless of the technicalities of the employment agreement. Clearly, there were utilitarian arguments—what would the effect on the company be if we were perceived to be taking an unjust or overly technical view in a dispute with the young widow of a beloved employee in a small town? However, it seemed to me, that there was a deeper issue of right and wrong. Fortunately, our corporate vice president of human resources overruled the decision, and both benefits were paid.

I tell this story not to demonstrate any unusual righteousness on my part, but to demonstrate what I believe most of us sense without knowing the source: doing the right thing is something beyond the use of instrumental reason and the employment of norms and maxims (including legal norms) to achieve an end. It involves the whole of one's substance, one's active participation in all of the reality of the world, not merely reliance on habits and customs.[254] Do we then live in some kind of moral anarchy, without norms, and in reliance on each person's intuition? Again, Buber provides a satisfying answer, consistent with something previously noted: all we can do is commit ourselves to the struggle to reconcile law and equity, rules and exceptions, and live the question.[255] Finally, we undertake the struggle not just in our solitary reflections (which may be self-deceiving) but from a second person standpoint, cognizant of our relationships with our opponents as well as our allies.

iii. Conflicts with Business Opponents

> The company has signed a definitive agreement to sell one of its divisions. The acquiring company has had trouble raising money for the purchase. The definitive agreement provides Seller may factor accounts

---

[254] Buber, *supra* note 184, at 135.

[255] *Id.*

> receivable of the division until the closing. In practice, what this means is that Seller sells the accounts receivable to a bank (a factor) for a small discount, and takes the cash out of the business. Under the framework of the agreement, it all should work out in the wash, because the post-closing adjustment, which compares the net assets of the division as of the closing with a base line net asset figure, should account for it. Acting on this legal right, the company has factored \$50 million in receivables, and so it will owe the Buyer that \$50 million (plus interest) in about six months when the parties resolve all the post-closing adjustment claims. On the day of the closing, Buyer advises the company that its financing is conditioned on the accounts receivable being there to help finance the business over that intervening six months, and because of what Seller did (perfectly permissible under the contract), \$50 million will be missing from the business. The Buyer will be in breach of loan covenants from the day it first owns the business, and perhaps even insolvent in the equity sense (unable to pay bills as they come due). Hence, it is threatening not to close.

What is unique among great business leaders is their ability to listen to their own lawyers and executives argue passionately why the company's position is right, and then make decisions that transcend the particular legal rights and duties in play at the time. While it is certainly possible this is a wholly consequential process, my casual empiricism is that it is not. In considering the opponent, the great business leader thinks of her not only as means, but as also as an end. This is because the leader puts herself, in reality or hypothetically, in an event of relation with the other side, and sees the dispute from the perspective of the other leader.

The preceding story was in fact the circumstance we faced as sellers in closing an acquisition valued at almost three-quarters of a billion dollars. As a result of prior disagreements, the deal had been re-negotiated to require the buyer to pay \$100 million in liquidated damages if it failed to close. For whatever reason, the buyer did not tell us about the problem it faced until late in the evening preceding the scheduled closing. I was at the law office where we were preparing the closing documents; the senior executives of the buyer were present, but our company's senior executives were not. We scheduled a conference call between the buyer's executives and our chief financial officer at 2:00 p.m. The arguments were like ships passing in the night. In particular, our CFO kept repeating the theme that the contract gave us the right to do what we did, and it was the buyer's fault if it did not read or understand the contract. The call ended in an impasse.

I was the working in-house lawyer for the company; my job was to get the deal closed. It was not to make fundamental decisions about whether to stand on our contract rights and litigate, or make a concession and close. I was sure that the buyer was not bluffing; unlike our other executives, I could see the sweat beads and the shaking hands during the two o'clock call. A solution was available: we could reverse the effect of the factoring, and put the cash back into the business, but it would mean losing the leverage that the CFO wanted in the post-closing adjustments by being the party owing the money (an instance of the Golden Rule in business: "he who has the gold rules"). I participated in a phone call with my boss, the company's general counsel, the CFO, and the company's chairman and chief executive officer, widely regarded as one of the great business leaders of his generation. I listened to the CFO argue his position to the CEO, why it was we had been justified in factoring the receivables under the contract, his distrust of the buyer's inclination to perform a fair post-closing adjustment, and his desire to have the leverage by holding the cash. The CEO listened, and quickly replied, in so many words, "look, whatever the contract said, I would have been upset with us too, if the other side had done that." Our internal impasse broke; we made the decision to put the cash back, and the deal closed.

It is important to understand that the CEO's reaction was not a foregone conclusion. Whether the decision itself was ethical, whether it emanated from some idea of moral duty or consequentialism, nevertheless, it was different than a purely legal calculation of rights and duties under the contract. And its essence was for just a moment, to consider not just the claim of the other, but the relation with the other.

iv. Conflicts Between Right and Right

> You are managing a fairly significant piece of litigation. Your view of the probability of an unfavorable outcome will likely determine both whether the case is disclosed to the public, and whether an accounting reserve is set (i.e. the estimate of liability is taken as a current expense). Intuitively, you know there is about a 75% chance the case will end up settling for a figure that is material to the company's earnings in a specific quarter, but almost no chance that it will threaten the long-term viability of the company.

The context here is not a direct conflict, but issues between people in an organization whose job responsibilities drive them toward different conclusions on particular issues. For example, think of the inherent conflict between the sales department and the credit department. What is the function of the sales department and how it is measured? The answer is: by selling products to customers. Of course, if the bill is not collectable, there is no profit and the sale was pointless. But if the sales department is measured on sales (or more significantly, sees its own success in terms of making sales), the collection of the proceeds is someone else's problem. Someone else is the credit department, which is measured on collections (or more significantly, sees its own success in terms of having a low bad debt as a percentage of sales). There is a natural conflict between sales and credit.

Consider the information technology (IT) department. Generally, the IT department is managed by a senior IT vice president in the corporate office. The IT department's job is, among other things, to insure dependability and security in the company's computer networks. That requires money. The job of the business division is to make profits, which involve increasing revenues and reducing costs. When the IT department relies on its functional expertise to incur costs in the business division, there is a natural conflict with the leader of the division whose job it is to reduce costs.

Lawyers are not immune from this kind of conflict. Using the hypothetical presented at the beginning of this section, let us now also assume the CEO believes the company's stock price will fall in the short term if the current earnings are required to reflect a charge for the outcome of the present litigation. Moreover, there are no other litigation charges for the quarter, and so disclosure of the litigation reserve that would be established will tell the other side not only how much the company expects to have to pay, but that the amount has already been reserved, so that future earnings will not be affected (although cash flow will be) if the case is settled up to that amount. On the other hand, the auditors insist that if the lawyers believe there is more than a 50% probability of an unfavorable outcome, and the amount can be reasonable estimated, that amount must be reflected as a charge to current earnings.

What are the implications of law and ethics in this situation? Under the securities laws, the company would be liable if it made a materially misleading statement or omitted to state a fact required to make a statement not misleading.[256] We may assume that, if litigation outcome is material, failure to disclose it would be an omission making the financial statements misleading. Moreover, under the Statement of Financial Accounting Standards No. 5 ("FAS 5"), part of the definition of generally accepted accounting principles ("GAAP"), if an event is probable and the amount of the loss is reasonably estimable, FAS 5 requires that the obligation be booked as an accrual (an expense, and hence a charge to earnings) on the income statement and a liability on the balance sheet.[257] Accountants and auditors use the word "probable" to indicate one of three different states of likelihood; the other two are "reasonably possible" and "remote," that future events will confirm the incurrence of a liability. "Probable" is defined as "[t]he future event or events are likely to occur."[258] Telling an auditor one has a better than even chance of losing a case in which the amount of the loss can be estimated is tantamount to incurring the expense. Lawyers, on the other hand, use loose language of probability to convey a sense of the outcome to their clients on a regular basis. "Your odds of winning are 50-50, 60-40, one in ten, etc." The ABA has attempted to cover these conflicting uses of language in its *Statement of Policy Regarding Lawyers' Responses to Auditors' Requests for Information* by claiming that accountants and lawyers simply use the word "probable" in different ways.[259]

---

[256] Dura Pharm., Inc. v. Broudo, 125 S. Ct. 1627, 1631 (2005) ("Rule 10b-5 forbids, among other things, the making of any 'untrue statement of material fact' or the omission of any material fact 'necessary in order to make the standards made . . . not misleading.'").

[257] AM. INST. OF CERTIFIED PUB. ACCOUNTANTS (AICPA) PROFESSIONAL STANDARDS, AU § 337C, para. 5.1(f), at 575 (1996), *available at* http://www.aicpa.org/download/members/div/auditstd/AU-00337C.pdf.

[258] *Id.* at para. 5.1(b)(i).

[259] *Id.* at para. 5.2 ("Concepts of probability inherent in the usage of terms like 'probable' or 'reasonably possible' or 'remote' mean different things in different contexts. Generally, the outcome of, or the loss which may result from, litigation cannot be assessed in any way that is comparable to a statistically or empirically determined concept of 'probability'. . . . Lawyers do not generally quantify for clients the 'odds' in numerical terms; if they do, the quantification is generally only undertaken in an effort to make

It is unclear what the ethical answer is, or even if this constitutes an ethics issue. The ABA policy provides enough cover for a lawyer to justify a conclusion that any outcome is not "probable" by disclaiming any meaning to the way lawyers refer to the probabilities of outcomes (the justification being that the amount of variability in the estimate means that the statement of probability is inherently unreliable). Lawyers, auditors, and CEOs will often butt heads over the answer not in any sense because they want to get to the right answer, but because they believe they have a professional responsibility to put the answer in a particular way. Accountants and auditors want to follow the dictates of GAAP; the lawyer wants to avoid prejudicing her ability to litigate the case to a favorable outcome; and in the face of conflicting views from the professional functions, the CEO is inclined not to take a charge to earnings anything that is not required (unless, of course, he views it as being to his advantage to take the charge, in which case several of the positions are reversed).

V. CONCLUSION

Obviously, Martin Buber never faced any of these particular situations. However, he did suggest a concept of ethical character that is as applicable in business as it is in any personal decision we might face. It starts with facing every bit of reality inherent in the situation—oneself, one's colleagues, one's adversary, the uncomfortable possibility that a rule does apply or does not apply, the uncomfortable possibility that one's most deeply held beliefs or desires are wrong, or might not be satisfied.[260]

I began my career as a litigator, and the way I approached conflict was structured by maxims and habits. Our goals were dictated by our clients' demands, and we worked within a constrained model, like rational frogs, employing instrumental legal reasoning to win the argument. I used to suggest that one of the differences between being a business litigator and a transactional lawyer was the familiarity with the turf. In business litigation, the business person is in the realm of the lawyer and his system. The maxims, habits, and customs are foreign to the business people. Data, such as hearsay, on which she might normally rely in making a decision, is legally irrelevant. The mode of discourse, as borne out by every pre-testimony preparation session between witness and lawyer, is artificial and designed not for explanation but for advantage.

Later in my career, when I became a transactional lawyer, the turf changed. In a business deal, the transactional lawyer is on the business turf. At least at first, the maxims, habits, and customs are foreign to one trained in the law. But after a while, those maxims, habits, and customs become clear. There is a sequence to the completion of an acquisition. There is appropriate disclosure, and an understanding, by and large, of the rules by which risk is allocated between buyer and seller. Nevertheless, our goals

---

meaningful, for limited purposes, a whole host of judgmental factors applicable at a particular time, with any intention to depict 'probability' in any statistical, scientific or empirically-grounded sense.").

[260] BUBER, *supra* note 184, at 134-35.

continued to be dictated by the clients' demands, and we employed the tools of our trade to accomplish them.

It was not until I was an in-house lawyer that the distinction between being a great lawyer and having ethical character began to become clear to me. That is not to say that lawyers cannot have great ethical character. Of course they can. But it arises outside of the mere application of maxims and habits. I remember feeling, and expressing to a former law firm colleague, that every bit of my personality, every bit of accumulated wisdom (such as it was) or experience, factored into the advice I was giving, and the decisions I made.

When I am faced with a difficult choice, I fear nothing like my ability to persuade myself. Kant understood that we can never really tell if the principle of our action is determined by our material wants and inclinations, or by recognition of the universality of the rightness in what we are choosing. I agree. Whether in our own minds, or in a group of like-minded executives, we are wholly capable of mistaking what makes us happy or fulfilled for what is right. And, the only check on the power of reason, and its thirst for rationality that produces lies, is openness to the insight and reality, however uncomfortable or distasteful or opposed to our own reasoned conclusions, that come from another.

Someplace Between Philosophy and Economics: Legitimacy and Good Corporate Lawyering[*]

Donald C. Langevoort[**]

INTRODUCTION

What attitude toward the law should a lawyer have when advising a client? That is one of the motivating questions . . . , and, of course, a central one that connects jurisprudence and professional responsibility.

People's answers will likely be influenced, implicitly at least, by what law they are thinking of when the question is posed. We can imagine many expressions of law that radiate a warm glow and readily incline one toward Hart's "internal" point of view grounded comfortably in duty and justice. Holmesian lawyers look callous and miserly when their advice with respect to this kind of law is simply about the odds of avoiding sanction.

But in the legal universe, how representative is this sample? This essay deals with the demands of responsible lawyering when one's client is a corporate or other business entity.[1] I suspect that to most business clients, many of the laws they encounter are mundane and, worse, suspicious in their origins. We would be naïve to think that laws always do more good than harm, or even that they are intended to do so. Too often, law in economic and commercial settings is the product of special interest haggling, political grandstanding, or bureaucratic sloth. In its totality, the bulk of commercial and regulatory law probably is mediocre at best. If this is the law we imagine, identifying the right posture for responsible legal advice gets much harder. To pose the question bluntly, what is the right way to advise a business person whose company is facing burdensome new regulation that is the product of effective lobbying by a trade group representing its competitors? Or with regard to new investor protection rules responding

---

[*] Originally published at 75 FORDHAM L. REV. 1615 (2006). Reprinted by permission.

[**] Thomas Aquinas Reynolds Professor of Law, Georgetown University Law Center. Thanks to Ben Zipursky and Heidi Li Feldman for helping me get started, to Mitt Regan for helpful comments on an earlier draft, and to the participants at the Fordham Symposium for a stimulating discussion.

[1] This has become a large enough subject now to have a casebook for itself. *See generally* MILTON C. REGAN, JR. & JEFFREY D. BAUMAN, LEGAL ETHICS AND CORPORATE PRACTICE (2005).

to some recent scandal, if it seems that compliance will cost those investors much more in diminished returns than they will ever realize in protection?[2]

I am by no means suggesting that ill-conceived or mediocre laws necessarily dominate the business landscape, just that they are frequent enough and, perhaps more importantly, that many businesspeople genuinely believe that they are quite frequent. Both jurisprudence and professional responsibility scholars ought to take this challenge fairly seriously—good advice, after all, depends on constructive engagement with the audience to which it is directed.

My aim in what follows is to articulate a role for the "good" corporate lawyer that is more capacious and appealing than that of the Holmesian legal risk calculator. But for the reasons just suggested, I find myself unable to accept that law has a strong normative claim merely because it is law, and, again, strongly suspect that most who inhabit the business world share that perspective. To be sure, I am saying nothing new here: The point I am making comes fairly close to what many others, including Stephen Pepper,[3] have argued. That posture, however, usually tends to set one off in an effort to distinguish among laws that have moral content and those that do not, such as malum in se versus malum prohibitum or criminal versus civil. As generalities, these distinctions do not work very well. And as a result, it is easy to backslide toward the entirely amoral perspective.

What I want to put on the table is a distinction that might have more traction, and which a good corporate lawyer could employ to engage her client in a constructive, appealing way. It involves substituting the sociologist's favorite word, legitimacy, for morality, in considering what follows when we think about the professional responsibility of corporate lawyers in terms of the corporation's pursuit of social legitimacy. In other words, suppose we think of the "inside view" of legal obligation not so much as a (normative) moral claim but as a (descriptive) societal expectation.

This distinction may seem flimsy, and may in the end prove to be no better than any of the prior efforts. Maybe it is simply a way of retelling the well-worn "lawyer as statesman" story. But I am intrigued by a number of different strands of contemporary legal and social science research wherein legitimacy is an increasingly useful concept, and how these strands might entwine in the corporate world. In corporate governance, for example, the "agency cost" perspective, which has come to dominate in legal scholarship, has a plausible sociology-based competitor in the idea of "resource dependency," which assumes that the organizational imperative is to gain resources from a variety

---

[2] *See generally* Roberta Romano, *The Sarbanes-Oxley Act and the Making of Quack Corporate Governance*, 114 YALE L.J. 1521 (2005). I do not go anywhere near as far as Romano in doubting Sarbanes-Oxley, but suspect that at least some of it is of questionable efficacy. *See* Donald Langevoort, *Internal Controls After Sarbanes-Oxley: Revisiting Corporate Law's "Duty of Care as Responsibility for Systems,"* 31 J. CORP. L. 949 (2006).

[3] Stephen L. Pepper, *Counseling at the Limits of the Law: An Exercise in Jurisprudence and Ethics of Lawyering*, 104 YALE L.J. 1545 (1995).

of public and private actors.[4] Gaining legitimacy in these interactions is key, which is why, for instance, directors might be chosen for their ability to negotiate the interactions rather than (as most corporate legal scholars assume) their ability to monitor. Recent sophisticated work in corporate social responsibility (CSR) picks up on this to demonstrate why CSR is likely a real behavioral phenomenon rather than the mere window-dressing cynics make it out to be.[5] Legitimacy also plays an important role in the social psychology of law-abidingness,[6] and of organizational compliance with law.[7] The economics of reputation and, more speculatively, the economics of identity[8] touch on it as well.

Underlying this effort is a suggestion about how morality and legitimacy relate, although I certainly claim no deep expertise in social theory outside the corporate world. As discussed more fully below, characteristic of economic activity is the need for high-velocity cooperative behavior. This behavior is burdened not only by the possibility of selfish opportunism, a well-recognized problem in law and economics, but by any disagreement about matters that increases transaction costs. To facilitate cooperative behavior, norms must evolve in economic settings that are neither so weak as to discourage trust nor so strong as to diminish incentives.[9] These norms, which in turn define legitimacy, are unlikely to be well-grounded in any coherent ethical philosophy because they are the product of compromise and are driven by conflicting, shifting social pressures. They tend more toward baseline than aspiration. The embedded relativism is easily criticized as falling short of the most revered expressions of moral philosophy and social justice.[10]

---

[4] *See* JEFFREY PFEFFER & GERALD R. SALANCIK, THE EXTERNAL CONTROL OF ORGANIZATIONS 258-62 (1978); Amy J. Hillman & Thomas Dalziel, *Boards of Directors and Firm Performance: Integrating Agency and Resource Dependence Perspectives*, 28 ACAD. MGMT. REV. 383, 388 (2003).

[5] *See generally* Cynthia A. Williams & John M. Conley, *An Emerging Third Way? The Erosion of the Anglo-American Shareholder Value Construct*, 38 CORNELL INT'L L.J. 493 (2005).

[6] *See generally* Tom R. Tyler, *Psychological Perspectives on Legitimacy and Legitimation*, 57 ANN. REV. PSYCH. 375 (2006). Useful collections of materials on this subject include THE PSYCHOLOGY OF RIGHTS AND DUTIES: EMPIRICAL CONTRIBUTIONS AND NORMATIVE COMMENTARIES (Norman J. Finkel & Fathali M. Moghaddam eds., 2005) [hereinafter The Psychology of Rights and Duties], and THE PSYCHOLOGY OF LEGITIMACY: EMERGING PERSPECTIVES ON IDEOLOGY, JUSTICE, AND INTERGROUP RELATIONS (John T. Jost & Brenda Major eds., 2001) [hereinafter THE PSYCHOLOGY OF LEGITIMACY].

[7] *See generally* Lauren B. Edelman & Mark C. Suchman, *The Legal Environments of Organizations*, 23 ANN. REV. SOC. 479 (1997).

[8] *See generally* George A. Akerlof & Rachel E. Kranton, *Identity and the Economics of Organizations*, 19 J. ECON. PERSP. 9 (2005).

[9] This oversimplifies, of course. A functionalist view of norms naturally runs into problems of stickiness and path dependency; it is doubtful that norms are truly efficient at any given point in time.

[10] Psychologists are particularly interested in why so many people accept the legitimacy of structures and institutions that operate to their immediate disadvantage, particularly uneven distributions of wealth. *See* James M. Olson & Carolyn L. Hafer, *Tolerance of Personal Deprivation, in* THE PSYCHOLOGY OF LEGITIMACY, *supra* note 6, at 157.

For this reason, lawyers and legal academics whose work is tied to the workings of markets and economic behavior—except when they act as social critics—shy away from a strongly moral conception of legal obligation. Market-driven activity rewards sensitivity to transaction costs, thus encouraging the natural inclination to negotiate. Of course, law can be seen as an effort to override these "morals of the marketplace." But those inclined toward the workings of the marketplace are likely to be ethical relativists to whom even the law is market-produced (that is, something resembling public choice theory) and thus having no special moral significance. Either because of special interests or lawmaker incompetence, they think, the law will often be inferior to what the market would do on its own, or with less heavy-handed regulatory interference. This is why pursuing a strong "inside view" agenda in a world inhabited by corporate lawyers and their clients is an uphill battle.

However, this is not cause for abject despair. What I am suggesting is that corporate lawyers and their clients are likely inclined towards pragmatism, not opportunism. The baseline might not be as appealing as we might want, but it is far better than nothing. My substitution of legitimacy for morality is just a pragmatic move designed to describe a form of professional responsibility that does not devolve into simple legal risk calculation. Instead, it involves the good lawyer in the second step of helping the corporate client assess the legitimacy of its behavior, which, as we shall see, is no small task.

I. "INSIDE-OUT" IN THE CORPORATION

Though I am not particularly well-read in the contemporary "inside view" debate, I assume that inside view proponents have as their baseline the existence of an inherent moral obligation to obey the law, so that resting behavior on the probability of detection/magnitude of sanction calculation is wrong. There is also a second claim commonly made (though not necessarily so): The moral content of at least some laws makes literal or technical compliance insufficient; instead, attention must be paid to the law's spirit or purpose.[11]

My assigned task is to relate this to the situation where the client is a corporation. In terms of the underlying corporate theory, there are really two separate questions. The easier question, for me, is whether the corporation has the right or freedom to act as anything other than a wealth-generator for its stakeholders (which to most corporations means its shareholders). This is certainly one of the great debates in corporate theory, with Milton Friedman as the canonical citation that it does not,[12] and Frank Easterbrook and Dan Fischel as evangelists for the view that the profit-maximizing constraint extends even to compliance with the law.[13]

---

[11] *See* W. Bradley Wendel, *Professionalism as Interpretation*, 99 NW. U. L. REV. 1167, 1168 (2005).

[12] *See* MILTON FRIEDMAN, CAPITALISM AND FREEDOM 133-34 (1962).

[13] *See* Frank H. Easterbrook & Daniel R. Fischel, *Antitrust Suits by Targets of Tender Offers*, 80 MICH. L. REV. 1155, 1168 (1982). For additional citations and a critique, *see* Cynthia A. Williams, *Corporate Compliance with the Law in the Era of Efficiency*, 76 N.C. L. REV. 1265 (1998).

Today, however, this debate has largely run out of steam.[14] To those who believe that natural persons have moral obligations of any sort, it is difficult to accept that these obligations could be deflected by the consensual act of investment in a legal entity and delegation to professional managers.[15] The more sophisticated view—that organizations take on characteristics separate and distinct from its stakeholders—lends itself naturally to a moral theory of distinct corporate rights and responsibilities.[16] So does the view that I prefer: that the corporation is a creature of the state whose nature and purposes are simply defined by law, from which a norm of law-abidingness follows easily. Those who still aggressively insist on shareholder wealth maximization as the only permissible goal of the corporation are either hard-core libertarians who refuse to accept that the firm is anything more than a consent-based private association of investors or, far more likely, instrumentalists, who claim that any permission to deviate from the goal of wealth maximization leads naturally to sloth and slack rather than exemplary behavior by those handling other people's money. The vast majority of instrumentalists do not quarrel with the view that the obligation to comply with the law overrides the pursuit of profits. They simply do not want us to consider this part of "corporate law."[17]

So far as corporate law itself is concerned, the law's primacy over strict profit-maximization is well recognized.[18] The business judgment rule prevails in a way that gives officers and directors permission to pursue moral or social goals so long as some possible (usually reputational) argument might be made that the corporation would benefit in the long run, which certainly protects law-abidingness. Many state laws go further, expressly authorizing "other regarding" activity by the corporation. And at least one well-known case indicates that the business judgment rule does not protect deliberate decisions not to obey the law.[19]

Thus, there is very little today to support the view that the corporation is required simply to be calculative in how it approaches the law. The separate question then is whether it is obliged to be law-abiding in anything more than calculative terms. In light of what was just said, "corporateness" should simply make no difference. The one authority that has thoroughly considered the specific question of acting "within the law" in recent years is the American Law Institute's *Principles of Corporate Governance,* which says clearly that the corporation "is obliged, to the same extent as a natural person,

---

[14] For a recent criticism of this view using conventional economic analysis, *see* Einer Elhauge, *Sacrificing Corporate Profits in the Public Interest,* 80 N.Y.U. L. REV. 733 (2005).

[15] Or if one takes a more managerialist view, it is hard to explain why managers gain freedom from moral claims on their behavior simply because they have raised capital externally.

[16] MEIR DAN-COHEN, RIGHTS, PERSONS AND ORGANIZATIONS: A LEGAL THEORY FOR BUREAUCRATIC SOCIETY 78 (1986).

[17] *See, e.g.,* Henry Hansmann & Reinier Kraakman, The *End of History for Corporate Law,* 89 GEO. L.J. 439 (2001).

[18] *See* Elhauge, *supra* note 14, at 756-62.

[19] *See* Miller v. AT&T Co., 507 F.2d 759, 762 (3d Cir. 1974).

to act within the boundaries set by law" regardless of whether or not such conduct enhances shareholder wealth.[20]

If so, then "corporateness" is unimportant to the main questions that motivate this Symposium, so that I could well end my contribution here. Whatever the lawyer is expected to do with respect to a human client, she should be expected to do with respect to a corporate client. But I will not end here, because there is something more pragmatic to say about corporate lawyering. The nature of ethical deliberation within an organization is in many ways different from the ethical deliberation of a natural person. To the extent that a lawyer's professional responsibility is something more than shrewd risk calculation (which I believe, but have nothing novel to offer as justification[21]), it follows that the good lawyer should take those differences into account in order to act responsibly. Fortunately, given my interests and expertise, this allows me to turn to the social sciences for insight as to what those differences might be.

As a starting point, consider the ethical decision making of the individual. There is rich psychological literature on this question, which I could not hope to capture fully. The older Kohlberg-style research claims that people vary in their stages of moral development—with good ethical reasoning dominating the decisions of those with more fully developed moral awareness and sensitivity. More recent research has stressed the automaticity of moral reactions,[22] which is only partially (and often unsuccessfully) adjusted by conscious deliberation. This suggests that some situations—particularly where empathy is triggered—will produce fairly strong inclinations to "do good," while others will prompt egocentric construals and forms of self-deception that make self-serving behavior more likely even among those who seem able, at the conscious level, to engage in sophisticated ethical reasoning.[23] Even at the individual level, then, it may well be a challenge for the lawyer to express an "inside" view of legal obligation that makes the client more likely to act appropriately.

---

[20] *Principles of Corporate Governance* § 2.01 cmt. G (1994). As Cynthia Williams has pointed out, there are certain aspects of corporate law (*e.g.*, formulations of the duty of care and indemnification rules) that are inconsistent with a strong corporate obligation to obey the law. *See generally* Williams, *supra* note 13. These can be explained in two separate ways that do not lead to the conclusion that the *Principles'* main statement is disingenuous. First (and to me more plausibly), these other rules reflect views about protecting directors from personal liability that go beyond the specific context of illegality. Second, they may subtly reflect a Holmesian view in which both corporations and individuals have *some* freedom to act in a calculative way. All the text says is that the corporation's obligations are the same as the natural person's, not that the natural person's obligation to obey the law is necessarily absolute.

[21] *See* Richard W. Painter, *The Moral Interdependence of Corporate Lawyers and Their Clients*, 67 S. CAL. L. REV. 507, 525 (1994).

[22] *See* Jonathan D. Cohen, *The Vulcanization of the Human Brain: A Neural Perspective on Interactions Between Cognition and Emotion*, 19 J. ECON. PERSP. 3, 10-13 (2005); Jonathan Haidt, *The Emotional Dog and Its Rational Tail: A Social Intuitionist Approach to Moral Judgment*, 108 PSYCHOL. REV. 814, 818 (2001).

[23] *See* Don A. Moore & George Lowenstein, *Self-Interest, Automaticity, and the Psychology of Conflict of Interest*, 17 SOC. JUST. RES. 189, 195-96 (2004); Ann E. Tenbrunsel & David M. Messick, *Ethical Fading: The Role of Self-Deception in Unethical Behavior*, 17 SOC. JUST. RES. 223 (2004).

Whatever the challenge at the individual level, the problem compounds many times over when we are dealing with organizational decision making. The importance of the effort also compounds because of the one key difference between individual and corporate clients: In the latter setting, there are no natural persons with unqualified authority to act as the client.[24] Many of the behavioral differences are well understood and frequently noted by business and legal scholars. For example, diffusion of responsibility in an organization reduces the likelihood that any given person or small group will be inclined to assume it. In this sense, structure and process (i.e., corporate governance) become inextricably bound up in corporate ethics in a way that we would not see with individuals. In fact, many post-Sarbanes-Oxley reforms in corporate governance go explicitly to questions of ethics. There is the requirement of a code of conduct for senior financial officers, and new internal controls requirements that force both lawyers and auditors to investigate the firm's ethical climate along with legal compliance.

My interests recently have focused on the cognitive dimension to this problem, about which much can be said. To summarize an argument I have made elsewhere, organizations develop strong or weak belief systems—sense-making devices that privilege certain inferences, construals, and explanations over others.[25] Often these are grouped under the heading of "corporate culture" as coordination mechanisms. Imagine two people who have to cooperate to get work done. Constant negotiation over what is happening, what to think about it, and how to proceed slows down the pace of work. To get work done, assumptions have to be made. And the taken-for-granted beliefs that permit the most work to get done are those that simplify, reduce anxiety and the potential for conflict, and motivate. My prediction is that perceptions that deflect hard ethical dilemmas (that is, rationalizations) are more adaptive than those that generate moral angst.

Now imagine what happens when tens of thousands of people must interact, rather than just two. The need for taken-for-granted beliefs to "grease" the endless interactions required for efficient coordinated effort expands mightily, especially if the firm is under competitive pressure. Put simply, "stories" about why what is happening is acceptable are functional on average, even though they may not be entirely realistic and may cause those inside the organization to ignore important risks. As I have argued elsewhere, at the very least the good corporate lawyer must maintain a cognitive distance from these organizational pressures even to be a good Holmesian legal risk calculator, much less to play a more ambitious professional role.[26]

---

[24] *See generally* William H. Simon, *Whom (or What) Does the Organization's Lawyer Represent?: An Anatomy of Intraclient Conflict*, 91 CAL. L. REV. 57 (2003).

[25] *See* Donald C. Langevoort, *Opening the Black Box of "Corporate Culture" in Law and Economics*, 162 J. INST. & THEO. ECON. 1 (2006); *See* also, *e.g.*, Donald C. Langevoort, *Resetting the Corporate Thermostat: Lessons from the Recent Financial Scandals About Self-Deception, Deceiving Others and the Design of Internal Controls*, 93 GEO. L.J. 285 (2004) [hereinafter Langevoort, *Lessons*].

[26] Donald C. Langevoort, *The Epistemology of Corporate-Securities Lawyering: Beliefs, Biases and Organizational Behavior*, 63 BROOK. L. REV. 629 (1997). For a very thoughtful application to the work of

II. BRINGING LEGITIMACY INTO THE CONVERSATION

To sociologists, belief systems "legitimate" perceptions, inferences, and behaviors; this is just another way of saying that they provide normative cover for the privileged beliefs. My point above is that corporate cultures will legitimate certain perceptions because they operate to grease interactive productivity, rather than introduce grit into the organizational machinery. This, it seems to me, says much about organizational responses to legal and ethical demands.

There is ample evidence, even at the individual level, that people's judgments about whether to comply with the law are heavily affected by their perceptions of the law's legitimacy as applied in a particular instance.[27] But legitimacy is a largely social construct—hence we would often expect fairly common patterns of legal compliance, with some legal claims having substantial legitimacy and others (e.g., speeding, certain copyright violations) resisted based on doubts about their legitimacy.

At the organizational level, corporate cultures have the capacity to influence perceptions of the law's legitimacy, especially when there is some ambiguity in what the law demands. On this point, we come very close to the subject of this Symposium, because it connects closely to the "inside view" discussion. As I suggested earlier, corporate cultures will sometimes offer agents an account that rationalizes marginal or "aggressive" compliance, or even noncompliance. This poses one of the most interesting dilemmas in professional responsibility: the appropriate interaction with clients (or clients' agents) who have formed a strongly critical or dismissive view of the law's demands, and to whom marginal compliance is thus ethically permissible.

Before turning to this question in more detail, I should note an important point about corporate cultures. As organizational sociologists point out, cultures vary in strength, and for the most part, it is unusual for a culture to emerge that overrides the more general cultural values that most agents bring to work with them. Most corporate cultures, in other words, are fairly weak and only fill in firm-specific gaps with respect to those broader values.[28] This is quite good news, because it operates to make firm-wide misbehavior more difficult. All other things being equal, agents resist acting contrary to their values and will do so only if strongly motivated, and firms pay a substantial cost in morale and good will if the motivation is too heavy handed.

That said, rationalized resistance is common enough.[29] This can be the product of a strong corporate culture (most likely when a strong culture is essentially a survival

---

inside counsel, *see* Sung Hui Kim, *The Banality of Fraud: Re-situating the Inside Counsel as Gatekeeper*, 74 FORDHAM L. REV. 983 (2005).

[27] Tom Tyler's work has emphasized this, in particular noting the fairness (procedural and otherwise) of the law's demands. *See, e.g.*, Tyler, *supra* note 6; Tom Tyler, *A Deference-based Perspective on Duty: Empowering Government to Define Duties to Oneself and to Others, in* THE PSYCHOLOGY OF RIGHTS AND DUTIES, *supra* note 6, at 137.

[28] *See generally* Edelman & Suchman, *supra* note 7.

[29] This is often the product of the slippery slope. *See, e.g.*, John M. Darley, *The Cognitive and Social Psychology of Contagious Organizational Corruption*, 70 BROOK. L. REV. 1177 (2005).

instinct), or just a gap-filler when more general cultural norms are not in play (e.g., when the law is fairly technical in its operation). Legal researchers who pay attention to organizational behavior have found many examples of this. David Spence's work in environmental compliance shows that a dominating reason for noncompliance is the corporate actors' belief that the laws are poorly crafted, unduly burdensome, and arbitrarily enforced.[30] This triggers a cascade of plausible excuses (utilitarian and otherwise) for cutting corners in the face of imperfect enforcement of those laws. With respect to the corporate financial reporting scandals, which had many different contributing causes, one likely contributor was a rejection in key segments of the business community during the 1990s of the legitimacy of technical accounting rules in producing valuable disclosure. Playing games with "Generally Accepted Accounting Principals" was at worst trivial and could often be rationalized as actually doing more good for the company than harm, especially in the early stages of the slide down the slippery slope toward corruption.[31]

So what does the good corporate lawyer do in the face of this? Put another way, what is the "inside view" when the law's legitimacy is doubted, as it so frequently is in the business community? Being largely unread in the contemporary jurisprudence literature, I will simply assume that critics have repeatedly made the point that laws vary substantially in how well they are crafted, what motivates them, and what balance of costs and benefits they have for society. Putting aside the too-easy case of evil or corrupt laws, there probably are numerous statutes and administrative regulations that generate more costs than benefits, either because they were ineptly drafted in the first place, were overly influenced by special interests, or have since become obsolete. Although the dominant view in jurisprudence is that literal compliance even with poorly crafted laws is obligatory, it is not at all clear to me that there is a compelling professional responsibility to search for its spirit or purpose in an effort to go any further. And the dominant view notwithstanding, many people would find a posture of strategic noncompliance morally acceptable on utilitarian grounds so long as the poor quality of the law is clear enough. I do not want to argue the point because I am sure that jurisprudence and professional responsibility scholars have debated it quite thoroughly as a general matter. I simply want to emphasize the professional dilemma it creates. To take an immediately pressing illustration, consider the many prophylactic requirements of the Sarbanes-Oxley Act, which are widely seen as a knee-jerk political reaction disproportionate to the severity of the underlying problems, costing shareholders (the primary intended beneficiaries) far more than any benefits it might generate. Numerous academics agree: Roberta Romano calls it "quack" corporate governance,[32] and even more moderate commentators have expressed doubts about whether any sensible cost-benefit calculation guided the

---

[30] *See generally* David B. Spence, *The Shadow of the Rational Polluter: Rethinking the Role of Rational Actor Models in Environmental Law*, 89 CAL. L. REV. 917 (2001).

[31] *See generally* Donald C. Langevoort, *Technological Evolution and the Devolution of Corporate Financial Reporting*, 46 WM. & MARY L. REV. 1 (2004).

[32] *See generally* Romano, *supra* note 2.

legislative process or the rule making that followed.[33] Over the last two years, corporate lawyers have had to assist their clients through the compliance process. What should be the touchstone, especially if such criticism is apt?

Of course, this concern is not specific to business law. But as noted earlier, I think that the business community is particularly sensitive to it, and business involvement in lawmaking through lobbying and other forms of influence is hardly conducive to a romanticized view of law's moral force. Disenchantment is more likely. If we turn specifically to corporate law, moreover, there is a strong academic view, and some statutes and doctrine in support, that the law of business associations is private law—the contractualization of nearly everything, so that all is negotiable, nothing fixed. As many critics of the trend have noted, such instability drains nearly all moral force out of the law, making it hard to discern an inside view. While this essay is no place to try to explain why this trend occurred, or how far the law has come to the purely contractual model, "thou shall not loot" may be the only practically immutable rule in corporation law. As today's executive compensation packages demonstrate, even that rule may be challenged at the margins. That leaves the good corporate lawyer without much of an inside view to work with on matters that are purely "corporate." Process and negotiation so often trump substantive fairness even in the one doctrinal subject area that used to be solidly fiduciary, the duties of loyalty and good faith.

III. LAWYERS AND LEGITIMACY

I have made a jumble of claims about corporations and their lawyers, which come down to the idea that the world in which they operate is so dominated by the necessity of compromise that a strongly moral view of legal obligation is off-putting. That the law itself, at least that regulating business behavior, is so often the product of compromise and flawed processes simply underscores that perception, leading to strongly held doubts that merely because something is the law, it has particular virtue. These doubts, rather than anything about the nature of the corporation, tempt corporate lawyers to adopt a Holmesian posture.

This suggests that an entirely amoral conception of professional responsibility will emerge, creating the dreaded race to the bottom where the lawyer is just a cynical legal risk calculator. While this is a real danger, I want to turn to the flip side of the notion of legitimacy in the hopes of checking the cynicism. As noted earlier, social legitimacy and prevalent norms fall short when measured against coherent expressions of ethics. But they are better than simple self-interest, because they reflect society's baseline demands from those participating in society and the economy. They are widely recognized within the business community. The idea that I want to put forth is that corporate lawyers are responsible for helping their clients understand and appreciate the relationship between legality and legitimacy, and that this is both a challenging and professionally rewarding task.

---

[33] *See, e.g.*, Robert Charles Clark, *Corporate Governance Changes in the Wake of the Sarbanes-Oxley Act: A Morality Tale for Policymakers, Too*, 22 GA. ST. L. REV. 251 (2005).

A reasonable fear at the outset is that legitimacy is little more than the most overused word in sociology, too fuzzy and manipulable, or that the pursuit of legitimacy is little more than public relations. That impression management techniques can provide cover for illegitimate behavior is certainly true, especially in the face of ambiguity. My prediction, however, is that truly illegitimate behavior is actually difficult to sustain, and that on average, a decision to persist in such behavior has negative returns for the firm. An interesting body of sociological work suggests that businesses for the most part act as if this is so, and have reasonably good "legitimacy instincts." Robert Kagan and his colleagues term this "social license"—the recognition that if conduct inexcusably falls short of societal demands, the firm will lose access to important resources and be disadvantaged.[34] This is so regardless of whether the conduct is law-abiding or not; something can be lawful but still illegitimate. But to the extent that the law tracks legitimacy, law-abidingness is a way of staying within social bounds. Moreover, this is not disconnected from legal risk itself—prosecutor, judge, and jury decisions are plausibly related to judgments about legitimacy, so that legal consequences can follow that would not if the behavior were illegal but not illegitimate. By way of example, concealment and deception are often tolerated in economic behavior. But if the concealment or deception is connected to seemingly offensive behavior, what was tolerable and commonly accepted receives a lightning bolt of liability—just ask Arthur Andersen or Bernie Ebbers. As noted earlier, more sophisticated understanding of CSR also builds on this idea, so that firms in a wide variety of settings (environmental compliance, consumer safety, etc.) seek to maintain their social license through a combination of impression management and real behaviors, with the latter having more sustainability.

So what is the lawyer's role here? If Kagan is correct that firms generally perceive the need to respect their social license, we have to inquire into why, sometimes, they lose sight of it.[35] There are two possibilities, each of which pulls in the lawyer. One is an agency cost problem: that the self-interest of some agents justifies causing the firm to take a social license (and legal liability) risk. The negative consequences may be stronger for the firm than for the individuals. The other, which I find more interesting, relates back to what was discussed earlier. The internal work of the firm requires cognitive

---

[34] *See, e.g.*, Neil Gunningham et al., *Social License and Environmental Protection: Why Businesses Go Beyond Compliance*, 29 LAW & SOC. INQUIRY 307 (2004); Robert A. Kagan et al., *Explaining Corporate Environmental Performance: How Does Regulation Matter?*, 37 LAW & SOC'Y REV. 51, 69 (2003) (discussing a mill manager's claim "that the sanctions it feared most for breaching regulations were not legal but informal sanctions imposed by the public and the media, and hence it was motivated less by avoiding regulatory violations per se as anything that could give you a bad name" (internal quotation marks omitted)); *see also* Williams & Conley, *supra* note 5; Jason Scott Johnston, *Signaling Social Responsibility: On the Law and Economics of Market Incentives for Corporate Environmental Performance* (U. Pa. Inst. for L. & Econ. Research, Paper No. 05-16, May 2005), *available at* http://srrn.com/abstract=725103. Business people's inclination to obey the law when the law's demands are properly framed is an important message of Ayres's and Braithwaite's well-known work on regulation. *See generally* IAN AYRES & JOHN BRAITHWAITE, RESPONSIVE REGULATION: TRANSCENDING THE DEREGULATION DEBATE (1992).

[35] *See* Kimberly D. Elsbach, *The Architecture of Legitimacy: Constructing Accounts of Organizational Controversies*, *in* THE PSYCHOLOGY OF LEGITIMACY, *supra* note 6, at 391.

simplification—belief systems—to achieve coordination. A natural incentive is to grease these interactions by deflecting moral doubts and anxieties that might otherwise burden them. Under certain circumstances, the internal culture may cast doubt on the legitimacy of legal demands in order to maintain internal coherence and productivity.[36]

Although this kind of rationalization will not necessarily be inaccurate, it is easy to see how it can also be myopic or self-serving, mindlessly justifying behavior that from an external perspective would cross the line. Sarbanes-Oxley is a good example. There are doubtlessly many aspects of the legislation that deserve skepticism, and many businesspeople who honestly believe that it is bad law. If unchecked, however, this attitude can lead to rationalizations that justify cutting corners and other forms of "cosmetic compliance,"[37] which can easily devolve into noncompliance. I suspect that the lawyer who pushes for a higher level of compliance because "it's the law" will not be persuasive unless she can (in true Holmesian fashion) also threaten a significant risk of detection and enforcement, and that posture fails when the risk diminishes, as it probably has already.

The legitimacy-oriented posture that I envision has two dimensions. First, it pushes back on organizational inferences and rationalizations that are essentially self-serving. Left to its own, an internal culture is likely to doubt the legitimacy of too much law. In essence, the lawyer needs to advocate so far as is plausible for the law's legitimacy, not out of any sense that the law is necessarily right but because it is so easy inside the culture to devalue it. Second, the good lawyer has to be sensitive to and engage the client's agents on those aspects of the law or regulation that reflect societal expectations of appropriate behavior—that is, legitimacy. To give a concrete example, the most hated portion of Sarbanes-Oxley in the business community is the requirement of audited internal controls.[38] Much of the increased costs comes from hard-to-justify intrusiveness on mundane matters such as personnel protocols and double-check mechanisms far removed from likely risks of malfeasance.[39] I would not expect a lawyer to push too hard here, even though that might be the regulatory expectation. But there are specific places where a failure of internal controls—for example, on managerial self-dealing—would be regarded as a sin of omission inconsistent with emerging societal expectations about senior executive accountability. The good lawyer has to fight here, because this goes to the legitimacy (not just compliance) of the systems of checks and balances in a public corporation, against managers primed to resist.

---

[36] This is, of course, not the only problem corporate lawyers face. They also face problems of information diffusion, which raise hard questions about lawyers' responsibility to "dig" for the truth when encountering cause for suspicion. *See generally* William H. Simon, *Wrongs of Ignorance and Ambiguity: Lawyer Responsibility for Collective Misconduct*, 22 YALE J. ON REG. 1 (2005).

[37] *See* Kimberly D. Krawiec, *Cosmetic Compliance and the Failure of Negotiated Governance*, 81 WASH. U. L.Q. 487 (2003).

[38] *See* William J. Carney, *The Costs of Being Public After Sarbanes-Oxley: The Irony of "Going Private,"* 55 EMORY L.J. 141 (2006).

[39] *See* Langevoort, *supra* note 2, at 959-60.

This brings me to a point I have made before.[40] Lawyers have to maintain a posture of cognitive independence from the internal belief systems of the corporation in order to do their jobs well. Being too close creates the risk that powerful organizational perceptions and inferences will spread and compromise the quality of the legal advice, regardless of how the goal of professional responsibility is articulated. Skilled corporate lawyers should not simply take this as a trite invitation toward an attitude of professional superiority but learn carefully how and why these belief systems can be so powerful. Only then will professional engagement be successful.

CONCLUSION

In the end, I confess, I am a Holmesian who believes that law and morality are only loosely coupled. More importantly, the business world to which I pay most of my professional attention is one in which the language of legitimacy has a much stronger pull on behavior than the language of morality. That makes me doubt that a project to promote a strong "inside view" of the law's demands generally would find much of a willing audience.

But I am also unwilling to give up on some way of engaging clients beyond the language of risk. Both lawyer[41] and legal academics signal much by the way we think and talk about responsibility: Being relentlessly descriptive can become a self-fulfilling prophecy to the extent that what is repeatedly identified as common or predictable is then gradually accepted as normative as well.[42] The "devolution" of the legal profession—in corporate practice, particularly[43]—may be the product of economic circumstances beyond our control, but it certainly does not help when the dominant social science methodology persistently treats lawyers and their clients as either economic opportunists or risk actuaries.

To be sure, a legitimacy-based vision of the lawyer's role is not very different from long-standing calls for lawyers to think about risks to their clients in terms broader than simple legal sanction. The payoff is not in the conception but in understanding precisely how and why agents of the corporation think about the law's demands—including the possibility that they mischaracterize or trivialize the legitimacy of the law in ways that are unwise. Countering those perceptions and inferences is hard, and takes sophistication, which makes the task deserving of professional respect. It requires study of why managers are tempted to violate the law, which has long been of interest to professional responsibility scholars. But perhaps less expectedly, it also requires study of why managers so frequently adhere to or exceed what the law demands, because that is

---

[40] *See supra* note 26 and accompanying text.

[41] *See* Tanina Rostain, *Ethics Lost: Limitations of Current Approaches to Lawyer Regulation*, 71 S. CAL. L. REV. 1273, 1336 (1998).

[42] *See, e.g.*, Moore & Lowenstein, *supra* note 23, at 195-96.

[43] *See* Ronald J. Gilson, *The Devolution of the Legal Profession: A Demand Side Perspective*, 49 MD. L. REV. 869 (1990).

where we will find the language, the beliefs, and the social influences from which advice in the business setting can be framed constructively, with an eye to legitimacy as well as legality. Perhaps as we learn more about the psychology, sociology, and economics of legitimacy and social license, good lawyers will get some help.

The Pivotal Role of the General Counsel in Promoting Corporate Integrity and Professional Responsibility[*]

Sarah Helene Duggin[**]

INTRODUCTION

In the complex, highly regulated world in which business corporations operate, corporate general counsel play a key role in promoting organizational integrity and ethical lawyering. The fiduciary and professional responsibilities of the general counsel[1] or chief legal officer[2] are explicit in the rules adopted by the Securities and Exchange

---

[*] Reprinted with permission of the Saint Louis University Law Journal © 2007 St. Louis University School of Law, St. Louis, Missouri. Sarah Helene Duggin, *The Pivotal Role of the General Counsel in Promoting Corporate Integrity and Professional Responsibility*, 51 St. Louis U. L.J. 989 (2007).

[**] Associate Professor of Law and Director, Law and Public Policy Program, Columbus School of Law, The Catholic University of America; formerly Vice President and General Counsel, National Railroad Passenger Corp.; Chief Legal Officer, University of Pennsylvania Health System; and Partner, Williams & Connolly, LLP. An earlier version of this paper was presented on January 5, 2007, at the American Association of Law Schools (AALS) annual meeting in Washington, D.C. My thanks to Professor Carol Needham, Chair of the Section on Professional Responsibility, for her creative ideas and for inviting me to participate in the panel on "Navigating Treacherous Waters: Initiating an Investigation, Going Up the Ladder and Reporting Out." Thanks, too, to Association of Corporate Counsel (ACC) Vice President and General Counsel Susan Hackett for her perceptive comments and for allowing me to access ACC's online library, to my colleague Professor Lisa Lerman for her insights, and to Sean Murphy of the Columbus School of Law Class of 2008 for his invaluable help with research for the article. As always, my abiding thanks to Kirk, Alex, and Bryant Renaud for their constant support and encouragement.

[1] While outside lawyers or law firms sometimes serve as general counsel to entities or their components, for purposes of this discussion, the term "general counsel" refers to a lawyer employed by a corporation or other organization to serve as its chief legal officer with responsibility for overseeing legal matters pertaining to the entity, including its governance, finance, and operations.

[2] The term "chief legal officer," customarily abbreviated "CLO," is employed in some organizations in lieu of the term "general counsel" because it is comparable to the terminology used for other executive functions, such as "chief executive officer," "chief financial officer," "chief operating officer," etc. "Chief legal officer" is also the terminology used by the Securities and Exchange Commission (SEC) in its Standards of Professional Conduct for Attorneys Appearing and Practicing Before the Commission in the Representation of an Issuer, 17 C.F.R. § 205 (2003).

Commission (SEC) pursuant to section 307 of the Sarbanes-Oxley Act of 2002.[3] They are also implicit in the August 2003 amendments to Model Rule of Professional Responsibility 1.13[4] adopted by the American Bar Association's (ABA) House of Delegates[5] pursuant to the recommendations of the ABA Task Force on Corporate Responsibility.[6] The real power and potential influence of the men and women who serve as corporate general counsel, however, goes far beyond the areas touched upon by these mandates. Enron and other corporate debacles illustrate all too well what happens when business managers fail to understand and honor their responsibilities. As advisors and liaisons to senior corporate officers, directors, boards, and board committees, general counsel have a great deal to do with the way business managers perceive both their particular legal obligations and corporate responsibility in general.[7] General counsel are ideally

---

[3] Sarbanes-Oxley Act of 2002, Pub. L. No. 107-204, 116 Stat. 745 (2002) (codified as amended in scattered sections of 11, 18, 28 and 29 U.S.C.). In section 307 Congress directed the SEC to issue rules:

> setting forth minimum standards of professional conduct for attorneys appearing and practicing before the Commission in any way in the representation of issuers, including a rule—
>
> (1) requiring an attorney to report evidence of a material violation of securities law or breach of fiduciary duty or similar violation by the company or any agent thereof, to the chief legal counsel or the chief executive officer of the company (or the equivalent thereof); and
>
> (2) if the counsel or officer does not appropriately respond to the evidence (adopting, as necessary, appropriate remedial measures or sanctions with respect to the violation), requiring the attorney to report the evidence to the audit committee of the board of directors of the issuer or to another committee of the board of directors comprised solely of directors not employed directly or indirectly by the issuer, or to the board of directors.

Id. at § 307; 15 U.S.C. 7245 (2000 & Supp. II).

[4] MODEL RULES OF PROF'L CONDUCT 1.13 (2003).

[5] *See* ABA HOUSE OF DELEGATES, RESOLUTIONS OF THE ABA HOUSE OF DELEGATES (Aug. 11-12, 2003), *available at* http://www.abanet.org/media/corpgov.pdf [hereinafter August 2003 ABA RESOLUTIONS].

[6] *See* American Bar Ass'n, Report of American Bar Association Task Force on Corporate Responsibility (Mar. 31, 2003), *available at* http://www.abanet.org/buslaw/corporateresponsibility/final_report.pdf [hereinafter Corporate Responsibility Task Force Report]. While the impetus for the SEC's Part 205 rules, much of the work of the ABA Task Force on Corporate Responsibility, and the August 2003 amendments to the Model Rules of Professional Conduct, arose primarily out of concerns over the role of lawyers representing public corporations, many other entities, including those in the not-for-profit sector, are subject to similar concerns. These concerns merit inclusion in work on reporting up and reporting out requirements, even though only issuers registered under federal securities laws are subject to the relevant SEC rules. *See, e.g.*, Susan Hackett, *It's Private Companies' Turn to Dance the Sarbox Shuffle* (Am. Corporate Counsel Ass'n, Washington, D.C.), Aug. 2003, available at http://www.acca.com/public/article/corpresp/sarbox_shuffle.pdf. While the principal focus of this article is on general counsel in public corporations, much of the discussion also applies to general counsel employed by private business entities and not-for-profit organizations.

[7] In addition to the challenges presented by the new regulatory measures, the renewed focus on legal compliance and corporate governance issues offers opportunities for corporate lawyers, particularly for general counsel, to raise attention to legal issues. "General counsel are both legal officers and corporate officers. Most of the time, General Counsel have to balance their legal roles and their business roles. Sarbanes-Oxley is a profound exception to this need for balance in the sense that, by rigorously applying their legal insight, general Counsel directly serve economic business objectives." Lawrence J. Stybel &

situated to serve as leaders in the struggle to define the parameters of corporate conscience. They can and should be held accountable for promoting integrity on the part of corporations and their constituents and for fostering professional responsibility on the part of corporate lawyers.

Despite the vital importance of general counsel in the corporate arena, a great deal remains to be explored about the nature of the office and the part general counsel will play in the emerging ethical landscape.[8] The purpose of this article is to offer an overview of the role of contemporary general counsel, with a particular focus on the specific responsibilities assigned to these individuals as chief legal officers pursuant to the SEC's Part 205 rules and implicit in Model Rule 1.13. The discussion emphasizes three points. First, corporate general counsel play multifaceted roles in the corporate legal environment, and their influence extends across a vast spectrum of corporate activity. Consequently, the ability of general counsel to perform their functions successfully in the new ethical landscape will significantly impact the effectiveness of regulatory efforts designed to promote corporate integrity and professional responsibility.

Second, the article suggests that it is not only what general counsel do that matters, but also how they do it. Corporate lawyers constantly face pressure to compromise professional judgment and abandon internal moral standards in the interest of fitting into business environments. They are urged to be team players in a game where winning depends on wealth maximization—corporate and individual. Measures designed to require ethical vigilance on the part of general counsel need to support broader values

---

Maryanne Peabody, *A New Balance of Power Means New Boardroom Opportunity for General Counsel*, OF COUNS., May 2004, at 9, 10.

[8] There are, however, a few excellent recent articles. *See, e.g.*, Deborah DeMott, *The Discrete Roles of General Counsel*, 74 FORDHAM L. REV. 955 (2006); Carl D. Liggio, Sr., *A Look at the Role of Corporate Counsel: Back to the Future—Or is it the Past?*, 44 ARIZ. L. REV. 621, 621-28 (2002) [hereinafter Liggio, *A Look at the Role of Corporate Counsel*]; E. Norman Veasey & Christine T. Di Guglielmo, *The Tensions, Stresses, and Professional Responsibilities of the Lawyer for the Corporation*, 62 BUS. LAW. 1 (2006). The ethical obligations of chief legal officers were also discussed in the Section on Professional Responsibility panel on "Navigating Treacherous Waters: Initiating an Investigation, Going Up the Ladder and Reporting Out" at the American Association of Law Schools January 2007 meeting in Washington, D.C., and a number of thoughtful articles were written a decade ago in connection with Emory University Law School's 1997 Randolph Thrower Symposium on the Role of the General Counsel. *See, e.g.*, Mary C. Daly, *The Cultural, Ethical, and Legal Challenges in Lawyering for a Global Organization: The Role of the General Counsel*, 46 EMORY L.J. 1057 (1997); Richard S. Gruner, *General Counsel in an Era of Compliance Programs and Corporate Self-Policing*, 46 EMORY L.J. 1113 (1997); Geoffrey C. Hazard, Jr., Ethical Dilemmas of Corporate Counsel, 46 Emory L.J. 1011 (1997) [hereinafter Hazard, *Ethical Dilemmas*]; Geoffrey C. Hazard, Jr., *Three Afterthoughts*, 46 EMORY L.J. 1053 (1997) [hereinafter Hazard, *Three Afterthoughts*]; James F. Kelley, The *Role of the General Counsel*, 46 EMORY L.J. 1197 (1997); Carl D. Liggio, *The Changing Role of Corporate Counsel*, 46 EMORY L.J. 1201, 1201-02 (1997) [hereinafter Liggio, *The Changing Role of Corporate Counsel*]; Howard B. Miller, *Law Risk Management and the General Counsel*, 46 EMORY L.J. 1223 (1997); Timothy P. Terrell, *Professionalism as Trust: The Unique Internal Legal Role of the Corporate General Counsel*, 46 EMORY L.J. 1005 (1997); Sally R. Weaver, *Ethical Dilemmas of Corporate Counsel: A Structural and Contextual Analysis*, 46 EMORY L.J. 1023 (1997)

and empower general counsel to act as "lawyer statesmen"[9] who offer insights that go beyond technical legal advice.

Third, given the importance of the general counsel function, in evaluating the efficacy of the rules governing corporate legal practice scholars, practitioners and regulators need to recognize the significance of the role of corporate general counsel and consider the impact of new legal rules and the practices they engender on those charged with so much of the responsibility for making these rules work.

Part I begins with an overview of the history of the corporate general counsel position and then outlines formal and informal roles contemporary general counsel play, concluding with a discussion of the importance of a broad vision of the role in fostering corporate integrity and professional ethics. Part II looks at the responsibilities of general counsel in connection with Sarbanes-Oxley and the 2003 amendments to the Model Rules of Professional Conduct.

In the interest of beginning a conversation, Part III focuses on two of the many areas that merit careful consideration concerning the role of general counsel in the struggle to promote corporate integrity and professional responsibility. The first section advocates caution with respect to the increasingly popular practice of retaining separate "independent" counsel to handle various corporate legal matters. It is clearly necessary for corporate boards to retain separate counsel in certain limited circumstances—e.g., in connection with special litigation committee decisions in shareholder derivative actions or internal investigations involving allegations of misconduct that implicates the general counsel. Overuse of this device, however, wastes resources, and, more importantly, threatens to undermine the authority and effectiveness of general counsel. Consequently, the article suggests consideration of an ethical rule pertaining to coordination of counsel absent extraordinary circumstances.

The second and final section of Part III turns to the critical need for ongoing attention to the relationship between general counsel and corporate directors. Lawyers and business managers alike need standards applicable to the intersection of their roles, both as a basis for guidance and as a source of authority to invoke as a bulwark against countervailing pressures that assault integrity and professionalism.[10] Accordingly, standards pertaining to general counsel attendance at board meetings and ongoing communication with independent directors have a great deal of merit. In addition, this article proposes a standard requiring chief legal officers to report to directors on the resignation or termination of in-house lawyers or outside counsel handling significant matters for a company and the reasons therefore.

---

[9] *See* Benjamin W. Heineman, Jr., *The Ideal of the "Lawyer Statesman,"* 22 ACC DOCKET 62, 64 (May 2004) (stating that general counsel "must have enough life experience, stature, and self-confidence to express honest, complex views even under the inevitable pressure for simple, short-term answers"); *Face Value: Where's the Lawyer?*, THE ECONOMIST, Mar. 20, 2004, at 73 (discussing former General Electric Company General Counsel Benjamin Heineman's view that an ideal general counsel is a "lawyer statesman" who "should be involved in everything from creating a 'culture of compliance and integrity' to engaging in public debate and fighting the current cynicism about business").

[10] *Cf.* Veasey & Di Guglielmo, *supra* note 8, at 21 (observing that new up-ladder reporting requirements "provide counsel with leverage to cause . . . corporate constituents to 'do the right thing'").

I. THE GENERAL COUNSEL IN CONTEMPORARY ENTITIES

The office of general counsel is an exciting and much sought-after position in the contemporary legal market.[11] General counsel function in the midst of the crossroads where business objectives, corporate governance standards, and rules of professional responsibility intersect. The following discussion briefly looks at some of the major historical trends that have defined the nature of the position and then turns to the role of general counsel in contemporary entities.[12]

A. Historical Trends in the Role of General Counsel

Over time, the star of in-house lawyers in corporate entities has risen and fallen. As noted legal historian Lawrence Friedman reports, in the second half of the nineteenth century—the time period when the corporate form became a hallmark of big business in the United States[13] corporate legal jobs were highly desirable.[14] "To be general counsel of a major railroad, after the Civil War, was to occupy a position of great prestige and enormous salary."[15] The potential rewards inspired many of the bar's best and brightest, including judges, to seek general counsel positions.[16]

Prestige and power continued to be associated with corporate counsel positions well into the twentieth century. Many senior corporate managers began their careers as in-house lawyers during this "golden age of corporate counsel."[17] Gradually, however, business school graduates took over the leadership of corporate America.[18] At a time when both the regulatory environment and financial transactions were significantly less complex than today, few senior managers perceived the need to devote corporate resources to law departments.[19] In-house positions became less desirable as compensation

---

[11] *See, e.g.*, Liggio, *A Look at the Role of Corporate Counsel, supra* note 8, at 632 & n.28; Janet Stidman Eveleth, *Life as Corporate Counsel*, 37 MD. B.J. 16, 18 (Jan.-Feb. 2004) (stating that "over the last 20 years, the role of general counsel has emerged as a popular area of practice").

[12] In recent years the role of general counsel has become increasingly important in many different kinds of entities. Even large law firms now have general counsel. *See* Geoffrey C. Hazard, Jr., *"Lawyer for Lawyers": The Emerging Role of Law Firm Legal Counsel*, 53 U. KAN. L. REV. 795, 795 (2005).

[13] *See* Sarah H. Duggin & Stephen M. Goldman, *Restoring Trust in Corporate Directors: The Disney Standard and the "New" Good Faith*, 56 AM. U. L. REV. 211, 220-21 (2006).

[14] LAWRENCE M. FRIEDMAN, A HISTORY OF AMERICAN LAW 490 (3d ed. 2005).

[15] *Id.; see also, e.g.*, DeMott, *supra* note 8, at 958-59; Liggio, *A Look at the Role of Corporate Counsel, supra* note 8, at 621-22; Liggio, The Changing Role of Corporate Counsel, supra note 8, at 1201-02.

[16] DeMott, *supra* note 8, at 958-59.

[17] Liggio, *A Look at the Role of Corporate Counsel, supra* note 8, at 621 (observing that during the first decades of the twentieth century, "75% of the CEOs of the major companies were lawyers compared to less than 5% today"); *see also* Liggio, *The Changing Role of Corporate Counsel, supra* note 8, at 1202.

[18] Liggio, *The Changing Role of Corporate Counsel, supra* note 8, at 1202.

[19] *See* FRIEDMAN, *supra* note 14, at 490; *see also* Liggio, *A Look at the Role of Corporate Counsel, supra* note 8, at 623 ("Compared to today, the 1950s and early 1960s were the land of legal simplicity.").

lagged and advancement opportunities steadily decreased.[20] As business managers turned to outside lawyers for legal advice, the prestige of in-house positions plummeted.[21] In the 1970s, however, the tide began to turn,[22] and in-house lawyers once again emerged as significant players in the corporate world.[23] As the practice environment evolved, the importance of general counsel within corporate structures became clear.

B. Emergence of the Contemporary Model

The ascendancy of the corporate law department during the last three decades resulted from the confluence of a variety of factors.[24] Professor Geoffrey Hazard notes that businesses experienced an increasing need for "continuous legal assistance, readily at hand and already familiar with the corporation's operations and legal environment."[25] As former Chief Justice Rehnquist observed in *Upjohn Co. v. United States*,[26] "corporations, unlike most individuals, 'constantly [needed to] go to lawyers to find out how to obey the law'";[27] by the early 1980s, corporate legal compliance was "hardly an

---

[20] *See* Liggio, *A Look at the Role of Corporate Counsel, supra* note 8, at 622-23; Liggio, *The Changing Role of Corporate Counsel, supra* note 8, at 1202-03. During this time period "the term 'house counsel' was one of double disparagement." Hazard, *Ethical Dilemmas, supra* note 8, at 1011. As Professor Regan points out, it was also during the first decades of the twentieth century that the "Cravath approach" sparked the development of the elite Wall Street firms that dominated corporate legal work for many years by providing high quality services to corporate clients, albeit at a high cost. MILTON C. REGAN, JR., EAT WHAT YOU KILL: THE FALL OF A WALL STREET LAWYER 23 (2004).

[21] *See* Liggio, *A Look at the Role of Corporate Counsel, supra* note 8, at 622 (noting that "few companies had internal legal departments"). Mr. Liggio also notes that the resources necessary to support an adequate legal library, particularly the cost of the books themselves, reinforced the role of large law firm lawyers as "gatekeepers of legal knowledge." *Id.* at 625. He cites the rapid development of technology during the last few decades as a tremendous leveling influence with respect to access to legal knowledge. *Id.* at 633-34.

[22] Abram Chayes and Antonia Chayes wrote an influential article describing this trend in 1985. *See* Abram Chayes & Antonia H. Chayes, *Corporate Counsel and the Elite Law Firm*, 37 STAN. L. REV. 277 (1985). They noted:

> A striking development in the legal profession over the last decade has been the rapid growth in both importance and size of the in-house, or corporate counsel. The traditional house counsel was a relatively minor management figure, stereotypically, a lawyer from the corporation's principal outside law firm who had not quite made the grade as partner. . . . The new breed of general counsel has left this stereotype behind.

Id. at 277 n.1.

[23] As Chayes and Chayes noted in 1985, the shift to in-house legal departments was "most pronounced among the largest corporations in the American economy . . . those that [had] traditionally been the anchor clients of the large, elite law firms." *Id.* at 278.

[24] As Professor DeMott has observed, this renaissance resulted from both demand and supply side factors. DeMott, *supra* note 8, at 961.

[25] Hazard, *Ethical Dilemmas, supra* note 8, at 1012; *see also* Liggio, *The Changing Role of Corporate Counsel, supra* note 8, at 1210 (noting the numerous functional roles of corporate counsel).

[26] 449 U.S. 383 (1981).

[27] *Id.* at 392.

instinctive matter."[28] At the time of the *Upjohn* decision, SEC and Internal Revenue Service (IRS) enforcement initiatives pursuant to the Foreign Corrupt Practices Act[29] were in full swing, the Watergate scandal had opened the eyes of law enforcement authorities and the public to questionable domestic political contributions by major corporations and their constituents,[30] and a burst of legislative activity had given birth to comprehensive regulatory systems applicable to corporate actors.[31] This was also the era of the litigation explosion. The number of civil actions against corporations dramatically increased in areas ranging from employment to products liability,[32] and class actions and shareholders' derivative suits emerged as effective weapons against powerful corporate behemoths.[33] Corporate managers learned from experience, and they, too, began to use litigation as an offensive weapon to pursue business objectives and as a defensive tool to combat hostile takeover attempts.[34]

At the same time, external economic factors made law firm representation increasingly expensive.[35] Familiarizing outside counsel with the details necessary to effective representation required large cash outlays[36] and diverted human resources from more economically productive business tasks. As legal fees became a larger part of corporate expenditures, managers also clamored for utilization of business-oriented approaches to contain rapidly expanding legal risks and concomitant counsel fees.[37] Perhaps most

---

[28] *Id.*

[29] Foreign Corrupt Practices Act of 1977, Pub. L. No. 95-213, 91 Stat. 1494 (1977).

[30] *See generally* Sarah Helene Duggin, *Internal Corporate Investigations: Legal Ethics, Professionalism and the Employee Interview*, 2003 COL. BUS. L. REV. 859, 872-73 (citing STEPHEN F. BLACK, INTERNAL CORPORATE INVESTIGATIONS § 1.01 at 1-1 (1998), and Arthur F. Mathews, *Internal Corporate Investigations*, 45 OHIO ST. L.J. 655, 655-56 (1984)).

[31] *See* Liggio, *The Changing Role of Corporate Counsel*, *supra* note 8, at 1204 (noting growth of "'alphabet soup' agencies" and passage of several comprehensive new laws). *See generally* Duggin, *supra* note 30, at 881-83.

[32] *See* Duggin *supra* note 30, at 881-83; Liggio, *The Changing Role of Corporate Counsel*, *supra* note 8, at 1203. *See generally* WALTER K. OLSON, THE LITIGATION EXPLOSION: WHAT HAPPENED WHEN AMERICA UNLEASHED THE LAWSUIT (1991).

[33] Duggin, *supra* note 30, at 881-83.

[34] Susanna M. Kim, *Dual Identities and Dueling Obligations: Preserving Independence in Corporate Representation*, 68 TENN. L. REV. 179, 199-200 (2001) (discussing the recent increase in the number of in-house attorneys and the corresponding benefits to corporations); Liggio, *A Look at the Role of Corporate Counsel*, *supra* note 8, at 624; Liggio, *The Changing Role of Corporate Counsel*, *supra* note 8, at 1203.

[35] Daly, *supra* note 8, at 1060 ("As the legal fees charged by law firms continued to rise, both corporate financial officers and general counsel perceived the fiscal and professional wisdom of making salaried lawyers responsible for the delivery of nonroutine, complex legal services, particularly those of a transactional character."); Liggio, *The Changing Role of Corporate Counsel*, *supra* note 8, at 1204-05 (noting that "[e]scalating costs, coupled with a distaste for lawyers generally, were a critical catalyst in propelling employed counsel into the forefront of the modern corporate hierarchy," and that many corporate executives believed that outside counsel overcharged for their services).

[36] *See* Daly, *supra* note 8, at 1060-61; *see also* Kim, *supra* note 34, at 199-200.

[37] Liggio, *The Changing Role of Corporate Counsel*, *supra* note 8, at 1206 (stating that "the business of the law is being addressed by a new breed of corporate counsel who are applying business techniques and

importantly, many corporate managers began to recognize, albeit sometimes grudgingly, the usefulness of involving lawyers early on in business initiatives.[38]

During the same time period, lawyers, too, were beginning to see the promising possibilities of in-house positions. As law firms demanded longer and longer workdays, lawyers looking for ways to escape the tyranny of the billable hour and the pressure to become rainmakers[39] were attracted to in-house positions.[40] This trend accelerated as compensation and benefit packages became increasingly lucrative[41] and the "affirmative self-assurance of corporate counsel [was] manifested in their own organizations, publications and special identity."[42] The creation of the American Corporate Counsel Association[43] in 1982 by a group of prominent general counsel evidenced this phenomenon.[44] Further, in an environment of increasing specialization, "employment by a single client bec[ame] simply another form of specialization."[45]

---

tools to management of the legal process") (citing Howard B. Miller, *Law Risk Management and General Counsel*, 46 EMORY L.J. 1223 (1997)); *see also id.* at 1204-05 (noting 1980s survey results reflecting high percentage of corporate executives who believed outside law firms overcharged their companies).

[38] Kim, *supra* note 34, at 202-03.

[39] *See, e.g.*, Liggio, *A Look at the Role of Corporate Counsel, supra* note 8, at 628.

[40] *See generally* Eveleth, *supra* note 11, at 18 (citing reports of more flexible hours, no need to bill time or compete to bring in clients, and better benefit packages as attractions of in-house counsel positions); Hazard, *Ethical Dilemmas, supra* note 8, at 1012 (noting the "growth of the large law firm, where the working environment for the average lawyer is not much different from, and often is worse than, that in corporate law departments" as one of several key factors); Liggio, *A Look at the Role of Corporate Counsel, supra* note 8, at 628. Professor DeMott discusses four hypotheses that may explain why general counsel positions have become far more attractive to members of the legal profession in recent years. DeMott, supra note 8, at 961. These hypotheses include (1) the "fit" between ability and position demands, (2) perceptions of in-house counsel positions as "launching pads" for transitions to other senior management positions, (3) increasing economic rewards, and (4) the contrast between the work experiences of law firm attorneys and their in-house counterparts. *Id.*

[41] Eveleth, *supra* note 11, at 18; Liggio, *A Look at the Role of Corporate Counsel, supra* note 8, at 627-28; Liggio, *The Changing Role of Corporate Counsel, supra* note 8, at 1206.

[42] Hazard, *Ethical Dilemmas, supra* note 8, at 1012.

[43] The Association of Corporate Counsel (ACC), originally called the American Corporate Counsel Association (ACCA), was formed on March 14, 1982. Liggio, *The Changing Role of Corporate Counsel, supra* note 8, at 1211. The principal founders were Carl Liggio of Ernst & Young, Robert Banks of Xerox Corporation, and S.T. Jack Brigham III of Hewlett-Packard. Daly, *supra* note 8, at 1063. The organization began with fifty members, Liggio, *The Changing Role of Corporate Counsel, supra* note 8, at 1211, but it now serves more than 20,000 members working in sixty-eight countries for more than 8,800 corporations, including all of the Fortune 100 companies and seventy-four of the Global 100 companies. *Ass'n of Corporate Counsel*, About ACC, http://www.acc.com/php/cms/index.php?id=28 (last visited June 25, 2007).

[44] *See* Daly, *supra* note 8, at 1063 ("They were determined to alter a perceived long-standing misallocation of power between legal departments and law firms in which in-house lawyers exercised little oversight or control over the outside attorneys whom they retained."); *see also* Liggio, *The Changing Role of Corporate Counsel, supra* note 8, at 1211.

[45] Hazard, *Ethical Dilemmas, supra* note 8, at 1012.

As companies began to hire lawyers and law firms for particular projects rather than affiliating with a few firms for nearly all of their work,[46] outside counsel "tend[ed] to become an executor of the general counsel's instructions, with decreasing scope for originality or independent judgment."[47] This phenomenon made in-house positions even more desirable for lawyers interested in opportunities to influence organizational behavior from the inside, rather than working as hired guns lining up for another shoot-out.[48] It is possible that the changing demographics of the legal profession—particularly the entry of large numbers of women and minority lawyers into the profession beginning in the 1960s—also made a difference.[49] In any event, as lawyers' perceptions of successful career paths evolved,[50] members of the profession began to understand the potential power and influence of in-house counsel in the business world.[51]

During the latter part of the twentieth century, corporations themselves were also becoming increasingly integral to the economic, social, and political life of ordinary Americans. In 1900 fewer than one percent of Americans held corporate stock, and

---

[46] *See, e.g.*, Liggio, *The Changing Role of Corporate Counsel, supra* note 8 (describing retention of outside counsel as "increasingly episodic"); *see also* Milton C. Regan, Jr., *Corporate Norms and Contemporary Law Practice*, 70 GEO. WASH. L. REV. 931, 933-40 (2002) (suggesting that expansion of in-house law departments and concomitant retention of outside counsel on a task basis rather than general retainer has had a major impact on large law firms and their lawyers).

[47] Chayes & Chayes, *supra* note 22, at 298. In recent years, a number of corporations have sought to reduce the number of law firms handling their work as a means of lessening the managerial burden on in-house counsel and obtaining more favorable billing arrangements. *See, e.g.*, Susan Hackett, *Inside Out: An Examination of Demographic Trends in the In-House Profession*, 44 ARIZ. L. REV. 609, 614 (2002). A return to the days of utilizing one or a few firms for the bulk of a corporation's legal work is unlikely, however, given the complexity of contemporary corporate entities and the impact of globalization.

[48] *See id.* at 294; Liggio, *The Changing Role of Corporate Counsel, supra* note 8, at 1209.

[49] The impact of the dramatic increase in the number of women in the legal profession during the last part of the twentieth century on the evolution of in-house counsel positions remains to be explored. Legal historian Lawrence Friedman notes that women were rare beasts in the bar until the 1960s.

> Then the tide turned, and dramatically. By the end of the century, about a quarter of the bar was made up of women, most of them rather young; and there were so many women in the pipeline—half or more of the law students in many schools—that the percentage of women lawyers was bound to rise, perhaps to majority status in the twenty-first century.

FRIEDMAN, *supra* note 14, at 538. Professor Friedman also notes a significant increase in the number of lawyers from racial and ethnic minority groups over the same time period. *Id.*; *see also* Liggio, *A Look at the Role of Corporate Counsel, supra* note 8, at 628 & n.22 (citing AM. CORP. COUNS. ASS'N, AMERICAN CORPORATE COUNSEL ASSOCIATION'S CENSUS OF IN-HOUSE COUNSEL: EXECUTIVE SUMMARY (Dec. 2001) (noting demographic changes and paucity of relevant information)). Still, however, ACC reports that in its 2006 member survey, 89% of respondents identified themselves as Caucasian and approximately two-thirds as male. *See* ACC 2006 Census of In-house Counsel, www.acc.com/resource/v8360 (last visited June 25, 2007).

[50] *See* DeMott, *supra* note 8, at 960-61 & *supra* note 40.

[51] *See* Kim, *supra* note 34, at 200-01; Liggio, *A Look at the Role of Corporate Counsel, supra* note 8, at 629; Liggio, *The Changing Role of Corporate Counsel, supra* note 8, at 1205.

in 1980 only thirteen percent were shareholders.[52] By 1998, however, more than fifty-two percent of Americans owned shares in corporations in one form or another.[53] The media chronicled daily the parts major business entities and their leaders played—not only in the nation's economic life, but in politics, philanthropic endeavors, and social arenas. A number of corporate executives even became well-known celebrities.[54] The increasing prominence of corporations and their leaders in society undoubtedly further enhanced the allure of in-house legal positions.

As the twentieth century drew to a close, in-house opportunities, particularly general counsel and deputy general counsel positions, had become extremely competitive for lawyers at all professional levels. Law firm partners, government officials, and, once again, even judges joined the ranks of corporate general counsel.[55] Ironically, law firms even began to create their own internal general counsel positions.[56] As a result of this dramatic shift, during the last quarter of the twentieth century, "[g]eneral counsel, not law firm partners [became] the 'statesmen' to chief executive officers (CEOs), confidently offering business as well as legal advice."[57]

C. The Multifaceted Roles of Contemporary General Counsel

In a heavily regulated, litigious world, the way in which entities deal with legal issues is critical to their survival and success, whether they are global corporations,

---

[52] *See* Duggin & Goldman, *supra* note 13, at 214 n.9 (citing THEODORE CAPLOW ET AL., THE FIRST MEASURED CENTURY: AN ILLUSTRATED GUIDE TO TRENDS IN AMERICA, 1900-2000 252-53 (2001), and U.S. Census Bureau, Statistical Abstract of the United States 2006, *available at* http://www.census.gov/prod/2005pubs/06statab/income.pdf (follow "Table 655" link)).

[53] *Id.*

[54] *See, e.g.*, Geraldine Fabrikant & Shelby White, *Personal Business; How the Other Half Gives*, N.Y. TIMES, Dec. 20, 1998, at § 3, at 1 (describing attitudes of Bill Gates, Ted Turner, and other celebrities toward philanthropy); Randy Kennedy, *When Scraping the Sky Makes a City Bleed*, N.Y. TIMES, Oct. 23, 1998, at B1 (discussing Donald Trump and his plans for new buildings); *Who Did the Best Job?*, FORBES, Jan. 13, 1997, at 91 (examining the accomplishments of Jack Welch and other well known executives).

[55] For example, in 2005, Sven Holmes, Chief Judge of the United States District Court for the Northern District of Oklahoma, left the federal bench to become vice chairman for legal affairs of KPMG, Inc. Lynnley Browning, *Openers: Suits, Here Comes the Judge*, N.Y. TIMES, Jan. 23, 2005, § 3, at 2; Carrie Johnson & Brooke A. Masters, *KPMG Hires Federal Judge*, WASH. POST., Jan. 21, 2005, at E1; *see also* DeMott, *supra* note 8, at 962 n.33. Other companies have successfully sought out former government officials, and even prosecutors, to serve as general counsel or in other senior in-house positions. *See, e.g.*, Emma Schwartz, *From Public to Private Employment: Companies Seek Exiting Government Lawyers for Hire*, LEGAL TIMES, Aug. 25, 2005; Joseph A. Slobodzian, *GCs for Tough Times: Companies Are Hiring Attorneys Who Have Been Prosecutors*, NAT'L L.J., Dec. 5, 2002, *available at* www.law.com/jsp/article.jsp?id=1038966824667.

[56] *See generally* Terry Carter, *Taking a Cue from the Corporate World, Law Firms Create Internal General Counsel Jobs*, ABA J., Aug. 2006, at 30; Elizabeth Chambliss & David B. Wilkins, *The Emerging Role of Ethics Advisors, General Counsel, and Other Compliance Specialists in Large Law Firms*, 44 ARIZ. L. REV. 559 (2002); Hazard, *supra* note 12.

[57] Daly, *supra* note 8, at 679.

local charities, or government agencies. Although empirical evidence is limited,[58] it is apparent that the influence of in-house counsel generally has grown as the significance of legal considerations has escalated in the strategic planning process.[59] In 1985 Professors Abram and Antonia Chayes concluded that "the general counsel has a personal role in defining alternatives, in strategic decisions, and even in tactical choices."[60] More recently, Professor Deborah DeMott suggested that, because his or her influence "may extend well beyond the bare bones of ensuring legal compliance,"[61] a corporate general counsel "may be uniquely well positioned to champion a transformation of the organizational culture that shapes how the corporation addresses its relationships with law and regulation."[62]

Commentators who have addressed the emerging contours of the general counsel function have described its component duties in terms of functional categories.[63] The

---

[58] The situation regarding general counsel today is little different from that in 1985 when Abram and Antonia Chayes noted that the empirical basis for analyses of the role of in-house counsel amounted to "little better than informed speculation." Chayes & Chayes, *supra* note 22, at 299; *see also* DeMott, *supra* note 8, at 957 ("Scholars using sophisticated social science methodologies have yet to investigate the environment and performance of general counsel to the extent that social scientists have explored law firms and relationships between clients and external counsel."). The ACC has perhaps the best compilation of information on the general counsel function in its "Virtual Library," which is available to members and with permission through the ACC website, http://www.acc.com.

[59] *See, e.g.*, Chayes & Chayes, *supra* note 22, at 281-83; DeMott, *supra* note 8, at 960; Liggio, *The Changing Role of Corporate Counsel*, *supra* note 8, at 1209.

[60] Chayes & Chayes, *supra* note 22, at 298.

[61] DeMott, *supra* note 8, at 955 (pointing out that general counsel's roles are "complex and interlinked").

[62] *Id.* at 955-56. Professor DeMott also notes, however, that "[w]hile a lawyer who serves as general counsel of a large corporation holds the clearly defined power associated with a hierarchical position in a large bureaucratic organization, the position itself is ambiguous in many ways that may prove troubling." *Id.* at 957; *see, e.g.*, Hazard, *Ethical Dilemmas*, *supra* note 8, at 1012 (noting that "clarity of the role does not necessarily imply clarity in ethical responsibilities"). Professor DeMott suggests that the tensions inherent in the general counsel position are often difficult to resolve, particularly when ethical demands require a general counsel to maintain professional independence from the entity he or she serves. *See id.* at 981; *see also, e.g.*, Sara A. Biro, Martine Petetin & Anthony E. Wales, *Identity Crisis: Managing a Legal vs. Business Role*, ACC EUROPE, 2005, at 10, *available at* http://www.acca.com/resource/index.php?key=7214 (noting that "[a] modern in-house lawyer expects to cope with paradoxes, inconsistencies and changing scenarios arising in a business . . . and needs to wear a different hat at different times"); Veasey & Di Guglielmo, *supra* note 8, at 10 (discussing tensions inherent in general counsel's relationships with other corporate agents).

[63] *See, e.g.*, JULIE A. BELL ET AL., IN-HOUSE COUNSEL AS MULTI-DISCIPLINARIAN 4, *available at* www.acca.com/resource/v6922 (describing "[e]xpanding [r]ings of [r]esponsibility" ranging from traditional responsibilities to "the convergence of management of compliance, risk and legal affairs—the 'Chief Risk Officer'"); Daly, *supra* note 8, at 681(identifying typical roles as: barrister, solicitor, business advisor, and statesman); DeMott, *supra* note 8, at 957 (identifying four principal roles as: legal advisor, officer, administrator, and corporate agent); Veasey & Di Guglielmo, *supra* note 8, at 5 (discussing roles of "legal advisor," "corporate officer and member of senior executive team," "administrator of the in-house legal department," and "corporate agent in dealings with third parties, including outside counsel").

following discussion takes a slightly different tack. It begins by delineating "formal" and "informal" responsibilities and then breaks down these functions into component parts. The purpose is to illustrate both the wide variety of the roles of contemporary general counsel and the many stages on which they play them.[64] Both formal and informal roles are important. While the formal tasks constitute the official responsibilities of general counsel, the ways in which general counsel operate informally—i.e., behind the scenes—can exert a great deal of influence on the attitudes of managers and employees toward lawyers and legal obligations.

1. Formal Functions

For purposes of this discussion, "formal" describes the kinds of tasks one might expect to find articulated in a general counsel's job description, as well as other responsibilities typically associated with the position. Many aspects of a general counsel's work are those traditionally expected of lawyers. Others, described here as "quasi-legal" roles, encompass less traditional tasks—e.g., compliance monitoring. These functions are often assigned to or undertaken by general counsel in response to evolving demands generated by regulation, litigation, and other changes in the milieu in which corporations operate. Yet another type of formal function encompasses managerial duties and non-legal business responsibilities.

a. Traditional Lawyering Roles

i. Legal Advisor

Perhaps the most widely recognized and far-reaching duty of contemporary general counsel is to provide legal advice to officers, directors, and other constituents acting on behalf of entities. Typically, this advice spans a broad spectrum of issues ranging from internal matters such as corporate governance, to external affairs such as transactions, litigation, and regulatory issues. In providing advice to entities and their constituents, general counsel have an obligation to know the business of their client entities intimately.[65] General counsel are often the first lawyers to hear of matters requiring legal input and the last to sign off before proposed actions become a reality.[66] In providing advice to the client, a general counsel "must be a futurist, a seer . . . us[ing] . . . legal

---

[64] *See* Ass'n of Corporate Counsel, Chair's Forum: Wearing More Hats Than a Hydra Has Heads—In-House Practitioners in Today's Corporate Environment . . . Anticipating the Challenges and Meeting the Demands in Today's Corporate Practice, Oct. 2004, *available at* http://www.acca.com/resource/v5570 (describing in-house counsel as lawyers "wearing more hats than a hydra has heads").

[65] *See* Liggio, *The Changing Role of Corporate Counsel, supra* note 8, at 1208; Irma S. Russell, *Keeping the Wheels on the Wagon: Observations on Issues of Legal Ethics for Lawyers Representing Business Organizations*, 3 WYO. L. REV. 513, 517 (2003).

[66] This is particularly true for the many general counsel who serve on corporate management or executive committees. *See infra* Part I.C.l.c.iv. General counsel are ultimately responsible to corporate boards, but ordinarily their line reporting relationships are with CEOs or other senior corporate managers. *See*

foresight to discern trends in the law and to predict how those trends will impact the company's business over time."[67]

In the course of their advice work, general counsel necessarily develop direct working relationships with senior managers. The quality of these relationships almost certainly affects the influence a general counsel exerts over an entity and its business managers. At the same time, there is an inherent danger that relationships that become too close may compromise the ability of general counsel to give objective legal advice, particularly when the advice appears to raise barriers to the accomplishment of business objectives.[68] There is evidence, however, that business managers realize the importance of seeking out candid legal advice in the post-Sarbanes-Oxley environment. A number of businesses have hired former prosecutors and even judges for their top legal positions in efforts to achieve better legal compliance.[69]

Part of the complexity of the role of legal advisor arises out of the general counsel's obligation to provide advice to directors as well as to officers. Despite the trend toward retention of independent counsel to advise boards and board committees on particular matters,[70] the general counsel is still the primary provider of legal advice to corporate boards and board committees as well as to the CEO and other senior corporate officers. This dual reporting responsibility can create tensions in situations that require general counsel to advise against actions recommended by senior managers, or to report troublesome acts or omissions by officers. The general counsel's ultimate responsibility, however, is always to the client, and the highest authority capable of speaking on behalf of a corporate client is ordinarily its board of directors.[71]

One of the principal areas in which general counsel provide advice is the corporate governance arena. While they are not "gatekeepers" in the same sense as accountants who perform audits,[72] general counsel often have the practical ability to change an entity's

ASS'N OF CORPORATE COUNSEL, ROLE OF THE GENERAL COUNSEL 24 (2005), *available at* http://www.acca.com/resource/v6685; Hackett, supra note 46, at 614; Veasey & Di Guglielmo, supra note 8, at 10.

[67] Liggio, *The Changing Role of Corporate Counsel, supra* note 8, at 1208.

[68] *See infra* Part I.D.; Russell, *supra* note 65, at 517-18 (noting that inside counsel "should recognize the inherent tendency to identify with his corporate client and guard against loss of independence"); DeMott, *supra* note 8, at 967-68; Veasey & Di Guglielmo, *supra* note 8, at 8-11 (discussing lawyer independence and related tensions); Weaver, *supra* note 8, at 1034 (observing that "Corporate counsel often acknowledge the increased effectiveness that they enjoy when senior management believes that they are 'team players,'" but noting potential downsides to "team player" role).

[69] *See supra* note 55 and accompanying text.

[70] *See infra* Part III.A.

[71] *See* MODEL RULES OF PROF'L CONDUCT R. 1.13(b) (2003). From a structural standpoint, general counsel ordinarily report to their company's CEOs, but they necessarily have a parallel reporting obligation to the board of directors as the company's highest authority. *See* DeMott, *supra* note 8, at 34; Hackett, *supra* note 46, at 614; Veasey & Di Guglielmo, *supra* note 8, at 8-9.

[72] *See* CORPORATE RESPONSIBILITY TASK FORCE REPORT, *supra* note 6, at 22. *See generally* John C. Coffee, Jr., *The Attorney as Gatekeeper: An Agenda for the SE C,* 103 COLUM. L. REV. 1293 (2003); Veasey & Di Guglielmo, *supra* note 8, at 28-30.

direction by raising objections to a planned course of action.[73] Even in the pre-Enron era, it took an unusually determined group of directors to vote to consummate a major transaction or proceed on other key matters when confronted with directly contrary advice by a company's general counsel—particularly in situations in which the general counsel was instrumental in structuring a major transaction or obtaining the legal opinions necessary for it to proceed. As Delaware's former Chief Justice E. Norman Veasey notes, "The finest service that the corporate lawyer can perform for the board is to guide it toward the adoption and consistent implementation of best practices that consistently ensure loyalty, good faith and due care" on the part of all constituents.[74]

ii. Educator

Another critical task of general counsel is to educate corporate constituents.[75] General counsel serve as educators at the highest levels of their organizations and set in motion the programs designed to alert employees at all levels to their legal obligations.[76] Education of client constituents is a core element of proactive lawyering[77] in American corporations that "animates entire legal departments."[78] As the principal in-house legal advisor for the client, a general counsel has the responsibility to find ways to inform business managers and constituents throughout the company about what they can and cannot lawfully do as they pursue business objectives.[79] This function is particularly

---

[73] *See* Chayes & Chayes, *supra* note 22, at 281 (discussing general counsel's "right and responsibility to insist upon early legal involvement in major transactions that raise significant legal issues").

[74] E. Norman Veasey, *Separate and Continuing Counsel for Independent Directors: An Idea Whose Time Has Not Come as a General Practice*, 59 BUS. LAW. 1413, 1417 (2004).

[75] *See, e.g.*, Chayes & Chayes, *supra* note 22, at 284; Eveleth, *supra* note 11, at 18.

[76] The part lawyers play in educating constituents of client organizations is too seldom emphasized in law school courses.

[77] *See* Kim, *supra* note 34, at 202; *see also, e.g.*, Robert J. Haft & Michele H. Hudson, *Specific Due Diligence Standards Imposed by SEC and Professional Rules, in* ROBERT J. HAFT, DUE DILIGENCE § 6:15 (2006) (citing Pereira v. Cogan, 294 B.R. 449 (S.D.N.Y. 2003), *vacated,* Pereira v. Farace, 413 F.3d 330 (2d Cir. 2005) (discussing a holding where a corporate general counsel breached his duty to advise the board of its obligations with respect to management and evaluation of corporate officers)). Dean Daly locates the origins of proactive lawyering early in American history. She cites Alexis de Tocqueville's 1831 account of observations that lawyers were the "American aristocracy," "naturally called upon to occupy most of the public stations." Daly, *supra* note 8, at 1068 (quoting ALEXIS DE TOCQUEVILLE, DEMOCRACY IN AMERICA 357 (Henry Reeve trans., 1862)). Professors Abram and Antonia Chayes connected proactive lawyering with what they call "programmatic prevention," an approach they believed could be effectively undertaken only by in-house lawyers. *See* Chayes & Chayes, *supra* note 22, at 284.

[78] Daly, *supra* note 8, at 1071; *see also, e.g., id.* at 1080 (observing that in global entities it is critical for U.S. lawyers to educate foreign constituents on proactive legal practice); John H. McGuckin, Jr., *The Ethical Dilemma of the In-House Counsel,* 25 L.A. LAW. 31 (2002) (discussing the proactive role of in-house counsel versus reactive position of outside counsel).

[79] *See* Eveleth, *supra* note 11, at 18 (observing that, among other tasks, most general counsel "train and educate company employees on legal issues"); Kelley, *supra* note 8, at 1198 (suggesting that the general

important when major new legal obligations—e.g., those created by Sarbanes-Oxley[80] come into existence.

The educative responsibilities of general counsel, like those of all in-house lawyers, arise in a variety of settings. As Professor Hazard has observed, in-house lawyers are particularly well suited to acquire "back channel" information.[81] Access to such information not only creates unique challenges,[82] it offers important opportunities to engage proactively in identifying potential legal problems and educating constituents about relevant legal obligations. In these and other circumstances, general counsel and staff members aware of potential problems arising in the conduct of daily corporate business and alert to out-of-the-ordinary events can engage in the kind of on-the-spot client education that can prevent major legal problems. In 1985, Professors Abram and Antonia Chayes described educative efforts as components of "programmatic prevention."[83] Today, "programmatic prevention" efforts usually are encompassed in compliance programs, but client education remains an integral part of proactive lawyering in all areas.

iii. Transactions Facilitator

The daily life of a modern business includes mergers, acquisitions, sales of assets, spin-off businesses, joint ventures, acquisition and transfer of intellectual property, real estate deals, procurement of goods and services, and a host of other transactions. These transactions often entail complex business structures and highly sophisticated financing arrangements with extensive legal consequences.[84] "[A]s key advisers to senior management [general counsel] usually participate in the negotiation, structuring and documentation of the corporation's significant business transactions."[85] As chief legal officers, they are responsible for managing inside lawyers and outside counsel

---

counsel's role in the compliance area is primarily to educate corporate managers). During the last several years, many law firms, trade associations, and other groups have provided a great deal of information through internet sites. *See, e.g.*, Gibson, Dunn & Crutcher LLP, Gibson Dunn Sarbanes-Oxley Resource Center, http://www.gibsondunn.com/news/firm/detail/id/762/?pubItemId=6638 (last visited June 25, 2007); Jones Day, Jones Day Memorandum, The Sarbanes-Oxley Act of 2002, http://www.jonesday.com/pubs/pubs_detail.aspx?pubID=S2368 (last visited June 25, 2007). It is unclear, however, whether and to what extent non-lawyer corporate constituents read these kinds of materials.

[80] *See* Roger C. Cramton, George M. Cohen & Susan P. Koniak, *Legal and Ethical Duties of Lawyers After Sarbanes-Oxley*, 49 Vill. L. Rev. 725 (2004).

[81] *See* Hazard, *Ethical Dilemmas, supra* note 8, at 1019 ("To put the point bluntly, a lawyer in independent practice is sheltered from the informal, back-channel information that flows around the company water cooler."); Weaver, *supra* note 8, at 1028.

[82] *See* Hazard, *Ethical Dilemmas, supra* note 8, at 1018-19.

[83] Chayes & Chayes, *supra* note 22, at 284.

[84] For example, tax considerations, regulatory clearances, and governance issues are just a few of the myriad questions that often arise in the context of corporate transactions.

[85] Corporate Responsibility Task Force Report, *supra* note 6, at 20.

working on transactions.[86] It is also the general counsel's role to advise directors whether shareholder approval is needed and, if so, what mechanisms will suffice to obtain the requisite approval.

The existence of corporate law departments should promote early legal involvement in proposed transactions.[87] While most business lawyers undoubtedly would like to be involved in significant transactions from their inception, simply having lawyers on hand does not necessarily produce this result. Even within an entity, the extent to which lawyers have access to business planning information is a function of both corporate culture and the degree of trust managers have in the capabilities of their in-house lawyers. However, the ready availability of in-house counsel at least puts these lawyers in position to get involved at earlier stages of transactions than outside lawyers.

iv. Advocate

When it comes to advocacy work, general counsel captain both the defensive and offensive teams for their client entities and marshal the resources to respond to legal actions ranging from routine civil claims to criminal investigations. To do so effectively, a general counsel must make predictions about the outcome of litigation and regulatory proceedings in many different jurisdictions.[88] The general counsel must safeguard the entity's interests and take steps to ensure that its lawyers adopt coherent and consistent stances in tribunals across the nation and throughout the world,[89] while simultaneously managing the costs of advocacy responsibly from an institutional point of view. In these endeavors, a general counsel bears responsibility for overseeing the ethical propriety of litigation on the entity's behalf and for requiring responsible, professional behavior on the part of the lawyers who represent the company.[90]

A general counsel's advocacy function also includes the role of liaison with governmental authorities. Many routine interactions between entity and government personnel take place without lawyers,[91] but others—for example, in situations in which government approval may make or break a business activity—should involve counsel. Participation of counsel is critical in those situations in which government actions may result in significant sanctions, especially when criminal proceedings are a risk.[92]

---

[86] Chayes & Chayes, *supra* note 22, at 281, 289-90.

[87] *See id.* at 281; DeMott, *supra* note 8, at 960-61; Hazard, *Ethical Dilemmas*, *supra* note 8, at 1019 (discussing availability of "back-channel information" to in-house counsel).

[88] *See supra* text accompanying note 67.

[89] *See infra* note 126 and accompanying text. *See generally* John K. VILLA, CORPORATE COUNSEL GUIDELINES §§ 4:1-4:24 (2005); Chayes & Chayes, *supra* note 22, at 293-94.

[90] *See* MODEL RULES OF PROF'L CONDUCT R. 3.1-3.7, 8.4 (2003); *see also* ASS'N OF CORPORATE COUNSEL, *supra* note 66, at 15.

[91] For example, routine discussions with customs officials, ordinary inspections by regulatory agencies, and many interactions in the environmental area all take place without a lawyer present.

[92] *See* Veasey & Di Guglielmo, *supra* note 8, at 6-7 (noting the government affairs role of some general counsel). *Cf.* Evan A. Davis, *The Meaning of Professional Independence*, 103 COLUM. L. REV. 1281, 1281

v. Investigator

The valiant prosecutors and intrepid defense attorneys of novels, television, and the silver screen often succeed because of their uncanny ability to unearth the critical facts that save the day and ensure that justice is done. While the reality may be far less glamorous, finding and sorting out the relevant facts is a key ingredient of all legal representation. When suspicions of significant problems with potentially serious legal consequences arise within organizations it is often the general counsel who persuades corporate constituents of the need to pursue the matter and initiates an internal investigation. The general counsel determines whether the inquiry will be handled in-house or by an outside law firm, a decision that is far more nuanced than is often appreciated. Key factors include ability to access information, an understanding of its significance in the context of the corporation's business and operations, and preservation of attorney-client privilege and work product protections. Even choosing among outside law firms requires thoughtful consideration. Thorough investigation and candid advice are essential, but some investigators pursue their charges so aggressively that they are more likely to destroy a company than cure its ills.[93] It is ordinarily the role of the general counsel to strike the necessary balance.

When lawyers conduct internal investigations for the purpose of providing legal advice and preparing for anticipated litigation, corporations and other entities have an opportunity to invoke attorney-client privilege and work product protections to safeguard the confidentiality of investigative findings.[94] The United States Supreme Court confirmed the availability of these protections to corporations in *Upjohn Co. v. United States*[95] in adjudicating a dispute over the confidentiality of the fruits of an

---

(2003) (suggesting that "the ethical rules for protecting the professional independence of the bar need to take into account the role of the legal profession as an independent bulwark between individuals or organizations and the political branches of government").

[93] *See* Letter from Board of Directors of the American Corporate Counsel Association to Johnathan G. Katz, Secretary, SEC (Apr. 7, 2003), *available at* www.sec.gov/rules/proposed/s74502/acca040703.htm. As the ACC has pointed out:

> CLOs [chief legal officers] regularly voice their concern that outside counsel hired by [a board committee] might have little guidance or commitment to working sensitively and productively with managers to uncover and remedy allegations. Such firms can mistakenly believe that their retention by a group of directors indicates a presumed hostility to any cooperation with or presumption of good faith behavior on the part of management. In the pursuit of their mission to uncover evidence of the reported allegations, they may employ scorched-earth investigation tactics that could unnecessarily degrade employee morale and dignity, inappropriately disrupt the business of the organization, or permanently burn bridges to any future relationship between "surviving" managers and lawyers who seek to work cooperatively with them.

Id.; *see also* Veasey & Di Guglielmo, *supra* note 8, at 31 (noting potential risks of initiating internal investigations).

[94] See Thomas G. Bost, *Corporate Lawyers After the Big Quake: The Conceptual Fault Line in the Professional Duty of Confidentiality*, 19 GEO. J. LEGAL ETHICS 1089, 1118 (2006); Duggin, *supra* note 30, at 892-93 and sources cited therein.

[95] 449 U.S. 383 (1981).

internal investigation of potential Foreign Corrupt Practices Act[96] violations by Upjohn's general counsel.[97] Since then, the subject of corporate attorney-client and work product protections has sparked tremendous controversy, particularly in the context of federal prosecution of business entities and other organizations.[98] Nevertheless, because of the special skills lawyers bring to bear in investigating potential legal violations and the concomitant availability of attorney-client and work product protections, the role of initiating and supervising internal investigations has become a recognized responsibility of general counsel.[99]

vi. Client Representative

In addition to doing the kinds of work lawyers find most familiar on behalf of corporations, general counsel often sit on the other side of the table as the embodiment of their organizational client. The role of client is not a part lawyers generally play. Like any other role it presents a unique set of challenges. As the client representative, a general counsel must focus on business objectives and other organizational goals,

---

[96] Foreign Corrupt Practices Act of 1977, Pub. L. No. 95-213, 91 Stat. 1494 (1977).

[97] Upjohn, 449 U.S. at 386.

[98] *See generally* Sarah Helene Duggin, *The Impact of the War Over the Attorney-Client Privilege on the Business of Health Care*, 22 J. CONTEMP. HEALTH L. & POL'Y 301, 304-27 (2006) (recounting struggle between the United States Department of Justice (U.S.D.O.J.) and other federal agencies with the ABA and an alliance of business associations and civil right groups over government insistence on corporate waiver of attorney-client and work product protections, because of the impact on individuals as well as entities). There were extensive ongoing protests over the policy embodied first in a memorandum from Deputy Attorney General Eric Holder. Memorandum from Eric H. Holder, Jr., Deputy Attorney General on Bringing Criminal Charges Against Corporations (June 16, 1999), *available at* http://www.usdoj.gov/criminal/fraud/docs/reports/1999/chargingcorps.html. The policy was later incorporated and made mandatory in a memorandum from Deputy Attorney General Larry Thompson. Memorandum from Deputy Attorney General Larry D. Thompson to Heads of Department Components, United States Attorneys on Principles of Federal Prosecution of Business Organizations (Jan. 20, 2003), *available at* http://www.usdoj.gov/dag/cftf/corporate_guidelines.htm. The U.S.D.O.J. retreated to some extent with respect to the Department's position on corporate waiver of these protections in response to the protests, Congressional inquiries, and a federal court decision excoriating the Department for its role in causing accounting powerhouse KPMG, Inc. to decline to advance counsel fees to executives unless they cooperated with prosecutors in a government investigation of the company. United States v. Stein, 435 F. Supp. 2d 330 (S.D.N.Y. 2006); *see also* Memorandum of Deputy Attorney General Paul J. McNulty to Heads of Department Components, United States Attorneys on Principles of Federal Prosecution of Business Organizations, Dec. 12, 2006, *available at* http://www.usdoj.gov/dag/speech/2006/mcnulty_memo.pdf. For discussion of the McNulty Memorandum and its impact, *see* Lisa Kern Griffin, *Compelled Cooperation and the New Corporate Criminal Procedure*, 82 N.Y.U. L. REV. 311, 312-28 (2007); Veasey & Di Guglielmo, *supra* note 8, at 32-33; John K. Villa, *The McNulty Memorandum: A Reversal in Practice or in Name Only?*, 25 ACC DOCKET 90 (2007).

[99] However, when the conduct of the general counsel or other senior lawyers is at issue or when there is a concern that problems may be pervasive among senior managers, it is clearly appropriate to call in independent counsel reporting directly to the board or a board committee. *See* Veasey & Di Guglielmo, *supra* note 8, at 30-33.

manage the costs of outside legal services in relation to their benefits, and ensure that the many different individual lawyers and law firms who represent the corporate client utilize strategies that make sense in terms of overall client objectives rather than focusing solely on particular cases or transactions.[100]

b. Quasi-Legal Roles

In recent years many general counsel have taken on new formal responsibilities consonant with the evolution of the legal environment in which corporations and other entities operate.[101] These tasks require a combination of skills, including both legal acumen and managerial ability. Two significant examples—compliance and ethics roles—are discussed below.[102]

i. Compliance Officer

Law enforcement actions against corporations and other entities were infrequent prior to the last few decades of the twentieth century. The incidents that led to the passage of the Foreign Corrupt Practices Act,[103] the Watergate scandal,[104] and a host of other events that took place during the tumultuous years of the late 1960s and 1970s, however, focused attention on the power of major corporations and the far-reaching consequences of corporate wrongdoing.[105] In response, the SEC and the IRS, followed by the Department of Justice and several other federal agencies, began to pursue civil sanctions against corporations and other entities.[106] Criminal prosecutions soon followed.[107] In 1991, the United States Sentencing Commission's publication of its

---

[100] Coordination is critical to large corporations, because it is all too easy for lawyers focused on success in discrete matters to pursue a strategy or take a position in litigation that may foreclose a different path in a more important matter. *See infra* note 126 and accompanying text.

[101] *See, e.g.*, Bell et al., *supra* note 63, at 4; DeMott, *supra* note 8, at 961-62.

[102] It is important to emphasize that ethical obligations apply to lawyers engaged in business activities and other extra-legal duties related to their representation of the client. *See* Villa, *supra* note 89, at § 3:3 ("To be safe, a lawyer who provides any legal services to the corporate client must assume that all of his conduct is governed by the ethical rules [of the legal profession]."). *See generally* GEOFFREY HAZARD, JR. & WILLIAM HODES, THE LAW OF LAWYERING §§ 17.7, 17.23, 17.24 (3d ed. 2001) (noting that in-house counsel are co-agents with entity managers and employees and "that in some situations an entity lawyer may have to exercise independent professional judgment to determine what is truly in the client's best interest—setting aside, if need be, the views of other highly placed agents"). For additional discussion of this point from the perspective of general counsel, *see* ASS'N OF CORPORATE COUNSEL, *supra* note 66, at 14-15.

[103] Foreign Corrupt Practices Act of 1977, Pub. L. No. 95-213, 91 Stat. 1494 (1977).

[104] *See* WILLIAM MEADE FLETCHER ET AL., FLETCHER CYCLOPEDIA OF THE LAW OF CORPORATIONS § 5.12 (2006) (discussing the impact of the Watergate scandal on public corporations).

[105] *See generally* Duggin, *supra* note 30, at 871-74.

[106] *Id.* at 871-73.

[107] *Id.* at 874-75.

Organizational Guidelines[108] made it quite clear that corporations and other entities were likely to be scrutinized by law enforcement officials and subjected to criminal sanctions where appropriate.[109]

As noted earlier,[110] a general counsel's responsibility for initiating compliance efforts and assisting corporations to develop resources and implement programs is an essential part of what Professors Abram and Antonia Chayes recognized in 1985 as "programmatic prevention."[111] A number of factors have contributed to the prominent place corporate compliance programs now occupy in corporate practice. First and foremost, of course, is the opportunity to deter and, if deterrence fails, discover wrongdoing.[112] Perhaps even more significant is the impact of the dramatic increase in civil enforcement actions and criminal prosecutions against corporations and their constituents that began in the late 1970s, and the importance of institutional compliance programs in persuading law enforcement officials not to prosecute, as well as the potential mitigating impact pursuant to the Organizational Guidelines.[113]

In many corporations, the general counsel serves as chief compliance officer.[114] In others, the compliance function is separate from the law department, and the role of the general counsel ranges from providing legal advice pertaining to compliance functions to hiring compliance officers and briefing senior managers and directors on compliance matters.[115] Whether or not the formal corporate compliance function reports directly to the general counsel,[116] the general counsel and other in-house lawyers play a major role in ensuring legal compliance throughout the entity. The "conception of the lawyer as a promoter of corporate compliance with law emanates from the basic values of the legal profession,"[117] and it is a vital responsibility of contemporary general counsel.

---

[108] U.S. SENTENCING GUIDELINES MANUAL CH. 8 (2007).

[109] The number of corporations prosecuted by federal authorities increased dramatically during the 1980s, see Mark A. Cohen, *Corporate Crime and Punishment: An Update on Sentencing Practice in the Federal Courts*, 1988-90, 71 B.U. L. REV. 247, 252 & n.12 (1991), and continued to increase steadily throughout the 1990s. U.S. SENTENCING COMMISSION, 2000 ANNUAL REPORT 45 (2000), *available at* http://www.ussc.gov/ANNRPT/2000/ar00toc.htm.

[110] *See supra* text accompanying note 83.

[111] Chayes & Chayes, *supra* note 22, at 284-89; *see also, e.g.*, Gruner, *supra* note 8, at 1124-26, 1142-46, 1157-58 (discussing "crime prevention" and information components of compliance function).

[112] *See* Gruner, *supra* note 8, at 1143-62.

[113] *See* U.S. SENTENCING GUIDELINES MANUAL, *supra* note 108, at § 8C2.5(g); *see also* Griffin, *supra* note 98, at 317-20; Gruner, *supra* note 8, at 1143-62.

[114] A 2003 ACC survey reflected that a significant percentage of general counsel oversee risk management and compliance functions. *See* ASS'N OF CORPORATE COUNSEL, *supra* note 66, at 26; *see also* Veasey & Di Guglielmo, *supra* note 8, at 6.

[115] *See id.*

[116] There are a number of reasons to separate the two functions. The most compelling is that, depending on how they are structured, attorney-client and work product protections often do not apply in the context of compliance programs.

[117] CORPORATE RESPONSIBILITY TASK FORCE REPORT, *supra* note 6, at 21.

ii. Corporate Ethics Officer

Many general counsel also have primary responsibility for resolving ethics issues relevant to corporate policies that go beyond legal compliance. For example, general counsel are often key contributors to the development of business conduct codes and other corporate ethics standards—e.g., rules governing the acceptance of gifts and gratuities or use of corporate vehicles and other resources.[118] Codes of conduct and business ethics policies require proactive education if they are to be effective. Employees must be informed about ethical requirements relevant to their jobs, including internal grievance procedures, limitations on personal matters such as financial investments, nepotism issues, and rules pertaining to interactions with people and entities outside the company.[119] In many corporations, the general counsel sets up a process for responding to ethics inquiries; acts as the ultimate arbiter of conflict-of-interest matters, questions involving business, and other ethics issues; and establishes procedures for notifying the company of ethics violations and disciplining errant constituents. Even when another official performs this function with respect to employees, because of their stature within the entity general counsel often handle issues pertaining to directors and senior managers.

c. Management and Other Extra-Legal Business Roles

The third category of duties often formally assigned to general counsel encompasses managerial responsibilities and extra-legal business roles. Examples of these kinds of functions are described below.

i. Manager of Law Department and Related Functions

Whatever other duties they have, virtually all general counsel serve as senior managers of corporate legal departments. They supervise financial and administrative functions and, most importantly, oversee the hiring and training of the in-house legal staff. It is the general counsel who sets the tone for the law department and who is ultimately responsible for setting the standards that govern how in-house lawyers represent the corporate client and deal with its constituents. As a department manager, the general counsel often has considerable leeway in establishing compensation and benefit packages for subordinate lawyers. He or she is the principal advocate for lawyers and other law department personnel within the corporation, and his or her willingness to support staff inevitably has a major impact on the respect other constituents accord to members of the law department and the extent to which they value their input. From an ethical

---

[118] *See* Gruner, *supra* note 8, at 1156-58; Veasey & Di Guglielmo, *supra* note 8, at 7 & n.14 (citing Daly, *supra* note 8, at 1084).

[119] *See* Gruner, *supra* note 8, at 1152-59 (exploring compliance function of general counsel); REGAN, *supra* note 46, at 934 (discussing corporate internalization of dispute resolution processes in areas such as sexual harassment); Veasey & Di Guglielmo, *supra* note 8, at 7 & n.14 (discussing role of general counsel as ethicist).

standpoint, the general counsel is a supervisory attorney within the meaning of the SEC's Part 205 rules and Model Rule 5.1.[120] As Professor Hazard noted a decade ago, a general counsel can profoundly affect the attitudes of in-house counsel by being open to talking with subordinates about "ethically troublesome situations . . . [and] taking responsibility for resolving" them.[121]

Depending on the structure of the particular organization, the functions a general counsel supervises may include document retention, equal employment opportunity, disciplinary proceedings, intellectual property management, risk management, and a host of other matters related to quasi-legal organizational functions. In many organizations the role of the law department is to oversee the provision of advice in these areas, but in other entities these functions report directly to the general counsel.[122] In recent years, the position of law department manager also has included encouraging and supporting pro bono work and bar activities by corporate counsel.[123]

ii. Manager of Outside Legal Resources

As the organization's chief legal officer, the general counsel oversees the retention and management of the outside lawyers and law firms engaged to represent the entity or to assist in legal matters. The general counsel has a great deal to do with setting the

---

[120] *See* 17 C.F.R. § 205.4 (2003); MODEL RULES PROF'L CONDUCT R. 1.0(c) & 5.1 (2003). Rule 1.0(c) defines "firm" or "law firm" to include "lawyers employed in the legal department of a corporation or other organization." *Id.* Rule 5.1 provides:

> (a) A partner in a law firm, and a lawyer who individually or together with other lawyers possesses comparable managerial authority in a law firm, shall make reasonable efforts to ensure that the firm has in effect measures giving reasonable assurance that all lawyers in the firm conform to the Rules of Professional Conduct.
>
> (b) A lawyer having direct supervisory authority over another lawyer shall make reasonable efforts to ensure that the other lawyer conforms to the Rules of Professional Conduct.
>
> (c) A lawyer shall be responsible for another lawyer's violation of the Rules of Professional Conduct if:
>
> (1) he orders or, with knowledge of the specific conduct, ratifies the conduct involved; or
>
> (2) the lawyer is a partner or has comparable managerial authority in the law firm in which the other lawyer practices, or has direct supervisory authority over the other lawyer, and knows of the conduct at a time when its consequences can be avoided or mitigated but fails to take reasonable remedial action.

Id.

[121] Hazard, *Ethical Dilemmas, supra* note 8, at 1022.

[122] According to a recent survey, employment/labor functions reported to 51.30% of general counsel surveyed, trademark and copyright functions to 75.4%, and patent functions to 42.1%. *See* ASS'N OF CORPORATE COUNSEL, *supra* note 66, at 26 (citing ALTMAN WEIL, ASS'N OF CORPORATE COUNSEL, 2003 SURVEY OF LAW DEPARTMENT BENCHMARKS SURVEY (2003)). Risk management functions reported to 33.7% of those surveyed. *Id.; see also* Veasey & Di Guglielmo, supra note 8, at 6-7 (describing roles of general counsel and noting that a number of general counsel also act as government affairs officers for their companies).

[123] *See* Hackett, *supra* note 46, at 616-17; *see also* Liggio, *The Changing Role of Corporate Counsel, supra* note 8, at 1211-13 (discussing the role of general counsel in encouraging lawyers to engage in bar activities).

tone for outside counsel relationships.[124] General counsel establish policies and practices that directly impact the terms and conditions of engagements, interactions with in-house lawyers and client constituents, billing practices, and many other aspects of the relationship of outside counsel to the client entity and its constituents.[125] These policy-making and oversight functions are particularly important in an era when few law firm lawyers are intimately familiar with client corporations. As Professor DeMott observes, "[T]he diffusion of corporate work among multiple law firms limits the breadth of any one firm's knowledge of the client, empowering general counsel in dealings with firms but reducing the capacity of any one firm to bring judgment to bear when more comprehensive insight into the corporation may be desirable."[126]

iii. Corporate Officer

Many, perhaps most, general counsel are corporate officers. Titles such as "vice president and general counsel" or "vice president, legal affairs" are common. A high percentage of general counsel also hold the office of corporate secretary.[127] As vice presidents and secretaries, in addition to their professional obligations, general counsel owe fiduciary allegiance to the corporation as officers.[128] In the performance of their duties, however, they may well be held to the ethical standards of conduct applicable to lawyers.[129]

iv. Management Committee Member

General counsel routinely sit on corporate management or executive committees. In this capacity, they are part of an elite group whose members guide both significant day-to-day management decisions and long-range planning. General counsel who function in this capacity have opportunities to learn about the operational issues and financial questions critical to client corporations. They also have the stature to gain access to the Chief Executive Officer (CEO), Chief Financial Officer (CFO) and other members of a company's senior management team. Consequently, this role offers the opportunity to influence significant corporate decisions as they are formulated and implemented.

---

[124] DeMott, *supra* note 8, at 970. Conversely, a general counsel's decision to retain or terminate an outside lawyer as counsel for an important, ongoing engagement may make or break a lawyer's career.

[125] ASS'N OF CORPORATE COUNSEL, *supra* note 66, at 32-34.

[126] DeMott, *supra* note 8, at 972; *see also* Chayes & Chayes, *supra* note 22, at 294; Eveleth, *supra* note 11, at 20; *supra* note 100. Depending on one's perspective, the net result of such changes may or may not be of overall benefit to the corporate client. *See, e.g.*, REGAN, *supra* note 46, at 933-36.

[127] One recent survey reported that 80.80% of general counsel also serve as corporate secretaries. *See* ASS'N OF CORPORATE COUNSEL, *supra* note 66, at 26 (citing ALTMAN WEIL, ASSOC. OF CORPORATE COUNSEL, 2003 SURVEY OF LAW DEPARTMENT BENCHMARKS SURVEY (2003)); *see also* Veasey & Di Guglielmo, *supra* note 8, at 8, 18 (discussing dual roles as well as the need for coordination between general counsel and secretary in companies in which different individuals perform these functions).

[128] *See, e.g.*, MODEL BUS. CORP. CODE § 8.42 (2005).

[129] *See supra* note 102.

v. Strategic Planner

For public corporations the strategic planning process necessarily involves consideration of legal issues.[130] Corporate initiatives may rise or fall on legal questions, and profits may depend heavily on tax consequences and other legal aspects of particular ventures or financing structures. As Professor Irma Russell notes, "[G]oal-setting and the evaluation of goals in light of legal consequences . . . [is an] integral part" of the strategic planning process for major corporations.[131] Both legal feasibility and risk levels are critical factors in the calculus of whether or not to proceed with new projects or redesign existing programs.[132] Involvement in the strategic planning process therefore affords general counsel and the in-house lawyers they supervise a chance to help shape business initiatives to meet legal requirements.

vi. Director

Some general counsel serve as corporate directors for the entities that employ them.[133] Service as a director of a client corporation, however, is "[a]mong the most controversial of the legal/business activities that U.S. lawyers undertake"[134] because lawyer-directors must navigate an ethical minefield.[135] A general counsel can bring a great deal of insight to a corporate board as a result of his or her intimate familiarity with the organization and sensitivity to the legal ramifications of business matters. At the same time, a general counsel who serves as a director risks losing the independent judgment that makes counsel valuable to the entity and becoming entangled in conflicts between the role of legal advisor and corporate decision maker.[136] The ability of the board to invoke the attorney-client privilege in seeking legal advice from the general counsel is also imperiled when the general counsel is a director.[137] In a 1998 formal opinion pertaining to the

---

[130] *See* Chayes & Chayes, *supra* note 22, at 282 (discussing formal participation of counsel in strategic planning); Liggio, *The Changing Role of Corporate Counsel, supra* note 8, at 1209-10; Russell, *supra* note 65, at 521-23.

[131] Russell, *supra* note 65, at 522.

[132] Liggio, *The Changing Role of Corporate Counsel, supra* note 8, at 1209 (discussing the role of general counsel in the corporate planning process).

[133] *See* ABA Comm. on Ethics & Prof. Responsibility, Formal Op. 98-410 (1998); ASSOC. OF CORPORATE COUNSEL, *supra* note 66, at 15; Villa, supra note 89, at § 3.32; Kim, supra note 34, at 182.

[134] Daly, *supra* note 8, at 1097.

[135] For a comprehensive analysis of the risks and benefits of lawyers' dual service as counsel and board members, *see* Kim, *supra* note 34. Professor Kim concludes that service as both counsel and director is risky because "[l]awyers who attempt to fill both roles simultaneously risk a loss of professional independence that can impair their ability to perform either role well." *Id.* at 260; *see also, e.g.*, ASS'N OF CORPORATE COUNSEL, *supra* note 66, at 15; Villa, *supra* note 89, at §§ 3:32, 6:23; Terrell, *supra* note 8, at 1006-07 (identifying ethical issues attendant upon a general counsel's service on his or her employer's board); Veasey & Di Guglielmo, *supra* note 8, at 15-17.

[136] *See* Kim, *supra* note 34, at 221-45.

[137] *Id.* at 239-42.

dual role of counsel and director, the ABA declined to prohibit lawyers from serving on the boards of client corporations.[138] The opinion, however, cautioned of the hazards of this role and the potential need to resign from the board and/or withdraw from the representation in the event of a conflict of interest.[139] General counsel are especially vulnerable to these ethical traps because their primary responsibility is to serve as their corporations' chief legal officers.

2. *Informal Roles of General Counsel*

One of the reasons that general counsel can be so influential in organizations is that, in addition to fulfilling their formal or official duties, they frequently play a variety of informal parts that have a less visible but sometimes even more powerful impact on client corporations and the way constituents view the corporation's lawyers. The following discussion focuses on these kinds of informal roles—those that do not appear in any job description but often comprise an important part of what a general counsel does and account for much of his or her influence.

a. Legal Services Marketer

As Carl Liggio, former General Counsel of Ernst & Young and a founder of the Association of Corporate Counsel, has observed, "Within the corporate hierarchy, the legal department is a cost center, not a profit center."[140] This is one reason lawyers are not always popular with corporate constituents. Many business managers—even those who hold to the highest standards of personal and corporate integrity—resent the cost of legal services and too often perceive lawyers as creators of obstacles rather than facilitators of business objectives.[141] Yet lawyers cannot successfully represent clients who do not seek their services and willingly confide in them. Consequently, to function effectively within a corporate structure, general counsel must persuade senior managers and others within their organizations that it makes sense to seek legal services early and often.[142] This task has evolved into an internal marketing function

---

[138] ABA Comm. on Ethics & Prof. Responsibility, Formal Op. 98-410 (1998).

[139] *See id. But see* Hazard, *Three Afterthoughts*, *supra* note 8, at 1053 (reflecting on possible benefits of lawyers' service on client boards); Kim, *supra* note 34, at 204 (discussing the upside of lawyers' service as directors); Veasey & Di Guglielmo, *supra* note 8, at 15 & note 41-43 (noting that there are benefits as well as disadvantages to service on client boards).

[140] Liggio, *The Changing Role of Corporate Counsel*, *supra* n. 8, at 1219.

[141] *See id.* (explaining that management often looks to corporate counsel to draw the difficult lines necessary to cut costs without jeopardizing "either the quality of service or the outcome of legal issues").

[142] *See* Robert L. Nelson & Laura Beth Nielsen *Cops, Counsel, and Entrepreneurs: Constructing the Role of Inside Counsel in Large Corporations,* 34 LAW & SOC. REV. 457, 477 (2000) (reporting that 43% of lawyers in a survey of forty-two attorneys "indicated that they market the law and lawyers to others in the corporation"); *see also* Veasey & Di Guglielmo, *supra* note 8, at 28-30 (discussing importance of general counsel as "persuasive counselor").

that necessitates both educating managers as to why early legal input makes sense and demonstrating the ability of lawyers to "add value" in business contexts.[143] While the sobering revelations of the corporate debacles of recent years should heighten awareness of the need for good legal counsel in business matters, internal marketing of legal services still remains an important component of in-house lawyers' responsibility, particularly for general counsel.

b. Ad Hoc Planning Advisor

Prior to World War II, before a Masters in Business Administration from an elite business school had become an important qualification for senior managers of major corporations, many organizations valued a legal education as a credential for business leaders.[144] Presumably this was because of respect for the rigorous approach to thinking that law schools instilled in their students and a belief that those capable of disciplined, logical analysis were well equipped to make business decisions.[145] Unfortunately, as noted earlier, during the middle decades of the last century the general view of the acumen and value of in-house lawyers diminished considerably.[146] In recent years, however, in-house lawyers have emerged as influential legal advisors to corporations and their constituents.

Today, general counsel and many other in-house lawyers, like their predecessors in the early part of the last century,[147] have become important resources for informal, as well as formal, corporate planning.[148] As in-house lawyers have earned respect for their ability to offer perceptive insights on a variety of subjects important to the business planning process, constituents have come to consult their in-house lawyers early in the course of corporate initiatives, often seeking their advice before a new project is formally proposed.[149] The exchanges that make these kinds of preliminary contacts possible arise out of a shared working environment that involves contacts in company meetings and social events, as well as chance encounters "at the water cooler."[150]

c. Ethics Counselor

Whether or not a general counsel serves as the official ethics officer for his or her company, as in the informal planning context, general counsel often serve as trustworthy

---

[143] *See* Kim, *supra* note 34, at 199-200; Weaver, *supra* note 8, at 1027.

[144] *See* FRIEDMAN, *supra* note 14, at 165-70.

[145] See *id.*

[146] *See supra* Part I.A.

[147] See *id.*

[148] Chayes & Chayes, *supra* note 22, at 283.

[149] *See* Chayes & Chayes, *supra* note 22, at 283-84 (noting importance of corporate counsel's role in the informal planning process—"a noteworthy extension of the development of anticipatory law"—as a result of regular contact with senior business managers).

[150] *See* Hazard, *Ethical Dilemmas, supra* note 8, at 1017-18; Weaver, supra n. 8, at 1028.

advisors or "wise counselors"[151] when thorny issues arise. Many ethical dilemmas have legal ramifications, but, even in corporate settings, not all ethical issues involve legal questions.[152] It is not at all uncommon for others to turn to a general counsel seeking moral or ethical guidance because of respect for his or her personal integrity and ability to think clearly. As Professor Russell observes, "Lawyers are routinely called upon to exercise moral judgment in advising clients. In the corporate setting, lawyers often become trusted advisers not only for their legal knowledge, but also for the practical wisdom they offer."[153]

d. Crisis Manager

From industrial accidents to security breaches, from insider trading to workplace violence, every organization has crises that range along a continuum from minor incidents to financial debacles to terrible human tragedy. Crises inevitably generate unwelcome consequences for organizations and the individuals connected with them. For public companies, media attention frequently creates adverse publicity, and adverse publicity often impacts stock prices. Depending on the nature of the underlying event, government investigators may arrive before it is even possible to sort out exactly what has happened. Customers and employees may require immediate assistance, and psychological, as well as physical, needs must be addressed. At times, human lives may be in danger, and the very survival of the entity may be at issue.

In crisis situations, while operations managers deal with physical events and financial personnel assess the extent of monetary harm, immediate steps must be taken to obtain accurate information, inform directors, employees, and other key stakeholders, coordinate media statements, deal with government authorities, investigate what happened, and take steps to mitigate damage to the entity's interests. Each of these steps has significant legal ramifications. In light of their legal expertise and leadership skills, general counsel are usually found in the midst of the fray, identifying what must be done and marshalling the resources necessary to do it.[154]

---

151 *See* Bruce A. Green, *Thoughts About Corporate Lawyers After Reading the Cigarette Papers: Has the "Wise Counselor" Given Way to the "Hired Gun"?*, 51 DEPAUL L. REV. 407, 407 & note 1 (citing Robert A. Kagan & Robert Eli Rosen, *On the Social Significance of Large Law Firm Practice*, 37 STAN. L. REV. 399, 410 (1985) (concerning the image of an "independent and influential counselor")).

152 *See* CORPORATE RESPONSIBILITY TASK FORCE REPORT, *supra* note 6, at 4 (noting that "the term 'corporate responsibility' also embraces ethical behavior beyond that demanded by minimum legal requirements"); Harold Williams, *Corporate Accountability and the Lawyer's Role*, 34 BUS. LAW. 7, 16 (1978) (observing that "[w]e tend to resort to legality often as a guideline; in that sense, ethics is on the wane and the age of the legal technician is in full flower," but "in . . . practices in which our justification is that they are 'legal,' we are in a position we can no longer defend").

153 Russell, *supra* note 65, at 518-19. *But see* DeMott, *supra* note 8, at 981 (noting that a CEO could reasonably believe that an outside attorney might be better able to serve in this counseling capacity because of the perception that he or she would "bring[] a greater measure of detachment to the exercise of judgment").

154 "Counsel who are able to balance the company's legal needs with the company's public relations, business operations, and other needs, . . . are vital to success" in addressing a crisis. John R. Parker, Jr.,

e. Arbitrator

Yet another informal role that general counsel often play is that of arbitrator among corporate factions.[155] While many different people may serve in this capacity within an organization, lawyers often have a skill set uniquely suited to identifying the issues at the core of internecine disputes and negotiating workable resolutions. As chief legal officers, general counsel are ideally situated to appreciate the impact of factionalization and the damage that it can do, particularly when disgruntled employees fairly or unfairly believe that their rights have been violated or that another group within the entity has engaged in inappropriate behavior. As lawyers trained in the art of negotiation, general counsel also have skills that often prove invaluable in resolving intracorporate disputes among business units or administrative departments.

D. The Desirability of a Broad Vision of the Role of General Counsel

Given the multifaceted roles contemporary general counsel play and the influence they exert, how these lawyers approach their responsibilities is at least as important as what they do. Professor Ralph Cramton notes that "compliant lawyers" contributed significantly to the corporate debacles of the last several years.[156] As Professor Thomas Bost writes, many lawyers lost their way because of a "dual failure of vision."[157] They lost sight of the corporation itself as their true client and they saw "their role in unacceptably narrow terms—as mere implementers or transaction engineers, rather than as broadly-gauged corporate counselors or advisers."[158] One of the principal goals of Sarbanes-Oxley, the Model Rules amendments, and other regulatory changes is to hold corporate lawyers more accountable and to prompt them to take a broader view of their responsibilities. Lawyers willing to help dishonest managers clothe improper actions in legalistic trappings betray the very foundations of the profession; those who willingly turn their heads away from improprieties are little better. Lawyers need to be proactive ethical actors capable of looking beyond the cribbed confines of technical legal questions

---

Hard Tale of a Soft Drink: Dealing With a Corporate Crisis—It's the Real Thing, BUS. L. TODAY, Jul.-Aug. 2004, *available at* http://www.abanet.org/buslaw/blt/2004-07-08/parker.shtml. For discussion of the roles counsel play in crisis situations, *see*, for example, ASS'N OF CORPORATE COUNSEL, *supra* note 66, at 40 (citing seven sources therein); Jay G. Martin, *Developing an Effective Crisis Management Plan for a Corporation*, 65 TEX. BAR J. 233, 237-38 (2002); Harvey L. Pitt & Karl A. Groskaufmanis, *When Bad Things Happen to Good Companies: A Crisis Management Primer*, 15 CARDOZO L. REV. 951, 956 (1994).

[155] *See* Veasey & Di Guglielmo, *supra* note 8, at 6 (discussing general counsel as mediator) (citing Michele D. Beardslee, *If Multidisciplinary Partnerships Are Introduced Into the United States, What Could or Should Be the Role of General Counsel?*, 9 FORDHAM J. CORP. & FIN. L. 1, 24 (2003)).

[156] *See, e.g.*, Roger C. Cramton, *Enron and the Corporate Lawyer: A Primer on Legal and Ethical Issues*, 58 BUS. LAW. 143, 144 (2003) ("[C]ompliant lawyers as well as greedy executives, lazy directors and malleable accountants are necessary for large corporate frauds to come to life and persist long enough to cause major harm.").

[157] Bost, *supra* note 94, at 1090.

[158] *Id.*

and willing to respond assertively to safeguard the integrity of their client entities when they encounter evidence of wrongdoing.[159] This is particularly true for general counsel, for they are invariably on the front lines in the corporate legal arena.

Empirical studies of the way in which in-house counsel function are scarce; however studies specifically focused on general counsel and their impact on the entities they serve are virtually non-existent,[160] but recent studies of in-house counsel generally, as well as a recent analysis of the ethical behavior of lawyers in large law firms, offer useful, if troubling, insights. For example, an article published shortly before the collapse of Enron, Robert Nelson, and Laura Nielson suggested that "inside counsel construct different professional roles for themselves depending on the circumstances."[161] They observed a reluctance to constrain business managers, despite general acceptance of this function as a necessary element of counsel's role in safeguarding the corporation.[162] Nelson and Nielson also found substantial behavioral reciprocity—i.e., the ways in which business people treated lawyers influenced lawyers' behavior and the attitudes of lawyers affected the behavior of other corporate constituents.[163]

Professors Nelson and Nielson reported that in-house lawyers "were eager to be seen as part of the company, rather than as obstacles to getting things done."[164] They were willing to "discount[] their gatekeeping function in corporate affairs" to do so,[165] although they did not wish to give up their identity as lawyers or the professional status accompanying this identity.[166] More than a year before Enron collapsed, Professors Nelson and Nielson presciently suggested that in-house lawyers too often "are subservient to management prerogatives . . . despite profound changes in the structural position of inside counsel, in the presence of law in the corporate environment and the ideology of management itself."[167]

---

[159] *See infra* note 178 and accompanying text.

[160] Professors Hugh and Sally Gunz have conjectured that the scarcity of studies may be a function of the employment of different methodologies by researchers in the sociology of the professions, ethics, and law. As a result, researchers have worked in "silos" with "little cross-fertilization." Hugh P. Gunz & Sally P. Gunz, *The Lawyer's Response to Organizational Professional Conflict: An Empirical Study of the Ethical Decision Making of In-House Counsel*, 39 AM. BUS. L.J. 241, 244-45 (2002).

[161] Nelson & Nielson, *supra* note 142, at 457. Professors Nelson and Nielson focused on four dimensions: "(1) the gatekeeping functions of corporate counsel; (2) how lawyers and executives view each other within the corporation; (3) the blending of legal and business advice; and (4) the distinctiveness of lawyers' identities," utilizing three ideal types: "cops," "counsel" and "entrepreneurs." *Id.* at 460, 462. Nelson and Nielson found that in-house counsel most frequently play the role of "counsel," but that they also acted from time to time as "cops" policing other corporate constituents or as "entrepreneurs" emphasizing business values and seeking to use law aggressively to generate profits. *Id.* at 464-66.

[162] *Id.* at 471.

[163] *Id.* at 490.

[164] *Id.* at 477.

[165] *Id.*

[166] Nelson & Nielson, *supra* note 142, at 477-78.

[167] *Id.* at 486.

Given the similarities between sizable corporate law departments and large law firms,[168] an ongoing study by Professor Kimberly Kirkland also offers relevant insights. Utilizing the work of sociologist Robert Jackall on corporate bureaucracies, Professor Kirkland conducted an empirical analysis of choices of norms by associates in large law firms.[169] She concluded that, much like corporate managers, large-firm lawyers tend to follow highly mutable norms: "the appropriate norms . . . are those of the people the lawyer is working for . . . at the time."[170] Professor Kirkland found that the "habit of mind" of these lawyers "is to discern the norm[s] 'appropriate' to the situation, not to judge the merits of any given norm."[171] Like Professor Jackall, Professor Kirkland warns that "[a] habit of mind that focuses on identifying what norms others would follow rather than on the content of the norms themselves will 'convert principles into guidelines, ethics into etiquette, [and] values into tastes.'"[172]

In the absence of specific research pertaining to general counsel, the observations of Professors Nelson, Nielson, and Kirkland offer some of the best available information. They suggest that lawyers in organizations are heavily influenced by the demands and objectives of the powerful players in their environments. Consequently, despite their sense of professional independence, it is sometimes difficult for lawyers to separate themselves and their professional ethical obligations from organizational objectives and the norms elevated by the most powerful players in those organizations. After a time, the line between ethical and unethical behavior becomes harder to see and easier to cross. It seems likely that general counsel are subject to the same kinds of influences.[173]

However, there is also some good news. As Professors Abram and Antonia Chayes observed, "The General Counsel sits close to the top of the corporate hierarchy as

---

[168] *See generally id.* (analyzing the changes in law firms and in-house counsel).

[169] *See* Kimberly Kirkland, *Ethics in Large Law Firms: The Principle of Pragmatism*, 35 U. MEM. L. REV. 631, 635-36 (2005).

[170] *Id.* at 638. Professor Kirkland applies Robert Jackall's approach to analyzing ethical decision by corporate managers in the context of ethical decision-making by lawyers employed as associates by large law firms. *Id.* at 635-36. She concludes that in large law firms, as in corporate settings, "morality becomes indistinguishable from the quest for one's own survival and advantage." *Id.* at 729 (quoting ROBERT JACKALL, MORAL MAZES: THE WORLD OF CORPORATE MANAGERS 204 (1988)).

[171] *Id.* at 638-39.

[172] *Id.* at 639 (quoting Jackall, *supra* note 170, at 204). Another study reported by Mark Suchman, although focused primarily on large-firm corporate litigators, noted that in-house counsel involved in the exercise exhibited only passing concern for legal norms of any kind and focused, instead, on the often challenging task of reconciling managerial ideals . . . with the vagaries of a court system that operates on starkly different principles. . . . [A]lthough they were often more willing than outside counsel to link ethics and morality, in-house counsel rarely framed this linkage as a question of their professional obligations as lawyers. Mark C. Suchman, *Working Without a Net: The Sociology of Legal Ethics in Corporate Litigation*, 67 FORDHAM L. REV. 837, 845 (1998) (emphasis added).

[173] The debate continues over whether in-house lawyers, including general counsel, are more likely to succumb to client pressures than outside counsel. *See, e.g.*, DeMott, *supra* note 8, at 967-68; Veasey & Di Guglielmo, *supra* note 8, at 11-13; *cf.* Hazard, Ethical Dilemmas, *supra* note 8, at 1019 (noting the possibility that constituents may retain outside counsel to provide advice on the basis of "selected facts").

a member of senior management."[174] Consequently, a general counsel should have the authority necessary to set high standards for the lawyers employed by his or her company. A strong general counsel who is a person of integrity is ideally situated to moderate the choice-of-norm phenomenon, create a positive role model, and require high ethical standards on the part of both the members of his or her department and the outside counsel the company retains. As Professor Timothy Terrell suggested several years before the most recent rash of corporate debacles,

> [w]hat every corporation needs is [a] sophisticated lawyer who respects not only the strong foundations of the law but the nature and significance of its constraints as well . . . . who can, in a very special . . . way, be trusted by everyone to bring a troublingly expansive sense of the law and our legal system . . . when corporate decisions are made.[175]

With this perspective in mind, the following discussion examines the role of general counsel pursuant to the professional conduct rules of the SEC's Part 205 and the amendments to Model Rule 1.13.

II. THE GENERAL COUNSEL AND THE TONE AT THE TOP IN THE POST-ENRON/SARBANES-OXLEY ERA

The events of the past several years have highlighted the importance of corporate general counsel with respect to legal compliance,[176] especially the role of the general counsel in responding appropriately to evidence of possible corporate wrongdoing.[177] A number of scholars and practitioners, including those who have served as in-house lawyers, would argue that corporate counsel have always had a responsibility to seek out and address entity failures to comply with the law.[178] It is also true, however, that earlier

---

[174] Chayes & Chayes, *supra* note 22, at 277; DeMott, *supra* note 8, at 964.

[175] Terrell, *supra* note 8, at 1009; *see also* Liggio, *A Look at the Role of Corporate Counsel, supra* note 8, at 630 (describing the "leader" model of general counsel); *see also, e.g., Face Value: Where's the Lawyer?, supra* note 9 (discussing former General Electric Co. general counsel Benjamin Heineman's ideal of general counsel as a "lawyer statesman").

[176] For discussion of the infamous corporate debacles at the beginning of the twenty-first century and their impact on lawyers, *see*, for example, Bost, *supra* note 94, at 1090; Cramton, Cohen & Koniak, *supra* note 80; Cramton, *supra* note 156; Lisa H. Nicholson, *Sarbox 307's Impact on Subordinate In-House Counsel: Between a Rock and a Hard Place,* 2004 MICH. ST. L. REV. 559 (2004).

[177] *See, e.g.*, Bost, *supra* note 94, at 1111; Cramton, *supra* note 156, at 186; DeMott, *supra* note 8, at 979.

[178] For example, in an article written several years before the Enron debacle and the subsequent enactment of Sarbanes-Oxley and the 2003 amendment to Model Rules 1.13 and 1.6, Professor Geoffrey Hazard stated:

> In a properly run law department, the general counsel is alert to back-channel information as well as to "official information" within the corporation. The general counsel knows that early interception of legally improper conduct is much easier than cleaning up a mess after the fact. The

incarnations of Model Rule 1.13 and state rules based on its provisions allowed leeway for corporate counsel to view their responsibilities much too narrowly, thereby closing their eyes to problems.[179] The amendments to Rule 1.13 and, for public companies, the SEC's Part 205 rules, impose specific requirements that make it very difficult for

---

> general counsel has made it clear, by deed as well as pronouncement, that his or her door is open for confidential discussion with any lawyer down the line who confronts an ethically troublesome situation. *The general counsel has also made it clear, by deed as well as pronouncement, that he or she will take to the CEO, or to the Board of [D]irectors if necessary, any matter requiring such a reference.* The general counsel must further make clear in the same way that, assuming the staff lawyers have been able to refer difficult problems to the head legal office, the incumbent in the office will take responsibility for resolving them. The general counsel knows that being open but tough-minded about ethical problems is much more effective than being sanctimonious.

Hazard, *Ethical Dilemmas, supra* note 8, at 1021-22 (emphasis added); *see also* Cramton, *supra* note 156, at 154-55 (suggesting that "[a]lthough the [pre-August 2003] Rule [did] not explicitly require an organization's lawyer to take a problem up the corporate ladder, that response [was] required in circumstances in which [the] action [was] the only one that [was] in the 'best interest of the organization"'). Professor Thomas Morgan stated:

> [S]ome critics of attorney conduct seem to assume that there was virtually no effective regulation of corporate attorneys prior to the federal Sarbanes-Oxley legislation. This is simply not true. . . . At least seven [of the Model Rules of Professional Conduct on which most state rules are based], taken individually and together, define what state law has understood to be a corporate attorney's duties in dealing with possible corporate crime or fraud.

The Role of Attorneys in Corporate Governance: Hearing Before the Subcommittee on Capital Markets, Insurance and Gov. Sponsored Enterprises, 108th Cong. 71-72 (2004) (statement of Professor Thomas D. Morgan). *But see* Bost, *supra* note 94, at 1089 ("[T]he past four years or so have witnessed a convulsion and consequent seismic shift in the roles, duties, expectations, and liabilities of corporate lawyers.").

[179] *See* Cramton, Cohen & Koniak, *supra* note 80, at 738 (discussing confusing language and structure of MRPC 1.13 prior to the August 2003 amendments); Cramton, *supra* note 156, at 145 (noting that as of 2002, ethical rules were "controverted, often ambiguous and provide[d] insufficient guidance to lawyers and inadequate protection to the public interest in preventing corporate frauds and illegalities."). As Professor Cramton has pointed out:

> The conduct of the inside and outside lawyers who represented Enron, Arthur Andersen, and the many financial institutions involved in the Enron scandal tell the same story that has been told to us by a long string of major financial frauds for fifty years: the professional ideal of "independent professional judgment" does not inform the behavior of some lawyers who represent large corporations in major transactions and high-stakes litigation. These lawyers take the position that they must do everything for the client that the client's managers want them to do, providing the conduct is permitted by law. The problem is that by constantly going to the edge of the law and taking a very permissive view of what the law permits, these lawyers gradually adopt a mindset that ignores and may eventually assist the client's managers in illegality that harms third persons and the client entity. These lawyers have confused the role of advocates in litigation or adversary negotiation with the need of corporate clients for independent, objective advice in the course of corporate decision-making. Current practices have resulted in a widespread problem, not just a failure of individual law firms.

Cramton, *supra* note 156, at 173 (citations omitted). *But see* Jill E. Fisch & Kenneth M. Rosen, *Is There a Role for Lawyers in Preventing Future Enrons?*, 48 VILL. L. REV. 1097, 1097 (2003) (concluding that the "Sarbanes-Oxley approach to corporate governance reform is flawed"); Thomas D. Morgan, *Sarbanes-*

lawyers who represent entities—particularly general counsel—to close their eyes and ears to problems.[180] Concomitant developments, such as the perception that corporate counsel are increasingly being named as defendants in civil enforcement proceedings, shareholder derivative actions, and even criminal prosecutions,[181] have also raised the stakes for the lawyers who hold these positions.

Since the dust began to settle in the aftermath of Enron's collapse, many corporate counsel have engaged in far-reaching efforts to establish internal controls designed to safeguard their clients both internally and externally.[182] Of course, Sarbanes-Oxley and SEC initiatives pursuant to the statute have provided powerful incentives for upgrading corporate integrity efforts. As the Association of Corporate Counsel's materials, trade publications, and other legal and general media articles reveal, compliance with Sarbanes-Oxley is a major concern for many corporate lawyers, especially general counsel.[183] A number of excellent scholarly articles and practical pieces have explored the nature and impact of the standards set forth in the SEC's Part 205 rules and the August 2003 amendments to Model Rules 1.13 and 1.6,[184] as well as the noisy withdrawal provisions

---

Oxley: A Complication, Not a Contribution, in the Effort to Improve Corporate Lawyers' Professional Conduct, 7 Geo. J. Legal Ethics 1, 2-11 (2003) (questioning the value of new ethics mandates).

[180] *See, e.g.*, Ass'n of Corporate Counsel, *supra* note 66, at 18-19 (noting "[e]xpanded ethics role of General Counsel under the Sarbanes-Oxley Act"); *After Sarbanes-Oxley: A Panel Discussion on Law and Legal Ethics in the Era of Corporate Scandal*, 17 Geo. J. Legal Ethics 67 (2003); Susan D. Carle et al., *The Evolving Legal and Ethical Role of the Corporate Attorney after the Sarbanes-Oxley Act of 2002, Panel Three: Ethical Dilemmas Associated with the Corporate Attorney's New Role*, 52 Am. U. L. Rev. 655 (2003); Karl A. Groskaufmanis, *Climbing "Up the Ladder": Corporate Counsel and the SEC's Reporting Requirement for Lawyers*, 89 Cornell L. Rev. 511 (2004); Morgan, *supra* note 179; Terry F. Moritz & Robert M. Oberlies, *Up the Ladder and Beyond: Attorney Conduct and Reporting Duties with Respect to Issuers, Auditors and the Commission under SEC Implementing Rules to the Sarbanes-Oxley Act of 2002*, 1402 PLI Corp 308 (2004).

[181] *See, e.g.*, Janet Langford Kelly, Susan R. Sneider & Kelly A. Fox, *The Relationship Between the Legal Department and the Corporation*, 1 Successful Partnering Between Inside and Outside Counsel § 16:36.3 (Feb. 2006) (describing general counsel as "the new white collar criminal"). For a detailed analysis of information available with respect to targeting of in-house counsel, *see* John K. Villa, SEC and Criminal Proceedings Against Inside Corporate Counsel (2005), *available at* http://www.acca.com/resource/v6063. *See also* DeMott, *supra* note 8, at 974-75 (discussing recent enforcement actions against general counsel and the specific predicaments of Franklin C. Brown, General Counsel of Rite Aid and James V. Derrick, Jr., General Counsel of Enron). A 2006 *Washington Post* article suggests, however, that "lawyers serving fraud-ridden companies have emerged relatively unscathed." Carrie Johnson, *Legal Penalties in Corporate Frauds Seldom Paid by Legal Advisers*, Wash. Post, Aug. 31, 2006, at D1.

[182] *See, e.g.*, Assoc. of Corporate Counsel, Emerging and Leading Practices in Sarbox 307 Up-the-Ladder Reporting and Attorney Professional Conduct Programs: What Companies and Law Firms Are Doing 1 (2003), *available at* http://www.acca.com/legres/corpresponsibility/attorney.php.

[183] *See, e.g., id.*

[184] *See, e.g.*, Carle et al., *supra* note 180; Cramton, Cohen & Koniak, *supra* note 80; Groskaufmanis, *supra* note 180; Morgan, *supra* note 180; Russell, *supra* note 65. For an earlier discussion of relevant issues, *see* Cramton, *supra* note 156. The SEC also received extensive commentary on its proposed Sarbanes-Oxley Rules that affords insights from a variety of perspectives. *See* SEC Final Rule: Implementation of Standards

the SEC proposed but never put into effect.[185] The following discussion highlights key points pertaining to the role of general counsel as chief legal officers.

In this context, it is important to realize that we are dealing not simply with professional ethics, but corporate governance issues as well. As the Report of the ABA Task Force on Corporate Governance emphasized, "Lawyers are and should be important participants in corporate governance and important contributors to corporate responsibility . . . . a prudent corporate governance program should call upon lawyers—notably the corporation's general counsel—to assist in the design and maintenance of the corporation's procedures for promoting legal compliance."[186] In a similar vein, in August 2003, the ABA House of Delegates resolved:

> Providing information and analysis necessary for [corporate] directors to discharge their oversight responsibilities, particularly as they relate to legal compliance matters, requires the active involvement of general counsel for the public corporation.[187]

The critical question is whether the applicable rules effectively empower general counsel to do what is asked of them.

A. The Role of the General Counsel Pursuant to SEC Provisions and the Model Rules

Following the Enron fiasco, there was a general consensus that some corporate lawyers were confused about the identity of their true client—the entity itself. In reality, of course, it simply may be that corporate lawyers were engaging in the kinds of choice-of-norm behavior described by Robert Jackall and Kimberly Kirland.[188] The SEC and the ABA have devoted a great deal of effort to devising ways to prod lawyers to report problems to corporate actors with the power to address and resolve them. General counsel—as chief legal officers—qualify as report recipients and are featured prominently in the SEC's Part 205 rules. The ABA Task Force on Corporate Responsibility, chaired by James Cheek of Tennessee, also discussed the role of general counsel, although the Model Rules amendments recommended by the Task Force and adopted

---

of Professional Conduct for Attorneys, Release Nos. 33-8185, 34-47276, IC-25919 (issued Jan. 29, 2003, effective Aug. 5, 2003) (reporting receipt of 167 timely comment letters).

[185] *See* Implementation of Standards of Professional Conduct for Attorneys, Securities Act Release, 67 Fed. Reg. 71670-71 (proposed Nov. 21, 2002), *available at* http://www.sec.gov/rules/proposed/33-8150.htm. In January 2003, the SEC proposed an alternative to the original noisy withdrawal provision that would have required issuers to inform the SEC of attorney withdrawals. *See* Implementation of Standards of Professional Conduct for Attorneys, Securities Act Release, 68 Fed. Reg. 6824 (proposed Jan. 29, 2003), *available at* http://www.sec.gov/rules/proposed/33-8186.htm.

[186] CORPORATE RESPONSIBILITY TASK FORCE REPORT, *supra* note 6, at 20-21 (emphasis added).

[187] AUGUST 2003 ABA RESOLUTIONS, *supra* note 5, at ¶ 4 (emphasis added).

[188] *See supra* Part III.B.

by the ABA House of Delegates do not specifically refer to general counsel or chief legal officers.[189] This section offers a brief overview of the Part 205 rules and Model Rule 1.13, as amended in August 2003, from the perspective of the general counsel.

1. General Counsel as Chief Legal Officers under the SEC's Part 205 Rules

The SEC's Part 205 rules apply to attorneys who represent registered issuers—i.e., publicly traded companies—and who are "appearing and practicing before the Commission."[190] The "appear or practice" language sweeps quite broadly, drawing in lawyers involved in many aspects of corporate representation, both in-house and outside.[191] Pursuant to the Part 205 rules, attorneys who appear or practice before the SEC, except those retained by chief legal officers or Qualified Legal Compliance Committees (QLCC) to investigate or assert a colorable defense to an alleged material violation,[192] must report evidence of material violations of law up the corporate ladder to the chief legal officer, or to both the chief legal officer and CEO, and the chief legal officer may in turn refer the report to a QLCC of the company's board of directors,[193] although relatively few entities have established QLCCs.[194] Thus, the reporting attorney must go through the general counsel—unless the attorney reasonably believes that a report to the chief legal officer or to the chief legal officer and CEO would be futile.[195] In that event, the attorney may report directly to the corporation's audit committee, another board committee comprised of independent directors, or to the full board if there is no committee of independent directors.[196]

As a chief legal officer, the general counsel of an issuer is deemed to be a supervisory attorney "appearing and practicing" before the SEC[197] with concomitant responsibility to make reasonable efforts to ensure that subordinate attorneys conform to applicable

---

[189] *See* Corporate RESPONSIBILITY TASK FORCE REPORT, *supra* note 6, at 34-40.

[190] 17 C.F.R. § 205.1 (2003)

[191] *See id.* at § 205.2(a); *see also* Implementation of Standards of Professional Conduct for Attorneys, Securities Act Release, 68 Fed. Reg. 6296, 6296 (Feb. 6, 2003) (to be codified at 17 C.F.R. § 205), *available at* http://www.sec.gov/rules/final/33-8185.htm.

[192] Lawyers acting in this capacity, however, are subject to the rules set forth in 17 C.F.R. §§ 205.3(b)(6) & (7) (2003).

[193] 17 C.F.R. § 205.3(b)(2) (2003)

[194] *See* Bost, *supra* note 94, at 1107 (citing Susan Hackett, QLCCs: *The In-House Perspective*, WALL ST. LAW., May 2004, *available at* http://www.acca.com/resource/v6355); Eli Rosen, *Resistances to Reforming Corporate Governance: The Diffusion of QLCCs*, 74 FORDHAM L. REV. 1251 (2005) (noting limited use of QLCCs and stating that as of September 30, 2005, 97.5% of issuers did not have QLCCs).

[195] 17 C.F.R. § 205.3(b)(4) (2003)

[196] *Id.* at §§ 205.3(b)(4) & (3)

[197] *Id.* at § 205.4(a). *See generally* VILLA, *supra* note 89, at § 8:6.

reporting requirements.[198] If and when the chief legal officer receives a report of a material violation, the chief legal officer must either refer the matter to a QLCC or conduct a reasonable inquiry to determine whether the purported material violation "has occurred, is ongoing, or is about to occur."[199] Unless the chief legal officer reasonably believes that there is no such material violation, the chief legal officer must "take all reasonable steps to cause the company to adopt an appropriate response"—i.e., endeavor to cause the company to stop the violation, try to prevent it from happening, or initiate steps to rectify the consequences of the violation.[200]

Whether or not he or she determines that a material violation has occurred, the chief legal officer must notify the reporting lawyer of his or her findings.[201] If the chief legal officer has found that a material violation has occurred, is ongoing, or is about to occur, the chief legal officer must advise the reporting attorney of the responsive actions undertaken.[202] If the reporting lawyer does not reasonably believe that the responsive actions are appropriate he or she must go to the audit committee, another committee of the board comprised of independent directors, or to the full board if there is no such committee.[203] If, after a reasonable time, the reporting attorney still does not reasonably believe the corporation has responded appropriately, the attorney must explain why to the chief legal officer, CEO, and/or directors to whom the attorney made the reports.[204] Ultimately, the reporting attorney may reveal "confidential information related to the representation" to the SEC without the corporation's consent if the attorney reasonably believes that this disclosure is necessary to prevent "a material violation that is likely to cause substantial injury to the financial interests or property of the issuer or investors," to prevent the corporation from committing or suborning perjury or to avert a fraud upon the Commission, or "to rectify consequences of a material violation by the issuer that caused, or may cause, substantial injury to the financial interest of the issuer or investors in the furtherance of which the attorney's services were used."[205] An attorney who believes that he or she has been discharged as a result of reporting evidence of a material violation as provided in the rules "may notify the [corporation's]

---

[198] 17 C.F.R. §§ 205.4(a), (b) (2003). However, attorneys under the direct supervision of chief legal officers—e.g., deputy general counsel—are not subordinate attorneys pursuant to the Part 205 rules. *Id.* at § 205.5(a). *See generally* VILLA, *supra* note 89, at § 8:6.

[199] 17 C.F.R. § 205.3(b)(2) (2003). The chief legal officer also has the option of referring the report to a QLCC and informing the reporting attorney of this referral. *Id.* at § 205.3(c)(2).

[200] *Id.* at § 205.3(b)(2)

[201] *Id.*

[202] *Id.* Appropriate responses include corporate action to prevent the violation or cause it to cease, remedial steps, and/or retention of a lawyer to investigate the matter with the consent of the board or a QLCC or other appropriate board committee. *Id.* at § 205.2(b).

[203] *Id.* at § 205.3(b)(3)

[204] 17 C.F.R. § 205(b)(9) (2003).

[205] *Id.* at § 205.3(d)(2).

board of directors or any committee thereof that he or she believes that he or she has been discharged for reporting evidence of a material violation."[206]

Of course, the optimal solution for lawyers and corporations alike would be to create an environment that obviates the necessity for reporting damaging information outside the client entity. It would be naïve, however, to assume that optimal results are likely in all situations. However, the general counsel, through his or her formal and informal interactions with business managers and other in-house and outside lawyers, is in an ideal position to foster an environment of integrity and legal compliance within the corporation.

If a chief legal officer is unsuccessful in efforts to get an entity to avert, cease, or remedy a material violation, however, like the reporting attorney, he or she has the option of resigning and/or reporting out relevant information.[207] It seems possible that a general counsel might choose to resign if the directors of the client corporation refused to address evidence of a material violation,[208] although that decision might well encompass economic considerations and other extra-professional standards.[209] It is harder to envision that a general counsel would elect to report out damaging information. To do so would not only go against client loyalty and constituent ties, but it could constitute professional suicide. What corporation or other organization would hire as its senior counsel an attorney who reported another entity and its senior managers to law enforcement authorities? Consequently, it is particularly important to empower general counsel to act internally to promote corporate integrity.

2. *Mandatory Reporting and Permissive Disclosure Pursuant to Model Rule 1.13*

Model Rule of Professional Responsibility 1.13 specifically pertains to representation of entities.[210] Since its inception, Rule 1.13 has provided that lawyers who represent corporations and other organizations must place allegiance to the entity over loyalty to constituents.[211] The August 2003 amendments to the rule add a presumptive reporting-up requirement and, in tandem with amendments to the client confidentiality provisions

---

[206] *Id.* at § 205.3(b)(10). *But see* VILLA, *supra* note 89, at § 8.11 (noting that the § 205.1 preemption of conflicting state ethics rules protects attorneys who disclose client confidences in such circumstances "only where the attorney has in fact acted as required by the rules and does so in good faith").

[207] 17 C.F.R. § 205.3(d)(2) (2003)

[208] *See* DeMott, *supra* note 8, at 967-68.

[209] *See Id.* at 967-69.

[210] MODEL RULES OF PROF. CONDUCT R. 1.13 (2003). The Model Rules of Professional Conduct came into existence on August 2, 1983. Since that time, Rule 1.13(a) has provided: "A lawyer employed or retained by an organization represents the organization acting through its duly authorized constituents." *Id.* at R. 1.13(a). For information pertaining to the Model Rules of Professional Conduct, see the website of the ABA Center for Professional Responsibility, http://www.abanet.org/cpr/mrpc/model_rules.html.

[211] *See* HAZARD & HODES, *supra* note 102, at § 17.2.

of Model Rule 1.6, identify circumstances in which reporting out otherwise confidential client information is permissible.[212]

Unlike the Part 205 rules, the up-ladder reporting obligation set forth in Model Rule 1.13(b) applies not only to public corporations but to all entities. The reporting duty arises when an attorney "knows" of conduct by a constituent "in a matter related to the representation that is a violation of a legal obligation to the organization, or a violation of law that might reasonably be imputed to the organization, and that is likely to result in substantial injury to the organization . . . ."[213] In such situations, "[u]nless the lawyer reasonably believes that it is not necessary in the best interest of the organization to do so," he or she must "refer the matter to higher authority in the organization, including, if warranted by the circumstances to the highest authority that can act on behalf of the organization . . . ."[214]

Model Rule 1.13(c) permits reporting information outside the corporation even if Rule 1.6 would not otherwise permit disclosure, but only if reporting up efforts have been unavailing, and, even then, only in the event of a clear violation of the law that "the lawyer reasonably believes . . . is reasonably certain to result in substantial injury to the organization, . . . but only if and to the extent the lawyer reasonably believes necessary to prevent" the injury.[215] This permissive disclosure provision does not apply to attorneys engaged to investigate or defend against alleged legal violations.[216] Of course, corporate counsel, like all attorneys operating under ethics laws substantially identical to the Model Rules, may invoke the longstanding confidentiality exceptions of Rule 1.6 to disclose information "to prevent reasonably certain death or substantial bodily harm,"[217] as well as to prevent the client from using the lawyer's services to further a crime or fraud,[218] or to "prevent, mitigate or rectify substantial injury to the financial interests or property of another" as a result of such misuse of the lawyer's services.[219] Ultimately, the lawyer may also withdraw from the representation and "proceed as the lawyer reasonably believes necessary to assure that the organization's highest authority is informed of the lawyer's . . . withdrawal."[220] Consistent with the SEC rule, the same

---

212 As Professors Hazard and Hodes observe, however, "[N]otwithstanding the Enron, WorldCom, and other scandals that gave rise to the important amendments to Rules 1.6 and 1.13 that were approved as a package by the ABA House of Delegates in 2003, . . . Rule 1.13 is still almost an entirely 'inward-looking rule.'" HAZARD & HODES, *supra* note 102, at § 17.2.

213 MODEL RULES OF PROF. CONDUCT R. 1.13(B) (2003); *see generally* HAZARD & HODES, *supra* note 102.

214 MODEL RULES OF PROF. CONDUCT R. 1.13(B) (2003).

215 *Id.* at R. 1.13(c).

216 *Id.* at R. 1.13(d).

217 *Id.* at R. 1.6(b)(1).

218 *Id.* at R. 1.6(b)(2).

219 MODEL RULES OF PROF. CONDUCT R. 1.6 (B)(3) (2003).

220 *Id.* at R. 1.13(e).

procedure applies to a lawyer who reasonably believes that he or she has been discharged because of his or her report.[221]

The role of the general counsel is implicit in the amendments to Rule 1.13, because the general counsel is precisely the type of "higher authority" to whom most in-house and outside lawyers would naturally report upon discovery of a significant problem likely to injure the client. Although neither Model Rule 1.13 nor the accompanying commentary specifies that a report to an entity's general counsel/chief legal officer is required, corporations and other entities can create such requirements through contractual provisions. The general counsel is also bound by the requirement to report up conduct likely to result in substantial injury to the organization. Since the scope of the general counsel's representation is arguably coextensive with the operation of the entity itself, the amendment underscores the general counsel's obligation to communicate about any such matters with the CEO and, ultimately, the board of directors.

3. Sarbanes-Oxley's Independent Counsel Provisions

In viewing the emerging ethical landscape from the perspective of general counsel, another provision of Sarbanes-Oxley is particularly worth noting. Section 301 of the statute amends section 10A of the Securities Act of 1934 to provide: "Each audit committee shall have the authority to engage independent counsel and other advisers, as it determines necessary to carry out its duties."[222] The statute further provides that payment for these services is to come from corporate funds.[223] Sarbanes-Oxley's independent counsel provisions underscore a trend that is already well established in corporate law. The impact of the increasing frequency of retention of independent counsel by directors, as well as the persistent practice of separate retention of counsel by other constituents is discussed below.[224]

B. The Critical Role of the General Counsel in Fostering a Climate Conducive to Reporting Up and Resolving Significant Legal Problems

The legal and professional standards established by the SEC's Part 205 rules and state ethics standards adopting and adapting amended Model Rule 1.13 define the boundaries of a new ethical framework, particularly for public companies. While both approaches require up-ladder reporting and permit limited external disclosure, whether these rules

221 *Id.*; *see supra* text accompanying note 206.

222 Sarbanes-Oxley Act of 2002, Pub. L. No. 107-204, § 301, 116 Stat. 745, 776 (2002). The term "separate" counsel is sometimes used interchangeably with "independent" counsel, but as Chief Justice Veasey and Ms. Di Guglielmo point out, in any given situation "independence" depends on "a context-specific inquiry." Veasey & Di Guglielmo, *supra* note 8, at 9. Separately retained counsel are not necessarily "independent."

223 *Id.* at § 301(m)(6).

224 *See supra* Part III.A.

will accomplish their intended objectives depends not only on their enforcement by external authorities but also on their internalization by members of the legal profession and the entities they serve. Internalization is less a function of paper policies and procedures than it is a product of institutional culture and the ability and willingness of those in charge to make the system work.[225] There is perhaps no more critical player in this process than the general counsel.

As head of the law department and the individual with the most direct and comprehensive responsibility for the legal aspects of an entity's operation,[226] the general counsel has a great deal to do with the much touted "tone at the top" of a corporation. There are some checks and balances built into the system—primarily in the Part 205 provisions mandating reports to the CEO or audit committee if chief legal officers fail to fulfill their responsibilities and the referral to the "highest authority" required in Model Rule 1.13 when lesser authorities have failed to mend their ways.[227] In reality, however, general counsel are likely to continue to exert great influence because of the practical difficulty of contacting CEOs and board members, and because of the extent to which most in-house and outside lawyers depend upon positive relationships with general counsel in doing and keeping their jobs or clients.

In light of the influence they exert, or have the potential to exert, in the corporate arena, it is reasonable to impose a major part of the responsibility for navigating the new ethical landscape on general counsel. Congress, the SEC, and, albeit less explicitly, the profession itself have placed significant trust in the ability of chief legal officers to accomplish this task. It remains to be seen whether the regulatory framework is adequate to empower general counsel to perform their ethical obligations[228] and to hold them accountable when they fail to do so.

III. BEGINNING A CONVERSATION: AREAS THAT MERIT CONSIDERATION WITH RESPECT TO THE GENERAL COUNSEL FUNCTION

The first part of this article touched upon the multifaceted formal and informal responsibilities of corporate general counsel, the significance of their role in promoting corporate integrity and the importance of a broad vision of the position in combating the kinds of choice-of-norm phenomena that may undermine the professional ethics of corporate lawyers as well as the integrity of other corporate constituents. The second section focused on the functions assigned to chief legal officers pursuant to the Part 205 rules and implicit in amended Model Rule 1.13. As lawyers, regulators, and legal

---

[225] Enforcement is critical. Enron, for example, had a business ethics code that was a work of art on paper. *See* Enron Code of Ethics, *available at* http://www.thesmokinggun.com/enron/enronethics1.html (last visited June 25, 2007).

[226] This is particularly true in light of most companies' relegation of outside counsel to episodic representation. *See supra* Part I.C.1.c.ii.

[227] MODEL RULES OF PROF. CONDUCT 1.13(B) (2003).

[228] As Professor Coffee has saliently observed, "Deterrence is easy, but empowerment is more complex." Coffee, *supra* note 72, at 1315.

scholars gain experience with the new rules, ongoing evaluation of their operation will be essential. This assessment should include analysis of their impact on general counsel, as well as other critical players. In an effort to initiate conversation on the role of general counsel, the following discussion briefly focuses on two of the many areas that merit ongoing consideration in the new ethical landscape: (1) the implications of the practice of hiring independent counsel to advise directors and other constituents and (2) general counsel-director relationships.

A. Separate Counsel Provisions and the Need for Counsel Coordination Provisions

On occasion, senior officers, business units, and other corporate constituents engage outside lawyers without the knowledge of the general counsel or law department. At one time, the frequency with which this phenomenon occurred reflected the extent of a general counsel's influence, the ways in which legal expenses were allocated and paid by various corporate components, and the extent to which corporate constituents believed that they could obtain better—or perhaps less "conservative"—advice or other assistance from outside lawyers.[229] More recently, it has become relatively common for corporate boards and board committees, particularly those comprised of independent directors, to retain separate counsel.[230] This latter phenomenon is related to developments such as the proliferation of shareholders' derivative actions and the use of special litigation committees to evaluate the claims and determine board responses to the litigation,[231] the necessity for independent assessment of management actions in connection with certain types of corporate combinations,[232] and, in the post-Enron world, the call for corporate-wide internal investigations of allegations of misconduct implicating general counsel along with other senior managers.[233]

While it is sometimes necessary, retention of separate counsel by corporate constituents can be antithetical to the best interests of the entity. Constituents are unlikely to obtain the best possible legal advice for the entity without law department involvement. This is not because they will hire inadequate lawyers, but because lawyers retained in this fashion often lack sufficient knowledge of the way in which a particular matter fits into the overall objectives of the entity. In some situations, they may not even be aware that they lack information material to their task. Lawyers are also at risk of receiving "selected" facts from constituents seeking to circumvent unfavorable advice from

---

[229] *See infra* text accompanying note 236.

[230] For discussion of the emergence of the practice and an evaluation of potential benefits and problems, *see* Geoffrey C. Hazard, Jr. & Edward B. Rock, *A New Player in the Boardroom: The Emergence of Independent Directors' Counsel*, 59 BUS. LAW. 1389 (2004); *see also* Veasey, *supra* note 74, at 1414-15 (suggesting that regular ongoing retention of separate counsel for directors or board committees is unnecessary).

[231] *See* Hazard & Rock, *supra* note 230, at 1391-92.

[232] *See id.*

[233] *See id.* at 1392.

in-house counsel or looking to pursue avenues outside permitted channels.[234] From an institutional point of view, uncoordinated efforts to attack problems often waste corporate resources and create the risk of inconsistent advice or litigation at odds with broader objectives. Perhaps most importantly, while it is easy to believe that "independent" counsel will bring objective analyses to bear on problems, there is no compelling reason to believe that the end result will be better from a business perspective or more likely to promote corporate integrity, and such engagements may cost a company a great deal in terms of human and financial resources.

Many commentators have emphasized that in-house counsel may be less independent than outside lawyers because they have only one client—their employer.[235] It is equally true, however, that outside counsel "may be retained on the basis of selected facts precisely to accommodate a response that provides a desired outside opinion."[236] With major economic interests at stake, more than one law firm has provided overly aggressive opinions to support a questionable transaction or an opinion supporting a manager's effort to circumvent "overly conservative" in-house counsel. The report of the ABA Task Force on Corporate Responsibility specifically notes that "[t]he competition to acquire and keep client business, [like] the desire to advance within the corporate executive structure, may induce lawyers to seek to please the corporate officials with whom they deal rather than to focus on the long-term interest of their client, the corporation."[237] Outside advice based on incomplete knowledge or a lack of understanding of the reasons in-house lawyers have insisted on particular courses of action, can draw corporations into dangerous waters. Finally, when constituents retain outside counsel without the help of in-house lawyers, they often pay more for services because they fail to negotiate favorable fee structures or they do not manage the engagement efficiently.

For public corporations, the new ethical framework may have the incidental effect of promoting coordination of counsel. The August 2003 Resolutions of the ABA House of Delegates advise that

> [a]ll reporting relationships of internal and outside lawyers for a public corporation [should] establish at the outset a direct line of communication with general counsel through which these lawyers are to inform the general counsel of material potential or ongoing violations of law by, and breaches of fiduciary duty to, the corporation.[238]

---

[234] *See* Hazard, *Ethical Dilemmas, supra* note 8, at 1019; *see also supra* note 173 and accompanying text.

[235] For informative discussions of the independence issue, *see* DeMott, *supra* note 8, at 967-68; Veasey & Di Guglielmo, *supra* note 8, at 11-12.

[236] Hazard, *Ethical Dilemmas, supra* note 8, at 1019.

[237] CORPORATE RESPONSIBILITY TASK FORCE REPORT, *supra* note 6, at 15.

[238] AUGUST 2003 ABA RESOLUTIONS, *supra* note 5, at ¶ 7(c).

This admonition is not, however, incorporated into the Model Rules, nor do the rules contain any other coordination-of-counsel provision applicable to lawyers representing entities.

The considerations relevant to retention of independent counsel by corporate boards and board committees comprised of independent directors are different. In this context, consultation of independent counsel offers distinct advantages because it affords access to legal advice free of the predilections or self-protective biases that may taint the advice of in-house lawyers and law firms with close relationships to the company. In some instances—e.g., decisions by special litigation committees pertaining to shareholders' derivative actions—statutory mandates require or, as a practical matter, necessitate consultation with independent counsel.[239] Similarly, the use of separate counsel allows independent directors to bypass general counsel potentially implicated in questionable corporate activities or unable to break free of the influence of CEOs or other senior managers. Retention of separate counsel aids in avoiding dangerous situations in which lawyers are called upon to evaluate their own prior work, so long as the outside counsel retained are truly independent.[240] This is presumably why Sarbanes-Oxley specifically provides that the audit committees of corporations or public companies must have authority to retain independent counsel at the corporation's expense.[241] A similar rationale underlies the ABA House of Delegates' August 2003 resolution that "[e]ngagements of counsel by the board of directors, or by a committee of the board, for special investigations or independent advice should be structured to assure independence and direct reporting to the board of directors or the committee."[242]

Nevertheless, even for boards and board committees there are also downsides to retaining separate counsel. For example, retaining separate counsel to conduct an internal investigation makes sense when independent directors need to evaluate the validity of claims in shareholders' derivative actions, when there is evidence of pervasive senior management problems, or when the conduct of the general counsel herself is in question.[243] Even so, many of the same kinds of problems applicable to constituent retention of counsel—advice based on an insufficient knowledge base, unnecessary redundancies in the performance of legal tasks, and significantly increased financial and human resource costs—may arise.[244] There is also a danger that directors may employ independent counsel in an effort to exonerate themselves when charges of wrongdoing

---

239 *See* Hazard & Rock, *supra* note 230, at 1390-91; Veasey, *supra* note 74, at 1414.

240 Vinson & Elkins found itself in a great deal of trouble as a result of an internal investigation conducted by firm lawyers into Enron matters in which the firm had provided legal advice. The firm was investigating not only the conduct of a major client, but its own. *See* Bost, *supra* note 94, at 1098; *see also* NEAL BATSON, FINAL REPORT OF NEAL BATSON, COURT-APPOINTED EXAMINER (2003), *available at* http://www.enron.com/corp/por/examinerfinal.html.

241 *See* Sarbanes-Oxley Act of 2002, Pub. L. No. 107-204, § 301, 116 Stat. 745, 776 (2002).

242 AUGUST 2003 ABA RESOLUTIONS, supra note 5, at ¶ 9.

243 *See* Hazard & Rock, *supra* note 230, at 1390; Veasey & Di Guglielmo, *supra* note 8, at 8-10.

244 *See* Hazard & Rock, *supra* note 230, at 1411-12; *supra* note 93.

arise, rather than to serve the best interests of the entity. In such cases the effect may be to salvage the directors at the expense of the company and its shareholders. Consequently, retention of separate counsel is far from a panacea.

In addition, when other counsel enter the mix—whether at the behest of directors or other constituents—the ties between officers, directors, and other key players and corporate general counsel may be weakened,[245] thereby making it more difficult for general counsel to address other legal issues. It certainly becomes more difficult to hold general counsel accountable for legal matters relevant to matters addressed by outside lawyers acting beyond their control and sometimes even without their knowledge. The ABA Task Force on Corporate Responsibility emphasized that "[t]he general counsel of a public corporation should have primary responsibility for assuring the implementation of an effective legal compliance system under the oversight of the board of directors."[246] It is unrealistic to expect any general counsel to oversee legal compliance effectively without assurance that lawyers retained to handle corporate business or investigate suspected wrongdoing coordinate with them in some fashion.

As a society we have become enamored of "independent" professionals. Independent counsel are only one species; others include "independent" doctors, consultants, prosecutors, examiners, testing laboratories, and many more. These independent professionals and entities can do a great deal of good, but they should not supplant those charged with the responsibility for ensuring the integrity of a corporation or any other institution.[247] Used judiciously, independent counsel provide invaluable services, but the trend toward employing lawyers who are not answerable to general counsel neither empowers general counsel to fulfill their obligations nor offers a basis to hold them fully accountable for corporate legal compliance or ethical behavior on the part of the lawyers who represent these entities.

In a recent article on the independent counsel phenomenon, Delaware's former Chief Justice E. Norman Veasey, a preeminent expert in corporate law who chaired the ABA's Ethics 2000 Commission, concurred with the ABA Task Force on Corporate Responsibility in cautioning against the idea that audit committees should retain separate counsel on an ongoing basis.[248] In Chief Justice Veasey's view:

---

[245] *See* DeMott, *supra* note 8, at 980 (discussing the impact of retention of independent counsel on general counsel's relationship to the Board and CEO).

[246] CORPORATE RESPONSIBILITY TASK FORCE REPORT, *supra* note 6, at 32.

[247] Moreover, even "independent" professionals are not always free of the problem of client confusion. *See id.* at 26 ("Too often, even when an outside adviser is formally engaged by the board of directors or by a committee of the board, the adviser's view of the senior executive officers as the client has influenced the advice rendered.").

[248] *See* CORPORATE RESPONSIBILITY TASK FORCE REPORT, *supra* note 6, at 24 n.54 (cautioning that "retention of counsel other than general corporate counsel to advise the board of directors or one or more of its committees . . . may result in less open communication, less constructive collaboration between directors and senior executive officers, and, ultimately, less effective oversight by the board of directors"); Veasey, *supra* note 74, at 1414-15; Veasey & Di Guglielmo, *supra* note 8, at 8-10 (noting that independence issues

> the real "heavy lifting" in this new world of corporate governance must generally be done by the general counsel and her in-house counsel staff, supplemented when necessary by the corporation's regular outside counsel. It is the general counsel . . . who must shape the quest for best practices by the board . . . one would expect that a highly professional general counsel would have the intellectual honesty to counsel directors when they should consider separate representation.[249]

Chief Justice Veasey's point is a compelling one. The judgment of outside counsel, while their services are often invaluable, should rarely substitute for the judgment of a general counsel whose sole professional responsibility is to represent one organization.[250]

Two conclusions flow from this analysis. First, incorporation of some type of coordination provision applicable to lawyers retained to represent entities with general counsel into Model Rule 1.13 merits serious consideration. The proviso could be applied unless the client entity's CEO, board, or a board committee directs otherwise, or the counsel retained in such circumstances reasonably believes that communication with the chief legal officer would imperil the well-being of the entity itself. Such a requirement would also strengthen the creation of lines of communication between all lawyers and corporate general counsel.[251] In the same vein, even when independent counsel must keep an entity's general counsel out of an investigative loop, as a matter of good governance practice, directors should still require investigating counsel to follow the company's standard practices with respect to billing to the extent that this does not interfere in the substance of the investigation.[252] Otherwise, the company loses the benefit of policies developed by those most expert at ensuring good quality, high-value legal products. This is particularly true when payment for separate counsel comes out of the law department's budget without any departmental oversight.

Second, it is essential to continue the current exploration of the relative merits of the retention of independent counsel by corporate boards and board committees. Assuming that the trend continues, it makes sense to consider the development of guidance to assist corporate directors in determining when retention of independent

---

apply to outside as well as in-house counsel and that "determining the independence of counsel requires a context-specific inquiry").

[249] Veasey, *supra* note 74, at 1414-15; *see also* Hazard & Rock, *supra* note 230, at 1402-03.

[250] As Chief Justice Veasey also notes:

> The independent directors must make the decision whether and when they need special outside counsel on a continuing basis. For this decision-making process they should be able to turn to the general counsel or to the corporation's regular outside counsel, who must have the professionalism and integrity to provide the directors with unvarnished, objective advice. If these counsels are not up to that task, they should be replaced.

Veasey, *supra* note 74, at 1418.

[251] *See* CORPORATE RESPONSIBILITY TASK FORCE REPORT, *supra* note 6, 36-38.

[252] These kinds of policies ordinarily address the level of detail required for billing, presentation of charges, limitations on expenses, and related matters.

counsel is appropriate and when such engagements are unnecessary or perhaps even counterproductive.

B. Ongoing Attention to the Relationship Between General Counsel and Corporate Directors

Good governance principles and professional responsibility on the part of corporate lawyers should operate in tandem to facilitate a healthy economic climate in which business managers, corporations, and corporate lawyers are mutually accountable. The work of Nelson and Nielson discussed earlier in this article reinforces the common sense proposition that the way people are treated influences the way they behave.[253] In particular, Professors Nelson and Nielson found that the business manager-lawyer relationship in in-house settings involves considerable reciprocity.[254] Similarly, Professor Kirkland, by adapting the approach Professor Jackall developed to study choices of norms in corporate settings, found that associates in large law firms often make decisions on the basis of perceptions of what it takes to survive and advance in a law firm environment rather than by evaluating the content of applicable norms on the basis of an internal moral compass.[255] These studies highlight the importance of aligning the objectives of both business managers and business lawyers with those of society. Shared objectives need to include a strong sense of the importance of complying with the law. In the end, perhaps the most useful aspect of Sarbanes-Oxley and the SEC implementing rules is not the resulting procedural mechanism but the clear message that norms are not fungible and that business managers and corporate attorneys need to work together to ensure corporate integrity.

Achieving the goal of prioritizing legal compliance in the corporate arena becomes possible when, as the Report of the ABA Task Force on Professional Responsibility emphasizes, lawyers, business people, courts, and legislatures recognize the integral interrelationship between corporate governance and the role of corporate lawyers.[256] Pursuant to Task Force recommendations, in August 2003, the ABA House of Delegates adopted several resolutions highlighting this relationship. Its proposals included injunctions that:

Public corporations should adopt practices in which:

a. The selection, retention, and compensation of the corporation's general counsel are approved by the board of directors.
b. General counsel meets regularly and in executive session with a committee of independent directors to communicate concerns regarding legal compli-

---

[253] *See supra* text accompanying notes 161-67.

[254] *See id.*

[255] *See supra* text accompanying notes 169-72.

[256] *See* CORPORATE RESPONSIBILITY TASK FORCE REPORT, *supra* note 6, at 9 & nn.20-21.

> ance matters, including potential or ongoing material violations of law by, and breaches of fiduciary duty to, the corporation.[257]

These resolutions delineate important strategies for enhancing the relationship between general counsel and corporate managers, but they could go farther. While, as the Task Force Report recognizes, corporations and other entities differ with respect to the structure of the reporting relationships of general counsel,[258] general counsel should always have a reporting relationship to the board, as well as to the CEO, and open lines of communication with independent directors. It needs to be crystal clear to all concerned that this should be a two-way process facilitated by directors as well as the general counsel. Without such clarity, the ability of the general counsel to safeguard the entity's best interests is necessarily compromised in important respects. Boards need to be educated about the ethical responsibilities of general counsel and all corporate lawyers, including those hired directly by the board or board members in their official capacity.

Second, general counsel or another senior attorney should ordinarily attend all plenary board meetings, as well as significant committee meetings.[259] General counsel are in the best position to assist directors in identifying legal obligations and to caution them against potential violations of the law. Given the breadth of matters in which public companies may be involved, even the most capable lawyer may not catch every issue. Nevertheless, the presence of counsel at board meetings offers the best possibility of minimizing such errors. It also provides opportunities for general counsel to educate directors as to relevant legal obligations. Although the calculus is somewhat different with respect to meetings of independent directors, the general counsel has a professional obligation with respect to all legal aspects of the corporation's operation and governance. Consequently, as Chief Justice Veasey and Ms. Di Guglielmo have recently suggested, it is generally a good idea for general counsel "to attend or at least be available to attend [independent director meetings], absent some personal involvement of counsel in the subject matter under discussion."[260] At a minimum, as the ABA

---

[257] AUGUST 2003 ABA RESOLUTIONS, *supra* note 5, at ¶ 7; *see also* REPORT OF THE NEW YORK CITY BAR ASS'N TASK FORCE ON THE LAWYER'S ROLE IN CORPORATE GOVERNANCE (Nov. 2006), 62 BUS. LAW. 427, 482-83 (2006) [hereinafter N.Y.C. BAR ASS'N TASK FORCE REPORT] (emphasizing the importance of general counsel's relationship with and access to the board).

[258] CORPORATE RESPONSIBILITY TASK FORCE REPORT, *supra* note 6, at 29; *see also* ASS'N OF CORPORATE COUNSEL, *supra* note 66, at 24 (citing data showing that a high percentage, but not all, of general counsel report directly to corporate boards as well as to senior managers).

[259] *See* Veasey & Di Guglielmo, *supra* note 8, at 17.

[260] *Id.* Independent directors may have concerns abut confidentiality vis-à-vis general counsel who report to CEOs, but it is incumbent upon general counsel to maintain the confidentiality of independent director meetings. Those who cannot do so should face termination. This is one of the necessary tensions inherent in the general counsel function. *See generally* Veasey & Di Guglielmo, *supra* note 8. *See also* DeMott, *supra* note 8, at 956-57; N.Y.C. BAR ASSOC. TASK FORCE REPORT, *supra* note 257, at 480-81.

Task Force recommends, general counsel should meet periodically with their company's independent directors in executive session.[261]

Third, general counsel should, as a matter of course, inform the board of changes in counsel employment or retention arrangements in the event of: (1) termination or resignation of the general counsel or another senior in-house counsel, or (2) the termination or withdrawal of a law firm handling major work for the entity in the course of the representation rather than at its completion. As a matter of good governance, it is not enough to simply rely on individual lawyers who believe they have been inappropriately discharged.[262] The board, or a committee of the board, should require information as to the reasons for termination, resignation, or withdrawal of lawyers who have previously played significant roles in corporate matters and inquire into matters that raise particular concerns. While most of these changes are unlikely to be related to concerns over corporate integrity, as a matter of good governance, directors should take steps to satisfy themselves of the reason for the discharge or withdrawal.

Corporate managers do not operate under the kinds of rules of professional responsibility applicable to lawyers. Nevertheless, lawyers are instrumental in advising boards and legislatures on good governance practices, and courts are in a position to comment on the practices of organizations that come before them in the course of litigation. The ABA Task Force on Corporate Responsibility made great strides in identifying good governance practices already in place in many organizations but sorely needed in others. It is important to continue this work in both the legal and corporate arenas.

CONCLUSION

As Professor Hazard noted ten years ago, "[T]he role of corporate counsel is among the most complex and difficult of those functions performed by lawyers."[263] This observation applies with particular force to general counsel, and, if anything, the role they play has become more complex during the past decade.[264] It is critical for the profession to recognize that general counsel are pivotal players in the new ethical landscape. As a New York City Bar Task Force recently emphasized, "Strengthening the role of the General Counsel should be a high priority in efforts to promote compliance with laws, including the securities laws."[265] Regulatory standards and ethical rules should empower general counsel to do their jobs and hold them accountable when they fail to meet their obligations.

---

261 CORPORATE RESPONSIBILITY TASK FORCE REPORT, *supra* note 6, at 32, 70.

262 *See supra* text accompanying notes 206 & 221.

263 *See* Hazard, *Ethical Dilemmas, supra* note 8, at 1011.

264 *See* DeMott, *supra* note 8, at 980 (noting the likelihood that the role of general counsel will continue to change over time); Veasey & Di Guglielmo, *supra* note 8, at 36 (observing that "[n]ot only lawyers but also directors and officers need to understand and appreciate the complexities and the ever-changing nature of the challenges faced by counsel for the corporation.").

265 N.Y.C. BAR ASS'N TASK FORCE REPORT, *supra* note 257, at 480-81.

Lawyers' Independence and Collective Illegality in Government and Corporate Misconduct, Terrorism, and Organized Crime[*]

Peter S. Margulies[**]

Lawyers' independence has been much celebrated but little observed.[1] This Article suggests that the fault lies with our amorphous definition of independence. By asking the concept of independence to perform too much work, actors in the legal system ignore the competing values at stake. Substituting a model of equipoise for the amorphous concept of independence will sharpen analysis of lawyers' overreaching.

A more workable concept than independence has particular relevance for collective illegality—including terrorism, organized crime, and government and corporate misconduct. Where groups interact, conspiracies to break the law can follow. In these days of pervasive law and legality, lawyers may find themselves drawn, knowingly or unknowingly, into the web.[2] Clarifying the lawyer's role in a concrete fashion can reduce collective illegality, without stifling legitimate risk-taking behavior.

Money, ideology, and politics are prime villains in the story of the decline of professional independence.[3] In the private sector, lawyers have financial incentives to do the

---

[*] Originally published at 58 RUTGERS L. REV. 939 (2006). Reprinted by permission of the author and Rutgers Law Review.

[**] Professor of Law, Roger Williams University School of Law. I thank Richard Delgado, John Leubsdorf, Nancy Moore, and participants at a workshop at St. John's University School of Law and a panel at the 2006 Law and Society Association Annual Meeting in Baltimore, Maryland for their comments.

[1] For a particularly cogent study, *see* Robert W. Gordon, *The Independence of Lawyers*, 68 B.U. L. REV. 1 (1988).

[2] *See* Peter Margulies, *The Virtues and Vices of Solidarity: Regulating the Roles of Lawyers for Clients Accused of Terrorist Activity*, 62 MD. L. REV. 173 (2003).

[3] For arguments that the legal profession has declined in independence and judgment, see ANTHONY T. KRONMAN, THE LOST LAWYER: FAILING IDEALS OF THE LEGAL PROFESSION (1993) (criticizing the decline of the "lawyer-statesman" and the increasing commercialization and politicization of the profession); DEBORAH L. RHODE, IN THE INTERESTS OF JUSTICE: REFORMING THE LEGAL PROFESSION (2000) (critiquing profession's thin commitment to serving the public interest); JEAN STEFANCIC & RICHARD DELGADO, HOW LAWYERS LOSE THEIR WAY: A PROFESSION FAILS ITS CREATIVE MINDS 52-54 (2005) (describing deadening routine and job dissatisfaction within legal profession); Peter Margulies, Progressive *Lawyering and Lost Traditions*, 73 TEX. L. REV. 1139 (1995) (review essay) (asserting that accounts of profession's decline pay

bidding of an organized crime kingpin, such as the late John Gotti,[4] or to align their efforts with corporate insiders, such as executives at Enron.[5] In government work, as the example of the lawyers who drafted the "torture memos" reflects, lawyers may heed the call of ideological allegiance, and become cheerleaders for their clients, if not accomplices.[6] For prosecutors, the cascade of concern about terrorism after September 11, accelerated by signaling from superiors such as former Attorney General Ashcroft, led to violations of constitutional norms.[7]

However, these cautionary tales mask counter-stories and disparate meanings of independence. In the criminal context, for example, permitting the courts to exercise broad discretion in defining defense counsel's independence can deprive the defendant of especially able legal help.[8] This deprivation gives the government a substantial strategic advantage. Independence can also become less an affirmative obligation of attorneys than an alibi, justifying the failure to hold the lawyer accountable for client wrongs.[9]

Rather than an amorphous invocation of independence, courts and commentators should focus on the conduct of lawyers as the interaction of branding and gatekeeping norms. All lawyers establish a brand—a distinctive professional identity. Establishing this brand serves constitutional and social interests. For example, a lawyer like the late William Kunstler, who defined his professional identity in opposition to the state, signaled his commitment to clients such as suspected terrorists who might otherwise be

---

insufficient attention to countervailing trends, such as the work of civil rights lawyers and the heightened inclusiveness of the profession).

[4] *See* United States v. Locascio, 6 F.3d 924 (2d Cir. 1993).

[5] Consider the problematic conduct of the lawyers advising Enron, who assisted executives in setting up partnerships to conceal Enron's liabilities. *See* Robert W. Gordon, *A New Role for Lawyers?: The Corporate Counselor After Enron, in* Lawyers' ETHICS AND THE PURSUIT OF SOCIAL JUSTICE 371 (Susan D. Carle ed., New York University Press 2005).

[6] *See* Memorandum for Alberto R. Gonzales, Counsel to the President, Re: Standards of Conduct for Interrogation under 18 U.S.C. §§ 2340-2340A (Aug. 1, 2002), in MARK DANNER, TORTURE AND TRUTH: AMERICA, ABU GHRAIB, AND THE WAR ON TERROR 115, 145 (2004) [hereinafter Gonzales Memo]. For commentary on the Gonzales Memo, see David Luban, *Liberalism, Torture, and the Ticking Bomb*, 91 VA. L. REV. 1425 (2005); *cf.* W. Bradley Wendel, *Legal Ethics and the Separation of Law and Morals*, 91 Cornell L. Rev. 67, 80-85 (2005) (critiquing torture memos); W. Bradley Wendel, *Professionalism as Interpretation*, 99 NW. U. L. REV. 1167 (2005) (same).

[7] *See* Peter Margulies, *Above Contempt?: Regulating Government Overreaching in Terrorism Cases*, 34 SW. U. L. REV. 449 (2005).

[8] Bruce A. Green, *"Through a Glass, Darkly": How the Court Sees Motions to Disqualify Criminal Defense Lawyers*, 89 COLUM. L. REV. 1201, 1209 (1989); *see infra* notes 98-115 and accompanying text.

[9] *See* RHODE, *supra* note 3, at 54 (arguing that lawyer's lack of accountability for client's actions is socially beneficial, since lawyers might otherwise be chilled in representing those without resources); Steven L. Schwarcz, *The Limits of Lawyering: Legal Opinions in Structured Finance*, 84 Tex. L. Rev. 1, 29 (2005) (outlining argument that declining to hold lawyer responsible for client's decisions facilitates client autonomy). *But see* Russell G. Pearce, *Model Rule 1.0: Lawyers are Morally Accountable*, 70 FORDHAM L. REV. 1805, 1808-09 (2002) (arguing that lawyers have a moral responsibility for their clients' actions).

virtually alone and universally despised.[10] The lawyers for the government who drafted the torture memos saw themselves as vindicating the Framers' vision of the separation of powers.[11] Corporate lawyers for Enron and the like viewed themselves as championing innovation in the financial markets, and creating value for shareholders consistent with a capitalist system of private property.[12] Branding can also promote the lawyer's financial interest and prestige, by attracting clients and giving the lawyer credibility with other political and economic actors.

As professionals, however, lawyers must balance branding with gatekeeping. While lawyers use branding to attract and maintain clients, gatekeeping norms cast the lawyer as an officer of the court who has an interest in law's integrity. To discharge her role as gatekeeper, the lawyer must be prepared to rock the client's boat, for example by "climbing the ladder" to inform the highest authority in the corporation of a corporate official's wrongdoing.[13] Gatekeeping norms may require or permit the lawyer to take action that prevents or rectifies misrepresentations to others.[14]

Neither branding nor gatekeeping is sufficient in isolation—norms of practice suggest the need for an equipoise or balance. Equipoise between branding and gatekeeping involves two cardinal elements in both advocacy and advice regarding alleged group wrongdoing—including terrorism, organized crime, and corporate and government misconduct. First, the lawyer should not have advance knowledge of a client's wrongdoing. A lawyer who has such knowledge risks becoming a witness at best,[15] and an accomplice at worst. Equipoise also requires that the attorney retain the ability to give balanced advice, including that most difficult subject of attorney-client interaction: "bad news" about the constraints the law places on the client's plans. Dispensing with bad news may facilitate a lawyer's efforts to build a brand, at least in the short term. In the longer term, however, as Enron's shareholders discovered, a lawyer's reluctance to say, "No," adversely affects both the client and the system's integrity.[16]

---

[10] *See* WILLIAM M. KUNSTLER, MY LIFE AS A RADICAL LAWYER 334-35 (1994).

[11] John C. Yoo, *War and the Constitutional Text*, 69 U. CHI. L. REV. 1639, 1654 (2002).

[12] *See* Milton C. Regan, Jr., *Ethics in Corporate Representation: Teaching Enron*, 74 FORDHAM L. REV. 1139 (2005); Schwarcz, *supra* note 9; William H. Simon, *Wrongs of Ignorance and Ambiguity: Lawyer Responsibility for Collective Misconduct*, 22 YALE J. ON REG. 1, 12-15 (2005).

[13] *See* MODEL RULES OF PROF'L CONDUCT R. 1.13(b) (2005).

[14] *See* MODEL RULES OF PROF'L CONDUCT R. 4.1(b) (2005) ("a lawyer shall not knowingly . . . fail to disclose a material fact when disclosure is necessary to avoid assisting a criminal or fraudulent act by a client . . ."). For discussions of gatekeeping, particularly with respect to the conduct of lawyers advising Enron, see John C. Coffee, Jr., *The Attorney as Gatekeeper: An Agenda for the SEC*, 103 COLUM. L. REV. 1293, 1305-11 (2003); Regan, *supra* note 12; Roger C. Cramton, *Enron and the Corporate Lawyer: A Primer on Legal and Ethical Issues*, 58 BUS. LAW. 143 (2002); Wendel, *Professionalism as Interpretation*, *supra* note 6; *cf.* Nancy B. Rapoport, *Enron and the New Disinterestedness—The Foxes Are Guarding the Henhouse*, 13 AM. BANKR. INST. L. REV. 521 (2005) (discussing conflicts of interest among investment bankers).

[15] *See* Judith A. McMorrow, *The Advocate as Witness: Understanding Context, Culture and Client*, 70 FORDHAM L. REV. 945 (2001).

[16] *See* Cramton, *supra* note 14; Regan, *supra* note 12; RHODE, *supra* note 3.

Focusing on the lawyer's lack of advance knowledge and ability to say "No" clarifies how we view lawyers' independence in a number of contexts, including disqualification of defense counsel in criminal cases, the regulation of prosecutors, and the propriety of legal advice that may lead to illegal conduct. Existing doctrine leads to asymmetry, not equipoise, between defense counsel and the state. Courts have been too eager to disqualify defense counsel, particularly in the area of so-called successive conflicts, involving lawyers' obligations to former clients. At the same time, courts have not been diligent enough in promoting accountability for prosecutors and government attorneys. Boiling down independence to freedom from prior knowledge and freedom to give bad news would reduce inappropriate disqualification of defense counsel, while preserving the remedy for lawyers whose continued representation of a client would undermine judicial integrity. Courts would also use their supervisory power to ensure that prosecutors and government lawyers do not obtain strategic advantage through an excess of branding. Finally, for advisers in and out of government, an equipoise approach would limit defenses based on advice of counsel, and increase the legal exposure of lawyers who violated the conditions of equipoise.

The Article is in six Parts. Part I unpacks the concept of independence, suggesting that it encompasses conflicting values that limit its utility. Part II advances the equipoise of branding and gatekeeping as an alternative. It focuses on the importance to both advocacy and legal advice of the two core equipoise factors: freedom from advance knowledge of alleged illegality, and freedom to give the client bad news. Part III addresses equipoise in the disqualification of defense counsel. Part IV deals with equipoise in regulating prosecutors. Part V outlines the use of equipoise in the provision of legal advice, focusing on the Enron lawyers, criminal defense lawyer Lynne Stewart's conviction for material support of terrorist activity, and the opinion rendered in the so-called "torture memos" by government lawyers. Finally, Part VI analyzes possible alternatives to the equipoise conception.

I. LAWYERS' INDEPENDENCE: CLARION CALL OR CONFLICT IN VALUES?

Lawyers have a distinctive role in a democratic republic that requires both solidarity with and detachment from client interests. As Talcott Parsons observed, lawyers act as intermediaries between the state and the private realm.[17] Judgment and deliberation are the calling cards of this intermediary status. Lawyers cannot be mere ministerial functionaries, taking their client's direction like commands for a word-processing program. For lawyers, as for other professionals, judgments articulated through deliberation with clients can make a difference, yielding client decisions and desires that may be different

---

[17] *See* Talcott Parsons, *A Sociologist Looks at the Legal Profession, in* ESSAYS IN SOCIOLOGICAL THEORY 384 (rev. ed. 1954), *cited in* Robert W. Gordon, *Corporate Law Practice as a Public Calling*, 49 MD. L. REV. 255, 255 n. 1 (1990).

from those the client brought to bear initially.[18] This kind of judgment is impossible when the lawyer lacks detachment from the client.

Professional judgment always takes into account abiding values and interests,[19] as does constitutionalism itself. In other systems of governance, actors within the system have a far more limited time horizon.[20] Left to their own devices, for example, most people unduly privilege present consequences or benefits, and unduly discount longer-term effects.[21] The idea of constitutionalism, which commits the polity in advance to long-term values such as liberty and equality, acts as a check on the expedient responses that government can employ in crises.[22] The lawyer's independence is another guarantor of longer-term perspective.

The lawyer must maintain independence from three sources of pressure: the client, the lawyer's own interests, and the state. To avoid undue influence from the client and the lawyer's self-interest, the lawyer accepts constraints by virtue of her membership in the legal profession. For example, to safeguard the lawyer's capacity for detached judgment, ethical rules bar the lawyer from entering into partnerships with members of other professions.[23] Moreover, lawyers as repeat players in the justice system have

---

[18] *See* KRONMAN, *supra* note 3; *cf.* Susan D. Carle, *Theorizing Agency*, 55 AM. U. L. REV. 307, 344-62 (2005) (discussing pragmatists' conception of agency as site of deliberation and interaction between self and others); *see also* BRIAN Z. TAMANAHA, REALISTIC SOCIO-LEGAL THEORY: PRAGMATISM AND A SOCIAL THEORY OF LAW xi (1997) (arguing for application of pragmatic values of interaction and dialogue to the study of law).

[19] *See generally* Ronald J. Gilson & Robert H. Mnookin, *Disputing Through Agents: Cooperation and Conflict Between Lawyers in Litigation*, 94 COLUM. L. REV. 509 (1994) (discussing incentives for lawyers, as "repeat-players" in litigation process, to cooperate, as well as countervailing incentives to perpetuate disputes).

[20] *Cf.* BENEDICT ANDERSON, IMAGINED COMMUNITIES 22-25 (rev. ed. 1991) (discussing preoccupation with the present that cuts across modern societies).

[21] *See* Christine Jolls, Cass R. Sunstein & Richard H. Thaler, *A Behavioral Approach to Law and Economics, in* BEHAVIORAL LAW AND ECONOMICS 13, 46 (Cass R. Sunstein ed., 2000) (discussing individuals' tendency to heavily discount future costs); *cf.* David Laibson, *Golden Eggs and Hyperbolic Discounting*, 112 Q. J. ECON. 443 (1997) (analyzing how individuals use "commitment mechanisms" such as insurance policies or savings plans to remedy tendency to unduly discount the future); Ted O'Donoghue & Matthew Rabin, *Doing It Now or Later*, 89 AM. ECON. REV. 103 (1999) (analyzing "present-biased preferences").

[22] *See* JED RUBENFELD, FREEDOM AND TIME: A THEORY OF CONSTITUTIONAL SELF-GOVERNMENT 163-76 (2001).

[23] *See* MODEL RULES OF PROF'L CONDUCT R. 5.4(b) (2005); *see also* George C. Nnona, *Multidisciplinary Practice in the International Context: Realigning the Perspective on the European Union's Regulatory Regime*, 37 CORNELL INT'L L.J. 115, 138-52 (2004) (arguing that law in Europe stresses theme of lawyer independence that has fueled opposition to multidisciplinary partnerships in United States); *cf.* Mary C. Daly, *Choosing Wise Men Wisely: The Risks and Rewards of Purchasing Legal Services in a Multidisciplinary Partnership*, 13 GEO. J. LEGAL ETHICS 217, 263-68 (2000) (discussing arguments for and against partnerships between lawyers and other professionals, while arguing that rhetoric has often concealed true dimensions of issue); Carol A. Needham, *Permitting Lawyers to Participate in Multidisciplinary Practices: Business as Usual or the End of the Profession As We Know It?*, 84 MINN. L. REV. 1315, 1317-19 (2000) (offering pragmatic test for conflicts of interest in multidisciplinary practices).

reputational interests to uphold.[24] Repeat player clients, including organizational entities such as corporations, also have long-term interests that lawyers should consider. For example, corporations depend on the good will of a range of stakeholders, including investors, employees, and customers.[25] A lawyer in thrall to large fees and the short-term perspectives of corporate insiders[26] undermines those long-term interests.

As lawyers accept constraints by virtue of their status as lawyers, however, they must also take care to avoid becoming mere proxies for state power. In some societies, lawyers define their roles solely in terms of compliance with the dictates of the state.[27] In a constitutional democracy, however, lawyers must act as a check on those dictates, even (or perhaps especially) when dealing with those targeted by the state and despised by society.[28]

The foregoing suggests that independence is a rhetorical construct that masks conflicting values. Moreover, emphasizing independence has some negative consequences that also demonstrate the inadequacy of the concept. I address each in turn.

First, the almost clinical detachment from clients that independence contemplates is difficult, if not impossible. Solidarity with clients is an ongoing reality of practice. Lawyers often develop affective ties with clients—criminal defense lawyers, for example, sometimes bond with clients on an emotional level, as clients face an uncertain future and a hostile jury pool.[29] Lawyers for corporations often, as in the case of Enron, are members of the same country clubs as the corporate officers who hire them and give them direction on the corporation's behalf.[30] "Political" lawyers may feel a sense of "positional solidarity" with clients, favoring the goals, such as the overthrow of despotic

---

[24] *See* Gilson & Mnookin, *supra* note 19.

[25] *Cf.* Liam Seamus O'Melinn, *Neither Contract Nor Concession: The Public Personality of the Corporation*, 74 GEO. WASH. L. REV. 201, 216-20 (2006) (discussing roots of American corporate law in law of religious and other nonprofit institutions); Susan J. Stabile, *A Catholic Vision of the Corporation*, 4 SEATTLE J. SOC. JUST. 181, 191-92 (2005) (discussing links between welfare of corporation and common good).

[26] This was a central problem with Enron's lawyers. *See* Regan, *supra* note 12.

[27] *See* Gerald J. Clark, *The Legal Profession in Cuba*, 23 SUFFOLK TRANSNAT'L L. REV. 413, 434 (1999) ("The Cuban lawyer has studied from childhood that the socialist state is the repository of all good for each individual."), *quoted in* Daniel Richman, *Community Courts and Community Justice: Commentary: Professional Identity: Comment on Simon*, 40 AM. CRIM. L. REV. 1609 n.2 (2003); Ethan Michelson, *The Practice of Law as an Obstacle to Justice: Chinese Lawyers at Work*, 40 L. & SOC'Y REV. 1, 20-21 (2006) (describing how client-selection practices of Chinese lawyers reinforce socio-economic norms).

[28] *See generally* Abbe Smith, *Criminal Responsibility, Social Responsibility, and Angry Young Men: Reflections of a Feminist Criminal Defense Lawyer*, 21 N.Y.U. REV. L. & SOC. CHANGE 433 (1994-95).

[29] *See* Charles J. Ogletree, Jr., *Beyond Justifications: Seeking Motivations to Sustain Public Defenders*, 106 HARV. L. REV. 1239, 1272-75 (1993) (discussing importance of defense lawyers' empathy with the accused); *See also* Smith, *supra* note 28; Michael E. Tigar, *Voices Heard in Jury Argument: Litigation and the Law School Curriculum*, 9 REV. LITIG. 177, 179-83 (1990) (discussing importance of empathy and regard for human voice in author's defense of radical lawyer charged with perjury and making false statements to federal agents).

[30] *See* Cramton, *supra* note 14.

regimes abroad and greater equality at home, that their clients espouse.[31] Speeches about lawyer's independence on Law Day will not eliminate these ties. Extolling independence will only engender further rationalizations of potentially compromised lawyer-client relationships, not force real reform.

Precisely because lawyer-client ties are strong, particularly in dealing with money and to a lesser extent ideology, the notion of independence may end up with the banal meaning it has typically had in lawyer regulation, namely that the lawyer, by virtue of being a lawyer, is not responsible for the client's misdeeds. This convenient nostrum allows lawyers to sleep at night, secure in the belief that they have not, for example, presided over the dissipation of the life savings of those victimized by corporate insiders' overreaching,[32] or actually ordered or participated in the mistreatment of detainees.[33] It also, not incidentally, shields lawyers from legal liability in such matters.[34] In this way, independence becomes a factual conclusion about lawyers' responsibility, not a normative prescription for greater lawyer engagement as an officer of the court.[35]

Second, the rhetoric of independence spurs negative externalities. Lawyers who are independent from clients lose the grounding in concrete cases—the discipline imposed by seeing matters through a client's eyes. For example, lawyers in charge of massive class actions who receive little input from clients risk an arrogance and lack of connection that can detract from their goals.[36] Historically, this excess of detachment has also been a risk for government lawyers dealing with counterterrorism issues. While the Department of Justice lawyers who endorsed a sweeping view of executive power over interrogation of detainees should have maintained greater distance from the concerns

---

[31] *See* Margulies, Virtues and Vices of Solidarity, *supra* note 2.

[32] *See* RHODE, *supra* note 3.

[33] *See* Stephen Gillers, *Legal Ethics: A Debate, in* THE TORTURE DEBATE IN AMERICA 236, 237-38 (Karen J. Greenberg ed., 2006).

[34] *See* Christopher Kutz, *The Lawyers Know Sin: Complicity in Torture, in* THE TORTURE DEBATE IN AMERICA 241, 243-44 (Karen J. Greenberg ed., 2006).

[35] *Cf.* James A. Cohen, *Lawyer Role, Agency Law, and the Characterization "Officer of the Court"*, 48 BUFF. L. REV. 349 (2000) (arguing that term "officer of the court" should be read consistently with agency law principles).

[36] *See* Derrick Bell, *Serving Two Masters: Integration Ideals and Client Interests in School Desegregation Litigation*, 85 YALE L.J. 470 (1976) (critiquing lawyers' approach to client views); Peter Margulies, *The New Class Action Jurisprudence and Public Interest Law*, 25 N.Y.U. REV. L. & SOC. CHANGE 487, 497-98 (1999) (discussing law reform efforts and class action litigation in context of desegregation of public education, prison reform, and deinstitutionalization of persons with mental illness); *see also* Anthony V. Alfieri, *Reconstructive Poverty Law Practice: Learning Lessons of Client Narrative*, 100 YALE L.J. 2107 (1991) (critiquing top-down model of poverty law, and arguing for more comprehensive client participation); *cf.* Peter Margulies, *Public Interest Lawyering and the Pragmatist Dilemma, in* RENASCENT PRAGMATISM: STUDIES IN LAW AND SOCIAL SCIENCE 220, 225-30 (Alfonso Morales ed., 2003) (arguing that instrumental concerns often marginalize dialogue with affected parties in public interest class actions). *But see* Charles F. Sabel & William H. Simon, *Destabilization Rights: How Public Law Litigation Succeeds*, 117 HARV. L. REV. 1015, 1029-33 (2004) (discussing use of judicial remedies in class actions to promote experimentation and innovation in public administration).

of their clients in the executive branch, earlier lawyers may have had too much distance, failing to follow up aggressively before September 11 on possible leads.[37] Lawyers should be able to see the long-term consequences of their clients' conduct, but should also be able to understand the depths of their clients' concerns.[38]

Even more seriously, independence for many lawyers is a goal that raises the question: Independence from whom? Lawyers for corporations who disdain the officers who typically represent the corporation may cozy up inappropriately to government regulators.[39] In other (or related) settings, such as criminal defense, independence from clients may lead to solidarity with the state. Solidarity of this kind, which reflects the dominant mode of practice in many less-than-democratic countries around the globe, is hardly a desirable trade-off.[40] The asymmetry of remedies that restore independence, such as disqualification, compounds this trend toward solidarity with the state: disqualification is a remedy courts reserve for defense counsel, since it has no effect on the more fungible procession of prosecuting attorneys employed by the government. In addition, judicial focus on the chimera of independence introduces distortions into the criteria for disqualification, for example, by overuse of disqualification and neglect of less intrusive procedures in the "successive" conflict area, in which a former client of a defense lawyer serves may serve as a government witness.[41]

II. BRANDING, GATEKEEPING, AND EQUIPOISE

The flaws of the independence concept suggest the need for a more workable alternative. To meet that need, this section advances an equipoise approach. The premise of the equipoise approach is that the legal profession experiences a tension between two kinds of commands: branding norms and gatekeeping norms. This tension occurs in both the advice and advocacy realms of law practice. Equipoise endeavors to keep both in balance. To understand the challenges of this balancing task, I first analyze the distinctive elements of branding and gatekeeping.

A. Branding

Professions and their members strive to establish a brand—a set of commitments embodied in a story that professionals tell themselves and share with relevant audiences. Branding can be instrumental—fulfilling particular goals such as the acquisition of money, status, and power—or constitutive—marking who lawyers are as a profession.

---

[37] *See* THE 9/11 COMMISSION REPORT 273 (2004), http://www.9-11commission.gov/report/911Report.pdf (asserting that law enforcement officials should have been more aggressive in obtaining authorization to search the laptop of Zacarias Moussaoui, who was apprehended at a flight school prior to September 11); *cf.* Peter Margulies, *Foreword: Risk, Deliberation, and Professional Responsibility*, 2 J. NAT'L SEC. L. & POL'Y 357 (2005).

[38] *See* KRONMAN, *supra* note 3 (discussing lawyer's integration of sympathy and detachment).

[39] *See* Schwarcz, *supra* note 9.

[40] *See* Smith, *supra* note 28.

[41] *See infra* notes 108-15 and accompanying text.

Branding also plays out on both a macro stage, involving the professional advantages of lawyers as a group, and on a micro level, involving the search for identity or strategic advantage by individual attorneys.

Scholars view branding as an effort to differentiate products along axes other than price.[42] Branding can develop consumer trust, as when consumers wary of participating in Internet commerce seek out retailers with a "bricks and mortar" presence, and pay more for the privilege.[43] Consumers also view branding, including branding among related products offered by a company, as reducing their risk and uncertainty.[44] When companies brand their products, consumers believe that companies have invested time, effort, and reputation in ensuring that consumers "know what they're getting." We see a comparable dynamic—albeit one that is not one-dimensionally instrumental—in the legal profession.

On a macro level, lawyers brand themselves through commitments such as the duty of confidentiality.[45] The elevation of confidentiality to a core professional norm symbolizes the importance of client-related information and the commitment the profession places on building client trust.[46] The lawyer's duty of confidentiality also serves to distinguish lawyers from members of other professions, such as accountants and investment bankers, who lack comparable obligations.

On a micro level, branding serves ideological and financial purposes. Consider the public reluctance of criminal defense attorneys, including radical attorneys like the late William Kunstler, to represent a client who seeks to cooperate with the state.[47] Consider also the eagerness of the lawyers who drafted the torture memos to embrace an all-encompassing vision of executive power. Branding of this kind signals clients with

---

[42] *See* David E.M. Sappington & Birger Wernerfelt, *To Brand or Not to Brand? A Theoretical and Empirical Question*, 58 J. BUS. 279, 283 (1985); *see also* Lance Eliot Brouthers & Kefeng Xu, *Product Stereotypes, Strategy and Performance Satisfaction: The Case of Chinese Exporters*, 33 J. INT'L BUS. STUD. 657, 661 (2002) (discussing branding strategies pursued by Chinese export companies that seek to transcend image of Chinese as low-price leaders).

[43] *See* Erik Brynjolfsson & Michael D. Smith, *Frictionless Commerce? A Comparison of Internet and Conventional Retailers*, 46 MGMT. SCI. 563, 578-79 (2000) (noting that Internet consumers appear willing to pay a premium for products from established retailers such as Tower Records or Powell Books, or from heavily advertised on-line retailers such as Amazon.com).

[44] *See* Cynthia A. Montgomery & Birger Wernerfelt, *Risk Reduction and Umbrella Branding*, 65 J. BUS. 31, 49-50 (1992) (discussing consumer perceptions of risk reduction in purchases linked with companies' practice of "umbrella branding," i.e., branding of related products).

[45] *See* MODEL RULES OF PROF'L CONDUCT R. 1.6 (2005) (providing, with some exceptions, that a law "shall not reveal information relating to the representation of a client. . . .").

[46] *See* Richard L. Abel, *Why Does the ABA Promulgate Ethical Rules?*, 59 TEX. L. REV. 639, 667-68 (1981) (arguing that self-interest of legal profession drives development of ethical norms); *cf.* Coffee, Jr., *supra* note 14, at 1307-08 (discussing branding virtues of confidentiality, while arguing that the profession overstates the importance of confidentiality regarding client communications that take place before client misconduct).

[47] *See* David Margolick, *Still Radical After All These Years: At 74, William Kunstler Defends Clients Most Lawyers Avoid*, N.Y. TIMES, July 6, 1993, at B1-B2 (quoting Kunstler as observing that his "purpose is to keep the state from becoming . . . all powerful").

particular agendas that the lawyer warrants their trust. In sending such signals, branding can bring fame and power, attract new clients, and solidify important relationships with persons or entities who fund legal representation. For example, lawyers who build a reputation based on rejection of cooperation are in a better competitive position to secure the business of organizations such as organized crime enterprises that depend on a code of silence to protect higher-ups. Similarly, a lawyer in government with a broad view of executive power may be kept "in the loop" when Administration officials shut out lawyers who are more nuanced in their perspective.[48]

Viewed less cynically, branding is also fundamental to professional culture in a democracy. Take the question of a criminal defendant's cooperation with the government.[49] For a radical lawyer like Kunstler, cooperation with the state bolstered the government's bid to become all-powerful, and eroded the check on the government posed by vigorous criminal defense.[50] Lawyers have a First Amendment right to hold such views.[51] Moreover, espousing such views acts as a powerful signaling device, assuring potential clients targeted by the government that the lawyer will resolutely represent their interests. Branding in this sense helps ensure that an unpopular client will view proceedings against him as fair, whatever the outcome. It also makes it more likely that this perception will be shared by the wider public audience, nationally and internationally, as well as persons who share various attributes of identity with the client.

B. Gatekeeping

While branding is important in lawyering, gatekeeping is also crucial. Gatekeeping refers to lawyers' observance of norms that protect the integrity of the legal system.[52]

---

[48] *See* Jane Mayer, *The Memo: How an Internal Effort to Ban the Abuse and Torture of Detainees Was Thwarted*, THE NEW YORKER, Feb. 27, 2006, at 32 (discussing efforts by Bush Administration, particularly Vice President Cheney's staff, to freeze out in-house dissenters on policy that rejected applicability of Geneva Conventions to suspected Al Qaeda detainees, and waxing influence of "true believers" in executive power).

[49] *See* Daniel C. Richman, *Cooperating Clients*, 56 OHIO ST. L.J. 69 (1995) (discussing cooperation and legal ethics); Michael A. Simons, *Vicarious Snitching: Crime, Cooperation, and "Good Corporate Citizenship"*, 76 ST. JOHN'S L. REV. 979, 992-95 (2002) (discussing federal prosecutors' insistence on cooperation of corporations in order to stave off indictment); Michael A. Simons, *Retribution for Rats: Cooperation, Punishment, and Atonement,* 56 VAND. L. REV. 1, 33-42 (2003) (arguing that cooperation can be reflection of remorse and atonement, instead of merely utilitarian calculus); Ian Weinstein, *Regulating the Market for Snitches*, 47 BUFF. L. REV. 563, 614 (1999) (discussing dynamics of cooperation with prosecutors, based on sentencing decisions of judges and other factors); *cf.* Ellen Yaroshefsky, *Cooperation with Federal Prosecutors: Experiences of Truth Telling and Embellishment*, 68 FORDHAM L. REV. 917 (1999) (describing incentives for embellishment and outright misrepresentation among cooperators).

[50] *See* Richman, *Cooperating Clients, supra* note 49, at 127 n.197.

[51] *Cf.* NAACP v. Button, 371 U.S. 415 (1963) (holding that First Amendment values can trump state bar regulations regarding aspects of representation touching on political speech).

[52] *Cf.* JOHN C. COFFEE, JR., GATEKEEPERS: THE PROFESSIONS AND CORPORATE GOVERNANCE 2-3 (2006) (discussing roles of lawyers, accountants, and other professionals in safeguarding integrity of financial system).

The law of lawyering calls upon all lawyers, whether defense or prosecution, public or private, to observe certain norms, such as refraining from counseling clients to engage in illegal conduct.[53] The regulation of conflicts of interest,[54] including the conflict of the lawyer serving as witness, similarly serves the interests of the legal system in avoiding confusion of roles. Duties of candor, including the duty of candor toward the tribunal,[55] also serve this gatekeeping function, imposing obligations on lawyers to guard against conduct that could skew the legal process, even when doing so may further branding efforts by yielding short-term success.[56] The SEC, pursuant to its authority under the Sarbanes-Oxley Act,[57] has also sought to enforce a gatekeeping role for lawyers in this situation, requiring that the lawyer go up the corporate ladder to inform officials of abuses, and that the lawyer be free to disclose fraudulent conduct that could cause substantial financial harm.[58]

Lawyers' gatekeeping is particularly important in addressing collective wrongdoing because the nature of groups can create substantial challenges to compliance with law. Groups can polarize in a fashion that promotes illegality, as group entrepreneurs encourage passionate followers with reductive narratives.[59] Members of the group feel that their membership hinges on accepting the narrative without dissent.[60] Cognitive dynamics that privilege short-term responses at the expense of deliberation about long-term goals can also promote polarization.[61] Branding behavior by lawyers can exacerbate this trend, legitimating the excesses of "group-think."[62] In contrast, lawyers'

---

[53] *See* MODEL RULES OF PROF'L CONDUCT R. 1.2(d) (2005).

[54] *See id.* at R. 1.7-1.12.

[55] *See id.* at R. 3.3.

[56] The requirement under Model Rule 4.1 that the lawyer disclose information necessary to prevent facilitation of a client crime or fraud is another gatekeeping rule. *See id.* at R. 4.1.

[57] *See* Sarbanes-Oxley Act of 2002, Pub. L. No. 107-204, §307, 116 Stat. 745; *cf.* Michael A. Perino, *Enron's Legislative Aftermath: Some Reflections on the Deterrence Aspects of the Sarbanes-Oxley Act of 2002*, 76 ST. JOHN'S L. REV. 671, 676-89 (2002) (expressing skepticism about deterrence value of Sarbanes-Oxley provisions).

[58] *See* 17 C.F.R. 205 (2003); *see also* Sung Hui Kim, *The Banality of Fraud: Re-Situating the Inside Counsel as Gatekeeper*, 74 FORDHAM L. REV. 983 (2005). New federal statutes that require lawyers to ascertain the merits of claims before raising them, such as Rule 11 of the Federal Rules of Civil Procedure or provisions of the new Bankruptcy Act, reflect comparable concerns, which may on occasion lead to undue chilling of lawyer advice and advocacy. *See supra* notes 55-57 and accompanying text (discussing how gatekeeping can skew lawyering toward state interests).

[59] *See* AMY CHUA, WORLD ON FIRE: HOW EXPORTING FREE MARKET DEMOCRACY BREEDS ETHNIC HATRED AND GLOBAL INSTABILITY (2003); CHARLES TILLY, THE POLITICS OF COLLECTIVE VIOLENCE 141 (2003); Peter Margulies, *Making "Regime Change" Multilateral: The War on Terror and Transitions to Democracy*, 32 DENV. J. INT'L L. & POL'Y 389 (2004).

[60] *See* Cass R. Sunstein, *Why They Hate Us: The Role of Social Dynamics*, 25 HARV. J.L. & PUB. POL'Y 429 (2002); Neal Kumar Katyal, *Conspiracy Theory*, 112 YALE L.J. 1307 (2003).

[61] *See* Kim, *supra* note 58.

[62] Prof. Yoo, the principal drafter of the torture memo, supplied not only ideological fervor but intellectual heft for his sweeping view of executive power. One can argue, of course, as the independence

gatekeeping can counteract polarization, invoking the constraints of law as both limits worth observing for their own sake and pragmatic obstacles that a competent decision-maker should take into account.[63]

C. Equipoise as a Working Approach

Describing the tension between branding and gatekeeping begs the question of how to integrate these two crucial lawyering moves. Two factors are crucial: 1) freedom from advance knowledge of client's wrongdoing, and 2) the ability to say "No." When lawyers

as alibi conception would have it, that had Professor Yoo demurred, the Administration would have found another lawyer to take his place. However, at such critical junctures, lawyers may not be entirely fungible. The Administration may have had difficulty in finding someone else with Prof. Yoo's compelling combination of ideology and intellect. Without such an individual, those expressing doubts about the Administration's course, such as the counselor for the State Department or the General Counsel for the Navy, may have had a better opportunity to block or at least mitigate the furious organizational momentum behind the Administration's coercive interrogation policy. *Cf.* Peter Margulies, *Legal Institutions and the War on Terror*, 60 U. MIAMI L. REV. 309 (2006) (rejecting ex ante authorizations of torture, such as those in the Department of Justice memo, but arguing that those using certain less serious forms of coercion should be able to present necessity defense to jury based on demonstrable proof that their actions save lives).

[63] At the same time, moreover, branding and gatekeeping are on some level reciprocal, not merely competing, norms. For example, in terrorism cases, including those involving detainees at Gitmo or elsewhere, the government may wish to limit the access of defense lawyers, and the ability of detainees to communicate to the outside world through their lawyers, and may propose special measures, such as attorney-client monitoring, to deal with these issues. *See* Teri Dobbins, *Protecting the Unpopular from the Unreasonable: Warrantless Monitoring of Attorney Client Communications in Federal Prisons*, 53 CATH. U. L. REV. 295 (2004); Margulies, *The Virtues and Vices of Solidarity*, *supra* note 2; Ellen S. Podgor & John Wesley Hall, *Government Surveillance of Attorney-Client Communications: Invoked in the Name of Fighting Terrorism*, 17 GEO. J. LEGAL ETHICS 145 (2004). However, if the government clamps down too hard, the result is a fatal decline in perceptions of legitimacy that undermines gatekeeping goals.

By the same token, every lawyer, no matter how aggressive the lawyer wishes to be in branding, needs some minimal level of good will from prosecutors and courts that compliance with gatekeeping norms will yield. This may be one reason why even "radical lawyers" will, in a pinch, represent cooperators, as Lynne Stewart, convicted last year of material support of terrorist activity, has on occasion done. *See* Skinner v. Duncan, 2003 U.S. Dist. LEXIS 10102 (S.D.N.Y. June 17, 2003), at *172 n. 82 (noting that Stewart had represented a cooperating witness in a state prosecution, and observing that, "[i]f representing a cooperator created a conflict [with representation of defendants in other cases], few if any criminal defense attorneys could be considered conflict free"). Indeed, Stewart represented a person who is arguably the best known cooperator of the last twenty-five years—Sammy "the Bull" Gravano, who turned state's evidence against the "Teflon Don" John Gotti, after a colorful career as Gotti's chief enforcer. *See* Margulies, *The Virtues and Vices of Solidarity*, *supra* note 2; *cf.* LoCascio v. United States, No. 00-CV-6015, 2005 U.S. Dist. LEXIS 29562 (E.D.N.Y. Nov. 16, 2005) (discussing evidence in the Gotti case). Gravano, subsequent to entering the federal witness protection program, apparently decided that the career change to law abiding citizen was too jarring, and allegedly embarked on a career path more suited to his talents, that of big-time Ecstasy dealer. The feds did not approve of his new career choice, and indicted him, at which point he retained Lynne Stewart; to Stewart's credit, she seemed to view him not as someone wearing the Scarlet Letter "S" for Snitch, as vigorous defense counsel branding might have required, but instead as a person in a bind who needed legal assistance.

retain these prerogatives, further sanctions risk tilting the system in the state's favor. When lawyers lack either attribute, sanctions of some kind are necessary to preserve equipoise. The following paragraphs discuss each factor in turn.

First, consider the freedom from advance knowledge of client wrongdoing. Lawyers who knowingly give advice that facilitates client wrongdoing violate a basic rule of legal ethics, embodied in Model Rule of Professional Conduct 1.2(d). Model Rule 1.2(d) prohibits lawyers from giving advice in this situation, precisely because of concerns about maintaining the lawyer's distinctive role. Knowingly giving advice in such a situation makes someone into an accomplice. An accomplice cannot easily sever links to fellow wrongdoers, and thus cannot provide legal advice, properly understood. Moreover, a lawyer who takes this path has, like Lynne Stewart in the conduct that led to her conviction on charges of lending material support to terrorist activity, sought to game the system—using the privileges and access that the legal system affords lawyers to achieve inappropriate ends that would be more difficult to achieve for a non-lawyer.[64] Tobacco industry lawyers exhibited similar strategic behavior by colluding over time with cigarette manufacturers to conceal adverse health studies by placing those studies under the attorneys' nominal supervision.[65]

The bench and bar have rightly sought to deprive those accused of collective wrongdoing of any strategic advantage derived from such manipulation. Established doctrines like the crime-fraud exception have long operated to ferret out lawyer-client communications used to facilitate illegal conduct, deeming them to be communications that society should not encourage through the cover of a privilege. Recent exceptions made to the duty of confidentiality in cases where the client used the lawyer's services in furtherance of a fraud have supplemented these venerable rules.[66]

Giving the client bad news is the other cornerstone of equipoise. Elihu Root, a giant in the New York bar at the turn of the century and a one-time Secretary of State, once famously observed that "half the practice of a decent lawyer consists of telling would-be clients that they are damned fools and should stop."[67] Lawyers who say "no" act as gatekeepers for the preservation of long-term perspectives and values. Rather than acquiescing in a scheme from a client that may be remunerative or expedient in the short term, lawyers at the very least should invite a discussion with clients about more sustainable approaches to accomplishing client goals. In a democratic republic, this kind of deliberation is precious, tempering insidious tendencies that can corrode institutions. The importance of such deliberation is one reason that lawyers and

---

[64] *See* Julia Preston, *Lawyer is Guilty of Aiding Terror*, N.Y. TIMES, Feb. 11, 2005, at A1.

[65] *Cf.* Burton v. R.J. Reynolds Tobacco Co., 177 F.R.D. 491, 496-98 (D. Kan. 1997) (rejecting claim of attorney-client privilege).

[66] *See* MODEL RULES OF PROF'L CONDUCT R. 1.6(b) (2004).

[67] *See* MARY ANN GLENDON, A NATION UNDER LAWYERS 37 (1994); *cf.* BRIAN Z. TAMANAHA, LAW AS A MEANS TO AN END: THREAT TO THE RULE OF LAW 142 (2006) (asserting that Root also gave lawyers seemingly contradictory advice to accommodate their clients whenever possible).

commentators continue to turn to the example of Brandeis as a lawyer who refused to sacrifice his professional reputation for short-term client approval.[68]

Rather than follow Brandeis's path, most lawyers shy away from giving clients bad news, for a range of reasons including money, power, and ideology. This was true in the corporate scandals that have periodically rocked the business community. For example, the law firm of Vinson & Elkins earned $165.2 million doing legal work for Enron between 1997 and 2001[69] as it set up "special purpose" entities for corporate officials, claiming subsequently that it had no knowledge that those officers were using the partnerships to enrich themselves and hide liabilities that should have been disclosed on the corporate balance sheet.[70] It was also true of the overreaching in the national security arena characteristic of the Bush Administration, in which lawyers neglected to mention the relevance of a crucial precedent—the Steel Seizure Case —to issues of executive power over rules governing interrogation or surveillance.[71] Equipoise is impossible when attorneys surrender to lucre's lure or group-think.

D. Equipoise in Advocacy and Advice

Group-think is fatal because equipoise is necessarily a pragmatic concept involving weighing of alternatives. It applies in both the advice and advocacy contexts. In each setting the lawyer seeking equipoise must consider the opportunity costs of conduct that overweighs either gatekeeping or branding behavior.

The case for equipoise is clearest in the advice context. Advance knowledge of wrongdoing in matters related to the lawyer's advice may make the lawyer an accomplice. Moreover, as Bradley Wendel has pointed out, the lawyer as advisor should follow a rule of reason that looks not only to the language of statutes governing, say, transactions designed for tax purposes, but also to common-sense views of what the legislature intended.[72] A narrow, parched view of legislative intent may give clients greater autonomy in the short term, but stoke mistrust among other stakeholders such as investors, voters, and even foreign states. This mistrust may ultimately make social

---

[68] *See* DAVID LUBAN, *Making Sense of Moral Meltdowns, in* LAWYERS' ETHICS AND THE PURSUIT OF SOCIAL JUSTICE 355, 369 (Susan D. Carle ed., New York University Press 2005) (discussing Brandeis); *cf.* John Leubsdorf, *Gandhi's Legal Ethics*, 51 RUTGERS L. REV. 1923, 1925-26 (1999) (describing how Gandhi's law practice demonstrated regard for the welfare of third parties, as well as clients); *but see* Clyde Spillenger, *Elusive Advocate: Reconsidering Brandeis as People's Lawyer, in id.* at 72 (arguing that Brandeis was excessively detached from client concerns).

[69] *See* Terry Maxon, *As the Rules Change, So Do Lawyers' Roles: Latest Report in the Enron Fallout Amplifies Calls for Watchdog Duty*, DALLAS MORNING NEWS, Dec. 7, 2003, at 1D (also noting that Vinson & Elkins earned $42.8 million from Enron in the year 2000 alone).

[70] *See* Regan, *supra* note 12.

[71] *See* Gillers, *supra* note 33, at 237-38 (criticizing Department of Justice Lawyers for ignoring Supreme Court's holding limiting executive power in *Youngstown Sheet & Tube Co. v. Sawyer*, 343 U.S. 579 (1952)); Luban, *Liberalism and Torture*, *supra* note 6 (same).

[72] *See* Wendel, *Professionalism as Interpretation*, *supra* note 6.

and political coordination impossible. However, a lawyer should not unduly discount the social utility of innovation in financial transactions, particularly where all parties are sophisticated repeat players.[73]

Additional caveats are required for the application of equipoise to advocacy. Here, the costs of excessive gatekeeping will be significant, while branding is aligned with core values of individual autonomy and government accountability.[74] Here, too, however, equipoise reconciles competing interests.

We should begin by acknowledging the force of arguments for branding in the advocacy context. Criminal defense, where the stakes are highest for the client and the need to check government overreaching is greatest, presents the most compelling case for aggressive branding behavior. As Justice White asserted, "[D]efense counsel has no . . . obligation to . . . present the truth. Our system assigns him a different mission . . . If he can confuse a witness, even a truthful one . . . that will be his normal course . . . [A]s part of the duty imposed on the most honorable defense counsel, we countenance or require conduct which in many instances has little, if any, relation to the search for truth."[75] By rigorously testing the government's proof, the criminal defense lawyer deters the state from hasty or cavalier resort to its monopoly on legitimate violence. Raising the costs of prosecution in this fashion has a prophylactic purpose, guarding against use of the criminal justice system against political enemies or disfavored groups.

Moreover, too much gatekeeping may already be a problem in criminal defense. Issues of branding and gatekeeping are difficult to separate from the status of criminal defense lawyers as "repeat players" in the legal system. In some respects, being a repeat player with interests beyond the fortunes of a particular case can undermine the lawyer's zeal. The literature is replete with arguments that lawyers encourage clients to settle or refrain from a "full-bore" defense in certain cases, because they are concerned that vigorous advocacy may not be worth the candle, and may try the patience of prosecutors and courts.[76] Lawyers may also view a "radical" defense, such as a theory that the government fabricated evidence to achieve political ends, as isolating them from sources of institutional support, including judges who may be in a position to sabotage sources of long-term funding.[77] In other settings, for instance military commissions, repeat player defense counsel, such as JAG officers, may be subject to command influence, or fear that zealous defense will harm their careers.

---

[73] *See* Schwarcz, *supra* note 9 (defending lawyers' writing of opinion letters regarding complex financial transactions).

[74] *Cf.* Fred C. Zacharias & Bruce A. Green, *Reconceptualizing Advocacy Ethics*, 74 GEO. WASH. L. REV. 1 (2005) (offering comprehensive view seeking to reconcile gatekeeping and advocacy).

[75] United States v. Wade, 388 U.S. 218, 256-58 (1967) (White, J., concurring and dissenting), *cited in* LISA G. LERMAN & PHILIP G. SCHRAG, ETHICAL PROBLEMS IN THE PRACTICE OF LAW 541-42 n.118 (2005).

[76] *See* Daryl K. Brown, *Rationing Criminal Defense Entitlements: An Argument from Institutional Design*, 104 COLUM. L. REV. 801 (2004); Richman, *Cooperating Clients*, *supra* note 49.

[77] *See generally* ROBERT E. PRECHT, DEFENDING MOHAMMAD: JUSTICE ON TRIAL (2003) (discussing institutional pressure in trial of defendants ultimately convicted of the 1993 World Trade Center bombing).

Even in the advocacy context, however, lawyers owe a duty to the legal system to avoid entanglements that cloud their roles. Keeping these roles separate avoids confusion for fact finders, thereby safeguarding the integrity of the system, while also preserving the leeway that the system offers to advocates to zealously represent defendants in criminal cases. The well-known rule against knowingly eliciting or failing to timely correct perjured testimony is one example.[78] In addition, the conflict of interest rules, as interpreted by courts in disqualification cases, protect the integrity of the advocate's role.[79]

To see how we can reconcile equipoise with an appropriate conception of the criminal defense lawyer's role in a democracy, consider the interaction of one of the two core equipoise factors—freedom from prior knowledge of the client's alleged wrongdoing—with the defense lawyer's choice of tactics. As Justice White's quote above suggests,[80] most criminal defense lawyers believe that it is permissible, if not required, to seek to discredit the testimony of an eye-witness, even when the lawyer knows that the witness's account is accurate. The defense lawyer can seek to impeach the witness by asking, for example, whether the witness is near-sighted.[81] We accept this dimension of the lawyer's role as an indispensable element of the state's constitutional obligation to prove a criminal defendant guilty beyond a reasonable doubt. However, on an equipoise view, criminal defense attorneys also accept reciprocal duties.

The advocate's right to act despite contrary knowledge entails an unspoken bargain—that the lawyer has obtained such knowledge *after* the fact, through a client approaching the lawyer with a legal problem, and not before or during commission of the illegal act. This precept preserves equipoise by separating the advocate's role from that of the accomplice or witness. It ensures that the advocate does not become unduly involved with clients' illegal conduct.[82] Prophylactic application of the lawyer as witness rule also gives lawyers an incentive to vigorously counsel clients to refrain from illegal behavior, in a fashion which may deter some illegal activity.

This protection of the distinctive attributes of the advocacy role also protects the integrity of the court. In the absence of such a prophylactic conception, a judicial proceeding risks becoming just another forum for collective wrongdoing, featuring a lawyer pre-selected by a client to get a close-up view of the facts as they unfold, the better to disarm the prosecution with a wink and a nod when the client is called to account.[83] A lawyer building a brand might seek such a forum. Moreover, the lawyer's

---

[78] MODEL RULES OF PROF'L CONDUCT R. 3.3 (2005).

[79] *See infra* notes 98-102 and accompanying text.

[80] *See supra* note 75 and accompanying text.

[81] The lawyer's ability to act despite contrary knowledge in this crucial advocacy situation contrasts with the lawyer's obligation in a transactional or pervasively regulated setting to withdraw. Similarly, a lawyer apprised by a client of the client's ongoing illegal activity has an obligation to advise the client to cease and desist, even though nonlawyers so apprised have no comparable obligation, although they may not actively assist.

[82] *See* McMorrow, *supra* note 15.

[83] The "unsworn witness" conception advanced by the Second Circuit overlaps to some degree with this focus on stripping the client of any possible strategic advantage gained by retaining a lawyer with advance

advance knowledge of the facts could conceivably enhance her functional value to the client. Whatever the functional effects, however, concern for judicial integrity would mandate deterrence of such strategic behavior.

Equipoise in both advocacy and advice addresses collective action problems and transaction costs. On the collective action front, lawyers face pressures to approve transactions and policies, such as the Bush administration's disregard of both international and domestic law on coercive interrogation of terror detainees, that push branding to the forefront. Lawyers who give advice are subject to a "race to the bottom"—a collective action problem in which lawyers compete for clients by signaling their willingness to tolerate conduct that is close to the line of legality, or indeed steps over it. Equipoise mitigates the branding behavior inspired by the race to the bottom dynamic.

At the same time, equipoise helps deal with the agency costs confronted by collective entities, including business organizations, government, and even groups that use terrorist tactics. In each context, a central problem is the gap that can develop between the entity's leaders and the entity's interests. Leaders, after all, are agents of the organizations they lead. However, if they overreach or pursue their own agenda, they injure the interests of the entity. For example, the corporate insiders who ran Enron, and retained counsel to advise the corporation on their bewilderingly complex financial dealings, apparently had an agenda that was *not* aligned with that of Enron's shareholders.[84] Similarly, the actions of the Bush administration in approving coercive means of interrogation have grievously injured the standing and moral strength of America throughout the world.[85]

Organized crime groups such as the Gambino crime family also have interests that depart from the short-term wishes of the kingpin.[86] For example, when John Gotti initially suggested that each of his associates defy the subpoena to appear before a grand jury, Gotti initially failed to recognize that one of his associates had received bail pending appeal that might be revoked if Gotti's associate was cited for contempt.[87] Losing the associate to prison would have been contrary to the interests of the organization. However, Gotti's lawyers failed to identify this problem. Gotti himself eventually had to point out the revocation of bail risk, observing in the process that the lawyers were taking "family" money but not providing value in return.[88] Similarly, organizations

knowledge. *See* United States v. Locascio, 6 F.3d 924, 933 (2d Cir. 1993). The lawyer's presence in the courtroom as an advocate for the defense encourages a circus atmosphere in the courtroom that undercuts the seriousness of the charges. The legal system deserves a lawyer who will not interact with the jury in a fashion that the record cannot capture about his outside-the-courtroom familiarity with the defendants. Such nonverbal cues confuse the system of roles on which the legal system depends.

[84] *See* Regan, *supra* note 12, at 1220-29 (discussing effort by Andrew Fastow, Enron's Chief Financial Officer, to conceal compensation received from partnership tied to Enron).

[85] *Cf.* Gillers, *supra* note 33 (critiquing torture memos).

[86] *See generally* United States v. Gotti, 771 F. Supp. 552 (E.D.N.Y. 1991), *aff'd sub nom.*

[87] *See id* at 557; United States v. Locascio, 6 F.3d 924 (2d Cir. 1993).

[88] *Gotti*, 771 F. Supp. at 557; *cf. id.* at 555-57 (discussing large sums of money Gotti had paid to lawyers to represent Gotti's associates).

such as the Palestinian group Hamas that use violence for political goals sometimes seek to downplay violence and stress greater political participation. When lawyers like Lynne Stewart side with those who seek renewed violence, they undermine this turn toward the political sphere.[89]

E. The Equipoise Model and Structural Protections

When considering how to safeguard the equipoise between branding and gatekeeping, courts and other players in the process should keep in mind two goals: 1) deterring departures from the equipoise norm, and, 2) stripping advocates, parties, and (where possible) advisers and their clients of the strategic advantages derived from those departures. Implementing these goals requires structural protections for the two freedoms identified above as central to equipoise: freedom of advance knowledge of wrongdoing, and freedom to provide the client with bad news.

Because equipoise deals with a range of lawyering tasks, including both advocacy and advice, remedies for failures of equipoise will necessarily be eclectic and pragmatic. A structural approach to policing lawyer's independence starts with courts' exercise of their inherent and supervisory authority over defense lawyers and prosecutors. In addition, appropriate remedies for failures of equipoise in the advice context will include subjecting lawyers to a higher risk of both civil and criminal liability, and limiting "advice of counsel" defenses that clients may seek to interpose to excuse overreaching.

In considering the pedigree of structural remedies, we can look to a wide range of sources. Remedies such as disgorgement and the constructive trust have long stood for the proposition that a fiduciary should relinquish the fruits of his wrongdoing.[90] Equitable interpretations of statutes, such as the New York Court of Appeals's holding in the classic of jurisprudence, *Riggs v. Palmer*,[91] that a murderer of a testator cannot take under the will, also embody the principle that no one should profit from his own wrong.

The remedial authority of federal courts in the domain of criminal procedure has followed a similar path.[92] In curbing law enforcement excesses, the [Supreme] Court has required concrete steps as a prophylactic measure. The Court's decision in *Miranda*

---

[89] *See Lawyer Denies Islamic Group Has Withdrawn Backing for Peace*, BBC SUMMARY OF WORLD BROADCASTS, June 24, 2000 (quoting Egyptian lawyer for faction of Islamic Group that wished to join civil society in Egypt as disputing Stewart's report that Islamic Group's leader, Sheik Abdel Rahman, had withdrawn his support for a cease-fire put in place after adverse international reaction to 1997 attack by the Islamic Group that resulted in the deaths of over 60 people at an Egyptian tourist site). *See generally* Andrew Kydd & Barbara F. Walter, *Sabotaging the Peace: The Politics of Extremist Violence*, 56 INT'L ORG. 263 (2002) (discussing collective action problem caused when governments and insurgents bid up violence through cycles of repression and terror).

[90] *See* Colleen P. Murphy, *Misclassifying Monetary Restitution*, 55 SMU L. REV. 1577, 1584-86 (2002) (discussing remedies).

[91] 22 N.E. 188, 191 (N.Y. 1889).

[92] This discussion draws heavily from the analysis in Margulies, *Above Contempt?*, *supra* note 7, at 484-87.

v. Arizona,[93] for example, requiring specific warnings to defendants in custody, addressed law enforcement officials' tendency to manipulate the fuzzier "totality of the circumstances" test.[94] Courts have also exercised their supervisory authority to regulate inappropriate conduct by federal prosecutors that undermines the integrity of legal processes or interferes with the relationship between a defendant and his attorney.[95] Structural protections for equipoise have also been a central theme in cases on disqualification of defense counsel.[96]

F. Summary

Achieving equipoise between branding and gatekeeping entails two virtues: freedom from advance knowledge of client wrongdoing, and freedom to give clients bad news. Equipoise applies to both advice and advocacy. Courts and other legal actors should tailor remedies for violations of equipoise in order to deter future departures and strip lawyers and clients of strategic advantages gained from failures of equipoise. The following sections address equipoise and remedies in concrete fashion.

III. DISQUALIFICATION OF DEFENSE COUNSEL

The disqualification of defense counsel offers a compelling case study in the challenges of achieving equipoise. Courts sometimes disqualify counsel who seem competent as a functional matter to represent a client's interests.[97] However, courts have also declined to disqualify defense counsel who exhibit material impediments to their ability to serve.[98] Viewing disqualification as a means of balancing branding and gatekeeping offers a coherent approach.

One reason judicial decisions regarding disqualification[99] seem incoherent is the formidable array of values they embody, including the defendant's Sixth Amendment

---

[93] 384 U.S. 436 (1966); *cf.* Dickerson v. United States, 530 U.S. 428 (2000) (re-affirming Miranda's viability as constitutional precedent).

[94] *See* Miranda v. Arizona, 384 U.S. 436, 444, 457 (1966).

[95] *See, e.g.,* United States v. Hammad, 858 F.2d 834 (2d Cir. 1988) (holding that court could invoke supervisory power to suppress evidence yielded by sham grand jury subpoena to target of investigation when target was represented by counsel); United States v. Ming He, 94 F.3d 782 (2d Cir. 1996) (holding that absent express waiver, prosecutor could not interview cooperating witness without counsel being present); *cf.* Sara Sun Beale, *Reconsidering Supervisory Power in Criminal Cases: Constitutional and Statutory Limits on the Authority of the Federal Courts*, 84 COLUM. L. REV. 1433 (1984) (arguing for clarification of judicial authority); Bruce A. Green & Fred C. Zacharias, *Regulating Federal Prosecutors' Ethics*, 55 VAND. L. REV. 381 (2002) (analyzing supervisory power).

[96] *See infra* notes 97-115 and accompanying text.

[97] *See* United States v. Gotti, 771 F. Supp. 552, 558 (E.D.N.Y. 1991).

[98] *See* Williams v. Meachum, 948 F.2d 863, 868 (2d Cir. 1991).

[99] Such exercises of power are part of a tapestry that also includes criminal prosecution of attorneys and legislation requiring that corporate attorneys exercise independent judgment in their dealings with corporate

rights, fairness to the government, and concern for the integrity of the legal process.[100] Disqualification of counsel promotes Sixth Amendment fair trial and right to counsel values because conflicted counsel may not be able to provide effective assistance. Courts can also invoke their general supervisory power to prevent and deter violation of professional norms regarding conflicts.[101] By reducing the accuracy and reliability of litigated outcomes in the criminal courts, such conflicts can damage not only the defendant, but the integrity of the legal system. Counsel's neglect of minimum gatekeeping requirements, including freedom from prior knowledge of client wrongdoing and freedom to give the client bad news, can also injure systemic integrity even without a clear functional impact on the lawyer's ability to represent the client.

At the same time, defense lawyers' independence is also threatened by the government's manipulation of the disqualification process and conflict of interest rules. The government has an incentive to seek disqualification when confronted with an attorney who may be only modestly conflicted, or whose conflict is purely speculative but whose acumen and energy is unquestioned.[102] In such situations, allowing the government to seek disqualification permits strategic behavior by the government.

A court that balances these interests should disqualify counsel where power differentials between clients or the presence of substantial financial incentives impinge on effective attorney-client deliberation, or where the lawyer has prior knowledge of wrongdoing. In such cases, courts should not defer to client waivers of conflicts, since

---

officers who may be violating their fiduciary duties to the corporation or defrauding the public. The insurance industry, *see* Aviva Abramovsky, *The Enterprise Model of Managing Conflicts of Interest in the Tripartite Insurance Defense Relationship*, 27 CARDOZO L. REV. 193 (2005), has also attracted scrutiny for what some commentators view as the insufficient independence of advocates paid by insurers to represent policyholders. On conflicts of interest of defense counsel, *see generally* Mark W. Shiner, *Note, Conflicts of Interest Challenges Post* Mickens v. Taylor: *Redefining the Defendant's Burden in Concurrent, Successive, and Personal Interest Conflicts*, 60 WASH. & LEE L. REV. 965 (200) (discussing relationship between conflicts of interest and ineffective assistance of counsel); Patrice McGuire Sabach, Note, *Rethinking Unwaivable Conflicts of Interest After United States v. Schwarz and Mickens v. Taylor*, 59 N.Y.U. ANN. SURV. AM. L. 89 (2003) (same).

[100] *See* Nancy J. Moore, *Conflicts of Interest in the Simultaneous Representation of Multiple Clients: A Proposed Solution to the Current Confusion and Controversy*, 61 TEX. L. REV. 211 (1982) (discussing competing values).

[101] To illustrate how courts resolve the clash in values inherent in disqualification cases, consider Glasser v. United States, 315 U.S. 60, 67-74 (1942), in which counsel's concurrent conflict, arising from his representation of co-defendants, resulted in a failure to cross-examine a key witness regarding the witness's lack of knowledge of one of the defendants. Such questioning may have highlighted one defendant's lack of guilt at the expense of the other defendant. Winnowing out such conflicts is particularly important, the Court has noted, because conflicts caused by concurrent representation can cause omissions, such as the failure to cross-examine in *Glasser*, that are particularly difficult for a reviewing court to detect.

[102] Courts allow prosecutors to seek the disqualification of defense counsel for a number of reasons: if conflicted counsel go forward without court consideration of the conflict, a defendant who has been found guilty can appeal based on ineffective assistance of counsel. Furthermore, the government, as much as the defendant and the court, has a stake in maintaining the integrity of the legal system. That being said, if the goal is securing conflict-free counsel and systemic integrity, allowing the government to seek defense counsel's disqualification creates significant agency costs.

other interests, including the integrity of the judicial process, are at stake. In cases that do not present these concerns, however, courts should appreciate that disqualification is more likely to confer an unearned strategic advantage on the government, and should consider measures less drastic than disqualification to deal with the problem.

Courts have struck the right note when the lawyer's financial dependence on a participant in the case indicated a failure of equipoise. For example, in supporting its motion to disqualify attorney Bruce Cutler from representation of the "Teflon Don," John Gotti, the government submitted evidence that Gotti had paid Cutler and another lawyer, Gerry Shargel, hundreds of thousands of dollars to represent a range of "family" clients.[103] Cutler's receipt of money—some of it, according to Gotti, "under the table"—immersed Cutler in advance knowledge of some of Gotti's illegal activities and made it impossible for Cutler to give Gotti bad news.[104] While Gotti was clearly not someone who enjoyed frustration, a lawyer's duty to avoid assisting illegal conduct under Rule 1.2(d) should trump that concern—otherwise the lawyer veers away from the lawyer's role, and moves dangerously close to the role of accomplice. Whether or not Cutler's lack of equipoise would have had a functional effect at Gotti's trial,[105] deterring such failures of equipoise justified Cutler's disqualification.[106]

---

[103] United States v. Gotti, 771 F. Supp. 552, 555-57 (E.D.N.Y. 1991), *aff'd sub nom.*

[104] For example, the government's tapes reveal that Shargel suggested that a Gotti associate plead guilty to avoid the need for Gotti and others to testify under a grant of immunity. *See* United States v. Gotti, 771 F. Supp. 552, 557 (E.D.N.Y. 1991). The decision reveals no mention by attorney Cutler that having the associate plead guilty to avoid the need for Gotti to testify would constitute obstruction of justice.

[105] *Cf.* LoCascio v. United States, No. 00-CV-6015, 2005 U.S. Dist. LEXIS 29562, at *19-21 (E.D.N.Y. Nov. 16, 2005) (denying writ based on alleged ineffective assistance of counsel for one of Gotti's co-defendants; court held that defendant had not demonstrated that defense lawyer's failing to ask questions of government witness designed to illustrate defendant's lack of substantial participation in alleged murder was "adverse effect" for purposes of finding ineffective assistance, where client had previously agreed to joint defense with kingpin and government had presented other evidence of the client's participation).

[106] In United States v. Schwarz, 283 F.3d 76 (2d Cir. 2002), the court correctly found that the defense lawyer's receipt of a retainer of $10 million from a police officers' union rendered the lawyer incapable of providing balanced advice on whether the defendant, a police officer accused of participating in the abuse of a man in custody, should offer a defense based on asserting that another officer had in fact participated in the abuse. *But see* Williams v. Meachum, 948 F.2d 863 (2d Cir. 1991) (holding that defendant's waiver of right to unconflicted counsel was effective where lawyer informed client that he could not mount "look-alike" defense because his office also represented the individual who would be identified in the course of the defense).

Courts have also enforced the equipoise norm where the lawyer arguably participated in illegal activity at the client's behest. Consider United States v. Merlino, 349 F.3d 144 (3d Cir. 2003), in which a long-time lawyer for an alleged kingpin of the Philadelphia Cosa Nostra visited the kingpin's former associate in jail, after the associate had agreed to testify for the government. The lawyer, Mr. Pinsky, handed the witness a letter from the kingpin saying, in essence, that all was forgiven, and that the associate should not hesitate to return to Philly upon his release. Lawyer Pinsky also offered the associate $100 for his jail commissary account. Despite these touching gestures, the Merlino Court upheld Pinsky's disqualification, ruling that his conduct created a risk that he, too, would be prosecuted, or at the very least might be called to testify at his client's trial on grounds that the lawyer's contact with the witness demonstrated his client's consciousness of guilt. Incidentally, the kingpin's substitute attorney upon Pinsky's disqualification

In other cases, however—particularly those involving so-called successive conflicts between a lawyer for a defendant and a former client whom the government might call as a witness—disqualification has undermined equipoise by aiding the prosecution. In *Wheat v. United States*,[107] for example, the Supreme Court, despite a defendant's waiver of any potential conflicts, upheld on speculative grounds the disqualification of counsel whom the defendant had retained after the lawyer had obtained an acquittal and a favorable plea agreement for defendants in related cases. The court was concerned that one of the previous defendants might be called by the government to testify against Wheat, and that Wheat's attorney would then have to cross-examine his former client. However, the court ignored the fact that the earlier defendant was unlikely to implicate Wheat,[108] and failed to explore the use of stand-by or substituted counsel for the purpose of cross-examination only. Wheat was subsequently convicted.[109] In upholding the conviction, the Supreme Court unduly discounted the risk that disqualifying counsel based on such speculative concerns gave the government a strategic advantage[110] by removing the one attorney with a demonstrated track record of successful representation.[111]

Disqualification in terrorism cases can pose the same risk of tilting the balance toward the government. In terrorism cases, even more than organized crime cases, the public's concern about the acts alleged may give the government an advantage before the trial even begins. To prevail in the face of this obstacle, defense counsel may need to be not merely competent, but extraordinary. Moreover, terrorism cases do not necessarily pose the equipoise problems exhibited in organized crime cases, in which a crime kingpin like Gotti controls the purse strings of the litigation[112] and defense lawyers are exposed

---

was Bruce Cutler, who had been disqualified a decade earlier from representing John Gotti; all of which goes to show that there are second acts in American law. *Cf.* Rubin v. Gee, 292 F.3d 397, 404-05 (4th Cir. 2002) (granting writ based on representation of petitioner in murder trial by two lawyers who had advised the client immediately following the homicide to act in manner that secured their fee but allowed jury to infer petitioner's guilt).

[107] 486 U.S. 153 (1988).

[108] *See* Green, *Through a Glass Darkly*, *supra* note 8, at 1209.

[109] Wheat v. United States, 486 U.S. 153, 164 (1988).

[110] The Court cited the institutional interest of the court in ensuring that lawyers appearing before it comply with the rules of professional conduct. However, given the speculative nature of the conflict in Wheat, it was far from clear that the disqualified lawyer had in fact violated the rules. *See* Green, *supra* note 8.

[111] *Cf.* United States v. Pizzonia, 415 F.2d 168, 186 (2006) (declining to disqualify counsel based on family relationship to alleged organized crime figures); with United States, *ex rel.* Stewart, on Behalf of Tineo v. Kelly, 870 F.2d 854, 857 (2d Cir. 1989) (holding that lawyer's prior representation of witness on unrelated matter constituted grounds of disqualification); United States v. Yannotti, 358 F. Supp. 2d 289, 297 (S.D.N.Y. 2004) (granting government's motion to disqualify attorney on grounds that government witness would testify about unrelated incident in which counsel allegedly urged witness to shoot another individual).

[112] *See* MODEL RULES OF PROF'L CONDUCT R. 1.8(f)(2) (2005) (a lawyer should not accept payment from someone other than the client unless "there is no interference with the lawyer's independence of professional judgment").

to advance information about possible wrongdoing. As a result, means less intrusive than disqualification, including stipulation,[113] waiver, and standby-counsel,[114] should be the primary tools for courts to assure defendants' Sixth Amendment rights and the integrity of the trial process.

Unfortunately, the court presiding over the single high-profile terrorism case to raise conflicts of interest issues disqualified defense counsel in circumstances that gave the government a strategic advantage. In *United States v. Rahman*,[115] the District Court disqualified famed political attorney William Kunstler from representing the "blind sheik," Sheik Abdel Rahman, and subsequently other defendants.[116] The government alleged that Abdel Rahman was guilty of seditious conspiracy, involving plans to attack the United States military and assassinate Egyptian President Mubarak.[117] The Court said that since the government had charged Abdel Rahman with directing the conspiracy and Kunstler's other clients, Siddig Ali and Ibrahim El-Gabrowny, with attempting to execute the plan through obtaining explosives and other overt acts, Kunstler could not represent all three.[118]

Here, under the functional view of representation endorsed both by the Model Rules[119] and by the Supreme Court in the *Wheat* case, the court may have been right. Following the functional model, the court observed that if Kunstler's theory of the case was that Abdel Rahman was unaware of the details of the conspiracy, Kunstler would elevate the Sheik's interests above those of his co-defendants.[120] Nor was this the end of Kunstler's problems. Kunstler later, in seeking to represent the more directly involved

---

113 *See* United States v. Perez, 325 F.3d 115 (2d Cir. 2003) (holding that defendant's informed consent to representation by lawyer who had employed him when defendant allegedly conceived of plan to smuggle cash into a foreign country, based on scheme of a previous client of attorney, was sufficient to waive conflict of interest, where government did not have to call attorney as a witness because defendant submitted an affidavit acknowledging that he was not traveling on business for the lawyer).

114 *See* U.S. v. Stein, 410 F. Supp. 2d 316, 330 (S.D.N.Y. 2006) (permitting law firm to represent defendant when a partner at firm had represented co-defendant now cooperating with the government, provided that firm hired stand-by counsel to cross-examine co-defendant should he take the stand, and implemented screening procedures to insulate partner from case).

115 837 F. Supp. 64 (S.D.N.Y. 1993); *cf.* United States v. Rahman, 189 F.3d 88, 103 (2d Cir. 1999) (affirming Abdel Rahman's conviction).

116 *See* United States v. Rahman, 861 F. Supp. 266, 276-78 (S.D.N.Y. 1994).

117 The evidence against the Sheik was strongest regarding plans for Mubarak's assassination, which was to take place during a visit of the Egyptian President to New York. *See* United States v. Rahman, 189 F.3d at 108, 117.

118 *Id.*; *see also* KUNSTLER, *supra* note 10, at 334-35 (discussing case).

119 *See* MODEL RULES OF PROF'L CONDUCT R. 1.7 (2005) (concurrent conflict—i.e., conflict between current clients—exists if "there is a significant risk that the representation of one or more clients will be materially limited by the lawyer's responsibilities to another client"); *id.* at R. 1.9 (stating that lawyer shall not represent a client in a matter "substantially related" to a matter in which the lawyer represented a former client, when the present client's interests are "materially adverse" to the former client's interests).

120 *See* United States v. Rahman, 837 F. Supp. 64, 66-68 (S.D.N.Y. 1993).

defendant, El-Gabrowny, also developed a potential "former client/witness" conflict.[121] If any of the other defendants, including the Sheik, had sought to testify, then Kunstler's cross-examination would have been limited by his obligations to his former clients. The court ruled that permitting stand-by counsel to cross-examine would not cure the problem, because Kunstler could still try to use privileged information to inform his opening and closing.[122]

In contrast, an equipoise view would have seen the forest, not the trees. On an equipoise view, there was no evidence that Kunstler had advance knowledge of the events described in the indictment, or lacked the ability to give his clients bad news. In fact, the news Kunstler apparently gave his clients was correct: that their best chance was to stick together,[123] and argue that the government had concocted the conspiracy case to punish the Sheik, who had been widely identified in the media as the inspiration for the first World Trade Center bombing in 1993.[124] The thinness of the government's evidence on whether the Sheik ever approved a concrete plan to bomb United States military installations dovetailed with this defense, as did the presence among the conspirators of an FBI informant. Just as importantly, Kunstler had an unparalleled track record of succeeding with this kind of defense theory. By taking Kunstler out of the equation, even given the functional justifications for doing so, the court deprived the defendants of their best chance for an acquittal. This result served the government's interests, but undermined equipoise.[125]

---

[121] *See* United States v. Rahman, 861 F. Supp. 266, 276-78 (S.D.N.Y. 1994).

[122] *Id.* at 278.

[123] *See* SUSAN P. SHAPIRO, TANGLED LOYALTIES: CONFLICTS OF INTEREST IN LEGAL PRACTICE 112 (2002) (noting that multiple defendants often prefer having "one person working toward a common goal"); *cf.* KENNETH MANN, DEFENDING WHITE-COLLAR CRIME: A PORTRAIT OF ATTORNEYS AT WORK 167-68 (1985) (discussing rationale for joint representation of multiple defendants).

[124] *See* Binny Miller, *Give Them Back Their Lives: Recognizing Client Narrative in Case Theory*, 93 MICH. L. REV. 485, 576 (1994).

[125] The conception of equipoise advanced here for defense counsel would also permit lawyers to brand themselves as not representing cooperators. *See generally* Richman, *Cooperating Clients*, *supra* note 49. Lawyers have legitimate reasons for avoiding collaborating with the government, which sound in overall concerns for the integrity of the system: snitches can manufacture information to sell their product in exchange for favorable treatment, telling prosecutors what they want to hear, rather than the unvarnished facts. Lawyers who do not wish to take part in such a process should not be forced to do so. The case law demonstrates, moreover, that defendants who wish to cooperate have pathways available, involving notice to the prosecutor or to the court, accompanied by appointment of stand-by counsel. *See* Weinstein, *supra* note 49. While these pathways are not perfect, their availability suggests that a rigid bar on lawyers' branding in this situation is not necessary. However, judges should vigorously dismantle systemic barriers to representation of cooperators that turn less on ideology and more on mammon. Rule 1.8(f), which regulates payments by third parties for legal services, should be more vigorously enforced by courts, to prevent the corruption of the lawyer's judgment caused by receipt of payment from a third party such as a mob kingpin involved in the acts giving rise to the charges against the client.

Refusing to represent cooperators should also be permissible for indigent legal services providers, such as public defenders' offices. *See* Kim Taylor-Thompson, *Individual Actors v. Institutional Players: Alternating Visions of the Public Defender*, 84 GEO. L.J. 2419, 2457-60 (1996). The problem here is not

IV. EQUIPOISE, PROSECUTORS, AND GOVERNMENT OVERREACHING

While equipoise generally counsels a lighter hand for courts considering disqualification of defense lawyers, it requires vigorous oversight of prosecutorial overreaching.[126] One problem with policing prosecutorial equipoise, however, is that courts have no convenient remedy that compares with the availability of disqualification for conflicted defense counsel. This lack of remedy for failures of equipoise is even more troubling for being real, not hypothetical: prosecutors in a significant number of terrorism cases post-9/11 have exhibited significant ethical flaws.[127]

Prosecutors' work involves the same dynamic of branding and gatekeeping that typifies defense lawyers, in a setting that creates collective action problems. Government misconduct in criminal cases is generally a collaborative enterprise, including signals from above, overreaching by investigators, and either acquiescence in factually uncertain declarations or outright misrepresentations by line prosecutors.[128] Prosecutors often experience the temptation to distinguish themselves with superiors and colleagues as aggressive and vigorous law enforcement officials. A prosecutor who is aggressive, including establishing a reputation as being willing to make a case even when investigators have used methods that are "close to the line" of legality, will establish relationships with investigative personnel that bring in more cases.[129] A prosecutor who brands herself as unduly cautious, in contrast, may get less interesting and important work.[130] Given this dynamic, prosecutors are subject to a "race to the bottom"[131] that discourages careful scrutiny of law enforcement practices. The tacit nature of the prosecutors' role in some of these cases does not make their conduct more appropriate—building

that cooperation is inherently wrong, but that any other policy encourages an inappropriate distribution of legal services for poor criminal defendants. If public defender's offices represented cooperators, they would risk being conflicted out of representing noncooperating defendants in the same case. This would mean that noncooperating defendants, who may end up going to trial, would end up being represented by assigned counsel. In state systems, in particular, assigned counsel often represent defendants for a flat fee. This mode of payment tends to place a premium on speedy settlement of a case, since the fee rarely covers the time and cost a lawyer puts in a trial. Assigned counsel with minimal flat fee payments have an incentive to cut corners in their trial efforts, in terms of the amount of investigation they do. *See* Brown, *supra* note 76. Defendants in this situation are more appropriately represented by legal aid offices, which often have an institutional commitment to high-quality trial representation in significant cases. *See* Smith, *supra* note 28; Ogletree, *supra* note 29.

[126] Prosecutorial ethics has long been a stepchild of professional responsibility. *See* Bruce A. Green, *Prosecutorial Ethics as Usual*, 2003 U. ILL. L. REV. 1573 (2003).

[127] *See* Margulies, *Above Contempt*, *supra* note 7.

[128] *Id.*

[129] *See* Daniel Richman, *Prosecutors and Their Agents, Agents and Their Prosecutors*, 103 COLUM. L. REV. 749, 799-801 (2003) (discussing interaction of local legal culture with national norms);

[130] *Id.*

[131] Solid Waste Agency v. United States Army Corps of Engineers, 531 U.S. 159, 179-180 (2001) (Stevens, J., dissenting) (arguing that strong federal environmental standards curb the race to the bottom among states eager to attract business by relaxing environmental standards).

in deniability is a frequent element of group wrongdoing, but one that the law should vigorously deter.[132]

Prosecutors are also subject to gatekeeping norms that exceed those applying to defense lawyers, including a duty to do justice.[133] In addition, prosecutors must refrain from gratuitous or prejudicial public comments about evidence.[134] Furthermore, as representatives of the state, prosecutors must temper their vigorous pursuit of suspected criminals with regard for the public interest.[135] Prosecutors are also subject to an array of substantive law rules, including requirements that they refrain from misrepresentations, including both affirmative statements and omissions, in pleadings submitted to the court, and that they hand over exculpatory evidence.[136]

In the face of these gatekeeping obligations, collective misconduct within law enforcement yields substantial agency costs. The rule of law depends less on sanctions than on overall perceptions of legitimacy.[137] By undermining legitimacy, government misconduct also undermines the commitments felt by ordinary citizens to obey the law. This concern is even more salient in the antiterrorism context. The international effort to defeat terrorism hinges on taking the moral high ground.[138] Evidence that the United States, which leads this effort, has targeted individuals based on religion, ethnicity, and immigration status impedes this vital work.

Unfortunately, threats to prosecutors' equipoise become even more intense in times of crisis, such as the anxiety that followed the September 11 attacks. Here, senior officials may send signals—sometimes subtle, and sometimes obvious—that prosecutors should avoid legal niceties and make cases in an aggressive fashion. Former Attorney General John Ashcroft's observation, echoing Bobby Kennedy's remark about organized crime, that Ashcroft would, if necessary, arrest suspected terrorists for "spitting

---

132 *See* CHRISTOPHER KUTZ, COMPLICITY: ETHICS AND LAW FOR A COLLECTIVE AGE 81-85 (2000); David Luban, *Making Sense of Moral Meltdowns, in* LAWYERS' ETHICS AND THE PURSUIT OF SOCIAL JUSTICE 354, 358-60 (Susan D. Carle ed., New York University Press 2005); Simon, *supra* note 12, at 12-15.

133 *See* MODEL RULES OF PROF'L CONDUCT R. 3.8 (2005) ("A prosecutor has the responsibility of a minister of justice and not simply that of an advocate"); *cf.* Green, *Prosecutorial Ethics, supra* note 126; Bruce A. Green & Fred C. Zacharias, *Regulating Federal Prosecutors' Ethics*, 55 VAND. L. REV. 381, 439-41 (2002) (discussing advantages of formal and informal regulation of prosecutors by courts).

134 *See* MODEL RULES OF PROF'L CONDUCT R. 3.8 (2005); *cf.* Lonnie T. Brown, Jr., *"May It Please the Camera, . . . I Mean the Court"—An Intrajudicial Solution to an Extrajudicial Problem*, 39 GA. L. REV. 83 (2004) (arguing for more vigorous judicial oversight regarding extrajudicial remarks by prosecutors and defense attorneys).

135 *See* Green, *supra* note 8.

136 *See* Brady v. Maryland, 373 U.S. 83 (1963).

137 *See* TOM R. TYLER, WHY PEOPLE OBEY THE LAW (1990) (discussing how participants' perceptions of the fairness of procedures affect legitimacy).

138 *Cf.* Catherine Powell, *The Role of Transnational Norm Entrepreneurs in the U.S. "War on Terrorism"*, 5 THEORETICAL INQUIRIES L. 47, 71-72 (2004) (discussing dialogue between transnational nongovernmental organizations and United States on human rights issues).

on the sidewalk,"[139] typifies this encouragement of aggressive prosecutorial branding. Ashcroft's willingness to comment publicly about defendants and evidence in pending cases—a willingness that triggered an admonition from a federal judge[140]—constituted a strong signal to prosecutors to relax their gatekeeping obligations. The result of this signaling has been a trend toward overreaching by prosecutors and other government lawyers, including inappropriate publicity, omissions and misrepresentations to courts, overcharging,[141] and withholding of exculpatory evidence.

To gauge how the war on terror has undermined equipoise in the prosecution context, consider the investigation of Portland lawyer Brandon Mayfield.[142] A report by the Depart of Justice's Inspector General recently revealed that prosecutors in the Mayfield case, in the course of investigating Mayfield for suspected participation in the Madrid train bombings of 2004, had submitted to the court an affidavit that asserted that Spanish authorities agreed with the fingerprint analysis of the FBI.[143] The FBI's analysis identified Mayfield's prints as a match for a print found at the scene of the terrorist attack.[144] As a result, a judge apparently approved a covert search of Mayfield's residence and Mayfield's detention for over two weeks as a material witness. In fact, however, FBI agents knew that Spanish authorities *disagreed* with the FBI's fingerprint analysis, and did not believe that Mayfield's prints were a match.[145] If the prosecutor knew what the FBI knew about the disagreement with the Spanish authorities, making a contrary assertion in the affidavit submitted to the court or failing to alert the judge upon discovering this discrepancy between the facts and the pleadings submitted would be a violation of Rule 3.3, which requires candor with the tribunal.[146]

---

[139] *See* Daniel C. Richman & William J. Stuntz, *Al Capone's Revenge: An Essay on the Political Economy of Pretextual Prosecution*, 105 COLUM. L. REV. 583, 599 (2005).

[140] *See* United States v. Koubriti, 305 F. Supp. 2d 723, 764-65 (E.D. Mich. 2003).

[141] For instance, the government initially charged Captain James Yee, a chaplain at Guantanamo, with inappropriate use of classified information, but eventually dismissed all charges. *See* David Cole, *Are We Safer?*, N.Y. REV. BKS., Mar. 9, 2006, at 15, 18. The government had initially charged Chaplain Yee, as well as three translators at Guantanamo who had all or most charges against them dropped, with being part of an espionage ring. *Id.*

[142] *See* Office of the Inspector General, U.S. Dep't of Justice, *A Review of the FBI's Handling of the Brandon Mayfield Case* (January 2006), at http://www.usdoj.gov/oig/special/s0601/final.pdf (last visited Mar. 6, 2006) [hereinafter OIG Rep't].

[143] *Id.*

[144] *Id.*; *cf.* Darryl K. Brown, *Rationing Criminal Defense Entitlements: An Argument From Institutional Design*, 104 COLUM. L. REV. 801, 823-24 (2004) (noting surprisingly weak reliability of fingerprint evidence).

[145] The FBI's focus on Mayfield, who was entirely unconnected to the Madrid attacks, may have stemmed from evidence relating to Mayfield's religion and professional associations: Mayfield was a practicing Muslim, and had represented a terrorism defendant in a completely unrelated family law case. *But see* OIG Rep't, *supra* note 142 (asserting that Mayfield's religious ties and professional experience played no role in law enforcement decisions).

[146] *See* MODEL RULES OF PROF'L CONDUCT R. 3.3 (2005). OIG cleared DOJ attorneys of any wrongdoing, *see* OIG Rep't, *supra* note 133, although this seems like a very charitable view, in light of the facts.

For an example of prosecutorial overreaching that continued through trial, consider *Koubriti v. United States.*[147] In *Koubriti,* a prosecutor failed to disclose exculpatory material, including material that suggested that the government's own experts believed that a drawing in defendants' possession was not a drawing of a missile base in preparation for an attack, but simply a crude map of the Middle East.[148] Over a year after obtaining convictions of the defendants, the prosecution's abuses came to light. The court ultimately granted the government's motion to vacate the convictions.[149]

Unfortunately, the court's decision in *Koubriti* stopped well short of the systemic focus merited by the misconduct in the case. Following the government's motion, the court largely pinned blame on the individual prosecutor. The court, while it had earlier admonished Attorney General Ashcroft for inappropriate public comments on the case,[150] failed to consider whether Ashcroft's signaling had created an institutional climate that eroded equipoise. Nor did the court consider the puzzling contrast between Ashcroft's specific public comments on evidence in the case and the absence of basic supervision of Justice Department personnel that *Koubriti* revealed.

Other court decisions exhibit a similarly narrow view of government misconduct in terrorism cases. In *United States v. Moussaoui,*[151] the Fourth Circuit expressed concern that prosecutors had failed to take appropriate measures to insulate themselves from other government agencies' interrogation of the high value Al Qaeda detainees whom Moussaoui[152] sought to depose, and had failed to timely inform the court of this problem.[153] The court imposed no sanctions on the government, either for undermining Moussaoui's fair trial rights by denying him access to the detainees or for the prosecutors' lack of insulation from the detainees' interrogation.[154] Similarly, the Fourth Circuit in

Moreover, from a law enforcement standpoint, the discrepancies in the affidavit could have been disastrous. If Mayfield had turned out to be factually guilty, the misrepresentations in the affidavit could have been considered both material and entered into in bad faith, thus requiring exclusion of evidence obtained through a search authorized in reliance on the affidavit. *See* Franks v. Delaware, 438 U.S. 154, 164-72 (1978) (discussing requirements for accuracy in affidavits supporting warrant applications).

[147] 336 F. Supp. 2d 676, 678 (E.D. Mich. 2004).

[148] United States v. Koubriti, 435 F. Supp. 2d 666, 670 (E.D. Mich. 2006).

[149] *See* Koubriti v. United States, 336 F. Supp. 2d at 682.

[150] *See* United States v. Koubriti, 305 F. Supp. 2d 723, 764-65 (E.D. Mich. 2003).

[151] No. 03-4792 (4th Cir. May 13, 2004), at http://www.ca4.uscourts.gov/moussaoui4792/pdf/034792orO40514.pdf (last visited Mar. 8, 2006).

[152] Moussaoui, whom the government at one point believed to be the so-called "twentieth hijacker" slated to participate in the September 11 attacks, pleaded guilty to terrorism charges after the Fourth Circuit declined to permit his lawyers to depose the detainees.

[153] *See* United States v. Moussaoui, No. 03-4792 at http://www.ca4.uscourts.gov/moussaoui4792/pdf/034792orO40514.pdf.

[154] While the District Court had struck the government's request for the death penalty to compensate for the government's refusal to make these detainees available for deposition by Moussaoui's lawyers, the Fourth Circuit reversed, allowing the government to provide summaries to the defense, despite the lack of vividness that makes such summaries a pale substitute for actual testimony, and despite the case law

Padilla v. Hanft[155] failed to appropriately sanction the government's lawyers, who had failed in their gatekeeping obligations by making arguments designed to manipulate the justice system.[156] The government's shifting of stories and relentless publicity about Padilla's alleged terrorist activities—four stories thus far, in advance of any hearing on the facts—have also thus far evaded judicial review or sanction.[157]

The weakness of judicial responses to prosecutorial overreaching stands in stark contrast to the courts' over-use of disqualification in policing the independence of defense attorneys.[158] On a macro level, this asymmetry in remedies erodes equipoise, giving the government even more leverage against the defense. Despite the institutional ties between prosecutors and the judiciary,[159] judges should develop a repertoire of structural measures for redressing the balance.

A structural approach to prosecutorial failures of equipoise would seek to deter the risk of overreaching by prosecutors, and deprive the government of any strategic advantage gained by such overreaching. Using the contempt power, the court could cite prosecutors and their superiors for contempt in cases involving egregious and repeated misconduct. Exercising its general supervisory authority,[160] as well as power to enforce Sixth Amendment guarantees, the court could strike counts that ratified

---

that suggests that access to witnesses is a central Sixth Amendment right. *See* United States v. Moussaoui, 382 F.3d 453 (4th Cir. 2004). The Fourth Circuit allowed the government's lawyers to maintain a pose of independence, even though the lawyers benefited in their preparation from access to the detainees. A more vigorous approach, echoing the District Court, would at least encourage the government's lawyers to say, "No" to their own clients.

155 432 F.3d 582 (4th Cir. 2005).

156 In *Padilla*, government lawyers had argued that the government could detain Padilla as an enemy combatant, even though those lawyers knew that if the Fourth Circuit agreed, the government would move quickly to moot out the dispute by transferring Padilla to a correctional facility and charging him with criminal violations. The court's remedies failed to match the seriousness of the government lawyers' disregard for the court's integrity. The Court declined to authorize Padilla's transfer—a pyrrhic gesture soon overruled by the Supreme Court. *See* Hanft v. Padilla, 126 S. Ct. 978 (2006). More compelling signals would have been sent if the Fourth Circuit had withdrawn its opinion, thereby depriving the government's lawyers of the victory they obtained by failing to disclose the government's plans to the court, *and* sanctioned the lawyers for their lack of candor.

157 Proceedings are pending in at least one other terrorism case where prosecutorial conduct has raised concerns. *See* United States v. Bin Laden, No. S7R 98 Cr. 1023 (KTD), 2005 U.S. Dist. LEXIS 1669 (S.D.N.Y. Feb. 7, 2005) (requiring evidentiary hearing on motion for new trial of associate of Bin Laden convicted for his role in the Kenya Embassy bombings, based on government's failure to disclose interviews with one of the government's prime witnesses).

158 *See supra* notes 103-16 and accompanying text.

159 Roberta K. Flowers, *An Unholy Alliance: The Ex Parte Relationship Between the Judge and the Prosecutor*, 79 NEB. L. REV. 251 (2000) (discussing patterns of tacit and active collaboration between courts and prosecutors).

160 *See* Margulies, *Above Contempt?, supra* note 7; *cf.* Green & Zacharias, *supra* note 95 (discussing scope of supervisory power). *But see* John Gleeson, *Supervising Criminal Investigations: The Proper Scope of the Supervisory Power of Federal Judges*, 5 J. L. & POL'Y 423, 428 (1997) (arguing that courts should narrowly construe supervisory power).

an inappropriately obtained strategic advantage. The District Court's striking of the government's request for the death penalty in the Moussaoui case, while reversed on appeal, is a strong example of a substantive remedy that sends a structural message. In other cases, the court could suppress evidence, such as evidence based on the National Security Agency (NSA) surveillance program[161] or evidence obtained after an inappropriately obtained judicial authorization for detention of a material witness.[162] The court could also order the government to investigate claims of possible misconduct, and submit a report to the court of its findings.[163] In each case, a structural approach would ensure that prosecutors guard against ongoing misconduct, and cultivate the fortitude necessary to tell governmental higher-ups the "bad news" about the applicability of constitutional rules.

V. EQUIPOISE AND LEGAL ADVICE

Equipoise also furnishes a useful model for questions concerning legal advice and collective wrongdoing. In situations including a lawyer's assistance to terrorist groups, government lawyers' advice on antiterrorism measures, and legal advice to corporate insiders regarding transactions of dubious legality, lawyers have ignored the line separating legal advice from accomplice conduct. Focusing on the two criteria of equipoise—freedom from prior knowledge of illegal conduct and freedom to give the client bad news—clarifies the location of the boundary between acting as a lawyer and assuming the role of an accessory to criminal acts. In such cases, courts and other players should adopt a structural approach that deters lawyers from reaping the branding benefits of ignoring equipoise.

The Enron lawyers provide a good starting point. These lawyers structured transactions ideally suited to the goals of corporate insiders such as Andrew Fastow, Enron's chief financial officer, using partnerships called "special purpose entities" (SPEs) to conceal liabilities that would scare off investors if they appeared on Enron's balance sheet.[164] The volume and frequency of the work done by at least one law firm—Vinson

---

[161] *See* Assoc. Press., U.S. *Is Ordered to Disclose Spying*, N.Y. TIMES, Feb. 22, 2006, at A16 (reporting on order of District Court delaying sentencing hearing for Abu Ali, who had been convicted on terrorism charges involving an alleged conspiracy to assassinate President Bush, pending a government report on use of NSA surveillance program to obtain evidence in the case).

[162] The court had such an opportunity in one pending case, but failed to take advantage of it, instead opting for a decision that imposed a less rigorous standard on the government. *See* United States v. Awadallah, 349 F.3d 42 (2d Cir. 2003) (holding that omissions in affidavit supporting application for material witness warrant did not require suppression of statements subsequently made by defendant to grand jury involving defendant's links to two of the September 11 attackers).

[163] *See In re* Material Witness Warrant, 214 F. Supp. 2d 356, 363 (S.D.N.Y. 2002) (requiring that government investigate and submit report on abusive interrogation of Egyptian national detained as material witness after September 11 based on false report that he had brought a radio transceiver to his hotel room near Ground Zero before the attacks).

[164] *See* Cramton, *supra* note 14, at 21.

& Elkins—for Enron, as well as the high percentage of the law firm's revenues taken up by Enron-related work, suggest that Vinson & Elkins had a stake in not merely doing routine legal work, but in advancing the fraudulent purposes of Enron insiders.[165] Indeed, as the District Court presiding over the Enron securities litigation has found, Vinson & Elkins repeatedly acted as a "co-author" of false and misleading disclosures made by Enron to the investing public.[166] Vinson & Elkins compounded its own failures of equipoise by serving as "independent counsel" for Enron, investigating problems with the same SPEs that it had helped create.[167] In this fashion, through delivering a clean bill of health to Enron on the special-purpose entities' role, the firm was able to continue to capitalize yet again on its abdication of gate-keeping responsibilities.

A structural approach to preserving equipoise between gatekeeping and branding would make the law firm liable as a principal in the Enron-related schemes. While the Supreme Court has held that the securities laws do not permit aiding and abetting liability,[168] a law firm can become so deeply integrated in a fraudulent scheme that it becomes an actor in its own right. Vinson & Elkins's dependence on Enron approached the financial dependence on John Gotti displayed by attorneys Cutler and Shargel. We should not treat Vinson & Elkins any better simply because it has an ampersand in its firm name or more branch offices. If proven to be principal actors in a scheme to defraud the public, Vinson & Elkins should have to disgorge all of the revenue it gained through its actions to members of the investing public who relied on those pronouncements. A structural approach would also mandate more affirmative action by counsel to alert the ultimate authority in the corporation, and, if necessary, disclose information to the public.

But a structural approach would not stop there. Other firms that lacked Vinson & Elkins's principal status nevertheless did work for Enron that raises questions about equipoise. For example, Milbank Tweed represented both banks *and* Enron in framing loans to the company as commodities trades.[169] While Milbank Tweed argued successfully to the court that this was merely the "normal activity of a law firm,"[170] a structural approach would subject the firm's "normal" practices to far more vigorous scrutiny. The mere fact that a law firm represents both a borrower and a lender should be a tip-off that the firm's work involved casting the transaction in a fashion that favored the company's

---

165 The high percentage of Vinson & Elkins's revenues accounted for by Enron, according to the court, was one factor distinguishing Vinson & Elkins from firms doing legal work for Enron on a more limited basis. *See In re* Enron Corp. Sec., No. H-01-3624, 2005 U.S. Dist. LEXIS 39927, at 45 (S.D. Tex. Dec. 5, 2005) (dismissing claims against Milbank Tweed Hadley & McCloy, whose work for Enron accounted for approximately 1% of firm revenues during a 5-year period).

166 *See In re* Enron Corp. Sec., 235 F. Supp. 2d 549, 705 (S.D. Tex. 2002).

167 *Id.*; *cf.* Regan, *supra* note 12, at 58 and accompanying text (discussing failure of Enron's lawyers).

168 *See* Cent. Bank of Denver, N.A. v. First Interstate Bank of Denver, N.A., 511 U.S. 164, 191 (1994).

169 *See In re* Enron Corp. Sec., 2005 U.S. Dist. LEXIS 39927, at 45.

170 *Id.* at 38.

balance sheet, rather than seeking the best terms for either party. When the parties to a loan have no incentive to bargain for best terms, someone else—investors or the taxpayers—will be left holding the bag. A structural approach, perhaps expanding the lawyer's duties as an evaluator under Rule 2.3,[171] would view the legal profession as having an institutional interest in discouraging the failures of gatekeeping that underwrite such dealings. Liability might be appropriate under the securities laws, to prevent the shareholders from bearing the risk of such less-than-arm's-length transactions.

Two other cases—both involving the war on terror—supply useful book-ends to this discussion of legal advice and collective illegality. One case involves attorney Lynne Stewart, who was convicted last year of material support of terrorist activity and making false statements to the government in matters arising out of her post-conviction representation of Sheik Abdel Rahman.[172] The other situation involves not a criminal defense lawyer, but government lawyers such as John Yoo[173] offering advice to the executive branch.[174]

Stewart's problems began in 2000 when she violated the administrative restrictions the government had placed on the Sheik's communication with the outside world, and informed the public in a press conference that the Sheik was renouncing a cease-fire that his organization, the Islamic Group, had entered into after a 1997 attack on tourists in Luxor, Egypt.[175] On the question of advance knowledge of collective wrongdoing, most damaging for the defense was Stewart's view, expressed during a visit with the Sheik, that a kidnapping in the Philippines for the ostensible purpose of securing the Sheik's

---

[171] *See* MODEL RULES OF PROF'L CONDUCT R. 2.3 (2005) (imposing duty to be candid on lawyer who produces legal work upon which the lawyer knows others will rely).

[172] *See* Julia Preston, *Lawyer is Guilty of Aiding Terrorists*, N.Y. TIMES, Feb. 11, 2005, at A1; *cf.* Margulies, *Virtues and Vices of Solidarity, supra* note 2, at 194-217 (discussing Stewart case); Alissa Clare, Note, *We Should Have Gone to Med School: In the Wake of Lynne Stewart, Lawyers Face Hard Time for Defending Terrorists*, 18 GEO. J. LEGAL ETHICS 651, 662-63 (2005) (arguing that Stewart's conviction will chill advocacy). For further discussion of 18 U.S.C. § 2339(a), (b), which bar the provision of material support to terrorist activity or designated foreign terrorist organizations, see *e.g.*, DAVID COLE, ENEMY ALIENS: DOUBLE STANDARDS AND CONSTITUTIONAL FREEDOMS IN THE WAR ON TERRORISM 75-79 (2003) (critiquing statute); *cf.* Robert M. Chesney, *Civil Liberties and the Terrorism Prevention Paradigm: The Guilty By Association Critique*, 101 MICH. L. REV. 1408, 1432-52 (2003) (book review) (supporting policy behind material support statute, but pointing out legal and policy concerns); Margulies, *The Virtues and Vices of Solidarity, supra* note 2, at 200-08 (discussing appropriate scope of material support provisions); Nina J. Crimm, *High Alert: The Government's War on the Financing of Terrorism and its Implications for Donors, Domestic Charitable Organizations, and Global Philanthropy*, 45 WM. & MARY L. REV. 1341, 1409-14 (2004) (discussing ramifications of statute for best practices in charitable giving).

[173] Yoo served in the Justice Department's Office of Legal Counsel, where he drafted memos on coercive interrogation and the definition of torture. He is currently a professor at the University of California at Berkeley.

[174] *See* David Luban, *Selling Indulgences: The Unmistakable Parallel Between Lynne Stewart and the President's Torture Lawyers,* SLATE, Feb. 14, 2005 http://www.slate.com/id/2113447 (last visited March 9, 2006).

[175] *See* Margulies, *Virtues and Vices of Solidarity, supra* note 2, at 183.

release was "very, very crucial."[176] This comment, while not indicating that Stewart had prior knowledge of the kidnapping or that Stewart contemplated that *specific* acts of violence would result from her efforts to disseminate the Sheik's message, constitutes evidence that Stewart would not have found violence of this kind unwelcome.

Stewart's problems with the other equipoise criterion—freedom to give the client bad news—emerged in response to the theory she advanced at trial that her press conference was part of a legal strategy to secure the Sheik's release, by increasing the pressure on Egyptian President Mubarak to intercede with the United States government on the Sheik's behalf.[177] It seems implausible that the Mubarak regime or the United States government would cave in to such pressure. Indeed, it would seem far more likely that the United States government would reject such an effort out of hand, leading to even more onerous restrictions on the Sheik. However, Stewart, in hundreds of pages of transcribed conversations with her client,[178] failed to give the Sheik this potential bad news. Stewart had become more concerned with branding—with establishing her solidarity with the Sheik's goals—and had abandoned even a modest gatekeeping role.[179]

A failure of equipoise is equally evident for government lawyers offering advice regarding potential government misconduct. Consider here the well-known example of John Yoo, Berkeley law professor and formerly of the Justice Department's Office of Legal Counsel, in preparing his memoranda for the President arguing that the United States was not bound by international law norms governing interrogation of detainees.[180] Yoo had the same lack of freedom from prior knowledge and lack of freedom to provide bad news as Stewart and the Enron lawyers.

It seems reasonable to infer that Yoo understood that his opinion was not being sought for purely academic reasons. Rather, his view would be the cornerstone of a policy based on the use of techniques that would otherwise be considered torture. The focus of Yoo's analysis on the exact contours of torture under American law demonstrates this problem of prior knowledge. Yoo's painstaking arguments that torture 1) required

---

[176] *See* Julia Preston, *Videotapes of Jailed Sheik, Hatred and Candy Bars*, N.Y. TIMES, Aug. 29, 2004, § 1, at 31 (discussing evidence at trial).

[177] *See* Clare, *supra* note 172, at 665.

[178] Transcripts of these conversations are available on Stewart's excellent web-site, http://www.lynnestewart.org.

[179] In Stewart's case, as with other criminal defendants, the issue of appropriate sentencing is distinct from the issue of culpability. *See* Julia Preston, *Cancer Delays Sentence of Lawyer in Terror Case*, N.Y. TIMES, Mar. 4, 2006, at B3 (discussing delays in sentencing caused by Stewart's illness). The author of this Article joined a number of academics in urging moderation in Stewart's sentencing, because of her long history of capable criminal defense work, the lack of evidence that she intended to facilitate specific acts of violence, and the chilling effect a harsh sentence might have on other members of the criminal defense bar. *See* Peter Margulies, et al., Letter Re. Lynne Stewart Sentencing, July 26, 2005 (on file with author); *cf.* Julia Preston, *Sheik's Lawyer, Facing 30 Years, Gets 28 Months, to Dismay of U.S.*, N.Y. TIMES, Oct. 17, 2006, at A1 (reporting on Stewart's sentence).

[180] *See* Gonzales Memo, *supra* note 6; *cf.* Jesselyn Radack, *Tortured Legal Ethics: The Role of the Government Advisor in the War on Terrorism*, 77 U. COLO. L. REV. 1, 23 n.154 (2006) (arguing that memo represented inappropriate view of government lawyer's role).

something akin to severe organ failure, and 2) required specific intent to inflict pain for its own sake, as opposed to a goal of inflicting pain to gain information, demonstrate that he knew he was setting boundaries that persons in operational tasks would be called upon to observe.[181] Moreover, Yoo failed to give the President the bad news that the Supreme Court's decision in *Youngstown*—the Steel Seizure Case—might complicate Yoo's analysis.[182] Indeed, Yoo did not mention *Youngstown* at all.[183] Yoo was more concerned about branding—about cementing his professional identity as a champion of executive power. In Yoo's case, as in Stewart's, ideology undermined equipoise.

Yoo, like Stewart and the Enron lawyers, argued that he was embarked on nothing more than the ordinary business of lawyering.[184] In practice, however, Yoo's disdain for the gatekeeping function lends his work a far more ominous cast. Yoo's stress on branding created sizable negative externalities for United States antiterrorism efforts by inflaming populations and communities whose cooperation the United States desperately needs.

In the government antiterrorism advice area, a structural approach might mandate consideration of contrary precedent and opportunity costs as a fundamental attribute of acceptable lawyering. Any such approach should also reconsider the barriers to criminal and tort liability based on the existence of "non-frivolous" legal claims. Yoo had undertaken as part of his branding activities to write a series of articles that conveniently supplied him with non-frivolous arguments.[185] Recognizing such branding efforts as dispositive of the question of frivolity is antithetical to the structural approach, which would require at least acknowledgment on a descriptive level of the current state of the law, regardless of the writer's ideology.

Moreover, a structural approach would aim to deprive perpetrators of government torture, particularly policymakers, of the strategic advantage they would gain from reliance on such a compromised legal opinion. Reliance on a legal opinion in this area creates a risk of moral hazard, as policymakers use the legal opinion to justify torture.[186] The way to minimize moral hazard is to construe narrowly any "advice of counsel"

---

[181] *Cf.* Gillers, *supra* note 33 (critiquing torture memo); Luban, *Liberalism, Torture, and the Ticking Bomb*, *supra* note 6 (same); Radack, *supra* note 180 (same).

[182] *See* Gillers, *supra* note 33, at 237-38.

[183] *Id.*; *see also supra* note 68 and accompanying text.

[184] *See* Radack, *supra* note 180, at 30.

[185] For an example of Yoo's perspective, see Yoo, *supra* note 11, at 1674, arguing that Presidential power in war is limited only by Congress's power of the purse. Of course, scholarly views that stress the prerogatives and institutional competence of the Executive are legitimate contributions to debate. *Cf.* Julian Ku & John Yoo, *Beyond Formalism in Foreign Affairs: A Functional Approach to the Alien Tort Statute*, 2004 SUP. CT. REV. 153 (2004) (arguing that Executive interpretation of statute providing remedies to aliens for violation of law of nations should control, in part because courts lack institutional competence in this arena). However, a scholarly position should not per se insulate an advisor from accountability for actions that risk grave harm to others.

[186] *See, e.g.*, Radack, *supra* note 180, at 3.

defense to charges of government misconduct. In the torture context, for example, courts construing possible defenses advanced by alleged perpetrators of torture should focus on objective, independent indicia of reasonableness, such as the extent and severity of the coercive tactics employed, the gravity of the harm prevented, and the availability of alternatives to coercive tactics.[187] Courts should instruct juries to reject as unreasonable legal advice that does not meet with accepted professional standards. Omissions in legal advice, such as the failure of the authors of the torture memos to cite the *Youngstown* case, should be evidence that the legal opinions could not be the basis for reasonable reliance.

Another element of a structural approach to legal advice is permitting or requiring greater disclosure by lawyers. When lawyers can blow the whistle on collective wrongdoing, one lawyer who asks herself tough questions can exert some leverage over otherwise intransigent organizations. A whistleblower at Enron, Sherron Watkins, who tellingly was not a lawyer, played a significant role in the process that led to public revelation of the abuses committed by corporate insiders.[188] In the scandal regarding the torture memos and the treatment of detainees at Guantanamo and in Iraq, unnamed military lawyers who approached a human rights attorney in New York played a substantial role. The ABA Model Rules of Professional Conduct currently permit disclosure when disclosure is necessary to prevent death or substantial bodily harm, or to prevent, mitigate, or rectify financial injury resulting from client fraud.[189] This result is a welcome trend, and a contrast to the previous regime in which the rules barred whistleblowing or disclosure except in situations involving a client crime that could result in death or substantial bodily harm.[190] In the government lawyer scenario, further leverage for gatekeeping could be obtained by reading the provisions permitting disclosure in cases of reasonably certain substantial bodily harm or death to include disclosure of a policy like the coercive interrogation program.

VI. COMPETING MODELS

To determine if the equipoise approach makes sense, one must consider competing approaches. One alternative model stresses client choice and autonomy. This view

---

[187] *See* Margulies, *Legal Institutions and the War on Terror*, *supra* note 62, at 317-18.

[188] *See* Luban, *Making Sense of Moral Meltdowns*, *supra* note 68, at 370.

[189] *See* MODEL RULES OF PROF'L CONDUCT R. 1.6(b) (2005). Permissive disclosure regarding financial harm extends only to cases where the client used the lawyer's services in furtherance of the fraud, as arguably occurred in the recent corporate debacles, not to lawyers subsequently retained to defend an individual against charges of fraud or other wrongdoing. Extending permissive disclosure regarding financial injury to this latter group—basically litigators and trial lawyers—would disturb equipoise by unduly elevating the gatekeeping role at the expense of core Fifth and Sixth Amendment guarantees.

[190] *See* Margaret Colgate Love, *The Revised ABA Model Rules of Professional Conduct: Summary of the Work of Ethics 2000*, 15 GEO. J. LEGAL ETHICS 441, 450-51 (2002).

would severely limit disclosure by the lawyer to prevent harm.[191] The choice model also suggests, with respect to conflicts of interest, that the client's informed consent may be obtained in virtually any situation, no matter how dire the attorney's conflict. The difficulty in this approach, however, is that it fails to address situations, like *United States v. Schwarz*,[192] in which financial or institutional factors undermine the lawyer's equipoise. In other areas of law, the legal system recognizes that certain decisions are problematic because cognitive biases or conflicting agendas make informed consent particularly difficult to obtain, or because systemic integrity or social welfare trump an individual's expressed wishes.[193] The client choice model fails to take these factors into account.

In the advice context, moreover, the client choice model ignores agency costs. When the client is a diffuse entity—the corporation or the government— the client's agents, such as self-dealing corporate insiders or overreaching government officials, may act contrary to the interests of their principal.[194] In this situation, gatekeeping by lawyers to compensate for this problem reduces agency costs, and actually *promotes* client autonomy.

The other alternative model is one I call the risk-averse approach.[195] This model privileges gatekeeping and looks to risk-aversion as a kind of tie-breaker when a client decision may have adverse social consequences. The problem with this approach is that sometimes risk aversion is not the appropriate strategy. In the days preceding September 11th, for example, government lawyers were unduly risk averse in not seeking a warrant to see the contents of Zacarias Moussaoui's laptop.[196] Access to this laptop would have given the government useful information about the scope of the conspiracy and some of its participants.[197] However, government lawyers refused to apply for a warrant out of concern that a court would reject their application.[198] By failing to define probable cause to include not only the probability, but also the gravity, of harm that a search might prevent,[199] the lawyers exalted gatekeeping to a level that upset equipoise. Similarly, an excess of risk-aversion would have stifled development of the legal rationales for the

---

[191] *See* Fred C. Zacharias, *Coercing Clients: Can Gatekeeping Rules Work?*, 47 B.C. L. Rev. 455, 458-59 (2006) (describing the view of proponents of a broad duty of confidentiality, that lawyer's threat of disclosure to prevent client from committing harm is form of "extortion").

[192] 283 F.3d 76 (2d Cir. 2002); *see supra* note 106 (discussing Schwarz).

[193] *See, e.g.*, Lars Noah, *Informed Consent and the Elusive Dichotomy Between Standard and Experimental Therapy*, 28 Am. J. L. & Med. 361, 382-88 (2002) (discussing difficulty of ensuring that patients understand risks and benefits of experimental treatments).

[194] *See* Regan, *supra* note 12 (discussing Enron).

[195] *See* Gordon, *A New Role for Lawyers*, *supra* note 5 at 25; Luban, *Moral Meltdowns*, *supra* note 68.

[196] *See* 9/11 Commission Report, *supra* note 37, at 273.

[197] *Id.*

[198] *Id.*

[199] *See* Craig S. Lerner, *The Reasonableness of Probable Cause*, 81 Tex. L. Rev. 951 (2003).

Lend-Lease program that assisted Britain prior to America's entry into World War II,[200] and for the Kennedy Administration's measured, yet effective, response to the Cuban Missile Crisis.[201] An equipoise model would encourage such inventive lawyering, rather than leave a client hamstrung in a situation of manifest exigency.

Moreover, a risk-averse approach heavily weighted toward gatekeeping in the representation of private parties will undermine core values by unduly extending the long arm of government. For constitutionalism to thrive, private parties need some space in which to make their own decisions. Lawyers' branding behavior helps to carve out that space. By discounting branding as a normative good, the risk-averse approach risks a dangerous conflation of state and private interests, in which state interests predominate. In contrast, equipoise preserves this space for clients.

VII. CONCLUSION

Lawyers' independence is a good slogan in times when lawyers have overreached. Episodes like Enron and the torture memos are compelling examples of lawyers' willingness to straddle the line separating legal from illegal activity, or even step over to the wrong side. Like many slogans, however, ultimately invocations of independence obscure more than they illuminate.

Much of the confusion stems from the disparate meanings of the concept of professional independence. Independence can be an apologia or alibi for lawyers whose clients have done bad things—"Don't blame me, I'm only the lawyer," is a convenient disclaimer. Independence also can be a call to virtue, but sometimes this virtue can end up being too detached from the real-world struggles of clients. Moreover, lawyers' independence can be a distressingly selective concept, with the end result being separation from clients, and a solidarity with the state that threatens the premises of our adversary system. This kind of threat to the adversarial zeal that helps actualize constitutional protections is most serious in the arena of criminal defense.

Rather than seek in quixotic fashion for the real meaning of independence, this Article suggests a more down-to-earth alternative: equipoise. The basis for the equipoise approach is the dynamic within lawyers and the legal profession between branding and

---

[200] *See* ROBERT H. JACKSON, THAT MAN: AN INSIDER'S PORTRAIT OF FRANKLIN D. ROOSEVELT 93-103 (John Q. Barrett ed., 2003). Then-Attorney General Jackson, after some public encouragement by distinguished private lawyers concerned about the Nazi threat, argued that the net value of the Lend-Lease deal, including the British bases leased to the United States, demonstrated that the American destroyers lent to Britain were not "essential" to the United States' defense, and therefore complied with congressional directives. *Id.* at 97. Regarding international law, Jackson argued that Hitler's aggression violated international agreements that Germany had signed, and that these treaties allowed countries such as the United States to assist victims of this aggression. *Id.* at 102-03; *cf.* Jonathan A. Bush, *"The Supreme . . . Crime" and Its Origins: The Lost Legislative History of the Crime of Aggressive War,* 102 COLUM. L. REV. 2324, 2406-09 (2002) (discussing contemporary analysis of crime of aggressive war under international law).

[201] *See* Richard N. Gardner, *Future Implications of the Iraq Conflict: Neither Bush nor the "Jurisprudes"*, 97 AM. J. INT'L L. 585, 587-88 (2003) (discussing the Kennedy Administration's quarantine rationale for imposing a blockade on Cuba).

gatekeeping. Branding entails attempts by both the profession and its practitioners to forge identities that assist in marketing legal services to prospective clients. On a broad scale, distinctive features of the legal profession such as the duty of confidentiality are a kind of branding effort. In a more individual light, attorneys may brand themselves as being eager to please clients by representing the client's associates, as in the organized crime setting, or as being eager to make cases brought to them by law enforcement agents, as in the prosecutorial context. Gatekeeping, in contrast, requires the lawyer to safeguard the public's interest in a fashion that may check and balance short-term client preferences, and eventually transform those preferences through dialogue.

A system with too much branding among lawyers results in crises of the kind that are familiar from the headlines on Enron and the torture memos. By the same token, a system that enforces gatekeeping excessively may give an advantage to the state that erodes constitutional protections. Equipoise seeks to navigate between these extremes.

The key conditions for equipoise are twofold: freedom from prior knowledge of client wrongdoing and freedom to give the client bad news. A lawyer who meets these conditions can do lawyer's work in a fashion that serves clients and democratic values. A lawyer whose work fails these conditions risks becoming an accomplice or a crony—roles that do not serve the rule of law, and ultimately disserve most clients, as well.

Faced with failures of equipoise, courts should adopt a structural approach. In the criminal defense area, this structural approach would often mean less judicial intervention than currently takes place regarding disqualification of defense lawyers. Too often, in such settings, judicial concern about lawyer independence gives the government an unearned advantage. Dealing with prosecutors, however, courts have typically not intervened sufficiently. Advancing equipoise requires ending this asymmetry. In the area of legal advice, structural remedies that preserve equipoise would involve limiting advice of counsel defenses, and expanding liability for attorneys who offer one-sided advice to corporate insiders or government officials.

Substituting equipoise for independence is a modest step. In and of itself, it will not guarantee an end to Enrons or the excesses of government attorneys in the war against terror. Nor will it guarantee effective assistance of counsel to criminal defendants. However, focusing on equipoise can dissipate some of the confusion wrought by invoking independence, and clear a path for future reform.

Beyond Cardboard Clients in Legal Ethics

*Katherine R. Kruse**

In the world of legal ethics, clients are most often constructed as cardboard figures interested solely in maximizing their own wealth or freedom at the expense of others.[1] Scour any professional responsibility textbook, and you will find examples of the ethical issues that arise when the pursuit of a client's interests requires a lawyer to harm innocent third parties, undermine the truth-seeking norms of the legal system, or both. The proliferation of these examples is no accident. Rather, it is a consequence of a choice by early legal ethicists to focus on the dilemma faced by a lawyer forced by professional duty to do something that would otherwise be wrong. To generate this kind of dilemma, legal ethicists had to posit hypothetical clients impervious to ordinary moral considerations, unconcerned with preserving their relationships with others and indifferent to their reputations in the community.

This article argues that the reliance on cardboard clients has disserved legal ethics by obscuring important issues of professional responsibility that cannot be examined in the simplified world of the standard professional responsibility hypothetical. Most notably, the reliance on cardboard clients has disabled legal ethicists from confronting a problem I call legal objectification. Legal objectification is the tendency of lawyers to view their clients as walking bundles of legal rights and interests rather than as whole persons whose legal issues often come deeply intertwined with other concerns—relationships, loyalties, hopes, uncertainties, fears, doubts, and values—that shape the objectives they bring to legal representation.

---

* Professor of Law, William S. Boyd School of Law, University of Nevada, Las Vegas. The following persons merit special thanks for facilitating invaluable discussion of these ideas and feedback on earlier drafts this article: Annette Appell, Susan Carle, David Luban, and Ted Schneyer. This article benefited greatly from presentation at the Law Speakers' Series at American University, Washington College of Law, the Clinical Research Forum at William S. Boyd School of Law, and the Potomac Valley Writers' Workshop.

[1] *See* Ann Shalleck, *Constructions of the Client Within Legal Education*, 45 Stan. L. Rev. 1731, 1737 (1993); Robert Rubinson, *Attorney Fact-Finding, Ethical Decision-Making and the Methodology of Law*, 45 St. Louis L.J. 1185 (2001).

The classic example of *Spaulding v. Zimmerman* is a case in point.[2] In *Spaulding*, a personal injury defense lawyer learned from his own medical expert that the plaintiff had suffered a heart aneurysm probably caused by the automobile accident at issue in the case.[3] The defense lawyer proceeded to settle the case without ever revealing to the plaintiff that his life was in danger. The court re-opened the settlement two years later when the aneurysm was discovered in a routine medical examination.[4] However, the court was careful to note that "no canon of ethics or legal obligation" had required the defense lawyer to inform the plaintiff of the life-threatening medical condition.[5]

For almost thirty years, legal ethicists have used the dramatic facts of *Spaulding* to discuss the boundaries of a lawyer's competing moral and professional duties when divulging confidential information could save a human life.[6] However, to use *Spaulding* to explore this moral and ethical dilemma, one must imagine a client who will not consent to disclose the confidential information. Lawyers are always ethically permitted to reveal confidential information if the client consents after consultation.[7] If the client in *Spaulding* were to consent to reveal the information—perhaps because the client shares the lawyer's concern for the value of human life—the lawyer's dilemma would disappear.

When the facts behind *Spaulding* are probed more deeply, it appears quite likely that the client would have consented to reveal the potentially life-saving information—that is, if his lawyer had consulted him.[8] The litigation in *Spaulding* arose from a car accident in the mid-1950s involving three families living in the same rural area of Minnesota.[9] The action was brought on behalf of 20-year-old David Spaulding, a passenger in the car driven by 19-year-old John Zimmerman.[10] When the accident occurred, Zimmerman had been transporting Spaulding and other employees of his father's road construction

---

[2] Spaulding v. Zimmerman, 116 N.W.2d 704 (1962).

[3] *Id.* at 707.

[4] *Id.* at 709.

[5] *Id.* at 710.

[6] *See* Roger C. Cramton & Lori P. Knowles, *Professional Secrecy and Its Exceptions:* Spaulding v. Zimmerman *Revisited*, 83 MINN. L. REV. 63, 65-66, 72 (1998). For many years, the public policy exception to permit disclosure to prevent harm to others was conditioned on "prevent[ing] *the client* from committing a *criminal act* that was reasonably certain to cause *imminent* death or substantial bodily harm." MODEL R. PROF'L CONDUCT 1.6(b)(1) (1983) (emphasis added). The most recent amendments to the ABA Model Rules omit the requirement that one's client be criminally culpable and permit disclosure "to prevent reasonably certain death or substantial bodily harm" regardless of whether the threat to life or bodily security arises from a criminal act. MODEL R. PROF'L CONDUCT 1.6(b)(1) (2002).

[7] MODEL R. PROF'L CONDUCT 1.6(a) (2002) ("A lawyer shall not reveal information relating to the representation of a client *unless the client consents after consultation*, except for disclosures that are impliedly authorized in order to carry out the representation, and except as stated in paragraph (b).") (emphasis added).

[8] Cramton & Knowles, *supra* note 6, at 94.

[9] *Id.* at 63-64.

[10] Spaulding, 116 N.W.2d, at 706-07.

business home from a worksite at dusk. Their car collided with a car occupied by the Ledermann family on their way to the county fair.[11] The accident was a tragic event for all three families. In addition to seriously injuring David Spaulding, the accident killed 12-year-old Elaine Ledermann, who was thrown from her car; killed John Zimmerman's brother James, also a passenger in his car; and broke the neck of John Zimmerman's father, Edward.[12] Given the close relationship between John Zimmerman and David Spaulding and the devastating loss his own family had already suffered, it is likely that Zimmerman would have consented—even wanted—to reveal medical information critically important to Spaulding's health and life.[13]

The more interesting moral and ethical question revealed by the facts in *Spaulding* is why a lawyer would make the decision not to reveal the confidential information without consulting his client. One likely answer is that the lawyer in *Spaulding* saw it as his job simply to maximize his client's legal and financial interests and did not consider the effect of the settlement on the client's other values or relationships.[14] In other words, the lawyer in *Spaulding* may have been guilty of legally objectifying his client—of viewing John Zimmerman narrowly as nothing more than a collection of legal and financial interests disconnected from the rest of his life.

Legal ethicists have not generally explored the problem of legal objectification revealed in *Spaulding*, nor could they. To create the dilemma legal ethicists wanted to discuss, John Zimmerman had to be constructed as a cardboard figure interested only in maximizing his legal interests and therefore unwilling to reveal confidential information that might increase the damages for which he was liable. Once Zimmerman is constructed as a cardboard figure, it is no longer possible to see—much less to confront—the problem of legal objectification also raised by the case. And this kind of oversight will always occur when legal ethicists rely on cardboard clients, because cardboard clients are constructed in theory from the very same narrowing assumptions that plague the problem of legal objectification in practice.

The construction of cardboard clients in legal ethics has other theoretical costs. Relying on the image of cardboard clients, legal ethicists have exaggerated the problem of over-zealous partisanship and proposed solutions that distort the balance between lawyers' professional obligations to clients and to the public. The alternative professional ideal most commonly proposed by legal ethicists—sometimes called the "lawyer-statesman model"—exhorts lawyers to conform their clients' projects to the public good even if that means manipulating or betraying their clients in the process.[15] Yet, reasonable persons often disagree about the content and application of moral standards. Lawyers who judge their clients' projects based on moral standards that the

---

[11] Cramton & Knowles, *supra* note 6, at 63.

[12] *Id.* at 64.

[13] *See* Cramton & Knowles, *supra* note 6, at 94. The authors based this conclusion in part on interviews with surviving members of the Zimmerman and Ledermann families. *Id.* at 91-92.

[14] *Id.* at 94-96.

[15] *See infra* Part II.C.

clients do not share can become guilty of moral overreaching. And the image of the moral lawyer responsible for enforcing the public good enables a systemic denial of the reality—glaringly obvious to non-lawyer observers—that lawyers often pursue their own self-interest at the expense of their clients.[16]

This article seeks to move legal ethics beyond cardboard clients by re-imagining how the ideals of professionalism could have developed if legal ethicists had diagnosed the problem of legal objectification and sought to cure it. Part I examines the theoretical history of legal ethics at the time of its post-Watergate fluorescence, showing how the assumptions of moral lawyers and cardboard clients arose from the way legal ethicists initially framed the interesting issues in legal ethics as conflicts between ordinary morality and role morality. *[Editors' note: we've deleted part I of this piece for space purposes, but you really should read it sometime.]* Part II re-examines the theoretical history of legal ethics to reveal an early interest in the problem of legal objectification that was never fully explored, and shows how contemporaneous movements in legal interviewing and counseling literature implicitly addressed the problem of legal objectification. Part III proposes a model of partisanship for three-dimensional clients that brings these divergent strands together and places fidelity to client values at the center of a lawyer's partisan duties. Part IV examines the limitations of the client valued-based model of representation proposed in Part III in the contexts of representing diminished capacity clients, representing organizational clients, and pursuing cause lawyering where mobilization around collective values is necessary to fight systemic injustice.

. . . .

II. THE ROAD NOT TAKEN: LEGAL OBJECTIFICATION AS THE CENTRAL PROBLEM OF LEGAL PROFESSIONALISM

A serious analysis of problem of legal objectification is a road not taken in legal ethics. But it is a road that could have been taken. This part traces its potential, noting that the earliest essay outlining the moral issues in legal professionalism identified the problem of legal objectification and called for a solution of limited deprofessionalization that would decrease the professional distance between lawyers and clients. A concurrent movement in the legal interviewing and counseling literature advocated a client-centered approach to legal representation that re-oriented the lawyer-client relationship in ways responsive to the problem of legal objectification. Had these threads come together, they could have redefined the problems with legal professionalism and suggested a different kind of solution.

A. Wasserstrom's Lost Concern for Legal Objectification

In 1975, Richard Wasserstrom published a groundbreaking essay that raised "two moral criticisms of lawyers," each of which "concern the lawyer-client relationship."[110]

[16] *See infra* Part III.E.

[110] Wasserstrom, *supra* note 21, at 1.

The first criticism was the familiar concern that in carrying out their professional role obligations, lawyers are required to further the interests of morally unworthy clients and to disregard the moral harm that partisan advocacy visits on others.[111] . . . . [T]his criticism of legal professionalism came to dominate the discourse as legal ethicists framed the moral issues in legal ethics as conflicts between role morality and ordinary morality.

Wasserstrom's second moral criticism is less familiar: that the lawyer-client relationship is itself morally suspect because lawyers tend to objectify their clients in legal terms and to treat them paternalistically.[112] "[F]rom the professional's point of view," he wrote, "the client is seen and responded to more like an *object* than a human being, and more like a *child* than an adult."[113] The problem of lawyer paternalism—treating a client "more like a child than an adult"—has received limited attention from legal ethicists.[114] However, the problem of lawyers' objectification of their clients—treating a client "more like an object than a human being"—has gone largely unnoticed as a moral problem in its own right.[115]

What is hardly ever discussed—perhaps hardly ever noticed—is that Wasserstrom viewed his two moral criticisms as aspects of a single underlying pathology.[116] It may seem a paradox, Wasserstrom noted, that a lawyer could be both excessively preoccupied with a client's concerns and inattentive to the client.[117] However, he explained, the lawyer accomplishes both by being "overly concerned with the *interest* of the client and at the same time fail[ing] to view the client as a *whole person*."[118] According to Wasserstrom, lawyers are not alone. All professionals tend to objectify their clients or patients by focusing attention on the subject matter of their expertise. Professionals in medicine, law, and psychiatry tend to view a client or patient "not as a whole person but a segment or aspect of a person—an interesting kidney problem, a routine marijuana possession case, or another adolescent with an identity crisis."[119] For lawyers, the problem of legal objectification arises from viewing clients narrowly in terms of their legal interests alone.

The tendency of lawyers as professionals to objectify their clients reveals the two kinds of moral disregard—for clients as whole persons and for anyone not a client—as

[111] *Id.* at 3-4.

[112] *Id.* at 1.

[113] *Id.* at 19 (emphasis added).

[114] Luban, *Paternalism, supra* note 22; William H. Simon, *Lawyer Advice and Client Autonomy: Mrs. Jones's Case,* 50 MD. L. REV. 213 (1991). *But see* David Luban, *Introduction,* THE ETHICS OF LAWYERS xi, xiv (1994) (noting that the issue of lawyers' paternalism toward clients has "attracted a much smaller philosophical literature" than the issue of harm caused by overzealous advocacy).

[115] For limited exceptions in early legal ethical literature, see Warren Lehman, *The Pursuit of a Client's Interests,* 77 MICH. L. REV. 1078 (1979); Simon, *Ideology of Advocacy, supra* note 22.

[116] Wasserstrom, *supra* note 21, at 1, 15.

[117] *Id.* at 16.

[118] *Id.* (emphasis added).

[119] *Id.* at 21.

different aspects of the same problem. The root of the problem lies in the narrow definition lawyers give to their client's objectives. Clients, it might be argued, come to lawyers with the capacity and desire to be moral; it is lawyers, with the analytical precision of their professional training, who slough off clients' non-legal concerns and focus only on the legally relevant aspects of the case. Consonant with their professional training, lawyers "issue-spot" their clients as they would the facts in a blue-book exam, reducing client objectives to bundles of legal rights and interests. Lawyers then pursue those legal interests in disregard of *both* clients' actual wishes *and* the harm caused to others. In the process, lawyers disregard their clients' inclinations to be cooperative, moral and socially responsible and encourage the self-seeking behavior that accompanies legal interest maximization.

The solution Wasserstrom proposed to this underlying pathology of legal professionalism was a kind of limited "deprofessionalization" of the lawyer-client relationship. He did not go very far in elaborating what deprofessionalization might mean, and he acknowledged that an adequate solution was difficult to envision because there were certain "important and distinctive competencies" that clients seek and lawyers possess. At the very end of his essay, Wasserstrom suggested that the key to solving the puzzle of limited deprofessionalization would have to "await an explicit effort to alter the ways in which lawyers are educated and acculturated to view themselves, their clients, and the relationships that ought to exist between them."[120]

B. Redefining the Problem: the Hidden Complicity of Lawyers in Shaping Client Objectives

In the view of early legal ethicists, lawyers' partisan loyalty and moral neutrality was the source of the moral and ethical problems that plagued legal professionalism. They defined the central problems of professionalism as stemming from lawyers' unquestioning deference to clients. It was clients who pushed their lawyers to the limits of the law where the lawyers were required by professional duty to transgress the dictates of ordinary morality.

However, if we view legal objectification as the central pathology of the legal profession, then pinning the problems on the standard's combination of partisan loyalty and moral neutrality is a misdiagnosis. If lawyers are responsible for transforming their clients from whole persons into bundles of legal interests, then lawyers are complicit in creating the conflicts between personal morality and professional role morality that the early ethicists observed. Lawyers are complicit because they are the ones who define the clients' objectives narrowly as legal interest maximization in the first place.

The idea that lawyers shape their clients' objectives based on a particular and professionalized perspective is supported by empirical research of the legal profession across a number of legal practice fields.[121] In one recent study, for example, lawyers and cli-

---

[120] *Id.*

[121] *See* AUSTIN SARAT & WILLIAM L. F. FELSTINER, DIVORCE LAWYERS AND THEIR CLIENTS: POWER AND MEANING IN THE LEGAL PROCESS (1995) (divorce); Tamara Relis, *"It's Not About the Money!": A Theory on*

ents in medical malpractice cases were surveyed to determine their view of plaintiffs' objectives in malpractice suits. When asked why plaintiffs sue, lawyers on all sides of litigation—representing doctors, hospitals and patients—"either immediately or ultimately described the issue as one of money—solely or primarily."[122] By contrast, the vast majority of medical malpractice plaintiffs did not cite money as their sole or even their primary motivation; and sixty-five percent of plaintiffs didn't mention money until they were prompted.[123] What plaintiffs said they wanted to gain by suing were admissions of responsibility, the prevention of harm to others, answers to their questions, retribution for misconduct, and apologies for the suffering caused by medical error.[124] The study concluded that the discontinuity between lawyer and client understandings of clients' objectives was due in part to the fact that "lawyers are trained to operate according to rights and rules, applying law to facts and placing people and occurrences into legal categories."[125] As a consequence, lawyers endeavored to fit their clients' more emotional goals "into legally cognizable categories—ultimately relating to monetary compensation alone."[126]

The problem of legal objectification was discussed in a pair of other early legal ethics article. In 1978, as one part of a sweeping critique of professional ideology, William Simon argued that lawyers who adhere to the dominant ideology of professionalism "impute certain basic aims to the client and . . . work to advance these imputed ends."[127] As Simon noted, the ends are defined on the basis of egoistic assumptions that "emphasize extreme selfishness."[128] Simon suggested that lawyers end up representing a "hypothetical person with only a few crude discrete ends" who bears little resemblance to the real client whose satisfaction relies on a complex balance of interrelated goals within the context of cooperative social relationships.[129] In an essay published a year later, Warren Lehman further developed Simon's point by analyzing how the lawyer's instrumentalist approach to legal advice based on the interests of a "standardized" client can distort the decision making of clients, whose deference to their lawyers' expertise may cause them to overvalue factors like the tax consequences of important life decisions.[130]

Misconceptions of Plaintiffs' Litigation Aims 68 U. PITT. L. REV. 701 (2007) (medical malpractice); Marvin W. Mindes & Alan C. Adcock, *Trickster, Hero, Helper: A Report on the Lawyer Image*, 1982 AMER. BAR FOUND. RESEARCH J. 177 (survey of lawyers and public on the image of lawyers).

[122] Relis, *supra* note 120, at 713.

[123] *Id.* at 721.

[124] *Id.* at 723.

[125] *Id.* at 740.

[126] *Id.* at 741.

[127] Simon, *Ideology of Advocacy*, *supra* note 22, at 53.

[128] *Id.* at 54.

[129] *Id.* at 55.

[130] Lehman, *supra* note 22, at 1088-89. Lehman relates two personal anecdotes in support of his point about tax consequences. In one, a client defers an intended gift until a more tax advantageous time, and ends up dying in a car crash without ever bestowing the gift. *Id.* at 1088. In the other, a widow recovering from alcoholism avoids going to a lawyer for advice on selling a house that has become an emotional

Lawyers' complicity in shaping their clients' objectives was also revealed—though not explicitly discussed—in Luban's discussion of custody blackmail in divorce cases. Luban offered custody blackmail as an example of "precisely the sort of hardball tactic that would be virtually impossible to justify without the standard conception."[131] He described it as a practice in which "the divorcing father (at the behest of his attorney) threatens to demand joint custody unless the mother reduces her financial demands."[132] It is beyond the bounds of morality, he argued, for "the zealous divorce lawyer [to] suggest[ ] custody blackmail to a father who has no desire for custody."[133] Such a lawyer "has wronged the wife and children, contributed to the social problem of emiserated divorced mothers, added to the general sexism of American society and abused the legal system."[134]

For Luban, custody blackmail was an example of the need for lawyers to break role and take moral charge of the legal representation by refusing to pursue a financial benefit for their clients at the cost of moral harm to others. However, custody blackmail is also precisely the sort of hardball tactic that it is difficult to imagine a divorcing father coming up with on his own. Luban's own description of the practice reveals the active participation of the divorce lawyer: the divorcing father makes the custody demand "at the behest of his attorney" who "suggests" it to him. It is implicit in the very definition of the tactic that the lawyer advances a claim for custody that the client *doesn't really want* to win. It is lawyers who begin legal representation by constructing their clients narrowly in the image of the clients' legal interests who are likely to come up with the tactic of custody blackmail in the first place.[135]

C. Re-defining the Solution: the Client-Centered Approach to Legal Representation

At about the same time Wasserstrom was making his call for "an explicit effort to alter the ways in which lawyers are educated and acculturated to view themselves, their clients, and the relationships that ought to exist between them,"[136] legal education was in the nascent stages of a movement with just those goals. Also undergoing fluorescence in the mid-1970s, the clinical legal education movement was in the midst of developing

and psychological burden to live in, fearful that she will be talked into delaying the sale to gain a tax advantage. *Id.* at 1089.

131 Luban, *Partisanship, Betrayal and Autonomy, supra* note 102, at 1016.

132 *Id.* at 1015.

133 *Id.* at 1018.

134 *Id.*

135 Because the practice of custody blackmail is an ethically marginal tactic, a lawyer who was morally disinclined to employ it could easily find support in professional standards of conduct. MODEL RULES OF PROFESSIONAL CONDUCT R. 4.4(a) ("In representing a client, a lawyer shall not use means that have no substantial purpose other than to embarrass, delay, or burden a third person").

136 Wasserstrom, *supra* note 22, at 23.

a curriculum for teaching the skills and values of lawyering in the context of live client representation.[137] However well cardboard clients worked to discuss dilemmas in the legal ethics classroom, they were ill-fitted to the clinical teaching context, in which law students developed relationships with actual clients and confronted the complexities of their clients' life situations in their fullest dimensions.

It was within the client interviewing and counseling literature designed for clinical teaching that a solution to the problem of legal objectification developed. The most prominent model of lawyering to emerge from the clinical legal education movement was the development of client-centered representation, an approach to lawyering that encouraged lawyers to conceptualize legal representation as problem-solving, to attend to clients' non-legal needs, and to include them in participatory decision-making on matters of legal strategy.[138] Client-centered representation is taught pervasively in law school clinical and lawyering skills courses and has since generated a rich body of practice and pedagogy-based scholarship about lawyering, much of which explores the internal dynamics of the lawyer-client relationship.[139]

The client-centered approach is directly responsive to the problem of legal objectification. It urges lawyers to unlearn the professional habit of "issue-spotting" their clients and to approach their clients as whole persons who are more than the sum of their legal interests. The hallmarks of the client-centered approach include understanding the client's problem from the client's point of view and shaping legal advice around the client's values.[140] Under the client-centered approach, hearing clients' stories and understanding their values, cares, and commitments is the first step—and a continuing duty—of legal representation.[141]

---

[137] The earliest clinical teaching materials focused on the acquisition of professional role by breaking down and analyzing the various aspects of legal representation that made up what Gary Bellow and Bea Moulton famously called "the lawyering process." Gary Bellow & Bea Moulton, The Lawyering Process: Materials for Clinical Instruction in Advocacy (1978). For a history of this pedagogical movement, see *Symposium: Celebrating* The Lawyering Process, 10 Clin. L. Rev. 1 (2003).

[138] David A. Binder, et al., Lawyers as Counselors: A Client-Centered Approach 2-15 (1991). For a comprehensive examination of the history and theoretical basis for this approach, see Robert D. Dinerstein, *Client-Centered Counseling: Reappraisal and Refinement*, 32 Ariz. L. Rev. 501 (1990). For a survey of the growth and development of the client-centered approach into a multiplicity of closely-related lawyering theories, see Katherine R. Kruse, *Fortress in the Sand: The Plural Values of Client-Centered Representation*, 12 Clinical L. Rev. 369 (2006).

[139] For a fuller description of the theories that have grown up in the critique, expansion and modification of the client-centered approach, see Kruse, *Fortress in the Sand, supra* note 137, at 375-99.

[140] Binder, et al. *supra* note 137, at 19-22. The client-centered approach is contrasted with more traditional approaches to lawyering, which "view client problems primarily in terms of existing doctrinal categories" and "seek the best 'legal' solutions to problems without fully exploring how those solutions meet clients' nonlegal as well as legal concerns." *Id.* at 17.

[141] For discussion of techniques for helping lawyers hear and understand their clients' stories and perspectives, see Jane Harris Aiken, *Striving to Teach "Justice, Fairness and Morality,"* 4 Clinical L. Rev. 1 (1997); Jane H. Aiken, *Provocateurs for Justice*, 7 Clinical L. Rev. 287 (2001); Susan Bryant, *The Five*

The client-centered approach also re-orients the lawyer-client relationship along the lines of limited de-professionalization foreshadowed by Wasserstrom's essay. In a highly professionalized conception of role, lawyers exercise maximum professional control over strategic decisions with minimal consultation from clients.[142] In client-centered representation, the focus on understanding clients' objectives more broadly and holistically than the sum of the clients' legal interests tends to break down the boundaries between legal and non-legal strategies for addressing clients' problems.[143] By contrast, the lawyer-statesman ideal proposed by legal ethicists reinforces a highly professionalized view of the lawyer-client relationship. In addition to using professional expertise to shape tactical and strategic decisions, lawyers are encouraged to make professional judgments about morality and the public good. Client influence and participation in representation decisions is seen as a threat to the independence that lawyers need to establish and maintain to play an effective role as mediator between clients' self-interested projects and the public interest.[144]

Although the client-centered approach has been seen as appropriate for the contexts in which it is primarily taught—law school clinical programs that serve poor and otherwise marginalized clients—it has been argued to have limited application in the circles of highly-paid lawyers for high-powered clients.[145] As legal ethics has matured as an academic discipline, legal ethicists have increasingly gravitated toward analyzing the scandals and pressures of practice in the big law firm, where the vision of "zeal at the margin" is "alive and well" and the conflicts between role morality and ordinary morality can most clearly be found.[146] Wasserstrom's early insight—that the amoral attitude lawyers exhibit toward others outside the lawyer-client relationship is connected to the way lawyers treat their clients—has been lost between the diverging paths of clinical scholarship and legal ethics.

Habits: Building Cross-Cultural Competence in Lawyers, 8 CLIN. L. REV. 65 (2001); Kimberly O'Leary, *Using "Difference Analysis" to Teach Problem-Solving*, 4 CLIN. L. REV. 65 (1997).

[142] DOUGLAS E. ROSENTHAL, LAWYERS AND CLIENTS: WHO'S IN CHARGE? 7-28 (1974) (contrasting traditional and client-participatory professional relationships).

[143] Kruse, *Fortress in the Sand, supra* note 137, at 392-94.

[144] Gordon, *supra* note 91.

[145] *See* Ellmann, *Lawyers and Clients*, 34 UCLA L. REV. 717, 718-19 (1987) (distinguishing contexts in which clients "enjoy economic leverage over their lawyers" from those in which lawyers' social status and expertise gives them power over clients). *See also* Dinerstein, *supra* note 137, at 521-23 (discussing whether "the historical relationship to poverty law mean[s] that client-centered counseling should be restricted to representation of poor people"); Kimberly E. O'Leary, *When Context Matters: How to Choose an Appropriate Client Counseling Model*, 4 T.M. COOLEY J. PRAC. & CLINICAL L. 103 (2001) (distinguishing practice settings in which client-centered practice is more or less appropriate).

[146] Douglas N. Frenkel, et al., *Introduction: Bringing Legal Realism to the Study of Ethics and Professionalism*, 67 FORDHAM L. REV. 697, 703 (1998) (summarizing conclusion of empirical study of large-firm litigators' ethical attitudes that the standard conception was "alive and well"). *See also* Luban, *Partisanship, Betrayal and Autonomy, supra* note 102, at 1016 ("The true haven of the standard conception, however, is large-firm practice").

III. LEGAL ETHICS FOR THREE-DIMENSIONAL CLIENTS

This Part weaves the insights of client-centered representation into legal ethics by proposing and defending a theoretical model of client value-based representation that re-defines the standard conception's principles of partisanship and neutrality in the context of three-dimensional clients who come to legal representation with a mixture of values, commitments, relationships, hopes, dreams and fears. It starts with the premise that client objectives are complex and multidimensional and places client values—as the client defines them—at the center of a lawyer's partisan duties. When the pursuit of a client's objectives is redefined in the context of three-dimensional clients, the standard conception's principles of partisan loyalty and moral neutrality look different. This Part argues that the redefined versions of partisan loyalty and moral neutrality survives the critiques that legal ethicists leveled at the extreme version of partisanship captured by "zeal at the margin" without succumbing to the dangers of moral elitism and moral overreaching that the lawyer-statesman model presents.

A. Putting Client Values at the Center of Legal Representation

In an early article on lawyer paternalism, David Luban provided a theoretical vocabulary of wants, values, and interests with untapped potential for addressing Wasserstrom's puzzle of limited deprofessionalization.[147] Wasserstrom noted that the idea of limited de-professionalization is difficult because clients come to lawyers for help with problems that really do require legal expertise. Although it is problematic to reduce a client to nothing more than a bundle of legal interests, legal issue-spotting is a core competency of lawyering and a necessary component of virtually all legal representation.[148] The puzzle is in figuring out how to "weaken the bad consequences" of lawyers' tendency to professionalize the lawyer-client relationship "without destroying the good that lawyers do."[149]

Luban's theoretical vocabulary re-defines client objectives in three dimensions, suggesting that client objectives are complex, ambiguous, and potentially conflicting. Luban theoretically distinguished three different aspects of a client's objectives, as follows:

- *Wants* are those things a client subjectively desires in the moment; they are like facts that exist but cannot be disputed.[150]
- *Values* are the desires with which a client most closely identifies, playing an important role in defining a client's larger life-plans and self-conceptions.[151]

---

[147] Luban, *Paternalism, supra* note 22.

[148] Model R. Prof'l Conduct 1.1, Cmt. par. [2].

[149] Wasserstrom, *supra* note 22, at 23.

[150] *Id.*

[151] *Id.* at 470.

- *Interests* are "generalizable means to any ultimate end."[152] They include freedom, wealth, health, power, and control over other people's actions.[153] Interests are not valuable in themselves, but as means by which we can satisfy our wants and actualize our values.[154]

According to Luban's analysis, the touchstone for a lawyer's appropriate intervention into client decision making is whether the intervention supports or undermines the client in actualizing her values.[155] The primacy of client values emerges from the way Luban analyzes what a lawyer should do when clients' wants, interests, and values conflict. Luban argued that lawyers are justified in paternalistically manipulating clients to promote the clients' *interests* in favor of the clients' *wants*.[156] If a client expresses the desire to deviate from the maximization of legal interests, Luban saw it as "the lawyer's job to express the conservative and restrained point of view" from the standpoint of the client's interests.[157] Because wants come and go, a lawyer who protects a client's interests can serve as a sort of "ego" to the client's "id"—getting clients past the fleeting wants that dominate their desires in the moment and keeping their future options open.[158] However, lawyers are not justified in paternalistically manipulating clients to further the client's interests in ways that override the client values.[159] Because values form the core of a client's personality, manipulating a client to act against the client's values is a violation of the client's personal integrity.[160] Such paternalistic intervention cannot be justified because interests are not valuable in themselves—they derive their value from their utility as means toward other ends.[161]

To place the actualization of client values at the center of legal representation would require lawyers to assist their clients in making decisions that are consistent with the clients' most important goals and life plans. As Luban and other philosophers have

---

[152] *Id.* at 471.

[153] *Id.* at 466, 471.

[154] *Id.* at 474.

[155] I have previously discussed respect for client values in terms of enhancing a client's autonomy. Kruse, *Fortress in the Sand, supra* note 137, at 399-414. When a lawyer overrides a client's wants in favor the client's interests, Luban calls it "justified paternalism." Luban, *Paternalism, supra* note 22, at 472. *But see* Simon, *Mrs. Jones' Case, supra* note 114, at 224 (arguing that refined versions of autonomy and paternalism converge in a view that would support a client in actualizing her own values).

[156] Luban, *Paternalism, supra* note 22, at 472-74.

[157] *Id.* at 493.

[158] *Id.* at 493. *See also id.* at 486 (arguing that the superiority of what he calls the Ideal of Prudence "lies in the flexibility of the goods I have termed 'interests' in realizing our ambitions, not in the intrinsic merits of money or power . . . in other words, in its breadth and not in its depth.")

[159] Luban, *Paternalism, supra* note 22, at 472-74.

[160] *Id.* at 473.

[161] *Id.* at ("[i]t is absurd . . . to assume that interests constitute the dominant values in a human life").

discussed, values are those things that are closest to the centers of our personalities, and which invest our lives with meaning.[162] Values play a dual role, both motivating our actions and shaping the way we define ourselves. Our values are in one sense normative—-they provide reasons for our actions.[163] But our values are also expressions of our identity—they define who we are. And the motivation that values provide for our actions is connected to the way they define who we are. We are motivated to live our lives in accordance with our values because it is through acting in accordance with our values that we become the persons we want to be.[164]

Living a life in accordance with our values is likely to be a process that unfolds over time through experiences of conflict and confrontation. In part, this is because of the diversity of values that can form the cores of our identities.[165] We may value a life of adventure or the life of the mind. We may value material success, family ties, or quality time spent with friends. Our values may be based in career choices, political commitments, projects that we have undertaken—anything by which we define ourselves. We may feel a "calling" to live out our values through commitments to particular ways of life—joining the Peace Corps, converting to a religion, even going to law school—and those commitments may be the source of commitment to political, religious or professional values. We may value ourselves through relationships and in community with others, and the ways in which these relationships and communities define us may be at the deepest core of our identities.[166] Because of this diversity, our values are likely to be internally inconsistent, forcing us to choose between them as we move through life. Practical choices—what career path to pursue, for example—will often bring our values into internal conflict, forcing us to prioritize and choose between them. It is through practical choices made in situations of value conflict that we are likely to discover, articulate and actualize the kind of persons we want to be.

Yet, the process of assessing and clarifying our values in situations of value conflict may be difficult. Our deepest values are often opaque; we may be motivated by underlying values that we don't explicitly recognize, but which can be seen over time to tie our choices together in recognizable patterns.[167] Moreover, our process of value

---

[162] *Id.* at 470; Bernard Williams, *Persons, Character and Morality, in* Moral Luck, *supra* note 25, at 1, 12-13 (describing "ground projects" through which we define our lives' success).

[163] Christine Korsgaard, The Sources of Normativity 8 (1996) (normative statements "make *claims* on us; they command, oblige, recommend or guide).

[164] For a discussion of this idea in the context of autonomy theory, see Kruse, *Fortress in the Sand, supra* note 137, at 404-05.

[165] *See* Thomas Nagel, *The Fragmentation of Value, in* Mortal Questions 128 (1979) (discussing values coming from different types of sources: personal obligations, rights, utility, perfectionist ends, and private commitments).

[166] Shaffer & Shaffer, *supra* note 94, at 98-108.

[167] Luban, *Paternalism, supra* note 22, at 470. In later work, Luban has suggested that many times we do not experience the things we care the most about as being chosen by us, but rather we feel as if our values have chosen us. David Luban, *Lawyers As Upholders of Human Dignity (When They Aren't Busy Assaulting It), in* Legal Ethics and Human Dignity, *supra* note 41, at 65, 76.

clarification may be distorted by short-term and reactionary emotions like anger, fear, and insecurity.[168] Or, we may succumb to rationalizations that sound like the articulation of our values, but which are really just excuses for doing what we want to do in the moment. Value clarification is a process of self-reflection—often triggered by experiences of confrontation and choice—that helps penetrate the fog of confusion that may attend practical choices in the face of uncertainty. Its purpose is to help us surface and order our values so that our lives will reflect our values and we can become the kind of persons we want to be.[169]

When clients come to lawyers for legal advice and representation, their legal issues are often entangled with values, projects, commitments, and relationships with others. Sometimes legal tasks may touch on a client's deeply held personal values, such as getting legal help to start up a business a client has always dreamed of having or helping a couple adopt a child. Sometimes legal action arises because a client has been harmed by the actions of others: the client has been fired from a job, hit by a car, or beaten by a spouse. Sometimes the client has been accused of treating others unjustly: sexually harassing an employee, reneging on a deal, negligently allowing harm to others, or committing a crime. Other times clients come to lawyers to overcome barriers to taking care of business as usual: a deal needs to be negotiated, property needs to be leased, or a permit needs to be obtained.

In discussions with clients, lawyers will inevitably emphasize and order information in ways that influence the client's choices.[170] Whether or not a lawyer discusses a client's other commitments, projects, relationships, and values, the client still experiences the legal interests within the context of these other considerations. The counseling approach the lawyer employs will put a thumb on the scale in favor of particular considerations. If the lawyer believes that her role is to maximize the client's legal interests, the lawyer will take an approach that emphasizes legal interests over other considerations. By contrast, lawyers who believe that their role is to shape representation around a client's values will give their clients space to clarify those values and make representation decisions that are consistent with those values.

As Luban pointed out, lawyers' tendency to focus on their clients' legal interests may be justified to the extent that it diverts clients from making impulsive decisions. If a client is experiencing loss, transition, or uncertainty about the future—such as in a divorce or in the aftermath of a serious life-changing injury—the protection of legal interests may be the most effective way to keep the client's future options open until she is able to adjust to dramatic changes in her life and sort her values out. Where the threatened loss will severely impair the client's ability to pursue options in the future—as

---

[168] Luban, *Paternalism, supra* note 22, at 473.

[169] Christina Korsgaard sees the process of "reflective endorsement" as central to our ability to act autonomously—to give authoritative law to ourselves. *See* KORSGAARD, SOURCES OF NORMATIVITY, *supra* note 162, at 129.

[170] *See* Simon, *Mrs. Jones's Case, supra* note 114 (describing how lawyers influence their clients' decision making even when they are ostensibly providing clients with information about legal interests).

in criminal cases where defendants face substantial loss of liberty or even death—there may be particularly strong imperatives to protect the client's legal interests to keep avenues open for the client's future ability to actualize her values.

However, legal interest-based counseling serves the actualization of the client's life goals only indirectly. Legal interests are not good in themselves; they are merely the channels by which clients can use the law to pursue and protect the things they value in life. Protecting a client's legal interests helps the client only because interests are generalized means toward *anyone's* ends. The temporary restraint on impulsive decision making that legal interests provide is valuable precisely because pursuing the wants of the moment may foreclose the client from actualizing more deeply-held values, goals, or life plans.

Counseling that proceeds on the assumption that client merely want to maximize their legal interests is far from neutral. In the context of legal representation—where the client may be confronting new opportunities or battling fear, uncertainty, anger or pain—counseling clients that they "should" do what is in their legal interests to do may distort the client's process of value clarification and encourage self-seeking choices.[171] Lawyers who say "this is what you should do"—when what they really mean is "this is what it is in your legal interests to do"—may encourage clients to press their legal interests further than the clients might otherwise be inclined to pursue them. Clients who might otherwise be motivated to act in the public interest may be dissuaded by their deference to a lawyer's professional expertise. Or, if a client is experiencing hurt or anger, knowing how the law can be used to defeat the interests of others may provide the client with a way to rationalize selfish choices at the expense of the client's better moral judgment. Just as lawyers may seek refuge in the excuse, "but that is not my job"; clients may seek refuge in the excuse, "but I'm just following legal advice."[172]

When a lawyer approaches legal representation as problem-solving endeavor shaped around the client's values, it helps to mitigate the distorting influence of legal interests and allow the client's values to provide a natural check on legal interest maximization. Like legal interests, appeals to client values—to the kind of person that a client wants to be—help curb impulsive, fearful, or vengeful decisions. However, rather than achieving this goal by appealing to a hypothetical client's standardized interests, client value clarification appeals directly to the client's own values. The purpose of value clarification in legal counseling is not to change the weight or priority of the client's values—though that might be a byproduct of the process. The purpose is to ensure that the client's representation decisions are consistent with and further the client's values.

The methods of client value clarification involve both actively listening to what the client wants and probing beneath the client's expressed desires. Client-centered interviewing literature, for example, suggests that the lawyer dedicate time early in a client's initial interview for open-ended questions and other active listening techniques

---

171 Lehman, *supra* note 22, at 188-89.

172 *See* Pepper, *Lawyers' Ethics in the Gap Between Law and Justice*, 40 S. TEX. L. REV. 181, 189-90 (1999).

that help the lawyer hear the client's problem in the client's own terms.[173] Hearing the client's story—as the client chooses to tell it—is a key component of understanding what the client values and what it is about the legal representation that will threaten or further those values.

Client value clarification may also require probing beneath the surface of a client's stated desires. As Lehman has suggested, when clients seek legal representation, their judgment and articulation of what they really want may be skewed: "We say we want justice when we want love. We say we were treated illegally when we were hurt. We insist on our rights when we have been snubbed or cut. We want money when we feel impotent."[174] Lehman noted that instead of inquiring about clients' deeper goals, most lawyers give instrumentalist advice on how to maximize outcomes based on a the desires of a hypothetical "'standard client' for whom lawyers are wont to model their services."[175] By contrast, lawyers interested in helping a client center decisions on the client's own values will help their clients contemplate how the decisions of the moment will affect the clients' development in the direction of becoming the kind of person each of them uniquely wants to be.

A. Partisan Loyalty for Three-Dimensional Clients

The centering of legal representation on client values suggests a more defensible ideal of partisanship than the "zeal at the margin" for cardboard clients that has occupied legal ethical critique. As we have seen, the moral theorists' critiques of the standard conception drew their force from their extreme interpretation of partisan loyalty as "zeal at the margin" for clients who want nothing other than to maximize their legal interests up to and beyond the moral limits in the law. When this conception of partisanship is replaced with an ideal based on helping clients actualize their own values, the critiques lose much of their force.

Hidden within the adversary system critique is a defense of partisanship conceived more broadly as shaping legal representation around a client's actual values and fashioning advocacy around the stories that clients would tell about themselves. For example, Luban's argument against the truth-finding efficacy of adversarial proceedings was based on the observation that lawyers use a client's *legal interests* as a starting point from which to develop facts and present evidence to a decision maker. The "theories of the case" that arise from this method are misleading because they are based, not on the client's actual perspective of what occurred, but on what it would be best—from the standpoint of the client's legal interests—to prove.[176] Under client-value centered partisanship,

---

[173] BINDER, ET AL., *supra* note 137, at 88-93.

[174] Lehman, *supra* note 22, at 1081.

[175] *Id.* at 1089.

[176] For a criticism of advocacy that proceeds from this perspective in disregard of a client's actual story, see Binny Miller, *Give Them Back Their Lives: Recognizing Client Narrative in Case Theory*, 93 MICH. L. REV. 485 (1994).

advocacy would be focused on finding ways connect clients' own stories to themes and values reflected in the law.[177] Luban conceded that developing facts from the actual perspectives of disputing *clients* (rather than from the standpoint of their competing *interests*) would support, rather than hinder, accurate truth-finding.[178] The same goes for the arguments from human dignity and legal rights. The adversary system, Luban conceded, could be defended quite strongly on grounds of human dignity,[179] precisely because providing the opportunity for a client to tell her own story is an important way of honoring her dignity.

In his later work, Luban has sketched just such an ideal of partisan advocacy based on upholding a client's dignity in which lawyers strive to match the case theory the lawyer presents—the legal story the lawyer tells about a client in negotiation or litigation—with the cares, commitments, and concerns that are most central to the client.[180] According to Luban, human dignity means "having a story of one's own"—having a subjective view of the world in which one is at the center.[181] Lawyers dignify their clients by giving voice to their clients: by "telling the client's story and interpreting the law from the client's viewpoint";[182] and "by giving the client voice and sparing the client the humiliation of being silenced and ignored."[183] A lawyer calibrating legal representation to a client's values would be much less likely to cynically manipulate the facts or stretch the law to extract anything it could be made to give, and much more likely to look for ways to legitimate the client's values by connecting them to values reflected in the law.

Client value-centered partisanship would also survive the role disposition theorists' critique. This critique, we can recall, is that the standard conception encourages lawyers to develop a professional disposition toward amorality, which dulls them to the harm they cause others and is ultimately unsatisfying to lawyers themselves. However, client value-centered partisanship would encourage the development of a very different disposition: a disposition based in the capacities for empathy and self-reflection.[184] To seriously undertake the task of centering representation on client values, lawyers

---

[177] *See, e.g., id.*; Robert D. Dinerstein, *A Meditation on the Theoretics of Practice*, 43 HASTINGS L.J. 971 (1992); Lucie White, *Subordination, Rhetorical Survival Skills, and Sunday Shoes: Notes on the Hearing of Mrs. G.*, 38 BUFF. L. REV. 1 (1990).

[178] *See* LUBAN, LAWYERS AND JUSTICE, *supra* note 32, at 73 ("the more perspectives we have, the better informed our judgment will be").

[179] *Id.* at 85-87.

[180] LUBAN, *Human Dignity*, *supra* note 166, at 68-73 (endorsing an even stronger argument in favor of partisan advocacy based on the honoring the story that the client has to tell). Luban finds particularly persuasive the account of adversary ethics offered by philosopher Alan Donagan as part of the Working Group on Legal Ethics. *Id.* at 819. *See* Alan Donagan, *Justifying Legal Practice in the Adversary System*, *in* THE GOOD LAWYER, *supra* note 22, at 123.

[181] LUBAN, *Human Dignity, supra* note 166, at 70-71.

[182] *Id.* at 70.

[183] *Id.* at 72.

[184] Markovits, *supra* note 66, at 273. The development of empathic understanding has long been a central component of the client-centered approach to interviewing and counseling. *See* BINDER, ET AL., *supra*

would endeavor to see the world as their clients see it. Unlike the disposition of amoral detachment, which is argued to be at the root of lawyer alienation and discontent,[185] empathy with clients has been noted as a source of internal motivation that can help sustain lawyers in their professional roles.[186]

In short, in the very places where "zeal at the margin" fails to stand up to the deeper scrutiny of the early legal ethicists' critiques, client value-centered partisanship survives. The critiques of the moral theorists are quite forceful when leveled against the extreme vision of partisanship captured by "zeal at the margin." Yet, if ideal partisanship is conceived as being centered on client value actualization, a more defensible—even honorable—version of partisan loyalty emerges.

B. Moral Neutrality for Three-Dimensional Clients

In addition to critiquing partisan loyalty, the early legal ethicists were critical of the moral neutrality of the lawyer-client relationship. However, the critiques of moral neutrality—like the critiques of partisan loyalty—were distorted by the assumption of morally corrupt cardboard clients who cared only about maximizing their wealth, freedom, or power over others. Because the early legal ethicists developed their ideal in a context defined by assumptions of moral lawyers and cardboard clients, they had in mind clients who were by definition devoid of moral constraint. And the lawyers they had in mind were by definition more suited to moral decision making than the cardboard clients they had constructed. Focusing on client value actualization requires a type of moral neutrality on the part of the lawyer; because the lawyer focuses on the client's values, the lawyer must put her own values to the side. However, the moral neutrality of client value-centered representation is not morally empty. Rather, it imports moral considerations into legal representation by drawing on the rich landscape of the client's values—including the client's moral values—that might otherwise be excised by the lawyer's focus on legal interests.

Not all outcomes of value clarification favor morality. Whether moral claims win out in the process of value clarification depends on how important moral values are to the person doing the clarifying. The process of value clarification will assist moral decision making for persons who have internalized the moral values about the way they ought to treat others. It may also assist persons who draw support for moral behavior from personal values such as being an upstanding citizen or good neighbor; in standing by their commitments, honoring their word; or maintaining their reputation in a community. But helping to clarify the values of a person with largely selfish values is likely to assist him in endorsing his own self-regarding behavior. The emotional core

---

note 137, at 40-42. Self-reflection has also been noted as a key component to successful communication between lawyers and clients. Bryant, *supra* note 140.

[185] *See generally* Postema, *Self-Image, supra* note 75.

[186] *See* Charles J. Ogletree, Jr., *Beyond Justifications: Seeking Motivations to Sustain Public Defenders,* 106 HARV. L. REV. 1239 (1993).

of Luban's moral activism is that standing by neutrally and allowing such a client to act on his selfish choices would be tantamount to condoning his mistreatment of others. Intervening to override the selfish choices of such a client might violate his autonomy and dignity, but it may at the same time be the only way to protect the autonomy and dignity of those who stand in harm's way.

The moral activist approach is defensible in the narrow circumstances toward which it was originally directed: the situation of a moral lawyer counseling a cardboard client. However, the moral activist solution is ill-suited to the representation of three-dimensional clients because the tactics of moral activism run directly contrary to the principles of respect for a client's values. The moral activist lawyer's focus is on conforming the client's behavior to the lawyer's conception of the public good. To achieve this end, moral activist lawyers employ increasingly aggressive tactics of persuasion, coercion, and even betrayal, which deliberately distort the client's decision making process.[187] The further along the scale the lawyer goes, the more likely it is that the lawyer is battling the client's deeply-held values. Less deeply-grounded resistance is likely to give way earlier in the process.

When lawyers and clients disagree about the morality of a course of action, the problems with moral activist counseling take on an added dimension. Like most people confronted with someone reluctant to act in accordance with what we see as the claims of morality, lawyers will have a tendency to believe that their clients are mistaken in their moral calculus. We can affirm on an intellectual level that our moral beliefs may reasonably differ from the moral beliefs of others. However, when we are confronted with someone who does not share our moral values, it is difficult for us to understand their view as reasonable. We are more likely to believe that we are right and that the other person has made a "moral mistake."[188] The belief that their clients are making a moral mistake will naturally tempt lawyers to intervene into their clients' decision making—perhaps even by strong tactics—to prevent what they view as a moral wrong. The stakes for the lawyer of gaining a client's compliance with the claims of morality—as the lawyer sees them—are especially high. Lawyers do not simply sit by and tolerate their clients' differing moral viewpoints; they act on them. The force of the role disposition theorists' critique of the standard conception is that being forced to *act* against their own values is damaging to lawyers.

The kind of moral neutrality that results from respect for another person's values helps to discipline lawyers' tendency to impose their own moral and value choices on

---

[187] As Luban describes it, moral activist client counseling

> may mean kindling the clients' consciences, but more often it will mean inventing alternative ways for clients to satisfy their interests. Sometimes it means persuading clients that the course of action they propose will harm them even when that is not necessarily so. In other instances, client counseling will require threatening to withdraw from a representation or refusing to follow a client's instructions. In the extreme cases, it means telling the client that if he does not back away from a course of action, the lawyer will blow the whistle on him.

Luban, Noblesse Oblige *Tradition*, *supra* note 90, at 737-38.

[188] Kruse, *Moral Pluralism*, *supra* note 105, at 402-07.

their clients in the guise of legal advice. If we assume three-dimensional clients, it is respect for client values that ensures the good that moral activism hopes to achieve by importing moral considerations into legal representation without succumbing to the danger of moral overreaching.

C. Beyond Moral Lawyers: Three-Dimensional Lawyers in the Arena of Legal Representation

If we take seriously the possibility that lawyers shape their clients' objectives in the direction of legal interest maximization, it raises a puzzling question for moral theorists: why would lawyers willingly create situations that provide them with deep role dissatisfaction? Ethicists concluded that lawyers were forced into the deeply dissatisfying kind of practice characterized by "zeal at the margin" by their partisan loyalty to clients who insisted that the lawyers pursue slash and burn tactics in the pursuit of immoral ends. However, if we accept the premise that lawyers construct their clients' objectives as legal interest maximization, we have to conclude that lawyers who practice "zeal at the margin" are at least partially responsible for their own misery. Part of the answer has to be that—just as clients are not solely motivated by the maximization of their legal interests—lawyers are not purely motivated by morality and a commitment to the public interest. Lawyers, like clients, are morally complex three-dimensional persons who bring a mix of reputational interests, personal relationships, values, cares and commitments into the arena of legal representation. And all of these factors may affect lawyers' decision making for better or for worse.

An examination of the moral complexity of lawyers is important for another reason as well. Even if we reject the moral elitist premise that underlies the lawyer-statesman model—that lawyers are morally superior to their clients—we might accept the more plausible assumption that lawyers are generally *better situated* than clients to make moral decisions in the specific arena of legal representation. As we have seen, in the arena of legal representation, clients' own resolution of their conflicting wants, values, and interests may be distorted by temporary conditions of anger, fear or insecurity. Because they are less personally and emotionally invested in the situations that lead to legal representation, lawyers are arguably better situated in legal representation to bring moral considerations to bear. However, to conclude that lawyers are better situated as moral decision makers in the arena of legal representation, we need to consider the ways in which lawyers' own wants, interests, and values compete with their moral and professional judgment.

First, and most obviously, the lawyer-client relationship involves a commercial exchange of services for fees, giving rise to an interest on the part of the lawyer in maximizing the financial return on a case. However the lawyer gets paid—by the billable hour, contingent on the outcome, or on a flat fee or contract—the lawyer will have a financial interest in how the representation proceeds. Hourly fees give the lawyer an interest in spending a lot of time on a case, especially if the client is a "deep pocket" with virtually unlimited resources to sink into legal representation. Consequently, a lawyer billing by the hour may have a financial interest in making an extravagant investment of time or resources in a task that produces only marginally better results for the client. Contingent fees give lawyers an interest in maximizing outcomes with as little investment of time as possible, and at any cost to others along the way. Flat fees or contracts give lawyers an interest in resolving the representation of each client as quickly as possible, providing an incentive to conclude or settle the matter whether or not the client has fully understood or bought into the terms of the settlement or agreement.

Moreover, lawyers have a legal interest in protecting themselves from malpractice lawsuits by advising clients to maximize legal interests and leaving a clear paper trail any time a client declines to follow that advice. Lawyers who fail to pursue a client's legal interests as far as it is possible to pursue them risk exposure to malpractice claims if the client suffers financial damage as a result of the decision. Even if a client has made an informed and reasonable decision not to pursue a possible avenue of relief, the lawyer may be concerned about liability in the event of the client's future change of heart. The commonly recommended "CYA" letters that lawyers sent to clients are designed to protect themselves against future malpractice suits any time a client decides to act against lawyer advice or the clients' own interests.[189]

Lawyers also have reputational interests at stake in legal representation. Lawyers may depend on their professional reputations to make their practices run smoothly, and may be subject to informal social sanctions for engaging in behavior that doesn't serve the values or interests of other members of their professional community.[190] In some cases, this pressure to conform to informal professional norms can support ethical behavior.[191] However, it can also work as a collective protectionist strategy to discriminate against lawyers who represent outsiders or who are themselves outsiders to the legal community.[192]

In addition lawyers, like their clients, have personal values, cares, and commitments that come into play in legal representation. Their personal identities may be defined in part by their ability to win, their sense of fair play, or even their ruthlessness or gritty determination. They may have ambitions for career advancement, such as the desire to make partner in a firm or to get an appointment as a judge. Preserving relationships inside and outside of professional circles may be personally important to them. They may have political commitments to practicing a certain kind of law or achieving a certain vision of social justice through their legal careers. They may value their families and the balance that they can achieve between work and home life. They may be members of religious communities or political organizations with accompanying values and commitments that interact with or affect the actions they take as lawyers. Any or all of these personal values and ambitions may affect lawyers' decisions in legal representation.

---

189 Karen Erger, *Cover Me: Documentation is More Than CYA*, 98 Ill. B.J. 316 (2008).

190 *See generally* Wendel, *supra* note 95.

191 *Id.* at 1968-69.

192 *Id.*

As critics have noted, the premise that lawyers are driven to overly zealous tactics by the loyal pursuit of client interests does not paint a particularly accurate picture of legal practice.[193] When examined more closely, it appears that lawyers engage in "zeal at the margin"—not because they are loyal to their clients—but because it serves their own interests to do so. Lawyers practicing in small communities are likely to curb the zeal of their advocacy to preserve their professional relationships and standing in the community.[194] Lawyers for relatively powerless one-shot clients are more than willing to manipulate their clients into taking deals that help maintain the lawyer's professional standing.[195]

Even in the place where the ruthless tactics of "zeal at the margin" seem to be a more accurate description of lawyers' practices—the large litigation firm—the lawyer's own drive to maximize profits by amassing billable hours provides at least as good an explanation as the premise that these lawyers are acting out of loyalty to their clients. At least, the assumption that big firm lawyers are driven by their own financial interests may better explain how the same lawyers who engage in scorched earth litigation tactics are also willing to gouge their own clients with questionable billing practices.[196]

In the arena of legal representation, lawyers and clients are thus differently situated, but it is difficult to conclude that one is better positioned than the other to engage in moral reasoning and decision making. The situations that lead clients to seek legal representation may incline clients to pursue their wants in favor of their values. Lawyers will generally have no particular investment in the situations in which their clients are embroiled. However, lawyers will inevitably have financial, reputational and personal interests that present their own form temptation to transgress moral and professional values. The principles of partisan loyalty and moral neutrality—redefined as attention to and deference to client value choices—can help check lawyers' own self-interested motivations in legal representation.

D. *Spaulding v. Zimmerman* in Three Dimensions

We are now in a position to return to *Spaulding v. Zimmerman*—the legal ethics classic in which the lawyer for a defendant in a personal injury automobile accident case chose not to inform the plaintiff that he suffered a life-threatening heart aneurysm—to explore the interests and motivations of the lawyer and the client in three dimensions.

---

[193] *See* Schneyer, *Standard Misconception*, *supra* note 22; Stephen Ellmann, *Lawyering for Justice in a Flawed Democracy*, 90 COLUM. L. REV. 116 (1990).

[194] Schneyer, *supra* note 22, at 156-47; Donald Landon, *Clients, Colleagues and Communities: The Shaping of Zealous Advocacy in Small Town Practice*, 1985 AM. B. FOUND. RES. J. 81.

[195] Schneyer, *supra* note 22, at 1544-45 (discussing Abraham Blumberg, *The Practice of Law as a Confidence Game*, 1 L & SOC'Y REV. 15 (1967)).

[196] Lisa G. Lerman, *Gross Profits?: Questions About Lawyer Billing Practices*, 22 HOFSTRA L. REV. 645 (1994); Lisa G. Lerman, *Blue-Chip Bilking: Regulation of Bill and Expense Fraud By Lawyers*, 12 GEO. J. LEGAL ETHICS 205 (1999); Susan Saab Fortney, *The Billable Hours Derbey: Empirical Data on the Problems and Pressure Points*, 33 FORDHAM URBAN L.J. 171 (2005).

As traditionally interpreted, *Spaulding* presents a moral and ethical dilemma for the lawyer: should the lawyer breach the professional duty of confidentiality to save a human life?[197] I have suggested that this interpretation of *Spaulding* has been driven by a theoretical interest in creating conflicts between role morality and ordinary morality, and that the more interesting ethical question raised by the real-life facts of *Spaulding* is why the lawyer felt entitled to settle the case without consulting his client about whether to reveal the potentially life-saving information.

I have argued that at the heart of the more interesting question in *Spaulding* is the problem of legal objectification: the lawyer was thinking only in terms of Zimmerman's legal interests. Certainly, it was contrary to Zimmerman's legal interests to volunteer otherwise confidential information that could increase the amount he owed in damages. The defense expert who examined Spaulding opined that the heart aneurysm could well have been caused by the automobile accident at issue in the litigation. And, if the doctor was right, it might well have affected the amount of money for which David Spaulding was willing to settle the case.[198] However, this narrow view of what was important to John Zimmerman overlooked his relationship with David Spaulding and other values that might have influenced Zimmerman to reveal the medical information to save the life of his neighbor and friend.

Had the lawyer been following a client value-based approach to legal representation, the situation would have been different. First, the lawyer would not have received the information about David Spaulding's heart aneurysm in the vacuum of legal interests. Because consistency with Zimmerman's long-term goals and deeply-held values would have been a central concern in the legal representation, the lawyer would have spent time at the beginning of the representation listening to John Zimmerman about hearing about the context of the lawsuit. When the information about Spaulding's heart aneurysm came across his desk, the lawyer would have been attuned to the importance of the information, not just to the legal case, but to Zimmerman's relationship with the Spaulding family. And he would have flagged it as an important issue to discuss with his client.

In discussing with John Zimmerman the question of whether to reveal the confidential information about David Spaulding's medical condition, the lawyer would explain to Zimmerman that he wasn't legally required to reveal the information and that revealing it might drive up the costs of settlement—perhaps even over the limits of the insurance policy. But the lawyer would also be prepared to help Zimmerman put his legal interests into the context of his other values and commitments. For example, the lawyer might probe to ensure that whatever decision Zimmerman made about divulging the information was consistent with Zimmerman's long-term values, perhaps asking Zimmerman how he would feel looking back on the decision from some vantage point in the future.

---

197 *See, e.g.* LUBAN, LAWYERS AND CLIENTS, *supra* note 32, at 149-50.

198 When the heart aneurysm was eventually discovered, it required corrective surgery that resulted in permanent and severe speech loss for David Spaulding. Cramton & Knowles, *supra* note 6, at 71.

From what we know about the real *Spaulding* case, that kind of discussion never took place. And *Spaulding* provides a window into the personal, financial, and reputational interests that may have prevented the discussion from occurring. Zimmerman's lawyer was hired and paid by the insurance company to represent Zimmerman, and the insurance contract most likely gave the insurance company rights to control certain aspects of the defense.[199] Although these contractual rights complicate the decision-making authority in the legal representation, they do not alleviate the lawyer's professional responsibility to consult with his client about important representation decisions, to share information that might create conflicting interests, and to protect Zimmerman's interests in the event of a conflict of interest with the insurance company.[200]

The lawyer's own interest in future business with the insurance company provided a powerful incentive for him to construe Zimmerman's objectives narrowly as legal interest maximization so that a conflict would not materialize. Zimmerman was a one-shot client that the lawyer was not likely to encounter again. The lawyer's long-term financial and reputational interests lay in protecting his relationship with the insurance company that hired and paid him.[201] If Zimmerman had insisted on revealing the confidential information, it might have negated the possibility of a settlement within the policy limits and created a financial conflict of interest between Zimmerman and the insurance company.[202] Even if the settlement stayed within the policy limits, Zimmerman's insistence on revealing the information might have created a conflict of interest requiring the lawyer to withdraw. It was certainly easier for the lawyer to construe John Zimmerman's objectives narrowly in terms of legal interests because, when narrowly construed, Zimmerman's legal interests remained in alignment with the legal interests of the insurance company.

It was also possible that part of the reason for overlooking Zimmerman's broader interests in this case was that the lawyer simply viewed the insurance company as the real party in interest and gave little thought to John Zimmerman as a client.[203] Of course, that does not answer the question of why the lawyer did not engage in a serious value-based discussion about revealing confidential information with representatives of the insurance company.[204] It is at least conceivable that, if consulted, representatives of the insurance company would direct the lawyer to reveal the information. After all, David Spaulding's

---

199 *Id.* at 90-91.

200 *See* RESTATEMENT (THIRD) OF LAW GOVERNING LAW. §134 (2000); ABA FORMAL OP. 01-421 (Feb. 16, 2001). For contrasting analyses of the difficulties of professional obligations in the insurance law context, see Thomas D. Morgan, *What Insurance Scholars Should Know About Professional Responsibility*, 4 CONN. INS. L.J. 1 (1997); Kent D. Syverud, *What Professional Responsibility Scholars Should Know About Insurance Law*, 4 CONN. INS. L.J. 17 (1997).

201 Cramton & Knowles, *supra* note 6, at 92-93.

202 *See* ABA FORMAL OP. 96-403 (Aug. 2, 1996).

203 Cramton & Knowles, *supra* at 93.

204 *Id.* at 93-94 (concluding that although it is possible that disclosure was discussed in the context of settlement offers with the insurance company "it is not clear . . . that the issue was the subject of pointed and meaningful consultation" and that "[t]he most likely conclusion is that the defense lawyers made this decision largely on their own.")

life hung in the balance, and that is a powerful counter-weight to the profit motive of even the most calculating profit-maximizer.[205] Even absent the long-term relationship with Spaulding that might have motivated Zimmerman to reveal the information, the lawyer might have assumed—at least presumptively—that the opportunity to save another human life was important to his insurance company client as well.

Finally, it is conceivable that even after consultation Zimmerman would have directed his lawyer not to reveal the information. He might have decided that he just couldn't do it to his family: the accident had killed his brother and broken his father's neck, the family was struggling to hold things together, and he just couldn't inflict a devastating financial blow to his mother and surviving family members. If so, the lawyer taking a client-value based approach might have faced something like the dilemma discussed by the early legal ethicists between whether to remain loyal to the duties of confidentiality or to follow the moral imperative to save a human life.

But the lawyer's dilemma at the conclusion of a client value-based discussion would not be the same dilemma envisioned by the early legal ethicists. The lawyer's dilemma would not arise out of the lawyer's solitary struggle over whether to break out of the impersonal demands of a professional role. Rather, the dilemma would arise in the context of overriding the decision of a three-dimensional client who had struggled through a difficult moral choice. Betraying another person with whom you stand in a relationship of trust and protection is qualitatively different than betraying a role obligation. And this difference cannot help but affect the lens through which the lawyer views his ordinary moral obligations. The lawyer who chooses to override his client's considered moral decision says, in essence: "You may not be willing to bring more hardship upon your family to save David Spaulding's life, but I am going to do it anyway without your permission and against your wishes." When the early legal ethicists talked about breaking out of bureaucratic professional roles to acknowledge the human suffering of third parties, this kind of personal betrayal was not what they had in mind.[206]

Although it is difficult to say with any confidence what the outcome of a lawyer-client dialogue with either Spaulding or the insurance company would have yielded, one thing is certain. A lawyer who felt a professional duty to shape legal representation around the client's values as well as to protect the client's legal interests would not have been prevented by the logic of legal objectification—buttressed by lawyer self-interest—that pre-empted the lawyer-client dialogue in the *Spaulding* case from occurring.

IV. BEYOND THREE-DIMENSIONAL CLIENTS IN LEGAL ETHICS

In the previous sections, I have argued that the problem of legal objectification poses a more central and important moral and ethical problem of legal professionalism than

---

[205] *Id.* at 94-95, quoting Stephen Pepper, *Counseling at the Limits of the Law: An Exercise in the Jurisprudence and Ethics of Lawyering*, 104 YALE L.J. 1545, 1606 (1995) ("I wonder why we assume that the middle-level manager in the defendant's insurance company . . . is likely to be more concerned with company profits (or with his own career advancement or security) than with the possible death of the plaintiff.")

[206] *See* LUBAN, LAWYERS AND JUSTICE, *supra* note 32, at 127.

the conflicts between role morality and professional morality on which legal ethics has historically focused. And I have argued that a client value-based model of legal representation provides an antidote against both the self-seeking behavior that legal objectification tends to promote and the danger of moral overreaching associated with the lawyer-statesman model. This Part examines representation in three contexts that challenge the client value-based ideal of representation I have proposed: the representation of clients with diminished capacity, the representation of organizational clients, and cause lawyering.

Each of the contexts examined in this Part poses a distinct problem in defining and ascertaining client objectives—both generally and in terms of client values. Implementing the methods of client value-based legal representation is neither simple nor straightforward in any of these contexts. However, I argue that a client value-based approach to representation is still valuable as a professional ideal to guide the behavior of lawyers. Each context provides reasons, temptations, and opportunities for lawyers to revert to either purely legal interest-based representation or representation shaped around the lawyer's own values. A professional ideal that exhorts lawyers to shape representation around *client* values—even when it is difficult to implement directly—provides a valuable check on lawyers' tendencies to either legally objectify their clients or impose their own values on the representation.

A. Representing Clients with Diminished Capacity

When lawyers represent children, the elderly, or other clients with diminished capacity, professional rules exhort them to "as far as reasonably possible, maintain a normal client-lawyer relationship with the client."[207] However, this is not always easy to do. Elderly, child, or developmentally disabled clients often lack the capacity to direct their lawyers.[208] The very process of determining how much autonomy to allow such clients can result in "circular lawyer-centric thinking" in which the lawyer abides by the client's choices as long as the lawyer agrees with them, and uses the client's disagreement about the client's interests as evidence that the client lacks competency to make an informed decision.[209]

One possibility for a lawyer representing a client with diminished capacity is to act as a de facto guardian, shaping representation around what the lawyer determines to be in the client's best interests.[210] However, the de facto guardian model has been criticized because it provides no constraints to check lawyer overreaching based on bias or conflicts of interest.[211] The problem is that what is "best" for a child, elderly,

---

[207] MODEL. R. PROF'L CONDUCT 1.14 (2002).

[208] *See generally* Paul R. Tremblay, *On Persuasion and Paternalism: Lawyer Decisionmaking and the Questionably Competent Client*, 1987 UTAH L. REV. 515 (1987).

[209] Jean Koh Peters, *The Roles and Content of Best Interests in Client-Directed Lawyering for Children in Child Protective Proceedings*, 64 FORDHAM L. REV. 1505, 1509 (1996).

[210] Tremblay, *supra* note 207, at 570.

[211] *Id.* at 575.

or other impaired client often rests on a value judgment. Allowing these judgments to be made on the basis of the lawyer's values runs the risk of imposing lawyer values on clients whose own values diverge from that of the lawyer. It thus exposes clients to decision-making based on "the personalities, values and opinions of the randomly chosen lawyers" in their cases.[212]

Another possibility is for the lawyer to determine an impaired client's objectives by reference to the client's legal interests.[213] Legal interests-based representation can help avoid the arbitrariness of "best interest" representation by grounding representation decisions in objectively determined legal rights. However, legal interests can also be based on conflicting or substantively unfair law.[214] Moreover, as with fully-functioning adult clients, the reduction of impaired clients to their legal interests results in a narrow and individualistic understanding of client objectives that overlooks significant non-legal reasons why clients might choose not to aggressively pursue their legal rights.[215] As scholars writing about the role of lawyers for children have argued, the narrow focus of legal interests overlooks social relationships that child clients may value and can isolate them from caregivers and communities in which they form their strongest psychological and emotional bonds.[216]

The kind of client value-based approach to legal representation proposed in Part III of this Article is difficult to implement directly in the case of impaired clients. The methods of active listening and probing to determine whether a decision is consistent with a client's deeply-held values may be difficult or impossible to carry out with clients who are impaired in their "ability to understand, deliberate upon, and reach conclusions about matters affecting the client's own well-being."[217] For example, elderly clients may not always be lucid, or their decisions may reflect distorted priorities.[218] Very young children may be unable to express their preferences, and even children who can express their opinions often lack the maturity and competence to direct their lawyers in complex decision making.[219]

However, when invoked as a professional ideal rather than as a methodology, client value-based representation provides a goal toward which lawyers can strive. For example,

---

212 Martin Guggenheim, *A Paradigm for Determining the Role of Counsel for Children*, 64 FORDHAM L. REV. 1399, 1415 (1996).

213 *Id.* at 1412 (arguing that when representing an impaired child client, lawyers should be guided by the legal rights the law grants the child).

214 Annette R. Appell, *Decontextualizing the Child Client: The Efficacy of the Attorney-Client Model for Very Young Children*, 64 FORDHAM L. REV. 1955, 1962-65 (1996) (critiquing Guggenheim's legal interest representation proposal).

215 Tremblay, *supra* note 207, at 551.

216 Annette R. Appell, *Children's Voice and Justice: Lawyering for Children in the Twenty-First Century*, 6 NEV. L.J. 692, 699 (2006).

217 MODEL R. PROF'L CONDUCT 1.14, cmt., par. [1] (2002).

218 *See, e.g.* Paul R. Tremblay, *Counseling Clients Who Weren't Born Yesterday: Age and the Attorney-Client Relationship*, 16 FAM. ADVOC. 24 (1993).

219 Guggenheim, *supra* note 211, at 1406-07.

comments to Model Rule 1.14 on diminished capacity clients suggest that lawyers can check "the consistency of a [client's] decision with the known long-term commitments and values of the client."[220] With elderly clients, lawyers are encouraged to gather information about the client's long-term commitments and values by consulting family members who have "known and perhaps lived with the client for years."[221] With children, the situation is different, because children have "not yet reached the point in life when their values have been revealed."[222] However, lawyers can view client competency as a "dimmer switch" that always allows access to some amount of information about the client's unique individuality, and to stay true to the interests and wishes of child clients to whatever degree the child's individuality can be expressed.[223]

B. Representing Organizational Clients

Like most of legal ethics, the analysis of legal ethics for three-dimensional clients is based on a paradigm of individual client representation. The question arises how a lawyering model based on individual client representation can translate to situations where the client is an organization, rather than a natural person. More particularly, the question arises whether a client-value based model makes any sense at all in the context of organizational clients. After all, it is natural persons who have hopes, dreams, fears, loyalties, commitments, and values that fill out the dimensions of their objectives beyond simple legal interest maximization.

The individual client model is used as a metaphor for the representation of organizational clients. Ethically, lawyers for organizations are required to treat the organization itself—a fictitious entity—as the client.[224] This means that the fictitious entity-client is supposed to decide the objectives of the representation and engage in the consultation required about how those objectives are to be pursued.[225] However, neither ethical standards nor lawyer training provide direction on how a lawyer is to go about ascertaining the objectives of a fictitious entity "embodied in a large and diffuse collection of people and information."[226] Lawyers are directed generally to defer to the decision-making of duly-authorized constituents of the organization—usually officers and directors—on matters involving policy, operations, and the assessment of risk.[227] And, most of the ethical heat in organizational client representation is generated by situations in which

---

220 MODEL R. PROF'L CONDUCT 1.14, cmt., par. [6] (2002).

221 Tremblay, *supra* note 207, at 569.

222 Guggenheim, *supra* note 211, at 1400.

223 *Id.*

224 MODEL R. PROF'L CONDUCT 1.13(a) (2002).

225 *See* MODEL R. PROF'L CONDUCT 1.2(a) (2002)(". . . a lawyer shall abide by a client's decisions concerning the objectives of representation and . . . shall consult with the client as to the means by which they are to be pursued.")

226 *See* Donald Langevoort, *The Epistemology of Corporate Securities Lawyering: Beliefs, Biases and Organizational Behavior*, 63 BROOK. L. REV. 629, 631 (1997).

227 MODEL R. PROF'L CONDUCT 1.13, cmt., par. [3] (2002).

the actions of individual constituents, like managers, expose the organization to substantial injury as a result of a legal violation.[228] In such situations, lawyers are directed to protect the best interests of the organization.

It could be argued that the easiest way for lawyers to separate the interests of the organizational client from the self-interest of managers and other constituents is to revert to simple legal interest analysis. The objectives of organizations, it might be argued, really are nothing more than the sum of their legal and financial interests. Hence, the problem of legal objectification that plagues the world of individual client representation creates significantly less concern in the organizational client context. In the organizational context, legal objectification helps lawyers accomplish what is best for the organization—as opposed to individual constituents—by ensuring that legal representation decisions protect and promote the organization's best interests.

However, the argument that organizational clients are nothing more than the sum of their legal interests is both too facile and somewhat suspect. It is too facile because organizations may well have objectives beyond the crude maximization of their freedom, wealth, and power over others. Organizations are complex entities with reputations, organizational cultures, relationships with outsiders, and ties with the community that create interests beyond the maximization of their profits.[229] The argument is also suspect because it too easily conflates the objectives of organizational clients with the profit motive of the lawyers who represent them. Lawyers whose financial success depends on billable hours have self-interested reasons to pursue every conceivable legal argument at their client's expense.[230] Lawyers' legal objectification of organizational clients may thus provide a convenient rationalization for the pursuit of the lawyer's own interests under the guise of zealous representation of client interests.

On the other hand, it could be argued that the lawyer-statesman model is the most promising ideal for guiding lawyers' professional role in the organizational client representation context. Responsible corporate decision-making that takes the organization's broader interests into account requires a range of viewpoints from both insiders who are assimilated into corporate culture and outsiders who can challenge it.[231] Within this mix of views, lawyers can play the role of the corporate conscience, questioning whether and how the proposed actions of the organization comport with the public interest.[232]

---

[228] MODEL R. PROF'L CONDUCT 1.13(b) (2002).

[229] JOANNE MARTIN, ORGANIZATIONAL CULTURE: MAPPING THE TERRAIN (2002).

[230] *See* Abram Chayes & Antonia H. Chayes, *Corporate Counsel and the Elite Law Firm*, 37 STAN. L. REV. 277, 296-97 (1985). *See also* Robert Gordon, *The Ethical World of Large-Firm Litigators: Preliminary Observations*, 67 FORDHAM L. REV. 709, 716-18, 725-26 (1998) (noting a disjuncture between large-firm litigators' view that clients want aggressive no-holds-barred representation and in-house counsels' view that clients want cost-efficiency).

[231] Donald Langevoort, *The Human Nature of Corporate Boards: Law, Norms, and the Unintended Consequences of Independence and Accountability*, 89 GEO. L.J. 797 (2001).

[232] Stephen Pepper, *Lawyers' Ethics in the Gap Between Law and Justice*, 40 S. TEX. L. REV. 181, 194-95 (1999); Russell G. Pearce, *The Legal Profession as a Blue State: Reflections on Public Philosophy, Jurisprudence and Legal Ethics*, 75 FORDHAM L. REV. 1339 (2006).

And the more intrusive methods of moral activist counseling do not present the same dangers of moral overreaching when lawyers operate as one voice among many in the organizational decision-making process.[233] However, the lawyer-statesman model poses its own problems of implementation in the corporate context. Although strong moral counseling seems more appropriate in settings where the client is a relatively powerful corporate entity, the lawyer is likely to be less comfortable raising moral considerations as part of legal representation in such contexts.[234] And, even in the corporate context some of lawyers' concerns with explicitly moral dialogue arise from skepticism that their "own view of morality" is not universally shared.[235]

The methods of client value-based representation present an alternative for lawyers representing organizational clients that lies somewhere between the crude assumptions of legal interest maximization and the moralistic approach of the lawyer-statesman model. As we have seen in the individual representation context, part of the purpose of client value clarification is to curb impulsive client decision-making that may be distorted by anger, fear, or insecurity and to ensure that legal representation furthers the clients' deeper and more fundamental values.[236] Lawyers in the corporate context can serve a similar function of checking the sometimes unrealistic optimism that tends to pervade business and corporate culture by raising measured and risk-averse concerns about the long-term consequences of proposed decisions.[237] And they can help promote and invite their organizational clients' voluntary compliance with legal regulation by being spokespersons with corporate management about the purposes and functions of legal regulations.[238]

Such inquiries invite the constituents with decision-making authority in an organization to consider the long-term goals and values of the organization and to consider how

---

[233] Pepper, *supra* note 233, at 194. *See also* LUBAN, *Human Dignity*, *supra* note 166, at 87 (arguing for an abolishment of the lawyer-client privilege for corporations because corporations do not have human dignity to violate by self-incriminatory disclosure).

[234] Pepper, *Ethics in the Gap*, *supra* note 233, at 194-95; Gordon, *supra* note 230, at 711; Mark Suchman, *Working Without a Net: The Sociology of Legal Ethics in Corporate Litigation,* 67 FORDHAM L. REV. 837, 843-44 (1998). *See also* LUBAN, *Human Dignity, supra* note 166, at 87 (acknowledging that his argument for abolishing the attorney-client privilege in the corporate context—though strong philosophically—has been viewed as "too fanciful to take seriously").

[235] In the words of one large-firm litigator, explaining why he would not engage his client in a moral dialogue:

> I personally would have a problem conveying my own view of the morality of the situation to a client. I think morality is a very slippery concept, primarily in the eye of the beholder.

Robert L. Nelson, *The Discovery Process as a Circle of Blame: Institutional, Professional, and Socio-Economic Factors That Contribute to Unreasonable, Inefficient, and Amoral Behavior in Corporate Litigation,* 67 FORDHAM L. REV. 773 (1998).

[236] *See supra* Part III.B.

[237] Langevoort, *Epistemology of Corporate-Securities Lawyering, supra* note 226; Suchman, *supra* note 234, at 844 (lawyers tend to assume that unethical behavior will carry long-term negative consequences).

[238] Donald C. Langevoort, *Someplace Between Philosophy and Economics: Legitimacy and Good Corporate Lawyering,* 75 FORDHAM L. REV. 1615 (2006).

the goals and values of the organization fit within the structure of legal regulations that govern corporate activity. And empirical analysis of the attitudes and reported behavior of corporate lawyers suggests that they often engage in some of the same counseling techniques designed in the individual client context to probe the consistency of a client's decision with the client's deeper values.[239] For example, researchers in one study concluded that, when counseling their business clients, lawyers tend to couch moral considerations in pragmatic or reputational concerns, such as asking a client what a proposed course of action would look like on the front page of the newspaper, or how it would be viewed by a judge or the jury.[240] Such appeals to reputation are not simply part of a pragmatic cost-benefit analysis or strategy for making the lawyer's moral judgment of the client more palatable. Rather, as Mark Suchman points out, "[t]he 'newspaper test' operates much like Mead's 'generalized other'—providing a social looking-glass that allows one . . . to see and judge oneself."[241]

C. Cause Lawyering

Finally, the representation of politically vulnerable, socially disadvantaged, and otherwise disempowered clients presents both a special case of the tension between legal interests-based representation and the dangers of moral overreaching associated with the lawyer-statesman ideal and unique challenges to a client value-based representation as a solution.

In one view, the representation of politically and socially disempowered client presents the most appropriate venue for a client value-based approach to legal representation. Because of their relative lack of legal sophistication, such clients are seen as particularly vulnerable to domination by their lawyers. [242] Moreover, the construction of client objectives in purely legal terms in the poverty law context is especially pernicious because it reinforces inequities built into the law itself. Because those without social advantage lack the power to influence the law-making process, the law that affects their lives is often created without taking their perspectives into account. A client value-based approach to legal representation holds out the promise of making law more responsive

---

[239] The empirical study to which this section refers—called *Ethics: Beyond the Rules*—was sponsored by the American Bar Association Section on Litigation, and invited a team of legal scholars, legal ethicists, and social scientists to study large firm litigators. Robert E. Nelson, et al., *Introduction: Bringing Legal Realism to the Study of Ethics and Professionalism*, 67 FORDHAM L. REV. 697, 701 (1998). The team interviewed both partners and associates at large law firms in two cities over extended weekends. *Id.* A year later, they interviewed groups of judges, plaintiffs' counsel, and in-house counsel in the same two cities. *Id.* at 702. The results were published in a series of articles in the FORDHAM L. REV.

[240] Gordon, *supra* note 230, at 733; Suchman, *supra* note 234, at 844-45.

[241] *Id.*

[242] *See* O'Leary, *supra* note 144; Pepper, *Ethics in the Gap*, *supra* note 233, at 194-95.

to the lived experience of clients by shaping legal representation around the values and narratives of clients. [243]

However, the conditions of poverty law practice pressure poverty lawyers in the direction of legal interest-based representation. The overwhelming need for legal services and the relentless demands to meet the immediate and often desperate needs of individual clients create pressures to process cases routinely and to settle them as quickly as possible.[244] To access the remedies that law offers politically vulnerable or socially disadvantaged clients, lawyers must slot them into categories that may be disconnected from the perspectives and circumstances of their lives.[245] And this pressure works against the ability of lawyers to use individual client representation to change the contours of the law. The incentive for more powerful repeat players like landlords, employers and banks is to settle cases that might make unfavorable law, while the incentives for one-shot individual clients are to maximize their tangible gain in the particular case by taking the deals they are offered.[246]

Moreover, the typical client value-based methods of overcoming legal interest-based representation through active listening and probing for client values are arguably insufficient to overcome the barriers created by social subordination. Even when poverty lawyers attempt to attend more holistically to the values of fewer individual clients—such as in law school clinic settings—the individual focus of representation in discrete cases has a tendency to isolate the client's objectives from the collective and community values required for reform of unjust laws and systems.[247] And, clients who seek legal services are often in crisis situations of eviction from housing, denial of benefits for life necessities, loss of parental rights, or deportation. Attention to the unique needs of such individual clients will often be synonymous with getting whatever remedy the law offers to alleviate the crisis.

To escape the endless grind of remedying injustice one client at a time, lawyers for politically and socially disadvantaged clients have engaged in what Stuart Scheingold and Austin Sarat call "cause lawyering."[248] In cause lawyering, the representation of individual clients is a means to the achievement of political ends that transcend the individual clients' financial or legal interests.[249] Cause lawyers choose or recruit clients to

---

[243] Anthony Alfieri, *Reconstructive Poverty Law Practice: Learning the Lessons of Client Narrative*, 100 YALE L.J. 2107 (1991); Lucie E. White, *Subordination, Rhetorical Survival Skills, and Sunday Shoes: Notes on the Hearing of Mrs. G.*, 38 BUFF. L. REV. 1 (1990).

[244] *See* Gary Bellow, *Turning Solutions Into problems: The Legal Aid Experience*, 34 NLADA BRIEFCASE 106 (1977).

[245] Alfieri, *Client Narrative, supra* note 243, at 2112-13; White, *Sunday Shoes, supra* note 243, at 27-29.

[246] Mark Galanter, *The Duty Not To Deliver Legal Services*, 30 MIAMI L. REV. 929, 938-40 (1976).

[247] Sameer Ashar, *Law Clinics and Collective Mobilization*, 14 CLINICAL L. REV. 355 (2008). *See also* William H. Simon, *Homo-Psychologicus: Notes on a New Legal Formalism*, 32 STAN. L. REV. 487 (1980).

[248] *See* STUART A. SCHEINGOLD & AUSTIN SARAT, SOMETHING TO BELIEVE IN: POLITICS, PROFESSIONALISM AND CAUSE LAWYERING (2006).

[249] *Id.* at 6-7.

fit the needs of the cause and put the needs of the cause over the needs of the individual clients who represent the class for whom the lawyers advocate.[250] Although the needs of individuals are subordinated to collective goals, the promise of cause lawyering is to effect reforms that will improve conditions for entire classes of persons affected by injustice embedded in the law itself.[251]

Cause lawyers are arguably an embodiment of the lawyer-statesman ideal.[252] The relative independence from client control and the ability to define and pursue public interest goals directly are consonant with the ideal of the lawyer who mediates between the client's interests and the public good. As Scheingold and Sarat put it, cause lawyers are "advocates not only, or primarily, for their clients but for causes and, one might say, for their own beliefs."[253]

However, the dangers of moral overreaching associated with the lawyer-statesman ideal also assert themselves in the context of cause lawyering. Perhaps the quintessential example of cause lawyering is the NAACP's campaign to desegregate public schools.[254] This campaign involved both a carefully-orchestrated legal challenge that resulted in the historic 1954 ruling in *Brown v. Board of Education*,[255] and a persistent decades-long effort to enforce and implement *Brown* through litigation in lower federal courts.[256] However, as Derrick Bell argued in one of the earliest critiques of Civil Rights lawyering, the lawyers' pursuit of the goal of *desegregated schools* became disconnected from the goal of *better quality education* that desegregation was designed to achieve.[257] Committed to the symbolic importance of desegregation, beholden to their middle-class donors, and disconnected from the experience of inner-city black families, national-level NAACP lawyers opposed local efforts by community groups and parents to structure settlements that would retain segregated school systems and require the investment of resources to improve the quality of inner-city schools.[258]

As in the context of representing clients with diminished capacity and representing organizational clients, a client value-based model of representation presents itself not so much as a method of representing individual clients, but as an professional ideal or "theory of practice" around which lawyers representing socially and politically

---

[250] LUBAN, LAWYERS AND CLIENTS, *supra* note 32, at 317.

[251] Lucie E. White, *Mobilization on the Margins of the Lawsuit: Making Space for Clients to Speak*, 16 N.Y.U. REV. L. & SOC. CHANGE 535, 535-37 (1987-88).

[252] *See, e.g.* LUBAN, LAWYERS AND CLIENTS, *supra* note 32, at 237-38 (connecting the Brandeis vision of the "people's lawyer" with public interest law practice). *See also* SCHEINGOLD & SARAT, *supra* note 155, at 9-17 (exploring the continuities and discontinuities of cause lawyering and the lawyer-statesman ideal).

[253] *Id.* at 9.

[254] Austin Sarat & Stuart Scheingold, *What Cause Lawyers Do* For, *and* To, *Social Movements: An Introduction*, *in* CAUSE LAWYERS AND SOCIAL MOVEMENTS 1, 4-7 (Sarat & Scheingold, eds. 2006).

[255] 347 U.S. 483 (1954).

[256] Derrick A. Bell, Jr., *Serving Two Masters: Integration Ideals and Client Interests in School Desegregation Litigation*, 85 YALE L.J. 470, 472-82 (1976).

[257] *Id.* at 487-88.

[258] *Id.* at 487-93.

disadvantaged clients strive to shape their representation.[259] The strategies of a new generation of lawyers practicing law for socially and politically disadvantaged clients seek greater participation from clients in the formation of collective goals, while at the same time recognizing that the clients' capacity for voicing collective values may have to be consciously created, rather than merely received.[260] Lucie White, for example, recounts ways to create space in the "margins" of a lawsuit for class members to discover and define a collective voice through speak-out events or street theater.[261] Lawyers have also formed alliances with community organizing groups, often playing a subordinate role in the definition of the legal services that would benefit the larger social movement.[262] These strategies seek to avoid the disengagement from client values that may result when the lawyer—a socially advantaged social and political actor—defines the "public interest" in isolation from the values and perspectives of the clients.[263]

CONCLUSION

The debates in theoretical legal ethics center around the way lawyers' roles should be conceived, and they both arise from and help define the way lawyers practice law. The early legal ethicists sought a definition of lawyers' professional "role morality" that would serve the theoretical purpose of generating conflicts between role morality and ordinary morality. But in starting from the standpoint of theory, I have argued, they misinterpreted practice. The lawyer behavior that looked to them like the overindulgence of client interests, I have argued, was really something else. It was really the lawyers' own legal objectification of their clients: the narrow construction of client objectives in terms of legal interests and the disengagement from client values. As a result of misdiagnosing the problems that plagued legal professionalism, legal ethicists proposed a solution—the "lawyer-statesman" model—that aggravates the problem of lawyer disengagement from client values by encouraging lawyers to shape legal representation around the lawyer's conception of morality and the public interest.

The client value-based approach to representation that this Article proposes asserts a faith in client values as a corrective for both the anti-social aspects of legal interest maximization and the hubris of the lawyer-statesman ideal. Attention to client values may not, in the end, provide salvation from the competitive and self-interested culture of American society. But if competition and self-interest are culturally pervasive, reliance on lawyers to transcend by appealing to their own personal values is just as idealistic

---

259 Ascanio Piomelli, *Appreciating Collaborative Lawyering*, 6 CLINICAL L. REV. 427, 429-31 (2000).

260 GERALD LOPEZ, REBELLIOUS LAWYERING: ONE CHICANO'S VISION OF PROGRESSIVE LAW PRACTICE (1992); Anthony V. Alfieri, *The Antinomies of Poverty Law and a Theory of Dialogic Empowerment,* 16 NYU REV. L. & SOC. CHANGE 659 (1987-88).

261 White, *Mobilization at the Margins*, *supra* note 251.

262 *See generally* CAUSE LAWYERS AND SOCIAL MOVEMENTS, *supra* note 253.

263 Lucie E. White, *Collaborative Lawyering in the Field?: On Mapping the Paths from Rhetoric to Practice,* 1 CLINICAL L. REV. 157 (1994).

a dream. The goal of shaping representation around the values of clients provides an opportunity for legal representation to redeem itself without compromising the core values of client loyalty and service that lie at the heart of legal professionalism. Before we give up on the professional values of client loyalty and service, we ought to see what it would be like if lawyers actually represented their clients, rather than zealously pursued their clients' legal interests.

Chapter 6

Lessons About Corporate Scandals

If you've made it this far in our book, then you're well-armed to think about more current corporate scandals. You've considered history (Chapter 1), some explanations for corporate scandals (Chapter 2), social science and human nature (Chapter 3), organizational governance and structure (Chapter 4), and ethics issues (Chapter 5). In this chapter, we ask you to think about what we can learn from prior scandals to use in analyzing current scandals—and to think about how you might avoid getting involved in situations that are likely to pressure you into some very bad decisions. After all, if we're going to read about you and your actions in the future, we'd like to read about how you conquered social pressure or ferreted out fraud, and not about what dastardly deeds you committed before your "perp walk."*

As a parting thought, take a look at something Jeff Skilling said, way back in 2000. We don't know whether he believed what he said, or whether he was just trying to put himself (and Enron) in a good light. But here's the quote:

> We're on the side of angels. We're taking on the entrenched monopolies. In every business we've been in, we're the good guys.**

Just remember: it's not that hard for you to talk yourself into believing that you're one of the good guys, too. We hope that, after you've had a chance to think about this chapter and the rest of the essays in the book (and on the web), you'll actually *be* one of the good guys.

* For a definition of "perp walk," see http://en.wikipedia.org/wiki/Perp_walk.

** http://www.chron.com/content/chronicle/special/01/enron/skilling/skilling.html (interview about Enron, BUSINESS WEEK, Feb. 12, 2000).

Protecting Financial Markets: Lessons from the Subprime Mortgage Meltdown

Steven L. Schwarcz[*]

INTRODUCTION

Congress has been holding hearings on threats to the financial system in response to the recent subprime[1] mortgage meltdown and its impact on the mortgage-backed and other asset-backed securities markets and on credit markets generally.[2] Central banks and governments worldwide have likewise expressed concern about this crisis and its potential systemic effects.

Initial remedial steps were focused on banks. The United States Federal Reserve Bank, for example, attempted to reduce the likelihood that this crisis might affect other financial markets and the economy by cutting both the discount rate, which is the interest rate the Federal Reserve charges a bank to borrow funds when a bank is

[**] Stanley A. Star Professor of Law & Business, Duke University School of Law; Founding/Co-Academic Director, Duke Global Capital Markets Center. E-mail: schwarcz@law.duke.edu. The author thanks Richard Bookstaber, Kathleen C. Engel, Alan Hirsch, Jonathan C. Lipson, Joseph H. Sommer, and participants in faculty workshops at Temple University; James E. Beasley School of Law, Duke Law School; The University of Tennessee (College of Law, College of Business Administration, and Corporate Governance Center); University of Utah S.J. Quinney College of Law; and University of Geneva Faculty of Law (Centre for Banking & Financial Law), and a workshop on "Structured Finance and Loan Modification" at the United States Federal Reserve Bank of Cleveland for comments. He also thanks Mark Covey for excellent research assistance.

[1] The term "subprime" includes both loans to borrowers of dubious creditworthiness and very large loans to otherwise creditworthy borrowers.

[2] *See, e.g., Systemic Risk: Examining Regulators' Ability to Respond to Threats to the Financial System: Hearing Before the H. Comm. on Financial Serv.*, 110th Cong. (2007), *available at* http://frwebgate.access.gpo.gov/cgi-bin/getdoc.cgi?dbname=110_house_hearings&docid=f:39903.pdf [hereinafter *Systemic Risk Hearing*]. As this Essay was going to press, Congress enacted and the President signed the Emergency Economic Stabilization Act of 2008, Pub. L. 110-343, enacted Oct. 3, 2008.

temporarily short of funds,[3] and the federal funds rate, which is the interest rate banks charge other banks on interbank loans.[4] The European Central Bank and other central banks similarly cut the interest rate they charge to borrowing banks.[5]

These steps, ironically, directly impacted banks but not the financial markets whose very fall was weakening banks.[6] In medical terms, it was as if a doctor were attempting to cure a patient by focusing on curing symptoms, not the underlying disease.[7] Changes in monetary policy may not work quickly enough—or may be too weak—to quell panics, falling prices, and the potential for systemic collapse.[8]

This somewhat anachronistic focus on banks, not markets, ignores new trends in the global marketplace. Increasingly, the financial system is characterized by disintermediation, which enables companies to access the ultimate source of funds, the capital markets, without going through banks or other financial intermediaries.[9] An exclusively bank-focused approach simply does not keep up with underlying changes in the financial system.[10] In a financially disintermediated world, the old protections are no longer reliable.

---

[3] *See* Greg Ip et al., *Stronger Steps: Fed Offers Banks Loans Amid Crisis*, WALL ST. J., Aug. 18-19, 2007, at A1.

[4] *See* Greg Ip, *Fed's Rate Cut Could Be Last For a While*, WALL ST. J., Nov. 1, 2007, at A1.

[5] *See* Randal Smith et al., *How a Panicky Day Led the Fed to Act: Freezing of Credit Drives Sudden Shift; Shoving to Make Trades*, WALL ST. J., Aug. 20, 2007, at A1.

[6] Ip et al., *supra* note 3 (observing that "the [Fed's] discount window's reach in the current crisis is limited by the fact that only banks can use it, and they aren't the ones facing the greatest strains").

[7] *Cf.* Steven L. Schwarcz, in *How Three Economists View a Financial Rescue Plan*, N.Y. TIMES, Sept. 22, 2008, at C4 (observing that the U.S. Treasury Department's proposal to use government money to purchase mortgage-backed securities held by banks and other financial institutions was "the first serious attempt by government to cure the underlying financial disease and not merely treat its symptoms," and also observing that financial institutions are in trouble "because of falling prices of mortgage-backed and other securities, requiring these institutions to market their securities down to the collapsed market prices . . . .").

[8] Mortimer B. Zuckerman, *Preventing a Panic*, U.S. NEWS & WORLD REP., Feb. 11, 2008, at 63 (observing that "[l]ower interest rates promoted by the Federal Reserve Bank cannot fully counter the forces of credit and liquidity contraction" caused by the subprime mortgage crisis); *see* Seth Carpenter & Selva Demiralp, *The Liquidity Effect in the Federal Funds Market: Evidence from Daily Open Market Operations*, 38 J. MONEY CREDIT & BANKING 901, 918-19 (2006) (concluding that although a change in monetary policy can begin to affect the cost of capital within a day, its full effects can take much longer); Serena Ng et al., *Fed Fails So Far in Bid to Reassure Anxious Investors*, WALL ST. J., Aug. 21, 2007, at A1.

[9] *See* Steven L. Schwarcz, *Enron and the Use and Abuse of Special Purpose Entities in Corporate Structures*, 70 U. CIN. L. REV. 1309, 1315 (2002). Capital markets are now the nation's and the world's most important sources of investment financing. *See* MCKINSEY GLOBAL INST., MAPPING THE GLOBAL CAPITAL MARKET THIRD ANNUAL REPORT 8 (2007), *available at* http://www.mckinsey.com/mgi/publications/third_annual_report/index.asp (reporting that as of the end of 2005, the value of total global financial assets, including equities, government and corporate debt securities, and bank deposits, was $140 trillion).

[10] Although there is some concern about capital levels at banks, the losses giving rise to this concern are not due to bad mortgage loans made by those banks but rather to investments in mortgage-backed securities or loans made to entities, such as hedge funds, holding mortgage-backed securities as assets. *See infra* note 64 (reporting on write-downs stemming from bad mortgage-backed securities); *see also* David

This Essay seeks to understand what new protections are needed by exploring why the subprime financial crisis occurred, notwithstanding the array of existing protections included in financial regulation, market norms and customs, and the market-discipline approach undertaken by the second Bush administration.[11] The Essay begins by identifying anomalies and obvious protections that failed to work. It then searches for lessons by examining various hypotheses of why these anomalies and failures occurred.

I. IDENTIFYING ANOMALIES AND FAILURES

The following represent anomalies arising from, and protections that failed to deter, the subprime mortgage meltdown: (A) disclosure provides investors with all the information they need to assess investments, yet many investors made poor decisions; (B) securitization and other forms of structured finance (collectively, "structured finance"), pursuant to which mortgage-backed and other forms of asset-backed securities are issued, are supposed to diversify and reallocate risk to parties best able to bear it, yet structured finance did not protect many investors in mortgage-backed securities; (C) the subprime mortgage meltdown originally related to subprime mortgage-backed securities markets, but it quickly infected the markets for prime mortgage-backed securities and other asset-backed securities;[12] (D) the second Bush administration expected that its market-discipline approach, along with existing protections, would be sufficient to protect against financial market instabilities, but this approach turned out to be insufficient; and (E) rating agencies purport to assess an investment's safety, but they failed to anticipate the defaults. As this Essay will show, most of the causes of these anomalies and failures can be attributed to conflicts of interest, investor complacency, and overall complexity, all exacerbated by cupidity.

Examining hypotheses of why these anomalies and failures may have occurred requires explanation of certain structured finance terminology. The issuer of mortgage-backed and other forms of asset-backed securities in structured finance transactions is typically a special-purpose vehicle, or "SPV" (also sometimes called a special-purpose entity, or "SPE").[13] These securities are customarily categorized as mortgage-backed securities ("MBS"), asset-backed securities ("ABS"), collateralized debt obligation ("CDO"), or ABS CDO.[14] MBS are securities whose payment derives principally or entirely

---

Wessel, *Magnifying the Credit Fallout*, WALL ST. J., Mar. 6, 2008, at A2 (discussing the erosion of the capital level at banks due to the falling value of bank-owned mortgage loans and mortgage-backed securities).

[11] *See* Anthony W. Ryan, Assistant Sec'y for Fin. Mkts., U.S. Dep't of the Treasury, Remarks Before the Managed Funds Association Conference (June 11, 2007) (transcript available at http://www.ustreas.gov/press/releases/hp450.htm) (discussing the market-discipline approach).

[12] For an explanation of the types of securities involved in the subprime financial crisis, see *infra* notes 14-26 and accompanying text.

[13] *See* JOHN DOWNES & JORDAN ELLIOT GOODMAN, DICTIONARY OF FINANCE AND INVESTMENT TERMS 662-63 (7th ed. 2006).

[14] There are arcane variations on the CDO categories, such as CDOs "squared" or "cubed," but these go beyond this Essay's analysis.

from mortgage loans owned by the SPV.[15] ABS are securities whose payment derives principally or entirely from receivables or other financial assets—*other than mortgage loans*—owned by the SPV.[16] Industry participants refer to transactions in which SPVs issue MBS or ABS as "securitization."[17]

The term "securitization" also technically includes CDO and ABS CDO transactions. CDO securities are backed by—and thus their payment derives principally or entirely from—a mixed pool of mortgage loans and/or other receivables owned by an SPV.[18] ABS CDO securities, in contrast, are backed by a mixed pool of ABS and/or MBS securities owned by the SPV, and thus their payment derives principally or entirely from the underlying mortgage loans and/or other receivables ultimately backing those ABS and MBS securities.[19] For this reason, ABS CDO transactions are sometimes referred to as "re-securitization."

Schematically, the distinctions among these categories can be portrayed as follows:

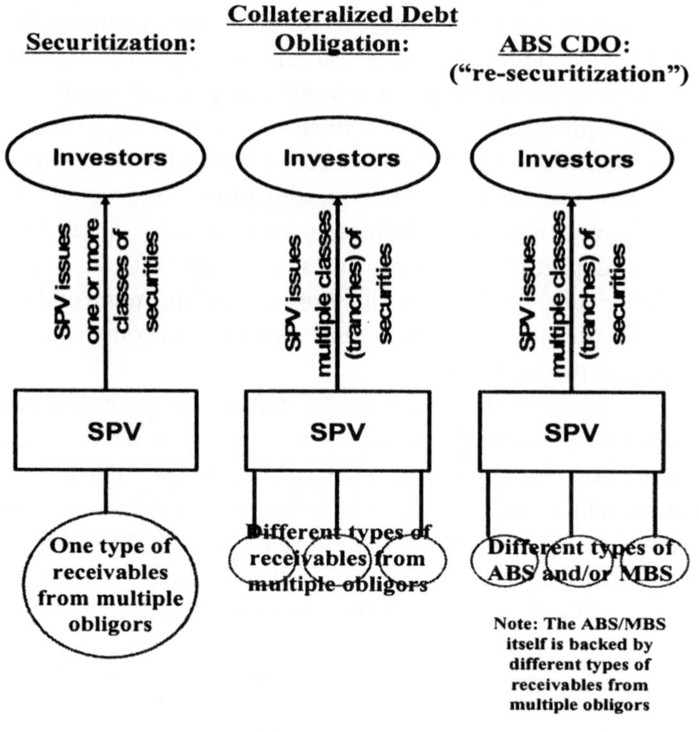

---

[15] *See* DOWNES & GOODMAN, *supra* note 13, at 434-35.

[16] *See id.* at 35.

[17] *See id.* at 630.

[18] *See id.* at 121.

[19] "Synthetic" CDOs, which do not appear to be relevant to this Essay's analysis, own derivative instruments, such as credit default swaps, rather than receivables, ABS, or MBS.

The classes, or "tranches," of MBS, ABS, CDO, and ABS CDO securities issued in these transactions are typically ranked by seniority of payment priority.[20] The highest priority class is called senior securities.[21] In MBS and ABS transactions, lower priority classes are called subordinated, or junior, securities.[22] In CDO and ABS CDO transactions, lower priority classes are usually called mezzanine securities[23]—with the lowest priority class, which has a residual claim against the SPV, called the equity.[24]

The senior and many of the subordinated classes of these securities are more highly rated than the quality of the underlying receivables.[25] For example, senior securities issued in a CDO transaction are usually rated AAA even if the underlying receivables consist of subprime mortgages, and senior securities issued in an ABS CDO transaction are usually rated AAA even if none of the MBS and ABS securities supporting the transaction are rated that highly. This is accomplished by allocating cash collections from the receivables first to pay the senior classes and thereafter to pay more junior classes (the so-called "waterfall" of payment).[26] In this way, the senior classes are highly overcollateralized to take into account the possibility, indeed likelihood, of delays and losses on collection.

The subprime financial crisis occurred because, with home prices unexpectedly plummeting[27] and adjustable-rate mortgage (ARM) interest rates skyrocketing,[28] many more borrowers defaulted than anticipated,[29] causing collections on subprime mortgages to

---

[20] *See* DOWNES & GOODMAN, *supra* note 13, at 749.

[21] *See id.* at 637.

[22] *See id.* at 369.

[23] *See id.* at 421.

[24] In MBS and ABS transactions, the term "equity" is not generally used because the company originating the securities (the "Originator") usually holds, directly or indirectly, the residual claim against the SPV. *See id.* at 491 (defining "originator").

[25] *See id.* at 121 (defining CDO as an investment-grade bond backed by a diversified pool of bonds including junk bonds). The equity class is generally not rated.

[26] *See* Investopedia, http://www.investopedia.com/terms/w/waterfallpayment.asp (last visited Sept. 20, 2008) (defining waterfall payment as "[a] type of payment scheme in which higher-tiered creditors receive interest and principal payments, while the lower-tiered creditors receive only interest payments. When the higher tiered creditors have received all interest and principal payments in full, the next tier of creditors begins to receive interest and principal payments.").

[27] *See* Kemba J. Dunham & Ruth Simon, *Refinancing May be Harder to Enjoy*, WALL ST. J., Nov. 24-25, 2007, at B1 (discussing the difficulty of refinancing due to tighter lending standards and falling home prices).

[28] Rick Brooks & Constance Mitchell Ford, *The United States of Subprime*, WALL ST. J., Oct. 11, 2007, at A1 (analyzing high-rate mortgages). Although rate increases on ARM loans (through rate re-sets) were not per se unexpected, the end of the liquidity glut made it harder for subprime borrowers to refinance into loans with lower, affordable interest rates. *See id.*

[29] Anthony B. Sanders, Bob Herberger Ariz. Heritage Chair Professor of Fin., Ariz. State Univ., Incentives and Failures in the Structured Finance Market: The Case of the Subprime Mortgage Market, Presentation to the Federal Reserve Bank of Cleveland Workshop: Structured Finance and Loan Modification (Nov. 20, 2007) (notes on file with author). *But cf.* Ruth Simon, *Rising Rates to Worsen Subprime*

plummet below the original estimates. Thus, equity and mezzanine classes of securities were impaired, if not wiped out, and in many cases even senior classes were impaired.[30] Investors in these securities lost billions,[31] creating a loss of confidence in the financial markets.[32]

II. SEARCHING FOR LESSONS

A. IF DISCLOSURE PROVIDES INVESTORS WITH ALL THE INFORMATION NEEDED TO ASSESS INVESTMENTS, WHY DID SO MANY INVESTORS MAKE POOR DECISIONS?

To explain this anomaly and failure, this Essay examines several hypotheses:

> ***Hypothesis**: The disclosure was inadequate because the depth of the fall of the housing market exceeded reasonable worst-case scenarios. Mortgage loans, which were the asset class supporting the MBS as well as a significant portion of the CDO and ABS CDO securities, therefore, turned out to be severely undercollateralized in many cases.*

Any failure to envision the worst-case scenario that resulted from the fall of the housing market may have reflected, to some extent, a failure to take a sufficiently long view of risk. Some explain the near collapse of Long-Term Capital Management (LTCM), a hedge fund that lost hundreds of millions of dollars in 1998, as a result of this type of failure.[33] Investors and other market participants looked to the recent past to form predictions about home prices,[34] but they did not always look to worst-case possibilities, such as the experience of the Great Depression.[35]

Mess, WALL ST. J., Nov. 24-25, 2007, at A1 (reporting that many mortgages defaulted even before interest rates increased).

[30] *See* Carrick Mollenkamp & Serena Ng, *Wall Street Wizardry Amplified Credit Crisis: A CDO Called Norma Left 'Hairball of Risk'; Tailored by Merrill Lynch,* WALL ST. J., Dec. 27, 2007, at A1 (reporting on the downgrade of one CDO's AAA rated tranches to junk status).

[31] *See id.*

[32] Reference in this article to "investors" means investors in capital market securities, not investors in the homes financed by the mortgage loans ultimately backing such securities.

[33] *See, e.g.*, Paul Krugman, *Rashomon in Connecticut: What Really Happened to Long-Term Capital Management?*, SLATE, Oct. 2, 1998, http://www.slate.com/toolbar.aspx?action=print&id=1908.

[34] Jack Guttentag, *Shortsighted About the Subprime Disaster*, WASH. POST, May 26, 2007, at F2 (explaining that because housing prices had been rising for a long period of time, it was assumed that they would continue to rise).

[35] *See* Christine Harper, *Death of VaR Evoked as Risk-Taking Vim Meets Taleb's Black Swan*, BLOOMBERG.COM, Jan. 28, 2008, http://www.bloomberg.com/apps/news?pid=20601109&sid=axo1oswvqx4s&refer=home (reporting that financial models at Merrill Lynch, Morgan Stanley, and UBS failed to foresee the decline in housing prices). *See generally* NASSIM TALEB, THE BLACK SWAN: THE IMPACT OF THE HIGHLY IMPROBABLE (2007) (discussing human tendency of failing to anticipate improbable events). One commentator suggests that the disclosure also did not adequately address the relatively illiquid nature of the securities: "It is true that the level of default was unusually high, but the bulk of the problem is coming from liquidity issues—no one wants to hold these [securities], and if you try to find [a buyer] you have to

These types of failures are inevitable, though, because the reasonableness of worst-case scenarios is assessed, necessarily, ex ante. It does not appear unreasonable, for example, to have viewed the Great Depression as unique.[36] As Monty Python memorably put it (in a different context), "Nobody expects the Spanish Inquisition!"[37]

Some failures to take a sufficiently long view of risk reflect behavioral bias due to associations with recent similar events.[38] Those failures are discussed separately.

***Hypothesis*: The disclosure was adequate, but many investors failed to read it carefully enough or appreciate what they were reading.**

This hypothesis has several possible sub-hypotheses explaining the ultimate failure. The first is over-reliance: investors may have relied heavily, and perhaps in some cases exclusively, on third parties, in making important investment decisions. For example, one commentator argues that investors over-relied on the underwriter or arranger selling them the securities:

> Investors have the prospectus to rely on, but the reality is that they have not taken any responsibility for reading the detail of the documentation or digesting the risks involved. These investors are still under the impression

---

trade them at a very low price." E-mail from Richard Bookstaber, author, A DEMON OF OUR OWN DESIGN, to author (Nov. 30, 2007, 08:11:08 EST) (on file with author). Lack of liquidity, however, appears to have been a standard disclosure item. *See, e.g.*, Soundview Home Loan Trust, Prospectus Supplement (WMC1) (Mar. 12, 2007), *available at* http://www.secinfo.com/dqTm6.uPa.htm:

> There is no assurance that . . . a secondary market [in the securities] will develop or, if it develops, that it will continue. Consequently, you may not be able to sell your [securities] readily or at prices that will enable you to realize your desired yield. The market values of the [securities] are likely to fluctuate; these fluctuations may be significant and could result in significant losses to you.

Id. at "Lack of Liquidity" subsection under "Risk Factors." I therefore believe that the problem was less issuer failure to disclose the illiquidity risk than investor failure to appreciate that disclosure. *See infra* notes 38-51 and accompanying text. Query, however, whether anyone knew—much less knew enough to disclose—the *extent* of the illiquidity problem. *See* Bookstaber, *supra* ("[N]o one knew how levered [sic] funds were, and therefore how quickly they would need to dump [securities] if they faced a market shock.").

36 *But cf.* Atif Mian & Amir Sufi, *The Consequences of Mortgage Credit Expansion: Evidence from the 2007 Subprime Mortgage Default Crisis* 1, 4 (Nat'l Bureau of Econ. Research, Working Paper No. 13936), *available at* http://www.nber.org/papers/w13936 (arguing that investors and rating agencies likely did not fully appreciate that the mortgage supply expansion itself was in part driving house price appreciation). In other words, Professors Mian and Sufi argue that home prices dropped radically, as a percentage, once mortgage money tightened, and that investors and rating agencies should have anticipated that possibility. *See id.*

37 *Monty Python's Flying Circus: The Spanish Inquisition* (BBC television broadcast Sept. 22, 1970), *available at* http://people.csail.mit.edu/paulfitz/spanish/script.html.

38 *See infra* notes 48-51 and accompanying text (discussing herd behavior and the availability heuristic).

> that the arranger will look after their interests and are yet to appreciate the need to negotiate what are highly complicated bilateral agreements.[39]

Because this interpretation of investor behavior flies in the face of *caveat emptor* ("buyer beware"), it seems dubious that investors would depend so heavily on sellers of securities, unless the underwriter/arranger's interests were aligned with that of the investors.[40] Those interests were somewhat aligned, however, in ABS CDO transactions where underwriters customarily purchased some portion of the equity tranches at least in part in order to demonstrate their (subsequently unjustified) confidence in the securities being sold. Ironically, this created a mutual misinformation problem: aligning the interests of sellers and investors actually worked against investor caution.

Investors also may have over-relied on rating-agency ratings, without necessarily engaging in, or at least fully performing, their own due diligence.[41] Even if investors performed their own due diligence, agency-cost conflicts[42] and lack of economy of scale[43] may have limited the extent to which they could have done a better job of assessing creditworthiness than the rating agencies.

Another sub-hypothesis is that, as a result of a market bubble, "many investors, swept up in the euphoria of the moment, failed to pay close attention to what they were buying."[44] Bubbles can start quite easily. If, for example, a particular stock unexpectedly gains in value, the losers (e.g., those shorting the stock) will tend to withdraw from that market, and the winners will tend to increase their investment, driving up the price even further. Soon, other winners are attracted to the stock, and other losers cut their losses and stop shorting the stock. This process is aided by commentators' explanations of why it is rational for the price to keep going up, and why the traditional relationship of price to earnings does not apply. Even investors who recognize the bubble as irrational may buy in, hoping to sell at the height of the bubble before it bursts.[45] In these ways, price movements can become somewhat self-sustaining.[46]

---

[39] Daniel Andrews, *The Clean Up: Investors Need Better Advice on Structured Finance Products*, 26 INT'L FIN. L. REV. 14, 14 (2007).

[40] This form of the hypothesis, of course, is now even more dubious as a predictor of (at least near-term) future investor reliance.

[41] This Essay later examines why rating agencies failed to anticipate the downgrades. *See infra* Part III.E.

[42] *See infra* notes 59-63 and accompanying text.

[43] Individual investors face relatively high costs to assess the creditworthiness of complex ABS, CDO, and ABS CDO securities, whereas rating agencies make this assessment on behalf of many individual investors, thereby achieving an economy of scale. *See infra* notes 52-53 and accompanying text (discussing the complexity of these types of transactions and the volume of associated disclosure documents).

[44] Alan S. Blinder, *Six Fingers of Blame in the Mortgage Mess*, N.Y. TIMES, Sept. 30, 2007, at BU 4.

[45] *See* Sam Segal, *Tulips Portrayed: The Tulip Trade in Holland in the 17th Century*, *in* THE TULIP: A SYMBOL OF TWO NATIONS 17-19 (Michael Roding & Hans Theunissen eds., 1993) (noting that all levels of the population from the weaver to the aristocrat were buying tulips at staggering prices in hopes of making a profit from the "tulip mania").

[46] RICHARD BOOKSTABER, A DEMON OF OUR OWN DESIGN: MARKETS, HEDGE FUNDS, AND THE PERILS OF FINANCIAL INNOVATION 169-70 (2007).

Bubbles are an old phenomenon. Compare the "tulip bubble" in seventeenth century Holland, in which certain tulips were highly prized, and their bulbs were sold for thousands of guilder. Almost everyone got caught up in the excitement of buying and selling tulip bulbs, usually on credit and with the intention of making a quick profit; but many who speculated on credit were left with crushing debts when the market finally crashed.[47] Occasional bubbles may well be an inevitable side effect of a market economy.

A third sub-hypothesis explaining investor actions is the notion of bounded rationality imposed by human cognitive limitations. Bubbles do not necessarily require individual investors to behave irrationally. In contrast, investors can make poor decisions, notwithstanding disclosure, because of their cognitive limitations. There are at least two ways in which this can occur. To some extent, investor failure in the subprime financial crisis may have resulted from herd behavior.[48] It may also have resulted from the availability heuristic, under which people overestimate the frequency or likelihood of an event when examples of, or associations with, similar events are easily brought to mind.[49] People typically overestimate the divorce rate, for example, if they can quickly find examples of divorced friends.[50] Similarly, once past financial crises recede in memory, and investors are making money, investors always "go for the gold."[51]

***Hypothesis*: The disclosure was inherently inadequate because the transactions were so complex that many investors could not understand them.**[52]

This hypothesis turns on the extraordinary complexity of CDO and ABS CDO transactions. The prospectus itself in a typical offering of these securities can be hundreds of

---

47 Segal, *supra* note 45, at 19.

48 *Cf.* Steven L. Schwarcz, *Rethinking the Disclosure Paradigm in a World of Complexity*, 2004 U. ILL. L. REV. 1, 14-15 (observing and explaining this behavior in a related context).

49 Paul Slovic et al., *Facts Versus Fears: Understanding Perceived Risk*, *in* JUDGMENT UNDER UNCERTAINTY: HEURISTICS AND BIASES 463, 465 (Daniel Kahneman et al. eds., 1982).

50 *Id.*

51 *Cf.* Larry Light, *Bondholder Beware: Value Subject To Change Without Notice*, BUS. WK., Mar. 29, 1993, at 34 (discussing that within years after the "Marriott split," investors favor higher interest rates over "event risk" covenants, once the examples of events justifying the covenants have receded in memory). "Bondholders can—and will—fuss all they like. But the reality is, their options are limited: Higher returns or better protection. Most investors will continue to go for the gold." *Id.*

52 *See, e.g.*, Aaron Lucchetti & Serena Ng, *Credit & Blame: How Rating Firms' Calls Fueled Subprime Mess*, WALL ST. J., Aug. 15, 2007, at A10 ("A lot of institutional investors bought [mortgage-backed] securities substantially based on their ratings [without fully understanding what they bought], in part because the market has become so complex."); *cf.* Blinder, *supra* note 44 (arguing that the MBS, especially the CDOs, "were probably too complex for anyone's good"); *see also* Malcolm Gladwell, *Open Secrets: Enron, Intelligence, and the Perils of Too Much Information*, NEW YORKER, Jan. 8, 2007, at 44-53 (distinguishing between transactions that are merely "puzzles" and those that are truly "mysteries"). To the extent complexity is merely a puzzle, investment bankers theoretically could understand it. *See id.* at 46 (stating why puzzles are easier to solve than mysteries).

pages long.[53] This hypothesis, if true, would extend the thesis in my article, *Rethinking the Disclosure Paradigm in a World of Complexity,*[54] beyond investors in an Originator's[55] securities to investors in an SPV's securities. Although that article concerned investors in an Originator's securities, the proposal of that article nonetheless can help to inform this analysis. That article proposes that investors in an Originator's securities be protected in a supplementary manner by restricting conflicts of interest in complex transactions for which disclosure would be insufficient.[56] The rationale is that, absent conflicts, the Originator's management will make decisions that more closely reflect the interests of the Originator's investors.

The same approach has potential application to investors in an SPV's securities, particularly when the SPV transaction is so complex (as some CDO and ABS CDO transactions apparently were) that disclosure would be insufficient. In that context, there are at least two ways in which material conflicts arise. For securities backed by subprime mortgages, the interests of mortgage originators, absent their taking a prior or pari passu ("equal and ratable") risk of loss,[57] are misaligned with that of investors in those securities.[58] To mitigate this type of conflict, perhaps mortgage originators should be required to take some risk of loss.

Secondly, agency-cost conflicts arise when the interests of individual investment bankers, who structure, sell, or invest in securities, are misaligned with the interests of the institutions for which they work.[59] For example, certain losses of institutional investors such as Bear Stearns appear to have resulted from losses in CDO investments by controlled or managed hedge funds.[60] If managers of those hedge funds were paid according to hedge-fund industry custom—in which "fund managers reap large rewards on the upside without a corresponding punitive downside"[61]—they would have

---

[53] The disclosure documents ordinarily consist of a prospectus and a prospectus supplement, each close to 200 pages long.

[54] Schwarcz, *supra* note 48, at 7.

[55] The term "Originator" is defined in footnote 24.

[56] Schwarcz, *supra* note 48, at 30. *See also id.* at 32-33 (showing how to identify these transactions, which are defined as "disclosure-impaired transactions").

[57] If mortgage originators take a risk of loss prior to, or pari passu (i.e., equal and ratable) with, investor risk of loss, their incentives would be aligned with investor incentives.

[58] *See infra* notes 70-83 and accompanying text.

[59] Most investors were institutions. *See* SEC. EXCH. COMM'N, STAFF REPORT: ENHANCING DISCLOSURE IN THE MORTGAGE-BACKED SECURITIES MARKETS (2003), http://www.sec.gov/news/studies/mortgagebacked.htm (reporting that investors in MBS are "overwhelmingly institutional").

[60] *See, e.g.*, Kate Kelly et al., *Two Big Funds At Bear Stearns Face Shutdown,* WALL. ST. J., June 20, 2007, at A1.

[61] James Surowiecki, *Performance-Pay Perplexes*, NEW YORKER, Nov. 12, 2007, at 34. Hedge funds sometimes impose a limited punitive downside by ensuring that managers who lose money may not receive future bonuses until they subsequently make money above a "high water mark." MARK J. P. ANSON, THE HANDBOOK OF ALTERNATIVE ASSETS 361 (2002). Generally, however, there is no clawback of past bonuses,

had significant conflicts of interest with the institutions owning the hedge funds.[62] To mitigate this type of conflict, these individuals should be paid in a manner that better aligns their interests with the interests of the institutions for which they work.

Restricting conflicts of interest, as a supplement to disclosure, is only a second-best solution. It would not solve the problem that, even absent conflicts, individual investment bankers might have insufficient incentives to try to completely understand the highly complex transactions in which they recommend their institutions invest. For example, such individuals might not choose to fully comprehend complex transactions because they view the possibility of losses as remote, or anticipate being in a new job if and when losses occurred, or simply feel safe following the herd of other bankers.[63]

There do not appear to be any perfect solutions to the problem of investor ignorance of complex transactions. Government already takes a somewhat paternalistic stance to mitigate disclosure inadequacy by mandating minimum investor sophistication for investing in complex securities; yet sophisticated investors and qualified institutional buyers (QIBs) are the very investors who lost the most money in the subprime financial crisis.[64] And any attempt by government to restrict firms from engaging in complex transactions would be highly risky because of the potential of inadvertently banning beneficial transactions.[65]

---

so these managers can go to another hedge fund where they will not be subject to this liability. *Id.* at 85 (reporting that "clawbacks are rare in the hedge fund world").

[62] In this regard, the reader should distinguish these conflicts of interest not only from the agency-cost problem discussed above but also from the potential conflict of interest between mortgage originators and investors discussed in footnotes 70-83 and accompanying text.

[63] *See, e.g.*, Schwarcz, *supra* note 48, at 2, 14-15. Outside of an institutional-industry context, there may be further misalignment of incentives because of higher employee turnover. *Id.* at 14 (observing that employee turnover reduces accountability).

[64] *See, e.g.*, Jenny Anderson, *Wall St. Banks Confront a String of Write-Downs*, N.Y. TIMES, Feb. 19, 2008, at C1 (reporting that "major banks . . . have already written off more than $120 billion of losses stemming from bad mortgage-related investments"); Randall Smith, *Merrill's $5 Billion Bath Bares Deeper Divide*, WALL ST. J., Oct. 6, 2007, at A4 (reporting a total of $20 billion in write-downs by large investment banks).

[65] *Cf. infra* note 74 and accompanying text (cautioning against "throwing out the baby with the bathwater"). Although otherwise beyond this article's scope, certain CDO products, the so-called CDOs "squared" and "cubed," might be worthy of special consideration because they are subject to "cliff risk," or suddenly losing 100% of their value. *See, e.g.*, MICHIKO WHETTEN & MARK ADELSON, NOMURA FIXED INCOME RESEARCH, CDOS-SQUARED DEMYSTIFIED 12-13 (2005), *available at* http://www.math.ust.hk/~maykwok/courses/MAFS521_07/CDO-Squared_Nomura.pdf; Janet Tavakoli, *Leverage and Junk Science: A Credit Crunch Cocktail*, TOTAL SECURITIZATION, Sept. 20, 2007. In this context, the tort law doctrine of "unavoidably unsafe products" may help to inform a regulatory analysis. In tort law, an "unavoidably unsafe product" is subject to strict liability unless its utility outweighs its risk. Joanne Rhoton Galbreath, Annotation, *Products Liability: What Is an "Unavoidably Unsafe" Product*, 70 A.L.R. 4th 16, § 3 (1989). For example, the vaccine for rabies is inherently dangerous, but rabies can result in death, so the vaccine is not subject to strict liability. RESTATEMENT (SECOND) OF TORTS § 402A cmt. k (1965).

Hypothesis: ***Even when disclosure is adequate and investors understand it perfectly (i.e., they have perfect knowledge of the risk), disclosure alone will be inadequate to address at least systemic risk in financial markets.***

Systemic risk is the risk that an economic shock such as market or institutional failure triggers (through a panic or otherwise) either by (i) the failure of a chain of markets or institutions or (ii) a chain of significant losses to financial institutions, resulting in increases in the cost of capital or decreases in its availability, often evidenced by substantial financial-market price volatility.[66] Disclosure alone will be inadequate to prevent systemic risk because, like a tragedy of the commons, the benefits of exploiting finite capital resources accrue to individual market participants, each of whom is motivated to maximize use of the resource, whereas the costs of exploitation, which affect the real economy, are distributed among an even wider class of persons.[67] Investors are therefore unlikely to care about disclosure to the extent it pertains to systemic risk.

Should disclosure therefore be supplemented to address systemic risk? I address this in a separate article,[68] proposing, among other things, a "market" liquidity provider of last resort to purchase securities in collapsing markets in order to mitigate market instability that would lead to systemic collapse. Such a liquidity provider would supplement disclosure by making its purchases at a deep enough discount to (i) make a profit, or at least be repaid, and (ii) mitigate moral hazard by impairing speculative investors.[69]

Summary: The discussion above suggests that multiple causes, viewed collectively, explain why so many investors make poor investment decisions notwithstanding disclosure. Some investors may have taken too short-sighted a view of risk in the housing market or have been swayed by the fact that, in recent memory, home prices had only been rising. Some investors may have simply followed the herd in their investments, while others—possibly recognizing the bubble forming in the market for CDO and ABS CDO securities—may have invested anyway, hoping prices would continue to rise and their investments would rise in value. Investors also may have relied excessively on credit ratings without performing their own due diligence. In the case of investments in ABS CDO transactions, investors additionally may have over-relied on the judgment of underwriters who had purchased portions of the "equity" tranches. Finally, certain of the CDO and ABS CDO transactions may have been so complex that disclosure was inherently inadequate.

---

66 *See* Schwarcz, *infra* note 68, at 196-97.

67 In other words, the externalities of systemic failure include social costs that can extend far beyond market participants. *Id.* at 208-09.

68 Steven L. Schwarcz, *Systemic Risk*, 97 GEO. L.J. 193 (2008), *available at* http://ssrn.com/abstract=1008326.

69 *Id.* at 228-30 & 248-49.

B. IS THERE SOMETHING STRUCTURALLY WRONG ABOUT HOW STRUCTURED FINANCE WORKED IN THE MORTGAGE CONTEXT?

For this anomaly, this Essay examines several hypotheses:

> ***Hypothesis:*** ***Structured finance facilitated an undisciplined mortgage lending industry characterized by ease of entrance by enabling mortgage lenders to sell off loans as they were made (a concept called "originate-and-distribute"). This created moral hazard to the extent that mortgage lenders did not have to live with the credit consequences of their loans. For that reason, probably exacerbated by the fact that mortgage lenders could make money on the volume of loans originated,[70] the underwriting standards of mortgage lenders fell.[71]***

Anecdotal evidence suggests this hypothesis is at least somewhat true.[72] One solution would be to limit the originate-and-distribute model.[73] However, that would be like "throwing out the baby with the bathwater," as an originate-and-distribute model is critical to the underlying funding liquidity of banks[74] as well as many corporations.[75]

---

[70] This may have been further exacerbated by certain mortgage lenders without balance-sheet assets simply advancing to borrowers the proceeds of selling the loans. Interview with Monoline Insurance executive (Oct. 18, 2007) (notes on file with author).

[71] *See, e.g.*, *Legislative and Regulatory Options for Minimizing and Mitigating Mortgage Foreclosures: Hearing Before the H. Comm. on Financial Serv.*, 110th Cong. 74 (2007) (statement of Ben S. Bernanke, Chairman, Fed. Reserve System), *available at* http://frwebgate.access.gpo.gov/cgi-bin/getdoc.cgi?dbname=110_house_hearings&docid=f:39540.pdf. There is also speculation that some mortgage-loan originators might have engaged in fraud by manipulating borrower income, and that some borrowers may have engaged in fraud by lying about their income, in each case to qualify borrowers for loans. *See, e.g.*, Vikas Bajaj, *A Cross-Country Blame Game*, N.Y. TIMES, May 8, 2007, at C4. If such fraud occurred, it would exacerbate but is unlikely to be significant enough to have caused the subprime financial crisis.

[72] *See* Gary B. Gorton, "The Panic of 2007," NBER Working Paper 14358 (2008), at 68 (stating that the originate-and-distribute model and resulting moral hazard are the "dominant explanation" for the financial panic). To some extent, the drop in underwriting standards under the originate-and-distribute model may reflect distortions caused by the recent liquidity glut, in which lenders competed aggressively for business and allowed otherwise defaulting borrowers to refinance. *See* Ravi Balakrishnan et al., *Globalization, Gluts, Innovation or Irrationality: What Explains the Easy Financing of the U.S. Current Account Deficit?* (Int'l Monetary Fund, Working Paper No. 07/160, 2007), *available at* http://www.imf.org/external/pubs/ft/wp/2007/wp07160.pdf (discussing this liquidity glut).

[73] This model is also referred to as "originate to distribute."

[74] *See, e.g.*, Joseph R. Mason, Assoc. Professor of Fin. & LeBow Research Fellow, Lebow Coll. of Bus., Drexel Univ., Presentation to the Federal Reserve Bank of Cleveland: Mortgage Loan Modification: Promises and Pitfalls (Nov. 20, 2007) (presentation notes on file with author) (showing that 58% of mortgage liquidity in the United States, and 75% of mortgage liquidity in California has come from structured finance).

[75] *See* Xudong An et al., *Value Creation Through Securitization: Evidence from the CMBS Market* 3 (SSRN Working Paper No. 1095645, 2008), *available at* http://papers.ssrn.com/sol3/papers.cfm?abstract_

A better solution, already discussed, would be to require mortgage lenders and other originators to retain a risk of loss.[76] In many non-mortgage securitization transactions, for example, it is customary for originators to bear a direct risk of loss by overcollateralizing the receivables sold to the SPV.[77] This is not always done in mortgage securitization because mortgage loans are inherently overcollateralized by the value of the real-estate collateral, and thus investors can effectively be overcollateralized even if the originator bears no risk of loss. However, originators should be required to retain a risk of loss to mitigate moral hazard. In this context, one might ask why investors and other parties, such as credit insurers, who ultimately bear the risk of loss in an originate-and-distribute model do not monitor the underlying loans. Although in theory they should, the practical limits suggested by this Essay—including complexity of disclosure, herd behavior, and, as will be discussed, possible excessive diversification of risk that undermines any given investor's incentive to monitor[78]—help to explain this failure to monitor.[79]

Some investors take comfort in the limited risk of loss imposed on mortgage originators through representations and warranties.[80] Representations and warranties, however, are not always effective because they are costly to enforce and become illusory when mortgage originators are unable, as in the current subprime mortgage meltdown, to pay damages for breach.[81] Prudent investors should insist that mortgage originators retain some direct risk of loss to mitigate moral hazard.[82] For this same reason, for example, banks buying loan participations insist that the bank originating the loan

id=1095645 (concluding that despite the recent mortgage crisis, securitization has created value in the financial markets).

[76] *See supra* text accompanying notes 57-58.

[77] *See* Vincent Ryan, *Debt in Disguise,* CFO MAG., Nov. 2007, at 80 (reporting that most securitization agreements include overcollateralization).

[78] *See infra* notes 87-89 and accompanying text.

[79] The failure to monitor also can be explained by systematic underestimation of the risk by all market players. *See, e.g.*, Oz Ergungor, The Mortgage Debacle and Loan Modification 7-8 (2008) (unpublished manuscript, on file with author).

[80] Sanders, *supra* note 29.

[81] *Cf. id.* (arguing that mortgage originators be required to post capital to backstop their representations and warranties for loans originated and then sold). Representations and warranties are even more patently illusory for mortgage originators lacking assets, who simply advance to borrowers the proceeds of selling the loans. *See supra* note 70.

[82] The market actually was beginning to adjust in this fashion shortly before the subprime mortgage crisis started. *See* Jon D. Van Gorp, Capital Markets Dispersion of Subprime Mortgage Risk 10 (Nov. 2007) (unpublished manuscript, on file with author) (observing that, at the beginning of 2007, "early payment default protection became standardized across the market," requiring loan originators to repurchase loans that fail to make any of their first two or three scheduled payments). Obligations to repurchase can become ineffective, however, when so many loans default that the obligor is unable to make its required repurchases. Ergungor, *supra* note 79, at 4-5.

retain a minimum portion, typically at least ten percent of the loan exposure, even if the loan itself is overcollateralized.[83]

Another possible solution is to regulate the loan underwriting standards applicable to mortgage lenders. This approach would be akin to the Federal margin regulations G, U, T, and X imposed in response to the 1929 stock market crash.[84] The then-falling stock values caused margin loans—that is, loans to purchase publicly-listed, or margin stock—to become undercollateralized, causing bank lenders to fail. To protect against a recurrence of this problem, the margin regulations require margin lenders to maintain two-to-one overcollateralization when securing their loans by margin stock that has been purchased, directly or indirectly, with the loan proceeds.[85]

Imposing a minimum real-estate-value-to-loan overcollateralization on all mortgage loans secured by the real estate financed would likewise protect against a repeat of the subprime mortgage problem. Unfortunately, though, it would have a high price, potentially impeding and increasing the cost of home ownership and imposing an administrative burden on lenders and government monitors.[86]

***Hypothesis*: Structured finance dispersed subprime mortgage risk so widely that there was no clear incentive for any given investor to monitor it.**

---

[83] In the author's experience, this observation is accurate. *Cf.* Blinder, *supra* note 44 (suggesting that mortgage loan originators "retain a share of each mortgage"); *also cf. supra* notes 40-41 and accompanying text (discussing underwriters retaining a portion of the equity when selling ABS CDO securities).

[84] *Cf.* Blinder, *supra* note 44 (suggesting a "suitability standard" for selling mortgage products and that all mortgage lenders be placed under federal regulation).

[85] 12 C.F.R. § 221.3 (2008).

[86] One might also consider imposing lending "suitability" standards and predatory-lending restrictions. For example, North Carolina's Home Loan Protection Act, among other things, mandates that lenders verify borrower income and also review the borrower's ability to repay the loan after introductory rates adjust upwards. N.C. GEN. STAT. § 24-1.1E (2007) (amended by 2008 N.C. Sess. Laws). The U.S. Congress also has considered mortgage suitability standards and anti-predatory lending restrictions. *See, e.g.*, Mortgage Reform and Anti-Predatory Lending Act, H.R. 3915, 110th Cong. (2007). There is dispute, however, over whether the North Carolina law has negatively impacted home ownership. *Compare* Raphael W. Bostic et al., *State and Local Anti-Predatory Lending Laws: The Effect of Legal Enforcement Mechanisms*, 60 J. ECON. & BUS. 47, 50 (2008) (lending evidence that anti-predatory lending laws have not curtailed credit mortgage markets), *and* Nanette Byrnes, *These Tough Lending Laws Could Travel*, BUS. WK., Nov. 5, 2007, at 70 (reporting that North Carolina's housing market has not, according to "academic studies," been negatively impacted), *and* ROBERTO G. QUERCIA ET AL., CTR. FOR COMMUNITY CAPITALISM, THE IMPACT OF NORTH CAROLINA'S ANTI-PREDATORY LENDING LAW: A DESCRIPTIVE ASSESSMENT (2003), http://www.planning.unc.edu/pdf/CC_NC_Anti_Predatory_Law_Impact.pdf (stating that since the law was passed, there has been a reduction in predatory loans, but there has been "no change in the cost of subprime credit or reduction in access to credit for high-risk borrowers"), *with* Byrnes, *supra* (reporting that groups such as the Mortgage Bankers Association argue that tough loan underwriting standards will prevent needy borrowers from obtaining mortgage loans). Some argue also that the "borrowers are not victims of inappropriate loan prospecting (such as predatory lending). Rather, they [or, at least, many] were willful participants." Sanders, *supra* note 29. *But cf.* Gretchen Morgenson, *Blame the Borrowers? Not So Fast*, N.Y. TIMES, Nov. 25, 2007, at BU 1.

Structured finance generally diversifies and reallocates risk, which is normally salutary.[87] Might it have excessively dispersed subprime risk?[88]

If this hypothesis is true, it would call into question whether incentives should be better aligned to promote monitoring, for example, by limiting the degree of risk dispersion. To some extent, this article already proposes a variant on that approach, by suggesting that loan originators in an originate-and-distribute model retain some minimum percentage or amount of risk.[89]

> ***Hypothesis:*** ***Structured finance can make it difficult to work out problems with an underlying asset class—in this case, for example, making it difficult to work out the underlying mortgage loans because the beneficial owners of the loans are no longer the mortgage lenders but a broad universe of financial-market investors. As a result, mortgage defaults result in unnecessarily high losses.***

News stories observe that homeowners have been unable to restructure or modify their loans because they cannot identify who owns the loans.[90] Laws protecting mortgage borrowers, however, suggest this concern may be overstated. For example, the federal Truth in Lending Act states that, "[u]pon written request by the obligor, the servicer shall provide the obligor, to the best knowledge of the servicer, with the name,

---

[87] DOUGLAS ELMENDORF, NOTES ON POLICY RESPONSES TO THE SUBPRIME MORTGAGE UNRAVELING 9 n.6 (2007), http://www.brookings.edu/~/media/Files/rc/papers/2007/09subprimemortgageunravelling/09useconomics_elmendorf.pdf. *See also* Darrell Duffie, *Innovations in Credit Risk Transfer: Implications for Financial Stability* 1-2 (BIS Working Paper No. 255, July 2008) (arguing that instruments that transfer credit risk improve financial stability by dispersing risk among investors), available at http://www.bis.org/publ/work255.pdf?noframes=1.

[88] The very assumption that structured finance reallocates risk to parties best able to bear it also may have failed in the subprime context. E-mail from Bookstaber, *supra* note 35 ("Rather than spreading the risk to those who were most comfortable holding the assets and taking the risk, many of the [holders] were 'hot money' hedge funds that would have to run for cover at the very time the risk taking function was most critical.").

[89] *See supra* text accompanying note 82 (arguing that prudent investors should insist that mortgage originators retain some direct risk of loss to mitigate moral hazard.

[90] Gretchen Morgenson, *More Home Foreclosures Loom as Owners Face Mortgage Maze*, N.Y. TIMES, Aug. 6, 2007, at A1. A somewhat related issue is that, at least heretofore, individual borrowers could not use Chapter 13 bankruptcy to restructure their home mortgage loan liabilities. *See* 11 U.S.C. §§ 1322(b)(2), 1332(b)(5) (2006). Bills have been introduced into both houses of Congress to amend Chapter 13 and allow for restructuring of home mortgages by bankruptcy courts. *See* Emergency Home Ownership and Mortgage Protection Act, H.R. 3609, 110th Cong. (2007); Helping Families Save their Homes in Bankruptcy Act, S. 1236, 110th Cong. (2007). In a corporate reorganization context, however, debtors can, with the lender's consent, use bankruptcy to restructure their secured-loan liabilities. *Cf.* 11 U.S.C. § 1123(a)(5) (2006) (listing the contents of a bankruptcy plan); 11 U.S.C. § 1126(c) (2006) (acceptance of a bankruptcy plan); § 1129(a)(7)-(8) (2006) (confirmation of a bankruptcy plan).

address, and telephone number of the owner of the obligation or the master servicer of the obligation."[91]

In theory, servicers bridge the gap between beneficial owners of the loans and the mortgage lenders. It is typical, for example, for originators of securitized mortgage loans, or a specialized servicing company such as Countrywide Home Loans Servicing LP, to act as the servicer for a fee.[92] In this capacity, the servicer ordinarily retains power to restructure the underlying loans, so long as restructuring changes are "in the best interests" of the investors holding the securities.[93] Subject to that constraint, the servicer may even change the rate of interest, the principal amount of the loan, or the maturity dates of the loan if, for example, the loan is in default or, in the servicer's judgment, default is reasonably foreseeable.[94]

In practice, though, even when a servicer has the power to restructure a mortgage loan and restructuring is in the best interests of investors, the servicer may be reluctant to engage in restructuring if there is uncertainty that the transaction will generate sufficient excess cash flow to reimburse the servicer's costs.[95] A mortgage loan servicer, for example, must "spend $750-$1000 to do a [loan] mod[ification] [and] can't charge the borrower."[96] If there is insufficient excess cash, neither can it charge the securitization trust.[97] By contrast, "all foreclosure costs are reimbursed."[98] Servicers also may sometimes prefer foreclosure over restructuring because the former is more ministerial and thus has lower litigation risk.[99] The litigation risk of restructuring is exacerbated by

---

[91] 15 U.S.C. § 1641(f)(2) (2006). Identification would be even less of a problem if the underlying receivables are not consumer assets, like mortgage loans, since the amounts involved in consumer receivables are typically relatively small.

[92] *See* JAMES A. ROSENTHAL & JUAN M. OCAMPO, SECURITIZATION OF CREDIT: INSIDE THE NEW TECHNOLOGY OF FINANCE 49-51 (1988) (explaining the general structure of a grantor trust when the originator of asset-backed securities services the pool of assets); Gretchen Morgenson, *Countrywide Is Upbeat Despite Loss*, N.Y. TIMES, Oct. 27, 2007, at C1 (reporting that Countrywide is the nation's largest loan servicer). In addition to a primary servicer, there are often other servicers involved in MBS transactions including a specialized servicer who services defaulted mortgage loans. *See* Mortgage Bankers Ass'n, Presentation to the Securities and Exchange Commission on the Proposed Asset-Backed Securities Rule (Sept. 23, 2004), *available at* www.sec.gov/rules/proposed/s72104/mba092304.ppt.

[93] Morgenson, *supra* note 90 (observing that a servicer might, for example, be permitted to restructure only five percent of the loans). Sometimes, however, the servicer is limited as to the percentage of loans in a given pool that can be restructured. *Id.*

[94] Financial Asset Securities Corp., Pooling and Service Agreement for Soundview Home Loan Trust Asset-Backed Certificates § 3.01 (Mar. 1, 2007), *available at* http://www.sec.gov/Archives/edgar/data/1386634/000088237707001029/d650626ex4_1.htm.

[95] Mason, *supra* note 74 (observing that servicers will prefer to foreclose, even if it is not the best remedy, when foreclosure costs, but not modification costs, are reimbursed).

[96] *Id.*

[97] *Id.*

[98] *Id.*

[99] Kathleen C. Engel, Assoc. Professor of Law, Cleveland-Marshall Coll. of Law, Presentation to the Federal Reserve Bank of Cleveland: Modifications of Loans in Securitized Pools: Obstacles and Options (Nov. 20, 2007) (notes on this presentation on file with author).

the fact that, in many MBS, CDO, and ABS CDO transactions, cash flows deriving from principal and interest are separately allocated to different investor tranches.[100] Therefore, a restructuring that, for example, reduces the interest rate would adversely affect investors in the interest-only tranche,[101] leading to what some have called "tranche warfare."[102]

Summary: The discussion above indicates there is little structurally wrong about how structured finance worked in the mortgage context. Although the originate-and-distribute model of structured finance may have created a degree of moral hazard, the model is critical to underlying funding liquidity. Moreover, the moral hazard cost can be mitigated if, as likely will occur in the future, investors learn from the subprime crisis and require mortgage originators to retain a direct risk of loss beyond the sometimes illusory risk borne through representations and warranties.

Structured finance can make it more difficult to address problems with the underlying financial assets, but the increased difficulty may be able to be managed. Parties should consider writing underlying deal documentation that sets clearer and more flexible guidelines and more certain reimbursement procedures for loan restructuring, especially when such restructuring is superior to foreclosure.[103] Investors (and servicers) should prefer foreclosure to restructuring if restructuring merely delays an inevitable foreclosure.[104]

There nonetheless is a residual structural concern insofar as structured finance may have dispersed subprime mortgage risk so widely that there is no clear incentive for any given investor to monitor the risk. Whether that has occurred is uncertain. Even if it has, the evil is not so much risk dispersion per se as the failure to align incentives sufficiently to promote monitoring.

C. Why Did a Problem with the Subprime Mortgage-Backed Securities Markets Quickly Infect the Markets for Prime Mortgage-Backed Securities and Other Asset-Backed Securities?[105]

Understanding this anomaly can help to expand an understanding of how market risk can become systemic. For this anomaly, this Essay examines several hypotheses:

---

[100] Van Gorp, *supra* note 82, at 7-8.

[101] The conflicts among tranches can become even more complicated because subprime MBS, CDO, and ABS CDO securities sometimes also include prepayment-penalty tranches, and the different tranches "have different priorities relative to one another for the purpose of absorbing losses and prepayments on the underlying subprime mortgage loans." *Id.* at 8.

[102] Telephone Interview with Alan Hirsch, Dir., N.C. Policy Office (Feb. 20, 2008) (describing tranche conflicts as a significant reason why servicers choose foreclosure over restructuring).

[103] In the current subprime crisis, of course, the underlying deal documentation is already in place. Because existing documentation cannot be easily renegotiated, the government might consider legislating changes. Any such changes that are subsidized in whole or part by government, however, could foster moral hazard, potentially making future homeowners more willing to take risks when borrowing.

[104] Engel, *supra* note 99.

[105] *Cf.* Andrews, *supra* note 39, at 15 (observing from the subprime financial crisis that "liquidity in markets for structured investments can disappear immediately as soon as there are any shocks—no buying or selling at all in an entire sector," though not explaining why this occurs). A somewhat related question

***Hypothesis**: The MBS, ABS, CDO, and ABS CDO markets are inherently tightly coupled, both within and among such markets.*

By "tight coupling," I mean the tendency for financial markets to move rapidly into a crisis mode with little time or opportunity to intervene.[106] Tight coupling could result from various mechanisms, even as elementary as investor panic, guilt-by-association, or loss of confidence.[107] In the subprime crisis, once investors realized that highly-rated subprime mortgage-backed securities could lose money, they began shunning all complex securitization products.[108] This pattern of behavior was particularly true with respect to asset-backed commercial paper—not surprisingly, since commercial paper is effectively a substitute for cash (albeit one that yields a return). Investor reaction also may have been magnified by the dramatic shift away from the liquidity glut of the past few years, which had obscured the problem of defaults by enabling defaulting borrowers to refinance with ease.[109]

Tight coupling also may have been caused by a type of adverse selection: investors were no longer sure which securitization investments or counterparties were good and which were bad (CDO and ABS CDO products being especially difficult to value[110]), so they stopped investing in all securitization products.[111] Incongruously, adverse selection may have been made worse by the otherwise salutary effect of securitization to disperse risk: investors were unable, in part exacerbated by the indirect holding system

might be why the U.S. domestic real estate collapse is having a significant impact overseas. The answer is that foreign investors purchased a significant amount of the CDO and ABS CDO securities backed (directly or indirectly) by such real estate. Jenny Anderson & Heather Timmons, *Why a U.S. Subprime Mortgage Crisis Is Felt Around the World*, N.Y. TIMES, Aug. 31, 2007, at C1.

106 Thanks to Rick Bookstaber for this term. Bookstaber himself borrows it from engineering nomenclature. *See Systemic Risk Hearing*, *supra* note 2, at 8 (statement of Richard Bookstaber).

107 *See, e.g.*, Paul Davies & Gillian Tett, *'A Flight to Simplicity': Investors Jettison What They Do Not Understand*, FIN. TIMES, Oct. 22, 2007, at 9.

108 *Cf.* Markus K. Brunnermeier, *Deciphering the 2007-08 Liquidity and Credit Crunch*, J. ECON. PERSP. (forthcoming 2008), *available at* http://www.princeton.edu/~markus/research/papers/liquidity_crunch_2007_08.pdf (speculating that when investors realized how difficult it was to value mortgage structured products, the volatility of all structured products increased).

109 *Cf. supra* note 72 and accompanying text (explaining that lenders competed aggressively for business during the recent liquidity glut, which allowed otherwise defaulting borrowers to refinance).

110 Many CDO and ABS CDO products are valued by models rather than market price because they are issued in private placements and not freely traded. Valuation models are imperfect because they are based on assumptions. *See* Floyd Norris, *Reading Write-Down Tea Leaves*, N.Y. TIMES, Nov. 9, 2007, at C1 (discussing the problems related to using valuation models). *See generally* Ingo Fender & John Kiff, *CDO Rating Methodology: Some Thoughts on Model Risk and its Implications* (Bank of Int'l. Settlements, Working Paper No. 163, 2004), *available at* http://www.bis.org/publ/work163.htm (discussing the problems associated with the valuation models used by rating agencies).

111 *See, e.g.*, Zuckerman, *supra* note 8, at 63 (stating that the "credit system has been virtually frozen," which poses a problem "since few people even know where the liabilities and losses are concentrated").

for securities under which third parties cannot readily determine who ultimately owns specific securities,[112] to ascertain to whom the risk was dispersed.

Finally, and incongruously, tight coupling can even result from mark-to-market, or "fair value," accounting. In its simplest form, this is the common requirement that a securities account be adjusted in response to a change in the market value of the securities. An investor, for example, may buy securities on credit from a securities broker-dealer, securing the purchase price by pledging the securities as collateral. To guard against the price of the securities falling to the point where their value as collateral is insufficient to repay the purchase price, the broker-dealer requires the investor to maintain a minimum collateral value. If the market value of the securities falls below this minimum, the broker-dealer will issue a "margin call" requiring the investor to deposit additional collateral, usually in the form of money or additional securities, to satisfy this minimum. Failure to do so triggers a default, enabling the broker-dealer to foreclose on the collateral.[113] Requiring investors to mark prices to market value in this fashion is generally believed to reduce risk.[114] Nonetheless, it can cause "perverse effects on systemic stability" during times of market turbulence, when forcing sales of assets to meet margin calls can depress asset prices, requiring more forced sales (which, in turn, will depress asset prices even more), causing a downward spiral.[115] The existence of leverage makes this spiral more likely and amplifies it if it occurs.[116] At least some portion of the subprime crisis appears to have been caused by this downward spiral.[117]

---

[112] Under the indirect holding system for securities, intermediary entities hold securities on behalf of investors. Issuers of the securities generally record ownership as belonging to one or more depository intermediaries, which in turn record the identities of other intermediaries, such as brokerage firms or banks, that buy interests in the securities. Those other intermediaries, in turn, record the identities of investors that buy interests in the intermediaries' interests. *See* Steven L. Schwarcz, *Intermediary Risk in a Global Economy*, 50 DUKE L.J. 1541, 1547-48 (2001). Because of this ownership chain, there is no single location from which third parties can readily determine who ultimately owns specific securities. *Id.* at 1583.

[113] ZVI BODIE ET AL., INVESTMENTS 78-79 (6th ed. 2005).

[114] *See, e.g.*, Gikas A. Hardouvelis & Panayiotis Theodossiou, *The Asymmetric Relation Between Initial Margin Requirements and Stock Market Volatility Across Bull and Bear Markets*, 15 REV. FIN. STUD. 1525, 1554-55 (2002) (finding a correlation between higher margin calls and decreased systemic risk, and speculating that higher margin calls may bleed the irrationality out of the market until only sound bets are left).

[115] *See* Rodrigo Cifuentes et al., *Liquidity Risk and Contagion* 2 (Bank of Int'l Settlements, Working Paper, 2004), *available at* http://www.bis.org/bcbs/events/rtf04shin.pdf; *see also* Clifford De Souza & Mikhail Smirnov, *Dynamic Leverage: A Contingent Claims Approach to Leverage for Capital Conservation*, J. PORTFOLIO MGMT. 25, 28 (Fall 2004) (arguing that, in a bad market, short-term pressure to sell assets to raise cash for margin calls can lead to further mark-to-market losses for remaining assets, which triggers a whole new wave of selling, the process repeating itself until markets improve or the firm is wiped out; and referring to this process as a "critical liquidation cycle").

[116] *Id.* at 26-27.

[117] Rachel Evans, *Banks Tell of Downward Spiral*, 27 INT'L FIN. L. REV. 16 (2008).

***Hypothesis:* Tight coupling resulted from convergence in hedge-fund quantitatively-constructed investment strategies.**[118]

Professors Khandani and Lo hypothesize that when a number of hedge funds experienced unprecedented losses during the week of August 6, 2007, they rapidly unwound sizable portfolios, likely based on a multi-strategy fund or proprietary-trading desk.[119] These initial losses then caused further losses by triggering stop/loss and de-leveraging policies.[120] To the extent this hypothesis has validity, hedge fund strategies, and not securitization or structured finance per se, are responsible for the subprime financial crisis.

Summary: The discussion above provides three explanations for why a problem with the subprime mortgage-backed securities markets quickly infected the prime markets.[121] Faced for the first time with the reality that highly-rated tranches of subprime MBS could lose money, investors appear to have lost confidence, shunning all complex securitization products. To this extent, future investors should try to better understand these types of investments so that confidence is built on a firmer foundation.

Adverse selection also helps to explain the rapid infection. Investors became uncertain which securitization products, and indeed which securitization counterparties, were good and which were bad. They therefore stopped investing in all securitization products. Adverse selection can be mitigated through information; in this case, by valuing the securities and ascertaining the holdings of securitization counterparties. However, because CDO and ABS CDO securities were not actively traded, and there was no established market price to which to mark them, these securities could not be valued at "market." Valuation, therefore, was priced off quantitative models. Marking-to-model,

---

[118] *Cf.* Schwarcz, *supra* note 68, at 202-04 (discussing the danger of converging hedge-fund investment strategies).

[119] Amir Khandani & Andrew W. Lo, *What Happened to the Quants in August 2007?* 2 (Soc. Sci. Research Network, Paper No. 1015987, 2007), *available at* http://papers.ssrn.com/sol3/papers.cfm?abstract_id=1015987.

[120] *Id.* Essentially, the authors argue that if shared models are wrong, an unanticipated error is shared by everyone.

[121] There also might have been amplifying mechanisms that exacerbated or expanded market losses. For example, highly leveraged hedge funds apparently borrowed money from banks and invested in significant amounts of MBS, CDO, and ABS CDO securities backed by subprime mortgages. *See, e.g.*, Paul Davies & Gillian Tett, *'A flight to simplicity': Investors Jettison What They Do Not Understand*, FIN. TIMES, Oct. 22, 2007, at 9 (reporting that hedge funds borrowed large amounts of money to invest in CDO securities). Failure of these hedge funds resulting from losses on these securities can affect the bank lenders. Another possible amplifying mechanism is that certain bank-sponsored investment conduits purchased AAA-rated CDO and ABS CDO securities with the proceeds of short-term commercial paper. As the CDO and ABS CDO securities were marked down in value and investors failed to roll over their commercial paper, the bank sponsors faced the prospect of having to make payments to the conduits pursuant to liquidity and credit-enhancement facilities. *See* Carrick Mollenkamp & Margot Patrick, *Credit Crunch: Citigroup Moves to Quell SIV Concerns*, WALL ST. J., Sept. 7, 2007, at C2 (reporting that Citibank was unable to raise money through the sale of asset-backed commercial paper); *see also infra* note 148 and accompanying text.

however, creates intrinsic valuation uncertainties, and indeed the valuations priced off those models proved hopelessly unreliable. The indirect holding system for securities also made it very difficult to ascertain whether CDO and ABS CDO securities were held by securitization counterparties, and as long as that system continues to dominate securities holdings, this difficulty will remain.

The third explanation is also related to valuation. Absent a real market, valuation of CDO and ABS CDO securities must, as indicated, be priced off quantitative models. It is critical, then, that the range of models used by investors be sufficiently diverse that errors in one model will not cut across all models.

D. WHY WAS THE MARKET-DISCIPLINE APPROACH INSUFFICIENT?

Under a market-discipline approach, the regulator's job is to ensure that the private sector exercises the type of diligence that enables markets to work efficiently.[122] Until recently, it appeared that a market-discipline approach worked well for the banking and securities-brokerage industries.[123] In the subprime context, however, this approach failed. To explain this failure, this Essay examines several hypotheses:

> ***Hypothesis:* Certain foundations of a market-discipline approach have rotted.**

Regulators implement a market-discipline approach by ensuring that market participants have access to adequate information about risks and by arranging incentives so that those who influence an institution's behavior will suffer if that behavior generates losses.[124] In the recent financial crisis, however, disclosure inadequately conveyed information about the risks for various reasons,[125] including that certain of the structured finance transactions were too complex to be adequately disclosed.[126] Furthermore, the incentives of managers did not appear to be fully aligned with those of their institutions; managers would not necessarily suffer and, more importantly, they would not expect

---

[122] *Cf.* Ben S. Bernanke, Chairman, Bd. of Governors, Fed. Reserve Sys., Remarks at the Federal Reserve Bank of Atlanta's 2006 Financial Markets Conference (May 16, 2006), *available at* http://www.federalreserve.gov/newsevents/speech/Bernanke20060516a.htm) (observing that, to the extent hedge funds are regulated solely through market discipline, government's "primary task is to guard against a return of the weak market discipline that left major market participants overly vulnerable to market shocks").

[123] *See, e.g.*, Albert J. Boro, Jr., Comment, *Banking Disclosure Regimes for Regulating Speculative Behavior*, 74 CAL. L. REV. 431, 471 (1986); Helen A. Garten, *Banking on the Market: Relying on Depositors to Control Bank Risks*, 4 YALE J. ON REG. 129, 129-30 & n.1 (1986).

[124] *See* sources cited *supra* note 123; *cf.* Ben S. Bernanke, Chairman, Bd. of Governors, Fed. Reserve Sys., Remarks at the New York University Law School (Apr. 11, 2007), *available at* http://www.federalreserve.gov/newsevents/speech/Bernanke20070411a.htm) ("Receivership rules that make clear that investors will take losses when a bank becomes insolvent should increase the perceived risk of loss and thus also increase market discipline. . . . In the United States, the banking authorities have ensured that, in virtually all cases, shareholders bear losses when a bank fails.").

[125] *See generally supra* Part III.A.

[126] *See supra* notes 52-54 and accompanying text.

to suffer, if their behavior generated losses to their institutions.[127] Additionally, in the context of systemic risk, there were fundamental misalignments between institutional and financial market interests.[128]

Market discipline also may have failed due to the simple human greed of market participants.[129] In the face of greed, market discipline is undermined by the availability heuristic[130] as well as the almost endemic shortage of funding for regulatory monitoring.

Market discipline alone, therefore, appears to be an insufficient approach.

> ***Hypothesis*: At least regarding systemic risk, market discipline is inherently suspect because no firm has sufficient incentive to limit its risk taking in order to reduce the danger of systemic contagion for other firms.**

Recall that the externalities of systemic failure include social costs that can extend far beyond market participants, resulting in a type of tragedy of the commons.[131] Thus, a firm that exercises market discipline by reducing its leverage will marginally reduce the overall potential for systemic risk; but if other firms do not also reduce their leverage, the first firm will likely lose net asset value relative to the other firms.[132]

Summary: The preceding discussion shows that a market-discipline approach must be supplemented and that market discipline is particularly suspect as a protection against systemic risk.

E. WHY DID THE RATING AGENCIES FAIL TO ANTICIPATE THE DOWNGRADES?

This failure is particularly problematic due to the extent of investor over-reliance on rating-agency ratings.[133] For this failure, this Essay examines several hypotheses:

---

[127] *See supra* notes 59-63 and accompanying text (observing potential agency-cost conflicts between investment bankers who structured, sold, or invested in securities and the institutions for which they worked).

[128] *See supra* notes 87-88 and accompanying text (arguing that structured finance may have dispersed subprime mortgage risk so widely that there was no clear incentive for any given investor to monitor it); *see also infra* text accompanying note 131 (observing that from the standpoint of systemic risk, a market-discipline approach is inherently suspect because no firm has sufficient incentive to limit its risk taking in order to reduce the danger of systemic contagion for other firms).

[129] *See* Roberta Romano, *A Thumbnail Sketch of Derivative Securities and Their Regulation*, 55 MD. L. REV. 1, 79 (1996) (discussing greed as a central factor that, in the hedge-fund context, transforms a successful hedging or moderately risky investment strategy into one of high-risk speculation). *But cf.* Bernanke, *supra* note 122 (suggesting a possible alternative psychological explanation, at least in the case of the failure of market-discipline with respect to LTCM's investors, that those "[i]nvestors, perhaps awed by the reputations of LTCM's principals, did not ask sufficiently tough questions about the risks that were being taken to generate the high returns"); *supra* note 39 and accompanying text (describing the "over-reliance" hypothesis).

[130] *See supra* notes 48-49 and accompanying text.

[131] *See generally supra* notes 65-67 and accompanying text.

[132] *See* Bookstaber, *supra* note 35.

[133] *See supra* text accompanying notes 41-43.

<u>Hypothesis</u>: Rating agencies failed due to conflicts of interest regarding compensation.

Rating agencies are customarily paid by the issuer of securities,[134] but investors rely heavily on their ratings.[135] This is technically a conflict, but it is not usually a material conflict because ratings are made independently of the fee received.[136] Furthermore, the reputational cost of a bad rating usually far exceeds the income received by giving the rating.[137]

In the subprime crisis, though, the conflict would have been more material than normal because ratings were given to numerous issuances of CDO and ABS CDO securities, with each issuance (and rating) earning a separate fee. Assuming arguendo this created a material conflict, there is no easy solution. The question of who pays for a rating is difficult. Historically, rating agencies made their money by selling subscriptions, but that may not generate sufficient revenue to allow rating agencies to hire the top-flight analysts needed to rate complex deals.[138] And even if there was an easy way to get investors to pay for ratings, that might create the opposite incentive: to err on the side of low ratings in order to increase the rate of return to investors, thereby increasing the cost of credit to companies.[139]

<u>Hypothesis</u>: Rating agencies failed to foresee that the depth of the fall of the housing market could, and indeed did, exceed their worst-case modeled scenarios.

This hypothesis begs the question of whether the rating agency models were reasonable, at least when viewed ex ante. That question is, effectively, identical to the earlier question of whether the failure by investors to envision the actual worst-case scenario may have reflected, to some extent, a failure to take a sufficiently long view of risk.[140] The earlier analysis proposed two possible answers: that the failure simply reflected a

---

134 Steven L. Schwarcz, *Private Ordering of Public Markets: The Rating Agency Paradox*, 2002 U. ILL. L. REV. 1, 15.

135 *See id.* at 3.

136 *See id.* at 16.

137 *See id.* at 14.

138 *See id.* at 16 n.94. For other possible ideas of how to avoid conflicts of interest in paying rating agencies, see Alan S. Blinder, *Economic View: The Case for a Newer Deal*, N.Y. TIMES, May 4, 2008, at BU 5 (noting ideas of his Princeton University colleagues, such as paying rating agencies with some of the securities they rate, or having a governmental entity pay rating agencies from the proceeds of a tax levied on issuers). Professor Blinder admits the difficulty of avoiding conflicts of interest, requesting that "[i]f you have a better idea, write your legislators." *Id.*

139 *Cf.* Steven L. Schwarcz, *Temporal Perspectives: Resolving the Conflict Between Current and Future Investors*, 89 MINN. L. REV. 1044, 1053-54 (2005) (observing that to the extent ratings affect not only new investors but also existing investors, the analysis is complicated by the inherent conflict between those two sets of investors).

140 *See supra* notes 33-38 and accompanying text.

failed judgment call, made ex ante, of what the worst-case could be like;[141] and that the failure also may have reflected behavioral bias caused by the availability heuristic.[142]

It is unlikely that the failure of rating-agency models reflected significant behavioral bias since these models are constructed by multiple trained and experienced analysts.[143] To the extent the failure reflected a failed ex ante judgment call, this type of failure may be inevitable—even for rating agencies—because the exercise of judgment involves an inherent risk of error. The hope is that rating agencies, through their institutional memory, will learn from experience and exercise better judgment in the future.

At least one commentator argues that the rating agency failure likely reflected an under-appreciation of how an oversupply of mortgage money was artificially driving up home prices in subprime areas.[144] This would be rather surprising, if true, given rating agency sophistication. It also is possible that the rating-agency models may have failed because of fraud in the borrower-income data.[145] To this extent, rating agencies may be stymied because they have little alternative in most cases but to accept as true the data they receive.[146]

***Hypothesis:* Rating agencies failed to fully appreciate the correlation in subprime mortgage loans when analyzing CDOs, especially ABS CDOs.**

Early CDOs and ABS CDOs had highly diversified underlying assets.[147] Later CDOs and ABS CDOs were still diversified but were more susceptible to a finance-based link in which prices of the underlying assets start to move in lockstep as investors hedge their exposure to those assets.[148] Furthermore, even though later ABS CDOs had significant diversification in the ABS and MBS securities included therein, there was an underlying

---

141 *See supra* text accompanying notes 34-37.

142 *See supra* notes 48-51 and accompanying text.

143 In order to qualify as a Nationally Recognized Statistical Rating Organization (NRSRO), the rating agency must employ "an adequate number of staff members with the education and experience necessary to competently evaluate an issuer's credit." Arturo Estrella et al., *Credit Ratings and Complementary Sources of Credit Quality Information* 51 (Bank for Int'l. Settlements, Basel Comm. on Banking Supervision Working Papers, Paper No. 3, 2000), *available at* http://www.bis.org/publ/bcbs_wp3.htm. *But cf.* Gerry McNamara & Paul Vaaler, A Management Research Perspective on How and Why Credit Assessors 'Get it Wrong' when Judging Borrowers (undated draft, on file with author) (suggesting that rating-agency models may have failed in part because of systematic biases resulting from behavioral factors).

144 *See* Mian & Sufi, *supra* note 36, at 24-25.

145 *See supra* note 71.

146 *See* Schwarcz, *supra* note 134, at 6 (observing that rating agencies do not, and cannot pragmatically, rate for fraud).

147 One explanation for the erosion of diversification is the growth of synthetics. *See infra* note 145.

148 *See also* Jody Shenn, *Overlapping Subprime Exposure Mask Risks of CDOs, Moody's Says*, BLOOMBERG.COM, Apr. 4, 2007, http://www.bloomberg.com/apps/news?pid=20601170&sid=aszosOrxVmjk&refer=home (reporting that the growth of synthetics in the CDO market has created situations where assets and the synthetic products derived from those assets are in the same CDO, causing the CDO to be exposed to the same risk twice); Bookstaber, *supra* note 35 (discussing this link).

correlation in the subprime mortgage loans backing the different MBS securities. Rating agencies, however, continued to use historical cash-flow models which did not anticipate the degree of price convergence or correlation of subprime loans.[149]

Summary: Rating agencies obviously failed to anticipate the worst-case scenario represented by the subprime meltdown. Although this failure might have resulted in part from conflicts of interest in the way rating agencies are paid, that is unlikely since payment is independent of the rating. Furthermore, the reputational cost of issuing bad ratings usually far exceeds the payment received. In any event, there is no easy solution to the dilemma of how rating agencies can be paid without creating conflicts with either issuers or investors.

A more likely explanation for the failure is that ratings are judgment calls by human beings, and mistakes inevitably will be made.[150] One might argue that rating agencies should be more conservative, or that government should mandate more conservative ratings, but overprotection itself has a cost. If rating agencies had used more conservative models requiring greater overcollateralization, those models would have been decried as wasteful if housing prices had not collapsed.

Whatever the reasons for the failure by rating agencies to anticipate the downgrades, it should be noted that rating agencies may not be perfect but the *idea* of rating agencies is important. Individual investors face relatively high costs to assess the creditworthiness of complex securities. Rating agencies can make this assessment on behalf of many individual investors, thereby achieving an economy of scale.[151]

CONCLUSION

This Essay has suggested various insights into protecting financial markets. Additional insight can be gained by recognizing that most of the causes of the anomalies and failures can be divided into three categories: (i) conflicts; (ii) complacency; or (iii) complexity.[152]

---

[149] *See The Role of Credit Rating Agencies in the Structured Finance Market: Hearing Before the Subcomm. on Capital Markets, Insurance and Government Sponsored Enterprises of the H. Comm. on Financial Servs.*, 110th Cong. 63 (2007) (statement of Mark Adelson, Member, Adelson & Jacob Consulting, LLC). Another possible hypothesis is that there has been rating-agency "grade inflation." *See* Charles W. Calomiris, Am. Enter. Inst. for Pub. Policy Research, Not (Yet) a 'Minsky Moment' 18 (2007), http://www.aei.org/doclib/20071010_Not(Yet)AMinskyMoment.pdf ("Grade inflation has been concentrated particularly in securitized products, where the demand is especially driven by regulated intermediaries."). However, even if there was grade inflation, the consequences are unclear since investors were probably not misled but simply did not care so long as the securities purchased were in fact rated investment grade.

[150] *Cf.* Standard & Poor's, *S&P Announces New Actions to Strengthen the Ratings Process*, Credit Wk., Feb. 13, 2008, at 12 (proposing various procedural review steps to minimize human failure in the ratings process and to increase the efficiency of, and public confidence in, credit ratings).

[151] *See supra* note 43.

[152] I am grateful to Professor Jonathan Lipson for suggesting these categories.

The first category, conflicts, is the most tractable. Once identified, conflicts can often be managed. For example, this Essay has shown that the excesses of the originate-and-distribute model can be managed by aligning the interests of mortgage lenders and investors by requiring the former to retain a risk of loss. Some conflicts, though, may be harder to manage in practice, such as conflicts in how rating agencies are paid.

The second category, complacency, is less tractable because solutions to complacent behavior can require changing human nature, an obviously impossible task. After a crisis, everyone focuses on avoiding that crisis in the future (though hopefully also avoiding the all-too-human tendency to fall into the rut of fighting the "last war"[153]). But bounded rationality makes investors forget such crises with alacrity.[154]

The subprime mortgage crisis appears to have discredited, though, at least one form of complacency: widespread investor obsession with securities that have no established market and, instead, are valued by being marked-to-model.

Other forms of complacency are rational and can only be addressed through structural changes. For example, investors will almost certainly continue to over-rely on rating-agency ratings, so long as the cost of making independent credit investigations remains high. If rating agencies continue to provide unreliable ratings, perhaps investors should consider whether innovative collective-action approaches, such as collective credit determinations by groups of investors, might prove more reliable.[155]

The third category, complexity, is least tractable.[156] Complexity can deprive investors and other market participants of the information needed for markets to operate effectively. It was responsible for the failure of disclosure in the subprime crisis. Even beyond disclosure, complexity is increasingly a metaphor for the modern financial system and its potential for failure, illustrated further by the tight coupling that causes markets to move rapidly into a crisis mode; the potential convergence in quantitatively-constructed investment strategies; the layers inserted between obligors on loans and other financial assets and the assets' beneficial owners, which make it difficult to work out underlying defaults;[157] and the problem of adverse selection, in which investors, uncertain which investments or counterparties are sound, begin to shun all investments. Solving problems of financial complexity may well be the ultimate twenty-first century market goal.[158]

---

[153] *Systemic Risk Hearing*, *supra* note 2, at 27 (statement of Steven L. Schwarcz, Stanley A. Star Professor of Law and Business, Duke University).

[154] *Cf. supra* note 51 and accompanying text (observing that investors quickly forget past financial crises and "go for the gold").

[155] Collective approaches, though, might face potential antitrust hurdles.

[156] *Cf.* Michael Mandel, *The Economy's Safety Valve*, BUS. WK., Oct. 22, 2007, at 36 ("In today's complex and globally integrated financial markets, it's almost impossible for regulators to plug every hole").

[157] *See, e.g.*, Hirsch, *supra* note 102 (observing that, because of these layers, the "instruments were so complex that no one followed the trail").

[158] *See, e.g.*, Steven L. Schwarcz, "Complexity as a Catalyst of Market Failure: A Law and Engineering Inquiry," unpublished manuscript on file with author, *available at* http://papers.ssrn.com/sol3/papers.cfm?abstract_id=1240863.

These categories are broad, but they do not capture everything. One might propose, for example, a fourth category: cupidity. Greed, however, is so ingrained in human nature and so intertwined with the other categories that it adds little insight to view it as a separate category.

These categories also do not capture the problem of systemic risk, whose uniqueness arises from a type of tragedy of the commons. Because the benefits of exploiting finite capital resources accrue to individual market participants whereas the costs of exploitation are distributed among an even wider class of persons, market participants have insufficient incentive to internalize their externalities. Government, however, can provide solutions, such as creating a market liquidity provider of last resort to purchase securities in collapsing markets (albeit at profitable discounts to minimize moral hazard) in order to mitigate market instability that would lead to systemic collapse.[159]

A final possible inquiry is to ask whether periodic financial market instabilities are harmful or, in the long run, possibly helpful to the economy. For example, perhaps the subprime financial crisis, or something like it, was needed to turn around the incentive-distorting liquidity glut of the past few years.[160] Financial market instabilities are believed to be acceptable if they are "relatively limited in scope," even if deep in their narrow impact.[161] Indeed, such instabilities "may serve as critical safety valves."[162] There are, however, two concerns. On a distributional level, market instabilities impact people, and in the subprime crisis many of those affected have been "low-income" individuals.[163] On a more fundamental level, there is "no guarantee that the next crisis won't spread and turn into the Big One, which undermines the whole financial system."[164]

---

[159] *See* Schwarcz, *supra* note 68, at pt. III.D.

[160] *Cf.* Balakrishnan et al., *supra* note 72, at 8 (discussing the liquidity glut).

[161] Mandel, *supra* note 156, at 34.

[162] *Id.*

[163] *Id.* at 36-37. That many of the affected individuals have been "low-income" individuals does not conflict with this Essay's earlier observation that QIBs are the investors who lost the most money in the subprime crisis. *See supra* text accompanying note 64. Low-income individuals lost money not as investors but as foreclosed homeowners.

[164] *Id.* at 37; *see also* Vikas Bajaj & Louise Story, *Mortgage Crisis Spreads Beyond Subprime Loans*, N.Y. TIMES, Feb. 12, 2008, at A1 (discussing the spread of the subprime crisis to other markets); *cf.* Michael D. Bordo et al., *Real Versus Pseudo-International Systemic Risk: Some Lessons from History* 10 (Nat'l Bureau of Econ. Research, Working Paper No. 5371, 1995), *available at* http://www.nber.org/papers/w5371.pdf (discussing how normal market expansions and contractions can turn into market crises in situations of "speculative mania").

Lessons from the Subprime Meltdown[*]

L. Randall Wray[**]

PART I: THE MINSKY MOMENT: CROSSING THE RUBICON

> *Over a protracted period of good times, capitalist economies tend to move from a financial structure dominated by hedge finance units to a structure in which there is a large weight to units engaged in speculative and Ponzi finance.* (Minsky 1992.)

Many recent writings on the subprime meltdown have referred to the work of the late Hyman Minsky, probably the most astute observer of the financial system of the past century. Some have even called the current situation a "Minsky moment" (Whalen 2007, Magnus 2007). This paper will argue that these commentators are correct—Minsky's writings can shed a lot of light on the current problems. However, most have not delved deeply enough into Minsky's insights. Indeed, exactly twenty years ago, Minsky wrote a prescient piece on securitization that can help us to analyze the evolution of financial markets that brought us to the present crisis.

Minsky always insisted that there are two essential propositions of his "financial instability hypothesis." The first is that there are two financing "regimes"—one that is consistent with stability and the other in which the economy is subject to instability. The second proposition is that "stability is destabilizing," so that endogenous processes will tend to move a stable system toward fragility. While Minsky is best known for his analysis of the downturn and crisis, he argued that the strongest force in a modern capitalist economy operates in the other direction—toward an unconstrained speculative boom. The current crisis is a natural outcome of these processes—an unsustainable explosion of real estate prices, mortgage debt and leveraged positions in collateralized securities. Unlike some popular explanations of the causes of the meltdown, Minsky

---

* From *Challenge*, vol. 51, no. 2 (March-April 2008): 40-68.

** Professor of Economics at the University of Missouri–Kansas City. The author thanks Yeva Nersisyan for research assistance and for producing all of the figures.

would not blame "irrational exuberance" or "manias" or "bubbles." Those who had been caught up in the boom behaved "rationally," at least according to the "model of the model" they had developed to guide their behavior. That model included the prospective course of asset prices, future income, behavior of policy-makers, and ability to hedge or shift risks onto others. It is only in retrospect that we can see the boom for what it was—mass delusion propagated in part by policy makers and those with vested interests who should have known better. However, a large part of the blame must be laid on the relative stability experienced over the past couple of decades—even if that is a rather unsatisfying place to lay blame, as no one would have preferred greater instability in order to avoid the current "Minsky moment." But the tranquility that made the boom possible also brought us to the current unstable situation.

The question that Minsky would ask is whether the current environment is one conducive to "it" happening again—that is, whether we are likely to fall into a debt deflation process that results in a great depression. It is likely that the current regulatory system with a "big government" and "big bank" will be sufficient to contain the repercussions. However, given the substantial human, social, and economic costs of a Fisher-type snowball of defaults, it is worth considering policy that might constrain the impulse toward asset price deflation. Further, it is time to rethink the New Deal reforms to create new institutional constraints to prevent "it" from happening again. This paper will conclude with some general recommendations for directions that policy might take.

1. Origins of the Crisis

> *What was recently seen as "creative" and "innovative" democratization of credit is now viewed as misguided and culpable bungling or worse.* Alex Pollock, Testimony before the Subcommittee on Financial Institutions and Consumer Credit, Committee on Financial Services, U.S. House of Representatives, Hearing on Subprime and Predatory Lending, March 27, 2007.
>
> *Sentiment just keeps getting more and more bleak. This week it's been all about fear overtaking greed.* James W Paulson, quoted in Michael M. Grynbaum, Stocks Plummet on "Ugly Week" for Investors, NEW YORK TIMES, November 22, 2007.

Irrational exuberance? No, the seeds of the current mortgage crisis were sown in the 1951 Treasury-Fed "Accord" that freed the central bank from its commitment to keep interest rates low. Henceforth, the Fed could use interest rate hikes to reduce perceived inflation pressures. Fortunately, rate hikes were relatively moderate and short-lived for the following two decades. Each rate hike caused problems in the commercial banking and thrift sectors because they were subject to Regulation Q interest rate ceilings, thus suffered "disintermediation" (deposit withdrawals) when market rates rose above legislated deposit rates. At the same time, usury laws throughout the nation also placed ceilings on lending rates, so the Fed could engineer "credit crunches" by pushing market rates toward the maximum permitted. In addition, other rules and regulations that dated to the New Deal financial reforms also constrained practice in an attempt to preserve safety and soundness. However, as Minsky argued long ago, financial institutions responded to each tight money episode by innovating, creating new practices and instruments that would evade constraints to make the supply of credit more elastic. In this manner, as time passed, the upside tendency toward speculative booms became ever more difficult to attenuate.

In addition, the Fed and elected policy makers gradually relaxed constraints, often in response to private initiative. New practices were validated and sometimes even encouraged to allow heavily regulated banks and thrifts to compete with lightly controlled markets. Thrift ownership rules were relaxed in the early 1970s, opening the way to the abuses that decimated the whole industry in the 1980s. The development of secondary markets in mortgages in the early 1980s was a reaction to the high interest rate monetarist experiment used by Volcker to fight stagflation. The Glass Steagall act that had separated commercial and investment banking was repealed in 1999, allowing commercial banks to engage in a wider range of practices so that they could better compete with their relatively unregulated Wall Street competitors. As Kregel (2007a) notes, in 1999 Congress approved the Gramm-Leach-Bliley Bank Reform Act, according to which "banks of all sizes gained the ability to engage in a much wider range of financial activities and to provide a full range of products and services without regulatory restraint"[1] (Kregel 2007a). As Minsky argued, at each step, deregulation allowed increasingly risky innovations that made the system more vulnerable.

Finally, it must be emphasized that deregulation and legal recognition of new practices were not, by themselves, sufficient to bring us to the present precipice. If these innovations had led to excessively risky behavior that generated huge losses, financial institutions would have been reluctant to retain them. As Minsky always argued, by preventing "it" (a debt deflation on the order of the 1930s collapse) from happening again, new practices and instruments were validated. The remarkable thing about the post-war period is the absence of depressions. While recessions occur with regularity, they are constrained; while financial crises arise from time-to-time, the fall-out is contained. This is due in part to the various reforms that date to the New Deal, but also

---

[1] According to Kregel (2007a), the Gramm-Leach-Bliley Bank Reform Act

- allowed banks to expand the range of their activities into areas previously preserved for investment banks, and allowed investment banks to expand their "commercial" banking activities.
- amended the Bank Holding Company Act of 1956 to permit the holding company owners of commercial banks to engage in any type of financial activity.
- allowed banks to own subsidiaries engaged in financial activities that were off-limits to commercial banks.

These changes allowed Countrywide Financial Corporation to own: a bank (overseen by the OTS); a broker-dealer trading US government securities and mortgage-backed securities; a mortgage servicing firm; a real estate closing services company; an insurance company; and three special-purpose vehicles to issue short-term commercial paper backed by Countrywide mortgages (Kregel 2007a).

to countercyclical movement of the "Big Government" budget, to lender of last resort activity of the "Big Bank" Fed, and to periodic bail-outs arranged by the Fed, by the government sponsored enterprises (GSEs), or by Congress.

In other words, irrational exuberance is just the end result of long-term policy-induced, and in turn policy-validated, financial innovations that stretched liquidity and enabled prices of real estate and of equity to reach unjustified and unsustainable levels. Blaming the "bubble" for the current crisis is rather like blaming the car for an accident—when we ought to take a good long look at the driver, and at the bartender who kept the whiskey flowing all evening before helping the drunk to his car after last call. To be sure, there isn't anything necessarily wrong with driving or with drinking, but separation of functions can be prudent. Further, the bartender bears some responsibility for maintaining that separation. Unfortunately, those in charge of the financial system have for a very long time encouraged a blurring of the functions, mixing drinking and driving while arguing that the invisible hand guided by self interest can keep the car on course. The current wreck is a predictable result.

2. Securitization

That which can be securitized will be securitized.

Securitization lowers the weight of that part of the financing structure which the Central Bank (Federal Reserve in the United States) is committed to protect.

The investment banker hires "econometricians" or financial economists to demonstrate that the risks of default on interest and principle of some class of the securities it proposes to issue are so small that these instruments deserve to have an investment rating that implies a low interest rate. Hyman Minsky, "Memo on Securitization," 1987.

Modern securitization of home mortgages began in the early 1980s, although as Robert Kuttner (2007) argues, securitized loans played a major role in the 1920s speculation that helped to bring on the 1930s collapse.[2] While securitization is usually presented as a technological innovation that came out of private sector initiative to spread risk, in reality—as Minsky (1987) argued—it was a response to policy initiated by Chairman Volcker in 1979. (See also Kuttner 2007.) This was the infamous experiment in monetarism, during which the Fed purportedly targeted money growth to fight inflation. The fed funds rate was pushed above 20% in full recognition that this would kill the

[2] Lewis Ranieri at Salomon Brothers is credited with the creation of mortgage securities, bundling mortgages and issuing bonds with the mortgages serving as collateral and providing interest to pay the bond holders. Wall Street later began to divide the packages of mortgages into tranches, with holders of the safest tranches paid first, and with the holders of the riskiest tranches the last to be paid. In recent years, the search for higher returns drove the demand for the riskiest tranches as well as for riskier mortgage pools, such as securitized subprimes.

thrift industry—which was stuck with a portfolio of fixed rate mortgages paying as little as 6% (Wray 1994). The whole industry had been constructed in the aftermath of the Great Depression on the promise that short term rates would be kept low so that the "three-six-three" business model (pay 3% on deposits, earn 6% on mortgages, and hit the golf course at 3 p.m.) would profit while offering safe repositories for deposits and keeping homeownership affordable for most families. In the new policy regime, however, no financial institution could afford to be stuck with long-term fixed-rate mortgages. Hence, regulators and supervisors "freed" the savings and loans to pursue higher return, and riskier, activities—with quite predictable consequences.

There is no need to recount the sordid details of that fiasco. (Wray 1994; Black 2005.) However, the long-term consequence was the recognition that the mortgage "market" had to change. In the beginning, it was the safer, conforming, loan that was securitized. Indeed, in the early 1990s there was widespread fear that the trend to securitization would leave behind low income, minority, and female borrowers. With lower credit scores, and with housing in less desirable neighborhoods, these borrowers would not meet the standards required by markets for packaged mortgages. Minsky (1987) was one of the few commentators who understood the true potential of securitization, however. In principle, all mortgages could be packaged into a variety of risk classes, with differential pricing to cover risk. Investors could choose the desired risk-return trade-off. Thrifts and other regulated financial institutions would earn fee income for loan origination, for assessing risk, and for servicing the mortgages. Wall Street would place the collateralized debt obligations (CDOs), slicing and dicing to suit the needs of investors. Far from excluding borrowers of moderate means, securitization contributed to an apparent democratization of access to credit, as homeownership rates rose to record levels over the coming decades.

Minsky (1987) argued that securitization reflected two additional developments. First, it was part and parcel of the globalization of finance, as securitization creates financial paper that is freed from national boundaries. German investors with no direct access to America's homeowners could buy a piece of the action in U.S. real estate markets. As Minsky was fond of pointing out, the unparalleled post-WWII depression-free expansion in the developed world (and even in much of the developing world) has created a global glut of managed money seeking returns. Packaged securities with risk weightings assigned by respected rating agencies were appealing for global investors trying to achieve the desired proportion of dollar-denominated assets. It would be no surprise to Minsky to find that the value of securitized American mortgages now exceeds the value of the market for federal government debt. The subprime problems thus quickly spread around the world—from a German bank (IKB) that required a bailout in July, to problems in BNP Paribas (France's biggest bank), and to a run on Northern Rock in the UK. Not even the central bank of China can escape losses!

The second development assessed by Minsky is the relative decline of the importance of banks (narrowly defined as financial institutions that accept deposits and make loans) in favor of "markets." (The bank share of all financial assets fell from around 50% in the 1950s to around 25% in the 1990s (Kregel 2007a). This development, itself, was encouraged by the experiment in monetarism (that decimated the regulated portion of the sector in favor of the relatively unregulated "markets"), but it was also spurred by continual erosion of the portion of the financial sphere that had been allocated by rules, regulations, and tradition to banks. The growth of competition on both sides of banking business—checkable deposits at non-bank financial institutions that could pay market interest rates; and rise of the commercial paper market that allowed firms to bypass commercial banks—squeezed the profitability of banking. Minsky (1987) observed that banks appear to require a spread of about 450 basis points between interest rates earned on assets less that paid on liabilities. This covers the normal rate of return on capital, plus the required reserve "tax" imposed on banks (reserves are non-earning assets), and the costs of servicing customers. By contrast, financial markets can operate with much lower spreads precisely because they are exempt from required reserve ratios, regulated capital requirements, and much of the costs of relationship banking.

To restore profitability in the aftermath of monetarism, banks and thrifts would earn fee income for loan origination, but by moving the mortgages off their books, they could escape reserve and capital requirements. They might continue to service the mortgages, earning additional fees. Investment banks would purchase the mortgages, securitize them, and sell them to investors. As Minsky (1987) argued, investment banks would pay ratings agencies to provide favorable ratings, and hire economists to develop models to demonstrate that interest earnings would more than compensate for risks. Later, Wall Street bankers would add other "credit enhancements" to the securities, such as large penalties for early payment and buy-back guarantees in the event of capital losses due to unexpectedly high delinquencies and foreclosures. As Minsky frequently said, the trick is to convince AAA borrowers to accept the terms appropriate to BBB borrowers, ensuring more than adequate returns to service the securities (the corollary is that profits can also be increased by convincing investors in lower-grade securities that the underlying BBB mortgages are just as safe as AAA mortgages—which is what the modelers were paid to do). However, Minsky was also quick to add that, for many borrowers there is no interest rate that can compensate for risk, because the higher the interest rate charged, the greater the probability of default. For example, an appropriate spread for a BBB-borrower might be 400 basis points higher than that for the highest rated borrower; however, at the higher monthly payments required, that borrower would be sure to default, so that no premium could compensate for the expected loss.

The problem is that the incentive structure in which mortgage originators operated generated conditions sure to create problems. In the aftermath of the equity market crash, investors looked for alternative sources of profits. Low interest rate policy by Greenspan's Fed meant that traditional money markets could not offer adequate returns. Investors lusted for higher risks, and mortgage originators offered subprimes and other "affordability products" with ever lower underwriting standards. Brokers were richly rewarded for inducing borrowers to accept unfavorable terms, which increased the value of the securities. New and risky types of mortgages—hybrid ARMs (called "2/28" and "3/27") that offered low teaser rates for two or three years, with very high reset rates, were pushed.[3] As originators would not hold the mortgages, there was little reason to worry about ability to pay. Indeed, since banks, thrifts, and mortgage brokers relied on fee income, rather than interest, their incentive was to increase through-put, originating as many mortgages as possible. By design, these "affordability products" were not affordable—at the time of reset, the homeowner would need to refinance, generating early payment penalties and more fees for originators, securitizers, holders of securities, and all others in the home finance food chain. Risk raters essentially served as credit enhancers, certifying that prospective defaults on subprimes would be little different from those on conventional mortgages—so that the subprime-backed securities could receive the investment-grade rating required so that insurance funds and pension funds could buy them. Chairman Greenspan gave the maestro seal of approval to the practice, urging homebuyers to take on adjustable rate debt. Ironically, this shift to "markets" reduced the portion of the financial structure that the Fed is committed to regulate, supervise, and protect—something that was celebrated rather than feared. The fate of homeowners was sealed by bankruptcy "reform" that makes it virtually impossible to get out of mortgage debt—a very nice "credit enhancement."[4]

One other credit enhancement played an essential role—mortgage insurance and the ABX index. Some of the subprime loans are covered by mortgage insurance; more importantly, insurance was sold on the securities themselves. Such insurers include MBIA of Armonk, NY (the world's largest insurer), AMBAC, FGIC Corp., and CFIG. The health of the insurers, in turn, is assessed by the ratings agencies (Moody's, Fitch) as well as by the ABX subprime index that tracks the cost of insuring against defaults on subprime securities. This index includes 20 asset-backed bonds with a low investment grade credit rating. If it declines, the cost of insurance rises. We will return to recent developments in the insurance market for subprimes below. However, it must be

---

[3] According to an analysis of $2.5 trillion worth of subprime loans performed for the *Wall Street Journal*, most of those who obtained subprime loans would have qualified for better terms. For example, in 2005, 55% and, in 2006, 61% of subprime borrowers had credit scores high enough to obtain conventional loans. Because brokers were rewarded for persuading borrowers to take on higher interest rates than those they qualified for, there was strong pressure to avoid conventional loans with lower rates. For example, at New Century Financial Corporation, "brokers could earn a 'yield spread premium' equal to 2% of the loan amount—or $8,000 on a $400,000 loan—if a borrower's interest rate was an extra 1.25 percentage points higher" (Brooks and Simon 2007). According to New Century's rate sheet, spreads for similar borrowers with similar loans depended on documentation, with "full docs" typically paying interest rates 60 to well over 100 basis points less than "stated docs"—even with the same high credit scores. (Rate sheet available at http://online.wsj.com/public/resources/documents/tretroSubPrimel107.html, accessed 12/31/2007.) This may also explain why brokers accepted little documentation from borrowers.

[4] However, in a ruling that has sent shockwaves through mortgage securities market, a federal judge in Ohio has thrown out 14 foreclosure cases, ruling that mortgage investors had failed to prove they actually owned the properties they were trying to seize (Morgenson 2007c). Because the securities are so complex, and documentation lax, the judge found their claims to the properties weak. Josh Rosner, a mortgage securities specialist said, "This is the miracle of not having securities mapped to the underlying loans. There is no repository for mortgage loans. I have heard of instances where the same loan is in two or three pools" (Morgenson 2007c). It is possible that this can prove to be one of the weak links in the slice-and-dice securities market.

noted that without affordable insurance, and without high credit ratings for the insurers themselves, the market for pools of mortgages would have been limited. As Richard and Gutscher (2007) write, "For more than 20 years, the safety of insurance has eased the way for elementary schools, Wall Street banks, and thousands of municipalities to sell debt with unquestioned credit quality." As the real estate market boomed, insurers "increased their guarantees of securities created from mortgages, including subprime loans to people with poor credit and home-equity loans" (Richard and Gutscher 2007). Insurers now guarantee $100 billion of securitized subprime mortgages—and many hundreds of billions of other bonds. For example, AMBAC guarantees more than half a trillion dollars worth of securities, and MBIA backs $652 billion of municipal and structured finance bonds. Insurance allowed the debts to gain the highest ratings—ensuring a deep market and low interest rate spreads (Richard and Gutscher 2007).

The combination of incentives to increase throughput, plus credit enhancements led to virtually no reluctance to purchase securities with the riskiest underlying debts. Ironically, while relationship banking had based loans on the relevant characteristics of the borrower (such as income, credit history, assets), the new arrangements appeared to offer a nearly infinite supply of impersonal mortgage credit with no need to evaluate borrower ability to repay. Instead, "quant models" based on historical data regarding default rates of purportedly similar borrowers would replace costly relationship banking, enhancing efficiencies and narrowing interest rate spreads (Kregel 2007b).

Markets responded in a manner that should have been anticipated. The subprime market bloomed, with increasingly risky instruments and practices. "Low doc" loans (less documentation required) evolved to "no docs" and to "liar loans" (borrowers were allowed and even encouraged to lie about income and other information relevant to the application process), and finally to "Ninja loans" (no income, no job, no assets). Risky mortgages were pooled and sliced into a variety of tranches to meet the risk-return profile desired by investors. Senior tranches would be paid first—if borrowers were able to service any part of the mortgage, the senior securities holders would receive income, making it appear that a security backed by exceedingly risky mortgages was actually quite safe. More junior, non-investment grade, tranches could be sold to hedge funds that would receive payments only if the senior securities were fully serviced. Because the historical experience of securities backed by nonconforming loans was very short, and because it (necessarily) coincided with an era of rapidly rising home prices, rating agencies felt justified in assigning low default probabilities on low docs, no docs, and NINJAs—warranting good prices for even the junior tranches. A nice virtuous cycle was created: such innovations expanded the supply of loans, fueled homebuying and drove up the value of real estate, which increased the size of loans required and justified rising leverage ratios (loan-to-value and loan-to-income) since homes could always be refinanced or sold later at higher prices if problems developed. The combination of low interest rates and rising real estate prices encouraged a speculative frenzy that would end only if rates rose or prices stopped rising. Of course, both events were inevitable, indeed, were dynamically linked because Fed rate hikes would slow speculation, attenuating rising property values and increasing risk spreads.

In sum, by 2000, the nature of the real estate finance market had changed in a fundamental manner so that it would evolve toward fragility. In the "old days" of the three-six-three model described above, banks and thrifts financed their positions in mortgages through their retail deposit liabilities. In principle, this exposed them to a maturity mismatch as deposits were short term while mortgages were long term. However, in practice, deposit withdrawals were relatively predictable so long as deposit insurance prevented bank runs, and so long as the Fed kept its interest rate target below legislated ceilings (Regulation Q) on deposit rates. Most withdrawals from one bank or thrift would end up in another bank or thrift, so an institution that faced a clearing drain could turn to the overnight interbank lending market (fed funds) to borrow reserves. Banks also had access to the discount window, while thrifts could turn to the Federal Home Loan Banks for funds. In this way, liquidity needs were met so that the "leverage ratio" of bank and thrift positions in loans was effectively one-to-one.[5] Growth rates of these institutions would be limited because any bank or thrift that tried to grow too fast would face a clearing drain—forcing it to borrow reserves (relatively more costly than cheap retail deposit sources of funds). Further, a credit crunch was caused whenever the Fed pushed the overnight rate target above Reg Q ceilings, causing "disintermediation" as depositors sought higher market returns. For these reasons, a runaway speculative boom in real estate was unlikely because financing was constrained by the institutional structure as well as by Fed countercyclical interest rate policy.

The Fed's experiment with monetarism from 1979-82 created both liquidity problems as well as solvency problems by raising interest rates (higher than 20%) far above Reg Q ceilings and far above earnings on mortgages. As discussed above, the long-term response was to move mortgages off bank and thrift balance sheets. In addition, Reg Q ceilings were eliminated, and new types of deposits such as large denomination negotiable CDs that paid market rates were created.[6] This freed banks and thrifts from local sources of retail deposits as they could always issue an essentially unlimited volume of CDs in national (and international "Eurodollar") wholesale markets. This also allowed them to grow at any desired rate—limited only by their ability to locate borrowers and their stomach for risk. This is why many thrifts were able to grow at annual rates of 1000% (and more) in the days leading up to the thrift crisis (Wray 1994). Finally, the expansion of the wholesale market in financial institution liabilities reintroduced the specter of runs on banks—manifested not by long lines of depositors trying to withdraw funds,

---

[5] While it is common to measure leverage ratios as the ratio of assets to equity (since losses on assets must come out of equity), the argument here is that, in an environment in which home mortgages are safe assets and in which positions in these assets are financed by issuing very stable retail deposits, the relevant measure is the ratio of mortgages to retail deposits. However, as discussed, the liquidity of these positions requires a stable interest rate environment, deposit insurance, and access to funds from the Fed or FHLB.

[6] See Wray 1994 for a discussion of the deregulations in the 1970s and 1980s, including the Monetary Control Act of 1980, which phased out interest rate ceilings, raised deposit insurance limits so that "hot money" jumbo CDs (issued in $100,000 denominations) were covered, overrode usury laws, and allowed thrifts to buy riskier assets.

but by runs on uninsured jumbo CDs. Thus, these developments encouraged behavior that simultaneously led to solvency issues *and* to liquidity problems—neither of which had been faced by regulated banks and thrifts on a large scale in the first three decades after the New Deal reforms.

The growth of securitization led to a tremendous increase of leverage ratios. While the "old model" of home finance involved a leverage ratio of one, the "new model" relies on leverage ratios of 15-to-1 and more, with the owners (for example, hedge funds and pension funds) putting up very little of their own money while issuing potentially volatile commercial paper or other liabilities to fund positions in the securitized mortgages.[7] This worked fine so long as the securities were deemed safe and liquid, which also ensured that the commercial paper and other liabilities issued to finance their purchase were safe and liquid. However, when losses on subprimes began to exceed expectations that had been based on historical experience, prices of securities began to fall. With big leverage ratios, owners faced huge losses, and began to deleverage by selling, putting more downward pressure on prices. Note that in a world of 15-to-1 leverage ratios, reducing exposure means that many multiples of CDOs relative to own funds must be sold (if equity is $1 billion, to reduce exposure by half requires sales of $7.5 billion if leverage is 15-to-1).The market for securitized mortgages dried up, as did the market for commercial paper.

Modeling by the Bank of England shows that a hypothetical portfolio of subprime mortgage credit default swaps (composed of AAA and AA subprime mortgages originated in 2006) lost 60% of value in July 2007 (Band of England 2007).

> These losses in RMBS [residential mortgage-backed securities] seemed to trigger a wider loss of confidence in all structured credit products and rating agencies' valuation models. A vicious spiral appeared to begin in which heightened uncertainty about the future value of complex assets and rising risk aversion caused many investors to want to sell but few to buy. Prices fell well outside the range of historical experience and in some cases there appeared to be no market-clearing price for some assets. Investors who had mistakenly made inferences about market and liquidity risk from credit ratings incurred large unexpected losses, contributing to further pressure to sell. (Bank of England 2007.)

Problems spread to other markets, including money market mutual funds and commercial paper markets, and banks became reluctant to lend even for short periods.

---

[7] As Chancellor (2007) reports, modern risk management techniques use historical volatility as a proxy for risk. As volatility falls, risk is presumed to fall, which induces managers to increase leverage ratios. As discussed in the next section, the period of "the great moderation" suggested that volatility would be permanently lower, hence, higher leverage ratios were deemed prudent. Chancellor reports research that indicates a hedge fund with only $10 million of its own funds could leverage that up to $850 million of collateralized mortgage obligations—a leverage ratio of 85 to 1.

By August, new issues of CDOs had fallen to one-sixth the average monthly volume experienced previously in 2007.

The "old" three-six-three home finance model worked only so long as policy acquiesced, and it failed when policy embarked on a risky Monetarist experiment. The new "originate and distribute" (as it is termed by the Bank of England) model is much less subject to control by policy, and is also less amenable to assistance when things go bad. Most of the players and activities are outside the traditional and direct control of the monetary authorities (including the Fed, the Comptroller, and the FDIC). Instead of a closely regulated industry, home finance has become a mostly unsupervised, highly leveraged, speculative activity—subject to fickle market expectations that are loosely grounded in highly complex valuation models based on relatively short historical runs. As Bank of England simulations show, the expected returns on asset backed securities are "highly sensitive to assumptions about default probability and correlation and rates of loss in the event of default" (Bank of England 2007). When confidence was shaken, prices swung widely, far outside the range of historical experience used in the quant models—and credit dried up. Other than standing by to act as lenders of last resort, there was not much that central bankers around the world could do. However, most of the players do not have direct access to the central bank, but rather rely on complex networks of back-up lines of credit, recourse, and hedges that represent at best contingent and multi-layered leveraging of bank access to central bank funding.

The problems would be sufficiently severe if they amounted to nothing more than a liquidity shortage. In that case, central bank lender of last resort operations could eventually settle markets, allowing prices to settle and interest rate spreads to narrow. However, as Kregel (2007a) argues, Ninja loans (as well as many of the low doc, no doc, and liar loans) are by definition Minsky's Ponzi schemes, in which payment commitments exceed income.[8] Interest must be capitalized into the loans until some point in the future when income rises or the house's price rises sufficiently that it can be sold to retire the loan. In an environment of slow or no growth of income for most Americans, it is clear that much of the financial structure depended on continued real estate appreciation to validate it—an inherently fragile situation. According to Kregel (2007b), even the senior tranches of many of the subprime mortgage pools have zero net present value because the borrowers will not be able to service the loans after interest rates reset. If the home finance structure is speculative and Ponzi, the problem is solvency, not simply liquidity. Yet, except for a few naysayers, most "experts" discounted the risks, arguing that real estate is not overvalued and debtors are not overburdened—until Countrywide floundered and problems snowballed across the country and around the world.

In the next section, we examine some reasons for the complacency.

[8] Others who have used Minsky's analysis of Ponzi positions to characterize the current situation include Buttonwood (2007), McCulley (2007; see also his earlier 2001 warning), Ash (2007), Magnus (2007), and Lahart (2007).

3. The Great Moderation—What, Me Worry?

> *At particular times a great deal of stupid people have a great deal of stupid money . . . At intervals . . . the money of these people—the blind capital, as we call it, of the country—is particularly large and craving; it seeks for someone to devour it, and there is a "plethora"; it finds someone, and there is "speculation"; it is devoured, and there is "panic."* Walter Bagehot, *Lombard Street,* quoted in Martin Wolf (2007).

> *New-Deal era has become a term of abuse. Who needs New Deal protections in the Internet age?* Robert Kuttner (2007).[9]

> *Financial markets, and particularly the big players within them, need fear. Without it, they go crazy.* Martin Wolf (2007).

In the last few years, a revised view of economic possibilities has been developed that goes by the name "the great moderation" (Bernanke 2004; Chancellor 2007). The belief is that due to a happy confluence of a number of factors, the world is now more stable. These factors include:

- Better monetary management by the world's major central banks that has dampened inflation and business cycle swings;
- Globalization that makes it easier to absorb shocks because effects are spread;
- Improvements in information technology that allow for better risk assessment and for timely communication;
- Rising profits and declining corporate leverage ratios that allow for higher equity prices;
- Securitization that enhances risk management, and allocates it to those better able to bear the risks; and
- Derivatives that can be used to hedge undesired risk.

Taken together, all of this implies that we live in a new economy that is far less vulnerable to "shocks." Further, central banks have demonstrated both a willingness and a capacity to quickly deal with, and to isolate, threats to the financial system. For example, according to conventional views, Chairman Greenspan was able to organize a successful response to the LTCM [Long Term Capital Management] crisis, and later rapidly lowered interest rates to steer the economy out of recession that was triggered by the equity market tumble. In the current period, Chairman Bernanke is supposed to have continued in the Greenspan tradition by responding to the subprime crisis by

[9] It is important to note that Kuttner's statement is his characterization of prevailing wisdom, not his belief.

"pumping liquidity"[10] into markets, by quickly lowering the fed funds rate, by taking some of the frown costs out of discount window borrowing—as a few of the major banks were induced to borrow unnecessary funds—and by lowering the penalty on such borrowing as the spread between the fed funds rate and the discount rate was lowered. Even as energy and food prices have pushed inflation up, the Fed made it clear that it remains on guard against any residual fall-out from mortgage losses. Thus, even after hints of problems during the summer of 2007, a carefully crafted conventional wisdom was created that a) any real estate mess will be contained, b) that house prices will recover sooner rather than later, and c) that impacts on the "real" economy will be small. Therefore, the stock market could safely continue to party like it is 1929; interest rate spreads could narrow because even the riskiest bets are relatively safe; income, down payments, loan-to-value ratios, and other conventional measures of ability to service debt didn't matter much because real estate asset price appreciation will make all bets good.

If Minsky were here, he would label this "A Radical Suspension of Disbelief"

As Alex Pollock testified before the US House of Representatives (Pollock 2007), "Booms are usually accompanied by a plausible theory about how we are in a 'new era' . . . . It is first success, and observing other people's success, which builds up the optimism, which creates the boom, which sets up the bust." The "radical suspension of disbelief" that allowed markets to ignore downside potential created "optimism and an euphoric belief in the ever-rising price of some asset class, in this case, houses and condominiums, providing a sure-fire way to make money for both lenders and borrows. They are inevitably followed by a hangover of defaults, failures, dispossession of unwise or unlucky borrowers, revelations of fraud and scandals, and late cycle regulatory and political reactions"[11] (Pollock 2007).

And, indeed, it is beginning to look like deja vu all over again. The 1980s thrift crisis was preceded by a tsunami of "innovations" that increased the supply of credit to every manner of swindle, egged-on not only by relaxed rules and supervision, but even by explicit encouragement of regulators, supervisors, and politicians (and by Alan Greenspan, who wrote a glowing letter in support of Charles Keating's exploits). Property appraisers willing to certify inflated values played a major role in that fiasco (just as they have in the current real estate boom and bust) (Wray 1994). We are still sorting

[10] This term is misleading as it implies that the Fed could simply fly Friedman's helicopters and drop bags of federal reserve notes. Actually, the Fed stood ready to lend reserves at the discount window and to supply them to the fed funds market through bond purchases to keep the fed funds rate on target. If a troubled bank was refused loans in the fed funds market, it could turn to the Fed's discount window to borrow at a penalty rate to meet liquidity needs. To modify a popular old saying, "you can't pump on a string"—the Fed could only supply the reserves desired by the market.

[11] Or, as Charles Kindleberger put it, "The propensity to swindle grows parallel with the propensity to speculate during a boom. The implosion of an asset price bubble always leads to the discovery of fraud and swindles." (Quoted in Pollock 2007.)

out the details of that mess two decades later (Black 2005). Similarly, the bursting of the equity market bubble at the beginning of this decade followed years of improper insider trading, "pump and dump" campaigns, and accounting fraud designed to raise stock prices—matters that will continue to tie up the courts for years to come.

Still, it is possible that we ain't seen nothin' yet. Many of the subprime loans are presumably relatively unencumbered by federal rules and regulations because they were made by mortgage brokers chartered and supervised by states. About half of all subprimes were made by such brokers. However, many states outlaw fraudulent practices, including predatory lending that burdens borrowers with loans they cannot afford. Indeed, it is suspected that part of the reason for the low doc and no doc loans was to give the brokers plausible deniability: they "didn't know" the borrowers couldn't afford the loans because they never collected the documents that would have been required to make the necessary calculations (JEC 2007)! There are also some hints that the Wall Street firms that sold the asset-backed securities were engaged in "pump and dump" strategies similar to those used by Wall Street during the New Economy boom, selling securities that they simultaneously were shorting, as they knew they were "trash."[12]

The players and the markets are intimately and dynamically connected in a way that fuels a growing snowball of problems. As discussed above, insurance on securitized mortgages and other bonds helped to validate high credit ratings assigned by credit raters; other enhancements such as penalties for early repayment, high mortgage rates, and draconian personal bankruptcy rules also helped to fuel the market for subprime-backed securities. However, as the subprime market unravels, fears spread to other asset-backed securities, including commercial real estate loans, and to other bond markets, such as that for municipal bonds. Markets are beginning to recognize that there are systemic problems with the credit ratings assigned by the credit ratings agencies. Further, they are realizing that if mortgage-backed securities, other asset-backed securities, and muni bonds are riskier than previously believed, then the insurers will have greater than expected losses. Ratings agencies are thus downgrading the credit ratings of the insurers. As the financial position of insurers is called into question, the insurance that guaranteed the assets becomes worthless—meaning that the ratings on bonds and securities must be downgraded. In many cases, investment banks have a piece of this action—they have either promised to take back mortgages, and they have assumed (or will do so) the losses of insurers as the lesser of two evils because the costs

---

[12] In a troubling piece, economist and sometime comic Ben Stein castigates Goldman Sachs, "whose alums are routinely Treasury secretaries, high advisers to presidents, and occasionally a governor or United States senator," and questioning whether Henry M. Paulson, Jr. should be running the Treasury after the questionable practices of the firm over the past few years. Stein argues that, while "Goldman Sachs was one of the top 10 sellers of C.M.O.'s for the last two and a half years" it "was also shorting the junk on a titanic scale through index sales—showing . . . how horrible a product it believed it was selling" (Stein 2007). Further, he even questions the motives of Jan Hatzius, a well-known economist at Goldman Sachs and a housing market bear who warns of impending crisis. According to Stein, this could be part of a strategy used by Goldman Sachs "to help along the goal of success at bearish trades in this sector and in the market generally." While that is almost certainly overstated, betting against performance of the securities you are creating does seem problematic.

assumed due to re-rating of securities after the bankruptcy of the insurers are higher than any hit to equity resulting from a take-over of the insurers.[13]

It is far too early to know how all of this will play out, but the past should have been some sort of guide to regulators and supervisors, who could have stepped in earlier, rather than standing idly by as they opined that it is impossible to identify a speculative bubble until after it bursts. Edward Gramlich tried to get Alan Greenspan to increase oversight of subprime lending as early as 2000, but could not penetrate the Chairman's ideological commitment to "free" markets (Krugman 2007). While it is true that many of the problem loans were originated by institutions outside the usual oversight of the Fed, Kuttner (2007) argues that the 1994 Home Equity and Ownership Protection Act did give the Fed authority to police underwriting standards, and directed the Fed "to clamp down on dangerous and predatory lending practices, including on otherwise unregulated entities such as sub-prime mortgage originators." If the Fed had acted on Gramlich's warnings in 2000, most of the damage could have been avoided—as it wasn't until 2001 that underwriting standards began to fall appreciably. In 2001, sub-primes accounted for 8.6% ($190 billion) of mortgage originations; this rose to 20% ($625 billion) in 2005. And in 2001, securitized sub-primes amounted to just $95 billion, growing to $507 billion by 2005 as the Fed slept at the wheel (JEC 2007, p. 18).

Even as questions were raised about rising risk, mortgage bankers successfully fought attempts by federal regulators to tighten rules on lending. According to Steven Pearlstein (2007), new federal guidelines were ready in December 2005, but were not implemented until September 2006, as "mortgage bankers fought the proposed rules with all the usual bogus arguments, accusing the agencies of 'regulatory overreach', 'stifling innovation' and substituting the judgment of bureaucrats for the collective wisdom of thousands of experienced lenders and millions of sophisticated investors." This delay allowed subprime lenders to make hundreds of billions of additional loans, many of which duped low income households into debt they cannot service. As late as November 1, 2007, HCL Finance, Inc. was still advertising on its website "Home of the 'No Doc' Loan," with a variety of options including "SISA" (stated income, stated assets), "NISA" (no income, stated assets), "NINA" (no income, no assets), "NEVA" (no income, no job, verify assets), and the famous NINJA (no income, no job, no assets) (https://broker.hclfinance.com/p/program_list.htm).

New York state Attorney General Andrew Cuomo has sued First American Corporation for colluding with mortgage lender Washington Mutual to overstate the value of homes. Internal emails purportedly show that executives at First America's subsidiary eAppraiseIT knowingly inflated appraisals to secure business from Washington Mutual (Barr 2007). Real estate appraisers across the country have complained that they were

[13] William Ackman, a hedge fund manager, argues that MBIA, the nation's largest bond insurer, could be bankrupt by February. In any case, he questions the triple-A rating of a firm that insures CDOs that have lost billions, forcing the biggest banks to take very large write-downs. Even the CEO of MBIA admits that "our triple-A rating is a fundamental driver of our business model"—meaning that business would dry up if the firm were downgraded. Many analysts are uncomfortable with a business model that *requires* a triple-A rating simply to stay in business (Nocera 2007).

strong-armed by lenders to inflate values; indeed, an industry group (Concerned Real Estate Appraisers from Across America) circulated a petition that was presented to Ben Hensen, Executive Director of the Appraisal Subcommittee of the Federal Financial Institutions Council, that enumerated unfair practices including:

- the withholding of business if we refuse to inflate values,
- the withholding of business if we refuse to guarantee a predetermined value,
- the withholding of business if we refuse to ignore deficiencies in the property,
- refusing to pay for an appraisal that does not give them what they want,
- black listing honest appraisers in order to use "rubber stamp" appraisers, etc.[14]

The petition concludes that "[w]e also believe that many individuals have been adversely affected by the purchase of homes which have been over-valued." There is little doubt that inflated appraisals played a major role in fueling the speculative boom—just as they had helped to create the S&L fiasco in the 1980s by rubber stamping values in "daisy chains" and other fraudulent schemes (Wray 1994).

The ratings agencies were also complicit because their ratings of the securities were essential to generating markets for risky assets.[15] Expressing twenty-twenty hindsight, Fitch now says that "poor underwriting quality and fraud may account for as much as one-quarter of the underperformance of recent vintage subprime RMBS" (Pendley et al. 2007). In a detailed examination of a sample of 45 subprime loans, Fitch found the appearance of fraud or misrepresentation in virtually every one; it also says that "in most cases" the fraud "could have been identified with adequate underwriting, quality control and fraud prevention tools prior to the loan funding." (Pendley et al. 2007.) Further, Fitch's investigation concluded that broker-originated loans have "a higher occurance of misrepresentation and fraud than direct or retail origination" (Pendley et al. 2007).

In 2000, Standard & Poor's had decided that "piggyback" mortgages, in which borrowers use a second loan (at a high interest rate) to obtain the money for a down payment are no more risky than standard mortgages[16] (Lucchetti and Ng 2007). Ratings agencies worked closely with the underwriters that were securitizing the mortgages to ensure ratings that would guarantee marketability. Further, they were richly rewarded for helping to market mortgages because fees were about twice as high as they were for

---

[14] http://www.appraiserspetition.com/.

[15] Some consultation between raters and securitizers was, of course, necessary to ensure that the pooled mortgages would find the appropriate market. Problems would arise only if the ratings were not appropriate to the pools.

[16] Incredibly, the riskier piggy-back loan arrangements allowed the borrowers to evade PMI (mortgage insurance) (Chancellor 2007)!

rating corporate bonds—the traditional business of ratings firms. Moody's got 44% of its revenue in 2006 from rating "structured finance" (student loans, credit card debt, and mortgages) (Lucchetti and Ng 2007). At first, ratings agencies limited the portion of piggybacks in a subprime mortgage pool to 20%; above that percent, a ratings penalty was imposed. However, buyers seeking higher returns soon began to accept pools with larger portions of riskier loans. In 2006 S&P studied the performance of such loans made in 2002 and found that piggybacks were 43% more likely to default. Still, however, S&P did not lower ratings on existing securities, although it did require underwriters to increase collateral on new mortgages portfolios. During the second half of 2006, Moody's noticed that an unusually large number of subprime borrowers were not even making their first payments. Finally, in summer 2007, Moody's and S&P began to slash ratings—sometimes by five notches, lowering ratings below investment grade BB (Lucchetti and Ng 2007). Angry investors wondered why it had taken them so long to act.

Re-rating of securities led inevitably to questions about the insurers. According to Frank Veneroso, current ABX index prices (that reflect risks in subprime mortgage-backed securities) suggest "well over a trillion dollars of subprime US mortgages will lose one half their value" (Veneroso 2007a). Moody's and Fitch are reviewing the ratings of the insurers, and the value of their stocks are plummeting—Ambac by 66% since June 1 and MBIA by 40%; ACA Capital Holdings, Inc. fell by 89%; bond insurers reported combined losses of $2.9 billion last quarter (Richard and Gutscher 2007). According to Richard and Gutscher (2007), derivative prices suggest that the probability of default has risen to 28% for MBIA and to 40% for Ambac. If the insurance guarantees are eliminated due to default of the insurers, $2.4 trillion of bonds could fall in value, according to their analysis. Ambac's insured securities backed by home equity lines of credit had already fallen by 15%; if the rest of the insured securities were to experience the same level of write-down, "it would reduce the value of the securities by $150 billion" (Richard and Gutscher 2007). According to the analysis by Richard and Gutscher, these write-downs were minimal—perhaps only a tenth of the write downs some of the Wall Street banks have been taking for similar mortgage pools. In other words, further write-downs are very likely. Estimates of the cushion that insurers currently have to weather losses is not comforting: MBIA has excess capital of only $550 million against $15.9 billion of CDOs backed by subprime mortgages; Ambac has about $1.15 billion on $29.3 billion of such CDOs and FGIC has $350 million against $10.3 billion of securities.

Henry Kaufman explains that a large part of the problem came from the use of quantitative risk models that relied on the assumption that past performance is a good guide to future performance (Kaufman 200). This requires that the *structure* of the economy and financial system has remained constant even as financial innovation proceeds and a tidal wave of risky assets floods the system. The models could not take account of systemic risk—Goldman Sachs said that according to its computer models, its losses on one of its global equity funds was a "25-standard deviation event," something that should happen once every 100,000 years (Tett and Gangahar 2007). Satyajit Das, a hedge fund consultant, quipped "People say these are one-in-a-100,000-years events but they seem to happen every year" (Tett and Gangahar 2007). In the case of these new instruments, models are based on data derived from only a few years' experience—and, as discussed above, that was an unusually good period for house prices. Further, since similar models are widely used, the models themselves drive the market—a type of "herding behavior" that was not anticipated and can have devastating results when all are simultaneously "selling out position," as Minsky would put it. James Norman, a managing director in Deutsche Asset Management's quantitative strategies group admitted "[q]uants are valuation-driven, and when there is a lot of selling, valuations don't matter" (Brewster 2007).

Martin Wolf (2007) nicely summarized the stages of a Minsky model of the transformation of the financial structure:

- Some "displacement" changes people's perception of the future;
- The changed perception leads to rising asset prices in the affected sector;
- Financial innovation provides easy credit to that sector, further fueling asset price appreciation;
- Overtrading in the sector, as markets provide a "fresh supply of 'greater fools'";
- Euphoria develops, more fools join in the fun;
- Warnings of those who cry "bubble" are ridiculed;
- Insider profit-taking by those who know better;
- Revulsion as those who stayed too long panic.

Figure 1a shows the virtuous cycle created over the course of the 1990s that led to the boom and subsequent bust. The "displacement" in this case was the economic stability encouraged financial innovations that "stretched liquidity" in Minsky's terminology; this plus competition urged financial institutions to increase leverage ratios, increasing credit availability. This is because for given expected losses, higher leverage raises return on equity. With easy credit, asset prices could be bid up, and rising prices encouraged yet more innovation and competition to further increase leverage. The virtuous cycle ensured that the financial system would move through the structures that Minsky labeled hedge, speculative, and finally Ponzi. As discussed, Ponzi finance requires asset price appreciation to validate it—but the virtuous cycle made Ponzi position-taking nearly inevitable.

Figure 1b shows the role played by the major participants in fueling the speculative frenzy.

Developers, real estate agents, and appraisers worked together to maximize home prices. Often the developer worked directly with a mortgage broker so that sufficient funding for inflated prices would be forthcoming; this also required complicity of appraisers to ensure home prices would warrant the mortgage foisted on the borrower. The broker also added the first set of enhancements, such as early payment penalties. Mortgages were then passed along to investment banks that would package them, slice

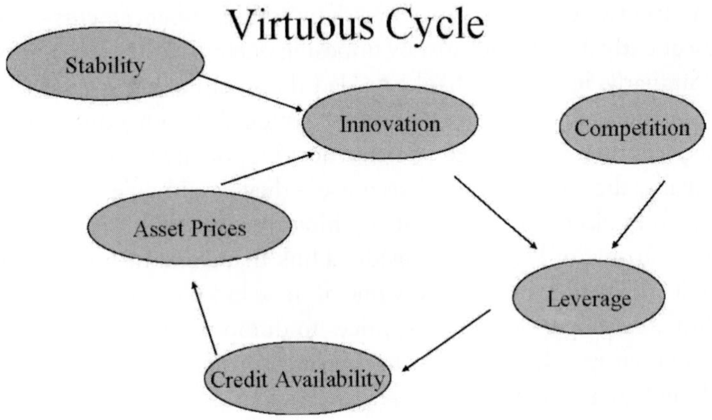

Figure 1a. The Virtuous Cycle

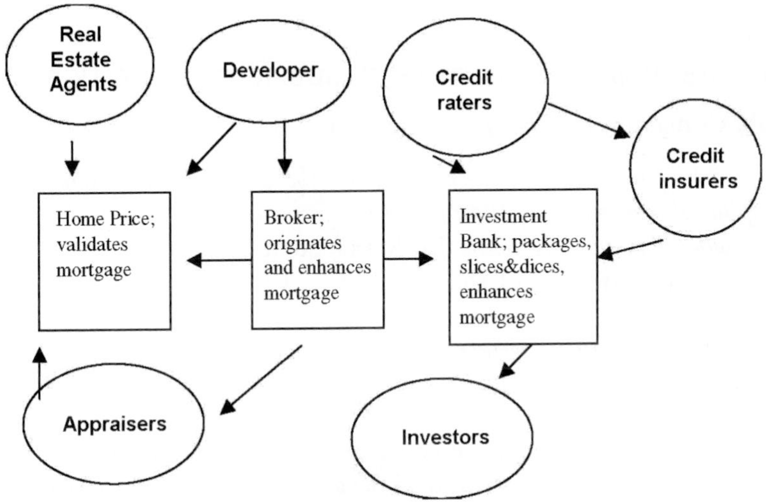

Figure 1b. The Major Players

them into tranches, and add further enhancements, such as those provided by credit rating agencies and insurers. "Trash" was thereby transformed into highly rated securities available for purchase by investors such as pension funds. It was the perfect system to fuel rising home prices, ever-increasing debt ratios, and deteriorating portfolios of unsuspecting investors: the incentives of developers, home sellers, and real estate agents were oriented to maximizing home prices; home appraisers and brokers worked together to facilitate this process, as they were rewarded by throughput—number of deals—but that in turn required that they service the needs of those invested in higher prices. Brokers had no interest in the actual riskiness of the mortgages; however, they did have an incentive to reduce apparent risk by adding enhancements—even if those would subsequently increase defaults by imposing onerous terms that borrowers could not meet. Similarly, investment banks needed the stamp of approval of credit rating agencies to provide a patina of safety; insurers removed any lingering doubts by guaranteeing the securities—with credit raters vouching for the financial strength of the insurers. Finally, the banks provided recourse—they would take the mortgage pools back onto their books at face value—if anything went wrong.

Each of the arrows of Figure 1b provides a link that could be broken, endangering the Ponzi scheme. Unfortunately, every one of these links is now at least weak: homes are not selling, developers are slashing prices to dump inventory, brokers are closing up shop, appraisers have been chastised, investment banks are holding mortgages they cannot sell (and are taking back some securities), investors are trying to sell out positions, ratings agencies are downgrading securities and the insurers, and the insurers are facing huge losses.

In Part II we will explore the possible consequences as well as possible policy responses.

PART II: THE MINSKY MOMENT: APRES SUBPRIME, LE DELUGE

1. Likely Consequences of the Meltdown

> *The rocket scientists who built models made the same mistakes as Long-Term Capital Management in 1998; they didn't factor in a convergence of correlation when things headed south.* T.J. Marta, quoted by Michael Mackenzie, Gillian Tett, and David Oakley (2007).

> *The subprime mortgage meltdown has economic consequences that will ripple through our communities unless we act.* Senator Charles Schumer(2007).

Before we can assess the likely consequences of the real estate meltdown, it is necessary to take stock of the current situation. That also entails an examination of the recent trends to see how we got to the present state.

First, it is useful to look at trends for aggregate household real estate value and for aggregate home mortgage liability, as shown in Figure 2. This shows that while real estate values easily doubled over the past decade, from $10 trillion in 1997 to well over $20 trillion by 2005, home mortgage liabilities rose even faster, from less than $2 trillion in 1997 to $10 trillion in 2005. (Indeed, between 2002-06, total credit grew by $8 trillion while GDP only grew by $2.8 trillion.) As is well known, average home prices have also been rising quickly. Figure 3 shows prices rose from around $150,000 in 1997 to a peak above $250,000 in 2005. Robert Shiller's (2007) data (which tries to track sales prices of individual houses) records even more spectacular gains, with the US real housing price index increasing by 85% between 1997 and 2006. Figure 4 shows that new homes for sale have risen sharply since 2002, easily exceeding anything experienced since 1980. While this was initially met by sufficient demand, for the past

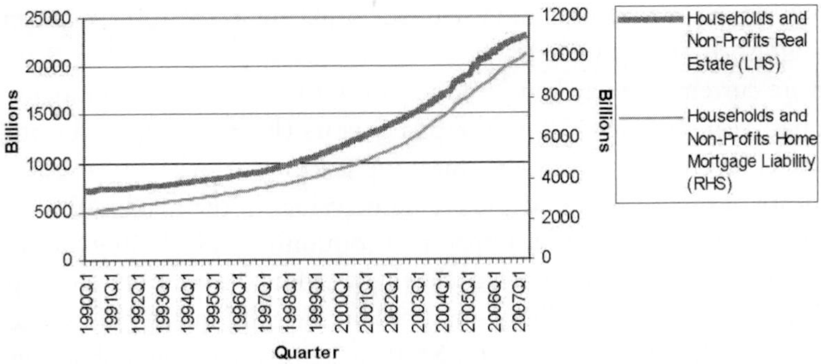

Figure 2. Households for Non-Profits Mortgage Liability and Real Estate

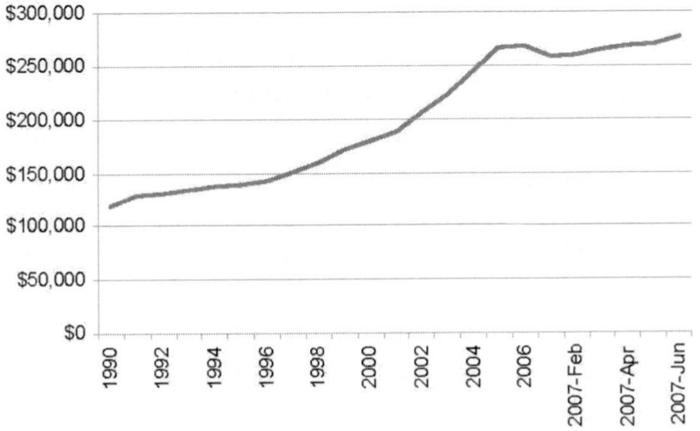

Figure 3. Average Price for Existing Homes

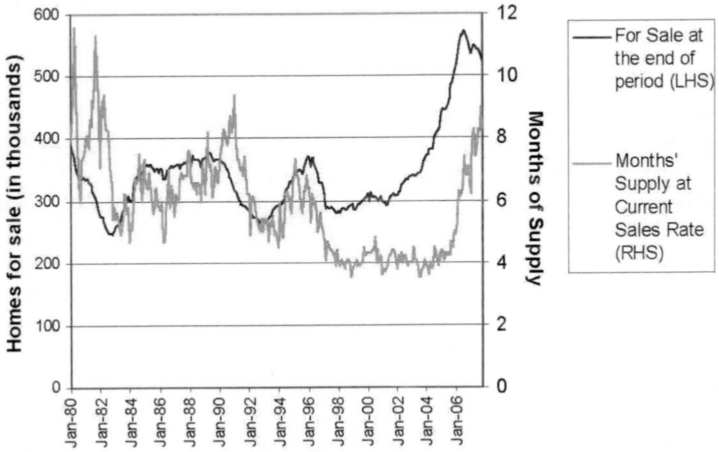

Figure 4. Home Production Has Outpaced Demand

Source: Bureau of the Census, U.S. Dept. of Commerce.

couple of years, excess supply has developed so that by early 2007, eight months of supply languished on the market.

There are currently more than 2 million vacant homes for sale, an increase of 7% over the past year, and up 57% in the past 3 years (Isidore 2007). Not only are the owners extremely motivated to sell—meaning prices are downward negotiable—but the inventory of unsold homes depresses home values in the neighborhood. Further, vacant homes have other negative impacts on communities, including increased crime and higher costs for local governments (clearing weeds and trash from vacant property). Predictably, house prices are falling—by 4.5% in the third quarter of 2007 compared to a year earlier, the biggest drop since S&P created its nationwide housing index in 1987. The Case-Shiller index of housing prices in 20 major cities declined by 4.9% in September compared with a year earlier, the steepest decline since April 1991 (AP 2007c). This was the ninth month in a row for declining house prices.

Nearly 3 million subprime homeowners face higher interest rates after resets that will occur in the next two years—which will increase the number of foreclosures and vacancies. The Fed has estimated that 500,000 of those will lose their homes after the resets (Reuters 2007c). A recent report by the U.S. Conference of Mayors projects another 1.4 million foreclosures and another 7% drop in real estate values over the next year (Reuters 2007d). The JEC conservatively expects an additional 2 million foreclosures by 2009, which will increase vacancies on the auction block, directly destroying over $100 billion of real estate wealth. Total costs will undoubtedly run higher as unemployment rises, and as neighborhoods suffer from vacancies and declining socioeconomic status—foreclosures not only lower the value of neighboring houses but also invite crime that leads to further losses.[17] In California, the foreclosure rate has reached 1 out of every 88 households, with foreclosure filings in the third quarter running four times the number filed a year ago (Reuters 2007d). California property values will fall by 16%, lowering property taxes by $3 billion, hurting local governments. The mayors predict that related problems such as neighborhood blight as well as crime will rise—at a time that state and local governments will be hard-pressed to afford to do anything about it.[18]

---

[17] Goldman Sachs is now projecting aggregate losses of around $400 billion on outstanding mortgages. This does not sound large relatively to occasional historical losses experienced in equity markets. However, the Goldman Sachs US Economic Research Group warns that is not a relevant analogy. Mortgage securities markets are highly leveraged, with 10 to 1 ratios not at all uncommon. If leveraged players (such as banks, broker-dealers, hedge funds, and GSEs) incur losses of $200 billion in these markets, they might need to scale-back balance sheets by $2 trillion (with a leveraged ratio often to one). Thus, while $200 billion (or $400 billion) is not large relative to the US economy or to US financial markets, $2 trillion (or $4 trillion) is. (U.S. Daily Financial Market Comment 2007). Veneroso (2007a) notes that estimates of total direct losses continue to rise—currently toward $500 billion, and it is likely that they will soon approach a more likely figure of $1 trillion.

[18] Jerry Abramson, Mayor of Louisville, Kentucky, put it this way: "What the mayors are most concerned about is what happens to those homes when the foreclosure begins and ultimately ends . . . . As the decrease in value occurs around homes that are being foreclosed on and left vacant or boarded, all of the sudden the property tax decreases. We've got to put more money into going in and policing the area.

Table 1
Mortgage Origination Statistics

	Total Mortgage Originations (Billions)	Subprime Originations (Billions)	Subprime Share in Total Originations (percent of dollar value)	Subprime Mortgage Backed Securities (Billions)	Percent Subprimes Securitized (percent of dollar value)
2001	$2,215	$190	8.6	$95	50.4
2002	$2,885	$231	8.0	$121	52.7
2003	$3,945	$335	8.5	$202	60.5
2004	$2,920	$540	18.5	$401	74.3
2005	$3,120	$625	20.0	$507	81.2
2006	$2,980	$600	20.1	$483	80.5

Source: Inside Mortgage Finance, The 2007 Mortgage Market Statistical Annual, Top Subprime Mortgage Market Players and Key Data (2006).

Table 1 provides mortgage origination statistics. Annual originations grew from $2.2 trillion in 2001 to nearly $4 trillion in 2003 before settling around a figure of about $3 trillion in the years 2004-06. Of that, subprime originations grew from just $190 billion in 2001 to $625 billion in 2005; as a percent of the dollar value of total originations, subprimes grew from 8.6% to 20% of the market. Over the same period, the percent of subprimes securitized increased from half to 80%. According to data reported by the JEC, the vast majority of such securitizations (83.4% in 2004) were undertaken by independent mortgage bankers (and only 2.6% by CRA-regulated lenders). So-called liar loans increased from a quarter of subprimes in 2001 to 40% in 2006. (Morgenson 2007a). Average *daily* trading in mortgage securities rose from $60 billion in 2000 to $250 billion by 2006. (Morgenson 2007a).

Table 2 shows the evolution of underwriting standards for subprime loans. The percent of such loans with adjustable rates rose from about 74% in 2001 to more than 93% in 2005; interest-only loans rose from zero to nearly 38% over the same period; and the low or no doc share rose from 29% to more than half. Data provided by the JEC shows that over the same period, hybrid adjustable rate mortgages (those with teaser rates for 2 or 3 years, after which loans would be reset at higher rates) rose from just under 60% of securitized subprimes in 2001 to nearly three-quarters by 2004 (JEC 2007, figure 12). In other words, the riskiest types of subprimes—ARMS and hybrid ARMS—were favorites with securitizers. From 2004-2006 (when lending standards were loosest) 8.4 million adjustable rate mortgages were originated, worth $2.3 trillion; of those, 3.2 million (worth $1.05 trillion) had "teaser rates" that were below market

We've got to put more money into going in and keeping them boarded up and as safe as can be possible." (Marketplace 2007).

Table 2
Underwriting Standards in Subprime Home-Purchase Loans

	ARM Share	IO Share	Low-No-Doc Share	Debt Payments-to-Income Ratio	Average Loan-to-Value Ratio
2001	73.8%	0.0%	28.5%	39.7%	84.04%
2002	80.0%	2.3%	38.6%	40.1%	84.42%
2003	80.1%	8.6%	42.8%	40.5%	86.09%
2004	89.4%	27.2%	45.2%	41.2%	84.86%
2005	93.3%	37.8%	50.7%	41.8%	83.24%
2006	91.3%	22.8%	50.8%	42.4%	83.35%

Source: Freddie Mac, obtained from the International Monetary Fund http://www.imf.org/external/pubs/ft/fmu/eng/2007/charts.pdf

and would reset in 2-3 years at higher rates[19] (Bianco 2007). The JEC also provides data that shows that riskier subprimes are much more likely to face prepayment penalties—apparently imposed to enhance credit ratings on the securitized mortgages. For example, the percent of prime ARMs originated in 2005 with prepayment penalties was just 15.4%; by contrast 72.4% of subprime ARMs carried a penalty. The typical penalty is six month's interest on 80% of the original mortgage balance, which could total $7500 for a $150,000 mortgage[20] (JEC 2007). In addition, the subprime ARM carried a 326 basis point premium over a prime ARM loan (JEC 2007, figure 15).

As underwriting standards fell, delinquency rates rose, as shown in Figure 5. Not surprisingly, delinquency rates for adjustable subprime loans rose fastest and farthest as troubles hit the real estate market over the course of 2006. Already, delinquency rates for such loans are reaching toward 20%. Figure 6 shows a similar increase for foreclosure rates, which reached nearly 8% for subprime adjustable rate loans in the beginning of 2007. Data presented by the JEC (2007, figure 14) shows that subprime loans of the most recent vintage (i.e., those made in 2007 and 2006) have much higher delinquency rates; further, delinquency rates seem to peak between 18 and 20 months after origination, meaning that the worst is probably still to come. During the third quarter of 2007, foreclosures reached nearly half a million, up 34% from the second quarter, and twice as high as the number for third quarter of2006 (AP 2007a). According to the Center for Responsible Lending, two-thirds of the foreclosures filed for the year ending June 30, 2007 involved subprime loans; Banc of America Securities reported that 93% of foreclosures completed during 2007 (through September) involved adjustable-rate loans that were made and securitized in 2006 (Morgenson 2007b).

---

[19] Of the $1 trillion dollars of teaser rate mortgages, $431 billion had initial interest rates at or below 2% (Bianco 2007).

[20] An example will help. A subprime hybrid adjustable rate mortgage on a $400,000 house might have initial payments of about $2200 per month for interest-only at a rate of 6.5%. After a reset, the payments rise to $4000 per month at an interest rate of 12% plus principal. (AP 2007a).

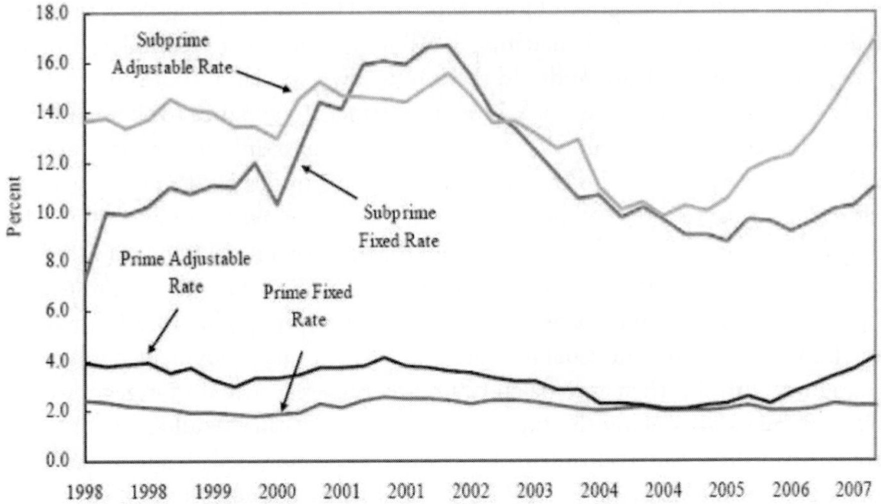

Figure 5. Comparisons of Prime vs Subprime Delinquency Rates, Total U.S. 1998-2007

Source: Mortgage Bankers Association.

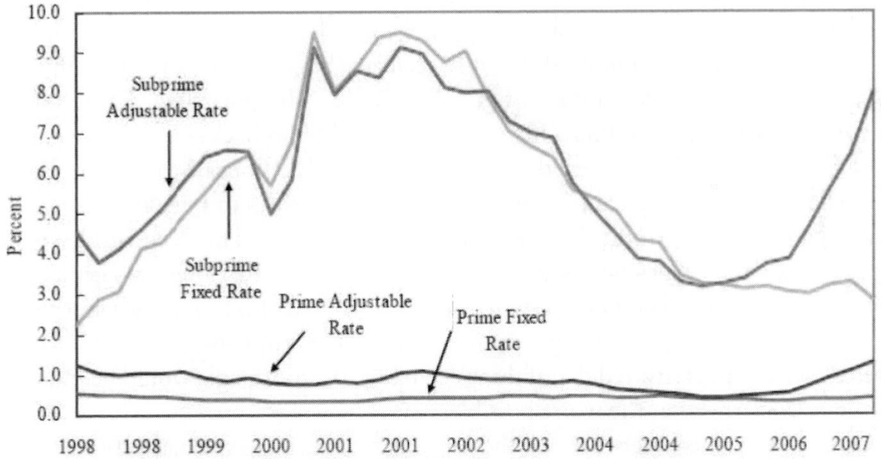

Figure 6. Comparisons of Prime vs Subprime Foreclosure Rates, Total U.S. 1998-2007

Source: Mortgage Bankers Association.

No one really knows who is bearing all the risks. Recall that securitization of mortgages was supposed to shift interest rate risk off the balance sheets of banks and thrifts. However, as mentioned above, among the institutions first impacted were foreign banks in Germany, the UK, and France. It is becoming increasingly apparent that American banks will be seriously affected because they promised to bear losses (through recourse) if the mortgages they securitized for originators sold below face value. According to

Floyd Norris (2007c), American Home Mortgage Holdings is suing Bank of America for reneging on swap deals it had made. While the details are complex, American Home made subprime loans and sold them to its own special purpose entities, which financed their purchases by issuing commercial paper. To enhance the demand for the paper, American Home obtained swap agreements from Bank of America and others that would cover losses if the entities had to sell mortgages for less than face value. Performing loans are now selling for 80% of face value, with nonperforming loans selling for as little as 54% of face value. Thus, banks took on risks and now face losses for loans they did not even originate, much less held! The problem is not restricted to subprime loans; even prime loans are experiencing sharply spiking foreclosure rates—something that is highly unusual in a period in which unemployment rates have not risen significantly. Further, as Whalen (2007) reports, securitized mortgages were also purchased by banks seeking the expected higher returns they would generate—often through specially created subsidiaries, that are now being bailed out by their bank owners that must assume the securities. Ironically, the financial instrument that was supposed to reduce bank risks has led to a situation in which banks now hold packages of mortgages originated by those who had no interest in evaluating the likelihood that debtors could service their debt.

In other words, banks abandoned relationship banking that allowed them to assess risk of borrowers as they turned to securitization and fee income, but now they hold the debt of borrowers whose risk was never evaluated by anyone. As an example, on November 5, Citigroup admitted that it had created a "liquidity-put," inserting a put option into CDOs backed by subprime mortgages. "The put allowed any buyer of these CDOs who ran into financing problems to sell them back—at original value—to Citi" (Loomis 2007). When the market for the CDOs began to dry up, holders of the liquidity-put returned $25 billion subprime securities to Citi, increasing Citi's total holdings of subprime related securities to $55 billion. This seems to have been the last straw for Chairman Charles Prince, who was forced to resign—replaced by Robert Rubin—as Citi announced write-downs of $8 to $11 billion. The whole idea of securitization was to get mortgages off the balance sheets of banks, but the "recourse" offered by these puts ensured that if things go badly, the mortgages would be right back on the balance sheets at the worst possible time.

Of course, homeowners are not the only ones suffering. As Bajaj (2007) reports, "Collateralized debt obligations—made up of bonds backed by thousands of subprime home loans—are starting to shut off cash payments to investors in lower-rated bonds as credit-rating agencies downgrade the securities they own . . . [this] is expected to accelerate in the months ahead." Moody's and Standard & Poor's are lowering the ratings on huge blocks of such bonds; as ratings decline, the trustees of the debt obligations are forced to discount the value of their portfolio. However, it takes "months for ratings downgrades to work their way through the system" (Bajaj 2007). As John Schiavetta, managing director at Derivative Fitch (responsible for rating the debt) says, "It's still the early stages of a very significant stress" (quoted in Bajaj 2007). This is forcing investment banks to write-down their assets: recent write-downs include those by Merrill Lynch ($8.4 billion), UBS ($3.4 billion), Citigroup ($1.3 billion) (Bajaj 2007; Hutchinson 2007). Bank of America's earnings on its fixed-income activities fell by 93% in the third quarter of2007; Citigroup's profits in all activities fell by 57% (Dash 2007).

Note that losses are not limited to the mortgage markets—Bank of America also lost $2 billion on credit cards due to rising personal bankruptcies, and is setting aside reserves for expected losses on its construction loans as the construction industry deteriorates. Citigroup now expects losses of $8 to $11 billion on its portfolio of $43 billion collateralized debt obligations (Norris 2007a). Goldman Sachs thinks the losses will be even larger, warning that write-downs at Citigroup will be $15 billion (Shell 2007). The top 10 global banks have already taken write-offs of $75 billion during 2007 (AP 2007a). JP Morgan has warned that large bank CDO losses could reach $77 billion, while aggregate losses would be $260 billion on such assets. According to the analysis, the losses on the "super-senior" or *safest* CDOs will be between 20% and 80%! A JP Morgan analyst wryly wrote that "One of the benefits of the securitization is the off-loading and global distribution of risk. Ironically, this is now a capital markets hazard, since no one is sure where subprime losses lurk" (Bloomberg 2007). Banks ended up holding so many of the CDOs because they could not sell them; other holdings came from promissory agreements and from seizures of collateral from hedge funds (Shen 2007). Lest one question the source, the JP Morgan team of CDO research was deemed to be the best, according to a poll by *Institutional Investor* (Bloomberg 2007). They believe that bond insurers face losses of $29 billion on CDOs they hold.

Problems are spilling over into the commercial paper market, where there is about $2.2 trillion outstanding, of which $1.2 trillion is backed by residential mortgages, credit card receivables, car loans, and other bonds (Morgenson and Anderson 2007). As ratings agencies have been downgrading issuers of commercial paper due to declining quality of the underlying assets, some money market funds have been forced to ban redemptions. As of mid November 2007, the dollar volume of asset-backed commercial paper has shrunk by about 30% since its peak in August. Because issuers cannot sell new paper, they have been forced to tap bank credit lines (Mackenzie et al. 2007). Problems have spread outside the U.S., with the European asset backed commercial paper market shrinking from a peak of $300 billion to about $170 billion in November.

The crisis is spreading to the commercial real estate market-securitized mortgages backed by commercial real estate are now carrying an interest rate spread of over 1500 basis points for BB tranches and new issues are down by 84% (Veneroso 2007a). The value of such securities was about $800 billion at the end of the first quarter of 2007, and some are projecting losses of at least $100 billion. Fitch has issued a warning about "overly optimistic expectations of future rental rates, sales growth and market growth" in the commercial property sector (Chittum and Forsyth 2007). RBS Greenwich Capital is predicting that US commercial property prices will fall 10-15% next year (Veneroso 2007a). Some analysts are predicting that there will soon be a run out of asset-backed commercial paper because no investors want to be caught holding such paper over year-end (Private communication, fixed income strategist). With perhaps half a trillion dollars worth of potentially worthless paper on the balance sheets of the biggest global banks, the fallout "could dwarf the nation's last big banking crisis—the failure of more than 1,000 savings and loans in the I 980s"—that required a $125 billion government bailout (AP 2007a).

Other markets are also affected. There are now rumors about the muni bond market—and as insurers are downgraded, the market for new issues will dry up. This calls to mind Minsky's well-known analysis of the 1966 credit crunch set off by problems in the muni bond market. Recent reports indicate that problems are also spreading to money-market funds that had been considered to be a safe haven. Indeed, money-market funds have been growing—to about $3 trillion on November 6, 2007, partly in reaction to liquidity and solvency problems in other asset markets. However, the ten largest managers of money funds had invested $50 billion in short term structured investment vehicles that are now losing money. As a result, Legg Mason had to invest $100 million in one of its funds, and arranged for $238 million in credit for two others (Harrington and Condon 2007). Bank of America might provide up to $600 million to prop up its funds (Harrington and Condon 2007). The Treasury is trying to arrange for an $80 billion fund to back-up SIVs, which typically borrowed by issuing short-term commercial paper in order to buy longer-dated assets such as bank bonds and mortgage-backed securities. So far, "fire sales" have reduced the average net asset value of SIV s by more than 30% (Harrington and Condon 2007).

Perhaps signaling further problems in both money market funds and in local government finance, the state of Florida had to suspend withdrawals from a state-operated investment pool as a run had eliminated 40% of its assets in two weeks (Associated Press 2007e). The pool operated much like a private money market fund, enabling cities, counties, and school districts to obtain higher returns on short-term investments, withdrawing funds as needed to pay wages and other operating costs. Problems began when $700 million in asset-backed commercial paper was downgraded that triggered a run. This is not likely to be the last run on an investment pool.

The FIRE (finance, insurance, and real estate) sector is shedding jobs as a result of the housing downturn. Through October 19, New York based financial services companies had cut 42,404 jobs in 2007 (Bajaj 2007). The Labor Department estimates that 100,000 financial services jobs have been lost nationwide (AP 2007a). Figure 7 shows the contributions to real GDP growth by components of the FIRE sector. During the recession at the beginning of this decade, the FIRE sector accounted for nearly all of the growth of real GDP; during the real estate boom from 2002, it accounted for 10% to 30% of annual GDP growth. The real estate sector alone (including rental leasing), accounted for half of real GDP growth during the recession, and then for about 20% of real GDP growth in the mid 2000s. As the sector slows, the impact on overall growth will be significant. Plummeting real estate values causes losses for suppliers to the home renovation market. Home Depot has reported a 26.8% drop in third quarter profits for 2007 (AP 2007b). Some analysts are projecting that GDP growth will fall to zero, and based on historical data that would mean 3 million job losses—fifty percent more

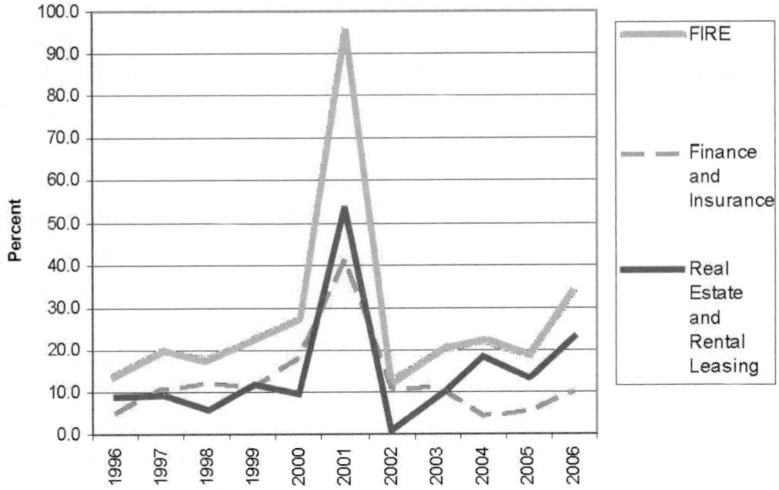

Figure 7. Contribution of FIRE Sector to Percent Change in Real Gross Domestic Product

Source: Bureau of Economic Analysis Industry Economic Accounts.

than the number of jobs lost during the past recession that followed the New Economy bust[21] (AP 2007a).

The crisis continues to spread internationally. Indeed, the first bank to fall was IKB in Germany—which apparently had a credit guarantee to a conduit equal to 40% of its assets—bailed out by a group of government-backed banks. In August, BNP Paribas in France had to stop investors from taking money out of three funds that had invested in American mortgage securities (Bajaj and Landler 2007). UBS lost 4.2 billion Swiss francs in the third quarter of 2007 due to its subprime holdings, and warned that it will have to write down more in the fourth quarter. UBS reported it is still holding $20.2 billion of "highly illiquid 'super senior' debt," as well as nearly $20 billion of residential mortgage-backed securities and collateralized debt obligations (Reuters 2007b). European banks have already taken charges of more than $40 billion on holdings in mortgage-backed securities (Werdigier 2007). Barclays is writing down $2.7 billion worth of assets due to losses on securities linked to the U.S. subprime crisis (Reuters 2007a). However, it still has a 5 billion pound exposure to collateralized debt obligations as well as 7.3 billion pounds of unsold leveraged finance underwriting positions (Reuters 2007a). While securitization in Europe has not proceeded on a scale that approaches what has occurred in the U.S., many are worried that the legal framework does not "provide authorities with the necessary tools for supervising cross-border

[21] While wages and jobs growth figures were not that bad during the fall, Norris (Nov 30, 2007) reports that the estimates are being revised. Official figures based on payrolls data were probably far too rosy—with average monthly jobs growth at 125,000. Household surveys, however, showed job losses. Recent revisions lowered growth of wage and salary income for the second quarter from 4.5% to just 1.6%; according to Norris, the jobs numbers will be similarly revised downward.

banking groups," and that they are ill-prepared to deal with a region-wide financial crisis[22] (Veron 2007). On November 22,2007 two French banks paid $l.5 billion to take over CIFG Holdings (a large bond insurance company operating in Europe) on fears that it would lose its AAA credit rating due to losses on mortgage loans (Landler and Werdigier 2007). CFIG had been created in 2001 by Natixis bank in order to move into exotic asset-backed securities; CFIG says it has direct exposure to $1.9 billion of residential mortgages. Dexia is expected to post an $871 million write-down for the third quarter of2007, most due to losses at CFIG. Swiss Re, a giant reinsurance company in Zurich also had to take big write-downs due to losses in mortgage-related securities (Werdigier 2007b).

As Richard Bookstaber says, conventional wisdom was that globalization of finance should have increased stability by distributing risks and allowing for diversification of asset holdings. However, in practice, "everybody tends to invest in the same assets and employ the same strategies" (Schwartz 2007). And, of course, they simultaneously sell out of the same assets. In late November the crisis spread to Asia, with panic withdrawals from money market funds and credit derivatives in search of safe government debt and insured deposit accounts. (Evans-Pritchard 2007) Even the Bank of China reported big losses from the $9.7 billion of subprime mortgage-backed securities it holds (Bloomberg News 2007). Japan's Mitsubishi UFJ Financial Group holds about $2.6 billion of such securities. Problems in Asia quickly circled the globe, returning to Europe, where spreads on low-grade bonds were climbing 10 basis points a day, causing the European Covered Bond Council to suspend trading in mortgage-backed securities (Bloomberg News 2007). The "Ted spread" (the spread between commercial Libor rates and US Treasury bills) rose to nearly 150 basis points, the highest since the 1987 stock market crash. HSBC Holdings announced on November 26 that it would bailout two of its structured investment vehicles (SIVs), returning $45 billion of assets to the bank's balance sheet. It had already written off $3.4 billion of bad consumer debt, and is expected to set aside another $12 billion.

It is difficult to project the possible impacts of the subprime meltdown on the continuing availability of credit. The initial impact led to a severe credit crunch, as Figure 8 below shows. Commercial paper interest rates immediately spiked, although stress was relieved by prompt lender of last resort intervention of the Fed, which supplied reserves on demand. Two of the biggest sources of credit to firms, commercial paper and commercial and industrial bank loans, retrenched by 9% between August and mid-November, the biggest drop on record since the Fed began tracking the volume of such credit in 1973 (Goodman 2007). There have been previous periods with downturns in these forms of credit—although none of them were this large—generally associated with recessions and economic slowdowns.

---

[22] One problem that we will not take up here is the absence of a Euroland treasury with the fiscal capacity equal to that of the U.S. Treasury. The individual Euro nations are constrained in their ability to bail-out a financial crisis and to protect depositors from losses, and the European Parliament's budget is too small.

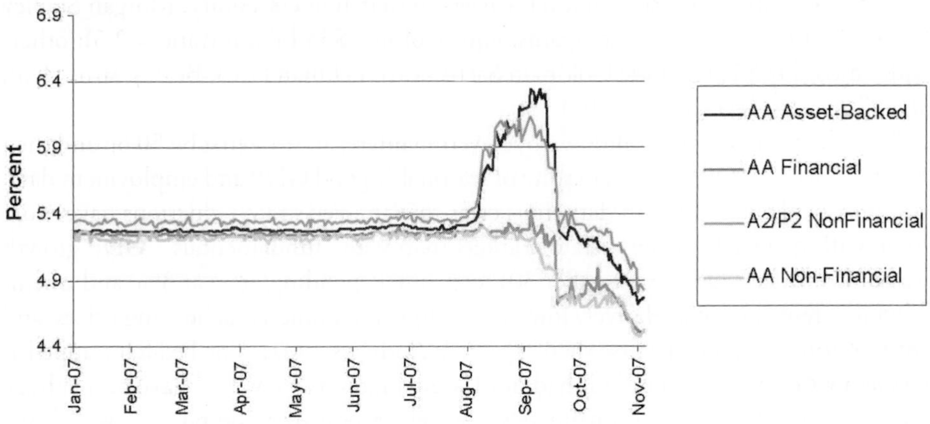

Figure 8. Commercial Paper Rates (30 Day)

Source: Federal Reserve Board Statistical Releases.

A rolling credit crunch hits market after market, and region after region. When it looks like liquidity problems are being attenuated in one market, the infection quickly spreads to another. S&P has downgraded 381 tranches of residential mortgage-related CDOs so far this year, and has another 709 on a watch list; Moody's downgraded 338 tranches and has kept 734 on its watch list for further downgrades (Wood 2007). New issues of mortgage backed securities have fallen to barely $20 billion; the spreads on BB tranches of the CMBX index have risen to 1500 basis points in November (Wood 2007). Even Larry Summers is now warning "there is the risk that the adverse impacts will be felt for the rest of this decade and beyond" and that "streams of data indicate how much more serious the situation is than was clear a few months ago" as "the housing sector may be in a free-fall" (Summers 2007). He goes on to note that the two-year Treasury bond rates dropped below 3%, that single family home construction could be down by 50% from peak, that house prices could fall by 25%, and that banks "will inevitably curtail new lending as they are hit by a perfect storm of declining capital due to mark-to-market losses, involuntary balance sheet expansion as various backstop facilities are called, and greatly reduced confidence in the creditworthiness of traditional borrowers as the economy turns downwards and asset prices fall" (Summers 2007).

The next shoe to drop could be a downgrading of investment banks due to problems in "level 3" assets. From November 15, banks have to divide their assets into three levels, depending on ease with which values can be determined from market prices. Level 1 assets have values determined by quoted prices in active markets. By contrast, level 3 assets do not have readily available markets, so their values are determined by the bank's own model (Hutchinson 2007). Banks have an interest in avoiding classification of too many assets as level 3; however, early reports by banks as of the end of August or September show that they total up 7.4% of total assets (Morgan Stanley), and are above 5% of total assets for Goldman Sachs, Lehman Brothers, Bear Stearns, and Citigroup.

More problematic is the ratio of level 3 assets to shareholders' equity: Morgan Stanley has $88 billion in level 3 assets against equity of just $35 billion (ratio = 2.5); others with ratios above 1.0 include Goldman Sachs (1.8), Lehman (1.6), Bear Stearns (1.6), and Citigroup (1.1) (Wood 2007).

The Fed reacted to the meltdown by lowering interest rates—first by 50 bp and then again by 25 bp on October 31, in spite of reasonably good GDP and employment data, and reasonably bad inflation data. It is clear that the Fed's rate reductions have more to do with financial and real estate markets than with "fundamentals." GDP growth was at 3.8 percent (as of September 30), consumer spending grew at 3%, and unemployment remained at a relatively low 4.7%. However, home sales, housing prices, and consumption all came in worse than expected (Andrews 2007). The Fed felt trapped at its October meeting because if it had not lowered rates, there would have been a huge selloff in equity markets; unfortunately, the celebration over the rate cut was short-lived: rate cuts at this point can merely confirm the market's suspicion that things are going badly. As of late November, markets are projecting about a 90% probability of further rate cuts in December, although Fed officials are proclaiming that is unlikely unless data worsen considerably before the next meeting.

It seems that the only sure thing is to bet against subprimes. Tellingly, a California hedge fund that shorted subprime mortgages earned a return greater than 1000% after fees during 2007. Andrew Lahde's Lahde Capital of Santa Monica might have made the greatest return of all time betting against residential mortgages; he is now putting his profits into bets against commercial real estate. John Paulson's New York-based Paulson&Co and a few others also earned returns well above 500% by shorting U.S. home loans.

There is a fairly large body of evidence that housing downturns precede recessions. Indeed, Edward Leamer (2007) has provocatively argued that what appears to be a business cycle is actually a housing cycle. Using a large number of measures, he claims to demonstrate that the so-called business cycle is actually a consumer-led cycle, and that the component of consumer spending that best "explains" the cycle (econometrically speaking) is housing. While I think this is probably overstated, there does appear to be a correlation, as shown in Figure 9, although causation could usually go the other way. Norris (2007b) notes that while the Fed was still forecasting at the end of November that the economy faces a slowdown but no recession, this would be "the first time ever that a housing slowdown this severe has not coincided with a recession. In fact, there has never been a [housing] slowdown of anything like this magnitude until after a recession was under way." He goes on to show that new-home starts are down by 47% compared with a similar period two years ago. Since the early 1960s there have only been three previous cycles when starts fell by at least a third: in 1974, 1980, and 1991—all of which occurred during recessions.

Finally, it must be remembered that the household sector was already in a precarious situation even before the meltdown, as documented in numerous studies published by colleagues at The Levy Economics Institute. Since 1996, households have persistently

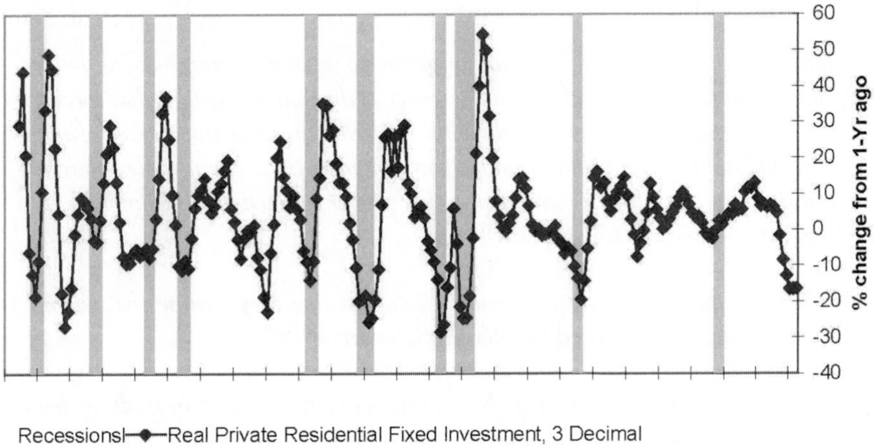

Figure 9. Correlation of Housing Sector Declines and Recessions: Real Private Residential Fixed Investment, 3 Decimal

Source: Federal Reserve Board of St. Louis.

spent more than their incomes, running up huge debt. During the internet boom, this could be justified because of all the financial wealth created by equity price appreciation; effectively, the private sector was borrowing against its capital gains. Of course, the stock market crash wiped out over $7 trillion of financial wealth—while almost all of the debt remained. More recently, the borrowing was even more directly related to rising housing wealth—as home equity cash-outs total $1.2 trillion since 2002 (equal to 46% of the growth of consumption over the period) (Wood 2007). As this source of finance dries up, the hit to consumption could be large. Further, as demonstrated by several Levy Institute Strategic Analyses, economic growth fueled by household consumption requires that indebtedness grows faster than income. Financial markets are demonstrably fickle—billions of dollars can be lost in a day. Ultimately, it is risky to back household debt with the expectation of continued appreciation of real estate values and stock prices. Perhaps the whole financial structure might be brought down in a wave of defaults, plummeting asset values, and bankruptcies. However, that is not required to turn a slow-down into a deep recession. All that must happen is that consumers finally retrench, and return to a normal pattern of "living within their means." All else equal, if the private sector were to reduce spending to, say, only 97 cents per dollar of income, this would lower GDP by half a dozen percentage points. And if the private sector were really spooked, it might reduce spending to 90 cents on the dollar—as it usually does in recession—taking a trillion and a half dollars out of GDP, leaving a huge demand gap that is unlikely to be fully restored by exploding budget deficits or by exports.

2. Policy and Reform

Implicit in the legislation which I am suggesting to you is a declaration of national policy. This policy is that the broad interests of the Nation require that special safeguards should be thrown around home ownership as a guarantee of social and economic stability, and that to protect home owners from inequitable enforced liquidation in a time of general distress is a proper concern of the Government. President Franklin D. Roosevelt (1933).

Sometimes financial crises are actually good because they cleanse the system. Marc Weidenmier, quoted by Nelson Schwartz (2007).

When Rome is burning, Emperor Nero must not benignly stand by fiddling, lest those careless with fire be encouraged toward future indiscretions. First things first. Teach lessons later. Later correct the bad regulating that encouraged and permitted excessively leveraged loans. Paul Samuelson (2007).

There is substantial evidence that financial markets succeed because of strong enforcement and regulation, not in spite of it. Linda Chatman Thomsen, Enforcement Chief for SEC, quoted in Carrie Johnson (2007).

Even as the financial crisis began to unfold, Wall Street mounted a major offensive against regulation to "secure America's competitiveness" (Johnson 2007). Fearing lawsuits by investors and wanting to protect accounting firms that had assisted in certifying the books of risky schemes, the Committee on Capital Markets Regulation (with the blessing of Treasury Secretary Henry Paulson) began its push to deregulate in fall 2006. The most important agenda items are to make it more difficult to pursue shareholder lawsuits and to repeal some sections of Sarbanes-Oxley, including the requirement that companies must review their safeguards that are designed to prevent fraud and mistakes. Deputy Assistant Attorney General Barry Sabin responded that "[e]liminating fraud is good for business" (Johnson 2007). Given the scope of the unfolding crisis, it is not clear that Wall Street will be able to hold off a growing demand for reregulation, because, as recognized by David Chavern (executive at the Chamber), "almost all significant laws and regulations are done in this country in times of crisis" (Johnson 2007). The best example, of course, was the policy response to the Great Depression.

There are two immediate policy issues facing us: first, what, if anything can be done to ameliorate the fall-out from the current crisis; second, what can be done to prevent recurrence of such a situation in the future? Both of these issues will require much study and debate. I can only offer some general statements that might warrant further research.

a. Policy to Deal with the Current Crisis

There are a number of initiatives designed to deal with the current crisis, some coming from the private sector while others are being pushed by policy makers. Among those considered are:

- As discussed above, the financial sector is setting up funds to maintain liquid markets for mortgage securities and asset-backed commercial paper. The Treasury-facilitated plan is that banks would put together $75 billion to stabilize prices. This is probably a good idea, although it will be successful only if losses can be contained—a rather unlikely scenario.
- The Fed has lowered interest rates. This is at least a movement in the right direction, although it will not help much. Because three-quarters of subprime VARs have pre-payment penalties (averaging six months interest payment on 80% of the original principle value), borrowers usually cannot afford to get out of their loans, thus, lower interest rates are not going to provide much relief to borrowers, and they only temporarily settle financial markets. Each rate cut is met with relief, but the market then clamors for another. As discussed below, resets must be limited and postponed.
- Time and economic growth go a long way in restoring financial health—if incomes can grow sufficiently, it becomes easier to service debt. This will require growth of aggregate demand. Recent growth has been fueled by exports, partly thanks to a depreciating dollar. Any U.S. slowdown will, however, be contagious and hurt exports. The private sector cannot be the main source of demand stimulus. The problem is that while the budget deficit will increase as the economy slows, this results from deterioration of employment and income (which lowers taxes and increases transfers)—thus it will not proactively create growth although it will help to constrain the depths of recession. It is not likely that the President and Congress (even with a change of administration) will embark on spending programs or big tax cuts. It is difficult to see how the U.S. can grow its way out of this problem.
- The House of Representatives is proposing legislation that would allow bankruptcy judges to modify mortgage terms to allow people to keep their homes. Congress needs to go farther, however. The recent "reform" of bankruptcy law was passed just in time to make it difficult to resolve this crisis, because the current code prohibits relief from mortgage debt. Thus, this law must be amended to allow those who had been subjected to predatory lending to escape subprime loans. Borrowers should only need to show that inability to service the debt is not their fault—that is, that they have a loan that the lender should have known they would not be able to service out of their incomes and assets at the time the loan was made. Whether the lender had that information is not relevant. The borrower should then be able to refinance the home at its current market value, and with the borrower's original equity (if any) intact. Only if the creditor can show that the borrower had defrauded the originator (through, for example, doctored W-2 forms or bank account statements) would the borrower be held liable for the original loan. The amendments to the bankruptcy code might be limited in application to loans for primary residences only, and up to a limited home value (such as median price for the SMSA). As President Roosevelt argued in announcing

his plan to save the "small homes," the goal would be to preserve homeownership, not to protect real estate speculators. The FHA and GSEs would be instructed to take the lead in refinancing these homes. The problem is that Fannie and Freddie are already experiencing their own problems. Freddie, itself, holds a huge volume of securitized subprimes, and has written these down from par to 90%—however, the AGX indices indicate they are worth only 70 or less. Freddie is also already below minimum capital requirements. (Veneroso 2007b).

- The Treasury is working with the mortgage industry to freeze interest rates, so that those who can afford mortgages before resets occur can keep their homes. (Reuters 2007c). This differs from the proposal made in the previous point, as it writes off as lost causes those who were enticed to take out loans they could not afford from the get-go. This is not equitable—brokers and other lenders should bear the costs of pushing expensive debt, and homeowners should be offered terms for which they *would* have qualified at the time the loan was originally made. Further, as Bianco (2007) has shown, most "teaser rate" hybrid loans have already reset (over 99% of the adjustable-rate mortgages with an initial interest rate of less than 3% had already reset by August 2007, with only 235,000 such mortgages left to reset in 2008 and beyond). Because almost half of all ARMs originated between 2004 and 2006 had reset by August, freezing rates on those mortgages is like closing the gate after the cows have escaped. Interest rate relief needs to be made retroactive. Admittedly, this is not easy due to the nature of the contracts.
- Roosevelt created an RFC-like agency, the Home Owners' Loan Corporation (HOLC), to take on the tasks of saving small homeowners. This successfully refinanced 20% of the nation's mortgages, issuing bonds to raise the funds. While about 20% of those loans eventually were foreclosed, the HOLC actually managed to earn a small surplus on its activities, which was paid to the Treasury when it was liquidated in 1951 (Pollock 2007). Clearly, there are lessons to be learned from that experience: refinance is preferable to foreclosure as it preserves homeownership and communities, while also saving money in the process.
- The JEC has also called for counseling of delinquent borrowers to prevent foreclosure. The federal government should provide the funds initially, and should sue predatory lenders to recover costs. Governor Schwarzenegger of California has allocated $1.2 million for a statewide public awareness program to inform homeowners about alternatives to foreclosure (Lifsher 2007).
- It appears that financial markets are expecting the federal government to step in should the subprime crisis spread to other securities, such as the muni bond market. Geraud Charpin of UBS AG wrote to investors that "[a] form of bailout would probably be worked out. A politically engineered solution will insure an acceptable way out where the innocent pensioner does not lose out and states are able to continue funding themselves and build more roads

> and schools" (quoted in Richard and Gutscher 2007). Of course, bail-outs validate bad behavior and encourage worse. However, Minsky (like Samuelson) would argue that a financial crisis is not the correct time to try to teach markets a lesson by allowing defaults to snowball until a generalized debt deflation and depression can "cleanse" the system. There is a fine line that must be walked, allowing the worst abusers (and especially the perpetrators of fraud) to lose while protecting the relatively innocent. Probably no one has put it any better than Mayor Abramson of Louisville, Kentucky when speaking about foreclosures in our nation's cities: "We're trying to find the individual who ultimately sold that mortgage to, or packaged it and now it's at Countrywide, or it's Wells Fargo, or it's Deutsche Bank, or U.S. National Bank, none of which have locations in most of our cities . . . . We'd like to see the Wall Street syndicators, who made enormous amounts of money off these exotic packagings that they've developed, work with their servicing organizations, like the Wells Fargos and the Countrywides, to give them the flexibility necessary to work with American citizens to get through this crisis by, if having to, leave the interest [rate] where it is, put the extra dollars on the back of the loan, and allow the folks to continue to live in the property, maintain the property, and keep the neighborhoods stable." Mayor Jerry Abramson, Louisville, Kentucky (Marketplace 2007).

Because financial markets cannot be allowed to learn lessons "the hard way," regulations and oversight must be strengthened to slow the next stampede toward a speculative bubble. We turn to such concerns in the next section.

b. Policy to Prevent "It" From Happening Again

As Shiller (2007) argues, the housing downturn of 1925-33, during which housing prices fell by 30%, provided an opportunity for a revolutionary policy response that restructured the housing sector in a manner that made it robust for two generations. This was also a major theme in Minsky's work. Reforms included creation of the Federal Home Loan Bank System that would discount mortgages in lender of last resort interventions modeled on the Federal Reserve System, and the creation of the Home Owners Loan Corporation (discussed above) to refinance mortgages. The real estate appraisal industry established the Appraisal Institute to create professional, national standards; Congress modified bankruptcy law to extend protection to homeownership; and the Federal Deposit Insurance Corporation was created to protect deposits and prevent runs that would close financial institutions that made mortgage loans. The Federal Housing Administration was created, which transformed the typical mortgage, from a very short (five year) loan with a balloon payment to the long-term fixed-rate, self-amortizing mortgage that two generations of Americans grew up with. Finally, Fannie Mae was created in 1938 to increase the supply of mortgages to households of moderate and middle-income means, to encourage standardization of terms and to guarantee mortgages. Shiller (2007) characterizes the official policy response today as "anemic in comparison," argues that we should be prepared for a housing collapse as large as that of 1925-33, and calls for thinking about big and fundamental changes to put the real estate sector back on more secure footing. In this section we examine policy changes to prevent Minsky's "it" from happening again.

- Congress is considering regulations on mortgage originators that would establish new licensing requirements, put restrictions on incentives for saddling borrowers with riskier loans, and provide liability for financial institutions that sell mortgages (Hulse 2007). In addition, Congress would set new standards to be met by originators regarding ability of borrowers to make payments. Unfortunately, it is not clear that Congress will apply these rules to state licensed mortgage brokers. Predictably, the mortgage industry has attacked the legislation as too intrusive. Consumer groups correctly argue that the proposals do not go far enough. The California State Assembly is also considering legislation to ban predatory lending practices, such as yield-spread premiums that induce brokers to push high interest rate loans (Lifsher 2007).
- Unscrupulous lending was a big part of the subprime boom, with little oversight of mortgage brokers and with substantial incentive to induce borrowers to take on more debt than they could handle, at interest rates that would reset at a level virtually guaranteed to generate delinquencies. The evidence is overwhelming that variable rate loans lead to more foreclosures; hybrid VARs are even more dangerous. There is a proper place for VARs and hybrid VARs, but not with the typical subprime borrower who has little reserve if things go bad. Speculative property "flippers" might not need protection from these risky financial instruments, but low income borrowers, and first-time buyers do. Congress should investigate limits to marketing of VARs and hybrids to low income borrowers and first time buyers.
- Pollock has called for a simple, standard, one-page disclosure of the loan terms, written in plain English. This summary should explicitly show all of the fees as well as the monthly payment under all likely scenarios (for example, after interest rate reset, and after the borrower's credit score deteriorates due to missed payments). Prepayment fees should be shown and explained. The primary borrower financial characteristics on which the loan is made should be shown—income, assets, down payment—as well as the home's market-assessed value and the loan to value ratio. The loan originator must sign a statement indicating that due diligence has been made to ensure accuracy of the disclosure. As the current crisis demonstrates, quick profits can be made for originators by duping borrowers and security purchasers, but social costs are too high to permit this to happen again.
- Predatory lending practices should be identified and banned. Predatory practices should be defined to include large pre-payment penalties, low "teaser" rates that reset at much higher rates, knowingly inducing a borrower to agree

to a higher interest rate than justified by the credit score, no doc and low doc loans, liar loans, and loan terms that the borrower will not be able to meet. Restrictions should be tighter when lending for a primary residence, than for a second or vacation home, or for commercial real estate. Ponzi and speculative loans (that rely on home price appreciation for validation) should not be permitted in the case of first time buyers, indeed, probably should not be permitted at all in the case of purchases of primary residences.

- Mortgage brokers must be supervised and regulated. Given that they originate mortgages that will be sold in national and international markets, federal oversight is necessary. Exactly what division in responsibilities will be made between state and federal supervision requires further study.
- As Martin Wolf and Henry Kaufman put it, fear must be reintroduced into markets. According to Kaufman, "It is therefore urgent that the Fed take the lead in formulating a monetary policy approach that strikes a balance between market discipline and government regulation. Until it does so, we will continue to see shocks of even greater intensity than the one now radiating outward from the quake in the U.S. subprime mortgage market." (Kaufman 2007.) Increased federal funding of investigation of fraud would help to strike some fear into the hearts of Wall Street.
- There should be losses, but, again, there must also be protection for the financial system as a whole and for the "innocent." Separating the "guilty" from the "wives and orphans" will not be easy—and the policy bias to save the system will mean that many of the guilty will have their losses "socialized." Where possible, policy should protect holders of financial institution liabilities but not the holders of equity. Policy should also avoid promotion of financial institution consolidation—a natural result of financial crises that can be boosted by policy-arranged bailouts. Minsky always preferred policy that would promote small-to-medium sized financial institutions. Unfortunately, policy makers who are biased toward "free markets" instinctively prefer to use public money to subsidize private institution take-overs of failing financial firms. The Roosevelt alternative should be adopted: temporary "nationalization" of failing institutions with a view to eventually return them to the private sector at a small profit to the U.S. Treasury. This is what Minsky advocated during the thrift crisis of the 1980s, but the administration of President Bush, senior, chose industry consolidation and public assumption of bad assets that resulted in Treasury losses. Policy should instead foster competition, with a bias against consolidation.

CONCLUSION: WHAT WE LEARNED FROM MINSKY

Have I learned from my mistakes? Yes, I believe I could repeat them all exactly the same.[23]

[23] Attributed to Kurt Vonnegut.

In response to the spreading subprime meltdown, the Bank of England has advocated "a greater focus on liquidity management, more rigorous stress testing, greater transparency in the composition and valuation of structured products and improved disclosure on institutions' risk exposures, including to off balance sheet vehicles" (Bank of England 2007). While these recommendations are surely welcome, they would have had little effect on the current outcome even if they had been in place in 2000. Notably absent is any enhanced regulation and oversight by central banks and other government supervisors, as the recommendations merely reflect the currently fashionable belief that if only markets function smoothly and with better information, all will be fine. This would perhaps work if the financial system were fundamentally stable.

Minsky, however, insisted that market processes are fundamentally destabilizing—an instability that is not due to inadequate transparency. The fundamental instability is upward—toward a euphoric expansion that cannot be tamed by better information or lower transactions costs. Indeed, even the Bank of England's own report makes it clear that in spite of warnings from "the Bank, the FSA and other official sector institutions" as well as from "market contacts" that risk was vastly underpriced, those operating in markets "were afraid to stand against the tide for fear of losing market Share"[24] (Bank of England 2007). Those familiar with Keynes will recall his statement that it is better to fail conventionally than to swim against the tide. Thus, one cannot look to market "reforms" for solutions to systemic problems—and blaming market participants for short-sightedness is not helpful.

Minsky used to argue that the Great Depression represented a failure of the small government, Laissez-faire economic model, while the New Deal promoted a Big Government/Big Bank highly successful model for financial capitalism. The current crisis just as convincingly represents a failure of the big-government, neoconservative (or, outside the U.S., what is called the neo-liberal) model. This model promotes deregulation, reduced supervision and oversight, privatization, and consolidation of market power. In the U.S., there has been a long run trend that favors "markets" over "banks," which has also played into the hands of neoconservatives. The current housing finance crisis is a prime example of the damage that can be done. The New Deal reforms transformed housing finance into a very safe, protected, business based on (mostly) small, local financial institutions that knew their markets and their borrowers. Homeownership was promoted through

---

[24] It is interesting that Northern Rock, the "poster child" for the spread of the U.S. subprime problems to the rest of the world, began as a mutual-form building society but converted to a stock-form U.K. bank in 1997. After conversion, it grew quickly with liabilities increasing from about 20 billion pounds in 1998 to nearly 120 billions in 2007. Those familiar with the US thrift crisis will notice the similarity: thrifts converted from mutuals after 1974, and then grew rapidly during the 1980s before spectacular failures that decimated the whole thrift industry. Northern Rock also proved that anything less than 100% deposit coverage is meaningless when a financial institution's solvency is called into question—with coverage equal to only 90%, Northern Rock faced a bank run that was calmed only when the government agreed to provide 100% coverage of deposits (remarkably, the Treasury agreed to indemnify the "Bank [Bank of England] against any losses and other liabilities arising from its role in providing finance to Northern Rock")—which was extended to all other financial institutions that might face liquidity problems. (Bank of England 2007).

long term, fixed rate, self-amortizing mortgages. Communities benefited, and households built wealth that provided a path toward middle class lifestyles (including college educations for baby-boomers and secure retirement for their parents). This required oversight by regulators, FDIC and FSLIC deposit insurance, and a commitment to relatively stable interest rates. The Big Government/Neocon model, by contrast, replaced the New Deal reforms with self-supervision of markets, with greater reliance on "personal responsibility" as safety nets were shredded, and with monetary and fiscal policy that is biased against maintenance of full employment and adequate growth to generate rising living standards for most Americans. The model is in trouble—and not just with respect to the mortgage mess, as the U.S. faces record inequality and destruction of the middle class, a healthcare crisis, an incarceration disaster, and other problems beyond the scope of this analysis (see Wray 2005 and Wray 2000).

Minsky's work provides guidance for development of a new model that is consistent with current realities. He teaches us that the modern financially complex economy is prone to speculative booms. Financial innovations stretch liquidity and increase leverage in a way that endangers solvency. Unfortunately, periods of relative stability hasten the process, encouraging the development of financially fragile structures. The Big Government and Big Bank help to put ceilings and floors on demand and income, as well as on asset prices. Again, however, by reducing volatility, leveraging is encouraged. Further, from his earliest work, Minsky recognized that private-led expansions are inherently more prone to creation of financial fragility because they imply deterioration of private balance sheets as borrowing tends to increase faster than ability to service debt out of income. For this reason, he advocated policy that would encourage consumption, but with a major impetus for growth coming from government spending. A government-led expansion would actually improve private sector balance sheets.

Minsky never really addressed a situation such as the one we have experienced since 1996, in which households consistently spend more than their incomes—although this analysis has shown that his work on financial instability can be extended to cover household finance. The housing sector boom has occurred in conjunction with a consumption-led boom (indeed the two were linked, as discussed), thus, household balance sheets have been doubly affected. Clearly, this is not a sustainable model for the long run, although it was sustained over the medium term by a confluence of supporting influences. Big government deficits kicked-in at the right time during the recession early this decade, to prop up income so that the consumption boom could resume. Socialization of risk through Big Bank (Fed) intervention helped to limit losses in financial markets in the increasingly frequent and severe financial crises experienced over the past two decades. Freeing financial markets and validating innovations increased the supply of credit to households, permitting what would have been otherwise impossibly stretched finances. However, all of this is leading to the inevitable crash.

We must return to a more sensible model, with enhanced oversight of financial institutions. We need to recreate a housing finance model that promotes stability rather than speculation. We need policy that promotes rising wages for the bottom half (or even three-quarters) of workers so that borrowing is less necessary to maintain middle class living standards. We need policy that promotes employment, rather than transfer payments—or worse, incarceration—for those left behind. Monetary policy must be turned away from using rate hikes to pre-empt inflation and toward a proper role: stabilizing interest rates, direct credit controls to prevent runaway speculation, and supervision. Minsky advocated support for small banks, and creation of a system of community development banks—the latter only partially achieved under President Clinton—as a viable alternative to the predatory lending practices that *did* increase the supply of credit to low income borrowers and neighborhoods, but which is resulting in foreclosures and vacancies.[25] As Keynes (1964) said, "Speculators may do no harm as bubbles on a steady stream of enterprise. But the position is serious when enterprise becomes the bubble on a whirlpool of speculation. When the capital development of a country becomes a by-product of the activities of a casino, the job is likely to be ill-done." Unfortunately, we turned American home finance over to Wall Street, which operated the industry as if it were a casino. Keynes warned that "[i]t is usually agreed that casinos should, in the public interest, be inaccessible and expensive." Instead, the price of admission to the American mortgage casino was cheap, but the potential losses are huge. Minsky called for "the creation of new economic institutions which constrain the impact of uncertainty is necessary," arguing that the "aim of policy is to assure that the economic prerequisites for sustaining the civil and civilized standards of an open liberal society exist. If amplified uncertainty and extremes in income maldistribution and social inequalities attenuate the economic underpinnings of democracy, then the market behavior that creates these conditions has to be constrained" (Minsky 1996).

REFERENCES

Andrews, Edmund. 2007. "Fed Lowers Key Interest Rate by a Quarter Point," *New York Times*. October 31. http://www.nytimes.com/2007/10/31/business/31cnd-fed.html.

Ash, Adrian. 2007. "Dr. Ponzi Goes to Congress," Mar 28.

Associated Press. 2007a. "Have We Seen Worse of Mortgage Crisis?" *New York Times*, November 24. http://www.nytimes.com/aponline/business/AP-DoomsdayScenario.html.

———. 2007b. "Home Depot Profit Down 26.8%," *York Times*, November 13. http://nytimes.com/aponline/business/AP-Earns-Home-Depot.html.

———. 2007c. "Home Prices Fall by 4.5 Percent in 3rd Quarter," *New York Times*, November 27. http://www.nytimes.com/aponline/business/AP-HomePrice-Index.html.

———. 2007d. "Florida Halts Withdrawals from Investment Pool," *New York Times*, November 2. http://www.nytimes.com/aponline/business/apeeinvest.html

———. 2007e. "Have We Seen Worse of Mortgage Crisis?" *New York Times*. November 24. www.nytimes.com/aponline/business/AP-DoomsdayScenario.html, accessed 11/24/2007.

Bajaj, Vikas. 2007. "Mortgage Security Bondholders Facing a Cutoff of Interest Payments," October 22. *New York Times*. November 25. http://www.nytimes.com/2007/10/22/business/22market.html.

Bajaj, Vikas and Edmund Andrews. 2007. "Reports Suggest Broader Losses from Mortgages." *New York Times*. October 25. http://www.nytimes.com/2007/10/25/business/25mortgage.html.

---

[25] See Papadimitriou and Wray (1998) for a summary of Minsky's policy proposals.

Bajaj, Vikas and Mark Landler. 2007. "Mortgage Losses Echo in Europe and on Wall Street," *New York Times.* August 10. http://www.nytimes.com/2007/08/10/business/10markets.html.

Bank of England. 2007. "Financial Stability Report," Issue No. 22, October.

Barr, Alistair. 2007. "First America Sued in Mortgage Appraisal Probe," MarketWatch. November 1. www.marketwatch.com/news/story/first-americans-target-suitover/story.aspx ... accessed 11/1/2007.

Bernanke, Ben S. 2004. "The Great Moderation," Speech given at the meeting of the Eastern Economic Association, Washington, DC, February 20. http://www.federalreserve.gov/Boarddocs/Speeches/2004/20040220/default.htm.

Bianco, James A. 2007. "Commentary: Why Subprime Is Not the Problem in the Capital Markets," August 29. Bianco Research L.L.C., www.biancoresearch.com.

Black, William. 2005. *The Best Way to Rob a Bank is to Own One.* Austin Texas: University of Texas at Austin.

Bloomberg News. 2007. "Bank of China Reports Heavy Exposure to Subprime Crisis," *New York Times,* August 24. http://www.nytimes.com/2007/08/24/business/worldbusiness/24wire-china.html.

Brooks, Rick and Ruth Simon. 2007. "As Housing Boomed, Industry Pushed Loans to a Broader Market," *Wall Street Journal,* December 3, p. AI.

Brewster, Deborah. 2007. "Liquidity Needs Throw Spanner in Quant Models," *Financial Times.* August 15, p. 14.

Burroughs, Eric. 2007. "Update 3-S&P Says State St-Managed CDO Liquidating Assets," Reuters, November 9. http://www.reuters.com/articlePrint?articleId-USL0954927220071109.

Buttonwood. 2007. "Ponzificating," March 17. *The Economist Newspaper,* p. 80.

Chancellor, Edward. 2007. "Ponzi Nation," February 7. *Institutional Investor.*

Chittum, Ryan and Jennifer S. Forsyth. 2007. "Fitch Sees Rising Shakiness in Commercial Mortgage Arena," *Wall Street Journal.* July 12, accessed at http://www.rgemonitor.com/blog/roubini/205212/ (December 3, 2007).

Concerned Real Estate Appraisers from across America. 2007. "Appraisers Petition," accessed August 14. www.appraiserspetition.com.

Dash, Eric. 2007. "Earnings Fall 32% at Bank of America," October 18. *New York Times.* November 25, 2007, http://www.nytimes.com/2007/10/18/business/18cndbank.html, accessed 10/22, 2007.

Evans-Pritchard, Ambrose. 2007. "Credit 'Heart Attack' Engulfs China and Korea," *Telegraph,* November 23. www.telegraph.co.uk/core/Content/ display Printable.jhtml, accessed 11/26/07.

Goldstein, Matthew. 2007. "Who's Profiting from the Subprime Bust," *Business Week.* March 8. http://www.businessweek.com/print/investor/content/mar2007/pi20070308_900631.htm.

Goodman, Peter S. 2007. "As Lenders Tighten Flow of Credit, Growth at Risk," *New York Times.* November 29. http://www.nytimes.com/2007/11/29/business/29lend.html.

Grynbaum, Michael M. 2007. "Stocks Plummet on 'Ugly Week' for Investors," *New York Times,* November 22. http://www.nytimes.com/2007/11/22/business/22markets.html.

Harrington, Shannon D. and Christopher Condon. 2007. "Bank of America, Legg Mason Prop Up Money Funds (update4)," Bloomberg.com. November 13. http://www.bloomberg.com/apps/news?pit=20670001&refer=worldwide&sid=aWWjLp ... (accessed 11/13/2007).

HCL Finance. 2007. Home of the "No Doc Loan." https://broker.hclfinance.com/p/program_list.htm, accessed 5/8/2007 and 11/1/2007.

Hill, F. Anita. 2007. "Women and the Subprime Crunch," *Boston Globe.* October 22. www.boston.cm/news/globe/editorial_opinion/oped/articles/2007/10/22/women_and_the_subprime_crunch ... accessed 10/24/07.

Hulse, Carl. 2007. "With Eye on '08, House Takes on Mortgage Rules," *New York Times,* November 15. http://www.truthout.org/docs_2006/printer_111507G.shtml.

Hutchinson, Martin. 2007."The Bear's Lair: Level 3 Decimation?" PrudentBear.com. October 29. http://prudentbear.com/index.php?option-com_content&view=frontpage&Itemid=6 ... (accessed 11/9/2007).

Isidore, Chris. 2007. "For Sale: 2 Million Empty Homes," October 26. CNNMoney. http://money.cnn.com/2007/10/26/news/economy/vacant_homes/inidex.htm.

Joint Economic Committee. 2007. *The Subprime Lending Crisis: The Economic Impact on Wealth, Property Values and Tax Revenues, and How We Got Here,* October. Senator Charles E. Schumer, Chairman and Rep. Carolyn B. Maloney, Vice Chair.

Johnson, Carrie. 2007. "Businesses Prepare to Mount a Concerted Attack on Regulation," *The Washington Post,* March 12, 2007, www.truthout.org/docs_2006/printer_031207s.shtml.

JP Morgan. 2007. "Banks may take $77 billion in CDO losses," November 27. mimeo.

Kaufman, Henry. 2007. "Our Risky New Financial Markets," *The Wall Street Journal.* August 15, p. A13.

Keynes, John Maynard. 1964. *The General Theory of Employment, Interest, and Money.* New York and London: Harcourt Brace Jovanovich.

Kregel, Jan. 2007a. "Financial Innovation and Crises - A Post-Keynesian-Minskyan Perspective," presentation given at the Noriss, Res Publica & Other Canon Conference, *Financial Crises In Capitalism: The Market Economy and Financial Crises: a Recurrent Theme,* Storsalen, Sormarka Conference Centre, August 27.

Kregel, Jan, 2007b. "Minsky's 'Cushions of Safety,' Systemic Risk and the Crisis in the U.S. Subprime Mortgage Market," draft, November 25.

Krugman, Paul. 2007. "A Catastrophe Foretold," *New York Times.* October 26. http://www.truthout.org/ docs_2006/printer_1026070.shtml.

Kuttner, Robert. 2007. "The Alarming Parallels between 1929 and 2007," *The American Prospect.* October 2. Testimony of Robert Kuttner Before the Committee on Financial Services, Rep. Barney Frank, Chairman, U.S. House of Representatives, Washington D.C. http://www.truthout.org/docs_2006/100307H.shtml.

Lahart, Justin. 2007. "In Time of Tumult, Obscure Economist Gains Currency," August 18. *The Wall Street Journal Online.* http://online.wsj.com/public/article-rint/SB118736585456901047.html, accessed 9/5/2007.

Lamothe, Keisha. 2007. "Foreclosures: Moving on Up," CNNMoney, November 1. http://money.cnn.com/2007/10/30/real_estate/foreclosure_activity/index.htm.

Landler, Mark and Julia Werdigier. 2007. "In Europe, Weathering the Credit Storm from U.S.," *New York Times.* November 24. http://www.nytimes.com/2007/11/24/business/worldbusiness/24subprime.html.

Leamer, Edward E. 2007. "Housing is the Business Cycle." Working Paper No. 13428, National Bureau of Economic Research, http://www.nber.org/papers/w13428.

Lifsher, Marc. 2007. "State Lawmakers Wade into Sub-prime Crisis," *The Los Angeles Times.* November 29, accessed at www.truthout.org/docs_2006/printer_112907T.shtml on 11/29/07.

Loomis, Carol. 2007. "Robert Rubin on the Job He Never Wanted," *Fortune,* CNNMoney. com. November 13. http/cnnmoney.printthis.clickability.com/pt/cpt?action=cpt&title= Robert+Rubin, accessed 11/22/2007.

Lucchetti, Aaron and Serena Ng. 2007. "How Rating Firms' Calls Fueled Subprime Mess," *The Wall Street Journal.* August 15, p. AI, A10.

Mackenzie, Michael, Gillian Tett, and David Oakley. 2007. "Crisis 'To Get Worse Before It Gets Better,'" *Financial Times.* November 8. FT. Com. http://www.ft.com/cms/s/0/a5db161e-8e3d, accessed 11/9/2007.

Magnus, George. 2007. "What This Minsky Moment Means for Business," August 23. *Financial Times,* p. 11.

Marketplace. 2007. "Cities Are Stuck in Mortgage Meltdown," November 27. http://market place.publicradio.org/display/web/2007/11/27/louisville_mayor_q/.

McCulley, Paul. 2001. "Capitalism's Beast of Burden," PIMCO Bonds. January. www.pimco. com/leftnav/featured+market+commentary/FF_01_200 ... accessed 9/5/2007.

———. 2007."The Plankton Theory Meets Minsky," Global Central Bank Focus, PIMCO Bonds. March. www.pimco.com/leftnav/featured+market+commentary/FF ... accessed 3/8/2007.

Minsky, Hyman P. 1987. "Securitization," Handout Econ 335A, Fall 1987. Mimeo, in The Levy Economics Institute archives.

———. 1986. *Stabilizing an Unstable Economy.* Yale University Press.

———. 1992. "The Financial Instability Hypothesis," Working Paper No. 74. Annandale-on-Hudson, New York: The Levy Economics Institute.

———. 1996. "Uncertainty and the Institutional Structure of Capitalist Economies," Working Paper No. 155, Annandale-on-Hudson: The Levy Economics Institute.

Morgenson, Gretchen. 2007a. "Crisis Looms in Market for Mortgages," *New York Times.* March 11. http://www.nytimes.com/2007/03/11/business/11mortgage.html.

Morgenson, Gretchen. 2007b. "Blame the Borrowers? Not So Fast," *New York Times.* November 25. http://www.nytimes.com/2007/11/25/business/25gret.html.

Morgenson, Gretchen. 2007c. "Foreclosures Hit a Snag for Lenders," *New York Times.* November 15. http://www.nytimes.com/2007/11/15/business/15lend.html.

Morgenson, Gretchen and Jenny Anderson. 2007. "Subprime Problems Spread into Commercial Loans," *New York Times.* August 15. http://www.nytimes.com/2007/08/15/business/15fund. html.

Nocera, Joe. 2007. "Short Seller Sinks Teeth into Insurer," *New York Times.* December 1. http:// www.nytimes.com/2007/12/01/business/01nocera.html.

Norris, Floyd. 2007a. "Reading the Tea Leaves of Financial Statements," *New York Times.* November 9. http://www.nytimes.com/2007/11/09/business/09norris.html.

Norris, Floyd. 2007b. "Economy May Defy Past and Disregard Housing," *New York Times.* November 24. http://www.nytimes.com/2007/11/24/business/24charts.html.

Norris, Floyd. 2007c."Who's Going to Take the Financial Weight," *New York Times.* October 26. http://www.nytimes.com/2007/10/26/business/26norris.html.

Norris, Floyd. 2007d. "The Case of the Vanishing Jobs," *New York Times.* November 30. http://norris.blogs.nytimes.com/2007 /11/30/the-case-of-the-vanashing-jobs/ ... accessed 12/3/2007.

Papadimitriou, Dimitri B. and L. Randall Wray.1998."The Economic Contributions of Hyman Minsky: Varieties of Capitalism and Institutional Reform," *Review of Political Economy,* 10(2), 199-225.

Parenteau, Robert W. 2007. "U.S. Household Deficit Spending: A Rendezvous with Reality," Public Policy Brief, No. 88. Annandale-on-Hudson, New York: The Levy Economics Institute.

Pearlstein, Steven. 2007. "'No Money Down' Falls Flat," *The Washington Post,* March 14, p. DOL

Pendley, M. Diane, Glenn Costello and Mary Kelsch. 2007. "The Impact of Poor Underwriting Practices and Fraud in Subprime RMBS Performance," FitchRatings, November 28. Accessed at www.rgemonitor.com/blog/economonitor/229372, on 11/29/2007.

Pollock, Alex J. 2007. "Subprime Mortgage Lending Problems in Context," Testimony to the Subcommittee on Financial Institutions and Consumer Credit, Committee on Financial Services, U.S. House of Representatives, Hearing on Subprime and Predatory Lending, March 27.

Reuters. 2007a. "Barclays to Write Down $2.7 Billion," *New York Times.* November 15. http://www.nytimes.com/reuters/business/business-barclays-trading.html.

Reuters. 2007b. "UBS Posts Larger-than-Expected Loss," *New York Times.* October 30. October 31, 2007, http://www.nytimes.com/reuters/business/business-ubsresults.html.

Reuters. 2007c. "U.S. Mortgage Industry Hashes Out Rate-freeze Plan," *New York Times.* December 1. http://www.nytimes.com/reuters/business/business-usasubprime.html.

Reuters. 2007d. "US Mayors Warn Worst of Mortgage Crisis Ahead," November 27. www.truthout.org/docs_2006/printer_112707N.shtml.

Richard, Christine and Cecile Gutscher. 2007. "MBIA, Ambac Downgrades May Cost Market $200 Billion (Update 2)," Bloomberg.com, November 15. http://www.bloomberg.com/apps/news?pid=20670001&refer=&sid=aqGYEJ40EJoE.

Roosevelt, Franklin D. 1933. "Message to Congress on Small Home Mortgage Foreclosures," April 13.

Roubini, Nouriel. 2007. "Steve Pearlstein of WaPo on Liar Loans, Teaser Loans, Stretch Loans, NINJA Loans and Other Mortgage Monstrosities," March 14.

Samuelson, Paul A. 2007. "The Financial Gods that Failed," Tribune Media Services, August 21. http://www.iht.com/articles/2007/08/21/opinion/edsamuelson.php.

Schumer, Charles. 2007. Press Release, New Joint Economic Committee Report Reveals Serious Local Economic Impact of Subprime Mortgage Fallout Across Country, April 11.

Schwartz, Nelson D. 2007. "One World, Taking Risks Together," *New York Times.* October 21. http://www.nytimes.com/2007/10/21/weekinreview/21 schwartz.html.

Shell, Adam. 2007. "Weakness in Banking Hammers Stocks," *USA Today.* November 20, p. 6B.

Shen, Jody. 2007. "Bank CDO Losses May Reach $77 Billion, JP Morgan Says (Update1)," Bloomberg.com. November 27. http://www.bloomberg.com/apps/news?pid=20601087&sid=aKx.Gintu5so&refer=home accessed and updated Dec 6, 2007.

Shiller, Robert 1. 2007. "A Time for Bold Thinking on Housing," *New York Times.* November 25. http://www.nytimes.com/2007//11/25/business/25view.html.

Stein, Ben. 2007. "The Long and Short of It at Goldman Sachs," *New York Times.* December 2. http://www.nytimes.com/2007/12/02/business/02every.html

Summers, Lawrence. 2007. "Wake Up to the Dangers of a Deepening Crisis," November 25. *FT.com,* http://www.ft.com/cms/s/0/b56079a8-9b71-11dc-8aad-0000779fd2ac.html. Accessed Dec 3, 2000.

Tett, Gillian and Anuj Gangahar. 2007. "System Error: Why Computer Models Proved Unequal to Market Turmoil," *Financial Times.* August 15. p. 7.

U.S. Daily Financial Market Comment. 2007. "Leveraged Losses: Why Mortgage Defaults Matter," U.S. Economic Research Group, Goldman Sachs, November 15. https://portal.gs.com.

Veneroso, Frank. 2007a. "On the Total Credit Losses Out There: Roubini's Analysis Says, Add another $100 billion in US commercial real estate losses," November 14. mimeo.

Veneroso, Frank. 2007b. "US Economy Watch: Larry Summers on the Current Financial Crisis and the Risk of Recession," November 26. mimeo.

Veron, Nicolas. 2007. "Is Europe Ready for a Major Banking Crisis?" *bruegelpolicybrief,* Issue 03, August. www.bruegel.org.

Werdigier, Julia. 2007a."HSBC Sets Bailout Plan for Assets of2 funds," *New York Times.* November 27. http://www.nytimes.com/2007/11/27 /business/worldbusiness/27bank.html.

Werdigier, Julia. 2007b. "Subprime Woes Hit Norwegian Brokerage," *New York Times.* November 29. http://www.nytimes.com/2007/11/29/business/worldbusiness/29bank.html.

Whalen, Charles. 2007. "The U.S. Credit Crunch of2007: A Minsky Moment," Public Policy Brief, No. 92. Annandale-on-Hudson, New York: The Levy Economics Institute.

Wolf, Martin. 2007. "In a World of Overconfidence, Fear Makes a Welcome Return," *Financial Times.* August 15, p. 9.

Wood, Christopher. 2007. "Cyclical Drumbeat," *Greed and Fear,* CLSA Asia-Pacific Markets. November 15.

Wray, L. Randall. 2000. "A New Economic Reality: Penal Keynesianism," *Challenge,* September-October, 31-59.

———. 1994. "The Political Economy of the Current US Financial Crisis," *International Papers in Political Economy,* vol. 1, no. 3.

———. 2004. "The Fed and the New Monetary Consensus: The Case for Rate Hikes, Part Two," Public Policy Brief No. 80. Annandale-on-Hudson, New York: The Levy Economics Institute.

———. 2005. "The Ownership Society: Social Security Is Only the Beginning ... "Public Policy Brief No. 82. Annandale-on-Hudson, New York: The Levy Economics Institute

*Extraordinary Circumstances: The Journey of a Corporate Whistleblower (Part 2)**

*Cynthia Cooper***

AN INSPIRING MEETING

It's November, 2002. When I check my voice-mail one morning, I have a message from Amanda Ripley, a reporter from *Time Magazine.* Because I have intentionally stayed out of the press so far, I ask my attorney Bob Muse to return *Time's* phone call. Bob calls me back several days later.

"Cynthia, *Time* is looking to do an article for their December edition on you, Sherron Watkins, and Coleen Rowley," he says, referring to the Enron and FBI whistle blowers. "I think you should give this interview." While I'm very reluctant, Bob believes that it's a tremendous opportunity to meet two other women who've faced similar challenges. My husband, Lance, is also encouraging me to do the interview. He thinks it will benefit people to hear all three of these personal stories. After talking with my family, I call Bob back. "I'll do it only if the others agree to the interview," I tell him. As it happens, I'm not the only one who wants to make sure the others are on board before signing on. We're all three reluctant, especially Coleen. While Sherron has resigned from Enron, Coleen is still an attorney in the FBI's Minneapolis office, and has less than two years until retirement.

The reporters work back and forth with the three of us until everyone agrees to the interview. They must move quickly to meet tight deadlines. Amanda Ripley, one of the *Time* reporters, is coming to Mississippi to interview my family and me over several days. She's professional, warm and congenial; any uncertainty I once had about reporters quickly dissipates. Two other reporters are interviewing Sherron and Coleen separately at their homes, and then all six of us will get together for a group interview. I'm eager to meet Sherron and Coleen. I know their names through the press, but little about

* From CYNTHIA COOPER, EXTRAORDINARY CIRCUMSTANCES: THE JOURNEY OF A CORPORATE WHISTLEBLOWER.

** President of Cynthia Cooper Consulting, and provides consulting and training services in internal audits, internal controls, governance and ethics.

their personal stories. I don't remember ever meeting a whistleblower before. I wonder if our experiences will be similar. Will we have anything in common?

It's early December, 2002. I'm flying to Minneapolis, where Coleen lives. Sherron is flying in from Texas. The three of us will have dinner with the reporters. In the morning, we'll have a roundtable discussion and a photographer will take our picture. "I hope I've made the right decision about going through with this interview," I tell my husband before leaving.

As Amanda and I walk into the hotel restaurant, Sherron is already waiting. She rises to greet me. We hug and have an instant casual rapport. Though we've never met, I feel somehow as if I already know her. After a few moments, Coleen arrives. Her demeanor is friendly but more formal, what I would expect from an FBI agent. We shake hands instead, and depart for dinner. I'm equally fascinated about meeting the three *Time* reporters, all women. As we sit at dinner, the conversation is easy and informal.

Sherron, 43, and Coleen, 48, are several years older than I am. They both seem more outspoken, but there's an immediate connection between us. While our stories and personalities are different, many of our experiences and challenges are similar. We will become friends and share advice based on what we went through. It's been only five months since this nightmare started for me, but Sherron has been living it longer.

Sherron was a vice president in Enron's Finance department when she warned Ken Lay, Enron's CEO, about shady accounting. Soon after, her boss Andy Fastow, Enron's CFO, seized the hard drive from her computer. She was moved out of her executive suite into a smaller run-down office with an old desk. Behind the scenes, executive management looked into firing her. As an e-mail by Enron's outside counsel to an Enron executive, written just two days after Sherron spoke to Ken Lay, stated, "Per your request, the following are some bullet thoughts on how to manage the case with the employee who made the sensitive report. . . . Texas law does not currently protect corporate whistle-blowers. The Supreme Court has twice declined to create a cause of action for whistleblowers who are discharged." Fearful for her personal safety, Sherron spoke with company security personnel about protection. She once received a call from someone blaming her for the fact that a senior Enron executive had taken his life shortly after the company's scandal broke. After less than a year, feeling isolated and frustrated that she was being given only busywork, Sherron left the company.

After the September 11 attacks, Coleen wrote a 13-page letter to then-FBI Director Robert Mueller. She also gave a copy of the letter to two Senators on the Senate Committee on Intelligence. The letter indicated that her office in Minneapolis had forwarded information to higher-ups related to a French-Moroccan, who had registered for flight school in the area, and that the information had not been properly addressed.

Coleen seems to have had a particularly difficult time. Disclosing internal FBI issues to Congress didn't go over well within the halls of the FBI. Loyalty is important in any organization, but especially so in law enforcement. She received nasty letters and phone calls, some that could be construed as threatening. One of Coleen's co-workers warned her that senior FBI personnel were talking about filing criminal charges against her. Coleen found herself faced with colliding values: loyalty to her superiors against what she believed was right and the obligation she felt to the American public. As she will say in her *Time* interview, "Loyalty to whoever you work for is extremely important. The only problem is, it's not *the* most important thing." Coleen will stay with the FBI until retirement, but before she leaves, she voluntarily takes a demotion, giving up her position as an attorney for her field office.

We all loved where we worked and had a strong belief in the value of our organizations. Sherron and I were both at the vice president level and had each been with our companies for around eight years. Coleen had worked with the FBI her entire career. She even dreamed of working as an FBI agent as a child when she organized her 5th grade girlfriends into a spy club. As an elementary school girl, she wrote the FBI for more information and soon learned that females weren't allowed to be agents. No matter, she was sure she would one day work for them anyway. By the time she grew up, the rules had changed, but she was one of the trailblazers, as there were still few female agents.

The photo shoot is the next morning. Coleen is a tri-athlete who is typically toting a gun wherever she goes. Wearing dresses and make-up is not her thing. But today, she agrees to make an exception. The hotel's racquetball court has been turned into a temporary studio. The photographer takes picture after picture, Coleen in the middle, Sherron and I to her sides. As he snaps away, he instructs us not to smile. I agree—the topic is too serious, and it would seem inappropriate. We're all surprised by the extent of the photo shoot. "I thought this was just going to be a snapshot for an article in the magazine," Coleen says as we leave.

It's early one Saturday morning in late December. I'm still in a deep sleep when the phone rings. Thinking it likely a family member, I roll over trying to shake the fog from my brain and pull the phone to my ear. "Cynthia, this is Jim Kelly with *Time Magazine.*" I try to compose myself and mask the fact I have just been awakened, as I listen to him say that we will be the 2002 Persons of the Year and that it will be announced first thing tomorrow morning. It is a call I will not forget. For an average citizen who has never been in the public eye, it is an incredibly humbling part of my journey. Beneath our photo, *Time* prints "The Whistleblowers," a term I don't much care for until my mother calls to tell me what one of the news stations is saying: Three snitches were named Persons of the Year. Maybe "whistleblower" isn't so bad after all, I think.

When *Time's* December issue comes out, the managing editor will write that the reporters were worried the night before the three of us met. "How would Rowley, famous for her fanny pack and 20-year-old-suits, get along with Watkins, who was bemoaning a lost airline bag containing a Hermes scarf? Would Cooper, who had stayed fiercely private since her name was leaked over the summer, have anything to say to anyone?" But he went on to note that the "worries were groundless." I admire these women for their tenaciousness and perseverance through tough times. Meeting them, I finally feel less alone. Lance will tell me that I returned from the meeting changed, "The person who left for Minneapolis isn't the same person who came home," he says.

From a personal perspective, meeting Sherron, Coleen and the *Time* reporters will be an incredible step forward for me. After the articles, my team and I receive many letters of encouragement. It will help me look beyond my own circumstances and begin to see how sharing this story might help others. What happened to Sherron, Coleen and me in our places of employment could have happened to anyone. In fact, most people have at one level or another identified wrongdoing or, like Betty Vinson and Troy Normand, felt pressured to do something they didn't believe was right. What happened to people in many companies involved in recent scandals will happen again, to other people, in other companies.

THE WHISTLEBLOWER PHENOMENON

Before being labeled a whistle blower, I hadn't given much thought to whistleblowers or what they go through, but now, I want to learn more. Are my experiences shared by others? I query whistleblowers on the Internet and find a multitude of articles, studies and books. I finally decide on a book titled *Whistleblowers: Broken Lives and Organizational Power* by Fred Alford. "Your book came today," Lance says. On its cover is a school of fish swimming in one direction with one fish swimming in the opposite. I read the back cover to Lance. "Alford argues that few whistleblowers recover from their experience, and that, even then, they live in a world very different from the one they knew before their confrontation with the organization." That's not encouraging.

I don't read far before it's clear that whistleblower studies offer a bleak outlook. "Of the several dozen whistleblowers I have talked with, most lost their houses," Alford writes. "Many lost their families. It doesn't happen all at once, but whistle blowers' cases drag on for years, putting a tremendous strain on families. Most whistle blowers will suffer from depression and alcoholism. Half of the whistle blowers examined by one study went bankrupt." Alford continues, "Most whistleblowers will be unable to retire. A typical fate is for a nuclear engineer to end up selling computers at Radio Shack."

A number of studies have shown that 50 to 66% of whistle blowers lose their jobs. For the most part, people who blow the whistle will leave their place of employment within a year. As Alford writes, "usually the whistleblower is not fired outright. The organization's goal is to disconnect the act of whistleblowing from the act of retaliation, which is why so much legislation to protect the whistle blower is irrelevant. The usual practice is to demoralize and humiliate the whistle blower, putting him or her under so much psychological stress that it becomes difficult to do a good job." And whether someone goes outside their organization or blows the whistle internally makes almost no difference in terms of retaliation.

Whistleblowers are typically shocked by how they are treated, and many say they wouldn't do it again. Everything I read is extremely negative. Is this destined to be my future?

"Will you stop reading that book?" Lance says.

"No." I read on. The reading is tough, but for me, the book is an enormous relief and empowerment. I realize that there's probably not a whistleblower alive who hasn't experienced what I've been through. Put a hundred other ordinary citizens in my place, and they would likely experience the same things. There is definitely some sort of a whistleblower phenomenon—step over the "invisible line," and you will experience it. There are many lessons within these pages. I realize I can either let these events continue to have a negative impact on my life or find a way to move in a positive direction.

I will continue to meet many other whistleblowers—some high-profile cases, others that received little or no public attention. Not one has a positive story to tell me about what happened to them afterward. Because some people view them as loose cannons, troublemakers whose loyalty is questionable, one of the biggest problems is finding new employment.

Late one afternoon at the office, a gentleman calls me and begins weeping uncontrollably. He says he devoted his career to his company, often at the expense of his wife and children, only to be laid off after blowing the whistle. "I've lost everything," he says. I encourage him as best I can and will later hear he is doing better.

After preparing a speech for some students, I walk through it with several friends. Each person cautions me not to discuss the trials of whistleblowers.

"It's too negative," one says.

"If you say some whistleblowers suffer from alcoholism or depression, people may think you suffer from alcoholism or depression," another says. "I would just leave it out."

I continue to include the consequences of bringing forward wrongdoing in my speeches because I think understanding is important to changing behavior. Laws will only go so far in protecting whistle blowers from being isolated, "laid off," or pressured. In fact, I've come to believe a free press can offer a balance of power and as much protection for whistleblowers as any law may provide. . . .

EPILOGUE[1]

Shaping the Next Generation

> Train up a child in the way he should go, and when he is old, he will not depart from it.
>
> Proverbs 22:6

In many ways this story is about human nature, about people and choices. It shows how power and money can change people, and how easy it is to rationalize, give in to fear, and cave under pressure and intimidation. It speaks of the importance of living a life of integrity and making decisions we can look back on without regret. It illuminates the value of developing strong boundaries, keeping our paths straight, and guarding against the temptations and trappings of material success.

Going through these events has made me more aware of the importance of teaching values to my own two daughters, now 18 and 6, and sharing this story with the next generation of leaders. "Good habits formed at youth make all the difference," wrote Aristotle. I want to make sure my children are able to recognize an ethical dilemma and

[1] From p. 362 of the text.

make the right choices. When I share this story with high-school and college students, I encourage them to put themselves in the shoes of others, think about the decisions they may have made, and envision how these events might have impacted their family, friends, and co-workers. What would you do, if like Betty Vinson or Troy Normand, your boss pressured you to do something you didn't believe was right? What if you were a high-level executive, like Scott Sullivan or Bernie Ebbers, used to being at the top of your profession, and your company wasn't going to meet quarterly earnings unless you fudged the numbers—just this once?

Most of the people who participated in the WorldCom fraud were ordinary, middle-class Americans. They had no prior criminal records and never imagined they would be confronted with such life-altering choices. They were mothers and fathers who went to work to support their families, spent their weekends going to their children's activities and to church, and were respected within their communities. *Wall Street Journal* reporter Susan Pulliam once told me that she was drawn to write about the WorldCom fraud because the people involved seemed so ordinary.

Often, I'm asked: "Were these bad people, or basically good people who made bad decisions?" Most people are honorable and want to do the right thing. But sometimes it's tough, even when the line between right and wrong is clear. I believe most of the employees who participated in the fraud were basically good people. But each of us is capable of making bad decisions. "We're all like clay pots that are cracked," Chip Henderson, my pastor says. "Not one of us is a perfect pot with no flaws or cracks." So how do good people lose their way so easily? "Think of a swimmer," Chip tells me. "In the pool, the lines on either side help him swim straight. But a tri-athlete swimming on the open water has no lines. He must pick a landmark and regularly look up at it to check his direction. If he doesn't, he'll easily find himself off-course."

There are many reasons people make poor choices. Betty Vinson and Troy Normand felt pressured and afraid that they would lose their jobs if they didn't go along. They also began to rationalize—if their boss told them to do it, it must be okay, and besides, they were just following orders. I think David Myers, the Controller, felt a sense of loyalty to his boss Scott Sullivan. Scott rationalized that he was trying to save the company. The employees involved initially told themselves the fraudulent entries would be a one-time thing and that there was likely an error that would correct itself. Once down the path, they felt trapped. Top-level executives, used to seeing their company win, felt a sense of pride, and didn't want WorldCom to fail on their watch. Greed may have been a factor for the executives who had their personal fortunes on the line.

I have come to believe that WorldCom outgrew the man most responsible for building it. The entrepreneur who builds a company is often not the best person to lead it as the company matures. But entrepreneurs sometimes have difficulty letting go and drawing a clear line between themselves and the company they've helped build. What does this story teach about leadership? About the influence executives at the top of a company have on the corporate culture? About the line between being an aggressive capitalist and committing fraud? If you overextend your personal investments, like Bernie Ebbers, how will it affect your ability to lead?

Young people may find it hard to imagine that they will ever find themselves in a position such as the employees who took part in the WorldCom fraud. Hopefully they won't. But we all face ethical choices and pressures daily: Give the money back to the cashier who gave too much change or keep it? Cheat on an exam or take it honestly? Fudge an expense report or tax return or file it truthfully? Keep our word or break a promise? The list is endless. "Every time you make a choice," wrote C. S. Lewis, "you are turning the central part of you, the part that chooses, into something a little different than it was before." The foundation of our character is laid brick by brick, decision by decision, in how we choose to live our lives.

We spend a lot of time teaching students math, science, and history, but we must also spend time teaching ethics and leadership. Some argue that you can't teach ethics at the high school or college level because values are primarily instilled at a young age. But character is not static. People can and do change throughout their lives, and by incorporating ethics into the curriculum, we can challenge students to think and help make sure they have the tools to recognize an ethical dilemma, think it through, and make the right decision.

As I talk to my children and students, I share what I've learned from this story and from talking with professors, ministers, and business professionals about what each of us can do to help sort through tough issues and make the right choices.

1. Know what you believe is right and wrong. Write down the values you will live by and what you will do if your values collide. Is your moral compass pointed in the right direction? Are your priorities in the right order? Goethe once wrote, "Things which matter most must never be at the mercy of things which matter least." Our priorities impact the choices we make.
2. When making decisions, apply the Golden Rule: Treat other people the way you would want to be treated. "If you lived each day as though it were your last, what would you do differently?," my pastor recently asked a group. "Would you speak more kindly? Love more deeply? Forgive more freely?" It is easy in the rush of the business world to forget the humanity of our daily encounters. The Golden Rule endures because it is such a central tenet of our existence. It comes as close as any value to being universally accepted, and, though worded differently, is incorporated in each of the world's major religions.
3. Guard against being lulled into thinking you're not capable of making bad decisions. Each of us is imperfect and must protect against giving in to temptation. Keep in mind that what is legal and what is ethical are sometimes different. For example, giving the WorldCom CEO loans to cover personal debt was legal at the time, but was it the right decision?
4. Ask yourself: Would I be comfortable with my decision landing on the front page of a newspaper? Would I be okay with my parents, professors, and mentors knowing about my choice? What are the potential consequences of my actions?

5. Practice ethical decision making every day. "Good and evil both increase at compound interest," wrote C.S. Lewis. "That is why the little decisions you and I make every day are of such infinite importance." Ask yourself, did the decisions I made today coincide with my values?
6. Discuss tough ethical dilemmas with others you respect—a professor, a parent, a friend. David Myers, the Controller, didn't share the pressure he was under at work with his wife or family. He kept it to himself. Since people often rationalize their decisions, it's important to get opinions from others who are removed from the situation.
7. Find your courage. Most people want to be part of a team. But groupthink can be dangerous, and the team can be like a herd of bison that follow one after another over the cliff's edge. A man once wrote a letter to me and said he and his wife try to teach their children that courage is not without fear. Courage is acting in the face of fear. If we practice finding our courage in smaller matters each day, we'll stand a better chance of keeping the courage of conviction when we come to the crossroads of more critical decisions.
8. Apply the same code of ethics whether at home, work, school, or a house of worship. Compartmentalizing can result in acting different ways in different environments instead of being one unified self.
9. Pay attention to your instincts. If something doesn't feel right, it may not be. Stop, step back, and re-evaluate the situation. Betty and Troy initially felt uncomfortable with what their bosses asked of them, even writing resignation letters, but they didn't act on those initial instincts.
10. Above being loyal to your superiors, be loyal to your principles. Don't assume that what superiors are telling you is right just because they are in positions of authority. Scott Sullivan assured Betty and Troy that they wouldn't get in trouble because they were just doing what they were told.

People are fascinated by the World Com story and the characters involved, but if we fail to focus on its lessons, apply them in our lives, and share them with our children and grandchildren, the story is of little value. The many recent corporate scandals are a backdrop for timeless lessons. Next month and next year, the company, cast of characters, and circumstances will be different, but the ethical dilemmas will continue.

In the end, life is about choices. Our challenge is to choose well. "There are really only two important points when it comes to ethics," the author John C. Maxwell writes. "The first is a standard to follow. The second is the will to follow it." We each have an opportunity to make a real difference in our world, whether through mentoring a child, teaching ethics in the classroom, sharing the lessons of our own experiences, or instilling values in our children so the next generation may benefit from what we've learned. Doing this is not merely a responsibility. It is a privilege, a gift of caring and guidance.

The Curious Incident of the Law Firm That Did Nothing in the Night-Time[*]

Nancy B. Rapoport[**]

"Is there any point to which you would wish to draw my attention?"
"To the curious incident of the dog in the night-time."
"The dog did nothing in the night-time."
"That was the curious incident," remarked Sherlock Holmes.[1]

In EAT WHAT YOU KILL,[2] Professor Milton Regan illustrates the lengths to which people will go to ignore egregiously bad conduct—in effect, "d[oing] nothing in the

* A review of MILTON C. REGAN, JR., EAT WHAT YOU KILL: THE FALL OF A WALL STREET LAWYER (University of Michigan Press, 2004). 10 LEGAL ETHICS 98 (2007) (reviewing MILTON C. REGAN, JR., EAT WHAT YOU KILL: THE FALL OF A WALL STREET LAWYER (Univ. of Michigan Press 2004)). Reprinted by permission.

** Gordon Silver Professor, William S. Boyd School of Law, University of Nevada, Las Vegas. I owe special thanks to my former University of Houston Law Center research assistant, Stephen Chen, who worked tirelessly on this book review while finishing his undergraduate studies at the University of Texas, and whose work was every bit as good as that of most first-year law students at any of the schools with which I have been associated. He is now about to graduate from at UH; some smart law firm should go ahead and hire him. He also wrote a dead-on accurate book review of this book: Stephen Chen, EAT WHAT YOU KILL: THE FALL OF A WALL STREET LAWYER (Ann Arbor, University of Michigan Press, 2005) (book review).

I owe thanks as well to two of my research assistants at Boyd, Robert Arroyo and Matt Seaton; and to Kelli Cline, Dr. Michele Follen, Jennifer Gross, Jeff Van Niel, and Morris Rapoport. Brad Wendel gets my thanks for two reasons: because he waited so patiently for this draft and because his suggestions made it better. I also want to thank two other groups for their very helpful comments: the faculty of the William S. Boyd School of Law, University of Nevada, Las Vegas (comments during a presentation of a related paper over a year ago), and the students in my Enron class at St. John's University School of Law's LL.M. in Bankruptcy Program (comments made during class discussions).

1 *Silver Blaze,* ARTHUR CONAN DOYLE, THE COMPLETE SHERLOCK HOLMES, VOLUME I 399, 413 (New York, Barnes & Noble Classics, 2003).

2 MILTON C. REGAN, JR., EAT WHAT YOU KILL: THE FALL OF A WALL STREET LAWYER (Ann Arbor, University of Michigan Press 2004) [hereinafter EAT WHAT YOU KILL].

night-time." Regan describes the rise and fall of John Gellene, a well-known bankruptcy lawyer who became a federal felon.[3]

> [I]n December 1996 federal prosecutors in Milwaukee obtained a grand jury indictment of Gellene. He was charged on two felony counts of making false declarations in the affidavits he had submitted to Judge Eisenberg. He also was charged on one felony count for using a false affidavit under oath to claim that Milbank was eligible to receive payment for its work on the bankruptcy. Each of the first two counts carried a penalty of up to five years in prison and a $250,000 fine. The third count was punishable by up to five years in prison and a $10,000 fine. Any prison sentence over a year would deprive Gellene of his right to vote, his ability to be a teacher, his eligibility to hold public office, and the opportunity to practice law. He was the first lawyer ever charged under federal criminal law for violating Bankruptcy Rule 2014.[4]

Gellene was convicted, and he served time for his misconduct.[5] The law firm at which he had been a partner—Milbank Tweed Hadley & McCloy ("Milbank")—was required to disgorge almost $2 million in fees and eventually settled a $100 million malpractice lawsuit.[6]

EAT WHAT YOU KILL is a marvelous book: a cautionary tale for all lawyers and law students, even if they will never practice bankruptcy law. There have been many interesting reviews of this book,[7] and most of them focus on Gellene's own characteristics.

---

[3] Mr. Gellene was found guilty of two counts of making false oaths in a bankruptcy proceeding, in violation of 18 U.S.C. § 152(3). He was convicted specifically of "knowingly and fraudulently" making false declarations under oath in two Rule 2014 bankruptcy applications. Twice he applied for an order approving his employment as attorney for the debtor; first, on February 18, 1994, the day he filed Bucyrus' Chapter 11 bankruptcy, and second, on March 28, 1994, after the hearing on his application, when he elaborated on potential conflicts of interest, as the bankruptcy court had requested. Those applications failed to list the senior secured creditor and related parties.

U.S. v. Gellene, 182 F .3d 578, 585-86 (7th Cir. 1999) (footnotes omitted). Gellene was also convicted of one court of perjury, *id.* at 590.

[4] EAT WHAT YOU KILL, *supra* n. 4, at 3.

[5] *Id.* at 287.

[6] Milton C. Regan, Jr., *Taking Law Firms Seriously,* 16 GEO. J. LEGAL ETHICS 155, 160 (2002).

[7] *See, e.g.,* Anthony V. Alfieri, *The Fall of Legal Ethics and the Rise of Risk Management,* 94 GEO. L.J. 1909 (2006); Stephen Lubet, *False Flats,* 19 GEO. J. LEGAL ETHICS 275 (2006); MARK A. SARGENT, *The Moral World of Corporate Lawyers,* 19 GEO. J. LEGAL ETHICS 289 (2006); Paul C. Saunders, *When Compensation Creates Culture,* 19 GEO. J. LEGAL ETHICS 295 (2006); Tanina Rostain, *Partners and Power: The Role of Law Firm Organizational Factors in Attorney Misconduct,* 19 GEO. J. LEGAL ETHICS 281 (2006) [hereinafter Rostain]; William H. Simon, *The Ethics Teacher's Bittersweet Revenge: Virtue and Risk Management,* 94 GEO. L.J. 1985 (2006); Bradley Wendel, *Ethical Lawyering in a Morally Dangerous World,* 19 GEO. J. LEGAL ETHICS 299 (2006) [hereinafter Wendel].

Some of them focus on the sort of pressure that high-caliber law firms put on their associates.

I'm interested in a slightly different question: what was there about Milbank that caused the partners to overlook such warning signs as (1) Gellene's failure to complete his paperwork to become admitted to the New York bar, which caused him to practice without a New York law license for several years; (2) his failure, as an experienced bankruptcy partner, to disclose a "potential"[8] conflict of interest to the bankruptcy court; (3) his failure to file timesheets unless he was fined for non-submission; and (4) his tendency to hunker down, take on all of the work himself, without asking for help or keeping others apprised of his workload? How many red flags did Milbank need to understand that Gellene was a liability as well as an asset?[9] In other words, was Milbank's failure to rid itself of Gellene an isolated instance of greed overcoming common sense, or was the failure a more systemic problem of how people in organizations behave?

I believe that Milbank's failure to act was a sort of co-dependency and that there are countless incidents of "ethical lapse" co-dependency in organizations, caused[10] not by simple greed, but by a combination of psychological and sociological factors that cause very bright people to do some very stupid things. John Gellene's story is but one example; Jeff Skilling, Andy Fastow, and Ken Lay of Enron provide other examples. History is replete with such examples. The American Bar Association (with ethics codes) and Congress often will react by attempting to legislate better behavior. Unfortunately, no amount of legislation is going to save us from the foibles of human nature. Until we understand the effects that cognitive dissonance, the diffusion of responsibility,[11] and

---

[8] The conflict in question was more than "potential." It was real.

[9] Gellene's tragic story—and Milbank's steadfast refusal to fire someone who had significant problems complying with law firm policy, the New York bar's requirements for admission, legal ethics generally, and the bankruptcy ethics rules relating to disclosure of conflicts—reminds me of the song we sing at Passover, *Dayenu*. *See, e.g.,* http://www.greatjewishmusic.com/Midifiles/Passover/Dayenu.htm. The point of *Dayenu* is that each gift that God gave us would have been sufficient in and of itself, but God kept giving us more and more. Gellene's (and Milbank's) story is a sort of anti-*Dayenu*: had Milbank fired Gellene when it had discovered that he had been representing himself as a duly admitted New York lawyer, *dayenu*; had Milbank fired Gellene when it had realized that the only way to force him to turn in a timesheet was to impose thousands of dollars in monthly fines, *dayenu*; had Milbank fired Gellene when it noticed that Gellene never, ever took time to participate in the summer associate mentorship program that he had agreed to do, *dayenu* (although I don't know of any firm that would fire someone just for that infraction); had Milbank fired Gellene after several annual reviews pointed out that he kept all of his work to himself, worked like a madman, and didn't ask for help, *dayenu*. By the time Milbank found out that it was going to lose (by default) a motion to disgorge $2 million in fees if it didn't act fast, it was too late.

[10] These incidents may be exacerbated by greed, but they aren't caused by greed.

[11] Partly in response to the highly publicized inaction of thirty-eight alleged witnesses of the death of Kitty Genovese in 1964, psychologists have conducted hundreds of field studies of helping behavior among strangers. Some of these focus on personal characteristics, such as age or sex, of the potential helper. Others focus on situational variables, such as how burdensome providing help would be. These sorts of studies can illuminate both what sorts of socialization processes abet altruism, and also how willing a well socialized person would be to trade off rectitude for, say, personal safety. Research along these lines might help rational-actor theorists decide in

social pressure[12] have on the human psyche, we can legislate behavior until the cows[13] come home, and we'll still see no changes in the way that people in organizations handle even the most glaring misbehavior.

I. ENRON AND THE HUMAN CONDITION

Many people have studied Enron,[14] and most point to a combination of loopholes in the legal and business worlds to explain what went wrong. After obsessing about Enron for years, though, I believe that the exploitation of loopholes was only a symptom of the problem, not a cause. Instead, I believe that human nature—especially that part of human nature that plays mind games, such as cognitive dissonance, diffusion of responsibility, and social pressure)—created the problems at Enron.

a. Cognitive Dissonance Generally

Although several academics have studied cognitive dissonance, Leon Festinger first defined it as

> [t]he psychological opposition of irreconcilable ideas (cognitions) held simultaneously by one individual, created a motivating force that would lead, under proper conditions, to the adjustment of one's belief to fit one's behavior—instead of changing one's behavior to fit one's belief (the sequence conventionally assumed).[15]

In short, cognitive dissonance is the mind's creation of a justification that can explain how a good person can do something very, very bad. Cognitive dissonance tells us

---

> which people, in which situations, and in what quantities, to alloy the self-interest model with a dollop of altruism.

Robert C. Ellickson, *Symposium on Post-Chicago Law and Economics: Bringing Culture and Human Frailty to Rational Actors: A Critique of Classical Law and Economics,* 65 CHI.-KENT L. REV. 23, 47-48 (1989) (footnotes omitted). *Cf.* Jeffrey J. Rachlinski, *Symposium on Law, Psychology, and the Emotions: The Limits of Social Norms,* 74 CHI.-KENT L. REV. 1537, 1556 (2000) ("Neither was Kitty Genovese really the victim of a callous, urban social norm. Rather, the presence of a passive group affected the bystander's interpretation of Genovese's plight.").

[12] *See, e.g.,* SOLOMON Asch, *Effects of Group Pressure Upon the Modification and Distortion of Judgments, in* READINGS IN SOCIAL PSYCHOLOGY 2 (G. Swanson, T. Newcomb, & E. Hartley (eds.), New York, Holt, 1952); Knud S. Larsen, *The Asch Conformity Experiment: Replication and Transhistorical Comparisons,* 5 J. SOC. BEHAV. & PERSONALITY 163 (1990).

[13] *Cf.* text accompanying n. 23, *infra.*

[14] Including me. *See* ENRON: CORPORATE FIASCOS AND THEIR IMPLICATIONS (New York, Foundation Press, Nancy B. Rapoport & Bala G. Dharan, eds., 2004) [hereinafter CORPORATE FIASCOS].

[15] LAUREN SLATER, OPENING SKINNER'S BOX: GREAT PSYCHOLOGICAL EXPERIMENTS OF THE TWENTIETH CENTURY 113 (New York, W.W. Norton) (2004) [hereinafter Slater] (citing LEON FESTINGER, A THEORY OF COGNITIVE DISSONANCE (Stanford, California, Stanford University Press, 1957)).

that, because the human mind can't tolerate acting in a way that contradicts a person's positive self-image, a person who does something unethical or immoral will come up with a "logical" explanation for that behavior. These explanations run the gamut, justifying everything from adultery ("if my spouse weren't distant, I wouldn't cheat") to embezzlement ("I'll pay it back tomorrow, and no one's being hurt") to murder ("he made me kill him").

One of Festinger's experiments involved asking a group of people to lie. He divided that group into two subgroups—one of the subgroups received $20 in exchange for telling the lie, and the other group received $1 in exchange for telling the lie. Festinger found that the members of the $1 payment group were

> far more likely to claim, after the fact, that they really believed the lie, than those who'd earned the twenty dollars. Why would that be? Festinger hypothesized that it is much harder to justify lying for a dollar; you are a good, smart person after all, and good, smart people don't do bad things for *no real reason*. Therefore, because you can't take back the lie, and you've already pocketed the measly money, you bring your beliefs into alignment with your actions, so as to reduce the dissonance between your self-concept and your questionable behavior. However, those folks who were paid twenty dollars to lie, they didn't change their beliefs; in effect they said, "Yeah, I lied, I didn't believe a word of what I said, but I got paid well." The twenty-dollar subjects experienced less dissonance; they could find a compelling justification for their fibs, and that justification had double-digits and a crisp snap.[16]

According to Festinger's theory, the smaller the payment, the more likely the creation of cognitive dissonance.[17]

---

[16] Slater, *supra*, at 117-18. In other words, cognitive dissonance occurs when someone doesn't want to admit that he did something bad for a bad reason (i.e., flat-out greed); instead, he'll "justify" his decision in order to believe that he did something objectively "bad" for a "good" reason. Who wants to say that he can be bought for a mere dollar? On the other hand, who among us can say that he will not be bought for *any* price?

[17] *Id.* at 118. I don't intend to discuss all of the literature on cognitive dissonance here. Other and better scholars have done that, and they have applied cognitive dissonance theory to lawyer behavior in far more elegant ways than I can. *See, e.g.*, David J. Luban, T*he Ethics of Wrongful Obedience,* in Ethics in Practice: Lawyers' Roles, Responsibilities, and Regulation (New York, Oxford University Press, Deborah L. Rhode ed., 2000). But even a cursory discussion of cognitive dissonance comes up with some unusual examples: the experiment by Landis in 1924, finding that 71% of subjects in his sample would chop off a rat's head if the experimenter asked them to do so; the experiment by Frank in 1944, in which subjects would do pretty much whatever the experimenter requested as long as the experimenter wore a white lab coat while making his request; Asch's superb experiment in which a group of actors could persuade an experiment's subject to disbelieve his own eyes and concur with the group's (wrong) conclusion about the length of some lines on paper; and, of course, Stanley Milbank's experiments using a fake electric shock machine to test his subjects' willingness to electrocute total strangers. Slater, *supra* n. 17, at 41-48. To see some film of the subjects in Milgram's experiment, see Enron: The Smartest Guys in the Room (Magnolia Home Entertainment 2005).

When I lecture about cognitive dissonance, I usually illustrate the theory by observing that only the theory of cognitive dissonance can explain why someone would go on a second date after the first date was horrendous. To explain the action of choosing to go out on date #2, the corresponding thought must be "I am a very good judge of people, so if I'm going out on a second date with this person after the first date was so miserable, it's because I believe that the person's behavior on date #1 was an aberration." People laugh at that example, but it's a very small step from that example to why someone might stay in an abusive relationship: "I'm not a masochist, so I must be with this person because the destructive behavior is not the 'real' him."

b. Cognitive Dissonance at Enron

I've written before about the cognitive dissonance at Enron.[18] Since the publication of our Enron book,[19] Andy Fastow and Jeff Skilling have begun serving time in federal prison, and Ken Lay likely would have joined them, but for his untimely death in 2005. Even though we know that not everyone who worked at Enron was a crook, a liar, or a cheat, we also know—or at least we have a reasonable understanding—that several of the deals were designed to generate the appearance of profits at the end of quarters or fiscal years.[20] As one classic Enron joke explains,

> Enron Capitalism: You have two cows. You sell three of them to your publicly listed company, using letters of credit opened by your brother-in-law at the bank, then execute a debt-equity swap with an associated general offer so that you get all four cows back, with a tax exemption for five cows. The milk rights of the six cows are transferred through an intermediary to a Cayman Island company secretly owned by the majority shareholder who sells the rights to all seven cows back to your listed company. The Enron annual report says the company owns eight cows, with an option on one more.[21]

In deal after deal, quarter after quarter, Enron was milking its fictitious cows for all they were ostensibly worth. There are several theories proposed to explain the behavior of Enron's officers and directors. Congress tended to explain the behavior as simple, unbridled greed,[22] and it tried to create negative incentives to offset this greed with

---

[18] *See, e.g., Enron,* Titanic, *and* The Perfect Storm, in CORPORATE FIASCOS, *supra* n. 16, at 927.

[19] *Id.*

[20] *See* Jeffrey D. Van Niel & Nancy B. Rapoport, *Dr. Jekyll & Mr. Skilling: How Enron's Public Image Morphed From the Most Innovative Company in the* Fortune 500 *to the Most Notorious Company Ever, in* CORPORATE FIASCOS, *supra* n. 16, at 77, 80-83.

[21] http://politicalhumor.about.com/library/blenronomics.htm (visited September 18, 2007).

[22] 148 CONG. REC. H5462-02, at H5466 (July 25, 2002).

Sarbanes-Oxley.[23] Others have suggested that Enron used political power to change the checks and balances on its accounting measures, as when Wendy Gramm's work at the Commodity Futures Trade Commission allowed Enron to use mark-to-market accounting on its energy deals.[24]

Enron's misdeeds weren't due to an absence of collective intelligence, because Enron regularly hired the best and the brightest (as did the late accounting firm Arthur Andersen).[25] As authors from Daniel Goleman[26] to Peter Salovey and John Mayer[27] have pointed out, though, IQ is not necessarily linked to EQ (emotional intelligence). IQ can tell a businessperson how to manipulate the rules to her advantage; EQ can tell her why she shouldn't do it.

A perfect example of Enron's failure to encourage more ethical decision-making is its exploitation of California's then-existing regulatory structure for round-trip electricity trading. According to several sources,[28] Enron traders shipped excess electricity out of California and then encouraged power plants to create false outages. Then, when California needed the electricity again, Enron[29] was able to import the out-of-California electricity at exorbitantly high prices.[30] The scheme looked something like this:[31]

---

23 *Id.* at H5464; PUBLIC COMPANY ACCOUNTING REFORM AND INVESTOR PROTECTION ACT OF 2002, Pub. L. No. 107-204, 116 Stat. 745 (codified in scattered sections of 11, 15, 18, 28, and 29 U.S.C. (2000)).

24 *See, e.g.,* Tim Fleck & Brian Wallstin, *Enron's End Run: To make a mess as big as the Enron debacle, you need some friends in high places—Texas Senator Phil Gramm and his wife, for instance,* DALLAS OBSERVER, Feb. 7, 2002. Mark-to-market accounting isn't a problem when the "market" to which the contract's estimated profits are accelerated and recorded in year one is a real market, with the ability to verify the calculation of those profits. Where Enron went wrong was in creating both the deal and the market itself, which allowed it to manipulate both sides of the equation: the contract's calculated profit and the market that set that profit.

25 Although Andersen's appeal of certain of the jury instructions to the United States Supreme Court was successful, *Arthur Andersen v. United States,* 544 U.S. 696 (2005), the decision came too late to save Andersen from destruction.

26 *See* DANIEL P. GOLEMAN, EMOTIONAL INTELLIGENCE (New York, Bantam Books, 2006); THE EMOTIONALLY INTELLIGENT WORKPLACE (San Francisco, Jossey Bass, Cary Cherniss & Daniel Goleman eds., 2001); DANIEL P. GOLEMAN, WORKING WITH EMOTIONAL INTELLIGENCE (New York, Bantam Books, 1998).

27 PETER SALOVEY, JOHN MAYER & MARC BRACKETT, EMOTIONAL INTELLIGENCE: KEY READINGS ON THE MAYER AND SALOVEY MODEL (Portchester, NY, Dude, 2004).

28 *See* Marc Lifsher & Elizabeth Douglass, *The Enron Verdicts: Californians See Poetic Justice,* L.A. Times, May 26, 2006, at A1; Timothy Egan, *Tapes Show Enron Arranged Plant Shutdown,* N.Y. TIMES, Feb. 4, 2005, at A12.

29 Other energy companies apparently also engaged in this sort of market manipulation.

30 Richard A. Oppel, Jr., *Enron's Many Strands; The Strategies: How Enron Got California To Buy Power It Didn't Need,* N.Y. TIMES, May 8, 2002, at C1; Michael W. Lynch & Adrian Moore, *Power Tripped: Energy Crisis, California,* REASON, June 1, 2001, at 33.

31 Jeffrey D. Van Niel, *Enron—The Primer, in* CORPORATE FIASCOS, *supra* n. 16, at 3, 22.

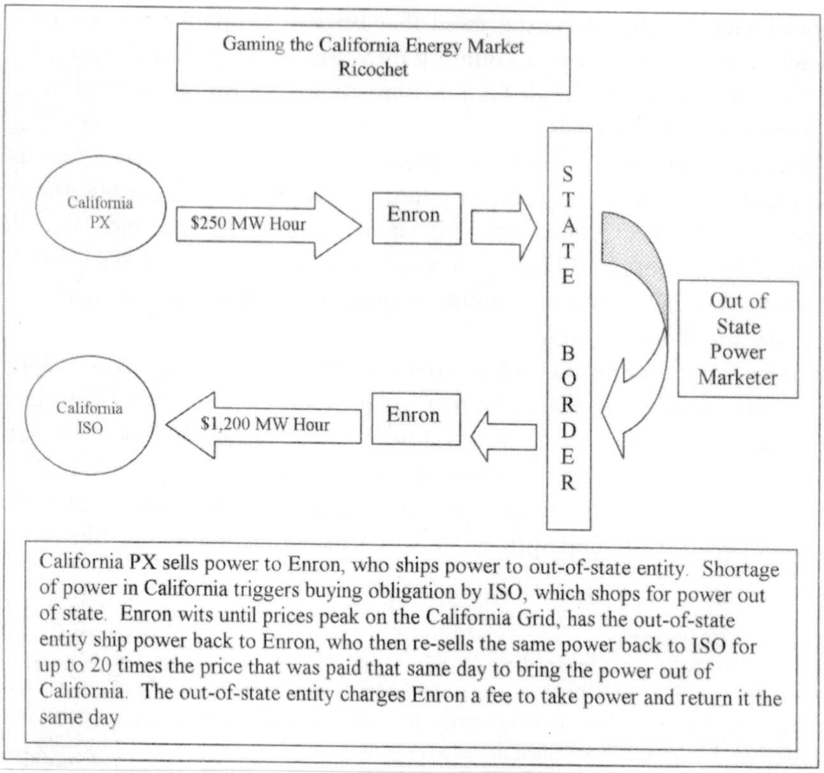

Source: Jeffrey D. Van Niel, *Enron—The Primer,* in ENRON: CORPORATE FIASCOS AND THEIR IMPLICATIONS 22 (2004).

Was the scheme *legal?* Had Enron not manipulated the supply of electricity out of, and then back into, California, then the answer is "sure": Enron was simply pricing the electricity so as to benefit its own shareholders. But was it *ethical*? Not by any stretch of the imagination.[32] Ask anyone who lived through the rolling brownouts of the California energy crisis.

Let's assume, though, that some of the people at Enron actually agonized over the "round-tripping" of electricity in California, as well as over Enron's business losses and the ridiculous deals designed to cover them up. In fact, there were many who expressed

[32] Had Enron (allegedly) not manipulated the demand for electricity by agreements, then the question of whether Enron's round-trip trading was ethical is much more difficult. Lawyers are supposed to find gaps and, yes, loopholes in regulations for the benefit of their clients. Still, the enormous profits generated by round-trip trading raise a related question: is there such a thing as too much profit?

their unease regarding those deals.[33] So then why did these smart people facilitate those deals, by participating in them[34] or by remaining silent about them?[35]

---

[33] *See generally* MIMI SCHWARTZ WITH SHARON WATKINS, POWER FAILURE: THE INSIDE STORY OF THE COLLAPSE OF ENRON (New York, Doubleday, 2003); *see also* Watkins's email to Lay, available at http://www.itmweb.com/f012002.htm.

[34] One possibility is that these very smart people had very poor moral reasoning skills. Maybe part of the problem at Enron was created by the relative youth of many of the key players: *see, e.g., Key Enron Executives' Penalties,* WASH. POST, Dec. 14, 2006, at D1; John S. Emshwiller, *'Benron' Behind Bars; An inside look at the life of Ben Glisan, Jr., the first Enron executive to go to jail,* WALL ST. J., Apr. 21, 2007, at A1, as well as a concomitant lag in their moral reasoning abilities, *see* ROBERT KEGAN, IN OVER OUR HEADS: THE MENTAL DEMANDS OF MODERN LIFE (Cambridge, Mass., Harvard University Press, 1998). My very-uneducated guess would place Fastow (and many of his colleagues) in stages one or two of Kohlberg's moral reasoning scale.

According to Kohlberg, moral reasoning progresses in relatively well-defined stages. In stage one, people decide to do or not do an act merely out of a desire to avoid punishment. *See* Nancy B. Rapoport, *Lord of the Flies (1963): The Development of Rules Within an Adolescent Culture, in* SCREENING JUSTICE—THE CINEMA OF LAW: FIFTY SIGNIFICANT FILMS OF LAW, ORDER AND SOCIAL JUSTICE 253 (Buffalo, William S. Hein & Co., Rennard Strickland, Teree Foster & Taunya Banks, eds. 2005) [hereinafter *Flies*]. Stage two decisions represent a *détente* or a *quid pro quo* between actors. *See* Michael D. Daneker, *Moral Reasoning and the Quest for Legitimacy,* 43 AM. U. L. REV. 49, 54 (1993) [hereinafter Daneker]; *cf.* MAPPING THE MORAL DOMAIN: A CONTRIBUTION OF WOMEN'S THINKING TO PSYCHOLOGICAL THEORY AND EDUCATION (Cambridge, Mass., Harvard University Press, Carol Gilligan et al. eds., 1988) [hereinafter MAPPING]; Carol Gilligan, *Getting Civilized,* 63 FORDHAM L. REV. 17 (1994); Carrie Menkel-Meadow, *What's Gender Got To Do With It?: The Politics and Morality of an Ethic of Care,* 22 N.Y.U. REV. L. & SOC. CHANGE 265, 276 & n. 39 (1996) (reviewing JOAN C. TRONTO, MORAL BOUNDARIES: A POLITICAL ARGUMENT FOR AN ETHIC OF CARE (N.Y., Routledge, 1993)); *see also* Pamela S. Karlan & Daniel R. Ortiz, *In a Diffident Voice: Relational Feminism, Abortion Rights, and the Feminist Legal Agenda,* 87 NW. U. L. REV. 858, 863, 870 (1993) (contrasting Kohlberg's theory of moral development with Gilligan's theory). Only after stage two does the concept of a social contract—a higher power than the relationship between two actors—start to come into play. In stage three, people enforce rules because the rules exist. The difference between stage three and stage four reasoning is that, in stage three, society enforces the rules because they exist, *see* Daneker, at 54-55; in stage four (the "law and order" stage), society enforces the rules because the rules have been enacted by the majority, which provides an independent rationale for the "rightness" of those rules, *id.* at 55. Stage five reasoning goes beyond majority rule to an articulable theory of rights (e.g., natural law), *id.* at 56, which allows stage five actors to factor in the rights of the minority, *id.* And the final stage, stage six, uses "universal ethical principles" to help the actor decide how to behave. *Id.* at 56 (footnotes omitted).

Once Enron started on its downhill track, by making riskier and more complicated deals in order to cover up its business failures, its executives were faced with a Hobbesian dilemma: take the losses, make the charges against earnings public, and reap the consequences, or come up with Rube Goldberg-like deals to disguise its problems. *See* Mary Flood, *Glisan Chips Away at Lay, Skilling Defense,* HOUSTON CHRON., March 23, 2006, at A1. (In all likelihood, Fastow's machinations enabled Enron to stay afloat far longer than it would have if Enron had come clean about its business failures at the time that the failures occurred.) I think that it's fair to assume that stage three-stage six reasoning didn't occur. In fact, I think that the key players at Enron stayed solidly in stage one. If the only reason to obey the rules is to avoid punishment, and if one discounts the risk of punishment by the likelihood of getting caught, then choosing to ignore the rules is a logical outgrowth of stage one reasoning. Bethany McLean and Peter Elkind didn't name their book *The Smartest Guys in the Room* by accident. *See* BETHANY MCLEAN & PETER ELKIND, THE SMARTEST GUYS IN THE ROOM: THE AMAZING RISE AND SCANDALOUS FALL OF ENRON (New York, Portfolio, 2003).

[35] "The only thing necessary for the triumph of evil is for good men to do nothing." Quotation attributed to Edmond Burke. *See* http://www.bartleby.com/66/18/9118.html, *but see* http://forum.quoteland.

c. Diffusion of Responsibility at Enron

Part of the answer must lie with the very human tendency to assume that "someone else" is taking care of the problem. The Powers Report to the Enron Board is a perfect example: the board blamed the accountants and the lawyers for Enron's downfall; the lawyers blamed the board and the accountants; and the accountants blamed the lawyers and the board.[36] None of these groups took responsibility for Enron's actions.

The classic example of diffusion of responsibility involves Kitty Genovese's murder on a warm, New York summer evening.[37] Genovese's murder took a long time to complete, and many people in many nearby apartments heard her cries for help, but no one called the police—on the assumption that someone else hearing her cries certainly must have called the authorities.[38] With everyone hoping that someone else was taking action, no one took any responsibility himself.

So it went at Enron. Various employees were uncomfortable with the shaky deals that Fastow and Skilling proposed,[39] but there are few examples of anyone at Enron calling "shenanigans"[40] on those deals. Sherron Watkins, in her now-famous memo, tried to get Ken Lay to own up to Enron's misdeeds—not because she was acting as a whistleblower, which she wasn't, but because she believed that Lay had not been involved in Enron's machinations. My guess is that Fastow et al. counted on this facet of human nature in structuring the deals. Certainly Skilling's "rank and yank" reviews of Enron employees encouraged people to keep their heads down and their opinions to themselves, as did the amount of fees going to the professionals representing Enron. But neither cognitive dissonance nor diffusion of responsibility can provide a complete explanation of what went wrong at Enron.

---

com/1/OpenTopic?a=tpc&s=586192041&f=099191541&m=4131014151 (suggesting that the quotation has been misattributed to Burke).

[36] Powers Report, available at http://i.cnn.net/cnn/2002/LAW/02/02/enron.report/powers.report.pdf; John C. Coffee, Jr., *Understanding Enron: "It's About the Gatekeepers, Stupid,"* reprinted in CORPORATE FIASCOS, *supra* n. 16, at 125-143.

[37] *Queens Woman is Stabbed to Death in Front of Home,* N.Y. TIMES, March 14, 1964, at 26.

[38] Martin Gansberg, *Thirty-Eight Who Saw Murder Didn't Call the Police,* N.Y. TIMES, March 27, 1964.

[39] MIMI SCHWARTZ WITH SHERRON WATKINS, POWER FAILURE: THE INSIDE STORY OF THE COLLAPSE OF ENRON 131-132 (New York, Doubleday, 2003) (2003); *see also* ROBERT BRYCE, PIPE DREAMS: GREED, EGO, AND THE DEATH OF ENRON (Oxford, Public Affairs, 2002); BRIAN CRUVER, ANATOMY OF GREED: THE UNSHREDDED TRUTH FROM AN ENRON INSIDER (Carroll & Graf, 2002); THE CROOKED E: THE UNSHREDDED TRUTH ABOUT ENRON (CBS television broadcast, Jan. 5, 2003).

[40] *Cf. South Park: Cow Days* (Comedy Central television broadcast, September 30, 1998) (Kyle calls "shenanigans" on a rigged carnival game). Brava to Jennifer Gross for finding this source.

d. Social Pressure at Enron

Social pressure played a large role in Enron's ability to keep its shady deals quiet. In Solomon Asch's famous experiment,[41] various actors were able to persuade the experimental subjects that the line that the subjects thought *was* identical to another line *wasn't* identical—even though the two lines were, in fact, exactly the same length.[42]

Even though the actors in the experiment were clearly wrong, the subject conformed to the social pressure in order to alleviate his own anxiety about the misidentification. If a subject can conform in a low-stakes situation, what likelihood was there that an Enron worker who "knew" that the deals weren't generating real money was going to speak out? Was someone at Enron likely to say that the Dabhol power plant in India could never generate a profit, or that Azurix in Houston was mathematically incapable of making money? Hardly.

Cognitive dissonance kept the lawyers, the accountants, the employees, and the board from recognizing that they had crossed the line repeatedly in their ill-fated attempts to keep Enron afloat. Even when they knew that something about the deals wasn't kosher, a combination of social pressure and diffusion of responsibility may have kept many of them from speaking out. Enron isn't unique—as the misadventures at WorldCom,[43] Tyco,[44] Global Crossing,[45] Hewlett-Packard,[46] Brocade,[47] and Dell[48] (among others) demonstrate. Milbank wasn't unique, either.[49]

---

41 Solomon Asch, *Effects of Group Pressure Upon the Modification and Distortion of Judgments, in* HAROLD S. GUETZKOW, GROUPS, LEADERSHIP AND MEN; RESEARCH IN HUMAN RELATIONS. REPORTS ON RESEARCH SPONSORED BY THE HUMAN RELATIONS AND MORALE BRANCH OF THE OFFICE OF NAVAL RESEARCH, 1945-1950 (New York, Holt, 1951).

42 *See* n. 14, *supra.*

43 *See, e.g.,* Jared Sanberg et al, *Disconnected: Inside WorldCom's Unearthing Of a Vast Accounting Scandal,* WALL ST. J., Jun. 27, 2002, at A1.

44 *See, e.g.,* Mark Maremont & Jerry Markon, *Leading the News: Former Tyco Executives Are Charged: New York Prosecutors Say Ex-CEO, Finance Officer Ran "Criminal Enterprise,"* WALL ST, J., Sept. 13, 2002, at A3.

45 *See, e.g.,* Simon Romero, *S.E.C. Scrutinizing Another Company,* N.Y. TIMES, Feb. 9, 2002, at A1.

46 *See, e.g.,* James B. Stewart, *The Kona Files: How an Obsession with Leaks Brought Scandal to Hewlett-Packard,* THE NEW YORKER, Feb. 19, 2007, at 152.

47 *See, e.g.,* Edward Iwata, *Former Brocade CEO Guilty of Backdating; Conviction is First in Nationwide Crackdown,* USA TODAY, Aug. 8, 2007, at B1.

48 *See, e.g.,* Michelle Quinn, *Earnings; Dell Reveals it Manipulated its Books,* L.A. TIMES, Aug. 17, 2007, at C1.

49 *See, e.g.,* Martha Neil, *Milberg Weiss on the Hot Seat: Should Law Firms Ever Be Indicted?,* 92 A.B.A. J. 34 (December 2006); *U.S. Supreme Court Denial of Review Ends Sidley & Austin Bid to Avoid Monetary Relief Issue in Age Bias Case,* U.S. FED NEWS, Oct. 2, 2006.

II. GELLENE, MILBANK, AND THE HUMAN CONDITION.

What makes EAT WHAT YOU KILL so interesting is its description of how Gellene's own insecurities managed to combine with Milbank's cavalier disregard for clear warning signs, thus creating a train wreck that sent Gellene to prison and Milbank to its malpractice insurer. Regan offers the two "prevailing explanations":

> The first is that Gellene was a moral rogue, an aberrant partner with a weakness for cutting corners when it suited his purposes. The second is that Gellene was the fall guy, someone pressured by his firm to conceal a conflict of interest so that Milbank could reap a reward of almost $2 million in fees. From this perspective, Gellene was done in by a corrupt organization. The first explanation blames Gellene's fall on flawed character; the second depicts him as the victim of circumstances that he couldn't resist.[50]

Of course, each explanation is incomplete. Neither "the person" nor "the situation" is the only explanation; rather, it's the synergistic combination of character and context that explains it.

a. Law Firms—The Context

To understand why Milbank overlooked Gellene's clear ethical lapses, EAT WHAT YOU KILL quite correctly begins with the social pressures that modern law firms face. Regan describes the three features of modern law firm life:

> Focusing on these questions directs attention to three features that are common to practice in modern large law firms. First, a shift to merit-based compensation and away from job security means that partners as well as associates are competitors in a tournament [that never ceases, even after someone becomes a partner] . . .
>
> . . . The common way to describe this system in the large firm is that you "eat what you kill." There are two main ways to be an entrepreneur who can compete successfully in a tournament organized around this principle. The first, and preferable, way is to be a "rainmaker": someone who develops contacts with clients that lead to regular business. The second is to cultivate a good relationship with a rainmaker, thereby gaining access to the work that his or her clients generate.[51]

---

[50] EAT WHAT YOU KILL, *supra* n. 4, at 6.

[51] EAT WHAT YOU KILL, *supra* n. 4, at 7-8. Regan goes on to list the other two attributes of modern large law firm life. First, ethical norms are established more within departments than firm-wide, leading to the very real chance that specialties will create their own, and possibly aberrant, ethics rules. The other attribute involves the fact that various groups within a firm will team up temporarily for particular client matters and then will disband, and that the goal of the temporary teams is simply to "win"—to get a good

In essence, then, the larger the law firm, the more important one's practice peers are in setting the social norms for that practice. Especially because the largest firms are, quite simply, too large to monitor everyone, life in large firms is lived at the departmental level, not the firm-wide level. And it was in the bankruptcy department that Gellene found himself, complete with a rainmaker (Larry Lederman) who needed a workhorse (Gellene).

> The particular move that ultimately begat the Gellene scandal was an effort to specialize in the representation of large corporate debtors in the bankruptcy reorganization process. Milbank had bankruptcy experience, but did most of its work on behalf of individual creditors: steady piecework, but not highly profitable. Directing reorganization on behalf of a large debtor, on the other hand, was a major project that could yield huge fees, ordered by the bankruptcy court and payable off the top of the estate. To move into this niche, it hired Larry Lederman, a "rainmaker" from the mergers and acquisitions powerhouse Wachtell, Lipton, Rosen & Katz, and gave him a free hand to wheel and deal. Gellene . . . saw Lederman as his ticket to continued success in the tournament. Economic pressures worked in grotesque synergy with his own psychological problems as Gellene committed his bizarre crime. Since even rainmakers are only a bad year away from unemployment, Lederman felt the same pressures. Consequently, when Gellene obliquely raised the possibility of a conflict on at least one occasion, Lederman either missed the point or chose to ignore it.[52]

---

result for the client—rather than to spend time thinking about firm-wide norms of ethical behavior. *Id.* Conley & Baker note the same pressures:

> Regan's (2004) depiction of Milbank, Tweed and the fall of John Gellene presents a vivid instance of the standard economic account of change in large law firms. By the late 1960s client companies were increasingly buffeted by the competitive pressures of globalization and a technology-driven decline in the life cycles of their products. As they looked for ways to cut costs, legal services were not exempt. Clients began to shop, in the process realizing that large firms were generally fungible and that work could be divided up among competing firms. As a consequence, whereas large firms had once sent one-line bills "for services rendered" that were paid without question, they were now forced to act like retailers, cutting prices to match the competition and even offering loss leaders. Firm profit margins fell as big-firm lawyers were suddenly thrust into the cutthroat global economy. Large corporate firms that had prospered for generations went out of business without warning.
>
> By Regan's account, the impact of these economic forces on the professional lives of Wall Street lawyers and the cultures of their firms was direct and dramatic. For the first time, law firm partners were forced to think like business managers.

John M. Conley & Scott Baker, *Fall From Grace or Business as Usual? A Retrospective Look At Lawyers on Wall Street and Main Street,* 30 L. & Soc. Inquiry 783, 798 (2005) [hereinafter *Fall From Grace*].

[52] *Fall From Grace, supra* n. 53, at 799-800.

I'm not the first (or the best) person to apply social science principles to Gellene's (and Milbank's) downfall.[53] But few people have taken that analysis beyond Gellene's own characteristics to view Milbank's complicity in his behavior, or to compare Milbank's inaction with the inaction that occurred at Enron. In order to understand how the situation at Milbank compared with the situation at Enron, we must still first examine how Gellene signaled that Milbank should have kept a closer watch on him.

b. What were Gellene's Signals to Milbank?

By all accounts, Gellene was a loner and an insanely hard worker.[54] And Milbank was aware of both of these characteristics, much as it was aware that Gellene didn't pay attention to the non-billable aspects of firm life. Even something as mundane as filling out his timesheets on a regular basis was apparently beneath Gellene, who was routinely as late as a month in turning them in.[55] Mentoring and recruiting functions also weren't his forte.[56] In sum, Gellene was a keep-his-head-down, focus-on-the-task-at-hand kind of lawyer: not unusual at a large firm, but perhaps more pathological than most.

When I say "pathological," I mean that Gellene was off the deep end in terms of understanding how his actions might relate to his professional conduct. Not every partner who submits very late timesheets needs psychological help, but every partner (or associate) who does so must recognize that he can't possibly recreate his timesheets accurately. Law firms tend to view slow timesheet submission as an accounting problem. I disagree. I view it as an ethics problem: late timesheets necessarily mean that the lawyer must "guess" how much time he spent on every matter, and thus those timesheets

---

[53] Brad Wendel has done a superb job of applying social science principles to Gellene. *See* Wendel, *supra* n. 9, at 302-08.

[54] Milbank's annual compensation committee reports on Gellene are studded with comments on his hard work from partners: "works tremendously hard"; "a very hard worker"; "tireless worker"; "overworked"; and "work[s] fiendishly hard."

> Colleagues also describe a lawyer who tended to take too much on himself without delegating responsibility to or involving others. . . . Barry Radick, cohead of the firm's bankruptcy practice, put it more vividly: He is a control freak and a loner. He refuses help; *we are concerned that he may get himself into trouble because he is working so hard.*

EAT WHAT YOU KILL, *supra* n. 4, at 53-54 (emphasis added).

[55] *Id.*

[56] . . . In a similar vein, the head of the firm's summer associate program reported in 1992 that Gellene had been "[f]ired as partner mentor this Summer—after 4 weeks had still not made a single contact with his Summer Associates." In 1994 the compensation committee was told, "The recruiting staff has determined, based on experience, that Gellene should not be asked to assist the Firm with recruiting or interviewing; he generally refuses or, if he agrees he then cancels." Gellene's intense immersion in his work thus gave rise to a tunnel vision that obscured anything he saw as not immediately relevant to the task at hand.

Id.

either systematically underbill or overbill[57] the clients. No matter on which side of the coin the "guesstimates" land, the end result is the same: the lawyer has lied about how he spent his time. And lies have an annoying tendency to multiply.[58]

Milbank was aware of something else about Gellene, at least after Gellene became a partner: he was practicing in New York without a license.

> Only a few months after earning partnership on January 1, 1989, [Gellene's] achievement was in jeopardy. In late May of that year, Milbank was conducting a routine check of the credentials of all its lawyers. It confirmed that he was a member of the New Jersey bar. The firm discovered however, that, contrary to his representation, Gellene was not listed as a member by the New York state bar. This in turn meant that his putative membership in the federal bar in New York City was invalid. In other words, for almost nine years Gellene had practiced law in New York without a license. When confronted with this discrepancy, Gellene did not immediately confirm that Milbank's information was correct. Eventually, however, he admitted that he had never completed the steps necessary to become a member of the New York bar.[59]

The portrait of Gellene thus falls into sharper focus: he was a loner, an insanely hard worker, and someone who believed that certain rules didn't apply to him. As Gellene's story unfolds, Milbank would also find out that Gellene was someone who would fail to disclose a conflict of interest to a court, fail to respond to a motion to disgorge fees in that case (the *Bucyrus* case) and, until he was cornered, fail to provide his fellow partners with undoctored versions of pleadings filed against him and the firm.

c. Cognitive Dissonance at Milbank[60]

If Gellene had so many problems, why did Milbank keep him on, first as an associate and then later as a partner? The likely answer is that Gellene was enough of a

---

[57] One of the problems with late timesheets is that every lawyer could easily make both types of mistakes: underbilling and overbilling. A lawyer will *under*bill when he forgets to bill for a matter on which he worked. The same lawyer will *over*bill when he recreates a late timesheet along the following lines: "well, I worked on this matter for seven days straight, and I probably put in ten-hour days, so I'll bill 70 hours for this matter." The odds are good that the lawyer didn't actually fill the entirety of those days with billable work. Underbilling cheats the law firm out of earned fees. Overbilling cheats the client—period.

[58] Oh what a tangled web we weave,
When first we practise to deceive!

Sir Walter Scott, *Marmion,* Canto vi, *Stanza* 17, available at http://www.quotationspage.com/quote/27150.html.

[59] *Id.* at 60.

[60] *Cf.* EAT WHAT YOU KILL, *supra* n. 4, at 304-05.

billing machine that he was profitable.[61] At some point, though, profit isn't enough of an answer.

Take Gellene's failure to take the time to complete his character and fitness requirements for the New York bar. That failure probably stemmed from the same tunnel vision that he had exhibited throughout his career. Milbank knew about Gellene's problems with his timesheets and with abandoning summer associates, and perhaps it could dismiss such mistakes as "merely internal" problems; however, Gellene's practice of law without a license created a problem externally for the firm.[62] The firm had tolerated other associates' failure to complete their character and fitness portions of bar applications,[63] so it would not have been unreasonable for Gellene to assume that the firm would tolerate his delay as well. And it did, in a manner of speaking.

Gellene completed his application and was sworn in some ten months after Milbank originally discovered the problem. The only action that Milbank took was to demote Gellene to "of counsel" for the rest of the year; Milbank reinstated him as a partner, but in a newer-partner compensation bracket, which rankled Gellene considerably.

What rationale could the management at Milbank give itself for retaining Gellene as a partner after realizing that he had knowingly practiced for years without a New York license? As Tanina Rostain correctly observes, "A fundamental purpose of law firm discipline should be to address the organizational factors, and specifically the dynamics of power, that contribute to individual wrongdoing."[64] Gellene wasn't the first Milbank lawyer who had neglected to finish the paperwork for admission to the New York bar. Why did Milbank look the other way, not just in Gellene's case, but in several Milbank lawyers' situations? One explanation is that Milbank was reluctant to admit that hiring Gellene (and the other lawyers) could have been a mistake. By rationalizing that Gellene had, ultimately, been admitted to the New York bar, Milbank could say that the delay in admission was merely due to overwork.

If my hypothesis is correct, Milbank certainly wouldn't be the only law firm that might pride itself on its sweatshop-like work conditions. Many (most?) of the largest firms use billable hours as a way to measure their associates' work ethic. It's a race to exhaustion, a race to sloppiness, and a race to malpractice, but it's a very macho race, nonetheless. And macho behavior is the norm at the top firms.[65]

---

[61] Someone more cynical than I might contend that Gellene was profitable enough, even with disgorgement and malpractice lawsuits filed against him, that the risk to the firm was worth it financially. *Cf. Ford Pinto Fuel-Fed Fires,* Center for Auto Safety, available at http://www.autosafety.org/article.php?did=522&scid=8.

[62] *Cf. id.* at 61. ("In all likelihood this failure was clue to a sense that he was too busy at the time with his clerkship duties to fill out the forms and make the trip to Albany—just as he later was too busy at Milbank to submit his billing records on time or help with summer associates.").

[63] *Id.*

[64] Rostain, *supra* n. 9, at 286.

[65] *See, e.g.,* MICHAEL H. TROTTER, PROFIT AND THE PRACTICE OF LAW: WHAT'S HAPPENED TO THE LEGAL PROFESSION 90 (Athens, Georgia, University of Georgia Press 1997) ("There is something in the system

d. Diffusion of Responsibility

Another problem endemic to organizations is diffusion of responsibility. Think of how many Milbank partners knew about Gellene's foibles generally, and how few of them took action. Regan describes the scene at Milbank when Gellene's partners discovered that he had not replied to the disgorgement motion in *Bucyrus*:

> Lichstein [one of Gellene's partners] was piqued that Lederman and Gellene had downplayed her earlier inquiries about a potential conflict. She suggested to Lederman that perhaps they should have taken her more seriously. Gellene nonetheless appeared composed during the meeting. He did not talk about the specifics of the JNL motion [for disgorgement of fees in the *Bucyrus* case]. . . . A response to the motion, he said, was due that coming Friday, February 28. He gave no indication of any problems with the response. The other Milbank partners apparently left the meeting feeling reassured that Gellene was on top of the situation, and that there was no danger to the firm.
>
> After the meeting, Lichstein continued to ask Gellene for the full set of papers associated with the motion. She would be happy, she said, to help with the response. Gellene said that he would prepare a draft response the next day, which she could then review before it was filed on Friday. As the day went on, Lichstein's exasperation mounted as her repeated calls to Gellene failed to result in receipt of the papers. At one point, Lichstein enlisted Barist [another partner] and asked for his help. Barist called Gellene, but the latter was not in his office.
>
> Finally, late that afternoon Lichstein sat down to read closely the only document she had, the memorandum of law. She was surprised by the fact that it referred to an accompanying affidavit of Andy Rahl dated December 12, 1996. That's odd, she thought. Why would a motion that had been filed in February be accompanied by an affidavit executed two months earlier? Lichstein then asked David Gelfand [another partner] to go up to Gellene's office to get a copy of the full set of papers. Gelfand had no more luck than she had, and came back empty-handed. Finally, early that evening, Lichstein phoned Gellene in his office and asked why the Rahl affidavit was dated in December. Gellene said that he would come down to talk to Lichstein and Gelfand.
>
> Gellene was quite distraught when he entered Lichstein's office. As Gelfand put it, "[W]hat happened next was a very difficult thing to witness." Gellene broke down in front of his colleagues. He felt terrible, he said, but he couldn't lie to Lichstein and Gelfand any longer. He said that the JNL motion papers had actually been served on him in December 1996, and that

that smacks of fraternity hazing. . . . The senior lawyers assume that younger lawyers would not answer the fire bell and work at night or weekends if necessary to get the job done.").

> he had later received a second set of papers filed on behalf of Bucyrus. He explained why the memorandum that he had given Lichstein had no date on the signature page: Gellene had whited it out. . . . [Gellene] had sought an extension of time to file a response [to the two motions]. The court, however, had denied his request. As a result, he had missed the deadline by about two weeks. Milbank thus faced the prospect that [the court] would rule that the firm had to return almost $2 million to Bucyrus.
>
> David Gelfand undertook a preliminary investigation of the matter on behalf of the firm. Milbank eventually called in the law firm of Sidley Austin to handle the matter. The February 14 deadline for responding to the JNL and Bucyrus motions had passed. Gelfand, however, prepared an affidavit stating that no one at the firm other than Gellene had been aware of the motions. The court then granted Milbank an extension of the time to reply until March 21.[66]

The motion to disgorge was, I believe, inevitable, based on Gellene's habit of playing things close to the vest. For a long time, Milbank had tolerated Gellene's habits, and even rewarded them: he wasn't fired after the firm discovered that he had been practicing without a license; he was fined a pittance when he turned in timesheets chronically late; and he was allowed to run large bankruptcy cases virtually by himself. What else could Milbank have expected would happen, given the extraordinary pressures that Gellene—and everyone else at Milbank—was under?

Milbank isn't an isolated firm, populated with bad actors. It is a large law firm, and it is run—like other law firms—by lawyers, few of whom have had any training as managers. Most law firms operate at a breakneck pace, with precious little time for thought about client matters, let alone law firm matters. I wouldn't be a bit surprised to find that the lawyers who worked with Gellene assumed that the firm either (1) knew about what was happening and was taking care of it, or (2) knew about what was happening and quietly approved of it. I also wouldn't be surprised to find out that the firm's management assumed that lawyers working more closely with Gellene would have alerted firm management if they thought that anything was amiss. After all, what behavior counts as normal in such a fast-paced environment?

e. Social Pressure

To the extent that Milbank, like other large law firms, is organized into departments by practice groups, those departments create powerful incentives to conform to practice group norms. In bankruptcy groups, for example, conflicts of interest can be interpreted very differently from how they would be interpreted in, say, commercial

---

[66] *Id.* at 212-14.

litigation departments, or in tax departments, etc.[67] Without input from other departments, there is a risk that the departmental group norms will override any firm-wide (or professional) norms.

> The result of all this is that teams can shape individual perceptions in powerful ways by creating a shared cognitive and moral universe. Members reinforce for one another the idea that their framework for interpreting events is accurate and reasonable. This process can result in "groupthink," a situation in which individuals arrive at a consensus without exploring all options or paying enough attention to information that challenges their framework. Group influence will be especially pronounced when members face stress and ambiguity, and when they perceive an external threat or adversary. It also may be especially potent when a project team is comprised of members from different organizations. The absence of a single entity with overall managerial responsibility in these cases may make it harder to prompt group members to view things from the standpoint of a broader organizational mission.
>
> The large-firm lawyer thus practices under conditions dramatically different from a quarter century ago. Firms are more loosely organized, partners are more akin to individual entrepreneurs, and competition is a relentless fact of life. These changes have been especially vivid at Wall Street firms, because they were the most insulated from competitive pressures for a good part of the twentieth century. All large firms, however, now inhabit a universe whose governing laws are those of the market.[68]

That competitive, never-say-die atmosphere was clear, and Gellene's behavior was consistent with that ethic as he began work on the *Bucyrus* case:

> Gellene... told Lederman, "I don't believe that we have to disclose that we represent Salovaara because he's not a creditor." Gellene testified that he had thought of Salovaara when preparing the declaration, but had told himself that "it's not related and he's not even a creditor." The latter conclusion apparently was based on the view that Salovaara individually was not someone to whom Bucyrus owed money. Gellene didn't share his reasoning on this

[67] I've based a large part of my career on my obsession about conflicts of interest in bankruptcy cases, especially in chapter 11 cases. *See, e.g.,* Nancy B. Rapoport, *Bankruptcy Ethics Issues for Solos and Small Firms, in* ATTORNEY LIABILITY IN BANKRUPTCY (Corinne Cooper, ed. & Catherine E. Vance, contributing ed., ABA 2006); Nancy B. Rapoport, *The Intractable Problem of Bankruptcy Ethics: Square Peg, Round Hole,* 30 HOFSTRA L. REV. 977 (2002); Nancy B. Rapoport, *Our House, Our Rules: The Need for a Uniform Code of Bankruptcy Ethics,* 6 AM. BANKR. INST. L. REV. 45 (1998); Nancy B. Rapoport, *Turning the Microscope on Ourselves: Self-Assessment by Bankruptcy Lawyers of Potential Conflicts of Interest in Columbus, Ohio,* 58 OHIO ST. L.J. 1421 (1997); Nancy B. Rapoport, *Seeing the Forest and the Trees: The Proper Role of the Bankruptcy Attorney,* 70 IND. L.J. 783 (1995); Nancy B. Rapoport, *Turning and Turning in the Widening Gyre: The Problem of Potential Conflicts of Interest in Bankruptcy,,* 26 CONN. L. REV. 913 (1994).

[68] *Id.* at 41-42.

> issue with anyone else at the time, because "we were in the middle of this fire drill to get everything done, and everybody was off doing something else. There was so much work to be done that everybody had to work on one thing and not really look at what somebody else was doing."[69]

Although it's possible that Gellene's failure to push the disclosure of the Salovaara relationship was part of some "nudge-nudge, wink-wink"[70] signaling from Lederman, Gellene was a partner at the time, and he was certainly capable of understanding that bankruptcy courts prefer to decide conflicts issues themselves, after full disclosure. Gellene was experienced enough to know that he

> had an ongoing obligation during the bankruptcy proceeding to inform the court if the firm developed new ties with any claimant. In asserting that Milbank had no connections to any party in interest other than those listed in his affidavit, Gellene already had crossed a crucial divide. To put it bluntly, he had lied to the court.[71]

He may have rationalized that lie on the grounds that everyone was feverishly busy with Bucyrus's first-day motions (cognitive dissonance thus rearing its ugly head), but he lied, nonetheless. And that lie, coupled with more lies and a cover-up, eventually sent him to prison. Would Gellene have lied about the conflict had he been working at a slower-paced law firm, or on a smaller case, or if he were a rainmaker on his own, not dependent on others' largesse for his assignments? It's hard to say. Those factors operated to make the decision to lie more likely, though.

III. CONCLUSION: THE INEVITABILITY OF HUMAN NATURE

Outside of most *Perry Mason* episodes, guilty people don't confess until they've been caught. After the jury verdict in the Ken Lay and Jeff Skilling cases, both defendants acted as if the verdicts were based on a simple factual misunderstanding:

> Speaking to reporters outside the courthouse, Lay expressed shock at the verdict and continued to maintain his innocence as his wife Linda stood by his side.
>
> "I firmly believe I am innocent of the charges," he said. "Despite what has happened I'm still a very blessed man." . . .
>
> Outside the courtroom after court was adjourned, Skilling said, "We fought a good fight. Some things work. Some things don't."

---

[69] *Id.* at 148.

[70] *See* http://en.wikipedia.org/wiki/Nudge_Nudge (explaining the origin of the phrase as part of a Monty Python skit).

[71] *Id.* at 155.

> "Obviously I'm disappointed, but that's the way the system works," he added."[72]

Each man stayed in character, with Lay maintaining that his inattention[73] and Fastow's greed caused Enron's downfall, and Skilling maintaining that ordinary people[74] couldn't understand why Enron had entered into such creative deals.

Gellene also had a theory for his downfall: a combination of his perfectionism and his inaction. Starting with his failure to finish his bar application, he explained:

> I think I have two things to say. First, is that I have not just for my adult life but before that I've been recognized as a person with gifts in terms of my intellect and my ability to deal with problems, and I've been very good and very competent at the kinds of problems presented [by] my clients in the practice of law and in academics and so on.
>
> And that is I think such a part of me and who I hold myself out to be and who I am that when I am confronted with mistake, an act of inadvertence that is stupid that I'm—it is very difficult for me to stand up and say I did a stupid thing.
>
> When I was a young lawyer, I did a very stupid thing. I got caught up in my work and I didn't fill out the forms, and as time went on it got more and more absurd and I could not stand up and say, I did something stupid. And when that first happened in my life in a traumatic way, I could not say it to myself and I could not say it to others so I hid it. I lied, and when it was discovered, I set about to repair it. It was a long process. Nine years ago it would have taken three weeks and it took almost a year later but I fixed it and moved on.
>
> When I did that with the state court, I didn't do it with the federal court, the other major court in New York City and I should have done that. And it would have been—certainly after the year that went on in my life with the New York bar, it would have been a very simple thing to do, but I was confronted again with the absurd stupidity of not filling out forms that thousands of lawyers fill out year in and year out and I couldn't stand up and say, I did this. I did something stupid so I didn't do it.[75]

Seeing a pattern in his own inaction, Gellene continued, in an effort to explain his actions in *Bucyrus*:

---

[72] Shaheen Pasha & Jessica Seid, *Lay and Skilling's day of reckoning: Enron ex-CEO and founder convicted on fraud and conspiracy charges; sentencing slated for September*, CNN MONEY, May 25, 2006, at http://money.cnn.com/2006/05/25/news/newsmakers/enron_verdict/index.htm.

[73] Somehow, Lay never realized that a CEO's inattention to business was itself problematic.

[74] I.e., jurors.

[75] *Id.* at 262-63.

> When I saw the [*Bucyrus*] papers in December, the same crushing weight of what I had experienced in May occurred again and it occurred at the culmination of a year that was personally and professionally very difficult and had created a sense of isolation from my colleagues, from my work, from things that I had invested thousands of hours in trying to give meaning to myself and to my life and I could not deal with it. I just fell apart during the month of December. I didn't work. I didn't do anything. I would sit at my desk.
>
> And only when I absolutely had to did I zip up all of that and for whatever time it took put a face before the world that didn't reveal what was going on with me. I did that and I've done that because through my adult life I have not been able to deal in a responsible and mature and forthright way with the imperfections that I like anyone else have and the shortcomings that I think any man or woman has in a world that's not perfect.[76]

More interesting than Gellene's self-psychoanalysis, though, is his rather offhand comment: "*on the one hand, you can see this pattern of behavior.*"[77] On this point, Gellene was absolutely correct. Milbank could have seen this pattern of behavior, had the right people connected the right dots. Although people saw Gellene's behavior with respect to timesheets and workaholism, that behavior was normal enough not to trigger any alerts. By the time that the abnormal behavior surfaced, in the guise of a motion to disgorge, it was too late.

In Enron's case, as well as in Milbank's case, misbehavior was an open secret. No matter how much Andy Fastow, or Jeff Skilling, or Ken Lay fooled themselves, others witnessed their machinations, and very few of them spoke out. Neither Enron nor Milbank did anything "in the night-time."

Some may argue that neither group spoke out because it was well-fed (read: greedy), but I hesitate to attribute simple greed as the sole answer. Using greed as the answer implies that the problem is cured when the guilty are spirited away.

Rather, I attribute the cause as the mind's ability to fool itself, not just in discrete circumstances, but for a prolonged period. Enron's workforce, as well as Milbank's workforce, was socialized to expect certain behavior—"work hard, play hard"—and certain consequences, such as interesting deals and a very comfortable standard of living. There weren't counter-examples valuing those who played by the rules. If the only myths of an organization involve overwork, outsmarting the opposition, and pushing the envelope, then few inside that organization will be able to withstand the pressure to conform. Those who want a different environment will leave. Those who stay will continue to be swayed by the group's norms.

"Do nothing in the night-time?" Actually, that's not curious at all.

---

[76] *Id.* at 263.

[77] *Id.* at 264 (emphasis added).